D0049586

THE RANDOM HOUSE CROSSWORD PUZZLE DICTIONARY

SECOND EDITION

THE RANDOM HOUSE CROSSWORD PUZZLE DICTIONARY

SECOND EDITION

Random House New York

Prepared for Random House, Inc., by Sachem Publishing Associates, Inc., Stephen P.
Elliott, President; Elizabeth J. Jewell, Managing Editor.

ISBN: 0-679-43376-7

0 9 8 7 6 5 4

Book design: Charlotte Staub
Manufactured in the United States of America

New York Toronto London Sydney Auckland

PREFACE

Although various word games and puzzles have existed almost since the beginnings of language, the modern crossword puzzle is a 20th-century innovation. The first newspaper crossword appeared on December 21, 1913, in the New York *World,* and this new type of word puzzle quickly captured the public's fancy. Within a decade, crossword puzzles were featured in most American newspapers, and they soon became the rage in England as well. Since the 1920s, crossword puzzles have been a standard feature of daily newspapers and have proved enormously popular when collected in book form.

Now found in almost every language and in variations ranging from theme puzzles to diagramless puzzles, crosswords are available for almost any age and vocabulary level. Those who solve crossword puzzles invariably relish the challenge of completing a puzzle, of "getting it right." When faced with a clue they cannot answer, they resist "cheating"—looking at the puzzle's solution. One way out of this difficulty is to consult a reference work, yet neither a dictionary nor an encyclopedia nor an almanac contains the necessary information in a useful, quick-reference format. A standard dictionary might give a few synonyms for a word, an encyclopedia would give information about countries or historical figures, and an almanac usually has information about sports figures or the Academy awards, but only a crossword puzzle dictionary combines in one handy volume the information that might be found in all three. Equally important, it does so without extraneous information and with the convenience of an arrangement by the number of letters in each word.

The Random House Crossword Puzzle Dictionary, drawing on the resources of the Random House dictionaries and thesauruses, with research into a host of other topics, answers the need of crossword puzzlers for one single-purpose reference work. In addition to general vocabulary and synonyms, there are entries covering history; the natural and physical sciences; literature; music, painting, and other arts; religion; mythology; sports; popular culture; and current affairs, among others. Highlighted boxed items provide easy-to-find detailed information on the continents and countries of the world, states of the United States, U.S. presidents, the months of the year, and other facts of special interest.

While *The Random House Crossword Puzzle Dictionary's* primary purpose is to meet the needs of the growing numbers of people who find crosswords both relaxing and challenging, even a cursory glance will demonstrate the book's usefulness as a reference for trivia buffs. From who won the Academy Award for best actress in 1970 (Glenda Jackson) to the name of a coffee grown in Jamaica (Blue Mountain), it's all here.

A volume of this scope is necessarily the work of many researchers, editors, and proofreaders. We would like to acknowledge the invaluable contributions made by Julianna Arbo, Suzanne Stone Burke, Francine Esposito, Gretchen Ferrante, Jan Jamilkowski, Rebecca Lyon, Julie E. Marsh, Blaine Merritt, Laurie Romanik, Christine Lindberg Stevens, and Diane Bell Surprenant; and by Patricia W. Ehresmann, Typographic Director and Production Manager, Random House, Inc., and Rita Rubin, Administrative Assistant.

HOW TO USE THIS BOOK

The main entries in *The Random House Crossword Puzzle Dictionary* are words or phrases likely to appear as crossword puzzle clues. Each entry consists of a clue word or phrase and a list of answer words, arranged first by the number of letters in each word and then alphabetically. For example, if the main entry—**banal**—is the clue for a five-letter answer, the answer—"trite"—will be found alphabetically listed under the five-letter answer words. For phrases, such as **contracted form,** the answer could be "digest," "summary," or "synopsis." Entries may also contain indented subheads and secondary subheads. If, for instance, the clue is a phrase, like **cotton fabric,** the word **cotton** will be found as a main entry in the dictionary, and **fabric** will be found as a subhead under it, with such possible answer words as "terry," "poplin," and "gingham." In some cases, the answer can be found in more than one place. For example, if the clue is **Mexican coin,** the answer could be found by looking under the main entry **Mexico** and the subhead **monetary unit,** or by looking under the main entry **coin/currency** and the subhead **of Mexico.**

Longer entries are set off in highlighted boxes so they can be found more quickly. All continents and countries of the world, states of the United States, presidents of the United States, and months of the year appear as boxed items, as do many other major entries.

There are also cross references for alternate spellings (**Epicaste** *see* **7** Jocasta) and very closely related items (**Epeans** *see* **5** Epeus—a look at **Epeus** reveals that **Epeans** are descendants of this king of the Peloponnesus).

The main entries, subheads, secondary subheads, and numbers all appear in boldface type; the answer words are in regular roman type. Most punctuation and accent marks have been omitted, since they are not used in puzzle answers; occasionally, apostrophes and other marks have been included in answers to make them more readable.

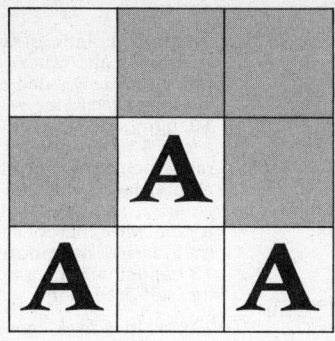

aardvark
  also: 7 ant bear 8 anteater
  family: 15 Orycteropodidae
  species: 15 Orycteropus afer
  order: 13 Tubulidentata
  native to: 6 Africa
  food: 4 ants 8 termites
  name comes from:
    9 Africaans
    meaning: 8 earth hog,
    earth pig

Aaron
  brother: 5 Moses
  father: 5 Amram
  mother: 8 Jochebed
  sister: 6 Miriam
  son: 5 Abihu, Nadab 7 Elea-
    zar, Ithamar
  wife: 8 Elisheba
  successor: 7 Eleazar
  deathplace: 3 Hor 8 Mount
    Hor
  priestly descendant of:
    8 Aaronite
  set up: 10 golden calf

Aaron, Henry (Hank)
  sport: 8 baseball
  position: 10 outfielder
  record: 8 homeruns
  team: 13 Atlanta Braves
    15 Milwaukee Braves
    16 Milwaukee Brewers

Aaron's Rod 21 miraculously
  blossomed
  yielded: 7 almonds
  herb: 21 Thermopsis
    caroliniana

Aatam *see* 4 Pima

Ab 16 fifth Hebrew month

Abaddon 4 hell 8 Appolyon

abaft 6 behind 11 to the rear
  of 12 to the stern of

Abagtha 6 eunuch
  served: 9 Ahasuerus

abandon 4 dash, drop, elan,
  jilt, junk, quit, stop 5 ardor,
  cease, forgo, gusto, leave, let
  go, scrap, verve, waive 6 desert, give up, spirit 7 discard,

forfeit, forsake, freedom 8 abdicate, evacuate, forswear, get
rid of, renounce, run out on
9 animation, cast aside, repudiate, surrender 10 depart
from, enthusiasm, exuberance,
relinquish, wantonness 11 discontinue, impetuosity, leave
behind, spontaneity, unrestraint 12 immoderation, intemperance, recklessness,
withdraw from
13 impulsiveness

abandoned 4 lewd, wild
5 loose 6 impure, jilted, sinful,
vacant, wanton, wicked 7 debased, immoral 8 cast away,
degraded, deserted, desolate,
forsaken, marooned, rejected,
unchaste 9 cast aside, debauched, discarded, dissolute,
neglected, reprobate, shameless 10 dissipated, left behind,
licentious, profligate, unoccupied 11 unrepentant 12 disreputable, incorrigible,
irreformable, relinquished, unprincipled 13 irreclaimable

abandon oneself to 7 yield
to 8 give in to, give up to
9 indulge in

Abantes
  tribe: 7 Euboean

Abaris
  origin: 5 Greek
  form: 4 sage

Abas
  mentioned in: 5 Iliad
  king of: 7 Argolis
  father: 6 Celeus 7 Lynceus
    9 Eurydamas
  mother: 8 Metanira
    12 Hypermnestra
  wife: 6 Aglaia
  son: 7 Proetus 8 Acrisius
  daughter: 7 Idomene
  changed into: 4 bird 6 lizard
  mocked: 7 Demeter
  protected by: 11 magic
    shield

  companion: 8 Diomedes
  killed by: 8 Diomedes

a bas 8 down with 11 to the
  bottom

abase 4 mock 5 shame 6 debase, defame, demean, humble, malign, vilify 7 cheapen,
degrade, mortify, put down,
vitiate 8 badmouth, belittle,
besmirch, bring low, cast
down, disgrace, dishonor
9 denigrate, devaluate, discredit, downgrade, humiliate
13 bring down a peg, cut
down to size

abash 4 dash 5 daunt 6 deject,
dismay 7 depress 8 dispirit
9 discomfit, embarrass 10 discompose, disconcert, discourage, dishearten

abashed 3 shy 5 cowed, fazed
7 ashamed, bashful, crushed,
daunted, humbled, subdued
8 confused, dismayed, over-
awed 9 chagrined, mortified
10 bewildered, confounded,
humiliated, nonplussed, taken
aback 11 dumbfounded, em-
barrassed, intimidated 12 disconcerted, disheartened
13 self-conscious

abashment 3 awe 6 wonder
9 confusion 12 discomfiture,
discomposure 13 embarrassment 14 disconcertment

abate 3 ebb 4 cool, dull, ease,
fade, slow, wane 5 allay,
blunt, lower, quell, quiet,
slack 6 dampen, go down,
lessen, pacify, recede, reduce,
soften, soothe, temper, weak-
en 7 assuage, curtail, decline,
dwindle, fall off, lighten, mollify, relieve, slacken, subside
8 decrease, diminish, fade
away, fall away, mitigate,
moderate, palliate, restrain, restrict, slack off, slow down,
taper off 9 alleviate

abatement 3 cut, ebb 5 break

1

6 ebbing, waning **8** decrease, discount, soothing **9** lessening, reduction, weakening **10** concession, mitigation, moderation, slackening, subsidence **11** assuagement, curtailment **13** mollification

Abba
 means: **6** father

Abbe Faria
 character in: **21** The Count of Monte Cristo
 author: **5** Dumas (pere)

abbey 6 cenoby, chapel, church, friary, priory **7** convent, nunnery **8** cloister, seminary **9** cathedral, hermitage, monastery

Abbey, Edwin Austin
 born: **14** Philadelphia PA
 artwork: **21** Quest of the Golden Grail **23** The Quest for the Holy Grail **37** Richard Duke of Gloucester and the Lady Anne

Abbott, Bud
 real name: **14** William A Abbott
 partner: **11** Lou Costello
 born: **12** Asbury Park NJ
 roles: **11** Who's on First **12** Buck Privates **13** Hold that Ghost **33** Abbott and Costello Meet Frankenstein

abbreviate 3 cut **4** clip, trim **6** reduce **7** abridge, curtail, cut down, shorten **8** boil down, compress, condense, contract, cut short, diminish, truncate **9** summarize, synopsize

abbreviated 5 brief, short **7** limited, summary **8** abridged **9** condensed, curtailed, shortened **10** compressed, summarized

abbreviation 5 brief **6** digest **7** cutting, pruning, summary **8** abstract, clipping, synopsis, trimming **9** lessening, reduction, short form **10** abridgment, diminution, shortening **11** abstraction, compression, contraction, curtailment, cutdown form, reduced form **12** condensation **13** condensed form, shortened form **14** compressed form, contracted form

Abderus
 father: **6** Hermes
 killed by: **5** mares **13** Diomedes mares

abdicate 4 cede, quit **5** forgo, waive, yield **6** abjure, give up, resign **7** abandon **8** abnegate, renounce **9** surrender **10** relinquish **15** vacate the throne

abdomen 3 gut, pot **5** belly, tummy **6** paunch, venter

7 stomach **8** pot belly **9** bay window **11** breadbasket, epigastrium **14** visceral cavity

Abdon 11 Hebrew judge
 father: **5** Micah **6** Achbor, Jehiel **7** Shashak
 city of: **5** Asher

abduct 5 seize, steal **6** kidnap **7** bear off **8** carry off, take away **10** run off with **11** make off with

Abduction from the Harem, The
 also: **25** Die Entfuhrung aus dem Serail
 opera by: **6** Mozart
 character: **5** Osmin **6** Blonde **8** Belmonte, Pedrillo **9** Constanze **10** Pasha Selim

Abdul-Jabbar, Kareem
 formerly: **11** Lew Alcindor **22** Lewis Ferdinand Alcindor
 sport: **10** basketball
 position: **6** center
 team: **8** LA Lakers **10** UCLA Bruins **14** Milwaukee Bucks **16** Los Angeles Lakers
 shot: **7** sky hook

Abednego
 companion: **6** Daniel
 friend: **8** Meschach, Shadrach
 former name: **7** Azariah

Abel
 father: **4** Adam
 mother: **3** Eve
 brother: **4** Cain, Seth
 killer: **4** Cain

Abel, Niels Henrik
 field: **11** mathematics
 nationality: **9** Norwegian
 theorem: **8** binomial
 theory of: **19** elliptical functions

Abe Lincoln in Illinois
 author: **14** Robert Sherwood
 director: **12** John Cromwell
 cast: **10** Alan Baxter, Mary Howard, Ruth Gordon (Mary Todd Lincoln) **11** Dorothy Tree, Minor Watson **12** Gene Lockhart **13** Howard da Silva, Raymond Massey (Abraham Lincoln)

Abelmeholah
 home of: **6** Elisha

aberrance 6 oddity **7** anomaly **8** rambling, straying **9** wandering **10** aberration **11** abnormality, peculiarity **12** eccentricity, irregularity **13** nonconformity

aberrant 3 odd **5** unusual **8** abnormal, atypical, peculiar, uncommon **9** anomalous, eccentric, irregular

aberration 5 lapse, quirk **6** lunacy, oddity **7** anomaly, madness **8** delusion, illusion,

insanity, mutation, rambling, straying **9** aberrance, aberrancy, curiosity, departure, deviation, exception, wandering **10** digression, distortion, divergence **11** abnormality, derangement, incongruity, mental lapse, peculiarity, singularity, strangeness **12** eccentricity, idiosyncrasy, irregularity, unconformity **13** hallucination, nonconformity, self-deception

abet 3 aid **4** back, goad, help, spur, urge **5** egg on **6** assist, incite, lead on, second, uphold, urge on **7** advance, endorse, promote, support, sustain **8** advocate, join with, sanction **9** encourage, instigate

abettor 4 ally **6** cohort **7** partner **9** accessory, associate, colleague **10** accomplice **11** confederate **12** collaborator

ab extra 11 from outside, from without

abeyance 5 delay, on ice, pause **6** hiatus, recess **7** latency **8** deferral, dormancy, inaction **9** cessation, remission **10** quiescence, suspension **11** adjournment **12** intermission, postponement **13** in cold storage, on a back burner, waiting period **14** discontinuance

abhor 4 hate, shun **5** scorn **6** detest, eschew, loathe **7** despise, disdain, dislike **8** execrate, recoil at **9** abominate, can't stand, shudder at **10** shrink from **11** can't stomach **12** be revolted by **13** be nauseated by, find repulsive

abhorred 5 hated **8** despised, detested, disliked **10** abominated

abhorrence 4 hate **5** odium, scorn **6** hatred **7** disdain, disgust, dislike **8** aversion, contempt, distaste, loathing **9** antipathy, revulsion **10** repugnance **11** abomination

abhorrent 4 foul, vile **6** odious **7** hateful **8** accursed **9** execrable, loathsome, repellent, repugnant, repulsive, revolting **10** abominable, despicable, disgusting, nauseating

Abiathar
 companion: **5** David
 father: **9** Ahimelech
 banished to: **7** Anatoth
 conspired to overthrow: **5** David

abide 3 sit **4** bear, last, live, stay, stop **5** brook, dwell, stand, tarry, visit **6** accept, endure, linger, remain, reside, suffer **7** sojourn, stomach **8** stand for, submit to, tolerate

abide by 4 obey **6** follow **8** accede to, adhere to, submit to **9** conform to **10** comply with **11** go along with

abiding 4 fast, firm **6** steady **7** durable, eternal, lasting **8** constant, enduring, unending **9** immutable, permanent, steadfast **10** changeless, continuing, unchanging, unshakable **11** everlasting **12** indissoluble, wholehearted **13** unquestioning

Abidjan
  capital of: 10 Ivory Coast

Abigail
  husband: 5 David, Nabal
  brother: 5 David

Abihu
  father: 5 Aaron
  mother: 8 Elisheba
  brother: 5 Nadab **7** Eleazar, Ithamar
  killed with: 5 Nadab
  accompanied to Mt Sinai: 5 Moses

Abijah
  father: 8 Rehoboam
  grandfather: 7 Solomon
  grandmother: 6 Naamah

ability 4 bent, gift **5** flair, knack, power, skill **6** acumen, genius, talent **7** faculty, knowhow, mind for **8** aptitude, capacity, facility **9** adeptness, expertise, potential **10** adroitness, capability, competence **11** proficiency **12** potentiality **13** qualification

Abimelech
  king of: 5 Gerar
  means: 15 the father is king
  father: 6 Gideon **8** Abiathar
  brother: 6 Jotham
  army commander: 7 Phichol

ab initio 16 from the beginning

Abinoam
  father: 4 Saul
  son: 5 Barak

ab intra 10 from inside, from within

Abishag
  comforted: 5 David

abject 3 low **4** base, mean, vile **6** sordid **7** ignoble **8** complete, cringing, hopeless, horrible, terrible, thorough, wretched **9** groveling, miserable **10** deplorable, despicable, spiritless **11** inescapable **12** contemptible

abjuration 7 refusal **8** eschewal **9** rejection **10** abnegation,

disclaimer, retraction **11** repudiation **12** renunciation

abjure 6 desert, give up, recant, reject **7** abandon, disavow **8** disallow, disclaim, forswear, renounce **9** repudiate **10** relinquish

ablaze 5 afire, eager, fiery **6** aflame, alight, ardent, fervid, on fire, red-hot **7** blazing, burning, excited, fervent, flaming, flushed, glowing, ignited, zealous **8** feverish, hopped-up, in flames, turned-on **10** passionate, switched-on **11** conflagrant, impassioned, intoxicated

able 3 apt, fit **4** good **5** adept **6** adroit, expert, fitted **7** capable, equal to, learned **8** adequate, skillful, talented **9** competent, effective, efficient, masterful, practiced, qualified **10** proficient **11** experienced **12** accomplished

able-bodied 5 beefy, hardy, husky, lusty, thewy **6** brawny, hearty, robust, rugged, strong, sturdy **8** athletic, muscular, powerful, stalwart, vigorous **9** herculean, strapping, well-built **15** broad-shouldered

ablution 4 bath, wash **7** bathing, washing **8** cleaning, lavation **9** cleansing **12** purification **13** ritual washing **17** ceremonial washing

Abnaki (Wabanaki)
  language family: 9 Algonkian **10** Algonquian
  tribe: 6 Micmac **8** Malecite **9** Penobscot **13** Norridegewock, Passamaquoddy
  location: 5 Maine **6** Canada, Quebec **7** Old Town **9** Norumbega **10** New England **12** New Brunswick

abnegate 5 forgo, waive **6** abjure, eschew, give up, refuse **7** abstain, forbear **8** renounce **9** repudiate **10** relinquish **11** deny oneself

abnegation 7 refusal **8** eschewal, giving up **9** rejection, sacrifice, surrender **10** abstinence, continence, forbearing, self-denial, temperance **11** forbearance, resignation **12** renunciation **14** relinquishment

Abner
  commanded: 9 Saul's army
  father: 3 Ner
  cousin: 4 Saul

abnormal 3 odd **4** rare **5** queer, weird **7** bizarre, curious, deviant, strange, unusual **8** aberrant, atypical, deformed, freakish, peculiar, uncommon **9** anomalous, eccentric, gro-

tesque, irregular, monstrous, unheard of, unnatural **10** inordinate, outlandish, unexpected **11** exceptional **12** unaccustomed **13** extraordinary **14** unconventional

abnormality 6 oddity **7** anomaly **9** aberrance, curiosity, deformity, deviation **10** aberration, perversion **11** peculiarity **12** eccentricity, idiosyncrasy, irregularity, malformation, unconformity

abode 3 pad **4** home, nest **5** house **7** address, habitat, lodging **8** domicile, dwelling **9** residence **10** habitation **13** dwelling place **14** living quarters

abolish 3 end **5** annul, erase, quash **6** cancel, repeal, revoke **7** blot out, nullify, rescind, squelch, vitiate, wipe out **8** abrogate, set aside, stamp out **9** eliminate, eradicate, extirpate, repudiate, terminate **10** annihilate, do away with, extinguish, invalidate, obliterate, put an end to **11** exterminate **18** declare null and void

abolishment 7 voiding **8** recision **9** abolition, annulment **10** extinction, rescinding, revocation **11** destruction, eradication **12** cancellation **13** doing away with, nullification

abolition 6 ending, repeal **9** annulment, vitiation **10** abrogation, extinction, rescinding, retraction, revocation **11** abolishment, dissolution, elimination, eradication, recantation, repudiation, termination **12** cancellation, invalidation **13** nullification

abominable 4 base, evil, foul, vile **5** awful, lousy **6** cursed, horrid, odious **7** hateful, heinous, hellish **8** accursed, damnable, horrible, infamous, terrible, wretched **9** abhorrent, atrocious, execrable, loathsome, miserable, repellent, repugnant, repulsive, revolting **10** deplorable, despicable, detestable, disgusting, unsuitable, villainous **11** ignominious **12** contemptible, disagreeable **13** reprehensible

abominate 4 hate **5** abhor, scorn **6** detest, loathe **7** despise **8** execrate **9** can't stand **10** recoil from, shrink from **11** can't stomach **12** be revolted by **13** find repugnant, find repulsive

abomination 4 evil, hate **6** hatred, horror, plague **7** bugbear, disgust, torment

8 anathema, aversion, disgrace, loathing **9** annoyance, antipathy, bete noire, obscenity, revulsion **10** abhorrence, affliction, defilement, repugnance **11** detestation

aboriginal 5 first, prime **6** native **7** ancient, endemic, primary **8** earliest, original, primeval **9** primitive **10** indigenous, primordial **13** autochthonous

aborigine 6 native **16** indigenous person **18** original inhabitant **19** primitive inhabitant

abort 3 end **4** fail, halt, stop **7** call off **8** miscarry **9** terminate

abortion 6 ending, fiasco **7** failure, halting **8** disaster **10** calling off **11** miscarriage, termination **16** fruitless attempt **19** unsuccessful attempt

abortive 4 vain **6** futile **7** sterile, useless **8** bootless **9** fruitless, nonviable, worthless **10** profitless, unavailing, unfruitful **11** ineffective, ineffectual, unrewarding **12** unproductive, unprofitable, unsuccessful **13** inefficacious

abound 4 gush, teem **5** swarm **6** thrive **7** run wild **8** be filled, be rich in, flourish, overflow **9** be flooded, luxuriate, spill over **10** be numerous **11** be plentiful, superabound, próliferate

abounding 4 rich, rife **5** ample **6** plenty **7** profuse, replete, teeming **8** abundant, brimming, swarming **9** bounteous, bountiful **11** overflowing, running over **14** more than enough

about 2 in, of, on **4** near **5** astir, circa **6** abroad, almost, around, circum, nearby, nearly **7** close to **9** proximate, regarding **10** concerning, in regard to **13** approximately, connected with **14** associated with

about-face 5 shift **6** switch **7** reverse **8** reversal **9** disavowal, turnabout, volte-face **10** retraction, rightabout, turnaround **11** recantation **13** change of heart **14** tergiversation

above 4 atop, over **5** aloft, north, supra **6** before, beyond, dorsal, excess, heaven, higher **7** earlier **8** in heaven, overhead, superior, upstairs **9** exceeding **10** surpassing

above all 4 most **9** most of

all **10** especially **12** particularly

aboveboard 4 just, open **5** blunt, frank, moral, plain **6** candid, direct, honest, public, square **7** artless, ethical, sincere, upright **8** revealed, straight, truthful, virtuous **9** disclosed, guileless, ingenuous, righteous **10** forthright, foursquare **11** unconcealed **12** on the up and up, plain-dealing, out in the open **13** square-dealing, undissembling **15** straightforward **16** straight-shooting

ab ovo 10 from the egg **16** from the beginning

abracadabra 5 charm, magic, spell **6** voodoo **7** sorcery **8** exorcism **10** hocus-pocus, invocation, magic spell, mumbo-jumbo, open sesame, witchcraft **11** incantation

abrade 3 rub **4** file, fray, fret, rasp **5** chafe, erode, grate, grind **6** scrape **8** irritate, wear down

Abraham
  former name: 5 Abram
  founded: 12 Hebrew nation
  father: 5 Terah
  wife: 5 Sarah, Sarai
    7 Keturah
  brother: 5 Haran, Nahor
  son: 5 Isaac **6** Midian
    7 Ishmael
  nephew: 3 Lot
  birthplace: 15 Ur of the Chaldees
  received: 17 law of circumcision
  sacrificed Isaac at: 6 Moriah
  burial place: 6 Hebron
  tomb buried in: 9 Machpelah

Abraham Lincoln
  author: 12 Carl Sandburg

Abraham's bosom 6 heaven

Abram see **7** Abraham

Abramovitz, Max
  architect of: 13 ALCOA Building (Pittsburgh PA, with Wallace Harrison) **15** Avery Fisher Hall (Lincoln Center NYC)

Abrams, Creighton
  served in: 4 WWII **10** Vietnam War
  rank: 16 army chief of staff

abrasion 6 lesion, scrape **7** chafing, erosion, grating, rubbing, scratch **8** friction, scouring, scraping **11** excoriation, scraped spot

abrasive 5 harsh, nasty, rough, sharp **6** biting, coarse **7** caustic, chafing, cutting, galling,

grating, hurtful, rasping **8** annoying **10** irritating **11** excoriating **16** grinding material, scouring material, scraping material

abreast 6 in rank **7** aligned **10** side by side **11** in alignment

abridge 3 cut **4** trim **5** limit **6** digest, lessen, reduce **7** curtail, cut down, shorten **8** compress, condense, decrease, diminish, pare down, restrict, take away, truncate **9** scale down, telescope **10** abbreviate

abridgment 6 digest **8** decrease **9** lessening, reduction, restraint **10** diminution, limitation, truncation **11** curtailment, diminishing, restriction **12** abbreviation, condensation **13** condensed form, shortened form

abroad 3 out **4** rife **5** astir, forth **7** at large, outside **8** overseas **9** all around **10** out of doors **13** in circulation, out of the house, round and about **15** making the rounds, out in the open air, out of the country

abrogate 3 end **4** junk, undo, void **5** annul, quash **6** abjure, cancel, negate, recall, repeal, revoke **7** abolish, nullify, rescind, retract, reverse, vitiate **8** dissolve, override, renounce, set aside, throw out, withdraw **9** repudiate, terminate **10** do away with, invalidate, put an end to **11** countermand

abrogation 6 repeal **7** junking **8** recision, reneging, reversal **9** abolition, annulment **10** rescinding, retraction, revocation **11** abolishment, going back on, repudiation **12** cancellation **13** nullification

abrupt 4 curt, rude **5** blunt, brisk, crisp, gruff, hasty, quick, rapid, rough, sharp, sheer, short, steep, swift **6** sudden **7** brusque, uncivil **8** impolite **9** impulsive **10** unexpected, unforeseen, ungracious **11** precipitate, precipitous, unannounced, unlooked for **12** discourteous **13** instantaneous, unanticipated, unceremonious

Absalom
  father: 5 David
  mother: 6 Maacah
  sister: 5 Tamar
  brother: 7 Solomon
    8 Adonijah
  half-brother: 5 Amnon

defeated at: **6** Gilead
killed by: **4** Joab

Absalom, Absalom!
  author: **15** William Faulkner
  character: **5** Henry **6** Judith
  10 Charles Bon **13** Rosa
  Coldfield **14** Quentin Compson, Shreve McCannon
  16 Goodhue Coldfield
  19 Colonel Thomas Sutpen
  20 Ellen Coldfield Sutpen

Absalom and Achitophel
  author: **10** John Dryden

abscond 3 fly **4** flee, skip
  5 split **6** escape, run off, vanish **7** make off, run away,
  take off **8** steal off **9** disappear,
  steal away **10** take flight

absence 3 cut **4** lack, want
  6 dearth **7** truancy **8** scarcity
  10 deficiency, scantiness
  11 absenteeism, nonpresence
  12 nonexistence **13** insufficiency, nonappearance, nonattendance **14** unavailability

Absence of Malice
  director: **13** Sydney Pollack
  based on story by: **11** Kurt
  Luedtke
  cast: **10** Bob Balaban, Paul
  Newman, Sally Field
  13 Melinda Dillon
  setting: **5** Miami

absent 3 cut, out **4** away,
  gone **5** blank, empty, vague
  6 dreamy, musing, truant, vacant **7** faraway, missing, out
  of it, removed, unaware
  8 heedless, keep away, stay
  away, tuned out **9** not appear,
  not show up, oblivious
  10 distracted, nonpresent, not
  present, out to lunch, play
  truant, unthinking **11** inattentive, preoccupied, unconscious **12** nonattendant

absentee 6 no show, truant
  10 nonpresent **11** nonattendee,
  nonpresence **12** nonattendant
  13 nonattendance

absenteeism 5 hooky
  7 truancy **11** nonpresence
  13 nonappearance **19** absence
  without cause

absent-minded 5 blank,
  vague **6** dreamy **9** oblivious
  10 abstracted, distracted
  11 preoccupied **14** out in left
  field **17** out of it

Absent Without Leave
  author: **12** Heinrich Boll

absinthe
  ingredient: **8** licorice, worm-
  wood **9** aromatics, star anise
  color: **11** yellow green
  substitute: **4** Ouzo **6** Pastis,
  Pernod **8** Anisette

absolute 4 full, pure, real,
  sure **5** sheer, total, utter
  7 certain, genuine, perfect, supreme **8** complete, decisive,
  definite, outright, positive, reliable, thorough **9** confirmed,
  out-and-out, unbounded, unlimited **10** conclusive, consummate, infallible, undeniable
  11 unequivocal, unmitigated,
  unqualified **12** unrestrained,
  unrestricted **13** unadulterated,
  unconditional **14** unquestionable **17** through and
  through

Absolute, Sir Anthony
  character in: **9** The Rivals
  author: **8** Sheridan

absolutely 5 truly **6** indeed,
  really, wholly **7** utterly **8** entirely **9** certainly, decidedly
  10 completely, definitely, positively, thoroughly **11** indubitably, undoubtedly **13** unequivocally **14** unquestionably
  15 unconditionally **17** without
  limitation

absolution 5 mercy **6** pardon
  7 amnesty, release **9** acquittal,
  clearance, quittance, remission **10** indulgence, liberation
  11 deliverance, exculpation,
  exoneration, forgiveness, vindication **12** dispensation

absolve 4 free **5** clear, loose
  6 acquit, exempt, pardon,
  shrive **7** deliver, forgive, release, set free **9** discharge, exculpate, exonerate, vindicate
  10 excuse from **13** find not
  guilty, judge innocent

absolved 5 freed **6** exempt,
  spared **7** cleared, excused
  8 forgiven, pardoned, released,
  relieved **9** acquitted **10** discharged, exonerated, vindicated **13** found innocent

absorb 3 fix **5** rivet **6** arrest,
  digest, engage, enwrap, ingest,
  occupy, soak up, suck up,
  take up **7** consume, drink in,
  engross, immerse **8** sponge
  up **9** fascinate, preoccupy,
  swallow up **10** assimilate
  11 incorporate

absorbed 4 deep **8** immersed,
  involved, soaked up, sucked
  up **9** blotted up, engrossed

absorbent 6 porous, spongy
  7 osmotic, thirsty **8** bibulous,
  pervious **9** permeable **10** ab-
  sorptive, penetrable **12** assimi-
  lative

absorbing 8 engaging, exciting **9** thrilling **10** engrossing,
  intriguing **11** captivating, fascinating, interesting

abstain 5 avoid, forgo **6** desist,

eschew, refuse, resist **7** decline, forbear, refrain

abstainer 3 dry **7** ascetic
  10 nondrinker, self-denier, teetotaler

abstemious 3 dry **5** sober
  7 ascetic, austere, sparing,
  spartan **8** teetotal **9** abstinent,
  continent, temperate **10** forbearing **11** abstentious,
  self-denying, straitlaced,
  teetotaling **12** nonindulgent
  15 self-disciplined

abstention 7 refusal **8** eschewal **9** avoidance, desisting, eschewing **10** abstaining,
  refraining, resistance **11** forbearance, holding back
  13 nonindulgence **14** denying
  oneself **16** nonparticipation

abstinence 8 chastity, sobriety **10** abstention, continence,
  discipline, self-denial, temperance **11** forbearance, self-
  control **13** nonindulgence, self-
  restraint

abstinent 3 dry **5** sober
  6 chaste **8** celibate, virginal
  9 continent **10** abstemious,
  forbearing

abstract 4 take **5** brief **6** arcane, digest, precis, remote,
  remove, resume, subtle
  7 abridge, extract, general, isolate, obscure, outline, summary, take out **8** abstruse,
  compress, condense, esoteric,
  profound, separate, synopsis,
  withdraw **9** imaginary, recondite, summarize, synopsize,
  theoretic, unapplied, visionary **10** abridgment, conceptual,
  dissociate, indefinite, intangible **11** generalized, impractical,
  nonspecific, theoretical
  12 condensation, hypothetical,
  intellectual **14** recapitulation

abstruse 4 deep **6** arcane, remote, subtle **7** complex, obscure **8** abstract, esoteric,
  profound, puzzling **9** enigmatic, recondite **10** perplexing **11** complicated
  12 unfathomable **16** incomprehensible

absurd 4 wild **5** crazy, funny,
  inane, kooky, silly **6** screwy,
  stupid **7** asinine, comical, foolish, idiotic **8** farcical **9** illogical, laughable, ludicrous,
  senseless **10** irrational, ridiculous **11** nonsensical **12** preposterous, unreasonable

absurdity 6 drivel, idiocy
  7 fallacy, inanity **8** delusion,
  nonsense **9** asininity, falsehood, silliness **10** buffoonery
  11 comicalness, foolishness

13 irrationality 14 ridiculousness 15 unbelievability 16 unreasonableness

Absyrtus *see* 8 Apsyrtus

Abu Dhabi
capital of: 18 United Arab Emirates

Abuja
capital of: 7 Nigeria

abundance 4 glut, heap 5 flood 6 bounty, excess, plenty, wealth 7 surfeit, surplus 8 plethora, richness 9 plenitude, profusion, repletion 10 cornucopia 11 copiousness, full measure, sufficiency

abundant 4 rich, rife 5 ample 6 enough, galore, lavish, plenty 7 copious, profuse, replete, teeming 8 brimming, prolific 9 abounding, bounteous, bountiful, luxuriant 10 sufficient

ab urbe condita 24 from the founding of the city

abuse 4 harm, hurt, slur 5 curse, scold 6 berate, carp at, defame, deride, ill-use, injure, injury, insult, malign, misuse, rail at, revile, tirade, vilify 7 assault, bawl out, beating, carping, censure, cruelty, cursing, exploit, harming, insults, railing, slander, torment, upbraid 8 badmouth, belittle, berating, denounce, derision, diatribe, ill-treat, maltreat, mistreat, reproach, ridicule, scolding, sneering, torments 9 castigate, criticism, criticize, denigrate, disparage, excoriate, invective 10 belittling, defamation, impose upon, imposition, oppression, speak ill of, upbraiding 11 castigation 12 exploitation, maltreatment, mistreatment, vilification 13 disparagement, misemployment, tongue-lashing 14 inveigh against, misapplication 15 take advantage of

abusive 4 rude, vile 5 cruel, gross, harsh 7 harmful, hurtful, obscene 8 critical, improper, reviling, scornful 9 injurious, insulting, maligning, offensive, vilifying 10 censorious, defamatory, derogatory, scurrilous, slanderous 11 acrimonious, castigating, deprecatory, disparaging, foulmouthed 12 vituperative

abusive word 5 curse 6 insult 7 epithet 9 blasphemy, expletive, invective, obscenity

abut 4 join, meet 5 touch 6 adjoin, border

abutment 4 prop, stay 5 brace, union 7 contact, meeting, support 8 buttress, junction, shoulder, touching 9 adjacency

abutting 6 next to 7 joining, meeting 8 adjacent, touching 9 bordering 10 contiguous, juxtaposed 12 conterminous

abysmal 4 deep, vast 7 endless, extreme, immense 8 complete, enormous, profound, thorough, unending 9 boundless 10 bottomless, incredible, stupendous 12 unfathomable, unbelievable, unimaginable

abyss 4 gulf, void 5 depth, gorge, gully, nadir 7 fissure 8 crevasse 9 vast chasm 13 bottomless pit

Abyssinia *see* 8 Ethiopia

Acacallis
father: 5 Minos
mother: 8 Pasiphae
son: 11 Amphithemis

acacia
family: 6 legume 11 leguminosae
also called: 5 thorn 6 mimosa, wattle

academic 4 moot 6 remote, school 7 bookish, erudite, general, learned 8 abstract, educated, pedantic, studious 9 scholarly 10 collegiate, scholastic, university 11 conjectural, educational, liberal-arts, presumptive, speculative, theoretical 12 hypothetical, ivory-towered, nontechnical, not practical 13 nonvocational, suppositional 14 nonspecialized 18 college-preparatory

Academus
origin: 8 Arcadian
owned: 6 estate
located in: 6 Athens
served as meeting place for: 12 philosophers

Academy Award *see box*

Acanthopolis
type: 8 dinosaur 10 ornithopod

Acastus
member of: 9 Argonauts
father: 6 Pelias
mother: 10 Phylomache
sister: 8 Alcestis
wife: 8 Cretheis
daughter: 7 Sterope 8 Laodemia, Sthenele

Acawai, Akawai
language family: 7 Cariban
location: 7 Guianas 12 South America

Accad
kingdom of: 6 Nimrod

location: 13 Plain of Shinar
captured by: 6 Sargon (I)

Acca Larentia
form: 7 goddess
corresponds to: 6 Dea Dia

accede 5 admit, grant 6 accept, permit 7 abide by, agree to, approve, concede, defer to, endorse, inherit, yield to 8 assent to, submit to 9 acquiesce, conform to, consent to, succeed to 10 comply with, concur with 11 acknowledge, subscribe to, surrender to

accede to the throne
4 keep 5 claim, usurp 6 ascend 7 possess, succeed 8 take over 9 be crowned 15 ascend the throne

accelerando
music: 15 becoming quicker

accelerate 4 rush, spur 5 hurry, impel 6 hasten, step up 7 advance, augment, further, promote, quicken, speed up 8 expedite 9 intensify 10 facilitate, to go faster 11 pick up speed, precipitate

accelerator 3 gas 4 goad, prod, spur 8 gas pedal 13 encouragement

accent 4 hint, tone 5 drawl, touch, twang 6 detail, stress 7 feature 8 emphasis, ornament, tonality, trimming 9 adornment, emphasize, highlight, punctuate, spotlight, underline 10 accentuate, inflection, intonation, modulation, underscore 11 enunciation 12 articulation 13 embellishment, primary stress, pronunciation

accentuate 6 accent, stress 7 feature, point up 9 emphasize, punctuate, underline 10 underscore

accentuation 6 accent, stress 8 emphasis

accept 3 buy 4 avow, bear 5 admit 6 assume 7 agree to, fall for, swallow 8 accede to, assent to 9 consent to, undertake 11 acknowledge, go along with

acceptable 4 fair, good, so-so 6 proper, worthy 8 adequate, passable, suitable 9 agreeable, allowable, tolerable 10 admissible 12 satisfactory

acceptable person
Latin: 12 persona grata

acceptance 6 belief, taking 7 consent, receipt 8 approval, sanction 9 accepting, agreement, receiving, reception 10 concession, permission

7

Academy Award
also called: 5 Oscar
1927-28:
actor: 12 Emil Jannings
actress: 11 Janet Gaynor
director: 12 Frank Borzage 14 Lewis Milestone
picture: 5 Wings
1928-29:
actor: 12 Warner Baxter
actress: 12 Mary Pickford
director: 10 Frank Lloyd
picture: 14 Broadway Melody
1929-30:
actor: 12 George Arliss
actress: 12 Norma Shearer
director: 14 Lewis Milestone
picture: 25 All Quiet on the Western Front
1930-31:
actor: 15 Lionel Barrymore
actress: 13 Marie Dressler
director: 12 Norman Taurog
picture: 8 Cimarron
1931-32:
actor: 12 Fredric March
actress: 10 Helen Hayes
director: 12 Frank Borzage
picture: 10 Grand Hotel
1932-33:
actor: 15 Charles Laughton
actress: 16 Katharine Hepburn
director: 10 Frank Lloyd
picture: 9 Cavalcade
1934:
actor: 10 Clark Gable
actress: 16 Claudette Colbert
director: 10 Frank Capra
picture: 18 It Happened One Night
1935:
actor: 14 Victor McLaglen
actress: 10 Bette Davis
director: 8 John Ford
picture: 17 Mutiny on the Bounty
1936:
actor: 8 Paul Muni
actress: 11 Luise Rainer
director: 10 Frank Capra
picture: 16 The Great Ziegfeld
1937:
actor: 12 Spencer Tracy
actress: 11 Luise Rainer
director: 10 Leo McCarey
picture: 15 Life of Emile Zola
1938:
actor: 12 Spencer Tracy
actress: 10 Bette Davis
director: 10 Frank Capra
picture: 20 You Can't Take It with You

1939:
actor: 11 Robert Donat
actress: 11 Vivien Leigh
director: 13 Victor Fleming
picture: 15 Gone with the Wind
1940:
actor: 12 James Stewart
actress: 12 Ginger Rogers
director: 8 John Ford
picture: 7 Rebecca
1941:
actor: 10 Gary Cooper
actress: 12 Joan Fontaine
director: 8 John Ford
picture: 19 How Green Was My Valley
1942:
actor: 11 James Cagney
actress: 11 Greer Garson
director: 12 William Wyler
picture: 10 Mrs Miniver
1943:
actor: 9 Paul Lukas
actress: 13 Jennifer Jones
director: 13 Michael Curtiz
picture: 10 Casablanca
1944:
actor: 10 Bing Crosby
actress: 13 Ingrid Bergman
director: 10 Leo McCarey
picture: 10 Going My Way
1945:
actor: 10 Ray Milland
actress: 12 Joan Crawford
director: 11 Billy Wilder
picture: 14 The Lost Weekend
1946:
actor: 12 Fredric March
actress: 17 Olivia de Havilland
director: 12 William Wyler
picture: 22 The Best Years of Our Lives
1947:
actor: 12 Ronald Colman
actress: 12 Loretta Young
director: 9 Elia Kazan
picture: 19 Gentleman's Agreement
1948:
actor: 15 Laurence Olivier
actress: 9 Jane Wyman
director: 10 John Huston
picture: 6 Hamlet
1949:
actor: 17 Broderick Crawford
actress: 17 Olivia de Havilland
director: 17 Joseph L Mankiewicz
picture: 14 All the King's Men
1950:
actor: 10 Jose Ferrer
actress: 12 Judy Holliday
director: 17 Joseph L Mankiewicz
picture: 11 All About Eve

1951:
actor: 14 Humphrey Bogart
actress: 11 Vivien Leigh
director: 13 George Stevens
picture: 17 An American in Paris
1952:
actor: 10 Gary Cooper
actress: 12 Shirley Booth
director: 8 John Ford
picture: 19 Greatest Show on Earth
1953:
actor: 13 William Holden
actress: 13 Audrey Hepburn
director: 13 Fred Zinnemann
picture: 18 From Here to Eternity
1954:
actor: 12 Marlon Brando
actress: 10 Grace Kelly
director: 9 Elia Kazan
picture: 15 On the Waterfront
1955:
actor: 14 Ernest Borgnine
actress: 11 Anna Magnani
director: 11 Delbert Mann
picture: 5 Marty
1956:
actor: 10 Yul Brynner
actress: 13 Ingrid Bergman
director: 13 George Stevens
picture: 26 Around the World in Eighty Days
1957:
actor: 12 Alec Guinness
actress: 14 Joanne Woodward
director: 9 David Lean
picture: 23 The Bridge on the River Kwai
1958:
actor: 10 David Niven
actress: 12 Susan Hayward
director: 16 Vincente Minnelli
picture: 4 Gigi
1959:
actor: 14 Charlton Heston
actress: 14 Simone Signoret
director: 12 William Wyler
picture: 6 Ben-Hur
1960:
actor: 13 Burt Lancaster
actress: 15 Elizabeth Taylor
director: 11 Billy Wilder
picture: 12 The Apartment
1961:
actor: 16 Maximilian Schell
actress: 11 Sophia Loren
director: 10 Robert Wise 13 Jerome Robbins
picture: 13 West Side Story

(continued)

Academy Award (*continued*)

1962:
actor: 11 Gregory Peck
actress: 12 Anne Bancroft
director: 9 David Lean
picture: 16 Lawrence of Arabia

1963:
actor: 13 Sidney Poitier
actress: 12 Patricia Neal
director: 14 Tony Richardson
picture: 8 Tom Jones

1964:
actor: 11 Rex Harrison
actress: 12 Julie Andrews
director: 11 George Cukor
picture: 10 My Fair Lady

1965:
actor: 9 Lee Marvin
actress: 13 Julie Christie
director: 10 Robert Wise
picture: 15 The Sound of Music

1966:
actor: 12 Paul Scofield
actress: 15 Elizabeth Taylor
director: 13 Fred Zinnemann
picture: 17 A Man for All Seasons

1967:
actor: 10 Rod Steiger
actress: 16 Katharine Hepburn
director: 11 Mike Nichols
picture: 19 In the Heat of the Night

1968:
actor: 14 Cliff Robertson
actress: 15 Barbra Streisand 16 Katharine Hepburn
director: 12 Sir Carol Reed
picture: 6 Oliver!

1969:
actor: 9 John Wayne
actress: 11 Maggie Smith
director: 15 John Schlesinger
picture: 14 Midnight Cowboy

1970:
actor: 12 George C Scott
actress: 13 Glenda Jackson
director: 17 Franklin Schaffner
picture: 6 Patton

1971:
actor: 11 Gene Hackman
actress: 9 Jane Fonda
director: 15 William Friedkin
picture: 19 The French Connection

1972:
actor: 12 Marlon Brando
actress: 11 Liza Minnelli
director: 8 Bob Fosse
picture: 12 The Godfather

1973:
actor: 10 Jack Lemmon
actress: 13 Glenda Jackson
director: 13 George Roy Hill
picture: 8 The Sting

1974:
actor: 9 Art Carney
actress: 12 Ellen Burstyn
director: 18 Francis Ford Coppola
picture: 12 The Godfather (Part II)

1975:
actor: 13 Jack Nicholson
actress: 14 Louise Fletcher
director: 11 Milos Forman
picture: 25 One Flew Over the Cuckoo's Nest

1976:
actor: 10 Peter Finch
actress: 11 Faye Dunaway
director: 13 John G Avildsen
picture: 5 Rocky

1977:
actor: 15 Richard Dreyfuss
actress: 11 Diane Keaton
director: 10 Woody Allen
picture: 9 Annie Hall

1978:
actor: 9 Jon Voight
actress: 9 Jane Fonda
director: 13 Michael Cimino
picture: 13 The Deer Hunter

1979:
actor: 13 Dustin Hoffman
actress: 10 Sally Field
director: 12 Robert Benton
picture: 14 Kramer vs Kramer

1980:
actor: 12 Robert De Niro
actress: 11 Sissy Spacek
director: 13 Robert Redford
picture: 14 Ordinary People

1981:
actor: 10 Henry Fonda
actress: 16 Katharine Hepburn
director: 12 Warren Beatty
picture: 14 Chariots of Fire

1982:
actor: 11 Ben Kingsley
actress: 11 Meryl Streep
director: 19 Richard Attenborough
picture: 6 Gandhi

1983:
actor: 12 Robert Duvall
actress: 15 Shirley MacLaine
director: 12 James L Brooks
picture: 17 Terms of Endearment

1984:
actor: 14 F Murray Abraham
actress: 10 Sally Field
director: 11 Milos Forman
picture: 7 Amadeus

1985:
actor: 11 William Hurt
actress: 13 Geraldine Page
director: 13 Sydney Pollack
picture: 11 Out of Africa

1986:
actor: 10 Paul Newman
actress: 12 Marlee Matlin
director: 11 Oliver Stone
picture: 7 Platoon

1987:
actor: 14 Michael Douglas
actress: 4 Cher
director: 18 Bernardo Bertolucci
picture: 14 The Last Emperor

1988:
actor: 13 Dustin Hoffman
actress: 11 Jodie Foster
director: 13 Barry Levinson
picture: 7 Rain Man

1989:
actor: 14 Daniel Day-Lewis
actress: 12 Jessica Tandy
director: 11 Oliver Stone
picture: 16 Driving Miss Daisy

1990:
actor: 11 Jeremy Irons
actress: 10 Kathy Bates
director: 12 Kevin Costner
picture: 16 Dances With Wolves

1991:
actor: 14 Anthony Hopkins
actress: 11 Jodie Foster
director: 13 Jonathan Demme
picture: 20 The Silence of the Lambs

1992:
actor: 8 Al Pacino
actress: 12 Emma Thompson
director: 13 Clint Eastwood
picture: 10 Unforgiven

1993:
actor: 8 Tom Hanks
actress: 11 Holly Hunter
director: 15 Steven Spielberg
picture: 14 Schindler's List

1994:
actor: 8 Tom Hanks
actress: 12 Jessica Lange
director: 14 Robert Zemeckis
picture: 11 Forrest Gump

1995:
actor: 11 Nicolas Cage
actress: 13 Susan Sarandon
director: 9 Mel Gibson
picture: 10 Braveheart

1996:
actor: 12 Geoffrey Rush
actress: 16 Frances McDormand
director: 16 Anthony Minghella
picture: 17 The English Patient

accepted 5 usual **6** common, normal **7** regular **8** approved, standard **9** confirmed, customary, universal **10** acceptable, agreed upon **11** established, time-honored **12** acknowledged, conventional

access 3 way **4** path, road **5** entry **6** avenue, course, entree **7** gateway, passage **8** entrance **10** admittance, an approach, passageway

accessible 5 handy, ready **6** at hand, nearby, on hand **8** possible **9** available, reachable **10** attainable, obtainable

accession 7 seizure **9** induction **10** arrogation, assumption, investment, taking over, usurpation **11** inheritance **12** inauguration, installation

accessory 4 plus **6** accent, cohort, detail **7** adjunct, partner **8** addition **9** adornment, assistant, associate, auxiliary, colleague, component, extension **10** accomplice, attachment, complement, decoration, supplement **11** confederate, contributor **13** accompaniment

accident 4 fate, luck **5** crash, fluke, wreck **6** chance, mishap **7** smashup **8** fortuity **9** collision, mischance **10** misfortune **11** good fortune, serendipity **12** happenstance, misadventure

accidental 6 chance, random **9** haphazard, unplanned, unwitting **10** fortuitous, incidental, unexpected, unforeseen

acclaim 4 hail, laud **5** cheer, exalt, extol, honor, kudos **6** bravos, praise, salute **7** applaud, commend, ovation **8** applause, cheering, eulogize, plaudits **9** celebrate, rejoicing **10** compliment, enthusiasm **11** acclamation, endorsement

acclamation 6 cheers, homage **7** acclaim, hurrahs, ovation, tribute **8** cheering, hosannas, plaudits **9** adulation **10** salutation **11** approbation

acclimate 5 adapt, inure **6** adjust **8** accustom **9** get used to, habituate, reconcile **11** accommodate **16** become seasoned to

acclimation 9 seasoning **10** adaptation, adjustment **11** habituation

acclimatize 5 adapt **6** attune **8** accustom **9** acclimate, get used to

acclivity 4 hill, rise **6** ascent **9** elevation **11** upward slope

accolade 5 award, honor, prize **6** praise, trophy **7** acclaim, tribute **8** citation **10** admiration, compliment, decoration **11** recognition, testimonial **12** commendation

accommodate 3 aid, fit **4** help, hold **5** adapt, board, house, lodge, put up **6** adjust, assist, billet, modify, oblige, supply **7** bed down, conform, contain, furnish, provide, quarter, shelter **8** accustom **9** acclimate, entertain, get used to, harmonize, lend a hand, reconcile

accommodating 4 kind **6** polite **7** helpful **8** gracious, obliging, yielding **9** courteous **10** hospitable, neighborly **11** considerate **12** conciliatory

accommodation 5 rooms **7** concord, housing **8** lodgings, quarters **9** agreement **10** adjustment, compromise, settlement **12** arrangements **14** reconciliation

accommodative 8 friendly **9** appeasing, pacifying, placatory **10** mollifying **11** peacemaking, reconciling **12** conciliatory

accompaniment 6 escort **7** support **8** ornament **9** accessory, adornment **10** incidental

accompany 5 guard, usher **6** attend, back up, convoy, escort, follow **7** conduct, support **8** chaperon

accomplice 4 aide, ally **5** crony **6** cohort, helper, stooge **7** abettor, comrade, partner **8** henchman, sidekick **9** accessory, assistant, associate, colleague, supporter **11** confederate, participant, subordinate **12** collaborator **13** co-conspirator **14** partner-in-crime

accomplish 2 do **6** attain, finish **7** achieve, execute, fulfill, get done, perform, produce, realize **8** carry out, complete, expedite, knock off **9** succeed at **10** bring about

accomplished 3 apt **4** able, deft, fine **6** adroit, expert, gifted, proved, proven **7** capable, eminent, skilled **8** accepted, effected, existing, finished, masterly, polished, realized, seasoned, skillful, talented **9** brilliant, completed, concluded, practiced, qualified **10** cultivated, proficient **11** consummated, established, experienced, well-trained

accomplishment 3 act **4** deed, feat, gift **5** skill **6** talent

7 exploit, success, triumph, victory **9** execution **10** attainment, capability **11** achievement, carrying out, culmination, fulfillment, proficiency, realization, tour de force **12** consummation

accord 4 cede, give, jibe **5** agree, allow, award, grant, match, tally **6** bestow, concur, render, square, tender, unison **7** concede, concert, conform, harmony, present, rapport **8** be in tune, bequeath, sympathy **9** agreement, harmonize, unanimity, vouchsafe **10** accordance, be in unison, comply with, conformity, consonance, correspond, uniformity

accordant 4 like **7** similar **8** parallel **10** consistent **11** homogeneous

accordingly 2 so **4** ergo, then, thus **5** hence **6** thence, whence **8** suitably **9** as a result, therefore, wherefore, whereupon **11** conformably, in due course, in which case **12** consequently **15** correspondingly

accost 3 nab **4** hail, halt, stop **5** greet **6** call to, salute, waylay **7** address, solicit **8** approach, confront **10** buttonhole **11** proposition

accouchement 10 childbirth **11** confinement

account 3 use **4** deem, hold, note, rank, rate, sake, tale **5** basis, books, cause, count, gauge, honor, judge, merit, score, story, think, value, weigh, worth **6** esteem, import, reason, reckon, record, regard, report, repute, view as **7** believe, clarify, dignity, explain, grounds, history, justify, recital, version **8** appraise, consider, estimate, megillah, standing **9** calculate, chronicle, narration, narrative, statement **10** accounting, commentary, illuminate, importance

accountable 6 guilty, liable **7** at fault, to blame **8** beholden, culpable **9** obligated **10** answerable, chargeable **11** blameworthy, responsible

accountant 3 CPA **7** actuary, auditor **10** bookkeeper **25** certified public accountant

account for 6 excuse **7** explain, justify **9** answer for

accounting 5 cause **6** answer, motive, reason **7** warrant **10** motivation **11** explanation

account rendered
French: 11 compte rendu

accoutrements 4 gear 7 apparel 8 supplies 9 equipment, trappings 11 accessories, furnishings 13 paraphernalia

Accra, Akkra
capital of: 5 Ghana

accredit 6 assign, credit 7 ascribe, certify, empower, endorse, license 8 sanction 9 attribute, authorize, guarantee 10 commission 19 officially recognize 22 furnish with credentials

accredited 8 ascribed, assigned, endorsed, licensed 9 authentic, certified, empowered 10 attributed, authorized, recognized, sanctioned 12 commissioned 20 officially recognized

accretion 4 rise 6 growth 7 accrual 8 addition, increase 9 expansion, extension, increment 10 supplement 11 enlargement 12 accumulation, augmentation 13 amplification

accrue 4 grow 5 add up, amass 6 pile up 7 build up, collect 8 increase 10 accumulate

accumulate 4 grow 5 amass, hoard 6 accrue, garner, gather, heap up, pile up, save up 7 collect, store up 8 assemble, cumulate 9 aggregate 10 congregate 14 gather together

accumulation 4 heap, mass, pile 5 hoard, stack, stock, store 6 pile-up, supply 7 accrual 8 amassing, hoarding 9 acquiring, gathering, stockpile 10 assemblage, collecting, collection 11 aggregation 13 agglomerating 14 conglomeration

accuracy 5 truth 6 verity 8 fidelity 9 exactness, precision 10 exactitude 11 correctness 12 accurateness, faithfulness

accurate 4 true 5 exact, right 7 careful, correct, perfect, precise 8 faithful, truthful, unerring 9 authentic, faultless 10 meticulous, scrupulous 11 punctilious 12 without error

accursed 4 base, foul, vile 6 cussed, horrid, odious 7 hellish 8 damnable, horrible, infamous 9 abhorrent, atrocious, execrable, loathsome, revolting 10 abominable, despicable, detestable, disgusting 12 contemptible

accusation 6 charge 8 citation

9 complaint 10 allegation, imputation, indictment 11 insinuation 13 incrimination

accuse 4 cite 5 blame 6 charge, indict 7 arraign, upbraid 8 reproach 10 take to task 13 call to account 22 lodge a complaint against

accuser 8 attacker 11 complainant 13 finger pointer

accustomed 3 set 5 fixed, prone, trite, usual 6 cliche, common, inured, normal, used to, wonted 7 general, given to, regular, routine 8 everyday, expected, familiar, habitual, hardened, ordinary, seasoned 9 customary, hackneyed, ingrained, prevalent, well-known 10 acclimated, habituated, prevailing 11 commonplace, established 12 conventional, familiarized

ace 2 A-1 3 top 4 star 5 crack, super 6 expert, master, tip-top, victor, winner 8 champion, medalist, terrific, top-rated 9 excellent, first-rate, headliner 10 first-class 11 crackerjack, outstanding 12 frontranking

Aceldama
means: 12 field of blood
purchased by: 5 Judas

Acerbas *see* 8 Sychaeus

acerbity 7 acidity, sarcasm 8 acridity, acrimony, pungency, sourness, tartness 9 nastiness, sharpness 10 bitterness 11 astringency, brusqueness 12 irascibility

aces 2 A-1 4 fine, tops 5 great, prime, super 6 grade-A, superb, tip-top 8 peerless, superior, terrific, top-notch 9 excellent, first-rate, marvelous, matchless, superfine, wonderful 10 first-class, tremendous 11 outstanding, superlative 13 extraordinary

Acesius
epithet of: 6 Apollo
means: 6 healer

Acessamenus
origin: 8 Thracian
mentioned in: 5 Iliad
form: 4 king

Acetes
origin: 6 Lydian
duty: 8 helmsman
protected: 8 Dionysus

Achaeus
founder of: 6 Achaea
father: 6 Xuthus
mother: 6 Creusa
brother: 3 Ion

Achan
punishment: 13 stoned to death

Acharnians
author: 12 Aristophanes
character: 7 Demigod 8 Lamachus 11 Dikaiopolis

Achates
mentioned in: 6 Aeneid
companion of: 6 Aeneas
position: 11 armorbearer

ache 4 hurt, need, pain, pang, want 5 covet, crave, mourn, smart, throb, yearn 6 be sore, desire, grieve, hanker, hunger, lament, sorrow, suffer, twinge 7 agonize, long for 8 soreness 10 discomfort

Achech
origin: 8 Egyptian
form: 8 creature
body of: 4 lion
wings of: 4 bird

Achelous
form: 3 god
habitat: 5 river
father: 7 Oceanus
mother: 6 Tethys
daughter: 6 Sirens 8 Castalia 10 Callirrhoe
defeated by: 8 Hercules
struggled over: 8 Deianira

Acheron
river in: 5 Hades
ferryman: 6 Charon
carries: 4 dead

Acheson, Dean
author of: 20 Present at the Creation

a cheval 7 by horse 11 on horseback

achieve 2 do 3 get, win 4 earn, gain 5 reach 6 attain, effect, finish, obtain 7 acquire, fulfill, procure, realize 8 arrive at, carry out, complete, dispatch 9 succeed in 10 accomplish, bring about, effectuate 11 bring to pass

achievement 3 act 4 coup, deed, fear 5 skill 6 effort 7 command, exploit, mastery 9 expertise 10 attainment 11 acquirement, fulfillment, realization, tour de force 14 accomplishment

achieve recognition 6 arrive, make it 7 succeed 8 make good 10 be somebody 11 reach the top

Achilles
mentioned in: 5 Iliad
father: 6 Peleus
mother: 6 Thetis
foster father: 7 Phoenix
grandfather: 6 Aeacus
teacher: 6 Chiron

charioteer: 9 Automedon
friend: 9 Patroclus
warrior in: 9 Trojan War
vulnerability: 4 heel
killed: 6 Hector
killed by: 5 Paris

Achish
king of: 4 Gath
gave refuge to: 5 David

Achomawi
language family: 5 Hokan
location: 8 Pit River **10** California **12** Shasta County
related to: 8 Atsugewi

Achsah
father: 5 Caleb
grandfather: 9 Jephunneh
husband: 7 Othniel

acid 4 sour, tart **5** acrid, harsh, nasty, sharp **6** biting, bitter, ironic **7** acerbic, caustic, crabbed, cutting, pungent **8** scalding, scathing, stinging, vinegary **9** acidulous, irascible, sarcastic, satirical, vitriolic **10** astringent, vinegarish **11** acrimonious

acidity 8 acerbity, pungency, sourness, tartness **9** sharpness **10** bitterness **11** astringency **13** nonalkalinity

Acis
lover: 7 Galatea
killed by: 10 Polyphemus

Acis and Galatea
opera by: 6 Handel

Acis et Galatee
opera by: 5 Lully

acknowledge 3 own **5** admit, allow, grant, yield **6** accede, accept, answer, assent, concur **7** concede, confess, own up to, reply to **8** call upon, thank for **9** recognize, respond to

acknowledged 7 acceded **8** accepted, admitted, answered, called on, conceded **9** replied to **10** agreed upon, called upon, recognized, thanked for **11** established, responded to

acknowledgment 5 reply **6** answer, credit, thanks **8** response **9** admission, gratitude **10** concession, confession **11** affirmation, recognition **12** appreciation, recognizance

acme 4 apex, peak **5** crest, crown **6** apogee, climax, height, heyday, summit, zenith **8** pinnacle **9** flowering, high point **11** culmination **12** highest point
Latin: 11 ne plus ultra

Acmon
companion: 8 Diomedes
changed into: 4 bird
defied: 9 Aphrodite

acolyte 3 fan **6** helper, novice **7** admirer, devotee, groupie **8** adherent, altar boy, follower **9** assistant, attendant

Acoma
language family: 6 Pueblo
location: 3 Ako **4** Acus **8** Valencia **9** New Mexico
noted for: 7 pottery

acorn
from: 3 oak
shape: 8 balanoid

a couvert 9 sheltered **10** under cover

acquaint 4 meet, tell **6** advise, inform, notify, reveal **7** apprise **8** disclose **9** divulge to, enlighten, introduce, make aware **11** familiarize

acquaintance 8 dealings **9** awareness, knowledge **10** cognizance, friendship **11** association, conversance, familiarity **12** relationship

acquiesce 5 admit, agree, allow, bow to, grant, yield **6** accede, assent, comply, concur, give in, submit **7** concede, conform, consent **10** capitulate, fall in with **13** resign oneself **16** reconcile oneself

acquiescence 5 leave **7** consent **8** approval, giving in, sanction **10** permission, submission **11** concurrence

acquiescent 7 willing **8** amenable, yielding **9** agreeable **10** submissive

acquire 3 get, win **4** earn, gain **6** attain, obtain, pick up, secure **7** achieve, capture, procure, realize **9** cultivate

acquirement 4 gain **5** prize **7** earning **10** attainment, obtainment, possession **11** achievement, acquisition, procurement

acquisition 4 gain **5** prize **8** property, purchase **10** attainment, obtainment, possession **11** achievement, acquirement, procurement

acquisitive 6 greedy **7** selfish **8** covetous, grasping **10** avaricious, possessive **13** materialistic

acquit 3 act **5** clear **6** behave, excuse, exempt, let off, pardon **7** absolve, comport, conduct, deliver, release, relieve, set free **8** liberate, reprieve

9 discharge, exculpate, exonerate, vindicate

Acraea
epithet of: 9 Aphrodite
means: 6 height

acre
one-fourth: 4 rood
one-half: 3 erf **5** erven
two-thirds: 5 cover
ten: 6 decare **7** furlong
one hundred: 7 hectare
one hundred twenty: 4 hide

Acres, Bob
character in: 9 The Rivals
author: 8 Sheridan

acrid 4 acid **5** harsh, nasty, sharp **6** biting, bitter, ironic, smelly **7** burning, caustic, pungent **8** stinging **9** sarcastic, satirical, vitriolic **10** irritating, malodorous **11** acrimonious **12** foul-smelling

acrimonious 4 sour **5** nasty, testy **6** bitchy, biting, bitter **7** caustic, cutting, peevish **8** venomous, spiteful **9** corrosive, irascible, rancorous, sarcastic, splenetic, vitriolic **10** ill-natured

acrimony 5 anger, scorn, spite **6** animus, rancor, spleen **7** ill will **8** asperity, derision **9** animosity, hostility, malignity **10** antagonism, bitterness, malignancy **12** hard feelings, spitefulness

Acrisius
king of: 5 Argos
father: 4 Abas
mother: 6 Aglaia
twin brother: 7 Proetus
daughter: 5 Danae
grandson: 7 Perseus
killed by: 7 Perseus

acrophobia
fear of: 7 heights

acrostic 6 cipher, puzzle **7** acronym

act 2 do **3** bit, gig, law **4** bill, deed, do it, fake, feat, move, play, pose, show, skit, step, work **5** edict, enact, feign, front, order, put-on **6** action, affect, behave, decree, stance **7** execute, exploit, go about, mandate, measure, operate, perform, portray, posture, press on, routine, statute **8** carry out, function, pretense, put forth, simulate **9** enactment, ordinance, represent **10** pretension, resolution **11** achievement, affectation, counterfeit, impersonate, legislation, performance, pretend to be **14** accomplishment

Actaeon
form: 6 hunter
father: 9 Aristaeus
mother: 7 Autonoe
changed into: 4 stag
transformed by: 5 Diana
killed by: 6 hounds
killed at: 9 Gargaphia

acting 5 drama 6 deputy, ersatz, pro tem 7 interim, theater 8 the stage 9 dramatics, simulated, surrogate, temporary 10 dramaturgy, stagecraft, substitute, the theater 11 dramatic art, officiating, provisional, thespianism 12 stage playing

actinium
chemical symbol: 2 Ac

action 3 act 4 deed, feat, move, step, suit, work 5 force, power 6 battle, combat, effect, effort, motion 7 exploit, process, warfare 8 activity, conflict, endeavor, exertion, fighting, movement, progress 9 adventure, execution, influence, operation 10 enterprise, excitement, performing, production 11 achievement, functioning, performance, prosecution 14 accomplishment

Actis
father: 6 Helius
mother: 5 Rhoda
crime: 10 fratricide
taught: 9 astrology
fled to: 5 Egypt
memorial: 16 Colossus of Rhodes

activate 4 stir 5 drive, impel, start 6 prompt, propel, turn on 7 actuate 8 energize, mobilize, motivate, vitalize 9 stimulate

activated 5 drive 7 started 8 impelled, in action, in effect, turned on 9 effective, energized, mobilized, operative, vitalized 10 stimulated 11 in operation

active 4 busy, spry 5 agile, alert, alive, peppy, quick 6 acting, at work, frisky, lively, nimble 7 engaged, in force, on the go, working, zealous 8 animated, diligent, forceful, occupied, spirited, vigorous 9 ambitious, assertive, effectual, energetic, go-getting, operative, sprightly, strenuous 10 aggressive, productive 11 functioning, imaginative, industrious 12 enterprising 13 indefatigable

active person 4 doer 6 dynamo 7 hustler 8 activist, go-getter

activist 4 doer 6 zealot 7 apos-tle 8 advocate, exponent 9 proponent, supporter

activity 4 fuss, stir 6 action, bustle, flurry, hustle, tumult 7 project, pursuit, venture 8 endeavor, exercise, exertion, function, goings on, movement, vivacity 9 agitation, animation, avocation, commotion 10 assignment, enterprise, hurly-burly, liveliness, occupation 11 undertaking 13 sprightliness

act of the faith
Spanish: 8 auto da fe, auto de fe

act of war 4 raid 6 attack, strike 7 assault, offense 8 invasion 10 aggression, hostile act

actor 3 ham 4 doer, star 6 player, walk on 7 starlet, trouper 8 thespian 9 bit player, performer 11 functionary, participant, perpetrator 14 dramatic artist 15 supporting actor
type: 4 hero 7 feature, leading 9 character 10 supporting

Actor
king of: 6 Phthia
father: 8 Myrmidon
mother: 8 Pasidice
brother: 6 Augeas
son: 7 Cteatus, Eurytus

actual 4 real, sure, true 7 certain, current, factual, genuine, present 8 bona fide, concrete, existent, existing, physical, tangible 9 authentic, confirmed, corporeal 10 legitimate, prevailing, true-to-life, verifiable

actuality 4 fact, life 5 being, truth 6 effect, living, verity 7 reality 8 existing 9 existence, plain fact, substance 10 brutal fact 11 point of fact

actually 5 truly 6 indeed, in fact, really, verily 9 genuinely, literally
Latin: 7 ex facto

actually existing
Latin: 6 in esse 7 de facto

actuary 5 clerk 9 tabulator 12 statistician

actuate 4 move, stir 5 cause, drive, impel, rouse 6 arouse, excite, incite, induce, prompt 7 animate, inspire, trigger 8 activate, motivate 9 influence, instigate, stimulate 10 bring about

acumen 6 wisdom 7 insight 8 keenness, sagacity 9 acuteness, ingenuity, smartness 10 astuteness, cleverness, per-ception, shrewdness 11 discernment 12 intelligence, perspicacity 13 sound judgment 15 clearheadedness

acute 4 keen 5 sharp 6 clever, fierce, peaked, severe 7 intense, very bad 8 critical, piercing, powerful 9 agonizing, ingenious, intuitive, sensitive, very great 10 discerning, perceptive 11 distressing, penetrating 12 excruciating, needle-shaped 14 discriminating

acuteness 6 acumen 8 keenness 9 sharpness, smartness 10 astuteness, cleverness, shrewdness

acute suffering 5 agony 7 anguish, torment, torture 8 distress

adage 3 saw 4 quip, wise 5 axiom, maxim, motto 6 cliche, dictum, old saw, saying, truism 7 epigram, precept, proverb 8 aphorism 9 platitude 11 observation

adagio
music: 4 slow

Adah
also: 9 Bashemath
husband: 4 Esau 6 Lamech
son: 5 Jabal, Jubal 7 Eliphaz

Adam
wife: 3 Eve
son: 4 Abel, Cain, Seth
home: 4 Eden
grandson: 4 Enas 5 Enoch

adamant 3 set 4 firm 5 fixed, rigid, tough 7 uptight 8 obdurate, resolute, stubborn 9 immovable, insistent, unbending 10 determined, hard as rock, inexorable, inflexible, unyielding 12 intransigent 14 uncompromising

Adamas
ally of: 7 Trojans
plotted against: 10 Antilochus
thwarted by: 8 Poseidon

Adamawa-Eastern
language family: 16 Niger-Kordofanian
group: 10 Niger-Congo
includes: 5 Sango, Zande

Adam Bede
author: 11 George Eliot
character: 8 Seth Bede 11 Dinah Morris, Hetty Sorrel 12 Martin Poyser 17 Arthur Donnithorne

Adams, Henry
author of: 6 Esther 9 Democracy 14 Chapters of Erie 24 History of the United States (Under the Jefferson and Adams Administration), The Education of Henry Ad-

ams **26** Mont-Saint Michel and Chartres **34** The Degradation of the Democratic Dogma

Adams, John *see box*

Adams, John Quincy *see box, p. 14*

Adams, Parson
character in: **13** Joseph Andrews
author: **8** Fielding

Adams, Richard
author of: **4** Maia **7** Shardik **12** Girl in a Swing **13** The Plague Dogs, Watership Down

Adam's Rib
director: **11** George Cukor
script by: **10** Ruth Gordon **11** Garson Kanin
cast: **8** Tom Ewell **9** Jean Hagen **10** David Wayne **12** Judy Holliday, Spencer Tracy **16** Katharine Hepburn

Adapa
origin: **8** Akkadian
form: **4** sage
forfeits: **4** food **5** water **11** immortality
offered by: **3** Anu
patron: **2** Ea

adapt 3 fit **4** suit **5** alter,

frame, shape **6** adjust, change, modify, rework **7** conform, convert, fashion, make fit, remodel, reshape **8** attune to **9** acclimate, harmonize, recompose, reconcile, transform **10** assimilate, coordinate **11** accommodate, acculturate **12** make suitable

adaptable 6 pliant, usable **7** unrigid **8** amenable, flexible, obliging **9** alterable, compliant, easygoing, malleable, tractable **10** adjustable, applicable, changeable, open-minded **11** conformable, serviceable **13** accommodating, accommodative

adaptation 5 shift **6** change **8** revision **9** refitting, reshaping, reworking **10** adjustment, alteration, conversion, remodeling **12** modification **13** metamorphosis

Adar 18 twelfth Hebrew month

add 4 join **5** affix, sum up, total **6** append, attach, join on, reckon, tack on **7** combine, compute, count up, enlarge, include **8** figure up, increase **9** calculate, enlarge by **10** increase by, supplement

Addams, Frankie
character in: **19** A Member of the Wedding
author: **15** Carson McCullers

Addams Family, The
character: **5** Gomez, Lurch **7** Pugsley **8** Morticia **9** Grandmama, Wednesday **11** Uncle Fester
cast: **9** John Astin **10** Lisa Loring, Ted Cassidy **11** Blossom Rock **12** Carolyn Jones, Jackie Coogan **13** Ken Weatherwax

add details 6 expand **7** clarify **9** elaborate, embellish **13** particularize

added 5 extra **6** joined **7** totaled **8** appended, attached, computed, included, joined on, reckoned, summed up, tacked on **9** counted up **10** additional, enlarged by, enumerated **11** increased by **13** supplementary

addendum 7 codicil **8** addition **9** appendage **10** attachment, postscript, supplement **12** afterthought

addict 3 fan, nut **4** buff, head, hook, user **5** freak, hound **6** junkie, submit, turn on, votary **7** acolyte, devotee, druggie, habitue **8** adherent **9** dope fiend, indulge in, surrender

addiction 5 craze, mania, quirk **6** fetish, hangup **8** fixation **9** cocainism, obsession **10** alcoholism, compulsion, dipsomania, morphinism **11** barbiturism, enslavement **12** addictedness, enthrallment **13** preoccupation

adding machine
invented by: **6** Pascal **9** Burroughs

Addis Ababa
capital of: **8** Ethiopia

Addison, Joseph
author of: **4** Cato **9** The Tatler **12** The Spectator **13** The Freeholder
co-author: **13** Richard Steele

addition 4 wing **5** annex, extra **6** adding **7** adjunct, joining **8** addendum, additive, annexing, increase, totaling **9** adjoining, appendage, appending, attaching, embracing, expansion, extending, extension, including, increment, reckoning, summation, summing up **10** counting up, increasing **11** enlargement, enumeration **12** appurtenance, augmentation, encompassing

additional 5 added, extra, spare **7** added on **8** appended

---

Adams, John
nickname: **19** Atlas of Independence
presidential rank: **6** second
party: **10** Federalist
state represented: **2** MA
defeated: **9** Jefferson
vice president: **9** Jefferson
cabinet:
  state: **8** (John) Marshall **9** (Timothy) Pickering
  treasury: **6** (Samuel) Dexter **7** (Oliver) Wolcott
  war: **6** (Samuel) Dexter **7** (James) McHenry
  attorney general: **3** (Charles) Lee
  navy: **8** (Benjamin) Stoddert
born: **2** MA **9** Braintree
  town now called: **6** Quincy
died/buried: **6** Quincy
education: **7** Harvard
religion: **9** Unitarian
author: **18** Discourses on Davila **20** Thoughts on Government
political career: **13** vice president **24** First Continental Congress **25** Second Continental Congress
  minister: **11** Netherlands **12** Great Britain
civilian career: **6** lawyer
notable events of lifetime/term: **9** XYZ Affair
  act: **9** Judiciary **16** Alien and Sedition
father: **4** John
mother: **7** Susanna (Boylston)
siblings: **5** Elihu **13** Peter Boylston
wife: **7** Abigail (Smith)
children: **7** Charles, Susanna **10** John Quincy (6th president) **13** Abigail Amelia **14** Thomas Boylston

Adams, John Quincy
  nickname: **14** Old Man Eloquent
  presidential rank: **5** sixth
  party: **4** Whig **10** Federalist **20** Democratic-Republican
  state represented: **2** MA
  defeated: **4** (Henry) Clay **7** (Andrew) Jackson **8** (William H) Crawford
  vice president: **7** (John C) Calhoun
  cabinet:
    state: **4** (Henry) Clay
    treasury: **4** (Richard) Rush
    war: **6** (Peter Buell) Porter **7** (James) Barbour
    attorney general: **4** (William) Wirt
    navy: **8** (Samuel Lewis) Southard
  born: **2** MA **9** Braintree
    town now called: **6** Quincy
  died: **2** DC **10** Washington
  buried: **2** MA **6** Quincy
  education:
    studied in: **5** Paris **9** Amsterdam **11** Latin School
    University of: **6** Leyden
    College: **7** Harvard
  religion: **9** Unitarian
  author: **7** Memoirs **14** Eulogy to Monroe, The Adams Papers **17** Eulogy to Lafayette **18** Letters from Silesia
  political career: **8** US Senate **19** Massachusetts Senate **24** US House of Representatives
    secretary of: **5** state
    minister: **6** Russia **7** Prussia **8** Portugal **11** Netherlands **12** Great Britain
  civilian career: **6** lawyer
  notable events of lifetime/term: **19** Pan-American Congress **20** Tariff of Abominations
  father: **4** John
  mother: **7** Abigail (Smith)
  siblings: **7** Abigail, Charles, Susanna **14** Thomas Boylston
  wife: **6** Louisa (Catherine Johnson)
  children: **4** John **14** Charles Francis **15** Louisa Catherine **16** George Washington

12 over-and-above **13** supplementary

additional feature 5 extra **7** adjunct **10** attachment, complement, supplement **12** appurtenance **13** accompaniment

additive 5 extra **8** addition **10** adulterant, supplement **12** augmentation, preservative

addle 5 mix up **6** muddle **7** confuse, nonplus, stupefy **8** befuddle

addled 5 silly **7** foolish, mixed-up, muddled **8** confused **9** befuddled, nonplused **10** nonplussed

add on 5 affix **6** append, attach, tack on **7** include **10** increase by

address 4 talk **5** greet, orate **6** salute, speech, talk to **7** lecture, oration, speak to, write to **8** dwelling, locality, location **9** discourse, statement

Address to the Deil
  author: **11** Robert Burns

add to 6 expand, extend, pad out **7** amplify, augment, bolster, enlarge **8** compound, increase, lengthen **10** strengthen, stretch out, supplement

Ade, George
  author of: **13** Fables in Slang **15** The College Widow **17** The County Chairman

Aden
  capital of: **10** South Yemen

adept 3 apt **4** able, good **6** adroit, expert, gifted, master **7** skilled **8** skillful **9** dexterous, ingenious, masterful, practiced **10** proficient **12** accomplished

adequacy 7 fitness **11** sufficiency **16** satisfactoriness

adequate 3 fit **4** so-so **5** ample **6** enough **7** fitting **8** passa-ble, suitable **9** tolerable **10** sufficient **12** satisfactory

a deux 6 for two **10** two at a time

ad extremum 6 at last **7** finally **12** to the extreme

ad fin 8 at the end **12** toward the end

adhere 3 fix **4** glue, hold, keep **5** cling, paste, stick **6** be true, cement, cleave, fasten, glue on, keep to **7** abide by, be loyal, stand by **8** maintain **9** stick fast **10** be constant, be faithful

adherence 6 fealty **7** loyalty **8** adhesion, devotion, fidelity **9** constancy, keeping to, obedience **10** allegiance, attachment, observance, stickiness **12** adhesiveness, faithfulness

adherent 3 fan **4** ally **5** gummy, pupil **6** sticky, viscid **7** acolyte, devotee, viscous **8** adhering, adhesive, advocate, champion, clinging, disciple, follower, partisan, sticking, upholder **9** supporter

adhesion 9 adherence **10** attachment, sticking to

adhesive 4 glue **5** epoxy, gummy, paste **6** cement, gummed, mortar, solder, sticky **7** stickum **8** adherent, adhering, clinging, sticking **12** mucilaginous, rubber cement

ad hoc 17 with respect to this **18** for this purpose only

ad hominem 8 to the man **17** against an opponent **20** appealing to prejudice

adieu 4 by-by, ciao, ta-ta **5** adios, aloha **6** bye-bye, goodby, so long **7** a demain, cheerio, goodbye, good day **8** a bientot, au revoir, farewell, godspeed, toodle-oo **10** take it easy **11** leavetaking, see you later, valediction **14** Auf Wiedersehen

ad infinitum 9 endlessly **10** infinitely, to infinity, unendingly **11** boundlessly, ceaselessly, limitlessly, unceasingly **12** continuously, interminably, without limit

ad initium 14 at the beginning

ad interim 13 in the meantime

adios 4 by-by, ciao, ta-ta **5** adieu, aloha **6** bye-bye, goodby, so long **7** a demain, cheerio, goodbye, good day **8** a bientot, au revoir, fare-

well, godspeed, toodle-oo
10 take it easy 11 leavetaking,
see you later, valediction
14 Auf Wiedersehen

adjacency 5 union 7 contact,
meeting 8 abutment, junction,
touching 11 proximation
13 juxtaposition

adjacent 6 beside, next to
8 abutting, touching 9 bordering, proximate 10 contiguous,
juxtaposed, next door to, tan-
gential 12 conterminous

adjoining 6 joined 7 joining
8 next-door, touching 9 connected 10 contiguous 14 interconnected

adjourn 3 end 4 move 5 close
6 put off, recess, remove, repair 7 dismiss, suspend 8 break
off, dissolve, postpone, withdraw 9 depart for, interrupt
11 discontinue

adjournment 6 recess 7 removal 8 abeyance 9 dismissal
10 suspension 12 postponement

adjudge 4 rule 5 judge 6 decide, decree, ordain, rule on,
settle, umpire 7 referee 8 consider 9 arbitrate, determine,
pronounce 10 adjudicate

adjudicate 4 rule 5 judge
6 settle 7 adjudge 9 arbitrate

adjunct 9 accessory, auxiliary,
secondary 10 complement, incidental, subsidiary, supplement 12 appurtenance

adjuration 4 oath, plea, suit
6 appeal 8 advising, entreaty
12 supplication

adjure 3 beg 5 plead 6 charge,
enjoin, exhort 7 beseech, command, entreat, implore, solicit 8 appeal to, petition
9 importune 10 supplicate

adjust 3 fix, set 4 move
5 adapt, alter, order 6 attune,
change, modify 7 conform
8 accustom, regulate 9 acclimate, reconcile 11 accommodate

adjustable 7 movable 9 adaptable, alterable 11 rectifiable,
regulatable 12 controllable

adjusting 8 adapting, altering
9 modifying 10 regulating
11 acclimating, controlling

adjusting device 5 lever, tun-
er, valve 6 handle 7 adapter
8 governor 9 modulator, regulator 11 control knob

adjustment 6 fixing 7 control,
setting 8 adapting, focusing
9 adjusting, alignment, regula-

tor 10 alteration, regulating,
regulation, settlement, settling
in 11 acclimation, orientation
12 modification 13 justification, rectification, straightening 14 reconciliation

adjutant 4 aide 9 assistant,
right hand 10 aide-de-camp
12 right-hand man

ad-lib 6 make up 9 improvise
11 extemporize 13 improvisa-
tion 14 speak impromptu
15 speak off the cuff 21 speak
extemporaneously 23 extemporaneous wisecrack

ad loc, ad locum 10 at the
place, to the place

Admah
    destroyed with: 5 Sodom
    6 Zeboim 8 Gomorrah

ad majorem Dei gloriam
    23 for the greater glory of
    God

Admete
    father: 10 Eurystheus
    received: 12 golden girdle
        belonged to: 4 Ares
        received from: 8 Hercules
        stolen from: 9 Hippolyte

Admeto, Re di Tessaglia
    also: 21 Admetus King of
    Thessaly
    opera by: 6 Handel

Admetus
    king of: 8 Thessaly
    member of: 9 Argonauts
    father: 6 Pheres
    wife: 8 Alcestis

administer 3 run 4 boss, give
5 apply 6 direct, govern, manage, tender 7 oversee 8 dispense 9 supervise 11 preside
over, superintend 12 administrate

administering 7 bossing, running, tending 8 managing
9 directing, executing 10 dispensing, governance, overseeing 11 carrying out,
supervising, supervision
14 administration, superintending

administrate 3 run 6 direct,
govern, manage 9 supervise
10 administer 11 superintend

administration 5 brass 8 officers 9 execution, governing,
tendering 10 executives, government, leadership, management, overseeing
11 application 12 dispensation,
distribution 13 administering,
governing body 15 superintendence

administrative 9 executive
10 management, managerial

11 supervisory 14 organizational

administrative head 7 manager 8 chairman, director
9 executive, president 10 supervisor 13 administrator
14 superintendent

admirable 6 worthy 8 laudable 9 estimable, venerable
11 commendable 12 praise-
worthy

Admirable Crichton, The
    author: 12 James M Barrie

admiration 5 honor 6 esteem,
praise 7 respect 8 approval
10 high regard, veneration
11 high opinion 12 commendation

admire 5 prize, value 6 esteem,
praise 7 respect

admirer 3 fan 5 swain 6 suitor,
votary 7 acolyte, devotee
8 adherent, advocate, champion, disciple, follower, partisan 9 attendant 10 aficionado

admissible 7 allowed 8 passable 9 allowable, permitted, tolerable, tolerated 10 acceptable,
admittable, legitimate 11 permissible

admission 3 fee 5 entry 6 access, assent, charge, entree,
tariff, ticket 8 entrance 10 admittance, concession, confession, profession 11 affirmation,
declaration, entrance fee
14 acknowledgment

admit 3 let 5 allow, grant, let
in, own up 6 induct, invest,
permit 7 support, concede,
confess, declare, profess, receive, welcome 8 let enter
11 acknowledge

admittable 7 allowed 9 allowable, permitted, tolerable, tolerated 10 acceptable,
admissible 11 permissible

admittance 5 entry 6 access,
entree 7 ingress 8 entrance
9 admission

admixture 4 mess 5 blend
6 jumble, medley 7 amalgam,
melange, mixture 8 compound,
mishmash 9 composite, confusion, potpourri 10 commixture, hodgepodge, salmagundi
11 combination, commingling,
gallimaufry 12 amalgamation,
intermixture 13 intermingling
14 conglomeration

admonish 4 warn 5 chide,
scold 6 advise, enjoin, rebuke,
tip off 7 caution, censure,
chasten, counsel, reprove, upbraid 8 reproach 9 criticize,
reprimand 10 put on guard,

take to task **11** remonstrate **13** call to account **16** rap on the knuckles

admonition 6 advice, rebuke **7** chiding, warning **8** reproach, scolding **9** reprimand **11** mild reproof **12** remonstrance **16** rap on the knuckles

admonitor 7 advisor **9** counselor **10** admonisher

Adnah
  deserted from: 4 Saul
  deserted to: 5 David
  fought against:
    10 Amalekites
  commander for:
    10 Jehosaphat

ado 4 fuss, stir, to-do **5** furor **6** bother, bustle, flurry, fracas, furore, hubbub, pother, racket, tumult, uproar **7** flutter, trouble, turmoil **9** agitation, commotion, confusion **10** hurlyburly

adobe 3 mud **4** clay, silt, tile **5** brick, marly **6** earthy **7** clayish **13** sun-dried brick

adolescence 5 teens, youth **7** puberty **10** pubescence

adolescent 3 lad **4** lass, teen **5** minor, youth **6** boyish, callow, lassie **7** babyish, girlish, puerile **8** childish, immature, juvenile, teenager, young man, youthful **9** fledgling, pubescent, schoolboy, stripling, young teen **10** schoolgirl, sophomoric, young woman **11** undeveloped

Adolf Hitler 9 der Fuhrer **10** der Fuehrer

Adonai 3 God **6** my Lord

Adonia
  event: 8 festival
  honors: 6 Adonis

Adonijah
  father: 5 David
  mother: 7 Haggith
  brother: 5 Amnon **7** Absalom, Chileab
  executed by: 7 Solomon
  conspired to overthrow:
    5 David

Adonis
  represents: 15 vegetation cycle
  father: 7 Cinyras
  mother: 6 Myrrha, Smyrna
  favorite of: 9 Aphrodite
  killed by: 4 boar
  festival in honor of:
    6 Adonia

adopt 3 use **4** take **6** accept, affect, assume, choose, employ, follow, take up **7** approve, embrace, espouse, utilize **9** con-

form to **11** acknowledge, appropriate

adorable 6 divine **7** darling, likable, lovable, winsome **8** charming, engaging, fetching, pleasing, precious **9** appealing **10** delightful **11** captivating **12** irresistible

adoration 5 honor **7** worship **8** devotion **9** adulation, reverence **10** exaltation, veneration, worshiping **11** idolization **13** glorification, magnification

adore 4 like, love **5** exalt, fancy, prize **6** admire, dote on, revere **7** cherish, glorify, idolize, worship **8** hold dear, venerate

adorer 3 fan **5** lover **7** admirer **8** follower **9** worshiper

adorn 5 array **6** bedeck **7** bejewel, deck out, furbish **8** beautify, decorate, ornament **9** embellish

adornment 6 attire, finery **7** jewelry **8** ornament **10** decoration **13** embellishment, ornamentation

ad patres 4 dead

Adrammelech 13 Sepharvite god
  father: 11 Sennacherib
  killed: 11 Sennacherib

Adrastea
  also: 7 Nemesis
  origin: 5 Greek
  goddess of: 17 divine retribution
  father: 9 Melisseus
  reared: 4 Zeus
  entrusted by: 4 Rhea

Adrastos see **8** Adrastus

Adrastus
  also: 8 Adrastos
  king of: 5 Argos
  son: 8 Aegialus
  leader of: 18 Seven against Thebes
  companions: 6 Tydeus **8** Capaneus **9** Polynices **10** Amphiaraus, Hippomedon **13** Parthenopaeus
  horse: 5 Arion

ad rem 9 pertinent **15** straightforward **17** without digression

Adrian, Edgar Douglas
  field: 8 medicine **10** physiology
  nationality: 7 British
  discovered function of:
    10 nerve cells
  awarded: 10 Nobel Prize

Adriana
  character in: 17 The Comedy of Errors
  author: 11 Shakespeare

adrift 4 lost **5** at sea **6** afloat, aweigh **8** confused, drifting, unmoored, unstable **9** perplexed, uncertain, unsettled **10** bewildered, irresolute, unanchored

adroit 3 apt **4** deft **5** slick **6** artful, clever, expert, facile, nimble **7** cunning, skilled **8** skillful **9** dexterous, masterful **10** proficient

adroitness 7 aptness **8** deftness, facility **9** dexterity, handiness **10** cleverness **11** proficiency **12** skillfulness
  French: 11 savoir-faire

adulation 7 fawning **8** flattery **9** adoration **11** fulsomeness **13** fulsome praise

adulatory 7 fulsome **8** admiring **10** flattering **13** complimentary

adult 3 big, man **5** elder, of age, woman **6** father, granny, mature, mother, parent, senior **7** grandma, grandpa, grownup, oldster **8** seasoned **9** developed, full-grown **11** experienced, grandfather, grandmother **13** senior citizen

adulterate 3 cut **4** thin **5** water **9** water down **10** depreciate **11** contaminate

adulterated 3 cut **6** impure, watery **7** debased, diluted, thinned, watered **8** doctored, weakened **11** watered down

adultery 9 carnality, cuckoldry **10** unchastity **11** fornication, promiscuity **14** unfaithfulness **17** marital infidelity **18** illicit intercourse **21** extramarital relations

adulthood 8 maturity, ripeness **10** full growth **11** age of reason

adumbrate 3 dim **6** darken, sketch **7** obscure, outline **8** intimate **9** prefigure **10** foreshadow, overshadow

adumbrated 3 dim **5** murky **7** shadowy **8** darkened **9** intimated **10** indistinct, prefigured **12** foreshadowed, overshadowed

advance 3 pre **4** gain, pass, step **5** add to, offer, prior **6** assign, binder, growth, move up, pay now, propel, send up **7** bring up, forward, further, improve, in front, lay down, press on, proffer, promote, upgrade, up front **8** foremost, increase, multiply, overture, previous, progress **9** go forward, promotion **10** furthering, move onward, prepayment, put up front

11 advancement, down payment, improvement, preliminary, proposition
12 breakthrough, bring forward, pay on account

advanced 7 extreme, far gone, radical **10** avant-guard **12** farther along, further along **14** industrialized

advanced in years 3 old **4** aged **5** hoary, older **7** ancient, antique, elderly **8** outmoded **9** senescent, venerable **10** antiquated, gray-haired

advancement 4 rise **5** boost **9** bettering, elevation, promotion **10** betterment, forwarding **11** improvement, progression

Advancement of Learning
   author: **12** Francis Bacon

advance slowly 4 inch **5** crawl, creep

advantage 3 aid **4** boon, edge, help **5** asset, clout **6** profit **7** benefit, comfort, service, success, support **8** blessing **9** dominance, upper hand **10** precedence **11** convenience, superiority

advantageous 6 useful **7** helpful **8** enviable, superior, valuable **9** favorable, fortunate **10** auspicious, beneficial, dominating, profitable

advent 5 onset, start **6** coming **7** arrival **9** appearing, beginning, emergence, opening up **10** appearance, occurrence **12** commencement

adventitious 5 alien **6** exotic **7** foreign, strange **9** adventive, extrinsic **10** accidental

adventure 5 quest **7** emprise, venture **8** escapade **10** enterprise **11** undertaking

adventurer 4 hero **7** heroine **8** romantic, vagabond **9** buccaneer, daredevil **11** giant-killer **12** dragonslayer, swashbuckler **16** soldier of fortune

Adventures of Robin Hood, The
   director: **13** Michael Curtiz **15** William Keighley
   cast: **8** Alan Hale (Little John) **10** Errol Flynn (Robin Hood) **11** Claude Rains (Prince John) **13** Basil Rathbone **17** Olivia de Havilland (Lady Marion)
   Oscar for: **5** score (Erich Wolfgang Korngold)

Adventures of Sherlock Holmes
   author: **16** (Sir) Arthur Conan Doyle

   character: **9** Mrs Hudson **10** Irene Adler **12** Dr John Watson **13** Mycroft Holmes **14** Sherlock Holmes **17** Inspector Lestrade, Professor Moriarty **21** Baker Street Irregulars

adventuresome 4 bold **6** daring **9** audacious, daredevil **11** adventurous

adventurous 4 bold **5** brave, risky **6** daring **7** valiant **8** intrepid, perilous **9** audacious, dangerous, hazardous **10** courageous **11** challenging, venturesome

adventurousness 6 daring **8** audacity, boldness **11** intrepidity

ad verbum 8 verbatim **9** to the word

adversary 3 foe **5** enemy, rival **8** opponent **10** antagonist, competitor

adverse 7 harmful, hostile **8** contrary, inimical, negative, opposing **9** difficult, injurious **10** pernicious, unfriendly **11** detrimental, unfavorable **12** antagonistic, unpropitious

adversity 3 woe **5** trial **6** mishap **7** bad luck, trouble **8** calamity, disaster, distress, hardship **9** suffering **10** affliction, ill-fortune, misfortune **11** catastrophe, tribulation

advertise 4 show, tout **5** vaunt **6** reveal **7** display **8** proclaim **9** broadcast, publicize **11** noise abroad

advertisement 5 blurb, flier, pitch, promo **6** notice, poster, want ad **7** leaflet, placard, trailer **8** circular, handbill **9** billboard, broadside, throwaway **10** commercial **12** announcement, classified ad, public notice

advice 4 news, view, word **6** report **7** account, counsel, message, opinion, tidings **8** guidance **10** advisement, suggestion **11** information **12** intelligence, notification **13** communication **14** recommendation

advisable 3 fit **4** best, wise **5** smart, sound **6** proper, seemly **7** fitting, prudent **8** a good bet, suitable **9** expedient, judicious **13** recommendable

advise 4 tell, urge, warn **6** enjoin, exhort, inform, notify, report **7** apprise, caution, commend, counsel, suggest **8** admonish **9** encourage, make known, recommend, suggest

to **10** give notice **11** communicate

advise against 8 dissuade **10** discourage, disincline

advisement 5 study **7** thought **12** deliberation **13** consideration

adviser, advisor 4 aide **5** coach, guide, tutor **6** mentor **7** monitor, teacher **8** director **9** admonitor, assistant, counselor, preceptor, surrogate **10** consultant, idea person, instructor

advisory 7 guiding, warning **10** admonitory, cautionary, counseling **11** informative, instructive **12** consultative, consultatory **13** informational

advisory board 7 cabinet, council **8** ministry

advocaat
   type: **7** liqueur
   origin: **7** Holland

advocacy 5 aegis **7** backing, defense, support **8** auspices, espousal **9** patronage, promotion **10** furthering, supporting **11** advancement, endorsement, pressing for, propagation, sponsorship **12** championship **14** campaigning for, recommendation

advocate 4 back, urge **5** favor **6** advise, backer, lawyer, patron **7** advance, apostle, counsel, endorse, espouse, further, pleader, promote, propose, push for, support **8** argue for, attorney, believer, champion, defender, press for, promoter, upholder **9** apologist, barrister, counselor, encourage, prescribe, propagate, proponent, recommend, solicitor, spokesman, supporter **10** mouthpiece, stand up for **11** campaign for, speak out for **12** legal adviser, propagandist, spokesperson **13** attorney-at-law

advocatus diaboli 14 devil's advocate

adz 2 ax **3** axe **5** addis **7** hatchet

Aeacides
   descendants of: **6** Aeacus

Aeacus
   form: **5** judge
   habitat: **5** Hades
   father: **4** Zeus
   mother: **6** Aegina
   brother: **12** Rhadamanthys
   wife: **6** Endeis
   son: **6** Peleus, Phocus **7** Telamon
   grandson: **8** Achilles

Aechmagoras
  father: **8** Hercules
  mother: **6** Phialo

Aedon
  father: **9** Pandareus
  sister: **8** Chelidon
  husband: **11** Polytechnus
  transformed into:
    11 nightingale
  transformed by: **4** Zeus

Aeetes
  king of: **7** Colchis
  custodian of: **12** Golden
    Fleece
  father: **6** Helios
  mother: **5** Perse
  sister: **5** Circe **8** Pasiphae
  wife: **5** Idyia **9** Asterodea
  son: **8** Absyrtus, Apsyrtus
  daughter: **5** Medea
    9 Chalciope

Aegaeon *see* **8** Briareus

Aegean Sea
  branch of: **13** Mediterranean
  islands: **5** Chios, Crete, Sa-
    mos **6** Euboea, Lesbos,
    Rhodes **8** Cyclades **10** Dode-
    canese **16** Northern Sporades
  rivers into: **6** Struma, Var-
    dar **7** Maritsa **8** Menderes
  surrounding countries:
    6 Greece, Turkey

Aegeon
  character in: **17** The Comedy
    of Errors
  author: **11** Shakespeare

Aegeria *see* **6** Egeria

Aegesta *see* **6** Egesta

Aegeus
  king of: **6** Athens
  son: **6** Medeus **7** Theseus

Aegialeus
  father: **8** Adrastus
  killed by: **8** Laodamas

Aegicores
  father: **3** Ion

Aegimius
  king of: **5** Doris **7** Dorians
  father: **5** Dorus
  son: **5** Dymas **9** Pamphylus

Aegina
  father: **6** Asopus
  mother: **6** Metope
  son: **6** Aeacus
  abducted by: **4** Zeus

Aeginaea
  epithet of: **7** Artemis
  means: **11** goat goddess

Aegiochus
  epithet of: **4** Zeus
  means: **11** aegis bearer

Aegipan
  form: **3** god **4** goat
  related to: **3** Pan

Aegir
  origin: **6** Nordic
  form: **5** giant
  god of: **3** sea
  wife: **3** Ran

aegis **4** wing **5** favor, guard
  6 surety **7** backing, shelter,
  support **8** advocacy, auspices,
  guaranty **9** patronage **10** protection **11** sponsorship
  12 championship, guardianship

Aegis
  form: **6** shield
  shield of: **4** Zeus **6** Athena

Aegisthus
  father: **8** Thyestes
  mother: **7** Pelopia
  cousin: **9** Agamemnon
  daughter: **7** Erigone
  seduced: **12** Clytemnestra
  killed by: **7** Orestes

Aegle
  member of: **8** Heliades
    10 Hesperides
  mother of: **6** Graces

Aegyptus
  king of: **5** Egypt
  father: **5** Belus
  twin brother: **6** Danaus
  number of sons: **5** fifty

Aella
  form: **6** Amazon
  gift: **9** swiftness
  killed by: **8** Hercules

Aello
  member of: **7** Harpies

aelurophobia
  fear of: **4** cats

Aemilia
  character in: **17** The Comedy
    of Errors
  author: **11** Shakespeare

Aeneas
  hero of: **4** Troy
  father: **8** Anchises
  mother: **5** Venus
  grandfather: **5** Capys
  son: **5** Iulus **7** Silvius
    8 Ascanius
  ancestor of: **6** Romans

Aeneas Silvius
  king of: **9** Alba Longa

Aeneid
  author: **6** Virgil
  character: **4** Gyas **5** Amata,
    Dares, Nisus **6** Arruns, Iar-
    bas, Lausus, Pallas, Salius,
    Turnus **7** Acestes, Allecto,
    Camilla, Celaeno, Drances,
    Evander, Harpies, Helenus,
    Juturna, Latinus, Lavinia,
    Tarchon, Trojans, Venulus,
    Virbius **8** Ascanius, Entellus,
    Euryalus, Messapus **9** Cloan-
    thus, Mezentius, Mnestheus,

Palinurus, Sergestus **10** An-
    dromache **12** Cumaean Sibyl
    gods: **4** Juno **5** Diana, Ve-
    nus **6** Vulcan **7** Jupiter,
    Neptune
    Queen of Carthage:
      4 Dido
    Aeneas' father: **8** Anchises
    Aeneas' mother:
      9 Aphrodite
    Aeneas' wife: **6** Creusa
    Aeneas' son: **5** Iulus
    *Aeneas meets in under-
      world:* **6** Charon **8** Cer-
      berus **9** Palinurus
  parts of the underworld:
    7 Elysium **8** Tartarus **9** Ivory
    Gate
    river: **4** Styx **5** Lethe
    Aeneas plucks: **11** Golden
      Bough
    Aeneas visits: **5** Crete, Delos
      6 Latium, Sicily, Thrace
      8 Carthage

Aenius
  ally of: **4** Troy
  killed by: **8** Achilles

Aeolides
  descendants of: **6** Aeolus

Aeolus
  ruler of: **5** winds
  founder of: **8** Aeolians
  father: **6** Hellen
  mother: **6** Orseis
  brother: **5** Dorus **6** Xuthus
  wife: **7** Enarete
  son: **5** Deion **6** Magnes
    7 Athamas, Misenus **8** Cre-
    theus, Macareus, Perieres,
    Sisyphus **9** Salmoneus
  daughter: **6** Calyce, Canace
    7 Alcyone **8** Cleobule, Per-
    imede, Pisidice

aerate **3** air **9** ventilate **10** mix
  with air **11** expose to air

aerial **3** air **4** airy **5** by air,
  lofty **6** dreamy, flying, unreal
  7 antenna, elusive, soaring,
  tenuous **8** airborne, ethereal,
  fanciful, in the air **9** ephemeral, imaginary, visionary
  10 by aircraft, from the air, of
  aircraft **11** atmospheric, impractical, wind-created **13** unsubstantial **15** capable of flight

aerobatic group **10** Blue
  Angels

aeronautics **6** flight, flying
  8 aviation

Aerope
  father: **7** Catreus, Cerheus
  husband: **6** Atreus
    10 Plisthenes
  sister: **9** Clymene
  son: **8** Menelaus
    9 Agamemnon

aerophobia
  fear of: **6** flying

aeroplane 5 plane 8 aircraft, airplane

Aesacus
 father: 5 Priam
 lover: 8 Hesperia

Aeschylus
 author of: 8 Oresteia 9 Agamemnon, Choephori (The Libation-bearers), Eumenides 11 The Persians 13 The Suppliants 15 Prometheus Bound 16 The House of Atreus 18 Seven Against Thebes

Aesculapius
 origin: 5 Roman
 god of: 7 healing 8 medicine
 corresponds to: 9 Asclepius

Aesepus
 mother: 9 Abarbarea
 twin brother: 7 Pedasus
 fought in: 9 Trojan War
 killed by: 8 Euryalus

Aesir
 also: 4 Asar
 origin: 12 Scandinavian
 leader: 4 Odin 5 Othin
 home: 6 Asgard
 conflicting with: 5 Vanir

aesthetic see 8 Esthetic

Aesyetes
 son: 7 Antenor

Aethalides
 member of: 9 Argonauts
 father: 6 Hermes
 trait: 6 memory

Aether
 origin: 5 Greek
 personifies: 3 air, sky

Aetheria
 member of: 8 Heliades
 father: 6 Helius
 mother: 7 Clymene

Aethra
 father: 8 Pittheus
 son: 7 Theseus

Aethylla
 brother: 5 Priam

Aetolus
 founder of: 7 Aetolia
 father: 8 Endymion
 brother: 5 Epeus, Paeon
 wife: 6 Pronoe
 son: 7 Calydon, Pleuron
 killed: 8 Laodocus

Afars and the Issas see 8 Djibouti

affability 9 geniality 10 amiability, cordiality 11 sociability 12 friendliness, pleasantness 13 compatibility

affable 4 open, warm 5 civil 6 genial 7 amiable, cordial 8 friendly, gracious, mannerly, pleasant, sociable 9 agreeable, congenial, courteous, easygo-

ing 10 compatible 11 good-humored, good-natured

affair 5 amour, event, party 6 effort, matter 7 concern, episode, liaison, pursuit, romance, shindig 8 activity, business, function, incident, interest, intrigue, occasion 9 adventure, festivity, happening, operation 10 love affair, occurrence, proceeding 11 celebration, transaction, undertaking 12 circumstance, relationship 14 social function 15 social gathering

affaire d'honneur 4 duel 13 affair of honor

affect 4 fake, move, stir 5 act on, adopt, alter, fancy, feign, put on, touch 6 assume, change, modify, regard 7 embrace, concern, imitate, impress 8 interest, relate to, simulate 9 impinge on, influence, pertain to, pretend to 10 tend toward 11 counterfeit

affectation 4 airs, sham 5 put-on 6 facade 8 false air, pretense 10 pretension 11 insincerity 13 artificiality, false mannerism

affected 4 vain 5 moved, phony, sorry, upset 6 harmed, unreal 7 assumed, changed, grieved, injured, pompous, stirred, studied, touched 8 impaired, mannered, troubled 9 acted upon, afflicted, concerned, conceited, contrived, impressed, pertinent, sorrowful, unnatural 10 artificial, distressed, influenced, interested, not genuine 11 pretentious 12 vainglorious

affectedness 4 airs 7 hauteur, tension 9 formality 10 constraint 11 haughtiness, pretensions 12 affectations 15 pretentiousness

affection 4 love 6 liking, malady, warmth 7 ailment, disease, illness 8 disorder, fondness, sickness 10 proclivity, tenderness

affectionate 4 fond, warm 6 ardent, caring, doting, loving, tender 11 warmhearted 13 demonstrative, tenderhearted

affectionate term 7 pet name 8 nickname 9 sobriquet 10 endearment

Affery
 character in: 12 Little Dorrit
 author: 7 Dickens

affettuoso
 music: 8 tenderly

affiance 6 engage, pledge

7 betroth 13 engage to marry 15 solemnly promise

affiancing 5 troth 8 pledging 9 betrothal 10 engagement

affiche 6 poster 12 public notice

affidavit 4 oath 8 document 11 affirmation 14 sworn statement

affiliate 3 arm 4 ally, join, part 5 merge, unite 6 branch 7 chapter, connect, consort 8 division 9 associate, colleague 10 amalgamate, fraternize 11 incorporate, subdivision 12 band together

affiliated 6 allied, joined, united 9 connected 10 associated 12 incorporated

affiliation 5 union 8 alliance 10 connection 11 association 12 relationship

affinity 4 bent 5 fancy 6 liking 7 leaning, rapport 8 fondness, homology, likeness, penchant, relation, sympathy, tendency 10 connection, partiality, proclivity, propensity, similarity 11 inclination, parallelism 13 compatibility

affirm 4 aver, avow, hold 5 claim 6 allege, assert, ratify, uphold 7 approve, confirm, contend, declare, endorse, profess, support, sustain, warrant 8 maintain, proclaim, validate

affirmation 6 avowal 7 consent 8 approval 11 declaration, endorsement 12 confirmation, ratification 13 certification

affirmative 3 yes 8 emphatic, positive 9 affirming, approving, assenting, ratifying 10 conclusive, concurring, confirming 11 affirmatory, categorical 12 confirmatory 13 corroborative

affix 3 fix, tag 4 glue, seal 5 add on, paste, put on, set to, stick 6 attach, fasten, tack on

afflict 5 beset 6 plague 7 oppress, torment 8 distress

afflicted 6 cursed 7 plagued 8 affected, troubled 9 tormented 10 distressed

affliction 4 pain 5 curse, trial 6 misery, ordeal 7 anguish, torment, trouble 8 calamity, distress, hardship 9 adversity 10 misfortune, oppression 11 tribulation 12 wretchedness

affluence 5 money 6 plenty, riches, wealth 7 success 10 prosperity 14 prosperousness, successfulness

affluent 4 rich 6 loaded
7 moneyed, wealthy, well-off
8 well-to-do 9 well-fixed
10 prosperous, well-heeled

afford 4 bear, give, lend, risk
5 grant, offer, yield 6 chance,
impart, manage, supply
7 command, furnish, provide,
support, sustain

affray 4 fray 5 brawl, melee
6 fracas 7 contest, scuffle
8 conflict 9 encounter
11 altercation

affright 4 fear 5 alarm, dread,
panic, scare 6 dismay, fright,
horror, terror 8 frighten

affront 4 slur 5 abuse, wrong
6 injury, insult, offend, slight
7 offense, outrage, provoke,
put-down 8 disgrace, dishonor,
ignominy, rudeness 9 indignity, insolence 11 discourtesy,
humiliation 12 ill-treatment,
impertinence 13 mortification
16 contemptuousness

afghan 5 shawl, throw 7 blanket 8 covering, coverlet

Afghanistan *see box*

aficionado 3 fan, nut 5 freak,
pupil 7 devotee, pursuer, student 8 disciple

afield 5 amiss 6 abroad, astray
10 off the mark 11 out of the
way 16 off the right track

afire 5 fiery 6 ablaze, aflame,
alight, ardent, fervid, fuming,
on fire 7 blazing, burning, fervent, flaming, flaring, glowing,
ignited, smoking, zealous
8 aflicker, in flames, inspired
10 flickering, smoldering

afloat 5 at sea 6 adrift, wafted
7 sailing, wafting 8 drifting,
floating

afoot 5 astir 8 underway 10 in
the works

a fortiori 10 all the more

afraid 5 sorry 6 scared
7 alarmed, anxious, chicken,
fearful, panicky, unhappy
8 cowardly, timorous 9 regretful, terrified 10 apologetic,
frightened 11 lily-livered
12 apprehensive, disappointed,
fainthearted 13 anxiety-ridden,
panic-stricken 14 chicken-
hearted, chicken-livered, terror-stricken

Afreet
also: 5 Afrit
origin: 7 Arabian
form: 5 demon

afresh 4 anew 5 again 11 from
scratch 16 from the beginning
Latin: 6 de novo

Africa *see box*

Africaine, L'
also: 14 The African Girl
opera by: 9 Meyerbeer

African Queen, The
director: 10 John Huston

cast: 12 Robert Morley
14 Humphrey Bogart
16 Katharine Hepburn
setting: 5 Congo
Oscar for: 5 actor (Bogart)

Afrit *see* 6 Afreet

Afghanistan
other name: 6 Ariana, Aryana
capital/largest city: 5 Kabul
others: 3 Rui 4 Jurm, Nani, Wama 5 Asmar, Balkh, Doshi,
Farah, Herat, Kunar, Makur, Maruf, Matun, Pahra,
Tagab, Tulak, Urgan 6 Chaman, Gardez, Ghazni, Haibak,
Kunduz, Nauzad, Panjao, Rustak, Sangan, Sarobi, Tukzar,
Washir 7 Andkhui, Baghlan, Bamiyan, Dilaram, Ghurian,
Girishk 8 Charikar, Faizabad, Kandahar 9 Jalalabad
10 Daulatabad, Pul-i-Khumri, Shibarghan 12 Mazar-i-
Sharif
government:
  parliament: 10 Loya-Jirgah
leader: 4 amir, emir 5 ameer, emeer 6 sharif, sherif
measure: 3 paw, sir 5 jerib, karoh 6 khurds 7 kharwar
monetary unit: 3 pul 5 abaze, riyal, rupee 6 abbasi,
  amania 7 afghani
weight: 3 pau, paw, ser, sir
lake: 13 Hamud-i-Helmand
mountain: 3 Koh 5 Safeo 6 Chagai, Pamirs 7 Nowshak
  8 Koh-i-Baba, Safed Koh, Sulaiman 9 Himalayas, Hindu
  Kush 11 Khwaja Amran, Paropamisus
highest point: 9 Istoro Nal
river: 4 Lora, Oxus 5 Cabul, Indus, Kabul, Kunar 6 Kok-
  cha, Kunduz 7 Hari Rud, Helmand, Helmund, Murghab,
  Taleqan 8 Amu Darya, Farah Rud, Harut Rud, Khash
  Rud 9 Arghandab
sea: 5 Darya
physical feature:
  desert: 8 Registan
  panhandle: 6 Wakhan
  pass: 6 Khyber
  wind: 9 Afghanets
people: 5 Aimak, Aymak, Kafir, Nuris 6 Baloch, Baluch,
  Chahar, Durani, Hasara, Hazara, Kaffir, Kirgiz, Pathan,
  Tajiks, Uzbeks 7 Beluchi, Belucki, Ghilzai, Pakhton, Pakhtun, Pashtun, Pukhtun, Pushtun, Sistani, Taimani, Taimuri 8 Jamshidi, Siah Push 9 Firuzkuhi, Safed Push,
  Safid Push
  dynasty: 8 Barakzai
  leader: 5 Najib 7 Mohmand 10 Najibullah 12 Babrak
    Karmal 14 Hafizullah Amin 17 Mohammad Zahir Shah,
    Mohammed Daoud Khan 18 Burhanuddin Rabbani
    Noor Mohammed Taraki
language: 4 Dari 5 Farsi 6 Afghan, Pashto, Pushtu 7 Balochi, Baluchi, Persian
religion: 5 Islam
place:
  dam: 6 Boghra 7 Kajakai 9 Arghandab
feature:
  clothing: 7 chaderi
  coat: 6 chapan
  dance: 5 attan
  game: 8 buz-kashi
  guest room: 5 hujra
  hat: 7 karakul
  head-cloth: 7 chawdar
  house with tower: 4 qala
  medicinal plant: 9 asafetida
  wrestling: 6 ghosai
food:
  potluck meal: 6 sohbat

Africa
  country: 4 Chad, Mali, Togo **5** Benin, Congo, Egypt, Gabon, Ghana, Kenya, Libya, Niger,
  Sudan, Zaire **6** Angola, Gambia, Guinea, Malawi, Rwanda, Uganda, Zambia **7** Algeria, Burundi, Comoros, Eritrea, Lesotho, Liberia, Morocco, Namibia, Nigeria, Reunion, Senegal, Somalia, Tunisia **8** Botswana, Cameroon, Djibouti, Ethiopia, Tanzania, Zimbabwe **9** Cape Verde,
  The Gambia, Mauritius, Swaziland **10** Ivory Coast, Madagascar, Mauritania, Mozambique,
  Seychelles **11** Burkina Faso, Sierra Leone, South Africa **12** Guinea-Bissau **13** Canary Islands,
  Western Sahara **15** South-West Africa **16** Equatorial Guinea **18** Sao Tome and Principe
  22 Central African Republic
  people: 2 Ga **3** Ibo, Kru, Luo, San, Tiv, Yao **4** Arab, Beja, Bobo, Boer, Fang, Hutu, Kota,
  Kuba, Luba, Nuba, Nuer, Nupe, Teda, Tibu, Zulu **5** Bemba, Dinka, Galla, Hausa, Kamba,
  Makua, Masai, Mende, Mongo, Negro, Pygmy, Rundi, Serer, Shona, Sotho, Swazi, Temne,
  Tigre, Tutsi, Wolof, Xhosa **6** Bateke, Berber, Fulani, Herero, Ibibjo, Kikuyu, Mau Mau, Nubian, Ovambo, Rwanda, Senufo, Sidamo, Somali, Tswana, Tuareg, Yoruba, Watusi **7** Ashanti,
  Baganda, Bambara, Bushmen, Chaamba, Makonde, Mashoma, Ndebele, Nilotic, Oshogbo,
  Songhai, Turkana **8** Khoikhoi, Mangbetu, Matabele **9** Africaner, Hottentot
  desert: 5 Namib **6** Sahara **8** Kalahari
  island: 5 Bioko, Pemba **6** Canary **7** Comoros, Madeira, Mayotte, Reunion **8** St Helena, Zanzibar **9** Ascension, Cape Verde, Mauritius **10** Madagascar, Seychelles
  ancient people/empire: 3 Oyo **4** Kush, Mali, Toro **5** Aksum, Benin, Ghana, Kongo, Mossi,
  Nubia, Wadai **6** Ankole, Tekrur **7** Ashanti, Buganda, Bunyoro, Dahomey, Songhai **8** Baguirmi,
  Carthage **10** Kanem-Bornu, Monomotapa **11** Ife and Benin
  ancient city: 5 Kilwa, Meroe **8** Timbuktu
  language: 4 Afar, Peul, Teda **5** Bantu, Bemba, Click, Hausa, Masai, Wolof **6** Arabic, Berber,
  French, Kanuri, Tsonga **7** Amharic, Khoisan, Lingala, Nilotic, Songhai, Swahili, Turkana
  8 Cushitic, Mandingo **9** Afrikaans
  river: 4 Juba, Nile, Sudd **5** Congo, Kasai, Niger **6** Kwango, Orange, Ubangi **7** Senegal, Zambezi **8** Blue Nile **9** White Nile
  lake: 4 Chad, Kivu, Tana **5** Assal, Nyasa **6** Albert, Edward, Kariba, Malawi, Nassar, Red Sea,
  Rudolf **8** Victoria **10** Tanganyika **12** Chott Melrhir
  falls: 8 Victoria
  mountain/mountain range: 3 Air **4** Bihu, Meru **5** Atlas, Elgon, Kenya **6** Hoggar **7** Ahaggar,
  Crystal, Tibesti, Toubkal **8** Cameroon **9** Emi Koussi, Munchinga, Ruwenzori **10** Futa Jallon
  11 Drakensberg, Kilimanjaro **13** Tibesti Massif
  lowest point: 17 Qattari Depression
  mineral/natural resource: 3 oil, tin **4** gold **5** ivory **6** cloves, copper, rubber **7** diamond, palm
  oil, uranium
  disease: 4 AIDS **7** malaria **9** bilharzia **11** yellow fever **16** sleeping sickness
  homeland: 5 Venda **6** Ciskei **8** Transkei **14** Bophuthatswana
  game reserve: 5 Tsavo **6** Kruger **8** Amboseli **9** Serengeti
  tree: 4 cork, teak **5** cedar, ebony, olive **6** acacia, baobab, okoume, rubber **7** juniper, oil palm
  8 date palm, mahogany, tamarisk **10** silk-cotton
  animal: 4 lion **5** bongo, hippo, hyena, zebra **6** jackal, monkey **7** buffalo, cheetah, giraffe, gorilla, leopard, wild pig **8** aardvark, antelope, elephant **9** crocodile **10** chimpanzee, rhinoceros
  11 wildebeeste **12** hippopotamus
  bird: 5 heron, stork **6** falcon **7** bustard, ostrich, pelican **8** flamingo, hornbill **10** kingfisher
  fly: 6 tsetse
  snake: 5 cobra, mamba **6** python

after 4 next, post **5** later **6** behind **9** afterward, following
10 conclusion, subsequent,
succeeding

aftereffect 6 result
11 consequence

After Hours
  director: 14 Martin Scorsese
  cast: 12 Griffin Dunne
  15 Rosanna Arquette

Afterlife
  god of: 4 Gwyn

aftermath 6 payoff, result, sequel, upshot **7** outcome **8** follow-up, offshoot **9** byproduct
11 consequence

afterpart 4 back, tail **6** far
end **7** back end, rear end, tail
end **8** backside, hind part
9 posterior

after the fact 4 late **5** tardy
7 belated, delayed, too late
10 behindhand, behind time

After the Fall
  author: 12 Arthur Miller

**after this, therefore be-
cause of it**
  Latin: 21 post hoc ergo propter hoc
  describes: 14 logical fallacy

afterword 4 coda **8** addendum,
epilogue **10** conclusion

Agacles
  king of: 9 Myrmidons

Agag
  king of: 10 Amalekites
  captured by: 4 Saul
  killed by: 6 Samuel

again 4 also, anew, more **7** besides **8** moreover, once more
10 in addition, repetition
11 another time, duplication,
furthermore **12** additionally
  Latin: 6 de novo

against 7 adverse, opposed
8 conflict, contrary, opposite
10 opposition **11** unfavorable

against an opponent
  Latin: 9 ad hominem

Against Our Will
    author: 16 Susan Brownmiller

against the property
    Latin: 5 in rem
    describes: 15 legal
        proceeding

against the thing
    Latin: 5 in rem

Agamede
    father: 6 Augeas
    husband: 6 Mulius
    gift: 7 healing
    healed with: 5 herbs

Agamemnon
    author: 9 Aeschylus
    mentioned in: 5 Iliad
    king of: 7 Mycenae
    leader of: 6 Greeks
    fought in: 9 Trojan War
    father: 6 Atreus
    brother: 8 Menelaus
    sister: 8 Anaxibia
    wife: 12 Clytemnestra
    daughter: 7 Electra 9 Iphi-
        genia 12 Chrysothemis
    son: 7 Orestes
    cousin: 9 Aegisthus
    captive: 9 Cassandra
    Clytemnestra's lover:
        9 Aegisthus
    killed by: 12 Clytemnestra

Aganippe 8 fountain
    location: 6 Greece 7 Helicon
    sacred to: 5 Muses

Aganus
    father: 5 Paris
    mother: 5 Helen

agape 4 agog 6 amazed, gap-
    ing 8 wide open 9 awestruck,
    stupefied 10 astonished,
    dumbstruck, spellbound
    11 dumbfounded 12 wonder-
    struck 13 flabbergasted

**Agassiz, Jean Louis
Rodolphe**
    field: 7 zoology
    worked on: 7 fossils 8 gla-
        ciers 14 classification

Agastrophus
    father: 5 Paeon
    killed by: 8 Diomedes

agate
    species: 6 quartz
    variety of: 10 chalcedony
    type: 3 eye 4 moss, onyx,
        ring 9 landscape
        13 fortification
    source: 4 Ider 6 Brazil
        7 Uruguay 9 Oberstein
        14 Rio Grande de Sul

Agathon
    father: 5 Priam

Agathyrsus
    father: 8 Hercules

Agave
    father: 6 Cadmus
    mother: 8 Harmonia

sister: 3 Ino 6 Semele
    7 Autonoe
husband: 6 Echion
son: 8 Pentheus

age 3 eon, era 4 date 5 epoch,
    phase, ripen 6 mature, mel-
    low, period, season 7 develop,
    forever, make old 8 life span,
    lifetime 9 adulthood, a long
    time, grow older, seniority
    10 generation, millennium
    11 stage of life, stage of time
    French: 6 siecle

aged 3 old 4 ripe 6 mature,
    mellow 7 ancient, as old as,
    elderly, ripened 8 enduring,
    grown old 9 developed, full-
    grown, long-lived

Agee, James
    author of: 10 Agee on Film
        17 A Death in the Family
        23 Let Us Now Praise Fa-
        mous Men
    screenwriter for: 15 The Af-
        rican Queen 19 The Night
        of the Hunter

Agelaus
    mentioned in: 5 Iliad
        7 Odyssey
    occupation: 8 herdsman
    father: 8 Hercules, Phradmon
    mother: 7 Omphale
    courted: 8 Penelope
    raised: 5 Paris
    employer: 5 Priam

ageless 7 classic, eternal 8 en-
    during, timeless

agency 5 force, means, power
    6 action, bureau, charge 8 ac-
    tivity 9 influence, mediation,
    operation 10 department, in-
    strument 12 intervention
    15 instrumentality

agenda 6 docket 7 program
    8 schedule 9 timetable

Agenor
    mentioned in: 5 Iliad
    king of: 9 Phoenicia
    father: 7 Antenor 8 Poseidon
    mother: 5 Libya 6 Theano
    twin brother: 5 Belus
    wife: 10 Telephassa
    son: 5 Cilix 6 Cadmus
        7 Phoenix
    daughter: 6 Europa
    gift: 7 bravery

agent 4 doer 5 cause, envoy,
    force, means, mover, power
    6 agency, author, deputy,
    worker 7 vehicle 8 advocate,
    emissary, executor, operator
    9 go-between, performer
    10 instrument, negotiator
    11 perpetrator 12 inter-
    mediary, practitioner
    14 representative

Age of Innocence, The
    author: 12 Edith Wharton
    character: 10 May Welland

12 Ellen Olenska 13 New-
land Archer

age-old 4 aged 7 ancient, an-
    tique, very old 9 venerable

agglomerate 4 clot, mass
    5 amass, bunch, clump, rally
    6 gather, heap up, muster, pile
    up 7 cluster, collect 8 assem-
    ble, condense, mobilize 10 ac-
    cumulate, collection
    12 accumulation, conglomer-
    ate, heap together, lump to-
    gether 14 conglomeration
    15 gather into a mass

agglomeration 4 heap, mass,
    pile 5 bunch, clump 7 cluster
    10 collection 12 accumulation
    14 conglomeration

aggrandize 5 bloat, exalt,
    widen 6 beef up, blow up, di-
    late, expand, extend, puff up,
    step up 7 amplify, broaden,
    build up, distend, enhance,
    enlarge, inflate, magnify,
    stretch 8 escalate, increase
    9 intensify 10 strengthen

aggrandizement 8 increase,
    widening 9 expansion, exten-
    sion 10 broadening, escalation,
    exaltation, stepping up 11 en-
    hancement, enlargement
    13 amplification, magnifica-
    tion 15 intensification

aggravate 3 vex 4 rile 5 anger,
    annoy 6 nettle, worsen 7 af-
    front, inflame 8 heighten, in-
    crease, irritate 9 intensify,
    make worse 10 exacerbate,
    exasperate

aggravating 7 irksome 9 in-
    flaming, vexatious, worsening
    10 irritating 11 heightening
    12 exacerbating, exasperating,
    intensifying

aggregate 3 mix 4 mass
    5 blend, union 7 mixture
    8 amassing, compound 9 com-
    posite, gathering, summation
    10 collection 11 combination
    12 accumulation, conglomer-
    ate 14 conglomeration

aggregation 3 mob 4 army,
    band, bevy, crew, gang, host,
    mass, pack 5 crowd, horde,
    swarm 6 throng 7 cluster
    9 multitude 10 collection

aggression 4 raid 7 assault, of-
    fense 8 act of war, invasion
    9 hostility, pugnacity 11 vi-
    ciousness 12 belligerence
    13 combativeness

aggressive 4 bold 5 harsh,
    pushy 7 dynamic, hostile, in-
    tense, vicious, warlike, war-
    ring, zealous 8 forceful,
    militant 9 ambitious, assailant,
    assertive, attacking, combative,
    energetic 10 pugnacious

11 belligerent, competitive, contentious, quarrelsome **12** antagonistic, enterprising **13** self-assertive **15** tending to attack

aggressiveness 9 hostility, pugnacity **10** antagonism **12** belligerence **13** combativeness

aggressor 7 invader **8** attacker **9** assailant **11** belligerent **12** antagonistic

aggrieved 3 sad **4** hurt **5** stung **6** abused, pained **7** injured, put upon, tearful, wounded, wronged **8** grieving, mournful, offended, saddened, troubled **9** affronted, disturbed, sorrowful **10** distressed, ill-treated, maltreated, persecuted **11** imposed upon **13** grief-stricken

aghast 6 amazed **7** shocked, stunned **8** appalled **9** astounded, horrified, terrified **10** astonished, fear-struck, frightened **12** horror-struck **13** thunderstruck

agile 4 keen, spry **5** alert, fleet, lithe, quick, swift **6** active, clever, limber, nimble, supple **8** athletic, graceful **9** dexterous

agility 8 alacrity, spryness **9** dexterity, quickness, swiftness **10** limberness, nimbleness **12** gracefulness

agitate 3 jar, mix **4** beat, goad, rock, stir **5** alarm, churn, shake, upset **6** excite, foment, stir up, work up **7** disturb, provoke, shake up, trouble **8** disquiet

agitated 6 uneasy **7** anxious, frantic, nervous **8** confused, seething **9** disturbed, perturbed, unsettled **10** disquieted, distracted, distraught **11** discomfited, discomposed **12** disconcerted

agitation 7 anxiety **9** confusion **10** discomfort, uneasiness **11** disquietude, distraction, nervousness **12** discomfiture, discomposure, perturbation

agitato
  music: **8** agitated

agitator 7 inciter **8** fomentor, inflamer, provoker **9** firebrand **10** incendiary, instigator **11** provocateur **12** rabble-rouser, troublemaker **13** mischief-maker, revolutionary **16** agent provocateur

Aglaia
  member of: **6** Graces
  father: **7** Jupiter
  mother: **8** Eurynome

  sister: **6** Thalia
    10 Euphrosyne
  husband: **4** Abas
  son: **7** Proteus **8** Acrisius
  daughter: **7** Idomene

Aglauros see **8** Agraulos

Aglaus
  father: **8** Thyestes
  mother: **5** naiad
  killed by: **6** Atreus

aglow 4 warm **5** fiery **6** ablaze, red-hot **7** blazing, glowing, radiant, shining

Agnes Grey
  author: **10** Anne Bronte
  character: **8** Mr Weston
    13 Rosalie Murray

agnostic 5 pagan **7** atheist, doubter, heathen, heretic, infidel, skeptic **10** empiricist, free spirit, secularist, unbeliever **11** disbeliever, freethinker, nonbeliever **14** doubting Thomas

ago 4 gone, over, past **5** since **6** gone by **7** earlier **8** backward **15** retrospectively

agog 5 astir **7** excited **8** thrilled, worked up **9** awestruck **10** enthralled **11** openmouthed

Agon
  ballet by: **10** Stravinsky

agonize 5 labor, sweat, worry **6** strain, suffer **7** anguish, wrestle **8** struggle

agonizing 6 severe **7** painful, racking **8** grievous, worrying **9** suffering, torturous **10** tormenting, unbearable **11** distressing, intolerable, unendurable **12** excruciating, insufferable

agony 3 woe **4** pain **5** trial **6** effort, misery, sorrow, strain, throes **7** anguish, anxiety, torment, torture **8** distress, striving, struggle **9** suffering **10** affliction **11** tribulation

Agony and the Ecstasy, The
  author: **11** Irving Stone

Agoraea
  epithet of: **6** Athena
  means: **16** of the marketplace

Agoraeus
  epithet of: **4** Zeus **6** Hermes
  means: **16** of the marketplace

agoraphobia
  fear of: **10** open spaces

Agraeus
  epithet of: **6** Apollo
  means: **6** hunter

agrarian 5 rural **7** farming **8** pastoral **11** agronomical, crop-raising **12** agricultural

Agraulos
  also: **8** Aglauros
  father: **7** Actaeus
  husband: **7** Cecropa
  daughter: **9** Pandrosos

agree 4 jibe **5** admit, allow, chime, grant, match, tally **6** accede, accept, accord, assent, concur, settle, square **7** concede, conform, consent, support **8** coincide, side with **9** harmonize, subscribe **10** correspond, think alike

agreeable 7 fitting **8** amenable, in accord, pleasant, pleasing, suitable **9** approving, complying, congenial **10** acceptable, concurring, consenting, gratifying **11** appropriate
  German: **9** gemutlich

agreeableness 7 amenity **9** geniality **10** amiability **11** sociability **12** pleasantness

agreed
  French: **7** d'accord

agreed upon 6 common, normal **8** accepted, approved **9** confirmed, customary **10** acceptable **11** established **12** acknowledged

agreement 4 deal, pact **6** accord **7** analogy, bargain, compact, concert, concord, harmony, promise **8** affinity, alliance, contract, covenant **10** accordance, compliance, conformity, settlement, similarity **11** arrangement, concordance, conformance **13** compatibility **14** correspondence

agricultural 4 farm **5** rural **7** farming **8** agrarian **9** gardening **11** agronomical, crop-raising **13** nonindustrial

agriculture 7 farming, tillage **8** agronomy **9** geoponics, husbandry **10** agronomics **11** crop-raising, cultivation **15** market gardening

Agriculture
  god of: **4** Dago **5** Dagan, Dagon, Picus **6** Saturn **12** Bonus Eventus
  goddess of: **5** Ceres **6** Brigit, Dea Dia, Vacuna

Agriope see **8** Eurydice

Agrius
  member of: **8** Gigantes
  form: **7** centaur
  mother: **5** Circe
  father: **8** Odysseus
  son: **9** Thersites
  attacked by: **8** Hercules

agronomics 7 farming, tillage **8** agronomy **9** geoponics **11** agriculture, crop-raising

agronomy 7 farming **9** gardening, husbandry **11** agriculture, cultivation

Agrotera
   epithet of: **7** Artemis
   means: **8** huntress

aground 5 stuck **6** ashore **7** beached **8** grounded, stranded **9** foundered

ague 5 chill, fever **7** malaria, shivers **12** sweating fits

Aguecheek, Sir Andrew
   character in: **12** Twelfth Night
   author: **11** Shakespeare

Agyius
   epithet of: **6** Apollo
   means: **15** god of the streets

Ah, But Your Land Is Beautiful
   author: **9** Alan Paton

Ah! Wilderness
   author: **12** Eugene O'Neill

Ahab
   character in: **8** Moby Dick
   author: **8** Melville

Ahab
   father: **4** Omri
   wife: **7** Jezebel
   son: **7** Ahaziah
   daughter: **8** Athaliah
   opposed: **6** Elijah
   killed by: **4** Aram

Ahasuerus
   known as: **6** Xerxes **8** Cyaxares
   wife: **6** Esther
   divorced: **6** Vashti
   son: **6** Darius
   eunuchs: **6** Biztha, Carcas, Zethar **7** Abagtha, Harbona, Mehuman
   servant: **7** Abagtha
   conqueror of: **7** Nineveh

Ahaz
   father: **6** Jotham

Ahaziah
   father: **4** Ahab **7** Jehoram
   mother: **7** Jezebel **8** Athaliah
   uncle: **7** Jehoram
   defeated by: **6** Hazael
   killed by: **4** Jehu
   died at: **7** Megiddo

ahead of time 5 early **6** before, in time, sooner **7** betimes, earlier **9** before now, in advance **10** beforehand, in good time **13** before the fact

Ahib 16 first Hebrew month

Ahiezer
   father: **11** Ammishaddai

Ahimelech
   father: **6** Ahitub
   son: **8** Abiathar
   killed by: **4** Saul
   friend: **8** Ahuzzath

Ahithophel
   counseled: **5** David
   rebelled with: **7** Absalom
   granddaughter: **9** Bathsheba

Ahuzzath
   friend: **9** Abimelech
   visited: **5** Isaac

Aias *see* **4** Ajax

aid 4 abet, alms, dole, help **5** serve **6** assist, foster, relief **7** advance, charity, further, promote, subsidy, support, sustain **8** donation, minister **9** allowance **10** assistance, contribute, facilitate **11** accommodate, helping hand **12** contribution

Aida
   opera by: **5** Verdi
   character: **4** Aida **6** Ramfis **7** Amneris, Radames **8** Amonasro, Rhadames

aide 5 gofer **6** deputy, helper **7** abettor, acolyte **8** adherent, adjutant, follower, retainer, sidekick **9** assistant, associate, auxiliary, man Friday **10** aide-de-camp, apprentice, girl Friday, lieutenant **11** helping hand, subordinate **12** right-hand man

aide-de-camp 4 aide **6** helper **8** adjutant **9** assistant, man Friday, right hand **12** right-hand man

aide memoire 4 memo, note **10** memorandum

aider 4 aide **6** helper **7** abettor **9** assistant **11** helping hand

Aidos
   origin: **5** Greek
   personifies: **10** conscience

Aiken, Conrad Potter
   author of: **6** Ushant **10** Blue Voyage **12** Reviewer's ABC **14** The Charnel Rose **15** Earth Triumphant

Aiken, Howard H
   field: **11** mathematics
   designed: **15** digital computer

ail 4 pain **5** annoy, be ill, upset, worry **6** be sick, bother, sicken **7** afflict, make ill, trouble **8** be infirm, be unwell, distress **12** be indisposed, fail in health

ailing 3 ill **4** sick **6** infirm, sickly, unwell **8** delicate

ailment 6 malady **7** disease, illness **8** disorder, sickness, weakness **9** complaint, infection, infirmity **10** affliction, disability, discomfort **13** indisposition

ailurophobia
   fear of: **4** cats

aim 3 try **4** beam, goal, mean, plan, seek, want, wish **5** essay, focus, level, point, sight, slant **6** aiming, design, desire, direct, intend, intent, object, scheme, strive, target **7** attempt, be after, purpose, take aim, train on **8** ambition, aspire to, endeavor **9** intention **10** aspiration, have in mind, have in view, work toward **11** have an eye to, line of sight **12** marksmanship

aim at 4 seek **6** pursue, target **8** aspire to, shoot for

aimless 6 chance, random **7** erratic, wayward **8** unguided **9** frivolous, haphazard, hit-or-miss, pointless, unfocus(s)ed **10** accidental, rudderless, undirected **11** purposeless, unorganized **12** inconsistent, unsystematic **13** directionless, unpredictable **14** indiscriminate

aine 5 elder **6** eldest

Ainsworth, William Harrison
   author of: **8** Boscobel, Crichton, Rookwood **9** Guy Fawkes **10** Old St Paul's **12** Jack Sheppard **13** Windsor Castle **16** The Flitch of Bacon, The Tower of London **17** The Miser's Daughter, The South Sea Bubble **20** The Lancashire Witches

Ainu
   language spoken in: **8** Hokkaido, Sakhalin

air, airs 3 lay, sky **4** aura, look, mood, puff, song, tell, tone, tune, vent, waft, wind **5** blast, carol, ditty, draft, ozone, style, swank, utter, voice, whiff **6** aerate, ballad, breath, breeze, expose, manner, melody, reveal, spirit, strain, zephyr **7** declare, display, divulge, exhibit, express, feeling, hauteur, quality **8** ambience, disclose, pretense, proclaim **9** arrogance, publicize, ventilate **10** appearance, atmosphere, make public **11** haughtiness, pretensions **12** affectations, affectedness, stratosphere **16** superciliousness
   god of: **5** Enlil
   goddess of: **6** Ninlil

airborne 5 aloft **6** aerial **8** in flight **12** off the ground

aircraft 3 jet, SST **4** bird **5** blimp, crate, plane **6** copter, glider **7** balloon, chopper, prop-jet, zepplin **8** airplane, jumbo jet **10** helicopter, whirlybird

air current 4 puff, wind

5 blast, draft, whiff **6** breeze, zephyr **11** breath of air

airdrome, aerodrome 7 airbase, airport, jet base **8** airfield **11** flying field **12** landing field

airfield 7 air base, airport, jet base **8** airstrip **11** flying field **12** landing field, landing strip

airfoil
insect: **4** wing

airless 8 stifling **10** overheated, sweltering **16** poorly ventilated

airplane *see box*

airport 5 field **7** air base, jet base **8** airdrome, airfield, airstrip **9** aerodrome **11** flying field **12** landing field, landing strip

airship 5 blimp **7** balloon **9** dirigible **19** lighter-than-air craft

airship, rigid dirigible
invented by: **8** Zeppelin

airstrip 6 runway **12** landing field, landing strip

air weapon
German: **9** Luftwaffe

airy 5 light, merry, sunny, windy **6** breezy, cheery, drafty, dreamy, jaunty, lively **8** cheerful, ethereal, fanciful, gossamer, illusory, spacious **9** idealized, imaginary, sprightly **10** frolicsome, immaterial **11** unrealistic **12** light-

hearted, light-of-heart **13** unsubstantial **14** well-ventilated

aisle 3 way **4** lane, path, walk **5** alley **6** avenue **7** passage, walkway **8** cloister, corridor **10** ambulatory, passageway

Aius Locutius
form: **5** voice
warned: **6** Romans
warned of: **14** Gallic invasion

ajar 4 open **5** agape **6** gaping **8** unclosed **10** partly open

Ajax
also: **4** Aias
called: **9** Great Ajax **10** Oilean Ajax **11** Locrian Ajax **13** Ajax the Lesser **14** Telamonian Ajax
king of: **7** Locrius
father: **6** Oileus **7** Telamon
mother: **8** Periboea
brother: **6** Teucer
author: **9** Sophocles
character: **8** Achilles, Odysseus **9** Agamemnon
   son: **9** Eurysaces
   slave: **8** Tecmessa
   seer: **7** Calchas
rescued body of: **8** Achilles
violated shrine of: **6** Athena
killed in: **9** shipwreck

Akawai *see* **6** Acawai

Akela
character in: **14** The Jungle Books
author: **7** Kipling

Akeldama *see* **8** Aceldama

Akh
origin: **8** Egyptian
transfiguration of: **4** dead

Akihito
position: **7** emperor **11** crown prince
reign name: **6** Heisei **17** Establishing Peace
family:
   father: **5** Showa **8** Hirohito
   mother: **6** Nagako
   wife: **7** Michiko
   children: **4** Hito **8** Narahito
schools: **6** Oxford **9** Gakushuin

akin 3 kin **4** like **5** alike **6** allied **7** kindred, related, similar, uniform **8** agreeing, parallel **9** analogous, congenial, connected, identical **10** affiliated, comparable, resembling **11** correlative **13** corresponding **14** consanguineous

Akkad *see* **5** Accad

Akutagawa, Ryunosuke
author of: **5** Kappa **8** Rashomon **13** The Hell Screen

a la 9 in honor of **13** in the manner of

Alabama *see box, p. 26*

Alabama, Alibamu
language family: **9** Muskogean
location: **5** Texas **9** Louisiana **10** Polk County **12** Alabama River
related to: **7** Koasati

alacrity 4 zeal **6** fervor **7** agility, avidity **8** dispatch **9** alertness, briskness, eagerness, readiness **10** enthusiasm, liveliness, nimbleness, promptness **11** willingness **13** sprightliness

Aladdin
character in: **27** Arabian Nights' Entertainments

Al Aiun, El Aaiun
capital of: **13** Western Sahara

a la mode 12 in the fashion, in the style of **13** in the manner of

Alarcon, Pedro Antonio de
author: **10** The Scandal **12** Captain Venom **14** El Nino de la Bola **19** The Three-Cornered Hat

alarm 4 fear **5** alert, panic, scare **6** appall, dismay, fright, terror, war cry **7** agitate, disturb, terrify, trouble, unnerve, warning **8** affright, distress, frighten **9** agitation, hue and cry, misgiving **11** trepidation **12** apprehension, perturbation **13** consternation

alarmed 6 afraid, scared

---

airplane 3 jet **4** bird **5** crate, plane **7** airship, prop-jet **8** aircraft **9** aeroplane **11** flying jenny **19** heavier-than-air craft **20** propeller-driven plane
   invented by:
      automatic pilot: **6** Sperry
      jet engine: **5** Ohain
      with motor: **12** Wilbur Wright **13** Orville Wright **14** Wright Brothers
      hydro: **7** Curtiss
   first: **5** Flyer
   part: **3** fin **4** flap, nose, tail, wing **5** cabin, cargo, pylon **6** rudder **7** aileron, cockpit, turbine **8** elevator, fuel tank, fuselage, throttle, turbofan, turbojet **9** empennage, propeller, turboprop **10** flight deck, power plant, stabilizer **11** landing gear **13** undercarriage
   kind: **3** MIG **4** Zero **5** Eagle, Gotha, Piper, Sabre **6** Boeing, Cessna, Fokker, Mirage **7** Concorde, Piper Cub **10** Beechcraft, Dornier Do-X **11** Piper Navajo **12** Lockheed Vega, Sopwith Camel **13** Boeing Clipper, Messerschmitt, Piper Cherokee, Super Fortress **14** Cessna Citation, Flying Fortress, Grumman Hellcat, Stratofortress **15** Hawker Hurrican **16** De Havilland Comet
   variation: **3** SST **4** STOL, VTOL **5** blimp, drone, VSTOL **6** bomber, glider **7** airship, fighter **8** zeppelin **10** hang glider, helicopter, supersonic
   battle: **8** dog fight

Alabama
abbreviation: 2 AL 3 Ala
nickname: 6 Cotton 12 Heart of Dixie, Yellowhammer
capital: 10 Montgomery
largest city: 10 Birmingham
others: 5 Selma 6 Athens, Dothan, Marion, Mobile 7 Decatur, Gadsden 8 Anniston 10 Huntsville, Tuscaloosa
colleges: 5 Miles 6 Auburn 7 Alabama 8 Tuskegee 9 Talladega 10 Huntingdon
explorer: 12 Hernan DeSoto
feature:
  festival: 11 Azalea Trail
  statue: 6 Vulcan
tribe: 5 Creek 6 Tohome 7 Alabamu, Alibamu, Koasati 8 Tuskegee
people: 8 Joe Louis 9 Hank Aaron, Hugo Black 10 Willie Mays 11 Helen Keller, Nat King Cole 13 George Wallace, William C Handy, William Gorgas
lake: 12 Guntersville
land rank: 11 twenty-ninth
physical feature:
  gulf: 6 Mexico
  highest point: 6 Cheaha
  highlands: 11 Appalachian
river: 3 Pea 5 Coosa 6 Mobile 7 Alabama 9 Tombigbee, Tennessee 10 Tallapoosa 13 Chattahoochee
state admission: 12 twenty-second
state bird: 7 flicker 12 yellowhammer
state fish: 6 tarpon
state flower: 8 camellia 9 goldenrod
state motto: 21 We Dare Defend Our Rights
state song: 7 Alabama
state tree: 20 southern longleaf pine

7 anxious, fearful, panicky, worried 8 dismayed 9 concerned, terrified 10 frightened 12 apprehensive 13 panic-stricken 14 terror-stricken

alarming 5 awful, dread 7 fearful 8 dreadful 10 horrifying, terrifying 11 frightening, hair-raising

alas
expresses: 4 pity 5 grief 6 sorrow 7 concern 9 weariness 11 unhappiness 12 wretchedness

Alaska *see box*

Alaskan Adventures
author: 8 Rex Beach

Alastor
epithet of: 4 Zeus 5 demon 11 avenging god
means: 7 avenger
father: 13 Neleus of Pylos
brother: 6 Nestor
wife: 9 Harpalyce
killed by: 8 Hercules

Albach-Retty, Rosemarie
real name of: 13 Romy Schneider

Albania *see box, p. 28*

Albanian
language family: 12 Indo-European
spoken in: 7 Balkans

Albee, Edward
author of: 3 Box 7 All Over 8 Seascape, Zoo Story 9 Tiny Alice 10 The Sandbox 16 A Delicate Balance, The American Dream 18 The Lady from Dubuque 21 The Ballad of the Sad Cafe, The Death of Bessie Smith 25 Who's Afraid of Virginia Woolf?
identified with: 18 theater of the absurd

Albeniz, Isaac
born: 5 Spain 9 Camprodon
composer of: 6 Iberia 12 The Magic Opal 13 Henry Clifford

Alberich
origin: 8 Teutonic
king of: 6 dwarfs
possessed treasure of: 8 Niblungs 9 Nibelungs
also possessed: 9 Tarnkappe

Albert, Eddie
real name: 21 Eddie Albert Heimberger
wife: 5 Margo

born: 12 Rock Island IL
roles: 8 Oklahoma 10 Brother Rat, Green Acres 11 Room Service 12 Roman Holiday 13 The Longest Day 16 The Heartbreak Kid 19 The Boys from Syracuse

Alberta
abbreviation: 4 Alta
capital/largest city: 8 Edmonton
others: 7 Calgary, Reddeer 10 Lethbridge 11 Medicine Hat
lakes: 5 Banff, Claire 6 Jasper 8 Waterton 9 Athabasca 11 Lesser Slave
rivers: 3 Bow 4 Milk 6 Oldman, Wapiti 9 Athabasca 12 Saskatchewan
religion: 13 Roman Catholic 20 United Church of Canada 22 Anglican Church of Canada
people: 5 Dutch 6 French, German 7 British, English 9 Ukrainian 12 Scandinavian

Albert Herring
opera by: 7 Britten

Alberti, Leon Battista
architect of: 15 Palazzo Rucellai 18 Church of Sant' Andrea, Temple Malatestiano 20 Church of San Sebastian 25 Church of Santa Maria Novella

Albertosaurus
type: 8 dinosaur, theropod
period: 10 Cretaceous

Albertson, Jack
born: 8 Malden MA
roles: 14 Chico and the Man 15 The Sunshine Boys 18 Days of Wine and Roses, The Subject Was Roses

Albion *see 7 England*

album 2 LP 4 book 6 record 8 register 9 portfolio, scrapbook

Albunea
origin: 5 Roman
form: 5 nymph
habitat: 8 fountain

Alcaeus
father: 9 Androgeus
mother: 9 Andromeda
grandfather: 5 Minos
brother: 9 Sthenelus

Alcaids
descendants of: 7 Alcaeus

Alcandre
husband: 7 Polybus
received: 5 Helen 8 Menelaus

Alceste
opera by: 5 Gluck

Alaska
  abbreviation: **2** AK **4** Alas
  nickname: **9** Great Land, Sourdough **12** Last Frontier
    20 Land of the Midnight Sun
  capital: **6** Juneau
  largest city: **9** Anchorage
  others: **4** Nome **5** Sitka **6** Barrow, Kodiak **7** Cordova,
    Douglas, Skagway **9** Fairbanks, Ketchikan
  feature: **5** Alcan **13** Alaska Highway
    national park: **13** Mount McKinley
  tribe: **3** Han **5** Aleut, Haida **6** Ahtena, Akkhas, Eskimo,
    Karluk, Tetlin **7** Amerind, Ingalik, Kayukon, Khotana,
    Kutchin, Tanaina, Tlingit, Tlinkit, Venetie **9** Tsimshian,
    Unakalett
  island: **4** Adak, Atka **5** Aleut **6** Kodiak, Unimak **7** Diomede,
    Nunivak **8** Aleutian, Pribilof **9** Alexander
  lake: **6** Naknek **7** Iliamna **8** Becharof **9** Teshekpuk
  land rank: **5** first
  mountain: **3** Ada **4** Muir **5** Coast **6** Alaska, Brooks **7** For-
    aker, St Elias **8** Aleutian, Wrangell **9** Blackburn
    highest point: **8** McKinley
  physical feature:
    bay: **7** Glacier, Prudhoe
    channel: **9** Gastineau
    glacier: **9** Malaspina
    pass: **8** Chilkoot
    peninsula: **5** Kenai **6** Alaska, Seward
    rapids: **10** Whitehorse
    sea: **6** Arctic **8** Beaufort
    strait: **6** Bering
  river: **5** Kobuk, Yukon **6** Copper, Noatak, Tanana **7** Koyu-
    kuk, Susitna **8** Colville **9** Kuskokwim, Matanuska,
    Porcupine
  state admission: **10** forty-ninth
  state bird: **15** willow ptarmigan
  state fish: **10** king salmon
  state flower: **11** forget-me-not
  state motto: **16** North to the Future
  state song: **11** Alaska's Flag
  state symbol: **9** bald eagle
  state tree: **11** sitka spruce

Alcestis
  author: **9** Euripides
  character: **6** Apollo **7** Adme-
    tus **8** Heracles, Thanatos

Alcestis
  father: **6** Pelias
  mother: **8** Anaxibia
    10 Phylomache
  husband: **7** Admetus
  son: **7** Eumelus **8** Hippasus
  returned from: **5** Hades
  returned by: **8** Hercules

Alchemist, The
  author: **9** Ben Jonson
  character: **4** Face **5** Surly
    6 Dapper, Subtle **7** Ananias,
    Drugger, Kastril, Love-wit
    9 Dol Common **10** Dame
    Pliant **16** Sir Epicure Mam-
    mon **20** Tribulation
    Wholesome

alchemy 5 magic **7** sorcery
  8 wizardry **10** conversion,
  witchcraft **11** magic appeal

13 transmutation **17** medieval
chemistry
  god of: **6** Hermes

Alcides *see* **8** Hercules

Alcidice
  husband: **10** Salmoneaus
  daughter: **4** Tyro

Alcimede
  father: **8** Phylacus
  mother: **7** Clymene
  husband: **5** Aeson
  son: **5** Jason

Alcimedon
  origin: **8** Arkadian
  mentioned in: **5** Iliad
  father: **7** Laerces
  daughter: **6** Philao
  captain of: **9** Myrmidons

Alcina
  opera by: **6** Handel
  character: **6** Alcina
    8 Ruggiero

Alcindor, Lew
  former name of: **17** Kareem
    Abdul-Jabbar

Alcinous
  origin: **5** Greek
  mentioned in: **7** Odyssey
  king of: **10** Phaeacians
  father: **10** Nausithous
  mother: **8** Periboea
  brother: **8** Rhexenor
  wife: **5** Arete
  son: **8** Laodamas
  daughter: **8** Nausicaa
  niece: **5** Arete

Alcis
  father: **10** Antipoenus
  sister: **9** Androclea

Alcithoe
  father: **6** Minyas
  mocked: **8** Dionysus

Alcmaeon
  father: **10** Amphiaraus
  mother: **8** Eriphyle
  brother: **11** Amphilochus
  wife: **10** Callirrhoe
  son: **7** Acarnan
    10 Amphoterus
  daughter: **9** Tisiphone
  commanded: **7** Thebans

Alcmaon
  father: **7** Thestor
  wounded by: **7** Glaucus
  killed by: **8** Sarpedon

Alcmene
  father: **9** Electryon
  mother: **9** Anaxo
  husband: **10** Amphitryon
    12 Rhadamanthys
  twin sons: **8** Hercules,
    Iphicles

alcohol 3 ale **4** beer, wine
  5 drink **6** liquor **7** whiskey
  9 the bottle
  Latin: **9** aqua vitae

alcoholic 3 sot **4** hard, lush,
  soak **5** drunk, rummy, souse,
  toper **6** barfly, boozer, strong
  7 guzzler, imbiber, tippler
  8 drunkard **9** distilled, fermented, inebriate **10** spirituous **11** dipsomaniac, hard
  drinker, inebriating, inebria-
  tive, whiskey head
  12 intoxicating

alcoholism 3 DT's **9** oeno-
  mania **10** dipsomania **12** intemperance **15** delirium
  tremens

Alcon
  form: **6** archer, Trojan
    7 warrior
  aided: **8** Hercules
  wounded: **8** Odysseus
  abducted: **13** Geryons cattle
  killed by: **8** Odysseus

Alcott, Louisa May
  author of: **7** Jo's Boys **9** Lit-

Albania
 other name: 8 Shqiperi 9 Shqiprija, Shqyptare
 capital/largest city: 6 Tirana, Tirane
 others: 3 Opp 4 Fier, Klos, Puka, Puke 5 Berat, Dukat,
  Korce, Kruje, Pecin, Peqin, Qukes, Rubic, Spash, Vlore
  6 Avlona, Bitsan, Dardhe, Durres, Karaje, Preshe, Valona
  7 Chimara, Coritza, Durazzo, Elbasan, Koritsa, Preyesa,
  Scutari, Shkoder 8 Tepeleni 11 Gjirokaster
 monetary unit: 3 lek 5 franc 6 qintar 7 quintar
 island: 6 Saseno
 lake: 4 Ulze 5 Matia, Ohrid 6 Prespa 7 Ochrida, Scutari,
  Shkoder 8 Ohridsko
 mountain: 5 Shala 6 Pindus 8 Koritnjk 12 Albanian Alps
 highest point: 10 Mount Korab
 river: 3 Mat 4 Arta, Drin 5 Byene, Erzen, Seman 6 Bojana,
  Bojane, Vijosa, Vijosa, Vijose 7 Drin-i-ci, Shkumbi
 sea: 6 Ionian 8 Adriatic
 physical feature:
  bay: 5 Vlore
  cape: 6 Glossa
  gulf: 4 Drin
  lagoon: 10 Kara Vastas
  peninsula: 6 Balkan
  promontory: 13 acroceraunium
  strait: 7 Otranto
  wind: 4 bora
 people: 3 Geg 4 Cham, Gheg, Gueg, Tosk 6 Arnaut, Arnout 8 Illyrian, Skipetar
  king: 3 Zog 9 Ahmet Zogu
  leader: 4 Alia 5 Hoxha 7 Berisha 10 Scanderbeg, Skenderbeg 13 Bishop Fan Noli
 language: 3 Geg 4 Cham, Gheg, Hish, Tosk 5 Greek
  8 Albanian
 religion: 5 Islam 7 Bektash 13 Roman Catholic 15 Eastern
  Orthodox
 place:
  square: 10 Skenderbeg
 feature:
  lute: 6 luhata
  soldier: 7 palikar
  stone house: 4 kula
 food:
  cheese: 8 kackaval

tle Men 11 Little Women
12 Eight Cousins, Flower
Fables 15 Aunt Jo's Scrap-
Bag 18 An Old-Fashioned
Girl

alcove 3 bay 4 nook 5 niche
6 corner, recess 7 cubicle,
opening 11 compartment

Alcyone
 also: 7 Halcyon
 father: 6 Aeolus
 husband: 4 Ceyx
 son: 6 Anthas
 transformed into:
  10 kingfisher

Alcyoneus
 form: 5 giant
 hurled: 5 stone
 victim: 8 Hercules
 killed by: 8 Hercules

Alda, Alan
 born: 9 New York NY

 father: 10 Robert Alda
 real name: 15 Alfonso
  D'Abruzzo
 roles: 4 MASH 9 Paper Lion
  12 Sweet Liberty 13 Betsy's
  Wedding, Hawkeye Pierce
  14 The Four Seasons
  16 Same Time Next Year,
  The Mephisto Waltz

Alden, Roberta
 character in: 17 An American
  Tragedy
 author: 7 Dreiser

al dente 10 to the tooth

alder 5 Alnus
 varieties: 3 Red 5 Black,
  Hazel, White, Witch 6 Oregon, Smooth, Yellow 7 Italian, Seaside 8 Japanese,
  Mountain, Speckled 9 Caucasian 10 Manchurian
  13 American green, European green

Aldiss, Brian W
 author of: 7 Non-Stop
  9 Greybeard 13 The Saliva
  Tree 19 Frankenstein Unbound, The Billion Year
  Spree, The Eighty Minute
  Hour

ale 4 beer, brew 5 stout
12 malt beverage 15 English
festival

Alea
 epithet of: 6 Athena
 means: 9 sanctuary

Alebion
 father: 8 Poseidon
 brother: 8 Dercynus
 killed by: 8 Hercules

Alecto
 member of: 6 Furies

alehouse 3 pub 6 saloon, tavern 7 taproom 11 public house

Aleichem, Sholom
 author of: 12 The Great
  Fair 14 Tevye's Daughter

Alembert, Jean le Rond d'
 field: 11 mathematics
 nationality: 6 French
 studied: 13 fluid dynamics
  18 celestial mechanics
  28 partial differential
  equations

Aleph and Other Stories
 author: 15 Jorge Luis Borges

alert 4 warn, wary 5 alarm,
aware, quick, siren 6 active,
inform, lively, nimble, notify,
signal 7 careful, heedful, on
guard, warning 8 diligent,
forewarn, keen-eyed, vigilant,
watchful 9 attentive, observant, sprightly, wideawake
10 perceptive 11 intelligent

alertness 8 alacrity, dispatch
9 awareness, readiness, vigilance 10 liveliness
12 watchfulness

Alethia
 origin: 5 Greek
 personifies: 5 truth

Aleus
 king of: 5 Tegea
 father: 7 Aphidas
 brother: 6 Pereus
 cousin: 6 Neaera
 wife: 6 Neaera
 son: 7 Cepheus 8 Lycurgus
  10 Amphidamas
 daughter: 4 Auge

Aleut
 language family: 6 Eskimo
 tribe: 4 Atka 8 Unalaska
 location: 6 Alaska 15 Shumagin Islands 17 Aleutian
  Peninsula
 noted for: 7 hunting

Aleutians
 islands: 3 Fox, Rat 4 Near

9 Andreanof **25** Islands of the Four Mountains
state: 6 Alaska
people: 6 Aleuts
language: 5 Atkan **9** Unalaskan

Alexander, Jane
real name: 11 Jane Quigley
born: 8 Boston MA
roles: 9 Testament **17** The Great White Hope **18** Eleanor and Franklin **19** All the President's Men

Alexander's Feast
author: 10 John Dryden

Alexander the Great
battle: 5 Issus **9** Gaugamela
birthplace: 5 Pella
conquered: 6 Darius, Persia
father: 8 Philip II
founded: 10 Alexandria
friend: 11 Hephaestion
general: 7 Cleitus **8** Philotas **9** Parmenion
horse: 10 Bucephalus
mother: 8 Olympias
nationality: 10 Macedonian
tutor: 9 Aristotle
wife: 6 Roxana

Alexandra *see* **9** Cassandra

Alexandrinus 16 Greek unical codex

alexandrite
species: 11 chrysoberyl
source: 8 Sri Lanka
color: 3 red **5** green

Alexiares
father: 8 Hercules
mother: 4 Hebe

Alexicacus
epithet of: 6 Apollo
means: 13 averter of evil

Alfader *see* **7** Alfadir

Alfadir
also: 7 Alfader
origin: 12 Scandinavian
epithet of: 4 Odin **5** Othin

Alfheim
origin: 12 Scandinavian
dwelling place of: 5 elves
location: 11 above ground

Alfie
director: 12 Lewis Gilbert
based on play by: 12 Bill Naughton
cast: 12 Michael Caine **14** Shelley Winters

alga, algae 6 fungus **8** pond scum
contains: 4 agar **5** algin **11** carrageenan, chlorophyll
type: 3 red **5** brown, green **9** blue-green, euglenids **11** golden-brown, yellow-green **15** dinoflagellates
forms: 4 kelp **5** dulse **7** diatoms, seaweed **8** plankton,

rockweed **9** Irish moss, stonewort

Alger, Horatio
author of: 10 Ragged Dick **11** Tattered Tom **12** Luck and Pluck

Algeria *see box*

Algiers
Arabic: 8 al-Jazair
building: 11 Great Mosque
capital of: 7 Algeria
center of city: 6 Casbah

Algeria
other name: 7 Algerie, Numidia, Pomaria **9** al-Djazair
capital/largest city: 7 Algiers
others: 4 Bona, Bone, Oran **5** Aflou, Arzew, Batna, Blida, Medea, Saida, Setif, Tenes **6** Abadla, Annaba, Aumale, Barika, Bechar, Bejaia, Benoud, Biskra, Bougie, Dellys, Djanet, Djelfa, Dzioua, Eloued, Frenda, Guelma, Skikda **7** Boghari, Mascara, Miliana, Negrine, Nemours, Ouargla, Tebessa, Tlemcen **8** Ghardaia, Laghouat **9** Touggourt **11** Constantine **12** Sidi-bel-abbes
division: 4 Oran **6** Annaba **7** Algiers **11** Constantine
leader: 3 bey, dey **6** disawa **9** beylerbey
measure: 3 pik **5** rebis, tarri **6** termin
monetary unit: 5 dinar **7** centime
weight: 4 rotl
lake: 5 Hodna **6** Sabkha **7** Cherqui, Fedjadj, Meirhir **10** Azzel Matti, Mekerrhane
mountain: 5 Aissa, Atlas, Aures, Dahra **6** Chelia **7** Ahaggar, Kabylia, Mouydir **8** Djurjura **9** Djurdjura, Tell Atlas **12** Saharan Atlas
highest point: 5 Tahat
river: 6 Shelif **7** Cheliff **8** Medjerda **15** Cheliffmedjerda
sea: 13 Mediterranean
physical feature: 14 Tropic of Cancer
desert: **6** Sahara
giant sand dune: **3** erg
grass: **4** diss **7** esparto
hill: **4** tell
oasis: **5** Mzab
oil field: **7** Edjeleh, El Gassi **10** Zarzaitine **13** Hassi Messaoud (happy spring), Tiguentourine
plain: **7** Cheliff, Mitidja
rocky plateau: **7** hammada
salt basin: **5** chott, shatt
wind: **7** sirocco
people: 4 Arab **6** Berber, Kabyle, Shawia, Tuareg **7** Haratin
author: **3** Dib **5** Camus, Fanon **6** Yacine
leader: **9** Bendjedid **10** Abd al-Qadir, Abd-al-Kadir, Abd-el-Kader **11** Boumedienne **13** Ahmed Ben Bella
ruler: **8** Jugurtha **9** Masinissa
language: 6 Arabic, Berber, French, Zenata **7** Senhaja
religion: 5 Islam
place:
monastery: **5** Ribat
ruins: **7** Djemila
feature:
camel: **6** mehari
cavalry man: **5** spahi **6** spahee
commune: **5** setif
dwelling: **6** gourbi
French settler/landowner: **5** colon **8** piednoir
holy man: **8** marabout
kingdom: **7** Numidia
native quarter: **6** casbah, kasbah
pirate: **7** corsair
ship: **5** xebec, zebec
slum: **10** bidonville
food:
dish: **8** couscous
fruit drink: **5** syrop
seasoning: **4** mint **5** anise, cumin **6** cloves, fennel, ginger, pepper **7** parsley, pimento **8** cinnamon **9** coriander

French: **5** Alger
hills: **5** Sahel
Roman: **7** Icosium
ruled by: **5** Turks **6** French
7 Berbers **10** Free French
14 Barbary Pirates
sea: **13** Mediterranean

Algonkian-Mosan
language branches: **5** Mosan
7 Kutenai **15** Algonkian-Ritwan

Algonkian-Ritwan
language family: **14** Algonkian-Mosan
subgroup: **3** Fox **4** Cree,
Sauk **5** Wiyot, Yurok
6 Ojibwa **7** Abenaki, Arapaho, Mohican **8** Cheyenne,
Delaware, Menomini
9 Blackfoot

Algonkin, Algonquin
language family: **9** Algonkian **10** Algonquian
tribe: **7** Abitibi **8** Algonkin
9 Nipissing **11** Temiscaming
location: **6** Canada **11** Ottawa
River
spirit of nature: **7** Manitou

Algonquian, Algonkian
tribe: **3** Fox, Sac **4** Cree,
Innu, Sauk **5** Miami **6** Abnaki, Atsina, Micmac,
Ojibwa, Ottawa, Pequot
7 Arapaho, Mahican, Mohegan, Mohican, Ojibway,
Shawnee **8** Algonkin, Cheyenne, Chippawa, Delaware,
Haaninin, Iliniwek, Illinois,
Kickapoo, Menomini, Merrimac, Powhatan, Puyallop
9 Algonquin, Blackfeet,
Blackfoot, Massasoit, Menominee, Menomonie, Mesquakie, Pennacook,
Penobscot, Pokanoket,
Twightwee, Wampanoag
10 Leni-Lenape, Potawatomi **11** Gros Ventres
12 Narragansett **17** Montagnais-Naskapi

algophobia
fear of: **4** pain

Algum 13 red sandalwood

Ali, Muhammad
formerly: **11** Cassius Clay
sport: **6** boxing
class: **11** heavyweight
won: **8** Olympics **16** heavyweight title

alias 9 pseudonym **11** assumed
name, nom de guerre

Ali Baba
character in: **27** Arabian
Nights' Entertainments

Alibamu see **7** Alabama

alibi 3 out **6** excuse **7** pretext
11 explanation **13** justification

Alice Adams
author: **15** Booth Tarkington
character: **6** Mr Lamb
11 Virgil Adams, Walter Adams **13** Arthur Russell,
Mildred Palmer

**Alice's Adventures in
Wonderland**
author: **12** Lewis Carroll
character: **5** Alice **7** Duchess
9 Mad Hatter, March Hare
10 Mock Turtle **11** Cheshire
Cat, White Rabbit **12** King
of Hearts **13** Queen of
Hearts

Alice Sit-by-the-Fire
author: **12** James M Barrie

alien 6 exotic, remote, unlike
7 distant, foreign, opposed,
strange **8** contrary, newcomer,
outsider, stranger **9** different,
estranged, foreigner, immigrant, not native, outlander,
separated, unrelated **10** dissimilar, outlandish **11** conflicting, incongruous,
unconnected **12** incompatible,
inconsistent **13** contradictory
German: **9** Auslander

alienate 7 divorce **8** estrange,
separate, turn away

alienation 5 exile **7** divorce
9 isolation **10** separation, withdrawal **13** repulsiveness

alight 4 land **6** get off **7** deplane, descend, detrain, get
down **8** come down, dismount **9** climb down, disembark, thump down, touch
down

align 4 ally, even, join, side
6 even up, line up **9** affiliate,
associate **10** straighten

alignment 7 allying, evening
9 evening up **13** straightening

alike 4 akin, even, same
5 equal **6** evenly **7** equally,
kindred, uniform **8** of a piece,
parallel **9** analogous, identical,
similarly, uniformly **10** equivalent, synonymous **11** homogeneous, identically
13 corresponding

Alisande (Sandy)
character in: **36** A Connecticut Yankee in King Arthur's
Court
author: **5** Twain

alive 4 spry **5** alert, aware, eager, quick, vital **6** active, extant, lively, living, viable
7 animate, in force, not dead
8 animated, possible, spirited,
vigorous **9** breathing, energetic, operative, vivacious
10 subsisting, unquenched

11 above ground, in existence,
in operation
14 unextinguished

alive to 5 alert, awake, aware
7 heedful, mindful **8** watchful
9 attentive, conscious, wideawake

alkaline 5 salty **7** antacid
9 nonacidic

alkaloid 7 alkaline, codeine,
guinine **8** morphine, nicotine
16 colorless complex

all 4 each, full, very **5** any of,
every, fully, total, utter,
whole **6** each of, entire, to a
man, utmost, wholly **7** highest, perfect, totally, utterly
8 any one of, complete, entirely, everyone, greatest, the
sum of, the total, the whole
9 every item **10** altogether,
completely, every one of,
everything, the total of, the
whole of **11** every member,
every part of, exceedingly, the
entirety

All About Eve
director: **17** Joseph L
Mankiewicz
cast: **10** Anne Baxter, Bette
Davis **11** Celeste Holm, Gary
Merrill **12** Thelma Ritter
13 George Sanders, Marilyn
Monroe
Oscar for: **7** picture **8** director **10** screenplay **15** supporting actor (George
Sanders)

Allan-a-Dale, Alan-a-Dale
character in: **9** Robin Hood

allargando
music: **13** getting slower

all around 6 abroad **7** all over
10 everywhere, far and wide
15 making the rounds

all-around 5 broad **6** adroit,
gifted **8** flexible **9** adaptable,
many-sided, versatile **11** wellrounded **12** ambidextrous,
multifaceted **13** comprehensive

allay 4 calm, dull, ease, hush
5 blunt, check, quell, quiet,
slake **6** lessen, pacify, quench,
reduce, smooth, soften,
soothe, subdue **7** appease, assuage, lighten, mollify, relieve,
slacken **8** diminish, mitigate,
moderate **9** alleviate, put to
rest **14** cause to subside

all but 6 almost, nearly **7** close
to **8** not quite **10** not far
from, very nearly **14** except
everyone, within an inch of
16 everything except

all by oneself 5 alone **7** unaided **9** on one's own **10** un-assisted **13** unaccompanied

all-consuming 3 hot **5** fiery **6** ardent, fervid, raging, red-hot **7** burning, fanatic, fervent, frantic, glowing, intense, zealous **8** frenzied **10** passionate **11** impassioned

allegation 5 claim **6** avowal, charge **9** assertion, statement **10** accusation, contention, indictment, profession **11** declaration

allege 3 say **4** aver, avow **5** claim, state **6** accuse, affirm, assert, charge, impugn, impute **7** contend, declare, profess **8** maintain

allegiance 6 fealty, homage **7** loyalty **8** devotion, fidelity **9** adherence, constancy, deference, obedience **12** faithfulness

allegory 5 fable **7** parable

allegro
  music: **4** fast

all-embracing 5 broad **6** all-out **7** general, overall **8** complete, sweeping, thorough **9** expansive, extensive, universal, unlimited **10** exhaustive, widespread **11** far-reaching, wide-ranging **12** all-inclusive, encyclopedic **13** comprehensive

Allen, Arabella
  character in: **14** Pickwick Papers
  author: **7** Dickens

Allen, Ethan
  served in: **16** Revolutionary War
  commander of: **17** Green Mountain Boys
  captured: **15** Fort Ticonderoga

Allen, Fred
  real name: **20** John Florence Sullivan
  born: **11** Cambridge MA
  roles: **11** What's My Line **16** The Fred Allen Show

Allen, Steve
  real name: **12** Stephen Allen
  wife: **12** Jayne Meadows
  nickname: **10** Mr Midnight
  born: **9** New York NY
  roles: **13** I've Got a Secret **14** The Tonight Show

Allen, William Hervey
  author of: **7** Israfel **14** Anthony Adverse

Allen, Woody
  author of: **11** Getting Even, Side Effects **15** Without Feathers
  real name: **22** Allen Stewart Konigsberg

  wife: **12** Louise Lasser
  born: **10** Brooklyn NY
  roles: **5** Zelig **7** Bananas, Sleeper **9** Annie Hall, Manhattan **16** Stardust Memories **19** Hannah and Her Sisters
  director of: **5** Zelig **7** Bananas, Sleeper **9** Annie Hall (Oscar), Interiors, Manhattan **16** Stardust Memories **19** Hannah and Her Sisters **20** The Purple Rose of Cairo

alleviate 4 dull, ease, quit **5** abate, allay, blunt, check, slake **6** lessen, quench, reduce, soften, subdue, temper **7** assuage, lighten, mollify, relieve, slacken **8** diminish, mitigate, moderate

alleviation 6 easing, relief **9** lessening **10** palliation

alley 4 lane **5** byway **7** passage, pathway **10** passageway **16** narrow back street

Alley Oop
  creator: **14** Vincent T Hamlin
  character:
    girlfriend: **4** Oola
    dinosaur: **5** Dinny
    king: **6** Guzzle
    scientist: **8** Dr Wonmug
  place:
    kingdom of: **3** Moo

All for Love
  author: **10** John Dryden
  character: **6** Antony, Caesar **7** Octavia **9** Cleopatra, Dolabella, Ventidius

All God's Chillun Got Wings
  author: **12** Eugene O'Neill
  character: **6** Mickey **9** Jim Harris **10** Ella Downey

alliance 4 pact **5** union **6** league, treaty **7** compact, company **9** agreement, coalition, concordat **10** federation **11** affiliation, association, confederacy, partnership **13** confederation **15** entente cordiale

allied 4 akin, like **5** alike, joint **6** united **7** cognate, kindred, related, similar **8** combined **9** corporate, federated **10** affiliated, associated, resembling **11** amalgamated **12** incorporated

all in 4 beat **5** spent, tired, weary **6** bushed, done in, pooped **7** drained, wearied, worn out **8** dog tired, fatigued, tired out **9** bone weary, dead tired, exhausted, played out

all in all 5 in sum **10** on the whole **20** when all is said and done

all-inclusive 5 broad **6** all-out, entire **7** general, overall **8** absolute, complete, sweeping, thorough **9** expansive, extensive, universal, unlimited **10** altogether, exhaustive, widespread **11** far-reaching, wide-ranging **12** all-embracing **13** comprehensive

All in the Family
  character: **10** Joey Stivic, Mike Stivic (Meathead) **11** Edith Bunker (Dingbat) **12** Archie Bunker **18** Gloria Bunker Stivic
  cast: **9** Rob Reiner **13** Jean Stapleton **14** Carroll O'Connor, Sally Struthers
  spinoffs: **5** Maude **12** Archie's Place **13** The Jeffersons

allocate 5 allot, allow **6** assign, budget **7** earmark **8** set aside **9** apportion, designate **11** appropriate

allocation 5 quota, share **7** measure, portion **8** division **9** allotment, meting out **10** dealing out **11** consignment, designation **12** apportioning, dispensation, distribution **13** apportionment

Allosaurus *see* **10** Antrodemus

allot 5 allow, grant **6** assign **7** appoint, consign, dole out, earmark, give out, mete out, provide **8** allocate, dispense, divide up **9** apportion, parcel out **10** distribute, portion out

allotment 5 grant, quota, share **6** ration **7** measure, portion **9** allowance **10** allocation **11** consignment **12** dispensation **13** apportionment, appropriation

all-out 5 broad, total **7** full-out, maximum **8** complete, sweeping, thorough **9** extensive, full-scale **11** unqualified, unremitting **12** all-embracing, all-inclusive **13** comprehensive, thoroughgoing

all over 5 ended, kaput **8** finished **9** concluded **10** everywhere **11** universally

All Over
  author: **11** Edward Albee

allow 3 let **4** give **5** allot, grant **6** assign, permit **7** agree to, approve, concede, provide **8** allocate, sanction **9** authorize

allowable 7 allowed **8** accepted **9** permitted, tolerable, tolerated **10** acceptable, admissible, admittable, authorized, sanctioned **11** permissible

allowance 5 grant **6** bounty, income, ration **7** annuity, payment, pension, stipend, subsidy **8** discount **9** allotment, deduction, reduction **10** concession **11** subtraction

allow to go 4 free **5** let go **6** excuse **7** dismiss, release, set free **8** liberate **9** discharge

allow to pass
   French: **13** laissez passer

alloy 3 mix **5** admix, blend **6** commix, dilute, fusion, impair **7** amalgam, combine, mixture **8** compound, intermix **9** admixture, composite, synthesis **10** adulterate, commixture, interblend **12** conglomerate

alloyed 5 mixed **6** impure **7** debased

All Quiet on the Western Front
   author: **18** Erich Maria Remarque
   character: **6** Muller, Tjaden **10** Paul Baumer **11** Albert Kropp, Haie Westhus **20** Stanislaus Katczinsky (Kat)
   director: **14** Lewis Milestone
   cast: **8** Lew Ayres **12** Louis Wolheim **14** Russell Gleason
   setting: **3** WWI
   Oscar for: **7** picture

all right 2 OK **3** yes **4** fair, hale, safe, well **6** hearty **7** healthy **8** properly, unharmed **9** certainly, correctly, uninjured **10** absolutely, acceptably, unimpaired **14** satisfactorily
   Spanish: **5** bueno

All Said and Done
   author: **16** Simone de Beauvoir

allspice
   botanical name: **7** pimenta, p dioica **12** p officinalis
   also called: **7** pimento
   origin: **7** Jamaica **16** Caribbean Islands
   flavor: **5** clove **6** nutmeg **8** cinnamon
   use: **6** baking

Allston, Washington
   born: **10** Waccamaw SC
   artwork: **9** The Deluge **13** Uriel in the Sun **16** Belshazzar's Feast, Moonlit Landscape **20** Spanish Girl in Reverie

All's Well That Ends Well
   author: **18** William Shakespeare
   character: **5** Diana **6** Helena **7** Bertram **8** Parolles **12** King of France **14** Duke of Florence **19** Countess of Rousillon

All That Jazz
   director: **8** Bob Fosse
   cast: **9** Ben Vereen **11** Ann Reinking, Cliff Gorman, Roy Scheider **12** Jessica Lange, Leland Palmer

All the King's Men
   author: **16** Robert Penn Warren
   character: **10** Jack Burden, Judge Irwin, Sadie Burke **11** Adam Stanton, Willie Stark **12** Annie Stanton
   director: **12** Robert Rossen
   cast: **9** Joanne Dru, John Derek **11** John Ireland **17** Broderick Crawford **19** Mercedes McCambridge
   Oscar for: **5** actor (Crawford) **7** picture **17** supporting actress (McCambridge)

all the more
   Latin: **9** a fortiori

All the President's Men
   author: **11** Bob Woodward **13** Carl Bernstein
   subject: **16** Watergate scandal
   newspaper: **14** Washington Post
   director: **11** Alan J Pakula
   cast: **10** Jack Warden **11** Hal Holbrook **12** Jason Robards, Martin Balsam **13** Dustin Hoffman (Carl Bernstein), Jane Alexander, Robert Redford (Bob Woodward)
   Oscar for: **12** screenwriter **15** supporting actor (Robards)

all the same 5 alike **7** however, uniform **8** unvaried **9** identical **11** homogeneous

all together 7 en masse, in a body **8** as a group, in a group, in unison
   French: **12** tout ensemble

all told 5 in sum, total **6** in toto **7** totally **8** as a whole **10** altogether

allude 4 hint **5** refer **7** mention, speak of, suggest **8** intimate **9** touch upon

allure 4 bait, lure **5** charm, tempt **6** entice, lead on, seduce **7** attract, beguile, enchant, glamour **8** intrigue **9** captivate, fascinate **10** attraction, enticement, temptation **11** enchantment, fascination

allurement 4 draw, lure **5** charm **9** magnetism **10** attraction **11** fascination

alluring 4 sexy **8** charming, enticing, magnetic **10** attractive **11** fascinating

allusion 4 hint **7** mention **9** reference **10** suggestion

Allworthy, Squire
   character in: **8** Tom Jones
   author: **8** Fielding

ally 5 unite **6** league **7** combine, partner **8** confrere **9** accessory, affiliate, associate, colleague **10** accomplice, join forces **11** confederate **12** band together, bind together, collaborator, join together

Allyson, June
   real name: **11** Ella Geisman
   husband: **10** Dick Powell
   born: **9** New York NY
   roles: **8** Good News **9** Interlude, The Shrike **11** Little Women **12** My Man Godfrey **16** The Stratton Story **18** The Glen Miller Story

Almagest
   author: **7** Ptolemy
   title means: **11** the greatest
   subject: **9** astronomy

Al Maghrib see **7** Morocco

almandite
   species: **6** garnet
   color: **3** red

Almaviva, Count and Countess
   author: **12** Beaumarchais
   characters in: **18** The Barber of Seville **19** The Marriage of Figaro

Almayer's Folly
   author: **12** Joseph Conrad

almighty 7 supreme **8** absolute, infinite **9** sovereign, unlimited **10** invincible, omnipotent **11** all-powerful **12** transcendent

Almira
   opera by: **6** Handel

almond 12 Prunus dulcis
   varieties: **4** Wild **5** Earth, Green, Sweet **6** Bitter, Desert, Indian **8** Tropical **9** Flowering **12** Dwarf Russian
   candy: **8** marzipan
   liqueur: **6** orgeat **7** ratafia

almost 5 about **6** all but, nearly **7** close to **8** not quite, well-nigh **9** just about **10** not far from, very nearly **11** practically, on the verge of **13** approximately **14** within an inch of

almost alike 5 close **7** similar **10** resembling **11** approaching, much the same **15** nearly identical

alms 3 aid **4** dole, gift **5** mercy **6** relief **7** charity, handout, largess, present, subsidy, tribute **8** donation, gratuity, offering, pittance **9** baksheesh **10** assistance

11 benefaction, beneficence
12 contribution

almshouse 6 asylum **9** poor-house, workhouse

almsman 5 tramp **6** beggar **9** mendicant **10** panhandler

Almug 13 red sandalwood

aloft 2 up **5** above, way up **6** high up, on high **7** sky-ward **8** in the air, in the sky, overhead **10** heavenward

Aloha state
nickname of: **6** Hawaii

Aloidae
name: **4** Otus **9** Ephialtes
form: **5** giant
father: **8** Poseidon
mother: **9** Iphimedia
raised by: **6** Aloeus

alone 4 only, sole **6** lonely, sin-gle, singly, solely, unique **7** forlorn, unaided **8** deserted, desolate, forsaken, isolated, lonesome, peerless, singular, solitary, uniquely **9** aban-doned, matchless, nonpareil, separated, unmatched, unri-valed **10** friendless, separately, singularly, solitarily, unass-isted, unattended, unequalled, unescorted **11** unsurpassed, without help **12** incomparable, unchaperoned, unparalleled, without peers **13** unaccom-panied, without others **14** sin-gle-handedly
Latin: **4** sola **5** solus
French: **4** seul

along 2 on **4** over **6** beside, during, onward **7** abreast, for-ward, through

alongside 2 at, by **6** beside, next to **7** abreast, close by **9** at the side **10** parallel to **12** collaterally, parallelwise **13** equidistantly

aloof 4 cold, cool **5** above, apart **6** chilly, formal, remote **7** distant, haughty, high-hat **8** detached, reserved **10** unso-ciable **11** at a distance, indif-ferent, standoffish, unconcerned **12** uninterested, unresponsive **13** unsympa-thetic **14** unapproachable

aloofness 7 reserve **8** coldness, coolness **9** formality **10** de-tachment, remoteness **11** haughtiness **12** indiffer-ence **13** unsociability **15** standoffishness

Alope
father: **7** Cercyon
son: **10** Hippothous
attacked by: **8** Poseidon

Alopecus
origin: **7** Spartan
form: **6** prince

aloud 7 audibly

alphabet 4 ABCs **6** schema **7** grammar, letters **8** elements **9** rudiments, tablature **10** characters, principles **13** writing system

Alphesiboea
also: **7** Arsinoe
form: **5** nymph
father: **4** Bias **7** Phegeus **9** Leucippus
mother: **9** Philodice
husband: **8** Alcmaeon
son: **6** Adonis
rejected: **8** Dionysus
nurse for: **7** Orestes

Alpheus
father: **7** Oceanus
mother: **6** Tethys
loved: **8** Arethusa
changed into: **5** river

Alphonse and Gaston
creator: **14** Frederick Opper
saying: **22** After you my dear Alphonse, No after you my dear Gaston

alpine 5 alpen, lofty **6** aerial **8** elevated, snow-clad, tower-ing **9** subalpine **10** alpestrine, sky-kissing, snow-capped **11** cloud-capped, mountainous **13** cloud-piercing, cloud-touch-ing **14** heaven-touching

Alps, Alpine
country: **5** Italy **6** France **7** Austria, Germany **10** Yu-goslavia **11** Switzerland **13** Liechtenstein
range: **6** Carnic, Graian, Ju-lian, Otztal **7** Bernese, Cot-tian, Pennine **8** Bavarian, Ligurian, Maritime, Rhae-tian **9** Dolomites, Lepontine **10** Hohe Tauern
peak: **4** Rosa **5** Eiger, Monch **8** Jungfrau **10** Kara-wanken, Matterhorn, Piz Bernina **13** Grossglockner
highest point: **5** Blanc
pass: **7** Brenner, Simplon, Splugen, Stelvio **9** Semmer-ing **10** St Gotthard **14** Great St Bernard
lake: **4** Como **6** Alpine, Ge-neva **7** Lucerne **8** Maggiore **9** Constance
resort: **7** Zermatt **8** Chamo-nix, Salzburg, St Moritz **9** Innsbruck **13** Berchtesgaden
wind: **6** foehns

already 5 early, so far **6** be-fore **8** formerly, hitherto, until now **10** heretofore, previously

already seen
French: **6** deja vu

also 3 and, too **4** more, plus **5** extra **6** as well **7** besides **8** moreover **9** including **10** in addition **12** additionally

Altaic
language branches: **6** Turkic **8** Tungusic **9** Mongolian

altar 5 bomos **6** hestia, scribis **7** eschara **8** credence **9** holy table, prothesis **10** Lord's table

Altar
constellation of: **3** Ara

Altdorfer, Albrecht
born: **7** Germany **10** Regensburg
artwork: **16** Susanna at the Bath **20** St George and the Dragon, Susannah and the Elders **24** Landscape with a Footbridge **39** The Battle of Alexander and Darius on the Issus

alter 4 vary **5** amend **6** change, modify, recast, revise **7** con-vert, remodel **9** transform **13** make different

alterable 7 unfixed **8** variable **9** adaptable **10** adjustable, changeable, modifiable **11** convertible

alteration 6 change **10** adjust-ment, conversion, remodeling **12** modification **13** transmuta-tion **14** transformation

altercation 3 row **4** spat **5** brawl, broil, fight, melee, scene **6** affray, fracas, rumpus, scrape **7** discord, dispute, quarrel, scuffle **8** argument **9** bickering, wrangling **10** fall-ing-out **11** controversy **12** disagreement

alter ego 4 twin **5** match **6** double **9** duplicate, other self, semblable **10** comple-ment, other image, second self, simulacrum **11** counter-part **12** Doppelganger

alternate 3 sub **4** vary **5** alter, proxy **6** backup, change, dep-uty, rotate, second **7** another, standby, stand-in **9** surrogate, take turns **10** every other, re-ciprocal, substitute, successive, understudy **11** alternating, consecutive, every second, in-terchange, intersperse, pinch hitter

alternative 6 choice, option, way out **8** recourse **9** selec-tion **10** substitute **11** other choice

Altes
origin: **5** Greek
mentioned in: **5** Iliad
king of: **7** Leleges
daughter: **7** Laothoe

Althaea
father: **8** Thestius
brother: **9** Plexippus
husband: **6** Oeneus
son: **6** Toxeus, Tydeus
8 Meleager
daughter: **5** Gorge **8** Deianira

Althaemenes
father: **7** Catreus
sister: **9** Apemosyne
killed: **7** Catreus **9** Apemosyne

although 3 but, yet **4** even
5 still **7** however **11** nonetheless **12** nevertheless
15 notwithstanding

altitude 4 apex **6** height, vertex, zenith **8** eminence, tallness **9** elevation, loftiness, sublimity **10** prominence

Altman, Robert
director of: **4** MASH
9 Nashville

altogether 5 fully, in all, in sum, quite **6** in toto, wholly **7** all told, totally, utterly **8** all in all, as a whole, entirely **9** in general, out and out, perfectly **10** absolutely, completely, in sum total, on the whole, thoroughly **12** all inclusive, collectively

altruism 7 charity **10** generosity **11** benevolence **12** philanthropy, public spirit
13 unselfishness **14** bigheartedness, charitableness
15 humanitarianism

altruistic 8 generous **9** unselfish **10** benevolent, charitable **12** humanitarian, largehearted **13** philanthropic **14** publicspirited

aluminum
chemical symbol: **2** Al

alumnus 8 graduate **12** male graduate **13** former student

Alverio, Rosita Dolores
real name of: **10** Rita Moreno

always 7 forever **8** evermore **9** eternally, every time, regularly **10** for all time, invariably **11** continually, incessantly, perpetually, unceasingly **12** consistently **13** everlastingly, unremittingly **14** forever and ever

Amadan
origin: **5** Irish
form: **5** fairy

Amadeus
director: **11** Milos Forman
cast: **8** Tom Hulce (Wolfgang Amadeus Mozart) **14** F Murray Abraham (Antonio Salieri)

choreography: 10 Twyla Tharp
Oscar for: **5** actor (Abraham) **7** picture **8** director

Amadis of Gaul
author: **16** Garcia de Montalvo
character: **6** Oriana, Perion **7** Elisena **8** Garinter, Lisuarte

Amado, Jorge
author of: **14** Tent of Miracles **15** Home Is the Sailor **19** Shepherds of the Night **24** Gabriela Clove and Cinnamon **25** Dona Flor and Her Two Husbands **30** The Two Deaths of Quincas Wateryell

Amahl and the Night Visitors
opera by: **7** Menotti

Amalek
father: **7** Eliphaz
mother: **6** Timnah
grandfather: **4** Esau
descendant of: **9** Amalekite

amalgam 5 alloy, blend, combo, union **6** fusion, league, merger **7** joining, mixture **8** alliance, compound, mishmash **9** admixture, composite **10** assemblage, commixture **11** combination **12** amalgamation, intermixture

amalgamate 3 mix **4** fuse **5** blend, merge, unify, unite **7** combine **8** coalesce, federate **9** commingle, integrate **10** synthesize **11** consolidate, incorporate **12** join together

Amalthaea
form: **4** goat **5** nymph
raised: **4** Zeus

Amarcord
director: **15** Federico Fellini
cast: **10** Bruno Zanin, Magali Noel **13** Pupella Maggio

amaretto
type: **7** liqueur
origin: **5** Italy
flavor: **6** almond
with vodka: **9** Godmother

Amaryllis
character in: **9** Ecologues
author: **6** Virgil
represented: **11** shepherdess

Amarynceus
origin: **5** Greek
mentioned in: **5** Iliad
king of: **7** Messene
ruled: **4** Elis
ruled with: **6** Augeas
killed by: **6** Nestor

Amasa
father: **6** Jether
mother: **7** Abigail
uncle: **5** David

commander for: **5** David
7 Absalom
killed by: **4** Joab

amass 6 gather, heap up, pile up **7** acquire, collect, compile, round up **8** assemble **10** accumulate

amassing 7 heaping, piling **8** piling up **9** aggregate, compiling, gathering **10** assemblage, assembling, collecting **11** compilation **12** accumulating

Amata
husband: **7** Latinus
daughter: **7** Lavinia

amateur 4 tyro **6** novice **7** dabbler **8** beginner, hobbyist, inexpert, neophyte **9** greenhorn, unskilled **10** dilettante, unpolished **13** inexperienced **14** unprofessional
15 nonprofessional

amateurish 5 inept **6** clumsy **7** awkward **8** inexpert, mediocre **9** unskilled, untrained **10** unskillful **11** incompetent, ineffective, unpracticed **13** inexperienced **14** unaccomplished, unprofessional

amatory 3 hot **4** fond, sexy **6** ardent, doting, erotic, loving, sexual, steamy, tender **7** adoring, amorous, devoted, fervent, sensual, sexed-up **8** lovesick, romantic, yearning **9** libidinal, loverlike, rapturous **10** infatuated, lascivious, passionate **11** impassioned, languishing

amaxophobia
fear of: **7** driving **8** vehicles

amaze 3 awe **4** daze, stun **5** shock **7** astound, stagger, stupefy **8** astonish, surprise **9** dumbfound **11** flabbergast

amazement 3 awe **5** shock **6** wonder **8** surprise **9** disbelief **11** incredulity **12** astonishment, bewilderment, stupefaction

Amaziah
father: **5** Joash
opposed: **7** Jehoash
captured at: **11** Bethshemesh
killed at: **7** Lachish

Amazon
occupation: **7** warrior
sex: **6** female
queen: **9** Hippolyta

amazonite
species: **8** feldspar

Amazonomachia
battle between: **6** Greeks
7 Amazons

ambassador 5 agent, envoy **6** consul, deputy, legate, nuncio **7** attache, courier **8** diplomat, emissary, minister **9** go-between **11** diplomatist **12** intermediary **13** consul general **14** representative

Ambassadors, The
author: **10** Henry James
character: **8** Strether, Waymarsh **10** Mrs Newsome **11** Mamie Pocock, Sarah Pocock **12** Maria Gostrey **15** Chadwick Newsome **17** Comtesse de Vionnet

amber
formed from: **5** resin
color: **6** yellow
Greek: **8** elektron

ambiance 3 air **4** aura, mood, tone **5** tenor **6** spirit, flavor, milieu, temper **7** climate, setting **9** character **10** atmosphere **11** environment **12** surroundings

ambiguity 9 vagueness **11** uncertainty **12** abstruseness, doubtfulness, equivocation **14** indefiniteness
French: **13** double entente

ambiguous 5 vague **7** cryptic, unclear **8** doubtful, puzzling **9** enigmatic, equivocal, uncertain **10** indefinite, misleading

ambition 3 aim **4** goal, hope, plan, push, zeal **5** dream, drive **6** design, desire, intent **7** longing, purpose **8** striving, yearning **9** objective **10** aspiration

ambitious 4 avid **5** eager **6** ardent, intent **7** arduous, zealous **8** aspiring, desirous **9** difficult, energetic, grandiose, strenuous **10** determined **11** industrious **12** enterprising

ambivalent 5 mixed **7** warring **8** clashing, confused, opposing, wavering **9** equivocal, undecided, unfocused **10** wishy-washy **11** conflicting, fluctuating, vacillating **13** contradictory

amble 6 ramble, stroll **7** meander, saunter **15** wander aimlessly

Ambler, Eric
author of: **11** The Levanter **12** A Kind of Auger **13** The Care of Time **14** The Night-Comers, Uncommon Danger **15** Journey Into Fear, The Dark Frontier **16** The Light of the Day **19** A Coffin for Dimitrios **22** The Siege of the Villa Lipp

Ambling Alp, The
nickname of: **12** Primo Carnera

ambrosial 5 balmy **8** fragrant, luscious, perfumed **9** delicious **13** sweet-smelling

ambrosia of the gods
4 food **5** drink **6** nectar **7** perfume

ambulance chaser 4 beak **6** lawyer **8** attorney **9** counselor **10** mouthpiece **12** legal advisor

ambulatory 6 mobile, moving **7** walking **10** up and about **11** peripatetic

ambush 4 trap **5** blind, cover **6** attack, entrap, hiding, lay for, waylay **7** assault **8** hideaway, surprise **9** ambuscade **11** concealment, hiding place **13** stalking-horse

Ameche, Don
real name: **17** Dominic Felix Amici
born: **9** Kenosha WI
roles: **6** Cocoon (Oscar) **13** Heaven Can Wait, Moon Over Miami, Silk Stockings **14** That Night in Rio **16** Down Argentine Way **18** The Three Musketeers **29** The Story of Alexander Graham Bell

Amelia
author: **13** Henry Fielding
character: **10** Dr Harrison **11** Mrs Atkinson **12** Miss Matthews **19** Captain William Booth

ameliorate 4 heal, help, mend **5** amend, fix up **6** better, perk up, pick up, reform, remedy, revise **7** advance, correct, improve, patch up, promote, rectify **8** palliate, progress **9** come along, get better **10** grow better **11** improve upon

ameliorative 8 remedial **9** improving **10** corrective, palliative **11** therapeutic **12** compensatory

amen 5 truly **6** it is so, so be it, verily **8** hear hear **9** let it be so, yes indeed **11** so shall it be **17** would that it were so

Amen
also: **4** Amon **5** Ammon
origin: **8** Egyptian
king of: **4** gods
worshiped at: **6** Thebes
personifies: **3** air **6** breath
represented by: **3** ram **5** goose
patron of: **6** Thebes
corresponds to: **4** Jove, Zeus **6** Amen Ra, Amon Ra **7** Jupiter

amenable 4 open **7** cordial, willing **8** obliging, yielding

9 agreeable, tractable **10** open-minded, responsive, submissive **11** acquiescent, complaisant, cooperative, persuadable, sympathetic **17** favorably disposed

amend 3 fix **4** mend **5** alter, emend **6** better, change, modify, polish, reform, remedy, revise **7** correct, develop, enhance, improve, perfect, rectify

amendment 6 change, reform **7** adjunct **8** addition, revision **10** alteration, correction, emendation **11** improvement **12** modification **13** rectification

amends 7 apology, defense, payment, redress **8** requital **9** atonement, expiation **10** recompense, reparation **11** explanation, restitution, restoration, retribution, vindication **12** compensation, satisfaction **13** justification, peace offering **14** acknowledgment **15** indemnification

amenity, amenities 8 civility, mildness, niceties **9** geniality, gentility **10** affability, amiability, courtesies, gentleness, politeness, refinement **11** gallantries, good manners **12** friendliness, graciousness, pleasantness **13** agreeableness

Amen Ra
also: **6** Amon Ra
origin: **8** Egyptian
god of: **8** universe
corresponds to: **4** Amen, Amon, Jove, Zeus **5** Ammon **7** Jupiter

America
author: **19** Stephen Vincent Benet

America, North see box, p. 36

America, South see box, p. 37

American, The
author: **10** Henry James
character: **8** Mrs Bread **10** Mr Tristram **11** Mrs Tristram **12** Noemie Nioche **13** Count Valentin **14** Claire de Cintre **17** Christopher Newman **25** Marquis Urbain de Bellegarde
setting: **5** Paris

American Caesar
author: **17** William Manchester

American Claimant, The
author: **9** Mark Twain

American Dreams
author: **11** Studs Terkel

American Graffiti
director: **11** George Lucas
cast: **9** Paul Le Mat, Ron

America, North
country: 4 Cuba 5 Haiti 6 Belize, Canada, Mexico, Panama 8 Honduras 9 Costa Rica, Guatemala, Nicaragua 10 El Salvador 12 United States 17 Dominican Republic
island: 5 Banks 6 Baffin, Kodiak 7 Bahamas, Bermuda 8 Victoria 9 Alexander, Anticosti, Ellesmere, Greenland, Vancouver 10 Aleutians, Cape Breton, Long Island, West Indies 11 Southampton 12 Newfoundland, Prince Edward 13 Prince of Wales 14 Queen Charlotte
mountain: 5 Coast, Rocky 6 Brooks 7 Cascade 9 Mackenzie 10 Bitterroot 11 Appalachian 12 Sierra Nevada
highest point: 8 McKinley
lowest point: 11 Death Valley
river: 3 Red 4 Ohio 5 Yukon 6 Copper, Fraser, Hudson, Nelson 8 Arkansas, Colorado, Columbia, Delaware, Missouri 9 Mackenzie 10 Coppermine, Sacramento, San Joaquin, St Lawrence 11 Connecticut, Mississippi
lake: 4 Erie 5 Huron 6 Carson, Walker 7 Nipigon, Ontario 8 Manitoba, Michigan, Reindeer, Superior, Winnipeg 9 Athabasca, Champlain, Great Bear, Great Salt 10 Great Slave 11 Yellowstone
animal: 3 bat, rat 4 bear, lynx, puma, wolf 5 bison, moose, skunk 6 beaver, musk ox 7 bighorn, caribou 8 sewellel 9 pronghorn, white goat
bird: 4 hawk 5 eagle, snipe 8 bobwhite, woodcock, wood ibis 9 blue heron, ptarmigan
sea: 6 Bering 7 Chukchi, Lincoln 8 Beaufort 9 Caribbean
religion: 7 Judaism 10 Protestant 13 Roman Catholic 27 Eastern Orthodox Christianity
people: 6 Eskimo 8 European 12 African Negro 14 American Indian
language: 6 French 7 English, Spanish

Howard 10 Candy Clark 11 Wolfman Jack 12 Harrison Ford 13 Cindy Williams 15 Richard Dreyfuss 17 MacKenzie Phillips

American in Paris, An
director: 16 Vincente Minnelli
cast: 8 Nina Foch 9 Gene Kelly 11 Leslie Caron, Oscar Levant 14 Georges Guetary
score: 14 George Gershwin
Oscar for: 7 picture

Americanization of Emily
director: 12 Arthur Hiller
script by: 14 Paddy Chayefsky
cast: 11 James Coburn, James Garner 12 Julie Andrews 13 Melvyn Douglas

American Tragedy, An
author: 15 Theodore Dreiser
character: 12 Roberta Alden 14 Clyde Griffiths, Sondra Finchley 15 Samuel Griffiths

America's Sweetheart
nickname of: 12 Mary Pickford

amethyst
species: 6 quartz
color: 6 purple
month: 8 February

Amfortas
leader of: 7 knights
in search of: 9 holy grail

ami, amie 6 friend

amiability 10 good nature, kindliness 12 agreeability, friendliness, pleasantness

amiable 6 genial, kindly, polite 7 affable, cordial, winning 8 amicable, charming, engaging, friendly, gracious, obliging, pleasant, pleasing, sociable 9 agreeable, congenial 10 attractive 11 good-natured

amicability 5 amity 7 concord 8 good will 9 affection 10 cordiality, friendship 12 friendliness 14 neighborliness

amicable 4 kind 5 civil 6 kindly, polite 7 amiable, cordial 8 amenable, friendly, sociable 9 agreeable, courteous, peaceable 10 benevolent, harmonious, neighborly 11 kindhearted

Amici, Dominic Felix
real name of: 9 Don Ameche

amicus curiae 17 a friend of the court

amigo, amiga 6 friend

Amis, Kingsley
author of: 8 Ending Up, Lucky Jim 10 Colonel Sun, Jake's Thing 11 I Like It Here, The Green Man 16 One Fat Englishman, Take A Girl Like You 18 Russian Hide-and-Seek, The Anti-Death League 20 That Uncertain Feeling

amiss 4 awry 5 askew, false, wrong 6 astray, faulty 7 falsely, mixed-up, off base, wrongly 8 faultily, improper, mistaken, untoward 9 erroneous, incorrect, out of line 10 fallacious, improperly, mistakenly, out of order, unsuitable, unsuitably, untowardly 11 erroneously, incorrectly 12 inaccurately 13 inappropriate 15 inappropriately

Amittai
son: 5 Jonah

amity 6 accord 7 concord, harmony 8 good will, sympathy 9 agreement 10 cordiality, fellowship, fraternity, friendship 11 brotherhood, cooperation 13 understanding

Ammishaddai
son: 7 Ahiezer

Ammon
father: 3 Lot
descendants: 9 Ammonites

Ammon see 4 Amen

Ammonite god 6 Molech, Moloch

ammunition 4 ammo, arms 5 shell 6 bullet, rocket 7 missile, torpedo 9 artillery, cartridge, small arms 11 iron rations 13 powder and shot

ammunition dump 7 arsenal 8 magazine 18 military storehouse, munitions warehouse

amnesia 4 daze 5 fugue 6 stupor 7 agnosia 8 blackout 9 memory gap 11 anterograde, trance state

amnesty 6 pardon 8 immunity, reprieve 10 absolution 11 forgiveness 14 reconciliation

amoeba, ameba 4 dyad, germ, mold 5 spore, virus 6 fungus 7 ciliate, microbe 8 bacteria, reovirus 9 bacterium, echovirus 13 microorganism
part: 7 nucleus 8 membrane 9 pseudopod 10 protoplasm 11 food vacuole 18 contractile vacuole
reproduction by: 7 fission

amok see 5 amuck

Amon see 4 Amen

America, South
country: **4** Peru **5** Chile **6** Brazil, Guyana **7** Bolivia, Ecuador, Uruguay **8** Colombia, Paraguay, Suriname **9** Argentina, Venezuela
city: **4** Lima **5** Quito **6** Bogota, Recife **7** Caracas **8** Salvador, Santiago, Sao Paulo **10** Montevideo **11** Buenos Aires, Porto Alegre **12** Rio de Janeiro **13** Belo Horizonte
island: **6** Chiloe, Chonos, Marajo **9** Galapagos **10** Wellington **11** Madre de Dios **13** Juan Fernandez, Reina Adelaida **14** Tierra del Fuego
sea: **9** Caribbean
lake: **5** Patos, Poopo, Mirim **6** Viedma **8** Titicaca **9** Maracaibo, San Martin **10** Concepcion
mountain: **6** Andes **9** Pakaraima **12** Monte Fitz Roy **14** Cerro Aconcagua, Monte Sarmiento **15** Serra dos Parecis **16** Monte San Valentin, Serra do Espinhaco
highest point: **9** Aconcagua
lowest point: **15** Peninsula Valdes
river: **3** Ica **4** Beni, Iaco, Jari, Meta, Napo **5** Abuna, Cauca, Chico, Iriri, Ituxi, Jurua, Jutai, Negro, Palma, Pardo, Purus, Tiete, Tigre, Xingu **6** Amazon, Arauca, Branco, Chubut, Cumina, Curaco, Cuyuni, Grande, Gurupi, Iguacu, Japura, Javari, Mamore, Maroni, Mortes, Parana, Salado, Vaupes **7** Bermejo, Caqueta, Deseado, Guapore, Jamunda, Juruena, Madeira, Mapuera, Maranon, Orinoco, Oyapock, Ucayali, Vichada **8** Amazonas, Araguaia, Colorado, Guaviare, Jamachim, Paraguay, Parnaiba, Putumayo, Tapajoz, Urubamba, Uruguay **9** Essequibo, Jaguaribe, Paranaiba, Saladillo, Sao Manuel, Tocantins **10** Courantyne **12** Sao Francisco
animal: **3** bat **4** bear, deer **5** llama, sloth, tapir **6** alpaca, monkey, ocelot, weasel **7** opossum, peccary, raccoon **8** capybara, javelina **9** armadillo
bird: **3** owl **4** hawk, rhea **5** eagle **6** condor, falcon, jabiru **7** hoatzin **8** flamingo **11** hummingbird
people: **6** Indian **7** African, Chibcha, Mestizo, Mulatto, Spanish **10** Araucanian, Portuguese
religion: **7** Judaism **10** Protestant **13** Roman Catholic
language: **5** Dutch **7** English, Spanish **10** Portuguese

among 2 at **3** mid **4** amid, with **6** amidst **7** amongst, between, betwixt **12** in the midst of

among other persons
Latin: **10** inter alios

among others 8 attended, escorted, in a crowd, in a group, together **11** accompanied

among other things
Latin: **9** inter alia

among themselves
Latin: **7** inter se

Amon Ra *see* **6** Amen Ra

Amopaon
mentioned in: **5** Iliad
form: **7** warrior
army: **6** Trojan
killed by: **6** Teucer

Amor *see* **5** Cupid

Amore dei Tre Re, L'
opera by: **10** Montemezzi

Amoretti
author: **13** Edmund Spenser

amorous 4 fond **6** ardent, doting, loving, tender **8** enamored, lovesick **10** passionate **11** impassioned **12** affectionate

amorousness 4 love **5** ardor **6** warmth **7** passion

amor patriae 10 patriotism **13** love of country

amorphous 5 vague **8** formless, unshapen **9** anomalous, shapeless, undefined **11** nondescript **12** undelineated **13** characterless, indeterminate

Amos
father: **4** Naum

Amos 'n' Andy
character: **8** Lightnin' **9** Amos Jones, Andy Brown **13** George (the King Fish) Stevens **15** Sapphire Stevens
cast: **8** Tim Moore **13** Ernestine Wade, Horace Stewart **14** Alvin Childress **15** Spencer Williams

amount 3 sum **4** bulk, mass **5** total **6** extent, volume **7** measure **8** quantity, sum total **9** aggregate, magnitude

amour 6 affair **7** liaison, romance **8** intrigue **10** love affair

amour propre 8 self-love **10** self-esteem **11** self-respect

Ampelos
form: **5** satyr

Ampere, Andre-Marie
field: **7** physics **11** mathematics
nationality: **6** French
founded: **15** electrodynamics **16** electromagnetism

Amphiaraus
father: **6** Oicles
mother: **12** Hypermnestra
wife: **8** Eriphyle
son: **8** Alcmaeon **11** Amphilochus
daughter: **9** Demonassa
member: **18** Seven against Thebes
charioteer: **5** Baton

amphibian 8 seaplane **10** hydroplane, vertebrate **14** aerohydroplane
kind: **4** frog, newt, toad **9** caecilian **10** salamander
young: **6** larvae **7** tadpole **8** polliwog

Amphidamas
king of: **7** Cythera
father: **5** Aleus
brother: **7** Cepheus
member of: **9** Argonauts

Amphilochus
form: **4** seer
father: **10** Amphiaraus
mother: **8** Eriphyle
brother: **8** Alcmaeon

Amphimachus
origin: **5** Greek
mentioned in: **5** Iliad
chief of: **6** Epeans
father: **13** Cteatus of Elis
killed by: **6** Hector

Amphimarus
father: **8** Poseidon
son: **5** Linus
vocation: **8** musician

Amphinome
form: **6** maiden
father: **6** Pelias
sister: **6** Evadne
deceived by: **5** Medea
killed: **6** Pelias

Amphinomus
suitor of: **8** Penelope

Amphion
father: **4** Zeus

mother: 7 Antiope
twin brother: 6 Zethus
wife: 5 Niobe
daughter: 7 Chloris
built: 11 Theban walls

Amphisbaena
form: 7 serpent
number of heads: 3 two

amphitheater 4 bowl 5 arena
7 gallery, stadium 8 coliseum
10 auditorium
Roman: 9 Colosseum

Amphithemis
also: 7 Garamas
father: 6 Apollo
mother: 9 Acacaelis
son: 8 Nausamon
9 Caphaurus

Amphitrite
origin: 5 Greek
goddess of: 3 sea
father: 6 Nereus
mother: 5 Doris
husband: 8 Poseidon

Amphitruo (Amphitryon)
author: 7 Plautus
character: 4 Zeus 7 Alcmena,
Jupiter, Mercury
10 Amphitryon

Amphitryon
father: 7 Alcaeus
grandfather: 7 Perseus
uncle: 9 Electryon, Sthenelus
wife: 7 Alcmene
son: 8 Iphicles
daughter: 8 Perimede

Amphitryon 38
author: 13 Jean Giraudoux

Amphius
ally of: 7 Trojans

amphora 3 jar, jug, urn 4 vase

Amphoterus
father: 8 Alcmaeon
mother: 10 Callirrhoe
brother: 7 Acarnan

ample 3 big 4 huge, vast,
wide 5 broad, large, roomy
6 enough, plenty 7 copious,
immense, liberal, profuse
8 abundant, adequate, ex-
tended, generous, spacious
9 bountiful, capacious, expansive, extensive, outspread,
plentiful 10 commodious, sufficient, voluminous 11 substantial 12 satisfactory 14 more
than enough

amplification 7 raising 8 increase, widening 9 expansion,
extension 10 developing, filling out, increasing 11 added
detail, development, elaboration, enlargement, expatiation,
fleshing out, heightening,
lengthening, rounding out
12 augmentation 13 magnification 14 aggrandizement
15 supplementation

amplify 5 add to, raise, widen
6 deepen, expand, extend
7 augment, broaden, develop,
enlarge, fill out 8 complete,
heighten, increase, lengthen
9 elaborate (on), expatiate, intensify 10 illustrate,
strengthen, supplement

amplitude 4 bulk, mass, size
5 range, reach, scope, sweep,
width 6 extent, volume 7 bigness, breadth, compass, expanse 8 fullness, plethora,
richness, vastness 9 abundance, dimension, largeness,
magnitude, plenitude, profusion 11 copiousness 12 completeness, spaciousness
13 capaciousness

amply 5 fully 6 richly 8 lavishly 9 copiously, liberally,
profusely 10 abundantly, adequately, completely, generously, thoroughly
11 bountifully, plentifully
12 sufficiently, unstintingly
14 satisfactorily

amputate 5 sever 6 cut off, excise, lop off, remove
9 dismember

Ampycides
epithet of: 6 Mopsus
means: 12 son of Ampycus

Amram
father: 4 Bani 6 Dishon
son: 5 Aaron, Moses
daughter: 6 Miriam

Amsterdam
airport: 8 Schiphol
canal: 11 Herengracht
13 Keizersgracht,
Prinsengracht
capital of: 7 Holland
11 Netherlands
landmark: 8 Oude Kerk
10 Nieuwe Kerk
museum: 7 Van Gogh
9 Stedelijk 11 Rijksmuseum
nickname: 16 Venice of the
North
waters: 6 Amstel 7 Ij River
9 Zuiderzee 10 Ijsselmeer
13 North Sea

amuck 4 amok, nuts 6 wildly
7 berserk, bonkers 8 crackers,
insanely 9 in a frenzy
10 frenziedly, maniacally
11 ferociously, murderously
14 uncontrollably

amulet 5 charm 6 fetish 8 talisman 10 lucky piece

Amulius
father: 5 Proca
brother: 7 Numitor

amuse 5 cheer 6 absorb, divert,
occupy, please 7 beguile, engross, enliven, gladden 8 interest 9 entertain

amusement 3 fun 4 game,
play 5 hobby, revel 7 delight,
pastime 8 pleasure 9 avocation, diversion, enjoyment,
merriment 10 recreation
11 distraction
13 entertainment

amusing 5 droll, funny, witty
7 comical, waggish 8 cheering,
farcical, humorous, pleasant,
pleasing 9 absorbing, beguiling, diverting 10 delightful,
engrossing 11 interesting,
pleasurable 12 entertaining

Amy, Gilbert
composer of: 9 Alpha-Beth
10 Epigrammes, Mouve-
ments 11 Antiphonies
12 Trajectories

Amyclas
father: 7 Amphion
10 Lacedaemon
mother: 5 Niobe 6 Sparta

Amymone
father: 6 Danaus
son: 8 Nauplius
lover: 8 Poseidon

Amyntor
king of: 8 Ormenium
father: 7 Ormenus
wife: 8 Cleobule
son: 7 Phoenix
daughter: 9 Astydamia
concubine: 6 Phthia
killed by: 8 Hercules

Amythaon
father: 4 Tyro
mother: 8 Cretheus
wife: 7 Idomene
son: 4 Bias 8 Melampus

An
origin: 8 Sumerian
god of: 6 heaven
corresponds to: 3 Anu

Anadyomene *see* 9 Aphrodite

anagram 4 code 6 cipher

Anakim 11 giant people

analects 8 extracts 9 gleanings 10 miscellany, selections
11 collectanea, miscellanea

Analects of Confucius, The
author: 9 Confucius

analeptic 9 stimulant
11 restorative

analgesic 4 drug 6 opiate
7 anodyne 8 narcotic 10 anesthetic, painkiller

analogous 4 akin, like 7 similar 8 parallel 10 comparable,
equivalent 11 correlative
13 corresponding

analogy 6 simile 8 likeness,
metaphor 10 comparison, similarity, similitude 11 correla-

tion, equivalence, parallelism, resemblance
14 correspondence

analysis 4 test **5** assay, brief, study **6** digest, precis, review, search **7** breakup, inquiry, outline, summary, therapy **8** abstract, judgment, synopsis, thinking **9** appraisal, breakdown, diagnosis, partition, reasoning, reduction **10** dissection, estimation, evaluation, resolution, separation **11** examination, observation, speculation **12** dissociation **13** investigation, psychotherapy **14** interpretation, psychoanalysis

analyst 5 judge **6** shrink, tester **8** examiner, observer **9** appraiser, estimator, evaluator **12** headshrinker, investigator **13** psychoanalyst

analytic, analytical 7 logical, testing **8** rational, studious **9** inquiring, organized, searching **10** diagnostic, systematic **14** problem-solving

analyze 5 assay, judge, study **6** search **7** examine **8** appraise, consider, diagnose, evaluate, question **9** reason out **11** investigate **12** think through

Anammelech 13 Sepharvite god

Ananais
　father: **8** Nebedeus
　wife: **8** Sapphira
　sent to: **4** Paul, Saul
　lied to: **5** Peter

anarchist 5 rebel **8** mutineer, nihilist **9** insurgent, terrorist **11** syndicalist **13** revolutionary

anarchy 5 chaos **6** utopia **8** disorder **11** lawlessness **13** the millennium **19** absence of government

Anastasia
　director: **13** Anatole Litvak
　cast: **10** Helen Hayes, Yul Brynner **12** Akim Tamiroff **13** Ingrid Bergman
　Oscar for: **7** actress (Bergman)

anathema 3 ban **5** curse, taboo **7** censure **11** abomination, malediction **12** condemnation, denunciation, proscription **13** unmentionable **15** excommunication

Anathema
　author: **14** Leonid Andreyev

anathematize 4 damn **7** accurse, condemn **8** execrate, maledict **9** abominate **13** excommunicate **17** hold in abomination

Anatolia *see* **7** Armenia

Anatolian
　language family: **12** Indo-European
　spoken in: **9** Asia Minor
　spoken by: **8** Hittites

anatomist 12 morphologist
　American: **5** Allen, Evans **7** Herrick **8** Stockard
　Arabian: **8** Avicenna
　British: **4** Owen **5** Hooke **6** Harvey
　Dutch: **10** Swammerdam
　French: **6** Buffon, Cuvier
　German: **5** Wolff **7** Schwann
　Greek: **5** Galen **9** Aristotle **10** Herophilus **12** Erasistratus
　Italian: **8** Malpighi
　Scottish: **5** Brown

anatomize 7 analyze, dissect **18** separate into pieces

anatomy 4 body **8** analysis **9** structure **10** dissection **11** examination

Anatomy Lesson, The
　author: **10** Philip Roth

Anatomy of a Murder
　director: **13** Otto Preminger
　cast: **8** Eve Arden **9** Lee Remick **10** Ben Gazzara **12** George C Scott, James Stewart, Kathryn Grant **14** Arthur O'Connell
　score: **13** Duke Ellington

Anatomy of Melancholy, The
　author: **12** Robert Burton

Anatosaurus
　type: **8** dinosaur **10** ornithopod
　period: **10** Cretaceous
　characteristic: **10** duck-billed
　location: **12** North America

Anax
　member of: **8** Gigantes
　son: **8** Asterius

Anaxarete
　form: **8** princess

Anaxibia
　father: **6** Atreus
　mother: **6** Aerope
　brother: **8** Menelaus **9** Agamemnon
　husband: **6** Nestor **9** Strophius
　son: **7** Pylades

Anaximander
　field: **11** mathematics
　nationality: **5** Greek
　doctrine: **11** single-world
　first: **22** geometric universe model

Ancaeus
　father: **8** Poseidon
　member: **9** Argonauts
　ship: **4** Argo
　vocation: **8** helmsman
　gift: **8** strength

ancestor 8 begetter, forebear **9** precursor, prototype **10** antecedent, forefather, forerunner, procreator, progenitor **11** predecessor

ancestry 4 line, race **5** house, stock **6** family, origin **7** descent, lineage **8** heredity, pedigree **9** ancestors, blood line, genealogy, parentage **10** derivation, extraction, family tree **11** progenitors

Anchesmius *see* **4** Zeus

Anchiale
　form: **5** nymph

Anchinoe
　father: **5** Nilus
　husband: **5** Belus
　son: **6** Danaus **8** Aegyptus

Anchisaurus
　type: **8** dinosaur
　location: **17** Connecticut Valley

Anchises
　prince of: **4** Troy
　father: **5** Capys
　mother: **8** Themiste
　grandfather: **9** Assaracus
　uncle: **8** Laomedon
　brother: **7** Laocoon
　son: **5** Lyrus **6** Aeneas

anchor 3 fix **4** hook, moor **5** affix, basis **6** fasten, secure **7** bulwark, defense, mooring, support **8** mainstay, security **9** safeguard **10** foundation **12** ground tackle

anchorage 3 key **4** bund, dock, pier, port, quay, slip **5** berth, haven, jetty, wharf **6** harbor, marina **7** dockage, mooring, seaport **9** harborage, roadstead

ancient 3 old **4** aged **5** early, hoary, Greek, olden, passe, Roman **6** age-old, bygone, old hat, remote **7** antique, archaic, very old **8** long past, obsolete, outmoded, primeval, timeworn **9** classical, out-of-date, primitive **10** antiquated, fossilized, Greco-Roman **11** obsolescent, prehistoric **12** old-fashioned, out-of-fashion

ancientness 8 great age **9** antiquity **11** advanced age

ancient times 9 antiquity **10** days of yore **12** the Golden Age

Ancile
　origin: **5** Roman
　form: **6** shield
　given to: **13** Numa Pompilius
　given by: **4** Mars
　purpose: **10** protection
　copied by: **8** Mamurius

ancillary 5 minor **7** adjunct

8 inferior 9 accessory, auxiliary, dependent, secondary
10 additional, subsidiary
11 subordinate, subservient
12 contributory
13 supplementary

Ancius
form: 7 centaur

Ancus Marcius
king of: 4 Rome

and 3 too 4 also, more, plus
10 in addition

andante
music: 4 even 14 moderately slow

Andean
language family: 16 Andean-Equatorial
group: 3 Ona 6 Aymara, Yahgan, Zaparo 7 Quechua
10 Araucanian

Andean-Equatorial
language branch: 6 Andean
10 Equatorial

Andersen, Hans Christian
author of: 10 Thumbelina
11 The Red Shoes 12 The Snow Queen, The Swineherd, The Tinder Box
14 The Nightingale 15 The Ugly Duckling 16 The Little Mermaid 18 The Little Match Girl 20 The Princess and the Pea 21 The Emperor's New Clothes 22 The Steadfast Tin Soldier 25 The Shepherdess and the Sweep

Anderson, Frances Margaret
real name of: 14 Judith Anderson

Anderson, Judith
real name: 23 Frances Margaret Anderson
born: 8 Adelaide 9 Australia
roles: 5 Medea 6 Hamlet, Salome 7 Macbeth, Rebecca 8 Kings Row 16 Cat on a Hot Tin Roof

Anderson, Maxwell
author of: 7 High Tor 8 Key Largo 9 Winterset 11 Valley Forge 14 Both Your Houses, Lost in the Stars, Mary of Scotland, What Price Glory? 17 Elizabeth the Queen 20 Knickerbocker Holiday

Anderson, Sherwood
author of: 9 Poor White
12 Beyond Desire, Dark Laughter, Horses and Men
13 Many Marriages, Winesburg Ohio 15 Death in the Woods 18 The Triumph of the Egg

Anderson, Sparky (George Lee)
sport: 8 baseball
position: 7 manager
team: 9 Minnesota 14 Cincinnati Reds

Andersonville
author: 15 MacKinlay Kantor

Andersson, Bibi
born: 6 Sweden 9 Stockholm
roles: 14 The Seventh Seal
16 Wild Strawberries
19 Scenes from a Marriage
20 Smiles of a Summer Night

Andes
Spanish: 20 Cordillera de los Andes
peak: 6 Pissis, Sajama, Sorata 7 Illampu 8 Cotopaxi, Illimani 9 Huascaran
10 Chimborazo 14 Cristobal Colon
highest point: 9 Aconcagua
volcano: 6 Sangay, Tolima
8 Cotopaxi 10 Tungurahua
country: 4 Peru 5 Chile
6 Panama 7 Bolivia, Ecuador 8 Colombia 9 Argentina, Venezuela
river: 5 Cauca 6 Amazon, Parana 7 Orinoco, Ucayali 9 Magdalena
lake: 5 Poopo 8 Titicaca
animal: 5 llama 6 alpaca, condor, huemul 10 chinchilla

And I Worked at the Writer's Trade
author: 13 Malcolm Cowley

Andorra *see box*

Andorra-la-Vella
capital of: 7 Andorra

and others 3 etc 4 et al 6 et alii 7 and so on 8 et cetera
10 and so forth, and the rest

And Quiet Flows the Don
author: 15 Mikhail Sholokov
character: 6 Piotra 7 Bunchuk, Natalia 14 Gregor Melekhov 16 Aksinia Astakhova

Andrea del Sarto
real name: 32 Andrea Domenico d'Agnolo di Francesco
born: 5 Italy 8 Florence
artwork: 7 Caritas 9 A Young Man 16 Birth of the Virgin, Journey of the Magi
19 Madonna of the Harpies, Portrait of a Sculptor

Andrea del Sarto
author: 14 Robert Browning

Andress, Ursula
husband: 9 John Derek
born: 5 Bern 11 Switzerland
roles: 3 She 4 Dr No 12 Casino Royale, Four for Texas

Andorra
other name: 13 Valls d'Andorra 16 Valleys of Andorra
capital/largest city:
14 Andorra-la-Vella
others: 3 Pal 5 Ramio
6 Ordino, Soldeu
7 Canillo, Certers 9 La Massana 11 Les Escaldes 16 San Julian de Loria
division: 6 Encamp, Ordino 7 Andorra, Camillo 9 La Massana, Sant Julia
heads of state:
13 Bishop of Urgel (Spain) 17 President of France
head of government:
11 First Syndic
monetary unit: 5 franc
6 peseta
lake: 11 Engolasters
mountain: 6 d'Etats
8 l'Estanyo, Pyrenees
10 Cataperdis
highest point: 11 Como Pedrosa
river: 6 Ariege, Valira
people: 7 Catalan
8 Andosian
language: 6 French
7 Catalan, Spanish
religion: 13 Roman Catholic
place: 12 Casa de la Vall
Moorish ruin: 4 Ceca, Meka
feature:
co-princes' representative: 7 vigueer, viguier
fiesta: 13 Bal de Morratxa
food payment to bishop: 9 la quistia

Andrew 7 apostle
brother: 5 Peter, Simon

Andrews, Dana
real name: 17 Carver Dana Andrews
brother: 12 Steve Forrest
born: 9 Collins MS
roles: 5 Laura 9 State Fair
12 Elephant Walk 13 A Walk in the Sun, Ox-Bow Incident 15 Two for the Seesaw 22 The Best Years of Our Lives

Andrews, Julie
real name: 19 Julia Elizabeth Wells
husband: 12 Blake Edwards
born: 7 England 14 Walton-on-Thames

roles: 10 My Fair Lady
11 Mary Poppins (Oscar)
14 Victor Victoria **15** The
Sound of Music

**Andreyev, Leonid
Nikolaevich**
author of: **3** S O S **5** Savva
7 Lazarus, Silence **8** Anath-
ema **10** To the Stars **11** The
Red Laugh **12** The Life of
Man **16** He Who Gets
Slapped **18** Love of One's
Neighbor **19** Seven That
Were Hanged

Andria
author: **7** Terence

Androclea
father: **18** Antipoenus of
Thebes

Androcles
origin: **5** Roman
position: **5** slave

Androcles and the Lion
author: **17** George Bernard
Shaw

Androgeus
father: **5** Minos
mother: **8** Pasiphae
son: **7** Alcaeus **9** Sthenelus
battled: **6** Athens

androgenous
14 hermaphroditic

Andromache
father: **6** Eetion
husband: **6** Hector
son: **6** Pielus **8** Astyanax, Molossus, Pergamus
9 Cestrinus
author: **9** Euripides
character: **6** Peleus, Thetis
7 Orestes **8** Menelaus
mistress of:
11 Neoptolemus
rival: **8** Hermione
son: **8** Molossus
setting: **8** Thessaly

Andromaque
author: **18** Jean Baptiste
Racine
character:
son: **8** Astyanax
king: **7** Pyrrhus
setting: **6** Epirus

Andromeda
father: **7** Cepheus
mother: **10** Cassiopeia
husband: **7** Perseus
son: **6** Mestor, Perses **7** Alcaeus, Heleius **9** Electryon,
Sthenelus
daughter: **10** Gorgophone
rescued from: **10** sea
monster
rescued by: **7** Perseus

Andromeda Strain, The
author: **15** Michael Crichton

androphobia
fear of: **3** men

Androsphinx
form: **6** sphinx
head of: **3** man

and so forth 3 etc **7** and so
on **8** et cetera **9** and others
10 and the rest

and so on 3 etc **8** et cetera
9 and others **10** and so forth,
and the rest

**And Then There Were
None**
director: **9** Rene Clair
based on novel by: **14** Agatha Christie
cast: **11** Roland Young
12 Louis Hayward, Walter
Huston **15** Barry Fitzgerald
remade as: **16** Ten Little
Indians

and thou, Brutus
Latin: **9** et tu Brute
spoken by: **12** Julius Caesar

Andvari
origin: **6** Nordic
form: **5** dwarf

Andy Capp
creator: **14** Reginald Smythe
character: **5** Vicar
wife: **3** Flo
plays: **7** snooker

Andy Griffith Show, The
character: **10** Andy Taylor,
Barney Fife, Goober Pyle,
Helen Crump, Opie Taylor
11 Floyd Lawson **12** Otis
Campbell **13** Aunt Bee Taylor, Howard Sprague
cast: **8** Hal Smith **9** Don
Knotts, Ron (Ronny) How-
ard **10** Jack Dodson
12 Andy Griffith, Anita Cor-
saut, Howard McNear
13 Frances Bavier, George
Lindsey
setting: **8** Mayberry
Andy's job: **7** sheriff

anecdote 4 tale, yarn **5** story
6 sketch **12** brief account,
reminiscence

anemic, anaemic 3 wan
4 dull, pale, weak **5** quiet
6 feeble, pallid **7** subdued
9 colorless **11** thin-blooded
13 characterless

anemone 4 lily **5** plant
6 flower

Anemotis
epithet of: **6** Athena
means: **5** winds

Anesidora
epithet of: **7** Demeter
means: **15** sender up of gifts

**anesthesia, anaesthesia,
anesthesis 6** stupor **8** numbness **11** insentience **13** loss of
feeling **15** unconsciousness

anesthetic, anaesthetic
4 drug **5** ether, local **6** caudal,
opiate, spinal **7** general **8** narcotic, procaine **9** analgesic, en-
flurane, halothane, lidocaine,
peridural **10** chloroform, iso-
flurane, painkiller, tetracaine,
thiopental **11** acupuncture,
laughing gas **12** nitrous oxide
15 sodium pentothal

anesthetize 4 dope, drug,
numb **6** deaden, sedate

anew 5 again, newly **6** afresh
8 once more **9** over again
11 from scratch
Latin: **6** de novo

**a new order of the ages is
born**
Latin: **17** novus ordo
seclorum
author: **6** Virgil
work: **8** Eclogues
motto of: **11** US great seal

angel 3 gem **4** doll **5** jewel,
power, saint **6** cherub, patron,
seraph, throne, virtue **7** sponsor **8** cherabim, seraphim,
treasure **9** archangel **10** benefactor, domination **11** underwriter **12** principality
14 celestial being, heavenly
spirit, messenger of God
15 financial backer

Angel, fallen 5 Satan **6** Azazel **7** Lucifer

angelic 4 good, pure **5** ideal
6 divine, lovely **7** saintly
8 adorable, beatific, cherubic,
ethereal, heavenly, innocent,
seraphic **9** angel-like, beautiful,
celestial, rapturous, spiritual
10 entrancing **11** enrapturing

Angelic Doctor
nickname of: **15** St Thomas
Aquinas

Angelico, Fra
real name: **13** Guido di
Pietro
born: **7** Vicchio **14** Castell
Vecchio
artwork: **12** Annunciation
15 Madonna Annalena
19 Descent from the Cross
21 Coronation of the Virgin **29** Madonna of the
Linen Drapers' Guild

Angelo
character in: **17** Measure for
Measure
author: **11** Shakespeare

Angel of Fire, The
also: **13** The Fiery Angel
opera by: **9** Prokofiev

anger 3 ire, vex **4** bile, fury,
gall, rage, rile **5** annoy, chafe,
pique, wrath **6** choler, dander,
enmity, enrage, hatred, madden, nettle, rankle, ruffle,

spleen, temper 7 incense, inflame, outrage, provoke, umbrage 8 acrimony, embitter, irritate, vexation 9 animosity, annoyance, displease, hostility, hot temper, ill temper, infuriate, petulance 10 antagonism, antagonize, exacerbate, exasperate, irritation, resentment 11 displeasure, indignation 12 exasperation, make bad blood 14 disapprobation 15 get one's dander up 16 cause ill feelings 18 ruffle one's feathers

Anger
   author: 9 May Sarton

Angerboda
   also: 9 Angrbodha, Angurboda
   origin: 12 Scandinavian
   form: 8 giantess
   children: 3 Hel 6 Fenrir, Fenris 11 Iormungandr, Jormungandr 14 Midgard Serpent

Angerona
   origin: 5 Roman
   goddess of: 7 anguish

angle 4 bend, cusp, edge, side, turn 5 focus, slant 6 aspect, corner 7 outlook 8 position 9 viewpoint 10 divergence, standpoint 11 perspective, point of view
   kind: 5 acute, right 6 obtuse 8 straight
   point: 6 vertex
   measure: 7 degrees

angled 4 bent 6 fished 7 crooked, slanted 8 diverged

Anglo-Frisian
   language family: 12 Indo-European
   branch: 8 Germanic
   group: 15 Western Germanic
   language: 7 English, Frisian

Angola *see box*

Angrbodha *see* 9 Angerboda

angry 3 mad 5 huffy, irate, riled, vexed 6 fuming, galled, piqued, raging 7 annoyed, boiling, burnt up, enraged, furious, hateful, hostile, nettled 8 incensed, inflamed, offended, outraged, petulant, provoked 9 affronted, indignant, irasci-

ble, irritated, resentful, splenetic, turbulent 10 displeased, embittered, infuriated 11 acrimonious, exasperated, ill-tempered 12 antagonistic

angst 5 dread 6 unease 7 anxiety 10 foreboding, uneasiness 12 apprehension

angstrom
   abbreviation: 1 A

Angstrom, Anders Jon
   field: 7 physics 9 astronomy
   founded: 12 spectroscopy
   mapped: 11 solar system
   angstrom unit: 17 wavelength of light

anguish 3 woe 4 pain 5 agony, grief 6 misery, sorrow 7 anxiety, despair, remorse, torment 8 distress 9 heartache, suffering

Anguish
   goddess of: 8 Angerona

anguished 6 pained 7 anxious, fearful 9 tormented 10 distressed 11 heartbroken

angular 4 bent, bony, lank, lean 5 gaunt, lanky, spare 6 jagged 7 crooked, scrawny 8 rawboned 13 sharp-cornered

Angurboda *see* 9 Angerboda

Angus Og
   origin: 5 Irish
   god of: 4 love 5 youth 6 beauty

Anicetus
   father: 8 Hercules
   mother: 4 Hebe

animadversion 4 flak 7 nagging, quibble 9 aspersion, criticism, pestering 12 faultfinding 14 censoriousness

animal 3 pet 5 beast, brute 6 mammal 8 creature, nonhuman, organism 9 quadruped
   group: 4 bird, fish, worm 6 insect, mammal, sponge 7 primate, reptile, rotifer 8 ruminant 9 amphibian 10 vertebrate 12 invertebrate

Animal Crackers
   director: 13 Victor Heerman
   cast: 5 Chico, Harpo, Zeppo 7 Groucho 11 Lillian Roth 12 Marx Brothers 14 Margaret Dumont
   song: 25 Hooray for Captain Spaulding

Animal Farm
   author: 12 George Orwell
   character: 5 Boxer 7 Mr Jones 8 Napoleon, Snowball

Animals in that Country, The
   author: 14 Margaret Atwood

Angola
   other name: 7 Bakongo 20 Portuguese West Africa
   capital/largest city: 6 Luanda
   others: 5 Dundo 6 Ambriz, Huambo, Lobito 7 Cabinda, Kampala, Malange, Malanje, Salazar 8 Benguela, Cassinga, Vila Luso 9 Ambrizete, Mocamedes 10 Mossamedes, Nova Lisboa, Silva Porto
   division: 3 Bie 4 Uige 5 Huila, Lunda, Zaire 6 Cunene, Huambo, Luanda, Moxico 7 Cabinda, Malanje 8 Benguela 9 Cuanza Sul, Mocamedes 11 Cuanza Norte 13 Cuando Cubango
   monetary unit: 6 escudo, macuta, macute 7 angolar, centavo
   mountain: 5 Chela 6 Loviti 16 Humpata Highlands
   highest point: 4 Moco
   river: 4 Cuvo 5 Congo, Cuito, Longa 6 Cassai, Coanza, Cuando, Cuanza, Cunene, Kunene, Kwango, Kwanza, Luando 7 Chiumbe, Cubango, Zambezi 11 Lungue-Bungo
   sea: 6 Indian 8 Atlantic
   physical feature:
      basin: 8 Okavango
      desert: 9 Mocamedes
      falls: 15 Catarata Ruacana, Duque de Braganca
      plain: 8 Planalto
      plateau: 4 Rand 5 Huila 11 Benguela Bie, Lunda Divide
   people: 5 Bantu, Kongo, Lundu 6 Chokwe, Herero, Mbundu, Ovambo 7 Bakongo, Kangela, Kikongo 8 Kimbundu, Kwangare 9 Ovinbundu 12 Nyaneka-Humbi
      leader: 13 Agostinho Neto 20 Jose Eduardo dos Santos
   language: 5 Bantu 8 Kimbundu, Oumbundu 9 Ovimbundu 10 Portuguese
   religion: 7 animism 10 Protestant 13 Roman Catholic
   place:
      fortress: 9 Sao Miguel
   feature:
      mahogany: 5 khaya
      weed: 6 archil

animate 4 fire, goad, move, stir, urge, warm **5** alive, impel, set on **6** arouse, excite, fire up, incite, moving, prompt, spur on, vivify, work up **7** actuate, enliven, inspire, provoke, quicken **8** activate, energize, vitalize **9** instigate, make alive, stimulate **10** invigorate, make lively **11** add spirit to **12** give energy to

animated 3 gay, hot **4** airy **5** brisk, quick, vivid **6** active, ardent, blithe, breezy, bright, elated, lively **7** buoyant, dynamic, fervent, glowing, vibrant, zealous, zestful **8** exciting, spirited, sportive, vigorous **9** ebullient, energetic, sprightly, vivacious **10** passionate **12** invigorating

animation 3 vim **4** fire, glow, life, zest **5** ardor, verve, vigor **6** action, gaiety, spirit **7** elation **8** activity, alacrity, buoyancy, vibrancy, vitality, vivacity **9** alertness, briskness, eagerness, good cheer **10** brightness, ebullience, enthusiasm, excitement, liveliness **12** exhilaration, sportiveness **13** sprightliness

animosity 4 hate **5** anger **6** enmity, hatred, malice, rancor, strife **7** dislike, ill will **8** acrimony **9** antipathy, hostility, malignity **10** antagonism, bitterness, resentment **11** malevolence **14** unfriendliness

animus 5 anger, spite, venom **6** enmity, hatred, malice, rancor **7** disdain, dislike, ill will **8** acrimony, bad blood **9** animosity, antipathy, hostility **10** antagonism, bitterness, ill feeling, resentment **12** hard feelings

anise
botanical name: **16** Pimpinella Anisum
origin: **5** Egypt, India **13** Mediterranean
flavor: **8** licorice
use: **5** cakes, fruit, rolls **7** cookies
plant with similar flavor: **9** star anise
legend:
   safeguards against: **7** evil eye **10** nightmares **11** indigestion
   antidote to: **12** scorpion bite

anisette
type: **7** liqueur
origin: **6** France
flavor: **5** anise
drink: **17** Suissesse cocktail
with gin: **8** Snowball **11** Bachio Punch
substitute for: **8** Absinthe

Ankylosaurus
type: **8** dinosaur **10** ornithopod
location: **12** North America
period: **10** Cretaceous
characteristic: **7** armored

Anna
husband: **5** Tobit
daughter: **4** Mary
sister: **4** Dido
corresponds to: **11** Anna Perenna
died by: **8** drowning

Annabel Lee
author: **13** Edgar Allan Poe

Anna Christie
author: **12** Eugene O'Neill
character: **6** Marthy **8** Mat Burke **19** Chris Christopherson
ship: **14** Simeon Winthrop

Anna Karenina
author: **10** Leo Tolstoy
character: **12** Count Vronsky **13** Alexei Karenin **15** Konstantin Levin **19** Kitty Shcherbatskaya **20** Prince Stepan Oblonsky
setting: **6** Moscow, Russia **12** St Petersburg
director: **13** Clarence Brown
cast: **9** May Robson **10** Greta Garbo (Anna Karenina) **13** Basil Rathbone (Karenin), Frederic March (Vronsky) **16** Maureen O'Sullivan **18** Freddie Bartholomew
earlier film version: **4** Love

annals 7 history, minutes, records **8** archives **9** registers **10** chronicles, chronology **13** yearly records **15** historical rolls **20** chronological records

Annam *see* **7** Vietnam

Anna Marie
character in: **16** Giants of the Earth
author: **7** Rolvaag

Anna of the Five Towns
author: **13** Arnold Bennett

Anna Perenna
origin: **5** Roman
goddess of: **9** longevity

anneal 6 harden, temper **7** toughen

Anne of Geierstein (or, The Maiden of the Mist)
author: **14** Sir Walter Scott

annex 3 add **4** grab, join **5** affix, merge, seize **6** adjoin, append, attach, tack on **7** acquire, connect, subjoin **8** addition **9** appendage **10** attachment **11** appropriate, expropriate, incorporate

Annfwn
also: **5** Annwn

origin: **5** Welsh
means: **8** paradise

Annie Hall
director: **10** Woody Allen
cast: **9** Carol Kane, Paul Simon **10** Woody Allen **11** Diane Keaton, Tony Roberts **13** Shelley Duvall **15** Colleen Dewhurst
Oscar for: **7** actress (Keaton), picture **8** director (Allen) **10** screenplay

annihilate 3 end **5** erase, waste **7** abolish, destroy, wipe out **8** decimate, demolish, lay waste **9** eradicate, extirpate, liquidate **10** extinguish, obliterate **11** exterminate

annihilation 9 abolition, wiping out **11** destruction, extirpation, laying waste, liquidation **12** obliteration **13** extermination

anniversary 4 fete **7** holiday, name day **8** birthday, feast day **9** centenary **10** centennial **11** bicentenary, celebration **12** bicentennial **13** commemoration, golden jubilee **16** sesquicentennial

Ann-Margret
real name: **16** Ann-Margret Olsson
husband: **10** Roger Smith
born: **6** Sweden **9** Valsjobyn
roles: **5** Tommy **12** Bye-Bye Birdie **15** Carnal Knowledge

anno mundi 19 in the year of the world

anno regni 19 in the year of the reign

annotate 5 gloss **6** remark **7** comment, explain, expound **8** construe, footnote **9** elucidate, explicate, interpret **10** commentate

annotation 4 note **5** gloss **6** remark **7** comment **8** exegesis, footnote **10** commentary, marginalia **11** elucidation, explication, observation

announce 5 augur **6** herald, reveal, signal **7** betoken, declare, divulge, give out, portend, presage, publish, signify, trumpet **8** disclose, foretell, proclaim **9** advertise, broadcast, harbinger **10** promulgate **11** disseminate

announcement 9 broadcast, statement **11** declaration **12** proclamation

annoy 3 irk, nag, tax, vex **4** gall, rile **5** harry, tease, worry **6** badger, bother, harass, heckle, hector, nettle, pester, plague, ruffle **7** disturb,

provoke, torment, trouble
8 distract, irritate **10** exasperate **13** inconvenience

annoyance 6 bother **8** irritant, nuisance, vexation **10** irritation **11** distraction, disturbance

annoyed 5 irked, upset, vexed **9** disturbed, irritated, perturbed **11** discomposed **12** disconcerted

Ann Sothern Show, The
   character: 6 Johnny **10** Olive Smith **11** James Devery, Katy O'Connor **13** Jason Macauley
   cast: 9 Don Porter **10** Ann Sothern, Ann Tyrrell **11** Ernest Truex **12** Jack Mullaney

annual 4 weed **5** plant **6** flower, serial **7** gazette, journal, reports **8** bulletin, magazine, notebook, periodic **9** vegetable **10** periodical, record book

annuity 6 income **7** pension, stipend **9** allowance

annul 4 undo, void **6** cancel, negate, recall, repeal, revoke **7** abolish, nullify, rescind, retract, reverse **8** abrogate, dissolve **10** invalidate

annulment 6 recall, repeal **7** undoing, voiding **8** reversal **9** abolition **10** abrogation, retraction, revocation **11** dissolution, repudiation **12** cancellation, invalidation **13** nullification

annus mirabilis 13 year of wonders

Annwn see **6** Annfwn

anodyne 4 balm **6** solace **7** comfort **9** comforter **10** palliative

anoint 3 oil **5** crown **6** ordain **8** put oil on **9** pour oil on

Anointed One 5 Jesus **7** Messiah

anomalous 3 odd **7** bizarre, strange **8** abnormal, atypical, peculiar **9** irregular, monstrous **11** incongruous **12** out of keeping

anomaly 6 oddity, rarity **9** deviation **10** aberration **11** abnormality, incongruity, peculiarity **12** eccentricity, irregularity **18** exception to the rule

anon 4 soon, then **5** again, later **7** by and by, shortly **8** tomorrow **9** afterward, presently **10** before long **11** immediately, in the future

anonymous 7 unnamed

8 nameless, unsigned **12** unidentified **13** bearing no name **14** unacknowledged **19** of unknown authorship

anoplura
   class: 8 hexopoda
   phylum: 10 arthropoda
   group: 11 sucking lice

another 4 else, more **5** extra, other **7** further, renewed **9** accessory, otherwise **10** additional **12** supplemental **13** something else, supplementary **14** different thing

Anouilh, Jean
   author of: 6 Becket **8** Antigone, Eurydice, Leocadia, L'hermine **11** Dear Antoine **14** Time Remembered **15** Le Bal des Voleurs, Thieves' Carnival **16** Point of Departure, Ring Round the Moon **19** Waltz of the Toreadors **20** L'Invitation au Chateau **23** Traveller Without Luggage

answer 3 say **4** fill, meet, suit **5** reply, serve, solve, write **6** be like, rejoin, retort **7** conform, fulfill, react to, resolve, respond **8** be enough, response, solution **9** be similar, rejoinder **10** be adequate, correspond, pass muster, resolution **11** acknowledge, explanation **12** be correlated, be equivalent, be sufficient, do well enough **14** acknowledgment, be satisfactory

answerable 6 liable **8** beholden **10** chargeable **11** accountable, responsible

Answer as a Man
   author: 14 Taylor Caldwell

ant
   caste: 4 male **5** queen **6** worker **7** soldier
   kind: 3 red **4** army, fire **5** dairy, thief **6** beggar, farmer, velvet, weaver **7** formica, janitor, pharaoh **8** honeypot, mushroom **9** Argentine, carpenter, cornfield, harvester, legionary **10** leaf cutter **11** little black **12** fungus grower, odorous house, southern fire **13** mound building **14** Texas harvester
   group of: 6 colony

Antaea
   epithet of: 4 Rhea **6** Cybele **7** Demeter
   means: 6 prayer

Antaeus
   form: 5 giant
   father: 8 Poseidon
   mother: 2 Ge
   gift: 13 invincibility

power derived from: 5 Earth
   crushed by: 8 Hercules
   crushed in: 3 air
   home: 6 Africa

antagonism 5 spite **6** animus, enmity, hatred, rancor, strife **7** discord, dislike, rivalry **8** aversion, clashing, conflict, friction **9** animosity, antipathy, hostility **10** bitterness, dissension, opposition, resentment **11** detestation

antagonist 3 foe **5** enemy, rival **7** opposer **8** attacker, opponent **9** adversary, assailant, disputant **10** competitor, contestant

antagonistic 7 hostile **8** contrary, inimical **9** rancorous **10** antisocial, unfriendly **11** belligerent **12** antipathetic, disputatious

antagonize 5 repel **6** offend **8** alienate, estrange

Antagoras
   occupation: 8 shepherd
   home: 3 Cos
   challenged: 8 Hercules

Antananarivo, Tananarive
   capital of: 10 Madagascar

Antarctica see box

ante 3 bet, pot **5** stake, wager **12** beginning bet

anteater 5 sloth **7** echidna **8** aardvark **9** armadillo

antecede 7 precede, predate **8** go before, preexist **10** anticipate

ante Christum 12 before Christ
   abbreviation: 2 AC

antedate 7 precede, predate **8** antecede, go before **9** come first **10** anticipate **12** happen before

Antediluvian 14 before the flood

antediluvian 7 antique, archaic **8** obsolete **10** antiquated

antelope 8 ruminant
   family: 7 Bovidae
   kind: 3 doe, gnu **4** buck, deer, fawn, kudu, oryx, roan **5** bongo, eland, moose, sable **6** dik-dik, duiker, impala, lechwe, nilgai **7** gazelle, gemsbok, gerenuk **8** bluebuck, bontebok, steinbok **9** blackbuck, sitatunga, springbok, waterbuck **10** four-horned **12** Klipspringer
   habitat: 4 Asia **6** Africa

Antelope State
   nickname of: 8 Nebraska

Antarctica
  division: 10 Wilkes
    Land 13 Marie Byrd
    Land, Queen Maud
    Land 14 Edith Ronne
    Land 17 Ellsworth
    Highland
  island: 4 Ross 5 Peter,
    Scott 6 Biscoe, Hearst
    7 Ballery, Charcot
    8 Adelaide, Elephant
    9 Alexander, Joinville,
    Roosevelt 10 Corona-
    tion, King George
    11 South Orkney
    13 South Shetland
  mountain: 8 Sentinel
    9 Pensacola 14 Trans-
    antarctic 23 Executive
    Committee Range
  valley: 6 Wright
  river: 4 Onyx
  natural resource/min-
    eral: 4 coal
  plant life: 4 moss 5 al-
    gae, fungi 6 lichen, pol-
    len 8 bacteria
  animal: 4 lice, mite,
    tick 5 whale 7 fur seal
    8 ross seal 9 crabeater
    11 weddell seal, wing-
    less fly
  bird: 4 skua 6 fulmar,
    petrel 7 penguin
    10 cape pigeon
  sea: 4 Ross 5 Davis
    6 Scotia 7 Weddell
    8 Amundsen
    14 Bellingshausen

antenna 6 aerial, feeler

anterior 5 front, prior 7 forward, in front 8 previous
9 precedent 10 antecedent
12 placed before

Anteros
  brother: 4 Eros
  avenger of: 14 unrequited
    love

Antevorta
  also: 6 Prorsa 7 Porrima
  form: 5 nymph
  member of: 7 Camenae
  gift: 8 prophecy

Anthas
  father: 8 Poseidon
  mother: 7 Alcyone

Anthea
  epithet of: 4 Hera
  means: 7 flowery

Antheil, George
  born: 9 Trenton NJ
  autobiography: 13 Bad Boy
    of Music
  composer of: 7 Volpone
    12 Helen Retires, Jazz Sym-

phony 13 Sonata Sauvage,
Transatlantic 14 Airplane
Sonata 15 Ballet Mecanique

anthem 4 hymn, song 5 carol,
ditty, music, paean, psalm
6 ballad, sacred 7 cantata
8 doxology 11 church music

Anthesteria
  origin: 5 Greek
  festival of: 4 wine 6 spring
    7 flowers

Antheus
  father: 7 Antenor
  killed by: 5 Paris

anthology 6 choice, digest
7 garland 8 analects, chapbook, extracts, treasury
9 gleanings, scrapbook 10 collection, compendium, miscellany, selections 11 collectanea,
compilation, florilegium, miscellanea 15 commonplace
book

Anthony Adverse
  author: 18 William Hervey
    Allen

anthophobia
  fear of: 7 flowers

anthropologist
  American: 4 Boas, Mead
    5 Lowie, Sapir 6 Geertz, Lin-
    ton, Morgan 7 Kroeber
    8 Benedict
  British: 5 Leach, Tylor
    6 Fortes, Leakey, Rivers
    14 Evans-Pritchard, Radcliffe-
    Brown
  French: 5 Mauss 8 Durkheim
    11 Levi-Strauss
  Polish: 10 Malinowski

anthropology
  term: 4 myth 6 custom, rit-
    ual 7 culture, kinship 8 arti-
    fact 9 ethnology, evolution,
    field work 11 ethnography
    16 natural selection
  type/related study: 5 legal,
    urban 6 social 7 applied,
    medical 8 cultural, eco-
    nomic, physical 9 political
    11 linguistics 12 human
    ecology 13 psychological
    19 structural-symbolist
  famous study: 3 San 4 Kung
    7 Eskimos, Samoans, Tasa-
    day 10 Aborigines 16 Pacific
    Islanders

anthropophobia
  fear of: 6 people

Antia
  husband: 7 Proetus
  daughter: 7 Lysippe
  slandered: 11 Bellerophon

antibiotic 4 drug 5 venom
6 poison 8 curative 9 antidotal,
antitoxic, pesticide 10 wonder
drug 11 insecticide, miracle
drug

kind: 8 neomycin, subtilin
  9 mycomycin 10 ampicillin,
  penicillin 12 erythromycin

antic, antics 5 larks, sport
6 pranks, tricks 9 escapades
10 buffoonery, skylarking,
tomfoolery 11 shenanigans
12 clownishness, monkey-
shines 14 practical jokes

anticipate 5 await 6 expect
7 count on, foresee, long for,
look for, predict 8 envision,
forecast, foretell 9 pin hope
on 10 look toward 13 look
forward to

anticipation 4 hope 10 expectancy 11 expectation,
preparation

anticlimax 7 letdown 8 comedown 14 disappointment

antidote 4 cure 6 remedy
9 antitoxin 10 antipoison, corrective 12 counteragent, coun-
tervenom 13 counterpoison
14 countermeasure

Antigone
  author: 9 Sophocles 11 Jean
    Anouilh
  character: 6 Ismene
    8 Tiresias
    father: 7 Oedipus
    mother: 7 Jocasta
    brother: 8 Eteocles
      9 Polynices
    sister: 6 Ismene
    uncle: 5 Creon
    cousin/lover: 6 Haemon
    defied: 5 Creon

Antigua and Barbuda *see
box, p. 46*

anti-intellectual 5 yahoo
7 lowbrow 9 ignoramus, vulgarian 10 illiterate, philistine

Antilochus
  father: 6 Nestor
  brother: 11 Thrasymedes
  friend: 8 Achilles

Antimachus
  origin: 5 Greek
  mentioned in: 5 Iliad
  chieftain of: 7 Trojans

antimony
  chemical symbol: 2 Sb

Antinous
  suitor of: 8 Penelope
  killed by: 8 Odysseus

Antiochus
  father: 8 Hercules
  mother: 4 Meda

Antiope
  form: 6 Amazon
  father: 7 Nycteus
  sister: 9 Hippolyte
  son: 6 Zethus 7 Amphion
    10 Hippolytus
  mistress of: 7 Theseus

Antigua and Barbuda
capital/largest city: **7** St John's
government:
member of: **26** West Indies Associated States
head of state: **14** British monarch **15** governor-general
island: **4** Long **5** Guana **7** Antigua, Barbuda, Redonda
highest point: **9** Boggy Peak
sea: **9** Caribbean
physical feature:
cove: **5** Royal
harbor/harbour: **7** English
people: **7** African, British **8** Lebanese **10** Portuguese
language: **7** English
religion: **8** Anglican, Moravian **13** Roman Catholic
feature: **15** Nelson's Dockyard

antipathetic 6 averse **7** hostile **8** inimical **9** rancorous **11** ill-disposed

antipathy 6 enmity, rancor **7** disgust, dislike, ill will **8** aversion, distaste, loathing **9** animosity, hostility, repulsion **10** abhorrence, antagonism, repugnance **14** unfriendliness

Antiphas
father: **7** Laocoon

Antiphates
origin: **5** Greek
mentioned in: **5** Iliad **7** Odyssey
father: **8** Melampus
chief of: **10** Laestrygon
occupation: **7** warrior **9** chieftain
killed by: **8** Leonteus

Antipholus
character in: **17** The Comedy of Errors
author: **11** Shakespeare

antiphony 6 chorus **7** refrain **8** response

Antiphus
origin: **5** Greek
mentioned in: **5** Iliad **7** Odyssey
form: **5** nymph
father: **5** Priam **10** Talaemenes
half-brother: **4** Isus
ally of: **4** Troy
devoured by: **10** Polyphemus

antipode 8 contrary, opposite **10** antithesis

Antipoenus
daughter: **5** Alcis **9** Androclea
home: **6** Thebes
descendant of: **6** Sparti

Antiquary, The
author: **14** Sir Walter Scott

antiquated 5 dated, passe **7** antique, archaic **8** obsolete, outdated, outmoded **9** out-of-date **11** obsolescent **12** old-fashioned

antique 3 old **5** curio, relic **6** rarity **7** bibelot, trinket **9** objet d'art **10** antiquated, memorabile **11** memorabilia

antiquities 6 relics **8** artifact **9** monuments

antiquity 7 oldness **8** great age **11** ancientness **12** ancient times

antiseptic 7 aseptic, sterile **8** germ-free **9** germicide **10** germ killer **11** bactericide **12** disinfectant, prophylactic

antisocial 7 asocial, hostile **8** menacing, retiring, unsocial **9** alienated **10** disruptive, rebellious, unfriendly, unsociable **11** belligerent, sociopathic **12** antagonistic, misanthropic

antithesis 7 inverse, reverse **8** antipode, contrary, contrast, converse, opposite

antithetical 8 contrary, opposing, opposite **10** discrepant, refutatory **11** conflicting, disagreeing **13** contradictory **14** countervailing, irreconcilable

antitoxin 5 serum **8** antidote **9** antivenom **12** counteragent **13** counterpoison

antler 4 horn, knob, rack **5** spike **6** shovel **8** deerhorn, troching
part: **3** bay **4** brow **5** crown, royal

ant lion
also: **8** lacewing **9** doodlebug
kind: **6** owlfly **9** dusty wing, mantidfly **12** spongillafly **13** brown lacewing, giant lacewing, green lacewing **14** beaded lacewing **15** ithonid lacewing **16** pleasing lacewing

Antonello da Messina
born: **5** Italy **7** Messina
artwork: **8** Ecce Homo **11** Three Angels **13** Il Condottiere (Portrait of a Man), Salvador Mundi **21** Saint Jerome in his Study

Antonio
character in: **12** Twelfth Night **19** The Merchant of Venice
author: **11** Shakespeare

Antonioni, Michelangelo
director of: **6** Blowup **8** The Night **10** The Eclipse **12** The Adventure, The Passenger **14** Zabriskie Point

Antony, Mark
also: **14** Marcus Antonius
member of: **11** triumvirate
other triumvirs: **7** Lepidus **8** Octavian (Caesar Augustus)
lover: **9** Cleopatra
cousin: **12** Julius Caesar
wife: **7** Octavia
battle: **6** Actium **8** Philippi **9** Pharsalus
invaded: **7** Parthia
died by: **7** suicide

Antony and Cleopatra
author: **18** William Shakespeare
character: **7** Octavia **9** Cleopatra **10** Mark Antony **14** Octavius Caesar
setting: **5** Egypt
Cleopatra bitten by: **3** asp

antonym 8 opposite **10** antithesis
abbreviation: **3** ant

Antrodemus
type: **8** dinosaur, therapod
also called: **10** Allosaurus
period: **8** Jurassic **10** Cretaceous

Anu
origin: **8** Akkadian
god of: **6** heaven
corresponds to: **2** An

Anubis
origin: **8** Egyptian
god of: **5** tombs **9** embalming
weigher of: **15** hearts of the dead
represented by head of: **6** jackal

Anunnaki
origin: **8** Sumerian
member of: **14** divine assembly
assembly headed by: **2** An **5** Enlil

anvil 5 block, incus **9** converter **11** transformer

anxiety 4 fear **5** alarm, angst, dread, worry **6** unease **7** anguish, concern, tension **8** disquiet, distress, suspense **9** misgiving **10** foreboding, solicitude, uneasiness **11** disquietude, fretfulness **12** apprehension

anxiety-ridden 7 anxious, fearful, nervous **10** distraught

11 worried sick
12 apprehensive

anxious 4 avid, keen **5** eager, tense **6** ardent, intent, uneasy **7** alarmed, earnest, fearful, fervent, fretful, itching, uptight, wanting, worried, zealous **8** desirous, troubled, yearning **9** anguished, concerned, disturbed, expectant, impatient **10** disquieted, distressed **11** overwrought **12** apprehensive

any 3 all, one **4** each, lone, sole, some **5** every **6** single, unique **8** anything, singular, solitary **9** something **10** individual, quantifier

anybody 3 any **6** anyone **8** anything

anyhow see **6** anyway

anything 3 any **4** some **5** aught **6** anyone **7** anybody

anyway 3 anyhow **8** sloppily **9** at any rate, in any case **10** carelessly, in any event, regardless **11** haphazardly, just the same, nonetheless **12** nevertheless **13** indifferently **14** without concern

anywhere 8 anyplace, wherever **11** wheresoever

Aoede
  muse of: **4** song

Ao-men see **5** Macao

A-1 3 ace **4** aces, fine, tops **5** great, prime, super **6** choice, grade-A, superb, tip-top **7** capital **8** sterling, superior, top-notch **9** excellent, first-rate, superfine **10** first-class, tremendous **11** crackerjack, outstanding, superlative

Aornis
  tributary of: **4** Styx

Aornum
  entrance to: **5** Hades
  used by: **7** Orpheus

Aotearoa see **10** New Zealand

apace 4 fast **7** flat-out, hastily, quickly, rapidly, swiftly **8** speedily **9** posthaste **10** at top speed **11** double-quick, on the double **12** lickety-split **13** expeditiously, precipitately **18** hell bent for leather

Apache
  language family: **10** Athabascan, Athapaskan
  band: **9** Jacarilla, Mescalero, San Carlos **13** White Mountain
  location: **7** Arizona **8** Oklahoma **9** New Mexico
  leader: **7** Cochise **8** Geronimo
  noted for: **8** basketry

apart 4 afar **5** alone, aloof, aside **6** cut off **7** asunder, distant **8** by itself, divorced, isolated, separate **9** by oneself, into parts, to one side **10** into pieces, separately

apartment 3 pad **4** flat **5** rooms, suite

Apartment, The
  director: **11** Billy Wilder
  cast: **10** Jack Lemmon, Ray Walston **13** Fred MacMurray **15** Shirley MacLaine
  Oscar for: **7** picture

apathetic 4 cold **7** unmoved **9** impassive, unfeeling **10** disengaged, impossible, phlegmatic, spiritless **11** emotionless, indifferent, passionless, uncommitted, unconcerned, unemotional **12** uninterested, unresponsive

apathy 8 coolness, lethargy, numbness **9** lassitude, unconcern **11** impassivity, inattention, passiveness **12** indifference **13** impassibility, lack of feeling **14** lack of interest **15** emotionlessness **16** unresponsiveness

apatite
  source: **5** Burma, Mogok

Apatosaurus see **12** Brontosaurus

ape 4 copy, echo, mock **5** mimic **6** follow, mirror, monkey, parody, parrot **7** emulate, imitate, primate **8** travesty **9** burlesque **10** caricature
  family: **8** Pongidae
  combining form: **8** pithecus
  study of: **11** pithecology
  kind: **6** gibbon **7** gorilla, siamang **9** orangutan **10** chimpanzee
  famous: **8** Godzilla, King Kong

Apemius
  epithet of: **4** Zeus
  means: **13** averter of ills

Apemosyne
  father: **7** Catreus
  brother: **11** Althaemenes
  ravished by: **6** Hermes
  killed by: **11** Althaemenes

Apepi see **7** Apophis

apercu 6 glance **7** glimpse, insight, outline, summary

aperture 3 gap **4** hole, rent, rift, slit, slot **5** chink, cleft, space **6** breach **7** fissure, opening, orifice **10** interstice

apex 3 cap, tip **4** acme, peak **5** crest, crown **6** apogee, climax, height, summit, vertex, zenith **8** pinnacle **11** culmina-

tion **12** consummation, highest point **13** crowning point

Aphareus
  king of: **8** Messenia
  father: **8** Perieres
  mother: **10** Gorgophone
  grandfather: **7** Perseus
  brother: **9** Leucippus
  wife: **5** Arene
  son: **4** Ides **7** Lynceus

aphasic 4 dumb, mute **12** inarticulate **17** incapable of speech

Aphesius
  epithet of: **4** Zeus
  means: **8** releaser

aphid
  variety: **3** pea **4** pine, rose **5** apple, grape, peach, tulip **6** cereal, cotton, potato, spruce **7** adelgid, cabbage **8** pear root **9** elm woolly, plant lice, water lily **10** gall-making, phylloxera

Aphidas
  father: **5** Arcas
  son: **5** Aleus

aphorism 5 adage, axiom, maxim **6** dictum, old saw, saying, slogan, truism **7** epigram, proverb **8** apothegm

aphrodisiac 4 sexy **6** carnal, erotic **7** fleshly, philter, raunchy **8** prurient **9** cantharis **10** love potion **11** cantharides, magic potion, stimulating

Aphrodite
  also: **6** Urania **7** Cyprian, Paphian **9** Cytherea **10** Anadyomene
  origin: **5** Greek
  goddess of: **4** love **6** beauty
  husband: **10** Hephaestus
  lover: **4** Ares
  son: **5** Lyrus **6** Deimos, Phobus, Rhodus **7** Priapus
  daughter: **8** Harmonia
  corresponds to: **5** Venus
  epithet: **6** Acraea, Scotia **7** Doritis, Erycina, Limenia **8** Melaenis, Nymphaea, Pandemos **9** Migonitis **11** Aphrogeneia, Apostrophia

Aphrogeneia
  epithet of: **9** Aphrodite
  means: **8** foam born

Apia
  capital of: **12** Western Samoa

apiary 4 hive **7** beehive

apiece 4 each **9** severally **12** individually, respectively

a pied 6 on foot **7** walking

Apis
  origin: **8** Egyptian
  also: **3** Hap **4** Hapi
  form: **4** bull
  from: **7** Memphis

father: 6 Apollo 9 Phoroneus
mother: 8 Teledice
sister: 5 Niobe
nephew: 5 Argus
rid Argos of: 8 serpents
killed by: 7 Aetolus
worshipped at: 7 Memphis

aplomb 5 poise 7 balance
8 calmness, coolness 9 composure, sang-froid, stability
10 confidence, equanimity
11 intrepidity, savoir faire
13 self-assurance, self-composure 14 self-confidence, self-
possession 15 level-headedness 16 imperturbability

Apocalypse Now
director: 18 Francis Ford
Coppola
based on: 15 Heart of
Darkness
novel by: 12 Joseph
Conrad
cast: 11 Martin Sheen
12 Marlon Brando, Robert
Duvall 16 Frederick Forrest
setting: 7 Vietnam

apocalyptic 4 dire 7 ominous
8 oracular 9 far-seeing, ill-boding, ill-omened, prescient, prophetic, revealing 10 disclosing,
eye-opening, foreboding, portentous, predictive, revelatory
11 prophetical 12 inauspicious,
revelational
15 prognosticative

apocryphal 7 dubious 8 disputed, doubtful, mythical, spurious 10 fabricated, fictitious,
unofficial, unverified
11 unauthentic, uncanonical
12 questionable, unauthorized
14 probably untrue 15 unauthenticated, unsubstantiated

apogee 3 top 4 acme, apex,
peak 5 crest, crown 6 climax,
summit, vertex, zenith 8 meridian, pinnacle 9 high point
11 culmination 12 highest
point

Apollo
also: 7 Phoebus, Pythius
9 Musagetes
origin: 5 Greek, Roman
god of: 5 light, music
6 beauty, poetry 7 healing
8 prophecy
father: 4 Zeus
mother: 4 Leto
twin sister: 7 Artemis
sons: 5 Iamus 8 Laodocus
9 Aristaeus, Asclepius,
Philammon 10 Polypoetes
corresponds to: 5 Paeon
8 Hyperion
epithet: 6 Loxias 7 Acesius,
Agraeus, Agyieus, Carneus,
Phyteus, Spodius 8 Gry-
naeus 9 Parnopius, Smin-
theus 10 Alexicacus,
Archegetes, Boedromius,

Delphinius 11 Argyrotoxus,
Epibaterius 12 Platanistius

Apollyon 4 hell 7 Abaddon

apologetic 5 sorry 8 contrite,
penitent 9 defensive, regretful
10 excusatory, mitigatory, remorseful 11 exonerative, extenuatory, vindicatory
12 apologetical 13 justificatory,
making excuses 15 self-
reproachful

Apologia pro Vita Sua
author: 15 John Henry Newman (Cardinal)

**Apologie for Poetrie (De-
fense for Poetry)**
author: 15 Sir Philip Sidney

apologist 7 pleader 8 advocate,
defender 9 supporter

apologize 9 beg pardon
11 make apology 13 express
regret

apology 6 excuse 7 defense
11 explanation, vindication
13 begging pardon,
justification

Apomyius
epithet of: 4 Zeus
means: 14 averter of flies

Apophis
also: 5 Apepi
form: 7 serpent
habitat: 8 darkness
destroyed daily by: 4 Dawn

Apophthegms New and Old
author: 12 Francis Bacon

apostasy 7 atheism, perfidy
8 unbelief 9 defection, disbelief, recreancy 10 disloyalty,
infidelity, irreligion 11 godlessness 13 double-dealing

apostate 6 bolter 7 heretic, seceder, traitor 8 defector, deserter, recanter, recusant,
renegade, turncoat 9 dissenter,
dissident, turnabout 10 backslider 13 nonconformist,
tergiversator

apostle 5 envoy 6 zealot 7 pioneer, witness 8 activist, advocate, disciple, emissary,
exponent, preacher 9 messenger, proponent, supporter
10 evangelist, missionary,
propagator 12 propagandist,
proselytizer, spokesperson

Apostle, The
author: 10 Sholem Asch

Apostles 4 John, Jude, Levi,
Paul 5 Jacob, James, Peter, Si-
mon 6 Andrew, Philip,
Thomas 7 Matthew 8 Barna-
bas, Matthais 9 Nathanael,
Thaddaeus 11 Bartholomew
12 James the Less 13 Judas
Iscariot

apostle to the Gentiles:
4 Paul
apostle to the English:
9 Augustine
apostle to the Irish:
7 Patrick
apostle to the Goths:
7 Ulfilas
apostle to the Germans:
8 Boniface
apostle to the French:
5 Denis
**apostle to the American In-
dians:** 9 John Eliot

Apostrophia
epithet of: 9 Aphrodite
means: 24 rejecter of sinful
passions

apothegm 5 adage, axiom,
maxim, motto 6 dictum 7 epigram, proverb 8 aphorism
9 catchword

apotheosis 7 epitome, essence
9 elevation 10 embodiment,
exaltation 11 deification
12 canonization, consecration,
enshrinement, idealization,
quintessence 13 dignification,
glorification, magnification
15 immortalization

Appalachian Spring
ballet by: 7 Copland

appall 4 stun 5 abash, alarm,
repel, shock 6 dismay, offend,
revolt, sicken 7 disgust, horrify, outrage, terrify, unnerve
8 frighten, nauseate
10 dishearten

appalled 6 aghast 7 alarmed,
shocked 8 dismayed, outraged,
repelled, revolted 9 disgusted,
horrified, nauseated

appalling 4 dire, grim 5 awful
6 horrid 7 fearful, ghastly
8 alarming, dreadful, horrible,
horrific, shocking, terrible
9 dismaying, frightful, repellent, repulsive, revolting, sickening 10 abominable,
disgusting, horrifying, nauseating, outrageous, terrifying
11 frightening, intolerable
12 insufferable
13 disheartening

apparatus 4 gear 5 gismo,
setup, tools 6 device, gadget,
outfit, system, tackle 7 machine 8 material, utensils
9 appliance, equipment, machinery, materials, mechanism 10 implements
11 contraption, contrivance,
instruments 12 organization
13 paraphernalia

apparatus criticus 8 exegesis
10 annotation 11 elucidation,
explication 14 interpretation

apparel 4 duds, garb, gear,
togs 5 array, dress, habit,

robes **6** attire **7** clothes, costume, raiment, threads, vesture **8** clothing, garments **9** equipment, trappings, vestments **13** accouterments

appareled 4 clad **5** robed **6** garbed, suited **7** attired, clothed, covered, dressed

apparent 4 open **5** clear, overt, plain **6** likely, marked, patent **7** blatant, evident, obvious, seeming, visible **8** clear-cut, distinct, manifest, probable **10** clear as day, ostensible, presumable **11** conspicuous, discernible, perceivable, perceptible, self-evident, unequivocal **12** unmistakable **14** understandable

apparently
  Latin: **7** ex facie

apparition 5 ghost, shade, spook **6** spirit, wraith **7** phantom, specter **8** phantasm, presence, revenant **10** phenomenon **13** manifestation **15** materialization

appeal 3 beg, SOS **4** plea, pull, suit **5** apply, charm, plead, sue to, tempt **6** adjure, allure, engage, entice, excite, invite, invoke **7** attract, beseech, entreat, implore, request, solicit **8** call upon, charisma, entreaty, interest, petition **9** fascinate **10** adjuration, attraction, supplicate **11** fascination **12** solicitation, supplication

appealing 7 likable, lovable **8** adjuring, charming, engaging, enticing, fetching, inviting, pleading, pleasing, tempting **10** attractive, entreating, requesting, soliciting **11** charismatic, petitioning **12** irresistable, supplicating

appear 4 look, seem, show **5** arise **6** crop up, emerge, loom up, show up, turn up **7** be clear, be plain, come out, perform, surface **8** be patent **9** be evident, be obvious **10** be apparent, be manifest **11** be published, come to light, materialize

appearance 4 look **5** guise, image **6** advent, aspect, coming **7** arrival, pretext **8** pretense **9** appearing, emergence, showing up, turning up **10** impression **11** outward show **13** manifestation **15** materialization

appear at 6 attend, show up **8** peform at

appease 4 calm, dull, ease, lull **5** abate, allay, blunt, quell, quiet, slake, still **6** pacify,

quench, solace, soothe, temper **7** assuage, compose, mollify, placate, relieve, satisfy **8** mitigate **9** alleviate **10** conciliate, propitiate **11** accommodate

appeasement 6 easing **7** abating, dulling **8** allaying, blunting, giving in **9** abatement, assuasion, quenching **10** mitigation, submission **11** alleviation, assuagement **12** conciliation, pacification, propitiation, satisfaction **13** accommodation, gratification, mollification

appellation 3 tag **4** name **5** title **6** handle **7** epithet, moniker **8** cognomen **9** sobriquet **11** designation, nom de guerre

append 3 add **4** join **5** affix **6** attach, hang on, tack on **7** subjoin, suspend **10** supplement

appendage 3 arm, leg **4** limb, tail **6** branch, feeler, member **7** adjunct **8** addition, offshoot, tentacle **9** accessory, auxiliary, extension, extremity **10** attachment, supplement

appendix 7 codicil **8** addendum, addition **10** back matter, postscript, supplement

appertain 7 apply to, concern, refer to **8** bear upon, be part of, belong to, inhere in, relate to **9** touch upon

appetite 4 zest **5** gusto **6** desire, hunger, liking, relish, thirst **7** craving, passion, stomach **8** fondness, penchant, yearning **10** proclivity **11** inclination

appetizer 6 canape, dainty, savory, tidbit **8** aperitif, cocktail, delicacy **9** antipasto **11** bonne bouche, hors d'oeuvre

appetizing 6 savory **8** alluring, enticing, inviting, tempting **9** appealing, palatable, succulent **10** attractive **11** tantalizing **13** mouth-watering

applaud 4 clap, hail, laud **5** extol **6** praise **7** acclaim, commend **8** eulogize **10** compliment **12** congratulate

applaudable 8 laudable **9** admirable, desirable, excellent **11** commendable, meritorious, outstanding **12** praiseworthy

applause 5 kudos **6** praise **7** acclaim, ovation **8** approval, clapping, plaudits **9** accolades **11** compliments

apple 5 Malus **15** Malus Sylvestris
  varieties/fruit: 4 Crab, Lodi

6 Pippin **7** Baldwin, Stayman, Winesap **8** Ben Davis, Cortland, Jonathan, McIntosh **9** Delicious **10** Rome Beauty **11** Granny Smith, Gravenstein, Northern Spy, Summer Rambo **12** Grimes Golden, York Imperial **13** Yellow Newtown **14** Stayman Winesap **15** Yellow Delicious **17** Esopus Spitzenberg, Yellow Transparent **19** Rhode Island Greening
  varieties/tree: 2 Wi **3** Kai, Kau, Sea, Wax **4** Cane, Java, Jew's, Pond, Rose, Star **5** Adam's, Baked, Belle, Blade, Chess, Conch, Malay, Melon, Thorn **6** Balsam, Indian, Mammee, Possum **7** Chinese, Custard, Dead Sea, Mexican **8** Elephant, Kangaroo, Otaheite, Paradise, Peruvian **11** Soulard crab, Toringo crab **12** Siberian crab
  beverage: 5 cider **8** Calvados **9** Applejack

apple brandy
  drink: 8 Jack Rose **12** Jack-in-the-Box
  with rum: 6 Bolero **8** Apple Pie

applejack
  type: 6 brandy
  origin: 6 Canada **10** New England
  flavor: 10 apple cider
  drink: 11 Frozen Apple **13** Harvard Cooler

Apple of discord
  color: 6 golden
  thrown by: 4 Eris
  awarded to: 9 Aphrodite
  awarded by: 5 Paris
  inscription: 13 for the fairest

apple of one's eye 11 pride and joy **15** light of one's life

applesauce 3 rot **4** bull, bunk **5** hokum, hooey **6** bunkum **7** baloney, hogwash, spinach **8** tommyrot **9** poppycock **12** fiddlesticks **13** horsefeathers **16** stuff and nonsense

Apples of the Hesperides
  color: 6 golden
  given to: 4 Hera
  kept by: 5 Ladon **10** Hesperides

appliance 4 gear **6** device **7** fixture, machine **9** apparatus, equipment, implement, mechanism **11** contraption, contrivance

applicable 3 apt, fit **6** useful **7** apropos, fitting, germane **8** relevant, suitable **9** adaptable, befitting, pertinent

applicant 7 hopeful 8 aspirant, claimant 9 candidate, job seeker, suppliant 10 petitioner

application 4 balm, form, suit, wash 5 claim, salve 6 appeal, lotion 7 request, unguent 8 dressing, entreaty, industry, ointment, petition, poultice, solution 9 assiduity, attention, diligence, emollient, putting on, relevance 10 commitment, dedication, pertinence 11 germaneness, persistence, requisition, suitability 12 appositeness, perseverance, solicitation 13 attentiveness

Appling, Luke (Lucius Benjamin)
nickname: 16 Old Aches and Pains
sport: 8 baseball
position: 9 shortstop
team: 15 Chicago White Sox

apply 3 fit, use 4 suit 5 adapt, lay on, put on, refer 6 devote, direct, employ, relate 7 address, pertain, request, utilize 8 dedicate, exercise, petition, practice, spread on 9 implement

apply oneself 6 attend 10 buckle down 13 give oneself to 15 give it all one has 16 put one's heart into

appoint 3 fix, set 4 name 5 equip 6 assign, choose, engage, fit out, select, settle, supply 7 arrange, furnish, provide 8 decide on, delegate, deputize, nominate 9 designate, determine, establish, prescribe 10 commission

appointment 3 job 4 date, post, spot 5 berth, place 6 naming, office 7 meeting, station 8 choosing, position 9 placement, selection, situation 10 assignment, engagement, nomination, rendezvous 11 designation, meeting time 13 commissioning

Appointment in Samarra
author: 9 John O'Hara
character: 8 Al Grecco, Caroline 11 Harry Reilly 13 Julian English

appointments 4 gear 6 outfit 8 equipage 9 equipment, furniture 11 furnishings 13 accouterments

apportion 5 allot, share 6 divide, ration 7 consign, deal out, dole out, mete out, prorate 8 allocate, disperse 9 parcel out, partition 10 measure out

apportioning 8 alloting, dividing 9 doling out, meting

out 10 allocating, consigning, dealing out, dispensing 12 distributing

apportionment 5 quota 6 ration 7 measure, portion 8 division 9 allotment 10 allocation 11 consignment 12 distribution, pro rata share

apposite 3 apt 7 apropos, fitting, germane 8 material, relevant, suitable 9 pertinent 10 applicable 11 appropriate

appositeness 9 relevance 10 pertinence 11 germaneness 15 appropriateness

appraisal 8 estimate, judgment 9 valuation 10 assessment, evaluation 14 estimated value

appraise 5 assay, judge, value 6 assess, review, size up 7 examine, inspect 8 evaluate

appreciable 7 evident, obvious 8 clear-cut, definite 10 detectable, noticeable, pronounced 11 discernible, perceivable, perceptible, significant, substantial 12 recognizable 13 ascertainable

appreciate 4 like 5 prize, savor, value 6 admire, esteem, relish 7 cherish, enhance, improve, inflate, realize, respect 8 perceive, treasure 9 recognize 10 comprehend, sympathize, understand 11 acknowledge

appreciation 4 rise 6 growth, liking, regard, relish, thanks 7 advance 8 sympathy 9 awareness, elevation, gratitude 10 admiration, cognizance 12 gratefulness, thankfulness 13 comprehension, understanding

apprehend 3 bag, nab, see 4 know 5 catch, grasp, seize, sense 6 arrest, collar 7 capture, discern, realize 8 perceive 9 recognize 10 comprehend, understand 12 take prisoner 15 take into custody

apprehension 5 alarm, dread, worry 6 arrest, dismay 7 anxiety, capture, concern, seizure 8 disquiet, distress, mistrust 9 misgiving, suspicion 10 foreboding, perception, uneasiness 11 premonition 12 presentiment 13 comprehension, understanding 16 apprehensiveness

apprehensive 6 afraid, scared, uneasy 7 alarmed, anxious, fearful, jittery, nervous, worried 9 concerned, misgiving 10 disquieted, distressed, suspicious 11 distrustful

apprehensiveness 5 dread, worry 6 dismay 7 anxiety 9 misgiving 10 foreboding, uneasiness 12 apprehension

apprentice 4 tyro 5 pupil 6 novice 7 learner, student 8 beginner, neophyte 19 indentured assistant

apprise 4 tell 6 advise, inform, notify 8 disclose 9 enlighten, make aware

approach 3 way 4 come, near, road 5 begin, equal, match 6 access, avenue, be like, method, system 7 advance, compare, passage, solicit 8 attitude, come near, draw near, embark on, gain upon, initiate, resemble, set about, sound out 9 come close, enter upon, procedure, technique, undertake 10 move toward, passageway 11 approximate

approachable 9 available, reachable 10 accessible

approbation 6 praise 7 acclaim, support 8 applause, approval, sanction 9 laudation 10 acceptance, compliment 11 endorsement 12 commendation, ratification 14 congratulation

appropriate 3 apt 4 take 5 allot 6 assign, proper, seemly 7 apropos, correct, earmark, fitting, germane 8 allocate, relevant, set apart, suitable 9 apportion, befitting, belonging, congruous, opportune, pertinent 10 confiscate, to the point, well-chosen, well-suited 11 expropriate 12 to the purpose 14 characteristic

appropriateness 7 aptness, fitness 9 congruity, propriety, relevance 10 pertinence 11 correctness, suitability

appropriation 6 taking 9 allotment 10 allocation, arrogation, usurpation 12 confiscation 13 expropriation, money set aside 16 misappropriation

approval 5 favor, leave 6 esteem, liking, regard 7 acclaim, consent, license, mandate, respect 8 sanction 9 agreement 10 acceptance, admiration, compliance, permission 11 approbation, concurrence, countenance, endorsement, good opinion 12 acquiescence, appreciation, confirmation 13 authorization 14 acknowledgment

approve 4 like, pass 5 allow 6 accept, affirm, defend, esteem, permit, praise, ratify, second, uphold 7 condone, confirm, endorse, respect, sustain **8** accede to, advocate, assent to, concur in, sanction **9** authorize, consent to **10** appreciate **11** countenance, go along with, rubber-stamp, subscribe to

approved 8 official **9** canonical **10** authorized, sanctioned

approving 9 endorsing, favorable **10** concurring **11** affirmative, sanctioning **12** appreciative

approximate 5 guess, rough **6** reckon **7** inexact, verge on **8** approach, border on, estimate, look like, relative, very near **9** estimated

approximately 5 circa **6** almost, around **7** close to **9** generally, just about **10** more or less, not far from, very nearly

appurtenance 4 wing **5** annex, extra **7** adjunct **8** addendum, addition **9** accessory, appendage, extension **10** attachment

Apres-midi d'un Faune, L' (The Afternoon of a Faun)
  author: 16 Stephane Mallarme

April *see box*

April Fool's Day
  French: 9 April Fish

April
  event: 11 Black Monday (13)
  flower: 5 daisy **8** sweet pea
  French: 5 Avril
  gem: 7 diamond
  German: 5 April
  holiday: 6 Easter **11** All Fool's Day (1) **13** April Fool's Day (1)
  Italian: 6 Aprile
  Latin: 7 Aprilis
  number of days: 6 thirty
  origin of name: 4 aper (wild boar) **6** aparas (following) **7** aperire (to open) **9** Aphrodite
  place in year:
    Gregorian: **6** fourth
    Roman: **6** second
  saying: 24 April is the cruellest month **27** April showers bring May flowers
  Spanish: 5 Abril
  zodiac signs: 5 Aries **6** Taurus

---

a priori 6 theory **7** opinion **11** of reasoning

apron 3 bib **5** smock **8** covering **10** stagefront

apropos 3 apt **6** seemly **7** correct, fitting, germane, related **8** relevant, suitable **9** befitting, congruous, opportune, pertinent **10** applicable, to the point, well-suited **11** appropriate **12** just the thing

apry
  type: 7 liqueur
  origin: 6 France
  flavor: 7 apricot

Apsyrtus
  also: 8 Absyrtus
  father: 6 Aeetes
  sister: 5 Medea
  killed by: 5 Medea

apt 5 prone **6** bright, clever, gifted, liable, likely, proper, seemly **7** apropos, fitting, germane, given to **8** inclined, relevant, suitable **9** befitting, congruous, opportune, pertinent **10** disposed to, well-suited **11** appropriate, intelligent, predisposed

aptitude 4 bent, gift, turn **5** flair, knack, skill **6** genius, talent **7** ability, faculty, leaning **8** capacity, facility, penchant, tendency **9** endowment, proneness, quickness **10** capability, cleverness, proclivity, propensity **11** inclination, proficiency **12** predilection **14** predisposition

aptness 4 bent, gift **5** flair, knack **6** talent **7** ability, faculty **8** aptitude, facility **11** suitability **15** appropriateness

Apuleius
  author of: 12 The Golden Ass **13** Metamorphoses

aqua 4 blue **5** water **6** bluish **9** turquoise **10** aquamarine **12** greenish-blue

aquamarine 4 aqua, blue **5** beryl **9** turquoise **12** greenish-blue
  color: 9 blue-green

aquaphobia
  fear of: 5 water

aquarelle 10 watercolor

Aquarius
  symbol: 11 water bearer **12** water-carrier
  planet: 6 Saturn, Uranus
  rules: 5 hopes **7** friends
  born: 7 January **8** February

aquatic 6 marine **7** abyssal, fluvial, neritic, oceanic, pelagic **8** littoral **9** thalassic **10** fluviatile, lacustrine

---

aquavit
  type: 6 spirit
  origin: 11 Scandinavia
  flavor: 4 dill **7** caraway **9** coriander
  drink: 5 Glogg

aqua vitae 7 alcohol **11** water of life

aqueduct 4 duct, race **7** channel, conduit **11** watercourse **18** artificial waterway

aqueous 4 damp **5** moist **6** liquid, serous, watery **7** hydrous **8** waterish **9** lymphatic

Aqueus
  epithet of: 4 Zeus
  means: 6 watery

Aquilo *see* **6** Boreas

Aquinas, St Thomas
  nickname: 13 Angelic Doctor
  followers: 8 Thomists
  author of: 15 Summa Theologica **21** Summa Totius Theologiae **34** Summa Catholicae Fidei contra Gentiles

Arab
  clothing: 3 fez **4** veil
  country: 4 Iraq, Oman **5** Egypt, Libya, Qatar, Sudan, Syria, Yemen **6** Jordan, Kuwait **7** Algeria, Bahrain, Lebanon, Morocco, Tunisia **11** Saudi Arabia **18** United Arab Emirates
  habitat: 6 desert
  Holy City: 5 Mecca **6** Medina
  language: 6 Arabic
  people: 7 Semitic
  religion: 6 Muslim **7** Islamic
  tribe: 4 Kurd **6** Berber, Nubian, Tuareg

Arabella
  opera by: 7 (Richard) Strauss

Arabia
  ancient name: 14 Jazirat al-Arab
  ancient people: 6 Sabean **8** Egyptian **10** Babylonian
  bounded by: 5 Syria **6** Jordan, Red Sea **10** Gulf of Aden, Gulf of Oman **11** Indian Ocean, Persian Gulf
  country: 4 Oman **5** Qatar, Yemen **6** Kuwait **11** Saudi Arabia **18** United Arab Emirates
  highest peak: 11 Jabal Shayib
  holy book: 5 Koran
  Holy City: 5 Mecca **6** Medina
  island: 7 Bahrain, Socotra **9** Laccadive
  language: 6 Arabic
  mineral/natural resource: 3 oil **4** goat **5** sheep, wheat **6** barley, millet **7** iron ore, granite **8** porphyry **9** manganese, petroleum

nomadic tribe: 5 Maaza
6 Ababda
prophet: 8 Muhammad
religion: 6 Muslim **7** Islamic
river: 4 Nile, Oxus **5** Indus
6 Tigris **9** Euphrates
sea: 3 Red **7** Arabian **11** Persian Gulf **13** Mediterranean

Arabian Nights
director: 17 Pier Paolo Pasolini
based on: 20 Thousand and One Nights
cast: 11 Franco Citti **13** Ninetto Davoli **14** Ines Pellegrina

Arabian Nights' Entertainments, The (The Thousand and One Nights)
author: 7 unknown
storyteller: 12 Scheherazade

Arabic
national language in: 4 Iraq
5 Syria **6** Jordan **7** Lebanon
11 North Africa **16** Arabian Peninsula
also spoken in: 6 Israel
12 North America, South America **17** Soviet Central Asia, Sub-Saharan Africa
language of: 5 Koran

arable 6 fecund **7** fertile
8 farmable, fruitful, plowable, tillable **10** cultivable, productive

Arachne
origin: 6 Lydian
challenged: 6 Athena
contest: 7 weaving
changed into: 6 spider

arachnid
class: 4 mite, tick **6** spider
8 scorpion **13** daddy-long-legs
phylum: 9 Arthropod
pairs of legs: 4 four
respiratory organ: 12 pulmonary sac, tracheal tube
dwelling: 4 land **5** water
body part: 15 anterior prosoma **20** posterior opisthosoma
way of feeding: 8 parasite, predator **9** scavenger

arachnophobia
fear of: 7 spiders

Aram *see* **5** Syria

Aramis
character in: 18 The Three Musketeers
author: 5 Dumas (pere)

Arapaho
language family: 9 Algonkian **10** Algonquian
tribe: 6 Atsine **11** Gros Ventres **15** Northern Arapaho, Southern Arapaho
location: 6 Plains **8** Colorado, Red River

related to: 8 Cheyenne
ceremony: 8 sun dance

Aras
first king of: 8 Phliasia

Arawak
language family: 8 Arawakan
tribe: 5 Taino **6** Igneri, Lucayo
location: 4 Cuba **5** Haiti
6 Guyana **8** Antilles, Colombia **9** Venezuela **12** South America

Arawakan
tribe: 6 Arawak **8** Boriquen
9 Borinquen

Arawn
lord of: 6 Annfwn

arbiter 5 judge **6** pundit, umpire **7** referee **9** authority **10** arbitrator **11** connoisseur

arbitrary 6 chance, random **7** summary, willful **8** absolute, despotic, fanciful, personal **9** frivolous, imperious, unlimited, whimsical **10** autocratic, capricious, peremptory, subjective **12** inconsistent, uncontrolled, unrestrained

arbitrate 5 judge **6** decide, settle, umpire **7** adjudge, mediate, referee **9** reconcile **10** adjudicate **12** bring to terms **13** sit in judgment

Arbitration, The
author: 8 Menander

arbitrator 5 judge **6** umpire
7 arbiter, referee **8** mediator **9** go-between, moderator **10** negotiator **11** adjudicator **12** intermediary

arbor 5 bower, folly, kiosk
6 gazebo, grotto **7** pergola **8** pavilion **9** belvedere **10** shaded walk **11** summerhouse

arc 3 bow **4** arch **5** curve
8 crescent, half-moon **10** semicircle

arcade 6 loggia, piazza **7** archway, areaway, gallery, skywalk **8** cloister, overpass **9** breezeway, colonnade, peristyle, underpass

Arcadia, The
author: 15 Sir Philip Sidney
character: 5 Mopsa **6** Pamela **7** Dametas, Gynecia, Zelmane **8** Basilius, Cecropia, Pyrocles **9** Amphialus, Musidorus, Philoclea, Plexistus

Arcadian stag *see* **8** Cerynean

Arcanan
father: 8 Alcmaeon
mother: 10 Callirrhoe
brother: 10 Amphoterus

arcane 6 mystic, occult **7** obscure **8** abstruse, esoteric, hermetic, mystical **9** enigmatic, recondite **10** mysterious

Arcas
father: 4 Zeus
mother: 8 Callisto
wife: 5 Erato
son: 6 Elatus
ancestor of: 9 Arcadians
set among: 5 stars
placed by: 4 Zeus

Arce
father: 7 Thaumas
sister: 4 Iris **7** Harpies
Zeus took: 5 wings
aided: 6 Titans

Arcesius
father: 4 Zeus
mother: 8 Euryodia
son: 7 Laertes
grandson: 8 Odysseus

arch 3 arc, bow, sly **4** bend, dome, main, span, wily **5** chief, curve, major, saucy, vault **7** cunning, primary, roguish **8** bow shape **9** curvature, designing, principal **10** curved span **11** mischievous

archaeologist
American: 7 Bingham
8 Douglass, Stephens
British: 5 Evans **6** Carter, Childe, Layard, Leakey, Petrie, Wooley **7** Lubbock, Ventris, Wheeler **9** Rawlinson **10** Pitt-Rivers **13** Caton-Thompson
Danish: 7 Thomsen, Worsaae
French: 5 Botta **8** Cousteau **11** Champollion
German: 5 Conze **7** Curtius **8** Dorpfeld, Koldewey **9** Grotefend **10** Schliemann **11** Winckelmann
Italian: 8 Fiorelli
Swedish: 4 Geer **9** Montelius

archaic 5 passe **6** bygone **7** ancient, antique **8** obsolete **9** out-of-date **10** antiquated **11** obsolescent **12** old-fashioned

archangel 5 Satan, Uriel **7** Gabriel, Michael, Raphael

arched 4 bent **5** bowed
6 curved

Archegetes
epithet of: 6 Apollo
means: 7 founder

Archelaus
father: 7 Temenus
descendant of: 8 Hercules

Archelochus
mentioned in: 5 Iliad
father: 7 Antenor
mother: 6 Theano
killed by: 14 Telamonian Ajax

Archemorus *see* **8** Opheltes

archenemy 3 foe 7 archfoe, bugbear, nemesis, scourge 8 opponent 9 adversary, assailant, bete noire, combatant, disputant 10 antagonist

archeology
  term: 3 dig 6 midden 9 earthwork 11 burial mound 17 aerial photography
  type: 7 salvage 8 American, medieval 9 classical, text-aided 10 Egyptology, industrial, underwater 11 Assyriology, prehistoric 12 Mesopotamian
  ages: 4 Iron 6 Bronze
    Old Stone Age: 11 Paleolithic
    Middle Stone Age: 10 Mesolithic
    New Stone Age: 9 Neolithic
  dating method: 5 cross 8 absolute, carbon-14 13 geochronology 16 dendrochronology 18 thermoluminescence 28 potassium-argon varved deposits
  site/artifact: 2 Ur 4 Giza, Troy 5 Copan, Crete, Delos, Minos 6 Amarna, Carnac, Nimrud, Nippur, Tiryns 7 Alalakh, Babylon, Ephesus, Knossos, Mycenae, Nineveh, Olympia, Pompeii, Rio Azul 8 Behistun, Kuyunjik, Pergamum, pyramids 9 Arikamedu, Hissarlik, Khorsabad, New Grange, Tarquinia, Woodhenge 10 Carchemish, Persepolis, Samothrace, Stonehenge 11 Herculaneum, Machu Picchu, Mohenjodaro 12 Easter Island, Hadrian's Wall, Olduvai Gorge, Rosetta Stone 13 Avebury Circle, Zimbabwe Ruins 14 Dead Sea Scrolls, Laocoon statues 15 temple of Artemis 16 Valley of the Kings 18 Ostrava-Petrokovice, Royal Palace of Minos
  tomb: 11 Tutankhamen 15 Ch'in Shih Huang Ti

Archeptolemus
  mentioned in: 5 Iliad
  father: 7 Iphitus
  charioteer of: 6 Hector

archer 6 bowman 8 spearman
  famous: 5 Cupid 9 Robin Hood 11 William Tell

Archer
  constellation of: 11 Sagittarius

Archer, Isabel
  character in: 18 The Portrait of a Lady
  author: 5 James

Archer, Miles
  character in: 16 The Maltese Falcon
  author: 7 Hammett

Archer, Newland
  character in: 17 The Age of Innocence
  author: 7 Wharton

Archer in Jeopardy
  author: 13 Ross MacDonald

archery
  athlete: 10 Linda Myers, Luanne Ryon 11 Darrell Pace

archetypal 5 model 7 classic 8 original 9 classical, exemplary 10 definitive, prototypal, protypical

archetype 5 model 7 classic 8 exemplar, original 9 prototype 12 prime example

Archias
  founder of: 8 Syracuse
  location: 6 Sicily
  descendant of: 8 Hercules

Archie
  creator: 10 Bob Montana 13 John Goldwater
  character: 5 Betty, Moose 6 Reggie 7 Sabrina 8 Big Ethel, Veronica 11 Mr Weatherby 12 Jughead Jones
  place: 9 Riverdale

Archimago
  character in: 15 The Faerie Queene
  author: 7 Spenser

Archipenko, Alexsandr
  born: 4 Kiev 6 Russia
  artwork: 8 Medranos 9 Gondolier, Medrano II, Pregnancy, The Bather 11 Boxing Match 12 Archipentura, Walking Woman 15 Geometric Statue 18 Wilhelm Furtwangler 19 Woman Combing Her Hair

architect 6 author, shaper 7 creator, deviser, founder, planner 8 designer, engineer 9 artificer, contriver, draftsman, innovator 10 instigator, originator, prime mover 13 master builder 16 building designer
  name 3 Pei 4 Hunt, Mead, Pope, Root, Wren 5 Hoban, Jones, Le Vau, McKim, Mills, Roche, Stone, Tange, White, Wyatt 6 Breuer, Fuller, Owings, Smirke, Wright 7 Bernini, Burnham, Gilbert, Gropius, Johnson, Latrobe, Mansart, Merrill, Renwick 8 Bramante, Harrison, Palladio, Saarinen, Skidmore, Sullivan, Yama-

saki 9 Jefferson 10 Richardson 11 Le Corbusier 12 Brunelleschi, Michelangelo 14 Mies van der Rohe 15 Hardouin-Mansart
  legendary first: 8 Daedalus
    designed: 18 Minotaur's Labyrinth
  Roman: 9 Vitruvius

architecture 5 style 6 design 11 structuring 12 construction 14 architectonics 16 structural design

archives 6 annals, museum, papers 7 library, records 9 documents 10 chronicles, depository 11 memorabilia

arctic 3 icy 5 gelid, polar 6 bitter, frigid, frozen 7 glacial, ice-cold 8 freezing, icebound 9 North Pole 10 frostbound 11 far-northern, hyperborean 13 septentrional

Arden, Eve
  real name: 13 Eunice Quedens
  born: 12 Mill Valley CA
  roles: 13 Mildred Pierce, Our Miss Brooks

ardent 4 keen 5 eager, fiery, lusty 6 fierce 7 earnest, fervent, intense, zealous 8 feverish, spirited, vehement 10 passionate 11 impassioned, tempestuous 12 enthusiastic

ardor 4 love, zeal 5 gusto, verve, vigor 6 fervor, spirit 7 feeling, passion, rapture 8 devotion 9 eagerness, intensity, vehemence 10 enthusiasm, excitement, fierceness 11 amorousness 12 feverishness

Ardrey, Robert
  author of: 17 The Social Contract

arduous 4 hard 5 heavy, tough 6 severe, tiring, trying 7 onerous 8 toilsome, vigorous 9 difficult, energetic, fatiguing, Herculean, laborious, strenuous, wearisome 10 burdensome, exhausting, formidable 11 troublesome

arduousness 5 trial 8 tough job 10 difficulty, rough going, uphill work 12 hard sledding, toilsomeness 13 laboriousness, wearisomeness

area 4 turf, zone 5 arena, field, range, realm, scope, space, tract 6 domain, extent, region, sphere 7 expanse, portion, section, stretch, terrain 8 district, locality, precinct, province 9 territory

Areithous
  origin: 5 Greek
  mentioned in: 5 Iliad
  king of: 7 Arcadia

son: **10** Menesthius
nickname: **7** maceman
weapon: **8** iron mace
killed by: **8** Lycurgus

Areius *see* **5** Areus

arena 4 area, bowl, ring
5 field, lists, realm, scene,
stage **6** circus, domain, sector,
sphere **7** stadium, theater
8 coliseum, platform, province **9** gymnasium, territory
10 hippodrome **11** battlefield,
marketplace **12** amphitheater,
battleground, playing field

Arendt, Hannah
author of: **10** On Violence
12 On Revolution **13** Life of
the Mind **17** The Human
Condition **19** Crises of the
Republic, Eichmann in Jerusalem **27** The Origins of
Totalitarianism

Arene
son: **4** Idas **7** Lynceus

**Arensky, Anton Stepanov-
ich (Antony)**
born: **6** Russia **8** Novgorod
composer of: **7** Tempest
13 Egyptian Night **18** Variations on Legend

Areopagitica
author: **10** John Milton

Ares
also: **8** Theritas
origin: **5** Greek
god of: **3** war
father: **4** Zeus
mother: **4** Hera
sister: **4** Hebe
son: **5** Molus **6** Cycnus, Deimos, Phobos, Tereus
8 Diomedes, Eurytion, Meleager, Oenomaus, Phlegyas,
Thestius **10** Ascalaphus
daughter: **7** Alcippe **8** Harmonia **9** Melanippe
11 Penthesilea
nurse: **5** Thero
corresponds to: **4** Mars
epithet: **8** Enyalius
14 Gynaecothoenas

Arete
father: **8** Rhexenor
husband: **8** Alcinous
daughter: **8** Nausicaa
personifies: **7** courage

Arethusa
form: **5** nymph
changed into: **6** spring
saved from: **7** Alpheus

Aretus
father: **5** Priam
killed by: **9** Automedon

Areus
also: **6** Areius
father: **4** Bias
mother: **4** Pero
brother: **6** Talaus **8** Leodocus

member of: **9** Argonauts
epithet of: **4** Zeus
means: **7** warlike

**Are You There, God? It's
Me, Margaret**
author: **9** Judy Blume

Argades
father: **3** Ion

Argeiphontes
also: **11** Argiphontes
epithet of: **6** Hermes
means: **13** slayer of Argus

argent 5 white **6** silver **7** shining, silvery

Argentina *see box*

Arges
member of: **8** Cyclopes

Argia
also: **5** Aegia
father: **7** Oceanus
mother: **6** Tethys
husband: **7** Polybus
son: **5** Argus

Argiope
form: **5** nymph
father: **8** Teuthras
husband: **6** Agenor
8 Telephus
son: **6** Cadmus
daughter: **6** Europa

Argiphontes *see*
12 Argeiphontes

Argive
pertaining to: **5** Argos

Argo
ship of: **4** Argo

argon
chemical symbol: **2** Ar

Argonauts
searchers for: **12** Golden
Fleece
leader: **5** Jason
ship: **4** Argo
sailed to: **7** Colchis

argot 4 cant **5** idiom, lingo,
slang **6** jargon, patois
10 vernacular

arguable 7 at issue **9** debatable **10** disputable **12** questionable **13** controversial,
problematical

argue 4 hold, show **5** claim,
imply, plead **6** assert, bicker,
debate, denote, evince, reason **7** contend, display, dispute, exhibit, express, point
to, quarrel, quibble, wrangle
8 indicate, maintain, manifest
11 demonstrate, expostulate,
remonstrate

argument 3 row **4** case, gist,
plot, spat, tiff **5** clash, fight,
story **6** debate, reason **7** dispute, outline, quarrel, summary **8** abstract, contents,

squabble, synopsis **9** bickering,
imbroglio **10** war of words
11 altercation, central idea,
controversy, embroilment
12 disagreement

argumentation 6 debate **7** dispute **8** argument **10** discussion

argumentative 5 testy **7** peevish, scrappy **8** contrary, petulant, snappish **9** combative,
fractious, litigious, querulous
11 belligerent, contentious,
quarrelsome **12** cantankerous,
disputatious

Argus
form: **5** giant
father: **7** Phrixus
mother: **9** Chalciope
builder of: **4** Argo
number of eyes: **10** one
hundred
epithet: **8** Panoptes

Argyra
form: **5** nymph
habitat: **6** spring
loved: **8** Selemnus

Argyrotoxus
epithet of: **6** Apollo
means: **18** lord of the silver
bow

aria 3 air **4** solo, song, tune
6 melody, number **7** arietta,
excerpt, section **9** selection
10 canzonetta **13** aria
cantabile

Aria
form: **5** nymph
son: **7** Miletus
fathered by: **6** Apollo

Ariadna *see* **7** Ariadne

Ariadne
also: **7** Ariadna
father: **5** Minos
mother: **8** Pasiphae
husband: **8** Dionysus
son: **8** Oenopion
gave thread to: **7** Theseus
deserted by: **7** Theseus

Ariadne auf Naxos
also: **14** Ariadne on Naxos
opera by: **7** (Richard) Strauss
character: **7** Bacchus, Theseus **8** Composer
10 Zerbinetta

Ariana *see* **11** Afghanistan

Ariane et Barbe-Bleu
also: **19** Ariadne and
Bluebeard
opera by: **5** Dukas
character: **7** Ariadne
9 Bluebeard

Arianrhod
origin: **5** Welsh
form: **7** goddess
brother: **7** Gwydion

Argentina
  name means: **6** silver
  capital/largest city: **11** Buenos Aires
  others: **4** Acha, Azul, Goya, Oran, Puan, Rosa **5** Jujuy, Junin, Lanus, Lujan, Metan, Monte,
    Salta, Tigre **6** Parana, Rufino, Zarate **7** Bolivar, Caseros, Cordoba, Dolores, Formosa, LaBanda,
    LaPlata, LaRioja, Mendoza, Neuquen, Posadas, Quilmes, Rafaela, Rosario, San Juan, Santa
    Fe, Tucuman **9** Catamarca, Rio Cuerto **10** Avellaneda, Corrientes **11** Bahai Blanca, Mar del
    Plata, Resistencia **17** Santiago del Estero **20** San Carlos de Bariloche
  division: **5** Andes, Chaco, Pampa **9** Patagonia **11** Mesopotamia **14** Tierra del Fuego
  measure: **4** sino **5** legua **6** cuadra, lastre **7** manzana
  monetary unit: **4** peso **7** centavo **9** argentino
  weight: **4** last **5** libra **7** quintal **8** tonelada
  island: **14** Tierra del Fuego
  lake: **6** Viedma **7** Cardiel, Fagnano, Musters **11** Buenos Aires, Mar Chiquita, Nahuel Huapi
  mountain: **4** Toro **5** Andes, Chato, Laudo, Potro **6** Bonete, Conico, Pissis, Rincon **8** Famatina,
    Murallon, Olivares, Tronador, Zapaleri **9** Aconcagua, Tupungato **10** Cordillera **13** Ojos del Sa-
    lado **15** Cerro Mercedario, Sierra de Cordoba
  highest point: **9** Aconcagua
  river: **4** Sali **5** Atuel, Chico, Coyle, Dulce, Limay, Negro, Plata, Teuco **6** Blanco, Chubut,
    Cuarto, Flores, Grande, Iguazu, Parana, Quinto, Salado **7** Bermejo, Deseado, Iguassu, Men-
    doza, Tercero, Tunuyan, Uruguay **8** Colorado, Paraguay, Picomayo, Senguerr **9** Pilcomayo
  sea: **8** Atlantic
  physical feature:
    falls: **6** Grande, Iguazu **7** Iguassu
    lowland: **5** chaco
    plains: **6** pampas
    plateau: **4** Puna **6** Parana
    salt flat: **14** Salinas Grandes
    volcano: **5** Lanin, Maipo **6** Domuyo **7** Peteroa
    wind: **5** Zonda **7** Pampero
  people: **3** Api **4** Lule **5** Vejoz **6** Abipon, Vilela **7** Guarani, Puelche, Ranquel, Taluhet **8** Quer-
    andi, Querendy
    artist: **6** Borges
    author: **4** Wast **6** Banchs, Borges **7** Lugones **9** Guiraldes, Hernandez **10** Echeverria
    leader: **4** Roca **5** Illia, Menem, Mitre, Peron, Rosas **6** Videla **7** Urquiza **8** Aramburu, Bel-
      grano, Eva Peron, Frondici, Galtieri **9** San Martin, Sarmiento **11** Isabel Peron
  language: **7** Spanish
  religion: **13** Roman Catholic
  place:
    opera house: **11** Teatro Colon
    world's southernmost town: **7** Ushuaia
  feature:
    bird: **6** chunga
    cowboy: **6** gaucho **7** vaquero
    dance: **5** samba, tango, zamba **6** cuando, gaucho **7** milonga **9** chacarera
    farm: **6** quinta
    knife: **5** facon
    metal straw: **8** bombilla
    ranch: **8** estancia
    school smock: **9** delantale
    shawl: **6** poncho
    trousers: **9** bombachas
    weapon: **4** bola
  food:
    cocktail: **7** clarito
    dish: **4** luna **7** criollo, puchero **8** chivitos, empanada **10** parrillada

mistress of: 7 Gwydion
son: 14 Llew Llew Gyffes
cursed: 14 Llew Llew
  Gyffes

arid 3 dry **4** dull **5** vapid **6** barren, dreary, jejune **7** dried-up,
parched, tedious **8** lifeless, pedantic **9** colorless, dry as dust,
waterless **10** desertlike, uninspired **13** unimaginative, uninteresting **15** drought-scourged

aridity 6 dearth **7** drought, dryness **8** aridness, dullness
  10 barrenness **12** lifelessness,
  rainlessness
  17 unimaginativeness

aridness 6 dearth **7** aridity,
  drought, dryness **8** dullness
  10 barrenness **12** lifelessness,
  rainlessness
  17 unimaginativeness

arid region 6 desert **9** wasteland **16** barren wilderness

Ariel
  author: **11** Shakespeare, Syl-
    via Plath
  character in: **10** The Tempest

Aries
  symbol: **3** ram
  planet: **4** Mars
  rules: **11** personality
  born: **5** April, March

Arimaspians
  member of: **9** Scythians
  number of eyes: **3** one

Arion
  form: **11** winged horse
  father: **8** Poseidon
  mother: **7** Demeter

Ariosto, Ludovico
  author of: **14** Orlando
    Furioso

Arisbe
  father: **6** Teucer
  husband: **5** Priam **8** Dardanus,
    Hyrtacus

arise 4 dawn, go up, rise,
  wake **5** awake, begin, climb,
  ensue, get up, mount, occur,
  set in, start **6** appear, ascend,
  crop up, emerge, result, wake
  up **7** emanate, stand up
  8 commence, spring up, stem
  from **9** originate **11** come to
  light

Aristaeus
  origin: **5** Greek
  god of: **9** husbandry **10** bee-
    keeping, winemaking
  father: **6** Apollo
  mother: **6** Cyrene
  wife: **7** Autonoe
  son: **7** Actaeon
  caused death of: **8** Eurydice

aristocracy 5 elite **6** gentry
  7 peerage, society **8** nobility
  9 beau monde **10** patricians,
  upper class, upper crust
  11 high society

aristocrat 4 duke, earl, lady,
  lord, peer **5** noble **7** Brahmin,
  duchess, grandee, marquis
  8 countess, marquess, nobleman **9** blue blood, gentleman,
  patrician **10** noblewoman
  11 gentlewoman **12** silk
  stocking

aristocratic 5 noble, regal,
  royal **6** lordly, titled **7** courtly,
  genteel, refined **8** highborn,
  highbred, wellborn **9** dignified,
  patrician **10** of high rank,
  upper-class **11** blue-blooded,
  gentlemanly **12** silk-stocking
  13 of gentle blood

Aristodemus
  member of: **10** Heraclidae
  father: **12** Aristomachus
  son: **7** Procles **11** Eurysthenes
  killed by: **9** lightning

Aristomachus
  member of: **10** Heraclidae
  son: **7** Temenus **11** Aristode-
    mus, Cresphontes
  granddaughter: **8** Hyrnetho
  invaded: **12** Peloponnesus

Aristophanes
  author of: **6** Plutus **8** The
    Birds, The Frogs, The Peace,
    The Wasps **9** The Clouds

10 Lysistrata, The Knights
13 Ecclesiazusae, The
  Acharnians

Aristotle
  author of: **7** Physics, Poetics
    8 On Plants, Politics, Rheto-
    ric, Sophisms **9** On the
    Soul **10** Generation **11** Met-
    aphysics **12** On the Heav-
    ens **14** Parts of Animals,
    Prior Analytics **17** Nicoma-
    chean Ethics **18** Posterior
    Analytics **23** On Beginning
    and Perishing

Arizona *see box*

ark 3 box **4** ship **5** barge,
  chest **8** flatboat **9** houseboat
  10 Noah's boat

Arkansas *see box*

Arkin, Alan
  born: **9** New York NY
  roles: **7** Catch-22 **13** Wait
    Until Dark **21** Last of the
    Red-Hot Lovers **23** The
    Heart Is a Lonely Hunter
    40 The Russians Are Com-
    ing The Russians Are
    Coming

Ark of the Covenant
  gold covering: **9** mercy seat
  12 propitiatory

arm, arms 4 guns **5** brace,
  crest, equip, prime **6** branch,
  outfit, sector **7** forearm, fortify, prepare, protect, section,
  weapons **8** armament, blazonry, division, firearms, insignia, materiel, offshoot,
  ordnance, weaponry **9** appendage, make ready, upper
  limb **10** coat of arms, department, detachment, obtain
  arms, projection, strengthen,
  take up arms **12** anterior
  limb **13** prepare for war
  14 heraldic emblem **18** furnish
  with weapons

armada 4 navy **5** fleet **8** flotilla,
  squadron **10** escadrille

armadillo
  family: **11** Dasypodidae
  order: **8** Edentata
  body: **5** armor **6** plates
  habitat: **12** South America,
    United States **14** Central
    America
  habit: **9** nocturnal

Armageddon 8 doomsday
  11 final battle **13** great conflict
  author: **8** Leon Uris

armagnac
  type: **6** brandy **7** liqueur
  origin: **6** France

Arizona
  abbreviation: **2** AZ **4** Ariz
  nickname: **11** Grand Canyon
  capital/largest city: **7** Phoenix
  others: **3** Ajo **4** Eloy, Mesa, Naco, Yuma **5** Globe, Leupp,
    Tempe **6** Bisbee, McNary, Salome, Toltec, Tucson **7** Cor-
    taro **8** Chandler, Glendale, Prescott **9** Flagstaff
    10 Scottsdale
  college: **11** Grand Canyon **12** Southwestern
  explorer: **8** Coronado **12** Marcos de Niza
  feature:
    dam: **6** Hoover **8** Coolidge **9** Roosevelt
    national park: **11** Grand Canyon **15** Petrified Forest
  tribe: **4** Hano, Hopi, Pima **6** Apache, Navaho, Navajo,
    Papago
  people: **7** Cochise **8** Geronimo **14** Barry Goldwater
  lake: **4** Mead **6** Havasu, Mohave, Mormon, Powell
    9 Roosevelt
  land rank: **5** sixth
  mountain: **5** White **6** Lemmon **7** Hualpai **8** Mazatzal
    9 Baldy Peak **13** Santa Catalina
    highest point: **13** Humphreys Peak
  physical feature:
    canyon: **5** Grand
    desert: **6** Sonora **7** Painted
    forest: **9** Petrified
  river: **4** Gila, Salt, Zuni **5** Verde **6** Puerco **8** Colorado
    12 Bill Williams **14** Little Colorado
  state admission: **11** forty-eighth
  state bird: **10** cactus wren
  state flower: **13** saguaro cactus
  state motto: **11** God Enriches
  state song: **7** Arizona
  state tree: **9** palo verde

armament 4 arms, guns
7 weapons **8** ordnance, weaponry **9** equipment, munitions **10** outfitting **13** military
might **16** war-making machine

Armenia *see box*

Armenian
   language family: 12 Indo-
   European
   spoken in: 4 USSR **6** Russia
   7 Armenia

Armida
   opera by: 5 Gluck, Haydn,
   Lully **6** Dvorak **7** Rossini
   10 Eszterhazy

Armies 7 Sabaoth

Armies of the Night
   author: 12 Norman Mailer

armistice 5 peace, truce
9 cease-fire **23** suspension of
hostilities

armlet 6 bangle **8** bracelet,
ornament

arm of the sea 5 bight, firth,
fjord (fiord), inlet **6** strait
7 channel, estuary, narrows

armoire 8 cupboard, wardrobe
12 clothespress

armor 4 mail **5** chain **6** shield
7 bulwark **10** coat of mail,
protection **11** suit of armor
18 protective covering

armorial bearings 4 arms
5 crest **10** coat of arms,
escutcheon

armory 7 arsenal **9** arms depot **13** ordnance depot

Arms and the Man
   author: 17 George Bernard
   Shaw

arms depot 6 armory **7** arsenal **13** ordnance depot
18 military storehouse

Armstrong, Henry
   sport: 6 boxing
   class: 11 lightweight
   12 welterweight

army 3 mob **4** band, bevy,
crew, gang, host, mass, pack
5 crowd, force, horde, swarm
6 legion, throng, troops **7** legions, militia **8** military, soldiers, soldiery **9** land force,
multitude **10** land forces
11 aggregation, fighting men
12 congregation **13** military
force **15** military machine

Arnaeus
   also: 4 Irus
   origin: 5 Greek
   mentioned in: 7 Odyssey
   form: 6 beggar **9** errandboy
   errandboy for: 16 Penelopes
   suitors

Arkansas
   abbreviation: 2 AR **3** Ark
   nickname: 4 Bear **9** Bowie Land **17** Land of Opportunity
   capital/largest city: 10 Little Rock
   others: 3 Coy, Cuy, Keo, Ola, Roe, Ulm **4** Alma, Bono,
   Casa, Dell, Diaz, Moro **5** Enola, Perla, Rondo **6** Alicia,
   Camden **8** El Dorado **9** Fort Smith, Jonesboro, Pine Bluff,
   Texarkana **10** Hot Springs **11** Blytheville **12** Fayetteville
   feature:
      national park: 10 Hot Springs
   tribe: 5 Caddo, Osage **6** Quapaw **7** Choctaw, Wichita
   8 Cherokee
   people: 8 Alan Ladd **10** Dick Powell **11** Bill Clinton
   16 Douglas MacArthur
   lake: 6 Beaver, Chicot, Conway, Nimrod **7** Greeson, Nor-
   fork **8** Maumelle, Ouachita **10** Bull Shoals **11** Greers
   Ferry **12** Blue Mountain
   land rank: 13 twenty-seventh
   mountain: 4 Blue **5** Ozark **6** Boston, Gaylor **7** Fourche
   8 Magazine, Ouachita
      highest point: 8 Magazine
   river: 3 Red **5** Black, White **6** Saline **7** Buffalo, Current
   8 Arkansas, Cossatot, Ouachita **9** St Francis **11** Mississippi
   state admission: 11 twenty-fifth
   state bird: 11 mockingbird
   state flower: 12 apple blossom
   state motto: 13 (Let) The People Rule
   state song: 8 Arkansas
   state tree: 13 shortleaf pine

Armenia
   other name: 5 Minni **6** Urartu **8** Anatolia
   former name: 31 Armenian Soviet Socialist Republic
   capital/largest city: 6 Erivan **7** Yerevan
   ancient capital: 3 Ani **8** Artashat, Artaxata
   others: 3 Van **5** Sivas **7** Trabzon **9** Kirovakan, Leninakan,
   Trabizond **13** Bitlisarzurum
   head of state: 9 President
   monetary unit: 5 ruble
   lake: 3 Van **5** Sevan, Urmia **8** Urumiyah
   mountain: 6 Ararat, Taurus **7** Aladagh **8** Karabakh
   highest peak: 12 Mount Aragats
   river: 3 Ara **4** Aras, Kura **5** Araks, Cyrus, Halys, Zanga
   6 Araxes, Razdan, Tigris **9** Euphrates **10** Kizil-Irmak
   physical feature:
      volcano: 7 Aragats
   people: 5 Armen, Ermyn, Gomer, Hadji
      apostle: 7 Gregory
      gypsy: 5 bosha
      hero: 4 haik **6** vartan
      leader: 26 Levon Akopovich Ter Petrosyan
      me: 3 ara
      saint: 5 Sahak **6** Mesrop
   language: 7 Russian **8** Armenian
   religion: 16 Armenian Orthodox
   feature:
      cap: 6 calpac
      fortress: 7 erebuni
      game: 7 barbout
      kingdom: 6 Urartu, Vannic **7** Cilicia, Sophene **8** Ardsruni
   food:
      bread: 4 peda
      cucumber: 4 guta
      dish: 7 lahvosh **9** paraghatz, sou-beoreg

Arne
   author: **20** Bjornstjerne
   Bjornson

Arne
   son: **6** Aeolus **7** Boeotus
   foster father: **9** Desmontes

Arne, Thomas Augustine
   born: **6** London **7** England
   composer of: **6** Alfred, Judith **8** Rosamond, Tom
   Thumb **10** Artaxerxes
   14 Love in a Village,
   Thomas and Sally

Arness, James
   real name: **12** James Aurness
   brother: **11** Peter Graves
   born: **13** Minneapolis MN
   roles: **8** Gunsmoke **10** Matt
   Dillon

Arnold, Matthew
   author of: **7** Thyrsis **10** Dover
   Beach **15** Sohrab and Rustum, The Scholar-Gypsy
   16 Empedocles on Etna
   17 Culture and Anarchy, Essays in Criticism **18** On
   Translating Homer

Arnold, Roseanne *see*
   Roseanne

aroma 4 odor **5** savor, scent,
   smell **7** bouquet **9** fragrance,
   redolence

aromatic 5 spicy **7** odorous, piquant, pungent, scented **8** fragrant, perfumed, redolent
   11 odoriferous

around 4 near **5** about, circa
   10 encircling, on all sides,
   roundabout **11** surrounding

**Around the World in
   Eighty Days**
   author: **10** Jules Verne
   director: **15** Michael
   Anderson
   character: **11** Phileas Fogg
   12 Passepartout
   cast: **10** Cantinflas, David
   Niven **12** Robert Newton
   15 Marlene Dietrich, Shirley
   MacLaine
   score: **11** Victor Young
   Oscar for: **5** score **7** picture

arouse 3 fan **4** goad, move,
   spur, warm, whet **5** pique,
   rouse, waken **6** awaken, bestir,
   excite, foment, foster, heat up,
   incite, kindle, stir up, wake
   up **7** provoke, quicken,
   sharpen **8** summon up
   9 stimulate

Arowhena
   character in: **7** Erewhon
   author: **6** Butler

arpeggio 5 chord, scale
   8 flourish **13** musical device

arraign 6 accuse, charge, impute, indict **7** censure **8** denounce **9** criticize

arrange 4 file, plan, plot, pose,
   rank, sort **5** adapt, array, fix
   up, group, order, range, score
   6 assort, design, devise, lay
   out, line up, map out, set out,
   settle **7** agree to, marshal, prepare, provide **8** classify, contrive, organize, schedule
   9 methodize **11** orchestrate,
   systematize

arrangement 5 order **8** arraying, disposal, grouping, ordering **10** assortment
   12 distribution, organization
   13 methodization **14** categorization, classification
   15 systematization
   German: **9** Ausgleich

arrangements 5 plans, score,
   terms **7** compact **8** measures
   9 agreement **10** adaptation,
   provisions, settlement
   12 preparations
   13 orchestration

arrant 4 rank **5** utter **7** extreme **8** flagrant, outright,
   thorough **9** confirmed, downright, egregious, notorious,
   out-and-out **11** undisguised,
   unmitigated **13** thoroughgoing

array 4 deck, garb, pose, rank,
   robe, show, wrap **5** adorn,
   align, dress, group, order,
   place, range **8** attire, bedeck,
   clothe, deploy, finery, fit out,
   outfit, parade, set out, supply
   7 apparel, arrange, display,
   marshal, raiment **8** clothing,
   garments, organize **9** pageantry **10** assortment, collection,
   exhibition, marshaling **11** arrangement, disposition

arrears 5 debit **9** liability
   10 balance due, obligation,
   unpaid debt **11** overdue debt
   12 indebtedness **15** outstanding debt

arrest 3 end, fix, nab **4** bust,
   halt, hold, slow, stay, stop
   5 block, catch, check, delay,
   pinch, rivet, roust, seize, stall
   6 absorb, collar, detain, engage, hinder, occupy, retard,
   secure **7** attract, capture, engross, inhibit, seizure, slowing,
   staying **8** blocking, checking,
   hold back, restrain, stoppage,
   stopping, suppress **9** apprehend, interrupt, retention
   10 inhibiting **11** holding back
   12 apprehension, take prisoner

Arrhenius, Svante August
   field: **7** physics **9** chemistry
   nationality: **7** Swedish

theory of: **24** electrolytic
   dissociation

arriere pensee 12 hidden motive **17** mental reservation

arrival 5 comer **6** advent, coming **7** entrant, visitor **8** approach, arriving, entrance,
   newcomer, visitant
   10 appearance

arrive 4 come, near **5** get to,
   occur, reach **6** appear, befall,
   happen, show up, turn up
   7 succeed **8** approach, make
   good

arrivederci, a rivederci
   7 goodbye **8** farewell **16** until
   we meet again

arrogance 5 scorn **6** egoism,
   vanity **7** bluster, conceit, disdain, swagger **8** contempt
   9 assurance, insolence, loftiness, vainglory **10** lordliness,
   pretension **11** braggadocio,
   haughtiness, presumption
   13 imperiousness **14** self-
   importance

arrogant 4 vain **6** lordly
   7 haughty, pompous **8** insolent, scornful **9** conceited, imperious **10** disdainful,
   egoistical, swaggering **11** egotistical, overbearing, overweening, pretentious
   12 contemptuous, presumptuous, self-assuming, supercilious, vainglorious **13** high-and-
   mighty, self-important

arrogate 5 adopt, claim, seize,
   usurp **6** assume **7** preempt
   8 take over **10** commandeer
   11 appropriate

arrogation 6 taking **7** seizure
   10 assumption, usurpation
   12 confiscation **13** appropriation, expropriation

arrow 3 bow **4** bolt, dart
   5 shaft **7** pointer **9** direction
   12 pointed shaft

Arrow
   constellation of: **7** Sagitta

Arrowsmith
   author: **13** Sinclair Lewis
   character: **10** Leora Tozer
   11 Max Gottlieb **12** Terry
   Wickett **14** Capitola Mc-
   Gurk **15** Gustaf Sondelius
   16 Martin Arrowsmith
   18 Dr Almus Pickerbaugh

arroyo 4 wadi **5** gorge, gully
   6 ravine, trench

arsenal 6 armory **7** weapons
   8 magazine **9** arms depot
   11 arms factory **13** ordnance
   depot **14** ammunition dump

arsenic
chemical symbol: **2** As

Arsenic and Old Lace
director: **10** Frank Capra
cast: **9** Cary Grant **10** Jack
Carson, Peter Lorre **13** Josephine Hull, Priscilla Lane,
Raymond Massey

Arsinoe *see* **11** Alphesiboea

Arsinous
son: **8** Aecamede

Arsippe
father: **6** Minyas
mocked: **8** Dionysus

ars longa, vita brevis 20 art
is long life is short

Ars Poetica
author: **5** Homer

art, arts 5 craft, knack, skill
6 genius **7** finesse, mastery,
methods **8** artistry, facility,
strategy **9** dexterity, expertise,
technique **10** fine points, humanities, principles, subtleties,
virtuosity
goddess of: **6** Athena, Athene, Pallas, Saitis **7** Minerva
11 Tritogeneia **12** Pallas
Athena **18** Alalcomenean
Athena

Artacia
origin: **5** Greek
mentioned in: **7** Odyssey
means: **6** spring
in the land of: **10** Laestrygon

Artegall
character in: **15** The Faerie
Queene
author: **7** Spenser

Artemis
also: **7** Cynthia **9** Astrateia
origin: **5** Greek
form: **6** virgin **7** goddess
8 huntress
habitat: **4** moon
mother: **4** Leto
twin brother: **6** Apollo
companion: **4** Opis **5** Oread
corresponds to: **5** Diana
6 Phoebe, Selene
11 Britomartis
epithet: **6** Orthia **7** Eurippa,
Laphria, Limnaea, Pyronia
8 Aeginaea, Agrotera, Calliste, Caryatis, Daphnaea
9 Hemerasia, Lygodesma
10 Polymastus
11 Leucophryne

Artemision
shrine of: **7** Artemis

artery 3 way **4** path, road,
vein **6** aorta **6** street **7** channel, highway **11** blood vessel

artful 3 apt, sly **4** able, deft,
foxy, wily **5** adept, quick,
sharp, smart **6** adroit, astute,
clever, crafty, gifted, shifty,
shrewd, subtle, tricky **7** cunning, knowing, politic **8** masterly, scheming, skillful,
talented **9** deceitful, deceptive,
designing, dexterous, ingenious, inventive, strategic, underhand **10** contriving,
diplomatic, proficient
11 imaginative, machinating,
maneuvering, resourceful
12 disingenuous

artfulness 5 guile **6** deceit
7 cunning, slyness **8** artifice,
foxiness, scheming, subtlety,
trickery, wiliness **10** craftiness **11** machination

Arthur
director: **11** Steve Gordon
cast: **11** Dudley Moore, John
Gielgud **12** Liza Minnelli
19 Geraldine Fitzgerald
Oscar for: **15** supporting actor (Gielgud)

Arthur
began: **10** Round Table
father: **14** Uther Pendragon
half-sister: **11** Morgan le Fay
home: **7** Camelot
island: **6** Avalon
knights: **3** Kay **6** Gareth, Gawain **7** Geraint **8** Bedivere,
Lancelot, Percival, Tristram
9 Launcelot
knights sought: **9** Holy Grail
mother: **7** Igraine, Ygaerne
nephew: **6** Modred
sword: **9** Excalibur
given by: **13** Lady of the
Lake
wife: **9** Guinevere
wizard: **6** Merlin

Arthur, Chester Alan *see*
box, p. 60

artichoke 14 Cynara Scolymus
varieties: **5** Globe **7** Chinese
8 Japanese **9** Jerusalem
14 White Jerusalem

article 4 item, part, term
5 count, essay, paper, piece,
point, story, theme, thing
6 clause, detail, matter, object,
review, sketch **7** portion, product, proviso, write-up **8** division **9** commodity, condition,
paragraph, provision, substance **10** commentary, particular **11** proposition, stipulation

articulate 4 join **5** hinge, state,
utter, voice **6** convey, facile,
fluent, hook up **7** connect, enounce, express **8** eloquent, organize **9** enunciate, formulate,
pronounce **10** enunciated, expressive, meaningful, speechlike **12** intelligible

articulation 5 hinge, joint
7 diction **8** juncture **9** elocution, utterance **10** connection
11 enunciation
13 pronunciation

artifact 4 tool **7** manmade
9 arrowhead

artifice 4 hoax, ruse, trap,
wile **5** blind, dodge, feint,
guile, trick **6** deceit, device,
tactic **7** cunning, slyness
8 foxiness, intrigue, maneuver,
scheming, trickery, wiliness
9 deception, duplicity, falsehood, imposture, ingenuity,
invention, stratagem **10** artfulness, cleverness, craftiness,
subterfuge **11** contrivance,
machination **13** inventiveness

artificer 7 artisan, deviser
9 contriver, craftsman

artificial 4 fake, mock, sham
5 false, phony, stagy **6** ersatz,
forced **7** feigned, labored,
manmade, stilted **8** affected,
mannered, specious, spurious
9 imitation, insincere, pretended, simulated, synthetic,
unnatural **10** factitious, nonnatural, theatrical **11** counterfeit **12** manufactured

artillery 6 cannon **7** big guns
8 ordnance **11** mounted guns

artisan 6 master **9** craftsman
10 technician
14 handicraftsman

art is long life is short
Latin: **18** ars longa vita
brevis

artist 6 expert, master
8 virtuoso

artistic 7 elegant, stylish
8 graceful, handsome, tasteful
9 aesthetic, exquisite
10 attractive

artistic ability 6 talent **7** mastery **8** artistry **10** virtuosity

artistry 5 taste, touch **6** talent
7 mastery **10** virtuosity
11 proficiency, sensibility
14 accomplishment

artless 4 open, pure, true
5 crude, frank, naive, plain
6 candid, honest, humble, simple **7** natural, sincere **8** innocent, trusting **9** guileless,
ingenuous, primitive, unadorned **10** inartistic, lacking
art, unaffected, untalented
11 open-hearted, undesigning
13 unpretentious **15** straightforward, unselfconscious,
unsophisticated

artlessness 6 candor **7** honesty, naivete **8** openness
9 frankness, sincerity **10** simplicity **11** naturalness
13 guilelessness, ingenuousness **14** unaffectedness

art object
French: **9** objet d'art

Arthur, Chester Alan
nickname: **4** Chet **16** The Gentleman Boss
presidential rank: **11** twenty-first
party: **10** Republican
state represented: **2** NY
defeated: **5** no-one
   succeeded upon death of: **8** Garfield
vice president: **4** none
cabinet:
   state: **6** (James Gillespie) Blaine **13** (Frederick Theodore) Frelinghuysen
   treasury: **6** (Charles James) Folger, (William) Windom **7** (Walter Quintin) Gresham **9** (Hugh) McCulloch
   war: **7** (Robert Todd) Lincoln
   attorney general: **8** (Benjamin Harris) Brewster, (Isaac Wayne) MacVeagh
   navy: **4** (William Henry) Hunt **8** (William Eaton) Chandler
   postmaster general: **4** (Timothy Otis) Howe **5** (Thomas Lemuel) James **6** (Frank) Hatton **7** (Walter Quinton) Gresham
   interior: **6** (Henry Moore) Teller **8** (Samuel Jordan) Kirkwood
born: **2** VT (or Canada) **9** Fairfield
died: **2** NY **11** New York City
buried: **2** NY **6** Albany
education:
   college: **5** Union
   studied: **3** law
religion: **12** Episcopalian
interests: **8** good food (an epicure) **13** salmon fishing
political career: **13** vice president **26** customs collector for New York
civilian career: **6** lawyer **7** teacher
military service: **8** Civil War
   quartermaster general of: **12** state militia (New York)
notable events of lifetime/term: **5** Panic (of 1883)
   Act: **9** Pendleton **16** Chinese Exclusion **19** Edmunds Anti-Polygamy
father: **7** William
mother: **7** Malvina (Stone)
siblings: **4** Jane, Mary **6** Almeda, George, Regina **7** Malvina, William **8** Ann Eliza
wife: **5** Ellen (Lewis Herndon)
   nickname: **4** Nell
children: **11** Chester Alan **12** Ellen Herndon **19** William Lewis Herndon

Art of Living, The
author: **11** John Gardner

Art of Love, The (Ars Amatoria)
author: **4** Ovid

arty 6 dainty **7** foppish **8** affected, highbrow, overnice, precious **9** dandified, overblown **10** effeminate **11** overrefined, pretentious **12** artsy-craftsy, bluestocking, high-sounding

Aruns
killer of: **7** Camilla

Arval
also: **13** Arval Brothers **14** Fratres Arvales
priests of: **6** Dea Dia
number of priests: **6** twelve

Arval Brothers *see* **5** Arval

Aryan
modern name: **13** Indo-European
origin: **10** North India **11** Central Asia
family of languages: **5** Hindi **7** Bengali, Panjabi **9** Sinhalese
religion: **8** Hinduism
originated: **11** caste system

Aryana *see* **11** Afghanistan

as 4 that, when **5** while **7** because, equally

Asa
father: **6** Abijah
grandfather: **8** Rehoboam
grandmother: **6** Maacah
deposed: **6** Maacah
defeated: **6** Baasha

as above
Latin: **7** ut supra

as a group 7 en masse, in a body **8** as a whole, together **11** all together

as a matter of form
Latin: **8** pro forma

Asar *see* **5** Aesir

as a result 2 so **5** due to **7** because **9** therefore, wherefore, whereupon **11** accordingly **12** consequently **13** in consequence

as a whole 8 all in all **10** altogether **19** all things considered
French: **6** en bloc

as below
Latin: **7** ut infra

Ascalabus
form: **5** youth
mocked: **7** Demeter
changed into: **6** lizard

Ascalaphus
occupation: **6** sentry **8** gardener
location: **10** underworld
father: **4** Ares
brother: **8** Ialmenus
member of: **9** Argonauts
killed by: **9** Deiphobus
changed into: **3** owl
changed by: **7** Demeter

Ascanius
also: **5** Iulus
father: **6** Aeneas
mother: **6** Creusa
founder of: **9** Alba Longa

ascend 4 rise **5** climb, mount, scale **7** inherit **9** succeed to

ascendancy, ascendance 4 edge, rule, sway **5** power, reign **7** command, control, mastery **8** whip hand **9** advantage, authority, dominance, influence, supremacy, upper hand **10** domination, leadership **11** preeminence, sovereignty, superiority **12** predominance

ascension 6 ascent, rising **7** scaling **8** climbing, mounting **10** ascendancy

ascent 4 rise **5** climb, grade, slope **6** rising **7** advance, incline, scaling, upgrade **8** climbing, gradient, mounting, progress **9** ascension **11** advancement, progression

ascertain 5 learn **6** detect, verify **7** certify, find out, unearth **8** discover **9** determine, establish, ferret out

ascertainable 10 detectable

11 discernible, perceivable, perceptible

ascetic 3 nun **4** monk, yogi **5** fakir, stern **6** hermit, strict **7** austere, dervish, eremite, recluse, Spartan **8** celibate, cenobite, rigorous, solitary **9** abstainer, anchorite, religious **10** abstemious, flagellant, self-denier **11** self-denying **13** self-mortifier **14** self-mortifying

Asch, Sholem
  author of: **4** Mary **5** Moses **8** A Village **10** The Apostle, The Prophet **11** The Nazarene, Three Cities **15** Song of the Valley **17** The God of Vengeance

Asclepiade
  descendants of: **9** Asclepius

Asclepius
  origin: **5** Greek
  god of: **7** healing **8** medicine
  father: **6** Apollo
  mother: **7** Coronis
  wife: **6** Epione
  son: **7** Machaon **10** Podalirius
  daughter: **4** Iaso **6** Hygeia
  nurse: **6** Trygon
  corresponds to: **11** Aesculapius
  epithet: **8** Cotyleus

ascribe 6 assign, credit, impute, relate **7** trace to **8** accredit, charge to **9** attribute

Ascus
  form: **5** giant
  helped: **8** Lycurgus
  chained: **8** Dionysus

asea 4 lost **6** addled, adrift **7** puzzled **8** confused **10** bewildered

Asenath
  father: **10** Potipherah
  husband: **6** Joseph
  son: **7** Ephraim **8** Manasseh

Asgard
  home of: **4** Asar **5** Aesir
  origin: **12** Scandinavian
  connected to earth by: **7** bifrost **13** rainbow bridge
  location of: **8** Valhalla

ash 4 dust **6** cinder **7** residue **12** powdered lava
  family: **5** olive
  genus: **8** Fraxinus
  climatic zone: **17** northern temperate
  varieties: **3** Pop, Red, Sea **4** Blue **5** Black, Green, Manna, Texas, Wafer, Water, White **6** Alpine, Ground, Shamel, Syrian, Velvet **7** Arizona, Modesto, Prickly **8** Carolina, Stinking **9** Evergreen, Flowering **10** Manchurian, Montebello **18** Yellow-topped mallee
  use: **4** fuel **6** timber **7** barrels **8** landscape **9** furniture **10** motor parts, sport goods
  most common species: **8** white ash

ashamed 3 shy **7** abashed, bashful, prudish **9** chagrined, mortified, squeamish **10** chapfallen, distressed, humiliated, shamefaced **11** crestfallen, discomfited, embarrassed **12** disconcerted **13** guilt-stricken **18** conscience-stricken

Ashby, Hal
  director of: **10** Being There, Coming Home

ashen 3 wan **4** gray, pale **5** livid, pasty **6** anemic, leaden, pallid **8** blanched

Asher
  father: **5** Jacob
  mother: **6** Zilpah
  brother: **3** Dan, Gad **4** Levi **5** Judah **6** Joseph, Reuben, Simeon **7** Zebulun **8** Benjamin, Issachar, Nephtali
  sister: **5** Dinah
  city in: **8** Manasseh
  descendant of: **8** Asherite

Ashkenaz
  father: **6** Japhet
  mother: **5** Gomer

Ashley, Lady Brett
  character in: **15** The Sun Also Rises
  author: **9** Hemingway

ashore 6 on land **7** aground **9** on dry land

Ashton-Warner, Sylvia
  author of: **5** Three **6** Myself **7** Teacher **8** Spinster **10** Greenstone

Ashtoreth
  origin: **7** Semitic
  corresponds to: **6** Inanna, Ishtar **7** Astarte, Mylitta

Ash-Wednesday
  author: **7** T S Eliot

ashy 3 wan **4** pale **5** ashen, pasty, white **6** pallid, sallow **7** ghastly, ghostly **8** blanched **9** colorless

Asia *see box, p. 62*

aside 4 away **5** apart **6** aslant, beside **7** whisper

As I Lay Dying
  author: **15** William Faulkner
  character:
    Bundren family: **4** Anse, Cash, Darl **5** Addie, Jewel **9** Dewey Dell

Asimov, Isaac
  author of: **6** I Robot **10** Foundation (trilogy) **12** Caves of Steel, Robots of Dawn **17** The Gods Themselves
  character: **12** Elijah Bailey **13** R Daneel Olivaw

asinine 5 silly **6** absurd, insane, stupid **7** foolish, idiotic, moronic, witless **9** brainless, imbecilic, senseless **10** halfwitted, irrational, muddlehead, ridiculous **11** lamebrained, thickheaded, thick-witted **12** dunderheaded, feebleminded, simpleminded, thickskulled

asininity 5 folly **8** dumbness **9** silliness, stupidity **10** imbecility **11** doltishness, foolishness **16** simplemindedness

as it should be
  French: **11** comme il faut

Asius
  origin: **5** Greek
  mentioned in: **5** Iliad
  king of: **7** Percote
  father: **8** Hyrtacus
  killed by: **9** Idomeneus

ask 3 beg, bid, sue **4** call, pump, quiz, seek, urge **5** apply, claim, grill, plead, press, query **6** appeal, charge, demand, desire, expect, invite, summon **7** beseech, entreat, implore, inquire, request, solicit **8** petition, question, sound out **10** supplicate **11** interrogate

Ask
  origin: **6** Nordic
  first: **3** man
  made from: **7** ash tree
  made by: **4** gods

askance 11 skeptically **12** disdainfully, suspiciously **13** distrustfully, mistrustfully **14** disapprovingly

askew 4 awry **6** aslant **7** crooked **8** cockeyed, lopsided, sleeping **9** crookedly

Askkimey *see* **6** Eskimo

aslant 4 awry **5** askew **7** crooked **8** cockeyed, lopsided **9** crookedly, obliquely, slantwise

asleep 6 dozing **7** napping **10** slumbering **13** taking a siesta **14** dead to the world

as much as this
  Latin: **8** quoad hoc

Asner, Ed
  born: **12** Kansas City KS
  roles: **5** Roots **8** Lou Grant **14** Rich Man Poor Man **18** Mary Tyler Moore Show

asocial 8 unsocial **9** nonsocial, reclusive **10** antisocial **12** misanthropic

Asia
country: **4** Iran, Iraq, Laos, Oman **5** Burma, China, India, Japan, Macao, Nepal, Qatar, Syria, Tibet, Yemen **6** Bhutan, Brunei, Cyprus, Israel, Jordan, Russia, Sikkim, Taiwan, Turkey **7** Armenia, Bahrain, Georgia, Kashmir, Lebanon, Myanmar, Vietnam **8** Cambodia, Hong Kong, Malaysia, Maldives, Mongolia, Pakistan, Sri Lanka, Thailand **9** Indonesia, Kirghizia, Singapore **10** Azerbaijan, Bangladesh, Kazakhstan, Kyrgyzstan, North Korea, South Korea, Tajikistan, Uzbekistan **11** Afghanistan, Saudi Arabia **12** North Vietnam, South Vietnam, Turkmenistan **13** Inner Mongolia **14** Papua New Guinea **15** Sinkiang-Uighur **18** United Arab Emirates
desert: **4** Gobi, Thar **6** Syrian **7** Arabian, Karakum **8** Kyzylkum **10** Takla Makan
island: **5** Kuril, Japan **6** Taiwan **7** Hai-nan **8** Sri Lanka **9** Indonesia: **3** Aru **4** Java, Sulu **5** Ceram, Sumba, Timor **6** Borneo, Flores **7** Celebes, Sumatra **8** Moluccas, Tanimbar **9** Halmahera, New Guinea **11** Philippines
ancient people/empire: **4** Elam, Thai **5** Akkad, Aryan, Indus, Khmer, Media, Shang **6** Mongol, Ohoman, Semite **7** Amorite, Assyria, Hwang Ho, Parthia, Persian **8** Sumerian **9** Babylonia, Dravidian, Sassanian **11** Hephthalite, Mesopotamia
ancient city: **2** Ur **5** Pagan, Sumer **6** Anyang **7** Ayuthia, Harappa **8** Mandalay **12** Mohenjo-daro
ancient leader: **5** Asoka, Kassi **6** Darius **9** Anawratha, Zoroaster **13** Cyrus the Great **17** Alexander the Great
religion: **5** Islam **6** Muslim, Shinto, Taoism **7** Jainism, Judaism **8** Buddhism, Hinduism **12** Christianity, Confucianism **13** Protestantism **16** Roman Catholicism
language: **5** Hindi **6** Arabic, French **7** Chinese, English, Russian, Spanish
   Chinese dialects: **2** Wu **3** Min **5** Hakka **8** Mandarin **9** Cantonese
river: **2** Ob **3** Amu, Hsi, Syr **4** Amur, Lena **5** Indus **6** Ganges, Mekong, Tigris **7** Hwang Ho, Salween, Yangtze, Yenisei **9** Euphrates, Irrawaddy **11** Brahmaputra **16** Tigris-Euphrates
lake: **6** Baikal **7** Aral Sea **8** Balkhash **10** Caspian Sea
mountain/mountain range: **5** Altai, Urals **6** Kunlon, Pamirs, Taurus, Zagros **8** Caucasus, Sulaiman, Tien Shan **9** Himalayas, Hindu Kush, Karakoram **10** Arakan Yoma
highest point: **12** Mount Everest
lowest point: **7** Dead Sea
mineral/natural resources: **3** oil, tin **4** coal, mica, talc, zinc **7** bauxite, iron ore, mercury **8** chromium, graphite, selenium, tungsten **9** manganese **10** natural gas
largest city: **8** Shanghai
vegetation: **3** fir, sal **4** moss, pine, teak **5** larch **6** bamboo, lichen, spruce **8** ironwood
animal: **3** elk, yak **4** bear, wolf **5** camel, panda, sable, takin, tiger **6** ermine, kuland **7** markhor **8** antelope, elephant, reindeer **9** arctic fox, polar bear
people: **4** Huis, Kurd, Thai, Turk **5** Aryan, Khmer, Malay, Tungu **6** Buryat, Chuang, Kalmyk, Mongol, Semite, Vighor **7** Baluchi, Burmese, Chinese, Chukchi, Persian, Russian, Tadzhik, Tibetan **8** Armenian, Filipino, Japanese **9** Dravidian **10** Han Chinese, Indonesian, Vietnamese

Asopus
form: **3** god
habitat: **5** river
father: **7** Oceanus
mother: **6** Tethys
wife: **6** Metope
son: **7** Ismenus, Pelagon

number of daughters:
6 twenty

asparagus
varieties: **4** Cape **6** Common, Garden, Smilax **7** Cossack **8** Prussian, Sprenger

aspect 3 air **4** look, side **5** angle, facet, point **7** feature **10** appearance **13** consideration

aspen 7 Populus
varieties: **7** Chinese, Quaking **8** European, Japanese **9** Trembling **12** Large-toothed

asperity 5 rigor **6** rancor **8** acrimony, hardship, severity **9** harshness, hostility, roughness **10** difficulty

Aspern Papers, The
author: **10** Henry James

aspersion 4 slur **5** abuse, smear **7** calumny, censure, obloquy, railing, slander **8** reproach, reviling **10** defamation, detraction **11** deprecation **12** vilification **13** disparagement

Asphalius *see* **8** Poseidon

Asphodel Fields
meadow of: **10** dead heroes

asphyxiate 5 choke **6** stifle **7** smother **9** suffocate **11** strangulate

aspirant 7 hopeful, nominee **9** applicant, candidate **10** competitor, contestant

aspiration 3 end **4** hope, mark, wish **6** design, desire, intent, object **7** craving, longing, purpose **8** ambition, daydream, endeavor, yearning **9** hankering, intention, objective

aspire 4 seek **5** aim at, covet, crave **6** desire, pursue **7** hope for, long for, pine for, wish for **8** yearn for **9** pant after **10** hunger over **11** hanker after, thirst after

ass 4 dolt, fool, jerk **5** booby, burro, dunce, idiot, moron, ninny **6** donkey, dum-dum, nitwit **7** half-wit, jackass **8** bonehead, imbecile, lunkhead, numskull **9** blockhead, lamebrain **10** dunderhead, nincompoop **11** male jackass

assail 5 fly at **6** attack **7** assault, lunge at, set upon **9** pitch into **11** descend upon

assailant 6 mugger **8** assailer, attacker, molester **9** aggressor, assaulter

assailer 8 attacker **9** aggressor, assailant, assaulter

Assamese
language family: **12** Indo-European
branch: **11** Indo-Iranian
group: **5** Indic
spoken in: **5** (northern) India

Assaracus
origin: **5** Greek
mentioned in: **5** Iliad
father: **4** Tros
son: **5** Capys
founder of: **10** royal house

assassin 6 hit man, killer, slayer **8** murderer **11** executioner

assassinate 4 kill, slay **6** murder, rub out **7** bump off **9** do to death, liquidate **10** put to death **11** exterminate

assault 4 push, raid **5** drive, fly at, foray, lunge, sally, siege, storm **6** assail, attack, charge, invade, strike, thrust **7** besiege, bombard, lunge at, offense, set upon **8** fall upon, invasion, storming, strike at, thrust at **9** assailing, lash out at, onslaught **10** aggression **11** bombardment

assaulter 6 mugger **8** assailer, attacker **9** aggressor, assailant

assay 3 try **4** rate, test **5** essay, prove **6** assess **7** analyze, attempt **8** appraise, endeavor, estimate, evaluate **9** undertake

assemblage 4 body, heap, herd, mass, pack, pile **5** batch, bunch, clump, flock, group, stock, store **6** throng **7** cluster, company **8** assembly, conclave **9** aggregate, amassment, gathering **10** collection **11** aggregation **12** accumulation, congregation

assemble 4 join, meet **5** amass, flock, rally **6** gather, heap up, muster, pile up, summon **7** collect, compile, connect, convene, convoke, marshal, round up **9** construct, fabricate **10** accumulate, congregate **11** fit together, put together **12** call together, come together **13** bring together, group together

assembly 4 body, herd, mass, pack **5** crowd, flock, group, troop **6** throng **7** cluster, company, council **8** conclave, congress **9** aggregate, gathering **10** assemblage, collection **11** aggregation, convocation, legislature **12** congregation

assembly hall 8 auditory **10** auditorium **11** concert hall, lecture hall, meeting hall

assent 5 agree, allow, grant, yield **6** accept, accord, comply, concur, permit **7** approve, concede, consent, defer to **8** approval, sanction **9** acquiesce, admission, agreement **10** acceptance, compliance, concession, fall in with

11 affirmation, approbation, concurrence, endorsement, recognition, subscribe to **12** acquiescence, confirmation, ratification, verification **13** corroboration **14** acknowledgment

assent to 4 okay **5** allow **6** accept, permit **7** approve **8** sanction, say yes to **9** agree with, authorize **11** acquiesce to, go along with

assert 4 aver, avow **5** argue, claim, state, swear **6** accent, affirm, avouch, insist, stress, uphold **7** advance, contend, declare, profess **8** advocate, maintain, propound, set forth **9** emphasize **10** put forward

assertion 5 claim **6** avowal, dictum **8** argument, averment **9** statement, upholding **10** allegation, contention **11** declaration, maintaining **12** protestation

assertion without proof
Latin: **9** ipse dixit

assertive 5 pushy **8** cocksure, decisive, emphatic, forceful, positive **9** confident, insistent, outspoken **10** aggressive **11** domineering, self-assured **12** strong-willed

assertiveness 10 insistence **11** forwardness **12** cocksureness, forcefulness, positiveness **13** agressiveness, outspokenness **14** self-confidence

assess 3 tax **4** levy **5** judge, value **6** charge **8** appraise, consider, estimate, evaluate, look over

assessment 3 fee, tax **4** dues, fine, rate, toll **6** charge, impost, tariff **8** judgment **9** appraisal **10** estimation, evaluation

asset 3 aid **4** boon, help, plus **7** benefit, service **9** advantage

assets 4 cash **5** goods, means, money **6** wealth **7** capital, effects **8** property, reserves **9** resources **10** belongings **11** possessions

asseverate 4 aver, avow **5** state, swear **6** affirm, assert, attest, avouch, insist **7** certify, contend, declare, protect **8** maintain, proclaim **9** emphasize, pronounce

as shown below
Latin: **7** ut infra

assiduity 8 industry, tenacity **9** diligence **10** dedication,

doggedness **11** application, persistence **13** determination

assiduous 6 dogged **7** earnest **8** constant, diligent, sedulous, tireless, untiring **9** laborious, steadfast, tenacious **10** determined, persistent, unflagging **11** hardworking, industrious, persevering, unremitting **13** indefatigable

assign 3 fix, set **4** give, name **5** allot, grant **6** charge, choose, invest **7** appoint, consign, entrust, mete out, specify **8** allocate, delegate, dispense, set apart **9** apportion, designate, determine, prescribe, stipulate **10** commission, distribute

assignation 4 date **5** tryst **7** meeting **10** rendezvous **11** appointment

assignment 3 job **4** duty, post, task **5** chore **6** lesson **8** exercise, homework **9** allotment **10** allocation, commission **11** appointment, designation **12** distribution **13** apportionment

assimilate 6 absorb, digest, imbibe, ingest, take in **9** integrate **10** metabolize **11** incorporate

Assiniboine, Assiniboin
language family: **6** Siouan
location: **9** Minnesota
12 Lake Winnipeg, Saskatchewan
related to: **7** Dakotas

assist 3 aid **4** abet, hand, help **5** boost, serve **6** back up, uphold, wait on **7** benefit, support, sustain **9** cooperate, lend a hand, reinforce **11** accommodate, collaborate, helping hand

assistance 3 aid **4** alms, help **6** relief **7** charity, service, stipend, subsidy, support **10** sustenance **11** cooperation, helping hand **12** contribution **13** collaboration, reinforcement **16** financial support

assistant 3 aid **4** aide, ally **5** aider **6** helper **7** partner **8** adjutant, co-worker, sidekick **9** accessory, associate, auxiliary, colleague, subaltern, supporter **10** accomplice, apprentice, cooperator, lieutenant **11** confederate, helping hand, subordinate **12** collaborator **15** second-in-command

associate 3 mix, pal, tie **4** ally, bind, chum, club, join, link, mate, pair, peer, yoke **5** buddy, crony, merge, unite **6** allied, couple, fellow, friend, hobnob, league, mingle, relate **7** combine, comrade, connect, consort, hang out, partner, related **8** confrere, co-worker, identify, intimate, sidekick **9** affiliate, colleague, companion, confidant, correlate, pal around, rub elbows, run around **10** accomplice, affiliated, fraternize **11** confederate, subordinate **12** collaborator

associated 6 allied, joined, united **9** connected **10** affiliated **11** amalgamated

association 3 tie **4** body, bond, club, meld **5** blend, group, union **6** clique, league **7** combine, company, linkage, mixture, society **8** alliance, intimacy, mingling, relation **9** coalition, community, relations, syndicate **10** assemblage, connection, federation, fellowship, fraternity, friendship, membership **11** affiliation, camaraderie, combination, confederacy, corporation, correlation, familiarity, partnership **12** acquaintance, friendliness, organization, relationship **13** collaboration, companionship, confederation, participation **14** fraternization, identification

assorted 5 mixed **6** motley, sundry, varied **7** diverse, various **9** different **11** diversified **13** heterogeneous, miscellaneous

assortment 5 array, stock, store **6** medley, motley **7** melange, mixture, sorting, variety **8** grouping, quantity **9** arranging, assorting, diversity, potpourri, selection **10** collection, hodgepodge, miscellany **11** arrangement, classifying, disposition **14** classification, conglomeration

as stated below
Latin: **7** ut infra

assuage 4 calm, ease **5** allay, quiet, still **6** lessen, pacify, soften, soothe, temper **7** appease, lighten, mollify, relieve **8** mitigate, tone down **9** alleviate **14** take the edge off

assuagement 6 easing, relief, solace **7** comfort **8** blunting, easement **9** abatement, lessening, tempering **10** mitigation **11** appeasement **13** mollification

assume 4 take **5** fancy, guess, infer, judge, seize, think, usurp **6** accept, deduce, gather, take on, take up **7** believe, imagine, presume, suppose, surmise, suspect **8** arrogate,

shoulder, take over, theorize **9** postulate, speculate, undertake **10** commandeer, conjecture, understand **11** appropriate, expropriate, hypothesize **14** take for granted

assumed 4 fake **5** bogus, false, phony **6** made-up **8** presumed, supposed **9** falsified **10** fictitious **11** make-believe, presupposed, pseudonymic **12** pseudonymous

assumed name 5 alias **7** pen name **9** pseudonym **13** false identity
French: **10** nom de plume **11** nom de guerre

assuming 4 bold **5** nervy, pushy **6** brazen, cheeky **7** forward, haughty **8** arrogant, insolent **9** audacious, presuming **11** overbearing **12** presumptuous **13** self-assertive

assumption 6 belief, taking, theory **7** premise, seizure **8** assuming, taking on, taking up **9** accepting, postulate **10** acceptance, arrogation, hypothesis, usurpation **11** postulation, presumption, shouldering, supposition, undertaking **13** appropriating **14** presupposition

assurance 3 vow **4** oath **5** poise **6** binder, pledge **7** promise **8** averment, boldness, coolness, sureness, warranty **9** certainty, certitude, guarantee **10** confidence, profession **11** affirmation, assuredness, word of honor **12** self-reliance **14** aggressiveness, self-confidence, self-possession

assure 5 vow to **6** clinch, ensure, secure **7** confirm, promise **8** pledge to **9** guarantee **11** make certain **14** give one's word to

assured 4 sure **5** fixed **6** poised, secure **7** certain, settled **8** positive **9** confident, undoubted **10** dependable, guaranteed **11** indubitable, irrefutable **12** indisputable **13** self-confident, self-possessed **14** unquestionable

Astaire, Fred
real name: **19** Frederick Austerlitz
partner: **12** Ginger Rogers
born: **7** Omaha NE
roles: **6** Top Hat **9** Funny Face, Let's Dance, Swing Time **10** Holiday Inn **12** Easter Parade, Royal Wedding, Shall We Dance **14** The Gay Divorcee

Astarte
origin: **7** Semitic
goddess of: **9** fertility **12** reproduction
habitat: **4** moon
corresponds to: **6** Inanna, Ishtar **7** Mylitta **9** Ashtoreth

aster 12 Callistephus
varieties: **4** Tree **5** Black, China, Heath **6** Annual, Golden, Mojave, Stoke's **7** Italian **8** Blue-wood **9** Tartarian, White wood **10** New England **11** White upland

Asteria
form: **8** Titaness
father: **5** Coeus
mother: **6** Phoebe
sister: **4** Leto
husband: **6** Perses
son: **8** Paropeus
daughter: **6** Hecate
changed into: **5** Delos **6** island

Asterion
also: **8** Asterius
father: **7** Cometes
member of: **9** Argonauts

Asterius
also: **8** Asterion
form: **5** giant **8** minotaur
king of: **5** Crete
father: **4** Anax **8** Tectamus **10** Cretan Bull, Hyperasius
mother: **8** Pasiphae
wife: **6** Europa
adopted sons: **5** Minos **8** Sarpedon **12** Rhadamanthys
daughter: **5** Crete
member of: **9** Argonauts

astern 3 aft **5** abaft **6** behind **9** to the rear

Asterodia
form: **5** nymph
type of nymph: **9** Caucasian

asteroid 6 debris **9** meteorite, planetoid

Asteropaeus
origin: **5** Greek
mentioned in: **5** Iliad
father: **7** Pelegon
ally of: **4** Troy
killed by: **8** Achilles

Asterope see **7** Sterope

astir 2 up **5** afoot, awake **6** active, roused **8** in motion, out of bed **10** up and about

astonish 4 daze, stun **5** amaze, shock **6** dazzle **7** astound, confuse, perplex, stagger, startle, stupefy **8** bewilder, confound, dumfound, surprise **9** electrify, overwhelm, take aback **10** strike dumb **11** flabbergast **15** make one's eyes pop **18** take one's breath away

astonishing 7 amazing **8** daz-

zling, shocking, striking
9 confusing, startling **10** astounding, impressive, perplexing, staggering, stupefying, surprising **11** bewildering, confounding **12** breathtaking, electrifying, overpowering, overwhelming

astonishment 3 awe **5** shock **6** wonder **8** surprise **9** amazement, confusion **10** perplexity, wonderment **12** bewilderment, stupefaction

Astor, Mary
   real name: 28 Lucille Vasconcellos Langhanke
   born: 8 Quincy IL
   roles: 6 Marmee **11** Little Women, The Great Lie
      15 Meet Me in St Louis
      16 The Maltese Falcon
      17 The Palm Beach Story
      18 The Prisoner of Zenda

astound 4 daze, stun **5** amaze, shock **6** dazzle **7** stagger, startle, stupefy **8** astonish, dumfound, surprise, take back **9** electrify, overwhelm **10** strike dumb **11** flabbergast **15** make one's eyes pop **18** take one's breath away

Astrabacus
   origin: 5 Greek **7** Spartan
   form: 6 prince
   found: 11 wooden image
      hidden by: **7** Orestes
      co-finder: **8** Alopecus

Astraea
   also: 6 Astrea
   goddess of: 7 justice
   father: 4 Zeus
   mother: 6 Themis

Astraeus
   form: 5 Titan
   consort of: 3 Eos
   father of: 4 wind **5** stars

astral 6 starry **9** celestial **12** astronomical

astraphobia
   fear of: 9 lightning

Astrateia *see* **7** Artemis

astray 3 off **5** amiss **6** afield **10** off the mark **12** off the course **16** off the right track

Astrea *see* **7** Astraea

astringent 4 acid, keen, sour, tart **5** brisk, sharp, stern, tonic **6** biting, severe **7** acerbic, austere, bracing, puckery, styptic **8** curative, incisive, piercing, salutary, stabbing, vinegary **10** antiseptic, salubrious **11** contracting, penetrating, restorative **12** invigorating

astrology 6 Zodiac **9** horoscopy, starcraft **10** astromancy,

astrometry, stargazing **11** genethliacs **13** mathematicals **14** astrodiagnosis
   belief in: 8 siderism
   term: 4 sign **5** house, trine **6** alnath, apheta, aspect **7** almuten, anareta, mansion, mundane, sextile **8** alkahest, nativity, quartile, synastry **9** planetary **10** opposition **11** conjunction

astronomer 4 Bode, Gold **5** Adams, Baade, Bayer, Bethe, Gould, Hoyle, Royer **6** Bessel, Halley, Hubble, Jansky, Kepler, Newton, Piazzi **7** Bradley, Celcius, Galileo, Huggins, Huygens, Kapteyn, Laplace, Ptolemy, Russell, Shapley, Slipher **8** Angstrom, Einstein, Herschel, Hevelius, Lacaille, Lemaitre, Mercator **9** Eddington, Leverrier **10** Copernicus, Hipparchus, Tycho Brahe **11** Aristarchus, Hertzsprung **13** Petrus Apianus

astronomy
   term: 5 comet, orbit **6** apogee, meteor, nebula, parsec, quasar **7** azimuth, eclipse, equinox, perigee, transit **8** aphelion, asteroid, ecliptic, meridian, solstice **9** meteorite, satellite **10** perihelion, precession **11** declination, occultation **12** perturbation, spectroscopy **16** celestial equator
   type/related study: 9 cosmogony, cosmology **10** astrometry, photometry **12** astrophysics **18** celestial mechanics
   see also: **4** star

Astrophel and Stella
   author: 15 Sir Philip Sidney

astute 3 sly **4** able, foxy, keen, wily **5** acute, sharp, smart **6** adroit, artful, bright, clever, crafty, shrewd, subtle **7** cunning, knowing, politic **9** designing, sagacious **10** discerning, keen-minded, perceptive **11** calculating, intelligent, penetrating **13** Machiavellian, perspicacious

astuteness 6 acumen **8** keenness **9** acuteness, smartness **10** cleverness, shrewdness **12** perspicacity

Astyanax
   also: 11 Scamandrius
   father: 6 Hector **9** Strophius
   mother: 10 Andromache
   thrown from: 11 Trojan walls
      thrown by: **6** Greeks
   slain by: 8 Menelaus

Astydamia
   father: 7 Amyntor
   husband: 7 Acastus

   daughter: 8 Laodamia
   abducted by: 8 Hercules

Asuncion
   capital of: 8 Paraguay

asunder 4 rent **5** apart **8** in pieces, to shreds **9** torn apart **11** broken apart

asylum 4 home **5** haven **6** harbor, refuge **7** retreat, shelter **8** madhouse, preserve **9** almshouse, orphanage, poorhouse, sanctuary **10** sanatorium, sanitarium **11** institution **13** children's home, state hospital **14** mental hospital **15** place of immunity **17** mental institution **23** eleemosynary institution

Asynjur
   origin: 12 Scandinavian
   goddesses of: 4 Asar **5** Aesir
   leader: 3 Fri **5** Frigg, Frija **6** Frigga

As You Like It
   author: 18 William Shakespeare
   character: 5 Celia (Aliena) **6** Audrey, Jaques, Oliver **7** Orlando **8** Rosalind (Ganymede) **9** Frederick **10** Touchstone

Atabyrian *see* **4** Zeus

at a distance 4 afar, away **5** above, aloof, apart **6** far off **9** separated

Atala
   author: 21 Francois Chateaubriand

Atalanta
   also: 8 Atalante
   form: 6 virgin **8** huntress
   father: 5 Iasus
   mother: 7 Clymene
   son: 13 Parthenopaeus
   wounded: 14 Calydonian boar
   lost race to: 10 Hippomenes

Atalanta in Calydon
   author: 24 Algernon Charles Swinburne

Atalante *see* **8** Atalanta

at any rate 6 anyhow, anyway **9** in any case **10** in any event

at cross purposes 7 counter, opposed **8** contrary, converse, inimical, opposite **9** disparate **10** at variance, discordant **11** conflicting **12** antithetical, incompatible **13** contradictory

Ate
   origin: 5 Greek
   form: 7 goddess
   personifies: 12 recklessness **16** divine punishment

at ease 4 calm, cool **6** at rest,

serene **7** content, relaxed, unmoved **8** composed **9** at leisure, confident, unruffled **10** complacent, nonchalant, unbothered, untroubled **11** comfortable, unconcerned

a tergo 9 at the back **10** from behind

at fault 6 guilty **8** culpable **10** implicated **11** blameworthy, responsible

at full length
Latin: **9** in extenso

Athabascan, Athapascan (Slave Indians)
language family: **10** Athabascan, Athapaskan
location: **6** Canada **14** Great Slave Lake
dominated by: **4** Cree
related to: **9** Chipewyan
tribe: **4** Dine **5** Slave **6** Apache, Navaho, Navajo **9** Mescalero **10** Athabascan

Athaliah
father: **4** Ahab
mother: **7** Jezebel
husband: **7** Jehoram
son: **7** Ahaziah

Athalie
author: **18** Jean Baptiste Racine

Athamas
king of: **6** Thebes
father: **6** Aeolus
wife: **3** Ino **7** Nephele
son: **5** Ptous **6** Leucon **7** Phrixus **8** Learchus **10** Melicertes
daughter: **5** Helle

at hand 4 near, nigh **5** close, handy, on tap, ready **6** nearby **7** close by **8** imminent **9** available, impending **10** accessible, convenient **11** at one's elbow, forthcoming **14** at one's disposal **15** within arm's reach

atheism 8 apostasy, unbelief **9** disbelief **10** irreligion **11** godlessness

atheist 7 infidel **10** unbeliever **11** disbeliever, nonbeliever **13** godless person

Athena
also: **6** Athene, Pallas, Saitis **11** Tritogeneia **12** Pallas Athena **18** Alalcomenean Athena
origin: **5** Greek
goddess of: **4** arts **6** wisdom **7** warfare **9** fertility
father: **4** Zeus **6** Triton
mother: **5** Metis
sprang from head of: **4** Zeus
raised by: **12** Alalcomeneus
symbol: **3** owl
corresponds to: **7** Minerva

epithet: 4 Alea **5** Meter, Xenia **6** Ergane, Itonia, Polias **7** Agoraea, Cissaea, Paeonia, Pronaus, Pronoea **8** Anemotis, Poliates, Zosteria **9** Oxyderces, Parthenia, Poliuchus, Promachus **10** Axiopoenus, Chalinitis, Cyparissia **11** Promachorma

Athens
capital of: **6** Greece
Greek: **7** Athinai
hills: **9** Acropolis **14** Hagios Georgios
landmark: **4** Stoa **9** Areopagus, Parthenon **10** Erechtheum, Propylaeum **17** Theater of Dionysus
marketplace: **5** Agora
mountain: **6** Parnes **8** Aigaleos, Hymettus **10** Pentelikon
named for: **6** Athena
port: **7** Piraeus
river: **7** Ilissus
sea: **6** Aegean **11** Saronic Gulf
square: **8** Syntagma (Constitution)

Athens Graces 4 Auxe **8** Hegemone

athirst 4 avid, keen **5** eager **6** raring **7** longing, panting **8** yearning

athlete 4 jock **8** champion **9** contender, sportsman **10** contestant, game player

athletic 5 burly, hardy, husky, manly **6** brawny, robust, strong, sturdy, virile **8** muscular, powerful, stalwart, vigorous **9** masculine, strapping **10** able-bodied

athletics 5 games **6** sports **8** exercise **9** exercises **10** gymnastics

at home 6 at ease, inside, shut in **7** indoors **8** confined **10** in the house **11** comfortable
French: **4** chez

Athos
character in: **18** The Three Musketeers
author: **5** Dumas (pere)

athwart 6 across **7** astride **8** sideways, sidewise **9** crossways, crosswise **12** transversely

Atlanta
baseball team: **6** Braves
basketball team: **5** Hawks
football team: **7** Falcons

Atlantean
pertaining to: **5** Atlas

Atlantic
pertaining to: **10** Titan Atlas

Atlantic City
director: **10** Louis Malle

cast: **8** Kate Reid **13** Burt Lancaster, Michel Piccoli, Susan Sarandon

at large 5 astir, loose **6** abroad **8** as a whole, at length **9** at liberty, in general **10** on the loose, unconfined **11** out and about **13** in circulation **14** around and about **15** making the rounds

Atlas
form: **5** Titan
father: **7** Iapetus
mother: **7** Clymene
brother: **9** Menoetius **10** Epimetheus, Prometheus
wife: **7** Pleione
daughters: **6** Hyades **7** Calypso **8** Pleiades **10** Hesperides
supported: **3** sky
identified with: **14** Atlas Mountains

Atlas Shrugged
author: **7** Ayn Rand
character: **8** John Galt **11** Hank Reardon **12** Dagny Taggart, James Taggart

at last
Latin: **10** ad extremum

at leisure 4 idle **7** off duty **8** inactive **9** at liberty **10** unemployed, unoccupied

Atli
origin: **12** Scandinavian
sister: **8** Brynhild
wife: **6** Gudrun, Kudrun **7** Guthrun
killed by: **6** Gudrun, Kudrun **7** Guthrun
represents: **6** Atilla

atmosphere 3 air **4** aura, feel, mood, tone **5** color **6** spirit **7** feeling, quality **8** ambience **11** environment **12** surroundings

atmospheric 3 air **4** airy **8** ethereal

at odds 6 unlike **8** contrary **9** different **10** at variance, discordant, discrepant, dissimilar **11** contrasting

at odds with 9 counter to **10** contrary to **14** at variance with

atom 3 bit, dot, jot **4** iota, mite, mote, whit **5** crumb, grain, scrap, shred, speck, trace **6** morsel, tittle **7** smidgen **8** fragment, particle **9** scintilla **10** smithereen

atomic 6 cobalt **7** fission, neutron, nuclear, uranium **8** hydrogen **9** molecular, plutonium, subatomic, unseeable **10** impalpable **11** fissionable, microcosmic, microscopic, superatomic **13** imperceptible, indiscernible, infinitesimal, thermonuclear

atom part 6 proton **7** neutron **8** electron

at once
French: **11** tout de suite

atone 6 pay for, redeem, repent, shrive **7** expiate **9** make up for **10** compensate, recompense, remunerate **12** do penance for **13** make amends for **17** make reparation for

atonement 6 amends, shrift **7** penance, redress **9** expiation **10** recompense, redemption, reparation, repentance **12** compensation, satisfaction **14** penitential act

at one's disposal 5 handy **6** at hand, on hand **9** available **10** accessible, convenient **11** at one's elbow, ready for use **13** at one's service

at one's elbow 5 handy **6** at hand, nearby **9** available **10** accessible, convenient

Atrax
father: **6** Peneus

at rest 5 quiet, still **6** asleep, at ease, serene **7** at peace, content **8** in repose **9** quiescent **10** motionless

Atreus
father: **6** Pelops
mother: **10** Hippodamia
sister: **7** Nicippe
wife: **6** Aerope
son: **8** Menelaus **9** Agamemnon **10** Plisthenes
daughter: **8** Anaxibia
killed: **6** Aglaus

Atridae
descendants of: **6** Atreus
family name of: **8** Anaxibia, Menelaus **9** Agamemnon **10** Plisthenes

atrium 4 hall **6** cavity **7** auricle **8** entrance **13** Roman entrance

atrocious 3 bad, low **4** dark, evil, rude, vile **5** black, cruel **6** brutal, savage, tawdry, vulgar **7** heinous, hellish, inhuman, uncouth, vicious **8** dreadful, enormous, fiendish, flagrant, grievous, horrible, infamous, infernal, pitiless, ruthless, terrible **9** barbarous, execrable, merciless, monstrous, nefarious, tasteless **10** diabolical, outrageous, villainous

atrociousness 6 infamy **7** cruelty **8** enormity, vileness **9** barbarity, brutality, depravity **11** heinousness, vicious-

ness **13** monstrousness, offensiveness **14** outrageousness

atrocity 6 horror **7** outrage **8** enormity, savagery, villainy **9** barbarism, barbarity, brutality **10** inhumanity **11** heinousness

atrophy 7 decline **8** decaying, drying up **9** lack of use, withering **10** emaciation, shriveling **11** wasting away **12** degeneration **13** deterioration

Atropos
member of: **5** Fates
cuts thread of: **4** life

Atsina (Gros Ventres, Haaninin)
language family: **9** Algonkian **10** Algonquian
location: **6** Canada **7** Montana **9** Milk River **12** Saskatchewan **13** Missouri River
related to: **7** Arapaho

attach 3 fix **4** join **5** affix, allot, annex **6** append, assign, couple, detail, secure **7** connect, destine, earmark **8** allocate, be fond of, fasten to, make fast **9** affiliate, associate, designate

attache 4 aide **5** envoy **6** consul **8** adjutant, diplomat, emissary, minister **9** assistant **10** ambassador, vice consul **11** diplomatist, subordinate **12** ambassadress **13** consul general

attachment 4 bond, love **6** fixing, liking, regard **7** adjunct, fixture, respect **8** addendum, addition, affinity, affixing, appendix, coupling, devotion, fondness, securing **9** accessory, affection, appendage, attaching, fastening **10** connection, friendship, supplement, tenderness **12** predilection

attack 3 fit **4** damn, go at **5** abuse, blame, fault, fly at, onset, spasm, spell **6** assail, charge, impugn, strike, stroke, tackle **7** assault, censure, lunge at, offense, seizure **8** denounce, fall upon, invasion, paroxysm **9** criticism, criticize, denigrate, disparage, incursion, offensive, onslaught, pitch into, undertake **10** aggression, impugnment **11** denigration **13** disparagement

attacker 6 mugger **7** accuser **8** assailer, opponent **9** adversary, aggressor, assailant **10** antagonist **11** belligerent

attain 3 win **4** earn, gain,

reap **5** reach **6** effect, obtain, secure **7** achieve, acquire, procure, realize **10** accomplish

attainable 6 at hand **9** available, reachable **10** accessible, achievable, realizable **11** within reach

attainment 5 skill **6** talent **7** earning, gaining, getting, mastery, success, winning **8** securing **9** acquiring, attaining, obtaining, procuring **10** competence **11** achievement, acquirement, acquisition, fulfillment, procurement, proficiency, realization **14** accomplishment

attempt 3 aim, try **4** seek **5** essay **6** attack, effort, hazard, strive, tackle, work at **7** assault, venture **8** endeavor **9** have a go at, onslaught, undertake **11** undertaking **12** make an effort, take a crack at, take a whack at

Attenborough, Richard
director of: **6** Gandhi (Oscar) **12** Young Winston **13** A Bridge Too Far

attend 4 go to, heed, mark, mind, note **5** serve, usher, visit **6** convoy, escort, follow, show up, squire, tend to **7** care for, conduct, observe, oversee, service **8** appear at, consider, frequent, harken to, listen to, wait upon **9** accompany **11** superintend
French: **4** oyez
cry used by: **10** court crier
preceded: **12** proclamation

attendance 4 gate **5** crowd, house **8** audience, presence **10** appearance, assemblage, being there

attendant 3 aid **6** escort, flunky, helper, lackey, menial **7** related, servant **8** adherent, chaperon, follower **9** accessory, assistant, companion, underling **10** associated, consequent **12** accompanying

attention 4 care, heed, mind, note, suit **5** court **6** homage, notice, regard, wooing **7** concern, respect, service, thought **8** civility, courtesy, devotion, wariness **9** alertness, deference, diligence, vigilance **10** observance, politeness **11** assiduities, compliments, gallantries **12** deliberation **13** concentration, consideration, contemplation **14** thoughtfulness

attentive 5 alert, awake **6** intent, polite **7** devoted, heedful, mindful, zealous **8** diligent, obliging **9** courteous, dedicated, listening, observant, wide awake **10** respectful, thoughtful **11** considerate, deferential, painstaking **13** accommodating

attentiveness 7 concern **8** devotion, industry **9** alertness, attention, diligence **10** commitment, dedication **11** application, devotedness, heedfulness, mindfulness **14** thoughtfulness

attenuate 6 dilute, impair, lessen, reduce, weaken **7** draw out, spin out **8** decrease, diminish, enervate, enfeeble **9** water down **10** adulterate

attest 4 show **5** prove **6** affirm, assert, assure, evince, verify **7** bear out, certify, confirm, declare, display, exhibit, support, swear to, testify, warrant **8** vouch for **11** bear witness, corroborate, demonstrate **12** substantiate

attestation 9 testimony **10** deposition **11** declaration

at the back
Latin: **6** a tergo

at the beginning
Latin: **9** ad initium

at the bottom
French: **6** au fond

At the Edge of the Body
author: **9** Erica Jong

at the end
Latin: **5** ad fin

at the place
Latin: **5** ad loc **7** ad locum

At the Sign of the Reine Pedauque
author: **13** Anatole France

attic 4 loft **6** garret **7** mansard **8** cockloft **10** clerestory
French: **7** grenier
German: **9** Dachboden
Spanish: **9** guardilla

attire 3 don **4** duds, garb, gown, robe, togs **5** array, dress **6** bedeck, clothe, finery, fit out, invest, outfit, rig out **7** apparel, clothes, costume, deck out, raiment, turn out **8** clothing, garments, glad rags, wardrobe **9** vestments **11** habiliments

Attis
also: **4** Atys
form: **5** youth
home: **7** Phrygia
loved: **6** Cybele
driven mad by: **6** Cybele

attitude 3 air **4** pose **6** manner, stance **7** outlook, posture **8** demeanor, position **11** disposition, frame of mind, perspective, point of view

attorney 4 beak **6** lawyer **7** counsel **8** advocate **9** barrister, counselor, solicitor **10** mouthpiece **12** legal adviser **14** member of the bar **15** ambulance chaser

attract 4 draw, lure, pull **5** cause, charm, evoke **6** allure, beckon, entice, induce, invite **7** bewitch, enchant, provoke **8** appeal to, interest **9** captivate, fascinate **11** precipitate

attraction 4 lure, pull **5** charm **6** allure, appeal **7** glamour **8** affinity, charisma, tendency **9** magnetism **10** enticement, inducement, temptation **11** captivation, enchantment, fascination **12** drawing power

attractive 4 chic, fair **6** lovely, pretty **7** elegant, likable, sightly, winning **8** alluring, becoming, charming, engaging, enticing, fetching, handsome, inviting, pleasant, pleasing, tasteful, tempting **9** agreeable, appealing, beautiful, seductive **10** bewitching, delightful, enchanting **11** captivating, charismatic, fascinating

attractiveness 5 charm **6** beauty **9** good looks **11** pulchritude **12** handsomeness

attribute 4 gift **5** facet, grace, lay to, trait **6** aspect, assign, credit, impute, talent, virtue **7** ability, ascribe, blame on, cause by, faculty, feature, quality, trace to **8** charge to, property **9** character, endowment, set down to **10** account for, attainment, derive from, saddle with **11** acquirement, bring home to, distinction **14** accomplishment, characteristic

attrition 4 loss **7** erosion **8** abrasion, decrease, friction, grinding, scraping **9** reduction **10** decimation **11** wearing away, wearing down **14** disintegration

attune 5 adapt **6** adjust, tailor **8** accustom **9** acclimate **11** acclimatize

attune to 3 fit **5** adapt **6** adjust **7** conform **9** harmonize **11** accommodate

at variance 7 counter, opposed **8** contrary, converse, inimical, opposite **9** disparate **10** discordant **11** conflicting **12** antithetical, incompatible **13** contradictory **15** at cross purposes

Atwood, Margaret
author of: **8** Survival **9** Surfacing **10** Bodily Harm, Lady

Oracle **11** Second Words **13** Life Before Man, Power Politics, The Circle Game **23** The Animals in That Country

at work 4 busy **5** in use **6** active **7** engaged, working **8** occupied

Atymnius
mentioned in: **5** Iliad
companion of: **8** Sarpedon
killed by: **10** Antilochus

atypical 7 unusual **8** abnormal, contrary, uncommon **9** anomalous, irregular, unnatural, untypical **10** nontypical **11** uncustomary, unlooked for **12** out of keeping **16** unrepresentative

Atys *see* **5** Attis

Auber, Daniel Francois Esprit
born: **4** Caen **6** France
composer of: **6** Haydee **7** La Macon **10** Fra Diavolo **12** Le Domino Noir **14** The Bronze Horse **16** Le Cheval de Bronze, The Crown Diamonds **17** La Muette de Portici **19** La Bergere Chatelaine **20** The Dumb Girl of Portici **22** Le Premier Jour de Bonheur **23** Les Diamants de la Couronne

auberge 3 inn **6** tavern

auburn 5 henna, tawny **6** russet **8** cinnamon, nutbrown **11** golden-brown, rust-colored **12** reddish-brown **13** copper-colored **15** chestnut-colored

Aucassin and Nicolette
author: **7** unknown

Auchincloss, Louis
author of: **10** Watchfires **11** The Dark Lady, The Partners **12** Second Chance, The Embezzler **14** A World of Profit **16** Powers of Attorney, Tales of Manhattan, The Country Cousin **17** The Rector of Justin **19** The Winthrop Covenant **20** Portrait in Brownstone

au contraire 13 on the contrary

au courant 8 up-to-date

auction 3 sale **7** bidding **8** offering

Auction Block, The
author: **8** Rex Beach

audacious 4 bold, pert, rash, rude, wild **5** bossy, brave, fresh, gutsy, risky, saucy **6** brazen, cheeky, daring, plucky **7** defiant, forward, valiant **8** assuming, fearless, heedless, impudent, insolent, intrepid, reckless, stalwart, unafraid, valorous **9** breakneck, daredevil, dauntless, desperate, foolhardy, hotheaded, imprudent, shameless, unabashed **10** courageous, outrageous, self-willed **11** adventurous, impertinent, injudicious, lionhearted, venturesome **12** death-defying, devil-may-care, discourteous, enterprising, presumptuous, stouthearted **13** disrespectful

audaciousness 6 daring **8** audacity, boldness **11** forwardness **13** assertiveness **14** aggressiveness **15** adventurousness

audacity 4 gall, grit, guts **5** brass, cheek, nerve, pluck, spunk, valor **6** daring, mettle **7** bravery, courage **8** backbone, boldness, chutzpah, rashness, temerity **9** brashness, derring-do, impudence, insolence **10** brazenness, effrontery **11** forwardness, presumption **12** fearlessness, impertinence, recklessness **13** bumptiousness, foolhardiness, shamelessness **15** venturesomeness

Auden, W H
author of: **11** Another Time, Thank You Fog **12** Homage to Clio, The Dyer's Hand **13** About the House, Journey to a War **15** For the Time Being, The Age of Anxiety **16** City Without Walls, Epistle to a Godson **17** In Memory of W B Yeats, Musee des Beaux Arts **20** The Dog Beneath the Skin **22** Forewords and Afterwords

Audhumbla
also: **8** Audhumla
origin: **12** Scandinavian
form: **3** cow
owner: **4** Ymir
birth from: **3** ice
uncovered: **4** Buri

Audhumla see **9** Audhumbla

audible 5 clear, heard **8** distinct **11** discernible, perceptible

audience 4 talk **5** house **6** market, parley, public **7** hearing, meeting **8** assembly, audition **9** following, interview, listeners, onlookers, reception **10** conference, discussion, readership, spectators **12** congregation, constituency, consultation

audit 5 check **6** go over, review, verify **7** balance, examine, inspect **10** inspection, scrutinize **11** examination, investigate, take stock of

12 scrutinizing, verification **13** investigation

audition 6 tryout **7** hearing **15** test performance

auditor 8 listener **10** accountant, bookkeeper **11** comptroller **17** financial examiner

auditorium 4 hall **5** arena **7** theater **8** auditory, coliseum **11** concert hall, lecture hall, meeting hall **12** assembly hall

Audrey
character in: **11** As You Like It
author: **11** Shakespeare

Audubon
author: **16** Robert Penn Warren

Audubon, John James
born: **8** Les Cayes **12** Santo Domingo
artwork: **14** Birds of America **34** Viviparous Quadrupeds of North America

Auel, Jean M
author of: **17** The Mammoth Hunters, The Valley of Horses **20** The Clan of the Cave Bear

Auerbach, Arnold (Red)
sport: **10** basketball
position: **5** coach
team: **13** Boston Celtics

au fait 6 expert, versed **11** experienced **13** knowledgeable

Aufklarung 13 enlightenment **16** the Enlightenment

au fond 9 basically, in reality **11** at the bottom

auf Wiedersehen 7 goodbye **8** farewell **16** until we meet again

Auge
priestess of: **6** Athena
father: **9** King Aleus
mother: **6** Neaera
son: **8** Telephus
assaulted by: **8** Hercules

Augean stables
owned by: **10** King Augeas
number of oxen: **13** three thousand
cleaned by: **8** Hercules
river running through: **7** Alpheus

Augeas
king of: **6** Epeans
realm: **4** Elis
member of: **9** Argonauts
brother: **5** Actor
son: **7** Eurytus, Phyleus **10** Agasthenes
daughter: **7** Agamede
grandson: **9** Polyxenus

auger 4 bore **5** drill **6** pierce **10** boring tool

aught 3 all, zip **4** love, nada, null, zero **6** naught **7** a cipher, nothing **8** goose egg **11** horse collar

augment 5 add to, boost, raise, swell, widen **6** deepen, expand, extend **7** amplify, build up, enlarge, inflate, magnify **8** flesh out, heighten, increase, lengthen **9** intensify

augmentation 5 boost, extra, raise **8** addition, increase, swelling, widening **9** deepening, expansion, extension, inflation **10** supplement **11** elaboration, enlargement, heightening, lengthening **13** amplification, magnification **15** intensification

augur 4 bode, seer **6** herald, oracle **7** diviner, portend, predict, presage, promise, prophet, signify **8** forecast, foretell, forewarn, intimate, prophesy **9** be a sign of **10** be an omen of, foreshadow, soothsayer **13** prognosticate **14** prognosticator

augury 4 omen, sign **5** token **6** herald **7** auspice, portent, promise, warning **8** prophecy **9** harbinger, precursor, sortilege **10** divination, forerunner, indication **11** forewarning, soothsaying **14** fortunetelling **15** prognostication

august 5 grand, lofty, noble, regal **6** solemn, superb **7** eminent, exalted, stately, supreme **8** glorious, imposing, majestic **9** dignified, estimable, grandiose, venerable **10** impressive, monumental **11** high-ranking, illustrious, magnificent **12** awe-inspiring **13** distinguished

August see box, p. 70

Augustine, St (of Hippo)
author of: **10** Civitas Dei **11** Confessions, Enchiridion **12** The City of God

augustness 7 dignity, majesty **8** eminence, nobility **9** loftiness **11** distinction **13** monumentality **15** illustriousness

August 1914
author: **23** Aleksandr Solzhenitsyn Jr

au naturel 4 nude **8** uncooked **15** in a natural state

Auntie Mame
author: **13** Patrick Dennis

Aunt Jo's Scrap-Bag
author: **15** Louisa May Alcott

August
  Anglo-Saxon: 10 Weod-
    Monath
  characteristic: 7 dog
    days
  flower: 5 poppy
  French: 4 Aout
  gem: 7 peridot **8** sardo-
    nyx **9** carnelian
  German: 6 August
  holiday:
    England/Scotland:
      11 Harvest Home (1)
    Italian: 6 Agosto
  number of days:
    9 thirty-one
  original name: 8 Sextilis
    12 Metageitnion
  origin of name: 6 Au-
    gere (Latin to open)
    8 Augustus (Roman
    emperor)
  place in year:
    Roman: **5** sixth
    Gregorian: **6** eighth
  Spanish: 6 Agosto
  zodiac sign: 3 Leo
    5 Virgo

**Aunt Julia and the
Scriptwriter**
  author: 16 Mario Vargas
    Llosa

au pair 4 maid **5** nanny **9** governess **13** mother's helper

aura 3 air **4** feel, mood
  5 aroma **7** essence, feeling,
  quality **8** ambience **9** character, emanation **10** atmosphere,
  suggestion

Aura
  companion of: 7 Artemis
  bore: 5 twins
    fathered by: **9** Dionysius
  changed into: 6 spring
    changed by: **4** Zeus

au revoir 7 goodbye **8** farewell **16** until we meet again

Aurness, James
  real name of: 11 James
    Arness

Aurora
  origin: 5 Roman
  goddess of: 4 dawn
  corresponds to: 3 Eos

Aurora Leigh
  author: 24 Elizabeth Barrett
    Browning

Ausgleich 10 compromise
  11 arrangement
  12 equalization

Auslander 5 alien **9** foreigner,
  outlander

auspice 4 omen, sign **6** augury **7** portent, warning
  10 indication
  15 prognostication

auspices 4 care **5** aegis
  6 charge **7** control, support
  8 advocacy, guidance **9** authority, influence, patronage
  10 protection **11** countenance,
  sponsorship **12** championship

auspicious 4 good **5** happy,
  lucky **6** benign, timely
  7 hopeful **9** favorable, fortunate, opportune, promising,
  red-letter **10** felicitous, heartening, propitious, reassuring,
  successful **11** encouraging

Austen, Jane
  author of: 4 Emma **10** Per-
    suasion **13** Mansfield Park
    15 Northanger Abbey
    17 Pride and Prejudice
    19 Sense and Sensibility

austere 5 rigid, spare, stark,
  stern **6** chaste, severe, simple,
  strict **7** ascetic, Spartan
  8 rigorous **10** abstemious,
  forbidding **11** self-denying,
  strait-laced

Austerlitz, Frederick
  real name of: 11 Fred
    Astaire

Australia *see box*

Austria *see box, p. 72*

Austroasiatic
  language subfamily: 5 Khasi,
    Munda **8** Annamite, Mon-
    Khmer **9** Palaung-Wa **10** Ni-
    cobarese **11** Semang-Sakai
    13 Annamite-Muong
  spoken in: 5 Burma, India
    7 Nicobar, Vietnam **8** Cam-
    bodia, Malaysia
    9 Kampuchea

authentic 4 pure, real, true
  5 valid **6** actual **7** factual, genuine **8** accurate, attested, bona
  fide, faithful, original, reliable,
  verified **9** veritable **10** accredited, dependable, legitimate **11** trustworthy
  12 unquestioned **13** authoritative, unadulterated

authenticate 6 attest, avouch,
  verify **7** certify, confirm, endorse, warrant **8** document,
  validate, vouch for **9** guarantee **11** corroborate
  12 substantiate

authenticated 7 genuine **8** attested, verified **9** validated
  10 accredited, vouched for
  13 substantiated

authentication 7 voucher
  10 validation **11** certificate
  12 verification **13** authorization, certification

author 4 poet **5** maker **6** father, framer, writer **7** creator,
  founder, planner **8** essayist, inventor, novelist, producer
  9 initiator, innovator, organizer **10** originator, playwright, prime mover
  16 short-story writer
    see author under each
    country

authoritarian 5 harsh **6** severe,
  strict, tyrant **7** austere, fascist
  8 autocrat, dogmatic, martinet **9** by the book, by the
  rule **10** inflexible, tyrannical,
  unyielding **11** dictatorial, doctrinaire **12** disciplinary, rule
  follower **14** disciplinarian, little dictator, uncompromising

authoritative 5 sound, valid
  6 lordly, ruling **7** factual,
  learned **8** arrogant, decisive,
  dogmatic, imposing, official,
  reliable **9** authentic, masterful,
  scholarly, sovereign **10** autocratic, commanding, definitive,
  dependable, imperative, impressive, peremptory, sanctioned, tyrannical
  11 dictatorial, trustworthy
  14 administrative

authoritativeness 6 belief
  9 authority **10** conviction
  11 credibility
  14 conclusiveness

authorities 6 expert, police,
  pundit **7** scholar **10** mastermind, specialist **11** connoisseur, officialdom **12** powers
  that be

authority 4 rule, sway **5** clout,
  force, might, power **6** esteem,
  weight **7** command, control,
  respect **8** dominion, prestige,
  strength **9** influence, supremacy **10** domination, importance **12** jurisdiction
  14 administration

authorization 7 license **8** approval, sanction **10** commission, imprimatur, permission
  11 entitlement **12** confirmation, legalization **13** accreditation, certification

authorize 5 allow **6** enable, invest, permit **7** approve, certify,
  charter, confirm, empower,
  entitle, license, warrant **8** accredit, sanction, vouch for
  9 give leave **10** commission

authorized 8 approved, official
  9 canonical **10** sanctioned

**Autobiography of Alice B
Toklas**
  author: 13 Gertrude Stein

**Autobiography of Miss
Jane Pittman, The**
  author: 13 Ernest J Gaines

Australia
other name: 9 Down Under
name means: 19 unknown southern land
capital: 8 Canberra
largest city: 6 Sydney
others: 3 Ayr **4** Yass **5** Dubbo, Perth **6** Albury, Cairns, Casino, Coburg, Darwin, Hobart **7** Bendigo, Geelong, Kogarah, Mildura, Mitcham, Whyalla **8** Adelaide, Ballarat, Bathurst, Brighton, Brisbane, Essendon, Randwick, Ringwood **9** Melbourne, Newcastle, Port Pirie, Toowoomba **10** Broken Hill, Kalgoorlie, Waggawagga, Wollongong **11** Collingwood, Rockhampton **12** Alice Springs
division: 8 Tasmania, Victoria **10** Queensland **13** New South Wales **14** South Australia **16** Western Australia **17** Northern Territory **26** Australian Capital Territory
head of state: 14 British monarch **15** governor general
measure: 4 arna, naut, saum
monetary unit: 4 dump, tray, zack **5** pound **6** dollar **8** shilling
island: 4 Cato, King **5** Cocos, Green, Timor **6** Barrow, Koolan **7** Coringa, Keeling, Neptune, Norfolk **8** Flinders, Kangaroo, Lacepede, Melville, Rottnest, Tasmania, Thursday **9** Admiralty
lake: 4 Eyre **5** Carey, Cowan, Frome, Moore, Wells **6** Austin, Barlee, Bulloo, Dundas, Harris, Mackay **7** Amadeus, Blanche, Everard, Torrens **8** Carnegie, Gairdner **9** MacDonald **10** Yammayamma **14** Disappointment
mountain: 3 Ise **4** Blue, Olga, Ossa, Zeil **5** Bruce, Snowy **6** Cradle, Doreen, Garnet, Gawler, Magnet, Morgan **7** Bongong, Gregory, Herbert **8** Augustus, Brockman, Cuthbert, Jusgrave, Mulligan, Surprise **9** Murchison, Woodroffe **14** Australian Alps **15** New England Range **18** Great Dividing Range
highest point: 9 Kosciusko
river: 3 Hay **4** Avon, Daly, Swan, Yule **5** Bullo, Comet, Drava, Naomi, Paroo, Roper, Yarra **6** Barcoo, Barwon, Bulloo, Culgoa, Degrey, Hunter, Isaacs, Murray, Norman **7** Darling, Derwent, Fitzroy, Georges, Gilbert, Lachlan, Staaten, Warrego **8** Belyando, Brisbane, Burdekin, Clarence, Drysdale, Flinders, Gascoyne, Georgina, Mitchell, Thompson, Victoria, Weeribee, Wooramel **9** Ashburton, Fortescue, Hawksbury, MacKenzie, Macquarie, Murchison, Saltwater **10** Diamantina, Shoalhaven **12** Murrambidgee
sea: 5 Coral, Timor **6** Indian, Tasman **7** Arafura, Pacific
physical feature:
  bay: **5** Bight, Shark **6** Botany **7** Moreton **11** Port Phillip
  cape: **4** Howe, York **5** Byron **9** Southeast
  channel: **5** Cowal **9** Anabranch, Billabong
  desert: **6** Arunta, Gibson, Stuart, Tanami **7** Simpson **10** Great Sandy **13** Great Victoria
  gulf: **8** Spencers **9** Van Dieman **11** Carpentaria **15** Joseph Bonaparte **20** Great Australian Bight
  peninsula: **4** Eyre
  reef: **12** Great Barrier
  strait: **4** Bass
people: 3 Abo **4** Koko, Mara, Wong **5** Anzac, Binge, Dieri, Maori, Myall **6** Aranda, Arunta, Aussie, Binghi, Digger, Kipper, Papuan **7** Arawong, Ilpirra **8** Antipode, Barkinji, Billijim, Euahlayi, Warragal, Warrigal **9** Aborigine **10** Australoid, Melanesian, Sandgroper
  actor: **9** Judy Davis, Mel Gibson, Paul Hogan **10** Bryan Brown
  author: **4** West **5** White **7** Russell **10** Richardson
  explorer: **4** Bass, Cook **6** Mawson, Tasman **7** Wilkins
  leader: **4** Holt **5** Hawke **7** Keating, Menzies, Whitlam
  nurse: **11** Sister Kenny
language: 7 English
religion: 7 Judaism **8** Anglican **10** Protestant **13** Roman Catholic
place: 7 outback **9** billabong **11** back country
  aborigine area: **9** Arhemland
  beach: **5** Manly
  dam: **4** Hume
possession: 12 Cocos Islands **13** Norfolk Island **16** Christmas Islands
feature:
  animal: **5** dingo **6** kelpie **7** wallaby **8** anteater, kangaroo **9** koala bear **18** duckbilled platypus
  bird: **3** emu **10** kookaburra
  cowboy: **6** waddie **8** jackaroo
  dance: **6** dreher
  flower: **7** boronia, fuchsia, waratah **9** coachwood **12** kangaroo paws
  game: **3** sye **10** tambaroora
  tree: **3** gum **10** eucalyptus
  weapon: **5** kiley, kyley **7** wommera **9** boomerang
food: 3 kai **6** tucker
  cake: **6** damper **7** brownie
  dish: **8** coolamon
  drink: **9** arkaloola
  fruit: **5** nonda **7** kumquat **11** desert-lemon

Austria

other name: 10 Osterreich

name means: 12 eastern state

capital/largest city: 6 Vienna

others: 4 Enns, Graz, Lech, Linz, Ried, Wels 5 Krems, Steyr, Traun 6 Leoben 7 Bregenz, Modling, Spittal, Villach 8 Bad Ischl, Dornbirn, Salzburg 9 Innsbruck, Semmering 10 Kapfenberg, Klagenfurt 11 Sankt Polten 14 Wiener Neustadt

division: 5 Tirol, Tyrol 6 Istria, Styria, Triest 7 Bohemia, Galicia, Moravia, Silesia 8 Bukowina, Dalmatia, Earniola, Gradisca 9 Earinthia 10 Burgenland, Vorarlberg 12 Lower Austria, Upper Austria

   Roman province: 6 Raetia 7 Noricum 8 Pannonia

government:
   legislature: 9 Bundesrat, Reichsrat 10 Herrenhaus, Reichsrath

head of government: 10 Chancellor

other leader: 7 emperor 12 burgomeister

measure: 4 fass, fuss, joch, mass, muth, yoke 5 halbe, linie, meile, metze, pfiff, punkt 6 achtel, becher, leipoa, seidel 7 dlafter, viertel 8 dreiling 12 futtermassel

monetary unit: 4 lira 5 crown, ducat, krone 6 florin, gulden, heller, zehner 8 albertin, groschen, kreutzer 9 schilling

weight: 4 marc, unze 5 denat, karch, stein 7 centner, pfennig 8 vierling 9 quantchen

lake: 6 Almsee 7 Fertoto, Mondsee 8 Bodensee, Traunsee 9 Constance 10 Neusiedler

mountain: 4 Alps 6 Stubai, Tirols, Tyrols 8 Eisenerz, Rhatikon 9 Dolomites, Kitzbuhel 10 Hohe Tauern 14 Silvretta Group

highest point: 13 Grossglockner

river: 3 Inn, Mur 4 Drau, Elbe, Enns, Iser, Kamp, Lech, Murz, Raab 5 Donau, Drava, Drave, March, Salza, Thaya, Traun 6 Danube, Moldau

physical feature:
   basin: 7 Styrian
   canal: 6 Danube
   mountain pass: 7 Brenner
   wind: 6 Foehen
   woods: 6 Vienna

people: 5 Poles 6 Croats, Czechs 7 Germans, Gypsies 8 Slovenes 10 Hungarians
   botanist: 6 Mendel
   composer: 5 Haydn 6 Czerny, Mahler, Mozart, Webern 7 Amadeus, Strauss 8 Bruckner, Schubert 9 Beethoven 10 Schoenberg
   emperor: 7 Charles, Francis 9 Ferdinand, Habsburgs, Hapsburgs 10 Franz Josef
   philosopher: 12 Wittgenstein
   psychiatrist: 5 Adler, Freud, Reich
   statesman: 10 Metternich 12 Kurt Waldheim

language: 5 Czech 6 German, Magyar 8 Croatian 9 Slovenian

religion: 7 Judaism 10 Protestant 13 Roman Catholic

place:
   boulevard: 3 Kai 11 Ringstrasse
   cathedral: 9 St Stephen
   city hall: 7 Rathaus
   fortress: 13 Hochosterwitz, Hohensalzburg
   imperial palace: 7 Hofburg
   monastery: 4 Melk 8 Gottweig 14 Klosterneuburg
   museum: 6 Mozart 9 Johanneum
   people's garden: 11 Volksgarten
   resort: 5 Baden 7 Bregenz 8 Bad Ischl 9 Innsbruck, Semmering

feature: 8 yodelers 11 ice grottoes
   clothing: 5 loden 10 lederhosen
   dance: 5 waltz 6 dreher 7 landler 13 schuhplattler 14 grand polonaise
   festival: 8 Salzburg
   horse: 10 Lippizaner
   pastry shop: 12 konditoreien

food:
   breaded veal cutlet: 15 Wiener schnitzel
   cake: 11 linzer torte, sacher torte
   cookie: 7 kipferl
   roll: 10 golatschen

autochthonous 5 first 6 native, primal 7 ancient 8 earliest, original, primeval
10 aboriginal, indigenous, primordial

autocracy 7 czarism, tyranny
8 autarchy, monarchy 9 Caesarism, despotism, Hitlerism, kaiserism, monocracy, Stalinism 10 absolutism 11 Bonapartism 12 dictatorship
14 tyrannical rule 15 totalitarianism 16 absolute monarchy

autocrat 5 ruler 6 despot, tyrant 7 monarch 8 dictator, overlord 13 absolute ruler

autocratic 8 despotic 9 czaristic, imperious, tyrannous
10 iron-handed, oppressive, repressive, tyrannical 11 dictatorial, monarchical
13 authoritarian

auto da fe, auto de fe
13 act of the faith 17 burning of heretics
  from: 18 Spanish Inquisition

autograph 4 mark, sign 5 x-mark 9 John Henry, signature 11 endorsement, handwriting, inscription, John Hancock 16 countersignature

Autolycus
  character in: 14 The Winter's Tale
  author: 11 Shakespeare

Autolycus
  form: 5 thief
  father: 6 Hermes
  mother: 6 Chione
  half-brother: 9 Philammon
  wife: 9 Amphithea
  daughter: 8 Anticlea
  grandson: 8 Odysseus
  gift: 12 invisibility 13 shape changing

automated 9 automatic
10 mechanical, mechanized
15 machine-operated

automatic 6 reflex 7 natural, routine 8 electric, habitual, inherent, unwilled 9 automated
10 mechanical, push-button, self-acting, self-moving 11 instinctive, involuntary, spontaneous, unconscious
12 uncontrolled 13 nonvolitional, self-operating 14 self-propelling

automaton 4 pawn, tool
5 patsy, robot 6 puppet, stooge 7 android, cat's-paw, fall guy, machine 10 fantoccino, marionette

Automedon
  charioteer of: 8 Achilles

automobile
  invented by:
    differential gear: 4 Benz

    electric: 8 Morrison
    gasoline: 6 Duryea
      7 Daimler
    muffler: 5 Maxim
    self-starter: 9 Kettering
  see also: car

Automobile state
  nickname of: 8 Michigan

Autonoe
  father: 6 Cadmus
  mother: 8 Harmonia
  sister: 3 Ino 5 Agave
    6 Semele
  husband: 9 Aristaeus
  son: 7 Actaeon
  daughter: 6 Macris

autonomous 4 free 9 sovereign 11 independent, self-reliant 13 self-governing
14 self-determined, self-sufficient

autonomy 7 freedom 8 home rule, self-rule 10 liberation
11 sovereignty 12 independence 14 self-government
17 self-determination

auto racing
  driver: 6 A J Foyt 7 Al Unser 8 Tom Sneva 9 Niki Lauda 10 Bobby Unser, Juan Fangio 11 Jack Brabham 12 Bobby Allison, Janet Guthrie, Richard Petty
  13 Jackie Stewart, Mario Andretti 14 Barney Oldfield, Cale Yarborough, Craig Breedlove 16 Johnny Rutherford

Autry, Gene
  horse: 8 Champion
  born: 7 Tioga TX
  roles: 11 Melody Ranch
    16 The Singing Cowboy
    19 Tumbling Tumbleweeds
    22 Springtime in the Rockies

autumn 4 fall 11 harvest time
12 Indian summer 15 autumnal equinox

auxiliary 6 backup, helper
7 partner, reserve 9 accessory, ancillary, assistant, associate, companion, emergency, secondary 10 accomplice, subsidiary, supplement
11 subordinate
13 supplementary

avail 3 aid, use 4 help 5 serve
6 assist, profit 7 benefit, purpose, service, success, utilize
9 advantage 10 usefulness

available 4 free, open 5 handy, on tap 6 at hand, on hand
9 in reserve 10 accessible, convenient, obtainable

avalanche 4 heap, mass, pile
5 flood 6 deluge 7 barrage, cascade, torrent 8 blizzard

9 cataclysm, rockslide, snowslide 10 earthslide, inundation 11 bombardment

Avalon
  island of: 8 Paradise
  burial place for: 6 heroes
    10 King Arthur

avant-garde 7 leaders 8 pioneers, vanguard 10 innovators 11 forerunners, originators, tastemakers
12 advance guard, trailblazers, trendsetters

avarice 5 greed 6 penury 8 rapacity, venality 9 parsimony
10 greediness, stinginess
11 miserliness 12 covetousness, graspingness 13 money-grubbing, niggardliness, penny-pinching 15 close-fistedness

Ave Maria 8 Hail Mary

avenge 5 repay 6 injure, punish 7 revenge 9 retaliate

Avengers, The
  character: 8 Emma Peel, Tara King 9 John (Jonathan) Steed
  cast: 9 Diana Rigg 12 Linda Thorson 13 Patrick Macnee

avenue 3 way 4 gate, path, road 5 means, route 6 access, chance, course, outlet 7 gateway, parkway, passage, pathway 8 approach 9 boulevard, concourse, direction, esplanade 10 passageway 11 opportunity 12 thoroughfare

aver 4 avow 5 state, swear
6 affirm, assert, avouch, insist, verify 7 certify, contend, declare, profess, protest 8 maintain, proclaim 9 emphasize, guarantee, pronounce, represent 10 asseverate

average 3 par 4 fair, mean, norm, so-so 5 ratio, usual
6 common, medial, median, medium, normal, not bad
7 the rule, typical 8 mediocre, midpoint, moderate, ordinary, passable, standard, standing, the usual 9 tolerable 10 mean amount 11 indifferent, rank and file 12 run-of-the-mill

averment 5 claim 6 avowal
8 argument 9 assertion, assurance 10 allegation, contention, profession 11 affirmation

averse 5 loath 7 opposed 8 inimical 9 reluctant, unwilling
10 indisposed, unamenable
11 disinclined, ill-disposed, unfavorable 12 antipathetic, recalcitrant

aversion 6 hatred, horror
7 disgust, dislike 8 distaste, loathing 9 animosity, antipa-

thy, hostility, prejudice, repulsion, revulsion **10** abhorrence, opposition, reluctance, repugnance **11** detestation **13** unwillingness **14** disinclination

avert 4 turn **5** avoid, deter, shift **7** beat off, deflect, fend off, keep off, prevent, ward off **8** preclude, stave off, turn away **9** forestall, frustrate, keep at bay, sidetrack **11** nip in the bud

aviary 4 cage **9** birdhouse, enclosure

aviation 6 flight, flying **11** aeronautics **12** aerodynamics

aviator, aviatrix 4 bird **5** flyer, pilot **6** airman, flyboy **7** birdman

avid 4 keen **5** eager, rabid **6** ardent, greedy, hungry **7** anxious, devoted, fanatic, intense, zealous **8** covetous, desirous, grasping **9** rapacious, voracious **10** avaricious, insatiable **11** acquisitive **12** enthusiastic

avidity 4 zeal **5** greed **6** fervor, hunger **8** rapacity, voracity **9** eagerness **10** enthusiasm, fanaticism, greediness **12** covetousness **15** acquisitiveness

Avignon Papacy 15 Babylonian Exile **19** Babylonian Captivity

avocado 9 dark green **13** alligator pear, tropical fruit
origin: 6 Mexico **12** South America **14** Central America
family: 9 Lauraceae
used to make: 9 guacamole

avocation 5 hobby **7** pastime **8** sideline **9** diversion **10** recreation **11** distraction **13** entertainment

Avogadro, Amedeo
field: 7 physics **9** chemistry
nationality: 7 Italian
formulated: 19 molecular hypothesis

avoid 4 shun **5** avert, dodge, elude, evade, skirt **6** escape, eschew **7** boycott, forbear, forsake **8** sidestep **10** fight shy of **11** refrain from **12** steer clear of

avoidance 7 eluding, evasion **8** shirking, shunning, skirting

avoid the issue 4 duck **5** dodge, evade, hedge, stall **10** equivocate **17** beat around the bush

a votre sante 12 to your health

avouch 5 argue, swear **6** af-

firm **7** declare **8** advocate, maintain

avow 3 own **4** aver **5** admit, state, swear **6** affirm, assert, reveal **7** confess, declare, profess **8** announce, disclose, proclaim **11** acknowledge

avowal 4 word **8** averment **9** admission, assertion, assurance, statement **10** confession, profession **11** affirmation, declaration **12** proclamation, protestation **14** acknowledgment

avowed 5 sworn **8** admitted, declared **9** confessed, professed **12** acknowledged, self-declared **14** self-proclaimed

await 6 attend, expect **7** look for **10** anticipate

awake 5 alert, aware, spark **6** arouse, awaken, bestir, excite, incite **7** alive to, heedful, inspire, mindful, provoke **8** open-eyed, vigilant, watchful **9** attentive, conscious, stimulate

Awake and Sing!
author: 13 Clifford Odets

awaken 3 fan **4** fire **6** arouse, excite, kindle, revive, stir up **9** stimulate

awakening 7 arising, arousal **8** sparking, stirring **11** stimulation

award 4 give **5** allot, allow, grant, honor, medal, prize **6** accord, assign, bestow, decree, trophy **7** appoint, concede, laurels, tribute **8** citation, confer on **10** decoration

aware 6 with it **7** alert to, alive to, awake to, mindful **8** apprised, informed, sensible, sentient **9** cognizant, conscious, tuned in to **10** conversant **11** enlightened **12** familiar with **13** knowledgeable

awareness 9 acuteness, alertness, appraisal, knowledge **10** cognizance, perception **11** familiarity, information, mindfulness, realization, recognition, sensibility **12** acquaintance **13** consciousness, understanding

away 3 far **4** gone **6** absent, at once, way off **8** distance **9** elsewhere

awe 3 cow **4** fear **5** abash, alarm, amaze, dread, panic, shock **6** dismay, fright, horror, terror, wonder **7** perturb, quaking, respect, terrify **8** astonish, disquiet, frighten **9** abashment, adoration, amazement, quivering, rever-

ence, solemnity, trembling **10** exaltation, intimidate, veneration **11** disquietude, trepidation **12** apprehension, astonishment, perturbation **13** consternation

awe-inspiring 5 giant, grand, great, noble **6** august, mighty **7** eminent, exalted, mammoth, sublime, supreme, titanic **8** colossal, enormous, gigantic, glorious, imposing, majestic, wondrous **9** excessive **10** impressive, incredible, monumental, prodigious, stupendous, tremendous **11** astonishing, extravagant, illustrious, magnificent, spectacular **12** breathtaking, over-whelming

awesome 6 solemn **7** amazing, fearful **8** alarming, dreadful, fearsome, majestic, wondrous **9** inspiring **10** formidable, perturbing, stupefying, terrifying **11** astonishing, disquieting, frightening, magnificent **12** breathtaking, intimidating, overwhelming

awestruck 6 humble **8** overcome **11** reverential

awful 3 bad, low **4** base, dire, mean, ugly **5** lousy **6** solemn **7** amazing, awesome, fearful, ghastly, heinous, hideous **8** alarming, dreadful, fearsome, gruesome, horrible, majestic, shocking, terrible, wondrous **9** appalling, frightful, monstrous, revolting **10** deplorable, despicable, formidable, horrendous, horrifying, stupefying, terrifying, unpleasant **11** displeasing, disquieting, distressing, redoubtable **12** awe-inspiring, contemptible, disagreeable **13** reprehensible

awfully 4 very **5** quite **8** horribly, terribly **9** extremely, immensely **10** dreadfully **11** excessively **13** exceptionally

awkward 5 inept **6** clumsy, touchy, trying **7** unhandy **8** bungling, delicate, inexpert, ticklish, ungainly, unwieldy **9** difficult, graceless, maladroit **10** blundering, cumbersome, unpleasant, unskillful **11** troublesome **12** embarrassing, inconvenient, unmanageable **13** disconcerting, uncomfortable, uncoordinated
French: 6 gauche

Awkward Age, The
author: 10 Henry James

awkwardness 9 gaucherie **10** clumsiness, difficulty, ineptitude **12** ungainliness, unwieldiness **13** embarrassment, inconvenience

awl 4 nail 6 gimlet 11 leather tool, sharp device

awning 4 hood 6 canopy 7 marquee 8 covering, sunshade

awry 5 amiss, askew, wrong 6 astray, uneven 7 crooked, twisted 8 unevenly 9 crookedly, obliquely 11 out of kilter

axe, ax 3 can 4 chop, fire, oust, sack 5 let go, split 6 bounce, cut out, delete, remove 7 cut down, dismiss 8 get rid of, tomahawk 9 discharge, terminate 11 send packing
  type: 4 pick 6 poleax 7 hatchet 8 tomahawk

Axe, The
  author: 12 Sigrid Undset

Axelrod, Julius
  field: 9 chemistry
  studied: 24 nerve-impulse transmission
  awarded: 10 Nobel Prize

axiom 3 law 5 basic 7 precept 9 postulate, principle 10 assumption 14 fundamental law

axiomatic 5 banal, given 6 cliche 7 assumed 8 accepted, manifest 9 apodictic 10 aphoristic 11 self-evident 12 demonstrable, epigrammatic, indisputable, unquestioned 13 incontestable, platitudinous

Axiopoenus
  epithet of: 6 Athena
  means: 12 just requital

axis 4 stem 5 pivot, shaft 7 compact, entente, spindle 8 alliance 9 alignment, coalition 10 center line 11 affiliation 12 pivotal point 13 confederation 14 line of rotation, line of symmetry

axle 3 bar, pin 5 shaft, wheel 7 spindle 8 crossbar 10 turning bar

ayah 4 maid 5 nurse

aye 3 yea, yes 11 affirmative

Aykroyd, Dan
  born: 6 Canada, Ottawa 7 Ontario
  roles: 12 Ghostbusters 13 Doctor Detroit, Trading Places 16 The Blues Brothers, Driving Miss Daisy, The Great Outdoors 17 Saturday Night Live

Aymara
  location: 4 Peru 7 Bolivia 12 South America

Ayres, Lew
  wife: 8 Lola Lane 12 Ginger Rogers
  born: 13 Minneapolis MN
  roles: 7 Holiday, The Kiss 9 Dr Kildare 25 All Quiet on the Western Front

azalea 12 Rhododendron
  varieties: 4 Cork, Mock, Snow 5 Coast, Dwarf, Early, Flame, Hiryu, Hoary, Luchu, Royal, Sims's, Swamp, Sweet, Torch 6 Alpine, Balsam, Clammy, Indian, Korean, Kurume, Kyushu, Oconee, Pontic, Smooth, Spider, Summer, Yellow 7 Alabama, Chinese, Maries's, Mt Amagi, Oldham's, Western 8 Five-leaf, Japanese, Piedmont, Rusticum, Yodogawa 9 Kirishima, Mayflower, Pink-shell, Rose-shell, Wild-thyme 10 Cumberland, Macranthum, Plum-leaved, White swamp 11 Gable hybrid, Ghent hybrid, Molle hybrid 12 Arnold hybrid, Florida flame, Sander hybrid 13 Indicum hybrid 15 Glenn Dale hybrid, Kaempferi hybrid, Knapp Hill hybrid 16 Rutherford hybrid 24 Rusticum Flore Pleno hybrid

Azan
  father: 5 Arcas
  mother: 5 Erato

Azariah
  also: 6 Uzziah
  father: 4 Jehu 5 Ethan 6 Nathan 7 Hilkiah, Jehoram, Johanan 11 Jehoshaphat
  son: 4 Joel
  known as: 8 Abednego
  companion: 6 Daniel
  friend: 7 Meshach 8 Shadrach
  succeeded: 5 Zadok

Azazel 9 scapegoat 11 fallen angel

Azerbaijan
  capital/largest city: 4 Baku
  others 9 Kirovabad
  division 24 Nagorno-Karabakh Territory 29 Nakhichevan Autonomous Republic
  head of state: 9 president
  government: 8 republic
  monetary unit: 5 manat
  mountain: 8 Caucasus
  sea: 7 Caspian
  people: 5 Azeri 11 Azerbaijani
  language: 6 Turkic
  religion: 6 Muslim

Aziz, Dr
  character in: 15 A Passage to India
  author: 7 Forster

Aztec (Nahua, Mexica)
  language family: 7 Nahuatl 10 Uto-Aztecan
  location: 6 Mexico, Puebla 8 Guerrero, Veracruz 9 Guatemala, Michoacan 11 Lake Texcoco 14 Central America
  leader: 9 Montezuma
  worshipped: 12 Quetzalcoatl
  capital: 12 Tenochtitlan

Azuela, Mariano
  author of: 8 The Flies 9 The Bosses 12 The Underdogs 26 Trials of a Respectable Family

azure 5 lapis 6 cobalt 7 sky blue 8 cerulean 9 clear blue, cloudless 11 lapis lazuli

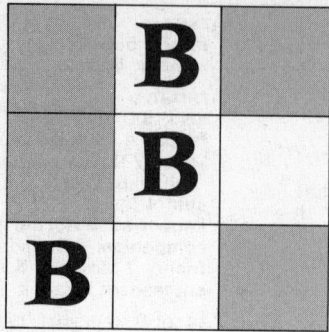

Baade, Walter
  field: **9** astronomy
  discovered: **15** Hidalgo
    asteroid

Baal 3 god **5** deity

Baal Merodach *see* **6** Marduk

Babbage, Charles
  field: **11** mathematics
  nationality: **7** British, English
  first: **15** actuarial tables
  inventor of: **13** adding ma-
    chine **18** calculating
    machine
  invented forerunner of:
    15 digital computer
  planned: **10** calculator

Babbitt 9 bourgeois
  10 conformist, middlebrow,
    philistine

Babbitt
  author: **13** Sinclair Lewis
  character: **11** Myra Babbitt,
    Seneca Deane **12** Paul Ries-
    ling **15** Mrs Tanis Judique
    22 George Folansbee Babbitt

babble 3 coo, din, gab, hum
  4 blab, talk **5** prate **6** burble,
  clamor, drivel, gabble, gibber,
  gurgle, hubbub, jabber, murmur **7** blabber, blather, chatter, prattle, twaddle **8** chitchat,
  rattle on **9** jabbering, murmuring **14** chitter-chatter

babbling 6 drivel, hubbub
  7 blabber, twaddle **8** burbling,
  gabbling, gurgling, nonsense
  9 clamoring, gibberish, jabbering, murmuring

babe 3 tot **4** baby **5** child
  6 infant

babe in arms 4 baby **6** infant **7** neonate, newborn

babe in the woods 8 innocent **9** fledgling, greenhorn
  10 tenderfoot

babel, Babel 3 din **6** bedlam,
  clamor, hubbub, tumult, uproar **7** turmoil **9** confusion

10 hullabaloo
11 pandemonium

Babel, Isaac
  author of: **9** Benia Krik
    11 Odessa Tales **13** The Red
    Cavalry

Babe Ruth
  nickname of: **16** George Her-
    man Ruth

Babe the Blue Ox
  character in: **10** Paul Bunyan

baboon 6 monkey
  breeding: **9** year round
  characteristic: **4** mane, pads
    6 muzzle
  diet: **6** plants **8** scorpion
    12 small animals
  dwelling: **5** Egypt, Sudan
    6 Africa, Arabia **7** Somalia
    8 Ethiopia
  family: **15** cercopithecidae
  habitat: **5** hills **6** plains
  largest genus: **6** Chacma
  most sacred: **6** Anobis
  smallest genus: **7** Western

babushka 4 baba, veil **5** scarf,
  stole **8** kerchief

baby 3 wee **4** babe, tiny
  5 dwarf, humor, pygmy, small,
  spoil, young **6** bantam, coddle,
  coward, infant, little, midget,
  minute, pamper, petite **7** crybaby, indulge, neonate
  8 dwarfish, sniveler **9** miniature, youngster **10** babe in
  arms, diminutive **11** mollycoddle, overindulge, pocket-sized

Baby
  nickname of: **12** Lauren
    Bacall

baby carriage 4 cart, pram
  6 cradle **12** perambulator

babyish 7 puerile **8** childish,
  immature, juvenile **9** infantile

babylike 3 wee **4** tiny **5** small
  9 infantile **10** diminutive

Babylonian Captivity
  13 Avignon Papacy **15** Babylonian Exile

Babylonian god 3 Bel
  6 Marduk

Babylonian Mythology *see*
box

Baby Roo
  character in: **13** Winnie-the-
    Pooh
  author: **5** Milne

Baby Snookums
  character in: **12** The
    Newlyweds

Bacall, Lauren
  real name: **15** Betty Joan
    Perske

Babylonian Mythology
  chief of gods: **6** Mar-
    duk **8** Merodach
    12 Baal Merodach
  demon: **6** Namtar
  goddess of air: **6** Ninlil
  goddess of death:
    10 Ereshkigal
  goddess of love/war/
    fertility: **6** Ananna, In-
    anna, Ishtar **7** Astarte,
    Mylitta **9** Ashtoreth
  god of air: **5** Enlil
  god of dead: **6** Nergal
  god of fire: **5** Ishum
  god of heaven: **2** An
    3 Anu
  god of moon: **3** Sin
  god of pastures/vegeta-
    tion: **6** Dumuzi
  god of pestilence: **4** Irra
  god of shepherds:
    6 Tammuz
  god of sun: **3** Utu
    7 Shamash
  god of wisdom: **4** Enki
  hero: **5** Ninib **7** Ninurta
  king: **9** Gilgamesh
  king of gods: **5** Enlil
  mother of gods:
    5 Nammu
  queen of heaven:
    6 Ishtar
  world of dead: **3** Kur

husband: 12 Jason Robards **14** Humphrey Bogart
nickname: 4 Baby
born: 9 New York NY
roles: 8 Applause, Key Largo **11** Dark Passage, The Big Sleep **12** Cactus Flower **16** To Have and Have Not **22** How to Marry a Millionaire

Bacchae
form: 11 priestesses
attendants of: 7 Bacchus
participants in: 11 Bacchanalia

Bacchae, The
author: 9 Euripides
character: 4 Zeus **5** Agave **6** Cadmus, Semele **8** Dionysus, Pentheus, Tiresias

bacchanal 4 orgy **5** feast, revel, spree **6** frolic **7** carouse, debauch, revelry, wassail **8** carnival, carousal, festival **10** debauchery, Saturnalia **11** merrymaking

Bacchanalia
festival honoring: 7 Bacchus

Bacchant
priest who worships: 7 Bacchus

Bacchante
also: 6 Thyiad
priestess who worships: 7 Bacchus

Bacchus
also: 5 Evius **8** Dionysus
god of: 4 wine **5** drama **9** fertility
father: 4 Zeus
mother: 6 Semele
son: 6 Phlias **7** Narcaus, Priapus **8** Oenopion
epithet: 6 Lyaeus **7** Bromius, Cresius **8** Thyoneus, Triambus **9** Pyrigenes **11** Dithyrambus, Mitrephorus

Bach, Carl (Karl) Philipp Emanuel
born: 6 Weimar **7** Germany
father: 19 Johann Sebastian Bach
composer of: 14 Prussian Sonata **19** Wurtembergian Sonata

Bach, Johann Sebastian
born: 7 Germany **8** Eisenach
composer of: 8 Chaconne **10** Giant Fugue, Inventions, Magnificat, Wedge Fugue **11** Dorian Fugue, Fiddle Fugue, Little Fugue **12** Corelli Fugue, French Suites, Fuga alla Giga, German Suites, St Anne's Fugue **13** Coffee Cantata, English Suites, St John Passion **14** Alla Breve Fugue, Easter Oratorio, Peasant Cantata,

Wedding Cantata **15** Jesu Meine Freude, Musical Offering **16** St Matthew Passion, The Art of the Fugue **17** Christmas Oratorio **18** Goldberg Variations **20** Brandenburg Concertos **22** The Well-Tempered Clavier **24** The Wise and Foolish Virgins **30** The Dispute Between Phoebus and Pan

Bach, Richard
author of: 25 Jonathan Livingston Seagull

bachelor 6 single **9** single man, unmarried **12** unmarried man

Bachelor Father
character: 9 Peter Tong **10** Kelly Gregg **12** Bentley Gregg **13** Ginger Farrell
cast: 10 Sammee Tong **12** John Forsythe **14** Noreen Corcoran **17** Bernadette Withers

bachelorhood 8 celibacy **13** baccalaureate **14** unmarried state

bacillus 3 bug **4** germ **7** microbe **8** pathogen **9** bacterium **13** microorganism

Bacis
origin: 8 Boeotian
form: 7 prophet

back *see box*

back away from 7 back off **11** retreat from **12** draw back from, withdraw from

backbiter 5 scold **6** carper, critic **7** reviler **8** vilifier **9** slanderer

backbiting 5 abuse, catty **6** gossip, malice **7** abusive, calumny, gossipy, hurtful, obloquy, slander **8** libeling, reviling **9** aspersion, cattiness, censuring, contumely, injurious, invective, malicious, maligning, vilifying **10** belittling, bitchiness, calumnious, defamation, defamatory, derogating, detracting, detraction, scandalous, scurrility, slanderous, traduction **11** badmouthing, denigrating, deprecating, disparaging, traducement **12** backstabbing, calumniation, vilification, vituperation **13** disparagement, maliciousness **16** scandal-mongering

backbone 4 grit, guts, sand **5** basis, chine, nerve, pluck, spine, spunk **6** dorsum, mettle, spirit **7** bravery, courage, resolve **8** firmness, mainstay, strength, tenacity **9** character, fortitude, manliness, vertebrae **10** foundation, resolution **11** intrepidity

back 3 aid, ebb **4** abet, gone, help, hind, late, past, rear, tail **5** after, guard, minor, rural, spine, tardy **6** affirm, assist, attest, behind, bygone, caudal, dorsal, dorsum, far end, former, hinder, hold up, praise, recede, recoil, remote, retire, return, revert, second, succor, tergal, uphold, verify **7** belated, bolster, certify, confirm, delayed, distant, earlier, elapsed, endorse, expired, far side, finance, not paid, overdue, promote, protect, rear end, rebound, retract, retreat, reverse, sponsor, support, sustain, tail end, warrant **8** advocate, backbone, hind part, hindmost, maintain, move away, obsolete, previous, sanction, secluded, turn tail, validate, vouch for, withdraw **9** afterpart, encourage, in arrears, out-of-date, patronize, posterior, reinforce, subsidize **10** retrogress, testify for, underwrite, untraveled **11** bear witness, corroborate, countenance, countrified, countryside, farthermost, furthermost, reverse side, undeveloped, unimportant, unpopulated **12** beat a retreat, hindquarters, spinal column, substantiate **13** take sides with

12 resoluteness, spinal column **13** dauntlessness, steadfastness **15** vertebral column **19** strength of character

back-country 4 farm **5** rural **6** rustic **7** farming **10** provincial

back down 7 back off **8** draw back, move away **9** withdrawn

backdrop 4 flat **7** curtain, scenery **10** background

backer 4 ally **5** angel **6** patron **7** sponsor **8** adherent, advocate, champion, follower, investor, promoter **9** financier, guarantor, supporter **10** wellwisher **11** underwriter

backfire 4 flop, miss **5** crash **6** fizzle, go awry **8** backlash, lay an egg, miscarry, ricochet **9** boomerang **10** bounce back, disappoint **11** come to grief, fall through **12** come to naught **13** come to nothing

background 3 set 4 past, rear
5 flats 6 milieu 7 context, history, rearing, setting 8 backdrop, breeding, distance, heritage, training 9 education, grounding, landscape, life story 10 experience, upbringing 11 antecedents, credentials, environment, mise-en-scene, preparation
13 circumstances

backhanded 7 awkward 8 reversed 9 insincere

backing 3 aid 4 core, help
5 aegis 6 succor 7 support
8 advocacy, interior, sanction
9 patronage, prompting 10 assistance, inner layer, sustenance 11 championing, cooperation, endorsement, helping hand, sponsorship
13 encouragement

backlash 4 flop, snag 5 crash, ravel 6 fizzle, go away, recoil
7 rebound 8 backfire, kick back, miscarry, ricochet, snap back 9 animosity, boomerang, hostility, reversion 10 antagonism, bounce back, opposition, resistance 11 come to grief, fall through 12 come to naught 13 come to nothing, counteraction, recalcitrance

backlog 5 hoard, stock, store
6 assets, excess, supply 7 nest egg, reserve, savings 9 abundance, amassment, inventory, reservoir, stockpile 12 accumulation 13 reserve supply
14 superabundance

back matter 5 index 8 addendum, appendix 10 supplement
12 bibliography

back off 7 retreat 8 back down, pull back, withdraw

backpack 4 hike, load
5 pouch 6 bundle 8 knapsack

backside 3 can 4 buns, butt, duff, prat, rear, rump, seat, tail 5 fanny 6 behind, bottom, settee, setter, sitter 7 keister, rear end 8 buttocks, derriere
9 fundament, posterior

backslide 5 lapse 6 revert
7 relapse 10 recurrence, regression 11 deteriorate
14 slip from virtue

back street 5 alley, byway
8 alleyway 13 secondary road

Back Street
    director:
      1941 version: 15 Robert Stevenson
      1961 version: 11 David Miller
    based on story by: 11 Fannie Hurst

cast:
    1932 version: 9 John Boles 10 Irene Dunne
    1941 version: 12 Charles Boyer 16 Margaret Sullavan
    1961 version: 9 John Gavin, Vera Miles 12 Susan Hayward

back talk 3 jaw, lip 4 gall, guff, rude, sass 5 cheek
8 pertness, rudeness 9 impudence, insolence, sassiness, sauciness 12 impertinence

Back to the Future
    director: 14 Robert Zemeckis
    cast: 11 Lea Thompson, Michael J Fox 16 Christopher Lloyd

backup 6 second 7 reserve, standby, stand-in 9 alternate, auxiliary, emergency, secondary 10 substitute, understudy
11 pinch-hitter
13 supplementary

back up 4 abet 6 assist, uphold 9 reinforce 11 corroborate

backward, backwards 3 shy
4 dull, slow 5 dense, tardy, timid, wrong 6 behind, ebbing, remiss, toward 7 bashful, impeded, laggard, messily, reverse, the rear 8 inverted, rearward, receding, reserved, retarded, reticent, reversed, sluggish 9 in retreat, in reverse, inside out, returning, slow-paced, to the past, to the rear, withdrawn 10 disorderly, improperly, regressive, retreating, retrograde, slow-witted, topsy-turvy, upside down
11 chaotically, undeveloped, withdrawing 12 wrong side out 13 retrogressive
15 uncommunicative
    French: 9 en arriere

backwash 4 burg, wake 6 result, sticks, upshot 7 boonies, outcome 8 frontier, tank town 9 aftermath, backwater, boondocks, provinces, upcountry 10 hinterland 11 aftereffect, backcountry, consequence

backwater 3 ebb 5 slack 7 retreat, reverse 8 holdback, stagnant, withdraw

backwoods 5 rural, wilds
6 rustic, simple, sticks 7 boonies, country 8 woodland
9 boondocks, rural area
10 hinterland, provincial
11 back-country, countryside, hinterlands 15 unsophisticated

bacon 3 pig 4 pork 6 gammon
8 porkslab 10 smoked pork
11 porkbellies
    measure: 6 rasher

Bacon, Francis
    author of: 6 Essays 11 New Atlantis 12 Novum Organum 14 Maxims of the Law 16 Instauratio Magna
    17 History of Henry VII
    18 De Sapientia Veterum
    20 Apophthegms New and Old 21 Advancement of Learning 25 Reading on the Statute of Uses

Bacon, Francis
    born: 6 Dublin 7 Ireland
    artwork: 15 Henrietta Moraes 35 Three Studies at the Base of a Crucifixion
    44 Studies After Velazquez' Portrait of Pope Innocent X

Bacon, Henry
    architect of: 15 Lincoln Memorial

bacteria 3 bug 4 germ 5 virus
7 microbe 8 bacillus, pathogen 13 microorganism

bactericide 9 germicide 10 antiseptic, germ killer
12 disinfectant

bacteriologist
    American: 4 Reed
    British: 7 Fleming
    German: 4 Koch 7 Behring, Ehrlich 10 Wassermann
    Japanese: 7 Noguchi
      8 Kitasato

bad *see* **box**

bad faith 7 perfidy, treason
8 betrayal 9 falseness, treachery, two timing 10 disloyalty
11 double-cross 13 breach of faith, double-dealing
14 unfaithfulness

badge 4 mark, seal, sign
5 brand, stamp, token 6 device, emblem, ensign, shield, symbol 7 earmark 8 hallmark, insignia 9 medallion

badger 3 nag, vex 4 bait, goad 5 annoy, beset, bully, chafe, harry, hound, tease
6 coerce, harass, hector, nettle, pester, plague 7 provoke, torment, trouble 8 irritate
9 persecute
    group of: 4 cete

Badger State
    nickname of: 9 Wisconsin

badinage 5 chaff 6 banter, joking 7 jesting, joshing, kidding, ragging, ribbing, waggery
8 chaffing, raillery, repartee, word play

bad judgment 5 folly 10 imprudence 11 foolishness
12 carelessness 13 senselessness 15 thoughtlessness
16 shortsightedness, unperceptiveness

bad 3 ill, sad, sin **4** base, dire, evil, foul, glum, grim, mean, poor, rank, sick, sour, vile **5** acrid, acute, angry, awful, cross, false, fetid, grave, harsh, lousy, moldy, nasty, risky, sorry, unfit, wrong **6** ailing, bitter, crimes, faulty, gloomy, guilty, infirm, odious, putrid, rancid, rotten, severe, sickly, sinful, touchy, tragic, turned, unwell, wicked, wrongs **7** baneful, beastly, corrupt, decayed, harmful, hurtful, immoral, joyless, lacking, naughty, not good, noxious, painful, searing, serious, spoiled, tainted, unsound, useless **8** below par, contrite, criminal, dreadful, grievous, inferior, menacing, mildewed, offenses, polluted, terrible, troubled, villainy, wretched **9** agonizing, dangerous, defective, deficient, erroneous, frightful, hazardous, imperfect, incorrect, injurious, irascible, irritable, loathsome, miserable, nefarious, obnoxious, offensive, regretful, repugnant, repulsive, revolting, sad events, sickening, troubling, unethical, unhealthy, unnerving, unwelcome, valueless **10** calamitous, decomposed, deplorable, detestable, disastrous, disgusting, distressed, disturbing, fallacious, immorality, inadequate, indisposed, melancholy, misfortune, nauseating, not correct, perfidious, putrescent, remorseful, second-rate, unpleasant, villainous, wickedness **11** detrimental, discouraged, distasteful, distractive, distressing, ineffective, inefficient, opprobrious, regrettable, substandard, troublesome, unpalatable **12** contaminated, disagreeable, discouraging, disreputable, excruciating, questionable, unprincipled, unproductive **13** below standard, disappointing, disheartening, harmful things, nonproductive, reprehensible, short-tempered **14** disappointment **15** disadvantageous, under the weather **18** conscience-stricken

---

bad luck 6 mishap **7** ill wind **8** bad break **9** adversity, mischance **10** ill fortune, misfortune

badly 5 wrong **6** basely, poorly, sorely, vilely **7** acutely, greatly, ineptly, not well, wrongly **8** faultily, horribly, severely, shoddily, sinfully, sloppily, terribly, very much, wickedly **9** corruptly, extremely, immorally, intensely, unsoundly **10** carelessly, criminally, dreadfully, improperly, wretchedly **11** defectively, deficiently, desperately, erroneously, exceedingly, frightfully, imperfectly, incorrectly, nefariously, offensively, unethically **12** disreputably, inadequately, villainously **13** incompetently, in the worst way **16** unsatisfactorily

bad manners 8 rudeness **9** surliness **10** incivility **11** boorishness, discourtesy **12** impoliteness

bad mark 4 blot **7** demerit **9** poor grade

badminton
  racket: **10** battledore
  racket used to hit: **4** bird **7** shuttle **11** shuttlecock
  Indian version: **5** poona
  stroke: **4** drop **5** clear, smash **7** service **13** backhand drive, forehand drive

badmouthing 5 barbs **7** insults, slander **9** criticism, insulting **10** slandering **11** criticizing

bad taste 9 crudeness, vulgarity **10** coarseness, garishness, tawdryness

bad tasting 4 sour **5** nasty **6** bitter **7** spoiled **9** medicinal, revolting **10** disgusting **11** unpalatable

bad-tempered 5 cross, testy **6** grumpy **7** grouchy **8** choleric, churlish **9** difficult, irascible, irritable **10** ill-natured **11** acrimonious **12** disagreeable

bad times 4 bust **5** slump **9** hard times, recession **10** depression

bad turn 4 harm, hurt **5** wrong **6** injury **7** ill turn **8** disfavor **9** injustice **10** disservice **11** discourtesy

Baekleland, Leo Hendrik
  field: **9** chemistry
  invented: **8** Bakelite **32** artificial light photographic paper

Baer, Max (Maximillian Adalbert)
  nickname: **17** Livermore Larruper
  sport: **6** boxing
  class: **11** heavyweight

Baeyer, Johann Friedrich Wilhelm Adolph von
  field: **9** chemistry
  nationality: **6** German
  synthesized: **6** indigo
  discovered: **13** phthalein dyes
  awarded: **10** Nobel Prize

baffle 3 bar **4** daze, dull, foil, stop **5** amaze, check, stump **6** deaden, muddle, puzzle, reduce, thwart **7** astound, confuse, inhibit, mystify, nonplus, perplex **8** astonish, befuddle, bewilder, confound, dumfound, minimize, restrain, surprise **10** disconcert

baffling 7 elusive **8** puzzling **9** confusing, enigmatic **10** mysterious, mystifying, perplexing **11** confounding **16** incomprehensible

bag 3 get, sag **4** hunt, kill, sack, take, trap **5** bulge, catch, droop, pouch, purse, shoot, snare **6** bundle, entrap, obtain, packet **7** acquire, capture, collect, ensnare **8** paper bag, protrude, suitcase **10** receptacle

bagatelle 6 trifle **7** nothing, trinket **10** knickknack, light music **11** unimportant

baggage 4 bags, gear **5** grips **6** trunks **7** bundles, effects, luggage, valises **8** movables, packages **9** apparatus, equipment, suitcases, trappings **10** belongings **11** impedimenta **13** accouterments, paraphernalia

baggy 4 limp **5** loose, slack **6** droopy, flabby, puffed **7** bloated, bulbous, flaccid, paunchy, sagging, swollen **9** unpressed, unshapely **12** loose-fitting

Baghdad
  capital of: **4** Iraq
  founder: **8** (Caliph) al-Mansur
  landmark:
    minaret: **10** Suq al-Ghazi
    mosque: **8** Madrasah **14** al-Mustansiriya
  means: **8** God-given
  river: **6** Tigris

Bagheera
  character in: **14** The Jungle Books
  author: **7** Kipling

bagnio 4 bath, stew **5** house **6** bordel, prison **7** brothel **8** bordello, cathouse **10** bawdy house, fancy house, whorehouse **13** sporting house **14** house of ill fame **16** house of ill repute **19** house of prostitution

Bagnold, Enid
  author of: **14** National Vel-

vet, The Chalk Garden
23 The Chinese Prime
Minister

Bagstock, Joe
character in: 12 Dombey and
Son
author: 7 Dickens

Bahamas
capital/largest city:
6 Nassau
others: 8 Freeport
9 Rock Sound
10 George Town
11 Mastic Point
12 Spanish Wells
head of state: 14 British monarch **15** governor general
island: 3 Cat **4** Long
5 Berry, Exuma **6** Andros, Bimini, Caicos,
Rum Cay **7** Crooked,
Harbour, Watling
9 Eleuthera, Mayaguana **10** Great Abaco
11 Grand Bahama,
Great Inagua, Great
Ragged, San Salvador
13 New Providence
sea: 8 Atlantic
9 Caribbean
physical feature:
strait: **7** Florida
swamp: **8** mangrove
people: 5 black **7** Haitian
language: 6 Creole
7 English
religion: 12 Christianity
place:
harbor: **9** Governors
naval base:
9 Mayaguana
feature:
key: **3** cay
native: **5** conch

Bahrain *see box*
bail 3 dip **4** bond, lade **5** ladle,
scoop, spoon **6** surety **9** guarantee **11** post bond for

bailiff 6 deputy **8** marshall,
overseer **9** assistant, constable
12 court officer

bailiwick 4 area, beat, turf
5 arena, orbit, place, realm
6 domain, sphere **7** compass
8 dominion, province **9** territory **10** department
12 neighborhood

Baird, Spencer Fullerton
field: 7 zoology
authority on: 5 birds
7 mammals
established: 30 US Commission of Fish and Fisheries

Bahrain
capital/largest city:
6 Manama
others: 5 Rifaa **7** Jidhafs **8** Muharraq
head of state/government: 4 emir
monetary unit: 4 fils
5 dinar
island: 5 Hawar, Jidda
6 Sitrah **7** Bahrain
9 Umm Nassan **10** alMuharraq **11** An Nabi
Salih
physical feature:
gulf: **7** Bahrain,
Persian
people: 4 Arab **6** Indian
7 Persian **8** American,
European **9** Pakistani
ruling family: **9** alKhalifa
language: 4 Urdu
5 Farsi **6** Arabic
7 English, Persian
religion: 5 Islam

laboratory at: 11 Woods
Hole MA

bait 3 vex **4** lure, ride, worm
5 annoy, bribe, harry, hound,
tease, worry **6** allure, badger,
come-on, harass, heckle, hector, magnet, needle **7** provoke,
torment **9** put bait on, tantalize **10** allurement, antagonize,
attraction, enticement, inducement, temptation

bake 3 fry **4** boil, burn, cook,
sear, stew **5** grill, roast, saute,
toast **6** braise, pan-fry, scorch,
simmer **7** parboil, swelter

Baked Bean State
nickname of:
13 Massachusetts

Baker, Norma Jean
Mortenson
real name of: 13 Marilyn
Monroe

Baking
goddess of: 6 Fornax

Balaam
father: 4 Beor
brother: 4 Bela
lived at: 4 Aram **6** Pethor
commanded by: 5 Balak
killed by: 6 Israel

Balak
father: 6 Zippor
commanded: 6 Balaam

Balakiref, Mily
born: 6 Russia **13** NijniNovgorod
member of: 7 Kutchka, The
Five

composer of: 6 Russia, Tamara, Thamar **7** Islamey
8 King Lear (overture)

balance, balances 3 pay
4 cool, mean, rest **5** poise, ratio, scale, sum up, tally, total,
tot up, weigh **6** aplomb,
equate, offset, parity, ponder,
reckon, scales, set off, square,
steady, weight **7** compare,
compute, harmony, opinion,
reflect, remnant, residue
8 cogitate, consider, contrast,
coolness, equality, estimate,
evaluate, judgment, leftover,
level off, parallel, presence,
symmetry **9** appraisal, calculate, composure, equipoise,
juxtapose, make level, remainder, stability, stabilize
10 amount owed, comparison,
counteract, deliberate, equanimity, evaluation, keep
steady, neutralize, proportion,
steadiness **11** equilibrium
12 counterpoise, equalization,
middle ground **13** compensate
for, consideration, judiciousness **14** amount credited, selfpossession, unflappability
15 level-headedness
16 imperturbability
constellation of: 5 Libra

balanced 4 fair, just **9** equitable, impartial **12** unprejudiced
13 disinterested

balance out 6 cancel, offset
9 make up for **10** neutralize
13 compensate for
14 counterbalance

Balanchine, George
choreographer of: 4 Agon
6 Jewels **8** Episodes, Ivesiana, Serenade **15** Concerto
Barocco **16** Allegro
Brillante

balcony 4 deck **5** boxes, foyer,
loges **6** loggia **7** portico, terrace, veranda **9** mezzanine

bald 4 bare, flat, open **5** blunt,
naked, plain, stark, utter
6 barren, simple, smooth
7 denuded, obvious **8** flagrant,
glabrous, hairless, outright,
treeless **9** depilated, out-andout, unadorned **11** categorical,
undisguised, unqualified, unvarnished **12** without cover
13 unembellished, unequivocable **15** straightforward

Balder
also: 5 Baldr **6** Baldur
origin: 6 Nordic
god of: 6 beauty **8** radiance
father: 4 Odin **5** Othin
mother: 3 Fri **5** Frigg, Frija
6 Frigga
twin brother: 5 Hoder, Hodur
killed by: 5 Hoder, Hodur

balderdash 3 rot **4** bosh, bull,

bunk **5** crock, trash **6** bunkum, drivel, hot air **7** twaddle **8** buncombe, claptrap, flummery, nonsense, tommyrot **9** gibberish, poppycock **10** double-talk, tomfoolery **11** obfuscation **16** stuff and nonsense

baldheaded 8 hairless **9** bald-pated, depilated **10** skin-headed **11** chrome-domed

Baldr
    see: **6** Balder

Baldung Grien, Hans
    born: **6** Alsace **10** Weyersheim
    artwork: **9** Todentanz **17** Death and the Maiden **19** Death Kissing a Maiden **21** The Bewitched Stable Boy **24** Rest on the Flight into Egypt

Baldur
    see: **6** Balder

Baldwin, James
    author of: **13** Giovanni's Room, The Amen Corner **14** Another Country **15** Just Above My Head, The Fire Next Time **17** Going to Meet the Man, Nobody Knows My Name, No Name in the Street **21** Blues for Mister Charlie, Go Tell It on the Mountain

bale 4 case, load, pack **6** bundle, packet, parcel **7** package **11** bound bundle

balefire 6 beacon **9** watchfire **10** signal fire

baleful 3 icy **4** cold, dire, evil **6** deadly, malign **7** baneful, furious, harmful, hurtful, ominous **8** sinister, spiteful, venomous **9** malicious, malignant **10** malevolent **11** cold-hearted, threatening

Balfe, Michael William
    born: **6** Dublin **7** Ireland
    composer of: **15** The Bohemian Girl, The Maid of Artois **17** I rivali di se stessi **18** The Siege of Rochelle

Balfour, David
    character in: **9** Kidnapped
    author: **9** Stevenson

Bali
    province of: **9** Indonesia
    capital: **8** Denpasar
    city: **10** Singaraja
    island: **11** Lesser Sunda
    highest peak: **6** Agoeng
    climate: **3** dry **7** monsoon
    tree: **8** waringin
    animal: **4** deer **5** tiger
    people: **7** Malayan
    religion: **8** Hinduism
    agriculture: **3** pig **4** corn,

rice **6** cattle, coffee **7** tobacco

Balius
    horse of: **8** Achilles
    gift: **11** immortality

balk 3 bar **4** foil, shun **5** block, check, demur, evade, shirk, spike, stall **6** baffle, defeat, derail, eschew, hinder, impede, recoil, refuse, resist, stymie, thwart **7** inhibit, prevent **8** draw back, hang back, hesitate, obstruct **9** forestall, frustrate **10** shrink from

Balkan 16 Forested mountain
    agriculture: **5** grain **6** cotton, grapes, olives **7** tobacco
    ancient people: **4** Slav **5** Greek, Roman **8** Illyrian, Thracian
    language: **9** Slovenian **10** Macedonian **14** Serbo-Croatian
    mountain: **6** Balkan, Massif **7** Rhodope **10** Carpathian **11** Dinaric Alps **13** Transylvanian
    religion: **5** Islam **8** Orthodox **13** Roman Catholic
    river: **6** Danube, Morava, Vardar
    sea boundary: **5** Black **6** Aegean, Ionian **8** Adriatic **13** Mediterranean
    state: **6** Greece, Turkey **7** Albania, Romania **8** Bulgaria **10** Yugoslavia

balky 6 mulish, ornery, unruly **7** restive, wayward, willful **8** contrary, perverse, stubborn **9** fractious, obstinate, pigheaded **10** rebellious, refractory **11** disobedient, intractable **12** recalcitrant, unmanageable

ball 3 hop, orb **4** prom, shot **5** dance, globe **6** pellet, soiree, sphere **7** bullets, globule **8** spheroid **9** cotillion, promenade **11** projectiles

Ball, Lucille
    husband: **9** Desi Arnaz
    children: **4** Desi **5** Lucie
    born: **11** Jamestown NY
    roles: **9** Here's Lucy, I Love Lucy **11** The Lucy Show

Balla, Giacomo
    born: **5** Italy, Turin
    artwork: **8** The Sewer **11** The Mad Woman **18** Speeding Automobile **20** Rhythm of the Violinist **22** Dynamism of a Dog on a Leash **26** The Street Light—Study of Light **29** Mercury Passing in Front of the Sun **40** Swifts Paths of Movement and Dynamic Sequences

ballad 3 lay **4** song **5** carol, ditty **6** chanty **8** folk song

12 rhyming story **13** narrative poem **14** narrative verse

Ballad of Reading Gaol, The
    author: **10** Oscar Wilde

Ballads and Poems
    author: **19** Stephen Vincent Benet

ballast 6 weight **7** balance, control **9** equipoise **10** ballasting, dead weight, makeweight, stabilizer **12** counterpoise **13** counterweight **14** counterbalance **19** stabilizing material

Ballesteros, Severiano
    nickname: **4** Seve
    sport: **4** golf
    nationality: **7** Spanish

ballet *see box, p. 82*

Ball of Fat
    author: **15** Guy de Maupassant

balloon 4 grow **5** belly, bloat **6** billow, blow up, dilate, expand **7** distend, enlarge, fill out, inflate, puff out **8** increase, swell out

ballot 4 poll, vote **5** slate **6** ticket, voting **7** polling **13** round of voting **16** list of candidates

ballyhoo 4 hype, puff, push, tout **6** herald, hoopla **7** buildup, promote, puffery, trumpet **8** proclaim **9** advertise, promotion, publicity, publicize **10** hullabaloo, propaganda **11** advertising **15** public relations

balm 5 cream, salve **6** balsam, lotion, solace **7** anodyne, comfort, unguent **8** curative, narcotic, ointment, sedative **9** comforter, emollient **10** palliative **11** restorative **12** tranquilizer

balmy 3 odd **4** calm, fair, mild, soft, warm **5** bland, kooky, weird **6** easing, gentle **7** calming, clement, summery **8** aromatic, fragrant, perfumed, pleasant, redolent, soothing **9** agreeable, ambrosial, eccentric, temperate **10** refreshing, salubrious

Balnibari
    fictional land in: **16** Gulliver's Travels
    author: **5** Swift

baloney 3 rot **4** bull, bunk **5** hokum, hooey, stuff **6** bunkum, hot air, humbug **7** hogwash, sausage, spinach **8** claptrap, nonsense, tommyrot **9** poppycock **10** applesauce **11** foolishness

ballet 4 Agon **5** Manon, Rodeo **6** Apollo, Parade **7** Giselle, Orpheus **8** Coppelia, Episodes, Ivesiana, Les Noces, Serenade, Swan Lake, The Doves **9** Anastasia, Fancy Free, Interplay, Petrushka, The Jewels **10** La Sylphide, Petrouchka **11** Billy the Kid, Lilac Garden, Soccer Dance, Symphony in C, The Firebird **12** Pillar of Fire, Sailor's Dance, Spring Waters, The Partisans **13** The Nutcracker **14** Romeo and Juliet **15** Concerto Barocco, Fall River Legend, The Rite of Spring **16** Allegro Brillante, La Fille Mal Gardee, Specter of the Rose **17** The Sleeping Beauty **18** Raymonda Variations **19** The Afternoon of a Faun, The Four Temperaments **24** Stravinsky Violin Concerto

  ballet company: 5 Kirov, Royal **7** Bolshoi, Joffrey **9** Mariinsky, Maryinsky **11** New York City **13** Ballets Russes **20** Dance Theater of Harlem **21** American Ballet Theater **22** National Ballet of Canada

  choreographer: 9 Hanya Holm, Lev Ivanov **10** John Weaver **11** Jules Perrot **12** Agnes de Mille, Igor Moiseyev, Marius Petipa, Michel Fokine **13** Jean Dauberval, Jerome Robbins, Leonid Massine **15** Arthur Saint-Leon **16** George Balanchine, Kenneth MacMillan **18** August Bournonville, Bronislava Nijinska, Jean Georges Noverre, Sir Frederick Ashton

  chorus: 8 ensemble **13** corps de ballet

  dancer: 9 Karen Kain **10** Anton Dolin, Marie Lieta, Serge Lifar **11** Allegra Kent, Anna Pavlova, Anthony Blum, Lucile Grahn, Lynn Seymour, Nadia Nerina **12** Fanny Cerrito, Marie Camargo, Peter Martins **13** Alicia Markova, Andre Eglevsky, Anthony Dowell, Carlotta Grisi, Frank Augustyn, Galina Ulanova, Margot Fonteyn, Marie Taglioni, Melissa Hayden, Patricia Neary, Rudolf Nureyev **14** Arthur Mitchell, Cynthia Gregory, Edward Villella, Gelsey Kirkland, Leonide Massine, Maria Tallchief, Suzanne Farrell, Vaslav Nijinsky **15** Jacques D'Amboise, Martine Van Hamel, Maya Plisetskaya, Natalia Makarova, Patricia McBride, Tamara Karsavina **16** Antoinette Sibley, Olga Spessivtseva **17** Alexandra Danilova, Marina Kondratieva **18** Mikhail Baryshnikov

  fast movement: 7 allegro

  first ballet: 22 Ballet Comique de la Reine

  impresario: 12 Marie Rambert **15** Ninette de Valois, Sergei Diaghilev

  kick: 9 battement

  modern dancer/choreographer: 8 Ted Shawn **9** Eliot Feld **10** Mary Wigman, Paul Draper, Twyla Tharp **11** Anna Sokolow, Antony Tudor, Eric Hawkins, Ruth St Denis **12** Martha Graham **13** Alwin Nikolais, Doris Humphrey, Isadora Duncan **14** Charles Weidman **15** Merce Cunningham

  position/step: 4 jete, plie, tour **5** saute **6** releve **7** en avant, fouette, on point, pas seul, turnout **8** batterie, cabriole, en dedans, en dehors, glissade **9** arabesque, developpe, en arriere, entrechat, pas de chat, pas-de-deux, pirouette **10** demi-pointe, port de bras, tour en l'air **11** rond de jambe, terre-a-terre **12** pas de bourree, saut de basque **17** changement de pieds

  principal female dancer: 9 ballerina **14** prima ballerina

  principal male dancer: 12 danseur noble

  skirt: 4 tutu

  slow movement: 6 adagio

  term: 4 coda **5** barre **6** ballon **14** divertissement

Baloo
  character in: 14 The Jungle Books
  author: 7 Kipling

balsam 3 fir **4** balm **5** cream, salve **7** unguent **8** ointment **9** Impatiens

varieties: 2 He **3** Fir, She **4** Rose, Wild **6** Garden **8** Zanzibar

Balsam, Martin
  born: 9 New York NY
  roles: 6 Psycho **7** Catch-22

15 A Thousand Clowns, On the Waterfront

Baltic
  language family: 12 Indo-European
  group: 11 Balto-Slavic
  subgroup: 7 Latvian **10** Lithuanian

Baltimore
  baseball team: 7 Orioles
  football team: 5 Stars

Baltimore, David
  field: 12 microbiology
  studied: 11 animal cells **13** viral genetics
  awarded: 10 Nobel Prize

Balto-Slavic
  language family: 12 Indo-European
  branch: 6 Baltic, Slavic

baluster 4 post, rail **6** column, pillar **7** support, upright **8** pilaster

balustrade 7 railing **8** baluster, banister, handrail

Balzac, Honore de
  author of: 7 Gobseck **10** La Vendetta **11** Cousin(e) Bette **12** Father Goriot, Le Cousin Pons, Le Pere Goriot **13** Lost Illusions **14** Eugenie Grandet, The Human Comedy **15** The Wild Ass's Skin **16** La Comedie Humaine **23** The Physiology of Marriage

Bamako
  capital of: 4 Mali

Bambi
  author: 11 Felix Salten
  character: 6 Faline, Flower **7** Thumper

bamboo 4 Sasa **7** Bambusa **9** Shibataea **10** Pseudosasa **11** Arundinaria **13** Phyllostachys **14** Chimonobambusa **15** Semiarundinaria
  varieties: 4 Moso **5** Arrow, Black, Dwarf, Giant, Hardy, Hedge, Henon, Meyer, Pygmy, Simon, Stake **6** Buddha, Common, Forage, Oldham, Sacred, Sickle, Square, Tonkin **7** Allgold, Beechey, Mexican **8** Calcutta, Feathery, Heavenly, Narihira **9** Canebrake, Castillon **10** Red-berried, Square-stem **11** Punting-pole **12** Alphonse Karr, Yellow-groove **13** Dwarf fern-leaf, Fern-leaf hedge, Oriental hedge **14** Chinese-goddess **16** Dwarf white-stripe **17** Silver-stripe hedge **18** Stripe-stem fern-leaf

bamboozle 3 con, gyp **4** coax, dupe, fool, gull, hoax, lure, rook, take **5** cheat, cozen, trick **6** delude **7** beguile, deceive, defraud, mislead, swindle **8** hoodwink **9** victimize

ban 3 bar **5** debar, taboo **6** banish, enjoin, forbid **7** barring, embargo, exclude **8** disallow, prohibit, stoppage, suppress **9** exclusion, interdict, proscribe, restraint **10** banishment, censorship **11** forbiddance, prohibition, restriction **12** interdiction, proscription

banal 4 dull **5** corny, stale, stock, tired, trite, vapid **6** jejune **7** humdrum, insipid, prosaic **8** bromidic, everyday, ordinary, shopworn **9** hackneyed **10** pedestrian, threadbare, unexciting, unoriginal **11** commonplace, stereotyped **12** cliche-ridden, conventional **13** platitudinous, unimaginative, uninteresting

banality 6 cliche **7** bromide **9** platitude, staleness, triteness **10** insipidity

banana 4 Musa
  varieties: 3 Fe'i **4** Fehi, Koae **5** Dwarf **6** Edible **7** Chinese **9** Flowering **10** Abyssinian, Ladyfinger **12** Canary Island, Chinese dwarf
  similar to: 8 plantain

Bananas
  director: 10 Woody Allen
  cast: 10 Woody Allen **12** Howard Cosell, Louise Lasser **15** Carlos Montalban

Bancroft, Anne
  real name: 23 Anna Maria Louise Italiano
  husband: 9 Mel Brooks
  born: 7 Bronx NY
  roles: 11 Mrs Robinson, The Graduate **15** The Pumpkin Eater, The Turning Point, Two for the Seesaw **16** The Miracle Worker (Oscar)

band 3 set **4** belt, body, club, crew, gang, hoop, join, pack, ring, sash **5** bunch, crowd, group, junta, party, strap, strip, swath, thong, troop, unite **6** caucus, circle, clique, collar, fillet, gather, girdle, league, ribbon, streak, stripe, throng **7** bandeau, binding, circlet, company, society **8** assembly, cincture, ensemble **9** multitude, orchestra, surcingle **10** fellowship, sisterhood **11** association, brotherhood, confederacy, consolidate **13** confederation

bandage 4 bind **5** dress **7** binding, plaster **8** compress, dressing

bandanna, bandana 5 scarf **8** kerchief **10** silk square **11** neckerchief **12** handkerchief

Bandar Seri Begawan
  capital of: 6 Brunei

bandeau 3 bra **4** band **6** fillet **7** binding, circlet **9** brassiere

bandit 4 thug **5** crook, thief **6** badman, outlaw, robber **7** brigand, burglar, footpad, ladrone **8** blackleg **9** desperado, road agent **10** highwayman

bandleader 6 master **7** maestro **8** director **9** conductor
  famous: 11 Glenn Miller, Tommy Dorsey **12** Lawrence Welk

Band of Merry Men
  followers of: 9 Robin Hood

band together 5 unify, unite **6** league **7** combine **10** join forces **11** consolidate

bandy 4 swap **5** trade **6** barter **7** shuffle **8** exchange **9** toss about **11** interchange **16** toss back and forth

bandying 4 swap **5** trade **8** exchange **9** tit for tat **10** quid pro quo **11** give and take

bane 3 woe **4** ruin **5** curse, toxin, venom **6** blight, burden, canker, plague, poison **7** scourge, torment, tragedy **8** calamity, disaster, downfall, nuisance **9** destroyer, detriment, ruination **10** affliction **13** pain in the neck **14** thorn in the side **16** fly in the ointment

baneful 4 evil **6** deadly, malign, woeful **7** harmful, noxious **8** venomous **9** injurious, malignant, poisonous **10** malevolent **11** destructive

bang 3 box, hit, pop, rap, tap **4** beat, blow, boom, clap, cuff, kick, lick, slam, slap, sock **5** burst, clout, crash, knock, smack, thump, whack **6** buffet, charge, report, thrill, thwack, wallop **7** delight **8** good time, headlong, pleasure, suddenly **9** enjoyment, explosion **10** crashingly, excitement

Bangkok, Bankok
  also: 9 Krung Thep
  capital of: 8 Thailand
  landmark: 5 Wat Po **11** Grand Palace **16** Wat Emerald Buddha
  means: 12 City of Angels
  nickname: 15 Venice of the East
  port: 8 Klongtoi
  river: 10 Chao Phraya

Bangladesh
  other name: 10 East Bengal **12** East Pakistan
  capital/largest city: 5 Dacca
  others: 6 Khulna, Sylhet **7** Comilla, Jessore, Rangpur, Saidpur **8** Jamalpur, Rajshahi **9** Madaripur **10** Chittagong **11** Narayanganj **12** Brahmanbaria
  monetary unit: 4 taka **5** paisa
  island: 10 Sundarbans
  mountain: 15 Chittagong Hills
  highest point: 10 Keokradong
  river: 5 Padna **6** Ganges, Meghna **10** Burhi Ganga, Karnaphuli **11** Brahmaputra
  physical feature:
    bay: 6 Bengal
  people: 7 Bengali
    guerrillas: 11 muktibahini
    leader: 6 Ershad **11** Ziaur Rahman **19** Sheikh Mujibur Rahman
  language: 6 Bihari **7** Bengali, English
  religion: 5 Hindu, Islam
  feature:
    clothing: 4 sari **5** lungi

bangle 3 fob **5** chain, charm **6** armlet, bauble, gewgaw, tinsel **7** bibelot, fribble, trinket **8** bracelet, gimcrack, ornament, wristlet **10** knickknack **11** junk jewelry **14** costume jewelry

Bangui
  capital of: 22 Central African Republic

banish 3 ban, bar **4** drop, oust **5** eject, erase, evict, exile, expel **6** deport, dispel, outlaw, reject, remove **7** cast out, discard, dismiss, exclude, put away, shut out, turn out **8** cast away, dislodge, drive out, get rid of, send away, shake off **9** discharge, eliminate, eradicate, extradite **13** excommunicate **14** send to Coventry

banished person 5 exile **6** emigre, pariah **7** outcast **8** deportee, expellee **10** expatriate **14** deported person **15** displaced person

banishment 3 ban **5** exile **6** ouster **7** removal **8** eviction

9 dismissal, exclusion, expulsion **11** deportation **12** expatriation **14** transportation **15** excommunication

Banjo Eyes
nickname of: **11** Eddie Cantor

Banjul, Bathurst
capital of: **9** The Gambia

bank 3 bar, row, tip **4** dike, dune, edge, file, flat, fund, heap, hill, keep, line, mass, pile, rank, reef, rise, save, side, tier, tilt **5** amass, array, brink, chain, knoll, mound, ridge, shelf, shoal, shore, slant, slope, stack, store, train **6** barrow, line up, margin, pile up, series, strand, string, supply **7** deposit, parapet, reserve, savings, shallow, terrace **8** keyboard, sandbank **9** exchequer, reservoir, stockpile **10** depository, embankment, repository, storehouse, succession **12** accumulation, trust company **14** savings and loan

Bank Dick, The
director: **10** Eddie Cline
cast: **8** W C Fields **9** Una Merkel **15** Cora Witherspoon

Bankhead, Tallulah
father: **16** William B Bankhead
born: **12** Huntsville AL
roles: **8** Lifeboat **14** The Little Foxes **17** The Skin of Our Teeth

banknote 4 bill **9** greenback **11** certificate, legal tender **12** currency note, treasury note **17** silver certificate

bank of pity
French: **11** mont-de-piete
literal name for:
10 pawnbroker

bankrupt 5 broke **6** busted, failed, ruined **8** depleted, indigent, in the red, wiped out **9** destitute, exhausted, insolvent, penniless **12** impoverished, without funds

Bankruptcy, A
author: **20** Bjornstjerne Bjornson

Banks, Ernie
nickname: **5** Mr Cub
sport: **8** baseball
noted for: **7** hitting
team: **11** Chicago Cubs

banner 4 flag **6** burgee, colors, ensign, record **7** leading, notable, pendant, pennant, winning **8** standard, streamer **9** red-letter **10** profitable

11 outstanding **14** most successful

Bannock
language family:
10 Shoshonean
location: **5** Idaho

banquet 4 dine **5** feast, revel **6** dinner, repast **9** symposium

Banquo
character in: **7** Macbeth
author: **11** Shakespeare

bantam 3 hen, wee **4** cock, fowl, tiny **5** dwarf, pygmy, runt, small, teeny, weeny **6** little, midget, minute, petite **7** chicken, dwarfed, rooster, stunted **9** miniature **10** diminutive, pocket-size, teenyweeny **11** Lilliputian, pocketsized

banter 3 kid, rib **4** dish, josh, mock, ride, twit **5** chaff, jolly, taunt, tease **6** joking, needle **7** jesting, joshing, kidding, ragging, ribbing, teasing, waggery **8** badinage, chaffing, raillery, repartee, word play

Banting, Frederick Grant
field: **8** medicine
nationality: **8** Canadian
extracted: **7** insulin
awarded: **10** Nobel Prize

Bantu
means: **9** the people
dwelling: **6** Africa
tribe: **5** Xosas, Zulus **6** Swazis **7** Basutos, Kalanga

baptism 9 beginning, immersion, sacrament **10** initiation, sprinkling **11** christening **12** introduction, purification **13** rite of passage **16** spiritual rebirth

baptize 3 dub **4** name **8** christen

bar 3 ban, pub, rib, rod **4** band, bank, beam, belt, bolt, cake, curb, flat, line, lock, oust, pale, pole, rail, reef, snag, spar, spit, stay, stop **5** block, catch, check, court, debar, eject, evict, exile, expel, forum, ingot, jimmy, lever, limit, shelf, shoal, slice, sprit, stake, stick, strip, taboo **6** banish, enjoin, fasten, forbid, impede, lounge, paling, ribbon, saloon, secure, streak, stripe, stroke, tavern **7** barrier, block up, canteen, cast out, close up, crowbar, exclude, grating, lock out, measure, prevent, sandbar, shallow, shut out, taproom **8** alehouse, crossbar, disallow, judgment, obstacle, obstruct, preclude, prohibit, restrain, restrict, tribunal **9** barricade, blackball, blacklist, hindrance, long ta-

ble, lunchroom, restraint, speakeasy **10** constraint, crosspiece, impediment, injunction, limitation **11** obstruction, public house, restriction **14** cocktail lounge, serving counter, stumbling block **15** legal profession

Bara, Theda
real name: **16** Theodosia Goodman
nickname: **7** The Vamp
born: **12** Cincinnati OH
roles: **6** Carmen, Salome **7** Camille **8** The Vixen **9** Cleopatra **13** A Fool There Was, Madame Du Barry

Barabbas 6 robber **8** murderer

Barak
father: **7** Abinoam
summoned by: **7** Deborah
defeated: **6** Sisera

barb 3 cut, dig, nib **4** cusp, jibe, snag, spur, tine **5** point, prong, spike **6** insult **7** affront, barbule, bristle, prickle, putdown, sarcasm, spicule **9** complaint, criticism **11** badmouthing

Barbados *see box*

barbarian 4 boor, hood, lout, punk **5** alien, bully, crude, rowdy, tough, yahoo **6** savage, vandal **7** boorish, hoodlum, lowbrow, peasant, ruffian, uncouth **8** hooligan **9** ignoramus, outlander, roughneck, vulgarian **10** delinquent, illiterate, philistine, provincial, troglodyte, uncultured **11** knownothing **12** uncultivated **15** unsophisticated **16** antiintellectual

barbaric 4 rude, wild **5** crude **6** coarse, savage, vulgar **7** boorish, uncouth, untamed **9** barbarian, barbarous **10** unpolished **11** ill-mannered, uncivilized

barbarism 7 cruelty **8** savagery **9** brutality **10** inhumanity **11** viciousness

barbarity 7 cruelty **9** brutality **10** savageness **12** ruthlessness

barbarous 4 mean **5** crass, crude, cruel, harsh, rough **6** brutal, coarse, vulgar **7** inhuman, vicious **8** barbaric, impolite **10** outrageous

barber 3 cut **4** trim **5** dress, shave, style **7** arrange, stylist, tonsure **10** haircutter **11** hairdresser

Barber, Samuel
born: **13** West Chester PA
composer of: **7** Vanessa **10** Dover Beach **16** Adagio for Strings **17** Capricorn

Barbados
  capital/largest city:
    10 Bridgetown
  others: **7** Oistins **8** Bos-
    cabel, Crab Hill, Hast-
    ings, Holetown,
    Portland, Worthing
    9 Bathsheba **10** Martin's
    Bay **11** Belleplaine
    12 Speightstown
  school: **10** Codrington
  head of state: **14** British
    monarch **15** governor
    general
  mountain: **6** Chalky
  highest point: **7** Hillaby
  river: **12** Constitution
  sea: **8** Atlantic
    9 Caribbean
  physical feature:
    bay: **4** Foul, Long
      8 Carlisle
    beach: **5** Crane
    gully: **12** Welchman
      Hall
    hill: **10** Cherry Tree
    point: **5** North, South
      6 Ragged **8** Harrison,
      Kitridge
  people: **5** Bajan
    9 Barbadian
    leader: **5** Adams
  language: **7** English
  religion: **8** Anglican
  place:
    airport: **7** Seawell
    castle: **8** Sam Lords
    church: **7** St Johns
  feature:
    sea crab: **7** shagger

Concerto **19** Anthony and
Cleopatra, The School for
Scandal

Barber of Seville, The
  author: **12** Beaumarchais
  opera by: **7** Rossini
  character: **6** Bazile, Figaro,
    Rosine, Rosina **8** Almaviva,
    Bartholo **9** Dr Bartolo
    13 Count Almaviva

barbette 5 mound **7** bastion,
rampart **8** platform **9** earthwork **10** breastwork

barbiturate 8 euphoria, hypnotic, sedative **10** depressive
13 anesthesiatic **14** barbituric
acid
  kind: **7** seconal **10** thiopental
    11 amobarbital **12** secobar-
    bital **13** phenobarbital

barbule 4 barb **11** feather part

Barchester Towers
  author: **15** Anthony Trollope
  sequel to: **9** The Warden
  character: **7** Mr Slope, Mrs
    Bold **8** Mr Arabin **9** Dr

Proudie, Mr Harding **10** Mrs
Proudie **11** Mr Quiverful
13 Canon Stanhope
17 Archdeacon Grantly
18 Signora Vesey-Neroni

bard 4 poet **6** rhymer, writer
8 epic poet, minstrel, poetizer
9 poetaster, rhymester, trouba-
dor, versifier **10** poet-singer
13 narrative poet

Bardell, Mrs
  character in: **14** Pickwick
    Papers
  author: **7** Dickens

Bardot, Brigitte
  husband: **10** Roger Vadim
  born: **5** Paris **6** France
  roles: **18** And God Created
    Woman

bare 4 bald, mere, nude, open,
show, thin, void, worn
5 basic, blank, empty, naked,
offer, plain, scant, stark, strip
6 denude, divest, expose, meager, peeled, reveal, simple, unclad, unmask, unveil, vacant
7 austere, exposed, hapless,
uncover, undrape, undress, unrobed **8** disrobed, in the raw,
marginal, stripped **9** endurable,
essential, unadorned, un-
clothed, uncolored, uncovered,
undressed, unsheathe **10** elementary, just enough, threadbare **11** fundamental,
supportable, undecorated, undisguised, unvarnished
12 unelaborated, unornamented **13** unembellished
15 straightforward

barefaced 4 bald, bold, flip
5 brash, fresh, sassy **6** brazen,
cheeky, snotty **7** forward
8 flippant, impudent, insolent,
palpable **9** shameless, unabashed **11** transparent

barefoot 6 unshod **8** shoeless
9 discalced **10** unsandaled
11 discalceate

Barefoot Boy
  author: **21** John Greenleaf
    Whittier

Barefoot in the Park
  director: **8** Gene Saks
  based on play by: **9** Neil
    Simon
  cast: **9** Jane Fonda
    12 Charles Boyer **13** Robert
    Redford

barely 4 just **6** almost, hardly
7 faintly, scantly **8** meagerly,
only just, scarcely, slightly
9 almost not, just about, sparingly **10** no more than **20** by
the skin of one's teeth

bareness 6 nudity **9** bleakness,
emptiness, nakedness
10 barrenness

Baresark
  origin: **12** Scandinavian
  form: **7** warrior
  trait: **7** courage

Baretta
  character: **7** Rooster **11** Billy
    Truman, (Det) Tony Baretta,
    (Lt) Hal Brubaker
  cast: **8** Tom Ewell **11** Robert
    Blake **12** Edward Grover
    15 Michael D Roberts
  Tony's pet: **8** cockatoo
    named: **4** Fred

barfly 3 sot **4** lush, soak
5 drunk, rummy, souse, toper
7 tippler **8** drunkard **9** alcoholic **11** dipsomaniac

bargain 4 deal, pact **5** steal
6 accord, barter, dicker, haggle, higgle, pledge, treaty
7 compact, entente, good buy,
promise **8** contract, covenant,
good deal **9** agreement, negotiate **10** settlement **11** arrangement, transaction
13 understanding
  French: **9** bon marche

bargain for 6 expect **7** foresee
8 envision, reckon on
11 contemplate

barge 4 bust, scow, ship
6 launch, vessel **7** freight,
intrude

barium
  chemical symbol: **2** Ba

bark 3 bay, cry, rub, yap, yip
4 flay, hide, howl, hull, husk,
peel, rind, roar, skin, woof,
yell, yelp **5** crust, scale, shout,
strip **6** abrade, arf-arf, bellow,
bow-wow, casing, cry out,
holler, scrape **7** howling
8 covering, periderm
9 sheathing

Barker, Lex
  real name: **25** Alexander
    Crichlow Barker Jr
  wife: **10** Arlene Dahl, Lana
    Turner
  born: **5** Rye NY
  roles: **6** Tarzan **11** La Dolce
    Vita

Barkis
  character in: **16** David
    Copperfield
  author: **7** Dickens

Barkley, Catherine
  character in: **15** A Farewell
    to Arms
  author: **9** Hemingway

Barlach, Ernst
  born: **5** Wedel **7** Germany
    8 Holstein
  artwork: **9** Expellees
    10 Seated Girl, Singing
    Man **11** Man in a Stock
    13 Mater Dolorosa **14** Crip-
    pled Beggar, The Hovering

One **16** Man Drawing a Sword **25** The Community of the Holy Ones

barn 4 mews **6** corral, stable

Barnabas
companion: **4** Paul

Barnaby Jones
character: **7** J R (Jedediah Romano) Jones **8** Lt Biddle **10** Betty Jones
cast: **9** Mark Shera **10** Buddy Ebsen, John Carter **13** Lee Meriwether

Barnaby Rudge
author: **14** Charles Dickens
character: **8** Mrs Rudge **9** Miss Miggs **10** John Willet **11** Dolly Varden **12** Emma Haredale **13** Edward Chester, Gabriel Varden **14** Reuben Haredale, Simon Tappertit, Sir John Chester **16** Dennis the Hangman, Geoffrey Haredale
subject: **11** Gordon riots

Barnard, Christiaan
field: **7** surgery **8** medicine
nationality: **12** South African
performed first: **15** heart transplant

Barnard, Edward Emerson
field: **9** astronomy
named for him: **12** red dwarf star

Barnes, Jake
character in: **15** The Sun Also Rises
author: **9** Hemingway

Barney Google
creator: **11** Billy DeBeck
character: **11** Snuffy Smith
baby: **5** Bunky
horse: **9** Spark Plug

Barney Miller
character: **8** (Det) Phil Fish **9** (Det) Ron Harris **10** (Det Wojo) Wojohowicz, (Det) Nick Yamana, (Officer) Carl Levitt **14** Inspector Luger, (Det) Arthur Dietrich
cast: **7** Jack Soo **8** Ron Carey, Ron Glass **9** Abe Vigoda, Hal Linden **11** Maxwell Gail **12** James Gregory **15** Steve Landesberg

Barnstock *see* **9** Branstock

Baroja y Nessi, Pío
author of: **15** Caesar or Nothing **23** The Struggle for Existence **26** Memorias de un Hombre de Accion

barometer
invented by: **10** Torricelli

baroque 6 florid, ornate **10** flamboyant **11** extravagant

Barrack-Room Ballads
author: **14** Rudyard Kipling

barracks 3 BOQ **4** base, camp **7** lodging **8** garrison

barrage 5 blast, burst, salvo, spray **6** ack-ack, deluge, shower, stream, volley **7** battery, torrent **8** shelling **9** cannonade, fusillade **10** outpouring **11** bombardment

barrel 3 keg, tub, tun, vat **4** butt, cask, drum, tube **8** hogshead
abbreviation: **3** bar, bbl

barren 3 dry **4** arid, dull **5** stale, waste **6** farrow, futile **7** austere, prosaic, sterile, useless **8** depleted, desolate, infecund **9** fruitless, infertile **10** lackluster, unfruitful **11** ineffectual, uninspiring, unrewarding **12** unproductive **13** uninformative, uninstructive, uninteresting

barrenness 8 bareness **9** bleakness, emptiness **10** desolation

barren wilderness 6 desert **9** wasteland

barricade 5 block, fence **7** barrier, bulwark, rampart **8** blockade, obstacle, obstruct **10** impediment **11** obstruction

Barrie, Sir James M
author of: **7** The Will **8** Mary Rose, Peter Pan **10** Dear Brutus **13** Quality Street **15** Margaret Ogilvie, The Wedding Guest **17** Alice Sit-By-the-Fire, The Little Minister **18** A Kiss for Cinderella, The Twelve-Pound Look **19** What Every Woman Knows **20** Shall We Join the Ladies?, The Admirable Crichton
character: **8** Peter Pan **10** Tinkerbell **11** Captain Hook
Darling children: **4** John **5** Wendy **7** Michael
nurse/Newfoundland dog: **4** Nana
setting: **14** Never-Never Land

barrier 3 bar **4** moat, wall **5** ditch, fence, hedge **6** hurdle, trench **7** rampart **8** blockade, handicap, obstacle **9** barricade, hindrance **10** difficulty, impediment, limitation **11** obstruction, restriction **13** fortification **14** stumbling block

Barrier, The
author: **8** Rex Beach

barring 3 but **4** save **6** except, saving **7** besides **9** excepting, excluding, other than **11** exclusive of

barrister 6 lawyer **7** counsel **8** advocate, attorney **9** counselor **10** mouthpiece **13** attorney-at-law

barroom 3 bar, pub, **6** bistro, lounge, saloon, tavern **7** taproom

barrow 4 heap, pile **5** mound **7** tumulus **8** handcart, pushcart **11** wheelbarrow

Barrow, Joe Louis
real name of: **8** Joe Louis

Barry, Gene
real name: **11** Eugene Klass
born: **9** New York NY
roles: **9** Burke's Law **11** Thunder Road **12** Bat Masterson **16** The Name of the Game **17** The War of the Worlds

Barry, John
served in: **16** Revolutionary War
commander of ship: **7** Raleigh **8** Alliance **9** Effingham, Lexington
ship captured: **6** Edward

Barry, Redmond
character in: **11** Barry Lyndon
author: **9** Thackeray

Barry, Sir Charles
architect of: **8** Cliveden **14** City Art Gallery (Manchester) **18** Houses of Parliament (London)

Barry Lyndon
author: **25** William Makepeace Thackeray
character: **12** Redmond Barry **14** Lord Bullingdon **17** Lady Honoria Lyndon (Countess of Lyndon) **19** Chevalier de Balibari
director: **14** Stanley Kubrick
cast: **9** Ryan O'Neal **11** Hardy Kruger **12** Patrick Magee **14** Marisa Berenson

Barrymore, Ethel
real name: **14** Ethel Mae Blythe
brother: **4** John **6** Lionel
born: **14** Philadelphia PA
roles: **11** A Doll's House **14** The Corn Is Green **16** Portrait of Jennie **19** Trelawney of the Wells **21** None But the Lonely Heart, Rasputin and the Empress

Barrymore, John
real name: **10** John Blythe
brother: **6** Lionel
sister: **5** Ethel
son: **17** John Drew Barrymore
daughter: **14** Diana Barrymore
nickname: **12** Great Profile

born: 14 Philadelphia PA
roles: 6 Hamlet **7** Don Juan
8 Moby Dick, Svengali
9 Richard IV **10** Grand Hotel **11** Beau Brummel
13 Dinner at Eight **17** Dr
Jekyll and Mr Hyde **21** Rasputin and the Empress

Barrymore, Lionel
real name: 12 Lionel Blythe
brother: 4 John
sister: 5 Ethel
born: 14 Philadelphia PA
roles: 7 The Jest **9** A Free
Soul (Oscar), Dr Kildare
11 Dr Gillespie **13** Peter Ibbitson, The Copperhead
21 Rasputin and the
Empress

Barsabbas *see* **6** Joseph

Barstad, John
character in: 16 A Tale of
Two Cities
author: 7 Dickens

Bart, Lily
character in: 15 The House
of Mirth
author: 7 Wharton

barter 4 swap **5** trade **8** exchange **11** interchange

Bartered Bride, The
opera by: 7 Smetana
character: 5 Jenik, Kecal,
Micha, Vasek **7** Marenka

Barth, John
author of: 7 Chimera
12 Giles Goat-Boy **15** The
End of the Road **16** The
Floating Opera, The Sot-
Weed Factor **17** Lost in the
Funhouse

Barthelme, Donald
author of: 7 Sadness **8** City
Life **9** Great Days, Snow
White **12** Sixty Stories
13 The Dead Father
15 Guilty Pleasures **18** Come
Back Dr Caligari **33** Unspeakable Practices Unnatural Acts

Bartholdi, Frederic-Auguste
born: 6 Alsace, Colmar
artwork: 13 Lion of Belfort
26 Liberty Enlightening the
World (Statue of Liberty)

Bartholo, Dr
character in: 18 The Barber
of Seville **19** The Marriage
of Figaro
author: 12 Beaumarchais

Bartholomew 7 apostle
also called: 9 Nathanael

Bartholomew Fair
author: 9 Ben Jonson

Bartok, Bela
born: 7 Hungary

15 Nagyszentmiklos
composer of: 9 Wrestling
11 Mikrokosmos **12** Divertimento **14** Cantata Profana
15 The Wooden Prince
20 Duke Bluebeard's Castle
21 The Miraculous
Mandarin

Bartolommeo, Fra
born: 5 Italy **8** Florence
real name: 31 Bartolommeo
di Pagolo del Fattorino
artwork: 5 Jonah **6** Isaiah
13 Salvator Mundi **15** The
Last Judgment **17** Vision of
St Bernard **24** Madonna
della Misericordia **30** The
Mystic Marriage of St
Catherine

Barton, Benjamin Smith
field: 6 botany
noted for first American:
14 botany textbook

Bartram, John
field: 6 botany
noted for first American:
12 hybrid plants

Baruch
father: 5 Judah **6** Neriah
friend and scribe of:
8 Jeremiah

basal 3 key **4** easy **5** basic, vital **6** simple **7** initial, minimal,
primary **8** cardinal **9** beginning, essential, intrinsic, necessary **10** elementary,
lower-level, simplified **11** fundamental, rudimentary **12** prerequisite **13** indispensable

bas bleu 12 bluestocking

base 3 bad, bed, key, low
4 camp, core, foul, mean,
post, root, vile **5** basis, dirty,
gross, heart, petty, place,
stand **6** abject, billet, bottom,
craven, ground, impure, locate, scurvy, sinful, sneaky,
sordid, source, vulgar, wicked
7 alloyed, corrupt, debased, essence, found on, ignoble, immoral, install, model on,
scrubby, situate, station, support **8** backbone, cowardly, degraded, depraved, garrison,
infamous, inferior, pedestal,
rudiment, shameful, spurious,
unworthy **9** dastardly, dissolute, establish, faithless, insidious, nefarious, principle
10 degenerate, derive from,
despicable, detestable, evil-
minded, foundation, groundwork, iniquitous, villainous
11 adulterated, disgraceful, ignominious, poor quality,
scoundrelly **12** black-hearted,
contemptible, dishonorable,
disreputable, installation, substructure, underpinning, unprincipled **13** discreditable,
reprehensible

baseball
athlete/coach: 6 Mel Ott, Ty
Cobb **7** Al Lopez, Cy Young,
Jim Rice **8** Al Kaline, Babe
Ruth, Lou Brock, Pete Rose,
Rod Carew, Vida Blue **9** Alvin Dark, Bob Feller, Bob
Gibson, Bowie Kuhn, Dizzy
Dean, Ford Frick, Gil
Hodges, Hank Aaron, Hank
Bauer, Jim Palmer, Jimmy
Foxx, Joe Morgan, Lou Gehrig, Luis Tiant, Nellie Fox,
Nolan Ryan, Ralph Houk,
Ron Guidry, Ted Turner,
Tom Seaver, Tommy John,
Yogi Berra **10** Boog Powell,
Connie Mack, Duke Snider,
Earl Weaver, Ernie Banks,
John McGraw, Lefty Grove,
Maury Wills, Ralph Kiner,
Roger Maris, Sparky Lyle,
Stan Musial, Whitey Ford,
Willie Mays **11** Billy Martin,
Carl Hubbell, Dave Kingman,
Don Drysdale, Frank
Thomas, George Brett,
George Weiss, Honus Wager,
Joe DiMaggio, Joe McCarthy,
Johnny Bench, Leo Durocher, Luke Appling, Mark Fidrych, Mike Schmidt, Pee
Wee Reese, Phil Rizzuto,
Rich Gossage, Sandy Koufax,
Ted Williams, Tris Speaker,
Warren Spahn **12** Branch
Rickey, Casey Stengel, Graig
Nettles, Dave Winfield, Dennis McLain, Dick Williams,
Eddie Mathews, Elston Howard, Gaylord Perry, George
Sisler, Ken Griffey Jr.,
Mickey Mantle, Satchel
Paige, Steve Carlton, Tommy
Lasorda **13** Catfish (Jim)
Hunter, Frank Robinson,
Reggie Jackson, Rocky Colavito, Rogers Hornsby, Roy
Campanella, Thurman Munson, Walter O'Malley, Willie
McCovey **14** Al Schoendienst,
Brooks Robinson, Jackie
Robinson, Keith Hernandez,
Peter Ueberroth, Sparky Anderson, Willie Stargell
15 Carl Yastrzemski, Charly
Gehringer, Harmon Killebrew, Rickey Henderson, Roberto Clemente **16** Christy
Mathewson, Darryl Strawberry **18** Fernando Valenzuela, George Steinbrenner
21 Kenesaw Mountain Landis
24 Grover Cleveland
Alexander

baseball leagues
National: 11 Chicago Cubs,
New York Mets **13** Atlanta
Braves, Houston Astros,
Montreal Expos **14** Cincinnati Reds, San Diego
Padres **16** St Louis Cardinals **17** Los Angeles Dodg-

ers, Pittsburgh Pirates **18** San Francisco Giants **20** Philadelphia Phillies **American: 9** Oakland A's **12** Boston Red Sox, Texas Rangers **13** Detroit Tigers **14** Minnesota Twins, New York Yankees **15** Chicago White Sox, Seattle Mariners, Toronto Blue Jays **16** Baltimore Orioles, California Angels, Cleveland Indians, Kansas City Royals, Milwaukee Brewers

baseball team *see box*

baseless 7 unsound **9** unfactual, unfounded **10** groundless, ungrounded **11** unjustified, unsupported **12** without basis **13** unjustifiable **14** uncorroborated **15** unsubstantiated

basement 5 below **6** bottom, cellar **15** underground room

baseness 7 lowness **8** meanness, vileness **9** depravity **11** ignobleness **14** iniquitousness **16** contemptibleness

base of operations
  Greek: 6 pou sto

bash 4 blow **5** blast, clout, crack, knock, party, whack **7** clopper **8** wingding **9** bacchanal

Bashemath *see* **4** Adah

bashful 3 shy **5** timid **6** demure, modest **8** blushing, reserved, reticent, retiring, sheepish, skittish, timorous **9** diffident, shrinking, uncertain **10** shamefaced **11** constrained, unconfident

bashfulness 7 shyness **10** diffidence **12** sheepishness **14** self-effacement **15** unassertiveness

basic 3 key **4** base, core **5** prime, vital **7** bedrock, primary **8** rudiment **9** essential, intrinsic **10** elementary, foundation **11** fundamental, rudimentary **12** foundational, prerequisite, underpinning

basically
  French: 6 au fond

basic ideas 6 basics **7** essence, factors, origins **8** elements, features **9** rudiments **10** principles **11** foundations

basic need 9 essential, necessity, requisite, vital part **10** key element, sine qua non

basic part 4 unit **5** element **9** component **10** ingredient **11** constituent **13** building block

basic quality 6 nature **7** essence **9** principle, substance **12** quintessence

---

---

basics 8 elements **9** rudiments **10** principles **11** nitty-gritty **12** fundamentals

basil
  also called: 6 tulasi
  botanical name: 6 Ocimum **8** O minimum **10** O basilicum
  means: 5 royal **6** kingly, lizard (basilisk)
  nickname: 14 kiss-me-Nicholas
  origin: 5 India
  sacred to: 6 Vishnu **7** Krishna, Lakshmi
  symbol of: 4 hate, love
  use: 10 vegetables

basilica 6 church **10** house of God **14** house of worship

Basilisk
  form: 6 dragon

basin 3 pan, tub, vat **4** bowl, dale, dell, font, glen, sink **5** gulch, gully, stoup **6** crater, hollow, lavabo, ravine, tureen, valley **7** dishpan, washtub **8** lavatory, sinkhole, washbowl **9** porringer, washbasin,

washstand **10** depression, finger bowl

basis, bases 4 base, root **6** ground **7** bedrock **9** essential, principle **10** foundation, touchstone **11** cornerstone, fundamental **12** underpinning **13** starting point

bask 5 revel, savor **6** relish, wallow **7** delight **8** sunbathe **9** luxuriate **11** warm oneself **12** soak up warmth, toast oneself

basket 5 crate **6** barrel, hamper **7** carrier, pannier **8** bassinet, canister

basketball
  athlete/coach: 7 K C Jones **8** Bob Cousy, Hal Greer, Joe Fulks, Pat Riley, Sam Jones **9** Bob McAdoo, Bob Pettit, Jerry West, Larry Bird, Rick Barry, Wes Unseld **10** Bill Walton, Danny Ainge, Dave Cowens, Earl Monroe, Elvin Hayes, John Wooden, Paul Arizin, Red Holzman, Willis

Reed **11** Alex English, Bill Bradley, Bill Lambeer, Bill Russell, Bill Sharman, Elgin Baylor, George Mikan, James Worthy, Kevin McHale, Lew Alcindor, Moses Malone, Red Auerbach, Walt Frazier **12** Calvin Murphy, Dolph Schayes, George Gervin, Isaiah Thomas, John Havlicek, Julius (Dr J) Erving, Lenny Wilkens, Patrick Ewing, Robert Parish **13** Connie Hawkins, David Robinson, Earvin (Magic) Johnson, Michael Jordan, Nate Archibald, Scottie Pippen **14** Charles Barkley, Hakeem Olajuwon, Shaquille O'Neal, Oscar Robertson **15** Billy Cunningham, Dave DeBusschere, Wilt Chamberlain **17** Kareem Abdul-Jabbar

basketball team *see box*

Basque
language spoken in: 5 Italy, Spain **6** France

bas-relief
Italian: 12 basso-rilievo

bass 3 low **4** alto **5** basso **7** harmony **8** baritone, bass clef

---

basketball team
league: 3 NBA **29** National Basketball Association
Atlanta: 5 Hawks
Boston: 7 Celtics
Charlotte: 7 Hornets
Chicago: 5 Bulls
Cleveland: 9 Cavaliers
Dallas: 9 Mavericks
Denver: 7 Nuggets
Detroit: 7 Pistons
Golden State: 8 Warriors
Houston: 7 Rockets
Indiana: 6 Pacers
Los Angeles: 6 Lakers **8** Clippers
Miami: 4 Heat
Milwaukee: 5 Bucks
Minnesota: 12 Timberwolves
New Jersey: 4 Nets
New York: 14 Knickerbockers
Orlando: 5 Magic
Philadelphia: 5 76ers **13** Seventy-sixers
Phoenix: 4 Suns
Portland: 12 Trail Blazers
Sacramento: 5 Kings
San Antonio: 5 Spurs
Seattle: 11 Supersonics
Toronto: 7 Raptors
Utah: 4 Jazz
Vancouver: 9 Grizzlies
Washington: 7 Bullets

---

bass
types: 3 sea **4** rock **5** black **6** calico **7** striped, sunfish
characteristic: 10 forked-tail **12** spiny-finned

Bassanio
character in: 19 The Merchant of Venice
author: 11 Shakespeare

basso-rilievo 9 bas-relief

Bast, Jacky and Leonard
characters in: 10 Howard's End
author: 9 E M Forster

bastard 6 impure **8** inferior, spurious **9** imperfect, irregular, love child **12** natural child **17** illegitimate child

bastardize 6 debase, weaken **7** degrade **9** downgrade

baste 3 sew **4** drip **5** roast **6** cudgel, flavor, stitch, thrash **15** temporary stitch

bastinado 4 beat, blow, cane, drub **5** whale **7** beating **8** drubbing

bastion 4 fort **5** tower **6** pillar **7** bulwark, citadel, rampart **8** barbette, fortress **10** breastwork, stronghold

bat 3 hit, rod **4** cane, clip, club, cuff, mace, slug, sock **5** baton, billy, knock, smack, staff, stick, whack **6** buffet, cudgel, mallet, strike, thwack, wallop **7** clobber **8** bludgeon **9** blackjack, truncheon **10** shillelagh

batch 3 lot **5** bunch, crowd, group, stock **6** amount, number **8** quantity **9** aggregate **10** collection

Bates, Alan
born: 7 England **9** Allestree **10** Derbyshire
roles: 8 The Fixer **10** Georgy Girl **12** King of Hearts **13** Zorba the Greek **16** An Unmarried Woman **22** Far From the Madding Crowd

Bates, Miss
character in: 4 Emma
author: 6 Austen

Bateson, William
field: 7 biology
nationality: 7 British
founded: 8 genetics

bath 3 dip, tub **4** wash **5** sauna **6** douche, shower **7** washing **8** ablution, lavement **9** cleansing, immersion, steam bath **10** irrigation
type: 2 hip **4** sitz **5** steam **6** shower, sponge **7** Turkish bath

bathe 3 dip, tub, wet **4** lave, soak, wash **5** douse **6** douche, shower, sponge **7** cleanse **8** irrigate

bathing 3 dip, tub **6** laving, plunge **7** washing **8** swimming **9** ablutions, immersion

bathos 4 corn, mush **5** slush **8** schmaltz **9** mushiness, soppiness **10** maudlinism, slushiness **11** false pathos, mawkishness **14** sentimentalism, sentimentality

bathroom 2 W C **3** can, loo **4** head, john **5** biffy **6** toilet **7** commode, latrine **8** facility, lavatory, men's room, restroom, washroom **10** ladies' room, powder room **11** water closet **14** little boys' room **15** little girls' room

Bathsheba
also: 8 Bathshua
father: 5 Eliam
husband: 5 David, Uriah
son: 7 Solomon
grandfather: 10 Ahithophel

Bathshua *see* **9** Bathsheba

Bathurst
see: Banjul

Batia
form: 5 nymph
father: 6 Teucer
husband: 8 Dardanus
son: 12 Erichthonius

Batman
character: 6 Alfred **7** Egghead, King Tut **8** Catwoman, The Joker **10** Bruce Wayne (Batman), Chief O'Hara, The Penguin, The Riddler **11** Dick Grayson (Robin) **13** Barbara Gordon (Batgirl) **17** Aunt Harriet Cooper **24** Police Commissioner Gordon
cast: 8 Adam West, Burt Ward **9** John Astin **10** Alan Napier, Eartha Kitt, Madge Blake **11** Cesar Romero, Julie Newmar, Victor Buono, Yvonne Craig **12** Frank Gorshin, Neil Hamilton, Stafford Repp, Vincent Price **13** Lee Meriwether **15** Burgess Meredith
city: 10 Gotham City
nickname: 9 Boy Wonder **10** Dynamic Duo **13** Caped Crusader
gimmick: 6 Batlab **8** Batphone **9** Batmobile, Batsignal

Bat Masterson
cast: 9 Gene Barry

baton 3 bat, rod **4** club, mace, wand **5** billy, crook, staff, stick **6** cudgel, fasces **7** crosier, scepter, war club **8** bludgeon, caduceus **9** billy club, truncheon **10** nightstick, shillelagh

Baton
  chariot**eer of: 10** Amphiaraus

batter 4 beat, lash, maul **5** break, crush, pound, smash, smite **6** beat up, buffet, mangle, pummel **7** clobber, shatter

battercake 6 waffle **7** biscuit, pancake

battered 4 shot **6** beat-up, ruined, shabby **8** decrepit **11** dilapidated **12** disreputable

battery 3 set **4** army, band, pack, team **5** block, cadre, force, group, suite, troop **6** caning, cannon, convoy, legion, lineup, outfit, series **7** beating, brigade, company, hitting, hurting, maiming, phalanx, section **8** armament, cannonry, clubbing, division, drubbing, flogging, ordnance, squadron, whipping, wounding **9** cudgeling, spearhead, strapping, thrashing

battle 3 war **4** bout, duel, feud, fray, meet **5** argue, brawl, clash, fight, siege **6** action, affray, combat, debate, engage, tussle **7** contend, contest, crusade, dispute, quarrel, warfare **8** campaign, conflict, skirmish, struggle **9** agitation, encounter, firefight **10** engagement **11** altercation, controversy **13** confrontation

Battle, final
  place: **10** Armageddon

battle cry 6 war cry **8** Geronimo, war whoop **9** Rebel yell

Battle Cry
  author: **8** Leon Uris

battlefield 5 arena, lists **8** the front, war arena **9** front line **10** battle line, no man's land **11** battlefront **12** battleground

battleground 5 arena, lists **11** battlefield, battlefront

Battle of the Books
  author: **13** Jonathan Swift

battle-ready 5 armed **7** arrayed **8** prepared **9** fortified

battleship 4 Iowa **5** Maine **6** Oregon **7** carrier, warship **8** Missouri **9** Ironsides, New Jersey, Wisconsin **10** bluishgray **11** Dreadnought **12** Constitution
  first: **7** Gloire
  largest: **6** Yamato

Battus
  ruler of: **5** Libya
  form: **7** peasant
  witness to: **11** cattle theft
  thief: **6** Hermes

turned to: **5** stone
cured of: **16** speech impediment

batty 4 nuts **5** crazy, loony, queer, wacko, wacky **6** cuckoo, crazed **7** bat-like, cracked

bauble 3 toy **4** bead **6** geegaw, trifle **7** trinket **8** gimcrack, ornament

Baucis
  form: **7** peasant
  home: **7** Phrygia
  husband: **8** Philemon
  offered hospitality to:
  4 Zeus **6** Hermes

Baudelaire, Charles
  author of: **13** Flowers of Evil **14** Les Fleurs du Mal

Baugh, Sammy
  nickname: **13** Slinging Sammy
  sport: **8** football
  position: **11** quarterback
  team: **18** Washington Redskins

Bauhin, Gaspard
  field: **6** botany
  nationality: **5** Swiss
  devised: **14** binomial system
  described: **14** ileocecal valve

Baum, Lyman Frank
  author of: **13** The (Wonderful) Wizard of Oz **18** Father Goose His Book, Mother Goose in Prose

Baum, Vicki
  author of: **8** Shanghai **10** Grand Hotel, Grand Opera **12** Men Never Know **13** A Tale from Bali, And Life Goes On

Baumer, Paul
  character in: **25** All Quiet on the Western Front
  author of: **8** Remarque

Baumgarner, James
  real name of: **11** James Garner

Bauto
  nurse of: **6** Celeus

bawdy 4 blue, lewd, sexy **5** dirty, gross, lusty **6** coarse, earthy, ribald, risque, sexual, vulgar **7** raunchy **8** immodest, improper, indecent, off-color **10** indecorous, indelicate, licentious, suggestive

bawdy house 7 brothel **8** bordello, cathouse **10** fancy house, whorehouse **13** sporting house **14** house of ill fame **16** house of ill repute **19** house of prostitution

bawl 3 cry **4** call, howl, roar, wail, weep, yell, yowl **5** shout **6** bellow, clamor, cry out, squall **7** blubber, call out

bawling out 6 rebuke **7** censure, chiding, reproof **8** reproach, scolding **9** reprimand **10** chewing out, upbraiding **11** castigation, reprobation **12** dressing-down, remonstrance **13** tongue-lashing

bawl out 5 scold **6** berate, rail at, rebuke, yell at **7** censure, chew out, reprove, upbraid **8** admonish, reproach **9** castigate, dress down, reprimand **10** take to task, tongue-lash **14** read the riot act

Bax, Arnold Edward Trevor
  born: **6** London **7** England
  composer of: **8** Tintagel **13** November Woods **14** Mater Ora Filium **15** The Garden of Fand **27** Overture to a Picaresque Comedy

Baxter, Anne
  grandfather: **16** Frank Lloyd Wright
  born: **14** Michigan City IN
  roles: **8** Applause **11** All About Eve **13** The Razor's Edge

Baxter, Jody
  character in: **11** The Yearling
  author: **8** Rawlings

Baxter, William Sylvanus
  character in: **9** Seventeen
  author: **10** Tarkington

bay 3 cry, yap **4** bank, bark, cove, gulf, howl, nook, road, yelp **5** basin, bayou, bight, fiord, firth, inlet, niche, sound **6** alcove, bellow, clamor, lagoon, recess, strait **7** barking, estuary, howling, narrows, yapping, yelling, yelping **9** bellowing **11** compartment **13** natural harbor

bay (at bay) 7 trapped **8** cornered

bay leaf
  botanical name: **12** Pimenta acris
  expression: **16** to win one's laurels
  from tree: **9** bay laurel
  transformation of:
    6 Daphne
  tree sacred to: **6** Apollo
  laurel berries called:
    10 bacca lauri
  source of:
    13 baccalaureate
  gives gift of: **8** prophecy
  helps girls win back: **12** errant lovers
  origin: **5** Italy
  protects against: **5** death **6** poison **7** sorcery **11** evil spirits
  symbol of: **7** victory (laurel wreath)
  use: **4** fish, fowl, meat, soup, stew

bayou 4 slew 5 creek, inlet, marsh, river, swamp 6 outlet, slough, stream 9 backwater 13 stagnant marsh

Bayou State
nickname of: 9 Louisiana 11 Mississippi

Bay Psalm Book
author: 9 John Eliot

Bay State
nickname of:
13 Massachusetts

bazaar, bazar 4 fair, mart 6 market 8 carnival, exchange 11 charity fair, charity sale, marketplace

Bazile
character in: 18 The Barber of Seville
author: 12 Beaumarchais

Bazzard, Deputy
character in: 22 The Mystery of Edwin Drood
author: 7 Dickens

B C
creator: 10 Johnny Hart
character: 3 Tor 4 Grog 5 Peter 8 anteater 10 Clumsy Carp 11 the Fat Broad
poet: 5 Wiley
era: 11 Neanderthal, prehistoric

be 4 last, live, stay 5 exist, occur 6 befall, endure, happen, remain 7 persist, subsist 8 continue 9 be present, take place 10 come to pass

be absent 4 miss 12 fail to attend

beach 5 coast, shore 6 strand 8 littoral, seashore 10 water's edge

Beach, Rex
author of: 6 The Net 7 Oh Shoot 8 Pardners 9 Going Some 10 Jungle Gold, The Barrier 11 Don Careless, The Spoilers 12 Son of the Gods 13 The Goose Woman, The Ne'er-do-well 15 The Auction Block 17 Alaskan Adventures

beached 7 aground 8 grounded, stranded 11 shipwrecked 12 washed ashore

beacon 4 beam 5 light 6 pharos, signal 7 seamark 8 bale-fire, landmark 9 watch fire 10 lighthouse, watchtower 11 lighted buoy

bead 3 dot 4 blob, drop, pill 5 speck 6 bubble, pellet 7 droplet, globule 8 particle, spherule

be adequate 2 do 6 answer 8 be enough 10 pass muster

12 be sufficient, do well enough 14 be satisfactory

be afraid of 4 fear 5 dread 7 cower at 8 cringe at 10 shrink from

beak 3 neb, tip 4 bill, nose, pike, prow 5 lorum, snout, spout 7 process, rostrum, snozzle 8 hooknose 9 headmaster, proboscis 10 magistrate

beaker 3 cup 5 glass 6 vessel 9 container

beam 3 ray 4 emit, glow, prop, spar, stud 5 brace, glare, gleam, glint, joist, shine, width 6 girder, rafter, streak, stream, timber 7 breadth, expanse, glimmer, glitter, radiate, trestle 8 transmit 9 broadcast, radiation

bean 9 Phaseolus
varieties: 3 Goa, Pea, Soy, Wax, Yam 4 Jack, Lima, Moth, Mung, Rice, Seim, Snap, Soja, Soya, Tick, Wild 5 Azuki, Black, Broad, Civet, Coral, Field, Green, Horse, Lubia, Pinto, Salad, Screw, Sewee, Sieva, Snail, Sword, Tonka 6 Butter, Castor, Common, French, Indian, Kaffir, Kidney, Lablab, Locust, Manila, Mescal, Nicker, Potato, Romano, Runner, Sacred, String, Tepary, Velvet, Winged, Wonder 7 Cluster, English, Sarawak, Windsor 8 Bovanist, Bush lima, Carolina, Cherokee, European, Egyptian, Hyacinth, Yard-long 9 Algarroba, Asparagus, Bonavista, Dwarf lima, Java glory 10 Dwarf sieva, Giant stock, Hottentot's 12 Italian queen, Scarlet flame 13 African locust, Florida velvet, Scarlet runner 14 Dutch case-knife 16 White Dutch runner

be a party to 3 aid 4 abet 7 support 9 connive in 11 cooperate in 13 be accessory to, participate in

be apparent 6 appear 7 be clear, be plain 8 be patent 9 be evident, be obvious 10 be manifest

bear 4 bend, drop, give, haul, have, lead, push, show, take, tend, tote, turn, wear 5 abide, admit, allow, apply, brace, brave, bring, brook, carry, curve, drive, force, hatch, press, refer, spawn, stand, whelp, yield 6 affect, aim for, convey, convoy, create, endure, escort, go with, harbor, invite, permit, relate, render, suffer, take on, uphold 7 bol-

ster, cherish, concern, conduct, contain, deliver, develop, deviate, display, diverge, exhibit, pertain, possess, produce, stomach, support, sustain, undergo, warrant 8 bear down, engender, generate, maintain, manifest, shoulder, submit to, tolerate, transfer, underpin 9 accompany, appertain, encourage, germinate, hold close, propagate, put up with, reproduce, touch upon, transport 10 bring forth, keep in mind 11 give birth to, hold up under

bear
combining form: 4 arct, ursi 5 arcto
constellation: 4 ursa 9 ursa major, ursa minor
family: 7 Ursidae
group of: 6 sleuth
kind: 3 sun 5 black, brown, koala, malay, panda, polar, sloth 6 kodiak, wombat 7 grizzly 9 roachback, silvertip 10 spectacled, thalarctos
male: 4 boar
mythological: 8 Callisto
order: 9 carnivora
young: 3 cub

beard 4 dare, defy, face, trap 5 brave 6 corner 7 stubble 8 bristles, confront, whiskers 10 bring to bay 16 five-o'clock shadow

bearded 5 bushy, hairy 6 shaggy 7 bristly, hirsute 8 unshaven 9 whiskered 11 bewhiskered

bear down 4 push 5 press 13 apply pressure

bear down upon 6 assail, attack, come at 7 assault 11 descend upon

Beardsley, Aubrey Vincent
born: 7 England 8 Brighton
artwork: 6 Salome 10 Lysistrata 12 Morte d'Arthur

Beard's Roman Women
author: 14 Anthony Burgess

bearer 5 Atlas 6 holder, porter 7 carrier 8 conveyer, producer 9 messenger 13 beast of burden 16 one holding a check
Spanish: 8 escudero, portador

bear fruit 4 bear 6 mature 7 develop, prosper 8 fructify

bearing 3 air 4 mien, port 5 sense 6 import, manner 7 concern, meaning 8 attitude, behavior, breeding, carriage, demeanor, presence, relation 9 producing, reference, relevance 10 conception, connection, deportment, importance, pertinence **11** application, association, comportment, germination, giving birth, procreation, propagation, reproducing **12** relationship, reproduction, significance **13** applicability

bearing no name 7 unnamed **8** unsigned **9** anonymous

bearings 3 way **6** course **8** position **9** direction **11** orientation **16** sense of direction

bearish 5 cross, gruff, surly, testy **6** crusty, sullen **7** brusque, crabbed, grouchy **8** churlish **9** crotchety, irascible **10** ill-humored, out of sorts **11** ill-tempered, pessimistic **12** cantankerous

bear off 5 seize, steal **6** abduct, convey, kidnap

bear out 5 prove **6** verify **7** confirm **11** corroborate **12** substantiate

Bear State
 nickname of: **8** Arkansas

bear up under 4 bear, take **5** abide, brave, brook, stand **6** endure, suffer **7** stomach, undergo, weather **9** go through, withstand

bear witness 4 back **6** attest **7** confirm, testify **11** corroborate, demonstrate **12** give evidence, substantiate

beast 3 cad, cur, pig, rat **4** ogre **5** brute, swine **6** animal, mammal, savage **8** creature **9** barbarian, quadruped

beastly 3 bad **4** vile **5** awful, cruel, gross, lousy, nasty **6** brutal, coarse, savage **7** bestial, brutish, inhuman, swinish **8** degraded, dreadful, terrible **9** barbarous, loathsome, monstrous **10** abominable, deplorable, disgusting, unpleasant **12** contemptible, disagreeable

beat 3 bat, hit, mix, rap, tap, way **4** area, bang, best, blow, cane, club, drub, flap, flog, flop, lick, maul, path, rout, slap, time, whip, zone **5** clout, count, crush, flail, knock, meter, outdo, pound, pulse, punch, quake, quell, realm, repel, route, shake, smack, smite, strap, throb, whack **6** accent, batter, course, defeat, domain, hammer, master, pummel, quiver, rhythm, rounds, stress, strike, stroke, subdue, switch, thrash, thwack, twitch, wallop **7** cadence, circuit, clobber, conquer, destroy, eclipse, flutter,

pulsate, put down, repulse, scourge, shellac, surpass, trounce, vibrate, win over **8** overcome, vanquish **9** excel over, fluctuate, go pit-a-pat, overpower, palpitate, pulsation, territory **10** win out over **11** predominate, prevail over, triumph over **14** stir vigorously

beat a retreat 6 beat it **7** back off **8** turn tail, withdraw **10** high tail it

beat around the bush 5 dodge, evade, hedge, stall **10** equivocate, mince words

beatific 4 rapt **6** divine, serene **7** angelic, exalted, saintly, sublime **8** blissful, ecstatic, glorious, heavenly **9** rapturous **10** enraptured **14** transcendental

beat it 2 go **3** out **4** away, scat, shoo **5** be off, leave, scram **6** begone, cut out, depart, get out, go away **7** get lost, vamoose **10** hit the road, make tracks

beatitude 5 bliss **7** ecstasy, rapture **8** euphoria, felicity **10** exaltation **11** blessedness, exaltedness, saintliness **13** transcendence **15** transfiguration

be at loggerheads 5 clash **7** quarrel **8** disagree

be at odds 6 differ **7** dispute, diverge **8** conflict, disagree

beat rhythmically 3 rap, tap **4** drum **6** tattoo **7** pulsate

Beatrice
 character in: **12** Divine Comedy
 author: **5** Dante

Beatrice
 character in: **19** Much Ado About Nothing
 author: **11** Shakespeare

Beatrice et Benedict
 opera by: **7** Berlioz

Beat the Clock
 host: **10** Bud Collyer

Beattie, Ann
 author of: **11** Distortions **14** Falling in Place **15** The Burning House **19** Secrets and Surprises **20** Chilly Scenes of Winter

Beatty, Warren
 real name: **11** Warren Beaty
 sister: **15** Shirley MacLaine
 born: **10** Richmond VA
 roles: **4** Reds **11** All Fall Down **13** Heaven Can Wait **14** Bonnie and Clyde **18** Splendor in the Grass

24 The Roman Spring of Mrs Stone
 director of: **4** Reds (Oscar)

beat up 3 mug **4** lick, maul, whip **6** batter, pummel **7** assault, clobber

beat-up 4 shot **6** shabby **7** worn-out **8** battered **10** broken-down **11** dilapidated

Beaty, Shirley MacLean
 real name of: **15** Shirley MacLaine

Beaty, Warren
 real name of: **12** Warren Beatty

beau, beaux 3 fop, guy, nob **4** buck, dude, love, stud, toff **5** blade, dandy, flame, lover, Romeo, spark, swain, swell, wooer **6** adorer, escort, fellow, fiance, garcon, squire, steady, suitor **7** admirer, beloved, courter, coxcomb, cupidon, Don Juan, gallant, playboy **8** cavalier, courtier, gay blade, Lothario, paramour, popinjay, true love, young man **9** betrothed, boyfriend, courtesan, gentleman, inamorato, ladies' man **10** sweetheart, young blood **15** gentleman caller, gentleman friend
 nickname of: **14** George Brummell

Beauchamp's Career
 author: **14** George Meredith

Beau Geste
 author: **6** P C Wren **15** Christopher Wren
 director: **14** William Wellman
 cast: **10** Gary Cooper, Ray Milland **12** Brian Donlevy, Susan Hayward **13** Robert Preston
   silent version starred: **12** Ronald Colman
 setting: **19** French Foreign Legion

Beaumarchais, Pierre Augustin Caron de
 author of: **18** The Barber of Seville **19** The Marriage of Figaro

beau monde 5 elite **6** gentry **7** society **10** upper class, upper crust **11** aristocracy, high society **15** beautiful people

Beaumont, Ned
 character in: **11** The Glass Key
 author: **7** Hammett

Beauregard, P G T (Pierre Gustave Toutant)
 served in: **8** Civil War
 side: **11** Confederate
 rank: **7** general

ordered firing on: 8 Ft
Sumter
battle: 7 Bull Run

beaut 4 lulu **5** daisy, dandy
6 beauty **7** stunner **8** knockout **10** good-looker

beautification 9 adornment
10 decoration **13** embellishment, ornamentation

beautiful 4 fair, fine **5** bonny,
great **6** comely, lovely, pretty,
seemly, superb, worthy **7** radiant **8** alluring, gorgeous,
handsome, pleasing, splendid,
very good **9** admirable, beauteous, enjoyable, estimable,
excellent, exquisite, first-rate,
ravishing, wonderful **10** attractive, stupendous **11** captivating, commendable,
fine-looking, good-looking, resplendent **15** pulchritudinous

beautify 4 do up **5** adorn,
grace **7** dress up, enhance,
gussy up, improve **8** ornament **9** embellish, glamorize

beauty 4 boon, doll **5** asset,
beaut, belle, grace, Venus
6 eyeful, looker **7** benefit, feature, goddess, stunner
8 knockout, radiance, splendor **9** advantage, good looks,
good thing **10** attraction, excellence, good-looker, loveliness **11** pulchritude
12 handsomeness, magnificence, resplendence
14 attractiveness
goddess of: 6 Graces **7** Gratiae **9** Aphrodite, Charities
god of: 5 Baldr **6** Apollo,
Balder, Baldur **7** Angus Og,
Phoebus, Pythias
9 Musagetes

Beauvoir, Simone de
author of: 12 The Mandarins,
The Second Sex **14** A Very
Easy Death, All Said and
Done, The Coming of Age,
The Prime of Life **17** Ethics
of Ambiguity **22** The Force
of Circumstance **25** Memoirs
of a Dutiful Daughter
34 Brigitte Bardot and the
Lolita Syndrome

beaver
young: 3 kit

Beaver State
nickname of: 6 Oregon

be blessed with 3 own
4 have **5** enjoy **7** possess
16 have the benefit of

because 2 so **3** for **4** that,
then, thus **5** cause, hence,
since **6** whence **7** whereas
8 inasmuch **9** therefore
10 seeing that **11** considering

Bechuanaland
now called: 8 Botswana

beck 3 bid **4** call **7** bidding,
summons **9** summoning

Becket
author: 11 Jean Anouilh
18 Alfred Lord Tennyson
director: 14 Peter Glenville
cast: 11 John Gielgud, Peter
O'Toole (King Henry II)
13 Richard Burton
(Becket)

Beckett, Samuel
author of: 4 Not I, Play,
Watt **6** Embers, Molloy
7 Endgame **8** That Time
9 Footfalls, Happy Days
10 Malone Dies **11** All that
Fall, The Lost Ones **13** The
Unnameable **15** Waiting for
Godot **16** Mercier and Cam-
ier **20** Murphy Krapp's Last
Tape **25** Stories and Texts
for Nothing

Beckmann, Max
born: 7 Germany, Leipzig
artwork: 6 Kasbek **7** Perseus
8 Acrobats, The Night **9** The
Actors **11** View of Genoa
12 Charnel House, The Argonauts, The Departure
13 Blindman's Buff, Family
Picture **14** Double Portrait
17 David and Bathsheba
18 Odysseus and Calypso
19 Sinking of the Titanic
20 Destruction of Messina
22 The Descent from the
Cross

beckon 4 call, coax, draw,
lure, pull **6** allure, entice, invite, motion, signal, summon,
wave at, wave on **7** attract,
gesture **11** gesticulate **14** crook
a finger at

be clear 6 appear **7** be plain
8 be patent **9** be evident, be
obvious **10** be apparent, be
manifest

becloud 3 fog **4** blur, hide,
veil **5** befog, cloud **6** muddle,
screen, shroud **7** confuse,
cover up, eclipse, obscure
8 confound, make hazy, overcast **9** obfuscate **10** camouflage, overshadow **14** make
indistinct

become 3 get **4** grow, suit,
turn **6** go with **7** enhance,
flatter, get to be **8** come to
be **9** agree with, begin to be
10 complement **11** be reduced
to, turn out to be

become apparent 4 dawn,
loom **5** arise **6** appear, crop
up, emerge, turn up **7** develop, surface

become bigger 4 grow

5 swell **6** expand **7** develop,
enlarge, inflate **8** increase

become irrational 5 break,
crack **7** crack up **9** break
down, fall apart, go berserk
10 go to pieces **11** lose control **12** lose one's mind

become one 3 wed **4** fuse
5 blend, marry, merge, unite
7 combine **8** coalesce **10** amalgamate **11** consolidate

become seasoned to
5 adapt, inure **6** adjust **8** accustom **9** acclimate, get used
to, habituate **15** learn to live
with

become smaller 6 lessen,
shrink **7** decline, dwindle,
shrivel **8** decrease, diminish

become visible 4 loom, show
6 appear, crop up, emerge,
show up, turn up **7** surface
11 come to light **12** come into
view

becoming 3 apt, fit **4** meet
6 pretty, proper, seemly, worthy **7** fitting **8** suitable **9** befitting, congenial, congruous,
enhancing, in keeping **10** attractive, compatible, consistent, flattering, harmonious
11 appropriate, good-looking

Becquerel, Antoine Henri
field: 7 physics
nationality: 6 French
discovered: 13 radioactivity
awarded: 10 Nobel Prize

bed 3 cot, hay **4** band, bank,
base, belt, bunk, crib, lode,
plot, sack, seam, zone **5** berth,
floor, layer, patch **6** bottom,
cradle, pallet **7** deposit, stratum **8** bedstead **10** foundation

bedazzle 4 daze **6** dazzle **7** astound, confuse, enchant, flus-
ter, nonplus, stagger, stupefy
8 befuddle, bewilder, confound, dumfound **9** captivate,
overpower, overwhelm **10** disconcert **11** flabbergast
19 sweep one off one's feet

bed chamber 7 bedroom,
boudoir

bed down 5 sleep **7** lie down,
sack out **8** doss down **10** hit
the hay, settle down **11** accommodate, hit the sack

bedeck 4 deck, trim **5** adorn,
array **7** garnish **8** decorate, ornament **9** embellish

be deficient in 4 fail, lack,
want **7** be scant **9** be short of
10 have too few

be deprived of 4 lack, lose,
want

be deserving of 4 earn, rate

5 merit 7 deserve 10 be worthy of 12 be entitled to

bedevil 3 dog 5 annoy, hound, worry 6 badger, harass, pester, plague 9 beleaguer

be devoted to 4 love 5 adore 6 dote on 7 cherish 8 be fond of

bedim 4 blur 6 darken 7 obscure

Bedivere
  character in: 16 Arthurian romance

bedizen 5 adorn, array 6 bedeck, rig out 7 bejewel, costume

bedlam 5 chaos 6 tumult, uproar 7 turmoil 8 madhouse 11 pandemonium

bed of justice
  French: 12 lit de justice

Bedouin, Beduin
  also: 4 Absi, Arab 5 nomad 7 bedawee
  Arabic: 6 badawi
    means: 13 desert dweller
  found in: 5 Egypt, Syria 6 Arabia 11 North Africa
  religion: 5 Islam

bedraggled 4 limp 5 dirty, dowdy, messy, seedy, soggy, tacky, tatty 6 blowsy, frowsy, frumpy, matted, ragtag, sloppy, soiled, untidy 7 unkempt 8 frumpish, sluttish, tattered 10 disarrayed, disordered, disheveled, slatternly, threadbare 11 disarranged 13 draggletailed 14 down-at-the-heels, out-at-the-elbows

bedridden 7 invalid 8 disabled, immobile 13 incapacitated

bedroom 7 boudoir, chamber 10 bedchamber

bedspread 5 quilt 8 bedcover, coverlet 9 comforter

bedstead 3 bed 8 bed frame 10 four poster

bee
  caste: 5 drone, queen 6 worker
  classification: 6 social 8 solitary
  communication: 13 dance language
  family: 6 Apidae 7 Apoidea 8 Bombidae 10 Andrenidae, Halictidae 11 Meliponidae, Xylocopidae 12 Megachilidae
  group of: 5 grist, swarm
  order: 11 Hymenoptera
  scent: 10 pheromones
  variety: 5 mason, miner 6 alkali, cuckoo 8 burrower, honeybee 9 bumblebee, car-

penter, plasterer 10 leafcutter 11 yellow-faced

beech 5 Fagus
  varieties: 4 Blue 5 Water 6 Copper, Purple 7 Cut-leaf, Weeping 8 American, European, Fern-leaf, Japanese

Beedle, William Franklin, Jr,
  real name of: 13 William Holden

beef 4 heft, kick, meat 5 brawn, gripe, steer 6 cattle, grouch, grouse 7 grumble 8 complain 9 bellyache, complaint, criticize, find fault

Beef State
  nickname of: 8 Nebraska

beefy 5 bulky, burly, hefty 6 brawny, robust 8 thickset 9 strapping

beehive 4 hive 6 apiary 9 busy place 10 powerhouse

Beehive State
  nickname of: 4 Utah

Beekeeping
  god of: 9 Aristaeus

Beelzebub
  character in: 12 Paradise Lost
  author: 6 Milton

be enough 2 do 6 answer 7 suffice

be entitled to 4 rate 5 merit 7 deserve 10 be worthy of 13 be deserving of

beer-bust 4 toot 5 binge, drunk, spree 6 bender 8 carousal 9 bacchanal

Beery, Noah
  brother: 7 Wallace
  son: 6 Noah Jr
  born: 12 Kansas City MO
  roles: 7 Lord Jim, The Dove 9 Beau Geste 10 The Sea Wolf 14 The Mark of Zorro

Beery, Wallace
  brother: 4 Noah
  nephew: 6 Noah Jr
  wife: 13 Gloria Swanson
  born: 12 Kansas City MO
  roles: 8 The Champ (Oscar) 9 The Bowery, Viva Villa 10 Grand Hotel 11 The Big House 13 Dinner at Eight 14 Treasure Island 15 The Mighty Barnum 16 A Message to Garcia

beet 12 Beta vulgaris
  varieties: 3 Red, Sea 4 Leaf, Wild 5 Sugar 6 Garden, Yellow 7 Spinach

Beethoven, Ludwig van
  born: 4 Bonn 7 Germany
  composer of: 5 Laube (sonata) 6 Egmont, Eroica (symphony no 3), Spring (sonata) 7 Fidelio, Leonore 8 Coriolan, Dramatic (sonata), Kreutzer (sonata), Pastoral (symphony no 6), The Storm 9 Moonlight (sonata), Pastorale (sonata), Waldstein (sonata) 10 Bagatellen, Great Fugue (no 133), Pathetique

beer 3 ale, keg, mum 4 bier, bock, brew, dark, faro, flip, gail, grog, gyle, hops, kvas, malt, mild, quas, scud, suds 5 chang, chica, draft, grout, kvass, lager, light, quass, scuds, stout, weiss 6 bitter, chicha, double, gatter, porter, spruce, stingo, swanky, swipes, wallop, zythum 7 bottled, cerveza, pangasi, pharaoh, Pilsner, tankard, taplash, tapwort 8 bock beer, cervisia, near beer, pilsener 10 malt liquor
  add to beer: 7 krausen
  bad/inferior beer: 4 tack 5 belch 6 swanky 7 taplash
  brand: 5 Beck's, Coors, Pabst, Piels 6 Miller, Molson, Stroh's 7 Schlitz 8 Bud Light, Michelob 9 Budweiser, Lowenbrau 10 Miller Lite, Molson Gold 13 Guinness Stout 15 Pabst Blue Ribbon
  cask: 4 butt
  cup: 3 mug 4 toby 5 glass, stein 6 flagon, seidel 7 tankard 8 schooner 9 blackjack
  hot beer and gin: 4 purl
  ingredient: 4 hops, malt 5 yeast 6 barley
  maker: 6 brewer 8 brewster, maltster
  mythological inventor: 9 Gambrinus
  quantity of: 3 keg 4 case 7 six-pack
  small beer: 4 tiff 5 grout
  sour beer: 4 kuas, kvas 5 quash, quass 8 beeregar
  thin beer: 6 pritch, swipes
  Tibetan beer: 5 chang
  warm beer and oatmeal: 6 storry
  with whiskey: 11 Boilermaker

(sonata), Spirit Trio
11 Grosse Fugue (no 133),
Harp Quartet (no 74), Na-
mensfeier **12** Appassionata
(sonata), Archduke Trio,
Konig Stephan **13** Ham-
merklavier (sonata), Missa
Solemnis **15** Emperor Concerto (No 5) **16** Christus am
Olberg, The Mount of Ol-
ives, The Ruins of Athens
17 Die Ruinen von Athen,
Die Weihe des Hauses
18 An die ferne Geliebte,
Rage over a Lost Penny
20 Rasoumoffsky Quartets
(no 59) **24** The Creatures of
Prometheus **25** Die Ge-
schopfe des Prometheus

beetle
  variety: 3 bog, may, sap
  4 bark, bean, flea, leaf,
  mold, moss, pill, rove, sand,
  stag **5** cedar, click, flour,
  grain, marsh, penny, tiger,
  water **6** beaver, diving,
  flower, fungus, ground, his-
  ter, lizard, spider, weevil
  7 bessbug, blister, burying,
  carrion, firefly, goldbug, goliath, ladybug, soldier **8** elephant, glowworm, hercules,
  Japanese, ladybird, tortoise
  9 ant loving, bombadier,
  burrowing, checkered, fruit-
  worm, goldsmith, grassroot,
  scavenger, tumblebug, whirligig **10** deathwatch, false
  clown, longhorned, mammal
  nest, shiptimber **11** reticu-
  lated, trout stream **12** ant-
  like stone, lightning bug
  13 feather winged, horseshoe crab

Beetle Bailey
  creator/artist: 9 Dik
  Browne **10** Mort Walker
  12 Bob Gustafson
  character: 5 Cosmo, Plato
  6 Killer, Lt Flap, Lt Fuzz
  10 Miss Buxley **12** Gen
  Halftrack **17** Sgt Orville
  Snorkel
    chef: 6 Cookie
  place: 10 Camp Swampy

be evident 6 appear **7** be
clear, be plain **8** be patent
9 be obvious **10** be apparent,
be manifest

befall 5 ensue, occur **6** betide,
chance, follow, happen
10 come to pass
11 materialize

befitting 3 apt, fit **5** right
6 decent, proper, seemly **8** becoming, relevant, suitable
11 appropriate

be fond of 6 dote on **11** be
devoted to **12** be in love with

before 3 ere, yet **5** afore,

ahead, prior **6** rather, sooner
7 already, earlier, vis-a-vis
8 erewhile, until now **9** in advance, in front of, in sight
of **10** face-to-face, previously

before Christ
  abbreviation: 2 BC
  Latin: 2 AC **12** ante Christum

beforehand 6 in time, sooner
7 earlier **9** in advance
11 ahead of time

before now 6 in time,
sooner **7** earlier **9** in advance

before the fact 6 in time
9 in advance **10** beforehand
11 ahead of time

before the public
  Latin: 11 coram populo

befoul 4 soil **5** dirty, smear,
stain, sully, taint **6** defile, poison **7** blacken, corrupt, pollute, tarnish **8** besmirch
9 desecrate **11** contaminate

befriend 4 help **5** assist, defend, succor, uphold **7** comfort, embrace, help out,
protect, stand by, stick by,
support, sustain, welcome
8 side with **9** give aid to, look
after **10** minister to **11** consort
with **13** associate with
14 fraternize with, sympathize
with **17** take under one's
wing

be friends 7 consort **9** associate, pal around **10** fraternize

befringe 3 hem **4** bind, edge,
trim **6** border **7** festoon
8 decorate

befuddle 4 daze **5** addle, mix
up **6** baffle, muddle, puzzle,
rattle **7** confuse, fluster, perplex, stupefy **8** bewilder, confound, unsettle **9** disorient,
inebriate, make drunk, make
tipsy **10** intoxicate, make
groggy **11** disorganize

beg 3 bum, sue **4** pray, shun
5 avert, avoid, cadge, dodge,
evade, mooch, parry, plead,
shirk **6** escape, eschew, hustle,
sponge **7** beseech, entreat,
fend off, implore, solicit **8** appeal to, petition, sidestep
9 importune, panhandle
10 supplicate

beg, bey 4 lord **6** prince
8 governor

beget 3 get **4** sire **5** breed,
cause, spawn **6** effect, father,
lead to **7** produce **8** engender,
generate, occasion, result in
9 call forth, procreate, propagate **10** bring about, give rise
to

begetter 4 sire **6** father **7** creator **9** generator **10** progenitor

beggar 3 bum, guy **4** chap
5 devil, tramp **6** baffle, fellow
7 almsman, moocher, sponger,
surpass **8** be beyond **9** challenge, mendicant
10 panhandler

Beggar 7 Lazarus

Beggar's Opera, The
  author: 7 John Gay
  form: 11 ballad opera
  character: 6 Lockit **10** Lucy
  Lockit **12** Polly Peachum
  15 Captain Macheath

begin 5 arise, found, start **6** be
born, crop up, emerge,
launch, set out **8** break out,
commence, embark on, initi-
ate **9** establish, institute, introduce, originate, undertake
10 burst forth, inaugurate
11 set in motion **16** take the
first step

beginner 4 babe, tyro **6** author, father, novice, rookie
7 creator, founder, learner,
starter, student **8** freshman,
neophyte **9** fledgling, greenhorn, initiator, organizer
10 apprentice, originator,
prime mover, tenderfoot
11 inaugurator **14** babe in the
woods

beginning 3 new **4** germ, seed
5 birth, onset, start **6** embryo,
novice, origin, outset, source,
spring **7** kickoff, student, untried **8** neophyte, zero hour
9 embryonic, inception, incipient, launching **10** foundation,
wellspring **11** preliminary,
springboard **12** commencement, fountainhead, inauguration, introduction
13 inexperienced, starting
point
  Latin: 12 terminus a quo

Beginning of Wisdom, The
  author: 19 Stephen Vincent
  Benet

Beginnings
  god of: 5 Janus

begone 3 out **4** away, scat,
shoo **5** be off, leave, scram
6 beat it, depart, get out, go
away **7** get lost, vamoose

begonia
  varieties: 3 Rex, Wax **4** Fern,
  King, Star, Wild **5** Hardy,
  Trout **6** Bamboo, Kidney,
  Shrimp, Winter, Zigzag
  7 Bedding, Dewdrop, Elm-
  leaf, Eyelash, Fuchsia, Leopard, Lily-pad, Swedish
  8 Climbing, Fern-leaf, Fire-
  king, Lorraine, Palm-leaf,
  Pond-lily, Star-lily, Trailing
  9 Alder-leaf, Angel-wing,
  Beefsteak, Calla-lily, Christmas, Crazy-leaf, Grape-leaf,

Grapevine, Hollyhock, Holly-leaf, Honey-bear, Iron-cross, Maple-leaf, Miniature, Pennywort, Trout-leaf, Whirlpool **10** Bronze-leaf, Castor-bean, Finger-leaf, Guinea-wing, Seersucker, Strawberry **11** Fairy-carpet, Lettuce-leaf, Painted-leaf **12** Blooming-fool, Elephant's Ear, Metallic-leaf **13** Peanut-brittle **14** Hybrid tuberous, Nasturtium-leaf, Youth-and-old-age **15** Winter-flowering **16** Manda's woolly-bear, Philodendron-leaf **17** Miniature pond-lily **18** Trailing watermelon

beg pardon 6 excuse **9** apologize **13** express regret, say one is sorry

be grateful 9 be obliged **10** appreciate, be beholden, be thankful **11** be obligated

begrime 4 soil **5** dirty, muddy, smear, stain, sully **6** smudge, soot up **7** besmear, tarnish

begrimed 5 dirty, grimy, muddy **6** filthy, grubby, soiled **7** unclean **8** unwashed **9** tarnished

begrudge 4 envy **5** covet **6** grudge, resent **11** be jealous of, hold against

beguile 4 dupe, hoax, lull, lure **5** amuse, charm, cheat, cheer, trick **6** delude, divert, occupy, please **7** bewitch, deceive, enchant, ensnare **8** distract, hoodwink **9** bamboozle, captivate, entertain **10** lead astray

beguiling 7 winning, winsome **8** charming, magnetic **9** appealing, disarming **10** bewitching, entrancing **11** captivating **12** ingratiating, irresistible

behalf 3 aid, for **4** part, side **5** favor **7** benefit, by proxy, defense, in aid of, support **8** interest

Behan, Brendan
  author of: 10 Borstal Boy, The Hostage **12** The Scarperer **14** The Quare Fellow **25** Confessions of an Irish Rebel

be handed down 4 pass **7** descend **11** be inherited

behave 3 act **13** acquit oneself, deport oneself **14** comport oneself, conduct oneself, control oneself

behavior 4 acts **5** deeds **6** action, habits, manner **7** actions, bearing, conduct, control **8** activity, attitude, demeanor,

practice, reaction, response **9** operation **10** deportment **11** comportment, functioning, performance, self-control

behead 9 decollate **10** decapitate, guillotine **15** bring to the block

behest 4 fiat **5** edict, order, say-so **6** charge, decree, ruling **7** bidding, command, dictate, mandate **9** direction, ultimatum **10** injunction **11** instruction

behind 4 rump, seat, slow **5** abaft, after, fanny **8** backward, buttocks, in back of **9** fundament, in arrears **11** to the rear of **12** hindquarters

behind closed doors 7 sub rosa **8** in secret, secretly **9** in private, privately

behindhand 4 late, slow **5** tardy **7** belated **8** backward **10** unpunctual

behind the times 5 passe **7** archaic **9** out-of-date **10** antiquated **12** old-fashioned

behind time 4 late, slow **5** tardy **7** belated, delayed **12** after the fact

behold 3 see **4** heed, look, mark, note, scan, view **5** watch **6** attend, gaze at, look at, notice, regard, survey **7** discern, examine, inspect, observe, stare at, witness **8** look upon **10** scrutinize **11** contemplate **12** pay attention

beholden 5 bound **6** liable **7** obliged **8** indebted **9** obligated **10** answerable, in one's debt **11** accountable, responsible **15** under obligation

behold the man
  Latin: 8 ecce homo
  said by: 13 Pontius Pilate
  spoken of: 6 Christ

behoove 4 suit **5** be apt, befit **6** become, be wise **7** benefit **8** be proper **9** be fitting **11** be advisable, be necessary **13** be appropriate **14** be advantageous

Behring, Emil Adolph von
  field: 12 bacteriology
  nationality: 6 German
  developed: 19 diphtheria antitoxin
  awarded: 10 Nobel Prize

beige 3 tan **4** ecru, fawn **6** greige **8** brownish

be ill 3 ail **6** be sick **8** be unwell **12** be indisposed **13** be in ill health

be in a class with 5 equal,

match **6** be up to **7** compare **8** approach **10** be as good as **11** compete with **12** be comparable, be on a par with **13** hold a candle to

being 4 core, life, soul **5** human **6** living, mortal, nature, person, psyche, spirit **7** essence, persona, reality **8** creature, existing **9** actuality, existence **10** individual, occurrence **11** subsistence

be inherited 4 pass **7** descend **12** be handed down

be in short supply 4 lack, want **8** be scanty, be scarce **9** fall short

be intemperate 7 carouse, debauch **9** dissipate **11** overindulge

be in tune 4 jibe **5** agree, match, tally **6** accord, square **7** conform **9** harmonize

Beirut, Beyrouth
  capital of: 7 Lebanon
  Phoenician name: 7 Berytus
  sea: 13 Mediterranean
  settled by: 11 Phoenicians

be jealous of 4 envy **6** resent **8** begrudge

Bekesy, Georg von
  field: 7 physics
  researched: 3 ear **7** cochlea, hearing
  awarded: 10 Nobel Prize

Bel 3 god **5** deity

Bela
  father: 4 Beor
  brother: 6 Balaam

belabor 6 rehash, repeat **7** dwell on **9** reiterate **11** pound away at **12** hammer away at, recapitulate **14** beat a dead horse

Bel-Ami
  author: 15 Guy de Maupassant

Belarus
  other name: 10 Belorussia **11** Byelorussia, White Russia
  capital/largest city: 5 Minsk
  head of state: 9 president
  government: 8 republic
  monetary unit: 5 ruble
  river: 5 Dvina **7** Dnieper
  physical feature: 13 Pripet Marshes
  people: 12 Byelorussian

Belasco, David
  author of: 7 DuBarry **15** Madame Butterfly **21** The Return of Peter Grimm **22** The Girl of the Golden West

belated 4 late, slow **5** tardy **6** behind **7** delayed, overdue, past due **8** deferred **10** behindhand, behind time, unpunctual **12** after the fact

belch 4 burp, emit, gush, spew, vent **5** eject, eruct, erupt, expel, issue, spout, spurt, vomit **7** cough up, issuing **8** disgorge, ejection, emission, eruption

9 discharge, roar forth, send forth **10** eructation

Belch, Sir Toby
character in: **12** Twelfth Night
author: **11** Shakespeare

beleaguer 3 vex **5** annoy **6** assail, badger, bother, harass,

hector, pester, plague **7** besiege, bombard **8** blockade, surround

bel-esprit 3 wit **12** intellectual

belfry 4 dome **5** spire **7** steeple **9** bell tower, campanile

Belgian Congo *see* **5** Zaire

Belgium
other name: 13 Gallia Belgica **15** Cockpit of Europe **16** Koninkrijk Belgie **17** Royaume de Belgique
capital/largest city: 8 Brussels **9** Bruxelles
others: 2 As **3** Aat, Ans, Ath, Hal, Huy, Mol, Spa **4** Aath, Amay, Asse, Boom, Bree, Doel, Gaud, Geel, Genk, Gent, Hoei, Lier, Looz, Mons, Vise, Waha, Zele **5** Aalst, Alost, Arlon, Ciney, Ecklo, Essen, Eupen, Evere, Genck, Ghent, Heist, Ieper, Jette, Jumet, Liege, Namur, Ronse, Tielt, Uccle, Vorst, Wezet, Ynoir, Ypres **6** Aarlen, Anvers, Bergen, Bilzen, Bruges, Deurne, Izegem, Leuven, Lierre, Merxem, Opwijk, Ostend **7** Antwerp, Ardooie, Berchem, Brabant, Hainaut, Herstal, Hoboken, Ixelles, Leliven, Limburg, Louvain, Malmedy, Mechlin, Roulers, Seraing, Tournai **8** Bastogne, Courtrai, Doorwick, Flanders, Kortrijk, Mouscron, Turnhout, Verviers, Waterloo **9** Antwerpen, Charleroi **10** Anderlecht, Borgerhout, Luxembourg, Quatrebras, Schaerbeek
school: 7 Louvain
division: 5 Liege, Namur **7** Antwerp, Brabant, Hainaut, Limburg **8** Flanders, Wallonia
head of state: 4 king
measure: 3 vat **4** aune, pied **5** carat **6** perche **8** boisseau
monetary unit: 5 belga, franc **7** brabant, centime, crocard
weight: 4 last **5** carat, livre **6** charge **7** chariot **8** esterlin
mountain: 8 Ardennes
highest point: 16 Signal de Botrange
river: 3 Lys **4** Dyle, Leie, Maas, Mark, Yser **5** Boucq, Demer, Lesse, Meuse, Nethe, Rupel, Senne **6** Dender, Escaut, Manjel, Ourthe, Sambre, Semois, Vesdre, Warche **7** Ambleve, Schelde, Scheldt
sea: 5 North
physical feature:
  canal: **4** Yser **5** Union **6** Albert **7** Campine
  cave: **7** Furfooz **8** Grenelle
  forest: **8** Ardennes
  plateau: **8** Hohevenn
people: 4 Remi **6** Nervii **7** Belgian, Fleming, Flemish **8** Walloons **9** Bellovaci
  artist: **5** Ensor **6** Rubens **7** Delvaux, Van Dyck, Van Eyck **8** Brueghel, Magritte
  author: **6** Coster **7** Simenon **9** Verhaeren **10** Conscience, Ghelderode **11** Maeterlinck
  composer: **6** Franck
  king: **6** Albert **7** Leopold **8** Baudouin
  leader: **5** Spaak **9** Tindemans
language: 5 Dutch **6** French, German **7** Flemish
religion: 13 Roman Catholic
place:
  battleground: **5** Bulge **8** Waterloo
  breadhouse: **9** Broodhuis
  castle: **5** Steen
  cathedral: **5** Ghent **13** Saint Rombauts
  city hall: **12** Hotel de Ville
  home for elderly women: **9** Beguinage
  museum: **9** Beaux Arts
  palace: **10** Gruuthuuse
features:
  horse: **9** Brabancon
  lace: **5** fichu **6** Bruges **7** Malines, Mechlin **8** Brussels
  lawn bowling: **6** boules
  linen: **7** brabant
  musical instrument: **8** carillon
  religious procession: **9** Holy Blood
  tapestry: **9** oudenarde
food:
  cheese: **9** Limburger
  gingerbread: **12** pain d'espices
  raisin bread: **8** cramique
  soup: **9** Waterzooi

Belgrade, Beograd
capital of: 10 Yugoslavia
landmark:
fortress: **10** Kalemegdan
parliament house:
9 Skupstina
name means: 11 white forest
river: 4 Sava **6** Danube
Roman fort: 10 Singidinum
Serbian: 7 Beograd

Belial
character in: 12 Paradise
Lost
author: 6 Milton

belie 4 defy, deny, mask
5 cloak **6** betray, negate, refute **7** conceal, falsify, gainsay **8** disguise, disprove
9 repudiate **10** camouflage,
contradict, controvert, invalidate **12** misrepresent

belief 4 view **5** faith, guess,
trust **6** theory **7** feeling, opinion **8** judgment, reliance **9** assurance, certitude, deduction,
inference **10** assumption, conclusion, confidence, conviction, firm notion, hypothesis,
impression, persuasion **11** expectation, presumption,
supposition

beliefs 5 canon, creed, dogma,
faith, tenet **6** ethics, gospel,
morals **8** doctrine, morality
9 principle, teachings **10** conviction, persuasion

believable 8 credible, knowable, possible **9** plausible, thinkable **10** acceptable, convincing,
imaginable, supposable
11 conceivable, perceivable

believe 4 hold **5** guess, infer,
judge, think, trust **6** assume,
credit, deduce, rely on **7** count
on, fall for, imagine, presume,
suppose, surmise, suspect,
swallow, swear by **8** be sure
of, consider, depend on, maintain, theorize **9** speculate
10 conjecture, presuppose, put
faith in **11** hypothesize

believe in 5 trust **6** accept, esteem **7** approve, go in for, respect **11** have faith in **16** have
confidence in

Believe It or Not
author: 13 Robert L Ripley

believer 7 admirer **8** advocate,
disciple, partisan **9** supporter
16 faithful adherent

be like 5 equal, match **8** approach, resemble

Bel-Imperia
character in: 17 The Spanish
Tragedy
author: 3 Kyd

Belinda
character in: 16 The Rape of
the Lock
author: 4 Pope

belittle 5 knock, scorn **6** deride, malign **7** disdain, put
down, run down, sneer at
8 minimize, mitigate, play
down, pooh-pooh **9** deprecate,
disparage, underrate **10** depreciate, undervalue **11** make
light of **13** underestimate
16 cast aspersions on

belittling 5 snide **10** derogatory **11** deprecating, disparaging, unfavorable
12 depreciating
15 uncomplimentary

Belize
other name: 15 British
Honduras
capital: 8 Belmopan
**largest city/former cap-
ital: 10** Belize City
head of state: 13 prime
minister **14** British
monarch **15** governor-
general
monetary unit: 6 dollar
island: 8 Turneffe
mountain range: 4 Maya
highest point: 12 Victoria Peak
river: 3 New **4** Moho
6 Belize, Monkey
sea: 9 Caribbean
physical feature:
gulf: **8** Honduras
peninsula: **7** Yucatan
swamp: **9** mangrove
people: 5 Mayan **6** Indian, Syrian **7** African,
Chinese **15** Spanish-
American
language: 7 English

---

bell 4 gong, peal **5** chime
6 tocsin **7** ringing **8** carillon
16 tintinnabulation

Bell, Alexander Graham
born: 8 Scotland
inventor of: 9 telephone
14 record cylinder
saying: 24 Mr Watson come
here I want you

Bellamann, Henry
author of: 8 King's Row

Bellamy, Edward
author of: 8 Equality
15 Looking Backward

Bellamy, Ralph
born: 9 Chicago IL
roles: 11 Ellery Queen, Mike

Barnett **13** The Awful
Truth **14** Detective Story
15 Man Against Crime,
State of the Union **19** Sunrise at Campobello

Bellarius
character in: 9 Cymbeline
author: 11 Shakespeare

Bellaston, Lady
character in: 8 Tom Jones
author: 8 Fielding

bell buoy 5 float **6** signal
13 channel marker

belle 4 star **5** queen **6** beauty
7 charmer **12** heart-stopper

Belle Dame Sans Merci, La
author: 9 John Keats

Bellefleur
author: 15 Joyce Carol Oates

Belle Helene, La
also: 14 Beautiful Helen
operetta by: 9 Offenbach

Bellerophon
form: 4 hero
brother: 8 Deliades
son: 11 Hippolochus
home: 7 Corinth
rode: 7 Pegasus
killed: 7 Chimera

Bell for Adano, A
author: 10 John Hersey
director: 9 Henry King
cast: 10 John Hodiak
11 Gene Tierney **13** William
Bendix

bellicose *see* **11** belligerent

belligerence, belligerency
9 animosity, hostility, pugnacity **10** aggression, antagonism
11 bellicosity **12** warmongering **13** combativeness **14** aggressiveness, unfriendliness

belligerent 7 fighter, hostile,
martial, warlike, warring **8** attacker, inimical **9** adversary,
aggressor, bellicose, combatant, combative, irascible, irritable, truculent **10** aggressive,
antagonist, pugnacious, unfriendly **11** bad-tempered, contentious, quarrelsome
12 antagonistic, cantankerous

belligerent state 3 foe **5** enemy **9** aggressor **13** hostile
nation

Bellini, Gentile
born: 5 Italy **6** Venice
father: 6 Jacopo
brother: 8 Giovanni
artwork: 24 The Miracle of
the True Cross **26** A Procession in St Mark's Square,
The Miracle at Ponte di
Lorenzo **27** St Mark Preaching in Alexandria **38** A
Procession of Relics in the
Piazza San Marco

Bellini, Giovanni (Giambellino)
born: **5** Italy **6** Venice
father: **6** Jacopo
brother: **7** Gentile
artwork: **8** St Jerome **16** Venus with a Mirror **18** St Francis in Ecstasy, The Madonna and Child **19** Allegory of Purgatory, The Agony in the Garden, The Barberini Madonna

Bellini, Jacopo
born: **5** Italy **6** Venice
son: **7** Gentile **8** Giovanni
artwork: **11** Crucifixion **16** Christ on the Cross **35** The Madonna and Child with Lionello d'Este

Bellini, Vincenzo
born: **5** Italy **7** Catania
composer of: **5** Norma, Zaira **8** Il Pirata **9** I Puritani **11** La Straniera **12** La Sonnambula **15** Bianca e Fernando

Bell Jar, The
author: **11** Sylvia Plath

Bellona
origin: **5** Roman
goddess of: **3** war
husband: **4** Mars
brother: **4** Mars
corresponds to: **4** Enyo

bellow 4 bawl, roar, yell **5** shout, whoop **6** holler, scream, shriek

Bellow, Saul
author of: **6** Herzog **13** Dean's December, Humboldt's Gift, Mosby's Memoirs **15** The Last Analysis **16** Mr Sammler's Planet **18** To Jerusalem and Back **25** The Adventures of Augie March

Bellows, George Wesley
born: **10** Columbus OH
artwork: **8** Lady Jean **11** Billy Sunday, Edith Cavell, Floating Ice, Up the Hudson **12** Forty-Two Kids **13** Men of the Docks **14** Rain on the River, Stag at Sharkey's **16** The Cliff Dwellers **18** Emma and her Children **21** Both Members of This Club

Bells Are Ringing
director: **16** Vincente Minnelli
cast: **9** Fred Clark **10** Dean Martin **12** Judy Holliday
song: **10** Just in Time **13** The Party's Over

Bells in Winter
author: **13** Czeslaw Milosz

Bells of St Mary's, The
director: **10** Leo McCarey
cast: **10** Bing Crosby (Father O'Malley) **12** Henry Travers **13** Ingrid Bergman
sequel to: **10** Going My Way
song: **20** Aren't You Glad You're You

bell tower 5 spire **6** belfry **7** steeple **9** campanile

Belluschi, Pietro
architect of: **21** Bank of America Building (San Francisco) **22** Juilliard School of Music (NYC) **31** Pan American World Airways Building (NYC, with Gropius)

bellwether 4 lead **5** doyen, guide, pilot **6** leader **8** director, shepherd **9** conductor, guidepost, precursor **10** forerunner, pacesetter **14** standard-bearer

belly 3 gut, yen **4** guts **5** taste, tummy **6** bowels, depths, desire, hunger, liking, paunch, vitals **7** abdomen, insides, midriff, stomach **8** appetite, interior, recesses **11** breadbasket

bellyache 4 beef, kick **5** gripe **6** grouch, grouse, squawk **7** grumble **8** complain **9** tummy ache **11** stomach ache **12** upset stomach

belong 6 go with **7** concern **8** attach to, be held by, be part of **9** be owned by, pertain to **10** be allied to **11** be a member of **12** be included in **15** be connected with, be the property of

belongings 4 gear, junk **5** goods, stuff **6** things **7** effects **8** movables **11** possessions **13** accouterments, paraphernalia **16** personal property

beloved 4 beau, dear, love, wife **5** loved, lover **6** adored, fiance, spouse, steady **7** admired, darling, dearest, fiancee, husband, revered **8** endeared, esteemed, loved one, precious **9** betrothed, boyfriend, cherished, respected, treasured **10** girlfriend, sweetheart

below 4 less **5** lower, under **6** in hell **7** beneath, on earth, short of **8** inferior, unworthy **9** at a low ebb, downwards **10** downstairs, downstream, second-rate, underneath **11** at a discount, at the foot of, indifferent, subordinate, underground

below par 3 bad **4** poor **8** inferior **9** imperfect **10** second-rate **12** below average, not up to snuff

below standard 3 bad **4** poor **5** lousy **6** faulty, shoddy **8** below par, inferior, slipshod, terrible **9** imperfect **10** second-rate **12** not up to snuff

Belshazzar
father: **9** Nabonidus **14** Nebuchadnezzar

belt 4 area, band, land, sash, zone **5** cinch, layer, strip **6** circle, girdle, region, stripe **7** country **8** district, encircle **9** waistband **10** cummerbund

Belteshazzar
Babylonian name of: **6** Daniel
friend: **7** Meshach **8** Abednego, Shadrach

Belus
king of: **7** Chemmis
father: **8** Poseidon
mother: **5** Libya
twin brother: **6** Agenor
wife: **8** Anchinoe
son: **6** Danaus **8** Aegyptus
daughter: **4** Dido

Belushi, John
born: **9** Chicago IL
roles: **9** Neighbors **11** Animal House **16** The Blues Brothers **17** Saturday Night Live

be manifest 6 appear **7** be clear, be plain **8** be patent **9** be evident, be obvious **10** be apparent

bemoan 3 rue **5** mourn **6** bewail, lament, regret **7** cry over **8** weep over **9** whine over **10** grieve over

bemused 5 dazed, fuzzy **7** muddled, stunned **8** confused **9** engrossed, stupefied **10** bewildered, dull-witted, thoughtful **11** preoccupied **12** absent-minded

be nauseated by 4 hate **5** abhor **6** detest, loathe **7** despise **8** execrate **9** abominate **11** can't stomach **13** be disgusted by, find repulsive, find revolting, find sickening

Benbow, Horace
character in: **9** Sanctuary
author: **8** Faulkner

Ben Casey
character: **12** Dr David Zorba, Dr Ted Hoffman **13** Nick Kanavaras **14** Dr Maggie Graham
cast: **8** Sam Jaffe **10** Nick Dennis **12** Harry Landers, Vince Edwards **14** Bettye Ackerman

bench 3 pew **4** seat **5** board, court, stool, table **6** settee **7** counter, take out, trestle **8** sideline, tribunal **9** judiciary, workbench, worktable **10** second team **11** judge's chair, substitutes **12** second string

Benchley, Peter
author of: **4** Jaws **7** The Deep

Benchley, Robert
author of: **14** From Bed to Worse **21** Benchley Beside Himself, My Ten Years in a Quandary

benchmark 4 norm **5** gauge, guide, model **7** example, measure **8** exemplar, paradigm, standard **9** criterion, principle, prototype, reference, yardstick **10** touchstone

bend 3 arc, bow **4** flex, hook, lean, loop, mold, sway, turn, warp, wind **5** crook, curve, defer, force, shape, stoop, twist, yield **6** accede, attend, buckle, coerce, compel, crouch, give in, relent, submit **7** bow down, contort, control, succumb **9** genuflect, influence, surrender **10** buckle down, capitulate **11** make crooked

Bend in the River, The
author: **9** V S Naipaul

Bendix, William
born: **9** New York NY
roles: **8** Hostages, Lifeboat **11** The Hairy Ape **13** A Bell for Adano **14** The Life of Riley **16** Guadalcanal Diary, The Babe Ruth Story

bend to one's own will
4 tame **5** break, train **6** master, subdue **8** overcome **10** discipline **12** show who's boss **18** have under one's thumb

beneath 5 below, lower, under **9** covered by **10** inferior to, underneath, unworthy of **11** subordinate, underground **16** below one's dignity

Benedick
character in: **19** Much Ado About Nothing
author: **11** Shakespeare

benedictine
type: **6** brandy, cognac **7** liqueur
flavor: **4** herb
with brandy: **5** B and B
with bourbon: **9** Twin Hills **13** Brighton Punch
with whiskey: **10** Frisco Sour

benediction 6 prayer **7** benison **8** blessing **10** invocation **12** consecration **13** closing prayer

benefaction 4 alms, gift **5** grant **7** charity **8** bestowal, donation, offering **9** endowment **10** almsgiving **12** contribution, dispensation, philanthropy

benefactor 5 angel, donor **6** backer, friend, helper, patron **7** sponsor **8** upholder **9** supporter **11** contributor **14** fairy godmother

beneficent 6 benign, kindly **7** liberal **8** generous, salutary **10** beneficial, benevolent, charitable **11** magnanimous **13** philanthropic

beneficial 6 useful **7** good for, healing, helpful **8** valuable **9** favorable, healthful **10** productive, profitable, propitious **12** advantageous, contributive

beneficiary 4 heir **7** grantee, heiress, legatee **8** receiver **9** inheritor, recipient

benefit 3 aid, use **4** gain, good, help **5** asset, avail, serve, value, worth **6** assist, behalf, better, profit **7** advance, be aided, service **8** be helped, be served, blessing, interest **9** advantage, do good for **10** be useful to, betterment, profit from **13** charity affair **18** charity performance

Benet, Stephen Vincent
author of: **7** America **8** Tiger Joy **11** Western Star **14** John Brown's Body, Thirteen O'Clock, Young Adventure **16** Five Men and Pompey **19** Tales Before Midnight, The Headless Horseman **20** The Beginning of Wisdom **24** The Devil and Daniel Webster

benevolence 7 charity **8** good will, kindness **9** benignity **10** compassion, generosity, kindliness, liberality **13** bountifulness **14** charitableness **15** humanitarianism, kindheartedness

benevolent 3 kin **6** benign, humane, tender **7** liberal **8** generous **9** benignant, bounteous, bountiful, unselfish **10** bighearted, charitable **11** considerate, kindhearted, warmhearted **12** humanitarian **13** compassionate, philanthropic

Bengali
language family: **12** Indo-European
branch: **11** Indo-Iranian
group: **5** Indic
spoken in: **5** (northern) India

Ben-Hur
author: **10** Lew Wallace
character: **4** Iras, Isas **5** Jesus **6** Esther **7** Messala **9** Balthasar, Simonides **11** Judah Ben-Hur
director: **12** William Wyler
cast: **11** Jack Hawkins, Ste-

phen Boyd **12** Hugh Griffith **14** Charlton Heston (Judah Ben-Hur)
setting: **9** Palestine
Oscar for: **5** actor (Heston) **7** picture **8** director **14** cinematography **15** supporting actor (Griffith)

benighted 4 dumb **5** crude, unhip **8** backward, ignorant, untaught **9** primitive, untutored **10** illiterate, uncultured, uneducated, uninformed, unlettered, unschooled **11** emptyheaded, know-nothing, uncivilized **12** uncultivated **13** unenlightened

benign 4 good, kind, mild, nice, soft **5** balmy, lucky **6** genial, gentle, humane, kindly, tender **7** affable **8** gracious, harmless, pleasant, salutary **9** favorable, healthful, innocuous, temperate **10** auspicious, benevolent, propitious **11** encouraging, kindhearted, softhearted **13** tender-hearted

benignant 4 kind **6** benign, humane, kindly, tender **9** forgiving **10** benevolent **11** kindhearted **13** compassionate, tenderhearted

benignity 8 good will, kindness **10** compassion, kindliness **11** benevolence **15** kindheartedness

Benin *see box*

Benito Cereno
author: **14** Herman Melville

Benjamin
father: **5** Jacob
mother: **6** Rachel
also known as: **6** Benoni
brother: **3** Dan, Gad **4** Levi **5** Asher, Judah **6** Joseph, Reuben, Simeon **7** Zebulun **8** Issachar, Naphtali
sister: **5** Dinah
descendant of: **11** Benjaminite

Bennet family
characters in: **17** Pride and Prejudice
members: **4** Jane, Mary **5** Kitty, Lydia **9** Elizabeth
author: **6** Austen

Bennett, Arnold
author of: **8** Accident **10** Clayhanger, Lord Raingo, Milestones, These Twain **11** Buried Alive **13** Hilda Lessways, Riceyman Steps **15** The Old Wives' Tale **18** Anna of the Five Towns

Benny, Jack
real name: **16** Benjamin Kubelsky
born: **10** Waukegan IL
roles: **12** Charley's Aunt

Benin
other name: 17 Republic of Dahomey
capital: 9 Porto-Novo
largest city: 7 Cotonou
others: 4 Pobe **5** Kandi, Kerou, Ketou, Porga **6** Abomey, Ouidah **7** Parakou, Savalou **8** Aplahoue
government: 30 Military Council of the Revolution
monetary unit: 5 franc **7** centime
lake: 5 Aheme **6** Nokoue
mountain: 7 Atakora
river: 4 Mono **5** Niger, Oueme **6** Couffo
sea: 8 Atlantic
physical feature:
   gulf: **6** Guinea
   plains: **6** Borgou
people: 3 Fon, Pla **4** Adja, Aizo, Mina, Peul **5** Pedah, Peuhl, Somba **6** Bariba, Fulani, Yoruba **8** Pilapila **9** Dahomeyan
language: 3 Fon **5** Dendi **6** Bariba, French, Fulani, Yoruba
religion: 5 Islam **6** tribal **7** animism **13** Roman Catholic
food:
   tapioca: **4** gari

13 Jack Benny Show, To Be or Not To Be **16** Artists and Models

Benoni *see* **8** Benjamin

Benson
   character: 5 Kraus **12** (Lt Gov) Benson DuBois **13** (Gov) Eugene Gatling
   cast: 10 James Noble **11** Inga Swenson **15** Robert Guillaume

bent 4 bias, gift, mind **5** bowed, flair, knack **6** angled, arched, curved, genius, liking, talent **7** ability, aptness, crooked, faculty, hunched, leaning, stooped, twisted **8** aptitude, capacity, facility, fondness, penchant, tendency **9** contorted, endowment **10** attraction, partiality, proclivity, propensity **11** disposition, inclination **12** predilection **14** predisposition

bent into folds 6 fluted, ridged **7** creased, grooved, pleated **8** crinkled, furrowed, puckered, wrinkled **10** corrugated

Benton, Robert
   director of: 14 Kramer vs Kramer (Oscar) **16** Places in the Heart

Benton, Thomas Hart
   born: 8 Neosho MO
   artwork: 7 Bubbles **8** Boomtown **9** Homestead **12** American Life **13** Arts of the West, Cotton Pickers **14** Threshing Wheat **19** Louisiana Rice Fields, The Lord Is My Shepherd

Benue-Congo
   language family: 16 Niger-Kordofanian
   group: 10 Niger-Congo
   includes: 3 Tiv **4** Zulu **5** Bantu, Jukun **6** Chwana, Nyanja **7** Kikongo, Luganda, Swahili

benumb 4 daze, dull **5** blunt **6** deaden **7** stupefy **15** make insensitive

Benvolio
   character in: 14 Romeo and Juliet
   author: 11 Shakespeare

Benz, Karl
   nationality: 6 German
   inventor of: 22 electric ignition engine **26** differential gear automobile
   built first practical: 10 automobile

be obvious 6 appear **7** be clear, be plain **8** be patent **9** be evident **10** be apparent, be manifest

be off 2 go **5** leave, scram **6** beat it, begone, cut out, depart, go away, set out **8** set forth, withdraw **10** make tracks

be of one mind 5 agree **6** accord, concur **10** think alike **11** see eye to eye

be of use 3 aid **4** help **5** serve **6** assist **7** benefit

be on a par with 5 equal **6** be up to **7** compare **10** be as good as **12** be comparable **14** be in a class with

be on the sick list 3 ail **5** be ill **6** be sick **8** be unwell **12** be indisposed **13** be in ill health **17** be under the weather

Beor
   son: 4 Bela **6** Balaam

Beothuk (Red Indians)
   location: 6 Canada **12** Newfoundland
   intermixed with: 7 Naskapi

Beowulf
   author: 7 unknown
   character: 4 Finn **5** Breca, Hnaef, Oslaf, Scyld **6** Wig-

laf **7** Guthlaf, Hengest, Higelac, Hrethel, Unferth **8** Aeschere, Heardred, Hondscio, Hrothgar **9** Hildeburh
   great hall: 6 Heorot
   monster: 7 Grendel **14** Grendel's mother
   tribe: 5 Danes, Geats **8** Frisians
   Beowulf tears from Grendel: 3 arm

bequeath 4 will **5** endow, leave **6** impart **7** consign **8** hand down

bequest 6 legacy **8** bestowal **9** endowment **10** settlement **11** inheritance

be part of 4 form **6** make up **8** belong to **9** appertain, pertain to **10** constitute

be patent 6 appear **7** be clear, be plain **9** be evident, be obvious **10** be apparent, be manifest

be pertinent to 4 bear **5** apply, refer **6** affect, relate **7** concern, pertain **9** appertain, touch upon

be plain 6 appear **7** be clear **8** be patent **9** be evident, be obvious **10** be apparent, be manifest

be pleased with 4 like **5** favor **7** approve

berate 5 scold **6** rail at, rebuke **7** bawl out, chew out, reprove, upbraid **8** reproach **9** castigate, criticize, reprimand **10** take to task, tonguelash

Berber
   language family: 11 Afroasiatic **13** Hamito-Semitic
   spoken in: 6 Sahara **11** North Africa

Berchta *see* **7** Perchta

bereave 3 rob **5** strip **6** divest **7** deprive **10** dispossess

Berecyntia *see* **6** Cybele

Berenice's Hair
   constellation of: 13 Coma Berenices

be resigned to 6 accept **8** tolerate

Beret
   character in: 16 Giants of the Earth
   author: 7 Rolvaag

be revolted by 4 hate **5** abhor **6** detest, loathe **7** despise **8** execrate **9** abominate **10** recoil from, shrink from **11** can't stomach **13** find repulsive

berg 4 floe **7** glacier, iceberg, icefloe
South African: 8 mountain
French: 4 neve **5** serac

Berg, Alban
born: 6 Vienna **7** Austria
composer of: 4 Lulu **7** Wozzeck

Bergen, Candace
father: 11 Edgar Bergen
born: 14 Beverly Hills CA
roles: 8 The Group **15** Carnal Knowledge

Berger, Thomas
author of: 7 The Feud **9** Neighbors **10** Vital Parts **11** Killing Time **12** Little Big Man, Sneaky People **15** Regiment of Women

Bergman, Ingmar
director of: 14 The Seventh Seal **16** Cries and Whispers, Wild Strawberries **17** Fanny and Alexander **19** Scenes from a Marriage **20** Smiles of a Summer Night

Bergman, Ingrid
born: 6 Sweden **9** Stockholm
roles: 8 Gaslight (Oscar) **9** Anastasia (Oscar), Joan of Arc, Notorious **10** Casablanca, Intermezzo, Spellbound **17** A Woman Called Golda, The Bells of St Mary's **19** For Whom the Bell Tolls **24** Murder on the Orient Express **25** The Inn of the Sixth Happiness

Berith, Berit, Brith, Brit
8 covenant **12** circumcision

Berle, Milton
real name: 15 Milton Berlinger
nickname: 11 Uncle Miltie **12** Mr Television
born: 9 New York NY
roles: 17 The Texaco Star Hour **18** Who's Minding the Mint **23** Always Leave Them Laughing

Berlin (East, West)
landmark: 14 Humboldt Castle **15** Gruenwald Castle **16** Berlin Opera House, Markisches Museum **21** Scharlottenburg Castle **29** Kaiser-Wilhelm-Gedachtniskirche
river: 5 Spree
square: 14 Alexander-Platz

Berlin, Elaine
real name of: 9 Elaine May

Berlinger, Milton
real name of: 11 Milton Berle

Berlioz, (Louis) Hector
born: 6 France **13** La Cote St Andre

composer of: 6 Rob Roy, Te Deum **7** Requiem, **8** Herminie, King Lear, Waverley **9** Cleopatra, Nuits d'Ete **10** Le Corsaire, Les Troyens, The Trojans **11** Sardanapale **13** Harold in Italy **14** Les Francs Juges, Romeo and Juliet **16** Benvenuto Cellini, Damnation of Faust, Le Carnaval Romain, L'Enfance du Christ **18** Beatrice et Benedict **20** Symphonie Fantastique **28** Symphonie Funebre et Triomphale

Bermuda
other name: 13 Somers Islands
capital/largest city: 8 Hamilton
others: 8 St George
head of state: 14 British monarch **15** governor general
island: 4 Boaz **5** Coney **7** Bermuda, Ireland, Watford **8** Somerset, St Davids **9** St Georges
highest point: 8 Town Hill
sea: 8 Atlantic
physical feature:
  harbor: **6** Castle
  hill: **5** Gibbs
people:
  discoverer: **14** Juan de Bermudez
language: 7 English
religion: 8 Anglican **10** Protestant **15** Church of England
feature:
  dancers: **6** Gombey

Bern
capital of: 11 Switzerland
landmark: 10 Clock Tower **12** Nydegg Church
river: 4 Aare

Bernard, Henriette-Rosine
real name of: 14 Sarah Bernhardt

Bernhardt, Sarah
real name: 22 Henriette-Rosine Bernard
nickname: 11 Divine Sarah
born: 5 Paris **6** France
roles: 6 Phedre **7** Hernani, Ruy Blas **8** King Lear **14** Queen Elizabeth **17** La Dame aux Camelias

Bernini, Gianlorenzo (Giovanni Lorenzo)
born: 5 Italy **6** Naples
father: 6 Pietro
artwork: 7 Montoya **8** Louis

XIV, Vigevano **10** Bellarmine, St Longinus **13** Cathedra Petri, Francis I d'Este, The Assumption **15** Apollo and Daphne **18** Costanza Buonarelli **19** The Rape of Proserpina **21** Saints Andrew and Thomas, The Ecstasy of St Theresa **24** Blessed Lodovica Albertoni **25** Aeneas Anchises and Ascanius
architect of: 12 Santa Bibiana **16** Piazza of St Peter's (Rome) **19** Palazzo Montecitorio **21** Sant' Andrea al Quirinale **22** Palazzo Chigi-Odescalchi **23** Fountain of the Four Rivers **24** Santa Maria dell' Assunzione

Bernoulli, Daniel
field: 11 mathematics
nationality: 5 Swiss
theory of: 5 gases **6** fluids **18** Bernoulli's Equation

Bernstein, Carl
author of: 12 The Final Days (with Bob Woodward) **19** All the President's Men (with Bob Woodward)
newspaper reporter for: 14 Washington Post

Bernstein, Leonard
born: 10 Lawrence MA
composer of: 4 Mass **7** Candide, Kaddish **8** Jeremiah **9** Facsimile, Fancy Free, On the Town **13** West Side Story, Wonderful Town **15** The Age of Anxiety, Trouble in Tahiti **16** Chichester Psalms

Beroe
father: 6 Adonis
mother: 9 Aphrodite
nurse of: 6 Semele

Berowne
character in: 16 Love's Labour's Lost
author: 11 Shakespeare

Berra, Yogi (Lawrence Peter Berra)
sport: 8 baseball
position: 5 coach **7** catcher
team: 14 New York Yankees

berry 3 egg **4** seed **5** fruit, grain, grape **6** dollar, kernel, tomato, banana **7** currant **8** allspice, bayberry, mulberry **9** blueberry, cranberry, raspberry **10** blackberry, gooseberry, peppercorn, strawberry **11** boysenberry, huckleberry, pomegranate **12** checkerberry
poisonous: 9 baneberry

Berryman, John
author of: 8 Recovery **9** Delusions **11** Love and Fame **12** 77 Dream Songs **13** The Dream Songs **16** Berryman's Sonnets **19** The Freedom of

the Poet **21** His Toy His
Dream His Rest **26** Homage
to Mistress Bradstreet

berserk 4 amok, wild **5** crazy
6 insane **7** frantic, violent
8 demented, deranged, frenzied, maniacal, wild-eyed
9 desperate **10** distracted, distraught **12** out of control

Berserker
origin: **6** Nordic
form: **7** warrior

berth 3 bed, job **4** bunk, dock,
pier, post, quay, slip, spot
5 haven, niche, place, wharf
6 billet, employ, office **8** position **9** anchorage, situation
11 appointment **12** resting
place **13** sleeping place

Berthollet, Claude Louis
field: **9** chemistry
nationality: **6** French
researched: **7** ammonia
8 chlorine

Bertram
character in: **20** All's Well
That Ends Well
author: **11** Shakespeare

Bertram family
characters in: **13** Mansfield
Park
members: **3** Tom **5** Julia,
Maria **6** Edmund **9** Sir
Thomas
author: **6** Austen

beryl
color: **5** green **6** yellow

Berzelius, Jons Jakob
field: **9** chemistry
nationality: **7** Swedish
developed: **15** chemical
symbols
discovered: **6** cerium **7** silicon, thorium **8** selenium, titanium **9** zirconium
founded: **15** modern
chemistry

be satisfactory 2 do **6** answer **7** suffice **8** be enough
10 be adequate, pass muster
12 be sufficient, do well
enough

be scant 4 lack, want **8** be
skimpy **9** fall short **14** be insufficient **15** be in short supply

beseech 3 beg **4** pray **6** adjure **7** entreat, implore **9** plead
with **10** supplicate

beset 3 dog, set **4** bead, deck,
stud **5** annoy, array, hem in,
hound, worry **6** assail, badger,
harass, pester, plague **7** bedevil, besiege, set upon **8** surround **9** beleaguer, embellish

be sick 3 ail **5** be ill **8** be unwell **12** be indisposed **13** be in
ill health

beside 2 by **4** near **5** saved
6 except, nearby, unless
7 abreast, barring, without
8 let alone **9** adjoining, alongside, aside from, other than
10 on a par with, side by
side **12** compared with, in addition to

beside oneself 4 wild
6 elated, joyful, joyous, raging **7** berserk, exalted, frantic,
furious, ranting **8** agitated,
blissful, distrait, ecstatic, frenetic, frenzied **9** delirious, in a
frenzy, overjoyed, rapturous
10 distracted, distraught, distressed, enraptured **11** carried
away, overwrought, trans-
ported **13** out of one's wits

besides 3 but **4** also, save **6** as
well, except, saving **7** barring
8 moreover **9** excepting, excluding, other than **11** exclusive of, furthermore

besiege 3 dog **5** annoy, beset,
hound **6** assail, badger, harass,
pester, plague **7** assault, bedevil **9** beleaguer **10** lay siege
to

besmear 4 soil **5** dirty, muddy,
smear, stain, sully **6** mess up,
slop up, smudge **7** begrime,
tarnish **8** besmirch

besmeared 5 dirty, grimy,
messy **6** grubby, smudgy
7 muddied, sullied **8** begrimed
10 besmirched

besmirch 4 soil **5** smear, stain,
sully, taint **6** defame, defile
7 blacken, corrupt, debauch,
degrade, slander, tarnish
8 discolor, disgrace, dishonor
9 discredit

besotted 5 drunk **6** sodden,
soused, wasted, zapped,
zonked **7** smashed **9** plastered
10 inebriated, infatuated
11 intoxicated **17** under the
influence **20** three sheets to
the wind

bespangle 3 dot **4** gild, star,
stud **5** adorn, jewel **6** bedeck
7 dress up, festoon, garnish
8 decorate, ornament **9** embellish **10** illuminate

bespatter 4 blot, soil, spot
5 decry, dirty, libel, smear,
stain, sully, taint **6** debase, defame, defile, smudge, splash
7 condemn, slander, smotter,
tarnish **8** denounce, reproach
9 deprecate, fling dirt **10** calumniate, disapprove

Bessemer, Sir Henry
nationality: **7** English
inventor of manufacturing
process for: **5** steel

best 3 top **4** most, pick

5 cream, elite **6** choice, finest,
nicest, utmost **7** hardest, largest **8** foremost, greatest, superior, topnotch **9** greetings,
loveliest, most fully, most of
all, unequaled, unrivaled
10 unexcelled **11** compliments,
unsurpassed **13** most competent, most desirable, most excellent **14** highest quality,
kindest regards

Best, Charles Herbert
field: **10** physiology
nationality: **8** Canadian
discovered: **7** insulin

best group 3 top **5** cream,
elite **6** choice **7** chosen few
10 select body **14** cream of
the crop, creme de la
creme

bestial 5 cruel **6** brutal, savage **7** beastly **8** barbaric, depraved, inhumane, ruthless
9 barbarous, merciless

bestir 4 goad, spur, stir, urge
5 rouse, speed **6** arouse, excite,
hasten **7** quicken **8** activate
9 get moving

bestir oneself 5 rouse **8** be
active **9** make haste **10** get up
early, lose no time **11** keep
moving **15** make short work
of **19** seize the opportunity

bestow 3 use **4** give, mete
5 apply, award, grant, lay on,
spend **6** accord, confer, devote,
donate, employ, expend, impart, occupy, render **7** consign,
consume, deal out, deliver,
hand out, present, utilize
8 dispense, give away **9** apportion **10** settle upon, turn
over to

bestowal 4 alms, gift **5** bonus,
favor, grant **6** reward **7** charity, present, tribute **8** donation, gratuity, offering
9 endowment **10** conferment,
recompense **11** benefaction
12 contribution, dispensation

best society
French: **10** grand monde

**Best Years of Our Lives,
The**
director: **12** William Wyler
based on story by:
15 MacKinlay Kantor
script: **14** Robert Sherwood
cast: **8** Myrna Loy **11** Dana
Andrews **12** Teresa Wright,
Virginia Mayo **13** Frederic
March, Harold Russell
15 Hoagy Carmichael
Oscar for: **5** actor (March)
7 picture **8** director

be sufficient 6 answer **7** suffice **8** be enough **10** be adequate, pass muster **12** do well
enough **14** be satisfactory

bet 4 ante, risk **5** stake, wager **6** chance, gamble, hazard, plunge **7** venture **8** make a bet **9** speculate **11** speculation

bete noir 5 bogey **6** plague **7** bugaboo, bugbear **8** anathema, bogeyman **9** annoyance **10** black beast

be thankful 8 thank God **10** appreciate **11** thank heaven **19** thank one's lucky stars

Bethe, Hans Albrecht
field: **7** physics
developed: **8** atom bomb
awarded: **10** Nobel Prize

be the same 5 agree, equal, match **6** equate **7** balance **11** be identical

Bethuel
son: **5** Laban

betide 4 fall **5** occur **6** befall, chance, happen **10** come to pass

betimes 5 early **10** in good time

betoken 4 show **5** augur **6** attest, denote **7** portend, presage, signify **8** foretell

betray 4 dupe, fink, jilt, show, tell **5** rat on, trick **6** expose, reveal, squeal, tell on, unmask **7** abandon, deceive, divulge, lay bare, let down, let slip, sell out, two-time, uncover, violate **8** blurt out, disclose, give away **9** play Judas **10** be disloyal **11** double-cross **12** be unfaithful **13** inform against, play false with **14** break faith with

betrayal 7 perfidy, telling, treason **8** bad faith, sedition, trickery **9** chicanery, deception, duplicity, falseness, treachery, two-timing, violation **10** disclosure, disloyalty, divulgence, revelation **11** double-cross **13** breach of faith, double-dealing **14** unfaithfulness

betrayal of trust 7 falsity, perfidy **8** apostasy, cheating **9** falseness, recreancy **10** disloyalty, infidelity **11** inconstancy **13** deceitfulness, double-dealing, faithlessness **14** unfaithfulness

Betrayer 13 Judas Iscariot

betroth 6 commit, engage, pledge **7** espouse, promise **8** affiance, contract

betrothal 5 troth **8** espousal **10** affiancing, betrothing, engagement

betrothed 6 fiance **7** engaged, fiancee **8** promised **9** affianced

Bettelheim, Bruno
author of: **15** Love Is Not Enough **16** The Informed Heart **20** The Uses of Enchantment

better 3 top **4** more **5** finer, outdo, raise **6** bigger, enrich, exceed, fitter, larger, longer, refine, uplift **7** advance, elevate, enhance, farther, forward, further, greater, improve, mending, promote, surpass, upgrade **8** heighten, improved, increase, outstrip, stronger, superior **9** cultivate, healthier, improving **10** preferable, recovering, strengthen **11** more healthy, progressing

bettering 9 elevation **10** betterment **11** advancement, improvement

betterment 4 good **6** reform **7** benefit **8** revision **9** advantage, amendment, promotion **10** correction, enrichment **11** advancement, improvement **12** amelioration, regeneration **13** rectification **14** reconstruction

better than average 2 A-1 **3** A-OK **4** aces, fine, good, tops **5** great, prime, super **6** choice, grade-A, superb **7** capital, special **8** peerless, sterling, superior, terrific, topnotch **9** excellent, first-rate, marvelous, matchless, wonderful **10** first-class, inimitable, preeminent, remarkable, tremendous **11** exceptional, outstanding, superlative **12** incomparable **13** extraordinary

between 4 amid **5** among, entre **6** amidst, atwixt, shared **7** betwixt, joining **9** in the midst **10** connecting

between ourselves
French: **9** entre nous
Latin: **8** inter nos

Between the Battles
author: **20** Bjornstjerne Bjornson

between themselves
Latin: **7** inter se

between us 9 entre nous, privately **14** confidentially **15** between you and me **16** between me and thee, between ourselves

betwixt and between 4 so-so **7** average **8** confused **9** in between, undecided **14** halfway between **21** neither one nor the other

Beulah, Land of
place in: **16** Pilgrim's Progress
author: **6** Bunyan

be unlike 4 vary **6** differ **7** deviate, diverge **8** conflict, disagree **12** be at variance, be discordant, be dissimilar

be unwell 3 ail **5** be ill **6** be sick **12** be indisposed **13** be in ill health

be unwilling to pursue
Latin: **13** nolle prosequi

bevel 4 blow, cant, ream, tool **5** angle, bezel, miter, mitre, slant, slope, snape, splay **6** aslant **7** incline, oblique **8** slanting

beverage 3 ade, ale, cup, nog, pop, tea **4** beer, brew, dram, grog, milk, soda, soup, wine **5** broth, cider, cocoa, draft, drink, juice, julep, lager, leban, punch, toddy, water **6** bishop, coffee, cordial, eggnog, liquid, liquor, potion **7** limeade, seltzer, spirits, wassail **8** aperitif, cocktail, highball, lemonade, libation, potation **9** champagne, chocolate, orangeade

Beverley, Constance de
character in: **7** Marmion
author: **5** Scott

Beverly Hillbillies, The
character: **11** Jed Clampett **12** Jane Hathaway, Jethro Bodine **14** Granny Clampett, Milton Drysdale **16** Ellie May Clampett
cast: **9** Irene Ryan, Max Baer Jr, Nancy Kulp **10** Buddy Ebsen **12** Donna Douglas **13** Raymond Bailey

Beverly Hills Cop
director: **11** Martin Brest
cast: **11** Eddie Murphy **13** Judge Reinhold, Lisa Eilbacher

bevy 4 band, body, herd, host, pack **5** brood, covey, crowd, drove, flock, group, horde, party, shoal, swarm **6** clutch, flight, gaggle, school, throng **7** company, coterie **9** gathering, multitude **10** assemblage, collection

bewail 3 rue **5** mourn **6** bemoan, lament, regret **7** cry over, deplore **8** moan over, weep over **10** grieve over

beware 4 mind **6** be wary **7** look out **8** take care, take heed **9** be careful **11** take warning, watch out for **12** be on the alert, guard against **15** take precautions

beware of the dog
Latin: 9 cave canem

bewhiskered 5 bushy, hairy
6 shaggy 7 bearded, bristly,
hirsute 8 unshaven
11 mustachioed

bewilder 5 addle, mix up
6 baffle, bemuse, muddle, puzzle 7 confuse, fluster, mystify,
nonplus, perplex, stupefy
8 befuddle 10 disconcert

bewildered 7 at a loss, up a
tree 8 all at sea, confused
9 perplexed 10 confounded,
nonplussed 12 disconcerted

bewilderment 9 confusion
10 perplexity, puzzlement
11 frustration 13 mystification

bewitch 4 jinx 5 charm,
spook 6 turn on 7 bedevil, beguile, delight, enchant 8 entrance 9 captivate, enrapture,
fascinate 12 cast a spell on
14 put under a spell

bewitched 7 charmed, seduced 8 beguiled 9 bedeviled,
enchanted, entranced 10 captivated, enraptured, fascinated,
spellbound 11 under a spell

Bewitched
character: 6 Endora, Serena
7 Maurice 9 Aunt Clara, Es-
merelda, Larry Tate 11 Uncle Arthur 12 Abner
Kravitz 13 Gladys Kravitz
14 Darrin Stephens 15 Tabitha Stephens 16 Samantha
Stephens
cast: 8 Dick York 9 Paul
Lynde 10 David White
11 Dick Sargent, Marion
Lorne, Sandra Gould
12 George Tobias, Maurice
Evans 13 Alice Ghostley
14 Agnes Moorehead
19 Elizabeth Montgomery

bewitching 8 alluring, charming, enticing, fetching, tempting 9 appealing, beguiling,
disarming, seductive 10 enchanting, entrancing 11 captivating, fascinating
12 irresistible

be worthy of 4 earn, rate
5 merit 7 deserve

bey, beg 4 lord 6 prince
8 governor

beyond 2 by 4 over, past
5 above, later, ultra 6 abroad,
except, yonder 7 beneath, besides, farther, further, outside,
passing 8 superior 9 exceeding,
hereafter 10 out of range, out
of reach 11 at a distance, in
addition to

Beyond Desire
author: 15 Maxwell Anderson

beyond hope 8 hopeless
9 desperate 10 despairing

Beyond Human Power
author: 20 Bjornstjerne
Bjørnson

beyond one's means 10 immoderate 11 extravagant
15 too high on the hog

beyond question 4 sure
6 surely 7 certain, decided, settled 9 certainly, decidedly
10 absolutely, positively
12 without doubt

Bharat (Varsha) see 5 India

Bhot see 5 Tibet

Bhutan see box

Bia
origin: 5 Greek
personifies: 5 force
father: 11 Titan Pallas
mother: 4 Styx
brother: 5 Zelos 6 Cratus
sister: 4 Nike

Biadice
husband: 8 Cretheus

Bianca
character in: 19 The Taming
of the Shrew
author: 11 Shakespeare

Bianchi, Mose
born: 5 Italy, Milan
artwork: 11 Snow in Milan
21 Return from the Festival

bias 4 bent, sway 5 angle,
slant 7 bigotry, feeling, leaning 8 tendency 9 fixed idea,
prejudice, proneness 10 narrow view, partiality, predispose, proclivity, propensity,
unfairness 11 inclination, intolerance 12 diagonal line,
one-sidedness, predilection
13 preconception 16 narrow-
mindedness, preconceived idea

Bias
father: 8 Amythaon
mother: 7 Idomene
brother: 8 Melampus
wife: 4 Pero 10 Iphianassa
son: 6 Talaus
daughter: 8 Anaxibia
secured: 6 cattle
cattle owned by:
8 Phylacus

biased 6 unfair, unjust 7 bigoted, slanted 8 inclined 9 arbitrary 10 intolerant, prejudiced
11 close-minded, opinionated
12 narrow-minded

bibelot 5 curio 7 trinket 8 ornament 9 objet d'art

bible 5 guide 6 manual
8 handbook 9 authority, guidebook 13 reference book

Bible 6 Gospel 7 the Book

Bhutan
other name: 7 Druk-Yul
15 Kingdom of Bhutan,
Land of the Dragon
capital/largest city:
6 Thimbu 7 Thimphu
others: 4 Paro
12 Phuntsholing
14 Wangdu Phedrang
government:
assembly: 7 Tsongdu
head of state/
government:
hereditary king:
10 dragon king, druk
gyalpo
other leader:
spiritual leader:
10 dharma raja
temporal ruler: 7 deb
raja
monetary unit: 5 paisa,
rupee 8 chetrums,
ngultrum
mountain: 5 Black
9 Himalayas 10 Chomo
Lhari
highest point: 10 Kula
Kangri
river: 4 Kuru, Paro
5 Machu, Manas, Pa-
chu, Torsa 6 Amochu,
Raidak, Tongsa 7 San-
kosh, Thinchu
physical feature:
plain: 5 Duars
people: 5 Monpa 6 Bhu-
tia 7 Tibetan 8 As-
samese, Nepalese
dragon people:
7 Drukpas
language: 5 Hindi,
Lhoke 7 Tibetan
8 Dzongkha, Nepalese
religion: 15 Tibetan
Buddhism
place:
fortress (dzong):
4 Paro 6 Bya Kar,
Tongsa 8 Tashi Cho
feature:
pony: 6 Tangun

8 good book, Holy Writ
10 Scriptures 11 bibliotheca,
the Good Book 13 holy scripture 14 Holy Scriptures, sacred
writings

Bible, books of
Old Testament: 3 Job
4 Amos, Ezra, Joel, Osee,
Ruth 5 Hosea, Jonah, Jonas,
Josue, Kings, Micah, Na-
hum, Tobit 6 Abdias, Ag-
geus, Baruch, Daniel, Esdras,
Esther, Exodus, Haggai, Isa-
iah, Isaias, Joshua, Judges,
Judith, Psalms, Samuel, Sir-

ach, Tobias, Wisdom
7 Ezekiel, Genesis, Habacuc,
Malachi, Micheas, Numbers,
Obadiah **8** Ezechiel, Habakkuk, Jeremiah, Jeremias,
Nehemiah, Proverbs **9** Leviticus, Maccabees, Machabees,
Malachias, Sophonias,
Zacharias, Zechariah,
Zephaniah **10** Chronicles
11 Deuteronomy, Song of
Songs **12** Ecclesiastes, Lam-
entations **13** Paralipomenon,
Song of Solomon **14** Ecclesiasticus **19** Canticle of
Canticles
New Testament: 4 Acts,
John, Jude, Luke, Mark
5 James, Peter **6** Romans
7 Hebrews, Matthew, Timothy **9** Ephesians, Galatians
10 Colossians, Revelation
11 Corinthians, Philippians
13 Thessalonians, Titus
Philemon
first five books called:
3 Law **5** Torah
10 Pentateuch
first seven books called:
10 Heptateuch

Bible scholar 7 biblist
9 biblicist

Bible version 6 The Way
7 Vulgate **8** Peshitta **9** Gutenberg, Jerusalem, King James
10 New English **11** New
American, Rheims-Douay **14**
The Living Bible **15** American
revised, revised standard

Biblical animal 7 unicorn

Biblical gemstone 6 ligure
7 sardius **8** sardonyx

Biblical instrument 7 sackbut

Biblical length
reed: 9 six cubits

Biblical measure 3 cab, cor
4 epah, omet, reed, seah
5 cubit, epheh, homer
6 shekel **9** half homer

Biblical personage 9
patriarch

Biblical plant 6 hyssop
12 Rose of Sharon

Biblical precept
Hebrew: 7 mitsvah, mitzvah

Biblical tree 5 algum, almug
6 storax **7** juniper **8** sycamire
10 gopherwood **11** shittim
wood **12** opobalsammum
13 red sandalwood

Biblical weed 4 tare **6** darnel

Biblical weight 6 talent

Biblicist 12 Bible scholar

Bibliotheca 5 Bible **14** sacred
writings

Biblist 12 Bible scholar

**Bickel, Ernest Frederick
McIntyre**
real name of: 13 Frederic
March

bicker 4 spar, spat **5** argue,
fight **6** haggle **7** dispute, quarrel, wrangle **8** disagree,
squabble

bickering 4 spat **5** fight **7** arguing, dispute, quarrel **8** argument, fighting **9** wrangling
10 quarreling, squabbling
12 disagreement

Bickford, Charles
born: 11 Cambridge MA
roles: 12 Anna Christie
13 Johnny Belinda **16** Song
of Bernadette **18** The Farmer's Daughter

bicycle 4 bike, ride **5** cycle,
moped **10** two-wheeler
invented by: 7 Starley

Bicycle Thief, The
director: 14 Vittorio De Sica
cast: 14 Lianella Carell
18 Lamberto Maggiorani

bid 3 ask, say, try **4** call, tell,
wish **5** greet, offer, order
6 beckon, charge, demand, direct, effort, enjoin, insist, invite, ordain, summon, tender
7 attempt, command, proffer,
propose, request, require **8** call
upon, endeavor, instruct, offering, proposal **10** invitation

bidding 4 beck, call **5** offer, order **6** behest, charge, demand,
offers **7** command, dictate,
mandate, request, summons
8 offering, proposal **9** direction, summoning, tendering
10 injunction, invitation, proffering **11** instruction

bide 4 stay, wait **5** abide,
dwell, stand, tarry **6** endure,
linger, remain, suffer **8** tolerate **9** put up with

Bierce, Ambrose
author of: 15 Can Such
Things Be? **16** In the Midst
of Life **19** The Devil's
Dictionary

Bierstadt, Albert
born: 7 Germany **8** Solingen
artwork: 11 Laramie Park
13 Mount Corcoran **17** The
Rocky Mountains **20** Discovery of the Hudson,
Storm on the Matterhorn
21 Sunrise Yosemite Valley
22 Settlement of California
31 Thunderstorm in the
Rocky Mountains

bifocal lenses
invented by: 8 Franklin

Bifrost
origin: 12 Scandinavian
form: 6 bridge

bridge of: 4 gods
made of: 7 rainbow
from: 6 Asgard
to: 5 earth

bifurcate 4 fork **5** split
6 branch, divide **7** diverge
8 separate

big 3 top **4** head, high, huge,
just, kind, main, vast **5** adult,
ample, bulky, chief, great,
grown, heavy, husky, large,
major, noble, prime, vital
6 heroic, humane, mature
7 eminent, grown-up, haughty,
hulking, immense, leading,
liberal, mammoth, massive,
notable, pompous, sizable,
weighty **8** abundant, arrogant,
boastful, bragging, colossal,
enormous, generous, gigantic,
gracious, princely **9** conceited,
grandiose, honorable, important, momentous, prominent,
strapping **10** benevolent, chivalrous, high-minded, monumental, prodigious
11 magnanimous, pretentious,
significant, substantial **12** considerable **13** consequential

Big Apple
nickname of: 11 New York
City

Big Bend State
nickname of: 9 Tennessee

Big Chill, The
director: 14 Laurence Kasdan
cast: 10 Kevin Kline **11** William Hurt

Big Daddy
character in: 16 Cat on a
Hot Tin Roof
author: 8 Williams

Big E
nickname of: 10 Elvin Hayes

Bigfoot 4 Yeti **9** Sasquatch
17 Abominable Snowman

big guns 4 VIPs **5** brass **6** cannon **7** bigwigs, top dogs **8** big
shots, ordnance **9** artillery
14 heavy artillery, high
mucky-mucks **15** important
people

bighearted 6 lavish **7** liberal
8 generous, handsome,
princely, prodigal **9** bounteous,
bountiful, unselfish **10** beneficent, benevolent, charitable,
free-handed, open-handed, unstinting **11** magnanimous,
open-hearted **12** humanitarian

bight 3 bay **4** bend, cave,
road

Biglow Papers
author: 18 James Russell
Lowell

Big Money, The
author: 13 John Dos Passos

bigness 4 bulk **8** enormity, hugeness **9** amplitude, great size, greatness, largeness, magnitude **11** massiveness

Big O, The
nickname of: **14** Oscar Robertson

bigoted 6 biased **10** intolerant, prejudiced **12** closed-minded, narrow-minded

bigotry 4 bias **6** racism **9** prejudice **10** unfairness **11** intolerance **14** discrimination **16** closed-mindedness, narrow-mindedness

Big Parade, The
director: **9** King Vidor
cast: **11** John Gilbert, Renee Adoree **14** Hobart Bosworth

big shot 3 VIP **4** name **5** mogul, nabob, wheel **6** big gun, bigwig, fat cat, tycoon **7** big deal, magnate, notable **8** somebody **9** big cheese, dignitary, personage **13** high-muck-a-muck, wheeler-dealer

Big Six
nickname of: **16** Christy Mathewson

Big Sky, The
author: **11** A B Guthrie Jr

Big Sky State
nickname of: **7** Montana

Big Sleep, The
author: **15** Raymond Chandler
director: **11** Howard Hawks
cast: **12** Elisha Cook Jr, Lauren Bacall **13** Dorothy Malone, Martha Vickers **14** Humphrey Bogart (Philip Marlowe)
setting: **10** Los Angeles

Big Train
nickname of: **13** Walter Johnson

Big Valley, The
character: **11** Nick Barkley **12** Audra Barkley, Heath Barkley **13** Jarrod Barkley **15** Victoria Barkley
cast: **9** Lee Majors **10** Linda Evans, Peter Breck **11** Richard Long **15** Barbara Stanwyck

bigwig 3 vip **7** big shot, notable **9** dignitary, personage

bikini 8 two-piece **11** bathing suit
topless: **8** monokini
type: **6** string

Bikini 5 atoll **9** Namu islet **10** West Pacific **15** Marshall Islands

Bilah, Bilhah
concubine of: **5** Jacob

son: 3 Dan **8** Maphtali, Naphtali
served: **6** Rachel

Bildad
friend: **3** Job **5** Elihu **6** Zophar **7** Eliphaz

bile 4 gall, rage **5** anger, venom, wrath **6** choler, spleen

bilge 3 rot **4** bosh, bull, bunk, tosh **5** hooey, tripe **6** drivel, humbug, jabber, piffle **7** baloney, hogwash, rubbish, twaddle **8** malarkey, nonsense **9** gibberish **10** balderdash **11** foolishness, jabberwocky **13** horsefeathers **16** stuff and nonsense

bilious 4 sick **5** angry, cross, huffy, nasty, testy **6** crabby, cranky, grumpy, queasy, sickly, touchy **7** grouchy, peevish **8** bilelike, greenish, nauseous, petulant, snappish **9** irritable, sickening **10** ill-humored, out of sorts **11** ill-tempered **12** cantankerous **13** short-tempered **15** green at the gills

bilk 3 gyp **4** dupe, gull, rook, take **5** cheat, cozen, trick **6** fleece, rip off **7** deceive, defraud, swindle **8** hoodwink **9** bamboozle, victimize

bill 3 act, fee, law **4** card, chit, list **5** tally **6** agenda, charge, decree, docket, poster, roster, ticket **7** account, catalog, charges, invoice, leaflet, measure, placard, program, statute **8** banknote, brochure, bulletin, calendar, circular, handbill, proposal, register, schedule **9** greenback, inventory, ordinance, reckoning, statement **10** regulation **12** treasury note **13** advertisement **17** silver certificate

billet 3 job **4** base, bunk, camp, digs, note, post **5** berth, house, lodge, place, put up **6** letter, office **7** bed down, lodging, quarter, shelter **8** domicile, dwelling, lodgment, position, quarters **9** residence, situation **11** accommodate, appointment **13** accommodation

billfold see **6** wallet

billiards
player: **11** Willie Hoppe **13** Minnesota Fats, Willie Mosconi

Bill of Divorcement, A
director: **11** George Cukor
cast: **11** Billie Burke **13** John Barrymore **16** Katharine Hepburn

billow 4 roll, wave **5** belly,

cloud, crest, surge, swell **6** puff up **7** balloon, breaker

Billy Budd
author: **14** Herman Melville
character: **8** Claggart **11** Captain Vere

billyclub 3 bat **5** billy, stick **8** bludgeon **9** truncheon

bin 3 box **4** cart, crib, silo **5** crate, frame, hatch **6** barrel, basket, bunker, hamper, holder, trough, vessel **9** container, inclosure **10** receptacle

binate 4 dual **6** double **7** coupled, two fold **14** growing in pairs

bind 3 rim, tie **4** edge, gird, glue, join, lash, rope, trim, wrap **5** affix, chafe, cover, cramp, force, frame, hitch, paste, stick, strap, tie up, truss **6** attach, border, coerce, compel, encase, fasten, fringe, oblige, secure, swathe **7** bandage, confine, require **8** encumber, obligate **9** prescribe **11** necessitate

binder 4 glue, roux **5** paste **6** cement **8** notebook **9** assurance, guarantee **11** down payment **12** earnest money **17** looseleaf notebook

binding 4 band, face, tape **5** valid **6** edging, ribbon **7** styptic **8** fastener, ligative **9** stringent **10** compulsory, obligatory, peremptory **12** constricting

binge 3 jag **4** bust, orgy, tear, toot **5** blast, drunk, fling, revel, spree **6** bender **7** carouse **8** beer-bust, carousal **11** bacchanalia **12** drunken spree

Bingham, George Caleb
born: **15** Augusta County VA
artwork: **13** Stump Speaking **17** The Trapper's Return **18** Verdict of the People **19** The Jolly Flatboatman **20** Raftsmen Playing Cards **31** Fur Traders Descending the Missouri

Bingley, Mr
character in: **17** Pride and Prejudice
author: **6** Austen

biochemist 17 biological chemist
American: **4** Cori **5** Bloch, Moore, Ochoa **7** Axelrod, Lipmann **8** Kornberg
English: **5** Krebs **6** Porter, Sanger **8** Mitchell
French: **5** Monod **7** Duclaux
German: **5** Lynen

biogenesis
discoverer: **12** Louis Pasteur

biography 3 bio **4** life, vita
6 memoir **7** account, history
9 life story

biologist
American: 6 Carson, Yerkes
7 Burbank **8** Delbruck
British: 6 Darwin, Huxley
7 Bateson, Medawar
French: 5 Jacob, Monod
7 Lamarck
German: 7 Schwann
Swiss: 6 Haller

biology
branch: 6 botany **7** zoology
classification: 15 Carolus
Linnaeus

birch 6 Betula
varieties: 3 Low, Red **4** Fire,
Gray **5** Black, Canoe, Dwarf,
Paper, River, Swamp, Sweet,
Water, White **6** Cherry, Yellow **7** Monarch **8** Mahogany, Old-field **10** West
Indian **13** European white,
Japanese white, Young's
weeping **14** Japanese
cherry

Birches
author: 11 Robert Frost

bird *see box*

Bird, Larry
sport: 10 basketball
position: 7 forward
team: 13 Boston Celtics

---

bird
anatomy: 3 bec, neb, nib **4** beak, bill, cere, crop, lora, lore, mala, nape, rump, tail, tuft,
wing **5** alula, crest, crown, flank, larum, lorum, pilea, rosta **6** breast, gullet, pecten, pileum,
pinion, syrinx, tarsus **7** ambiens, crissum, gizzard, rostrum **8** gigerium, pectines, scapular
9 auchenium, gastraeum **10** cordylanus
aquatic/water: 3 auk, cob, ern, mew **4** cobb, coot, duck, erne, gony, gull, ibis, loon, rail,
shag, skua, sora, swan, teal, tern **5** booby, cahow, crane, diver, goose, grebe, heron, murre,
ousel, rotch, snipe, solan, stilt, stork **6** avocet, curlew, cygnet, dipper, fulmar, gannet, godwit, hagdon, jabiru, jacana, osprey, petrel, plover, puffin, rotche, scoter, wigeon **7** anhinga,
bidcock, bittern, bustard, dovekey, dovekie, finfoot, mallard, moorhen, pelican, penguin, seriema, skimmer, widgeon **8** alcatras, baldpate, dabchick, flamingo, murrelet, umbrette **9** albatross, baptornis, cormorant, gallinule, guillemot, kittiwake, phalarope, snakebird, spoonbill
10 gaviformes, kingfisher, shearwater, sheathbill, yellowlegs **13** whooping crane
bird cage/home: 4 cote, mews, nest **5** roost **6** aviary, volary, volery **7** rookery
bird of freedom: 9 bald eagle
bird of ill-omen: 5 raven
bird of Jove: 5 eagle
bird of June: 7 peacock
bird of Minerva: 3 owl
bird of peace: 4 dove
bird of prey: 3 owl **4** gled, hawk, kite **5** buteo, eagle, glead, glede, harpy, saker **6** condor, ela-
net, elenet, falcon, musket, osprey, raptor **7** buzzard, goshawk, harrier, kestrel, stooper, vulture **8** caracara **9** accipiter, gyrfalcon, peregrine **11** accipitrine, lammergeier
bird of wonder/rebirth: 7 phoenix
carrion-eater: 4 aura **5** urubu **6** condor **7** buzzard, vulture
class: 4 Aves
combining form: 3 avi **4** orni **5** ornis **6** ornith **7** ornitho **8** ornithes
crow family: 3 daw, jay, kae **4** crow, rook **5** crake, raven **6** chough, corbie, magpie **7** corvine,
jackdaw
duck family: 4 clee, coot, lory, smew, teal, wood **5** eider, goose **6** scoter **7** gadwall, mallard,
Muscovy, pintail, pochard **8** baldpate, redshank, shoveler **9** merganser **10** bufflehead,
canvasback
extinct: 3 auk, jib, moa **4** dodo, jibi, mamo **5** didus **8** Diatryma **9** aepyornis, apatornis, gastor-
nis, hespornis, solitaire **11** archaeornis
flightless: 3 emu, ihi, moa **4** dodo, gorb, kagu, kiwi, rhea, weka **5** nandu **6** callow, kakapo,
moorup, ratite, takahe **7** apteryx, horling, ostrich, peacock, penguin, roatelo **8** notornis
9 cassowary
game: 4 duck, guan, rail, sora, teal **5** brant, goose, quail, snipe **6** chukar, colima, grouse, pigeon, plover, turkey **7** bustard, chicken, flapper, gadwall, mallard, pintail, prairie, widgeon
8 baldpate, bobwhite, moorfowl, pheasant, shoveler, tragopan, wildfowl, woodcock **9** merganser, partridge, ptarmigan **10** canvasback
group of birds: 3 nye **4** bank, bevy, cast, nide, sord **5** aerie, brood, covey, drove, flock,
plump **6** covert, flight, gaggle, litter, spring
largest: 7 ostrich **11** lammergeier
legendary: 3 roc **6** simurg **7** phoenix, simurgh **9** feng-huang, feng-hwang
loss of feathers: 7 molting
smallest: 11 hummingbird
nocturnal: 3 owl **5** cahow, owlet, potoo **7** bullbat, dorhawk **8** guacharo, nightjar **9** nighthawk,
thickknee **10** goatsucker **11** nightingale
pet: 4 myna **5** mynah **6** canary, parrot, pigeon **8** cockatoo, lovebird, parakeet
plumage: 8 ptilosis
poultry: 3 hen **4** duck **5** goose **6** pigeon, turkey **7** chicken, rooster **8** pheasant **14** Cornish
game hen
talking: 4 myna **5** mynah **6** parrot

Birdman of Alcatraz
director: **17** John
Frankenheimer
cast: **10** Karl Malden **12** Edmond O'Brien, Neville
Brand, Thelma Ritter
13 Burt Lancaster (Robert
Stroud)

Bird of Paradise
constellation of: **4** Apus

Birds, The
author: **12** Aristophanes

character: **4** Iris **5** Meton
8 Basileia, Cinesias **9** Euel-
pides **10** King Tereus, Prometheus **12** Peithetairos

Birds, The
director: **15** Alfred Hitchcock
based on story by:
15 Daphne du Maurier
cast: **9** Rod Taylor **11** Tippi
Hedren **12** Jessica Tandy
16 Suzanne Pleshette
setting: **10** California

Birds Fall Down, The
author: **15** Dame Rebecca
West

Birkin, Rupert
character in: **11** Women in
Love
author: **8** Lawrence

Birmingham
football team: **9** Stallions

Birmingham, Stephen
author of: **8** Our Crowd

---

wingless: 4 kiwi, weka **7** apteryx
young: 4 eyas, gull **5** chick, piper, poult, squab **6** gorlin, pullus **7** flapper, nestler **8** birdikin,
nestling **9** fledgling
of Africa: 4 coly, fink, taha, tock **5** crane, paauw **6** barbet, bulbul, cuckoo, jabiru, quelea,
whidah **7** courser, finfoot, marabou, ostrich, touraco **8** hornbill, oxpecker, parakeet, umbrette **9** beefeater, broadbill, francolin, napecrest, trochilus **10** hammerhead, weaverbird
of Antarctic/Arctic: 3 auk **4** gull, knot, skua, xema **5** brant, murre, rotch **6** dunlin, falcon,
fulmar, jaeger, rotche **7** dovekey, dovekie, penguin **8** grayling **9** guillemot, gyrfalcon, ptarmigan **10** sheathbill
of Asia: 4 kora, myna, ruff, smew **5** mynah, pewit, pitta **6** bulbul, chukar, drongo, dunlin,
hoopoe, linnet **7** boobook, courser, hill tit, lapwing, peacock, sirgang **8** accentor, dotterel,
hornbill, leaf bird, parakeet, tragopan, wheatear **9** brambling, francolin, muted swan
of Australia: 3 emu **4** kahu, kiwi, koel, koil, lory **5** arara, galah, lowan, pitta **6** drongo, leipoa **7** boobook, bustard, figbird, grinder, waybung **8** bellbird, bushlark, cockatoo, ganggang,
lorikeet, lyrebird, megapode, manucode, morepork, parakeet, platypus **9** bowerbird, cassowary, coachwhip, cockatiel, frogmouth, pardalote, thornbird **10** kookaburra
of Central America: 4 guan, ibis **5** booby, macaw **6** barbet, jabiru, quezal, toucan **7** bittern,
cotinga, jacamar, quetzal, tinamou **8** curassow, puffbird, troupial
of Cuba: 6 trogon **8** tocororo **14** bee hummingbird
of England: 4 kite, rook **9** cormorant **11** carrion crow
of Europe: 3 dar, mag, mew, nun **4** clee, gled, mall, merl, pope, rook, ruff, shag, smew,
wren **5** amsel, crake, egret, finch, glede, merle, ousel, ouzel, pewit, pipit, stilt, stork, swift,
tarin, terek, whaup **6** cuckoo, dunlin, godwit, grouse, hoopoe, linnet, martin, merlin, missel,
redleg, roller, siskin, thrush **7** bittern, bustard, jackdaw, kestrel, lapwing, martlet, ortolan,
redwing, ruddock, skylark, sparrow, starnel, wagtail, wryneck **8** bee eater, blackcap, brantail,
daychick, dotterel, garganey, nightjar, nuthatch, peesweep, redstart, reedling, starling, thros-
tle, wheatear, whimbrel, whinchat, whinshat, woodcock **9** brambling, chaffinch, crossbill,
field fare, gallinule, sheldrake, stonechat **10** chiffchaff, goatsucker, kingfisher, lammergeir,
turtledove **11** lammergeier, nightingale, wallcreeper **12** capercaillie
of Hawaii: 2 io **3** ava, ioa, iwa, poe **4** nene, iiwi, koae, mamo, moho, omao **6** parson
7 frigate
of India: 4 baya, kala, koel, koil **5** sarus, shama **6** argala, bulbul, homrai, luggar **7** peacock
8 adjutant, amadavat, pheasant, tragopan **11** red hornbill
of Jamaica: 7 vervain
of Java: 7 sparrow **8** rice bird **9** fruit dove
of Madagascar: 6 drongo **7** anhinga, kirombo, roatelo
of Mexico: 6 jacana
of New Guinea: 9 cassowary **14** bird of paradise
of New Zealand: 3 ihi, kea, moa, poe, tui **4** huia, kaka, kaki, kiwi, koko, kuku, ruru, titi,
weka **6** kakapo **7** apteryx **8** morepork, notornis
of North America: 3 ani, auk, tit **4** coot, crow, dove, ibis, lark, loon, pape, rook, sora, stib,
swan, tern, wamp, wren **5** booby, brant, colin, crane, egret, finch, grebe, junco, murre,
quail, robin, snipe, swift, veery, vireo **6** chebec, cuckoo, curlew, darter, dunlin, fulmar,
grouse, hagdon, magpie, martin, oriole, phoebe, plover, shrike, thrush, towhee, turkey, ver-
din, willet **7** anhinga, bittern, blue jay, catbird, flicker, goshawk, grackle, lapwing, pelican,
sparrow, swallow, tanager, warbler **8** bluebird, bobolink, bobwhite, cardinal, grosbeak, killdeer, nuthatch, poorwill, starling, thrasher, titmouse, wheatear **9** blackbird, chickadee, crossbill, goldfinch, gyrfalcon, nighthawk, partridge, sandpiper, snakebird **10** bufflehead,
kingfisher, meadowlark, woodpecker **11** hummingbird, mockingbird **12** whippoorwill
of South America: 3 ara, hia **4** anna, guan, jacu, loro, mitu, rhea, soco, toco, yeni **5** egret,
macaw, potoo, sylph **6** barbet, chatja, chunga, cracid, jabiru, motmot, sappho, toucan **7** car-
iama, cotinga, hoatzin, jacamar, limpkin, manakin, seriema, tinamou, warrior **8** boatbill, caracara, curassow, guacharo, hoactzin, screamer, tapacolo, tapaculo, terutero, troupial
9 campanero, trumpeter **11** scarlet ibis
of West India: 3 ani **4** tody

11 The Grandees 14 The Right People 15 Life at the Dakota

Birnbaum, Nathan
real name of: 11 George Burns

birth 5 blood, start, stock 6 family, origin, source, strain 7 bearing, descent, genesis, lineage 8 ancestry, breeding, delivery 9 beginning, being born, emergence, genealogy, inception, parentage 10 background, beginnings, childbirth, derivation, extraction 11 confinement, parturition 12 commencement

Birth of a Nation, The
director: 10 D W Griffith
cast: 8 Mae Marsh 11 Lillian Gish 14 Henry B Walthall

Birth of Tragedy, The
author: 18 Friedrich Nietzsche

birthstones
January: 6 garnet
February: 8 amethyst
March: 6 jasper 10 aquamarine, bloodstone
April: 7 diamond 8 sapphire
May: 5 agate 7 emerald
June: 5 pearl 7 emerald 9 moonstone 11 alexandrite
July: 4 onyx, ruby 8 star ruby
August: 7 peridot 8 sardonyx 9 carnelian
September: 8 sapphire 10 chrysolite 12 star sapphire
October: 4 opal 5 beryl 10 aquamarine, tourmaline
November: 5 topaz
December: 4 ruby 6 zircon 9 turquoise

biscuit 3 bun 4 cake, roll 5 cooky, scone, wafer 6 bisque, cookie, muffin, parking, simnel 7 cracker, dogbone 8 hardtack, zwieback 9 pale-brown 10 crisp bread, quick bread 15 unglazed pottery

bisect 5 cross, split 8 cut in two 9 cut in half, intersect

bishop 4 abba, pope 5 punch 6 cleric, despot, priest 7 pontiff, prelate, primate 8 overseer 9 clergyman, patriarch 10 chesspiece, high priest of Rome: 4 pope
Greek: 9 episkopos
means: 8 overseer
district: 7 diocese
headdress: 5 miter, mitre

Bismarck, Otto von
nickname: 14 Iron Chancellor
unified: 7 Germany

chancellor/minister for: 15 Emperor William I
policy: 12 "iron and blood"

bison 4 urus 6 wild ox, wisent 7 aurochs, buffalo
native to: 6 Europe 12 North America

Bissau
capital of: 12 Guinea-Bissau

Bisset, Jacqueline
real name: 22 Jacqueline Fraser Bisset
born: 7 England 9 Weybridge
roles: 5 Class 7 Airport, The Deep 11 Day for Night 12 Anna Karenina 16 The Mephisto Waltz 24 Murder on the Orient Express

bistro 3 bar 4 cafe 6 tavern 7 cabaret 9 nightclub 10 supper club
French: 9 estaminet

bit 3 dab 4 chip, drop, iota, mite, snip, whit 5 crumb, grain, pinch, scrap, shred, speck, spell, trace 6 dollop, moment, morsel, paring, trifle 7 droplet, granule, shaving, smidgen 8 fragment, particle 9 short time 10 short while, small piece, smithereen, sprinkling
type: 5 auger, drill 6 gimlet, wimble 7 bradawl 11 brace and bit

bitch 3 nag 5 botch, brood, cheat, fault, shrew, spoil, witch, whine 6 kvetch, virago 7 blunder, bungle, grouse 8 complain, harridan 9 complaint, female dog, termagant

bitchy 4 mean 5 catty, cruel, nasty 6 wicked 7 hateful, vicious 8 spiteful 9 heartless, malicious 10 backbiting, malevolent, vindictive

bite 3 bit, dab, dig, nip 4 gnaw, grip, snip 5 champ, crumb, gnash, prick, scrap, shred, smart, speck, sting, taste 6 morsel, nibble, pierce 7 eat into 8 mouthful, stinging, take hold 10 small piece, tooth wound 12 small portion

biting 5 harsh, sharp 6 bitter 7 caustic, cutting, mordant, nipping 8 piercing, scathing, smarting, stinging 9 sarcastic, trenchant, withering 12 sharp-tongued

Biton
father: 7 Cydippe

bit player 5 extra 6 walk on 14 minor character

bitte 6 please 12 you're welcome 14 I beg your pardon

bitter 4 acid, mean, sour, tart

5 acrid, angry, cruel, harsh, sharp 6 biting, morose, severe, sullen 7 acerbic, caustic, crabbed, painful 8 grievous, piercing, scornful, smarting, spiteful, stinging, wretched 9 rancorous, resentful 10 astringent 11 distressing

bitterness 5 anger, scorn, spite 6 animus, rancor, spleen 7 ill will 8 acerbity, acrimony, sourness 9 animosity, harshness, hostility, malignity, sharpness 10 antagonism, malignancy 11 astringency 12 hard feelings, spitefulness 14 unpleasantness

bitters
type: 6 spirit
flavor: 6 orange 7 gentian
brand: 9 Angostura

bivalve 4 clam 5 pinna 6 cockle, mussel, mollusk, scallop 8 mollusca 9 pelecypod 13 lamellibranch

bivouac 4 camp 5 tents 10 campground, encampment

bizarre 3 odd 5 kinky, kooky, queer, weird 7 strange, unusual 8 freakish 9 fantastic, grotesque 10 outlandish

Bizet, Georges
real name: 26 Alexandre Cesar Leopold Bizet
born: 5 Paris 6 France
composer of: 4 Roma (suite) 6 Carmen, Patrie 8 Djamileh 11 Don Procopio, L'Arlesienne 12 Jeux d'enfants, Pearl Fishers 14 Children's Games 15 Ivan the Terrible 16 Le Docteur Miracle 18 The Fair Maid of Perth

Biztha 6 eunuch

Bjornson, Bjornstjerne
author of: 4 Arne 7 The King 8 Magnhild 9 A Happy Boy, In God's Way, Lame Hulda, The Editor 10 King Sverre 11 A Bankruptcy, The Bankrupt 12 Sigurd Slembe 14 Arnljot Gelline, Beyond Our Power 15 The Fisher Maiden, The Newly Married 16 Beyond Human Might, Sigurd the Bastard 17 Between the Battles 20 Mary Stuart in Scotland 24 Paul Lange and Tora Parsberg 27 Flags Are Flying in Town and Port

blab 3 rat 6 babble, tattle 7 blabber, prattle 9 tell tales 13 spill the beans 20 let the cat out of the bag

blabber 3 gab, gas, yak 4 blab, bull 5 prate 6 babble, drivel, gabble, gibber, gossip, jabber 7 blather, chatter, palaver, prattle, twaddle **8** blah-blah, chitchat, idle talk **9** jabbering **10** mumbo-jumbo **12** gobbledegook **14** chitter-chatter

blabbermouth 6 gabber, gossip, prater **7** blabber **8** bigmouth, busybody, gossiper, informer, jabberer, liverlip, prattler, quidnunc **9** chatterer **10** chatterbox, talebearer, tattletale **11** rumormonger **12** gossipmonger **13** scandalmonger

black, Black 3 bad, dim, jet **4** dark, evil, grim, inky **5** angry, ebony, murky, Negro, raven, sable **6** dismal, gloomy, somber, sullen, wicked **7** colored, furious, hostile, stygian, sunless, swarthy **8** moonless **9** coal-black, lightless, nefarious, unlighted **10** calamitous **11** dark-skinned, threatening **12** Afro-American **13** unilluminated

Black Arrow, The
author: **20** Robert Louis Stevenson

blackball 3 ban, bar, cut **4** snub **5** debar **6** banish, outlaw, reject **7** boycott, exclude, keep out, shut out **8** pass over, turndown **9** blacklist, ostracize, proscribe **11** vote against **12** cold-shoulder **14** send to Coventry

black beast
French: **9** bete noire

blackberry 5 Rubus
variety: **4** Sand **5** Swamp **7** Cut-leaf, Pacific, Running, Sow-teat **9** Evergreen **13** Parsley-leaved **18** Evergreen thornless

Blackberry Winter
author: **12** Margaret Mead

blackbird 4 crow **5** raven, slave **6** thrush **7** cowbird, grackle, redwing **8** song bird **9** slave ship **11** slave trader **17** kidnapped islander, plantation laborer
kind: **9** red-winged **12** yellow-headed
family: **8** Turdidae **9** Icteridae

Blackboard Jungle, The
director: **13** Richard Brooks
based on novel by: **10** Evan Hunter
cast: **9** Glenn Ford, Vic Morrow **11** Anne Francis **12** Louis Calhern, Paul Mazursky, Richard Kiley **13** Sidney Poitier **14** Warner Anderson

Black Boy
author: **13** Richard Wright

blacken 5 libel, smear, stain,

sully **6** befoul, darken, defame, defile, revile, vilify **7** slander, tarnish **8** besmirch, disgrace, dishonor **9** denigrate, discredit **10** stigmatize

Blackfoot, Blackfeet
language family: **9** Algonkian **10** Algonquian
tribe: **6** Bloods, Kainah, Piegan, Pikuni **7** Siksika
location: **6** Canada **7** Alberta, Montana **12** Saskatchewan

blackguard 3 cad, rat, SOB **5** knave, louse, rogue, scamp **6** rascal **7** bastard, villain **9** miscreant, scoundrel

blackhearted 4 base, vile **6** sinful, wicked **7** ignoble **10** despicable, evil-minded, villainous **11** scoundrelly **12** unprincipled **13** reprehensible

blackjack
also known as: **9** twenty-one
French: **9** vingt-et-un
play against: **6** dealer
additional card: **3** hit

Black Lamb and Grey Falcon
author: **15** Dame Rebecca West

Black Land, The see **5** Egypt

blackleg 7 cheater **8** swindler **9** trickster

blacklist 3 ban, bar **4** shun **5** debar **6** reject **7** exclude, lock out, shut out **8** preclude **9** blackball, ostracize

blacklisting 7 boycott **8** spurning **9** exclusion, ostracism, rejection **12** blackballing

black magic 7 sorcery **10** witchcraft

blackmail 5 force **6** coerce, extort, payoff **7** squeeze, tribute **8** threaten **9** extortion, hush money, shakedown

black mark 4 blot **5** stain **6** bruise **7** blemish, demerit **9** contusion

Blackmore, Richard Doddridge
author of: **10** Lorna Doone **11** Springhaven **13** The Maid of Sker

black mountain see **10** Montenegro

Black Narcissus
author: **11** Rumer Godden
director: **13** Michael Powell **17** Emeric Pressburger
cast: **4** Sabu **11** David Farrar, Deborah Kerr, Jean Simmons
setting: **9** Himalayas

blackness 4 dark **5** gloom, shade **7** dimness **8** darkness

Blackpool, Stephen
character in: **9** Hard Times
author: **7** Dickens

Black Prince, The
author: **11** Iris Murdoch

Blackstone, Sir William
author of: **12** Commentaries (on the Laws of England)

Black Uhlan
nickname of: **12** Max Schmeling

Blackwater State
nickname of: **8** Nebraska

Blackwell, Elizabeth
first American: **11** woman doctor

bladder 3 bag, sac **4** cyst **5** pouch **7** blister, pustule, saccule, utricle **10** receptacle

blade 4 leaf **5** frond, knife, razor, sword **6** cutter, needle, switch **7** scalpel **10** sled runner **11** cutting edge, skate runner

blah 4 bosh, dull, flat, guff, soso **5** bland, ho-hum, hooey, vapid **6** boring, bunkum, dreary, hot air, humbug **7** blather, eyewash, humdrum, nothing, tedious, twaddle **8** claptrap, lifeless, listless, nonsense **9** gibberish **10** balderdash, monotonous, pedestrian **11** uninspiring **13** characterless, unimaginative, uninteresting, unstimulating

Blaik, Earl H
sport: **8** football
position: **5** coach
team: **4** Army **9** Dartmouth
military rank: **7** colonel

Blair, Eric Arthur
real name of: **12** George Orwell

Blake, Robert
real name: **28** Michael James Vijencio Gubitosi
born: **8** Nutley NJ
roles: **7** Baretta, Our Gang **8** Red Ryder **11** In Cold Blood **12** Little Beaver **23** Tell Them Willie Boy Is Here **24** The Treasure of Sierra Madre

Blake, William
born: **6** London **7** England
author of: **6** Milton, Tiriel **9** Jerusalem **13** The Book of Thel **14** Prophetic Books **15** The Book of Urizen **16** Songs of Innocence **17** Songs of Experience **21** Little Lamb Who Made Thee **23** Marriage of Heaven and Hell, Tiger Tiger Burning Bright
artwork: **6** Milton **9** Book of

Job, Jerusalem **11** The Four Zoas **12** Book of Urizen, Divine Comedy **16** Songs of Innocence **17** Songs of Experience **23** Marriage of Heaven and Hell

blamable 10 censurable, deplorable, punishable, reprovable **11** blameworthy **12** reproachable **13** reprehensible

Blamauer, Karoline
real name of: **10** Lotte Lenya

blame 4 onus **5** fault, guilt **6** accuse, burden, charge, rebuke **7** censure, condemn, reproof, reprove **8** reproach **9** castigate, criticism, criticize, liability **10** accusation, disapprove **11** castigation, culpability **12** condemnation, denunciation, remonstrance **13** find fault with, recrimination **14** accountability, responsibility **15** hold responsible

blameless 5 clear **8** innocent, spotless **9** guiltless, not guilty, unspotted, unstained, unsullied, untainted **10** inculpable, not at fault, unblamable **11** unblemished, uncorrupted **13** unimpeachable **14** irreproachable, not responsible

blameless in life
Latin: **12** integer vitae

blame on 7 trace to **8** charge to **9** set down to **11** attribute to **14** lay at the door of

blameworthy 8 blamable **10** censurable, deplorable, punishable, reprovable **12** reproachable **13** reprehensible

blanch 4 fade **6** bleach, whiten **7** lighten **8** turn pale

blanched 3 wan **4** pale **5** ashen, faded **6** chalky, pallid **8** bleached **9** bloodless

bland 4 blah, calm, dull, even, flat, mild **5** balmy, quiet, vapid **6** benign, smooth **7** calming, humdrum, nothing, prosaic, tedious **8** moderate, peaceful, soothing, tiresome, tranquil **9** peaceable, temperate, unruffled **10** monotonous, unexciting, untroubled **11** uninspiring **13** nonirritating, uninteresting, unstimulating

blandish 4 coax, lure, urge **5** charm, tempt **6** cajole, entice, prompt **7** blarney, flatter, wheedle **8** inveigle, persuade

blandishment, blandishments 7 blarney, coaxing **8** cajolery, flattery **9** sweet talk, wheedling **12** ingratiation, inveiglement

Blandois, Monsieur
character in: **12** Little Dorrit
author: **7** Dickens

blank 3 gap **4** dull, idle, void **5** clean, clear, empty, inane, plain, space **6** futile, hollow, unused, vacant, vacuum, wasted **7** useless, vacancy, vacuous **8** unmarked **9** emptiness, fruitless, valueless, worthless **10** empty space, hollowness, profitless **11** meaningless, thoughtless, unrewarding **12** inexpressive **14** expressionless

blanket 4 coat, film **5** cloak, cover, quilt, throw **6** afghan, carpet, mantle, veneer **7** coating, overlay **8** covering, coverlet **9** comforter

blare 4 honk, peal, roar **5** blast **6** bellow, scream **7** resound, trumpet

blarney 4 fibs, line **5** pitch, spiel **6** hot air **7** coaxing, fawning, snow job, stories **8** cajolery, flattery **9** hyperbole, wheedling **10** inveigling, overpraise, sweet words **12** exaggeration, honeyed words **13** blandishments, overstatement

blase 4 full **5** bored, jaded **6** gorged **7** glutted **9** apathetic, satisfied, saturated, surfeited, unexcited, unmovable **10** insouciant, nonchalant, spiritless, world-weary **11** indifferent, unconcerned **12** uninterested **14** unenthusiastic

Blasko, Bela
real name of: **10** Bela Lugosi

blaspheme 5 curse, swear **6** revile **7** profane **10** take in vain

blasphemous 7 godless, impious, profane, ungodly **10** irreverent **11** irreligious **12** sacrilegious

blasphemy 7 cursing, impiety **8** swearing in **9** profanity, sacrilege **11** impiousness, irreverence, profanation

blast 4 bomb, boom, bore, gale, gust, honk, peal, roar, rush, toot **5** blare, bleat, burst, level, shell, surge **6** bellow, blow up, report, scream, shriek **7** explode, resound, torpedo **8** dynamite, eruption **9** discharge, explosion, loud noise **10** detonation **11** sound loudly

blasting material 3 TNT **8** dynamite **9** explosive

blatant 4 loud **5** cheap, clear, crass, crude, gross, harsh,

noisy, overt **6** brazen, coarse, tawdry, vulgar **7** blaring, glaring, obvious, uncouth **8** flagrant, piercing, unsubtle **9** clamorous, deafening, obtrusive, offensive, prominent, tasteless, ungenteel, unrefined **10** indelicate, unpolished **11** conspicuous, ill-mannered, undignified **12** ear-splitting, unmistakable

blather 4 stir **7** chatter, prattle **8** nonsense **9** commotion

Blatty, William P
author of: **11** The Exorcist

Blaue Reiter 10 Blue Riders
group of: **13** German artists

blaze 3 ray **4** beam, burn, fire, glow, rush **5** blast, burst, flame, flare, flash, glare, gleam, shine **6** flames **7** glisten, glitter, shimmer, torrent **8** eruption, outbreak, outburst, radiance **9** explosion **10** brightness, brilliance, effulgence **12** resplendence **13** conflagration

blazer 4 coat **6** jacket **12** sports jacket

blazing 3 hot **5** fiery, afire **6** firing, on fire **7** burning, flaming, flaring, glaring, glowing, intense, shining **8** bursting, bleaming, shooting, shouting **9** brilliant

Blazing Saddles
director: **9** Mel Brooks
cast: **9** Mel Brooks **10** Alex Karras, Dom DeLuise, Gene Wilder **11** Slim Pickens **12** Harvey Korman, Madeline Kahn **13** Cleavon Little, John Hillerman **15** David Huddleston

blazon 5 blare, boast **7** trumpet **8** proclaim **10** coat of arms, make public **16** armorial bearings

blazonry 4 arms **5** crest **6** blazon **8** insignia **10** coat of arms **14** heraldic emblem **16** heraldic bearings

bleach 4 fade **6** blanch, whiten **7** lighten, wash out **8** make pale

bleak 3 icy, raw **4** bare, cold, grim **5** chill **6** barren, biting, bitter, dismal, dreary, frosty, gloomy, somber, wintry **7** nipping **8** desolate, piercing **9** cheerless, windswept **10** depressing, forbidding **11** distressing, unpromising **13** weather-beaten

Bleak House
author: **14** Charles Dickens
character: **2** Jo (the crossing

sweeper) **4** Nemo **5** Guppy, Krook **6** Bucket, Guster **7** Snagsby **8** Ada Clare, Chadband **9** Miss Flite **10** Mrs Jellyby, Turveydrop **11** Dr Woodcourt, Lady Dedlock, Tulkinghorn **12** John Jarndyce **13** Captain Rawdon **14** Harold Skimpole **15** Esther Summerson, Richard Carstone **19** Sir Leicester Dedlock
satire of: 3 law **6** courts **8** chancery
case: 19 Jarndyce and Jarndyce

bleakness 8 bareness, grimness **10** barrenness, desolation, dreariness, gloominess **13** cheerlessness

bleat 3 baa, cry, maa **5** whine **7** whimper

bleb 6 bubble **7** blister

bleed 3 run, tap **4** leak, soak **5** drain, valve **6** fleece, suffer **7** diffuse, extract, **8** let blood **9** draw blood, sacrifice **10** hemorrhage, overcharge **12** phlebotomize

Blefuscu
fictional land in: 16 Gulliver's Travels
author: 5 Swift

blemish 3 mar, zit **4** blot, blur, flaw, mark, spot **5** spoil, stain, sully, taint **6** blotch, defect, smirch, smudge **7** tarnish **9** disfigure **12** imperfection **13** disfigurement

blend 3 mix **4** fuse **5** merge, unite **6** fusion, go well, merger, mingle **7** amalgam, combine, mixture **8** coalesce, compound, mergence, mingling **9** harmonize **10** amalgamate, complement, concoction **11** combination, incorporate, intermingle

bless 4 give **5** endow, favor, grace, guard, honor **6** anoint, bestow, hallow, oblige, ordain **7** baptize, benefit, protect, support **8** dedicate, sanctify **9** watch over **10** consecrate

blessed 4 holy **5** happy, lucky **6** adored, graced, joyful, joyous, sacred **7** endowed, favored, revered **8** blissful, hallowed **9** fortunate, venerated, wonderful **10** felicitous, sanctified **11** consecrated

Blessed Damozel, The
author: 20 Dante Gabriel Rossetti

blessedness 5 bliss **8** felicity **9** beatitude **11** saintliness

blessing 4 gain, gift, good

5 favor, grace, leave **6** bounty, profit, regard **7** backing, benefit, consent, support **8** approval, sanction **9** advantage, hallowing **10** dedication, good wishes, invocation, permission **11** benediction, concurrence, good fortune **12** consecration, thanksgiving **14** sanctification

blessings 4 joys **5** gifts **6** favors **7** success **8** benefits, delights **10** advantages **11** good fortune

Blifil, Master
character in: 8 Tom Jones
author: 8 Fielding

Bligh, Captain William
character in: 17 Mutiny on the Bounty
authors: 4 Hall **8** Nordhoff

blight 3 pox, rot **4** harm, kill, ruin, rust **5** blast, crush, curse, decay, smash, spoil, wreck **6** cancer, canker, dry rot, fungus, injure, mildew, plague, thwart, wither **7** cripple, destroy, scourge, shrivel **8** demolish **9** frustrate **10** affliction, corruption, pestilence **12** plant disease **13** contamination

Blimber, Dr
character in: 12 Dombey and Son
author: 7 Dickens

blind 4 dull, ruse **5** cover, dodge, front, shade **6** hidden, insane, obtuse, screen **7** obscure, pretext, unaware **8** disguise, heedless, ignorant, mindless, unseeing **9** concealed, deception, senseless, sightless, sun shield, unfeeling, unknowing, unmindful, unnoticed **10** camouflage, insouciant, irrational, masquerade, neglectful, subterfuge, unthinking **11** inattentive, incognizant, indifferent, insensitive, smoke screen, unconcerned, unconscious, unobservant, unobserving **12** imperceptive, uncontrolled, undiscerning, uninterested, unnoticeable, unperceptive, unreasonable **13** unenlightened **14** uncontrollable **15** uncomprehending

blind alley 7 closure, dead-end, impasse **8** blockade, cul-de-sac, dead lock, no escape **9** hindrance, stone wall **10** impassable, standstill **11** obstruction

blinder 4 hood **5** blind, shade **6** screen **7** blinker **9** blindfold

blindfold 6 darken **7** bandage, blinder, obscure **8** covering heedless, reckless **11** strike blind

blind seer 8 Tiresias

blink 4 wink **5** flash, shine, waver **6** falter, flinch, squint **7** flicker, glimmer, shimmer, sparkle, twinkle **9** nictitate, vacillate

blinker(s) 3 eye **6** peeper **7** blinder, flasher, goggles **8** black eye **13** warning signal

blintz, blintze 4 blin **5** crepe **6** blints **7** pancake

blip 3 dot, tap **4** spot **5** bleep, image **6** censor **7** replace

bliss 3 joy **4** glee **6** heaven, luxury **7** delight, ecstasy, rapture **8** gladness, paradise **9** happiness **10** exaltation, jubilation **12** exhilaration

blissful 5 happy **6** divine, joyful, joyous **7** blessed, sublime **8** beatific, ecstatic, glorious, heavenly **9** rapturous

blithe 3 gay **4** airy, glad **5** blind, happy, jolly, merry, sunny **6** casual, cheery, jaunty, jovial, joyous, lively **7** gleeful, radiant **8** carefree, careless, cheerful, debonair, exaltant, heedless, mirthful, uncaring **9** ebullient, sprightly, unfeeling, unmindful **10** blithesome, frolicking **11** indifferent, insensitive, thoughtless, unconcerned, unconscious **12** lighthearted **13** inconsiderate

Blithedale Romance, The
author: 18 Nathaniel Hawthorne

blithesome 3 gay **5** light, merry, sunny **6** breezy, jaunty, lively **7** buoyant **8** animated, carefree, cheerful **11** free and easy

Blixen-Finecke, Karen
real name of: 11 Isak Dinesen

blizzard 4 blow, gale **5** blast **6** flurry, squall **7** tempest **8** snowfall **9** snowstorm **11** winter storm

Blizzard State
nickname of: 11 South Dakota

bloat 5 swell **6** blow up, dilate, expand, puff up **7** balloon, distend, enlarge, inflate

blob 4 daub, drop, mass **7** globule, splotch

bloc 4 body, ring, wing **5** cabal, group, union **6** clique **7** combine, faction **8** alliance **9** coalition **11** combination

Bloch, Ernest
born: 6 Geneva **11** Switzerland

composer of: 7 Macbeth, Solomon **8** Baal Shem, Schelomo **13** Sacred Service **14** Avodath Hakdesh, Israel Symphony **16** American Symphony **19** Concerto Symphonique **20** Voice in the Wilderness

block 3 bar, jam **4** cube, form, halt, mold **5** brick, check, choke, shape **6** hinder, impede, re-form, square, stop up, thwart **7** barrier, prevent, reshape **8** blockade, blockage, obstacle, obstruct **9** hindrance **10** impediment **11** obstruction **12** interference

blockade 3 bar, dam **4** dike **5** block, check, levee **6** hurdle **7** barrier, parapet, rampart **8** blockage, obstacle, obstruct, stockade, stoppage **9** barricade, hindrance, roadblock **10** checkpoint, earthworks, impediment **11** obstruction, restriction **13** fortification

blockage 3 jam **8** obstacle **9** hindrance **10** impediment **11** obstruction

blockhead 3 ass **4** clod, dolt, fool, yutz **5** booby, dummy, dunce, idiot, klutz, moron, ninny **6** dum-dum, nitwit **7** fathead, half-wit, jackass **8** bonehead, dumb-dumb, dumm kopf, imbecile, lunkhead, mushhead, numskull **9** harebrain, lamebrain, simpleton **10** chowerhead, dunderhead, nincompoop, noodlehead **12** featherbrain

block out 3 hew **5** carve **6** chisel, devise, map out, sculpt, sketch **7** outline **8** indicate **9** formulate

block up 3 bar **4** clog **6** stop up **7** brick up **9** barricade

blond, blonde 4 fair, gold, pale **5** light **6** flaxen, golden, yellow **8** light tan **9** yellowish **10** fair-haired **11** fair-skinned **12** light-colored

Blonde Bombshell
nickname of: **10** Jean Harlow

Blondell, Joan
husband: **8** Mike Todd **10** Dick Powell
born: **9** New York NY
roles: **8** The Champ **11** Blonde Crazy, Gold Diggers, The Blue Veil **14** Blondie Johnson, The Public Enemy **20** A Tree Grows in Brooklyn

Blondie
creator: **9** Chic Young

character:
husband: **15** Dagwood Bumstead
children: **6** Cookie **9** Alexander **12** Baby Dumpling
boss: **6** Julius **9** Mr Dithers
boss's wife: **4** Cora
neighbor: **11** Herb Woodley **14** Tootsie Woodley
dog: **5** Daisy

blood 4 gore **5** birth, stock **6** family, source, spirit, temper **7** descent, lineage, passion **8** ancestry, heritage, vitality **9** lifeblood **10** extraction, family line, vital fluid, vital force **11** temperament **13** consanguinity **14** vital principle

Blood, field of 8 Aceldama

Blood, Sweat and Tears
author: **17** Winston S Churchill

bloodless 4 pale **5** ashen **6** anemic, pallid **7** insipid **8** blanched, lifeless, peaceful **9** colorless, deathlike, washed out

bloodline 6 family **8** ancestry, pedigree **9** genealogy **10** family tree

Bloodline
author: **13** Sidney Sheldon

bloodshed 4 gore **6** murder, pogrom **7** carnage, killing, slaying **8** butchery, massacre **9** blood bath, blood feud, slaughter **10** mass murder **12** bloodletting, manslaughter **15** spilling of blood

Bloodsmoor Romance, A
author: **15** Joyce Carol Oates

bloodstone
month: **5** March

blood system
part: **5** blood, liver **6** spleen **9** lymph node **10** bone marrow

bloodthirsty 5 cruel **6** bloody, brutal, fierce, savage **7** bestial, demonic, inhuman, vicious **8** barbaric, demoniac, fiendish, pitiless, ruthless **9** atrocious, barbarous, cutthroat, heartless, homicidal, merciless, murdering, murderous **10** demoniacal, sanguinary **11** sanguineous

blood vessel 4 vein **5** aorta **6** artery **7** carotid **9** capillary
prefix: **5** angio

Blood Wedding
author: **19** Federico Garcia Lorca

bloody 3 red **4** gory, rude, vevy **5** cruel, lurid **6** cursed, damned **7** crimson, scarlet

8 bleeding **9** merciless, murderous **10** sanguinary

Bloody Shame *see* **10** Virgin Mary (drink)

bloom 3 bud **4** glow, grow, zest **5** flare, flush, prime, shine, vigor **6** beauty, flower, heyday, luster, sprout, thrive **7** blossom, burgeon, develop, prosper, succeed **8** fare well, flourish, fructify, radiance, rosiness, strength **9** bear fruit, flowerage, flowering, germinate **10** blossoming **11** florescence, flourishing

Bloom, Claire
real name: **11** Claire Blume
husband: **10** Rod Steiger
born: **6** London **7** England
roles: **6** Charly **9** Limelight **10** Richard III **15** Look Back in Anger **26** The Spy Who Came in from the Cold

Bloom, Leopold and Molly
characters in: **7** Ulysses
author: **5** Joyce

bloomers 8 knickers, trousers **9** plus fours, underwear **10** underpants **15** knickerbockers

blooming 3 fit **4** pert, rosy **5** utter **6** abloom, robust, strong **7** healthy **8** vigorous **9** healthful **10** blossoming **11** flourishing **12** efflorescent, fit as a fiddle **15** picture of health

blooper 4 goof, slip **5** boner, botch, error, fluff, gaffe, lapse **6** bobble, booboo, slip-up **7** blunder, mistake, screwup

blossom 4 grow **5** bloom **6** flower, thrive **7** burgeon, develop **8** flourish, progress

Blossomed miraculously
9 Aaron's rod

blossoming 5 bloom **8** blooming, thriving **9** flowering **10** burgeoning, developing **11** florescence, flourishing

blot 3 dry **4** flaw, mark, spot **5** smear, stain, taint **6** absorb, blotch, remove, smirch, smudge, soak up, stigma, take up **7** bad mark, blemish, splotch **8** besmirch **13** discoloration

blotch 4 blot, mark, spot **7** splotch

Blot on the 'Scutcheon, The
author: **14** Robert Browning

blot out 5 erase **6** remove, rub out **7** abolish, eclipse, expunge **9** eliminate, eradicate **10** obliterate

blotting out 7 eclipse, erasing **9** expunging, wiping out **11** eradicating, eradication **12** annihilation, obliterating, obliteration **13** overshadowing

blouse 4 coat **5** drape, tunic, shirt, smock **6** camise, billow **7** blouson **8** casaquin

blow 3 box, hit, jab, pop **4** bang, bash, belt, cuff, gale, gust, honk, jolt, play, puff, sock, toot, wind **5** blast, burst, clout, crack, knock, punch, shock, smack, sound, storm, thump, upset, whack **6** exhale, rebuff, squall, wallop **7** breathe, explode, tempest, tragedy, whistle **8** calamity, disaster, expel air, reversal **9** detriment, windstorm **10** affliction, misfortune **11** catastrophe **14** disappointment

blow from the hand
French: **10** coup de main

blowhard 6 gascon **7** boaster, bragger, egotist **8** braggart **9** big talker **11** braggadocio

blow of mercy
French: **11** coup de grace

blow out 5 burst **7** rupture **10** extinguish

blowsy, blowzy 5 messy **6** frowzy, mussed, sloppy, untidy **7** unkempt **10** disarrayed, disheveled, disordered, disorderly, in disorder **11** disarranged

blow up 5 bloat, burst **6** billow, dilate, expand **7** balloon, distend, enlarge, explode, inflate, puff out **8** dynamite, swell out **12** lose one's cool **14** lose one's temper

Blowup
director: **21** Michelangelo Antonioni
cast: **8** Verushka **10** Sarah Miles **13** David Hemmings **15** Vanessa Redgrave

blowy 5 gusty, windy **6** breezy **7** squally **8** blustery

blubber 3 cry, fat, sob **4** bawl, flab, wail, weep **6** boohoo

Blubber
author: **9** Judy Blume

bludgeon 3 bat, hit **4** club **5** billy, clout, stick **6** cudgel **7** clobber **9** billyclub, truncheon

blue 3 low, sad **4** aqua, down, navy **5** azure **6** bluish, cobalt, gloomy, indigo, morose **7** doleful **8** cerulean, dejected, downcast, sapphire **9** depressed, turquoise **10** aqua-

marine, despondent, melancholy **11** downhearted, lapis lazuli, ultra-marine **12** disconsolate **14** down in the dumps, down in the mouth

Blue Angel, The
director: **17** Josef von Sternberg
based on novel by: **12** Heinrich Mann
cast: **10** Kurt Gerron **12** Emil Jannings **15** Marlene Dietrich (Lola-Lola)
song: **18** Falling in Love Again

Bluebeard
characteristic: **9** many wives

bluebell 9 Mertensia **18** Mertensia Virginica **21** Campanula rotundifolia
variety: **7** English, Spanish **8** Virginia **10** Australian, California **11** Clanwilliam

blueberry 9 Vaccinium
variety: **3** Low **4** Male **5** Swamp **7** Lowbush, Sourtop, Western **8** Creeping, Elliott's, Highbush, Low sweet **9** Late sweet, Rabbiteye **10** Velvet-leaf **13** Black highbush

blueblood 4 peer **5** noble **8** nobleman **9** patrician, socialite **10** aristocrat, noblewoman **14** peer of the realm

blue-blooded 5 noble, regal, royal **6** titled **7** courtly **8** highbred, wellborn **9** patrician **10** upper-class **12** aristocratic, of royal blood

blue bloods 5 elite **8** nobility **9** haut monde **10** patricians **11** aristocracy, high society **14** creme de la creme

bluegrass 3 Poa
varieties: **3** Big **4** Wood **5** Rough, Texas **6** Annual, Canada **7** Bulbous, English **8** Kentucky, Sandberg **10** Rough-stalk

Bluegrass State
nickname of: **8** Kentucky

Blue Hen State
nickname of: **8** Delaware

Blue Knight, The
author: **14** Joseph Wambaugh

Blue Law State
nickname of: **11** Connecticut

blue-pencil 3 cut **4** edit, trim **6** censor, cut out, delete, digest, reduce **7** abridge, shorten **8** boil down, condense, pare down **9** expurgate **10** abbreviate

blueprint 4 plan **5** chart **6** design, scheme **7** diagram **9** schematic

Blue Riders
German: **11** Blaue Reiter
group of: **7** artists

blues 5 dumps **8** doldrums **10** depression, low spirits, melancholy **11** despondency

bluestocking
French: **7** bas bleu

bluff 3 lie **4** bank, bold, crag, curt, dupe, fake, fool, hoax, liar, open, peak, sham **5** blunt, boast, cliff, faker, frank, fraud, ridge, rough **6** abrupt, candid, crusty, delude, direct, humbug **7** bluffer, boaster, brusque, deceive, fake out, mislead, pretend **8** bragging, headland, headlong, palisade, pretense **9** bamboozle, deception, idle boast, outspoken, precipice, pretender **10** escarpment, forthright, promontory, subterfuge **11** braggadocio, counterfeit, plainspoken **13** unceremonious, straightforward

bluffer 5 bluff, faker, fraud, phony **6** humbug **9** pretender

bluish 7 off-blue **12** somewhat blue

Blume, Claire
real name of: **11** Claire Bloom

Blume, Judy
author of: **5** Wifey **6** Deenie **7** Blubber, Forever **19** Then Again Maybe I Won't **22** It's Not the End of the World **26** Tales of a Fourth Grade Nothing **27** Are You There God? It's Me Margaret

Blumenbach, Johann Friedrich
field: **7** anatomy **10** physiology
nationality: **6** German
father of: **20** physical anthropology

blunder 4 goof, slip **5** boner, error, gaffe **6** booboo, bumble, bungle, slip up **7** faux pas, mistake, stagger, stumble **8** flounder **9** gaucherie **11** impropriety, make a booboo **12** indiscretion

blunt 4 curt, dull, numb, open **5** frank, rough, thick **6** abrupt, benumb, candid, deaden, dulled, soften, weaken **7** brusque, lighten, stupefy **8** edgeless, explicit, mitigate, moderate, tactless **9** outspoken, unpointed **10** to the point

11 insensitive, unsharpened **15** straightforward

bluntness 6 candor **10** directness **14** forthrightness **15** plainspokenness

blur 3 dim, fog, run **4** blot, haze, veil **5** bedim, befog, cloud, smear **6** blotch, darken, smudge, spread **7** becloud, obscure, splotch **9** confusion, obscurity

blurb 2 ad **4** rave, spot **5** brief **10** commercial **13** advertisement

blurred 3 dim **5** vague **6** blurry **7** smeared **10** ill-defined, indefinite, indistinct

blurt out 4 blab, sing **7** confess, divulge, let slip **8** give away **9** come clean

blush 5 color, flush **6** redden **7** grow red, turn red **8** rosy tint **9** reddening

blushing 3 coy, red **4** rosy **5** fresh, timid **6** demure, modest **7** colored, bashful, flushed, glowing **8** blooming, sheepish **9** rosaceous **10** embarrassed **11** flourishing

bluster 4 brag, crow, rant **5** bluff, boast, bully, gloat, noise, storm **7** bombast, bravado, crowing, protest, ranting, swagger **8** boasting, gloating, threaten **9** noisy talk **10** swaggering **14** boisterousness

blustery 5 blowy, gusty, windy **6** breezy **7** squally

Blythe, Ethel Mae
    real name of: 14 Ethel Barrymore

Blythe, John
    real name of: 13 John Barrymore

Blythe, Lionel
    real name of: 15 Lionel Barrymore

Boadicea
    Latin name: 8 Boudicca
    queen of: 5 Iceni
    husband: 10 Prasutagus
    ruled: 7 Norfolk (England)
    fought: 6 Romans
    died: 7 suicide

Boanerges
    means: 13 sons of thunder
    name given to: 4 John **5** James

boar
    group of: 7 sounder

board 3 bed **4** deal, feed, food, slat **5** enter, get on, house, lodge, meals, panel, plank, put up **6** batten, billet, embark, go onto **7** council, quarter **8** tribunal **9** clapboard, directors **10** daily meals

board game 4 Clue, Life, ludo **5** chess **7** Othello **8** checkers, cribbage, dominoes, draughts, fanorona, Monopoly, Scrabble **9** Alquerque **10** backgammon **14** Trivial Pursuit **15** Chinese checkers
    Egyptian: 5 Senat
    Korean: 5 Nyout, Pa-tok
    Indian: 7 pachisi **8** parchesi, shatranj **9** ashtapada **10** shaturanga
    Japanese: 2 Go **3** I-go **5** Shogi
    Chinese: 6 Ma-jong, wei-ch'i **7** Ma-jongg
    Swedish: 6 tablut

boast 4 brag, crow, have **5** vaunt **6** flaunt **7** contain, exhibit, possess, show off, talk big **15** blow one's own horn

boaster 6 gascon **7** bragger, egotist **8** blowhard, braggart **9** big talker **11** braggadocio

boastful 5 cocky **7** crowing, pompous, swollen **8** bragging, cocksure, inflated, puffed up, vaunting **9** conceited **11** braggadocio, exaggerated, pretentious **12** vainglorious

boastfulness 7 conceit, egotism **8** bragging **9** cockiness, immodesty, pomposity, vainglory **10** self-praise **11** braggadocio **12** cocksureness

boastful soldier
    Latin: 14 miles gloriosus

boat 4 ship **5** craft **6** vessel

Boaz
    father: 5 Salma **6** Salmon
    wife: 4 Ruth
    son: 4 Obed
    kinsman of: 5 Naomi **9** Elimelech

bob 3 cut, hop, nod **4** clip, crop, dock, duck, leap, trim **5** dance, shear **6** bounce **7** shorten

Bobadill
    character in: 19 Every Man in His Humour
    author: 6 Jonson

bobbin 3 pin **4** coil, cord, reel **5** quill, spool **6** piping **7** ratchet, spindle, torchon **8** cylinder

bobcat 3 cat **4** lynx **7** wildcat

Bob Cummings Show, The
    later name: 11 Love That Bob
    character: 10 Bob Collins **14** Chuck MacD... **15** Charmaine (...

Shultz **17** Margaret MacDonald
    cast: 9 Ann B Davis **11** Bob Cummings **13** Dwayne Hickman **14** Rosemary DeCamp

Bob Newhart Show, The
    character: 12 Elliot Carlin, Emily Hartley, Howard Borden **13** Jerry Robinson, Robert (Bob) Hartley **20** Carol Kester Bondurant
    cast: 9 Bill Daily, Jack Riley **11** Peter Bonerz **13** Marcia Wallace **16** Suzanne Pleshette

Boccaccio, Giovanni
    author of: 10 Filostrato, Il Filocopo **11** Life of Dante **12** The Decameron

Boccherini, Luigi
    born: 5 Italy, Lucca
    composer of: 8 La Divina **9** The Aviary **10** Clementina **11** L'Uccelliera

Boccioni, Umberto
    born: 5 Italy **12** Reggio Emilia **16** Reggio di Calabria
    artwork: 10 Elasticity **12** The City Rises **15** Charge of Lancers **18** Dynamism of a Cyclist, The Forces of a Street **21** Fusion of Head and Window **30** Unique Forms of Continuity in Space

Bock, Hier
    field: 6 botany
    nationality: 6 German
    founded: 12 modern botany
    classified: 6 plants
    author of: 15 Neu Kreutterbuch

Bocklin, Arnold
    born: 5 Basel **7** Germany
    artwork: 13 Pan in the Reeds **16** The Isle of the Dead

Bod *see* **5** Tibet

bode 4 omen **5** augur **6** herald **7** betoken, ominate, point to, portend, predict, presage, signify **8** forecast, foretell, precurse **9** foreshadow, prefigure

bodega 9 warehouse **12** grocery store

bodice 3 top **5** stays, waist **6** bolero, corset, girdle **7** corsage **8** camisole, corselet **9** stomacher **10** underwaist

bodily 8 corporal, physical

Bodily Harm
    author: 14 Margaret Atwood

bodkin 3 awl **4** pick, tool **5** auger, borer, drill, point, probe **6** dagger, lancet, needle, ...ner **7** hair pin, piercer ...ncheon, stiletto

body 3 mob 4 bloc, bulk, form, mass 5 being, build, force, frame, group, shape, stiff, thing, torso, trunk 6 corpse, figure, league, person, throng 7 cadaver, carcass, combine, council, faction, remains, society 8 assembly, cohesion, congress, deceased, main part, majority, physique, quantity 9 coalition, multitude, stiffness, thickness 10 federation 11 brotherhood, consistency 13 confederation

Body and Soul
director: 12 Robert Rossen
cast: 10 Anne Revere 11 Hazel Brooks, Lilli Palmer 12 John Garfield 13 William Conrad

bodybuilder 12 Charles Atlas 20 Arnold Schwarzenegger

Boedromius
epithet of: 6 Apollo
means: 7 rescuer

Boeotus
father: 8 Poseidon
mother: 4 Arne

Boer, Boor 6 farmer 9 Afrikaner
language: 9 Afrikaans
ancestry: 5 Dutch
inhabitants of: 9 Transvaal 11 South Africa 15 Orange Free State

Boethius, Anicius Manlius Severinus
also called: 5 Boece
author of: 23 Consolation of Philosophy

Boffin
character in: 15 Our Mutual Friend
author: 7 Dickens

bog 3 fen 4 mire, sink 5 marsh, swamp 6 morass 7 be stuck 8 quagmire, wetlands 9 marshland, swampland

Bogaerde, Derek Van den
real name of: 11 Dirk Bogarde

Bogarde, Dirk
real name: 19 Derek Van den Bogaerde
born: 6 London 7 England 9 Hempstead
roles: 6 Victim 7 Darling 10 The Servant 13 Death in Venice 14 Song Without End, The Night Porter 16 A Tale of Two Cities

Bogart, Humphrey
nickname: 5 Bogie
wife: 12 Lauren Bacall
born: 9 New York NY
roles: 8 Key Largo 10 Casablanca, High Sierra 11 The Big Sleep 14 The Caine Mu-

tiny 15 The African Queen (Oscar) 16 The Maltese Falcon, To Have and Have Not 18 The Petrified Forest 27 The Treasure of the Sierra Madre

Bogdanovich, Peter
director of: 4 Mask 9 Paper Moon 18 The Last Picture Show

boggle 3 shy 4 balk, muff 5 botch, demure, hover, waver 6 bungle, shrink, wobble 7 blunder, stumble 8 flounder, frighten, hesitate, hold back 9 overwhelm 11 make a mess of

boggy 3 wet 4 soft 5 foggy, mossy, soggy 6 marshy, spongy, swampy 7 squashy

Bogie
nickname of: 14 Humphrey Bogart

Bogota
capital of: 8 Colombia

bogus 4 fake, sham 5 dummy, false, phony 6 ersatz, forged, pseudo 7 feigned, pretend 8 spurious 9 imitation, simulated, synthetic 10 artificial, fraudulent 11 counterfeit, make-believe

Boheme, La
also: 12 Bohemian Life
opera by: 7 Puccini
character: 4 Mimi 7 Colline, Musetta, Rodolfo 8 Marcello 9 Schaunard

bohemian, Bohemian 6 hippie 7 beatnik 10 unorthodox 13 nonconformist 14 unconventional

Bohr, Niels
field: 7 physics
nationality: 6 Danish
developed: 8 atom bomb 13 quantum theory, uranium theory

Boiardo, Matteo Maria
author of: 17 Orlando Innamorato

boil 4 brew, burn, foam, fume, rage, rant, rave, sore, stew, toss 5 chafe, churn, froth, storm 6 bubble, fester, quiver, seethe, simmer, sizzle, well up 7 abscess, bristle, parboil, pustule, smolder 8 furuncle 9 carbuncle, fulminate

boil down 3 cut 6 reduce 7 abridge, cut down, shorten 8 condense, contract 10 abbreviate

boiler 6 copper, geyser, heater, kettle 7 alembic, caldron, furnace

Boilermaker, the
nickname of: 20 James Jackson Jeffries

boisterous 4 loud, wild 5 noisy, rowdy 6 unruly 9 clamorous, out-of-hand 10 disorderly, uproarious 12 obstreperous, uncontrolled, unrestrained

boite, boite de nuit 7 cabaret 9 nightclub

Bojer, Johan
author of: 12 Folk by the Sea, The Emigrants 14 The Great Hunger, The Power of a Lie 16 Last of the Vikings

bold 3 hot 4 loud, rude 5 brash, brave, fiery, fresh, saucy, vivid 6 brazen, cheeky, daring, flashy, heroic 7 defiant, forward, valiant 8 colorful, creative, fearless, impudent, insolent, intrepid, spirited, stalwart, striking, unafraid, valorous 9 audacious, daredevil, dauntless 10 courageous 11 eye-catching, imaginative, impertinent, indomitable, lionhearted, unshrinking 12 stouthearted 13 adventuresome

boldfaced 5 brash, saucy 6 brassy, brazen 7 forward 8 immodest, impudent, insolent 9 audacious, barefaced, shameless, unabashed

boldness 4 grit 5 nerve, pluck, spunk 6 daring, mettle 7 bravery, courage 8 audacity 9 brashness, hardihood 10 brazenness 13 audaciousness, determination, self-assurance 14 courageousness 15 adventurousness

Bolger, Ray
born: 12 Dorchester MA
roles: 9 Scarecrow 10 On Your Toes 13 The Wizard of Oz, Where's Charley

Bolivia *see box, p. 118.*

Bolkonsky, Andrei
character in: 11 War and Peace
author: 7 Tolstoy

Boll, Heinrich
author of: 8 The Clown 12 The Safety Net 18 Absent Without Leave 21 Group Portrait With Lady 27 The Lost Honor of Katharina Blum 28 Missing Persons and Other Essays

bolster 3 aid 4 help 5 add to, brace 6 assist, cradle, hold up, pillow, prop up, uphold 7 cushion, shore up, support, sustain 8 buttress, maintain,

Bolivia
named for: **12** Simon Bolivar
capital:
   administrative: **5** La Paz
   legal: **5** Sucre

largest city: **5** La Paz

others: **3** Ivo **4** Icla, Itau, Mojo, Saya, Yaco, Yato, Yura **5** Cliza, Llica, Oruro, Quime, Uyuni, Zongo **6** Guaqui, Potosi, Tiraja, Tupiza **8** Pulacayo **9** Santa Cruz **10** Chuquisaca, Cochabamba **11** Vallegrande, Villa Montes

school: **6** Xavier **8** St Andrew **12** San Francisco

division: **6** Valles **7** Oriente, Valleys **8** Montanas **9** Altiplano

measure: **6** league **7** celemin

monetary unit: **7** centavo **13** peso boliviano

weight: **5** libra, marco

lake: **5** Poopo **7** Allagas, Coipasa, Rogagua **8** Titicaca **10** Desaguader

mountain: **4** Jara **5** Andes, Cusco, Cuzco **6** Pupuya, Sajama, Sorata, Sunsas **7** Illampu **8** Illimani, Mururata, Sansimon, Santiago, Zapaleri **12** Eastern Range, Western Range **18** Cordillera Oriental **20** Cordillera Occidental

highest point: **8** Ancohuma

river: **4** Beni, Yata **5** Abuna, Lauca, Orton **6** Blanco, Ichilo, Itenez, Madidi, Mamore, Mizque, Yacuma **7** Guapore, Machupo **8** Inambari, Itonamas **9** Pilcomayo, Rio Grande, San Miguel **11** Desaguadero, Madre de Dios

physical features:
   lowlands: **6** Llanos
   plateau: **9** Altiplano
   swamp: **6** Izozog
   valley: **5** Yunga
   volcano: **7** Ollague

people: **6** Aymara **7** mestizo, Quechua
   author: **7** Mendoza **8** Arguedas **11** Costa du Rels
   leader: **5** Busch, Sucre **6** Candia, Ortuno, Zamora **7** Bolivar **9** Melgarejo, Paz Zamora, Santa Cruz **10** Barrientos, Estenssoro

language: **6** Aymara **7** Quechua, Spanish

religion: **13** Roman Catholic

place:
   church: **9** St Francis, St Michael **10** San Lorenzo
   monument: **11** La Coronilla
   ruins: **10** Tiahuanaco
   tower: **6** Chulpa

feature:
   animal: **5** llama **6** alpaca, vicuna
   bar/club: **7** boliche
   boat: **5** balsa
   dance/song: **5** cueca **7** huainos, pasillo **8** morenada **9** taquirari **10** palla-palla **11** cacharpayas, waka-tokonis
   devil dance: **8** Diablado
   guitar: **8** charango
   skirt: **7** pollera
   wind instrument: **4** kena, sicu **5** erque, quena, tarka **6** pututu **9** pinquillo

food:
   chicken dish: **14** picante de pollo
   corn: **4** mote
   corn drink: **3** api **14** chicha taratena
   dish: **11** plato paceno **14** sajta de gallina
   dried meat: **7** charque
   pancakes: **7** bunulos
   potato: **5** chuno

shoulder **9** reinforce **10** strengthen

bolster one's spirits 5 cheer **7** cheer up, comfort, hearten **8** inspirit **9** buoy one up, encourage

bolt 3 bar, fly, peg, pin, rod, run **4** dart, dash, flee, gulp, jump, leap, lock, roll, rush, tear, wolf **5** bound, brand, catch, dowel, flash, hurry, latch, rivet, scoot, shaft, speed **6** fasten, gobble, hasten, hurtle, length, secure, spring, sprint, stroke **8** fastener **12** swallow whole

bolt down 4 wolf **5** scarf **6** devour, gobble **8** gulp down

bomb 3 dud, egg **4** bust, fail, flop, mine **5** lemon **6** fiasco, fizzle **7** bombard, grenade, failure, washout

bombard 5 beset, hound, shell, worry **6** assail, attack, batter, harass, pepper, pester, strafe **7** assault, barrage, besiege **8** fire upon **9** cannonade

bombardment 5 blitz, siege **7** air raid, assault, barrage, bombing **10** blitzkrieg

bombast 3 pad **4** puff, rant **6** cotton **7** bluster, fustian, palaver **8** boasting, flummery, rhapsody, tall talk, verbiage **9** bavardage **10** balderdash **12** braggadocio, exaggeration **13** magniloquence, overstatement **14** grandiloquence **17** sesquipedalianism

bombastic 5 tumid, windy, wordy **6** padded, turgid **7** pompous, verbose **8** inflated **12** magniloquent **13** grandiloquent

Bombay
area: **7** Trombay **8** Salsette **12** Bombay Island
called: **14** Gateway to India
creek: **7** Bassein
landmark: **9** High Court **13** Taj Mahal Hotel **14** Gateway of India **16** Victoria Terminus **17** Rajabai Clock Tower
rock formation: **10** Deccan Trap
sea: **7** Arabian

Bona Dea
also: **5** Fauna
origin: **5** Roman
goddess of: **8** chastity **9** fertility
worshipped by: **5** women
father: **6** Faunus
brother: **6** Faunus
husband: **6** Faunus

bona fide 4 real, true **5** legal **6** actual, honest, lawful **7** genuine, sincere **9** authentic, honorable **10** legitimate **11** in good faith

bon ami 5 lover **10** good friend

bonanza 8 gold mine, windfall

Bonanza
character: **3** Ben **4** Adam, Hoss **5** Candy **7** Hop Sing **9** Little Joe
family: **10** Cartwright
cast: **10** Dan Blocker **11** David Canary, Lorne Greene **13** Michael Landon, Victor Sen Yung **14** Pernell Roberts
ranch: **9** Ponderosa

Bonanza State
nickname of: **7** Montana

bon appetit 14 hearty appetite

Bonario
character in: **7** Volpone
author: **6** Jonson

bonbon 5 candy, sweet **7** fondant **9** sweetmeat **10** confection, sugar candy **13** confectionery **14** chocolate cream

bond, bonds 3 tie **4** cord, knot, link, rope **5** irons, scrip, union **6** chains, pledge **7** compact, fetters, promise **8** affinity, bindings, manacles, security, shackles **9** agreement, guarantee, handcuffs **10** allegiance, attachment, connection, fastenings, obligation **11** certificate, stipulation

Bond, James
actor: **10** Roger Moore **11** Sean Connery **12** Peter Sellers **13** George Lazenby, Timothy Dalton
appears in: **4** Dr No **9** Moonraker, Octopussy **10** Goldfinger **11** Thunderball **12** A View To A Kill **13** Live and Let Die **15** For Your Eyes Only **16** The Spy Who Loved Me, You Only Live Twice **18** Diamonds Are Forever, From Russia with Love, Never Say Never Again, The Living Daylights **22** The Man with the Golden Gun **26** On Her Majesty's Secret Service
author: **10** Ian Fleming
drink: **12** vodka martini **16** shaken not stirred
employer: **3** MI-6 **20** British Secret Service
foe: **7** Blofeld, SPECTRE
office staff: **1** M, Q **14** Miss Moneypenny
university: **6** Oxford
wife: **5** Tracy

bondage 4 yoke **6** chains **7** fetters, serfdom, slavery

8 shackles **9** captivity, servitude, vassalage **11** enslavement

bone
comprise: **8** skeleton
contain: **6** marrow **9** cartilage **11** blood vessel
fitted together by: **5** joint
held by: **8** ligament
pulled by: **6** muscle
specific: **3** rib **4** ulna **5** femur, skull, tibia **6** carpal, fibula, pelvis, radius, sacrum, tarsal **7** humerus, patella, scapula, sternum **8** clavicle, vertebra **9** vertebrae

bone chilling 3 icy **4** cold **5** harsh, sharp **6** arctic, biting, bitter, frigid **7** cutting, glacial **8** piercing, stinging **11** penetrating **15** teeth-chattering

bonehead 3 ass **4** clod, dolt, fool **5** booby, dunce, idiot, moron, ninny **6** dimwit, nitwit **7** fathead, half-wit **8** dumb-dumb, imbecile, lunkhead **9** blockhead, lamebrain, numbskull **10** dunderhead, nincompoop **11** chowderhead

boner 4 goof, slip **5** error **6** boo-boo, slip-up **7** blooper, blunder, mistake

boneyard 4 dump **7** ossuary **8** Boot Hill, cemetery, junkyard **9** graveyard **10** churchyard **12** burial ground **13** burying ground

Bonheur, Rosa
real name: **19** Marie Rosalie Bonheur
born: **6** France **8** Bordeaux
artwork: **12** The Horse Fair **23** Ploughing in the Nivernais

bonjour 5 hello **7** good day

Bonjour Tristesse
author: **14** Francoise Sagan

bon marche 7 bargain

bon mot 4 quip **7** epigram **9** witticism

Bonn
capital of: **11** West Germany
landmark: **10** Bundeshaus **11** Munsterkerk
museum: **18** Ludwig van Beethoven
river: **5** Rhine
Roman fort: **15** Castra Bonnensia

Bonnard, Pierre
born: **6** France **16** Fontenay-aux-Roses
artwork: **8** Intimist, Luncheon **9** The Review **13** Nude in the Bath, The Open Window, Women with a Dog **14** After the Shower, Farm at Le Cannet **16** The

Breakfast Room **17** The Terrasse Family **22** Figure Before a Fireplace

bonne amie 5 lover **6** friend **10** good friend

bonne nuit 9 good night

bonnet 3 cap, hat **4** cowl, hood, sail **5** cover, toque **7** chapeau, commode **8** headgear **9** headdress

Bonnie and Clyde
director: **10** Arthur Penn
cast: **11** Faye Dunaway (Bonnie Parker), Gene Hackman **12** Warren Beatty (Clyde Barrow) **15** Michael J Pollard

bonny 4 fair **6** comely, lovely, pretty, seemly **7** winning, winsome **8** engaging, fetching, handsome, pleasing **9** beautiful, exquisite, ravishing **10** attractive

bon soir 9 good night **11** good evening

bonus 4 gift **5** prize **6** bounty, reward **7** benefit, premium **8** dividend, gratuity **10** honorarium

Bonus Eventus
also: **7** Eventus
origin: **5** Roman
god of: **4** luck **10** prosperity **11** agriculture

bon vivant 7 epicure, gourmet **8** gourmand, sybarite **10** gastronome

bony 4 lean **5** gaunt, lanky, spare **6** skinny **7** angular, scrawny **11** full of bones **12** skin-and-bones

boo 3 pan **4** hiss **5** taunt **6** deride, heckle, revile **7** catcall **8** ridicule **9** criticize, shout down **11** give the bird **16** give the raspberry

boo-boo 4 goof, slip **5** boner, error **6** slip-up **7** blunder, mistake

boobtube 2 TV **3** box **8** idiot box **13** television set

booby 4 bird, dope, fool **5** dummy, dunce, idiot, moron, ninny **6** dimwit, gannet, nitwit **7** fathead, halfwit **8** bonehead, dumb-dumb, imbecile, lunkhead, numskull **9** blockhead, lamebrain, simpleton **10** nincompoop **11** chowderhead

Booby, Lady
character in: **13** Joseph Andrews
author: **8** Fielding

boodle 4 loot, swag **5** booty, bribe, crowd, graft, group

7 plunder **10** collection
11 stolen goods

Boog
nickname of: **10** John Powell

boohoo 3 cry, sob **4** bawl,
weep **7** blubber **9** shed tears

book 4 bill, file, list, note,
opus, post, tome **5** album, enter, index, slate **6** accuse,
charge, engage, enroll, indict,
insert, line up, record, tablet,
volume **7** catalog, procure,
program, put down, reserve
8 mark down, notebook, register, schedule, treatise **9** bound
work, write down **10** arrange
for **11** publication, written
work **16** make reservations

bookish 7 erudite, learned,
stilted **8** academic, educated,
informed, literary, pedantic,
studious, well-read **9** scholarly
11 pedagogical, impractical
12 intellectual

bookkeeper 5 clerk **7** auditor
10 accountant **11** comptroller

booklet 5 folio **7** leaflet, program **8** brochure, circular,
pamphlet

Book of Common Prayer
author: **10** Joan Didion

Book of Lights, The
author: **10** Chaim Potok

Book of Manuel
author: **13** Julio Cortazar

Book of Odes
author: **9** Confucius

Book of psalms 12 psalter

Book of Sand, The
author: **15** Jorge Luis Borges

Book of the Duchess, The
author: **15** Geoffrey Chaucer

boom 3 bar **4** bang, beam,
gain, grow, push, roar, spar
5 blast, boost, shaft, spurt
6 growth, rumble, thrive,
thrust, upturn **7** advance, develop, prosper, thunder, upsurge **8** flourish, increase
9 expansion, good times

Boom Boom
nickname of: **15** Bernie
Geoffrion

boomerang 5 kalie, kiley, ky-
lie, wango **6** atlatl, recoil
7 rebound, womerah, woom-
era **8** backfire, ricochet, trom-
bush **9** bound back, solitaire
10 projectile

Boomer State
nickname of: **8** Oklahoma

boon 3 fun, gay **4** gift **5** favor,
jolly, merry **6** kindly **7** benefit,
bequest **8** blessing, donation,

offering, pleasant **9** advantage,
congenial, convivial, endowment **11** full of cheer, good-
natured

boon companion 3 pal
4 chum **5** buddy, crony
6 friend **7** comrade **8** confrere,
intimate **9** confidant **10** bosom
buddy

boondocks 4 bush, veld **6** Podunk, sticks **7** boonies, country, outback **8** frontier
9 backwater, backwoods, provinces **10** hinterland **11** back-
country, countryside
12 squaresville **13** nowheres-
ville **14** wide open spaces

Boone, Richard
born: **12** Los Angeles CA
roles: **5** Medic **6** Hombre
7 Paladin **8** The Alamo
11 The Shootist **12** Ten
Wanted Men, The Desert
Fox **17** Have Gun Will
Travel

boonies 6 sticks **7** country
9 backwoods, boondocks, provinces **10** hinterland
11 countryside

boor 3 oaf **4** hick, lout, rube
5 brute, churl, yokel **6** rustic
7 bumpkin, hayseed, peasant
9 vulgarian **10** clodhopper,
philistine **11** guttersnipe

boorish 4 rude **5** crude
6 coarse, gauche, oafish, rustic, vulgar **7** loutish, uncouth
9 unrefined **10** unpolished
11 peasantlike

boorishness 8 rudeness **9** surliness, vulgarity **10** bad manners, coarseness, incivility,
oafishness **12** churlishness,
impoliteness

boost 4 hike, laud, lift, plug,
push, rise **5** add to, extol,
heave, hoist, pitch, raise,
shove **6** expand, foster, free
ad, growth, pickup, praise, upturn, urge on **7** acclaim, advance, develop, elevate,
enlarge, forward, further, improve, nurture, promote, root
for, support, sustain, upsurge,
upswing **8** addition, applause,
good word, increase, pro-
pound **9** expansion, increment,
promotion **10** compliment,
give a leg up, stick up for
11 development, enlargement,
improvement, speak well of

boot
French: **9** chaussure

booth 3 pen **4** coop, nook,
tent **5** hutch, stall, stand, table **7** counter **9** cubbyhole, enclosure **11** compartment

Booth, Shirley
real name: **15** Thelma Booth
Ford
born: **9** New York NY
roles: **5** Hazel **13** The Matchmaker **19** Come Back Little
Sheba (Oscar)

bootleg 5 hooch **7** illegal, illicit **8** unlawful **9** moonshine
12 football play

bootless 6 futile **7** useless
11 ineffective, ineffectual
12 unproductive, unprofitable

bootlick 4 fawn **5** toady
6 cringe, grovel **7** flatter,
truckle

bootmaker 7 cobbler
9 shoemaker

booty 4 gain, loot **5** prize
6 boodle, spoils **7** pillage,
plunder, takings **8** pickings,
winnings

booze 4 bout, soak **5** drink,
hooch, spree **6** guzzle, liquor,
tipple **7** alcohol, spirits, swizzle **8** cocktail **10** intoxicant
14 drink like a fish
type: **3** gin, rum, rye **4** beer,
wine **5** vodka **6** scotch
7 bourbon, whiskey

boozer 3 sot **4** lush **5** drunk,
souse, toper **7** tippler **8** drunkard **9** alcoholic, inebriate
11 hard drinker

bordello, bordel 4 stew
5 house **6** bagnio **7** brothel
8 cathouse **10** bawdy house,
fancy house, whorehouse
13 sporting house **14** house of
ill fame **16** house of ill repute **19** house of prostitution

border 3 hem, rim **4** abut,
bind, brim, curb, edge, join,
line, pale, trim **5** brink, flank,
frame, limit, skirt, touch,
verge **6** adjoin, fringe, margin
8 befringe, be next to, boundary, frontier, outskirt **9** extremity, perimeter, periphery
13 circumference

borderline 4 open **5** vague
7 halfway, inexact, obscure,
unclear **8** marginal **9** ambiguous, equivocal, uncertain, undecided, unsettled
10 ambivalent, indefinite
11 indefinable, problematic
13 indeterminate

bore 4 drag, drip, sink, tire
5 drill, drive, weary **6** burrow,
pierce, tunnel **7** caliber, exhaust, fatigue, wear out
8 gouge out **9** hollow out
10 wet blanket **14** inside
diameter

Boreadae
decendants of: **6** Boreas

Boreal
pertaining to: **6** Boreas

Boreas
origin: **5** Greek
personifies: **9** north wind
father: **8** Astraeus
mother: **3** Eos
twin sons: **5** Zetes **6** Calais
daughter: **6** Chione
9 Cleopatra

bored 5 jaded **7** wearied
12 discontented, uninterested

boredom 6 tedium **8** doldrums,
dullness, monotony **9** weariness **11** tediousness
French: **5** ennui

Borges, Jorge Luis
author of: **8** The Aleph
10 Labyrinths **11** Dreamtigers **13** The Book of Sand
18 A Personal Anthology, In
Praise of Darkness **19** Doctor Brodie's Report, Fervor
of Buenos Aires **25** A Universal History of Infamy

Borghild
origin: **12** Scandinavian
mentioned in: **8** Volsunga
husband: **7** Sigmund

Borgia, Alfonso de 16 Pope
Callistus III

Borgia, Rodrigo de 15 Pope
Alexander VI

Borglum, (John) Gutzon
born: **10** Bear Lake ID
artwork: **7** Lincoln **18** Mt
Rushmore Memorial, The
Mares of Diomedes

Borgnine, Ernest
real name: **18** Ermes Effron
Borgnine
wife: **11** Ethel Merman
born: **8** Hamden CT
roles: **5** Marty (Oscar) **8** Barabbas **11** McHale's Navy
12 The Wild Bunch **13** The
Dirty Dozen **17** Bad Day at
Black Rock **18** From Here
to Eternity **20** The Poseidon
Adventure

boring 4 dull, flat **5** stale **6** tiring **7** humdrum, insipid, tedious **8** tiresome **9** wearisome
10 monotonous, unexciting
11 repetitious **13** uninteresting

boring tool 3 bit **5** auger,
drill **11** brace and bit

Borinquen see **10** Puerto Rico

Boriquen, Borinquen
language family: **8** Arawakan
location: **10** Puerto Rico
related to: **5** Taino

Boris Godunov
author: **16** Alexander Pushkin
opera by: **10** Mussorgsky

12 Shostakovich **14** Rimsky-Korsakov
character: **6** Dmitri, Feodor,
Maryna **7** Gregory, Grigory
8 Basmanov, Otrepyev

born 6 innate **7** natural **9** delivered, intuitive **12** brought
forth

Born, Max
field: **7** physics
nationality: **7** British
worked on: **13** quantum
theory
awarded: **10** Nobel Prize

borne 6 afloat, braved **7** carried, endured **9** put up with,
tolerated **11** gone through,
went through **12** given birth
to

Borneo see **box**

Born Yesterday
director: **11** George Cukor
cast: **12** Judy Holliday
13 William Holden **17** Broderick Crawford
Oscar for: **7** actress (Holliday)

Borodin, Alexander
born: **6** Russia **12** St
Petersburg
member of: **7** The Five
composer of: **8** Bogatyri
10 Prince Igor **25** In the
Steppes of Central Asia

boron
chemical symbol: **1** B

borough 4 burg, town **5** borgo,
shire **6** county, parish **7** village **8** district, precinct, province, township **12** municipality
of New York City: **5** Bronx
6 Queens **8** Brooklyn
9 Manhattan **12** Staten
Island

Borromini, Francesco
architect of: **10** San Carlino
17 Palazzo Falconieri
20 Sant' Ivo della Sapienza
23 Oratory of San Filippo
Neri **24** Collegio di Propaganda Fide **26** San Carlo
alle Quattro Fontane (Rome)

borrow 3 get, use **4** copy,
take **5** filch, steal, usurp **6** obtain, pilfer, pirate **7** acquire
10 commandeer, plagiarize,
take on loan **11** appropriate

Borrow, George Henry
author of: **8** Lavengro **9** Romany Rye, Wild Wales
10 The Zincali **15** The Bible
in Spain

Bors
character in: **16** Arthurian
romance

Bosch, Hieronymus
real name: **13** Jerome van

Borneo
other name: **10** Kalimantan
largest city: **12** Bandjermasin
others: **5** Kumai **6** Sambas, Sampit **7** Malinau, Pagatan,
Sanggau, Sintang, Tarakan **8** Ketapang **9** Pontianak
10 Balikpapan
division of island:
independent: **6** Brunei
Malaysian state: **5** Sabah **7** Sarawak
part of Indonesia: **10** Kalimantan
measure: **7** gantang
weight: **4** para **6** chapah
mountain: **4** Iran, Raja, Raja **5** Saran **6** Kapuas, Muller, Nijaan,
Tebang **8** Kinibalu, Schwaner
highest point: **8** Kinabalu
river: **4** Arut, Iwan **5** Bahau, Berau, Kajan, Padas, Pawan
6 Barito, Kapuas, Rajang, Sebuku **7** Kahajan, Mahakam,
Mendawi **8** Pembuang
sea: **4** Java, Sulu **7** Celebes **10** South China
physical feature:
bay: **5** Adang, Kumai **6** Sampit
cape: **3** Aru **4** Datu **5** Lojar **6** Puting, Sambar **7** Selatan
port: **4** Miri **5** Balik, Papan **6** Brunei **9** Pontianak
12 Bandjermasin
strait: **8** Macassar
people: **4** Iban **5** Bukat, Dajak, Dayak, Dusan, Malay,
Punan **6** Illano **7** Bakatan, Chinese, Illanum
language: **5** Malay **6** tribal **7** Chinese, English
religion: **5** Islam **7** animism **12** Christianity
feature:
tree: **5** kapor, kapur **7** billian

Aeken **17** Jeroen Anthoiszoon
artwork: 7 Hay-Wain **11** Ship of Fools **14** The Crucifixion **19** Adoration of the Kings **21** The Crowning with Thorns **26** The Garden of Earthly Delights

bosh 3 rot **4** bunk **6** bunkum, drivel **7** twaddle **8** claptrap, nonsense, tommyrot **10** balderdash, tomfoolery **11** foolishness **16** stuff and nonsense

bosky 5 bushy, drunk, shaded, tipsy, treed **6** wooded

Bosnia-Herzegovina
capital/largest city: 8 Sarajevo
others: 4 Neum **5** Tuzlal **6** Citluk, Kupres, Lenica, Mostar **8** Prijedor **9** Banja Luka, Bijeljina **10** Srebrenica **12** Bosanski Brod, Siroki Brijeg
head of state: 9 president
monetary unit: 5 dinar
mountain: 11 Dinaric Alps
river: 3 Una **4** Sava **5** Bosna, Drina, Vrbas **7** Neretva
sea: 8 Adriatic
people: 4 Serb **5** Croat **6** Muslim **8** Yugoslav
language: 13 Serbo Croatian
religion: 11 Sunni Muslim **15** Serbian Orthodox

bosom 4 bust, core, dear, soul **5** chest, close, heart, midst **6** breast, center, spirit **7** beloved, nucleus **8** intimate **9** cherished **11** inner circle

bosom buddy 4 chum **5** crony **6** cohort **7** best pal, comrade **8** alter ego, intimate, sidekick **9** companion, confidant **10** best friend

bosomy 5 busty, buxom **6** zaftig **11** full-figured **13** large-breasted

boss 4 head, push **5** chief, order **6** leader, master **7** command, foreman, kingpin, manager **8** employer **9** big cheese, executive **10** supervisor **13** administrator **14** superintendent

bossy 3 cow **9** imperious **10** commanding, tyrannical **11** dictatorial, domineering

Boston
airport: 5 Logan
area: 7 Back Bay **10** Bunker Hill, Fenway Park **11** Faneuil Hall **14** Kennedy Library, Old North Church
baseball team: 6 Red Sox
basketball team: 7 Celtics
dish: 10 baked beans
hockey team: 6 Bruins
landmark: 10 Beacon Hill
leader: 7 Brahmin
nickname: 8 Bean town
river: 7 Charles

Bostonians, The
author: 10 Henry James

Boston Strong Boy
nickname of: 13 John L Sullivan

Boswell, James
author of: 22 The Life of Samuel Johnson

botanist
American: 6 Barton, Torrey **7** Bartram
Austrian: 6 Mendel
Dutch: 7 DeVries
German: 4 Bock, Cohn
Scottish: 5 Brown
Swedish: 8 Linnaeus
Swiss: 6 Bauhin

botch 3 err, mar **4** blow, fail, flop, flub, goof, hash, mess, muff, ruin **5** spoil **6** bungle, foul up, fumble **7** blunder, butcher, failure, louse up **8** butchery **9** mismanage **11** make a mess of

bother 3 ado, irk, nag, tax, try, vex **4** care, drag, fret, fuss, load, onus, stir **5** annoy, harry, trial, upset, worry **6** dismay, flurry, harass, pester, racket, rumpus, strain, stress, tumult **7** attempt, disturb, problem, trouble **8** disquiet, distress, hardship, headache, irritate, nuisance, vexation **9** aggravate, commotion, hindrance **10** affliction, difficulty, impediment, irritation **11** aggravation, disturbance, encumbrance **12** make an effort **13** inconvenience, pain in the neck **14** responsibility

bothersome 6 taxing, vexing **8** annoying **9** worrisome **10** disturbing **11** aggravating, disquieting, distressing, troublesome **12** inconvenient

Botswana *see box*

Botticelli, Sandro
real name: 30 Alessandro di Mariano dei Filipepi
born: 5 Italy **8** Florence
artwork: 12 Birth of Venus **14** Mystic Nativity **16** Calumny of Apelles **18** Adoration of the Magi **22** Pallas Subduing a Centaur **25** The Madonna of the Magnificat

bottle 3 jar **4** vial **5** flask, phial **6** carafe, flagon, vessel **7** canteen

bottleneck 3 bar, jam **4** clog, stop **5** block **6** detour **7** barrier, embolus **8** blockage, embolism, gridlock, obstacle, stoppage, thrombus **10** congestion, impediment, infarction **11** costiveness, obstruction

Botswana
other name: 12 Bechuanaland
capital/largest city: 8 Gaborone **9** Gaberones
others: 5 Kanye, Orapa, Tsane **6** Serowe **7** Lobatse, Lobotsi, Mochudi, Palapye, Thamaga **10** Molepolole **11** Francistown, Selebi-Pikwe
monetary unit: 4 pula, rand
lake: 3 Dow, Xau **5** Ngami
highest point: 11 Tsodilo Hill
river: 4 Nata, Okwa **5** Chobe, Nosob **6** Cuando, Molopo, Shashi **7** Cubango, Limpopo **8** Botletle, Okovango **9** Okovanggo
physical feature:
  desert: 8 Kalahari
  salt pans: 10 Makarikari
  swamp: 8 Okavango
people: 5 Bantu **6** Tswana **7** Bakatla, Bakwena, Bushman **8** Bamalete, Baralong, Batawana, Batlokwa, Botswana **10** Bamangwato **11** Bangwaketse
language: 5 Bantu, Click **6** Tswana **7** English, Khoisan **8** Setswana
religion: 7 animism **10** Protestant **12** Christianity

bottom 3 can **4** base, core, foot, gist, root, rump, seat, sole **5** basis, belly, cause, fanny, heart, lower **6** center, deeper, depths, ground, lowest, origin, source, spring **7** deepest, essence **8** backside, buttocks, pedestal, riverbed **9** beginning, fundament, principle, rudiments, substance, underpart, underside **10** foundation, mainspring, wellspring **12** quintessence

Bottom
character in: 21 A Midsummer Night's Dream
author: 11 Shakespeare

bottomless 4 deep **7** abysmal **8** profound **11** measureless **12** immeasurable, unfathomable

Boucher, Francois
born: 5 Paris **6** France
artwork: 9 The Rising

13 Madame Boucher, Reclining Girl **16** Evening Landscape, Rinaldo and Armida, The Toilet of Venus **17** Chinese Tapestries, The Triumph of Venus **18** The Setting of the Sun

boudoir 7 bedroom **10** bedchamber **12** dressing room

bough 4 limb **6** branch

bougie 3 dip, wax **5** light, taper **6** candle, cierge, tallow

boulder, bowlder 3 nob **4** crag, knob, rock **5** block, stone **6** gibber **7** dornick **8** megalith

boulevard 6 avenue **7** parkway **9** concourse

bouleversement 7 turmoil **9** confusion, upsetting **11** overturning

bounce 3 bob, hop, pep **4** bump, life **5** bound, thump, verve, vigor **6** energy, jounce, recoil, spirit **7** rebound **8** dynamism, ricochet, vitality, vivacity **9** animation **10** liveliness

bouncing 3 big **4** full **5** jolly, large, lusty, plump **6** chubby, lively, robust, strong **7** healthy **8** animated, vigorous **12** in good health

bound 3 bob, orb, rim **4** area, edge, jump, leap, line, mark, pale, romp, sure, tied **5** dance, fated, hedge, limit, orbit, range, realm, vault **6** border, bounce, define, domain, doomed, forced, fringe, gambol, liable, prance, region, spring, tied up **7** certain, compass, confine, covered, encased, enclosed, flounce, going to, in bonds, limited, obliged, rebound, secured, trussed, wrapped **8** beholden, boundary, confined, destined, district, encircle, fastened, province, required, resolute, resolved, surround, tethered **9** bailiwick, committed, demarcate, extremity, periphery, territory **10** determined, restrained **11** demarcation **12** circumscribe

Boundaries
  god of: 8 Terminus

boundary 3 rim **4** edge, line, pale **6** border, margin **7** barrier **8** frontier, landmark **9** extremity, periphery **11** demarcation **12** dividing line

boundary line 4 edge **5** bound **6** border **8** sideline

bounder 3 cad, rat **4** heel

5 knave, louse, rogue **6** rascal, rotter **7** caitiff, dastard, villain **9** scoundrel **10** blackguard

Bounderby, Mr
  character in: 9 Hard Times
  author: 7 Dickens

boundless 4 vast **7** endless, immense **8** infinite, unending **9** limitless, perpetual, unbounded, unlimited **10** without end **11** everlasting, measureless **12** immeasurable, incalculable, unrestricted **13** inexhaustible

bounteous, bountiful 4 free, full, rich **5** ample, large **6** lavish **7** copious, liberal, profuse, teeming **8** abundant, generous, prolific **9** abounding, plenteous, plentiful, unsparing **10** beneficent, benevolent, charitable, munificent, unstinting **11** magnanimous, overflowing

Bountiful, Lady
  character in: 17 The Beaux Stratagem
  author: 8 Farquhar

bountifulness 10 liberality, generosity **11** benevolence, magnanimity, munificence **14** charitableness **15** humanitarianism

bounty 3 aid **4** gift, help **5** bonus, favor, grant **6** giving, reward **7** charity, present, tribute **8** bestowal, donation, gratuity **9** endowment **10** almsgiving, assistance, generosity, liberality, recompense **11** benefaction, benevolence, munificence **12** contribution, philanthropy **14** charitableness, openhandedness

bouquet 4 odor **5** aroma, scent, spray **7** essence, garland, nosegay, perfume **9** fragrance **11** boutonniere

bouquet garni
  ingredient: 5 basil, thyme **6** celery, savory **7** bay leaf, chervil, parsley **8** rosemary, tarragon

bourbon
  variety of: 7 whiskey
  origin: 7 America
  ingredient: 4 corn
  type: 7 blended **8** straight
  drink: 9 Mint Julep **10** Boston Sour **11** John Collins **12** Old Fashioned
  with Benedictine: 9 Twin Hills
  with brandy and Benedictine: 13 Brighton Punch
  with Cointreau: 10 Temptation
  with rum: 14 Artillery Punch
  with sloe gin: 9 Black Hawk

with Southern Comfort: 14 Blended Comfort
  with triple sec: 10 Chapel Hill
  with vermouth: 9 Allegheny

bourgeois 6 square **7** Babbitt, burgher **8** commoner, ordinary **11** middle-class **12** conventional **13** unimaginative

Bourgeois Gentleman, The
  author: 7 Moliere
  character: 6 Lucile, Nicole **7** Cleonte, Dorante **8** Covielle, Dorimene **14** Madame Jourdain **16** Monsieur Jourdain

Bourget, Charles Joseph Paul
  author of: 11 The Disciple **12** A Cruel Enigma **14** The Night Cometh

Bourgh, Lady Catherine de
  character in: 17 Pride and Prejudice
  author: 6 Austen

Bourjaily, Vance
  author of: 11 The Violated **14** The End of My Life **18** Brill Among the Ruins **22** Now Playing at Canterbury

Bourne Identity, The
  author: 12 Robert Ludlum

bout 4 fray, term, tilt, turn **5** brush, clash, cycle, fight, match, set-to, siege, spell, spree **6** affair, battle, course, period, series **7** contest, go-round, scuffle, session, tourney **8** conflict, interval, skirmish, struggle **9** encounter **10** contention, engagement **11** boxing match, embroilment

boutonniere 4 posy **7** nosegay **16** buttonhole flower

bow 3 arc **4** bend, knot, prow, stem **5** agree, curve, defer, front, stoop, yield **6** archer, comply, curtsy, give in, kowtow, relent, salaam, submit, weapon **7** concede, succumb, crescent **9** acquiesce, genuflect, surrender **10** capitulate, forward end **12** genuflection, knuckle under

Bow, Clara
  nickname: 6 It Girl
  born: 10 Brooklyn NY
  roles: 2 It **7** Mantrap **12** The Wild Party

bowdlerize 6 censor **9** expurgate **10** blue-pencil

bow down 5 yield **6** give in, submit **9** surrender **10** capitulate **12** knuckle under

bowed 4 bent **6** arched,

curved, nodded **7** hunched, stooped

bowels 3 gut, pit **4** core, guts, womb **5** abyss, belly, bosom, heart, midst **6** depths, hollow, vitals **7** innards, insides, stomach, viscera **8** entrails, interior, recesses **10** intestines **11** vital organs **13** innermost part

Bowen, Elizabeth
author of: **8** Eva Trout, The Hotel **10** To the North **11** Bowen's Court, Little Girls, The Cat Jumps **12** A World of Love **15** The Heat of the Day, The House in Paris **18** The Death of the Heart

Bowen's Court
author: **14** Elizabeth Bowen

bower 4 jack, joker, nook **5** arbor **6** alcove, anchor, pandal **7** bedroom, chamber, cottage, enclose, retreat, sanctum, shelter **8** dwelling, snuggery

Bowie, David
real name: **16** David Robert Jones
born: **6** London **7** England
roles: **9** Cat People, The Hunger **20** The Man Who Fell to Earth **24** Merry Christmas Mr Lawrence

Bowie Land, Bowie State
nickname of: **8** Arkansas

bowl 4 boat **5** arena, basin **6** cavity, hollow, tureen, valley, vessel **7** dishful, helping, portion, stadium **8** coliseum, deep dish **9** container, porringer **10** depression, receptacle **12** amphitheater

bowler 11 Earl Anthony

bowling
variation: **7** tenpins **8** duckpins, fivepins **10** candlepins
term: **4** miss **5** frame, spare, split **6** strike **10** gutterball
perfect score: **12** three hundred

bow-shape 3 arc **4** arch, bend **5** curve **9** curvature

bow to 5 yield **6** give in, give up, submit **9** acquiesce

box 3 bat, hit, rap **4** belt, cuff, slap, spar **5** booth, caddy, chest, crate, fight, punch, stall, whack **6** buffet, carton, coffer, strike, thwack **8** thumping **9** container **10** receptacle **11** compartment **13** exchange blows

boxer 7 Max Baer **8** Joe Louis **10** Barney Ross, Gene Tunney, Joe Frazier, Joe Walcott, Leon Spinks **11** Archie Moore, Jack

Dempsey, Jack Johnson, Jake LaMotta, Larry Holmes, Muhammad Ali, Sonny Liston **12** Benny Leonard, James Corbett, John Sullivan, Johnny Dundee, Max Schmeling, Mickey Walker, Primo Carnera, Roberto Duran, Thomas Hearns **13** Carmen Basilio, Ezzard Charles, George Foreman, James Jeffries, Rocky Graziano, Rocky Marciano **14** Bob Fitzsimmons, Floyd Patterson, Henry Armstrong **15** Maxie Rosenbloom, Sugar Ray Leonard **16** Sugar Ray Robinson

boy 3 lad **5** youth **8** man child **9** male child, stripling, youngster
French: **6** garcon

Boy
character in: **6** Tarzan
author: **9** Burroughs

boycott 5 spurn **6** reject **7** exclude **8** spurning **9** blackball, blacklist, exclusion, ostracism, ostracize, rejection **12** blackballing, blacklisting

Boyd, James
author of: **5** Drums **8** Long Hunt **9** Roll River **10** Marching On

Boyd, William
born: **13** Hendrysburg OH
roles: **15** Hopalong Cassidy

Boyer, Charles
born: **6** Figeac, France
roles: **7** Algiers **8** Conquest, Gaslight **10** Back Street **11** Lost Horizon **16** The Garden of Allah **19** All This and Heaven Too

boyfriend 3 man **4** beau, date **5** flame, lover, swain, wooer **6** escort, fellow, old man, squire, steady, suitor **7** admirer, beloved, Don Juan **8** cavalier, Lothario, paramour, truelove, young man **9** companion, inamorato **10** sweetheart **15** gentleman caller

boyish 5 boyey, fresh **6** callow, tender **7** boylike, puerile **8** childish, immature, innocent, juvenile, youthful **9** childlike **10** sophomoric

Boylan, Blazes
character in: **7** Ulysses
author: **5** Joyce

Boyle, Robert
field: **9** chemistry
nationality: **7** British
father of: **9** chemistry
advocated: **20** experimental approach
established: **9** Boyle's Law

boylike 5 fresh, young **6** boy-

ish, callow **7** puerile **8** childish, immature, innocent, juvenile, youthful **9** childlike

Boys Town
director: **12** Norman Taurog
cast: **9** Henry Hull **12** Mickey Rooney, Spencer Tracy (Father Flanagan)
Oscar for: **5** actor (Tracy)
sequel: **13** Men of Boys Town

Boy Wonder
nickname of: **5** Robin **6** Mel Ott

brace 3 duo **4** pair, prop, stay **5** shore, strut, truss **6** bracer, couple, hold up, prop up, steady **7** bolster, bracket, fortify, prepare, shore up, support, sustain, twosome **8** buttress **9** reinforce, stanchion **10** strengthen **13** reinforcement

bracelet 6 armlet, bangle

bracer 10 stiff drink, stimulator, wristguard **11** invigorator **12** strengthener, strong drink

Brachiosaurus
type: **8** dinosaur, sauropod
location: **10** East Africa **12** United States
period: **8** Jurassic

bracing 8 arousing, reviving **10** energizing, fortifying, refreshing **11** restorative, stimulating **12** exhilarating, invigorating **13** strengthening

Brack, Judge
character in: **11** Hedda Gabler
author: **5** Ibsen

bracken 4 fern **5** brake, brush, ferns **10** underbrush **11** undergrowth

bracket 4 prop, rank, stay **5** brace, class, group, range, shore, strut, truss **6** prop up, status **7** shore up, support **8** category, classify, division, grouping **9** designate, stanchion **10** categorize **11** designation **14** classification

brackish 4 salt **5** briny, salty **6** saline

Bracknell, Lady Augusta
character in: **27** The Importance of Being Earnest
author: **5** Wilde

bract 4 leaf

Bradbury, Ray
author of: **13** Dandelion Wine, Fahrenheit 451 **17** The Illustrated Man **20** The Martian Chronicles **27** Something Wicked This Way Comes

Bradford, Barbara Taylor
author of: **17** A Woman of
Substance

Bradford, Richard
author of: **15** Red Sky at
Morning

Bradley, Bill (William Warren)
nickname: **10** Dollar Bill
sport: **10** basketball
team: **13** New York Knicks
elected: **7** Senator
  from: **9** New Jersey

Bradstreet, Anne
author of: **35** The Tenth
Muse Lately Sprung Up in
America

Brady Bunch, The
character: **3** Jan **4** Greg
  5 Alice, Bobby, Cindy, Peter **6** Marcia **9** Mike Brady
  10 Carol Brady
cast: **8** Eve Plumb **9** Ann B
  Davis **10** Robert Reed, Susan
  Olsen **13** Barry Williams
  14 Mike Lookinland
  16 Maureen McCormick
  17 Christopher Knight, Florence Henderson

brag 4 crow **5** boast, vaunt
7 big talk, crowing, talk big
8 boasting, bragging **10** exaggerate, self-praise **12** boastfulness, exaggeration **15** blow
one's own horn **19** pat oneself
on the back

Brage *see* **5** Bragi

**Bragg, William Henry and
William Lawrence**
field: **7** physics
nationality: **7** British
determined: **16** crystal
structure
  by: **15** X-ray diffraction
established: **9** Bragg's Law
awarded: **10** Nobel Prize

braggadocio 5 pride **6** egoism,
vanity **7** bluster, conceit, swagger **9** cockiness, vainglory
10 pretension **14** self-
importance

braggart 7 boaster, bragger
8 blowhard **9** big talker

Bragi
also: **5** Brage
origin: **6** Nordic
god of: **5** music **6** poetry
father: **4** Odin **5** Othin
wife: **4** Idun **5** Iduna, Ithun
  6 Ithunn
mother: **3** Fri **5** Frigg, Frija
  6 Frigga

Brahe, Tycho
field: **9** astronomy
nationality: **6** Danish
built: **11** observatory

Brahman
country: **5** India

religion: **8** Hinduism
system: **5** caste
rank: **7** highest
function: **6** leader, priest
  7 teacher

Brahms, Johannes
born: **7** Germany, Hamburg
composer of: **7** Rinaldo
  10 Rain Sonata **11** Tri-
  umphlied, Volkslieder
  12 Thuner-Sonate **13** German Requiem, Song of Destiny, Song of Triumph
  14 Schicksalslied, Song of
  the Fates, Tragic Overture
  15 Gesang der Parzen, Hungarian Dances **19** Liebes-
  lieder Waltzes, Meistersinger
  Sonata **24** Academic Festival
  Overture **31** Variations on
  the St Anthony Chorale

braid 4 knit, lace **5** plait, ravel,
twine, twist, weave **7** entwine,
wreathe **9** interlace
10 intertwine

brain
part: **7** medulla **8** cerebrum
  9 pituitary **10** cerebellum

brainchild 8 creation **9** invention **12** original work
15 imaginative work

braininess 6 genius **9** smartness **10** brightness, brilliance,
cleverness **12** intelligence

brainless 4 dumb **6** stupid
7 asinine, foolish, idiotic, moronic, witless **8** mindless **9** imbecilic **10** half-witted
11 lamebrained **12** feeble-
minded, simple-minded

brain power 4 mind **9** intellect **12** intelligence **14** mental
capacity

Brainworm
character in: **19** Every Man
  in His Humour
author: **6** Jonson

brainy 5 smart **6** bright, clever
9 brilliant **11** intelligent

brake 4 curb, drag, halt, rein,
slow, stay, stop **5** check **6** arrest **7** control **9** restraint
10 constraint **11** reduce speed

Bramante, Donato
architect of: **9** Tempietto
  14 Belvedere Court (the Vatican), Palazzo Caprini
  19 Santa Maria della Pace
  21 Santa Maria della Grazie

bramble 4 bush, vine **5** rough,
shrub **7** thicket **8** prickers
13 raspberry bush **14** blackberry bush

Bramble, Matthew
character in: **14** Humphry
  Clinker
author: **8** Smollett

Bran
origin: **5** Welsh
king of: **7** Britain
habitat: **3** sea
saint in: **12** Christianity
brother: **9** Evnissyen
  10 Manawyddan
sister: **7** Branwen
head buried in: **6** London

branch 3 arm, leg **4** fork, limb,
part, wing **5** bough, prong,
spray **6** agency, bureau, divide,
feeder, member, office, ramify **7** channel, chapter, diverge, radiate, section,
segment **8** division, offshoot,
separate, shoot off **9** bifurcate,
component, extension, tributary **10** department **11** subdivision **12** ramification

branched 6 forked, parted
7 divided **8** extended **9** spread
out

Branchus
father: **6** Apollo
power of: **6** augury
power given by: **6** Apollo

Brancusi, Constantin
born: **7** Romania **13** Pestisani
  Gorj
artwork: **4** Fish **7** Chimera,
  The Kiss, The Seal **9** Sorceress **10** Adam and Eve, Prometheus **11** Bird in Space,
  Prodigal Son **12** Flying Turtle, Sleeping Muse **13** Endless Column **20** Sculpture
  for the Blind

brand 4 blot, kind, make,
mark, sear, sign, slur, sort,
spot, type **5** class, grade, label,
smear, stain, stamp, taint
6 burn in, emblem, smirch,
stigma **7** blemish, quality, variety **8** besmirch, disgrace **9** discredit, trademark
10 imputation, stigmatize
11 manufacture

brandish 4 wave **5** shake,
swing, wield **6** flaunt, waggle
7 display, exhibit, show off
8 flourish

brand new 5 fresh, young
6 unused

Brando, Marlon
born: **7** Omaha NE
roles: **8** Sayonara **10** The
  Wild One, Viva Zapata
  12 Julius Caesar, The Godfather (Oscar refused)
  13 Apocalypse Now **15** On
  the Waterfront (Oscar)
  16 Last Tango in Paris
  17 Mutiny on the Bounty
  21 A Streetcar Named Desire

brandy 6 cognac, grappa, kahlua, kirsch, metaxa **8** Calvados,
Tia Maria **9** applejack, Slivovitz **12** Grand Marnier, Peter

Heering **14** forbidden fruit
French: **8** eau de vie

Brangwen, Ursula and Gudrun
characters in: **11** Women in Love
author: **8** Lawrence

Branstock
also: **9** Barnstock
origin: **12** Scandinavian
mentioned in: **8** Volsunga
form: **3** oak **4** tree
location: **7** Volsung
house of: **7** Volsung
Odin (Othin) thrusts:
4 Gram **5** sword

Brant, Captain Adam
character in: **22** Mourning Becomes Electra
author: **6** O'Neill

Branwen
origin: **5** Welsh
brother: **4** Bran
husband: **10** Matholwych
son killed by: **9** Evnissyen

Braque, Georges
born: **6** France **18** Argenteuil sur Seine
artwork: **7** Atelier, Grand Nu (Great Nude), The Echo **8** The Table **13** The Portuguese **14** Man with a Guitar **16** Violin and Palette, Violin and Pitcher **18** Woman with a Mandolin

brash 4 bold, rash, rude **5** fresh, hasty, sassy **6** brazen, cheeky, madcap **7** forward **8** careless, heedless, impudent, reckless **9** foolhardy, impetuous, imprudent, know-it-all **10** incautious **11** impertinent, precipitous, smart-alecky **12** unconsidered **13** overconfident

brashness 4 gall **5** brass, cheek, nerve **8** audacity, boldness, chutzpah, temerity **10** brazenness, effrontery **11** forwardness, presumption

Brasilia
capital of: **6** Brazil

brass 4 gall, sand, VIPs **5** cheek, nerve **8** audacity, boldness, chutzpah, officers, temerity **9** impudence **10** brazenness, effrontery **11** forwardness, presumption

Brass, Sampson
character in: **19** The Old Curiosity Shop
author: **7** Dickens

brass instrument 4 tuba **5** bugle **6** cornet **7** trumpet **8** trombone **9** euphonium **10** French horn, sousaphone
ancient: **3** lur **7** Alphorn,

buisine, serpent **10** ophicleide

brass tacks 4 crux, meat **7** details **9** realities, substance **10** essentials **11** nitty-gritty **15** sum and substance

brassy 4 bold **5** brash, cocky, sassy, saucy **6** brazen **7** forward **8** arrogant, impudent, insolent, overbold **9** barefaced, outspoken, shameless, unabashed **10** unblushing **11** impertinent

brat 3 imp **4** chit **5** whelp **6** hoyden, rascal **9** rude child **12** spoiled child

Brauhaus 6 tavern **7** brewery

Brautigan, Richard
author of: **15** Sombrero Fallout **18** The Hawkline Monster **21** Trout Fishing in America **38** The Pill Versus the Springhill Mine Disaster

bravado 7 big talk, blowing, bluster, bombast, bravura, crowing, puffery, swagger **8** boasting, bragging **9** cockiness **10** swaggering **11** braggadocio **12** boastfulness **13** show of courage

brave 4 bear, dare, defy, face, game, take **5** abide, brook, gutsy, stand **6** breast, endure, gritty, heroic, plucky, spunky, suffer **7** doughty, stomach, sustain, undergo, valiant, weather **8** confront, fearless, intrepid, stalwart, tolerate, unafraid, valorous **9** challenge, dauntless, outbrazen, put up with, stand up to, undaunted, withstand **10** courageous **11** lionhearted, unflinching, unshrinking **12** stouthearted

brave deed 4 feat **7** exploit **9** heroic act **11** achievement

Brave New World
author: **12** Aldous Huxley
character: **4** John **11** Bernard Marx **12** Lenina Crowne, Mustapha Mond

bravery 4 grit **5** pluck, spunk, valor **6** daring, mettle, spirit **7** courage, heroism **8** audacity, boldness **11** intrepidity **12** fearlessness **13** dauntlessness

Bravo, The
author: **19** James Fenimore Cooper

brawl 3 row **4** fray, tiff **5** broil, clash, fight, melee, scrap, set-to **6** battle, fracas, ruckus, rumpus, uproar **7** dispute, quarrel, scuffle, wrangle **8** squabble **9** imbroglio **11** altercation, embroilment

brawn 5 might, power **7** muscles, stamina **8** strength **9** beefiness, huskiness **10** robustness, ruggedness, sturdiness **19** muscular development

brawny 5 burly, husky **6** mighty, robust, rugged, strong, sturdy **8** muscular, powerful **9** strapping

Bray, Madeline
character in: **16** Nicholas Nickleby
author: **7** Dickens

brazen 4 bold, open **5** brash, saucy **6** brassy, cheeky **7** forward **8** arrogant, immodest, impudent, insolent **9** audacious, barefaced, boldfaced, shameless, unabashed

brazenness 4 gall **5** brass, cheek, nerve **8** audacity, boldness, chutzpah **9** impudence **10** effrontery, fowardness **11** presumption

Brazil *see box*

Brazil
director: **12** Terry Gilliam
cast: **8** Ida Lowry **9** Kim Greist **12** Robert De Niro **13** Jonathan Pryce

Brazilian Bombshell
nickname of: **13** Carmen Miranda

Brazzaville
capital of: **5** Congo

breach 3 gap **4** gash, hole, rent, rift, slit **5** break, chink, cleft, crack, split **7** crevice, failure, fissure, neglect, opening, rupture **8** defiance, trespass **9** disregard, violation **10** infraction **11** dereliction **12** disobedience, infringement **13** noncompliance, nonobservance, transgression

breach of faith 7 perfidy **8** bad faith, betrayal **9** falseness, treachery, two-timing **10** disloyalty **11** double-cross **13** double-dealing

breach of order 4 riot **6** fracas, mutiny, ruckus, uproar **7** turmoil **8** uprising **9** commotion, rebellion **10** dissension **11** disturbance, pandemonium **18** disturbance of peace

breach of trust 7 falsity, perfidy **9** falseness, treachery **10** disloyalty, infidelity **13** deceitfulness, double-dealing

bread 3 rye **4** food, pita **5** bucks, dough, money, wheat **6** staple **9** sourdough **10** livelihood, sustenance **11** staff of life **12** pumpernickel

bread and butter 3 job **6** ca-

Brazil

capital: 8 Brasilia

former capital: 12 Rio de Janeiro

largest city: 8 Sao Paulo

others: 5 Bahia, Belem **6** Recife, Sabara, Santos **7** Vitoria **8** Salvador **9** Ouro Preto, Paranagua **10** Diamantina **11** Porto Alegre **13** Belo Horizonte, Cruzeiro do Sul

school:
   junior high: **7** ginasio
   senior high: **7** colegio

measure: 2 pe **4** moio, sack, vara **5** braca, legoa, milha, tonel **6** canada, cuarto, quarto, tarefa **7** garrafa **8** alqueire

monetary unit: 3 joe **4** reis **5** dobra **7** centara, halfjoe, milreis **8** cruzeiro

weight: 3 bag **4** onca **5** libra **6** arroba, oitava **7** quilate, quintal **8** tonelada

island: 6 Maraca, Marajo **7** Bananal, Cardoso, Caviana, Mexiana **8** Comprida

lake: 4 Aima, Feia **5** Mirim **13** Logo dos Platos

mountain: 3 Mar **5** Geral, Organ, Piaui **6** Acarai, Gurupi, Parima, Urucum **7** Amambai, Carajas, Gradaus, Oragaos, Roraima **8** Bandeira, Itatiaja, Roncador, Tombador **9** Pacaraima, Sugar Loaf **10** Tumuc-Humac

highest point: 7 Neblina

river: 3 Apa, Ica **4** Doce, Geio, Ivai, Jari, Para, Paru, Sono, Tefe **5** Abuna, Anaua, Apore, Capim, Claro, Corua, Icana, Iriri, Itapi, Jurua, Jutai, Manso, Negro, Pardo, Piaui, Preto, Tiete, Turvo, Urubu, Verde, Xingu **6** Ajuana, Amazon, Arinos, Balsas, Branco, Canuma, Contas, Cuiaba, Demini, Grajau, Grande, Gurupi, Ibicui, Iguacu, Japura, Javari, Mearim, Mortes, Mucuri, Parana, Purpus, Ronuro, Sangue, Tacutu, Tibagi, Uatuma, Uaupes **7** Corumba, Iguassu, Madeira, Madiera, Orinoco, Paraiba, Sucuriu, Tapajos, Taquari, Teodoro, Uruguai, Uruguay, Velhass **8** Araguaia, Padauiri, Paracatu, Paraguay, Parnaiba, Solimoes, Tarauaca **9** Tocantins **12** Sao Francisco

sea: 8 Atlantic

physical feature:
   bay: **9** All Saints
   cape: **4** Frio **6** Blanco, Buzios, Gurupy, Orange **7** Saotome **8** Saoroque
   dam: **6** Furnas **7** Peixoto
   estuary: **4** Para
   rain forest: **5** selva
   waterfall: **6** Guaira, Iguacu **7** Iguassu **11** Paulo Afonso

people: 2 Ge **4** Anta **5** Acroa, Arara, Araua, Bravo, Carib, Guana, Negro **6** Arawak, Caraja **7** Carayan, Javahai, Tariana **8** Botocudo, Chambioa **9** Caucasian, mamelucos, mulattoes **10** Portuguese **11** Tupi-Guarani
   architect: **8** Niemeyer
   artist: **6** Segall **9** Portinari **10** Cavalcenti
   author: **5** Amado, Bilac, Ramos **6** Freyre
   composer: **10** Villalobos
   discoverer: **6** Cabral
   leader: **6** Aranha, Branco, Collor, Franco, Geisel, Medici, Vargas **7** Goulart
   sculptor: **11** Aleijadinho

language: 10 Portuguese

religion: 10 Protestant **13** Roman Catholic

place:
   beach: **7** Ipanema **9** Boa Viagem **10** Copacabana

feature:
   bird: **4** mitu **5** mitua
   dance: **5** frevo, samba **6** maxixe **9** bossa nova
   fish: **7** piranha
   gourd: **4** cuia
   plantation: **7** fazenda
   slums: **7** favelas
   tree: **5** icica **6** ucuuba **7** arariba

food:
   dish: **6** vatapa **8** feijoada
   dried salted beef: **7** charque
   drink: **4** acai **9** cafezinho
   tea: **4** mate
   turtle soup: **16** cas quinho de mucua

reer, living **7** calling **8** business, vocation **9** life's work **10** livelihood **14** means of support

Bread and Wine
author: **13** Ignazio Silone

breadbasket 3 gut **5** belly, tummy **6** paunch **7** abdomen, labonza, midriff, Midwest, stomach **11** solar plexus

breadth 4 area, size, span **5** range, reach, scope, width **6** extent, spread **7** compass, expanse, measure, stretch **8** latitude, wideness **9** broadness **10** dimensions **13** extensiveness

break *see box*

breakable 5 frail, shaky **6** flimsy **7** brittle, crumbly, fragile **8** delicate

break apart 7 crumble, shatter **8** collapse **9** fall apart **12** disintegrate, fall to pieces

breakdown 6 mishap **7** crackup, decline, failure **8** analysis, collapse, disorder, division **12** detailed list **13** deterioration **14** categorization

break down 6 divide **7** dissect **8** collapse, separate **9** decompose **11** deteriorate

breaker 4 cask, wave **6** comber **7** crusher **8** boat cask **9** destroyer

break faith with 6 betray **7** do wrong **9** play false **11** double-cross **12** be unfaithful **13** be treacherous **16** sell down the river

Breakfast at Tiffany's
author: **12** Truman Capote
director: **12** Blake Edwards
cast: **10** Buddy Ebsen **12** Mickey Rooney, Patricia Neal **13** Audrey Hepburn (Holly Golightly), George Peppard
score: **12** Henry Mancini
song: **9** Moon River

Breakfast Club, The
director: **10** John Hughes
cast: **10** Ally Sheedy **13** Emilio Estevez, Molly Ringwald **18** Anthony Michael Hall

Breakfast of Champions
author: **12** Kurt Vonnegut

break free 4 bolt, flee, skip **6** escape **7** get away, make off, run away **9** cut and run **10** fly the coop **12** make a getaway

breakfront 5 hutch **7** cabinet **8** bookcase, cupboard **12** china cabinet

break in 5 train **7** intrude **8** accustom, initiate **9** acclimate, interrupt **10** burglarize **12** indoctrinate

break-in 5 theft **7** robbery **8** burglary, stealing **12** burglarizing **13** housebreaking **19** breaking and entering

Breaking Away
director: **10** Peter Yates
screenplay: **11** Steve Tesich
cast: **10** Paul Dooley **11** Daniel Stern, Dennis Quaid **13** Barbara Barrie **16** Jackie Earle Haley **17** Dennis Christopher

setting: **7** Indiana **11** Bloomington

break loose 4 bolt, flee, skip **6** escape **7** get away, make off **9** cut and run **10** fly the coop **12** make a getaway

breakneck 4 rash **5** risky **8** reckless, very fast **9** dangerous, daredevil **12** death-defying

break of day 4 dawn **5** sunup **7** dawning, sunrise **8** daybreak **11** crack of dawn

break off 3 end **4** halt **5** cease **6** recess **7** adjourn, snap off, suspend **8** conclude, shut down **11** discontinue

breakout 6 escape, flight **7** getaway **10** decampment

break out 4 bolt, skip **5** begin, erupt **6** escape **7** bust out, get away **10** burst forth, fly the coop **12** make a getaway

Break the Bank
host: **9** Bert Parks **10** Bud Collyer

break the habit 4 kick, quit, stop **6** eschew, give up **8** renounce, withdraw **14** quit cold turkey

breakthrough 7 advance **11** advancement, improvement, penetration, step forward

breakup 5 split **7** crackup **9** dispersal, splitting **10** separation **14** disintegration

break with 5 leave **8** be untrue, part from **10** be disloyal **11** divorce from **12** fall away from, separate from

breast 4 bust, core **5** bosom, chest, heart **10** very marrow
Italian: **5** petto

breastwork 7 bastion, rampart **8** barbette **9** earthwork **13** fortification

breath 4 wind **6** spirit **9** animation, breathing, lifeblood, life force **10** exhalation, inhalation, vital spark **11** divine spark, respiration, vital spirit **12** vitalization

breathe 4 gasp, huff, pant, puff **5** utter **6** impart, murmur **7** respire, whisper **9** draw in air **10** draw breath **15** inhale and exhale

breathe in 6 inhale **7** inspire, respire

breathe out 4 huff, pant, puff **6** exhale, expire **7** respire

breathing 4 live **5** alive **6** living **7** animate **11** respiratory **13** drawing breath

---

break 3 cap, end, fly, gap, off, run, top **4** beat, bust, chip, dash, defy, flee, gash, halt, hole, rend, rent, rest, rift, rive, ruin, snap, stop, tame, tear, tell **5** burst, cease, cleft, crack, crush, erupt, excel, lapse, occur, outdo, pause, sever, shirk, smash, split, train **6** appear, better, breach, chance, cleave, detach, divide, escape, exceed, happen, hiatus, ignore, inform, lessen, master, powder, recess, reveal, soften, subdue, sunder, weaken **7** control, cushion, destroy, disobey, divulge, eclipse, fissure, fortune, give out, lighten, neglect, opening, pull off, respite, run away, rupture, shatter, surpass, suspend, tear off, violate, wipe out **8** announce, bankrupt, burst out, cracking, demolish, diminish, disclose, disjoint, division, fracture, fragment, go beyond, interval, outstrip, overcome, proclaim, renege on, separate, shut down, slip away, splinter **9** dismember, disregard, granulate, interlude, interrupt, make a dash, pulverize, splitting, transcend **10** discipline, disconnect, fall back on, fly the coop, fracturing, impoverish, infringe on, make public, overshadow, separation, shattering, take flight, wrench away **11** discontinue, get away from, opportunity, pay no heed to **12** be derelict in, disintegrate, intermission, interruption, make a getaway, stroke of luck **13** strap for funds **14** bend to one's will, take the force of **15** take to one's heels

Breathless
director: **14** Jean-Luc
Goddard
written by: **16** Francois
Truffaut
cast: **10** Jean Seberg
16 Jean-Paul Belmondo
setting: **5** Paris

breathtaking 7 amazing, awesome **8** exciting **9** startling
10 surprising **11** astonishing

Brecht, Bertolt
author of: **13** Mother Courage **15** Drums in the Night
18 The Threepenny Opera
21 St Joan of the Stockyards **23** The Caucasian
Chalk Circle **27** The Resista-
ble Rise of Arturo Ui
29 The Private Life of the
Master Race

Breck, Alan
character in: **9** Kidnapped
author: **9** Stevenson

breech 4 rump, seat **6** behind
8 buttocks, haunches, hind
part **9** fundament, posterior
12 hindquarters

breeches 5 pants **8** trousers

breed 4 bear, grow, kind, race,
sire, sort, type **5** beget, cause,
order, raise, spawn, stock
6 family, father, foster, lead
to, mother, strain **7** develop,
nurture, produce, promote,
species, variety **8** generate,
multiply, occasion **9** cultivate,
give forth, procreate, propagate, reproduce **10** bring forth,
give rise to **11** proliferate
16 produce offspring

breeding 4 line **5** grace **6** mating, polish **7** bearing, descent,
growing, lineage, manners,
raising, rearing **8** ancestry,
courtesy, hatching, heredity,
pedigree, spawning, training
9 begetting, bloodline, genealogy, gentility, parentage, producing **10** background,
extraction, family tree, generation, politeness, production,
refinement, upbringing **11** cultivation, germination, multiplying, procreation,
propagation **12** reproduction

breeze 4 flit, pass, sail, waft
5 coast, float, glide, sweep
6 zephyr **9** light gust, light
wind **10** gentle wind, puff of
wind

breezy 3 gay **4** airy, pert, spry
5 blowy, brisk, fresh, gusty,
light, merry, peppy, sunny,
windy **6** bouncy, casual, frisky,
jaunty, lively **7** buoyant,
squally **8** animated, blustery,
carefree, cheerful, debonair,

spirited **9** energetic, resilient,
sprightly, vivacious, windswept **10** blithesome **11** free
and easy

Brennan, Walter
born: **12** Swampscott MA
roles: **8** Kentucky **12** Come
and Get It, The Westerner
13 The Real McCoys **16** To
Have and Have Not

Brent, George
real name: **18** George Brendan Nolan
wife: **11** Ann Sheridan
14 Ruth Chatterton
born: **7** Ireland
14 Shannonsbridge
roles: **7** Jezebel **11** Dark Victory, The Great Lie
17 Forty-Second Street

Bres
origin: **5** Irish
king of: **7** Ireland

Breton, Andre
author of: **5** Nadja **21** Manifesto of Surrealism

Breuer, Marcel
architect of: **17** IBM Research Center (La Gaude
France) **18** UNESCO headquarters (Paris) **25** St John's
Abbey and University (Col-
legeville MN) **26** Whitney
Museum of American Art
(NYC)

brevity 9 briefness, pithiness,
quickness, shortness, terseness
10 transience **11** conciseness
12 ephemerality, impermanence, succinctness

brew 3 ale **4** beer, boil, cook,
form, make, plan, plot, soak
5 begin, drink, hatch, ripen,
start, steep, stout **6** cook up,
devise, foment, gather, porter,
scheme, seethe **7** arrange, concoct, ferment, mixture, prepare, produce, think up
8 beverage, contrive, initiate
9 formulate, germinate, originate **10** concoction, malt
liquor

brewery
German: **8** Brauhaus

Brian de Bois, Sir
character in: **7** Ivanhoe
author: **5** Scott

Briareus
also: **7** Aegaeon
member of: **13** Hecatonchires

bribe 5 graft **6** buy off, grease,
pay off, payola, suborn **9** hush
money **10** inducement **11** illegal gift **15** grease the hand of,
grease the palm of
French: **7** douceur

bric-a-brac 7 baubles,

gewgaws **8** bibelots, trinkets
9 gimcracks, kickshaws, ornaments **11** knickknacks

Brick
character in: **16** Cat on a
Hot Tin Roof
author: **8** Williams

Bricks
god of: **5** Kulla

bridal 7 nuptial, wedding
8 marriage **11** matrimonial

Bridehead, Sue
character in: **14** Jude the
Obscure
author: **5** Hardy

Bride of Lammermoor, The
author: **14** Sir Walter Scott
character: **10** Lady Ashton,
Lucy Ashton, Ravenswood
14 Laird of Bucklaw **16** Sir
William Ashton

Brideshead Revisited
author: **11** Evelyn Waugh
character: **5** Celia, Julia
8 Cordelia **9** Sebastian
10 Brideshead (Bridey), Rex
Mottram **12** Boy Mulcaster,
Charles Ryder **13** Lady
Marchmain, Lord March-
main **14** Anthony Blanche

bridge 3 tie **4** band, bind,
bond, link, span **5** cross,
unify, union **6** go over **7** catwalk, connect, liaison, viaduct **8** alliance, overpass,
traverse **9** cross over **10** connection, passageway **11** association, reach across **12** extend
across

bridge
derived from: **5** whist
variation: **14** contract bridge
partnership: **9** East/West
11 North/South
cards/hand: **8** thirteen
no cards of a suit: **4** void
one card of a suit:
9 singleton
two cards of a suit:
9 doubleton
rule book by: **5** Goren

**Bridge of San Luis Rey,
The**
author: **14** Thornton Wilder
character: **5** Clara, Jaime
6 Manuel, Pepita **7** Esteban,
Viceroy **8** Uncle Pio **11** La
Perichole **14** Brother Juniper **20** Marquesa de
Montemayor

**Bridge on the River Kwai,
The**
director: **9** David Lean
based on story by: **12** Pierre
Boulle
cast: **11** Jack Hawkins
12 Alec Guinness **13** Wil-

liam Holden **14** Sessue
Hayakawa
Oscar for: 5 actor (Guinness) **7** picture

Bridges, Beau
real name: 21 Lloyd Vernet
Bridges III
father: 5 Lloyd
brother: 4 Jeff
born: 12 Los Angeles CA
roles: 5 Space **8** Norma Rae
11 The Landlord **25** The
Other Side of the Mountain

Bridges, Jeff
father: 5 Lloyd
brother: 4 Beau
born: 12 Los Angeles CA
roles: 4 Tron **7** Starman
8 King Kong **10** Jagged
Edge **13** Kiss Me Goodbye
14 Against All Odds **18** The
Last Picture Show

Bridges, Lloyd
son: 4 Beau, Jeff
born: 12 San Leandro CA
roles: 7 Sea Hunt **8** Airplane,
High Noon

Bridges at Toko-ri, The
author: 13 James Michener

Bridget
character in: 19 Every Man
in His Humour
author: 6 Jonson

Bridge Too Far, A
author: 13 Cornelius Ryan

Bridgetown
capital of: 8 Barbados

bridle 3 gag **4** curb, rule
5 check **6** arrest, direct, draw
up, flinch, hinder, manage,
master, muzzle, rear up, recoil **7** control, harness, inhibit,
repress **8** draw back, restrain,
restrict, suppress **9** constrain,
restraint **11** bit and brace,
head harness

brief 4 case **5** hasty, pithy,
quick, short, swift, terse **6** advise, inform, precis, resume
7 capsule, compact, concise,
defense, limited, prepare, summary **8** abridged, abstract, argument, fill in on, fleeting,
instruct, succinct **9** condensed,
curtailed, momentary, shortened, temporary, thumbnail,
transient **10** abridgment, compressed, contention, describe
to, short-lived, summarized,
transitory **11** abbreviated
12 legal summary

brief account 6 precis, sketch
7 outline, summary **8** anecdote

brier, briar 4 Rosa **5** Rubus,
thorn **6** Smilax **7** bramble
varieties: 3 Cat, Dog, Hag,
Saw **4** Bull **5** Green, Horse,
Sweet **7** Jackson **8** Austrian

9 Sensitive **14** Austrian
copper

brigade 4 crew, team, unit
5 corps, force, group, squad
6 legion, outfit **7** company
9 regiments, squadrons
10 army groups, battalions,
contingent, detachment

Brigadoon
director: 16 Vincente
Minnelli
based on Broadway hit by:
14 Lerner and Loewe
cast: 9 Gene Kelly **10** Van
Johnson **11** Cyd Charisse

brigand 5 thief **6** bandit, gunman, looter, outlaw, pirate,
robber, vandal **7** corsair, hoodlum, ruffian, rustler, spoiler
8 marauder, pilferer, pillager
9 buccaneer, cutthroat, desperado, despoiler, plunderer, privateer **10** highwayman

bright 3 gay **4** glad, good,
keen, rosy, sage, warm,
wise **5** acute, alert, aware,
grand, great, happy, jolly,
merry, quick, sharp, smart,
sunny, vivid **6** astute,
blithe, brainy, clever,
gifted, joyful, joyous,
lively, shrewd **7** beaming,
blazing, capable, glowing,
healthy, hopeful, intense,
lambent, radiant, shining
8 cheerful, dazzling, exciting, gleaming, luminous,
lustrous, profound, splendid, talented **9** brilliant,
competent, effulgent, excellent, favorable, ingenious,
inventive, masterful, promising, sagacious, sparkling,
wide-awake **10** auspicious,
discerning, glittering, optimistic, perceptive, proficient, propitious,
prosperous, remarkable,
shimmering, successful
11 clearheaded, illuminated, illustrious, intelligent, light-filled,
magnificent, outstanding,
quick-witted, resourceful,
resplendent **12** exhilarating

brighten 4 lift **5** boost, cheer,
light **6** buoy up, lift up, perk
up **7** animate, enliven, gladden, lighten **9** make happy,
stimulate **10** illuminate

bright-eyed 5 alert, awake
9 wide-awake **12** on the qui
vive

Bright Flows the River
author: 14 Taylor Caldwell

brightness 4 glow **5** glare,
gleam, shine **6** dazzle, luster
7 glitter, sparkle **8** radiance
9 lightness **10** brilliance, luminosity **12** intelligence

bright spot 3 joy **6** solace
7 comfort **8** pleasure
13 consolation

Brigit
origin: 5 Welsh
goddess of: 4 fire **6** wisdom
9 fertility, household
11 agriculture

**Brigitte Bardot & the Lolita
Syndrome**
author: 16 Simone de
Beauvoir

Brill Among the Ruins
author: 14 Vance Bourjaily

brilliance, brilliancy 4 gift,
glow **5** blaze, gleam, sheen,
shine **6** acuity, dazzle, genius,
luster, talent, wisdom **7** glitter,
shimmer, sparkle **8** grandeur,
keenness, radiance, sagacity,
splendor **9** alertness, awareness, greatness, ingenuity, intensity, quickness, sharpness,
smartness, vividness **10** braininess, brightness, capability,
cleverness, competence, effulgence, excellence, luminosity,
perception, profundity,
shrewdness **11** discernment,
distinction, proficiency **12** intelligence, magnificence, resplendence **13** inventiveness,
masterfulness **15** clearheadedness, illustriousness,
resourcefulness

brilliant see **6** bright

brim 3 fill, lip, rim **5** brink,
flood, ledge, verge **6** border,
fill up, margin, well up
8 overflow

brimless hat 3 cap **5** beret
6 beanie **11** stocking cap, tam
o'shanter

brimming 4 full **7** flooded,
teeming **8** overfull, swarming
11 overflowing

Brimo
origin: 5 Greek
form: 7 goddess
corresponds to: 6 Hecate
7 Demeter **10** Persephone

brine 6 the sea **8** sea water
9 salt water **12** salt solution
14 saline solution **16** pickling
solution

bring 4 bear, make, take, tote
5 begin, carry, cause, fetch,
force, start **6** compel, convey,
create, effect, induce **7** deliver,
produce, sell for, usher in

8 convince, engender, generate, initiate, persuade, result in **9** accompany, institute, originate, transport **10** bring about

bring about 2 do **4** form, open **5** begin, cause, found, set up, start **6** attain, create, effect, lead to **7** achieve, execute, produce **8** carry out, generate, initiate, organize **9** establish, institute, succeed at **10** accomplish, effectuate, inaugurate **11** bring to pass, precipitate **18** bring into existence

bring back 6 return **7** restore **8** recreate **9** surrender **10** return with

bring down a peg 5 abase **6** humble **7** mortify **9** humiliate **13** cut down to size

bring down to earth 10 disenchant **11** disenthrall, disillusion, open the eyes **13** break the spell **14** burst the bubble **20** shatter one's illusions

bring forth 4 bear **5** breed, elicit, evoke, hatch, spawn, whelp **7** deliver, produce **9** reproduce **10** make appear **11** give birth to

bring home to 7 blame on, clarify **11** attribute to **15** place emphasis on

bringing together 7 joining, wedding **8** amassing **9** combining, gathering, including **10** assembling, collecting **12** accumulating **13** incorporating

Bringing Up Baby
director: **11** Howard Hawks
cast: **9** Cary Grant **14** Charlie Ruggles **16** Katharine Hepburn

Bringing Up Father
creator: **13** George McManus
character: **5** Jiggs **6** Maggie
  daughter: **5** Rosie
  brother-in-law: **5** Bimmy
place: **11** Dinty Moore's
favorite dish: **20** corned beef and cabbage

bring into being 4 bear, form, make **5** erect, hatch, spawn, whelp **6** create, design, devise, invent, render **7** concoct, deliver, develop, fashion, produce **8** contrive, generate **9** construct, fabricate, formulate, originate **10** bring forth **11** give birth to

bring into existence 4 form **5** begin, set up, start **6** create **8** organize **9** establish, institute **10** bring about, inaugurate

bring into line 5 adapt **6** adjust **7** conform, shape up **9** harmonize, reconcile **10** discipline **11** accommodate **13** whip into shape

bring into question 11 cast doubt on **18** throw suspicion upon

bring into relief 6 accent, stress **7** dwell on, feature, point up **9** emphasize, press home, underline **10** accentuate, underscore

bring low 5 abase, shame **6** humble **8** cast down **9** denigrate, humiliate

bring off 4 gain **6** attain, effect, secure **7** achieve **10** accomplish

bring to an end 5 cease **6** finish **8** break off, conclude **9** call a halt, terminate **11** discontinue

bring to a standstill 3 end **4** halt, stay, stop **5** block, check **6** arrest **12** bring to a halt

bring to bay 4 trap, tree **6** corner **8** confront, hunt down

bring to bear 5 apply **6** employ **7** utilize **9** implement

bring together 5 amass **6** gather, muster **7** collect, marshal, round up **8** assemble **10** accumulate

bring to light 6 expose, reveal, unveil **7** clarify, divulge, explain, uncover **8** disclose **9** explicate, make known, make plain **10** illuminate, make public

bring to one's senses 3 jar **5** alarm, alert, shock **9** make aware

bring to pass 5 cause **6** create, effect **8** carry out **10** bring about, effectuate

bring to terms 6 settle **7** mediate **9** arbitrate, reconcile

bring to view 5 dig up **6** reveal **7** exhibit, uncover, unearth **8** disclose, retrieve **10** come up with

bring word 4 tell **6** advise, convey, inform, notify, relate, reveal **7** divulge, publish **8** announce, disclose, proclaim **9** apprise of, broadcast, make known, publicize **11** communicate

brink 3 rim **4** bank, brim, edge **5** point, shore, skirt, verge **6** border, margin **9** threshold

briny 4 salt **5** salty **6** saline

brio, con
music: **9** with vigor **10** with spirit

Briseis
origin: **5** Greek
mentioned in: **5** Iliad
father: **18** Briseus of Lyrnessus
husband: **5** Mynes
captured by: **8** Achilles
caused: **7** quarrel
  between: **8** Achilles **9** Agamemnon

Briseus
origin: **5** Greek
mentioned in: **5** Iliad
daughter: **7** Briseis
death by: **7** suicide

Brisingamen 8 necklace
origin: **12** Scandinavian
trait: **5** magic
owned by: **5** Freia, Freya

brisk 4 busy, spry **5** alert, fresh, peppy, quick, swift **6** active, breezy, lively, snappy **7** bracing, chipper, dynamic, rousing **8** animated, bustling, spirited, stirring, vigorous **9** energetic, sprightly, vivacious, vivifying **10** refreshing **11** stimulating **12** exhilarating, invigorating

briskness 3 pep **5** vigor **6** energy **8** alacrity, spryness **9** quickness, swiftness **13** sprightliness

bristle 4 hair **5** quill **7** stiffen, whisker

bristles 5 barbs **6** quills **7** stubble **8** prickles, whiskers

bristletail
variety: **7** jumping **8** firebrat **9** primitive **10** nicoletiid, silverfish

bristly 5 rough **6** barbed, coarse **7** prickly, stubbly **8** unshaven **9** whiskered **11** bewhiskered

Britannia see 7 England

British 6 Breton, Briton **7** English **8** Brittany

British Columbia
bordered by: **5** Idaho, Yukon **6** Alaska **7** Montana **10** Washington **12** Pacific Ocean, United States **20** Northwest Territories
country: **6** Canada
Indian: **5** Haida **6** Nootka, Salish **8** Kwakiutl **9** Tsimshian **10** Bella Coola
island: **9** Vancouver **14** Queen Charlotte
mountain: **5** Coast, Rocky **7** Cascade **8** Columbia

11 Cordilleran **14** Cassiar Omineca
nickname: 2 BC
park: 7 Glacier
rank in size: 5 sixth
river: 6 Fraser
section: 8 province

British Guiana *see* **6** Guyana

British Honduras *see* **6** Belize

British Mythology
god of rebirth/afterlife: 4 Gwyn
chief of gods: 5 Woden
island of paradise: 6 Avalon

Britomart
character in: 15 The Faerie Queene
author: 7 Spenser

Britomartis
origin: 6 Cretan
goddess of: 7 hunters, sailors **9** fishermen
father: 4 Zeus
mother: 5 Carme
corresponds to: 7 Artemis **8** Dictynna

Briton 4 Celt **6** Celtic **7** British

Brittany
coast: 5 Armor
country: 6 France
inhabitant: 5 Celts **6** French, Romans
interior: 6 Argoat
land form: 9 peninsula
language: 6 Breton
other name: 5 Breiz **6** Breton **8** Bretagne

Britten, (Edward) Benjamin
born: 7 England **9** Lowestoft
composer of: 8 Gloriana **9** Billy Budd **10** Paul Bunyan, War Requiem **11** Curlew River, Peter Grimes, Winter Words **12** Owen Wingrave, The Poet's Echo **13** Albert Herring, Death in Venice **14** The Prodigal Son, Turn of the Screw **15** Phantasy Quartet **17** A Ceremony of Carols, A Charm of Lullabies, Sinfonia da Requiem, The Rape of Lucretia **18** Holderlin Fragments **20** Cantata Misericordium **21** A Midsummer Night's Dream, Sonnets of Michelangelo **22** The Burning Fiery Furnace

brittle 7 crumbly, fragile, friable **9** breakable, frangible

Brize
form: 6 gadfly
sent by: 4 Hera
sent to annoy: 2 Io

Brizo
origin: 5 Greek
goddess of: 7 sailors

prophesied through: 6 dreams

broach 4 pose **6** launch, open up, submit **7** advance, bring up, mention, propose, suggest, touch on **9** institute, introduce

broad 4 full, open, wide **5** ample, clear, large, plain, rangy, roomy, thick **7** general, immense, obvious, sizable **8** extended, spacious, sweeping **9** capacious, expansive, extensive, inclusive, outspread, universal, unlimited **10** undetailed **11** far-reaching, nonspecific, wide-ranging **12** all-embracing, encyclopedic **13** comprehensive

broadcast 4 beam, show, talk **5** cable, radio, relay **7** program, send out **8** televise, transmit **9** statement **10** distribute **11** disseminate, put on the air **12** announcement

broaden 5 boost, raise, swell, widen **6** dilate, expand, extend **7** advance, amplify, augment, build up, develop, distend, enlarge, improve, stretch **8** increase **9** intensify, reinforce, spread out **10** strengthen, supplement

broadened 7 dilated, swelled, swollen, widened **8** enlarged, expanded, extended **9** distended, spread out

broad-minded 7 liberal **8** amenable, catholic, flexible, tolerant, unbiased **9** receptive, unbigoted **10** charitable, open-minded, undogmatic **11** magnanimous **12** unprejudiced, unprovincial

Broadway Joe
nickname of: 9 Joe Namath

Brobdingnag
fictional land in: 16 Gulliver's Travels
author: 5 Swift

Brobdingnagian 4 huge **5** giant **7** immense, mammoth **8** colossal, enormous, gigantic **10** gargantuan, tremendous **11** elephantine

broccoli 9 vegetable **12** Brassica rapa **16** Brassica oleracea (Botyris Group) **17** Brassica septiceps
variety: 6 Turnip **7** Italian **9** Asparagus, Sprouting

brochure 5 flier **6** folder **7** booklet, leaflet **8** circular, handbill, pamphlet **9** throwaway

Brockton Blockbuster
nickname of: 13 Rocky Marciano

Broglie, Louis Victor de
field: 7 physics
nationality: 6 French
developed: 13 wave mechanics
awarded: 10 Nobel Prize

broil 3 fry **4** bake, burn, cook, sear **5** parch, roast, toast **6** scorch **7** blister

broiler 3 hot, pan **4** rack **5** grill **6** cooker **8** scorcher **12** young chicken

broke 8 bankrupt, strapped, wiped out **9** insolvent, penniless **10** down and out **12** impoverished, on one's uppers, without funds **16** strapped for funds

broken 4 torn **5** rough, split, tamed **6** ruined, uneven **7** crushed, damaged **8** bankrupt, in pieces, ruptured **9** fractured, separated, shattered **10** incomplete **11** fragmentary, interrupted

Broken Commandment, The
author: 14 Toson Shimazaki

broken-down 6 beat-up, ruined **7** rickety, worn-out **8** battered, decrepit **10** ramshackle **11** dilapidated **12** deteriorated

broken-hearted 3 sad **6** gloomy, woeful **7** crushed, doleful, forlorn, unhappy **8** dejected, desolate, downcast, mournful, wretched **9** depressed, long-faced, miserable, sorrowful, woebegone **10** despairing, despondent, melancholy **11** heartbroken **12** disconsolate, inconsolable

Brom Bones
also: 12 Brom Van Brunt
character in: 23 The Legend of Sleepy Hollow
author: 6 Irving

Brome
form: 5 nymph
cared for: 8 Dionysus

Bromfield, Louis
author of: 11 Early Autumn, Malabar Farm **12** The Rains Came **13** Mrs Parkington, Night in Bombay **14** Wild Is the River **15** The Green Bay Tree **31** The Strange Case of Miss Annie Spragg

bromide 6 cliche **8** banality **9** platitude **10** stereotype **11** trite phrase **19** hackneyed expression

bromidic 4 dull **5** banal, corny, stale, tired, trite, vapid **6** jejune **7** humdrum, insipid **8** ordinary **9** hackneyed **10** pedestrian, unexciting, unoriginal **13** platitudinous, unimaginative

bromine
  chemical symbol: **2** Br

Bromius
  epithet of: **8** Dionysus
  means: **7** thunder

Bronson, Charles
  real name: **16** Charles Buchinsky
  wife: **11** Jill Ireland
  born: **11** Ehrenfeld PA
  roles: **9** Death Wish **13** The Dirty Dozen **14** The Great Escape **16** Battle of the Bulge, The Valachi Papers **19** The Magnificent Seven

Bronte, Anne
  author of: **9** Agnes Grey **23** The Tenant of Wildfell Hall

Bronte, Charlotte
  author of: **7** Shirley **8** Jane Eyre, Villette **12** The Professor

Bronte, Emily
  author of: **16** Wuthering Heights

Brontes
  member of: **8** Cyclopes

brontophobia
  fear of: **7** thunder

Brontosaurus
  also: **11** Apatosaurus
  type: **8** dinosaur, sauropod
  period: **8** Jurassic

Bronx Bull
  nickname of: **11** Jake La Motta

bronze 3 tan **5** metal **8** brownish, chestnut **10** reddish-tan **12** reddish-brown **13** copper-colored

brooch 3 pin **5** clasp

brood 4 chew, fret, mope, mull, sulk **5** cover, dwell, hatch, spawn, worry, young **6** chicks, family, litter **7** agonize, sit upon **8** children, incubate **9** offspring **10** hatchlings

brook 3 run **4** bear, rill, take **5** abide, allow, creek, stand **6** accept, endure, stream, suffer **7** rivulet, stomach **8** tolerate **9** put up with, streamlet

Brooks, Gwendolyn
  author of: **4** Riot **10** Annie Allen **14** Family Pictures

Brooks, James L
  director of: **17** Terms of Endearment (Oscar)

Brooks, Mel
  real name: **14** Melvin Kaminsky

wife: 12 Anne Bancroft
  born: **10** Brooklyn NY
  director of/roles: **11** High Anxiety, Silent Movie **12** The Producers **14** Blazing Saddles **17** Young Frankenstein **20** The History of the World

Brooks, Richard
  director of: **11** Elmer Gantry, In Cold Blood **16** Cat on a Hot Tin Roof, Sweet Bird of Youth **19** The Blackboard Jungle

broom 4 bush **5** besom, brush, whisk **7** sweeper

Broteas
  father: **8** Tantalus
  devotee of: **6** Cybele
  denied divinity of: **7** Artemis

broth 5 stock **8** bouillon, consomme **9** clear soup

brothel 4 stew **5** house **6** bagnio, bordel **8** bordello, cathouse **10** bawdy house, fancy house, whorehouse **11** maison close **13** maison de passe, sporting house **14** house of ill fame **16** house of ill repute **19** house of prostitution

brother 3 pal **4** chum, monk, peer **5** buddy, friar **6** cleric **7** comrade, kinsman, partner, sibling **8** confrere, landsman, monastic, relative, relation **9** associate, colleague, companion, fellowman **10** countryman **11** male sibling **12** fellow member **13** fellow citizen
  French: **5** frere

brotherhood 4 club **5** amity, lodge **10** fellowship, fraternity, friendship **11** association

Brother Juniper
  character in: **21** The Bridge of San Luis Rey
  author: **6** Wilder

Brothers Karamazov, The
  author: **10** Dostoevsky **17** Fyodor Dostoyevsky
  character: **4** Ivan **6** Dmitri **7** Alyosha (Alexey), Zossima **8** Katerina **9** Grushenka **10** Smerdyakov **15** Fyodor Karamazov

brougham 3 car **8** carriage **10** automobile

brought 6 caused **7** carried, fetched, sold for **8** conveyed **9** conducted, convinced, persuaded

brow 3 rim **4** brim, edge, side **5** brink, verge **6** border, margin **8** boundary, forehead **9** periphery

browbeat 3 cow **5** abash, bully, cower **6** badger, harass,

hector **7** henpeck **8** bulldoze, domineer, frighten, threaten **9** terrorize, tyrannize **10** intimidate

browbeater 5 bully **6** despot **7** coercer **9** oppressor, tormenter, tormentor **11** intimidator, petty tyrant

browbeating 8 bullying **11** threatening, tyrannizing **12** intimidation

brown 3 bay, dun, fry, tan **4** buff, cook, drab, fawn, puce, roan, rust **5** beige, camel, cocoa, hazel, khaki, saute, tawny, toast, umber **6** auburn, bronze, brunet, coffee, copper, ginger, russet, sorrel, walnut **8** brunette, chestnut, cinnamon, mahogany **9** chocolate, olive drab **10** terra-cotta **11** dirt-colored, sand-colored **12** liver-colored

Brown, Angeline
  real name of: **14** Angie Dickinson

Brown, Berenice Sadie
  character in: **19** A Member of the Wedding
  author: **9** McCullers

Brown, Charles Brockden
  author of: **6** Ormond **7** Wieland **11** Edgar Huntly **12** Arthur Mervyn

Brown, Claude
  author of: **16** The Children of Ham **25** Manchild in the Promised Land

Brown, Dee
  author of: **15** Creek Mary's Blood **24** Bury My Heart at Wounded Knee

Brown, Helen Gurley
  author of: **19** Sex and the Single Girl
  editor of: **12** Cosmopolitan

Brown, Helen Hayes
  real name of: **10** Helen Hayes

Brown, Jim (Jimmy)
  sport: **8** football
  position: **8** fullback
  team: **15** Cleveland Browns
  actor in: **10** Dirty Dozen

Brown, Robert
  field: **6** botany
  nationality: **8** Scottish
  established: **16** Brownian movement

Brown Bomber
  nickname of: **8** Joe Louis

Browne, Dik
  creator/artist of: **9** Hi and Lois **12** Beetle Bailey **16** Hagar the Horrible

Browne, Sir Thomas
author of: **9** Urn Burial
12 Hydriotaphia **13** Religio
Medici **16** The Garden of
Cyrus

brownie 3 elf **4** cake, puck
5 fairy, pixie **6** sprite
10 leprechaun

Browning, Elizabeth Barrett
author of: **11** Aurora Leigh
14 How Do I Love Thee
16 Casa Guidi Windows
24 Sonnets from the
Portuguese

Browning, Robert
author of: **8** Sordello **10** Par-
acelsus **11** Pippa Passes
13 Fra Lippo Lippi, My Last
Duchess **14** Andrea del
Sarto **17** The Ring and the
Book **20** The Pied Piper of
Hamlin **29** Soliloquy of the
Spanish Cloister **30** Childe
Roland to the Dark Tower
Came

brownish 3 tan **5** taupe
6 bronze **8** chestnut **13** copper-
colored

Brownlow, Mr
character in: **11** Oliver Twist
author: **7** Dickens

Brownmiller, Susan
author of: **14** Against Our
Will

Brown's Descent
author: **11** Robert Frost

browse 3 eat **4** feed, scan,
skim **5** graze **6** nibble, peruse,
survey **7** dip into, pasture
8 look over **9** check over
11 look through **13** glance
through

Bruckner, Anton
born: **7** Austria **9** Ansfelden
composer of: **6** Te Deum
7 Psalm CL **11** Grosse
Messe **16** Romantic Symphony **26** Intermezzo for
String Quartet

Brueghel, Pieter (the Elder)
born: **5** Breda **8** Flanders
nickname: **14** Peasant Bruegel
son: **11** Jan Brueghel
artwork: **9** Blue Cloak, The
Months **10** Dulle Griet (Mad
Meg) **12** Fall of Icarus,
Peasant Dance, Tower of
Babel **14** Children's Games,
The Misanthrope **15** Return
of the Herd **16** Hunters in
the Snow **17** The Triumph
of Death **19** Peasant Wedding Dance **21** Peasant Wedding Banquet, The Magpie
on the Gallows **22** Massacre
of the Innocents **23** The
Blind Leading the Blind,
The Fall of the Rebel
Angels

Brueghel, Jan
born: **8** Brussels, Flanders
nickname: **6** Velvet
father: **13** Pieter Bruegel
artwork: **12** Four Elements
13 Village Street **15** The
Garden of Eden (with Rub-
ens) **17** The Battle of
Arbela

**Brueghel, Pieter (the
Younger)**
born: **8** Brussels, Flanders
nickname: **12** Hell Brueghel
19 The Infernal Brueghel
father: **13** Pieter Bruegel (the
Elder)
artwork: **11** Village Fair
14 The Crucifixion **16** The
Burning of Troy

Brugh, Spangler Arlington
real name of: **12** Robert
Taylor

bruise 3 mar **4** hurt, mark
5 abuse, wound **6** damage, injure, injury, offend **7** blacken,
blemish **8** discolor **9** black
mark, contusion
13 discoloration

bruit 3 din **5** noise, rumor
6 clamor, hubbub, racket, report, uproar **7** clangor **10** clattering, noise about **11** voice
abroad

Brunei
capital/largest city:
17 Bandar Seri
Begawan
others: **4** Labi **5** Badas,
Danau, Muara, Seria
6 Bangar, Tutong
7 Kampong **10** Kuala
Abang, Kuala Balai
11 Kuala Belait
head of state/govern-
ment: **6** sultan
island: **6** Borneo
8 Sipitang
mountain: **6** Teraja **9** Ulu
Tutong
highest point: **10** Pagon
Priok
river: **6** Belait, Brunei,
Tutong **9** Temburong
sea: **10** South China
physical feature:
bay: **6** Brunei
people: **4** Iban **5** Dayak,
Malay **7** Chinese,
Kadazan
language: **4** Iban **5** Malay **7** Chinese, English
religion: **5** Islam
6 Taoism **7** animism
8 Buddhism
12 Christianity
feature: **3** oil

Brunelleschi, Filippo
architect of: **10** San Lorenzo **11** Pazzi Chapel (Santa
Croce), Pitti Palace **12** Santo
Spirito **14** Badia Fiesolana
15 Duomo of Florence
16 Palazzo Quaratesi
21 Santa Maria degli An-
geli **22** Ospedale degli Innocenti **23** Dome of Florence
Cathedral

brunet, brunette 4 dark
5 black **9** brown-eyed, dark
brown **10** dark-haired
11 brown-haired, dark-
skinned **12** olive-skinned
16 dark-complexioned

Brunhild
origin: **8** Germanic
Scandinavian: **8** Brynhild
character in:
14 Nibelungenlied
queen of: **8** Isenland
husband: **7** Gunther
won by: **9** Siegfried

brunt 5 force **6** impact, stress,
thrust **8** violence **9** full force,
main shock

brush 4 bush, dust, fern, wash
5 clean, copse, flick, graze,
groom, paint, run-in, scrub,
sedge, set-to, shine, sweep,
touch, whisk **6** battle, bushes,
caress, duster, forest, fracas,
polish, shrubs, stroke
7 bracken, cleanse, dusting,
grazing, meeting, scuffle,
thicket, varnish **8** skirmish,
woodland **9** encounter, shrubbery, woodlands **10** engagement, underbrush,
whiskbroom **11** bush country,
undergrowth **12** bristled tool
13 confrontation
type: **4** hair, nail, shoe,
wash **5** paint, scrub, tooth
7 clothes

brush aside 6 slight **7** neglect
8 pass over **9** disregard

brush-off 3 cut **4** snub
5 brush **6** rebuff, slight **7** put-
down, squelch **9** disregard, rejection **11** repudiation **12** cold
shoulder

brusque 4 curt, rude, tart
5 bluff, blunt, gruff, harsh,
rough, short **6** abrupt, crusty
7 bearish **8** impolite, ungentle
10 ungracious **12** discourteous
13 unceremonious

Brussels
canal: **9** Charleroi
10 Willebroek
capital of: **7** Belgium
cathedral: **26** Saint Michel
and Sainte Gudule
early name: **10** Bruoc-sella
means: **16** marshy
settlement
Flemish: **7** Brussel

French: 9 Bruxelles
headquarters of: 3 EEC
4 NATO 12 Common Market 25 European Economic
Community
landmark: 11 Royal Palace
15 Palace of Justice 17 Palace of the Nation
province: 7 Brabant
river: 5 Senne, Zenne
square: 11 Grande Place

brutal 5 crude, cruel, harsh
6 bloody, coarse, fierce, savage 7 brutish, hellish, inhuman, vicious 8 barbaric,
pitiless, ruthless 9 atrocious,
barbarous, heartless, merciless,
unfeeling 10 demoniacal
11 hardhearted, remorseless
12 bloodthirsty

brutality 7 cruelty 8 ferocity,
savagery 9 barbarity, harshness 10 inhumanity, savageness 11 brutishness,
viciousness 12 ruthlessness

brute 5 beast, demon, devil,
fiend, swine 6 animal, savage
7 monster 9 barbarian 10 wild
animal 11 cruel person
12 dumb creature

brutish 5 cruel, feral 6 bloody,
brutal, fierce, savage 7 inhuman 8 barbaric 9 barbarous,
ferocious, unfeeling
11 remorseless

brutishness 8 ferocity, savagery 9 barbarity, brutality
10 bestiality, coarseness, inhumanity, savageness 11 viciousness 15 remorselessness

Brutus
also: 12 Marcus Brutus
character in: 12 Julius
Caesar
author: 11 Shakespeare

Bruxelles see 8 Brussels

Bryan, C D B
author of: 12 Friendly Fire
24 Ugly Scenes Beautiful
Women

Bryant, Bear (Paul)
sport: 8 football
position: 5 coach
team: 7 Alabama 11 Crimson
Tide

Brynhild
origin: 12 Scandinavian
Germanic: 8 Brunhild
husband: 6 Gunnar
won by: 6 Sigurd
position: 8 Valkyrie

Brynhildr Sigrdrifa see
9 Sigrdrifa

Brynner, Yul
real name: 10 Taidje Khan
born: 14 Sakhalin Island
roles: 9 Anastasia, West
World 11 The King and I

(Oscar) 18 The Ten Commandments 19 The Magnificent Seven 20 The Brothers
Karamazov 23 Invitation to
a Gunfighter

Brythonic
language family: 12 Indo-European
group: 5 Welsh 6 Breton
7 Cornish, Pictish

Bschliessmayer, Oskar
Josef
real name of: 11 Oskar Werner

Bubba Smith
nickname of: 17 Charles
Aaron Smith

bubble, bubbles 4 bleb, boil,
fizz, foam 5 froth 6 burble, fizzle, gurgle, seethe 7 air ball,
blister, droplet, globule, sparkle 9 percolate 10 effervesce
13 effervescence

bubbliness 9 fizziness, foaminess 10 ebullience, enthusiasm, frothiness, liveliness
11 high spirits
13 effervescence

bubbling 5 fizzy, foamy
6 frothy 7 fizzing, foaming
9 sparkling 12 effervescent

bubbly 5 fizzy, foamy 6 frothy,
lively 7 fizzing, foaming
9 champagne, sparkling 12 effervescent, high-spirited

Bubona
origin: 5 Roman
protectress of: 4 cows, oxen

buccaneer 6 pirate 7 corsair
9 privateer 10 freebooter

Buchan, John (Baron
Tweedsmuir)
author of: 10 John Macnab
11 Greenmantle, Pilgrim's
Way 17 John Burnet of
Barns 18 The Thirty-Nine
Steps

Buchanan, Daisy
character in: 14 The Great
Gatsby
author: 10 Fitzgerald

Buchanan, Edgar
born: 13 Humansville MO
roles: 5 Shane, Texas 7 Arizona 8 Cimarron 9 McLintock 13 Penny Serenade
17 Petticoat Junction
18 Ride the High Country

Buchanan, James see box,
p. 136

Bucharest
capital of: 7 Romania,
Rumania
founder: 5 Bucur
landmark: 8 Scinteia 13 Village Museum
river: 9 Dimbovita
Rumanian: 9 Bucuresti

Buchinsky, Charles
real name of: 14 Charles
Bronson

buck 3 man 4 beau, deer,
dude, kick, male 5 dandy
6 dollar, oppose 7 coxcomb
8 cavalier, gay blade 9 go
against 10 young blood

Buck
character in: 16 The Call of
the Wild
author: 6 London

Buck, Pearl S
author of: 8 The Exile
9 Other Gods 10 Dragon
Seed 12 The Good Earth
13 A House Divided

bucket 3 can, hod, tub 4 cask,
pail 5 scoop 6 vessel 7 pailful,
pitcher, scuttle 9 container
10 receptacle

Buckeye State
nickname of: 4 Ohio

buckle 3 sag 4 bend, clip, curl,
hasp, hook, warp 5 bulge,
catch, clasp 6 cave in, couple,
fasten, secure 7 contort, crinkle, crumple, distort, wrinkle
8 belly out, collapse, fastener

buckle down 6 attend 12 apply oneself

Buckley, William F Jr
author of: 11 Who's on
First? 15 God and Man at
Yale, God Save the Queen

Buck Rogers
creator: 14 Richard Calkins
character: 5 Alura, Buddy,
Dercu, Kayla, Wilma 6 Ardala 10 Killer Kane

bucolic 4 idyl, poem 5 idyll,
rural 6 poetic, rustic 7 eclogue,
idyllic, peasant 8 pastoral,
shepherd

Bucolion
father: 8 Laomedon
son: 7 Aesepus
wife: 9 Abarbarea

bud 4 open 5 shoot 6 flower,
sprout 7 blossom, burgeon,
develop

Bud, Rosa
character in: 22 The Mystery
of Edwin Drood
author: 7 Dickens

Budapest
area: 4 Buda, Pest 5 Obuda
capital of: 7 Hungary
cathedral: 13 Saint Matthias
hill: 10 Castle Hill
island: 6 Csepel
river: 6 Danube
Roman town: 8 Aquincum

Buddenbrooks
author: 10 Thomas Mann

Buchanan, James
nickname: **7** Old Buck
presidential rank: **9** fifteenth
party: **8** Democrat
state represented: **2** PA
defeated: **7** (John Charles) Fremont **8** (Millard) Fillmore
vice president: **12** (John Cabell) Breckinridge
cabinet:
  state: **4** (Lewis) Cass **5** (Jeremiah Sullivan) Black
  treasury: **3** (John Adams) Dix **4** (Howell) Cobb **6** (Philip Francis) Thomas
  war: **4** (Joseph) Holt **5** (John Buchanan) Floyd
  attorney general: **5** (Jeremiah Sullivan) Black **7** (Edwin McMasters) Stanton
  navy: **6** (Isaac) Toucey
  postmaster general: **4** (Horatio) King, (Joseph) Holt **5** (Aaron Venable) Brown
  interior: **8** (Jacob) Thompson
born: **11** Cove Gap PA (near Mercersburg)
died/buried: **11** Lancaster PA
education:
  Academy: **8** Old Stone
  College: **9** Dickinson
  studied: **3** law
religion: **12** Presbyterian
political career: **13** state assembly **24** US House of Representatives
  secretary of: **5** State
  minister: **6** Russia **12** Great Britain
civilian career: **6** lawyer
notable events of lifetime/term: **5** Panic (of 1857) **11** English Bill, Pony Express
  raid by: **9** John Brown
  raid on: **12** Harper's Ferry
  Supreme Court case: **9** Dred Scott
father: **5** James
mother: **9** Elizabeth (Speer)
siblings: **4** Jane, John, Mary **5** Maria, Sarah **7** Harriet **9** Elizabeth **11** Edward Young **12** William Speer **16** George Washington
wife: **4** none
children: **4** none

Buddha
also called: **5** Butsu
born: **ll** Kapilavastu
father: **ll** Suddhodhana
founded: **8** Buddhism
means: **15** enlightened one
message: **6** dharma
name for: **l7** Siddhartha Gautama
son: **6** Rahula
tree: **2** bo **5** bodhi
wife: **9** Yasodhara

Buddhism
action: **5** karma
branch: **8** Mahayana **9** Theravada **l2** Great Vehicle **l4** way of the elders
doctrine: **6** duhkha **7** nirvana **9** suffering **l3** eightfold path **l5** four noble truths **l7** pratityasamutpada
founded by: **6** Buddha **l7** Siddhartha Gautama
monk: **7** bhikshu
nun: **9** bhikshuni

rebirth: **7** samsara
religious community: **6** sangha

buddy **3** pal **4** chum, mate **5** amigo, crony **6** cohort, fellow, friend **7** brother, comrade, partner **8** confrere, intimate, playmate, sidekick **9** associate, colleague, companion, confidant **10** playfellow **11** confederate

buddy-buddy **5** close, palsy **6** chummy **8** friendly, intimate **10** palsy-walsy

budge **4** move, push, roll, stir, sway **5** shift, slide **6** change **8** convince, dislodge, persuade **9** dislocate, influence

budget **4** cost, plan **5** funds, means **6** moneys, ration **7** arrange **8** allocate, schedule **9** allotment, allowance, apportion, resources **10** allocation, portion out **12** spending plan **13** financial plan

budgetary **6** fiscal **8** economic, monetary **9** financial, pecuniary

buenas noches **9** good night

bueno **4** good

Buenos Aires
capital of: **9** Argentina
landmark: **11** Teatro Colon **16** Saavedra Monument, San Martin Theater **17** Wildestein Gallery, Witcomb Art Gallery **18** Church of El Salvador **27** Christopher Columbus Monument
park: **7** Palermo
people: **8** portenos
  means: **15** people of the port
river: **12** Rio de la Plata

buff **3** bug, fan, nut, rub, tan **4** swab **5** freak, hound, mavin, sandy, straw, tawny **6** addict, dauber, polish, smooth, the raw **7** admirer, burnish, devotee, leather **8** bare skin, follower, polisher **9** nakedness, yellowish **10** aficionado, enthusiast **11** buffalo hide, connoisseur **14** yellowish-brown

buffalo **5** bison **6** puzzle **7** mystify **l0** intimidate
kind: **7** African **l0** Asian water
African: **l4** syncerus caffer
Asian water: **l4** bubalus bubalis

Buffalo
football team: **5** Bills
hockey team: **6** Sabres

buffer **6** bumper, fender, shield **7** cushion **9** protector

buffet **3** box, hit, jab, rap **4** bang, beat, bump, cuff, meal, push, slap **5** baste, knock, pound, shove, thump **6** pummel, strike, supper, thrash, thwack, wallop **7** cabinet, counter **8** credenza **9** cafeteria, sideboard **ll** smorgasbord

Buffone, Carlo
character in: **22** Every Man out of His Humour
author: **6** Jonson

buffoon **3** wag **4** fool, zany **5** clown, comic, joker, mimic, Punch **6** jester, madcap **7** Pierrot **8** comedian, funnyman **9** harlequin, pantaloon, prankster, trickster **10** Scaramouch, silly-billy **11** merry-andrew, punchinello, Scaramouche

buffoonery **6** antics, comedy **7** foolery, inanity **8** zaniness **9** asininity, horseplay, silliness, slapstick **10** tomfoolery **11** foolishness, loutishness

12 clownishness, monkey-shines, prankishness **14** clowning around, playing the fool

bug 3 nag **4** flaw, germ **5** annoy, fault, virus **6** badger, bother, defect, insect, pester **7** wiretap **8** drawback, listen in, weakness **9** eavesdrop, Hemiptera **11** Heteroptera **variety: 3** bat, bed, red **4** gnat, lace, leaf, seed, toad **5** negro, plant, shore, stilt, stink, water **6** ambush, damsel, fungus, pirate, ripple **7** boatman, stainer **8** assassin, burrower, creeping **9** royal palm **10** leaf footed **11** ashgray leaf, backswimmer, broadheaded, jumping tree, velvet water **12** velvety shore, water strider, water treader **13** jumping ground, water measurer, water scorpion **14** scentless plant **17** terrestrial turtle

bugaboo 5 scare **6** fright **7** anxiety

bugbear 4 ogre **5** bogey **6** goblin **7** bugaboo **8** bogeyman **9** bete noire

buggy 4 cart **5** wagon **7** vehicle **8** carriage **10** conveyance

bugle 4 horn **10** instrument

Bugs Bunny
creator: 15 Leon Schlesinger
character: 9 Elmer Fudd
voice of: 8 Mel Blanc
saying: 10 what's up doc

build 4 body, form, make, mold, open **5** begin, brace, erect, forge, found, put up, raise, renew, set up, shape, start, steel **6** create, extend, figure, harden, launch **7** amplify, augment, develop, enhance, enlarge, fashion, greaten, improve, produce **8** embark on, increase, initiate, multiply, physique **9** construct, establish, fabricate, institute, intensify, originate, reinforce, structure, undertake **10** inaugurate, strengthen, supplement **11** manufacture, put together **12** construction

building 7 edifice **9** structure **12** construction

building front 6 facade **8** frontage

build up 5 amass **7** develop, promote **8** increase **10** accumulate

Bujold, Genevieve
born: 6 Canada **8** Montreal
roles: 4 Coma **9** Monsignor, Obsession **12** King of

Hearts **21** Anne of the Thousand Days

Bujumbura
capital of: 7 Burundi

Bul 17 eighth Hebrew month

bulb 3 bud **4** corm, seed **5** plant, tuber **8** swelling

Bulfinch, Charles
architect of: 7 Capitol (Washington DC) **16** Hartford City Hall (CT) **23** Massachusetts State House (Boston)
style: 7 Federal

Bulgakov, Mikhail
author of: 9 Black Snow **13** The White Guard **14** The Heart of a Dog **19** The Days of the Turbins **21** The Master and Margarita

Bulgaria *see box*

bulge 3 bag, sag **4** bump,

lump **5** curve, swell **6** excess **7** distend, project, puff out, sagging **8** protrude, stand out, stick out, swelling, swell out **9** bagginess **10** projection, prominence, protrusion **12** protuberance

bulk 4 body, mass, most, size **6** extent, volume, weight **7** bigness, measure **8** enormity, hugeness, main part, majority, quantity **9** amplitude, greatness, largeness, magnitude, major part, plurality, substance **10** better part, dimensions, lion's share **11** greater part, massiveness, proportions **13** preponderance

bulky 3 big **4** huge **5** large **6** clumsy **7** awkward, hulking, immense, lumpish, massive, sizable, unhandy **8** enormous, ungainly, unwieldy **9** capacious, extensive **10** cumber-

Bulgaria
capital/largest city: 5 Sofia
others: 3 Lom **4** Rila, Ruse **5** Aytos, Butan, Byclu, Elena, Iskra, Stara, Varna **6** Burgas, Devnia, Dulovo, Levsky, Pernik, Pleuna, Pleven, Plevna, Shumen, Shumla, Sliven, Slivno, Widden, Yambol, Zagora **7** Gabrovo, Karlovo, Plovdiv, Sistova, Tirnova **8** Khaskovo, Rustchuk, Svishtov **9** Ruse Vidin, Silistria **11** Kolorovgrad **12** Dimitrovgrad
school: 5 Sofia **7** Plovdiv **13** Veliko Turnovo
measure: 3 oka, oke **5** krine, lekhe, likhe
monetary unit: 3 lev **8** stotinki
weight: 3 oka, oke **5** tovar
mountain: 3 Kom **5** Botev, Pirin, Sapka **6** Balkan, Sredna **7** Vikhren **11** Rila-Rhodope
highest point: 6 Musala **8** Musallah
river: 3 Lom, Vit **4** Arda, Osma **5** Isker, Iskur, Mesta **6** Danube, Marica, Ogosta, Struma, Yantra **7** Maritsa, Stryama, Tundzha
sea: 5 Black
physical feature:
    cape: **5** Emine, Sabla **7** Kuratan
    gulf: **5** Burga
    plateau: **6** Danube
    resort: **9** Pyassatzi **13** Slunchev Bryay
    valley: **7** Maritsa
people: 4 Slav, Turk **5** Gypsy, Pomak, Tatar **6** Bulgar, Slavic **7** Chuvash **9** Cheremiss **10** Macedonian
language: 9 Bulgarian
religion: 5 Islam **24** Bulgarian Eastern Orthodox
place:
    church: **9** St Nedelja
    monastery: **4** Rila **6** Rilski
    monument: **7** Red Army
    mosque: **10** Banya Bashi
    museum: **21** Revolutionary Movement
    square: **5** Lenin
    valley of roses: **8** Kazanluk
feature:
    dance: **4** horo
    holiday: **12** St Georges Day
    newspaper: **17** Rabot Nichesko Delo
food:
    stew: **8** giuvetch

some, voluminous
12 unmanageable

bull 2 ox **4** male
male of the: 3 elk **4** seal
5 moose, whale **6** bovine
8 elephant
constellation of: 6 Taurus
Spanish: 4 toro

bulldoze 3 cow **4** bump, fell,
push, rage, raze **5** abash,
bully, drive, force, level, press,
shove **6** coerce, hector, jostle,
propel, subdue, thrust **7** buffalo, dragoon, flatten **8** bludgeon, browbeat, domineer,
shoulder **9** push about, tyrannize **10** intimidate

Bullen, Frank T
author of: 19 Told in the
Dry Watches **22** The Cruise
of the Cachalot

bullet 4 ball, lead, shot, slug
7 missile **8** buckshot

bulletin 4 note **6** report **7** account, message, release **8** dispatch **9** statement
10 communique, news report
12 notification
13 communication

Bullet Park
author: 11 John Cheever

bull fighter 6 torero **7** mata-
dor, picador **8** toreador **10** El
Cordobes **15** Miguel
Dominguin

Bullion State
nickname of: 8 Missouri

Bullitt
director: 10 Peter Yates
cast: 9 Don Gordon **12** Robert Duvall, Robert Vaughn,
Steve McQueen **16** Jacqueline Bisset
setting: 12 San Francisco

bullock 2 ox **4** beef, bull
5 steer

bullocks 4 kine, oxen **5** beefs,
bulls **6** beeves, cattle, steers

bull session 3 rap **4** talk
7 gabfest, palaver **8** dialogue
9 discourse **10** discussion
12 conversation
13 confabulation

bull's-eye 5 black **6** center
7 exactly **8** on target **9** dead
center, precisely

bully 3 cow **4** good **5** annoy,
swell, tough **6** cheers, coerce,
despot, harass, hurrah, hurray **7** coercer, right on, ruffian, tread on **8** browbeat,
bulldoze, domineer, frighten,
ride over, well done **9** oppressor, terrorize, tormentor, tyrannize **10** browbeater,
intimidate **11** intimidator

bullying 7 torment **8** coercion
9 despotism **10** harassment,
tormenting **11** browbeating,
domineering, tyrannizing
12 intimidation

bulrush 5 plant, sedge **7** cattail,
papyrus

bulwark 5 guard **7** barrier, parapet, rampart, support, de-
fense **8** mainstay **9** earthwork
10 embankment

Bulwer-Lytton, Edward
author of: 6 Harold, Pelham,
Rienzi **9** Richelieu **13** The
Coming Race **16** Kenelm
Chillingly **18** The Last of
the Barons **20** The Last
Days of Pompeii

bum 3 beg **4** grub, hobo
5 cadge, idler, mooch, tramp
6 borrow, loafer, sponge
7 drifter, vagrant **8** derelict,
vagabond

bumble 6 bungle **7** blunder,
stagger, stumble **8** flounder

Bumble
character in: 11 Oliver Twist
author: 7 Dickens

bumcombe, bunkum 3 rot
4 bosh, bunk **6** drivel **7** twaddle **8** nonsense, tommyrot
10 balderdash **16** stuff-and-
nonsense

bump 3 hit, jar, rap **4** bang,
blow, butt, hump, jolt, knob,
knot, lump, node, poke, slam,
slap, sock **5** bulge, clash,
crack, crash, gnarl, knock,
punch, shake, smack, smash,
thump, whack **6** bounce, buffet, impact, jostle, jounce,
nodule, rattle, strike, wallop
7 collide, run into **8** swelling
9 collision, crash into, smash
into **11** excrescence
12 protuberance

bump into 4 meet **7** collide,
run into **9** encounter

bumpkin 3 oaf **4** boor, lout
5 churl, yokel **8** ship beam
10 clodhopper

bump off 4 do in, kill, slay
6 murder, rub out **7** execute,
gun down **8** dispatch **11** assassinate **12** take for a ride

bumptious 4 bold **5** cocky,
pushy **6** brazen **7** forward,
haughty **8** arrogant, boastful,
cocksure, impudent, insolent
9 bodacious, conceited, obtrusive **10** aggressive, swaggering **11** impertinent,
overbearing **12** presumptuous
13 overconfident, self-assertive

bumptiousness 4 gall
5 cheek **8** audacity, boldness

9 impudence **11** forwardness,
presumption **12** impertinence
13 obtrusiveness **17** self-
assertiveness

bumpy 5 lumpy, rocky, rough
6 uneven **10** undulating

bun 4 coil, knot, roll **8** soft
roll **9** sweet roll

Bunaea
epithet of: 4 Hera
refers to: 6 temple

bunch 3 lot, mob **4** band, bevy,
gang, heap, herd, host, knot,
mass, pack, pile, team **5** array,
batch, clump, crowd, flock,
group, shock, stack, tribe,
troop **6** amount, bundle,
gather, huddle, number,
string **7** cluster, collect, company **8** assemble, assembly,
quantity **9** gathering, multitude **10** assortment, collection,
congregate **12** accumulation

bundle 3 lot **4** bale, bind, heap,
mass, pack, pile, wrap **5** array,
batch, bunch, group, sheaf,
stack, truss **6** amount, packet,
parcel **7** package **8** quantity
9 multitude **10** assortment, collection **11** tie together
12 accumulation

Bundren family
characters in: 11 As I Lay
Dying
member: 4 Anse, Cash, Darl
5 Addie, Jewel **9** Dewey Dell
author: 8 Faulkner

bungalow 5 cabin, house,
lodge **7** cottage

bungle 3 mar **4** flub, goof,
miff, ruin **5** botch, spoil **6** foul
up, mess up, muddle **7** blunder, butcher, do badly, louse
up, screw up **8** misjudge
9 mismanage, misreckon
10 miscompute **11** make a
mess of, misestimate
12 miscalculate

Bunin, Ivan Alekseyevich
author of: 10 The Village
15 The Elagin Affair **17** The
Life of Arseniev **28** The
Gentleman from San
Francisco

bunk 3 bed, cot, rot **4** bull
5 berth, hokum, hooey, stuff
6 bunkum, hot air, humbug,
pallet **7** baloney, blather, bombast, hogwash, inanity, malarky, spinach **8** claptrap,
nonsense, tommyrot **9** poppycock **10** applesauce, balderdash **11** foolishness **16** stuff
and nonsense

Bunsen, Robert Wilhelm
nationality: 6 German
inventor of: 9 gas burner

10 photo meter **12** Bunsen burner, spectroscope **24** electromechanical battery

Bunshaft, Gordon
  architect of: 10 Lever House (NY) **23** Beinecke Rare Book Library (Yale) **33** Hirshhorn Museum and Sculpture Garden (Washington DC) **34** Lyndon Baines Johnson Memorial Library (Austin TX)

Bunus
  father: 6 Hermes
  mother: 9 Aleidamea
  raised temple honoring:
    4 Hera
    location of temple:
      7 Corinth

Bunyan, John
  author of: 10 The Holy War **16** Pilgrim's Progress **25** The Life and Death of Mr Badman **33** Grace Abounding to the Chief of Sinners

buona notte 9 good night

buona sera 11 good evening

buon giorno 7 good day **11** good morning

Buono, Victor
  born: 10 San Diego CA
  roles: 11 The Stranger **12** Four for Texas **22** Hush Hush Sweet Charlotte **26** Whatever Happened to Baby Jane

buoy 4 bell, lift **5** boost, cheer, float, raise **6** beacon, uplift **7** cheer up, elevate, gladden, lighten **8** brighten **10** keep afloat **14** floating marker

buoyancy, buoyance 4 glee **6** gaiety **7** jollity **8** gladness, vivacity **9** animation, good humor, joviality, lightness, sunniness **10** brightness, cheeriness, enthusiasm, floatiness, joyousness **11** good spirits **12** cheerfulness, exhilaration, floatability **14** weightlessness **16** lightheartedness

buoyant 3 gay **4** glad **5** happy, jolly, light, merry, peppy, sunny **6** afloat, breezy, bright, elated, joyful, joyous, lively **7** hopeful **8** animated, carefree, cheerful, floating, sportive **9** energetic, floatable, sprightly, vivacious **10** blithesome, optimistic, weightless **11** exhilarated, free and easy **12** enthusiastic, lighthearted

buoyed 6 elated **7** exalted, pleased **8** elevated **9** confident, heartened, reassured **10** inspirited

buoy up 4 warm **6** assure,

uplift **7** comfort, hearten, inspire **8** inspirit, reassure **9** encourage

Buphagus
  father: 7 Iapetus
  slain by: 7 Artemis
  epithet of: 8 Hercules
  means: 7 ox-eater

Burbank, Luther
  field: 7 biology
  developed: 13 plant breeding

burble 6 babble, bubble, gurgle, murmur **8** babbling

Burce, Suzanne
  real name of: 10 Jane Powell

Burchill, Mr
  character in: 19 The Vicar of Wakefield
  author: 9 Goldsmith

burden 3 tax, try, vex **4** care, load, onus, pack **5** cargo **6** hamper, hinder, strain, stress, weight **7** afflict, anxiety, freight, oppress, trouble **8** encumber, handicap, hardship, load with, obligate, overload **9** press down, weigh down **10** saddle with **11** encumbrance **14** responsibility

Burden, Jack
  character in: 14 All the King's Men
  author: 6 Warren

burden of proof
  Latin: 12 onus probandi

burdensome 4 hard **5** heavy **6** tiring **7** arduous, onerous **8** wearying **9** Herculean, laborious **10** exhausting

bureau 6 agency, branch, office **7** cabinet, commode, dresser, service, station **8** division **10** chiffonier, department **14** administration, chest of drawers

bureaucrat 8 mandarin, official, politico **9** penpusher **10** politician **11** apparatchik, functionary, rubber stamp **12** civil servant, officeholder **13** public servant

burgee 4 flag **6** banner, colors, ensign **7** pennant

burgeon 3 wax **4** blow, grow, open **5** bloom **6** expand, flower, spread, thrive **7** augment, blossom, develop, enlarge, prosper, shoot up, succeed **8** escalate, flourish, fructify, increase, mushroom, spring up **9** bear fruit **10** effloresce **11** proliferate

Burgess, Anthony
  author of: 2 MF **13** Man of Nazareth, Time for a Tiger

14 Enderby Outside, The Wanting Seed **16** A Clockwork Orange, Beard's Roman Women **17** Nothing Like the Sun **20** The End of the World News

burgher 7 citizen **9** bourgeois **11** townsperson

burglar 3 cat **4** yegg **5** thief **6** robber **7** prowler **8** pilferer **9** cracksman, purloiner **12** housebreaker **14** secondstory man

burglary 5 theft **6** felony **7** break-in, larceny, robbery **8** filching, stealing **9** pilfering **10** purloining **13** housebreaking **19** breaking and entering

burgundy 3 red **4** wine **5** color **13** reddish-purple

Burgundy
  ancient city: 5 Autun
  city: 5 Dijon
  district: 5 Youne **6** Nievre **7** Cote d' Or **12** Saone-et-Loire
  French: 9 Bourgogne
  location: 6 France
  river: 5 Rhone, Saone
  tribe: 9 Burgundii

Buri
  origin: 12 Scandinavian
  first: 3 god
  revealed by: 8 Audhumla **9** Audhumbla

burial 5 rites **7** funeral **9** interment, obsequies **10** entombment, inhumation

burial ground 7 ossuary **8** boneyard, Boot Hill, catacomb, cemetery **9** graveyard **10** churchyard, necropolis **12** potter's field

buried 4 laid, sunk **6** hidden **7** covered, inhumed, immured **9** concealed, deep sixed **10** laid to rest **11** underground

Burke, Francis
  character in: 21 The Master of Ballantrae
  author: 9 Stevenson

Burkina Faso *see* Upper Volta

burlap 3 bag **4** hemp, jute **5** cloth **6** fabric **8** material

burlesque 5 farce, spoof **6** comedy, parody, satire **7** mockery, takeoff **8** ridicule, travesty **10** buffoonery, caricature **15** slapstick comedy

burly 3 big **5** beefy, bulky, hefty, large **6** brawny, stocky, strong, sturdy **7** hulking, sizable **8** thickset **9** ponderous, strapping

Burma *see* **7** Myanmar

burn 3 nip, tan **4** bite, char, fire, glow, hurt, pain, sear, skin **5** be hot, blaze, brown, chafe, flame, flare, flash, parch, prick, scald, singe, smart, smoke, sting **6** abrade, bronze, flames, ignite, kindle, nettle, scorch, scrape, suntan, tingle, wither **7** blister, consume, cremate, flicker, oxidize, prickle, shrivel, smolder, sunburn, swelter **8** abrasion, be ablaze, be on fire, charring, irritate, kindling **9** be flushed, reddening, set fire to, set on fire, use as fuel **10** be feverish, be in flames, blistering, incandesce, incinerate, irritation, smoldering **12** incineration **13** reduce to ashes

burnable 9 flammable, ignitable **10** combustible **11** combustible, inflammable **13** conflagrative

Burne-Jones, Sir Edward Coley
born: 7 England **10** Birmingham
artwork: 11 Laus Veneris **15** The Golden Stairs **16** The Mirror of Venus **18** The Star of Bethlehem **28** King Cophetua and the Beggar Maid

burner, gas
invented by: 6 Bunsen

Burnett, Carol
born: 12 San Antonio TX
roles: 14 The Four Seasons **19** The Carol Burnett Show

Burnett, Frances H
author of: 20 Little Lord Fauntleroy

Burney, Fanny
author of: 7 Camilla, Diaries, Evelina

Burnham, Daniel Hudson
partner: 16 John Wellborn Root

architect of: 7 Rookery **12** Union Station (Washington DC) **15** Calumet Building **16** Flatiron Building (NYC), Reliance Building **17** Monadnock Building **25** World's Columbian Exposition

burning 3 hot **5** acrid, afire, aglow, eager, fiery, sharp **6** aflame, ardent, biting, fervid, heated, raging, red-hot **7** blazing, boiling, caustic, earnest, fanatic, fervent, flaming, flaring, frantic, glowing, ignited, intense, kindled, painful, pungent, sincere, smoking, zea-

lous **8** flashing, frenzied, piercing, resolute, sizzling, smarting, stinging, tingling **9** corroding, prickling **10** astringent, compelling, flickering, irritating, passionate, smoldering **11** impassioned **12** all-consuming

burnish 3 wax **4** buff **5** rub up, shine **6** polish, smooth

burnished 5 shiny **6** bright, buffed, shined **8** lustrous, polished, smoothed

burnoose 4 cape, robe **5** cloak **6** mantle **7** pelisse

burn out 3 pop **4** blow **7** exhaust **10** exhaustion, extinguish

Burns, George
real name: 14 Nathan Birnbaum
wife: 11 Gracie Allen
born: 9 New York NY
roles: 5 Oh God **12** Going in Style **15** The Sunshine Boys **17** Burns and Allen Show

Burns, Robert
author of: 8 To a Louse, To a Mouse **11** A Red Red Rose, Tam O'Shanter **12** Auld Lang Syne **16** Address to the Deil, Coming Thro the Rye **17** Holy Willie's Prayer **20** Flow Gently Sweet Afton **22** My Heart's in the Highlands **23** The Cotter's Saturday Night **32** Poems Chiefly in the Scottish Dialect

Burnt Norton
author: 7 T S Eliot

burp 5 belch, eruct **10** eructation

burr 4 buhr, rock **5** notch, stone **9** whetstone **13** pronunciation

Burr
author: 9 Gore Vidal

Burr, Raymond
born: 6 Canada **14** New Westminster **15** British Columbia
roles: 8 Ironside **10** Perry Mason, Rear Window

burro 3 ass **4** mule **6** donkey, onager **7** jackass

Burroughs, Edgar Rice
author of: 15 Tarzan of the Apes

Burroughs, William S
author of: 5 Queer **6** Junkie **13** The Naked Lunch

Burroughs, William Seward
nationality: 8 American
inventor of: 13 adding machine
grandson: 17 William S Burroughs (author)

burrow 3 den, dig **4** cave, hole, lair **6** covert, dugout, furrow, tunnel **8** excavate, scoop out **9** hollow out

Burrows, Abe
author of: 41 How to Succeed in Business without Really Trying

bursa 3 bag, sac **5** pouch, purse **6** cavity

bursar 6 purser **7** cashier **9** paymaster, treasurer **10** cashkeeper

burst 3 fly, pop, run **4** bang, bust, rend, rush **5** barge, blast, break, crack, erupt, split, spout **6** blow up, detach, divide, sunder **7** disjoin, explode, rupture, shatter, torrent **8** breaking, break out, cracking, crashing, detonate, eruption, fly apart, fracture, fragment, outbreak, separate, splinter **9** break open, discharge, explosion, gush forth, pull apart, splitting, tear apart **10** detonation, disconnect, outpouring, shattering **11** spring forth **12** disintegrate

burst forth 5 arise, begin, erupt, start **6** arrive, emerge **8** break out, commence

Burstyn, Ellen
real name: 14 Edna Rae Gillooly
born: 9 Detroit MI
roles: 11 The Exorcist **16** Same Time Next Year **18** The Last Picture Show **26** Alice Doesn't Live Here Anymore (Oscar)

Burton, Richard
real name: 22 Richard Walter Jenkins Jr
wife: 15 Elizabeth Taylor
born: 5 Wales **11** Pontrhydfen Wales
roles: 6 Becket, Hamlet **7** Camelot, The Robe **9** Cleopatra **14** My Cousin Rachel **19** The Night of the Iguana, The Taming of the Shrew **21** Anne of the Thousand Days **25** Who's Afraid of Virginia Woolf **26** The Spy Who Came in from the Cold

Burton, Robert
author of: 22 The Anatomy of Melancholy

Burundi
capital/largest city:
9 Bujumbura
others: 5 Ngozi 6 Bururi,
Gitega, Kitega, Rutana,
Ruyigi 7 Kibumbu,
Muyinga
monetary unit: 5 franc
7 centime
lake: 7 Rugwero 8 Tshohoha 10 Tanganyika
mountain: 9 Nyamisana
highest point:
8 Nyarwana
river: 6 Akanya, Ruvuvu,
Ruzizi 8 Rukagera
10 Malagarasi
people: 3 Twa 4 Hutu
5 Bantu, Batwa, Pygmy,
Tutsi 6 Bahutu, Watusi
7 Barundi
language: 6 French
7 Kirundi, Swahili
religion: 5 Islam 7 animism 11 Protestant
13 Roman Catholic
feature:
king: 4 mwam
food:
coffee: 7 Arabica

Burushaski
language spoken in: 7 Kashmir

bury 4 hide 5 cache, cover, inter 6 encase, engulf, entomb,
inhume 7 conceal, cover up,
enclose, immerse, secrete
8 submerge, submerse 13 lay in
the grave 17 consign to the
grave

Bury My Heart at
Wounded Knee
author: 8 Dee Brown

bush 4 veld 5 brush, hedge,
plant, shrub, woods 6 forest,
jungle 7 barrens 9 shrubbery,
woodlands

bush country 5 scrub, wilds
7 outback 10 wilderness

bushed 4 beat 5 all in, spent,
tired, weary 6 done it,
pooped 7 drained, wearied,
worn out 8 dog tired, fatigued,
tired out 9 dead tired, exhausted, played out

bushel
abbreviation: 2 bu 4 bush

bushes 5 brush 6 shrubs
9 brushwood, shrubbery
10 underbrush 11 undergrowth

bushy 5 hairy 6 fluffy, shaggy
7 hirsute 9 overgrown

business 3 job 4 case, duty,
firm, line, shop, task, work

Bush, George Herbert
Walker
presidential rank:
10 forty-first
party: 10 Republican
state represented:
2 TX 5 Texas
defeated: 7 (Michael)
Dukakis
defeated by: 7 (Bill)
Clinton
vice president: 6 (James
Danforth) Quayle
born: 8 Milton MA
education: 4 Yale
7 Andover
religion: 12 Episcopalian
vacation spot: 5 Maine
13 Kennebunkport
political career: 13 vice
president 14 represen-
tative 21 Ways and
Means Committee
   ambassador to: 2 UN
   13 United Nations
   chairman of: 27 Re-
   publican National
   Committee
   head of: 3 CIA
   liaison with: 5 China
civilian career: 3 oil
14 Zapata Offshore
military career: 5 pilot
6 US Navy
vice president under:
12 Ronald Reagan
**notable events of life-
time/term:** 7 Gulf War
14 Persian Gulf War
20 Operation Desert
Storm
   *Supreme Court ap-
   pointments:* 11 David
   Souter 14 Clarence
   Thomas
   invasion of: 6 Panama
father: 15 Prescott
Sheldon
mother: 13 Dorothy
Walker
wife: 13 Barbara Pierce
children: 4 John, Neil
5 Robin (died 1953)
6 George, Marvin
7 Dorothy

5 chore, field, place, point,
store, topic, trade 6 affair, career, living, matter, office,
racket 7 affairs, calling, company, concern, dealing, factory,
mission, problem, pursuit, subject, venture 8 activity, commerce, function, industry,
position, province, question,
vocation 9 procedure, situation,
specialty 10 assignment, bargaining, employment, enterprise, livelihood, occupation,
profession, walk of life 11 cor-

poration, negotiation, partnership, transaction, undertaking
13 establishment, manufacturing, merchandising 14 bread
and butter, responsibility

businesslike 7 careful, correct,
orderly, regular, serious 8 diligent, sedulous, thorough 9 assiduous, efficient, organized,
practical 10 methodical, systematic 11 industrious, painstaking 12 professional

Busiris
king of: 5 Egypt
father: 8 Poseidon
mother: 10 Lysianassa

Busoni, Ferruccio
born: 5 Italy 6 Empoli
composer of: 8 Turandot
10 Arlecchino 11 Doctor
Faust, Doktor Faust 12 Die
Brautwahl 14 Comedy Over-
ture 25 Fantasia
Contrappuntistica

bus station 5 depot 8 terminal,
terminus

Bus Stop
director: 11 Joshua Logan
cast: 9 Don Murray 10 Betty
Field 13 Eileen Heckart, Marilyn Monroe 14 Arthur
O'Connell

bust 3 nab 4 head, raid 5 bosom, chest, seize 6 arrest,
breast, collar 7 capture 9 apprehend, sculpture 12 take prisoner 15 take into custody

Buster Brown
creator: 10 RF Outcault
bulldog: 4 Tige
trademark: 9 sailor hat
10 wide collar

bustle 3 ado, fly 4 dash, flit,
fuss, rush, stir, tear, to-do
5 hurry 6 bestir, flurry, hustle,
pother, scurry, tumult 7 be
quick, fluster, flutter, press on,
scamper, scuttle 8 activity, be
active, scramble 9 agitation,
commotion, make haste 10 excitement, hurly-burly

busy 4 full 6 active, employ,
engage, intent, occupy, on
duty, work at 7 engaged, labor
at, slaving, toiling, working
8 absorbed, bustling, employed,
laboring, occupied 9 engrossed,
in harness, strenuous 10 hard
at work 11 industrious 12 be
absorbed in, keep occupied
13 be engrossed in

busybody 3 pry 5 snoop 6 gossip 7 blabber, meddler, Paul
Pry 8 telltale 10 chatterbox,
newsmonger, talebearer, tattletale 12 blabbermouth 13 scandalmonger

busy place 4 hive 6 warren 7 anthill, beehive

but 3 yet 4 save, than that 5 if not, still 6 except, saving, unless 7 however, outside, that not 9 excepting, other than, otherwise 10 except that 14 on the other hand

Butch Cassidy and the Sundance Kid
director: 13 George Roy Hill
cast: 10 Paul Newman (Butch) 13 Katharine Ross (Etta Place), Robert Redford (The Kid)
score: 13 Burt Bacharach
Oscar for: 5 score
song: 27 Raindrops Keep Fallin' on My Head

butcher 4 goof, kill, muff, ruin, slay 5 botch, purge, spoil 6 boggle, bungle, fumble, hack up, hit man, killer, mess up, murder 7 louse up, screw up 8 assassin, decimate, homicide, massacre, murderer 9 liquidate, manhandle, mishandle, slaughter 10 annihilate, hatchet man, liquidator 11 assassinate, exterminate, make a mess of, slaughterer 12 exterminator, mass-murderer 15 homicidal maniac

butchery 4 flop, mess 5 botch 8 massacre 9 slaughter

Butes
father: 6 Boreas 7 Pandion
mother: 8 Zeuxippe
brother: 8 Lycurgus 10 Erechtheus
sister: 6 Procne 9 Philomela
son: 4 Eryx
priest of: 6 Athena 8 Poseidon
member of: 9 Argonauts
stricken with: 8 insanity
enticed by: 6 Sirens
leaped into: 3 sea
rescued by: 9 Aphrodite

Butkus, Dick (Richard Marvin)
sport: 8 football
position: 10 linebacker
team: 12 Chicago Bears

Butler, Rhett
character in: 15 Gone With the Wind
author: 8 Mitchell

Butler, Samuel
author of: 7 Erewhon 8 Hudibras 16 The Way of All Flesh 20 The Elephant in the Moon

butt 3 end, hit, jab, ram, rap 4 buck, bump, bunt, dupe, goat, mark, push, slap, stub 5 knock, shank, shove, smack, stump, thump 6 bottom, buffet, jostle, object, strike, target, thrust, thwack, victim 8 blunt end 13 laughingstock

buttercup 10 Ranunculus
variety: 4 Tall 5 Early 6 Common 7 Bermuda, Bulbous, Persian 8 Colombia, Creeping 11 Yellow water

butterfingered 5 inept 6 clumsy 7 awkward 8 bungling 9 maladroit 10 ungraceful

butterfly
pupa: 9 chrysalis 10 chrysalids 11 chrysalides
variety: 4 blue 5 giant, nymph, satyr, snout, tiger, zebra 6 alpine, apollo, arctic, kalima 7 alfalfa, budwing, dogface, monarch, peacock, viceroy 9 Baltimore, bathwhite, brimstone, christmas, metalmark, orange tip, wood nymph 10 Parnassian 11 painted lady, spring azure 12 blue mountain, cabbage white, clouded white, silver stripe, white admiral 13 chalkhill blue, mourning cloak, pearl crescent 14 American copper, gulf fritillary, tailed birdwing 15 longtail skipper, regal fritillary 16 black swallowtail, black veined white, camberwell beauty, green veined white, Leonardus skipper, red-spotted purple 18 orchard swallowtail 19 European swallowtail 20 spicebush swallowtail, variegated fritillary 21 great purple hairstreak, questionmark anglewing, white admiral wood nymph

butter up 4 coax 6 cajole 7 flatter, wheedle 8 soft-soap

buttocks 4 buns, butt, rear, rump, seat 5 fanny, nates 6 behind, bottom 7 keister, rear end 8 backside, derriere, haunches 9 fundament, posterior 12 hindquarters

buttonhole 4 halt, slit, stop 6 accost, waylay 7 solicit 8 approach, confront

button one's lip 7 keep mum 10 keep silent 16 keep one's trap shut 18 keep one's lips sealed

Buttons, Red
real name: 11 Aaron Chwatt
born: 9 New York NY
roles: 8 Sayonara 13 The Longest Day 20 The Poseidon Adventure 23 They Shoot Horses Don't They

buttress 4 arch, prop, stay 5 boost, brace, shore, steel 6 prop up 7 bolster, shore up, support 8 abutment, shoulder 9 reinforce, stanchion 10 strengthen

buxom 5 plump 6 bosomy, chesty, robust, zaftig 9 strapping 10 voluptuous 13 largebreasted, well-developed

buy 3 get 4 deal, gain 5 bribe 6 buy off, obtain, pay for, suborn 7 acquire, bargain, corrupt, procure 8 invest in, purchase 9 influence

buy and sell 4 deal 5 trade 6 market

buy off 5 bribe 6 pay off 13 grease the palm

Buzi
son: 7 Ezekiel

Buz Sawyer
creator: 8 Roy Crane
sidekick: 7 Sweeney

Buzuhov, Pierre
character in: 11 War and Peace
author: 7 Tolstoy

buzz 3 hum 4 whir 5 drone 6 murmur 7 whisper

by 4 near, over, past 5 along 6 beside, beyond, during, toward 7 through 8 alongside 10 concerning, on or before 11 according to, no later than

by air
French: 8 par avion

Byam, Roger
character in: 17 Mutiny on the Bounty
authors: 4 Hall 8 Nordhoff

Byblis
father: 7 Miletus
mother: 6 Cyanea
twin brother: 6 Caunus
loved: 6 Caunus
changed into: 8 fountain

by few words
Latin: 12 paucis verbis

bygone 4 past 5 olden 6 former, gone by, of yore 7 ancient, earlier 8 departed, obsolete, previous 10 antiquated

by horse
French: 7 a cheval

Byington, Spring
born: 17 Colorado Springs CO

roles: 7 Jezebel **11** Little Women **13** December Bride, Heaven Can Wait **17** Mutiny on the Bounty **20** The Devil and Miss Jones, You Can't Take It with You **26** The Charge of the Light Brigade

by itself 4 solo **5** alone, aloof, apart **8** isolated **13** unaccompanied

Byng, Admiral
character in: 7 Candide
author: 8 Voltaire

by oneself 4 solo **5** alone, aloof **8** isolated **10** solitarily **13** unaccompanied
Latin: 4 sola **5** solus

by operation of law
Latin: 8 ipso jure

bypass 4 go by **5** avert, avoid, dodge **8** go around **10** circumvent **12** detour around

bypath 3 way **4** lane **5** alley, byway, track, trail **6** bypass **7** footway, pathway, towpath, walkway **8** back road, dirt road, footpath, shortcut, side road **10** beaten path, bridle path, garden path

by-product 8 offshoot **9** aftermath **16** incidental result

by right
Latin: 6 de jure

Byron, Lord (George Gordon)
author of: 7 Don Juan, Manfred **10** The Corsair **19** The Vision of Judgment **20** The Prisoner of Chillon **23** Childe Harold's Pilgrimage

byrrh
type: 8 aperitif
origin: 6 France
flavor: 6 orange **7** quinine

bystander 6 viewer **7** watcher, witness **8** attender, beholder, looker-on, observer, onlooker, passerby **9** spectator

by the book 9 by the rule **13** authoritarian **16** according to Hoyle

by the fact itself
Latin: 9 ipso facto

by the grace of God
Latin: 9 Dei gratia

by the law itself
Latin: 8 ipso jure

by the month
Latin: 9 per mensem

by the rule 9 by the book **11** as specified **13** authoritarian

by the skin of one's teeth 6 barely, hardly **8** only just, scarcely **11** by an eyelash

by the very nature of the deed
Latin: 9 ipso facto

by the way
French: 9 en passant

by virtue and arms
Latin: 13 virtute et armis
motto of: 11 Mississippi

byway 4 lane **5** alley **6** detour, street **8** shunpike

by what right?
Latin: 7 quo jure

byword 3 law, saw **4** rule **5** adage, axiom, maxim, motto, truth **6** dictum, saying, slogan **7** precept, proverb **8** aphorism, apothegm **9** catchword, pet phrase, principle, watchword **10** shibboleth

Byzantine 6 complex **8** scheming **9** expedient, intricate **13** Machiavellian

Byzas
founder of: 9 Byzantium
father: 8 Poseidon

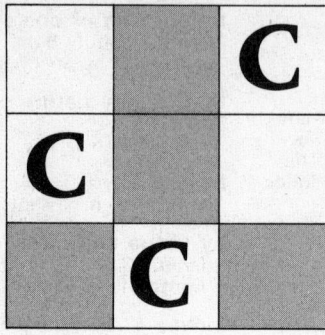

Caan, James
born: **9** New York NY
roles: **9** Funny Lady
10 Brian's Song, Rollerball
12 Brian Piccolo, The Godfather **13** Sonny Corleone
17 Cinderella Liberty

Caanthus
father: **7** Oceanus
sister: **5** Melia
killed by: **6** Apollo

cab 4 hack, taxi **7** taxi cab

Cab 15 Biblical measure

cabal 4 band, plan, plot, ring
5 junta **6** design, league,
scheme **7** faction **8** intrigue
10 connivance, conspiracy
11 combination, machination

cabalistic 6 arcane, mystic, occult, secret **7** cryptic, obscure,
strange **8** abstruse, esoteric,
mystical **10** mysterious, unknowable **11** inscrutable
12 impenetrable, supernatural,
unfathomable
16 incomprehensible

cabaret 4 cafe, club **6** bistro
9 nightclub **10** supper club
French: **5** boite **11** boite de
nuit

Cabaret
director: **8** Bob Fosse
based on stories by:
20 Christopher Isherwood
cast: **8** Joel Grey **11** Fritz
Wepper, Helmut Griem, Michael York **12** Liza Minnelli
(Sally Bowles) **14** Marisa
Berenson
Oscar for: **7** actress (Minnelli) **8** director **15** supporting actor (Grey)
song: **12** The Money Song

cabbage 16 Brassica oleracea
(Capitata Group)
varieties: **3** Cow **4** Deer,
Head, Wild **5** John's, Savoy,
Skunk **6** Celery **7** Chinese
9 Flowering, Tronchuda

10 Portuguese **11** Yellow
skunk **12** Western skunk

Cabecar
language family:
10 Talamancan
location: **9** Costa Rica **12** Sixaola River **14** Central America, Talamanca Plain
intermixed with: **6** Bribri

Cabell, James Branch
author of: **6** Jurgen **12** The
High Place **14** Figures of
Earth **17** The Cream of the
Jest

cabin 3 hut **4** room **5** hutch,
lodge, shack **6** shanty **7** cottage **8** bungalow, log cabin,
quarters **9** stateroom
11 compartment

cabinet 3 box **4** case, file
5 chest **6** bureau **7** council
8 advisors, cupboard, ministry
10 breakfront, counselors, receptacle **11** china closet
13 advisory board **14** chest of
drawers

cable 4 cord, line, rope, wire
5 chain, wires **6** hawser
7 mooring **8** wire line, wire
rope **12** electric wire **16** overseas telegram

Cable, George W
author of: **8** Dr Sevier **13** Old
Creole Days **15** The
Grandissimes

cablegram 4 wire **5** cable
7 message **8** wireless **16** overseas telegram

Cabot, Ephraim
character in: **18** Desire Under
the Elms
author: **6** O'Neill

Caca
origin: **5** Roman
goddess of: **6** hearth
corresponds to: **5** Vesta

Cacambo
character in: **7** Candide
author: **8** Voltaire

cache 4 heap **5** hoard, stock,
store **8** hideaway **9** stockpile
11 hiding place, secret place

cachet 4 mark, seal **5** stamp,
wafer **6** design, slogan
7 capsule

cackle 7 chatter **10** harsh
laugh **11** shrill laugh
sound made by: **3** hen
4 chicken

cacophonous 5 harsh **6** offkey **7** grating, jarring, raucous **8** off-pitch, screechy, strident **9** dissonant, out of tune,
unmusical **10** discordant
11 unmelodious **12** inharmonious, nonmelodious
13 disharmonious

cacophony 7 discord **9** harshness **10** disharmony,
dissonance

cactus *see box*

Cacus
form: **5** giant
father: **6** Vulcan
eats: **3** men
killed by: **8** Hercules

cad 3 cur, rat **4** heel, lout
5 churl, knave, louse, rogue
6 rascal, rotter **7** bounder, caitiff, dastard, villain **9** scoundrel

cadaver 4 body **5** stiff
6 corpse **7** remains **8** dead
body, deceased

cadaverous 4 pale **5** ashen,
gaunt **6** chalky, pallid
7 deathly, ghastly **8** blanched
9 bloodless, deathlike
10 corpselike

caddisfly
variety: **5** micro **8** northern
9 fingernet, primitive, snailcase **10** longhorned, trumpetnet, tubemaking
11 netspinning

Caddoan
tribe: **6** Pawnee
14 Chahiksichhiks

cactus
  varieties: **3** Cob, Sun **4** Ball, Cane, Chin, Claw, Club, Comb, Crab, Hook, Lace, Leaf, Moon, Rose, Star, Toad, Vine, Yoke **5** Agave, Apple, Brain, Chain, Coral, Crown, Devil, False, Giant, Leafy, Melon, Paper, Plain, Prism, Snake, Spice, Torch **6** Barrel, Button, Cholla, Dagger, Dollar, Easter, Hatpin, Hot-dog, Myrtle, Nipple, Old-man, Orchid, Peanut, Pencil, Ribbon, Spider **7** Cushion, Eve's pin, Feather, Hatchet, Hat-rack, Jumping, Old-lady, Popcorn, Rainbow, Rattail, Redbird, Serpent, Thimble, Whisker **8** Cinnamon, Dumpling, Fishbone, Fishhook, Flapjack, Gold lace, Golf-ball, Hedgehog, Old-woman, Polka-dot, Pond-lily, Snowball, Snowdrop, Starfish, Tortoise, Turk's-cap **9** Bird's nest, Chain-link, Christmas, Cow-tongue, Electrode, Fire-crown, Hairbrush, Lamb's-tail, Mistletoe, New old-man, Organ-pipe, Porcupine, Red orchid, Sea-urchin, Spineless, Teddy-bear, Toothpick, Totem-pole, Turk's-head, White chin **10** Bluebarrel, Candelabra, Cotton-pole, Easter-lily, Golden ball, Golden-star, Living-rock, Powder-puff, Silver ball, Strawberry, Unguentine, White torch, Wickerware **11** Frilled lace, Grizzly-bear, Joseph's coat, Large barrel, Scarlet ball, Woolly torch **12** Dancing-bones, Golden barrel, Mule-crippler, Scarlet crown, Thanksgiving **13** Colombian ball, Creeping-devil, Dutchman's pipe, Peruvian apple, Peruvian torch, Silver cluster **15** Golden bird's nest **16** Mexican dwarf tree **17** Burbank's spineless **18** Fishhook pincushion

caddy 3 box, can, tin **5** chest **6** coffer

cadence 4 beat, lilt **5** meter, pulse, swing, tempo, throb **6** accent, rhythm **7** measure

Caderousse
  character in: **21** The Count of Monte Cristo
  author: **5** Dumas (pere)

cadet 5 plebe **7** recruit, student **11** youngest son **14** military student

cadge 3 beg, bum **5** mooch **6** hustle, peddle, sponge **7** solicit, scrounge **9** panhandle

cadmium
  chemical symbol: **2** Cd

Cadmus
  form: **6** prince
  realm: **9** Phoenicia
  father: **6** Agenor
  mother: **10** Telephassa
  brother: **5** Cilix **7** Phoenix
  sister: **6** Europa
  wife: **8** Harmonia
  son: **8** Illyrius **9** Polydorus
  daughter: **3** Ino **5** Agave **6** Semele **7** Autonoe
  introduced to the Greeks: **7** writing
  founded: **6** Thebes
  planted: **12** dragons teeth

Caduceus
  staff of: **7** Mercury

Caeneus
  also: **6** Caenis
  member of: **9** Argonauts
  gift: **15** invulnerability
  former identity: **6** Caenis

Caenis
  also: **7** Caeneus
  father: **6** Elatus
  violated by: **8** Poseidon
  changed into: **3** man
  subsequent identity: **7** Caeneus

caesar, Caesar 5 ruler **6** despot, tyrant **7** emperor **8** autocrat, dictator

Caesar, Julius *see box*

Caesar, Sid
  partner: **11** Imogene Coca
  born: **9** Yonkers NY
  roles: **15** Your Show of Shows

Caesar and Cleopatra
  author: **17** George Bernard Shaw

Caesar or Nothing
  author: **9** Pio Baroja

caesura 5 break, pause **6** hiatus **12** interruption

cafe 3 bar, inn **5** diner **6** bistro, eatery, nitery, tavern **7** automat, beanery, cabaret **9** cafeteria, chophouse, hash house, lunchroom, nightclub **10** restaurant, supper club **11** bar and grill, coffeehouse, discotheque **12** luncheonette
  French: **9** estaminet

cafe au lait 10 light brown **14** coffee with milk

cafe noir 11 black coffee

cage 3 pen **4** coop **5** pen in **6** coop up, encage, lock up, shut in **7** confine, impound **8** imprison, restrain, restrict **9** enclosure

cagey 3 sly **4** foxy, keen, wary, wily **5** alert, chary, leery, sharp **6** artful, crafty, shifty, shrewd **7** careful, cunning, heedful, prudent **8** cautious, discreet, watchful

Cagliari
  capital of: **8** Sardinia

Cagney, James
  nickname: **5** Jimmy
  born: **9** New York NY
  roles: **7** Ragtime **14** The Public Enemy **17** Yankee Doodle Dandy (Oscar) **19** Man of a Thousand Faces

Cagney and Lacey
  cast: **8** Tyne Daly **11** Sharon Gless

Cahita
  tribe: **5** Yaqui

Cain
  father: **4** Adam
  mother: **3** Eve
  brother: **4** Abel, Seth
  home: **4** Eden
  son: **5** Enoch
  killed: **4** Abel
  traveled to: **3** Nod

Caesar, Julius
  adopted son: **8** Octavian **14** Caesar Augustus
  author of: **13** On the Civil War **14** On the Gallic War
  battle: **4** Zela **5** Munda **7** Durazzo, Thapsus **8** Mytilene **9** Pharsalus **11** Dyrrhachium
  conquered: **4** Gaul
  crossed: **7** Rubicon (river)
  defeated: **6** Pompey
  lover: **9** Cleopatra
  member of: **16** First Triumvirate
  murdered by: **5** Casca **6** Brutus **7** Cassius
  murdered on: **11** Ides of March
  other triumvirs: **6** Pompey **7** Crassus
  saying: **9** Et tu Brute? (Even you Brutus?) **12** Veni vidi vici (I came I saw I conquered)
  wife: **7** Pompeia **8** Cornelia **9** Calpurnia

Caine, Michael
real name: 24 Maurice Joseph Micklewhite
born: 6 London 7 England
roles: 4 Zulu 5 Alfie
6 Sleuth 9 Deathtrap 13 Educating Rita 14 The Ipcress File

Caine Mutiny, The
author: 10 Herman Wouk
director: 13 Edward Dmytryk
cast: 7 May Wynn 9 Lee Marvin 10 E G Marshall, Jose Ferrer, Van Johnson 13 Fred MacMurray, Robert Francis 14 Humphrey Bogart (Captain Queeg)

Caingua *see* 7 Guarani

Cairo
Arab camp: 8 al-Fustat
Arabic: 9 al-Qahirah
capital of: 5 Egypt
island: 5 Rodah
7 Zamalik
landmark:
mosque: 7 al-Azhar
11 Muhammed Ali
statue: 8 Ramses II
museum: 8 Egyptian
river: 4 Nile
Roman fortress:
7 Babylon
rulers: 5 Turks 7 British, Saladin 8 Fatimids
9 Mamelukes 11 Ismail Pasha, Muhammed Ali
12 Ottoman Turks
university: 7 Al-Azhar
8 Ain Shams, American

Cairo, Joel
character in: 16 The Maltese Falcon
author: 7 Hammett

caitiff 3 cad, cur, rat 4 heel 5 churl, knave, louse, rogue 6 rascal, rotter 7 bounder, dastard, villain 9 scoundrel 10 blackguard

cajole 4 coax 7 beguile, deceive, flatter, wheedle 8 blandish, inveigle, persuade

cajolery 7 blarney, coaxing, fawning 8 flattery, promises, soft soap 9 adulation, sweet talk, wheedling 10 enticement, inveigling, persuasion 11 beguilement 12 blandishment

cake 3 bar, bun, dry 4 lump, mass 5 block, crust, tort 6 cookie, eclair, gateau, harden, pastry, 7 congeal, cupcake, thicken 8 compress, solidify 9 coagulate, sweet roll 11 consolidate

Cakes and Ale
author: 16 W Somerset Maugham

cakewalk 5 cinch, dance 9 promenade 12 dance contest

calaboose 3 pen 4 jail, stir 6 prison 7 slammer 8 hoosegow

Calah
founder: 6 Nimrod

Calais
origin: 5 Greek
member of: 9 Argonauts
father: 6 Boreas
mother: 8 Orithyia
twin brother: 5 Zetes

calamitous 5 fatal 6 tragic, woeful 7 adverse, baleful, harmful, ruinous, unlucky 8 dreadful 9 blighting 10 disastrous, pernicious 11 cataclysmic, deleterious, destructive, detrimental, distressful, unfortunate 12 catastrophic

calamity 3 ill, woe 4 blow, ruin 5 trial 6 misery, mishap 7 bad luck, failure, ill wind, reverse, scourge, tragedy, trouble, undoing 8 disaster, distress, downfall, hardship 9 adversity, cataclysm, mischance 10 affliction, ill fortune, misfortune 11 catastrophe, tribulation 13 sea of troubles 15 stroke of ill luck

calando
music: 22 getting weaker and slower

Calchas
vocation: 10 soothsayer
father: 7 Thestor
burial place: 6 Notium

calcium
chemical symbol: 2 Ca

calculate 4 mean, plan 5 add up, aim at, count, judge, sum up 6 design, devise, figure, intend, reckon 7 compute, measure, predict, project, surmise, work out 8 estimate 9 ascertain, determine 10 conjecture

calculated 7 planned 10 deliberate, purposeful, thought out 11 intentional, prearranged 12 premeditated

calculating 3 sly 4 foxy, wily 6 artful, crafty, shrewd, tricky 7 cunning, devious 8 plotting, scheming 9 designing 10 contriving, intriguing 12 manipulative 13 Machiavellian

calculating machine
invented by: 7 Babbage

calculation 6 answer, result 8 figuring, judgment 9 reckoning 10 estimation 11 computation

calculator 6 abacus 7 counter, thinker 8 computer, reckoner

Calcutta
captured by: 5 Clive
founded by: 23 British East India Company
landmark: 10 Jain Temple 12 Howrah Bridge, Indian Museum 16 Botanical Gardens, Victoria Memorial 17 Zoological Gardens 18 Dakshineswar Temple
opposite city: 6 Howrah
river: 7 Hooghly
state: 10 West Bengal

Calder, Alexander
born: 14 Philadelphia PA
sculptures also called:
7 mobiles
artwork: 3 Man 5 Whale 6 Spiral 10 Teodelapio 12 Ticket Window 13 La Grande Voile 14 The Brass Family 23 Lobster Traps and Fish Tail

Calderon de la Barca, Pedro
author of: 12 Life Is a Dream

caldron, cauldron 3 pot 6 boiler, kettle

Caldwell, Erskine
author of: 10 Georgia Boy 11 Tobacco Road 14 God's Little Acre

Caldwell, Taylor
author of: 12 Answer as a Man 13 A Pillar of Iron 14 Great Lion of God 17 Testimony of Two Men, The Devil's Advocate 19 Bright Flows the River 20 Glory and the Lightning 22 The Captains and the Kings 24 Dear and Glorious Physician

Caleb
father: 8 Jepunneh
brother: 5 Kenaz
daughter: 6 Achash
nephew: 7 Othniel
descendant: 8 Calebite

Caleb Williams
author: 13 William Godwin

Caledonia *see* 8 Scotland

calendar 4 list 5 chart, diary, table 6 agenda, docket 7 day book, program 8 register, schedule

Caletor
origin: 5 Greek
mentioned in: 5 Iliad
cousin: 6 Hector
killed by: 14 Telamonian Ajax

calf **4** veal **5** dogie **6** weaner
7 leg part
   young of: **3** cow **4** bull, seal
   5 whale **8** elephant

Calgary
   hockey team: **6** Flames

Calhern, Louis
   real name: **13** Carl Henry
   Vogt
   born: **10** Brooklyn NY
   roles: **8** King Lear **12** Julius
   Caesar **15** Annie Get Your
   Gun **16** The Asphalt Jungle
   20 The Magnificent Yankee

Calhoun, Rory
   real name: **20** Francis Timothy Durgin
   born: **12** Los Angeles CA
   roles: **8** The Texan **21** Treasure of Pancho Villa
   22 How to Marry a Millionaire, Requiem for a
   Heavyweight

Caliban
   character in: **10** The Tempest
   author: **11** Shakespeare

caliber **4** bore, rank **5** gifts,
merit, place, power, scope,
skill, worth **6** repute, talent
7 ability, quality, stature **8** capacity, diameter, eminence,
position, prestige **10** capability,
competence, estimation, excellence, importance, promi-
nence, reputation
11 achievement, distinction

California *see box*

Calinieff, Martin
   real name of: **13** Michael
   Callan

Calinky State
   nickname of: **13** South
   Carolina

calisay
   type: **7** liqueur
   origin: **5** Spain **9** Catalonia
   flavor: **5** herbs **7** quinine

Calkins, Richard
   creator/artist of: **10** Buck
   Rogers

call **3** ask, bid, cry, dub, tag
4 bawl, buzz, hail, name,
need, plea, ring, roar, stop,
term, yell **5** cause, claim, label, order, phone, rally, right,
shout, style, title, visit **6** appeal, ask for, bellow, charge,
clamor, cry out, decree, demand, direct, drop in, excuse,
gather, halloo, holler, invite,
invoke, know as, muster, notice, outcry, pray to, reason,
scream, stop by, summon
7 collect, command, contact,
convene, convoke, declare, entitle, entreat, grounds, refer
to, request, require, specify,
stop off, summons, warrant

California
   abbreviation: **2** CA **3** Cal **5** Calif
   nickname: **6** Golden **8** Eldorado **12** Promised Land
   capital: **10** Sacramento
   largest city: **10** Los Angeles
   others: **4** Lodi **5** Azusa, Chico, Chino, Indio **6** Blythe, Carmel, Covina, Eureka, Fresno, Lompoc, Merced, Oxnard,
   Pomona, Sonoma, Tulare **7** Alameda, Anaheim, Burbank,
   Gardena, Needles, Oakland, Salinas, Vallejo, Visalia **8** Al-
   tadena, Berkeley, Palo Alto, Pasadena, Redlands, San
   Diego, Stockton **9** Cucamonga, Long Beach **11** Palm
   Springs, Santa Monica **12** Beverly Hills, San Francisco,
   Santa Barbara
   college: **3** USC **4** UCLA **5** Mills **6** Pitzer, Pomona **7** Caltech,
   Chapman, Scripps **8** Stanford, Whittier **10** Occidental,
   Pepperdine
   explorer: **6** Cortez
   feature:
      amusement park: **10** Disneyland **15** Knotts Berry Farm
      area: **9** Hollywood **15** Fishermans Wharf
      dam: **6** Hoover, Shasta **7** Boulder
      island prison: **8** Alcatraz
      mill: **7** Sutters
      national park: **7** Redwood, Sequoia **8** Yosemite **11** Kings
      Canyon **14** Channel Islands, Lassen Volcanic
      parade: **4** Rose
      prison: **6** Folsom **10** San Quentin
   tribe: **4** Hupa, Pomo, Yana, Yuki **5** Karok, Maidu, Miwok,
   Wappo, Wiyot, Yurok **6** Patwin, Shasta, Tolowa, Yokuts
   7 Chumash, Luiseno, Salinan, Serrano **8** Diegueno
   people: **6** Sutter **10** Earl Warren **11** Robert Frost
   13 George S Patton, John Steinbeck **14** William Saroyan
   island: **4** Goat, Mare **7** Anacapo, Channel **8** Alcatraz, Catalina, Coronado **9** Farallone
   lake: **4** Mono, Soda **5** Clear, Eagle, Owens, Tahoe **6** Salton,
   Tulare **7** Almanor **8** Elsinore **9** Berryessa
   land rank: **5** third
   mountain: **4** Muir **5** Coast **6** Lassen, Shasta, Wilson **7** Cascade, Klamath, Palomar, Whitney **10** Peninsular, Transverse **12** Sierra Nevada
      highest point: **7** Whitney
   physical feature:
      bay: **8** Monterey, San Diego **12** San Francisco
      cape: **9** Mendocino
      desert: **6** Mohave, Mojave **8** Colorado
      fault: **10** San Andreas
      glacier: **8** Palisade
      sea: **6** Cortez **7** Pacific
      tree: **7** redwood
      valley: **5** Death
      volcano: **6** Lassen
      wind: **7** Collada **8** Santa Ana
   president: **13** Richard M Nixon, Ronald W Reagan
   river: **3** Eel, Mad, Pit **4** Kern **5** Kings, Owens, Putah,
   Smith, Stony **6** Little, Merced, Salmon **7** Feather, Klamath, Rubicon, Russian, Salinas, Trinity, Truckee **10** Sacramento, San Jacinto, San Joaquin, Stanislaus
   state admission: **11** thirty-first
   state bird: **21** California Valley quail
   state fish: **21** California golden trout
   state flower: **11** golden poppy
   state motto: **6** Eureka (I have found it)
   state song: **18** I Love You California
   state symbol: **11** grizzly bear
   state tree: **17** California redwood
   baseball team: **6** Angels, Padres **7** Dodgers
   basketball team: **6** Lakers **8** Clippers **19** Golden State
   Warriors
   football team: **4** Rams **7** Raiders **8** Chargers **11** Forty-
   Niners

8 announce, appeal to, assemble, christen, entreaty, identify, instruct, look in on, occasion, petition, proclaim **9** crying out, designate, direction, pay a visit, telephone **10** describe as, invitation, supplicate **11** declaration, instruction **12** announcement, call together, characterize, proclamation, supplication **13** justification

Callan, Michael
　real name: 15 Martin Calinieff
　born: 14 Philadelphia PA
　roles: 9 Cat Ballou **10** The Interns **18** Gidget Goes Hawaiian, The Flying Fontaines **23** The Magnificent Seven Ride

call for 4 need **6** demand, pick up **7** request, require

call forth 4 spur **5** evoke, raise **6** arouse, awaken, excite, incite, invoke, kindle, stir up **7** command, conjure, provoke **8** summon up **9** make aware, stimulate **10** make appear

Callidice
　form: 5 queen
　realm: 10 Thesprotia
　husband: 8 Odysseus
　son: 10 Polypoetes

calling 3 job **4** line, work **5** craft, field, forte, trade **6** career, crying, living, metier, outcry **7** hailing, mission, passion, yelling **8** activity, business, devotion, function, province, shouting, vocation **9** bellowing, crying out, first love, hallooing, life's work, screaming, specialty **10** assignment, attachment, dedication, employment, enthusiasm, livelihood, occupation, profession, walk of life **14** bread and butter, means of support, specialization

calling off 6 ending **7** halting **8** giving up **11** termination **12** backing out of, cancellation

calling oneself thus
　French: 9 soi-disant

Calliope
　member of: 5 Muses
　presided over: 10 epic poetry
　father: 4 Zeus
　mother: 9 Mnemosyne
　son: 7 Orpheus

Callipolis
　father: 9 Alcathous

Callirrhoe, Callirhoe
　father: 6 Oeneus **8** Achelous
　husband: 4 Tros **8** Alcmaeon
　son: 4 Ilus **8** Ganymede **10** Amphoterus

ended plague in: 7 Calydon
death by: 9 sacrifice

Calliste
　epithet of: 7 Artemis
　means: 7 fairest

Callisto
　form: 5 nymph
　attended: 7 Artemis
　loved: 4 Zeus
　changed into: 4 bear
　killed by: 7 Artemis

call off 3 end **4** halt **5** abort **6** cancel, give up **8** postpone **9** back out of, terminate **10** summon away **12** dispense with

Call of the Wild, The
　author: 10 Jack London
　dog: 4 Buck
　master: 12 John Thornton

callous 4 cold, hard **5** cruel, horny, tough **6** inured **8** hardened, uncaring **9** apathetic, heartless, unfeeling **11** hardhearted, indifferent, insensitive **12** thick-skinned, unresponsive **13** dispassionate, unsympathetic **14** pachydermatous

call out 3 cry **4** bawl, hail, yell **5** shout **6** bellow, cry out, holler, summon **9** challenge

callow 3 raw **5** crude, green, naive **7** artless, awkward, puerile, shallow, untried **8** childish, ignorant, immature, juvenile **9** infantile **10** sophomoric, uninformed, unschooled, unseasoned **11** uninitiated **13** inexperienced **15** unsophisticated

call to 4 hail **5** greet **6** accost, salute **7** address, shout at

call to account 5 chide, scold **6** accuse, charge, rebuke **7** arraign, bawl out, censure, chasten, reprove, upbraid **8** admonish, denounce, reproach **9** criticize, dress down, reprimand **10** take to task **11** remonstrate

call to arms 6 war cry **9** battle cry **11** rallying cry

call to order 4 open **6** muster **7** convene, convoke

call upon 3 ask, bid **4** urge **5** visit **6** charge, enjoin, exhort, invite, invoke **7** beseech, entreat, request, require **8** appeal to, petition, summon up **9** encourage **11** acknowledge

callused 4 hard **5** horny, tough **8** hardened **12** thick-skinned **14** pachydermatous

calm 4 cool, ease, mild **5** allay, balmy, bland, quell, quiet, still **6** becalm, gentle, lessen,

pacify, placid, reduce, repose, sedate, serene, smooth, soothe, subdue **7** assuage, collect, compose, cool off, halcyon, mollify, pacific, placate, relaxed, relieve **8** composed, coolness, diminish, mitigate, moderate, peaceful, serenity, tranquil, unshaken **9** alleviate, collected, composure, impassive, placidity, quietness, stillness, unexcited, unruffled **10** cool-headed, motionless, simmer down, smoothness, unagitated, untroubled **11** impassivity, passionless, restfulness, self-control, tranquility, tranquilize, undisturbed, unflappable, unperturbed **12** peacefulness, tranquillity, windlessness **13** imperturbable, self-possessed, stormlessness **14** self-possession **16** imperturbability

calmness 5 poise **6** aplomb **8** coolness, serenity **9** composure, placidity, sangfroid, stillness **10** equanimity, steadiness **11** self-control, tranquility **12** peacefulness, tranquillity **14** presence of mind, self-possession **16** imperturbability

Calpurnia
　character in: 12 Julius Caesar
　author: 11 Shakespeare

calumnious 8 libelous **9** maligning, vilifying **10** defamatory, derogatory, slanderous **11** disparaging

calumny 4 barb, slur **5** libel, smear **6** malice **7** slander **8** innuendo **9** aspersion **10** backbiting, defamation, derogation, revilement **11** denigration, deprecation, insinuation **12** backstabbing, calumniation, depreciation, vilification **13** animadversion, disparagement, malicious lies

calvados
　type: 6 brandy
　origin: 6 France **8** Normandy
　flavor: 5 apple
　aged in: 3 oak

Calvary 8 Golgotha
　means: 10 skull place

Calyce
　father: 6 Aeolus
　mother: 7 Enarete
　son: 8 Endymion

Calydonian boar
　sent by: 5 Diana
　killed by: 8 Meleager

Calydonian hunt
　pursuit of: 4 boar

Calypso
　form: 5 nymph

home: 6 Ogygia
father: 10 Titan Atlas
detained: 8 Odysseus
   for: **10** seven years

calyx 4 husk **5** sepal

cam 3 cog **4** disk **8** cylinder
10 projection
  located on: 5 shaft, wheel
  motion: 7 rocking **8** circular
  12 back and forth

camaraderie 7 jollity **8** bonhomie, good will **10** affability,
clubbiness, fellowship, friendship **11** brotherhood, comradeship, sociability **12** congeniality, conviviality,
friendliness **13** companionship,
esprit de corps **14** good-
fellowship

Camarasaurus
  type: 8 dinosaur, sauropod
  location: 12 United States
  period: 8 Jurassic

Cambodia *see box*

Cambria *see* **5** Wales

cambric 5 cloth, linen **6** cotton, fabric **8** material

camel
  called: 13 beast of burden
  15 ship of the desert
  chews: 3 cud
  group: 4 herd
  habitat: 4 Asia **6** Africa,
  desert
  kind: 7 Arabian **8** Bactrian
  9 dromedary
  number of humps: 3 one,
  two
  species: 6 mammal
  type of: 8 ruminant
  young: 4 calf

camellia
  varieties: 5 Silky **6** Common
  8 Mountain, Sasanqua

Camenae
  means: 11 foretellers
  form: 6 nymphs **7** deities
  gift: 8 prophecy
  names: 6 Egeria **8** Carmenta
  9 Antevorta, Postvorta
  habitat: 8 fountain
  correspond to: 5 Muses

camera
  invented by:
    Kodak: **6** Walker
    7 Eastman
    Polaroid: **4** Land
    photography: **6** Niepce,
    Talbot **8** Daguerre
    film, celluloid: **6** Edison
    11 Reichenbach
    film, transparent: **7** East-
    man, Goodwin
    color photo: **4** Ives

Cameroon *see box*

Camilla
  form: 5 woman
  occupation: 7 warrior
  father: 7 Metabus
  mother: 7 Casmila
  fought with: 6 Turnus
  fought against: 6 Aeneas

Camille
  also: 17 La Dame aux
  camelias
  author: 14 Alexander Dumas
  (fils)
  character: 6 Nanine **11** Ar-

Cambodia
  other name: 7 Camboja
  8 Cambodge
  9 Kampuchea
  capital/largest city:
  8 Pnom-Penh
  others: 3 Som **4** Ream
  5 Takeo **6** Kampot, Kra-
  tie, Pursat **7** Kohnieh,
  Kompong, Kracheh,
  Rovieng, Samrong
  8 Siem Reap, Sisophon
  10 Battambang, Stung
  Treng **11** Kompong
  Cham **12** Krungkoh
  Kong **13** Sihanoukville
  head of state: 4 King
  monetary unit: 3 sen
  4 quan, riel **6** puttan
  7 piaster
  weight: 4 mace, tael
  island: 4 Kong, Rong
  lake: 8 Tonle Sap
  mountain: 3 Pan **7** Dangrek, Dong Rek **8** Cardamom, Elephant
  highest point: 10 Phnom
  Aoral, Phnom Aural
  river: 3 San, Sen
  5 Sreng **6** Bassac,
  Chinit, Mekong, Po-
  rong, Pursat, Srepok
  7 Kamlong, Sekhong
  8 Tonle Sap
  physical feature:
    bay: **10** Kompongsom
    cape: **5** Samit
    gulf: **4** Siam
    8 Thailand
  people: 4 Cham, Thai
  5 Khmer **7** Chinese
  10 Vietnamese
    leader: **6** Pol Pot
    8 Sihanouk
  language: 5 Khmer
  6 French **9** Cambodian
  10 Vietnamese
  religion: 7 animism
  8 Buddhism
  12 Christianity
  places:
    ruins/temple: **6** Ang-
    kor **9** Angkor Wat
  feature:
    Communist group:
    10 Khmer Rouge

Cameroon
  capital: 7 Yaounde
  largest city: 6 Douala
  others: 3 Wum **4** Bali,
  Buea, Edea, Tiko
  5 Kumba, Lomie,
  Mamfe **6** Garona, Mar-
  oua **7** Batouri, Dschang,
  Ebolowa, Foumban
  8 Victoria **10** N'Gaoun-
  dere, N'Kongsamba
  monetary unit: 5 franc
  7 centime
  island: 5 Nanny
  8 Fernando
  lake: 4 Chad
  mountain: 5 Mbabo
  7 Bambuto, Kapsiki,
  Mandara **8** Batandji
  9 Atlantika
  highest point:
  8 Cameroon
  river: 3 Dja, Lom **4** Faro,
  Mbam, Vina **5** Benue,
  Campo, Cross, Kadei,
  Mbere, Nyong, N'Goko,
  Sanga, Shari **6** Djerem,
  Ivindo, Logone, Sanaga
  sea: 8 Atlantic
  physical feature:
    cape: **10** Debundscha
    gulf: **6** Guinea
    plateau: **7** Adamawa
    8 Mambilla
  people: 3 Abo, Edo, Ibo
  4 Beti, Bulu, Ekoi, Ijaw,
  Sara **5** Bantu, Bassa,
  Kirdi, Pygmy, Tikar
  6 Bamoun, Donala,
  Ewondo, Fulani, Ibibio
  7 Bakweri **8** Bamileke
    Fulani chief:
    7 Lamidos
  language: 4 Bulu
  5 Bantu, Bassa, Hausa
  6 Douala, Ewondo,
  French, Fulani
  7 English **8** Bamileke,
  Fulfulde
  religion: 5 Islam **7** animism **12** Christianity
  places:
    home of prime minis-
    ter: **7** Schloss

---

mand Duval **17** Marguerite
Gautier (Camille)
director: 11 George Cukor
cast: 10 Greta Garbo (Camille) **12** Henry Daniell, Robert Taylor (Armand)
14 Elizabeth Allan, Laura
Hope Crews **15** Lionel
Barrymore

Camillo
character in: 14 The Winter's
Tale
author: 11 Shakespeare

Camirus
origin: **5** Greek
grandfather: **6** Helios, Helius

camisole 3 top **4** slip **6** jacket
10 underwaist

camouflage 4 hide, mask,
veil **5** blind, cloak, cover,

front **6** screen, shroud **7** conceal, cover up **8** disguise
10 masquerade, subterfuge
11 concealment

camouflaged 6 hidden,
masked **7** cloaked **8** shrouded
9 concealed, disguised

camp 4 tent **5** tents **7** bivouac,
lodging, rough it **8** army base,
barracks, quarters **10** pitch a
tent

campaign 3 run **4** push
5 drive, stump **6** action, effort
7 crusade **8** endeavor, move-

Canada
capital: **6** Ottawa
largest city: **8** Montreal
others: **4** Hull **5** Banff, Laval **6** Dawson, Guelph, London, Oshawa, Quebec, Regina, Sarnia,
Val d'or **7** Calgary, Halifax, Moncton, Nanaimo, Sudbury, Toronto, Welland, Windsor **8** Edmonton, Hamilton, Kingston, Moose Jaw, Victoria, Winnipeg **9** Saskatoon, Vancouver
10 Port Arthur, Sherbrooke **11** Fredericton **12** Niagara Falls, Peterborough, Prince Albert,
Prince George **13** Charlottetown **21** St Catherines Stratford
school: **3** UBC **5** Laval **6** McGill, Queens **7** Toronto **8** McMaster, Montreal **9** Concordia, Dalhousie **11** Simon Fraser
division: **5** Yukon **6** Quebec **7** Alberta, Ontario **8** Manitoba **10** Nova Scotia **12** Newfoundland,
New Brunswick, Saskatchewan **15** British Columbia **18** Prince Edward Island **20** Northwest
Territories
New division: **7** Nunavut
head of state: **14** British monarch **15** governor general
measure: **3** ton **5** minot, perch, point **6** arpent **7** chainon
island: **4** Read **5** Banks, Bylot, Coats, Devon, Grand, Manan, Parry, Sable **6** Baffin, Breton,
Mansel, Middle **7** Belcher **8** Bathurst, Magdalen, Victoria **9** Anticosti, Ellesmere, Vancouver
10 Campobello, Manitoulin **11** Southampton **14** Queen Charlotte
lake: **4** Cree, Erie, Gras, Seul **5** Garry, Huron, Rainy **6** Louise, St John **7** Abitibi, Dubawnt,
Nipigon, Ontario, Testlin **8** Kootenay, Manitoba, Okanagan, Reindeer, Superior, Winnipeg
9 Athabaska, Great Bear, Nipissing **10** Great Slave, Mistassini **12** Winnipegosis
mountain: **5** Coast, Royal **6** Robson, Skeena **7** Cariboo, Cascade, Purcell, Rockies, Selkirk, St
Elias **8** Columbia, Hazelton, Monashee **9** Mackenzie, Notre Dame, Tremblant **10** Laurentian,
Richardson, Shickshock **14** Jacques Cartier
highest point: **5** Logan
river: **3** Hay, Red **4** Peel **5** Liard, Peace, Slave, Yukon **6** Albany, Fraser, Nelson, Nicola, Ottawa, Skeena, St John, Thames, Thelon **7** St Marys **8** Columbia, Gatineau, Kootenay, Petawawa, Saguenay **9** Athabasca, Athapaska, Churchill, Mackenzie, Richelieu **10** Coppermine, St
Lawrence **11** Assiniboine, **12** Saskatchewan
sea: **6** Arctic **7** Pacific **8** Atlantic, Labrador
physical features:
 bay: **5** Basin, Fundy, Hecla, James, Minas **6** Baffin, Griper, Hudson, Ungava **8** Georgian
 canal: **3** Soo **7** Welland **10** Wellington
 cape: **5** Canso
 falls: **7** Niagara **9** Horseshoe
 gulf: **10** St Lawrence
 pass: **8** Chilkoot
 peninsula: **5** Gaspe **7** Boothia **8** Labrador, Melville
 plain: **11** Barren lands
 port: **6** Quebec **7** St Johns **8** Hamilton, Victoria **9** Churchill
 strait: **5** Cabot, Davis, Dease **6** Hecate, Hudson **7** Georgia **9** Belle Isle **10** Juan de Fuca
people: **5** Inuit **6** Canuck, Eskimo, French **7** English
 explorer: **5** Cabot **6** Fraser, Joliet **7** Cartier, LaSalle, Selkirk **8** Thompson **9** Champlain,
 MacKenzie, Marquette
 leader: **4** King, Riel **5** Clark **6** Borden **7** Laurier, Trudeau **8** Campbell, Chretien, Mulroney
 9 Macdonald, St Laurent **11** Diefenbaker
language: **6** Eskimo, French **7** English
religion: **8** Anglican **13** Roman Catholic **20** United Church of Canada
places:
 battlefield: **15** Plains of Abraham
 national park: **4** Yoho **5** Banff **6** Jasper **7** Glacier **8** Kootenay **9** Elk Island **10** La Mauricie,
 Revelstoke **11** Wood Buffalo **12** Prince Albert **13** Waterton Lakes
 resort: **5** Banff **10** Lake Louise
feature:
 airport: **6** Gander
 emblem: **9** maple leaf
 fish: **5** charr, trout
 flower: **10** Juneflower
 police: **8** Mounties **12** Royal Mounted
food:
 soup: **7** rubaboo

ment **9** offensive, operation **11** electioneer, whistle-stop **12** battle series, beat the drums, solicit votes

campanile 6 belfry **9** bell tower

campari
type: 7 bitters **8** aperitif
origin: 5 Italy

Campe
form: 8 old woman
occupation: 6 jailer
place: 8 Tartarus

campground 7 bivouac **8** tent city **16** temporary shelter

Campin, Robert
born: 8 Flanders
also known as/identified with: 14 Master of Merode **16** Master of Flemalle
artwork: 10 St Veronica, The Trinity **13** The Entombment **16** Merode Altarpiece (Merode Triptych) **17** The Virgin and Child **18** The Thief on the Cross

Camptosaurus
type: 8 dinosaur **10** ornithopod
location: 12 North America
period: 8 Jurassic
characteristic: 10 duck-billed

Camus, Albert
author of: 4 L'ete **6** Summer **7** The Fall **8** Caligula, The Rebel **9** The Plague **11** A Happy Death, The Stranger **12** Cross Purpose **17** The Myth of Sisyphus

can 3 tin **4** buns, fire, rump, seat **5** fanny, put up **6** bottom **8** backside, buttocks, preserve **9** container, fundament, give the ax

Canaan
father: 3 Ham
brother: 4 Cush
grandfather: 4 Noah
known as: 12 promised land
see also **6** Israel

Canace
father: 6 Aeolus
brother: 8 Macareus
death by: 7 suicide

Canada *see box*

canaille 6 proles, rabble **8** riffraff **9** commoners, hoi polloi **11** proletariat **13** great unwashed

canal 4 duct, tube **7** channel, conduit, passage **8** aqueduct

Canaletto
real name: 20 Giovanni Antonio Canal
born: 5 Italy **6** Venice
artwork: 18 The Stonemason's Yard

canard 4 hoax **5** rumor **7** slander **9** falsehood **12** exaggeration

---

Canary Islands
other name: 14 Fortunate Isles **15** Isles of the Blest
named for: 3 dog **5** canis **6** canine
capital: 9 Las Palmas **19** Santa Cruz de Tenerife
largest city: 9 Las Palmas
others: 4 Icod **6** Laguna **7** Orotava **8** Arrecife, Valverde **12** San Sebastian
government: 16 overseas province
of: **5** Spain
measure: 8 fanegada
monetary unit: 6 peseta
island: 4 Roca **5** Clara, Ferro, Lobos, Rocca **6** Gomera, Hierro **7** Inferno, La Palma **8** Graciosa, Tenerife **9** Lanzarote **10** Lanzarotte **11** Gran Canaria **13** Fuerteventura
mountain: 6 La Cruz **8** El Cumbre, Tenerife
highest point: 5 Teide, Teyde
sea: 8 Atlantic
people: 7 Spanish
language: 7 Spanish
religion: 13 Roman Catholic

---

canasta
number of players: 4 four
cards/hand: 6 eleven
meld: 12 three of a kind
wild card: 5 deuce, joker

Canberra
capital of: 9 Australia
territory: 13 New South Wales **26** Australian Capital Territory
lake: 13 Burley Griffin

cancel 4 void **5** annul, erase, quash **6** delete, offset, recall, recant, repeal, revoke **7** abolish, call off, nullify, rescind, retract, vitiate **8** abrogate, call back, set aside **9** repudiate **10** balance out, blue-pencil, do away with, invalidate, neutralize **11** countermand **12** dispense with **13** compensate for **14** counterbalance **18** declare null and void

cancellation 6 repeal **9** abolition **10** abrogation, efface-

ment, rescinding, revocation **11** abolishment, eradication, repudiation, termination

cancer 3 rot **6** plague **7** sarcoma, scourge **8** neoplasm, sickness **9** carcinoma **10** malignancy **14** malignant tumor **15** malignant growth

Cancer
symbol: 4 crab
planet: 4 Moon
rules: 4 home **6** family
born: 4 July, June

Cancer Ward, The
author: 21 Aleksandr Solzhenitsyn

candelabrum 7 menorah **8** dikerion **9** girandole, trikerion **11** candlestick **12** candleholder

Candia *see* **5** Crete

candid 4 fair, free, just, open **5** blunt, frank, plain **6** direct, honest **7** genuine, natural, relaxed, sincere, unposed **8** informal, outright, truthful **9** downright, impromptu, outspoken **10** forthright **11** plainspoken, spontaneous, unvarnished **14** extemporaneous **15** straightforward

Candida
author: 17 George Bernard Shaw

candidate 7 hopeful, nominee **8** aspirant, eligible **9** applicant, contender, job seeker **10** competitor, contestant **11** possibility **12** office seeker

Candid Camera
host: 9 Allen Funt
co-host: 11 Bess Myerson **12** Durward Kirby **13** Arthur Godfrey

Candide
author: 8 Voltaire
character: 6 Martin **7** Cacambo **8** Pangloss **9** Cunegonde **11** Admiral Byng **17** Thunder-ten-Tronckh

candidness 6 candor **7** honesty, openness **9** frankness, sincerity **10** directness **12** truthfulness **13** guilelessness

candle 3 dip, wax **5** light, taper **6** bougie, cierge, tallow **9** rush light

candleholder, candlestick
6 sconce **7** menorah **8** dikerion **9** girandole, trikerion **10** chandelier **11** candelabrum

candor 7 honesty **8** fairness, justness, openness **9** bluntness, frankness, sincerity **10** directness **11** artlessness **12** impartiality, truthfulness **14** forthrightness **15** plainspokenness **19** straightforwardness

candy 3 bar 4 kiss 5 cream, fudge, jelly, sweet, taffy 6 bonbon, comfit, dainty, nougat, sweets, toffee 7 brittle, caramel, fondant, gumdrop, praline 8 lollipop 9 chocolate, jellybean, sweetmeat 10 confection 12 all-day sucker 13 confectionery, peanut brittle

cane 3 hit, rap, rod, tan 4 beat, drub, flog, lash, whip 5 baste, flail, smite, staff, stick, whack 6 strike, switch, thrash, wallop 7 trounce 12 walking stick

cane 11 Arundinaria
   varieties: 4 Dumb, Wild 5 Arrow, Sugar 6 Rattan, Switch, Tobago, Tonkin 7 Tsingli 8 Southern 11 Spotted dumb 12 Chinese sweet 14 Yellow-leaf dumb

Canea
   capital of: 5 Crete

Canens
   father: 5 Janus
   mother: 7 Venilia
   betrothed to: 5 Picus
   cried over: 5 Picus
   death by: 6 crying

Canephora
   form: 7 maidens
   carried: 7 baskets

Canetti, Elias
   author of: 8 Auto da Fe 12 Tower of Babel 14 Crowds and Power 15 The Torch in My Ear 16 Kafka's Other Trial, The Tongue Set Free

Caniff, Milton
   creator/artist of: 10 Dickie Dare 11 Steve Canyon 14 The Gay Thirties 18 Terry and the Pirates

canine 3 cur, dog, fox, pup 4 mutt, wolf 5 hound, hyena, puppy 6 coyote, cuspid, jackal 7 mongrel 8 eyetooth

canker 4 sore 5 ulcer 6 blight, cancer, lesion 9 mouth sore 12 inflammation

Cannibal Galaxy, The
   author: 12 Cynthia Ozick

cannon 3 bit, gun 4 bone 5 carom 6 mortar 7 battery 8 field gun, howitzer, ordnance 9 artillery 10 field piece, mounted gun, pickpocket

Cannon
   character: 11 Frank Cannon
   cast: 13 William Conrad

Cannon, Dyan
   real name: 19 Samille Diane Friesen

   husband: 9 Cary Grant
   born: 8 Tacoma WA
   roles: 6 Shamus 9 Deathtrap 13 Heaven Can Wait 15 Such Good Friends 19 Bob & Carol & Ted & Alice 23 Revenge of the Pink Panther

cannonade 5 burst, salvo 6 volley 7 barrage, battery 8 shelling 9 fusillade 11 bombardment

canny 4 foxy, wary, wily, wise 5 cagey, sharp 6 artful, astute, clever, crafty, shrewd, subtle 7 careful, cunning, knowing 8 skillful 9 judicious, sagacious 10 convincing 11 circumspect, intelligent 13 perspicacious

Cano, Alonso
   born: 5 Spain 7 Granada
   artwork: 16 Granada Cathedral (facade) 18 Madonna of the Rosary 20 Immaculate Conception 23 The Seven Joys of the Virgin

canoe 4 boat 5 bungo, kayak 6 dugout 7 pirogue

canoeing
   athlete: 11 Marcia Smoke

canon 3 law 4 code, rule 5 dogma, edict, model, order 6 decree 7 pattern, precept, statute 8 doctrine, standard 9 bench mark, criterion, ordinance, principle, yardstick 10 regulation, touchstone

canonical 6 proper 8 accepted, approved, official orthodox 9 authentic, customary 10 authorized, legitimate, recognized, sanctioned 12 conventional 13 authoritative

Canonization, The
   author: 9 John Donne

canopy 4 hood 5 cover 6 awning, tester 8 covering

Canova, Antonio
   born: 5 Italy 8 Possagno
   artwork: 7 Perseus 12 Venus Victrix (Pauline Bonaparte Borghese) 14 Cupid and Psyche 16 Letizia Bonaparte 17 Daedalus and Icarus

Cansino, Margarita Carmen
   real name of: 12 Rita Hayworth

cant 4 sham, talk 5 argot, lingo, slang 6 humbug, jargon 8 parlance, pretense 9 hypocrisy 10 lip service, vernacular 11 insincerity 15 pretentiousness 17 sanctimoniousness

cantabile
   music: 7 flowing, singing 8 songlike

cantaloupe 5 fruit, melon 9 muskmelon

cantankerous 4 mean 5 cross, huffy, short, sulky, surly, testy 6 cranky, crusty, grumpy, morose, sullen, touchy 7 bearish, crabbed, fretful, grouchy, peevish, waspish 8 choleric, churlish, contrary, snappish 9 irascible, irritable, splenetic 10 ill-humored, ill-natured 11 contentious, ill-tempered, quarrelsome 12 disagreeable 13 argumentative

cantatrice 6 singer 9 chanteuse 10 songstress 18 professional singer

canteen 2 PX 4 club 5 flask 6 bottle 10 commissary 11 pocket flask 12 post exchange

canter 4 gait, lope, trot 6 gallop, singer, whiner

Canterbury Tales, The
   author: 15 Geoffrey Chaucer
   starting point: 9 Southwark, Tabard Inn
   goal:
      tomb of: 6 Becket
   character/tale: 3 Nun 4 Cook, Dyer, Monk 5 Canon, Friar, Reeve, Webbe 6 Knight, Miller, Parson, Squire, Yeoman 7 Shipman, Tapicer 8 Franklin, Maniple, Merchant, Pardoner, Prioress, Summoner 9 Carpenter, Ploughman 10 Wife of Bath 11 Haberdasher 13 Clerk of Oxford, Sergeant of Law 14 Doctor of Physic

Canthus
   member of: 9 Argonauts

Cantor, Eddie
   real name: 21 B Edward Israel Iskowitz
   nickname: 9 Banjo Eyes
   wife: 9 Ida Tobias
   born: 9 New York NY
   roles: 7 Whoopee 8 Kid Boots 9 Banjo Eyes

cantor of a synagogue
   Hebrew: 5 hazan

Cantos
   author: 9 Ezra Pound

can't stand 4 hate 5 abhor 6 detest, eschew, loathe 7 despise 8 execrate 9 abominate, can't abide 11 can't stomach 14 hate the sight of

can't stomach 4 hate 5 abhor 6 detest, loathe 7 despise 8 execrate 9 abominate, can't abide, can't stand

10 shrink from **13** find repulsive

canvas 4 duck **7** painting **8** painting **9** sailcloth, tarpaulin, tent cloth

canvass 4 poll, scan, sift **5** study, tally **6** survey **7** analyze, discuss, examine, explore, inquiry, inquire, inspect, solicit **8** analysis, campaign, scrutiny **10** evaluation, scrutinize **11** enumeration, exploration, inquire into, investigate, take stock of **13** give thought to, investigation

canyon 3 col, cut, gap **4** draw, pass, wadi, wash **5** break, chasm, cleft, crack, gorge, gulch, gully, notch **6** arroyo, coulee, defile, divide, ravine, valley **7** fissure, opening **8** corridor, crevasse, water gap

cap 3 lid, top **4** seal **5** cover, outdo **6** better, exceed, top off **7** surpass **8** headgear, outstrip **9** headdress **10** visored hat

capability 3 art **4** gift **5** flair, knack, power, skill **6** talent **7** ability, faculty, know-how **8** capacity, efficacy, facility **9** potential **10** attainment, competence, competency **11** proficiency **12** potentiality **13** qualification

capable 3 apt **4** able, deft **5** adept **6** adroit, artful, clever, expert, gifted **7** skilled **8** masterly, skillful, talented **9** competent, effective, ingenious **10** proficient **11** efficacious, intelligent **12** accomplished

capable of assuming legal responsibility
Latin: **8** sui juris

Capable of Honor
author: **10** Allan Drury

capable of managing one's own affairs
Latin: **8** sui juris

capacious 3 big **4** huge, vast, wide **5** ample, broad, large, roomy **7** mammoth, massive **8** gigantic, spacious **9** expansive, extensive **10** commodious, expandable, tremendous, voluminous **13** amplitudinous

capaciousness 9 amplitude, roominess **12** spaciousness **14** commodiousness

capacitate 5 allow **6** enable, permit **7** empower, qualify **8** make able

capacity 4 mind, role, room, size **5** gifts, limit, might, power, range, scope, space **6** extent, talent, volume

7 ability, faculty **8** aptitude, facility, function, judgment, position, sagacity, strength **9** amplitude, endowment, intellect, potential **10** brain power, capability **11** discernment **12** intelligence, perspicacity **15** maximum contents

Capaneus
member of: **18** Seven against Thebes
father: **9** Hipponous
mother: **8** Astynome
wife: **6** Evadne
son: **9** Sthenelus
crime: **9** blasphemy
destroyed by: **4** Zeus

caparison 5 adorn, equip **6** bedeck **9** equipment, trappings

cape 4 spit **5** cloak, manta, point, shawl **6** mantle, poncho, serape, tabard, tongue **7** pelisse **8** headland **9** peninsula **10** promontory

Capek, Karel
author of: **3** R U R **8** Hordubal, Krakatit **9** The Mother **13** Power and Glory **18** The War with the Newts

caper 3 hop **4** jape, jump, lark, leap, romp, skip **5** antic, bound, fling, frisk, prank, spree, stunt, trick **6** bounce, cavort, frolic, gambol, prance **7** caprice **8** escapade **9** adventure, high jinks **10** carrying on **11** shenanigans **14** monkey business

Cape Verde *see box*

capital 4 cash, fine **5** great, money, super **6** center, riches, superb, wealth **7** supreme **9** excellent, financing, first-rate, majuscule, matchless, principal, resources **10** cash on hand, first-class **11** large letter, wherewithal **12** headquarters **13** working assets **14** available means **15** investment funds, upper-case letter

capital city (of countries) *see box, p. 154*

capital city (of states) *see* **13** state capitals

capitalism 14 free enterprise

capitalist 5 mogul **6** tycoon **8** investor **9** financier, plutocrat **14** businessperson

capitalize 4 back, fund **5** stake **7** exploit, finance, support, trade on, utilize **8** bankroll, cash in on, profit by **9** subsidize **11** foot the bill **13** make the most of **17** turn an honest penny **23** strike while the iron is hot **24** make hay while the sun shines

Cape Verde
capital: **5** Praia
largest city: **7** Mindelo
others: **6** Sal Rei **7** Espargo **8** Assomada, Palmeira, Tarrafal **9** Pedra Lume, Sao Filipe **10** Nova Sintra, Santa Maria **11** Porto Ingles **13** Ribeira Grande **16** Vila de Nova Sintra **18** Vila de Ribeira Brave
division: **9** Solavento **10** Barlavento **14** Leeward Islands **15** Windward Islands
monetary unit: **6** escudo **7** centavo
island: **3** Sal **4** Fogo, Maio, Razo **5** Brava, Secos **6** Branco **8** Boa Vista, Sao Tiago **10** Santa Luzia, Santo Antao, Sao Nicolau, Sao Vicente
mountain: **4** Fogo
highest point: **4** Cano **10** Pico de Cano
sea: **8** Atlantic
physical feature:
volcano: **4** Cano
people: **6** Creole **7** mulatto **8** Africans **9** Europeans **10** Portuguese
language: **7** Crioulo **10** Portuguese **13** Verdean Creole
religion: **13** Roman Catholic

capitalize on 7 exploit, utilize **8** profit by **13** turn to account **14** use to advantage

capitol 10 statehouse **11** legislature **15** government house

capitulate 5 yield **6** accede, give in, give up, relent, submit **7** succumb **8** cry quits **9** acquiesce, surrender **11** come to terms, sue for peace **15** lay down one's arms **17** acknowledge defeat, hoist the white flag

capitulation 8 giving in, giving up, quitting, yielding **9** surrender **10** submission

Capote, Truman
author of: **11** In Cold Blood **12** A Tree of Night **19** Breakfast at Tiffany's
character: **14** Holly Golightly

Capp, Al
real name: **18** Alfred George Caplin
creator/artist of: **8** Li'l Abner

Capra, Frank
director of: **11** Lady for a Day, Lost Horizon **15** State of the Union **17** Arsenic and Old Lace, It's a Wonderful Life, Mr Deeds Goes to Town (Oscar) **18** It Happened One Night (Oscar) **20** You Can't Take It with You (Oscar) **23** Mr Smith Goes to Washington

caprice 3 fad **4** lark, whim **5** antic, caper, craze, fancy, fling, prank, quirk, spree, stunt **6** notion, oddity, vagary **7** impulse **8** crotchet, escapade **10** erraticism **11** peculiarity **12** eccentricity, idiosyncrasy

capricious 6 fickle, fitful, quirky, uneven **7** erratic, fad-dish, flighty **8** fanciful, skittish, unstable, unsteady, variable, wavering **9** eccentric, impulsive, mercurial, uncertain, undecided **10** changeable, indecisive, irresolute **11** vacillating **12** inconsistent **13** irresponsible **15** shilly-shallying

capriciousness 7 caprice **10** fickleness **11** instability **12** irresolution **13** impulsiveness, inconsistency

Capricorn
symbol: **4** goat
planet: **6** Saturn
rules: **6** career
born: **7** January **8** December

capsicum peppers
origin: **15** tropical America
variety: **7** cayenne, paprika **9** red pepper **11** chili pepper, chili powder, curry powder, sweet pepper
use: **5** chili, curry, pizza **8** barbecue **9** paprikash

capsize 5 upset **6** invert **7** tip over **8** flip over, keel over, overturn, turn over **10** turn turtle

capsule 4 case, pill **6** ampule **7** cockpit **8** covering **9** spore case **12** condensation

captain 4 boss, head **5** chief, pilot **6** leader, master, old man **7** headman, skipper **9** chieftain, commander **10** commandant **12** chief officer **16** company commander **17** commanding officer

Captain Blood
director: **13** Michael Curtiz

capital city (of countries)
of **Afghanistan: 5** Kabul
of **Albania: 6** Tirana, Tirane
of **Algeria: 7** Algiers
of **Andorra: 14** Andorra-la-Vella
of **Angola: 6** Luanda
of **Antigua and Barbuda: 7** St John's
of **Argentina: 11** Buenos Aires
of **Armenia: 6** Erivan **7** Yerevan
of **Australia: 8** Canberra
of **Austria: 6** Vienna
of **Azerbaijan: 4** Baku
of **the Bahamas: 6** Nassau
of **Bahrain: 6** Manama
of **Bangladesh: 5** Dacca
of **Barbados: 10** Bridgetown
of **Belarus: 5** Minsk
of **Belgium: 8** Brussels **9** Bruxelles
of **Belize: 8** Belmopan
of **Benin: 9** Porto-Novo
of **Bermuda: 8** Hamilton
of **Bhutan: 6** Thimbu **7** Thimphu
of **Bolivia: 5** Sucre
of **Bosnia-Herzegovina: 8** Sarajevo
of **Botswana: 8** Gaborone **9** Gaberones
of **Brazil: 8** Brasilia **12** Rio de Janeiro
of **Brunei: 17** Bandar Seri Begawan
of **Bulgaria: 5** Sofia
of **Burkina Faso: 11** Ouagadougou
of **Burundi: 9** Bujumbura
of **Cambodia: 8** Pnom-Penh
of **Cameroon: 7** Yaounde
of **Canada: 6** Ottawa
of **the Canary Islands: 9** Las Palmas **19** Santa Cruz de Tenerife

of **Cape Verde: 5** Praia
of **the Central African Republic: 6** Bangui
of **Chad: 8** Fort-Lamy, N'Djamena
of **Chile: 8** Santiago
of **China: 6** Peking
of **Colombia: 6** Bogota
of **Comoros: 6** Moroni
of **the Congo: 11** Brazzaville
of **Costa Rica: 7** San Jose
of **Crete: 5** Canea **8** Iraklion
of **Croatia: 6** Zagreb
of **Cuba: 6** Havana **8** Le Habana
of **Cyprus: 7** Nicosia
of **Czechoslovakia/Czech Republic: 6** Prague
of **Denmark: 10** Copenhagen
of **Djibouti: 8** Djibouti
of **the Dominican Republic: 12** Santo Domingo **14** Ciudad Trujillo
of **Ecuador: 5** Quito
of **Egypt: 5** Cairo
of **El Salvador: 11** San Salvador
of **England: 6** London
of **Equatorial Guinea: 6** Malabo
of **Eritrea: 6** Asmara
of **Estonia: 7** Tallinn
of **Ethiopia: 10** Addis Ababa
of **Fiji: 4** Suva
of **Finland: 8** Helsinki **11** Helsingfors
of **France: 5** Paris
of **the Gabon Republic: 10** Libreville
of **The Gambia: 6** Banjul **8** Bathurst
of **Georgia: 7** Tbilisi
of **Germany (East): 10** East Berlin
of **Germany (West): 4** Bonn
of **Ghana: 5** Accra, Akkra
of **Greece: 6** Athens

of **Greenland: 3** Nuk **8** Godthaab, The Point
of **Grenada: 9** St Georges
of **Guatemala: 13** Guatemala City
of **Guinea: 7** Conakry
of **Guinea-Bissau: 6** Bissau
of **Guyana: 10** Georgetown
of **Haiti: 12** Port-au-Prince
of **Honduras: 11** Tegucigalpa
of **Hong Kong: 8** Victoria
of **Hungary: 8** Budapest
of **Iceland: 9** Reykjavik
of **India: 8** New Delhi
of **Indonesia: 7** Jakarta **8** Djakarta
of **Iran: 6** Tehran **7** Teheran
of **Iraq: 7** Baghdad
of **Ireland: 6** Dublin
of **Israel: 9** Jerusalem
of **Italy: 4** Roma, Rome
of **the Ivory Coast: 7** Abidjan
of **Jamaica: 8** Kingston
of **Japan: 3** Edo **5** Tokyo
of **Java: 7** Jakarta **8** Djakarta
of **Jordan: 5** Amman
of **Kazakhstan: 7** Alma-Ata
of **Kenya: 7** Nairobi
of **Kiribati: 6** Tarawa
of **Korea (North): 9** Pyongyang
of **Korea (South): 5** Seoul
of **Kuwait: 10** Kuwait City
of **Kyrgyzstan: 7** Bishkek (Frunze)
of **Laos: 9** Viengchan, Vientiane
of **Latvia: 4** Riga
of **Lebanon: 6** Beirut **8** Beyrouth
of **Lesotho: 6** Maseru
of **Liberia: 8** Monrovia
of **Libya: 7** Tripoli

of **Liechtenstein: 5** Vaduz
of **Lithuania: 5** Vilna **6** Kausas **7** Vilnius
of **Luxembourg:**
   10 Luxembourg
of **Macedonia: 6** Skopje
of **Madagascar:**
   10 Tananarive
   12 Antananarivo
of **Malawi: 8** Lilongwe
of **Malaysia: 11** Kuala
   Lumpur
of **Maldives: 4** Male
of **Mali: 6** Bamako
of **Malta: 8** Valletta
of **Mauritania: 10** Nouakchott
of **Mauritius: 9** Port Louis
of **Mexico: 10** Mexico City
of **Moldova: 8** Chisinau,
   Kishinev
of **Monaco: 11** Monaco-Ville
of **Mongolia: 9** Ulan Bator
of **Montenegro: 7** Cetinje
   8 Titograd **9** Podgorica
of **Morocco: 5** Rabat
   6 Rabbat
of **Mozambique: 6** Maputo
   15 Lourenco Marques
of **Myanmar: 6** Yangon
   7 Rangoon
of **Namibia: 8** Windhoek
of **Nauru: 13** Yaren District
of **Nepal: 8** Katmandu
   9 Kathmandu
of **Netherlands: 8** The Hague
   9 Amsterdam
of **New Guinea: 11** Port
   Moresby
of **New Zealand:**
   10 Wellington
of **Nicaragua: 7** Managua
of **Niger: 6** Niamey
of **Nigeria: 5** Abuja, Lagos
of **Norway: 4** Oslo
   11 Christiania
of **Oman: 6** Masqat, Muscat

of **Pakistan: 9** Islamabad
of **Panama: 10** Panama City
of **Paraguay: 8** Asuncion
of **Peru: 4** Lima
of **the Philippines: 6** Manila
of **Poland: 6** Warsaw
of **Portugal: 6** Lisbon
of **Puerto Rico: 7** San Juan
of **Qatar: 4** Doha **7** al-Dawha
of **Romania: 9** Bucharest
of **Russia: 6** Moscow
of **Rwanda: 6** Kigali
of **Samoa (American): 8** Pago
   Pago
of **Samoa (Western): 4** Apia
of **San Marino: 9** San
   Marino
of **Sao Tome and Principe:**
   7 Sao Tome
of **Sardinia: 8** Cagliari
of **Saudi Arabia: 6** Riyadh
of **Scotland: 9** Edinburgh
of **Senegal: 5** Dakar
of **Seychelles: 8** Victoria
of **Sicily: 7** Palermo
of **Sierra Leone: 8** Freetown
of **Sikkim: 7** Gangtok
of **Singapore: 9** Singapore
of **Slovakia: 10** Bratislava
of **Slovenia: 9** Ljubljana
of **the Solomon Islands:**
   7 Honiara
of **Somalia: 9** Mogadishu
   10 Mogadiscio
of **South Africa: 8** Cape
   Town, Pretoria
   12 Bloemfontein
of **Spain: 6** Madrid
of **Sri Lanka: 7** Colombo
of **the Sudan: 8** Khartoum
of **Suriname: 10** Paramaribo
of **Swaziland: 7** Mbabane
of **Sweden: 9** Stockholm
of **Switzerland: 4** Bern
of **Syria: 8** Damascus
of **Taiwan: 6** Taipei

of **Tajikistan: 8** Dushanbe
of **Tanzania: 11** Dar es
   Salaam
of **Thailand: 6** Bankok
   7 Bangkok **8** Thonburi
   9 Ayutthaya
of **Tibet: 5** Lassa, Lhasa
of **Togo: 4** Lome
of **Tonga: 9** Nukualofa
of **Trinidad and Tobago:**
   11 Port of Spain
of **Tunisia: 5** Tunis
of **Turkey: 6** Ankara
of **Turkmenistan:**
   9 Ashkhabad
of **Tuvalu: 8** Funafuti
of **Uganda: 7** Kampala
of **Ukraine: 4** Kiev
of **United Arab Emirates:**
   8 Abu Dhabi
of **United States: 12** Washington DC
of **Upper Volta:**
   11 Ouagadougou
of **Uruguay: 10** Montevideo
of **Uzbekistan: 8** Tashkent
of **Vanuatu: 4** Vila
of **Venezuela: 7** Caracas
of **Vietnam: 5** Hanoi
   6 Saigon
of **Wales: 7** Cardiff
of **Western Sahara: 6** Al
   Aiun **7** El Aaiun
of **Western Samoa: 4** Apia
of **Yemen (North): 4** Sana
   5 Sanaa
of **Yemen (South): 4** Aden
   14 Madinat al-Shaab
of **Yugoslavia: 7** Beograd
   8 Belgrade
of **Zaire: 8** Kinshasa
of **Zambia: 6** Lusaka
of **Zimbabwe: 6** Harare
   9 Salisbury

---

cast: 10 Errol Flynn **12** Lionel Atwill **13** Basil Rathbone **17** Olivia de Havilland

Captain Hook
  character in: 8 Peter Pan
  author: 6 Barrie

Captain Horatio Hornblower
  author: 10 C S Forester

Captains Courageous
  author: 14 Rudyard Kipling
  director: 13 Victor Fleming
  cast: 12 Mickey Rooney,
  Spencer Tracy **13** John Carradine, Melvyn Douglas
  15 Lionel Barrymore
  18 Freddie Bartholomew
  Oscar for: 5 actor (Tracy)

Captain's Daughter, The
  author: 16 Alexander Pushkin

Captain Video and His Video Rangers
  character: 7 Dr Pauli **9** The
  Ranger **12** Captain Video
  cast: 7 Al Hodge **10** Hal
  Conklin **11** Don Hastings
  13 Richard Coogan
  slogan: 29 Guardian of the
  Safety of the World
  villain: 4 Atar **7** Nargola
  8 Dahoumie, Kul of Eos
  9 Dr Clysmok **12** Heng Foo
  Seeng **14** Mook the Moon
  Man
  gimmick: 5 Tobor **9** Discatron **11** Atomic Rifle
  16 Barrier of Silence, Radio
  Scillograph **17** Cosmic Ray
  Vibrator **18** Opticon Scillometer **19** Cloak of Invisibility, Trisonic Compensator
  spaceship: 6 Galaxy

caption 5 title **6** legend
  7 heading, subhead **8** headline,
  subtitle **11** explanation

captious 4 mean **5** picky,
  testy **6** ornery **7** carping, cutting, peevish **8** caviling, contrary, niggling, perverse,
  petulant, picayune, snappish
  9 fractious, querulous **10** belittling, censorious, nitpicking
  11 deprecating **12** cantankerous, faultfinding
  13 hypercritical

captivate 4 lure **5** charm
  6 dazzle, enamor, seduce **7** attract, bewitch, delight, enchant, win over **8** enthrall
  9 carry away, enrapture, fascinate, hypnotize, infatuate,
  mesmerize, transport **13** turn
  the head of **14** take the fancy
  of

captivated 7 charmed, pleased **9** delighted, enchanted **10** enraptured, enthralled, spellbound

captivating 7 winning, winsome **8** adorable, charming, dazzling, engaging, fetching, magnetic **9** appealing, beguiling, disarming **10** attractive, bewitching, delightful, enchanting, entrancing **11** enthralling, fascinating, mesmerizing **12** ingratiating, irresistible

captive 5 caged **6** penned **7** hostage **8** confined, enslaved, interned, locked up, prisoner **9** oppressed **10** imprisoned, subjugated **12** incarcerated

captivity 7 bondage, holding, slavery **9** servitude **10** detainment /12 imprisonment

capture 3 bag, nab **4** bust, grab, snag, take, trap **5** catch, grasp, pinch, seize, snare **6** arrest, collar, taking **7** bagging, ensnare, procure, seizure, snaring **8** catching, trapping **9** apprehend, collaring, ensnaring, lay hold of **12** apprehension, laying hold of, take prisoner **14** taking prisoner **15** take into custody

Capulet family
  characters in: 14 Romeo and Juliet
  author: 11 Shakespeare

Capys
  father: 9 Assaracus
  son: 7 Laocoon **8** Anchises
  grandson: 6 Aeneas
  founded: 5 Capua
  warned against: 11 Trojan horse

car 4 auto, heap **5** buggy, coach, diner, motor **6** boxcar, hot rod, jalopy, wheels **7** flivver, machine, sleeper, vehicle **8** carriage **9** tin lizzie **10** automobile **12** motor vehicle
  kind: 4 coal **5** cable, horse, motor **6** cattle, dining, parlor, street **7** baggage, freight, Pullman, railway **8** sleeping

Car
  father: 9 Phoroneus
  mother: 5 Cerdo
  founder of: 6 Megara

carabiniere 9 policeman

Caracas
  birthplace of: 12 Simon Bolivar
  capital of: 9 Venezuela
  founder: 13 Diego de Losada
  museum: 7 Bolivar **8** Criolan **11** Colonial Art, Raul Santana
  river: 6 Guaire

carafe 5 flask **6** bottle, vessel **9** container

carapace 4 case **5** shell **6** lorica, shield **7** carapax **8** calipash, covering **11** turtle shell

Caravaggio, Michelangelo Merisi da
  born: 5 Italy **10** Caravaggio
  artwork: 12 Young Bacchus **14** Burial of St Lucy **16** Raising of Lazarus **17** The Supper at Emmaus **18** Calling of St Matthew, The Life of St Matthew **20** St Matthew and the Angel **21** The Conversion of St Paul **23** The Crucifixion of St Peter **30** The Beheading of St John the Baptist

caravan 4 band, file, line **5** queue, train, troop **6** coffle, column, convoy, parade, string **7** company, cortege, retinue **9** cavalcade, chain gang, entourage, motorcade **10** procession, wagon train

caravansary 3 inn **5** hotel **8** hostelry

caraway
  botanical name: 10 Carum carvi
  origin: 6 Europe **9** Asia Minor **14** the Netherlands
  liqueur: 6 Kummel
  candy-covered caraway
    seeds: 6 comfit **12** whiskykiller
  use: 4 pork, soup, stew **8** rye bread

carbohydrate
  consists of: 5 water **6** carbon, oxygen **8** hydrogen **13** carbon dioxide
  kinds: 5 sugar **6** simple, starch, xylose **7** complex, glucose, lactose, maltose, sucrose **8** dextrose, fructose **9** cellulose

carbon 4 coal, coke, copy **8** charcoal **9** lampblack
  chemical symbol: 1 C

carbon copy 5 clone **7** replica **9** duplicate, facsimile **12** reproduction

carbonize 4 burn, char, sear **5** singe **6** scorch **10** incinerate

carbuncle 4 boil, sore **11** excrescence **12** inflammation

carcass 4 body, bouk, husk, wall **5** shell, stiff, trunk **6** corpse **7** cadaver, carrion, remains **8** dead body, fireball, skeleton **9** framework

carcinoma 5 tumor **6** cancer **8** neoplasm **10** malignancy **15** malignant growth

card 4 bill **6** ticket **7** program **8** postcard
  kind: 7 calling, get-well, playing **8** birthday, business, greeting **9** Christmas, Valentine

cardamon
  botanical name: 19 Elettaria cardamomum
  origin: 4 Asia **5** India **13** southeast Asia
  related to: 6 ginger
  color: 5 black
  use: 5 curry **7** dessert **12** Danish pastry

Cardea
  origin: 5 Roman
  goddess of: 6 family **10** door hinges

Cardew, Cecily
  character in: 27 The Importance of Being Earnest
  author: 5 Wilde

card game *see box*

Cardiff
  capital of: 5 Wales

cardigan 5 corgi **6** jacket, wampus **7** sweater **10** Welsh corgi

cardinal 3 key, top **4** head, main **5** basic, chief, first, prime, vital **6** cherry, claret **7** carmine, central, deep-red, highest, leading, primary, scarlet **8** blood-red, dominant, foremost, greatest **9** essential, intrinsic, necessary, paramount, principal, uppermost **10** elementary, preeminent, underlying **11** fundamental, outstanding, predominant, wine-colored **13** indispensable, most important

care 4 heed, load, mind, want, wish **5** grief, pains, worry **6** bother, charge, desire, effort, misery, regard, sorrow, strain, stress **7** anguish, anxiety, caution, concern, control, custody, keeping, sadness, thought, trouble **8** distress, hardship, nuisance, pressure, vexation **9** annoyance, attention, be worried, diligence, exactness, heartache, vigilance **10** affliction, management, precaution, protection, solicitude **11** application, be concerned, bother about, carefulness, supervision, tribulation, unhappiness **12** ministration, trouble about, watchfulness **13** attentiveness, consideration **14** be interested in, circumspection, discrimination, fastidiousness, meticulousness, responsibility, scrupulousness **17** conscientiousness

card game 3 loo, war 4 brag, fish, skat, vint 5 ombre, poker, rummy, whist 6 boston, bridge, casino, chemmy, ecarte, euchre, go fish, hearts, memory, piquet, pocher 7 bezique, canasta, cooncan, Old Maid, plafond, primero 8 baccarat, conquian, cribbage, gin rummy, napoleon, patience, pinochle, slapjack 9 blackjack, pelmanism, solitaire, spoil five, twenty-one 11 chemin de fer, crazy eights 13 concentration 14 contract bridge 16 beggar-my-neighbor, trente et quarante
   card names: 3 ace 4 fool, jack, king, trey 5 joker, queen
   combination of cards: 4 meld
   one hand or round: 5 trick
   rulebook by: 5 Hoyle
   suits: 4 club 5 heart, spade 7 diamond
    French: 5 coeur, pique 6 trefle 7 carreau
    German: 4 grun, herz, piks 5 karos, treff 6 eichel 7 schelle
    Italian: 5 coppa, cuori, fiori, spada 6 denaro, picchi, quadri 7 bastone
    Spanish: 3 oro 4 copa 5 basto 6 espada

Careas 6 eunuch

careen 3 tip, yaw 4 lean, list, sway, tilt, veer 5 heave, slant, slope 7 capsize 8 lean over, overturn

career 3 job 4 line, work 7 calling, pursuit 8 activity, business, lifework, vocation 10 employment, livelihood, occupation, profession, walk of life

care for 4 like, mind, tend 5 fancy 7 oversee 8 attend to, wait upon 9 look after, watch over 10 minister to, provide for

carefree 3 gay 4 glad 5 happy, jolly, sunny 6 breezy, elated, jaunty, joyous 7 buoyant, gleeful, radiant, relaxed, smiling 8 careless, cheerful, jubilant, laughing 9 easygoing 10 full of life, optimistic, untroubled 11 free-and-easy 12 happy-go-lucky, light-hearted, without

worry 13 in high spirits 23 without a worry in the world
   French: 9 sans souci

careful 4 fine, nice, wary 5 alert, chary, exact, fussy 7 correct, guarded, heedful, mindful, on guard, precise, prudent, tactful 8 accurate, cautious, diligent, discreet, vigilant, watchful 9 attentive, concerned, judicious, observant, regardful 10 fastidious, meticulous, particular, scrupulous, solicitous, thoughtful 11 circumspect, painstaking, punctilious 13 conscientious

carefulness 7 caution 10 steadiness 12 deliberation 14 circumspection

careless 3 lax 4 rash 5 messy, slack 6 casual, sloppy, untidy 7 inexact, offhand 8 heedless, mindless, slapdash, slipshod, slovenly 9 forgetful, imprecise, incorrect, negligent, unmindful 10 disorderly, inaccurate, neglectful, nonchalant, unthinking, untroubled 11 indifferent, thoughtless, unconcerned 12 absentminded, devil-may-care 13 inconsiderate, lackadaisical

carelessness 6 laxity 7 neglect 9 messiness, slackness 10 inaccuracy, negligence, sloppiness, untidiness 11 imprecision, inexactness 12 heedlessness, indiscretion, slovenliness 13 unmindfulness 14 disorderliness 15 thoughtlessness 16 absentmindedness, irresponsibility

Care of Time, The
   author: 10 Eric Ambler

caress 3 hug, pat, pet 5 clasp, touch 6 cuddle, fondle, stroke 7 embrace, petting, toy with 8 fondling, stroking 11 gentle touch

caretaker 6 keeper, porter, warden 7 curator, janitor, steward 8 overseer, watchman 9 concierge, custodian 10 gatekeeper 14 superintendent

careworn 7 haggard, worried 8 fatigued, troubled 11 pessimistic

cargo 4 load 5 goods 6 burden, lading 7 freight 8 shipment 11 consignment, merchandise

Carib
   language family: 7 Cariban
   location: 7 Guianas 9 Caribbean, Venezuela 12 South America
   custom: 11 cannibalism

Cariban
   tribe: 5 Carib 6 Acawai, Akawai

Caribbean 3 sea
   channel: 7 Yucatan
   city: 6 Havana 7 San Juan 8 Santiago 10 Guantanamo 12 Port au Prince 13 Santo Domingo 15 Charlotte Amalie
   Indian: 5 Carib 6 Arawak
   island: 4 Cuba 5 Aruba, Haiti, Nevis 6 Cayman, Nassau, Tobago, Virgin 7 Antigua, Bahamas, Barbuda, Curacao, Grenada, Jamaica, Leeward 8 Anguilla, Dominica, Trinidad, Windward 9 Saint John 10 Guadeloupe, Hispaniola, Martinique, Montserrat, Puerto Rico, Saint Kitts, Saint Lucia 11 Saint Thomas 12 Saint Vincent 14 Lesser Antilles 15 Greater Antilles 19 Dominican Republic, Netherlands Antilles
   language: 6 gullah 10 papiamento
   product: 3 rum 5 fruit, spice, sugar 6 coffee

caricature 4 mock 6 parody, satire 7 lampoon, mockery, takeoff 8 satirize, travesty 9 absurdity, burlesque 10 distortion 12 exaggeration

Carker
   character in: 12 Dombey and Son
   author: 7 Dickens

Carlisle, Kitty
   real name: 13 Katherine Conn
   husband: 8 Moss Hart
   born: 12 New Orleans LA
   roles: 13 She Loves Me Not 14 To Tell the Truth 16 A Night at the Opera 19 Murder at the Vanities

Carlton, Steve (Steven Norman)
   nickname: 5 Lefty
   sport: 8 baseball
   position: 7 pitcher
   team: 20 Philadelphia Phillies

Carlyle, Thomas
   author of: 8 Cromwell 14 Sartor Resartus 17 Frederick the Great 19 The French Revolution 20 Heroes and Hero-Worship

Carmanor
   king of: 5 Crete
   purified: 6 Apollo 7 Artemis

Carme
   daughter: 11 Britomartis

Carmen
   author: 14 Prosper Merimee
   opera by: 5 Bizet
   setting: 7 Seville

character: **7** Don Jose **9** Es-
camillo, Frasquita

Carmen Jones
director: **13** Otto Preminger
based on opera by: **5** Bizet
(Carmen)
adaptation by: **18** Oscar
Hammerstein II
cast: **11** Pearl Bailey
14 Harry Belafonte **16** Dorothy Dandridge

Carmenta
origin: **5** Roman
member of: **7** Camanae
protectress of: **10** childbirth
husband: **7** Evander
son: **7** Evander

carmine 3 red **6** cherry **7** crimson, deep red, scarlet **8** blood
red **9** bright red

carnage 8 butchery, massacre
9 blood bath, slaughter

carnal 4 lewd **6** erotic, impure,
sexual, sinful, wanton
7 fleshly, immoral, lustful, sensual **8** prurient, sensuous, unchaste, venereal **9** lecherous,
salacious **10** lascivious, libidinous, voluptuous

Carnegie, Dale
author of: **33** How To Win
Friends and Influence
People

carnelian
species: **6** quartz

Carnera, Primo
nickname: **13** the Ambling
Alp
sport: **6** boxing
class: **11** heavyweight

Carneus
epithet of: **6** Apollo
alludes to: **11** cornel trees

Carney, Art
real name: **26** Arthur William Matthew Carney
partner: **13** Jackie Gleason
born: **13** Mount Vernon NY
roles: **8** Ed Norton **13** Harry
and Tonto (Oscar) **15** The
Honeymooners

carnival 4 fair, fete, gala **6** circus **7** holiday, jubilee **8** festival, jamboree, sideshow
9 Mardi Gras **11** celebration

carnivore 3 cat, dog, fox
4 bear, lion, lynx, mink,
puma, wolf **5** civet, dingo,
fossa, hyena, otter, panda,
skunk, tayra, tiger **6** badger,
bobcat, coyote, ferret, grison,
hyaena, jackal, jaguar, marten,
olingo, weasel **7** polecat, raccoon, suricat **8** aardwolf, kinkajou, mongoose **9** meat eater,
wolverine **10** cacomistle, coatimundi, flesh eater

carnivorous 9 predatory
10 meat-eating, predaceous
11 flesh-eating

Carnus
occupation: **4** seer
seer of: **6** Apollo
killed by: **10** Heraclidae

carol 4 hymn, noel, sing
5 paean **6** warble **8** canticle
9 song of joy **12** song of
praise

Caroline Islands
district: **3** Yap **4** Truk **5** Pa-
lau **6** Ponape
inhabitant: **10** Polynesian
11 Micronesian
island: **3** Yap **6** Ponape,
Ulithi **8** Nukuroro
10 Babelthuap
14 Kapinamarangi
language: **7** English
10 Polynesian
11 Micronesian
ocean: **7** Pacific

carom 6 bounce, strike **7** collide, rebound, **8** billiard,
ricochet **9** bounce off

Caron, Leslie
born: **6** France **19** Boulogne-
Billancourt
roles: **4** Gaby, Gigi, Lili
5 Fanny **11** Father Goose
13 Daddy Longlegs **14** The
L-Shaped Room **17** An
American in Paris

Carothers, Wallace Hume
field: **9** chemistry
discovered: **5** nylon

carousal 4 orgy **5** binge,
drunk, spree **7** debauch **9** bacchanal **10** debauchery,
saturnalia

carouse 5 drink, party, quaff,
revel **6** guzzle, imbibe, tipple
7 roister, wassail **8** live it up
9 make merry **10** go on a
binge **11** make whoopee

Carousel
director: **9** Henry King
based on: **6** Liliom
adaptation by: **21** Rodgers
and Hammerstein
cast: **12** Gordon MacRae
(Billy Bigelow), Shirley
Jones **15** Cameron Mitchell
song: **9** Soliloquy **11** If I
Loved You **19** You'll Never
Walk Alone

carp 3 nag **5** cavil, chide, decry, knock **6** deride, impugn,
jibe at, pick on **7** censure,
condemn **8** belittle, complain,
reproach **9** criticize, deprecate,
disparage, fault-find, find
fault **10** disapprove

Carpaccio, Vittore
born: **5** Italy **6** Venice
artwork: **13** Two Courtesans

18 The Dream of St Ursula
19 The Legend of St Ursula
21 St Augustine in his
Study **24** St George Killing
the Dragon **28** St Augustine's Vision of St Jerome
29 The Arrival of St Ursula
at Cologne

carpal
bone of: **5** wrist

carpe diem 11 seize the day
15 enjoy the present

carpenter 6 fitter, joiner
7 builder **8** repairer **10** wood-
worker **12** cabinetmaker
ant: **10** camponotus
bee: **8** xylocopa
bird: **10** woodpecker
fish: **10** hammerhead
moth: **10** prinoxysus

Carpenter, Harlean
real name of: **10** Jean
Harlow

carper 6 critic **7** caviler **9** nitpicker **11** fault-finder

carpet 3 mat, rug **5** cover,
layer, sheet **7** blanket, mat-
ting **8** covering

Carpetbaggers, The
author: **13** Harold Robbins

Carpo
origin: **5** Greek
member of: **5** Horae
goddess of: **11** summer fruit

Carpophorus
epithet of: **7** Demeter
10 Persephone
means: **11** fruit bearer

Carr, Emily
born: **6** Canada **8** Victoria
15 British Columbia
artwork: **3** Sky **8** Big Raven
14 Blunden Harbour, Kis-
piax Village **15** Woods and
Blue Sky **17** Forest Landscape II **36** Cape Mudge An
Indian Family with Totem
Pole

Carra, Carlo
born: **5** Italy **9** Quargneto
artwork: **13** Lot's Daughters
16 Metaphysical Muse
20 Patriotic Celebration
29 The Funeral of the Anarchist Galli

Carradine, David
father: **4** John
half-brothers: **5** Keith
6 Robert
born: **11** Hollywood CA
roles: **6** Kung Fu **13** Bound
for Glory **14** The Serpent's
Egg

Carradine, John
real name: **21** Richmond
Reed Carradine
son: **5** David, Keith **6** Robert

born: 18 Greenwich Village NY
roles: 9 Cleopatra, Kidnapped **10** Stagecoach **12** Count Dracula **15** The Invisible Man **18** Captains Courageous, The Three Musketeers

Carradine, Keith
father: 4 John
brother: 6 Robert
half-brother: 5 David
born: 10 San Mateo CA
roles: 9 Nashville **10** Pretty Baby

Carraway, Nick
character in: 14 The Great Gatsby
author: 10 Fitzgerald

Carrere, John Merven
partner: 14 Thomas Hastings
architect of: 19 House Office Building (Washington DC) **20** New York Public Library, Senate Office Building (Washington DC) **21** Henry Clay Frick mansion (now Frick Collection NYC)
style: 18 French neo-classical, Spanish Renaissance

carriage 3 air, rig **4** mien **5** buggy, coach, poise, wagon **6** aspect, manner **7** bearing, posture, vehicle **8** attitude, behavior, demeanor, presence **10** appearance, conveyance, deportment **11** comportment

Carrie
author: 11 Stephen King

carried away 7 excited, frantic, seduced **8** ecstatic, frenzied, overcome **9** delirious **10** fascinated, infatuated **11** transported

carrier 3 bus, car **4** rack, wave **5** agent, barge, plane, coach, drain, ferry, train, truck, wagon **6** bearer, boxcar, pigeon, porter **7** airline, channel, mailman, postman, trucker, vehicle **8** airplane, aircraft, carriage, catalyst, railroad **9** messenger **11** transmitter, wheelbarrow

carrion 5 bones, offal, waste **6** corpse, refuse **7** cadaver, carcass, garbage, remains, wastage **8** crowbait, dead body, leavings

Carroll, Leo G
born: 6 Weedon **7** England
roles: 6 Topper **7** Rebecca **9** Suspicion **10** Spellbound **11** Cosmo Topper **15** A Christmas Carol, The Man from UNCLE, The Paradine Case **16** Father of the Bride, North by Northwest

Carroll, Lewis
real name: 22 Charles Lutwidge Dodgson
author of: 11 Jabberwocky **22** Through the Looking Glass **28** Alice's Adventures in Wonderland

carrousel 4 ride, tray **8** conveyor **9** quadrille, whirligig **10** tournament **12** merry-go-round

carry 3 lug, run **4** bear, cart, haul, lift, move, prop, ship, take, tote **5** brace, bring, fetch, offer, print, shift, stock **6** convey, hold up, supply, uphold **7** conduct, deliver, display, publish, release, support, sustain **8** displace, maintain, shoulder, transfer, transmit **9** broadcast, transport **10** keep on hand **11** communicate, disseminate

carry away 4 lure **6** abduct, kidnap, seduce **7** attract **9** captivate, fascinate, infatuate, transport

carry off 5 seize, steal **6** abduct, kidnap **7** bear off **9** succeed at **11** get away with

carry out 2 do **6** effect, wind up **7** achieve, execute, fulfill, perform, realize **8** complete, conclude, dispatch **9** discharge, dispose of, succeed at **10** accomplish, bring about **11** bring to pass

carry through 6 effect, finish **7** achieve, develop, execute, fulfill, perform, realize **8** complete, conclude **9** discharge **10** accomplish, consummate, effectuate, perpetuate **13** put into effect

Carson, Rachel Louise
field: 7 biology
studied: 9 pollution
author of: 12 Silent Spring **14** The Sea Around Us **15** The Edge of the Sea

Carstone, Richard
character in: 10 Bleak House
author: 7 Dickens

cart 3 gig, lug **4** bear, dray, haul, move, take, tote, trap **5** bring, carry, fetch, truck, wagon **6** barrow, convey **7** schlepp, tumbrel **8** curricle, transfer, transmit **9** transport **10** handbarrow, transplant, two-wheeler **11** wheelbarrow
kind: 2 go **3** dog, tip **4** dump, hand, push

carte blanche 7 license **9** a free hand, free reign **10** blank check **12** open sanction **13** full authority **18** unconditional power

cartel 4 pool **5** chain, trust **7** combine **8** monopoly **9** syndicate **10** consortium, federation **11** corporation

Carter, Charles
real name of: 14 Charlton Heston

Carter, James Earl, Jr *see box, p. 160*

Carthage *see* **7** Tunisia

carton 3 box **4** case **5** crate **9** container **11** packing case **12** cardboard box, packing crate **18** cardboard container

Carton, Sydney
character in: 16 A Tale of Two Cities
author: 7 Dickens

cartoon 5 comic **6** design, satire, sketch **7** drawing, funnies, picture **8** animated **10** caricature, comicstrip

cartoonist 6 artist, drawer **7** gagster **12** caricaturist
famous: 6 Al Capp, C C Beck, Ted Key **8** Herblock (Herbert L. Block), Jim Davis, Roy Crane **9** Bud Fisher, Chic Young, Dik Browne, Frank King, Hal Foster, Ham Fisher, Walt Kelly **10** Bob Montana, Harold Gray, Johnny Hart, Mort Walker, Paul Conrad, Thomas Nast, Walt Disney **11** Alex Raymond, Bill Mauldin, Dale Messick, David Levine, Ding Darling, Elzie C. Segar, Hank Ketcham, Max Beerbohm, Rollin Kirby **12** Brad Anderson, Chester Gould, Garry Trudeau, James Thurber, Jeff MacNelly, Jules Feiffer, Milton Caniff, Rube Goldberg, Rudolph Dirks, Virgil Partch **13** Charles Addams, Charles Schulz, George McManus, Honore Daumier, Joseph Keppler, Saul Steinberg **14** Homer Davenport, William Hogarth **15** Ernie Bushmiller, Patrick Oliphant, Richard Outcault **16** Benjamin Franklin, George Cruikshank

cartridge 3 dud **4** case, tape **5** blank, shell **6** holder **7** capsule, package **8** cassette, cylinder **9** container

Cartwright, Edmund
nationality: 7 English
inventor of: 9 power loom **18** wool-combing machine

carve 3 hew, saw **4** etch, form, hack, mold, rend, turn, work **5** allot, cleve, cut up, model, shape, slash, slice, split **6** chisel, divide, incise, sculpt

Carter, James Earl, Jr
  nickname: 3 Hot **5** Jimmy **7** Hotshot
  presidential rank: 11 thirty-ninth
  party: 10 Democratic
  state represented: 2 GA **7** Georgia
  defeated: 4 (Gerald R) Ford **8** (Eugene) McCarthy
  vice president: 7 (Walter Frederick "Fritz") Mondale
  cabinet:*state:* **5** (Cyrus R) Vance **6** (Edmund S) Muskie-
    treasury: **6** (G William) Miller **10** (W Michael) Blumen-
    thal*defense:* **5** (Harold) Brown*attorney general:*
    4 (Griffin B) Bell **9** (Benjamin R) Civiletti*interior:*
    6 (Cecil D) Andrus*agriculture:* **8** (Robert S) Bergland-
    commerce: **5** (Juanita Morris) Kreps **9** (Philip M)
    Klutznick*labor:* **8** (F Ray) Marshall*HEW:* **6** (Patricia
    Roberts) Harris **8** (Joseph A) Califano (Jr)*HUD:* **6** (Patri-
    cia Roberts) Harris **8** (Moon) Landrieu*transportation:*
    5 (Brockman) Adams **11** (Neil E) Goldschmidt*education:*
    10 (Shirley) Hufstedler
  born: 2 GA **6** Plains
  education: 14 US Naval Academy **26** Georgia Southwestern
    College **28** Georgia Institute of Technology
  religion: 15 Southern Baptist
  interests: 5 track **6** tennis **7** fishing, hunting **8** football, soft-
    ball **10** basketball **12** cross country **13** square dancing
    17 collecting bottles*music:* **8** folk rock **9** classical
  author: 13 Why Not the Best?
  political career: 12 state senator*governor of:* **7** Georgia
  civilian career: 12 peanut farmer
  military service: 6 US Navy
  notable events of lifetime/term: 6 SALT II **9** Love Canal,
    recession **18** Habitat for Humanity*deaths at:* **9** Jonestow-
    n*eruption of:* **13** Mount St Helens*first baby from:*
    8 test tube*hostages taken in:* **4** Iran*nuclear accident:*
    15 Three Mile Island*pipeline:* **5** Alcan*scandal/investiga-
    tion:* **6** Abscam **9** Bert Lance, Koreagate **11** Billy
    Carter*Supreme Court case:* **5** Bakke*treaty:* **11** Panama
    Canal **16** Camp David Accords
  father: 11 James Earl Sr
  mother: 7 Lillian (Gordy)*nickname:* **11** Miss Lillian
  siblings: 6 Gloria **17** William "Billy" Alton **19** Ruth Carter
    Stapleton
  wife: 8 Rosalynn (Smith)
  children: 7 Amy Lynn **11** John William (Jack) **12** James
    Earl III (Chip) **13** Donnel Jeffrey (Jeff)
  first lady: 36 Presidential Commission on Mental Health*au-
    thor:* **19** First Lady from Plains

Caryatis
  epithet of: 7 Artemis
  means: 15 of the walnut tree

Casablanca
  director: 13 Michael Curtiz
  cast: 10 Peter Lorre **11** Claude
    Rains (Louis), Conrad Veidt,
    Paul Henreid (Victor Laslo)
    12 Dooley Wilson (Sam),
    13 Ingrid Bergman (Ilsa
    Lund) **14** Humphrey Bogart
    (Rick) **17** Sydney Greenstreet
  Oscar for: 7 picture
  song: 12 As Time Goes By

Casanova 3 cad, rip **4** beau,
  lech, roue, wolf **5** lover, Romeo, swain, wooer **6** chaser,
  lecher, suitor **7** admirer, bounder, Don Juan, gallant, rounder
  8 cavalier, Lothario, lover boy,
  paramour **9** ladies' man, libertine, womanizer **10** lady-killer,
  profligate **11** philanderer

Casby
  character in: 12 Little Dorrit
  author: 7 Dickens

cascade 4 fall, gush, pour, rush
  5 chute, falls, surge **6** plunge,
  rapids, tumble **7** Niagara **8** cataract **9** waterfall

case 3 bin, box **4** plea, suit,
  tray **5** cause, chest, cover,
  crate, event **6** action, affair,
  appeal, carton, debate, injury,
  jacket, matter, sheath, victim
  7 cabinet, concern, disease, dispute, episode, example, hearing, housing, inquiry, invalid,
  lawsuit, overlay, patient, wrapper **8** argument, business, covering, envelope, incident,
  instance, sufferer **9** condition,
  container, happening, incidence, sheathing, situation
  10 litigation, occurrence, proceeding, protection, receptacle,
  sick person **11** controversy
  12 circumstance, illustration

case in point 7 example **8** instance **12** illustration

**Case of Sergeant Grischa,
The**
  author: 11 Arnold Zweig

Casey
  nickname of: 20 Charles Dil-
    lon Stengel

cash 5 bills, bread, coins,
  dough, money **6** change, redeem **8** currency, exchange
  9 bank notes **10** paper money
  11 legal tender **13** turn into
  money **14** coin of the realm

cashier 6 banker, bursar,
  purser, teller **9** treasurer
  10 bank teller

Carver, George Washington
  field: 9 chemistry
  worked in: 11 agriculture
  studied: 6 peanut **7** soybean
    11 sweet potato

7 engrave, fashion, pattern,
  quarter **8** block out, dissever
  9 apportion, sculpture

carving 5 cameo **8** intaglio,
  triptych **9** sculpture

Carya
  origin: 8 Laconian
  form: 6 maiden
  home: 7 Laconia
  changed into: 10 walnut tree
  changed by: 8 Dionysus

cash register
invented by: **5** Ritty

casing 4 skin **5** frame
9 sheathing

Casino Royale
author: **10** Ian Fleming

cask 3 keg, tub, tun, vat
4 butt, pipe **6** barrel
8 hogshead

casket 4 case, pall **5** chest
6 coffer, coffin **8** jewel box
11 sarcophagus

Cask of Amontillado, The
author: **13** Edgar Allan Poe
character: **9** Fortunato,
Montresor

Cassandra
also: **9** Alexandra
father: **5** Priam
mother: **6** Hecuba
brother: **5** Paris
concubine of: **9** Agamemnon
son: **6** Pelops **9** Teledamus
cursed by: **6** Apollo
violated by: **4** Ajax
killed by: **12** Clytemnestra

Cassatt, Mary
born: **15** Allegheny City PA
artwork: **6** La Loge **7** The
Bath **11** The Cup of Tea
12 After the Bath, Woman
Bathing **14** Gathering Fruit
15 Reading Le Figaro
20 Girl Arranging Her Hair,
Woman and Child Drawing

Cassavetes, John
wife: **12** Gena Rowlands
born: **9** New York NY
roles/films: **8** Husbands
10 The Tempest **13** Rosemary's Baby, The Dirty
Dozen **23** A Woman Under
the Influence

casserole 4 dish, food, mold
6 tureen, vessel **8** saucepan

Cassio
character in: **7** Othello
author: **11** Shakespeare

Cassiopeia
husband: **7** Cepheus
daughter: **9** Andromeda
offended: **7** Nereids

Cassius
also: **12** Caius Cassius
character in: **12** Julius
Caesar
author: **11** Shakespeare

Cass Timberlane
author: **13** Sinclair Lewis
character: **11** Bradd Criley
24 Jinny Marshland
Timberlane

cast 3 set, sow **4** fire, form,
hurl, look, mien, mint, mold,
pick, shed, toss **5** fling, heave,
model, pitch, shape, shoot,

sling, stamp, throw **6** actors,
assign, casing, choose, direct,
launch, let fly, propel, sculpt,
spread, troupe **7** appoint, company, deposit, diffuse, pattern,
players, project, scatter **8** catapult, disperse **9** broadcast, circulate, discharge, launching,
semblance **10** appearance, distribute, impression, performers, propulsion **11** disseminate,
give parts to **16** dramatis
personae

Castalia
origin: **5** Greek
sacred: **6** spring
location: **14** Mount Parnassus
sacred to: **5** Muses **6** Apollo
source of: **11** inspiration

Castalides see **5** Muses

cast aside 4 junk, shed **6** desert, reject **7** abandon, discard,
forsake, neglect **8** get rid of,
renounce, throw out **9** repudiate, throw away
11 discontinue

cast a spell on 5 charm
7 bewitch, conjure, enchant
8 entrance **11** work magic on

cast aspersions on 5 knock,
scorn **6** deride, malign **7** disdain, put down, run down,
sneer at **8** belittle, pooh-pooh
9 criticize, disparage **13** find
fault with

castaway 3 bum **4** hobo, waif
5 exile, leper, nomad, rover,
stray **6** outlaw, pariah **7** Ishmael, outcast, vagrant **8** deportee, derelict, renegade,
unperson, vagabond, wan-
derer **9** foundling, nonperson
10 expatriate **11** beachcomber,
offscouring, untouchable
12 down-and-outer **15** knight-
of-the-road

cast away 4 junk **6** launch,
propel, reject **7** abandon, discard, toss out **8** get rid of,
pitch out, throw out **9** throw
away

cast down 5 abase, droop,
lower **6** abased, deject, droopy,
humble, sadden **7** depress,
humbled, lowered **8** bring low,
dejected, disgrace, saddened
9 depressed, disgraced, humiliate **10** brought low, dishearten, humiliated
11 crestfallen **12** disheartened

caste 4 rank **6** status **7** lineage,
station **8** position **9** condition
Hindu: **5** sudra, varna
6 vaisya **7** brahman
9 kshatriya

castigate 5 chide, scold **6** berate, punish, rebuke **7** bawl
out, censure, chasten, chew

out, correct, reprove, upbraid
8 admonish, chastise, penalize,
reproach **9** criticize, dress
down, reprimand **10** discipline,
take to task **15** call on the
carpet **16** haul over the coals

castigation 9 reprimand
10 chastening, correction, discipline, penalizing, punishment **12** chastisement

Castiglione, Baldassare
author of: **20** The Book of
the Courtier

castle 4 hall, keep **5** manor,
tower, villa **6** palace **7** chateau, citadel, mansion **8** fortress **10** stronghold

Castle, The
author: **10** Franz Kafka
character: **1** K

Castle of Otranto, The
author: **13** Horace Walpole
character: **6** Conrad **7** Alfonso, Manfred, Matilda
8 Isabella, Theodore **12** Father Jerome

Castle Rackrent
author: **14** Maria Edgeworth

cast off 4 shed **6** reject **7** discard, set sail, toss out **8** throw
off, throw out **9** repudiate,
throw away **11** weigh anchor

Castor and Pollux
also: **8** Dioscuri **10** Polydeuces, Tyndaridae
form: **8** twin sons
mother: **4** Leda
father: **4** Zeus
sister: **5** Helen
12 Clytemnestra
members of: **9** Argonauts
protectors of: **6** seamen

cast out 4 oust **5** eject, evict,
exile, expel **6** banish, reject
7 discard, dismiss, turn out
8 drive out, send away, throw
out

cast up 4 spew **5** eject, expel,
vomit **6** spew up **7** cough up,
throw up **8** disgorge

casual 4 cool, so-so **5** blase,
vague **6** chance, random,
sporty **7** offhand, passing, relaxed **8** informal **9** easygoing,
haphazard, non-dressy, unplanned **10** accidental, fortuitous, incidental, nonchalant,
unarranged, undesigned, undirected, unexpected, unforeseen **11** half-hearted,
indifferent, unlooked for
13 lackadaisical, serendipitous,
unintentional **14** indiscriminate, unpremeditated

Casuals of the Sea
author: **12** William McFee

casualty 6 injury, victim **7** injured **8** fatality

casuistry 5 guile **6** deceit **7** fallacy, sophism **8** subtlety **9** Jesuitism, quibbling, sophistry **10** nitpicking **12** equivocation, pettifoggery, speciousness **13** deceptiveness, hair-splitting **14** sophistication

casus belli 10 cause of war

Casy, Jim
character in: 16 The Grapes of Wrath
author: 9 Steinbeck

cat *see* **box**

cataclysm 4 blow **7** debacle **8** calamity, disaster, upheaval **11** catastrophe, devastation

cataclysmic 4 dire **6** tragic **7** ruinous **10** calamitous, disastrous **12** catastrophic, earth-shaking

catacomb 4 tomb **7** ossuary **8** cemetery **10** passageway **12** burial ground

Cataebates
epithet of: 4 Zeus
means: 9 descender

catafalque 3 box **4** pall **6** casket, coffin

catalog, catalogue 4 file, list, post, roll **5** index **6** record, roster **7** listing **8** classify, register, syllabus, tabulate **9** directory, enumerate, inventory

Catamitus *see* **8** Ganymede

Cat and Mouse
author: 11 Gunter Grass

catapult 4 cast, hurl, toss **5** fling, heave, pitch, shoot, sling, throw **6** hurtle, propel **9** slingshot **13** hurling engine

cataract 5 falls, flood **6** deluge, rapids **7** cascade, torrent **8** downpour **9** waterfall **10** inundation

catastrophe 4 blow **5** havoc **6** mishap, ravage **7** debacle, scourge, tragedy **8** calamity, disaster **9** cataclysm **10** affliction, misfortune **11** devastation

catastrophic 6 tragic **7** ruinous **10** calamitous, disastrous **11** cataclysmic

catcall 3 boo **4** gibe, hiss, hoot, jeer **7** whistle **8** heckling **9** raspberry **10** Bronx cheer

catch 3 bag, bat, get, hit, nab **4** bait, bang, belt, bump, bust, dupe, feel, find, fool, grab, hasp, haul, hoax, hook, lock, lure, make, snag, snap, spot, take, trap **5** booty, break, charm, clasp, crack, get to,

cat 3 pet **4** puss, whip **5** kitty, pussy, tabby **6** feline, kitten, mouser, tomcat
anatomy: 3 paw **4** loin, nape, rump, tail **5** break, flank, shank **6** feeler **7** dewclaw, leather, whisker **8** vibrissa **10** metatarsus
breed/kind: 3 tom **4** coon, Eyra, lion, lynx, Manx, puma **5** alley, civet, hyena, kitty, Korat, tabby, tiger **6** Angola, angora, bobcat, cougar, jaguar, ocelot, serval **7** Burmese, caracal, cheetah, leopard, linsang, Maltese, panther, Persian, polecat, Siamese, Turkish, wildcat **8** Balinese, Cheshire, Egyptian, ringtail **9** Himalayan, shorthair **10** Abyssinian, chinchilla **11** Russian blue **13** tortoise-shell
combining form: 5 aelur, ailur, felin **6** aeluro, ailuro, felino
Egyptian goddess of: 4 Bast
extinct: 10 saber-tooth
family: 7 Felidae
famous: 6 Morris **8** Cheshire, Garfield, Kilkenny **9** Mehitabel **10** Heathcliff
fastest: 7 cheetah
fear of: 12 aelurophobia, ailurophobia
female: 5 queen **7** lioness, tigress **8** wheencat **9** grimalkin
genus: 5 Felis
grinning: 8 Cheshire
group: 7 clowder, clutter
group of kittens: 6 kendle, kindle
lover: 11 aelurophile, ailurophile
male: 3 gib, tom **6** tomcat
ring-tailed: 6 serval **10** cacomistle
tailless: 4 Manx
young: 6 kitten

grasp, hitch, latch, prize, reach, seize, sense, smack, smite, snare, trick, whack, yield **6** allure, arrest, betray, buffet, collar, corner, corral, dazzle, deceit, delude, descry, detect, expose, fasten, fathom, kicker, snatch, strike, take in, turn on, unmask **7** attract, bewitch, capture, closure, deceive, delight, discern,

enchant, ensnare, find out, gimmick, mislead, rasping, seizure **8** catching, come upon, contract, coupling, discover, drawback, enthrall, hoodwink, overtake, perceive, pickings, surprise **9** apprehend, bamboozle, captivate, carry away, enrapture, fastening, intercept, lay hold of, play false, recognize, transport **10** comprehend, understand **11** take captive **12** break out with, come down with, disadvantage, seize and hold, take off guard **14** stumbling block **15** take into custody **18** become infected with

catch-as-catch-can 7 cursory **9** haphazard, hit-or-miss, unplanned **10** disorderly, incomplete **11** superficial, unorganized **12** disorganized, unsystematic

Catcher in the Rye, The
author: 10 J D Salinger
character: 15 Holden Caulfield

catching 10 contagious, infectious **12** communicable **13** transmittable

catch on to 3 get **5** grasp, savvy **6** absorb, digest, fathom, pick up **10** assimilate, comprehend, get the idea, understand

catch sight of 3 see **4** espy **6** behold, descry, detect, notice **7** discern, make out, observe, pick out **8** perceive

Catch-22
author: 12 Joseph Heller
character: 9 Yossarian

catchword 5 motto **6** byword, cliche, slogan, war cry **8** password **9** battle cry, guide word, pet phrase, watchword **10** shibboleth

categorical 4 flat, sure **7** certain, express **8** absolute, definite, emphatic, explicit **10** pronounced, unreserved **11** unequivocal, unqualified **12** unmistakable **13** unconditional

categorically 10 absolutely, definitely, positively **12** conclusively

categorization 5 order **11** arrangement **14** classification

category 5 class, group **8** division, grouping **14** classification

cater 5 humor **6** pamper, pander, please **7** gratify, indulge, satisfy

caterpillar 4 moth, worm **5** larva **7** cutworm, tractor, webworm **8** hangworm, silkworm, wortworm **9** butterfly, woolybear **10** astragalus

caterwaul 3 cry **4** bawl, howl, wail, yelp **5** whine **6** clamor, scream, shriek, squawk, squeal **7** screech **10** rend the air

catfish 4 barb **5** banjo **6** dorado, madtom, mudcat, sucker **7** ariidae, bluecat **8** bagridae, bullhead, claridae, electric, flathead **9** siluridae **10** channel cat, cuttlefish, mochocidae, plotosidae, spotted cat **11** ictaluridae, pimelodidae, schilbeidae **12** aspredinidae, ostariophysi **14** malapteruridae **16** trichomycteridae

Catfish
    nickname of: 9 Jim Hunter

catharsis 7 purging, release, venting **9** cleansing **12** purification

Catharsius
    epithet of: 4 Zeus
    means: 8 purifier

cathartic 5 purge **6** physic **8** aperient, evacuant, laxative **9** castor oil, purgative, purifying

cathedral 3 see **6** church, temple **7** lateran **8** basilica, official **9** authority **10** pontifical **Italian: 5** duomo

Cather, Willa
    author of: 9 A Lost Lady, My Antonia, One of Ours, O Pioneers! **13** My Mortal Enemy **16** Shadows on the Rock, The Song of the Lark **18** The Professor's House **23** Sapphira and the Slave Girl **26** Death Comes for the Archbishop

cathode ray tube
    abbreviation: 3 CRT
    invented by: 7 Crookes

catholic, Catholic 5 broad **7** liberal **9** universal, worldwide **12** all-embracing, all-inclusive **13** comprehensive

cathouse 4 stew **5** house **6** bagnio, bordel **7** brothel **8** bordello **10** bawdy house, fancy house, whorehouse **13** sporting house **14** house of ill fame **16** house of ill repute **19** house of prostitution

Cat Jumps, The
    author: 14 Elizabeth Bowen

catlike 5 catty, lithe **7** sinuous **8** stealthy **14** light on the feet

Catlin, George
    born: 13 Wilkes-Barre PA
    artwork: 16 Gallery of Indians

catnap 3 nap **4** doze **6** siesta, snooze **10** forty winks, light sleep

Cato
    author: 13 Joseph Addison

Cat on a Hot Tin Roof
    author: 17 Tennessee Williams
    director: 13 Richard Brooks
    cast: 8 Burl Ives (Big Daddy) **10** Jack Carson, Paul Newman (Brick) **14** Judith Anderson **15** Elizabeth Taylor (Maggie)

Catreus
    king of: 5 Crete
    father: 5 Minos
    mother: 8 Pasiphae
    son: 11 Althaemenes
    daughter: 6 Aerope **7** Clymene **9** Apemosyne
    grandson: 8 Menelaus

cats-eye
    species: 11 chrysoberyl
    source: 8 Sri Lanka

cat's paw 4 dupe, pawn, tool **5** patsy **7** fall guy

cattle 4 cows, kine, oxen **5** beefs, bulls, stock **6** beeves, calves, dogies, steers **8** bullocks, milk cows **9** livestock
    family: 7 Bovidae
    group of: 5 drove
    kind: 2 ox **3** yak **4** Zebu **5** Angus **6** Ankole, Jersey **7** Brahman **8** Ayrshire, Guernsey, Hereford, Highland, Holstein **9** Charolais **12** water buffalo **13** Texas Longhorn **16** English Shorthorn, Holstein-Friesian
    young: 4 calf **6** heifer **8** yearling

Catton, Bruce
    author of: 22 A Stillness at Appomattox

catty 4 mean **7** catlike **8** spiteful **9** malicious, malignant **10** malevolent

catwalk 6 bridge **7** walkway **10** passageway

Caucasian
    language branch: 5 Ubykh **9** Daghestan **10** Circassian **11** Khartvelian

Caucon
    brought mysteries to: 8 Messenia

caucus 6 parley, powwow **7** council, meeting, session **8** assembly, conclave **10** conference

caudal 4 back, tail **7** tail-end

cauldron *see* **7** caldron

Caulfield, Holden
    character in: 18 The Catcher in the Rye
    author: 8 Salinger

Caulfield, Joan
    real name: 21 Beatrice Joan Caulfield
    born: 8 Orange NJ
    roles: 8 Dear Ruth **17** My Favorite Husband

Caunus
    brother: 6 Byblis

causation 4 root **5** cause **6** author, origin, reason, source **7** creator, genesis **8** etiology, inventor, stimulus **9** generator, invention **10** antecedent, conception, mainspring, originator **11** determinant, inspiration, origination

cause 4 goal, make, root, side **5** ideal, impel, tenet **6** belief, create, effect, incite, lead to, motive, object, origin, reason, source, spring, stir up **7** genesis, grounds, incline, inspire, produce, provoke, purpose **8** etiology, generate, motivate, occasion, stimulus **9** incentive, principle, stimulate **10** aspiration, bring about, conviction, foundation, give rise to, inducement, initiation, mainspring, motivation, persuasion, prime mover **11** bring to pass, inspiration, instigation, precipitate, provocation

cause of war
    Latin: 10 casus belli

cause to appear 6 expose, reveal **7** uncover **8** disclose **12** bring to light **13** bring into view

caustic 4 tart **5** acrid, harsh, sharp **6** biting, bitter **7** burning, cutting, erosive, gnawing **8** scathing, stinging **9** corroding, corrosive, sarcastic **10** astringent **11** acrimonious

caution 4 care, heed, warn **5** alarm, alert **6** advise, caveat, exhort, notify, regard, tip-off **7** concern, thought, warning **8** admonish, forewarn, prudence, wariness **9** alertness, restraint, vigilance **10** admonition, discretion, precaution **11** carefulness, forewarning, guardedness, heedfulness, mindfulness **12** deliberation, watchfulness **14** circumspection, put on one's guard

cautionary 7 warning **8** advisory **10** admonitory **11** admonishing

cautious 4 wary **5** alert, cagey **7** careful, guarded, prudent **8** discreet, vigilant, watchful

9 attentive, judicious **11** circumspect

cavalcade 5 troop **6** column, parade **7** caravan, retinue **10** procession

Cavalcade
director: **10** Frank Lloyd
based on play by: **10** Noel Coward
cast: **10** Clive Brook **11** Ursula Jeans **12** Diana Wynyard **13** Herbert Mundin **15** Margaret Lindsay
Oscar for: **7** picture

cavalier 3 fop **4** beau **5** blade, cocky, dandy, swell **6** hussar, lancer **7** cursory, dragoon, gallant, haughty, offhand, playboy **8** arrogant, courtier, gay blade, horseman, uncaring **9** easygoing **10** cavalryman, disdainful, nonchalant **11** indifferent, thoughtless

cavalry 7 hussars, lancers **8** dragoons **10** mounted men **11** horse troops **13** horse soldiers, mounted troops

cavalryman 6 hussar, lancer **7** dragoon **8** cavalier, horseman **12** horse soldier, horse trooper **14** mounted soldier

cave 3 den **4** lair, sink **6** burrow, cavern, cavity, dugout, grotto, hollow
growth: **10** stalactite, stalagmite
explorer: **9** spelunker

caveat 5 alarm, alert, aviso **6** tip-off **7** caution, red flag, warning **8** high sign, red light **10** admonition, danger sign, yellow jack **11** forewarning **12** admonishment, flea in the ear **13** word to the wise **20** handwriting on the wall

caveat emptor 17 let the buyer beware

cave canem 14 beware of the dog

cave in 6 buckle, fall in, give up, submit **7** crumple, give way, implode **8** collapse **10** capitulate **12** fall to pieces

Cavendish, Henry
field: **7** physics **9** chemistry
nationality: **7** British
discovered: **8** hydrogen
determined composition of: **3** air **5** water **10** nitric acid
method: **19** Cavendish experiment

cavernous 4 huge, vast **5** roomy **6** gaping **7** chasmal, immense, yawning **8** cavelike, enormous, spacious **10** tremendous

cavil 6 deride **7** nitpick, quib-

ble **8** belittle, complain **9** criticize, deprecate, discredit, disparage, faultfind, find fault **12** pick to pieces

cavity 3 dip, pit **4** bore, dent, hole, sink **5** basin, niche **6** burrow, crater, hollow, pocket, tunnel **7** opening, orifice, vacuity **8** aperture **9** concavity **10** depression, excavation

cavort 4 play, romp **5** bound, caper, frisk **6** frolic, gambol, prance

Cawdor
author: **15** Robinson Jeffers

Caxtons, The
author: **12** Bulwer Lytton

Cayster
river in: **5** Lydia

Cayuga
language family: **9** Iroquoian
location: **4** Ohio **6** Canada **7** New York **8** Oklahoma **9** Wisconsin
branch of: **10** Six Nations **19** Iroquois Confederacy, League of the Iroquois

cease 3 end **4** halt, pass, quit, stop **5** abate, pause **6** desist, finish **7** adjourn, die away, forbear, suspend **8** break off, conclude, leave off **9** terminate **11** abstain from, discontinue, refrain from **12** bring to an end

cease-fire 5 truce **9** armistice

ceaseless 7 endless, eternal **8** constant, enduring, unending **9** continual, incessant, permanent, perpetual, unceasing **10** continuous, protracted **11** everlasting, never-ending, unremitting **12** interminable **13** uninterrupted

cease to be 3 die, end **6** die out, expire, vanish **9** disappear, evaporate **13** become extinct

Cebriones
father: **5** Priam
brother: **6** Hector
charioteer for: **6** Hector

Cecilia (Memoirs of an Heiress)
author: **11** Fanny Burney

Cecrops
also: **8** Cecropia
form: **3** man **6** dragon
founder of: **6** Attica
king of: **6** Attica
father: **14** King Erechtheus
brother: **6** Metion, Orneus
wife: **8** Aglaurus
son: **11** Erysichthon
daughter: **5** Herse **8** Aglaurus **9** Pandrasos
renamed Attica: **8** Cecropia

Cedalion
occupation: **5** smith
forge owner: **10** Hephaestus
served as guide for: **5** Orion

cedar 6 Cedrus
varieties: **3** red **4** pink, salt **5** Atlas, giant, white **6** Alaska, Cyprus, ground, Mlanje **7** Bermuda, incense, Russian, Spanish **8** Barbados, cigar-box, creeping, Japanese, stinking **10** Ozark white, Port Orford, swamp white, western red, West Indian, Willowmore **11** Clanwilliam, Colorado red, southern red **13** Atlantic white, southern white **14** Chilean incense, Formosa incense **17** California incense

cede 4 give **5** grant, leave, yield **6** tender **7** abandon, deliver, release **8** hand over, transfer **9** deliver up, surrender **10** relinquish

cedez
music: **8** slow down

Cedreatis
epithet of: **7** Artemis
means: **14** of the cedar tree

Cedric the Saxon
character in: **7** Ivanhoe
author: **5** Scott

ceiling 3 top **4** roof **5** cover, limit **6** canopy, cupola, lining **7** maximum **8** altitude **10** upperlimit

Celaeno
member of: **7** Harpies **8** Pleiades

Celebes
also: **8** Sulawesi
bordered by: **6** Borneo **8** Moluccas **10** Celebes Sea, Kalimantan **12** Flores Strait **14** Makassar Strait
city: **4** Poso **6** Manado **7** Kendari, Madjene **8** Bonthain, Donggala, Makassar **9** Gorontalo
location: **9** Indonesia
people: **4** Bugi, Laki, Mori, Muna, Napu, Palu, Peso, Seko, Wana **5** Besoa, Buton, Toala **6** Bungku, Butung, Parigi, Sadang, Sangir, Toland **7** Banggai, Bolaang, Kabaena, Loinang, Toradja **8** Balantak, Buginese, Mongondu, Rongkong, Sanghike **9** Gorontalo **11** Makassarese
province: **13** North Sulawesi, South Sulawesi **15** Central Sulawesi **17** Southeast Sulawesi

celebrate 4 laud **5** bless, cheer, exalt, extol, honor **6** hallow,

praise, revere 7 acclaim, applaud, commend, glorify, observe **8** proclaim, sanctify, venerate **9** broadcast, ritualize, solemnize **10** consecrate **11** commemorate **13** ceremonialize

celebrated 5 famed, noted **6** famous, prized **7** eminent, honored, notable, revered **8** lionized, renowned **9** acclaimed, important, prominent, respected, treasured, venerable, well-known **11** illustrious, outstanding **13** distinguished

Celebrated Jumping Frog of Calaveras County, The
   author: **9** Mark Twain

celebration 4 fete, gala **5** feast, party **6** ritual **7** jubilee, revelry **8** carnival, ceremony, festival **9** festivity, hallowing **10** ceremonial, observance **13** commemoration, solemnization **14** sanctification **15** memorialization

celebrity 3 VIP **4** fame, name, note, star **5** glory, wheel **6** bigwig, renown **7** big shot, notable, stardom **8** eminence, luminary **9** dignitary, notoriety, personage **10** notability, popularity, prominence **11** distinction, personality **12** famous person, person of note

celerity 5 haste, hurry, speed **6** hustle **8** alacrity, dispatch, fast clip, fastness, legerity, rapidity **9** briskness, quickness, swiftness **10** expedition, snappiness, speediness **12** precipitance **14** lightning speed **15** expeditiousness

celery seed
   also called: **8** smallage
   origin: **13** Mediterranean
   use: **4** soup **5** salad, sauce **6** pickle **10** vegetables

celestial 3 sky **5** solar **6** astral, divine **7** angelic, elysian, stellar, sublime **8** beatific, blissful, empyrean, ethereal, hallowed, heavenly, seraphic **9** planetary, unearthly **12** astronomical, otherworldly, paradisiacal

celestial being 3 god **5** angel, deity **7** goddess **8** divinity **11** divine being

Celestial City
   place in: **16** Pilgrim's Progress
   author: **6** Bunyan

Celia (Aliena)
   character in: **11** As You Like It
   author: **11** Shakespeare

celibacy 8 chastity **9** virginity **10** abstinence, continence **12** bachelorhood, spinsterhood

celibate 4 pure **5** unwed **6** chaste, single **8** bachelor, spinster, virginal **9** abstinent, continent, unmarried

Celine, Louis-Ferdinand
   author of: **12** Guignol's Band **25** Death on the Installment Plan, Journey to the End of the Night

cell
   part: **7** nucleus **8** membrane **9** cytoplasm
   made of: **3** fat **4** salt **5** water **7** protein **9** compounds **12** carbohydrate
   theory of: **7** (Rudolf) Virchow, (Theodor) Schwann

cellar 3 den **4** cave **6** dugout **8** basement **10** downstairs

Cellini, Benvenuto
   born: **5** Italy **8** Florence
   artwork: **7** Cosimo I, Perseus **13** Bindo Altoviti **18** The Crucified Christ **20** Nymph of Fontainebleau
   autobiography: **22** Life of Benvenuto Cellini

Celsius
   abbreviation of: **1** C

Celt 4 Gaul, Kelt, Manx, Scot **5** Irish, Welsh **6** Breton, Briton, chisel **8** Scottish **10** Highlander

Celtic
   language group: **6** Gaelic **9** Brythonic
   family: **12** Indo-European
   language of: **5** Gauls

cement 3 fix, set **4** bind, fuse, glue, join, seal, weld **5** paste, stick, unite **6** mortar, secure **8** concrete

cemetery 7 ossuary **8** boneyard, Boot Hill, catacomb **9** graveyard **10** churchyard, necropolis **12** burial ground, memorial park, potter's field **13** burying ground

Cenaean see **4** Zeus

Cenchrias
   father: **8** Poseidon
   mother: **6** Pirene
   killed by: **7** Artemis

Cenci, The
   author: **18** Percy Bysshe Shelley

cenobite 4 monk **7** ascetic **8** celibate **9** religious

censor 4 blip, edit **5** amend, judge, purge **6** critic, delete, excise **7** amender, clean up **8** black out, examiner, reviewer, suppress **9** expurgate, inspector **10** blue-pencil, bowdlerize, expurgator, suppressor **11** bowdlerizer, faultfinder, scrutinizer

12 investigator **17** custodian of morals **25** guardian of the public morals

censorious 5 picky **7** abusive, carping **8** critical **10** defamatory **12** faultfinding

censurable 8 blamable **10** deplorable, punishable, reprovable **11** blameworthy **12** reproachable **13** reprehensible

censure 3 pan, rap **5** chide, scold **6** berate, rebuke **7** bawl out, chew out, chiding, condemn, reproof, reprove, upbraid **8** admonish, denounce, reproach, scolding **9** castigate, complaint, criticism, criticize, reprehend, reprimand **10** admonition, bawling-out, chewing-out, disapprove, upbraiding **11** castigation, disapproval, reprobation **12** condemnation, dressing-down, remonstrance **13** tongue-lashing **14** disapprobation **16** rap on the knuckles, take over the coals
   god of: **5** Momos, Momus

census 3 tax **4** data, list, poll **5** count **6** amount, number **11** enumeration **12** registration

Centaur
   form: **3** man **5** horse **7** monster **16** half-man half-horse
   constellation of: **9** Centaurus
   famous: **6** Chiron
   represents: **11** Sagittarius

Centaurus
   father: **5** Ixion
   mother: **7** Nephele
   father of: **8** Centaurs

Centennial
   author: **13** James Michener

Centennial State
   nickname of: **8** Colorado

center, centre 3 fix, hub, mid **4** axis, core, crux **5** focus, heart, pivot, point **6** direct, gather, middle **7** address, essence, nucleus **8** converge, interior **9** middle **10** focal point **11** concentrate

centered 4 even, true **5** right **7** focused **8** straight **10** pinpointed **12** concentrated

centigrade 5 scale **6** degree **7** celcius **11** thermometer

centigram
   abbreviation of: **2** cg

centiliter
   abbreviation of: **2** cl

Centimani see **13** Hecatonchires

centimeter
   abbreviation of: **2** cm

centipede 4 boat **5** shrub
6 earwig, insect **8** chilopod,
multiped **9** arthropod
13 muehlenbeckia

central 3 key **4** main **5** basic,
chief, focal, inner, major,
prime **6** inmost, middle
7 leading, midmost, pivotal,
primary **8** dominant, foremost,
interior **9** essential, paramount, principal **10** middlemost **11** fundamental,
predominant **13** most
important

**Central African
Republic**
  other name: 11 Ubangi-
    Chari **20** Central Afri-
    can Empire
  **capital/largest city:
    6** Bangui
  others: 3 Obo **4** Bria,
    Ippy **5** Birao, Bouar,
    Kembe, Ndele, Ngoto,
    Paoua, Rafai, Zemio
    6 Baboua, Bakala, Bo-
    zoum, Mbaiki **7** Bam-
    bari, Grimari,
    Zemongo **9** Bangassou,
    Berberati, Bossangoa,
    Fort-Sibut
  monetary unit: 5 franc
    7 centime
  lake: 4 Chad
  mountain: 5 Karre,
    Tinga **6** Mongos **9** Dar
    Challa
  **highest point:
    11** Kayagangiri
  river: 4 Bomu, Nana
    5 Chari, Kotto, Mbari,
    Mpoko, Ouaka
    6 Chinko, Lobaye,
    Mbomou, Ubangi
    11 Upper Sangha
  people: 4 Baya, Sara
    5 Banda, Bwaka,
    Sango **6** Azande, Yak-
    oma **7** Banziri, Mandjia,
    Nzakara
  language: 5 Sango,
    Zande **6** French
  religion: 5 Islam **7** ani-
    mism **12** Christianity
    13 Roman Catholic
  place:
    plaza: **13** Edouard
      Renard
  food:
    tapioca: **6** manioc
      7 cassava

Central America *see box*

Central Amerind
  language branch: 9 Oto-Man-
    gue **10** Uto-Aztecan
    11 Kiowa-Tanoan

Central America
  land form: 7 isthmus
  countries: 6 Belize, Panama **8** Honduras **9** Costa Rica, Gua-
    temala, Nicaragua **10** El Salvador
  bordered by: 6 Mexico, **8** Colombia **12** Caribbean Sea,
    North America, Pacific Ocean, South America
  capital city: 7 Managua, San Jose **8** Belmopan **10** Panama
    City **11** San Salvador, Tegucigalpa **13** Guatemala City
  river: 3 New **4** Axul, Coco, Sico, Tuma, Ulua, Wawa
    5 Aguan, Chepo, Hondo, Lempa, Wauks **6** Chixoy,
    Grande, Pasion, Patuca, Sulaco, Waspuk **7** Motagua, Pau-
    laya, San Juan, Sarstun, Segovia **8** Kukalaya **9** Choluteca,
    Escondido **10** Chucunague **11** Prinzapolca
  lake: 5 Gatun, Guija, Yojoa **7** Atitlan, Managua **9** Nicara-
    gua, Peten Itza
  mountain: 4 Maya, Pija **5** Colon, Huapi, Minas, Pando
    6 Blanco **7** Dipilto, Gongora, San Blas **8** Brewster, Dar-
    iense, Isabelia, San Pablo, Santa Ana **9** Esperanza
    14 Chirripo Grande
  people: 3 Mam **5** Zambo **6** Indian, Ladino, Quiche **7** mes-
    tizo **8** Miskitas **10** Black Carib, Cakchiquel
  animal: 5 tapir **6** agouti **7** opossum, peccary **8** anteater,
    kinkajou, marmoset **9** armadillo, porcupine, tree sloth
    12 howler monkey, spider monkey **14** capuchin monkey

central city 8 core city, downtown **9** inner city, urban area
10 metropolis **16** business district, metropolitan area

central idea 3 nut **4** core,
crux, gist, meat **5** heart,
theme **6** kernel **7** essence
9 main point

centralization 5 focus **11** convergence **13** concentration,
consolidation

centralize 5 focus, unify
6 center, gather **7** collect, compact **8** center on, coalesce,
converge, pinpoint **9** integrate
10 congregate **11** concentrate,
consolidate

central part 4 core, crux, gist,
pith **5** heart **6** center, kernel
7 nucleus

century
  abbreviation of: 4 cent
  French: 6 siecle

cephalopod 5 squid **7** mollusk,
octopus **8** nautilus **10** cuttlefish

Cephalus
  father: 6 Hermes
  mother: 5 Herse
  brother: 5 Ceryx
  wife: 7 Clymene, Procris

Cephas *see* **5** Peter

Cepheus
  king of: 8 Ethiopia
  wife: 10 Cassiopeia
  daughter: 9 Andromeda

Cerambus
  form: 6 beetle

ceramic ware 5 china, glass
7 pottery **8** crockery **9** chinaware, glassware, porcelain,

stoneware **10** enamelware
11 earthenware

ceratopsid
  type of: 8 dinosaur
  member: 10 Torosaurus
    11 Monoclonius, Tricera-
    tops **13** Protoceratops, Styra-
    cosaurus **14** Psittacosaurus

Ceratosaurus
  type of: 8 dinosaur
  period: 8 Jurassic

Cerberus
  form: 3 dog
  father: 6 Typhon
  mother: 7 Echidna
  sibling: 5 Hydra **7** Orthrus
    8 Chimaera **10** Nemean
    lion **12** Theban Sphinx
  number of heads: 5 three
  guarded: 10 Underworld

Cercopes
  race of: 6 Gnomes

Cercyon
  king of: 7 Arcadia
  daughter: 5 Alope

cereal 4 corn, oats, rice, seed
5 grain, grass, gruel, plant,
wheat **6** barley, pablum **7** oatmeal, pabulum **8** porridge

cerebellum
  part of: 5 brain
  controls: 7 balance
    8 movement

cerebrum
  part of: 5 brain
  controls: 6 seeing **7** hearing,
    tasting **8** deciding, feelings,
    learning, smelling, thinking,
    touching **9** awareness
    11 remembering

ceremonial 4 rite **6** formal, ritual **7** liturgy, service **8** ceremony **9** formality, sacrament **10** liturgical, observance **11** celebration, ritualistic

ceremonialize 7 observe **9** celebrate, ritualize **11** commemorate

ceremonious 5 exact, fussy, rigid, stiff **6** formal, proper, solemn **7** careful, correct, pompous, precise **8** starched **9** dignified **10** methodical, meticulous **11** punctilious

ceremony 4 rite **6** custom, nicety, ritual **7** amenity, decorum, pageant, service **8** function, protocol **9** etiquette, formality, propriety **10** observance, politeness **11** celebration, formalities **13** commemoration

Cerenkov, Pavel Alekseevich
  field: **7** physics
  nationality: **7** Russian
  discovered: **12** cause of
    light **14** Cerenkov effect

Ceres
  origin: **5** Roman
  goddess of: **11** agriculture
  corresponds to: **7** Demeter

certain 4 sure **5** valid **6** secure **7** assured, express, settled, special **8** absolute, cocksure, definite, positive, reliable, specific **9** confident, convinced, satisfied **10** conclusive, individual, inevitable, particular, undeniable, undisputed, undoubtful, undoubting, unshakable **11** indubitable, inescapable, irrefutable, unalterable, unequivocal, unqualified **12** indisputable, unchangeable, unmistakable, well-grounded **13** bound to happen, incontestable **14** unquestionable **16** incontrovertible

certainly 5 truly **6** indeed, surely **7** for sure **8** of course **9** decidedly **10** absolutely, definitely, positively **11** indubitably, undoubtedly **13** unequivocally, without a doubt **14** unquestionably **21** beyond a shadow of a doubt

Certain Smile, A
  author: **14** Francoise Sagan

certainty 4 fact **5** faith, trust **6** belief, surety **7** reality, sure bet **8** sureness **9** actuality, assurance, certitude, sure thing **10** confidence, conviction **11** presumption **12** positiveness **13** inevitability **14** conclusiveness, inescapability **17** authoritativeness

certificate 4 deed **6** permit **7** diploma, license, voucher **8** document, warranty **9** affida-

vit **10** credential **11** testimonial **13** authorization **14** authentication

certification 7 voucher **8** approval **10** validation **11** endorsement **12** confirmation, ratification, verification **13** authorization, corroboration **14** authentication, substantiation

certify 4 aver **5** swear, vouch **6** assure, attest, ratify, second, verify **7** confirm, declare, endorse, support, warrant, witness **8** notarize, sanction, validate **9** authorize, guarantee, testify to **10** underwrite **11** corroborate **12** authenticate, give one's word, substantiate

certitude 5 faith, trust **6** belief, surety **8** reliance, sureness **9** assurance, certainty **10** confidence **12** positiveness **14** conclusiveness

cerulean 4 blue **5** azure **6** cobalt **7** sky blue **9** clear blue

Cervantes Saavedra, Miguel de
  author of: **20** Don Quixote de la Mancha

Cerynean stag
  also: **12** Arcadian stag
  home: **7** Arcadia
  captured by: **8** Hercules

Ceryx
  herald of: **4** gods
  father: **6** Hermes
  mother: **5** Herse
  brother: **8** Cephalus

Cesar Birotteau
  author: **14** Honore de Balzac

cessation 3 end **4** halt, stay, stop **5** pause **6** ending, recess **7** ceasing, halting, respite **8** quitting, stopping, surcease **9** desisting **10** concluding, leaving off, suspension **11** adjournment, breaking off, termination **12** interruption **13** coming to a halt, discontinuing **14** discontinuance

c'est la vie 9 that's life **10** such is life

Cestrinus
  father: **7** Helenus
  mother: **10** Andromache

Cestus
  girdle of: **5** Venus

cetacean 4 apod **5** whale **6** beluga, mammal **7** cetacea, dolphin, dowfish, grampus, narwhal **8** porpoise, sturgeon **9** blue whale **11** baleen whale, killer whale

Cetinje
  capital of: **10** Montenegro

Ceto
  father: **6** Pontus
  mother: **4** Gaea
  brother: **7** Phorcys
  husband: **7** Phorcys
  mother of: **6** Graeae
    7 Gorgons
  children called: **8** Phorcids

Ceylon see **8** Sri Lanka

Ceyx
  father: **9** Eosphorus
  wife: **7** Alcyone

Cezanne, Paul
  born: **6** France **13** Aix-en-Provence
  artwork: **7** Bathers **11** Card Players **13** The Black Clock, The Railway Out **14** Uncle Dominique **15** La Maison du Pendu **16** The Suicide's House **17** Grandes Baigneuses **19** Woman with a Coffee Pot **36** Mont-Sainte-Victoire with Large Pine Trees

Chabrier, (Alexis) Emmanuel
  born: **6** Ambert, France
  composer of: **6** Espana **7** L'Etoile **10** Gwendoline **13** Marche Joyeuse **14** Le Roi Malgre Lui **18** King Despite Himself **19** Une Education Manquee

Chad
  other name: **5** Tchad
  capital/largest city: **8** Fort-Lamy, N'Djamena
  others: **3** Ati, Bol, Lai, Mao **4** Fada, Faya, Sarh **5** Mongo **6** Abeche, Bongor **7** Largeau, Moundou **8** Moussoro
  monetary unit: **5** franc **7** centime
  lake: **4** Chad
  mountain: **7** Tibesti, Touside
  highest point: **9** Emi Koussi
  river: **5** Chari **6** Logone **8** Bahraouk
  physical feature:
    plateau: **6** Ennedi
  people: **4** Arab, Daza, Maba, Sara, Teda, Tubu **5** Barma, Hakka, Kreda, Massa **6** Fulani, Kotoko, Toubou, Wadaii **7** Kamadja, Kanembu, Moundan
  language: **4** Sara **5** Turku **6** Arabic, French
  religion: **5** Islam **7** animism **12** Christianity

Chadband
character in: 10 Bleak House
author: 7 Dickens

Chadic
language family: 11 Afroasiatic 13 Hamito-Semitic
includes: 5 Hausa
spoken in: 6 Africa 8 Lake
Chad

Chadwick, James
field: 7 physics
nationality: 7 British
discovered: 7 neutron
awarded: 10 Nobel Prize

chafe 3 rub 4 boil, burn, foam,
fume, rage, rasp 6 abrade,
rankle, scrape, seethe
7 scratch 9 be annoyed 11 be
irritated

chaff 3 bug, kid, rag, rib
4 josh, junk, pods, razz, ride,
slag, twit 5 dross, hulls, husks,
jolly, trash, waste 6 banter,
debris, litter, refuse, rubble,
shells, shoddy, shucks 7 kidding, ragging, remnant, residue, ribbing, rubbish,
waggery 8 badinage, chaffing,
leavings, raillery, ridicule
9 sweepings 9 give and take

chaffing 6 banter 7 jesting,
joshing, kidding, ragging, ribbing, waggery 8 badinage,
raillery

chafing 5 harsh 6 fuming
7 rasping, rubbing 8 abrading,
abrasive 10 irritating

Chagall, Marc
born: 6 Liosno, Liozno,
Russia
artwork: 8 Birthday, Cock-
crow 9 The Circus, The Red
Sun 10 The Juggler 11 Over
Vitebsk 12 The Violinist
14 Double Portrait, I and
the Village 16 The Jewish
Wedding 17 Lovers with
Rooster 20 Paris Through
My Window

chagrin 5 shame 6 dismay
8 distress 11 humiliation
13 embarrassment,
mortification

chagrined 7 abashed,
ashamed 9 mortified 10 humiliated 11 embarrassed

Chahiksichhiks see 6 Pawnee

chain 3 fob 5 cable, links
7 shackle 8 necklace 10 metal
links 11 linked cable
abbreviation: 2 ch

Chain, Ernst Boris
field: 12 biochemistry
nationality: 7 British
discovered: 10 penicillin
worked with: 6 Florey
7 Fleming
awarded: 10 Nobel Prize

Chained Lady
constellation of:
9 Andromeda

chains 3 tie 4 bind, lash,
moor 5 bonds, irons, tie up,
train 6 fasten, fetter, secure,
series, string, tether 7 bondage, fetters, manacle, serfdom,
shackle, slavery 8 leg irons,
manacles, sequence, shackles
9 handcuffs, servitude, thralldom 10 put in irons, succession 11 enslavement,
subjugation

chair 4 seat 5 bench, couch, sedan stool 6 chaise, lounge,
rocker, settee, throne 7 conduct, ottoman 11 preside
over 16 presiding officer

chairman 4 head 5 chair, emcee 6 leader 7 manager,
speaker 8 director 9 chairlady,
executive, moderator 10 chairwoman, supervisor 11 chair-
person, toastmaster
13 administrator 16 presiding
officer 18 master of
ceremonies

Chair of Forgetfulness
form: 4 seat
made of: 5 stone
location: 10 Underworld

chaise 3 gig 4 shay 5 chair
6 daybed, lounge 7 calesin
8 carriage, duchesse

chalcedony 3 gem 4 onyx,
opal, sard 5 agate, prase 6 jasper, plasma, quartz, silica
7 catseye, mineral, opaline,
sardius 8 hematite, sardonyx
9 carnelian 10 bloodstone, heliotrope 11 chrysoprase
12 semiprecious 14 silicon
dioxide

Chalcis
father: 6 Asopus
mother: 6 Metope

Chaldean 4 seer 5 magic
6 Syriac 7 Aramaic, semitic
8 magician 9 astrology, enchanter, Nabonidus 10 astrologer, Babylonian, soothsayer
12 Nabopolassar
14 Nebuchadnezzar

chalice 3 cup 5 grail 6 goblet,
vessel

Chalinitis
epithet of: 6 Athena
means: 7 bridler

chalk 4 draw 6 crayon, pastel,
sketch 9 limestone

chalk up 4 earn 5 score 6 attain, charge, credit 7 achieve,
ascribe

chalky 3 wan 4 pale 5 ashen,
white 6 pallid 7 powdery
8 blanched 9 bloodless

challenge 3 bid, tax, try
4 dare, defy, gage, test
5 doubt, trial 6 demand, impute, summon 7 defiant, dispute, summons 8 question
15 take exception to 20 fling
down the gauntlet

chamber 4 diet, hall, room
5 board, court, house, salon
6 office, parlor 7 bedroom,
boudoir, council 8 assembly,
congress 9 apartment

Chamberlain, Owen
field: 7 physics
developed: 8 atom bomb
awarded: 10 Nobel Prize

Chamberlain, Richard
real name: 24 George Richard Chamberlain
born: 12 Los Angeles CA
roles: 6 Shogun 9 Dr Kildare
10 Wallenberg 13 The
Thorn Birds 17 The Bourne
Identity 21 The Count of
Monte Cristo

Chamberlain, Wilt (Wilton Norman)
nickname: 6 Dipper 12 Wilt
the Stilt
sport: 10 basketball
position: 5 coach 6 center
team: 16 Los Angeles Lakers
17 Philadelphia 76ers
20 Philadelphia Warriors,
San Francisco Warriors
21 San Diego Conquistadors

chambermaid
French: 14 femme de
chambre

chambord
type: 7 liqueur
origin: 6 France
flavor: 9 raspberry

chameleon 4 newt 6 lizard
8 renegade, turncoat 10 fickleness 14 changeableness

champ 4 bite, chew, gnaw
5 chomp, crush, grind,
munch 6 crunch 8 champion

champagne
type: 4 wine
drink: 7 the Pope
with white wine: 8 Cold
Duck
with orange juice: 6 Mimosa
measure: 6 magnum 8 jero-
boam, rehoboam 9 baltha-
zar 10 methuselah,
salmanazar
14 Nebuchadnezzar

Champaigne, Philippe de
born: 7 Belgium 8 Brussels
artwork: 6 Ex Voto 17 Cardinal Richelieu 26 The Adoration of the Shepherds

champion 3 aid 4 abet, back
6 backer, defend, master, uphold, victor, winner 7 espouse,

paragon, promote, support
8 advocate, defender, fight for, laureate, promoter, speak for, upholder **9** battle for, conqueror, protector, supporter **10** stand up for, vanquisher **11** protagonist, title holder

Champion
  constellation of: **7** Perseus

championship 3 cup **5** crown, title **7** backing, defense, support, winning **8** advocacy, espousal

Chamyne
  epithet of: **7** Demeter

chance 3 try **4** fall, fate, luck, risk **5** lucky, occur **6** befall, danger, gamble, happen, hazard, random **7** attempt, destiny, fortune, turn out, venture **8** accident, jeopardy, occasion **9** come about, fortunate, unplanned **10** accidental, fortuitous, likelihood, likeliness, providence, undesigned, unexpected, unforeseen **11** opportunity, possibility, probability, speculation, unlooked for **12** happenstance **13** unintentional **14** unpremeditated

chance upon 4 find, meet **7** learn of, run into **8** come upon, discover **9** encounter, light upon **10** happen upon **11** stumble upon

chancy 4 iffy **5** dicey, risky **6** touchy, tricky **7** dubious, erratic, unsound **8** doubtful **9** hazardous, uncertain, whimsical **10** capricious, precarious **11** speculative, venturesome **13** problematical, unpredictable

chandelier 11 hanging lamp **12** candleholder **15** lighting fixture

Chandler, Jeff
  real name: **10** Ira Grossel
  born: **10** Brooklyn NY
  roles: **7** Cochise **11** Broken Arrow **17** Merrill's Marauders

Chandler, Raymond
  author of: **11** The Big Sleep **14** The Long Goodbye **16** Farewell My Lovely
  character: **13** Philip Marlowe
  screenplay: **13** The Blue Dahlia **15** Double Indemnity **17** Strangers on a Train

Chaney, Lon
  real name: **12** Alonso Chaney
  son: **9** Creighton (Lon Chaney Jr)
  nickname: **19** Man of a Thousand Faces
  born: **17** Colorado Springs CO
  roles: **14** The Unholy Three **18** Tell It to the Marines **20** Hunchback of Notre Dame, The Phantom of the Opera

Chaney, Lon Jr
  real name: **9** Creighton
  father: **3** Lon
  born: **14** Oklahoma City OK
  roles: **6** Lennie **8** The Mummy **10** The Wolf Man **12** Of Mice and Men, Son of Dracula **20** Frankenstein's Monster

change 4 swap, turn, vary **5** alter, coins, shift, trade **6** modify, mutate, recast, reform, silver, switch **7** convert, novelty, remodel, replace, restyle, shuffle, variety, veering **8** pin money, swapping, transfer **9** deviation, diversion, exception, restyling, transform, transmute, turn about, variation **10** alteration, conversion, difference, remodeling, reorganize, revolution, small coins, substitute **11** fluctuation, pocket money, reformation **12** metamorphose, modification, substitution **13** make different, metamorphosis, revolutionize, transmutation, transposition **14** reorganization, transformation **15** transfiguration

changeable 6 fickle, fitful **7** erratic, flighty, mutable, varying **8** unstable, unsteady, variable, volatile **9** deviating, irregular, mercurial, uncertain **10** capricious, inconstant, modifiable, reversible **11** alternating, convertible, fluctuating, vacillating **13** transformable

change in plan
  French: **8** demarche

changeless 4 fast **5** fixed **6** stable **7** abiding, certain, durable, eternal, lasting **8** constant, enduring **9** immutable, steadfast, unvarying **10** unshakable **11** everlasting, unalterable **12** indissoluble

changelessness 9 certainty, constancy, stability **10** durability, permanence **12** immutability **13** steadfastness

change of heart 10 conversion **16** change of attitude

changeover 10 conversion

channel 3 cut **4** gash, lead, send **5** guide, route, steer **6** convey, course, direct, furrow, groove, gutter, strait, trough **7** narrows, passage **11** watercourse **21** avenue of communication

Channing, Carol
  born: **9** Seattle WA
  roles: **10** Hello Dolly **22** Gentlemen Prefer Blondes, Thoroughly Modern Millie

chanson 4 song

Chanson de Roland
  also: **12** Song of Roland
  author: **7** unknown
  character: **4** Aude **6** Turpin **7** Ganelon, Marsile, Olivier **11** Charlemagne, Twelve Peers
  foe: **8** Saracens

chant 3 ode **4** hymn, lied, sing, song **5** carol, croon, dirge, elegy, psalm, theme, trill, troll **6** chorus, intone, melody, monody, strain **7** chanson, chorale, descant **8** canticle, doxology, threnody, vocalize **9** homophony, monophony, offertory, plainsong **11** Gloria Patri **14** Gregorian chant

chanteuse 6 singer (female)

Chants de Maldoror, Les
  author: **18** Comte de Lautreamont

Chaon
  father: **5** Priam
  mother: **6** Hecuba
  brother: **5** Paris **6** Hector **7** Helenus
  sister: **8** Polyxena **9** Cassandra

chaos 4 mess **5** furor **6** bedlam, jumble, muddle, tumult, uproar **7** turmoil **8** disarray, disorder, upheaval **9** agitation, commotion, confusion **10** turbulence **11** pandemonium **12** discomposure **14** disarrangement **15** disorganization

Chaos
  origin: **5** Greek
  personifies: **9** confusion

chaotic 7 jumbled, mixed-up, muddled, tangled **8** confused **9** confusing, illogical, turbulent **10** disjointed, incoherent, in disarray **11** unorganized **12** disorganized **13** disharmonious

chap 3 boy, dry, guy, jaw, lad, man, rap **4** chop, gent **5** bloke, buyer, crack, knock, split **6** fellow, redden, split, stroke **7** fissure, roughen **8** customer **9** purchaser

chapbook 7 garland **8** treasury **9** anthology **10** collection **11** florilegium

chapeau 3 hat

chapel 6 church, shrine **7** oratory **9** sanctuary **10** house of God, tabernacle **14** place of worship

chaperon, chaperone
  5 guard, watch **6** duenna, es-

cort **7** oversee **8** guardian, shepherd **9** accompany, attendant, custodian, protector, safeguard **11** keep an eye on

chaperoned 7 oversaw **8** attended, escorted **10** supervised **11** accompanied

chapfallen 6 droopy **8** cast down, dejected **9** depressed

chaplain 4 abbe **5** padre, rabbi, vicar **6** cleric, curate, father, parson, pastor, priest, rector **7** Holy Joe **8** minister, preacher, reverend, sky pilot **9** churchman, clergyman **12** ecclesiastic

chaplet 4 band **6** fillet, wreath **7** circlet, coronet

Chaplin, Charlie
real name: **24** Sir Charles Spencer Chaplin
nickname: **14** the Little Tramp
wife: **10** Oona O'Neill **15** Paulette Goddard
daughter: **9** Geraldine
born: **6** London **7** England
director of/roles: **6** The Kid **8** The Tramp **9** Limelight **10** City Lights **11** Modern Times, The Gold Rush **15** Monsieur Verdoux **16** The Great Dictator

Chaplin, Geraldine
father: **14** Charlie Chaplin
mother: **17** Oona O'Neill Chaplin
born: **13** Santa Monica CA
roles: **12** The Hawaiians **13** Doctor Zhivago

chapter 3 era **4** body, part, span, unit **5** group, phase **6** branch, clause, period **7** episode, portion, section **8** division **9** affiliate **11** subdivision

Chapters of Erie
author: **10** Henry Adams

char 4 burn, sear **5** singe **6** scorch **9** carbonize **10** incinerate

character 4 part, role, self **5** being, honor **6** makeup, nature, person, traits, weirdo **7** honesty, oddball, persona **8** goodness, morality, original, specimen **9** eccentric, integrity, odd person, qualities, rectitude **10** attributes, individual, one-of-a-kind **11** personality, uprightness **13** individuality, moral strength **15** distinctiveness **16** dramatis personae

characteristic 4 mark **5** trait **6** aspect **7** earmark, feature, quality, typical **8** property, symbolic **9** attribute, mannerism, specialty, trademark **10** emblematic, indicative

11 distinctive, peculiarity **14** distinguishing, representative

characterization 8 portrait **9** depiction, picturing, portrayal **11** delineation, description **12** representing **14** representation

characterize 4 mark **5** class **6** define, depict, typify **7** earmark, portray **8** classify, describe, indicate **9** designate, represent **11** distinguish

characterless 4 weak **5** vague **6** anemic **11** nondescript **13** indeterminate **14** expressionless

Characters of Shakespeare's Plays, The
author: **14** William Hazlitt

Charcot, Jean Martin
nationality: **6** French
father of: **9** neurology

Chardin, Jean Baptiste Simeon
born: **5** Paris **6** France
artwork: **7** The Kiss **8** The Grace **14** Young Governess **16** The Copper Cistern **17** Attributes of Music **19** Attributes of the Arts **28** Rayfish Cat and Kitchen Utensils

charge 3 ask, bid, fee **4** care, cost, duty, fill, heap, lade, levy, load, pack, pile, rate, rush, toll **5** beset, blame, debit, exact, onset, order, price, stack, storm, stuff **6** accuse, advice, amount, assail, assess, assign, attack, come at, demand, direct, enjoin, impute, indict, sortie, summon **7** ascribe, assault, bidding, command, control, custody, dictate, expense, keeping, payment, require **8** call upon, instruct, storming **9** attribute, complaint, direction, enjoining, onslaught **10** accusation, allegation, assessment, indictment, injunction, management, protection **11** arraignment, incriminate, instruction, safekeeping, supervision **12** delay payment, guardianship, jurisdiction **14** administration, lay the blame for, request payment **15** superintendence **16** put on one's account

chargeable 6 liable **10** answerable **11** responsible

charged 5 taxed, tense **6** blamed, filled, levied, loaded, priced **7** accused, ordered, uptight **8** assessed, attacked, exhorted, mandated, prepared **9** commanded, entrusted

10 accusation, allegation, indictment

Charge of the Light Brigade, The
author: **18** Alfred Lord Tennyson
director: **13** Michael Curtiz
cast: **10** David Niven, Errol Flynn, Nigel Bruce **11** Donald Crisp **13** Patric Knowles **15** Henry Stephenson **17** Olivia de Havilland
setting: **6** Russia

charger 5 horse, mount, steed **6** vessel **7** accuser, platter **8** warhorse

charge with 5 trust **6** assign, commit **7** consign, entrust **8** delegate, hand over, turn over **9** authorize

Chariclo
husband: **6** Chiron
son: **8** Tiresias
companion of: **6** Athena

chariot 3 car **5** buggy **7** phaeton, vehicle **8** carriage

Charioteer
constellation of: **6** Auriga

Chariots of Fire
director: **10** Hugh Hudson
cast: **7** Ian Holm **8** Ben Cross (Harold Abrahams) **11** John Gielgud, Nigel Havers **12** Ian Charleson (Eric Liddell)
Oscar for: **5** score (Vangelis) **6** script **7** picture

Charis
member of: **6** Graces
husband: **10** Hephaestus

charisma 5 charm **6** allure, appeal **7** glamour **8** presence, witchery **9** magnetism, sex appeal **10** bewitchery **11** enchantment, fascination **14** attractiveness

charitable 4 kind **6** giving, kindly **7** lenient, liberal **8** generous, gracious, tolerant **9** bounteous, bountiful, forgiving, indulgent **10** almsgiving, benevolent, munificent, open-handed **11** considerate, kind-hearted, magnanimous, sympathetic, warmhearted **12** eleemosynary, sympathizing **13** philanthropic, understanding

charitableness 10 liberality **11** benevolence, generousity **12** philanthropy **13** bountifulness **14** openhandedness **15** humanitarianism

Charites see **6** Graces

charity 3 aid **4** alms, fund, gift, help, love **6** bounty, giving **7** handout **8** altruism, donating, good will, goodness, humanity, kindness, offering, sympathy **9** benignity, donations, endowment, tolerance **10** alms-giving, assistance, compassion, generosity **11** benefaction, benevolence, fundraising, munificence **12** graciousness, philanthropy **13** contributions, financial help, love of mankind **14** open-handedness

charlatan 4 fake **5** cheat, fraud, quack **7** cozener **8** deceiver, imposter, impostor, swindler **9** trickster **10** mountebank **16** confidence artist

Charles, Nick and Nora
  characters in: 10 The Thin Man
  author: 7 Hammett

Charles O'Malley
  author: 12 Charles Lever

Charleston 5 dance **13** ballroom dance
  capital of: 9 W Virginia

Charlie's Angels
  character: 10 Jill Monroe, John Bosley, Kris Munroe **12** Kelly Garrett **13** Sabrina Duncan **15** Charlie Townsend
  cast: 10 Cheryl Ladd, David Doyle **11** Jaclyn Smith, Kate Jackson **18** Farah Fawcett-Majors
  voice of Charlie: 12 John Forsythe

Charlotte's Web
  author: 7 E B White

Charly
  director: 11 Ralph Nelson
  based on story by: 11 Daniel Keyes (Flowers for Algernon)
  cast: 10 Leon Janney, Lilia Skala **11** Claire Bloom **13** Dick van Patten **14** Cliff Robertson
  Oscar for: 5 actor (Robertson)

charm 4 draw, grip, lure, take **5** magic, spell **6** allure, amulet, bauble, cajole, engage, please, seduce, turn on **7** attract, beguile, bewitch, conjure, delight, enchant, gratify, sorcery, trinket, win over **8** charisma, enthrall, entrance, ornament, talisman **9** captivate, enrapture, fascinate, magnetism **10** allurement, attraction, cast a spell, lucky piece **11** conjuration, enchantment, fascination, incantation, work magic on

charmer 4 vamp **5** belle, siren **9** enchanter, temptress **11** en-

chantress, femme fatale, spellbinder

charming 6 lovely **7** likable, winning, winsome **8** alluring, engaging, enticing, fetching, graceful, magnetic, pleasing **9** agreeable **10** attractive, bewitching, delightful, enchanting, entrancing **11** captivating, charismatic, enthralling, fascinating **12** irresistible

charmless 4 dull **5** blunt **6** dreary **9** repulsive, unlikable, unlovable **10** unpleasant **12** disagreeable, unattractive

Charon
  father: 6 Erebus
  mother: 3 Nyx
  occupation: 8 ferryman
  river: 4 Styx

Charops
  epithet of: 8 Hercules
  means: 14 with bright eyes

Charpentier, Gustave
  born: 6 Dieuze, France
  composer of: 6 Julien, Louise **18** Impressions of Italy

chart 3 map **4** plan, plot **5** draft, graph, table **6** design, draw up, lay out, map out, scheme, sketch **7** diagram, outline **8** tabulate **9** blueprint, delineate **10** tabulation

charter 3 let **4** deed, hire, rent **5** grant, lease **6** employ, engage, permit **7** compact, license **8** contract, covenant, sanction **9** agreement, authority, authorize, franchise **10** commission, concession

Charterhouse of Parma, The
  author: 23 Marie Henri Beyle Stendhal
  character: 8 Marietta **10** Count Mosca **11** Clelia Conti **14** Gina Pietranera **16** Fabrizio del Dongo

chartreuse
  type: 7 liqueur
  origin: 6 France **15** Carthusian monks
  flavor: 4 herb
  color: 5 green **6** yellow
  with apricot brandy:
    13 Golden Slipper
  with gin: 5 Bijou **9** Green Lady

chary 3 shy **4** wary **5** alert, cagey, leery **7** careful, guarded, heedful, prudent, sparing **8** cautious, hesitant, vigilant, watchful **10** economical, suspicious **11** circumspect, distrustful

Charybdis
  form: 7 monster

  father: 8 Poseidon
  mother: 4 Gaea
  identified with: 9 whirlpool

chase 3 dog **4** hunt, oust, rout, shoo, tail **5** drive, evict, hound, quest, stalk, track, trail **6** dispel, follow, pursue, shadow **7** cast out, go after, hunting, pursuit, repulse, scatter **8** pursuing, run after, send away, stalking, tracking **9** drive away, following **11** put to flight, send packing

Chase, Chevy
  real name: 19 Cornelius Crane Chase
  born: 9 New York NY
  roles: 8 Foul Play, Vacation **10** Caddyshack **17** Saturday Night Live

chasm 3 gap, pit **4** gulf, hold, rift **5** abyss, break, cleft, crack, gorge, gulch, split **6** breach, cavity, crater, divide, ravine **7** fissure **8** crevasse

chasseur 6 hunter

chaste 4 pure **5** clean **6** decent, modest, severe, strict **7** austere, classic, precise, sinless **8** virginal, virtuous **9** continent, righteous, unadorned, unsullied, untainted, wholesome **10** immaculate, restrained **11** clean-living, uncorrupted **12** unornamented **13** unembellished

chasten 5 chide, scold **6** berate, punish, rebuke **7** censure, reprove, upbraid **8** admonish, chastise, reproach **9** reprimand **10** discipline, take to task

chastened 7 humbled **8** contrite, penitent **9** repentant **10** remorseful **18** conscience-stricken

chastise 4 beat, flog, whip **5** chide, roast, scold, spank, strap **6** berate, punish, rebuke, thrash **7** censure, chasten, correct, reprove, scourge, upbraid **8** admonish, call down, penalize, reproach **9** castigate, criticize, reprimand **10** discipline, take to task, tongue-lash **15** call on the carpet **16** fulminate against, haul over the coals

chastisement 10 correction, discipline, punishment **11** castigation **12** reprimanding

chastity 6 purity **8** celibacy **9** innocence, virginity **10** abstinence, continence, singleness **12** bachelorhood, spinsterhood **14** abstemiousness
  goddess of: 5 Diana, Fauna **7** Artemis, Bona Dea

chasuble 6 casual **7** garment **8** vestment

Chasuble, Reverend Canon
character in: **27** The Importance of Being Earnest
author: **5** Wilde

chat 3 gab, rap **4** talk **5** prate **7** chatter, palaver, prattle **8** chitchat, converse **10** chew the fat, chew the rag, rap session **11** talk session **12** conversation **13** confabulation **16** heart-to-heart talk

chateau 4 wine **6** castle, estate **7** mansion **8** chatelet **12** country house

Chateaubriand, Francois Rene
author of: **4** Rene **5** Atala **10** Los Natchez, The Martyrs **19** Memoires d'Outretombe **24** Memoirs from Beyond the Tomb

Chateau d'If
prison in: **21** The Count of Monte Cristo
author: **5** Dumas (pere)

Chateaupers, Phoebus de
character in: **23** The Hunchback of Notre Dame
author: **4** Hugo

chattel 4 gear **6** things **7** effects **8** movables **9** trappings **10** belongings **13** accouterments, paraphernalia **15** personal effects **19** personal possessions

chatter 3 gas **4** blab, talk **5** clank, click, prate **6** babble, gabble, gibber, gossip, jabber, patter **7** blabber, blather, clatter, palaver, prattle, talking, twaddle **8** blabbing, chitchat, idle talk, talk idly **11** confabulate **14** chitterchatter

chatterbox 6 gabber, gasbag, gossip, talker **7** babbler, tattler, windbag **8** jabberer, prattler, tell tale **9** chatterer **10** talebearer, tattle tale **12** blabbermouth, blatherskite, hot-air artist **13** chatterbasket

chatty 5 gabby, gassy, gushy, talky, windy **7** gossipy, gushing, prating, verbose, voluble **8** babbling, chatting, effusive **9** garrulous, jabbering, talkative **10** blabbering, longwinded, loquacious **11** looselipped **12** loose-tongued **13** tongue-wagging

Chaucer, Geoffrey
author of: **18** The Canterbury Tales, Troilus and Criseyde **19** The Book of the Duchess **20** The Legend of Good Women, The Parlement of Fowles

Chauchoin, Claudette Lily
real name of: **16** Claudette Colbert

chauffeur 6 driver

chaussure 4 boot, shoe **8** footwear

chauvinism 8 jingoism **10** flagwaving, militarism, patriotism **11** nationalism **15** ethnocentricity, superpatriotism

cheap 4 base, easy, mean, poor **5** close, gaudy, petty, tacky, tight **6** common, flashy, meager, paltry, shabby, shoddy, sordid, stingy, tawdry, trashy, two-bit, vulgar **7** ignoble, immoral, miserly **8** costless, gimcrack, indecent, inferior, wretched **9** inelegant, low-priced, penurious, worthless **10** despicable, economical, effortless, in bad taste, reasonable, second-rate **11** inexpensive, tightfisted **12** contemptible

Cheaper by the Dozen
author: **14** Frank B Gilbreth (with Ernestine Gilbreth Carey)

cheat 3 con, gyp **4** bilk, dupe, fake, foil, fool, gull, hoax, rook, take **5** cozen, crook, fraud, quack, shark, trick **6** baffle, betray, defeat, delude, dodger, escape, fleece, humbug, outwit, thwart **7** deceive, defraud, mislead, swindle **8** chiseler, deceiver, hoodwink, imposter, impostor, swindler **9** bamboozle, charlatan, con artist, frustrate, trickster, victimize **10** circumvent, mountebank **11** short-change **13** break the rules, double-crosser

check 3 bar, end, fit, gag **4** curb, halt, hold, jibe, mesh, rein, slow, stay, stop, test **5** agree, block, brake, chime, choke, limit, probe, stall, study, tally **6** arrest, bridle, impede, look at, muzzle, peruse, rein in, retard, review, search, survey, thwart **7** barrier, conform, control, examine, explore, harness, inhibit, inspect, perusal, prevent, smother **8** hold back, look into, look over, obstacle, obstruct, restrain, scrutiny, stoppage, suppress **9** cessation, constrain, frustrate, harmonize, hindrance, restraint **10** circumvent, constraint, correspond, impediment, inspection, limitation, prevention, repression, scrutinize **11** examination, exploration, investigate, obstruction, prohibition, restriction, take stock of

13 investigation **18** bring to a standstill

checkered 4 pied **6** fitful, motley, seesaw, uneven, varied **7** checked, dappled, mottled, piebald **9** irregular, up-anddown **10** inconstant, variegated **11** fluctuating, vacillating **12** parti-colored

checkmate 4 rout, stop **6** corner, defeat, outwit, stymie, thwart **8** deadlock **9** frustrate, overthrow **11** countermove

cheder, heder 12 Jewish school

cheek 4 jowl **5** brass, nerve **8** audacity, boldness, temerity **9** arrogance, brashness, impudence, insolence **10** brazenness, effrontery **11** forwardness **12** impertinence

cheep 4 peep **5** chirp, tweet **7** chirrup, chitter, twitter

cheer 3 cry, fun, joy **4** glee, hail, hope, root, warm, yell **5** bravo, shout **6** assure, buoy up, gaiety, hooray, hurrah, huzzah, shriek, uplift **7** acclaim, animate, comfort, delight, enliven, fortify, gladden, hearten, inspire, revelry **8** brighten, buoyance, buoyancy, gladness, optimism, pleasure, reassure, vivacity **9** animation, assurance, encourage, festivity, geniality, joviality, merriment, rejoicing **10** joyfulness, jubilation, liveliness **11** acclamation, high spirits, hopefulness, merrymaking, reassurance **13** encouragement

cheerful 3 gay **4** airy, glad **5** happy, jolly, merry, sunny **6** blithe, breezy, bright, cheery, elated, jaunty, jovial, joyful, joyous, lively **7** buoyant, gleeful **8** gladsome, pleasant **9** agreeable, sparkling, sprightly **10** optimistic **11** in high humor **12** high-spirited, lighthearted

cheerfulness 5 gaity **7** jollity **8** buoyancy, optimism **9** joviality, merriment **10** brightness, cheeriness **11** high spirits **16** lightheartedness

cheerless 3 sad **4** dull, glum, gray, grim **5** bleak **6** dismal, dreary, gloomy, morose, rueful, solemn, somber, sullen, woeful **7** austere, doleful, forlorn, joyless, sunless, unhappy **8** dejected, desolate, dolorous, downcast, funereal, mournful **9** miserable, saturnine, woebegone **10** depressing, despondent, dispirited, lugubrious, melancholy, spiritless, uninviting **11** comfortless, downhearted **12** disconsolate, heavy-hearted

Cheers
location: 3 bar **6** Boston
character: 4 Norm **5** Cliff, Coach, Woody **5** Lilith **7** Rebecca **9** Sam Malone **13** Carla Tortelli, Diane Chambers
cast: 9 Ted Danson **11** George Wendt, Rhea Perlman, Shelley Long **12** Kirstie Alley **13** Kelsey Grammer **14** Woody Harrelson **16** John Ratzenberger

cheer up 5 pep up **6** buoy up **7** comfort, enliven, hearten **8** brighten, inspirit **9** bolster up, encourage **18** bolster one's spirits

cheery 3 gay **5** happy, jolly, merry, sunny **6** bright, joyful **9** sprightly **12** lighthearted

Cheeryble Brothers
nephew: 5 Frank
characters in: 16 Nicholas Nickleby
author: 7 Dickens

cheese
French: 7 fromage
kind: 4 bleu, blue, brie, edam, feta, jack **5** brick, colby, cream, gouda, Swiss **6** romano, samsoe **7** cheddar, cottage, fontina, gjetost, gruyere, limburg, munster, ricotta, sapsago, stilton **8** American, bel paese, cheshire, emmental, muenster, parmesan, port wine, raclette **9** camembert, jarlsberg, limburger, port salut, provolone, roquefort **10** caerphilly, Danish blue, Gloucester, gorgonzola, mozzarella, neufchatel **11** emmenthaler, liederkranz, petit suisse, port du salut, wensleydale **12** monterey jack

Cheever, John
author of: 8 Falconer **10** Bullet Park **16** The Enormous Radio, The World of Apples **17** The Wapshot Scandal **19** The Wapshot Chronicle **20** The Way Some People Live **22** Oh What a Paradise It Seems

Chekhov, Anton
author of: 6 Ivanov **10** The Sea Gull, Uncle Vanya **15** The Three Sisters **16** The Cherry Orchard

Chelciope
father: 6 Aeetes
mother: 5 Idyia
sister: 5 Medea
husband: 7 Phrixus

son: 5 Argus, Melas **8** Phrontis **9** Thessalus **10** Cytissorus

Chelidon
sister: 5 Aedon
brother-in-law: 11 Polytechnus
changed into: 7 swallow
changed by: 7 Artemis

chemical symbols
actinium: 2 Ac
aluminum: 2 Al
antimony: 2 Sb
argon: 2 Ar
arsenic: 2 As
barium: 2 Ba
boron: 1 B
bromine: 2 Br
cadmium: 2 Cd
calcium: 2 Ca
carbon: 1 C
chlorine: 2 Cl
chromium: 2 Cr
cobalt: 2 Co
columbium: 2 Cb
copper: 2 Cu
fluorine: 1 F
gold: 2 Au
hafnium: 2 Hf
helium: 2 He
hydrogen: 1 H
iodine: 1 I
iron: 2 Fe
krypton: 2 Kr
lead: 2 Pb
lithium: 2 Li
magnesium: 2 Mg
manganese: 2 Mn
mercury: 2 Hg
molybdenum: 2 Mo
neon: 2 Ne
nickel: 2 Ni
nitrogen: 1 N
oxygen: 1 O
phosphorus: 1 P
platinum: 2 Pt
plutonium: 2 Pu
potassium: 1 K
radium: 2 Ra
radon: 2 Rn
rhodium: 2 Rh
rubidium: 2 Rb
silicon: 2 Si
silver: 2 Ag
sodium: 2 Na
sulfur: 1 S
thorium: 2 Th
tin: 2 Sn
titanium: 2 Ti
tungsten: 1 W
uranium: 1 U
xenon: 2 Xe
zinc: 2 Zn
zirconium: 2 Zr

chemise 4 slip **5** dress, shift, shirt, smock **6** blouse **7** garment **8** camisole, lingerie, unbelted **12** undergarment

chemist
American: 4 Urey **5** Tatum **6** Carver **7** Axelrod, Lipmann, Pauling **8** Kornberg, Langmuir, McMillan **9** Carothers **10** Baekleland
British: 4 Davy **5** Boyle, Chain, Soddy **6** Dalton, Ramsay **7** Faraday **8** Smithson **9** Cavendish, Priestley, Wollaston
Dutch: 4 Hoff
French: 5 Curie, Le Bel **6** Cuvier, Dulong **7** Pasteur **9** Gay-Lussac, Lavoisier **10** Berthollet **11** Joliot-Curie
German: 4 Hahn **5** Krebs **6** Baeyer, Wohler **7** Glauber, Ostwald
Italian: 8 Avogadro
Russian: 9 Mendeleev **10** Mendeleyev
Scottish: 5 Dewar
Swedish: 7 Scheele **9** Arrhenius, Berzelius
Swiss: 6 Muller

Chemosh 10 Moabite god

Chennault, Claire L
served in: 4 WWII **15** Sino-Japanese War
commander of: 12 Flying Tigers
general in: 12 Army Air Force
air advisor to: 13 Chiang Kai-shek

cherchez la femme 15 look for the woman

cherie 4 dear **10** sweetheart

cherish 4 love **5** honor, nurse, prize, value **6** dote on, esteem, revere, succor **7** care for, idolize, nourish, nurture, shelter, sustain **8** hold dear, treasure, venerate **10** appreciate, take care of

cherished 4 dear **5** loved **7** beloved, darling, dearest **8** favorite, held dear, precious **9** treasured

Cherokee
language family: 9 Iroquoian
location: 7 Alabama, Georgia **8** Oklahoma, Virginia **9** Tennessee **13** North Carolina, South Carolina
associated with: 12 Trail of Tears
scholar: 7 Sequoya

cherry
varieties: 3 pie, pin, rum **4** bing, bird, duke, fire, sand, sour, wild **5** black, brush, choke, dwarf, Higan, Naden, sweet **6** bitter, Brazil, ground, Indian, Madden, Oregon, Taiwan, winter **7** bastard, Cayenne, Morello, Nanking, Potomac, prairie, rosebud, sargent, Spanish, St

Lucie, wild red, Windsor, Yoshino **8** Barbados, Catalina, oriental, perfumed, Suriname **9** christmas, cornelian, evergreen, Jerusalem, wild black **10** west indian **11** downy ground, Hansen's bush, holly-leaved, western sand **12** clammy ground, European bird, Japanese bush, purple ground **13** European dwarf **14** European ground, false Jerusalem, purple-leaf sand **15** Australian brush **17** Japanese cornelian, Japanese flowering, north Japanese hill
drink: 6 kirsch

cherry brandy 6 kirsch
12 Peter Heering

Cherry Orchard, The
author: 12 Anton Chekhov
character: 4 Anya, Gaev
5 Fiers, Varya, Yasha **7** Pischin **8** Dunyasha, Lopakhin, Trofimov **9** Charlotta
16 Madame Ranevskaya

cherub 4 amor **5** angel, child, cupid, youth **6** moppet **8** cherubim **13** heavenly being

cherubic 7 angelic **8** innocent **9** spiritual

Cherubin
character in: 19 The Marriage of Figaro
author: 12 Beaumarchais

chervil
botanical name: 20 Anthriscus cerefolium
origin: 6 Europe, Russia
use: 4 soup **5** salad **11** fines herbes, potato salad

Chesapeake
author: 13 James Michener

Cheshire Cat
character in: 28 Alice's Adventures in Wonderland
author: 7 Carroll

chess *see box*

chest
Italian: 5 petto

Chester, Edward
character in: 12 Barnaby Rudge
author: 7 Dickens

chesterfield 4 coat, sofa
5 couch **8** overcoat
9 davenport

Chesterton, G K (Gilbert Keith)
author of: 20 The Man Who Was Thursday **24** The Napoleon of Notting Hill **25** The Innocence of Father Brown

---

chess
also called: 9 Royal Game
chess champion:
4 Euwe, Fine, Tahl
6 Karpov, Lasker
7 Fischer, Kashdan, Smyslov, Spassky
8 Alekhine, Kasparov, Philador, Steinitz **9** Anderssen, Botvinnik, Petrosian, Reshevsky
10 Capablanca
French: 6 echecs
German: 11 schachspiel
horizontal rows: 4 rank
international chess federation: 4 FIDE
patron goddess/muse:
6 Caissa
piece: 4 king, pawn, rook **5** queen **6** bishop, castle, knight **8** chessman, material
Russian: 8 shakhmat
Spanish: 7 Ajedrez
term: 3 pin **4** fork, hole **5** check, tempo **6** center **7** isolani, outpost **8** castling, majority, open file, queening, zugzwang **9** checkmate, en passant, promotion **10** fianchetto **11** zwischenzug
tied game: 4 draw **9** stalemate
vertical rows: 4 file

---

chestnut 8 Castanea
varieties: 4 Cape, Wild **5** Horse, Water **6** Guiana, Marron **7** Chinese, Spanish **8** American, Eurasian, European, Japanese, Red horse **10** Dwarf horse, Moreton Bay **11** Common horse **12** Chinese water **13** European horse, Japanese horse **15** California horse

chestnut-colored 6 auburn, russet, sienna **8** cinnamon, nut-brown **11** golden-brown, rust-colored **12** reddish-brown

chest of drawers 5 chest **6** bureau, lowboy **7** cabinet, commode, dresser, highboy, tallboy **10** chiffonier

cheval 5 horse

chevalier 4 lord **5** cadet, noble **6** knight **7** gallant **8** cavalier

Chevalier, Maurice
born: 5 Paris **6** France
roles: 4 Gigi **5** Fanny **6** Can-Can **13** The Love Parade,

---

The Merry Widow **18** Love in the Afternoon

chew 4 gnaw **5** champ, crush, grind, munch **6** crunch, nibble **8** ruminate **9** masticate

Chew
character in: 21 The Master of Ballantrae
author: 9 Stevenson

chewing-out 6 rebuke **7** censure, chiding, reproof **8** reproach, scolding **9** reprimand **10** bawling-out, upbraiding **11** castigation, reprobation **12** dressing-down, remonstrance **13** tongue-lashing

chew noisily 4 gnaw **5** chomp, gnash, grind, munch **6** crunch

chew out 5 scold **6** berate, rail at, rebuke **7** bawl out, reprove, upbraid **8** reproach **9** castigate, reprimand **10** take to task, tongue-lash **14** read the riot act

chew the fat 3 gab, gas **4** blab, chat, talk **5** prate **6** gossip, patter **7** blather, chatter, palaver, prattle, twaddle **8** chitchat, converse, talk idly **10** chew the rag **11** confabulate **14** chitterchatter

chew the rag 3 gab, gas, jaw, rap **4** chat, chin, talk **5** prate **7** chatter, palaver, prattle **8** chitchat, converse **10** chew the fat **11** confabulate

Cheyenne
language family: 9 Algonkian **10** Algonquian
location: 6 Platte **7** Montana, Wyoming **8** Oklahoma, Red River **9** Minnesota **11** South Dakota
allied with: 7 Arapaho

Cheyenne
character: 6 Smitty **13** Cheyenne Bodie
cast: 7 L Q Jones **11** Clint Walker

chez 4 with **6** at home

Chiang Kai-shek
leader of: 5 China **6** Taiwan
ally: 9 Sun Yat-sen
party: 10 Kuomintang **11** Nationalist
defeated by: 10 Communists
wife: 12 Soong Mei-ling

Chibcha (Muisca)
location: 6 Bogota, Panama **8** Colombia **12** South America
associated with: 8 El Dorado

Chibchan
language family: 13 Macro-Chibchan
group: 4 Cuna, Paya, Rama **5** Lenca, Xinca **7** Chibcha

chic 5 natty, ritzy, smart, swank 6 classy, modish, snazzy, swanky 7 elegant, stylish, voguish 11 fashionable

Chicago
author: 12 Carl Sandburg

Chicago *see box*

chicanery 4 ruse, wile 5 craft, fraud, guile 6 deceit, duping 7 cunning, gulling, knavery, roguery 8 artifice, cozenage, trickery, villainy 9 deception, duplicity, rascality, sophistry 10 craftiness, hocus-pocus, humbuggery, subterfuge 11 hoodwinking 12 pettifoggery 13 double-dealing

chichi 4 arty 5 fussy, showy 6 flashy, frilly, garish, prissy, vulgar 7 finical, pompous, splashy 8 affected, gimcrack, overnice, precious, sissyish 9 arty-tarty, grandiose, nasty-nice 10 flamboyant 11 overrefined, pretentious 12 artsy-craftsy, ostentatious

chick
group of: 5 brood 6 clutch

Chickasaw
language family: 10 Muskhogean
location: 8 Oklahoma 9 Tennessee 11 Mississippi
related to: 7 Choctaw
member of: 19 Five Civilized Tribes

chicken, chickenhearted 3 hen 4 cock, fowl 5 layer, timid 6 afraid, coward, craven, pullet, scared, yellow 7 caitiff, dastard, fearful, gutless, rooster 8 cowardly, poltroon, timorous 9 flinching, fraidy-cat, shrinking 11 lily-livered, yellow-belly 12 fainthearted 13 pusillanimous, yellow-bellied 22 showing the white feather

chickenheartedness 8 timidity 9 cowardice 10 yellowness 11 fearfulness, poltroonery 12 timorousness 13 pusillanimity 16 faintheartedness

chide 5 scold 6 berate, rebuke 7 censure, chasten, reprove, upbraid 8 admonish, denounce, reproach 9 criticize, find fault, reprimand 10 take to task

chief 3 key 4 boss, head, lord, main 5 first, major, prime, ruler 6 leader, master, ruling 7 captain, highest, leading, monarch, primary, supreme 8 cardinal, chairman, crowning, director, dominant, foremost, greatest, overlord, overseer 9 chieftain, commander, governing, number-one, paramount, potentate, principal, sovereign, uppermost 10 prevailing, ringleader, supervisor 11 outstanding, predominant 12 preponderant 13 administrator

chief good
Latin: 11 summum bonum

chiefly 5 first 6 mainly, mostly 8 above all 9 expressly, in the main, most of all, primarily 10 especially 11 principally 12 particularly 13 predominantly

chieftan 4 boss, head 6 leader 7 captain, head man

chiffonier 6 bureau 7 dresser 8 cupboard 14 chest of drawers

chignon 3 bun 4 knot, roll 6 hairdo 9 hairpiece, hairstyle

child 3 boy, kid, lad, son, tad, tot 4 baby, girl, lass, tyke 5 youth 6 infant, moppet 7 toddler 8 daughter, juvenile 9 little one, offspring, youngster

childbearing 5 birth 11 parturition

childbirth 8 delivery 11 confinement, parturition
French: 12 accouchement
goddess of: 4 Upis 5 Parca 6 Lucina, Matuta 7 Artemis 8 Ilithyia 10 Eileithyia

Childe Harold's Pilgrimage
author: 21 George Gordon Lord Byron

Childe Roland to the Dark Tower Came
author: 14 Robert Browning

childhood 5 youth 7 boyhood 8 girlhood 10 school days 11 adolescence, nursery days

childish 5 naive, silly 6 callow, simple 7 asinine, babyish, foolish, puerile 8 immature, juvenile 9 infantile 10 adolescent

childlike 8 childish, immature, innocent 9 ingenuous

child prodigy
German: 10 Wunderkind

children 4 boys, kids, sons, tads, tots 5 girls, issue, young 6 babies, result, youth 7 infants, product, progeny 9 daughters, juveniles 11 descendants

Children of God
author: 12 Vardis Fisher

Children of Paradise
director: 11 Marcel Carne
cast: 7 Arletty 11 Albert Remay 14 Pierre Brasseur 17 Jean-Louis Barrault

Child's Garden of Verses, A
author: 20 Robert Louis Stevenson

Chile *see box, p. 176*

chill, chilly 3 icy, nip, raw 4 bite, cold, cool, keen 5 aloof, brisk, crisp, fever, harsh, nippy, sharp, stiff, stony 6 arctic, biting, bitter, frigid, frosty, frozen, wintry

---

Chicago
airport: 5 O'Hare 6 Midway
baseball team: 4 Cubs 8 White Sox
basketball team: 5 Bulls
downtown area: 4 Loop
football team: 5 Bears
fort: 8 Dearborn
hockey team: 10 Black Hawks
lake: 4 Wolf 7 Calumet 8 Michigan
landmark: 10 Meigs Field, Sears Tower 12 Board of Trade, Comiskey Park, Humboldt Park, Soldier Field, Wrigley Field 13 Shedd Aquarium 15 Lincoln Monument, Merchandise Mart, Newberry Library, Wrigley Building 16 Adler Planetarium 17 Holy Name Cathedral, John Hancock Center 18 Mercantile Exchange, Prudential Building 20 Midwest Stock Exchange 21 Art Institute of Chicago 23 Museum of Contemporary Art 26 Museum of Science and Industry 27 Field Museum of Natural History
mayor: 5 Byrne, Daley 10 Washington
nickname: 9 Windy City
river: 7 Chicago 10 Des Plaines
street: 11 Wacker Drive 13 Chicago Skyway 14 Lake Shore Drive
university: 6 DePaul, Loyola 9 Roosevelt 12 Northwestern 29 Illinois Institute of Technology

Chile

other name: 6 Tchile

name means: 21 deepest part of the Earth

capital/largest city: 8 Santiago

others: 4 Boco, Cuya, Lebu, Lota, Ocoa, Tome 5 Angol, Arica, Cobya, Talca 6 Arauco, Calama, Curico, Gatico, Osorno, Ovalle, Serena, Temuco, Vicuna, Yumbel, Yungay 7 Caldera, Chillan, Copiapo, Iquique, Valdiva 8 Coquimbo, Rancagua, Santiago, Vallenar 9 Cauquenes 10 Concepcion, Coquembana, Valparaiso, Vina del Mar 11 Antofagasta, Puerto Montt, Punta Arenas, San Bernardo

measure: 4 vara 5 legua, linea 6 cuadra, fanega

monetary unit: 4 peso 5 libra 6 condor, escudo

weight: 5 grano, libra 7 quintal

island: 3 Luz 4 Prat 5 Byron, Guafo, Hoste, Mocha, Nueva, Nunez, Vidal 6 Chiloe, Chonos, Dawson, Easter, Lennox, Piazzi, Picton, Quilan, Riesco, Stosch, Talcan 7 Angamos, Campana, Hanover, Hermite, Pajaros, Refugio, Tranqui 8 Chauques, Clarence, Huamblin, Nalcayec, Navarino, Traiguen 13 Juan Fernandez 14 Tierra del Fuego

lake: 5 Ranco 6 Yelcho 7 Puyehue, Rupanco 8 Cochrane 10 General Paz, Llanquihue 11 Buenos Aires

mountain: 4 Maca, Toro 5 Chato, Maipo, Maipu, Paine, Potro, Pular, Torre, Yogan 6 Apiwan, Burney, Conico, Jervis, Poquis, Rincon 7 Chaltel, Copiapo, Fitzroy, Palpana, Velluda 8 Cochrane, Tronador, Yanteles 9 Tupungato

highest point: 13 Ojos del Salado

river: 3 Loa 4 Laja, Yali 5 Alhue, Azapa, Bravo, Bueno, Elqui, Lauca, Lluta, Maipo, Maule, Puelo, Rahue, Rapel, Stata, Vitor 6 Biobio, Camina, Choapa, Choros, Cisnes, Colina, Huasco, Limari, Morado, Palena, Poscua, Tolten 7 Copiapo 8 Valdivia

sea: 7 Pacific

physical features:
  bay: 4 Cook, Eyre, Nena, Tarn 5 Lomas, Otway, Sarco 6 Darwin, Inutil, Moreno, Stokes, Tongoy 7 Dyneley, Inglesa, Skyring 8 Desolate
  cape: 4 Dyer, Horn 6 Choros, Falsos, Hornos, Quilan, Tablas 7 Deseado 10 Tres Montes
  channel: 5 Ancho, Cheap 6 Beagle 8 Cockburn, Moraleda
  desert: 7 Atacama
  gulf: 5 Ancud, Guafo, Penas 6 Arauco
  isthmus: 5 Ofqui
  peninsula: 5 Hardy, Lacuy 6 Taitao, Tumbes
  point: 4 Toro 5 Gallo, Liles, Lobos, Loros, Morro, Talca, Tetas, Vieja 6 Cachos, Galera, Molles 7 Angamos, Lavapie
  strait: 6 Nelson 8 Magellan
  volcano: 5 Lanin, Maipo 6 Antuco, Llaima, Oyahue, Tacora 7 Peteroa, Socomap

people: 3 Ona 4 Auca, Inca, Onan 6 Arauca, Chango, Yahgan 7 Mapuche, mestizo, Moluche, Pampean, Patagon, Puegian, Ranquel 8 Alikuluf, Picunche, Tsonecan
  author: 5 Bello 6 Donoso, Neruda 7 Mistral
  conqueror: 7 Valdiva
  explorer: 8 Magellan
  leader: 7 Allende 8 O'Higgins, Pinochet 9 San Martin 10 Alessandri

language: 7 Spanish

religion: 13 Roman Catholic

places:
  copper mine: 12 Chuquicamata
  resort: 8 Portillo 10 Vina del Mar

possession: 12 Easter Island 20 Juan Fernandez Islands

feature:
  cowboy: 5 huaso
  dance: 5 cueca 6 pequen 9 resbalosa
  shrub: 5 litre
  slum: 9 callempas
  tree: 5 rauli
  wind instrument: 4 sicu

food:
  drink: 5 pisco 6 chicha
  hot red pepper: 3 aji
  meat pie: 8 empanada
  soup: 7 cazuela 8 caldillo

7 callous, coolish, cutting, glacial, hostile, iciness, rawness, shivery **8** coolness, uncaring **9** crispness, frigidity, sharpness, unfeeling **10** forbidding, frostiness, unfriendly **11** indifferent, passionless, penetrating **12** unresponsive

chilled 4 cold, iced **6** cooled, frozen **7** frosted **8** hardened **10** dispirited **11** discouraged **12** refrigerated

chilling 3 icy, raw **5** nippy, on ice **6** frigid **7** bracing, cooling **10** unfriendly

Chillingworth, Roger
character in: **16** The Scarlet Letter
author: **9** Hawthorne

chime 4 gong, peal, ring, toll **5** knell, sound **6** jingle, tinkle **7** pealing, ringing **8** carillon, ding-dong, tinkling, tollings **10** set of bells **14** tintinnabulate **16** tintinnabulation

Chimene
character in: **6** The Cid
author: **9** Corneille

chimera 5 dream, fancy **6** bubble, mirage **7** fantasy, monster, phantom **8** daydream, delusion, idle whim, illusion **9** pipe dream **10** self-deceit, she-monster **12** will-o'-the-wisp **13** castle in Spain, fool's paradise, hallucination, self-deception **14** castle in the air **24** figment of one's imagination

Chimera
form: **7** monster
father: **6** Typhon
mother: **7** Echidna
breathes: **4** fire

Chimera
author: **9** John Barth

chimerical 6 absurd, unreal **7** utopian **8** delusive, ethereal, fabulous, fanciful, illusory, mythical quixotic **9** fantastic, imaginary, visionary **10** impossible, phantasmal, **11** nonexistent

chimney 4 flue, tube, vent **5** cleft, gully, spout, stack **6** funnel, hearth **7** opening **9** stovepipe **10** smokestack

chimpanzee 3 ape **6** animal, baboon, monkey

chin 3 gab, jaw, rap **4** chat, talk **7** chatter, palaver **8** chitchat, converse **10** chew the fat, chew the rag **11** confabulate

china 6 dishes, plates **7** pottery **8** crockery **9** chinaware, porcelain, stoneware, table-

ware **11** ceramic ware, earthenware **14** cups and saucers

China *see box, p. 178*

China Syndrome, The
director: **12** James Bridges
cast: **9** Jane Fonda **10** Jack Lemmon, Scott Brady **14** Michael Douglas
setting: **17** nuclear power plant

Chinatown
director: **13** Roman Polanski
cast: **10** John Huston **11** Faye Dunaway **13** Jack Nicholson
Oscar for: **5** story **10** screenplay

chinaware 6 dishes, plates **7** pottery **8** crockery **9** porcelain, stoneware, tableware **11** ceramic ware, earthenware **14** cups and saucers

chine 5 spine **6** dorsum **8** backbone

Chinese book of divination 6 I Ching

Chingachgook
character in: **13** The Pathfinder **20** The Last of the Mohicans
author: **6** Cooper

chink 3 cut, gap **4** gash, hole, rent, rift, ring, slit **5** break, clank, cleft, clink, crack, fault, split **6** breach, jangle, jingle, rattle, tinkle **7** crevice, fissure, opening **8** aperture

Chinook (Flathead)
language family: **9** Chinookan
location: **7** Pacific **10** Washington
ritual: **15** head deformation

Chinookan
tribe: **7** Chinook **8** Flathead

chintzy 5 cheap, close, dowdy, tacky, tatty, tight **6** frowzy, frumpy, shabby, sleazy, stingy **7** miserly **8** grudging, schlocky, stinting **9** niggardly, penurious **11** closefisted **12** parsimonious **13** penny-pinching

Chione
father: **6** Boreas **9** Daedalion
mother: **8** Orithyia
son: **9** Autolycus, Philammon

chip 3 bit, cut, hew **4** chop, gash, hack, nick **5** chunk, crumb, flake, scrap, shred, slice, split, wafer **6** chisel, morsel, paring, sliver **7** cutting, shaving, whittle **8** fragment, splinter

chipmunk 6 chippy, gopher, rodent **8** chipmuck, squirrel **14** ground squirrel **16** chipping squirrel

chipper 3 gay **4** pert, spry **5** alive, brisk, peppy **6** frisky, jaunty, lively **8** animated, carefree, cheerful, spirited **9** easygoing, energetic, sprightly, vivacious **12** high-spirited, light-hearted

Chippewa (Ojibwa, Ojibway)
language family: **9** Algonkian **10** Algonquian
tribe: **4** Cree **6** Ottawa **8** Chippewa **10** Missisauga
location: **6** Canada **9** Lake Huron **11** North Dakota **12** Lake Superior, Niagara Falls
leader: **7** Pontiac

CHiPS
character: **8** (Officer) Jon Baker **10** (Sgt) Joe Getraer **16** (Officer) Frank (Ponch) Poncherello
cast: **10** Robert Pine **11** Erik Estrada, Larry Wilcox

Chirico, Giorgio de
born: **5** Volos **6** Greece
artwork: **15** Enigma of the Hour **19** Enigma of an Afternoon **21** Enigma of an Autumn Night **22** Nostalgia of the Infinite **32** The Melancholy and Mystery of a Street

Chiron
also: **7** Cheiron
form: **7** centaur
father: **6** Cronos, Cronus, Kronos
mother: **7** Philyra
wife: **8** Chariclo
daughter: **6** Endeis
grandson: **6** Peleus
occupation: **7** teacher

chirp 4 peep, sing **5** cheep, chirr, tweet **7** chirrup, chitter, peeping, twitter **8** cheeping

chirrup 4 peep **5** cheep, chirp, tweet **7** chitter, twitter

chisel 3 cut, gyp **4** gull, hoax, rook, tool **5** blade, cheat, slice **6** incise
type: **4** cape, cold, wood **7** v-shaped

Chisel
constellation of: **6** Caelum

chiseler 4 fake **5** cheat, fraud, quack **7** cheater **8** swindler

Chislev 16 ninth Hebrew month

chit 3 IOU, tab **4** note **5** check **7** voucher

chitchat 3 gab **4** chat **5** prate **6** drivel, gossip **7** chatter, palaver, prattle **8** converse **9** small talk **10** chew the fat, chew the rag **11** confabulate **13** confabulation

China

other name: 3 PRC **13** Middle Kingdom **14** Flowery Kingdom **22** People's Republic of China

capital: 6 Peking **7** Beijing

largest city: 8 Shanghai

others: 3 Bai, Noh **4** Ahpa, Amoy, Fuyu, Guma, Hami, Huma, Ipin, Kian, Kisi, Lini, Loho, Luta, Moho, Moyu, Niya, Noho, Omin, Rima, Saka, Sian, Taku, Tali, Tayu, Wuhu, Yaan **5** Chiai, Fusin, Kirin, Koklu, Linyu, Macao, Penki, Shasi, Soche, Taian, Talai, Tihwa, Tuyun, Wuhan, Wusih, Yenan, Yenki, Yulin, Yumen **6** Anshan, Antung, Canton, Dairen, Fuchau, Fuchow, Fushun, Hankow, Harbin, Ilhasa, Kalgan, Loyang, Lushun, Mukden, Nanhai, Ningpo, Singan, Sining, Taipei, Tsinan, Yangku, Yunnan **7** Fuskhih, Hanyang, Kunming, Lanchow, Lioyang, Mengtze, Nanking, Nanning, Paoshan, Peiping, Soochow, Taiyuan, Tatshan, Urumchi, Urumsti, Waichow, Wuchang, Yenping **8** Chinchow, Fengkiek, Fengtien, Hangchow, Kingchow, Nanchang, Shanghai, Shenyang, Siangtan, Tientsin, Tungchow, Wanchuan, Wanhsien **9** Chungking, Kiangling, Tsingyuan **10** Chiangling, Port Arthur

school: 5 Futan **6** Peking **7** Nanking **8** Hangchow **9** Sun Yat-sen **16** Cheng-tu Technical

division:
  province: **5** Honan, Hunan, Hupei, Kansu **6** Anhwei, Fukien, Shansi, Shensi, Yunnan **7** Kiangsi, Kiangsu **8** Chekiang, Kweichow, Shantung, Szechwan, Tientsin, Tsinghai **9** Kwangtung, Manchuria

measure: 3 cho, fan, fen, pau, tou, tun, yan, yin **4** chek, chih, fang, kish, papa, quei, shih, teke, tsan, tsun **5** catty, chang, ching, sheng, shing **6** chupak, gungli, kungho, kungmu, tching **7** kungfen, kungyin **8** kungchih, kungshih, **9** kungching

monetary unit: 4 cash, cent, fyng, mace, tael, tiao, yuan **5** sycee **12** jen nin piao pu

weight: 3 fan, fen, hao, kin, ssu, tan, yin **4** chee, chin, dong, shih, tael, tsin **5** catty, chien, picul, tchin, tsien **6** kungli **7** haikwan, kungfen, kungssu, kungtun **8** kungchin **9** candareen **10** kupingtael

island: 4 Amoy **5** Macao, Matsu, Namki, Taipa **6** Chusan, Hainan, Pratas, Quemoy, Taiwan, Tinian, Yuhwan **7** Coloane, Formosa, Hungtow, Tungsha **8** Ching Hai, Chouchan, Kulangsu

lake: 3 Tai **4** Chao, Na-mu **5** Kaoyu, Oling, Telli **6** Bamtso, Bornor, Ebinor, Erhhai, Khanka, Lopnor, Namtso, Poyang **7** Chaling, Hungtse, Karanor, Kokonor **8** Hulunnor, Montcalm, Taroktso, Tellinor, Tienchih, Tsinghai, Tungting

sea: 6 Yellow **9** East China **10** South China

physical features:
  bay: **7** Laichow **8** Hangchow
  cape: **7** Olwanpi
  channel: **5** Bashi
  desert: **4** Gobi **5** Ordos, Shamo **7** Alashan **10** Takla Makan
  dry lake: **6** Lopnor
  gulf: **5** Pohai **6** Chihli, Tonkin **7** Pechili **8** Liaotung
  peninsula: **6** Leichu **7** Luichow **8** Liaotung
  plateau: **5** Loess **7** Tibetan
  port: **4** Amoy, Wuhu **5** Aigun, Shasi **6** Antung, Canton, Chefoo, Dairen, Ichang, Ningpo, Pakhoi, Swatow, Wuchow **7** Foochow, Hunchun, Luichow, Nanking, Samshui, Santuao, Soochow, Wenchow, Yinkkow, Yungkia **8** Changsha, Hangchow, Kiukiang, Kongmoon, Shanghai, Tengyueh, Tientsin, Tsingtao, Wanhsien **9** Kwangchow, Weihaiwei **10** Tsingkiang
  strait: **6** Hainan, Taiwan **7** Formosa

people: 3 Han, Yis **4** Huis, Lolo, Miao, Pu-is **5** Hakka, Hoklo, Seres, Sinic **6** Cataia, Chuang, Johnny, Korean, Manchu, Mongol, Serian, Uighun **7** Sinaean, Tibetan
  leader: **9** Sun Yat-sen, Zhou Enlai **10** Kublai Khan, Mao Tse-tung **11** Genghis Khan **12** Deng Xiaoping **13** Chiang Kai-shek
  philosopher: **6** Lao-tzu **9** Confucius

language: 7 Chinese **8** Mandarin, Shanghai **9** Cantonese

religion: 5 Islam **6** Taoism **8** Buddhism **12** Christianity, Confucianism

place:
  palace: **6** Summer **8** Imperial **13** Forbidden City
  ruins: **9** Ming Tombs
  square: **9** Tiananmen
  wonder: **9** Great Wall

feature:
  boat: **4** junk
  conspirators: **10** Gang of Four
  dynasty: **3** Han, Sui **4** Chou, Ch'in, Ming, Sung, T'ang **5** Ch'ing, Shang **6** Manchu
  military academy: **7** whompoa
  watercolor: **8** shan shiu

Chitimacha
  language family: **6** Tunica
  location: **9** Louisiana
  noted for: **8** basketry

chitter 4 peep **5** cheep, chirp,
  tweet **7** chatter, chirrup,
  twitter

chitter-chatter 3 gab **4** blab
  6 babble, drivel, gabble, jabber **7** blabber, prattle, twaddle **8** chitchat **9** jabbering
  16 idle conversation

chivalrous 6 polite **7** courtly,
  gallant **8** mannerly

chivalry 8 courtesy **9** gallantry
  10 knighthood, politeness
  11 courtliness

Chivery, Young John
  character in: **12** Little Dorrit
  author: **7** Dickens

chivy 3 nag **4** hunt, race **5** annoy, chase, chevy, hound,
  trail, worry **6** badger, bother,
  harass, pursue **7** scamper,
  torment

Chlidanope
  form: **5** Naiad

Chloe
  epithet of: **7** Demeter
  means: **5** green

chloride 7 muriate **8** chemical,
  compound

chlorine
  chemical symbol: **2** Cl

Chloris
  father: **7** Amphion
  mother: **5** Niobe
  daughter: **4** Pero

chocolate 5 brown, candy, cacao, cocoa, drink **6** bon bon
  10 confection

Choctaw
  language family:
    10 Muskhogean
  location: **7** Alabama
    11 Mississippi
  related to: **9** Chickasaw

Choephoroe
  author: **9** Aeschylus
  character: **6** Furies **7** Electra,
    Orestes, Pylades **8** Aegis-
    thus **12** Clytemnestra

choice 3 say **4** A-one, best,
  fine, pick, vote **5** array, elite,
  prime, prize, stock, store,
  voice **6** better, opting, option,
  select, supply, tip-top **7** display, special, variety **8** choosing, deciding, decision,
  superior **9** excellent, exclusive,
  first-rate, preferred, selection,
  top drawer **10** assemblage, assortment, collection, consummate, discretion, first-class,
  preferable, preference, well-
  chosen **11** alternative, appoint-

ment, exceptional, superlative
  13 determination,
  extraordinary

choice food 5 treat **8** delicacy

choicest part
  French: **14** creme de la
    creme

choir 4 band **5** quire **6** angels,
  chorus **7** chorale, singers
  10 choristers

Choirboys, The
  author: **14** Joseph Wambaugh

choke 3 dam, gag **4** clog, plug
  5 block, check, dam up, stuff
  6 arrest, bridle, hamper,
  hinder, impede, plug up, retard, stifle, stop up **7** congest,
  garrote, inhibit, repress,
  smother **8** blockade, hold
  back, obstruct, restrain, strangle, suppress, throttle **9** constrain, constrict, suffocate
  10 asphyxiate

choler 3 ire **4** fury, rage **5** anger, wrath **6** spleen, temper

choleric 3 mad **5** angry, irate,
  testy, vexed **6** cranky, grumpy,
  shirty, touchy **7** enraged, furious, grouchy, peevish, waspish **8** snappish, wrathful
  9 dyspeptic, indignant, irritable, irascible, splenetic **10** infuriated, short-fused
  11 contentious, hot-tempered,
  ill-tempered, thin-skinned
  12 cantankerous, sour-
  tempered **13** quick-tempered,
  short-tempered

choose 3 opt **4** like, pick, take,
  wish **5** adopt, elect **6** decide,
  desire, intend, opt for, prefer,
  see fit, select **7** call out, embrace, espouse, extract, fix
  upon, pick out, resolve **8** decide on, settle on **9** determine,
  single out **10** be inclined
  13 commit oneself **14** make
  up one's mind

choosy 5 fussy, picky **7** finicky **9** selective **10** fastidious,
  particular **14** discriminating

chop 3 cut, hew, hit, lop
  4 blow, chip, crop, cube, dice,
  fell, gash, hack **5** cut up,
  mince, slash, slice, split,
  swipe, whack **6** cleave, cutlet,
  stroke, sunder **8** fragment, rib
  slice **9** cotelette, pulverize

Chopin, Frederic Francois
  born: **6** Poland
    12 Zelazowawola
  companion: **10** George Sand
  composer of: **5** Etude **7** Bal-
    lade **8** Berceuse, Cat Valse,
    Dog Valse, Fantasie **9** Ecos-
    saise **10** Barcarolle **11** Min-
    ute Valse **15** Andante
    Spianato, Heroic Polonaise

(No 6), Raindrop Prelude,
  Winter Wind Etude
  16 Shepherd Boy Etude
  17 Impromptu Fantasie,
    Rondo a la Krakowiak
  18 Revolutionary Etude
  20 Butterfly's Wings Etude

choral ode
  Greek: **7** parodos **8** stasimon

chord 4 cord, line, note, tone
  5 music, triad **6** accord, string,
  tendon **7** cadence, emotion,
  feeling, harmony **9** harmonize

chore 3 job **4** duty, task, work
  5 stint **6** burden, errand,
  strain **8** farm task, small job
  10 assignment **13** household
  task **14** responsibility

choreography 5 dance
  12 stage dancing **16** dance
  composition

chorister 6 singer **7** changer
  8 choirboy

chortle 5 laugh **7** chuckle

chorus 5 choir, unity **6** accord,
  unison **7** concert, concord, refrain **8** glee club, one voice,
  response **9** antiphony, consensus, unanimity **11** concordance **12** singing group

chosen 5 elite **6** picked, sorted
  7 elected **8** selected **9** picked
  out

Chosen, The
  author: **10** Chaim Potok

Choson see **5** Korea

Chouans, The
  author: **14** Honore de Balzac

chough
  group of: **10** chattering

Chowbok
  character in: **7** Erewhon
  author: **6** Butler

Christ, the see **5** Jesus

christen 3 dip, dub **4** name
  6 launch **7** baptize, immerse
  8 dedicate, sprinkle **9** designate

Christian
  character in: **16** Pilgrim's
    Progress
  author: **6** Bunyan

Christian, Fletcher
  character in: **17** Mutiny on
    the Bounty
  authors: **4** Hall **8** Nordhoff

Christian, Linda
  real name: **16** Blanca Rosa
    Welter
  husband: **11** Tyrone Power
    12 Edmund Purdom
  born: **6** Mexico **7** Tampico
  roles: **6** Athena **15** Slaves of
    Babylon **18** Green Dolphin
    Street

Christiania
  capital of: **6** Norway

Christie, (Dame) Agatha
  author of: **7** Curtain **12** The Mousetrap **14** Death on the Nile **15** The Mirror Crack'd **16** Ten Little Indians **19** Murder at the Vicarage **20** And Then There Were None **22** What Mrs Mc-Gillicuddy Saw! **23** The Murder of Roger Ackroyd **24** Murder on the Orient Express, Witness for the Prosecution **27** The Mysterious Affair at Styles
  character: **10** Jane Marple **13** Hercule Poirot

Christie, Julie
  born: **5** Assam, India **6** Chukua
  roles: **7** Darling (Oscar), Shampoo **9** Billy Liar **11** Heat and Dust **13** Doctor Zhivago, Fahrenheit 451, Heaven Can Wait **18** Mc-Cabe and Mrs Miller **22** Far From the Madding Crowd

Christine
  author: **11** Stephen King

Christmas
  also: **4** Noel, Yule **8** Yuletide
  feature/symbol: **4** bell, star, tree **5** angel, gifts, holly **6** candle, carols, creche, manger, sleigh, wreath **7** Yule log **8** presents **9** evergreen, mistletoe, snowflake, stockings **10** Santa Claus

Christmas, Joe
  character in: **13** Light in August
  author: **8** Faulkner

Christmas Carol, A
  author: **14** Charles Dickens
  character: **7** Tiny Tim **8** Fezziwig **11** Bob Cratchit **12** Marley's Ghost **15** Ebenezer Scrooge
    ghosts of: **13** Christmas Past **15** Christmas Future **16** Christmas Present
  director: **17** Brian Desmond Hurst
  cast: **10** Jack Warner **11** Alastair Sim (Ebenezer Scrooge), Mervyn Johns **14** Michael Hordern **16** Kathleen Harrison

Chrome Yellow
  author: **12** Aldous Huxley

chromium
  chemical symbol: **2** Cr

chronic 7 abiding, lasting **8** constant, enduring, habitual, periodic **9** confirmed, continual, ingrained, perennial, recurrent, recurring

10 continuous, deep-rooted, deep-seated, inveterate, persistent, persisting **12** intermittent, longstanding

chronicle 3 log **4** epic, list, note, post, saga **5** diary, enter, story **6** annals, docket, record, relate, report **7** account, history, journal, narrate, recount, set down **8** archives **9** narrative **10** chronology

Chronicles of England, Scotland, and Ireland
  author: **16** Raphael Holinshed

chronological 5 dated **6** serial **7** ordered, sequent **10** sequential, succeeding, successive **11** consecutive, progressive, time-ordered **12** chronometric, chronoscopic **13** chronographic

chronology 6 annals, record **7** history **9** chronicle **13** order of events

chronometer 5 clock **8** horologe **9** timepiece

chrysanthemum
  varieties: **3** Max **4** Corn **5** Daisy, Tansy **6** Nippon **7** Garland **8** Florist's, Tricolor **10** Portuguese

Chrysaor
  father: **8** Poseidon
  mother: **6** Medusa
  brother: **7** Pegasus

Chryseis
  father: **7** Chryses
  concubine of: **9** Agamemnon

Chryses
  priest of: **6** Apollo
  daughter: **8** Chryseis

Chrysippus
  father: **6** Pelops
  abducted by: **5** Laius
  half-brother: **6** Atreus **8** Thyestes

chrysoberyl
  variety: **7** cat's-eye **11** alexandrite

chrysolite 4 iron, lava **5** beryl, green, stone **6** yellow **7** mineral, olivine, peridot **8** silicate **9** magnesium **10** aquamarine

chrysoprase
  species: **6** quartz
  color: **5** green

Chrysothemis
  father: **9** Agamemnon
  mother: **12** Clytemnestra
  brother: **7** Orestes
  sister: **7** Electra **9** Iphigenia
  daughter: **5** Rhoeo

Chthonian
  form: **5** deity **6** spirit
  habitat: **10** underworld

Chthonius
  member of: **6** Sparti
  epithet of: **4** Zeus
  means: **15** of the underworld

Chuang-tzu, Chwang-tse
  author: **9** Chuang-tzu

chubby 3 fat **5** buxom, plump, podgy, pudgy, stout, tubby **6** chunky, flabby, fleshy, portly, rotund, stocky, zaftig **7** paunchy **8** heavyset, roly-poly, thickset **9** corpulent **10** overweight **15** pleasingly plump

chuck 3 pat, pet, tap **4** cast, toss **5** fling, heave, pitch, sling, throw **6** tickle

chuckle 5 cluck, laugh **6** clumsy **7** cackle, chortle, snicker

chum 3 pal **5** buddy, crony **6** cohort, friend **7** comrade **8** intimate, playmate, sidekick **9** companion, confidant **10** bosom buddy, playfellow **11** close friend

chummy 5 close, palsy **7** devoted **8** familiar, friendly, intimate **9** congenial **10** buddy-buddy, palsy-walsy **12** affectionate

chump 4 dolt, dupe, fool, goof, goon, head **5** champ, munch **6** sucker **9** blockhead

chunk 3 gob, wad **4** clod, hunk, lump, mass **5** batch, block, piece **6** nugget, square

chunky 5 beefy, dumpy, lumpy, pudgy, squat, stout, thick **6** chubby, portly, stocky, stodgy, stubby **7** squabby **8** heavyset, thickset **11** thickbodied

church 4 cult, sect **5** faith **6** belief, chapel, mosque, temple **7** service **8** basilica, religion **9** cathedral, devotions, synagogue **10** house of God, Lord's house, persuasion, tabernacle **11** affiliation **12** denomination **13** divine worship **14** house of worship

Church, Frederick Edwin
  born: **10** Hartford CT
  artwork: **14** Andes of Ecuador, Falls of Niagara (Niagara Falls) **18** The Heart of the Andes **19** Morning in the Tropics

Churchill, Frank
  character in: **4** Emma
  author: **6** Austen

Churchill, Sarah
  father: **19** Sir Winston Churchill
  born: **6** London **7** England
  roles: **12** Royal Wedding

Churchill, Winston Spencer
born: **7** England **14** Blenheim Palace
father: **8** Randolph
mother: **12** Jennie Jerome
wife: **16** Clementine Hosier
daughter: **5** Sarah
school: **6** Harrow **9** Sandhurst
captured by: **5** Boers
position: **13** prime minister
author of: **11** Marlborough, My Early Life **14** The World Crisis **17** The Second World War **35** A History of the English-Speaking Peoples

churchly 8 clerical, pastoral, priestly **9** parochial **11** ministerial **14** ecclesiastical

churchman 5 vicar **6** bishop, cleric, curate, deacon, parson, pastor, priest, rector **7** prelate **8** chaplain, minister, preacher **9** clergyman **12** ecclesiastic

church official 5 elder **6** beadle, deacon **9** presbyter

churchyard 8 cemetery **9** graveyard **12** burial ground **13** burying ground

churl 3 cad, oaf **4** boor, lout **7** bounder

churlish 4 rude, sour, tart **5** crude, surly, testy **6** crusty, sullen **7** bearish, bilious, boorish, brusque, crabbed, grouchy, ill-bred, uncivil, uncouth, waspish **8** arrogant, captious, choleric, impolite, impudent, insolent, petulant **9** dastardly, insulting, irascible, irritable, obnoxious, rancorous, splenetic **10** unmannerly **11** ill-mannered, ill-tempered, quarrelsome **12** contemptible, discourteous

churn 4 beat, foam, rage, roil, roll, toss, whip **5** heave, shake, swirl, whisk **6** stir up **7** agitate, disturb, pulsate, shake up, vibrate **8** convulse **9** palpitate

chute 5 rapid, slide, slope **7** incline, passage **9** parachute

chutzpa, chutzpah 4 gall **5** brass, cheek, nerve **8** audacity, boldness, temerity **9** brashness, impudence **10** brazenness, effrontery **11** forwardness, presumption

Chwatt, Aaron
real name of: **10** Red Buttons

ciao 2 hi **5** hello **6** so long **7** goodbye **11** see you later

Cicero, Marcus Tullius
lived in: **11** ancient Rome
noted as: **6** author, lawyer, orator **9** statesman **11** philosopher **12** letter writer
position: **6** aedile, consul **7** praetor
author of: **9** De finibus, De oratore **10** De amicitia, De officiis **11** De re publica, De senectute, In Catilinam **14** De natura deorum, Pro lege Manilia **23** Tusculanae Disputationes

cicerone 5 guide, pilot **8** conductor **9** explainer

cicisbeo 5 lover

Cid, The
also: **11** Poema del Cid
author: **7** unknown **15** Pierre Corneille
character: **7** Chimene **8** Rodrigue
Cid also called: **14** el Cid Campeador **18** Rodrigo Diaz de Bivar
horse: **7** Babieca

ci-devant 6 former **7** retired **10** heretofore

cierge 3 dip, wax **5** light, taper **6** bougie, candle, tallow

cigar 4 toby **5** claro **6** corona, havana, maduro, stogie **7** cheroot **8** panatela, panetela, perfecto **9** cigarillo, panatella
ingredient: **11** tobacco leaf
part: **6** binder, filler **7** wrapper
made in: **4** Cuba **6** Havana
kept in: **7** humidor

cigarette, cigaret 3 cig, fag **4** biri **5** smoke **6** gasper, reefer **10** coffin nail
ingredient: **3** tar **7** menthol, tobacco **8** nicotine

Cilissa
nurse of: **7** Orestes

Cilix
father: **6** Agenor
sister: **6** Europa
searched for: **6** Europa

Cilla
brother: **5** Priam
killed by: **5** Priam

Cillus
charioteer of: **6** Pelops

Cimabue
real name: **11** Cenni di Pepi
born: **5** Italy **8** Florence
artwork attributed: **18** The S Trinita Madonna **29** Madonna Enthroned with St Francis **45** Madonna and Child Enthroned with Angels and Prophets

Cimarron
author: **10** Edna Ferber
director: **13** Wesley Ruggles
cast: **10** Irene Dunne, Richard Dix **13** Estelle Taylor
Oscar for: **7** picture **10** screenplay

Cimarron Strip
character: **8** (US Marshal) Jim Crown **9** Mac Gregor **12** Francis Wilde **17** Dulcey Coopersmith
cast: **10** Randy Boone **12** Jill Townsend, Percy Herbert **13** Stuart Whitman

Cimino, Michael
director of: **11** Heaven's Gate **13** The Deer Hunter (Oscar)

Cimmerian
mentioned by: **5** Homer
form: **10** Westerners
live in: **8** darkness

cinch 4 band, snap **5** girth **6** clinch, ensure, girdle, shoo-in **8** lead-pipe **9** pull tight, sure thing **11** piece of cake

Cincinnati
baseball team: **4** Reds
football team: **7** Bengals

cincture 4 band, belt, cord, sash **6** girdle

cinder 3 ash **4** slag **5** ashes, dross, ember **6** embers, scoria **8** clinkers, iron slag **10** burned coal, burned wood

Cinderella
author: **7** unknown
source: **8** Perrault
character: **14** Fairy Godmother, Handsome Prince **15** Ugly Stepsisters **16** Wicked Stepmother
coach: **7** pumpkin
horses: **9** white mice
footman: **4** frog
loses: **12** glass slipper

cinema 5 films **6** flicks, movies **7** theater **14** motion pictures, moving pictures

cinnamon 5 spice
botanical name: **20** Cinnamomum zeylanicum
variety: **6** cassia, Ceylon **10** zeylanicum
color: **4** buff **5** tawny **6** auburn **8** nut-brown **11** golden-brown, yellow-brown **12** reddish-brown **13** chestnut-brown **14** yellowish-brown
origin: **5** China **7** Vietnam **9** Indonesia **10** East Indies

Cinyras
king of: **6** Cyprus
son: **5** Melus
daughter: **6** Myrrha
introduced worship of: **9** Aphrodite
crime: **6** incest
death by: **7** suicide

cipher 3 nil, zip **4** code, zero **5** aught **6** naught, nobody **7** anagram, nothing, nullity **8** acrostic, goose egg **9** nonentity, obscurity **10** cryptogram **11** cryptograph

Cipus
  origin: **5** Roman
  occupation: **7** praetor

Circe
  form: **11** enchantress
  father: **6** Helios
  mother: **5** Perse
  brother: **6** Aeetes
  son: **6** Agrius **7** Latinus **9** Telegonus
  home: **5** Aeaea
  turned men into: **4** pigs **5** swine

circle **3** orb, set **4** belt, curl, gird, girt, halo, hoop, knot, loop, reel, ring, turn **5** arena, bound, cabal, crowd, curve, cycle, field, girth, group, hem in, orbit, pivot, range, reach, realm, round, sweep, swing **6** border, bounds, clique, cordon, corona, course, domain, girdle, region, sphere **7** circlet, circuit, company, compass, coterie, enclose, envelop, hedge in, revolve, ringlet, society, theater **8** dominion, encircle, province, sequence, surround **9** bailiwick, encompass, territory, wind about **10** move around, revolution, ring around **11** curve around, progression **12** circumrotate, circumscribe **13** revolve around **14** circumnavigate

Circle **6** gilgal

circlet **4** band, halo, ring **5** tiara **6** diadem, fillet, wreath **7** chaplet, coronet, ringlet

circuit **3** lap, run **4** area, beat, edge, tour, trek, walk **5** jaunt, limit, round, route **6** border, bounds, course, margin, sphere **7** compass, confine, journey **8** circling, frontier, orbiting, pivoting **9** excursion, extremity, perimeter, revolving, territory **10** revolution **13** circumference **14** distance around

circuitous **7** devious, turning, winding **8** circular, indirect, rambling, tortuous, twisting **10** meandering, roundabout, serpentine **12** labyrinthine **14** circumlocutory

circular **4** bill **5** flier, round **6** curved, notice, rotary **7** coiling, curling, leaflet, rocking, rolling, rounded, turning, winding **8** bulletin, gyrating, handbill, pivoting, spinning, twirling **9** revolving, spiraling, swiveling, throwaway **10** circuitous, ring-shaped **12** announcement **13** advertisement

circulate **4** flow **5** issue, strew **6** circle, course, spread, travel **7** give out, go forth, journey, publish, radiate, scatter **8** announce, disperse, go around, put about **9** broadcast, get abroad, make known, move about, publicize **10** distribute, make public, move around, pass around, put forward **11** disseminate, pass through, visit around **13** make the rounds

circulation **4** flow **6** motion **7** flowing **8** circling, rotation **9** diffusion, radiation **10** dispersion **11** propagation **12** distribution, promulgation, transmission **13** dissemination

circulatory system
  part: **4** vein **5** heart **6** artery **9** capillary **15** lymphatic vessel
  carries: **6** plasma **9** platelets **13** red blood cells **15** white blood cells

circumcision
  Hebrew: **4** Brit **5** Berit, Brith **6** Berith

circumference **3** rim **4** edge **5** girth **6** border, bounds, fringe, girdle, limits, margin **7** circuit, compass, outline **8** boundary **9** extremity, perimeter, periphery **14** distance around

circumlocution **8** rambling, verbiage **9** garrulity, verbosity, wordiness **10** digression, meandering **14** discursiveness, long-windedness, roundaboutness

circumlocutory **5** wordy **7** diffuse, verbose **8** rambling **9** wandering **10** digressive, discursive, maundering, roundabout

circumnavigate **5** skirt **6** bypass, circle **8** encircle, go around **10** circumvent

circumnavigation **8** circling, skirting **9** bypassing **11** going around **12** encirclement **13** circumvention

circumscribe **3** fix **4** curb **5** check, hem in, limit **6** bridle, circle, corset, define, impede **7** confine, enclose, outline **8** encircle, restrain, restrict, surround **9** constrain, delineate, encompass, proscribe

circumscribed **6** narrow **7** limited **10** restricted

circumscription **5** limit **7** outline **9** hemming in, restraint **10** constraint **11** confinement **12** encirclement **14** restrictedness

circumspect **4** sage, wary **5** alert **7** careful, guarded, prudent **8** cautious, discreet, vigilant, watchful **9** judicious, sagacious, wide-awake **10** deliberate, discerning, particular, thoughtful **13** contemplative, perspicacious **14** discriminating

circumspection **4** care, heed **7** caution **8** prudence **10** discretion, precaution, steadiness **11** carefulness, heedfulness, mindfulness **12** deliberation

circumstance **4** fact, item **5** event, point, thing **6** detail, factor, matter, ritual **7** element **8** ceremony, incident, splendor **9** condition, formality, happening, pageantry **10** brilliance, occurrence, particular, phenomenon **11** vicissitude **12** happenstance, magnificence, resplendence **14** state of affairs

circumstances **5** state **9** situation **11** environment **16** living conditions

circumstantial **4** full **6** minute **7** deduced, hearsay, implied, precise **8** accurate, complete, detailed, explicit, inferred, presumed, thorough **9** secondary **10** blow-by-blow, evidential, exhaustive, extraneous, incidental, particular, unabridged **11** conjectural, inferential, provisional **12** nonessential

circumvent **4** miss, shun **5** avoid, dodge, elude, evade, skirt **6** bypass, circle, escape, outwit, thwart **8** go around **9** frustrate **12** keep away from **14** circumnavigate

circumvention **7** dodging, ducking, eluding, evasion **9** avoidance, bypassing **11** frustration **12** sidestepping

circus **4** ring **5** arena **6** big top, circle, uproar **8** carnival, coliseum **9** spectacle **10** exhibition, hippodrome **11** ampitheater **12** intersection
  act: **5** clown, flyer **7** acrobat, juggler, trapeze **8** side show **9** lion tamer, menagerie **10** equestrian **13** flying trapeze
  famous: **6** Astley **12** Cirque d'Hiver **15** Barnum and Bailey **16** Ringling Brothers

Cissaea
  epithet of: **6** Athena
  means: **10** ivy goddess

Cist
  form: **9** sacred box
  used for: **8** utensils

cistern **3** box, tub, vat **4** tank,

well 6 cavity, vessel 8 aqueduct 9 reservoir

citadel 4 fort 7 bastion, rampart 8 fortress 10 stronghold 13 fortification

citation 4 cite 5 award, honor, kudos, medal, quote 7 example, excerpt, extract, passage 8 instance 9 quotation 12 commendation, illustration 14 official praise

cite 4 name, note 5 honor, quote 6 praise 7 advance, commend, mention, present, refer to, specify 8 allude to, document, indicate 9 enumerate, exemplify 12 bring forward 13 give as example

Cithaeron
  brother: 7 Helicon
  crime: 6 murder
  changed into: 8 mountain

Cithaeronian see 4 Zeus

citified 5 urban 6 urbane 12 cosmopolitan 13 sophisticated

citizen 6 native 7 denizen, subject 8 national, resident 10 inhabitant
  French: 7 citoyen

Citizen Kane
  director: 11 Orson Welles
  script: 11 Orson Welles 17 Herman J Mankiewicz
  cast: 11 Orson Welles 12 Joseph Cotten 13 Everett Sloane 14 Agnes Moorehead
  score: 15 Bernard Herrmann
  sled: 7 Rosebud

citizenry 4 folk 6 people, public 7 society 8 populace 9 community 10 population

citoyen 7 citizen

citrine
  species: 6 quartz
  color: 6 yellow

citron 3 rue 4 lime, rind 5 lemon 6 cedrat, orange, yellow 8 Rutaceae 9 tangerine 10 watermelon 12 citrus medica
  Jewish: 6 ethrog

city 4 burg, town 7 big town 8 denizens, township 9 residents 10 metropolis 11 inhabitants, megalopolis, townspeople 12 municipality 16 incorporated town, metropolitan area

city hall
  French: 12 hotel de ville

City Life
  author: 15 Donald Barthelme

City Lights
  director: 14 Charles Chaplin
  cast: 8 Hank Mann 10 Harry

Myers 14 Charlie Chaplin 16 Virginia Cherrill

City of God, The (De Civitate Dei)
  author: 11 St Augustine

City of the Lion see 9 Singapore

city slicker 4 dude 8 urbanite 11 cosmopolite 12 sophisticate

City Without Walls and Other Poems
  author: 7 W H Auden

Ciudad Trujillo
  capital of: 17 Dominican Republic

Civ 17 second Hebrew month

civic 5 local 6 public 8 citizen's, communal 9 community

civil 3 lay 4 city 5 civic, state 6 genial, polite, public 7 affable, amiable, citizen, cordial, secular 8 citizen's, communal, decorous, gracious, mannerly, obliging 9 civilized, community, courteous, municipal 10 individual, neighborly, respectful 11 gentlemanly, nonmilitary 12 conciliatory, well-mannered

Civil Disobedience
  author: 17 Henry David Thoreau

civilian 9 lay person 14 private citizen 17 nonmilitary person 18 nonuniformed person

civility 4 tact 7 manners, respect 8 courtesy 10 affability, amiability, cordiality, good temper, politeness 11 good manners 12 graciousness, pleasantness 13 agreeableness, courteousness 14 respectfulness

civilization 7 culture, society 10 refinement 11 cultivation, worldliness 13 enlightenment 14 sophistication

civilize 5 edify, teach, train 6 inform, polish, refine 7 culture, develop, educate, elevate 8 humanize, instruct 9 cultivate, enlighten 11 acculturate 12 sophisticate

civil law
  Latin: 9 jus civile

clad 6 garbed 7 arrayed, attired, clothed, dressed 9 outfitted

Claggart
  character in: 9 Billy Budd
  author: 8 Melville

claim 3 ask 4 avow, call, plea, take 5 exact, right, title 6 access, affirm, allege, assert, avowal, charge, demand, pick up 7 call for, collect, command, declare, profess, re-

quest 8 exaction, insist on, maintain, proclaim 9 assertion, ownership, seek as due, statement 10 allegation, lay claim to, pretension, profession 11 affirmation, declaration, postulation, requirement 12 proclamation, protestation

claimant 6 suitor 9 applicant, pretender 10 petitioner

clairvoyant 7 psychic 8 divining, oracular 9 prescient, prophetic 10 telepathic 11 foreknowing, telekinetic 12 extrasensory, precognitive, psychometric 13 psychokinetic, second-sighted

clam 4 vise 5 clamp, clasp 6 dollar, marine 7 bivalve, mollusk
  kind: 5 pismo, razor 6 butter, quahog 7 geoduck, steamer 10 little neck 11 cherrystone
  part: 4 foot, palp 5 gills, shell, valve 6 mantle, siphon 7 sinuses 8 ligament
  habitat: 3 mud 4 sand
  relative: 6 mussel, oyster

clamber up 5 climb, mount, scale 10 scramble up, struggle up

clamminess 4 damp 7 wetness 8 dampness, dankness 10 stickiness, sweatiness

clammy 3 wet 4 damp 5 pasty, slimy 6 sticky, sweaty 10 perspiring 11 cold and damp

clamor 3 cry, din 4 call, howl, yell 5 blast, chaos, noise, shout, storm 6 bedlam, bellow, cry out, hubbub, jangle, outcry, racket, rumpus, tumult, uproar 7 bluster, call out, clangor, thunder 8 brouhaha, shouting 9 commotion, hue and cry 10 hullabaloo, vociferate, wild chorus

clamorous 4 loud 5 noisy 10 boisterous, uproarious

clamp 4 clip, grip, vise 5 brace, clasp 6 clench, clinch, fasten, secure 7 bracket 8 fastener

clan 4 gang, knot, line, ring 5 breed, cabal, crowd, group, guild, house, party, stock 6 circle, league, strain 7 company, dynasty, lineage, society 8 alliance, pedigree 10 fraternity 11 affiliation, association, brotherhood, family group, lineal group 12 tribal family

clandestine 6 covert, hidden, masked, secret, veiled 7 cloaked, furtive, private 8 secluded, sneaking, stealthy 9 concealed, secretive, underhand 10 undercover, unrevealed **11** underground, underhanded, undisclosed **12** confidential **13** surreptitious

clang 3 din **4** bong, gong, peal, toll **5** chime, clank, clash, knell **6** jangle **7** clangor, resound, ringing, tolling **8** clashing **10** resounding, ring loudly

clangor 3 din **5** noise **6** clamor, hubbub, jangle, racket, uproar

clank 5 chink, clang, clash, clink **6** jangle, rattle **7** clangor, clatter **8** clashing

clannish 4 cold **5** aloof **6** narrow **7** distant, insular **8** cliquish, snobbish **9** exclusive, parochial, sectarian **10** provincial, restricted, unfriendly **11** unreceptive

Clan of the Cave Bear, The
  author: **9** Jean M Auel

clap 3 bat, hit, rap, tap **4** bang, bump, cast, cuff, dash, hurl, peal, push, roar, rush, slam, slap, swat, toss **5** burst, clack, crack, drive, fling, force, pitch, shove, smack, smite, thump, whack **6** buffet, plunge, propel, strike, thrust, thwack, wallop **7** applaud, clatter **9** explosion **11** set suddenly

claptrap 3 rot **4** bosh, bull, bunk, sham, **5** bilge, hokum, hooey, stuff, trash, tripe **6** bunkum, drivel, hot air, humbug, tinsel **7** baloney, blarney, fustian, hogwash, spinach, twaddle **8** buncombe, nonsense, quackery, tommyrot **9** gaudiness, poppycock, staginess **10** applesauce, flapdoodle, tawdriness, tomfoolery **12** foolishness **15** pretentiousness **16** stuff and nonsense

claque 10 sycophants **15** cheering section

Clare, Ada
  character in: **10** Bleak House
  author: **7** Dickens

claret 3 red **7** carmine, deep red, red wine **8** blood-red, Bordeaux, cardinal **11** purplish red, wine-colored

clarification 10 commentary **11** elucidation, explanation, explication **14** further comment
  French: **15** eclaircissement

clarify 5 clear, purge, solve **6** purify, refine **7** clear up, explain, lay open, resolve **9** elucidate, explicate, make clear, make plain **10** illuminate **11** disentangle, shed light on

12 bring to light **18** make understandable

clarinet 4 wind **8** woodwind **11** transposing
  mouthpiece: **4** reed
  ancestor: **9** chalumeau
  musician: **12** Benny Goodman

clarion 5 acute, clear, sharp **6** shrill **7** blaring, ringing **8** distinct, piercing, resonant, sonorous, stirring **10** commanding, compelling, imperative **11** high-pitched

Clarissa Harlowe
  author: **16** Samuel Richardson
  character: **8** Miss Howe **11** John Belford **14** Robert Lovelace **20** Colonel William Morden

clarity 6 purity **8** lucidity, radiance **9** clearness, exactness, plainness, precision **10** brightness, brilliance, directness, effulgence, glassiness, luminosity, simplicity **12** explicitness, translucence, transparency **15** intelligibility **17** comprehensibility

Clark, Mark W
  served in: **3** WWI **4** WWII **9** Korean War
  rank: **22** allied commander in Italy **24** commander of forces in Korea **30** chief of staff of army ground forces **42** commander of Allied occupation forces in Austria
  president of: **7** Citadel

Clark, Walter Van Tilburg
  author of: **16** The Ox-Bow Incident

Clarke, Arthur C
  author of: **10** (2010) Odyssey Two **13** (2001) A Space Odyssey, Childhood's End

clash 4 bang, boil, feud, fray, tiff **5** argue, clang, clank, crash, fight, set-to **6** battle, combat, fracas, jangle, rattle, tussle **7** clangor, clatter, contend, contest, discord, dispute, grapple, jarring, quarrel, wrangle **8** conflict, crashing, friction, skirmish, squabble, struggle **9** altercate, encounter, lock horns **10** antagonism, difference, disharmony, dissidence, opposition **11** cross swords **12** disagreement **13** exchange blows

clash of arms 5 fight **6** battle, combat **8** conflict, skirmish, struggle **9** encounter **10** engagement

clash with 9 fight with **12** do battle with **14** contend against **15** cross swords with

clasp 3 hug **4** bolt, clip, grip, hasp, hold, hook, link, lock, snap **5** catch, clamp, grasp, latch, press **6** buckle, clinch, clutch, couple, fasten, secure **7** coupler, embrace, grapple, squeeze **8** fastener **9** fastening

clasp in the arms 3 hug **4** hold **6** enfold **7** embrace

class 3 set **4** form, kind, rank, rate, size, sort, type **5** brand, breed, caste, genre, genus, grade, group, index, label, order, state **6** circle, clique, codify, course, lesson, number, sphere, status **7** arrange, catalog, section, session, species, station, variety **8** category, classify, division, pedigree, position **9** condition, designate **10** categorize, pigeonhole, social rank **11** set of pupils **13** social stratum **14** classification **15** departmentalize, graduating group

classic, classical 4 epic **5** model **6** heroic **7** ageless, paragon **8** absolute, accepted, enduring, masterly **9** archetype, excellent, exemplary, first-rate, prototype **10** archetypal, consummate, definitive, first-class, Greco-Roman, prototypal **11** masterpiece, outstanding, traditional **12** ancient Greek, ancient Roman, standard work **13** authoritative, distinguished **14** distinguishing **17** first-class example

classification 4 kind, rank, sort, type **5** class, genus, group, order **6** family, series **7** section, species **8** category, classing, division, grouping, labeling, ordering, taxonomy **9** arranging, gradation **10** assortment, organizing **11** arrangement, designation, disposition **12** categorizing, codification, organization **14** categorization **15** systematization

classified 5 secret **6** sorted **7** classed **8** assorted **10** restricted **11** categorized **12** confidential

classify 3 tag **4** list, rank, rate, size, type **5** brand, class, grade, group, index, label, order, range **6** assort, codify, number, ticket **7** arrange, catalog **8** organize **9** segregate **10** categorize, pigeonhole **11** distinguish

classy 4 chic, posh, tony **5** nifty, nobby, ritzy, smart, swank, swell **6** dressy, modish, spiffy, swanky **7** elegant, genteel, opulent, refined, stylish **8** cultured, polished, tasteful

9 high-class **10** ultrasmart **11** fashionable, in good taste **12** aristocratic, well-mannered

clatter 4 bang **5** clack, clang, clank, clash, clink, clump, crash **6** clamor, jangle, racket, rattle **7** chatter **8** crashing, rattling

clattering 3 din **6** clamor, hubbub, racket, uproar **7** clangor

Claude
real name: **12** Claude Gellee
also called: **14** Claude Lorraine
born: **6** France **8** Chamagne
artwork: **7** The Mill **16** Hagar and the Angel **18** Ascanius and the Stag, The Enchanted Castle **27** The Rest on the Flight into Egypt **31** The Embarkation of the Queen of Sheba

Claudel, Paul
author of: **6** L'Otage **10** The Hostage **13** Partage de Midi **15** The Satin Slipper **20** Tidings Brought to Mary

Claudia Quinta
freed: **12** grounded ship
feat proved: **8** chastity

Claudio
character in: **17** Measure for Measure **19** Much Ado About Nothing
author: **11** Shakespeare

Claudius
character in: **6** Hamlet
author: **11** Shakespeare

Claudius the God
author: **12** Robert Graves

clause 4 term **7** article, proviso **8** covenant **9** condition, provision **11** proposition, stipulation **13** specification **14** simple sentence

claustrophobia
fear of: **12** closed spaces **14** confined spaces

Clavell, James
author of: **6** Shogun, Tai-Pan **7** King Rat **9** Whirlwind **10** Noble House

clavicle
bone of: **10** collarbone

claw 3 paw **4** foot, grip, maul, tear **5** seize, slash, talon **6** clutch, pincer, scrape **7** scratch **8** lacerate **10** animal nail

Clay, Cassius
former name of: **11** Muhammad Ali

Clayburgh, Jill
born: **9** New York NY
roles: **9** Semi-Tough **12** Starting Over **16** An Unmarried Woman, North Dallas Forty **21** I'm Dancing as Fast as I Can

Clayhanger Trilogy, The
author: **13** Arnold Bennett

clean 3 mop **4** dust, fine, neat, pure, tidy, trim, wash **5** bathe, clear, fresh, moral, order, scour, scrub, sweep **6** bathed, chaste, decent, neaten, tidy up, vacuum, washed **7** cleaned, cleanse, healthy, launder, orderly, perfect, scoured, shampoo, upright **8** cleansed, decorous, flawless, innocent, sanitary, scrubbed, spotless, unsoiled, virtuous, well-made **9** exemplary, faultless, honorable, laundered, stainless, undefiled, unspotted, unstained, unsullied, untainted, wholesome **10** immaculate, uninfected, unpolluted **11** unblemished **13** unadulterated **14** uncontaminated

cleaner, cleanser 4 soap **5** borax **6** washer **7** ammonia, janitor **8** purifier, scrubber **9** detergent **14** scouring powder

cleaning 7 bathing, washing **8** scouring **9** cleansing, going-over, scrubbing, tidying up **10** laundering

cleanse 3 rid **4** free, wash **5** bathe, clean, clear, erase, flush, scour, scrub **7** absolve, deliver, expunge, launder, release, shampoo **8** sweep out, unburden **9** expurgate

clean-shaven 6 smooth **9** unbearded **11** unwhiskered **12** smooth-shaven

cleansing 7 bathing, healing, purging, washing **8** flushing, scouring **9** expunging, purifying, scrubbing **10** absolution

cleanup 4 gain **6** profit **8** windfall
baseball: **12** fourth batter

clear *see box*

clearance 4 room, sale **6** margin, permit **7** removal **8** clearing **10** offsetting **11** elimination **13** authorization, certification

clear as day 5 plain **7** obvious **8** apparent, clear-cut, manifest **11** self-evident

clear-cut 4 open **5** exact, lucid, plain **6** patent **7** evident, express, obvious, precise **8** definite, detailed, distinct, explicit, manifest **10** clear as day, unconfused, undeniable **11** appreciable, conspicuous, self-evident, substantial,

---

clear 3 rid **4** fair, free, keen, make, open **5** alert, clean, empty, gauzy, lucid, plain, sharp, sunny **6** acquit, bright, patent, remove, serene, unstop, wholly **7** absolve, audible, audibly, certain, clearly, evident, express, fly over, glowing, halcyon, hop over, lighten, obvious, plainly, radiant, unblock **8** apparent, brighten, clear-cut, dazzling, definite, distinct, entirely, explicit, gleaming, leap over, luminous, manifest, pass over, pellucid, positive, skip over, unhidden **9** all the way, bound over, brilliant, cloudless, exculpate, exonerate, sparkling, unblocked, unclouded, unimpeded, unmuddled, vindicate, wide-awake **10** articulate, become fair, completely, diaphanous, discerning, distinctly, glistening, pronounced, unconfused, undeniable, unobscured **11** crystalline, inescapable, self-evident, translucent, transparent, unambiguous, unconcealed, undisguised, unequivocal, unqualified **12** articulately, intelligible, recognizable, unencumbered, unmistakable, unobstructed **14** comprehensible **15** distinguishable, straightforward

---

unambiguous, undisguised, unequivocal, well-defined **12** crystal-clear, unmistakable **14** comprehensible, understandable **15** straightforward

clearheaded 5 acute, alert, awake, aware, sharp **6** astute **8** rational, sensible **9** on the ball, practical, realistic, wide-awake **10** discerning, insightful, on one's toes, on the stick, perceptive **13** perspicacious

clearheadedness 7 insight **8** sagacity **9** alertness, sharpness **10** perception **11** discernment **12** perspicacity

clearing 5 glade

clearly 6 surely **7** plainly **8** markedly, palpably, patently **9** assuredly, certainly, decidedly, evidently, obviously **10** distinctly, manifestly, noticeably, observably, undeniably **11** beyond doubt, indubitably, perceptibly, undoubtedly **12** recognizably, unmistakably **13** unequivocally **14** beyond question, unquestionably

clearly expressed 8 coherent **10** articulate **11** unambiguous **12** intelligible

clearness 7 clarity **10** brightness, brilliance **12** explicitness **15** unmistakability

clear-sighted 4 sage, wise **5** acute, sharp **6** astute, shrewd **8** piercing **9** judicious, sagacious, sensitive **10** discerning, perceptive **11** intelligent, keen-sighted, penetrating **12** sharp-sighted **13** perspicacious

clear up 6 settle **7** clarify, unsnarl **8** untangle **11** disentangle **12** uncomplicate **13** straighten out

Cleary, Beverly
  author of: **6** Ramona **7** Fifteen **12** Henry Huggins **13** Jean and Johnny **15** Beezus and Ramona **16** Sister of the Bride

cleat 5 block, chock, spike, wedge **6** batten **7** bollard

cleavage 3 gap **4** rent, rift, slit **5** cleft, crack, notch, split **6** furrow, trench, trough **7** crevice, fissure, opening **8** crevasse

cleave 3 cut, hew **4** chop, fuse, hack, hold, open, part, plow, rend, rive, slit, tear **5** cling, crack, halve, sever, slash, slice, split, stick, unite **6** adhere, be true, bisect, cut off, detach, divide, furrow, sunder, uphold **7** abide by, chop off, disjoin, lay open, stand by **8** be joined, break off, hold fast, separate **9** disengage, dismember

cleaver 3 axe **4** tool **5** knife ridge

cleft 3 gap **4** rent, rift, slit **5** break, crack, notch, split **6** breach, cloven, cranny, divide, forked, furrow, trench, trough **7** crevice, divided, fissure, notched, opening, slotted **8** aperture, bisected, branched, cleavage, crevasse, division **10** separation **11** indentation

clemency 5 mercy **7** charity **8** humanity, kindness, leniency, mildness, softness, sympathy **9** tolerance **10** compassion, indulgence, moderation, temperance **11** benevolence, forbearance, magnanimity **12** mercifulness, pleasantness **13** forgivingness

clement 4 kind, mild, warm **5** balmy **6** benign, gentle, humane **7** lenient **8** merciful, tolerant **9** not severe, not strict **10** benevolent **13** compassionate

clench 3 set **4** grip **5** clasp, tense **6** clinch, clutch **7** stiffen, tighten **8** fasten on, hold fast **11** grasp firmly, strain tight **12** close tightly

Clennam, Arthur
  character in: **12** Little Dorrit
  author: **7** Dickens

Cleobis
  mother: **7** Cydippe
  brother: **5** Biton

Cleodaeus
  father: **6** Hyllus
  mother: **4** Iole
  grandfather: **8** Hercules

Cleone
  father: **6** Asopus

Cleopas see **4** Mary

Cleopatra
  queen of: **5** Egypt
  father: **7** Ptolemy
  brother/husband: **7** Ptolemy
  lover: **10** Mark Antony **12** Julius Caesar
  son: **9** Caesarion **15** Alexander Helios **19** Ptolemy Philadelphos
  daughter: **15** Cleopatra Selene
  death by: **3** asp **7** suicide

Cleopatra
  director:
    1934 version: **13** Cecil B DeMille
    1963 version: **17** Joseph L Mankiewicz
  cast:
    1934 version: **13** Henry Wilcoxon, Warren William **16** Claudette Colbert
    1963 version: **11** Rex Harrison **13** Richard Burton, Roddy McDowall **15** Elizabeth Taylor

Cleothera
  father: **9** Pandareus

clergy 6 rabbis **7** clerics, pastors, priests **8** ministry, prelates, the cloth **9** churchmen, clergymen, clericals, ministers, pastorate, preachers, rabbinate, the church, the pulpit **10** priesthood **14** the first estate

clergyman 5 padre, rabbi **6** cleric, father, parson, pastor, priest **7** prelate **8** chaplain, minister, preacher, reverend, sky pilot **9** churchman **13** man of the cloth

cleric 6 parson, pastor **8** chaplain, preacher **9** churchman,

clergyman 13 man of the cloth

clerical 6 cleric, filing, office, typing **7** clerkly **8** churchly, of clerks, pastoral, priestly **10** accounting, rabbinical **11** bookkeeping, ministerial **13** recordkeeping **14** ecclesiastical

clerical worker 5 clerk **6** typist **9** file clerk **10** bookkeeper, keypuncher **12** office worker **13** data processor

clerk 6 typist **8** salesman **9** file clerk **10** bookkeeper, salesclerk, saleswoman **11** salesperson **12** office worker

Cleta
  member of: **6** Graces
  worshipped at: **6** Sparta

Cleveland
  baseball team: **7** Indians
  basketball team: **9** Cavaliers
  football team: **6** Browns

Cleveland, Grover *see box*

clever 4 able, cute, deft, keen **5** acute, quick, sharp, smart, witty **6** adroit, artful, astute, bright, crafty, expert, shrewd **8** creative, humorous, original **9** ingenious, inventive **11** imaginative, intelligent, quick-witted, resourceful

cleverly 6 deftly **7** sharply, smartly, wittily **8** adroitly, artfully, craftily, expertly **10** creatively, humorously **11** ingeniously, inventively **13** imaginatively, intelligently

cleverness 3 wit **6** acumen **8** ableness, deftness, keenness **9** expertise, ingenuity, quickness, sharpness, smartness **10** adroitness, artfulness, astuteness, brightness, craftiness **12** intelligence, skillfulness **13** inventiveness **15** imaginativeness, quick-wittedness

clew see **4** clue

Clew
  thread in: **9** Labyrinth
  showed way to: **7** Theseus
  given by: **7** Ariadne

cliche 3 saw **6** old saw **7** bromide **8** banality, old story **9** platitude **10** stereotype **11** trite phrase

cliche-ridden 5 corny, stale, tired, trite, vapid **6** jejune **8** bromidic **9** hackneyed **10** unoriginal **13** platitudinous, unimaginative

click 3 tap **4** clap, snap **5** clack, clink, crack **6** rattle **7** crackle

Clide
  form: **5** nymph
  habitat: **5** Naxos

Cleveland, Grover
  name at birth: 22 Stephen Grover Cleveland
  nickname: 5 Grove
  presidential rank: 12 twenty-fourth, twenty-second
  party: 8 Democrat
  state represented: 2 NY
  defeated: 4 (Simon) Wing **6** (Benjamin Franklin) Butler, (James Baird) Weaver, (James Gillespie) Blaine, (John Pierce) St John **7** (John) Bidwell **8** (Belva Ann Bennett) Lockwood, (Benjamin) Harrison
  vice president: 9 (Adlai Ewing) Stevenson, (Thomas Andrews) Hendricks
  cabinet:
    state: **5** (Richard) Olney **6** (Thomas Francis) Bayard **7** (Walter Quinton) Gresham
    treasury: **7** (Daniel) Manning **8** (John Griffin) Carlisle **9** (Charles Stebbins) Fairchild
    war: **6** (David Scott) Lamont **8** (William Crowninshield) Endicott
    attorney general: **5** (Richard) Olney **6** (Judson) Harmon **7** (Augustus Hill) Garland
    interior: **5** (Hoke) Smith, (Lucius Quintus Cincinnatus) Lamar, (William Freeman) Vilas **7** (David Rowland) Francis
  born: 2 NJ **8** Caldwell
  died/buried: 2 NJ **9** Princeton
  education:
    high school: **16** Liberal Institute
  religion: 12 Presbyterian
  interests: 7 fishing **8** shooting **13** gun collecting
  political career:
    mayor of: **7** Buffalo
    governor of: **7** New York
  civilian career: 6 lawyer
  notable events of lifetime/term: 5 Panic (of 1893) **10** gold crisis (of 1895)
    Act: **6** Tariff **14** Dawes Severalty **18** Interstate Commerce
    strike: **7** Pullman
  father: 13 Richard Falley
  mother: 4 Anne (Neal)
  siblings: 7 Ann Neal **9** Mary Allen **11** Susan Sophia, William Neal **12** Richard Cecil **13** Rose Elizabeth **14** Lewis Frederick **20** Margaret Louise Falley
  wife: 7 Frances (Folsom)
  children: 4 Ruth **6** Esther, Marion **13** Francis Grover, Richard Folsom

client 5 buyer **6** patron **7** advisee, shopper **8** customer **9** purchaser **17** person represented

cliff 3 tor **4** crag **5** bluff, ledge **8** palisade **9** precipice **10** promontory

Cliff Dwellers *see* **6** Pueblo

Clift, Montgomery
  real name: 21 Edward Montgomery Clift
  nickname: 5 Monty
  born: 7 Omaha NE
  roles: 9 The Search **10** The Heiress, The Misfits **14** A Place in the Sun **18** From Here to Eternity, Suddenly Last Summer

climactic 7 crucial **8** critical, dramatic **11** sensational, suspenseful

climate 3 air **4** mood, tone **5** pulse **6** spirit, temper **7** quality, weather **8** ambience, attitude **9** character, condition **10** atmosphere **11** disposition, frame of mind, weather zone **12** usual weather **13** weather region **14** general feeling, weather pattern

climax 4 acme, apex, peak **5** crown **6** crisis, height, summit **8** best part, pinnacle **9** high point **10** denouement **11** culmination **12** highest point, turning point **13** critical point, crowning point, decisive point, supreme moment **18** moment of revelation

climb 4 go up, rise **5** mount, scale **6** ascend, ascent, come up **8** climbing **9** clamber up **10** scramble up

climb down 6 go down **7** descend **8** back down, come down

clinch 3 cap, fix, win **4** bind, bolt, grip, nail **5** cinch, clamp, clasp, close, crown, grasp, screw **6** assure, clutch, couple, decide, fasten, obtain, secure, settle, verify, wind up **7** confirm, grapple **8** complete, conclude, make fast, make sure **9** culminate, establish, finish off **10** grab hold of, hold firmly **12** seize and hold **13** ensure victory

cling 3 hug **4** fuse, grip, hold **5** clasp, grasp, stick **6** adhere, be true, cleave, clutch **7** stand by **8** hang on to, hold fast, hold on to, maintain **9** stay close **10** be constant, be faithful, grab hold of

clinging 6 sticky **7** holding **8** adherent, adhering, adhesive, clasping, cleaving, grasping, gripping, sticking **9** hanging on, holding on **11** holding fast **12** grabbing hold

clinic 9 infirmary **10** polyclinic **13** medical center **15** outpatients' ward

Clinis
  form: 3 man
  home: 11 Mesopotamia
  loved by: 6 Apollo **7** Artemis

clink 4 ting **5** clack, clank, click **6** jangle, jingle, rattle, tinkle **11** ring sharply

clinkers 4 duds, slag **5** dross, flops **6** cinder, scoria **8** failures

Clinton, William Jefferson
see box p. 188

Clio
  muse of: 7 history

clip 3 bob, cut, fix **4** crop, grip, hook, snip, trim **5** clamp, clasp, shear **6** attach, buckle, clinch, couple, cut off, cut out, fasten, paring, secure, staple **7** cutting, shorten **8** clipping, cropping, cut short, fastener, shearing, snipping

clipper 4 boat, ship **6** cutter, shears **8** aircraft, airplane, sailboat, scissors **9** racehorse

clipping 7 cutting, pruning, snippet **8** trimming

clique 3 set **4** clan, gang **5** crowd, group **6** circle **7** coterie, faction

cliquish 4 cold **5** aloof **7** distant **8** clannish, snobbish **9** exclusive **10** unfriendly **11** unreceptive

Clite
  father: 6 Merops

Clinton, William Jefferson
original last name: **6** Blythe
nickname: **4** Bill
presidential rank: **11** forty-second
party: **10** Democratic
state represented: **2** AR
8 Arkansas
defeated: **4** (George) Bush
4 (Robert) Dole
vice president: **4** (Albert) Gore
cabinet:
  state: **8** (Madeleine) Albright **11** (Warren) Christopher
  treasury: **5** (Robert) Rubin **7** (Lloyd) Bentsen
  attorney general: **4** (Janet) Reno
  defense: **5** (William) Cohen
  interior: **7** (Bruce) Babbitt
  labor: **5** (Robert) Reich
  HUD: **8** (Henry) Cisneros
born: **2** AR **4** Hope
education: **6** Oxford **7** Yale Law **10** Georgetown
honor: **13** Rhodes scholar
political career:
  governor of: **8** Arkansas
  attorney general of: **8** Arkansas
notable events of lifetime/term: **5** NAFTA **6** Bosnia **10** Whitewater **13** Anti-crime Bill, **15** Branch Davidians
Supreme Court appointments: **13** Stephen Breyer **17** Ruth Bader Ginsburg
father: **13** William Blythe
mother: **21** Virginia Cassidy Blythe
stepfather: **12** Roger Clinton
sibling: **12** Roger Clinton
wife: **13** Hillary Rodham
children: **7** Chelsea

husband: **7** Cyzicus
killed by: **7** hanging, suicide

cloak 4 cape, hide, mask, robe, veil, wrap **5** cover, tunic **6** mantle, screen, shield, shroud **7** conceal, curtain, pelisse, secrete **8** burnoose, disguise **10** camouflage **11** concealment

cloaked 7 covered, muffled, wrapped **9** disguised

cloaking 7 masking, veiling **8** covering **9** obscuring **10** disguising

cloakroom 8 anteroom, coatroom

clobber 3 hit **4** beat, belt, drub, lick, maul, rout, slug, sock, trim, whip **5** clout, pound, punch, smash, smear, whack **6** batter, beat up, strike, subdue, thrash, wallop **7** conquer, shellac, trounce **8** beat up on, lambaste

clock 5 watch **8** horologe **9** timepiece **11** chronometer

Clockwork Orange, A
author: **14** Anthony Burgess
director: **14** Stanley Kubrick
cast: **12** Patrick Magee **13** Adrienne Corri **15** Malcolm McDowell

clod 3 oaf, wad **4** boor, dolt, dope, glob, hunk, lout, lump, rube **5** chunk, clown, clump, dummy, dunce, moron, yokel **7** bumpkin, fathead **8** imbecile, numskull **9** blockhead, ignoramus, simpleton

clodhopper 3 oaf **4** boot, clod, hick, lout, rube, slob **5** booby, clown, yokel **6** galoot, lubber, lummox, rustic **7** bumpkin, hayseed, peasant, plowboy, redneck **8** clodpole, lunkhead **9** heavy shoe, hillbilly **10** provincial

clog 4 stop **5** block, check, choke, close, dam up **6** stop up

7 barrier, congest **8** blockage, obstacle, obstruct, stoppage **9** restraint **10** impediment **11** obstruction

clogged 6 choked, halted, jammed **7** clotted, impeded **8** choked up, filled up, hampered, hindered, restrained **10** encumbered, obstructed, overloaded

cloister 4 stoa, walk **5** abbey, aisle **6** arcade, closet, coop up, friary, hole up, immure, shut up, wall up **7** conceal, confine, convent, embower, gallery, nunnery, passage, portico, seclude, walkway **8** shut away **9** colonnade, courtyard, monastery, promenade, sequester **10** ambulatory, passageway

cloistered 5 alone, aloof, apart **6** hidden **7** immured, recluse **8** closeted, confined, detached, isolated, secluded, secreted, separate, solitary **9** concealed, insulated, sheltered, withdrawn **11** dissociated, sequestered

clone 4 copy **5** robot **6** double **7** android, replica **9** automaton, duplicate, replicate **10** carbon copy **12** doppelganger **13** identical copy

close *see box*

closed 6 secret **7** private **9** exclusive

closed-minded 5 rigid **7** adamant, uptight **8** obdurate, stubborn **9** hidebound, obstinate, pig-headed, unbending **10** inflexible, unyielding **12** intransigent **14** uncompromising

close 3 end, hot, pen **4** akin, clog, fast, fill, firm, fuse, halt, join, keen, link, near, neat, nigh, plug, shut, stop, trim, warm **5** alert, block, cease, dense, fixed, humid, muggy, pen in, sharp, short, solid, stuff, tight, unite **6** allied, at hand, clog up, coop up, couple, ending, fill in, fill up, finale, finish, hard by, intent, jammed, loving, narrow, nearby, next to, plug up, recess, secure, shut in, shut up, smooth, stingy, stop up, stuffy, windup **7** adjourn, careful, close up, closing, compact, confine, connect, cramped, crowded, devoted, dismiss, enclose, intense, miserly, pinched, seal off, shut off, similar, stuffed, suspend, teeming **8** attached, blockade, break off, conclude, confined, familiar, friendly, grudging, imminent, intimate, leave off, obstruct, populous, shut down, squeezed, stagnant, stifling, stinting, swarming, thorough, vigilant, watchful **9** attentive, congested, impending, niggardly, penurious, scrimping, terminate **10** almost like, completion, compressed, conclusion, nearly even, nip-and-tuck, resembling, restricted, sweltering, ungenerous **11** almost alike, approaching, approximate, close-fisted, discontinue, forthcoming, impermeable, in proximity, inseparable, nearly equal, neighboring, suffocating, termination, tight-fisted, well-matched **12** bring to an end, impenetrable, parsimonious, unventilated **13** bring together, near to the skin, penny-pinching, uncomfortable **14** thick as thieves

Close Encounters of the Third Kind
director: **15** Steven Spielberg
cast: **8** Teri Garr **13** Melinda Dillon **15** Richard Dreyfuss **16** Francois Truffaut
score: **12** John Williams

closefisted 4 mean **5** cheap, close, mingy, tight **6** stingy **7** miserly **8** grudging **9** niggardly, penurious **10** economical, ungenerous **11** close-handed, tightfisted **12** parsimonious **13** penny-pinching

close-fitting 4 snug **5** tight **9** skintight **11** constricted, form-fitting **12** constricting, tight-fitting **15** like a second skin

close friend 3 pal **4** chum, mate **5** buddy, crony **6** cohort **7** best pal **8** alter ego, intimate **9** companion, confidant **10** bosom buddy **17** intimate confidant

close loudly 4 bang, clap, slam

closely 6 keenly **7** alertly, sharply **8** intently **9** carefully, heedfully, intensely **10** diligently, vigilantly, vigorously, watchfully **11** attentively

close-mouthed 3 shy **4** cool **5** terse **7** bashful, distant **8** reserved, reticent, retiring, taciturn **9** diffident, secretive, withdrawn **11** tight-lipped **15** uncommunicative

closeness 8 meanness, nearness **10** stinginess **11** familiarity, miserliness **15** tightfistedness

close of day 3 eve **4** dusk, even **6** sunset **7** evening, sundown **8** eventide, gloaming, twilight **9** nightfall

closet 2 WC **4** eury, safe **5** ambry, cuddy **6** covert, hidden, locker pantry, secret, toilet **7** cabinet, private **8** coatroom, cupboard, imprison, secluded **9** cloakroom, storeroom, visionary **11** speculative, theoretical, unpractical, water closet

close tightly 3 set **4** seal, slam **5** latch **6** clench, secure **13** press together

close to 4 near **6** almost, around **9** just about **12** on the point of **13** approximately

closure 3 lid, tap **4** bung, cork, plug, stop **5** cover **6** ending, faucet, finish, spigot **7** barring, bolting, closing, cloture, locking, sealing, stopper **8** securing, shutting, stoppage **9** cessation **10** conclusion, stoppering **11** termination **14** discontinuance **15** discontinuation

clot 3 gob **4** lump, mass **7** congeal, thicken **8** embolism, solidify, thrombus **9** coagulate, occlusion **11** coagulation

Cloten
character in: **9** Cymbeline
author: **11** Shakespeare

cloth 5 goods **6** fabric **7** textile **8** dry goods, material **9** yard goods **10** piece goods

clothe 3 don **4** case, coat, deck, garb, robe, veil, wrap **5** array, cloak, cloud, cover, drape, dress **6** attire, bedeck, encase, enwrap, outfit, rig out, screen, shroud **7** bedizen, costume, deck out, envelop, sheathe, swaddle **8** accouter

clothed 4 clad **5** robed **6** draped **7** cloaked, couched, covered, dressed, mantled, wearing **8** equipped, provided **9** expressed, furnished

clothes 4 duds, garb, rags, togs, wear **5** dress **8** attire, finery **7** apparel, costume, raiment, regalia **8** clothing, ensemble, garments, wardrobe **11** habiliments

clotheshorse 3 fop **5** dandy, model **12** Beau Brummell, fashion plate, man of fashion, sharp dresser **14** woman of fashion

clothing see **7** clothes

Clotho
member of: **5** Fates
spinner of: **12** thread of life

cloud 3 dim, mar **4** blur, hide, veil **5** blind, cloak, cover, muddy, shade, sully, upset **6** darken, impair, muddle, screen, shadow, shroud **7** conceal, confuse, curtain, distort, disturb, eclipse, obscure, tarnish **8** overcast **9** discredit, make vague **10** overshadow **11** cast doubt on **14** call to question **19** place under suspicion

cloudburst 6 deluge **8** downpour, rainfall **9** rainstorm

clouded 3 dim **5** dusky, murky **7** blurred, obscure, sullied, tainted, unclear **8** confused, darkened, obscured **10** ill-defined, indistinct

cloudless 4 fair **5** clear, sunny **6** bright **7** halcyon **8** sunshiny **9** unclouded **10** unobscured

Clouds
goddess of: **3** Fri **5** Frigg, Frija **6** Frigga

Clouds, The (Nephelai)
author: **12** Aristophanes
character: **8** Just Plea, Socrates

10 Unjust Plea **11** Strepsiades **12** Pheidippides

cloudy 4 dark, gray, hazy **5** murky, vague **6** dreary, gloomy, leaden, veiled **7** clouded, obscure, sunless, unclear **8** confused, nebulous, overcast **9** confusing, undefined **10** indefinite, mysterious **11** overclouded

Clouet, Jean
born: **8** Flanders
artwork attributed: **13** Guillaume Bude **16** Madame de Canaples, Man with Gold Coins **17** The Count of Brissac, The Dauphin Francis **22** Man with a Book by Petrarch

clout 3 box, hit, jab **4** bash, belt, blow, pull, sock **5** crack, knock, punch, smack, thump, whack **6** wallop **9** influence **10** importance

clove
botanical name: **16** Eugenia aromatica **18** Syzygium aromaticum
origin: **5** Pemba **7** Far East **8** Moluccas, Zanzibar **9** Mauritius **10** Madagascar
use: **3** ham **8** pickling, pomander **16** yellow vegetables

cloven 5 cleft, split **7** divided, notched, slotted **8** bisected

clover 9 Trifolium
varieties: **3** bur, elk, hop, low, pin, red **4** bush, holy, Kura, musk, owl's, tick **5** Alyce, Hubam, lucky, sweet, water, white **6** Alsike, cow hop, indoor, Korean, Ladino, yellow **7** Bukhara, crimson, Italian, mammoth, Mexican, Persian, prairie **8** Japanese, large hop, reversed, small hop, stinking **9** Hungarian **10** strawberry, toothed bur, white Dutch, white sweet **11** yellow sweet **12** silky prairie, subterranean, white prairie **13** European water **16** strawberry-headed

clown 3 wag, wit **4** card, fool, jest, joke, mime, zany **5** comic, cut up, joker **6** jester, madcap **7** buffoon **8** comedian, humorist **9** harlequin, kid around **10** comedienne, fool around **11** funny person, merry-andrew

clownishness 6 antics **10** buffoonery, tomfoolery **12** monkeyshines **14** playing the fool

cloy 3 gag **4** bore, glut, pall, sate, tire **5** choke, weary **6** benumb, overdo **7** exhaust, satiate, surfeit **8** nauseate, saturate

cloying 5 sweet **6** sugary **9** excessive, satiating **10** saccharine

club 3 bat, hit **4** bash, beat, flog, slug **5** billy, flail, group, guild, lay on, lodge, stick, union **6** batter, buffet, cudgel, league, pommel, pummel, strike **7** society **8** alliance, bludgeon, sorority **9** billyclub, clubhouse, truncheon **10** fraternity, shillelagh, sisterhood **11** affiliation, association, brotherhood, country club

clubhouse 4 club, hall **5** lodge **11** locker rooms **12** meeting house

clue 3 cue, key **4** clew, hint, mark, sign **5** guide, scent, trace **7** glimmer, inkling, pointer **8** evidence **9** indicator, inference **10** indication, intimation, suggestion **11** insinuation

clump 4 bulb, bump, knob, knot, lump, mass, plod, thud **5** batch, bunch, clomp, clunk, copse, group, grove, plunk, shock, stamp, stomp, thump, tramp **6** lumber **7** cluster, thicket **9** aggregate **10** assemblage, collection

clumsiness 9 gawkiness **10** ineptitude **11** awkwardness **12** carelessness, ungainliness **13** gracelessness, maladroitness

clumsy 5 bulky, crude, gawky, inept, rough **6** klutzy **7** awkward, unhandy **8** bungling, careless, ungainly, unwieldy **9** graceless, makeshift, maladroit, unskilled **10** blundering, cumbersome, ungraceful **11** heavy-handed **12** illcontrived, unmanageable **14** butterfingered **21** like a bull in a china shop

cluster 4 band, bevy, heap, herd, knot, mass, pack, pile **5** amass, batch, block, bunch, clump, crowd, flock, group, sheaf, shock, swarm **6** gather, muster, throng **7** collect, company **8** assemble, converge **9** aggregate **10** accumulate, assemblage, collection, congregate **12** accumulation, congregation **13** agglomeration **14** conglomeration

cluster around 6 gather **7** collect **10** congregate **12** herd together **13** flock together

clutch 3 hug **4** grip, hold **5** clasp, grasp **6** clench **7** cling to, embrace, squeeze **8** hang on to

clutter 4 fill, heap, mess, pile **5** chaos, strew **6** jumble, litter, tangle **7** scatter **8** disarray, disorder **9** confusion **10** hodgepodge

cluttered 5 messy **7** chaotic, crowded, jumbled, muddled **8** confused, littered **9** scattered **10** disordered, disorderly

Clymene
  origin: 5 Greek
  mentioned in: 5 Iliad
  form: 5 nymph
  habitat: 5 ocean
  father: 6 Mimyas, Minyas **7** Catreus, Oceanus
  mother: 6 Tethys
  husband: 7 Iapetus **8** Cephalus, Phaethon, Phylacus
  son: 4 Oeax **5** Atlas **8** Iphiclus, Phaethon **9** Palamedes **10** Epimetheus, Nausimedon, Prometheus
  daughter: 8 Alcimede
  attended: 11 Helen of Troy
  sold to: 8 Nauplius
  beloved of: 3 Sun

Clymenus
  king of: 10 Orchomenus
  grandfather: 7 Phrixus
  son: 7 Erginus
  daughter: 9 Harpalyce
  violated: 9 Harpalyce
  home: 7 Arcadia

Clytemnestra
  father: 9 Tyndareus
  mother: 4 Leda
  brother: 6 Castor, Pollux
  sister: 5 Helen **8** Timandra
  cousin: 8 Perilaus
  husband: 9 Agamemnon
  son: 7 Orestes
  daughter: 7 Electra, Erigone **9** Iphigenia **12** Chrysothemis
  lover: 9 Aegisthus
  killed: 9 Agamemnon
  killed by: 7 Orestes

Clytie
  form: 5 nymph
  habitat: 5 water
  loved: 6 Apollo
  changed into: 10 heliotrope

Clytius
  member of: 8 Gigantes
  father: 8 Laomedon
  brother: 5 Priam
  companion of: 5 Jason
  killed by: 8 Hercules

coach 3 bus **5** drill, guide, sedan, stage, teach, train, tutor **6** advise, direct, mentor **7** omnibus, trainer **8** carriage, instruct **9** limousine, preceptor **10** automobile, four-in-hand, motor coach, stagecoach **11** four-wheeler, second class **12** economy class **14** private teacher **16** athletic director

coachman 3 fly **4** jehu, whip **5** pilot **6** driver **10** charioteer

Coactrice 14 poisonous snake

coagulate 3 gel, set **4** clot,

jell **6** curdle, harden **7** congeal, jellify, thicken **8** solidify

coagulation 3 gob **4** clot, mass **8** clotting, curdling, thrombus **10** thickening

coal 4 ash, bass, char, coke, coom, culm, dust, fuel, slag, smut, swad **5** ember **6** cannel, cinder **7** lignite, clinker **8** charcoal **10** fossil fuel **11** charred wood
  box: 3 hod **7** scuttle
  made from: 6 carbon
  type: 4 hard, soft **7** lignite **10** anthracite, bituminous
  mining method: 4 deep **8** opencast **10** strip auger **11** underground
  mine: 5 drift, shaft, slope, strip
  size: 3 egg, nut, pea **5** stove

coal-black 3 jet **4** dark, inky **5** black, ebony, raven, sable **9** pitch-dark

coalesce 3 mix **4** ally, form, fuse, join, meld **5** blend, merge, unify, unite **6** cohere **7** combine **9** become one, integrate **10** amalgamate, join forces **11** agglutinate, consolidate **12** band together, come together **14** form an alliance

coalition 5 union **6** fusion, league **7** society **8** alliance **9** syndicate **10** federation **11** affiliation, association, combination, confederacy, partnership **12** amalgamation **13** agglomeration, consolidation **14** conglomeration

Coal Miner's Daughter
  director: 12 Michael Apted
  cast: 9 Levon Helm **11** Sissy Spacek (Loretta Lynn) **13** Tommy Lee Jones **14** Beverly D'Angelo
  Oscar for: 7 actress (Spacek)
  screenplay: 10 Tom Rickman

Coaluitecan
  tribe: 6 Payaya

coarse 4 lewd, rude, vile **5** crass, crude, dirty, gross, harsh, rough **6** common, nubbly, odious, ribald, shaggy, sordid, vulgar **7** boorish, bristly, brutish, ill-bred, loutish, obscene, prickly, uncouth **8** impolite, improper, indecent, scratchy **9** bristling, inelegant, offensive, repulsive, revolting, sandpaper, unrefined **10** disgusting, indecorous, indelicate, lascivious, licentious, scurrilous, unladylike, unpolished **11** foul-mouthed, illmannered **12** lacking taste **13** rough-textured, ungentlemanly

coarse-grained 5 crude, harsh,

nubby, rough **6** coarse, grainy, shaggy **7** bristly **8** scratchy **9** unrefined **13** rough-textured

coarseness 9 crudeness, grossness, roughness, vulgarity **10** indelicacy, inelegance **11** boorishness **16** lack of refinement

coast 4 skim, slip, waft **5** drift, float, glide, shore, slide, sweep **6** strand **7** seaside **8** glissade, littoral, seaboard, seacoast, seashore **9** shoreline

coaster 3 mat **4** ship, sled, tray **5** wagon **6** cradle, glider, slider **8** toboggan **9** tray stand **13** decanter stand, roller coaster

coat 3 fur **4** hair, hide, pelt, wrap **5** cover, glaze, layer, paint, smear **6** blazer, enamel, encase, jacket, spread **7** coating, encrust, envelop, lacquer, overlay, plaster, slicker, topcoat **8** covering, laminate, mackinaw, overcoat, raincoat **9** whitewash **10** mackintosh, sports coat

coating 4 coat, film, skin **5** layer, sheet **6** veneer **7** overlay **8** covering, envelope

coat of arms 4 arms **5** crest **6** creast **8** insignia **9** blaconwry **10** escutcheon **14** heraldic emblem **16** armorial bearings

coat of mail 4 mail **5** armor **9** chain mail **11** suit of armor

Coat of Varnish, A
author: **6** C P Snow

coax 6 cajole **7** wheedle **8** butter up, inveigle, soft-soap, talk into **9** sweet-talk

cobalt 4 blue **5** azure **7** element, sky blue **10** bright blue **12** greenish blue
chemical symbol: **2** Co

Cobb, Lee J
born: **9** New York NY
roles: **10** Willy Loman **12** The Virginian **14** Twelve Angry Men **15** On the Waterfront **16** Death of a Salesman

Cobb, Ty (Tyrus Raymond)
nickname: **12** Georgia Peach
sport: **8** baseball
position: **8** outfield
team: **13** Detroit Tigers

cobbler 3 pie **9** bootmaker, shoemaker **12** shoe repairer **16** deepdish fruit pie

cobra
also: **3** asp **5** mamba **11** hooded snake
native to: **4** Asia **6** Africa

kind: 4 king **6** hooded, Indian **8** Egyptian
enemy: **8** mongoose

Coburn, Charles
born: **10** Savannah GA
roles: **9** Boss Tweed **17** The More the Merrier

Coburn, James
born: **8** Laurel NE
roles: **11** In Like Flint, Our Man Flint **14** The Great Escape **19** The Magnificent Seven

Coca, Imogene
partner: **9** Sid Caesar
born: **14** Philadelphia PA
roles: **15** Your Show of Shows

Cocalus
king of: **6** Sicily

Coccygius
epithet of: **4** Zeus
means: **6** cuckoo

cock 3 tip **4** knob **5** raise, valve **6** faucet, handle, perk up **7** rooster, stand up **8** cockerel, male bird, set erect **9** bristle up **11** chanticleer **13** turn to one side **16** raise the hammer of **17** draw back the hammer

cockade 4 knot **5** badge **6** ribbon **7** rosette **8** ornament **10** party badge

Cockade State
nickname of: **8** Maryland

cock-and-bull story 3 fib, lie **4** myth, yarn **5** fable **7** fiction, untruth, whopper **9** fairy tale, falsehood, fish story, invention, tall story **11** fabrication **13** prevarication

Cockcroft, John Douglas
field: **7** physics
nationality: **7** British
developed: **24** Cockcroft-Walton generator
worked with: **6** Walton
awarded: **10** Nobel Prize

cockeyed 3 mad **4** awry, wild **5** askew, crazy, goofy, inane, nutty, weird **6** absurd, aslant, insane, tilted **7** crooked, foolish, twisted **8** lopsided, sideways **9** irregular, off-center, senseless **10** cockamamie, out of whack, ridiculous, unbalanced **11** nonsensical **12** asymmetrical, preposterous

Cockpit of Europe see **7** Belgium

cockscomb 4 comb **5** crest **7** celosia, coxcomb **8** amaranth, caruncle

cocksure 4 pert, smug, vain

5 brash, cocky, pushy **6** cheeky, snooty **8** arrogant, positive **9** assertive, audacious, bumptious, conceited **10** aggressive, swaggering **11** overbearing, self-assured, swellheaded **13** overconfident, self-confident

cocktail 5 drink, fruit, horse **6** shrimp **10** docked tail, semiformal
type: **4** grog **6** brandy, gibson, gimlet, mai tai, rob roy, zombie **7** gin fizz, martini, sidecar, stinger **8** daiquiri, highball, hot toddy, pink lady **9** cuba libre, hurricane, gin rickey, manhattan, margarita, mint julep, rusty nail **10** bloody mary, tom collins **11** boilermaker, gin and tonic, grasshopper, screwdriver, sloe gin fizz **12** black russian, old-fashioned, tom and jerry, whiskey sour **13** planter's punch **15** brandy alexander
mixer: **4** soda **5** tonic, water **7** bitters, seltzer **9** ginger ale
garnish: **4** lime **5** lemon, olive, orange, twist **16** maraschino cherry

cocktail lounge 3 bar **6** saloon, tavern **7** gin mill, taproom

cocky 5 brash, saucy **6** jaunty **8** arrogant, cocksure, impudent **9** conceited, egotistic **10** swaggering

Cocles see **8** Horatius

Coco, James
born: **9** New York NY
roles: **11** Sancho Panza **13** Man of La Mancha **21** Last of the Red Hot Lovers

cocoa 5 brown, cacao **9** chocolate **12** hot chocolate

cocoon
covering for: **5** larva
stage: **5** pupal
made of: **4** silk

Cocteau, Jean
author of: **7** Orpheus **8** Antigone **12** Blood of a Poet **18** The Infernal Machine **19** Les Enfants Terribles, Les Parents Terribles **20** The Beauty and the Beast

Cocytus
river in: **5** Hades

coddle 3 pat, pet **4** baby **5** humor, spoil **6** caress, cuddle, dote on, fondle, pamper **7** indulge **11** mollycoddle

code 4 laws **5** rules **6** cipher **7** statute **8** precepts **9** ordinance, standards **10** crypto-

gram, guidelines, principles
11 cryptograph, proprieties,
regulations **13** secret writing
14 secret language

codger 5 crank, miser **6** oddity,
old man **9** eccentric, odd
person

codicil 5 rider **8** addendum, addition, appendix **9** extension,
subscript **10** postscript, supplement **11** added clause

codify 4 rank, rate **5** grade,
group, index, order **7** arrange,
catalog **8** classify, organize,
tabulate **9** methodize **10** categorize, coordinate, regularize
11 systematize

coelenterate 5 coral, hydra,
polyp **6** Medusa **7** acaleph, radiate **8** acalephe **9** jellyfish
10 sea anemone
  habitat: 5 ocean **9** salt water

Coelophysis
  type: 8 dinosaur, therapod
  location: 7 Arizona
  period: 8 Triassic

coequal 5 equal **10** coordinate
16 equally important

coequality 6 parity **8** equality,
evenness, sameness **10** uniformity **11** equivalency
14 correspondence

coerce 3 cow **4** make **5** bully,
drive, force **6** compel, oblige
7 dragoon **8** browbeat, bulldoze, pressure, threaten
9 constrain, strong-arm
10 intimidate

coercer 5 bully **9** oppressor,
tormenter, tormentor
10 browbeater **11** intimidator,
petty tyrant

coercion 5 force **6** duress
7 threats **8** bullying, pressure
10 compulsion, constraint
11 browbeating
12 intimidation

coercive 8 enforced, forcible
10 compulsory, obligatory
11 threatening

Coeus
  form: 5 Titan
  father: 6 Uranus
  mother: 4 Gaea
  daughter: 4 Leto **7** Asteria

coexist with 12 go hand in
hand, go side by side, live together **13** go hand in glove

coffee 6 Coffea **13** Coffea
arabica
  varieties: 4 Java, Kona,
  Wild **5** Irish, Mocha **6** Almond, Common **7** Arabian,
  Arabica, Robusta, Vanilla
  8 Liberian, Liberica, Zanzibar **9** Colombian **11** French
  Roast, Wild robusta **13** De-

caffeinated **20** Jamaican
Blue Mountain
  beverage: 6 kahlua **8** es-
  presso **10** cafe au lait,
  cappuccino
  small cup: 9 demitasse

coffee (black)
  French: 8 cafe noir **10** cafe
  nature

coffee brandy 6 Kahlua **8** Tia
Maria

coffee with milk
  French: 10 cafe au lait

coffer 3 box **4** case **5** chest
9 strongbox **10** depository, repository **13** treasure chest

coffers 5 safes **6** vaults **8** treasury **9** cash boxes **11** money
supply

coffin 3 box **4** pall **6** casket
10 catafalque **11** sarcophagus

cog 3 cam, lie **4** gear **5** cheat,
cozen, tenon, tooth, wedge,
wheel **8** small boat
10 projection

cogent 5 sound, valid **6** potent **7** weighty **8** forceful,
powerful **9** effective, trenchant **10** compelling, convincing,
persuasive, undeniable
11 meritorious, well-founded
12 well-grounded
16 incontrovertible

cogitate 5 study, think, weigh
6 ponder **7** reflect **8** meditate,
mull over, ruminate **9** think
over **10** deliberate, think
about **11** contemplate, reflect
upon **18** consider thoroughly

cogito ergo sum 18 I think
therefore I am
  said by: 9 Descartes

cognac
  type: 6 brandy **7** liqueur
  origin: 6 France
  brand: 7 Bisquit, Martell
  8 Hennessy **10** Remy Martin **11** Courvoisier
  label: 2 VO (very old), VS
  (very special), XO (extra
  old) **3** XXO (extra
  old) **4** VSOP (very superior
  old pale) **8** Napoleon (5 year
  premium)
  drink: 9 Andalusia
  with Cointreau: 10 Rolls
  Royce
  with Triple Sec: 7 Chicago
  10 Rolls Royce
  with vodka: 7 Cossack

cognate 5 akin, like **5** alike,
close **7** kindred, related, similar **8** familial, parallel, relative **9** affiliate **10** derivative
11 consanguine

cognition 7 knowing **9** awareness, knowledge **11** familiar-

ity **13** comprehension,
understanding

cognizance 4 heed, note
5 grasp **6** notice, regard
8 scrutiny **9** attention, awareness, cognition, knowledge
10 perception **11** familiarity,
observation, recognition, sensibility **12** apprehension
13 comprehension, consciousness, understanding

cognizant 5 aware **6** posted
7 knowing, mindful **8** familiar,
informed, versed in **9** conscious **10** acquainted, conversant, instructed
11 enlightened **13** knowledgeable, understanding

cognomen 4 name **6** handle
7 epithet, moniker, surname
11 appellation, designation

cognoscenti 6 judges **7** ex-
perts **8** insiders **11** authorities
12 connoisseurs **14** those in
the know

cohere 3 fit, set **4** bind, fuse,
glue, hold, jibe, join **5** agree,
cling, match, stick, tally,
unite **6** cement, concur,
square **7** combine, conform,
congeal **8** coalesce, coincide,
dovetail, solidify **9** coagulate,
harmonize **10** correspond
11 consolidate, synchronize
12 hold together **13** stick
together

coherence 5 logic, unity
7 clarity, concord, harmony
8 cohesion **9** congruity **10** accordance, conformity, conso-
nance **11** consistency,
rationality **12** organization

coherent 5 clear, lucid **7** logical, orderly **8** cohesive, rational **9** congruous, connected, in
keeping, organized **10** articulate, consistent, harmonious,
meaningful, systematic **11** in
agreement **12** intelligible
13 corresponding **14** comprehensible, understandable

cohesion 4 bond **5** union, unity **7** bonding **8** adhesion
10 attraction, solidarity

cohesive 3 set **5** solid **6** sticky
7 viscous **8** cemented, coherent, cohering, sticking **9** connected **11** indivisible,
inseparable **12** consolidated
13 agglutinative

Cohn, Ferdinand Julius
  field: 6 botany
  nationality: 6 German
  founded: 12 bacteriology

Cohn, Robert
  character in: 15 The Sun
  Also Rises
  author: 9 Hemingway

cohort 3 pal 4 chum 5 buddy, crony 6 fellow, friend 7 comrade 8 follower, myrmidon 9 associate, companion 10 accomplice

coif 3 cap 4 hood, veil 6 beggin, burlet, hairdo 8 biggonet, coiffure, skull cap 9 head-dress

coiffed 6 capped, styled 7 dressed 8 arranged

coiffeur 7 stylist 11 hairdresser 15 male hairdresser

coiffure 2 DA, GI 3 bob, bun 4 Afro, coif, perm, shag, trim, wave 6 hairdo 7 beehive, blow-cut, comb-out, flattop, haircut, pageboy, upsweep 8 cold wave, cornrows, ducktail 9 hairstyle, permanent, pompadour

coil 4 curl, loop, ring, roll, wind 5 braid, twine, twist 6 circle, spiral, writhe 7 entwine 8 encircle

coin 4 mint 5 hatch, money, piece 6 change, create, devise, invent, make up, silver, strike 7 concoct, dream up, think up 8 conceive 9 fabricate, originate

coin/currency *see box*

coincide 3 fit 4 jibe, meet 5 agree, cross, match, tally 6 accord, concur, square 7 conform 8 converge, dovetail 9 harmonize 10 correspond 11 synchronize 12 be concurrent, come together 19 occur simultaneously

coincidence 4 fate, luck 6 chance 8 accident 11 concurrence, synchronism 12 happenstance 22 simultaneous occurrence

coincident 10 coexistent, concurrent 12 contemporary, simultaneous 15 contemporaneous

---

coin/currency
 of Afghanistan: 3 pul 5 abaze, riyal, rupee 6 abbasi, amania 7 afghani
 of Albania: 3 lek 5 franc 6 qintar 7 quintar
 of Algeria: 5 dinar 7 centime
 of Andorra: 5 franc 6 peseta
 of Angola: 6 escudo, kwanza, macuta, macute 7 angolar, centavo
 of Argentina: 4 peso 7 centavo 9 argentino
 of Armenia: 5 ruble
 of Australia: 4 dump, tray, zack 5 pound 6 dollar 8 shilling
 of Austria: 4 lira 5 crown, ducat, krone 6 florin, gulden, heller, zehner 8 albertin, groschen, kreutzer 9 schilling
 of Azerbaijan: 5 manat
 of Bahrain: 5 dinar
 of Bangladesh: 4 taka 5 paisa
 of Belarus: 5 ruble
 of Belgium: 5 belga, franc 7 brabant, centime, crocard
 of Benin: 5 franc 7 centime
 of Bhutan: 5 paisa, rupee 7 chetrum 8 ngultrum
 of Bolivia: 4 peso 7 centavo 9 boliviano
 of Bosnia-Herzegovina: 5 dinar
 of Botswana: 4 pula, rand
 of Brazil: 3 joe 4 reis 5 dobra 7 centara, halfjoe, milreis 8 cruzeiro
 of Bulgaria: 3 lev 8 stotinki
 of Burkina Faso: 5 franc 7 centime
 of Burundi: 5 franc 7 centime

 of Cambodia: 3 sen 4 quan, riel 6 puttan 7 piaster
 of Cameroon: 5 franc 7 centime
 of Canary Islands: 6 peseta
 of Cape Verde: 6 escudo 7 centavo
 of Central African Republic: 5 franc 7 centime
 of Chad: 5 franc 7 centime
 of Chile: 4 peso 5 libra 6 condor, escudo
 of China: 4 cash, cent, fyng, mace, tael, tiao, yuan 5 sycee 12 jen nin piao pu
 of Colombia: 4 peso, real 6 condor, peseta 7 centavo
 of Comoros: 5 franc 7 centime
 of Congo: 5 franc 7 centime
 of Costa Rica: 5 colon 6 colone 7 centimo
 of Crete: 7 drachma
 of Croatia: 5 dinar
 of Cuba: 4 peso 7 centavo 8 cuarenta
 of Cyprus 4 para 5 pound
 of Czechoslovakia/Czech Republic: 5 crown, ducat 6 heller, koruna
 of Denmark: 3 one, ora, ore 4 fyrk 5 krone 8 frederik, skilling 9 rigsdaler
 of Djibouti: 5 franc 7 centime
 of Dominican Republic: 3 oro 4 peso 6 franco
 of Ecuador: 5 sucre 7 centavo
 of Egypt: 4 fils, kees, para 5 asper, dinar, fodda, gersh, girsh, medin, pound, riyal 6 ahmadi, dirham, foddah, guinea, junayh, maidin,

 medine, medino 7 piaster, piastre, tallard 8 bedidlik, millieme
 of El Salvador: 4 peso 5 colon 7 centavo
 of England: 3 ora 4 rial 5 achey, crown, groat, noble, pence, penny, pound 6 bawbee, florin, guinea 7 angelet, hapenny 8 farthing, shilling, sixpence, tuppence, tuppenny 13 pound sterling
 of Equatorial Guinea: 6 ekuele, peseta 7 centimo
 of Estonia: 3 lat 4 sent 5 kroon 7 estmark
 of Ethiopia: 4 besa, birr, harf 5 amole, girsh 6 dollar, kharaf, levant, pataca, talari 7 ashrafi, menelik, plaster, tallero 12 maria theresa
 of Fiji: 6 dollar
 of Finland: 4 mark 5 penni 6 markka 7 markkaa
 of France: 5 franc 7 centime 8 napoleon
 of Gabon Republic: 5 franc 7 centime
 of the Gambia: 5 pound 6 butbut, dalasi
 of Georgia: 5 ruble
 of Germany: 4 mark 7 Ostmark, pfennig 12 Deutsche mark
 of Ghana: 4 cedi, cidi 5 ackey
 of Greece: 5 lepta 7 drachma
 of Greenland: 3 ore 5 krone
 of Guatemala: 4 peso 7 centavo, quetzal

 (continued)

coin/currency (*continued*)

of Guinea: 4 iliy, syli 5 franc 6 cauris
 of Guinea-Bissau: 4 peso 6 escudo 7 centavo
 of Haiti: 6 gourde 7 centime
 of Honduras: 4 peso 7 centavo, lempira
 of Hungary: 4 gara 5 balas, krone, pengo 6 filler, forint, gulden, korona, ongara, ungara
 of Iceland: 5 aurar, eyrir, krona 6 kronur
 of India: 3 lac, pie 4 anna, fels, lakh, pice, tara 5 abidi, crore, paisa, rupee
 of Indonesia: 3 sen 6 rupiah
 of Iran: 3 pul 4 asar, gran, lari, rial 5 bisti, daric, dinar, larin, shahi, toman 6 stater 7 ashrafi, kasbeke, pahlavi
 of Iraq: 4 fils 5 dinar
 of Ireland: 3 rap 4 real 5 pence, pound 6 turney 8 shilling
 of Israel: 3 mil 5 agora, agura, pound, pruta 6 agorot, shekel
 of Italy: 4 lira, lire, tara 5 grano, paoli, paolo, scudo, soldo 6 danaro, denaro, ducato, sequin 7 testone 8 zecchino 9 centesimi
 of Ivory Coast: 5 franc 7 centime
 of Jamaica: 7 quattie
 of Japan: 2 bu 3 mon, rin, rio, sen, shu, yen 4 cash, mibu, oban 5 koban, obang, tempo 6 cobang, ichebu, ichibu, itzebu, kogang 7 itzeboo, itziboo
 of Jordan: 4 fils 5 dinar
 of Kazakhstan: 5 ruble
 of Kenya: 4 cent 5 pound 8 shilling
 of Kiribati: 4 cent 6 dollar
 of Korea: 3 woh, won 4 chun, hwan, kwan
 of Kuwait: 4 fils 5 dinar
 of Kyrgyzstan: 3 som
 of Laos: 2 at 3 att, kip
 of Latvia: 3 lat 4 latu 6 rublis, santim 7 kapeika, santima
 of Lebanon: 5 livre, pound 7 piastre
 of Lesotho: 4 cent, rand 6 maloti
 of Liberia: 4 cent 6 dollar
 of Libya: 5 dinar
 of Liechtenstein: 5 franc 6 rappen 7 franken
 of Lithuania: 3 lit 5 litas, marka 6 centas, fennig

7 ostmark, skatiku 8 auksinas, skatikas
 of Luxembourg: 5 franc 7 centime
 of Macao: 3 avo 6 pataca, pataco
 of Macedonia: 5 denar
 of Madagascar: 5 franc 7 centime
 of Malawi: 6 kwacha 7 tambala
 of Malaysia: 3 sen, tra 4 taro, trah 7 ringgit, tampang
 of Maldives: 5 laree, rupee 7 rufiyaa
 of Mali: 5 franc 7 centime
 of Malta: 4 cent 5 grain, grano, pound
 of Mauritania: 5 khoum 7 ouguiya
 of Mauritius: 4 cent 5 rupee
 of Mexico: 4 onza, peso 5 adobe, claco, tlaco 6 azteca, cuarto, dinero 7 centavo, piaster
 of Moldova: 5 ruble
 of Monaco: 5 franc 7 centime
 of Mongolia: 5 mongo, mungo 6 tugrik 7 tughrik
 of Montenegro: 4 para 6 florin 7 perpera
 of Morocco: 4 flue, okia, rial 5 floos, franc, okieh, ounce 6 dirham, miskal 8 mouzouna
 of Mozambique: 6 escudo 7 centavo, metical
 of Myanmar: 3 pya 4 kyat
 of Namibia: 4 cent, rand
 of Nauru: 4 cent 6 dollar
 of Nepal: 4 anna, pice 5 mohar, rupee
 of the Netherlands: 4 doit, oord, raps 5 crown, daler, rider, ryder 6 florin, gulden, stiver, suskin 7 daalder, ducaton, escalan, escalin, guilder, stooter, stuiver 8 albertin, ducatoon 9 dubbeltje 12 rijksdaalder 13 albertustaler
 of New Guinea: 4 kina, toea
 of New Zealand: 4 cent 6 dollar
 of Nicaragua: 4 peso 7 centavo, cordoba
 of Niger: 5 franc 7 centime
 of Nigeria: 4 kobo 5 naira
 of Norway: 3 ore 5 krone 6 kroner

 of Oman: 3 gaj, gaz 4 rial 5 baiza, ghazi 7 mahmudi
 of Pakistan: 4 anna, pice 5 paisa, rupee
 of Panama: 4 cent 6 balboa 9 centesimo
 of Paraguay: 4 peso 7 centimo, guarani
 of Peru: 3 sol 5 libra 6 dinero, reseta 7 centavo
 of the Philippines: 4 peso 6 conant, peseta 7 centavo
 of Poland: 4 abia 5 dalar, ducat, grosz, marka, zloty 6 fening, groszy, gulden, halerz, korona 8 groschen
 of Portugal: 3 avo, joe 4 peca, real 5 conto, crown, dobra, indio, justo, rupia 6 escudo, macuta, octave, pataca, testad, tostao, vintem 7 angalar, centavo, crusado, miereis, moidore, testone 8 equipaga, johannes
 of Qatar: 5 riyal 6 dirham
 of Rumania: 3 ban, lei, leu, lev, ley 4 bani 5 uncia 6 triens
 of Russia: 5 altin, bisti, copec, genga, grosh, kopek, ruble, shaur 6 abassi, copeck, grivna, kopeck, piatak, rouble 7 poltina, valiuta 8 auksinas, deneshka, imperial, polushka 9 poltinnik 10 altininink, chervonets
 of Rwanda: 5 franc 7 centime
 of San Marino: 4 lira, lire 9 centesimi
 of Samoa: 4 tala
 of Sao Tome and Principe: 5 dobra 6 escudo 7 centavo
 of Sardinia: 7 carline
 of Saudi Arabia: 5 girsh, gursh, pound, riyal
 of Scotland: 3 ecu 4 demy, doit, lion, mark, rial, ryal 5 bodle, broad, groat, plack, rider, turne 6 bawbee, folles 7 unicorn 8 atchison, hardhead 9 halfpenny 11 bonnetpiece
 of Senegal: 5 franc 7 centime
 of Sicily: 5 litra, oncia, uncia 6 carlin 7 carline, oncetta

of Sierra Leone: 4 cent **5** leone
of Singapore: 4 cent **6** dollar
of Slovakia: 6 koruna
of Slovenia: 5 tolar
of Solomon Islands: 4 cent **6** dollar
of Somalia: 4 besa **6** somalo **8** shilling **9** centesimi
of South Africa: 4 cent, pond, rand **5** pound **6** florin **7** daalder **9** krugerand
of Spain: 3 cob **4** duro, peso, real **5** dobla **6** cuarto, dinero, doblon, escudo, peseta **7** alfonso, centimo, pistole, realdor **8** doubloon
of Sri Lanka: 4 cent **5** rupee
of Sudan: 5 dinar, pound **7** piastre
of Suriname: 4 cent **7** guilder
of Swaziland: 4 rand **9** lilangeni
of Sweden: 3 ore **5** krona, krone **7** carolin **8** skilling **9** rigsdaler
of Switzerland: 5 franc,
rappe **6** hallar, rappen **7** angster, centime, duplone **8** baetzner, blaffert
of Syria: 4 lira **5** pound **6** talent **7** piaster
of Taiwan: 4 yuan **6** dollar
of Tajikistan: 5 ruble
of Tanzania: 4 cent **8** shilling
of Thailand: 2 at **3** att **4** baht **5** cutty, fuang, tical **6** pynung, salung, satang **11** bullet money
of Tibet: 5 tanga
of Togo: 5 franc **7** centime
of Tonga: 6 paanga, seniti
of Trinidad and Tobago: 4 cent **6** dollar
of Tunisia: 5 dinar **6** dollar **7** millime
of Turkey: 4 lira, para **5** akcha, asper, attun, kurus, pound, rebia **6** akcheh, sequin, zequin **7** aetilik, beshlik, pataque, piaster **8** medjidie, zecchino
of Turkmenistan: 5 ruble
of Tuvalu: 4 cent **6** dollar
of Uganda: 4 cent **8** shilling
of Ukraine: 6 grivna **10** karbovanet
of United Arab Emirates: 3 fil **6** dirham
of Uruguay: 4 peso **9** centesimo, centisimo
of Uzbekistan: 5 ruble
of Vanuatu: 5 franc **6** dollar
of Venezuela: 4 peso, real **5** medio **6** fuerte **7** bolivar, centimo **8** morocota **10** venezolano
of Vietnam: 2 xu **4** dong **7** piaster
of Western Samoa: 4 sene, tala
of Yemen: 4 fils, rial **5** dinar, riyal
of Yugoslavia: 4 para **5** dinar
of Zaire: 5 zaire **6** makuta
of Zambia: 5 ngwee **6** kwachaof **of Zimbabwe: 4** cent **6** dollar

coincidental 6 chance **9** unplanned **10** accidental, contiguous, synchronal **11** concomitant, synchronous **12** happenstance, simultaneous

cointreau
type: 7 liqueur
variety: 7 curacao **9** triple sec
origin: 6 France
flavor: 6 orange
drink: 8 Applecar
with bourbon: 10 Temptation
with brandy: 7 Sidecar
with cognac: 10 Rolls Royce
with gin: 7 Florida **9** White Lady **13** Sweet Patootie **14** Flying Dutchman
with rum: 8 Acapulco **10** Casa Blanca **11** Beachcomber **12** Blue Hawaiian
with rye: 10 Temptation
with tequila: 9 Margarita
with whiskey: 16 Canadian Cocktail

Colavito, Rocky (Rocco Domenico)
sport: 8 baseball
team: 16 Cleveland Indians

Colbert, Claudette
real name: 22 Claudette Lily Chauchoin
born: 5 Paris **6** France
roles: 8 Tovarich **9** Cleopatra **14** Palm Beach Story **18** It Happened One Night (Oscar)

cold *see box*

cold-blooded 4 evil, hard **5** cruel, harsh, stiff, stony **6** brutal, flinty, formal, frigid, inured, savage, steely **7** callous, demonic, inhuman, passive, satanic, unmoved **8** detached, fiendish, hardened, inhumane, pitiless, reserved, ruthless, uncaring **9** barbarous, heartless, impassive, merciless, unfeeling, unpitying, unstirred **10** deliberate, diabolical, disdainful, impervious, implacable, unfriendly, unmerciful, villainous **11** calculating, hardhearted, indifferent, insensitive, passionless, unconcerned, unemotional, unexcitable **12** bloodthirsty, contemptuous, uninterested, unresponsive **13** disinterested, unimpassioned, unimpressible, unsympathetic **16** unimpressionable

cold-hearted 5 cruel **9** heartless, unfeeling **11** hard-hearted **13** unsympathetic

cold 3 icy, old **4** cool, dead, flat, hard **5** aloof, brisk, chill, crisp, cruel, faded, faint, gelid, harsh, nippy, polar, sharp, stale, stiff, stony **6** arctic, biting, bitter, chilly, cooled, frigid, frosty, frozen, inured, numbed, remote, severe, snappy, steely, wintry **7** callous, chilled, cutting, distant, frosted, glacial, haughty, nipping, passive, unmoved **8** chilling, coolness, detached, freezing, hardened, piercing, reserved, reticent, stinging, uncaring, unheated, unloving, unwarmed **9** apathetic, heartless, impassive, insensate, unfeeling, unstirred **10** disdainful, forbidding, impervious, insensible, phlegmatic, unfriendly **11** frozen stiff, indifferent, passionless, penetrating, unconcerned, unconscious, unemotional, unexcitable **12** antipathetic, bone-chilling, inaccessible, supercilious, uninterested, unresponsive **13** uninteresting, unsympathetic **14** marrow-chilling, unapproachable **15** teeth-chattering, uncommunicative, undemonstrative **16** chilled to the bone, unimpressionable **18** chilled to the marrow

coldness 5 chill **7** iciness
9 aloofness **10** chilliness, frostiness **12** indifference **13** unfeelingness **14** unfriendliness
15 hardheartedness

Cole, Thomas
born: **7** England **13** Bolton-le-
Moors
artwork: **8** The Ox-Bow
15 The Voyage of Life **17** The
Course of Empire

coleoptera
class: **8** hexopoda
phylum: **10** arthropoda
group: **6** beetle, weevil

Coleridge, Samuel
author of: **9** Kubla Khan
10 Christabel **14** Dejection An
Ode, Lyrical Ballads (with
Wordsworth) **19** Biographia
Literaria **26** The Rime of the
Ancient Mariner

Colette (Sidonie)
author of: **4** Gigi, Sido **5** Cheri
8 Claudine **11** La Vagabonde
14 The Evening Star

coliseum 4 bowl **5** arena **6** circus **7** stadium, theater **10** hippodrome **12** amphitheater
14 exhibition hall

collaborate 4 join **5** unite **6** assist, team up **7** collude **9** cooperate **10** join forces **12** work
together **14** work side by side

collaborationist 6 puppet
7 traitor **8** quisling

collaborator 4 ally **6** puppet
7 traitor **8** co-worker, quisling,
teammate **9** associate, colleague, co-partner
11 confederate

collapse 4 coma, fail, fall, flop,
fold **5** faint, swoon **6** attack,
buckle, cave-in, fizzle **7** break
up, crack-up, crumple, failure,
give way, seizure **8** be in vain,
buckling, downfall, flounder,
keel over, take sick **9** become
ill, break down **10** be stricken,
break apart, run aground
11 fall through **12** disintegrate,
falling apart, fall helpless, fall
to pieces **13** come to nothing,
sudden illness **14** disintegration
17 become unconscious

collapsed 4 limp **7** caved in,
compact **8** deflated, fallen in,
folded up **13** disintegrated

**Collapse of the Third Re-
public, The**
author: **14** William L Shirer

collapsible 7 folding **8** foldable
10 deflatable

collar 3 nab **4** eton, grab
5 catch, fichu, pinch, seize
6 arrest, bertha **7** capture **9** apprehend, neckpiece **12** take
prisoner **15** take into custody

collate 5 order **6** bestow, verify
7 compare **8** assemble, organize
9 integrate **11** put together

collateral 4 bond **5** extra
6 pledge, surety **7** warrant
8 parallel, security, warranty
9 accessory, ancillary, auxiliary,
guarantee, insurance,
secondary **10** additional,
incidental, supporting, supportive **11** endorsement, subordinate **12** contributory
13 supplementary

collation 3 tea **4** meal **5** lunch
6 brunch, repast, sermon **7** address, reading **8** hotchpot, luncheon, treatise **10** comparison
11 description

colleague 4 mate **6** fellow
7 partner **8** confrere, co-
worker, teammate **9** associate,
co-partner **11** confederate
12 collaborator, fellow worker

collect 3 get **4** calm, meet
5 amass, raise, rally **6** gather,
heap up, muster, obtain, pick
up, pile up, summon **7** call for,
compile, compose, control,
convene, marshal, prepare, receive, solicit **8** assemble, gather
up, scrape up **9** aggregate, get
hold of **10** accumulate, congregate **11** concentrate, get
together

collectanea 8 analects, treasury **9** anthology, gleanings
10 collection, miscellany, selections **11** miscellanea

collected 4 calm, cool **5** quiet
6 placid, poised, serene, steady
8 composed, peaceful, tranquil
9 confident, unruffled **10** cool-
headed, restrained **11** levelheaded, self-assured,
undisturbed, unemotional, unflappable, unperturbed
12 even-tempered **13** self-
possessed **14** self-controlled

collection 3 mob **4** bevy, body,
gift, heap, mass, pack, pile
5 array, bunch, clump, crowd,
drove, flock, group, hoard,
store, swarm **6** corpus, jumble,
muster, throng **7** cluster, clutter, variety **8** amassing, assembly, oblation, treasury
9 anthology, gathering, offertory, receiving **10** assemblage,
assortment, hodgepodge, mis-

cellany, soliciting **11** aggregation, compilation
12 accumulating, accumulation

collective 5 joint **6** common,
mutual, united **7** unified
8 combined, gathered **9** aggregate, composite **10** cumulative,
integrated **11** accumulated,
cooperative

collector 6 grouper **7** dustman
8 antiquer, compiler, composer,
gatherer, zamindar **9** assembler
10 garbageman **11** anthologist

Collector, The
author: **10** John Fowles

college 7 academy **8** seminary
9 institute **10** university
11 institution

college-preparatory 4 prep
8 academic **11** liberal-arts
12 nontechnical

collegiate 8 academic **10** scholastic, university **11** educational

collembola
class: **8** hexopoda
phylum: **10** arthropoda
group: **10** springtail

collide 3 hit **4** meet **5** clash,
crash, smash **7** crack up, diverge, run into **8** bump into,
conflict, disagree **9** knock into
10 meet head on **11** beat
against **13** hurtle against, strike
against

Collins, Mr
character in: **17** Pride and
Prejudice
author: **6** Austen

Collins, Wilkie
author of: **6** No Name **12** The
Moonstone **15** The Woman
in White

collision 4 bump **5** clash, crash,
fight, smash **6** battle, combat,
impact **7** smash-up **8** accident,
conflict, skirmish, struggle
9 encounter **10** engagement
11 clash of arms

colloquial 5 homey, plain **6** casual, chatty, common, folksy
8 everyday, familiar, homespun, informal, ordinary,
workaday **9** idiomatic **10** vernacular **14** conversational

colloquy 4 chat, talk **6** caucus,
parley **7** council, palaver, seminar **8** commerce, congress,
converse, dialogue **9** commun-

ion, discourse **10** conference, discussion, rap session **11** interchange, intercourse **12** conversation **13** confabulation

collude 4 plot **7** connive **8** conspire, intrigue **9** cooperate **11** collaborate

collusion 5 fraud **7** treason **8** intrigue **10** complicity, connivance, conspiracy **13** collaboration **15** secret agreement **17** guilty association

Colman, Ronald
  born: 7 England **8** Richmond
  roles: 9 Beau Geste **10** Arrowsmith **11** A Double Life (Oscar), Lost Horizon **16** A Tale of Two Cities

cologne 5 scent **7** essence, perfume **9** fragrance **11** toilet water

Colomba
  author: 14 Prosper Merimee

Colombia *see box*

Colombo
  capital of: 8 Sri Lanka

colon 4 coin **6** farmer, vitals **7** pioneer, planter, settler, viscera **9** hemistich, intestine **15** plantation owner, punctuation mark

colonize 5 found, plant **6** gather, settle **7** migrate **8** establish **10** infiltrate

colonnade 3 row **4** stoa **5** porch **6** arcade, piazza **7** portico, terrace **8** cloister **9** peristyle

colony 3 set **4** band, body **5** flock, group, swarm **7** mandate **8** dominion, province **9** community, territory **10** dependency, possession, settlement **12** protectorate **14** satellite state

colophon 6 design, device, emblem **7** insigne **8** insignia **11** inscription

color 3 dye, hue **4** bias, burn, cast, glow, mood, tint, tone, warp, wash **5** bloom, blush, chalk, drift, flame, flush, force, paint, sense, shade, slant, stain, taint, tinge, twist **6** affect, aspect, crayon, effect, import, intent, redden, spirit, stress **7** distort, feeling, meaning, pervert, pigment, redness, skin hue **8** dyestuff, rosiness **9** go crimson, influence, intention, prejudice **10** intimation **11** connotation, implication, insinuation **12** become florid, pigmentation, significance **17** natural complexion

Colorado *see box, p. 198*

Colombia
  other name: 6 Darien **10** New Granada
  capital/largest city: 6 Bogota
  others: 3 Ten **4** Amza, Buga, Cali, Mitu, Muzo, Paez, Sipi, Tado, Tolu, Yari **5** Bello, Chinu, Guapi, Neiva, Pasto, Tulua, Tunja **6** Cucuta, Ibaque, Lorica, Quibdo, Sangil, Tumaco **7** Cartago, Ipiates, Leticia, Palmira, Pereira, Popayan **8** Girardot, Maganque, Medellin, Monteria **9** Cartagena, Manizales **10** Santa Marta **11** Bucaramanga **12** Barranquilla, Buenaventura
  school: 5 Andes, Valle **20** Instituto Caro y Cuervo **21** Industrial de Santander
  measure: 4 vara **7** azumbre, celemin
  monetary unit: 4 peso, real **6** condor, peseta **7** centavo
  weight: 3 bag **4** saco **5** libra **7** quintal
  island: 4 Baru **5** Naipo **6** Fuerte **7** Gorgona, Malpelo **8** Cusachon **9** San Andres **11** Providencia
  lake: 4 Tota
  mountain: 5 Abibe, Andes, Baudo, Chita, Cocuy, Huila, Pasto **6** Ayapel, Perija, Purace, Tolima, Tunahi **7** Chamusa, del Ruiz **8** Oriengal **10** Santa Marta **17** Central Cordillera, Eastern Cordillera, Western Cordillera
  highest point: 14 Cristobal Colon
  river: 3 Uva **4** Bita, Meta, Muco, Sinu, Tomo, Yari **5** Cauca, Cesar, Isana, Mesai, Nechi, Pauto, Sucio **6** Amazon, Arauca, Ariari, Atrato, Atroto, Caguan, Pattia, Yapura **7** Apapois, Caqueta, Guainia, Inirida, Truando, Vichada **8** Casanare, Guaviara, Putumayo **9** Magdalena
  sea: 7 Pacific **9** Caribbean
  physical feature:
    cape: **4** Vela **5** Aguja, Marzo, Punta **7** Augusta **8** Gallinas
    falls: **10** Tequendama
    gulf: **5** Uraba **6** Cupica, Darien, Tibuga **8** Tortugas
    inlet: **6** Tumaco
    plains: **6** Ilanos
    point: **6** Cruces, Lacruz, Solano **8** Caribana, Gallinas
  people: 4 Boro, Cuna, Duit, Hoka, Macu, Muso, Muzo, Paez, Tama, Tapa **5** Carib, Catio, Choco, Cofan, Cogui, Cubeo, Guane, Haida, Mocoa, Paeze, Pijao, Seona, Yagua **6** Arawak, Betoya, Calima, Colima, Ingano, Mirana, Saliva, Tahami, Ticunu, Tucano, Tunebo, Witoto, Yahuna **7** Achagua, Andaqui, Chibcha, Chimila, Churoya, Guahibo, Guajiro, Panches, Puinave, Puitoto, Quechua, Shuswap, Tairona, Telembi **8** Coconuco, Guarauno, mestizos, Motilone, Puinavis, Quimbaya, Sinsigas **9** Cocanucos, Coconucan, mulattoes, Panaquita **10** Bellacoola
    leader: **7** Bolivar
  language: 7 Spanish
  religion: 13 Roman Catholic
  place:
    museum: **4** Gold **8** Colonial
    palace: **11** Inquisition
  feature:
    dance: **7** bambuco **8** merengue
    game: **4** tejo
    guitar: **5** tiple
    poncho: **5** ruana
    shoes: **10** alpargatas
    shoulder bag: **7** carriel
    tree: **8** arboloco
    woven hat: **5** jipas

---

colored 4 dyed, hued **5** dusky **6** biased, shaded, tinged, tinted **7** blushed, excused, flushed, glossed, labeled, painted, stained **8** affected, labelled, reddened **9** chromatic, distorted, pigmented **10** influenced, prejudiced **12** complexioned **13** characterized **14** misrepresented

colorful 3 gay **4** loud **5** showy, vivid **6** bright, florid, unique **7** dynamic, graphic, unusual, vibrant, zestful **8** animated, forceful, spirited, vigorous

Colorado

abbreviation: 2 CO 4 Colo
nickname: 10 Centennial
capital/largest city: 6 Denver
others: 4 Vail 5 Aspen, Delta, Lamar, Ouray 6 Arvada, Aurora, Denver, Golden, Pueblo, Salida 7 Alamosa, Boulder, Durango, Greeley, Manassa, Manitou 8 Gunnison, Loveland, Trinidad 9 Purgatory, Silverton, Telluride 11 Central City 12 Cripple Creek 13 Grand Junction 15 Colorado Springs
college: 5 Regis 6 Denver 7 Boulder 17 US Air Force Academy
feature: 11 Four Corners 15 Garden of the Gods 17 Continental Divide
  national monument: 8 Dinosaur 14 Great Sand Dunes
  national park: 5 Estes 9 Mesa Verde 13 Rocky Mountain
tribe: 3 Ute 7 Arapaho 8 Cheyenne
people: 11 Jack Dempsey 12 Ralph Edwards 14 Scott Carpenter 18 Douglas Fairbanks Sr
lake: 6 Frozen
land rank: 6 eighth
mountains: 5 Longs, Rocky 7 San Juan 9 Pikes Peak 14 Sangre de Cristo
  highest point: 6 Elbert
physical feature:
  canyon: 5 Black
  gorge: 5 Royal
  plains: 5 Great
  wind: 7 Chinook
river: 4 Gila 5 Yampa 6 Platte 7 Dolores 8 Apishapa, Arikaree, Arkansas, Gunnison 9 Rio Grande 10 Purgatoire
state admission: 12 thirty-eighth
state bird: 11 lark bunting
state flower: 22 Rocky Mountain columbine
state motto: 24 Nothing Without Providence
state song: 22 Where the Columbines Grow
state tree: 18 Colorado blue spruce

9 brilliant, full-toned, vivacious 10 compelling, variegated 11 distinctive, interesting, many-colored, picturesque 12 multicolored, particolored

coloring 3 dye 4 tint 5 color, shade, stain 10 coloration, complexion

colorless 3 wan 4 ashy, drab, dull, flat, pale 5 ashen, dingy, faded, pasty, vapid, white 6 anemic, boring, dreary, grayed, pallid, sallow, sickly, undyed 7 ghastly, ghostly, insipid, natural, neutral, prosaic 8 blanched, bleached, lifeless, ordinary, whitened 9 bloodless, washed out 10 cadaverous, lackluster, monotonous, spiritless, unanimated, unexciting, uninspired 11 commonplace 13 uninteresting

Color Purple, The
author: 11 Alice Walker
director: 15 Steven Spielberg
cast: 11 Danny Glover 12 Adolph Caesar, Oprah Winfrey 13 Margaret Avery 14 Whoopi Goldberg

colors 4 flag, jack 6 banner, ensign, pennon 7 pennant 8 standard

colossal 4 huge, vast 5 giant, grand, great 6 mighty 7 extreme, immense, mammoth, massive, titanic 8 enormous, gigantic, imposing 9 exceeding, excessive 10 incredible, inordinate, monumental, prodigious, tremendous 11 extravagant, spectacular 12 awe-inspiring, overwhelming

Colossus of Rhodes
statue of: 6 Apollo

colt 4 foal 5 horse 6 novice 8 equuleus, yearling 9 fledgling, youngster
constellation of: 8 Equuleus

columbium
chemical symbol: 2 Cb

Columbo
character: 9 Lt Columbo
cast: 9 Peter Falk

column 3 row 4 file, line, post 5 pylon, queue, shaft, train 6 parade, pillar, string 7 caravan, phalanx, support, upright 8 pilaster 9 cavalcade,

formation 10 procession 11 vertical row 12 vertical list

columnist 6 writer 7 analyst
famous: 7 Heloise 8 Dear Abby, Herb Caen 9 HL Mencken, Jack Smith 10 Ann Landers 11 Miss Manners 15 Abigail van Buren

coma 6 stupor, torpor 8 collapse 15 unconsciousness

Comaetho
form: 9 priestess
father: 9 Pterelaus
loved: 10 Amphitryon
lover: 10 Melanippus
killed by: 10 Amphitryon

Comanche
language family: 10 Shoshonean
location: 5 Texas 6 Kansas, Mexico 8 Oklahoma
noted as: 8 horsemen

comatose 3 lax 4 dull, idle, lazy 5 inert 6 leaden, torpid 7 drugged, languid, passive 8 inactive, indolent, lifeless, listless, slothful, sluggish 9 apathetic, catatonic, lethargic, stuporous 10 cataleptic, insensible, narcotized, phlegmatic, spiritless 11 indifferent, unconcerned, unconscious 12 unresponsive

comb 4 card, tuft 5 curry, dress, groom, plume, scour, style 6 search 7 arrange, explore, panache, ransack, topknot 8 head tuft, hunt over, untangle 9 cast about, cockscomb, currycomb 11 look through 14 rummage through

combat 5 clash, fight 6 action, attack, battle, oppose, resist 7 contest, go to war, wage war 8 conflict, fighting, skirmish, struggle 9 encounter 10 contention, engagement, war against 11 come to blows, grapple with, make warfare, work against 12 do battle with, march against 13 confrontation 14 military action

Combat
character: 4 Caje (Caddy Cadron) 8 Kirby (Pvt) Braddock 9 Doc Walton, (Lt) Gil Hanley 12 (Sgt) Chip Saunders
cast: 9 Jack Hogan, Rick Jason, Vic Morrow 12 Shecky Greene, Steven Rogers 13 Pierre Jalbert

combatant 7 fighter, soldier, warrior 9 man-at-arms 10 serviceman 11 fighting man

combating 8 battling, clashing, fighting, opposing 9 waging war 10 contention, contesting, opposition, struggling **11** doing battle **13** grappling with **17** coming to blows with

combative, **6** bantam **8** militant **9** agonistic, bellicose **10** aggressive, pugnacious **11** belligerent, contentious **12** antagonistic

combativeness 9 hostility, pugnacity **10** antagonism **12** belligerence **14** aggressiveness **15** contentiousness

combination 3 mix **5** alloy, blend, union **6** fusion, league, medley, merger, mixing **7** amalgam, joining, mixture, pooling, variety **8** alliance, blending, compound **9** coalition, composite, synthesis **10** assortment, coalescing, federation **11** association, composition, confederacy **12** amalgamation **13** confederation

combine 3 mix **4** fuse, join, pool **5** blend, merge, unify, unite **6** couple, league, mingle **8** compound **9** commingle **10** amalgamate, synthesize **11** consolidate, incorporate

combo 4 band **5** group **11** aggregation, combination

comb out 4 curl **5** dress **7** arrange, unsnarl **8** untangle

combustible 8 burnable **9** flammable, ignitable **10** combustive, incendiary **11** inflammable **13** conflagrative

combustion 6 firing **7** burning, flaming **8** ignition, kindling **12** incineration **13** conflagration

combustive 8 burnable **9** flammable, ignitable **11** combustible, inflammable **13** conflagrative

come 2 be, go **3** bud **4** fall, loom, rise **5** arise, issue, occur, range, reach **6** appear, arrive, be made, drop in, emerge, extend, follow, happen, impend, show up, spread, spring, turn up **7** advance, descend, emanate, stretch **8** approach, draw near, go toward, grow to be **9** be a native, germinate, take place **10** be imminent, move toward **11** be a resident, be in the wind, materialize, originate in, spring forth

come about 5 occur **6** chance, happen **7** turn out **10** come to pass

come afterward 5 ensue **6** derive, follow, result **7** succeed

come apart 6 detach **7** disjoin, unstick **8** separate

come back 5 rally **6** answer, retort, return **7** rebound **8** recovery

Come Back Little Sheba
  director: **10** Daniel Mann
  based on play by: **11** William Inge
  cast: **10** Terry Moore **12** Shirley Booth **13** Burt Lancaster
  Oscar for: **7** actress (Booth)

come clean 4 sing **5** own up **7** confess **14** unbosom oneself **18** make a clean breast of

come close to 7 verge on **8** approach, border on **11** approximate, nearly equal

comedian 3 wag **4** fool, zany **5** clown, comic, cutup, joker **6** jester, madcap **7** buffoon **8** humorist, jokester **9** prankster **10** comedienne, comic actor **14** practical joker

comedown 4 drop **8** lowering **10** anticlimax

come down 4 dive, drop, fall, sink **6** plunge, tumble **7** descend, plummet **8** decrease

come down a peg 5 deign, stoop **6** unbend **7** descend **10** condescend **12** lower oneself **13** humble oneself

comedy 3 fun, wit **5** farce, humor **6** banter, joking, pranks, satire **7** foolery, jesting **8** drollery, raillery, travesty **9** burlesque, cutting up, horseplay, silliness **10** buffoonery, pleasantry, tomfoolery **13** fooling around

Comedy of Errors, The
  author: **18** William Shakespeare
  character: **6** Aegeon, Dromio **7** Adriana, Aemilia, Luciana, Solinus **10** Antipholus

come face to face with 4 meet **8** confront **9** encounter

come first 7 precede, predate **8** antecede, antedate, go before **10** anticipate

come into being 4 dawn, show **5** arise, begin, occur, set in, start **6** appear, be born, crop up, emerge, sprout **8** commence, spring up **9** germinate, originate **11** come to light

come into port 4 dock **5** berth

come into view 4 show **6** appear, come up, emerge, show

up **7** surface **11** come to light **13** become visible

come loose 5 let go **6** detach, loosen **7** slip off **8** break off, separate, unfasten **9** break away **10** come undone, come untied, disconnect **11** come unglued, come unstuck

comely 4 fair, nice **5** bonny **6** pretty, proper, seemly, simple **7** correct, fitting, natural, sightly, winning, winsome **8** becoming, blooming, charming, decorous, engaging, fetching, pleasant, pleasing, suitable, tasteful **9** agreeable, appealing, wholesome **10** attractive, unaffected **11** well-favored

come near 4 loom, near **6** appear **8** approach **9** draw close **10** move toward

come-on 4 bait, hook, lure, trap **5** decoy, snare **6** magnet **9** seduction **10** allurement, attraction, bewitchery, enticement, inducement, seducement, temptation **12** inveiglement

comestibles 5 foods **7** edibles **8** victuals **10** foodstuffs, provisions

Cometes
  lover of: **8** Aegialia

come to a decision 6 decide, settle **7** resolve **8** conclude **9** determine

come to an understanding 5 agree **6** settle **11** come to terms **12** agree to marry **16** reach an agreement

come to a standstill 4 halt, quit, stop **5** abate, cease **7** die away **8** quit cold

come to blows 5 fight **7** contest **8** do battle **9** square off **12** start to fight

come together 4 meet **5** flock, group, rally **6** gather **7** collect, convene **8** assemble **10** congregate **11** get together

come to light 4 dawn **5** arise **6** appear, crop up, emerge, evolve, show up, turn up, unfold **7** develop, surface, turn out

come to nothing 4 fail, flop, fold **6** fizzle **8** be in vain, collapse **9** break down **11** fall through **12** come to naught **17** fail to materialize

come to pass 5 ensue, occur **6** arrive, befall, follow, happen **9** take place

come to terms 5 agree, yield **6** give up, settle **7** succumb **8** contract, cry quits **9** make a deal, negotiate, surrender **10** capitulate, compromise **11** come to grips, meet halfway, sue for peace **13** resign oneself **14** strike a bargain **15** lay down one's arms **16** reach an agreement **17** acknowledge defeat, hoist the white flag **18** split the difference

come unglued 6 detach, loosen **8** separate **9** fall apart **11** come unstuck

come unstuck 4 lift **6** detach, loosen **8** break off, unfasten **9** break away, come apart, come loose, fall apart **11** come unglued

come up 4 rise **5** arise **7** quicken, sharpen **8** heighten, increase **9** intensify **10** accelerate, strengthen **12** be referred to

come upon 4 find, meet **7** learn of, run into **8** discover **9** encounter

comfit 5 candy, sweet **9** sweetmeat **10** confection, sugar candy **13** confectionery

comfort 4 calm, ease, help **5** cheer, peace, quiet **6** luxury, relief, solace, soothe, succor, warmth **7** cheer up, compose, console, hearten **8** coziness, opulence, pleasure, reassure, serenity, snugness **9** bolster up, comforter, composure, encourage, well-being **10** cheering up, relaxation **11** consolation, contentment, reassurance **12** satisfaction **13** encouragement, gratification **14** quiet one's fears **16** source of serenity **17** lighten one's burden **18** bolster one's spirits

Comfort, Alex
author of: **11** The Joy of Sex **12** More Joy of Sex

comfortable 4 cozy, easy **6** at ease, at home, serene **7** relaxed **8** adequate, pleasant, suitable **9** agreeable, congenial, contented **10** giving ease, gratifying, untroubled **11** pleasurable, undisturbed **12** satisfactory **16** free from distress

comforter 4 balm, puff **5** quilt, scarf **6** afghan, solace **7** anodyne, blanket, comfort, soother **8** coverlet **10** palliative

comic, comical 4 rich **5** droll, funny, merry, silly, witty **6** absurd, jocose, jovial **7** amusing, jocular, risible **8** farcical, humorous, mirthful **9** facetious, laughable, ludi-

crous, whimsical **10** ridiculous **11** nonsensical **12** nimble-witted

coming 4 next **6** advent, future, in view, to come **7** arrival, nearing **8** approach, arriving, imminent, on the way **9** advancing, emergence, imminence, impending, in the wind, proximity **10** appearance, occurrence, subsequent **11** approaching, forthcoming, prospective **12** on the horizon **13** materializing

Coming Home
director: **8** Hal Ashby
cast: **9** Bruce Dern, Jane Fonda, Jon Voight **15** Robert Carradine
Oscar for: **5** actor (Voight) **7** actress (Fonda) **10** screenplay

Coming into the Country
author: **10** John McPhee

Coming of Age, The
author: **16** Simone de Beauvoir

Coming of Age in Samoa
author: **12** Margaret Mead

Coming Race, The
author: **18** Edward Bulwer-Lytton

command 3 bid, get **4** boss, call, draw, fiat, grip, head, hold, lead, rule **5** edict, evoke, grasp, guide, order, power **6** adjure, behest, charge, compel, decree, demand, direct, elicit, enjoin, govern, incite, induce, kindle, manage, ordain, prompt, summon **7** call for, conduct, control, deserve, extract, inspire, mastery, provoke, receive, require, summons **8** call upon, instruct, motivate **9** authority, call forth, direction, directive, governing, knowledge, ordinance, supervise, ultimatum **10** administer, be master of, domination, injunction, leadership, management **11** familiarity, instruction, superintend, supervision **12** have charge of **13** comprehension, understanding **14** administration **17** have authority over

commandant 7 captain **9** commander **12** chief officer

commandeer 4 take **5** seize, usurp **8** shanghai **11** appropriate, expropriate

commander 4 boss, head **5** chief, ruler **6** leader **7** manager **8** director **9** conductor

commanding 4 head **5** chief, grand, lofty **6** ruling, senior, strong **7** dynamic, leading,

ranking, stately **8** forceful, gripping, imposing, powerful, striking, towering **9** arresting, directing, governing, important, prominent **10** compelling, dominating, impressive **11** controlling, significant **13** authoritative, distinguished, overshadowing

commandment
Hebrew: **7** mitsvah, mitzvah

comme il faut 6 proper **7** fitting **12** as it should be

commemorate 4 hail, mark **5** extol, honor **6** hallow, revere, salute **7** acclaim, glorify, observe **8** venerate **9** celebrate, solemnize **11** acknowledge, memorialize, pay homage to **12** pay tribute to

commence 5 begin, start **8** get going, initiate **10** get started, inaugurate, originated

commencement 4 dawn **5** birth, onset, start **6** outset **7** genesis, morning **9** beginning, first step, inception **10** graduation, initiation **11** origination **12** inauguration **13** graduation day **20** graduation ceremonies

commend 2 OK **4** back, give, laud **5** extol **6** commit, confer, convey, praise **7** acclaim, approve, consign, endorse, entrust, stand by, support **8** delegate, give over, hand over, pass over, relegate, transfer **13** speak highly of

commendable 6 worthy **7** notable **8** laudable **9** admirable, deserving, estimable, exemplary, honorable **10** creditable **11** meritorious **12** praiseworthy

commendation 5 honor **6** praise **7** support **8** approval **10** acceptance **11** acclamation, approbation

commendatory 8 admiring, praising **9** laudatory, praiseful **10** plauditory **13** complimentary **14** congratulatory

commensurate, commensurable 4 even, meet **5** equal **6** square **7** fitting **8** balanced, in accord, parallel, relative, suitable **10** comparable, compatible, consistent, equivalent **11** appropriate, in agreement **13** corresponding, proportionate **14** on a proper scale

comment 4 note, word **6** remark **7** clarify, discuss, explain, expound **8** expand on **9** assertion, criticism, elucidate, shed light, statement, talk about, touch upon, utterance

10 annotation, expression, reflection **11** elucidation, explanation, explication, observation **13** clarification **15** exemplification

commentary 6 review **8** critique, scholium, treatise **9** criticism **10** exposition **11** explanation, explication **12** dissertation **14** interpretation **16** explanatory essay

commentator 6 critic, writer **7** speaker **8** panelist, reporter, reviewer **9** columnist, explainer **10** newscaster **11** interpreter, news analyst

comment upon 7 clarify, clear up, explain **8** spell out **9** delineate, elucidate, explicate, interpret, make plain **10** illuminate, illustrate **14** throw light upon

commerce 5 trade **6** barter **7** trading, traffic **8** business, exchange, industry **12** mercantilism **16** buying and selling
  god of: 6 Hermes **7** Mercury

commercial 2 ad **5** sales, trade **8** business **10** mercantile, sales pitch **12** profit-making **13** advertisement **16** buying-and-selling

commingle 3 mix **4** fuse **5** blend, merge, unify **7** combine **10** amalgamate

commiserate 7 feel for **8** show pity **10** grieve with, lament with **13** express sorrow **14** sympathize with **15** share one's sorrow **17** have compassion for

commiseration 4 pity **8** sympathy **10** compassion, tenderness **13** fellow feeling

commission *see box*

commissioner 5 envoy, trier **7** officer, pristaw **8** delegate, official **9** authority, commissar

commissioning 10 assignment, delegation **11** appointment, designation, entrustment **13** authorization

commit 2 do **3** act, put **4** bind, pull **5** enact, place **6** assign, decide, effect, engage, intern, pursue **7** confine, consign, deliver, deposit, entrust, execute, perform, pull off, resolve **8** carry out, give over, obligate, practice, transact, transfer **9** determine **10** make liable, perpetrate **13** participate in **16** institutionalize

commitment 3 vow **4** bond, word **5** stand **6** pledge **7** promise **8** decision, delivery,

---

commission 3 act, bid, cut, fee **4** duty, hire, name, rank, role, task **5** board, doing, order, piece, power, proxy, trust **6** agency, assign, charge, direct, employ, engage, office **7** appoint, certify, charter, conduct, council, empower, license, mandate, mission, portion, rake-off, stipend, warrant **8** capacity, contract, delegate, dividend, document, exercise, function, position **9** acting out, allotment, allowance, authority, authorize, committal, committee **10** assignment, commitment, committing, delegation, deputation, entrusting, percentage, performing **11** appointment, carrying out, certificate, performance, transacting **12** officer's rank, perpetration **13** authorization, written orders **14** give the go-ahead **15** representatives **16** piece of the action **17** appointment papers, grant officer's rank

---

transfer, warranty **9** assurance, detention, guarantee, liability, restraint **10** assignment, giving over, internment, obligation, resolution **11** confinement, consignment, dispatching **12** imprisonment **13** determination, incarceration **14** responsibility **18** institutionalizing

commit oneself 3 act **7** resolve **8** dedicate, obligate **9** determine

---

committed 6 active, liable **8** confined, detained, interned **9** concerned, delivered, entrusted, obligated **10** interested, responsive **11** responsible **17** institutionalized

committee 4 body, jury **5** bench, board, group, junta, table **6** bureau, soviet **7** cabinet, council **9** gathering, syndicate **10** assemblage **12** organization

commode 6 bureau **7** cabinet, dresser **9** washstand **14** chest of drawers

commodious 5 ample, large, roomy **8** spacious **9** capacious, uncramped **11** unconfining

commodity 4 ware **5** asset, goods, stock **6** staple **7** chattel, holding, product **8** property **9** advantage, belonging **10** possession **11** convenience, merchandise **14** article of trade **17** article of commerce

common *see box*

commoners 5 plebs **6** masses **8** plebians

common law
  Latin: **13** lex non scripta

commonly 5 often **6** widely **7** as a rule, usually **8** normally, of course **9** generally, in general, most often, popularly, regularly, routinely **10** by and large, familiarly, frequently, habitually, informally, ordinarily, repeatedly **11** customarily **13** traditionally **14** by force of habit, conventionally, for the most part **15** in most instances **17** generally speaking

common people 5 demos, plebs **6** masses **8** populace

---

common 3 bad, low **4** base, lewd, mean, rude, vile **5** brash, cheap, crass, crude, gross, joint, lowly, minor, plain, stock **6** brazen, brutal, coarse, lesser, normal, old-hat, public, ribald, shared, simple, smutty, tawdry, vulgar **7** average, boorish, callous, general, ignoble, ill-bred, loutish, low-bred, obscene, obscure, popular, prosaic, regular, routine, settled, uncouth, unknown, worn-out **8** communal, everyday, familiar, frequent, homespun, impolite, informal, mediocre, middling, nameless, ordinary, plebeian, shameful, standard, workaday, worn thin **9** bourgeois, customary, deficient, household, low-minded, moth-eaten, obnoxious, offensive, pervasive, shameless, tasteless, unexalted, universal, unnoticed, unrefined, well-known **10** collective, colloquial, despicable, dime-a-dozen, inglorious, threadbare, unblushing, uncultured, unpolished, widespread **11** disgraceful, established, ill-mannered, insensitive, middle-class, oft-repeated, subordinate, traditional, unimportant, widely known, without rank **12** contemptible, conventional, disagreeable **13** garden-variety, insignificant **15** undistinguished

9 hoi polloi, plebeians
11 bourgeoisie

commonplace 3 old **4** dull
5 adage, banal, stale, trite,
usual **6** cliche, old-hat, truism
7 bromide, general, humdrum,
regular, routine, worn-out
8 banality, everyday, familiar,
ordinary, standard, worn thin
9 customary, hackneyed,
moth-eaten, platitude **10** pedestrian, threadbare, un-
original, widespread
11 oft-repeated, stereotyped,
traditional **12** received idea,
run-of-the-mill **13** unimaginative, uninteresting

commonplace book 9 anthology, gleanings, scrapbook

Common Sense
author: **11** Thomas Paine

common-sense 5 sound
8 everyday, sensible **9** mother
wit, practical, pragmatic, realistic **10** no-nonsense **11** down-
to-earth, levelheaded,
serviceable, utilitarian
12 matter-of-fact

commonwealth 5 state **6** nation **8** republic
Latin: **10** res publica

commotion 3 ado **4** fuss, stir,
to-do **5** furor **6** bustle, racket,
ruckus, tumult, uproar **7** clatter, turmoil **9** agitation **10** excitement, hullabaloo
11 disturbance **12** perturbation

communal 5 joint **6** common,
mutual, public, shared **9** community **10** collective

commune 3 gab, rap, yak
4 chat, chin, talk **5** visit
6 babble, confer, gossip, parley, powwow **7** chatter, palaver, prattle **8** converse,
schmooze **9** discourse **10** chew
the fat, chew the rag **11** communicate, confabulate
14 shoot the breeze

communicable 8 catching
10 contagious, infectious
12 transferable **13** transmissible, transmittable

communicate 3 say **4** give,
show, talk, tell **5** state, write
6 advise, convey, impart, notify, pass on, relate, reveal
7 declare, divulge, exhibit,
mention, publish, signify
8 announce, converse, disclose,
inform of, proclaim, transmit
9 apprise of, bring word,
broadcast, make known, publicize **10** correspond

communication 4 news, note,
wire **5** cable **6** letter, missal,
report **7** liaison, message, missive, notices, rapport, writing

8 bulletin, dispatch, document,
speaking, telegram **9** broadcast,
cablegram, directive, statement **10** communique **11** declaration, information
12 conversation, intelligence,
proclamation, radio message
13 telephone call
14 correspondence

communicative 4 open
5 frank **6** candid, chatty **7** voluble **8** friendly, outgoing, sociable **9** revealing, talkative
10 expressive, forthright, free-
spoken, loquacious, revelatory,
unreserved **11** informative

communion, Communion
6 accord **7** concord, harmony,
rapport, sharing **8** affinity,
sympathy **9** agreement **12** the
Eucharist **13** communication,
contemplation

communique 4 note, wire
5 aviso, cable, flash **6** report,
letter, notice **7** epistle, message, missive, release, telegram **8** bulletin, dispatch
9 directive, statement
10 memorandum **12** announcement, intelligence, notification **13** communication

Communist 3 red **6** soviet
7 comrade, marxist **8** Leninist
9 bolshevik, socialist **10** bol-
shevist **12** totalitarian

Communist Manifesto
author: **8** Karl Marx
15 Friedrich Engels

community 4 area, folk, town
5 arena, field, group, range,
realm, scope **6** locale, people,
public, sphere, suburb **7** quarter, society **8** affinity, district,
environs, likeness, populace,
province, sameness, vicinity
9 agreement, citizenry **10** population, similarity **11** environment, social group
12 commonwealth, neighborhood, surroundings

commute 4 ride, trip **5** alter
6 adjust, change, redeem,
soften, switch, travel **7** convert, journey, replace, reverse
8 diminish, exchange, mitigate **9** alleviate, supersede,
transform, transmute, trans-
pose **10** substitute **11** transfigure **12** metamorphose,
transmogrify

comodo
music: **9** leisurely

Comoros *see box*

compact 4 bond, cram, deal,
pack, pact, snug, tidy **5** close,
dense, press, small, stuff **6** little, treaty **7** bargain, crammed,
pressed, squeeze, stuffed **8** alliance, compress, contract, cove-

---

Comoros
other name: **26** lost
pearls of the Indian
Ocean
capital/largest city:
6 Moroni
others: **6** Bambao
7 Fomboni **8** Dzaoudzi
9 Mutsamudu
11 Mitsamiouli
monetary unit: **5** franc
7 centime
island: **6** Moheli **7** An-
jouan, Mayotte
12 Grande Comoro
highest point: **7** Kartala
8 Karthala
sea: **6** Indian
physical feature:
channel:
10 Mozambique
people: **4** Arab **5** Bantu,
Malay **7** African
8 Malagasy
language: **6** Arabic,
French **7** Swahili
8 Malagasy
religion: **5** Islam **13** Roman Catholic

---

nant **9** agreement, clustered,
concordat **10** compressed
11 arrangement, pack closely
12 concentrated **13** tightly
packed, understanding

compactness 7 density
8 snugness **9** smallness **10** lit-
tleness **11** compression
13 concentration

companion 3 pal **4** chum,
mate **5** buddy, crony **6** escort,
friend, helper **7** comrade **9** assistant, associate, attendant

companionable 6 social
7 amiable, cordial **8** friendly,
sociable **9** agreeable, congenial, convivial

companionate 4 warm **6** genial **7** cordial **8** amicable,
friendly, platonic, suitable
9 accordant, agreeable, consonant, easygoing, nonsexual,
spiritual, unfleshly **10** compatible, concordant, harmonious
11 nonphysical, passionless,
warm-hearted **12** affectionate
13 companionable

companionship 4 pals
5 chums **7** buddies, company,
friends **8** comrades **10** associates, companions, fellowship,
friendship **11** camaraderie,
comradeship, familiarity, sociability **17** close acquaintance,
friendly relations

company 3 mob **4** band, firm,

gang **5** bunch, group, guest, party **6** guests, outfit, people, throng **7** callers, concern, friends, society, visitor **8** assembly, comrades, presence, visitors **9** gathering, multitude, syndicate **10** assemblage, companions, fellowship, friendship **11** camaraderie, comradeship, corporation, sociability **12** conglomerate, congregation **13** companionship, establishment **15** business concern

comparable 4 like, up to **5** close, equal **6** akin to **7** similar **8** as good as, parallel **9** a match for, analogous **10** equivalent, on a par with, tantamount **11** approaching, approximate **12** commensurate, in a class with **13** commensurable

comparative 4 near **8** relative **11** approximate

compare 5 equal, liken, match **6** be up to, equate, relate **7** vie with **8** approach, contrast **9** correlate **11** compete with **12** be on a par with **13** hold a candle to **14** be in a class with **20** draw a parallel between

compare notes 6 confer **7** consult **8** talk over **13** exchange views

comparison 7 analogy, kinship **8** contrast, equality, likeness, parallel, relation **10** connection, similarity **11** correlation, resemblance **13** comparability

compartment 3 box, pew **4** brig, cell, crib, hold, hole, nook, room **5** berth, booth, cabin, crypt, niche, stall, vault **6** alcove, bunker, closet **7** chamber, cubicle, section **8** anteroom, roomette **9** cubbyhole **10** pigeonhole **11** antechamber

compass 5 bound, range, reach, scope, sweep **6** domain, extent **8** boundary, province **13** circumference

Compass, Mariner's Compass
  constellation of: **5** Pyxis

Compasses, Pair
  constellation of: **8** Circinus

compassion 4 pity **5** heart **7** empathy, feeling **8** humanity, sympathy **10** tenderness **13** commiseration, fellow feeling **17** tender-heartedness
  Latin: **12** misericordia

compassionate 4 kind **6** humane **7** pitying **8** merciful

10 benevolent, charitable **11** kindhearted, sympathetic **13** tender-hearted

compatibility 6 accord **7** concord, harmony, rapport **8** affinity **9** agreement, unanimity **12** congeniality **14** like-mindedness

compatible 3 apt, fit **6** seemly **7** fitting **8** in accord, suitable **9** congenial, in harmony, in keeping **10** like-minded **11** appropriate

compel 4 make **5** drive, force **6** oblige **7** require **11** necessitate

compelled 4 must **5** bound, urged **6** driven, forced **7** coerced, obliged, pressed **8** commanded, dragooned, enforced, impelled, obsessed, pressured, required **11** constrained, overpowered

compelling 7 driving, dynamic **8** forceful **10** commanding **12** overwhelming

compel obedience to 5 force **6** coerce **7** enforce **8** carry out, insist on **10** administer

compendium 4 list **5** brief **6** apercu, digest, precis, survey **7** abstract, capsule, catalog, epitome, summary **8** syllabus, synopsis **9** catalogue **11** abridgement, compilation **12** condensation

compensate 3 pay **5** cover, repay **6** make up, offset, redeem, square **7** balance, pay back, redress **9** indemnify, reimburse **10** make amends, recompense, remunerate **14** counterbalance **15** make restitution

compensation 3 fee, pay **4** gain **5** wages **6** income, profit, return, reward, salary **7** payment, redress **8** benefits, earnings, gratuity **9** indemnity, repayment **10** recompense, settlement **11** restitution **12** remuneration, satisfaction **13** consideration, reimbursement

compete 3 vie **5** fight **6** battle, combat, oppose **7** contend, contest **8** be rivals **9** lock horns, match wits

competence 5 skill **7** ability, know-how, mastery **8** ableness **9** expertise **10** capability, competency, expertness **11** proficiency

competent 3 fit **6** expert, versed **7** skilled, trained **8** skillful **9** efficient, practiced, qualified **10** dependable, profi-

cient **11** experienced, responsible, trustworthy

competition 4 game **5** event, match, rival **7** contest, rivalry, tourney **8** conflict, opponent, struggle **9** contender **10** contention, opposition, tournament

competitive 8 fighting, opposing, striving **9** combative **10** aggressive, contending

competitor 5 rival **7** fighter **8** opponent **9** adversary, contender **10** contestant, opposition

compilation 4 body **5** group **9** collating, garnering, gathering, mustering **10** assemblage, assembling, assortment, collecting, collection, compendium, marshaling **11** aggregating, aggregation, marshalling **12** accumulating, accumulation

compile 5 amass **6** garner, gather, heap up, muster **7** collate, collect, marshal **8** assemble **10** accumulate

complacent 4 smug **6** at ease **7** content **9** contented **10** self-secure, unbothered, untroubled **13** self-satisfied

complain 3 nag **4** beef, carp, kick, moan, pick **5** cavil, gripe, whine **6** grouch, grouse, squawk **7** grumble **9** bellyache, criticize, find fault **15** state a grievance

complaint 4 beef, kick **5** gripe **6** malady, squawk, tirade **7** ailment, illness, protest **8** debility, disorder, sickness **9** criticism, grievance, infirmity, objection **10** impairment **12** faultfinding **15** dissatisfaction

complaisance 7 pliancy **8** docility **10** affability, amiability, compliance **12** acquiescence

complaisant 4 warm **7** affable, amiable, cordial **8** friendly, gracious, obliging, pleasant, pleasing **9** agreeable, compliant, congenial, easygoing **10** solicitous **11** good-humored, good-natured

Compleat Angler, The
  author: **11** Izaak Walton

complement 3 cap **5** crown, match, total, whole **7** balance, perfect **8** ensemble, entirety, parallel, round out **9** aggregate, companion **10** completion, consummate, full amount, full number, supplement **11** counterpart, rounding-out **12** consummation **14** required number

complementary 7 matched
8 integral, opposite 9 companion 10 additional, compatible, completing 11 correlative
12 interrelated, supplemental
13 correspondent, corresponding

complete 3 cap, end 4 full
5 crown, total, utter, whole
6 entire, finish, intact, settle, wrap up 7 achieve, execute, fulfill, perfect, perform, plenary, settled 8 absolute, achieved, carry out, conclude, executed, round out, thorough, unbroken 9 discharge, make whole, performed, polish off, terminate, undivided
10 accomplish, carried out, complement, conclusive, consummate, unabridged 11 consummated 12 accomplished

completed 4 done 5 ended, whole 6 closed, entire, filled
7 matured, through
8 achieved, finished, realized
9 concluded, executed, fulfilled, perfected 10 terminated, wrapped up 11 consummated
12 accomplished

completeness 8 fullness, richness 9 wholeness 10 perfection 12 thoroughness

completion 3 end 5 close
6 ending, finish, windup
7 closing 9 finishing 10 concluding, conclusion, expiration 11 fulfillment, terminating, termination
12 consummation

complex 4 maze 5 mixed
6 knotty, system 7 network, tangled 8 compound, involved, manifold, multiple, puzzling
9 aggregate, composite, difficult, enigmatic, fixed idea, intricate, obsession
10 perplexing, variegated
11 bewildering, complicated
12 conglomerate, labyrinthian, labyrinthine, multifarious
13 preoccupation

complexion 3 hue 4 look, tone 5 color, guise, image, slant 6 aspect 7 outlook 8 coloring 9 character 10 appearance, coloration, impression
11 countenance, skin texture
12 pigmentation, skin coloring

complexity 6 puzzle 9 intricacy, obscurity 10 bafflement, involution, perplexity
11 crabbedness, elaboration, involvement 12 complication, entanglement 15 inextricability 17 unintelligibility
19 incomprehensibility

compliance 6 assent 7 pliancy
8 docility, giving in, meekness, yielding 9 deference, obedi-

ence, passivity 10 conforming, conformity, submission 12 acquiescence, complaisance
13 nonresistance

compliant 8 flexible, yielding
9 agreeable 10 submissive

complicate 4 knot 5 ravel, snarl 6 muddle, tangle 7 confuse, involve 8 confound, entangle 11 make complex
13 make difficult, make intricate

complicated 7 complex 8 involved 9 elaborate, intricate

complication 4 snag 5 hitch
7 dilemma, problem 8 drawback, handicap, obstacle, quandary 9 hindrance 10 difficulty, impediment, perplexity
11 aggravation, obstruction, predicament 12 disadvantage
14 stumbling block

complicity 8 abetment, intrigue, plotting, schemery, scheming 9 collusion, finagling 10 connivance, conspiracy 11 confederacy, contrivance, implication, involvement 12 entanglement

compliment 5 honor, kudos
6 homage, praise 7 tribute
8 flattery 9 adulation, laudation 11 acclamation 12 commendation 14 congratulation

complimentary 4 free 6 gratis
8 admiring, praising 9 adulatory, extolling, laudatory, panegyric, praiseful 10 flattering, gratuitous, plauditory 12 appreciative, commendatory
13 without charge
14 congratulatory

compliments 4 best, laud
5 exalt, extol, toast 6 homage, praise, salute 7 applaud, commend, regards 8 respects
9 greetings 10 best wishes, good wishes 11 salutations
13 felicitations
15 congratulations

comply 3 bow 4 bend, meet, mind, obey 5 defer, yield
6 accede, adhere, follow, give in, submit 7 abide by, conform, consent, fulfill, observe, satisfy 9 acquiesce, surrender

component 4 item, part
5 piece 6 detail, member, module 7 element, modular, segment 8 material 9 composing, elemental, essential, intrinsic
10 elementary, ingredient, particular 11 constituent, fundamental 13 component part

component part 4 item, part
5 piece 6 detail, member
7 element 10 ingredient, par-

ticular 11 constituent, fundamental

comport 3 act 4 bear 5 carry
6 acquit, behave, deport
7 conduct

comportment 7 bearing, conduct 8 attitude, behavior, carriage, demeanor, presence
9 acquittal 10 appearance, deportment

comport oneself 3 act 6 behave 13 acquit oneself
14 conduct oneself

compose 4 calm, form, lull, make 5 frame, quell, quiet, relax, shape, write 6 create, devise, make up, pacify, settle, soothe 7 collect, fashion, placate 8 be part of, belong to, comprise, conceive, modulate
9 formulate 10 constitute

composed 4 calm, cool
5 quiet 6 at ease, placid, poised, sedate, serene, steady
8 peaceful, tranquil 9 collected, quiescent, unexcited, unruffled 10 controlled, coolheaded, restrained, unagitated, untroubled 11 level-headed, undisturbed, unemotional, unflappable, unperturbed
12 even-tempered 13 dispassionate, imperturbable
15 undemonstrative

composer 4 bard, poet 6 author, writer 7 creator 8 musician, producer 10 compositor, typesetter

composite 6 mosaic 7 blended
8 combined, compound
10 compounded

composition 4 form, opus, work 5 essay, etude, piece
6 design, layout, make-up, making 7 forming, framing, product, shaping 8 creating, creation, devising, exercise
9 framework, structure
10 concoction, fashioning, organizing, production 11 arrangement, combination, compilation, formulation, preparation 12 constitution, organization 13 configuration

compos mentis 4 sane
13 mentally sound

composure 4 calm, cool, ease
5 poise 6 aplomb 7 control, dignity 8 calmness, coolness, patience, serenity 9 sangfroid 10 equanimity
11 self-control 13 selfassurance, self-restraint
14 cool-headedness, selfpossession, unexcitability, unflappability 15 levelheadedness 16 even-temperedness, imperturbability

compound 3 mix **4** fuse, make **5** add to, alloy, blend, boost, mixed, union, unite **6** devise, fusion, mingle **7** amalgam, amplify, augment, blended, combine, complex, concoct, enlarge, magnify, mixture, prepare **8** combined, heighten, increase **9** composite, fabricate, formulate, reinforce **10** synthesize **11** combination, complicated, composition, incorporate, put together **12** conglomerate **14** conglomeration

comprehend 3 dig, get **5** catch, grasp, savvy **6** absorb, digest, fathom **7** make out **8** conceive, perceive **9** penetrate **10** appreciate, assimilate, understand

comprehensible 5 clear, plain **7** evident **8** apparent **11** unambiguous **12** intelligible

comprehension 5 grasp **7** insight **9** awareness **10** conception, perception **11** realization **12** acquaintance, appreciation, apprehension **13** consciousness, understanding

comprehensive 4 full **5** broad **7** copious, general, overall **8** complete, sweeping, thorough **9** expansive, extensive, universal **10** exhaustive, widespread **11** compendious **12** all-embracing, all-inclusive

compress 4 cram, pack **5** press **6** reduce, shrink **7** abridge, bandage, compact, curtail, plaster, shorten, squeeze **8** condense, dressing **10** abbreviate

compressed 5 dense **6** jammed, packed **7** crowded **8** squashed, squeezed **9** compacted **12** concentrated

compressed form 6 digest **7** summary **8** cake form, synopsis **10** shortening **11** abridgement, contraction, curtailment **12** abbreviation, condensation

compression 9 narrowing, squeezing, stricture, tightness **10** compaction, constraint **12** constriction

compressor 4 pump **7** presser, reducer **8** squeezer **9** compactor, condenser

comprise 4 form **6** make up **7** compose, contain, include **8** be made of **9** consist of **10** constitute **12** be composed of

compromise 4 risk **5** agree, truce **6** settle **7** balance, compact, imperil **8** endanger, undercut **9** agreement, discredit, embarrass, implicate, make a deal, prejudice **10** adjustment, jeopardize, settlement **11** arrangement, come to terms, happy medium, make suspect, meet halfway **12** conciliation **13** accommodation, rapprochement **14** make vulnerable, strike a bargain **16** mutual concession **18** split the difference **21** come to an understanding
    German: 9 Ausgleich

compromising 7 risking **8** settling **9** adjusting **10** bargaining **11** give and take, making a deal **12** embarrassing, jeopardizing **13** accommodating, coming to terms **14** meeting halfway

Compsognathus
    type: 8 dinosaur, theropod
    characteristic: 8 smallest
    location: 6 Europe **7** Bavaria
    period: 8 Jurassic

Compson, Quentin
    character in: 14 Absalom Absalom **18** The Sound and the Fury
    author: 8 Faulkner

Compson family
    characters in: 18 The Sound and the Fury
    member: 5 Benjy, Caddy, Jason **7** Candace, Quentin **8** Benjamin
    author: 8 Faulkner

compte rendu 6 record, report, review **7** account **15** account rendered

comptroller 7 auditor **9** treasurer **10** accountant, bookkeeper, controller

compulsion 5 force **6** demand, duress, urging **8** coercion, pressure **9** necessity **10** obligation **11** domineering, requirement

compulsive 6 driven, hooked **7** driving, fanatic **8** addicted, habitual **9** compelled, obsessive **10** compelling **14** unable to resist, uncontrollable

compulsory 7 binding **8** coercive, demanded, enforced, forcible, required **9** mandatory, requisite **10** compulsive, imperative, obligatory **11** unavoidable **12** prescriptive

compunction 5 demur, qualm, shame **6** regret, unease **7** anxiety, concern, remorse, scruple **9** misgiving **10** contrition **16** pang of conscience

computation 5 tally, total **8** figuring **9** numbering, reckoning **10** numeration **11** calculation, enumeration

compute 3 add **5** add up, sum up, tally, total **6** figure, reckon **7** count up, work out **9** ascertain, calculate, figure out

computer 5 adder **9** processor **10** calculator
    language: 3 ADA **4** LOGO **5** ALGOL, BASIC, COBOL **6** PASCAL **7** FORTRAN
    term: 2 PC **3** bit, CAD, CAM, CPU, RAM, ROM **4** boot, byte, chip, hack **5** drive, input, modem, pixel, queue **6** analog, glitch, hacker, memory, online, output **7** digital, network, offline, program **8** database, hardware, lightpen, printout, software, terminal **9** interface, mainframe **10** binary code, floppy disk **12** minicomputer **13** microcomputer, word processor **14** microprocessor

comrade 3 pal **4** ally, chum **5** buddy, crony **6** friend **7** partner **8** confrere, co-worker, helpmate, intimate **9** associate, colleague, companion, confidant **10** bosom buddy **11** confederate **12** collaborator **13** boon companion
    Russian: 8 tovarich

comradeship 8 alliance **10** fellowship, friendship **11** association, camaraderie **13** companionship

comte 5 count

Comte Ory, Le
    also: 8 Count Ory
    opera by: 7 Rossini
    character: 13 Countess Adele

Comus
    author: 10 John Milton

Comus
    origin: 5 Roman
    god of: 7 revelry **8** drinking

con 3 gyp **4** anti, bilk, coax, fool, gull, hoax, lure, rook **5** cheat, cozen, felon, trick **6** delude **7** against, beguile, convict, defraud, mislead, swindle **8** hoodwink, jailbird, prisoner, yardbird **9** bamboozle

Conakry
    capital of: 6 Guinea

concatenation 4 link **5** union **6** hookup **7** joining, linking, reunion **8** coupling, junction **10** bracketing, confluence, connection **11** conjunction **12** interlinking **15** interconnection **16** interassociation **18** intercommunication

concave 6 hollow, sunken
8 indented 9 depressed
13 curving inward

conceal 4 hide, mask 5 cloak,
còver 6 screen, shield 7 cover
up, obscure, secrete 8 disguise 10 camouflage, keep
secret

concealed 5 blind, doggo
6 covert, hidden, latent,
masked, perdue, secret, veiled
7 cloaked, covered, obscure,
unknown, wrapped 8 abstruse,
shrouded, ulterior 9 disguised,
incognito 11 clandestine

concealment 5 cover 6 hiding
7 hideout, masking 8 covering,
hideaway 9 screening, secreting, secretion 10 covering up,
under cover

concede 3 own 4 cede 5 admit,
agree, allow, grant, yield
6 accept, give up, resign,
tender 7 abandon, confess, deliver 8 hand over 9 acquiesce,
recognize, surrender, vouchsafe 10 relinquish 11 acknowledge, be persuaded

conceit 5 pride 6 vanity 7 ego
trip, egotism 8 bragging, self-
love 9 vainglory 10 self-
esteem 12 boastfulness 14 self-
importance

conceited 4 smug, vain
7 stuck-up 8 arrogant, boasting, bragging, puffed up
9 bombastic, overproud, strutting 11 egotistical, swell-
headed 12 vainglorious
13 self-important

conceivable 8 credible, knowable, possible 9 thinkable
10 believable, imaginable, supposable 11 perceivable

conceive 4 form 5 frame,
hatch, start 6 create, invent
7 concoct, dream up, imagine,
produce, think of, think up
8 consider, contrive, envisage,
envision, initiate 9 originate
10 comprehend, understand

concentrate 4 mass 5 amass,
bunch, focus, hem in 6 center,
gather, heap up, reduce
7 close in, cluster, pay heed,
thicken 8 assemble, attend to,
condense, converge, fasten
on 10 accumulate, congregate
11 bring to bear 12 direct
toward

concentrated 5 dense
7 crowded, focused, thought
8 centered 10 compressed

concentration 4 mass 5 focus
7 cluster 9 diligence, gathering, reduction 10 absorption,
assemblage, collection, intentness, thickening 11 aggrega-

tion, boiling down,
convergence, deep thought,
engrossment 12 accumulation
13 concentrating, consolidation 14 centralization

concept 4 idea, view 5 image
6 belief, notion, theory
7 opinion, surmise, thought
9 postulate 10 conviction, hypothesis, impression
11 supposition

conception 4 idea 5 birth, image, start 6 notion 7 forming,
genesis, inkling, picture 8 creating, devising, hatching 9 beginning, formation, imagining,
inception, invention, launching 10 conceiving, concocting,
initiation, perception 11 envisioning, formulation, originating 12 apprehension
13 fertilization, understanding
16 becoming pregnant

conceptual 8 abstract 9 visionary 11 conjectural, ideological,
speculative, theoretical 12 experimental, hypothetical
15 impressionistic

concern 3 job 4 care, duty,
firm, heed 5 chore, house,
store, touch, worry 6 affair, affect, charge, matter, occupy,
regard 7 anxiety, apply to,
company, disturb, involve,
mission, trouble 8 bear upon,
business, distress, interest, relate to 9 attention, pertain to
10 disconcert, enterprise, solicitude 11 appertain to, corporation, disturbance, involvement,
undertaking 12 apprehension
13 consideration, establishment 14 thoughtfulness

concerned 5 upset 6 active,
caring, uneasy 7 alarmed, anxious, engaged, fearful, worried 8 involved, troubled
9 attentive, committed, disturbed 10 disquieted, distressed, interested, solicitous
12 apprehensive
13 participating

concerning 2 of, on, re 3 for
4 as to, over, upon 5 about,
anent 7 apropos 8 engaging,
touching, worrying 9 affecting,
involving, mattering, regarding 10 relating to, respecting

concert 5 union, unity 6 accord, settle 7 concord, harmony 8 teamwork
9 agreement, congruity, unanimity 10 accordance, complicity 11 association,
cooperation 13 collaboration
14 correspondence 18 musical
performance

concerted 5 joint 6 united
7 planned 8 by assent
10 agreed upon 11 coopera-

tive, prearranged 12 premeditated 13 predetermined

concert hall 9 music hall
10 auditorium 12 symphony
hall

concession 5 lease 6 assent
8 giving in, yielding 9 admission, franchise, privilege
10 adjustment, compromise,
indulgence 12 acquiescence,
modification
14 acknowledgment

Conch
form: 7 trumpet
made of: 5 shell
owned by: 7 Tritons

Conchobar
origin: 5 Irish
king of: 6 Ulster
nephew: 10 Cuchulainn

concierge 7 janitor 9 custodian 10 doorkeeper

conciliate 6 pacify 7 appease,
placate 9 make peace, reconcile 11 accommodate

conciliation 11 appeasement,
peacemaking 12 propitiation
13 accommodation
14 reconciliation

conciliatory 8 friendly 9 appeasing, pacifying, placatory
10 mollifying, reassuring
11 peacemaking, reconciling
13 accommodative

concise 5 brief, pithy, short,
terse 7 compact 8 succinct
9 condensed 10 to the point
11 abbreviated

conciseness 7 brevity 9 terseness 11 compactness 12 condensation, succinctness

conclave 6 parley, powwow
7 council, meeting, session
8 assembly 10 conference, convention 11 convocation 13 secret council

conclude 3 end 4 halt, stop
5 close, infer, judge 6 decide,
deduce, effect, finish, gather,
reason, settle 7 arrange, resolve, surmise 8 break off,
carry out, complete 9 determine, terminate 10 accomplish 11 bring to pass,
discontinue 12 draw to a close

concluded 5 bound, ended,
guess 6 closed, judged 7 decided, deduced, expired, settled, wound up 9 completed
10 culminated, determined, restrained, terminated

conclusion 3 end 5 close 6 finale, finish, result, upshot,
windup 7 finding, outcome
8 decision, judgment 9 agreement, deduction, final part, inference, summation

10 completion, denouement, resolution, settlement, working out **11** arrangement, presumption, termination **13** determination

conclusive 5 clear **6** patent **7** certain, obvious **8** absolute, decisive, definite, manifest, palpable **9** clinching **10** compelling, convincing, undeniable **11** categorical, determining, inescapable, irrefutable **12** demonstrable, unanswerable **13** incontestable, unimpeachable **14** unquestionable **16** incontrovertible

concoct 3 mix **4** brew **5** frame, hatch **6** cook up, create, devise, invent, make up **7** think up **8** compound, contrive **9** fabricate, formulate

concoction 4 brew **5** blend **6** jumble, medley **7** mixture **8** compound, creation **9** invention, potpourri **11** contrivance, fabrication **14** conglomeration

concomitant 7 related **9** accessory, attendant, connected, corollary, secondary **10** additional **12** accompanying, contributing, supplemental **13** complementary

concord 5 amity, peace **6** accord **7** harmony **8** goodwill **9** agreement **10** friendship **11** amicability, cooperation **16** cordial relations **19** mutual understanding

concordance 5 index **6** accord **7** concord **9** agreement, consensus, unanimity **17** meeting of the minds

concordant 6 unison **7** calming **8** agreeing, unifying **9** assenting, consonant **10** concurrent, harmonious

concordat 4 pact **8** covenant **9** agreement

Concordia
   origin: 5 Roman
   goddess of: 5 peace
      7 harmony

concourse 7 conflux, joining, linkage, meeting **8** junction **9** amassment **10** assembling, concursion, confluence **11** aggregation, association, convergence **12** congregation, focalization **13** concentration **14** conglomeration **15** flowing together **16** flocking together

concrete 4 real **5** solid **6** cement **7** express, factual, precise **8** definite, distinct, explicit, material, specific, tangible **10** particular **11** fused stones, substantial **12** alloyed rocks

concupiscence 4 itch, lust **6** desire **7** craving, lechery, longing, passion **8** appetite, hot pants, lewdness, satyrism **9** horniness, lubricity, prurience, randiness **10** wantonness **11** goatishness, libertinism, lustfulness **12** sexual desire **13** lecherousness **14** lasciviousness, libidinousness

concur 5 agree, match, tally **6** square **7** conform **8** coincide, hold with **9** be uniform **10** be in accord, correspond **11** go along with **12** go hand in hand

concur in 7 approve **9** agree with **11** go along with

concurrence, concurrency 6 accord **7** concord, consent, harmony **8** approval **9** agreement, consensus, unanimity **10** acceptance, conformity **11** affirmation, coexistence, coincidence, conjuncture, cooperation, synchronism **12** acquiescence **13** collaboration, mutual consent **14** correspondence **15** working together **17** meeting of the minds **22** simultaneous occurrence

concurrent 5 at one **6** allied **7** aligned **8** agreeing, matching **9** congenial, congruous, consonant **10** coexisting, coincident, coinciding, compatible, harmonious **11** in agreement, sympathetic, synchronous **12** commensurate, contemporary, in accordance, simultaneous **13** correspondent, of the same mind **15** contemporaneous

concurring 8 agreeing **10** consenting **11** affirmative, in agreement, synchronous **12** coincidental, simultaneous **13** corresponding

concussion 3 jar **4** blow, bump **5** clash, shock **6** buffet, impact **7** shaking **8** pounding **9** agitation, collision **11** brain injury

condemn 4 damn, doom **5** decry **6** rebuke **7** censure **8** denounce, sentence **9** criticize, proscribe, reprehend **10** disapprove

condemnation 6 rebuke **7** censure, reproof **8** judgment, reproach, sentence **9** criticism **10** conviction, punishment **11** disapproval **12** denunciation, reprehension **14** disapprobation **20** pronouncement of guilt

condensation 6 digest **9** re-

duction **10** abridgment **13** shortened form **16** condensed version

condense 3 cut **4** trim **6** digest, reduce **7** abridge, compact, liquefy, shorten, thicken **8** boil down, compress, contract, pare down **10** abbreviate, blue-pencil **11** concentrate, consolidate, precipitate

condensed form 6 digest **7** summary **8** synopsis **10** shortening **11** abridgment, compression, contraction, curtailment **12** abbreviation

condescend 5 deign, stoop **6** submit, unbend **7** descend, disdain **9** patronize **10** look down on, talk down to **12** come down a peg, lower oneself **13** humble oneself

condescending 7 high-hat **8** superior **9** disdainful **11** overbearing, patronizing

condescension 4 airs **7** disdain, hauteur, modesty **8** humility **9** deference, loftiness **10** humbleness **11** haughtiness **12** graciousness **13** self-abasement **14** self-effacement **19** patronizing attitude **20** assumption of equality **21** high-and-mighty attitude

condign 3 due **4** fair, just, meet **5** right **6** earned, proper, worthy **7** fitting, merited **8** deserved, suitable **9** warranted **11** appropriate

condiment 4 herb **5** sauce, spice **8** dressing, flavorer, seasoner **9** seasoning
   kind: 3 bay **4** dill, mace, mint, sage, salt **5** caper, clove, curry, onion, thyme **6** catsup, garlic, ginger, nutmeg, pepper, pickle, relish **7** caraway, chutney, ketchup, mustard, parsley, oregano, paprika, pimento, tabasco, vinegar **8** cardamon, marjoram, turmeric **9** pimpernel **10** bell pepper, mayonnaise

condition 3 fit **4** term **5** adapt, equip, ready, shape, state, train **6** demand, fettle, malady, status, tone up **7** ailment, prepare, problem, proviso **8** accustom, position, standing **9** agreement, complaint, provision, requisite, situation **10** limitation, make used to, put in shape **11** arrangement, contingency, malfunction, reservation, restriction, stipulation **12** prerequisite **13** circumstances, qualification, state of health **14** state of affairs **15** physical fitness

conditional 7 limited 9 dependent, qualified, tentative 10 contingent, restricted 11 provisional, stipulative 16 with reservations

condolence 4 pity 6 solace 7 comfort 8 sympathy 10 compassion 11 consolation 13 commiseration

Condon, Richard author of: 11 Winter Kills 18 Death of a Politician 22 The Manchurian Candidate

condonation 11 forgiveness, overlooking 12 disregarding 13 putting up with

condone 6 excuse, forget, ignore, pardon, wink at 7 absolve, forgive, justify, let pass 8 overlook 9 disregard, put up with

conduce 3 aid 4 help, lead, tend 5 bring, favor, guide 6 effect 7 advance, forward, further, promote 10 contribute

conducive 7 helpful 8 salutary 9 favorable, promotive 10 beneficial 11 expeditious 12 contributive, contributory, instrumental 19 calculated to produce 22 helpful in bringing about

conduct 3 act 4 bear, lead, rule, ways 5 carry, chair, deeds, enact, guide, pilot, steer, usher 6 action, attend, behave, convey, convoy, direct, escort, govern, manage, manner 7 carry on, comport, control, execute, marshal, operate, perform 8 behavior, carry out, dispatch, guidance, regulate, transact 9 accompany, direction, discharge, look after, supervise 10 administer, deportment, government, leadership, management 11 comportment, generalship, preside over, superintend, supervision 14 administration

conduct oneself 3 act 6 behave 13 acquit oneself 14 comport oneself

conductor 3 cad 5 guide 6 carman, escort, leader 7 cathode, channel, maestro, manager 8 aqueduct, batonist, cicerone, conveyor, director, operator, stickman, trainman 9 collector, drum major 10 impresario, supervisor 11 choirmaster, transmitter 13 concert master

conduit 4 duct, main, pipe, tube 5 canal, drain, flume, sewer 6 gutter, trough 7 channel, passage 8 aqueduct 11 watercourse

cone 5 bevel, shape, spire 6 bobbin, conoid, funnel 7 pyramid, volcano 8 pyramid kind: 3 fir 4 pine 5 larch 7 conifer, retinal 8 ice cream

confabulate 4 chat, talk 6 confer, patter 7 chatter, discuss 8 chitchat, converse, talk idly

confabulation 4 chat, talk 8 chitchat 10 conference, discussion 12 conversation

confection 3 jam 5 candy 6 pastry 7 dessert 8 conserve, delicacy 9 preserves, sweetmeat 10 sugar candy

confectionery 5 candy 6 sweets 7 goodies, pasties 10 sugar candy, sweetmeats

confederacy, Confederacy 3 CSA 4 band, bloc 5 guild, union 6 fusion, league 7 combine, society 8 alliance, the South 9 coalition, syndicate 10 federation 11 association 13 confederation 14 Southern states 18 secessionist states 26 Confederate States of America

confederate 4 ally 5 merge, unite 6 cohort, helper 7 abettor, comrade, partner 8 coalesce, coworker 9 accessory, affiliate, associate, colleague, companion 10 accomplice, cooperator, join forces 11 consolidate, helping hand 12 band together, collaborator, right hand man 17 fellow conspirator

Confederates author: 14 Thomas Keneally

confederation 4 band 5 guild, union 6 fusion, league 7 combine, society 8 alliance 9 coalition, syndicate 10 federation 11 association, confederacy

confer 4 give 5 award 6 accord, parley 7 consult, discuss, palaver 8 converse 9 present to 10 bestow upon 12 compare notes, talk together 15 hold a conference 18 deliberate together

conference 4 talk 6 parley 7 council, meeting, seminar 8 conclave 9 symposium 10 convention, discussion 12 consultation, deliberation

conferment 4 gift 5 award 8 bestowal 12 presentation

confess 4 avow, sing 5 admit, own up 6 expose, reveal 7 declare, divulge, lay bare 8 blurt out, disclose 9 come clean, make known 11 acknowledge 12 bring to light 14 unbosom oneself 18 make a clean breast of

confessed 6 avowed 8 admitted 9 professed 12 self-declared 14 self-proclaimed

confession 6 avowal, shrift 9 admission 10 disclosure, divulgence, revelation 11 declaration 12 confessional 14 acknowledgment

Confessions of an English Opium Eater author: 15 Thomas DeQuincey

Confessions of Nat Turner, The author: 13 William Styron

confidant, confidante 5 crony 6 friend 8 intimate 10 bosom buddy 15 trusty companion

confide 6 impart, reveal 7 confess, divulge, lay bare, let in on, let know 8 disclose 9 make known 12 tell secretly 13 tell privately 14 unbosom oneself

confidence 4 grit, guts 5 faith, nerve, pluck, spunk, trust 6 belief, daring, mettle, secret, spirit 7 courage 8 audacity, boldness, credence, intimacy, reliance 9 certainty, certitude 10 conviction 11 intrepidity 12 self-reliance 13 private matter, self-assurance 14 faith in oneself 17 inside information

confidence man 5 cheat 6 con man 8 swindler 9 charlatan, trickster 10 mountebank

confident 4 bold, sure 5 cocky 6 daring, secure 7 assured, certain 8 cocksure, intrepid, positive 9 convinced, dauntless, expectant 10 optimistic 11 self-assured, self-reliant 13 sure of oneself

confidential 5 privy 6 secret 7 private 8 hush-hush 9 top-secret 10 classified 11 undisclosed 12 off-the-record 16 not to be disclosed

confidentially 7 sub rosa 8 in secret, secretly 9 privately 16 between ourselves 17 behind closed doors French: 9 entre nous

confiding 6 trusty 7 reliant 8 trustful, trusting 9 confident 11 trustworthy

configuration 4 form 6 design, makeup 11 arrangement, composition

confine 3 pen, tie 4 bind, cage, hold, jail, keep 5 limit 6 coop up, govern, keep in, lock up, shut in, shut up 7 fence in, impound 8 imprison, regulate, restrain, restrict 9 sequester 11 incarcerate 13 hold in custody

confined 5 close, tight 6 jailed, narrow 7 cramped 8 locked up 10 imprisoned, restricted

confinement 7 custody, lying in 9 cooping up, detention, restraint 10 childbirth, constraint, limitation, shutting in 11 parturition, restriction 12 accouchement, imprisonment 13 incarceration 15 circumscription

confines 4 edge 6 border, bounds, limits 7 margins 8 precinct 10 boundaries 13 circumference

confirm 5 prove 6 accept, clinch, ratify, uphold, verify 7 agree to, approve, bear out, certify, sustain 8 make firm, validate 9 authorize, establish 11 acknowledge, corroborate, make binding, make certain 12 authenticate, substantiate

confirmation 5 proof 6 assent 8 approval, sanction 9 agreement 10 acceptance, validation 11 affirmation, endorsement 12 ratification, verification 13 corroboration 14 authentication, substantiation

confirmed 3 set 5 fixed 7 chronic 8 hardened, verified 9 ingrained, validated 10 deep-rooted, deep-seated, inveterate, proven true 11 established 12 corroborated 13 authenticated, dyed-in-the-wool, substantiated

confiscate 4 take 5 seize 7 impound, possess, preempt 8 take over 9 sequester 10 commandeer 11 appropriate, expropriate

confiscation 7 seizure 10 impounding, preemption 13 appropriation, commandeering, expropriation

conflagration 4 fire 5 blaze 7 bonfire, inferno 8 conflict, fighting, wildfire 9 brush fire, firestorm, holocaust 10 forest fire, raging fire, wall of fire 11 sea of flames 12 sheet of flame

conflagrative 8 burnable 9 flammable, ignitable 10 combustive, incendiary 11 combustible, inflammable

conflict 4 fray 5 clash, fight,

melee, set-to 6 action, battle, combat, fracas, oppose, strife, tussle 7 collide, discord, dissent, scuffle, warfare 8 disagree, division, friction, skirmish, struggle, variance 9 encounter, hostility 10 antagonism, be contrary, difference, dissension, engagement 12 disagreement 13 confrontation 14 be inharmonious 15 be contradictory
  Spanish: 9 mano a mano

conflicting 7 warring 8 clashing, opposing 10 ambivalent 13 contradictory

confluence 5 union 7 conflux, joining, linkage, meeting 8 junction, juncture 9 concourse, gathering 10 assembling, concursion 11 association, convergence 13 concentration 14 coming together 15 flowing together

conform 3 fit 4 obey 5 adapt 6 adjust, follow 8 adhere to, jibe with, submit to 9 agree with, reconcile, tally with 10 be guided by, comply with, fall in with, square with 11 acquiesce in 12 correspond to

conformable 8 amenable 9 agreeable, malleable 10 submissive 12 in compliance

conformance 7 harmony 9 agreement 10 accordance, compliance, conformity 13 compatibility

conformation 4 form 5 build, shape 6 figure 7 anatomy 9 formation, framework, structure 11 arrangement 13 configuration

conformist 12 well-adjusted 13 unadventurous

conformity 6 accord, assent 7 harmony 8 likeness 9 agreement, obedience 10 compliance, observance, similarity, submission, uniformity 11 resemblance 12 acquiescence 14 correspondence 15 conventionality

confound 5 amaze, mix up 6 baffle, puzzle, rattle 7 astound, confuse, fluster, mystify, nonplus, perplex, startle 8 astonish, bewilder, dumfound, surprise, unsettle 10 disconcert 11 flabbergast 16 strike with wonder, throw off the scent

confounded 8 confused 10 bewildered, nonplussed 11 dumbfounded 12 disconcerted

confraternity 4 body 5 guild,

union 7 society 8 sodality 9 confrairy 11 association, brotherhood

confrere 3 pal 4 ally, chum 5 buddy 6 friend 7 brother, comrade, partner 9 associate, colleague

confront 4 dare, defy, face, meet 5 brave 8 cope with, face up to 9 challenge, encounter, withstand

confrontation 5 clash, run-in, set-to 6 battle, combat, debate 7 contest, dispute, face-off 8 conflict, showdown, skirmish 9 encounter 10 engagement, opposition 11 controversy 17 face-to-face meeting
  Spanish: 9 mano a mano

Confucius
  author of: 10 Book of Odes 11 The Analects

confuse 3 addle, befog, mix up, stump 6 baffle, muddle, puzzle, rattle 7 fluster, mistake, mystify, nonplus, perplex 8 befuddle, bewilder, confound, unsettle 10 discompose, disconcert 11 make unclear 12 make baffling 14 make perplexing 17 throw into disorder

confused 5 fazed 6 addled 7 abashed, baffled, chaotic, jumbled, mixed-up, muddled, tangled 8 rambling 9 befuddled, illogical, perplexed, unsettled 10 bewildered, disjointed, distracted, incoherent, nonplussed 11 dumbfounded 12 disconcerted, disorganized 13 disharmonious, heterogeneous

confusing 7 addling 8 baffling, blinding, blurring, dizzying, jumbling, mixing up, muddling 9 deranging, mistaking 10 befuddling, disorderly, flustering, mystifying, perplexing, stupefying 11 bewildering, confounding 13 disconcerting, unintelligible

confusion 4 mess, riot 5 chaos, snarl 6 bedlam, hubbub, jumble, muddle, tangle, tumult, uproar 7 clutter, ferment, turmoil 8 disarray, disorder, madhouse, shambles, upheaval 9 abashment, commotion 10 bafflement, hodgepodge, hullabaloo, perplexity, puzzlement, untidiness 11 disturbance, pandemonium 12 bewilderment, discomposure, stupefaction 13 mystification 14 disarrangement, disconcertment 15 disorganization
  French: 14 bouleversement

confutation 6 denial
7 counter **8** negation, rebuttal
10 refutation **13** contradiction

confute 4 deny **5** rebut **6** impugn, oppose, refute
7 counter, gainsay **10** contradict, controvert **12** be contrary to

congeal 3 set **4** clot, jell **6** curdle, freeze, harden **7** stiffen, thicken **8** solidify **9** coagulate **10** gelatinize

congenial 4 like **6** genial, social **7** affable, cordial, kindred, related, similar **8** agreeing, amenable, gracious, pleasant, pleasing, sociable **9** agreeable, convivial **10** compatible, consistent, harmonious, well-suited **11** sympathetic **13** companionable, corresponding
French: 9 en rapport
German: 9 gemutlich

congeniality 7 harmony, rapport **8** affinity **11** sociability
12 conviviality, friendliness, pleasantness **13** compatibility
14 like-mindedness

congenital 6 inborn, inbred, innate, native **7** natural **8** inherent **9** ingrained, inherited, intrinsic **10** hereditary

congested 6 filled, gorged, jammed, packed **7** crowded **9** saturated **10** overcrowded

congestion 3 jam, mob
4 mass **5** snarl **6** pile-up
8 crowding **10** bottleneck
11 obstruction
12 overcrowding

conglomerate 4 heap, mass, pile **5** amass, blend, stack **7** mixture **8** assemble **9** aggregate **10** accumulate, assemblage **12** accumulation
16 large corporation

conglomeration 6 jumble, medley **7** mixture **8** mishmash **9** aggregate, potpourri **10** assortment, collection, hodgepodge **11** aggregation, combination **13** agglomeration

Congo *see box*

congratulate 4 hail **6** salute
10 compliment, felicitate, wish

one joy **11** rejoice with
18 give one's best wishes
28 wish many happy returns of the day

congratulations 6 salute
9 blessings, greetings **10** best wishes, good wishes **11** well-wishing **13** felicitations
24 many happy returns of the day

congregate 4 mass **5** amass, flock, swarm **6** gather, throng **7** cluster, collect **8** assemble **12** come together **13** crowd together

congregation 5 crowd, flock, group, horde, laity **6** parish, throng **8** assembly, audience, brethren **9** gathering, multitude **12** parishioners
16 church membership **17** religious assembly

congress, Congress 4 diet
6 caucus **7** council **8** assembly **9** delegates, gathering **10** conference, convention, parliament **11** legislature **14** federal council **15** discussion group, legislative body, national council, representatives
17 chamber of deputies

Congreve, William
author of: **11** Love for Love
15 The Double-Dealer
16 The Mourning Bride, The Way of the World

congruity 7 harmony **9** agreement, coherence **10** consonance **11** consistency
12 congeniality **13** compatibility **14** correspondence
15 appropriateness

congruous 4 meet **6** seemly
7 apropos **8** becoming, relevant, suitable **9** congenial, consonant, in keeping **10** harmonious **11** appropriate, in agreement **13** corresponding

conifer
means: **11** cone bearing
order: **11** coniferales
class: **10** gymnosperm
kind: **3** fir, yew **4** pine **5** cedar, larch, pinal **6** ginkgo, pinale, spruce, torrey **7** cypress, hemlock, juniper, redwood, sequoia **8** softwood
9 evergreen

Coningsby
author: **16** Benjamin Disraeli

conjectural 7 reputed **8** abstract, academic, doubtful, putative, supposed, surmised
11 inferential, speculative, theoretical **12** hypothetical
13 suppositional
14 supposititious

conjecture 4 idea, view

Congo
   other name: **10** Moyen Congo **11** Middle Congo
   capital/largest city: **11** Brazzaville
   others: **3** Ewo **4** Boko **5** Epena, Kayes, Kelle, Okoyo, Sembe **6** Dongou, Komono, Makoua, Matadi, M'Binda, M'Vouti, Ouesso, Sibiti, Zanaga **7** Cabinda, Dolisie, Etoumbi, Gamboma, Kinkala, Loubomo, Loudima, Madingo, Mossaka, Souanke **8** Djambala, Impfondo, Kibangou, Madingou, Mindouli **9** Mossendjo **11** Fort-Rousset, Pointe-Noire **17** Mayombe Escarpment
   school: **13** Marien Ngoubai
   monetary unit: **5** franc **7** centime
   lake: **5** Mweru, Tumba **6** Albert, Nyanza, Upemba **7** Leopold **11** Stanley Pool
   highest point: **6** Leketi
   river: **3** Dja **4** Uele **5** Alima, Congo, Kasal, Kwilu, Lulua, Ngoko, Niari, Sanga, Swilu, Wamba, Zahir, Zaire **6** Kwango, Kwenge, Loange, Lobaye, Lomami, Ogooue, Ubangi **7** Aruwima, Kouilou, Lualaba, Luapula, N'Gounie **8** Itimbiri, Likouala, Lubilash
   sea: **8** Atlantic
   physical feature:
      plateau: **6** Bateke
   people: **3** Rua **4** Akka, Susa, Teke, Vili **5** Amadi, Bantu, Figot, Kongo, Mantu, Pygmy, Sanga, Warua, Zambi **6** Ababua, Bafyot, Bateke, Mbochi, Nzambi, Wabuma **7** Bacongo, Bakongo, Bangala, Batetla, Manyema **10** Binga Pygmy
      discoverer: **3** Cam
   language: **4** Susu **5** Bantu, Fiote **6** French, Kituba **7** Bangala, Lingala
   religion: **5** Islam **7** animism **10** Protestant **13** Roman Catholic
   place:
      church: **9** Saint Anne
      stadium: **5** Eboue
   feature:
      tree: **5** limba

5 fancy, guess, infer, judge, think **6** augury, notion, reckon, theory **7** imagine, opinion, presume, suppose, surmise **8** estimate, forecast, judgment, theorize **9** calculate, deduction, guesswork, inference, speculate, suspicion **10** assumption, guestimate, hypothesis, presuppose **11** guess-timate, hypothesize, speculation, supposition **13** shot in the dark

conjoin 4 join, knit, link **5** touch, unite **7** combine, connect, overlap **8** together **9** associate

conjoined 6 joined, linked, united **7** knitted, meeting **8** combined, touching **9** connected **10** associated **11** overlapping **14** joined together

conjugal 6 wedded **7** marital, married, nuptial, spousal **9** connubial **11** matrimonial

conjugate 4 join, pair, yoke **5** mated, unite, yoked **6** couple, joined, paired, united **7** connect, coupled, related **9** connected **10** paronymous

conjunction 5 union **7** joining, meeting **11** association, coincidence, combination, concurrence

conjuration 5 charm, spell, trick **11** incantation

conjure 5 allay, charm, raise **6** invoke, summon **7** bewitch, command, enchant **8** call away, call upon **9** call forth **10** cast a spell, make appear **13** make disappear **15** practice sorcery

conjurer 6 wizard **8** magician

conk 3 die, hit **4** bean, blow, fail, head **5** decay, faint, sleep, stall **6** fungus, strike **7** bracket **8** knock out **9** break down **10** straighten

Conn, Katherine
  real name of: **13** Kitty Carlisle

connect 3 tie **4** join **5** hinge, merge, unite **6** attach, couple, relate **7** combine, compare **9** associate, correlate **14** fasten together

connected 4 tied **6** joined, merged, united **7** coupled **8** abutting, adjacent, attached, combined, touching **9** bordering, proximate **10** connecting, contiguous, juxtaposed **12** conterminous **16** fastened together

connected group 5 cycle **6** series **8** sequence **11** progression

---

Connecticut
  abbreviation: 2 CT **4** Conn
  nickname: 6 Nutmeg **7** Blue Law **9** Freestone **12** Constitution **18** Land of Steady Habits
  capital/largest city: 8 Hartford
  others: 4 Avon **6** Bethel, Canaan, Cos Cob, Darien, Hamden, Mystic, Sharon, Storrs **7** Ansonia, Bristol, Danbury, Enfield, Madison, Meriden, Milford, Niantic, Norwalk, Norwich, Shelton, Tolland, Windsor **8** Guilford, New Haven, Simsbury, Stamford, Westport **9** Greenwich, Naugatuck, New London, Stratford, Waterbury **10** Bridgeport, Manchester, New Britain, Torrington **11** Wallingford
  college: 4 Yale **7** Trinity **8** Hartford, St Joseph, Wesleyan **9** Fairfield **10** Bridgeport, Quinnipiac **11** Sacred Heart **12** U S Coast Guard
  feature: 10 Charter Oak
    museum: **8** PT Barnum
    seaport: **6** Mystic
    theater: **27** American Shakespeare Festival
  tribe: 6 Pequot **7** Mohegan, Niantic **10** Quinnipiac
  people: 8 PT Barnum **9** John Brown **10** Nathan Hale **11** Noah Webster **12** Thomas Hooker **19** Harriet Beecher Stowe
  lake: 10 Candlewood
  land rank: 11 forty-eighth
  mountain: 4 Bear **7** Taconic
    hills: **10** Berkshires
    highest point: **8** Frissell
  physical feature: 15 Long Island Sound
  river: 6 Thames **9** Naugatuck **10** Housatonic **11** Connecticut
  state admission: 5 fifth
  state bird: 5 robin
  state flower: 14 mountain laurel
  state motto: 30 He Who Transplanted Still Sustains
  state song: 12 Yankee Doodle
  state tree: 8 white oak

Connecticut Yankee in King Arthur's Court, A
  author: 9 Mark Twain
  character: 5 Sandy **6** Merlin **8** Alisande, Clarence **11** Morgan le Fay **12** Hello-Central **18** Sir Kay the Seneschal

connection 3 kin, tie **4** bond, link **5** nexus **6** family, friend **7** contact, coupler, kinfolk, kinsman, linkage **8** affinity, alliance, coupling, junction, kinsfolk, relation, relative **9** associate, connector, fastening **10** attachment, kith and kin **11** association, correlation **12** acquaintance, relationship **13** flesh and blood, interrelation

Connelly, Marc
  author of: 16 The Green Pastures
    with Frank Elser: **19** The Farmer Takes a Wife
    with George S Kaufman: **5** Dulcy **11** To the Ladies **17** Beggar on Horseback, Merton of the Movies

---

Connery, Sean
  real name: 13 Thomas Connery
  born: 8 Scotland **9** Edinburgh
  roles: 6 Marnie **14** Robin and Marian **15** The Untouchables **16** The Molly Maguires **20** The Man Who Would Be King **28** Darby O'Gill and the Little People
    James Bond: **4** Dr No **10** Goldfinger **11** Thunderball **16** You Only Live Twice **18** Diamonds Are Forever, From Russia with Love, Never Say Never Again

connivance 4 plot **5** cabal **6** design, scheme **8** intrigue **9** collusion **10** complicity, conspiracy **11** machination

connive 3 aid **4** abet, plan, plot **5** allow **6** wink at **7** collude **8** conspire **10** be a party to **13** be accessory to, lend oneself to **14** shut one's eyes to **17** be in collusion with, cooperate secretly

conniving 4 wily **6** artful,

crafty **7** cunning **8** plotting, scheming **9** designing **10** intriguing **11** calculating

connoisseur 5 judge, maven, mavin **6** expert **7** epicure, gourmet **9** authority **11** cognoscente **17** person of good taste

Connolly, Maureen
nickname: **8** Little Mo
sport: **6** tennis

Connor, Dale
creator/artist of: **9** Mary Worth

connotation 5 drift **6** import, spirit **8** coloring **9** evocation, undertone **10** intimation, suggestion **11** implication, insinuation **12** significance

connote 5 imply **6** hint at **7** suggest **8** intimate **9** insinuate **11** bring to mind

connubial 6 wedded **7** marital, married, nuptial **8** conjugal **11** matrimonial

conquer 4 beat, best, drub, lick, rout, rule, trim, whip **5** floor, quell **6** defeat, humble, master, occupy, subdue, thrash **7** possess, win over **8** overcome, surmount, vanquish **9** overpower, rise above, subjugate **11** prevail over, triumph over **14** get the better of

conqueror 6 victor, winner **7** subduer **8** champion **10** subjugator, vanquisher **12** conquistador

conquest 3 fan **4** sway **5** lover **6** adorer, defeat **7** captive, mastery, triumph, victory, winning **8** adherent, follower, whip hand **9** upper hand **10** ascendancy, conquering, domination, overcoming **11** acquisition, subjugation **12** vanquishment **17** captured territory

Conrad, Joseph
real name: **29** Josef Teodor Konrad Korzeniowski
author of: **6** Chance **7** Lord Jim, Typhoon, Victory **8** Nostromo **11** Almayer's Folly **14** The Secret Agent **15** Heart of Darkness **16** Under Western Eyes **21** An Outcast of the Islands **23** The Nigger of the Narcissus

consanguine 4 akin **7** cognate, kindred, related **8** relative

consanguineous 3 kin **4** akin **7** kindred, related **9** connected **21** having a common ancestor

conscience 8 scruples **10** moral sense, principles **15** ethical feelings **20** sense of right and wrong

conscience-stricken 6 guilty **7** ashamed **8** contrite, penitent **9** chastened, regretful, repentant **10** remorseful **13** guilt-stricken

conscientious 5 exact **6** honest **7** careful, dutiful, ethical, upright **10** fastidious, meticulous, particular, scrupulous **11** painstaking, responsible, trustworthy **12** consciable **14** high-principled

conscious 5 aware **7** alert to, alive to, awake to, studied **8** noticing, sensible, sentient **9** cognizant, in the know, observing **10** calculated, deliberate, discerning, perceiving **12** apperceptive, premeditated **13** knowledgeable

consciousness 4 mind **6** senses **8** feelings, thoughts **9** awareness **10** cognizance, perception **11** discernment, sensibility

conscript 3 PFC **4** boot, hire, levy **5** draft **6** call up, employ, engage, enlist, enroll, induct, muster, rookie, seaman, select, take on **7** draftee, impress, private, recruit **8** enlistee, inductee, mobilize, register, selectee, shanghai **9** conscribe **11** buck private

consecrate 5 bless **6** hallow **7** glorify **8** sanctify **10** make sacred **11** immortalize **13** declare sacred

consecrated 4 holy **7** blessed **8** hallowed **10** sanctified

consecutive 6 in turn, serial **8** unbroken **10** continuous, sequential, successive **11** progressive **13** uninterrupted **19** following one another

consensus 6 accord **7** concord **9** unanimity **11** concurrence **13** common consent **14** general opinion **15** majority opinion **16** general agreement

consent 5 agree, allow, yield **6** accede, accept, accord, assent, concur, permit, ratify, submit **7** approve, concede, concord, confirm, endorse **8** approval, sanction **9** acquiesce, agreement **10** acceptance, fall in with, permission **11** concurrence, endorsement, willingness **12** acquiescence, confirmation, ratification

Consenting Adults
author: **12** Peter DeVries

consent to 2 OK **4** okay

6 permit **7** approve **8** accede to **10** concur with **11** acquiesce to, go along with **14** give the go-ahead

consequence 3 end **4** note **5** avail, fruit, issue, value, worth **6** import, moment, result, sequel, upshot **7** account, gravity, outcome **9** aftermath, influence, magnitude, outgrowth **10** importance, notability, prominence, usefulness **11** development, distinction, seriousness **12** significance

consequent 7 ensuing **8** eventual **9** following, resulting

consequential 7 crucial, epochal **8** historic **9** important, momentous **10** meaningful **11** significant

consequently 2 so **4** ergo, then **5** and so, hence, later **9** as a result, therefore **11** accordingly **12** subsequently

conservation 4 care **6** upkeep **9** husbandry **10** careful use, protection **11** maintenance, safekeeping **12** preservation

conservative 5 quiet **6** square **7** old-line **8** cautious, moderate, undaring **9** right-wing **10** nonliberal, unchanging **11** reactionary, right-winger, traditional **13** unprogressive **15** middle-of-the-road **16** opponent of change **17** middle-of-the-roader **22** champion of the status quo

conservatoire 11 music school **12** conservatory, music academy

conservatory 7 nursery **8** hothouse **9** arboretum **10** glasshouse, greenhouse **11** music school **12** music academy **13** conservatoire

conserve 4 save **5** guard **7** care for, cut back, husband, use less **8** maintain, not waste, preserve **9** safeguard **12** use sparingly

consider 4 deem, hold, note **5** gauge, honor, judge, opine, study, think, weigh **6** ponder, regard, review **7** believe, examine, pay heed, respect **8** appraise, envision, hold to be, mull over **9** be aware of, reflect on **10** bear in mind, cogitate on, think about **11** contemplate **12** deliberate on **17** make allowances for **18** turn over in one's mind

considerable 4 tidy **5** ample, great, large **6** goodly **7** notable, sizable **8** not small **9** estimable, important **10** impressive, noteworthy, noticeable, of some size, remarkable **11** a good deal of, significant, substantial

considerably 5 amply **7** greatly, largely, notably, sizably **9** estimably **10** abundantly, noticeably, remarkably **13** significantly, substantially

considerate 4 kind **6** kindly **7** mindful **8** obliging **9** attentive, concerned **10** solicitous, thoughtful

consideration 4 heed, tact **5** cause, honor, point, study **6** factor, ground, motive, notice, reason, regard, review **7** concern, respect, thought **8** interest, judgment **9** attention **10** advisement, cogitation, inducement, kindliness, meditation, reflection, solicitude **11** examination **12** deliberation **13** contemplation **14** thoughtfulness **15** considerateness

consider closely 7 pay heed **11** concentrate **12** pay attention **13** put one's mind to **21** give one's full attention

considered 5 mused **6** deemed, heeded, judged, mulled **7** advised, express, honored, noticed, studied, thought, weighed, willful **8** believed, esteemed, looked on, pondered, regarded, supposed **9** reflected, respected, ruminated **10** considered, deliberate, looked upon, thought out **11** deliberated, entertained, intentional **12** contemplated, premeditated, thought about

consign 5 remit **6** assign, commit, convey, remand **7** deliver, entrust **8** delegate, hand over, relegate, transfer **9** commend to **11** deposit with

consignment 8 delivery, shipment, transfer **10** assignment, committing, consigning, delegation, depositing, entrusting, relegation **11** handing over **12** goods for sale, goods shipped **19** goods sent on approval

consist 3 lie **6** reside **7** contain, include **10** be made up of **11** to be found in **13** be comprised of **14** to be composed of

consistency, consistence 4 body **5** unity **6** makeup **7** density, harmony, texture **8** firmness **9** agreement, coherence, congruity, stiffness, structure, thickness, viscosity **10** accordance, conformity, connection, uniformity

11 compactness, composition, persistence **12** construction, faithfulness, steady effort **13** compatibility, steadfastness **14** correspondence **16** uniform standards **19** constant performance, undeviating behavior

consistent 4 meet **6** steady **7** regular, unified **8** agreeing, constant, of a piece, suitable **9** congenial, congruous, consonant **10** compatible, harmonious, persistent, unchanging **11** in agreement, undeviating **13** correspondent **16** conforming to type

consolation 4 help **5** cheer **6** relief, solace, succor **7** comfort, support **8** easement, soothing, sympathy **10** condolence **11** alleviation, assuagement **13** encouragement

Consolation of Philosophy (De Consolatione Philosophiae)
    author: **31** Anicius Manlius Severinus Boethius

console 4 calm, ease **5** cheer **6** soothe, succor **7** comfort, support, sustain **10** lament with, sympathize **11** condole with **13** express sorrow **15** commiserate with **18** express sympathy for

consolidate 4 fuse, join **5** merge, unify, unite **6** league **7** combine, fortify **8** coalesce, compress, condense, federate, make firm, make sure, solidify **9** integrate, make solid **10** amalgamate, centralize, strengthen **11** concentrate, incorporate **12** band together **13** bring together

consolidation 5 union **6** fusion, merger **8** alliance **9** coalition **11** unification **12** amalgamation **13** agglomeration **14** conglomeration

consomme 4 soup **5** broth **9** madrilene

consonance 5 amity, unity **6** accord, unison **7** concord, harmony, oneness **9** agreement, coherence, congruity, unanimity **10** accordance, conformity, congruence, consonancy **11** concordance, consistency, homogeneity **13** compatibility **14** correspondence, like-mindedness

consonant 8 in accord **9** agreeable, congruous, in harmony **10** concordant, consistent **11** in agreement

consort 3 mix **4** club, mate, wife **6** mingle, spouse **7** hang out, husband, pair off, partner **8** go around, sidekick

9 accompany, associate, companion, other half, pal around, rub elbows **10** fraternize **11** keep company

conspicuous 5 clear, great, plain **6** famous, patent **7** eminent, evident, glaring, notable, obvious **8** distinct, flagrant, glorious, manifest, renowned, splendid, striking **9** arresting, brilliant, memorable, notorious, prominent, well-known **10** celebrated, easily seen, remarkable **11** illustrious, outstanding, standing out **13** distinguished, easily noticed, highly visible

conspicuousness 9 celebrity, flagrance, notoriety **10** prominence, visibility **11** obviousness **13** noticeability

conspiracy 4 plot **7** treason **8** intrigue, sedition **9** collusion, treachery **10** connivance, secret plan **11** machination **12** criminal plan **14** treasonous plan

conspirator 7 plotter, schemer, traitor **8** conniver **9** intriguer **10** subversive

conspire 5 unite **6** concur, scheme **7** collude, combine, connive **8** intrigue **9** cooperate, machinate **11** plot treason **12** work together

Constable, John
    born: **7** England **12** East Bergholt
    artwork: **10** The Haywain **12** Cloud Studies **14** Hadleigh Castle **39** Salisbury Cathedral from the Bishop's Grounds

constancy 6 fealty **7** loyalty **8** devotion **9** fixedness, stability **10** allegiance, permanence **12** faithfulness, immutability **13** dependability, invariability, steadfastness **15** trustworthiness **16** unchangeableness

constant 4 even, true **5** fixed, loyal **6** stable, steady, trusty **7** abiding, devoted, endless, eternal, regular, staunch, uniform **8** diligent, enduring, faithful, resolute, stalwart, unbroken, unvaried **9** ceaseless, continual, immutable, incessant, permanent, perpetual, steadfast, sustained, unceasing, unfailing **10** dependable, invariable, persistent, unchanging, unflagging, unswerving, unwavering **11** everlasting, never-ending, trustworthy, unalterable, undeviating, unrelenting **12** interminable, tried-and-true **13** uninterrupted

Constant Nymph, The
director: 14 Edmund
Goulding
cast: 11 Alexis Smith
12 Charles Boyer, Joan Fontaine 14 Brenda Marshall

constellation *see box*

consternation 5 alarm, panic, shock 6 dismay, fright, horror, terror 11 trepidation
12 apprehension

constituent 4 atom, part
5 piece, voter 6 factor, member 7 elective, element, essence 8 electing, integral, making up 9 component, formative, principal, supporter
10 appointing, ingredient

constitute 4 form, make, name 5 found, set up 6 create, invest, make up 7 appoint, compose, empower, produce
8 compound, delegate 9 authorize, establish, institute
10 commission

constitution 6 figure, health, make-up, mettle 7 charter, stamina, texture 8 physique, strength, vitality 9 basic laws, formation, structure 10 figuration 11 composition 12 construction 13 configuration
16 governing charter 17 physical condition 21 fundamental principles

constitutional 4 turn, walk
5 basic 6 inborn, ramble, stroll, vested 7 natural, organic 8 inherent, internal, physical 9 chartered, intrinsic
10 congenital 11 fundamental

Constitution State
nickname of: 11 Connecticut

constrain 4 curb, urge 5 check, crush, drive, force, quash

6 coerce, compel, oblige, subdue 7 confine, enforce, put down, repress, restrain, restrict, suppress 9 fight down, necessity, strong-arm 14 put the screws on

constrained 3 shy 5 timid
6 forced 7 bashful 8 reserved, reticent 9 compelled, diffident
10 restricted 11 embarrassed

constraint 5 force 6 duress
7 reserve 8 coercion, pressure
9 restraint 10 compulsion, diffidence, inhibition, obligation
11 enforcement
13 necessitation

constrict 4 bind 5 choke, cramp, pinch 6 shrink
7 squeeze 8 compress, contract, strangle 11 strangulate

constriction 7 binding, choking 8 cramping, pinching
9 narrowing, shrinking, squeezing, stricture, tightness
10 constraint, strangling
11 compression, contraction

construct 4 form, make
5 build, erect, frame, set up, shape 6 create, design, devise
7 arrange, fashion 8 organize
9 fabricate, formulate

construction 4 form, make
5 build, style 6 format 7 edifice, raising, reading, rearing, version 8 building, creation, erecting 9 rendition, structure
10 fashioning, production
11 composition, elucidation, explanation, explication, fabrication, manufacture 12 conformation, constructing
13 configuration 14 interpretation 15 putting together

constructive 5 handy 6 useful

7 helpful 8 valuable 9 practical 10 beneficial, productive
12 advantageous

construe 4 read, take 7 explain, make out 8 decipher
9 elucidate, figure out, interpret, translate 10 comprehend, understand

Consuelo
author: 10 George Sand

consul 5 envoy 8 emissary, minister 14 foreign officer, representative 15 diplomatic agent

Consul, The
opera by: 7 Menotti
character: 10 Magda Sorel

consult 6 confer, parley, regard 7 refer to 8 consider, talk over 9 inquire of 11 ask advice of, have an eye to
12 compare notes 13 exchange views 15 discuss together, seek counsel from, take into account 16 seek the opinion of
18 deliberate together

consultant 6 expert 7 adviser, advisor, counsel 9 discusser

consultation 7 council, hearing, meeting, palaver 9 interview 10 conference, discussion 12 deliberation

consumable 6 edible 7 eatable 10 comestible

consume 3 eat 4 gulp 5 drain, eat up, spend, use up, waste
6 absorb, devour, expend, guzzle, ravage 7 deplete, destroy, drink up, engross, exhaust
8 demolish, lay waste, squander 9 devastate, dissipate, swallow up 10 annihilate

consumed 4 used 5 burnt, drank, drunk, eaten, spent
6 used up, wasted 7 drained, outworn 8 absorbed, burned up, expended, perished 9 destroyed, engrossed, exhausted, swallowed 10 squandered
11 annihilated

consume greedily 6 devour
7 stuff in 8 bolt down, gobble up, gulp down, wolf down
12 swallow whole 13 eat ravenously 14 eat voraciously

consumer 4 user 5 buyer, drain 6 client, patron, waster
7 spender 8 customer 9 purchaser 10 dissipater, squanderer

consummate 2 do 5 sheer, total, utter 6 effect, finish
7 achieve, execute, fulfill, perfect, perform, realize, supreme 8 absolute, carry out, complete, finished, thorough
9 faultless 10 accomplish,

---

constellation 4 host 5 group, rally 6 circle, galaxy, nebula, spiral, throng 7 cluster, company, pattern 9 gathering 10 assemblage, collection 12 spiral nebula 13 configuration 14 island universe
name: 3 Ara, Leo 4 Apus, Crux, Grus, Lynx, Lyra, Pavo, Vela 5 Aries, Cetus, Draco, Hydra, Indus, Lepus, Libra, Lupus, Mensa, Musca, Norma, Orion, Pyxis, Virgo 6 Antlia, Aquila, Auriga, Bootes, Caelum, Cancer, Carina, Corvus, Crater, Cygnus, Dorado, Fornax, Gemini, Hydrus, Octans, Pictor, Pisces, Puppis, Scutum, Taurus, Tucana, Volans 7 Cepheus, Columba, Lacerta, Pegasus, Perseus, Phoenix, Sagitta, Serpens, Sextans 8 Aquarius, Circinus, Equuleus, Eridanus, Hercules, Leo Minor, Scorpius, Sculptor 9 Andromeda, Centaurus, Delphinus, Monoceros, Ophiuchus, Reticulum, Ursa Major, Ursa Minor, Vulpecula 10 Canis Major, Canis Minor, Cassiopeia, Chamaeleon, Horologium, Triangulum 11 Capricornus, Sagittarius, Telescopium 12 Microscopium 13 Canes Venatici, Coma Berenices 14 Camelopardalis, Corona Borealis 15 Corona Australis, Piscis Austrinus 18 Triangulum Australe

bring about, undisputed **11** unmitigated **12** accomplished, unquestioned **13** unconditional **17** through-and-through

consummation 3 end **5** close **6** finish **9** execution **10** attainment, completion, conclusion **11** achievement, culmination, fulfillment, realization **14** accomplishment

consumption 2 TB **3** use **7** using up **9** consuming, depletion **10** exhaustion **11** expenditure, utilization **12** exploitation, tuberculosis

Consus
  origin: 5 Roman
  god of: 11 good counsel, horse racing
  protector of: 5 grain
  corresponds to: 3 Ops

contact 4 join, meet **5** reach, touch, union **7** connect, meeting **8** abutment, junction, touching **9** adjacency, get hold of **10** connection **11** association **13** communication **14** get in touch with **15** communicate with

contagion 7 disease **8** epidemic, outbreak **9** infection, spreading **13** contamination

contagious 8 catching **9** spreading **10** infectious, spreadable **12** communicable **13** transmittable

contain 4 curb, hold **5** check **6** embody, hold in **7** control, embrace, enclose, include, inhibit, involve, repress **8** hold back, keep back, restrain, suppress **11** accommodate, incorporate **12** keep the lid on **16** keep within bounds

container 3 bag, box, can, jar, vat **4** pail **6** barrel, bottle, bucket, carton, holder, vessel **10** receptacle

containment 7 control **9** restraint, retention

contaminate 4 foul, soil **5** dirty, spoil, taint **6** befoul, blight, debase, defile, infect, poison **7** corrupt, pollute **8** besmirch **10** adulterate, make impure

contamination 5 filth **7** fouling, soiling **8** dirtying, foulness, impurity, spoiling **9** dirtiness, poisoning, polluting, pollution, putridity **10** defilement **11** uncleanness **12** adulteration

Conte, Richard
  real name: 18 Nicholas Peter Conte
  born: 12 Jersey City NJ

roles: **8** Barabbas **13** A Bell for Adano **24** The Greatest Story Ever Told

contemplate 4 note, plan, scan **5** weigh **6** expect, gaze at, intend, ponder, regard, survey **7** examine, imagine, inspect, observe, project, stare at, think of **8** aspire to, envision, mull over, ruminate **9** muse about **10** anticipate, cogitate on, have in view, meditate on, think about **11** reflect upon **12** deliberate on **13** consider fully, look at fixedly, look forward to **14** speculate about **15** view attentively

contemplation 5 study **6** gazing, musing, seeing, survey **7** looking, reverie, thought, viewing **8** scanning, thinking **9** pondering **10** cogitation, inspection, meditation, reflection, rumination **11** examination, observation **12** deliberation **13** consideration

contemplative 6 musing **7** pensive **8** studious **9** engrossed **10** cogitative, meditative, reflective, ruminating, thoughtful **11** speculative **13** introspective, lost in thought

contemporaneous 6 coeval **10** coexistent, coincident, concurrent **11** synchronous **12** contemporary, simultaneous

contemporary 3 new **4** late **6** modern, recent, with-it **7** current **8** advanced, brand-new, up-to-date **9** coexistent, coincident, concurrent, newfangled, present-day **11** ultramodern **12** simultaneous **13** of the same time, up-to-the-minute **15** contemporaneous

contempt 4 hate **5** scorn, shame **6** hatred **7** disdain, disgust **8** aversion, derision, disfavor, disgrace, dishonor, distaste, ignominy, loathing, ridicule **9** antipathy, disregard, disrepute, revulsion **10** abhorrence, repugnance **11** detestation, humiliation

contemptible 3 low **4** base, mean, vile **5** cheap **6** abject, paltry, shabby **8** shameful, unworthy, wretched **9** miserable, repugnant, revolting **10** despicable, detestable, disgusting **11** ignominious

contemptuous 6 lordly **7** haughty, pompous **8** arrogant, derisive, insolent, scornful, snobbish **10** disdainful **12** supercilious **13** condescending, disrespectful

contemptuousness 5 scorn **7** disdain **8** contempt, rudeness **9** arrogance, insolence

contend 3 vie, war **4** aver, avow, hold, spar **5** argue, claim, clash, fight **6** allege, assert, battle, combat, debate, insist, jostle, strive, tussle **7** compete, contest, declare, dispute, grapple, quarrel, wrestle **8** be a rival, maintain, propound, skirmish, struggle **10** put forward

content 4 area, core, gist, load, size, text **5** cheer, happy, heart, ideas, peace **6** at ease, at rest, matter, please, serene, thesis, volume **7** appease, comfort, essence, gratify, insides, meaning, pleased, satisfy, suffice, unmoved **8** capacity, make easy, pleasure, serenity, thoughts **9** contented, gratified, happiness, satisfied, set at ease, substance **10** complacent, untroubled **11** comfortable, contentment, peace of mind, unconcerned **12** satisfaction **13** gratification

contented 5 happy **6** at ease, serene **7** at peace, content, pleased **9** gratified, satisfied **11** comfortable

contentedness 4 ease **5** peace **7** comfort, content **8** pleasure, serenity **9** happiness **11** contentment **12** satisfaction **13** gratification

contention 5 clash, fight **6** battle, combat, strife **7** contest, discord, dispute, rivalry **8** argument, conflict, disunity, fighting, friction, skirmish, struggle, variance **9** assertion, encounter, wrangling **10** dissension, quarreling **11** competition, discordance **12** disagreement **13** confrontation

contentious 5 angry, cross **7** bateful, scrappy **8** captious **9** bellicose **10** pugnacious **11** belligerent, competitive, quarrelsome **12** cantankerous, disputatious **13** argumentative, controversial

contentment 4 ease **5** peace **7** comfort, content **8** pleasure, serenity **9** happiness **12** satisfaction **13** contentedness, gratification

conterminous 8 abutting, adjacent, touching **9** bordering **11** right beside **14** contiguous with

contest 3 war **4** bout, game **5** fight, match **6** battle, combat, debate, oppose, vie for **7** dispute, rivalry, tourney

8 conflict, fight for, object to, struggle **9** battle for, challenge, combat for, encounter **10** compete for, contend for, controvert, engagement, tournament **11** competition, struggle for **12** argue against **14** call in question

contestant 5 rival **6** player **7** entrant, fighter **8** competer, prospect **9** combatant, contender **10** challenger, competitor

context 6 milieu **7** climate, meaning, setting **8** ambience **9** framework, precincts, situation **10** atmosphere, background, conditions, connection **11** environment **12** relationship, surroundings **13** circumstances **16** frame of reference

contiguous 5 close, handy **6** nearby **7** close-by, tangent **8** abutting, adjacent, next-door, touching **9** adjoining, bordering, in contact **10** juxtaposed **11** neighboring **12** conterminous

continence 6 purity **8** chastity, sobriety **10** abstinence, moderation, temperance **11** forbearance **13** self-restraint

continent 4 Asia, pure **6** Africa, chaste, Europe **8** celibate, land mass, mainland, virginal **9** abstinent, Australia, temperate **10** abstemious, Antarctica **12** North America, South America

contingency 7 urgency **8** accident **9** emergency, extremity **10** likelihood **11** possibility, predicament **15** unforeseen event

contingent 9 dependent, subject to **11** conditioned **12** controlled by

continual 7 endless, eternal **8** constant, frequent, habitual, unbroken, unending **9** ceaseless, incessant, perennial, perpetual, recurring, unceasing **10** continuous, persistent **11** everlasting, never-ending, oft-repeated, unremitting **12** interminable **13** uninterrupted

continually 3 aye **4** ever **6** always, steady **7** endless, eternal, forever, on and on **8** steadily **9** recurring **10** constantly, frequently, repeatedly

continuance 4 stay, term **6** extent, period **7** lasting **8** duration **9** extension **10** continuing, permanence **11** adjournment, persistence,

protraction **12** continuation, perseverance, prolongation

continuation 6 sequel **8** addition, sequence **9** extension **10** continuing, supplement **11** continuance, protraction **12** prolongation

continue 4 go on, last, stay **5** abide **6** drag on, endure, extend, keep on, keep up, remain, resume, stay on **7** carry on, persist, proceed **9** persevere

continued 6 kept on, kept up, lasted, went on **7** endured **8** extended **9** carried on, persisted, proceeded, prolonged **10** persevered, protracted

continuing 6 steady **7** abiding, eternal, ongoing **8** constant, enduring, extended, unbroken, unending **9** ceaseless, incessant, perpetual, prolonged **10** dragged out, persistent, protracted **11** persevering, unremitting **12** interminable **13** uninterrupted

continuity 4 flow **5** chain **9** continuum **10** succession **11** continuance, progression **12** continuation

continuous 6 linked, steady **7** endless, eternal, lasting **8** constant, enduring, unbroken **9** ceaseless, connected, continual, extensive, incessant, perpetual, prolonged, unceasing **10** continuing, persistent, protracted, successive **11** consecutive, everlasting, persevering, progressive, unremitting **12** interminable **13** uninterrupted

continuum 4 flow **5** chain **8** sequence **10** continuity, succession **11** continuance, progression **12** continuation

contort 4 bend, warp **5** twist **6** deform **7** distort **11** be misshapen

contorted 4 bent **7** crooked, twisted **8** deformed **9** distorted

contortion 7 bending **8** twisting **10** distortion **11** crookedness

contour 4 form **5** lines, shape **6** figure **7** outline, profile **10** silhouette **11** physiognomy

contraband 11 bootlegging **13** smuggled goods **14** illegal exports, illegal imports **15** unlicensed goods **17** black-marketeering **18** prohibited articles **19** unlawful trafficking

contract 3 get **4** pact, take **5** agree, incur **6** absorb, assume, narrow, pledge, reduce,

shrink, treaty **7** acquire, compact, develop, dwindle, promise, shorten, tighten **8** compress, condense, covenant, engender **9** constrict, enter into, negotiate, undertake **11** arrangement, come to terms **12** draw together, make a bargain **13** become smaller, legal document **15** sign an agreement **16** written agreement

contracted form 6 digest **7** summary **8** synopsis **9** short form **11** abridgement, compression **12** abbreviation, condensation

contraction 8 decrease **9** drawing in, lessening, narrowing, reduction, shrinkage **10** shortening, shriveling, tightening **11** compression **12** abbreviation, condensation, constriction

contradict 4 deny **5** belie, rebut **6** impugn, oppose, refute **7** confute, counter, dispute, gainsay **8** disprove **10** controvert **12** be contrary to, disagree with

contradiction 6 denial **7** counter **8** negation, rebuttal **10** refutation **11** confutation **12** disagreement

contradictory 8 contrary, opposing **10** discrepant, dissenting, refutatory **11** conflicting, disagreeing **12** antithetical, inconsistent **14** countervailing, irreconcilable

contradistinction 8 contrast **10** difference **13** dissimilarity

contraption 6 device, gadget **9** apparatus, invention **11** contrivance

contrariety 9 deviation **10** difference, divergence **13** contradiction

contrary 5 balky **7** adverse, counter, froward, hostile, opposed, wayward, willful **8** converse, inimical, opposite, stubborn, untoward **9** disparate, obstinate, unfitting **10** at variance, discordant, headstrong, refractory, unsuitable **11** conflicting, disagreeing, intractable, unfavorable **12** antagonistic, antithetical, disagreeable, inauspicious, incompatible, recalcitrant, unpropitious **13** contradictory **15** at cross purposes, unaccommodating

contrast 6 depart, differ **7** deviate, diverge **8** variance **9** disparity **10** comparison, difference, divergence, unlikeness **11** distinction **12** disagree with **13** differentiate, dissimilarity **15** differentiation, set in opposition

contrasting 8 clashing, dividing, opposing **9** comparing, differing **10** discordant, juxtaposed **14** distinguishing **15** differentiating

contravene 4 deny **5** annul, fight, spurn **6** abjure, breach, combat, disown, negate, offend, oppose, reject, resist **7** disobey, exclude, gainsay, infract, nullify, violate **8** abrogate, disclaim, overstep **9** overreach, repudiate **10** act against, contradict, infringe on, transgress **12** encroach upon **15** trespass against

contretemps 4 spat **5** clash, set-to **7** dispute, quarrel **8** argument, squabble **10** difference, falling out **12** disagreement **18** embarrassing mishap

contribute 4 give **5** endow, grant **6** bestow, confer, donate, lead to **7** advance, forward, hand out, present **9** bear a part, influence **11** have a hand in **13** be conducive to **14** help bring about

contribution 4 alms, gift **5** grant **7** charity, subsidy **8** bestowal, donation, offering **9** endowment **11** benefaction **12** dispensation

contributive 8 valuable **9** favorable **10** beneficial

contributory 9 accessory, ancillary, auxiliary **13** supplementary

contrite 6 rueful **7** humbled **8** penitent **9** chastened, regretful, repentant, sorrowful **10** apologetic, remorseful **18** conscience-stricken

contrition 6 regret **7** penance, remorse **9** atonement, penitence **10** repentance **11** compunction **12** self-reproach **18** qualms of conscience

contrivance 4 plan, plot, tool **5** gizmo, trick **6** design, device, doodad, gadget **7** machine, measure **8** artifice, intrigue **9** apparatus, implement, invention, mechanism, stratagem **10** instrument **11** contraption, machination, thingamajig

contrive 4 plan, plot **6** create, design, devise, invent, manage, scheme **7** concoct **8** maneuver **9** improvise **11** devise a plan **17** effect by stratagem

contrived 7 labored, studied **8** mannered **9** unnatural **10** artificial

contriver 7 creator, deviser **8** designer, inventor **9** architect

control 4 curb, rule, sway **5** brake, steer **6** bridle, charge, govern, manage, master, subdue **7** command, contain, mastery, repress **8** dominate, dominion, regulate, restrain, restrict **9** authority, direction, reign over, restraint, supervise **10** domination, management, manipulate, regulation **11** superintend, supervision, suppressant **12** have charge of, jurisdiction

controlled 5 ruled **6** curbed, steady, swayed **7** checked, managed, powered, servile, subdued **8** directed, governed, held back, kept down, reserved, verified **9** commanded, contained, dominated, moderated, regulated, repressed **10** authorized, regimented, restrained, supervised **11** manipulated

controlling 6 ruling **8** dominant **9** governing **10** commanding **11** influencing, predominant **13** predominating

controversial 7 at issue **8** arguable **9** debatable, polemical **10** disputable **12** questionable **13** causing debate **15** widely discussed **16** open to discussion

controversy 6 debate **7** dispute, quarrel, wrangle **8** argument, squabble **10** contention, discussion, dissension **11** altercation **12** disagreement

controvert 4 deny **5** belie, rebut **6** negate, oppose, refute **7** confute, dispute, gainsay, protest **8** confound, disprove, question **9** challenge, disaffirm **10** contradict, contravene, invalidate **12** give the lie to

contumacious 6 unruly **7** froward **8** contrary, factious, insolent, mutinous, perverse **9** fractious, seditious **10** headstrong, rebellious, refractory **11** disobedient, intractable **12** ungovernable, unmanageable **13** disrespectful, insubordinate

contumely 5 abuse, insult, scorn **7** disdain, obloquy **8** contempt, diatribe, reproach, rudeness **9** arrogance, insolence, invective, pomposity **10** opprobrium, scurrility **11** brusqueness, haughtiness **12** billingsgate, vituperation **15** overbearingness

contusion 4 hurt, mark, sore **5** mouse **6** bruise, injury, shiner **7** blemish **8** abrasion,

black eye **9** black mark **13** discoloration **16** black-and-blue mark

conundrum 5 poser, rebus **6** enigma, puzzle, riddle **7** arcanum, mystery, paradox, problem, puzzler, stopper, stumper **11** brain-teaser **13** Chinese puzzle

convalesce 4 mend **5** rally **6** revive **7** improve, recover, restore **8** progress **9** get better **10** recuperate

convalescence 7 recruit **8** recovery **11** restoration **12** recuperation **14** return to health

convene 6 gather, muster, summon **7** collect, convoke, round up **8** assemble **12** call together, come together, hold a session **13** bring together

convenience 3 use **4** ease **6** chance **7** benefit, comfort, service, utility **8** facility, pleasure **9** appliance, enjoyment, handiness, work saver **10** usefulness **11** opportunity **12** availability, satisfaction, suitable time **13** accessibility, accommodation

convenient 5 handy **6** at hand, nearby, suited, useful **7** adapted, helpful **8** suitable **9** easy to use **10** beneficial **11** serviceable **12** advantageous **16** easily accessible

convent 7 nunnery **8** cloister **13** society of nuns

convention 4 code **6** caucus, custom **7** meeting, precept **8** assembly, conclave, congress, practice, propriety, protocol, standard **9** formality, gathering **10** conference, social rule **11** convocation

conventional 5 usual **6** common, normal, proper **7** regular, routine **8** accepted, orthodox, standard **9** customary **11** traditional

converge 4 meet **5** focus **8** approach **11** concentrate **12** come together **13** bring together

convergence 6 accord **8** junction **9** congruity **10** confluence **12** meeting place **14** correspondence

conversant 4 up on **5** aware **6** au fait **7** erudite, privy to, skilled, tutored **8** familiar, informed, sensible, sentient **9** au courant, cognizant, practiced **10** acquainted, proficient **12** well-informed **13** knowledgeable

conversation 3 rap **4** chat,

talk **7** gabfest, palaver **8** chit-chat, dialogue **9** discourse, tete-a-tete **11** bull session **13** confabulation
Italian: **13** conversazione

Conversation, The
director: **18** Francis Ford Coppola
cast: **10** John Cazale **11** Gene Hackman **13** Allen Garfield

conversational 6 casual, chatty **8** everyday, informal **9** idiomatic **10** colloquial, vernacular

conversazione 12 conversation

converse 3 gab, jaw, rap **4** chat, chin, talk **7** palaver, reverse **8** chitchat, contrary, opposite **10** antithesis, chew the fat, chew the rag **11** confabulate **13** speak together **14** shoot the breeze

conversely 12 contrariwise **14** antithetically, on the other hand

conversion 6 change **10** changeover **12** modification **13** change of heart, metamorphosis, transmutation **14** transformation **15** change in beliefs, transfiguration **16** change of religion

convert 4 turn **6** change, modify, novice **8** neophyte **9** proselyte, transform **11** proselytize

convex 7 bulging, rounded **11** protuberant **13** curved outward

convey 4 bear, cede, deed, give, move, tell, will **5** bring, carry, grant, leave **6** impart, relate, reveal **7** conduct, consign, deliver, divulge **8** bequeath, disclose, dispatch, transfer, transmit **9** confide to, make known, transport **11** communicate

conveyance 3 bus, car, rig, van **4** cart **5** buggy, truck, wagon **7** vehicle **8** carriage, carrying, movement, transfer **9** conveying, transport **12** transmission **14** transportation

convict 3 con **4** doom **5** felon **7** condemn **8** jailbird, prisoner, yardbird **10** find guilty **11** prove guilty **13** declare guilty

conviction 4 view, zeal **5** ardor, creed, dogma, faith, fever, tenet **6** belief, fervor **7** opinion **8** doctrine, judgment, position **9** assurance, certainty, certitude, intensity, principle, viewpoint **10** per-

suasion **11** earnestness **13** steadfastness

convince 4 sway **6** assure **7** satisfy, win over **8** persuade **9** influence **11** bring around, prevail upon

convincing 5 sound, valid **6** cogent, potent **7** evident **8** assuring, forceful, powerful **9** plausible **10** persuading, persuasive, satisfying

convivial 5 merry **6** genial, jovial **7** affable, festive **8** friendly, sociable **9** agreeable, fun-loving **10** gregarious **13** companionable

convocation 6 caucus, muster, roster **7** council, meeting, roundup **8** assembly, conclave, congress **9** gathering **10** conference, convention **11** ingathering

convoke 4 meet, open **6** gather, muster **8** assemble, converse **11** call to order **12** call together

convolute 4 coil, wave, wavy, wind **5** twirl, twist **6** coiled, rolled, spiral, tangle **7** contort, sinuous, twisted **8** involved, spiraled **9** intricate **11** complicated **12** turn and twist

convolution 4 coil, maze **5** twist **7** coiling, winding **8** twisting **9** labyrinth, sinuosity **10** contortion, undulation **11** sinuousness **12** tortuousness

convoy 5 fleet, usher **6** column, escort **7** conduct **9** accompany, formation, safeguard **10** armed guard, protection

convulse 4 rock, stir **5** laugh, shake, spasm, wring **6** excite **7** agitate, disturb, perturb, trouble **8** double up

convulsion 3 fit **5** spasm **6** tumult **7** seizure **8** outburst, paroxysm **9** agitation, commotion **10** contortion **11** disturbance

convulsive 6 fitful **7** hurtful, rending, shaking **8** exciting, stirring **9** agitating, epileptic, spasmodic, troubling **10** disturbing

Conway, Tim
real name: **18** Thomas Daniel Conway
born: **12** Willoughby OH
roles: **11** McHale's Navy **16** Carol Burnett Show **17** The Steve Allen Show

coo 6 babble, gurgle, murmur **20** whisper sweet nothings

Coogan, Jackie
real name: **16** Jack Leslie Coogan
wife: **11** Betty Grable
born: **12** Los Angeles CA
roles: **6** The Kid **9** Tom Sawyer **11** Oliver Twist, Peck's Bad Boy **15** Huckleberry Finn

cook 3 fix **4** chef, fire, heat, make **5** occur **6** cookie, doctor, happen, seethe **7** concoct, falsify, prepare, process **8** work well **9** improvise
method: **3** fry **4** bake, boil, brew, sear, stew **5** baste, broil, grill, poach, roast, saute, scald, shirr, steam **6** braise, coddle, simmer **7** parboil **8** barbecue **9** fricassee

Cooke, Alistair
author of: **14** One Man's America **18** A Generation on Trial **26** Around the World in Fifty Years
TV host of: **18** Masterpiece Theatre

cooked sufficiently 4 done **5** ready **7** al dente **11** done to a turn

cookie 3 bar, gal, gul **4** cake, cook **5** wafer **6** person **7** biscuit, brownie **10** shortbread
type: **4** oreo **6** sugar **7** oatmeal **8** macaroon, molasses **9** girl scout, tollhouse **10** gingersnap, lorna doone **12** peanut butter **13** chocolate chip

cooking, fine/gourmet
French: **12** haute cuisine

cooking term 3 a la, cut, dot, fry **4** bake, beat, boil, chop, coat, cube, dice, dust, flan, fold, lard, roux, sear, snip, stew, toss, whip **5** aspic, au jus, baste, blend, bread, broil, brush, candy, cream, crepe, devil, dough, flake, glace, glaze, grate, grill, knead, plank, puree, roast, saute, scald, score, shirr, steep, stock, torte **6** au lait, blanch, braise, coddle, devein, dredge, fillet, flambe, fondue, render, simmer, skewer, sliver **7** a la mode, compote, crouton, garnish, goulash, liquefy, parboil, precook, preheat, rissole, scallop, stir-fry **8** aperitif, au gratin, barbecue, conserve, consomme, julienne, marinate, pot roast **9** brochette, demitasse, drippings, forcemeat, fricassee, lyonnaise, macedoine **10** caramelize, cracklings
boneless strips of meat/fish: **6** fillet
clear soup: **8** bouillon, consomme

cubed toasted bread:
   7 crouton
food cooked and served in foil or paper: 11 en
   papillote
fruit preserve with nuts/raisins: 8 conserve
fruits in syrup: 7 compote
in the fashion: 7 a la mode
remove veins: 6 devein
skewered meat: 5 kebab
   9 brochette
small cup of black coffee:
   9 demitasse
thin strips: 6 sliver **8** julienne
with cheese: 8 au gratin
with ice cream: 7 a la mode
with juice/with its own juices: 5 au jus
with milk: 6 au lait

cook up 3 mix **4** brew
   5 hatch **6** create, devise, invent, make up **7** concoct, think up **8** compound, contrive **9** fabricate, formulate

cool 3 icy **4** calm, cold **5** aloof, chill **6** chilly, frosty, offish, serene **7** distant, not warm **8** composed, lose heat, make cool, reserved **9** collected, impassive, uncordial, unexcited **10** become cool, cool-headed, deliberate, nonchalant, unfriendly, unsociable, untroubled **11** indifferent, standoffish, undisturbed, unemotional, unflappable **12** slightly cold, somewhat cold, unresponsive **13** dispassionate, imperturbable, self-possessed

cooler 3 ade, can, fan, jug
   4 coop, icer, jail **5** drink, icier **6** calmer, icebox, lockup, prison **11** refrigerant **12** refrigerator **14** air conditioner

Cool Hand Luke
   director: 15 Stuart Rosenberg
   cast: 8 J D Cannon **10** Jo Van Fleet, Lou Antonio, Paul Newman **12** Anthony Zerbe, Dennis Hopper **13** George Kennedy **14** Strother Martin
   Oscar for: 15 supporting actor (Kennedy)

Coolidge, Calvin *see box*

coolness 5 chill **7** dislike
   8 distance **9** aloofness, composure, sangfroid **10** chilliness, detachment, frostiness **11** impassivity **12** indifference **13** lack of emotion, lack of feeling **14** unfriendliness **15** emotionlessness, standoffishness **16** imperturbability, unresponsiveness

coop 3 car, mew, pen, sty
   4 auto, cage, cote **5** cramp, hutch **6** encase, prison **7** con-

---

Coolidge, Calvin
   name at birth: 18 John Calvin Coolidge
   nickname: 9 Silent Cal
   presidential rank: 9 thirtieth
   party: 10 Republican
   state represented: 2 MA
   succeeded: 7 Harding
   defeated: 5 (Frank Thomas) Johns, (Herman P) Faris, (John William) Davis **6** (William Zebulon) Foster **7** (Gilbert O) Nations, (William James) Wallace **10** (Robert Marion) La Follette
   vice president: 4 none (first term) **5** (Charles Gates) Dawes
   cabinet:
      state: **6** (Charles Evans) Hughes **7** (Frank Billings) Kellogg
      treasury: **6** (Andrew William) Mellon
      war: **5** (Dwight Filley) Davis, (John Wingate) Weeks
      attorney general: **5** (Harlan Fiske) Stone **6** (Charles B) Warren **7** (John Garibaldi) Sargent **9** (Harry Micajah) Daugherty
      navy: **5** (Edwin) Denby **6** (Curtis Dwight) Wilbur
      postmaster general: **3** (Harry Stewart) New
      interior: **4** (Hubert) Work, (Roy Owen) West
      agriculture: **4** (Howard Mason) Gore **7** (Henry Cantwell) Wallace, (William Marion) Jardine
      commerce: **6** (Herbert Clark) Hoover **7** (William Fairfield) Whiting
      labor: **5** (James John) Davis
   born: 2 VT **13** Plymouth Notch
   died: 2 MA **11** Northampton
   buried: 2 VT **8** Plymouth
   education:
      College: **7** Amherst
      later studied: **3** law
   religion: 17 Congregationalist
   vacation spot: 10 Black Hills
   author: 32 The Autobiography of Calvin Coolidge
   political career: 13 vice president
      state senator/lieutenant governor/governor of: **2** Ma **13** Massachusetts
   civilian career: 6 lawyer **17** bank vice president **18** newspaper columnist
   notable events of lifetime/term: 22 Pennsylvania coal strike
      Act: **8** Volstead **10** Boulder Dam **11** Immigration **17** Japanese Exclusion
      bribery case: **8** Elks Hill
      conference: **11** Geneva Naval
      flight by: **16** Charles Lindbergh
      Lindbergh's plane: **15** Spirit of St Louis
      Pact: **13** Kellogg-Briand
      trial: **6** Scopes **12** Scopes monkey
   quote: 35 (After all) the chief business of America is business **43** Spend less than you make and make more than you spend
   father: 10 John Calvin
   mother: 8 Victoria (Josephine Moor)
      stepmother: **8** Caroline (Brown)
   sibling: 13 Abigail Gratia
   wife: 5 Grace (Anna Goodhue)
   children: 4 John **6** Calvin

---

fine **8** imprison **9** enclosure
11 cooperation, cooperative

Cooper, Gary
   real name: 16 Frank James Cooper
   born: 8 Helena MT

roles: 8 High Noon (Oscar)
   9 Beau Geste **12** Sergeant York (Oscar), The Virginian **15** A Farewell to Arms **17** Mr Deeds Goes to Town **19** For Whom the Bell Tolls, The Cowboy and the

Lady **20** The Pride of the Yankees **22** North West Mounted Police

Cooper, James Fenimore
author of: **6** The Spy **8** The Bravo, The Pilot **9** Wyandotte **10** The Prairie **11** The Pioneers, The Red Rover **13** The Deerslayer, The Pathfinder, The Water-Witch **20** Leatherstocking Tales, The Last of the Mohicans
character: **4** Cora **5** Alice, Magua, Uncas **7** Hawkeye **11** Natty Bumppo **12** Chingachgook

cooperate 4 join **5** unite **7** go along, pitch in, share in **8** take part **9** join hands **10** act jointly, bear part in, join forces **11** collaborate, participate **12** pull together, work together **14** work side by side

cooperation 7 concert, detente **8** teamwork **9** agreement **10** accordance **11** concurrence, cooperating, give and take, joint action **13** collaboration, participation **15** pulling together, working together

coop up 3 pen **4** cage **5** pen in **6** closet, encage, shut in **7** confine, impound **8** restrain, restrict

coordinate 4 mesh **5** equal, match, order **6** relate **7** arrange, coequal **8** organize, parallel **9** correlate, harmonize **11** correlative, systematize **16** equally important

coordination 4 bond **5** skill **6** accord **7** harmony, liaison **10** adaptation, adjustment **12** equalization, organization **15** synchronization

cop 3 bag, nab, rob, win **4** bull, grab, take **5** bobby, catch, filch, pinch, snare, steal, swipe **6** peeler, pilfer, snatch **7** capture **8** gendarme, purchase **9** policeman **11** acquisition, policewoman **13** police officer

cope 4 face, spar **6** hurdle, manage, strive, tussle **7** contend, wrestle **8** struggle **11** hold one's own

copious 4 full **5** ample **6** lavish **7** liberal, profuse **8** abundant, generous **9** bountiful, extensive, plenteous, plentiful

copiousness 6 bounty, plenty, wealth **7** surfeit **8** fullness, plethora **9** abundance, ampleness, plenitude, profusion **10** lavishness, oversupply

Copland, Aaron
born: **10** Brooklyn NY
composer of: **5** Rodeo **9** Quiet City **10** Statements **11** Billy the Kid **12** Connotations **13** Dance Symphony, El Salon Mexico, The Tender Land **15** Outdoor Overture **17** Appalachian Spring **18** Music for a Great City, Music for the Theater

Copley, John Singleton
born: **8** Boston MA
artwork: **11** Samuel Adams **19** The Siege of Gibraltar **21** The Boy with the Squirrel **22** Brook Watson and the Shark, The Death of Major Pierson **26** The Death of the Earl of Chatham

copper
chemical symbol: **2** Cu

copper-colored 5 henna **6** auburn, russet **11** golden-brown, rust-colored **12** reddish-brown

coppice 4 bosk, wood **5** bluff, copse, firth, grove **6** forest, growth **7** boscage, thicket

Coppola, Francis Ford
director of: **12** The Godfather (Part I) (Part II, Oscar) **13** Apocalypse Now, The Cotton Club **15** The Conversation

Copreus
father: **6** Pelops
son: **10** Periphetes
herald of: **14** King Eurystheus

copse 5 brush, clump, grove **6** forest **7** coppice, thicket **8** woodland

copy 3 ape **4** fake, sham, text **5** clone, mimic, story, Xerox **6** follow, mirror, parody, repeat **7** emulate, forgery, imitate, replica **8** likeness **9** duplicate, facsimile, imitation, photostat, reportage, reproduce **10** carbon copy, manuscript **11** counterfeit, make a copy of **12** reproduction **14** representation **15** written material

coquette 4 vamp **5** flirt, tease **12** heart-breaker

coquettish 3 coy **9** kittenish **11** flirtatious

Cor 15 Biblical measure

Cora see **10** Persephone

coral 3 red **4** fire, pink, rose **5** horny, polyp, snake **7** orange, sea fan **8** acropora, hydrozoa, staghorn **9** gorgonian **10** sea feather **12** coelenterata

coram populo 8 publicly **15** before the public

corban 8 offering

Corbett, James (John)
nickname: **12** Gentleman Jim
sport: **6** boxing
class: **11** heavyweight

cord 5 braid, twine **8** thin rope **11** heavy string
abbreviation: **2** cd

Cordelia
character in: **8** King Lear
author: **11** Shakespeare

cordial 4 warm **6** genial, hearty **7** affable, amiable, sincere **8** friendly, gracious **9** heartfelt **11** good-natured **12** affectionate, wholehearted

cordiality 6 warmth **8** goodwill **9** affection, geniality, sincerity **10** affability, amiability, heartiness **11** amicability, earnestness **12** friendliness, graciousness, pleasantness **13** agreeableness

cordial relations 5 amity **6** accord **7** concord, harmony **8** goodwill **9** agreement **10** friendship **11** amicability **15** entente cordiale

cordon 4 cord, ring, rope **6** circle **8** encircle

cordon bleu 4 bird **5** finch **7** waxbill **10** red cheeked **11** estrildidae
school for: **5** chefs **7** cooking
where: **5** Paris **6** France
founded by: **13** Marthe Distell
means: **10** blue ribbon

core 3 nub **4** crux, gist, guts, meat, pith **5** heart **6** center, kernel **7** essence, nucleus **9** substance **10** brass tacks **11** central part, nitty-gritty **13** essential part, innermost part **15** sum and substance

Corelli, Arcangelo
born: **5** Imola, Italy
composer of: **7** La Folia (sonata No 12) **14** Concerti Grossi

Coresus
form: **6** priest
father: **6** Asopus
loved: **10** Callirrhoe
rejected by: **10** Callirrhoe

coriander
botanical name: **17** Coriandrum sativum
origin: **13** Mediterranean
color: **5** brown, white **6** yellow
flavor: **4** sage **5** cumin **7** caraway **9** lemon peel
candy: **6** comfit

Corinth, Lovis
born: **6** Tapiau **7** Prussia
artwork: **6** Salome **8** Ecce

Homo **10** Apocalypse **29** The Walchensee with a Yellow Field

Corinthus
founder of: **7** Corinth
possible father: **4** Zeus **8** Marathon

Coriolanus
author: **18** William Shakespeare
character: **8** Cominius, Virgilia, Volumnia **12** Junius Brutus, Titus Lartius **14** Tullus Aufidius **15** Menenius Agrippa, Sicinius Velutus **22** Caius Marcius Coriolanus

cork 3 bob, oak **4** bark, bung, plug, seal, stop **5** check, close, float **7** confine, filling stopper, stopple **8** restrain, suppress **10** insulation

corker 3 ace **4** whiz **7** stopper **8** clencher, striking, top notch **9** excellent, humdinger **10** remarkable **11** astonishing

corkscrew 4 coil, curl **5** twist **6** spiral **7** winding **10** serpentine **12** bottle opener

Corleone family
characters in: **12** The Godfather
author: **4** Puzo
member: **5** Sonny **7** Don Vito, Freddie, Michael

corn 4 cure **5** grain **6** callus **7** Zea Mays **8** preserve, schmaltz **9** vegetable
varieties: **3** Pod **4** Crow, Dent, Rice, Sand **5** Broom, Flint, Kafir, maize, Sugar, Sweet **6** Indian, Turkey **8** Egyptian, Squirrel
bread/cake: **4** pone **7** hoecake **8** tortilla **9** hushpuppy **10** johnnycake
beverage: **7** bourbon, whiskey

Corncracker State
nickname of: **8** Kentucky

Corneille, Pierre
author of: **5** Cinna, Le Cid, Medea, Medee **6** Horace, The Cid **8** Nicomede **9** Polyeucte

Cornelius, Peter von (van)
born: **7** Germany **10** Dusseldorf
artwork: **12** Last Judgment **24** The Wise and Foolish Virgins **30** The Four Horsemen of the Apocalypse

Cornell, Katharine
nickname: **21** first lady of the theater
born: **6** Berlin **7** Germany
roles: **8** Dear Liar **9** Saint Joan **18** Antony and Cleopa-

tra **26** The Barretts of Wimpole Street

corner 3 fix, jam, nab **4** bend, grab, hole, nail, nook, spot, trap **5** angle, seize **6** collar, pickle, plight, scrape **7** dead end, dilemma, impasse **10** blind alley, pigeonhole **11** predicament

cornerstone 4 base **5** basis **9** principle **10** foundation **11** fundamental

cornet 4 cone, horn **7** trumpet **9** cornopean

Cornhuskers, The
author: **12** Carl Sandburg

Cornhusker State
nickname of: **8** Nebraska

cornice 4 drip **5** ancon, crown **7** molding, valance **8** astragal

Cornopian see **8** Hercules

Cornwallis, Charles
also: **10** second Earl **13** first Marquess
nationality: **7** British
served in: **5** India **7** Ireland **18** American Revolution
battle: **8** Yorktown **10** Brandywine
captured: **10** Charleston **12** Philadelphia
surrendered at: **8** Yorktown

Cornwell, David
real name of: **11** John Le Carre

corny 5 banal, hokey, inane, stale, tired, trite, vapid **6** jejune, square **7** fatuous, insipid **8** bromidic, ordinary, shopworn **9** hackneyed **10** threadbare, unoriginal **11** commonplace, stereotyped **12** cliche-ridden, old-fashioned **13** platitudinous, unimaginative **15** unsophisticated

Coroebus
form: **4** hero
home: **5** Argos
father: **6** Mygdon
built: **6** temple
temple honored: **6** Apollo
killed: **5** Poena
killed by: **8** Diomedes

corona 4 halo, ring **5** cigar **6** circle, nimbus

coronet 5 tiara **6** diadem **7** chaplet, circlet **10** small crown

Coronis
form: **5** nymph **8** princess
father: **9** Phylegyas
husband: **6** Ischys
son: **9** Asclepius
cared for: **8** Dionysus
killed by: **6** Apollo

Coronus
king of: **7** Lapiths
father: **7** Caeneus
son: **8** Leonteus
daughter: **10** Anaxirrhoe
companion: **5** Jason

Corot, Jean-Baptiste-Camille
born: **5** Paris **6** France
artwork: **9** Pastorale **11** Ville d'Avray, Woman in Blue **15** Woman with a Pearl **16** The Farnese Garden, Woman in the Studio **21** Memory of Mortefontaine **23** Souvenir de Mortefontaine

corporal 6 bodily **8** physical **9** corporeal

corporation 7 combine, company **9** syndicate **11** association **14** conglomeration

corporeal 6 bodily, mortal **7** worldly **8** material, physical **11** perceptible **12** nonspiritual

corps 4 band, crew, team **5** force, party, squad, troop **6** outfit

corpse 4 body **5** stiff **7** cadaver, remains **8** dead body

corpselike 4 pale **5** ashen **6** pallid **9** bloodless, deathlike **10** cadaverous

corpulent 3 fat **5** dumpy, hefty, obese, plump, pudgy, stout **6** chubby, chunky, fleshy, portly, rotund **7** lumpish, well-fed **8** roly-poly **10** overweight, well-padded

corral 4 herd **5** pen in **6** shut in **7** enclose, fence in, round up

correct 3 fit, fix **4** true **5** alter, amend, chide, exact, right, scold **6** adjust, berate, change, modify, proper, punish, rebuke, remedy, repair, revamp, revise, rework, seemly **7** censure, chasten, factual, fitting, improve, lecture, perfect, precise, rectify, reprove **8** accurate, admonish, becoming, chastise, flawless, regulate, suitable, unerring **9** castigate, dress down, faultless, make right, reprimand **10** acceptable, discipline, take to task **11** appropriate **12** conventional **16** haul over the coals, read the riot act to

correction 6 change **8** revision **10** adjustment, alteration, discipline, emendation, punishment **11** castigation, improvement, reformation **12** chastisement, modification **13** rectification

corrective 7 counter **8** remedial 9 improving 10 palliative, rectifying 11 reformatory, restorative, therapeutic 12 ameliorative, compensatory 13 counteractive 16 counterbalancing

correctness 8 accuracy 9 exactness, precision, propriety, rightness 10 exactitude, seemliness 11 suitability 12 becomingness, flawlessness 13 acceptability

Correggio
real name: 14 Antonio Allegri
born: 5 Italy 6 Emilia 9 Correggio
artwork: 5 Danae 12 Jupiter and Io 14 Leda and the Swan 17 The Rape of Ganymede 21 The Madonna of St Francis 23 Adoration of the Shepherds 28 Mystic Marriages of St Catherine

correlate 7 compare, connect 8 parallel 10 correspond

correlation 8 parallel 10 comparison, connection 14 correspondence

correlative 4 akin 7 related 8 agreeing, parallel 9 analogous 10 comparable, connecting, equivalent 13 corresponding

correspond 3 fit 4 jibe, suit 5 agree, match, tally 6 accord, be like, concur, equate, square 7 conform 8 coincide, dovetail, parallel 9 harmonize 11 communicate, drop a line to, keep in touch

correspondence 4 mail 7 analogy, letters 8 epistles, missives, relation 9 bulletins 10 dispatches, similarity 11 association, communiques, resemblance

corresponding 4 akin 5 alike, equal 7 similar 8 agreeing, matching, tallying 9 according 10 equivalent 11 correlative 12 proportional

corridor 3 way 4 hall, road 5 aisle 6 artery 7 hallway, passage 8 approach 10 passageway

Corridors of Power
author: 6 C P Snow

corroborate 4 back 5 prove 6 affirm, back up, uphold, verify 7 bear out, certify, confirm, endorse, support, sustain 8 validate 9 vindicate 12 authenticate, substantiate

corroborated 6 backed, proved, proven, upheld 7 factual 8 affirmed, backed up,

borne out, verified 9 certified, confirmed, supported, sustained, validated 10 vindicated 11 well-founded 12 well-grounded 13 authenticated, substantiated

corroboration 5 proof 7 support 8 evidence 10 validation 11 affirmation, endorsement, vindication 12 confirmation, verification 13 certification, documentation 14 authentication, substantiation

corroborative 7 proving 9 affirming, backing up, upholding, verifying 10 bearing out, concurring, confirming, supporting, validating 11 affirmative 12 confirmative 14 substantiating

corrode 4 rust 7 oxidize 12 disintegrate

corrosive 4 acid 7 burning, caustic, erosive, mordant 8 abrasive 9 corroding 11 destructive

corrugated 6 fluted, ridged 7 creased, grooved, pleated 8 crinkled, furrowed, puckered, wrinkled 10 crenulated

corrupt 3 low 4 base, evil, mean 5 shady 6 debase, poison, seduce, sinful, wicked 7 crooked, debased, debauch, deprave, immoral, pervert, subvert 8 depraved 9 dishonest, unethical 10 fraudulent, iniquitous 11 contaminate 12 dishonorable, unprincipled, unscrupulous

corruption 4 vice 5 fraud, graft 7 bribery 8 iniquity 9 decadence, depravity, looseness, turpitude 10 debauchery, degeneracy, dishonesty, immorality, perversion, sinfulness, wickedness, wrongdoing 11 malfeasance

corsair 6 pirate, sea dog, Viking 7 brigand, sea wolf 8 marauder, picaroon, sea rover 9 buccaneer, plunderer, privateer, sea looter, sea robber 10 Blackbeard, freebooter 11 Captain Kidd 14 Long John Silver

corset 5 laces 6 girdle 8 corselet 17 foundation garment

Corsica 6 island
located in: 16 Mediterranean Sea
capital: 7 Ajaccio
colony of: 4 Rome
purchased by: 6 France
birthplace of: 8 Napoleon
industry: 7 tourism 10 wine making 12 sheep raising, cheese making

Corsican Brothers, The
author: 14 Alexandre Dumas (pere)

Cortazar, Julio
author of: 7 Rayuela 9 A Model Kit, Bestiario, Hopscotch 10 The Winners 12 Book of Manuel, End of the Game 15 All Fires the Fire 18 We Love Glenda So Much

cortege 4 line 5 court, staff, suite, train 6 column, escort, parade, string 7 caravan, company, retinue 9 cavalcade, entourage, following, motorcade 10 attendants, procession 17 funeral procession

corundum
variety: 4 ruby 8 sapphire, star ruby 12 star sapphire

coruscate 4 beam 5 flash, gleam 7 glimmer, glitter, shimmer, sparkle

Corybant
attendant of: 6 Cybele

Corycia
form: 5 nymph
bore son to: 6 Apollo

Corynetes
also: 8 Pelasgus
epithet of: 10 Periphetes
means: 12 cudgel bearer

Coryphaeus
epithet of: 4 Zeus
means: 7 highest

Corythosaurus
type: 8 dinosaur 10 ornithopod
period: 10 Cretaceous
characteristic: 10 duck-billed

Corythus
father: 5 Priam
mother: 6 Oenone
adopted son: 8 Telephus
loved: 5 Helen
killed by: 5 Priam
birthplace of: 8 Dardanus

Cosby, Bill
born: 14 Philadelphia PA
roles: 4 I Spy 12 The Cosby Show 19 Mother Juggs and Speed, Uptown Saturday Night

Cosby Show, The
character: 4 Rudy, Theo 6 Denise, Sondra 7 Vanessa 13 Clair Huxtable, (Dr) Cliff (Heathcliff) Huxtable
cast: 9 Bill Cosby, Lisa Bonet 14 Sabrina LeBeauf 15 Tempestt Bledsoe 18 Malcolm Jamal-Warner 19 Keshia Knight Pulliam, Phylicia Ayers-Rashad

Cosi fan tutte
also: **11** So Do They All
16 Women Are Like That
opera by: **6** Mozart
character: **7** Despina **8** Ferrando **9** Dorabella, Guglielmo **10** Don Alfonso, Fiordiligi

Cosmetas
epithet of: **4** Zeus
means: **7** orderer

cosmetic 5 paint, rouge
6 powder **7** mascara, surface
8 artifice, eyeliner, lipstick
9 cold cream, eye shadow
10 foundation, nail polish
11 beautifying **13** eyebrow
pencil

cosmic 4 vast **7** immense **8** colossal, enormous, infinite
9 grandiose, universal **10** stupendous, widespread **12** interstellar **14** interplanetary
16 extraterrestrial

cosmopolitan 6 urbane
7 worldly **8** traveler **11** broad-minded, worldly-wise
12 globetrotter, sophisticate
13 international, sophisticated

cosmos 5 stars **8** universe
9 macrocosm **10** starry host
13 vault of heaven

Cossack 7 czarist, Russian,
trooper **8** horseman **10** cavalry
man

cosset 3 pet **6** caress, coddle,
fondle, pamper

cost 3 fee, run, tab **4** bill,
harm, hurt, loss, pain, take,
toll **5** fetch, go for, price,
value, worth **6** amount, burden, charge, come to, damage,
injure, injury, outlay **7** bring
in, expense, penalty, sell for,
set back **8** amount to, distress
9 face value, sacrifice, suffering, valuation, weigh down
11 expenditure, market price

Costa-Gavras, Constantine
director of: **7** Missing

Costard
character ‘in: **16** Love's Labour's Lost
author: **11** Shakespeare

Costa Rica *see box*

Costello, Lou
real name: **21** Louis Francis
Cristillo
partner: **9** Bud Abbott
born: **10** Paterson NJ
roles: **11** Who's on First

costly 4 dear **5** steep, stiff
7 harmful **8** damaging, precious **9** expensive **10** disastrous, exorbitant, high-priced
11 deleterious, extravagant
12 catastrophic

Costa Rica
name means: **9** rich coast
other name: **19** Land of Eternal Spring
capital/largest city: **7** San Jose
others: **5** Canas, Limon, Vesta **6** Boruca, Nicoya **7** Cartago,
Golfito, Heredia, Liberia, Negrita **8** Alajuela, Colorado,
Guapiles **9** Turrialba **10** Puntarenas
measure: **4** vara **5** cafiz, cahiz **6** fanega, tercia **7** cajuela,
cantaro, manzana **10** caballeria
monetary unit: **5** colon **7** centimo
weight: **3** bag **4** caja **5** libra
island: **4** Cano, Coco
lake: **6** Arenal
mountain: **4** Poas **5** Barba, Irazu **6** Blanco **7** Central, Gongora **9** Talamanca, Turrialba **10** Guanacaste
highest point: **14** Chirripo Grande
river: **4** Poas **5** Irazu **6** Matina **7** San Juan, Sixaola, Tenoria **8** Tarcoles
sea: **7** Pacific **9** Caribbean
physical feature:
  bay: **7** Salinas **8** Coronada
  cape: **5** Velas **6** Blanco **8** Matapalo **10** Santa Elena
  crater: **4** Poas
  gulf: **5** Dulce **6** Nicoya **8** Papagayo
  hot springs spa: **12** Agua Caliente
  peninsula: **3** Osa **6** Nicoya
  point: **5** Judas **6** Blanca, Burica, Quepos **7** Cahuito, Galonos, Guionos, Llerena
  valley: **8** Tarcoles **10** Reventazon
people: **4** Voto **6** Boruca, Bribri, Guaymi **7** Guatuso, mestizo, Spanish
  explorer: **8** Columbus, Coronado
language: **7** Spanish
religion: **13** Roman Catholic
place:
  shrine: **18** Our Lady of the Angels
  theater: **14** Teatro Nacional
feature:
  barbecue: **5** asado
  dance: **6** torito **9** botijuela, zapateado **11** baile suelto
  17 punto guanacasteco
  drum: **8** quijonga
  gourd: **4** caro
  outdoor concerts: **7** retreta
  plantation: **5** finca
  wind instrument: **8** chirimia
food:
  hearts of palm salad: **7** palmito
  pudding: **10** tamal asado

Costner, Kevin
born: **2** CA **10** Los Angeles
films: **3** JFK **9** Silverado
10 Bull Durham **12** The
Bodyguard **13** Field of
Dreams, A Perfect World
15 The Untouchables
16 Dances With Wolves
24 Robin Hood: Prince of
Thieves

costume 4 garb **5** dress **6** attire, livery, outfit **7** apparel,
clothes, raiment, uniform
8 clothing, garments

costuming 8 disguise
10 masquerade

cot 3 bed, hut, pen **4** coop,
crib **5** cover, stall **7** cottage

cotelette 3 cut **4** chop **5** slice
6 cutlet

coterie 3 set **4** band, camp,
clan, club, crew, gang
5 crowd, group **6** circle,
clique **7** faction

cottage 3 cot, hut **5** lodge,
shack **6** chalet **8** bungalow

Cotten, Joseph
born: **12** Petersburg VA
roles: **8** Gaslight **11** Citizen
Kane, The Third Man
12 Duel in the Sun
14 Shadow of a Doubt
15 Journey into Fear
16 Portrait of Jennie **23** The
Magnificent Ambersons

cotton 9 Gossypium
varieties: 3 bog 4 tree,
wild 6 kidney, levant,
upland 8 lavender 9 sea
island 11 Arizona wild
fabric: 4 duck, jean,
lawn, pima 5 baize,
chino, denim, drill,
khaki, lisle, pique,
scrim, terry, twill
6 burlap, calico, canvas,
chintz, dimity, madras,
muslin, nankin, oxford,
poplin, sateen 7 batiste,
buckram, cambric, flannel, fustian, gingham,
holland, jaconet, oilskin, organdy, percale,
ticking 8 chambray,
cretonne, sheeting
9 crinoline, sailcloth
10 broadcloth, hopsacking, printcloth, seersucker, terrycloth
11 cheesecloth, dotted
Swiss

Cotton Club, The
director: 18 Francis Ford
Coppola
cast: 9 Diane Lane 11 Richard Gere 12 Gregory Hines

cotton gin
invented by: 7 Whitney

Cotton State
nickname of: 7 Alabama

cottonwood 7 Populus
16 Populus deltoides
varieties: 5 black, Jack's,
swamp 7 Fremont 9 Rio
Grande 10 Wislizenus
11 Great Plains

Cottus
member of: 13 Hecatonchires

Cotyleus
epithet of: 9 Asclepius
means: 13 of the hip joint

Cotys, Cotytto
origin: 8 Thracian
form: 7 goddess
corresponds to: 6 Cybele
11 Great Mother

couch 3 put 4 sofa, word 5 divan, draft, frame, state, utter,
voice 6 daybed, draw up,
lounge, phrase, settee 7 express 8 love seat, set forth
9 davenport 12 chesterfield

cougar 3 cat 4 lion, puma
7 panther 9 catamount
12 mountain lion

cough 4 hack 6 tussis
9 pertussis

cough up 3 pay 5 eject, expel
7 deliver 8 disgorge, hand
over 9 surrender 11 regurgitate

Coulomb, Charles Augustin de
field: 7 physics
nationality: 6 French
invented: 14 torsion balance
discovered: 16 inverse square
law

council 5 board, panel, synod
7 cabinet, chamber 8 assembly,
colloquy, conclave, congress,
ministry 9 committee, gathering, sanhedrin 10 conference,
convention 11 convocation
12 congregation
15 representatives

counsel 4 urge, warn 6 advice,
advise, charge, lawyer,
prompt 7 call for, caution,
opinion, suggest 8 admonish,
advocate, attorney, guidance,
instruct 9 barrister, counselor,
recommend, solicitor 10 advisement, suggestion 12 consultation 14 recommendation

counsel house
German: 7 Rathaus

Counsellor-at-Law
director: 12 William Wyler
based on play by: 9 Elmer
Rice
cast: 11 Bebe Daniels, Doris
Kenyon 12 Isabel Jewell
13 John Barrymore, Melvyn
Douglas, Onslow Stevens

counselor, counsellor 5 tutor 6 lawyer, mentor 7 adviser 8 advocate, attorney,
minister 9 barrister, solicitor
10 instructor

counselor-at-law 6 lawyer
8 advocate, attorney 9 barrister, solicitor 10 mouthpiece

count 4 deem, hold, lord, rate,
tell 5 add up, judge, noble,
tally, total 6 impute, look on,
matter, number, reckon, regard 7 ascribe, include, tick
off 8 consider, estimate, look
upon, numerate 9 attribute,
enumerate, numbering, reckoning 10 numeration 11 calculation, computation,
enumeration
German: 4 Graf
French: 5 comte
Italian: 5 conte

countenance 3 aid, air 4 back,
face, help, look, mien 5 build,
favor 6 aspect, permit, traits,
uphold, visage 7 advance, approve, condone, endorse, forward, further, profile,
promote, support, work for
8 advocacy, advocate, approval, auspices, champion,
contours, features, presence,

sanction 9 promotion 10 appearance, assistance, expression, silhouette
11 approbation, physiognomy
12 championship, moral support 13 encouragement

counter 3 bar, man 4 defy,
disk 5 piece, stand, table
6 buffet, contra, offset, oppose,
resist 7 against, get even, hit
back, opposed, pay back, reverse 8 contrary, fountain, opposite 9 fight back, retaliate
11 conflicting 13 contradictory

counteract 4 curb, undo
5 check, fight 6 defeat, hinder,
negate, offset, oppose, resist,
thwart 7 assuage, nullify, repress 8 overcome, restrain
9 alleviate, frustrate, overpower 10 annihilate, contravene, neutralize

counteraction 8 negation
10 offsetting, opposition
13 contravention, nullification
14 neutralization

counteractive 7 adverse 8 inimical 10 corrective 11 unfavorable 12 antagonistic,
neutralizing

counteractor 7 negator 9 nullifier, offsetter 11 neutralizer

counteragent 8 antidote 9 antitoxin 10 antipoison 11 double agent

counterbalance 5 amend,
check 6 cancel, offset, redeem,
set off 7 correct, rectify
8 atone for, equalize, make
good, outweigh 9 make up
for 10 balance out, neutralize,
outbalance, recompense
12 compensation

counterfeit 4 copy, fake,
sham 5 bogus, fraud, phony
6 ersatz, forged 7 feigned, forgery 8 spurious 9 facsimile,
imitation, simulated 10 artificial, fraudulent, substitute
11 make-believe

Counterfeiters, The
author: 9 Andre Gide

countermand 4 void 5 annul,
quash 6 cancel, recall, repeal,
revoke 7 abolish, nullify, rescind, retract, reverse 8 abrogate, call back, disenact,
override, overrule, set aside,
withdraw, write off
12 disestablish

counterpart 4 copy, mate,
twin 5 equal, match 6 double,
fellow 8 parallel 9 duplicate
11 correlative 12 doppelganger 13 correspondent, spitting
image

counterpoise 7 balance 9 stability 11 equilibrium

countersign 4 sign **7** certify, confirm, endorse **8** validate **9** authorize **11** corroborate **12** authenticate

countess
  French: **8** comtesse
  Italian: **8** contessa

countless 6 myriad, untold **7** endless **8** infinite **9** limitless, unlimited **10** numberless, unnumbered **11** innumerable, measureless **12** immeasurable, incalculable **13** multitudinous

Count of Monte Cristo, The
  author: **14** Alexandre Dumas (pere)
  character: **6** Albert, Haydee, Morrel **7** Fernand (Comte de Morcerf) **8** Danglars, Mercedes **9** Abbe Faria, Valentine, Villefort **10** Caderousse, Maximilian **12** Edmond Dantes
  prison: **10** Chateau d'If

count on 6 expect **7** hope for **10** anticipate

countrified 5 rural **6** rustic **9** backwoods **15** unsophisticated

country 4 area, farm, land **5** realm, rural, state **6** nation, people, public, region, rustic, simple, sticks **7** boonies, farming, kingdom, natives, scenery, terrain **8** citizens, district, homeland, populace **9** backwoods, boondocks, community, landscape, territory **10** fatherland, native land, native soil, population, provincial, rural areas **11** farming area, hinterlands, inhabitants, nationality **12** commonwealth **15** unsophisticated

Country Cousin
  author: **16** Louis Auchincloss

Country Girl, The
  director: **12** George Seaton
  based on play by: **13** Clifford Odets
  cast: **10** Bing Crosby, Grace Kelly **11** Anthony Ross **13** William Holden
  Oscar for: **7** actress (Kelly)

countryman 4 hick, rube **5** yokel **6** farmer, rustic **7** bumpkin, hayseed, peasant **8** landsman **10** clodhopper, compatriot, provincial

Country of the Pointed Firs, The
  author: **15** Sarah Orne Jewett

country place 4 farm **5** manor **6** estate

countryside 6 sticks **7** boonies **9** backwater, backwoods, boondocks, rural area **10** hinterland

count up 3 add **5** tally, total **6** reckon **7** compute **9** calculate

count upon 6 expect **7** foresee **10** anticipate

coup 3 act **4** blow, deed, feat **6** stroke **12** master stroke

coup de grace 9 deathblow **11** mercy stroke **12** decisive blow **15** finishing stroke
  literally: **11** blow of mercy

coup de main 14 surprise attack **17** sudden development
  literally: **15** blow from the hand

coup d'etat 6 mutiny **8** uprising **9** overthrow, rebellion **10** revolution, subversion

coup de theatre 15 theatrical trick

coup d'oeil 11 quick glance
  literally: **14** stroke of the eye

Couperin, Francois (Le Grand)
  born: **5** Paris **6** France
  composer of: **9** La Sultane, Les Fastes (de la grande et ancienne) **13** Concert Royaux **16** Apotheose de Lulli, Pieces de Clavecin **17** Lecons des Tenebres **20** Les Follies Francoises **31** Le Parnasse on l'Apotheose de Corelli

couple 3 duo, tie **4** bind, join, link, pair, yoke **5** hitch **6** fasten **7** connect, doublet, twosome **10** man and wife **11** man and woman **14** husband and wife

coupler 4 link, lock **5** clasp, hitch **6** buckle **8** fastener **9** fastening

Couples
  author: **10** John Updike

coupling 5 clasp, hatch **6** hookup, yoking **7** joining, pairing **8** hitching **9** attaching, fastening **10** attachment, connecting, connection

courage 4 grit, guts, sand **5** nerve, pluck, spunk, valor **6** daring, mettle **7** bravery **8** boldness **9** derring-do, fortitude **11** intrepidity **12** fearlessness **13** dauntlessness **16** stoutheartedness

courageous 4 bold **5** brave, manly **6** dogged, heroic **7** dashing, doughty, gallant, valiant **8** fearless, intrepid, resolute, stalwart, unafraid, valorous **9** dauntless **10** chivalrous **11** indomitable **12** boldspirited **13** stronghearted

Courbet, Jean Desire Gustave
  born: **6** France, Ornans
  artwork: **16** The Artist's Studio, The Stonebreakers **17** The Burial at Ornans **19** The Peasants of Flagey **25** Self-Portrait with a Black Dog

courier 4 mule **5** envoy **6** herald, legate, runner **7** Gabriel, mailman, Mercury, postman **8** emissary **9** go-between, harbinger, messenger, postrider **11** herald angel, internuncio

course 3 run, way **4** flow, gush, mode, path, pour, race, road **5** march, orbit, round, route, surge, track **6** action, circle, method, policy, stream **7** channel, circuit, classes, conduct, lessons, passage, subject **8** behavior, lectures, sequence **9** direction, procedure, unfolding **10** curriculum, racecourse, trajectory **11** development, progression

court 3 bar, woo **4** hall, quad, seek, suit, yard **5** bench, manor, plaza, staff, train **6** atrium, castle, homage, induce, invite, palace, pursue, wooing **7** address, attract, chateau, cortege, council, flatter, hearing, meeting, provoke, retinue, session **8** advisers, assembly, audience, blandish, fawn upon, pander to, respects, run after **9** entourage, following **10** attendants, quadrangle **13** solicitations

Courtenay, Tom
  born: **4** Hull **7** England
  roles: **9** Billy Liar **10** The Dresser **36** The Loneliness of the Long Distance Runner

courteous 4 kind, mild **5** civil **6** polite **7** refined, tactful **8** gracious, mannerly, well-bred **10** diplomatic, respectful, soft-spoken **11** considerate, well-behaved **12** well-mannered

courtesy 5 favor **7** manners, regards, respect **8** civility, kindness, respects **9** deference, gallantry, gentility **10** indulgence, politeness, refinement **11** cultivation **12** graciousness **13** consideration

courtier 4 beau **7** gallant **8** cavalier **9** attendant **18** gentleman-in-waiting

Courtier, The
  author: **21** Baldassare Castiglione

Court Jester
  director: **11** Melvin Frank **12** Norman Panama

cast: 9 Danny Kaye 11 Glynis Johns 13 Basil Rathbone 14 Angela Lansbury

courtly 5 suave 6 polite 7 elegant, gallant, genteel, refined, stately 8 debonair, decorous, highbred, ladylike, mannerly, polished 9 civilized, courteous, dignified 10 chivalrous 11 blue-blooded, gentlemanly 12 aristocratic 14 silk-stockinged

courtship 4 suit 6 wooing 14 keeping company

Courtship of Eddie's Father, The
character: 4 Tina 10 Tom Corbett 12 Eddie Corbett, Norman Tinker 13 Mrs Livingston
cast: 9 Bill Bixby 11 Brandon Cruz, James Komack 12 Miyoshi Umeki 15 Kristina Holland

Courtship of Miles Standish, The
author: 24 Henry Wadsworth Longfellow
character: 9 John Alden, Priscilla

courtyard 4 area, quad 9 curtilage, enclosure 10 quadrangle

cousin 7 kinsman 8 relation, relative 9 kinswoman

Cousin Bette
author: 14 Honore de Balzac
character: 6 Crevel 7 Adeline 10 Baron Hulot 11 Mme Marneffe 13 Hortense Hulot, Marechal Hulot 14 Lisbeth Fischer 23 Count Wenceslas Steinbock

Cousin Pons
author: 14 Honore de Balzac

Cousy, Bob
nickname: 12 Mr Basketball
sport: 10 basketball
position: 5 guard
team: 13 Boston Celtics

couturier, couturiere 8 designer 9 midinette 10 dressmaker, seamstress

cove 3 bay 5 inlet 6 lagoon 7 estuary

covenant 3 vow 4 bond, oath, pact 6 pledge, treaty 7 bargain, promise 8 contract 9 agreement 15 solemn agreement
Hebrew: 4 Brit 5 Berit, Brith 6 Berith

Covenant, The
author: 13 James Michener

cover see box

coverage 7 payment 8 analy-

cover 3 cap, lid, top 4 case, hide, hood, mask, veil, wrap 5 cloak, cross, guard, lay on, put on, quilt 6 asylum, clothe, defend, embody, enwrap, jacket, refuge, report, screen, sheath, shield, shroud, take in, tell of 7 binding, blanket, conceal, contain, defense, embrace, envelop, include, involve, obscure, overlay, protect, put over, secrete, sheathe, shelter, wrapper, write up 8 comprise, deal with, describe, disguise, envelope, pass over, traverse 9 chronicle, comforter, eiderdown, encompass, sanctuary 10 camouflage, comprehend, encasement, protection 11 concealment, hiding place

sis 9 indemnity, reporting 10 protection, publishing 11 description 12 broadcasting 13 reimbursement

covered 4 clad 6 hidden 7 aimed at, cloaked, guarded, insured 8 included, overlaid, screened 9 blanketed, concealed, protected, sheltered, traversed 10 overspread

covering 6 casing, sheath 7 wrapper 8 envelope, wrapping 11 descriptive, explanatory 12 introductory

coverlet 5 quilt, throw 6 afghan, spread 7 blanket 9 bedspread, comforter

Coverly, Sir Roger de
character in: 12 The Spectator
authors: 6 Steele 7 Addison

covert 6 hidden, secret, veiled 7 sub rosa, unknown 9 concealed, disguised 11 clandestine 13 surreptitious

cover up 4 hide, mask, veil 6 hush up 7 conceal 8 disguise, keep back, suppress, withhold 9 gloss over, whitewash

cover-up 4 mask 5 blind 6 screen 8 disguise 9 whitewash 11 concealment

covet 4 want 5 crave, fancy 6 desire 7 long for

covetous 6 greedy 7 craving, envious, jealous, lustful, selfish 8 desirous, grasping, yearning 9 mercenary, rapacious 10 avaricious

covetousness 4 envy 5 greed 7 avarice 8 jealousy, rapacity 10 greediness 12 graspingness 13 mercenariness

covey 4 bevy 5 flock, group 6 family

cow 4 beef 5 abash, bossy, bully, deter, scare 6 bovine, cattle, dismay 7 terrify 8 browbeat, bulldoze, frighten, threaten 9 terrorize 10 discourage, dishearten, intimidate, make cringe
young: 4 calf 6 heifer

coward 3 cad 5 sissy 6 craven 7 caitiff, chicken, dastard, milksop 8 poltroon 11 Milquetoast, mollycoddle, yellowbelly

Coward, Sir Noel
author of: 8 Hay Fever 9 Cavalcade 10 Sigh No More 12 Blithe Spirit, Private Lives 14 In Which We Serve, Nude with Violin 15 Design for Living

cowardliness 8 timidity 10 yellowness 12 irresolution 13 pusillanimity, spinelessness 18 chicken-heartedness

cowardly 5 shaky, timid 6 afraid, craven, yellow 7 anxious, fearful, gutless, nervous 8 timorous 9 dastardly, tremulous 10 frightened 11 lily-livered 12 apprehensive, fainthearted, uncourageous 13 pusillanimous, yellow-bellied 14 chicken-hearted

Cowardly Lion
character in: 13 The Wizard of Oz
author: 4 Baum

cowboy 6 drover, gaucho 7 vaquero 8 buckaroo 10 roughrider 12 broncobuster, cattle-herder

cowed 5 fazed 7 abashed, crushed, subdued 8 dismayed 11 intimidated 12 disconcerted 14 under one's thumb

cower 5 crawl, quail, toady 6 cringe, flinch, grovel, recoil, shrink 7 tremble, truckle 8 bootlick, draw back

cowl 4 cope, hood 5 cloak

Cowley, Malcolm
author of: 12 Exile's Return 16 A Second Flowering 27 And I Worked at the Writer's Trade 28 The Dream of the Golden Mountains

coworker 7 partner 8 teammate 9 associate, colleague 10 accomplice 11 confederate 12 collaborator

Cowper, William
author of: **7** The Task **11** The
Cast-Away

Cowperwood, Frank
character in: **8** The Titan
12 The Financier
author: **7** Dreiser

coxcomb 3 fop **4** beau
5 dandy **8** popinjay

coy 3 shy **5** timid **6** demure,
modest **7** bashful, prudish
8 blushing, sheepish, skittish,
timorous **9** diffident, kittenish,
shrinking **10** coquettish,
overmodest

Coyote State
nickname of: **11** South
Dakota

cozen 3 con, gyp **4** bilk, coax,
dupe, gull, rook **5** cheat,
trick **6** fleece **7** deceive, defraud, swindle, wheedle
9 bamboozle, victimize

cozener 4 fake **5** cheat, fraud,
quack **6** con man **8** deceiver,
swindler **9** charlatan, trickster
10 mountebank **13** confidence
man

coziness 6 warmth **7** comfort
8 intimacy, snugness
11 contentment

cozy 4 easy, snug **5** comfy,
homey **7** restful **8** homelike,
relaxing **9** gemutlich, simpatico **11** comfortable **16** snug as
a bug in a rug
French: **6** intime

Cozzens, James Gould
author of: **12** Guard of
Honor **15** By Love Possessed

CPA 7 auditor **10** accountant,
bookkeeper **25** certified public
accountant

crab 4 carp **5** crank, gripe,
grump **6** grouch, grouse
8 complain, sourball **9** shellfish **10** crustacean,
curmudgeon
constellation of: **6** Cancer

Crabbe, Buster
real name: **20** Clarence Linden Crabbe
nickname: **16** King of the
Serials
born: **9** Oakland CA
roles: **6** Tarzan **10** Buck Rogers **11** Flash Gordon
15 King of the Jungle

crabbed 4 mean, sour
6 cranky, morose **7** grouchy,
peevish, pinched **8** churlish,
spiteful **9** irascible, irritable,
rancorous

crabby 5 cross, testy **6** cranky,
touchy **7** grouchy, peevish
8 petulant, snappish **9** irritable **10** ill-humored, out of

sorts **11** ill-tempered
12 cantankerous

crack 3 gag, jab, pop **4** chip,
clap, gash, gibe, jest, joke,
quip, rent, rift, slit, snap
5 break, burst, cleft, split,
taunt **6** cleave, insult, report
7 crackle, crevice, fissure, give
way, rupture, thunder **8** fracture, splinter **9** break down,
wisecrack, witticism **10** go to
pieces

cracked 3 mad **4** daft, nuts
5 crazy, nutty **6** crazed, insane **8** demented, deranged,
unhinged **10** unbalanced
12 mad as a hatter **13** off
one's rocker, out of one's
head **14** off one's trolley
15 mad as a March hare

cracker 5 snack, wafer **7** biscuit, redneck **10** party favor
11 backsettler
12 backwoodsman

crackerjack 2 A-1 **3** ace **4** a-
one, fine **5** super **6** superb,
tip-top **8** splendid, terrific
9 excellent, fantastic, first-rate,
wonderful **10** first-class

Cracker State
nickname of: **7** Georgia

crackle 4 snap **5** craze, crink
9 crepitate

crackpot 3 nut, odd **4** fool,
kook **5** balmy, crank, flake,
freak, kinky, kooky, loony,
nutty, wacko **6** freaky, insane,
looney, madman, maniac,
weirdo **7** dingbat, foolish, lunatic, oddball **9** character, eccentric, screwball
11 impractical

cracksman 4 yegg **7** burglar
10 cat burglar **14** second-story
man

crackup 5 crash, smash, split,
wreck **6** mishap, pileup
7 breakup, debacle, smashup
8 accident, calamity, collapse,
disaster **9** breakdown, collision, splitting **10** exhaustion,
shellshock **11** catastrophe,
prostration **14** disintegration

cradle 3 hug **4** crib, font, rock
6 cuddle, enfold, origin,
source, spring **7** nursery, snuggle **8** bassinet, fountain
10 birthplace, wellspring
12 fountainhead

craft 3 art **4** boat, ruse, ship,
wile **5** guile, knack, plane,
skill, trade **6** deceit, vessel
7 ability, calling, cunning,
know-how, mastery, perfidy,
pursuit **8** airplane, artifice,
business, commerce, deftness,
fineness, industry, intrigue,
trickery, vocation **9** adeptness,

chicanery, deception, duplicity,
expertise, technique **10** adroitness, artfulness, competency,
craftiness, employment, expertness, handicraft, occupation
11 proficiency

craftiness 4 ruse, wile **5** guile
7 cunning, slyness **8** artifice,
foxiness, scheming, trickery,
wiliness **9** chicanery **10** artfulness **11** machination

craftsman 4 hand **5** smith
6 worker, wright **7** artisan
8 mechanic

crafty 3 sly **4** foxy, wily
5 canny, sharp **6** artful, astute,
shifty, shrewd, tricky **7** cunning, devious **8** guileful, plotting, scheming **9** deceitful,
deceptive, designing, dishonest,
underhand, unethical **10** intriguing, perfidious, suspicious **11** calculating

crag 3 tor **4** rock **5** bluff, cliff
9 precipice

craggy 5 rocky, rough, sheer,
steep, stony **6** abrupt, jagged,
ragged, rugged, snaggy
7 scraggy **8** bouldery **9** rock-
bound **10** rock-ribbed
11 precipitous

Crain, Jeanne
born: **9** Barstow CA
roles: **5** Pinky **6** Margie
9 State Fair **17** Cheaper by
the Dozen **19** A Letter to
Three Wives

cram 3 jam **4** fill, pack
5 crowd, force, grind, press,
stuff **7** congest, squeeze
8 compress **9** overcrowd, study
hard

Cram, Ralph
architect of: **17** US Military
Academy (West Point)
29 Cathedral of Saint John
the Divine (NYC)
style: **13** Gothic Revival

crammed 4 full **6** filled,
packed **7** studied, stuffed
9 jam-packed **11** overflowing,
well-stocked

cramp 4 pang **5** block, check,
crick, limit, spasm **6** hamper,
hinder, stitch, stymie, thwart
7 prevent, seizure **8** handicap,
obstruct, restrain, restrict
9 frustrate **12** charley horse

cramped 5 close, tight **6** narrow **7** compact, pinched
8 confined **10** compressed, restrained, restricted

Cranach, Lucas (Lukas)
(the Elder)
born: **7** Kronach, Germany
artwork: **6** Luther **10** Adam
and Eve **11** Crucifixion
14 Apollo and Diana

15 Rest on the Flight
18 The Judgment of Paris
22 Duke and Duchess of Saxony

Cranaus
king of: 6 Athens, Attica
wife: 6 Pedias
daughter: 6 Atthis, Cranae
renamed Athens: 6 Attica

cranberry 9 Vaccinium
19 Vaccinium vitis-idaea
20 Vaccinium macrocarpon
varieties: 3 bog 4 rock, tree
5 large, small 8 American,
European, highbush, moun-
tain 10 Australian

crane 4 bird, boom 5 davit,
heron 7 derrick 10 wading
bird
group of: 5 sedge, siege
constellation of: 4 Grus

Crane, Bob
born: 11 Waterbury CT
roles: 12 Colonel Hogan, Hogan's Heroes

Crane, Hart
author of: 9 The Bridge
14 White Buildings

Crane, Ichabod
character in: 23 The Legend
of Sleepy Hollow
author: 6 Irving

Crane, Roy
creator/artist of: 9 Buz Sawyer, Wash Tubbs 11 Captain
Easy

Crane, Stephen
author of: 11 The Open
Boat 20 The Red Badge of
Courage 23 Maggie: A Girl
of the Streets 24 The Bride
Comes to Yellow Sky

Cranford
author: 10 Mrs Gaskell

cranium 4 head 5 skull 6 noggin 8 brain box, brainpan
9 brain case

crank 4 turn, whim 5 brace,
winch 6 grouch, handle 7 fanatic 8 crotchet 9 eccentric

cranky 5 cross, testy 6 crabby,
touchy 7 bearish, grouchy,
peevish, waspish 8 captious,
petulant 9 crotchety, irascible,
splenetic 10 ill-humored, out
of sorts 11 ill-tempered
12 cantankerous

cranny 3 gap 4 nook, slit
5 break, chink, cleft, crack,
notch, split 7 crevice, fissure
8 cleavage

crash 3 din 4 bang, boom,
bump, dash, ruin 5 crack,
slump, smash, wreck 6 hurtle,
invade, pileup, plunge, racket,
slip in, topple, tumble
7 bumping, clangor, clatter,

collide, crackup, decline, failure, hitting, intrude, setback,
shatter, smashup, sneak in
8 accident, smashing, toppling,
tumbling 9 collision, recession 10 bankruptcy, depression, shattering

crass 5 crude, cruel, gross
6 coarse, oafish, vulgar
7 boorish 8 uncaring 9 inelegant, unfeeling, unrefined
10 unpolished 11 hardhearted,
insensitive 13 unsympathetic

crassness 9 crudeness, grossness, vulgarity 10 coarseness,
inelegance, oafishness
11 boorishness 13 insensitivity

Crataeis
daughter: 6 Scylia

Cratchit, Bob
character in: 15 A Christmas
Carol
author: 7 Dickens

crate 3 box, car 4 auto, case,
pack 5 plane 6 jalopy, pallet
8 airplane 9 container

crater 3 pit 4 hole 6 cavity
10 depression

Cratus
origin: 5 Greek
personifies: 8 strength

cravat 3 tie 5 ascot, scarf,
stock 7 necktie 11 neckerchief

crave 4 need, want 5 covet
6 desire 7 hope for, long for,
pine for, require, sigh for,
wish for 8 yearn for 9 hunger
for, lust after, thirst for
11 hanker after, have a yen
for 13 have a fancy for

craven 3 low 4 base 5 timid
6 scared, yellow 7 fearful, low-
down 8 cowardly, timorous
9 dastardly 10 frightened
11 lily-livered 12 mean-
spirited 13 pusillanimous
14 chicken-hearted

craving 3 yen 4 need 6 desire,
hunger, thirst 7 longing
9 hankering

Crawford, Broderick
real name: 24 William Broderick Crawford
wife: 11 Jan Sterling
born: 14 Philadelphia PA
roles: 6 The Mob 10 The Interns 12 Of Mice and Men
13 Born Yesterday, Highway
Patrol 14 All the King's
Men (Oscar)

Crawford, Henry
character in: 13 Mansfield
Park
author: 6 Austen

Crawford, Joan
real name: 17 Lucille Fay Le
Sueur

husband: 12 Franchot Tone
18 Douglas Fairbanks Jr
daughter: 6 Cheryl
9 Christina
born: 12 San Antonio TX
biography: 13 Mommie
Dearest
roles: 8 The Women
10 Grand Hotel 13 Mildred
Pierce (Oscar) 26 What Ever
Happened to Baby Jane

crawl 4 drag, inch, poke,
worm 5 creep, mosey
6 squirm, wiggle, writhe
7 slither, wriggle

Crawley, Rawdon
character in: 10 Vanity Fair
author: 9 Thackeray

crayon 5 chalk, draft 6 pastel,
pencil, sketch 7 drawing
8 charcoal

craze 3 fad 4 rage 5 furor,
mania 6 dement 7 derange,
passion, unhinge
11 infatuation

crazed 3 mad 6 insane
7 cracked, lunatic 8 demented,
deranged

crazy 3 mad, odd 4 avid, daft,
gaga, keen, nuts, wild 5 nutty,
rabid, silly, weird 6 absurd,
far-out, insane, stupid, unwise 7 berserk, bizarre,
cracked, excited, foolish, frantic, idiotic, strange, touched,
unusual, zealous 8 demented,
deranged, maniacal, peculiar,
uncommon, unhinged 9 fanatical, foolhardy, imprudent,
laughable, senseless 10 hysterical, infatuated, outrageous,
passionate, ridiculous, unbalanced 11 smitten with 12 enthusiastic, mad as a hatter
13 out of one's head 15 mad
as a March haré

creak 4 rasp 5 grate, grind
6 scrape, scream, squeak
7 screech

Creakle
character in: 16 David
Copperfield
author: 7 Dickens

cream 3 top 4 beat, best, drub
5 elite 6 choice, flower 7 the
pick, trounce 8 greatest, off-
white 14 creme de la creme

Cream, Arnold Raymond
real name of: 10 Joe Walcott

cream of the cream
French: 14 creme de la
creme

Cream of the Jest, The
author: 17 James Branch
Cabell

creamy 5 thick, foamy
6 smooth, yellow 8 emulsive

crease 4 fold **5** crimp, pleat, ridge **6** furrow, pucker, ruffle, rumple **7** crimple, crinkle, wrinkle **9** corrugate **11** corrugation

create 4 form, make, mold **5** cause, erect, found, set up **6** design, devise, invent **7** appoint, concoct, develop, fashion **8** conceive, contrive, organize **9** construct, establish, fabricate, formulate, institute, originate

creation 5 world **6** making, nature **8** building, devising, erection, founding **9** all things, formation, handiwork, invention **10** brainchild, conception, concoction, fashioning, production **11** development, fabrication, institution, origination **12** construction **13** establishment

Creation
author: **9** Gore Vidal

creative 8 fanciful, original **9** ingenious, inventive **11** imaginative, resourceful

creator 5 maker **6** author, father, framer **7** founder **8** begetter, designer, inventor, producer **9** architect, generator, initiator **10** originator

creature 3 man **4** bird, fish **5** beast, human **6** animal, insect, mammal, mortal, person **7** critter, reptile **9** earthling, quadruped **10** individual, vertebrate **12** invertebrate

credence 5 faith, trust **6** belief, credit **8** reliance **9** certainty, certitude **10** confidence **11** reliability **13** believability **14** acceptableness, dependableness **15** trustworthiness

credentials 6 permit **7** diploma, license, voucher **9** reference **11** certificate, testimonial **13** authorization

credenza 5 shelf, table **6** buffet **8** bookcase **9** sideboard

credible 6 likely **7** tenable **8** possible, probable, reliable **9** plausible, thinkable **10** believable, dependable, imaginable, reasonable **11** conceivable, trustworthy

credit 3 buy **4** time **5** glory, honor, trust **6** accept, assign, esteem, rely on **7** acclaim, ascribe, believe, fall for, swallow **9** allowance, attribute, recognize **10** prepayment **11** acknowledge, recognition **12** commendation **14** acknowledgment

creditable 6 worthy **8** laudable **9** admirable, estimable,

reputable **11** commendable, meritorious, respectable **12** praiseworthy

credo 4 code, rule **5** maxim, motto, tenet **8** doctrine **10** philosophy

credulous 5 naive **8** gullible, trusting **9** believing **12** overtrustful, unsuspecting, unsuspicious **13** unquestioning **15** unsophisticated

Cree
language family: **9** Algonkian **10** Algonquian
tribe: **10** Plains Cree **13** Woodlands Cree
location: **6** Canada **8** Manitoba
related to: **8** Chippewa

creed 5 dogma **6** belief, canons, gospel **8** doctrine

creek 3 run **4** rill **5** brook **6** branch, spring, stream **7** freshet, rivulet **10** millstream, small river

Creek
language family: **10** Muskhogean
location: **7** Alabama, Florida, Georgia **11** Mississippi
leader: **8** Red Eagle **15** William McIntosh **20** Alexander McGillivray

Creek Mary's Blood
author: **8** Dee Brown

creep 4 inch, worm **5** crawl, sneak, steal **6** dawdle, squirm, writhe **7** slither, wriggle

creeper 3 ivy **4** bird, iron, vine, worm **5** snake **7** climber, crawler, grapnel, trailer

creepy 4 eery **5** eerie, scary **6** crawly, spooky, uneasy **12** apprehensive

cremate 4 burn, char, fire, sear **5** roast **6** ignite, kindle, scorch **8** enkindle **10** incinerate **11** conflagrate **17** consume with flames

creme de banane
type: **7** liqueur
flavor: **6** banana
color: **6** yellow

creme de cacao
type: **6** brandy **7** liqueur
origin: **6** France
flavor: **9** chocolate
color: **5** brown, white
drink: **11** Fifth Avenue
with rum: **6** Panama
with tequila: **8** Toreador
with vodka: **9** Ninotchka **11** Russian Bear **12** Velvet Hammer, White Russian

creme de cassis
type: **7** liqueur
origin: **6** France **8** Burgundy

flavor: **12** black currant
with gin: **8** Parisian

creme de fraise
type: **7** liqueur
flavor: **10** strawberry

creme de framboise
type: **7** liqueur
flavor: **9** raspberry

creme de la creme 3 top **4** best **5** cream, elite **6** choice, flower **8** choicest, very best **12** choicest part **15** cream of the cream

creme de menthe
type: **7** liqueur
flavor: **4** mint
color: **5** green, white
with brandy: **7** Stinger
with cream: **11** Grasshopper
with gin: **6** Caruso, Virgin

creme de noyau
type: **7** liqueur
flavor: **6** almond

creme de violette
type: **7** liqueur
flavor: **7** violets
color: **8** lavender

creme Yvette
type: **7** liqueur
origin: **12** United States
flavor: **7** violets
with gin: **9** Union Jack

Crenna, Richard
born: **12** Los Angeles CA
roles: **9** Death Ship **13** Our Miss Brooks, The Real McCoys

Creole 6 patois **7** criollo, dialect, Haitian **10** West Indian

Creole State
nickname of: **9** Louisiana

Creon
king of: **6** Thebes **7** Corinth
father: **9** Lycaethus, Menoeceus
sister: **7** Jocasta
daughter: **6** Creusa, Glauce
nephew: **7** Oedipus **8** Eteocles **9** Polynices
niece: **6** Ismene **8** Antigone
defeated: **18** Seven against Thebes

crescendo
music: **22** gradually getting louder
abbreviation: **5** cresc

crescent 3 arc, bow **4** arch **5** curve **8** half-moon

crescit eundo 15 it grows as it goes
motto of: **9** New Mexico

Cresius
epithet of: **8** Dionysus
means: **6** Cretan

Cresphontes
member of: **8** Heraclid

father: **12** Aristomachus
brother: **7** Temenus
11 Polyphontes
wife: **6** Merope
father-in-law: **8** Cypselus
son: **7** Aepytus
controlled: **8** Messenia
invaded: **12** Peloponnesus

Cressida
also: **8** Criseyde **9** Crisseyde
based on characters of:
7 Bryseis **8** Chryseis
setting: **9** Trojan War
loved: **7** Troilus
deserted Troilus for:
8 Diomedes

crest 3 tip, top **4** apex, arms,
comb, peak, tuft **5** crown,
plume **6** emblem, height, summit **7** topknot **8** pinnacle
10 coat of arms, escutcheon

crestfallen 8 dejected, downcast **9** depressed, woebegone
10 despondent, dispirited
11 discouraged, downhearted,
low-spirited **12** disappointed,
disheartened

Creta
daughter: **8** Pasiphae

Cretaceous period
dinosaur from: **9** Euhelopus,
Iguanodon **10** Allosaurus,
Antrodemus **11** Anatosaurus,
Ankylsaurus, Deinonychus,
Gorgosaurus, Triceratops
12 Lambeosaurus, Ornithomimus **13** Albertosaurus, Corythosaurus, Hypselosaurus,
Hypsilophodon, Palaeoscincus, Protoceratops, Stru-
thiomimus, Styracosaurus,
Tyrannosaurus **14** Psittacosaurus, Thescelosaurus
15 Parasaurolophus,
Procheneosaurus

Cretan bull
also: **15** Marathonian bull
form: **4** bull
son: **8** Minotaur
captured on: **5** Crete
captured by: **8** Hercules
roamed: **8** Marathon
recaptured by: **7** Theseus

Cretan Mythology
goddess of fishermen/hunt-
ers/sailors: **11** Britomartis
corresponds to Greek:
7 Artemis
goddess of the sea:
8 Dictynna
maze: **9** labyrinth
monster: **8** Minotaur

Crete *see box*

Cretheis
husband: **7** Acastus
killed by: **6** Peleus

Cretheus
founder of: **6** Iolcus
father: **6** Aeolus
mother: **7** Enarete
brother: **9** Salmoneus
wife: **4** Tyro
son: **5** Aeson **6** Pheres
8 Amythaon
companion: **6** Aeneas

Creusa
also: **6** Glauce
father: **5** Creon, Priam **8** Cychreus **10** Erechtheus
mother: **6** Hecuba
husband: **6** Aeneas **7** Telamon
son: **3** Ion **8** Ascanius
bride of: **5** Jason
killed by: **5** magic, Medea

crevasse 3 gap **4** rift **5** abyss,
break, chasm, cleft, gorge,
gulch, gully, split **6** breach, divide **7** fissure

crevice 4 rent, rift, slit
5 chasm, cleft, crack, split
6 breach **7** fissure **8** crevasse,
fracture

crew 3 mob **4** band, body,
herd, mass, pack, team
5 corps, force, group, hands,
horde, party, squad, troop
6 seamen, throng **7** company,
sailors **8** mariners **9** multitude,
seafarers **10** assemblage,
complement

crib 3 bed, bin, cot, hut, key
4 pony **5** cheat, shack, stall,
steal **6** creche, manger **7** purloin **8** bassinet **10** plagiarize

cribbage
score kept on: **5** board
points/game: **8** sixty-one
third hand: **4** crib

Crich, Gerald
character in: **11** Women in
Love
author: **8** Lawrence

Crichton, Michael
author of: **5** Congo **6** Sphere
9 Rising Sun **12** Jurassic
Park **14** The Terminal Man
18 The Andromeda Strain
20 The Great Train
Robbery

cricket *see box*

cricket
variety: **4** bush, cave, sand,
tree **5** camel, field, house
6 ground **9** Jerusalem,
pygmy mole

Cries and Whispers
director: **12** Ingmar Bergman
cast: **10** Liv Ullmann **12** Ingrid Thulin **16** Harriet
Andersson

crime 3 sin **4** tort **5** wrong
6 felony **7** misdeed, offense,
outrage **8** foul play, iniquity,
villainy **10** misconduct, wrongdoing **11** abomination, lawbreaking, malfeasance,
misdemeanor **13** transgression

Crime and Punishment
author: **16** Fyodor Dostoevsky
character: **5** Sonya **6** Dounia
7 Porfiry **9** Razumihin
11 Raskolnikov

Crete
other name: **5** Kriti **6** Candia
capital/largest city: **5** Canea **8** Iraklion
others: **3** Hag **4** Lato **5** Khora, Sitia, Zakro **6** Anoyia, Candia, Khania, Lisamo, Mallia, Meleme, Retimo **7** Malerni
8 Kastelli, Nikolaos, Sphakion **9** Heraclion, Heraklion, Re-
thymnon, Tympakion **11** Palaiophora
government: division of: **6** Greece
monetary unit: **7** drachma
mountain: **3** Ida **5** Dikte, Phino **6** Juktas **7** Lasithi, Madaras **8** Leuka Ori, Theodore, Thriphte **9** Psiloriti
highest point: **3** Ida
sea: **5** Crete **6** Aegean **13** Mediterranean
physical feature:
bay: **4** Suda **5** Kanca **6** Kisamo, Mesara
cape: **4** Buza **5** Liano **6** Salome, Sidero, Spatha **7** Stavros **8** Lithinon, Sidheros
gulf: **6** Khania **9** Merabello
people: **7** Candiot, Cretans, Minoans **9** Caphtorim, Sphak-
iots **11** Philistines
artist: **7** El Greco
author: **11** Kazantzakis
conqueror: **8** Metellus
king: **5** Minos
language: **5** Greek **6** Minoan **7** Linear A, Linear B
religion: **14** Greek Orthodoxy
place:
ruins: **15** Palace at Knossos

cricket
  players/team: 6 eleven
  equipment: 3 bat **4** bail,
  ball **5** stump **6** wicket
  position: 5 gully, mid on,
  slops **6** bowler, long on,
  mid off **7** batsman, fine
  leg, long off **8** third man
  9 mid wicket, square leg
  10 cover point, extra
  cover, silly mid on
  11 silly mid off **12** wicket
  keeper **13** deep mid
  wicket **16** backward
  short leg
  lines: 7 creases
  period of play: 4 over
  7 innings
  championship game:
  9 test match
  England/Australia match:
  8 the Ashes

criminal 4 hood **5** crook, felon,
wrong **6** guilty, outlaw
7 crooked, culprit, illegal, illicit,
lawless **8** culpable, offender,
unlawful, wasteful **9** felonious,
senseless, wrongdoer **10** abominable, delinquent, indictable,
lawbreaker, malefactor, outrageous, villainous **11** blameworthy, disgraceful,
lawbreaking **12** transgressor

crimp 4 curl, fold, kink, wave
5 clamp, flute, frill, frizz **7** crinkle, frizzle, wrinkle **8** obstacle

crimple 4 curl **6** pucker **7** crinkle, crumple, wrinkle
9 corrugate

crimson 3 red **5** blush, flush
6 redden **7** carmine, scarlet

cringe 4 duck **5** cower, dodge,
quail, toady **6** blench, flinch,
grovel, recoil, shrink **7** truckle

cringing 6 abject **7** fawning, ignoble, servile, wincing **8** cowering, toadying **9** flinching,
groveling, shrinking, sniveling

crinkle 5 crush **6** rumple, rustle
7 crumple, wrinkle

crinkly 4 wavy **5** curly, kinky
6 crimpy, frizzy **7** cockled,
crimped, crimply, puckery, ruffled, rumpled, twisted, wrinkly
8 crimpled, frizzled, puckered,
wrinkled **9** shriveled

crinoline 4 hoop **5** skirt **9** hoopskirt, petticoat **10** underskirt

Criophorus
  epithet of: 6 Hermes
  means: 9 ram bearer

cripple 4 gimp, halt, harm,
maim, stop **6** damage, impair
7 disable **8** make lame, paralyze **9** hamstring **10** debilitate,
inactivate **12** incapacitate

crisis 6 climax **9** emergency

crisp 5 brisk, fresh, nippy,
sharp, terse, witty **6** candid,
chilly, crispy, lively, snappy
7 bracing, brittle, crunchy,
pointed **8** incisive **9** energetic,
sparkling, vivacious **10** refreshing **12** invigorating

crisscross 4 awry **5** cross **8** confused, traverse

Crisseyde see **8** Cressida

Cristillo, Louis Francis
  real name of: 11 Lou Costello

criterion 3 law **4** norm, rule
5 gauge, model **7** example,
measure **8** standard **9** guidepost, precedent, principle,
yardstick **10** touchstone

critic 5 judge, mavin, scold
6 carper, censor, expert, rapper
7 analyst, arbiter, knocker, reviler **8** attacker, vilifier, virtuoso **9** authority, backbiter,
detractor, evaluator **10** antagonist, criticizer **11** cognoscente,
commentator, connoisseur,
faultfinder

critical 5 fussy, grave, hairy,
picky, risky, vital **6** urgent
7 carping, crucial, finicky,
judging, nagging, serious **8** caviling, decisive, perilous, pressing **9** dangerous, harrowing,
hazardous, judicious, momentous, sensitive **10** analytical,
censorious, derogatory, diagnostic, nitpicking, precarious
11 disparaging **12** disapproving,
faultfinding

critical situation 3 jam **4** mess
6 crisis, pickle **7** straits, trouble
8 hot water **9** deep water
10 difficulty **11** predicament

critical stage 6 climax, crisis
9 emergency

critical success
  French: 13 succes d'estime

criticism 4 fire, flak, slam
5 blame, knock **6** review **7** censure, comment **8** analysis, critique, judgment **9** aspersion,
stricture **10** commentary, evaluation **12** faultfinding

criticize 4 carp, fuss, pick
5 cavil, nag at **7** censure, nitpick, reprove **8** denounce, reproach **9** disparage

critique 6 review **8** analysis

Crna Gora see **10** Montenegro

croak 3 caw, die **4** kill, moan,
roup **7** grumble, kick off
8 complain, harsh cry **13** kick
the bucket

Croatia
  capital/largest city: 5 Zagreb
  others: 4 Knin **5** Split, Zadar
  6 Osijek, Rijeka (Fiume)
  7 Vukovar, Sibenik **8** Karlo-
  vac, Varazdin, Vinkovci
  9 Dubrovnik **10** Kostajnica
  head of state: 9 president
  government: 9 democracy
  monetary unit: 5 dinar
  mountain: 10 Julian Alps
  11 Styrian Alps
  sea: 8 Adriatic
  people: 5 Serbs **6** Croats
  7 Muslims **9** Yugoslavs
  language: 8 Croatian **10** Serbo
  Croat
  religion: 17 Catholic Christian,
  Orthodox Christian

Crocetti, Dino Paul
  real name of: 10 Dean Martin

crocodile 4 croc **6** cayman, ga-
vial, lizard **7** reptile, asurian

crock 3 jar, pot **9** container

crockery 5 china **6** dishes,
plates **7** pottery **8** clayware
9 chinaware, tableware **11** ceramic ware, earthenware
14 cups and saucers

Crock of Gold
  author: 13 James Stephens

crocus
  varieties: 4 fall, wild **5** dutch
  6 autumn, scotch **7** Chilean,
  saffron **8** tropical **9** celandine
  12 iris-flowered

Crocus
  form: 5 youth
  changed into: 12 saffron plant

Crome Yellow
  author: 12 Aldous Huxley

Crommyonian sow
  also: 5 Phaea
  killed by: 7 Theseus

Cromwell, Oliver
  also: 13 Lord Protector
  served in: 15 English Civil
  War
  fought against: 8 Charles I
  9 Cavaliers
  fought for: 10 Parliament,
  Roundheads
  regiment: 9 Ironsides
  battle: 6 Naseby, Oxford
  7 Preston **11** Marston Moor

crone 3 hag **5** witch **6** beldam
7 beldame, old wife

Cronia
  festival in: 6 Athens

Cronus
also: 6 Cronos, Kronos
form: 5 Titan
father: 6 Uranus
mother: 4 Gaea
sister: 4 Rhea
wife: 4 Rhea
son: 4 Zeus 5 Hades
8 Poseidon
daughter: 4 Hera 6 Hestia
7 Demeter
corresponds to: 6 Saturn

crony 3 pal 4 ally, chum,
mate 5 buddy 6 bunkie, cohort, friend 7 comrade
8 bunkmate, intimate, ship-
mate, sidekick 9 accessory, associate, companion, old
friend 10 accomplice, bosom
buddy 11 confederate 12 acquaintance, collaborator
13 coconspirator

Cronyn, Hume
wife: 12 Jessica Tandy
born: 6 London 7 Canada,
Ontario
roles: 13 The Fourposter
17 Phantom of the Opera
19 Sunrise at Campobello

crook 3 arc, bow 4 bend, hook,
thug, turn 5 angle, cheat,
curve, knave, thief, twist
6 bandit, outlaw, robber
7 burglar 8 criminal, swindler
9 curvature, embezzler

crooked 4 awry, bent, wily
5 askew, bowed, shady
6 crafty, curved, hooked,
shifty, sneaky, spiral, warped,
zigzag 7 corrupt, sinuous,
twisted, winding 8 criminal,
deformed, tortuous, twisting,
unlawful 9 deceitful, deceptive,
dishonest, distorted, nefarious,
unethical 10 fraudulent, meandering, perfidious, serpentine
11 underhanded 12 dishonorable, unscrupulous

crookedness 10 dishonesty
11 deviousness 13 deceitfulness, double-dealing

Crookes, William
nationality: 7 British
invented: 8 thallium 10 radi-
ometer 11 Crookes tube

croon 3 hum 4 sing 6 murmur,
warble

crop 3 bob, cut, lop 4 clip,
snip, trim 5 prune, shear,
yield 6 growth 7 harvest, reaping 8 cut short, gleaning
9 gathering 10 production

crop-raising 7 farming, tillage
11 agriculture 12 agribusiness,
truck farming 15 market
gardening

crop up 5 arise, ensue, occur
6 appear 7 develop, surface
11 come to light

croquet
equipment: 4 hoop 6 mallet,
wicket
variation: 5 roque
term: 5 rover

Crosby, Bing
real name: 17 Harry Lillis
Crosby
partner: 7 Bob Hope 10 Hedy
Lamarr 13 Dorothy Lamour
nickname: 8 Der Bingle
wife: 8 Dixie Lee 12 Kathryn
Grant
born: 8 Tacoma WA
roles: 10 Going My Way (Oscar), Holiday Inn 11 High
Society 14 The Country Girl,
White Christmas 17 The
Bells of St Mary's
22 Christmas in Connecticut
Road to: 3 Rio 4 Bali
7 Morocco 8 Hong Kong,
Zanzibar 9 Singapore

cross 3 mad, mix 4 crux,
ford, meet, rood 5 angry,
blend, erase, gruff, surly,
testy, trial 6 burden, cancel, cranky, delete, go
over, hybrid, ordeal, shirty,
touchy 7 amalgam, an-
noyed, athwart, grouchy,
oblique, peevish, trouble,
waspish 8 captious, chol-
eric, churlish, contrary,
crucifix, distress, intermix,
pass over, petulant, snappish, traverse 9 adversity,
crotchety, half-breed, hybridize, intersect, irascible,
irritable, querulous, splenetic, strike out, suffering
10 affliction, difficulty, ill-
humored, interbreed, mis-
fortune, obliterate, out of
sorts, transverse 11 combination, ill-tempered, in-
tractable, tribulation
12 cantankerous, disagreeable, intersecting

crossbar 3 bar 4 spar 5 sprit
6 stripe

crossbreed 3 mix 8 intermix
9 hybridize 10 interbreed

cross-fertilize 9 hybridize

crossing 4 pass 7 mixture, passage 8 blocking, opposing, traverse 9 thwarting
10 traversing 11 hybridizing,
intersection 13 hybridization

cross over 4 span 5 cross
6 bridge 8 traverse

crosspiece 3 bar 4 spar 5 sprit

cross-pollinate 9 hybridize

crossroad 12 intersection,
turning point

cross swords 5 clash, fight
6 battle, combat, tussle 7 contend, contest 8 skirmish

crossways 7 athwart
12 transversely

crosswise 6 across 7 athwart
8 sideways, traverse
10 transverse

crotchet 4 bent, whim 5 habit,
quirk, trait 6 foible, hang-up,
oddity, vagary, whimsy 7 caprice 8 quiddity 9 mannerism
10 erraticism 11 peculiarity
12 eccentricity, idiosyncrasy,
irregularity 14 characteristic

crotchety 3 odd 5 fussy
6 cranky 7 erratic, grouchy
8 contrary, peculiar 9 eccentric

Crotopus
king of: 5 Argos
daughter: 8 Psamathe
killed: 8 Psamathe

Crotus
father: 3 Pan
skilled in: 7 archery
companion of: 5 Muses

crouch 4 bend, duck 5 cower,
squat, stoop 6 cringe, recoil,
shrink 9 hunch over
10 hunker down 11 scrooch
down, scrunch down

crow 3 daw, jay, kae 4 blow,
brag, rook 5 boast, crake, exult, gloat, raven, strut, vaunt
6 cackle, chough, corbie, magpie 7 corvine, jackdaw, rejoice,
swagger, triumph, trumpet
8 jubilate 14 cock-a-doodle-doo
group of: 6 murder

Crow
constellation of: 6 Corvus

Crow
language family: 6 Siouan
tribe: 9 River Crow
12 Mountain Crow
location: 7 Montana,
Wyoming
related to: 7 Hidatsa

crowbar 3 bar, pry 5 jimmy,
lever

crowd 3 jam, mob, set 4 cram,
gang, herd, host, mass, push
5 crush, flock, group, horde,
press, shove, surge, swarm
6 circle, claque, clique, gather,
huddle, legion, throng 7 cluster, coterie, elbow in,
squeeze 8 assemble 9 gathering, multitude 10 assemblage,
congregate 11 concentrate
12 congregation

Crowd, The
director: 9 King Vidor
cast: 9 Bert Roach 11 James

Murray **15** Eleanor
Boardman

crowded 4 full **6** filled,
jammed, mobbed, packed
7 crammed, teeming **8** swarming, thronged **9** congested,
jampacked **11** overflowing

crowd out 8 displace
9 overwhelm

crown 3 cap, top **4** acme, apex,
head, pate, peak **5** crest, tiara
6 climax, diadem, noggin,
noodle, summit, top off,
wreath, zenith **7** chaplet, circlet, coronet, fulfill, garland,
perfect, royalty **8** complete,
monarchy, pinnacle, round
out **11** sovereignty

Crowne, Lenina
character in: **13** Brave New
World
author: **6** Huxley

crowning point 3 cap, tip
4 apex, peak **6** summit, vertex,
zenith **8** pinnacle

crown of thorns 4 bane
5 cross **6** burden, ordeal **7** torment **8** vexation **10** affliction
11 tribulation

crow over 5 gloat **9** brag
about **10** boast about

crucial 5 grave **6** knotty, urgent **7** serious, weighty **8** critical, decisive, pressing
9 essential, important, momentous **11** determining,
significant

Crucible, The
author: **12** Arthur Miller

crude 3 raw **5** crass, gross,
rough **6** coarse, vulgar **7** obscene, sketchy, uncouth **9** imperfect, tasteless, unrefined
10 incomplete, unfinished, unpolished, unprepared **11** uncompleted, undeveloped,
unprocessed

crudeness 7 rawness **8** bad
taste **9** crassness, grossness,
obscenity, vulgarity **10** coarseness, indelicacy
13 tastelessness

cruel 6 brutal, savage **7** inhuman, vicious **8** inhumane, pitiless, ruthless, sadistic
9 heartless, merciless, unfeeling **10** unmerciful **11** cold-
blooded, hardhearted, remorseless **15** uncompassionate

cruelty 6 sadism **8** ferocity,
savagery **9** barbarity, brutality
10 bestiality, inhumanity
11 viciousness **12** ruthlessness
13 heartlessness

cruet 3 jar, jug **6** bottle **7** ur-
ceole **9** dispenser

cruise 4 sail, scud, skim
5 coast, drift, float, glide,
sweep **6** stream, voyage **7** sea-
fare **8** navigate

Cruise, Tom
original name: **21** Thomas
Cruise Mapother
born: **2** NY **8** Syracuse
wife: **10** Mimi Rogers **12** Nicole Kidman
films: **4** Taps **6** Top Gun
7 The Firm, Rain Man
8 Cocktail **10** Far and
Away **11** Endless Love, A
Few Good Men **12** The Outsiders **13** Risky Business
15 The Color of Money
16 All the Right Moves
21 Born on the Fourth of
July

crumb 3 bit **5** grain, scrap,
shred, speck **6** morsel, sliver
8 fragment, particle

crumble 5 crush, decay, grate,
grind **6** powder **8** fragment,
splinter **9** decompose, pulverize **12** disintegrate

crumbly 7 brittle, friable
9 breakable

Crummles, Vincent
character in: **16** Nicholas
Nickleby
author: **7** Dickens

crummy 5 awful, lousy **6** rotten **8** terrible

crumple 4 fall **5** crush **6** cave
in, crease, pucker, rumple
7 crimple, crinkle, wrinkle
8 collapse **9** corrugate

crunch 4 chew, gnaw **5** chomp,
gnash, grind, munch
9 masticate

Cruncher, Jerry
character in: **16** A Tale of
Two Cities
author: **7** Dickens

crunchy 3 dry **5** crisp **6** crispy
7 crackly

crusade, Crusade 5 drive,
rally **8** movement

crusader, Crusader 6 knight,
zealot **7** pilgrim, Templar
8 champion **11** Hospitaller

crush 4 mash **5** break, press,
quash, quell, smash **6** enfold,
quench, squash, subdue
7 crumble, crumple, embrace,
put down, shatter, squeeze,
squelch **8** compress, overcome,
suppress **9** granulate, overpower, overwhelm, pulverize
10 extinguish

crushed 3 sad **5** cowed **6** broken, mashed, woeful
7 abashed, doleful, forlorn,
pressed, put down, quashed,
quelled, smashed, subdued

8 crumbled, crumpled, dejected, desolate, overcame,
overcome, quenched, squashed,
squeezed, wretched **9** flattened,
miserable, squelched, woebegone **10** compressed, despondent, pulverized, suppressed
11 overpowered, over-
whelmed **12** disconsolate, extinguished, inconsolable
13 broken-hearted

crushing 7 mashing **8** decisive,
quelling, smashing **10** shattering **11** humiliating, putting
down, stamping out, suppression **12** obliterating, overwhelming **13** pulverization

crust 4 coat, gall, hull, rind,
scab **5** brass, nerve, shell
6 harden **7** coating **8** chutzpah,
covering, pie shell **9** impudence **11** pastry shell

crustacean 4 crab, flea
5 louse, prawn **6** isopod,
shrimp **7** lobster **8** barnacle,
crawfish, crayfish **9** shellfish,
water flea

crusty 4 curt **5** blunt, gruff,
rough, short, stern, surly,
testy **6** abrupt, crabby, cranky,
shirty, snippy, sullen
7 brusque, peevish, waspish
8 choleric, snappish, snippety
9 irascible, splenetic **10** ill-
natured **11** ill-tempered
13 short-tempered

crux 3 nub **4** core, gist **5** basis,
heart **7** essence **9** essential
10 brass tacks **11** nitty-gritty

cry 3 beg, sob, sue **4** bawl, call,
hawk, howl, keen, moan,
plea, roar, wail, weep, yell,
yelp **5** blare, cheer, groan,
mourn, plead, shout, utter,
whoop **6** appeal, bellow, blazon, boohoo, clamor, hurrah,
huzzah, lament, outcry,
prayer, scream, shriek, snivel
7 blubber, call out, exclaim,
implore, request, screech,
trumpet, whimper **8** entreaty,
petition, proclaim **9** advertise,
importune **10** adjuration, promulgate **11** exclamation
12 solicitation, supplication

Cry, the Beloved Country
author: **9** Alan Paton
locale: **11** South Africa

cry out 4 bark, bawl, call,
howl, roar, yell **5** shout **6** bellow, clamor, holler **7** exclaim
8 proclaim **9** ejaculate

cry over 5 mourn **6** bemoan,
bewail, lament

crypt 4 tomb **5** vault **8** catacomb **9** mausoleum, sepulcher

cryptic 4 dark **5** vague **6** arcane, hidden, occult, secret
7 obscure, strange **8** esoteric,

mystical, puzzling **9** ambiguous **10** cabalistic, mysterious, perplexing **11** enigmatical

cryptogram 4 code **6** cipher

cryptograph 4 code **6** cipher, encode

crystal 3 ice **5** clear, flake, glass, lucid **6** quartz **7** diamond **8** stemware **9** glassware, snowflake, watch part **10** rhinestone **11** transparent

crystallize 3 fix, gel **4** firm, jell **5** candy **6** harden **8** solidify **9** granulate

Csonka, Larry (Lawrence Richard)
 nickname: **9** Lawnmower

sport: 8 football
position: 8 fullback
team: 13 Miami Dolphins, New York Giants

Cteatus
 origin: **5** Greek
 mentioned in: **5** Iliad
 father: **5** Actor
 mother: **7** Molione

Ctesippus
 father: **8** Hercules
 suitor of: **8** Penelope

Ctesius
 epithet of: **4** Zeus
 means: **9** god of gain

cub 3 boy, pup **4** bear, lion **5** scout, whelp **6** novice **8** re-

porter **9** youngling, youngster **10** apprentice

Cuba *see box*

cubbyhole 4 nook **5** niche **6** cranny **10** pigeonhole **11** compartment

cube of deep-fried pork
 American Spanish: **10** cuchifrito

cubic centimeter
 abbreviation: **4** cu cm

cubic dekameter
 abbreviation: **5** cu dkm

cubic foot
 abbreviation: **4** cu ft

Cuba
 other name: **18** pearl of the Antilles
 capital/largest city: **6** Havana **8** Le Habana
 others: **5** Bauta, Colon, Duabi, Guane, Manes **6** Baines, Bayamo, Gibara, Guines, Mayari **7** Antilla, Baracoa, Fomento, Holguin, Holquin, Jiguani, Niquero, Palmira, Sanhuis **8** Artemisa, Camaguey, Cardenas, Guaimaro, Guayabal, Marianao, Matanzas, Nuevitas, Varadero, Yaguajay **9** Cabaiguan, Camajuani, Cienfuego **10** Cienfuegos, Guanabacoa, Guantanamo, Manzanillo, Santa Clara **11** Campechuela, Pinar del Rio, Puerto Padre **12** Ciego de Avila **13** Sagua de Tanamo **14** Sancti Spiritus, Santiago de Cuba **17** Aguada de Pasajeros, Consolacion del Sur
 measure: **4** vara **5** bocoy, cocoy, tarea **6** cordel, fanega **10** caballeria
 monetary unit: **4** peso **7** centavo **8** cuarenta
 weight: **5** libra **6** tercio
 island: **5** Pines, Pinos **6** Sabana **8** Camaguey, Juventud **9** Canarreos **17** Jardines de la Reina
  cay: **4** Coco **5** Largo **6** Romano **7** Guajaba, Rosareo, Sabinal **8** Cantiles **9** San Felipe **10** Santa Maria
 mountain: **6** Copper **7** Cristal, Maestra, Organos **8** Camaguey, Trinidad **9** Las Villas **11** Pinar del rio **12** Guaniguanico **14** Sancti-Spiritus
 highest point: **8** Turquino
 river: **4** Zaza **5** Cauto **8** San Pedro
 sea: **8** Atlantic **9** Caribbean
 physical feature:
  bay: **4** Nipe, Pigs **6** Jiguey **8** Cochinos **10** Buena Vista, Guantznamo
  cape: **4** Cruz **5** Maisi **8** Lucrecia **10** Corrientes, San Antonio
  channel: **8** Nicholas **9** Old Bahama
  falls: **3** Toa **7** Agabama, Caburni
  gulf: **6** Mexico **7** Cazones **8** Anamaria, Batabano **12** Guancanayabo
  inlet: **4** Broa **10** Corrientes
  peninsula: **6** Zapata
  point: **7** Guarico
  swamp: **6** Zapata
 people: **5** Carib, Negro, Taino, white **6** Arawak **7** Ciboney, mestizo **8** Ciboneye
  conqueror: **9** Velazquez
  explorer: **8** Columbus
  leader: **6** Castro **7** Batista **10** Che Guevara
 language: **7** Spanish
 religion: **13** Roman Catholic
  cult: **6** Chango, Yemaya
 places:
  castle: **5** Morro
  cathedral: **8** Santiago
 feature:
  dance: **5** conga, rumba **6** danzon, rhumba **8** guaracha, pachanga
  harvest: **5** zafra
  peasant: **7** guajiro
  tree: **5** jique, jiqui
  witch doctor: **7** nanigos
 food:
  dish: **6** paella
  drink: **4** pina

cubic inch
abbreviation: **4** cu in

cubicle 3 bay **4** cell, nook
5 booth, niche **6** alcove, recess

cubic meter
abbreviation: **3** cu m

cubic millimeter
abbreviation: **4** cu mm

cubic yard
abbreviation: **4** cu yd

cubit 15 Biblical measure

cuchifrito 19 cube of deep-
fried pork

Cuchulainn
origin: **5** Irish
hero of: **6** Ulster
uncle: **9** Conchobar
guarded house of: **10** Smith
Culan
killed by: **6** Lugaid

cuckoo 3 ani **4** bats, bird, fool,
gaga, nuts **5** balmy, batty,
crazy, daffy, dotty, goofy,
loony, nutty, silly, wacky
6 screwy **7** idiotic **9** screwball
12 crackbrained **13** off one's
rocker **14** off one's trolley

cucumber 14 Cucumis sativus
varieties: **3** bur **4** mock, star,
wild **6** bitter **7** prickly, serpent **9** squirting **13** African
horned

cuddle 3 pet **5** clasp **6** caress,
curl up, fondle, huddle, nestle,
nuzzle **7** cling to, embrace, lie
snug, snuggle

Cuddly Dudley
nickname of: **11** Dudley
Moore

cudgel 4 club **5** baton, staff,
stick **8** bludgeon **9** billy club,
blackjack, truncheon **10** shillelagh **12** quarterstaff

cue 3 key, tip **4** clue, hint,
sign **6** signal **7** inkling **10** intimation, suggestion
11 insinuation

cuff 3 box, hit, rap **4** blow
5 clout, smack, thump,
whack **6** thwack, wallop

cui bono 10 for what use, of
what good **15** for whose
benefit

cuisine 4 fare, food, menu
5 table **6** viands **7** cookery,
cooking, edibles **8** victuals, vittles **11** comestibles

Cukor, George
director of: **7** Camille **8** Adam's Rib, Gaslight, The
Women **10** My Fair Lady
(Oscar) **11** A Double Life, A
Star Is Born, Little Women
13 Born Yesterday, Dinner
at Eight **14** Romeo and Ju-

liet **16** David Copperfield
18 A Bill of Divorcement
20 The Philadelphia Story

cul-de-sac 6 pocket **7** dead-
end, impasse **10** blind alley

cull 4 junk, pick, sift, take
5 dross, glean, scrap, trash,
waste **6** choose, divide, garner,
gather, jetsam, reject, second,
select, winnow **7** castoff, collect, discard, excerpt, extract,
leaving **8** abstract, scouring,
separate **9** segregate

culminate 3 cap, end, top
5 crown, end up **6** climax, finish, result, top off, wind up
8 complete, conclude **9** terminate **10** consummate

culmination 4 acme, apex,
peak **6** apogee, climax, height,
zenith **7** epitome **8** pinnacle
10 conclusion **11** fulfillment,
realization **12** consummation

Culp, Robert
born: **10** Berkeley CA
roles: **4** I Spy **20** Greatest
American Hero

culpability 4 onus **5** blame,
fault, guilt **9** liability **14** accountability, responsibility

culpable 6 guilty, liable **7** at
fault, to blame **8** blamable
10 censurable **11** blameworthy

culprit 5 felon **6** sinner **8** criminal, evildoer, offender **9** miscreant, wrongdoer
10 lawbreaker, malefactor
12 transgressor

cult 4 sect **7** faction, zealots
8 admirers, devotees, devotion **9** disciples, followers
10 admiration

cultivable 6 arable **7** fertile, friable **8** farmable, plowable,
tillable

cultivate 3 dig, hoe, sow
4 farm, grow, plow, seek, till,
weed **5** court, plant, spade
6 enrich, garden **7** acquire, advance, develop, elevate, enhance, improve

cultivated 3 dug **4** fine, grew,
hoed **6** farmed, forked, sought,
spaded, tilled, weeded
7 courted, planted **8** advanced,
cultured, elevated, enhanced,
enriched, finished, improved,
polished **9** developed

cultivation 5 grace **6** polish,
sowing **7** farming, manners,
tilling **8** agronomy, planting
9 elevation, gardening, gentility, good taste, husbandry
10 refinement **11** agriculture

culture 3 art **5** music **7** the
arts **8** learning **9** erudition,
knowledge **10** enrichment, lit-

erature, refinement **12** civilization **13** enlightenment
15 accomplishments

Culture and Anarchy
author: **13** Matthew Arnold

cultured 7 elegant, erudite,
genteel, learned, refined
8 polished, well-bred, well-
read **11** enlightened **12** accomplished, well-educated
13 sophisticated

culvert 5 ditch, drain, sewer
6 trench **7** channel, conduit,
fox-hole

Cumaean sibyl
prophetess of: **5** Cumae
guided: **6** Aeneas

cumbersome 5 bulky, hefty
6 clumsy **7** awkward **8** cumbrous, ungainly, unwieldy
9 ponderous **12** unmanageable

cum grano salis 15 not too
seriously **16** with a grain of
salt

cumin
botanical name: **14** Cuminum
cyminum
other name: **6** comino, jir-
aka, kummel
origin: **5** Egypt
family: **7** parsley
symbol of: **5** greed
guards against straying:
7 pigeons **8** chickens,
husbands
use: **4** fish, meat, rice, soup,
stew **5** bread, curry
6 cheese **7** pickles, sausage
8 potatoes **11** chili powder

cum laude 10 with praise

**cummings, e e (Edward
Estlin)**
author of: **12** in just spring
15 The Enormous Room
17 Tulips and Chimneys
18 Chansons Innocentes

Cummings, Robert
real name: **29** Clarence Robert Orville Cummings
born: **8** Joplin MO
roles: **8** King's Row **14** Dial
M for Murder **18** The Bob
Cummings Show

cumulate 5 amass **6** gather,
heap up, pile up
10 accumulate

cumulative 7 amassed, piled
up **8** additive, heaped up
9 aggregate **10** collective
12 accumulative, conglomerate

Cunegonde
character in: **7** Candide
author: **8** Voltaire

Cunina
origin: **5** Roman
goddess of: **15** sleeping
infants

cunning 3 art, sly 4 foxy, wily 5 canny, craft, guile, knack, skill 6 artful, crafty, deceit, genius, shifty, shrewd, talent, tricky 7 ability, devious, finesse, slyness 8 aptitude, artifice, deftness, foxiness, guileful, subtlety, trickery, wiliness 9 chicanery, deceitful, deception, deceptive, dexterity, duplicity, ingenious, underhand 10 adroitness, artfulness, cleverness, craftiness, expertness, shrewdness 11 deviousness 13 Machiavellian
  god of: 6 Hermes

Cunning Little Vixen, The
  opera by: 7 Janacek

cup 3 cup 5 glass, grail, stein 6 beaker, goblet, vessel 7 chalice, tankard 8 schooner
  abbreviation: 1 c

Cup
  constellation of: 6 Crater

Cupava
  companion of: 6 Aeneas

cupbearer of gods
  8 Ganymede

cupboard 6 buffet, bureau, closet 7 armoire, cabinet 9 sideboard, storeroom 10 chiffonier 11 china closet 12 clothespress

Cupid
  also: 4 Amor
  origin: 5 Roman
  god of: 4 love
  mother: 5 Venus
  corresponds to: 4 Eros

cupidity 5 greed 7 avarice, avidity 8 rapacity 10 greediness 11 selfishness 12 covetousness, graspingness 13 concupiscence, insatiability, rapaciousness 14 avariciousness 15 acquisitiveness

cupola 4 dome, roof 5 tower, vault 6 belfry, turret 7 ceiling

cur 3 cad 4 mutt 5 rogue 6 rascal, varlet, wretch 7 mongrel, varmint, villain 9 scoundrel 10 blackguard

curacao
  type: 7 liqueur
  origin: 19 Netherlands
    Antilles
  flavor: 6 orange
  with gin: 8 Blue Moon, Napoleon 9 Blue Devil 14 Flying Dutchman
  with rum: 6 Mai-Tai 8 Blue Lady 12 Blue Hawaiian
  with vodka: 8 Aqueduct

curate 5 vicar 6 cleric, deacon, parson, pastor, priest, rector 8 minister, preacher 9 churchman, clergyman 12 ecclesiastic

curative 4 balm 7 healing 11 restorative

curator 5 doyen 6 keeper 8 director, overseer 9 caretaker, custodian

curb 3 rim 4 edge, rein 5 brink, check, ledge, limit 6 border, bridle, halter, retard, slow up 7 control, harness, inhibit, repress, slacken 8 hold back, moderate, restrain, restrict, slow down, suppress 9 curbstone, hindrance, restraint 10 decelerate, limitation 11 restriction, retardation

curdle 3 rot 4 clot, curd, sour, turn 5 decay, go bad, go off, spoil 7 clabber, congeal, ferment, putrefy, thicken 8 putresce, solidify 9 coagulate 11 deteriorate

cure 3 dry 4 heal, salt 5 smoke 6 remedy 8 antidote, make well, preserve 10 corrective

cure-all 4 balm 6 elixir, remedy 7 panacea 10 catholicon

cured 5 dried 6 healed, mended, smoked 8 made well, remedied 9 preserved, recovered

Curetes
  form: 8 demigods
  attendants of: 4 Zeus

Curiatii *see* 7 Horatii

Curie, Marie Sklodowska and Pierre
  field: 7 physics 9 chemistry
  discovered: 6 radium 8 polonium 13 radioactivity
  awarded: 10 Nobel Prize

curio 7 bibelot, trinket 9 bric-a-brac, objet d'art

curiosity 5 freak, sight 6 marvel, oddity, prying, rarity, wonder 7 novelty 8 interest, nosiness 10 phenomenon, rare object 11 questioning 15 inquisitiveness

curious 3 odd 4 nosy, rare 5 funny, novel, queer, weird 6 prying, quaint, unique 7 bizarre, strange, unusual 8 peculiar, singular, snooping, uncommon 9 inquiring, searching 11 inquisitive, questioning

Curitis
  epithet of: 4 Juno
  means: 10 of the spear

curl 4 coil, lock, wave, wind 5 crimp, frizz, swirl, twirl, twist 6 spiral 7 frizzle, ringlet, scallop 8 curlicue 9 corkscrew

curled 3 set 5 kinky, waved, wound 6 coiled, frizzy spiral

7 crimped, frizzed, twisted 8 crinkled, scrolled 9 curlicued

curlicue 4 coil 5 twist 6 spiral 8 flourish

curly 4 wavy 5 kinky 6 frizzy 7 rippled 8 crinkled 9 ringleted

curmudgeon 4 crab 5 crank, grump 6 grouch 8 grumbler, sourball

currant 5 Ribes
  varieties: 3 red 5 black, fetid, skunk, squaw, stink 6 alpine, cherry, common, garden, Indian, Sierra 7 Buffalo 8 Missouri, mountain, swamp red 9 chaparral, wild black 11 northern red 12 bristly black 13 American black, European black, northern black, white-flowered 15 California black

currency 4 cash, coin 5 bills, money, vogue 7 coinage 9 bank notes 10 acceptance, popularity, prevalence 12 predominance, universality

current 3 now 4 flow, flux, mood, tide 5 draft, drift, trend 6 modern, spirit, stream, with-it 7 feeling, in style, in vogue, popular, present 8 existing, tendency, up-to-date 9 prevalent, zeitgeist 10 atmosphere, present-day, prevailing 11 inclination 12 contemporary, undercurrent

current of air 4 wind 5 draft 6 breeze, zephyr

curricle 3 gig 4 cart, trap 6 chaise 8 carriage

curry powder
  origin: 5 India
  ingredient: 5 cumin 6 cloves 8 capsicum, turmeric 9 coriander, fenugreek, red pepper 13 cayenne pepper
  use: 5 kebab, kebob, kofta, malai 6 kormas 7 curries, pea soup 8 meat loaf, vindaloo, zucchini 11 potato salad

curse 3 vex 4 bane, cuss, damn, oath 5 blast, cross, swear, trial 6 burden, ordeal, plague, whammy 7 afflict, condemn, evil eye, scourge, swear at, torment, trouble 8 anathema, denounce, execrate, swearing, vexation 9 annoyance, blasphemy, damnation, evil spell, expletive, obscenity, profanity 10 affliction, execration, misfortune 11 imprecation, malediction, tribulation 12 anathematize, denunciation

cursory 5 brief, hasty, quick, swift 6 casual, random 7 hurried, offhand, passing 8 careless 9 desultory, haphazard

11 inattentive, perfunctory, superficial

curt 4 rude **5** bluff, blunt, gruff, short, terse **6** abrupt, crusty, snappy **7** brusque, summary **8** petulant **10** peremptory

curtail 3 cut **4** clip, trim **6** reduce **7** abridge, shorten **8** condense, contract, cut short, decrease, diminish, pare down **10** abbreviate

curtailed 3 cut **7** checked, concise, cut back, reduced, slashed **8** abridged, cut short **9** shortened **10** retrenched

curtailment 7 cutback, cutting, halting, pruning **8** clipping, decrease, trimming **9** lessening, reduction, restraint **10** limitation, shortening **11** abridgement, contraction **12** abbreviation, condensation

curtain 3 end **4** mask, veil **5** blind, cover, drape, shade, sheet **6** screen, shroud **7** conceal, drapery, hanging **8** portiere

Curtis, Tony
real name: **15** Bernard Schwartz
wife: **10** Janet Leigh
daughter: **8** Jamie Lee
born: **9** New York NY
roles: **7** Houdini, Trapeze **12** The Great Race **13** Some Like It Hot **14** The Defiant Ones **16** The Great Imposter **18** The Boston Strangler **22** The Sweet Smell of Success

Curtius
also: **6** Marcus
volunteered as: **17** sacrificial victim

Curtiz, Michael
director of: **10** Casablanca (Oscar), The Sea Hawk **12** Captain Blood **13** Mildred Pierce **14** Life with Father **17** Yankee Doodle Dandy **24** The Adventures of Robin Hood (with William Keighley) **26** The Charge of the Light Brigade **34** The Private Lives of Elizabeth and Essex

curtsy, curtsey 3 bob, bow, dip **5** honor **6** homage **9** obeisance, reverence **11** bend the knee

curvature 3 arc **4** arch, bend **5** crook **6** bowing

curve 3 arc, bow **4** arch, bend, coil, hook, loop, turn, wind **5** crook, twist **6** spiral, swerve

curved 4 bent **5** bowed **6** arched, looped, turned

curved span 3 bow **4** arch, dome **5** vault **6** bridge

Curve of Binding Energy, The
author: **10** John McPhee

curving 4 bent **5** bowed **6** arched **7** bending, looping, turning, winding **8** twisting

curving inward 6 hollow, sunken **7** concave **8** hollowed **9** depressed

curving outward 5 bowed **6** convex **7** bulging, rounded **8** bellying **11** protuberant

Cuscatlan see **10** El Salvador

Cush
father: **3** Ham
grandfather: **4** Noah
brother: **6** Canaan
son: **6** Nimrod
Hebrew for: **8** Ethiopia

cushion 3 mat, pad **4** damp **5** quiet **6** dampen, deaden, muffle, pillow, soften, stifle **7** bolster **8** suppress

Cushitic
language family: **11** AfroAsiatic **13** Hamito-Semitic
branch: **6** Somali **8** Gallinya
spoken in: **7** Somalia **8** Ethiopia, Tanzania

cusp 4 apex, barb, horn, peak **5** angle, point, tooth **6** corner

custard 4 flan, fool **5** creme **6** junket **7** dessert, pudding **8** flummery **10** blanc-mange, zabaglione

Custer, George A
served in: **8** Civil War **10** Indian Wars
side: **5** Union
battle: **13** Little Big Horn
defeated: **11** Black Kettle
defeated by: **10** Crazy Horse

custodian 6 duenna, keeper, warden **7** janitor **8** chaperon, guardian, watchman **9** attendant, caretaker, chaperone, concierge **14** superintendent

custody 4 care **5** watch **6** charge **9** detention **10** possession, protection **11** confinement, safekeeping, trusteeship **12** conservation, guardianship, preservation

custom 4 form, mode **5** habit, usage **7** fashion **10** convention

customarily 7 as a rule, usually **8** commonly, normally **9** generally, regularly **10** frequently, habitually, ordinarily **13** traditionally

customary 5 usual **6** common, normal, wonted **7** general, regular, routine, typical **8** everyday, habitual, ordinary

10 accustomed **11** traditional **12** conventional

customer 5 buyer **6** client, patron **7** habitue, shopper **9** purchaser

customs 4 duty, levy, toll **6** excise, tariff **9** import tax **10** assessment

cut 3 mow, saw **4** chop, clip, crop, cube, dice, fall, gash, hack, move, nick, pare, part, rent, rive, slit, snip, snub, trim **5** carve, cross, lance, mince, piece, prune, sever, share, shave, shear, slash, slice, split, wound **6** bisect, course, delete, divide, furrow, hollow, ignore, incise, pierce, reduce, sunder, trench **7** abridge, channel, curtail, decline, dissect, opening, passage, portion, section, segment **8** condense, contract, decrease, diminish, incision, lacerate **9** abatement, intersect, lessening, reduction, shrinkage **10** abbreviate, diminution, excavation, shortening **11** contraction, curtailment, indentation

cut and run 4 bolt, flee, skip **6** escape **7** abscond, get away, make off, run away **8** slip away **9** break free **10** break loose, fly the coop **12** make a getaway

cut apart 7 dissect **9** anatomize

cutback 8 decrease, trimming **9** reduction **11** abridgement, curtailment

cut back 4 trim **5** prune **6** reduce **7** abridge, curtail **8** decrease

cut costs 4 save **5** skimp, stint **6** scrimp **7** husband **8** conserve **9** economize **15** tighten one's belt

cut down 4 kill, trim **5** limit **6** lessen, reduce **7** abridge, curtail, destroy, disable, remodel, shorten **8** condense, decrease, diminish, restrict **10** abbreviate

cut-down form 6 digest, precis **7** summary **8** synopsis, trimming **10** shortening **11** abridgement, contraction, curtailment **12** abbreviation, condensation

cut down to size 5 abase
6 humble 7 mortify 8 belittle,
bring low, disgrace 9 humiliate 13 bring down a peg

cute 5 sweet 6 dainty, pretty
7 darling, lovable 8 adorable,
handsome, precious 9 beautiful 10 attractive

cut expenses 4 save 5 skimp,
stint 6 scrimp 8 conserve
9 economize 12 pinch pen-
nies 15 tighten one's belt

cut in half 5 halve 6 bisect

cut in two 5 halve, sever
6 bisect

cutlet 3 cut 4 chop 5 slice
9 cotelette, croquette

cut off 4 dock, trim 5 apart,
sever 6 detach, remove 7 chop
off, divorce, isolate 8 amputate, divorced, isolated, separate 10 disconnect

cut out 2 go 4 blow, exit 5 be
off, erase, leave, scram, split
6 beat it, delete, depart, escape, excise, go away, remove,
set out 7 abolish 8 designed,
get rid of, set forth 9 eliminate 10 do away with, hit the
road, make tracks 11 exterminate, take a powder

cut short 4 clip, crop, dock,
trim 7 abridge, shorten
8 truncate 10 abbreviate

cutter 4 boat 5 blade, hewer,
knife 6 sledge, sleigh, tailor
11 cutting edge

cutthroat 5 cruel 6 outlaw
7 brigand, hoodlum, ruffian
8 ruthless 9 merciless

cutting 3 raw 4 acid, cold
5 harsh, nasty, sharp 6 biting,
bitter 7 acerbic, caustic, nipping, pruning, searing 8 clipping, derisive, piercing,
scathing, smarting, snubbing,
stinging, trimming 9 reduction,
sarcastic, stringent 11 abridgement, acrimonious, compression, contraction, curtailment,
disparaging, penetrating
12 abbreviation, condensation

cutting edge 5 blade 8 vanguard 9 forefront

cutting off 8 severing 9 severance 10 detachment, separation 13 disconnection,
disengagement

cutting remark 3 dig 4 gibe,
jeer 5 taunt

Cuttle
character in: 12 Dombey and
Son
author: 7 Dickens

cut up 4 chop, hack, maim,
rend 5 caper, carve, halve,
mince, slash, slice, split
6 cleave, deface, deform, divide 7 portion, quarter 8 dissever, mutilate 9 apportion,
kid around 10 fool around
11 clown around, play the
fool

Cuvier, Georges
field: 7 geology, zoology
nationality: 6 French
founded: 12 paleontology
18 comparative anatomy

Cyane
form: 5 nymph 8 princess
violated by: 6 father
unsuccessful rescuer of:
10 Persephone

Cyaxares see 9 Ahasuerus

Cybele
also: 9 Dindymene 10 Berecyntia, Magna Mater
11 Great Mother 12 Mater
Turrita 17 Great Idaean
Mother
origin: 8 Phrygian 9 Asia
Minor
goddess of: 6 nature
priest: 5 Galli 10 Corybantes
corresponds to: 3 Ops
4 Rhea
epithet: 6 Antaea

Cychreus
king of: 7 Salamis
father: 8 Poseidon
mother: 7 Salamis
daughter: 6 Glauce

Cyclades 3 Dos, Zea 4 Keos,
Nios, Sira, Syra 5 Delos, Melos, Naxos, Paros, Siros, Syros,
Tenos, Tinos 6 Andros
7 Amorgos, islands, Kythnos
13 Aegean islands

cycle 3 run 6 series 8 sequence 10 succession 11 progression 14 connected group

cyclone 4 gale, gust, wind
5 storm 7 tornado, twister, typhoon 9 whirlwind, windstorm
Australian: 10 willy-nilly

Cyclone (Cy)
nickname of: 15 Denton True
Young

Cyclops, Cyclopes
form: 5 giant
number of eyes: 3 one
father: 6 Uranus
mother: 2 Ge
blinded by: 8 Odysseus

Cycnus
father: 4 Ares
killed in: 4 duel
killed by: 8 Hercules
changed into: 4 swan

Cydippe
priestess of: 4 Hera
location: 5 Argos
father: 7 Ochimus
son: 5 Biton 7 Cleobis

cylinder 3 can, tin 4 drum,
pipe, roll, tube 5 spool 6 barrel, column, pillar, piston,
platen, roller 13 piston
chamber

cylindrical 5 round 6 tarete
7 tubular 8 columnar

Cyllene
form: 5 nymph
nursed: 6 Hermes

Cyllenian
pertains to: 6 Hermes
12 Mount Cellene

Cymbeline
author: 18 William
Shakespeare
character: 6 Cloten, Imogen
7 Iachimo, Pisanio 9 Bellarius 17 Leonatus Posthumus

Cymodoce
mentioned in: 6 Aeneid
form: 4 ship
fleet of: 6 Aeneas
changed by: 6 Cybele
changed into: 8 sea nymph

Cymru see 5 Wales

cynic 7 scoffer, skeptic 9 pessimist 10 misogynist 11 faultfinder, misanthrope

cynical 8 derisive, sardonic,
scoffing, scornful, sneering
9 misogynic, sarcastic, skeptical 12 misanthropic

Cynortes
father: 7 Amyclas
mother: 7 Diomede

Cynosura
nurse of: 4 Zeus

Cynthia see 7 Artemis

Cynurus
father: 7 Perseus

Cyparissia
epithet of: 6 Athena
means: 14 cypress goddess

Cyparissus
killed: 4 stag
changed into: 11 cypress tree

cypress 8 Taxodium
9 Cupressus
varieties: 3 toy 4 bald, berg,
pond 5 false, Gowen, Mo-
doc, Piute 6 Bhutan, Hinoki,
Lawson, MacNab, Nootka,
Sawara, summer, Tecate
7 African, Arizona, Italian,
Mexican, Sargent 8 Cuya-
maca, golf-ball, Monterey,
mourning, Siskiyou, standing 9 Guadalupe, Mendo-
cino, Montezuma, red
summer, Santa Cruz 10 Portuguese, tennis-ball
12 Chinese swamp
18 rough-barked Arizona
19 smooth-barked Arizona

Cyprian see 9 Aphrodite

Cyprus
biblical name: 6 Kittim
capital/largest city:
    7 Nicosia
city: 6 Paphos **7** Kyrenia,
    Larnaca **8** Limassol
    9 Famagusta
monetary unit: 4 para
    5 pound
mountain: 7 Kyrenia,
    Troodos
highest point: 7 Olympus
river: 6 Pedias
sea: 13 Mediterranean
physical feature:
    bay: **8** Episkopi
    cape: **4** Gata **5** Greco
        7 Andreas, Arnauti
        9 Kormakiti
    peninsula: **6** Karpas
    plain: **8** Mesaoria
        9 Messaoria
people: 5 Greek, Turks
    9 Cypriotes
    ruler: **5** Turks **6** Greeks,
        Romans **7** British
        9 Egyptians, Lusignans,
        Venetians **10** Byzan-
        tines **11** Phoenicians
language: 5 Greek
    7 Turkish
religion: 5 Islam **6** Muslim
    13 Greek Orthodoxy
    16 Eastern Orthodoxy

Cypselus
king of: 7 Arcadia
father: 7 Aepytus
daughter: 6 Merope
son-in-law: 11 Cresphontes
grandson: 7 Aepytus

Cyrano de Bergerac
director: 13 Michael Gordon
author: 13 Edmond Rostand
cast: 10 Jose Ferrer (Cyrano),
    Mala Powers **13** William
    Powers
character: 6 Roxane **22** Chris-
    tian de Neuvillette
setting: 5 Paris
Oscar for: 9 best actor (Ferrer)

**Cyrano de Bergerac,
Savinien**
author of: 25 Voyages to the
    Moon and the Sun
play based on his life by:
    13 Edmond Rostand

Cyrene
father: 7 Hypseus
mother: 6 Creusa
lover: 6 Apollo
son: 5 Idmon **9** Aristaeus

Cytherea *see* **9** Aphrodite

Cytissorus
father: 7 Phrixus
mother: 9 Chalciope
brother: 5 Argus, Melas
    8 Phrontis

cytology
    study of: 5 cells

czar, tsar 4 king **5** ruler **6** cae-
    sar, despot, tyrant **7** emperor,
    monarch **8** dictator, overlord
    9 potentate, sovereign

czarina 7 empress

czaristic 10 autocratic **11** all-
    powerful, dictatorial,
    monarchical

Czechoslovakia *see box*

Czechoslovakia/Czech Republic see Slovakia
capital/largest city: 5 Praha **6** Prague
others: 2 As **4** Asch, Brno, Cheb, Most **5** Brunn, Nitra,
    Opava, Plzen, Tabor, **6** Aussig, Bilina, Kladno, Kosice, Pil-
    sen, Presov, Sadowa, Trnava, Vsetin **7** Budweis, Jihlava,
    Liberec, Olomouc, Ostrava, Teplitz **8** Carlsbad, Jachymov,
    Karlsbad **9** Pressburg **10** Austerlitz, Bratislava, Koniggratz
    11 Reichenberg
university: 7 Charles
division: 7 Bohemia, Moravia, Silesia **8** Ruthenia, Slovakia
measure: 3 Lan **4** Mira **5** Korec, Liket, Stopa **6** Merice,
    Strych
monetary unit: 5 crown, ducat **6** heller, Koruna
mountain: 3 Erz, Ore **5** Giant, Tatra **6** Sumava **7** Sudeten,
    Sudetes **8** Krkonose **10** Carpathian
highest point: 7 Gerlach **11** Gerlachovka
river: 2 Uh, **3** Mze, Vag, Vah **4** Dyje, Eger, Elbe, Gran,
    Hron, Ipel, Iser, Labe, Nisa, Oder, Odra, Ohre, Olse,
    Waag **5** Becva, Dunaj, March, Nitra, Slana, Tisza **6** Dan-
    ube, Moldau, Morava, Ondava, Sazava, Torysa, Vltava
    7 Laborec, Luznice **8** Berounka
physical feature:
    plateau: **8** Bohemian **11** Sudetenland
people: 4 Slav **5** Czech **6** Slovak **8** Bohemian, Moravian
    author: **5** Capek, Hasek, Havel **7** Kundera, Seifert
    composer: **6** Dvorak **7** Janacek, Martinu, Smetana
    director: **11** Milos Forman
    philosopher/reformer: **8** Comenius, John Huss
language: 5 Czech **6** German, Magyar, Slovak **7** Russian
    9 Hungarian
religion: 6 Uniate **8** Lutheran **9** Orthodoxy **13** Roman
    Catholic
place:
    castle: **8** Hradcany
    cathedral: **7** St Vitus **10** St Nicholas
    resort/spa: **8** Carlsbad, Piestany **9** Marienbad **10** Luha-
        covice **11** Karlovy Vary **14** Marianske Lazne
    square: **9** Wenceslas
feature:
    dance: **5** polka **6** redowa, talian **7** furiant
    gymnastics festival: **11** spartakiada
    song: **7** Ma Vlast
food:
    beer: **6** pilsen
    sausage: **5** parky **6** vursty

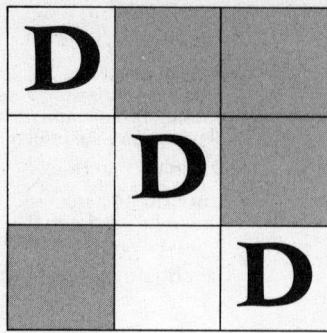

dab 3 bit, pat, tap **6** stroke
7 smidgen, soupcon

dabble 5 slosh **6** fiddle, putter,
splash **7** spatter, toy with
8 sprinkle

dabbler 7 amateur, trifler
10 dilettante **12** experimenter
15 nonprofessional

da capo
music: **22** repeat from the
beginning
abbreviation: **2** D C

Dacca
capital of: **10** Bangladesh

d'accord 2 OK **6** agreed
7 granted

Dactyls
also: **7** Daktyls
dwellers of: **8** Mount Ida

dad 2 da, pa **3** pop **4** papa,
pops, sire **5** daddy, pappy, pater **6** father, parent **11** the old
man

Daedala
festival in: **7** Boeotia

Daedalion
father: **9** Eosphorus
mother: **10** Phosphorus
daughter: **6** Chione
leaped off: **9** Parnassus
changed into: **4** hawk

Daedalus
occupation: **9** architect
father: **6** Metion
son: **5** Iapyx **6** Icarus
nephew: **5** Talos **6** Perdix
killed: **5** Talos
built: **9** labyrinth
for: **5** Minos
made: **5** wings

daffodil 9 Narcissus **24** Narcissus pseudonarcissus
varieties: **3** sea **6** winter
8 Peruvian **9** petticoat
13 hoop-petticoat

daft 3 mad **4** loco **5** balmy,
batty, crazy, daffy, dizzy,
goofy, loony, nutty, silly,
wacky **6** cuckoo, insane,
screwy **7** foolish, lunatic,
witless

Dagan
origin: **12** Mesopotamian
god of: **5** earth **11** agriculture
corresponds to: **5** Dagon

dagger 4 dirk, snee **5** blade,
knife **6** weapon **7** poniard
8 stiletto

Dagon
origin: **10** Philistine,
Phoenician
god of: **5** earth **11** agriculture
corresponds to: **5** Dagan

Daguerre, Louis J M
nationality: **6** French
inventor of: **11** photography
13 daguerreotype

dahlia
varieties: **3** sea **4** tree **6** common, garden **7** bedding
8 bell tree **10** candelabra

Dahomey, Republic of *see*
5 Benin

daily 7 diurnal, per diem **9** cir-
cadian, quotidian

Daimler, Gottlieb
nationality: **6** German
inventor of: **10** carburetor,
motorcycle **14** gasoline engine **18** gasoline automobile **25** compression ignition
engine

daimyo 4 lord **10** feudal lord

dainty 4 fine **5** fussy, tasty
6 choice, choosy, lovely,
pretty, savory **7** choosey, elegant, refined **8** delicate, pleasing **9** beautiful, delicious,
exquisite **10** attractive, fastidious, particular

Daira
father: **7** Oceanus

dais 5 stage **6** podium **7** rostrum **8** platform

daisy 6 Bellis **23** Chrysanthemum frutescens **25** Chrysanthemum leucanthemum
varieties: **4** blue, cape, high,
lazy **5** crown, giant, globe,
oxeye, Paris, veldt, white
6 butter, Easter, Nippon,
shasta, sleepy, Tahoka **7** African, English, painted, seaside, turfing **8** Dahlberg,
mountain, panamint **9** Bar-
berton, Englemann, Swan
River, Transvaal **10** Kingfisher, Michaelmas, Portuguese **11** Clanwilliam,
Livingstone, Namaqualand
12 Boston yellow, double
orange **15** blue-eyed African

Daisy Miller
author: **10** Henry James
character: **10** Giovanelli
12 Winterbourne

Dakar
capital of: **7** Senegal

Dakota (Sioux)
language family: **6** Siouan
tribe: **5** Teton **6** Lakota, Na-
kota, Santee **7** Yankton
8 Sisseton, Wahpeton, Wici-
yela **9** Wahpekute, Yankto-
nai **11** Mdewakanton
location: **7** Montana **9** Minnesota **11** North Dakota,
South Dakota
leader: **4** Gall **10** Crazy
Horse **11** Sitting Bull **13** Ja-
shunca-Uiteo
noted for: **15** military
prowess
deity: **10** Wakan Tanka

Daktyls *see* **7** Dactyls

dale 4 dell, dene, glen, vale
6 dingle, hollow, valley

D'Alembert
author of: **12** Encyclopedia

Dali, Salvador
born: **5** Spain **7** Figuras
artwork: **10** Last Supper
17 Atomic Leda and Swan
19 Persistence of Memory
22 Accommodations of De-

sire **24** Christ of St John of
the Cross

Dalibor
opera by: **7** Smetana
character: **6** Milada

Dallas
airport: **23** Dallas-Fort
Worth Regional
basketball team:
4 Mavs **9** Mavericks
football team:
7 Cowboys
landmark: **15** Turtle
Creek Park **16** Museum
of Fine Arts **19** Dallas
Theater Center
25 Margo Jones Memo-
rial Theater
river: **7** Trinity
stadium: **10** Cotton Bowl
university: **3** SMU
13 Bishop College
17 Southern Methodist

Dallas
character: **7** JR Ewing **9** Jack
Ewing, Jenna Wade, Jock
Ewing, Miss Ellie, Ray
Krebbs **10** Bobby Ewing
11 Christopher, Cliff Barnes,
Mandy Winger, Mark Grai-
son **12** Digger Barnes
13 Clayton Farlow, John
Ross Ewing, Sue Ellen Ew-
ing **16** Donna Culver Krebs
17 Pamela Barnes Ewing
22 Eleanor Southworth
Ewing
cast: **8** John Beck **9** Dack
Rambo, Linda Gray
10 Howard Keel **11** Larry
Hagman, Steve Kanaly, Su-
san Howard **12** Ken Ker-
cheval, Patrick Duffy
16 Barbara Bel Geddes, Priscilla Presley **17** Victoria
Principal
ranch: **9** Southfork
business: **3** oil **8** Ewing Oil

dalliance 6 affair, toying **7** romance **8** fiddling, trifling
10 flirtation, lovemaking

dally 3 toy **4** play **5** flirt **6** dawdle, loiter, trifle

Dalmatia *see* **10** Yugoslavia

Dalton, John
field: **7** physics **9** chemistry
nationality: **7** British
formulated: **12** atomic theory
first: **18** atomic weights table
described: **14** color blindness

dam 3 bar, cow **4** clog, mare,
plug, stop, wall **5** bitch, block,
check **6** bridle, hinder, hold

in, impede, plug up, stanch,
stop up **7** barrier, block up,
confine, congest, inhibit, repress, stopper, stuff up
8 blockade, hold back, obstruct, restrain **9** barricade,
hindrance **11** obstruction

damage, damages 3 mar
4 cost, harm, hurt, loss **6** impair, injure, injury, ravage
10 impairment, reparation, settlement **11** destruction
12 compensation, despoliation

damaging 7 harmful, hurtful,
ruinous **9** injurious **11** destructive, detrimental

Damascus
ancient kingdom:
8 Aramaean
Arabic: **7** Dimashq
capital of: **5** Syria
monastery: **22** Suleiman
the Magnificent
mosque: **5** Great
7 Umayyad
mount: **6** Qasyun
museum: **8** National
9 Qasr al-Azm
river: **4** Awaj **6** Barada
rulers: **5** Arabs, Timur
6 Romans **7** Mongols,
Saladin **8** Assyrian
9 Caliphate, Seleucids
12 Ottoman Turks
15 Byzantine Empire
17 Alexander the Great
tomb: **7** Saladin

Damastes *see* **10** Procrustes

Dame Pliant
character in: **12** The
Alchemist
author: **6** Jonson

Damia
spirit of: **9** fertility

damn 4 doom **5** blast **6** rail at
7 censure, condemn **8** denounce **9** criticize, disparage

damned 4 lost **6** cursed,
darned, doomed, fallen **7** doggone, dratted, godless **8** accursed, doggoned
9 condemned, execrated, reprobate **12** unregenerate

Damocles
offended: **9** Dionysius
seated under: **14** suspended
sword

Damon
friend: **7** Pythias

damp 3 wet **4** curb, dank,
dash, dewy, dull, mist
5 check, foggy, humid, misty,

moist, muggy, rainy, soggy,
spoil **6** clammy, deaden, hamper, hinder, reduce, soaked,
sodden **7** depress, drizzly, inhibit, sopping, wettish **8** dankness, diminish, dripping,
humidity, moisture, restrain
9 mugginess, restraint
10 clamminess, discourage
14 discouragement

dampen 3 wet **7** moisten, wet
down

dampen one's spirits
5 daunt, unman **6** deject **7** depress **10** discourage,
dishearten

damper 4 curb **8** obstacle
9 hindrance, restraint **10** constraint, impediment, wet blanket **14** discouragement

damsel 4 girl, lass **6** maiden
9 young lady

damselfly
varieties: **8** forktail **10** civil-
bluet **11** black-winged,
broad-winged **12** narrow-
winged, spread-winged, violet dancer

dam up 4 clog, plug **5** block,
choke **6** plug up, stop up
7 congest **8** obstruct

Damysus
member of: **8** Gigantes

Dan
means: **5** judge
father: **5** Jacob
mother: **6** Bilhah
brother: **3** Gad **4** Levi
5 Asher, Judah **6** Joseph,
Reuben, Simeon **7** Zebulun
8 Benjamin, Issachar,
Naphtali
sister: **5** Dinah
descendant of: **6** Danite

Dana *see* **4** Danu

Dana, Richard Henry
author of: **21** Two Years Before the Mast

Danae
form: **6** maiden
father: **8** Acrisius
mother: **8** Eurydice
imprisoned by: **8** Acrisius
lover: **4** Zeus
son: **7** Perseus

Danai
members of: **6** Greeks
7 Argives

Danaides
daughters of: **6** Danaus
number of daughters: **5** fifty

Dan August
character: **9** (Sgt) Joe Rivera
14 (Sgt) Charles Wilentz
16 (Chief) George
Untermeyer
cast: **9** Ned Romero **10** Nor-

man Fell **12** Burt Reynolds
15 Richard Anderson

Danaus
ruler of: **5** Argos
father: **5** Belus
twin brother: **8** Aegyptus
daughters called: **8** Danaides
number of daughters: **5** fifty

dance *see* box

dance of death
French: **12** danse macabre

Dandelion Wine
author: **11** Ray Bradbury

dander 5 anger, Irish **6** temper

Dandie Dinmont terrier
24 soft-coated wheaten terrier,
Staffordshire bull terrier, West
Highland white terrier

dandy 3 fop **4** beau, dude,
fine **5** beaut, great, super,
swell **6** beauty, superb **7** coxcomb, peacock **8** terrific **9** excellent **12** clotheshorse

danger 4 risk **5** peril **6** hazard,
menace, threat **8** jeopardy
12 endangerment

dangerous 5 hairy, risky
6 chancy, unsafe **8** menacing,
perilous **9** hazardous **10** pre-

carious **11** threatening,
treacherous

danger signal 5 alarm, alert
7 red flag, warning

dangle 3 sag **4** drag, hang,
sway **5** droop, swing, trail
6 depend **7** draggle, hang out,
suspend **8** hang down, hang
over **9** oscillate

Daniel
Babylonian name:
12 Belteshazzar
companion: **7** Meshach
8 Abednego, Shadrach

Daniel Boone
character: **5** Mingo **6** Yadkin
11 Cincinnatus, Israel
Boone, Jemima Boone
12 Rebecca Boone
cast: **6** Ed Ames **10** Fess Parker **11** Albert Salmi, Dal
McKennon, Darby Hinton
13 Patricia Blair **18** Veronica
Cartwright

Danielovitch, Issur
real name of: **11** Kirk
Douglas

dank 3 wet **4** cold, damp **5** humid, moist, muggy, soggy
6 chilly, clammy, sodden,
sticky

danke 8 thank you

danke schon 16 thank you
very much

dankness 4 damp **7** wetness
8 dampness, humidity **9** humidness, moistness, mugginess **10** clamminess

Danner, Blythe
born: **14** Philadelphia PA
roles: **8** Betrayal **15** The
Great Santini **16** Man
Woman and Child

Danny Deever
story in: **18** Barrack-Room
Ballads
author: **14** Rudyard Kipling

Danny Thomas Show, The
character: **6** Clancy **12** Uncle
Tonoose **13** Danny Williams,
Linda Williams, Rusty Williams, Terry Williams
16 Mrs Kathy Williams
18 Uncle Charley Halper
cast: **9** Sid Melton **10** Rusty
Hamer **11** Hans Conried
12 Marjorie Lord, Penney
Parker **13** Sherry Jackson
16 Angela Cartwright

danse macabre 12 dance of
death

Dante (Alighieri)
author of: **9** Vita Nuova
15 The Divine Comedy
Divine Comedy Part I:
10 The Inferno

---

dance 3 hop **4** ball, jump, leap, prom, reel, skip **5** lindy,
party, polka, twist **6** bounce, cavort, frolic, gambol, prance,
square **7** fox-trot, perform **8** cakewalk **9** jitterbug **10** Charleston **11** Boston waltz **12** choreography, Virginia reel **15** hesitation waltz
Renaissance/17th century: 3 jig **5** galop, gigue **6** branle,
pavane, redowa **7** bourree, gavotte, lancers, lavolta, mazurka **8** canaries, chaconne, courante, galliard, rigadoon,
rigaudon, tourdion **9** allemande, passepied, polonaise, sar-
abande **10** danse basse, danse haute
18th century: 6 minuet **9** cotillion **11** contre danse
12 country dance
19th century: 5 waltz **9** quadrille
early 1900's: 7 foxtrot, one-step, two-step **8** bunny hug
10 turkey trot **11** grizzly bear
1920's: 5 tango **6** shimmy, toddle **10** Charleston **11** black
bottom
1930's: 4 shag **5** conga, rumba, samba, Suzy-Q **7** pecking
8 big apple, lindy hop, trucking **9** jitterbug
1940's: 5 mambo **6** cha-cha
1950's and 1960's: 4 frug, go-go **5** twist **6** monkey
9 rock-'n'-roll
1970's: 5 disco
Argentine: 5 tango
Austrian: 13 schuhplattler
Balinese: 6 legong
Brazilian: 5 samba **6** maxixe
Cuban: 5 conga, rumba **6** cha-cha
Czech: 5 polka
Dominican: 8 marengue, merengue
folk: 6 Morris **7** maypole
French: 6 can-can **8** galliard **9** ecossaise
German: 11 schottische
Indian: 6 kathak **8** manipuri **9** kathakali **13** bharata nat
yam
Japanese: 6 bugaku **7** dengaku **8** sarugaku
dance/theater: **2** no **3** noh **6** kabuki
Mexican: 3 hat
Polish: 7 mazurka **9** krakoviak, polonaise **11** varsovienne
Scottish: 5 sword
Siamese: 10 wayang wong
Spanish: 4 jota **6** bolero **8** flamenco **9** sevillana
10 seguidilla
modern dancer/choreographer: 4 Juba **8** Ted Shawn
9 Eliot Feld, Gene Kelly, Ray Bolger **10** Mary Wigman,
Paul Draper, Twyla Tharp **11** Anna Sokolow, Antony Tu-
dor, Eric Hawkins, Fred Astaire, Irene Castle, Ruth St
Denis **12** Bill Robinson, Ginger Rogers, Martha Graham,
Vernon Castle **13** Alwin Nikolais, Doris Humphrey, Isadora Duncan **14** Charles Weidman **15** Merce Cunningham
see also: **6** ballet

Divine Comedy Part II:
  9 Purgatory
Divine Comedy Part III:
  8 Paradise
  heroine: 8 Beatrice

Dantes, Edmond
  character in: 21 The Count
    of Monte Cristo
  author: 5 Dumas (pere)

Danton, Ray
  born: 9 New York NY
  roles: 14 I'll Cry Tomorrow
    18 The George Raft Story
    27 The Rise and Fall of
    Legs Diamond

Danu
  also: 4 Dana
  origin: 5 Irish
  mother of: 14 Tuatha De
    Danann

Danvers, Mrs
  character in: 7 Rebecca
  author: 9 Du Maurier

Daphnaea
  epithet of: 7 Artemis
  means: 11 of the laurel

Daphne
  form: 5 nymph
  father: 5 Ladon **6** Peneus
  pursued by: 6 Apollo
    9 Leucippus
  changed into: 7 bay tree

Daphnephoria
  festival of: 6 Apollo

Daphnis
  occupation: 7 cowherd
    8 shepherd
  father: 6 Hermes
  originated: 14 pastoral poetry
  blinded by: 5 Nomia

Daphnis and Chloe
  characters in: 12 Greek
    romance
  author: 6 Longus

Daphnis et Chloe
  ballet by: 5 Ravel
  choreographer: 12 Michel
    Fokine

dapper 4 neat, trim **5** natty,
  smart **6** jaunty, modish, spiffy,
  sporty, spruce **7** stylish

dapple 3 dab, dot **4** spot
  6 mottle

dappled 7 flecked, mottled,
  spotted **10** variegated

Darcy, Fitzwilliam
  character in: 17 Pride and
    Prejudice
  author: 6 Austen

Dardanus
  father: 4 Zeus
  mother: 7 Electra
  twin brother: 6 Iasion
  wife: 6 Myrina
  son: 12 Erechthonius
  ancestor of: 7 Trojans

dare 3 bet **4** defy **5** taunt
  7 venture **9** challenge
  11 provocation

daredevil 4 bold, rash **5** risky
  8 heedless, reckless **9** audacious, breakneck, risk-taker
  11 adventurous **12** death-
  defying, devil-may-care
  13 adventuresome

daredevilry 6 daring **8** rashness **9** derring-do **10** imprudence **12** carelessness,
  heedlessness, recklessness
  13 foolhardiness

Dares
  companion of: 6 Aeneas
  noted for: 6 boxing

Dares Phrygius
  priest of: 10 Hephaestus

Dar es Salaam
  former capital of: 8 Tanzania

Darien *see* **8** Colombia

daring 4 bold, game **5** brave
  6 plucky **7** bravery, courage,
  gallant, valiant **8** audacity,
  boldness, intrepid **9** audacious,
  dauntless, undaunted **10** courageous **11** adventurous, venturesome **13** audaciousness
  15 adventurousness

daring deed 4 feat **7** exploit
  11 achievement

dark 3 dim **4** deep, evil, inky
  5 angry, black, bleak, dingy,
  dusky, murky, night, shady
  6 dismal, dreary, gloomy, hidden, opaque, secret, somber,
  sullen, wicked **7** evening, joyless, obscure, ominous, shadowy, sunless **8** eventide,
  frowning, hopeless, overcast,
  sinister, twilight **9** concealed,
  nightfall, nighttime, sorrowful **10** forbidding **11** threatening **12** discouraging
  13 disheartening

darken 3 dim, dye **4** tint
  5 cloud, color **6** sadden
  7 blacken, obscure **8** dispirit

darkened 3 dim **5** dusky, unlit **6** cloudy, gloomy
  7 clouded **9** blackened, tenebrous, unlighted **10** blacked
  out **13** unilluminated

darkening 7 eclipse, shading
  8 clouding, lowering **9** obscuring, shadowing **10** blackening
  12 clouding over

Dark Frontier, The
  author: 10 Eric Ambler

dark-hued 5 black, dusky,
  ebony, raven **6** somber
  7 swarthy

Dark Is Light Enough, The
  author: 14 Christopher Fry

Dark Lady, The
  author: 16 Louis Auchincloss

Dark Laughter
  author: 16 Sherwood
    Anderson

darkness 4 dusk **5** night,
  shade **7** dimness, evening
  8 eventide, twilight **9** blackness, nightfall, nighttime

Darkness at Noon
  author: 14 Arthur Koestler

Darkness Visible
  author: 14 William Golding

Dark Victory
  director: 14 Edmund
    Goulding
  cast: 10 Bette Davis
    11 George Brent **12** Ronald
    Reagan **14** Humphrey Bo-
    gart **19** Geraldine Fitzgerald
  remade as: 11 Stolen Hours

darling 4 cute, dear, love
  5 loved, sweet **6** adored,
  lovely **7** beloved, dearest, lovable **8** adorable, charming, precious **9** cherished **10** attractive,
  enchanting, sweetheart
  11 captivating

Darling
  director: 15 John Schlesinger
  cast: 11 Dirk Bogarde **13** Ju-
    lie Christie **14** Laurence
    Harvey
  Oscar for: 6 script **7** actress
    (Christie)

Darling, Wendy
  character in: 8 Peter Pan
  author: 6 Barrie

darn 4 damn, dang, dash, drat,
  mend **5** blast, patch, sew up
  6 hang it, stitch **7** consarn,
  doggone, goldang **8** confound
  10 confound it

Darnay, Charles
  character in: 16 A Tale of
    Two Cities
  author: 7 Dickens

darnel 12 Biblical weed

Darnell, Linda
  real name: 20 Monetta
    Eloyse Darnell
  born: 8 Dallas TX
  roles: 12 Blood and Sand,
    Forever Amber **14** The Mark
    of Zorro **17** Unfaithfully
    Yours

Darren, James
  real name: 13 James Ercolani
  born: 14 Philadelphia PA
  roles: 6 Gidget **13** The Time
    Tunnel

dart 3 run **4** bolt, dash, flit,
  jump, leap, race, rush, tear
  5 bound, fling, hurry, spear,
  spurt **6** hasten, spring, sprint
  7 javelin, missile **10** projectile

D'Artagnan
character in: **18** The Three Musketeers
author: **5** Dumas (pere)

Dartle, Rosa
character in: **16** David Copperfield
author: **7** Dickens

Darwin, Charles
author of: **15** The Descent of Man **18** The Origin of Species **20** The Voyage of the Beagle
studied: **16** Galapagos Islands
field: **6** nature **7** biology
nationality: **7** British
theory of: **9** evolution **16** natural selection
ship: **6** Beagle

Dascylus
member of: **9** Argonauts
father: **5** Lycus

dash 3 bit, run, zip **4** bolt, dart, drop, elan, foil, hurl, race, ruin, rush, slam, tear, zeal **5** bound, crash, flair, fling, hurry, oomph, pinch, smash, speed, spoil, throw, touch, verve, vigor **6** dampen, energy, hasten, pizazz, spirit, splash, sprint, thrust, thwart **7** a little, panache, shatter, soupcon, spatter **8** splatter, splinter, vivacity **9** animation, frustrate **10** disappoint, discourage

dashing 4 bold **5** brave **6** daring, plucky **7** gallant **8** fearless, spirited, unafraid **9** audacious, impetuous **10** courageous **13** swashbuckling

dash one's hopes 5 daunt, unman **6** deject **7** depress **8** dispirit **10** discourage, dishearten

Dashwood, Elinor and Marianne
characters in: **19** Sense and Sensibility
author: **6** Austen

DaSilva, Howard
real name: **17** Harold Silverblatt
born: **11** Cleveland OH
roles: **8** Oklahoma **12** Sergeant York **14** The Great Gatsby **20** Abe Lincoln in Illinois

Dass, Secunda
character in: **21** The Master of Ballantrae
author: **9** Stevenson

dastard 3 cad **6** coward, craven **7** bounder, caitiff, chicken **8** poltroon **11** yellowbelly

dastardly 3 low **4** base, mean, vile **6** sneaky **8** cowardly, shameful **9** atrocious **10** despicable

data 4 dope, info **5** facts **7** dossier, figures **8** evidence **9** documents **11** information

Datchery, Mr
character in: **22** The Mystery of Edwin Drood
author: **7** Dickens

date 3 age, era **5** court, epoch, stage **6** escort, period **7** partner, take out **9** companion, originate **10** engagement, rendezvous **11** appointment

date 18 Phoenix dactylifera
varieties: **5** cliff **6** Ceylon **7** Chinese **9** Jerusalem **12** Canary Island

dated 5 passe **6** old hat **8** obsolete, outmoded **9** out-of-date **10** antiquated **12** old-fashioned **13** unfashionable

daub 4 blot, coat, soil, spot **5** cover, dirty, paint, smear, stain **6** blotch, smirch, smudge **7** splotch

Daudet, Alphonse
author of: **6** Sappho **15** The Woman of Arles **17** Letters from My Mill **18** Tartarin of Tarascon

Daughter of the Regiment, The
opera by: **9** Donizetti

Daumier, Honore
born: **6** France **10** Marseilles
artwork: **7** Bathers **9** Gargantua **12** Men of Justice **13** Bluestockings **14** The Washerwoman **16** The Good Bourgeois **18** The Legislative Body **19** Professors and Pupils **20** Stories from Antiquity **21** The Third-Class Carriage

daunt 3 cow **4** dash, faze **5** abash, alarm, scare **6** deject, dismay, menace, subdue **7** depress, unnerve **8** affright, browbeat, frighten, threaten **10** discourage, dishearten, intimidate

dauntless 4 bold **5** brave, gutsy **6** daring, heroic **7** gallant, valiant **8** fearless, resolute, unafraid, valorous **10** courageous **12** stouthearted

dauntlessness 4 grit, guts, sand **5** nerve, pluck, spunk, valor **6** daring, mettle **7** bravery, courage, resolve **8** boldness **9** fortitude **10** resolution **12** fearlessness, resoluteness **16** stout-heartedness

Davers, Lady
character in: **6** Pamela
author: **10** Richardson

David
king of: **6** Israel
father: **5** Jesse
wife: **6** Maacah, Michal **7** Abigail, Ahinoam, Haggith **9** Bathsheba
son: **5** Amnon **7** Absalom, Chileab, Solomon **8** Adonijah
daughter: **5** Tamar
brother: **5** Eliab **7** Shammah **8** Abinadab
sister: **7** Abigail
friend: **5** Abner **8** Jonathan
nephew: **5** Amasa
city of: **9** Bethlehem, Jerusalem
anointed by: **6** Samuel
killed: **7** Goliath
wrote: **6** Psalms
comforter: **7** Abishag
conspirators against: **4** Joab **8** Abiathar, Adonijah
pertaining to: **7** Davidic

David, Jacques-Louis
born: **5** Paris **6** France
artwork: **13** Mme de Verninac **15** The Death of Marat **19** The Oath of the Horatii **23** The Coronation of Napoleon **26** View of the Luxembourg Gardens **31** The Intervention of the Sabine Women

David Copperfield
author: **14** Charles Dickens
character: **3** Ham **6** Barkis, Mr Dick **7** Creakle **8** Traddles **9** Mr Spenlow, Uriah Heep **10** Aunt Betsey, Little Em'ly, Mr Micawber, Rosa Dartle, Steerforth **11** Dora Spenlow, Little Emily, Mr Murdstone, Mr Wickfield, Mrs Gummidge **13** Clara Peggotty **14** Agnes Wickfield, Betsey Trotwood
director: **11** George Cukor
cast: **8** W C Fields **10** Madge Evans **11** Frank Lawton, Roland Young **13** Basil Rathbone, Edna May Oliver **15** Lionel Barrymore **16** Maureen O'Sullivan **18** Freddie Bartholomew

David Harum
author: **19** Edward Noyes Westcott

Davies, Arthur Bowen
born: **7** Utica NY

artwork: 5 Dream **8** Unicorns **9** Crescendo **13** Every Saturday **15** Dancing Children, Sacramental Tree **17** Along the Erie Canal **18** Leda and the Dioscuri

Davies, Marion
  real name: 19 Marion Cecilia Douras
  lover: 21 William Randolph Hearst
  born: 10 Brooklyn NY
  roles: 12 Cain and Mable **13** Runaway Romany **15** Tillie the Toiler

Davis, Bette
  real name: 18 Ruth Elizabeth Davis
  husband: 11 Gary Merrill
  born: 8 Lowell MA
  roles: 7 Jezebel (Oscar) **9** Dangerous (Oscar), The Letter **10** Now Voyager, The Old Maid **11** All About Eve, Dark Victory **14** Of Human Bondage, The Little Foxes **18** The Petrified Forest **22** Hush Hush Sweet Charlotte **26** What Ever Happened to Baby Jane?

Davis, H L
  author of: 14 Honey in the Horn

Davis, Ossie
  wife: 7 Ruby Dee
  born: 9 Cogdell GA
  author: 16 Purlie Victorious
  roles/films: 7 Jamaica **15** A Raisin in the Sun **18** No Time for Sergeants **19** Cotton Comes to Harlem

Davis, Sammy Jr
  wife: 8 May Britt
  group: 14 Will Master Trio
  born: 9 New York NY
  autobiography: 7 Yes I Can
  roles: 11 Mr Wonderful **12** Porgy and Bess **20** The Benny Goodman Story

Davis, Stuart
  born: 14 Philadelphia PA
  artwork: 4 Visa **9** Eggbeater **11** Lucky Strike, Ready to Wear **11** Owh! In Sao Pao **12** The Mellow Pad **14** Colonial Cubism **15** Cigarette Papers

Davy, Humphrey
  field: 9 chemistry
  nationality: 7 British
  isolated: 5 boron **6** barium, sodium **7** calcium **8** chlorine **9** magnesium, potassium, strontium
  invented: 8 Davy lamp **10** miner's lamp

dawdle 4 idle, loaf **5** dally, delay **6** loiter **10** dillydally **12** putter around **13** procrastinate

dawdler
  French: 7 flaneur

dawdling
  French: 8 flanerie

dawn 4 rise **5** begin, birth, occur, start, sunup **6** advent, appear, Aurora, emerge, origin, strike, unfold **7** develop, sunrise **8** commence, daybreak, daylight **9** beginning, emergence, inception, unfolding **12** commencement
  god of: 8 Heimdall
  goddess of: 3 Eos **6** Aurore, Matuta

dawning 5 sunup **7** morning, sunrise **8** daybreak, daylight

Dawn Patrol, The
  director: 14 Edmund Goulding
  cast: 10 David Niven, Errol Flynn **11** Donald Crisp **13** Basil Rathbone **14** Melville Cooper **15** Barry Fitzgerald

day 3 age **4** date, time **5** epoch **6** period

Day, Clarence (Jr)
  author of: 14 God and My Father, Life with Father, Life with Mother

Day, Doris
  real name: 18 Doris von Kappelhoff
  born: 12 Cincinnati OH
  autobiography: 19 Doris Day Her Own Story
  roles: 10 Pillow Talk **12** Calamity Jane **13** The Pajama Game **15** Move Over Darling, The Doris Day Show **23** Please Don't Eat the Daisies

daybed 5 couch **6** lounge **12** chaise longue

day book 5 diary **6** agenda **7** journal **8** calendar, schedule

daybreak 4 dawn **5** sunup **7** sunrise

daydream 4 muse **5** fancy **7** fantasy, imagine, reverie **9** fantasize **10** wool-gather **14** castle in the air

Day for Night
  director: 16 Francois Truffaut
  cast: 15 Jean-Pierre Leaud **16** Francois Truffaut, Jacqueline Bisset, Jean-Pierre Aumont
  Oscar for: 11 foreign film

daylight 4 dawn **5** sunup **7** morning, sunrise **8** full view, openness, sunlight, sunshine

Days and Nights
  author: 17 Konstantin Simonov

day's end 3 eve **4** dusk, even **6** sunset **7** evening, sundown **8** gleaming, twilight **9** nightfall

Days of Heaven
  director: 14 Terrence Malick
  cast: 9 Linda Manz **10** Sam Shepard **11** Brooke Adams, Richard Gere
  Oscar for: 14 cinematography

Days of Wine and Roses
  director: 12 Blake Edwards
  cast: 9 Lee Remick **10** Jack Lemmon **11** Jack Klugman **15** Charles Bickford
  score: 12 Henry Mancini

daze 4 numb, stun **5** amaze, shock **6** benumb, dazzle, excite, muddle, stupor **7** astound, confuse, stagger, startle, stupefy **8** astonish, bewilder, surprise **9** disorient, electrify **11** flabbergast **12** astonishment, bewilderment, blow one's mind **14** discombobulate

dazed 5 woozy **6** groggy **7** confused, dazzled, stunned **9** befuddled, stupefied **10** bewildered, punch-drunk

dazzle 3 awe **4** blur, daze **5** blind **6** excite **7** confuse, overawe **9** electrify, overpower, overwhelm

dazzling 7 radiant **8** blinding **9** sparkling **10** impressive, staggering **11** coruscating **12** breathtaking, electrifying, overwhelming **14** flabbergasting

deacon 6 cleric **9** churchman, clergyman **12** ecclesiastic

deactivate 6 defuse **9** switch off **10** neutralize

dead, the dead 4 beat, cold, dull, flat **5** depth, exact, midst, quiet, spent, tired, total, utter, vapid **6** entire, middle, unused **7** defunct, expired, extinct, insipid, precise, useless, utterly, worn-out **8** abruptly, absolute, complete, deceased, entirely, inactive, lifeless, obsolete, perished, stagnant, suddenly, thorough, unerring **9** exhausted, inanimate, inorganic **10** absolutely, completely, lackluster, unemployed, unexciting **11** ineffectual, inoperative **12** unproductive, unprofitable
  Latin: 8 ad patres
  god of: 6 Osiris **7** Veiovis

dead body 5 stiff **6** corpse **7** cadaver, remains

deaden 4 dope, drug, dull, mute, numb **5** abate, blunt **6** lessen, muffle, soothe, subdue, weaken **7** assuage, smother **8** diminish, mitigate, moderate **9** alleviate **11** anesthetize

deadened 5 muted **6** dulled, numbed **7** muffled, subdued

Dead Father, The
author: **15** Donald Barthelme

Dea Dia
origin: **5** Roman
goddess of: **11** agriculture
corresponds to: **13** Acca Laurentia

deadlock 7 impasse **8** standoff **9** stalemate **10** standstill

deadly 3 wan **4** dull **5** ashen, awful, fatal, fully, undue **6** boring, lethal, mortal, pallid **7** awfully, baneful, destroy, extreme, ghostly, tedious, totally **8** dreadful, entirely, horribly, terrible, terribly, tiresome **9** excessive, malignant, wearisome **10** cadaverous, completely, implacable, inordinate, relentless, thoroughly **11** destructive, unrelenting

deadpan 5 sober **8** detached **9** impassive **11** unemotional **13** straight-faced

dead ringer 4 copy, mate, twin **6** double **9** duplicate **11** counterpart **13** spitting image

Dead Souls
author: **12** Nikolai Gogol

dead to the world 6 asleep **7** out cold **9** konked out **10** fast asleep, slumbering **11** sound asleep

dead weight 7 ballast **9** inert mass

Dead Zone, The
author: **11** Stephen King

deal 3 act **4** give, hand **5** round, see to, trade, treat **6** behave, handle, market **7** bargain, concern, deliver, dole out, give out, mete out, oversee **8** consider, dispense **9** agreement, apportion **10** administer, distribute, **11** arrangement **12** distribution **13** apportionment

dealer 5 agent **6** monger, trader, vendor **8** merchant **10** trafficker **11** distributor

dealing, dealings 5 trade **7** traffic **8** business, practice **9** relations, treatment **12** transactions

dealing out 8 dividing **9** allotting, bestowing **10** conferring, consigning, dispensing **12** apportioning, distributing

Dea Marica see **6** Marica

Dean, Dizzy (Jay Hanna)
sport: **8** baseball
position: **7** pitcher
team: **16** St Louis Cardinals
part of: **12** Gashouse Gang
brother: **4** Paul

Dean, James (Jimmy)
real name: **14** James Byron Dean
born: **8** Marion IN
roles: **5** Giant **10** East of Eden **18** Rebel Without a Cause

Deane, Seneca
character in: **7** Babbitt
author: **5** Lewis

Dean's December
author: **10** Saul Bellow

dear 4 love **5** angel, loved **6** costly **7** beloved, darling **8** esteemed, favorite, precious **9** cherished, expensive, respected **10** sweetheart
French: **5** cheri **6** cherie

Dear Antoine
author: **11** Jean Anouilh

Dear Brutus
author: **12** James M Barrie

dearest 7 beloved, darling

dearth 4 lack **7** paucity **8** scarcity, shortage **10** deficiency

death, Death 5 dying **6** demise **7** decease, passing **9** departure **10** expiration, grim reaper
goddess of: **3** Hel **7** Berchta, Perchta **10** Ereshkigal

Death Be Not Proud
author: **9** John Donne

death blow
French: **11** coup de grace

Death Comes for the Archbishop
author: **11** Willa Cather
character: **7** Jacinto **9** Kit Carson **16** Bishop Jean Latour **20** Father Joseph Vaillant

death-dealing 5 fatal **6** lethal, mortal **7** killing **11** destructive

death-defying 4 bold, rash **5** risky **6** daring **8** reckless **9** audacious, breakneck, daredevil

Death in the Family, A
author: **9** James Agee

Death in Venice
director: **15** Luchino Visconti
author: **10** Thomas Mann
cast: **9** Mark Burns **11** Dirk Bogarde **14** Marisa Berenson

deathless 7 eternal **8** immortal **9** perpetual **11** everlasting

deathlike 3 wan **4** pale **5** ashen **6** pallid **7** ghastly

9 bloodless **10** cadaverous, corpselike

deathly 4 very **7** extreme, intense **8** terrible **9** extremely **12** overwhelming **15** resembling death

Death of a Salesman
director: **12** Laslo Benedek
author: **12** Arthur Miller
character: **4** Biff **5** Happy, Linda **7** Bernard, Charley **8** Uncle Ben **10** Willy Loman
cast: **13** Frederic March, Kevin McCarthy **14** Mildred Dunnock **15** Cameron Mitchell

Death of Ivan Ilyich, The
author: **10** Leo Tolstoy

Death of the Gods, The
author: **17** Dmitri Merejkowski

Death of the Heart
author: **14** Elizabeth Bowen

Death on the Nile
author: **14** Agatha Christie

Death Takes a Holiday
director: **14** Mitchell Leisen
cast: **11** Guy Standing **13** Evelyn Venable, Frederic March (Death)

Death Valley Days
host: **12** Robert Taylor, Ronald Reagan **13** Dale Robertson **14** Stanley Andrews

debacle 4 rout, ruin **5** havoc, wreck **8** collapse, disaster, downfall **9** breakdown, cataclysm, overthrow, ruination **10** bankruptcy **11** catastrophe, devastation, dissolution **12** vanquishment **14** disintegration

debar 3 ban **6** reject **7** exclude, keep out **8** preclude, prohibit **9** blackball, blacklist

debark 4 land

debarment 7 removal **8** omission **9** exception, exclusion, exemption, rejection **11** elimination, prohibition **12** nonadmission

debase 5 lower **6** befoul, defile **7** corrupt, degrade **8** disgrace, dishonor **9** desecrate **10** adulterate **11** deteriorate **16** impair the worth of **18** reduce the quality of

debased 4 vile **6** impure **7** corrupt, defiled, lowered **8** degraded, depraved **9** debauched, disgraced, dissolute, perverted **10** degenerate, dissipated **11** adulterated

debasement 9 decadence, depravity **10** corruption, de-

bauchery, degeneracy,
immorality, perversion
13 dissoluteness

debatable 4 iffy **6** unsure
7 dubious **8** arguable, doubtful **9** uncertain, undecided
10 disputable **12** questionable
13 problematical

debate 5 argue **6** ponder **7** discuss, dispute, reflect **8** argument, cogitate, consider, hash
over **10** cogitation, deliberate,
discussion, meditation, reflection, think about **12** deliberation, meditate upon
13 consideration

debauch 4 orgy **5** revel, spree
6 debase **7** carouse, corrupt,
deprave, revelry, subvert
8 carousal **9** bacchanal **10** lead
astray, saturnalia

debauched 4 lewd **6** wanton
7 corrupt, debased, immoral
8 degraded, depraved, perverse,
vitiated **9** abandoned, corrupted, dissolute, lecherous,
led astray, perverted, reprobate, shameless **10** degenerate,
dissipated, lascivious, libidinous, licentious, profligate
12 disreputable

debauchery 6 excess **11** dissipation **12** immoderation, intemperance **14** self-indulgence

DeBeck, Billy
  creator/artist of: 12 Barney
  Google **20** Parlor Bedroom
  and Sink

debilitate 6 weaken **7** wear
out **8** enervate **10** devitalize,
make feeble **17** deprive of
strength

debilitated 5 frail **6** feeble, infirm **7** worn out **8** delicate,
weakened **9** enervated
11 devitalized

debilitation 8 handicap, weakness **9** infirmity **10** affliction,
disability, impairment, inadequacy **11** disablement

debility 7 fatigue, frailty **8** as-
thenia, handicap, senility,
weakness **9** infirmity, lassitude,
weakening **10** affliction, enervation, exhaustion, feebleness,
impairment, invalidism, sickliness **11** decrepitude,
prostration

Debir
  conqueror: 7 Othniel

debit 4 debt **6** red ink **7** account, payable **9** liability
10 balance due, obligation
11 ledger entry, shortcoming

debonair 5 suave **6** dapper,
jaunty, urbane **7** buoyant, elegant, genteel, refined **8** care-

free, charming, gracious, well-
bred **9** sprightly **11** free and
easy **12** lighthearted
13 sophisticated

Deborah 11 Hebrew judge
  companion: 7 Rebekah
  summoned: 5 Barak

debouch 5 drain **6** emerge, let
out **7** flow out **9** discharge

debris 4 crap, junk **5** dreck,
dregs, dross, ruins, scrap,
trash, waste **6** litter, rubble,
shards **7** clutter, garbage, rubbish **8** detritus, wreckage
9 fragments

debt 4 bill **5** debit **7** arrears
9 liability **10** obligation **15** deferred payment, that which is
owed

debunk 4 bare **5** strip **6** expose,
send up, show up, unmask
7 deflate, lampoon, take off,
uncloak, uncover **8** ridicule,
satirize **9** burlesque, demystify,
disparage **13** demythologize

Debussy, Claude Achille
  born: 6 France **15** St Germain-en-Laye
  composer of: 5 La Mer
  6 Gigues, Iberia, Images
  8 Estampes **9** Nocturnes,
  Printemps **11** Clair de Lune
  13 En Blanc et Noir
  15 Children's Corner, L'Enfant prodigue **16** La Demoiselle Elue, Suite
  Bergamasque **17** Rondes de
  Printemps, The Blessed Damozel **18** Pelleas et Melisande **24** The Girl with the
  Flaxen Hair **26** Prelude a
  l'apres-midi d'un faune
  28 Prelude to the Afternoon
  of a Faun

debut 9 coming out
12 presentation

decadence 5 decay **7** decline
10 corruption, debasement, degeneracy, immorality **12** degeneration **13** deterioration

decadent 7 corrupt, debased,
immoral **8** decaying, depraved,
perverse **9** debauched, dissolute, perverted **10** degenerate
  French: 11 fin de siecle

Decalogue 15 Ten
Commandments

Decameron, The
  author: 17 Giovanni
  Boccaccio

decamp 7 move off, run away,
take off **8** march off, sneak
off

decampment 6 escape, flight
7 getaway

decant 4 pour **7** draw off, pour
out

decanter 6 bottle, carafe,
vessel

decathlon winner 11 Bruce
Jenner

Decatur, Stephen
  served in: 11 Algerine War,
  Barbary Wars **13** Tripolitan
  War **19** War of Eighteen
  Twelve
  **commander of ship:
  12** United States
  defeated ship: 10 Macedonian (British)
  saying: 22 "Our country right
  or wrong"

decay 3 rot **5** spoil **7** corrode,
putrefy, rotting **8** spoiling
9 decompose **12** disintegrate,
putrefaction **13** decomposition
  goddess of: 4 Hour **5** Horae

decayed 3 bad **6** putrid, rotted,
rotten, ruined **7** corrupt, gone
bad, spoiled **10** decomposed
12 deteriorated
13 disintegrated

deceased see **4** dead

deceit 5 fraud **8** cheating,
trickery **9** duplicity **10** dishonesty, trickiness **11** fraudulence **13** double-dealing
15 underhandedness
17 misrepresentation

deceitful 5 false **6** crafty,
sneaky, tricky **7** cunning
9 dishonest, insincere **11** duplicitous, treacherous, underhanded **12** hypocritical
13 double-dealing,
untrustworthy

deceitfulness 5 fraud **7** cunning, slyness **9** falseness, hypocrisy, treachery
10 craftiness, dishonesty,
sneakiness, trickiness **11** insincerity **15** underhandedness
17 untrustworthiness

deceive 3 con **4** fool **5** cheat,
put on, trick **6** delude **7** defraud, mislead, swindle

deceiver 4 fake **5** cheat, fraud,
quack **6** con man **7** cozener
8 impostor, swindler **9** charlatan, trickster **10** mountebank
13 confidence man

decelerate 5 brake **8** slow
down

deceleration 7 braking,
slowing

December see box, p. 248

decency 7 decorum, modesty
9 propriety **14** respectability
15 appropriateness

decent 4 fair, nice **5** ample
6 proper, seemly **7** correct, fitting **8** adequate, gracious,
obliging, passable, suitable

December
event: 11 Pearl Harbor (7), Winter solstice (21, 22)
flower: 5 holly 9 narcissus
French: 8 Decembre
gem: 4 ruby 6 zircon 9 turquoise
German: 8 Dezember
holiday: 8 Hanukkah 9 Boxing Day (26), Christmas (25) 16 Saint Nicholas Day (6)
Italian: 8 Dicembre
number of days: 9 thirty-one
origin of name: 5 decem (Latin meaning ten)
place in year:
  Gregorian: 7 twelfth
  Roman: 5 tenth
  Julian: 7 twelfth
Spanish: 9 Diciembre
Zodiac sign: 9 Capricorn 11 Sagittarius

---

9 courteous 10 acceptable, sufficient 11 appropriate 12 satisfactory 13 accommodating

deception 5 fraud, trick 7 cunning 8 artifice, illusion, trickery 9 duplicity, treachery 10 trickiness 11 fraudulence, insincerity 13 double-dealing

deceptive 5 phony 9 dishonest 10 fraudulent, misleading

deceptiveness 5 fraud 11 fraudulence

decibel
abbreviation: 2 dB

decide 4 rule 5 elect, judge 6 choose, decree, select, settle 7 resolve 9 determine

decided 4 firm 7 certain 8 clear-cut, definite, emphatic, resolute 9 assertive 10 deliberate, determined, unwavering 12 indisputable, strong-willed, unhesitating, unmistakable 14 unquestionable

decidedly 9 certainly 10 absolutely 11 indubitably, undoubtedly 12 indisputably, unmistakably 13 unequivocally 14 unquestionably

decidedness 7 purpose, resolve 10 resolution 12 resoluteness 13 determination 14 purposefulness

decide on 5 adopt, elect 6 choose, opt for, select, settle 7 appoint, arrange, embrace, espouse, pick out

8 settle on 9 determine, establish, single out

decigram
abbreviation: 2 dg

deciliter
abbreviation: 2 dL

decimate 6 reduce 7 destroy 8 massacre 9 slaughter 13 greatly reduce

decimeter
abbreviation: 2 dm

decipher 5 solve 6 decode, deduce, render 7 decrypt, dope out, explain, make out, unravel 8 construe, untangle 9 interpret, translate 12 cryptanalyze

decision 6 decree, ruling 7 finding, outcome, purpose, resolve, verdict 8 judgment 10 conclusion, resolution 12 resoluteness 13 determination 14 purposefulness

decisive 4 firm 5 final 8 absolute, definite, positive, resolute 10 conclusive, convincing, definitive, determined, undeniable 12 indisputable

decisive blow 9 deathblow 11 coup de grace

decisiveness 7 purpose, resolve 10 resolution 12 resoluteness 14 purposefulness

decisive point 3 nut 4 core, crux, gist 5 basis, heart 6 kernel 7 essence 9 essential

deck 4 garb, trim 5 adorn, array, dress, prank 6 clothe, doll up, enrich, outfit, tog out 7 apparel, bedizen, festoon, furbish, garnish, gussy up 8 accouter, beautify, ornament, spruce up 9 embellish

Decker, Mary
sport: 7 running
married name: 6 Slaney

deck out 5 adorn, array, dress 6 attire, clothe, fit out, outfit, rig out 7 costume

declaim 4 rail 5 orate 6 recite 7 inveigh 9 sermonize 11 pontificate

declaration 6 avowal, notice 8 document 9 assertion, statement, testimony 10 deposition 11 affirmation, attestation, publication 12 announcement, notification, proclamation 14 acknowledgment

declare 4 show 6 affirm, reveal 7 express 8 announce, proclaim 9 pronounce

declare null and void 6 cancel, repeal, revoke 7 abolish, rescind, retract 8 abrogate, set

aside 9 repudiate 10 invalidate 11 countermand

declare untrue 4 deny 9 repudiate 10 contradict

decline 3 ebb 4 drop, fail, flag, sink, wane 5 decay, slump, spurn 6 balk at, eschew, lessen, refuse, reject, weaken, worsen 7 dwindle 8 decrease, diminish, downfall 9 downgrade, downswing 11 deteriorate 13 deterioration

Decline and Fall
author: 11 Evelyn Waugh

Decline and Fall of the Roman Empire, The
author: 12 Edward Gibbon

declivity 4 drop 5 slant, slope 6 plunge 7 descent

decompose 3 rot 5 decay, spoil 7 putrefy 8 separate 10 go to pieces 12 disintegrate

decomposed 6 putrid, rotted, rotten 7 decayed, spoiled 9 putrefied 13 disintegrated

decontaminate 6 purify 9 disinfect, sterilize

decor 13 ornamentation

decorate 4 trim 5 adorn, array, honor 7 festoon, garnish 8 beautify, ornament 9 embellish

decorated 5 fancy 6 decked, ornate 7 adorned, trimmed 8 bedecked 9 bemedaled, bedizened, garnished 10 ornamented 11 embellished

decoration 4 trim 5 award, badge, medal 6 emblem, ribbon 7 garnish 8 ornament, trimming 9 adornment 13 embellishment, ornamentation 14 beautification

decorous 3 fit 6 decent, polite, proper, seemly 7 correct 8 becoming, mannerly, suitable 9 dignified 10 respectful 11 appropriate

decorum 4 tact 5 taste 7 dignity 8 good form 9 gentility, propriety 10 politeness 14 respectability

decoy 4 bait, lure 5 plant, snare 6 allure, come-on, entice 10 enticement, inducement 11 smoke screen

decrease 4 drop, ease, loss 5 abate, taper 6 lessen, reduce 7 cutback, decline, dwindle, fall-off, slacken, subside 8 diminish 9 abatement, dwindling, lessening, reduction 10 de-escalate, diminution 12 de-escalation

decree 3 law 5 edict, order

6 dictum, ruling **7** command, mandate, statute **8** proclaim **9** authorize **12** proclamation

decrepit 7 rickety **8** battered **10** broken-down **11** dilapidated

decrescendo
music: **22** gradually getting softer
abbreviation: **4** decr

decry 7 censure, condemn **8** denounce **9** criticize, deprecate, disparage

Dedalus, Stephen
character in: **7** Ulysses **30** Portrait of the Artist as a Young Man
author: **5** Joyce

dedicate 6 commit, devote, launch, pledge **7** address, present **8** inscribe

dedication 8 devotion **10** commitment **11** devotedness **16** prefatory address **20** prefatory inscription

Dedlock, Sir Leicester and Lady
characters in: **10** Bleak House
author: **7** Dickens

deduce 5 infer **6** gather, reason **8** conclude **10** comprehend, understand

deduct 4 take **6** remove **8** subtract, take from, withdraw **10** decrease by

deduction 5 guess **6** belief, credit, rebate **7** removal **8** analysis, decrease, discount, judgment, markdown, rollback **9** abatement, allowance, exemption, gathering, inference, lessening, reasoning, reduction **10** assumption, concession, conclusion, diminuition, hypothesis, reflection, taking away, withdrawal **11** calculation, presumption, speculation, subtraction, supposition **13** comprehension, consideration, understanding **14** interpretation

Dee, Ruby
real name: **14** Ruby Ann Wallace
husband: **10** Ossie Davis
born: **11** Cleveland OH
roles: **15** A Raisin in the Sun **16** Purlie Victorious

Dee, Sandra
real name: **13** Alexandra Zuck
husband: **10** Bobby Darin
born: **9** Bayonne NJ
roles: **6** Gidget **12** A Summer Place **15** Tammy Tell Me True

deed 3 act **4** feat **5** title **6** action, effort **11** achievement **14** accomplishment

deeds are manly, words are womanish
Italian: **24** fatti maschii parole femine
motto of: **8** Maryland

deem 4 hold, view **5** judge, think **6** regard **7** believe **8** consider

de-emphasize 8 play down **9** underplay

deep 3 far, sea **4** dark, late, lost, rich, wise **5** far in, midst, ocean, vivid **6** astute, strong **7** extreme, intense, learned **8** absorbed, immersed, involved, profound, resonant, sonorous **9** engrossed, sagacious **10** discerning **11** intelligent **13** philosophical

Deep, The
author: **13** Peter Benchley

deeply 6 richly **7** acutely, gravely, greatly, vividly **8** entirely **9** intensely, seriously **10** completely, profoundly, resonantly, sonorously, thoroughly **12** passionately

deeply felt 6 ardent, fervid **7** earnest, fervent, intense, sincere, zealous **9** heartfelt **10** passionate **11** impassioned **12** wholehearted

deepness 10 profundity

deep-rooted 7 abiding, lasting **8** enduring **9** confirmed, ingrained

deep-seated 7 abiding, lasting **8** enduring **9** confirmed, ingrained

deep thought 10 absorption, brown study, intentness **11** engrossment **13** concentration

deep water 3 jam **4** mess **5** ocean **6** pickle **7** trouble **8** distress **10** difficulty **11** dire straits, predicament **12** over one's head

deer
young: **4** fawn
female: **3** doe

Deer Hunter, The
director: **13** Michael Cimino
cast: **10** John Cazale, John Savage **11** Meryl Streep **12** Robert De Niro **17** Christopher Walken
Oscar for: **7** picture **8** director **15** supporting actor (Walken)

Deerslayer, The
author: **19** James Fenimore Cooper

first of: **20** Leatherstocking Tales
character: **4** Hist **5** Hetty **6** Judith **10** Hurry Harry **11** Natty Bumppo (Deerslayer) **12** Chingachgook, Thomas Hutter

de-escalate 5 limit **6** lessen, narrow **8** contract, minimize

deface 3 mar **4** mark, scar **5** spoil **6** bruise, damage, impair, injure **9** disfigure

de facto 4 real **6** actual, really **8** actually

defalcate 8 embezzle **14** misappropriate

defamation 5 libel **7** calumny, slander **12** vilification **13** disparagement

defamatory 8 libelous **9** vilifying **10** calumnious, derogatory, slanderous **11** disparaging

defame 5 libel **6** malign, vilify **7** degrade, slander **8** derogate **9** denigrate, discredit, disparage **10** calumniate

Defarge, Madame
character in: **16** A Tale of Two Cities
author: **7** Dickens

default 10 nonpayment

defeat 4 foil, loss, rout **5** cream, crush, elude, quell **6** baffle, thwart **7** conquer, setback, shellac, trounce **8** confound, overcome, vanquish **9** frustrate, overpower, overthrow, overwhelm, thwarting **11** frustration **14** disappointment

defeated 4 beat **5** upset **6** beaten, bested, licked, routed **7** outdone, whipped, worsted **8** overcame **9** conquered, overthrew, put to rout **10** frustrated, overthrown **11** overpowered, overwhelmed **12** hors de combat

defect 4 flaw, scar, spot **5** break, crack, fault, stain **6** blotch, foible **7** blemish, default, failing, frailty **8** omission, weakness **10** deficiency **11** shortcoming **12** imperfection **14** incompleteness

defective 6 broken, faulty, flawed **7** lacking, wanting **8** abnormal, impaired **9** deficient, imperfect, subnormal **10** inadequate, out of order **11** inoperative **12** insufficient

Defence of Poetry
author: **18** Percy Bysshe Shelley

defend 5 guard **6** secure, shield, uphold **7** endorse, protect, shelter, stand by, support, sustain **8** advocate, champion, maintain, preserve **9** safeguard

defender 8 advocate, champion, guardian, upholder **9** protector, supporter

Defender of the Faith
Latin: **13** Fidei Defensor
title of: **17** English sovereigns

Defenders, The
character: **10** Joan Miller **14** Helen Donaldson, Kenneth Preston **15** Lawrence Preston
cast: **10** E G Marshall, Robert Reed **11** Joan Hackett, Polly Rowles

defense 4 care **5** guard **7** custody, support **8** advocacy, security **9** barricade, safeguard, upholding **10** protection, stronghold **11** maintenance, safekeeping **12** preservation **13** fortification, justification

defenseless 7 unarmed **8** helpless **10** on one's back, vulnerable, weaponless **11** unprotected, unresisting

defensible 3 fit **5** valid **6** proper **7** tenable **8** sensible, suitable **9** allowable, excusable **10** admissible, condonable, forgivable, pardonable, vindicable **11** justifiable, permissible, supportable, warrantable

defer 4 obey **5** delay, table, yield **6** accede, give in, put off, shelve, submit **7** respect, suspend **8** postpone **10** capitulate

deference 5 honor **6** esteem, regard **7** respect **9** obedience, reverence **12** capitulation · **13** consideration

deferential 5 civil **6** polite **7** dutiful **8** obedient, reverent **9** courteous, regardful **10** respectful, submissive **11** acquiescent, considerate, reverential

deferment 4 stay **5** delay **9** extension **12** postponement

deferral 5 pause **6** hiatus, recess **8** abeyance **10** suspension **12** postponement **14** discontinuance

defiance 9 hostility, obstinacy, rebellion **12** disobedience **14** rebelliousness

defiant 4 bold **9** truculent **10** aggressive, rebellious **11** disobedient, provocative

Defiant Ones, The
director: **13** Stanley Kramer
cast: **10** Tony Curtis **11** Lon Chaney Jr **12** Cara Williams **13** Charles McGraw,

Sidney Poitier, Theodore Bikel
Oscar for: **10** screenplay

deficiency 4 flaw **6** defect **7** failing, frailty **8** shortage, weakness **10** inadequacy **11** shortcoming **12** imperfection **13** insufficiency

deficient 4 weak **6** flawed **7** lacking, short on **8** inferior **9** defective **10** inadequate **11** substandard **12** insufficient **14** unsatisfactory

deficit 8 shortage **9** shortfall **10** deficiency

de fide 10 of the faith

defile 4 soil **5** dirty, smear, spoil, stain, taint **6** befoul, debase **7** degrade, profane, tarnish **8** besmirch, disgrace, dishonor **9** desecrate

defiled 5 dirty **6** fouled, impure, soiled **7** debased, dirtied, stained, sullied, tainted, unclean **8** befouled, polluted, ravished, smirched, violated **9** blackened, corrupted, tarnished **10** besmirched **12** contaminated

define 5 state **7** clarify, explain, specify **8** describe, spell out **9** delineate, designate

definite 3 set **4** sure **5** exact, fixed **7** certain, precise **8** clearcut, positive

definitely 5 truly **6** indeed, surely **7** for sure, no doubt **9** assuredly, certainly, decidedly, doubtless, expressly **10** absolutely, decisively, explicitly, positively, undeniably **11** indubitably, inescapably, unavoidably, undoubtedly **12** unmistakably **13** categorically, unequivocally **14** unequivocally, unquestionably **16** incontrovertibly

definiteness 8 sureness **9** certainty, precision **10** exactitude **11** unambiguity

definition 6 limits **7** clarity, purpose **11** description **15** distinctiveness

definitive 5 exact **7** decided, perfect **8** complete, decisive, reliable **10** conclusive, consummate

deflate 6 reduce **7** flatten **8** contract **9** devaluate

deflect 6 divert, swerve

Defoe, Daniel
author of: **6** Roxana **11** Colonel Jack **12** Moll Flanders **14** Robinson Crusoe **23** A Journal of the Plague Year

DeForest, Lee
invented/worked on: **10** audion tube, television **13** sound pictures

deform 3 mar **4** maim **5** twist **6** mangle **7** contort, distort **9** disfigure

deformation 9 deformity **10** distortion **12** malformation **13** disfigurement

deformed 6 marred, warped **7** defaced, mangled, spoiled, twisted **8** crippled **9** misshapen, monstrous **10** disfigured

deformity 12 malformation

defraud 3 con **4** bilk, rook **5** cheat **6** fleece, rip off **7** swindle

defray 3 pay **5** cover **11** foot the bill

deft 3 apt **4** able, sure **5** quick **6** adroit, expert **8** skillful **9** dexterous

deftness 5 knack, skill **7** ability **8** facility **9** adeptness, dexterity, handiness **10** adroitness, competency **11** proficiency **12** skillfulness

defunct 4 dead **7** extinct

defy 5 spurn **6** oppose, resist **7** disdain **8** confront **9** challenge, disregard, withstand

degage 4 easy **8** detached **10** disengaged **13** unconstrained

Degas, (Hilaire Germain) Edgar
born: **5** Paris **6** France
artwork: **14** The Ballet Class, The Morning Bath **15** Ballet Rehearsal **16** The Millinery Shop **17** The Glass of Absinth **23** Woman with Chrysanthemums **30** The Little Fourteen-Year-Old Dancer

degeneracy 9 decadence, depravity **10** debasement, debauchery, immorality, perversion **11** dissolution

degenerate 3 rot **4** base, sink, vile **5** decay **6** revert, wanton, wicked, worsen **7** corrupt, debased, decline, go to pot, immoral, pervert, vicious **8** decadent, degraded, depraved **9** abandoned, backslide, debauched, dissolute, perverted **10** dissipated, go downhill, profligate, retrograde, retrogress **11** deteriorate, hit the skids **12** disintegrate

degeneration 7 decline **9** depravity **10** corruption, debasement, immorality, perversion **11** degradation, dissolution, viciousness **13** deterioration

degradation 8 disgrace
11 humiliation

Degradation of the Democratic Dogma, The
author: **10** Henry Adams

degrade 5 lower, shame **6** debase, demote **7** corrupt **8** disgrace, dishonor

degraded 4 vile **6** wicked
7 corrupt, debased, lowered
8 depraved, shameful, unworthy **9** debauched, perverted, reprobate **10** degenerate
11 undignified
12 unregenerate

degrading 3 low **6** menial
8 shameful **11** humiliating

degree 4 mark, step, unit
5 grade, level, order, phase, point, stage **8** division, interval
abbreviation: **3** deg

De Guiche, Lillian
real name of: **11** Lillian Gish

de gustibus non est disputandum 29 there is no disputing about tastes

De Havilland, Joan de Beauvoir
real name of: **12** Joan Fontaine

De Havilland, Olivia
sister: **12** Joan Fontaine
born: **5** Japan, Tokyo
roles: **7** Melanie **10** The Heiress (Oscar) **11** The Snake Pit **12** Captain Blood, To Each His Own (Oscar)
14 Anthony Adverse, My Cousin Rachel **15** Gone With the Wind, Hold Back the Dawn **16** Light in the Piazza **22** Hush Hush Sweet Charlotte **24** The Adventures of Robin Hood

dehydrate 3 dry **5** parch **6** dry out

dehydrated 3 dry **7** parched, thirsty **8** dried-out **9** shriveled
10 desiccated

Deianira
father: **6** Oeneus
mother: **7** Althaea
brother: **8** Meleager
husband: **8** Heracles
killed: **8** Heracles

Deicoon
father: **8** Hercules
mother: **6** Megara
killed by: **8** Hercules

Deidamia
father: **9** Lycomedes
lover: **8** Achilles
son: **11** Neoptolemus

deification 7 worship **8** idolatry **10** exaltation
13 glorification

deify 5 exalt **7** glorify, idolize, worship

Deighton, Len
author of: **4** SS-GB **14** The Ipcress File **15** Funeral in Berlin **16** Catch a Falling Spy

deign 4 deem **5** stoop **6** see fit
7 consent **8** think fit
10 condescend

Dei gratia 15 by the grace of God

Deimos
origin: **5** Greek
father: **4** Ares
mother: **9** Aphrodite
brother: **6** Phobus
personifies: **4** fear

Deino
member of: **6** Graeae, Graiae

Deinonychus
type: **8** dinosaur
period: **10** Cretaceous

Deiope
father: **11** Triptolemus

Deiphobe
form: **5** sibyl
father: **7** Glaucus

Deiphobus
father: **5** Priam
mother: **6** Hecuba
brother: **6** Hector
wife: **5** Helen
killed by: **8** Menelaus

Deipyle
father: **8** Adrastus
husband: **6** Tydeus
son: **8** Diomedes

Deipylus
grandfather: **5** Priam

Deirdre
origin: **5** Irish
husband: **6** Naoise
father-in-law: **6** Usnach
uncle: **9** Conchobar

Deirdre of the Sorrows
author: **19** John Millington Synge

deity, the Deity 3 god **4** idol
7 goddess, godhead, Jehovah
8 Almighty, divinity, immortal, Olympian

deja vu 11 already seen

dejected 3 low, sad **4** blue, down **7** doleful, unhappy
8 desolate **9** depressed, sorrowful **10** despondent, dispirited, spiritless **11** discouraged, downhearted, low-spirited
12 disconsolate, disheartened

dejection 5 gloom **7** sadness
10 depression, low spirits, melancholy **11** despondency
15 dispiritedness, downheartedness

dejeuner 5 lunch

de jure 7 by right **14** according to law

dekagram
abbreviation: **3** dkg

dekaliter
abbreviation: **3** dkL

dekameter, decameter
abbreviation: **3** dkm

Dekker, Thomas
author of: **11** Westward Ho! (with John Webster) **20** The Shoemaker's Holiday

de Kooning, Willem
born: **9** Rotterdam **14** The Netherlands
artwork: **5** Woman **8** Painting **15** Woman and Bicycle

Delacroix, Eugene
born: **6** France **18** Charenton-St Maurice
artwork: **8** Paganini
14 Women of Algiers
15 Massacre at Chios
16 The Barque of Dante
19 Chopin and George Sand **20** Dante and Virgil in Hell **22** Liberty at the Barricades, The Death of Sardanapalus

Delaroche, Paul
born: **5** Paris **6** France
artwork: **24** The Death of Queen Elizabeth, The Death of the Duke of Guise,
26 The Execution of Lady Jane Grey **36** Children of Edward Imprisoned in the Tower

Delaunay, Robert
born: **5** Paris **6** France
artwork: **5** Disks **6** Cities, Rhythm **7** Runners, Windows **10** Cathedrals **11** City of Paris, Eiffel Tower
14 The Cardiff Team
19 Cosmic Circular Forms
28 Simultaneous Prismatic Windows

Delaware *see box, p. 252*

Delaware (Lenni-Lenape)
language family: **9** Algonkian **10** Algonquian
tribe: **5** Munsi, Unami
6 Munsee **11** Unalachtigo
location: **7** New York **8** Delaware **9** Manhattan, New Jersey **10** Long Island
12 Pennsylvania, Staten Island
leader: **7** Tamanen, Tammany
deity: **11** Kitanitowet

delay 4 slow, stay **5** check, table, tarry **6** dawdle, detain, hamper, hinder, hold up, impede, linger, put off, retard, shelve **7** inhibit, slowing, sus-

Delaware
  abbreviation: 2 DE 3 Del
  nickname: 5 First 7 Blue Hen, Diamond
  capital: 5 Dover
  largest city: 10 Wilmington
  others: 5 Acoma, Lewes 6 Easton, Newark, Smyrna 7 Briston, Elsmere, Milford 8 Claymont 9 New Castle 10 Georgetown
  college: 6 Wesley 10 Brandywine, Wilmington 12 Goldey Beacom
  feature: 10 Winterthur 15 Old Swedes Church 17 E I du Pont de Nemours
  tribe: 4 Leni 5 Lenni 6 Lenape, Munsee
  people: 10 Howard Pyle
  island: 7 Fenwick
  land rank: 10 forty-ninth
  physical feature:
    bay: 8 Delaware, Rehoboth
    sea: 8 Atlantic
    river: 8 Delaware 9 Christina, Nanticoke 10 Brandywine
  state admission: 5 first
  state bird: 14 blue hen chicken
  state flower: 12 peach blossom
  state motto: 22 Liberty and Independence
  state song: 11 Our Delaware
  state tree: 13 American holly

pend 8 dawdling, obstruct, postpone, reprieve, stoppage, tarrying 9 deferment, lingering, loitering 10 suspension 12 postponement, prolongation 13 procrastinate

delayed 4 late 6 put off, slowed 7 held up, stalled, tarried 8 arrested, deferred, detained, retarded 9 postponed, slackened 12 dillydallied 14 procrastinated 15 dragged one's feet

Delbruck, Max
  field: 7 biology 17 molecular genetics
  researched: 20 genetic recombination
  awarded: 10 Nobel Prize

delectable 8 pleasant 9 agreeable, delicious, enjoyable 10 delightful, gratifying 11 pleasurable

delegate 4 give, name 5 agent, envoy, proxy 6 assign, charge, deputy 7 entrust 8 give over, transfer 9 authorize, designate 10 commission 14 representative

delegation 11 designation, entrustment 13 authorization, commissioning

delete 3 cut 4 omit 5 erase 6 cancel, remove

deleterious 7 harmful, hurtful, ruinous 9 dangerous, injurious 11 destructive, detrimental

Delia
  festival of: 6 Apollo

deliberate 4 easy, slow, wary 5 weigh 6 confer, debate 7 careful, discuss, examine, express, planned, prudent, willful 8 cautious, cogitate, consider, measured, meditate, mull over 9 leisurely, unhurried 10 calculated, considered, purposeful, thoughtful 11 circumspect, contemplate, intentional, prearranged 12 premeditated

deliberate together 6 confer 7 consult, discuss

deliberation 4 care 6 debate 10 conference, discussion, steadiness 11 calculation, carefulness, forethought 13 premeditation 14 circumspection

Delibes, C P (Clement Philibert) Leo
  born: 6 France 14 St Germain-du-Val
  composer of: 5 Lakme 6 Sylvia 8 Coppelia 10 Le Roi l'a dit

delicacy 4 tact 5 taste 7 frailty 8 accuracy, elegance, fineness, softness, weakness 9 fragility, frailness, lightness, precision 10 perfection, smoothness 11 savoir-faire, sensibility, sensitivity, unsoundness 13 consideration, exquisiteness, sensitiveness 14 discrimination

delicate 4 fine, soft 5 frail, muted 6 ailing, dainty, feeble, flimsy, infirm, minute, savory, sickly, touchy, unwell 7 careful, elegant, fragile, refined, subdued, tactful 8 detailed, luscious, tasteful, ticklish, weakened 9 breakable, delicious, difficult, exquisite, palatable, sensitive, toothsome 10 appetizing, diplomatic, fastidious, perishable, precarious, scrupulous 11 debilitated

Delicate Balance, A
  author: 11 Edward Albee

delicious 5 tasty 6 joyful, savory 8 charming, luscious, pleasant 9 palatable 10 appetizing, delectable, delightful 11 pleasurable 13 mouth-watering

delight 3 joy 5 amuse, charm, cheer, revel 6 please 7 enchant, gratify, rapture 8 pleasure 9 enjoyment, fascinate, happiness 13 gratification

delighted 6 elated 7 pleased 8 ecstatic 9 enchanted 10 captivated, enraptured, enthralled

delightful 6 peachy 7 amiable, amusing 8 charming, engaging, pleasing 9 agreeable, congenial, enjoyable 10 enchanting 11 pleasurable 12 entertaining

delight in 4 love 5 adore, eat up, enjoy, fancy, savor 6 dote on, relish 7 cherish 8 treasure 10 appreciate

Delilah
  lover: 6 Samson
  betrayed: 6 Samson

delineate 4 draw 5 draft 6 define, depict, design, lay out, sketch 7 outline, portray 8 describe 9 represent 12 characterize

delineation 9 depiction, portrayal 11 description 12 illustration 14 representation 16 characterization

delineavit 6 he drew (this) 7 she drew (this)

delinquency 7 misdeed 10 misconduct, negligence 11 dereliction, misbehavior 19 neglect of obligation

delinquent 3 due 4 late 6 remiss 7 hoodlum, misdoer, overdue 8 derelict 9 in arrears, miscreant, negligent, wrongdoer 10 neglectful

delirious 6 raving 7 excited, frantic 8 ecstatic, frenzied 10 incoherent 11 carried away 13 hallucinating

delirium 5 fever 6 frenzy, raving 7 madness, ranting 8 insanity 10 brain fever

Deliro
character in: 22 Every Man Out of His Humour
author: 6 Jonson

Delisle, Guillaume
field: 9 geography
nationality: 6 French
founder of: 15 modern geography

Delius, Frederick
born: 7 England 8 Bradford
composer of: 5 Paris 6 Koanga 7 Eventyr, Irmelin 8 Sea-Drift 9 Brigg Fair 10 Appalachia 11 A Mass of Life, Sur les Cimes 17 Fennimore and Gerda 20 North Country Sketches 22 A Village Romeo and Juliet, Over the Hills and Far Away

deliver 3 aim, say 4 bear, deal, free, give, save 5 bring, carry, throw, utter 6 convey, direct, launch, rescue, strike 7 release, set free 8 give over, hand over, liberate, proclaim, turn over 9 surrender 10 emancipate

deliverance 6 rescue 7 release 9 salvation 10 liberation 12 emancipation

Deliverance
director: 11 John Boorman
author: 11 James Dickey
cast: 8 Ronny Cox 9 Jon Voight, Ned Beatty 12 Burt Reynolds
song: 13 Dueling Banjos

deliver up 4 cede, give 5 grant, yield 8 fork over, hand over, transfer 9 surrender 10 relinquish

delivery 8 transfer 11 transferral, transmittal 12 transmission

dell 4 dale, dene, glen, vale 5 glade 6 dingle, hollow, valley

Della Robbia, Luca
born: 5 Italy 8 Florence
artwork: 8 Cantoria (Singing Gallery) 12 The Ascension 13 Altman Madonna 15 Madonna and Child, The Resurrection

Dello Joio, Norman
born: 9 New York NY
composer of: 7 The Ruby 12 Psalm of David 15 New York Profiles, The Trial at Rouen, Triumph of St Joan 20 Proud Music of the Storm, The Lamentation of Saul

Delon, Alain
born: 6 France, Sceaux
roles: 10 Purple Noon, The Leopard 13 The Black Tulip

14 Is Paris Burning?
19 Rocco and His Brothers

Delphic
pertains to: 6 Apollo, Delphi

Delphic oracle
oracle of: 6 Apollo
located at: 6 Delphi
priestess: 6 Pythia

Delphinia
festival of: 6 Apollo

Delphinius
epithet of: 6 Apollo
means: 7 dolphin

Delphinus
function: 12 intermediary persuaded Amphitrite to marry: 8 Poseidon

Delphus
father: 8 Poseidon
mother: 8 Melantho

Delphyne
also: 6 Python
form: 7 monster
guarded: 4 Zeus 5 chasm
location: 6 Delphi
killed by: 6 Apollo

Del Rio, Dolores
real name: 21 Lolita Dolores Negrette
born: 6 Mexico 7 Durango
roles: 11 The Fugitive 13 Madame duBarry 15 Flying Down to Rio, Journey into Fear, Maria Candelaria

Delta Wedding
author: 11 Eudora Welty

delude 3 con 4 dupe, fool 5 put on, trick 7 deceive, mislead

deluge 4 bury, glut 5 drown, flood, spate, swamp 6 engulf 7 barrage, torrent 8 inundate, overflow, submerge 10 inundation

DeLuise, Dom
born: 10 Brooklyn NY
roles: 5 Fatso 6 The End 11 Silent Movie 14 Blazing Saddles

delusion 8 illusion 9 misbelief 10 aberration 11 derangement 13 hallucination, irrationality, misconception, self-deception

Delusions, Etc. of John Berryman
author: 12 John Berryman

deluxe 4 fine, posh 5 grand 6 choice, classy 7 elegant 8 splendid 9 luxurious

delve 5 probe 6 search 7 examine, explore 8 look into

demagogue 6 ranter 7 hothead, spouter 8 agitator, fomenter, inflamer 9 firebrand,

haranguer 10 incendiary, malcontent, tub-thumper 12 rabble-rouser, troublemaker

demand 4 call, need, want 5 exact, order 7 command, require 11 requirement

demanding 4 hard 5 harsh, rigid 6 strict 8 exacting 9 difficult

demantoid
species: 6 garnet

demarche 4 gait, plan

demean 5 lower, shame 6 debase, humble 7 degrade 8 disgrace 9 humiliate

demeanor 6 manner 7 bearing, conduct 8 behavior, presence 10 appearance, deportment 11 comportment

demented 3 mad 4 nuts 5 crazy 6 crazed, cuckoo, insane 7 lunatic 8 deranged

dementia praecox
13 schizophrenia

dementophobia
fear of: 8 insanity

demesne 4 land 5 realm 6 domain, estate 8 property

Demeter
origin: 5 Greek
goddess of: 5 earth 9 fertility
protectress of: 8 marriage 11 social order
father: 6 Cronus
mother: 4 Rhea
daughter: 10 Persephone
corresponds to: 5 Brimo, Ceres 8 Despoena
epithet: 5 Chloe, Lusia, Mysia 6 Antaea, Erinys, Stiria 7 Chamyne, Thesmia 8 Stiritis 9 Anesidora, Thermasia 11 Carpophorus 13 Thesimophorus

Demetrius
character in: 21 A Midsummer Night's Dream
author: 11 Shakespeare

DeMille, Cecil B
director of: 9 Cleopatra 18 The Ten Commandments 22 The Greatest Show on Earth

Demiphon
form: 4 king
sacrificed: 7 maidens
to prevent: 6 plague

demise 3 end 4 fall, ruin 5 death 7 decease, passing 8 collapse 10 expiration

demobilization 7 release 9 discharge 10 disbanding

demobilize 7 disband, release 9 discharge

Democoon
father: **5** Priam
birth: **12** illegitimate
killed by: **8** Odysseus

democracy 8 equality, fairness

Democracy
author: **10** Henry Adams

Democracy in America
author: **19** Alexis de
Tocqueville

Democratic Party
symbol: **6** donkey
president belonging to:
4 Polk **6** Carter, Pierce, Truman, Wilson **7** (Lyndon
Baines) Johnson, Jackson,
Kennedy **8** Buchanan, Van
Buren **9** Cleveland, (Franklin
D) Roosevelt

**Democratic Republican
Party**
president belonging to:
5 (John Quincy) Adams
6 Monroe **7** Madison
9 Jefferson

demode 8 outmoded
13 unfashionable

Demodocus
minstrel of: **8** Alcinous

Demogorgon
object of: **3** awe **4** fear

demoiselle 4 girl

demolish 4 raze, ruin **5** level,
total, wreck **7** destroy
9 devastate

demolition 6 razing **8** leveling,
wrecking **11** destruction

demon 5 devil, fiend **7** monster **8** go-getter

Demonassa
father: **10** Amphiaraus
mother: **8** Eriphyle
husband: **10** Thersander
son: **9** Tisamenus

demonic, demoniacal 6 hec-
tic **7** frantic, hellish **8** devilish,
fiendish, frenzied

demonstrable 7 evident **8** apparent, manifest, palpable
11 supportable

demonstrate 4 show **5** march,
prove, teach **6** parade, picket,
reveal **7** display, exhibit, explain **8** describe, manifest
9 establish **10** illustrate

demonstration 5 march, rally
6 parade **7** display **9** picketing
10 exhibition, exposition,
expression **12** illustration, presentation **13** manifestation

demonstrative 7 gushing **8** effusive **12** affectionate

demonstrativeness 9 gushi-

ness **12** effusiveness,
emotionalism

Demophon
father: **7** Theseus
mother: **7** Phaedra
brother: **6** Acamas
wife: **7** Phyllis

Demophoon
father: **6** Celeus
mother: **8** Metanira
nursed by: **7** Demeter

demoralize 8 dispirit **9** undermine **10** disconcert, discourage, dishearten **11** disorganize

**de mortuis nil nisi bonum
26** of the dead say nothing
but good

demos 5 plebs **6** masses
7 commons **8** populace
9 commoners

demote 4 bust **7** degrade

**Dempsey, Jack (William
Harrison)**
nickname: **13** Manassa
Mauler
sport: **6** boxing
class: **11** heavyweight

demur 5 qualm **6** object **7** protest, scruple **8** disagree **9** misgiving, objection
10 hesitation **11** compunction

demure 3 shy **4** prim **6** modest **7** bashful **8** reserved

demurrer 5 doubt, qualm
7 dissent, protest, scruple
8 objector, question, rebuttal
9 challenge, exception, misgiving, objection, protester,
protestor, stricture **11** compunction **12** remonstrance

den 4 lair **5** haunt, study
6 hotbed **7** hangout, library,
retreat, shelter **9** sanctuary

denial 7 refusal **9** disavowal,
disowning, rejection
10 disclaimer

denigrate 4 soil **5** abuse,
smear, sully **6** defame, dump
on, malign, revile, vilify **7** asperse, blacken, degrade, run
down, slander, traduce
8 backbite, badmouth, belittle,
besmirch, tear down **9** call
names, discredit, disparage,
downgrade **10** calumniate,
stigmatize

De Niro, Robert
born: **9** New York NY
roles: **10** Raging Bull (Oscar),
Taxi Driver **11** Mean
Streets **13** The Deer Hunter
14 New York New York,
The Godfather II **15** The
King of Comedy, True
Confessions **17** Bang the
Drum Slowly

denizen 7 dweller **8** resident
10 inhabitant

Denmark *see box*

Dennis, Patrick
author of: **10** Auntie Mame

Dennis, Sandy
real name: **16** Sandra Dale
Dennis
born: **10** Hastings NE
roles: **12** Any Wednesday
15 A Thousand Clowns
18 Up the Down Staircase
25 Who's Afraid of Virginia
Woolf?

Dennis the Hangman
character in: **12** Barnaby
Rudge
author: **7** Dickens

Dennis the Menace
creator: **11** Hank Ketcham
character: **9** Mrs Elkins
10 John Wilson **12** Eloise
Wilson, George Wilson,
Joey McDonald, Martha
Wilson **13** Alice Mitchell,
Henry Mitchell, Tommy An-
derson **14** Dennis Mitchell
dog: **4** Ruff
cast: **8** Gil Smith, Jay North
10 Billy Booth, Gale Gordon, Sara Seeger **11** Gloria
Henry, Irene Tedrow, Sylvia
Field **12** Joseph Kearns
15 Herbert Anderson

denomination 4 name, sect,
size **5** class, value **8** category,
grouping **10** persuasion
11 designation

denotation 4 mark, name,
sign **6** symbol **7** meaning
10 indication

denote 4 mark, mean, name
6 signal **7** signify **8** indicate

denouement 3 end **6** finale,
upshot **7** outcome **8** solution
10 conclusion **11** termination

denounce 6 accuse, vilify
7 censure, condemn **9** criticize

denouncement 7 censure
12 condemnation,
denunciation

de novo 4 anew **5** again
6 afresh **16** from the
beginning

dense 4 dull, dumb, slow
5 close, heavy, thick **6** stupid
7 compact, crowded, intense
8 ignorant **9** dimwitted
10 compressed **11** thickheaded **12** concentrated,
impenetrable

Densher, Merton
character in: **17** The Wings
of the Dove
author: **5** James

density 4 mass **6** weight

Denmark

other name: 17 Kongeriget Danmark

capital/largest city: 9 Kobenhavn **10** Copenhagen

others: 3 Hov **4** Hals, Koge, Nibe, Ribe, Soro **5** Arhus, Kosor, Vejle **6** Aarhus, Abenra, Alborg, Dorsor, Dragor, Nyberg, Odense, Skagen, Struer, Viborg **7** Aalborg, Esbjerg, Horsens, Kolding, Morsens, Randers **8** Ballerup, Elsinore, Gentofte, Glostrup, Hillerod, Naestred, Roskilde, Slagelse **9** Haderslev, Helsingor, Svendborg **10** Fredericia **13** Frederikshavn

school:
university institute of: **18** Theoretical Physics
folk high school: **14** folkehojskoler
continuation school: **11** efterskoler

division: 3 Fyn **7** Jutland, Lolland **9** Schleswig, Sjaelland

measure: 3 ell, fod, mil, pot **4** alen, favn, last, rode **5** album, anker, kande, linje, paegl, tomme **6** achtel, paegel, skeppe **7** landmil, oltonde, ortonde, skieppe, viertel **8** fjerding **9** ottingkar **10** korntonmde

monetary unit: 3 one, ora, ore **4** fyrk **5** krone **8** frederik, skilling **9** rigsdaler

weight: 2 es **3** lod, ort, vog **4** last, mark, pund, unze **5** carat, kvint, pound, quint, tonde **6** toende **7** centner, lispund, quintin **8** lispound, skippund **9** skibslast, skippound **10** bismerpund

island: 2 Oe **3** Als, Fyn, Mon, Rum, Thy **4** Aaro, Aero, Fano, Fohr, Moen, Mors, Romo **5** Baago, Faero, Faroe, Funen, Laeso, Samso, Sando **6** Amager, Sandoy, Sejero, Sudero **7** Faeroes, Falster, Hesselo, Laaland, Lolland, Seeland, Zealand **8** Bornholm, Eysturoy, Sudhuroy **9** Greenland, Langeland, Sjaelland **10** Vendsyssel

lake: 6 Arreso

hill: 12 Ejer Bavnehoj **14** Himmelbjaerget

highest point: 12 Yding Skovhoj

river: 3 Asa **4** Holm, Omme, Stor **5** Skive, Susaa, Varde **6** Gelsaa, Gudena, Vorgod **7** Gudenaa, Lilleaa, Lonborg

sea: 5 North **6** Baltic **7** Oresund **8** Atlantic, Kattegat **9** Skagerrak

physical feature:
fjord: **3** Ise **4** Isse **5** Lamme
inlet: **3** Ise **5** Fjord, Vejle **6** Nissum, Odense **7** Horsens, Logstor **8** Limfjord, Mariager
peninsula: **7** Jutland
strait: **7** Otesund **8** Kattegat **9** Skagerrak

people: 4 Dane, Jute **5** Angle **6** Cimbri, Eskimo, German, Ostmen, Teuton, Viking **12** Scandinavian
astronomer: **10** Tycho Brahe
author: **11** Isak Dinesen **21** Hans Christian Andersen
founder: **4** Axel **7** Absalon
king: **4** Hans, Knud **6** Canute **8** Frederik **9** Christian **10** Gorm the Old **15** Harold Bluetooth
philosopher: **11** Kierkegaard
physicist: **9** Niels Bohr
queen: **9** Margrethe **12** Thyra Danebod
sculptor: **11** Thorvaldsen
teacher: **4** Kold

language: 4 Odan **6** Danish, German **8** Faeroese **11** Greenlander

religion: 19 Evangelical Lutheran

place:
airport: **7** Kastrup
castle: **7** Egeskov **8** Kronborg **13** Frederiksborg
museum: **6** Rebild **9** Glyptotek **11** Thorvaldsen **15** Rosenborg Castle
park: **10** Langelinie **13** Tivoli Gardens
royal palace: **11** Amalienborg
statue: **13** Little Mermaid
stock exchange: **5** Borse **6** Borsen

feature:
dance: **6** sextur
drink: **5** glogg **7** aquavit

food:
beer: **6** Tuborg **9** Carlsberg
cheese: **3** Ost **4** Blue, Tybo **5** Esrom, Samso **6** Samsoe **7** Havarti, Mycella
meat patty: **11** frikadeller
pudding: **15** rodgrod med flode

7 opacity **8** dullness, solidity **9** stupidity, thickness **10** obtuseness, opaqueness **11** compactness

dent 3 pit **4** nick **6** hollow **10** depression **11** indentation

denude 4 bare **5** strip **6** divest **7** lay bare **8** unclothe

denuded 4 bare **5** naked **6** barren **8** stripped **9** unclothed, uncovered

denunciation 7 censure **12** condemnation, denouncement **13** attack against

Denver
   basketball team: 7 Nuggets
   football team: 4 Gold
      7 Broncos

deny 6 refuse, refute **7** disavow **8** disallow, disclaim **9** disaffirm **10** contradict

deny oneself 5 avoid, forgo **6** eschew, give up, refuse **7** abstain, forbear **8** renounce **9** sacrifice

deny responsibility 7 disavow

Deo gratias 13 thanks be to God

Deo volente 10 God willing

DePalma, Brian
   director of: 6 Carrie
      13 Dressed to Kill

depart 2 go **4** exit **5** leave **7** deviate, digress

departed 4 dead, gone, late, left, past, went **6** at rest, bygone **7** gone off **8** gone away **10** passed away **11** gone to glory **12** late-lamented **20** gone the way of all flesh

depart for 8 leave for **9** adjourn to, set off for, set out for **10** head toward, move toward

depart hastily 3 fly **4** flee **6** decamp, escape **7** abscond **9** skedaddle

department 4 unit **6** branch, bureau, sector **7** section **8** district, division, province

departure 4 exit **5** going **6** exodus **7** leaving **9** deviation **10** digression, divergence

depend 4 rely, rest **5** count, hinge **6** hang on

dependable 4 sure, true **5** loyal **6** steady, trusty **7** trusted **8** faithful, reliable **9** steadfast, unfailing **11** trustworthy

dependence 5 trust **8** reliance **10** confidence, dependency

dependency 10 dependence

dependent 7 reliant

depict 4 draw, limn **5** carve, chart, draft, paint **6** define, detail, map out, recite, record, relate, sculpt, sketch **7** diagram, narrate, picture, portray, recount **8** describe **9** chronicle, delineate, dramatize, represent, verbalize **10** illustrate **12** characterize

depiction 6 sketch **7** drawing, picture **8** portrait **9** picturing, portrayal **11** delineation **12** illustration **14** representation **16** characterization

deplete 5 drain, use up **6** lessen, reduce **7** consume, exhaust **8** decrease **10** impoverish

depleted 5 empty, spent, waste **6** barren, used up **7** drained, emptied, reduced, worn out **8** bankrupt, consumed, expended, lessened **9** exhausted, infertile **10** unfruitful

depletion 5 drain **7** using up **8** decrease **9** lessening, reduction **10** exhaustion **11** consumption

deplorable 5 awful **8** wretched **9** miserable **11** blameworthy **13** reprehensible **17** deserving reproach

deplore 5 mourn **6** bemoan, bewail, lament **7** censure, condemn **9** grieve for **12** disapprove of

deport 3 act **4** oust **5** carry, exile, expel **6** banish, behave **7** cast out **10** expatriate **14** conduct oneself

deported person 2 DP **5** exile **8** deportee **10** expatriate **14** banished person

deportment 7 conduct **8** behavior, demeanor **11** comportment

depose 4 oust **6** unseat **8** dethrone **16** remove from office

deposit 3 put **4** pile **5** place **7** put down, set down **8** sediment **10** accumulate **11** down payment, give in trust, installment **12** accumulation **14** partial payment

deposition 7 deposit **9** statement, testimony **11** declaration **12** accumulation

depository 4 bank, safe **5** vault **6** museum **7** library **8** archives **10** storehouse

depot 4 dump **8** terminal, terminus **10** bus station **15** railroad station **20** military storage place

depraved 4 vile **6** wicked **7** corrupt, debased **8** degraded **9** debauched, perverted **10** degenerate

depravity 8 vileness **9** decadence **10** corruption, debasement, debauchery, degeneracy, immorality, perversion, wickedness **11** degradation, dissolution

deprecate 7 condemn, protest **8** belittle, object to, play down **10** depreciate **15** take exception to

deprecated 7 defamed, put down **8** despised **9** belittled, derogated, disdained

deprecation 4 slur **5** abuse **7** protest, put-down **9** aspersion **10** aspersions, belittling, defamation, derogation **11** disapproval **12** condemnation **13** disparagement

deprecatory 8 critical **9** maligning, vilifying **10** belittling, defamatory, derogatory, slanderous **11** disparaging **12** disapproving

depreciate 5 scorn **7** run down **8** belittle, diminish **9** denigrate, disparage, downgrade, lose value **13** reduce in value, lower the value

depreciation 5 scorn **7** disdain **8** contempt **9** criticism, deflation **10** belittling, disrespect **11** devaluation **13** disparagement

depredation 4 sack **6** rapine, ravage **7** looting, pillage, plunder, robbery, sacking **8** spoiling **9** marauding **10** brigandage, ravishment, spoliation **11** desecration, devastation, freebooting, laying waste

depress 5 lower **6** deject, lessen, reduce, sadden, weaken **7** cut back **8** diminish, dispirit **9** press down **10** dishearten **14** lower in spirits

depressed 3 sad **4** blue **7** unhappy **8** dejected, downcast **10** despondent, dispirited, melancholy **11** low-spirited **12** disconsolate, inconsolable

depressing 3 sad **6** gloomy **8** lowering **9** dejecting, saddening **10** oppressing **11** casting down, dispiriting, melancholic, pushing down **12** discouraging, pressing down, weighing down **14** causing sadness

depression 5 gloom **6** dimple, hollow **7** sadness **9** dejection, recession **10** desolation, melancholy **11** despondency, indentation, melancholia

14 discouragement **15** down-heartedness, economic decline

deprive 5 strip **6** divest **8** take from **10** confiscate, dispossess

deprived 8 divested, stripped **11** handicapped **12** dispossessed, impoverished **13** disadvantaged **15** underprivileged

deprive of honor 5 abase, shame, sully **6** defame **7** blacken, tarnish **8** disgrace, dishonor **9** discredit **10** stigmatize

deprive of strength 6 hinder, weaken **7** disable, wear out **8** enervate, enfeeble, handicap **10** debilitate, devitalize

de profundis 13 from the depths

depth 6 timbre **8** deepness **10** profundity **19** downward measurement **24** perpendicular measurement

depths 4 deep **6** bowels **8** interior, recesses

deputation 9 committee **10** commission, delegation **15** representatives

deputize 6 assign **7** appoint **8** delegate **10** commission

deputy 4 aide **5** agent, envoy, proxy **6** second **8** delegate, emissary, minister **9** alternate, assistant, go-between, messenger, middleman, surrogate **10** ambassador, substitute **11** pinch hitter **12** spokesperson **14** representative **15** second-in-command

DeQuincey, Thomas
  author of: **19** The English Mail-Coach **31** On the Knocking at the Gate in Macbeth **32** Confessions of an English Opium-Eater

derail 3 bar **4** balk, foil **5** block, check, spike **6** hinder, impede, thwart **7** inhibit, prevent **8** obstruct **14** throw off course

deranged 5 crazy **6** insane **8** demented **10** irrational, unbalanced

derangement 6 lunacy **7** madness **8** insanity **9** craziness **11** peculiarity **13** irrationality, mental illness **14** mental disorder

Der Bingle
  nickname of: **10** Bing Crosby

Derek, Bo
  husband: **4** John
  roles: **3** Ten (10) **6** Bolero, Tarzan

derelict 3 bum **4** hobo

5 tramp **6** remiss **7** outcast, vagrant **8** careless, deserted **9** abandoned, negligent **10** delinquent, neglectful

dereliction 7 failure, neglect **9** disregard **10** negligence **11** delinquency **13** noncompliance, nonobservance

De rerum natura
  author: **9** Lucretius

deride 4 mock **5** scoff, scorn **7** sneer at **8** ridicule

de rigueur 11 fashionable **16** strictly required

derision 5 scorn **7** disdain, mockery **8** ridicule, sneering

derivation 5 stock **6** origin, source **7** descent, getting, lineage **8** ancestry, deriving, heritage **9** acquiring, etymology, parentage **10** background, beginnings, extraction **21** historical development

derive 4 gain **5** arise, enjoy, glean **6** obtain **7** descend **8** stem from **9** originate

dermaptera
  class: **8** hexapoda
  phylum: **10** arthropoda
  group: **6** earwig

dermatitis 4 rash **6** eczema **9** psoriasis **12** inflammation

Dern, Bruce
  born: **9** Chicago IL
  roles: **6** Marnie, Tattoo **10** Coming Home, Family Plot **11** Black Sunday **13** The Wild Angels **14** The Great Gatsby **22** The King of Marvin Gardens

dernier 4 last **5** final **8** ultimate

dernier cri 9 latest cry **10** latest word **13** latest fashion

derogate 4 blot **5** taint **6** smirch **8** disgrace **9** disparage

derogation 4 blot **5** odium, stain **7** blemish **8** contempt, disfavor, disgrace, ignominy **9** disesteem, disrepute **10** disrespect **11** humiliation **13** disparagement

derogatory 9 injurious **10** belittling **11** disparaging, unfavorable **12** unflattering **15** uncomplimentary

derrick 3 rig **5** crane, hoist, tower **9** framework
  kind: **3** oil **6** sheers **7** gin-pole
  part: **3** gin, leg **4** boom, mast **6** pulley **7** guy line

derring-do 6 daring **8** audacity, boldness **11** daredevilry **12** daredeviltry, recklessness **15** venturesomeness

dervish 5 fakir **6** Muslim **7** ascetic

De Sapientia Veterum
  author: **12** Francis Bacon

Descartes, Rene
  author of: **17** Discourse on Method
  field: **11** mathemathics
  nationality: **6** French
  developed: **18** analytical geometry
  quote: **13** Cogito ergo sum **18** I think therefore I am

descend 3 dip **4** drop, pass **5** slant, slope, swoop **6** go down, invade **7** incline **8** come down, inherited **11** come in force **12** be handed down, move downward

descendant 5 issue **7** progeny **9** offspring

descend upon 6 assail, attack, charge **7** assault, set upon **12** bear down upon

descent 4 drop, fall, raid **5** slant, slope **6** origin **7** assault, decline, lineage **8** ancestry **9** declivity, incursion **10** coming down **11** sneak attack, sudden visit

describe 4 draw **5** trace **6** depict, detail, recite, relate **7** explain, mark out, narrate, outline, portray, recount, speak of **9** delineate **10** illustrate **12** characterize

description 3 ilk **4** kind, sort, type **5** brand, class, genus **6** manner, nature **7** account, species, variety **9** depiction, narration, portrayal **12** illustration **16** characterization

descry 3 see **4** spot **6** behold, notice **7** discern, observe, pick out **8** discover **12** catch sight of

Desdemona
  character in: **7** Othello
  author: **11** Shakespeare

desecrate 6 defile **7** profane, violate **8** dishonor

desecration 8 dishonor **9** violation **10** defilement **11** profanation

desert 3 dry **4** arid, wild **5** leave, waste **6** barren **7** abandon, forsake **8** desolate, untilled **9** infertile, wasteland **10** arid region **11** run away from, uninhabited **12** uncultivated **16** barren wilderness

deserted 4 AWOL, left **5** empty **6** lonely, vacant **7** cast off, forlorn, reneged **8** defected, desolate, forsaken, marooned **9** abandoned, absconded **12** quit one's post **14** left in the lurch

desertedness 9 emptiness **10** desolation **13** uncrowdedness

Deserted Village, The
author: **15** Oliver Goldsmith

desertion 8 quitting **9** forsaking **11** abandonment **14** relinquishment

desertlike 3 dry **4** arid **5** sandy **6** barren **7** dried up, parched **9** waterless

deserts 3 due **5** worth **6** reward **7** payment

deserve 4 rate **5** merit **7** warrant **9** earn as due **10** be worthy of, qualify for **12** be entitled to **13** be deserving of

deserving 6 worthy **9** qualified

deserving reproach 8 blamable **10** deplorable, punishable, reprovable **11** blameworthy **12** reproachable **13** reprehensible

De Sica, Vittorio
director of: **15** The Bicycle Thief **27** The Garden of the Finzi-Continis

desiccate 5 dry up, parch **6** wither **7** shrivel **9** dehydrate

design 3 aim, end **4** draw, form, goal, plan, plot **5** draft, motif, set up **6** devise, intend, scheme, sketch, target **7** destine, diagram, drawing, fashion, outline, pattern, project, purpose **8** conceive, intrigue **9** blueprint, intention, objective **11** arrangement **14** draw up plans for

designate 4 call, name, term **5** elect, label **6** assign, choose, select **7** appoint, signify, specify **8** identify, indicate, nominate, pinpoint

designation 5 label **6** naming **10** delegation **11** appointment **13** specification **14** identification

designer 7 creator, deviser, planner **9** contriver **10** originator

designing 4 wily **6** artful, crafty **7** cunning **8** plotting, scheming **9** conniving

desirable 4 fine **8** in demand, pleasing **9** advisable **10** beneficial **11** worth having **12** advantageous

desire 4 need, urge, want, wish **5** crave **6** ask for, hunger, thirst **7** craving, longing, long for, request **8** yearning,

yearn for **9** hunger for, thirst for

Desire Under the Elms
author: **12** Eugene O'Neill
character: **4** Eben **5** Peter **6** Simeon **11** Abbie Putnam **12** Ephraim Cabot

desirous 4 avid, keen **5** eager **7** hopeful, longing, wishful **8** yearning

desist 4 stop **5** cease **6** lay off **7** suspend **8** leave off **11** discontinue, refrain from

Desk Set
director: **10** Walter Lang
cast: **8** Gig Young **11** Dina Merrill **12** Joan Blondell, Spencer Tracy **16** Katharine Hepburn

Desmontes
foster son: **4** Arne

desolate 3 sad **4** bare, ruin **5** bleak, empty **6** barren, grieve, ravage, sadden **7** depress, destroy, forlorn **8** dejected, demolish, deserted, distress, downcast, forsaken, lay waste, wretched **9** abandoned, depressed, devastate, miserable, sorrowful **10** despondent, discourage, dishearten, melancholy **11** downhearted, uninhabited

desolating 6 tragic **7** ruinous **8** dreadful, grievous, terrible **10** calamitous, horrendous **11** devastating **12** catastrophic

desolation 4 ruin **6** misery, sorrow **7** sadness **8** bareness, distress, solitude **9** bleakness, dejection, emptiness, seclusion **10** barrenness, depression, dreariness, loneliness, melancholy, wilderness **11** destruction, devastation, unhappiness **12** solitariness

despair 5 gloom, trial **6** burden, ordeal **9** lose heart **10** depression, have no hope **11** despondency, lose faith in **12** hopelessness **14** discouragement

despair of 5 doubt **8** give up on **10** have no hope

desperado 4 thug **5** rowdy **6** bandit, gunman, outlaw **7** brigand, convict, hoodlum, ruffian **8** criminal, fugitive, hooligan **9** terrorist **10** lawbreaker

desperate 4 dire, rash, wild **5** grave, great **6** daring, urgent **7** extreme, frantic, serious **8** critical, hopeless, reckless, wretched **9** dangerous, incurable **10** beyond hope, despairing, despondent

Desperate Hours, The
director: **12** William Wyler
cast: **8** Gig Young **11** Dewey Martin, Martha Scott **13** Arthur Kennedy, Frederic March **14** Humphrey Bogart

Desperately Seeking Susan
director: **14** Susan Seidelman
cast: **7** Madonna **15** Rosanna Arquette

desperation 7 despair **12** hopelessness, recklessness

despicable 4 base, mean, vile **10** detestable, outrageous **11** disgraceful **12** contemptible **13** reprehensible

despise 5 abhor, scorn **6** detest, loathe **7** contemn, disdain, dislike **10** look down on

Despoena
origin: **5** Greek
father: **8** Poseidon
mother: **7** Demeter
corresponds to: **10** Persephone

despoil 3 rob **4** loot **6** ravage **7** pillage, plunder

despoiler 6 looter, robber, vandal **7** brigand **8** pillager **9** plunderer

despondency 5 gloom **6** dismay **7** despair, sadness **9** dejection, pessimism **10** depression, desolation, low spirits, melancholy **11** melancholia **12** hopelessness **14** discouragement **15** downheartedness

despondent 3 low **4** blue, down **8** dejected, downcast, hopeless **9** depressed **11** discouraged, downhearted **12** disconsolate, disheartened

despot 6 tyrant **8** autocrat, dictator **9** oppressor

despotic 9 imperious **10** autocratic, tyrannical **11** dictatorial **13** authoritarian

despotism 7 tyranny **9** autocracy **10** absolutism

dessert 3 pie **4** cake, nuts, tart **5** fruit, sweet **8** ice cream **11** final course

destination 3 aim, end **4** goal, plan **6** object, target **7** purpose **8** ambition **9** objective **11** journey's end

destiny 3 lot **4** fate **5** karma, moira **6** future, kismet **7** fortune **9** necessity
goddess of: **5** Fates, Morae, Parca **6** Moerae, Moirai, Parcae

destitute 4 poor **5** broke, needy **6** busted **8** indigent **9** penniless **15** poverty-stricken

destitution 4 lack, want **6** penury **7** beggary, poverty **9** indigence, privation **11** extreme want **13** pennilessness **14** impoverishment

destroy 4 ruin **5** waste, wreck **6** ravage **8** demolish **9** devastate

destroy completely 3 end **7** abolish, wipe out **8** lay waste **9** eradicate, extirpate, liquidate **10** annihilate, obliterate **11** exterminate

destroyer 4 bane **6** blight, killer **7** gunboat, warship **10** affliction **11** annihilator

destruct 3 gut **4** raze, ruin **5** wreck **7** despoil, destroy, wipe out **8** decimate, demolish, desolate, pull down, tear down **9** devastate **10** lay in ruins

destruction 4 ruin **5** havoc **8** wreckage, wrecking **10** demolition **11** devastation

destructive 7 harmful, hurtful, ruinous **8** damaging **9** injurious **11** detrimental, devastating **15** not constructive

Destry Rides Again
  director: 14 George Marshall
  based on a story by: 8 Max Brand
  cast: 12 Brian Donlevy, James Stewart **15** Marlene Dietrich **16** Charles Winninger
  song: 35 See What the Boys in the Back Room Will Have

desultory 6 casual, chance, fitful, random **7** aimless, cursory **9** haphazard **10** without aim **11** unconnected

detach 5 sever **6** loosen **7** unhitch **8** separate, unfasten **9** disengage **10** disconnect **11** disentangle

detached 4 fair **5** aloof **7** distant, neutral, severed **8** reserved, unbiased **9** impartial, objective, separated, uncoupled, unhitched **10** disengaged, fair-minded, unfastened **11** indifferent, unconnected **12** disconnected, unprejudiced **13** disinterested, dispassionate
  French: 6 degage

detachment 4 unit **5** force **8** coolness, fairness, severing **9** aloofness, isolation, severance **10** cutting off, neutrality, separation **11** objectivity **12** impartiality, indifference **13** disconnection, disengagement, preoccupation **16** special task force

detail 4 fact, iota, item **6** as-

pect, relate **7** appoint, feature, itemize, recount, respect, specify **9** component, delineate, designate, enumerate **10** detachment, particular **11** special duty **13** assign to a task, particularize **14** special service **20** particular assignment

detailed 6 minute **8** itemized, thorough **10** item by item **12** point by point

detailed list 9 breakdown **11** itemization **14** categorization

detain 4 hold, slow, stop **5** delay **6** arrest, hinder, retard, slow up **7** confine **8** slow down **13** keep in custody

detainment 7 custody, holding **9** detention **11** confinement **12** imprisonment **13** incarceration

detect 3 see **4** espy, note, spot **5** catch **6** notice **7** observe, uncover **8** discover, perceive

detectable 10 noticeable **11** appreciable, discernible, perceivable, perceptible **13** ascertainable

detective 2 PI **6** shamus, sleuth **7** gumshoe **10** private eye **12** investigator **19** special investigator

detention 7 custody, holding **9** keeping in **10** detainment **11** confinement, holding back **12** imprisonment **13** incarceration

deter 4 stop **5** daunt **6** divert, hinder, impede **7** prevent **8** dissuade **10** discourage

deteriorate 3 ebb **4** fade, wane **5** decay, lapse **6** worsen **7** crumble, decline, fall off **10** degenerate **12** disintegrate

deteriorated 6 shabby **7** rickety **8** decaying, worsened **9** crumbling **10** broken-down, tumble-down **11** dilapidated, in disrepair **13** disintegrated

deterioration 5 decay, lapse **6** fading, waning **7** decline **9** crumbling, decadence, worsening **12** degeneration, dilapidation **14** disintegration

determination 4 grit **5** pluck, power, spunk **6** fixing **7** finding, resolve, verdict **8** boldness, decision, judgment, settling, solution, tenacity **9** reasoning, resolving **10** conclusion, resolution **11** determining, persistence **12** perseverance, resoluteness **13** act of deciding, steadfastness **16** stick-to-it-iveness

determine 5 learn **6** affect, decide, detect, settle **7** control, find out, resolve **8** conclude, discover, regulate **9** ascertain, establish, figure out, influence **15** come to a decision, give direction to

determined 7 dead set, decided, settled **8** found out, obdurate, resolute, stubborn **9** obstinate, tenacious **10** figured out, ascertained, established **15** come to a decision

deterrent 4 curb **5** check **9** hindrance, restraint **14** discouragement

detest 4 hate **5** abhor **6** loathe **10** despise **10** recoil from **16** dislike intensely

detestable 4 vile **6** odious **7** hateful **9** abhorrent, loathsome, obnoxious, offensive, repulsive, revolting **10** disgusting, unpleasant **12** disagreeable

detestation 4 hate **6** hatred **7** disgust, dislike **8** aversion, distaste, loathing **9** antipathy, repulsion, revulsion **10** abhorrence, repugnance

dethrone 4 oust **6** depose, unseat

detonate 4 fire **5** blast, burst, erupt, go off, shoot **6** blow up, ignite, report, set off **7** explode **8** touch off **9** discharge, fulminate

detonation 5 blast, burst **6** report **9** discharge, explosion

detour 5 skirt **6** bypass, byroad, divert **7** digress **9** deviation, diversion **10** digression

detract 5 lower **6** lessen, reduce **8** diminish **12** subtract from, take away from

detraction 4 flaw **11** shortcoming **12** disadvantage

detractor 5 enemy **6** critic **8** opponent **9** adversary, belittler, slanderer **10** antagonist, bad mouther, disparager

detriment 4 harm, loss **6** damage, injury **10** impairment **12** disadvantage

detrimental 7 adverse, harmful **8** damaging **9** injurious **10** pernicious **11** deleterious, destructive, unfavorable **15** disadvantageous

Detroit
  baseball team: 6 Tigers
  basketball team: 7 Pistons
  football team: 5 Lions
  hockey team: 8 Redwings

de trop 7 too many, too

much **8** in the way **9** not wanted

Deucalion
father: **10** Prometheus
mother: **7** Pronoia
wife: **6** Pyrrha
son: **6** Hellen
founded: **9** human race
after: **6** deluge

deus ex machina 15 god from a machine **18** improbable solution

Deus vobiscum 12 God be with you

Deus vult 8 God wills (it) cry of: **9** Crusaders

devaluate 6 lessen, reduce **7** deflate, degrade **10** depreciate

devaluation 4 drop **7** decline **12** depreciation

devalue 5 lower, taint **6** debase, defile, infect **7** cheapen, corrupt, degrade, pervert, pollute, revalue **8** mark down **9** devaluate, underrate, write down **10** adulterate, degenerate, demonetize, depreciate, remonetize **11** contaminate

devastate 4 ruin **5** level, spoil, waste, wreck **6** ravage **7** despoil, destroy **8** demolish, desolate, lay waste

devastating 7 ruinous **8** damaging **9** injurious **10** calamitous, disastrous **11** cataclysmic, destructive, detrimental **12** catastrophic

devastation 4 ruin **9** ruination **10** demolition **11** destruction

develop 4 grow **5** print, ripen **6** evolve, expand, finish, flower, mature, pick up, unfold **7** acquire, advance, amplify, augment, broaden, build up, convert, enlarge, improve, process, turn out **8** contract, energize **9** cultivate **10** come to have **11** come to light, elaborate on

development 5 event **6** growth, result **7** advance, history **8** progress **9** evolution

deviant 4 warp **5** shift **7** deviate, pervert **8** aberrant, abnormal **9** deflected, divergent

deviate 4 part, vary, veer **5** stray **6** depart, swerve, wander **8** go astray **9** sidetrack, turn aside

deviation 6 change **7** veering **8** rambling, straying **9** wandering **10** aberration, digression, divergence **11** abnormality, fluctuation

device 4 plan, plot, ploy, ruse, wile **5** angle, trick **6** design, gadget, scheme **7** gimmick **8** artifice, strategy **9** apparatus, invention, mechanism, stratagem **11** contraption, contrivance

devil, the Devil 3 guy **5** rogue, Satan, thing **6** Azazel, fellow, wretch **7** hellion, Lucifer, ruffian, serpent, villain **8** creature **9** Archfiend, Beelzebub, scoundrel **11** unfortunate **12** spirit of evil **13** mischief-maker **16** prince of darkness

Devil and Daniel Webster, The
author: **19** Stephen Vincent Benet
director: **15** William Dieterle
character: **5** Devil **7** Webster **9** Mr Scratch
cast: **10** James Craig **11** Anne Shirley **12** Edward Arnold, Walter Huston
score: **15** Bernard Herrmann
Oscar for: **5** score
also titled: **18** All That Money Can Buy

devilish 4 evil **6** wicked **7** demonic, heinous, impious, satanic, vicious **8** demoniac, fiendish **9** nefarious **10** demoniacal, diabolical, villainous

devil-may-care 4 bold, rash, wild **5** risky **6** daring, rakish **8** heedless, reckless **9** audacious, daredevil

devil's advocate
Latin: **16** advocatus diaboli

Devil's Advocate
author: **14** Taylor Caldwell

Devil's Disciple, The
author: **17** George Bernard Shaw

Devine, Andy
real name: **16** Jeremiah Schwartz
born: **11** Flagstaff AZ
roles: **7** Jingles **9** Andy's Gang **14** Wild Bill Hickok

devious 3 sly **4** wily **6** sneaky, tricky **7** crooked **9** deceitful, dishonest **11** treacherous **12** dishonorable **13** doubledealing

devise 4 plot **5** forge, frame **6** design, invent, map out **7** concoct, prepare, think up **8** block out, conceive, contrive **9** construct, formulate

deviser 6 author, framer **7** creator, planner **8** inventor **9** architect, contriver **10** originator

devitalize 4 kill **6** deaden, weaken **8** enervate **10** debilitate

devoid 5 empty **6** barren **7** lacking, wanting, without **8** bereft of **9** destitute **11** unblest with

devote 5 apply **6** direct **7** address, utilize **8** dedicate **10** consecrate, give over to **11** concentrate **15** give oneself up to **22** center one's attentions on

devoted 4 fond, true **5** loyal **6** ardent, loving **7** earnest, staunch, zealous **8** adhering, faithful **9** dedicated, steadfast **10** passionate, unwavering **17** strongly committed

devotedness 8 devotion **10** commitment, dedication **13** attentiveness **17** earnest attachment

devoted to luxury 9 sybaritic **10** hedonistic, voluptuous

devotee 3 fan **6** rooter **7** booster **8** adherent, advocate, champion, disciple, follower **10** aficionado, enthusiast **11** afficionado

devotion, devotions 4 love, zeal **5** ardor, piety **6** fealty, regard **7** loyalty **8** fondness, holiness **9** adherence, godliness, reverence **10** allegiance, commitment, concern for, dedication, devoutness, meditation **11** religiosity **12** faithfulness, spirituality **13** attentiveness, prayer service **15** religious fervor **17** earnest attachment **19** religious observance

De Voto, Bernard A
author of: **21** Across the Wide Missouri

devour 7 stuff in **8** bolt down, gobble up, gulp down, knock off, wolf down **9** go through **10** read widely **14** eat voraciously **15** absorb oneself in, consume greedily **16** read compulsively, take in ravenously **17** become engrossed in

devout 5 pious **6** ardent **7** earnest, fervent, intense, serious, zealous **8** orthodox, reverent **9** religious **10** passionate, worshipful

devoutness 5 piety **8** devotion, holiness **9** godliness, reverence **12** spirituality **15** religious fervor

DeVries, Hugo
field: **6** botany
nationality: **5** Dutch
researched: **8** heredity, mutation

DeVries, Peter
author of: **16** Consenting Adults **24** Slouching Toward Kalamazoo

dew 8 moisture 12 condensation 18 droplets of moisture

Dewar, James
field: 7 physics 9 chemistry
nationality: 8 Scottish
liquified: 8 hydrogen
solidified: 8 hydrogen
developed: 7 cordite
10 Dewar flask 12 liquid oxygen

Dewey, George
served in: 18 Spanish-American War
battle: 9 Manila Bay
destroyed: 12 Spanish fleet

Dewhurst, Colleen
husband: 12 George C Scott
born: 6 Canada 8 Montreal
roles: 12 The Nun's Story
18 Desire Under the Elms
22 A Moon for the Misbegotten

De Wilde, Brandon
born: 10 Brooklyn NY
roles: 3 Hud 5 Shane 11 All Fall Down

dewy 4 damp 5 moist 7 bedewed

Dexamenus
form: 7 centaur
king of: 6 Olenus

dexterity 8 deftness, facility 9 handiness 10 adroitness, nimbleness 11 manual skill, proficiency

dexterous 4 able, deft 5 agile, quick 6 active, adroit, gifted, nimble 8 skillful 9 efficient, ingenious 11 resourceful

Dhegiha
tribe: 5 Omaha

Dia
father: 7 Eioneus
husband: 5 Ixion
son: 9 Pirithous

diabolic, diabolical 4 evil, foul 6 wicked 7 baleful, demonic, heinous, impious, satanic, vicious 8 devilish, fiendish 9 monstrous, nefarious 10 malevolent, villainous

diadem 4 halo 5 crown 7 circlet, coronet 8 headband

diagnosis 5 study 8 analysis, scrutiny 11 examination 13 investigation, medical report 16 scientific report 22 conclusion from symptoms, specification of illness

diagonal line 4 bias 5 angle, slant

diagram 3 map 4 plan 5 chart 6 sketch 7 drawing, outline 9 breakdown 11 line drawing 12 illustration 14 representation 15 rough projection

dialect 5 argot, idiom, lingo 6 jargon, patois 8 localism 10 vernacular 11 regionalism 13 colloquialism, provincialism 15 language variety

Dial M for Murder
director: 15 Alfred Hitchcock
based on play by: 14 Frederick Knott
cast: 10 Grace Kelly, Ray Milland 14 Robert Cummings

dialogue, dialog 4 talk 5 lines 6 parley, speech 8 conclave 10 conference 12 conversation 14 verbal exchange 15 personal meeting 16 formal discussion

diamond
characteristic: 7 hardest
color: 4 blue, pink 9 blue-white 12 canary yellow
element: 6 carbon
famous: 4 Hope 6 Jonker 8 Cullinan, Idol's Eye, Kohi-Noor 9 Excelsior 12 Star of Africa 13 Star of the East 17 Star of Sierra Leone
quality: 3 cut 4 fire 5 color 7 clarity 10 brilliance
source: 5 Congo, India 6 Africa, Borneo, Brazil, Guyana 8 Tanzania 9 Australia, Venezuela 11 South Africa, Soviet Union 12 South America 15 South West Africa
weight: 5 carat, point

Diamond State
nickname of: 8 Delaware

Diana
origin: 5 Roman
goddess of: 4 moon 6 slaves 7 hunting
protectress of: 5 women
corresponds to: 6 Phoebe 7 Artemis
epithet: 10 Nemorensis
means: 10 of the grove

Diana of the Crossways
author: 14 George Meredith
character: 9 Mr Warwick 11 Diana Merion, Percy Dacier 12 Lady Dunstane 14 Thomas Redworth 15 Lord Dannisburgh

diaphanous 5 filmy, gauzy, lucid, sheer 6 flimsy, limpid 8 gossamer, pellucid 11 translucent, transparent

diary 3 log 7 daybook, journal 9 chronicle 12 daily journal 14 day-to-day record

Diary of Anne Frank, The
author: 9 Anne Frank
director: 13 George Stevens
cast: 6 Ed Wynn 9 Lou Jacobi 10 Diane Baker 13 Millie Perkins, Richard

Beymer 14 Shelley Winters (Mrs Van Daan) 17 Joseph Schildkraut (Father Frank)
Oscar for: 17 supporting actress (Winters)

Diasia
festival of: 4 Zeus

diatribe 6 tirade 9 contumely, invective 11 castigation 12 vituperation 13 stream of abuse 14 bitter harangue 18 accusatory language 19 violent denunciation

dice 4 chop, cube 5 bones, cubes, cut up, mince
singular: 3 die

Dice
also: 4 Dike
origin: 5 Greek
member of: 5 Horae
goddess of: 7 justice
father: 4 Zeus
mother: 6 Themis

Dick, Mr
character in: 16 David Copperfield
author: 7 Dickens

Dickens, Charles
author of: 9 Hard Times 10 Bleak House 11 Oliver Twist 12 Barnaby Rudge, Dombey and Son, Little Dorrit 14 Pickwick Papers 15 A Christmas Carol, Our Mutual Friend 16 A Tale of Two Cities, David Copperfield, Martin Chuzzlewit, Nicholas Nickleby 17 Great Expectations 19 The Old Curiosity Shop 22 The Mystery of Edwin Drood

dicker 4 deal 6 haggle, higgle, outbid 7 bargain, chaffer, quibble, wrangle 8 beat down, talk down, underbid 9 negotiate 17 drive a hard bargain

Dickey, James
author of: 9 The Zodiac 11 Deliverance 16 Strength of Fields 17 Buckdancer's Choice

Dickinson, Angie
real name: 13 Angeline Brown
husband: 13 Burt Bacharach
born: 6 Kulm ND
roles: 8 Rio Bravo 11 Police Woman 13 Dressed to Kill 19 The Sins of Rachel Cade

Dick Tracy
creator: 12 Chester Gould
character: 8 BO Plenty, Moonmaid 12 Gravel Gertie 13 Sparkle Plenty 16 Jeremiah Truehart
wife: 12 Tess Truehart
daughter: 11 Bonny Braids
assistant: 9 Pat Patton

protege: **6** Junior
villain: **5** Itchy **6** B-B Eyes
7 Flattop, Flyface, Measles, Mumbles, The Brow,
The Mole **8** The Blank
9 Pruneface, The Midget,
The Rodent
equipment: 16 two-way
wristradio

Dick Van Dyke Show, The
character: 9 Alan Brady, Rob
Petrie **11** Jerry Helper,
Laura Petrie, Sally Rogers
12 Buddy Sorrell, Melvin
Cooley, Millie Helper
13 Ritchie Petrie
cast: 9 Rose Marie **10** Carl
Reiner, Jerry Paris **13** Larry
Matthews, Richard Deacon
14 Mary Tyler Moore,
Morey Amsterdam **17** Ann
Morgan Guilbert

dictate 4 rule **5** edict, order
6 decree, dictum, direct, enjoin, impose, ordain, ruling,
urging **7** bidding, counsel, lay
down, mandate **8** set forth
9 determine, ordinance, prescribe, prompting, pronounce,
stricture **11** exhortation, inclination, requirement

dictator 4 czar, duce **6** caesar,
despot, fuhrer, kaiser, tyrant
7 emperor **8** autocrat **13** absolute ruler
Argentinian: 5 Peron
German: 6 Hitler
Italian: 9 Mussolini
Russian: 5 Lenin **6** Stalin
Spanish: 6 Franco

dictatorial 6 lordly **7** haughty,
willful **8** absolute, arrogant,
despotic **9** arbitrary, imperious,
unlimited **10** autocratic, peremptory, tyrannical **11** categorical, domineering,
magisterial, overbearing
12 supercilious, unrestricted
13 authoritative **17** inclined to
command

diction 7 wording **8** delivery,
rhetoric, verbiage **9** elocution
10 intonation, use of idiom,
vocabulary **11** enunciation,
phraseology, verbal style
12 articulation **13** choice of
words, pronunciation **16** turn
of expression **17** command of
language **18** manner of
expression

dictum 3 saw **4** fiat **5** adage,
axiom, edict, maxim, order
6 decree, saying, truism **7** dictate, precept, proverb **11** commandment **13** pronouncement
15 dogmatic bidding **22** authoritative statement

Dictynna
origin: 6 Cretan
goddess of: 3 sea

corresponds to:
11 Britomartis

Dictys
occupation: 9 fisherman
found: 5 chest
containing: **5** Danae
7 Perseus

didactic 7 donnish, preachy
8 academic, edifying, pedantic,
tutorial **9** doctrinal, homiletic,
pedagogic **10** expository, moralizing **11** educational, instructive, lecturelike, overbearing
12 prescriptive **17** inclined to
lecture

didactics 8 teaching **9** education, teachings **10** pedagogics
11 instruction

Diderot, Denis
author of: 12 Encyclopedia
13 Rameau's Nephew

Didion, Joan
author of: 8 Salvador
10 White Album **14** Play It
as It Lays **19** A Book of
Common Prayer **24** Slouching Toward Bethlehem

Dido
queen of: 8 Carthage
father: 5 Mutto
brother: 9 Pygmalion
sister: 4 Anna
husband: 8 Sychaeus
lover: 6 Aeneas
corresponds to: 6 Elissa

Dido and Aeneas
opera by: 7 Purcell
character: 4 Dido (Queen of
Carthage) **6** Aeneas

Didymaea
festival of: 4 Zeus **6** Apollo

Didymus *see* **6** Thomas

die 3 ebb, rot **4** ache, fade, fail,
long, pass, stop, wane **5** croak,
yearn **6** depart, expire, go flat,
pass on, perish, recede, run
out, wither **7** be eager, decline, die away, go stale, run
down, subside **8** fade away,
melt away, pass away, pass
over, wear away **9** be anxious,
break down, lose force, lose
power, meet death **10** degenerate, want keenly **11** come to
an end, suffer death **12** wish
ardently **13** come to one's
end, desire greatly, go to
one's glory, kick the bucket
14 leave this world, pine with
desire, become inactive
15 slowly disappear **I7** become
inoperative
plural: 4 dice

die away 4 fade **5** abate,
cease **8** diminish

die down 5 abate **7** subside
8 diminish, slack off

die out 6 vanish **9** cease to be,
disappear **13** become extinct

Diesel, Rudolf
field: 11 engineering
invented: 12 Diesel engine

diet 5 board, synod **7** edibles,
nurture **8** congress, victuals
9 nutriment, nutrition **10** assemblage, convention, parliament, provisions, sustenance
11 comestibles, convocation,
legislature, nourishment, subsistence **12** eating habits, eat
sparingly **13** eating regimen,
lawmaking body **14** eat judiciously **15** eat abstemiously,
eat restrictedly, general assembly **16** limitation of fare, regulate one's food **17** bicameral
assembly **18** nutritional regimen, representative body, restrict one's intake

Dietrich, Marlene
real name: 22 Maria Magdalene Dietrich
born: 7 Germany
roles: 8 Lola Lola **11** Blonde
Venus **12** The Blue Angel
15 Rancho Notorious
16 Destry Rides Again, The
Garden of Allah **17** The
Scarlet Empress **24** Witness
for the Prosecution

Dietrich von Bern
origin: 8 Germanic
king of: 10 Ostrogoths
Latin name: 9 Theodoric

Diety 3 Bel, God **4** Baal **6** Marduk, Molech, Moloch, Yahweh **7** Chemosh, Jehovah
10 Anammelech
11 Adrammelech

Dieu et mon droit 13 God
and my right
motto of: 18 royal arms of
England

differ 5 demur **7** dispute, dissent **8** be unlike, contrast, disagree **9** take issue **10** be
distinct, depart from, stand
apart **11** be disparate, deviate
from, diverge from **12** be at
variance, be dissimilar, stand
opposed

difference 4 spat **5** clash, setto **7** dispute, quarrel **8** argument, contrast, squabble **9** deviation, disparity, variation
10 divergence, falling out, unlikeness **11** contrariety, contretemps, discrepancy,
distinction **12** disagreement
13 contradiction, dissimilarity,
dissimilitude **17** contradistinction, lack of resemblance

different 4 rare **6** divers, sundry, unique, unlike **7** bizarre,
diverse, foreign, several,
strange, unusual, various

8 aberrant, atypical, distinct, manifold, not alike, peculiar, separate, singular, uncommon **9** anomalous, disparate, divergent, other than, unrelated **10** dissimilar, individual, variegated **11** contrasting, distinctive, diversified, not ordinary **12** not identical **13** miscellaneous **14** unconventional

differential 8 contrast **11** distinction

differentiate 6 set off **8** contrast, separate, set apart **11** distinguish, draw the line **12** discriminate **13** make different

differentiation 8 contrast **10** comparison, separation **11** discernment, distinction

differing 6 unlike **7** variant **8** distinct, opposing **9** deviating, disparate, dissident, divergent **10** dissenting, dissimilar **11** contrasting, disagreeing

difficult 4 grim, hard **5** hairy, rough, tough **6** knotty, thorny, trying, unruly, uphill **7** arduous, complex, forward, not easy, onerous, tedious, willful **8** critical, exacting, perverse, stubborn, ticklish, toilsome **9** demanding, enigmatic, fractious, Herculean, intricate, laborious, obstinate, Sisyphean, strenuous, wearisome **10** burdensome, exhausting, fastidious, formidable, inflexible, perplexing, unyielding **11** bewildering, complicated, hard to solve, intractable, troublesome **12** hard to manage, hard to please, obstreperous, rambunctious, recalcitrant, unmanageable **13** hard to satisfy, problematical, unpredictable **14** hard to deal with **15** unaccommodating

difficulty 3 jam **4** mess, snag **5** trial **6** crisis, muddle, pickle, puzzle **7** barrier, dilemma, problem, straits, trouble **8** hot water, obstacle, quandary, tough job **9** deep water, hindrance, intricacy **10** impediment, perplexity, rough going, uphill work **11** arduousness, obstruction, predicament **12** hard sledding **13** laboriousness **14** stumbling block **15** troublesomeness **17** critical situation

diffidence 7 reserve, shyness **8** meekness, timidity **9** hesitancy, timidness **10** constraint, humbleness, insecurity, reluctance **11** bashfulness **12** introversion, sheepishness, timorousness **14** extreme modesty **15** unassertiveness **19** lack

of self-assurance, retiring disposition

diffident 3 shy **6** modest **7** anxious, bashful **8** doubtful, hesitant, reserved, reticent, retiring **11** distrustful, unassertive **12** apprehensive

diffuse 5 wordy **7** verbose **8** rambling **9** desultory, dispersed, scattered, spread out, wandering **10** digressive, discursive, disjointed, long-winded, maundering, meandering, roundabout **14** circumlocutory, extended widely, unconcentrated, vaguely defined **15** not concentrated **18** lacking conciseness

diffuseness 8 rambling **9** prolixity, verbosity, wandering, wordiness **10** dispersion **11** indirection **14** circumlocution, long-windedness

diffusion 6 spread **8** rambling, verbiage **9** dispersal, prolixity, verbosity, wordiness **10** maundering, scattering **11** indirection, profuseness **14** circumlocution, discursiveness, disjointedness, roundaboutness

dig 3 jab **4** gibe, jeer, poke, prod, slur **5** aside, drive, gouge, punch, taunt **6** exhume, thrust **7** put-down, salvage, unearth **8** disinter, excavate, pinpoint, retrieve, scoop out **9** extricate, find among, hollow out **10** come up with, excavation, wry comment **11** bring to view **12** verbal thrust **13** cutting remark, search and find

digest 3 dig **5** grasp **6** absorb, fathom, precis, resume **7** realize, summary **8** abstract, dissolve, synopsis **10** abridgment, appreciate, assimilate, comprehend, understand **12** condensation, take in wholly **14** take in mentally

digestive system
component: **5** liver, mouth, teeth **6** tongue **7** stomach **8** appendix, pancreas **9** esophagus, intestine **11** gall bladder **13** salivary gland

dig in 4 root **5** embed, imbed, plant **6** anchor **7** pitch in **8** entrench, go to work **10** begin to eat **12** apply oneself

digit 3 one, six, two, toe **4** five, four, nine, unit, zero **5** light, seven, three **6** cipher, figure, finger, number **7** integer, numeral

dignified 5 proud **6** august, proper **7** upright **8** decorous, reserved **9** honorable **10** upstanding **11** circumspect **13** distinguished **14** self-respecting

dignify 5 raise **6** uplift **7** elevate, inflate, promote

dignitary 3 VIP **7** notable **8** luminary **9** personage **12** person of note

dignity 5 honor **7** decorum, majesty, station **9** loftiness, solemnity **10** augustness, importance **11** comportment, stateliness **12** high position, lofty bearing **13** proud demeanor **14** self-possession

digress 5 stray **6** back up, wander **7** deviate **8** divagate **9** turn aside **15** go off on a tangent **17** depart from subject

digression 6 detour **8** straying **9** departure, deviation, diversion, wandering **10** divagation, divergence, side remark **12** obiter dictum

digressive 7 diffuse **9** wandering **10** disjointed, maundering, roundabout **11** off the point **14** circumlocutory

dig up 6 locate **7** find out, root out, uncover, unearth **8** discover **9** ferret out **12** bring to light

dike 4 bank **5** levee, ridge **10** embankment

Dike *see* **4** Dice

dikerion 11 candelabrum, candlestick **12** candleholder

dilapidated 4 shot **6** beat-up, ruined, shabby **7** rickety, rundown, worn-out **8** battered, decaying, decrepit **10** broken-down, ramshackle, tumble-down **11** in disrepair **12** deteriorated, falling apart **15** falling to pieces

dilate 5 swell, widen **6** expand, extend **7** broaden, distend, enlarge, inflate, puff out **9** make wider

dilation 8 swelling, widening **9** expansion **10** broadening, distension, distention

dilatory 4 lazy, slow **5** tardy **6** remiss **8** dawdling, indolent, slothful, sluggish **9** negligent, reluctant **10** phlegmatic **13** lackadaisical **15** inclined to delay, procrastinating

dilemma 4 bind **6** crunch, plight **7** impasse, problem **8** deadlock, quandary **9** stalemate **11** predicament **13** Hobson's choice **15** difficult choice

dilettante 7 amateur, dabbler, trifler 12 experimenter 16 cultured hobbyist

diligence 4 zeal 8 industry 10 commitment, dedication 11 persistence 12 perseverance

diligent 6 active 7 careful, earnest, patient, zealous 8 plodding, sedulous, studious, thorough, untiring 9 assiduous, concerted 10 persistent 11 hardworking, industrious, painstaking, persevering 12 pertinacious 15 well-intentioned

dill
   botanical name: 17 Anethum graveolens
   origin: 9 Asia Minor 13 Mediterranean
   family: 7 parsley
   guards against: 7 Evil Eye 10 witchcraft
   use: 6 sauces 7 pickles 10 vegetables

Dillon, Matt
   roles: 3 Tex 10 Rumblefish 12 The Outsiders

dillydally 3 lag 4 idle, loaf 5 dally, delay 6 dawdle, loiter 8 kill time 9 waste time 10 fool around 13 procrastinate

Dilsey
   character in: 18 The Sound and the Fury
   author: 8 Faulkner

dilute 4 thin, weak 6 reduce, temper, watery, weaken 7 diffuse, diluted, thin out 8 decrease, diminish, make weak, mitigate, weakened 9 attenuate, liquidify, water down 10 add water to, adulterate, thinned out 11 adulterated, make thinner, watered down

diluted 4 weak 6 dilute, watery 8 weakened 10 thinned out 11 adulterated, watered down

dilution 8 thinning 9 weakening 12 watering down

dim 3 low 4 hazy, soft, weak 5 dusky, faint, foggy, murky, muted, vague 6 blurry, feeble, gloomy, remote 7 blurred, clouded, muffled, shadowy 8 darkened, nebulous, obscured 9 not bright, tenebrous 10 adumbrated, ill-defined, indefinite, indistinct, intangible 13 unilluminated

DiMaggio, Joe
   nickname: 9 Joltin Joe
   sport: 8 baseball
   position: 8 outfield
   team: 14 New York Yankees
   wife: 13 Marilyn Monroe

dime-a-dozen 6 common 7 humdrum 8 ordinary, workaday 9 plentiful 10 ubiquitous 11 commonplace 12 easy to come by 13 garden-variety 15 undistinguished

dimension, dimensions 4 bulk, mass, size 5 range, scope, width 6 extent, height, length, volume, weight 7 measure 9 amplitude, greatness, magnitude, thickness 10 importance, proportion 11 massiveness 12 measurements 14 physical extent

diminish 3 ebb 4 wane 5 abate, lower 6 lessen, narrow, reduce, shrink 7 decline, dwindle, fall off, shorten, shrivel, subside 8 decrease, peter out 9 be reduced 11 make smaller 13 become smaller

diminuendo
   music: 22 gradually getting softer
      abbreviation: 3 dim

diminution 6 ebbing, waning 7 decline 8 decrease, lowering 9 dwindling, lessening, reduction, shrinkage 10 falling off, shortening, shriveling, subsidence 11 petering out, slacking off

diminutive 3 wee 4 tiny 5 elfin, short, small, teeny 6 little, minute, petite, slight 7 pet name, stunted 8 dwarfish, half-pint, nickname 9 miniature, short form 10 pocket-size, undersized, vest-pocket 11 lilliputian, small-scale, unimportant 13 insignificant 14 inconsiderable

Dimmesdale, Arthur
   character in: 16 The Scarlet Letter
   author: 9 Hawthorne

dimness 4 dusk 5 gloom, shade 8 darkness 14 indistinctness

dimwit 4 fool 5 dummy, dunce, idiot, moron 6 cretin, nitwit 7 dingbat, dullard, dumbell, pinhead 8 dumbbell, dummkopf, imbecile, meathead, numskull 9 birdbrain, blockhead, ding-a-ling, lamebrain, numbskull, simpleton 11 chowderhead, knucklehead

dim-witted 4 dull, dumb 5 dense 6 stupid 7 foolish, idiotic, moronic, witless 8 retarded 9 cretinous, imbecilic

din 4 stir, to-do 5 bruit 6 babble, clamor, hubbub, racket, ruckus, tumult, uproar 7 clangor 9 commotion 10 clattering, hullabaloo

Dinah
   father: 5 Jacob
   mother: 4 Leah
   brother: 3 Dan, Gad 4 Levi 5 Asher, Judah 6 Joseph, Reuben, Simeon 7 Zebulun 8 Benjamin, Issachar, Naphtali
   violated by: 7 Shechem

Dindymene see 6 Cybele

dine 3 eat, sup 4 feed 5 feast, lunch 6 fall to, supper 7 banquet, partake 9 breakfast, eat dinner 10 break bread, gluttonize, have dinner 11 gourmandize 14 take sustenance

Dine see 6 Navajo

Dinesen, Isak
   real name: 18 Karen Blixen-Finecke
   author of: 9 Last Tales 11 Out of Africa 12 Winter's Tales 16 Seven Gothic Tales

dinghy 5 skiff 7 rowboat 8 sailboat 9 small boat

dingy 4 dull 5 dusty, grimy, murky, tacky 6 dismal, dreary, gloomy, shabby 12 dirty and drab

dining room
   French: 12 salle a manger

dinner 4 food, meal 5 beano, feast 6 repast, supper 7 banquet
   French: 8 dejeuner 10 table d'hote

Dinner at Eight
   director: 11 George Cukor
   author: 10 Edna Ferber 14 George S Kaufman
   cast: 8 Lee Tracy 10 Jean Harlow 11 Billie Burke 12 Wallace Beery 13 John Barrymore, Marie Dressler 15 Lionel Barrymore

dinosaur *see box*

dint 4 push, will 5 drive, force, labor, might, power 6 charge, effort, energy, strain, stress 8 endeavor, exertion, strength, struggle 10 insistence 12 forcefulness 13 determination 14 relentlessness

diocese 3 see 7 eparchy 9 bishopric 14 church district
   jurisdiction of: 6 bishop

Diomedes
   king of: 6 Thrace
   father: 4 Ares 6 Tydeus
   mother: 6 Cyrene 7 Deipyle
   member of: 7 Epigoni
   kept: 9 wild mares
   fed mares on: 10 human flesh
   death planned by: 8 Hercules

dinosaur
  means: 14 fearfully great, terrible lizard
  subclass: 11 Archosauria
  characteristic: 7 diapsid **14** teeth in sockets, two-arched skull **18** three-element pelvis
  group: 11 Saurischian **13** Ornithischian
    flesh-eating biped: **8** therapod
    plant-eating quadruped: **8** sauropod
    plant-eating biped: **10** ornithopod
    armored: **10** ceratopsid
  of Africa: 9 Iguanodon **13** Brachiosaurus **17** Heterodontosaurus
  of Asia: 13 Hypselosaurus, Protoceratops
  of Europe: 9 Iguanodon **12** Plateosaurus **13** Compsognathus, Hypselosaurus, Hypsilophodon
  of North America: 10 Diplodocus, Edmontonia, Nodosaurus **11** Anatosaurus, Anchisaurus, Gorgosaurus, Monoclonius, Saurolophus, Scolosaurus, Stegosaurus, Triceratops **12** Ankylosaurus, Camarasaurus, Camptosaurus, Coelophysics, Lambeosaurus, Paleoscincus **13** Brachiosaurus, Styracosaurus, Tyrannosaurus **14** Thescelosaurus **15** Parasaurolophus, Procheneosaurus
  of South America: 12 Pisanosaurus
  fictional: 6 Barney **12** Jurassic Park

Dione
  consort of: 4 Zeus

Dionysia
  festival of: 8 Dionysus

Dionysus *see* **7** Bacchus

Diores
  father: 10 Amarynceus
  fought against: 7 Trojans

Dioscuri *see* **15** Castor and Pollux

dip 4 bail, dish, dunk, sink, skim, soak **5** droop, ladle, scoop, slope, spoon **6** dabble, dish up, peruse, shovel **7** decline, descend, dish out, run over **8** drop down, glance at, submerge, turn down **13** study slightly **14** immerse briefly, lift by scooping, try tentatively **15** incline downward

dip into 4 scan, skim **5** ladle **6** browse, peruse **7** deplete **8** look over **13** glance through, make inroads in

Diplodocus
  type: 8 dinosaur, sauropod
  period: 8 Jurassic
  location: 12 North America

diplomacy 4 tact **5** craft, skill **7** finesse **8** delicacy, prudence, subtlety **10** artfulness, discretion **11** maneuvering, savoir-faire **13** statesmanship **14** foreign affairs **16** artful management **18** foreign negotiation **21** international politics

diplomat 5 envoy **6** consul **7** attache **8** emissary, minister **9** statesman **10** ambassador, negotiator **12** interlocutor **13** tactful person

acceptable: 12 persona grata
unacceptable: 15 persona non grata

diplomatic 5 adept, suave **6** artful, urbane **7** attuned, politic, prudent, tactful **8** discreet **9** sensitive, strategic **13** ambassadorial **14** foreign-service **15** state-department

Dipolia
  festival of: 4 Zeus
  location: 6 Athens
  slaughter of: 2 ox

Dipper
  nickname of: 15 Wilt Chamberlain

Dipsas
  form: 7 serpent

dipsomaniac 3 sot **4** lush, soak, wino **5** drunk, rummy, souse, toper **6** barfly, boozer **7** tippler **8** drunkard **9** alcoholic, inebriate

diptera
  class: 8 hexapoda
  phylum: 10 arthropoda
  group: 7 true fly

Dirae *see* **6** Furies

dire 4 grim **5** awful, grave **6** dismal, urgent, woeful **7** crucial, extreme, fearful, ominous, ruinous **8** critical, dreadful, horrible, terrible **9** appalling, desperate, harrowing, ill-boding, ill-omened **10** calamitous, disastrous, portentous **11** apocalyptic, cataclysmic **12** catastrophic, inauspicious

direct 3 aim **4** head, lead, urge **5** blunt, clear, focus, frank, guide, order, pilot, usher **6** advise, candid, charge, enjoin, handle, head-on, honest, manage **7** address, command, conduct, control, earmark, forward, level at, oversee, pointed, sincere, train at **8** explicit, indicate, instruct, navigate, personal **9** conduct to, designate, firsthand, intend for, supervise **10** administer, face-to-face, forthright, point-blank, show the way, unmediated **11** plain-spoken, point the way, point toward, preside over, superintend **15** straightforward

direction 3 aim, way **4** bent, care, path **5** drift, order, route, track, trend **6** charge, course, recipe **7** bearing, command, control, current **8** guidance, headship, tendency **9** alignment **10** guidelines, leadership, management, regulation **11** inclination, instruction, line of march, supervision **12** line of action, prescription, surveillance **13** line of thought **14** administration, point of compass **15** superintendence

directive 5 ukase **8** bulletin **9** statement **10** communique **11** declaration **12** instructions, proclamation **13** communication

directly 4 soon **6** at once, openly **7** exactly, frankly **8** candidly, honestly, in person, promptly, straight **9** forthwith, precisely, presently, right away **10** face-to-face, in a beeline, personally **11** immediately, momentarily **12** in plain terms, not obliquely, unswervingly **13** unambiguously, unequivocally **14** as the crow flies **15** in a straight line **16** as soon as possible **17** on a straight course, straightforwardly

directness 6 candor **9** bluntness, frankness **10** candidness **14** forthrightness **19** straightforwardness

direct opposite 7 reverse **8** converse **10** antithesis

director 4 boss, head **5** chief **6** leader, master **7** curator, foreman, manager **8** chairman, governor, overseer **9** commander, conductor, organizer **10** controller, supervisor **13** administrator **14** superintendent

dirge 6 lament **7** requiem **8** threnody **9** death song **10** burial hymn, death march **11** funeral song **13** mournful sound **19** mournful composition

dirigo 7 I direct
motto of: **5** Maine

dirk 3 sny **4** snee, stab **5** knife, skean **6** dagger, skiver **7** poniard
origin: **8** Scotland

Dirks, Rudolph
creator/artist of: **12** Hans and Fritz **17** Captain and the Kids **19** The Katzenjammer Kids

dirt 3 mud **4** dust, loam, mire, muck, scum, slop, smut, soil, soot **5** dross, earth, filth, grime, humus, offal, rumor, slime, trash **6** gossip, ground, refuse, sludge, smudge **7** garbage, rubbish, scandal, slander **8** impurity, leavings, vileness **9** excrement, indecency, obscenity, profanity, sweepings **10** foul matter, moral filth, scurrility **11** pornography, scuttlebutt, squalidness **12** scabrousness **13** salaciousness **14** defamatory talk **15** filthy substance, unclean language **17** sensational expose

dirt-cheap 6 a steal **7** bargain **11** inexpensive **14** very reasonable **15** bargain-basement

dirty 4 base, foul, hard, lewd, mean, soil, spot, vile **5** grimy, messy, muddy, nasty, smear, stain, sully **6** coarse, filthy, grubby, mess up, muck up, risque, rotten, shabby, slop up, smudge, smudgy, smutty, soiled, sordid, untidy, vulgar **7** begrime, besmear, blacken, corrupt, crooked, devious, illegal, illicit, immoral, low-down, muddied, obscene, pollute, squalid, sullied, tarnish, unclean **8** befouled, begrimed, indecent, off-color, polluted, prurient, scabrous, unwashed **9** besmeared, deceitful, difficult, dishonest, tarnished, unsterile **10** despicable, fraudulent, licentious, perfidious, unpleasant, villainous **11** distasteful, treacherous **12** contemptible, disagreeable, dishonorable, pornographic, unscrupulous **14** morally unclean

Dirty Dozen, The
director: **13** Robert Aldrich
cast: **8** Jim Brown **9** Lee Marvin **10** Robert Ryan, Trini Lopez **11** Clint Walker **13** George Kennedy **14** Charles Bronson, Ernest Borgnine, John Cassavetes, Richard Jaeckel **16** Donald Sutherland

Dis
also: **8** Dis Pater
means: **5** Hades
god of: **10** underworld
corresponds to: **5** Orcus, Pluto

disability 5 minus **6** defect **8** handicap, weakness **9** infirmity, unfitness **10** affliction, impairment, impediment, inadequacy **11** shortcoming **12** debilitation, disadvantage **16** disqualification

disable 6 damage, hinder, impair, weaken **7** cripple **8** handicap **12** incapacitate

disabled
French: **12** hors de combat

disabuse 8 set right **9** relieve of **10** disenchant **11** disillusion, set straight

disaccord 7 discord **10** disharmony **12** disagreement **15** incompatibility

disacknowledge 4 deny **6** disown **7** disavow **8** disallow, disclaim **9** repudiate

disadvantage 4 flaw **6** burden **7** trouble **8** drawback, handicap, hardship, nuisance, weakness **9** detriment, hindrance, in arrears, weak point **10** impediment **12** weak position **13** inconvenience **16** fly in the ointment

disadvantaged 8 deprived, emergent, emerging, troubled **10** struggling **11** handicapped **12** impoverished **14** underdeveloped **15** underprivileged

disadvantageous 7 harmful **9** injurious **11** detrimental, inadvisable, inexpedient, undesirable, unfavorable, unfortunate

disaffect 4 wean **8** alienate, estrange **10** drive apart

disaffected 5 upset **7** hostile **8** agitated, inimical **9** alienated, disturbed, estranged, withdrawn **10** unfriendly **11** belligerent, discomposed, disgruntled, quarrelsome **12** antipathetic, discontented, dissatisfied **14** irreconcilable

disaffection 7 dislike **8** aversion, distaste **9** antipathy **10** alienation, discontent, disloyalty **12** estrangement

disaffirm 4 deny **5** annul **6** disown **7** decline, disavow **8** abnegate, disclaim, forswear, renounce **9** repudiate **15** wash one's hands of

disaffirmation 6 denial **9** annulment, disavowal **10** abnegation, disclaimer

11 repudiation **12** renunciation **13** contradiction

disagree 4 vary **5** clash, upset **6** depart, differ **7** deviate, diverge, make ill **8** be unlike, conflict, distress **9** discomfit **10** disconcert, stand apart **11** be injurious, fail to agree, not coincide **12** be at variance, be discordant, be dissimilar **13** cause problems **14** be unreconciled **15** be at loggerheads, differ in opinion **16** oppose one another, think differently

disagreeable 5 cross, harsh, nasty, surly, testy **7** grating, grouchy, peevish **8** churlish, petulant **9** difficult, irascible, irritable, obnoxious, offensive, repellent, repugnant, repulsive, unamiable, unwelcome **10** disgusting, ill-natured, uninviting, unpleasant **11** acrimonious, bad-tempered, displeasing, distasteful, ill-tempered, uncongenial, unpalatable **13** uncomfortable

disagreeing 6 at odds **7** deviant, varying **8** clashing **9** deviating, differing, disputing **10** quarreling **11** conflicting **13** at loggerheads

disagreement 5 clash, fight **7** discord, dispute, quarrel **8** argument, squabble, variance **9** deviation, disaccord, disparity, diversity **10** difference, divergence, falling-out, unlikeness **11** discrepancy, incongruity **13** dissimilarity, dissimilitude, lack of harmony **15** incompatibility **16** misunderstanding

disallow 4 deny, veto **6** abjure, forbid, refuse, reject **8** prohibit **9** repudiate

disallowance 4 veto **6** denial **7** refusal **9** rejection **11** prohibition, repudiation

disallowed 6 vetoed **7** abjured, refused **8** rejected **9** forbidden **10** repudiated **12** inadmissible, unacceptable

disappear 2 go **3** end **4** exit, fade, flee **5** leave **6** be gone, depart, die out, retire, vanish **8** be no more, fade away, melt away, withdraw **9** evaporate **12** be lost to view, cease to exist, leave no trace **13** cease to appear, cease to be seen **14** become obscured, cease to be known, pass out of sight **15** vanish from sight

disappearance 9 vanishing **11** evanescence **16** passing from sight

disappoint 4 foil **6** hinder, sadden, thwart **7** chagrin, let down, mislead **9** frustrate **10** dishearten **11** disillusion

disappointing 11 frustrating **12** unfulfilling **13** dissatisfying **14** unsatisfactory

disappointment 3 dud **4** bomb, loss **6** defeat, fiasco, fizzle **7** failure, letdown, setback, washout **8** disaster **9** the knocks **11** frustration **13** unfulfillment, unrealization **15** disillusionment, dissatisfaction

disapprobation 7 censure **8** disfavor **9** criticism, disesteem, objection **11** disapproval, displeasure **12** condemnation **15** dissatisfaction

disapprove 4 veto **5** decry **6** refuse, reject **7** censure, condemn, deplore, dislike **8** denounce, disallow, object to, turn down **9** criticize, deprecate, disparage, frown upon **10** think ill of **13** look askance at, regard as wrong **14** discountenance, refuse assent to **15** take exception to **16** find unacceptable, view with disfavor

disapprove of 7 censure, condemn, deplore **8** object to

disarm 4 move, sway **5** charm **6** entice **7** attract, bewitch, enchant, win over **8** convince, persuade **9** captivate, fascinate, influence, prevail on

disarming 7 melting, winning, winsome **8** charming, magnetic **9** appealing, beguiling, ingenuous, seductive **10** bewitching, entrancing **11** captivating **12** ingratiating, irresistible

disarrange 5 mix up, upset **6** jumble, mess up, muddle, ruffle, rumple **7** confuse, scatter **8** disarray, dishevel, disorder, displace, put askew, scramble **11** disorganize **13** put out of order **14** turn topsy-turvy

disarranged 5 messy **6** mussed, sloppy, untidy **7** jumbled, ruffled, rumpled, tousled, unkempt **8** uncombed **9** cluttered **10** disarrayed, disheveled, disordered, disorderly, in disorder **11** in a shambles

disarrangement 4 mess **5** chaos, mix-up, upset **6** jumble, mixing, muddle **7** clutter **8** disarray, disorder, scramble, shambles **9** confusion, messiness, messing up **10** disharmony, disruption, sloppiness, untidiness **12** dishevelment

14 disorderliness **15** disorganization, heaping together

disarray 5 chaos, mix-up, upset **6** jumble **7** clutter **8** disorder, scramble, shambles **9** confusion, messiness **10** disharmony, sloppiness, untidiness **12** dishevelment **14** disarrangement **15** disorganization

disarrayed 5 messy **6** mussed, sloppy, untidy **7** chaotic, jumbled, mixed up **10** disheveled, disordered, disorderly, in disorder **11** disarranged

disarticulate 6 detach **7** unhinge **8** disjoint, disunite, separate **9** disengage, dislocate **10** disconnect **13** put out of joint

disarticulated 5 apart **7** divided **8** unhinged **9** disunited, separated **10** disengaged, disjointed, dislocated, unattached **11** unconnected **12** disconnected **13** helter-skelter

disassemble 7 disband, scatter **8** disperse **9** knock down, take apart

disassociate 7 divorce **8** separate **10** disconnect **12** disaffiliate

disassociation 5 break, split **6** schism **7** divorce **8** division **10** separation

disaster 4 harm **5** wreck **6** blight, fiasco **7** scourge, tragedy, trouble **8** accident, calamity **9** adversity, cataclysm, ruination **10** misfortune **11** catastrophe, great mishap **12** misadventure

disastrous 4 dire **5** fatal **6** tragic **7** adverse, hapless, harmful, ruinous **8** dreadful, grievous, ill-fated, terrible **9** harrowing **10** calamitous, desolating, horrendous, ill-starred **11** destructive, devastating, unfortunate **12** catastrophic, inauspicious

disavow 4 deny **6** abjure, disown, recant, reject **7** gainsay, retract **8** denounce **9** repudiate **10** contradict

disavowal 6 denial **8** demurrer **9** rejection **10** abjuration, disclaimer, refutation **11** repudiation **13** contradiction

disband 7 adjourn, dismiss, scatter **8** disperse, dissolve **11** disassemble

disbelief 5 doubt **7** dubiety **8** distrust, mistrust, unbelief **10** skepticism **11** incredulity **12** doubtfulness **14** lack of credence

disbelieve 5 doubt **6** refuse, reject **7** suspect **8** discount, distrust **9** discredit, unbelieve **10** misbelieve

disbeliever 7 atheist, skeptic **8** apostate

disbursable 7 payable **9** available, spendable **10** expendable

disburse 6 lay out, pay out **7** fork out **8** allocate, shell out **10** distribute

disbursement 6 outlay **7** payment **8** spending **9** paying out **10** dispensing **11** expenditure **12** dispensation, distribution

discard 4 drop, dump, junk, shed **5** scrap **6** remove, shed **7** abandon, weed out **8** get rid of, jettison, throw out **9** cast aside, dispose of, eliminate, throw away **10** relinquish **11** thrust aside **12** dispense with, have done with **14** throw overboard

discarded 6 dumped, junked **7** cast off, dropped **8** deserted, forsaken, rejected, scrapped **9** abandoned, cast aside, tossed out **10** jettisoned, left behind, thrown away

discern 3 see **4** espy **6** behold, descry, detect, notice **7** make out, observe, pick out **8** perceive **9** ascertain **12** catch sight of

discernible 7 visible **8** apparent **10** detectable, noticeable **11** perceivable, perceptible

discerning 4 sage, wise **5** acute, sharp **6** astute, shrewd **8** piercing **9** judicious, sagacious, sensitive **10** perceptive **11** intelligent, keen-sighted, penetrating **12** clear-sighted, sharp-sighted **13** perspicacious **14** discriminating

discernment 6 acumen, senses **7** insight **8** feelings, sagacity, thoughts **10** cognizance, discretion, perception **11** distinction **13** consciousness, judiciousness **14** discrimination **15** differentiation

discharge 3 axe, can **4** emit, fire, flow, free, gush, ooze, oust, sack, shot **5** blast, burst, eject, expel, exude, issue, let go, shoot **6** bounce, firing, launch, lay off, let fly, propel, report, set off **7** cashier, dismiss, explode, fire off, project, release, seepage, set free, trigger **8** activate, detonate, drainage, emission, get rid of, liberate, throw off, touch off **9** allow to go, exploding, explosion, firing off, fusillade, give forth, pour forth, secretion, send forth, terminate **10** activating, detonating, detonation, triggering **11** send packing, suppuration **13** give the gate to, walking papers **14** demobilization **15** release document **16** remove from office

disciple 3 nut **5** freak, pupil **7** admirer, convert, devotee, pursuer, student **8** adherent, believer, follower, neophyte, partisan **9** proselyte, supporter **10** aficionado **11** afficionado

Disciple, The
  author: **11** Paul Bourget

disciplinarian 8 martinet **13** authoritarian **16** stickler for rules, strict taskmaster

disciplinary 8 punitive **9** punishing **10** corrective **13** authoritarian

discipline 5 drill, prime, rigor, train **6** method, punish **7** break in, chasten, regimen **8** chastise, drilling, instruct, practice, training **9** schooling **11** preparation **14** indoctrination **15** prescribed habit, teach by exercise **16** course of exercise

disclaim 4 deny **6** disown **7** decline, disavow **8** abnegate, forswear, renounce **9** disaffirm, repudiate

disclaimer 6 denial **8** demurrer **9** disavowal **10** abnegation **11** repudiation **12** renunciation

disclose 4 bare, leak, show, tell **6** expose, impart, reveal, unveil **7** divulge, lay bare, publish, uncover **9** broadcast, make known **10** make public **11** communicate **12** bring to light **13** allow to be seen, bring into view, cause to appear

discolor 4 spot **5** stain, tinge **6** bleach, streak **7** tarnish

discoloration 4 blot, mark, spot **5** smear, stain **6** blotch, bruise, smudge **7** blemish **9** contusion

discolored 4 doty **5** dingy, dirty, faded, livid **6** soiled, tinged **7** bruised, stained **9** tarnished

discomfit 5 upset **6** thwart **7** chagrin **8** confound, distress **9** embarrass, frustrate **10** disconcert

discomfited 5 upset **6** uneasy **7** ashamed **8** thwarted **9** chagrined, ill at ease **10** dis-

tressed **11** embarrassed **12** disconcerted

discomfiture 7 anxiety **9** agitation, confusion **10** uneasiness **11** disquietude, distraction, nervousness **12** discomposure, perturbation **13** embarrassment

discomfort 3 try **4** ache, hurt, pain **5** trial **6** misery **7** malaise, trouble **8** disquiet, distress, hardship, nuisance, soreness, vexation **9** annoyance, discomfit, embarrass **10** affliction, discompose, irritation, make uneasy **11** disquietude

discompose 5 abash, upset **6** rattle **7** agitate, confuse, disturb, fluster, nonplus, perturb, trouble, unnerve **8** disquiet, distract, distress, unsettle **9** discomfit, embarrass **10** disconcert

discomposed 5 upset **6** jolted, rocked, shaken, uneasy **7** anxious, nervous, worried **8** agitated, confused, troubled **9** disturbed, flustered, perturbed **10** disquieted, distracted **11** discomfited, uncollected

discomposure 6 flurry **7** anxiety **8** disquiet **9** agitation, confusion **10** discomfort, uneasiness **11** awkwardness, disquietude, distraction, nervousness **12** discomfiture, perturbation **13** embarrassment **17** self-consciousness

disconcert 5 abash, annoy, upset **6** raffle, ruffle **7** agitate, confuse, disturb, nonplus, perturb, trouble **8** unsettle **10** discompose

disconcerted 5 fazed, upset **7** annoyed, rattled, ruffled **8** agitated, confused, troubled **9** disturbed, perturbed, thrown off, unsettled **10** distracted, nonplussed

disconcertment 8 rattling **9** abashment, agitation, confusion **11** disturbance **12** discomposure

disconnect 6 detach **8** separate, uncouple **9** disengage

disconnected 5 split **6** cut off **7** jumbled, mixed-up, severed **8** confused, detached, rambling **9** illogical, separated, uncoupled **10** disengaged, disjointed, incoherent, irrational, unattached, unfastened **12** disorganized

disconnection 8 severing **9** severance **10** cutting off,

detachment, separation **13** disengagement

disconsolate 3 sad **4** blue, down **6** woeful **7** crushed, doleful, forlorn, unhappy **8** dejected, desolate, downcast, wretched **9** depressed, miserable, sorrowful, woebegone **10** despondent, dispirited, melancholy **11** discouraged, low-spirited, pessimistic **12** heavy-hearted, inconsolable **13** brokenhearted **14** down in the dumps, down in the mouth

discontent 9 displease **10** discomfort, disgruntle **11** displeasure, unhappiness **15** dissatisfaction

discontented 5 bored **7** fretful, unhappy **9** miserable, regretful **10** displeased, malcontent **11** disgruntled **12** dissatisfied

discontinuance 3 end **4** halt, stop **6** ending, recess **7** ceasing, halting **8** abeyance, giving up, quitting, stoppage, stopping, surcease **9** cessation, desisting **10** concluding, leaving off, suspension **11** abandonment, breaking off, termination

discontinue 3 end **4** drop, quit, stop **5** cease **6** desist, give up **7** abandon, abstain, suspend **8** break off, leave off **9** interrupt, terminate **10** put an end to

discontinuous 8 discrete, episodic, sporadic **9** segmented, spasmodic **10** occasional **11** interrupted **12** disconnected, intermittent

discord 6 strife **7** dispute **8** clashing, conflict, disunity, division, friction **9** cacophony, harshness, wrangling **10** contention, disharmony, dissension, dissonance, quarreling **11** being at odds, differences, discordance **12** disagreement, grating noise **13** lack of concord **15** incompatibility **16** unpleasant sounds
  goddess of: **4** Eris **9** Discordia

discordance 6 strife **7** discord, dispute **8** clashing, conflict, disunity, division, friction **9** wrangling **10** contention, disharmony, dissension, quarreling **12** disagreement **15** incompatibility

discordant 6 at odds **9** disparate, dissonant **10** at variance, discrepant **11** conflicting, disagreeing **12** unharmonious

Discordia
  origin: **5** Roman

goddess of: 7 discord
corresponds to: 4 Eris

discount 3 cut **5** break **6** rebate **7** cut rate **9** abatement, allowance, deduction, exemption, reduction **10** concession **11** subtraction

discountenance 7 condemn, despise, disdain, dislike **8** object to **9** frown upon **10** disapprove, think ill of **12** look down upon **13** look askance at, regard as wrong **14** hold in contempt **15** take exception to

discourage 4 do in **5** daunt, deter, unman **6** deject, dismay **7** depress, unnerve **8** decimate, dispirit, dissuade, keep back, restrain **9** disparage, prostrate **10** dishearten, disincline, divert from **13** advise against, dash one's hopes **17** dampen one's spirits

discouraged 3 low **7** daunted **8** dejected, downcast, hopeless **9** depressed **10** despondent, dispirited **11** downhearted, pessimistic **12** disconsolate, disheartened

discouragement 4 curb **5** gloom, worry **6** damper, dismay **7** despair **8** obstacle **9** dejection, hindrance, pessimism, restraint **10** constraint, depression, impediment, low spirits, melancholy, moroseness **11** despondency **12** hopelessness, lack of spirit **13** consternation **15** downheartedness

discourse 3 gab **4** chat, talk **5** essay **6** confer, sermon, speech **7** address, discuss, lecture, oration **8** colloquy, converse, dialogue, diatribe, harangue, treatise **10** discussion **11** intercourse **12** conversation, dissertation, talk together **16** formal discussion

Discourse on Method
author: 13 Rene Descartes

discourteous 4 rude **5** fresh, surly **6** cheeky **7** boorish, illbred, uncivil, uncouth **8** impolite, impudent, insolent **9** uncourtly, ungallant **10** ill-behaved, ungracious, unladylike, unmannerly **11** ill-mannered, impertinent **13** disrespectful, ungentlemanly

discourtesy 8 rudeness **9** impudence, insolence **10** incivility **11** boorishness **12** impoliteness

discover 3 see **4** find, spot **5** dig up **6** detect, locate, notice **7** discern, find out, learn of, realize, root out, uncover, unearth **8** come upon, per-

ceive **9** ascertain, determine, ferret out, light upon, recognize **10** chance upon **11** gain sight of, stumble upon **12** bring to light

discredit 4 deny, slur **5** abuse, smear, sully, taint **6** debase, defame, demean, reject, smirch, vilify **7** degrade, dispute, tarnish, vitiate **8** disallow, disgrace, dishonor, disprove, question **9** challenge, disparage, undermine **10** prove false, stigmatize **16** shake one's faith in **17** drag through the mud

discreditable 8 shameful, shocking **9** appalling **10** outrageous, scandalous **11** disgraceful, ignominious **12** dishonorable, disreputable

discreet 6 polite **7** careful, politic, prudent, tactful **8** cautious **9** judicious, sensitive **10** diplomatic, thoughtful **11** circumspect

Discreet Charm of the Bourgeoisie, The
director: 10 Luis Bunuel
cast: 11 Fernando Rey
   14 Delphine Seyrig, Stephane Audran
Oscar for: 11 foreign film

discrepancy 3 gap **8** variance **9** disparity **10** difference, divergence **11** discordance, incongruity **12** disagreement **13** dissimilarity, inconsistency

discrepant 6 at odds **8** contrary, opposing **9** disparate **10** at variance, discordant, dissimilar, refutatory **11** conflicting, contrasting, disagreeing **12** antithetical, inconsistent **13** contradictory **14** countervailing, irreconcilable

discrete 7 several, various **8** detached, distinct, separate **9** different **10** unattached **11** disjunctive, independent **12** disconnected, unassociated **13** discontinuous

discretion 4 tact **6** acumen, option **8** judgment, prudence, sagacity, volition **9** good sense **10** preference **11** discernment, inclination **12** good judgment, predilection **13** judiciousness, sound judgment **14** discrimination **15** power of choosing **16** individual choice

discretionary 8 optional **9** voluntary **10** nonbinding **11** nonrequired, unnecessary **12** nonrequisite, unimperative **13** nonobligatory

discriminate 7 disdain **8** separate **11** distinguish **12** disfranchise **13** differentiate

discriminating 5 acute **6** astute, biased, shrewd **7** bigoted, refined **9** judicious, sensitive **10** cultivated, discerning, fastidious **11** intelligent, prejudicial **13** perspicacious **15** differentiating

discrimination 4 bias **5** taste **6** acumen **7** bigotry **8** inequity, judgment, keenness, sagacity **9** prejudice **10** astuteness, discretion, favoritism, refinement, shrewdness **11** discernment, distinction **12** perspicacity **21** differential treatment

discursive 7 diffuse **8** rambling **9** wandering **10** circuitous, digressive, long-winded, meandering, roundabout

discursiveness 8 rambling **10** digression, meandering **14** circumlocution

discuss 6 debate, parley, review **7** dissect, examine, speak of **8** consider, talk over **9** talk about **13** converse about, exchange views **14** discourse about

discussion 3 rap **4** talk **6** debate, parley, powwow, review **7** inquiry **8** analysis, argument, colloquy, dialogue, scrutiny **9** discourse **10** hashing-out **11** disputation **12** deliberation **13** consideration, investigation

disdain 4 snub **5** abhor, scorn, spurn **6** deride, detest, loathe **7** despise, dislike **8** contempt, distaste **9** frown upon **10** abhorrence, brush aside, disrespect **11** intolerance **12** icy aloofness, look down upon **14** deem unbecoming, discountenance

disdained 7 derided, scorned, spurned **8** abhorred, despised **10** deprecated, disparaged **14** held in contempt

disdainful 4 cold **5** aloof **7** haughty, high-hat **8** derisive, scornful, superior **11** overbearing, patronizing **12** contemptuous, supercilious **13** condescending

disease 6 malady **7** ailment, illness **8** sickness **9** ill health, infirmity **10** affliction **15** morbid condition **16** physical disorder

disembark 4 land **7** deplane, detrain, pile out **10** leave a ship **11** get off a ship

disenchant 6 put off **7** turn off **8** alienate, disabuse, turn away **9** undeceive **11** disenthrall, disillusion **12** open one's eyes **13** break the spell

15 burst one's bubble **16** bring down to earth

disencumber 8 unburden **9** disburden, extricate **11** disentangle

disengage 5 sever **6** detach **7** disjoin **8** separate **9** extricate **10** disconnect

disengaged 7 unmoved **8** detached **9** apathetic, disjoined, separated **11** indifferent, uncommitted, unconcerned **12** disconnected, unresponsive French: **6** degage

disengagement 6 apathy **8** severing **9** severance, uncondern **10** detachment, separation **12** indifference **13** disconnection **16** unresponsiveness

disentangle 4 free **6** detach, loosen, remove **7** unravel **9** extricate

disenthrall 9 undeceive **10** disenchant **11** disillusion **12** open one's eyes **13** break the spell **15** burst one's bubble **16** bring down to earth

disesteem 7 dislike **8** disfavor **9** disrepute **11** disapproval, displeasure **14** disapprobation

disfavor 5 odium **7** dislike, ill turn **8** disgrace, ignominy **9** disesteem, disregard **10** disrespect, disservice, harmful act **11** disapproval, discourtesy, displeasure **14** disapprobation **15** dissatisfaction **16** unacceptableness

disfigure 3 mar **4** maim, scar **5** cut up **6** damage, deface, deform, impair **7** blemish, scarify **8** make ugly, mutilate

disfigurement 4 blot, flaw, mark, scar, spot **6** blotch, defect **7** blemish **12** imperfection

disfranchise, disenfranchise 15 deprive of a right **19** discriminate against

disgorge 4 spew **5** eject, expel, spout, vomit **6** cast up, spew up **7** cough up, throw up **8** dislodge **9** discharge **10** vomit forth **11** regurgitate

disgrace 4 blot **5** abase, shame, stain, taint **6** debase, smirch **7** blemish, degrade, eyesore, scandal, tarnish **8** contempt, derogate, disfavor, dishonor, ill favor, reproach **9** discredit, disparage, disrepute, embarrass, humiliate **13** embarrassment, in the doghouse **14** bring shame upon

disgraceful 3 low **4** base, mean, vile **6** odious **8** infamous, shameful, shocking, un-

seemly, unworthy **9** appalling, degrading, obnoxious **10** despicable, detestable, inglorious, outrageous, scandalous, unbecoming **11** ignominious, opprobrious **12** dishonorable, disreputable **13** discreditable, reprehensible

disgruntled 5 sulky, testy, vexed **6** grumpy, shirty, sullen **7** grouchy, peevish **8** petulant **9** irritated **10** displeased, malcontent **12** discontented, dissatisfied

disguise 4 garb, hide, mask, pose, sham, veil **5** blind, cloak, cover, feign, getup, guise **6** facade, muffle, screen, shroud, veneer **7** conceal, cover-up, dress up, falsify **8** pretense, simulate **9** costuming, dissemble, gloss over **10** camouflage, false front, masquerade **11** concealment, counterfeit **12** misrepresent **13** false identity **15** false appearance

disguised 6 masked, veiled **7** cloaked **9** dressed up, incognito **10** undercover **11** camouflaged **14** unrecognizable

disgust 5 repel **6** appall, hatred, offend, put off, revolt, sicken **7** dislike **8** aversion, contempt, distaste, loathing, nauseate **9** antipathy, disrelish, repulsion, revulsion **10** abhorrence, repugnance **11** detestation, displeasure **12** disaffection **13** be repulsive to, cause aversion **15** turn one's stomach

disgusting 4 vile **5** hasty **6** horrid, odious **7** hateful **9** abhorrent, appalling, loathsome, offensive, repellent, repugnant, repulsive, revolting, sickening **10** abominable, despicable, nauseating **13** reprehensible

dish 4 dole, fare, food **5** ladle, place, plate, scoop, serve, spoon **6** recipe, saucer, vessel **7** bowlful, dishful, edibles, helping, platter, portion, serving **8** dispense, plateful, transfer, victuals **10** comestible **11** shallow bowl

dishabille 7 undress **8** bathrobe, disarray, disorder, informal, negligee **9** housecoat

disharmonious 7 chaotic **8** clashing, confused **9** dissonant, illogical **10** discordant, incoherent **11** conflicting, contentious **12** incompatible **13** heterogeneous

disharmony 5 chaos **6** strife **7** discord **8** clashing, conflict,

disarray, disunity, division, friction **9** cacophony, confusion, disaccord, harshness **10** contention, dissension, dissonance **11** discordance **12** disagreement, grating noise **15** disorganization, incompatibility

dishearten 4 dash, faze **5** abash, crush, daunt **6** deject, dismay, sadden **7** depress **8** dispirit **10** discourage

disheartened 3 low **6** dismal **8** dejected, desolate, downcast **9** depressed **10** despondent, dispirited **11** discouraged **12** disconsolate

disheartening 4 dark **7** adverse **8** hopeless **11** dispiriting **12** discouraging, inauspicious

disheveled 5 messy **6** blowsy, frowzy, mussed, sloppy, untidy **7** ruffled, rumpled, tousled, unkempt **8** uncombed **10** bedraggled, disarrayed, disorderly, in disorder **11** disarranged

dishevelment 5 chaos, mix-up, upset **6** jumble **7** clutter **8** disarray, disorder, scramble, shambles **9** messiness **10** sloppiness, untidiness **14** disarrangement **15** disorganization

dishonest 5 false **7** corrupt, crooked **8** cheating, specious, spurious, two-faced **9** deceitful, deceptive, faithless, insincere, not honest **10** fraudulent, mendacious, misleading, perfidious, untruthful **11** underhanded **12** disingenuous, falsehearted, unprincipled, unscrupulous **13** untrustworthy

dishonesty 8 cheating **9** duplicity, falseness, mendacity **10** corruption **11** crookedness **12** speciousness **14** untruthfulness

dishonor 4 blot **5** abase, odium, shame, stain, sully **6** debase, defame, infamy, insult, slight, stigma **7** affront, blacken, blemish, degrade, offense, scandal, tarnish **8** disfavor, disgrace, ignominy **9** discredit, disparage, disrepute, humiliate, ill repute **10** derogation, stigmatize **11** discourtesy, humiliation **12** bring shame on **14** public disgrace

dishonorable 4 base **7** debased, ignoble **8** shameful **10** despicable **12** contemptible, disreputable **13** reprehensible

dishonorableness 4 blot **5** odium, shame, stain **6** stigma **7** blemish **8** disfavor, disgrace, ignominy **9** discredit, disrepute, ill repute **10** derogation **11** humiliation

dishonoring 8 disgrace **10** debasement **11** degradation, humiliation

dish up 3 dip **5** ladle, serve, spoon **7** dish out, serve up

disillusion 6 clue in **8** disabuse **9** undeceive **10** disenchant **11** disenthrall **13** break the spell, open the eyes of **14** burst the bubble **16** bring down to earth

disinclination 8 aversion **9** hesitancy **10** reluctance **13** indisposition, unwillingness

disincline 5 deter **8** dissuade, keep back, restrain **10** discourage, divert from **13** advise against **16** attempt to prevent

disinclined 5 loath **6** averse **8** hesitant **9** reluctant, unwilling **10** indisposed

disinfect 6 purify **7** cleanse **8** sanitize **9** kill germs, sterilize **13** decontaminate **15** destroy bacteria

disinfectant 9 germicide **10** antiseptic, germ killer **11** bactericide

disinherit 6 cut off, disown **15** deprive of rights

disintegrate 7 break up, crumble, shatter **8** splinter **9** fall apart **10** break apart, go to pieces

disintegration 4 ruin **5** decay **7** breakup, erosion **8** biolysis **9** crumbling **10** dispersion, dissolving, separation **11** decomposing **12** falling apart **13** decomposition, deterioration, pulverization

disinter 5 dig up **6** exhume **7** unearth

disinterest 6 apathy **9** disregard, unconcern **12** indifference

disinterested 7 neutral, outside **8** unbiased **9** impartial **10** impersonal, uninvolved **12** free from bias, unprejudiced **13** dispassionate

disinterment 9 digging up **10** exhumation, unearthing

disjecta membra 15 disjointed parts **16** scattered members

disjoin 4 part, undo **5** break, sever **6** detach, divide **8** disunite, separate **9** disengage

disjoint 6 detach **7** unhinge **8** disunite, separate **9** dislocate **10** disconnect **13** disarticulate

disjointed 5 apart, split **7** chaotic, divided, jumbled, mixedup, tangled **8** confused, detached, rambling **9** illogical, spasmodic **10** incoherent, irrational, unattached **11** unconnected **12** disconnected, disorganized **13** discontinuous, disharmonious, helter-skelter, heterogeneous **14** disarticulated

disjointedness 8 rambling **11** indirection **14** discursiveness **16** disconnectedness

disjointed parts
Latin: **14** disjecta membra

disk, disc 3 cam **4** aten, coin, dial, face, plow, puck **5** plate, wafer, wheel **6** harrow, record, sequin **7** discuss **8** diskette **9** cultivate, videodisc **11** discotheque
type: 4 hard **5** fixed **6** floppy **8** magnetic **10** Winchester

dislike 4 hate **5** abhor, scorn **6** animus, detest, enmity, hatred, loathe, malice, rancor **7** despise, disdain, disgust, not like **8** aversion, distaste, loathing, object to **9** abominate, animosity, antipathy, hostility, repulsion, revulsion **10** abhorrence, antagonism, repugnance **11** abomination, detestation **12** disaffection

disliked 5 hated **7** loathed, unloved **8** abhorred, despised, detested **10** abominated

dislike intensely 4 hate **5** abhor **6** detest, loathe **7** despise **9** abominate **10** recoil from

dislocate 6 uproot **7** unhinge **8** disjoint, disunite, separate **9** disengage **10** disconnect **13** disarticulate, put out of joint

dislodge 4 oust **5** eject, expel **6** dig out, dispel, remove, uproot **7** disturb **8** displace, force out **9** extricate **11** disentangle

disloyal 6 untrue **8** recreant **9** faithless, seditious, undutiful **10** inconstant, perfidious, subversive, traitorous, unfaithful **11** treacherous, treasonable **12** dishonorable

disloyalty 7 falsity, perfidy, treason **8** apostasy, betrayal, sedition **9** falseness, rebellion, recreancy, treachery **10** infidelity, subversion **11** inconstancy **12** insurrection **13** breach of trust, deceitfulness, double-dealing, faithlessness **14** lack of fidelity, perfidiousness, unfaithfulness **15** betrayal of trust, breaking of faith **18** subversive activity

dismal 3 sad **4** drab, grim, poor **5** awful, bleak **6** dreary, gloomy, morbid, rueful, somber, woeful **7** abysmal, doleful, forlorn, joyless, unhappy, very bad, visaged **8** dejected, desolate, dolorous, downcast, dreadful, hopeless, horrible, mournful, terrible **9** cheerless, depressed, long-faced, sorrowful, woebegone **10** abominable, despondent, in the dumps, lugubrious, melancholy **11** pessimistic **12** disconsolate, disheartened, heavy-hearted **13** unmentionable **14** down-in-the-mouth

dismantle 5 strip **6** denude, divest **9** take apart

dismay 3 cow **5** abash, alarm, daunt, dread, panic, scare **6** appall, fright, horror, put off, terror **7** anxiety, concern, horrify, unnerve **8** affright, distress, frighten **10** disappoint, discourage, dishearten, intimidate **11** disillusion, trepidation **12** apprehension, exasperation, intimidation, perturbation **13** consternation **14** disappointment, discouragement **15** disillusionment

dismayed 7 abashed, daunted **8** appalled **10** confounded, nonplussed **12** disconcerted

dismember 4 limb **6** hack up **8** disjoint **16** tear limb from limb

dismiss 3 can **4** fire, free, oust, sack **5** let go **6** bounce, excuse, reject **7** adjourn, cashier, disband, discard, release **8** disclaim, disperse, dissolve, lay aside, liberate, pink-slip, set aside **9** disregard, eliminate, repudiate, send forth, terminate **10** permit to go **11** send packing **12** allow to leave, put out of a job, put out of mind **14** give the heave-ho **17** remove from service, give walking papers **19** discharge from office

dismissal 6 firing **7** release **9** discharge, dispersal, disregard **10** disclaimer **11** adjournment, repudiation

Disney, Walt
creator/artist of: **10** Donald Duck **11** Mickey Mouse

disobedience 8 defiance **9** rebellion **10** resistance **13** noncompliance, nonconformity **14** rebelliousness

disobedient 6 unruly **7** defiant, froward, haughty, wayward **8** contrary, mutinous, perverse, stubborn **9** fractious, insurgent, obstinate, seditious, undutiful

10 disorderly, rebellious, refractory, unyielding **11** intractable **12** noncompliant, recalcitrant, ungovernable, unmanageable, unsubmissive **13** insubordinate

disobey 4 defy **5** break **6** ignore, resist **7** violate **8** overstep **9** disregard **10** infringe on, transgress **11** go counter to **12** rebel against

disoblige 5 annoy **6** bother **7** trouble **13** inconvenience

disobliging 4 rude **8** churlish **9** unhelpful **13** inconsiderate

disorder 4 mess, riot **5** chaos **6** fracas, jumble, malady, muddle, ruckus, uproar **7** ailment, clutter, disease, illness, turmoil **8** disarray, sickness **9** commotion, complaint, confusion **10** affliction, disruption, dissension **11** disturbance **13** indisposition, minor uprising **14** disarrangement **15** disorganization

disordered 7 jumbled **8** confused, messed up **9** haphazard **11** disarranged **12** disorganized

disorderliness 4 mess **5** chaos **6** muddle **8** disarray **9** confusion **10** disruption **14** disarrangement **15** disorganization

disorderly 3 bad **4** wild **5** messy, noisy, rowdy **6** sloppy, unruly, untidy **7** chaotic, jumbled, lawless, riotous, unkempt, wayward **8** careless, confused, improper, pell-mell, rowdyish, slipshod, slovenly, unlawful, unsorted **10** boisterous, disheveled, disordered, disruptive, rebellious, straggling, topsy-turvy **11** disarranged **12** disorganized, disreputable, obstreperous, unrestrained, unsystematic **13** helter-skelter, undisciplined **14** rough-and-tumble, unsystematized

disorganization 4 mess **5** chaos, upset **6** jumble, muddle **7** clutter **8** disarray, disorder, shambles **9** confusion, messiness **10** disharmony, disruption, sloppiness, untidiness **12** dishevelment **14** disarrangement, disorderliness

disorganize 5 mix up, upset **6** jumble, mess up, muddle **7** confuse, scatter **8** disarray, disorder, put askew, scramble **10** disarrange **13** put out of order **14** turn topsy-turvy

disorganized 5 messy, upset **7** chaotic, jumbled, mixed-up, muddled **8** confused, rambling **9** haphazard, illogical **10** disordered, disorderly, incoherent,

in disarray, irrational **12** unsystematic **16** at sixes and sevens

disoriented 7 mixed-up **8** confused, unstable **10** distracted, out of joint, out of touch **11** not adjusted

disown 6 reject **7** cast off, disavow, forsake **8** denounce, disclaim, renounce **9** repudiate **10** disinherit **17** refuse to recognize **19** refuse to acknowledge

disparage 4 mock **6** demean, slight **7** put down, run down **8** belittle, derogate, ridicule **9** denigrate, discredit, underrate **10** depreciate, undervalue **11** detract from

disparaged 7 ran down **9** belittled, ridiculed **10** denigrated, deprecated **11** depreciated

disparagement 6 abuse, libel **7** slander **8** ridicule **9** criticism **10** belittling, defamation, derogation, detraction **11** denigration, putting down **12** vilification **17** defamatory remarks

disparaging 5 snide **10** belittling, derogatory **11** unfavorable **15** uncomplimentary

disparate 6 at odds, unlike **9** different **10** at variance, discordant, discrepant, dissimilar **11** contrasting

disparity 3 gap **8** contrast, imparity, variance **10** difference, divergence, inequality, unlikeness **11** discrepancy, incongruity **12** disagreement, dissemblance **13** contradiction, disproportion, dissimilarity, dissimilitude, inconsistency

dispassion 6 apathy **8** coolness **10** detachment **12** indifference

dispassionate 4 calm, cool, fair **6** serene **7** neutral, unmoved **8** composed, detached, unbiased **9** collected, impartial, unexcited, unruffled **10** impersonal, uninvolved **11** levelheaded, undisturbed, unemotional **12** unprejudiced **13** disinterested, imperturbable

dispatch 4 item, kill, post, slay **5** flash, haste, piece, speed, story **6** finish, letter, murder, report, settle, wind up **7** bump off, execute, forward, message, missive, send off **8** alacrity, bulletin, carry out, celerity, complete, conclude, expedite, massacre, rapidity **9** finish off, quickness, slaughter, swiftness **10** communique, expedition, prompt-

ness, put an end to, put to death **11** assassinate, news account **12** send on the way **14** execute quickly, summarily shoot, swift execution **15** make short work of, transmit rapidly **16** carry out speedily, dispose of rapidly **18** telegraphic message **21** official communication

Dis Pater *see* 3 Dis

dispel 4 rout **5** allay, expel, repel **6** banish, remove **7** diffuse, dismiss, resolve, scatter **8** drive off **9** dissipate, drive away, eliminate **10** put an end to **11** disseminate **13** make disappear

dispensable 8 nonvital **9** accessory, extrinsic, secondary **10** disposable, expendable, extraneous **11** superfluous, unessential, unimportant, unnecessary **12** nonessential

dispensation 6 decree **8** approval, bestowal, division **9** allotment, diffusion, exemption, meting out **10** allocation, conferment, credential, dealing out, dispensing, permission, reparation **11** consignment, designation **12** apportioning, distribution, remuneration **13** authorization, dissemination

dispense 6 confer **7** dole out, mete out **8** allocate **9** apportion **10** administer, distribute

dispense with 4 drop, dump, junk, shed **5** scrap **6** shelve **7** abandon, discard **9** dispose of

dispensing 9 bestowing, doling out, meting out **10** allocating, conferring **12** distributing

dispersal 7 breakup, parting **9** dismissal **10** breaking up, scattering **12** distributing, distribution

disperse 4 rout **6** dispel **7** diffuse, disband, scatter, send off **8** drive off **9** dissipate **10** distribute **11** disseminate **13** send scurrying **16** spread throughout

dispersed 7 diffuse **9** scattered, spread out **10** dissipated **11** distributed **14** extended widely, unconcentrated

dispersion 9 dispersal **10** disbanding, scattering **11** dissipation **12** distribution

dispirit 5 cloud **6** darken, deject, sadden **7** depress **10** demoralize, dishearten

dispirited 3 sad **4** blue, down, glum **5** moody **6** morose

7 forlorn, unhappy **8** dejected, downcast, listless **9** cheerless, depressed **10** melancholy **11** crestfallen, demoralized, discouraged, downhearted, pessimistic **12** disconsolate, disheartened **14** down in the dumps, down in the mouth, unenthusiastic

dispiriting 4 cold, dark **6** chilly, dismal, gloomy **9** dampening **10** depressing **12** discouraging **13** disheartening

displace 4 bump, move, oust **5** shift **6** unseat **7** replace **8** crowd out, dislodge, force out, supplant **9** dislocate, supersede

displaced person 2 DP **5** exile **6** emigre **7** refugee **8** expellee **10** expatriate

display 4 show **6** reveal **7** exhibit **8** manifest **10** exhibition **11** demonstrate, make visible **12** presentation **13** bring into view, demonstration, manifestation **15** put in plain sight

display case 7 cabinet, vitrine **8** showcase

displease 3 irk **5** annoy, pique **6** offend **7** disturb, incense, provoke **8** irritate

displeasing 8 annoying **9** loathsome, offensive, repellent, repugnant **10** irritating **11** distasteful, distressing **12** disagreeable

displeasure 5 wrath **7** dislike **8** vexation **9** annoyance **10** irritation **11** disapproval, indignation **15** dissatisfaction

disport 3 act **4** play, romp **5** amuse, caper, sport **6** divert, frolic, gambol **7** display, pastime **9** amusement, entertain **10** recreation **13** entertainment

disposal 5 array, order, power **7** command, control, dumping, junking, pattern, ridding **8** grouping, riddance **9** authority, clearance, direction, placement **10** discarding, government, management, regulation, settlement **11** arrangement, destruction, disposition, supervision **12** distribution, organization, throwing away **13** authorization, configuration, juxtaposition **14** administration

dispose 4 rank **5** array, order, place **7** arrange, deal out, incline **8** classify, get rid of, motivate, organize **9** be willing **10** distribute

dispose of 4 dump **5** scrap **6** unload **7** discard **8** get rid

of, throw out **9** cast aside, throw away

disposition 6 nature, spirit **7** control **8** bestowal, grouping, tendency **9** placement **11** arrangement, inclination, temperament **12** distribution, organization **14** predisposition **15** final settlement

dispossess 4 oust **5** evict, expel **8** take away, take back **9** deprive of

disproportionate 7 unequal **9** disparate **10** dissimilar, unbalanced

disprove 6 refute **9** discredit **10** controvert

disputable 7 dubious **8** doubtful **9** debatable, uncertain **12** questionable **14** controvertible

disputant 5 rival **7** opposer **8** opponent **9** adversary **10** antagonist, competitor, contestant

disputation 6 debate, review **8** argument, dialogue **10** discussion

dispute 4 feud **5** argue, clash, doubt **6** debate, impugn **7** quarrel, wrangle **8** argument, question, squabble **9** bickering, challenge **10** contradict **11** altercation, controversy **12** disagreement

disputed 6 argued **8** wrangled **9** debatable, in dispute, quarreled **10** in question, unverified **12** questionable **13** controversial **15** unsubstantiated

disqualification 5 minus **8** handicap **10** disability **11** shortcoming **13** ineligibility

disqualify 7 disable **9** make unfit **17** declare ineligible, deny participation

disquiet, disquietude 3 awe **6** unease **7** anxiety **8** distress **9** agitation **10** uneasiness **11** fretfulness, trepidation **12** apprehension, discomposure, perturbation **13** consternation

disquieted 6 uneasy **7** anxious, worried **9** concerned **10** distressed **12** apprehensive

disquieting 6 vexing **8** annoying **9** troubling, upsetting **10** bothersome, disturbing, irritating, perturbing, unsettling **11** distressing **13** disconcerting

disquisition 8 tractate, treatise **9** discourse, monograph **12** dissertation

disregard 6 ignore **8** overlook **11** pay no heed to **13** lack of respect **14** take no notice of **15** lack of attention **16** willful oversight

disregardful 8 careless, heedless **9** unmindful **11** insensitive, thoughtless **13** inconsiderate

disreputable 5 shady **8** infamous, shameful, shocking **9** notorious **10** scandalous **11** disgraceful **12** dishonorable, unprincipled **14** not respectable, of bad character

disrespect 8 contempt, dishonor, rudeness **9** disregard **11** discourtesy, irreverence **12** impoliteness

disrespectful 4 rude **8** impolite **11** impertinent **12** contemptuous, discourteous

disrobe 5 strip **7** undress **16** divest of clothing

disrupt 5 upset **9** interrupt **13** interfere with **17** throw into disorder

disruption 5 upset **8** disorder **9** confusion **11** disturbance **12** interference, interruption **14** disarrangement **15** disorganization

dissatisfaction 4 veto **7** protest **9** rejection **10** discontent **11** disapproval, displeasure, unhappiness

dissatisfied 7 unhappy **10** displeased **12** discontented

dissect 5 study **7** analyze, lay open **8** cut apart, separate **9** anatomize, break down

dissemble 4 hide, mask **5** feign **7** conceal **8** disguise **10** camouflage **11** dissimulate

disseminate 6 spread **7** diffuse, scatter **8** disperse **9** broadcast, circulate

dissemination 9 diffusion, dispersal, spreading **10** scattering **12** broadcasting, distribution

dissension 7 discord, dispute **8** conflict, disunity, division **9** rebellion **10** contention, disharmony, quarreling **11** discordance **12** disagreement **14** rebelliousness

dissent 6 object, oppose **7** discord, protest **8** disagree **10** difference, dissension, opposition **12** disagreement **14** withhold assent **16** withhold approval

dissenter 5 rebel **9** dissident, protester **13** nonconformist

dissenting 9 differing, dissident **11** disagreeing

dissertation 6 memoir, thesis **8** tractate, treatise **9** discourse, monograph **12** disquisition

disservice 4 harm, hurt **5** wrong **6** injury **7** bad turn **9** injustice

dissever 3 saw **4** hack, rend **5** carve, sever, slash, slice, split **6** cleave, divide **8** disunite, separate

dissident 5 rebel **8** agitator, opposing **9** differing, dissenter **10** dissenting **11** disagreeing

dissimilar 6 unlike **8** distinct **9** different, disparate

dissimilarity 8 contrast, variance **9** disparity **10** difference, dissonance, divergence, inequality, unlikeness **11** discrepancy **12** disagreement **13** inconsistency **17** lack of resemblance

dissimilitude 8 variance **9** disparity **10** difference, unlikeness **11** incongruity **12** disagreement **17** lack of resemblance

dissimulate 4 hide, mask **7** conceal **8** disguise **9** dissemble **10** camouflage

dissipate 5 waste **6** dispel **7** carouse, deplete, scatter **8** disperse, misspend, squander **11** fritter away, overindulge **13** be intemperate **14** spend foolishly

dissipated 6 wasted **8** misspent **9** abandoned, debauched, dispelled, dispersed, dissolute, scattered **10** squandered **11** intemperate **12** disreputable **13** frittered away

dissipater 5 waste **7** wastrel **8** prodigal **10** profligate, squanderer **11** spendthrift

dissipation 6 excess **7** wasting **9** dispersal **10** debauchery, dispelling, scattering **11** dissolution, loose living **12** immoderation, intemperance **14** disintegration, frittering away, self-indulgence

dissociate 8 separate **10** disconnect **12** break off with

dissociation 7 breakup **10** separation

dissolute 5 loose **7** corrupt, immoral **9** abandoned, debauched **10** dissipated **12** unrestrained

dissolution 9 annulment **10** separation **11** termination **14** disintegration

dissolve 3 end, run **4** fade, melt, thaw, void **5** annul, sever **6** finish, render, soften, vanish **7** break up, disband, liquefy, thaw out **8** abrogate, conclude, evanesce **9** disappear, dissipate, terminate **10** deliquesce **12** disintegrate **13** dematerialize

dissonance 5 clash **7** discord **9** cacophony, harshness **10** difference, disharmony **11** discordance **12** disagreement **13** dissimilarity

dissonant 5 harsh **7** grating, hostile, jarring, raucous, warring **8** clashing, jangling **10** discordant, discrepant **11** cacophonous, disagreeing, incongruent, incongruous, unmelodious **12** incompatible, inconsistent, inharmonious **13** contradictory **14** irreconcilable

dissuade 9 urge not to **10** discourage **13** advise against, persuade not to

distance 3 gap **4** span **7** reserve, stretch **8** coldness, coolness, interval **9** aloofness, formality, restraint, stiffness **11** reservation **16** intervening space

distant 3 far **4** cold, cool **5** aloof **6** far-off, remote **7** faraway **8** detached, reserved **10** far-removed, restrained, unfriendly **11** standoffish **17** not closely related

Distant Mirror, A
author: **15** Barbara W Tuchman

distaste 7 disgust, dislike **8** aversion **9** antipathy **10** repugnance **11** displeasure

distasteful 9 loathsome, repugnant **10** disgusting, unpleasant **11** displeasing **12** disagreeable

distastefulness 13 offensiveness **14** unpleasantness **16** disagreeableness

distasteful work 8 drudgery **11** menial labor

distend 5 bloat, bulge, swell **6** billow, expand **7** inflate, puff out **8** swell out

distended 4 full, taut **5** puffy, tumid **7** blown up, bloated, dilated, swelled, swollen **8** enlarged, expanded, extended, inflated, patulant **9** edematous, stretched

distill 7 draw out, extract **8** condense, vaporize **9** draw forth, evaporate

distillate 7 essence, extract

11 concentrate **13** concentration

distilled 9 condensed, extracted, vaporized **10** evaporated

distinct 5 clear, lucid, plain **7** diverse, supreme **8** clear-cut, definite, explicit, separate **9** different **10** dissimilar, individual **11** unmitigated, well-defined **12** not identical, unmistakable **13** extraordinary **14** unquestionable

distinction 6 renown **8** contrast, eminence **9** greatness **10** difference, excellence, importance, notability, prominence, separation **11** discernment, preeminence, superiority **12** differential **14** discrimination **15** differentiation

distinctive 6 unique **7** special **8** atypical, original, singular, uncommon **9** different **10** individual **13** extraordinary **14** characteristic

distinctiveness 7 clarity **9** character **10** definition, uniqueness **11** personality **13** individuality

distingue 13 distinguished

distinguish 6 decide, define **7** discern **8** set apart **9** single out **10** make famous **12** characterize, discriminate **13** differentiate, make prominent, make well known **14** make celebrated **15** make distinctive, note differences

distinguished 5 grand, great **6** famous, superb **7** elegant, eminent, notable, refined **8** renowned, splendid **9** acclaimed, dignified, distingue, prominent **10** celebrated **11** illustrious, magnificent
French: **9** distingue

distort 6 deform **7** contort **8** misshape **9** disfigure **11** misconstrue **12** misrepresent **15** twist out of shape, twist the meaning

distorted 4 awry **5** askew **6** belied, loaded, warped **7** altered, colored, crooked, twisted **8** cockeyed, deformed, wrenched **9** contorted, falsified, grotesque, irregular, misshapen, misstated, perverted **13** unsymmetrical **14** misrepresented **15** misproportioned

distortion 7 skewing **8** twisting **10** aberration, caricature **11** crookedness, deformation **12** malformation **17** misrepresentation

distract 5 amuse, craze,

worry **6** divert, madden **7** agitate, confuse, disturb, perplex, torment, trouble **8** bewilder, disorder **9** entertain

distracted 3 mad **4** wild **6** amused, crazed, insane, raving **7** frantic, pleased, puzzled **8** agitated, confused, deranged, diverted, frenzied, harassed, heedless, occupied **9** disturbed, stirred up **10** bewildered, distraught, irrational **11** entertained, turned aside

distraction 5 fazed, upset **6** frenzy **7** frantic, madness, pastime, rattled, ruffled **8** agitated, confused **9** amusement, diversion, unsettled **10** distraught, distressed, nonplussed, recreation **11** desperation **12** disconcerted **13** entertainment **14** mental distress

distractive 9 confusing **10** disturbing, unsettling **11** distressing, troublesome

distraught 3 mad **7** anxious, frantic **8** agitated, frenzied, seething **10** distracted, distressed **13** beside oneself

distress 4 need, pain, want **5** agony, upset **6** danger, grieve **7** anguish, disturb, torment, torture, trouble **14** acute suffering

distressed 5 upset **7** anxious, fearful, frantic, grieved, unhappy, worried **8** agitated, troubled **9** anguished, concerned, disturbed, tormented **10** distracted, distraught

distressing 5 acute **7** nagging, painful **8** grievous **9** agonizing, upsetting **10** disturbing, tormenting, unpleasant **11** displeasing, troublesome, unfortunate **13** uncomfortable

distribute 5 allot, class **6** divide, parcel **7** arrange, catalog, deliver, dole out, give out, scatter **8** classify, dispense, disperse, separate, tabulate **9** apportion, circulate, methodize, spread out **11** disseminate, systematize

distribution 7 sorting **8** division, grouping **9** allotment, spreading **10** allocation, dispersion, scattering **11** arrangement, circulation, disposition **12** organization **13** apportionment, dissemination

distribution center
 French: **8** entrepot

district 4 area, ward **6** parish, region **8** precinct **12** neighborhood

distrust 5 doubt **7** suspect

8 question **9** misgiving, suspicion **11** lack of faith

distrustful 3 shy **4** wary **5** leery **7** dubious, jealous **8** cautious, doubtful, doubting **9** diffident **10** suspicious, untrusting **11** incredulous, mistrustful **12** disbelieving

disturb 5 annoy, upset, worry **6** bother **7** disrupt, perturb, trouble **8** distress, unsettle **9** dislocate, interrupt, intrude on **10** disarrange **11** disorganize

disturbance 5 upset, worry **6** bother, hubbub, ruckus, tumult, uproar **7** rioting, turmoil **8** disorder, distress, outbreak **9** annoyance **11** distraction **12** interruption, perturbation

disturbance of peace 4 riot **6** fracas, ruckus, uproar **7** turmoil **8** disorder **9** commotion **13** breach of order

disturbed 5 upset **6** uneasy **7** annoyed, anxious, nervous, rattled **8** agitated, confused, troubled **9** perturbed **10** disquieted **11** discomfited **12** disconcerted

disunion 7 divorce **8** division **9** secession **10** separation **14** disintegration

disunite 4 part **6** divide **7** divorce **8** separate **9** disengage **10** disconnect **12** disintegrate **13** disarticulate

disunited 6 parted **8** diverged, divorced, unallied **9** came apart, dispersed, separated **10** uncombined **13** disassociated

disunity 6 strife **7** discord **8** clashing, conflict, division, friction **9** wrangling **10** contention, dissension, separation **11** being at odds, discordance **12** disagreement **15** incompatibility

ditat Deus 11 God enriches
 motto of: **7** Arizona

ditch 3 pit **4** junk **5** scrap **6** hollow, trench **7** abandon, discard **8** get rid of **10** excavation

dither 4 flap, fuss **5** tizzy, waver, whirl **6** bother, flurry, lather, quiver, shiver, thrill **7** fluster, tremble, twitter **8** hesitate **9** agitation, commotion, confusion, vacillate, vibration **10** excitement

Dithyrambus
 epithet of: **8** Dionysus
 means: **20** child of the double door

ditty 3 lay **4** song, tune **6** ballad **7** refrain

Dius Fidius
 origin: **5** Roman
 god of: **5** oaths **11** hospitality **20** international affairs
 corresponds to: **6** Sancus
 10 Semo Sancus

divagation 8 straying **9** wandering **10** digression, divergence

divan 4 book, hall, poem, room, salon, seat, sofa **5** couch, court **6** canape, daybed, leewan, lounge, settee **7** chamber, council, ottoman, davenport

dive 4 dash, fall, jump, leap **5** lunge **6** plunge **7** gin mill **9** honky-tonk, shabby bar **15** sleazy nightclub

Diver, Dick and Nicole
 characters in: **16** Tender Is the Night
 author: **10** Fitzgerald

diverge 6 differ, swerve **7** deflect, deviate **8** be at odds, conflict, disagree, separate, split off

divergence 7 parting **8** conflict, rambling, straying, variance **9** deviation, disparity, wandering **10** difference, separation **11** discrepancy, incongruity **13** dissimilarity, inconsistency

divergent 8 separate **9** different **11** conflicting, disagreeing **12** drawing apart, splitting off

diverse 6 sundry, varied **8** eclectic, far-flung, opposite **9** different, differing, disparate **10** dissimilar **11** conflicting, of many kinds **13** contradictory

diversified 6 divers **7** various **8** manifold **9** different, unrelated **13** miscellaneous

diversify 4 vary **7** diffuse **8** divide up **9** spread out, variegate

diversion 5 hobby **7** pastime **9** amusement, avocation **10** deflection **11** distraction, drawing away **12** turning aside
 French: **14** divertissement

diversity 7 variety **8** variance **10** assortment, difference **13** heterogeneity

divert 5 amuse **7** deflect **8** distract **9** entertain, sidetrack, turn aside

diverting 7 amusing **10** deflecting **11** distracting **12** entertaining, sidetracking

divertissement 9 diversion **13** entertainment

divest 3 rid 4 free 5 strip 7 deprive, disrobe, peel off, take off 8 get out of 10 dispossess 14 remove clothing

divest oneself of 6 give up 7 take off 8 get rid of, give over, hand over, put aside, strip off 9 surrender 10 relinquish

divide 4 part, sort 5 share, split 7 arrange, deal out, divvy up 8 allocate, classify, disunite, separate 9 apportion, partition 10 distribute, put in order

divide and rule
Latin: 14 divide et impera
maxim of: 11 Machiavelli

divided 5 apart, split 6 parted 8 meted out 9 disunited, separated 10 unattached 11 apportioned 12 disconnected, portioned out

divide et impera 13 divide and rule
maxim of: 11 Machiavelli

divide in two 5 halve, split 6 bisect 8 cut in two, separate 9 cut in half 10 break in two 11 split in half 18 split down the middle

dividing line 4 edge 5 brink, verge 6 border, margin 8 boundary 9 threshold

divination 5 guess 6 augury 8 prophecy 10 conjecture, foreboding, prediction, prescience 11 premonition, soothsaying 15 prognostication

divine 4 holy 5 guess 6 fathom, sacred 7 predict, surmise, suspect 8 forecast, foretell, heavenly, prophesy 9 admirable, celestial, excellent, marvelous, wonderful

divine being 3 god 5 deity 7 goddess 8 divinity 14 celestial being

Divine Comedy
author: 14 Dante Alighieri
part: 7 Inferno 8 Paradiso 10 Purgatorio
guide: 6 Virgil 8 Beatrice

diviner 4 seer 5 augur 10 soothsayer 14 prognosticator

Divine retribution
goddess of: 7 Nemesis 8 Adrastea

Divine Sarah
nickname of: 14 Sarah Bernhardt

divinity 3 god 5 deity 7 goddess 8 holiness, religion, theology 9 theosophy 12 science of God 14 celestial being

division 4 part, unit, wing 5 split 6 branch 7 discord, divider, section 8 disunion, variance 9 partition 10 department, difference, divergence, separation 11 splitting up 12 disagreement

divorce 4 rift 5 split 6 breach, divide 7 rupture 8 disunite, separate 9 segregate 10 dissociate, separation

divulge 4 tell 6 impart, relate, reveal 8 disclose 9 make known 11 communicate

divulgence 7 telling 8 exposure 9 imparting 10 disclosure, giving away, laying open, revelation 13 communication 15 bringing to light 17 bring out in the open

divulge to 4 tell 6 advise, inform, notify, reveal 7 apprise 8 acquaint, disclose 9 enlighten, make aware 11 familiarize 13 spill the beans 20 let the cat out of the bag

Dix, Otto
born: 7 Germany 11 Unterhausen
artwork: 6 The War 7 The City 12 The Procuress 15 Sylvia von Harden 18 Parents of the Artist 39 Prague Street—Dedicated to My Contemporaries

Dixie Dugan
creator: 8 J P McEvoy 13 John H Striebel

dizzy 5 fleet, giddy, quick, rapid, shaky, swift 6 whirly 7 confuse, reeling 8 bewilder, unsteady 9 make giddy 11 lightheaded, vertiginous 12 make unsteady

Djawa see 4 Java

Djebel al-Tarik see 9 Gibraltar

Djibouti see box

do 3 act 4 fare 5 clean, cover, get on, serve, visit 6 behave, finish, look at, stop in 7 achieve, arrange, carry on, conduct, execute, fulfill, make out, perform, prepare, proceed, suffice 8 be enough, carry out, complete, conclude, organize 10 accomplish, administer, bring about, put in order 13 travel through 14 be satisfactory, comport oneself, conduct oneself

do a favor 4 help 6 assist, oblige 7 help out 11 accommodate, do a kindness

do away with 3 end 4 junk, kill, void 5 erase, quash 6 banish, cancel, cut out, give

---

Djibouti
other name: 16 French Somaliland 39 The French Territory of the Afars and the Issas
capital/largest city: 8 Djibouti
others: 5 Obock 6 Dikhil 8 Tadjoura 9 Ali-Sabieh
monetary unit: 5 franc 7 centime
lake: 4 Abbe 5 Assal
mountain: 5 Gouda
highest point: 9 Moussa Ali
sea: 3 Red
physical feature:
gulf: 4 Aden 8 Tadjoura
strait: 11 Bab el-Mandeb
people: 4 Afar, Arab 5 Issas 6 French 8 European
language: 4 Afar 6 Arabic, French, Somali
religion: 5 Islam

---

up, remove, repeal, revoke, rub out 7 abolish, blot out, nullify, rescind, weed out, wipe out 8 abrogate, stamp out, throw out 9 eliminate, eradicate, terminate 10 annihilate, put an end to 11 exterminate

Dobbin, Captain William
character in: 10 Vanity Fair
author: 9 Thackeray

Dobie Gillis, The Many Loves of
character: 11 Zelda Gilroy 13 Maynard G Krebs 14 Herbert T Gillis, Milton Armitage, Winifred (Winnie) Gillis 15 Thalia Menninger 19 Chatsworth Osborne Jr
cast: 9 Bob Denver 11 Frank Faylen, Sheila James, Tuesday Weld 12 Warren Beatty 13 Dwayne Hickman 14 Florida Friebus, Stephen Franken
Dobie imitated pose of: 7 Thinker

do business 4 deal 5 trade 10 buy and sell

docile 4 tame 7 willing 8 obedient, obliging 9 agreeable, compliant, tractable 10 manageable 11 complaisant

docility 7 pliancy 8 meekness 9 passivity 10 placidness 12 acquiescence, complaisance 13 nonresistance

dock 4 crop, join, pier, quay
5 berth, wharf **6** couple, cut
off, deduct, hook up, link up
7 landing **8** cut short **10** waterfront **12** come into port
13 subject to loss **14** fasten
together

dock 5 Rumux
varieties: 3 Bur **4** Sour
5 Green **6** Golden **7** Prairie,
Spinach, Tanner's, Western
8 Patience **9** Purple-wen
10 Giant water

docket 4 bill, card, list
5 slate **6** agenda, lineup, roster **7** program **8** calendar,
schedule **9** timetable **14** things
to be done **15** order of
business

doctor 2 GP, MD **3** PhD **5** alter, treat **6** change **7** dentist,
falsify, surgeon **9** internist, os-
teopath, physician **10** podia-
trist, tamper with
11 pathologist **12** gynecologist,
obstetrician, pediatrician, psychiatrist, veterinarian
15 ophthalmologist **17** apply
medication to **19** general practitioner, medical practitioner

Doctor Brodie's Report
author: **15** Jorge Luis Borges

Doctor Faustus
author: **10** Thomas Mann
18 Christopher Marlowe

Doctor Grimshaw's Secret
author: **18** Nathaniel
Hawthorne

Doctor J
nickname of: **12** Julius
Erving

Doctorow, E L
author of: **7** Ragtime **15** The
Book of Daniel

Doctor's Dilemma, The
author: **17** George Bernard
Shaw

Doctor Zhivago
director: **9** David Lean
author: **14** Boris Pasternak
cast: **10** Omar Sharif (Zhivago), Rod Steiger **12** Alec
Guinness, Tom Courtenay
13 Julie Christie (Lara)
14 Rita Tushingham
15 Ralph Richardson
16 Geraldine Chaplin

doctrinaire 5 rigid **6** mulish
8 absolute, dogmatic, stubborn **9** arbitrary, imperious,
pigheaded **10** bullheaded, inflexible, pontifical **11** dictatorial, opinionated, overbearing,
stiff-necked **12** narrow-
minded **13** authoritarian
14 disciplinarian

doctrinal 8 didactic, dogmatic,
edifying, tutorial **11** educa-

tional, instructive
12 prescriptive

doctrine 5 dogma, tenet **6** belief, gospel **7** precept **8** teaching **9** principle **10** conviction,
philosophy

document 6 back up, record,
verify **7** certify, support **9** legal
form **10** instrument **12** give
weight to, substantiate **13** official paper

documentation 5 proof **7** support **8** evidence **12** verification **13** corroboration
14 substantiation

doddering 4 weak **6** feeble, senile **7** shaking **8** decrepit
9 tottering, trembling

dodge 4 duck, wile **5** avoid,
elude, evade, hedge, trick
6 device, swerve **7** fend off
8 sidestep **9** jump aside, stratagem, turn aside **10** equivocate **11** machination

dodging 7 ducking, eluding,
evading **8** shunning **12** sidestepping **13** circumventing

Dodgson, Charles Lutwidge
real name of: **12** Lewis
Carroll

Dodoma
capital of: **8** Tanzania

Dodonian
epithet of: **4** Zeus

Dodsworth
director: **12** William Wyler
author: **13** Sinclair Lewis
character: **4** Fran **12** Arnold
Israel **14** Edith Cortright,
Renee de Penable **15** Samuel Dodsworth **16** Kurt von
Obersdorf **17** Major Clyde
Lockert
cast: **9** Mary Astor, Paul Lukas **10** David Niven **12** Walter Huston **14** Ruth
Chatterton

doer 6 dynamo **7** hustler **8** activist, go-getter **12** active
person

doff 4 bare, drop, junk, shed
5 scrap, strip **6** put off, remove **7** abandon, cast off, discard, disrobe, take off, toss
off, undress **8** throw off, throw
out **9** eliminate, step out of
10 do away with

dog *see box, p. 278*

Dogberry
character in: **19** Much Ado
About Nothing
author: **11** Shakespeare

Dog Day Afternoon
director: **11** Sidney Lumet
cast: **8** Al Pacino **10** John
Cazale **14** Charles Durning

dogged 8 stubborn **9** tenacious
10 determined, persistent
11 unremitting

dogie 4 calf **14** motherless calf

dogies 6 calves, cattle
16 motherless calves

dogma 5 credo, tenet **7** beliefs
8 doctrine **9** teachings **10** philosophy, principles
11 convictions

dogmatic 6 biased **8** stubborn
9 arbitrary, doctrinal, imperious, obstinate **10** prejudiced
11 dictatorial, domineering,
opinionated

Dog Star
constellation of:
Hunting Dogs: **13** Canes
Venatici
Larger Dog: **10** Canis
Major
Smaller Dog: **10** Canis
Minor

dogwood 6 Cornus
varieties: **5** Brown, Creek,
False, Giant, Silky, Stiff
6 Pagoda, Poison **7** Chinese
8 American, Jamaican,
Mountain, Panicled, Red-
osier, Siberian, Tatarian
9 Blood-twig, Flowering,
Tartarian **10** Golden-twig,
West Indian **11** Round-
leaved **13** White Mountain

Doha, al-Dawha
capital of: **5** Qatar

do in 4 kill **6** murder **7** destroy,
exhaust, tire out

Doktor Faust
opera by: **6** Busoni
character: **5** Faust **14** Duchess of Parma
14 Mephistopheles

dolce
music: **7** sweetly

dolce far niente 18 pleasing
inactivity **20** it is sweet to do
nothing

dolce vita 9 sweet life

Dol Common
character in: **12** The
Alchemist
author: **6** Jonson

doldrums 5 blues, dumps,
gloom **10** depression,
melancholy

dole 4 deal, give **5** share **6** parcel **7** charity, handout, wel-
fare **9** allotment **10** allocation
13 apportionment

doleful 3 sad **6** dismal, dreary,
gloomy, woeful **7** joyless, unhappy **9** sorrowful

dolente
music: **9** sorrowful

dog 3 cur, pup 4 heel, mutt 5 beast, puppy 6 canine 7 mongrel, villain 9 scoundrel 10 blackguard

  Alaskan: 5 husky 8 malamute, malemute

  anatomy: 3 hip, lip, pad, paw, toe 4 arch, back, hock, loin, rump, stop 5 cheek, crest, croup, flews, skull 6 carpus, dewlap, muzzle, stifle, tarsus 7 brisket, cushion, knuckle, occiput, pastern, withers 8 heelknob, shoulder 10 metacarpus, metatarsus

  Australian: 5 dingo 8 warragal

  barkless: 7 basenji

  breed:

    herding group: 5 pulik 6 briard, collie 13 bearded collie 14 German Shepherd 15 Belgian malinois, Belgian sheepdog, Belgian tervuren 16 Shetland sheepdog 18 Cardigan Welsh corgi, Old English sheepdog, Pembroke Welsh corgi 19 Australian cattle dog, Bouviers des Flandres

    hound group: 6 beagle, borzoi, saluki 7 basenji, harrier, whippet 9 dachshund, greyhound 10 bloodhound, otter hound 11 Afghan hound, basset hound, Ibizan hound 12 pharaoh hound 14 Irish wolfhound 15 English foxhound 16 American foxhound 17 Norwegian elkhound, Scottish deerhound 18 Rhodesian ridgeback 20 black and tan coonhound

    nonsporting group: 6 poodle 7 bulldog 8 chow chow, keeshond 9 dalmatian, lhasa apso 10 keeshonden, schipperke 11 Bichon frise 13 Boston terrier, French bulldog 14 Tibetan spaniel, Tibetan terrier

    sporting group: 6 vizsla 7 pointer 8 Brittany 10 weimaraner 11 Irish setter 12 field spaniel, Gordon setter 13 cocker spaniel, English setter, Sussex spaniel 14 Clumber spaniel 15 golden retriever 17 Irish water spaniel, Labrador retriever 19 flat-coated retriever 20 American water spaniel, curly-coated retriever, English cocker spaniel, Welsh springer spaniel 22 Chesapeake Bay retriever, English springer spaniel 23 German wirehaired pointer 24 German shorthaired pointer 25 wirehaired pointing griffon

    terrier group: 10 fox terrier 11 bull terrier, Skye terrier 12 Cairn terrier, Irish terrier, Welsh terrier 13 border terrier 14 Norfolk terrier, Norwich terrier, wire fox terrier 15 Airedale terrier, Lakeland terrier, Scottish terrier, Sealyham terrier 16 Kerry blue terrier, smooth fox terrier 17 Australian terrier, Bedlington terrier, Manchester terrier 18 miniature schnauzer 20 Dandie Dinmont terrier 24 soft-coated wheaten terrier, Staffordshire bull terrier, West Highland white terrier 28 American Staffordshire terrier

    toy group: 3 pug 7 Maltese, shih tzu 8 papillon 9 chihuahua, pekingese, toy poodle 10 pomeranian 12 Japanese chin, silky terrier 13 affenpinscher 15 Brussels griffon 16 Italian greyhound, Yorkshire terrier 17 English toy spaniel, Manchester terrier, miniature pinscher

    working group: 5 akita, boxer 7 mastiff, samoyed 8 kuvaszok 9 great Dane, St Bernard 10 komondorok, rottweiler 11 bullmastiff 12 Newfoundland 13 great Pyrenees, Siberian husky 14 giant schnauzer 15 Alaskan malamute 16 doberman pinscher 17 standard schnauzer 18 Bernese mountain dog, Portuguese water dog

Buster Brown's: 4 Tige

Chinese: 7 shih tzu

coach: 9 dalmatian

combining form: 3 cyn 4 cani, cyno

constellation: 12 Canis Majoris

Dorothy's: 4 Toto

family: 7 Canidae

FDR's: 4 Fala 5 Falla

female: 3 dam, gip, gyp 4 slut 5 bitch, brach 7 brachet

genus: 5 Canis

group: 4 pack 5 leash 6 kennel

"His Master's Voice": 6 Nipper

Hungarian: 4 puli 6 kuvasz, vizsla

Indian: 5 dhole

Japanese: 5 akita

Little Orphan Annie's: 5 Sandy

male: 3 dog

movie/TV: 4 Asta, Lady 5 Benji, Tramp 6 Lassie 9 Old Yeller, Rin Tin Tin

mythical: 8 Cerberus

Nixon's: 8 Checkers

Punch and Judy's: 4 Toby

Russian: 6 borzoi 7 samoyed

star: 6 Sirius 8 Canicula

Welsh: 5 corgi

wild: 5 adjag, dhole, dingo, guara, rabid 6 jackal 7 agouara 8 cimarron

young: 3 pup 5 puppy, whelp

dole out 4 give, mete **5** allot **6** parcel **7** portion **8** allocate, dispense **9** apportion **10** distribute

doling out 7 dealing **9** allotment, parceling **10** allocation, assignment **12** distribution **13** apportionment

Dolius
  epithet of: **6** Hermes
  means: **6** crafty
  form: **5** slave
  given to: **8** Penelope

doll 5 dolly, dummy, honey **6** beauty, puppet **7** darling, rag doll **8** baby doll, figurine, golliwog **9** teddy bear **10** marionette, sweetheart **11** pretty child

dollar 3 one **4** bean, bill, buck, coin, note, skin, yuan **5** money, tater, token **6** single **7** ironman, smacker **8** cartwheel, simolean

Dollar A Second
  host: **9** Jan Murray

Dollar Bill
  nickname of: **11** Bill Bradley

dollop 3 dab **4** blob, dash, lump **11** small amount

Doll's House, A
  author: **11** Henrik Ibsen
  character: **8** Krogstad **10** Nora Helmer **13** Torvald Helmer

dolly 3 toy **4** cart, doll **9** plaything **15** wheeled platform

Dolon
  mentioned in: **5** Iliad
  father: **7** Eumedes
  killed by: **8** Diomedes, Odysseus

dolor 5 grief **6** sorrow **7** anguish, sadness

dolorous 3 sad **6** rueful, woeful **7** doleful, tearful, unhappy **8** dejected, downcast, grievous, mournful, pathetic, pitiable, wretched **9** anguished, cheerless, harrowing, miserable, sorrowful, woebegone **10** calamitous, despondent, lamentable, melancholy **11** distressing **12** disconsolate, heavy-hearted **13** grief-stricken

Dolphin
  constellation of: **9** Delphinus

Dolphin, The
  author: **12** Robert Lowell

dolt 4 clod, fool, jerk **5** idiot, moron **6** nitwit **7** half-wit, jackass **8** bonehead, imbecile, numskull **9** blockhead

doltish 4 dumb, slow **5** thick **6** simple, stupid **7** asinine, foolish, idiotic, moronic, wit-

less **8** ignorant, retarded **9** brainless, imbecilic **10** half-witted, slow-witted **12** dunderheaded, muddleheaded, simpleminded **13** rattlebrained **14** featherbrained

domain 4 area, fief, land **5** field **6** empire, estate, region, sphere **7** kingdom **8** dominion, property, province **9** bailiwick, territory

Dombey and Son
  author: **14** Charles Dickens
  character: **4** Paul **5** Toots **6** Carker, Cuttle **8** Florence, Mr Dombey **9** Dr Blimber, Walter Gay **11** Joe Bagstock, Susan Nipper **12** Cousin Feenix, Edith Granger, Solomon Gills

dome
  Italian: **5** duomo

Domenichino
  real name: **16** Domenico Zampieri
  born: **5** Italy **7** Bologna
  artwork: **11** Hunt of Diana **16** Monsignor Agucchi **18** The Four Evangelists, The Life of St Cecilia **23** Last Communion of St Jerome **30** Landscape with Tobias and the Angel

domestic 4 cook, maid, tame **6** butler, native **7** endemic, servant **8** homemade, houseboy **9** attendant, home-grown **10** indigenous, not foreign **11** housebroken, native-grown, not imported **12** domesticated, hearth-loving **13** household help

domesticated 4 tame **11** housebroken

domicile 4 home **5** house **8** dwelling **9** residence **14** legal residence

dominance 4 edge **8** hegemony **9** advantage, authority, upper hand **10** precedence **11** preeminence, superiority

dominant 5 chief, major **6** ruling **8** superior **9** principal **10** commanding **11** controlling, outstanding **13** authoritative, most important, most prominent

dominate 4 rule **5** dwarf **6** direct, govern **7** command, control **8** domineer **9** tower over **11** preside over

dominating 6 lordly, ruling **7** topmost **8** dominant **9** directing, governing, principal, prominent **10** commanding **11** controlling, domineering, outstanding **12** advantageous

13 authoritative, most important **15** most outstanding

domination 4 rule **5** power **7** command, control, mastery **9** authority **11** superiority

domineer 7 control **8** dominate, lord over **9** dictate to, tyrannize

domineering 8 arrogant, despotic, dogmatic **9** imperious **10** commanding, oppressive, tyrannical **11** dictatorial, overbearing **13** authoritative

Dominican Republic see box, p. 280

dominion 4 land, rule **5** realm **6** domain, empire, region **7** command, mastery **9** authority, supremacy, territory **11** sovereignty **12** jurisdiction
  Hindu: **3** raj

Dominus 3 God **4** Lord

Dominus vobiscum 16 the Lord be with you

don 4 wear **5** put on **6** pull on **7** dress in, get into

Don
  origin: **5** Welsh
  form: **7** goddess
  son: **7** Gwydion
  daughter: **8** Arianrod

dona 4 lady **5** madam

Dona Flor and Her Two Husbands
  author: **10** Jorge Amado

Donalbain
  father: **6** Duncan
  brother: **7** Malcom

Donald Duck
  creator: **10** Walt Disney
  character:
    girlfriend: **5** Daisy
    nephew: **4** Huey **5** Dewey, Louie
    uncle: **7** Scrooge

Donar
  origin: **8** Germanic
  god of: **7** thunder

donate 4 give **6** bestow **7** present **8** bequeath **10** contribute **11** make a gift of

Donatello
  real name: **15** Donato di Niccolo
  born: **5** Italy **9** Florence
  artwork: **5** David **6** St Mark **7** Zuccone **8** Jeremiah, St George **11** Gattamelata **12** Mary Magdalen **19** Judith and Holofernes, St John the Evangelist **22** Cavalcanti Annunciation

donation 4 gift **7** present **12** contribution

Dominican Republic
capital/largest city: 12 Santo Domingo **14** Ciudad Trujillo
others: 4 Azua, Bani, Moca, Pena, Polo **5** Bonao, Cotui, Nagua, Neiba, Nizao, Sosua **6** Higuey, La Vega, Oviedo **7** Sanchez **8** Barahona, Santiago **11** Puerto Plata **17** San Pedro de Macoris **21** San Francisco de Macoris
measure: 3 ona **5** tarea **6** fanega
monetary unit: 3 oro **4** peso **6** franco
island: 5 Beata, Saona **8** Altovelo, Catalina **10** Hispaniola
lake: 10 Enriquillo
mountain: 4 Tina **5** Gallo, Neiba **7** Baoruco, Central **8** Bahoruco, Oriental **13** Sententrional
highest point: 6 Duarte
river: 4 Yuna **5** Ozama **11** Yaque del Sur **13** Yaque del Norte
sea: 8 Atlantic **9** Caribbean
physical feature:
  bay: **4** Ocoa, Yuma **5** Neiba **6** Rincon, Samana **7** Isabela **8** Calderas, Escocesa
  cape: **5** Beata, Falso **6** Cabron, Engano **7** Caucedo, Isabela, Macoris
  valley: **4** Real **5** Neyba
people: 5 Negro, Taino **6** Indian **7** mulatto, Spanish **9** Caucasian
  discoverer: **8** Columbus
language: 6 French **7** English, Spanish
religion: 13 Roman Catholic
feature:
  dance: **8** merengue
  religious pilgrimage: **8** romerias
food:
  dessert: **8** pinonate
  fish/meat pastry: **10** pastelitos
  stew: **8** sancocho

Don Careless
  author: 8 Rex Beach
Don Carlos
  author: 14 Johann Schiller
  opera by: 5 Verdi
  character: 7 Rodrigo **8** Philip II **9** Don Carlos **13** Princess Eboli **15** Grand Inquisitor **17** Elizabeth de Valois
Dondi
  creator: 8 Gus Edson **10** Irwin Hasen
  dog: 7 Queenie
done 5 ready **8** finished, prepared **9** completed **12** cooked enough **18** cooked sufficiently
done for 4 dead, gone, over, sunk **5** all up, ended, kaput, spent **6** beaten, doomed, ruined **7** all over, damaged, through **8** finished **9** exhausted
done in 4 beat **5** all in, slain, spent, tired, weary **6** bushed, killed, pooped **7** drained, wearied, worn out **8** dog tired, fatigued, murdered, tired out **9** bone weary, dead tired, played out **10** knocked off
Don Giovanni
  also: 7 Don Juan **15** The Rake Punished

  opera by: 6 Mozart
  setting: 7 Seville
  character: 7 Masetto, Zerlina **9** Donna Anna, Leporello **10** Don Ottavio **11** Donna Elvira **15** The Commendatore
Donizetti, Gaetano
  born: 5 Italy **7** Bergamo
  composer of: 10 Anna Bolena, La Favorita **11** Don Pasquale **12** Elixir of Love, Maria Stuarda **13** L'elisir d'amore, Marino Faliero, Torquato Tasso **14** Lucrezia Borgia **15** Roberto Devereux **16** Linda di Chamounix **17** Lucia di Lammermoor **21** Daughter of the Regiment
Don Juan 3 man **4** beau, wolf **5** Romeo, swain, wooer **6** fellow, squire, steady, suitor **7** admirer, courter, gallant, pursuer **8** Casanova, lothario, lover boy, paramour, young man **9** boyfriend, Lochinvar **10** lady-killer **15** gentleman caller
Don Juan
  author: 21 George Gordon Lord Byron

character: 6 Haidee **9** Donna Inez **10** Donna Julia
donkey 3 ass **4** fool, mule **5** burro, idiot **7** jackass
Donlevy, Brian
  wife: 12 Marjorie Lane
  born: 7 Ireland **9** Portadown
  roles: 9 Beau Geste **15** The Great McGinty **21** Two Years Before the Mast
Donn, Arabella
  character in: 14 Jude the Obscure
  author: 5 Hardy
donna 4 lady **5** madam
Donna Reed Show, The
  character: 9 Jeff Stone, Mary Stone **10** Donna Stone **11** Dr Alex Stone, Midge Kelsey, Trisha Stone **12** Dr Dave Kelsey
  cast: 8 Bob Crane, Carl Betz **9** Ann McCrea, Donna Reed **12** Paul Peterson **13** Patty Peterson **14** Shelley Fabares
Donne, John
  author of: 7 Sermons **10** The Ecstasy, The Extasie **11** Holy Sonnets **15** Death Be Not Proud, Songs and Sonnets, The Canonization **20** Paradoxes and Problems **30** A Valediction Forbidding Mourning
donnish 7 preachy **8** academic, didactic, pedantic **9** pedagogic
Donnithorne, Arthur
  character in: 8 Adam Bede
  author: 5 Eliot
donnybrook 3 row **4** fray **5** brawl, fight, melee, set-to **6** affray, dustup, fracas, ruckus, rumpus **7** ruction, scuffle **8** skirmish **10** free-for-all **19** knock-down-and-drag-out
donor 5 giver **10** benefactor **11** contributor **12** humanitarian **14** philanthropist
do-nothing 5 idler **6** loafer **14** good-for-nothing
do not prosecute
  Latin: 13 nolle prosequi
do not repeat
  Latin: 12 non repetatur
Don Pasquale
  opera by: 9 Donizetti
  character: 6 Norina **7** Ernesto **11** Dr Malatesta
Don Quixote de la Mancha
  also: 38 El ingenioso hidalgo Don Quijote de la Mancha
  author: 17 Miguel de Cervantes (Saavedra)
  character: 10 Pedro Perez

11 Sancho Panza **17** Dulcinea del Toboso
horse: 9 Rosinante
musical: 13 Man of La Mancha

doodad 5 gizmo **6** device, gadget **8** ornament **9** doohickey **10** decoration **11** contraption, contrivance, thingamabob, thingamajig **15** whatchamacallit

doohickey 5 gizmo, thing **6** device, dingus, gadget, object, widget **7** dojiggy, whatsis **8** dojigger **9** thingummy **11** thingamabob, thingamajig **14** thingamadoodle **15** whatchamacallit

Dooley, Thomas Anthony
founded: 6 MEDICO **31** Medical International Corporation
worked in: 13 Southeast Asia

Doolittle, Eliza
character in: 9 Pygmalion **10** My Fair Lady
author: 4 Shaw

doom 3 end, lot **4** fate, ruin **5** death, judge **7** condemn, convict, destiny, portion, verdict **8** judgment **10** Armageddon **11** destruction, Judgment Day **13** consign to ruin, end of the world, pronouncement **15** resurrection day, the Last Judgment **17** mark for demolition

doomed 5 fated **6** damned, ruined **8** ill-fated **9** condemned

doomsday 11 Judgment Day **13** Day of Judgment, end of the world **15** the Last Judgment

do one's best 3 try **6** strive **7** attempt **8** endeavor, go all out **9** take pains **12** make an effort **13** give all one has **15** knock oneself out

Doonesbury
creator: 12 Garry Trudeau
character: 2 B D **5** Honey, Rufus **6** Calvin **7** Boopsie **9** Uncle Duke **12** Joanie Caucus **14** Mark Slackmeyer **18** Michael J Doonesbury

door 4 exit **5** entry **6** egress, portal **7** hallway, ingress **8** entrance **11** entranceway

Door hinges
goddess of: 6 Cardea

doorway 5 entry **7** ingress, opening **8** entrance

Doorways
god of: 5 Janus

dope 3 tip **4** drip, drug, fool, jerk, nerd, news **5** creep, drugs, dummy, klutz, scoop **6** sedate, uppers **7** downers, opiates **8** additive **9** narcotics, narcotize, substance **10** antiseptic, astringent, medication **11** anesthetize, preparation **12** disinfectant **17** inside information

dope fiend 4 head, user **5** doper, freak **6** addict, junkie **7** hophead **8** cokehead **10** dope addict, drug abuser, drug addict

do penance 5 atone **7** expiate **10** make amends

dopey 4 dumb **6** leaden, stupid, torpid **7** asinine, idiotic, witless **8** comatose, mindless, sluggish **9** brainless, lethargic **10** dull-witted, slow-witted, slumberous **11** blockheaded, thickheaded **12** simple-minded

Doppelganger 6 double **13** ghostly double
literally: 12 double-walker

Doppler, Christian Johann
field: 7 physics
nationality: 8 Austrian
discovered: 13 Doppler Effect

Dorcas
also called: 7 Tabitha
revived by: 5 Peter
hometown: 5 Joppa

Doris
father: 7 Oceanus
mother: 6 Tethys
husband: 6 Nereus
mother of: 7 Nereids

Doritis
epithet of: 9 Aphrodite
means: 9 bountiful

dormancy 7 latency **8** inaction **10** inactivity, quiescence, somnolence **11** hibernation

dormant 4 idle **8** inactive, sleeping **9** quiescent, somnolent **11** hibernating

Dorothy
character in: 13 The Wizard of Oz
author: 4 Baum

Dorset, Bertha and George
characters in: 15 The House of Mirth
author: 7 Wharton

dorsum 5 chine, spine **8** backbone

Dorus
father: 6 Apollo, Hellen
mother: 6 Orseis, Phthia
killed by: 7 Aetolus

dose 2 OD **3** cut, nip **4** dram, pill, shot, slug **5** quota, share, slice **6** amount, needle, ration, tablet **7** capsule, measure, portion, section, segment **8** division, overdose, quantity **9** allotment, allowance, daily dose, injection **10** percentage

Dos Passos, John
author of: 3 U S A **11** The Big Money **13** Three Soldiers **16** Nineteen Nineteen **17** Manhattan Transfer **22** The Forty-Second Parallel

dossier 4 file **5** brief **6** record **9** portfolio **14** detailed report

Dostoevsky, Fyodor Mikhailovich
author of: 8 The Idiot **9** The Double **10** The Gambler **12** The Possessed **18** Crime and Punishment **20** The Brothers Karamazov **23** Notes from the Underground

dot 3 dab **4** mark, spot **5** fleck, point, speck **6** dapple, period **9** small spot

dotage 8 senility **15** second childhood **16** feeblemindedness

dote 8 be senile, fuss over

dote on 5 adore, prize, spoil, value **6** pamper **7** cherish, indulge **8** fuss over, treasure **15** lavish affection

doting 4 fond **6** loving **9** indulgent, pampering **12** affectionate

double 4 dual, twin **5** clone **6** paired **7** replica, two-part **8** two-sided **9** ambiguous, duplicate **10** dead ringer **11** again as much, counterpart, meant for two, twice as much **12** twice as great **13** multiply by two, spitting image **15** increase twofold
German: 12 Doppelganger

Double, The
author: 16 Fyodor Dostoevsky

double-cross 5 rat on **6** betray, do dirt, tell on, turn in **7** abandon, deceive, let down, sell out, two-time **8** denounce, inform on, run out on, snitch on **9** play Judas **10** be disloyal **13** be treacherous, inform against, play false with **14** break faith with **16** blow the whistle on, sell down the river

double-crosser 5 cheat **7** traitor **8** betrayer, deceiver, informer

Double-Dealer, The
author: 15 William Congreve

double-dealing 5 false **6** deceit, sneaky, tricky **7** crooked, devious, perfidy **8** bad faith, betrayal, disloyal **9** deceitful, duplicity, falseness, treachery, two-timing **10** disloyalty, perfidious, sneakiness **11** crookedness, double-cross, duplicitous, treacherous **12** dishonorable **13** breach of faith, faithlessness

double entendre 12 off-color joke, risque remark **18** ambiguous statement

double entente 9 ambiguity

Double Indemnity
   director: **11** Billy Wilder
   cast: **13** Fred MacMurray
   15 Barbara Stanwyck, Edward G Robinson
   script: **9** James Cain **15** Raymond Chandler

Double Life, A
   director: **11** George Cukor
   cast: **10** Signe Hasso **12** Edmond O'Brien, Ronald Colman **14** Shelley Winters
   Oscar for: **5** actor (Colman)
   script: **10** Ruth Gordon
   11 Garson Kanin

double meaning 9 ambiguity
   French: **13** double entente
   14 double entendre

doublet 4 pair **5** tunic **6** couple, jacket **10** two of a kind

double-talk 4 bunk, jazz **5** hokum **6** bunkum, drivel, gabble, jabber **7** baloney, blather, palaver, prattle, twaddle **8** flimflam, flummery, nonsense **9** gibberish **10** balderdash, hocus-pocus, mumbo jumbo **11** obfuscation **12** gobbledygook

double-walker
   German: **12** Doppelganger

Double X
   nickname of: **9** Jimmy Foxx

doubt 5 qualm **6** wonder **7** suspect **8** distrust, mistrust, question **9** misgiving, skeptical, suspicion **10** be doubtful, indecision **11** uncertainty **12** apprehension **13** feel uncertain **14** waver in opinion **15** have doubts about **16** lack confidence in, lack of conviction

Doubter see **6** Thomas

doubtful 5 vague **7** dubious, obscure, suspect, unclear **9** tentative, uncertain, undecided, unsettled **10** hesitating, irresolute, suspicious **11** unconvinced **12** inconclusive, questionable

doubtfulness 5 doubt **7** dubiety **8** distrust, mistrust, unbelief **9** disbelief, suspicion **10** skepticism **11** incredulity **14** lack of credence

Doubting see **6** Thomas

doucement
   music: **6** gently

douceur 3 tip **5** bribe **8** gratuity **9** sweetness

dough 4 cash, duff, spud **5** bread, crust, money, paster **6** batter, change, leaven, noodle **8** doughboy **11** infantryman

doughnut 4 cake, tire **5** bagel, torus **6** cymbal, dunker, sinker **7** beignet, cruller, twister

doughty 4 bold **5** brave **6** strong **8** fearless, intrepid, unafraid **9** confident, dauntless **10** courageous, determined **12** stout-hearted

Douglas, Archibald
   character in: **7** Marmion
   author: **5** Scott

Douglas, Kirk
   real name: **17** Issur Danielovitch
   son: **7** Michael
   born: **11** Amsterdam NY
   roles: **8** Champion **9** Spartacus **10** The Vikings **11** Lust for Life **14** Detective Story, Seven Days in May **17** The Glass Menagerie, Young Man with a Horn **18** Letter to Three Wives **22** Mourning Becomes Electra

Douglas, Lloyd C
   author of: **7** The Robe
   23 The Magnificent Obsession

Douglas, Melvyn
   real name: **23** Melvyn Edouard Hesselberg
   wife: **12** Helen Gahagan
   born: **7** Macon GA
   roles: **3** Hud **9** Ninotchka **10** Being There

Douglas, Michael
   father: **4** Kirk
   roles: **4** Coma **10** Wall Street **11** Star Chamber **14** Jewel of the Nile **15** Fatal Attraction (Oscar) **16** The China Syndrome **17** Romancing the Stone

dour 4 sour **6** gloomy, morose, solemn, sullen **9** cheerless **10** forbidding, unfriendly

Douras, Marion Cecilia
   real name of: **12** Marion Davies

douse 4 soak **5** souse **6** drench **7** immerse **8** saturate, submerge **15** plunge into water

Dove, Noah's
   constellation of: **7** Columba

Dover Beach
   author: **13** Matthew Arnold

dovetail 4 jibe, join **5** match, tally, unite **8** coincide **9** harmonize **11** fit together **12** interlocking

dowager 5 widow **6** relict **7** elderly

dowdy 4 drab **5** tacky **6** frumpy, shabby, sloppy **8** slovenly **12** unattractive

dowel 3 peg, pin, rod **4** pole **5** stick **7** spindle

down 3 ill **4** blue, deck, drop, fell, gulp, sick **5** drink, floor **6** ailing **7** put away, swallow **8** dejected, downcast, feathers **9** depressed **10** dispirited **12** disheartened

down-and-out 4 sick **5** broke **9** penniless **12** impoverished, on one's uppers **13** incapacitated **15** under the weather

downcast 3 low, sad **4** blue **7** unhappy **8** dejected **9** cheerless, depressed **11** discouraged **12** disconsolate, disheartened

downfall 4 fall, ruin **6** shower **8** collapse, downpour **9** rainstorm, ruination **10** rain shower **11** destruction

downgrade 4 drop **5** lower **6** debase **7** decline, descent, way down **8** belittle, minimize **9** declivity, denigrate, devaluate **10** depreciate

downhearted 3 sad **7** unhappy **8** dejected, downcast **9** depressed, sorrowful **10** dispirited **11** discouraged **12** disheartened

downheartedness 5 gloom **6** dismay **7** despair, sadness **9** dejection, pessimism **10** depression, low spirits, melancholy **11** despondency **12** hopelessness **14** discouragement

down in the dumps 4 blue, glum **6** gloomy **7** in a funk **9** depressed **10** despondent **13** in the doldrums

down in the mouth 3 sad **6** dismal, woeful **7** joyless, unhappy **8** dejected, downcast **9** depressed, sorrowful, woebegone **10** lugubrious **12** disconsolate

downpayment 6 binder **7** advance, deposit **9** money down

downpour 6 shower **9** rainstorm **10** cloudburst, rain shower

downright 4 open **5** blunt, frank, total, utter **6** candid, direct, honest, really **7** in truth, plainly, sincere, utterly **8** absolute, actually, complete

9 out-and-out **10** aboveboard, completely, thoroughly **12** unmistakably **13** thoroughgoing, unequivocally **15** straightforward

Downright
    character in: **19** Every Man in His Humour
    author: **6** Jonson

downstairs 5 below **6** cellar **8** basement **10** first floor **11** ground floor

down the drain 4 gone, lost **9** up in smoke **12** out the window

down-to-earth 5 crass, plain, sober, solid **6** casual, coarse, earthy, simple **7** relaxed **8** informal, sensible **9** practical, pragmatic, realistic **10** hardheaded, hard-boiled, nononsense **11** plain-spoken, substantial **12** matter-of-fact, unidealistic **13** unsentimental

downtown 9 inner city, urban area **10** center city, metropolis **16** business district, metropolitan area

downtrodden 9 exploited, oppressed **10** tyrannized **11** subservient **12** harshly ruled

downturn 3 dip, sag **4** drop, fall, skid, slip **5** slide, slump **6** plunge, waning **7** decline, reverse, setback **8** decrease **9** downslide, downswing, downtrend, dwindling, recession **10** depression, diminution **12** degeneration **13** deterioration

Down Under see **9** Australia

down with
    French: **4** a bas

downy 4 soft **5** fuzzy, nappy, plumy, quiet **6** fleecy, fluffy **7** cunning, knowing **8** feathery **9** featherbed

do wrong 3 err, sin **8** go astray **9** misbehave **10** transgress

Doyle, Sir Arthur Conan
    author of: **13** The Sign of Four **15** A Study in Scarlet, The White Company **25** The Hound of the Baskervilles **26** Adventures of Sherlock Holmes
    character: **12** Dr John Watson **13** Mycroft Holmes **14** Sherlock Holmes **17** Inspector Lestrade, Professor Moriarty

doze 3 nap **6** catnap, siesta, snooze **10** forty winks, light sleep **12** sleep lightly

dozy 4 lazy **6** drowsy, sleepy

7 languid **9** lethargic, somnolent

D P 5 exile **6** emigre **7** outcast, refugee **8** deportee **10** expatriate **14** banished person, deported person **15** displaced person **16** political refugee

drab 4 dull, gray **5** dingy **6** dismal, dreary, gloomy, somber **9** cheerless, dull brown **10** lackluster

drabness 8 dullness **9** dinginess **10** dreariness, gloominess **13** colorlessness

Dracula
    author: **10** Bram Stoker
    character: **8** Dr Seward **10** Mina Murray **12** Count Dracula, Dr Van Hesling, Lucy Westenra **14** Arthur Holmwood, Jonathan Harker

draft 4 drag, gulp, haul, pull, wind **5** drink **6** breeze, induct, sketch **7** diagram, outline, swallow **9** conscript, induction **10** money order **11** postal order, rough sketch **12** conscription, current of air **15** military service **16** drawing from a cask **18** preliminary version **22** call for military service

drafty 6 breezy, chilly

drag 3 lug **4** bore, haul, pull **5** bring, crawl, trail **6** dredge **7** be drawn **9** inch along **10** creep along, move slowly, spoilsport, wet blanket **11** party-pooper

Dragnet
    character: **8** (Sgt) Ed Jacobs **9** (Sgt) Ben Romero, (Sgt) Joe Friday **10** (Officer) Bill Gannon, (Officer) Frank Smith
    cast: **8** Jack Webb **9** Herb Ellis **11** Harry Morgan **12** Ben Alexander **14** Barney Phillips **16** Barton Yarborough
    setting: **10** Los Angeles

Dragon 14 Leviathan
    constellation of: **5** Draco

drag on 4 last **6** endure, keep on, keep up **7** persist **8** continue **9** persevere

drag one's feet 5 crawl, creep **6** dawdle **9** waste time **10** move slowly **13** procrastinate

dragonfly
    varieties: **5** biddy **6** darner **7** skimmer **8** clubtail, grayback **9** amberwing **12** elisa skimmer

Dragon Seed
    author: **10** Pearl S Buck

Dragon's teeth
    sown by: **6** Cadmus
    location: **6** Thebes
    grew into: **8** warriors

dragoon 5 bully, force **6** coerce, compel **7** trooper **8** browbeat, bulldoze, cavalier, horseman, pressure **9** strongarm **10** cavalryman **12** horse soldier, horse trooper **14** mounted soldier

drag through the mud 5 smear, sully, taint **6** debase, defame, smirch, vilify **7** degrade, tarnish, vitiate **8** disgrace, dishonor **9** discredit, disparage **10** stigmatize

drain 3 sap **4** drag, pipe, tube **5** empty, sewer, use up **6** outlet, strain **7** channel, conduit, debouch, deplete, flow out, pump off **8** empty out **9** depletion, discharge, dissipate **10** impoverish

drainage 4 flow **9** discharge

drained 4 beat **5** all in, empty, spent, tired, weary **6** bushed, done in, pooped, used up **7** emptied, wearied, worn out **8** consumed, depleted, dog tired, expended, fatigued, finished, tired out **9** dead tired, enervated, exhausted, played out

Drake, Stan
    creator/artist of: **21** The Heart of Juliet Jones

Drake, Temple
    character in: **9** Sanctuary
    author: **8** Faulkner

dram
    abbreviation: **2** dr

drama 4 play **6** acting **8** the stage **9** direction, vividness **10** excitement, the theater **11** mise-en-scene **15** dramatic quality, intense interest, theatrical piece
    god of: **7** Bacchus

dramatic 8 striking **9** climactic, emotional **10** theatrical **11** sensational, suspenseful **12** melodramatic **13** for the theater

dramatics 6 acting **7** emoting **9** theatrics **10** dramaturgy, stagecraft **11** hamming it up, histrionics, thespianism

dramatis personae 4 cast **6** actors **7** players **10** performers **16** cast of characters, list of performers

dramaturgy 5 drama **7** theater **10** stagecraft **11** dramatic art

Drambuie
    type: **7** liqueur

origin: **8** Scotland
flavor: **5** herbs, honey
with scotch: **9** Rusty Nail

Drances
enemy of: **6** Turnus

drape 4 deck, garb, veil, wrap
5 adorn, array, cloak, cover,
dress **6** attire, bedeck, enrobe,
enwrap, shroud, swathe, wrap
up **7** apparel, bedight, envelop,
festoon, sheathe, swaddle
8 enshroud, enswathe

drastic 4 dire, rash **7** bizarre,
extreme, radical **8** dreadful
9 dangerous **10** outlandish
11 deleterious

Dravidian
language group: **3** Kui
5 Ghond, Tamil **6** Teluga
8 Kanarese **9** Malayalam
spoken in: **5** India **6** Ceylon
8 Sri Lanka

draw 3 get, tie, tow **4** drag,
etch, haul, limn, lure, pick,
pull, take **5** charm, draft,
drain, evoke, infer, write **6** allure, come-on, deduce, elicit,
entice, extend, make up, siphon, sketch **7** attract, distort,
draw out, extract, make out,
pick out, pull out, pump out,
stretch, suck dry, take out,
wrinkle **8** contract, deadlock,
elongate, protract **9** attenuate,
pull along, stalemate **10** attraction, bring forth, enticement, inducement, make
appear **14** make a picture of

draw away 2 go **5** leave **6** go
back, shrink **7** retreat
8 withdraw

drawback 8 handicap, obstacle **9** detriment, hindrance
10 impediment **12** disadvantage **14** stumbling block

draw back 6 flinch, recoil
7 back off, retreat **8** move
away, withdraw

draw close 3 hug **4** come,
near **6** arrive, enfold **7** embrace **8** approach, come nigh,
gain upon **10** move toward

drawers 5 pants **6** shorts
7 panties **8** bloomers, calzoons,
trousers **9** pantalets, underwear **10** underpants

draw forth 5 evoke **6** elicit
7 distill, extract

drawing 5 study **6** sketch
7 lottery, picture **9** depiction,
selection **11** delineation
12 illustration

drawing apart 8 dividing
9 diverging **10** separating
12 splitting off

drawing out 9 expansion, extension **10** elongation, stretching **11** attenuation,
lengthening, protraction
12 prolongation

drawing power 4 pull **6** allure, appeal **9** magnetism
10 attraction, enticement
11 fascination

drawing room 5 salon **6** parlor **10** living room **11** sitting
room **13** reception room

drawn out 4 long **7** lengthy
8 extended **9** elongated, prolonged **10** lengthened,
protracted

draw out 5 educe, evoke
6 elicit, expand, extend, extort **7** distill, enlarge, extract,
prolong, spin out, stretch
8 elongate, lengthen, protract
9 attenuate, call forth
10 stretch out

draw the line 5 limit **8** contrast, separate **12** fix a boundary **13** differentiate

draw to a close 3 end **6** finish **8** conclude **11** come to an
end

draw together 4 herd, mass,
pack **5** bunch, crowd, flock,
group **6** gather, huddle **7** cluster, collect, tighten **8** assemble,
compress, contract **9** constrict
10 congregate

draw up 3 map **5** draft **6** make
up, map out **7** charter, diagram, outline **9** blueprint

draw up plans 5 draft **6** design, sketch **7** outline

dray 4 cart **5** wagon **7** tipcart,
tumbrel **8** dumpcart

dread 4 fear **5** awful **6** fright,
terror **7** anguish, anxiety,
cower at, fearful **8** alarming,
cringe at **10** be afraid of, horrifying, shrink from, terrifying **11** fearfulness, frightening,
trepidation **12** apprehension
20 anticipate with horror

dreaded object
French: **9** bete noire

dreadful 5 awful **6** tragic
7 fearful **8** alarming, horrible,
shocking, terrible **9** frightful
11 distressing

dream 3 joy **4** goal, hope,
muse, wish **5** think **6** desire,
vision **7** delight, fantasy, hope
for, incubus, reverie, think
up **8** consider, pleasure, prospect **9** nightmare **11** expectation, have as a goal **13** look
forward to, lost in thought

Dream Merchants, The
author: **13** Harold Robbins

**Dream of the Golden
Mountains, The**
author: **13** Malcolm Cowley

Dreams
god of: **6** Icelus, Oniros
7 Oneiros **8** Morpheus
9 Phantasus

Dream Songs, The
author: **12** John Berryman

dream up 5 frame, hatch
6 create, invent **7** concoct
8 conceive, contrive

dreamy 4 airy **5** blank, empty,
vague **6** absent, musing, unreal **8** ethereal, fanciful, illusory, soothing **9** fantastic,
wonderful **10** delightful
11 preoccupied, unrealistic
13 unsubstantial **14** out of this
world

dreariness 9 bleakness **10** desolation, dismalness, gloominess, melancholy
13 cheerlessness

dreary 3 sad **4** drab **5** bleak
6 dismal, gloomy **7** forlorn
8 mournful **9** cheerless **10** depressing, melancholy

dregs 6 rabble **7** deposit,
grounds, residue **8** canaille,
riffraff, sediment **9** settlings,
worst part **11** lower depths

Dreiser, Theodore
author of: **8** The Titan
12 Sister Carrie, The Financier **17** An American
Tragedy

drench 3 wet **4** soak **5** douse
8 saturate

dress 4 curl, deck, do up,
garb, gown, robe, trim
5 adorn, frock, groom, treat
6 attire **7** apparel, arrange,
bandage, cleanse, clothes,
comb out, costume, garnish
8 clothing, decorate, ornament **9** disinfect, embellish
12 put on clothes **13** clothe
oneself

Dressed to Kill
director: **12** Brian De Palma
cast: **10** Nancy Allen
11 Keith Gordon **12** Michael
Caine **14** Angie Dickinson

dressed up 7 adorned, duded
up **8** costumed, dolled up,
tarted up **9** decorated, disguised, in costume **10** ornamented **11** embellished

dresser 6 bureau **7** cabinet,
commode **8** cupboard **10** chiffonier **14** chest of drawers

dressing-down 6 rebuke
7 censure, chiding, reproof
8 reproach, scolding **9** reprimand **10** bawling-out,

chewing-out, upbraiding
11 castigation, reprobation
12 remonstrance **13** tongue-lashing

dressing-gown
French: 13 robe-de-chambre

dressmaker 9 couturier, midinette **10** couturiere, seamstress

dress up 5 adorn **6** doll up
7 enhance, improve **8** beautify, ornament, spruce up **9** embellish, embroider, smarten up
10 exaggerate

Dreyfuss, Richard
born: 10 Brooklyn NY
roles: 4 Jaws **6** Tin Men
8 Stakeout **14** The Goodbye Girl (Oscar) **15** Moon Over Parador **16** American Graffiti **24** Down and Out in Beverly Hills **29** Close Encounters of the Third Kind **31** The Apprenticeship of Duddy Kravitz

dribble 4 drip, kick **6** bounce
7 drizzle, trickle **11** fall in drops, run bit by bit

driblet 4 drip, drop, tear
7 droplet, globule

dried up 4 arid **7** drained, parched **9** prunelike, shriveled **10** dehydrated, desiccated

drift 3 aim **4** flow, gist, heap, mass, pile **5** amass, amble, sense **6** course, gather, object, pile up, ramble, stream, wander **7** current, meander, meaning, purpose, scatter
8 movement **9** direction, intention, objective **10** accumulate **11** implication, peregrinate **12** accumulation, be borne along

drifter 3 bum **4** hobo **5** idler, tramp **6** loafer **8** derelict, vagabond **16** ne'er-do-well

drill 4 bore **5** punch, train
6 pierce **8** exercise, practice, puncture, training, work with **10** boring tool, repetition **11** instruction **17** repeated exercises
type: 4 hand **5** twist **8** electric

drilling 4 rote **6** boring **8** practice, training **9** schooling **10** discipline **11** preparation

drink 3 sip **4** gulp, swig
5 booze, taste, toast **6** absorb, imbibe, ingest, salute, take in **7** alcohol, swallow **8** beverage, libation **9** partake of, the bottle **10** alcoholism **11** drunkenness **15** alcoholic liquor **17** liquid refreshment
type of: 3 cup, fix **4** fizz, flip, mull, puff, sour **5** daisy, julep, punch, shrub, sling,

smash **6** cooler, frappe, rickey **7** cobbler, stinger **8** highball

drinker 3 sot **4** lush, wino
5 dipso, drunk, rummy, souse **6** bibber, boozer, sponge **7** guzzler, imbiber, tippler, waterer **8** drunkard **9** alcoholic, inebriate

drink in 6 absorb, digest, soak up, take in **10** assimilate **14** immerse oneself

Drinking
god of: 5 Comus

drinking spree 4 orgy, toot
5 binge, drunk **6** bender **8** beer-bust, carousal **9** bacchanal

drink up 4 gulp **5** quaff **6** absorb, guzzle, soak up **7** consume, swallow

drip 3 ass **4** bore, jerk, nerd
5 creep, dummy, klutz **6** splash **7** dribble, drizzle, trickle **8** sprinkle

dripping 3 wet **4** damp
5 soggy **6** soaked, sodden **10** soaking wet

drive 4 goad, lead, mean, move, prod, push, ride, rush, spur, urge **5** force, guide, impel, motor, press, steer, surge **6** coerce, compel, incite, intend, outing **7** advance, conduct, go by car, impulse, operate, suggest **8** ambition, campaign, motivate **9** excursion, insinuate, trip by car, urge along **10** motivation

drive apart 8 alienate, estrange **9** disaffect

drive away 4 rout, shoo
5 chase, deter, repel **6** rebuff **7** repulse **8** alienate **11** put to flight, send packing

drive home 7 impress **8** hammer at

drivel 5 drool **6** babble, ramble, slaver **7** dribble, slobber **8** babbling, nonsense, rambling **9** gibberish **12** talk nonsense **13** senseless talk, talk foolishly

drive out 4 fire **5** chase, depel, eject, evict, exile, expel, force, roust **6** compel, remove **7** dismiss, repulse **8** discharge, exorcise

driver 6 cowboy, drover
8 herdsman **9** chauffeur

drizzle 3 fog **4** mist, rain
7 dribble **8** sprinkle

drizzly 3 wet **4** damp **5** foggy, misty, rainy

Dr Jekyll and Mr Hyde
author: 20 Robert Louis Stevenson
character: 5 Poole **10** Mr Utterson **13** Dr Henry Jekyll **14** Dr Hastie Lanyon

Dr Kildare
character: 14 Dr James Kildare **18** Dr Leonard Gillespie
cast: 13 Raymond Massey
18 Richard Chamberlain
hospital: 12 Blair General

Dr No
author: 10 Ian Fleming

Dr Strangelove or How I Learned to Stop Worrying and Love the Bomb
director: 14 Stanley Kubrick
cast: 9 Peter Bull **10** Keenan Wynn **11** Slim Pickens **12** George C Scott, Peter Sellers **14** James Earl Jones, Sterling Hayden

Dr Zhivago
author: 14 Boris Pasternak
character: 4 Lara
setting: 17 Russian Revolution

droll 5 funny **7** offbeat, strange **8** humorous **9** eccentric, laughable, whimsical **12** oddly amusing

drollery 3 wit **5** humor **6** banter, comedy, whimsy **7** jesting

Dromio
character in: 17 The Comedy of Errors
author: 11 Shakespeare

drone 3 hum **4** buzz, whir
5 idler **6** loafer **7** vibrate **8** parasite **9** murmuring, vibration **10** lazy person

drool 6 drivel, slaver **7** dribble, slobber **8** salivate **15** water at the mouth

droop 3 dim, sag **4** flag, sink
5 lower **6** weaken, wither **8** diminish, hang down **9** lose vigor **14** hang listlessly **15** incline downward

droopy 4 bent, blue, down, limp **5** baggy, bowed, slack **6** dashed, pining **7** doleful, sagging, subdued **8** cast down, dangling, dejected, downcast **9** depressed **10** despairing, despondent, dispirited, spiritless, world-weary **11** downhearted, hanging down, languishing **14** down in the mouth

drop 3 can, dab **4** bead, dash, deck, dive, drip, fall, fell, fire, omit, sack, sink, tear **5** abyss, floor, leave, lower, pinch, slide, slope, smack, trace **6** give up, lessen, plunge **7** abandon, decline, descend, descent, dismiss, dribble, driblet, dwindle, forsake, globule, plummet, slacken, smidgen, soupcon, trickle **8** decrease, diminish, leave out, lowering **9** declivity, discharge, knock down, precipice, terminate **10** sprinkling **12** bring to an end **13** fail to include **15** cease to consider, fail to pronounce

drop anchor 4 dock, moor **5** tie up

drop in 4 call, come **5** visit **6** appear, come by, look in, show up, stop by, turn up **7** stop off **9** pay a visit

droplet 4 bead, drip, tear **7** driblet, globule **8** spherule

droplets of moisture 3 dew, fog **4** mist **5** sweat **12** condensation

drop out 4 quit **5** leave **6** resign, retire

dross 4 scum, slag **5** waste **6** cinder, scoria **8** clinkers, impurity

drought, drouth 4 lack, need, want **6** dearth **7** aridity, paucity **8** scarcity, shortage **10** deficiency, dry weather, lack of rain **13** insufficiency

drover 6 cowboy, driver **7** cowpoke **8** herdsman, shepherd **10** cowpuncher

drown 4 soak **5** flood **6** deluge, drench, engulf **7** immerse **8** inundate, overcome, submerge **9** overpower, overwhelm, suffocate, swallow up **10** asphyxiate

drowse 3 nap, nod **4** doze, laze **5** dover, drone, sleep **6** snooze **7** slumber **8** languish **10** sleepiness

drowsy 4 dozy, lazy, slow **5** tired **6** sleepy **7** languid **8** hypnotic, listless, sluggish, soothing **9** lethargic, somnolent, soporific

drub 3 hit **4** beat, cane, flog, whip **5** whale **6** thrash **9** bastinado

drubbing 6 caning **7** beating, licking, tanning **9** trouncing **11** shellacking

drudge 4 grub, hack, plod, toil **5** labor, slave **6** lackey, menial, toiler **7** grubber **8** inferior, struggle **9** underling **11** subordinate

drudgery 4 toil **5** grind **7** travail **8** hack work **11** menial labor **15** distasteful work

Druk-Yul *see* **6** Bhutan

drum 3 din, keg, rap, tap, tub **4** beat, cask, roar, roll **5** expel, force **6** barrel, harp on, rumble, tattoo **7** dismiss, pulsate **8** drive out, hammer at **9** discharge, drive home, reiterate **11** beat a tattoo, din in the ear, reverberate

Drums
    author: **9** James Boyd

Drums Along the Mohawk
    author: **14** Walter D Edmonds
    character: **4** Lana **9** Blue Black, John Wolff **11** Joseph Brant, Mark Demooth **12** Mrs McKlennan **13** Gilbert Martin **20** Magdelena Borst Martin

drunk 3 sot **4** bust, lush, soak **5** binge, rummy, souse, tipsy, toper **6** barfly, bender, looped, sodden, soused, stewed, zapped, zonked **7** smashed **8** beer-bust, besotted, carousal **9** alcoholic, plastered **10** inebriated **11** dipsomaniac, intoxicated **13** drinking spree, under the influence

drunkard 3 sot **4** lush, soak, wino **5** rummy, souse, toper **6** barfly **9** alcoholic **11** dipsomaniac

drunkenness 10 alcoholism **11** inebriation **12** intoxication

Drury, Allen
    author of: **14** Capable of Honor, Return to Thebes **15** The Promise of Joy **16** Advise and Consent **19** Come Nineveh Come Tyre

dry 4 arid, blot, dull, wipe **5** droll **6** boring, low-key **7** deadpan, parched, tedious, thirsty **8** rainless **9** dehydrate, desiccate, shrivel up, wearisome **10** dehydrated, monotonous **13** uninteresting

Dryad
    form: **5** deity, nymph
    location: **5** woods

Dryas
    father: **8** Lycurgus
    killed by: **8** Lycurgus

dry as dust 4 arid, dull, sere **7** parched **8** pedantic, withered **9** shriveled **13** unimaginative

Dryden, John
    author of: **10** All for Love **11** Mac Flecknoe **14** Annus Mirabilis **15** Alexander's Feast, Marriage-a-la-Mode **20** Absalom and Achitophel, Essay on Dramatic Poesy, The Hind and the Panther

22 Fables Ancient and Modern

dry goods 5 cloth, goods **6** fabric **8** material **9** yard goods **10** piece goods

dryness 7 aridity, drought **8** aridness **11** dehydration

Dryope
    form: **5** nymph
    changed into: **6** poplar

Dry Salvages
    author: **7** T S Eliot

dry up 6 wither **7** shrivel **9** dehydrate, desiccate, evaporate

dual 6 double **7** twofold, twopart

dub 4 call, name **5** label **6** knight **7** baptize **8** christen, nickname **9** designate

dubiety 5 doubt **8** unbelief **9** disbelief **10** skepticism **11** incredulity **12** doubtfulness **14** lack of credence

Dubin's Lives
    author: **14** Bernard Malamud

dubious 5 shady **6** unsure **7** suspect **8** doubtful **9** skeptical, uncertain **10** suspicious, unreliable **11** unconvinced **12** questionable, undependable **13** untrustworthy

Dublin
    brewery: **8** Guinness
    capital of: **7** Ireland
    Irish: **8** Dubh Linn (black pool) **15** Baile Atha Cliath (town of the Hurdle Ford)
    landmark: **10** Four Courts **11** Custom House **12** Abbey Theater, Christ Church, Dublin Castle **13** Leinster House **18** Kilmainham **19** St Patrick's Cathedral
    mountain: **7** Wicklow
    museum: **8** National **10** James Joyce
    park: **7** Phoenix
    river: **6** Liffey
    rulers: **7** English, Vikings
    scene of: **12** Easter Rising (1916)
    university: **14** Trinity College

Dubliners
    author: **10** James Joyce

DuBois, Blanche
    character in: **21** A Streetcar Named Desire
    author: **8** Williams

Du Bois, W E B
    founded: **5** NAACP
    author of: **19** The Souls of Black Folk

Dubonnet
    type: **8** aperitif
    origin: **6** France

ingredient: 7 quinine, red
wine
with gin: 3 BVD **8** Napoleon
with rum: 10 Bushranger

duc 4 duke

Duccio di Buoninsegna
born: 5 Italy **6** Sienna
artwork: 6 Maesta **18** The
Rucellai Madonna
(attributed)

duce, il duce 6 despot, tyrant
8 dictator **9** Mussolini

Duchamp, Marcel
born: 6 France **8** Normandy
10 Blainville
artwork: 5 LHOOQ **9** Given
That **11** Etant Donnes
12 Bicycle Wheel **13** The
Large Glass (The Bride
Stripped Bare by Her Bache-
lors Even) **24** Nude Descending a Staircase **37** The King
and Queen Surrounded by
Swift Nudes

Duchess of Malfi, The
author: 11 John Webster
character: 6 Bosola **7** Antonio **8** Giovanna **9** Ferdinand **11** The Cardinal

duck 4 clee, coot, lory, smew,
teal, veer **5** avoid, dodge,
drake, eider, elude, evade,
goose, ruddy, shirk, stoop
6 canard, canvas, crouch, gannet, Peking, scoter, swerve
7 gadwall, mallard, Muscovy,
pintail, pochard **8** baldpate,
freckled, redshank, shelduck,
shoveler, sidestep, submerge
9 merganser, whistling **10** bufflehead, canvasback **11** wood
steamer **13** give the slip to
male: 5 drake
group of: 5 brace

Duck Soup
director: 10 Leo McCarey
cast: 5 Chico, Harpo, Zeppo
7 Groucho (Rufus T Firefly)
12 Louis Calhern, Raquel
Torres **14** Margaret Dumont
setting: 9 Freedonia

duct 4 pipe, tube **6** vessel
7 channel, conduit

ductile 6 docile, pliant, supple
7 elastic, plastic, pliable, ten-
sile **8** amenable, bendable,
flexible, formable, moldable,
shapable, swayable **9** adaptable, compliant, malleable,
tractable **10** extensible, manageable, submissive **11** complaisant, manipulable,
stretchable, susceptible

dud 3 dog **4** bomb, bust, flop,
hash **5** botch, lemon, loser
6 bummer, fiasco, fizzle
7 clinker, debacle, failure,

washout **11** lead balloon, miscarriage **14** disappointment

dude 3 fop **4** beau **5** dandy
7 peacock **11** city dweller, city
slicker **12** Beau Brummell

Dudevant, Aurore
real name of: 10 George
Sand

duds 4 togs **5** flops **6** attire
7 apparel, clothes, fizzles,
threads **8** clothing, failures,
garments

due 4 owed **5** ample, owing
6 enough, proper, unpaid
7 fitting, merited **8** adequate,
becoming, deserved, expected,
plenty of, rightful, suitable
9 in arrears, scheduled **10** sufficient **11** appropriate,
outstanding

duel
French: 15 affaire d'honneur

Duel, The
author: 15 Alexander Kuprin

duenna 8 guardian **9** attendant,
chaperone, custodian,
protector

dues 4 fees **7** charges
10 assessment

Duessa
character in: 15 The Faerie
Queene
author: 7 Spenser

duet 3 duo, two **4** pair **6** couple **7** twosome

Dufy, Raoul
born: 6 France **7** Le Havre
artwork: 7 The Palm **15** Riders in the Wood **16** Chateau
and Horses **18** Deauville
Racetrack, Posters at
Trouville

dugout 3 den **4** cave **5** canoe
6 cavity, hollow **7** shelter

Duino Elegies
author: 16 Rainer Maria
Rilke

Dukas, Paul
born: 5 Paris **6** France
composer of: 6 La Peri
18 Ariane et Barbe-Bleue
19 Ariadne and Bluebeard
22 The Sorcerer's Apprentice

duke
French: 3 duc

Duke
nickname of: 9 John Wayne

Duke, Patty (Patty Duke
Astin)
real name: 13 Anna Marie
Duke
husband: 9 John Astin
born: 10 Elmhurst NY
roles: 11 Helen Keller **16** The

Miracle Worker, The Patty
Duke Show, Valley of the
Dolls

Dukenfield, William Claude
real name of: 8 W C Fields

Duke Snider
nickname of: 11 Edwin
Snider

dulcet 7 lyrical, musical, tuneful **8** pleasing, sonorous **9** melodious **11** mellifluous

Dulcinea del Toboso
character in: 10 Don Quixote
author: 9 Cervantes

dull 4 slow **5** blunt, dense,
muted, quiet, thick, trite,
vapid **6** boring, obtuse, stupid
7 muffled, not keen, prosaic,
subdued, vacuous **8** deadened,
inactive, not brisk, not sharp
9 dimwitted **10** indistinct, lackluster, uneventful **13** unimaginative, uninteresting

Dull
character in: 16 Love's Labour's Lost
author: 11 Shakespeare

dullard 4 dolt **5** dummy,
dunce **6** nitwit **7** halfwit
8 dumbbell, imbecile

Dullea, Keir
born: 11 Cleveland OH
roles: 12 David and Lisa
18 Butterflies Are Free
27 Two Thousand One: A
Space Odyssey

dullness 6 idiocy, tedium
8 dumbness, lethargy, monotony, slowness **9** bluntness, ignorance, stupidity, vapidness
10 boringness, imbecility, obtuseness **11** tediousness
13 dim-wittedness **15** thick-
headedness

dull-witted 5 dazed, fuzzy
7 bemused, muddled, stunned
8 confused **9** stupefied

Dulong, Pierre-Louis
field: 7 physics **9** chemistry
nationality: 6 French
discovered: 19 nitrogen
trichloride
studied: 4 heat **13** atomic
weights

duly 6 on time **8** properly, suitably **9** correctly **10** deservedly,
punctually, rightfully **13** appropriately **15** at the proper
time

Dumaine
character in: 16 Love's Labour's Lost
author: 11 Shakespeare

Dumas, Alexandre (fils)
author of: 7 Camille **11** Le
Demi-Monde **17** La Dame

aux Camelias **21** The Lady
of the Camellias
Camille inspired: 10 La Traviata
opera by: **5** Verdi

Dumas, Alexandre (pere)
author of: 17 The Queen's
Necklace **18** The Three Musketeers **19** The Man in the
Iron Mask **21** The Count of
Monte Cristo **22** The Vicomte de Bragelonne

Du Maurier, Daphne
author of: 7 Rebecca **10** Jamaica Inn **11** Don't Look
Now **14** My Cousin Rachel
15 Frenchman's Creek
19 The House on the Strand

Du Maurier, George
author of: 6 Trilby **10** The
Martian **13** Peter Ibbetson

dumb 3 mum **4** dull, mute
5 dense, dopey **6** silent, stupid **7** foolish, aphasic **8** aphasiac **9** dim-witted
13 unintelligent **17** incapable
of speech

dumbbell 3 oaf **4** clod, dolt,
dope, fool **5** booby, clown,
dummy, dunce, idiot, moron
6 dimwit, nitwit **7** dullard,
halfwit **8** dumb-dumb, dummkopf, imbecile, lunkhead,
meathead, numskull **9** birdbrain, blockhead, ignoramus,
lamebrain, numbskull, simpleton **10** noodlehead

dumb-dumb 3 ass **4** dope,
fool **5** booby, dunce, idiot,
moron, ninny **6** dimwit, nitwit **7** halfwit **8** bonehead, imbecile, lunkhead, numskull
9 blockhead, lamebrain, numbskull **10** nincompoop

dumbfound, dumfound
4 stun **5** amaze **7** startle **8** astonish **11** flabbergast

dumbfounded 5 agape
6 amazed **7** stunned **9** astounded, stupefied **10** astonished, speechless **11** openmouthed **13** flabbergasted

dumbness 6 idiocy **8** dullness
9 asininity, stupidity, thickness **10** imbecility **11** witlessness **12** wordlessness
14 speechlessness
15 thickheadedness

dumbstruck 5 agape **6** amazed,
gaping **7** riveted **9** awestruck,
stupefied **10** speechless
11 electrified, open-mouthed
13 flabbergasted

dummy 3 oaf **4** dolt, form
5 clown, idiot, klutz, model
6 figure **9** blockhead, mannequin, simpleton **10** dunderhead **11** chowderhead,
knucklehead

dump 3 hut **4** hole, toss
5 empty, hovel, shack
6 shanty, unload **8** get rid of,
junkyard **9** dispose of **10** refuse pile **11** rubbish heap

dumpy 5 squat **7** lumpish
13 short and stout

Dumuzi
origin: 8 Sumerian
god of: 8 pastures
10 vegetation
consort of: 6 Inanna

Dunaway, Faye
real name: 18 Dorothy Faye
Dunaway
born: 8 Bascom FL
roles: 6 Barfly, Milady **7** Network (Oscar) **8** The Champ
9 Chinatown **13** Mommie
Dearest **14** Bonnie and
Clyde **15** Towering Inferno
17 The Four Musketeers
18 The Three Musketeers

Duncan
character in: 7 Macbeth
author: 11 Shakespeare

Duncan, Sandy
born: 11 Henderson TX
roles: 8 Peter Pan **9** Funny
Face **12** The Boyfriend

dunce 4 fool **5** dummy, idiot,
moron **6** dimwit, nitwit **8** imbecile, numskull **9** blockhead,
numbskull, simpleton

Dunciad, The
author: 13 Alexander Pope

dunderhead 3 ass **4** dolt, fool
5 booby, dunce, idiot, moron,
ninny **6** dimwit, nitwit **7** dullard, fathead, halfwit **8** bonehead, dumb-dumb, imbecile,
lunkhead, numskull **9** blockhead, dumb bunny, lamebrain,
numbskull **10** nincompoop
11 chowderhead

dune 4 bank **5** mound **8** sandbank, sandpile

dunk 3 dip, sop **4** duck, soak
5 bathe, douse, drown, slosh,
souse, steep **6** deluge, drench,
engulf, plunge **7** baptize, immerse **8** inundate, saturate,
submerge

Dunne, John Gregory
author of: 11 Dutch Shea Jr
18 Quintana and Friends

Dunnock, Mildred
born: 11 Baltimore MD
roles: 8 Baby Doll **12** The
Nun's Story **14** The Corn Is
Green **16** Butterfield Eight,
Cat on a Hot Tin Roof,
Death of a Salesman

duo 4 pair **5** combo **6** couple
7 twosome **11** combination

duomo 4 dome **9** cathedral

dupe 4 fool, pawn **5** patsy,
trick **6** humbug, sucker **7** cat's
paw, deceive, fall guy, mislead **8** hoodwink **9** bamboozle

duplicate 4 copy **5** clone,
match **6** repeat **7** replica
8 parallel **9** facsimile, imitation, make again, photocopy,
photostat **10** carbon copy
12 reproduction

duplicity 5 fraud, guile **6** deceit **7** cunning **9** deception,
falseness **10** dishonesty
13 deceitfulness

Du Pont Labs
founder: 17 E I du Pont de
Nemours
inventor of: 5 nylon

Duquesnoy, Francois
born: 8 Brussels, Flanders
nickname: 11 Il Fiammingo
artwork: 8 St Andrew **9** St
Susanna

dur
musical term: 5 major **8** major key

durability 7 stamina
8 strength **9** endurance, toughness **10** sturdiness

durable 5 sound, tough
6 strong, sturdy **7** lasting
8 enduring **11** long-wearing,
substantial

Durand, Asher Brown
born: 18 Jefferson Village NJ
artwork: 14 Kindred Spirits

Durant, Will and Ariel
authors of: 20 The Story of
Philosophy **21** Rousseau and
Revolution **22** The Story of
Civilization

Durante, Jimmy
real name: 19 James Francis
Durante
nickname: 10 Schnozzola
15 Inka Dinka Doo Man
born: 9 New York NY
roles: 5 Jumbo **21** It's a Mad
Mad Mad Mad World

duration 4 term **6** extent, period **11** continuance
12 continuation

Durdles
character in: 22 The Mystery
of Edwin Drood
author: 7 Dickens

Durer, Albrecht
born: 7 Germany
9 Nuremberg
artwork: 10 Adam and Eve,
Apocalypse, The Triumph
11 Wehlsch Pirg **12** Four
Apostles, Large Passion,
Melancholia I **13** Castle of
Trent **15** Life of the Virgin
18 St Jerome in his Study
19 Virgin with the Siskin

21 Christ Among the Doctors **22** Knight Death and the Devil **24** Crowned Death on a Thin Horse **25** The Feast of the Rose Garlands **28** The Festival of the Rose Garlands

duress 5 force **6** threat **8** coercion, pressure **10** compulsion, constraint

Durgin, Francis Timothy
real name of: **11** Rory Calhoun

during litigation
Latin: **12** pendente lite

Durocher, Leo
nickname: **9** Leo the Lip
sport: **8** baseball
position: **7** manager
team: **11** Chicago Cubs **13** New York Giants **15** Brooklyn Dodgers
saying: **18** Nice guys finish last

Durrenmatt, Friedrich
author of: **5** Traps **8** The Visit **9** The Pledge, The Quarry **13** The Physicists **21** The Judge and His Hangman **27** The Marriage of the Mississippi

Durrie, James and Henry
character in: **21** The Master of Ballantrae
author: **9** Stevenson

dusk 6 sunset **7** sundown **8** twilight **9** nightfall

dusky 3 dim **4** dark **5** murky **6** cloudy, gloomy, veiled **7** swarthy **8** dark-hued

dust 4 dirt, lint **5** brush, motes **8** sprinkle

duster 3 rag **4** coat, robe **5** brush, cloth, whisk **9** housecoat **10** whisk broom

Dutch Guiana see **8** Suriname

Dutch Shea, Jr
author: **16** John Gregory Dunne

dutiful 5 loyal **8** diligent, faithful, obedient **9** compliant **13** conscientious

duty 3 tax **4** levy, onus, task **6** charge, excise, tariff **7** customs **8** business, function, province **10** assignment, obligation **14** responsibility

Duval, Armand
character in: **7** Camille
author: **5** Dumas (fils)

Duvall, Robert
born: **10** San Diego CA
roles: **4** MASH **11** Godfather II **12** The Godfather **13** Apocalypse Now, Tender Mercies (Oscar) **15** The Great Santini, True Confessions **18** To Kill a Mockingbird

Duvall, Shelley
born: **9** Houston TX
roles: **6** Popeye **9** Nashville **10** The Shining, Three Women **15** Brewster McCloud

Dvorak, Antonin
born: **11** Nelahozeves **14** Czechoslovakia
composer of: **5** Dumky **6** Hymnus, Te Deum **8** Carnival (overture) **10** St Ludmilla **11** Stabat Mater **15** American Quartet, From the New World (Symphony in E Minor) **16** The Specter's Bride **17** The Bells of Zlonice

dwarf 3 dim, elf, imp **4** baby, tiny **5** fairy, gnome, pixie, pygmy, small, troll **6** bantam, goblin, petite, sprite **8** diminish **9** miniature **10** diminutive, leprechaun, overshadow

dwarfish 3 wee **4** tiny **5** pygmy, short, small **6** bantam, little, midget **7** compact, squatty **10** diminutive, undersized **13** foreshortened

dwell 4 live **5** abide **6** harp on, reside **7** inhabit **10** linger over

dwelling 4 home **5** abode, house **8** domicile **9** residence **10** habitation

dwelling place 4 home **5** abode, house **7** habitat, lodging **8** domicile **9** residence **10** habitation **14** living quarters

dwell on 6 accent, stress **7** feature, iterate **9** emphasize, press home

dwindle 4 fade, wane **6** lessen, shrink **7** decline **8** decrease, diminish **13** become smaller

dye 4 tint **5** color, shade, stain **8** coloring **10** coloration

dyed-in-the-wool 9 confirmed, ingrained **10** deep-rooted, inveterate **11** established

dyestuff 14 coloring matter

Dymas
home: **4** Troy
fought with: **6** Aeneas
fought against: **6** Greeks

dynamic 5 vital **6** active **7** driving **8** forceful, powerful, vigorous **9** energetic

dynamism 3 pep **4** life **5** verve, vigor **6** energy, spirit **8** vitality, vivacity **9** animation **10** liveliness

dynamite 4 raze, ruin **5** blast, trash, wreck **6** blow up, charge **7** destroy, shatter, wipe out **8** decimate, demolish **9** devastate, dismantle, eradicate, explosive **10** annihilate, extinguish, obliterate **11** exterminate

dynamo 4 doer **7** hustler **8** activist, go-getter **9** generator **12** active person **14** bundle of energy, mover and shaker

Dynasts, The
author: **11** Thomas Hardy
subject: **17** Napoleon Bonaparte

dynasty 4 line **5** crown, reign **6** regime **7** lineage, regency **8** dominion, hegemony, kingship, monarchy, regnancy **9** authority **10** government, suzerainty **11** ruling house **12** jurisdiction **14** administration

Dynasty
character: **9** Dex Dexter, Jeff Colby **12** Alexis (Morel Carrington Colby) Dexter **14** Adam Carrington **15** Blake Carrington **16** Amanda Carrington, Steven Carrington **17** Krystle Carrington **18** Dominique Devereaux, Krystina Carrington **21** Fallon Carrington Colby
cast: **9** John James **10** Linda Evans **11** Joan Collins **12** John Forsythe
setting: **6** Denver **8** Colorado
hotel: **8** La Mirage

dyspeptic 4 mean **6** crabby, grumpy, ornery, shirty, touchy **7** grouchy, waspish **8** choleric **9** crotchety, fractious, irascible, irritable **10** ill-humored, ill-natured **11** bad-tempered, contentious, hot-tempered **12** cantankerous, sour-tempered **13** short-tempered

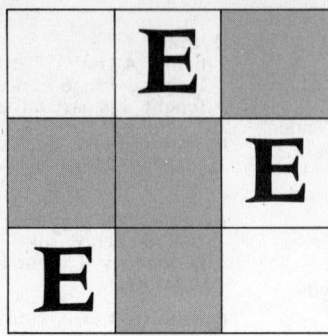

Ea
  origin: **8** Akkadian
  god of: **6** wisdom
  father: **4** Apsu
  son: **6** Marduk **8** Merodach
    12 Baal Merodach
  corresponds to: **4** Enki

each 5 every **6** apiece **7** that
one, this one **8** everyone, separate **12** respectively

Eagels, Jeanne
  born: **12** Kansas City MO
  roles: **4** Rain **8** Jealousy
    9 The Letter **13** Sadie
    Thompson **14** Man Woman
    and Sin

eager 4 agog, avid, keen **6** ardent, fervid, intent, raring
7 athirst, earnest, excited, fervent, intense, longing, zealous **8** desirous, diligent,
resolute, spirited, yearning
9 ambitious, hungering, impatient, thirsting **10** aggressive,
passionate **11** hardworking,
impassioned, industrious, persevering **12** enterprising,
enthusiastic

eagerly 6 avidly, keenly **8** ardently, desiring, fervidly, intently **9** anxiously, earnestly,
fervently, zealously
16 enthusiastically

eagerness 4 zeal, zest **5** ardor
6 fervor **7** avidity **9** readiness
10 enthusiasm **11** willingness

eagle
  young: **6** eaglet

Eagle
  constellation of: **6** Aquila

Eakins, Thomas
  born: **14** Philadelphia PA
  artwork: **11** Agnew Clinic
    13 Mrs Edith Mahon **14** The
    Gross Clinic **24** Max Schmitt
    in a Single Scull

ear
  section: **5** inner, outer
    6 middle

part: 4 drum **5** anvil, canal
    6 hammer **7** cochlea, stir-
    rup **8** hair cell **14** eustachian
    tube

earl 4 lord, peer **5** noble
    8 nobleman
  wife: **8** countess

earlier 6 before, in time,
sooner **9** before now, in advance **10** beforehand **11** ahead
of time **13** before the fact

earliest 5 first **6** oldest, primal
7 ancient, initial, primary,
soonest **8** original, primeval
9 beginning, primitive **10** aboriginal, indigenous
11 fundamental

Earl of Baltimore
  nickname of: **10** Earl Weaver

Earl the Pearl
  nickname of: **10** Earl Monroe

early 5 first **6** primal **7** ancient,
archaic, betimes, initial, too
soon, very old **8** primeval **9** in
advance, premature, primitive
10 beforehand, in good time,
primordial **11** ahead of time,
prehistoric, prematurely

Early Autumn
  author: **14** Louis Bromfield

early man 6 Peking **9** Cro-
Magnon, Steinheim **11** Neanderthal **18** Trobriand
Islanders **24** Australopithecus
robustus **25** Australopithecus
africanus

earmark 3 tag **4** band, hold,
sign **5** allot, label, stamp, token, trait **6** aspect, assign
7 feature, put away, quality,
reserve **8** allocate, property,
set aside **9** attribute, designate **11** peculiarity, singularity **14** characteristic

earn 3 get, net **4** draw, gain,
make, rate, reap **5** clear,
merit **6** attain, pick up, secure **7** achieve, collect, deserve, realize, receive,

warrant **9** bring home **12** be
entitled to

earn as due 4 rate **5** merit
7 deserve **10** be worthy of
12 be entitled to **13** be deserving of

earnest 4 firm **5** eager, fixed,
grave, sober, staid **6** ardent,
fervid, honest, intent, sedate,
solemn, stable, steady, urgent
7 devoted, fervent, intense, serious, sincere, zealous **8** constant, diligent, resolute,
spirited, vehement **9** ambitious, assiduous, heartfelt, insistent **10** deeply felt,
determined, passionate, purposeful, thoughtful **11** hardworking, impassioned,
industrious, persevering
12 enthusiastic, wholehearted

earnest attachment 4 love
6 regard **7** concern **8** devotion,
fondness **9** reverence **10** commitment, dedication **11** devotedness **13** attentiveness

earnest request 4 plea **6** appeal **8** entreaty, petition
11 importunity **12** supplication

earnings 3 pay **5** wages **6** income, salary **7** payment, profits **8** proceeds, receipts
12 compensation

Earnshaw, Catherine
  character in: **16** Wuthering
    Heights
  author: **6** Bronte

ear-splitting 7 blaring **8** piercing **9** clamorous, deafening
10 thunderous

earth 3 sod **4** clay, dirt, dust,
land, loam, soil, turf
6 ground **7** topsoil
  god of: **3** Geb, Keb **5** Dagan,
    Dagon **10** Trophonius
  goddess of: **2** Ge **4** Gaea,
    Gaia **6** Hecate, Hekate,
    Tellus

earthen pot
  Spanish: **4** olla

earthenware 5 china **7** pottery **8** clayware, crockery **11** ceramic ware

earthly 6 bodily **7** mundane, secular, ungodly, worldly **8** feasible, material, physical, possible, temporal **9** corporeal, practical **10** imaginable **11** conceivable, terrestrial **12** nonspiritual **13** materialistic

earthquake 5 quake, seism, shock **6** tremor **8** tremblor, upheaval **11** earth tremor

earth tremor 5 quake, seism, shock **6** tremor **8** tremblor, upheaval **10** earthquake

earthy 5 bawdy, crude, dirty, funky, gross, lusty, rough **6** coarse, filthy, ribald, robust, smutty, vulgar **7** obscene, peasant, raunchy **8** indecent **9** primitive, unrefined **10** unblushing, uncultured **12** uncultivated

Earwicker family
  characters in: **13** Finnegans Wake
  author: **5** Joyce

earwig
  variety: **5** black **6** little **10** long horned

ease 4 calm, rest, slip **5** abate, allay, poise, quiet, slide, still **6** aplomb, lessen, luxury, pacify, plenty, relief, repose, solace, soothe **7** assuage, comfort, console, leisure, lighten, mollify, relieve **8** diminish, easement, easiness, facility, maneuver, mitigate, palliate, security, serenity **9** abundance, affluence, alleviate, composure, disburden, readiness **10** confidence, prosperity, relaxation **11** assuagement, naturalness, peace of mind, restfulness **12** tranquillity, unconstraint **13** luxuriousness, move carefully, relaxed manner **14** effortlessness, handle with care, unaffectedness

easement 4 ease **6** relief, solace, succor **7** comfort **8** soothing **10** right of way **11** assuagement

easily 5 by far **6** freely, surely **7** clearly, handily, lightly, plainly, readily **8** facilely, smoothly, with ease **9** certainly **10** far and away, undeniably **11** beyond doubt, undoubtedly **12** effortlessly, with facility **13** without a hitch **14** beyond question, without trouble **17** without difficulty **23** beyond the shadow of a doubt

easily embarrassed 3 shy **5** timid **7** bashful **8** blushing, skittish, timorous **9** diffident, shrinking **11** constrained, unconfident

easily noticed 5 clear, plain **6** patent **7** evident, glaring, obvious, visible **8** flagrant, striking **9** arresting, prominent **10** noticeable **11** conspicuous, outstanding

easily ruffled 9 emotional, excitable **11** hot-tempered **13** quick-tempered

easiness 4 ease **10** equanimity, simplicity **11** naturalness **12** indifference **13** impassiveness

East, the 4 Asia **9** the Orient **10** the Far East **11** the Near East **17** Eastern Hemisphere

East Bengal see
  10 Bangladesh

East Berlin
  capital of: **11** East Germany

East Coker
  author: **7** T S Eliot

Eastern Slavic
  language family: **12** Indo-European
  group: **11** Balto-Slavic
  branch: **6** Slavic
  language: **7** Russian **9** Ukrainian **12** White Russian

Easter Parade
  director: **14** Charles Walters
  based on musical by: **12** Irving Berlin
  cast: **9** Ann Miller **11** Fred Astaire, Judy Garland **12** Peter Lawford

East Germany see Germany, East

Eastman, George
  nationality: **8** American
  founder of: **14** Eastman Kodak Co
  inventor of: **9** Kodak film **11** Kodak camera **20** transparent photo film

East of Eden
  author: **13** John Steinbeck
  director: **9** Elia Kazan
  cast: **8** Burl Ives **9** James Dean **10** Jo Van Fleet **11** Julie Harris **13** Raymond Massey
  Oscar for: **17** supporting actress (Van Fleet)

East wind
  associated with: **5** Eurus **9** Volturnus

Eastwood, Clint
  born: **14** San Francisco CA
  roles: **7** Firefox, Rawhide **10** Dirty Harry, Hang Em High, Unforgiven **11** Magnum Force, The Dead Pool **12** Coogan's Bluff, Kelly's Heroes, Sudden Impact **13** A Perfect World **14** Play Misty for Me **15** In The Line of Fire, Where Eagles Dare **17** A Fistful of Dollars, Any Which Way You Can, High Plains Drifter **18** Escape from Alcatraz, For a Few Dollars More **21** Two Mules for Sister Sara **23** The Good the Bad and the Ugly
  mayor of: **6** Carmel

easy 4 calm, mild, open, soft **5** cushy, frank, light, naive **6** benign, calmly, candid, docile, easily, gentle, secure, serene, simple **7** lenient, natural, not hard, relaxed, restful, wealthy **8** affluent, carefree, composed, friendly, gracious, gullible, informal, outgoing, painless, peaceful, pleasant, scarcely, serenely, tranquil, unforced, well-to-do, yielding **9** compliant, indulgent, leisurely, luxurious, tractable, unworried **10** effortless, peacefully, permissive, unaffected, untroubled **11** comfortable, comfortably **12** not difficult, unsuspicious **13** accommodating, unconstrained

easygoing 4 calm **6** casual **7** offhand, patient, relaxed **8** carefree **9** unruffled, unworried **10** insouciant, nonchalant **11** unconcerned, unexcitable **12** even-tempered, happy-go-lucky, mild-tempered

Easy Rider
  director: **12** Dennis Hopper
  cast: **10** Karen Black, Peter Fonda **11** Luana Anders **12** Dennis Hopper, Robert Walker **13** Jack Nicholson

easy to use 7 adapted, helpful **9** adaptable **10** convenient **11** serviceable **12** advantageous

eat 3 sup **4** bolt, dine, feed, gulp, rust, take **5** feast, lunch **6** devour, gobble, ingest, nibble **7** consume, corrode **8** dispatch, dissolve, wear away, wolf down **9** breakfast, take a meal, waste away **10** break bread, gormandize **14** take sustenance **15** take nourishment

eatable 4 food **6** edible **8** fit to eat **10** comestible, consumable

eat away 4 rust **5** erode **7** corrode, oxidize

eating habits 4 diet **13** eating regimen

eating regimen 4 diet **12** eating habits

eat into 4 bite **5** erode **6** nibble **7** consume, corrode **8** wear away **9** swallow up

eat one's fill 5 feast, gorge **6** pig out **7** banquet **12** stuff oneself

eat rapidly 4 bolt, gulp, wolf **5** scarf **6** gobble **12** swallow whole

eat up 5 enjoy, savor **6** devour, relish **7** consume, swallow **9** delight in, rejoice in **13** be pleased with, get a kick out of **14** take pleasure in

eat voraciously 6 cram in, devour, gobble **7** stuff in **8** bolt down, gulp down, wolf down **10** gormandize **12** swallow whole

eau, eaux 5 water

eau de vie 6 brandy **11** water of life

eavesdrop 3 bug, pry, spy, tap **5** snoop **6** attend, harken **7** monitor, wiretap **8** listen in, overhear **9** bend an ear **11** cock one's ear **14** strain one's ears **15** prick up one's ears

ebb 5 abate, go out **6** go down, lessen, recede, shrink, weaken **7** decline, dwindle, retreat, slacken, subside **8** decrease, diminish, fade away, fall away, flow away, flow back, move back, withdraw **9** waste away **10** degenerate **11** deteriorate

ebony 3 jet **4** dark, inky **5** black, raven, sable **8** hardwood **9** coal-black **15** Diospyros Ebenum
 varieties: 5 Green, Texas **8** Macassar, Mountain **10** East Indian, Queensland

Ebsen, Buddy
 real name: 23 Christian Rudolph Ebsen Jr
 born: 12 Belleville IL
 roles: 12 Barnaby Jones, Davy Crockett **21** The Beverly Hillbillies

ebullience 3 zip **7** elation **8** buoyancy **9** animation **10** enthusiasm, exuberance, joyousness, liveliness **11** high spirits **12** exhilaration **13** effervescence

ebullient 6 elated, joyful, joyous **9** exuberant **11** exhilarated **12** effervescent, enthusiastic, high-spirited

ecce homo 12 behold the man
 said by: 13 Pontius Pilate
 spoken of: 6 Christ

eccentric 3 nut, odd **4** kook, rash, sick **5** curio, flake, funny, kooky, nutty, queer, weird **6** freaky, insane, quaint, unique, weirdo **7** bizarre, curious, erratic, oddball, offbeat, strange, unusual, weirdie **8** aberrant, abnormal, crackpot, freakish, peculiar, quixotic, singular, uncommon **9** character, irregular, odd person, off center, parabolic, psychotic, screwball, unnatural, whimsical **10** capricious, elliptical, outlandish, unorthodox **13** extraordinary **14** unconventional

eccentricity 6 oddity, whimsy **7** caprice **9** deviation, queerness **10** aberration **11** abnormality, peculiarity, strangeness **12** idiosyncrasy, irregularity

ecclesiastic, ecclesiastical 5 rabbi, vicar **6** cleric, curate, deacon, parson, pastor, priest, rector **7** prelate **8** chaplain, churchly, clerical, minister, pastoral, preacher **9** churchman, clergyman, episcopal, parochial, religious

Echecles
 father: 5 Actor
 wife: 8 Polymela
 raised child of Polymela and: 6 Hermes

echelon 4 file, line, rank, rung, tier **5** grade, level **6** office **8** position **9** authority, hierarchy

Echemus
 king of: 7 Arcadia
 father: 7 Cepheus
 wife: 8 Timandra
 son: 8 Laodocus
 delayed: 18 Heraclidan invasion
 killed: 6 Hyllus

Echetus
 king of: 6 Epirus
 daughter: 8 Amphissa
 blinded: 8 Amphissa

Echidna
 form: 7 monster
 mother of: 5 Hydra **6** Sphinx **7** Chimera **8** Cerberus
 slain by: 5 Argus

echinoderm 9 sea animal
 characteristic: 10 spiny shell
 form: 6 radial
 kind: 6 cystid **7** crinoid **8** starfish **9** sea urchin **10** basket star **11** sea cucumber

Echion
 member: 6 Sparti
 wife: 5 Agave
 son: 8 Pentheus

echo 3 ape **4** copy, ring **5** match **6** follow, mirror, parrot, repeat **7** imitate, reflect, resound **9** parallel, simulate **9** duplicate, reproduce, take after **11** reverberate **13** reverberation

Echo
 form: 5 nymph
 location: 8 mountain
 loved: 9 Narcissus
 loved by: 3 Pan
 changed into: 4 echo

eclair 6 pastry **7** dessert **9** creampuff

eclaircissement 11 explanation **13** clarification, (the) Enlightenment

eclipse 3 dim **4** hide, loss, mask **5** cloak, cover, excel, outdo **6** darken, exceed **7** blot out, conceal, erasing, masking, obscure, surpass, veiling, wipe out **8** cloaking, clouding, covering, outrival, outshine **9** darkening, shadowing, transcend **10** obliterate, overshadow, tower above **11** blotting out, diminishing, eradicating, obscuration **12** annihilation, obliteration **13** overshadowing

eclogue 4 idyl, poem **5** idyll **7** bucolic **8** dialogue, pastoral

Eclogues
 author: 6 Vergil, Virgil

ecole 6 school

economic 6 fiscal **8** material, monetary **9** budgetary, financial, pecuniary **10** productive **12** distributive

economical 5 chary, cheap **6** frugal, modest, saving **7** careful, prudent, sparing, spartan, thrifty **8** economic **9** low-priced, niggardly, penurious, scrimping **10** reasonable **11** closefisted, tightfisted **12** parsimonious

economic decline 8 downturn **9** recession **10** depression

economics
 term: 3 GNP **5** labor **7** capital, Marxism, surplus **8** property **9** commodity, Communism, inflation, Keynesian, recession **10** capitalism, monetarist, supply-side **11** bourgeoisie, central bank, competition, consumption, marketplace, proletariat, stagflation **12** distribution, econometrics, fiscal policy, interest rate, laissez-faire, mercantilism **14** federal deficit, macroeconomics, microeconomics, monetary policy **17** trickle-down the-

ory **20** gross national product

economist
  American: **6** George, Hansen, Sumner, Veblen **7** Commons **8** Friedman, Laughlin **10** Schumpeter
  British: **4** Mill **5** Smith **6** Keynes **7** Malthus, Ricardo **8** Marshall
  French: **3** Say **7** Quesnay
  German: **4** Marx **7** Schacht
  Italian: **6** Pareto
  Scottish: **5** Smith

economize 4 save **5** pinch, skimp, stint **6** scrimp **7** husband **8** be frugal, conserve, cut costs **9** be prudent **10** avoid waste **11** cut expenses **12** be economical, use sparingly **14** be parsimonious **15** practice economy, tighten one's belt

economizing 10 conserving **11** cutting down **13** penny-pinching **14** belt-tightening **15** pinching pennies **18** tightening one's belt

economy 6 thrift **8** prudence **9** frugality **10** providence **11** thriftiness **15** financial status, productive power

ecstasy 3 joy **5** bliss **6** frenzy, thrill, trance **7** delight, emotion, madness, rapture **8** delirium, gladness, pleasure **9** happiness, transport **10** enthusiasm, exultation

ecstatic 4 glad, rapt **5** happy **6** elated, joyful, joyous **7** exalted, excited **8** blissful **9** delighted, delirious, ebullient, entranced, overjoyed, rapturous **10** enraptured **11** transported **12** enthusiastic **13** beside oneself

Ecuador *see box*

ecumenical 6 global **7** general **8** catholic **9** communist, planetary, universal, worldwide **10** heavenwide **11** communalist **12** all-embracing, all-including, all-inclusive, all-pervading, collectivist, cosmopolitan **13** communitarian, comprehensive, international

eczema 4 rash **8** eruption **10** dermatitis **12** inflammation

eddy 6 vortex **9** maelstrom, whirlpool **14** countercurrent

Eddy, Nelson
  partner: **17** Jeanette MacDonald
  born: **12** Providence RI
  roles: **9** Rose Marie **15** Naughty Marietta **16** Northwest Outpost

---

Ecuador
  name means: **7** equator
  other name: **5** Quito
  capital: **5** Quito
  largest city: **9** Guayaquil
  others: **4** Jama, Loja, Napo, Puyo, Tena **5** Guano, Manta, Pajan, Pinas, Piura, Pojan, Yaupi **6** Ambato, Cuenca, Ibarra, Tulcan, Zaruma **7** Azogues, Cayambe, Guamote, Guapulo, Machala, Pelileo, Pillaro, Salinas **8** Riobamba **10** Esmeraldas, Portoviejo
  division: **5** Costa **6** Sierra **7** Oriente
  measure: **5** libra **6** cuadra, fanega
  monetary unit: **5** sucre **7** centavo
  weight: **5** libra
  island: **4** Puna, Wolf **5** Colon, Mocha, Pinta **6** Baltra, Chaves, Darwin, Pinzon, Rabida, Wenman **7** Isabela, La Plata, Sante Fe, Tortuga **8** Espanola, Floreana, Genovesa, Marchena, Santiago **9** Culpepper, Galapagos, Santa Cruz **10** Fernandina, Santa Maria **11** San Salvador **12** San Cristobal
  mountain: **5** Andes **6** Condor, Sangay **7** Cayambe **8** Antisana, Cotopaxi **9** Cotacachi, Pichincha
  highest point: **10** Chimborazo
  river: **4** Coca, Mira, Napo **5** Cocoa, Daule, Paute, Pindo, Tigre **6** Blanco, Guayas, Tumbes, Zamora **7** Conambo, Curaray, Jubones, Pastaza, Puyango **8** Aguarico, Bobonaza, Cononaco, Naranjal, Putumayo **9** San Miguel **10** Esmeraldas, Nangaritza **12** Guaillabamba
  sea: **7** Pacific
  physical feature:
    bay: **5** Manta **7** Isabela **9** Elizabeth **11** Santa Elenas **15** Ancon de Sardinas
    cape: **4** Rosa **6** Pasado **8** Marshall, Puntilla **10** San Lorenzo
    channel: **7** Jambeli
    gulf: **9** Guayaquil, Pichincha
    peninsula: **10** Santa Elena
    point: **4** Jama **5** Essex **6** Galera **9** Albemarle **10** Christobal
  people: **4** Cara, Cixo, Inca **5** Ardan, Aucas, Macoa, Maina, Palta, Quitu, Yumbo **6** Canelo, Jibaro, Jivaro, Puruha **7** Cayapas, Jivaros, mestizo, mulatto **8** Barbacoa, Colorado, Montuvio, Serranos **9** Montubios
    artist: **4** Egas **8** Santiago **9** Caspicara **10** Guayasamin
    author: **6** Espejo **14** Carrera Andrade
    conqueror: **7** Pizarro **10** Benalcazar **11** Huayna-Capac
    god: **5** umina
    leader: **6** Alfaro, Flores **10** Plaza Lasso, Rocafuerte **12** Garcia Moreno **13** Velasco Ibarra
  language: **6** Jibaro **7** Quechua, Spanish
  religion: **13** Roman Catholic
  feature:
    animal: **6** vicuna
    dictator: **8** caudillo
    estate: **8** hacienda
    festival: **5** Yamor
    hat: **6** Panama **8** jipijapa, toquilla
    tree: **5** balsa
  food:
    baked guinea pig: **3** cuy
    corn tamale: **6** humita
    drink: **6** chicha
    marinated raw shrimp/fish: **7** ceviche, seviche
    potato/cheese patty: **11** llapingacho
    potato soup: **5** locro

Eden 8 Paradise
see also: 4 Adam

edentate 5 manis, sloth 7 ant-bear 8 aardvark, anteater 9 armadillo, toothless

Edgar Huntly
author: 20 Charles Brockden Brown

edge 3 hem, rim 4 bind, inch, line, side, trim 5 bound, brink, creep, limit, sidle, slink, sneak, steal, verge 6 border, fringe, margin 7 contour, outline 9 extremity, periphery, threshold 12 boundary line, dividing line, move sideways

Edgeworth, Maria
author of: 7 Belinda 11 The Absentee 14 Castle Rackrent

edging 3 hem 4 trim 5 limit 6 border, fringe, margin, ruffle 7 binding, curbing, salvage 8 boundary, fringing, trimming

edgy 5 sharp, testy 7 anxious, nervous 8 snappish 9 excitable, impatient, irascible, irritable 10 highstrung

edible 7 eatable 10 comestible, consumable, digestible 12 fit to be eaten, nonpoisonous 13 safe for eating

edict 3 law 4 bull, fiat 5 order, ukase 6 decree, dictum, ruling 7 command, dictate, mandate, statute 9 enactment, manifesto, ordinance, prescript 10 injunction, regulation 12 proclamation, public notice 13 pronouncement 14 pronunciamento

edification 8 guidance, teaching 9 direction, education, elevation, uplifting 11 advancement, information, instruction 13 enlightenment 14 indoctrination

edifice 8 building 9 structure 12 construction

edify 5 teach 6 inform 7 educate, improve 8 instruct 9 enlighten

edifying 8 didactic, tutorial 11 educational, instructive 12 enlightening

Edinburgh
bay: 12 Firth of Forth
capital of: 8 Scotland
Celtic: 11 Dune-eideann (Eidin's Fort)
church: 7 St Giles
landmark: 14 Holyrood Palace 15 Edinburgh Castle
port: 5 Leith
rocks: 10 Castle Rock 11 Arthur's Seat

Edison, Thomas Alva
nickname: 17 Wizard of Menlo Park
inventor of: 6 (wax cylinder) record 9 light bulb, (quadruplex) telegraph 10 phonograph 11 kinetoscope, stock ticker 14 movie projector 16 incandescent lamp 18 automatic telegraph (transmitter and receiver) 21 flexible celluloid film 22 alkaline storage battery

edit 5 adapt, emend 6 censor, polish, redact, revise 7 abridge, clean up, correct, expunge, rewrite, touch up 8 annotate, condense, copy-edit, rephrase 9 expurgate 10 blue-pencil, bowdlerize

edition 4 book, copy, kind 5 issue 6 number 7 imprint, version 8 printing 9 redaction

editor 2 ed 6 writer 7 newsman, reviser 8 compiler, redactor 10 journalist

Edmonds, Walter D
author of: 8 Rome Haul 19 Drums Along the Mohawk

Edmonton
hockey team: 6 Oilers

Edmontonia
type: 8 dinosaur 10 ornithopod
location: 12 North America

Edmund Campion
author: 11 Evelyn Waugh

Edom
name given: 4 Esau
descendants: 8 Edomites

Edson, Gus
creator/artist of: 5 Dondi 8 The Gumps

Ed Sullivan Show, The
regular cast: 17 June Taylor Dancers 23 Ray Bloch and His Orchestra
noted appearances: 7 Beatles, Bob Hope 10 Walt Disney 12 Elvis Presley 14 Martin and Lewis

educate 5 coach, edify, teach, train, tutor 6 inform, school 7 develop 8 civilize, instruct 9 enlighten

education 5 study 7 culture 8 learning, pedagogy, teaching, training, tutelage 9 didactics, erudition, knowledge, schooling 10 pedagogics 11 cultivation, edification, information, instruction, scholarship 13 enlightenment

Education of Henry Adams, The
author: 10 Henry Adams

educe 5 evoke 6 elicit, extort 7 draw out, extract 8 bring out 9 draw forth 12 bring to light

Edward II
author: 18 Christopher Marlowe

Edwards, Blake
director of: 3 SOB, Ten 14 The Pink Panther, Victor Victoria 18 Days of Wine and Roses 19 Breakfast at Tiffany's

Edwards, Vince
real name: 18 Vincent Edward Zoimo
roles: 8 Ben Casey 13 Devil's Brigade 14 The Desperadoes 15 Three Faces of Eve

Edwin Drood, The Mystery of
author: 14 Charles Dickens
character: 7 Durdles, Mr Tatar, Rosa Bud 8 Mr Sapsea 10 John Jasper, Mr Datchery 11 Mr Grewgious 12 Mr Crisparkle 13 Deputy Bazzard 14 Helena Landless, Miss Twinkleton, Mr Honeythunder 15 Neville Landless

eel
young: 5 elver

eerie 3 odd 5 queer, weird 6 creepy, spooky, uneasy 7 bizarre, fearful, ghostly, ominous, strange, uncanny 10 mysterious, portentous 11 frightening 12 apprehensive

Eetion
king of: 6 Thebes 7 Cilicia
daughter: 10 Andromache

Eeyore
character in: 13 Winnie-the-Pooh
author: 5 Milne

efface 4 raze 5 erase 6 cancel, delete, excise, rub out 7 blot out, destroy, expunge, wipe out 9 eradicate, extirpate 10 annihilate, obliterate

effect, effects 4 fact, gist, make 5 cause, drift, force, goods, power, tenor, truth 6 action, assets, attain, create, impact, import, intent, result, sequel, things, upshot, weight 7 achieve, essence, execute, meaning, outcome, perform, produce, purport, reality, realize 8 carry out, chattels, efficacy, function, holdings, movables, validity 9 actuality, aftermath, execution, furniture, influence, intention, operation, outgrowth, trappings 10 accomplish, bring about, impression 11 commodities, consequence, development, enforcement, general idea, impli-

cation, possessions
12 significance
14 accomplishment

effective 4 real **6** active, actual, cogent, moving, potent, strong, useful **7** capable, current, dynamic, telling **8** a reality, eloquent, forceful, forcible, incisive, powerful, striking **9** activated, competent, effectual, efficient, operative **10** compelling, convincing, impressive, persuasive, productive, successful **11** efficacious, influential, in operation, serviceable

effectiveness 5 power **6** effect, impact **7** potency **8** efficacy, strength **9** influence **10** efficiency, usefulness **14** serviceability

effectual 6 acting, active, useful **7** working **8** adequate **9** effective, efficient, operative **11** efficacious, functioning

effectuate 6 effect **7** achieve, execute, realize **8** carry out, complete **9** discharge **10** accomplish, consummate, perpetrate **12** carry through **13** put into effect

effeminate 7 unmanly **8** sissyish, womanish **9** sissified

effervesce 4 fizz, foam **5** froth **6** bubble, fizzle **7** sparkle

effervescence 3 zip **4** dash, fizz, life **5** froth, vigor **6** fizzle, gaiety, spirit **7** foaming **8** bubbling, buoyancy, vitality, vivacity **9** animation, fizziness **10** bubbliness, bubbling up, ebullience, enthusiasm, liveliness

effervescent 3 gay **5** fizzy, merry **6** bubbly, lively **7** fizzing, foaming **8** animated, bubbling **9** ebullient, exuberant, sparkling, vivacious **13** irrepressible

effete 5 spent **6** barren, wasted **7** sterile, worn-out **8** decadent, depraved **9** enervated, exhausted **10** degenerate, unprolific **12** unproductive

efficacious 9 effective, effectual, efficient

efficacy 6 impact **10** efficiency **13** effectiveness

efficiency 5 skill **6** energy **8** efficacy, facility **9** apartment **10** competence **11** proficiency **13** effectiveness

efficient 3 apt **7** capable **8** skillful **9** competent, effective, effectual **10** productive, proficient, timesaving, un-

wasteful, work-saving **11** crackerjack, efficacious, workmanlike **12** businesslike

effigy 4 doll **5** dummy, image **6** puppet, statue **8** likeness, straw man **9** mannequin, scarecrow **10** marionette **14** representation

effluence 6 efflux **7** outflow, outpour **8** effluent **9** discharge

effluent 5 waste **6** efflux, sewage **7** outflow **9** effluence

effluvium 4 aura, odor, ooze, . reek **5** vapor **6** efflux, flatus · **8** outgoing

efflux 7 outflow **8** effluent, emission **9** discharge, effluence

effort 3 try **4** toil, work **5** force, labor, pains, power **6** energy, strain, stress **7** attempt, travail, trouble **8** endeavor, exertion, industry, struggle **11** elbow grease

effortless 4 easy **6** facile, simple, smooth **8** graceful, painless **12** not difficult **13** uncomplicated

effortlessness 4 ease **8** easiness, facility **9** readiness **12** painlessness

effrontery 4 gall **5** brass, cheek, nerve **8** audacity, temerity **9** arrogance, brashness, impudence, insolence **10** brazenness **11** presumption **12** impertinence **13** shamelessness
   Yiddish: 7 chutzpa **8** chutzpah

effulgence 6 dazzle **8** radiance, splendor **10** brilliance **12** resplendence

effulgent 6 bright **7** radiant **8** dazzling, splendid **9** brilliant **11** resplendent

effusive 5 gushy **6** lavish **7** copious, gushing, profuse **9** ebullient, expansive, exuberant **10** unreserved **11** extravagant, free-flowing, overflowing **12** unrestrained

eft 4 newt **5** again **6** lizard **9** afterward

egalitarian 10 democratic **11** equal-rights **14** constitutional

egalite 8 equality

Egeria
   also: 7 Aegeria
   member of: 7 Camenae
   husband: 13 Numa Pompilius
   instructed: 13 Numa Pompilius

Egesta
   also: 7 Aegesta
   home: 4 Troy

   position: 5 slave
   sold by: 8 Laomedon
   rescued by: 9 Aphrodite

egg 3 ova, roe **4** bomb, goad, mine, oval, ovum, seed, spur **6** embryo, fellow, incite, person **7** albumen **9** instigate, stimulate

Eggar, Samantha
   born: 6 London **7** England
   roles: 12 The Collector, Walking Stick **15** Doctor Doolittle, The Lady in the Car **16** The Molly Maguires

egghead 8 highbrow **13** intellectual

Eggleston, Edward
   author of: 15 The Circuit Rider **19** The Hoosier Schoolboy **22** The Hoosier Schoolmaster

egg on 4 abet, back, goad, spur **6** exhort, incite **8** talk into **9** encourage

egg-shaped 4 oval **5** ovoid **7** oviform **10** elliptical

Egmont
   author: 12 Johann Goethe

egocentric 8 egoistic **11** egomaniacal, egotistical, on an ego trip, self-seeking, self-serving **12** narcissistic, self-absorbed, self-centered, self-involved, self-obsessed **13** self-concerned **14** megalomaniacal, stuck on oneself **18** wrapped up in oneself

egoism 6 vanity **8** self-love **10** narcissism **14** self-absorption, self-importance **16** overweening pride, self-centeredness

egoist 10 narcissist, selfish one **13** selfish person **18** self-centered person

Egoist, The
   author: 14 George Meredith

egoistic 7 selfish **12** narcissistic, self-centered

egotism 6 vanity **7** conceit **8** bragging, smugness **9** arrogance, immodesty, vainglory **10** self-praise **11** braggadocio **12** boastfulness

egotist 6 gascon **7** boaster, peacock **8** blowhard, braggart **9** swaggerer **11** braggadocio

egotistic 4 vain **10** egocentric **12** self-centered **13** self-important

egregious 5 gross **7** extreme, glaring, heinous **8** flagrant, grievous, shocking **9** monstrous, notorious **10** outrageous **11** intolerable **12** insufferable

Egypt

other name: 3 UAR 5 Kemet 6 To-meri 11 The Two Lands 12 The Black Land

capital/largest city: 5 Cairo

others: 3 Tor 4 Edfu, Gaza, Giza, Idfu, Said, Suez 5 Altur, Aswan, Tanta 6 Boolak, Dumyat, Faiyum, Quseir, Safaga, Sallum 7 Alemein, Memphis, Raschid, Rosetta, Zagazig 8 Damietta, Hurghada, Ismailia, Mansurah 10 Alexandria

school: 5 Cairo 7 Al-Azhar 8 American

division: 5 Lower, Nubia, Upper

measure: 3 apt, dra, hen, rob 4 arab, dira, draa, khet, nief, ocha, roub, theb, wudu 5 abdat, ardab, cubit, farde, fedan, keleh, kerat, kilah, sahme 6 artaba, aurure, baladi, kantar, keddah, robhah, schene 7 choryos, daribah, malouah, roubouh, toumnah 8 kassabah, kharouba 10 diramimari, diribaladi

monetary unit: 4 fils, kees, para 5 asper, dinar, fodda, gersh, girsh, medin, pound, riyal 6 ahmadi, dirham, foddah, guinea, junayh, maidin, medine, medino 7 piaster, piastre, tallard 8 bedidlik, millieme

weight: 3 kat, ket, oka, oke 4 dera, heml, khar, okia, rotl 5 artal, artel, deben, kerat, minae, minas, okieh, pound, ratel, uckia 6 hamlah, kantar 7 drachma, quintal

island: 4 Roda 6 Philae 7 Shadwan 11 Elephantine

lake: 4 Edku, Idku 5 Qarun 6 Maryut, Moeris, Nasser 7 Manzala 8 Burullus, Mareotis

mountain: 5 Sinai, Uekia 6 Gharib 13 Shayib al-Banat

highest point: 8 Katerina 9 Katherina

river: 4 Bahr, Nile

   Nile branch: 7 Rosetta 8 Damietta

sea: 3 Red 13 Mediterranean

physical feature:
   cape: 4 Sudr 5 Banas 8 Rasbanas
   desert: 3 Tih 5 Dakla, Scete, Sinai, Skete 6 Libyan, Nubian, Sahara 7 Arabian
   gulf: 4 Suez 5 Aqaba
   isthmus: 4 Suez
   oasis: 4 Siwa 6 Dakhel, Dakhla, Kharga 7 Farafra, Khargeh 8 Bahariya 9 Bahariyeh 12 Wahel-Khargeh
   peninsula: 5 Sinai 6 Pharos
   plain: 7 Asaseff
   plateau: 3 Tih

people: 3 Kem 4 Arab, Copt, Misr, Wafd 5 Gippy, Gyppy, Gypsy, Nilot 6 Ababda, Berber, Hyksos, Nubian, Tasian 7 Mizraim, Pharian 8 Badarian, Bisharin, Memphian
   leader: 5 Jawar, Sadat 6 Nasser 7 Mubarak, Saladin 10 King Farouk 11 Ismail Pasha, Mohammed Ali, Tawfiq Pasha
   pharaoh: 5 Khufu, Menes, Zoser 6 Khafre, Ptulol, Ramses 8 Horemheb, Menkaure 9 Akhenaten, Amenemhet, Amenhotep 10 Mentuhotep 11 Tutankhamen
   queen: 9 Cleopatra, Nefertari, Nefertiti 10 Hatshepsut, Hetepheres

language: 6 Arabic, French 7 English
   for liturgy: 6 Coptic

religion: 5 Islam 18 Coptic Christianity
   ancient god: 2 Ra 3 Geb, Nut, Shu 4 Aton, Atum, Isis, Ptah, Seth 5 Horus, Thoth 6 Anubis, Hathor, Osiris, Tefnut 8 Nephthys

place:
   dam: 4 Sadd, Sudd 5 Aswan 6 Assuan
   mosque: 5 Rifai 9 Alabaster 11 Sultan Hasan
   palace: 6 Kubbeh
   pyramids: 4 Giza 5 Khufu 6 Cheops 7 Saqqara
   ruins: 5 Miroe 6 Abydos, Sphinx, Thebes 7 Memphis 8 Berenice 9 Abu Simbel 13 Valley of Kings, Valley of Tombs
   temple: 4 Idfu 5 Edoon, Luxor, Thoth 6 Abydos, Karnak, Osiris 7 Dendera

feature:
   dynasty: 5 Saite 7 Ayyubid, Fatimid 8 Mameluke 9 Ptolemaic
   long robe: 10 gallabiyea
   peasant: 6 fellah 8 fellahin 9 fellaheen
   sacred bird: 4 benu, ibis 5 bennu
   sailboat: 7 felucca
   statue: 6 Sphinx 15 Colossi of Memnon

food:
   bean: 5 lotus
   beer: 6 zythum
   bread: 6 herisa
   dish: 3 ful
   drink: 4 bosa, boza 5 bozah

egress 4 exit, vent **5** issue
6 escape, outlet, way out
7 leakage, outflow, seepage
8 aperture **9** departure, discharge **10** passage out,
withdrawal

Egypt *see box*

Egyptian
  language family: 11 Afro-Asi-
    atic **13** Hamito-Semitic
  later form: 6 Coptic

Egyptian cross 4 ankh

Egyptian Mythology *see
box*

Ehrlich, Paul
  field: 12 bacteriology
  nationality: 6 German
  studied: 6 toxins **8** immunity
    10 antitoxins
  discovered: 9 salvarsan
  coined term:
    12 chemotherapy
  awarded: 10 Nobel Prize

Ehud 11 Hebrew judge

Eichenor
  mentioned in: 5 Iliad
  father: 8 Polyidus
  fought with: 6 Greeks
  slain by: 5 Paris

Eichmann in Jerusalem
  author: 12 Hannah Arendt

eiderdown 4 puff **5** cover,

quilt **8** coverlet **9** comforter
10 featherbed

Eight and a half, 8 1/2
  director: 15 Federico Fellini
  cast: 10 Anouk Aimee
    16 Claudia Cardinale
    19 Marcello Mastroianni

Eighteen Seventy-Six, 1876
  author: 9 Gore Vidal

Eijkman, Christiaan
  nationality: 5 Dutch
  discovered: 19 antineuritic
    vitamin
  researched: 8 beriberi
  awarded: 10 Nobel Prize

Eileithyia
  also: 8 Ilithyia
  origin: 5 Greek
  goddess of: 10 childbirth
  father: 4 Zeus
  mother: 4 Hera
  corresponds to: 6 Lucina

Einstein, Albert
  field: 7 physics
  theory of: 10 relativity
    14 uranium fission
  awarded: 10 Nobel Prize

Eioneus
  son: 6 Rhesus
  daughter: 3 Dia

Eire *see* **7** Ireland

Eisenhower, Dwight David
see box, p. 298

ejaculate 4 howl, yell, yelp
5 shout **6** bellow, cry out
7 exclaim **10** vociferate

ejaculation 3 cry **4** howl, yell,
yelp **5** shout **6** bellow, outcry,
shriek, squeal **7** screech
11 exclamation **12** vociferation

eject 4 emit, oust, spew
5 evict, exile, expel, exude,
spout **6** banish, bounce, deport, remove **7** cast out, kick
out, spit out, turn out **8** disgorge, drive out, force out,
throw out **9** discharge
10 dispossess

ejection 4 gush **5** spurt
6 ouster **7** issuing, removal
8 emission, eruption, eviction
9 dismissal, expelling, expulsion **10** banishment **11** throwing out

Ekdal, Hjalmar
  character in: 11 The Wild
    Duck
  author: 5 Ibsen

eke 3 add **4** also **7** augment,
enlarge, stretch **8** increase,
lengthen, likewise, moreover
10 in addition, supplement

elaborate 5 fancy, gaudy,
showy **6** expand, flashy, garish, ornate **7** clarify, complex,
elegant, labored, specify **8** involved, overdone **9** embellish,
intricate **10** add details
11 complicated, painstaking
12 ostentatious **13** particularize

elaborate on 6 expand **7** amplify, develop **9** embellish
10 supplement **11** expatiate on

elaboration 11 added detail,
rounding out **12** augmentation **13** amplification,
embellishment

Elaine
  character in: 16 Arthurian
    romance

Elais
  father: 5 Anius
  mother: 7 Dorippe
  changed things into: 3 oil

elan 4 dash, zeal **5** flair, verve,
vigor **6** energy, spirit **8** vivacity **9** animation **10** enthusiasm

eland 3 elk **8** antelope
11 taurotragus

elapse 4 go by, pass **5** lapse
6 pass by, roll by, slip by
7 glide by, slide by **8** slip
away **9** intervene

Elara
  mother of: 6 Tityus

elastic 6 pliant, supple **7** pliable, rubbery, springy **8** flexible, tolerant, yielding
9 adaptable, recoiling, resil-

Egyptian Mythology
  deities: 6 Ennead
  eight gods: 3 Heh **6** Ogdoad
  goddess of evil: 7 Sekhmet
  goddess of fertility: 2 Io **4** Isis
  goddess of law/righteousness: 4 Maat
  goddess of love/joy/music/dance: 6 Hathor
  goddess of sky: 3 Nut
  goddess personifying sky: 6 Hathor
  god of bricks: 5 Kulla
  god of creation: 4 Ptah
  god of dead/Nile: 6 Osiris
  god of earth: 3 Geb, Keb
  god of ocean: 3 Nun **4** Nunu
  god of sun: 2 Ra, Re **5** Horus
    corresponds to Greek: **10** Harcorates
  god of tombs/embalming: 6 Anubis
  god of wisdom/magic/learning: 5 Thoth
    corresponds to Greek: **6** Hermes
  immortal spirit: 2 Ka
  judge of dead: 6 Osiris
  king of dead: 6 Osiris
  king of gods: 4 Amen, Amon **5** Ammon **6** Amen Ra,
    Amon Ra
    corresponds to Greek: **4** Zeus
    corresponds to Roman: **4** Jove **7** Jupiter
  personification of femininity: 5 Neith
    corresponds to Greek: **6** Athena
  ram god: 5 Khnum
  vulture: 7 Nekhbet

Eisenhower, Dwight David
nickname: 3 Ike
 changed name from: 21 David Dwight Eisenhower
presidential rank: 12 thirty-fourth
party: 10 Republican
state represented: 2 NY
defeated: 4 (Eric) Hass, (Harry Flood) Byrd 5 (Farrell)
 Dobbs 6 (Darlington) Hoopes, (William Ezra) Jenner
 7 (Stuart) Hamblen, (Thomas Coleman) Andrews 8 (Enoch
 Arden) Holtwick, (Vincent William) Hallinan 9 (Adlai Ewing) Stevenson
vice president: 5 (Richard Milhous) Nixon
cabinet:
 state: 6 (Christian Archibald) Herter, (John Foster)
  Dulles
 treasury: 8 (George Magoffin) Humphrey, (Robert Bernard) Anderson
 defense: 5 (Thomas Sovereign) Gates (Jr) 6 (Charles Erwin) Wilson 7 (Neil Hesler) McElroy
 attorney general: 6 (William Pierce) Rogers 8 (Herbert)
  Brownell (Jr)
 postmaster general: 11 (Arthur Ellsworth) Summerfield
 interior: 5 (Douglas) McKay 6 (Frederick Andrew) Seaton
 agriculture: 6 (Ezra Taft) Benson
 commerce: 5 (Sinclair) Weeks 7 (Frederick Henry) Mueller, (Lewis Lichtenstein) Strauss
 labor: 6 (Martin Patrick) Durkin 8 (James Paul) Mitchell
 HEW: 5 (Oveta Culp) Hobby 6 (Marion Bayard) Folsom
  8 (Arthur Sherwood) Flemming
born: 9 Denison TX
died: 12 Washington DC
buried: 9 Abilene KS
education: 9 West Point 17 US Military Academy
religion: 12 Presbyterian
interest: 4 golf 6 flying 7 fishing, hunting 8 football,
 painting
vacation spot: 2 CA 11 Palm Springs
author: 11 Waging Peace 15 Crusade in Europe 16 Mandate for Change 27 At Ease: Stories I Tell to Friends
political career: 4 none (prior to presidency)
civilian career:
 president of: 18 Columbia University
military service: 7 general 9 World War I 10 World War
 II 16 Army Chief of Staff
 supreme commander of: 6 Allies 15 European Defense
  (NATO) 18 US occupation forces (Europe)
 head of: 18 Joint Chiefs of Staff
notable events of lifetime/term: 4 D-Day, NATO
 Acts: 11 Civil Rights
 battle of the: 5 Bulge
 conference: 7 Big Four 10 NATO Summit 11 Paris
  Summit
 Cuba taken over by: 11 Fidel Castro
 invasion: 8 Normandy
 trial/execution of: 14 Ethel Rosenberg 15 Julius
  Rosenberg
 USSR shot down: 9 U-Two plane
father: 10 David Jacob
mother: 3 Ida (Elizabeth Stover)
siblings: 3 Roy 4 Earl, Paul 5 Edgar 6 Arthur, Milton
wife: 5 Marie (Geneva Doud)
 nickname: 5 Mamie
children: 10 Doud Dwight 15 John Sheldon Doud

ient 10 rebounding, responsive 11 complaisant,
stretchable 12 recuperative
13 accommodating

elate 5 cheer, exalt 6 excite,
lift up, please 7 animate, delight, elevate, enliven, gladden, gratify, inspire
10 exhilarate

elated 4 glad 5 happy, proud
6 joyful, joyous 7 exalted, excited, gleeful, pleased 8 animated, blissful, ecstatic,
jubilant 9 overjoyed, rejoicing
10 delightful 11 exhilarated
13 in high spirits 18 flushed
with success

elation 3 joy 4 glee 5 pride
7 triumph 8 gladness 9 happiness 10 excitement, exultation,
jubilation 12 cheerfulness

Elatus
father: 5 Arcas
son: 6 Pereus 10 Polyphemus

elbow grease 4 work 5 force,
labor 6 effort, energy, muscle
8 exertion, hard work
11 application

elbow in 4 push 5 force, press,
shove 6 horn in 7 crowd in

**El Cordobes (Manuel Beni-
tez Perez)**
sport: 12 bullfighting

elder 4 head 5 older 6 senior
8 old-timer 9 firstborn, patriarch, presbyter 14 church official 15 church dignitary
French: 4 aine

elder, elderberry 8 Sambucus
varieties: 3 Box 4 Blue
5 Dwarf, Sweet 6 Ground,
Poison, Yellow 8 American,
European, Stinking 10 Red-
berried 11 American red,
European red 15 Pacific
Coast red

elderly 3 old 4 aged 9 venerable 11 over the hill 13 past
one's prime

Eldorado
nickname of: 10 California

Eleanor and Franklin
author: 11 Joseph P Lash

Eleazar
father: 4 Dodo 5 Aaron,
Elind, Mahli 6 Parosh
7 Phineas 8 Abinadab
mother: 8 Elisheba
brother: 5 Abihu, Nadab
7 Ithamar
succeeded: 5 Aaron

elect 4 pick 5 adopt 6 choose,
opt for, select, take up 7 embrace, espouse, fix upon, pick
out 8 decide on, settle on
9 single out

election 4 poll, vote 6 choice, option, voting 7 resolve 8 decision 9 balloting, selection 10 resolution 11 alternative 13 determination

electioneer 3 run 5 stump 8 campaign 11 whistle-stop 12 beat the drums, solicit votes

elective 8 optional 9 selective, voluntary 11 not required 12 open to choice, passed by vote 13 discretionary, not obligatory

Electra
 author: 9 Euripides, Sophocles
 character: 7 Orestes, Pylades
 8 Dioscuri 9 Aegisthus
 12 Clytemnestra
 father: 9 Agamemnon
 mother: 12 Clytemnestra
 brother: 7 Orestes
 sister: 9 Iphigenia
 12 Chrysothemis
 husband: 7 Pylades
 son: 5 Medon 9 Strophius

electric 7 dynamic, rousing 8 exalting, exciting, spirited, stirring 9 inspiring, thrilling 10 full of fire 11 galvanizing, power-driven, stimulating 12 electrifying, soul-stirring

electric battery
 invented by: 5 Volta

electricity measure 3 ohm 4 volt, watt 5 joule 6 ampere 10 horsepower

Electric Kool-Aid Acid Test, The
 author: 8 Tom Wolfe

Electrides
 form: 7 islands
 color: 5 amber

electrify 4 daze, stir, stun 5 amaze, rouse 6 dazzle, excite, fire up, thrill 7 animate, astound, quicken, startle 8 astonish, surprise 9 fascinate, galvanize, stimulate 18 take one's breath away

electrifying 8 dazzling, shocking, stunning 10 astounding, stupefying 11 astonishing

electromagnet
 invented by: 8 Sturgeon

Electryon
 king of: 7 Mycenae
 father: 7 Perseus
 mother: 9 Andromeda
 brother: 6 Mestor 9 Sthenelus
 wife: 5 Anaxo
 son: 9 Licymnius
 daughter: 7 Alcmene
 grandson: 8 Hercules

eleemosynary 10 altruistic, beneficent, benevolent, chari-

table 13 philanthropic 15 non-profitmaking

elegance 5 class, grace, taste 6 purity 7 balance 8 delicacy, grandeur, richness, symmetry 10 refinement 12 gracefulness 13 exquisiteness, luxuriousness, sumptuousness

elegant 4 fine, rich 5 grand 6 classy, dapper, lovely, ornate, polite, urbane 7 classic, courtly, genteel, refined, stylish 8 artistic, charming, debonair, delicate, graceful, gracious, handsome, polished, tasteful, well-bred 9 beautiful, dignified, exquisite, luxurious, sumptuous 10 attractive, cultivated 11 fashionable, symmetrical 16 well-proportioned

elegiac 3 sad 8 funereal, mournful 10 melancholy

elegy 7 requiem, sad poem 11 funeral song 14 melancholy poem 16 lament for the dead 17 poem of lamentation, song of lamentation 22 melancholy piece of music

Elegy Written in a Country Churchyard
 author: 10 Thomas Gray

Elektra *see* 7 Electra

element, elements 3 air 4 fire 5 earth, water 6 basics, member, milieu 7 essence, factors, origins 8 original 9 basic part, basic unit, component, rudiments 10 basic ideas, ingredient, principles, simple body 11 constituent, environment, foundations, native state, subdivision 13 building block, component part, natural medium 14 natural habitat

elemental 5 basal, basic 10 elementary 11 fundamental, rudimentary

elementary 4 easy 5 basal, basic, crude, first, plain 6 simple 7 primary 8 original 9 elemental, primitive 11 fundamental, rudimentary, undeveloped 13 uncomplicated

elephant
 group of: 4 herd

elephantine 4 huge 7 immense, mammoth, titanic 8 colossal, enormous, gigantic 9 ponderous 10 gargantuan, tremendous 14 Brobdingnagian

Elephant Man, The
 director: 10 David Lynch
 cast: 8 John Hurt 11 John Gielgud, Wendy Hiller 12 Anne Bancroft 14 Anthony Hopkins

Eleusinia
 origin: 5 Greek
 form: 8 festival

Eleusinian mysteries
 in memory of: 10 Persephone
 in honor of: 7 Bacchus, Demeter
 celebrated at: 6 Athens 7 Eleusis
 founded by: 8 Eumolpus
 god of: 7 Bacchus

Eleutherius
 epithet of: 4 Zeus
 means: 12 god of freedom

elevate 4 lift 5 boost, cheer, elate, heave, hoist, raise 6 better, excite, lift up, move up, perk up, refine, uplift 7 advance, animate, dignify, enhance, ennoble, improve, inspire, promote, upraise 8 heighten 9 place high 10 exhilarate, raise aloft

elevated 4 high 5 lofty 6 raised 7 exalted 8 improved, uplifted 9 prominent 10 heightened

elevation 4 hill, lift, rise 5 boost 6 ascent, height 8 altitude, mountain 9 acclivity, bettering, high place, promotion 10 prominence, refinement 11 advancement, cultivation, improvement

elevator 4 cage, lift, silo, wing 5 hoist 7 granary 10 dumbwaiter

elevator brake
 invented by: 4 Otis

elf 4 puck 5 fairy, gnome, pixie, troll 6 goblin, sprite 7 brownie, gremlin 9 hobgoblin 10 leprechaun

elfin 3 wee 4 tiny 7 pixyish 9 fairylike 10 diminutive

Elgar, Sir Edward William
 born: 7 England 10 Broadheath
 composer of: 8 Falstaff 9 Cockaigne, Froissart 10 Caractacus, The Kingdom 11 The Apostles 14 The Black Knight, The Light of Life 16 Enigma Variations 19 Pomp and Circumstance, The Banner of St George 30 Scenes from the Bavarian Highlands

Eli
 son: 6 Hophni 7 Phineas
 home: 6 Shiloh

Eli, Eli, Lama sabachthani
 means: 31 My God My God why hast thou forsaken me?

elicit 5 cause, educe, evoke, exact, fetch, wrest 6 derive, extort **7** draw out, extract **9** call forth, draw forth **10** bring forth **12** bring to light

Elicius
  origin: **5** Roman
  epithet of: **7** Jupiter

elide 4 omit, slur **5** annul **6** delete **7** neglect **8** slur over, suppress **9** eliminate, strikeout **10** abbreviate

Eliezar
  father: **5** Moses
  mother: **8** Zipporah
  brother: **7** Gershom

eligible 6 proper **7** fitting **8** suitable **9** desirable, qualified **10** acceptable, applicable, authorized, worthwhile **11** appropriate

Elihu
  brother: **5** David
  friend: **3** Job **6** Bildad, Zophar **7** Eliphaz

Elijah
  opposed: **4** Ahab, Baal **7** Jezebel
  successor: **6** Elisha

Elimelech
  wife: **5** Naomi

eliminate 4 drop, omit, oust **5** eject, erase, exile, expel **6** banish, cut out, delete, except, reject, remove, rub out **7** abolish, cast out, dismiss, exclude, weed out **8** get rid of, leave out, stamp out, throw out **9** eradicate **10** annihilate, do away with **11** exterminate

Eliot, George
  real name: **13** Mary Anne Evans
  author of: **6** Romola **8** Adam Bede **11** Middlemarch, Silas Marner **17** The Mill on the Floss

Eliot, John
  author of: **12** Bay Psalm Book

Eliot, T S
  author of: **9** East Coker, Gerontion, Hollow Men **11** Burnt Norton, Dry Salvages **12** Ash Wednesday, Four Quartets, The Waste Land **13** Little Gidding, The Sacred Wood **16** The Family Reunion **20** Murder in the Cathedral **27** Sweeney Among the Nightingales **28** The Love Song of J Alfred Prufrock

Eliphaz
  father: **4** Adah, Esau
  friend: **3** Job **5** Elihu **6** Bildad, Zophar

Elisabeth *see* **9** Elizabeth

Elisha
  home: **11** Abelmeholah
  succeeded: **6** Elijah

Elissa
  origin: **10** Phoenician
  corresponds to: **4** Dido

elite 3 top **4** best **5** cream **6** choice, flower **7** bigwigs, society, the pick, wealthy **8** big shots, notables **9** haut monde **10** blue bloods, personages, select body, upper class **11** aristocracy, celebrities, high society **14** creme-de-la-creme

elixir 7 essence, extract, spirits **8** tincture **11** concentrate **17** alcoholic solution

Eliza
  character in: **14** Uncle Tom's Cabin
  author: **5** Stowe

Elizabeth
  husband: **9** Zacharias, Zechariah
  son: **14** John the Baptist

Elizabeth I
  queen of: **7** England
  father: **10** Henry Tudor **14** Henry the Eighth
  mother: **10** Anne Boleyn
  sister: **4** Mary **10** Bloody Mary
  brother: **14** Edward the Sixth
  advisor: **5** Cecil **8** Burghley **10** Walsingham
  suitor: **5** Essex **6** Dudley **9** Leicester
  victory over: **13** Spanish Armada

Elizabeth II
  father: **14** George the Sixth
  mother: **9** Elizabeth
  husband: **17** Philip Mountbatten
  son: **6** Andrew, Edward **7** Charles
  daughter: **4** Anne

Elizabeth the Queen
  author: **15** Maxwell Anderson

elk
  group of: **4** gang

Ellas *see* **6** Greece

Elli
  origin: **12** Scandinavian
  personifies: **5** aging
  defeated: **4** Thor
  sport: **9** wrestling

Ellice Islands *see* **6** Tuvalu

Ellington, Duke
  real name: **22** Edward Kennedy Ellington
  born: **12** Washington DC
  composer of: **10** Mood Indigo **14** Creole Love Call, Creole Rhapsody, Hot and Bothered

17 Concerto for Cootie **18** Black and Tan Fantasy

Elliot family
  characters in: **10** Persuasion
  member: **4** Anne **7** William **9** Elizabeth, Sir Walter
  author: **6** Austen

Ellison, Harlan
  author of: **7** Paingod **10** Spider Kiss **13** A Boy and His Dog **16** Deathbird Stories **19** Approaching Oblivion **20** Alone Against Tomorrow

Ellison, Ralph
  author of: **12** Invisible Man

elm 5 Ulmus
  varieties: **3** red **4** bush, cork, rock, vase, wych **5** cedar, Dutch, dwarf, globe, wahoo, water, white **6** Exeter, horned, Jersey, moline, Scotch, willow, winged **7** Belgian, Chinese, Cornish, English, Holland **8** American, fern-leaf, Guernsey, Japanese, Siberian, slippery, tabletop, wheatley **9** September **10** camperdown, Chichester, Huntingdon, smooth-leaf **11** small-leaved **13** European white

Elmer Gantry
  author: **13** Sinclair Lewis
  director: **13** Richard Brooks
  cast: **10** Dean Jagger **11** Jean Simmons **12** Shirley Jones **13** Arthur Kennedy, Burt Lancaster
  Oscar for: **5** actor (Lancaster) **17** supporting actress (Jones)

elocution 6 speech **7** diction, oratory **10** intonation **11** enunciation **12** articulation **13** pronunciation **14** public speaking

Elohim 3 God

Eloisa to Abelard
  author: **13** Alexander Pope

Elon 11 Hebrew judge

elongate 6 extend **7** draw out, prolong **8** lengthen, protract **10** stretch out

elongated 4 long **8** drawn out, extended **9** prolonged **10** attenuated, lengthened, protracted **12** stretched out

eloquence 5 force, grace **7** fluency, oratory **8** rhetoric **9** elocution, speakwell, vividness **10** expression **11** silver tongue
  god of: **4** Ogma **6** Ogmios **7** Mercury

eloquent 5 vivid **6** moving, poetic **8** emphatic, forceful, spir-

ited, stirring, striking
10 articulate, passionate, persuasive **11** impassioned

Elpenor
 companion of: **7** Ulysses
 8 Odysseus

El Salvador *see box*

Elscheimer, Adam
 born: **7** Germany **15** Frankfurt am Main
 artwork: **17** Tobias and the Angel **21** The Stoning of St Stephen **24** Rest on the Flight into Egypt

else 3 and, too **4** also, more **5** if not, other **7** besides, instead **9** different, otherwise **10** additional, contrarily, in addition

elsewhere 4 away **6** except **7** absence, not here

Elsinore
 castle in: **6** Hamlet
 author: **11** Shakespeare

Elton, Mr
 character in: **4** Emma
 author: **6** Austen

elucidate 6 detail **7** clarify, clear up, explain, expound **8** describe, spell out **9** delineate, explicate, interpret, make plain **10** illuminate, illustrate **11** comment upon **14** throw light upon

elucidation 7 account **10** commentary **11** description, explanation, explication **13** clarification **14** interpretation **15** exemplification

elude 4 shun **5** avoid, dodge, evade **6** escape, slip by **10** circumvent, fight shy of **11** get away from, keep clear of

eluding 7 dodging, ducking, evading, evasion **8** avoiding **9** avoidance **12** escaping from, sidestepping **13** circumventing **15** getting away from

Elul 16 sixth Hebrew month

elusive 4 foxy, wily **6** crafty, shifty, tricky **7** evasive **8** baffling, puzzling, slippery **11** hard to catch, hard to grasp

elusory 4 wily **6** shifty **7** devious, dodging, elusive, evasive, hedging **8** slippery **9** ambiguous, deceitful, deceptive, equivocal **10** misleading **12** equivocating

Elvsted, Thea
 character in: **11** Hedda Gabler
 author: **5** Ibsen

elysian 7 sublime **8** blissful, empyreal, empyrean, ethereal, heavenly **9** celestial, unearthly **12** otherworldly, paradisiacal

Elysium
 also: **17** islands of the blest
 afterworld of the: **7** blessed

Elytis, Odysseus
 real name: **19** Odysseus Alepoudelis
 author of: **10** Seemly It Is **20** Heroic and Elegiac Song

emaciated 4 lank, lean, thin **5** gaunt **6** sickly, skinny, wasted **7** haggard, scrawny, wizened **8** skeletal, starving, underfed **10** cadaverous **14** undernourished

emanate 4 flow, rise, stem, well **5** exude, issue **6** spring **7** give off, proceed **8** come from **9** come forth, originate, send forth

emanation 6 coming **7** arising, flowing, issuing **8** effusion **9** effluence, radiation, springing **10** exhalation **11** coming forth

emancipate 4 free **7** manumit, release, set free, unchain **8** liberate, unfetter **9** unshackle **12** set at liberty

emancipation 7 freedom, liberty **10** liberation **11** manumission **12** independence

emasculate 4 geld **5** alter **6** soften, weaken **8** castrate **9** undermine **10** devitalize

Emathion
 father: **8** Tithonus
 mother: **3** Eos
 brother: **6** Memnon

El Salvador
 other name: **9** Cuscatlan
 capital/largest city: **11** San Salvador
 others: **6** Cutuco, Izalco **7** Corinto, Metapan **8** Acajutla, Libertad, Santa Ana, Usulutan **9** San Miguel, Sonsonate **10** San Vicente, Santa Tecla **11** Union-Cutuco **12** Chalatenango
 school: **15** Jose Simeon Canas **16** Alberto Masferrer
 measure: **4** vara **5** cafiz, cahiz **6** fanega **7** batella, botella, cantara, manzana
 monetary unit: **4** peso **5** colon **7** centavo
 weight: **3** bag **4** caja **5** libra
 lake: **5** Guiha, Guija **8** Ilopango **10** Coatepeque
 mountain: **6** Izalco
 highest point: **8** Santa Ana
 river: **5** Jiboa, Lempa, Lopaz **6** Torola **7** de la Paz **9** Goasoaran **17** Grande de San Miguel
 sea: **7** Pacific
 physical feature:
  bay: **10** Jiquilisco
  coast: **6** Balsam
  gulf: **7** Fonseca
  point: **7** Amapala **8** Remedios
  valley: **7** Hamacas
 people: **5** Lenca, Pipil **6** Indian, Mangue **7** mestizo, Spanish **9** Matagalpa
  artist: **8** Salarrue **10** Mejia Vides
  author: **8** Salarrue **14** Antonio Gavidia
  conqueror: **8** Alvarado
  leader: **6** Osorio **8** Jose Arce **13** Matias Delgado **15** Manuel Rodriguez **17** Hernandez Martinez
  philosopher/journalist: **9** Masferrer
 language: **7** Spanish
 religion: **13** Roman Catholic
 place:
  ruins: **7** Tazumal
 feature:
  blouse: **9** volcanena
  dance: **7** pasillo **15** los historiantes
  drum: **8** huehuetl
  estate: **5** finca
  musical instrument: **7** caramba
 food:
  bread: **10** quesadilla
  cheese pancake: **6** pupusa

Emaux et Camees
　author: **16** Theophile Gautier

Embalming
　god of: **6** Anubis

embankment 4 bank, dike, wall **5** levee

embargo 3 ban **8** shutdown, stoppage **10** impediment, inhibition, injunction, quarantine, standstill **11** prohibition, restriction **12** interdiction, proscription **16** restraint of trade

embark 5 begin, board, start **6** launch, set out **7** enplane, entrain **8** commence, go aboard **9** board ship, enter upon

embark on 5 begin, start **8** approach, commence, initiate, set about **9** enter upon, undertake

embarras de richesses 13 overabundance **21** embarrassment of riches

embarrass 4 faze **5** abash, shame, upset **6** rattle **7** agitate, chagrin, confuse, fluster, mortify, nonplus **8** distress **9** discomfit **10** discompose, disconcert **13** make ill at ease **14** discountenance **17** make self-conscious

embarrassed 7 abashed **8** red-faced **9** chagrined, mortified **10** nonplussed **11** discomfited **13** self-conscious

embarrassing 7 awkward **8** confused, crushing **9** bothering **10** disturbing, mortifying, unpleasant **12** demoralizing, discomfiting **13** discomforting, disconcerting, uncomfortable

embarrassment 4 blot **5** stain **6** smirch **7** blemish, scandal, tarnish **8** disgrace **9** discredit **19** financial difficulty

embarrassment of riches
　French: **19** embarras de richesses

embattled 8 fighting **9** embroiled, fortified **11** battle-ready, hard-pressed

embed 3 fix, set **4** bond **5** plant **6** fasten **8** ensconce **9** establish

embedded 3 set **5** fixed **6** bonded **7** engaged, planted **8** immersed, inserted **9** ensconced **11** established

embellish 4 gild **5** adorn, color **6** set off **7** dress up, enhance, fancy up, garnish, gussy up **8** beautify, decorate, ornament **9** elaborate, embroider **10** exaggerate

embellished 6 ornate **7** adorned, flowery **8** brocaded **9** decorated **10** beautified, elaborated, ornamented, rhetorical **11** embroidered

embellishment 5 frill **6** accent **7** garnish **8** furbelow, ornament, trimming **9** adornment **10** decoration, embroidery **11** elaboration **14** beautification **15** fuss and feathers

ember 3 ash **4** slag **6** cinder **7** clinker **8** live coal

embezzle 4 bilk, rook **5** cheat, filch **6** fleece **7** defraud, swindle **9** defalcate **14** misappropriate

embezzler 5 cheat, crook, thief **8** swindler

Embezzler, The
　author: **16** Louis Auchincloss

embitter 4 sour **6** rankle **7** envenom **10** make bitter **11** make cynical **13** make rancorous, make resentful **15** make pessimistic

embittered 6 soured **7** cynical **9** rancorous, resentful **11** acrimonious

Embla
　origin: **12** Scandinavian
　first: **5** woman
　made by: **4** gods
　made from: **4** tree

emblem 4 sign **5** badge **6** design, device, symbol **7** insigna **8** colophon, hallmark

emblematic 7 typical **8** symbolic **10** indicative **11** distinctive **14** characteristic, representative

embodiment 7 epitome, essence **14** representation **15** exemplification, personification

embody 4 fuse **5** blend, merge **6** typify **7** collect, contain, embrace, express, include, realize **8** manifest, organize **9** exemplify, personify, represent, symbolize **10** assimilate **11** consolidate, incorporate **12** substantiate

embolden 7 fortify, hearten, inspire **8** inspirit **9** encourage

emboldened 6 poised **7** assured, unfazed **9** confident, heartened, unabashed **10** courageous, encouraged, inspirited

embonpoint 9 plumpness, stoutness **15** in good condition

emboss 4 knob, knot, stud **5** adorn, chase **6** indent **7** engrave, exhaust **8** decorate

embossed 4 bold **6** raised

7 adorned, antique, knotted **8** engraved, indented **9** decorated, exhausted

embrace 3 hug **5** adopt, clasp, cover, grasp **6** accept, embody **7** contain, espouse, include, involve **8** comprise **9** encompass **10** comprehend **11** consolidate, incorporate

embroider 5 color **7** dress up **9** elaborate, embellish, fabricate **10** exaggerate **11** romanticize

embroidery 8 tapestry **9** adornment, gros point **10** crewelwork, decoration, needlework, petit point **11** imagination **12** exaggeration **13** ornamentation

embroil 4 trap **6** enmesh **7** ensnare, involve **8** entangle **10** complicate

embroiled 8 enmeshed **9** embattled, entangled **11** hard-pressed

embroilment 3 row **4** fray, tilt **5** brawl, brush, clash, melee **6** fracas, ruckus, rumpus, uproar **7** scuffle **8** conflict, disorder, struggle **9** confusion, imbroglio **10** contention **11** altercation **12** entanglement

embryo 3 bud, egg **4** germ **5** fetus, larva, ovule **6** budding, source **8** immature, rudiment **9** beginning **11** rudimentary, undeveloped

embryonic 5 rough **6** unborn **7** nascent **8** immature, inchoate **9** beginning, imperfect, incipient **10** incomplete, unfinished **11** rudimentary, undeveloped

emend 6 change, revise **7** correct, improve, rectify

emendation 8 revision **10** alteration, correction **11** improvement

emerald
　species: **5** beryl
　source: **4** Muzo **5** Egypt, India **6** Chivor **8** Colombia, Rhodesia, Zimbabwe **11** South Africa, Soviet Union **13** Ural Mountains
　color: **5** green

Emerald City
　setting in: **13** The Wizard of Oz
　author: **4** Baum

Emerald Isle see **7** Ireland

emerge 3 run **4** dawn, emit, flow, gush, loom, pour, rise **5** arise, issue **6** appear, come up, crop up, escape, stream, turn up **7** develop, surface **9** come forth, discharge

11 come to light 12 come into view 13 become visible 14 become apparent, become manifest

emergence 4 dawn 7 dawning 10 appearance 11 development 13 coming to light, manifestation 15 materialization

emergency 5 pinch 6 crisis 7 urgency 8 exigency 11 contingency, predicament 16 unforeseen danger

Emergency
  character: 8 (Dr) Joe Early, (Paramedic) John Gage 9 (Paramedic) Roy DeSoto 11 (Nurse) Dixie McCall 13 (Dr) Kelly Brackett
  cast: 10 Bobby Troup, Kevin Tighe 11 Julie London 12 Robert Fuller 16 Randolph Mantooth

Emerson, Ralph Waldo
  nickname: 13 Sage of Concord
  author of: 4 Fate 6 Brahma, Nature 10 Friendship, The Rhodora 12 Compensation, Self-Reliance 14 The Concord Hymn 18 The American Scholar
  philosophy:
    17 Transcendentalism

emeute 4 riot

emigrant 6 emigre 8 wanderer, wayfarer 10 expatriate

Emigrants, The
  author: 10 Johan Bojer

emigrate 4 move, quit 5 leave 6 depart, remove 7 migrate

emigration 5 exile 6 exodus 12 expatriation

emigre 2 DP 5 alien, exile 7 evacuee, refugee 8 defector, emigrant, expellee, fugitive 9 immigrant 10 expatriate 15 displaced person 16 political refugee

Emile
  author: 19 Jean Jacques Rousseau
  treatise on: 9 education

Emilia
  character in: 7 Othello
  author: 11 Shakespeare

eminence 4 fame, hill, note, peak, rise 5 bluff, cliff, glory, knoll, ridge 6 height, repute, summit, upland 7 hillock, hummock 8 mountain, standing 9 celebrity, elevation, greatness, high place, high point 10 excellence, importance, notability, prominence, promontory, reputation 11 distinction, preeminence

12 elevated rank, high position, public esteem 15 conspicuousness

eminence grise 15 unofficial power
  literally: 12 gray eminence

eminent 3 top 5 grand, great, noted 6 famous, signal, utmost 7 exalted, notable, unusual 8 elevated, esteemed, glorious, imposing, laureate, renowned 9 important, memorable, paramount, prominent, well-known 10 celebrated, noteworthy, preeminent, remarkable 11 high-ranking, illustrious, outstanding 13 distinguished, extraordinary

emir 4 amir, Arab, Turk 5 chief, emeer, ruler 6 leader, prince 9 chieftain, commander, dignitary

emissary 5 agent, envoy 6 deputy, herald, legate 7 courier 8 delegate 9 go-between, messenger 10 ambassador 14 representative

emission 5 fumes, smoke, waste 8 ejection, emitting, impurity, issuance, voidance 9 discharge, emanation, excretion, expulsion, extrusion, pollutant 10 sending out 11 throwing out 12 transmission

emit 4 beam, give, shed, vent 5 expel, issue 7 cast out, excrete, secrete, send out 8 dispatch, throw out, transmit 9 discharge, give forth, pour forth

Emma
  author: 10 Jane Austen
  character: 7 Mr Elton 9 Miss Bates, Mrs Weston 11 Jane Fairfax 12 Harriet Smith, Robert Martin 13 Emma Woodhouse 14 Frank Churchill 15 George Knightley

Emmanuel 7 Messiah 11 Jesus Christ
  means: 9 God with us

emollient 3 oil 4 balm 5 balmy, cream, salve 6 lotion 7 calming, easeful, healing, unguent 8 allaying, lenitive, ointment, relaxing, soothing 9 assuasive, lubricant, relieving 10 palliative 11 alleviative, restorative

emolument 3 fee, pay 4 gain, wage 6 income, profit, salary 7 benefit, stipend 9 advantage 10 honorarium 12 compensation, remuneration

emotion 4 fear, hate, heat, love, zeal 5 anger, ardor,

pride 6 fervor, sorrow, warmth 7 concern, despair, passion, sadness 8 jealousy 9 agitation, happiness, sentiment, vehemence 10 excitement 12 satisfaction

emotional 4 warm 5 fiery 6 ardent, moving 7 fervent, zealous 8 stirring, touching 9 excitable, impetuous, thrilling, wrought-up 10 highstrung, hysterical, passionate, responsive, vulnerable 11 impassioned, sentimental, tearjerking 12 enthusiastic, heartwarming, heart-rending, soul-stirring 13 demonstrative, temperamental 14 hypersensitive

emotionalism 8 hysteria 9 gushiness, hysterics, melodrama, theatrics 11 mawkishness 13 melodramatics, show of emotion 14 sentimentality 17 demonstrativeness

emotionless 6 stolid 7 unmoved 9 apathetic, impassive, unfeeling 11 passionless, unemotional

emperor, empress 4 czar, king, shah 5 queen, ruler 6 caesar, kaiser, mikado, sultan 7 czarina, monarch, sultana 9 sovereign 14 dowager empress

Emperor Jones, The
  author: 12 Eugene O'Neill
  character: 4 Jeff 8 Smithers 11 Brutus Jones

Emperor's New Clothes, The
  author: 21 Hans Christian Andersen

emphasis 6 accent, stress, weight 7 feature 10 focal point 12 accentuation, underscoring

emphasize 6 accent, stress 7 dwell on, feature, iterate, point up 9 press home, punctuate, underline 10 accentuate, underscore

emphatic 4 flat 6 marked, strong 7 certain, decided, express, telling 8 absolute, decisive, definite, distinct, forceful, striking, vigorous 9 assertive, insistent, momentous 10 pronounced, undeniable, unwavering, unyielding 11 categorical, conspicuous, significant, unequivocal, unqualified 12 unmistakable

empire 4 rule 5 realm 6 domain 8 dominion, imperium 11 sovereignty 12 commonwealth

Empire State
nickname of: **7** New York

Empire State of the South
nickname of: **7** Georgia

Empire Strikes Back, The
director: **13** Irvin Kershner
cast: **10** Kenny Baker, Mark
Hamill (Luke Skywalker)
11 David Prowse, Peter
Mayhew **12** Alec Guinness,
Carrie Fisher (Princess Leia),
Harrison Ford (Han Solo)
14 Anthony Daniels (C3P0)
16 Billy Dee Williams
(Lando Calrissian)
sequel to: **8** Star Wars
sequel: **15** Return of the Jedi

empirical 9 firsthand, practical,
pragmatic **12** experiential,
experimental

employ 3 use **4** hire **5** apply
6 devote, engage, occupy, retain, take on **7** service, utilize
8 exercise, keep busy, put to
use **9** make use of **10** commission, employment
12 retainership

employee 6 member, worker
8 hireling **9** job holder, underling **10** wage earner

employer 4 boss, firm **6** outfit
7 company **8** business **10** proprietor **12** organization
13 establishment

employment 3 job, use **4** line,
task, work **5** chore, field,
trade, using **6** employ **7** calling, pursuit, service **8** business, exercise, exertion,
vocation **9** employing **10** engagement, occupation, profession **11** application,
utilization **13** preoccupation

emporium 5 store **6** bazaar,
market **9** warehouse **10** large
store **12** general store **15** department store

empower 4 vest **5** allow, endow **6** enable, invest, permit
7 license **8** delegate, sanction
9 authorize **10** commission

empress 5 queen, ruler **7** czarina, monarch, sultana
9 sovereign

emprise 7 venture **9** adventure **10** enterprise
11 undertaking

emptied 6 used up **7** drained,
vacated **8** consumed, depleted,
finished **9** evacuated,
exhausted

emptiness 4 void **6** vacuum
7 vacancy **8** bareness **10** barrenness, desolation, hollowness

empty 4 bare, dump, flow,
idle, void **5** banal, drain, inane **6** futile, hollow, vacant

7 aimless, debouch, insipid,
pour out, shallow, trivial, vacuous **8** evacuate **9** discharge,
frivolous, worthless **10** unoccupied **11** meaningless, purposeless, unfulfilled,
uninhabited **13** insignificant

empty space 3 gap **4** void
5 blank **6** cavity, lacuna, vacuum **7** vacancy

Empusae
form: **7** monster
eats: **3** man

empyrean 7 elysian, sublime
8 blissful, heavenly **9** celestial
12 paradisiacal

emu
also: **4** emeu
form: **4** bird
characteristic: **9** nonflying,
three toed

emulate 3 ape **4** copy **5** mimic,
rival **6** follow **7** imitate

emulative 5 model
9 exemplary

enable 3 aid **5** allow **6** assist,
permit **7** benefit, empower,
qualify, support **8** make able
10 capacitate, facilitate
15 make possible for

enact 4 pass **6** decree, ratify
7 approve **8** proclaim, sanction **9** authorize, institute, legislate **11** pass into law **12** vote
to accept

enactment 3 law **4** bill **5** canon, edict, ukase **6** decree
7 statute **9** ordinance, prescript **11** legislation **12** proclamation, ratification

Enalus
loved: **7** Phineis
saved by: **7** dolphin

enamel 4 coat **5** paint **7** coating **12** glossy finish, tooth
coating

enamor 5 charm **6** allure, attach, draw to, excite **7** bewitch, enchant **8** enthrall,
entrance **9** captivate, enrapture, fascinate, infatuate
12 take a fancy to

enamored 6 in love **7** amorous **8** lovesick **10** infatuated

en arriere 8 backward

en avant 6 onward **7** forward

en bloc 8 as a whole

encage 3 pen **4** cage **5** pen in
6 coop up, lock up, shut in
7 confine **8** restrain
11 incarcerate

encamp 4 camp **7** bivouac
9 set up camp **10** pitch a tent

encampment 4 camp **5** tents
7 bivouac **8** tent city

encase 4 wrap **5** cover **6** enfold, enwrap **7** enclose, envelop, sheathe

enceinte 8 pregnant

Enceladus
form: **5** giant
hit by: **5** stone
stone flung by: **6** Athena
location: **6** Sicily
buried under: **9** Mount Etna

enchain 7 enslave, shackle
8 enthrall **11** put in chains
13 hold in bondage

enchant 5 charm **7** bewitch,
delight **8** enthrall, entrance
9 captivate, enrapture, fascinate, hypnotize, mesmerize,
transport **14** cast a spell over
16 place under a spell

enchanted 7 charmed,
pleased **9** bewitched, delighted,
entranced **10** captivated, enraptured, enthralled, spellbound **11** under a spell

enchanting 8 charming, pleasant **9** agreeable, wonderful
10 bewitching, delightful, entrancing **11** captivating, enthralling, fascinating,
hypnotizing **12** spellbinding
15 casting a spell on **17** casting a spell over

enchantment 5 spell **6** allure,
appeal **9** magnetism **10** attraction **11** captivation, fascination

enchantress 4 vamp **5** siren,
witch **7** charmer, vampire
9 sorceress, temptress **10** seductress **11** femme fatale

Enchiridion
author: **11** St Augustine

encircle 4 gird, ring, wall
5 fence, hem in **6** circle, girdle **7** enclose, wreathe **8** surround **9** encompass
12 circumscribe

enclose, inclose 4 ring **6** circle, girdle, insert, wall in
7 close in, fence in, include
8 encircle, surround **9** encompass, send along
12 circumscribe

enclosed area 4 quad **5** court,
patio **6** atrium **9** courtyard
10 quadrangle

enclosure 3 sty **4** cage, coop,
jail, wall **5** fence, hedge, stall
6 corral, kennel, pigsty **7** pad-
dock, wrapper **8** envelope,
stockade **9** cartridge, inclosure
10 receptacle

encomium 5 paean **6** eulogy
7 plaudit, tribute **8** citation

9 laudation, panegyric
11 acclamation

encompass 4 hold, ring
5 cover, hem in **6** circle, embody, girdle, take in, wall in
7 contain, embrace, enclose, fence in, include, involve, touch on **8** comprise, encircle, surround **11** incorporate
12 circumscribe

encounter 4 bout, face, meet
5 brush, clash, fight **6** affray, battle, combat, endure, fracas, suffer **7** run into, sustain, undergo **8** come upon, confront, meet with, skirmish **9** clash with **10** chance upon, engagement, experience **11** grapple with **12** do battle with, meet and fight, skirmish with
13 confrontation **14** contend against, engage in combat, hostile meeting **18** come face to face with

Encounters with the Archdruid
   author: **10** John McPhee

encourage 3 aid **4** help, spur, sway **5** boost, cheer, egg on, favor, impel, rally **6** assist, exhort, foster, induce, prompt
7 advance, forward, further, hearten, inspire, promote
8 embolden, inspirit, reassure
10 give hope to

encouragement 4 lift **5** boost
6 praise **7** backing, support
11 approbation, encouraging, reassurance **12** shot in the arm **13** reinforcement

encroach 6 invade **7** impinge, intrude, overrun, violate **8** infringe, overstep, trespass
9 break into, interfere
10 transgress **11** make inroads

encumber 3 tax **4** lade, load
6 burden, hinder, impede, saddle **8** handicap, load down, obstruct, slow down **9** weigh down **13** inconvenience

encumbrance 4 load, onus
6 burden **9** hindrance **10** impediment **11** obstruction
13 inconvenience

Encyclopedia
   author: **9** D'Alembert
   12 Denis Diderot

encyclopedic 5 broad **7** erudite **9** scholarly, universal
10 exhaustive **11** wideranging **13** comprehensive
15 all-encompassing

end 3 aim **4** edge, goal, halt, kill, ruin, stop **5** cease, close, death, issue, limit, scrap
6 border, demise, design, effect, ending, finale, finish, object, result, run out, upshot,

windup **7** destroy, outcome, purpose, remnant **8** boundary, conclude, fragment, leave off, leftover, terminus **9** cessation, eradicate, extremity, finish off, intention, objective, terminate
10 annihilate, completion, conclusion, denouement, expiration, extinction, extinguish, put an end to, settlement
11 consequence, culmination, destruction, exterminate, fulfillment, termination **12** annihilation, consummation, draw to a close **13** extermination
.**19** bring down the curtain

éndanger 4 risk **6** expose, hazard **7** imperil **8** threaten
10 compromise, jeopardize
11 put in danger

endear 8 make dear **10** ingratiate **11** make beloved

endearment 7 pet name
9 sweet talk **10** loving word
12 sweet nothing **13** fond utterance

endeavor 3 aim, job, try
4 seek, work **5** essay, labor
6 aspire, career, effort, strive, work at **7** attempt **8** exertion, interest, striving, struggle, vocation **9** take pains, undertake **10** do one's best, enterprise, occupation **11** undertaking **12** make an effort
13 preoccupation

ended 4 done, over **6** ceased, closed, halted, runout **7** expired, stopped, wound up
8 finished, over with, resulted
9 completed, concluded, destroyed **10** terminated **11** annihilated **12** discontinued, exterminated

Endeis
   father: **6** Sciron
   husband: **6** Aeacus
   son: **6** Peleus **7** Telamon
   stepson: **6** Phocus

Enderby
   author: **14** Anthony Burgess

end from which
   Latin: **12** terminus a quo

ending 3 end **5** close **6** finale, finish, windup **9** cessation
10 completion, conclusion, expiration **11** culmination, termination **12** consummation

ending point
   Latin: **14** terminus ad quem

Ending Up
   author: **12** Kingsley Amis

endless 7 eternal **8** constant, infinite, unbroken, unending
9 boundless, continual, perpetual, unlimited **10** continuous, persistent, without end **11** everlasting, measureless, never-

ending **12** interminable
13 uninterrupted

endlessly 7 forever **10** constantly **11** ceaselessly, continually, perpetually
12 continuously
   Latin: **11** ad infinitum

endocrine system
   component: **5** ovary **6** testes, thymus **7** adrenal, thyroid
   9 pituitary **11** parathyroid

endocuticle
   consists of: **6** chitin

end of the century
   French: **11** fin de siecle

End of the Road, The
   author: **9** John Barth

end of the world 8 doomsday **10** Armageddon **11** Judgment Day **13** Day of Judgment **15** the Last Judgment

End of the World News, The
   author: **14** Anthony Burgess

endorse, indorse 2 OK
4 back, sign **6** affirm, ratify, second **7** approve, certify, support **8** advocate, champion, sanction, validate, vouch for
9 authorize, recommend
11 countersign, stand behind, subscribe to **14** lend one's name to

endorsement 2 OK **7** support
8 approval **9** signature **10** acceptance **12** commendation, ratification **14** seal of approval **16** official sanction

endow 4 will **5** award, bless, equip, favor, grace, grant, leave **6** accord, bestow, confer, invest, supply **7** furnish, provide **8** bequeath, settle on

endowed 6 graced **7** blessed, favored **8** bestowed, enriched, provided **10** bequeathed

endowment 4 gift **5** award, flair, grant **6** legacy, talent
7 ability, bequest, faculty
8 aptitude, donation **9** attribute **10** capability **11** benefaction, natural gift

end to which
   Latin: **14** terminus ad quem

endue 5 dress, endow, equip, indue, put on **6** bestow, clothe, outfit, supply **7** furnish

endurable 8 bearable **9** tolerable **11** sustainable

endurance 7 stamina
8 strength, tenacity **9** fortitude, hardihood, stability **10** durability, permanence, resolution
11 durableness, persistence
12 immutability, perseverance,

staying power **13** tenaciousness **14** changelessness
16 stick-to-itiveness

endure 4 bear, last, live
5 brave, brook, stand **6** live
on, remain, suffer **7** persist,
prevail, sustain, undergo,
weather **8** continue, cope
with, tolerate **9** go through,
withstand **10** experience
11 bear up under, countenance

enduring 7 abiding, durable,
eternal, lasting **8** constant, unending **9** immutable, permanent, steadfast **10** changeless,
continuing, unchanging
11 everlasting, long-lasting
12 indissoluble

Endymion
author: **9** John Keats
form: **5** youth
father: **8** Aethlios
mother: **6** Calyce
loved by: **4** Moon **6** Selene
son: **5** Epeus, Paeon
7 Aetolus
number of daughters: **5** fifty
granddaughter: **7** Hyrmina

enemy 3 foe **5** rival **7** nemesis
8 armed foe, attacker, opponent **9** adversary, assailant, detractor **10** antagonist,
competitor

Enemy of the People, An
author: **11** Henrik Ibsen

energetic 5 alert, brisk, peppy,
zippy **6** active, lively, robust
7 dynamic **8** animated, forceful, restless, spirited, vigorous
9 go-getting **11** hard-working,
high-powered, industrious,
quick-witted **12** enthusiastic

energize 7 animate, enliven,
quicken **8** vitalize **9** galvanize,
stimulate **10** invigorate,
strengthen

energy 2 go **3** pep, vim, zip
4 elan, zeal, zest **5** drive,
force, power, verve, vigor
6 hustle **8** dynamism, vitality,
vivacity **9** animation **10** enterprise, liveliness

enervate 3 fag **4** bush, tire
5 weary **6** tucker, weaken
7 deplete, disable, exhaust, fatigue, wash out **8** enfeeble
9 prostrate **10** debilitate, devitalize **13** sap one's energy

enervated 5 spent **6** effete,
wasted **7** languid, worn-out
8 fatigued, listless, sluggish,
unmanned, unnerved, weak-
ened **9** enfeebled, exhausted,
lethargic, washed out **11** debilitated, devitalized,
emasculated

enervation 7 fatigue **9** tiredness, weariness **10** exhaustion

en famille 11 in the family

Enfants Terribles, Les
author: **11** Jean Cocteau

enfant terrible 16 indiscreet
person **17** incorrigible child
19 irresponsible person

enfeeble 3 sap **6** impair,
weaken **8** enervate
10 debilitate

enfin 7 finally **8** in the end
12 in conclusion

enfold 4 veil, wrap **5** cloak,
cover **6** encase, enwrap,
shroud **7** blanket, contain, embrace, enclose, envelop,
sheathe **8** surround

enforce 5 apply, exact **6** defend, impose **7** execute, support **8** carry out, insist on
9 implement **10** administer

enforcement 5 force **6** duress
7 defense, support **8** coercion,
pressure **9** execution **10** compulsion, constraint, imposition
obligation **11** carrying out
13 necessitation, strengthening **14** implementation

engage 4 hire **6** absorb, combat, employ, occupy, pledge,
retain, secure, take on **7** betroth, engross, involve, partake, promise, war with
8 affiance, embark on, set
about, takepart **9** enter into,
fight with, undertake **10** commission **11** busy oneself, participate **12** give battle to
15 take into service

engaged 5 hired, in use **6** active, took on **7** partook,
pledged, secured **8** absorbed,
employed, involved, occupied,
promised, retained, took part
9 affianced, betrothed, engrossed, undertook **10** em-
barked on **11** entered into,
particpated **15** took into
service

engagement 3 gig, job **4** bout,
date, duty, fray, post **5** banns,
berth, brush, fight, troth **6** action, battle, billet, combat
7 contest, meeting, scuffle
8 conflict, position, skirmish
9 betrothal, encounter, situation **10** affiancing, commitment, employment, obligation
11 appointment, arrangement

engage pleasantly 5 amuse,
charm **6** divert, please **7** beguile, delight **8** enthrall, interest **9** entertain

engaging 7 likable, lovable,
winning, winsome **8** charming,
fetching, pleasing **9** agreeable,
appealing, disarming **10** attractive, enchanting **11** captivating **12** ingratiating

Engels, Friedrich
author of: **18** Communist
Manifesto (with Karl Marx)

engender 5 beget, breed,
cause **7** produce **8** generate,
occasion **10** bring about, give
rise to **11** precipitate

engine
inventor:
of compression ignition:
7 Daimler
of electric ignition: **4** Benz
of gas (compound):
10 Eickemeyer
of gasoline: **7** Brayton,
Daimler
of piston steam: **4** Watt
8 Newcomen

engineer 5 pilot **6** driver, hog-
ger **7** builder, hoghead, planner **8** maneuver, motorman,
operator **10** accomplish

England *see box*

Engles, Friedrich
author of: **18** Communist
Manifesto (with Karl Marx)

English, Julian
character in: **20** Appointment
in Samarra
author: **5** O'Hara

English Mail-Coach, The
author: **15** Thomas
DeQuincey

engrave 3 cut **4** etch **5** carve,
stamp **6** chisel **7** decorate,
stipple

engraving 3 cut, die **5** print,
stamp **7** etching, gravure
9 woodblock **11** copperplate,
lithography **12** photogravure

engross 4 hold **6** absorb, arrest, engage, occupy, take up
7 immerse, involve
9 preoccupy

engrossed 4 busy, deep **6** intent **7** engaged **8** absorbed, immersed, involved, occupied
11 preoccupied

engrossing 8 engaging, exciting **9** absorbing, arresting,
thrilling **10** intriguing **11** captivating, fascinating,
interesting

engrossment 9 immersion
10 absorption, intentness
11 involvement **13** concentration, preoccupation

engulf 4 bury **5** swamp **6** deluge **7** envelop, immerse, overrun **8** inundate, submerge
9 swallow up

enhance 4 lift **5** add to, boost,
raise **7** augment, elevate, magnify **8** heighten, redouble
9 embellish, intensify
10 complement

England
other name: 6 Albion 7 Britain 9 Britannia 12 Great Britain
capital/largest city: 6 London
others: 3 Ely 4 Bath, Deal, Hull, Ryde, Ware, York 5 Blyth, Brent, Derby, Dover, Erith, Flint, Leeds, Ripon, Truro, Wigan 6 Barnet, Bolton, Bootle, Camden, Durham, Ealing, Exeter, Henley, Jarrow, Leyton, Oldham, Oxford, Yeovil 7 Bristol, Bromley, Burnley, Chelsea, Croydon, Enfield, Grimsby, Halifax, Hornsey, Ipswich, Lambeth, Newport, Norwich, Preston, Salford, 8 Bradford, Brighton, Cornwall, Coventry, Dewsbury, Hastings, Plymouth 9 Greenwich, Liverpool, Newcastle, Sheffield 10 Birmingham, Manchester 15 Stratford-on-Avon
school: 4 Eton 5 Leeds, Rugby 6 Harrow, London, Oxford 9 Cambridge, Sandhurst 23 London School of Economics
division: 4 Avon, Kent 5 Devon, Essex, 6 Dorset, Durham, Surrey, Sussex 7 Norfolk, Suffolk 8 Cheshire, Cornwall, Somerset 9 Hampshire, Wiltshire, Yorkshire 10 Derbyshire, East Sussex, Humberside, Lancashire, Merseyside, Shropshire, West Sussex 11 Oxfordshire, Tyne and Wear 12 Bedfordshire, Lincolnshire, Warwickshire, West Midlands 13 Hertfordshire, Staffordshire, West Yorkshire 14 Cambridgeshire, Leicestershire, Northumberland, North Yorkshire, South Yorkshire 15 Buckinghamshire, Gloucestershire, Nottinghamshire 16 Northamptonshire 20 Hereford and Worcester
head of state: 4 king 5 queen 7 monarch
measure: 3 cut, lea, pin, rod, ton, tun, vat 4 acre, bind, butt, comb, coom, foot, gill, goad, hand, hank, heer, hide, inch, last, line, mile, nail, pace, palm, peck, pint, pipe, pole, pool, rood, rope, sack, seam, span, trug, typp, wist, yard, yoke 5 bodge, chain, coomb, cubit, digit, float, floor, fluid, hutch, jugum, minim, ounce, perch, point, prime, quart, skein, stack, truss 6 barrel, bovate, bushel, cranne, fathom, firkin, gallon, hobbet, hobbit, league, manent, oxgang, pottle, runlet, square, strike, sulung, thread, tierce 7 auchlet, furlong, kenning, quarter, rundlet, seamile, spindle, tertian, virgate 8 carucate, chaldron, hogshead, landyard, puncheon, quadrant, standard
monetary unit: 3 ora 4 rial 5 ackey, crown, groat, noble, pence, penny, pound, sprat, unite 6 bawbee, florin, guinea, seskin 7 angelet, hapenny, shilling, sixpence, tuppence
weight: 3 bag, kip, tod, ton 4 keel, last, mast, maun 5 barge, fagot, grain, pound, score, stone, truss 6 bushel, cental, fangot, fother, fotmal, pocket 7 quarter, sarpler
island: 3 Man 4 Holy 5 Farne, Lundy, Wight 6 Coquet, Mersea, Scilly, Thanet, Tresco, Walney 7 Bardsey, Channel, Hayling, Ireland, Sheppey 8 Anglesea, Anglesey, Foulness, Holyhead
lake: 8 Grasmere 9 Ennerdale, Ullswater, Wastwater 10 Buttermere, Windermere 12 Derwentwater 13 Coniston Water
mountain: 5 Black 7 Pennine, Snowdon 8 Cambrian, Cumbrian
 hill: 6 Formby, Lizard, Mendip 7 Brendon, Cemmaes, Trevose
highest point: 11 Scafell Pike
river: 3 Cam, Dee, Don, Esk, Exe, Lea, Nen, Ure, Wye 4 Aire, Avon, Eden, Lune, Nene, Nidd, Ouse, Penk, Tame, Tees, Till, Tyne, Wear, Yare 5 Anker, Colne, Deben, Stour, Swale, Tamar, Tawar, Trent, Tweed 6 Humber, Kennet, Mersey, Rother, Severn, Thames, Wharfe, Witham 7 Derwent, Parrett, Waveney, Welland 8 Torridge 9 Yorkshire 12 Wensum Ribble
sea: 5 Irish, North 6 Celtic 8 Atlantic
physical feature:
 bay: 3 Tor 4 Lyme, Wash 5 Start 6 Mounts 7 Bigbury 8 Bideford, Cardigan, Falmouth, Tremadoc, Weymouth
 chalk cliffs: 5 Dover
 channel: 6 Solent 7 Bristol, English 8 Spithead
 firth: 6 Solway
 forest: 5 Arden 6 Exmoor 8 Dartmoor, Sherwood
 point: 4 Naze 5 Lynas, Morte, Sales 6 Dodman, Lizard, Prawle 8 Hartland, Landsend
 region: 5 Weald 8 Midlands 10 West Riding 11 North Riding 12 Lake District
 valley: 4 Coom, Eden, Tees, Tyne 5 Combe, Coomb 6 Coquet
people: 4 Celt, Pict 5 Jutes, Norse, Saxon 6 Angles, Briton, Norman, Viking
 artist: 6 Romney, Turner 7 Hogarth 8 Reynolds, Rossetti 9 Constable 12 Gainsborough
 author: 3 Kyd 4 Bede, Hume, Pope, Shaw 5 Auden, Bacon, Blake, Burke, Byron, Defoe, Donne, Eliot, Hardy, Joyce, Keats, Scott, Swift, Waugh, Wilde, Woolf 6 Austen, Bronte, Bunyan, Conrad, Dryden, Jonson, Milton, Newton, Ruskin, Sterne, Thomas 7 Boswell, Chaucer, Dickens, Kipling, Marlowe, Shelley, Spenser, Walpole 8 Browning, Fielding, Lawrence, Sheridan, Smollett, Tennyson, Trollope 9 Churchill, Coleridge, Stevenson, Thackeray 10 Galsworthy, Richardson, Thomas More, Wordsworth 11 Shakespeare
 king: 4 Hal 5 Cnut, John, Lear 5 Henry, James 6 Alfred, Arthur, Canute, Edmund, Edward, Egbert, George, Harold 7 Charles, Richard, Stephen, William 9 Cymbeline 18 Richard Coeur de Lion 19 Richard the Lionheart
 leader: 4 Eden, Grey, Lamb, Peel, Pitt 5 Heath 6 Attlee, Wilson 7 Baldwin, Balfour, Canning, Fitzroy, Spencer, Stanley, Walpole 8 Disraeli, Stanhope, Thatcher 9 Cavendish, Churchill, Gladstone, Grenville, MacDonald, Macmillan 10 Palmerston, Wellington 11 Chamberlain, Douglas-Home, Lloyd George
 queen: 3 Mab 4 Anne, Bess, Jane, Mary 7 Eleanor 8 Boadicea, Victoria 9 Catherine, Charlotte, Elizabeth, Guinivere 10 Bloody Mary 11 Jane Seymour

(continued)

England (*continued*)
  language: 7 English
  religion: 6 Jewish 8 Anglican 9 Methodist, Unitarian 13 Roman Catholic 15 Church of
  England
  place:
    bridge: 5 Tower 6 London 11 Westminster
    cathedral: 4 York 6 Exeter 7 St Pauls 8 St Albans 9 Salisbury 10 Canterbury, Winchester
      16 Westminster Abbey
    clock: 6 Big Ben
    fortification: 12 Hadrian's Wall
    museum: 4 Tate 7 British 9 Ashmolean 17 Madame Tussauds Wax
    palace: 7 St James, Windsor 10 Buckingham 12 Hampton Court
    racetrack: 5 Ascot
    ruins: 10 Stonehenge
    street: 5 Fleet 12 Threadneedle 16 Piccadilly Circus
    tower: 6 London
  feature:
    dance: 6 morris
  food:
    bacon: 6 gammon, rasher 7 streaky
    beer: 5 grout, stout
    cookie: 7 biscuit
    dessert: 6 trifle 11 plum pudding
    dish: 12 fish and chips 14 Cornish pasties 15 bubble and squeak 16 Yorkshire pudding
    drink: 3 ale, tea 6 squash

---

enhancement 11 heightening, improvement 15 intensification

Enid
  character in: 12 The Mabinogion 15 Idylls of the King 16 Arthurian romance
  author: 8 Tennyson

enigma 6 puzzle, riddle, secret 7 mystery 8 question 9 conundrum 10 perplexity

enigmatic, enigmatical 7 cryptic, elusive 8 baffling, puzzling 9 ambiguous, equivocal, secretive 10 mysterious, perplexing 11 inscrutable, paradoxical 12 unfathomable 14 indecipherable

Eniopeus
  mentioned in: 5 Iliad
  charioteer of: 6 Hector
  slain by: 8 Diomedes

enjoin 3 ask, ban, bar, beg, bid 4 urge, warn 6 advise, charge, direct, forbid 7 command, counsel, entreat 8 admonish, call upon, instruct, prohibit, restrain, restrict 9 interdict, proscribe

enjoy 3 own 4 have, like 5 eat up, fancy, savor 6 admire, relish 7 possess 9 delight in, rejoice in 10 appreciate 11 think well of 13 be blessed with, be pleased with, get a kick out of 14 take pleasure in 16 have the benefit of

enjoyable 8 pleasant, pleasing 9 agreeable, fun-filled, rewarding 10 delightful, gratifying, satisfying 11 pleasurable

enjoyment 3 fun, joy 4 zest 5 gusto, right 6 relish 7 benefit, delight 8 blessing, exercise, good time, pleasure 9 advantage, amusement, diversion, happiness, privilege 10 possession, recreation 11 prerogative 12 satisfaction 13 entertainment, gratification

Enki
  origin: 8 Sumerian
  god of: 6 wisdom
  habitat: 5 water
  corresponds to: 2 Ea

Enkidu
  origin: 8 Sumerian
  servant of: 9 Gilgamesh
  friend of: 9 Gilgamesh

enlarge 4 grow 5 add to, swell, widen 6 expand, extend 7 amplify, augment, broaden, develop, expound, inflate, magnify 8 elongate, increase, lengthen, multiply 9 discourse, elaborate, expatiate

enlarged 7 swollen, widened 8 expanded, extended, inflated 9 amplified, broadened, distended, elongated, magnified

enlargement 6 growth 8 addition, increase, swelling, widening 9 expansion, extension, inflation 10 broadening, elongation 11 development, elaboration, expatiation, lengthening 12 augmentation 13 amplification, magnification 14 multiplication

enlighten 5 edify 6 advise, inform, wise up 7 apprise, clarify, educate 8 civilize, instruct 9 make aware 10 illuminate 12 sophisticate

enlightenment 8 learning 9 erudition, knowledge 11 edification, instruction
  French: 15 Eclaircissement
  German: 10 Aufklarung

Enlil
  origin: 8 Sumerian
  king of: 4 gods
  god of: 3 air
  son: 5 Ninib 7 Ninurta

enlist 4 join 6 engage, enroll, join up, obtain, secure, sign up 7 procure, recruit 8 register 9 volunteer 19 gain the assistance of

enlistment 9 signing up 10 admittance, enrollment, recruiting

enliven 4 fire 5 pep up, renew 6 excite, vivify, wake up 7 animate, cheer up, quicken 8 brighten, vitalize 10 make lively, rejuvenate

enlivened 7 revived 8 animated, vivified 9 refreshed 11 invigorated

en masse 7 in a body 8 as a group, as a whole, in a group, together 11 all together

enmesh 4 trap 5 catch, snare, snarl 6 tangle 7 embroil, ensnare, entwine, involve 8 entangle

enmity 6 animus, hatred, malice, rancor, strife 7 ill will

8 acrimony, bad blood **9** animosity, antipathy, hostility **10** bitterness

Ennead 7 dieties
  origin: **8** Egyptian
  number: **4** nine

ennoble 5 raise **6** refine **7** dignify, elevate

Ennomus
  vocation: **6** angler
  joined: **7** Trojans

Ennosigaeus
  epithet of: **8** Poseidon
  means: **11** earth shaker

ennui 6 apathy, tedium **7** boredom, languor **9** lassitude, weariness **12** indifference, listlessness
  Latin: **12** taedium vitae

Enoch
  father: **4** Cain **5** Jared
  son: **10** Methuselah
  grandfather: **4** Adam

Enoch Arden
  author: **18** Alfred Lord Tennyson
  character: **8** Annie Lee **9** Philip Ray **10** Miriam Lane

enormity 8 baseness, evilness, hugeness, vastness, vileness, villainy **9** depravity, immensity, largeness, malignity **10** wickedness **11** heinousness, viciousness **12** enormousness **13** atrociousness, monstrousness, offensiveness **14** outrageousness

enormous 4 huge, vast **7** immense, mammoth, massive, titanic **8** colossal, gigantic **10** gargantuan, prodigious, tremendous **11** elephantine **14** Brobdingnagian

enormousness 8 enormity, hugeness, vastness **9** amplitude, immensity, largeness **11** massiveness

Enormous Room, The
  author: **10** e e cummings

Enos
  father: **4** Seth
  grandfather: **4** Adam

enough 5 ample, amply **6** plenty **7** copious **8** abundant, adequate, passably **9** tolerably **10** abundantly, adequately, competence, plentitude, reasonably, sufficient **11** ample supply, full measure, sufficiency **12** sufficiently **14** satisfactorily

enounce 8 set forth **9** enunciate **10** articulate

en passant 8 by the way **9** in passing

enrage 5 anger **6** madden **7** incense, inflame **9** aggravate, infuriate **11** make furious **13** make one see red **14** throw into a rage **17** make one's blood boil

enraged 3 mad **5** angry, irate **7** angered, furious, violent **8** incensed, inflamed, maddened, provoked **9** irritated **10** aggravated, infuriated **11** exasperated

en rapport 8 in accord **9** congenial **10** in sympathy **11** in agreement

enrapture 5 charm **6** thrill **7** beguile, bewitch, delight, enchant **8** enthrall, entrance, hold rapt **9** captivate, transport

enraptured 4 rapt **8** beatific, blissful, ecstatic **9** delighted, enchanted **10** enthralled **11** transported

enravel 5 snare, snarl, twist **6** enmesh, tangle **7** ensnare, ensnarl, entwine **8** entangle **10** intertwine

enrich 5 adorn, endow **6** refine **7** elevate, enhance, fortify, improve, upgrade **8** make rich **9** embellish **10** ameliorate **11** make wealthy **15** feather one's nest

enroll 4 join **5** admit, enter **6** accept, engage, enlist, join up, sign up, take on **7** recruit **8** register

enrollment 6 roster **9** enrolling, signing up **10** admittance, enlistment, recruiting **12** registration **13** matriculation

en route 8 on the way **9** in transit, on the road

ensconce 4 bury, hide, seat **5** lodge **6** settle **7** conceal, secrete, shelter **9** establish

ensemble 5 getup **6** attire, outfit, troupe **7** company, costume **8** assembly, entirety, grouping, totality **9** aggregate

ensign 4 flag, jack, mark, sign **5** badge **6** banner, colors, emblem, pennon, symbol **7** pennant **8** insignia, standard

enslave 6 addict, subdue **7** capture, control, enchain, shackle **8** dominate, enthrall **9** indenture, subjugate **13** hold in bondage, put in shackles

enslavement 4 yoke **6** chains, thrall **7** bondage, serfdom, slavery **9** captivity, servitude, thralldom, vassalage **11** subjugation

ensnare 4 trap **5** catch **6** en-

mesh, entrap, tangle **7** enravel **8** entangle

Ensor, James
  born: **6** Ostend **7** Belgium
  artwork: **8** Intrigue **19** Bourgeois Living Room **25** Entry of Christ into Brussels **26** The Tribulations of St Anthony **29** Self-Portrait Surrounded by Masks

enstatite
  source: **5** Burma, Mogok

ensue 6 derive, follow, result **7** succeed **10** come to pass **13** come afterward

ensuing 8 eventual **9** following, resulting **10** consequent, succeeding

en suite 6 in a set **9** in a series **12** in succession

ensure, insure 5 guard **6** assure, clinch, secure **7** protect, warrant **8** be sure of, make safe, make sure **9** guarantee, safeguard **13** make certain of

entail 6 demand **7** call for, include, involve, require **8** occasion **11** incorporate, necessitate

entangle 4 trap **5** catch, mix up, snare, snarl **6** enmesh, foul up, muddle, tangle **7** confuse, embroil, enravel, ensnare, involve **8** encumber **9** embarrass, implicate **10** complicate, compromise, intertwine

entanglement 5 mixup, snarl **6** foul-up, muddle **7** problem **9** confusion, imbroglio **10** difficulty, entrapment **11** embroilment **12** complication

Entellus
  vocation: **5** boxer
  home: **6** Sicily
  defeated: **5** Dares

entente 4 pact **6** accord, treaty **7** compact **8** alliance, covenant **9** agreement, consensus, unanimity **10** consortium **12** conciliation **13** rapprochement, understanding **14** likemindedness

entente cordiale 21 friendly understanding

enter 4 go in, join, list, post **6** arrive, come in, record **8** enlist in, enroll in, inscribe, pass into, set out on, trespass **9** penetrate, sign up for **10** embark upon, take part in

enterprise 4 push, task, zeal **5** drive, vigor **6** daring, effort, energy, spirit **7** attempt, program, project, venture **8** ambition, boldness, campaign, endeavor, industry **9** alertness,

eagerness, ingenuity, operation **10** enthusiasm, initiative
11 undertaking, willingness
14 aggressiveness
15 adventurousness

enterprising 4 bold, keen
5 alert, eager **6** active **7** earnest, zealous **8** intrepid **9** ambitious, energetic, inventive,
wide-awake **10** aggressive
11 hardworking, industrious,
self-reliant, up-and-coming,
venturesome **12** enthusiastic

entertain 4 heed **5** admit,
amuse, charm **6** absorb, divert,
foster, harbor, please, ponder,
regale **7** beguile, delight, dwell
on, engross, imagine, nurture,
support **8** consider, enthrall,
interest, muse over, play host
10 cogitate on, give a party,
have guests, keep in mind,
think about **11** contemplate
13 keep open house

entertainer 4 host **5** actor
6 amuser, artist, dancer,
singer **7** hostess **8** magician,
musician **9** performer

entertaining 3 fun **7** amusing,
hosting **8** charming, pleasing
9 beguiling, diverting, enjoyable **10** delightful, hostessing
11 playing host **12** having
guests **14** having people in

entertainment 3 fun **4** play
7 novelty, pastime **8** good
time, pleasure **9** amusement,
diversion, enjoyment **10** recreation **11** distraction
12 satisfaction
French: **14** divertissement

enter upon 5 begin **6** assume
9 undertake

enthrall, enthral 5 charm,
rivet **6** seduce, thrill **7** beguile,
bewitch, enchant, enslave
8 entrance, intrigue, transfix
9 captivate, enrapture, fascinate, hypnotize, overpower,
spellbind, subjugate, transport
13 keep in bondage **14** put
into slavery

enthralled 4 rapt **8** beguiled,
enslaved **9** bewitched, enchanted, entranced, in bondage, intrigued **10** captivated,
enraptured, fascinated,
hypnotized, spellbound,
subjugated

enthusiasm 4 love, rage, zeal,
zest **5** ardor, craze, hobby,
mania **6** fervor, relish **7** elation, passion **8** devotion, interest, keenness **9** diversion,
eagerness **10** excitement, exuberance, hobbyhorse **11** distraction, pet activity
12 anticipation

enthusiast 3 bug, fan, nut

4 buff **5** freak **6** addict **7** devotee, fanatic **10** aficionado

enthusiastic 5 eager **6** ardent,
fervid **7** fervent, zealous
8 spirited **9** exuberant **10** passionate, unstinting **11** unqualified **12** wholehearted

entice 4 coax, lure **5** tempt
6 allure, incite, induce, seduce **7** attract, beguile, wheedle **8** inveigle, persuade

enticement 4 bait, draw, lure
6 allure **9** seduction, siren
song **10** attraction,
temptation

entire 4 full **5** gross, total,
whole **6** in toto, intact **8** absolute, complete, thorough,
unbroken **9** undamaged
10 unimpaired **12** all-inclusive

entirely 5 fully **6** wholly **7** totally, utterly **10** absolutely, altogether, completely,
thoroughly **12** unreservedly
13 unqualifiedly
French: **9** tout a fait

entitle 3 dub, tag **4** call, name
5 allow, label, style, title
6 enable, permit **7** qualify
9 authorize, designate **12** make
eligible

entity 4 body **5** being, thing
6 matter, object **7** article
8 creature, presence, quantity
9 real thing, structure, substance **10** individual

entomb 4 bury **5** inter
7 confine

entombment 6 burial **9** interment **10** inhumation

**Entommeures, Frere Jean
des**
character in: **22** Gargantua
and Pantagruel
author: **8** Rabelais

entourage 5 court, staff, suite,
train **6** convoy, escort **7** cortege, retinue **9** followers, following **10** associates,
attendants, companions

entrails 4 guts **5** offal **6** bowels **7** innards, insides, viscera
10 intestines

entrance 4 door, gate **5** charm,
entry, way in **6** access, entree,
portal **7** beguile, bewitch, delight, doorway, gateway, gladden, ingress, opening
8 approach, coming in, enthrall **9** captivate, enrapture,
fascinate, hypnotize, mesmerize, spellbind, transport **10** admittance, appearance,
passageway **12** introduction

entranced 4 rapt **7** charmed
8 beguiled **9** enthralled, rapturous **10** enraptured, fascinated,

spellbound **11** carried away,
transported

entranceway 5 entry, foyer,
way in **7** doorway, ingress
8 entryway **9** front hall,
vestibule

entrancing 6 lovely **8** adorable,
charming **9** appealing, beautiful, beguiling, disarming
10 bewitching, delightful
11 captivating, fascinating
12 irresistible

entrap 3 bag, nab **4** hook,
land, nail **5** catch, snare,
tempt **6** allure, collar, drag in,
draw in, entice, rope in, seduce, suck in **7** beguile, capture, ensnare **8** inveigle

entreat 3 beg **6** adjure, enjoin,
exhort **7** beseech, implore, request **8** appeal to, petition
9 importune, plead with
10 supplicate

entreaty 4 plea **6** appeal,
prayer **8** petition **11** importunity **12** supplication

entree 4 pull **5** entry **6** access
7 ingress **8** entrance, main
dish **9** admission **10** acceptance, admittance, main
course

entremets 8 side dish

entrench, intrench 3 fix, set
4 root **5** dig in, embed, plant
6 anchor **7** implant, ingrain,
install, solidly **8** ensconce
12 establish

entrenched leaders 11 ruling
class **12** powers that be
13 Establishment **14** power
structure

entre nous 9 between us, privately **14** confidentially **15** between you and me
16 between me and thee, between ourselves **18** in strict
confidence

entrepot 5 depot **9** warehouse
18 distribution center

entrepreneur 7 manager **8** director **9** organizer **10** impresario **11** coordinator

entrust, intrust 5 trust **6** assign, commit **7** consign **8** delegate, hand over, turn over
9 authorize **10** charge with

entrustment 10 delegation
13 authorization,
commissioning

entry 3 way **4** door, gate, item,
memo, note **5** foyer, way in
6 access, entree, minute, portal, record **7** account, doorway, gateway, ingress, jotting
8 approach, entrance **9** admission, vestibule **10** admittance,

appearance, competitor, contestant, memorandum, passageway **11** entranceway **12** entrance hall, introduction, registration

entwine, intwine 4 fold, lace, wind **5** braid, plait, twine, twist, weave **9** interlace **10** interweave

enumerable 6 finite **7** limited **11** denumerable

enumerate 3 add **4** cite, list **5** add up, count, sum up, tally, total **6** detail, number, relate **7** count up, recount, specify, tick off **8** numerate, spell out, tabulate

enumeration 4 list **5** tally **7** account, listing **8** adding up, addition, citation, tallying, totaling **9** checklist, detailing, numbering, reckoning, summing up **10** counting up, recounting, tabulation, ticking off **11** spelling out

enunciate 5 sound, speak, voice **8** vocalize **10** articulate **15** utter distinctly **16** pronounce clearly

enunciation 6 accent, speech **7** diction **9** utterance **12** articulation **13** pronunciation

envelop 4 hide, veil, wrap **5** cloak, cover **6** encase, enfold, engulf, enwrap, shroud, swathe **7** blanket, conceal, contain, enclose, obscure, sheathe, swaddle **8** encircle, surround **9** encompass

envelope 5 cover **6** jacket **8** covering, wrapping

envenom 4 sour **6** rankle **8** embitter **13** make poisonous

enviable 5 lucky **8** salutary **9** agreeable, covetable, desirable, excellent, fortunate **10** beneficial **12** advantageous

envious 5 green **7** jealous **8** covetous, grudging, spiteful **9** jaundiced, resentful

enviousness 4 envy **8** jealousy **10** resentment **12** covetousness **13** resentfulness **19** the green-eyed monster

environment 5 scene **6** locale, medium, milieu **7** climate, element, habitat, setting **8** ambience **9** situation **10** atmosphere, background **12** surroundings **13** circumstances
   French: **11** mise en scene

environs 6 exurbs **7** suburbs **8** vicinity **9** outskirts, precincts **11** outer limits **12** outlying area **15** surrounding area

envisage 5 fancy **7** dream of, dream up, imagine, picture **8** conceive, envision **9** conjure up, visualize **11** contemplate **13** conceptualize **14** have a picture of **16** picture to oneself

envoy 5 agent **6** deputy, legate **7** attache, courier **8** delegate, emissary, minister **9** messenger, middleman **10** ambassador **12** intermediary **14** representative

envy 5 greed, spite **6** resent **8** begrudge, grudging, jealousy **10** resentment **11** be jealous of, enviousness, malevolence **12** covetousness **13** resentfulness **16** be spiteful toward **19** the green-eyed monster

enwrap 6 absorb, engage, enrobe **7** engross, envelop **9** preoccupy

Enyalius
   epithet of: **4** Ares
   means: **14** slayer of heroes

Enyeus
   king of: **6** Scyrus

Enyo
   origin: **5** Greek
   goddess of: **3** war
   companion of: **4** Ares
   member of: **6** Graeae, Graiae
   corresponds to: **7** Bellona

enzyme 7 protein **8** molecule **13** macromolecule
   function: **8** catalyst
   acts on: **9** substrate
   kind: **5** amino, malic **6** lactic, lipase, pepsin, rennin, urease **7** amylase, glucose, trypsin **8** aldehyde, glutamic, glycolic, lipozyme, thrombin, xanthine **9** cellulase **12** ribonuclease

eon 3 age, era **8** eternity, long time **9** many years **15** one billion years

Eos
   origin: **5** Greek
   goddess of: **4** dawn
   father: **8** Hyperion
   mother: **5** Theia
   brother: **6** Helios
   sister: **6** Selene
   husband: **8** Astraeus, Tithonus **10** Eosophorus
   son: **6** Memnon **8** Phaethon, Zephyrus **10** Eosophorus
   horse: **6** Lampos **8** Phaethon
   mother of: **5** stars, winds
   corresponds to: **6** Aurore **7** Hermera

Epaphus
   king of: **5** Egypt
   father: **4** Zeus
   mother: **2** Io
   wife: **7** Memphis

   daughter: **5** Lybia **10** Lysianassa

Epeans see **5** Epeus

Epeus
   king of: **12** Peloponnesus
   father: **8** Endymion, Panopeus
   brother: **5** Paeon **7** Aetolus
   wife: **10** Anaxirrhoe
   noted for: **9** cowardice
   built: **11** Trojan horse
   helped by: **6** Athena
   descendants: **6** Epeans

Epheh 15 Biblical measure

ephemeral 5 brief **7** passing **8** fleeting, flitting, fugitive, temporal **9** fugacious, momentary, temporary, transient **10** evanescent, fly-by-night, inconstant, nondurable, short-lived, transitory, unenduring **11** impermanent **21** here today gone tomorrow

ephemeroptera
   class: **8** hexapoda
   phylum: **10** arthropoda
   group: **6** mayfly

Ephialtes
   form: **5** giant
   member of: **7** Aloidae
   father: **8** Poseidon
   mother: **9** Iphimedia
   brother: **5** Oteus

Ephraim
   father: **6** Joseph
   mother: **7** Asenath
   brother: **8** Manasseh
   blessed by: **5** Jacob
   descendant of: **10** Ephraimite

Ephraimi 16 Greek unical codex

Epibaterius
   epithet of: **6** Apollo
   means: **9** seafaring

epic 4 saga **5** drama, great, noble **6** fabled, heroic **7** exalted, storied **8** fabulous, imposing, majestic **9** legendary **10** heroic poem, superhuman

Epicaste see **7** Jocasta

epicure 7 glutton, gourmet **8** gourmand, hedonist, sybarite **9** bon vivant **10** gastronome

epicurean 4 rich **6** lavish **7** gourmet, sensual **8** hedonist, Lucullan, sybarite **9** libertine, luxurious, sybaritic **10** hedonistic, sensualist, voluptuary, voluptuous **11** intemperate **13** self-indulgent

epidemic 4 rife **6** plague **7** rampant, scourge **8** catching, outbreak, pandemic **9** contagion, infection, pervasive, prevalent **10** infectious, pesti-

lence, prevailing, widespread
11 far-reaching

Epigoni
  sons of: **18** Seven against
  Thebes

epigram 4 quip **5** adage,
maxim **6** bon mot **8** aphorism,
apothegm **9** witticism

epilogue 4 coda **5** rider **7** codicil **8** addendum **9** afterword
10 supplement **12** final
section

Epimetheus
  father: **7** Iapetus
  brother: **5** Atals **9** Menoetius
  10 Prometheus
  wife: **7** Pandora
  daughter: **6** Pyrrha

Epione
  husband: **9** Asclepius

episcopal 8 churchly, diocesan,
pastoral **12** ecclesiastic(al)

episode 4 part **5** event, scene
6 affair, period **7** chapter, passage, section **8** incident **9** adventure, happening,
milestone **10** experience, occurrence **11** installment

Episode of Sparrows, An
  author: **11** Rumer Godden

episodic 7 halting **8** rambling
9 segmented, wandering
10 digressive, discursive,
meandering **13** discontinuous

epistle 6 letter **7** message, missive **10** encyclical

**Epistle to a Godson and
Other Poems**
  author: **7** W H Auden

Epistle to Dr Arbuthnot
  author: **13** Alexander Pope

Epithalamion
  author: **13** Edmund Spenser

epithet 5 curse **6** insult **8** nickname **9** blasphemy, expletive,
obscenity, sobriquet **10** ascription **11** appellation,
designation

Epithet *see box*

epitome 4 peak **5** ideal,
model **6** height **7** essence,
summary **9** summation
10 embodiment **12** typifica-
tion **14** representation **15** exemplification, sum and
substance

e pluribus unum 12 out of
many one
  motto of: **12** United States

epoch 3 age, era **4** time **6** period **8** interval

epochal 7 weighty **8** historic
9 important, momentous
11 significant **13** consequential

Eppie
  character in: **11** Silas Marner
  author: **5** Eliot

Epstein, Sir Jacob
  born: **9** New York NY
  artwork: **4** Adam **7** Genesis
  8 Ecce Homo, Einstein
  9 Rock Drill **10** Visitation
  11 Night and Day, Paul
  Robeson **12** Behold the
  Man, Joseph Conrad
  13 Haile Selassie **14** Con-
  summatum Est **19** Social
  Consciousness **20** Monument
  to Oscar Wilde, St Michael
  and his (the) Devil

equable 4 calm, even **5** sunny
6 placid, serene, stable,
steady **7** regular, uniform
8 constant, pleasant, tranquil,
unvaried **9** agreeable, easygoing, unruffled **10** consistent,
dependable, unchanging
11 good-natured, predictable,
unexcitable, unflappable
12 even-tempered
13 imperturbable

equably
  Latin: **9** pari passu

equal 4 even, like, peer
5 match **7** matched, the same,
uniform **8** balanced, be even
to, equalize, jibe with, of a
piece, parallel **9** agree with,
identical, tally with **10** accord
with, comparable, equate with,
equivalent, square with, tantamount **11** balance with, be

Epithet
  of **Aphrodite: 6** Acraea, Scotia **7** Doritis, Erycina, Limenia
  8 Melaenis, Nymphaea, Pandemos **9** Migonitis **11** Aphrogeneia, Apostrophia
  of **Apollo: 6** Loxias **7** Acesius, Agraeus, Agyieus, Carneus,
  Phyteus, Spodius **8** Grynaeus **9** Parnopius, Smintheus
  10 Alexicacus, Archegetes, Boedromius, Delphinius
  11 Argyrotoxus, Epibaterius **12** Platanistius
  of **Ares: 8** Enyalius **14** Gynaecothoenas
  of **Argus: 8** Panoptes
  of **Artemis: 6** Orthia **7** Eurippa, Laphria, Limnaea, Pyronia **8** Aeginaea, Agrotera, Calliste, Caryatis, Daphnaea
  9 Hemerasia, Lygodesma **10** Polymastus **11** Leucophryne
  of **Asclepius: 8** Cotyleus
  of **Athena: 4** Alea **5** Meter, Xenia **6** Ergane, Itonia, Polias
  7 Agoraea, Cissaea, Paeonia, Pronaus, Pronoea **8** Anemotis, Poliates, Zosteria **9** Oxyderces, Parthenia, Poliuchus,
  Promachus **10** Axiopoenus, Chalinitis, Cyparissia
  11 Promachorma
  of **Cybele: 6** Antaea
  of **Demeter: 5** Chloe, Lusia, Mysia **6** Antaea, Erinys, Stiria **7** Chamyne, Thesmia **8** Stiritis **9** Anesidora, Thermasia **11** Carpophorus **12** Thesmophorus
  of **Dionysus: 6** Lyaeus **7** Bromius, Cresius **8** Thyoneus,
  Triambus **9** Pyrigenes **11** Dithyrambus, Mitrephorus
  of **Hera: 6** Anthea, Bunaea **8** Henioche **9** Prodromia
  of **Hercules: 7** Charops **8** Buphagus **9** Ipoctonus
  of **Hermes: 6** Dolius **8** Agoraeus **9** Spelaites **10** Criophorus
  11 Argiphontes **12** Argeiphontes, Psychopompus
  of **Icelus: 8** Phobetor
  of **Juno: 6** Moneta **7** Curitis, Pronuba, Sospita
  of **Jupiter: 5** Ultor **7** Elicius, Pluvius
  of **Mopsus: 9** Ampycides
  of **Nestor: 7** Nelides
  of **Odin: 7** Alfader, Alfadir
  of **Odysseus: 10** Laertiades
  of **Persephone: 11** Carpophorus
  of **Pheriphetes: 9** Corynetes
  of **Poseidon: 11** Ennosigaeus, Hippocurius **12** Prosclystius
  of **Rhea: 6** Antaea
  of **Sinis: 12** Pityocamptes
  of **Vulcan: 8** Mulciber
  of **Zeus: 5** Areus, Soter **6** Aqueus, Areius, Nemean, Philus
  7 Alastor, Apemius, Ctesius, Lycaeus, Polieus, Stenius
  8 Agoraeus, Aphesius, Apomyius, Cappotas, Cosmetas, Dodonian, Herceius, Leucaeus, Tropaean **9** Aegiochus,
  Chthonius, Coccygius, Hecaleius, Lecheates, Mechaneus
  10 Cataebates, Catharsius, Coryphaeus, Homagyrius, Laphystius, Meilichius **11** Eleutherius **12** Panhellenius

the same as, correlative, counterpart, symmetrical **12** commensurate, correspond to, proportional **13** be identical to, corresponding, evenly matched, one and the same

equality 6 parity **7** balance, justice **8** evenness, fair play, fairness, sameness **10** similarity, uniformity **11** equivalency **12** impartiality **13** fair treatment **14** correspondence
  French: **7** egalite

Equality
  author: **13** Edward Bellamy

Equality State
  nickname of: **7** Wyoming

equalization 7 balance **9** stability **11** equilibrium
  14 counterbalance
  German: **9** Ausgleich

equalize 7 balance **9** make equal **11** make uniform
  13 compensate for

equal to 3 fit **4** able, up to **5** adept **7** capable **8** adequate, master of **9** competent, qualified

equanimity 4 cool **5** poise **6** aplomb **8** calmness, coolness **9** composure, sangfroid **10** steadiness **11** self-control, tranquility **12** tranquillity **14** presence of mind, self-possession **16** imperturbability

equate 5 liken, match **7** average, balance, compare, even out **8** equalize, equal out **9** think of as **10** consider as **14** be commensurate, be equivalent to **17** be proportionate to

Equatorial
  language family: **16** Andean-Equatorial
  group: **8** Arawakan **11** Tupi-Guarani

Equatorial Guinea *see* box

equilibrium 7 balance **8** symmetry **9** equipoise, stability **14** sense of balance

equip 3 rig **5** stock **6** fit out, outfit, supply **7** appoint, furnish, prepare, provide **8** accoutre **9** caparison, provision

equipage 4 gear **6** outfit **8** carriage **9** equipment **13** accoutrements

equipment 4 gear **5** stuff **6** tackle **8** equipage, material, materiel, supplies **9** apparatus **11** furnishings, outfittings **13** accoutrements, paraphernalia

equipoise 7 balance **9** stability **11** equilibrium

equitable 3 due **4** fair, just **6** proper **8** unbiased **9** impartial **10** evenhanded, reasonable **12** unprejudiced

equity 4 cash **5** value **6** assets, profit **7** justice **8** fairness, justness **9** cash value **10** investment **12** fair dealings, impartiality **14** evenhandedness, fairmindedness, reasonableness

equivalency 6 parity **7** balance **8** equality **10** coequality, uniformity **14** correspondence

equivalent 4 even, peer **5** equal, match **8** of a piece, parallel **9** the same as **10** comparable, tantamount **11** correlative, counterpart, equal amount

equivocal 4 hazy **5** vague **7** dubious **8** doubtful **9** ambiguous, enigmatic, imprecise, qualified, uncertain, undecided **10** ambivalent, indefinite, suspicious **11** nonspecific **12** undetermined **13** indeterminate

equivocate 5 dodge, evade, fudge, hedge, stall **9** pussyfoot **10** mince words **11** be ambiguous, prevaricate **13** avoid the issue **16** straddle

---

Equatorial Guinea
  other name: **13** Spanish Guinea
  capital/largest city: **6** Malabo
  others: **4** Bata **9** Rio Benito
  division: **5** Bioko **7** Rio Muni
  monetary unit: **6** ekuele, peseta **7** centimo
  island: **5** Bioko **6** Pagalu **7** Corisco **11** Chico Elobey **12** Grande Elobey
  mountain: **5** Mitra
  highest point: **11** Santa Isabel
  river: **5** Mbini
  physical feature:
    gulf: **6** Guinea
  people: **4** Bubi, Fang **5** Benge, Combe **6** Bujeba **10** Fernandino
    explorer: **2** Po
    leader: **12** Nguema Biyogo
  language: **4** Bubi, Fang **7** Spanish **13** pidgin English
  religion: **7** animism **10** Protestant **13** Roman Catholic

---

the fence **17** beat around the bush

equivocating 6 shifty **7** devious, dodging, elusive, elusory, evasive, hedging **8** stalling **9** ambiguous, deceptive, equivocal **10** misleading **11** dissembling

era 3 age **4** time **5** epoch **6** period **8** interval

eradicate 5 erase **6** remove **7** abolish, blot out, destroy, expunge, wipe out **8** get rid of **9** eliminate, extirpate, liquidate **10** annihilate, do away with, extinguish, obliterate **11** exterminate

eradication 7 erasure, removal **9** abolition **11** blotting out, destruction, elimination **12** obliteration

erase 6 delete, remove, rub out **7** expunge, scratch **8** wipe away **9** eliminate, eradicate, strike out

Erasistratus
  field: **10** physiology
  nationality: **5** Greek
  described: **5** brain, heart

Erasmus, Desiderius
  author of: **14** Encomium Moriae **16** The Praise of Folly

Erato
  muse of: **10** love poetry

Ercolani, James
  real name of: **11** James Darren

Erebus
  location: **10** underworld
  means: **8** darkness

Erechtheus
  king of: **6** Athens
  father: **7** Pandion
  wife: **9** Praxithea
  son: **6** Metion, Orneus, Sicyon **7** Cecrops **8** Pandorus, Thespius **9** Eupalamus
  daughter: **6** Creusa **7** Otionia, Procris **8** Chthonia, Orithyir **10** Protogonia

erect 5 build, put up, raise, rigid, stiff **6** unbent **7** stand up, upright **8** straight, vertical **9** construct, unstooped **12** place upright

erection 7 raising **8** building **9** putting up **11** fabrication **12** construction

eremite 4 monk **6** hermit **7** ascetic, recluse **9** anchorite, religious

Ereshkigal
  origin: **8** Akkadian, Sumerian
  goddess of: **5** death
  consort of: **6** Nergal

Ereuthalion
  mentioned in: **5** Iliad
  vocation: **7** warrior
  home: **7** Arcadia
  dueled with: **6** Nestor

Erewhon
  author: **12** Samuel Butler
  title anagram of: **7** nowhere
  character: **5** Higgs **6** Strong
  7 Chowbok **8** Arowhena

Ergane
  epithet of: **6** Athena
  means: **6** worker

ergo 4 work **6** hence **7** because **9** therefore
  11 accordingly

Eriboea
  husband: **6** Aloeus

Erigone
  father: **7** Icarius **9** Aegisthus
  mother: **12** Clytemnestra
  brother: **6** Aletes
  death by: **7** suicide

Eriking
  origin: **8** Germanic
  12 Scandinavian
  form: **6** spirit
  personifies: **6** nature
  works: **8** mischief

Erin *see* **7** Ireland

Erin go bragh 14 Ireland
forever

Erinys
  also: **6** Furies
  epithet of: **7** Demeter
  means: **4** fury

Eris
  origin: **5** Greek
  goddess of: **7** discord
  brother: **4** Ares
  threw: **14** apple of discord
  corresponds to: **9** Discordia

Eritrea
  capital/largest city:
  6 Asmara
  others: **5** Assab, Keren
  6 Ghinda **7** Massawa
  formerly division of:
  8 Ethiopia
  river: **5** Mareb
  highest point: **5** Soira
  strait: **11** Bab el Mandeb
  sea: **3** Red
  language: **7** Amharic
  religion: **5** Islam **6** Coptic,
  Muslim

ermine 3 fur **4** duty, rank
  6 weasel **7** ermalin **8** position

Ernani
  opera by: **5** Verdi
  setting: **6** Aragon
  character: **6** Ernani
  11 Donna Elvira

Ernst, Max
  born: **5** Bruhl **7** Germany
  co-founder of: **7** Dadaism
  10 Surrealism

artwork: **7** Moon Man
  8 Lady Bird **11** A Little
  Calm, Femme Oiseau
  12 The Whole City **13** The
  Table Is Set, Totem and Taboo **14** Lunar Asparagus

erode 5 spoil, waste **6** ravage
  7 corrode, despoil, eat away
  8 wear away **12** disintegrate

Eros
  origin: **5** Greek
  god of: **4** love
  mother: **9** Aphrodite
  corresponds to: **4** Amor
  5 Cupid

erosion 8 abrasion, ravaging
  9 corrosion **10** eating away
  11 wearing away, wearing
  down

erosive 7 burning, caustic
  9 corrosive

erotic 3 hot **4** lewd, sexy
  5 bawdy, lusty **6** ardent, carnal, impure, ribald, risque,
  sexual, wanton **7** amatory,
  amorous, obscene, raunchy
  8 immodest, indecent, unchaste **9** salacious **10** lascivious, passionate, suggestive

err 3 sin **6** mess up, slip up
  7 blunder, do wrong **8** go
  astray **9** be in error, misbehave **10** transgress **12** make a
  mistake, miscalculate **13** slip
  from grace

errand 4 duty, task **6** office
  7 mission **10** assignment

errant 5 wrong **6** arrant,
  astray, erring, roving **7** erratic,
  wayward **8** mistaken, straying
  9 incorrect, wandering, wayfaring **11** adventurous

errare humanum est 12 to
  err is human

erratic 3 odd **5** queer **6** fitful
  7 strange, unusual, wayward
  8 aberrant, abnormal, peculiar,
  shifting, unstable, variable
  9 eccentric, unnatural **10** capricious, changeable **11** vacillating **12** inconsistent
  13 unpredictable

erroneous 5 false, wrong **6** all
  wet, faulty, untrue **7** off base,
  unsound **8** mistaken, spurious
  9 incorrect, unfounded **10** fallacious, inaccurate **12** full of
  hot air **13** unsupportable

error 4 flaw **5** boner, botch,
  fault **6** boo-boo, bungle, howler **7** blooper, fallacy, mistake
  9 oversight **10** inaccuracy
  13 misconception **14** miscalculation **15** misapprehension
  16 misunderstanding
  17 misinterpretation

ersatz 4 fake, sham **5** bogus,

phony **9** imitation, pretended,
  synthetic **10** artificial, not genuine **11** counterfeit

Erse 4 Celt, Gael, Scot **5** Irish
  6 Celtic, Gaelic **7** Ireland
  8 Scottish **10** Highlander

erstwhile 2 ex **4** past **6** bygone, former **8** previous

eruct 4 burp **5** belch

eructation 4 burp **5** belch

erudite 4 wise **7** learned, sapient **8** cultured, literate, wellread **9** scholarly **10** cultivated,
  thoughtful, well-versed **11** intelligent **12** well-educated,
  well-informed, well-reasoned

erudition 5 skill **7** culture
  8 learning, literacy **9** education, expertise, knowledge,
  schooling **10** refinement
  11 cultivation, learnedness,
  scholarship **12** book learning
  13 enlightenment

Erulus
  king of: **5** Italy
  mother: **7** Feronia
  gift: **10** three lives

erupt 4 emit, gush, vent
  5 eruct **6** blow up **7** explode
  8 break out, throw off **9** ejected, discharge, flow forth,
  pour forth **10** belch forth,
  burst forth

eruption 4 rash **6** eczema
  7 flare-up, gushing, venting
  8 ejection, emission, outbreak,
  outburst **9** blowing up, discharge, explosion, festering
  10 dermatitis, outpouring
  11 breaking out **12** flowing
  forth, inflammation, pouring
  forth **13** belching forth, bursting forth

Erving, Julius
  nickname: **7** Doctor J
  sport: **10** basketball
  position: **7** forward
  team: **11** New York Nets
  15 Virginia Squires **25** Philadelphia Seventy Sixers

Erycina
  epithet of: **9** Aphrodite

Erymanthian boar
  form: **4** boar
  plagued: **7** Arcadia
  captured by: **8** Hercules

Erysichthon
  cut sacred tree of:
  7 Demeter

Erytheis
  member: **10** Hesperides
  changed into: **3** elm

erythrophobia
  fear of: **8** blushing

Eryx
  vocation: **5** boxer

challenged: 8 Hercules
killed by: 8 Hercules

Esau
  also called: 4 Edom
  father: 5 Isaac
  mother: 7 Rebekah
  twin brother: 5 Jacob
  wife: 6 Judith 8 Makalath
  son: 7 Eliphaz
  birthright sold to: 5 Jacob

escadrille 6 armada 8 flotilla, squadron

escalate 4 rise 5 boost, mount, swell 6 ascend, expand, extend, step up 7 advance, amplify, broaden, elevate, enlarge, magnify 8 increase 9 intensify 10 accelerate, aggrandize

Escalus
  character in: 17 Measure for Measure
  author: 11 Shakespeare

escapade 4 lark 5 antic, caper, fling, prank, revel, spree, trick 7 caprice 8 mischief 9 adventure 11 high old time

escape 4 bolt, exit, flee, flow, gush, leak, seep, shun, skip 5 avert, avoid, dodge, elude, issue, skirt 6 efflux, egress, emerge, eschew, exodus, flight, stream 7 abscond, emanate, getaway, leakage, make off, outflow, outpour, run away, seepage 8 breakout, emission, outburst, slip away, steal off 9 be emitted, break free, cut and run, discharge, diversion, effluence, pour forth 10 break loose, decampment, fly the coop 11 avoid danger, deliverance, distraction, extrication, safe getaway 12 make a getaway

escargot 5 snail

escarpment 4 bank, crag 5 bluff, cliff, ridge, slope 8 headland, palisade 9 precipice 10 promontory

eschew 4 shun 5 avoid, forgo 6 give up 7 forbear 9 keep shy of 11 abstain from 12 steer clear of

eschewal 7 refusal 8 forgoing, shunning 9 avoidance 10 abnegation, abstention, self-denial 11 forbearance 13 nonindulgence 16 nonparticipation

escort 4 date, take 5 guard, guide, train, usher 6 squire 7 company, conduct, cortege, retinue 8 chaperon 9 companion, conductor, entourage 10 attendants, lead the way

escritoire 4 desk 5 table 9 secretary 10 secretaire 11 writing desk

escutcheon 4 arms 5 crest 6 shield 10 coat of arms 16 armorial bearings

Eskimo (Eskimantsic, Askki-mey, Inuit, Yuit)
  tribe: 5 Aleut
  location: 6 Alaska, Arctic, Canada 9 Greenland
  noted for: 7 fishing 9 mechanics

Eskimo-Aleut
  language branch: 5 Aleut, Yupik
  spoken in: 6 Alaska 7 Siberia 15 Aleutian Islands

Esmeralda
  character in: 23 The Hunchback of Notre Dame
  author: 4 Hugo

esoteric 6 arcane, covert, hidden, occult, secret, veiled 7 cloaked, cryptic, obscure, private 8 abstruse, mystical 9 concealed, enigmatic, recondite 10 inviolable, mysterious 11 inscrutable, undisclosed 12 confidential 16 incomprehensible

espanol 7 Spanish 13 Spanish person 15 Spanish language

especial *see* 7 special

especially 6 really 7 notably 9 expressly, intensely, primarily, unusually 10 singularly, uncommonly 11 exclusively, principally 12 particularly, specifically 13 exceptionally, outstandingly 15 extraordinarily

espiegle 7 playful, roguish

espieglerie 12 playful trick

esplanade 4 mall, path, walk 5 drive 9 boardwalk 10 quadrangle

espousal 7 backing, support, wedding 8 adoption, advocacy, marriage, taking up 9 betrothal, promotion 10 supporting 12 championship

espouse 3 wed 4 back, tout 5 adopt, boost, marry 6 take up 7 embrace, further, promote, support 8 advocate, champion, side with 10 stand up for

espressivo
  music: 12 expressively
  abbreviation: 4 espr

esprit de corps 10 fellowship, group pride, group unity, high morale, solidarity, team spirit 11 camaraderie

espy 3 see, spy 4 spot, view 6 behold, descry, detect, locate, notice 7 discern

essay 3 try 5 paper, theme, tract 6 effort, take on 7 article,

attempt, venture 8 critique, endeavor, treatise 9 editorial, undertake 10 commentary, experiment 11 make a stab at, undertaking 12 dissertation, take a crack at, take a fling at 14 make an effort at 16 short composition

Essay on Criticism, An
  author: 13 Alexander Pope

Essay on Man, An
  author: 13 Alexander Pope

Essays
  author: 12 Francis Bacon

Essays in Criticism
  author: 13 Matthew Arnold

esse 5 being 9 existence

essence 4 core, germ, gist, pith, soul 5 heart, point, scent 6 elixir, nature, spirit 7 cologne, extract, meaning, perfume, spirits 8 tincture 9 fragrance, lifeblood, principle, substance 11 concentrate, toilet water 12 basic quality, quintessence, significance 15 sum and substance

essential, essentials 3 key 4 main 5 basic, vital 6 basics, needed 7 crucial, leading 8 cardinal, inherent 9 basic need, important, ingrained, intrinsic, necessary, necessity, principal, requisite, rudiments, vital part 10 key element, principles 11 fundamental, nitty-gritty 12 fundamentals 13 indispensable

essential ingredient 9 necessity 10 sine qua non 22 indispensable component

establish 3 fix 4 form, open, show 5 begin, found, prove, set up, start 6 create, settle, uphold, verify 7 confirm, implant, install, justify, situate, sustain, warrant 8 initiate, organize, validate 9 institute 10 bring about, inaugurate, make secure 11 corroborate, demonstrate 12 authenticate 16 win acceptance for 18 bring into existence

established 6 common 7 regular 8 accepted, familiar 9 customary 10 recognized

establishment, Establishment 4 firm 5 plant 6 office, outfit, system 7 company, concern, factory 8 building, business, creation, founding 9 formation, setting up 10 foundation 11 corporation, development, instituting, institution, ruling class 12 organization, powers that be 13 bringing about

estaminet 4 cafe 6 bistro

estate 4 rank, will **5** class, grade, manor, money, order, state **6** assets, legacy, status, wealth **7** bequest, fortune, station **8** compound, holdings, property **9** condition, situation **10** belongings, plantation **11** inheritance **12** country place

esteem 4 deem, hold **5** honor, judge, prize, think, value **6** admire, reckon, regard, revere **7** believe, cherish, respect **8** approval, consider, estimate, look up to, treasure, venerate **9** calculate, reverence **10** admiration, set store by, veneration **12** appreciation **13** think highly of **16** favorable opinion, hold in high regard **18** attach importance to

esteemed 5 great, noted **6** prized, valued, worthy **7** admired, eminent, honored, notable, revered **9** admirable, important, respected **10** looked up to, preeminent **11** illustrious **13** distinguished, well thought of **14** highly regarded

Estella
  character in: **17** Great Expectations
  author: **7** Dickens

Estevez, Ramon
  real name of: **11** Martin Sheen

Esther
  author: **10** Henry Adams

Esther
  Persian name of: **8** Hadassah
  father: **7** Abihail
  grandfather: **6** Shimei
  cousin: **8** Mordecai
  husband: **9** Ahasuerus
  displaced: **6** Vashti
  enemy: **5** Haman

Esther Waters
  author: **11** George Moore

esthetic 7 refined **8** artistic **9** sensitive **10** cultivated, fastidious **12** aesthetic **14** discriminating

estimable 4 good **6** prized **7** admired, revered **8** laudable **9** admirable, honorable, important, reputable, respected, treasured **10** worthwhile **11** commendable **12** praiseworthy **14** highly regarded

estimate 4 view **5** assay, guess, judge, opine, think, value **6** assess, belief, figure, reckon **7** believe, opinion, surmise **8** appraise, conclude, consider, evaluate, judgment, thinking **9** appraisal, calculate, reckoning **10** assessment, conjecture, evaluation **11** calculation

estimation 4 view **6** belief, esteem, regard **7** opinion, respect **8** approval, judgment **9** appraisal, reckoning **10** admiration, evaluation **13** consideration

estimator 7 analyst **8** assessor **9** appraiser, evaluator **10** calculator

Estonia *see box*

estop 3 bar **4** fill, plug, stop **7** prevent **8** obstruct

esto perpetua 17 may she live forever
  motto of: **5** Idaho

Estragon
  character in: **15** Waiting for Godot
  author: **7** Beckett

estrange 4 part **8** alienate **9** disaffect **10** antagonize, dissociate, drive apart

estranged 5 aloof **6** cut off **7** distant **8** detached, divorced

---

Estonia
  capital/largest city:
  7 Tallinn
  others: **5** Narva, Paide, Parnu, Tartu, Valga
  6 Dorpat **7** Petseri
  8 Paldiski **11** Kohtla-Jarve
  government: **8** republic
  measure: **3** tun **4** elle, liin, sund, toll, toop
  5 verst **6** sagene, versta
  7 kulimet **8** tonnland
  monetary unit: **3** lat
  4 sent **5** kroon
  7 estmark
  weight: **4** lood, nael, puud
  island: **4** Dago, Muhu
  5 Kihnu, Oesel, Saare
  6 Sarema, Vormsi
  7 Hiiumaa **8** Saaremaa
  lake: **5** Pskov **6** Peipus
  9 Vortsjarv
  highest point:
  8 Munamagi
  river: **3** Ema **5** Narva, Parnu
  sea: **6** Baltic
  physical feature:
    gulf: **4** Riga **5** Parnu
    7 Finland
    strait: **4** Irbe
  people: **4** Esth, Finn
  5 Aesti **6** Jewish **8** Estonian **9** Ukrainian
  11 Belorussian
  language: **5** Tartu
  10 Finno-Ugric
  religion: **8** Lutheran

---

9 alienated, separated **10** unfriendly

estrangement 8 coolness **10** alienation **12** disaffection

estuary 5 firth, inlet **10** river mouth, tidal basin

etagere 7 whatnot **11** open shelves

etc (&c) 4 et al **7** and so on, whatnot **8** et cetera, whatever **9** and others **10** and so forth, and the rest

etch 3 cut, fix **5** carve, stamp **7** corrode, engrave, impress, scratch

Eteocles
  father: **7** Oedipus
  mother: **7** Jocasta
    10 Euryganeia
  uncle: **5** Creon
  brother: **9** Polynices
  sister: **6** Ismene **8** Antigone
  son: **8** Laodamas
  slain by: **9** Polynices

eternal 7 abiding, endless **8** constant, immortal, infinite, timeless, unending **9** ceaseless, continual, perpetual **10** persistent, relentless, without end **11** everlasting, never-ending **12** interminable **13** uninterrupted

eternity 4 Zion **6** Heaven **7** forever, nirvana **8** infinity, paradise **11** ages and ages, endlessness, eons and eons, immortality **12** New Jerusalem, the hereafter, the next world **13** the afterworld **14** the world to come, time without end **15** everlasting life

Ethan Frome
  author: **12** Edith Wharton
  character: **5** Zeena **7** Zenobia **12** Mattie Silver

Ethanim 18 seventh Hebrew month

ether 5 ester, ethyl, ozone, vapor **7** diethyl, solvent **10** anesthetic **11** refrigerant

ethereal 4 airy, rare **6** aerial **7** elusive, refined, sublime **8** delicate, rarefied **9** celestial, exquisite, unearthly, unworldly

ethical 4 fair, just **5** moral, right **6** decent, kosher, proper **7** correct, fitting, upright **8** virtuous **9** honorable **10** aboveboard, scrupulous **15** straightforward **17** open and aboveboard

ethical feelings 9 integrity **10** conscience, moral sense **16** incorruptibility

ethics, ethic 8 morality **9** integrity, moral code **10** conscience, principles **11** moral values, sense of duty **14** moral standards, rules of conduct

Ethics of Ambiguity
author: **16** Simone de Beauvoir

Ethiopia *see box*

ethnic 6 native, racial, unique **8** cultural, national, original **10** indigenous

ethnic group *see box, p. 318*

etiquette 5 usage **7** decorum, manners **8** behavior, courtesy, good form, protocol **9** amenities, gentility, good taste **10** civilities, politeness **11** conventions, proprieties **15** rules of behavior

etoile 4 star

Ettarre
character in: **16** Arthurian romance

ET The Extra-Terrestrial
director: **15** Steven Spielberg
cast: **10** Dee Wallace
11 Henry Thomas, Peter Coyote **13** Drew Barrymore **17** Robert MacNaughton

et tu, Brute 13 and thou Brutus
spoken by: **12** Julius Caesar

etymology 7 history **10** derivation

Etzel
origin: **8** Germanic
mentioned in:
14 Nibelungenlied
represents: **6** Attila
wife: **9** Kriemhild

Euaechme
parent: **8** Megareus
husband: **9** Alcathous

Euboean *see* **7** Abantes

Eubuleus
father: **9** Trochilus
helped: **7** Demeter

Eucharist 8 viaticum **9** Communion, sacrament **13** Holy Communion

euchre
number of players: **3** two **4** four **5** three
derived from: **8** triomphe
five tricks won: **5** march
jack of trump: **10** right bower
second highest trump: **9** left bower

Euclid
field: **11** mathematics
nationality: **5** Greek
founder of: **8** geometry
author of: **8** Elements

Eugene Onegin
author: **16** Alexander Pushkin

Ethiopia
Biblical name: **4** Cush
other name: **9** Abyssinia
capital/largest city: **10** Addis Ababa
others: **3** Edd **4** Axum, Bako, Dori, Goba, Gore, Thio **5** Adola, Adowa, Aduwa, Aksum, Assab, Awash, Dimtu, Elfud, Harar, Jidda, Jimma, Kecha, Meroe, Mojjo **6** Antalo, Asmara, Dessye, Dunkur, Gondar, Harrar, Makale, Napata **7** Ankober, Gambela, Gardula, Magdala, Massawa, Nakamti **8** Dire Dawa, Lalibala, Mustahil
school: **13** Haile Selassie
division: **5** Tigre **6** Amhara, Ogaden
former division: **7** Eritrea
measure: **3** tat **4** cubi, kuba **5** derah, messe **6** cabaho, sinjer, sinzer, tanica **7** entelam, farsakh, farsang, ghebeta
monetary unit: **4** besa, birr, harf **5** amole, girsh **6** dollar, kharaf, levant, pataca, talari **7** ashrafi, menelik, plaster, tallero **12** maria theresa
weight: **3** pek **4** kasm, natr, oket, rotl **5** alada, artal, mocha, neter, ratel, wakea **6** wogiet **8** farasula **9** mutagalla
island: **6** Dahlak
lake: **3** Abe **4** Tana **5** Abaya, Shola, Tanna, Tsana, Tzana, Zeway **6** Dambea, Dembea **7** Rudolph **8** Stefanie **11** The Blue Nile
mountain: **4** Amba, Batu, Guge, Guna, Talo **5** Ahmar, Choke **9** Rasdashan
highest point: **9** Ras Deshen
river: **3** Omo **4** Baro, Dawa, Gibe, Gila, Juba **5** Abbai, Akoho, Albai, Awash, Fafan, Mareb, Mofer, Rahad, Webbe **6** Tekeze **7** Tacazze, Takkaze **8** Gashgash, Shebante **11** The Blue Nile
sea: **3** Red
physical feature:
desert: **17** Danakil Depression
falls: **7** Tisisat **8** Blue Nile
valley: **4** Rift
people: **4** Afar, Agau, Beja, Doko, Kafa, Kala, Saho, Shoa **5** Afara, Agows, Galas, Galla, Negro, Tigre **6** Abigar, Amhara, Annuak, Gondar, Hamite, Harari, Sidama, Sidamo, Somali, Tigrai, Wolamo **7** Cushite, Danakil, Donakus, Falasha, Somalis **8** Assamite, Blemmyes **10** Abyssinian, Troglodyte
leader: **7** Menelik **8** Mengistu **13** Haile Selassie
language: **3** Giz **4** Afar, Agow, Geez, Saho **5** Geeze, Ghese, Smali, Tigre **6** Arabic, Harari **7** Amharic, English, Italian, Russian **8** Gallinya, Irob-Saho, Tigrinya
religion: **5** Islam **7** Falasha, Judaism **18** Ethiopian Orthodoxy
place:
cathedral: **8** St George
hall: **6** Africa
palace: **7** Jubilee **9** Menelik II
park: **4** Lion
feature:
flower: **7** brayera
game: **5** dulla **8** shum-shir
garment: **4** toga **5** kamis **6** barnos, chamma, netela, shamma
tree: **4** koho, koso **5** cusso
food:
banana: **4** musa **6** ensete
beer: **5** talla
bread dish: **6** injera
cereal: **4** teff
honey liquor: **3** tej
spicy sauce: **3** wat

ethnic group

of Afghanistan: 5 Aimak, Aymak, Kafir, Nuris **6** Baloch, Baluch, Chahar, Durani, Hasara, Hazara, Kaffir, Kirgiz, Pathan, Tajiks, Uzbeks **7** Beluchi, Belucki, Ghilzai, Pakhton, Pakhtun, Pashtun, Pukhtun, Pushtun, Sistani, Taimani, Taimuri **8** Jamshidi, Siah Push **9** Firuzkuhi, Safed Push, Safid Push

of Albania: 3 Geg **4** Cham, Gheg, Gueg, Tost **6** Arnaut, Arnout **8** Illyrian, Skipetar

of Algeria: 4 Arab **6** Berber, Kabyle, Shawai, Tuareg **7** Haratin

of Andorra: 7 Catalan

of Angola: 5 Bantu, Kongo, Lundu **6** Chokwe, Herero, Mbundi, Ovambo **7** Bakongo, Kangela, Kikongo **8** Kimbundu, Kwangare **9** Ovinbundu **12** Nyaneka-Humbi

of Antigua and Barbuda: 7 African, British **8** Lebanese **10** Portuguese

of Argentina: 3 Api **4** Lule **5** Vejoz **6** Abipon, Vilela **7** Guarani, Puelche, Ranquel, Taluhet **8** Querandi, Querendy

of Armenia: 5 Armen, Ermyn, Gomer, Hadji

of Australia: 3 Abo **4** Koko, Mara, Wong **5** Anzac, Bieri, Binge, Maori, Myall **6** Aranda, Arunta, Aussie, Binghi, Digger, Kipper, Papuan **7** Arawong, Billjim, Ilpirra **8** Antipode, Barkinji, Euahlayi, Warragal, Warrigal **9** Aborigine **10** Austroloid, Melanesian, Sandgroper **12** Jindyworobak

of Austria: 4 Pole **5** Croat, Czech, Gypsy **6** German **7** Slovene **9** Hungarian

of Azerbaijan: 5 Azeri **11** Azerbaijani

of the Bahamas: 5 black **7** Haitian

of Bahrain: 4 Arab **6** Indian **7** Persian **8** European **9** Pakistani

of Bangladesh: 7 Bengali

of Barbados: 5 Bajan **9** Barbadian

of Belarus: 12 Byelorussian

of Belgium: 4 Remi **6** Nervii **7** Belgian, Fleming, Flemish, Walloon **9** Bellovaci

of Benin: 3 Fon, Pla **4** Adja, Aizo, Mina, Peul **5** Pedah, Peuhl, Somba **6** Bariba, Fulani, Yoruba **8** Pilapila **9** Dahomeyan

of Bhutan: 5 Monpa **6** Bhutia **7** Tibetan **8** Assamese, Nepalese

of Bolivia: 6 Aymara **7** mestizo, Quechua

of Borneo: 4 Iban **5** Bukat, Dajak, Dayak, Dusan, Malay, Punan **6** Illano **7** Bakatan, Chinese, Illanum

of Bosnia-Herzegovina: 4 Serb **5** Croat **8** Yugoslav

of Botswana: 5 Bantu **7** Tswana **7** Bakatla, Bakwena, Bushman **8** Bamalete, Baralong, Batawana, Batlokwa, Botswana **10** Bamangwato **11** Bangwaketse

of Brazil: 2 Ge **4** Anta **5** Acroa, Arara, Araua, Bravo, Carib, Guana, Negro **6** Arawak, Caraja **7** Carayan, Javahai, mulatto, Tariana **8** Botocudo, Chambioa, mameluco **9** Caucasian **10** Portuguese **11** Tupi-Guarani

of Brunei: 4 Iban **5** Dayak, Malay **7** Chinese, Kadazan

of Bulgaria: 4 Slav, Turk **5** Gypsy, Pomak, Tatar **6** Bulgar, Slavic **7** Chuvash **9** Cheremiss **10** Macedonian

of Burkina Faso: 4 Bobo, Lobi, Samo **5** Bella, Bissa, Dyula, Fulbe, Hausa, Mande, Marka, Mossi, Puchl **6** Fulani, Senufo, Tuareg **7** Grunshi, Voltaic, Yatenga **8** Mandingo **9** Gourounsi **15** Bunsansi Gambaga

of Burundi: 3 Twa **4** Hutu **5** Bantu, Batwa, Pygmy, Tutsi **6** Bahutu, Watusi **7** Barundi

of Cambodia: 4 Cham, Thai **5** Khmer **7** Chinese **10** Vietnamese

of Cameroon: 3 Abo, Edo, Ibo **4** Beti, Bulu, Ekoi, Ijaw, Sara **5** Bantu, Bassa, Kirdi, Pygmy, Tikar **6** Bamoun, Donala, Ewondo, Fulani, Ibibio **7** Bakweri **8** Bamileke

of Canada: 6 Canuck, Eskimo, French, Innuit **7** English

of the Canary Islands: 7 Spanish

of Cape Verde: 6 Creole **7** African, mulatto **8** European **10** Portuguese

of Central African Republic: 4 Baya, Sara **5** Banda, Bwaki, Sango **6** Azande, Yakoma **7** Banziri, Mandjia, Nzakara

of Chad: 4 Arab, Daza, Maba, Sara, Teda, Tubu **5** Barma, Hakka, Kroda, Massa **6** Fulani, Kotoko, Toubou, Wadaii **7** Kamadja, Kanembu **8** Moundang

of Chile: 3 Ona **4** Auca, Inca, Onan **6** Arauca, Chango, Yahgan **7** Mapuche, mestizo, Moluche, Pampean, Patagon, Puegian, Ranquel **8** Alikuluf, Picunche, Tsonecan

of China: 3 Han, Yis **4** Huis, Lolo, Miao, Pu-is **5** Hakka, Hoklo, Seres, Sinic **6** Cataia, Chuang, Johnny, Korean, Manchu, Mongol, Serian, Uighun **7** Sinaean, Tibetan

of Colombia: 4 Boro, Cuna, Duit, Hoka, Macu, Muso, Muzo, Paez, Tama, Tapa **5** Carib, Catio, Choco, Cofan, Cogui, Cubeo, Guane, Haida, Mocoa, Paeze, Pijao, Seona, Yagua **6** Arawak, Betoya, Calima, Colima, Ingano, Mirana, Saliva, Tahami, Ticunu, Tucano, Tunebo, Witoto, Yahuna **7** Achagua, Andaqui, Chibcha, Chimila, Churoya, Guahibo, Guajiro, mestizo, mulatto, Panches, Puinave, Puitoto, Quechua, Shuswap, Tairona, Telembi **8** Coconuco, Guarauno, Motilone, Puinavis, Quimbaya, Sinsigas **9** Cocanucos, Coconucan, Panaquita **10** Bellacoola

of Comoros: 4 Arab **5** Bantu, Malay **7** African **8** Malagasy

of the Congo: 3 Rua **4** Akka, Susa, Teke, Vili **5** Amadi, Bantu, Figot, Kongo, Mantu, Pygmy, Sanga, Warua, Zambi **6** Ababua, Bafyot, Bateke, Mbochi, Nzambi, Wabuma **7** Bacongo, Bakongo, Bangala, Batetla, Manyema **10** Binga Pygmy

of Costa Rica: 4 Voto **6** Boruca, Bribri, Guaymi **7** Guatuso, mestizo, Spanish

of Crete: 6 Cretan, Minoan **7** Candiot **8** Sphakiot **9** Caphtorim **10** Philistine

of Croatia: 4 Serb **5** Croat **8** Yugoslav

of Cuba: 5 Carib, Negro, Taino **6** Arawak **7** Ciboney, mestizo **8** Ciboneye **9** Caucasian

of Czechoslovakia/Czech Republic: **4** Slav **5** Czech **6** Slovak **8** Bohemian, Moravian

of Denmark: 4 Dane, Jute **5** Angle **6** Cimbri, Eskimo, German, Ostmen, Teuton, Viking **12** Scandinavian

(continued)

ethnic group (*continued*)

of Djibouti: 4 Afar, Arab **5** Issas **6** French **8** European
of Dominican Republic: 5 Negro, Taino **6** Indian **7** mulatto, Spanish **9** Caucasian
of Ecuador: 4 Cara, Cixo, Inca **5** Ardan, Aucas, Macoa, Maina, Palta, Quitu, Yumbo **6** Canelo, Jibaro, Jivaro, Puruha **7** Cayapas, Jivaros, mestizo, mulatto **8** Barbacoa, Colorado, Montuvio, Serranos **10** Montubious
of Egypt: 3 Kem **4** Arab, Copt, Misr, Wafd **5** Gippy, Gyppy, Gypsy, Nilot **6** Ababda, Berber, Hyksos, Nubian, Tasian **7** Mizraim, Pharian **8** Badarian, Bisharin, Memphian
of El Salvador: 5 Lenca, Pipil **6** Indian, Mangue **7** mestizo, Spanish **9** Matagalpa
of England: 4 Celt, Jute, Pict **5** Norse, Saxon **6** Angles, Briton, Norman, Viking
of Equatorial Guinea: 4 Bubi, Fang **5** Benge, Combe **6** Bujeba **10** Fernandino
of Estonia: 4 Esth, Finn **5** Aesti **6** Jewish **8** Estonian **9** Ukrainian **11** Belorussian
of Ethiopia: 3 Afar, Agau, Beja, Doko, Kafa, Kala, Saho, Shoa **5** Afara, Agows, Galas, Galla, Negro, Tigre **6** Abigar, Amhara, Annuak, Gondar, Hamite, Harari, Sidama, Sidamo, Somali, Tigrai, Wolamo **7** Cushite, Danakil, Donakus, Falasha **8** Assamite, Blemmyes **10** Abyssinian, Troglodyte
of Fiji: 6 Fijian, Indian **7** Chinese **10** Melanesian, Polynesian **11** Micronesian
of Finland: 3 Jew, Vod, Vot, Yak **4** Avar, Finn, Hame, Lapp, Turk, Veps **5** Fioun, Gypsy, Ijore, Inger, Suomi, Vepse, Zyrin **6** Magyar, Ostiak, Ostyak, Tarast, Tavast, Ugrian **7** Lappish, Mordvin, Permiak, Samoyed, Uralian **8** Cheremis, Estonian, Karelian, Livonian, Swekoman **9** Tavastian **11** Karjalaiset, Suomalaiset
of France: 5 Frank
of the Gabon Republic: 4 Fang **6** Adouma, Bakota, Bateke, Echira, Okande, Omyene **7** Eshiras **8** Bandjabi, Bapounou
of the Gambia: 4 Fula, Jola **5** Foula, Wolof **6** Fulani **8** Mandingo, Serahuli **9** Seranuleh
of Georgia: 5 Azeri **7** Russian **8** Armenian, Georgian, Ossetian
of Germany: 3 Hun **4** Slav, Sorb, Wend **5** Saxon
of Ghana: 2 Ga **3** Ewe **4** Akan, Akim, Akra, Aksa **5** Ahafo, Brong, Inkra **7** Akwapim, Ashanti, Dagomba, Maprusi **11** Mole-Dagbani
of Gibraltar: 6 Jewish **7** British, Italian, Maltese, Spanish **10** Portuguese
of Greece: 5 Greek **6** Achean, Dorian, Ionian **7** Aeolian, Hellene
of Greenland: 3 Ita **6** Eskimo **8** European
of Grenada: 5 Negro **6** Indian
of Guatemala: 3 Mam **4** Chol, Itza, Ixil, Maya **5** Xinca **6** Caribe, Quiche **7** ladinos, mestizo, Pocomam **13** Guatemaltecos
of Guinea: 4 Koma, Loma, Nalu, Susu, Toma **5** Kissi, Manon **6** Fulani, Guerzi **7** Landoma, Malinke **8** Kouranke, Landuman **11** Kissi-Sherbo **12** Guerze-Kpelle
of Guinea-Bissau: 6 Fulani **7** Balanta, Balante, mulatto **8** Mandingo, Mandyako
of Guyana: 6 Akawai, Arawak, Creole, Taruma **7** African, Chinese, mulatto **10** Portuguese
of Haiti: 5 Taino **7** African, mulatto
of Honduras: 4 Maya, Paya, Sumo, Ulva **5** Carib, Lenoa, Pipil **6** Tauira **7** Jicaque, mestizo, Miskito **8** Mosquito
of Hong Kong: 5 Hakka, Haklo, Punti, Tanka **7** British, Chinese **8** American, Japanese **9** Cantonese **10** Portuguese
of Hungary: 3 Hun **4** Serb **5** Croat, Gypsy **6** Cigany, Magyar, Slovak, Ugrian
of Iceland: 6 Celtic, Viking **8** Norseman **9** Norwegian
of India: 2 Ao **3** Gor **4** Bhil **5** Aryan **6** Badaga, Pathan **7** Sherani **9** Dravidian **10** Andamanese
of Indonesia: 4 Dyak **5** Batak, Dayak, Malay **6** Battak, Papuan, Toraja **7** Chinese, Igorots **8** Acehnese, Achinese, Balinese, Javanese, Madurese, Sudanese **11** Minang Kabau
of Iran: 3 Lur, Tat **4** Arab, Kurd, Turk **5** Medes **6** Galcha, Gilani, Jewish, Shugni **7** Baluchi, Persian **8** Armenian, Bactrian, Bartangi, Parthian, Scythian **9** Bakhtiari **11** Azerbaijani, Mazandarani
of Iraq: 4 Arab, Kurd **7** Bedouin
of Ireland: 4 Celt, Erse, Gael **5** Irish **6** Celtic **9** Hibernian
of Israel: 3 Jew **4** Arab **5** Druze **10** Circassian
of Italy: 5 Latin **6** Sabine **7** Italian, Lombard **8** Etruscan
of Ivory Coast: 3 Abe, Dan, Kru, Kwa **4** Akan, Bete, Dida, Guro, Koua, Lobi, Wobe **5** Abron, Abure, Attie, Baule, Guere, Mande, Mossi **6** Baoule, Lagoon, Senufo, Senufu **7** Kroumen, Malinke, Voltaic **8** Dan-Gouro **10** Anyi-Baoule **11** Lobi-Kulango **12** Agnis-Ashanti
of Jamaica: 7 African, Chinese **10** East Indian
of Japan: 3 Eta **6** Korean **8** Japanese, Okinawan **10** Buramkumin
of Java: 5 Krama, Kromo **6** Kalang **8** Javanese, Madurese, Sudanese
of Jordan: 4 Arab, Kurd **7** Bedouin, Checher **8** Armenian, Assyrian **10** Circassian **11** Palestinian
of Kazakhstan: 6 Kazakh
of Kenya: 3 Luo **4** Arab, Meru **5** Bantu, Elgey, Galla, Kamba, Kisii, Luhya, Masai, Nandi, Tugen **6** Kikuyu, Ogaden, Somali **7** Baluyha, Hamitic, Hilotic, Kipsigi, Swahili, Turkana **8** Kalenjin, Marakwet
of Kiribati: 8 Banabans **10** Polynesian **11** Micronesian
of Korea: 6 Korean
of Kuwait: 4 Arab **5** Iraqi, Saudi **6** Indian **7** Bedouin **8** Egyptian **9** Pakistani **11** Palestinian
of Kyrgyzstan: 5 Uzbek **6** Kyrgyz **7** Kirghiz
of Laos: 2 Lu **3** Kha, Lao, Man, Meo, Tai, Yao, Yun **4** Miao, Thai **5** Hmong **8** Lao Teung **10** Phoutheung
of Latvia: 3 Kur, Liv **4** Balt, Cour, Lett **7** Latgale, Latvian, Russian, Zemgale

(*continued*)

ethnic group (*continued*)

of Lebanon: 4 Arab **9** Canaanite **10** Phoenician **11** Palestinian

of Lesotho: 4 Zulu **5** Bantu, Tembu **6** Basuto **7** Basotho

of Liberia: 2 Gi **3** Gio, Kra, Kru, Kwa, Vai, Vei **4** Gola, Kroo, Krou, Loma, Mano, Toma **5** Bassa, Gibbi, Gissi, Grebo **6** Gbande, Kpelle, Kpuesi, Krooby, Kruman **7** Krooboy, Krooman **8** Mandingo **15** Americo-Liberian

of Libya: 4 Arab, Tebu **6** Berber, Tuareg **7** Gaetuli **8** Getulans, Harratin

of Liechtenstein: 8 Alamanni, Alemanni

of Lithuania: 4 Balt, Lett, Pole **5** Zhmud **6** Jewish, Litvak **7** Aistian, Russian, Yatvyag **10** Lithuanian, Samogitian **11** Belorussian

of Luxembourg: 6 French, German **12** Luxembourger

of Macao: 6 Macaon **7** Chinese **10** Portuguese

of Macedonia: 4 Turk **8** Albanian **10** Macedonian

of Madagascar: 4 Arab, Bara, Hova **5** Malay **6** Merina, Tanala **7** African **8** Betsileo, Mahafaly, Malagasy, Sakalava **9** Antaimoro, Antaisaka, Antandroy, Tsimihety **10** Indonesian, Polynesian **13** Betsimisaraka

of Malawi: 3 Yao **4** Sena **5** Bantu, Lomwe, Ngoni **6** Cheiva, Maravi, Ngonde, Nyanja **7** Tumbuka

of Malaysia: 4 Iban **5** Dayak, Malay **6** Indian **7** Chinese, Kadazan **9** Pakistani, Sri Lankan **10** Bangladesh, Indonesian

of Maldives: 4 Arab **6** Indian **9** Sinhalese **10** Singhalese

of Mali: 3 Bwa **4** Fula, Kyan, Moor, Peul **5** Dogon, Dyula, Fulbe, Marka **6** Berber, Dognon, Fulani, Senufo, Tuareg **7** Bembara, Fellata, Malinke, Miniaka, Songhai, Soninke **8** Khasonke, Mandingo, Senoulfo

of Malta: 7 Maltese

of Mauritania: 4 Arab, Fula, Moor **5** Black, Fulbe, Wolof **6** Bafour, Berber, Fulani **7** African, Soninke, Tukulor **8** Sarakole **9** Sarakolle **10** Toucouleur **12** Halphoolaren

of Mauritius: 6 Creole, French, Indian **7** African, Chinese **8** European **13** Indo-Mauritian

of Mexico: 3 Ixe, Mam, Mie, Ser **4** Chol, Cora, Jova, Meco, Mixe, Pame, Pima, Roto, Seri, Teca, Teco, Texo, Xova **5** Aztec, Chizo, Chora, Mayan, Nahua, Opata, Otomi, Zoque **6** Eudeve, Indian, Mixtec, Pueblo, Toltec, Zotzil **7** Chincha, mestizo, Nahuatl, Nayarit, Spanish, Tehueco, Tepanec, Totonac, Zacatec, Zapotec **8** Lagunero, Mazateca, Tezcucan, Totonaco, Tzapotec, Yucateco, Zacateco, Zapoteca **9** Tlascalan **10** Coahuiltec, Cuitlateco, Tarahumara

of Moldova: 7 Gagauzi **8** Moldovan **9** Moldovian

of Monaco: 6 French **7** Italian **10** Monegasque

of Mongolia: 5 Oirat, Tungu **6** Buryat, Darbet, Khoton, Mongol **7** Kazakhs, Khalkha **8** Tuvinian **9** Dariganga

of Montenegro: 4 Serb, Slav **11** Montenegrin

of Morocco: 4 Arab, Moor **6** Berber, French **7** Spanish

of Mozambique: 3 Yao **5** Bantu, Chopi, Lomue, Lomwe, Macua, Makua, Ngoni, Nguni, Shona **6** Maravi, Thouga **7** Maconde, Makonde **10** Portuguese

of Myanmar: 4 Shan **7** Burmese, Siamese

of Namibia: 4 Nama **5** Bantu **6** Damara, Herero, Ovambo, Tswara **7** Bushman, Colored **8** Okavango **9** Hottentot

of Nauru: 7 Chinese **10** Melanesian, Polynesian **11** Micronesian

of Nepal: 3 Rai **4** Aoul **5** Limbu, Magar, Murmi, Newar, Tharu **6** Gurkha, Gurung, Nepali, Sherpa, Tamang **7** Bhutias, Kiranti **8** Gorkhali, Nepalese

of the Netherlands: 5 Dutch **7** Frisian **9** Hollander **10** Surinamese **12** Netherlander **13** South Moluccan

of New Guinea: 5 Pygmy **6** Papuan **7** Negrito **10** Melanesian

of New Zealand: 3 Ati **5** Arawa, Dutch, Maori **7** British, Ringatu **10** Polynesian

of Nicaragua: 4 Mico, Mixe, Rama, Smoo, Ulva **5** Cukra, Diria, Lenca, Sambo, Toaca **6** Mangue **7** mestizo, Miskito **8** Mosquito **9** Matagalpa

of Niger: 4 Daza, Idjo, Idyo, Idzo, Peul, Teda **5** Hausa, Warri **6** Djerma, Fulani, Kanuri, Songha, Toubou, Tuareg **13** Djerma-Songhai

of Nigeria: 3 Abo, Aro, Djo, Ebo, Edo, Ibo, Ijo, Tiv, Vai **4** Beni, Bini, Eboe, Efik, Egba, Ejam, Ekoi, Idyo, Igbo, Ijaw, Nupe **5** Angas, Benin, Gwari, Hausa **6** Chamba, Fulani, Ibibio, Kanuri, Yoruba **11** Hausa-Fulani

of Norway: 4 Lapp **5** Samme **6** Nordic, Viking

of Oman: 4 Arab

of Pakistan: 5 Sindi, Wazir **6** Afridi, Bengal, Mahsud, Pàthan, Puktun, Sindhi **7** Baluchi, Brahuis, Punjabi, Pushtun, Sherani **8** Khattack, Shinwari, Yusefazi **11** Mohammedzai

of Panama: 4 Cuna **5** Choco **6** Guaymi **7** mestizo

of Qatar: 4 Arab **6** Pushtu, Yemeni **7** Baluchi, Iranian **9** Pakistani

of Rumania: 6 Dacian **8** Romanian, Rumanian

of Russia: 4 Slav **5** Kulak **6** Jewish, Soviet, Velika **7** Chukchi, Cossack, Latvian, Russian, Turkmen **8** Armenian, Estonian, Georgian, Siberian, Ukrainian **10** Lithuanian **11** Belorussian

of Rwanda: **3** Twa **4** Hutu **5** Batwa, Pygmy, Tutsi **6** Bahutu, Watusi **7** Batutsi

of Samoa: 6 Samoan **10** Polynesian

of San Marino: 7 Italian **11** San Marinese

of Sao Tome and Principe: 7 African **10** Portuguese **11** Cape Verdean

of Saudi Arabia: 4 Arab **7** Bedouin

of Scotland: 4 Gael, Pict, Scot **5** Norse

(*continued*)

ethnic group (*continued*)

of Senegal: 4 Lebu, Peul, Soce **5** Diola, Dyola, Foula, Laobe, Peulh, Serer, Wolof **6** Fulani, Serere **7** Bambara, Malinke, Tukuler, Tukulor **8** Mandingo

of Seychelles: 5 Asian **6** Creole, French, Indian **7** African, Chinese

of Sicily: 5 Elymi, Sican, Sicel **6** Sicani, Siculi

of Sierra Leone: 3 Vai **4** Kono, Loko, Susu **5** Bulom, Kissi, Limba, Mande, Mendi, Temne **6** Creole, Fulani, Syrian **7** Gallina, Koranko, Kuranko, Sherbro, Yalunka **8** Lebanese, Mandingo

of Sikkim: 4 Rong **5** Bhote **6** Bhotia, Bhutia, Indian, Lepcha **7** Tibetan **8** Nepalese **9** Mongoloid

of Singapore: 5 Malay **6** Indian **7** Chinese **9** Malaysian, Pakistani, Sri Lankan

of Slovakia: 5 Czech **6** Slavik, Slovak **9** Hungarian

of Slovenia: 7 Slovene

of the Solomon Islands: 7 Chinese **8** European **10** Melanesian, Polynesian

of Somalia: 3 Sab **4** Asha **5** Galla **6** Hawiya, Isbaak, Somali **7** Danakil, Hamitic, Marehan, Samaale, Shuhali **8** Rahanwin

of South Africa: 4 Boer, Yosa, Zulu **5** Asian, Bantu, Namas, Nguni, Pondo, Sotho, Swazi, Tembu, Venda **6** Damara, Kaffir **7** African, British, Bushmen, English, Swahili **8** Bechuana, Coloured, Khoikhoi, San Xhosa **9** Afrikaner, Hottentot

of Spain: 4 Pict **5** Diego, Gente, Latin **6** Basque, Espana **7** Catalan, Espanol, Iberian **8** Galician, Gallegos, Maragato

of Sri Lanka: 5 Malay, Tamil, Vedda **6** Veddah, Weddah **7** Burgher, Mahinda, Malabar **8** Eurasian **9** Cingalese, Dravidian, Sinhalese **10** Ginghalese **12** Bandaranaike

of the Sudan: 3 Bor, Dor, Fur **4** Arab, Bari, Beri, Bobo, Daza, Egba, Fula, Golo, Nuba, Nuer, Poul, Sere **5** Anuak, Bongo, Dinka, Fulah, Hausa, Joluo, Junje, Mosgu, Mossi, Negro, Tibbu, Volta **6** Acholi, Azande, Gurusi, Hamite, Lotuho, Makari, Nilote, Nubian, Senufo, Surhai, Taureg **7** Balante, Baqqara, Gubayna, Jaaliin, Nilotes, Shilluk, Songhai, Songhay, Songhoi, Sourhai **8** Kababish, Mandingo, Menkiera **9** Sarakille **10** Gurmantshi, Shaiquiyya

of Suriname: 4 Boni, Bush, Trio **5** Djuka, Dutch **6** Creole, Wayana **7** African, Chinese **10** Amerindian, Boschneger, West Indian **11** Asian Indian

of Swaziland: 5 Asian, Bantu, Swazi **10** Eurafrican

of Sweden: 4 Lapp **5** Norse, Swede **6** Viking

of Switzerland: 5 Swiss, **6** Franks **8** Alamanni, Alemanni, Italians **12** Rhaeto-Romans

of Syria: 4 Arab, Kurd, Turk **5** Alawi, Aptal, Druse, Druze **6** Afshar, Aissor, Aushar, Avshar, Awshar **7** Amorite, Ansarie, Bedouin, Nosaris, Saracen, Shemite **8** Ansarieh, Armenian **9** Ansariyah **10** Circassian **12** Khachaturian

of Taiwan: 4 Yami **5** Hakka, Hoklo **7** Chinese, Malayan **9** Fukienese, Taiwanese **10** Indonesian, Polynesian **12** Kwangtungese

of Tajikistan: 5 Tajik, Uzbek **7** Tadzhik

of Tanzania: 2 Ha **4** Arab, Gogo, Goma, Haya, Hehe **5** Asian, Bantu, Masai **6** Arusha, Chagga, Sukuma, Wagogo, Wagoma **7** African, Makonde, Sambara, Sandawe, Shirazi, Swahili, Wabunga, Zongora **8** Nyakyusa, Nyamwezi

of Thailand: 3 Lao, Mon **4** Lawa, Shan, Thai **5** Malay **6** Indian, Khymer **7** Chinese, Siamese **9** Cambodian **10** Vietnamese

of Tibet: 5 Asian, Balti, Bodpa, Drupa **6** Bhotia, Champa, Drokpa, Khamba, Khambu, Mongol, Panaka, Sherpa, Tangut **7** Bhotiya, Bhutani, Gyarung, Taghlik, Tibetan

of Togo: 3 Ana, Ewe, Twi **4** Mina **5** Hausa **6** Akposa, Kabrai **7** Bassari, Cabrais, Kabrais, Ouatchi **8** Konkomba, Kotokoli, Lotokoli

of Tonga: 10 Polynesian

of Trinidad and Tobago: 5 Irish **6** French, Syrian **7** African, Chinese, English, Spanish **8** European, Lebanese **10** East Indian, Portuguese, Venezuelan **11** Asian Indian **13** Latin American

of Tunisia: 4 Arab **6** Berber, Jewish

of Turkey: 4 Arab, Kurd, Turk **6** Seljuk

of Turkmenistan: 7 Turkmen **10** Turkmenian

of Tuvalu: 6 Samoan **10** Polynesian

of Uganda: 4 Alur, Gisu, Soga, Teso **5** Ateso, Bantu, Chiga, Ganda, Langi, Lango, Nkole, Pygmy **6** Acholi, Ankole, Bagisu, Bakega, Basoga, Batoro **7** Baganda, Banyoro, Bunyoro, Hamitic, Lugbara, Nilotic, Sudanic **9** Nyoro-Toro **10** Banyankole, Karamojong

of Ukraine: 7 Russian **9** Ukrainian

of United Arab Emirates: 4 Arab **6** Indian **7** African, Iranian **9** Pakistani **10** South Asian

of Uruguay: 4 Yaro **5** Swiss **6** Indian **7** Italian, mestizo, Russian, Spanish **8** Charruas

of Uzbekistan: 5 Uzbek

of Vanuatu: 8 European **10** Melanesian, Polynesian **11** Micronesian

of Venezuela: 4 Bare, Pume **5** Bello, Carib, pardo, zambo **6** Arawak, Creole, Timote **7** Charoya, Guahibo, Kaliana, mestizo, mulatto, Otomaca, Timotex **8** Caquetio, Guarauno, Matilone **11** Maquiritare

of Vietnam: **3** Hoa, Man, Meo, Tai, Tay **4** Cham, Kinh, Nung, Thai **5** Khmer, Malay, Muong **7** Chinese **8** Annamese, Annamite **9** Cambodian **10** montagnard, Vietnamese

of Wales: 4 Celt, Kelt **5** Cymry, Kymry, Welsh **7** Brython, Silures, Taffies **8** Awabokal, Cambrian **9** Siluridan

of Western Sahara: 4 Arab **6** Berber

of Western Samoa: 6 Samoan **10** Melanesian, Polynesian

of Yemen: 4 Arab **5** Zaidi **6** Shafai, Yemeni **8** Yemenite

of Yugoslavia: 4 Serb, Slav **5** Croat **7** Bosnian, Slovene **8** Albanian, Croatian **9** Hungarian **10** Macedonian **11** Montenegrin **13** Herzegovinian

(*continued*)

ethnic group (*continued*)
of Zaire: 4 Kuba, Luba, Yaka **5** Bantu, Bashi, Bemba, Kongo, Lulue, Lunda, Mongo, Pygmy **6** Azande, Baluba, Watusi **7** Bakongo, Nilotes, Tshokwe **8** European, Mangbetu, Sudanese
of Zambia: 4 Lozi **5** Bantu, Bemba, Ngoni, Tonga
of Zimbabwe: 3 Ila **4** Sena **5** Asian, Bantu, Bemba, Sotho, Tongo, white **6** Indian **7** Barotse, Chinese, English, Mashoma, Mashona, Ndebele **8** Coloured, Japanese, Matabele **9** Afrikaner **10** Balakwakwa

opera by: 11 Tchaikovsky
character: 4 Olga **6** Lensky, Onegin **7** Tatyana **12** Prince Gremin, Tatyana Larin **14** Vladimir Lensky

Eugenie Grandet
author: 14 Honore de Balzac
character: 5 Nanon **7** Charles, Eugenie **11** Mme d'Aubrion

Euhelopus
type: 8 dinosaur, sauropod
period: 10 Cretaceous

Euhemerism
theory of: 9 Euhemerus
reduced deification of: 4 gods

Euippe
origin: 5 Roman
form: 6 maiden
parent: 6 Daunus
husband: 8 Diomedes
changed into: 5 horse

eulogize 4 hail, laud, tout **5** boost, exalt, extol **7** acclaim, commend, glorify, magnify **9** celebrate **10** compliment, panegyrize **12** pay tribute to, praise highly

eulogy 5 paean **6** homage **7** hosanna, plaudit, tribute **8** citation, encomium **9** laudation, panegyric **10** high praise **11** acclamation

Eumedes
father: 5 Dolon
companion of: 6 Aeneas
vocation: 6 herald

Eumelus
member of: 7 Trojans
commander of:
   13 Thessalonians
lost race to: 8 Diomedes
wife: 8 Iphthime
companion: 6 Aeneas

Eumenides
author: 9 Aeschylus
character: 6 Apollo, Athene, Furies **7** Orestes *see* **6** Furies

Eumolpus
king of: 6 Thrace
father: 8 Poseidon
mother: 6 Chione
son: 7 Ismarus
founded: 19 Eleusinian mysteries
supported accusations of: 9 Phylonome

Euneus
father: 5 Jason
mother: 9 Hypsipyle

Eunice
son: 7 Timothy

Eunomia
member of: 5 Horae
personifies: 5 order

Eunomus
father: 10 Architeles
cup bearer of: 6 Oeneus
slain by: 8 Hercules

Eunuch 6 Biztha, Careas, Zethar **7** Abagtha, Harbona, Mehuman

euphemism 11 prudishness, refined term **12** delicate term, overdelicacy **13** prudish phrase **14** mild expression, overrefinement

Euphemus
father: 8 Poseidon
mother: 6 Europa
aided: 9 Argonauts

Euphorbus
father: 8 Panthous
brother: 9 Hyperenor, Polydemas
fought with: 7 Trojans

euphoria 7 ecstasy, elation, rapture **9** well-being

Euphorion
father: 8 Achilles
mother: 5 Helen

Euphrosyne
member of: 6 Graces

Euphues
character in: 20 Euphues and His England **22** Euphues The Anatomy of Wit
author: 4 Lyly

Euripides
author of: 3 Ion **5** Medea **6** Hecuba **7** Electra, Orestes **8** Alcestis, Heracles **10** Andromache, Heraclidae, Hippolytus, Phoenissae, The Bacchae **13** The Suppliants **14** The Trojan Women **16** Iphigenia in Aulis **17** Iphigenia in Tauris **21** The Children of Heracles

Eurippa
epithet of: 7 Artemis
means: 18 delighting in horses

Europa
also: 6 Europe
father: 6 Agenor
mother: 10 Telephassa
brother: 5 Cilix **6** Cadmus **7** Phoenix
son: 5 Minos **8** Sarpedon **12** Rhadamanthus
daughter: 5 Crete
abducted by: 4 Zeus

Europe *see* **6** Europa

Europe *see* **box**

Eurotes
father: 5 Myles

Eurus
origin: 5 Greek
personifies: 8 east wind **13** southeast wind

Euryale
member of: 7 Gorgons

Eurybates
companion of: 8 Odysseus

Eurybia
father: 6 Pontus
mother: 4 Gaea
mated with: 5 Crius

Eurydice
also: 7 Agriope
form: 5 dryad
husband: 7 Orpheus
daughter: 8 Themiste
pursued by: 9 Aristaeus

Euryganeia
son: 8 Eteocles **9** Polynices

Eurylochus
companion of: 8 Odysseus

Eurynome
father: 7 Oceanus
mother: 6 Tethys
sister: 6 Thetis
daughters: 6 Graces

Eurypylus
origin: 5 Greek
occupation: 7 warrior
father: 8 Poseidon, Telephus
mother: 8 Astyoche
uncle: 5 Priam
killed by: 8 Hercules **11** Neoptolemus

Eurysaces
father: 14 Telamonian Ajax
mother: 8 Tecmessa
inherited: 6 shield

Eurysthenes
origin: 7 Spartan
father: 11 Aristodemus
twin brother: 7 Procles
shared: 6 throne
shared throne with: 7 Procles

Eurystheus
king of: 6 Tiryns **7** Mycenae
father: 9 Sthenelus
mother: 7 Nicippe
cousin: 8 Hercules
son: 9 Perimedes
imposed: 6 labors
   number of labors:
   6 twelve
   imposed on: 8 Hercules

Europe
   country: 5 Italy, Malta, Spain, Wales **6** France, Greece, Latvia, Monaco, Norway, Poland, Russia, Sweden **7** Albania, Andorra, Armenia, Austria, Belarus, Belgium, Croatia, Denmark, England, Estonia, Georgia, Germany, Hungary, Iceland, Ireland, Romania, Ukraine **8** Bulgaria, Portugal, Scotland, Slovakia, Slovenia **9** Lithuania, Macedonia, San Marino **10** Azerbaijan, Luxembourg, Yugoslavia **11** Byelorussia, Netherlands, Switzerland, Vatican City **13** Czech Republic, Liechtenstein **14** Czechoslovakia **17** Bosnia-Herzegovina
   city: 4 Bern, Bonn, Oslo, Rome **5** Paris, Sofia, Vaduz **6** Athens, Dublin, Lisbon, London, Madrid, Monaco, Moscow, Prague, Tirana, Vienna, Warsaw **7** Cardiff **8** Belgrade, Brussels, Budapest, Helsinki, Valletta **9** Amsterdam, Bucharest, Edinburgh, Reykjavik, San Marino, Stockholm **14** Bratislava, Copenhagen, Luxembourg **14** Andorra la Vella
   river: 3 Don **4** Ebro, Elbe, Oder **5** Loire, Neman, Rhine, Rhone, Seine, Tagus, Volga **6** Danube, Thames **7** Dnieper, Pechora, Vistula **8** Dniester
   island: 3 Man **4** Skye **5** Crete, Malta **6** Faeroe, Sicily **7** Corsica, Iceland, Ireland **8** Balearic, Sardinia **12** British Isles
   mountain/mountain range: 4 Alps **7** Balkans **8** Caucasus, Pyrenees **9** Apennines **11** Carpathians **12** Sierra Nevada
   highest point: 11 Mount Elbrus
   lowest point: 10 Caspian Sea
   sea: 4 Aral, Azov, Kara **5** Black, North, White **6** Aegean, Baltic **7** Caspian, Marmara **8** Adriatic **13** Mediterranean
   people: 3 Hun **4** Gael, Pict, Serb **5** Celts, Croat, Danes, Dutch, Jutes, Kymry, Marur, Poles, Scots, Slavs, Tatar, Welsh **6** Czechs, Franks **7** Basques, Britons, Gypsies, Iberian, Magyars, Slovaks, Slovene **8** Alamanni, Cossacks, Tyrolean, Walloons
   language: 5 Czech **6** Danish, German, French, Polish, Slovak **7** English, Italian, Romance, Russian, Spanish, Swedish **8** Germanic **9** Bulgarian, Portugese **11** Balto-slavic
   religion: 5 Islam **6** Jewish, Muslim **8** Anglican, Lutheran **9** Methodist **10** Protestant **12** Presbyterian **13** Dutch Reformed, Greek Orthodox, Roman Catholic **15** Church of England, Eastern Orthodox
   holiday: 11 Bastille Day, National Day **12** Guy Fawkes Day **13** Liberation Day, St Patricks Day **14** Queens Birthday **15** Independence Day **19** Heroes of the Republic

Eurytion
   form: 7 centaur
   father: 4 Ares **5** Actor
   companion of: 6 Aeneus
   guarded cattle of: 6 Geryon
   killed by: 6 Peleus **8** Hercules

Eurytus
   form: 5 giant
   father: 5 Actor **7** Auglaus **8** Melaneus
   twin brother: 7 Cteatus
   noted for: 7 archery
   slain by: 8 Hercules

Euterpe
   member of: 5 Muses
   muse of: 5 music **11** lyric poetry

evacuate 4 quit **5** leave **6** desert, remove, vacate **7** abandon, forsake, move out, take out **8** order out **12** withdraw from

evade 4 duck, shun **5** avoid, dodge, elude, hedge, parry **6** escape, eschew **7** fend off **8** sidestep **10** circumvent, equivocate **12** steer clear of

Evadne
   father: 6 Pelias **8** Poseidon
   mother: 6 Pitana
   sister: 9 Amphinome
   husband: 8 Capaneus

evaluate 4 rate **5** assay, gauge, judge, value, weigh **6** assess, size up **8** appraise, estimate

evaluation 4 test **8** analysis, judgment **9** appraisal **10** assessment, estimation

evaluator 5 judge **6** critic, tester **7** analyst, arbiter **8** assessor, reviewer **9** appraiser, estimator

Evander
   father: 6 Hermes **9** Carmentis
   mother: 6 Themis
   daughter: 4 Roma
   allied with: 6 Aeneas

evanesce 6 vanish **8** fade away, pass away **9** disappear, dissipate, evaporate

evanescence 9 vanishing **10** fading away **12** ephemerality **13** disappearance **14** transitoriness

evanescent 8 fleeting **9** ephemeral, transient **10** short-lived, transitory

Evangeline
   author: 24 Henry Wadsworth Longfellow
   character: 17 Gabriel Lajeunesse **23** Evangeline Bellefontaine

evangelist 4 John, Luke, Mark **7** apostle, Matthew **8** disciple, minister, preacher, reformer **9** apostolic, missioner, soulsaver **10** missionary, revivalist **12** Bible Thumper, propagandist, proselytizer **17** religious crusader

Evan Harrington
   author: 14 George Meredith
   character: 6 Louisa **10** Jack Raikes **11** Rose Jocelyn **12** Tom Cogglesby **13** Count de Saldar, Juliana Bonner **14** Caroline Strike **15** Andrew Cogglesby, Ferdinand Laxley, Melville Jocelyn **16** Countess de Saldar, Harriet Cogglesby **21** Melchisedek Harrington

Evans, Dame Edith
   born: 6 London **7** England
   roles: 8 Tom Jones **11** A Doll's House **13** The Whisperers **14** The Chalk Garden **27** The Importance of Being Earnest

Evans, Mary Anne
   real name of: 11 George Eliot

Evans, Maurice
   born: 6 Dorset **7** England **10** Dorchester
   roles: 9 Saint Joan **13** Rosemary's Baby **14** Man and Superman, Romeo and Juliet **15** Heartbreak House, Planet of the Apes **17** The Devil's Disciple **18** Gilbert and Sullivan **19** Androcles and the Lion

evaporate 5 dry up 6 dispel, vanish 7 scatter 8 dissolve, evanesce, fade away, melt away, vaporize 9 dehydrate, desiccate, disappear, dissipate

evasion 7 dodging, ducking, eluding 8 shunning 9 avoidance 12 sidestepping 13 circumventing, shrinking from 15 attempt to escape

evasive 6 shifty 7 devious, dodging, elusive, elusory, hedging 9 ambiguous, deceitful, deceptive, equivocal 10 misleading 11 dissembling 12 equivocating

Eva Trout
author: 14 Elizabeth Bowen

eve 4 dusk 6 female, sunset 7 evening, sunset 8 eventide 9 day before

Eve
husband: 4 Adam
son: 4 Abel, Cain, Seth
home: 4 Eden

Evelina
author: 11 Fanny Burney

even 4 calm, fair, flat, just, true 5 equal, flush, level, plane, plumb 6 placid, smooth, square, steady 7 balance, equable, flatten, regular, the same, uniform 8 balanced, constant, equalize, matching, parallel, straight, unbiased 9 equitable, identical, impartial, make flush, unruffled, unvarying 10 straighten, unwavering 11 make uniform, unexcitable 12 even-tempered, make parallel 13 dispassionate

evening 3 eve 4 dusk, even 6 sunset 7 day's end, sundown 8 eventide, gloaming, twilight 9 nightfall 10 close of day

evenly matched 5 equal 8 of a piece 9 identical 10 well suited 13 one and the same

evenness 7 balance 8 calmness, equality, fairness, flatness, sameness 9 placidity 10 regularity, smoothness, steadiness, uniformity 11 equivalency

event 4 bout, game 7 contest, episode 8 incident, occasion 9 happening, milestone 10 experience, occurrence, tournament 11 competition

even-tempered 4 calm 6 serene 7 equable, patient 11 good-natured, unflappable 12 mild-tempered, well-adjusted

eventful 7 crucial, epochal, fateful, notable, weighty

8 critical, exciting, historic 9 important, memorable, momentous, thrilling 10 noteworthy 11 significant 13 consequential, unforgettable

eventide 4 dusk 6 sunset 7 evening, sundown 8 gloaming, twilight 9 nightfall

eventual 5 final, later 6 coming, future 7 ensuing 8 imminent, ultimate, upcoming 9 following, impending, resulting 10 consequent, subsequent 11 prospective

eventually 6 one day 7 finally 8 in the end, sometime 10 ultimately 12 in the long run 13 sooner or later 17 in the course of time 20 when all is said and done

Eventus see 12 Bonus Eventus

even up 3 tie 5 align 8 make even 10 straighten

Evenus
father: 4 Ares
mother: 8 Demonice
daughter: 8 Marpessa

Eve of St Agnes, The
author: 9 John Keats

ever 5 at all 6 always 7 forever 9 at any time, eternally, in any case 10 at all times, constantly 11 incessantly, perpetually 12 continuously

Everdene, Bathsheba
character in: 22 Far From the Madding Crowd
author: 5 Hardy

Everes
son: 8 Tiresias

Everglade State
nickname of: 7 Florida

evergreen 3 fir, yew 4 pine 5 heath, holly 6 jujube, laurel, myrtle, needle, privet 7 arbutus, casiope, conifer, jasmine, juniper 8 camellia, hawthorn, oleander, rosemary 9 mistletoe, sugarbush 11 conebearing 12 rhododendrum

Evergreen State
nickname of: 10 Washington

everlasting 7 durable, endless, eternal, lasting, tedious, undying 8 constant, immortal, infinite, timeless, tiresome 9 ceaseless, continual, incessant, perpetual, unceasing, wearisome 10 continuous, ever-living 11 long-lasting, never-ending 12 imperishable, interminable 14 indestructible

evermore 6 always 7 forever 9 eternally 10 for all time 13 everlastingly

ever upward
Latin: 9 excelsior
motto of: 7 New York (state)

everybody
French: 11 tout le monde

everyday 4 dull 5 daily, stock, trite, usual 6 common, square 7 mundane, regular, routine 8 familiar, ordinary, workaday 9 customary, hackneyed, quotidian 11 commonplace, day after day, established, stereotyped 12 conventional, run-of-the-mill 13 unimaginative

Everyman
author: 7 unknown
character: 3 God 5 Death, Goods 6 Beauty 7 Kindred 8 Strength 9 Good Deeds, Knowledge, Messenger 10 Fellowship

every man for himself
French: 12 sauve qui peut

Every Man in His Humour
author: 9 Ben Jonson
character: 6 Kitely 7 Bridget 8 Bobadill, Wellbred 9 Brainworm, Downright 13 Edward Knowell 14 Justice Clement

Every Man out of His Humour
author: 9 Ben Jonson
character: 6 Deliro 7 Fungoso, Sordido 9 Maciliente, Sogliardo 10 Puntarvolo 12 Carlo Buffone 15 Fastidious Brisk

everyone
French: 11 tout le monde

everywhere 7 all over 10 every place, far and near, far and wide, throughout 11 extensively, in all places, universally 12 the world over, ubiquitously 14 to the four winds

evict 4 oust 5 eject, expel 6 remove 7 kick out, turn out 8 dislodge, get rid of, throw out 10 dispossess

evidence 4 fact, sign 5 proof, token 7 exhibit, grounds 9 testimony 10 indication 11 affirmation 12 confirmation, illustration 13 corroboration, documentation, material proof 14 authentication, substantiation 15 exemplification

evident 5 clear, plain 6 patent 7 certain, obvious, visible 8 apparent, manifest, tangible 10 noticeable, undeniable 11 conspicuous, perceptible 12 demonstrable, unmistakable 14 unquestionable 24 plain as the nose on your face

evidently 7 clearly, plainly **9** assumedly, certainly, doubtless, obviously **10** apparently, undeniably **11** doubtlessly **12** unmistakably **14** unquestionably **16** to all appearances

evil 3 bad, sin **4** base, vice, vile **5** venal **6** sinful, wicked **7** heinous, immoral, vicious **8** baseness, iniquity, sinister **9** depravity, malicious, malignant, nefarious, turpitude **10** corruption, immorality, iniquitous, malevolent, pernicious, villainous, wickedness, wrongdoing **12** black-hearted, unprincipled, unscrupulous **goddess of: 7** Sekhmet

evildoer 6 sinner **7** culprit, villain **9** miscreant, wrongdoer **10** malefactor **12** transgressor

evil-minded 4 base **5** nasty **6** wicked **7** ignoble, immoral **8** depraved **10** despicable, iniquitous, villainous **12** dishonorable, unprincipled

evilness 6 malice **7** cruelty **8** villainy **9** barbarity, malignity **10** sinfulness, wickedness

evince 4 show **6** convey, reveal **7** display, exhibit, express **11** communicate, demonstrate **12** give evidence

Evius see **7** Bacchus

Evnissyen
origin: 5 Welsh
brother: 4 Bran
10 Manawyddan
sister: 7 Branwen
caused: 3 war
between: 5 Irish **7** British
killed: 6 nephew

evoke 4 stir **5** rouse, waken **6** arouse, awaken, call up, elicit, excite, induce, invite, invoke, summon **7** produce, provoke, suggest **9** call forth, conjure up, stimulate **10** bring forth

evolution 4 rise **6** change, growth **8** fruition, increase **9** expansion, unfolding **10** maturation **11** development, enlargement, progression **13** metamorphosis
founder of theory:
13 Charles Darwin
forerunner of theory:
12 Charles Lyell **18** Chevalier de Lamarck

evolve 4 grow **5** ripen **6** expand, mature, unfold, unroll **7** develop, enlarge **8** increase

Ewell, Tom
real name: 14 Yewell Tompkins
born: 11 Owensboro KY
roles: 8 Adam's Rib **9** State

Fair **14** The Great Gatsby **16** Tender Is the Night, The Seven Year Itch

ewer 3 jug, urn **5** basin **6** vessel **7** pitcher

Ewing, Patrick
sport: 10 basketball
team: 13 New York Knicks
15 Georgetown Hoyas

exacerbate 3 irk **5** anger **6** deepen, worsen **7** inflame, magnify, provoke, sharpen **8** heighten, increase, irritate **9** aggravate, intensify **10** exaggerate **12** fan the flames **16** pour oil on the fire **17** add insult to injury **18** add fuel to the flames **19** rub salt into the wound

exact 4 take, true **5** claim, force, mulct, right, wrest **6** compel, demand, extort, strict **7** careful, correct, extract, literal, precise, require, squeeze **8** accurate, clear-cut, exacting, explicit, specific **9** on the head, on the nose **10** methodical, meticulous, scrupulous, systematic **11** painstaking, punctilious, to the letter, unequivocal

exacting 4 hard **5** harsh, rigid, stern, tough **6** severe, strict, trying **7** arduous **8** critical **9** demanding, difficult, hardnosed, strenuous, unbending, unsparing **10** hard-headed, meticulous, no-nonsense

exactly 4 just **5** fully, quite, truly **6** indeed, just so, wholly **7** quite so **8** entirely, of course, strictly **9** assuredly, certainly, correctly, literally, precisely **10** absolutely, accurately, definitely, explicitly, that's right **12** specifically

exactness 8 accuracy **9** precision **10** exactitude **12** accurateness

exact satisfaction 6 avenge, punish **7** get back, get even, revenge **9** retaliate **14** get one's own back

exaggerate 5 boast **6** overdo **7** amplify, lay it on, magnify, stretch **9** embellish, embroider, enlarge on, overstate **11** hyperbolize

exaggerated 7 extreme, intense **10** inordinate, overstated **14** overemphasized

exalt 4 laud **5** cheer, elate, extol, honor **6** praise, uplift **7** acclaim, applaud, commend, elevate, ennoble, glorify, inspire, magnify, worship **8** venerate **9** celebrate, stimulate

10 exhilarate, make much of **12** pay tribute to

exaltation 4 high **5** bliss, glory, honor **6** praise **7** dignity, ecstasy, elation, rapture, tribute, worship **8** grandeur, nobility, praising **9** happiness, panegyric, transport **10** eulogizing, exultation, veneration **11** celebration, deification **12** exhilaration

exalted 2 up **5** grand, happy, lofty, noble **6** august, elated, lordly **7** excited, notable **8** blissful, ecstatic, elevated, glorious, inspired, uplifted **9** dignified, honorable, rapturous, venerable **10** heightened **11** high-ranking, illustrious, magnificent

exaltedness 5 bliss **6** height **7** ecstasy, elation, heights, rapture **8** highness, nobility **9** elevation, loftiness, transport

examination 4 exam, quiz, test **5** assay, audit, final, orals, probe, study **6** review, survey **7** midterm, perusal **8** analysis, scrutiny **10** inspection **11** looking over **13** investigation **15** physical checkup

examine 4 pump, quiz, scan, test, view **5** audit, grill, probe, query, study **6** peruse, ponder, review, survey **7** explore, inspect, observe **8** consider, look into, look over, question **10** scrutinize **11** inquire into, interrogate, investigate, take stock of

examiner 6 tester **8** inquirer, reviewer, surveyor **12** interrogator, investigator

example 5 ideal, model **6** sample **7** paragon, pattern **8** exemplar, specimen, standard **9** archetype, prototype **11** case in point **12** illustration **14** representation **15** exemplification

exasperate 3 bug, irk, vex **4** rile **5** anger, annoy, chafe, pique **6** bother, enrage, harass, madden, offend, rankle, ruffle **7** incense, provoke, turn off **8** irritate **9** aggravate, infuriate **15** try one's patience

exasperating 7 irksome **8** annoying **9** vexatious **10** irritating **11** infuriating

ex cathedra 12 from the chair **13** with authority **22** from the seat of authority

excavate 3 dig **4** mine **5** dig up, gouge **6** burrow, cut out, dig out, furrow, groove, quarry, tunnel **7** uncover, unearth **8** scoop out **9** hollow out **11** make a hole in

excavation 3 dig, pit **4** hole, mine, sump **5** ditch, grave, shaft, space **6** cavity, dugout, trench, trough **7** digging, opening

exceed 4 pass **5** excel **6** go over, outrun, overdo **7** outpace, outrank, surpass **8** go beyond, outreach, outrival, outstrip, surmount **9** come first, overshoot, transcend **10** be superior **11** predominate

exceedingly 4 very **6** vastly **7** greatly, notably **9** amazingly, eminently, extremely, supremely, unusually **10** enormously, especially, unwontedly, very highly **11** excessively **12** immeasurably, impressively, inordinately, preeminently, surpassingly **13** astonishingly, outstandingly, superlatively **15** extraordinarily

excel 5 outdo **6** exceed **7** prevail, surpass **8** outrival, outstrip **9** rank first **10** tower above **11** predominate, take the cake **20** walk off with the honors

excellence 5 merit **7** quality **8** eminence **9** greatness **10** perfection **11** distinction, high quality, preeminence, superiority **13** transcendence

excellent 4 aces, A-one, fine, tops **5** great, nifty, prime, super, swell **6** bang-up, choice, grade A, superb **7** capital, classic, notable **8** peerless, sterling, superior, terrific, top-notch **9** admirable, exemplary, firstrate, matchless, superfine, wonderful **10** first-class, preeminent, tremendous **11** exceptional, outstanding, superlative

excelsior 10 ever upward motto of: **7** New York (state)

Excelsior State
nickname of: **7** New York

except 3 ban, bar, but **4** omit, save **6** enjoin, excuse, exempt, reject, remove, saving **7** barring, besides, exclude, shut out **8** count out, disallow, pass over **9** eliminate, excepting, excluding, other than **11** exclusive of

excepted 6 exempt **7** excused **8** excluded **11** not included

exception 6 oddity, rarity **7** anomaly, removal **8** omission **9** debarment, deviation, exclusion, exemption, isolation, rejection, seclusion

10 difference, leaving out, separation **11** elimination, peculiarity, repudiation, segregation, shutting out, special case **12** disallowment, irregularity, renunciation **13** inconsistency

exceptional 3 odd **4** rare **5** great, queer **6** unique **7** special, strange, unusual **8** aberrant, abnormal, atypical, freakish, peculiar, singular, superior, terrific, uncommon, unwonted **9** anomalous, excellent, irregular, marvelous, unheard of, unnatural, wonderful **10** first-class, inimitable, noteworthy, out-of-sight, phenomenal, remarkable **11** outstanding **12** incomparable **13** extraordinary, unprecedented **17** better than average

**exception to the rule
7** anomaly **11** abnormality **12** irregularity

excerpt 4 part **5** piece **7** extract, portion, section **8** abstract, fragment **9** quotation, selection **13** quoted passage

excess 4 glut **5** extra, flood, spare **7** residue, surfeit, surplus, too much **8** fullness, overflow, plethora **9** avalanche, excessive, profusion, remainder, repletion **10** inundation, lavishness, oversupply **11** undue amount **13** overabundance **14** superabundance

excessive 5 undue **6** excess **7** extreme, profuse, too much **8** needless **9** senseless **10** immoderate, inordinate **11** exaggerated, extravagant, superfluous, unnecessary **12** overabundant, unreasonable **16** disproportionate

excessively 5 enorm **7** greatly **9** extremely, intensely **11** exceedingly, fanatically **12** boisterously, exorbitantly, inordinately **14** overabundantly

exchange 4 swap **5** trade **6** barter, switch **8** bandying, trade off **9** tit for tat **10** quid pro quo **11** convert into, giveand-take, interchange, reciprocate, reciprocity

exchange blows 3 box **5** clash, fight **6** battle, combat, tussle **7** contend, contest, grapple **8** skirmish **11** cross swords

**exchange of viewpoints
6** debate, parley **8** dialogue **10** conference, discussion

exchange views 6 confer, debate **7** consult, discuss **8** consider, talk over **12** compare notes

excise 3 tax **4** duty **6** cut off, cut out, impost, remove **7** extract **8** pluck out **9** eradicate, surcharge

excitable 4 edgy **5** jumpy **7** jittery, nervous **8** feverish, frenzied, skittish **9** flappable, hotheaded **10** highstrung, passionate **11** combustible, inflammable

excite 4 fire, move, whet **5** evoke, pique, rouse, waken **6** arouse, awaken, elicit, foment, incite, kindle, spur on, stir up, thrill **7** agitate, animate, inflame, provoke **8** energize **9** electrify, galvanize, instigate, stimulate, titillate **13** get a kick out of

excited 4 daft **5** afire, astir **6** ablaze **7** aroused **8** agitated, ecstatic, frenzied, inflamed, turned on **9** disturbed, stirred up **10** magnetized **11** electrified

excitement 3 ado **4** flap, stir, to-do **5** furor, kicks **6** action, flurry, frenzy, hoopla, thrill, tumult **7** elation, ferment, flutter, turmoil **8** activity, brouhaha, interest **9** adventure, agitation, animation, commotion, fireworks **10** enthusiasm **11** stimulation

exciting 5 spicy **6** moving, risque **7** rousing, zestful **8** dazzling, stirring **9** affecting, impelling, inspiring, thrilling **11** hair-raising, provocative, sensational, stimulating, titillating **12** breathtaking, electrifying **13** spine-tingling

exclaim 4 howl, yell **5** shout **6** bellow, cry out **7** call out **8** proclaim **9** ejaculate **10** vociferate

exclamation 3 cry **4** howl, yell, yelp **5** shout **6** bellow, outcry, shriek, squeal **7** screech **9** expletive **11** ejaculation **12** interjection, vociferation

exclude 3 ban, bar **4** omit, oust **5** eject, evict, expel **6** banish, except, forbid, refuse, reject, remove **7** boycott, keep out, rule out, shut out **8** disallow, leave out, prohibit, set aside, throw out **9** blackball, repudiate **13** shut the door on

excluding 3 but **4** save **6** except, saving **7** banning, barring, besides **9** excepting, other than **10** keeping out

exclusion 6 ouster **7** barring, refusal, removal **8** ejection, eviction **9** debarment, dismissal, expelling, expulsion, rejection, restraint **10** banish-ment, keeping out, preclusion, prevention **11** prohibition, throwing out **12** nonadmission

exclusive 4 full, posh, sole **5** aloof, total **6** closed, entire, single **7** private **8** absolute, clannish, cliquish, complete, snobbish, unshared **9** undi-vided, selective **10** restricted **11** restrictive

exclusive of 3 but **4** save **6** except, saving **7** barring, be-sides **9** excepting, excluding, other than

excommunicate 3 ban **4** oust **5** eject, expel **6** banish, re-move **8** unchurch **12** anathematize

excommunication 3 ban **6** ouster **8** anathema **10** ban-ishment **12** proscription

excoriate 4 flay **5** curse **6** be-rate, revile **7** censure **8** de-nounce, execrate **9** skin alive

excrescence 4 bump, hump, knob, knot, lump **5** bulge, gnarl **6** nodule **8** swelling **10** protrusion **12** protuberance

excrete 4 void **5** expel **8** evac-uate **9** discharge, eliminate

excruciating 5 acute **6** fierce, severe **7** cutting, extreme, in-tense, racking, violent **9** ago-nizing, exquisite, torturous **10** lacerating, tormenting, un-bearable **11** unendurable **12** insufferable

exculpate 5 clear **6** acquit, ex-cuse, pardon **7** absolve **9** ex-onerate, let one off, vindicate

excursion 4 hike, ride, tour, trek, trip, walk **5** drive, jaunt, sally, tramp **6** cruise, flight, junket, outing, ramble, sortie, stroll, voyage **10** expedition **12** pleasure trip

excusatory 9 defensive **10** apologetic **11** extenuatory, vindicatory **13** justificatory

excuse 4 free **5** alibi, clear, spare **6** acquit, defend, exempt, let off, pardon, reason **7** ab-solve, condone, defense, ex-plain, forgive, indulge, justify, release **8** argument, bear with, mitigate, overlook, palliate, pass over **9** disregard, excul-pate, exemption, exonerate, extenuate, gloss over, let one off, relieve of, vindicate, whitewash **10** absolution **11** exoneration, vindication **12** apologize for **13** justifica-tion **16** make allowance for **17** accept one's apology

execrable 4 vile **5** awful

8 dreadful, terrible **9** atrocious, revolting **10** abominable

execrate 4 hate **5** abhor **6** de-test, loathe **7** despise **9** abomi-nate, can't stand, excoriate **10** shrink from **11** can't stom-ach **12** be revolted by **13** be nauseated by, find repulsive **15** be disgusted with **20** regard with repugnance

execration 4 hate **6** hating **7** disgust **8** loathing **9** despis-ing, repulsion, revulsion **10** repugnance **11** abomina-tion, detestation

execute 2 do **3** act **4** kill, play, slay **5** enact **6** effect, murder, render **7** achieve, enforce, ful-fill, perform, realize, sustain **8** carry out, complete, massa-cre **9** discharge **10** accomplish, administer, consummate, effec-tuate, perpetrate, put to death **11** assassinate **12** carry through **13** put into effect

execution 5 doing **7** killing, slaying **9** discharge, effecting, rendition **10** completion **11** achievement, carrying out, fulfillment, performance, real-ization, transaction **14** accom-plishment, administration, implementation, interpretation, putting to death

executioner 6 hit man, killer, slayer **7** butcher, hangman **8** assassin, murderer

Executioner's Song, The author: 12 Norman Mailer

executive 7 manager **8** chair-man, director, overseer **9** pres-ident **10** leadership, managerial, supervisor **11** di-rectorial, supervisory **13** ad-ministrator **14** administrative, superintendent

executives 7 leaders **8** manag-ers, officers **9** directors **13** governing body **14** administration

executor 4 doer **5** agent **9** per-former **13** administrator

exegesis 10 exposition **11** ex-planation **14** interpretation **18** explication de texte

exemplar 5 ideal, model **7** ex-ample, pattern **8** original, stan-dard **9** archetype, prototype

exemplary 5 ideal, model **6** sample **7** typical **8** laudable, sterling **9** admirable, emula-tive, estimable, nonpareil **10** noteworthy **11** commenda-ble, meritorious **12** illustrative, praiseworthy **14** characteristic, representative

exemplification 7 epitome, es-

sence, example **8** citation, evi-dence **10** embodiment **11** case in point **12** illustration **13** documentation **14** repre-sentation **15** personification

exemplify 6 depict, embody, typify **8** instance **9** epitomize, personify, represent **10** illus-trate **11** demonstrate **12** characterize

exempli gratia 6 such as **10** for example **19** for the sake of example **abbreviation: 2** eg

exempt 4 free **5** clear, freed, spare **6** except, excuse, im-mune, pardon, spared **7** ab-solve, cleared, excused, release, relieve **8** absolved, ex-cepted, relieved **9** not liable, privilege **10** privileged

exemption 6 excuse **7** expense, freedom, release **8** immunity **9** allowance, deduction, excep-tion **10** absolution **12** dispensation

exercise 3 use **4** show **5** apply, drill, exert, teach, train, tutor, wield **6** employ, school, warm-up **7** break in, develop, dis-play, execute, exhibit, per-form, prepare, program, utilize, workout **8** accustom, aerobics, carry out, ceremony, movement, practice, training **9** discharge, inculcate, school-ing **10** daily dozen, discipline, employment, gymnastics, iso-metrics **11** application, demon-strate, give lessons, performance, utilization **12** calisthenics **14** do calisthenics

exert 3 use **5** apply, wield **6** employ, expend **7** utilize **8** exercise, put forth, resort to **9** discharge, make use of **11** put in action, set in motion

exertion 4 toil, work **5** labor, pains **6** effort, energy **7** travail, trouble **8** activity, endeavor, industry, strength, struggle **11** application, elbow grease

ex facie 9 on the face **10** ap-parently **11** from the face

ex facto 8 actually **15** accord-ing to fact

exhalation 4 puff **6** breath, wheeze, whoosh **10** expira-tion **12** breathing out

exhale 4 huff, pant, puff **6** ex-pire **7** breathe, respire **10** breathe out

exhaust 3 fag, tax **4** bush, poop, tire **5** drain, empty, spend, use up **6** expend, fin-ish, strain, weaken **7** consume, deplete, disable, draw off, draw out, fatigue, wear out **8** enervate, overtire **9** dissipate **10** debilitate, devitalize, run through **13** sap one's energy

exhausted 4 beat, gone **5** all in, spent **6** bushed, done in, pooped, used up **7** drained, emptied, wearied, worn out **8** bankrupt, consumed, depleted, expended, fatigued, finished, tired out **9** dead tired, enervated, played out **11** devitalized **12** impoverished

exhausting 5 tough **6** tiring, uphill **7** arduous **8** toilsome **9** difficult, fatiguing, Herculean, laborious, Sisyphean, wearisome **10** burdensome

exhaustion 7 fatigue, using up **8** draining, spending **9** depletion, tiredness, weariness **10** enervation **11** consumption

exhaustive 6 all-out **7** indepth **8** complete, profound, sweeping, thorough **9** intensive **12** all-embracing, all-inclusive **13** comprehensive

exhibit 3 air **4** show **5** flaunt, parade, reveal, unveil **7** display **8** brandish **9** put on view **10** exhibition, exposition, make public **11** demonstrate **12** bring to light **13** public showing

exhibition 4 show **5** array **7** display, exhibit, showing **9** unveiling **10** exposition **13** demonstration, public showing

exhibitionist 7 flasher, show-off **15** attention-seeker

exhilarate 4 lift **5** cheer, elate **6** excite, perk up **7** animate, delight, enliven, gladden, hearten, quicken **9** stimulate **10** invigorate

exhilaration 6 gaiety **7** delight, elation **8** gladness, vivacity **9** animation **10** exaltation, excitement, joyousness, liveliness **11** high spirits **16** lightheartedness

exhort 3 bid **4** goad, prod, spur, urge **5** egg on, press **6** advise, enjoin **7** beseech, implore **8** admonish, advocate, appeal to, persuade **9** encourage, plead with, recommend **14** give a pep talk to

exhortation 6 sermon, urging **7** bidding, lecture, pep talk **8** dictates, harangue, prodding **9** prompting

exhumation 9 digging up **12** disinterment **13** disentombment

exhume 5 dig up **8** disinter

exigency 3 fix, jam **5** needs, pinch **6** crisis, pickle, plight, scrape, strait **7** demands **8** hardship, quandary **9** emergency, extremity, urgencies **10** difficulty **11** constraints, contingency, necessities, predicament **12** circumstance, requirements

exigent 5 vital **6** urgent **8** critical, exacting, pressing **9** demanding, difficult, necessary

exile 2 DP **4** oust **5** eject, expel **6** banish, deport, emigre, pariah **7** outcast, refugee **8** drive out, expellee **9** expulsion **10** banishment, expatriate

Exile, The
    author: **9** Pearl Buck

exiled person 5 exile **6** emigre **7** outcast **8** expellee **10** expatriate

Exile's Return
    author: **13** Malcolm Cowley

exist 4 last, live, stay **5** abide, ensue, occur **6** endure, happen, obtain, remain **7** breathe, prevail, survive

existence 4 life **5** being **7** reality **8** presence, survival **9** actuality, animation, endurance **11** continuance, materiality, subsistence, tangibility

existent 4 real **5** alive **6** actual, extant, living **7** present **8** existing, tangible **9** surviving, to be found **11** in existence

existing 4 real **5** being **6** actual, extant, living **7** ongoing, present **9** existence, surviving, to be found **10** continuing, prevailing **11** established, in existence **12** accomplished

exit 4 blow **5** go out, leave, split **6** cut out, depart, egress, escape, exodus, way out **7** retreat **8** withdraw **9** departure **10** withdrawal **11** take a powder

ex libris 15 out of the books of **16** from the library of

ex nihilo nihil fit 25 out of nothing nothing is made **27** nothing is created from nothing

exocuticle
    consists of: **9** sclerotin

exodus 4 exit **5** exile **6** flight, hegira **9** departure, migration **10** emigration, going forth

Exodus
    author: **8** Leon Uris
    story of founding of: **6** Israel

exonerate 4 free **5** clear **6** ac-

quit **7** absolve, forgive **9** exculpate, vindicate **12** find innocent

exoneration 8 clearing **10** absolution **11** exculpation, vindication

exorbitant 4 dear **5** undue **6** costly **7** extreme **8** enormous **9** egregious, excessive, expensive, out-of-line **10** high-priced, inordinate, oppressive, outrageous, overpriced **11** extravagant **12** extortionate, preposterous, unreasonable

exorcise 5 expel **7** cast out **8** get rid of

Exorcist, The
    author: **18** William Peter Blatty
    director: **15** William Friedkin
    cast: **8** Lee J Cobb **10** Linda Blair **11** Jason Miller, Max von Sydow **12** Ellen Burstyn
    Oscar for: **10** screenplay

exoskeleton
    of insect: **5** shell **8** body wall
    part: **10** epicuticle, exocuticle **11** endocuticle

exoteric 4 open **6** public, simple **7** popular **8** exterior, external, outsider

exotic 5 alien **6** quaint, unique **7** foreign, strange, unusual **8** colorful, peculiar, striking **9** different, not native **10** from abroad, intriguing, outlandish, unfamiliar **11** exceptional **13** not indigenous

expand 4 grow, open **5** swell, widen **6** dilate, evolve, extend, fatten, spread, unfold, unfurl, unroll **7** amplify, augment, develop, distend, enlarge, inflate, magnify, stretch, unravel **8** heighten, increase, multiply **9** outspread, spread out **10** aggrandize

expanded 4 grew **5** grown **7** dilated, swelled, swollen, widened **8** enlarged, extended, unfolded, unfurled, unrolled **9** augmented, broadened, increased, outspread, spread out, stretched **10** heightened **11** aggrandized

expanse 4 area **5** field, range, reach, space, sweep **6** extent **7** breadth, compass, stretch **9** magnitude

expansion 6 growth **8** dilation, increase, swelling, widening **9** enlarging, extension, spreading **10** amplifying, distention, magnifying, stretching **11** development, enlargement, lengthening, multiplying

12 augmentation
13 amplification

expansive 4 free, open, vast, wide **5** broad **6** genial **7** affable, amiable, general, liberal **8** effusive, generous, outgoing **9** bounteous, bountiful, capacious, extensive, exuberant **10** voluminous **11** extroverted, far-reaching, uninhibited, unrepressed, wide-ranging **12** unrestrained **13** comprehensive

expatiate 6 expand **7** amplify, enlarge, expound **9** discourse, elaborate

expatriate 2 DP **5** exile **6** emigre, pariah **7** outcast, refugee **15** displaced person

expatriation 5 exile **9** expulsion **10** banishment

expect 5 guess, trust **6** assume, demand, plan on, reckon **7** believe, count on, foresee, hope for, imagine, look for, presume, require, suppose, surmise **8** envision, reckon on, rely upon **9** calculate **10** anticipate, bargain for, conjecture, reckon upon **11** contemplate **13** look forward to

expectancy 11 expectation **12** anticipation

expectant 4 agog **5** eager, ready **7** anxious, hopeful, waiting **9** expecting **10** looking for, optimistic **12** anticipating, apprehensive

expectation 4 hope **5** trust **6** belief, chance **8** prospect, reliance **9** assurance **10** confidence, expectancy, likelihood **11** presumption **12** anticipation **13** contemplation

expedient 4 help, wise **5** means **6** resort, tactic, useful **7** benefit, helpful, measure, politic, selfish, stopgap **9** advantage, advisable, conniving, desirable, effective, judicious, makeshift, opportune, practical, strategem **10** beneficial, instrument, profitable, worthwhile **11** calculating, selfseeking, self-serving **12** advantageous **14** self-interested

expedite 4 rush **5** hurry **6** hasten **7** advance, forward, further, promote, quicken, speed up **8** dispatch **10** accelerate, facilitate **11** precipitate, push through

expedition 4 trek **6** voyage **7** journey, mission **8** campaign, voyagers **9** explorers, travelers, wayfarers **10** enterprise **11** adventurers, exploration

expeditious 4 fast **5** alert, awake, hasty, quick, rapid, ready, swift **6** prompt, snappy, speedy **7** instant **8** punctual **9** effective, immediate **10** bright-eyed **11** efficacious

expel 4 fire, oust, sack, spew, void **5** eject, evict, exile **6** banish, bounce, remove **7** cashier, cast out, dismiss, drum out, excrete **8** dislodge, drive out, evacuate, force out, throw out **9** discharge, eliminate

expellee 2 DP **5** exile **14** banished person **15** displaced person

expend 3 pay **4** give **5** drain, empty, spend, use up **6** donate, lay out, pay out **7** consume, exhaust, fork out, wear out **8** disburse, dispense, shell out, squander **9** dissipate, go through **10** contribute

expendable 7 payable **9** available, forgoable, spendable **10** consumable, extraneous **11** disbursable, dispensable, replaceable, superfluous **12** nonessential **14** relinquishable

expended 5 spent **6** used up **7** drained, emptied, paid out **8** consumed **9** disbursed, exhausted **10** dissipated

expenditure 3 use **4** cost **5** price **6** charge, outlay, output **7** payment **8** exertion, expenses, spending **9** expending, paying out **10** employment, money spent **11** application, consumption **12** disbursement

expense 4 cost, rate **5** drain, price **6** amount, charge, figure, outlay **9** depletion, quotation

expensive 4 dear **6** costly **9** excessive **10** exorbitant, high-priced, immoderate, overpriced **11** extravagant **12** uneconomical, unreasonable **15** beyond one's means

experience 3 see **4** bear, feel, know, meet, view **5** doing, event, sense **6** affair, behold, endure, suffer **7** episode, observe, sustain, undergo **8** exposure, incident, perceive, practice, training **9** adventure, encounter, go through, happening, seasoning, withstand **10** occurrence **11** familiarity, live through, observation **17** personal knowledge **18** firsthand knowledge

experienced 4 able, wise **6** expert, master **7** capable, knowing, skilled, trained, veteran **8** seasoned **9** competent, efficient, practical, qualified **10** well-versed **11** worldly-

wise **12** accomplished **13** sophisticated

experiential 9 empirical, firsthand, practical

experiment 4 test **5** assay, flier, trial **6** feeler, try out **7** analyze, examine, explore, venture **8** analysis, research **11** examination, investigate **12** seek proof for, verification **13** investigation **14** mess around with

experimental 3 new **4** test **5** fresh, rough, trial **7** radical **9** tentative **10** conceptual, firstdraft **11** conjectural, speculative **13** developmental, trial-and-error

experimentation 7 testing **8** analysis, research **10** experiment **11** examination, exploration **13** investigation, trial and error

experimenter 6 tester **10** researcher **15** experimentalist

expert 3 ace, apt, pro, wiz **4** able, deft, whiz **5** adept, crack, doyen, maven, mavin, shark **6** adroit, artist, facile, master, wizard **7** artiste, capable, perfect, skilled, trained, veteran **8** masterly, skillful, virtuoso **9** authority, competent, masterful, practiced, qualified **10** first-class, pastmaster, proficient, specialist **11** connoisseur, crackerjack, experienced **12** accomplished, professional **13** knowledgeable **French: 6** au fait

expertise 5 savvy, skill **7** know-how **10** expertness **12** special skill **14** specialization **15** professionalism

expertness 5 savvy, skill **7** ability, know how **8** training **9** expertise **10** capability, competence, experience **11** proficiency **12** special skill **13** qualification **14** accomplishment, specialization **15** professionalism

expiate 7 appease **8** atone for **13** make amends for **16** pay the penalty for

expiation 6 amends, shrift **7** penance **9** atonement **11** appeasement **16** paying the penalty

expiration 3 end **5** death, dying, demise, ending, finish **7** passing, closing **8** decrease, exhaling **10** conclusion **11** termination **12** breathing out

expire 3 die, end **5** cease, lapse **6** finish, perish, run out **7** decease, kick off, succumb

8 conclude, pass away 9 terminate 11 come to an end, discontinue 13 kick the bucket 14 give up the ghost

expired 4 dead, died 6 lapsed, ran out, run out 7 defunct, laspsed 8 deceased, lifeless, perished 10 passed away 11 came to an end, come to an end 14 gave up the ghost

explain 6 fathom 7 clarify, clear up, justify, resolve 8 describe, spell out 9 elucidate, explicate, interpret, make clear, make plain 10 account for, illuminate, illustrate 11 demonstrate, rationalize 14 give a reason for 20 give an explanation for

explainer 6 critic 7 analyst 8 reviewer 10 translator 11 commentator, interpreter

explanation
French: 15 eclaircissement

explicate 7 analyze, clarify, develop, explain 8 annotate 9 elucidate, interpret 10 elucidated, illuminate, illustrate

explication 8 analysis 10 commentary 11 elucidation, explanation 12 illumination 13 clarification 14 interpretation

explication de texte 8 exegesis 11 explanation 14 interpretation 17 literary criticism

explicit 5 blunt, clear, exact, frank, plain 6 candid, direct 7 certain, express, pointed, precise 8 absolute, definite, distinct, specific 9 outspoken 10 unreserved 11 categorical, unequivocal, unqualified 15 straightforward 16 clearly expressed

explicitness 7 clarity 9 clearness, precision 11 unambiguity

explode 5 belie, blast, burst, erupt, go off 6 blow up, expose, refute, set off 7 destroy 8 detonate, disprove 9 discredit, repudiate 10 invalidate, prove false, prove wrong 11 burst loudly 12 utter noisily 14 burst violently, express noisily 18 discharge violently 19 burst out emotionally

exploit 4 feat 5 abuse 6 misuse 7 utilize 8 profit by, put to use 9 adventure, brave deed, heroic act, make use of 10 daring deed 11 achievement 12 capitalize on 14 accomplishment, use to advantage 15 take advantage of 16 make selfish use of 21 take unfair advantage of 22 turn to practical account

exploited 6 abused 7 ill used, misused 11 downtrodden 15 took advantage of 16 taken advantage of

exploration 5 probe 7 inquiry 8 scrutiny 9 discovery 10 expedition, experiment 11 examination 12 scouting trip 13 investigation

explore 3 try 5 plumb, probe, scout 6 survey, try out 7 analyze, examine, feel out, pry into 8 look into, research, traverse 9 delve into, penetrate, range over 10 scrutinize, search into, travel over 11 inquire into, investigate, reconnoiter 14 experiment with

explorer *see box*

explosion 3 fit 4 clap 5 blast, burst, crack 6 report 7 tantrum 8 eruption, outbreak, outburst, paroxysm 9 blowing up, discharge 10 detonation 11 fulmination

explosive 5 shaky, tense 6 touchy 7 keyed up 8 critical, perilous, strained, ticklish, unstable, volatile 9 dangerous, emotional 10 ammunition, precarious 12 pyrotechnics

exponent 6 backer 8 advocate, champion, defender, promoter 9 expounder, proponent, spokesman, supporter 12 propagandist

export 7 send out 8 dispatch 10 sell abroad 11 foreign sale 12 ship overseas

expose 4 bare, risk, show 5 brand, offer, strip 6 betray, denude, divest, hazard, let out, reveal, submit 7 display, divulge, exhibit, imperil, let slip, subject, uncover, unearth 8 denounce, disclose, endanger 10 jeopardize, reveal to be 12 acquaint with, bring to light 16 leave unprotected

expose 6 baring 8 exposure 10 divulgence, revelation

exposed 4 open 5 bared 8 divulged, laid open, revealed, unmasked 9 denounced, disclosed, displayed, uncovered, unearthed 11 unprotected, unsheltered

exposition 4 expo, fair, mart, show 6 bazaar, market 7 account, display, exhibit, picture 8 exegesis 9 trade fair, trade show 10 commentary, exhibition, world's fair 11 description, elucidation, explanation, explication 12 illustration, presentation 13 clarification, demonstration 14 interpretation

expostulate 5 argue 6 enjoin, exhort, object, reason 7 caution, counsel, protest 8 forewarn 9 plead with 11 remonstrate 13 cry out against, reason against 14 inveigh against

exposure 4 view 5 vista 6 expose 7 outlook 8 frontage, prospect 9 divulging, unmasking 10 disclosure, divulgence, laying bare, laying open, reve-

---

explorer
American: 4 Byrd, Pike 5 Boone, Clark, Lewis, Peary, Perry
Australian: 4 Hume 5 Sturt 6 Stuart 8 Mitchell
British: 4 Bell, Cook, Park 5 Baker, Bligh, Bruce, Cabot, Davis, Drake, Grant, Puget, Scott, Smith, Speke 6 Baffin, Burton, Hudson, Lander 7 Raleigh, Stanley 8 Franklin 9 Frobisher, MacKenzie, Vancouver 11 Livingstone
Danish: 6 Bering 7 Niebuhr
Dutch: 6 Tasman 7 Barents, Le Maire 8 Schouten 10 Linschoten
French: 6 Joliet 7 Cartier, Jolliet, La Salle 9 Champlain, Marquette 12 Bougainville
Italian: 8 Columbus 9 Marco Polo, Verrazano 15 Amerigo Vespucci
Moslem: 10 Ibn Battuta
Norwegian: 8 Amundsen
Portuguese: 3 Cam, Cao 4 Dias, Diaz 6 Cabral, Da Gama 7 Almeida 8 Covilhao, Magellan 11 Albuquerque 23 Prince Henry the Navigator
Russian: 10 Middendorf 11 Przhevalsky
Spanish: 6 Balboa, Cortes, De Soto 7 Pizarro 8 Coronado, Orellana, Valdivia 11 Ponce de Leon
Swedish: 12 Nordenskjold
Viking: 10 Eric the Red 11 Leif Ericson

lation, subjection, submission, uncovering **11** perspective **12** public notice **15** bringing to light

expound 6 defend, uphold **7** explain **8** describe **9** elucidate, explicate, hold forth, make clear

express 3 say **4** fast, show, word **5** clear, couch, exact, lucid, plain, quick, rapid, speak, state, swift, utter, vivid, voice **6** convey, direct, evince, phrase, relate, reveal **7** certain, declare, divulge, exhibit, nonstop, precise **8** definite, describe, disclose, evidence, explicit, forceful, specific, vocalize **9** high-speed, make known, verbalize **10** articulate, particular **11** categorical, communicate, unequivocal **12** put into words

expression 4 look, mien, term, tone, word **5** idiom, style **6** airing, aspect, phrase, saying **7** emotion, meaning, stating, telling, venting, voicing, wording **8** language, locution, phrasing, relating, speaking, uttering **9** assertion, eloquence **10** appearance, modulation **11** countenance, declaration, enunciation, phraseology **12** articulation, setting forth, turn of phrase **13** communication

expressionless 5 blank, empty **6** vacant **7** deadpan **12** inexpressive

expressive 5 vivid **6** moving **7** telling **8** eloquent, forceful, poignant, powerful, striking **9** effective **10** compelling, indicative, meaningful, thoughtful **11** significant **14** characteristic

expressly 7 clearly, plainly **9** decidedly, pointedly, precisely, specially **10** definitely, distinctly, explicitly **12** particularly, specifically **13** categorically, unequivocally **18** in no uncertain terms

express sorrow 3 cry **4** weep **6** grieve, lament **7** condole, console **10** sympathize **11** commiserate

expropriate 4 take **5** seize **8** take over **10** commandeer, confiscate **11** appropriate

expropriation 7 seizure **10** arrogation, taking over **12** confiscation **13** commandeering

expulsion 5 exile **6** ouster **7** ousting, removal **8** ejection, eviction **9** debarment, discharge, dismissal, exclusion, expelling **10** banishment

11 elimination, prohibition, throwing out **12** proscription

expunge 5 erase **6** delete, efface, rub out **7** blot out, destroy, wipe out **9** eradicate, strike out **10** obliterate

expurgate 3 cut **4** blip, edit **5** purge **6** censor, cut out, delete, excise, remove **8** bleep out **10** blue-pencil, bowdlerize

exquisite 4 fine **5** dainty **6** choice, lovely, superb **7** elegant, perfect **8** delicate, flawless, peerless, precious, splendid **9** admirable, excellent, faultless, matchless **10** consummate, fastidious, impeccable, meticulous **11** superlative **12** incomparable **14** discriminating

exquisiteness 6 beauty **8** delicacy, elegance, fineness **10** loveliness, perfection **12** flawlessness

extant 6 living **7** present **8** existent, existing **9** surviving, to be found **11** in existence

Extasie, The
  author: **9** John Donne

extemporaneous 5 ad-lib **7** offhand **9** extempore, impromptu **10** improvised, off the cuff, unprepared **11** extemporary, spontaneous, unrehearsed **12** without notes **13** without notice **14** unpremeditated **15** spur-of-the-moment **19** off the top of one's head

extemporary 5 ad-lib **9** extempore, impromptu **10** improvised, off the cuff, unprepared **14** extemporaneous **19** off the top of one's head

extempore 5 ad-lib **7** offhand **9** impromptu **10** improvised, off the cuff, unprepared **11** extemporary, unrehearsed **12** without notes **14** extemporaneous, unpremeditated **15** spur-of-the-moment **19** off the top of one's head

extemporize 5 ad-lib **6** make up **9** improvise **14** speak impromptu **15** speak off the cuff

extend 4 give **5** grant, offer, widen **6** bestow, expand, impart, put out, spread, submit **7** advance, amplify, augment, broaden, draw out, enlarge, hold out, proffer, prolong, stretch **8** continue, elongate, increase, lengthen, protract, reach out **10** make longer, stretch out **12** stretch forth

extended 4 long **7** widened **8** drawn out, enlarged, ex-

panded, thorough, unfolded, unfurled **9** broadened, continued, extensive, prolonged, spread out **10** lengthened, protracted, widespread **12** stretched out **13** comprehensive

extending 8 full form **9** expansion **10** drawing out, elongation, proffering, stretching **11** enlargement, lengthening **12** putting forth

extension 3 arm **4** wing **5** annex, delay **6** branch, length, outlay **7** adjunct **8** addition, appendix, increase **9** appendage, expansion, outgrowth **10** drawing out, proffering **11** enlargement, lengthening **12** continuation, postponement, prolongation

extensive 4 huge, long, vast, wide **5** broad, great, large **7** lengthy **8** enormous, extended, far-flung, thorough **9** capacious, universal **10** protracted, voluminous **12** all-inclusive, considerable **13** comprehensive

extensiveness 4 span **5** range, reach, scope **6** extent, spread **7** breadth, compass, expanse, stretch

extent 4 area, size, time **5** range, reach, scope, sweep **6** amount, degree, length **7** breadth, compass, expanse, stretch **8** duration **9** amplitude, magnitude **10** dimensions

extenuate 6 excuse, temper **7** explain, justify, qualify **8** mitigate, moderate

extenuating 9 lessening, tempering **10** mitigating, moderating, qualifying **11** attenuating, diminishing, explanatory, justifiable

exterior 4 face, skin **5** alien, outer, shell **6** exotic, facade, finish, manner **7** bearing, coating, foreign, outside, outward, surface **8** covering, demeanor, external **9** extrinsic, outer side, outermost **10** extraneous **11** superficial

exterminate 3 zap **4** kill **5** erase, waste **7** abolish, destroy, expunge, root out, wipe out **8** demolish, massacre **9** eliminate, eradicate, slaughter **10** annihilate, extinguish

external 5 alien, outer **7** foreign, outside, outward, surface **8** exterior **9** extrinsic, outermost **10** extraneous **11** superficial

extinct 4 dead, gone, lost **6** put out **7** defunct, died out, gone out **8** quenched, vanished **12** extinguished

extinction 5 death **7** eclipse **9** wiping out **11** destruction, eradication **13** disappearance

extinguish 3 end, zap **4** dash, do in, kill **5** crush, douse, quash **6** cancel, dispel, put out, quench, stifle **7** abolish, blow out, destroy, smother, wipe out **8** demolish, snuff out **9** eliminate, eradicate, suffocate

extinguished 6 put out **7** gone out **8** quenched **15** no longer burning

extirpate 5 erase **7** abolish, destroy, extract, pull out, root out, wipe out **8** demolish **9** eradicate **10** annihilate, extinguish, obliterate **11** exterminate

extol 4 laud **6** praise **7** acclaim, applaud, commend, glorify **8** eulogize **9** celebrate **10** compliment **16** sing the praises of

extort 5 educe, exact **6** coerce, elicit **7** extract **9** shake down

extortion 5 force, graft **6** payola, ransom **7** threats, tribute **8** coercion **9** blackmail, hush money, shakedown **14** forced payments

extortionate 5 undue **7** extreme **9** excessive, out-of-line **10** exorbitant, inordinate **12** unreasonable

extra 4 more **5** spare **7** adjunct, further, surplus **9** accessory, auxiliary, redundant, unusually **10** additional, attachment, complement, especially, remarkably, uncommonly **11** superfluous, unnecessary **12** additionally, appurtenance, particularly, supplemental **13** exceptionally **15** extraordinarily

extract 3 get **4** cite, cull **5** educe, evoke, exact, gleen, juice, quote, wrest **6** choose, deduce, derive, elicit, obtain, pry out, remove, select **7** copy out, distill, draw out, essence, excerpt, passage, pull out, root out, take out **8** abstract, bring out, citation, pluck out, press out, separate **9** extirpate, extricate, quotation, selection **10** distillate, squeeze out **11** concentrate

extraction 5 stock **7** descent, removal **8** ancestry **10** derivation, drawing out, pulling out

extraneous 5 alien **6** exotic **7** foreign, strange **9** extrinsic, unrelated **10** immaterial, incidental, irrelevant, not ger-

mane **11** superfluous **12** adventitious, inadmissible, nonessential, not pertinent **13** inappropriate

extraordinary 3 odd **4** rare **5** queer **6** unique **7** amazing, notable, strange, unusual **8** uncommon **9** fantastic, monstrous, unheard of **10** incredible, phenomenal, remarkable **11** exceptional **12** unbelievable **13** inconceivable

extraterrestrial 6 cosmic **10** outer-space **12** interstellar, otherworldly **14** interplanetary

extravagance 5 folly, waste **6** excess **7** caprice **9** absurdity **10** profligacy **11** prodigality, squandering, unrestraint **12** immoderation, improvidence, overspending, recklessness, wastefulness **13** excessiveness **14** capriciousness **16** inordinate outlay, unreasonableness

extravagant 4 wild **6** absurd, costly, unreal **7** foolish **8** fabulous, lavishly, prodigal, spending, wasteful **9** excessive, expensive, fantastic, highflown, imprudent **10** exorbitant, high-priced, immoderate, inordinate, openhanded, outlandish, outrageous, overpriced, profligate **11** improvident, spendthrift, squandering **12** overspending, preposterous, unreasonable, unrestrained

extravaganza 4 fair **5** opera **6** ballet **7** pageant **8** carnival, operetta **9** spectacle, stage show **10** exposition, vaudeville **11** opera bouffe, spectacular **12** Broadway show, opera comique, son et lumiere, wild west show **14** phantasmagoria **17** sound and light show

extreme 3 end **5** depth **6** excess, height, severe **7** intense, radical, unusual **8** advanced, boundary, farthest, uncommon **9** excessive, extremity, nth degree, outermost, very great **10** avant-garde, immoderate, inordinate, outrageous **11** exaggerated, extravagant, most distant **13** extraordinary

extremely 4 very **5** quite **7** awfully **8** terribly **9** curiously, intensely, unusually **10** abnormally, especially, freakishly, peculiarly, remarkably, singularly, uncommonly **11** exceedingly, excessively, unnaturally **12** immoderately, surprisingly **13** exceptionally **15** extraordinarily

extremely painful 7 racking **9** agonizing, torturous **10** tor-

menting, unbearable **11** intolerable, unendurable **12** excruciating, insufferable

extremity 3 arm, end, leg, tip, toe **4** edge, foot, hand, limb **5** bound, brink, limit, reach **6** border, finger, margin **7** confine, extreme **8** boundary, terminus **9** outer edge, periphery

extricate 4 free **5** loose **6** get out, rescue **7** deliver, release **8** liberate, untangle **9** disengage **11** disencumber, disentangle **12** wriggle out of

extrication 6 escape **7** loosing, release **10** liberation **11** deliverance **13** disengagement **15** disentanglement

extrinsic 5 alien **7** foreign **9** accessory **10** accidental, extraneous, incidental **11** dispensable **12** nonessential

extrovert 7 show-off **13** exhibitionist **14** life of the party **17** hail-fellow-well-met

extroverted 8 outgoing, sociable **9** expansive **10** gregarious **12** unrestrained

extrude 4 spew **5** eject, expel **7** project, push out **8** force out, protrude, stickout **9** thrust out

exuberance 3 zip **4** elan, life, zeal **5** vigor **6** energy, spirit **8** buoyancy, vitality, vivacity **9** animation, eagerness **10** enthusiasm, excitement, liveliness **13** effervescence, sprightliness

exuberant 4 lush, rich **5** eager **6** lavish, lively **7** copious, excited, profuse, zealous **8** abundant, animated, spirited, vigorous **9** bounteous, energetic, luxuriant, plenteous, plentiful, sprightly **12** enthusiastic **13** superabundant

exudation 3 sap, tar **4** ooze **5** pitch, sweat **7** leakage, seepage **8** bleeding, drainage **9** discharge, excretion

exude 4 drip, emit, ooze **5** sweat **7** secrete **9** discharge

exult 4 crow **5** gloat, glory **7** rejoice **8** be elated **10** be jubilant, jump for joy **11** be delighted **13** be exhilarated **15** be in high spirits

exultant 5 happy **6** elated, joyful **7** crowing **8** boasting, ecstatic, euphoric, gloating, jubilant **9** rapturous, rejoicing **10** triumphant

exultation 3 joy **7** elation, ovation, rapture, triumph **9** rejoicing **10** jubilation

Eyck, Jan van
  born: **8** Flanders, Maaseyck
    10 Maastricht
  artwork: **9** Timotheos
    15 Ghent Altarpiece **18** Ad-
    oration of the Lamb, The
    Man in a Red Turban, The
    Virgin in a Church **20** The
    Arnolfini Marriage **24** Ar-
    nolfini Wedding Portrait
    29 The Madonna with
    Chancellor Rolin **30** The
    Madonna with Canon van
    der Paele

eye **3** orb **4** scan, view **5** sight,
  study, taste, watch **6** behold,
  gaze at, look at, peeper, regard, survey, take in, vision

  7 inspect, observe, stare at
  8 eyesight, glance at **10** perception, scrutinize
  14 discrimination
    part: **4** iris, lens, rods
    5 cones, nerve, pupil **6** cor-
    nea, muscle, retina **11** blood
    vessel

eyeful **4** doll **5** beaut, peach,
  Venus **6** beauty **7** stunner
  8 knockout **10** good-looker
  13 beautiful girl **14** beautiful
  woman

eyeglass, eyeglasses **4** lens
  5 specs **6** eyecup, lenses
  7 goggles, monocle **8** cheaters,
  contacts, pincenez **9** lorgnette
  10 spectacles

Eye of the Needle
  author: **10** Ken Follett

eyesight **4** eyes **5** sight
  6 vision

eyewitness **5** gaper, gazer
  6 gawker, viewer **7** witness
  8 attester, attestor, beholder,
  informer, looker-on, observer,
  onlooker, passerby **9** bystander, spectator, testifier
  10 rubberneck

Ezekiel
  father: **4** Buzi

Ezra
  father: **7** Seraiah

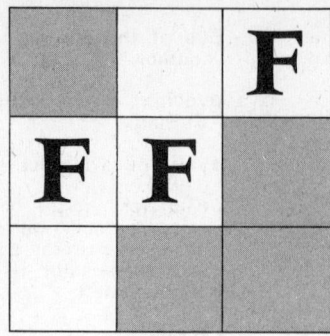

Fabares, Ruby Bernadette Nanette
real name of: 13 Nanette Fabray

fable 3 fib, lie **4** hoax, myth, tale, yarn **6** legend **7** fiction, leg-pull, parable, romance, untruth, whopper **8** allegory **9** fairy tale, falsehood, invention, tall story **11** fabrication

fabled 6 unreal **7** storied **8** fabulous, fanciful, mythical **9** imaginary, legendary **10** fictitious **12** mythological

Fables
author: 16 Jean de La Fontaine

Fabray, Nanette
real name: 28 Ruby Bernadette Nanette Fabares
partner: 9 Sid Caesar
born: 10 San Diego CA
roles: 7 Baby Nan **12** The Band Wagon **13** Sid Caesar Hour **15** High Button Shoes, Our Gang comedies

fabric *see box*

fabricate 4 fake, form **5** build, erect, feign, forge, frame, hatch, shape **6** design, devise, invent, make up **7** compose, concoct, falsify, fashion, produce, trump up **8** assemble, contrive, simulate **9** construct,

embroider, formulate **11** counterfeit, manufacture

fabrication 3 fib, lie **4** myth, yarn **5** fable **6** makeup **7** fiction, forgery, untruth **8** building, creation, erection **9** fairy tale, falsehood, invention **10** assemblage, concoction, fashioning, production **11** composition, manufacture **12** constructing, construction **13** prevarication **16** cock-and-bull story

Fabritius, Carel
real name: 13 Carel Pietersz
born: 14 Midden-Beemster, The Netherlands
artwork: 11 View of Delft **12** The Goldfinch **19** The Raising of Lazarus

fabulous 5 great **6** fabled, superb **7** amazing, storied **8** fanciful, invented, mythical, smashing **9** fantastic, imaginary, legendary, marvelous, wonderful **10** apocryphal, astounding, fictitious, incredible, stupendous **11** astonishing, spectacular **12** mythological, unbelievable **13** extraordinary

facade 4 face, mask **6** veneer **8** frontage, pretense **9** front view **10** false front **13** building front

face 3 air, mug, pan **4** coat, gall, grit, look, pout, puss, sand **5** brass, cheek, cover, front, image, nerve, pluck, spunk **6** aspect, daring, facade, kisser, mettle, repute, visage **7** bravado, dignity, front on, grimace, obverse, overlay, surface **8** boldness, confront, features, forepart, frontage, good name, overlook, prestige **9** encounter, hardihood, impudence, semblance **10** appearance, confidence, effrontery, expression, give toward, look toward, reputation,

---

fabric 5 cloth, frame, stuff **6** makeup **7** textile, texture **8** dry goods, material **9** framework, structure, substance, yard goods **10** foundation **12** organization, substructure **14** infrastructure, superstructure

  cotton: 4 duck **5** denim, drill, scrim, terry **6** burlap, calico, canvas, chintz, dimity, madras, muslin, oxford, poplin **7** batiste, buckram, flannel, gingham, organdy, percale, ticking **8** chambray **9** crinoline, sailcloth **10** broadcloth, printcloth, seersucker **11** cheesecloth, dotted Swiss

  linen: 6 canvas, damask **7** butcher, cambric **8** birds-eye **9** huckaback

  natural: 4 jute, silk, wool **5** linen **6** cotton **8** asbestos

  silk: 3 raw **4** tram **7** organza **8** organzie **9** organzine

  synthetic: 5 nylon, orlon, rayon **6** olefin **7** acetate, acrylic **9** polyester

  type: 4 felt, lace, lame **5** crepe, gauze, moire, serge, voile **6** damask, faille, jersey, melton, velour, velvet **7** brocade, chiffon, flannel, foulard, gingham, taffeta **8** chenille, corduroy, tapestry **9** gabardine, velveteen

  wool: 4 felt **5** crepe, serge, tweed, twill **6** boucle, covert, faille, melton, woolen **7** challis, doeskin, Donegal, worsted **8** homespun, Shetland **9** Astrakhan, gabardine, sharkskin **10** hopsacking **11** Harris tweed, herringbone

    from goats: **8** cashmere

    sheep: **4** Iraqi **6** Hirrik, merino, Romney, Somali **7** Lincoln **8** Cotswold, Tatarian **9** Hampshire, Southdown **10** Corriedale, Dorset Down, Dorset Horn, Shropshire, Sikkim Bera **13** Hampshire Down

    other wool-bearing animals: **5** camel, llama **6** alpaca, vicuna

---

turn toward **11** countenance, physiognomy, self-respect

Face
character in: **12** The Alchemist
author: **6** Jonson

facet 3 cut **4** part, side **5** angle, phase, plane **6** aspect **7** surface

facetious 5 comic, droll, funny, witty **6** clever, jocose, joking, jovial **7** amusing, comical, jesting, jocular, playful **8** humorous **12** wisecracking

face-to-face 6 direct **8** personal **9** firsthand

facile 3 apt **4** glib **5** adept, handy, quick, slick **6** adroit, artful, casual, clever, fluent, smooth **7** cursory, shallow **8** careless, skillful **10** effortless, proficient **11** superficial

facilitate 3 aid **4** ease **6** foster, help in, smooth **7** advance, forward, further, lighten, promote, speed up **8** expedite, simplify **10** accelerate, make easier

facility 3 aid **4** bent, ease **5** knack, means, skill **7** aptness, fluency **8** deftness, easiness, resource **9** advantage, appliance, dexterity, readiness **10** adroitness, capability, competence, efficiency, expertness, smoothness **11** convenience, proficiency **14** effortlessness, practicability

facsimile 4 copy **5** clone **7** replica, reprint **8** likeness **9** duplicate, imitation, photostat **10** transcript **12** reproduction

fact 3 act **4** deed **5** event, truth **6** verity **7** reality **8** incident, specific **9** actuality, certainty, happening, thing done **10** occurrence, particular **12** circumstance

faction 3 set **4** bloc, gang, ring, sect, side, unit **5** cabal, clash, group, split **6** breach, circle, clique, schism, strife **7** combine, coterie, discord, rupture, section **8** conflict, division, minority, sedition **9** rebellion **10** contention, disruption, dissension, dissidence, insurgency, quarreling **11** subdivision **12** disagreement **13** splinter group **15** incompatibility

factious 7 warring **8** divisive, fighting, mutinous **9** alienated, bickering, combative, estranged **10** contending, rebellious **11** belligerent, contentious, disaffected, disagreeing, dissentious, quarrelsome **12** disputatious **13** at

loggerheads, insubordinate **15** insubordinate **16** at sixes and sevens

factitious 4 sham **5** phony **9** pretended, synthetic, unnatural **10** artificial **12** manufactured

factor 4 part **5** cause **6** reason **7** element **9** component, influence **11** constituent **12** circumstance **13** consideration

factory 4 mill, shop **5** plant, works **8** workshop **11** manufactory

factotum 8 handyman **9** gal Friday, guy Friday, man Friday **10** girl Friday **12** right-hand man **15** jack-of-all-trades

factual 4 real, true **5** exact, plain **6** actual **7** certain, correct, genuine, literal **8** accurate, concrete, definite, faithful **9** authentic, unadorned **10** scrupulous, verifiable

faculty, faculties 4 bent, gift, wits **5** flair, knack, power, skill **6** genius, reason, talent **7** quality **8** aptitude, capacity, function, penchant, teachers **9** adeptness, endowment **10** capability, professors **12** mental powers, skillfulness **13** teaching staff

fad 4 mode, rage, whim **5** craze, fancy, mania, vogue **6** whimsy **7** fashion **10** dernier cri, latest word **11** latest thing

faddish 2 in **6** trendy **10** innovative **11** fashionable

fade 3 die, dim, ebb **4** blur, dull, fail, flag, pale, wane **5** droop, taper **6** bleach, lessen, recede, whiten, wither **7** crumble, decline, dwindle, fall off, grow dim, shrivel **8** diminish, dissolve, evanesce, languish, make pale, melt away, pass away **9** disappear dissipate, evaporate, lose color

fade away 3 die, ebb **6** recede **7** subside **8** diminish

faded 4 drab, dull, pale **5** dingy **6** grayed **7** died out **8** bleached, dwindled, whitened, withered **9** colorless, shriveled, washed out

Faerie Queene, The
author: **13** Edmund Spenser
character: **3** Una **5** Guyon **6** Duessa **8** Artegall, Gloriana (the Faerie Queen) **9** Archimago, Britomart **12** Prince Arthur **14** Red Cross Knight

Fafnir
origin: **12** Scandinavian

form: **6** dragon
father: **8** Hreidmar
brother: **5** Otter, Regin
killed: **8** Hreidmar
killed by: **6** Sigurd

fag 4 bush, butt, poop, tire, weed **5** weary **6** tucker **7** exhaust **9** cigarette

Fagin
character in: **11** Oliver Twist
author: **7** Dickens

Fahrenheit
abbreviation: **1** F

Fahrenheit 451
author: **11** Ray Bradbury

Fahrenheit, Gabriel Daniel
field: **7** physics
nationality: **6** German
invented: **16** thermometer scale **18** alcohol thermometer, mercury thermometer

fail 3 die, ebb **4** bomb, flag, flop, fold, wane **5** abort, crash, droop, flunk **6** desert, slip up **7** decline, dwindle, forsake, founder, give out, go under, let down, misfire **8** be in vain, collapse, fade away, languish, lay an egg, miscarry **9** disappear, fall short, fizzle out **10** end in smoke, go bankrupt, not succeed, run aground **11** be stillborn, come to grief, deteriorate, fall through, go up in smoke, miss the mark **12** come to naught, turn out badly **13** come to nothing **15** go out of business **16** meet one's Waterloo, meet with disaster

fail at 11 fall short of **12** be defeated in, not succeed at **16** be unsuccessful at

failed
French: **6** manque

failing 4 weak **5** shaky **6** defect, ebbing, waning **7** folding, frailty **8** drooping, flagging, giving up, slipping, weakness **9** deficient, dwindling, giving out, weakening, weak point **10** deficiency, going under **11** shortcoming **12** unsuccessful **13** insufficiency

fail to include 4 drop, omit **8** leave out

failure 3 dud **4** bomb, flop, mess, ruin **5** botch, crash, loser **6** fizzle, mishap, muddle **7** decline, default, failing, folding, misfire, washout **8** collapse, downfall **9** breakdown, ruination **10** bankruptcy, ne'er-do-well

Fainall, Mrs
character in: **16** The Way of the World
author: **8** Congreve

faint 3 dim, low 4 pale, soft, thin, weak 5 dizzy, faded, frail, giddy, muted, small, swoon, timid 6 dulcet, feeble, little, meager, remote, slight, subtle, torpid 7 fearful, fragile, languid, muffled, obscure, pass out, worn out 8 black out, collapse, cowardly, delicate, drooping, fatigued, timorous 9 exhausted, inaudible, lethargic, whispered 10 indistinct 11 lightheaded, lily-livered, vertiginous 13 inconspicuous 17 lose consciousness

fainthearted 4 weak 5 timid 6 feeble 8 cowardly 10 irresolute 11 halfhearted, indifferent, lily-livered

faintheartedness 9 cowardice 12 cowardliness, yellow streak 13 pusillanimity, yellow feather 17 pusillanimousness 18 chickenheartedness

fair 4 fine, just, pale, so-so 5 blond, bonny, sunny 6 bright, comely, creamy, decent, honest, justly, kosher, lovely, medium, pretty, proper, square 7 average, legally, not dark, upright 8 adequate, candidly, carnival, honestly, mediocre, middling, moderate, ordinary, passable, pleasant, rainless, squarely, sunshiny, unbiased 9 beautiful, cloudless, equitable, ethically, honorable, honorably, impartial, justified, objective, tolerable, unclouded 10 aboveboard, attractive, evenhanded, exhibition, legitimate, pretty good, reasonable, truthfully 11 indifferent, respectable 12 forthrightly, light-colored, light-skinned, on the up-and-up, run-of-the-mill, satisfactory, unprejudiced 13 disinterested, dispassionate 19 according to the rules

Fair, A A
pseudonym of: 18 Erle Stanley Gardner

Fairbanks, Douglas
real name: 17 Douglas Elton Ulman
wife: 12 Mary Pickford
son: 18 Douglas Fairbanks Jr
born: 8 Denver CO
roles: 9 Robin Hood 11 The Iron Mask 14 The Black Pirate, The Mark of Zorro 16 The Thief of Bagdad 18 The Three Musketeers 23 The Private Life of Don Juan

Fairbanks, Douglas Jr
father: 16 Douglas Fairbanks
wife: 12 Joan Crawford
born: 9 New York NY
roles: 8 Gunga Din 12 Little

Caesar 15 Sinbad the Sailor 16 That Lady in Ermine 17 Catherine the Great 18 The Prisoner of Zenda 19 The Corsican Brothers

fair dealing 7 honesty 8 fairness 15 trustworthiness

Fairfax, Gwendolen
character in: 27 The Importance of Being Earnest
author: 5 Wilde

Fairfax, Jane
character in: 4 Emma
author: 6 Austen

Fairfax, Mrs
character in: 8 Jane Eyre
author: 6 Bronte

Fair Land, Fair Land
author: 11 A B Guthrie Jr

fairly 5 fully 6 justly, rather, really 7 rightly 8 actually, honestly, passably, properly, somewhat, squarely 9 equitably, honorably, so to speak, tolerably 10 absolutely, completely, moderately, positively, reasonably 11 impartially, objectively 12 evenhandedly, legitimately 15 dispassionately 19 in a manner of speaking
Latin: 9 pari passu

fairness 7 balance, honesty, justice 8 equality, fair play 11 objectivity 12 impartiality 14 even-handedness 16 equal opportunity

fair play 7 justice 8 equality, fairness 12 impartiality 16 equal opportunity

fair-skinned 4 pale 5 blond, light 6 blonde 17 light-complexioned

fairy 3 elf 5 pixie 6 sprite 10 leprechaun

fairy tale 3 fib 4 myth 5 fable 6 legend 7 fantasy, fiction 8 tall tale 9 invention 11 fabrication 16 cock-and-bull story
German: 7 Marchen

fait accompli 16 accomplished fact, thing already done

faith 4 sect 5 creed, trust 6 belief, church, fealty 7 loyalty, promise 8 credence, fidelity, reliance, religion, security 9 assurance, certainty, certitude, constancy 10 confidence, conviction, obligation, persuasion

faithful 4 true 5 close, exact, loyal, tried 6 honest, strict, trusty 7 devoted, factual, precise, similar, staunch, upright 8 accurate, constant, lifelike, reliable, resolute, truthful 9 steadfast 10 dependable,

scrupulous, true-to-life, unswerving, unwavering, verifiable 11 trustworthy 13 conscientious, incorruptible

faithfulness 6 fealty 7 loyalty 8 devotion, fidelity 9 constancy 10 allegiance 11 reliability 13 steadfastness

faithless 5 false 6 fickle 8 disloyal 10 inconstant, perfidious, unreliable 11 treacherous 13 untrustworthy

faithlessness 5 doubt 7 perfidy 9 disbelief, falseness, treachery 10 disloyalty, fickleness, infidelity, skepticism 11 inconstancy 13 unreliability 14 perfidiousness, unfaithfulness

fake 4 hoax, ruse, sham 5 bogus, dodge, dummy, faker, false, feign, forge, fraud, phony, put-on, quack, trick 6 deceit, forged, humbug, poseur, pseudo 7 falsify, forgery, not real, pretend, trump up 8 artifice, contrive, deceiver, delusion, imposter, invented, simulate, specious, spurious 9 charlatan, concocted, contrived, deception, dissemble, fabricate, imitation, imposture, pretender, simulated 10 artificial, fabricated, fictitious 11 contrivance, counterfeit, dissimulate, fabrication, make-believe

faker 5 fraud, phony 6 humbug 8 imposter 9 charlatan, pretender

fakir 5 Hindu 6 Muslim 7 ascetic, dervish

falcon 5 hobby, saker 6 desert, lanner, merlin 7 goshawk, kestrel, prairie, shaheen, tiercel 8 caracara, falconet 9 gyrfalcon, peregrine

Falcon and the Snowman, The
author: 13 Robert Lindsey
director: 15 John Schlesinger
cast: 8 Sean Penn (Andrew Daulton Lee, the Snowman) 13 Timothy Hutton (Christopher John Boyce, the Falcon)

Falconer
author: 11 John Cheever

Falconet, Etienne-Maurice
born: 5 Paris 6 France
artwork: 9 The Bather 12 Bathing Nymph 13 Milo of Crotona, Peter the Great 19 Pygmalion and Galatea

falconry 7 hawking
equipment: 4 lure 5 cadge 6 jesses 7 creance

Falk, Lee
creator/artist of: **10** The Phantom **19** Mandrake the Magician

Falk, Peter
born: **9** New York NY
roles: **7** Columbo **9** Murder Inc **12** The Great Race **13** Murder by Death **17** The Cheap Detective **19** Pocketful of Miracles **21** It's a Mad Mad Mad Mad World, Robin and the Seven Hoods

fall, falls 3 die, ebb, err, sin **4** drop, plop, ruin, slip, wane **5** droop, lapse, occur, slope, slump, spill **6** autumn, crop up, defeat, happen, perish, plunge, topple, tumble **7** be slain, be taken, capture, cascade, cheapen, come off, crumple, decline, descend, descent, falling, plummet, sinking, succumb **8** cataract, collapse, come down, decrease, diminish, disgrace, downfall, drop down, dropping, go astray, hang down, lowering **9** crash down, overthrow, reduction, surrender, take place, waterfall **10** capitulate, come to pass, corruption, debasement, depreciate, diminution, subsidence, subversion, transgress **11** be destroyed, harvest time **12** capitulation, depreciation, Indian summer **15** loss of innocence

Fall, The
author: **11** Albert Camus

Falla, Manuel de
born: **5** Cadiz, Spain
composer: **11** El Amor Brujo, La Atlantida, La Vida Breve, Life Is Short **14** Fantasia Betica **15** Love the Magician **19** The Three-Cornered Hat **21** El sombrero de tres picos **25** Nights in the Gardens of Spain

fallacious 5 false, wrong **6** faulty, flawed, untrue **8** delusive, mistaken **9** deceptive, erroneous, illogical, incorrect **10** inaccurate, misleading, untruthful

fallacy 4 flaw **5** catch, error, fault **7** mistake, pitfall **8** delusion, illusion **9** misbelief **10** faultiness **11** false belief, false notion **13** inconsistency, misconception **15** misapprehension

fall apart 5 decay **7** break up, crumble, shatter **8** fragment, splinter **10** go to pieces **11** fragmentize **12** disintegrate

fall away 4 fade, wane **5** abate **7** drop off, slacken, subside **8** mitigate, taper off

fall back 6 recede **7** back off, retreat

fallen 4 dead **5** loose, slain **6** ousted, ruined, sinful **7** debased, deposed, dropped, immoral, spilled, toppled, tumbled **8** sprawled **9** butchered, disgraced, massacred, turned out **10** discharged, overthrown **11** slaughtered

fallen short
French: **6** manque

fall for 7 believe, swallow

fall guy 4 dupe, pawn, tool **5** patsy **7** cat's-paw

fallible 5 frail, human **6** faulty, mortal, unsure **9** imperfect **10** unreliable

fall in drops 4 drip, rain **7** dribble, drizzle **8** sprinkle

falling apart 6 ruined, shabby **7** rickety, run-down **8** decaying, decrepit **9** crumbling **10** broken-down, collapsing, ramshackle, tumbledown **11** dilapidated **13** deteriorating

Falling in Place
author: **10** Ann Beattie

falling into decay 6 ruined, shabby **7** rotting, run-down **8** decrepit **9** crumbling, moldering **10** broken-down, tumbledown **11** dilapidated, in disrepair **13** deteriorating

falling off 3 ebb **4** fall, wane **7** decline **8** decrease **9** dwindling, lessening, reduction **10** diminution **13** deterioration

falling out 4 spat **7** dispute, quarrel **8** argument, squabble **10** difference **12** disagreement

fall in with 6 concur **7** conform **8** accede to **9** acquiesce **11** go along with

fall off 4 drop, wane **6** lessen, plunge, reduce, topple **7** decline, drop off, plummet, slacken, subside **8** decrease, diminish, moderate, peter out

Fall of the House of Usher, The
author: **13** Edgar Allan Poe
character: **8** Narrator **13** Madeline Usher, Roderick Usher

fallow 4 arid, idle **5** inert **6** barren, unused **7** dormant, unsowed, worn out **8** depleted, inactive, untilled **9** exhausted, unplanted **10** unfruitful **12** uncultivated, unproductive

fall short 6 be less, fail at, give up **9** be lacking, lag behind **10** have too few **11** fail to reach, miss the mark **12** be inadequate **14** be insufficient

fall to one's lot 4 fall **5** occur **6** befall, chance, happen **7** turn out **9** come about **10** come to pass

fall upon 5 fly at **6** assail, attack, dive at **7** embrace, lunge at, set upon **8** thrust at, tuck into

false 4 fake, sham **5** bogus, phony, wrong **6** ersatz, faulty, forged, pseudo, tricky, unreal, untrue **7** devious, feigned, inexact, invalid, unsound **8** delusive, disloyal, mistaken, spurious, two-faced **9** deceitful, deceiving, deceptive, dishonest, erroneous, faithless, imitation, incorrect, unfounded **10** apocryphal, artificial, factitious, fallacious, inaccurate, inconstant, misleading, not correct, perfidious, traitorous, unfaithful, untruthful **11** counterfeit, make-believe, treacherous **12** hypocritical **13** double-dealing

false front 4 mask, sham, show **6** facade, screen, veneer **8** pretense

false-hearted 8 two-faced **9** deceitful, deceiving, faithless **10** perfidious **13** double-dealing, untrustworthy

falsehood 3 fib, lie **5** lying, story **6** canard, deceit **7** fiction, figment, perfidy, perjury, untruth, whopper **8** bad faith, white lie **9** deception, duplicity, hypocrisy, invention, mendacity **10** dishonesty, distortion, inaccuracy **11** dissembling, fabrication, insincerity **12** misstatement, two-facedness **13** deceptiveness, dissimulation, double-dealing, falsification **17** misrepresentation

falseness 5 fraud **6** deceit **7** perfidy **9** duplicity, treachery **10** dishonesty **12** spuriousness **13** deceitfulness, double-dealing, faithlessness **14** untruthfulness

falsified 5 false, phony **6** forged, made-up **7** assumed **10** fictitious

falsify 4 fake **5** belie, rebut **6** doctor, misuse, refute **7** confute, distort, pervert **8** disprove **10** tamper with **12** misrepresent

Falstaff
opera by: **5** Verdi
character: **4** Anne **6** Fenton, Pistol **7** Dr Caius **8** Bardolph **11** Dame Quickly **12** Mistress Ford, Mistress Page **15** Mistress Quickly, Sir John Falstaff

Falstaff, Sir John
   character in: 22 The Merry
   Wives of Windsor
   author: 11 Shakespeare

falter 3 lag 4 halt, reel 5 demur, waver 6 dodder, mumble, shrink, teeter, totter 7 shamble, shuffle, stagger, stammer, stumble, stutter 8 hesitate 9 fluctuate, vacillate 10 dillydally 11 be undecided 12 be irresolute, show weakness 14 blow hot and cold

fame 4 note 5 glory 6 renown, repute 7 laurels 8 eminence, prestige 9 celebrity, notoriety 10 notability, popularity, prominence, reputation 11 distinction, preeminence 15 illustriousness

famed 5 noted 6 famous 7 notable 8 renowned 9 prominent, well-known 10 celebrated

familiar 3 pal 4 bold, chum, cozy, free, snug 5 buddy, close, crony, known, stock, usual 6 chummy, common, friend 7 forward, general 8 accepted, amicable, at home in, everyday, frequent, friendly, habitual, informal, intimate, ordinary, seasoned, versed in 9 abreast of, brotherly, confidant, customary, fraternal, gemutlich, intrusive, simpatico, skilled in, well-known 10 accessible, accustomed, acquainted, apprised of, conversant, proverbial, unreserved 11 cognizant of, commonplace, impertinent, traditional 12 confidential, conventional, hand and glove, no stranger to, proficient at 13 boon companion, companionable, disrespectful 15 taking liberties

familiarity 4 ease 5 amity, skill 7 know-how, mastery 8 coziness, intimacy 9 closeness, impudence, indecorum, knowledge, unreserve 10 casualness, chumminess, cognizance, disrespect, experience, fellowship, fraternity, friendship 11 association, brotherhood, conversance, forwardness, impropriety, informality, naturalness, presumption, proficiency 12 acquaintance, impertinence, unconstraint, undue liberty, unseemliness 13 brotherliness, comprehension, intrusiveness, understanding, undue intimacy 16 acquaintanceship

familiarize 5 edify, teach, tutor 6 inform, school, season 7 educate 8 accustom, acquaint, instruct 9 enlighten,

habituate, inculcate 11 acclimatize

family 3 kin, set 4 clan, kind, line, race 5 blood, breed, brood, class, group, house, issue, order, stock, tribe 7 dynasty, kinfolk, kinsmen, lineage, progeny 8 ancestry, category, division, kinsfolk 9 forebears, genealogy, offspring, parentage, relations, relatives 10 extraction, kith and kin 11 forefathers 14 classification
   goddess of: 6 Cardea

Family Affair
   character: 4 Jody 5 Buffy, Cissy 8 Mr (Giles) French 9 Bill Davis
   cast: 10 Brian Keith 11 Anissa Jones, Kathy Garver 14 Sebastian Cabot 15 Johnnie Whitaker

family line 7 lineage 8 ancestry 9 blood line, genealogy, parentage

Family Moskat, The
   author: 19 Isaac Bashevis Singer

Family Reunion, The
   author: 7 T S Eliot

Family Ties
   character: 4 Nick 5 Ellen 6 Skippy 10 Alex Keaton 11 Elyse Keaton 12 Andrew Keaton, Steven Keaton 13 Mallory Keaton 14 Jennifer Keaton
   cast: 9 Marc Price 11 Michael J Fox, Tina Yothers 12 Michael Gross 14 Justine Bateman 20 Meredith Baxter-Birney

family tree 7 lineage 8 ancestry, pedigree 9 blood line, genealogy

famine 4 lack, want 6 dearth 7 paucity, poverty 8 scarcity 9 depletion 10 deficiency, exhaustion, famishment, meagerness, scantiness, starvation 11 destitution, half rations, short supply 13 acute shortage, extreme hunger, insufficiency

famish 6 hunger, starve

famous 5 noted 7 eminent, notable 8 far-famed, renowned, well-known 9 notorious, prominent 10 celebrated 11 conspicuous, illustrious 13 distinguished

famous person 4 name, star 7 notable 8 luminary, somebody 9 celebrity, personage, superstar 11 personality

fan 3 bug, nut 4 buff 5 fiend, freak 6 addict, rooter, zealot

7 booster, fanatic 8 follower, partisan

fanatic 5 crazy 6 maniac, zealot 7 hothead, radical 8 activist, militant 9 extremist 10 enthusiast 24 member of the lunatic fringe

fanaticism 6 fervor 8 activism, zealotry 9 dogmatism, extremism, monomania, obsession 10 enthusiasm, radicalism 11 extreme zeal, militantism 12 intemperance 13 ruling passion 15 opinionatedness

fancied 5 liked 6 dreamt, took to, unreal 7 assumed, desired, dreamed, thought 8 imagined, supposed 9 conceived, imaginary, preferred

fanciful 3 odd 6 unreal 7 bizarre, curious, flighty, unusual 8 fabulous, humorous, illusory, mythical, quixotic, romantic 9 eccentric, fantastic, imaginary, invective, legendary, visionary, whimsical 10 apocryphal, capricious, chimerical, fictitious 11 imaginative

fanciful talk 7 blarney 9 hyperbole, tall tales 11 fish stories 12 exaggeration

fancy 3 yen 4 fine, idea, like, want 5 crave, dream, enjoy, favor, opine, showy, taste, think 6 assume, custom, deluxe, desire, florid, liking, notion, ornate, relish, rococo, take it, take to, vagary, vision, whimsy 7 baroque, caprice, conceit, dream of, elegant, fantasy, figment, gourmet, imagine, leaning, longing, long for, picture, presume, reverie, special, suppose, surmise, suspect, unusual 8 be fond of, crotchet, daydream, fondness, illusion, not plain, penchant, superior, weakness, yearn for 9 elaborate, epicurean, expensive, hankering, superfine 10 be bent upon, conceive of, conjecture, decorative, high-priced, ornamental, partiality 11 distinctive, exceptional, extravagant, gingerbread, hanker after, have a mind to, imagination, inclination 12 have an eye for, predilection 13 be pleased with, take a liking to

fancy house 4 stew 5 house 6 bagnio 7 brothel 8 bordello, cathouse 10 bawdy house, whorehouse 13 sporting house 14 house of ill fame 16 house of ill repute 19 house of prostitution

fang 4 claw, nail, root, take, tang, tusk 5 prong, seize, tooth **6** obtain **7** capture, procure **8** eyetooth **9** chelicera

fanny 4 buns, rump, seat **6** behind, bottom **8** backside, buttocks **9** fundament

Fanny
    author: **9** Erica Jong

Fanny
    character in: **13** Joseph Andrews
    author: **8** Fielding

fan out 7 scatter **8** disperse **9** spread out

fantasize 5 dream, fancy **7** imagine **8** daydream

fantastic 3 mad, odd **4** huge, wild **5** antic, crazy, great, queer, weird **6** absurd, superb **7** amazing, bizarre, extreme, strange **8** enormous, fabulous, fanciful, freakish, illusory, quixotic, romantic, terrific **9** grotesque, imaginary, marvelous, visionary, wonderful **10** chimerical, far-fetched, incredible, irrational, outlandish, ridiculous, tremendous **11** extravagant, implausible, sensational **12** preposterous, unbelievable

fantasy 4 mind **5** dream, fancy **6** mirage, notion, vision, whimsy **7** caprice, chimera, fiction, figment, phantom, reverie **8** daydream, illusion, phantasm **9** imagining, invention, nightmare, unreality **10** apparition **11** fabrication, imagination, make-believe, supposition **13** hallucination, realm of dreams, visionary idea

Fantasy Island
    character: **6** Tattoo **8** Mr Roarke
    cast: **16** Herve Villechaize, Ricardo Montalban

far 4 afar, much **6** deeply, remote, way-off, yonder **7** distant, greatly **11** beyond range, out-of-the-way **12** considerably, immeasurably, incomparably

Faraday, Michael
    field: **7** physics **9** chemistry
    worked in: **11** electricity
    developed: **9** generator **12** electrolysis
    liquified: **8** chlorine
    discovered: **6** carbon **7** benzene **24** electromagnetic induction
    named for him: **5** farad

far and near 10 every place, everywhere, far and wide **11** in all places

far and wide 10 every place, everywhere, far and near **11** in all places

Far Away and Long Ago
    author: **8** W H Hudson

farce 4 sham **6** parody **7** mockery **8** drollery, nonsense, pretense, travesty **9** absurdity, burlesque, horseplay, low comedy **10** buffoonery, tomfoolery **11** broad comedy, make-believe **12** harlequinade **14** ridiculousness

farceur 3 wag **5** joker

farcical 5 droll, funny, silly **6** absurd, stupid **7** asinine, comical, foolish **8** humorous **9** laughable, ludicrous, senseless **10** irrational, ridiculous

fare 2 do **3** fee **4** diet, food, menu **5** board, get on, rider, table **6** charge, client, manage **7** make out, perform, regimen, turn out **8** customer, get along, victuals **10** provisions **11** comestibles, ticket price **12** food and drink, passage money **15** paying passenger **20** cost of transportation

farewell 6 so long **7** good-bye, parting **8** Godspeed **9** departing, departure **11** leave-taking, parting wish, valediction **17** parting compliment
    French: **5** adieu **8** au revoir
    German: **14** auf Wiedersehen
    Hawaiian: **5** aloha
    Italian: **4** ciao **5** addio **11** arrivederci
    Japanese: **8** sayonara
    Latin: **4** vale
    Spanish: **5** adios

Farewell to Arms, A
    author: **15** Ernest Hemingway
    character: **13** Frederic Henry **16** Catherine Barkley

far-fetched 7 dubious **8** doubtful, strained, unlikely **10** cockamamie, improbable **11** implausible **12** preposterous, unconvincing

Far From the Madding Crowd
    author: **11** Thomas Hardy
    character: **10** Fanny Robin, Gabriel Oak **12** Sergeant Troy **14** Farmer Boldwood **17** Bathsheba Everdene
    setting: **6** Wessex

farina 4 meal, mush **5** flour **6** cereal, pollen, starch **8** semolina

farm 3 sow **4** plow, reap **5** plant, ranch, tract **6** grange, spread **7** harvest **9** cultivate **10** plantation **11** till the soil **12** country place

farmable 6 arable **7** friable **8** plowable, tillable **10** cultivable

farm animal 2 ox **3** cow, ewe, hen, hog, pig, ram, sow **4** bull, goat **5** beast, brute, horse, sheep **7** chicken, rooster

farm boundaries
    god of: **8** Silvanus, Sylvanus

farmer 6 grower, raiser, reaper **7** granger, planter, rancher **8** agrarian **9** harvester **10** agronomist, husbandman **12** sharecropper **13** agriculturist, truck gardener **15** tiller of the soil

farming
    god of: **4** Thor

far-off 6 remote **7** distant, faraway **11** unreachable **12** inaccessible **13** unforeseeable

farouche 3 shy **6** fierce, sullen **10** unsociable

far-out 3 mad **4** wild **5** crazy, weird **7** bizarre, strange **10** outlandish **14** fantastic

Far Pavilions, The
    author: **6** M M Kaye

Farragut, David
    served in: **8** Civil War **10** Mexican War **19** War of Eighteen Twelve
    captured: **9** Mobile Bay **10** New Orleans
    saying: **30** Damn the torpedoes full speed ahead

far-reaching 4 wide **5** broad **8** sweeping **9** expansive, extensive, universal, unlimited **11** wide-ranging

Farrell, James T
    author of: **11** Judgment Day **12** Studs Lonigan, Young Lonigan **29** The Young Manhood of Studs Lonigan

far-removed 6 far-off, remote **7** distant, faraway

farrow 6 barren **7** piglets, sterile **9** infertile **10** unpregnant

Farrow, Mia
    real name: **27** Maria de Lourdes Villier Farrow
    father: **10** John Farrow
    mother: **16** Maureen O'Sullivan
    husband: **11** Andre Previn **12** Frank Sinatra
    born: **12** Los Angeles CA
    roles: **5** Zelig **11** John and Mary, Peyton Place **12** The Hurricane **13** Rosemary's Baby **14** The Great Gatsby **16** Allison MacKenzie **19** Hannah and Her Sisters **20** The Purple Rose of Cairo

far side 4 back **7** reverse **8** back side

Far Side, The
    creator/artist: **10** Gary Larson

farsighted 4 wise **5** acute
6 shrewd **7** prudent **9** farseeing, hyperopic, judicious, prescient, provident
10 forehanded, foreseeing
11 clairvoyant, levelheaded

farther 6 beyond, deeper,
longer **7** further, remoter
9 lengthier **10** more remote
11 more distant, more
removed

farthermost 7 extreme **8** farthest, furthest **11** furthermost,
most distant

farthest 3 end **4** most **7** extreme, longest **8** furthest, re-
motest, ultimate **9** uttermost
11 farthermost, furthermost

fascia 4 band, sash **5** board,
strip **6** fillet, girdle, ribbon, tissue **7** bandage **8** membrane
9 dashboard

fascinate 5 charm, rivet **6** absorb, allure **7** beguile, bewitch,
delight, enchant, engross
8 enravish, enthrall, entrance,
transfix **9** captivate, enrapture,
overpower, spellbind **14** hold
spellbound

fascinating 8 alluring, charming, gripping, riveting **9** absorbing, beguiling
10 bewitching, delightful, enchanting, engrossing, entrancing **11** captivating, enthralling,
interesting **12** overpowering,
spellbinding

fascination 4 draw, lure
5 charm **6** allure **9** magnetism
10 attraction **11** captivation

fascism 6 Nazism **9** autocracy,
oligarchy **10** plutocracy
11 corporatism, police state
13 corporativism **14** corporate
state **15** totalitarianism **17** national socialism **21** right-wing
dictatorship

fascist 9 right-wing **10** repressive, tyrannical **11** dictatorial,
doctrinaire

fashion 3 air, fad, hew, way
4 form, make, mode, mold,
rage **5** carve, craze, forge,
frame, habit, shape, style,
tenor, trend, usage, vogue
6 create, custom, design, devise, manner **7** compose, pattern, produce **8** attitude;
behavior, contrive, demeanor
9 construct, fabricate **10** convention **11** manufacture

fashionable 2 in **3** hip **4** chic
5 smart **6** modish, with-it
7 current, in style, in vogue,
popular, stylish, voguish **9** in
fashion **10** all the rage,
prevailing
French: **9** de rigueur

fashionable world
French: **10** grand monde

fashion designer 4 (Christian)
Dior **5** Kenzo, (Jean) Patou
6 Adolfo, Lanvin, Poiret,
(Coco) Chanel **7** Galanos, Hal-
ston, Missoni, (Pierre) Bal-
main **8** Givenchy **9** Courreges,
Mary Quant, Valentino
10 Balenciaga, Mainbocher,
Perry Ellis **11** Calvin Klein,
Emilio Pucci, Ralph Lauren
12 Liz Claiborne, Lucien Le-
long, Norman Norell, Pierre
Cardin, Schiaparelli **13** Karl
Lagerfeld, Rudi Gernreich
14 Pauline Trigere **15** Claire
McCardell **16** Gloria Vander-
bilt, Yves Saint-Laurent
Empress Eugenie's:
5 (Charles Frederick) Worth
Marie Antoinette's: 10 Rose
Bertin
Empress Josephine's:
19 Louis Hippolyte Leroy

fashioned 4 made **5** built
6 formed, framed, molded,
shaped, styled **7** adapted,
crafted, created, devised, managed, modeled **9** contrived,
patterned **11** constructed
12 accommodated

fashion plate 4 dude **5** dandy
12 Beau Brummell, clotheshorse, man of fashion, sharp
dresser **14** woman of fashion

fast 4 firm, taut, true, wild
5 ahead, brisk, fleet, fully,
hasty, loose, loyal, quick,
rapid, rigid, swift, tight
6 famish, firmly, flying, rakish,
secure, speedy, stable, starve,
steady, wanton, winged
7 abiding, devoted, durable,
fasting, fast day, fixedly, hastily, hurried, immoral, lasting,
lustful, quickly, rapidly, solidly, soundly, staunch, swiftly,
tightly **8** constant, enduring,
faithful, fastened, go hungry,
immodest, reckless, resolute,
securely, speedily, unfading
9 debauched, dissolute, hurriedly, immovable, immovably,
in advance, permanent, resistant, steadfast **10** completely,
dissipated, firmly tied, lascivious, licentious, profligate, starvation, stationary, unswerving,
unwavering **11** accelerated, expeditious, extravagant, intemperate, pleasure-mad,
tenaciously **12** hunger strike,
ineradicable, lickety-split

Fast, Howard
author of: **9** Spartacus
11 Freedom Road **13** The
Immigrants **15** Citizen Tom
Paine

fasten 3 bar, fix, pin, tie, wed
4 bind, bolt, clip, fuse, hold,

hook, join, lash, link, lock,
moor, snap, weld, yoke **5** affix, clamp, clasp, dowel, focus,
hitch, close, latch, rivet,
screw, stick, truss, unite **6** adhere, anchor, attach, button,
cement, couple, direct, pinion,
secure, solder, tether **7** connect **8** dovetail **11** put together

fastener 3 peg, pin, tie **4** clip,
glue, grip, hook, line, nail,
snap, tack **5** catch, clamp,
clasp, cleat, latch, screw, strap,
truss **6** buckle, button, cement,
staple, thread, zipper
7 bracket **8** barrette **9** fastening, safety pin, thumbtack
10 clothespin, connection,
hook and eye

fastening 4 snap **5** clasp
8 coupling **9** attaching **10** attachment, connection

fasten together 3 tie **4** dock,
join **6** couple, hook up, link
up

fastidious 5 fussy, picky
6 choosy, dainty, proper,
queasy **7** finicky **8** exacting,
precious **9** difficult, squeamish
10 meticulous, particular
11 overprecise, overrefined,
persnickety **12** hard to please,
overdelicate **13** hypercritical

Fastidious Brisk
character in: **22** Every Man
out of His Humour
author: **6** Jonson

fastidious connoisseur 7 epicure, gourmet **9** bon vivant
10 gastronome

fastidiousness 4 care **12** ex-
actingness **14** discrimination
15 persnicketiness

fat 4 full, oily **5** beefy, fatty,
flush, heavy, obese, palmy,
plump, pudgy, stout, suety
6 chubby, fleshy, grease,
greasy, portly, rotund **7** copious, fertile, lumpish, paunchy,
replete, stuffed **8** abundant,
blubbery, chockful, fruitful,
thickset, unctuous **9** animal
fat, corpulent, fortunate, lucrative, plenteous, plentiful, rewarding **10** overweight,
potbellied, productive **11** well-
stocked **12** remunerative

fatal 6 deadly, lethal, mortal
7 ruinous **8** terminal, virulent
10 calamitous, disastrous
11 destructive **12** catastrophic,
causing death

fatalism 8 stoicism **11** resignation **12** acquiescence, helplessness **13** powerlessness
14 predestination

fatality 5 death **8** casualty **9** le-
thality, mortality **10** deadli-

ness, malignancy
11 banefulness

fatal woman
French: 11 femme fatale

fate 3 lot 4 doom 5 karma,
moira 6 effect, future, kismet,
upshot 7 chances, destiny, fortune, outcome, portion
8 prospect 10 providence
11 consequence 12 will of
heaven 14 predestination

fated 4 sure 5 bound, meant
6 doomed 7 certain 8 destined

fateful 5 fatal 7 crucial, ominous 8 critical, decisive 9 momentous 10 disastrous,
portentous 11 significant

Fates
also: 5 Morae 6 Moerae,
Moirai, Parcae
named: 6 Clotho 7 Atropos
8 Lachesis
goddesses of: 7 destiny
number of goddesses:
5 three
called: 12 weird sisters
parents: 4 Zeus 5 Night
6 Themis

father 3 dad, pop 4 abbe, cure,
papa, sire 5 beget, begin,
daddy, found, hatch, maker,
padre, pater 6 author, create,
design, old man, parson, pastor, priest 7 creator, founder
8 ancestor, begetter, designer,
engender, forebear, inventor,
preacher 9 architect, confessor,
originate, procreate 10 forefather, male parent, originator,
progenitor
French: 4 pere

Father 4 Abba

Father, The
author: 16 August Strindberg

Father Knows Best
character: 11 Jim Anderson
13 Betty Anderson (Prin-
cess), Kathy Anderson (Kitten) 15 James Anderson Jr
(Bud) 16 Margaret Anderson
cast: 9 Billy Gray, Jane
Wyatt 11 Robert Young
12 Lauren Chapin 13 Elinor
Donahue

fatherland 6 Heimat, patria,
patrie 8 homeland 10 birthplace, motherland, native land,
native soil 13 mother country,
native country

fatherly 6 benign, kindly,
tender 8 parental, paternal
9 indulgent 10 beneficent,
benevolent

father of his country
Latin: 12 Pater Patriae

father of stars / wind
8 Astraeus

Father of the Bride
director: 16 Vincente
Minnelli
cast: 11 Billie Burke, Joan
Bennett, Leo G Carroll
12 Spencer Tracy 15 Elizabeth Taylor
sequel: 21 Father's Little
Dividend

father of the family
Latin: 13 paterfamilias

Father of the Rivers see
4 Nile

Fathers and Sons
author: 12 Ivan Turgenev
character: 5 Katya, Pavel
6 Arkady, Vasily 8 Bazaroff,
Fenichka 9 Kirsanoff
15 Madame Odintzoff

fathom 5 probe 6 divine, follow 7 hunt out, root out, uncover, unravel 8 discover
9 ferret out, figure out, penetrate 10 comprehend, understand 16 get to the bottom of

fathom
abbreviation: 4 fath

fatigue 3 fag 4 bush, tire
5 drain, weary 6 tedium,
tucker, weaken 7 exhaust, languor, wear out 8 enervate,
overtire 9 heaviness, lassitude,
tiredness, weariness 10 debilitate, drowsiness, enervation,
exhaustion 12 debilitation, listlessness 13 overtiredness

fatigued 4 beat 5 all in, jaded,
spent, tired, weary 6 bushed,
done in, fagged, pooped
7 worn out 8 dog-tired, weakened 9 dead tired, enervated,
exhausted, overtaxed 10 overworked 11 debilitated, tuckered out

fatiguing 6 tiring 7 arduous,
tedious 8 tiresome 9 wearisome 10 exhausting

Fatima
character in: 9 Bluebeard

**fatti maschii, parole fem-
ine** 29 deeds are manly words
are womanish
motto of: 8 Maryland

fatty 4 oily 5 lardy, suety
6 greasy 7 buttery 8 blubbery
9 shortened

fatuous 5 inane, silly, vapid
6 obtuse, simple, stupid 7 asinine, foolish, idiotic, moronic,
puerile, vacuous, witless 8 besotted, imbecile 9 brainless,
senseless 10 ridiculous

faucet 3 tap 4 cock 5 spout,
valve 6 nozzle, outlet, spigot
7 bibcock

Faulkland
character in: 9 The Rivals
author: 8 Sheridan

Faulkner, William
author of: 7 The Bear 8 Sar-
toris 9 Sanctuary, The Hamlet 10 The Reivers 11 As I
Lay Dying 13 Light in Au-
gust 15 Absalom Absalom!
17 Intruder in the Dust
18 The Sound and the Fury
fictional county:
13 Yoknapatawpha

fault 3 bug, sin 4 flaw, slip,
snag 5 blame, crime, error,
guilt, stain, taint, wrong 6 defect, foible, glitch, impugn
7 blemish, blunder, censure,
failing, frailty, misdeed, mistake, offense, reprove 8 drawback, weakness 9 criticize,
infirmity, oversight, weak
point 10 deficiency, impediment, negligence, peccadillo,
wrongdoing 11 culpability,
dereliction, misdemeanor,
shortcoming 12 imperfection,
indiscretion 13 answerability,
transgression 14 accountability,
responsibility

faultfind 3 nag 4 beef, carp,
kick 5 cavil, gripe, knock
6 deride, squawk 7 nitpick
8 complain 9 criticize

faultfinder 3 nag 4 bear, crab
5 crank 6 carper, censor, critic,
grouch 7 caviler, grouser
8 quibbler, sorehead 9 deroga-
tor, detractor, Mrs Grundy,
nitpicker 10 bellyacher, complainer, curmudgeon, fuddy-
duddy, fussbudget

faultfinding 4 beef, kick
5 gripe 6 squawk 7 beefing,
carping, griping, kicking, nagging 9 complaint, criticism,
squawking 10 nitpicking
11 complaining, criticizing

faultless 5 ideal 7 correct, perfect 8 accurate, flawless 9 exemplary 10 immaculate,
impeccable 11 unblemished
13 unimpeachable 14 irre-
proachable, without blemish

faulty 3 bad 4 awry 5 amiss,
false, wrong 7 injured, unsound 8 impaired, inferior,
mistaken 9 defective, deficient,
erroneous, imperfect, incorrect 10 inadequate, out of order, unreliable
14 unsatisfactory

faun
form: 5 deity
location: 5 rural

Fauna see 7 Bona Dea

Faunus
origin: 5 Roman
form: 5 deity

location: 5 woods
also called: 5 Inuus **6** Fatuus
king of: 6 Latium
father: 5 Picus
son: 7 Latinus
corresponds to: 3 Pan

Faure, Gabriel Urbain
born: 6 France **7** Pamiers
composer of: 5 Dolly **6** Pavane **7** Ballade, Mirages, Requiem, Shylock **8** Penelope
9 Fantaisie, Promethee
12 Le Jardin Clos **13** La Chanson d'Eve **14** La Bonne Chanson **18** L'Horizon Chimerique, Pelleas et Melisande **21** Masques et Bergamasques

Faust
author: 12 Johann Goethe
character: 6 Wagner
8 Gretchen **10** Homunculus
11 Helen of Troy
14 Mephistopheles

Faust
opera by: 6 Gounod
character: 9 Valentine
10 Marguerite
14 Mephistopheles

Faustulus
vocation: 8 herdsman, shepherd
raised: 5 Remus **7** Romulus

faute de mieux 24 for lack of something better

faux pas 4 goof **5** boner, error, gaffe, lapse **6** boo-boo, howler, slip-up **7** blooper, blunder, mistake **9** false step **11** impropriety **12** indiscretion

favela 4 slum **10** shanty town

Favell, Jack
character in: 7 Rebecca
author: 9 Du Maurier

Favonius
origin: 5 Roman
personifies: 8 west wind

favor 3 aid **4** abet, back, gift, help, like **5** be for, fancy, humor **6** assist, esteem, foster, oblige, pamper, prefer, succor, uphold **7** approve, commend, endorse, go in for, indulge, kind act, memento, present, service, support **8** advocacy, approval, courtesy, espousal, good deed, good turn, goodwill, largesse, look like, resemble, sanction, side with, souvenir **9** encourage, patronage, patronize, smile upon, take after, use gently **10** act of grace, use lightly **11** accommodate, approbation, be partial to, benefaction, countenance, good opinion **12** be the image of, championship, commendation, dispensation,

kindly regard **13** accommodation, goodwill token

favorable 4 fair, good, kind **6** benign, timely **7** helpful, hopeful **8** amicable, friendly, salutary **9** approving, conducive, opportune, promising **10** auspicious, beneficial, convenient, propitious **11** predisposed, serviceable, sympathetic **12** advantageous, commendatory, well-disposed

favorable opinion 6 esteem, regard **7** respect **8** approval **10** admiration **12** appreciation

favorably disposed 7 willing **8** amenable, inclined, obliging **9** agreeable **11** sympathetic

favorite 3 pet **5** fancy, jewel **6** choice **7** darling, special **9** best-liked, preferred **11** front-runner, most popular **13** fair-haired one **14** apple of one's eye

favoritism 4 bias **10** partiality **12** one-sidedness, partisanship

Fawley, Jude and Drusilla
characters in: 14 Jude the Obscure
author: 5 Hardy

fawn 5 toady **6** pander **7** flatter, truckle **8** pay court **9** be servile, seek favor **12** be obsequious, bow and scrape

fawning 7 servile **8** flattery, toadying **9** adulating, adulation, truckling **10** flattering, obsequious **11** sycophantic **12** ingratiating **14** obsequiousness

faze 4 fret **5** abash, daunt, upset, worry **6** bother, flurry, rattle **7** disturb, fluster, perturb **8** confound **10** discomfit, embarrass **10** discompose, disconcert

fazed 5 upset **7** abashed, ruffled **8** agitated, bothered, confused **9** chagrined, unsettled **10** confounded, distracted, nonplussed **11** embarrassed **12** disconcerted

FBI, The
character: 10 Arthur Ward **21** Inspector Lewis Erskine
cast: 12 Philip Abbott **16** Efrem Zimbalist Jr

fealty 7 loyalty **8** devotion, fidelity **9** adherence, constancy **10** allegiance, attachment **12** faithfulness

fear 3 awe **4** care **5** alarm, bogey, dread, panic, qualm, worry **6** dismay, esteem, fright, horror, phobia, revere, terror, threat, wonder **7** anxiety, bugaboo, bugbear, con-

cern, quaking, specter **8** affright, venerate **9** cowardice, nightmare, reverence, shudder at, tremble at **10** be afraid of, be scared of, feel awe for, foreboding, take fright, veneration **11** trepidation **12** apprehension, perturbation **13** consternation **14** be frightened of

fearful 4 dire **5** awful, dread, eerie, lurid, timid **6** afraid, aghast, horrid, scared, uneasy **7** alarmed, anxious, ghastly, macabre, nervous, ominous, panicky, worried **8** alarming, dreadful, horrible, shocking, sinister, skittish, terrible, timorous **9** appalling, concerned, diffident, frightful, tremulous **10** formidable, frightened, portentous, terrifying **11** distressing, frightening, intimidated **12** apprehensive, fainthearted **13** panic-stricken **14** chicken-hearted

fearfulness fear **5** alarm, dread, panic **6** fright, terror **7** anguish, anxiety **8** timidity **11** trepidation **12** apprehension

fearless 4 bold **5** brave **6** daring, gritty, heroic, plucky **7** doughty, gallant, valiant **8** intrepid, unafraid, valorous **9** audacious, confident, dauntless, unabashed, undaunted **10** courageous, undismayed **11** adventurous, indomitable, lionhearted, unflinching, unshrinking, venturesome, without fear **12** stout-hearted

fearlessness 4 grit **5** pluck, valor **7** bravery, courage **8** boldness **10** confidence **13** dauntlessness

Fear of Flying
author: 9 Erica Jong

feasible 6 viable **7** fitting, politic **8** possible, suitable, workable **9** advisable, desirable **10** achievable, attainable, reasonable **11** appropriate, conceivable, practicable

feast 4 dine, fete **5** festa, gorge **6** bounty **7** banquet, holiday, jubilee, surplus **8** feast day, festival **9** bacchanal, saint's day **10** gluttonize, gormandize, have a feast, rich supply **11** celebration, eat one's fill, elegant meal, wine and dine

feat 3 act **4** deed, task **6** action, stroke **7** exploit, triumph **8** maneuver **9** adventure **10** attainment, enterprise **11** achievement, performance, tour de force **14** accomplishment

feather 4 down, kind, sort
5 adorn, eider, plume, quill
7 bristle, plumage, variety
9 character, turn an oar

featherbrained 4 dumb
5 silly 6 simple, stupid 7 foolish, witless 9 brainless
12 muddleheaded, simple-
minded 13 rattle-brained
14 scatterbrained

feather in one's cap
5 honor 6 credit 11 distinction

feather one's nest 6 enrich
15 fill one's pockets

feature, features 3 see
4 mark, star 5 fancy, trait
6 aspect, play up, visage
7 display, earmark, imagine,
picture, present, quality 8 envision, hallmark, headline,
main item, property 9 attribute, character, highlight, specialty, spotlight 10 conceive
of, lineaments 14 characteristic

February *see box*

Fechner, Gustav Theodore
nationality: 6 German
founder of: 22 experimental
psychology

fecit 6 he made (it) 7 she made
(it)

feckless 3 lax 5 slack 6 re-

February
event: 4 Lent 5 Purim
8 Leap year 9 Mardi
Gras 12 Ash Wednes-
day, Groundhog Day
(2)
flower: 6 violet
8 primrose
French: 7 Fevrier
gem: 8 amethyst
German: 7 Februar
holiday: 9 Candlemas
(2) 13 Valentine's Day
(14) 14 Chinese New
Year 16 Lincoln's Birth-
day (12) 19 Washing-
ton's Birthday (22)
Italian: 8 Febbraio
Latin: 6 Februa
number of days:
10 twenty-nine (every 4
years) 11 twenty-eight
origin of name:
7 Februus
Roman god of:
12 purification
place in year:
Gregorian: 6 second
Roman: 7 twelfth
Spanish: 7 Febrero
Zodiac signs: 6 Pisces
8 Aquarius

---

miss 8 careless, heedless
9 negligent, worthless 10 neglectful 11 thoughtless
13 irresponsible

Fecundity
goddess of: 5 Freia, Freya

Federalist Party
president belonging to:
5 Adams 10 Washington

federate 5 unite 7 combine
12 join together

federation 5 union 6 league
7 combine 8 alliance 9 coalition, syndicate 10 sisterhood
11 association, brotherhood,
confederacy 12 amalgamation
13 confederation

fee 4 fare, hire, toll, wage
5 price 6 charge, salary, tariff
7 payment, stipend 8 emolument 10 commission, honorarium 12 compensation,
remuneration 13 consideration

feeble 4 flat, lame, poor, puny,
tame, thin, weak 5 faint, frail,
vapid 6 ailing, flabby, flimsy,
infirm, meager, paltry, senile,
sickly, slight 7 fragile, insipid
8 decrepit, delicate, disabled,
impotent, weakened 9 colorless, declining, doddering, enervated, enfeebled, forceless,
not strong, powerless 10 inadequate, spiritless, wishy-
washy 11 debilitated, ineffective, ineffectual

feeble-minded 4 dull 6 senile,
stupid 7 moronic 8 backward,
childish, retarded 9 imbecilic,
senseless, subnormal 10 half-
witted, weak-minded 12 mentally slow

feeble-mindedness 6 dotage,
idiocy 8 dullness, senility,
slowness 9 denseness, stupidity 11 retardation

feed 3 eat 4 fare, fuel, mash
5 cater, feast, graze 6 devour,
fodder, forage, foster, viands
7 augment, bolster, consume,
gratify, nourish, nurture, pasture, satisfy, support, sustain
8 maintain, take food, victuals 9 encourage, foodstuff,
provender 10 minister to, provisions, strengthen 11 comestibles, nourishment, wine and
dine

feeder 6 branch 7 channel
9 tributary

feel 3 paw, see 4 know
5 grope, press, probe, reach,
sense, think, touch 6 finger,
fumble, handle, makeup, notice 7 believe, discern, feeling,
observe, palpate, texture
8 perceive 9 be aware of, be
moved by, character, sensa-

tion 10 comprehend, experience, manipulate, suffer from,
understand 11 be convinced,
be stirred by, be touched by,
composition

feel aversion toward 4 hate
5 abhor 6 detest 7 despise
9 abominate, can't abide, can't
stand 11 can't stomach 12 be
revolted by 13 find repugnant,
find repulsive 14 view with
horror

feeler 7 antenna 8 proposal,
tentacle 10 experiment 12 trial
balloon

feel indebted 10 appreciate,
be beholden, be grateful
13 feel obligated

feeling 4 aura, pity, view, zeal
5 ardor, gusto, sense, verve
6 fervor, spirit, thrill, warmth
7 concern, emotion, opinion,
passion 8 attitude, instinct, reaction, response, sympathy
9 affection, awareness, intuition, sensation, sentiment, vehemence 10 atmosphere,
compassion, enthusiasm,
impression 11 earnestness, inclination, point of view, sensibility, sensitivity

feeling life is wearisome
Latin: 12 taedium vitae

feelings 3 ego 5 pride 8 emotions, passions 10 self-esteem
13 sensibilities, sensitivities
16 susceptibilities

feel pain 4 ache, hurt 5 smart
6 suffer 7 agonize 9 be in agony 11 be tormented 12 be in
distress

Feenix, Cousin
character in: 12 Dombey and
Son
author: 7 Dickens

feet 4 dogs, pads, paws
5 hoofs 6 hooves 8 gunboats,
tootsies

feign 4 fake, sham 5 forge, put
on 6 affect, assume, cook up,
invent, make up 7 concoct,
pretend 8 simulate 9 fabricate
11 counterfeit, make a show
of, make believe

feigned 4 fake, sham 5 bogus,
phony 6 ersatz 8 spurious
9 imitation, insincere, pretended, simulated 10 artificial
11 counterfeit, make-believe

feint 4 hoax, mask, move, pass,
ploy, ruse, wile 5 blind, bluff,
dodge, trick 6 gambit 7 pretext 8 artifice, maneuver, pretense 9 stratagem
10 subterfuge 13 feigned
attack

Feldman, Marty
born: 6 London 7 England
roles: 11 Silent Movie
17 Young Frankenstein
24 The Last Remake of
Beau Geste

feldspar
varieties: 8 sunstone 9 amazonite, moonstone

felicitate 4 hail 6 salute
10 wish one joy 11 rejoice
with 12 congratulate 18 give
one's best wishes 28 wish
many happy returns of the
day

felicitations 3 joy 6 cheers
9 blessings, greetings 10 best
wishes, good wishes 11 compliments, salutations 12 pat on
the back 15 congratulations
24 many happy returns of the
day

felicitous 3 apt 5 happy 6 joyful, joyous 7 fitting, germane,
well-put 8 inspired, pleasing,
relevant, suitable, well-said
9 effective, fortunate, pertinent 10 propitious, well-
chosen 11 appropriate

felicity 5 bliss, charm, grace,
knack, skill 6 heaven, nicety
7 aptness, delight, ecstasy, fitness 8 paradise 9 beatitude,
happiness 12 blissfulness 13 effectiveness 15 appropriateness

Felix the Cat
creator: 11 Pat Sullivan

fell 4 raze 5 level 7 cut down,
destroy, hew down 8 demolish 9 knock down, prostrate

Feller, Bob (Robert)
nickname: 11 Rapid Robert
sport: 8 baseball
position: 7 pitcher
team: 16 Cleveland Indians

Fellini, Federico
director of: 8 Amarcord, Casanova, La Strada 11 La
Dolce Vita 15 Nights of Cabiria 18 Juliet of the Spirits

fellow 3 boy, guy, man, pal
4 chap, chum, dude, mate,
peer 5 equal 6 friend 7 comrade, consort 8 coworker 9 associate, colleague, companion
10 compatriot

fellow-conspirator 4 ally
6 cohort 7 abettor 8 henchman 9 accessory 11 confederate 12 collaborator

fellow creature 6 mortal, person 10 individual

fellow feeling 6 regard 7 kinship 8 affinity, fondness 10 attraction, partiality

fellowship 5 amity 7 society

8 intimacy 10 affability, cordiality, fraternity, friendship
11 amicability, association,
brotherhood, comradeship, familiarity, sociability 12 friendliness 13 companionship

felon 5 crook, cruel, thief
6 fierce, outlaw, wicked
7 convict, illegal, villain,
whitlow 8 criminal, gangster,
jailbird, murderer 10 lawbreaker, malefactor 11 public
enemy 12 inflammation

felony 5 arson, crime 6 murder 7 assault, misdeed, offense,
robbery 8 burglary 9 blackmail 10 kidnapping, wrongdoing 12 capital offense

female 3 cow, dam, hen, sow
4 girl, mare 5 bitch, tabby,
woman 6 heifer 7 distaff,
womanly 8 feminine, ladylike
9 womanlike

feminine 4 soft 5 woman
6 dainty, female, gentle 7 distaff, girlish, womanly 8 delicate, ladylike 10 femalelike,
like a woman 14 of the female sex

femininity 8 softness 10 femaleness, gentleness 11 girl-
ishness, womanliness
12 feminineness 13 female
quality

femme 4 wife 5 woman

femme de chambre 9 lady's
maid 11 chambermaid

femme fatale 4 vamp 5 siren
7 charmer 10 fatal woman, seductress 11 enchantress

femur
bone of: 5 thigh 8 upper leg

fen 3 bog 4 moor, sump
5 marsh, swale, swamp 6 bottom, morass, slough 7 lowland, wetland 8 quagmire

fence 3 pen 4 coop, duel, gird,
rail 5 hedge, hem in 6 corral,
secure, wall in 7 barrier, confine, palings 8 encircle, palisade, stockade, surround
9 barricade, encompass
11 cross swords

fencing
equipment: 4 epee, foil,
mask 5 saber, sword
8 plastron
part of weapon: 5 blade,
forte, guard 6 foible, handle,
medium, pommel
term: 3 hit 5 prime, sixte,
touch 6 octave, quarte,
quinte, tierce 7 on guard,
seconde, septime
deceptive move: 5 feint
movement: 4 beat 5 lunge,
parry 6 double, fleche,

thrust 7 advance, cutover,
recover, retreat, riposte
9 disengage 11 froissement

fend 2 do 5 avert, avoid, parry,
repel, shift 6 manage 7 keep
off, make out, provide, repulse, support, survive, ward
off 8 push away

fender 3 pad 4 curb 5 guard
6 buffer, bumper, shield,
sluice 7 cushion, railing
9 fireguard, protector 10 cow-
catcher, fire screen, protection,
wheel guard

fend off 5 avert, dodge, evade,
parry, repel 6 escape 7 ward
off 8 sidestep, stave off

fennel
botanical name: 17 Foenicu-
lum vulgare
family: 7 parsley
varieties: 3 dog 4 wild
5 giant 8 Florence 9 com-
mon dog 11 common
giant
mythical aid to: 9 fortifier
11 aphrodisiac, slenderizer
12 rejuvenation, stops hiccups 16 restores eyesight
use: 4 duck, fish 5 bread,
rolls 7 chicken 8 apple pie
16 seafood casserole

Fenrir
also: 6 Fenris
origin: 12 Scandinavian
form: 4 wolf 7 monster
father: 4 Loki
mother: 9 Angerboda, An-
grbodha, Angurboda
sister: 3 Hel
brother: 11 Iormungandr,
Jormungandr 14 Midgard
Serpent
ate: 4 Odin 5 Othin
killed by: 5 Vidar

Fenris see 6 Fenrir

Fenton
character in: 22 The Merry
Wives of Windsor
author: 11 Shakespeare

feral 4 wild 6 brutal, deadly,
ferine, fierce, savage 7 bestial,
untamed, vicious 9 ferocious
12 uncultivated
14 undomesticated

Ferber, Edna
author of: 5 Giant, So Big
8 Cimarron, Show Boat
9 Ice Palace, Stage Door
(with George S Kaufman)
13 Dinner at Eight (with
George S Kaufman), Sara-
toga Trunk 14 The Royal
Family (with George S
Kaufman)

Ferdinand
character in: 10 The Tempest
author: 11 Shakespeare

Ferdinand
character in: **16** Love's Labour's Lost
author: **11** Shakespeare

Ferd'nand
creator: **3** Mik **13** Dahl
Mikkelsen

Feria
origin: **5** Roman
form: **7** holiday

Fermat, Pierre de
field: **11** mathematics
nationality: **6** French
discovered: **16** analytic
geometry

ferment 4 foam, mold, sour,
turn **5** froth, yeast **6** enzyme,
fester, leaven, seethe, tumult,
unrest, uproar **7** agitate, inflame, smolder, turmoil **8** bubble up, disquiet **9** agitation,
commotion, leavening **10** disruption, effervesce, turbulence
11 be turbulent, fomentation

fermented 6 soured, worked
7 seethed **8** agitated

Fermi, Enrico
field: **7** physics
nationality: **7** Italian
developed: **10** atomic bomb
20 uranium fission theory
awarded: **10** Nobel Prize

fern *see box*

fernet-branca
type: **8** aperitif
origin: **5** Italy
flavor: **4** herb

Fern Hill
author: **11** Dylan Thomas

ferocious 6 brutal, deadly,
fierce, savage **7** bestial, brutish, enraged, violent **8** fiendish, maddened, ravening,
ruthless **9** atrocious, barbarous,
merciless, murderous, predatory, rapacious **10** relentless
11 cold-blooded
12 bloodthirsty

ferocity 7 cruelty **8** savagery
9 barbarity, brutality, harshness **10** fierceness, inhumanity, savageness **11** brutishness,
viciousness **12** ruthlessness

Ferrer, Jose
real name: **33** Jose Vincente
Ferrer de Otero y Cintron
wife: **8** Uta Hagen **15** Rosemary Clooney
born: **8** Santurce **10** Puerto
Rico
roles: **7** I Accuse **9** Joan of
Arc **11** Moulin Rouge, Ship
of Fools **14** The Caine Mutiny **16** Cyrano de Bergerac
(Oscar), Lawrence of Ara-
bia **24** The Greatest Story
Ever Told

fern
varieties: **3** air, cup, lip, man, oak, saw **4** ball, blue, claw,
deer, dish, felt, fire, gold, hand, iron, king, lace, lady,
male, moss, nest, pine, sago, tara, tree, wall, wart,
wood **5** beard, beech, chain, cloak, fancy, glade, glory,
grape, grass, hedge, holly, marsh, plume, royal, strap,
swamp, sweet, sword, table, water, whisk **6** adder's, bamboo, basket, Boston, button, carrot, coffee, cotton, cuplet,
dagger, ladder, meadow, mother, ribbon, shield, silver,
tongue, turnip, winter **7** bladder, boulder, brittle, bulblet,
crested, emerald, feather, Fee's lip, fragile, Goldie's, hack-
saw, Halberd, hammock, leather, New York, ostrich, parsley, peacock, rainbow, walking **8** bear-foot, bear's-paw,
cinnamon, climbing, elk's-horn, fishtail, floating, florist's,
fragrant, hairy lip, Hartford, licorice, mosquito, Nebraska,
Savannah, snuffbox, soft tree, staghorn **9** asparagus,
bird's-nest, black tree, blond tree, Christmas, common
cup, deer's-foot, downy wood, flowering, glossy cup,
hare's foot, long beech, sensitive, vegetable, Venus hair,
viscid lip, wavy cloak, woolly lip **10** Alabama lip, Boott's
wood, broad beech, deer-tongue, Duff's sword, erect
sword, five-finger, hay-scented, lady ground, maidenhair,
scented oak, shoestring, silver tree, silver-back, silver-lace,
silver-leaf, slender lip, strawberry, upside-down, woolly
tree **11** Braun's holly, coastal wood, Coville's lip, crested
felt, crested wood, dwarf Boston, elephant-ear, Fendler's
lip, hart's-tongue, interrupted, Jamaica gold, leatherleaf,
leatherwood, narrow beech, netted chain, Northern oak,
Parry's cloak, Pursh's holly, rabbit's-foot, rattlesnake,
Sierra water, walking leaf **12** Adder's-tongue, American
wall, berry bladder, Clinton's wood, Dudley's holly, Eaton's shield, English hedge, Hawaiian tree, Java staghorn,
limestone oak, mountain wood, Northern lady, resurrection, Southern lady, squirrel-foot, toothed sword, Western
holly, Western sword **13** California lip, Cleveland's lip,
Dudley's shield, European chain, fan maidenhair, Fendler's cloak, Florida ribbon, leathery grape, Malay climbing, mountain holly, Northern holly, prickly shield,
Prince-of-Wales, spinulose wood, Tasmanian tree, triangle
water, Virginia chain, wild bird's nest **14** Anderson's
holly, Australian tree, bulblet bladder, California gold,
common staghorn, dissected grape, dwarf asparagus, hen-
and-chickens, imbricate sword, silver-king tree, West Indian tree **15** American parsley, California cloak, California holly, Delta maidenhair, East Indian holly, European
parsley, mountain bladder, mountain parsley **16** black-
stemmed tree, daisy-leaved grape, Farley maidenhair, Tassel maidenhair, Tracy's maidenhair **17** Bermuda maidenhair, brittle maidenhair, climbing bird's nest, walking
maidenhair **18** Aleutian maidenhair, American maidenhair, Barbados maidenhair, Northern maidenhair, Trailing
maidenhair, Triangular staghorn **20** Australian maidenhair, California maidenhair

ferret out 5 dig up **6** detect
7 find out, root out, uncover,
unearth **8** discover
9 ascertain

fertile 4 rich **5** loamy **6** fecund **8** creative, fruitful, original, prolific **9** fructuous,
ingenious, inventive, luxuriant, plenteous **10** fecundated,
fertilized, fructified, generative,
productive, vegetative
11 imaginative, resourceful
12 reproductive

Fertility
god of: **7** Bacchus, Mutinus
8 Lupercus, Picumnus
goddess of: **4** Isis **5** Fauna
6 Athena, Athene, Brigit,
Libera, Pallas, Saitis, Tellus
7 Astarte, Berchta, Bona
Dea, Demeter, Perchta
11 Tritogeneia **12** Pallas
Athena **16** Alalcomean
Athena

fertilize 6 enrich, manure
8 fructify **9** fecundate, polli-

nate **10** impregnate, inseminate

fertilizer 4 dung, muck **5** guano **6** manure, potash **7** compost **8** bonemeal, dressing **10** enrichener **14** superphosphate

fervent 4 keen **5** eager, fiery **6** ardent, devout, fervid, fierce, hearty, heated **7** burning, earnest, intense, zealous **8** spirited, vehement **9** heartfelt **10** passionate **11** impassioned, warmhearted **12** enthusiastic, wholehearted

fervid 5 eager **6** ardent, raging **7** burning, earnest, fanatic, fervent, intense, zealous **8** spirited **10** passionate **11** impassioned **12** all-consuming

fervor 4 fire, zeal, zest **5** ardor, gusto, piety, verve **6** warmth **7** passion **9** animation, eagerness, intensity, vehemence **10** devoutness, enthusiasm, heartiness **11** earnestness, seriousness **14** purposefulness

Feste
character in: **12** Twelfth Night
author: **11** Shakespeare

fester 3 rot, vex **4** fret, gall, grow, rile **5** chafe, pique **6** nettle, plague, rankle **7** blister, form pus, inflame, putrefy, smolder, torment **8** irritate, ulcerate **9** intensify, suppurate

festering 6 putrid **7** rotting **8** infected, inflamed, rankling **10** putrefying **11** suppurating

festina lente 15 make haste slowly

festival 4 fete, gala **5** feast **6** fiesta **7** gala day, holiday, jubilee **8** carnival, jamboree **11** celebration, festivities

festival of see box

festive 3 gay **4** gala **5** jolly, merry **6** festal, joyous **7** larkish, playful **8** sportive **9** convivial **10** frolicsome **11** celebratory **12** lighthearted

festivity 3 joy **4** fete, gala **5** feast, mirth **6** fiesta, gaiety, levity **7** fanfare, jollity, jubilee, revelry **8** festival, jamboree **9** merriment, rejoicing **11** celebration, merrymaking

festoon 3 lei **4** swag **5** chain, curve **6** wreath **7** garland, hanging **8** decorate

fetch 3 get **4** cost **5** bring, go for, yield **6** afford, obtain **7** procure, realize, sell for **8** amount to, retrieve

fetching 6 divine, lovely **8** adorable, becoming, charming, engaging, pleasing **9** appealing **10** attractive, delightful **11** captivating

fete 4 gala **5** feast, party, treat **6** regale **7** banquet, holiday **8** carnival, festival **9** bal masque **11** celebration, garden party, wine and dine **13** fete champetre

fete champetre 11 garden party **15** outdoor festival

fetid 4 foul, gamy, rank **5** fusty, moldy, musty, nasty **6** putrid, rancid, rotten **7** noisome, stenchy, tainted **8** mephitic, stifling, stinking **9** stenchful **10** malodorous **11** ill-smelling, suffocating

fetish 4 idol, joss **5** charm, craze, image, mania, totem **6** amulet, scarab **7** passion **8** idee fixe, talisman **9** obsession **10** golden calf, phylactery **11** magic object **12** superstition **13** preoccupation

fetter 4 bind, bond, cage, curb, yoke **5** chain, tie up **6** duress, hamper, hinder, hobble, impede, shut in, tether **7** confine, durance, manacle, pin down, shackle, tie down, trammel, truss up **8** bracelet,

Festival of
Adonis: **6** Adonia
Apollo: **5** Delia **8** Didymaea **9** Delphinia **12** Daphnephoria
Athena: **6** Lenaea **8** Diipolia **9** Pyanepsia **11** Oschophoria
Attica: **13** Rural Dionysia **14** Lesser Dionysia
Bacchus: **11** Bacchanalia
Boeotians: **7** Daedala **13** Little Doedala
Demeter: **5** Haloa
Dionysus: **5** Haloa **8** Dionysia
flowers: **11** Anthesteria
Greeks: **6** Heraea **9** Pyanepsia **11** Scirophoria, Skirophoria **13** Thesmorphoria
Persephone: **5** Haloa
Roman: **8** Floralia, Matralia **9** Lemuralia, Liberalia **10** Larentalia, Lupercalia, Matronalia, Parentalia, Saturnalia
spring: **11** Anthesteria
wine: **11** Anthesteria
Zeus: **6** Diasia **8** Didymaea

encumber, handcuff, hold back, restrain **9** hindrance, restraint **13** put into bilbos **15** bind hand and foot

feud 3 row **4** fuss, spat, tiff **5** argue, brawl, clash, set-to **6** affray, bicker, breach, enmity, fracas, schism, strife **7** discord, dispute, faction, ill will, quarrel, rupture, wrangle **8** argument, bad blood, be at odds, clashing, conflict, disagree, squabble, vendetta **9** animosity, bickering, hostility **10** falling out **11** altercation, controversy **12** disagreement, hard feelings

Feud, The
author: **12** Thomas Berger

feudal lord
Japanese: **6** daimyo

Feuerbach, Anselm
born: **6** Speyer **7** Germany
artwork: **9** Iphigenia **15** Judgment of Paris, Plato's Symposium **18** The Fall of the Titans

fever 4 fire, heat **5** ardor, craze, flush, furor **6** desire, frenzy, warmth **7** ferment, illness, pyrexia **8** delirium, sickness **9** agitation **10** enthusiasm, excitement **11** temperature **12** restlessness

feverish 3 hot **5** fiery **6** ardent, red-hot **7** burning, excited, fanatic, febrile, fervent, fevered, flushed, parched, pyretic, zealous **8** frenzied, inflamed, restless **9** impatient, overeager, wrought-up **10** high-strung, passionate **11** impassioned

few 4 rare, some, thin **5** scant **6** meager, paltry, scanty, scarce, skimpy, sparse, unique **7** handful, limited, not many, several, unusual **8** exiguous, piddling, sporadic, uncommon **9** hardly any **10** infrequent, occasional **11** scarcely any, small number **13** infinitesimal, insignificant **14** inconsiderable

Fezziwig
character in: **15** A Christmas Carol
author: **7** Dickens

fiance, fiancee 6 future **7** engaged, pledge **8** intended, promised **9** affianced, betrothed, bride-to-be, groom-to-be **10** bride-elect, groom-elect

fiasco 4 bomb, flop **5** botch **6** fizzle **7** debacle, washout **8** disaster **10** nonsuccess

fiat 3 act, law **4** rule **5** edict, order, ukase **6** decree, dictum,

ruling 7 command, mandate
11 commandment

fiat lux 15 let there be light

fib 3 lie **5** hedge **7** fiction, untruth **8** white lie **9** half-truth, invention **10** equivocate **11** fabrication, harmless lie, prevaricate **13** falsification, prevarication, tell a white lie **15** stretch the truth **17** misrepresentation

fiber 4 hemp, jute, silk **5** fibre, linen, nylon, rayon, shred, sinew, sisal **6** cotton, dacron, manila, nature, strand, thread **7** quality, texture **8** filament **9** character, polyester, structure

fibrolite
　source: 5 Burma, Mogok

fibula
　bone of: 8 lower leg

fickle 5 giddy **6** fitful **7** erratic, flighty **8** shifting, unstable, unsteady, variable, volatile, wavering **9** frivolous, mercurial, spasmodic, whimsical **10** capricious, changeable, inconstant, irresolute, unreliable **11** fluctuating, light-headed, vacillating **12** inconsistent **13** feather-headed, unpredictable, untrustworthy **14** featherbrained

fiction 3 fib, lie **4** play, tale, yarn **5** fable, novel **7** fantasy, forgery, novella, romance, whopper **8** tall tale **9** falsehood, invention, narrative **10** concoction, short novel, short story **11** fabrication, imagination, made-up story **12** storytelling **13** prevarication **16** cock-and-bull story

fictional 6 made-up **8** invented, literary, mythical **9** storybook **10** fictitious **11** theoretical **12** hypothetical

fictitious 4 fake, sham **5** bogus, false, phony **6** forged, made-up, unreal, untrue **7** assumed, feigned **8** fanciful, invented, mythical, spurious **9** imaginary, legendary, simulated, trumped-up, unfounded **10** apocryphal, artificial, fabricated, fraudulent, not genuine **11** counterfeit **14** supposititious

fiddle 3 bow, saw, toy **4** fool **5** cheat, dally, fraud **6** dawdle, monkey, potter, putter, tamper, trifle, violin **7** falsify, finagle, fritter, swindle **9** deception **10** fool around, mess around **12** monkey around

Fidei Defensor 18 Defender of the Faith
　title of: 17 English sovereigns

Fidelio
　opera by: 9 Beethoven
　character: 5 Rocco **7** Leonora (Fidelio), Pizarro **8** Fernando **9** Florestan

fidelity 5 honor **6** fealty **7** honesty, loyalty, probity **8** accuracy, devotion **9** adherence, closeness, constancy, exactness, good faith, integrity, precision, sincerity **10** allegiance, exactitude **11** earnestness, reliability, staunchness **12** faithfulness, truthfulness **14** correspondency **15** trueheartedness, trustworthiness

Fides
　origin: 5 Roman
　personifies: 9 good faith

fidget 4 fret, fuss, jerk, stew, toss **5** chafe, worry **6** jiggle, squirm, twitch, wiggle, writhe **7** twiddle, wriggle

fidgety 5 antsy, fussy, jerky, jumpy **6** uneasy **7** jittery, nervous, restive, squirmy, twitchy, unquiet **8** restless **9** impatient, irritable, tremulous **12** apprehensive

fief 4 land **6** domain, estate **9** territory

field 3 lea **4** area, grab, lawn, line, mead, turf, yard **5** arena, catch, court, front, glove, green, heath, lists, orbit, range, reach, realm, scope, sward, sweep **6** circle, common, course, domain, extent, meadow, pick up, region, sphere **7** acreage, calling, diamond, expanse, pasture, run down, stretch **8** clearing, province, retrieve, spectrum **9** bailiwick, grassland, territory **10** department, occupation, profession **12** battleground

Field, Sally
　born: 10 Pasadena CA
　roles: 5 Sybil **6** Gidget **8** Norma Rae (Oscar) **9** Punchline, Surrender **12** The Flying Nun **14** Murphy's Romance **15** Absence of Malice **16** Places in the Heart (Oscar) **18** Smokey and the Bandit

Fielding, Cecil
　character in: 15 A Passage to India
　author: 7 Forster

Fielding, Henry
　author of: 6 Amelia **7** Shamela **8** Tom Jones, Tom Thumb **12** Jonathan Wild **13** Joseph Andrews

Field of Blood 8 Aceldama

Fields, W C
　real name: 23 William Claude Dukenfield
　born: 14 Philadelphia PA
　roles: 5 Poppy **8** Micawber **11** The Bank Dick **16** David Copperfield **17** My Little Chickadee **27** Never Give a Sucker an Even Break

Fields of Mourning
　location: 10 underworld
　inhabited by: 14 shades of lovers
　　lovers who died by:
　　7 suicide

Fields of Visions, The
　author: 12 Wright Morris

fiend 5 beast, brute, demon, devil, Satan **6** dybbuk **7** incubus, monster, villain **8** succubus **9** barbarian, hellhound, scoundrel **10** evil spirit **12** wicked person **14** devil incarnate **16** prince of darkness

fiendish 4 evil, foul **5** cruel **6** wicked **7** demonic, heinous, impious, satanic, vicious **8** barbaric, demoniac, devilish **9** monstrous, nefarious **10** demoniacal, diabolical, villainous

fierce 4 fell, wild **5** cruel, feral, fiery **6** brutal, fervid, raging, savage, strong **7** enraged, extreme, fearful, fervent, furious, intense, leonine, untamed, violent **8** horrible, menacing, powerful, ravening, ravenous, terrible, tigerish, uncurbed, vehement **9** barbarous, bellicose, ferocious, impetuous, merciless, truculent, unbridled, voracious **10** immoderate, inordinate, passionate **11** threatening **12** bloodthirsty, overpowering, overwhelming, unrestrained
　French: 8 farouche

fierceness 4 zeal **7** passion **8** ferocity, wildness **9** pugnacity, vehemence **10** savageness

fiery 5 afire, angry, irate **6** ablaze, alight, ardent, fervid, fierce, red-hot, torrid **7** blazing, burning, febrile, fervent, fevered, flaming, glaring, glowing, peppery, pyretic, violent, zealous **8** choleric, feverish, flashing, headlong, inflamed, spirited, vehement, wrathful **9** excitable, hotheaded, impetuous, impulsive, irascible, irritable **10** full of fire, high-strung, mettlesome, passionate **11** hottempered, impassioned, precipitate **12** enthusiastic

fiesta 4 fete, gala **5** feast, party **6** picnic **7** funfair **8** carnival, feast day, festival, jamboree **9** saint's day **10** block

fig 348

party, observance, street fair **11** celebration **13** commemoration **15** festive occasion

fig 5 Ficus
varieties: **3** keg, sea **4** bush, cape, Java, Zulu **5** cedar, clown, Congo, rusty **6** common, Devil's, exotic, golden, Indian, Kaffir, Mysore, sacred **7** Barbary, cluster, oakleaf, spotted, weeping **8** climbing, creeping, Dracaena, mulberry, sycamore **9** Hottentot, mistletoe, strangler **10** East Indian, fiddleleaf, glossy-leaf, little-leaf, Moreton Bay, Philippine **11** Port Jackson **16** West Indian laurel

Figaro
character in: **18** The Barber of Seville **19** The Marriage of Figaro
author: **12** Beaumarchais

fight 3 box, row, war **4** bout, duel, feud, fray, grit, spar, spat, tiff, tilt, wage **5** argue, brawl, brush, clash, event, joust, match, melee, pluck, round, scrap, set-to **6** battle, bicker, combat, engage, fracas, mettle, oppose, resist, spirit, strife, tussle **7** carry on, conduct, contend, contest, discord, dispute, go to war, quarrel, repulse, scuffle, tourney, wage war, wrangle **8** confront, dogfight, gameness, skirmish, squabble, struggle **9** bickering, encounter, pugnacity, scrimmage, toughness, wrangling **10** contention, difference, dissension, prizefight, strive with, tournament **11** altercation, armed action, battle royal, bellicosity, clash of arms, controversy **12** belligerency, do battle with, rise up in arms, struggle with **13** armed conflict, combativeness, confrontation, exchange blows, pitched battle

fight back 7 counter, get even, hit back, pay back **9** retaliate **10** strike back **13** counterattack

fighter 5 boxer **7** soldier, sparrer, warrior **8** pugilist, scrapper **9** combatant **10** militarist **11** belligerent

fighting 3 war **4** fray **5** brawl, melee **6** action, battle, bicker, combat, rumpus, tumult, tussle **7** contest, dispute, quarrel, warfare **8** battling, brawling, conflict, skirmish, squabble **9** bickering, disputing **10** engagement, quarreling, squabbling **11** clash of arms, controversy, hostilities

Fighting Marine
nickname of: **10** Gene Tunney

fighting men 4 army **6** legion, troops **7** legions, militia **8** military, soldiers, soldiery **13** military force **15** military machine

fighting spirit 9 animosity, hostility, pugnacity **10** antagonism **11** bellicosity **12** belligerence **14** aggressiveness

fight shy of 5 avoid, dodge, elude, evade, skirt **6** escape **8** sidestep

figment 5 fable, fancy, story **6** canard **7** fantasy, fiction, product **8** creation **9** falsehood, invention **10** concoction **11** fabrication

figuration 4 form **7** outline **9** formation, structure **12** constitution

figurative 6 florid, ironic, ornate **7** flowery **8** humorous, symbolic **9** satirical **10** not literal **11** allegorical **12** hyperbolical, metaphorical

figure, figures 3 cut, man, sum **4** body, cast, cost, foot, form, mark, plan, rate, sign, sums **5** add up, adorn, build, count, digit, force, frame, guess, judge, motif, price, shape, think, total, tot up, value, woman **6** amount, appear, assess, cipher, design, device, emblem, factor, leader, number, person, reckon, schema, symbol **7** anatomy, believe, compute, contour, count up, diagram, drawing, imagine, notable, numeral, outline, pattern, presume, suppose **8** appraise, be placed, eminence, estimate, ornament, physique, presence **9** calculate, character, diversify, embellish, have a part, personage, play a part, quotation, variegate **10** arithmetic, conjecture, shine forth, silhouette **11** be mentioned, be prominent **12** calculations, computations, illustration

figurehead 4 tool **5** dummy, front, token **6** cipher, puppet **8** ornament **9** nonentity

figure out 6 reckon **7** compute, find out, work out **8** discover, ascertain, calculate, determine

figure roughly 5 guess **6** reckon **8** estimate **11** approximate, make a stab at

figure up 3 add **5** add up, total, tot up **6** reckon **7** compute, count up **9** calculate

figurine 7 bibelot **8** ornament **9** statuette

Fiji *see box*

filament 4 hair, line, wire **5** fiber, fibre **6** cilium, ribbon, strand, string, thread

filbert 7 Corylus
varieties: **3** red **4** cork, Momi, plum **5** azure, China, giant, Greek, joint, Nikko, noble, white **6** alpine, balsam, Fraser, Korean, needle, Scotch, silver, summer **7** cascade, Douglas, lowland, Spanish **8** Algerian, Japanese, Sakhalin, Southern **9** Himalayan, Shasta Red **10** dwarf Nikko, Santa Lucia **11** bristle-cone **13** Pacific silver **14** Southern balsam

filch 3 cop, rob **4** copy, crib, hook, lift **5** boost, heist, steal, swipe **6** pilfer, pirate **7** purloin **8** arrogate **10** plagiarize **11** appropriate, expropriate

file 3 row **4** data, line, list, rank, tier **5** apply, chain, index, put in, queue, store

6 drawer, folder, record, stacks, string **7** catalog, dossier, put away, records, request **8** archives, classify, petition **9** catalogue, chronicle
type: 4 mill, nail, rasp, wood **5** round **9** half-round **13** three-cornered

filial 7 dutiful, sonlike **10** daughterly, respectful

fill 3 act **4** cram, glut, lade, load, meet, pack, puff, sate **5** crowd, gorge, lay by, lay in, serve, stock, store **6** answer, assign, blow up, charge, dilate, do duty, expand, infuse, make up, occupy, outfit, supply, take up **7** distend, execute, furnish, inflate, pervade, preside, provide, satiate, satisfy, suffuse, surfeit **8** carry out, function, permeate, saturate **9** discharge, provision, replenish **10** full amount, impregnate, overspread

filled in 7 stood in **9** completed, **11** substituted

filled out 6 marked **7** matured **9** completed

fillet 4 band **5** slice, strip **6** ribbon **7** bandeau, circlet

fillip 3 tap **4** flip, snap, toss **5** flick, tonic **6** buffet **8** stimulus

Fillmore, Millard *see box*

fill with air 5 bloat **6** billow, blow up, expand **7** balloon, distend, inflate, puff out **8** swell out

fill with dread 5 alarm, panic **6** dismay **7** perturb, terrify, unnerve **8** disquiet, frighten

fill with gloom 6 darken, sadden **8** dispirit

fill with wonder 3 awe **5** amaze **7** astound **8** astonish **9** fascinate

film, films 4 coat, haze, mist, skin, veil **5** cloud, flick, movie, sheet, shoot **6** cinema, flicks, movies, screen **7** coating **8** membrane

filmy 3 dim **4** fine, hazy, thin **5** gauzy, misty, sheer, wispy **8** cobwebby, finespun, gossamer **10** diaphanous

fils 3 son

filter 4 leak, ooze, seep **5** drain, exude, sieve **6** effuse, purify, refine, screen, strain **7** clarify, cleanse, dribble, trickle, well out **8** filtrate, strainer

filth 3 mud **4** dirt, dung, mire, muck, slop, smut **5** feces, offal, slime, slush, trash **6** ma-nure, ordure, refuse, sewage, sludge **7** carrion, excreta, garbage, squalor **8** impurity, lewdness, ribaldry, vileness **9** excrement, grossness, indecency, nastiness, obscenity, pollution **10** corruption, defilement, immorality, indelicacy, putridness **11** pornography, squalidness **13** contamination **14** suggestiveness

filthy 4 foul, vile **5** black, dirty, grimy, gross, messy, nasty **6** grubby, impure, odious, soiled **7** defiled, dirtied, obscene, smirchy, squalid, unclean **8** befouled, slovenly, unwashed **9** repulsive **10** besmirched, disgusting **12** contaminated

finagle 3 con, gyp **4** plot, rook **5** cheat, mulct, trick **6** chisel, fleece, scheme, wangle **7** defraud, swindle **8** engineer, intrigue, maneuver

final 4 last, rear **6** ending, latest **7** closing, extreme **8** complete, decisive, finished, hindmost, rearmost, terminal, thorough, ultimate **10** concluding, conclusive, definitive, exhaustive, hindermost **11** irrevocable, terminating **12** unappealable, unchangeable **13** determinative
French: 7 dernier

finale 3 end **5** close, finis **6** finish, windup **7** curtain **8** epilogue, last part, swan song **10** conclusion **11** culmination, termination

final limit
Latin: 14 terminus ad quem

finally 6 lastly **10** eventually, inexorably, ultimately **11** inescapably **12** conclusively, definitively, in conclusion **16** incontrovertibly
French: 5 enfin
Latin: 10 ad extremum

Fillmore, Millard
presidential rank: 10 thirteenth
party: 4 Whig
state represented: 2 NY
defeated: 5 no one
succeeded upon death of: **6** Taylor
vice president: 4 none
cabinet:
State: **7** (Daniel) Webster, (Edward) Everett
Treasury: **6** (Thomas) Corwin
War: **6** (Charles Magill) Conrad
Attorney General: **10** (John Jordan) Crittenden
Navy: **6** (William Alexander) Graham **7** (John Pendleton) Kennedy
Postmaster General: **4** (Nathan Kelsey) Hall **7** (Samuel Dickinson) Hubbard
Interior: **6** (Alexander Hugh Holmes) Stuart
born: 7 Locke NY
died/buried: 9 Buffalo NY
education:
college: **4** none
studied: **3** law
religion: 9 Unitarian
interests: 5 civic
first chancellor of University of: **7** Buffalo
founder: **22** Buffalo General Hospital **24** Buffalo Historical Society
author: 21 Millard Fillmore Papers
political career: 13 state assembly, Vice President **24** US House of Representatives
civilian career: 6 lawyer (New York Supreme Court) **7** teacher **10** wool carder **12** cloth dresser
notable events of lifetime/term: 25 Compromise of Eighteen-Fifty
act: **13** Fugitive Slave
father: 9 Nathaniel
mother: 6 Phoebe (Millard)
siblings: 5 Cyrus, Julia **11** Phoebe Maria **12** Almon Hopkins, Calvin Turner **13** Charles DeWitt **14** Darius Ingraham, Olive Armstrong
wife: 7 Abigail (Powers) **8** Caroline (Carmichael McIntosh)
children: 11 Mary Abigail **13** Millard Powers

final section 4 coda **5** rider **6** ending **7** last act **8** addendum, epilogue **9** afterword **10** conclusion

final settlement 8 solution **11** disposition

finance 6 pay for **7** banking **8** accounts **9** economics **10** underwrite

financial backer 5 angel **6** patron **7** sponsor **9** supporter **10** benefactor

financial support 7 backing, subsidy **10** assistance **12** contribution

financier 5 angel **6** backer, banker, broker **7** rich man **10** capitalist **11** millionaire, underwriter

Financier, The
    author: **15** Theodore Dreiser
    character: **12** Aileen Butler, Edward Butler **15** Henry Cowperwood **16** Frank A Cowperwood **23** Lillian Semple Cowperwood

Finch, Peter
    real name: **15** Peter Ingle-Finch
    born: **6** London **7** England
    roles: **7** Network (Oscar) **11** Lost Horizon **12** The Nun's Story **15** The Pumpkin Eater **18** Sunday Bloody Sunday

Finchley, Sondra
    character in: **17** An American Tragedy
    author: **7** Dreiser

find 3 get, see, win **4** earn, espy, gain, meet, rule, spot **5** award, catch, dig up, judge, learn **6** attain, come by, decide, decree, detect, expose, locate, regain **7** achieve, acquire, adjudge, bargain, bonanza, discern, get back, godsend, good buy, hit upon, procure, recover, uncover, unearth **8** bump into, come upon, discover, disinter, lucky hit, meet with, retrieve, windfall **9** ascertain, determine, discovery, encounter, pronounce, repossess **10** adjudicate **11** acquisition

fin de siecle 8 decadent **15** end of the century

find fault 3 nag **4** beef, carp **5** blame, cavil, gribe **6** grouse, squawk **7** nitpick **8** complain **9** bellyache, criticize, disparage **10** disapprove

find guilty 5 blame **6** indict **7** condemn, convict **8** sentence **9** implicate

finding 6 decree, ruling **7** verdict **8** decision

find innocent 5 clear **6** acquit **9** exonerate

find out 5 learn **6** detect, locate **7** uncover, unearth **8** discover **9** ascertain, determine, establish

find repulsive 4 hate **5** abhor **6** detest, loathe **7** despise **8** execrate, recoil at **9** abominate

fine 4 airy, chic, fair, keen, neat, nice, rare, thin **5** bonny, clear, dandy, gauzy, mulct, nifty, sharp, sheer, silky, small, smart, sunny, swell **6** assess, bonnie, bright, charge, choice, comely, dainty, flimsy, ground, lovely, minute, modish, pretty, silken, slight, spiffy, subtle, superb **7** damages, elegant, forfeit, fragile, penalty, perfect, powdery, precise, refined, slender, stylish, tenuous **8** cobwebby, delicate, ethereal, flawless, gossamer, handsome, penalize, pleasant, polished, powdered, rainless, skillful, splendid, superior, tasteful **9** admirable, beautiful, brilliant, cloudless, excellent, exquisite **10** assessment, attractive, consummate, diaphanous, fastidious, pulverized, swimmingly **11** excellently, exceptional, lightweight, magnificent, transparent, well-favored **12** accomplished **13** hairsplitting, unsubstantial
    music: **3** end

fine clothes 8 glad rags **10** Sunday best **16** best bib and tucker

fine-looking 4 fair **5** bonny **6** bonnie, comely, lovely, pretty, seemly **8** gorgeous, handsome **9** beauteous, beautiful, exquisite, ravishing **10** attractive **11** resplendent **15** pulchritudinous

fineness 6 beauty **8** delicacy, elegance, thinness **10** perfection, smoothness **12** flawlessness **13** exquisiteness

fine points 3 art **7** finesse, nuances **8** niceties **10** subtleties **11** refinements **12** distinctions

finer 6 better **8** superior

finery 6 frills, tinsel **7** baubles, gaudery, gewgaws **8** frippery, spangles, trinkets **9** trappings, trimmings **13** paraphernalia

finesse 4 ruse, tact, wile **5** craft, dodge, guile, savvy **7** cunning **8** artifice, delicacy, intrigue, trickery **9** deception, stratagem **10** artfulness, discretion, subterfuge
    French: **11** savoir-faire

fine workmanship 8 delicacy **9** precision **13** craftsmanship

finger 3 paw **4** feel, poke **5** digit, punch, thumb, touch **6** caress, feeler, handle **7** pointer, squeeze, toy with, twiddle **8** play with **10** manipulate

finicky 5 fussy, picky **6** choosy **8** niggling **10** fastidious, meticulous, nitpicking, overprecise, particular, pernickety **11** persnickety **14** discriminating, overparticular

finish 3 end **4** coat, face, gild, goal, kill, last, seal, stop **5** cease, close, glaze, use up **6** clinch, defeat, devour, ending, finale, settle, veneer, wind up **7** achieve, coating, consume, curtain, destroy, fulfill, get done, lacquer, realize, surface, varnish **8** carry out, complete, conclude, dispatch, epilogue, exterior, get rid of, knock off, make good **9** discharge, eradicate, objective, polishing, terminate **10** accomplish, completion, conclusion, consummate, denouement **11** discontinue, exterminate, termination

finished 4 full **5** ended, final, ideal, whole **6** entire, urbane **7** classic, elegant, perfect, refined, shapely, skilled, trained, well-set **8** complete, flawless, polished, well-bred **9** beautiful, completed, concluded, exquisite, faultless **10** consummate, cultivated, impeccable **11** consummated **12** accomplished

finishing stroke 9 death blow
    French: **11** coup de grace

finish off 4 kill, slay **7** destroy, execute, wipe out **8** complete, dispatch **9** eradicate, polish off **10** annihilate **11** exterminate

finite 7 bounded, limited
8 confined, temporal **9** countable **10** measurable, restricted, short-lived, terminable
13 circumscribed

Finland *see box*

Finn
also: 5 Fionn **13** Fionn MacCumal
origin: 5 Irish
king of: 4 gods **14** Tuatha De Danann
son: 6 Ossian
father: 5 Cumal **6** Comhal

Finnegan's Wake
author: 10 James Joyce
family: 9 Earwicker

Finney, Albert
wife: 10 Anouk Aimee
born: 7 England, Salford
roles: 5 Annie **7** Scrooge **8** Tom Jones **10** The Dresser **12** Shoot the Moon **13** Two for the Road **17** Under the Volcano **29** Saturday Night and Sunday Morning

Finnish Mythology *see*
21 Scandinavian Mythology

Finno-Ugric
language family: 6 Uralic
Finnic group: 4 Lapp **6** Votyak, Zyryan **7** Finnish, Mordvin, Permian **8** Estonian **9** Cheremiss
Ugric group: 5 Vogul **6** Ostyak **7** Ob-Ugric **9** Hungarian

Fionn, Fionn MacCumal *see*
4 Finn

fiord, fjord 5 firth, inlet
7 estuary

fir 4 pine **5** cedar, larch **6** alpine, balsam, linden, spruce **7** conifer, cypress, douglas **9** evergreen

Firbolg
origin: 5 Greek, Irish
defeated by: 9 Fomorians
ousted by: 4 gods **14** Tuatha De Danann

fire *see box*

Fire and Ice
author: 11 Robert Frost

firearm 3 gun, rod **5** piece, rifle **6** pistol **7** shotgun **8** revolver **10** machine gun **12** shooting iron **13** submachine gun **20** Saturday-night special

---

Finland
other name: 5 Suomi **15** Suomen Tasavalta
capital/largest city: 8 Helsinki **11** Helsingfors
others: 3 Aba, Abo, Kem **4** Kemi, Ouli, Oulu, Ouou, Pori, Vasa **5** Enare, Espoo, Kotka, Lahti, Rauma, Turku, Vaasa **6** Imatra, Kuopio **7** Joensuu, Kajaani, Kokkola, Mikkeli, Tampere, Tapiola **9** Jyvaskyla, Mariehamn, Rovaniemi **12** Lappeenranta
measure: 5 kannu, verst **6** fathom, kannor **8** otlinger, skalpund, tunnland
monetary unit: 4 mark **5** penni **6** markka
island: 5 Aland, Karlo **6** Aaland **7** Hailuto **9** Vallgrund **10** Ahvenanmaa
lake: 3 Juo, Muo **4** Kemi, Kiui, Nasi, Oulu, Puru, Pyha, Simo **5** Enara, Enare, Hauki, Inari, Kalla, Lappa, Lesti, Puula, Saima **6** Ladoya, Lentua, Saimaa, Sounne, Syvari **7** Koitere, Nilakka, Pielien **9** Kallavesi, Pielavesi
mountain: 7 Laltiva **10** Saari Selka
highest point: 6 Haltia **11** Haldetsokka
river: 4 Kala, Kemi, Kymi, Oulu, Pats, Simo, Teno **5** Ivalo, Lotta, Ounas, Siika, Torne **6** Iijoki, Lapuan, Muonio, Pasvik, Tornoi, Vuoski **7** Kitinen **8** Kokemaki
sea: 6 Baltic **8** Atlantic
physical feature:
  gulf: **7** Bothnia, Finland
  isthmus: **7** Karelia
  peninsula: **13** Fennoscandian
people: 3 Jew, Vod, Vot, Yak **4** Avar, Finn, Hame, Lapp, Turk, Veps **5** Fioun, Gypsy, Ijore, Inger, Suomi, Vepse **6** Magyar, Ostiak, Ostyak, Tarast, Tavast, Ugrian, Zyrian **7** Lappish, Mordvin, Permiak, Samoyed, Uralian **8** Cheremis, Estonian, Karelian, Livonian, Swekoman **9** Tavastian **11** Karjalaiset, Suomalaiset
  athlete: **10** Paavo Nurmi
  composer: **8** Sibelius
  designer: **9** Marimekko
language: 4 Avar, Lapp **5** Karel, Ugric, Vogul **6** Magyar, Ostyak, Tarast **7** Finnish, Olonets, Samoyed, Swedish **8** Estonian **10** Olonetsian
religion: 19 Evangelical Lutheran
place:
  canal: **6** Saimaa
  castle: **10** Saint Olaf's **11** Olavinlinna
  fortress: **8** Sveaborg **11** Suomenlinna
  memorial: **8** Sibelius
  pine ridge: **10** Punkaharju
feature:
  game: **9** pesapallo
food:
  dish: **11** Karelian pie
  fruit: **16** yellow cloudberry
  liqueur: **9** Mesimarja

---

fire 3 can, vim **4** bake, boot, burn, cook, dash, dump, elan, hurl, oust, sack, stir **5** ardor, blaze, eject, flame, flare, flash, force, gusto, let go, light, power, punch, rouse, salvo, shell, shoot, spark, verve, vigor **6** arouse, bounce, depose, excite, fervor, foment, genius, ignite, incite, kindle, luster, spirit, stir up, vivify, volley **7** animate, bombard, bonfire, cashier, dismiss, inferno, inflame, inspire, project, quicken, sniping, trigger **8** enfilade, fervency, inspirit, radiance, splendor, vivacity **9** broadside, cannonade, discharge, eagerness, fusillade, galvanize, holocaust, instigate, intensity, stimulate, vehemence **10** brilliance, effulgence, enthusiasm **11** bombardment, earnestness, inspiration **13** conflagration, sharpshooting **15** imaginativeness
  god of: 4 Loki **5** Ishum **6** Vulcan **10** Hephaestus, Hephaistos
  goddess of: 6 Brigit

firefight 5 clash 6 battle, combat 8 skirmish

firefly 8 glowworm, lampyrid 9 candlefly 12 lightning bug

Fire Next Time, The
author: 12 James Baldwin

fire off 5 eject, shoot 6 launch 8 detonate 9 discharge

Fireside Theatre
host: 9 Jane Wyman 11 Frank Wisbar, Gene Raymond

Firestarter
author: 11 Stephen King

fire up 4 fuel, rile 5 anger, light, rouse 6 arouse, excite, ignite, incite, kindle 7 animate, enthuse, inspire 8 activate, energize, irritate, vitalize 9 galvanize, stimulate

firm 4 bent, fast, grim, hard, taut 5 close, dense, fixed, house, rigid, rocky, solid, stiff, stony, tight, tough 6 dogged, flinty, intent, moored, rooted, secure, stable, steady, steely 7 compact, company, dead set, decided, earnest, serious, settled, staunch 8 anchored, business, constant, definite, fearless, obdurate, resolute, resolved, unshaken 9 confirmed, hardnosed, immovable, obstinate, steadfast, tenacious, unbending 10 adamantine, compressed, determined, inexorable, inflexible, invincible, persistent, unwavering, unyielding 11 corporation, established, partnership, unalterable, unfaltering, unflinching 12 conglomerate, indissoluble, organization 13 establishment

firmament 3 air, sky 5 ether, space, vault 6 canopy, welkin 7 heavens, the blue, the void 10 outer space

firmness 8 tenacity 9 obstinacy 10 resolution 11 persistence, staunchness 12 resoluteness 13 determination, inflexibility, steadfastness

first 4 head, main 5 basic, prime, start, vital 6 before, eldest, maiden, outset, primal, rather, sooner 7 highest, leading, premier, primary, ranking, supreme 8 earliest, foremost, original, primeval, superior 9 beginning, essential, inception, initially, paramount, primitive, principal 10 aboriginal, elementary, preeminent, preferably, primordial 11 fundamental, rudimentary 12 commencement, introduction, introductory

first among equals
Latin: 16 primus inter pares

first appearance 4 dawn 5 debut 9 beginning 12 introduction

firstborn 5 elder, older 6 eldest, oldest

Firstborn, The
author: 14 Christopher Fry

First Circle
author: 23 Aleksandr Solzhenitsyn Jr

first god see 8 god, first

firsthand 6 direct 8 personal 9 empirical 10 unmediated 12 experimental

First Lady of the Theater
nickname of: 10 Helen Hayes 16 Katharine Cornell

first-line 4 main 5 chief 7 primary 8 foremost

first moving thing
Latin: 12 primum mobile

first-rate 3 ace 4 A-one, best, fine, tops 5 crack, elite, great, prime 6 choice, finest, select 7 top-hole 8 splendid, superior, top-notch, very good 9 admirable, estimable, excellent, exclusive, nonpareil, top drawer, topflight, wonderful 10 noteworthy, stupendous 11 commendable, outstanding 12 above-average, incomparable 13 distinguished

First State
nickname of: 8 Delaware

first step 5 start 9 beginning 12 commencement

firth 5 fjord, inlet 7 estuary

fiscal 8 economic, monetary 9 budgetary, financial, pecuniary

fish 3 net 4 cast, hook, hunt 5 angle, grope, seine, trawl, troll 6 ferret, search 7 rummage

fish see box

Fisher, Bud
creator/artist of: 11 Mutt and Jeff

Fisher, Carrie
father: 11 Eddie Fisher
mother: 13 Debbie Reynolds
role: 12 Princess Leia
films: 7 Shampoo 8 Star Wars 12 This Is My Life 16 The Blues Brothers 17 When Harry Met Sally 18 The Return of the Jedi 19 The Empire Strikes Back, Hannah and Her Sisters
author: 20 Postcards from the Edge

Fisher, Ham
creator/artist of: 10 Joe Palooka

fish
class: 7 Agnatha 12 Osteichthyes 14 Chondrichthyes
fin: 4 anal, tail 6 caudal, dorsal, median, paired, pelvic 7 adipose, ventral 8 pectoral
kind: 3 cod, eel, gar, ray 4 bass, carp, hake, opah, pike, tuna 5 brill, perch, shark, skate, sword, trout 6 bichir, blenny, marlin, minnow, mullet, salmon, tarpon 7 anchovy, catfish, dogfish, dolphin, hagfish, herring, lamprey, piranha, sunfish 8 bluefish, cavefish, crayfish, flounder, goldfish, lungfish, mackerel, menhaden, moray eel, pilchard, sea horse, squirrel, sturgeon 9 killifish, pygmy goby, swordfish 10 coelacanth, flying fish, paddlefish, rabbit fish, rocksucker, whale shark 11 anemonefish, electric eel, electric ray, lanternfish, long-nose gar 13 butterflyfish 14 largemouth bass
part: 3 fin 4 gill 5 scale 6 cirrhi 10 gas bladder 11 swim bladder 12 rete mirabile
shellfish:
　crustacean: 4 crab 6 shrimp 7 lobster 8 blue crab, king crab, snow crab 9 langouste 11 langoustine 13 Dungeness crab, horseshoe crab
　mollusk: 4 clam 6 mussel, oyster, quahog 8 surf clam 9 horse clam, razor clam 11 geoduck clam
young: 3 fry 10 fingerling

Fisher, Vardis
  author of: **10** The Mothers
  13 Children of God **17** The
  Testament of Man

fisherman 5 eeler **6** angler,
caster, jacker, netter, seiner
7 trawler, troller **8** piscator
9 flycaster, Waltonian **17** the
compleat angler

Fishermen
  goddess of: **11** Britomartis

Fishes
  constellation of: **6** Pisces

fish story 3 fib, lie **7** fiction,
whopper **9** falsehood, tall
story **16** cock-and-bull story

fishy 3 odd **4** dull **5** blank,
queer, shady, weird **6** vacant
7 dubious, strange, suspect
8 doubtful, peculiar, slippery
9 dishonest **10** farfetched,
glassy-eyed, improbable, suspicious, unreliable **11** exaggerated, extravagant
12 questionable, unscrupulous
14 expressionless

fission 7 atomize **8** breaking,
cleavage, scission **9** severance,
splitting **10** breaking up, sun-
derance **12** disseverance,
reproduction

fissure 3 gap **4** rift, slit
5 chink, cleft, crack, gully,
split **6** breach, cranny, groove,
hiatus **8** aperture, cleavage

fit *see* **box**

fitful 4 weak **6** broken, random,
uneven **7** erratic **8** listless, off-
and-on, periodic, sporadic, unsteady, variable **9** irregular,
spasmodic **10** capricious,
changeable, convulsive
11 fluctuating **12** disconnected,
intermittent

fitness
  Hebrew: **7** kashrut **8** kashruth

fit out 4 robe **5** array, dress,
equip **6** attire, clothe, supply
7 appoint, prepare

fitting 3 apt **4** meet **6** proper,
seemly **8** decorous, suitable
9 congruous **11** appropriate
  French: **11** comme il faut

fit to be eaten 6 edible
9 palatable **10** comestible, consumable, digestible

fit together 4 join **5** hinge,
unite **6** hook up **7** connect
8 dovetail **9** interlock
10 articulate

Fitzgerald, Barry
  real name: **20** William Joseph Shields
  born: **6** Dublin **7** Ireland
  roles: **10** Going My Way

11 The Quiet Man **19** How
Green Was My Valley

FitzGerald, Edward
  author of: **24** The Rubaiyat
  of Omar Khayyam
  (translation)

Fitzgerald, F Scott
  wife: **10** Zelda Sayre
  author of: **10** The Crack-Up
  13 The Last Tycoon **14** The
  Great Gatsby **16** Tender Is
  the Night **18** This Side of
  Paradise **24** The Beautiful
  and the Damned

Fitzgerald, George Francis
  field: **7** physics
  nationality: **5** Irish
  theory of: **24** electromagnetic
  radiation

Fitzgerald, Geraldine
  born: **6** Dublin **7** Ireland
  roles: **11** Dark Victory **12** Ah
  Wilderness, Rachel Rachel
  15 Watch on the Rhine
  16 Wuthering Heights
  24 Long Day's Journey into
  Night

**Fitzsimmons, Bob (Robert
Prometheus)**
  sport: **6** boxing

FitzSimons, Maureen
  real name of: **12** Maureen
  O'Hara

fit 4 able, good, hale,
meet, ripe, suit, well,
whim **5** adapt, agree, alter,
burst, equal, equip, hardy,
match, ready, right, shape,
sound, spasm, spell, train
6 access, accord, adjust, become, concur, enable, in
trim, mature, primed,
proper, robust, seemly,
strong, timely, worthy
7 adapted, apropos, capable, caprice, conform, correct, empower, fashion,
healthy, prepare, qualify,
rectify, seizure, toned up,
trained **8** apposite, becoming, coincide, crotchet,
decorous, eligible, graduate,
grand mal, outbreak, out-
burst, paroxysm, petit mal,
prepared, relevant, suit-
able **9** calibrate, competent,
consonant, deserving, efficient, explosion, harmo-
nize, initiated, opportune,
pertinent, qualified **10** acceptable, applicable, capacitate, convenient,
convulsion, correspond,
seasonable **11** appropriate,
capacitated

Five, The
  group of: **16** Russian
  composers
  member: **3** Cui **7** Borodin
  9 Balakirev **10** Mussorgsky
  14 Rimsky-Korsakov

Five Easy Pieces
  director: **11** Bob Rafelson
  cast: **10** Karen Black
  11 Fannie Flagg **12** Susan
  Anspach **13** Jack Nicholson
  14 Billy Breen Bush, Sally
  Struthers

Five Men and Pompey
  author: **19** Stephen Vincent
  Benet

five-o'clock shadow 5 beard
7 stubble **8** bristles, whiskers

fix 3 jam, put, set **4** bind,
make, mend, mess, moor,
spot **5** place, rivet **6** adjust, anchor, attach, decide, fasten,
harden, impose, muddle,
pickle, plight, repair, scrape,
secure, settle **7** congeal, connect, correct, dilemma, impasse, implant, patch up,
prepare, rebuild **8** assemble,
hot water, make fast, make
firm, quandary, regulate, renovate, set right, solidify **9** establish, prescribe, retaliate,
stabilize **10** difficulty **11** consolidate, involvement, predicament **12** entanglement

fixation 5 quirk **6** fetish
7 complex **8** crotchet, delusion **9** monomania, obsession
13 preoccupation

fixed 3 set **4** fast, firm **5** rigid,
still **6** intent, rooted, stable,
steady **8** constant, fastened,
resolute, unpliant **9** immovable, unbending **10** determined, inflexible, motionless,
persistent, stationary,
unwavering

fixed idea 4 bias **5** slant **9** obsession **13** preconception
  French: **8** idee fixe

fixedness 8 firmness **9** constancy, stability **10** immobility **12** immutability
16 unchangeableness

fixed regard 7 staring **9** diligence **10** absorption, intentness **11** engrossment
13 concentration

Fixer, The
  author: **14** Bernard Malamud

fixing 6 repair **7** mending,
mooring, placing, putting, setting **8** deciding, imposing,
righting, riveting, settling,
trimming **9** adjusting, anchor-
ing, attaching, fastening, hardening, preparing, repairing
10 adjustment, assembling,

congealing, connecting, correcting, implanting, rectifying, regulating, regulation **11** determining, prescribing, solidifying, stabilizing **12** establishing **13** consolidating

fixture 6 addict **7** devotee, habitue, regular **8** equipage **9** apparatus, appendage, appliance, equipment **10** attachment **11** appointment **12** appurtenance **13** paraphernalia

fix up 4 plan **6** design, devise **7** arrange, prepare **8** renovate, schedule

fix upon 4 pick **6** choose, opt for, select **7** call out, extract, pick out

fizz 4 foam **5** froth **7** bubbles **11** carbonation **13** effervescence

fizziness 9 foaminess **10** bubbliness, frothiness **13** effervescence

fizzing 6 bubbly **7** foaming **8** bubbling **9** sparkling **12** effervescent, effervescing

fizzle 3 dog, dud **4** bomb, fail, flop, hiss, mess **5** abort, botch **6** bubble, fiasco, gurgle, muddle, turkey **7** failure, founder, misfire, sputter, washout **8** collapse, disaster, miscarry

fizzy 6 bubbly **8** bubbling **9** sparkling **12** effervescent

flabbergast 4 stun **5** amaze, shock **6** puzzle **7** astound, stagger, stupefy **8** astonish, bewilder, bowl over, confound, overcome **9** dumbfound

flabbergasted 5 agape **6** amazed, gaping **9** awestruck, stupefied **10** astonished, dumbstruck, spellbound **11** dumbfounded **12** hornswoggled **13** thunderstruck

flabby 4 lame, limp, soft, weak **5** baggy, slack **6** doughy, effete, feeble, flimsy, floppy, spongy **7** flaccid **8** impotent, listless, yielding **9** enervated, inelastic **10** spiritless **11** adulterated, emasculated

flag 3 ebb, sag **4** fade, fail, pall, sink, tire, wane, warn, wave, wilt **5** abate, faint, slump **6** banner, colors, dodder, emblem, ensign, signal, totter **7** decline, give way, pennant, subside, succumb **8** grow weak, languish, Old Glory, standard, streamer **9** grow weary, Union Jack **12** Stars and Bars **15** Stars and Stripes

flagellant 7 ascetic **8** penitent **13** self-mortifier

flagon 3 gun, jug, mug **4** ewer **5** flask, stein **6** bottle, carafe, vessel **7** canteen **8** schooner

flagrant 5 gross, sheer **6** arrant, brazen, crying **7** blatant, glaring, heinous, obvious **8** immodest **9** audacious, barefaced, flaunting, monstrous, notorious, shameless **10** outrageous, scandalous **11** conspicuous

Flaherty, Margaret (Pegeen)
character in: 24 Playboy of the Western World
author: 5 Synge

flail 4 beat, lash, whip **5** swing **6** thresh **7** scourge

flair 4 bent, dash, feel, gift **5** knack, style, taste, touch, verve **6** genius, talent **7** faculty, feeling, panache **8** aptitude, capacity **9** ingenuity **11** discernment

flake 3 bit **4** chip, peel **5** fleck, layer, patch, scale, sheet, strip **7** chip off, crumble, peel off, shaving **8** scale off

flaky 4 bats, gaga, nuts **5** balmy, batty, crisp, daffy, dotty, goofy, loony, nutty, scaly, short, wacky **6** scabby, screwy, scurfy **8** scabious, squamous **9** eccentric **10** flocculent

flamboyant 4 wild **5** gaudy, jazzy, showy **6** flashy, florid, garish, ornate, rococo **7** baroque, dashing **8** colorful, exciting **10** theatrical **11** sensational **12** ostentatious

flame 4 beau, fire, glow **5** ardor, blaze, blush, flare, flash, flush, glare, gleam, light, lover, spark, swain **6** fervor, ignite, kindle, redden, warmth **7** passion **8** fervency **9** affection, boyfriend, intensity **10** enthusiasm, excitement, girlfriend, sweetheart **13** conflagration

flaming 5 afire, fiery **6** ablaze, alight, ardent, bright, fervid, stormy **7** blazing, burning, fervent, glaring, glowing, igneous, intense, shining, violent **8** flagrant, vehement **9** brilliant, egregious **10** passionate, smoldering **11** conspicuous, inflammable

flammable 7 igneous **10** combustive, incendiary **11** combustible, inflammable

flan 3 pie **4** gust, puff, tart

6 expand, pastry **7** custard, dessert **12** creme caramel

flanerie 8 dawdling, idleness

flaneur 5 idler **6** loafer **7** dawdler

flank 3 hip **4** edge, line, loin, side, wing **5** cover, skirt **6** border, fringe, haunch, screen, shield

Flannagan, John Bernard
born: 7 Fargo ND
artwork: 6 New One, Not Yet **9** Beginning **11** Dragon Motif **15** Triumph of the Egg **16** Jonah and the Whale

flap 3 bat, fly, tab **4** bang, beat, flop **5** apron, shake, skirt **6** lappet **7** agitate, banging, flutter, vibrate **9** oscillate

flare 4 burn, glow **5** blaze, erupt, flame, flash, glare, gleam, taper, torch, widen **6** blow up, dilate, expand, ignite, signal, spread **7** bell out, broaden, distend, explode, stretch **8** boil over, break out **9** coruscate **10** incandesce

flash 4 glow, wink **5** blaze, blink, burst, flame, flare, glare, gleam, jiffy, shake, shine, spark, touch, trice **6** minute, moment, second, streak **7** flicker, glimmer, glisten, glitter, instant, sparkle **8** instance, outburst, radiance **9** coruscate **10** occurrence **11** coruscation, fulmination, scintillate **13** incandescence

Flash Gordon
creator: 8 Dan Berry **11** Alex Raymond **12** Austin Briggs
character:
companion: 4 Dale

flashy 4 loud **5** gaudy, jazzy, showy, smart **6** garish, sporty, tawdry, tinsel, vulgar **7** raffish **8** dazzling **9** bedizened **10** flamboyant, tricked out **11** pretentious **12** ostentatious

flask 6 bottle **7** canteen **9** container

flat, flats 3 low **4** dead, dull **5** clear, equal, flush, level, marsh, plain, plane, prone, shoal, shoes, stale, total, vapid **6** direct, planar, smooth, supine **7** blowout, exactly, insipid, laid low, leveled, levelly, loafers, prairie, regular, shallow **8** absolute, complete, definite, lowlands, positive, puncture, thorough, unbroken **9** apartment, downright, precisely, prostrate, reclining, recumbent, tasteless **10** flavorless, horizontal, peremptory

11 unequivocal, unpalatable, unqualified 12 deflated tire, horizontally, unmistakable

flatfish 3 ray 4 sole 5 brill, fluke 6 turbot 7 halibut, sand dab, sunfish, teleost 8 flounder

Flathead *see* 5 Salis 7 Chinook

flatness 8 dullness 9 levelness, staleness 10 insipidity 13 tastelessness 14 flavorlessness

flatten 4 deck, even, fell 5 crush, floor, level, plane 6 defeat, ground, smooth 7 deflate 8 compress, overcome 9 overwhelm, prostrate

flatter 4 fool, laud 5 court, extol, honor, toady 6 become, cajole, delude 7 adulate, beguile, deceive, mislead, wheedle 8 blandish, bootlick, butter up, eulogize, soft-soap 9 brown-nose, sweet-talk, truckle to 10 compliment, overpraise, panegyrize

flatterer 5 toady 6 fawner, yes man 8 eulogist, truckler, wheedler 9 sycophant 10 bootlicker 11 lickspittle 13 apple-polisher

flattering 7 lauding 8 praising 9 extolling, favorable, laudatory 10 gratifying 13 complimentary

flattering attention 5 court 7 fawning

flattery 6 eulogy 7 blarney, fawning, snow job 8 cajolery, encomium, jollying, soft soap, toadying, toadyism 9 adulation, panegyric, servility, truckling, wheedling 10 sycophancy 12 blandishment 14 obsequiousness

Flaubert, Gustave
    author of: 8 Salammbo 12 Madame Bovary 21 A Sentimental Education 24 The Temptation of St Anthony

flaunt 3 air 4 brag, wave 5 boast, sport, strut, vaunt 6 blazon, dangle, parade 7 exhibit, show off 8 brandish, flourish 9 advertise, broadcast

flavor 4 aura, lace, soul, tang, tone 5 gusto, imbue, savor, spice, style, tenor 6 aspect, infuse, lacing, relish, season, spirit 7 essence, instill 8 ambience, piquancy 9 attribute, seasoning

flavorful 4 rich 5 nutty, sapid, spicy, tangy, tasty, zesty 6 savory 7 peppery, piquant 8 aro-

matic 9 palatable, toothsome 10 appetizing

flavoring 4 herb, salt 5 spice 6 pepper 7 essence, extract, vanilla 8 additive, seasoner 9 chocolate, condiment, seasoning

flavorless 4 dull, flat, thin, weak 5 bland, stale, vapid 6 watery 7 insipid 9 tasteless

flaw 3 mar 4 blot, harm, spot, vice 5 error, fault, speck, stain 6 blotch, deface, defect, foible, impair, injure, injury, smudge, weaken 7 blemish, failing, fallacy, frailty, mistake 8 weak spot, weakness 9 deformity, disfigure 10 compromise, defacement 11 shortcoming 12 imperfection 13 disfigurement

flawed 6 faulty 8 impaired 9 defective, imperfect

flawless 5 sound 7 perfect 9 errorless, faultless 10 immaculate, impeccable

flawlessness 8 accuracy 10 perfection 11 correctness 14 immaculateness

flay 4 bark, pare, peel, skin 5 scalp, scold, strip 6 assail, fleece, punish, rebuke 7 plunder, upbraid 9 castigate, excoriate 11 decorticate

flea
    varieties: 3 bat, dog, rat 5 mouse 6 rodent 9 carnivore 10 sticktight

fleck 3 dot, jot 4 drop, mark, mole, spot 5 flake, speck 6 bespot, dapple, mottle, streak, tittle 7 blemish, freckle, spatter, speckle, stipple 8 particle, small bit 9 bespeckle 10 besprinkle

Fledermaus, Die
    also: 6 The Bat
    operetta by: 7 (Johann) Strauss
    character: 5 Adele, Falke, Frank 6 Alfred 8 Rosalinda 14 Prince Orlofsky 18 Baron von Eisenstein

fledgling 4 tyro 6 novice 8 beginner, freshman 9 greenhorn 10 apprentice, tenderfoot

flee 4 shun, skip 5 avoid, dodge, elude, evade, split 6 decamp, desert, vanish 7 abscond, fly away, make off 8 speed off 9 cut and run, disappear 10 fly the coop

fleece 3 gyp 4 bilk, dupe, gull, rook, wool 5 cheat, cozen, trick 7 deceive, defraud, swindle 9 bamboozle, victimize

fleet 3 run 4 band, fade, fast, flow, navy, skim, spry, swim, unit 5 agile, array, brief, creek, drift, float, hasty, inlet, light, quick, rapid, shift, ships, short, swift 6 abound, active, armada, nimble, number, speedy, sudden, vanish 7 caravan, cursory, hurried 8 flotilla, squadron 9 disappear, momentary, transient 10 evanescent, transitory 11 expeditious 13 instantaneous

fleeting 5 brief, quick 7 passing 8 flitting, fugitive, temporal 9 ephemeral, fugacious, momentary, temporary, transient 10 evanescent, perishable, transitory 11 impermanent, precarious, unenduring

Fleming, Alexander
    field: 12 bacteriology
    nationality: 7 British
    discovered: 10 penicillin
    awarded: 10 Nobel Prize

Fleming, Henry
    character in: 20 The Red Badge of Courage
    author: 5 Crane

Fleming, Ian
    author of: 4 Dr No 9 Moonraker 10 Goldfinger 11 Thunderball 12 Casino Royale 13 Live and Let Die 15 For Your Eyes Only 16 The Spy Who Loved Me, You Only Live Twice 18 From Russia with Love
    character: 1 M, Q 6 Oddjob 7 SPECTRE (organization) 9 James Bond 14 Miss Moneypenny 15 Auric Goldfinger

Fleming, Victor
    director of: 13 The Wizard of Oz 14 Treasure Island 15 Gone With the Wind (Oscar) 18 Captains Courageous

flesh 3 fat, man 4 body, meat, pulp 5 brawn, power, vigor 6 embody, fatten, people 7 fatness, fill out, mankind, realize 8 humanity, physique, strength 9 carnality, substance 10 sensuality 11 materiality 13 individualize, particularize

flesh and blood 3 kin 4 real 5 a body, child 6 family 7 kindred 8 children 9 corporeal, offspring, relations, relatives 10 kith and kin 11 substantial

flesh-eating 9 predatory 10 predaceous 11 carnivorous

fleshy 3 fat 5 beefy, obese,

plump, stout, tubby **6** chubby, portly, rotund, stocky **7** paunchy **8** roly-poly, thickset **9** corpulent, succulent **10** overweight, potbellied

Fletcher, Louise
 born: 12 Birmingham AL
 roles: 17 The Cheap Detective **25** One Flew Over the Cuckoo's Nest (Oscar)

Fletcher, Susannah Yolande
 real name of: 12 Susannah York

flex 4 bend **5** curve

flexible 4 mild, soft **5** lithe **6** docile, genial, gentle, limber, pliant, supple **7** amiable, ductile, elastic, plastic, pliable, springy **8** bendable, yielding **9** adaptable, compliant, malleable, resilient, tractable **10** changeable, extensible, manageable, responsive, submissive **11** complaisant

Flibbertigibbet
 character in: 10 Kenilworth
 author: 5 Scott

flick 4 film **5** brush, graze, movie, sweep, whisk

flicker 4 flit, glow, sway **5** blaze, flame, flare, flash, gleam, glint, shake, spark, throb, trace, waver **6** quaver, quiver, waggle **7** flutter, glimmer, glisten, glitter, modicum, pulsate, shimmer, sparkle, tremble, vestige, vibrate, wriggle **8** undulate **9** coruscate, fluctuate, oscillate, scintilla, vacillate

Flickertail State
 nickname of: 11 North Dakota

flicks 5 films **6** cinema, grazes, movies, sweeps, whisks **7** brushes

flier 4 bill **5** pilot **6** notice **7** aviator, leaflet, venture **8** brochure, bulletin, circular, handbill **10** experiment **12** announcement **13** advertisement

flight 4 rout, rush, wing **5** flock **6** escape, exodus, flying, hegira **7** fleeing, retreat, soaring, winging **8** squadron **10** withdrawal **11** aeronautics

flighty 5 dizzy, giddy **6** fickle **8** quixotic, reckless, unstable, volatile **9** frivolous, mercurial, whimsical **10** capricious, changeable, inconstant, indecisive, irresolute **11** harebrained, impractical, light-headed, thoughtless **13** irresponsible **14** scatterbrained

flimsy 4 poor, thin, weak **5** cheap, filmy, frail, gauzy, petty, sheer **6** feeble, shabby, shoddy, sleazy, slight, trashy **7** foolish, fragile, ill-made, shallow, trivial **8** cobwebby, delicate, gossamer, trifling **9** frivolous, worthless **10** diaphanous, inadequate, jerrybuilt, ramshackle **11** dilapidated, superficial **13** unsubstantial

flinch 3 fly, shy **4** jerk **5** cower, quail, quake, start, wince **6** blench, cringe, falter, quaver, quiver, recoil, shiver, shrink **7** contort, grimace, retreat, shudder

fling 2 go **3** try **4** ball, bash, cast, dash, emit, hurl, lark, toss **5** eject, expel, heave, pitch, sling, spree, trial **6** let fly, propel **7** attempt **8** bit of fun **11** precipitate

Flintstones, The
 character: 7 Pebbles **8** Bamm Bamm **11** Betty Rubble **12** Barney Rubble **14** Fred Flintstone **15** Dino the Dinosaur, Wilma Flintstone
 voice: 8 Alan Reed, Mel Blanc **10** Don Messick **12** Bea Benaderet, Gerry Johnson **13** Jean Vander Pyl
 city: 7 Bedrock
 creator: 12 Hanna-Barbera

Flintwinch
 character in: 12 Little Dorrit
 author: 7 Dickens

flinty 4 cold, hard **5** cruel, harsh, stern, stony **6** inured, steely **7** callous **8** hardened **10** unyielding **11** hardhearted, insensitive

flip 3 tap **4** bold, pert, spin, toss, turn **5** brash, flick, fresh, throw, thumb **6** cheeky, fillip **8** impudent, insolent, turn over **9** unabashed

flippant 4 glib, pert, rude **5** brash, lippy, saucy **6** cheeky, nimble **7** voluble **8** impudent, insolent, trifling **9** bumptious, frivolous, talkative **11** impertinent **12** presumptuous **13** disrespectful

Flipper
 character: 8 Bud Ricks **10** Sandy Ricks **11** Porter Ricks
 cast: 10 Brian Kelly, Luke Halpin **11** Tommy Norden
 Flipper played by: 4 Suzy

flirt 3 toy **4** play, vamp **5** dally, tease **6** trifle **8** coquette **12** heartbreaker

flit 4 dart, scud, skim, wing

5 speed **6** hasten, scurry **7** flicker, flutter

Flitch of Bacon, The
 author: 16 William Ainsworth

Flite, Miss
 character in: 10 Bleak House
 author: 7 Dickens

flivver 3 car **4** auto, heap **5** motor **6** jalopy, wheels **7** machine, vehicle **8** motorcar **9** tin lizzie **10** automobile

float 3 bob **4** waft **5** drift, hover, slide **6** bear up, buoy up, hold up, launch **8** levitate

floating 4 free **5** awash, loose **6** adrift, afloat, errant **7** buoyant, wafting **8** drifting **9** fluctuant, wandering **10** unattached

flock 2 go **3** mob, run **4** band, bevy, gang, herd, mass, pack, rush **5** bunch, crowd, crush, drove, group, surge, troop **6** clique, gather, huddle, muster, stream, throng **7** cluster, company, coterie **8** converge **9** gathering, multitude **10** assemblage, collection, congregate **11** aggregation **12** congregation
 of fish: 6 school
 of game birds: 5 covey
 of geese: 6 gaggle
 of insects: 5 swarm
 of lions: 5 pride
 of seals or whales: 3 pod
 of young birds: 5 brood

flocks
 god of: 3 Pan

flock together 6 gather, mingle **7** convene **8** assemble **9** associate **10** congregate

flog 4 beat, cane, club, cuff, drub, hide, lash, maul, whip **5** birch, flail, smite, strap **6** cudgel, paddle, strike, switch, thrash **7** scourge **8** lambaste **9** horsewhip **10** flagellate

flood 4 flow, glut, gush, tide **6** deluge, drench, shower, stream **7** cascade, current, torrent **8** downpour, flow over, inundate, overflow, saturate, submerge, wash over **9** overwhelm **10** cloudburst, inundation, outpouring, oversupply
 period before: 12 antediluvian

Flood
 author: 16 Robert Penn Warren

flooded 6 flowed, surged **7** deluged, glutted, overran, swamped **8** drenched, engulfed **9** inundated, outpoured, washed out **10** downpoured, overflowed

floor 4 base, deck, fell, tier **5** level, stage, story **6** bottom, ground **7** minimum, parquet **8** base rate, flooring, pavement **9** prostrate

flop 4 bomb, bust, drop, fail, fold, plop **5** close **6** fiasco, fizzle, topple, tumble, turkey **7** failure, go under, shutter, washout **8** disaster, lay an egg **14** disappointment

Flora
origin: **5** Roman
goddess of: **7** flowers

floral 6 bloomy **7** verdant **8** blossomy **9** botanical **10** herbaceous

Floralia
origin: **5** Roman
form: **8** festival

Florence *see box*

florescence 5 bloom **9** flowerage **10** blossoming

florid 4 rosy **5** gaudy, ruddy, showy **6** blowsy, hectic, ornate, rococo **7** baroque, flowery, flushed, reddish **8** inflamed, red-faced, rubicund, sanguine **9** elaborate **10** flamboyant, ornamented **12** ostentatious **13** grandiloquent

Florida *see box*

florilegium 7 garland **8** chapbook, treasury **9** anthology

Florizel
character in: **14** The Winter's Tale
author: **11** Shakespeare

floruit 12 he flourished **13** she flourished

flotilla 5 fleet **6** armada

Flotow, Friedrich von
born: **7** Germany **11** Mecklenburg
composer of: **6** Martha **11** Die Matrosen **19** Alessandro Stradella

flotsam 4 junk **6** debris, refuse **7** garbage **8** castoffs

flounce 3 hem **4** edge, leap, skip, trim, trip **5** bound, caper, frill, stamp, stomp, storm, strut **6** bounce, edging, fringe, gambol, prance, ruffle, sashay, spring **7** valance **8** furbelow, ornament, skirting, trimming

flounder 4 fish, flop, halt, limp **5** lurch, waver **6** falter, hobble, muddle, totter, tumble, wallow, welter **7** blunder,

---

Florence
artist: **6** Giotto **7** Cimabue **8** Ghiberti **9** Donatello **10** Michelozzi **11** della Robbia **12** Brunelleschi, Michelangelo
capital of: **7** Tuscany **15** Firenze province
cathedral / church: **10** San Lorenzo, San Miniato, Santa Croce **18** Santa Maria del Fiore
Italian: **7** Firenze
landmark: **5** Pieta **6** Uffizi **8** Bargello **11** Pitti Palace **12** Ponte Vecchio **13** Boboli Gardens **14** Loggia dei Lanzi, Palazzo Vecchio **19** Piazza della Signoria **22** Baptistry of San Giovanni, Ospedale degli Innocenti
mountain: **9** Apennines
religious reformer: **10** Savonarola
river: **4** Arno
ruler: **5** Goths **6** Medici, Romans **8** Lombards **9** Etruscans **15** Byzantine Empire
tomb of: **7** Galileo, Rossini **11** Machiavelli **12** Michelangelo **15** Lorenzo de Medici

---

Florida
abbreviation: **2** FL **3** Fla
nickname: **6** Flower **8** Sunshine **10** Peninsular
capital: **11** Tallahassee
largest city: **12** Jacksonville
others: **4** Tice **5** Cocoa, Miami, Ocala, Tampa **7** Hialeah, Orlando, Palatka, Sebring **8** Sarasota **9** Bradenton, Palm Beach, Pensacola **10** Clearwater **11** Brooksville, Coral Gables, Gainesville, St Augustine **12** Daytona Beach, Ft Lauderdale, St Petersburg
college: **4** Nova **5** Barry, Miami, Tampa **6** Eckerd **7** Rollins, Stetson
explorer: **11** Ponce de Leon
feature:
  amusement park: **5** Epcot **10** Marineland **11** Disney World
  canal: **5** Miami **7** Tamiami
  museum: **8** Ringling
  national park: **10** Everglades
tribe: **3** Ais **5** Ocale, Utina **6** Calusa, Chatot, Potano **7** Timucua **8** Seminole
people: **5** conch **7** cracker, Osceola
island: **7** Bahamas, Sanibel **8** Biscayne
  key: **4** Long, Vaca, West **5** Largo **7** Big Pine **8** Biscayne **9** Sugarloaf
lake: **4** Dora **6** Apopka, Harney, Jessup, Newnan **7** Ledwith **8** Arbuckle **9** Kissimmee **10** Okeechobee
land rank: **12** twenty-second
physical feature:
  bay: **8** Biscayne **9** Apalachee **10** Waccasassa
  cape: **5** Sable **7** Kennedy **9** Canaveral
  gulf: **6** Mexico
  sea: **8** Atlantic
  springs: **6** Silver **7** Rainbow
  swamp: **10** Everglades, Okefenokee
river: **6** Banana, Indian **7** Aucilla, Manatee, Scambia, St Johns, Suwanee **9** Ochlawaha **12** Apalachicola
state admission: **13** twenty-seventh
state bird: **11** mockingbird
state fish: **16** Atlantic sailfish
state mammal: **7** dolphin
state flower: **13** orange blossom
state motto: **12** In God We Trust
state song: **11** Swanee River **14** Old Folks at Home
state tree: **13** sabal palmetto **15** cabbage palmetto

shamble, stagger, stumble
8 flatfish, hesitate, struggle

Flounder, The
　author: **11** Gunter Grass

flourish 4 curl, dash, grow,
pomp, rant, show, turn
5 bloom, bluff, get on, shake,
strut, sweep, swing, swish,
twirl, twist, wield **6** flaunt,
flower, hot air, parade, splash,
thrive, waving **7** blossom, bravado, burgeon, cadenza, fanfare, fustian, glitter, prosper,
shaking, succeed, swagger
8 boasting, brandish, curlicue,
fare well, get ahead, swinging,
vaunting, wielding **9** agitation,
grace note, thrashing **10** decoration **11** braggadocio, brandishing, fanfaronade,
ostentation **12** appoggiatura
13 embellishment, magniloquence, swashbuckling
14 grandiloquence

flourishing 8 swinging, swish-
ing, thriving, wielding
9 flaunting **10** prospering, successful **11** brandishing

flout 3 rag **4** defy, mock, twit
5 chaff, scorn, spurn, taunt
6 gibe at, insult

flow 3 jet, run **4** flux, gush,
pass, pour, rush, seep, tide
5 drain, drift, float, flood,
glide, issue, spout, spurt,
surge, sweep, swirl, train
6 abound, course, deluge, efflux, effuse, filter, plenty, rapids, stream **7** cascade, current,
debouch, torrent, well out
8 effusion, millrace, plethora,
sequence **9** abundance, discharge, effluence, emanation
10 outpouring, succession
11 debouchment, progression

flower 3 bud **4** best, blow,
open, pick, posy **5** bloom,
cream, elite, ripen **6** mature
7 blossom, bouquet, burgeon,
develop, nosegay, prosper
8 flourish **11** aristocracy

flower arranging, art of
　Japanese: **7** ikebana

Flower Fables
　author: **15** Louisa May Alcott

flowering 4 peak **5** bloom
6 height, heyday **8** blooming,
maturing **10** blossoming, developing, prospering
11 flourishing

Flowering Judas
　author: **19** Katherine Anne
　Porter

flowers
　goddess of: **5** Flora

Flowers of Evil
　author: **17** Charles Baudelaire

Flower State
　nickname of: **7** Florida

flowery 5 fancy **6** floral, florid,
ornate **8** blooming **10** blossoming, burgeoning, euphuistic, figurative, florescent,
ornamental, rhetorical **11** embellished **12** efflorescent, magniloquent **13** grandiloquent

Flowery Kingdom see
5 China

flowing 4 flux **5** fluid **6** ebbing,
fluent, smooth **7** current, copious, gliding, running **8** abundant **9** liquefied, plentiful
10 continuity, pouring out,
proceeding

fluctuate 4 sway, vary, veer
5 shift, swing, waver **6** dawdle, falter, wobble **8** hesitate,
undulate **9** alternate, oscillate,
vacillate **10** dillydally

fluctuation 5 shift **6** change
7 veering **8** shifting, swinging
9 deviation, variation **11** alternation, oscillation, vacillation

flue 3 net **4** barb, down, pipe,
tube, vent **5** fluff, fluke, shaft
6 funnel **7** channel, chimney,
passage **9** smokejack

fluent 4 glib **5** vocal **6** facile
7 voluble **8** effusive, eloquent
9 garrulous, talkative **10** articulate, effortless

fluff 3 err, nap **4** down, flub,
fuzz, lint, miss, puff, slip,
soft **5** botch, floss, froth,
primp **6** forget **7** blunder
8 feathers

fluffy 5 downy, fuzzy, nappy,
wooly **6** fleecy, woolly
8 feathery

fluid 6 liquid, watery **7** unfixed
8 flexible, floating, shifting, solution, unstable **9** adaptable,
liquefied, unsettled **10** adjustable, changeable, indefinite

fluid ounce
　abbreviation: **4** fl oz

fluke 3 hap **5** freak **6** chance
7 miracle **8** accident, windfall
9 mischance **11** vicissitude
12 stroke of luck

flummery 7 dessert, pudding
9 gibberish **10** doubletalk,
mumbo jumbo **11** obfuscation

flunky 6 lackey, menial, minion **7** servant **9** attendant,
underling

fluorine
　chemical symbol: **1** F

flurry 3 ado **4** fuss, gust, heat,
puff, stir **5** alarm, fever, flush,
haste, panic **6** breeze, bustle,
pother, rattle, shower, squall,

tumult **7** agitate, confuse, disturb, fidgets, fluster, flutter,
perturb **8** confound, disquiet
9 agitation, commotion, confusion **10** discompose, disconcert, turbulence
11 disturbance, hurry-scurry,
trepidation **12** discomposure,
perturbation, restlessness

flush 4 even, glow, swab, tint,
wash **5** bloom, blush, color,
elate, flood, level, rinse, scour,
scrub, shock, spray **6** access,
dampen, deluge, douche,
drench, excite, puff up, quiver,
redden, sponge, thrill, tremor
7 animate, flutter, glowing,
impulse, moisten, redness,
wash out **8** rosiness, rosy
glow, squarely, strength
9 freshness, make proud, ruddiness **10** exultation,
jubilation

flushed 3 hot, red **4** rosy,
ruby **5** aglow, **6** florid, torrid
7 crimson, excited, scarlet
8 blushing, feverish
10 prosperous

flushed with success
5 proud **6** elated

fluster 4 daze **5** shake, upset
6 dither, flurry, hubbub, muddle, ruffle **7** agitate, confuse,
disturb, flutter, perplex, perturb, startle, turmoil **8** befuddle, bewilder **9** agitation,
commotion, confusion, discomfit **10** discompose, disconcert
12 bewilderment, discomfiture,
discomposure
14 discombobulate

flute 4 fife, fold, pipe, roll,
tube, wind **5** crimp **6** furrow,
groove **7** piccolo, whistle **8** recorder **9** wine glass **14** champagne glass

flutter 3 bob **4** flap, flit, soar,
stir, wave, wing **5** hurry,
shake, throb **6** flurry, quiver,
ripple, thrill, tremor, wobble
7 beating, flitter, fluster, pulsate, tremble, twitter **8** flap-
ping, tingling **9** agitation,
commotion, confusion, palpitate, sensation, vibration
12 perturbation

fluvial 7 aquatic

fluviatile 7 aquatic

flux 4 flow, tide **5** flood
6 course, motion, stream, unrest **7** current **8** mutation,
shifting **10** alteration, transition **11** fluctuation **12** modification **14** transformation

fly 4 flap, flee, sail, skip, soar,
wave, wing **5** coast, float,
glide, hover, hurry, split,
swoop **6** hasten, hustle **7** flut-

ter, run away, take off, vibrate **8** take wing, undulate

fly
  varieties: 3 bat, bot **4** blow, deer, dung, gnat, horn, moth, rust, sand **5** beach, black, crane, dance, drone, flesh, fruit, horse, house, march, marsh, midge, mydas, punky **6** bee fly, cactus, maggot, pomace, robber, stable, tsetse, warble, window **7** chalcid, seaweed, skipper, soldier, tachima **8** lousefly, mosquito, stiletto **9** leaf miner **10** flatfooted, fungus gnat, humpbacked **11** thickheaded **14** black scavenger

fly apart 5 burst **6** blow up **7** explode, shatter **8** detonate, fragment

fly at 6 assail, attack

fly-by-night 5 shady **6** shifty **7** crooked **8** unstable, untrusty **9** dishonest **10** unreliable **12** disreputable, undependable **13** irresponsible, untrustworthy

Flying Dutchman, The
  opera by: 6 Wagner
  character: 4 Erik **5** Senta **6** Daland **11** The Dutchman

Flying Fish
  constellation of: 6 Volans

Flying Nun, The
  character: 9 Sister Ana **11** Sister Sixto **13** Carlos Ramirez **14** Mother Superior **15** Sister Bertrille **16** Sister Jacqueline
  cast: 10 Sally Field **12** Alejandro Rey, Linda Dangcil, Marge Redmond **14** Shelly Morrison **17** Madeleine Sherwood

fly in the ointment 5 hitch **7** problem, trouble **8** drawback, nuisance **9** hindrance **10** impediment **12** disadvantage

Flynn, Errol
  real name: 17 Leslie Thomas Flynn
  born: 6 Hobart **8** Tasmania
  roles: 10 The Sea Hawk **12** Captain Blood **14** Too Much Too Soon **15** The Sun Also Rises **24** The Adventures of Robin Hood **26** The Charge of the Light Brigade

fly off the handle 6 see red

fly the coop 4 bolt, flee **6** escape, run off **7** abscond, get away, make off, run away, skip out, take off

foal 4 cade, colt **5** filly, young **9** fledgling

foam 4 fizz, head, scum, suds **5** froth, spume **6** lather **7** sparkle **8** bubbling **13** effervescence

foaming 5 sudsy **6** bubbly, frothy **7** lathery **8** bubbling, frothing

foamy 5 fizzy **6** frothy **7** lathery **8** bubbling **9** sparkling **12** effervescent

fob 5 chain, medal, strap **6** ribbon **8** ornament **9** medallion

focal 3 key **4** main **5** chief **7** central, pivotal **8** foremost **9** principal

Foch, Ferdinand
  served in: 3 WWI
  nationality: 6 French
  rank: 7 marshal **16** commander-in-chief
  battle: 5 Marne, Somme

Foch, Nina
  real name: 20 Nina Consuelo Maud Fock
  born: 6 Leyden **11** Netherlands
  roles: 9 Spartacus **14** Executive Suite, Song to Remember **17** An American in Paris, My Name Is Julia Ross **18** The Ten Commandments

Fock, Nina Consuelo Maud
  real name of: 8 Nina Foch

focus 3 aim, fix, hub **4** core **5** haunt, heart **6** adjust, center, direct, middle, resort **7** nucleus, retreat **8** converge **9** limelight, spotlight **10** rendezvous **11** concentrate **12** headquarters

focusing 6 aiming **9** adjusting, centering, directing **10** adjustment, converging **11** pinpointing **13** concentrating

fodder 4 feed, food **6** forage, silage **7** rations **9** provender

foe 5 enemy, rival **8** attacker, opponent **9** adversary, assailant, combatant, contender, disputant **10** antagonist, competitor

fog 3 dim **4** daze, haze, smog, soup **5** brume, cloud **6** darken, muddle, stupor, trance **7** confuse, obscure, pea soup, perplex **8** bewilder **9** murkiness **10** cloudiness **12** bewilderment

Fogg, Phileas
  character in: 26 Around the World in Eighty Days
  author: 10 Jules Verne

foggy 3 dim **4** dark, hazy **5** dusky, filmy, fuzzy, misty, murky, musty, soupy, vague **6** cloudy, smoggy, spacey

7 brumous, clouded, obscure, shadowy, unclear **8** confused, nebulous, overcast, vaporous **9** beclouded **10** indistinct

foible 4 kink **5** quirk **6** defect, whimsy **7** failing, frailty **8** crotchet, weak side, weakness **9** infirmity **10** deficiency **11** shortcoming **12** imperfection

Foible
  character in: 16 The Way of the World
  author: 8 Congreve

foil 3 nip **4** balk, film, leaf **5** check, flake, match, sheet, wafer **6** hinder, lamina, set off, thwart **7** enhance, prevent **8** backdrop, contrast **9** frustrate **10** antithesis, complement, supplement **11** correlative, counterpart

foist 6 impose, unload **7** palm off, pass off

fold 3 hug, lap, pen, sty **4** bend, curl, sect, tuck, wrap, yard **5** clasp, close, crimp, flock, group, layer, pleat **6** corral, crease, dog-ear, double, encase, enfold, furrow, gather, parish, pucker, ruffle, rumple, wrap up **7** crinkle, crumple, embosom, embrace, entwine, envelop, flounce, overlap, wrinkle **8** barnyard, compound, doubling, stockade **9** community, corrugate, enclosure **12** congregation

folder 7 booklet, leaflet **8** brochure, circular, pamphlet **9** portfolio

foliage 6 leaves **7** leafage, verdure

folklore 5 myths **6** fables **7** legends **10** traditions

folks 3 kin **6** family, people **7** kinsmen, parents **8** everyone **9** relatives **10** kith and kin

folksy 6 casual, chatty **8** familiar, friendly, homespun, informal, sociable **10** neighborly **14** conversational **15** unsophisticated

folk tale
  German: 7 Marchen

Follett, Ken
  author of: 14 Eye of the Needle **15** On Wings of Eagles, The Key to Rebecca **22** The Man from St Petersburg

follow 3 dog **4** copy, heed, hunt, mind, note, obey, tail **5** aim at, chase, grasp, hound, stalk, trace, track, trail, watch **6** attend, notice, pursue, regard, shadow, take up **7** cherish, emulate, imitate, observe, replace, succeed **8** practice, supplant **9** accompany, cultivate, prosecute **10** comprehend, understand

follower 3 fan **4** tail **5** pupil, toady **6** chaser, hunter, shadow, stooge **7** admirer, apostle, convert, devotee, protege, pursuer, servant, stalker **8** adherent, advocate, disciple, hanger-on, henchman, parasite, partisan, retainer, servitor **9** accessory, attendant, dependent, proselyte, satellite, supporter, sycophant

following 4 next **5** below, suite, train **6** public **7** ensuing, retinue **8** audience **9** adherents, clientele, entourage, partisans, patronage **10** attendance, consequent, sequential, subsequent, succeeding, successive **11** consecutive

Follow the Fleet
   director: 12 Mark Sandrich
   cast: 11 Fred Astaire **12** Ginger Rogers **13** Randolph Scott **21** Harriet Hilliard Nelson
   song: 13 We Saw the Sea **13** Let Yourself Go **24** Let's Face the Music and Dance

follow-up 7 ensuing **8** sequence **9** aftermath **10** subsequent

folly 6 idiocy, levity **7** inanity, mistake **8** nonsense, trifling **9** absurdity, asininity, frivolity, giddiness, silliness **10** imbecility, imprudence, tomfoolery **11** doltishness, fatuousness, foolishness **12** indiscretion **13** brainlessness, irrationality, senselessness

foment 4 goad, spur, urge **5** rouse **6** arouse, excite, foster, incite, kindle, stir up **7** agitate, inflame, promote, provoke, quicken **8** irritate **9** aggravate, galvanize, instigate, stimulate **10** exacerbate

Fomorian
   origin: 5 Irish
   form: 5 demon **6** pirate
   habitat: 3 sea
   raided: 7 Ireland
   personifies: 13 hostile nature

fond 5 naive **6** ardent, doting, loving, tender **7** amorous, devoted **8** desirous, enamored, harbored, held dear **9** cherished, indulgent, preserved, sustained **10** infatuated, passionate **11** impassioned, sentimental **12** affectionate

16 overaffectionate

Fonda, Henry
   wife: 16 Margaret Sullavan
   son: 5 Peter
   daughter: 4 Jane
   born: 13 Grand Island NE
   roles: 7 Jezebel, Warlock **8** Fail Safe **10** Fort Apache, In Harm's Way, The Best Man, The Lady Eve **12** On Golden Pond (Oscar) **13** Mister Roberts, Ox-Bow Incident, The Longest Day **14** Twelve Angry Men, Young Mr Lincoln **16** Advise and Consent, Battle of the Bulge, How the West Was Won, The Grapes of Wrath **18** The Boston Strangler **19** My Darling Clementine, The Immortal Sergeant **21** Sometimes a Great Notion

Fonda, Jane
   father: 5 Henry
   brother: 5 Peter
   husband: 9 Ted Turner, Tom Hayden **10** Roger Vadim
   born: 9 New York NY
   roles: 5 Julia, Klute (Oscar) **10** Barbarella, Coming Home (Oscar) **11** A Doll's House **12** Any Wednesday, On Golden Pond **13** China Syndrome **17** Barefoot in the Park **23** They Shoot Horses Don't They?

Fonda, Peter
   father: 5 Henry
   sister: 4 Jane
   born: 9 New York NY
   roles: 7 The Trip **9** Easy Rider **13** The Wild Angels

fondle 3 hug, pet **5** spoon **6** caress, cuddle, nestle, nuzzle, smooch, stroke **7** embrace, make out **10** bill and coo

fondness 4 bent, care, love **5** ardor, fancy **6** desire, liking **7** passion **8** devotion, penchant, weakness **9** affection **10** attachment, partiality, preference, propensity, tenderness **11** amorousness, inclination **12** predilection **14** susceptibility

fond utterance 9 sweet talk **10** endearment **12** sweet nothing

Fons
   origin: 5 Roman
   god of: 7 springs

fons et origo 15 source and origin

Fontaine, Joan
   real name: 25 Joan de Beauvoir de Havilland
   sister: 17 Olivia de Havilland
   husband: 11 Brian Aherne
   born: 5 Japan, Tokyo
   roles: 3 Ivy **7** Ivanhoe, Re-

becca **8** Casanova, Gunga Din, Jane Eyre, The Women **9** Suspicion (Oscar) **12** The Devil's Own **15** Frenchman's Creek, September Affair **16** Tender Is the Night, The Constant Nymph

Fontanne, Lynn
   husband: 10 Alfred Lunt
   born: 6 London **7** England
   roles: 8 The Visit **9** Quadrille, The Pirate **10** The Sea Gull **13** O Mistress Mine **15** Design for Living **18** The Great Sebastians **19** The Taming of the Shrew

food 4 chow, feed, grub **5** board **6** fodder, forage, silage, viands **7** edibles, nurture, pasture, rations **8** eatables, victuals **9** nutrition, pasturage, provender **10** provisions, sustenance **11** comestibles, nourishment, subsistence

food, miraculous 5 manna

fool 3 ass, con, oaf **4** bilk, clod, dolt, dupe, gull, hoax, jest, joke **5** cheat, chump, clown, cozen, cut up, dummy, dunce, feign, goose, idiot, klutz, moron, ninny, tease, trick **6** diddle, fleece, frolic, humbug, jester, nitwit, rip off, stooge **7** beguile, buffoon, deceive, defraud, half-wit, Pierrot, pretend **8** bonehead, dummkopf, flimflam, hoodwink, imbecile, lunkhead, meathead, numskull **9** bamboozle, blockhead, harlequin, ignoramus, numbskull, simpleton **10** dunderhead, nincompoop, scaramouch **11** Punchinello

fool around 3 toy **4** idle **5** clown, dally **6** dawdle, loiter, trifle

foolhardy 4 rash **5** brash, hasty **6** madcap **8** careless, heedless, reckless **9** daredevil, hotheaded, impetuous, imprudent, impulsive **10** headstrong, incautious **11** harebrained, thoughtless

foolish 5 inane, silly **6** absurd, stupid, unwise **7** asinine, fatuous, idiotic, moronic, witless **9** brainless, imbecilic, imprudent, ludicrous, senseless **10** boneheaded, incautious, indiscreet, ridiculous **12** preposterous **13** irresponsible, unintelligent

foolishness 5 folly **6** idiocy, lunacy **8** unwisdom **9** absurdity, asininity, puerility, silliness, stupidity **10** imbecility, imprudence **11** fatuousness, witlessness **12** childishness, extravagance, indiscretion brainlessness, senselessness **14** ridiculousness **15** injudiciousness **16** irresponsibility, preposterousness

Fool of Quality, The
   author: **11** Henry Brooke

foot 3 dog, pad, paw **4** base, hoof **6** bottom, tootsy **7** trotter **8** infantry **10** foundation
   abbreviation: **2** ft

football
   athlete/coach: **8** Don Shula, Jim Brown, Kyle Rote, Lou Groza, Y A Tittle **9** Amos Stagg, Bart Starr, Bob Griese, Chuck Noll, Dan Marino, Don Hutson, Earl Blaik, Jerry Rice, Joe Namath, Len Dawson, Lou Little, O J Simpson, Red Grange, Tom Landry **10** Bear Bryant, Bruce Smith, Bubba Smith, Dick Butkus, Joe Montana, Joe Paterno, Ken Stabler, Larry Brown, Otto Graham, Sammy Baugh, Troy Aikman, Walter Camp, Weeb Ewbank **11** Ahmad Rashad, Craig Morton, Deacon Jones, Deion Sanders, Earl Morrall, Ernie Nevers, Floyd Little, Gayle Sayers, George Halas, Jan Stenerud, Jim Plunkett, John Riggins, Knute Rockne, Larry Csonka, Merlin Olsen, Paul Hornung, Pete Rozelle, Reggie White, Richard Todd, Tony Dorsett **12** Bud Wilkinson, Earl Campbell, Franco Harris, Frank Gifford, George Blanda, Joe Thiesmann, Johnny Unitas, Lance Alworth, Ozzie Newsome, Raymond Berry, Roman Gabriel, Walter Payton, William Perry **13** Ara Parseghian, Eric Dickerson, Fran Tarkenton, Roger Staubach, Terry Bradshaw, Vince Lombardi **14** Bronco Nagurski, Lawrence Taylor, Lydell Mitchell, Sonny Jurgensen **15** Norm Van Brocklin

football bowl games 3 Sun **4** Rose **5** Aloha, Gator, Peach, Sugar, Super **6** Citrus, Copper, Cotton, Fiesta, Orange **7** Holiday, Liberty **10** Bluebonnet, California **12** Independence

football leagues
   National Football League (NFL): **11** New York Jets **12** Buffalo Bills, Chicago Bears, Detroit Lions **13** Dallas Cowboys, Denver Broncos, Houston Oilers, Miami Dolphins, New York Giants **14** Atlanta Falcons, Los Angeles Rams **15** Cleveland Browns, Green Bay Packers, Seattle Seahawks **16** Kansas City Chiefs, Minnesota Vi-

kings, New Orleans Saints, Phoenix Cardinals (formerly St Louis), San Diego Chargers **17** Cincinnati Bengals, Indianapolis Colts (formerly Baltimore), Los Angeles Raiders (formerly Oakland) **18** New England Patriots, Philadelphia Eagles, Pittsburgh Steelers, Tampa Bay Buccaneers, Washington Redskins **23** San Francisco Forty-niners

United States Football League (USFL): 10 Denver Gold **12** Chicago Blitz **14** Baltimore Stars, Boston Breakers **15** Houston Gamblers, Oakland Invaders, Oklahoma Outlaws, Tampa Bay Bandits **16** Arizona Wranglers, Memphis Showboats, Michigan Panthers, Orlando Renegades, Portland Breakers

17 Jacksonville Bulls, Los Angeles Express, New Jersey Generals, Philadelphia Stars **18** Washington Federals **19** Birmingham Stallions **21** San Antonio Gunslingers

football team *see box*

footfall 3 pad **4** pace, step **5** tread **8** footstep

foothold 4 grip, hold **7** support **8** purchase

footloose 4 free **8** carefree **9** fancy-free **10** unattached **11** uncommitted **12** unencumbered

footnote 5 gloss **9** reference **10** annotation **11** explanation **12** afterthought

footpad 5 thief **6** bandit, mugger, outlaw, robber **10** highwayman

---

football team (NFC)
   Arizona: 9 Cardinals
      stadium: **8** Sun Devil
      formerly in: **7** St. Louis
   Atlanta: 7 Falcons
      stadium: **11** Georgia Dome
   Carolina: 8 Panthers
      stadium: **8** Carolina
   Chicago: 5 Bears
      stadium: **12** Soldier Field
   Dallas: 7 Cowboys
      stadium: **5** Texas
   Detroit: 5 Lions
      stadium: **17** Pontiac Silverdome
   Green Bay: 7 Packers
      stadium: **9** Milwaukee **12** Lambeau Field
   Minnesota: 7 Vikings
      stadium: **9** Metrodome
   New Orleans: 6 Saints
      stadium: **18** Louisiana Superdome
   New York: 6 Giants
      stadium: **6** Giants
   Philadelphia: 6 Eagles
      stadium: **8** Veterans
   Saint Louis: 4 Rams
      stadium: **7** TWA Dome
      formerly in: **10** Los Angeles
   San Francisco: 11 Forty-Niners
      stadium: **15** Candlestick Park
   Tampa Bay: 10 Buccaneers
      stadium: **5** Tampa

   Washington: 8 Redskins
      stadium: **14** Robert F Kennedy

football team (AFC)
   Buffalo: 5 Bills
      stadium: **4** Rich
   Cincinnati: 7 Bengals
      stadium: **10** Riverfront
   Cleveland: 6 Browns
      stadium: **9** Municipal
   Denver: 7 Broncos
      stadium: **8** Mile High
   Houston: 6 Oilers
      stadium: **9** Astrodome
   Indianapolis: 5 Colts
      stadium: **11** Hoosier Dome
      formerly in:
      9 Baltimore
   Jacksonville: 7 Jaguars
      stadium: **8** Municipal
   Kansas City: 6 Chiefs
      stadium: **9** Arrowhead
   Miami: 8 Dolphins
      stadium: **9** Joe Robbie
   New England: 8 Patriots
      stadium: **7** Foxboro
   New York: 4 Jets
      stadium: **6** Giants
   Oakland: 7 Raiders
      stadium: **8** Coliseum
      formerly in: **10** Los Angeles
   Pittsburgh: 8 Steelers
      stadium: **11** Three Rivers
   San Diego: 8 Chargers
      stadium: **10** Jack Murphy
   Seattle: 8 Seahawks
      stadium: **8** Kingdome

footpath 4 lane, ramp 5 jetty, trail 8 sidewalk

foot soldiers 8 infantry 10 fusilliers, musketeers

footstool 6 buffet 7 hassock, ottoman 8 footrest

footwear
French: 9 chaussure

fop 4 beau, dude 5 dandy, swell 7 coxcomb 8 popinjay 9 prettyboy 11 Beau Brummel

foppish 4 vain 5 gaudy, showy 6 ornate 7 finical 8 affected, dandyish 9 dandified 12 ostentatious 13 overelaborate

forage 4 feed, food, hunt, raid, seek 6 fodder, ravage, search, silage 7 despoil, explore, pasture, plunder, rummage 8 scavenge, scrounge 9 pasturage, provender 10 provisions

foray 4 raid 5 sally 6 attack, inroad, invade, ravage, thrust 7 pillage, plunder, venture 8 invasion 9 incursion 10 expedition 11 depredation

forbear 4 quit, stop 5 cease, forgo 6 desist, endure, eschew, forego, give up, suffer 7 abstain, refrain 8 abnegate, renounce, tolerate

forbearance 4 pity 5 mercy 6 pardon 8 clemency, eschewal, leniency, meekness, mildness, patience 9 endurance, tolerance 10 abstention, abstinence, continence, indulgence, moderation, submission, temperance 11 longanimity, resignation 12 mercifulness

forbearing 6 denial 7 lenient, refusal 8 eschewal, tolerant 9 indulgent 10 abnegation, abstention, abstinence, permissive, refraining 13 nonindulgence 16 nonparticipation

forbid 3 ban, bar 4 veto 5 taboo 6 enjoin, hinder, impede, oppose, refuse, reject 7 exclude, gainsay, inhibit, obviate, prevent 8 disallow, obstruct, preclude, prohibit, restrain 9 interdict, proscribe

forbiddance 3 ban 5 taboo 7 barring, embargo 9 exclusion, interdict 11 prohibition 12 interdiction, proscription

forbidden 5 taboo 6 banned 8 debarred 10 prohibited, proscribed
German: 8 verboten

forbidden fruit
type: 6 brandy 7 liqueur
origin: 7 America

flavor: 5 honey 6 orange 10 grapefruit

forbidden marriage
goddess of: 4 Lofn

forbidding 4 dour, grim, ugly 6 odious 7 hideous, ominous 8 horrible, sinister 9 abhorrent, offensive, repellent, repulsive 10 unfriendly, unpleasant 11 prohibitive, prohibitory, threatening 12 disagreeable, inhospitable 14 unapproachable

force 3 pry, vim 4 army, body, coax, crew, drag, gang, make, pull, push, team, unit, urge 5 break, clout, corps, drive, group, impel, might, power, press, squad, value, vigor, wrest 6 coerce, compel, duress, effect, elicit, energy, enjoin, extort, impact, import, impose, induce, oblige, propel, stress, thrust, weight, wrench 7 cogency, intrude, meaning, obtrude, potency, require, squeeze, stamina 8 charisma, coercion, division, efficacy, emphasis, momentum, persuade, pressure, squadron, strength, validity, violence, vitality 9 animation, battalion, constrain, magnetism, overpower, puissance 10 attraction, compulsion, constraint, detachment 11 necessitate, weightiness 12 significance 13 effectiveness
Latin: 3 vis

forced 5 slave 7 binding, coerced, labored, obliged 8 affected, enslaved, grudging, mannered, required, strained 9 compelled, impressed, insincere, mandatory, unwilling 10 artificial, compulsory, obligatory 11 constrained, involuntary

forceful 5 pithy, valid, vivid 6 cogent, potent, robust, strong, virile 7 dynamic, intense 8 emphatic, powerful, puissant, vigorous 9 effective, energetic 10 impressive

forceless 4 weak 8 impotent

force measurement 4 dyne 6 newton 7 poundal

Force of Circumstance
author: 16 Simone de Beauvoir

Force of Destiny, The
also: 17 La Forza del Destino
opera by: 5 Verdi
character: 7 Leonora 8 Don Carlo 9 Don Alvaro

forcible 8 coercive 10 compulsory

ford 3 car 4 span, wade 5 cross, edsel, shoal 6 bridge, model T, stream 7 passage 8 crossing, tin lizzy

Ford, Gerald Rudolph *see box*

Ford, Glenn
real name: 11 Gwyllyn Ford
wife: 13 Eleanor Powell
born: 6 Canada, Quebec
roles: 4 Rage 5 Gilda, Jubal 6 Santee 8 Cimarron 11 The Rounders 14 Is Paris Burning? 17 Interrupted Melody 18 Don't Go Near the Water 19 The Blackboard Jungle 23 Teahouse of the August Moon

Ford, Harrison
born: 9 Chicago IL
roles: 7 Frantic, Witness 8 Star Wars 11 Blade Runner 15 Return of the Jedi 16 American Graffiti 19 Raiders of the Lost Ark 20 The Empire Strikes Back 30 Indiana Jones and the Temple of Doom

Ford, John
author of: 13 Perkin Warbeck 17 'Tis Pity She's a Whore 19 The Lover's Melancholy

Ford, John
director of: 10 Stagecoach 11 The Informer (Oscar), The Quiet Man (Oscar) 12 The Hurricane, The Searchers 13 Grapes of Wrath (Oscar), Mister Roberts (with Mervyn LeRoy), The Lost Patrol 17 The Long Voyage Home 19 How Green Was My Valley (Oscar), My Darling Clementine 27 The Man Who Shot Liberty Valence

Ford, Thelma Booth
real name of: 12 Shirley Booth

Ford and Mistress Ford
characters in: 22 The Merry Wives of Windsor
author: 11 Shakespeare

fore 5 front 7 frontal 8 anterior, headmost

forearm 4 ulna 5 prime, ready 7 prepare

forebear 8 ancestor, begetter 10 antecedent, procreator, progenitor

foreboding 4 omen 5 dread 6 augury, boding 7 portent 9 intuition, misgiving 10 prescience, prognostic 11 premonition 12 apprehension, presentiment

Ford, Gerald Rudolph
  born: 17 Leslie Lynch King Jr
  adopted by/named after: 10 stepfather
  nickname: 5 Jerry 7 Mr Clean
  presidential rank: 12 thirty-eighth
  party: 10 Republican
  state represented: 2 MI
  defeated: 5 no one
  elected to neither: 10 presidency 14 vice presidency
  vice president: 11 (Nelson A) Rockefeller
  cabinet:
    state: 9 (Henry A) Kissinger
    treasury: 5 (William E) Simon
    defense: 8 (Donald H) Rumsfeld 11 (James) Schlesinger
    attorney general: 4 (Edward H) Levi 5 (William B)
      Saxbe
    interior: 6 (Rogers Clark Ballard) Morton, (Thomas S)
      Kleppe 8 (Stanley K) Hathaway
    agriculture: 4 (Earl Lauer) Butz 6 (John A) Knebel
    commerce: 4 (Frederick B) Dent 6 (Rogers Clark Ballard)
      Morton 10 (Elliot L) Richardson
    labor: 5 (W J) Usery (Jr) 6 (John T) Dunlop 7 (Peter J)
      Brennan
    HEW: 7 (F David) Mathews 10 (Caspar W) Weinberger
    HUD: 4 (James T) Lynn 5 (Carla Anderson) Hills
    transportation: 7 (William T) Coleman (Jr) 8 (Claude S)
      Brinegar
  born: 7 Omaha NE
  education:
    University: 8 Michigan
    Law School: 4 Yale
  religion: 12 Episcopalian
  interests: 4 golf 6 boxing, skiing 8 football, swimming
  vacation spot: 2 CO 4 Vail
  author: 21 Portrait of the Assassin (with John R Stiles)
    27 A Time To Heal: An Autobiography
  political career: 13 vice president 19 House minority
    leader 24 US House of Representatives
  civilian career: 6 lawyer
    assistant football coach at: 4 Yale
  military service: 6 US Navy 10 lieutenant, World War II
  notable events of lifetime/term: 9 recession
    12 Bicentennial
    assassination attempts on: 4 Ford
    clemency for: 12 draft dodgers, draft evaders
    kidnapping/trial/conviction of: 11 Patty Hearst
    scandal: 8 Lockheed 10 Hays Affair
    talks: 4 SALT
  quotes: 19 I am a Ford not a Lincoln 41 Indebted to no
    man—the president of all the people 50 Our long na-
    tional nightmare is over Our constitution works
  father:
    natural: 15 Leslie Lynch King
    adoptive: 17 Gerald Rudolph Ford
  mother: 7 Dorothy (Gardner King Ford)
  siblings:
    half-brothers: 12 James Francis 13 Thomas Gardner
      14 Richard Addison
  wife: 9 Elizabeth (Bloomer Warren)
    nickname: 5 Betty
  children: 4 John 5 Susan 6 Steven 7 Michael

10 antecedent, originator, procreator, progenitor
12 primogenitor

forefront 4 fame, head, lead
8 vanguard 9 celebrity

foreign 5 alien 6 exotic, remote 7 distant, strange, unknown, unusual 8 imported
9 barbarous, extrinsic, irregular, unrelated 10 extraneous,
heathenish, introduced, irrelevant, outlandish, unfamiliar
11 incongruous, inconsonant,
unconnected 12 antipathetic,
inadmissible, inapplicable, incompatible, inconsistent
13 inappropriate
16 uncharacteristic

Foreign Correspondent
director: 15 Alfred Hitchcock
cast: 10 Joel McCrea, Laraine
Day 13 George Sanders
14 Robert Benchley 15 Al-
bert Basserman, Herbert
Marshall

foreigner 5 alien, pagan
6 emigre 8 newcomer, out-
sider, stranger 9 barbarian, immigrant, nonnative, outlander
German: 9 Auslander

foreign officer 6 consul 8 diplomat, minister 10 ambassador 14 representative
15 charge d'affaires

foreknowledge 9 intuition,
prevision 10 prescience
11 premonition 12 anticipation, apprehension, clairvoyance, precognition,
presentiment

foreman 4 boss 7 manager
8 chairman, overseer 9 president, spokesman 10 supervisor 11 coordinator
14 superintendent

foremost 4 head, main 5 chief,
vital 7 capital, leading, supreme 8 cardinal 9 essential,
paramount, principal
10 preeminent

forerunner 4 omen, sign 5 token 6 augury, herald 7 portent, presage 8 ancestor
9 harbinger, precursor, prototype 10 progenitor, prognostic 11 predecessor,
premonition

foresee 5 augur 6 divine, expect 7 predict, presage 8 envision, prophesy 10 anticipate
13 prognosticate

foreshadow 5 augur 7 presage,
promise 9 prefigure

foresight 6 wisdom 8 planning,
prudence, sagacity 9 prevision
10 discretion, precaution, prescience, providence, shrewdness 12 anticipation,

forecast 5 augur 6 augury, divine, expect 7 outlook, portend, predict, presage, project
8 envisage, envision, prophesy 9 calculate, prevision,
prognosis 10 anticipate, conjecture, prediction, prescience,

projection 11 extrapolate
12 anticipation, precognition,
presentiment 13 prognosticate
15 prognostication

forefather 6 author 8 ancestor,
begetter 9 patriarch, precursor

clairvoyance, perspicacity, precognition, preparedness **13** premeditation **14** farsightedness

forest 4 bush, wood **5** copse, grove, stand, woods **6** jungle **7** thicket **8** wildwood, woodland **10** timberland, wilderness

forestall 5 avert, avoid, block, deter **6** thwart **7** head off, obviate, prevent, ward off **8** preclude **10** anticipate, circumvent, counteract

Forester, C S (Cecil Scott)
author of: **6** The Gun **14** A Ship of the Line **15** Payment Deferred, The African Queen **24** Captain Horatio Hornblower

forests
god of: **3** Pan **7** Silenus, Virbius

foretell 5 augur **6** divine **7** portend, predict, presage **8** prophesy, soothsay **9** apprehend **13** prognosticate

forethought 4 heed **7** caution **8** prudence, sagacity, wariness **10** discretion, precaution, providence, shrewdness **11** carefulness **12** anticipation, deliberation **13** consideration, premeditation **14** circumspection, farsightedness

forever 6 always **9** eternally, undyingly **10** constantly **11** ceaselessly, continually, incessantly, perpetually, unceasingly **12** interminably **13** everlastingly, unremittingly **Latin: 11** in perpetuum

forewarn 4 bode **5** alert **6** advise, notify, signal, tip off **7** caution, portend, presage, prewarn **8** cry havoc

foreword 7 preface, prelude **8** preamble, prologue **12** introduction

Forewords and Afterwords
author: **7** W H Auden

for example
Latin: **2** eg **13** exempli gratia

forfeit 4 fine, miss **5** waive, waste, yield **6** waiver **7** damages, default, let slip, penalty **8** squander **9** surrender **10** assessment

Forfeit
author: **11** Dick Francis

forge 4 copy, form, make **5** clone, shape **6** devise, hearth, smithy **7** falsify, fashion, furnace, imitate, produce, turn out **8** contrive, simulate **9** fabricate, ironworks **11** counterfeit, manufacture

forgery 4 copy, fake, hoax, sham **5** clone, fraud **7** cloning **9** deception, imitation **11** counterfeit, fraudulence **13** falsification **14** counterfeiting **17** misrepresentation

forget 6 slight **7** neglect **8** overlook, pass over **9** disregard

forgetful 6 remiss **7** out of it **8** amnesiac, careless, heedless, mindless **9** negligent, oblivious, unmindful **10** neglectful **11** inattentive

forget-me-not 8 Myosotis
varieties: **5** white **6** alpine, garden **7** Chinese **8** creeping

forgive 5 clear **6** acquit, excuse, pardon **7** absolve, condone, release, set free **8** overlook, reprieve **9** discharge, exculpate, exonerate

forgiveness 6 pardon **7** amnesty **9** remission **10** absolution

forgiving 6 benign, kindly **8** excusing **9** benignant, pardoning **11** kindhearted

forgo, forego 4 skip **5** waive, yield **6** eschew, give up **8** abnegate, renounce **9** sacrifice, surrender **10** relinquish

fork 4 bend, stab **5** angle, elbow, split **6** branch, crotch, divide, impale, pierce, ramify, skewer **7** diverge, trident **8** division **9** bifurcate, pitchfork **10** divergence, separation **11** bifurcation **12** intersection

forked 5 cleft **6** horned, zigzag **7** angular, divided, pronged **8** branched **9** ambiguous, deceitful, equivocal **10** bifurcated

For Kicks
author: **11** Dick Francis

fork out 5 spend **6** expend **8** disburse, dispense

for lack of something better
French: **12** faute de mieux

forlorn 4 lone **6** abject, bereft, dismal, dreary, lonely **7** unhappy **8** bereaved, dejected, deserted, desolate, forsaken, helpless, hopeless, lonesome, pathetic, pitiable, solitary, wretched **9** abandoned, depressed, desperate, destitute, forgotten, miserable, woebegone **10** despairing, despondent, dispirited, friendless **11** comfortless **12** disconsolate, inconsolable **13** brokenhearted

form *see box*

formal 4 cool, prim **5** aloof,

fancy, fixed, grand, legal, rigid, smart, stiff **6** dressy, lawful, proper, solemn, strict **7** distant, outward, pompous, prudish, regular, settled, stilted, stylish **8** decorous, definite, explicit, external, official, positive, reserved, starched **9** customary **10** ceremonial, inflexible, prescribed **11** ceremonious, highfalutin, perfunctory, punctilious, ritualistic, standoffish, straitlaced **12** conventional **13** authoritative **14** uncompromising

formal discussion 6 debate, parley **8** dialogue **10** conference

formality 4 rite **6** custom, motion, ritual **7** decorum, reserve **8** ceremony, coolness **9** etiquette, propriety, punctilio **10** ceremonial, convention **15** conventionality

Forman, Milos
director of: **7** Amadeus (Oscar), Ragtime **25** One Flew

---

form 3 cut, hew, way **4** body, cast, kind, make, mode, mold, plan, rite, rule, sort, trim, type **5** being, brand, build, carve, class, forge, found, frame, genre, genus, guise, habit, image, model, order, phase, set up, shape, stamp, style, usage **6** aspect, chisel, create, custom, design, devise, fettle, figure, manner, matrix, person, ritual, sculpt, system **7** acquire, anatomy, compose, conduct, contour, decorum, develop, fashion, fitness, harmony, liturgy, manners, outline, pattern, produce, species, variety **8** ceremony, comprise, contract, likeness, physique, practice, presence, roughhew, symmetry **9** character, construct, establish, etiquette, fabricate, framework, propriety, sculpture, semblance, structure **10** appearance, constitute, deportment, figuration, proceeding, proportion, regularity **11** arrangement, description, incarnation, manufacture, orderliness, shapeliness **12** denomination **13** configuration, manifestation **15** conventionality

Over the Cuckoo's Nest (Oscar)

formation 3 set **6** makeup **7** genesis **8** building, creation **9** structure **10** generation, production **11** arrangement, composition, development, fabrication, manufacture **12** organization **13** configuration, constellation, establishment

formative 7 plastic, shaping **9** sensitive **10** accessible **11** susceptible **13** determinative **14** impressionable

former 2 ex **4** gone, past **5** olden, prior **6** bygone, gone by, lapsed, of yore, whilom **7** ancient, earlier, elapsed, oldtime, quondam **8** anterior, previous **9** aforesaid, erstwhile, preceding **10** antecedent, firstnamed **14** aforementioned **French: 8** ci-devant

formerly 4 once **5** of old **6** ere now, lately, of yore, whilom **7** long ago **8** hitherto **9** anciently **10** originally, previously

former student 6 alumna **7** alumnus, dropout **8** graduate

formidable 6 taxing **7** awesome, fearful, mammoth, onerous **8** alarming, dreadful, imposing, menacing, terrific **9** dangerous, demanding, difficult **10** forbidding, impressive, portentous, terrifying **11** threatening **12** overpowering, overwhelming

formless 5 vague **9** amorphous, shapeless

Formosa see **6** Taiwan

formula 4 cant, plan, rule **5** chant **6** cliche, recipe, saying, slogan **7** precept **9** blueprint, guideline, platitude, principle, rigmarole **10** pleasantry **11** incantation **12** prescription

formulate 5 draft, frame, state **6** define, devise, invent **7** compose, itemize, specify **11** systematize **13** particularize

Fornax
  origin: 5 Roman
  goddess of: 6 baking

fornication 8 adultery

for one's country
  Latin: 9 pro patria

Forrest, Nathan Bedford
  served in: 8 Civil War
  side: 11 Confederate
  known for: 12 cavalry raids

forsake 4 deny, drop, flee, quit **5** leave, spurn, waive,

yield **6** abjure, depart, desert, give up, reject, resign, vacate **7** abandon, cast off, disavow, discard, lay down **8** abdicate, disclaim, go back on, jettison, part with, renounce **9** repudiate, surrender **10** relinquish

forsaken 4 bare **5** empty **8** deserted, desolate, rejected **9** abandoned, discarded, neglected **11** uninhabited

Forsete see **7** Forseti

Forseti
  also: 7 Forsete
  origin: 12 Scandinavian
  god of: 7 justice
  father: 5 Baldr **6** Balder, Baldur
  mother: 5 Nanna
  dwelling place: 7 Glitnir

Forster, E M (Edward Morgan)
  author of: 7 Maurice **10** Howard's End **14** A Room with a View **15** A Passage to India **17** The Longest Journey **22** Where Angels Fear to Tread
  member of: 15 Bloomsbury Group

forswear, foreswear 4 deny **5** spurn **6** abjure, disown, eschew, give up, recant, reject, revoke **7** disavow, gainsay, retract **8** abdicate, disclaim, renounce, take back **9** disaffirm, repudiate **10** contravene

Forsyte Saga, The
  author: 14 John Galsworthy
  trilogy including: 5 To Let **10** In Chancery **16** The Man of Property
  character: 3 Jon **4** June **5** Fleur **6** Dartie **7** Annette **8** Winifred **9** Old Jolyon **11** Young Jolyon **12** Irene Forsyte **13** Soames Forsyte **14** Philip Bosinney

Forsythe, John
  real name: 17 John Lincoln Freund
  born: 12 Penn's Grove NJ
  roles: 5 Topaz **7** Dynasty, Madame X **11** In Cold Blood **14** Bachelor Father, Charlie's Angels **15** Blake Carrington **16** And Justice for All **19** The Trouble with Harry **23** Teahouse of the August Moon

fort 4 base, camp **6** castle **7** bastion, bulwark, citadel, station **8** fastness, garrison **10** stronghold

forte 4 bent **5** knack, skill **8** strength **9** specialty **11** proficiency
  music: 4 loud
  abbreviation: 1 f

forth 5 ahead **6** onward **7** outward

forthcoming 5 handy, on tap **6** at hand **7** helpful **8** imminent **9** available, impending **10** accessible, obtainable, openhanded **11** approaching, cooperative, prospective

for the greater glory of God
  Latin: 19 ad majorem Dei gloriam

for the public good
  Latin: 14 pro bono publico

for the time being
  Latin: 10 pro tempore

For the Time Being
  author: 7 W H Auden

for this purpose only
  Latin: 5 ad hoc

forthright 4 open **5** blunt, frank **6** candid, direct, openly **7** bluntly, frankly, up-front **8** candidly, directly, straight **9** outspoken **10** truthfully **11** outspokenly, plain-spoken **15** straightforward **17** straightforwardly

forthrightness 6 candor **7** honesty **8** openness **9** frankness, sincerity **19** straightforwardness

forthwith 6 at once, pronto **7** quickly **8** directly, in a jiffy, promptly, right off **9** instantly **11** immediately **12** straightaway

fortification 5 tower **7** bastion, bulwark, citadel, rampart **8** fortress, garrison **9** earthwork **10** breastwork, stronghold

fortify 4 lace **5** boost, brace, cheer **6** buoy up, enrich, harden, secure, shield, urge on **7** build up, bulwark, hearten, protect, shore up, stiffen, support, sustain **8** buttress, embolden, garrison, reassure **9** encourage, reinforce, stimulate **10** invigorate, strengthen

fortissimo
  music: 8 very loud
  abbreviation: 2 ff

fortitude 4 dash, grit, guts, sand **5** nerve, pluck, spunk, valor **6** daring, mettle, spirit **7** bravery, courage, heroism, prowess **8** backbone, boldness, firmness, tenacity **9** endurance, hardihood **10** resolution **11** intrepidity **12** fearlessness, resoluteness **13** dauntlessness, determination

Fortitude
  author: 11 Hugh Walpole

Fort-Lamy
capital of: **4** Chad

fortress 7 bastion, bulwark, citadel, rampart **8** buttress **9** acropolis **10** stronghold

Fortress, The
author: **11** Hugh Walpole

fortuitous 5 happy, lucky, stray **6** casual, chance, random **9** haphazard, hit-or-miss **10** accidental, incidental, undesigned, unexpected, unintended, unpurposed **11** inadvertent **12** adventitious **13** serendipitous, unintentional **14** unpremeditated

fortuity 6 chance **8** accident **12** happenstance

Fortuna
origin: **5** Roman
goddess of: **7** fortune
corresponds to: **5** Tyche

fortunate 4 fair, rich, rosy **5** happy, lucky, palmy **6** benign, bright, timely **7** blessed, booming, favored, halcyon, well-off **8** well-to-do **9** favorable, opportune, promising **10** auspicious, convenient, felicitous, profitable, propitious, prosperous, successful **11** encouraging, flourishing **12** advantageous, providential

Fortunate Isles *see* **13** Canary Islands

Fortunato
character in: **20** The Cask of Amontillado
author: **3** Poe

fortune, fortunes 3 lot **4** doom, fate, luck, mint, pile, star **5** means **6** chance, estate, income, kismet, riches, wealth **7** bonanza, capital, destiny, godsend, portion, revenue **8** accident, fatality, gold mine, good luck, lady luck, opulence, property, treasure, windfall **9** affluence, haphazard, substance **10** prosperity, providence **12** circumstance **13** circumstances
goddess of: **5** Tyche **7** Fortuna

Fortunes of Nigel, The
author: **14** Sir Walter Scott

fortuneteller 4 seer **5** augur, Gypsy, sibyl **6** medium, oracle **7** palmist, prophet **8** magician **10** soothsayer **11** chiromancer, clairvoyant **12** crystal gazer

for two
French: **5** a deux

Forty Days of Musa Dagh, The
author: **11** Franz Werfel

42nd Parallel, The
author: **13** John Dos Passos

Forty-Second Street
director: **10** Lloyd Bacon
cast: **9** Guy Kibbee, Una Merkel **10** Dick Powell, Ruby Keeler **11** Bebe Daniels, George Brent **12** Ginger Rogers, Warner Baxter
choreographer: **13** Busby Berkeley
song: **15** Young and Healthy **17** Forty-second Street **19** Shuffle Off to Buffalo **28** You're Getting to Be a Habit with Me

Forty Thieves, The
author: **7** unknown
character: **7** Ali Baba
code word: **10** Open Sesame

forty winks 3 nap **4** doze **6** catnap, snooze

forum 6 medium, outlet **7** rostrum, seminar **8** platform **9** symposium **10** colloquium

forward, forwards 3 out **4** back, bold **5** ahead, brash, fresh, relay, sassy **6** assist, brazen, cheeky, hasten, onward, pass on, send on, spread **7** advance, frontal, further, go-ahead, promote, quicken, reroute **8** anterior, champion, immodest, impudent, insolent, up-to-date **9** advancing, barefaced, intrusive, offensive, presuming, readdress, shameless **10** accelerate, unmannerly **11** impertinent, progressive **12** enterprising, presumptuous **13** overconfident
French: **7** en avant

forwardness 4 gall **5** brass, cheek **8** audacity, boldness **10** brazenness, effrontery **11** presumption **13** bumptiousness, obtrusiveness

for what use
Latin: **7** cui bono

For Whom the Bell Tolls
author: **15** Ernest Hemingway
director: **7** Sam Wood
character: **5** Maria, Pablo, Pilar **6** Andres, Rafael **7** Anselmo, El Sordo **8** Augustin, Fernando **12** Robert Jordan
cast: **10** Gary Cooper **12** Akim Tamiroff **13** Ingrid Bergman, Joseph Calleia, Katina Paxinou **15** Arturo de Cordova
score: **11** Victor Young
Oscar for: **17** supporting actress (Paxinou)

for whose benefit
Latin: **7** cui bono

For Your Eyes Only
author: **10** Ian Fleming

Fosse, Bob
director of: **5** Lenny **7** Cabaret (Oscar) **11** All That Jazz

fossil 4 fogy, rock **5** fogey, oldie, relic, stone **7** imprint, antique **9** remainder **13** petrification

foster 3 aid **4** back, feed, rear, tend **5** favor, nurse, raise **6** foment, harbor, mother, rear up, take in **7** advance, bring up, care for, cherish, forward, further, nourish, nurture, promote, protect, support, sustain **8** advocate, befriend, hold dear, sanction, side with, treasure **9** encourage, patronize, stimulate **11** accommodate, countenance

Foster, Alicia Christian
real name of: **11** Jodie Foster

Foster, Harold
creator/artist of: **6** Tarzan **13** Prince Valiant

Foster, Jodie
real name: **21** Alicia Christian Foster
born: **9** Bronx NY
roles: **9** Tom Sawyer **10** Taxi Driver **11** Bugsy Malone

Foster, Stephen Collins
born: **15** Lawrenceville PA
composer of: **11** Swanee River **13** Camptown Races **16** Beautiful Dreamer **17** My Old Kentucky Home, The Old Folks at Home **27** Jeanie with the Light Brown Hair

Foucault, Jean Bernard Leon
field: **7** physics
nationality: **6** French
proved: **19** Earth spins on its axis
measured: **15** velocity of light
named for him: **16** Foucault currents

foul *see box*

foul-mouthed 4 lewd, rude, vile **5** dirty, gross **6** coarse, filthy, vulgar **7** abusive, obscene, profane **9** offensive **10** indelicate

foul play 5 crime **6** murder **8** violence **9** treachery

foul-smelling 4 rank **5** acrid, fetid, musty **6** putrid, smelly **7** noisome, reeking **8** stinking **10** malodorous

foul up 3 mar **4** goof, muff, ruin **5** botch, mix up, spoil **6** bungle, mess up, muddle **7** blunder, butcher, confuse, louse up, screw up **9** mismanage

foul 3 wet **4** base, clog, evil, lewd, soil, vile **5** dirty, foggy, grimy, gross, gusty, misty, muddy, murky, nasty, rainy, sully, taint **6** choked, cloudy, coarse, defile, filthy, grubby, odious, putrid, risque, scurvy, smelly, smutty, soiled, sordid, stormy, tangle, turbid, vulgar, wicked **7** abusive, begrime, drizzly, ensnare, hateful, heinous, impeded, obscene, pollute, profane, smeared, squalid, squally, stained, sullied, tangled, unclean **8** begrimed, besmirch, blustery, ensnared, entangle, immodest, indecent, infamous, stinking, unseemly **9** atrocious, besmeared, entangled, insulting, loathsome, monstrous, nefarious, notorious, obnoxious, repulsive, revolting **10** abominable, bedraggled, detestable, disgusting, encumbered, flagitious, indelicate, malodorous, putrescent, scurrilous, villainous **11** blasphemous, disgraceful **12** contemptible

---

found 4 base, rear, rest **5** build, erect, raise, set up, start **6** create, ground, locate, settle **7** develop, sustain **8** colonize, organize **9** construct, establish, institute, originate

foundation 3 bed **4** base, foot, fund, rock, root **5** basis, cause **6** bottom, cellar, ground, motive, origin, reason, source **7** charity, premise, purpose, support **8** basement, creation, pedestal **9** endowment, rationale **10** assumption, groundwork, settlement **11** benefaction, institution **12** commencement, installation, philanthropy, substructure, underpinning **13** establishment, justification **14** infrastructure, understructure

foundational 3 key **4** base, core **5** basic, prime **7** primary **9** essential **10** elementary

foundation garment 6 corset, girdle **8** corselet

founder 4 fall, limp, reel, sink, trip **5** abort, drown, lurch, swamp **6** author, father, go down, go lame, hobble, per-

ish, plunge, sprawl, topple, tumble **7** break up, builder, capsize, creator, go under, planner, stagger, stumble, succumb **8** collapse, miscarry **9** architect, organizer, shipwreck **10** originator, strategist **12** disintegrate

foundered 4 sank **6** failed **7** beached, swamped **8** capsized, went down **9** collapsed

founding 5 birth **8** creation, settling **9** beginning **11** institution, origination **12** introduction, organization **13** establishment

found on 6 base on **7** model on **8** stem from **10** derive from **11** establish on

fountain 3 jet **4** flow, gush, well **5** birth, cause, spout **6** cradle, feeder, origin, reason, source, spring **7** genesis **8** purveyor, supplier **9** beginning, reservoir, upswelling **10** derivation, wellspring

fountainhead 4 font **6** origin, source, spring **9** beginning **10** wellspring

Fountainhead, The author: **7** Ayn Rand

fourgon 3 van **7** tumbril

Four Horsemen of the Apocalypse, The author: **19** Vicente Blasco Ibanez based on: **10** Revelation

400 Blows, The director: **16** Francois Truffaut cast: **10** Albert Remy **13** Claire Maurier **14** Patrick Auffray **15** Jean-Pierre Leaud

Four Quartets author: **7** T S Eliot

Four-Season Recreation State nickname of: **7** Vermont

fowl 3 hen **4** cock, duck, game **5** banty, capon, chick, goose, quail **6** bantam, grouse, pigeon, turkey **7** chicken, cornish, leghorn, poultry **8** duckling

Fowles, John author of: **8** Mantissa, The Magus **10** The Aristos **12** Daniel Martin, The Collector **13** The Ebony Tower **25** The French Lieutenant's Woman

fox 9 scavenger young: **3** kit, pup group of: **5** leash, skulk

Fox (Mesquakie, Red Earth People) language family: **9** Algonkian **10** Algonquian location: **4** Iowa **9** Wisconsin allied with: **4** Sauk **8** Kickapoo

Fox, Fontaine creator/artist of: **16** Toonerville Folks **18** Toonerville Trolley

foxglove 9 digitalis varieties: **5** false, rusty **6** common, yellow **7** Grecian, Mexican **10** downy false **12** willow-leaved

foxiness 5 guile **7** cunning, slyness **8** artifice, trickery, wiliness **10** craftiness, shrewdness

fox-trot 5 dance **13** ballroom dance

Foxx, Jimmy (James Emory) nickname: **7** Double X sport: **8** baseball team: **12** Boston Red Sox **21** Philadelphia Athletics

Foxx, Redd real name: **16** John Elroy Sanford born: **9** St Louis MO roles: **13** Sanford and Son **19** Cotton Comes to Harlem

foxy 3 sly **4** wily **5** canny, sharp, slick **6** artful, astute, clever, crafty, shifty, shrewd, sneaky, tricky **7** cunning, devious, oblique **8** guileful, scheming, stealthy **9** conniving, deceitful, deceptive, designing, insidious, underhand **10** intriguing

foyer 4 hall **5** lobby **6** loggia **8** anteroom **9** vestibule **11** antechamber

fracas 3 row **4** fray, to-do **5** brawl, broil, clash, fight, melee, scrap **6** battle, ruckus, rumpus, strife, uproar **7** scuffle **9** imbroglio **10** donnybrook, free-for-all **11** altercation, embroilment

fraction 3 bit, few **4** chip **5** crumb, piece, ratio, scrap **6** morsel, trifle **7** cutting, portion, section, segment, shaving **8** fragment, particle, quotient **10** proportion **11** subdivision

fractious 5 cross, huffy **6** shirty, touchy, unruly **7** fretful, grouchy, peevish, pettish, waspish, wayward, willful **8** contrary, perverse, petulant, shrewish, snappish **9** irascible, irritable, querulous **10** rebellious, refractory

11 quarrelsome 12 disputatious, recalcitrant, unmanageable

fracture 4 rend, rift 5 break, crack, fault, sever, split 6 breach, cleave 7 disrupt, rupture, shatter 8 cleavage, division 9 severance 10 separation

Fra Diavolo, ou L'Hotellerie de Terracine
  also: 31 Brother Devil or The Inn at Terracina
  comic opera by: 5 Auber
  character: 7 Lorenzo, Zerlina 11 Lady Allcash, Lord Allcash 17 Marquis di San Marco

fragile 4 soft, weak 5 crisp, frail 6 dainty, feeble, flimsy, infirm, sleazy, slight, tender

7 brittle, crumbly, friable, rickety, shivery 8 decrepit, delicate 9 breakable, ephemeral, frangible, splintery 10 evanescent, tumbledown 11 dilapidated 13 unsubstantial

fragility 7 frailty 8 delicacy, weakness 9 frailness 10 feebleness 11 brittleness 12 frangibility

fragment 3 bit 4 chip, snip 5 crumb, cut up, piece, scrap, shard, shred, trace 6 chop up, divide, morsel 7 break up, crumble, portion, remnant, section, segment, shatter, vestige 8 disunite, fraction, separate, splinter, survival 12 disintegrate

fragmentary 6 broken, choppy 7 scrappy 8 detached

9 piecemeal, scattered, segmented 10 disjointed, fractional, incomplete, unfinished 12 disconnected

Fragonard, Jean-Honore
  born: 6 France, Grasse
  artwork: 8 The Swing 10 Stolen Kiss, The Bathers, The Warrior 12 Le Billet Doux 14 Progress of Love 16 La Chemise Enlevee 18 Storming the Citadel 40 Coresus Sacrificing Himself to Save Callirhoe

fragrance 4 aura, balm 5 aroma, scent 7 bouquet, incense, perfume 9 redolence, sweetness

fragrant 5 balmy, spicy 7 odorous 8 aromatic, perfumed, redolent 11 odoriferous

---

France
  other name: 4 Gaul
  anthem: 14 La Marseillaise
  capital/largest city: 5 Paris
  others: 4 Nice 5 Brest, Lille, Lyons, Rouen, Vichy 6 Amiens, Calais, Cannes, Carnac, Cognac, Dieppe, Grasse, Nantes, Prades, Rheims 7 Antibes, Avignon, Bayonne, Dunkirk, Le Havre, Les Baux 8 Bordeaux, Boulogne, Chartres, Grenoble, Poitiers, Toulouse 9 Cherbourg, Roquefort 10 La Rochelle, Marseilles, Saint-Denis, Strasbourg 12 Saint-Nazaire 13 Aix-en-Provence, Fontainebleau
  school: 8 Grenoble, Saint Cyr, Sorbonne 10 Montpelier
  division: 5 Anjou, Bearn, Berry, Maine, Savoy 6 Alsace, Artois, Marche, Poitou 7 Gascony, Guienne, Picardy 8 Auvergne, Bordeaux, Brittany, Burgundy, Dauphine, Flanders, Lorraine, Lyonnais, Normandy, Provence, Touraine 9 Aquitaine, Champagne, Languedoc 11 Ile de France 12 Bourbonnaise, Franche-Comte
  measure: 3 pot, sac 4 aune, mine, muid, pied, velt 5 arpen, carat, ligne, minot, pinte, point, pouce, velte 6 arpent, hemine, league, quarte, setier
  monetary unit: 5 franc 7 centime
  weight: 3 sol 4 gros, kilo, once 5 carat, livre, pound, tonne 6 gramme 7 tonneau 8 esterlin 9 esterling
  island: 2 Re 3 Yeu 4 Cite 5 Groix, Hyere 6 Comoro, Oleron, Tahiti, Ushant 7 Corsica, Leeward, Reunion 8 Windward 10 Guadeloupe, Martinique 12 New Caledonia
  lake: 6 Annecy, Cazaux, Geneva
  mountain: 4 Jura 5 Pelat 6 Vosges 8 Ardennes, Pyrenees 10 French Alps 11 Pic Montcalm
  highest point: 5 Blanc 9 Mont Blanc
  river: 3 Lys 4 Yser 5 Aisne, Eiser, Isere, Loire, Meuse, Rhine, Rhone, Saone, Seine 7 Garonne, Gironde
  sea: 5 North 8 Atlantic 13 Mediterranean
  physical feature:
    bay: 6 Biscay 7 Arachon
    beach: 5 Omaha
    cape: 5 Hague, Talma
    channel: 7 English 8 La Manche
    gulf: 4 Lion
  people: 6 Franks
    artist: 5 Corot, David, Degas, Manet, Monet 6 Braque, Ingres, Millet, Renoir, Seurat 7 Cezanne, Daumier, Gauguin, Matisse, Utrillo 8 Pissarro 9 Delacroix, Fragonard, Gericault
    author: 4 Gide, Hugo, Zola 5 Camus, Dumas 6 France, Proust, Racine, Sartre, Villon 7 Moliere 8 Rabelais, Rousseau, Voltaire 9 Corneille, Descartes, Giraudoux, Montaigne 10 Baudelaire
    composer: 5 Bizet, Ravel, Satie 6 Franck, Gounod 7 Berlioz, Debussy, Poulenc
    king: 5 Henri, Louis 6 Clovis, Philip 7 Charles 9 Hugh Capet 11 Charlemagne 13 Louis Philippe 14 Henry of Navarre
    leader: 6 Danton, Petain 7 Colbert, Mazarin 8 de Gaulle, D'Estaing, Pompidou 9 Joan of Arc, Richelieu 10 Mitterrand 11 Robespierre 17 Napoleon Bonaparte

Fragrant Harbor *see* 8 Hong Kong

frail 4 puny, weak 6 feeble, flimsy, infirm, sleazy, slight, weakly 7 brittle, crumbly, fragile, rickety, shivery 8 decrepit, delicate, fallible 9 breakable, frangible, splintery 10 perishable, vulnerable 11 dilapidated 13 unsubstantial

frailness 8 delicacy, weakness 9 fragility 11 unsoundness

frailty 3 sin 4 flaw, vice 5 fault 6 defect, foible 7 blemish, failing 11 fallibility 12 imperfection 14 susceptibility

Fra Lippo Lippi
  author: 14 Robert Browning

frame 3 rim, set 4 body, case, cast, form, make, mold, mood, plan 5 build, draft, hatch, humor, set up, shape, state 6 border, casing, design, devise, edging, figure, indite, invent, map out, nature, scheme, sketch, system, temper 7 anatomy, backing, chassis, concoct, contour, housing, outline, setting 8 attitude, conceive, contrive, mounting, organize, physique, skeleton 9 formulate, structure 11 disposition, scaffolding, systematize, temperament 12 constitution, construction

frame of mind 4 mood 7 climate 8 attitude 10 atmosphere 11 disposition

framer 6 author, shaper 7 creator, planner 10 formulator

framework 5 shell, truss 7 carcass 8 skeleton, template 9 structure 10 foundation 11 scaffolding 14 infrastructure

Framley Parsonage
  author: 15 Anthony Trollope

France *see box*

France, Anatole
  real name: 30 Jacques Anatole Francois Thibault
  author of: 5 Thais 12 Golden Verses 13 My Friend's Book, Penguin Island 17 The Gods Are Athirst 20 The Revolt of the Angels 25 Le Crime de Sylvestre Bonnard 27 At the Sign of the Reine Pedauque

franchise 5 grant, right 6 ballot 7 charter, freedom, license

---

  queen: 7 Eugenie 9 Josephine 13 Marie de Medici 15 Marie Antoinette
language: 6 French
religion: 5 Islam 7 Judaism 8 Huguenot 10 Protestant 13 Roman Catholic
place:
  cathedral: 6 Rheims 8 Chartres 9 Madeleine, Notre Dame 10 Sacre-Coeur 14 Sainte-Chapelle 15 Mont-Saint-Michel
  chapel: 8 Ronchamp
  gardens: 9 Tuileries
  hall of mirrors: 16 Galerie des Glaces
  museum: 6 Louvre
  palace: 6 Elysee 10 Luxembourg, Versailles 12 Grand Trianon, Petit Trianon, 13 Fontainebleau
  prison: 8 Bastille
  racetrack: 6 Le Mans 7 Auteuil 10 Longchamps
  resort: 3 Pau 5 Vichy 6 Cannes, Menton 7 Antibes, Mentone, Riviera 8 Biarritz, Chamonix, Grenoble 9 Cote d'Azur 11 Aix-les-Bains
  section of Paris: 8 Left Bank 9 Right Bank 10 Montmartre, Rive Droite, Rive Gauche 12 Latin Quarter
  street: 13 Champs-Elysees 17 Place de la Concorde
  woods: 14 Bois de Boulogne 15 Bois de Vincennes
possession: 12 French Guiana
  island: 6 Futuna, Hoorne, Wallis 7 Reunion 8 Miquelon 10 Guadeloupe, Martinique 11 Saint Pierre 12 New Caledonia 15 French Polynesia
feature:
  airport: 4 Orly 9 Le Bourget 15 Charles de Gaulle
  bicycle race: 12 Tour de France
  dance: 5 gavot 6 branle, canary, cancan 7 boutade, gavotte
  fortification: 11 Maginot Line
  holiday: 11 Bastille Day
  monument: 13 Arc de Triomphe 14 Tomb of Napoleon
  national theater: 16 Comedie Francaise
  sightseeing boat: 12 bateau mouche
  tower: 6 Eiffel
food:
  cheese: 4 bleu, Brie 6 bonbel 7 boursin 8 Muenster 9 camembert, marcillat, port-salut, Roquefort 11 coulommiers
  dessert: 6 mousse
  dish: 4 pate 5 crepe 6 canape, quiche 7 souffle 8 escargot, piperade, pot au feu 9 cassoulet, tournedos 14 pate de foie gras
  drink: 6 cognac 8 bordeaux, burgundy 9 champagne
  french fries: 12 pommes frites
  pastry: 7 brioche 8 napoleon 9 croissant
  soup: 8 a l'oignon 13 bouillabaisse
  steak: 7 bifteck

8 immunity, suffrage **9** privilege **10** permission **11** prerogative **13** authorization

Franciosa, Anthony
  real name: 14 Anthony Papales
  born: 9 New York NY
  wife: 14 Shelley Winters
  roles: 12 The Naked Maja
  13 A Hatful of Rain, Long Hot Summer, Name of the Game, Wild Is the Wind
  15 Assault on a Queen

Francis, Dick
  author of: 4 Bolt, Risk **5** Nerve, Proof **6** Banker, Reflex **7** Break In, Enquiry, Forfeit, Rat Race **8** Dead Cert, For Kicks, Slayride, Trial Run, Twice Shy, Whip Hand **9** Bonecrack, The Danger, Knockdown **10** Blood Sport, High Stakes, In the Frame **11** Smokescreen **12** Flying Finish

Franck, Cesar
  born: 5 Liege **7** Belgium
  composer of: 4 Ruth **5** Hulda **6** Psyche **7** Rebecca **8** Ghiselle **9** Les Djinns **10** Les Eolides, Redemption **13** La Tour de Babel, Les Beatitudes, The Beatitudes **16** Le Chasseur Maudit **17** The Accursed Hunter

Franglais 13 French-English **14** French-American

frank 4 bold, free, open **5** clear, plain, round **6** candid, direct, honest, patent **7** artless, evident, genuine, natural, sincere, up-front **8** apparent, distinct, explicit, manifest **9** downright, ingenuous, outspoken **10** aboveboard, forthright, unreserved **11** plainspoken, transparent, unambiguous, undisguised, unequivocal **12** unmistakable **15** straightforward

Frank, Anne
  author of: 19 The Diary of Anne Frank

Frankenstein
  author: 17 Mary Godwin Shelley
  character: 7 Clerval, Justine, William **9** Elizabeth **10** The Monster **12** Robert Walton **18** Victor Frankenstein

Franklin, Benjamin
  author of: 20 Poor Richard's Almanack
  inventor of: 12 lightning rod **13** bifocal lenses, Franklin stove

frankness 6 candor **7** honesty **8** openness **9** bluntness, sincer-

ity **10** directness **11** artlessness **13** guilelessness **14** forthrightness **19** straightforwardness

frantic 3 mad **4** wild **5** crazy, rabid **6** hectic, insane, raging, raving **7** berserk, excited, furious, nervous, violent **8** agitated, deranged, frenetic, frenzied **9** delirious **10** distracted, distraught, infuriated **11** impassioned, overwrought **12** ungovernable

fraternal 6 hearty, loving, social **7** devoted, kindred, related **8** amicable, friendly **9** brotherly **11** warmhearted **12** affectionate **14** consanguineous

fraternity 4 clan, club **5** union **6** circle, clique, league **7** company, coterie, kinship, society **8** alliance **9** coalition **10** federation **11** association, brotherhood, confederacy, propinquity **13** brotherliness, consanguinity, interrelation

Fraternity
  author: 14 John Galsworthy

fraternize 3 mix **5** unite **6** concur, hobnob, mingle **7** combine, consort **8** coalesce **9** associate, cooperate, harmonize, pal around, socialize **10** sympathize **11** confederate

Fratres Arvales *see* **5** Arval

frau 4 lady, wife **12** married woman

fraud 4 fake, hoax, hype, ruse, sham **5** cheat, craft, guile, knave, quack, rogue, trick **6** deceit, humbug, rascal **7** swindle **8** artifice, cheating, cozenage, impostor, swindler, trickery **9** charlatan, chicanery, con artist, deception, duplicity, imposture, pretender, stratagem, swindling, treachery **10** dishonesty, mountebank, subterfuge **11** counterfeit, fourflusher, machination **13** dissimulation

fraudulence 6 deceit **8** trickery **9** deception **13** deceitfulness, deceptiveness **17** misrepresentation

fraudulent 4 sham, wily **5** bogus, false **6** crafty, tricky **7** crooked, cunning, knavish **8** cheating, guileful, spurious **9** deceitful, deceptive, dishonest **11** counterfeit, treacherous, underhanded **12** dishonorable, unprincipled

fraught 4 full **5** heavy, laden **6** filled, loaded **7** charged, replete, teeming **8** attended,

pregnant **9** abounding **11** accompanied

fraulein 9 young lady **14** unmarried woman

Fraunhofer, Joseph von
  field: 7 physics
  nationality: 6 German
  established: 12 spectroscopy

fray 3 rub **4** fret, fuss, riot, spat, tiff **5** brawl, chafe, fight, melee, ravel, set-to **6** battle, combat, fracas, rumble, rumpus, strain, tatter, tumult, tussle **7** contest, dispute, frazzle, quarrel, scuffle, warfare, wear out, wrangle **8** conflict, skirmish, squabble **9** bickering, commotion **10** contention, dissension, engagement **11** altercation, controversy **12** disagreement

Frazer, Sir James G
  author of: 14 The Golden Bough

freak 3 fad, odd **4** kink, turn, whim **5** craze, fancy, humor, queer, quirk, sport, twist **6** marvel, oddity, vagary, whimsy, wonder **7** anomaly, bizarre, caprice, erratic, monster, strange, unusual **8** crotchet, mutation, peculiar **9** curiosity, deviation **10** aberration **11** abnormality, monstrosity **12** irregularity

freakish 3 odd **5** queer, weird **7** bizarre, strange, unusual **8** peculiar, singular, uncommon **9** eccentric, fantastic **10** outlandish **13** extraordinary

Frederick
  character in: 11 As You Like It
  author: 11 Shakespeare

Frederick I
  nickname: 10 Barbarossa
  position: 16 Holy Roman Emperor
  dynasty: 12 Hohenstaufen
  wife: 7 Beatrix
  battle: 7 Legnano

Frederick II
  position: 12 king of Sicily **13** king of Germany **16** Holy Roman Emperor
  battle: 8 Bouvines

Frederick the Great
  nickname: 8 Old Fritz
  position: 13 King of Prussia
  invaded: 7 Silesia
  war: 13 Seven Years' War **18** Austrian Succession

free *see* box

free-and-easy 6 breezy, casual, jaunty **7** buoyant, relaxed **8** debonair, informal

free 3 big, lax **4** able, bold, easy, idle, idly, open, save **5** clear, extra, let go, loose, rid of, spare **6** daring, devoid, exempt, giving, gratis, lavish, parole, ransom, redeem, unbond, uncage, wanton **7** allowed, assured, forward, liberal, loosely, manumit, release, unchain, unleash **8** at no cost, careless, costless, devoid of, familiar, fearless, generous, handsome, immune to, informal, let loose, liberate, prodigal, released, unfasten **9** abandoned, audacious, available, boundless, bounteous, bountiful, confident, delivered, discharge, disengage, dissolute, expansive, extricate, footloose, lacking in, leisurely, liberated, permitted, unblocked, unbridled, unchained, unclogged, unimpeded, unmuzzled, unshackle **10** autonomous, bighearted, carelessly, chargeless, emancipate, gratuitous, licentious, manumitted, munificent, openhanded, unattached, unconfined, unfettered, unhampered, unoccupied, unreserved, unshackled **11** emancipated, enfranchise, independent, uncluttered, uncommitted, uninhibited, unrepressed **12** enfranchised, overfamiliar, uncontrolled, unencumbered, unobstructed, unrestrained **13** complimentary, unceremonious, unconstrained

12 lighthearted, presumptuous, unrestrained **13** unconstrained

freed 6 exempt, loosed, spared **7** cleared, excused **8** absolved, let loose, released, relieved **11** emancipated

freedom 4 play **5** range, scope, sweep, swing **6** candor, margin **7** abandon, license, release **8** autonomy, boldness, latitude, openness, rudeness **9** bluntness, frankness, impudence, indecorum **10** directness, disrespect, liberation **11** abandonment, forwardness, impropriety, informality, manumission, naturalness, sovereignty, unrestraint **12** emancipation, impertinence, unconstraint **13** downrightness **14** unreservedness **15** enfranchisement

Freedom of the Poet, The
    author: **12** John Berryman

free-flowing 7 copious, gushing, profuse **8** effusive

free-for-all 3 row **4** fray **5** brawl, fight, melee, scrap **6** affray, fracas, ruckus, tussle **7** rhubarb, ruction, wrangle **9** brannigan **10** donnybrook

free from bias 7 neutral **9** impartial, unbigoted **12** unprejudiced **13** disinterested

free from moisture 3 dry **4** arid, sere **5** parch **6** dry out **7** parched **8** dried out, rainless **9** dehydrate **10** dehydrated, desertlike, desiccated

free hand 12 carte blanche, open sanction **13** full authority

free rein 12 carte blanche, open sanction **13** full authority

free-spoken 6 chatty **7** voluble **9** talkative **10** loquacious, unreserved **13** communicative

Free State
    nickname of: **8** Maryland

Freestone State
    nickname of: **11** Connecticut

Free to Choose
    author: **14** Milton Friedman (with Rose Friedman)

Freetown
    capital of: **11** Sierra Leone

freeze 3 nip **4** bite, cool, halt, stop **5** chill, frost, sting **6** arrest, benumb, harden, pierce **7** ceiling, congeal, terrify **8** glaciate, solidify **11** anesthetize, refrigerate, restriction

freezing 3 icy **6** arctic, frigid **7** glacial

Frege, Gottlieb
    field: **11** mathematics
    nationality: **6** German
    founded: **13** symbolic logic

Freia see **5** Freya

freight 4 haul, lade, load, ship **5** cargo, carry, goods **6** burden, charge, convey, lading **7** baggage, cartage, luggage, portage **8** transmit, truckage **9** transport **10** conveyance **13** transshipment

Freischutz, Der
    also: **11** The Marksman
    opera by: **5** Weber
    character: **3** Max **6** Agathe, Caspar, Samiel

Freki
    origin: **12** Scandinavian
    form: **4** wolf
    owner: **4** Odin **5** Othin
    received: **4** food
    exception: **4** meat
    fellow wolf: **4** Geri

French, Daniel Chester
    born: **8** Exeter NH
    artwork: **7** (seated) Lincoln (at Lincoln Memorial) **21** The Minute Man of Concord

French-American
    French: **9** Franglais

French civil code 12 Code Napoleon

French Connection, The
    director: **15** William Friedkin
    cast: **11** Fernando Rey, Gene Hackman (Popeye Doyle), Roy Scheider
    Oscar for: **5** actor (Hackman) **7** editing, picture **8** director **10** screenplay
    sequel: **21** The French Connection II

French-English
    French: **9** Franglais

French Guinea see **6** Guinea

French Indonesia see **7** Vietnam

French is spoken here
    French: **18** ici on parle francais

French Lieutenant's Woman, The
    director: **10** Karel Reisz
    author: **10** John Fowles
    cast: **9** Leo McKern **11** Hilton McRae, Jeremy Irons, Meryl Streep
    script: **12** Harold Pinter

French national anthem 12 Marseillaise

French national theater 16 Comedie Francaise

French parliament
    formal sessions: **12** lit de justice

French Somaliland see **8** Djibouti

French Sudan, Soudan see **4** Mali

French Togoland see **4** Togo

frenzied 3 mad **4** wild **7** excited, frantic, furious **8** agitated, ecstatic **9** delirious

frenzy 3 fit **4** fury **5** craze, furor, mania, state **6** access **7** mad rush, madness, seizure, turmoil **8** delirium, hysteria, outburst **9** obsession, transport **11** distraction

Frenzy
director: **15** Alfred Hitchcock
cast: **8** Jon Finch **10** Anna
Massey **11** Barry Foster
16 Barbara Leigh-Hunt

frequency 9 iteration **10** recurrence, regularity, repetition **11** persistence, reiteration

frequent 5 daily, haunt, usual
6 common, wonted **7** regular
8 constant, everyday, familiar,
habitual, numerous, ordinary,
resort to **9** continual, customary, incessant, perpetual, recurrent **10** accustomed
11 reiterative

frequently 5 often **7** usually
8 ofttimes **9** generally **10** constantly, habitually, ordinarily,
repeatedly **11** continually, customarily, incessantly, perpetually, recurrently

frere 4 monk **5** friar **7** brother

Frescobaldi, Girolamo
born: **5** Italy **7** Ferrara
composer of: **13** Fiori Musicali **14** Musical Flowers

fresh *see box*

freshen 4 wash **5** brace, calve,
clean, groom, renew **6** air out,

---

breeze, desalt, revive **7** cool
off, sweeten **8** renovate, spruce
up **9** deodorize

freshet 5 crest, flood
11 overflowing

Freshman, The
director: **9** Sam Taylor
12 Fred Newmeyer
cast: **11** Harold Lloyd **13** Jobyna Ralston **14** Brooks
Benedict

Fresnel, Augustin Jean
field: **7** physics
nationality: **6** French
worked in: **6** optics

fret 3 eat, rub, vex **4** fray,
fume, gall, gnaw, mope, pine,
pout, stew, sulk **5** brood,
chafe, erode, sulks, worry
6 abrade, lament, ruffle, tatter
7 agonize, corrode, fidgets
8 disquiet, distress, irritate,
vexation, wear away **9** annoyance, excoriate **10** irritation
11 displeasure, peevishness
12 discomposure

fretful 5 cross, huffy, sulky,
tense **6** cranky, shirty, touchy
7 grouchy, nervous, peevish,
pettish, waspish **8** contrary,
petulant, snappish **9** crotchety,
irritable, querulous **11** complaining **12** cantankerous

fretfulness 5 worry **6** unease
7 anxiety **10** crankiness
11 peevishness **12** irritability

Freud, Sigmund
lived in: **6** Vienna
collaborator: **6** Breuer
disciple: **4** Jung **5** Adler
daughter: **4** Anna
method: **15** free association
19 dream interpretation
coined: **2** id **8** superego
14 psychoanalysis
author of: **13** Totem and Taboo **22** Interpretation of
Dreams **37** Group Psychology and the Analysis of the
Ego, Jokes and Their Relation to the
Unconscious

Freund, John Lincoln
real name of: **12** John
Forsythe

Frey
also: **5** Freyr
origin: **12** Scandinavian
god of: **5** peace **8** marriage
10 prosperity
race: **5** Vanir
father: **5** Niord, Njord
home: **7** Alfheim

Freya
also: **5** Freia
origin: **8** Teutonic
goddess of: **4** love **6** beauty
9 fecundity
race: **5** Vanir

---

leader of: **9** Valkyries
father: **5** Niord, Njord

Fri *see* **5** Frigg

friable 7 crumbly **9** breakable,
frangible

friar
French: **5** frere

Friar Lawrence
character in: **14** Romeo and
Juliet
author: **11** Shakespeare

Friar Tuck
character in: **9** Robin Hood

friary 5 abbey **6** priory **8** cloister **9** hermitage, monastery

friction 6 strife **7** chafing, discord, grating, quarrel, rubbing **8** abrasion, bad blood,
conflict, fretting **9** animosity,
attrition, hostility **10** antagonism, contention, dissension,
dissidence, opposition, resentment, resistance **12** disagreement **13** counteraction

Friday
character in: **14** Robinson
Crusoe
author: **5** Defoe

Friday
from: **5** Freya, Frigg
heavenly body: **5** Venus
French: **8** vendredi
Italian: **7** venerdi
Spanish: **7** viernes
German: **7** freitag

Friedan, Betty
author of: **19** The Feminine
Mystique
co-founder of: **3** NOW
28 National Organization for
Women

Friedkin, William
director of: **11** The Exorcist
19 The French Connection
(Oscar)

Friedman, Milton
author of: **12** Free to Choose
(with Rose Friedman)
20 Capitalism and Freedom

Friedrich, Caspar David
born: **7** Germany
10 Greifswald
artwork: **22** The Cross on
the Mountains **26** Man and
Woman Gazing at the
Moon, The Ruined Monastery of Eldena, Two Men
Contemplating the Moon

friend *see box*

friendliness 5 amity **8** bonhomie, good will **9** geniality
10 affability, amiability, cordiality, fraternity **11** amicability, camaraderie, sociability
14 neighborliness
16 companionability

---

fresh 3 fit, hot, new
4 bold, cool, fair, keen,
late, pert, pure, rare, rosy,
rude **5** alert, brisk, chill,
clear, green, nervy, novel,
ready, ruddy, sassy, saucy,
stiff, sweet **6** active, biting,
brassy, brazen, bright,
cheeky, lively, modern, recent, rested, snotty,
unique, unused, unworn
7 bracing, cutting, forward,
glowing, just out, nipping,
strange, uncured, undried,
unfaded, untried, unusual
8 assuming, blooming,
brand-new, creative, flippant, gleaming, impudent,
insolent, original, stinging,
unabated, undimmed, unsalted, unsmoked, unwilted,
up-to-date **9** energetic, inventive, obtrusive, refreshed, sparkling,
undecayed, unpickled, unspoiled, unwearied, wholesome **10** meddlesome, newfangled, refreshing,
unfamiliar, unimpaired,
unwithered **11** flourishing,
invigorated, modernistic,
smart-alecky, untarnished
12 presumptuous,
unaccustomed

friend 3 pal 4 ally, beau, chum, date, mate 5 amigo, buddy, crony, lover 6 backer, cohort, escort, fellow, intime, minion, patron 7 brother, comrade, consort, partner 8 adherent, advocate, confrere, coworker, defender, favorite, follower, henchman, intimate, mistress, myrmidon, paramour, partisan, playmate, retainer, sidekick, soul mate 9 associate, bedfellow, colleague, companion, confidant, copartner, supporter 10 benefactor, encourager, playfellow, well-wisher 12 acquaintance
   French: 3 ami 4 amie 9 bonne amie
   Spanish: 5 amiga, amigo

friendly 4 kind 6 allied, ardent, benign, chummy, clubby, genial, kindly, loving, social 7 affable, amiable, cordial, devoted, helpful 8 amicable, familiar, generous, gracious, intimate, salutary 9 brotherly, convivial, favorable, fortunate, fraternal, opportune 10 accessible, auspicious, beneficial, hospitable, neighborly, not hostile, propitious 11 kindhearted, sympathetic, warmhearted 12 advantageous, affectionate 13 companionable

Friendly Fire
   author: 8 C D B Bryan

Friendly Islands see 5 Tongo

Friendly Persuasion
   director: 12 William Wyler
   author: 12 Jessamyn West
   cast: 10 Gary Cooper 11 Richard Eyer 12 Marjorie Main 14 Anthony Perkins, Dorothy McGuire
   score: 14 Dimitri Tiomkin

friendly understanding
   French: 15 entente cordiale

friend of the court
   Latin: 12 amicus curiae

friendship 5 amity 6 accord, comity 7 concord, harmony 8 close tie, goodwill, intimacy, sympathy 10 consonance, cordiality, fellowship, fraternity 11 brotherhood, comradeship, familiarity 12 amicableness 13 companionship, understanding 14 neighborliness 16 acquaintanceship

Friesen, Samille Diane
   real name of: 10 Dyan Cannon

Frigg
   also: 3 Fri 5 Frija 6 Frigga
   origin: 8 Teutonic
   goddess of: 3 sky 6 clouds 8 marriage
   husband: 4 Odin 5 Othin
   race: 4 Asar 5 Aesir

Frigga see 5 Frigg

fright 4 fear, funk 5 alarm, dread, panic, scare 6 dismay, horror, terror, tremor 7 anxiety, concern, flutter, quaking 8 cold feet 9 misgiving, quivering, the creeps 10 the jitters, the willies 11 disquietude, palpitation, trepidation 12 apprehension, intimidation, perturbation 13 consternation

frighten 5 alarm, daunt, scare, shock 6 affray, excite 7 agitate, horrify, petrify, startle, terrify 8 disquiet 9 terrorize 10 intimidate

frightened 6 afraid, scared 7 alarmed, panicky 9 horrified, petrified, terrified 10 terrorized

frightening 5 awful, dread 7 fearful 8 alarming, dreadful 10 horrifying, terrifying 11 hair-raising

frightful 5 awful, lurid, nasty 6 grisly, horrid 7 baleful, extreme, fearful, ghastly, hideous, macabre, ogreish 8 alarming, dreadful, fearsome, freakish, gruesome, horrible, horrific, shocking, sinister, terrible, terrific 9 appalling, loathsome, monstrous, offensive, repellent, repulsive, revolting 10 abominable, detestable, disgusting, horrendous 12 insufferable

frigid 3 icy, raw 4 cold, cool, prim 5 aloof, bleak, gelid, stiff 6 biting, bitter, chilly, formal, frosty 7 austere, cutting, distant, glacial, nipping 8 freezing, piercing 10 forbidding 11 straitlaced 12 unresponsive

frigidity 7 iciness 8 coldness 9 aloofness 10 frostiness 16 unresponsiveness

Frija see 5 Frigg

frill 3 air 6 edging, fringe, ruffle 7 flounce 8 falderal, frippery, furbelow, ornament 9 gathering, mannerism 10 decoration 11 affectation, superfluity 13 embellishment

fringe 3 hem, rim 4 edge, mane 5 limit, skirt 6 border, edging, margin, tassel 7 enclose, outline, selvage 8 deco-

rate, frontier, skirting, surround, trimming 9 embellish, periphery

frisk 3 hop 4 jump, lark, leap, romp, skip, trip 5 bound, caper, cut up, dance, sport 6 bounce, cavort, frolic, gambol, prance, search, spring 7 disport, examine, inspect, ransack 8 look over

frisky 4 spry 5 agile, peppy 6 active, lively, nimble 7 jocular, playful, waggish 8 animated, mirthful, prankish, spirited, sportive 9 vivacious 10 frolicsome, rollicking

fritter 4 blow 5 use up, waste 7 deplete 8 fool away, idle away, squander 9 dissipate

fritter away 4 blow 5 waste 6 misuse 8 misspend, squander 9 dissipate

fritter away time 4 idle 6 dawdle 10 dillydally

Fritzi Ritz
   also named: 5 Nancy
   creator: 15 Ernie Bushmiller 16 Larry Whittington
   character: 4 Phil 5 Nancy 6 Sluggo

frivolity 3 fun 4 jest, play 5 folly, sport 6 levity, whimsy 7 abandon 8 airiness, dallying, frippery 9 emptiness, flippancy, giddiness, lightness 10 fickleness, triviality, wantonness 11 flightiness 15 thoughtlessness

frivolous 4 airy, vain 5 barmy, dizzy, empty, inane, light, minor, petty, silly 6 flimsy, frothy, paltry, slight, stupid 7 fatuous, flighty, foolish, trivial, witless 8 careless, flippant, heedless, niggling, piddling, trifling 9 brainless, imprudent, pointless, senseless, unserious, worthless 10 insouciant 11 extravagant, harebrained, impractical, improvident, nonsensical, superficial, unimportant 13 insignificant, rattlebrained 14 shallowbrained

frizzle 4 curl 5 crimp

frock 4 coat, gown, robe, suit 5 cloak, dress, smock 6 blouse 7 cassock, soutane 8 chasuble, surplice, vestment 9 clericals 10 canonicals

frog 3 pad, pod 4 knot, wood 5 frosh, hitch, track 6 holder, peeper, toggle 7 crawler, croaker, cushion, leopard, tadpole 8 bullfrog, fastener, pickerel, pollywog 9 amphibian, plow frame 12 flower holder

Frogs, The
   author: 12 Aristophanes

character: 5 Pluto 6 Charon 7 Bacchus 8 Dionysus, Hercules, Xanthias 9 Aeschylus, Euripides

Froissart, Jean
author of: 8 Meliador 10 Chronicles

frolic 3 fun 4 lark, play, romp, skip 5 act up, antic, caper, frisk, mirth, prank, sport, spree 6 cavort, gaiety, gambol 7 disport, jollity, make hay 8 escapade 9 amusement, festivity, joviality, merriment 10 buffoonery, pleasantry, recreation, skylarking, tomfoolery 11 merrymaking 13 entertainment

frolicsome 5 antic, jolly, merry 6 cheery, jaunty, lively 7 playful 8 cheerful, mirthful, prankish 9 sprightly 12 lighthearted

Frollo, Claude
character in: 23 The Hunchback of Notre Dame
author: 4 Hugo

from 2 de, ex, of 3 for, fro 5 off of, out of 7 against 8 starting 9 beginning

from abroad 5 alien 6 exotic 7 foreign 8 imported

fromage 6 cheese

from behind
Latin: 6 a tergo

From Here to Eternity
director: 13 Fred Zinnemann
author: 10 James Jones
cast: 9 Donna Reed 11 Deborah Kerr 12 Frank Sinatra, George Reeves 13 Burt Lancaster 14 Ernest Borgnine 15 Montgomery Clift
setting: 11 Pearl Harbor
Oscar for: 7 picture 8 director 12 screenwriter 15 supporting actor (Sinatra) 17 supporting actress (Reed)

from inside
Latin: 7 ab intra

from outside
Latin: 7 ab extra

From Russia With Love
author: 10 Ian Fleming

from scratch 4 anew 14 from ground zero 16 from the beginning 20 from fresh ingredients

from side to side 4 over, sway 5 cross 7 athwart, swaying, zigzag 12 back and forth

from the beginning
Latin: 5 ab ovo 6 de novo 8 ab initio

from the chair
Latin: 10 ex cathedra

from the depths
Latin: 11 de profundis

from the face
Latin: 7 ex facie

from the fact
Latin: 7 de facto

from the founding of the city
Latin: 13 ab urbe condita

from the library of
Latin: 8 ex libris

from the seat of authority
Latin: 10 ex cathedra

front 3 air, top 4 face, fore, head, lead, mask, mien 5 first 6 facade, give on, regard 7 bearing, initial, look out 8 anterior, carriage, demeanor, presence, pretense, trenches, vanguard 9 beginning, semblance

Front, The
director: 10 Martin Ritt
cast: 10 Lloyd Gough, Woody Allen, Zero Mostel 13 Joshua Shelley, Michael Murphy 16 Herschel Bernardi

frontage 7 outlook 8 exposure, prospect

frontier 4 edge 5 march, verge 6 border, limits 7 extreme, marches 8 boundary, confines, outposts 9 backlands, backwoods, outskirts, perimeter 10 hinterland 11 territories

front matter 8 foreword 9 title page 12 introduction 15 table of contents 20 introductory material

Front Page, The
author: 8 Ben Hecht 16 Charles MacArthur
director: 11 Billy Wilder 14 Lewis Milestone
actor: 9 Mae Clarke, Mary Brian, Pat O'Brien 10 Jack Lemmon, David Wayne 12 George E Stone, Carol Burnett 13 Adolphe Menjou, Allen Garfield, Susan Sarandon, Walter Catlett, Walter Matthau 14 Charles Durning 15 Andrew Pendleton, Vincent Gardenia 19 Edward Everett Horton
character: 4 Earl 5 Burns, Grant, Hildy, Peggy 6 Walter 7 Hartman, Johnson 8 Williams

frost 4 rime 5 chill 7 iciness 8 coolness, distance 9 aloofness, cold spell, frigidity 10 chilliness, glaciality 13 inhospitality 14 unfriendliness

Frost, Robert
author of: 7 Birches 10 Fire

and Ice, Home Burial 11 Mending Wall 13 Brown's Descent 15 The Road Not Taken 17 After Apple-Picking 21 The Death of the Hired Man 30 Stopping by Woods on a Snowy Evening

frostiness 3 nip 4 bite 5 chill 7 iciness 8 coldness, coolness 9 crispness, frigidity, hoariness, sharpness 10 chilliness, wintriness

frosting 3 mat 4 trim 5 glass, icing 7 cooling, topping 8 chilling, divinity, freezing, trimming 13 embellishment, ornamentation

frosty 3 icy 4 cold, cool 5 bleak, chill, hoary 6 frigid, wintry 8 freezing

froth 4 bosh, fizz, foam, fume, head, scum, suds, surf 5 spume, trash, yeast 6 lather, trivia 7 bubbles, rubbish 8 flummery, frippery, nonsense, trumpery, whitecap 9 frivolity 10 balderdash, triviality 12 fiddle-faddle

frothy 5 fizzy, foamy, light 6 bubbly 7 trivial 9 frivolous 15 inconsequential

froward 5 balky 6 unruly 7 wayward, willful 8 contrary, perverse, stubborn 9 difficult, fractious, obstinate 10 headstrong, refractory 11 disagreeing, intractable 12 recalcitrant 13 contradictory 15 unaccommodating

frown 4 fret, mope, muse, pout, sulk 5 glare, scowl 6 glower, ponder 14 discountenance

frowning 4 dark 5 angry 6 gloomy, somber, sullen 8 scowling 9 glowering

frown upon 7 condemn, dislike 8 object to 14 discountenance

frowsy, frowzy 5 fusty, musty, stale 6 sloppy, untidy 7 tousled, unkempt 8 slovenly

frozen 3 icy 4 cold, iced, numb 5 chill, gelid, polar 6 arctic, chilly, cooled, wintry 7 chilled, clogged, glacial, stymied 8 benumbed, hibernal, icebound 10 obstructed, stalemated 11 frostbitten, immobilized 12 refrigerated

fructify 5 bloom 6 sprout, thrive 7 blossom, prosper, succeed 8 flourish

frugal 4 slim 5 scant, tight 6 skimpy, stingy 7 ascetic, sparing, thrifty 9 niggardly, penny-wise **10** abstemious, economical, unwasteful **12** parsimonious

frugality 6 thrift **7** economy **8** prudence, stinting **9** parsimony **10** scantiness, stinginess **11** thriftiness **12** cheeseparing **13** niggardliness, penny-pinching **16** parsimoniousness

fruit 4 crop **5** award, issue, yield, young **6** effect, profit, result, return, reward, upshot **7** benefit, harvest, outcome, produce, product, progeny, revenue **8** earnings **9** advantage, emolument, offspring, outgrowth **10** production **11** consequence **12** remuneration

fruitful 6 fecund **7** fertile **8** blooming, prolific, yielding **9** effective **10** productive, profitable, successful **11** efficacious **12** advantageous, fructiferous

fruition 8 maturity, ripeness **10** attainment **11** achievement, fulfillment, realization **12** consummation, satisfaction **13** actualization, gratification **15** materialization

fruitless 4 arid, vain **5** empty, inept **6** barren, futile, hollow **7** sterile, useless **8** abortive, bootless, nugatory **9** infertile, pointless, worthless **10** profitless, unavailing, unprolific **11** incompetent, ineffective, ineffectual, inoperative, purposeless, unrewarding **12** unproductive, unprofitable, unsuccessful **13** inefficacious

fruit trees
goddess of: **6** Pomona

frumpy 4 drab **5** dowdy **8** slovenly **10** slatternly **12** unattractive

frustrate 3 bar **4** balk, foil **5** block, check, upset **6** baffle, cancel, defeat, hinder, impede, thwart **7** counter, cripple, fluster, inhibit, nullify, prevent **8** dispirit, obstruct, prohibit, suppress **9** forestall, hamstring, undermine **10** circumvent, disappoint, disconcert, discourage, dishearten

frustration 6 defeat **7** balking, chagrin, failure, foiling, letdown **8** futility **9** hindrance, thwarting **10** bafflement, inhibition, nonsuccess **11** obstruction **12** discomfiture, interference **13** contravention, counteraction **14** disappointment, nonfulfillment **15** dissatisfaction

fry 4 cook **5** brown, grill, saute **7** frizzle **9** fricassee

Fry, Christopher
author of: **9** Yard of Sun **12** The Firstborn **13** Venus Observed **20** The Dark Is Light Enough **21** The Lady's Not for Burning

frying pan 3 wok **6** frypan **7** browner, griddle, skillet

fuchsia
varieties: **4** cape, tree **5** hardy **10** California **11** honeysuckle

fuddled 5 bosky, dopey, drunk, tipsy **6** boozed, groggy **7** maudlin, muddled, sozzled, tippled **8** confused **9** stupefied **10** inebriated **11** intoxicated

fudge 3 lie **4** bosh, fake **5** candy, cheat, evade, hedge, hunch, patch, welch **7** falsify, penuche **8** divinity

fuel 3 fan, gas, oil **4** coal, feed, fire, wood **5** light, means, stoke **6** charge, fill up, fodder, ignite, incite, kindle **7** impetus, inflame, sustain **8** activate, energize, gasoline, material, recharge, stimulus **9** petroleum, stimulate **10** ammunition, motivation, sustenance **11** inspiration, wherewithal

fugitive 4 hobo **5** brief, exile, hasty, nomad, rover, short, tramp **6** errant, fading, flying, loafer, outlaw **7** cursory, elusive, erratic, escaped, escapee, fleeing, hurried, passing, refugee, runaway, summary, vagrant **8** apostate, deserter, escaping, fleeting, flitting, renegade, shifting, unstable, vagabond, volatile, wanderer **9** ephemeral, fugacious, itinerant, momentary, straggler, temporary, transient, uncertain **10** evanescent, expatriate, short-lived, transitory **11** impermanent

Fugitive, The
character: **9** Donna Taft **11** Fred Johnson (one-armed man) **12** (Lt) Philip Gerard **13** (Dr) Richard Kimble
cast: **10** Barry Morse, Bill Raisch **12** David Janssen **15** Jacqueline Scott

fuhrer, Fuhrer, der fuhrer 4 Nazi **6** Hitler, leader, tyrant **8** dictator **11** Adolf Hitler

fulfill 2 do **4** heed, keep, meet, obey, suit **6** answer, effect, follow, redeem **7** achieve, execute, observe, perfect, perform, realize, satisfy **9** discharge, establish, implement **10** accomplish, consummate, effectuate

fulfillment, fulfilment 7 delight **8** crowning, pinnacle, pleasure **9** execution, happiness **10** attainment, completion **11** achievement, contentment, culmination, realization **12** effectuation, satisfaction **13** contentedness, establishment, gratification **14** accomplishment, implementation

Fulks, Sarah Jane
real name of: **9** Jane Wyman

full 3 big **4** rich, very, wide **5** ample, broad, flush, laden, large, plump, quite, round, sated, total, whole **6** entire, gorged, intact, loaded, mature, packed, rotund **7** brimful, crammed, exactly, fraught, glutted, heaping, maximum, perfect, plenary, replete, shapely, stuffed, teeming **8** brimming, bursting, complete, resonant, swarming, thorough **9** abounding, capacious, perfectly, precisely, saturated, surfeited **10** unabridged, voluminous

full amount 3 all, sum **5** total, whole **8** entirety, totality **9** aggregate **10** complement

full-bodied 3 fat **4** rich **5** ample, lofty **6** hearty, mature, robust **9** flavorful **10** meaningful

Fuller, R Buckminster
architect of: **10** US Pavilion (Expo '67 Montreal) **13** Dymaxion House
form: **12** geodesic dome

full-fledged 5 adept **6** expert, mature **7** skilled, trained **8** complete, masterly, schooled **9** qualified, topflight **10** proficient **11** experienced **13** authoritative

full form 9 extension **10** elongation **11** enlargement **12** augmentation **13** amplification

full-grown 4 ripe **5** adult, manly, of age, matured, womanly **9** developed

full measure 6 enough, plenty **7** abundance, plenitude **10** competence **11** sufficiency

Full Moon
author: **11** P G Wodehouse

fullness 7 satiety **8** richness **9** amplitude, roundness, satiation **12** completeness **14** voluminousness

full of fire 7 rousing **8** electric, exciting, spirited **9** thrilling **11** galvanizing, stimulating **12** electrifying, soul-stirring

full of life 5 vital 8 animated, spirited, vigorous 9 ebullient, energetic, exuberant, vivacious

full of pep 5 vital 6 lively 8 animated

full of vim and vigor 5 peppy 6 lively 11 invigorated

full view 7 the open 8 daylight, openness

fully 5 amply, quite 6 richly, wholly 7 totally, utterly 8 entirely 9 copiously, perfectly 10 abundantly, altogether, completely, positively, throughout 11 plentifully 12 sufficiently 13 substantially

fully realized 7 perfect 8 achieved, complete, executed, finished 9 completed, perfected, performed 11 consummated 12 accomplished

fulminate 4 boil, rage, rant 7 explode 8 denounce

fulminate against 5 roast 6 berate 7 scourge 8 call down, chastise 9 castigate

fulmination 7 violent 8 bursting, eruption 9 discharge, explosion

fulsome 3 fat 4 foul 5 suave 6 lavish, odious 7 cloying, lustful, noisome, obscene 8 overdone, unctuous 9 excessive, obnoxious, offensive, repulsive, tasteless 10 disgusting, obsequious

Fulton, Robert
nationality: 8 American
inventor of: 9 steamboat (Clermont), submarine 13 marine torpedo

fumble 3 err, mar 4 blow, muff 5 grope, spoil 6 bobble, boggle, bollix, bungle, goof up, mess up, muddle 7 butcher, louse up, screw up 9 mishandle

fume 3 gas 4 boil, burn, emit, foam, haze, puff, rage, rant, rave, reek, waft 5 exude, scent, smell, smoke, stink, vapor 6 billow, exhale, miasma, seethe, stench 7 carry on, explode, flame up, flare up, smolder 10 exhalation

fun 3 gas 4 ball, game, jest, lark, play, romp, trip 5 antic, blast, cheer, mirth, prank, sport, spree 6 frolic, gaiety, joking 7 jollity, revelry, whoopee 8 escapade, good time, pleasure 9 amusement, diversion, enjoyment, horseplay, joviality, merriment 10 buffoonery, recreation, relaxation, skylarking, tomfool-

ery 11 distraction, playfulness, waggishness 13 entertainment

Funafuti
capital of: 6 Tuvalu

function 3 act, job 4 duty, fete, gala, help, role, task, work 5 feast, field, niche, party, place, power, range, scope, serve 6 affair, behave, do duty, office, operate, perform, purpose 8 activity, business, capacity, ceremony, occasion, province 9 festivity, objective, operation, reception 13 entertainment

functional 6 useful 7 working 8 operable 9 operative, practical 11 serviceable, utilitarian

functionary 8 employee, official 10 bureaucrat 13 administrator

functioning 5 in use 6 active, at work, usable 7 working 9 effectual, operating, operative

fund 3 pot 4 bank, foot, lode, mine, pool, vein, well 5 endow, float, fount, hoard, kitty, stock, store 6 pay for, spring, supply 7 finance, nest egg, reserve, savings, support 8 treasure 9 endowment, patronize, reservoir 10 foundation, investment, repository, storehouse, underwrite 12 accumulation

fundament 3 can 4 buns, rump, seat 5 fanny 6 behind, bottom 7 backside, buttocks, haunches 9 posterior 12 hindquarters

fundamental 3 key 4 ABC's, base, main 5 axiom, basic, basis, chief, first, major, vital 7 central, crucial, element, primary 8 cardinal, integral 9 component, essential, necessary, principal, principle, requisite 10 elementary, foundation, groundwork, underlying 11 cornerstone 13 indispensable

funds 4 cash, jack, pelf 5 bread, dough, lucre, means, money, moola 6 assets, income, wampum, wealth 7 capital, scratch 8 finances, property 9 resources 11 wherewithal

funeral 4 wake 5 rites 6 burial 7 requiem 9 cremation, interment, obsequies 10 entombment, inhumation

funeral song 5 dirge, elegy

6 lament 7 requiem 8 threnody 11 lamentation

funereal 3 sad 4 grim 5 weepy 6 dismal, dreary, gloomy, solemn, somber, woeful 7 doleful 8 desolate, dirgeful, grieving, mournful 9 cheerless, woebegone 10 depressing, lachrymose, lugubrious 13 brokenhearted

fun-filled 5 happy 6 joyful, joyous 8 pleasant, pleasing 9 enjoyable 10 delightful 11 pleasurable

Fungoso
character in: 22 Every Man Out of His Humour
author: 6 Jonson

fungus, fungi 4 mold, myco, rust, smut 5 ergot, yeast 6 mildew 7 truffle 8 mushroom 9 toadstool 11 thallophyte

fun-loving 5 jolly, merry 6 genial, jovial 7 affable 8 sociable 9 convivial 10 gregarious

funnel 4 cone, duct, flue, pipe, pour 5 focus, shaft 6 direct, filter, siphon 7 channel, chimney, conduit 8 stovepipe 10 smokestack, ventilator 11 concentrate

funny 3 odd 5 antic, comic, droll, merry, queer, weird, witty 6 absurd, jocose 7 amusing, bizarre, comical, curious, jesting, jocular, offbeat, strange, unusual, waggish 8 farcical, humorous, mirthful, peculiar, sporting, uncommon 9 diverting, facetious, hilarious, laughable, ludicrous 10 outlandish, ridiculous

Funny Girl
director: 12 William Wyler
cast: 8 Lee Allen 10 Kay Medford, Omar Sharif 11 Anne Francis 13 Walter Pidgeon 15 Barbra Streisand (Fanny Brice)
score: 9 Jule Styne 10 Bob Merrill
sequel: 9 Funny Lady
song: 6 People 18 Don't Rain on My Parade

funnyman 3 wag, wit 4 card, fool, mime, zany 5 clown, comic, joker 6 jester, madcap 7 buffoon 8 comedian, humorist, jokester 9 harlequin

fuoco, con
music: 8 with fire

fur 3 fox 4 down, hair, lamb, mink, pelt, seal 5 coney, lapin, otter, sable 6 beaver, fleece, jaguar, kit fox, nutria, rabbit, red fox 7 blue fox, cheetah, leopard, muskrat, opossum, raccoon **8** black fox, cross fox, squirrel, white fox **9** silver fox **10** animal skin, chinchilla **11** karakul lamb, Persian lamb **13** broadtail lamb **14** mouton-dyed lamb

furbelow 5 frill **6** fringe **7** falbala, flounce **8** trimming

furbish 4 buff **5** renew, shine **6** polish **7** burnish **8** renovate

Furiae see **6** Furies

Furies
   also: **5** Dirae **6** Erinys, Furiae, Semnai **7** Allecto, Erinyes, Megaera **9** Eumenides, Tisiphone
   corresponds to: **3** Ker

furious 3 mad **4** wild **5** angry, fiery, irate, rabid **6** enrage, fierce, fuming, raging, savage, stormy **7** intense, rampant, violent **8** frenetic, frenzied, heedless, maddened, provoked, reckless, up in arms, vehement, wrathful **9** fanatical, irascible, turbulent **10** infuriated, passionate, tumultuous, unbalanced **11** tempestuous **12** ungovernable, unrestrained

furl 4 coil, curl, fold, roll, wrap **5** truss **6** curl up, fold up, furdle, roll up, spiral

furlong
   abbreviation: **3** fur

furnace 4 kiln, oven **5** forge, stove **6** boiler, heater **11** incinerator

Furnace
   constellation of: **6** Fornax

furnish 3 arm, rig **4** gird, give, vest **5** array, dress, endow, equip, favor, fit up, grant, stock **6** fit out, outfit, purvey, render, supply **7** appoint, indulge, prepare, provide **8** accoutre, bestow on **9** provision **11** accommodate

furnishings 9 equipment **11** accessories **12** haberdashery

furnish room for 5 lodge, put up **6** billet **7** shelter **11** accommodate

furniture 7 effects **8** chattels, movables, property **11** possessions **12** appointments

furor 3 fad **4** flap, rage, to-do, word **5** craze, mania, noise, thing, vogue **6** fervor, frenzy, hoopla, lunacy, raving, uproar **7** fashion, madness, passion **8** brouhaha, insanity, reaction **9** agitation, commotion, obsession, transport **10** dernier cri, enthusiasm, excitement, fanaticism

furrow 3 cut, dig, rut **4** knit, line, plow, rift, seam **5** cleft, crack, ditch, ridge, track **6** crease, groove, pucker, trench, trough **7** channel, crevice, fissure, wrinkle **10** depression **11** corrugation

furry 4 soft **5** downy, hairy, scary **6** cuddly, fleecy, pelted, shaggy **8** fearsome, horrible **11** hair-raising

further 3 aid, new, too, yet **4** also, back, help, more **5** again, extra, favor, fresh, other, spare, speed **6** abroad, assist, back up, beyond, foster, hasten, oblige, to boot, yonder **7** advance, afar off, besides, farther, forward, promote, quicken, stand by, work for **8** champion, expedite, likewise, moreover **9** accessory, ancillary, auxiliary, encourage, propagate **10** accelerate, additional, strengthen **11** accommodate **12** additionally, contributory, supplemental **13** supplementary

furtherance 3 aid **4** help, lift **5** favor **6** succor **7** advance, defense, support **8** advocacy, interest **9** patronage, promotion **10** assistance **11** advancement, cooperation, countenance **12** championship

furthering 3 aid **6** aiding, growth **8** abetting, advocacy, espousal **9** assisting, fostering, promoting, promotion **10** assistance, supporting **11** advancement, encouraging, propagating, propagation **12** accelerating, acceleration, encouragement **13** strengthening

furthermore 3 too **4** also **6** as well, to boot **7** besides **8** likewise, moreover **10** in addition **12** additionally

furthermost 7 extreme **8** farthest **11** farthermost

furtive 3 sly **4** wily **5** shady **6** covert, crafty, hidden, masked, secret, shifty, sneaky, unseen, veiled **7** cloaked, elusive, evasive, private **8** secluded, shrouded, skulking, sneaking, stealthy **9** collusive, secretive, underhand **10** mysterious, undercover, unrevealed **11** clandestine **12** confidential **13** surreptitious **14** conspiratorial

fury 3 fit, hag, ire, pet **4** gall, huff, rage, snit **5** force, might, shrew, vixen, wrath **6** attack, choler, frenzy, spleen, virago

7 assault, bluster, dudgeon, hellcat, tantrum **8** acerbity, acrimony, ferocity, outburst, severity, she-devil, spitfire, violence **9** intensity, termagant, vehemence, virulence **10** excitement, fierceness, turbulence **11** impetuosity

Fury
   form: **8** divinity
   sex: **6** female
   mother: **4** Gaea
   father: **6** Uranus
   born of the blood of: **6** Uranus
   Greek name: **6** Erinys **7** Erinyes **9** Eumenides
   Roman name: **5** Dirae **6** Furiae

fuse 4 join, link, meld, melt, weld, wick **5** blend, merge, smelt, torch **6** league, mingle, solder **7** combine **8** coalesce, federate, ignition, solidify **9** associate, detonator **10** amalgamate, assimilate **11** confederate, consolidate, incorporate, intermingler

fusillade 4 hail, rain **5** salvo, spray **6** volley **7** barrage, battery **8** drumfire, enfilade **9** broadside, cannonade **11** bombardment

fusion 5 blend, union **6** league **7** combine, melding, melting, merging **8** alliance, blending, compound, smelting **9** coalition, synthesis **10** commixture, dissolving, federation **11** association, coalescence, combination, commingling, confederacy, unification **12** amalgamation, intermixture, liquefaction **13** agglomeration, confederation

fuss 3 ado, nag **4** carp, fool, fret, fume, pomp, spat, stew, stir, tiff, to-do **5** annoy, cavil, labor, setto, worry **6** bother, bustle, excite, fidget, flurry, hubbub, hustle, niggle, pester, pother, potter, putter, rattle, scurry, tinker **7** agitate, confuse, dispute, fluster, flutter, nitpick, quarrel, quibble, perturb, trouble, turmoil **8** ceremony **9** agitation, commotion, confusion **10** disconcert, hurlyburly, turbulence **11** disturbance, superfluity **12** perturbation **15** ceremoniousness
   Yiddish: **7** tzimmes

fuss over 6 dote on

fussy 4 busy **6** ornate **7** finical, finicky, nervous **8** bustling, critical, exacting **9** assiduous, cluttered, crotchety, demanding, squeamish **10** compulsive, fastidious, meticulous, nitpicking, old-maidish, particular, scrupulous **11** painstaking, persnickety

fusty 5 moldy, musty, stale **6** foisty, rancid, stuffy **8** obsolete **9** out of date **10** malodorous **12** old fashioned

Futabatei, Shimei
  author of: **16** The Drifting (Floating) Cloud

futile 4 idle, vain **5** empty, petty **7** trivial, useless **8** abortive, bootless, nugatory, trifling **9** frivolous, fruitless, valueless, worthless **10** profitless, unavailing **11** ineffective, ineffectual, unimportant **12** unprofitable, unsuccessful **13** insignificant

future 4 hope **5** after, later **6** coming, latter, morrow, offing, to come **7** by-and-by, ensuing, outlook **8** eventual, prospect, tomorrow, ultimate **9** following, hereafter, impending, projected **10** in prospect, subsequent, succeeding **11** anticipated, expectation, opportunity, prospective **12** anticipation
  Spanish: 6 manana

Future Shock
  author: **12** Alvin Toffler

fuzz 4 down, lint **5** fluff

fuzzy 3 dim **4** hazy **5** downy, foggy, linty, misty, murky, vague, wooly **6** fluffy, frizzy, woolly **7** blurred, obscure, shadowy, unclear **8** confused **9** pubescent **10** indefinite, indistinct

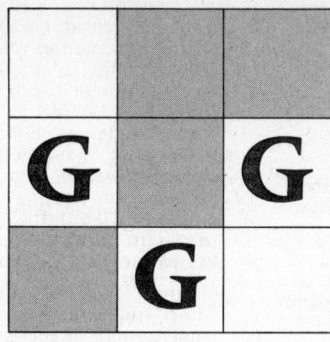

gab 3 jaw, rap **4** blab, chat
5 prate **6** babble, gibber, gossip, jabber, patter **7** baloney, blarney, blather, chatter, prattle **8** chitchat, idle talk, talk idly **10** balderdash
12 conversation

gabble 3 rap **4** blab **5** prate
6 babble, drivel, gossip, jabber **7** blather, chatter, prattle twaddle **8** babbling, chitchat, idle talk **9** gibbering, jabbering **10** blathering, chattering
14 chitterchatter

gabfest 3 rap **4** chat, talk
7 palaver **8** chitchat **10** discussion **12** conversation
13 confabulation

gable 4 edge, peak, roof, wall
6 detail, dormer, pinion **7** aileron **8** pediment, triangle

Gable, Clark
 real name: 17 William Clark Gable
 wife: 13 Carole Lombard
 nickname: 7 The King
 born: 7 Cadiz OH
 roles: 7 Red Dust **8** Saratoga
 10 The Misfits **11** Rhett Butler **15** Gone With the Wind **18** It Happened One Night (Oscar)

Gabo, Naum
 real name: 17 Naum Neemia Pevsner
 born: 6 Russia **7** Brainsk
 founder: 14 Constructivism
 artwork: 6 Column **11** Spiral Theme **16** Sculptural Models **19** Kinetic Construction **24** Variations of Spheric Theme

Gabon Republic *see box*

Gabor, Eva
 mother: 5 Jolie
 sister: 5 Magda **6** Zsa Zsa
 born: 7 Hungary **8** Budapest
 roles: 4 Gigi **10** Green Acres
 12 My Man Godfrey **13** A Royal Scandal, Forced Land-

ing **15** Youngblood Hawke
18 The Truth About Women **20** The Last Time I Saw Paris

Gabor, Sari
 real name of: 11 Zsa Zsa Gabor

Gabon Republic
 capital/largest city:
 10 Libreville
 others: 4 Oyem **5** Bongo, Kango **6** Mitzic, Moanda, Mouila, Omvane **7** Makokou, Mounana **9** Lambarene **10** Port-Gentil **11** Franceville
 monetary unit: 5 franc **7** centime
 lake: 7 Anengue, Azinguo
 mountain: 5 Mpele **7** Chaillu, Cristal, Mikongo **8** Balaquri, Birougou
 highest point: 8 Iboundji
 river: 4 Como **6** Abanga, Ivindo, Ogooue **7** Ngounie
 sea: 8 Atlantic
 physical feature:
  cape: **5** Lopez
 people: 4 Fang **6** Adouma, Bakota, Bateke, Echira, Okande, Omyene **7** Eshiras **8** Bandjabi, Bapounou
  leader: **3** Mba **5** Bongo
  philanthropist: **16** Albert Schweitzer
 language: 6 French
 religion: 5 Islam **7** animism **10** Protestant **13** Roman Catholic
 feature:
  tree: **6** okoume
 food: 6 manioc **9** Dika bread

Gabor, Zsa Zsa
 real name: 9 Sari Gabor
 mother: 5 Jolie
 sister: 3 Eva **5** Magda
 husband: 10 Nick Hilton
 13 George Sanders
 born: 7 Hungary **8** Budapest
 roles: 4 Lili **11** Moulin Rouge **14** Lovely To Look At **20** The Story of Three Loves

Gaboriau, Emile
 author of: 9 File No 113

Gaborone, Gaberones
 capital of: 8 Botswana

Gabriel 9 archangel
 means: 8 man of God
 11 God is strong
 spoke to: 4 Mary **9** Zacharias, Zechariah

Gad
 father: 5 Jacob
 mother: 6 Zilpah
 brother: 3 Dan **4** Levi
 5 Asher, Judah **6** Joseph, Reuben, Simeon **7** Zebulun **8** Benjamin, Issachar, Naphtali
 sister: 5 Dinah
 descendant of: 6 Gadite

gadget 4 tool **6** device, doodad, jigger **7** gimmick, novelty **9** accessory, doohickey **10** attachment **11** contraption, contrivance, thingamabob, thingamajig

Gaea
 also: 2 Ge **4** Gaia
 origin: 5 Greek
 goddess of: 5 earth
 husband: 6 Uranus
 children: 6 Pontus, Titans, Uranus **7** Cyclops, Erinyes
 9 mountains
 13 Hecatonchires
 son: 6 Nereus **7** Iapetus, Oceanus
 daughter: 4 Rhea **5** Theia
 6 Phoebe, Tethys, Themis
 9 Mnemosyne
 corresponds to: 6 Tellus

Gaelic
language family: 12 Indo-European
branch: 6 Celtic
subgroup: 4 Manx **5** Irish **8** Scottish

gaffe 4 goof **5** boner **6** boo-boo **7** blunder **11** impropriety **12** indiscretion
French: 7 faux pas **9** gaucherie

gag 4 hoax, hush,, jest, joke, stop **5** block, choke, heave, retch **6** muffle, muzzle, stifle **7** cloture, foolery, silence, smother **8** stoppage, suppress **9** horseplay, restraint **13** facetiousness

Gaia *see* **4** Gaea

gaiety, gayety 3 fun **4** show **5** mirth **6** frolic, tinsel **7** elation, glitter, jollity, spirits **8** airiness, frippery, trumpery, vivacity **9** amusement, animation, brummagem, gaudiness, merriment, showiness **10** brightness, brilliance, garishness, jauntiness, joyousness, liveliness **11** celebration, merrymaking **12** cheerfulness, colorfulness, exhilaration, sportiveness **13** effervescence, sprightliness

gain, gains 3 add, bag, get, hit, net, win **4** jump, leap, plus, reap **5** bloom, bonus, fetch, glean, put on, reach, wages, yield **6** attain, come to, gather, income, obtain, pick up, profit, return, salary, secure, thrive **7** achieve, acquire, blossom, capture, collect, improve, procure, produce, prosper, recover, revenue **8** addition, arrive at, black ink, dividend, earnings, flourish, increase, overtake, proceeds, winnings **9** accretion, advantage, increment **10** attainment **11** improvement **12** accumulation, compensation, remuneration

Gaines, Ernest J
author of: 33 The Autobiography of Miss Jane Pittman

gainful 4 rich **6** paying **9** lucrative **10** productive, profitable **12** remunerative

gainfully 8 usefully **10** profitably **11** lucratively **12** productively **14** remuneratively

gain recognition 9 establish

gainsay 4 deny **6** abjure, oppose, refute **7** disavow, dispute **9** repudiate **10** contradict, controvert

Gainsborough, Thomas
born: 7 England, Sudbury

artwork: 10 The Blue Boy **14** The Morning Walk **15** Mr and Mrs Andrews, The Hon Mrs Graham **16** Viscount Ligonier **26** Peasant Girl Gathering Sticks

gait 4 pace, step, walk **5** tread **6** stride **7** bearing **8** carriage **10** deportment
French: 8 demarche

gaiter 4 boot, shoe, spat, vamp **5** chaps, strad **6** gaskin, hugger, puttee **7** legging **8** cuttikin, overshoe

gala 3 gay **5** grand, party **7** benefit, festive, opulent **8** festival, majestic, splendid **9** festivity, glamorous, sumptuous **10** ceremonial, fancy-dress, glittering **11** celebration, celebratory, magnificent, spectacular, star-studded
French: 4 fete

Galahad
character in: 16 Arthurian romance

Galatea
form: 6 maiden, statue **8** sea nymph
father: 6 Nereus
mother: 5 Doris
courted by: 10 Polyphemus
lover: 4 Acis
killed: 4 Acis
statue carved by: 9 Pygmalion
brought to life by: 9 Aphrodite
son: 6 Paphos

gale 3 fit **4** blow, gust, stir **6** flurry, squall, tumult, uproar **7** cyclone, tempest **8** eruption, outbreak, outburst **9** agitation, commotion, windstorm

Galeus
form: 6 lizard
father: 6 Apollo

Galileo Galilei
nationality: 7 Italian
inventor of: 6 sector **11** thermometer
studied: 6 motion **8** pendulum
discovered: 18 Jupiter's satellites
constructed: 9 telescope
formulated: 18 law of falling bodies
author of: 8 Dialogue **10** Discourses **18** The Starry Messenger

Galinthias
handmaiden of: 7 Alcmene

gall 3 bug, irk, vex **4** bile, flay, fret, miff, rile **5** anger, annoy, brass, chafe, cheek, gripe, nerve, score, sting, venom

6 abrade, bruise, enrage, harass, injure, nettle, offend, rancor, ruffle, spleen **7** affront, incense, provoke, rub sore **8** acrimony, audacity, boldness, irritate, rudeness, temerity **9** animosity, assurance, displease, excoriate, impudence, insolence, malignity, sauciness, virulence **10** bitterness, brazenness, effrontery, exacerbate **11** presumption

gallant 3 fop **4** bold, dude, game, stud **5** blood, brave, dandy, gutsy, noble, suave, swell **6** daring, heroic, kindly, plucky, polite, urbane **7** courtly, dashing, valiant **8** cavalier, fearless, gay blade, intrepid, mannerly, obliging, resolute, stalwart, valorous, well-bred **9** attentive, courteous, dauntless **10** chivalrous, courageous, thoughtful **11** considerate, gentlemanly, lionhearted **12** stouthearted

gallantries 10 attentions **11** compliments **12** pleasantries

gallantry 4 grit, sand **5** nerve, pluck, valor **6** daring, mettle, spirit **7** bravery, courage, dashing, heroism, prowess, suavity **8** chivalry, courtesy, urbanity **9** derring-do, fortitude, gentility **10** politeness **11** courtliness, intrepidity **12** fearlessness, resoluteness **13** attentiveness, dauntlessness, determination **14** courageousness

gallery 4 stoa **5** salon **6** arcade, loggia, piazza **7** balcony, passage, portico **8** cloister, corridor **9** bleachers, colonnade, mezzanine, triforium **10** ambulatory, grandstand, passageway

Gallia Belgica *see* **7** Belgium

galliano
type: 7 liqueur
origin: 5 Italy
flavor: 5 herbs, spice
color: 6 yellow
with creme de cacao: 14 Golden Cadillac
with rum: 9 Bossa Nova
with vodka: 16 Harvey Wallbanger

gallinule 3 hen **4** coot, fowl, rail, sora **7** moorhen **8** dabchick, hyacinth, rallidae, ricebird, swamphen

Gallipoli
director: 9 Peter Weir
cast: 7 Mark Lee **8** Bill Kerr **9** Mel Gibson **11** Robert Grubb

gallivant, galavant 3 gad **4** kite, roam, rove **5** jaunt, range, stray **6** ramble, travel, wander **7** gallant, meander, traipse, **8** gad about **9** philander

gallon
abbreviation: **3** gal

gallop 3 fly, hie, jog, run **4** bolt, dart, dash, flit, race, rush, scud, skim, trot, whiz **5** bound, hurry, scoot, shoot, speed, whisk **6** hasten, scurry, spring, sprint **7** mad dash, scamper, scuttle, tear off **8** fast clip, fast gait **9** skedaddle

Galloping Ghost
nickname of: **9** Red Grange

gallows 4 rope **5** noose **6** gibbet, halter **8** scaffold

galore 7 aplenty, to spare

galosh, galoche 4 boot, clog, shoe **6** arctic, patten, rubber **8** overshoe

Galsworthy, John
author of: **5** To Let **6** Strife **7** Justice **9** Loyalties **10** In Chancery **11** The Skin Game **13** A Modern Comedy **14** The Forsyte Saga **15** End of the Chapter **16** The Man of Property **22** Indian Summer of a Forsyte

Galt, John
character in: **13** Atlas Shrugged
author: **4** Rand

galvanize 4 fire, move, stir, wake **5** rally, rouse, treat **6** arouse, awaken, charge, excite, foment, spur on, thrill **7** inspire, provoke, quicken **8** activate, energize, vitalize **9** electrify, stimulate

galvanizing 7 rousing **8** electric, exciting, spirited **9** inspiring, thrilling **11** stimulating **12** electrifying, soul-stirring

Galveston Giant
nickname of: **11** Jack Johnson

Gamaliel
father: **6** Simeon **8** Pedahzur
grandfather: **6** Hillel
taught: **4** Paul

Gambia, The see box

gambit 4 ploy, ruse **5** feint, trick **6** scheme **8** artifice, maneuver **9** stratagem

gamble 3 bet **4** back, risk **5** flyer, wager **6** chance, hazard, toss-up **7** trust in, venture **9** speculate **11** speculation, uncertainty

gambler 5 dicer, shark, sharp, sport **6** banker, bettor, bookie, dealer, player **7** hustler

8 gamester, hazarder **10** speculator

Gambler, The
author: **16** Fyodor Dostoevsky
character: **6** Astley, Polina **10** The General **11** Mlle Blanche **15** Marquis de Grieux **16** Alexey Ivanovitch **22** Antonida Tarasyevitchev

gambol 3 hop **4** leap **5** bound, caper, frisk, sport, vault **6** bounce, cavort, frolic, prance, spring **7** disport, rollick

game see box, p. 382

gamete 3 egg **4** ovum **5** sperm **6** oocyte, zygote **8** germ cell, oosphere **12** spermatozoan, spermatozoon

Gamow, George
field: **7** physics **9** cosmology
proponent of: **13** big bang theory
deciphered: **11** genetic code
proposed: **13** quantum theory
established: **17** Gamow-Teller theory

Gamp, Sarah
character in: **16** Martin Chuzzlewit
author: **7** Dickens

gamut 3 ken **5** reach, scope, sweep **6** extent **7** compass, purview

Gandhi
director: **19** Richard Attenborough

Gambia, The
capital/largest city: **6** Banjul **8** Bathurst
others: **5** Bakau, Basse, Mansa **7** Bintang, Brikama, Kuntaur **10** Georgetown
monetary unit: **5** butut, pound **6** dalasi
island: **7** Ft James, St Mary's **8** Elephant
river: **3** Bao **6** Gambia **7** Bintang, Nianija **9** Sandougou
sea: **8** Atlantic
people: **4** Fula, Jola **5** Foula, Wolof **6** Fulani **8** Mandingo, Serahuli **9** Seranuleh
language: **4** Fula **5** Wolof **6** Fulani **7** English, Malinke **8** Mandingo
religion: **5** Islam **10** Protestant **13** Roman Catholic

---

cast: **11** Ben Kingsley **13** Candice Bergen
Oscar for: **5** actor (Kingsley) **7** picture

gang 3 mob **4** band, body, crew, pack, pals, ring, team **5** chums, crowd, flock, group, party, relay, shift, squad, troop **6** clique, outfit **7** buddies, company, coterie, cronies, friends, phalanx **8** comrades **9** coworkers, neighbors **10** associates, classmates, companions, contingent, detachment **11** schoolmates

gangster 4 goon, hood, thug **5** crook, felon, tough **6** bandit, gunman **7** hoodlum, mafioso, mobster, ruffian **8** criminal, hooligan **9** racketeer

Gant, Eugene
character in: **17** Look Homeward Angel, Of Time and the River
author: **5** Wolfe

Ganymede
also: **9** Catamitus
cupbearer of: **4** gods

gap 3 cut **4** gash, hole, rent, rift, slit, slot, void **5** abyss, break, chasm, chink, cleft, crack, gulch, gully, notch, pause **6** breach, canyon, cavity, divide, hiatus, lacuna, ravine, recess, vacuum, valley **7** crevice, fissure, interim, opening **8** aperture, crevasse, fracture, interval, puncture **9** disparity, interlude **10** difference, divergence **12** intermission, interruption

gape 4 gasp, gawk, gaze, ogle, part, peer, yawn **5** split, stare **6** cleave, expand **7** fly open **8** wide open, separate **10** rubberneck

gaping 6 astare **7** gawking, staring, yawning **13** rubbernecking

Garamas see **11** Amphithemis

garb 3 rig **4** gear, gown, robe, suit, togs **5** dress, getup, habit **6** attire, finery, livery, outfit **7** apparel, clothes, costume, raiment, uniform, vesture **8** clothing, garments, vestment, wardrobe **9** trappings **11** habiliments

garbage 4 dirt, junk **5** offal, swill, trash, waste **6** debris, litter, refuse **7** carrion, rubbish **9** sweepings

garble 5 mix up **6** jumble **7** confuse, distort **8** fragment

Garbo, Greta
real name: **21** Greta Louisa Gustaffson

game 3 bad, fun 4 golf, halt, lame, lark, play, polo, pool, prey, romp 5 antic, brave, cocky, darts, gimpy, jacks, match, rugby, sport, spree 6 boccie, boxing, daring, frolic, gaiety, gambol, heroic, plucky, quarry, soccer, spunky, squash, tennis 7 archery, bowling, contest, crooked, croquet, curling, fencing, frisbee, gallant, hawking, hunting, hurling, jai alai, limping, pastime, tourney, valiant, willing 8 baseball, crippled, deformed, disabled, fearless, football, handball, hobbling, intrepid, lacrosse, ping pong, resolute, skittles, spirited, valorous, wild fowl 9 amusement, badminton, billiards, dauntless, diversion, festivity, merriment, wrestling 10 basketball, courageous, determined, horseshoes, ice-skating, lawn tennis, recreation, tournament, volleyball 11 competition, distraction, merrymaking, racquetball, table tennis, unflinching 12 shuffleboard 13 entertainment, incapacitated, roller-skating
  board game: 4 Clue, Life, ludo 5 chess 7 Othello 8 checkers, cribbage, dominoes, draughts, fanorona, Monopoly, Scrabble 10 backgammon 14 Trivial Pursuit
    Chinese: 6 Ma-jong, wei-ch'i 7 mahjong 8 Mah-jongg
    Egyptian: 5 Senat
    Indian: 7 pachisi 8 parchesi, shatranj 9 ashtapada, parcheesi 10 shaturanga
    Japanese: 2 Go 3 I-go 5 Sho-gi
    Korean: 5 Nyout, Pa-tok
    Swedish: 6 tablut
  card game: 3 loo, war 4 brag, fish, skat, vint 5 ombre, poker, rummy, tarot, whist 6 boston, bridge, casino, chemmy, ecarte, euchre, go fish, hearts, memory, piquet, pocher 7 bezique, canasta, cooncan, old maid, plafond, primero 8 baccarat, conquian, cribbage, gin rummy, napoleon, patience, pinochle, slapjack 9 blackjack, pelmanism, solitaire, spoil five, twenty-one 11 chemin de fer, crazy eights 13 concentration 14 contract bridge 16 beggar-my-neighbor, trente et quarante

born: 6 Sweden 9 Stockholm
roles: 4 Love 7 Camille 8 Conquest, Mata Hari 9 Ninotchka 10 Grand Hotel 12 Anna Christie, Anna Karenina 13 Queen Cristina, Two-Faced Woman 14 The Painted Veil 16 Flesh and the Devil

Garcia Lorca, Federico
author of: 5 Yerma 12 Blood Wedding, Gypsy Ballads 19 House of Bernarda Alba

Garcia Marquez, Gabriel
author of: 9 Leaf Storm 23 The Autumn of the Patriarch 25 One Hundred Years of Solitude

garcon 3 boy 6 waiter 7 servant

garden 4 Eden, lawn, plot, yard 7 Arcadia 8 paradise 10 Gethsemane
type: 4 herb, rock, rose 5 truck 6 flower, formal 7 kitchen 9 botanical, vegetable

gardenia
varieties: 5 crape 9 butterfly

Garden of Cypress, The
author: 15 Sir Thomas Browne

Garden of the Finzi-Continis, The
director: 14 Vittorio De Sica
author: 11 Rumer Godden
cast: 10 Fabio Testi 11 Romolo Valli 12 Helmut Berger 14 Dominique Sanda 15 Lino Capolicchio
Oscar: 11 foreign film

Garden of the West
nickname of: 6 Kansas

garden party
French: 13 fete champetre

gardens
god of: 9 Vertumnus
goddess of: 5 Venus

Garden State
nickname of: 9 New Jersey

garden variety 5 plain 6 common, simple 7 regular 8 everyday, familiar, ordinary 11 commonplace

Gardner, Ava
husband: 9 Artie Shaw 12 Frank Sinatra, Mickey Rooney
born: 12 Smithfield NC

roles: 7 Mogambo 8 Show Boat 9 Mayerling, Naked Maja 10 On the Beach 15 The Sun Also Rises 18 Snows of Kilimanjaro 19 The Barefoot Contessa, The Night of the Iguana

Gardner, Erle Stanley
character: 9 Paul Drake 10 Perry Mason 11 Della Street 14 Hamilton Burger
also wrote as: 6 A A Fair

Gardner, John
author of: 7 Grendel 12 October Light 14 Nickel Mountain, The Art of Living, The King's Indian 17 Michelsson's Ghosts 20 The Sunlight Dialogues, The Wreckage of Agathon

Gareth
character in: 16 Arthurian romance

Garfield, James Abram *see box*

Garfield, John
real name: 15 Julius Garfinkle
born: 9 New York NY
roles: 6 Juarez 10 Humoresque 11 Body and Soul 26 The Postman Always Rings Twice

Garfinkle, Julius
real name of: 12 John Garfield

Gargamelle
character in: 22 Gargantua and Pantagruel
author: 8 Rabelais

Gargantua and Pantagruel
author: 16 Francois Rabelais
character: 7 Panurge 10 Gargamelle, Grangosier, Picrochole 23 Frere Jean des Entommeures

gargantuan 4 huge, vast 5 great 7 hulking, immense, mammoth, massive, titanic 8 colossal, enormous, gigantic, lubberly, towering 9 herculean, monstrous, overgrown 10 prodigious, stupendous, tremendous 11 elephantine 13 amplitudinous

Gargaphia
death place of: 7 Actaeon

Gargery, Joe
character in: 17 Great Expectations
author: 7 Dickens

garish 4 loud 5 cheap, gaudy, showy 6 brassy, bright, flashy, tawdry, tinsel, vulgar 7 blatant, glaring 9 flaunting, obtrusive 11 pretentious 12 ostentatious 13 overelaborate

Garfield, James Abram
presidential rank: **9** twentieth
party: **10** Republican
state represented: **2** OH
defeated: **3** (Neal) Dow **6** (James Baird) Weaver, (John Wolcott) Phelps **7** (Winfield Scott) Hancock
vice president: **6** (Chester Alan) Arthur
cabinet:
  state: **6** (James Gillespie) Blaine
  treasury: **6** (William) Windom
  war: **7** (Robert Todd) Lincoln
  attorney general: **8** (Isaac Wayne) MacVeagh
  navy: **4** (William Henry) Hunt
  postmaster general: **5** (Thomas Lemuel) James
  interior: **8** (Samuel Jordan) Kirkwood
born: **2** OH **6** Orange **8** log cabin
died: **9** Elberon NJ
  died by: **13** assassination
buried: **11** Cleveland OH
education:
  seminary: **6** Geauga
  college: **5** Hiram (Eclectic Institute) **8** Williams
  studied: **3** law
religion: **17** Disciples of Christ
political career: **8** US Senate (declined seat) **11** state Senate **24** US House of Representatives
civilian career: **6** lawyer **7** teacher **11** lay preacher
military service: **6** US Army **8** Civil War **12** major general
notable events of lifetime/term:
  exposure of: **15** Star Route frauds
father: **7** Abraham
mother: **5** Eliza (Ballou)
siblings: **4** Mary **5** James **6** Thomas **9** Mehitabel
wife: **8** Lucretia (Rudolph)
  nickname: **5** Crete
children: **4** Mary **5** Abram, Eliza **6** Edward **12** James Rudolph **13** Harry Augustus, Irvin McDowell

garland 3 bay, lei **4** halo **5** crown **6** corona, diadem, fillet, laurel, wreath **7** chaplet, circlet, coronet, festoon **8** chapbook, headband, treasury **9** anthology **10** collection **11** florilegium

Garland, Hamlin
author of: **18** Main-Travelled Roads **20** Rose of Dutcher's Coolly

Garland, Judy
real name: **11** Frances Gumm
husband: **7** Sid Luft **16** Vincente Minnelli
daughter: **9** Lorna Luft **12** Liza Minnelli
costar: **12** Mickey Rooney
born: **13** Grand Rapids MN
roles: **7** Dorothy **11** A Star Is Born, Babes in Arms **12** Easter Parade **13** The Wizard of Oz **14** The Harvey Girls **15** A Child Is Waiting, Meet Me in St Louis

garlic
botanical name: **13** Allium sativum

origin: **4** Asia **13** Mediterranean
charm against: **7** poverty, witches **13** whooping cough
use: **4** fish, fowl, meat **5** salad **10** vegetables **13** Italian dishes, salad dressing
varieties: **4** crow, hog's, wild **5** bear's, false, field, giant, grace, mouse, stag's, sweet **6** levant **7** serpent, society, Spanish, striped **8** daffodil, oriental **11** great-headed, round-headed **16** fragrant-flowered

Garm
origin: **12** Scandinavian
form: **8** watchdog
watches over: **3** Hel
location: **8** Niflheim

garment, garments 4 garb, gear, togs **5** dress, habit **6** attire, outfit **7** apparel, clothes, costume, raiment **8** clothing, vestment **10** habiliment

garner 4 reap **5** amass, hoard **6** gather, heap up **7** acquire,

collect **8** assemble **10** accumulate

Garner, James
real name: **15** James Baumgarner
born: **8** Norman OK
roles: **8** Maverick, Sayonara **11** Jim Rockford **12** Bret Maverick, Hour of the Gun **13** Darby's Rangers, Rockford Files **14** Murphy's Romance, Victor Victoria **23** Support Your Local Sheriff **25** The Americanization of Emily

garnet
varieties: **6** syrope **9** almandite, demantoid, hessonite, rhodolite **12** grossularite
month: **7** January

Garnett, David
author of: **11** Lady into Fox

garnish 4 deck, gild, trim **5** adorn, array **6** bedeck, doll up, set off **7** festoon, furbish, smarten **8** beautify, decorate, emblazon, ornament, spruce up, trimming **9** adornment, embellish, embroider **10** decoration **13** embellishment

garret 4 loft **5** attic

garrison 4 fort **5** guard **6** patrol, secure **7** battery, bivouac, brigade, platoon, station **8** division, regiment, squadron **10** detachment, escadrille **13** fortification

garrulity 8 verbiage **9** loquacity, prosiness, verbosity, wordiness **13** talkativeness

garrulous 5 gabby, windy, wordy **6** chatty **7** gossipy, prating, verbose, voluble **8** babbling, chattery, effusive **9** prattling, talkative **10** loquacious

Garry Moore Show, The
cast: **9** Allen Funt, Denise Lor, John Byner, Ken Carson **11** Chuck McCann, Marion Lorne **12** Carol Burnett, Durward Kirby, Jackie Vernon, Pete Barbutti **13** Dorothy Loudon

Garson, Greer
born: **7** Ireland **10** County Down
roles: **10** Mrs Miniver (Oscar) **11** Madame Curie **12** Her Twelve Men **13** Mrs Parkington, Random Harvest **14** Goodbye Mr Chips **16** That Forsyte Woman **17** Pride and Prejudice **19** Sunrise at Campobello

gas 4 fuel, fume **5** vapor **6** petrol **7** essence

gascon 7 boaster, bragger, egotist **8** blowhard, braggart **9** swaggerer **11** braggadocio

gasconade 4 brag, crow **5** boast **7** bravado **8** boasting **11** braggadocio

gash 4 hack, rend, rent, slit, tear **5** carve, cleft, crack, lance, slash, slice, split, wound **6** cleave, incise, pierce **7** dissect, fissure, quarter **8** incision, lacerate

Gaskell, Elizabeth
author of: **4** Ruth **8** Cranford **10** Mary Barton **13** North and South **24** The Life of Charlotte Bronte

Gaslight
director: **11** George Cukor
cast: **10** Terry Moore **12** Charles Boyer **13** Dame May Whitty, Ingrid Bergman **14** Angela Lansbury **15** Halliwell Hobbes

Gasoline Alley
creator: **9** Bill Perry, Frank King **10** Dick Moores
character: **3** Eve **4** Adam, Hope **6** Clovia, Gideon, Nubbin **7** Chipper, Gabriel **10** Walt Wallet
wife: **14** Phyllis Blossom
children: **4** Judy **5** Corky **7** Skeezix
daughter-in-law: **9** Nina Clock
dog: **5** Punky

gasp 4 gulp, pant, puff **5** blurt **6** suck in, wheeze **10** vociferate

Gasterocheires
companions of: **7** Proteus

gastronome 7 epicure, gourmet **9** bon vivant

gastronomy 9 epicurism

gastropod, gasteropod 4 slug **5** cowry, snail, whelk **6** cowrie, limpet, nerite **7** abalone, mollusk **8** univalve

gate 3 tap **5** crowd, house, valve **6** portal, sluice, spigot **7** doorway **8** audience, hatchway **9** turnstile **10** attendance

gateau 4 cake **7** dessert

gatekeeper 5 guard **6** porter **8** watchman

Gates, Horatio
served in: **16** Revolutionary War **18** French and Indian War
battle: **6** Camden **8** Saratoga
defeated: **8** Burgoyne
defeated by: **10** Cornwallis

gateway 4 adit **5** entry **6** access, portal **7** doorway, opening **8** entrance, entryway **10** passageway

Gath 14 Philistine city

gather 4 fold, mass **5** amass, group, infer, learn, pleat, shirr, stack **6** assume, deduce, heap up, muster, pile up, pucker, ruffle **7** cluster, collect, convene, marshal, observe **8** assemble, conclude **9** stockpile **10** accumulate, congregate, understand **11** concentrate

gathering 3 mob **4** gang, pack **5** bunch, crowd, crush, drove, flock, horde, party, press **6** throng **7** company, meeting, roundup, turnout **8** assembly, conclave **9** concourse, multitude **10** assemblage, collection, conference, convention **11** aggregation, convergence, convocation **12** accumulation, congregation **13** concentration

gather together 4 herd **5** amass, hoard, rally **6** muster **7** collate, collect, compile, marshal, round up, sweep up **8** assemble, shepherd **9** aggregate, stockpile **10** accumulate, congregate

Gatling, Richard Jordan
nationality: **8** American
inventor of: **10** machine gun **16** steam-powered plow

gatophobia
fear of: **4** cats

gauche 5 inept **6** clumsy, oafish **7** awkward, boorish, illbred, uncouth **8** bungling, plebeian, tactless **9** inelegant, maladroit, tasteless, unrefined **10** blundering, uncultured, ungraceful, unmannerly, unpolished **11** proletarian **13** ungentlemanly

gaucherie 5 gaffe **7** blunder, faux pas **11** impropriety **12** indiscretion

Gaudeamus igitur 22 Let us therefore be joyful

gaudy 4 loud, sham **5** cheap, showy, vivid **6** flashy, flimsy, garish, tawdry, tinsel, vulgar **7** glaring, intense **8** colorful, dazzling, lustrous, striking **9** brilliant, sparkling, tasteless, worthless **10** bespangled, glittering **11** pretentious **12** ostentatious

gauge, gage 4 rate, size **5** guess, judge, meter **6** assess **7** adjudge, measure **8** appraise, estimate, evaluate, standard **9** ascertain, calculate, criterion, yardstick **11** measurement
type: **4** ring **5** bevel

Gauguin, Paul Eugene Henri
born: **5** Paris **6** France
artwork: **9** Nevermore **12** The

Tahitians **13** The White Horse **15** The Yellow Christ **18** Horsemen on the Beach **23** The Vision after the Sermon (Jacob Wrestling with the Angel) **25** Be in Love and You Will Be Happy **26** The Spirit of the Dead Watching **36** Where Do We Come From? Who Are We? Where Do We Go?
book: **6** Noa Noa

Gaul *see* **6** France

gaunt 4 bony, grim, lank, lean, slim, thin **5** bleak, lanky, spare **6** barren, meager, skinny, wasted **7** haggard, pinched, scraggy, scrawny, slender, spindly, starved **8** deserted, desolate, forsaken, rawboned, skeletal, withered **9** emaciated, shriveled **10** cadaverous, forbidding **14** spindle-shanked

Gauss, Carl Friedrich
field: **7** physics **9** astronomy **11** mathematics
nationality: **6** German
worked in: **9** magnetism **11** electricity **12** number theory
named for him: **9** Gauss's Law

Gautier, Marguerite
character in: **7** Camille
author: **5** Dumas (fils)

Gautier, Theophile
author of: **6** La Peri **7** Giselle **8** Albertus **11** Young France **13** Emaux et Camees **16** Enamels and Cameos **20** Mademoiselle de Maupin, The Romance of the Mummy
doctrine: **14** Art for art's sake

gauzy 5 filmy, sheer **6** flimsy, sleazy **10** diaphanous **11** translucent, transparent

gave up 4 quit **5** ceded **7** dropped, forsook, yielded **8** forswore, resigned **9** abandoned, abdicated, forfeited, renounced **11** surrendered **12** discontinued, relinquished

Gawain
character in: **16** Arthurian romance

gawk 4 gape, gaze, peer **10** rubberneck

gawky 6 clumsy, klutzy **7** awkward, lumpish **8** bungling, fumbling, lubberly, ungainly, unwieldy **9** all thumbs, graceless, ham-fisted, ham-handed, maladroit **10** blundering, ungraceful

gay 3 fun **4** airy, glad **5** happy, jolly, merry, showy, sunny, vivid **6** blithe, bright, cheery, elated, frisky, genial, jaunty, jocose, jovial, joyful, joyous, lively, social **7** buoyant, chipper, coltish, dashing, festive, gleeful, glowing, intense, jocular, playful, smiling, waggish **8** animated, cheerful, colorful, exultant, gladsome, humorous, jubilant, lustrous, skittish, spirited, splendid, sportive, volatile **9** brilliant, convivial, frivolous, hilarious, rejoicing, sparkling, sprightly, sumptuous, vivacious **10** flamboyant, frolicsome, glittering, insouciant, theatrical, variegated **12** effervescent, lighthearted, multicolored

Gay, John
author of dialogue/lyrics
for: **15** The Beggar's Opera

Gay, Walter
character in: **12** Dombey and Son
author: **7** Dickens

gay blade 3 fop **4** beau **5** blade, dandy **7** playboy **8** cavalier **9** ladies' man **12** boulevardier, man-about-town

Gay Divorcee, The
director: **12** Mark Sandrich
cast: **10** Alice Brady, Erik Rhodes **11** Betty Grable, Fred Astaire **12** Ginger Rogers **19** Edward Everett Horton
song: **11** Continental, Night and Day

Gay-Lussac, Joseph
field: **7** physics **9** chemistry
nationality: **6** French
discovered: **24** law of combining gas volumes
invented: **10** hydrometer

Gaynor, Mitzi
real name: **20** Franceska Mitzi Gerber
husband: **8** Jack Bean
born: **9** Chicago IL
roles: **8** Les Girls **10** Golden Girl **12** Anything Goes, South Pacific **14** The Joker Is Wild **32** There's No Business Like Show Business

gaze 3 eye **4** gape, ogle, peek, peer, scan **5** glare, lower, stare, study, watch **6** behold, glance, glower, peruse, regard, survey **7** examine, inspect, observe, witness **8** look long, pore over, scrutiny **10** rubberneck, scrutinize **11** contemplate

gaze at 4 view **5** watch **6** behold, look at **7** stare at **8** look upon **11** contemplate

Gazza Ladra, La
also: **17** The Thieving Magpie
opera by: **7** Rossini

Ge *see* **4** Gaea

gear 3 cam, rig **4** duds, garb, togs **5** dress, tools **6** attire, outfit, tackle, things **7** apparel, clothes, rigging **8** clothing, cogwheel, flywheel, garments, material, property **9** apparatus, equipment, trappings **10** belongings, implements **11** accessories, instruments **12** contrivances **13** accoutrements, paraphernalia

Geb
also: **3** Keb
origin: **8** Egyptian
god of: **5** earth
daughter: **4** Isis
son: **6** Osiris
sister: **3** Nut

Gedaliah
means: **14** Jehovah is great
father: **6** Ahikam, Pashur **8** Jeduthun
descendant: **9** Zephaniah

Geer, Will
born: **11** Frankfort IN
roles: **7** Grandpa **10** The Waltons **11** In Cold Blood

Gehenna 4 hell

Gehrig, Lou (Henry Louis)
nickname: **9** Iron Horse
sport: **8** baseball
position: **9** first base
team: **14** New York Yankees

Geisman, Ella
real name of: **11** June Allyson

Geist 4 mind **6** spirit

gelatin 4 agar, glue **5** aspic, gelee, jelly **6** glutin, pectin **7** protein, sericin

gelatinize 3 set **4** jell **7** congeal, stiffen, thicken **9** coagulate

gelatinous 7 colloid, viscous **8** muculent **9** jelly-like

geld 5 alter **8** castrate **10** emasculate

gelid 3 icy **6** frigid, frozen **8** freezing

Gelonus
father: **8** Hercules

gem *see box*

Gemini
symbol: **5** twins
planet: **7** Mercury
rules: **14** communications
born: **3** May **4** June

Gemini Contenders, The
author: **12** Robert Ludlum

Gem State
nickname of: **5** Idaho

gemutlich 4 easy **9** agreeable, congenial, simpatico **11** comfortable

gendarme 9 policeman

gender 3 sex **4** kind, male, sort, type **5** class **6** female, neuter **8** feminine **9** masculine

Gendre, Louis
real name of: **12** Louis Jourdan

genealogy 4 line **5** birth, house, stock **7** lineage **8** ancestry, pedigree **9** parentage **10** derivation, extraction

Gene Autry Show, The
cast: **10** Pat Buttram
horse: **8** Champion
theme song: **20** Back in the Saddle Again

general 5 basic, broad, usual, vague **6** common, normal,

gem 4 dear, doll, rock **5** beaut, bijou, jewel, peach, prize **6** marvel, wonder **8** treasure
type: **4** jade, opal, ruby, sard **5** agate, amber, beryl, coral, pearl, topaz **6** garnet, pyrope, quartz, spinel, zircon **7** apatite, cat's-eye, citrine, diamond, emerald, jadeite, kunzite, olivine, peridot **8** amethyst, corundum, feldspar, hematite, lazurite, nephrite, sapphire, steatite, sunstone **9** almandite, amazonite, carnelian, demantoid, enstatite, fibrolite, malachite, moonstone, morganite, rhodolite, scapolite, spodumene, tiger's-eye, turquoise **10** aquamarine, bloodstone, chalcedony, hessionite, rose quartz, tourmaline **11** alexandrite, chrysoberyl, chrysocolla, chrysoprase, lapis lazuli, rock crystal, topaz quartz **12** grossularite

public, wonted **7** blanket, current, generic, inexact, natural, overall, popular, regular, typical **8** everyday, frequent, habitual, ordinary, pandemic, sweeping **9** customary, extensive, imprecise, panoramic, prevalent, universal, worldwide **10** accustomed, collective, ecumenical, prevailing, widespread **11** unspecified **12** conventional, nonexclusive, nontechnical **13** comprehensive, miscellaneous

General Electric Theater
host: **12** Ronald Reagan

general idea 4 gist **5** drift, tenor **6** effect, import **7** purport **10** impression **11** implication

generality 6 cliche, truism **9** platitude **12** universality

14 collectiveness **17** miscellaneousness **18** indiscriminateness

generalization 3 law **5** axion **7** bromide **9** inference, statement

generalize 5 infer, judge **8** conclude

generally 5 often **6** always, mainly, mostly **7** as a rule, chiefly, largely, usually **9** currently, typically **10** frequently, habitually, ordinarily, repeatedly **11** extensively, principally, universally

general/military leader *see box*

generate 4 bear, coin, form, make, sire **5** beget, breed, cause, frame, spawn, yield **6** create, evolve, father, induce, invent **7** develop, fash-

ion, produce **8** contrive, engender, fructify, occasion **9** construct, fabricate, fecundate, fertilize, institute, originate, procreate, propagate, reproduce **10** effectuate, impregnate **11** proliferate

generation 3 kin **4** clan, line, race **5** breed, house, issue, stock, tribe **6** family, growth, strain **7** genesis, lineage, progeny **8** breeding, creation **9** begetting, causation, evolution, formation, offspring **10** production **11** development, engendering, origination, procreation, propagation **12** impregnation, reproduction **13** fertilization, proliferation

generic 6 common **7** general **8** sweeping **9** universal **10** collective **11** generalized, unspecified **12** nonexclusive **13** comprehensive **14** nonrestrictive

generosity 6 bounty **7** charity **8** altruism, courtesy, kindness, largesse **9** abundance, nobleness **10** liberality **11** benevolence, hospitality, magnanimity

generous 5 ample, large, lofty, noble **6** humane, lavish **7** copious, liberal **8** abundant, effusive, obliging, princely, prodigal **9** bounteous, bountiful, honorable, plenteous, plentiful, plethoric, unselfish, unstinted **10** altruistic, beneficent, benevolent, bighearted, charitable, freehanded, freegiving, high-minded, hospitable, munificent, openhanded, ungrudging, unstinting **11** considerate, extravagant, magnanimous, overflowing **12** humanitarian, largehearted, unrestricted **13** accommodating, philanthropic

genesis 4 rise, root **5** birth **6** origin **8** creation **9** begetting, beginning, inception **10** generation **11** engendering **12** commencement

geneticist
American: **5** Temin **6** Morgan, Muller

genetics
science of: **8** heredity
researcher: **6** Mendel

Genetyllis
origin: **5** Greek
protectress of: **6** births

Genghis Khan
also: **11** Jenghiz Khan
name means: **14** universal ruler
position: **13** Mongol emperor

---

general/military leader
American:
Revolutionary War: **3** (Light Horse Harry) Lee **5** Allen, Barry, Gates, Jones, Wayne **6** Arnold, Greene, Marion, Morgan **10** Washington
War of 1812: **4** Hull **5** Perry, Scott **7** Decatur
Mexican War: **5** Scott **6** Kearny
Civil War: **3** Lee **5** Early, Grant, Meade **6** Thomas, (JEB) Stuart **7** Forrest, Pickett, Sherman, (Stonewall) Jackson **8** Farragut, Sheridan **9** McClellan **10** Beauregard, Longstreet
Indian Wars: **6** Custer **7** Houston **10** Crazy Horse
WWI: **4** Sims **8** Mitchell, Pershing
WWII: **4** King **5** Clark **6** Arnold, Halsey, Nimitz, Patton **7** Bradley, Merrill **8** Marshall, Stilwell **9** Chennault, Doolittle, MacArthur **10** Eisenhower, Wainwright
Korean War: **5** Clark **9** MacArthur
Vietnam War: **6** Abrams **12** Westmoreland
Gulf War: **11** Schwarzkopf
British: **4** Byng, Haig, Howe, Slim **5** Wolfe **6** French, Gordon, Harris, Nelson, Wavell **7** Allenby, Clinton, Dowding, Wingate **8** Braddock, Burgoyne, Cromwell, Jellicoe, Lawrence **9** Alexander, Kitchener **10** Cornwallis, Montgomery, Wellington **11** Marlborough, Mountbatten
Carthagenian: **8** Hannibal **13** Hamilcar Barca
French: **3** Ney **4** Foch **5** Murat **6** Giraud, Joffre, Petain, Roland **7** Nivelle **8** De Gaulle, Montcalm, Napoleon **9** Lafayette **10** Bernadotte
German: **5** Kluck **6** Moltke, Paulus, Rommel, Scheer **7** Blucher, Goering, Tirpitz **8** Bismarck, Goebbels, Guderian **9** Rundstedt **10** Falkenhayn, Hindenburg, Kesselring, Ludendorff, Schlieffen **17** Frederick the Great
Israeli: **5** Dayan
Japanese: **10** Tojo Hideki **15** Yamamoto Isoroku
Macedonian: **7** Ptolemy **8** Philip II **9** Alexander (the Great)
Norman: **7** William (the Conqueror)
Roman: **5** Sulla **6** Brutus, Pompey, Seneca, Trajan **7** Crassus, Hadrian, Lepidus **8** Gracchus, Octavian (Caesar Augustus), Tiberius **9** Vespasian **10** Flamininus, Mark Antony **11** Gaius Marius **12** Julius Caesar **15** Cassius Longinus, Scipio Africanus **18** Tarquinius Superbus
Russian: **6** Zhukov **7** Kutuzov, Voronov **8** Brusilov, Kerensky, Kornilov, Samsonov **9** Bagration **10** Timoshenko, Vasilevsky

defeated: 6 Russia **10** Chin
empire
occupied: 6 Peking

genial 3 gay **4** glad, kind, warm
5 civil, happy, jolly, merry,
sunny **6** bright, cheery, hearty,
jaunty, jocund, jovial, joyful,
joyous, kindly, lively, social
7 affable, amiable, chipper, cordial, festive **8** cheerful, friendly,
gracious, mirthful, pleasant,
sociable **9** agreeable, congenial,
convivial, courteous, expansive, sparkling, vivacious
10 neighborly **12** lighthearted
13 companionable

geniality 10 affability, cordiality
11 sociability **12** conviviality,
friendliness **13** expansiveness

genius 3 ace, wit **4** bent, gift,
mind, whiz **5** brain, flair,
knack **6** expert, master, wisdom **7** faculty, insight, prodigy
8 aptitude, judgment, penchant, sagacity, wizardry **9** ingenuity, intuition, invention
10 mastermind, perception,
proclivity, propensity **11** imagination, percipience **12** intelligence, predilection
13 understanding

Genius, The
    author: 15 Theodore Dreiser

genius loci 16 guardian of a
place

genre 4 kind, sort, type
5 breed, class, genus, group,
order, style **6** school **7** fashion,
species, variety **8** category, division **11** description
14 classification

genteel 4 tony **5** civil, elite,
ritzy, swank, swell **6** modish,
poised, polite, urbane
7 courtly, elegant, high-hat, refined, stylish **8** cultured, decorous, ladylike, mannerly,
polished, well-bred **9** courteous, high-class, high-toned, patrician **10** cultivated, well-
spoken **11** fashionable,
gentlemanly, highfalutin, overrefined, pretentious **12** aristocratic, silk-stocking,
thoroughbred

gentian 8 Gentiana
    varieties: 5 blind, green, horse
    6 alpine, bottle, closed, Si-
    erra, yellow **7** crested,
    fringed, prairie, spurred **8** Ca-
    tesby's, soapwort, stemless
    9 Mendocino **10** pine barren

gentil 4 kind **5** noble **6** gentle

gentile
    Yiddish: 3 goy

man: 7 shegetz
woman: 6 shiksa

gentility 6 polish **7** decorum,
suavity **8** breeding, chivalry, civility, courtesy, urbanity **9** gallantry, propriety, punctilio
10 refinement **11** cultivation,
savoir-faire **12** mannerliness

gentle 3 low **4** calm, easy,
kind, meek, mild, soft, tame
5 balmy, bland, light, quiet
6 benign, broken, docile,
kindly, placid, serene, slight,
smooth, tender **7** lenient, pacific, subdued **8** harmless, merciful, moderate, peaceful,
tolerant, tranquil **9** indulgent,
temperate, tractable **10** manageable, thoughtful, untroubled
11 considerate, sympathetic
12 domesticated **13** compassionate, tenderhearted
    French: 6 gentil

gentleman 3 don, guy, man,
one **4** chap, gent **5** swell **6** fellow, person, squire **7** esquire,
hidalgo **8** cavalier **9** caballero,
chevalier, patrician **10** aristocrat, individual

Gentleman Jim
    nickname of: 12 James
    Corbett

gentlemanly 6 polite **7** courtly,
gallant, refined **8** cultured, decorous, mannerly, polished,
well-bred **9** courteous, dignified
10 cultivated

Gentleman's Agreement
    director: 9 Elia Kazan
    based on novel by: 12 Laura
    Z Hobson
    cast: 10 Anne Revere **11** Ce-
    leste Holm, Gregory Peck
    12 John Garfield **14** Dorothy
    McGuire
    Oscar for: 7 picture **17** sup-
    porting actress (Holm)

Gentlemen Prefer Blondes
    author: 9 Anita Loos

gentleness 8 calmness, docility,
mildness, serenity, tameness
10 compassion, tenderness
12 mercifulness, peacefulness,
tractability

gentle wind 4 waft **6** breath,
breeze, zephyr

gently 6 easily, kindly, meekly,
mildly, softly, tamely **7** amiably, lightly **8** benignly, placidly,
smoothly, tenderly **9** gradually
10 delicately, moderately,
pleasantly, soothingly **15** compassionately, sympathetically

gentry 5 elite **7** society **8** nobility **10** blue bloods, gentlefolk
11 aristocracy, aristocrats

genuflect 4 bend **6** kowtow

genuine 4 open, pure, real,
true **5** frank, naive, plain, solid
6 actual, candid, honest,
proven, simple **7** artless, earnest, natural, sincere **8** bona
fide, sterling, true-blue **9** authentic, guileless, heartfelt, ingenuous, simon-pure,
unalloyed, veritable **10** legitimate, unaffected **13** unadulterated **15** straightforward,
unsophisticated

genuineness 7 honesty
9 frankness, sincerity **10** candidness, simplicity **11** artlessness **13** guilelessness
14 unaffectedness
19 straightforwardness

genus 4 kind, sort, type **5** class,
group **7** variety **8** category, division **14** classification

geologist
    British: 4 Hall
    German: 6 Werner
    Scottish: 6 Hutton

geoponics 7 tillage **8** agronomy
9 husbandry **10** agronomics
11 agriculture, cultivation

**George Burns and Gracie
Allen Show, The**
    character: 9 Mr Beasley (Mail-
    man) **11** Harry Morton
    13 Blanche Morton
    theme song: 8 Love Nest

Georgetown
    capital of: 6 Guyana

Georgia *see box, p. 388*

Georgia Peach
    nickname of: 6 Ty Cobb

Georgics, The
    author: 6 Vergil, Virgil
    called: 17 agricultural poems

Georgia
    capital/largest city:
    7 Tbilisi
    others: 6 Batumi **7** Kuta-
    isi, Rustavi, Sukhumi
    division: 7 Ossetia **8** Ab-
    khazia, Adzharia
    head of state: 9 president
    government: 8 republic
    monetary unit: 5 ruble
    mountain: 8 Caucasus
    river: 4 Kura **5** Rioni
    sea: 5 Black
    people: 5 Azeri **7** Russian
    8 Armenian, Georgian,
    Ossetian **9** Abkhazian
    language: 8 Georgian
    religion 14 Georgian
    Church **15** Russian
    Orthodox

Georgia
  abbreviation: 2 GA
  nickname: 5 Peach 7 Cracker 21 Empire State of the South
  capital/largest city: 7 Atlanta
  others: 4 Rome 5 Jesup, Macon 6 Albany, Athens, Dalton, Plains, Sparta 7 Augusta, Conyers, Cordele, Decatur, Griffen, Vidalia 8 Columbus, LaGrange, Marietta, Moultrie, Savannah, Valdosta, Waycross 9 Brunswick 11 College Park, Gainesville, Thomasville 13 Andersonville
  college: 4 Tift 5 Clark, Emory, Paine 6 Mercer 7 Atlanta, Spelman 8 Wesleyan 9 Morehouse 10 Agnes Scott 11 Georgia Tech
  explorer: 15 James Oglethorpe
  feature: 16 Little White House
    amusement park: 19 Six Flags Over Georgia
    national cemetery: 13 Andersonville
    national monument: 8 Ocmulgee 11 Fort Pulaski 13 Fort Frederica
  tribe: 5 Creek, Guale, Yuchi 6 Chiaha, Oconee, Uchean 7 Yamasee 8 Hitchiti
  people: 6 Ty Cobb 7 cracker 10 Bobby Jones 11 Juliette Low 15 Erskine Caldwell 16 Margaret Mitchell 18 Joel Chandler Harris
  island: 3 Sea 6 Jekyll, Sapelo 7 Ossabaw 10 Cumberland
  lake: 6 Lanier, Martin 7 Harding, Nottely 8 Bankhead, Hartwell, Sinclair
  land rank: 11 twenty-first
  mountain: 5 Stone 7 Lookout 8 Kennesaw 9 Blue Ridge 11 Alleghenies 13 High Point Peak
    highest point: 17 Brasstown Bald Peak
  physical feature:
    sea: 8 Atlantic
    springs: 4 Warm
    swamp: 10 Okefenokee
  president: 11 Jimmy Carter
  river: 3 Pea 5 Flint 6 Etowah, Oconee, Pigeon 7 Conecuh, Satilla, St Mary's, Tugaloo 8 Altamaha, Ocmulgee, Ogeechee, Savannah, Suwannee 9 Chattooga 13 Chattahoochie
  state admission: 6 fourth
  state bird: 13 brown thrasher
  state fish: 14 largemouth bass
  state flower: 12 Cherokee rose
  state motto: 6 Wisdom 20 Justice and Moderation
  state song: 7 Georgia
  state tree: 7 live oak

Ge-Pano-Carib
  language branch: 7 Macro-Ge 10 Macro-Carib 11 Macro-Panoan

gephyrophobia
  fear of: 7 bridges

Geraint
  character in: 16 Arthurian romance

geranium 11 Pelargonium
  varieties: 3 ivy 4 fish, lime, mint, pine, rock, rose, show, wild 5 apple, fancy, house, lemon, regal, zonal 6 almond, alpine, cactus, jungle, nutmeg, orange 7 apricot, bedding, coconut, feather, hanging, knotted, polecat 8 crowfoot, fern-leaf, horsehoe 9 beefsteak, oak-leaved 10 California, gooseberry, peppermint, strawberry, sweetheart, village-oak 11 grape-leaved, herb-scented, maple-leaved, rose-scented 12 silver-leaved, southernwood, sweet-scented 13 black-flowered, pansy-flowered, pheasant's-foot 14 Lady Washington, little-leaf rose 15 mint-scented rose 16 Martha Washington 17 English finger-bowl

Gerber, Franceska Mitzi
  real name of: 11 Mitzi Gaynor

Gerd, Gerda
  origin: 12 Scandinavian
  husband: 4 Frey 5 Freyr

Gere, Richard
  roles: 5 Yanks 10 Breathless, Cotton Club 12 Days of Heaven 14 American Gigolo 19 Looking for Mr Goodbar 22 An Officer and a Gentleman

Geri
  origin: 12 Scandinavian
  form: 4 wolf
  owner: 4 Odin 5 Othin
  received: 4 food
  exception: 4 meat
  fellow wolf: 5 Freki

germ 3 bud, bug, egg 4 ovum, root, seed 5 ovule, spark, spore, virus 6 embryo, origin, source, sprout 7 microbe, nucleus, seed bud 8 bacillus, offshoot, rudiment 9 bacterium, beginning 12 fountainhead 13 microorganism

German 3 Hun 4 balt, Goth 5 boche, heine, jerry, kraut, Saxon 6 Teuton 7 tedesco 8 Prussian, Teutonic 9 deutscher
  article: 3 das, dem, den, der, des, die, ein 4 eine
  empire: 5 reich
  man: 4 herr
  storm and stress: 13 sturm und drang
  thank you: 5 danke 10 danke schon
  toast: 6 prosit
  woman: 4 frau 8 fraulein

German-Dutch
  language family: 12 Indo-European
  branch: 8 Germanic
  group: 15 Western Germanic
  language: 9 Low German 10 High German

germane 3 apt, fit 6 native, proper 7 apropos, fitting, related 8 material, relative, relevant, suitable 9 connected, intrinsic, pertinent 10 applicable 11 appropriate 12 appertaining

germaneness 9 relevance 10 pertinence 13 applicability 15 appropriateness

Germanic
  language family: 12 Indo-European
  group: 6 Gothic 15 Western Germanic

Germanic Mythology see box

German is spoken here
  German: 25 hier wird Deutsch gesprochen

German literary movement (18th cent) 13 sturm und drang

Germanic Mythology
chief of gods: 5 Wotan
corresponds to Scandinavian: **4** Odin
dwarf:
  15 Rumpelstiltskin
dwarves: 8 Niblungs
  9 Nibelungs
emperor: 15 Dietrich
  von Bern
epic: 14 Nibelungenlied
**goddess of clouds/sky/
  marriage: 3** Fri **5** Frigg,
  Frija **6** Frigga
goddess of death/fertility: 7 Berchta, Perchta
**goddess of love/
  beauty/fecundity:
  5** Freya
**goddess of moon/
  witch: 5** Holle
god of thunder: 5 Donar
**god of winter sports:
  4** Ullr **5** Uller
hero: 6 Sigurd
  9 Siegfried
heroine: 6 Gudrun, Kudrun **7** Guthrun **8** Brunhild **9** Kriemhild
king: 7 Siggeir
**king of dwarves:
  8** Alberich
**knight of the holy
  grail: 9** Lohengrin
**magic cloak:
  9** Tarnkappe
maidens: 9 Valkyries
nature spirit: 7 Eriking
nymph: 7 Lorelei, Lurelei
water spirit: 3 Nix

Germany *see box*

Germany, East *see box*

Germany, West *see box,*
p. 390

germicide 11 bactericide
12 disinfectant

Germinal
  author: 9 Emile Zola

germinate 3 bud **4** blow,
  open **5** bloom, shoot **6** flower,
  push up, sprout **7** blossom,
  burgeon, develop **8** generate,
  spring up, vegetate

germination 9 sprouting
  11 propagation

Gershom
  means: 13 stranger there
  father: 5 Moses
  mother: 8 Zipporah
  brother: 12 Eliezar

Gershwin, George
  born: 10 Brooklyn NY

Germany
capital: 6 Berlin
government leader: 10 chancellor, Helmut Kohl
monetary unit: 12 Deutsche mark
people: 3 Hun **4** Slav, Sorb, Wend **5** Saxon
  artist: **4** Marc **5** Durer **7** Barlach, Cranach, Gropius, Holbein **9** Grunewald **14** Mies van der Rohe
  author: **4** Mann, Marx **5** Grass **6** Brecht, Elsner, Goethe **7** Johnson, Lessing **8** Hochhuth
  composer: **4** Bach **5** Weill **6** Brahms, Handel, Wagner **7** Strauss **8** Schumann **9** Beethoven, Hindemith **11** Mendelssohn
  conductor: **5** Henze **6** Walter **9** Klemperer **11** Furtwangler, Stockhausen
  historical leader: **6** Hitler, Kaiser **8** Bismarck **10** Barbarossa
  Prussian noble: **6** Junker
  religious leader: **6** Luther
language: 6 German **10** High German **11** Hochdeutsch
religion: 8 Lutheran **10** Protestant **13** Roman Catholic **17** Evangelical Church
food:
  bread: **12** pumpernickel
  dish: **9** lebkuchen **15** wiener schnitzel
  dumpling: **6** knodel
  frankfurter: **15** wiener wurstchen
  fruit bread: **7** stollen
  ham: **11** Westphalian
  potato salad: **14** kartoffelsalat
  pot roast: **11** sauerbraten
  sausage: **5** wurst **9** blutwurst, bratwurst **10** brockwurst, knackwurst, leberwurst
  sole: **8** seezunge

Germany, East
capital/largest city: 10 East Berlin
others: 4 Jena **5** Halle, Waren **6** Erfurt, Weimar **7** Cottbus, Dresden, Leipzig, Meissen, Potsdam, Rostock, Schwedt, Wannsee, Zwickau **9** Frankfurt, Magdeburg **10** Angermunde, Warnemunde, Wittenberg **11** Neustrelitz **13** Karl-Marx-Stadt (Chemnitz)
school: 8 Humboldt
division: 6 Saxony **9** Thuringia **11** Brandenburg, Mecklenburg **12** Saxony-Anhalt
government: 11 Volkskammer (Peoples' Chamber)
monetary unit: 4 mark **7** Ostmark, pfennig
lake: 6 Muritz
mountain: 3 Ore **4** Harz **10** Erzgebirge
highest point: 11 Fichtelberg
river: 4 Elbe, Oder **5** Havel, Saale, Spree **6** Neisse, Warnow
sea: 6 Baltic
physical feature:
  forest: **10** Thuringian
place: 10 Berlin Wall **17** Checkpoint Charlie
  castle: **9** Sans Souci
  church: **8** St Thomas **12** Thomaskirche
  city center: **13** Karl Marx Platz **14** Alexanderplatz, Neubrandenberg
  comic opera: **12** Komische Oper
  gate: **11** Brandenburg
  museum: **7** Zwinger **8** Pergamon **10** Goethe Haus
  opera house: **18** Deutsche Staatsoper
feature:
  china: **7** Dresden
  fair: **7** Leipzig
  theater company: **16** Berliner Ensemble

Germany, West

capital: 4 Bonn

largest city: 10 West Berlin

others: 4 Kiel 5 Essen, Mainz, Trier 6 Aachen, Bochum, Bremen, Kassel, Lubeck, Minden, Munden, Munich 7 Cologne, Hamburg, Hanover, Krefeld, Munster 8 Augsburg, Biberach, Dortmund, Duisberg, Duisburg, Freiburg, Mannheim, Solingen 9 Darmstadt, Karlsruhe, Nuremberg, Oldenburg, Stuttgart, Wiesbaden, Wuppertal 10 Dusseldorf, Heidelberg, Steingaden 11 Saarbrucken 12 Oberammergau 13 Gelsenkirchen 15 Frankfurt am Main 16 Mulheim an der Ruhr

school: 4 Bonn 7 Hamburg 10 Heidelberg 16 Ludwig-Maximilian

division: 4 Saar 5 Baden, Hesse 6 Bremen 7 Bavaria 9 Rhineland 10 Palatinate, Westphalia 11 Lower Saxony, Wurttemberg 17 Schleswig-Holstein

head of government: 10 chancellor

monetary unit: 4 mark 7 pfennig 12 Deutsche mark

island: 11 East Frisian 12 North Frisian

lake: 9 Constance 11 Inner Alster, Outer Alster

mountain: 4 Harz 8 Feldberg 11 Black Forest 12 Bavarian Alps

highest point: 9 Zugspitze

river: 3 Ems 4 Elbe, Main, Nahe, Ruhr, Saar, Wese 5 Rhine, Weser 6 Danube, Neckar 7 Moselle, Pegnitz

sea: 5 North 6 Baltic

physical feature:
  canal: 4 Kiel 10 Mittelland
  forest: 5 Black 7 Bohemia 9 Teu Toburg

place: 17 Checkpoint Charlie
  botanical garden: 18 Pflantzen und Blumen
  boulevard: 14 Kurfurstendamm
  church: 12 Frauenkirche (Cathedral of Our Lady) 13 Kaiser Wilhelm 16 Gadachtniskirche
  city center: 11 Marienplatz
  fortress: 9 Marksburg
  fountain: 14 Schoner Brunnen
  garden: 10 Englischer
  hall: 9 Beethoven
  museum: 8 Residenz 9 Durer Haus 12 Schatzkammer 14 Alte Pinakothek
  opera house: 18 Deutsches Opern Haus
  park/zoo: 18 Hagenbecks Tierpark
  residential district: 11 Hansa Vierte 12 Hanse Viertel
  resort (on Baltic): 10 Travemunde
  theater: 9 Cuvillies

feature:
  beer cellar: 11 bierkellern
  beer garden: 10 biergarten
  beer hall: 10 bierhallen
  beer room: 10 bierstuben
  cars: 3 BMW 7 Porsche 10 Volkswagen 12 Mercedes-Benz
  children: 6 kinder
  city hall: 5 Romer 7 Rathaus
  festival: 11 Oktoberfest
  folk songs: 11 volkslieder
  kitchen: 5 kuche
  old city: 8 Altstadt
  pre-Lent carnival: 8 Fasching
  secondary school: 9 gymnasium
  states: 6 lander
  wine street: 11 Weinstrasse

partner/lyricist: 11 Ira Gershwin

composer of: 9 Funny Face 11 Of Thee I Sing 12 Porgy and Bess 13 Cuban Overture 14 Rhapsody in Blue 15 Strike Up the Band 17 An American in Paris

Gertrude

character in: 6 Hamlet

author: 11 Shakespeare

Gervin, George

nickname: 6 Iceman

sport: 10 basketball

team: 15 San Antonio Spurs

Geryon

form: 7 monster

father: 8 Chrysaor

mother: 10 Callirrhoe

home: 7 Erythea

possessed: 6 cattle

color of cattle: 3 red

herdsman: 8 Eurytion

dog: 7 Orthrus

killed by: 8 Heracles

cattle stolen by: 8 Heracles

Gesta Romanorum

author: 7 unknown

gestation 9 evolution, pregnancy 10 epigenesis, generation, incubation, maturation 11 development, propagation

gesticulate 3 nod 4 wink 5 nudge, shrug 6 beckon, motion, signal 8 indicate 9 pantomime

gesture 3 nod 4 sign, wave, wink 5 nudge, shrug, touch 6 beckon, motion, signal 8 courtesy, dumb show, flourish, high sign 9 formality, pantomime 13 demonstration

get 3 bag, fix, net, wax, win 4 beat, coax, earn, gain, grab, grip, grow, have, hear, move, reap, sway, take, turn 5 annoy, catch, fetch, glean, grasp, learn, reach, seize, sense, upset 6 arrive, attain, baffle, become, collar, come by, come to, enlist, entrap, fathom, follow, induce, obtain, pick up, pocket, prompt, puzzle, secure, snatch, suborn, take in, turn to 7 achieve, acquire, capture, confuse, contact, dispose, ensnare, go after, incline, inherit, mystify, perplex, prepare, procure, realize, receive, wheedle, win over 8 bewilder, confound, contract, irritate, perceive, persuade 9 influence, transport 10 comprehend, disconcert, predispose, understand

get a kick out of 4 like 5 eat

up, enjoy, fancy, savor **6** rel-ish **10** appreciate

getaway 6 escape, exodus, flight **10** decampment

get done 2 do **6** finish **8** complete **10** accomplish

get even 6 avenge **7** counter, hit back, pay back, revenge **9** retaliate

Gethsemane 6 garden

get into 3 don **5** enter, put on

get in touch with 5 reach **7** contact

get lost 4 scat, shoo **5** be off, leave, scram **6** beat it, begone, depart, go away **7** vamoose

get one's dander up 4 gall, rile **5** anger **6** enrage, madden, nettle, ruffle **7** incense, inflame, outrage **9** infuriate

get out of bed 4 rise **5** arise **12** rise and shine

get rid of 4 drop, dump, junk, shed **5** ditch, scrap **6** banish, cut out, delete, remove, unload **7** abolish, discard, weed out **8** jettison, stamp out, throw out **9** eliminate, eradicate **10** annihilate **11** exterminate

Get Smart
  character: 5 Hymie (CONTROL robot) **7** Agent 99, Carlson, Starker **8** Larrabee, The Chief (Thaddeus) **12** Maxwell Smart (Agent 86) **15** Conrad Siegfried
  cast: 8 Don Adams **9** King Moody **10** Stacy Keach **11** Dave Ketchum, Dick Gautier, Edward Platt **12** Bernie Kopell **13** Barbara Feldon **14** Robert Karvelas
  Max worked for:
    7 CONTROL
  foe: 4 KAOS

get the better of 4 foil, rout **5** crush, quell **6** baffle, defeat, thwart **7** conquer **8** confound, overcome **9** frustrate, overthrow

get the upper hand of 5 quell **6** master **7** conquer **8** dominate, overcome, surmount

get the worst of 4 fail, fall, lose

Getting Even
  author: 10 Woody Allen

get to 5 reach **8** approach

get-together 2 do **3** bee **4** meet **5** agree, party, visit **6** affair, gather, hobnob **7** meeting **8** assemble, assembly **9** gathering

getup 3 rig **6** attire, outfit **7** costume **8** disguise, ensemble

get up 4 find, rise **5** arise, rouse, stand **8** assemble

get used to 5 adapt, inure **6** adjust **8** accustom **9** acclimate, habituate

gewgaws 7 baubles, doodads, trifles **8** trinkets **9** bric-a-brac, gimcracks, kickshaws, ornaments **11** knickknacks

Ghana *see box*

ghastly 3 wan **4** grim, ugly **5** ashen, pasty, weird **6** dismal, glassy, grisly, horrid, odious, pallid **7** fearful, ghostly, haggard, hideous, uncanny **8** blanched, dreadful, gruesome, horrible, shocking, spectral, terrible **9** appalling, colorless, deathlike, frightful, ghostlike, loathsome, repellent, repulsive, revolting **10** cadaverous, corpselike, forbidding, horrendous, lackluster, terrifying

Ghiberti, Lorenzo
  born: 5 Italy **8** Florence
  artwork: 9 St Matthew, St Stephen **15** Gates of Paradise (baptistry doors) **16** St John the Baptist **19** The Sacrifice of Isaac

ghost 4 hint **5** demon, shade, spook, trace **6** goblin, shadow,

sprite, wraith **7** banshee, chimera, phantom, specter **8** phantasm **9** hobgoblin, phantasma, semblance **10** apparition, suggestion **12** Doppelganger **13** manifestation **15** materialization

Ghost and Mrs Muir, The
  character: 11 Candice Muir, Martha Grant **12** Jonathan Muir **13** Claymore Gregg **14** Mrs Carolyn Muir **18** Captain Daniel Gregg
  TV cast: 8 Reta Shaw **9** Hope Lange **13** Edward Mulhare **14** Harlen Carraher, Kellie Flanagan **19** Charles Nelson Reilly
  setting: 11 Gull Cottage
  director: 17 Joseph L Mankiewicz
  movie cast: 8 Edna Best **11** Gene Tierney, Rex Harrison **13** George Sanders

Ghostbusters
  director: 11 Ivan Reitman
  screenplay: 10 Dan Ackroyd **11** Harold Ramis
  cast: 10 Bill Murray, Dan Ackroyd **11** Harold Ramis **15** Sigourney Weaver

ghostly 4 pale **5** eerie, weird **6** spooky, unreal **7** ghastly, phantom, shadowy, uncanny **8** illusive, spectral **9** unearthly **10** phantasmal, wraithlike

---

Ghana
  other name: 9 Gold Coast
  capital/largest city: 5 Accra, Akkra
  others: 3 Oda **4** Axim, Fian, Keta, Tala, Tema **5** Bawku, Enchi, Lawra, Legon, Sampa, Yapei **6** Dunkwa, Karaga, Kpandu, Kumasi, Nsawam, Obuasi, Swedru, Tamale, Tarkwa, Wasipe **7** Antubia, Damongo, Mampong, Prestea, Sekondi, Sunyani, Winneba **8** Akosombo, Kintampo, Takoradi **9** Cape Coast **15** Sekondi-Takoradi
  school: 6 Kumasi **9** Cape Coast
  monetary unit: 4 cedi **5** ackey
  lake: 5 Volta **8** Bosumtwi
  mountain: 12 Akwapim Hills
  highest point: 8 Afadjato
  river: 3 Oti, Pra **4** Daka, Tano **5** Afram, Volta **7** Ankobra, Kulpawn **10** Black Volta, White Volta
  sea: 8 Atlantic
  physical feature:
    gulf: **6** Guinea
  people: 2 Ga **3** Ewe **4** Akan, Akim, Akra, Aksa **5** Ahafo, Brong, Inkra **7** Akwapim, Ashanti, Dagomba **8** Mamprusi **11** Mole-Dagbani
  language: 2 Ga **3** Ewe, Gur, Kwa, Twi **5** Fanti, Hausa **7** Dagomba, English
  religion: 5 Islam **7** animism **13** Roman Catholic
  feature:
    castle: **14** Christiansborg
    dam: **8** Akosombo
    national dress: **5** kente

11 phantomlike
12 supernatural

ghostly double
German: **12** Doppelganger

Ghosts
author: **11** Henrik Ibsen
character: **7** Manders **12** Oswald Alving **14** Jacob Engstrand, Mrs Helen Alving **15** Regina Engstrand

ghoulish 5 eerie, scary, weird **7** demonic, hellish, macabre, ogreish, satanic **8** diabolic, fiendish, gruesome, infernal, sinister **9** monstrous **10** horrifying, zombielike **11** hair-raising, necrophilic

Giacometti, Alberto
born: **11** Switzerland **12** Stampa-Tessin
artwork: **3** Dog **7** The Cage **8** Caroline **10** City Square **11** Head of Diego, Man Pointing **14** Reclining Woman **17** The Palace at Four Am **19** Hands Holding the Void

Gianni Schicchi
opera by: **7** Puccini
character: **11** Buoso Donati

giant 3 big **4** huge **5** titan **7** Goliath, spanker, thumper, whopper **8** behemoth, colossus, strapper **9** Gargantua **14** Brobdingnagian

Giant
director: **13** George Stevens
author: **10** Edna Ferber
cast: **9** James Dean **10** Chill Wills, Rock Hudson **11** Jane Withers **12** Carroll Baker **15** Elizabeth Taylor
setting: **5** Texas
Oscar for: **8** director

Giant *see* **8** Gigantes

giant people 6 Anakim

Giants in the Earth
author: **9** O E Rolvaag
character: **3** Ole **5** Beret **8** Per Hanea **9** Anna Marie **12** Hans Kristian **15** Peder Victorious

gibber 3 gab **4** blab **5** prate **6** babble, gabble, jabber **7** blabber, blather, chatter, prattle **8** chitchat

gibberish 4 blab, bosh **6** babble, drivel, gabble **7** blather, twaddle **8** nonsense **10** balderdash, double-talk, flapdoodle, hocus-pocus, mumbo-jumbo **12** gobbledegook

Gibbon, Edward
author of: **33** The (History of the) Decline and Fall of the Roman Empire

gibbous 6 convex, curved,

humped **7** bulging, rounded, swollen **8** swelling **10** humpbacked, protuberant

Gibbs family
characters in: **7** Our Town
member: **6** George **7** Rebecca
author: **6** Wilder

gibe, jibe 3 rag **4** jeer, mock, quip, razz, twit **5** chaff, flout, knock, toast, scoff, sneer, taunt **6** deride, needle, rail at **7** mockery, poke fun, sarcasm **8** brickbat, derision, ridicule, taunting **9** criticism, wisecrack

Gibraltar
other name: **11** rock of Tarik **13** Djebel al-Tarik **15** rock of Gibraltar
largest city: **9** Gibraltar
government: **18** British crown colony
head of government: **15** governor general
mountain: **6** Misery
sea: **13** Mediterranean
physical feature:
bay: **5** Ceuta, Rosia, Sandy **6** Catlan **9** Algeciras
cliffs: **17** Pillars of Hercules
people: **6** Jewish **7** British, Maltese, Spanish **8** Italians **10** Portuguese
language: **7** English, Spanish
feature: **12** King's Bastion
gardens: **7** Alameda

Gibson, Mel
roles: **6** Mad Max **9** Gallipoli, The Bounty **12** Lethal Weapon **14** The Road Warrior **26** The Year of Living Dangerously

Giddens, Regina
character in: **14** The Little Foxes
author: **7** Hellman

giddy 5 dizzy, faint, silly **6** fickle, fitful **7** awesome, erratic, flighty, muddled, reeling **8** careless, dizzying, fainting, fanciful, reckless, swimming, unsteady, volatile, whirling **9** befuddled, frivolous, impulsive, mercurial, whimsical **10** capricious, changeable, inconstant **11** hare-brained, harumscarum, lightheaded, thoughtless, vacillating, vertiginous

12 inconsistent, overpowering **13** irresponsible, rattlebrained

Gide, Andre
author of: **13** The Immoralist **15** Strait Is the Gate **17** The Counterfeiters **18** Lafcadio's Adventure (The Vatican Swindle) **19** The Pastoral Symphony

Gideon 11 Hebrew judge
father: **5** Joash, Ophra
son: **9** Abimelech
also called: **9** Jerubbaal

Gidget
character: **5** Larue **10** Anne Cooper, John Cooper **16** Francine (Gidget) Lawrence **21** Professor Russ Lawrence
cast: **9** Don Porter **10** Peter Deuel, Sally Field **11** Betty Conner **13** Lynette Winter

Gielgud, Sir John
born: **6** London **7** England
roles: **6** Arthur, Becket, Hamlet **7** Macbeth **9** Saint Joan **26** The Barretts of Wimpole Street **27** The Importance of Being Earnest

gift 3 aid, dot, fee, sop, tip **4** alms, bent, boon, dole, help, turn **5** award, bonus, bribe, craft, dower, dowry, favor, flair, forte, graft, grant, knack, power, prize, skill **6** genius, legacy, talent, virtue **7** aptness, bequest, faculty, handout, largess, premium, present, quality, tribute **8** aptitude, capacity, donation, facility, gratuity, offering, property **9** attribute, endowment, expertise, ingenuity **10** adroitness, capability, competency **11** benefaction, proficiency **12** contribution **13** consideration, qualification

gifted 4 able, deft **5** adept, crack, handy, quick, slick **6** adroit, bright, clever, expert, facile, master, wizard **7** capable, skilled **8** finished, masterly, polished, superior, talented **9** brilliant, ingenious, inventive, practiced, qualified **10** proficient **11** crackerjack, experienced, resourceful **12** accomplished

Gift From the Sea, The
author: **19** Anne Morrow Lindbergh

gig 3 job **4** trap **5** stint **6** chaise **7** dogcart **8** carriage, curricle **10** engagement

Gigantes
single member: **5** giant
father: **6** Uranus
mother: **4** Gaea

heads of: 3 men
bodies of: 8 serpents
attacked: 4 gods

gigantic 4 huge, vast **5** bulky, jumbo **6** mighty **7** hulking, immense, lumpish, mammoth, massive, titanic **8** colossal, enormous, lubberly, towering, unwieldy **9** herculean, monstrous, ponderous, strapping **10** gargantuan, prodigious, stupendous, tremendous, voluminous **11** elephantine

Gigantomachia
war of: 6 giants

giggle 6 cackle, hee-hee, simper, tee-hee, titter **7** chuckle, snicker, snigger, twitter

Gigi
director: 16 Vincente Minnelli
based on story by: 7 Colette
cast: 8 Eva Gabor **11** Leslie Caron **12** Louis Jourdan **15** Hermione Gingold, Jacques Bergerac **16** Maurice Chevalier
score: 14 Lerner and Loewe
Oscar for: 7 picture **8** director
song: 4 Gigi **15** I Remember It Well **25** Thank Heaven for Little Girls **29** The Night They Invented Champagne

Gilbert, Cass
architect of: 14 US Customs House (NYC) **17** Woolworth Building (NYC) **20** Supreme Court Building (Washington DC) **21** Minnesota State Capitol (St Paul) **22** George Washington Bridge

Gilbert, John
real name: 11 John Pringle
wife: 9 Ina Claire **11** Leatrice Joy **13** Virginia Bruce
born: 7 Logan UT
roles: 4 Love **12** The Big Parade **13** The Merry Widow **15** A Woman of Affairs **16** Flesh and the Devil

Gilbert, William
field: 7 physics
nationality: 7 British
father of: 11 electricity
named for him: 27 CGS unit of magnetomotive force

Gilbert, W S, and Sullivan, Arthur Seymour
composers of: 7 Ivanhoe **8** Iolanthe, Patience **9** Ruddigore, The Mikado **11** H M S Pinafore, Princess Ida, The Sorcerer, Trial by Jury **12** The Grand Duke **13** The Gondoliers, Utopia Limited **19** The Yeoman of the Guard **20** The Pirates of Penzance **24** Thespis or The Gods Grown Old

Gilbert Islands *see* **8** Kiribati

Gil Blas (of Santillane)
author: 11 Alain LeSage
character: 6 Scipio **11** Don Alphonso

Gilbreth, Frank B, Jr
author of: 17 Cheaper by the Dozen (with Ernestine Gilbreth Carey)

gild 4 bend **5** slant, twist **7** cover up, stretch, touch up **10** exaggerate

Gilded Age, The
authors: 9 Mark Twain **19** Charles Dudley Warner

gilded youth
French: 13 jeunesse doree

Gileadite password
10 Shibboleth

Giles Goat-Boy
author: 9 John Barth

Gilgal 5 wheel **6** circle

Gilgamesh
origin: 8 Sumerian
king of: 4 Uruk **5** Erech
servant: 6 Enkidu

gill
abbreviation: 2 gi

Gilligan's Island
character: 7 Skipper (Jonas Grumby) **8** Gilligan **9** Mrs Howell (Lovey), Professor (Roy Hinkley) **11** Ginger Grant **14** Mary Ann Summers **17** Thurston Howell III
cast: 9 Bob Denver, Dawn Wells, Jim Backus **10** Alan Hale Jr, Tina Louise **14** Natalie Schafer, Russell Johnson
ship: 6 Minnow

Gillooly, Edna Rae
real name of: 12 Ellen Burstyn

Gills, Solomon
character in: 12 Dombey and Son
author: 7 Dickens

Gilyak
language spoken in: 4 Amur **8** Sakhalin

gimcrack 5 bijou, curio **6** bauble, gewgaw, trifle **7** trinket, whatnot **8** kickshaw, ornament **9** bagatelle, plaything **10** knickknack **11** contrivance, thingamabob, thingamajig

gimmick 4 plan, ploy, ruse, wile **5** angle, dodge, stunt **6** design, device, gadget, scheme **7** wrinkle **9** stratagem **10** subterfuge **11** contrivance

gin *see box, p. 394*

ginger 3 pep, tan **5** brown, spice **6** energy
varieties: 3 red **4** wild **5** crape, crepe, shell, torch, white **6** canton, common, Kahili, orchid, spiral, yellow **9** butterfly **10** small shell, variegated
botanical name: 8 Zingiber **12** Z officinales
Sanskrit: 9 singabera
origin: 4 Asia **5** China, India **7** Jamaica
use: 6 tongue **7** vinegar **9** beef stock **11** baked dishes, gingerbread **12** chicken stock

gingerly 6 warily **7** charily, timidly **8** daintily **9** carefully, finically, guardedly, heedfully, mincingly, prudently **10** cautiously, delicately, discreetly, hesitantly, vigilantly, watchfully **11** squeamishly **12** fastidiously, suspiciously **13** circumspectly

gingham 5 cloth **6** cotton, fabric, striped **8** chambray **9** checkered

gin mill 4 dive **9** honky-tonk, roadhouse

Ginnungagap
origin: 12 Scandinavian
void filled with: 4 mist
between: 9 Nifelheim **10** Muspelheim

Ginsberg, Allen
author of: 4 Howl **7** Kaddish **10** Planet News **11** Mind Breaths **16** The Fall of America **20** Reality and Sandwiches

Giono, Jean
author of: 6 Regain **7** Colline, Harvest **13** Hill of Destiny **18** The Hussar on the Roof

Giordano, Umberto
born: 5 Italy **6** Foggia
composer of: 6 Fedora **8** Mala Vita **13** Andrea Chenier **14** Madame Sans-Gene

Giorgione da Castelfranco
born: 5 Italy **12** Castelfranco
artwork: 10 The Tempest **13** Ordeal of Moses, Sleeping Venus **17** Judgment of Solomon **19** The Concert Champetre (disputed) **20** The Three Philosophers **23** Adoration of the Shepherds

Giotto di Bondone
born: 5 Italy **8** (near) Florence
artwork attributed: 17 Ognissanti Madonna **31** Presentation of Christ in the Temple **32** St Francis Surrounded by his Brothers

gin
  origin: 11 Netherlands
  ingredient: 6 grains 12 juniper berry
  type: 6 Geneva 8 Plymouth 9 London dry
  drink: 5 Allen 6 Gibson, gimlet 7 Belmont, Bennett, gin
    Fizz, swizzle 8 Pink Lady 9 Gin Rickey 10 Tom Collins
    11 Alabama Fizz, gin and tonic 12 Grand Passion 14 Ca-
    sino Cocktail
  with anisette: 8 Snowball 11 Bachio Punch
  with apricot brandy: 14 Boston Cocktail
  with brandy: 15 Bermuda Highball
  with Chartreuse: 5 Bijou 9 Green Lady
  with cherry brandy: 14 Singapore Sling
  with Cointreau: 7 Florida 9 White Lady 13 Sweet Pa-
    tootie 14 Flying Dutchman
  with creme de cacao: 9 Alexander
  with creme de cassis: 8 Parisian
  with creme de menthe: 6 Caruso, Virgin
  with creme Yvette: 9 Union Jack
  with Curacao: 8 Blue Moon, Napoleon 9 Blue Devil
    14 Flying Dutchman
  with Dubonnet: 3 BVD 8 Napoleon
  with Grand Marnier: 7 Red Lion
  with grapefruit juice: 8 Salty Dog
  with kirsch, kirschwasser: 7 Florida 10 Lady Finger
  with onions: 6 Gibson
  with orange juice: 5 Abbey 13 Orange Blossom
  with Pernod: 7 Dubarry
  with rum: 3 BVD
  with scotch: 12 Barbary Coast
  with sherry: 11 Renaissance
  with strawberries: 10 Bloodhound
  with Swedish Punch: 5 Biffy
  with vermouth: 5 Bijou, Bronx, Tango 6 Caruso 7 Ber-
    muda, Cabaret, Martini 10 Bloodhound
  with vodka: 15 Russian Cocktail

Giovanelli
  character in: 11 Daisy Miller
  author: 5 James

Giovanni's Room
  author: 12 James Baldwin

Giraffe
  constellation of:
    14 Camelopardalis

girandole 11 candelabrum,
  candlestick 12 candleholder

Girardon, Francois
  born: 6 France, Troyes
  artwork: 13 Bathing
    Nymphs 14 Galley of
    Apollo, Virgin of Troyes
    16 Rape of Persephone
    17 (tomb for) Cardinal Rich-
    elieu 23 Apollo Tended by
    the Nymphs

Giraudoux, Jean
  author of: 5 Bella 6 Judith,
    Ondine, Racine 7 Electra
    12 Amphitryon 38 15 Tiger
    at the Gates 18 Madwoman
    of Chaillot 20 My Friend
    from Limousin

gird 3 pen, tie 4 belt, girt,
  loop, ring 5 brace, hem in,
  hitch, steel, strap, truss 6 circle, fasten, girdle, harden, secure, wall in 7 besiege,
confine, enclose, fortify, hedge
in, prepare, stiffen, sustain,
tighten 8 blockade, buttress,
encircle, lay siege, surround
9 encompass 10 strengthen
12 circumscribe

girder 4 beam 5 brace, truss
  6 binder, rafter 7 support, tie-
  beam

girdle 3 hem 4 band, belt, ring,
  sash 5 girth, hedge, stays
  6 bodice, circle, corset 7 baldric, circlet, contour 8 boundary, cincture, corselet
  9 surcingle, waistband
  10 cummerbund 12 waist
  cincher 17 foundation garment

girl 4 bird, cook, help, lass,
  maid, minx, miss 5 angel,
  chick, nymph, wench 6 damsel, kitten, lassie, maiden, pigeon, virgin 7 baggage,
  colleen, darling, fiancee, ingenue, nymphet 8 daughter,
  domestic, handmaid, lady love,
  mistress, scullion 9 affianced,
  betrothed, inamorata, lady's

maid, soubrette 10 sweetheart
11 maidservant
  French: 10 demoiselle, jeune
  fille

girl Friday 4 aide 6 helper
  9 assistant, secretary 10 amanuensis 12 office worker 23 administrative assistant

girlfriend 6 steady 7 beloved,
  sweetie 8 best girl 10 one and
  only, sweetheart

Girl in a Swing
  author: 12 Richard Adams

girlish 8 girl-like, maidenly,
  youthful 10 maidenlike

**Girl of the Golden West,
The**
  opera by: 7 Puccini
  setting: 8 Gold Rush
    10 California
  character: 6 Minnie 7 John-
    son, Sheriff

girt 4 belt, bind, gird, ring
  5 bound, girth 6 belted, circle,
  girdle, ringed 7 circled, gir-
  dled 9 encircled

girth 5 cinch 9 perimeter
  10 saddle band
  13 circumference

Giselle
  ballet by: 4 (Adolphe Charles)
    Adam

Gish, Lillian
  real name: 12 Lillian Gishi
    15 Lillian de Guiche
  born: 13 Springfield OH
  roles: 8 La Boheme 10 Enoch
    Arden 11 Annie Laurie, In-
    tolerance, Way Down East
    12 Duel in the Sun 13 Scar-
    let Letter 14 Broken Blos-
    soms 16 Portrait of Jennie
    17 Orphans of the Storm,
    The Birth of a Nation

Gissing, George
  author of: 5 Demos 13 New
    Grub Street 14 The Nether
    World

gist 4 core, crux, meat, pith
  5 drift, force, heart, sense,
  tenor, theme 6 burden, center,
  effect, import, kernel, marrow,
  spirit 7 essence, purport
  8 main idea 9 main point,
  substance 11 implication
  12 significance

Giuki
  also: 5 Gjuki
  origin: 12 Scandinavian
  mentioned in: 8 Volsunga
  form: 4 king
  wife: 8 Grimhild
  daughter: 6 Gudrun, Kudrun
    7 Guthrun
  son: 6 Gunnar

Giukung
  also: 7 Gjukung

origin: 12 Scandinavian
family member of: 5 Giuki, Gjuki

Giulio Romano
architect of: 12 Palazzo del Te
style: 9 Mannerist

give *see box*

give aid to 4 help **6** assist, succor **7** help out **8** befriend **9** look after **10** minister to

give a leg up 3 aid **4** help, lift **5** boost, hoist, raise **6** assist **7** elevate

give and take 8 exchange **10** compromise **11** interchange, reciprocity

give a pep talk to 4 goad, prod, spur **5** press **6** exhort **9** encourage

give a reason for 7 clarify, clear up, explain, justify **9** elucidate **10** account for

give as security 4 pawn **6** pledge **7** deposit, pay down, put down

give away 6 bestow, betray, donate, reveal **7** hand out

give birth 4 bear **5** hatch **6** create, invent **7** deliver, develop **9** originate **10** bring forth

give confidence to 7 inspire **8** embolden, inspirit **9** encourage

give courage 5 brace **6** buck up **7** hearten **8** inspirit, motivate

give energy to 7 animate, enliven **8** activate, energize, vitalize **9** stimulate **10** invigorate

give enjoyment 5 amuse, charm **6** divert, please **7** be-

guile, delight **8** enthrall **9** entertain

give forth 4 emit, gush **5** exude, issue **7** send out **8** throw off, transmit **9** discharge

give full attention 7 pay heed **8** fasten on **11** concentrate

give in 5 defer, yield **6** accede, cave in, submit **7** succumb **9** surrender **10** capitulate **12** knuckle under

give in to 7 yield to **9** indulge in, partake of **16** abandon oneself to

give leave 3 let **5** allow **6** permit **8** sanction **9** authorize **14** give permission

give moral support to 3 aid **4** abet, back, help **6** assist, uphold **7** support, sustain **8** sanction **9** encourage

given 3 apt **4** wont **5** prone **6** likely, wonted **7** awarded, donated, granted, offered **8** accorded, bestowed **9** committed, conferred, entrusted, presented **10** accustomed, handed over, in the habit **11** contributed **13** furnished with, made a donation, presented with **17** made a contribution

give new life to 3 fan **4** fire **6** awaken, revive **8** revivify **10** rejuvenate **11** reincarnate

give oneself to 8 dedicate **10** buckle down, consecrate

give one's word 3 vow **5** swear **6** assure, pledge **7** certify, promise, warrant **9** guarantee

give one walking papers 3 axe, can **4** fire, oust, sack **5** let go **6** bounce, lay off **7** cashier, dismiss, release

8 get rid of **9** discharge, terminate **11** give the gate, send packing

give out 4 quit, tell, tire **6** assign, inform, reveal, run out **7** divulge, dole out, mete out **8** allocate, announce, disclose, dispense, proclaim **9** apportion, broadcast, parcel out **10** distribute, make public, portion out **11** disseminate

give over 4 cede **5** yield **9** surrender **10** relinquish

give permission 3 let **5** allow **6** accede, permit **7** approve **8** sanction **9** acquiesce, authorize, give leave

give rise to 4 sire **5** breed, cause **6** lead to **7** produce **8** engender, generate, occasion **9** call forth **10** bring about

give support to 3 aid **4** abet **5** serve **6** defend, prop up, second **7** bolster, comfort, sustain **8** buttress, champion **10** contribute, minister to, provide for, stick up for

give the go-ahead 4 okay **5** order **6** direct **7** appoint, charter, empower **8** contract **9** authorize **10** commission

give the lie to 5 belie **8** disprove **9** repudiate **10** contradict, controvert

give the raspberry 3 boo, pan **4** razz **6** deride, hoot at **8** ridicule **11** give the bird **17** give the Bronx cheer

give the right to 5 allow **6** permit **7** entitle, qualify **9** authorize

give the slip 4 duck **5** avoid, dodge, elude, evade

give up 4 cede, drop, lose, quit, skip **5** forgo, let go, waive, yield **6** eschew, resign **7** abandon, forfeit, forsake **8** abdicate, forswear, renounce **9** sacrifice, surrender **10** relinquish **11** discontinue

give up the ghost 3 die **6** expire, pass on, perish **7** decease **8** pass away **15** breathe one's last

give vent 4 free **5** let go **7** release **8** let loose, liberate **12** give free rein

give way 4 fall **6** buckle, cave in **7** crumple **8** collapse **10** break apart

giving birth 7 bearing **8** creating, creation, delivery, hatching **9** inventing, invention **10** childbirth, delivering

---

give 3 buy, pay, tip **4** bend, ease, emit, hire, lend, show, sink **5** admit, allot, allow, apply, award, bribe, deign, endow, grant, issue, leave, offer, relax, utter, voice, yield **6** accord, addict, afford, assign, attach, bestow, bounce, commit, confer, convey, devote, donate, enable, enrich, hand to, impart, loosen, notify, open on, permit, recede, relent, render, shrink, supply, tender, unbend, vest in **7** concede, consign, deliver, entrust, fork out, furnish, hand out, let know, present, proffer, provide, requite, retreat, slacken **8** announce, bequeath, collapse, dispense, exchange, fork over, hand over, lead on to, make over, move back, put forth, shell out **9** apportion, break down, dispose of, equip with, favor with, look out on, present to, pronounce, subscribe, surrender, vouchsafe **10** articulate, become soft, compensate, contribute, deliquesce, distribute, recompense, remunerate, resilience, supply with **11** communicate, flexibility, provide with, springiness

11 originating, origination, parturition

giving up 7 refusal **8** dropping, quitting, yielding **9** resigning **10** abandoning, abdicating, abdication, abstinence, continence, forbearing, forfeiting, forfeiture, self-denial **11** abandonment, forswearing, resignation **12** renunciation, surrendering **14** relinquishment

gizmo 4 tool **6** device, doodad, gadget **9** apparatus, implement, invention, mechanism **10** instrument **11** contraption, contrivance, thingamabob, thingamajig

Gjuki *see* **5** Giuki

Gjukung *see* **7** Giukung

glacial 3 icy, raw **4** cold **5** chill, gelid, polar **6** arctic, biting, bitter, frigid, frosty, frozen, wintry **7** hostile **8** freezing, inimical, piercing **9** congealed **10** disdainful, unfriendly **12** antagonistic, bone-chilling, contemptuous

Glackens, William James born: **14** Philadelphia PA artwork: **9** Promenade **11** Chez Mouquin **15** Nude with an Apple **16** Washington Square (A Holiday in the Park) **17** Luxembourg Gardens

glad 5 happy **6** elated, joyful, joyous **7** elating, gleeful, pleased, tickled **8** blissful, cheerful, cheering, pleasing, rejoiced **9** contented, delighted, joy-giving **10** delightful, entrancing, gratifying **11** exhilarated, tickled pink **12** exhilarating

gladden 5 cheer, elate **6** please **7** animate, cheer up, delight, enliven, gratify, hearten, rejoice **8** inspirit, pleasure **9** make happy **10** exhilarate

gladdened 5 happy **6** joyful, joyous **8** cheerful

glade 4 dell, glen, lawn, vale, wood **5** grove, marsh, vista **6** canada, hollow, valley **7** opening **8** clearing

gladness 3 joy **4** glee **5** bliss, cheer, mirth **7** delight, gaiety, jollity **8** pleasure **9** happiness **10** joyfulness **11** contentment **12** cheerfulness

glad rags 5 array **6** attire, finery **10** Sunday best

Gladsheim origin: **12** Scandinavian

palace of: **4** Odin **5** Othin location: **8** Valhalla

gladsome 3 gay **5** happy, merry **6** cheery, joyful, joyous **8** cheerful **12** lighthearted

glamor, glamour 5 charm, magic **6** allure **7** glitter, romance **8** illusion **9** adventure, challenge, magnetism **10** excitement **11** enchantment, fascination **14** attractiveness

glamorous, glamourous 8 alluring, charming, dazzling, exciting, magnetic **10** attractive, bewitching, enchanting **11** captivating, charismatic, fascinating

glance 4 kiss, peek, peep, scan, skim, slip **5** brush, graze, shave, touch **6** bounce, careen, squint **7** glimpse, rebound **8** ricochet **9** brief look, quick look, quick view French: **6** apercu

glance through 4 scan, skim **6** browse, peruse **7** dip into **8** look over **9** check over

gland part of: **15** endocrine system type: **4** duct **8** ductless kind: **3** oil **5** sweat **7** adrenal, thyroid **8** pancreas **9** pituitary **11** parathyroid ductless gland secretes: **8** hormones

glare 4 glow **5** blaze, flame, flare, flash, gleam, glint, gloss, lower, scowl, sheen **6** dazzle, glower **7** flicker, glimmer, glisten, glitter, radiate, shimmer, sparkle, twinkle **8** radiance **9** angry look, black look, dirty look **10** brightness, harsh light, luminosity **12** resplendence

glaring 4 rank **5** gross, harsh, vivid **6** arrant, bright, strong **7** blatant, flaring, intense, obvious **8** blinding, dazzling, flagrant, piercing **9** audacious, brilliant, egregious **10** glittering, outrageous, shimmering **11** conspicuous, penetrating, resplendent, unconcealed, undisguised **12** unmistakable

Glasgow, Ellen author of: **10** Vein of Iron **12** Barren Ground **13** In this Our Life, Sheltered Life **18** They Stooped to Folly **20** The Romantic Comedians

glass 6 beaker, goblet **7** chalice, tumbler **10** tumblerful type of: **4** fizz, sour **5** flute, tulip **6** jigger, sherry **7** balloon, collins, cordial, red wine, snifter **8** cocktail, highball **9** champagne, white

wine **10** hollow-stem, pousse cafe **12** old-fashioned

glasshouse 7 nursery **8** hothouse **10** greenhouse **12** conservatory

glassiness 7 clarity **8** dullness, flatness **9** shininess **10** brilliance, luminosity **12** lifelessness, transparency

Glass Key, The author: **15** Dashiell Hammett character: **9** Shad O'Rory **10** Janet Henry, Opal Madvig, Paul Madvig **11** Ned Beaumont **12** Senator Henry **13** Bernie Despain

Glass Menagerie, The director: **12** Irving Rapper author: **17** Tennessee Williams character: **5** Laura **6** Amanda **12** Tom Wingfield cast: **9** Jane Wyman **11** Kirk Douglas **13** Arthur Kennedy **16** Gertrude Lawrence

glassware 5 agata **6** aurene **7** crystal, favrile, steuben, vitrics **8** amerina, stemware worker: **7** glazier

glassy 4 dull **5** clear, shiny **6** glazed, smooth **8** lifeless **10** glittering **11** transparent

Glauber, Johann Rudolf field: **9** chemistry nationality: **6** German prepared: **12** tartar emetic **13** sodium sulfate (Glauber's salt) **16** hydrochloric acid

Glauce *see* **6** Creusa

Glaucus god of: **3** sea father: **5** Minos ally of: **7** Trojans loved by: **5** Circe **6** Scylla **10** Amphitrite

glaze 4 blur **5** gloss **6** enamel, finish **7** grow dim, varnish **8** film over **9** glass over

glazed 4 iced **5** filmy **6** coated, glassy, shined, smooth **7** glossed, sugared **8** enameled, lustrous, polished **9** burnished, varnished

Glazunoff, Alex K (Glazunov, Alexander Konstantinovich) born: **6** Russia **12** St Petersburg composer of: **10** Chopiniana, The Seasons **11** Stenka Razin **13** Hymn to Pushkin **15** Memorial Cantata

gleam 3 bit, jot, ray **4** beam, drop, glow, hint, iota **5** blink, flare, flash, glare, glint, gloss, grain, sheen, shine, spark, speck, trace **6** luster, streak

7 flicker, glimmer, glimpse, glisten, glitter, inkling, shimmer, sparkle, tiny bit, twinkle **8** least bit, radiance **9** coruscate **10** brightness, brilliance, effulgence **11** coruscation, scintillate

gleaming 5 clear, shiny **6** bright, flashy, glossy **7** shining, radiant **8** dazzling, glinting, luminous, lustrous, polished, splendid **9** brilliant, burnished, sparkling **10** glistening

glean 4 cull **5** amass **6** gather, pick up **7** harvest **10** accumulate **13** piece together **14** scrape together

gleanings 8 analects, extracts **10** miscellany, selections **11** collectanea, miscellanea **15** commonplace book

Gleason, Jackie
    real name: 18 Herbert John Gleason
    nickname: 15 Mr Saturday Night
    born: 10 Brooklyn NY
    roles: 5 Gigot **6** The Toy **10** The Hustler **11** Life of Riley, The Poor Soul **12** Ralph Kramden **15** Joe the Bartender, The Honeymooners **17** Don't Drink the Water, Jackie Gleason Show, The Time of Your Life **22** Requiem for a Heavyweight **24** Reggie Van Gleason the Third

glebe 3 sod **4** clod, land, plot, soil **5** earth, field **6** termon **8** kirktown **10** church land

glee 3 joy **5** mirth, verve **6** gaiety **7** delight, ecstasy, jollity, rapture **8** gladness, hilarity, laughter **9** joviality, merriment **10** exultation, jocularity, joyfulness, joyousness, liveliness **11** playfulness **12** cheerfulness, exhilaration, sportiveness **13** jollification, sprightliness

glee club 6 chorus **12** singing group **13** choral society

gleeful 3 gay **4** glad **5** happy, jolly, merry **6** elated, jocund, jovial, joyful, joyous, lively **7** festive **8** blissful, cheerful, exultant, mirthful **9** delighted **11** exhilarated **12** lighthearted

Gleipnir
    origin: 12 Scandinavian
    chain that bound: 6 Fenrir, Fenris

glen 4 dale, dell, vale **6** bottom, hollow

Glencaire Cycle
    author: 12 Eugene O'Neill

glib 4 oily **5** gabby, quick, ready, suave **6** facile, fluent, smooth **7** devious, voluble **8** flippant, slippery, unctuous **9** insincere, talkative

glide 3 run **4** flow, roll, sail, skim, slip, soar **5** coast, drift, float, issue, skate, slide, steal **6** elapse, stream **7** proceed **8** glissade

glider 5 swing **7** aviator **9** sailplane **10** hydroplane

glimmer 3 bit, ray **4** beam, drop, glow, hint **5** blink, flare, flash, glare, gleam, grain, shine, speck, trace **7** flicker, glimpse, glisten, glitter, shimmer, sparkle, twinkle **9** coruscate, scintilla **10** flickering, intimation **11** scintillate

glimpse 3 see, spy **4** espy, peek, peep, spot **6** glance, peek at, peep at, squint **9** brief look, quick look, quick view **12** catch sight of, fleeting look
    French: 6 apercu

Glinka, Mikhail Ivanovich
    born: 6 Russia **8** Smolensk
    composer of: 12 Ivan Sussanin, Karaminskaya **13** Jota Aragonesa **18** Russlan and Ludmilla

glint 4 gaze, look, peep **5** flash, gleam, sheen, shine, stare **6** glance **7** appear, glimmer, glimpse, glisten, glitter, shimmer, sparkle, twinkle **9** coruscate **11** scintillate

glissade 5 coast, glide, slide

glissando
    music: 7 sliding

glisten 4 glow **5** flash, gleam, glint, shine **7** flicker, glimmer, glister, glitter, radiate, shimmer, sparkle, twinkle **9** coruscate **11** scintillate

glitter 4 fire, glow, pomp, show **5** flare, flash, gleam, glint, sheen, shine **6** luster, thrill, tinsel **7** beaming, display, glamour, glimmer, glisten, radiate, sparkle, twinkle **8** grandeur, radiance, splendor **9** pageantry, showiness **10** brilliance, excitement, refulgence **11** electricity

glittering 6 bright **7** radiant, shining **8** luminous, lustrous **9** brilliant, sparkling **11** coruscating

gloaming 4 dusk **7** evening **8** twilight

gloat 4 bask, brag **5** exult, strut, vaunt **7** revel in, swagger, triumph **8** crow over **9** glory over

global 5 world **6** all-out **7** general **9** planetary, unbounded, universal, unlimited, worldwide **10** widespread **13** comprehensive, international **16** intercontinental

globe 3 orb **4** ball **5** Earth, world **6** planet, sphere **7** globule **8** spheroid, spherule **9** biosphere

globule 4 ball, bead, bleb, blob, drop **5** globe **6** bubble, pellet, sphere **7** blister, droplet **8** particle, spheroid

glogg
    type: 5 punch
    origin: 6 Sweden

gloom 3 woe **4** dark, dusk, murk **5** blues, dolor, grief, shade **6** misery, sorrow **7** despair, dimness, sadness, shadows **8** darkness, distress, doldrums **9** blackness, dejection, dinginess, duskiness, murkiness, obscurity **10** cloudiness, depression, gloominess, low spirits, melancholy, mopishness, moroseness, oppression **11** despondency, forlornness, unhappiness **12** hopelessness **13** cheerlessness **16** disconsolateness, heavy-heartedness

gloomy 3 dim, sad **4** dark, dour, down, dull, glum, grim, mopy, sour **5** dusky, moody, mopey, murky, shady **6** cloudy, dismal, dreary, morbid, morose, shaded, somber **7** doleful, forlorn, shadowy, sunless, unhappy **8** dejected, desolate, downcast, frowning, funereal, overcast **9** cheerless, depressed, heartsick, miserable, sorrowful, woebegone **10** chapfallen, despondent, dispirited, ill-humored, melancholy **11** comfortless, crestfallen, discouraged, downhearted, low-spirited, pessimistic **12** disconsolate, disheartened, heavy-hearted **13** in the doldrums **14** down in the dumps, down in the mouth

Gloria in Excelsis Deo
    22 Glory in the highest to God

Gloriana
    character in: 15 The Faerie Queene
    author: 7 Spenser

Gloriana
    opera by: 7 Britten
    character: 10 Elizabeth I **11** Earl of Essex

glorification 7 worship **8** devotion **9** adoration, adulation

10 exaltation, veneration
13 magnification

glorify 4 laud 5 adore, deify, exalt, extol, honor 6 praise, revere 7 beatify, dignify, elevate, ennoble, idolize, worship 8 canonize, enshrine, sanctify, venerate 9 celebrate, glamorize 10 consecrate 11 apotheosize, immortalize, romanticize

glorious 4 fine 5 grand, great, noble, noted 6 august, divine, famous, superb 7 eminent, glowing, honored, notable, radiant, shining, stately, sublime, supreme 8 dazzling, gorgeous, imposing, lustrous, majestic, renowned, splendid 9 beautiful, brilliant, dignified, excellent, marvelous, sparkling, wonderful 10 celebrated, delightful, impressive, preeminent 11 illustrious, magnificent, resplendent 12 praiseworthy 13 distinguished

glory 4 fame, mark, name 5 boast, honor, revel, vaunt 6 esteem, homage, praise, renown, repute 7 dignity, majesty, worship 8 blessing, eminence, grandeur, nobility, prestige, splendor 9 adoration, celebrity, gratitude, solemnity, sublimity 10 admiration, excellence, notability, veneration 11 benediction, distinction, preeminence, stateliness 12 magnificence, resplendence, thanksgiving 14 impressiveness 15 illustriousness

Glory in the highest to God
Latin: 19 Gloria in Excelsis Deo

gloss 4 glow, mask, veil 5 cloak, color, glaze, gleam, japan, sheen, shine 6 enamel, excuse, luster, polish, veneer 7 cover up, lacquer, shimmer, varnish 8 annotate, disguise, mitigate, radiance 9 whitewash 10 annotation, brightness, brilliance, commentary, smooth over 11 explain away, explanation, rationalize 12 luminousness, treat lightly 14 interpretation

gloss over 4 hide, mask, veil 7 conceal, cover up 9 dissemble, whitewash 12 misrepresent

glossy 5 photo, shiny, showy, silky, sleek, slick 6 bright, satiny, smooth 7 picture, shining 8 gleaming, lustrous, magazine, polished 9 burnished

glove 3 kid 4 cuff, mitt 5 catch, thumb 6 gusset, mitten, muffle 7 chevron 8 gauntlet

glow 4 fill, heat 5 ardor, bloom, blush, color, flush, gleam, gusto, shine 6 fervor, thrill, tingle, warmth 7 flicker, glimmer, glisten, glitter, radiate, shimmer, smolder, twinkle 8 radiance 9 eagerness, intensity, radiation, reddening, vividness 10 brightness, enthusiasm 11 earnestness

glower 4 pout, sulk 5 frown, glare, lower, scowl, stare

glowing 3 hot, red 4 rave 5 ruddy, vivid 6 ardent, bright, florid, raving 7 fervent, flaming, flushed 8 ecstatic, exciting 9 rhapsodic, thrilling 10 passionate 11 luminescent, sensational, stimulating 12 enthusiastic

Glubbdubdrib
fictional land in: 16 Gulliver's Travels
author: 5 Swift

Gluck, Christoph Willibald (von)
born: 7 Bavaria 8 Neumarkt
composer of: 5 Orfeo 6 Armide 7 Alceste 13 Paride ed Elena 14 Echo et Narcisse 17 Iphigenie en Aulide 18 Iphigenie en Tauride

glue 3 fix, gum 5 affix, epoxy, paste, putty, stick 6 adhere, cement, fasten, mortar 7 plaster, stickum 8 adherent, adhesive, concrete, fixative, mucilage 11 agglutinate

gluey 5 gooey, gummy, mucid, ropey, slimy, tacky, thick, 6 sticky, viscid 7 stringy, viscous 8 adhesive 12 mucilaginous

glum 6 gloomy, morose 8 dejected 9 cheerless 10 melancholy 14 down in the mouth

glut 4 bolt, clog, cram, drug, fill, gulp, jade, load, sate 5 choke, flood, gorge, stuff 6 burden, deluge, devour, excess, gobble 7 congest, overeat, satiate, surfeit, surplus 8 gobble up, obstruct, overdose, overfeed, overload, plethora, saturate 9 gormandize, oversupply, saturation 11 obstruction, superfluity 13 overabundance, supersaturate 14 superabundance

glutinous 5 gluey, bummy, mucid, ropey, slimy, tacky, thick 6 sticky, viscid 7 viscous 8 adhesive 10 gelatinous 12 musilaginous

glutton 3 hog, pig 6 gorger 7 stuffer 8 gourmand 9 chowhound, overeater 10 bellyslave 11 gormandizer, trencherman

gluttonous 6 greedy 7 hoggish, piggish, swinish 8 edacious, grasping, ravening, ravenous 9 excessive, voracious 10 insatiable, omnivorous 11 intemperate

gluttony 8 rapacity, voracity 10 overeating 11 gourmandism, hoggishness, piggishness 12 gormandizing, intemperance, ravenousness 13 voraciousness

gnarled 6 knotty, rugged, snaggy 7 crooked, knotted, nodular, twisted 8 leathery, wrinkled 9 contorted, distorted 11 full of knots 13 weather-beaten

gnash 4 gnaw 5 chomp

gnat 7 no-see-um
group of: 5 cloud, horde

gnaw 4 bite, chew, fret, gall 5 chafe, chomp, eat at, grate, graze, munch, worry 6 browse, crunch, harrow, nibble, rankle 7 torment, trouble 8 distress, nibble at, ruminate 9 eat away at, masticate

gnome 3 elf 4 pixy 5 dwarf, troll 6 goblin, sprite 10 leprechaun

gnostic 4 sage, wise 6 clever, shrewd 7 knowing 8 mandaean, simonian 10 insightful

gnothi seauton 11 know thyself

gnu 7 brindle 8 antelope 10 wildebeest
type: 5 C gnou 9 C taurinus 12 Connochaetes

go *see box*

goad 4 move, prod, push, spur, urge, whet 5 drive, egg on, impel, press, prick, set on 6 arouse, exhort, fillip, incite, motive, propel, stir up 8 pressure, stimulus 9 constrain, incentive, stimulant, stimulate 10 cattle prod, inducement, motivation 11 instigation

goal 3 aim, end 4 home, mark, wire 5 point, score, tally 6 design, intent, object, target 7 end line, purpose 8 ambition, goal line, terminus 9 intention, objective 10 finish line

go along with 5 usher 6 assent, convoy, escort 8 accede to, shepherd 9 accompany, agree with, chaperone, consent to 10 comply with

go 3 act, end, fit, fly, pep, run, try, vim **4** blow, dash, elan, fare, flee, flow, jibe, lead, life, pass, quit, stir, turn, wend, work **5** agree, begin, be off, blend, drive, force, get on, lapse, leave, reach, scram, slide, split, steam, tally, trial, verve, vigor, whirl **6** accord, beat it, be used, belong, chance, decamp, depart, effort, elapse, energy, expire, extend, mettle, pass by, repair, result, retire, spirit **7** advance, attempt, be given, be known, comport, fall out, glide by, move out, operate, perform, proceed, slip off, take off, turn out, vamoose, work out **8** ambition, endeavor, function, move away, progress, slip away, sneak off, spread to, start for, steal off, vitality, vivacity, withdraw **9** animation, harmonize, terminate, transpire **10** enterprise, experiment, initiative

go ashore 4 land **6** debark **9** disembark

go astray 3 err, sin **6** wander **7** deviate, do wrong **9** misbehave **10** transgress **13** fall from grace

goat *see box*

Goat, Horned Goat
  constellation of:
  11 Capricornus

goat god 3 Pan **5** satyr

go away 3 ebb **4** fade, scat, wane **5** abate, leave, scram **6** depart, lessen, retire **8** withdraw **9** disappear

gob 3 dab, tar **4** clot, glob, lump, mass **6** sailor **7** Jack Tar

go back 6 return **7** retreat

gobble 3 caw **4** bolt, gulp, wolf **5** raven, stuff **6** cackle, devour, gabble, gaggle **8** bolt down, cram down, gulp down

gobbledygook 4 bosh, bunk, cant, tosh **6** jargon **7** rubbish, twaddle **8** buncombe, nonsense, tommyrot **9** gibberish, moonshine **10** balderdash, double-talk, hocus-pocus, mumbo jumbo **11** foolishness **12** fiddle-faddle

gobble up 6 devour **8** bolt down, gulp down, wolf down

go before 7 precede, predate **8** antecede, antedate **9** come first, go ahead of **10** anticipate

go-between 5 agent, envoy, fixer, proxy **6** deputy, second **7** arbiter **8** delegate, emissary, mediator **9** messenger, middleman, moderator **10** arbitrator, interceder, negotiator **12** intermediary **13** intermediator **14** representative

goblet 3 cup **5** glass **6** vessel **7** chalice

goblin 4 ogre **5** bogey, demon, troll **7** gremlin **8** bogeyman

Gobseck
  author: **14** Honore de Balzac

go by 4 pass **6** elapse, pass by, roll by, rush by, slip by **7** glide by, slide by **8** slip away

go by car 4 ride **5** drive, motor

go-cart 4 cart **5** buggy **6** barrow **8** carriage, handcart, pushcart, stroller **11** wheelbarrow

go crimson 4 burn, glow **5** blush, color, flame, flush **6** redden

goat 3 kid **4** buck, butt **5** billy, nanny **6** victim **7** fall guy **9** scapegoat **11** whipping boy **13** laughingstock
  breed: 6 Angora, Chamal, Nubian, Saanen **7** Granada **8** La Mancha **10** Toggenburg **11** Anglo-Nubian **12** French Alpine **13** British Alpine
  combining form: 4 aego **5** capri
  family: 7 Bovidae
  female: 3 doe **5** capra, nanny **7** doeling
  genus: 5 Capra
  goat-boy: 5 Giles
  goat-milk cheese: 7 chevret
  goat-man: 5 satyr
  god: 3 Pan **5** satyr **7** Aegipan
  group of: 4 herd **5** tribe
  hair: 5 kasha, tibet
  hair of Angora goat: 6 mohair
  male: 4 buck **5** billy
  meat: 7 cabrito
  star: 7 capella
  young: 3 kid

God, god 4 Lord **5** Allah, deity, Jeveh **6** Elohim, Yahweh **7** Holy One, Jehovah, Skaddai **8** divinity, the Deity **9** Our Father **10** the Creator, the Godhead **11** divine being, God Almighty, the Almighty **13** the Omnipotent, the Omniscient **14** the All-Merciful, the Man Upstairs **15** the Supreme Being
  Hebrew: 6 Adonai
  Latin: 7 Dominus

god, first
  origin: **12** Scandinavian
  known as: **7** Forsete, Forseti

God and Man at Yale
  author: **17** William F Buckley Jr

God and my right
  French: **14** Dieu et mon droit
  motto of: **18** royal arms of England

God be with us
  German: **10** Gott mit uns

God be with you
  Latin: **12** Deus vobiscum

Godbole, Professor
  character in: **15** A Passage to India
  author: **7** Forster

Goddard, Jean-Luc
  director of: **10** Breathless

Goddard, Paulette
  real name: **10** Marion Levy
  husband: **14** Charlie Chaplin **15** Burgess Meredith **18** Erich Maria Remarque
  born: **11** Great Neck NY
  roles: **11** Modern Times, Unconquered **15** So Proudly We Hail **16** Standing Room Only, The Great Dictator **19** Diary of a Chambermaid

Goddard, Robert Hutchings
  nationality: **8** American
  inventor of: **12** rocket engine **22** liquid propellant rocket

Godden, Rumer
  author of: **8** The River **14** Black Narcissus, Kitchen Madonna **16** The Peacock Spring **18** In This House of Brede, The Greengage Summer **19** An Episode of Sparrows **23** The Battle of Villa Fiorita

God enriches
  Latin: **9** ditat Deus
  motto of: **7** Arizona

Godfather, The
  author: **9** Mario Puzo
  family: **8** Corleone
  director: **18** Francis Ford Coppola
  cast: **8** Al Pacino (Michael) **9** James Caan (Sonny)

10 John Marley **11** Diane
Keaton **12** Marlon Brando
(Don Vito Corleone), Richard Conte, Robert Duvall
14 Sterling Hayden **17** Richard Castellano
Oscar for: **5** actor (Brando)
7 picture **10** screenplay
sequel: **18** The Godfather
Part II

Godfather, The, Part II
director: **18** Francis Ford
Coppola
cast: **8** Al Pacino **10** John
Cazale, Talia Shire **11** Diane
Keaton **12** Lee Strasberg,
Robert DeNiro, Robert
Duvall
Oscar for: **7** picture
10 screenplay **15** supporting
actor (DeNiro)
sequel to: **12** The Godfather

godforsaken 5 bleak **6** lonely,
remote **8** deserted, desolate,
wretched **9** abandoned,
neglected

god from a machine
Latin: **13** deux ex machina

God is with us
German: **10** Gott mit uns

godless 4 evil **6** wicked
7 heathen, impious, profane,
ungodly **8** agnostic, depraved
9 atheistic **10** unhallowed
11 blasphemous, irreligious,
unrepentant, unrighteous
12 sacrilegious,
unsanctified

godlessness 7 atheism **8** apostasy, unbelief **9** disbelief
10 irreligion

godlike 4 holy **5** godly, pious
6 deific, divine, sacred **8** immortal, olympian

godliness 5 piety **8** devotion,
holiness **9** reverence **10** devoutness **12** spirituality

godly 4 good, holy **5** moral,
pious **6** devout, divine, sacred
7 devoted, saintly **8** faithful,
hallowed, reverent **9** believing,
God-loving, pietistic, religious,
righteous, spiritual **10** Godfearing, sanctified **11** consecrated, pure in heart,
reverential

God of Vengeance, The
author: **10** Sholem Asch

go down 3 ebb **4** drop, fade,
wane **5** abate, lower, slide
6 lessen, plunge, reduce,
weaken **7** descend, plummet,
slacken, subside **8** decrease, diminish, moderate

God Save the Queen
author: **17** William F Buckley
Jr

God's Grace
author: **14** Bernard Malamud

God's Little Acre
author: **15** Erskine Caldwell

Godthaab
capital of: **9** Greenland

God willing
Latin: **10** Deo volente

God wills it
Latin: **8** Deus vult
cry of: **9** Crusaders

Godwin, William
author of: **13** Caleb Williams **35** An Enquiry Concerning Political Justice

Goes, Hugo van der
born: **5** Ghent **8** Flanders
artwork: **7** The Fall **14** The
Lamentation **19** The Death
of the Virgin **21** The Adoration of the Magi **22** The
Adoration of the Child
26 The Adoration of the
Shepherds

Goethe, Johann
author of: **5** Faust **6** Egmont
24 The Sorrows of Young
Werther **29** Wilhelm Meister's Apprenticeship

go-getter 4 doer **7** hustler
8 achiever, live wire

go-getting 7 driving, dynamic
8 forceful, hustling **9** ambitious, assertive, energetic
10 aggressive **11** hard-driving,
hard-working, industrious

Gogol, Nikolai
author of: **7** The Nose **9** Dead
Souls **10** Taras Bulba **11** The
Overcoat **19** The Inspector-
General

go hand in hand 5 match,
tally **6** concur, square **7** coexist **9** accompany

go hungry 4 fast **6** famish,
starve **7** abstain

Going My Way
director: **10** Leo McCarey
cast: **10** Bing Crosby (Father
O'Malley) **12** Gene Lockhart **15** Barry Fitzgerald
Oscar for: **4** song **5** actor
(Crosby) **7** picture **8** director
15 supporting actor
(Fitzgerald)
song: **15** Swinging on a Star

gold 3 bar **4** gilt **5** aurum, ingot **6** beauty, nugget, purity,
yellow **7** bullion **8** goodness,
goodwill, humanity, kindness
11 beneficence
chemical symbol: **2** Au

gold and silver
Spanish: **9** oro y plata
motto of: **7** Montana

Gold Bug, The
author: **13** Edgar Allan Poe

Gold Coast see **5** Ghana
11 Sierra Leone

golden 4 best, gilt, rosy **5** blest,
blond, great, happy, palmy
6 bright, gilded, joyous, timely **7** aureate, halcyon, rich-
est, shining **8** beatific,
glorious, happiest, splendid
9 favorable, opportune, priceless, promising **10** auspicious,
delightful, propitious, seasonable **11** exceptional, flourishing,
resplendent **12** advantageous,
bright-yellow
13 extraordinary

Golden Age
first age of: **3** man
world ruled by: **6** Cronus,
Saturn

Golden Ass, The
author: **14** Lucius Apuleius
character: **4** Milo **5** Fotis
6 Lucius **8** Charites, Pam-
phile **9** Lepolemus
10 Thrasillus

Goldenberg, Emmanuel
real name of: **15** Edward G
Robinson

Golden Bough, The
branch of: **9** mistletoe
sacred to: **10** Proserpina
used by: **6** Aeneas
at shrine of: **5** Diana
7 Virbius
author: **15** Sir James G
Frazer

Golden Bowl, The
author: **10** Henry James
character: **8** Mr Verver
12 Maggie Verver, Mrs As-
singham **13** Prince Amerigo
14 Charlotte Stant

Golden Boy
nickname of: **11** Paul
Hornung

golden brown 3 tan **5** tawny,
toast **6** sienna **7** tobacco
8 chestnut

Golden Cockerel, The
also: **8** Le Coq d'Or **15** Zolo-
toy Petushok
opera by: **14** Rimsky-
Korsakov
character: **9** King Dodon
14 Queen of Shemaka

golden egg-layer
form: **5** goose
made of: **4** gold

Golden Fleece
made of: **4** gold
kept at: **7** Colchis
kept by: **10** King Aeetes
stolen by: **5** Jason
9 Argonauts
accomplice: **5** Medea

Golden Legend
author: **13** William Caxton

goldenrod 8 Solidago
varieties: **5** sweet, white
6 Wreath **7** seaside **8** bluestem, European
10 California

Golden State
nickname of: **10** California

golden youth
French: **13** jeunesse doree

goldfinch
group of: **5** charm

Goldfinger
director: **11** Guy Hamilton
author: **10** Ian Fleming
cast: **9** Gert Frobe (Auric Goldfinger) **10** Bernard Lee (M) **11** Lois Maxwell (Miss Moneypenny) **12** Harold Sakata (Oddjob), Shirley Eaton **13** Honor Blackman (Pussy Galore), Sean Connery (James Bond, 007)

Golding, William
author of: **8** Free Fall **13** A Moving Target **14** Lord of the Flies, Rites of Passage **15** Darkness Visible

gold mine 7 bonanza
10 mother lode

Gold Rush, The
director: **14** Charlie Chaplin
cast: **9** Mack Swain, Tom Murray **11** Georgia Hale **14** Charlie Chaplin (Little Tramp)
setting: **5** Yukon

Goldsmith, Oliver
author of: **18** She Stoops to Conquer, The Deserted Village **19** The Vicar of Wakefield

Goldstein, Elliott
real name of: **12** Elliott Gould

goldwasser
form: **7** liquor
origin: **6** France **7** Germany
flavor: **4** herb **5** spice **7** caraway
flecked with: **8** gold leaf

golf *see box*

golfer 8 Ben Hogan, Lee Elder, Sam Snead **9** Carol Mann, Hale Irwin, Patty Berg, Tom Watson **10** Betsy Rawls, Bobby Jones, Deane Beman, Gary Player, Hubie Green, Jim Demaret, Judy Rankin, Lee Trevino, Nancy Lopez **11** Ben Crenshaw, Billy Casper, Byron Nelson, Calvin Peete, Donna Caponi, Gene Sarazen, Julius Boros, Tom Weiskopf, Walter Hagen **12** Arnold Palmer, Jack Nicklaus, Joanne Carner, Johnny Miller, Mickey Wright, Sandra Haynie **14** Cary Middlecoff, Kathy Whitworth **16** Roberto DeVicenzo **19** Susie Maxwell Berning **20** Severiano Ballesteros **21** Babe Didrikson Zaharias

Golgotha 7 Calvary
means: **10** skull place

Goliath
killed by: **5** David

golliwogg 3 toy **4** doll **9** plaything

Gomer
father: **7** Diblaim
husband: **5** Hosea

Gomer Pyle USMC
character: **5** Bunny **7** Frankie **9** Corp Boyle **11** Duke Slayter, (Sgt) Vince Carter
cast: **9** Jim Nabors, Roy Stuart **10** Ted Bessell **11** Frank Sutton **12** Ronnie Schell **13** Barbara Stuart

Gomorrah
destroyed with: **5** Sodom **6** Zeboim **10** Admah

Gondoliers, The
operetta by: **18** Gilbert and Sullivan
character: **4** Luiz **5** Tessa **7** Casilda **8** Gianetta **13** Marco Palmieri **15** Duke of Plaza-Toro **16** Giuseppe Palmieri

gone 3 ago, out **4** away, dead, left, lost, past **6** absent, ruined, used up **7** defunct, died out, extinct, missing **8** departed, finished, hopeless, vanished **11** disappeared

Goneril
character in: **8** King Lear
author: **11** Shakespeare

Gone With the Wind
author: **16** Margaret Mitchell
character: **5** Mammy **6** Big Sam, Prissy **7** Dr Meade **10** Ellen (Robillard) O'Hara **11** Gerald O'Hara, Honey Wilkes, India Wilkes **12** Ashley Wilkes, Aunt Pittypat, Belle Watling **13** Scarlett O'Hara, Tarleton twins **15** Mrs Merriweather **21** Melanie Hamilton Wilkes
Scarlett's husband: **11** Rhett Butler **12** Frank Kennedy **15** Charles Hamilton
Scarlett's children: **4** Emma, Wade **6** Bonnie
Scarlett's sister: **7** Carreen, Suellen
director: **13** Victor Fleming
cast: **9** Ona Munson **10** Clark Gable (Rhett Butler) **11** Evelyn Keyes, Vivien Leigh (Scarlett O'Hara) **12** Leslie Howard (Ashley Wilkes) **13** Ann Rutherford **14** Hattie McDaniel (Mammy), Thomas Mitchell (Gerald O'Hara) **16** Butterfly McQueen (Prissy) **17** Olivia de Havilland (Melanie Hamilton Wilkes)
score: **10** Max Steiner
Oscar for: **7** actress (Leigh), picture **8** director **12** screenwriter **17** supporting actress (McDaniel)
producer: **14** David O Selznick

---

golf
average number strokes to reach a hole: **3** par
ball in another's path: **6** stymie
championship: **6** US Open **9** Grand Slam **11** British Open **17** Masters' Tournament
club: **4** iron, wood **6** driver, putter **7** brassie **8** long iron **9** sand wedge, short iron **10** middle iron **13** pitching wedge
club carrier: **6** caddie
course also called: **5** links
golf ball formerly called: **6** guttie **8** feathery
hole scored in one stroke: **3** ace **9** hole-in-one
one stroke less than par: **6** birdie
one stroke more than par: **5** bogey
part of the course: **3** cup, tee **4** hole **5** apron, green, rough **6** bunker, hazard **7** fairway **8** sand trap
position: **3** lie
stance: **4** open **6** closed, square **7** address
two strokes less than par: **5** eagle
type of competition: **5** match **6** stroke
uprooted turf: **5** divot
warning cry: **4** fore

good 3 ace, fit, new **4** best, boon, fine, full, gain, kind, pure, real **5** ample, crack, favor, great, large, merit, moral, pious, prize, right, solid, sound, sunny, valid, value, worth **6** adroit, choice, devout, entire, genial, honest, humane, kindly, lively, newest, profit, proper, seemly, select, tiptop, useful, virtue, wealth, worthy **7** adapted, benefit, capable, capital, dutiful, fitting, genuine, godsend, healthy, orderly, service, sizable, skilled, success, upright, welfare **8** adequate, becoming, blessing, bonafide, cheerful, complete, decorous, gracious, innocent, interest, kindness, obedient, obliging, pleasant, precious, reliable, salutary, skillful, smartest, sociable, splendid, suitable, thorough, topnotch, valuable, virtuous, windfall **9** admirable, advantage, agreeable, authentic, convivial, deserving, efficient, enjoyable, enjoyment, excellent, exemplary, expensive, favorable, first-rate, happiness, healthful, honorable, priceless, qualified, religious, righteous, unsullied, untainted, wholesome, wonderful **10** altruistic, beneficent, beneficial, benevolent, excellence, first-class, legitimate, proficient, prosperity, sufficient, worthwhile **11** appropriate, commendable, considerate, improvement, substantial, sympathetic, well-behaved **12** advantageous, considerable, praiseworthy, satisfactory **13** companionable, conscientious, righteousness
   French: 3 bon **4** bien
   Spanish: 5 bueno
   German: 3 gut

Good as Gold
  author: **12** Joseph Heller

Good Book 5 Bible

good breeding 5 grace **6** polish **7** manners **9** gentility **10** refinement **11** cultivation

good buy 4 deal **5** steal **7** bargain

good-by, good-bye 3 bye **6** bye-bye, bye now, so long **7** parting, send-off **8** farewell, Godspeed **9** departure **10** separation **11** be seeing you, leave-taking, see you later **12** God be with you **15** till we meet again
  French: 5 adieu **8** au revoir
  German: 14 auf Wiedersehen
  Hawaiian: 5 aloha
  Italian: 4 ciao **5** addio **11** arrivederci
  Japanese: 8 sayonara
  Latin: 4 vale
  Spanish: 5 adios **12** hasta la vista

Goodbye, Darkness
  author: **17** William Manchester

Goodbye, Mr Chips
  director: **7** Sam Wood
  author: **11** James Hilton
  cast: **11** Greer Garson, Paul Henreid (von Henreid), Robert Donat
  Oscar for: **5** actor (Donat)
  character: **7** Mr Chips

10 Mrs Wickett **12** Kathy Bridges
  school: **10** Brookfield

Goodbye Girl, The
  director: **11** Herbert Ross
  based on play by: **9** Neil Simon
  cast: **11** Marsha Mason **13** Quinn Cummings **15** Richard Dreyfuss
  Oscar for: **5** actor (Dreyfuss)

Good Companions, The
  author: **11** J B Priestley

good counsel
  god of: **6** Consus

good day
  French: 7 bonjour
  German: 8 guten tag
  Spanish: 10 buenos dias
  Italian: 10 buon giorno

good deal 3 buy **5** steal **7** bargain

good deed 8 kindness **11** benefaction **12** philanthropy
  Hebrew: 7 mitsvah, mitzvah

Good Earth, The
  author: **10** Pearl S Buck
  character: **4** O-Lan **6** Nung En **7** Nung Wen, The Fool **8** Wang Lung **11** Pear Blossom **12** Lotus Blossom
  director: **14** Sidney Franklin
  cast: **8** Keye Luke, Paul Muni **10** Tilly Losch **11** Jessie Ralph, Luise Rainer

14 Walter Connolly **15** Charley Grapewin
  Oscar for: **7** actress (Rainer)

good feelings 8 good will **11** benevolence **12** friendliness

good form 9 etiquette, good taste **10** politeness **11** good manners

good-for-nothing 5 idler **6** loafer **7** useless **9** no-account, shiftless, worthless

good fortune 4 luck **7** bonanza **8** fortuity, lady luck, windfall **9** blessings **10** lucky break

good friend
  French: 6 bon ami **9** bonne amie

good health 5 vigor **7** fitness **8** vitality **10** robustness

Goodhue, Bertram Grosvenor
  architect of: **13** St Bartholomew (NYC) **14** St Thomas Church (NYC) **25** Chapel at US Military Academy (West Point), National Academy of Sciences (Washington DC) **28** Nebraska State Capitol Building (Lincoln)
  style: **13** Gothic Revival **15** Spanish Colonial

good humor 10 affability, amiability, cheeriness, kindliness, mellowness **12** cheerfulness, complaisance, pleasantness **15** kindheartedness

good-humored 4 mild, warm **6** cheery, genial, gentle, kindly, mellow **7** affable, amiable **8** cheerful, pleasant **9** congenial, easygoing **11** complaisant

good-looker 3 fox **4** doll, hunk **5** beaut, Venus **6** Adonis, beauty, eyeful **7** stunner **8** knockout **11** handsome Dan

good-looking 4 fair, foxy, sexy **5** bonny **6** comely, lovely, pretty **8** alluring, clean-cut, gorgeous, handsome, stunning **9** beauteous, beautiful, exquisite, ravishing **10** attractive, bewitching, enchanting **11** captivating, eye-catching, well-favored **15** pulchritudinous

good looks 6 beauty **10** comeliness, loveliness **11** pulchritude **12** handsomeness **14** attractiveness

good luck
  Yiddish: 8 mazel tov

goodly 4 tidy **5** ample, large **7** sizable **11** substantial **12** considerable

Goodman, Theodosia
real name of: **9** Theda Bara

good manners 8 courtesy
9 amenities, etiquette, gentility **10** politeness, refinement

good name 4 face **5** image
10 reputation **11** self-respect

good nature 6 warmth **9** geniality, good humor **10** affability, amiability, cordiality, likability **12** complaisance, pleasantness **13** agreeableness

good-natured 4 warm
5 sunny **6** genial, kindly **7** affable, amiable **8** cheerful, friendly, obliging, pleasant **9** agreeable, congenial, easygoing **11** complaisant, good-humored, warm-hearted **13** accommodating

goodness 3 boy, gee, hey, say, wow **5** favor, honor, mercy, merit, piety, value, worth, wowee **6** profit, purity, virtue **7** benefit, decorum, gee whiz, heavens, honesty, probity, service **8** boy-oh-boy, devotion, gracious, kindness, morality **9** advantage, innocence, integrity, land alive, landsakes, nutrition, propriety, rectitude **10** generosity, kindliness, sakes alive, usefulness **11** benevolence, nourishment **12** virtuousness **13** righteousness, wholesomeness **14** heavens to Betsy

good night
French: **7** bon soir **9** bonne nuit
German: **9** gute nacht
Spanish: **12** buenas noches
Italian: **10** buona notte

good opinion 6 esteem, regard **7** respect **8** approval **10** admiration

good person 4 dear, love **5** angel **7** darling **10** sweetheart

goods 4 gear **5** cloth, stock, wares **6** fabric, things **7** effects, fabrics **8** chattels, material, movables, property, textiles **9** inventory, trappings **11** commodities, furnishings, merchandise, possessions **13** appurtenances, paraphernalia

good sense 6 brains, wisdom **8** judgment **12** intelligence

good taste 10 refinement **11** cultivation, discernment **14** discrimination

good-tempered 5 sunny **7** amiable, smiling **8** cheerful **12** sweet-natured

good time 3 fun **9** amusement, diversion, enjoyment **13** entertainment

good times 4 boom **8** fat years

good turn 5 favor **7** service **8** good deed

goodwill 5 amity **8** kindness **9** benignity **10** cordiality, kindliness **11** amicability, benevolence **12** friendliness **15** kindheartedness

good wishes 4 best **5** favor **6** regard **7** consent, regards **8** approval, blessing, respects, sanction **11** compliments

Goodwood, Caspar
character in: **18** The Portrait of a Lady
author: **5** James

good word 6 praise **10** compliment **11** approbation **12** commendation **14** congratulation

Goodyear, Charles
nationality: **8** American
developed: **16** vulcanized rubber

goof 3 err **4** boob, flub, fool, mess **5** botch, error, gum up **6** bollix, boo-boo, bungle, fumble, slip up **7** blunder, mistake **9** oversight

Goolagong Cawley, Evonne
sport: **6** tennis
heritage: **19** Australian Aborigine

go on all fours 5 crawl, creep

goose
young: **7** gosling
group of: **5** flock, skein **6** gaggle

goose egg 3 nil, zip **4** zero **5** aught **6** cipher, naught **7** nothing **11** horse collar

go over 5 audit, check **6** review **7** examine, inspect **10** scrutinize **11** investigate

Gopher State
nickname of: **9** Minnesota

Gorbachev, Mikhail Sergeyevich
party: **9** Communist
country: **4** USSR **6** Russia **31** Union of Soviet Socialist Republics
born: **9** Stavropol **10** Privolnoye **16** Krasnogvardeisky
education: **21** Moscow State University
political career: **9** Politburo **16** General Secretary **20** Agriculture Secretary **23** Stavropol Communist Party **35** Deputy Supreme Soviet Central Committee

policy: **8** glasnost **11** perestroika
distinguishing characteristic: **19** strawberry birthmark (head)
wife: **15** Raisa Maksimovna
occupation: **7** teacher
daughter: **5** Irisa
occupation: **6** doctor **9** physician

Gorcey, Leo
born: **9** New York NY
roles: **4** Spit **10** Bowery Boys **11** Dead End Kids

Gordimer, Nadine
author of: **11** July's People **12** The Lying Days **13** A Guest of Honor **15** Burger's Daughter **16** A Soldier's Embrace **21** The Late Bourgeois World
award: **10** Nobel Prize

Gordon, Ruth
real name: **15** Ruth Gordon Jones
husband: **11** Garson Kanin
born: **11** Wollaston MA
roles: **11** Where's Poppa? **13** Rosemary's Baby **14** Harold and Maude **17** Inside Daisy Clover **20** Abe Lincoln in Illinois

gore 5 blood **7** carnage **8** butchery **9** bloodshed, slaughter

Gore, Albert
born: **10** Washington (DC)
wife: **6** Tipper **13** Mary Elizabeth
children: **5** Sarah **6** Albert **7** Karenna, Kristin
education: **7** Harvard **10** Vanderbilt
profession: **10** journalist
author of: **17** Earth in the Balance
political career: **6** Senate **13** vice president **22** House of Representatives

Gorgas, William Crawford
field: **8** medicine
position: **18** army surgeon general
conquered: **7** malaria **11** yellow fever
location: **11** Panama Canal

gorge 3 gap, ire **4** bolt, cram, craw, dale, dell, fill, glen, glut, gulp, pass, sate, vale **5** abyss, anger, blood, chasm, cleft, gulch, gully, mouth, stuff, wrath **6** canyon, defile, devour, gobble, gullet, hatred, hollow, muzzle, nausea, ravine, throat **7** disgust, indulge, overeat, satiate **8** crevasse **9** animosity, esophagus, repulsion, revulsion **10** gluttonize, gormandize, repugnance **11** overindulge

gormandize, repugnance
11 overindulge

gorgeous 4 fine, rich **5** grand
6 bright, costly, lovely **7** elegant, opulent, shining **8** dazzling, glorious, imposing,
splendid, stunning **9** beautiful,
brilliant, exquisite, luxurious,
ravishing, sumptuous **10** attractive, glittering, impressive
11 good-looking, magnificent,
resplendent, splendorous
13 splendiferous

Gorgons
form: **7** maidens **8** monsters
names: **6** Medusa, Stheno
7 Euryale, Sthenno
father: **7** Phorcys
mother: **4** Ceto
protectress: **6** Graeae, Graiae
hair of: **6** snakes
hands of: **5** brass
turned viewers to: **5** stone

Gorgophone
father: **7** Perseus
mother: **9** Andromeda
husband: **7** Oebalus **8** Perieres
son: **9** Leucippus

Gorgosaurus
type: **8** dinosaur, theropod
location: **7** Alberta **12** North
America
period: **10** Cretaceous

Gorgythion
mentioned in: **5** Iliad
father: **5** Priam
killed by: **6** Teucer

gorilla
group of: **4** band

Gorky, Arshile
real name: **21** Vosdanig Manoog Adokian
born: **7** Armenia
11 Khorkomvari
artwork: **5** Agony **15** Diary
of a Seducer **17** Making the
Calendar **21** The Artist and
his Mother, Water of the
Flowery Hill **22** The Liver is
the Cock's Comb

Gorky, Maxim (Maksim)
real name: **25** Alekseimaksimovich Peshkov
author of: **7** V I Lenin
11 My Childhood **14** The
Lower Depths **18** The Small
Town Okurov **20** City of the
Yellow Devil, Twenty-six
Men and a Girl **27** The Life
of Matthew Kozhemyakin

gormandize 5 feast, raven
6 devour

Gortys
father: **10** Stymphalus
12 Rhadamanthys

gory 5 scary **6** bloody, creepy

9 murderous **10** horrifying,
sanguinary, terrifying
11 bloodsoaked, ensanguined,
frightening **12** bloodstained,
bloodthirsty **13** bloodcurdling

gospel, Gospel 5 credo,
creed **8** doctrine **11** the good
news, the last word **12** the final word **13** the whole truth,
ultimate truth
the first four books of the
New Testament: **4** Luke,
John, Mark **7** Matthew

Gospel writers 4 John, Luke,
Mark **7** Matthew **9** synoptist

gospodin 2 Mr **6** Mister

gossamer 5 filmy, gauzy,
sheer **8** cobwebby **10** diaphanous **13** insubstantial

gossip 4 news **6** babble, report,
tattle **7** comment, hearsay,
prattle, scandal, twaddle **8** idle
talk **10** backbiting **12** tittle-
tattle **13** newsmongering

gossiper 3 pry **4** blab **5** prate,
snoop, yenta **6** gabble, magpie,
meddle, tattle **7** babbler, meddler, prattle, snooper, tattler
8 busybody **9** chatterer
10 chatterbox, newsmonger,
talebearer, tattletale **11** rumormonger **12** blabbermouth, gossipmonger **13** scandalmonger

go stale 3 die

Go Tell It on the Mountain
author: **12** James Baldwin

Gothic
language family: **12** Indo-
European

go through 4 bear **6** endure,
suffer **7** sustain, undergo **9** encounter, withstand
10 experience

go to 3 see **5** visit **6** attend
8 appear at, frequent

go to bed 6 retire, turn in
7 lie down, sack out **8** flake
out **9** hit the hay **10** call it a
day, hit the sack **11** catch
some z's

go to pieces 5 break, crack
7 break up, crack up, crumble,
give way, shatter **8** splinter
9 break down, fall apart
11 lose control **12** disintegrate

go to work on 6 attack,
tackle **8** set about **9** undertake

go to wrack and ruin 5 decay **7** crumble **9** fall apart
12 disintegrate

Gotterdammerung 17 Twilight of the Gods
see: **8** Ragnarok

Gott mit uns 11 God be with
us, God is with us

gouge 5 carve, drill, scoop
6 chisel, extort **10** overcharge

gouge out 5 drill **6** hollow
8 carve out, scoop out **9** chisel
out, hollow out **10** whittle out

Gould, Chester
creator/artist of: **9** Dick
Tracy

Gould, Elliott
real name: **16** Elliott
Goldstein
wife: **15** Barbra Streisand
born: **10** Brooklyn NY
roles: **4** MASH **13** Little Murders **14** The Long Goodbye
15 California Split, Getting
Straight **19** Bob & Carol &
Ted & Alice

Goulding, Edmund
director of: **10** Grand Hotel
11 Dark Victory **13** The
Dawn Patrol

go under 4 fail, fall, sink **9** go
belly up **10** go bankrupt

Gounod, Charles Francois
born: **5** Paris **6** France
composer of: **5** Faust **6** Gallia, Sappho, Te Deum
8 Cinq-Mars, Mireille **9** La
Colombe, Polyeucte **10** Mors
et Vita **11** Marie Stuart, Stabat Mater **13** La Reine de
Saba **14** Romeo and Juliet
16 La Nonne Sanglante, Philemon et Baucis **17** La Tribute de Zamora **18** Le
Medecin Malgre Lui

gourd 9 Cucurbita **13** Cucurbita
pepo
varieties: **3** ash, ivy, rag,
wax **4** club **5** snake, white
6 bitter, bottle, dipper,
sponge, teasel, viper's **7** figleaf, Malabar, serpent, trumpet **8** calabash, hedgehog,
Missouri **9** dishcloth
10 goareberry, gooseberry,
knob-kerrie, silver-seed
11 sugar-trough **12** Hercules'-club **14** scarlet-fruited

gourmand 7 glutton **8** big
eater **9** bon vivant, chowhound **11** gormandizer,
trencherman

gourmet 7 epicure **9** bon vivant **10** gastronome **11** connoisseur, gastronomer
12 gastronomist

gourmet cooking
French: **12** haute cuisine

Gourmont, Remy de
author of: **18** A Night in
Luxembourg

gout 5 style, taste
10 preference

govern 3 run **4** boss, curb,
form, head, lead, rule, sway,
tame **5** check, guide, pilot,
steer **6** bridle, direct, manage
7 command, control, incline,
inhibit, oversee **8** dominate,
restrain **9** influence, supervise
10 administer, discipline, hold
in hand **11** hold in check, superintend **13** be at the helm
of **14** pull the strings **16** keep
under control **17** exercise authority **18** be in the driver's
seat

governed 3 led **5** ruled
6 guided **7** steered, subject
8 directed **9** dependent
10 controlled, supervised
12 administered
13 superintended

governing 6 ruling **7** curbing,
guiding, heading, leading,
swaying **8** bridling, checking,
managing, piloting, reigning,
steering **9** directing, inclining
10 inhibiting, management,
overseeing **11** controlling, influencing, restraining, supervision **13** administering
14 administrating, administration, superintending

governing body 10 government, management, parlia-
ment **12** powers that be
14 administration **16** board of
directors, board of governors
18 executive committee

government 3 law **4** rule
5 state **6** regime **7** command,
control **8** dominion, guidance
9 authority, direction **10** domination, management, regulation **11** supervision
13 governing body, statesmanship **14** administration

governor
Turkish: **3** beg, bey

Gowan
character in: **12** Little Dorrit
author: **7** Dickens

go with 6 convey, convoy, escort **7** conduct **9** accompany

gown 4 robe **5** dress, frock
10 nightdress

goy 6 non-Jew **7** Gentile

**Goya (y Lucientes, Fran-
cisco Jose de)**
born: **5** Spain **13** Fuente de
todos
artwork: **8** Proverbs **10** Dis-
parates **11** Tauromaquia
12 Los Caprichos, The Naked Maja **15** Majas on a
Balcony **17** The Disasters of
War **21** Charles IV and his
Family

grab 3 bag, nab **4** grip, hold,
pass **5** catch, clasp, grasp,
lunge, pluck, seize **6** clutch,
collar, snatch **7** capture

grace 4 deck, love, tact, trim
5 adorn, charm, endow, exalt,
favor, honor, mercy, merit,
piety, skill, taste **6** beauty, bedeck, enrich, pardon, polish,
set off, virtue **7** charity, culture, decorum, dignify, dress
up, elevate, enhance, garnish,
glorify, manners, smarten,
suavity **8** beautify, clemency,
decorate, elegance, felicity, flu-
idity, God's love, holiness, lenience, ornament, reprieve,
sanctity, spruce up, urbanity
9 embellish, endowment, etiquette, exemption, extra time,
God's favor, good looks, propriety **10** aggrandize, comeliness, devoutness, excellence,
indulgence, refinement **11** cultivation, forgiveness, lissomeness, pulchritude, saintliness,
willowiness **12** dispensation,
gracefulness, mannerliness,
mercifulness **14** accomplishment, divine goodness
French: **11** savoir faire

graceful 5 lithe **6** comely, limber, lovely **7** elegant, lissome,
shapely, sinuous, willowy
8 delicate **9** beautiful, lithesome, sylphlike **10** attractive
11 light-footed

gracefulness 8 delicacy, fluid-
ity **10** suppleness
11 lissomeness

graceless 5 gawky, inept
6 clumsy **7** awkward **10** ungraceful **11** heavy-handed

Graces
also: **7** Gratiae **9** Charities
goddesses of: **6** beauty
father: **4** Zeus
mother: **8** Eurynome
names: **4** Auxo **5** Cleta
6 Aglaia, Thalia **7** Phaenna
8 Hegemone **10** Euphrosyne

gracious 2 my **3** boy, gee,
wow **4** kind **5** civil, mercy, oh
boy **6** benign, humane, kindly,
polite, tender, ye gods **7** affable, amiable, clement, cordial,
courtly, gee whiz, lenient, my
stars **8** friendly, goodness,
merciful, obliging, pleasant
9 benignant, courteous, landsakes **10** benevolent, charitable, chivalrous, hospitable
11 good heavens, good natured, kindhearted **13** compassionate **14** heavens to Betsy

gradation 4 step **5** stage **6** degree **7** shading **8** grouping, ordering **9** arranging
11 arrangement **12** organization **14** classification

grade 4 bank, even, hill, mark,
ramp, rank, rate, sort, step
5 brand, caste, class, level, order, pitch, place, slope, stage,
value **6** degree, estate, rating,
smooth, sphere, status **7** flatten, incline, quality, station
8 classify, gradient, position,
standing **9** acclivity, condition,
declivity, intensity

grade-A 2 A-1 **4** aces, a-one,
fine, tops **5** grade, great,
prime, super **6** choice, superb,
tip-top **7** capital **8** peerless,
sterling, superior, top-notch
9 excellent, first-rate, matchless, superfine **10** first-class,
preeminent, tremendous
11 outstanding, superlative

**Gradgrind, Thomas and
Louisa**
characters in: **9** Hard Times
author: **7** Dickens

gradient 4 ramp, tilt **5** pitch,
slant, slope **6** ascent **7** incline,
leaning **9** steepness
11 inclination

gradual 4 slow **6** gentle,
steady **7** regular **8** measured
9 graduated, piecemeal
10 continuous, deliberate,
drop-by-drop, inch-by-inch,
step-by-step, successive **11** incremental, progressive **13** imperceptible, slow-but-steady
14 little-by-little

graduate 5 grade **6** alumna
7 alumnus, mark off **9** calibrate **10** measure out **14** grant
a degree to, receive a
degree

Graduate, The
director: **11** Mike Nichols
cast: **12** Anne Bancroft (Mrs
Robinson) **13** Dustin Hoffman, Katharine Ross
14 Murray Hamilton, William Daniels
score: **17** Simon and
Garfunkel
Oscar for: **8** director

Graeae
also: **6** Graiae
goddesses of: **3** sea
number: **5** three
names: **4** Enyo **5** Deino
9 Pemphredo
father: **7** Phorcys
mother: **4** Ceto
sisters: **7** Gorgons
protectresses of: **7** Gorgons
personified: **6** old age
three shared: **6** one eye
8 one tooth
eye stolen by: **7** Perseus
corresponds to: **4** Enyo

Graeme, Alison
character in: **21** The Master
of Ballantrae
author: **9** Stevenson

Graf 5 count

graft 3 bud 4 join, last, slip, swag 5 booty, infix, inset, plant, scion 6 bribes, payola, splice, spoils, sprout 7 bribery, implant, ingraft, payoffs, plunder, rake-off 8 kickback 9 hush money 10 corruption, transplant 12 implantation 13 inserted shoot

Graham, Bruce
architect of: 17 John Hancock Center (Chicago)

Grahame, Kenneth
author of: 19 The Wind in the Willows

Graiae see 6 Graeae

grain 3 bit, dot, jot, rye 4 atom, corn, dash, iota, mite, oats, seed, whit 5 crumb, grist, maize, ovule, pinch, spark, speck, touch, trace, wheat 6 barley, cereal, kernel, millet, morsel, pellet, tittle, trifle 7 granule, modicum 8 fragment, molecule, particle 9 scintilla
abbreviation: 2 gr
god of: 7 Robigus
goddess of: 6 Ribigo

Grain Coast see 11 Sierra Leone

Grainger, Percy Aldridge
born: 9 Australia, Melbourne
composer of: 14 Country Gardens 17 Handel in the Strand 19 Rosenkavalier Ramble

gram
abbreviation of: 1 g

Gram
origin: 12 Scandinavian
mentioned in: 8 Volsunga
form: 5 sword
owned by: 7 Sigmund
used by: 6 Sigurd
killed: 6 Fafnir

grand 2 A-1 3 big 4 fine, full, good, head, huge, keen, main 5 chief, fancy, great, large, lofty, noble, regal, royal, showy, super, swell 6 august, choice, groovy, kingly, lordly, superb 7 dashing, elegant, exalted, haughty, mammoth, opulent, pompous, queenly, stately, sublime, supreme 8 arrogant, complete, elevated, fabulous, glorious, imperial, imposing, majestic, palatial, princely, real cool, real gone, smashing, splendid, striking, terrific 9 admirable, dignified, excellent, first-rate, grandiose, luxurious, marvelous, principal, sumptuous, wonderful 10 impressive, monumental, out-of-sight 11 highfalutin, magnificent,

pretentious, sensational 12 ostentatious 13 comprehensive, distinguished

Grand Canyon State
nickname of: 7 Arizona

grande dame 9 great lady

grandee 5 noble 8 nobleman 9 blue blood 10 aristocrat

Grandees
author: 17 Stephen Birmingham

grandeur 4 fame, pomp 5 glory, state 6 luster 7 dignity, majesty 8 eminence, nobility, splendor 9 celebrity, loftiness, solemnity, sublimity 10 augustness, excellence, importance 11 distinction, stateliness 12 magnificence, resplendence 14 impressiveness

Grand Hotel
author: 9 Vicki Baum
character: 9 Miss Flamm 12 Baron Gaigern 14 Dr Otternschlag, Otto Kringelein 27 Herr Generaldirektor Preysing 32 Elisaveta Alexandrovna Grusinskaya
director: 14 Edmund Goulding
cast: 10 Greta Garbo 12 Joan Crawford, Wallace Beery 13 John Barrymore 15 Lionel Barrymore
setting: 6 Berlin

Grand Illusion
director: 10 Jean Renoir
cast: 5 Dalio 7 Carette 9 Dita Parlo, Jean Gabin 13 Pierre Fresnay 16 Erich von Stroheim

grandiloquent 5 lofty 6 florid, turgid 7 flowery, pompous, stilted, swollen 8 inflated 9 bombastic, grandiose, highflown 10 rhetorical 11 highfalutin, pretentious 12 highsounding, magniloquent

grandiose 5 grand 7 pompous, splashy 8 affected 9 highflown 10 flamboyant, theatrical 11 extravagant, highfalutin, pretentious

Grand Marnier
type: 6 brandy, cognac 7 liqueur
origin: 6 France
flavor: 6 orange
with gin: 7 Red Lion

grand monde 10 great world 11 best society 16 fashionable world

grand prix 10 grand prize

grand prize
French: 9 grand prix

Grange, Red (Harold)
nickname: 14 Galloping Ghost
sport: 8 football
team: 11 U of Illinois 12 Chicago Bears

Granger, Edith
character in: 12 Dombey and Son
author: 7 Dickens

Grangosier
character in: 22 Gargantua and Pantagruel
author: 8 Rabelais

Granite State
nickname of: 12 New Hampshire

grant 4 boon, cede, gift, give 5 admit, allot, allow, award, endow, favor, yield 6 accord, assign, bestow, confer, donate, permit 7 agree to, bequest, concede, consent, deal out, largess, present, subsidy, tribute 8 accede to, allocate, bestowal, dispense, donation, gratuity, offering 9 allotment, allowance, apportion, consent to, endowment, vouchsafe 10 assignment, concession, indulgence 11 benefaction 12 contribution, presentation 13 appropriation

Grant, Cary
real name: 23 Archibald Alexander Leach
wife: 10 Dyan Cannon 13 Barbara Hutton
born: 7 England 8 Bristol
roles: 6 Topper 9 Dream Wife, Houseboat 10 Indiscreet 11 Blonde Venus, Father Goose 13 To Catch a Thief 14 Bringing Up Baby, Monkey Business, The Bishop's Wife 15 She Done Him Wrong 16 North by Northwest 17 Arsenic and Old Lace, I Was a Male War Bride 18 Operation Petticoat 20 The Philadelphia Story 21 None But the Lonely Heart

Grant, Lee
real name: 21 Lyova Haskell Rosenthal
born: 9 New York NY
roles: 7 Shampoo 10 Plaza Suite 11 Peyton Place, The Landlord 14 Detective Story 19 In the Heat of the Night 20 Divorce American Style

Grant, Ulysses Simpson
see box

granted
French: 7 d'accord

grantee 8 receiver 9 recipient 11 beneficiary

Grant, Ulysses Simpson
real name: 17 Hiram Ulysses Grant
nickname: 3 Sam **4** Lyss **27** Unconditional Surrender Grant
presidential rank: 10 eighteenth
party: 10 Republican
state represented: 2 IL
defeated: 5 (David) Davis, (James) Black **6** (Charles)
O'Conor **7** (Horace) Greeley, (Horatio) Seymour **9** (William Slocomb) Groesbeck
vice president: 5 (Thomas W) Ferry (acting) **6** (Henry)
Wilson (died in office 1875), (Schuyler) Colfax
cabinet:
  state: **4** (Hamilton) Fish **9** (Elihu Benjamin) Washburne
  treasury: **7** (Alexander Turney) Stewart, (Benjamin
  Helm) Bristow, (Lot Myrick) Morrill **8** (George Sewall)
  Boutwell **10** (William Adams) Richardson
  war: **4** (Alphonso) Taft **7** (James Donald) Cameron,
  (John Aaron) Rawlins, (William Worth) Belknap
  attorney general: **4** (Alphonso) Taft, (Ebenezer Rockwood) Hoar **7** (Amos Tappan) Akerman **8** (George
  Henry) Williams **10** (Edwards) Pierrepont
  navy: **5** (Adolph Edward) Borie **7** (George Maxwell)
  Robeson
  postmaster general: **5** (James Noble) Tyner **6** (Marshall)
  Jewell **8** (James William) Marshall, (John Angel James)
  Creswell
  interior: **3** (Jacob Dolson) Cox **6** (Columbus) Delano
  8 (Zachariah) Chandler
born: 15 Point Pleasant OH
died: 15 Mount McGregor NY
buried: 9 New York NY
education: 9 West Point **17** US Military Academy
religion: 9 Methodist
author: 24 Personal Memoirs of US Grant **30** Around the
World with General Grant
political career:
  secretary of: **3** War (interim appointment)
civilian career: 6 farmer
military service: 6 US Army **8** Civil War **10** Mexican War
18 Illinois Volunteers **20** Commander of Union Army
notable events of lifetime/career: 5 Panic (of 1873)
11 Black Friday (gold panic) **16** Custer's Last Stand
  Act: **10** Salary Grab
  conspiracy: **11** Whiskey Ring
  scandal: **14** Credit Mobilier
quote: 60 "No terms except unconditional and immediate
surrender can be accepted"
father: 9 Jesse Root
mother: 6 Hannah (Simpson)
siblings: 5 Clare **10** Orvil Lynch **11** Mary Frances **13** Samuel Simpson, Virginia Paine
wife: 5 Julia (Boggs Dent)
children: 5 Ellen **9** Jesse Root **13** Frederick Dent **14** Ulysses Simpson

---

grant immunity to 4 free
5 clear, spare **6** except, excuse,
exempt **7** absolve, release, relieve **9** privilege

grantor 5 giver **8** bestower
10 benefactor

granulate 5 crush **6** powder
9 pulverize **11** crystallize

granulated 6 ground
7 crushed **8** powdered **10** pulverized **12** crystallized

granule 5 grain **7** crystal
8 particle

grape *see box*

Grapes of Wrath, The
  author: 13 John Steinbeck
  character: 4 Noah **6** Connie,
  Ma Joad, Pa Joad **7** Jim
  Casy, Tom Joad **12** Rose of
  Sharon
  director: 8 John Ford
  cast: 10 Henry Fonda
  11 Jane Darwell **12** Dorris

Bowden **13** John Carradine
15 Charley Grapewin
Oscar for: 17 supporting actress (Darwell)

graphic 4 seen **5** clear, drawn,
lucid, vivid **6** visual **7** painted,
printed, visible, written **8** distinct, explicit, forcible, lifelike,
pictured, striking **9** pictorial,
realistic, trenchant **10** expressive **11** descriptive, picturesque **12** illustrative

grappa
  type: 6 brandy **7** liqueur
  origin: 5 Italy
  made from: 9 grape
  pulp

grapple 4 face, grip, hold,
meet **5** catch, clasp, fight,
grasp, seize **6** breast, clutch,
combat, engage, fasten, tackle,
take on **7** contend, grapnel,
wrestle **8** confront, deal with,
do battle, make fast, struggle
9 encounter, large hook, lay
hold of **11** hold tightly

---

grape 5 Vitis **13** Vitis
vinifera
  varieties: 3 cat, red, sea
  4 amur, blue, bush,
  cape, rock, sand, tail
  5 bear's, bunch, frost,
  Javan, sugar, veldt
  6 canyon, Damson,
  Miller, Oregon, pigeon,
  possum, summer, winter **7** African, Bullace,
  catbird, chicken, Concord, Spanish **8** European, mountain
  9 evergreen, panhandle,
  river-bank **10** silverleaf **11** southern fox
  13 sweet mountain
  wine: 5 Gamay **6** Cayuga, Duriff, Merlot,
  Muscat, Shiraz **7** Barbera, Catawba **8** Baco
  Noir, Dolcetto, Labrusca, Nebbiolo, Verduzzo **9** Aglianico,
  Fume Blanc, Huxelrebe,
  Pinot Noir, Primitivo,
  Trebbiano, Zinfandel
  10 Chardonnay, Sangiovese **11** Chenin
  Blanc, Petite Sirah,
  Pinot Bianco, Seyval
  Blanc **13** Cabernet
  Franc, Montepulciano
  14 Sauvignon Blanc
  15 Gewurtztraminer
  17 Cabernet Sauvignon
  20 Johannisberg
  Riesling

grasp 3 get, ken **4** grab, grip, hold, sway, take **5** catch, clasp, infer, power, range, reach, savvy, scope, seize, sense, skill, sweep **6** clinch, clutch, deduce, fathom, follow, master, snatch, take in, talent **7** catch at, compass, control, embrace, grapple, mastery, seizing, seizure **8** clutches, gripping, perceive **9** handclasp, knowledge, seize upon **10** comprehend, perception, understand **13** comprehension, understanding

grasping 5 venal **6** greedy **7** hoggish, miserly, selfish, wolfish **8** covetous **9** mercenary, predatory, rapacious **10** avaricious **11** acquisitive

graspingness 5 greed **7** avarice **8** rapacity, venality **10** greediness **12** covetousness

grass *see box*

Grass, Gunter
author of: 6 Floods **8** Dog Years **10** The Tin Drum **11** Cat and Mouse, The Flounder **16** Local Anaesthetic **18** The Meeting at Telgte **20** From the Diary of a Snail **33** Headbirths or The Germans Are Dying Out

grasshopper
variety: 5 pygmy **6** meadow, monkey **7** katydid **10** band winged, cone headed, long-horned, slant-faced **11** bush katydid, leaf-rolling, short-

horned **12** shield-backed, spur-throated

grassland 3 lea **4** farm, vale, veld **5** field, pampa, plain, range, veldt **6** meadow **7** pasture, prairie, savanna **8** farmland, flatland, savannah **10** plantation

grate 3 irk, jar, rub, vex **4** bars, burr, pampa, plain, gall, rasp **5** annoy, chafe, clack, grill, grind, mince, shred **6** abrade, gnaw at, hearth, jangle, rankle, scrape, scream, screen **7** firebed, firebox, grating, lattice, scratch, screech **8** irritate **9** fireplace, pulverize **10** exasperate, firebasket **11** latticework

grateful 7 obliged **8** beholden, indebted, thankful **9** gratified, obligated **12** appreciative

gratefulness 6 thanks **9** gratitude **12** appreciation, thankfulness

Gratiae *see* **6** Graces

Gratiano
character in: 19 The Merchant of Venice
author: 11 Shakespeare

gratification 3 joy **4** glee, kick **5** bliss **6** relish, solace, thrill **7** comfort, delight, ecstasy, elation, rapture **8** gladness, humoring, pleasing, pleasure, soothing **9** enjoyment, happiness, transport **10** indulgence, jubilation, satisfying **11** contentment, enchantment **12** exhilaration, satisfaction

gratified 5 happy **7** content, pleased **9** satisfied **11** comfortable

gratify 4 suit **5** amuse, favor, humor **6** coddle, divert, pamper, please, regale, soothe, thrill, tickle **7** appease, delight, enchant, flatter, gladden, indulge, refresh, satisfy **8** enthrall, entrance, interest, recreate **9** enrapture, entertain, transport **10** compliment, exhilarate

gratifying 8 humoring, pleasant, pleasing, soothing **9** agreeable, enjoyable, indulging, pampering, rewarding **10** delightful, satisfying **11** pleasurable

grating 4 bars, fret, grid **5** grate, harsh, raspy **6** creaky, grille, shrill **7** jarring, lattice, rasping, raucous, squeaky, tracery, trellis **8** abrasive, annoying, filigree, fretwork, gridiron, jangling, piercing,

---

grass
varieties: 3 cup, cut, dog, eel, elk, mat, nut, oat, oil, pin, rib, rye, Uva **4** barn, bear, bent, blue, chee, cord, crab, deer, fish, hair, lace, love, Lyme, moor, Nard, palm, Para, rice, rush, silk, star, tape, worm, yard **5** arrow, Bahia, beach, beard, Brome, Carib, China, cloud, curly, Ditch, fever, goose, lemon, Means, Melic, Mondo, natal, quack, sedge, shave, shore, Smilo, spike, squaw, Sudan, sword, Vasey, wheat, white, witch, zebra **6** Aleppo, alkali, basket, Bengal, Buffel, Canary, carpet, Dallis, Dudder, finger, gallow, Guinea, Indian, Korean, Manila, Napier, orange, orchid, Pampas, Rescue, Rhodes, ribbon, ripple, scurvy, signal, starry, switch, Tobosa, velvet, vernal, viper's, Zoysia **7** Bermuda, Brahman, Bristle, Buffalo, Esparto, Harding, Johnson, Kleberg, Pangola, poverty, pudding, quaking, Ravenna, sea lyme, serpent, tall oat, Wallaby, Widgeon **8** Angleton, blue-eyed, blue love, Boer love, elephant, fountain, hairy cup, lazy-man's, molasses, Ree wheat, sand love, scorpion, tuber oat **9** blue conch, centipede, common rye, hairy crab, hare's-tail, Hungarian, Malojilla, Mascarene, Oregon rye, rancheria, tall wheat, water star, yellow nut **10** Amur silver, beavertail, big quaking, blue finger, citronella, English rye, false wheat, golden-eyed, Indian rice, Italian rye, Korean lawn, Kuma bamboo, purple-eyed, rabbit-foot, rabbit-tail, reed canary, tufted hair, Washington, western rye, yellow-eyed **11** annual beard, branched cup, desert wheat, domestic rye, dwarf meadow, feather love, giant finger, green needle, Lehmann love, Nepal silver, Pentz finger, prairie cord, ringed beard, St Augustine, sweet vernal, Texas needle, Texas winter, weeping love **12** Common carpet, crested wheat, crinkled hair, European dune, Indian basket, Japanese lawn, Japanese love, Korean velvet, perennial rye, slender wheat, squirreltail, western wheat **13** American beach, Australian rye, billion-dollar, European beach, Himalaya fairy, Japanese sedge, little quaking, Paraguay Bahia, plains bristle, Siberian wheat **14** African Bermuda, bluebunch wheat, Japanese carpet, Pensacola Bahia, perennial veldt, pubescent wheat, Saint Augustine, stiff-hair wheat **15** European feather, Wilmington Bahia **16** creeping windmill, Pacey's English rye **17** Australian feather, intermediate wheat, Mediterranean salt, Transvaal dog-tooth **18** Australian windmill, California blue-eyed, Mexican everlasting **19** Fairway crested wheat **20** standard crested wheat

scraping, strident **9** offensive, vexatious **10** discordant, gate of bard, irritating, unpleasant **11** cacophonous, displeasing, high-pitched **12** disagreeable, exacerbating, exasperating

grating noise 7 discord, rasping **8** grinding **9** cacophony, harshness **10** disharmony, dissonance

gratis 4 free **10** gratuitous, on the house **13** complimentary, without charge

gratitude 6 thanks **10** obligation **11** recognition **12** appreciation, beholdenness, gratefulness, thankfulness, thanksgiving **14** acknowledgment

gratuitous 4 free **6** gratis, wanton **7** donated, willing **8** baseless, unproven **9** unfounded, voluntary **10** free of cost, groundless, irrelevant, unasked for, unprovoked **11** conjectural, impertinent, presumptive, spontaneous, uncalled for, unjustified, unwarranted **13** complimentary, unrecompensed

gratuity 3 tip **4** gift **8** donation **French: 7** douceur **9** pourboire

Graustark
   author: **20** George Barr McCutcheon

grave 4 dour, sage, tomb **5** acute, crypt, mound, quiet, sober, staid, vault, vital **6** gloomy, sedate, solemn, somber, urgent **7** crucial, earnest, ossuary, serious, subdued, weighty **8** catacomb, cenotaph, critical, frowning, pressing **9** dignified, important, long-faced, mausoleum, momentous, sepulcher **10** thoughtful **11** burial ground, grim visaged, significant **13** consequential, philosophical **16** last resting place, place of interment **music: 6** solemn **7** serious

Graves, Robert
   author of: **9** I Claudius, King Jesus **14** Claudius the God **15** The White Goddess **16** Goodbye to All That

graveyard 7 charnel, ossuary **8** boneyard, boot hill, cemetery **10** churchyard, necropolis **12** memorial park, potter's field **13** burying ground

gravitate 4 fall, head, move, sink, tend **6** settle **7** be drawn, descend, incline **8** converge, zero in on **9** be prone to **10** lean toward

gravity 4 pull **6** danger, import, moment **7** concern, dignity, urgency **8** calmness, enormity, grimness, serenity, sobriety **9** emergency, magnitude, solemnity, staidness **10** attraction, gloominess, importance, sedateness, solemnness, somberness **11** consequence, earnestness, gravitation, seriousness **12** significance, tranquillity **13** consideration, crucial nature **14** critical nature, pull of the earth, thoughtfulness **16** mutual attraction

gray, grey 3 dun **4** ashy, dark, drab, pale **5** ashen, foggy, hoary, misty, murky, slate **6** cloudy, dismal, gloomy, silver, somber **7** clouded, grayish, grizzly, neutral, silvery, sunless **8** overcast **9** cheerless, pearl-gray **10** depressing, gray-haired, gray-headed **11** dove-colored, hoary-headed **12** mouse-colored, silver-haired **13** salt and pepper

Gray, Harold
   creator/artist of: **17** Little Orphan Annie

Gray, Thomas
   author of: **32** Elegy Written in a Country Churchyard

grayness 4 murk **6** pallor **8** drabness **9** bleakness **10** somberness

Grayson, Kathryn
   real name: **19** Zelma Kathryn Hedrick
   born: **14** Winston-Salem NC
   roles: **8** Show Boat **10** Kiss Me Kate **13** Anchors Aweigh, The Desert Song **15** The Vagabond King

graze 3 rub **4** crop, rasp, skim, skin **5** brush, grind, swipe **6** abrade, browse, bruise, glance, scrape **7** pasture, scratch **8** abrasion, eat grass **16** turn out to pasture

grease 3 fat, oil **4** balm, lard **5** salve **6** anoint, tallow **7** unguent **8** ointment **9** drippings, lubricant, lubricate

grease the palm 3 tip **5** bribe **6** buy off, pay off

greasy 3 fat **4** oily, waxy **5** fatty, lardy, slick **7** buttery **8** slippery, slithery **10** lardaceous, oleaginous

great *see box*

Great Ajax
   origin: **5** Greek
   hero of: **9** Trojan War

greater 4 more **5** finer **6** better, bigger, larger **8** superior

Great Escape, The
   director: **11** John Sturges
   cast: **11** James Coburn, James Garner **12** Steve McQueen **13** David McCallum **14** Charles Bronson **15** Donald Pleasance **19** Richard Attenborough
   setting: **7** Germany, POW camp

greatest 4 best, most **5** ultra **6** picked, select, utmost **7** extreme, highest, maximal, maximum, noblest, supreme **8** champion **9** first-rate **11** superlative, unsurpassed

Greatest Show on Earth, The
   director: **13** Cecil B DeMille
   cast: **11** Betty Hutton, Cornel Wilde **12** James Stewart

great 3 apt, big **4** able, a-one, fine, good, high, huge, kind, many, vast, well **5** chief, crack, grand, grave, gross, heavy, large, noble, noted, super, swell **6** adroit, choice, expert, famous, groovy, humane, loving, strong, superb **7** crucial, decided, eminent, extreme, grandly, immense, leading, mammoth, notable, serious, titanic, weighty **8** abundant, colossal, critical, enormous, esteemed, fabulous, generous, gigantic, glorious, gracious, manifold, renowned, skillful, smashing, splendid, superbly, superior, terrific, very well **9** boundless, countless, cyclopean, excellent, fantastic, first-rate, important, marvelous, momentous, monstrous, prominent, unlimited, wonderful **10** altruistic, celebrated, gargantuan, high-minded, inordinate, out-of-sight, prodigious, proficient, pronounced, remarkable, splendidly, stupendous, tremendous, voluminous **11** crackerjack, excellently, extravagant, illustrious, magnanimous, magnificent, outstanding, sensational, significant, superlative, wonderfully **12** considerable **13** consequential, distinguished, inexhaustible, magnificently, multitudinous **14** out of this world

Greece

other name: 5 Ellas 16 Hellenic Republic

capital/largest city: 6 Athens

others: 4 Enor 5 Canea, Corfu, Pylos, Volos 6 Delphi, Patras, Sparta 7 Chalcis, Corinth, Olympia, Piraeus 8 Salonika, Thessaly 9 Epidaurus, Gallipoli 10 Herakleion 11 Hermoupolis

school: 5 Crete 6 Athens, Patras, Thrace 8 Ioannina, Salonika

division: 6 Attica, Epirus, Thrace 7 Boeotia 8 Thessaly 9 Macedonia

measure: 3 pik 4 bema, piki, pous 5 baril, chous, cubit, diote, doron, maris, pekhe, podos, pygon, xylon 6 acaena, bacile, barile, cotula, dichas, gramme, hemina, koilon, lichas, milion, orgyia, palame, pechys, schene, xestes 7 amphora, bacvhel, chenica, choenix, cyathos, diaulos, metreta, stadium, stremma 8 condylos, daktylos, dekapode, dolichos, medimnos, medimnus, metretes, palaiste, plethron, plethrum, stathmos 9 hemiekton, oxybaphon

monetary unit: 5 lepta 7 drachma

weight: 3 mna, oke 4 mina, obol 5 livre, pound 6 diobol, kantar, obolos, obolus, talent 7 chalcon, drachma 8 diobolon

island: 3 Ios 5 Chios, Corfu, Crete, Delos, Melos, Naxos, Paros, Samos, Syros, Tenos, Thera, Zante 6 Andros, Euboea, Ionian, Ithaca, Lemnos, Lesbos, Patmos, Rhodes, Skyros, Thasos 7 Mykonos 8 Cyclades, Mytilene, Skiathos, Skopelos 9 Alonnisos 10 Cephalonia, Dodecanese, Samothrace 16 Northern Sporades

lake: 5 Karla, Volve 6 Copais, Kopais, Prespa, Voweis 8 Ioannina, Koroneia, Vistonis 9 Trichonis, Vegoritis

mountain: 3 Ida 4 Idhi, Oeta, Oite, Ossa 5 Athos 6 Ithome, Peleon, Pelion, Pindus 7 Grammos, Helicon, Rhodope 8 Hymettos, Smolikas, Taygetos, Taygetus 9 Parnassus 10 Hagion Oros, Lycabettus, Pentelicus

highest point: 7 Olympus

river: 4 Arta 6 Peneus, Struma, Vardar 7 Hellada, Maritsa 8 Achelous, Aliakmon

sea: 5 Crete 6 Aegean, Ionian 7 Mirtoon 13 Mediterranean

physical feature:
gulf: 7 Corinth, Saronic
peninsula: 6 Balkan 10 Chalcidice 12 Peloponnesus
plain: 7 Boeotia 8 Thessaly
plateau: 7 Arcadia
valley: 5 Nemea

people: 5 Greek 6 Achean, Dorian, Ionian 7 Aeolian, Hellene
artist: 7 El Greco
author: 5 Homer 6 Hesiod, Pindar 8 Menander 9 Aeschylus, Euripides, Sophocles 11 Kazantzakis 12 Aristophanes
god: 4 Ares, Hera, Leto, Zeus 5 Cupid 6 Apollo, Cronus, Hermes, Hestia 7 Artemis, Demeter 8 Dionysus, Poseidon 9 Aphrodite 10 Hephaestus, Persephone 12 Pallas Athena 13 Phoebus Apollo
historian: 9 Herodotus 10 Thucydides
king: 11 Constantine
lawmaker: 5 Draco, Solon 8 Lycurgus, Pericles
leader: 10 Papandreou
mathematician: 6 Euclid 10 Archimedes, Pythagoras
mythological: 5 Atlas, Helen, Jason, Medea, Paris 6 Hector, Medusa 7 Ariadne, Chimera, Pandora, Pegasus, Perseus, Theseus 8 Achilles, Heracles, Minotaur, Odysseus 9 Agamemnon, Andromeda, Iphigenia, King Minos 10 Prometheus 11 Bellerophon
orator: 11 Demosthenes
philosopher: 5 Plato 8 Socrates 9 Aristotle
physician: 11 Hippocrates
sculptor: 5 Myron 7 Phidias 10 Praxiteles
tycoon: 7 Onassis

language: 5 Greek

religion: 14 Greek Orthodoxy

place:
ruins: 5 Delos, Pella, Pylos, Samos 6 Delphi, Sparta, Thebes, Tiryns 7 Corinth, Eleusis, Elevsis, Knossos, Mycenae, Olympia 9 Acropolis, Epidaurus, Parthenon 13 Palace of Minos

feature:
coffeeshop: 7 kaphene
marketplace: 5 agora
port 7 Piraeus
presidential guard: 7 Evzones
village square: 7 plateia

food:
dish: 7 mousaka 8 moussaka, souvlaka, dolmades, souvlakia 10 shish kabob
liquor: 4 ouzo
wine: 7 retsina

13 Dorothy Lamour, Gloria Grahame **14** Charlton Heston
Oscar for: **7** picture

Great Expectations
author: **14** Charles Dickens
character: **3** Pip **7** Estella **9** Compeyson, Mr Jaggers **10** Joe Gargery **12** Abel Magwitch, Miss Havisham **13** Herbert Pocket
director: **9** David Lean
cast: **9** John Mills **11** Martita Hunt **12** Alec Guinness, Bernard Mills **13** Valerie Hobson **16** Francis L Sullivan

Great Gatsby, The
author: **16** F Scott Fitzgerald
character: **9** Jay Gatsby **11** Tom Buchanan **12** Myrtle Wilson, Nick Carraway **13** Daisy Buchanan

Great God Brown, The
author: **12** Eugene O'Neill

Great Idean Mother see
6 Cybele

great lady
French: **10** grande dame

Great Lake 4 Erie **5** Huron **7** Ontario **8** Michigan, Superior

Great Land
nickname of: **6** Alaska

greatly 6 vastly **7** largely, notably **8** markedly, mightily, very much **9** immensely **10** abundantly, enormously, infinitely, powerfully, remarkably **12** considerably, immeasurably, tremendously

great mishap 5 wreck **6** blight, fiasco **7** tragedy **8** calamity, disaster **9** cataclysm, ruination **11** catastrophe

greatness 8 eminence, nobility **9** loftiness **10** excellence, importance, notability, prominence **11** preeminence, superiority **12** magnificence **15** illustriousness

Great Profile
nickname of: **13** John Barrymore

Great Railway Bazaar, The
author: **11** Paul Theroux

great world
French: **10** grand monde

Great Ziegfeld, The
director: **14** Robert Z Leonard
cast: **8** Myrna Loy **10** Fanny Brice **11** Frank Morgan, Luise Rainer (Anna Held) **13** Virginia Bruce, William Powell
Oscar for: **7** actress (Rainer), picture

grebe 4 bird, fowl, loon **5** diver **6** dipper **7** henbill **8** dabchick **9** hell-diver **10** water witch

Grecco, Al
character in: **20** Appointment in Samarra
author: **5** O'Hara

Greco, El Greco
real name: **23** Domenikos Theotokopoulos
born: **5** Crete **6** Candia
artwork: **7** Espolio (Disrobing of Christ), Laocoon **12** View of Toledo **19** Cleaning of the Temple **20** Healing of the Blind Man **21** Burial of the Count Orgaz **27** Christ Stripped of his Garments **28** San Ildefonso at his Writing Desk **29** Cardinal Fernando Nino de Guevara **42** Christ Driving the Money-Changers from the Temple

Greece see box

greed 7 avarice, avidity, craving **8** cupidity, rapacity **11** itching palm, money-hunger, piggishness, selfishness **12** covetousness **13** rapaciousness **14** avariciousness

greediness 7 avarice **8** gluttony, rapacity, voracity **12** covetousness, graspingness **15** acquisitiveness

greedy 4 avid **5** eager **6** ardent, hungry **7** anxious, burning, craving, fervent, hoggish, piggish, selfish, swinish, wolfish **8** covetous, famished, grasping, ravenous **9** devouring, impatient, mercenary, predatory, rapacious, thirsting, voracious **10** avaricious, gluttonous, insatiable **11** acquisitive, money-hungry **12** gormandizing

Greek
language family: **12** Indo-European
ancient branch: **5** Doric, Ionic **6** Aeolic

Greek alphabet see box

Greek Anthology, The
author: **8** Cephalas, Meleager

Greek measure 4 mina **5** cubit **6** obolos, talent **7** drachma, stadion

Greek Mythology see box, p. 412

Greek uncial codex 4 Syri **6** Regius **8** Ephraemi **9** Laudianus, Vaticanus **10** Sinaiticus **11** Basiliensis **12** Alexandrinus, Sangallensis **13** Koridethianus

green 3 raw **4** jade, lawn, lime, turf **5** crude, heath, ol-

ive, rough, sward, young **6** callow, campus, common, tender, unripe **7** awkward, emerald, verdant, verdure **8** greenish, gullible, ignorant, immature, inexpert, not cured, not dried, pea-green, sea-green, unsmoked, untanned, unversed **9** blue-green, credulous, grassplot, lime-green, unfledged, unskilled, untrained **10** aquamarine, chartreuse, golf course, grass-green, greensward, kelly-green, olive green, uninformed, unmellowed, unpolished, unseasoned **11** cobalt green, forest green, undeveloped, yellow-green **12** easily fooled, green-colored, not fully aged, putting green, village green **13** inexperienced, undisciplined **14** underdeveloped **15** unsophisticated

Green Acres
character: **7** Mr Haney **8** Eb Dawson **10** Fred Ziffel, Sam Drucker **11** Doris Ziffel, Hank Kimball, Lisa Douglas **20** Oliver Wendell Douglas
cast: **8** Eva Gabor, Fran Ryan **9** Alvy Moore, Frank Cady, Tom Lester **10** Pat Buttram **11** Eddie Albert **13** Barbara Pepper, Hank Patterson
pig: **6** Arnold
town: **11** Hooterville

green at the gills 6 queasy, sickly **7** bilious **8** nauseous **9** nauseated, sickening

greenback 4 bill **8** banknote **12** treasury note **15** legal-

Greek alphabet
a: **5** alpha
b: **4** beta
ch/kh: **3** chi
d: **5** delta
e: **3** eta **7** epsilon
g: **5** gamma
i: **4** iota
k: **5** kappa
l: **6** lambda
m: **2** mu
n: **2** nu
o: **5** omega **7** omicron
p: **2** pi
ph: **3** phi
ps: **3** psi
r: **3** rho
s: **5** sigma
t: **3** tau
th: **5** theta
x: **2** xi
y: **7** upsilon
z: **4** zeta

tender note **17** silver certificate

Green Bay
 football team: **7** Packers

Green Bay Tree, The
 author: **14** Louis Bromfield

Greene, Graham
 author of: **11** The Third Man **12** Brighton Rock, Ways of Escape **14** The Human Factor **16** Monsignor Quixote, **17** The End of the Affair, The Ministry of Fear, Travels with My Aunt **19** The Heart of the Matter, The Power and the Glory

Greene, Joe
 nickname: **7** Mean Joe
 sport: **8** football
 position: **7** lineman
 team: **18** Pittsburgh Steelers

Greene, Lorne
 born: **6** Canada, Ottawa **7** Ontario
 roles: **5** Adama **7** Bonanza **11** Peyton Place **12** Autumn Leaves, The Buccaneer **13** Ben Cartwright **16** The Silver Chalice **19** Battlestar Galactica

Greene, Nathanael
 served in: **16** Revolutionary War
 rank: **16** brigadier general **20** quartermaster general
 battle: **7** Cowpens, Trenton **12** Eutaw Springs, Hobkirk's Hill **18** Guilford Court House

green-eyed monster 4 envy **8** jealousy **12** covetousness

Green for Danger
 director: **13** Sidney Gilliat
 cast: **7** Leo Genn **9** Sally Gray **11** Alastair Sim **12** Rosamund John, Trevor Howard

greenhorn 4 rube, tyro **6** novice, rookie **7** learner **8** beginner, neophyte, newcomer **9** fledgling **10** apprentice, tenderfoot **14** babe in the woods

Green Hornet, The
 character: **4** Kato **9** Britt Reid (The Green Hornet)
 cast: **8** Bruce Lee **11** Van Williams
 car: **11** Black Beauty
 creator: **11** Bert Whitman
 sidekick: **4** Kato

Green House, The
 author: **16** Mario Vargas Llosa

Greening of America, The
 author: **12** Charles Reich

greenish 6 sickly **7** bilious

Greek Mythology
 afterworld of the blessed: **7** Elysium
 amber islands: **10** Electrides
 architect of labyrinth: **8** Daedalus
 blood-sucking monster: **5** Lamia
 cupbearer to the gods: **8** Ganymede **9** Catamitus
 dragon: **8** basilisk
 drink of the gods: **6** nectar
 eagle/lion monster: **7** griffin, griffon, gryphon
 enchantress: **5** Circe
 female warrior: **6** Amazon
 fire-breathing monster: **7** Chimera
 first man: **12** Alalcomeneus
 food/drink/perfume of the gods: **8** ambrosia
 the Furies: **5** Dirae **6** Erinys, Furiae, Semnai **7** Erinyes **9** Eumenides
  names: **7** Allecto, Megaera **9** Tisiphone
 goat god: **7** Aegipan
 goddess of beauty: **6** Graces **7** Gratiae **9** Charities
  names: **4** Auxo **5** Cleta **6** Aglaia, Thalia **7** Phaenna **8** Hegemone **10** Euphrosyne
 goddess of childbirth: **8** Ilithyia **10** Eileithyia
  corresponds to Roman: **6** Lucina
 goddess of the dawn: **3** Eos
  corresponds to Roman: **6** Aurora
 goddesses of destiny: **5** Fates, Morae **6** Moerae, Moirai
  names: **5** Moira **6** Clotho **8** Lachesis
  corresponds to Roman: **6** Parcae
 goddess of discord: **4** Eris
  corresponds to Roman: **9** Discordia
 goddess of divine punishment/recklessness: **3** Ate
 goddess of divine retribution: **8** Adrastea
 goddess of the earth: **2** Ge **4** Gaea, Gaia
  corresponds to Roman: **6** Tellus
 goddess of earth/fertility: **7** Demeter
  corresponds to Roman: **5** Ceres
 goddess of earth/Hades: **5** Brimo **6** Hecate, Hekate
 goddess of fortune: **5** Tyche
  corresponds to Roman: **7** Fortuna
 goddess of healing: **4** Iaso
 goddess of health: **6** Hygeia
  corresponds to Roman: **5** Salus
 goddess of the hearth: **6** Hestia
  corresponds to Roman: **5** Vesta
 goddess of justice: **4** Dice, Dike **6** Astrea **7** Astraea
 goddesses of literature/the arts: **5** Muses **7** the Nine **8** Pierides **10** Castalides
  names: **4** Clio **5** Aoede, Erato, Mneme **6** Melete, Thalia, Urania **7** Euterpe **8** Calliope **9** Melpomene **10** Polyhymnia **11** Terpsichore
  corresponds to Roman: **7** Camenae
  muse of astronomy: **6** Urania
  muse of dancing/choral song: **11** Terpsichore
  muse of history: **4** Clio
  muse of idyllic poetry/comedy: **6** Thalia
  muse of love poetry: **5** Erato
  muse of meditation: **6** Melete
  muse of memory: **5** Mneme
  muse of music/lyric poetry: **7** Euterpe
  muse of poetry/epic: **8** Calliope
  muse of sacred music/dance: **10** Polyhymnia
  muse of song: **5** Aoede
  muse of tragedy: **9** Melpomene
 goddess of love/beauty: **6** Urania **7** Cyprian, Paphian **8** Cytherea **9** Aphrodite **10** Anadyomene
  corresponds to Roman: **5** Venus
 goddess of memory: **9** Mnemosyne
 goddess of the night: **3** Nox, Nyx
 goddess of peace: **5** Irene
  corresponds to Roman: **3** Pax
 goddess of the rainbow: **4** Iris

goddess of sailors: 5 Brizo
goddess of the sea: 10 Amphitrite
goddesses of the sea: 6 Graeae, Graiae
 names: 4 Enyo 5 Deino 9 Pemphredo
goddesses of seasons/growth/decay/social order:
 4 Hour 5 Horae
 names: 4 Dice, Dike 5 Carpo, Irene 6 Thallo 7 Eunomia
goddess of spring flowers: 6 Thallo
goddess of summer fruit: 5 Carpo
goddess of victory: 4 Nike
 corresponds to Roman: 6 Athena 8 Victoria
goddess of war: 4 Enyo
 corresponds to Roman: 7 Bellona
goddess of wisdom/fertility/arts/warfare: 6 Athena,
 Athene, Pallas, Saitis 11 Tritogeneia 12 Pallas Athena
 18 Alalcomenean Athena
 corresponds to Roman: 7 Minerva
goddess of youth/spring: 4 Hebe
god of beekeeping/winemaking/husbandry: 9 Aristaeus
god of censure/ridicule: 5 Momos, Momus
god of dreams: 6 Icelus, Oniros 7 Oneiros 8 Morpheus
god of earth: 10 Trophonius
god of Eleusinian mysteries: 7 Bacchus
god of erotic desire: 7 Himeros
god of fire/metalworking/handicrafts: 10 Hephaestus,
 Hephaistos
 corresponds to Roman: 6 Vulcan
god of the heavens: 4 Zeus
 corresponds to Roman: 4 Jove 7 Jupiter
 corresponds to Egyptian: 4 Amen, Amon 5 Ammon
 6 Amen Ra, Amon Ra
god of light/healing/music/poetry/prophecy/beauty:
 6 Apollo
god of love: 4 Eros
 corresponds to Roman: 4 Amor 5 Cupid
god of male power/procreation: 7 Priapus
 corresponds to Roman: 7 Mutinus
god of marriage: 5 Hymen 9 Hymenaeus
 corresponds to Roman: 8 Talassio
god of medicine/healing: 9 Asclepius
 corresponds to Roman: 11 Aesculapius
god of oaths: 6 Horcus
god of recovery from illness: 11 Telesphorus
god of sea/caused earthquakes: 8 Poseidon
 corresponds to Roman: 7 Neptune
god of shepherds/flocks/pastures/forests: 3 Pan
 7 Sinoeis
god of sleep: 6 Hypnos, Hypnus
 corresponds to Roman: 6 Somnus
god of the sun: 6 Helios 8 Hyperion
 corresponds to Roman: 3 Sol
god of the underworld: 6 Infiri
god of war: 4 Ares 8 Theritas
 corresponds to Roman: 4 Mars
god of wine/fertility/drama: 5 Evius 7 Bacchus
 8 Dionysus
Gorgon monster: 6 Medusa
hundred-headed monster: 5 Ladon 8 Typhoeus
islands of the blessed: 10 Hesperides
man/horse monster: 7 centaur
messenger of gods/god of roads/commerce/invention/
 cunning/thieves: 6 Hermes
 corresponds to Roman: 7 Mercury
monster that asked riddles: 6 Sphinx
monsters that turn people to stone: 7 Gorgons
moon goddess/huntress/virgin: 6 Phoebe, Selene
 7 Artemis
 corresponds to Roman: 5 Diana
 corresponds to Cretan: 11 Britomartis
nine-headed water serpent: 5 Hydra
nymph: 7 Calypso

(continued)

Greenland *see box, p. 415*

Green Mansions
 author: 8 W H Hudson
 character: 4 Rima 5 Nu-
 flo 6 Mr Abel

Greenmantle
 author: 10 John Buchan

Green Mountain State
 nickname of: 7 Vermont

Greenough, Horatio
 born: 8 Boston MA
 artwork: 16 George
 Washington 18 The
 Chanting Cherubs

Green Pastures, The
 author: 12 Marc
 Connelly

Greenstreet, Sydney
 born: 7 England
 8 Sandwich
 roles: 9 The Fat Man
 10 Casablanca 16 The
 Maltese Falcon 19 Pas-
 sage to Marseilles

green with envy 7 envious,
 jealous 8 covetous

greet 4 hail, meet 5 admit
 6 accept, accost, salute 7 receive, speak to, welcome 9 ,
 smile upon, recognize 10 bid
 welcome

greeting 6 salute 7 welcome
 8 saluting 9 reception, welcoming 10 salutation 12 introduction, presentation

greetings 4 best 5 hello 7 regards 8 respects 10 best
 wishes, good wishes, salutation 11 compliments, remembrance, well-wishing
 13 felicitations
 Latin: 5 salve

gregarious 6 genial, lively, social 7 affable 8 friendly, outgoing, sociable 9 convivial,
 talkative, vivacious 11 extroverted 13 companionable

gremlin 3 imp 5 demon,
 gnome 6 goblin

Grenada *see box, p. 415*

grenade 7 missile 9 pineapple

Grendel
 character in: 7 Beowulf
 author: 7 unknown

Grewgious, Mr
 character in: 22 The Mystery
 of Edwin Drood
 author: 7 Dickens

Grey, Joel
 real name: 8 Joel Katz
 born: 13 Cleveland Ohio
 roles: 7 Cabaret, George M
 13 Come September 23 The
 Seven Percent Solution

Greek Mythology (*continued*)
- **one-eyed giant: 7** Cyclops
- **oracle of Apollo: 13** Delphic oracle
- **personification of death: 4** Mors **8** Thanatos
- **personification of punishment/revenge: 5** Poena, Poine
- **personification of soul: 6** Psyche
- **physician to gods of Olympia: 5** Paeon
- **prophetess: 9** Alexandra, Cassandra
- **queen of heaven: 4** Hera, Here
  - *corresponds to Roman:* **4** Juno
- **race of gods: 6** Titans
  - *names:* **4** Rhea, Thia **5** Coeus, Crius **6** Cronus, Phoebe, Tethys, Themis **7** Iapetus, Oceanus **8** Hyperion **9** Mnemosyne
- **river god: 6** Asopus, Peneus, Simois **7** Inachus, Pelegon **8** Achelous
- **river in Hades: 4** Styx **5** Lethe **7** Acheron, Cocytus
  - *ferryman:* **6** Charon
  - *river of forgetfulness:* **5** Lethe
- **ruler of the winds: 6** Aeolus
- **satyr/god of the forest: 7** Silenus
- **sea god: 6** Nereus, Triton **7** Glaucus, Phorcys, Proteus
- **sea monster: 6** Scylla
- **seer: 6** Mopsus **8** Tiresias
- **serpent: 6** dipsas
- **serpent of darkness: 5** Apepi **7** Apophis
- **seven against Thebes: 6** Tydeus **8** Adrastus, Capaneus **9** Polynices **10** Amphiaraus, Hippomedon **13** Parthenopaeus
- **seven sisters: 8** Pleiades
  - *names:* **4** Maia **6** Merope **7** Alcyone, Celaeno, Electra, Sterope, Taygete
- **sorceress: 5** Medea
- **spirits of disease/evil/old age/death: 5** Keres
- **three-headed dog that guards underworld: 8** Cerberus
- **twins: 8** Dioscuri **15** Castor and Pollux
- **two-headed serpent: 11** Amphisbaena
- **underworld: 5** Hades, Pluto
  - *corresponds to Roman:* **3** Dis **5** Orcus **8** Dis Pater
- **underworld darkness: 6** Erebus
- **underworld spirit: 9** Chthonian
- **virgin huntress: 8** Atalanta, Atalante
- **whirlpool: 9** Charybdis
- **winged horse: 5** Arion **7** Pegasus
- **woman/beast monster: 6** Python **8** Delphyne
- **woman/bird monster: 5** Harpy
- **woman/serpent monster: 7** Echidna
- **wood nymph: 5** dryad

Grey, Zane
  author of: 18 Valley of Wild Horses **20** The Spirit of the Border **21** Riders of the Purple Sage, The Last of the Plainsmen

greyhound
  group of: 5 leash

Greystoke, Lord
  real identity of: 6 Tarzan

griddle cake 6 blintz, waffle **7** crumpet, hot cake, pancake **8** corncake, flapcake, flapjack **10** battercake **11** flannel cake **13** buckwheat cake
  French: 5 crepe **12** crepe suzette
  German: 11 pfannkuchen

Hungarian: 10 palacsinta
Indian: 8 chapatty

Gride, Arthur
  character in: 16 Nicholas Nickleby
  author: 7 Dickens

grief 3 woe **4** care **5** agony, worry **6** burden, misery, ordeal, sorrow **7** anguish, anxiety, concern, despair, remorse, sadness, trouble **8** distress, grieving, hardship, nuisance, vexation **9** grievance, heartache, suffering **10** affliction, desolation, discomfort, heartbreak **11** despondency, tribulation **12** wretchedness **13** inconvenience

griefstricken 7 joyless, unhappy **8** saddened, wretched **9** sorrowful **13** brokenhearted

Grieg, Edvard Hagerup
  born: 6 Bergen, Norway
  composer of: 5 I Host **8** Bergljot, In Autumn, Peer Gynt **11** Lyric Pieces **12** Landjaenning **14** Fra Holbergs Tid, Lyriske Stykker **15** Sigurd Jorsalfar **16** From Holberg's Time **17** Recognition of Land **18** Foran Sydens Kloster **22** At a Southern Convent Gate

grievance 4 beef, hurt **5** wrong **6** injury **7** outrage **8** hardship, iniquity **9** complaint, injustice **10** affliction, bone to pick, disservice

grieve 3 cry, rue, sob **4** moan, pain, wail, weep **5** be sad, mourn **6** bemoan, deject, harass, lament, sadden, sorrow **7** afflict, agonize, depress, oppress, torture **8** disquiet, distress **10** discomfort **11** be anguished

grieve over 5 mourn **6** bemoan, bewail, lament **7** cry over **8** moan over, weep over

grievous 3 sad **5** acute, grave, harsh, heavy **6** severe, tragic, woeful **7** crucial, glaring, harmful, heinous, painful, serious, very bad **8** critical, shameful, shocking **9** agonizing, appalling, atrocious, monstrous, nefarious, sorrowful **10** burdensome, calamitous, deplorable, iniquitous, lamentable, outrageous, unbearable **11** destructive, distressing, intolerable, significant **12** insufferable **13** heartbreaking

griffin
  also: 7 griffon, gryphon
  form: 7 monster
  head of: 5 eagle
  wings of: 5 eagle
  body of: 4 lion
  guards of: 4 gold
  location: 7 Scythia

Griffith, Andy
  real name: 20 Andrew Samuel Griffith
  born: 8 Mt Airy NC
  roles: 7 Matlock **13** Will Stockdale **15** A Face in the Crowd, Angel in My Pocket **18** No Time for Sergeants **19** The Andy Griffith Show

Griffith, D W
  director of: 11 Intolerance

Greenland
  alternate name: 14 Kalaalit Nunaat
  capital/largest city: 3 Nuk **8** Godthaab, The Point
  others: 4 Etah, Nord **5** Thule **6** Ivigut, Umanak **7** Godhavn, Ivigtut **10** Nanortalik **11** Julianehaab **12** Angmagssalik, Sukkertoppen **14** Christianshaab
  government: 20 home rule under Denmark
  monetary unit: 3 ore **5** krone
  island: 5 Disko
  mountain: 5 Forel, Payer **7** Khardyu **8** Peterman **15** Petermannsbjerg
  highest point: 9 Gunnbjorn **16** Gunnbjornsfjaeld
  sea: 6 Arctic **9** Greenland
  physical feature: 9 Inland Ice
    bay: **5** Disko **6** Baffin **8** Melville
    cape: **4** Jaal **6** Grivel, Walker **8** Bismarck, Brewster, Farewell, Lowenorn **11** Morris Jesup
    glacier: **10** Jacobshavn
    strait: **5** Davis **7** Denmark
  people: 3 Ita **6** Eskimo **8** European
    explorer: **10** Eric the Red
  language: 6 Danish, Eskimo **11** Greenlandic
  religion: 19 Evangelical Lutheran
  feature:
    airbase: **4** Etah **5** Thule
    animal: **7** caribou

14 Broken Blossoms **17** Orphans of the Storm, The Birth of a Nation

Griffith, Hugh
  born: 5 Wales **8** Anglesey **10** Marian Glas
  roles: 6 Ben-Hur **8** Lucky Jim, Tom Jones

griffon *see* **7** griffin

grill 3 fry **4** cook, grid, pump, quiz, sear **5** broil, query **7** broiler, grating, griddle **8** gridiron, question **9** crossbars **11** interrogate **12** cross-examine

grim 4 foul, hard, ugly **5** cruel, harsh, lurid, stern, sulky **6** brutal, fierce, gloomy, grisly, grumpy, horrid, morose, odious, severe, somber, sullen **7** austere, ghastly, hideous, inhuman, macabre, squalid, vicious **8** dreadful, fiendish, gruesome, horrible, resolute, scowling, shocking, sinister **9** appalling, ferocious, frightful, heartless, loathsome, merciless, obstinate, repellent, repugnant, repulsive, revolting **10** determined, forbidding, implacable, inexorable, relentless, unyielding

grimace 4 face **5** scowl, smirk, sneer **6** glower **7** wry face
  French: 4 moue

grime 4 dirt, dust, smut, soil, soot **5** filth **6** smudge

Grimhild
  origin: 12 Scandinavian

mentioned in: 8 Volsunga
form: 9 sorceress
husband: 5 Giuki, Gjuki
daughter: 6 Gudrun, Kudrun **7** Guthrun
son: 6 Gunnar
tricked Sigurd to marry: 6 Gudrun, Kudrun **7** Guthrun

Grimm Brothers (Jakob and Wilhelm)
  editors of: 15 Hansel and Gretel **16** Grimm's Fairy Tales

grim reaper 5 death **12** angel of death

grim-visaged 8 frowning, scowling **9** long-faced **10** stern-faced

grin 4 beam **5** smile, smirk **6** rictus, simper **11** crack a smile

grind 4 file, grit, mill, rasp, whet **5** chore, crush, gnash, grate **6** abrade, drudge, polish, powder, scrape **7** crammer, hard job, plodder, sharpen, slavery **8** bookworm, drudgery **9** granulate, pulverize, triturate

Gringoire
  character in: 23 The Hunchback of Notre Dame
  author: 4 Hugo

grip 3 bag **4** grab, hilt, hold **5** clasp, grasp, rivet, seize **6** clench, clutch, handle, retain, snatch, valise **7** attract, control, impress, mastery, satchel **8** clutches, hold fast, suitcase **9** gladstone, handclasp, handshake, retention, spellbind **10** domination, perception

gripe, gripes 4 beef, carp, fret, kick, pain, pang, rail **5** cavil, colic, spasm, whine **6** cramps, grouch, grouse, kvetch, mutter, squawk, twinge, twitch **7** grumble, protest, whining **8** complain, distress, grousing, bellyache, complaint, find fault, grievance, grumbling **10** affliction

Grisham, John
  author of: 7 The Firm **9** The Client **10** The Chamber **11** A Time to Kill **15** The Pelican Brief
  movie:
    7 The Firm
      actors: **9** Tom Cruise **11** Gene Hackman
    15 The Pelican Brief
      actors: **12** Julia Roberts **16** Denzel Washington
    9 The Client
      actors **13** Tommy Lee Jones, Susan Sarandon

grisly 4 foul, gory, grim **5** lurid **6** horrid, odious **7** ghastly, hideous, macabre **8** dreadful, gruesome, horrible, shocking, sinister **9** abhorrent, appalling, frightful, loathsome, repellent, repugnant, repulsive, revolting **10** abominable, forbidding, horrendous

Grenada
  other name: 11 Isle of Spice
  capital/largest city: 9 St Georges
  others: 8 Sauteurs
  head of state: 14 British monarch **15** governor general
  island: 8 Windward **9** Carriacon **10** Grenadines
  lake: 10 Grand Etang
  highest point: 11 St Catherine
  sea: 9 Caribbean
  physical feature:
    bay: **9** St Georges'
  people: 5 Black, Negro **6** Indian
    discoverer: **8** Columbus
  language: 7 English
  religion: 8 Anglican **10** Protestant **13** Roman Catholic
  food:
    spice: **4** mace **6** nutmeg

grit 3 rub **4** dirt, dust, guts, muck, rasp, sand, soot **5** filth, gnash, grate, nerve, pluck, spunk **6** crunch, mettle, scrape **7** courage, stamina **8** backbone, tenacity **9** fortitude **10** doggedness, resolution **12** perseverance **13** determination, grind together

Grizzly Bear State
  10 California

groan 4 howl, moan, roar, wail **5** bleat, crack, creak, whine **6** bellow, bemoan, lament, manifest, murmur, squeak **7** grumble, screech, whimper **8** complain

grocery store
  Spanish: **6** bodega

groggy 5 dazed, dizzy, dopey, shaky, woozy **6** addled, punchy **7** muddled, reeling, stunned **8** confused, sluggish, unsteady **9** befuddled, lethargic, perplexed, stupefied **10** bewildered, punch-drunk, staggering

groom 4 comb, wash **5** boots, brush, curry, dress, drill, preen, prime, primp, train, valet **6** flunky, lackey, spouse **7** clean up, consort, develop, educate, footman, freshen, hostler, husband, prepare, refresh, rub down, servant **8** exercise, initiate, make neat, make tidy, practice, spruce up **9** currycomb, make ready, stableboy **10** bridegroom, manservant **12** indoctrinate **13** livery servant

groove 3 cut, rut, use **4** rule **5** flute, habit, score, usage **6** custom, furrow, gutter, hollow, trench **7** channel, cutting, scoring **8** practice **9** procedure **10** beaten path, convention **11** corrugation **12** fixed routine, second nature

grope 3 paw **5** probe **6** finger, fumble **7** fish for, venture **9** feel about **11** feel one's way, move blindly, try one's luck **13** search blindly

Gropius, Walter
  architect of: **5** Fagus (factory) **7** Bauhaus (Dessau) **13** Pan Am Building (NYC) **31** Harvard University Graduate Center

gross 3 bag, big, fat **4** bulk, earn, huge, lewd, mass, rank, reap, vast **5** bulky, crude, great, heavy, large, obese, plain, sheer, total, utter, whole **6** carnal, coarse, earthy, entire, pick up, ribald, smutty, sordid, take in, vulgar **7** glar-

ing, heinous, immense, lump sum, massive, obscene, obvious, titanic, uncouth **8** colossal, complete, enormous, flagrant, gigantic, improper, indecent, manifest, unseemly, unwieldy **9** aggregate, downright, egregious, lecherous, monstrous, offensive, unrefined **10** gargantuan, indelicate, lascivious, licentious, outrageous, overweight, prodigious, stupendous **11** unequivocal, unmitigated, unqualified

Grossel, Ira
  real name of: **12** Jeff Chandler

grossness 7 obesity **8** hugeness, lewdness, ribaldry **9** crudeness, heaviness, indecency, obscenity, roughness, vulgarity **10** coarseness, indelicacy, inelegance **14** lasciviousness

grossularite
  species: **6** garnet

Gros Ventre *see* **7** Hidatsa

grotesque 3 odd **4** wild **5** antic, weird **6** absurd, exotic, far-out, rococo, way-out **7** baroque, bizarre, strange **8** deformed, fanciful, peculiar **9** contorted, distorted, eccentric, fantastic, misshapen, odd-shaped, unnatural **10** outlandish **11** extravagant, incongruous **12** preposterous

grotto 4 cave **6** burrow, cavern, hollow, recess, tunnel **8** catacomb

grouch 3 cry **4** beef, carp, crab, fret, kick, mope, pout, rail, sulk **5** cavil, crank, gripe, growl, moper, whine **6** grouse, mutter, pouter **7** grumble, killjoy, protest **8** complain, grumbler **9** bellyache, find fault **10** complainer, curmudgeon, spoilsport, wet blanket

grouchy 5 cross, testy **6** crabby, cranky, grumpy, touchy **8** snappish **10** ill-humored, out of sorts **11** ill-tempered **12** cantankerous **13** short-tempered

ground, grounds 3 set, sod **4** area, base, call, dirt, farm, land, loam, soil, turf, yard **5** acres, basis, beach, cause, dregs, drill, earth, field, found, lawns, realm, teach, train **6** campus, domain, estate, excuse, inform, motive, object, reason, region, secure, settle, sphere, strand **7** account, confirm, deposit, dry land, educate, founder, gardens, habitat, prepare, purpose, support, terrain **8** district, exercise, firm

land, initiate, instruct, occasion, organize, practice, premises, property, province, sediment, the earth **9** arguments, bailiwick, establish, fix firmly, institute, principle, rationale, settlings, territory **10** discipline, inducement, real estate, terra firma **11** pros and cons **12** indoctrinate **14** considerations

grounded 5 based **6** kept in, taught **7** aground, beached, bounded, drilled, founded, secured, trained **8** informed, prepared, stranded **9** foundered, initiated **10** kept at home, instructed, restricted **11** disciplined, established **12** washed ashore **13** indoctrinated

grounding 8 training **9** education **10** background, experience **11** preparation **14** indoctrination **15** familiarization

groundless 4 idle **5** empty, false **6** faulty, flimsy, unreal, untrue **8** baseless, needless, unproved **9** erroneous, illogical, imaginary, unfounded **10** chimerical, fallacious, gratuitous **11** uncalled for, unjustified, unsupported, unwarranted **13** unjustifiable, without reason

groundwork 4 base, root **5** basis **6** cradle, ground, origin, source, spring **7** bedrock, footing, grounds, taproot **8** keystone, learning, planning, practice, training **9** spadework **10** foundation **11** cornerstone, fundamental, preparation **12** fundamentals, underpinning **14** apprenticeship, indoctrination

group 3 set **4** band, clan, file, gang, herd, pack, sift, size, sort **5** align, bunch, class, crowd, flock, grade, hoard, index, party, place, range, swarm, tribe, troop **6** assign, branch, circle, clique, family, hobnob, league, line up, mingle, throng **7** arrange, catalog, cluster, combine, company, consort, coterie, faction, marshal, section, species, variety **8** classify, division, graduate, organize, register **9** associate, gathering **10** assemblage, collection, coordinate, detachment, fraternity, fraternize **11** aggregation, alphabetize, association, brotherhood, subdivision **12** congregation **14** classification, representation

Group, The
  author: **12** Mary McCarthy

grouping 7 sorting **8** arraying, ordering **10** assemblage, assortment **11** arrangement, disposition **12** distribution, organization

group of performers 6 troupe **7** company **8** ensemble

Group Portrait of a Lady author: **12** Heinrich Boll

grouse 4 beef, crab, fret, fume, fuss, kick **5** gripe **6** grouch, mutter, squawk, take on **7** carry on, grumble **8** complain, gamebird **9** bellyache

grove 4 bosk **5** brake, copse **6** forest, pinery, timber **7** coppice, orchard, thicket, wood lot **8** wildwood, woodland **9** shrubbery **10** plantation

grovel 4 fawn **5** cower, crawl, stoop, toady **6** cringe, kowtow, snivel **7** flatter, truckle **12** bow and scrape **13** demean oneself, humble oneself **14** lick the boots of

groveling 6 abject **7** fawning, servile **8** cowering, crawling, cringing, toadying **9** kowtowing, truckling **11** bootlicking **17** bowing and scraping

grow 3 bud, sow, wax **4** boom, farm, rise, till **5** bloom, breed, plant, raise, ripen, surge, swell, widen **6** become, expand, extend, flower, garden, mature, spread, sprout, thrive **7** advance, amplify, blossom, develop, enlarge, fill out, get to be, improve, magnify, produce, prosper, shoot up, stretch, succeed **8** come to be, flourish, fructify, increase, mushroom, progress, spring up, vegetate **9** cultivate, germinate, propagate, skyrocket **10** aggrandize

Growing Up in New Guinea author: **12** Margaret Mead

growl 4 fret, snap **5** croak, grind, gripe, groan, grunt, snarl, whine **6** grouse, murmur, mutter, rumble **7** grumble **8** complain, talk back

grown-up 3 big, man **4** lady, ripe **5** adult, of age, woman **6** mature, senior **7** worldly **9** full-blown, full-grown, gentleman **11** full-fledged **13** sophisticated

growth 4 crop, hump, lump, rise **5** gnarl, prime, surge, swell, tumor **6** sowing, spread **7** advance, harvest, produce, success **8** increase, maturity, planting, progress **9** expansion, extension, flowering, increment **10** burgeoning, mature-

ness, production, prospering **11** advancement, cultivation, development, enlargement, excrescence, flourishing, improvement, propagation **12** augmentation, mass of tissue **13** amplification
   goddess of: **4** Hour **5** Horae

Groza, Lou
   nickname: **6** The Toe
   sport: **8** football
   team: **15** Cleveland Browns

grub 3 bum, dig **4** food, toil, worm **5** cadge, dig up, larva, mooch, slave **6** drudge, sponge **7** rummage

grubber 5 slave **6** drudge, toiler **7** laborer

grubby 4 foul **5** dirty, grimy, messy, muddy, nasty, seedy, tacky **6** beat-up, filthy, frowzy, frumpy, shabby, shoddy, sloppy, smudgy, soiled, sordid **7** squalid, unclean, unkempt **8** begrimed, slovenly, unwashed **9** besmeared **10** bedraggled

grudge 4 envy **5** pique, spite **6** animus, hatred, malice, rancor, resent **7** dislike, ill will **8** aversion, begrudge **9** animosity **10** resentment **11** malevolence **12** hard-feelings

grudging 7 envious **8** hesitant, spiteful **9** reluctant, resentful, unwilling **10** ungenerous **13** penny-pinching

grueling 4 hard **6** brutal, tiring **7** racking **9** fatiguing, punishing, torturous **10** exhausting

gruesome 4 gory, grim **5** awful **6** grisly, horrid **7** fearful, ghastly, hideous, macabre **8** horrible, shocking, terrible **9** frightful, loathsome, repellent, repulsive, revolting **10** forbidding, horrendous, horrifying **13** bloodcurdling, spine-chilling

gruff 4 curt, rude, sour, tart **5** bluff, blunt, harsh, husky, raspy, rough, sharp, short, stern, sulky, surly **6** abrupt, croaky, crusty, grumpy, hoarse, ragged, sullen **7** bearish, brusque, caustic, crabbed, cracked, grouchy, peevish, throaty, uncivil, waspish **8** churlish, guttural, impolite, snarling, strident **9** bristling, insulting **10** ill-humored, ill-natured, ungracious **11** ill-tempered **12** discourteous

grumble 4 fret **5** chafe, gripe, growl **6** grouch, grouse, mutter **8** complain **9** find-fault

grump 4 crab **5** crank

6 grouch **8** grumbler, sourball **10** curmudgeon

grumpy 4 sour **5** moody, sulky, surly, testy **6** crabby, cranky, crusty, sullen **7** grouchy, peevish, pettish **8** churlish **9** irritable, splenetic **10** ill-humored, out of humor, out of sorts **11** disgruntled, ill-disposed, ill-tempered **12** cantankerous

grunt 3 cry **4** bark, call, gasp, howl **5** burro, croak, groan, snort, utter **6** bellow, grouch, mumble, murmur, mutter, shriek **7** howling, whisper **8** complain **9** ululation **11** foot soldier, infantryman

Grunwald, Matthais (Grunewald, Mathis)
   real name: **23** Mathis Gothardt Neithardt
   born: **7** Germany **8** Wurzburg
   artwork: **14** The Crucifixion **15** The Resurrection **20** Altarpiece at Isenheim

Grushenka
   character in: **20** The Brothers Karamazov
   author: **11** Dostoyevsky

Gryce, Percy
   character in: **15** The House of Mirth
   author: **7** Wharton

Grynaeus
   epithet of: **6** Apollo

gryphon see **7** griffin

Guam see box, p. 418

Guarani (Caingua)
   language family: **7** Guarani
   location: **6** Brazil **8** Paraguay **9** Argentina **12** South America
   allied to: **4** Tupi

guarantee, guaranty 4 avow, bail, bond, pawn, word **5** swear **6** affirm, allege, assure, attest, avowal, insure, pledge, surety **7** deposit, endorse, promise, sponsor, testify, voucher, warrant **8** contract, covenant, security, vouch for, warranty **9** agreement, answer for, assurance, insurance, testimony **10** collateral, underwrite **11** affirmation, endorsement, word of honor **12** give one's word

guard 4 mind, save, tend **5** watch **6** attend, convoy, defend, escort, patrol, picket, screen, secure, sentry, shield, warder **7** conduct, defense, protect, shelter **8** defender, garrison, guardian, keep safe, preserve, security, sentinel, watchdog, watchman **9** bodyguard, concierge, custodian, guardsman, protector, safe-

Guam

capital: 5 Agana
largest city: 8 Tamuning
others: 4 Agat, Apra, Toto, Yigo 5 Magua 6 Dededo, Merizo 8 Inarajan, Mangilao, Mongmong, Sinajana, Talofofo, Tamuning 9 Barrigada, Finegayan, Santa Rita
member of: 7 Mariana (islands)
mountain: 5 Tenjo
highest point: 6 Lamlam
sea: 7 Pacific 10 Philippine
people: 7 Spanish 8 American, Chamorro, Filipino 11 Micronesian
explorer: 8 Magellan
ruler: 5 Japan, Spain 12 United States
language: 7 English 8 Chamorro
religion: 16 Roman Catholicism
feature: 7 typhoon 9 coral reef
Air Force base: 8 Andersen
product: 5 copra 6 banana, papaya

guard, watch over 10 doorkeeper, gatekeeper, protection 12 preservation 13 keep watch over

guard against 6 beware 10 look out for 11 take warning, watch out for

guarded 4 wary 5 cagey, chary, leery 7 careful, heedful, mindful, prudent 8 cautious, discreet, hesitant 9 in custody, protected, tentative 10 restrained, suspicious, under guard 11 circumspect, on one's guard

guardian 5 guard 6 convoy, escort, keeper, patrol, patron, picket, sentry, warden, warder 7 curator, trustee 8 advocate, champion, defender, sentinel, shepherd, wardsman, watchdog 9 attendant, bodyguard, caretaker, conductor, custodian, preserver, protector, safeguard, vigilante 10 benefactor 11 conservator 13 friend at court, guardian angel 14 legal custodian

guardian of a place
Latin: 10 genius loci

guardianship 4 care 6 charge 7 custody, keeping 10 protec-

tion 11 safekeeping, supervision, trusteeship

Guatemala *see box*

guava 7 Psidium 16 Psidium guineense
varieties: 5 apple 6 common, purple, yellow 7 Cattley, Chilean 9 pineapple 10 Costa Rican, strawberry 13 yellow cattley 16 purple strawberry, yellow strawberry

Gubitosi, Michael James Vijencio

real name of: 11 Robert Blake

Gudrun

also: 6 Kudrun 7 Guthrun
origin: 12 Scandinavian
mentioned in: 8 Volsunga
father: 5 Giuki, Gjuki 6 Hertel
mother: 8 Grimhild
brother: 6 Gunnar
husband: 4 Atli 6 Herwig, Sigurd
killed: 4 Atli
corresponds to: 9 Kriemhild

Guerrillas

author: 9 V S Naipaul

guess 4 deem, view 5 fancy, judge, opine, think 6 assume, belief, deduce, divine, gather, reckon, regard, theory 7 believe, daresay, feeling, imagine, opinion, predict, suppose, surmise, suspect, venture 8 conclude, estimate, theorize 9 postulate, speculate, suspicion 10 assumption, conjecture, divination, hypothesis, prediction 11 hypothesize, make a stab at, postulation, presumption, speculation, supposition

guesswork 7 surmise 10 con-

Guatemala

capital/largest city: 13 Guatemala City
others: 4 Ocos 5 Coban, Vieja 6 Chahal, Chisec, Cuilco, Flores, Iztapa, Jalapa, Salama, Solola, Tacana, Tecpan, Yaloch, Zacapa 7 Antigua, Cuilapa, Jutiapa, San Jose 8 Progreso 9 Escuintla, Tiquisate 10 Livingston 11 Totonicapan 13 Puerto Barrios, Quezaltenango 14 San Pedro Carcha 16 Chichicastenango
school: 9 San Carlos
measure: 4 vara 6 cuarta, tercia 7 cajuela, manzana 10 caballeria
monetary unit: 4 peso 7 centavo, quetzal
weight: 4 caja 5 libra
lake: 5 Dulce, Guija, Peten 6 Izabal 7 Atitlan 9 Amatitlan, Peten Itza
mountain: 4 Agua, Mico 5 Fuego, Madre 6 Pacaya, Tacana 7 Atitlan, Toliman 8 La Candon, Las Minas 10 Acatenango, Santa Maria 12 Cuchumatanes
highest point: 8 Tajumuko 9 Tajamulco
river: 4 Azul 5 Bravo, Dulce, Lapaz 6 Belize, Chixoy, Negino, Pasion, Samala 7 Chiapas, Motagua, Sarstun, Sastoon 8 Polochic, Rio Dulce, Sarstoon 10 Usumacinta
sea: 7 Pacific 8 Atlantic 9 Caribbean
physical feature:
  bay: 8 Amatique
  gulf: 8 Honduras
people: 3 Mam 4 Chol, Itza, Ixil, Maya 5 Xinca 6 Caribe, Quiche 7 ladinos, mestizo, Pocomam 13 Guatemaltecos
language: 6 Quiche 7 Spanish
religion: 13 Roman Catholic
place:
  church: 10 Santo Tomas
  ruins: 5 Mayan, Tikal 8 Uaxactun
feature:
  bird: 7 quetzal
  clarinet: 8 chirimta
  dance: 5 elson 8 guarimba
  flute: 3 xul
  military dictator: 8 Caudillo
food:
  dish: 6 pepian 10 enchiladas 13 gallo en chicha
  fruit: 4 anay

jecture, hypothesis **11** supposition **13** shot in the dark

guest 5 diner **6** caller, client, friend, inmate, lodger, patron, roomer **7** boarder, company, habitue, invitee, patient, visitor **8** customer **9** sojourner **10** frequenter **14** paying customer

Guest, Edgar A
author of: **12** A Heap of Livin'

Guest, Judith
author of: **14** Ordinary People

guffaw 4 howl **6** scream **10** belly laugh, horse laugh

Guglielmi, Rodolfo
real name of: **16** Rudolph Valentino

Guicciardini, Francesco
author of: **13** Storia d'Italia

guidance 3 tip **4** clue, help, hint, lead **6** advice, escort **7** conduct, counsel, pointer **8** auspices **9** direction **10** leadership, management, protection, suggestion **11** information, instruction, supervision **12** intelligence **13** enlightenment

guide 4 lead, rule **5** model, pilot, steer, usher **6** beacon, convoy, direct, escort, govern, handle, leader, manage, marker, master, mentor **7** adviser, command, conduct, control, example, marshal, monitor, oversee, pattern, steerer, teacher **8** chaperon, cicerone, director, engineer, helmsman, landmark, lodestar, maneuver, polestar, regulate, shepherd, signpost **9** accompany, attendant, conductor, counselor **10** manipulate

guidebook 5 bible **6** manual **8** Baedeker, handbook **13** reference book

Guidry, Ron (Ronald Ames)
nickname: **18** Louisiana Lightning
sport: **8** baseball
position: **7** pitcher
team: **14** New York Yankees

guild 5 order, union **6** league **7** company, society **8** alliance **9** coalition **10** craft union, federation, fraternity, labor union, sisterhood, trade union **11** association, brotherhood, confederacy, corporation

Guildenstern
character in: **6** Hamlet
author: **11** Shakespeare

guile 5 craft, fraud **6** deceit, tricks **7** cunning, slyness **8** ar-

tifice, strategy, trickery, wiliness **9** chicanery, deception, duplicity, treachery **10** artfulness, craftiness, dishonesty, hanky-panky, stratagems, trickiness **11** fraudulence **13** sharp practice

guileless 4 open **5** frank, naive **6** candid, honest, simple **7** artless, natural, sincere **8** harmless, innocent, truthful **9** ingenuous, innocuous **10** aboveboard, unaffected **11** undesigning, unoffending **15** straightforward, unselfconscious, unsophisticated

guilelessness 6 candor **9** innocence, sincerity **10** candidness, directness **11** artlessness **13** ingenuousness

guilt 3 sin **4** blot, vice **5** shame, wrong **6** infamy, stigma **7** misdeed **8** disgrace, dishonor, misdoing, trespass **9** black mark, turpitude **10** guiltiness, misconduct, sinfulness, wrongdoing **11** criminality, culpability, degradation, delinquency, dereliction, humiliation, misbehavior, self-disgust **13** transgression

guiltless 4 good, pure **5** clean **6** chaste **7** angelic, sinless **8** innocent, unfallen, virtuous **9** blameless, childlike, fault-

less **10** immaculate, inculpable, unblamable **11** uncorrupted
French: **12** sans reproche

guilt-stricken 7 ashamed

guilty 5 sorry, wrong **6** erring, sinful **7** ashamed, corrupt, hangdog, immoral **8** blamable, contrite, criminal, culpable, penitent, sheepish **9** offensive, regretful, repentant **11** blameworthy **18** conscience-stricken

Guilty Pleasures
author: **15** Donald Barthelme

Guinea see box

Guinea-Bissau see box, **p. 420**

Guinevere
character in: **16** Arthurian romance
husband: **6** Arthur
lover: **8** Lancelot

Guinness, Sir Alec
born: **6** London **7** England
roles: **8** Star Wars **11** Oliver Twist **13** Doctor Zhivago **14** Our Man in Havana, The Ladykillers **15** A Passage to India, Ben Obi Wan Kenobi, Lavender Hill Mob **16** Lawrence of Arabia **17** Great Expectations **21** Kind Hearts and Coronets **22** Tinker Tailor Soldier Spy **23** The

---

Guinea
other name: **12** French Guinea **13** Rivieres du Sud
capital/largest city: **7** Conakry
others: **4** Boke, Fria, Labe **5** Beyla **6** Dabola, Kankan, Kindia **7** Dubreka, Siguiri **8** Kerouane **9** Kouroussa, Nzerekore
measure: **7** jacktan
monetary unit: **4** iliy, syli **5** franc **6** cauris
weight: **4** akey, piso, uzan **5** benda, seron **6** quinto **8** aguirage
island: **3** Los **5** Tombo **7** Tristao
mountain: **4** Loma **6** Tamgue **11** Fouta Djalon
highest point: **5** Nimba
river: **4** Milo **5** Kogon, Niger **6** Bafing, Faleme, Gambia **7** Kolente, Senegal **8** Konkoure, Tinkisso **13** Great Scarcies
sea: **8** Atlantic
physical feature:
  cape: **5** Verga
people: **4** Koma, Loma, Nalu, Susu, Toma **5** Kissi, Manon **6** Fulani, Guerzi **7** Landoma, Malinke **8** Kouranke, Landuman **11** Kissi-Sherbo **12** Guerze-Kpelle
language: **5** Fulbe, Mande **6** Arabic, French, Fulani **7** English
religion: **5** Islam **7** animism
feature:
  plant: **11** globeflower
  tree: **4** akee **5** dalli

Guinea-Bissau
other name: 16 Portuguese Guinea
  capital/largest city: 6 Bissau
  others: 4 Buba 5 Catio, Farim 6 Bafata, Bolama, Cacheu, Cacine, Dandum, Mansoa 7 Bissora, Bubaque, San Joav 9 Fulacunda 10 Nova Lamego 11 Madina do Boe, Madine do Boe, Sao Domingos
  monetary unit: 4 peso 6 escudo 8 centavos
  island: 4 Roxa 6 Orango 7 Bijagos, Formosa
  river: 4 Geba 6 Cacheu, Mansoa 7 Corubal
  sea: 8 Atlantic
  people: 6 Fulani 7 Balanta, Balante, mulatto 8 Mandingo, Mandyako
  language: 5 Fulah 7 Balante, Crioulo 8 Mandingo 10 Portuguese 21 Cape Verde-Guinea Creole
  religion: 5 Islam 7 animism 12 Christianity

Bridge on the River Kwai (Oscar)

guise 4 garb, mode 5 dress, habit 6 attire 7 apparel, clothes, costume, fashion 8 clothing, disguise, pretense 10 masquerade

Gujarati
  language family: 12 Indo-European
  branch: 11 Indo-Iranian
  group: 5 Indic
  spoken in: 5 (northern) India

Gulag Archipelago, The
  author: 23 Aleksandr Solzhenitsyn Jr

gulch 3 gap 4 rift 5 abyss, chasm, cleft, crack, gorge, gully, split 6 arroyo, breach, divide, ravine 8 crevasse

gulf 4 cove, rent, rift 5 abyss, chasm, cleft, firth, fjord, gully, inlet, split 6 canyon, lagoon 7 estuary, opening 8 crevasse 10 separation

gull 3 gyp 4 dupe, rook 5 cozen, trick 7 deceive, defraud, sea gull, sea bird, swindle 9 bamboozle, victimize

gullet 3 maw 4 craw, crop 5 belly, gorge, tummy 6 dewlap, throat 7 abdomen, channel, stomach, weasand 9 beer belly, esophagus

gullible 5 green, naive 6 simple 8 innocent, trustful, trusting 9 credulous 11 easily duped 12 easily fooled, overtrusting, unsuspicious 13 easily cheated, inexperienced 14 easily deceived 15 unsophisticated

Gulliver's Travels
  author: 13 Jonathan Swift
  character: 14 Lemuel Gulliver
  visited: 6 Laputa, Yahoos 8 Blefuscu, Lilliput, Luggnagg 9 Balnibari 10 Houyhnhnms 11 Brobdingnag 12 Glubbdubdrib

gully 3 gap 5 ditch, gorge, gulch 6 defile, furrow, gutter, ravine, trench 7 channel 11 small canyon, small valley, watercourse 13 drainage ditch

gulp 4 bolt, swig, wolf 5 quaff, swill 6 devour, guzzle 7 swallow, toss off 8 mouthful

gulp down 4 bolt 6 devour, gobble 7 swallow 8 gobble up, wolf down

gum 3 wax 5 latex, resin 6 chicle 8 mucilage 10 Eucalyptus
  varieties: 3 cup, red 4 blue, cape, gray, rose, snow, sour 5 apple, black, cider, coral, giant, gully, Karri, Manna, sugar, swamp, sweet 6 cotton, Deane's, desert, gimlet, salmon, snappy, Tupelo 7 Barbary, cabbage, Fuchsia, maiden's, Morocco, scarlet, spotted 8 Formosan, Lehmann's, mountain, scribbly, spinning 9 forest red, Murray red, steedman's 10 Australian, candle-bark, red-spotted, Sydney blue, Timor white, tumble-down, urn-fruited 11 Blakely's red, blue weeping, salmon white, small-leaved, strickland's 12 lemon-scented, red-flowering, silver-dollar 13 American sweet, Oriental sweet, Tasmanian blue, Tasmanian snow 14 yellow-flowered 15 Omeo round-leaved, round-leaved snow 16 rough-barked manna, scarlet-flowering 17 heart-leaved silver 20 silver-leaved mountain

Gumm, Frances
  real name of: 11 Judy Garland

gummed 5 glued, gummy, stuck 6 sticky 8 adhering, adhesive

Gummidge, Mrs
  character in: 16 David Copperfield
  author: 7 Dickens

gummy 5 gluey, gooey, gunky 6 gloppy, sticky, viscid 7 rubbery, viscous 8 adhesive 10 gelatinous 12 mucilaginous

gumption 3 zip 4 dash, push 5 drive, spunk, verve 6 energy, hustle, pizazz, spirit 7 courage 10 enterprise, get-up-and-go, initiative 12 forcefulness 14 aggressiveness 15 resourcefulness

gumshoe 4 dick 6 shamus 9 detective 10 private eye 12 investigator

gun 3 aim, gat, rod, try 4 Colt, hunt, iron 5 piece, rifle, shoot 6 cannon, Magnum, mortar, musket, pistol 7 attempt, carbine, firearm, Gatling, go after, Long Tom, shotgun 8 howitzer, ordnance, revolver 9 automatic, Big Bertha, derringer, equalizer, flintlock, forty-five, twenty-two, Remington 10 fieldpiece, machine gun, six-shooter, three-fifty, Walther PPK, Winchester 11 blunderbuss, thirty-eight, trusty-rusty 12 fowling piece, muzzle loader, shooting iron 13 Kentucky rifle 14 artillery piece, Smith and Wesson
  invented by:
    breechloader: 8 Thornton
    magazine: 9 Hotchkiss
    silencer: 5 Maxim

Gunga Din
  story in: 18 Barrack-Room Ballads
  author: 14 Rudyard Kipling
  director: 13 George Stevens
  cast: 8 Sam Jaffe 9 Cary Grant 12 Joan Fontaine 14 Victor McLaglen 18 Douglas Fairbanks Jr
  setting: 5 India
  remade as: 13 Soldiers Three 14 Sergeants Three

gunman 6 bandit, outlaw, robber, sniper 7 hoodlum 9 assailant, desperado, holdup man

Gunn, Ben
  character in: 14 Treasure Island
  author: 9 Stevenson

Gunnar
  origin: 12 Scandinavian
  father: 5 Giuki, Gjuki
  mother: 8 Grimhild
  sister: 6 Gudrun, Kudrun 7 Guthrun
  wife: 8 Brynhild
  Brynhild won by: 6 Sigurd

Gunsmoke
  character: **3** Sam (the bartender) **8** Doc (Dr Galen) Adams **10** Quint Asper **11** Newly O'Brien **12** Chester Goode, Festus Haggen, Kitty Russell (Miss Kitty) **18** Marshall Matt Dillon **24** Clayton Thaddeus (Thad) Greenwood
  cast: **9** Ken Curtis **10** Buck Taylor, Roger Ewing **11** Amanda Blake, James Arness **12** Burt Reynolds, Dennis Weaver, Glenn Strange, Milburn Stone
  setting: **9** Dodge City
  saloon: **10** Longbranch

Guns of August, The
  author: **15** Barbara W Tuchman

Guns of Navarone, The
  director: **12** J Lee Thompson
  based on novel by: **15** Alistair MacLean
  cast: **10** David Niven **11** Gregory Peck, James Darren **12** Anthony Quinn, Stanley Baker **13** Anthony Quayle

Gunther
  origin: **8** Germanic
  mentioned in: **14** Nibelungenlied
  king of: **8** Burgundy
  wife: **8** Brunhild
  sister: **9** Kriemhild
  killed by: **9** Kriemhild

Guppy
  character in: **10** Bleak House
  author: **7** Dickens

Gurdin, Natasha
  real name of: **11** Natalie Wood

gurgle 5 plash **6** babble, bubble, burble, murmur, ripple **7** sputter **8** bubbling, gurgling

guru 5 guide **6** leader, master **7** teacher **9** preceptor **10** instructor

gush 3 gab, gas, jet, run **4** blab, bull, rush, well **5** issue, prate, spout, spurt **6** babble, burble, drivel, hot air, splash, squirt, stream **7** baloney, blather, blabber, chatter, pour out, prattle, rubbish, torrent, twaddle **8** nonsense, outburst, rattle on **10** outpouring **11** mawkishness **12** emotionalism **14** sentimentalism, talk effusively **16** run off at the mouth

gushiness 12 effusiveness, emotionalism **17** demonstrativeness

gushing 6 lavish **7** pouring, profuse **8** effusive, spurting

10 flattering **11** free-flowing **12** demonstrative, unrestrained **16** overenthusiastic

gushy 8 effusive **12** unrestrained **13** demonstrative **16** overenthusiastic

gussy up 5 adorn **7** dress up, enhance **8** beautify, decorate, ornament **9** embellish

gust 3 fit **4** blow, puff, wind **5** blast, burst, draft **6** breeze, flurry, squall, zephyr **8** outbreak, outburst, paroxysm **9** explosion

Gustaffson, Greta Louisa
  real name of: **10** Greta Garbo

Guster
  character in: **10** Bleak House
  author: **7** Dickens

gusto 3 joy **4** zeal, zest **5** savor **6** fervor, relish **7** delight **8** appetite, pleasure **10** enthusiasm **12** appreciation, exhilaration, satisfaction

gusto, con
  music: **9** with style, with taste

gusty 5 blowy, windy **6** breezy **7** squally **8** blustery

gut 4 raze **5** belly, clean, level, tummy **6** bowels, paunch, ravage **7** abdomen, consume, midriff, stomach, viscera **8** entrails, lay waste **9** bay window, beer belly, spare tire **10** disembowel, eviscerate, intestines, midsection **11** breadbasket

guten abend 11 good evening

Gutenberg
  nationality: **6** German
  inventor of: **11** movable type
  printer of: **14** Gutenberg Bible

guten morgen 11 good morning

guten tag 7 good day

Guthrie, A B Jr
  author of: **6** Arfive **9** The Big Sky **10** The Way West **13** The Last Valley **16** Fair Land Fair Land, The Blue Hen's Chick, The Thousand Hills

Guthrun *see* **6** Gudrun

Gutman, Casper
  character in: **16** The Maltese Falcon
  author: **7** Hammett

guts 4 dash, grit **5** nerve, pluck, spunk **6** bowels, daring, mettle,

spirit, vitals **7** bravado, bravery, courage, gizzard, innards, insides, viscera **8** audacity, backbone, boldness **9** fortitude **10** intestines **11** intrepidity

gutsy 4 game **5** brave **6** heroic, plucky **7** doughty, valiant **8** fearless, intrepid, stalwart, unafraid, valorous **9** dauntless, undaunted **10** courageous **11** lionhearted, unflinching **12** stouthearted

guttural 3 low **4** deep **5** gruff, harsh, husky, raspy, thick **6** hoarse **7** throaty **8** croaking **12** inarticulate

guy 3 boy, joe, kid, man **4** body, chap, dude, gent, rope **5** bloke, human, joker **6** fellow, hombre, person **8** blighter, upholder **9** supporter **10** individual

Guyana
  name means: **12** land of waters
  other name: **13** British Guiana
  capital/largest city: **10** Georgetown
  others: **7** Charity **8** Hyde Park, Rosignol **9** Jonestown, Mackenzie
  island: **6** Leguan **8** Wakenaam
  mountain: **5** Amuku, Ariwa, Kamoa **6** Akarai, Kanuku **7** Caburai **9** Pacaraima
  highest point: **7** Roraima
  river: **5** Waini **6** Barama **7** Amakura, Baruima, Berbice **8** Demerara, Mazaruni, Rupununi **9** Essequibo **10** Burro-Burro
  ocean: **8** Atlantic
  physical feature:
    falls: **5** Great, Tiger **7** Kamaria **8** Kaieteur **9** Serikoeng **10** Surwakwima **15** Fredrik Willem IV
  people: **6** Akawai, Arawak, Creole, Taruma **7** African, Chinese, mulatto **10** Portuguese
  language: **5** Hindi **7** English
  religion: **5** Hindu, Islam **8** Anglican **13** Roman Catholic

Guy Fawkes
author: **16** William Ainsworth

Guy Mannering
author: **14** Sir Walter Scott

Guyon
character in: **15** The Faerie Queene
author: **7** Spenser

Guys and Dolls
director: **17** Joseph L Mankiewicz
based on story by: **11** Damon Runyon
cast: **10** Stubby Kaye **11** Jean Simmons **12** Frank Sinatra, Marlon Brando, Vivian Blaine
setting: **11** New York City
score: **12** Frank Loesser
song: **11** Luck Be a Lady **12** Guys and Dolls **26** Sit Down You're Rocking the Boat

guzzle 4 bolt, swig **5** quaff, swill **6** devour, imbibe, tipple **7** toss off **8** gulp down

guzzler 5 drunk **6** boozer **7** imbiber, tippler **8** devourer, drunkard **9** alcoholic

Gwawl
origin: **5** Welsh
mentioned in: **10** Mabinogion
rival of: **5** Pwyll
sought hand of: **8** Rhiannon

Gwydion
origin: **5** Welsh
son: **14** Llew Llaw Gyffes
sister: **9** Arianhrod
lover: **9** Arianhrod

Gwyn
origin: **7** British
god of: **7** rebirth **9** afterlife

Gyas
companion of: **6** Aeneas

Gyes see **5** Gyges

Gygaea, Gyge
form: **5** nymph
location: **4** lake

Gyges
also: **4** Gyes
member of: **13** Hecatonchires

gymnasium 5 arena **6** circus **7** stadium **10** hippodrome

gymnast 10 Olga Korbut **13** Mary Lou Retton, Nadia Comaneci

gymnastics 9 exercises **10** acrobatics **11** contortions **16** physical training

Gynaecothoenas
epithet of: **4** Ares
means: **17** feasted by the women

gynophobia
fear of: **5** women

gyp 3 con **4** bilk, burn, fake, hoax, rook, scam, soak **5** cheat, cozen, fraud, phony, trick **6** diddle, fleece, humbug, ripoff **7** con game, defraud, swindle **8** flimflam, hoodwink **9** bamboozle, deception

gypsy
Italian: **7** zingara, zingaro

gyrate 5 swirl, twirl, wheel, whirl **6** circle, rotate, spiral **7** revolve **9** pirouette **10** spin around

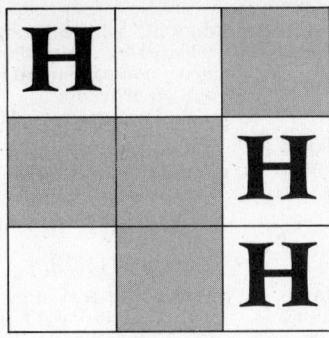

habeas corpus 11 have the body **23** produce the person in court
    legal writ guards against: 19 illegal imprisonment

habiliments 4 garb, wear **5** dress **6** attire, outfit **7** clothes, costume, raiment, regalia **8** clothing, wardrobe **9** vestments

habit 3 rut, way **4** garb, gear, robe, rule, wont **5** dress, trait **6** attire, custom, groove, livery, manner, outfit **7** apparel, clothes, costume, garment, leaning, raiment, routine, uniform, vesture **8** clothing, fondness, habitude, practice **9** mannerism, trappings **10** beaten path, convention, observance, partiality, proclivity, propensity **11** habiliments, inclination, peculiarity **12** predilection, second nature **13** accoutrements, fixed practice **14** matter of course, predisposition **15** behavior pattern

habitat 3 pad **4** digs, home, spot, zone **5** abode, haunt, place, range, realm, roost **6** domain, locale, milieu, region **7** housing, lodging, setting, terrain **8** domicile, dwelling, home base, lodgment, precinct, quarters **9** territory **10** habitation **11** environment, natural home **12** place of abode **13** dwelling place **14** stamping ground **15** natural locality **17** native environment

habitation 3 pad **4** digs, home **5** abode, haunt, house, roost **6** colony **7** habitat, housing, lodging, shelter, tenancy **8** domicile, dwelling, lodgment, quarters **9** community, occupancy, residence **10** occupation, settlement **12** place of abode **13** dwelling place, temporary stay **16** place of residence

Habit of Being, The
    author: 15 Flannery O'Connor

habitual 5 fixed, usual **6** common, normal, wonted **7** chronic, natural, regular, routine, typical **8** addicted, constant, expected, familiar, frequent, periodic, repeated **9** confirmed, continual, customary, incessant, ingrained, perpetual, recurrent **10** accustomed, deep-rooted, deep-seated, inveterate, methodical, systematic **11** established, traditional **12** conventional, second nature **14** by force of habit

habitual practice 4 wont **5** habit **6** custom

habituate 5 adapt, drill, imbue, inure, train **6** harden, school, season **7** break in, instill **8** accustom, initiate **9** inculcate **10** discipline, make used to **12** indoctrinate

habitue 7 regular **10** frequenter **13** regular patron **15** frequent visitor **16** constant customer

hack 3 cab, cut, hew, nag **4** bark, chip, chop, gash, plug, rasp, slit, taxi **5** coach, cut up, notch, slash, slice, whack **6** cleave, mangle **7** hackney, taxicab **8** lacerate, mutilate **9** cart horse, dray horse, scribbler, workhorse **10** cough drily, cut roughly, draft horse, hired horse, shaft horse **11** common horse, penny-a-liner **12** hackney coach, worn-out horse **13** carriage horse **16** grubstreet writer **18** horse-drawn carriage

hackle 3 peg **4** card, comb, hack, hook, ruff **5** curry, plume, quill **6** heckle, mangle **7** bristle, feather, plumage

Hackman, Gene
    born: 15 San Bernardino CA
    roles: 8 Superman **11** Popeye Doyle **14** Bonnie and Clyde **15** The Conversation **19** The French Connection (Oscar) **20** The Poseidon Adventure

hackneyed 4 dull, worn **5** banal, inane, stale, stock, trite, vapid **6** common, jejune **7** cliched, humdrum, insipid, routine, worn-out **8** bromidic, ordinary, shopworn, well-worn **9** moth-eaten **10** pedestrian, threadbare, uninspired **11** commonplace, stereotyped **12** conventional **13** platitudinous, unimaginative

Hadassah 6 Esther

Hades 4 hell
    also: 5 Pluto **10** lower world, Underworld
    corresponds to: 5 Orcus
    god of: 5 Orcus, Pluto
    goddess of: 6 Hecate, Hekate

Haemon
    father: 5 Creon
    loved: 8 Antigone
    died at tomb of: 8 Antigone
    death by: 7 suicide

Haenigsen, Harry
    creator/artist of: 5 Penny **7** Our Bill

hafnium
    chemical symbol: 2 Hf

hag 3 bat, nag **4** drab, fury **5** biddy, crone, frump, harpy, shrew, vixen, witch **6** beldam, gorgon, ogress, virago **7** hellcat **8** battle-ax, harridan **9** termagant

Hagar
    servant of: 5 Sarah
    husband: 7 Abraham
    son: 7 Ishmael

Hagar the Horrible
    creator: 9 Dik Browne

Hagen
    origin: 8 Germanic

mentioned in:
14 Nibelungenlied
killed by: 9 Kriemhild
killed: 9 Siegfried

haggard 4 beat, wild, worn 5 gaunt, spent, tired, upset, weary 6 bushed, fagged, pooped, raging, wasted 7 ranting 8 careworn, drooping, fatigued, flagging, frenzied, harassed, harrowed, overcome, toilworn, wild-eyed 9 exhausted, woebegone 10 hollow-eyed 11 debilitated, overwearied, overwrought, tuckered out, wild-looking 12 tired-looking

Haggard, H Rider
author of: 3 She 17 King Solomon's Mines

haggle 6 barter, bicker, dicker, higgle 7 bargain, dispute, quarrel, quibble, wrangle 8 beat down, squabble

Hagiographa
Hebrew: 7 Ketubim

hagiographer 19 writer of saints' lives

Hagman, Larry
mother: 10 Mary Martin
born: 13 Weatherford TX
roles: 6 Dallas 7 J R Ewing 15 I Dream of Jeannie

Hagno
origin: 8 Arcadian
form: 5 nymph
location: 6 spring

Hahn, Otto
field: 9 chemistry
nationality: 6 German
discovered: 13 protoactinium 14 nuclear isomers
awarded: 10 Nobel Prize

Haida
language family: 6 Masset, Na-Dene 10 Skidegatta
tribe: 7 Kaigani
location: 6 Alaska 15 British Columbia 21 Queen Charlotte Islands
related to: 7 Tlingit 9 Tsimshian
associated with: 9 totem pole 13 wood sculpture

hail 4 call 5 cheer, exalt, extol, greet, hello, honor, shout 6 accost, call to, esteem, salute 7 acclaim, address, applaud, commend, glorify, receive, shout at, usher in, welcome 8 cry out to, eulogize, greeting 9 accosting 10 calling out, compliment, panegyrize, salutation 11 make welcome
German: 4 heil
Latin: 5 salve

Hailey, Arthur
author of: 5 Hotel 6 Wheels 7 Airport 12 In High Places 14 Final Diagnosis 16 The Moneychangers

hail-fellow-well-met 8 familiar, friendly, intimate, outgoing, sociable 9 extrovert 10 gregarious

Hail Mary
Latin: 8 Ave Maria

Hail the Conquering Hero
director: 14 Preston Sturges
cast: 10 Ella Raines 12 Eddie Bracken 14 Raymond Walburn 15 William Demarest 16 Franklin Pangborn

hail to victory
German: 8 Sieg Heil

hair 3 fur, mop 4 coat, down, iota, mane, pelt, wool 5 bangs, curls, locks 6 fleece 7 tresses 8 ringlets 12 narrow margin

haircut, hairdo 3 bob, bun, cut 4 Afro, clip, crop, perm, shag, trim 5 bangs, braid, butch, swirl 6 boogie, mohawk 7 beehive, chignon, cornrow, crewcut, flattop, fuzz cut, natural, pachuco, page boy, pigtail, shingle, tonsure 8 bouffant, brushcut, coiffure, ducktail, ponytail, razorcut 9 barbering, hairstyle, permanent, pompadour 10 feathercut, french knot

haircutter 6 barber 11 hairdresser, hair stylist

hairdresser 8 coiffeur 9 coiffeuse 10 beautician, haircutter 11 beauty salon 12 beauty parlor
  French: 8 coiffeur

hair-raising 8 exciting 9 thrilling 10 terrifying 11 astonishing 12 breathtaking, electrifying

hairsplitting 4 fine 6 minute, subtle 7 carping 8 caviling, delicate, hairline, niggling 9 minuscule, quibbling 10 nitpicking, unapparent 12 faultfinding, overcritical 13 imperceptible, inappreciable, infinitesimal 15 inconsequential

hairy 5 bushy, furry, wooly 6 fleecy, pilose, shaggy, woolly 7 hirsute

Hairy Ape, The
author: 12 Eugene O'Neill

Haiti *see box*

Hakenkreuz 11 hooked cross 12 Nazi swastika

Haiti
name means: 15 mountainous land
other name: 12 Santo Domingo
capital/largest city: 12 Port-au-Prince
others: 5 Aquin, Furcy, Limbe 6 Hinche, Jacmel, St Marc 7 Jeremie, Leogane, Saltrou 8 Gonaives, Kenscoff, Les Cayes 10 Cap-Haitien
monetary unit: 6 gourde 8 centimes
island: 5 Vache 6 Gonave, Tortue 7 Navassa, Tortuga 8 Caymites 10 Hispaniola 14 Grande Cayemite 15 Greater Antilles
lake: 8 Saumatre
mountain: 4 Nord 5 Cahos 6 Macaya, Noires 7 Lahotte 8 Troudeau
highest point: 7 La Selle, Laselle
river: 9 Guayamoul 10 Artibonite
sea: 8 Atlantic 9 Caribbean
physical feature:
  gulf: 6 Gonave
  passage: 8 Windward
people: 5 Taino 7 African, mulatto
  discoverer: 8 Columbus
  liberator: 19 Toussaint Louverture
  ruler: 8 Duvalier
language: 6 Creole, French, patois
religion: 6 voodoo 13 Roman Catholic
feature:
  dance: 5 mambo
  festival: 9 Mardi Gras
  fortress: 10 La Ferriere 24 Citadelle du Roi Christophe
  security force: 8 bogeymen 15 Tontons Macoutes
food:
  sweet potato: 6 batata

Hakluyt, Richard
  author of: **7** Voyages
  15 Hakluyt's Voyages

HAL
  character in: **14** Two Thousand One (2001)
  author: **6** Clarke

Halas, George
  nickname: **8** Papa Bear
  sport: **8** football
  position: **5** coach
  team: **12** Chicago Bears

halcyon 4 calm, fair **5** happy, quiet, sunny **6** blithe, golden, hushed, joyous, placid, serene **7** pacific **8** carefree, cheerful, peaceful, tranquil **9** cloudless, contented, reposeful, unclouded, unruffled **10** unagitated, untroubled

Halcyon see **7** Alcyone

hale 3 fit **4** well **5** hardy, sound **6** hearty, robust, rugged, sturdy **7** healthy, in shape **8** vigorous **9** energetic, in the pink, strapping **10** ablebodied, robustious **12** in fine fettle

Hale, Edward Everett
  author of: **21** The Man Without a Country

Hale, George Ellery
  field: **9** astronomy
  initiated: **20** Mt Palomar Observatory
  invented:
    17 spectroheliograph

Halevy, Ludovic
  author of: **17** The Abbe Constantin

Haley, Alex
  author of: **5** Roots

Haley, Jack
  born: **8** Boston MA
  roles: **6** Tin Man **13** The Wizard of Oz

half 4 part, some **6** all but, barely, fairly, feebly, halved, in part, meager, partly, rather, scanty, skimpy, slight, weakly **7** divided, faintly, limited, partial, portion, section **8** fraction, middling, moderate, passable, passably, slightly **9** deficient, imperfect, partially, tolerable, tolerably **10** fractional, inadequate, incomplete, moderately, relatively **12** fifty percent, inadequately, insufficient, pretty nearly **13** after a fashion, comparatively **14** insufficiently

half-asleep 6 drowsy, groggy, unwary **7** out-of-it, unaware **8** sluggish **9** not-with-it, oblivious

half-hearted 4 cold, cool,

tame **5** blase, faint **7** languid, passive **8** listless, lukewarm **9** apathetic, lethargic **10** ambivalent, irresolute, lackluster, phlegmatic, spiritless, unaspiring **11** indifferent, perfunctory **13** lackadaisical **14** unenthusiastic

half homer 15 Biblical measure

half-moon 3 arc, bow **4** arch **5** curve **8** crescent

halfway 6 almost, in part, medial, medium, middle, midway, nearly, partly, rather **7** midmost **8** somewhat **9** partially, to a degree **10** middlemost, moderately **11** equidistant, in the middle **12** intermediate, pretty nearly, to some extent **13** in some measure **18** between two extremes

half-wit 4 dolt, dope, fool **5** dummy, dunce, idiot, moron, ninny **6** dimwit, nitwit **7** dullard **8** dumb-dumb, imbecile, numskull **9** blockhead, numbskull, simpleton **10** nincompoop **15** mental defective, mental deficient

half-witted 4 dumb **5** silly **6** stupid **7** asinine, foolish, idiotic, moronic **9** dimwitted, imbecilic, senseless **11** lamebrained **12** feebleminded, simple-minded

Halirrhothius
  father: **8** Poseidon
  mother: **6** Euryte
  raped: **7** Alcippe
  killed by: **4** Ares

Halitherses
  origin: **6** Ithaca
  form: **4** seer

hall 5 entry, foyer, lobby **6** arcade **7** chamber, gallery, hallway, passage **8** anteroom, club room, corridor, entrance **9** vestibule **10** auditorium, dining hall, passageway **11** antechamber, banquet hall, concert hall, waiting room **12** amphitheater, assembly room, meeting place **13** reception room

Hall, Diane
  real name of: **11** Diane Keaton

Hall, James
  field: **7** geology **9** chemistry
  nationality: **7** British
  founded: **12** geochemistry
    19 experimental geology

Hall, James Norman
  author of: **17** Mutiny on the Bounty
  co-author: **15** Charles Nordhoff

Hallel 6 praise **16** liturgical prayer

Haller, Albrecht von
  field: **7** biology
  nationality: **5** Swiss
  founded: **15** modern neurology

Haller, Harry
  character in: **11** Steppenwolf
  author: **5** Hesse

Halley, Edmund
  field: **9** astronomy
  nationality: **7** British
  discovered: **12** Halley's Comet

hallmark 4 sign **5** badge, stamp **6** device, emblem, symbol **14** characteristic

Hall of Fame see box, p. 426

halloo 3 cry **4** call, hail, yell **5** shout **6** cry out, holler

hallow 5 bless **7** respect **8** dedicate, sanctify, venerate **10** consecrate

hallowed 4 holy **6** sacred **7** blessed, honored **9** beatified, dedicated **10** sacrosanct, sanctified **11** consecrated

hallucination 5 dream **6** mirage, vision **7** chimera, fantasy, figment **8** delusion, illusion **9** nightmare **10** aberration, apparition **14** phantasmagoria

hallway 4 hall **7** passage **8** corridor, entryway **10** passageway

halo 6 aurora, corona, luster, nimbus **7** aureole, dignity, majesty **8** grandeur, holiness, radiance, sanctity, splendor **9** solemnity, sublimity **11** ring of light **12** chromosphere, luminousness, magnificence, resplendence **13** spiritual aura **15** illustriousness

Haloa
  event: **8** festival
  origin: **5** Greek
  honoring: **7** Demeter **8** Dionysus **10** Persephone

Hals, Franz
  born: **7** Antwerp, Holland
  artwork: **9** Gypsy Girl **10** Hille Bobbe (The Witch of Haarlem) **13** The Jolly Toper **14** Jacobus Zaffius **15** The Merry Company **19** The Laughing Cavalier **22** Portrait of a Standing Man **24** The Regents of the Almshouse **26** Yonker Ramp and his Sweetheart **28** The Regentesses of the Almshouse **33** The Banquet of the St George Civic Guard

Halsey, William F
  served in: **3** WWI **4** WWII

Hall of Fame

author: 3 Poe 5 Paine, Stowe 6 Bryant, Cooper, Holmes, Irving, Lanier, Lowell, Motley 7 Clemens, Emerson, Parkman, Thoreau, Whitman 8 Bancroft, Whittier 9 Hawthorne

aviation: 3 Six 4 Bell, Byrd, Lear, Luke, Post, Ryan 5 Beech, Eaker, Glenn, LeMay, Piper, Reeve 6 Arnold, Boeing, Cessna, Fokker, Hughes, Levier, Rogers, Spaatz, Sperry, Towers, Trippe, Wright, Yeager 7 Chanute, Earhart, Goddard, Langley, Shepherd, Twining 8 Mitchell, Northrup, Sikorsky 9 Armstrong, Chennault, Lindberg, Mcdonnell 12 Rickenbacker

baseball: 3 Ott 4 Bell, Cobb, Dean, Ford, Foxx, Hoyt, Kell, Mack, Mays, Mize, Rice, Ruth, Ward, Wynn 5 Aaron, Anson, Baker, Banks, Berra, Carey, Duffy, Faber, Gomez, Grove, Hafey, Irvin, Kelly, Lemon, Lloyd, Paige, Reese, Rusie, Terry, Vance, Wheat, Young 6 Alston, Barrow, Bender, Cuyler, Dickey, Feller, Frisch, Galvin, Gehrig, Gibson, Goslin, Grimes, Haines, Herman, Hooper, Hunter, Kaline, Keeler, Kelley, Koufax, Lajoie, Mantle, Musial, Schalk, Sewell, Sisler, Snider, Tinker, Wagner, Wilson, Youngs 7 Averill, Appling, Beckley, Hubbell, Jackson, Leonard, McCovey, Nichols, O'Rourke, Pennock, Roberts, Stengel, Traynor, Vaughan, Waddell, Wallace, Wilhelm 8 Bancroft, Boudreau, Clemente, Comiskey, DiMaggio, Drysdale, Jennings, McCarthy, Radbourn, Robinson, Thompson, Williams 9 Alexander, Delahanty, Greenberg, Mathewson 10 Campanella, Maranville

basketball: 4 Gola, Page, Reed, West 5 Cousy, Fulks, Greer, Hyatt, Lucas, Mikan 6 Barlow, Baylor, Cooper, Foster, Hanson, Holman, Pettit, Philip, Ramsey, Roosma, Sedran, Wooden 7 Beckman, Bradley, Johnson, Kurland, Pollard, Russell, Schmidt, Sharman 8 Borgmann, Endacott, Lapchick, Schommer 9 Robertson, Steinmetz, Vandivier 11 Chamberlain, Debusschere

business: 4 Ford, Kroc, Land, Luce, Vail 5 Beech, Deere, Heinz 6 Batten, Carrier, Cooper, Disney, du Pont, Edison, Hilton, Lowell, Mellon, Morgan, Penney, Schwab 7 Bechtel, Merrill, Peabody, Proctor, Whitney 8 Carnegie, Eastman, Franklin 9 Baekeland, Kettering, McCormick 10 Vanderbilt 11 Rockefeller 12 Westinghouse

football: 3 Mix, Ray 4 Bell, Carr, Ford, Hein, Huff, Hunt, Lane, Lary, Mara, Otto, Owen 5 Baugh, Berry, Brown, Clark, Davis, Fears, Green, Gregg, Groza, Guyon, Halas, Henry, Jones, Layne, Lilly, Lyman, Moore, Musso, Neale, Olsen, Perry, Pihos, Ringo, Starr 6 Atkins, Badgro, Blanda, Butkus, Connor, Dudley, Ewbank, Gatski, George, Graham, Grange, Healey, Herver, Hewitt, Hinkle, Hirsch, Hutson, Kinard, Langer, Lanier, Matson, McAfee, Motley, Namath, Nevers, Parker, Reeves, Rooney, Sayers, Strong, Taylor, Thorpe, Tittle, Trippi, Turner, Unitas, Upshaw, Walker, Willis, Wilson 7 Alworth, Battles, Bidwell, Canadeo, Donovan, Edwards, Gillman, Gifford, Hubbard, Lambeau, Lavelli, Leemans, Luckman, McNally, Millner, Schmidt, Trafton, Tunnell 8 Adderley, Bednarik, Driscoll, Fortmann, Kiesling, Lombardi, Marshall, Mitchell, Nagurski, Nitschke, Stautner, Stydahar, Van Buren, Warfield 9 Conzelman, Jurgensen, Marchetti, McElhenny, Michalske, Nomellini, Tarkenton 10 Robustelle, Waterfield 11 Chamberlain, Van Brocklin 12 Christiansen 13 Wohciechowicz

golf: 4 Berg, Ford, Hope, Wood 5 Boros, Brady, Burke, Dutra, Evans, Hagen, Hogan, Jones, Shute, Smith, Snead 6 Armour, Barnes, Casper, Cooper, Diegel, Dudley, Ghezzi, Harper, Little, McLeod, Nelson, Ouimet, Palmer, Picard, Runyan, Travis 7 Demaret, Guldahl, Harbert, Littler, Mangrum, Revolta, Sarazen, Travers 8 Anderson, Harrison, Zaharias 9 De Vicenzo, Hutchinson, McDermott 10 Middlecoff 11 Cruickshank

scientist: 4 Gray 5 Gibbs, Henry, Maury 6 Carver 7 Agassiz, Audubon, Burbank, Newcomb 8 Mitchell 9 Michelson

theater: 4 Drew, Kerr 5 Brook, Hecht, Kelly, Simon 6 Prince 7 Dunnock, Youmans 8 Kingsley, Lansbury, Meredith, Sondheim 9 MacArthur 11 Bloomgarden

---

rank: 12 fleet admiral

battle: 9 Leyte Gulf 11 Philippines 14 Solomon Islands

halt 3 end 4 balk, curb, foil, quit, rest, rout, stay, stem, stop, wait 5 abate, block, brake, break, cease, check, close, crush, delay, pause, quash, quell, stall, tarry 6 bridle, cut off, defeat, draw up, hamper, hinder, impede, linger, pull up, recess, rein in, scotch, subdue, thwart, wind up 7 heave to, inhibit, prevent, put down, repress, respite, squelch, suspend, time out 8 break off, breather, choke off, don't move, hang fire, interval, knock off, leave off, overturn, prohibit, restrain, restrict, shut down, suppress, vanquish 9 cessation, frustrate, interlude, interrupt, overthrow, terminate 10 call it a day, extinguish, shut up shop, standstill, suspension 11 come to a halt, come to a stop, discontinue, hold in check, termination 12 intermission, interruption, throttle down 13 spike one's guns 14 breathing spell, discontinuance

halting 6 ending 7 curbing 8 episodic, hesitant, stopping 9 faltering, stumbling 10 calling off, discursive, suspending 11 restraining, terminating 13 discontinuous 14 calling a halt to, putting a stop to

halting place
Spanish: 6 posada

halutz 7 pioneer 26 person who emigrates to Israel

halve 6 bisect 9 cut in half 10 split in two 13 divide equally

Ham
character in: 16 David Copperfield
author: 7 Dickens

Ham
father: 4 Noah
brother: 4 Shem 7 Japheth
son: 3 Put 4 Cush 6 Canaan 7 Misraim
descendant of: 6 Hamite

Hamadryad
form: 5 dryad
spirit of: 4 tree

Haman
served: 9 Ahasuerus

Hamill, Mark
born: 9 Oakland CA

roles: 8 Star Wars **13** Luke Skywalker **15** Return of the Jedi **20** The Empire Strikes Back

Hamilton
capital of: **7** Bermuda

Hamilton, Charles
character in: **15** Gone With the Wind
author: **8** Mitchell

Hamilton, Iain
composer of: **6** Aurora **7** Alastor **8** Sinfonia **9** Pharsalia **11** The Bermudas **18** Threnos In Time of War **20** The Royal Hunt of the Sun **21** The Catiline Conspiracy

Hamilton, Margaret
real name: **23** Margaret Hamilton Meserve
born: **11** Cleveland OH
roles: **4** Cora **13** The Wizard of Oz **23** The Wicked Witch of the West

Hamito-Semitic
language also known as: **11** Afro-Asiatic
branch: **6** Berber, Chadic **7** Semitic **8** Cushitic, Egyptian

hamlet 4 burg **7** village **8** hick town, tank town **10** crossroads **11** whistle stop **12** onehorse town, small village **13** jerkwater town

Hamlet
author: **18** William Shakespeare
character: **7** Horatio, Laertes, Ophelia **8** Claudius, Gertrude, Polonius, The Ghost **11** Rosencrantz **12** Guildenstern
skull: **6** Yorick
castle: **8** Elsinore
setting: **7** Denmark
director: **15** Laurence Olivier
cast: **11** Basil Sydney, Felix Aylmer, Jean Simmons **12** Eileen Herlie **15** Laurence Olivier
Oscar for: **5** actor (Olivier) **7** picture

Hamlet, The
author: **15** William Faulkner
character: **4** Eula, Jody **6** Labove **8** Ab Snopes **9** V K Ratliff **10** Flem Snopes, Mink Snopes, Will Varner **11** Isaac Snopes **12** Henry Armstid

Hamlin, Vincent T
creator/artist of: **8** Alley Oop

hammer 3 hit, tap **4** bang, form, make, nail **5** drive, forge, knock, pound, punch,

shape, whack **6** pummel, rammer, strike **7** beat out, fashion
type: **4** claw, jack, tack **5** gavel, steam **6** mallet, sledge **8** ballpeen **10** pile driver **12** upholsterers

Hammer, Mike
detective created by: **14** Mickey Spillane

hammered 6 banged, beaten, shaped **7** knocked, pounded, whipped, wrought **8** battered, repeated **10** terrorized

Hammett, Dashiell
author of: **10** Red Harvest, The Thin Man **11** The Glass Key **12** The Dain Curse **16** The Maltese Falcon
character: **8** Sam Spade **11** Miles Archer, Nick Charles, Nora Charles **13** Continental Op

hamper 3 gag **4** balk, curb, stem **5** block, check, stall **6** fetter, hinder, hog-tie, hold up, impede, muzzle, retard, thwart **7** inhibit, prevent, shackle **8** encumber, handicap, obstruct, restrain, restrict **9** frustrate **13** interfere with

Hampton, Hope
nickname: **22** The Duchess of Park Avenue
born: **14** Philadelphia PA
roles: **8** Star Dust **13** Lawful Larceny, The Road to Reno **16** The Price of a Party

hamstring 6 impair, muscle, tendon **7** cripple, disable **8** handicap **10** debilitate

Hamsun, Knut
author of: **3** Pan **6** August, Hunger **8** Victoria **9** Mysteries, Vagabonds **16** Children of the Age **18** The Growth of the Soil

Hananiah see **8** Shadrach

hand, hands 3 aid, man, paw **4** care, fist, give, help, hold, lift, mitt, palm, pass **5** guide, power, reach **6** assist, charge, convey, helper, menial, script, worker **7** command, control, custody, deliver, keeping, laborer, ovation, present, support, workman **8** auspices, dominion, employee, guidance, handyman, hired man, longhand, meat-hook **9** assistant, associate, authority, hired hand **10** assistance, domination, management, minister to, penmanship, possession, turn over to, workingman **11** calligraphy, furnish with, handwriting, supervision **12** jurisdiction **13** member of a crew **15** burst of applause,

manual extremity, round of applause

handbag 3 bag **4** grip **5** purse **6** clutch, valise **7** satchel **8** moneybag, reticule **10** pocketbook, portmanteau

handbill 5 flier **6** notice **7** leaflet **8** bulletin, circular **12** announcement **13** advertisement

handbook 5 bible **6** manual **9** guidebook **13** reference book

hand by hand
Spanish: **9** mano a mano

handcart 4 cart **6** barrow **8** pushcart **10** handbarrow **11** wheelbarrow

handcuffs 5 cuffs, irons **6** chains **7** fetters **8** manacles, shackles **9** bracelets

hand down 4 will **5** leave **6** hand on, pass on **8** bequeath

Handel, George Frederick (Georg Friedrich)
born: **5** Halle **7** Germany
composer of: **4** Nero, Saul **5** Serse, Silla, Siroe, Teseo **6** Admeto, Alcina, Almira, Esther, Flavio, Jeptha, Joseph, Ottone, Samson, Semele, Xerxes **7** Amadigi, Athalia, Deborah, Lotario, Messiah, Rinaldo, Rodrigo, Solomon, Tolomeo **8** Atalanta, Berenice, Hercules, Scipione, Theodora **9** Agrippina, Radamisto, Rodelinda, Tamerlano **10** Alessandro, Belshazzar, Floridante, Water Music **12** Giulio Cesare, Il Pastor Fido, Muzio Scevola **13** Israel in Egypt, Riccardo Primo **14** Acis and Galatea, Fireworks Music **15** Alexander's Feast, Judas Maccabaeus **16** Hornpipe Concerto **19** Julius Caesar in Egypt, Ode for St Cecilia's Day **22** The Royal Fireworks Music **23** Hallelujah Organ Concerto, The Harmonious Blacksmith **24** The Triumph of Time and Truth

handful 7 minimum, modicum **10** scattering, smattering, sprinkling, thimbleful, tiny amount **11** scant amount, small number **13** small quantity

Handful of Dust, A
author: **11** Evelyn Waugh

handgun 3 rod **5** piece, rifle **6** pistol, weapon **7** firearm, shotgun **8** revolver **9** automatic, twenty-two **12** shooting iron **20** Saturday night special

handicap 4 curb **5** limit **6** burden, defect, hamper, hinder, impede, retard, thwart **7** bar-

rier, inhibit, repress, shackle
8 deafness, drawback, encumber, hold back, lameness, obstacle, restrain, restrict, suppress **9** blindness, detriment **10** difficulty, impediment, inhibition, limitation **11** encumbrance, restriction, shortcoming **12** disadvantage **13** inconvenience **14** stumbling block

handicapped 7 limited **8** burdened, disabled, held back, hindered, impaired, retarded **10** encumbered, restrained, restricted **13** disadvantaged

handicrafts
  god of: **10** Hephaestus, Hephaistos

handicraftsman 7 artisan
10 handworker **12** handicrafter

handiness 7 utility **8** deftness **9** dexterity **10** adroitness, usefulness **11** convenience **12** availability **13** accessibility

hand in glove 5 as one **10** side by side **13** close together

handle 3 paw, ply, run, tag, use **4** feel, grip, hilt, hold, knob, name, poke, pull, sell, work **5** carry, grasp, guide, knead, pilot, pinch, shaft, shank, steer, swing, touch, treat **6** caress, deal in, employ, finger, fondle, manage, market, pick up, stroke **7** care for, command, conduct, control, massage, moniker, operate, paw over, trade in, utilize **8** cognomen, deal with, maneuver **9** traffic in **10** manipulate, take care of **11** appellation, merchandise **12** offer for sale **13** bring into play

Handley Cross
  author: **18** Robert Smith Surtees

handout 4 alms, dole **7** freebie **19** something for nothing

hand out 4 give **5** grant **6** bestow, confer, donate **7** dole out, mete out, present **8** dispense **9** apportion **10** contribute, distribute

hand over 4 cede **5** grant, yield **6** give up, tender **7** abandon, release **8** transfer **9** deliver up, surrender **10** relinquish

handsome 4 fair **5** ample, bonny, noble **6** benign, comely, lovely, pretty **7** elegant, liberal, sightly, sizable, stately **8** abundant, generous, gracious, imposing, merciful, princely, splendid, stunning,

tasteful **9** beauteous, beautiful, bountiful, exquisite, unselfish **10** attractive, benevolent, bighearted, impressive, sufficient, well-formed **11** fine-looking, good-looking, magnanimous **12** considerable, easy to look at, humanitarian **13** compassionate, easy on the eyes **16** well-proportioned

handy 4 deft, near, nigh **5** adept, on tap **6** adroit, at hand, clever, expert, on call, on hand, useful, wieldy **7** capable, helpful, skilled **8** skillful **9** available, competent, dexterous, easy to use, efficient, practical **10** accessible, convenient, manageable, obtainable, proficient **11** at one's elbow, close at hand, in readiness, ready to hand, serviceable **12** accomplished **14** nimble-fingered **15** within easy reach **16** easily accessible **17** at one's beck and call

hang 3 bow, sag **4** drop, gist, rest **5** affix, hinge, knack, lie in, lower, lynch, point, trail **6** append, attach, dangle, depend **7** incline, meaning, suspend, thought **8** lean over, let droop, repose in, string up, turn upon **9** be pendant, be pendent **11** be dependent, be subject to, bend forward, swing freely **12** be contingent, bend downward **13** revolve around **15** die on the gallows, fasten from above **16** execute by hanging, send to the gallows

hangdog 6 abject **7** ashamed **8** defeated, degraded, hopeless, resigned, wretched **9** miserable **10** browbeaten, chapfallen, humiliated, shamefaced **11** crestfallen, embarrassed, intimidated **13** guilty-looking

hang down 3 sag **5** droop

hanger-on 7 admirer, groupie **8** follower **9** sycophant

hanging object
  Japanese: **8** kakemono

hang loosely 3 bag, sag **5** droop

hangout 3 den **5** haunt

hang out 3 mix **4** live **5** dwell **6** hobnob, loiter, mingle, reside **7** consort **9** associate, be friends, pal around, run around **10** fraternize, hang around **11** keep company

hanker after 4 want **5** covet, crave, fancy **6** desire **7** long for, pine for **8** aspire to, yearn for **9** lust after **11** have a yen for, have an eye on, hunger after, thirst after

hankering 3 yen **4** itch, urge **6** aching, desire, hunger, pining, thirst **7** craving, longing **8** yearning

Hanna-Barbera
  creators of: **8** Yogi Bear **14** The Flintstones

Hannah
  husband: **7** Elkanah
  son: **6** Samuel

Hanoi
  capital of: **7** Vietnam **12** North Vietnam
  river: **3** Red **4** Yuan **7** Song Koi
  delta: **6** Tonkin
  airport: **6** Gia Lam

Hans Brinker
  author: **5** (Mary Elizabeth Mapes) Dodge
  character: **4** Raff **5** Gleck, Hilda **6** Gretel **7** Boekman, Mevrouw

Hansel and Gretel
  author: **13** Grimm Brothers (Jakob and Wilhelm)
  opera by: **11** Humperdinck
  character: **5** Witch

Hans Kristian
  character in: **16** Giants of the Earth
  author: **7** Rolvaag

Hanson, Howard
  born: **7** Wahoo NE
  composer of: **5** Sacra (symphony No 5) **6** Nordic (symphony No 1) **7** Requiem (symphony No 4) **8** Romantic (symphony No 2) **10** Merry-Mount

Hap see **4** Apis

haphazard 6 casual, chance, fitful, random **7** aimless, chaotic **8** careless, on-and-off, slapdash, sporadic **9** arbitrary, hit-or-miss **10** accidental, disordered, disorderly, fortuitous, undesigned, undirected, unthinking **11** purposeless, unorganized **12** disorganized, unmethodical, unsystematic **14** indiscriminate, unpremeditated **15** catch-as-catch-can

Hapi see **4** Apis, Nile

hapless 5 lousy **6** cursed, jinxed, no-good, rotten, woeful **7** forlorn, unhappy, unlucky **8** accursed, hopeless, ill-fated, luckless, wretched **9** miserable **10** ill-starred **11** star-crossed, unfortunate

happen 5 arise, ensue, occur **6** appear, befall, betide, crop up, result **7** turn out **8** become of, spring up **9** be borne by, be the case, come about, eventuate, take place, transpire **10** be one's fate, come to pass **11** be endured by **12** be suffered by **13** be one's fortune, fall to one's lot, present itself

happening 4 case **5** event **6** advent, affair, matter **7** episode **8** accident, incident, occasion **9** adventure, incidence **10** experience, occurrence, proceeding **11** vicissitude **12** circumstance, happenstance **20** just one of those things

happenstance 4 luck **6** chance **8** accident, fortuity

happiness 3 joy **4** glee **5** bliss, cheer, mirth **6** gaiety **7** comfort, content, delight, ecstasy, elation, jollity, rapture **8** blessing, felicity, gladness, pleasure **9** beatitude, enjoyment, merriment, rejoicing, transport **10** cheeriness, exuberance, exultation, jubilation **11** blessedness, contentment, high spirits **12** cheerfulness, satisfaction **13** gratification **16** lightheartedness, sense of well-being

happy 3 fit, gay **4** glad, meet **5** lucky **6** elated, joyful, joyous, timely **7** content, fitting, gleeful, pleased, tickled **8** blissful, cheerful, cheering, ecstatic, exultant, jubilant, pleasant, pleasing **9** agreeable, contented, delighted, exuberant, favorable, fortunate, gratified, opportune, overjoyed, rapturous, rhapsodic **10** auspicious, convenient, delightful, felicitous, gratifying, propitious, seasonable **11** exhilarated, tickled pink, transported **12** advantageous **13** in high spirits **15** in seventh heaven

Happy Days
  character: 6 Arnold, Fonzie **10** Ralph Malph **11** Potsie Weber **12** Chachi Arcola **14** Pinky Tuscadero **15** Chuck Cunningham **16** Alfred Delvecchio, Arthur Fonzarelli, Howard Cunningham, Joanie Cunningham, Leather Tuscadero, Marion Cunningham, Richie Cunningham
  cast: 8 Roz Kelly **9** Donny Most, Erin Moran, Pat Morita, Ron Howard, Scott Baio, Tom Bosley **10** Al Molinaro, Marion Ross, Suzi Quatro **12** Henry Winkler **13** Anson Williams, Gavan O'Herlihy **15** Randolph Roberts

happy-go-lucky 6 blithe **7** buoyant, flighty, relaxed **8** carefree, careless, feckless, heedless, skittish **9** easygoing,

unworried **10** insouciant, nonchalant, optimistic, untroubled **11** free-and-easy, unconcerned **12** devil-may-care, light-hearted **13** irresponsible **14** scatterbrained **23** without a worry in the world

harangue 6 speech, tirade **7** lecture, oration **8** diatribe, scolding **9** contumely, sermonize **12** denunciation, vituperation

Harare
  capital of: 8 Zimbabwe

harass 3 cow, irk, vex **4** bait, ride **5** annoy, beset, bully, harry, hound, tease, worry **6** attack, badger, bother, heckle, hector, pester, plague **7** assault, bedevil, besiege, disturb, torment **8** browbeat, distress, irritate **9** persecute **10** discommode, exasperate, intimidate **14** raid frequently

harbinger 4 clue, omen **5** token **6** herald, symbol **7** portent **8** signaler **9** announcer, first sign, precursor **10** forerunner, indication, proclaimer

Harbonna 6 eunuch

harbor 3 bay **4** cove, dock, feel, goal, hide, hold, keep, pier, port, quay **5** basin, ha-

ven, house, inlet, lodge, wharf **6** asylum, billet, foster, lagoon, refuge, retain, shield, take in **7** care for, cling to, conceal, nurture, protect, quarter, retreat, shelter **8** hideaway, keep safe, maintain, muse over, terminus **9** brood over, sanctuary **11** concealment, destination, hiding place **12** give refuge to **13** bear in the mind, terminal point **18** protected anchorage

harbors
  god of: 8 Portunus
  goddess of: 6 Matutu

Harcorates *see* **5** Horus

hard *see* **box**

hard-and-fast 3 set **6** strict **7** binding **8** exacting, rigorous **9** mandatory, unbending **10** compelling, compulsory, inflexible, obligatory, undeniable, unyielding **11** irrevocable, unalterable, unremitting **12** indisputable **13** incontestable **14** uncompromising

Hardcastle family
  characters in: 18 She Stoops to Conquer
  author: 9 Goldsmith

hard drinker 3 sot **4** lush, soak, wino **5** drunk, rummy,

---

hard 3 sad **4** cold, firm, mean, ugly **5** cruel, eager, harsh, heavy, rigid, rough, solid, stern, stiff, stony, tight, tough **6** bitter, brutal, fierce, firmly, keenly, knotty, severe, steely, strict, strong, sullen, thorny, unkind **7** angrily, arduous, callous, closely, complex, cryptic, eagerly, earnest, harmful, heavily, hostile, hurtful, inhuman, intense, onerous, sharply, solidly, tightly, to heart, vicious, violent, willing, zealous **8** animated, baffling, critical, diligent, exacting, fiercely, forceful, forcibly, hardened, intently, involved, pitiless, powerful, puzzling, rocklike, ruthless, severely, spirited, spiteful, steadily, strongly, stubborn, untiring, venomous, vigorous **9** arduously, assiduous, bellicose, confusing, difficult, earnestly, energetic, furiously, Herculean, insulting, intensely, intricate, laborious, malicious, merciless, painfully, rancorous, seriously, strenuous, stringent, unbending, unpliable, unsparing, violently, wearisome **10** burdensome, diligently, forcefully, formidable, impervious, implacable, inexorable, inflexible, lamentable, melancholy, oppressive, perplexing, persistent, powerfully, relentless, resolutely, rigorously, tormenting, unbearable, unflagging, unfriendly, unpleasant, untiringly, unyielding, vigorously, vindictive **11** acrimonious, agonizingly, assiduously, belligerent, bewildering, complicated, distressing, emotionally, hardhearted, industrious, insensitive, intolerable, laboriously, persevering, troublesome, unceasingly, unmalleable, unrelenting, unremitting, unsparingly **12** antagonistic, cantankerous, determinedly, disagreeable, enterprising, impenetrable, persistently, relentlessly, thick-skinned, unfathomable, unflaggingly **13** conscientious, disheartening, distressfully, energetically, indefatigable, industriously, with much anger **14** uncompromising, with much sorrow **15** conscientiously **16** with all one's might **18** with strong feelings

souse, toper **6** barfly, boozer **7** guzzler, imbiber, tippler **8** drunkard **9** alcoholic **11** dipsomaniac **14** problem drinker **16** two-fisted drinker

harden 3 dry, gel, set **4** cake, fire, firm **5** adapt, adjust, blunt, enure, inure, steel **6** anneal, freeze, season, temper **7** calcify, callous, congeal, fortify, petrify, stiffen, thicken, toughen **8** accustom, solidify **9** fossilize, make tough, reinforce **10** discipline, invigorate, strengthen **11** crystallize, turn to stone **12** restrengthen **13** make unfeeling

hard feelings 5 anger **6** grudge, hatred, rancor **7** ill

will **8** acrimony **9** animosity, hostility **10** antagonism, bitterness **12** spitefulness

hardheaded 4 cool **5** balky **6** astute, mulish, poised, shrewd **7** willful **8** contrary, sensible, stubborn **9** immovable, objective, obstinate, pigheaded, practical, pragmatic, realistic, unbending, unfeeling **10** coolheaded, impersonal, inflexible, refractory, self-willed, unyielding **11** down-to-earth, intractable, tough-minded, unemotional, unflappable **14** self-controlled

hardhearted 4 cold, hard, mean **5** cruel, stony **6** brutal **7** callous, inhuman **8** pitiless,

ruthless, uncaring **9** heartless, merciless, unfeeling, unpitying, unsparing **11** coldblooded, indifferent, insensitive, remorseless, unforgiving **12** cruelhearted, thick-skinned **13** unsympathetic

hardihood 4 grit **5** pluck, spunk **6** mettle **7** courage **8** strength **9** endurance, fortitude **10** resolution **12** resoluteness

Harding, Warren Gamaliel *see box*

hardly 4 just, only **6** barely, rarely **7** faintly, in no way **8** not often, not quite, scarcely **9** almost not, by no means **10** in no manner, uncommonly **12** certainly not, infrequently **13** not by any means **15** not by a great deal

hardnosed 4 hard **5** harsh, rigid, stern, tough **6** severe, shrewd, strict **8** critical, hardline, exacting, stubborn **9** demanding, unbending, unsparing **10** hardheaded, inflexible, no-nonsense, unyielding **11** calculating, intractable **12** unsentimental **14** uncompromising

Hardouin-Mansart, Jules architect of: **8** Orangery (Versailles) **12** Chateau du Val (St Germain-en-Laye), Grand Trianon (Versailles), Place Vendome (Paris) **15** Chateau de Clagny (Versailles) **16** Galerie des Glaces (Hall of Mirrors at Versailles), Les Invalides (Church of the Dome, Paris)

hard-pressed 7 harried, put-upon **9** embattled **10** overworked

hardship 3 woe **4** load **5** agony, grief **6** burden, misery, ordeal, sorrow **7** problem, travail, trouble **8** handicap **9** adversity, privation, suffering **10** affliction, difficulty, misfortune **11** cross to bear, encumbrance, tribulation, unhappiness **12** wretchedness

hard sledding 8 tough job **10** difficulty, tough going, uphill work **11** arduousness **13** laboriousness

hard times 4 bust **5** slump **8** bad times **9** recession **10** depression

Hard Times author: **11** Studs Terkel

Hard Times author: **14** Charles Dickens character: **9** Sissy Jupe **10** Mrs Sparsit **11** Mr Boun-

---

Harding, Warren Gamaliel
  presidential rank: **11** twenty-ninth
  party: **10** Republican
  state represented: **2** OH
  defeated: **3** (James Middleton) Cox, (William Wesley) Cox **4** (Eugene Victor) Debs **7** (Aaron Sherman) Watkins **8** (Robert Charles) Macauley **11** (Parley Parker) Christensen
  vice president: **8** (Calvin) Coolidge
  cabinet:
    state: **6** (Charles Evans) Hughes
    treasury: **6** (Andrew William) Mellon
    war: **5** (John Wingate) Weeks
    attorney general: **9** (Harry Micajah) Daugherty
    navy: **5** (Edwin) Denby
    postmaster general: **3** (Harry Stewart) New **4** (Hubert) Work, (William Harrison) Hays
    interior: **4** (Albert Bacon) Fall, (Hubert) Work
    agriculture: **7** (Henry Cantwell) Wallace
    commerce: **6** (Herbert Clark) Hoover
    labor: **5** (James John) Davis
  born: **9** Corsica OH (now Blooming Grove)
  died: **2** CA (while in office) **12** San Francisco
  buried: **8** Marion OH
  education:
    College: **11** Ohio Central
  religion: **7** Baptist
  interests: **5** poker
    played musical instrument: **6** cornet **7** helicon
  political career: **8** US Senate **15** Ohio State Senate
    lieutenant governor of: **4** Ohio
  civilian career: **9** publisher **13** schoolteacher **15** newspaper editor **17** insurance salesman
  notable events of lifetime/term:
    Act: **21** Fordney-McCumber Tariff
    peace treaty with: **7** Austria, Germany, Hungary
    scandal: **10** Teapot Dome (oil)
    Treaty: **9** Five-Power, Nine-Power **16** Four-Power Pacific
  father: **11** George Tryon
  mother: **6** Phoebe (Elizabeth Dickerson)
    stepmother: **4** Mary (Alice Severns) **6** Eudora (Kelley Luvisi)
  siblings: **11** George Tryon **12** Mary Clarissa **14** Charity Malvina, Phoebe Caroline **15** Abigail Victoria **16** Charles Alexander, Eleanor Priscilla
  wife: **8** Florence (Kling DeWolfe)
  children:
    illegitimate daughter: **21** Elizabeth Ann Christian (by mistress Nan Britton)

derby **12** Tom Gradgrind
14 James Harthouse
15 Louisa Gradgrind,
Thomas Gradgrind **16** Stephen Blackpool

hard to catch 4 foxy, wily
6 crafty, shifty, tricky **7** elusive, evasive **8** slippery

hard to grasp 7 elusive **8** baffling, puzzling, slippery **9** difficult **10** perplexing
16 incomprehensible

hard to manage 6 unruly
7 froward, willful **8** perverse,
stubborn **9** difficult, fractious,
obstinate **10** inflexible, refractory, unyielding **11** intractable **12** obstreperous,
unmanageable

hard to please 5 fussy, picky
7 exigent, finicky **8** critical
10 fastidious, meticulous,
particular

hard to understand 7 complex **9** difficult, intricate
10 perplexing **11** bewildering,
complicated

Hardwick, Elizabeth
author of: **11** Simple Truth
12 A View of My Own
15 Sleepless Nights **20** Seduction and Betrayal

Hardwicke, Sir Cedric
born: **3** Lye **7** England
roles: **14** On Borrowed Time
21 Livingstone and Stanley
36 A Connecticut Yankee in
King Arthur's Court

hardwood 4 wood **8** leadwood
kind: **3** ash, elm, oak **4** teak
5 beech, birch, maple
6 cherry, linden, walnut
7 hickory **8** mahogany, rose-
wood, sycamore

hardworking 8 diligent, sedulous **9** assiduous **11** industrious, persevering
12 enterprising
13 conscientious

hardy 3 fit **4** hale **5** tough
6 hearty, mighty, robust, rugged, strong, sturdy **7** healthy
8 stalwart, vigorous **9** strapping **10** able-bodied **12** in fine
fettle **13** physically fit **15** in
good condition

Hardy, Oliver
partner: **10** Stan Laurel
born: **8** Harlem GA
roles: **8** Pardon Us **9** Saps at
Sea **10** Way Out West

Hardy, Thomas
author of: **10** The Dynasts
14 Jude the Obscure **20** The
Return of the Native
21 Tess of the D'Urbervilles
22 Far from the Madding

Crowd, The Mayor of
Casterbridge
mythical county: **6** Wessex

hare
constellation of: **5** Lepus
group of: **4** down, husk

harebrained 5 silly, wacko,
wacky **7** asinine, flighty, foolish **8** skittish **9** dimwitted,
senseless **10** half-witted
11 empty-headed **12** simple-
minded **13** rattlebrained
14 featherbrained,
scatterbrained

Haredale, Reuben
character in: **12** Barnaby
Rudge
author: **7** Dickens

harem 5 serai **6** purdah, serail,
senana, zenana **8** love nest,
seraglio

Hargreaves, James
nationality: **7** English
inventor of: **13** spinning
jenny

Harker, Jonathan
character in: **7** Dracula
author: **6** Stoker

harlot 3 pro **4** bawd, doxy,
jade, pros, slut, tart **5** whore
6 chippy, wanton **7** jezebel,
trollop **8** call girl, mistress,
strumpet **9** courtesan, kept
woman **10** prostitute **11** fallen
woman **12** painted woman,
scarlet woman, streetwalker

Harlow, Jean
real name: **16** Harlean
Carpenter
nickname: **15** Blonde
Bombshell
born: **12** Kansas City MO
roles: **7** Red Dust **8** Riffraff,
Saratoga **9** Bombshell, China
Seas **11** Hell's Angels, Libeled Lady **13** Dinner at
Eight

harm 3 ill, mar, sin **4** evil,
hurt, maim, pain, ruin, vice
5 abuse, agony, havoc, spoil,
wound, wrong **6** damage, debase, deface, ill-use, impair,
injure, injury, malice, misuse,
trauma **7** blemish, cripple, degrade, scourge **8** aggrieve, calamity, hardship, iniquity,
maltreat, mischief, villainy
9 adversity, detriment, disfigure, suffering, undermine
10 defacement, immorality,
impairment, misfortune, sinfulness, wickedness **11** destruction, devastation, malevolence
12 do violence to **13** deterioration, maliciousness

harmful 3 bad **7** adverse, baneful, hurtful, ruinous **8** damaging **9** dangerous, injurious,
unhealthy **10** pernicious

11 deleterious, destructive, detrimental, unhealthful, unwholesome
17 counterproductive

harmless 4 mild, safe **6** benign, gentle **7** sinless **8** innocent, nontoxic **9** blameless,
guiltless, incorrupt, innocuous,
peaceable **10** not hurtful
11 inoffensive **12** not dangerous **15** unobjectionable

harmlessness 6 safety **9** innocence **10** gentleness **11** non-
toxicity **12** nonvirulence
13 innocuousness
15 inoffensiveness

Harmon, Young John
character in: **15** Our Mutual
Friend
author: **7** Dickens

Harmonia
father: **4** Ares
mother: **9** Aphrodite
husband: **6** Cadmus
daughter: **3** Ino

Harmonides see **9** Phereclus

harmonious 5 sweet **6** dulcet
7 amiable, cordial, unified
8 amicable, friendly, in accord,
matching **9** agreeable, congenial, in harmony, melodious
10 compatible, consistent, euphonious, likeminded **11** coordinated, harmonizing, in
agreement, mellifluous, sympathetic **12** synchronized
13 sweet-sounding **17** agreeably combined

harmonize 3 fit **4** jibe, mesh
5 agree, blend, chime, tally
6 accord, adjust, attune **7** conform **8** be in tune **9** reconcile
10 complement, correspond,
go together **13** sing in
harmony

harmony 5 amity, order, peace,
unity **6** accord **7** balance, concord **8** matching, symmetry,
sympathy **9** agreement, unanimity **10** conformity, fellowship, friendship, proportion
11 amicability, cooperation,
correlation, parallelism
12 congeniality, coordination,
mutual regard **13** compatibility, mutual fitness **14** like-
mindedness **15** organic totality **17** good understanding
19 harmonious relations,
pleasing consistency **21** concurrence in opinions

Harmony
goddess of: **9** Concordia

harness 4 curb, rein, tugs,
yoke **5** lines, reins, rig up
6 bridle, collar, employ, halter,
muzzle, straps, tackle, traces
7 exploit, hitch up, utilize
8 restrain **9** caparison, trap-

Harold
author: **18** Edward Bulwer-Lytton

pings **12** put in harness, render useful **13** control and use, turn to account **14** make productive **22** direct to a useful purpose

Harold
author: **18** Edward Bulwer-Lytton

Harper, Joe
character in: **9** Tom Sawyer
author: **5** Twain

Harphlyce
father: **8** Clymenus
husband: **7** Alastor
vocation: **8** huntress
violated by: **8** Clymenus
killed by: **8** Clymenus
9 shepherds

Harpina
father: **6** Asopus
son: **8** Oenomaus

harp on 7 dwell on **9** reiterate **18** repeat persistently

Harpy
form: **7** monster
head of: **5** woman
body of: **4** bird
father: **7** Thaumas
mother: **7** Electra
names: **5** Aello **7** Celaeno, Ocypete, Podarge

harridan 3 hag **5** crone, shrew, witch **6** virago **8** battle-ax, old crone **12** mean old woman

harried 5 upset **7** worried **8** harassed, troubled **10** distraught

Harris, Joel Chandler
author of: **10** Uncle Remus (His Songs and Sayings)

Harris, Julie
real name: **14** Julia Ann Harris
born: **18** Grosse Pointe Park MI
roles: **6** Harper **10** East of Eden, I Am a Camera **11** The Haunting **14** A Shot in the Dark, The Hiding Place **19** The Last of Mrs Lincoln **21** The Member of the Wedding **22** Requiem for a Heavyweight **27** And Miss Reardon Drinks a Little

Harris, Richard
born: **7** Ireland **8** Limerick
roles: **7** Camelot **8** Cromwell **15** A Man Called Horse **16** The Molly Maguires, This Sporting Life **17** Mutiny on the Bounty, The Guns of Navarone **20** The Cassandra Crossing **26** The Return of a Man Called Horse

Harris, Roy
composer of: **16** Folksong Symphony **17** American Por-

traits **27** When Johnny Comes Marching Home (overture)

Harrison, Benjamin see box

Harrison, Lou
born: **10** Portland OR
composer of: **8** Rapunzel, Solstice **13** Changing World **15** Four Strict Songs, Johnny Appleseed **17** The Perilous Chapel **19** Almanac of the Seasons **22** At the Tomb of Charles Ives

Harrison, Peter
architect of: **11** Brick Market (Newport RI), King's Chapel (Boston) **14** Redwood Library (Newport RI), Touro Synagogue (Newport RI)

Harrison, Rex
real name: **21** Reginald Carey Harrison
nickname: **8** Sexy Rexy
wife: **10** Kay Kendall **11** Lilli Palmer **13** Rachel Roberts
born: **6** Huyton **7** England
roles: **9** Cleopatra **10** My Fair Lady (Oscar) **12** Blithe Spirit **14** Doctor Dolittle **16** The Foxes of Harrow **17** Unfaithfully Yours **18** The Ghost and Mrs Muir **20** Anna and the King of Siam

Harrison, Wallace K
architect of: **13** Lincoln Center (NYC) **14** Socony Building (NYC) **17** Rockefeller Center (NYC) **22** Metropoli-

Harrison, Benjamin
nickname: **3** Ben **9** Little Ben
presidential rank: **11** twenty-third
party: **10** Republican
state represented: **2** IN
defeated: **4** (Clinton Bowen) Fisk **6** (James Langdon) Curtis **7** (Robert Hall) Cowdrey **8** (Albert) Redstone, (Alson Jenness) Streeter, (Belva Ann Bennett) Lockwood **9** (Grover) Cleveland
vice president: **6** (Levi Parsons) Morton
cabinet:
  state: **6** (James Gillespie) Blaine, (John Watson) Foster
  treasury: **6** (Charles) Foster, (William) Windom
  war: **6** (Stephen Benton) Elkins **7** (Redfield) Proctor
  attorney general: **6** (William Henry Harrison) Miller
  navy: **5** (Benjamin Franklin) Tracy
  postmaster general: **9** (John) Wanamaker
  interior: **5** (John Willock) Noble
  agriculture: **4** (Jeremiah McLain) Rusk
born: **11** North Bend OH
died/buried: **14** Indianapolis IN
education:
  prep school: **14** Farmer's College
  University: **21** Miami University of Ohio
  later studied: **3** law
religion: **12** Presbyterian
interests: **7** fishing, hunting **8** swimming
author: **17** This Country of Ours **20** Views of An Ex-President
political career: **8** US Senate
  city attorney: **12** Indianapolis
  reporter of: **19** Indiana supreme court
  secretary of: **31** Republican state central committee
civilian career: **6** lawyer **12** law professor
military service: **8** Civil War **16** brigadier general
notable events of lifetime/term:
  Act: **16** Dependent Pension, Sherman Anti-Trust **21** Sherman Silver Purchase
  Tariff: **8** McKinley
father: **9** John Scott
mother: **9** Elizabeth (Ramsey Irwin)
siblings: **8** Mary Jane **9** John Irwin, John Scott **10** Anna Symmes, James Irwin **12** James Findlay **13** Carter Bassett **14** Archibald Irwin
  half sisters: **9** Elizabeth **13** Sarah Lucretia
wife: **4** Mary (Scott Lord Dimmick) **8** Caroline (Lavinia Scott)
children: **9** Elizabeth, Mary Scott **15** Russell Benjamin

tan Opera House (NYC)
25 United Nations Headquarters (NYC) **34** Nelson A
Rockefeller Empire State
Plaza (Albany NY), ALCOA
Building (Pittsburgh, with
Max Abramovitz)

Harrison, William Henry
see box

harrowing 7 fearful, painful
8 alarming, chilling **9** traumatic, upsetting **10** disturbing,
terrifying, tormenting **11** distressing, frightening
13 bloodcurdling

harry 3 irk, vex **4** bait, gall,
raid, ride, sack **5** annoy, beset,
bully, haunt, hound, tease,
worry **6** badger, bother, harass, heckle, hector, pester,
plague **7** disturb, pillage, plunder, torment, trouble **8** distract, distress, irritate
9 terrorize **10** exasperate, intimidate **16** attack repeatedly

harsh 4 hard, mean **5** cruel,
raspy, rough, sharp, stern
6 bitter, brutal, hoarse, severe,
shrill, unkind **7** abusive, caustic, glaring, grating, jarring,
rasping, raucous, squawky
8 piercing, pitiless, ruthless,
scratchy, strident, ungentle
9 Draconian, heartless, merciless, too bright, unmusical,
unsparing **10** discordant, overbright, unpleasant, vindictive
11 cacophonous, hardhearted
12 uncharitable, unharmonious

harshness 5 rigor **7** cruelty,
discord **9** brutality, cacophony,
raspiness, roughness, sternness,
stridency **10** dissonance, shrillness, unkindness **12** ungentleness **13** heartlessness
14 unpleasantness
15 hardheartedness

Hart, Johnny
    creator/artist of: 2 B C
    13 The Wizard of Id

Hart, Moss
    author of: 15 Once in a Lifetime **20** You Can't Take It
    with You (with George S
    Kaufman) **21** The Man Who
    Came to Dinner (with
    George S Kaufman)

Harte, Bret
    author of: 20 The Luck of
    Roaring Camp **22** The Outcasts of Poker Flat

Hartford
    hockey team: 7 Whalers

Harthouse, James
    character in: 9 Hard Times
    author: 7 Dickens

Hartley, Vivian Mary
    real name of: 11 Vivien
    Leigh

harum-scarum 5 giddy
6 wildly **7** erratic, flighty, foolish **8** careless, confused **9** aimlessly, haphazard, impetuous,
impulsive, unplanned, unsettled **10** bewildered, recklessly,
unreliable **11** haphazardly,
harebrained, impulsively
12 absent-minded, capriciously,
disorganized, inconsistent, undependable **13** rattlebrained
14 featherbrained,
scatterbrained

harvest 3 cut, mow **4** crop,
gain, pick, reap **5** amass, fruit,
pluck, yield **6** gather, haying,
mowing, output, result, return,
reward **7** benefit, collect, cutting, picking, produce, product, reaping **8** fruition,
gleaning, proceeds **9** aftermath, amassment, gathering,
outgrowth **10** accumulate, collection, harvesting **12** accumulation **13** season's growth

harvest time 4 fall **6** autumn
8 maturity **12** Indian summer

Harvey
    director: 11 Henry Koster
    based on play by: 9 Mary
    Chase
    cast: 8 Peggy Dow **12** James
    Stewart (Elwood P Dowd)
    13 Cecil Kellaway, Josephine Hull
    Oscar for: 17 supporting actress (Hull)

Harvey, Laurence
    real name: 19 Larushka
    Misch Skikne
    wife: 16 Margaret Leighton
    born: 9 Lithuania, Yomishkis
    roles: 7 Darling **12** Life at
    the Top, Room at the Top
    14 Of Human Bondage,
    Summer and Smoke **16** Butterfield Eight **17** Walk on
    the Wild Side

Harvey, William
    field: 7 anatomy

Harrison, William Henry
    nickname: 6 Old Tip **22** The Washington of the West
    presidential rank: 5 ninth
    party: 4 Whig
    state represented: 2 OH
    defeated: 6 (James G) Birney **8** (Martin) Van Buren
    vice president: 5 (John) Tyler
    cabinet:
        state: **7** (Daniel) Webster
        treasury: **5** (Thomas) Ewing
        war: **4** (John) Bell
        attorney general: **10** (John Jordan) Crittenden
        navy: **6** (George Edmund) Badger
        postmaster general: **7** (Francis) Granger
    born: 2 VA **17** Charles City County **18** Berkeley plantation
    died: 12 Washington DC
    buried: 11 North Bend OH
    education: 16 privately tutored (at home)
        College: **13** Hampden-Sydney (did not graduate)
        later studied: **8** medicine
    religion: 12 Episcopalian
    political career: 8 US Senate **11** state Senate **24** US House
        of Representatives
        governor of: **16** Indiana Territory
        minister: **8** Columbia
    civilian career: 6 farmer **7** soldier
    military service: 6 US Army **12** major general **19** War of
        Eighteen Twelve
        battle: **6** (the) Thames **8** Lake Erie **10** Tippecanoe
    notable events of lifetime/term: 24 Land Act of Eighteen
        Hundred
        campaign slogan: **21** Tippecanoe and Tyler too
        treaty of: **10** Greenville
    father: 8 Benjamin
    mother: 9 Elizabeth (Bassett)
    siblings: 3 Ann **4** Lucy **5** Sarah **8** Benjamin **9** Elizabeth
        13 Carter Bassett
    wife: 4 Anna (Tuthill Symmes)
    children: 8 Benjamin **9** John Scott **10** Mary Symmes
        11 Anna Tuthill **12** James Findlay, William Henry
        13 Carter Bassett, Lucy Singleton **16** Elizabeth Bassett,
        John Cleves Symmes

Hasen, Irwin
  nationality: **7** British
  discovered: **18** circulation of
  blood

Hasen, Irwin
  creator/artist of: **5** Dondi
  9 Goldbergs **11** Wonder
  Woman **12** Green Lantern

hash out 6 review **7** discuss
8 consider, talk over

hasp 4 lock **5** catch, clasp,
latch **7** closure **8** fastener

Hassam, (Frederick) Childe
  born: **12** Dorchester MA
  artwork: **13** Southwest Wind
  14 Summer Sunlight, Washington Arch **15** Against the
  Light **23** Boston Commons
  at Twilight

hassle 3 bug, row, vex **5** annoy, fight, harry, hound,
scrap, set-to **6** badger, battle,
bother, harass, tussle **7** contest, dispute, quarrel **8** argument, conflict, squabble,
struggle **9** persecute

hassock 4 boss, pess, seat, tuft,
weed **5** bunch, chair, group,
trush **6** buffet, plants, tuffet
7 ottoman, tussock **9** footstool,
vegetable

hasta la vista 6 good-by, so
long **7** goodbye **12** until I see
you **16** until we meet again

hasta manana 13 until tomorrow **14** see you tomorrow

haste 4 rush **5** hurry, speed
8 celerity, dispatch, rapidity,
rashness **9** fleetness, quickness,
swiftness **10** expedition, speediness, undue speed **11** hur-
riedness **12** recklessness
13 careless hurry, impetuous-
ness, impulsiveness,
precipitation

hasten 3 fly, run **4** bolt, dart,
dash, flit, jump, race, rush
5 egg on, hurry, impel, speed,
whisk **6** hustle, incite, scurry,
sprint, urge on **7** advance,
drive on, hurry on, hurry up,
promote, quicken, scamper,
scuttle, speed up **8** expedite,
make time **10** accelerate, lose
no time **11** go full blast, precipitate, push forward **12** step
on the gas **13** go on the double **14** step right along **15** go
like lightning, make short
work of, work against time
20 go hell-bent for leather

hastily 4 fast **5** apace **6** pronto,
rashly **7** quickly **8** promptly,
speedily **9** hurriedly, like a
shot, posthaste, summarily
10 carelessly, heedlessly, recklessly, too quickly **11** impetuously, impulsively, on the
double **12** lickety-split,

straightaway **13** precipitately,
thoughtlessly **18** hell-bent for
leather **20** like greased lightning, on the spur of the
moment

Hastings, Thomas *see*
  17 Carrere, John Merven

hasty 4 fast, rash **5** brief, fleet,
quick, rapid, swift **6** abrupt,
prompt, rushed, speedy **7** cursory, hurried, passing **8** fleeting, headlong, heedless,
reckless **9** impetuous, impulsive, momentary **10** breathless **11** precipitate, superficial,
unduly quick **12** quick as a
wink **19** without
deliberation

hat
  French: **7** chapeau

hatch 4 plan, plot **5** frame
6 cook up, create, design, devise, evolve, invent, make up
7 concoct, dream up, fashion,
produce, think up **8** conceive,
contrive **9** construct, fabricate,
formulate, improvise, originate **10** bring forth **11** give
birth to, manufacture

hatchlings 5 brood, young
6 chicks **9** offspring

hate 5 abhor, dread, venom
6 animus, detest, enmity,
hatred, loathe, malice, rancor
7 be sorry, despise, dislike,
wince at **8** acrimony, aversion,
be sick of, distaste, execrate,
loathing **9** abominate, animosity, antipathy, be tired of, dis-
liking, hostility, not care to
10 abhorrence, be averse to,
feel sick at, recoil from, repugnance, resentment, shrink
from **11** abomination, be hostile to, be reluctant, be unwilling, detestation,
malevolence, wish to avoid
12 be repelled by **14** have no
taste for, hold in contempt,
revengefulness, vindictiveness
16 bear malice toward, have
no stomach for **17** feel disinclined to, not have the heart
to **19** regard as distasteful

hateful 4 evil, foul, mean,
ugly, vile **5** nasty **6** odious,
sinful, wicked **7** heinous **8** infamous, scornful **9** abhorrent,
atrocious, loathsome, monstrous, obnoxious, offensive,
repellent, repugnant, revolting,
sickening **10** abominable, deplorable, despicable, detestable,
disdainful, disgusting, forbidding, full of hate, irritating,
unbearable, unpleasant, villainous **11** distasteful, intolerable,
unendurable **12** contemptible,
contemptuous, insufferable
13 objectionable

Hathor
  origin: **8** Egyptian
  goddess of: **3** joy **4** love
  symbol: **4** ears, head **5** horns
  patron of: **5** dance, music
  personifies: **3** sky

Hat on the Bed, The
  author: **9** John O'Hara

hatred 4 hate **5** venom **6** animus, enmity, malice, rancor
7 disgust, dislike, ill will **8** acrimony, aversion, bad blood,
distaste, loathing **9** animosity,
antipathy, hostility, revulsion
10 abhorrence, antagonism,
bitterness, repugnance, resentment **11** abomination, detestation, malevolence
14 revengefulness,
vindictiveness

haughtiness 4 airs **5** pride
7 conceit, hauteur **8** snobbery
9 arrogance **10** snootiness
13 condescension **14** disdainfulness, high-handedness
16 superciliousness

haughty 5 aloof **6** lordly,
snooty, uppish, uppity **7** high-
hat, stuck-up **8** arrogant,
scornful, snobbish **9** conceited,
officious **10** disdainful, high-
handed, hoity-toity **11** highfalutin, overbearing, overly
proud, patronizing, swell-
headed **12** contemptuous
13 condescending, high and
mighty

haul 3 bag, lug, tow, tug
4 cart, drag, draw, gain, jerk,
move, pull, swag, take, tote,
yank **5** booty, bring, carry,
catch, fetch, heave, truck,
yield **6** convey, profit, remove,
reward, spoils, wrench **7** capture, takings **9** transport

haunches 4 buns, rear, rump,
seat **5** nates **7** rear end **8** buttocks **9** fundament, posterior
12 hindquarters

haunt 3 vex **5** beset, worry
6 live in, obsess, plague, prey
on **7** disturb, terrify, torment,
trouble, weigh on **8** distress,
frequent, frighten **9** hang out
at, preoccupy, terrorize
10 hang around, hover about,
loiter near, visit often **11** beat
a path to **12** linger around

haunts 3 den **4** cave, hole, lair,
nest **6** burrow **7** hangout
8 hideaway **9** waterhole
10 rendezvous **12** meeting
place **14** gathering place
15 stamping grounds

Hauptmann, Gerhart
  author of: **10** Before Dawn,
  The Weavers

haute couture 11 high
fashion

haute cuisine 11 fine cooking **14** gourmet cooking

hauteur 5 swank **7** conceit, disdain **8** snobbery **9** arrogance, loftiness **10** snootiness **11** haughtiness **12** affectedness, snobbishness **13** condescension **14** disdainfulness, high-handedness **16** superciliousness **19** patronizing attitude

haut monde 5 elite **10** blue bloods, upper class, upper crust **11** aristocracy, high society **14** creme de la creme

Havana
  capital of: 4 Cuba
  gulf: 6 Mexico
  landmark: 15 Cabaret Parisien **16** Castillo del Morro **17** Castillode la Punta, Jose Marti Monument **18** Castillo de la Atares, Castillo de la Fuerza, Garcia Lorca Theater **19** Maximo Gomez Monument **21** Latinamericano Stadium **22** Academy of Science of Cuba
  river: 10 (Rio) Almendares
  Spanish: 8 La Habana

Havasupai, Supai
  location: 7 Arizona **11** Grand Canyon
  related to: 7 Yavapai **8** Hualapai

have 3 buy, eat, get, own, use **4** bear, fool, gain, gull, hold, host, keep, make, must **5** beget, carry, cheat, drink, enjoy, force, grasp, ought, smoke, trick **6** accept, affirm, compel, harbor, obtain, outwit, permit, retain, suffer **7** achieve, acquire, defraud, exhibit, possess, realize, receive, swindle **8** comprise, maintain, manifest, outsmart, perceive, tolerate **9** encompass, encounter, partake of, recognize, victimize **10** comprehend, experience, understand

have a fancy for 4 want **5** covet, crave **6** desire **7** long for, wish for **8** yearn for **11** hanker after, have a yen for

have a go at 3 try **6** hazard, tackle **7** attempt **8** give a try **9** undertake **10** give a whirl **12** take a crack at, take a whack at

have a good opinion of 5 favor **6** admire, revere **7** approve, respect **9** believe in **10** appreciate

have a hand in 7 advance, forward **9** influence **10** take part in **12** contribute to **13** be conducive to, participate in **14** help bring about

have an eye on 4 want **5** covet, crave, fancy **6** desire **7** long for, pine for **8** aspire to, yearn for **9** lust after **11** have a yen for

have a yen for 4 want **5** covet, crave **6** desire **7** long for, wish for **8** yearn for **9** lust after **11** hanker after **13** have a fancy for

have bearing on 5 apply, refer **6** relate **7** concern, pertain **9** appertain, touch upon **13** be pertinent to, have respect to

have done with 4 drop, junk, shed **7** abandon, discard **9** dispose of **10** relinquish **12** dispense with

have faith in 5 trust **6** rely on **9** believe in **16** have confidence in

have guests 8 play host **9** entertain **10** give a party **13** keep open house **16** offer hospitality

Have Gun Will Travel
  character: 6 Hey Boy **7** Hey Girl, Paladin
  cast: 6 Lisa Lu **7** Kam Tong **12** Richard Boone
  setting: 12 San Francisco **13** Hotel Carleton

have in mind 4 mean, want, wish **6** desire, intend **10** think about

haven 4 port **5** cover **6** asylum,

Hawaii
  abbreviation: 2 HI
  nickname: 5 Aloha **15** Sandwich Islands **20** Paradise of the Pacific
  capital/largest city: 8 Honolulu
  others: 3 Ewa **4** Aiea, Hana, Hilo, Laie, Paia **5** Kapaa, Kapaa, Lihue, Maili **6** Kailua, Kekaha **7** Kahului, Kaneohe, Lanikae, Wahiawa, Waianae, Wailuku
  college: 9 Chaminade, Hawaii Loa **12** Brigham Young **13** Hawaii Pacific
  explorer: 4 Cook **7** Gaetano
  feature:
    district: 7 Lahaina
    national park: 9 Haleakala **15** Hawaii Volcanoes
  people: 9 Hiram Fong **10** Polynesian **11** Sanford Dole **12** Daniel Inouye
  island name: 4 Kure **9** Kahoolawe
    big isle: 6 Hawaii
    friendly isle: 7 Molokai
    garden isle: 5 Kauai
    gathering place: 4 Oahu
    house of the sun: 9 Haleakala
    mystery isle: 6 Niihau
    pineapple isle: 5 Lanai
    valley isle: 4 Maui
  lake: 5 Waiau
  land rank: 12 forty-seventh
  mountain: 3 Kea, Loa **5** Kaala **6** Kohala, Kohala, Koolau **7** Kamakou, Waianae **8** Maunaloa **9** Lanaihale
    highest point: 8 Maunakea
  physical feature:
    bay: 5 Pohue **6** Halawa, Kiholo, Mamala **7** Kamohio, Kaneohe, Waiagua **8** Kawaihae, Maunalua
    beach: 7 Waikiki
    canyon: 6 Waimea
    channel: 3 Aua **5** Kaiwi **6** Kalohi **7** Pailolo
    crater: 7 Kilauea **9** Punchbowl
    desert: 3 Kau
    harbor: 5 Pearl
    promontory: 11 Diamond Head
    valley: 3 Iao **5** Manoa
    volcano: 7 Kilauea **8** Maunakea, Maunaloa **9** Haleakala
  state admission: 8 Fiftieth
  state bird: 4 nene **13** Hawaiian goose
  state flower: 5 lehua **11** red hibiscus **15** scarlet hibiscus
  state motto: 44 The Life of the Land is Perpetuated in Righteousness
  state song: 11 Hawaii Ponoi **12** Our Own Hawaii
  state tree: 5 kukui **9** candlenut

harbor, refuge **7** hideout, retreat, shelter **8** hideaway **9** sanctuary

have no hope 6 give up **7** despair **11** be desperate

have plenty 6 abound, be rich **8** flourish, overflow **10** be numerous, have enough **11** be plentiful **14** be well supplied **18** have more than enough

have the body
Latin: **12** habeas corpus
legal writ guards against: **19** illegal imprisonment

have too few 4 lack, want **7** be scant **9** fall short **13** be deficient in, have a dearth of **14** have a paucity of **15** be in short supply, have a scarcity of, not have enough of

having life 5 alive, vital **6** living, viable **7** animate

having the means 3 fit **4** able **6** fitted **7** capable, equal to **8** adequate **9** qualified **12** being solvent **20** having the wherewithal

Havisham, Miss
character in: **17** Great Expectations
author: **7** Dickens

havoc 4 ruin **5** chaos **8** calamity, disaster, disorder, upheaval **9** cataclysm, ruination **11** catastrophe, destruction, devastation **12** wrack and ruin **16** widespread damage

Hawaii *see box, p. 435*

Hawaii
author: **13** James Michener

Hawaiian swimmer 14 Duke Kahanamoku

Hawaii Five-O
character: **4** Kono **5** Wo Fat **8** Ben Kokua **11** Chin Ho Kelly **13** Danny Williams **14** Steve McGarrett
cast: **4** Zulu **7** Kam Fong **8** Jack Lord **11** Khigh Dhiegh **12** Al Harrington **14** James MacArthur

hawk 4 bird, sell, vend **6** falcon, peddle **8** militant **9** accipiter, warmonger
young: **4** eyas
group of: **4** cast

Hawk, Sir Mulberry
character in: **16** Nicholas Nickleby
author: **7** Dickens

Hawkes, John
author of: **10** Second Skin **11** The Cannibal, The Lime Twig **12** The Beetle Leg **15** The Blood Oranges

Hawkeye State
nickname of: **4** Iowa

Hawkins, Jim
character in: **14** Treasure Island
author: **9** Stevenson

Hawkline Monster, The
author: **16** Richard Brautigan

Hawks, Howard
director of: **8** Red River, Rio Bravo, Scarface **11** The Big Sleep **12** Sergeant York **13** His Girl Friday **14** Bringing Up Baby **16** To Have and Have Not, Twentieth Century

Hawn, Goldie
husband: **12** Gus Trinkonis
born: **12** Washington DC
roles: **7** Laugh-In, Shampoo **8** Foul Play **12** Cactus Flower **15** Private Benjamin **18** Butterflies Are Free

hawser 4 line, rope **5** cable **7** mooring

hawthorn 9 Crataegus
varieties: **5** water, yeddo **6** Indian **7** English

Hawthorne, Nathaniel
author of: **13** The Marble Faun **14** Twice-told Tales **16** The Scarlet Letter **20** Mosses from an Old Manse **24** The House of the Seven Gables

Haydee
character in: **21** The Count of Monte Cristo
author: **5** Dumas (pere)

Haydn, Franz Joseph *see box*

Hayes, Elvin
nickname: **4** Big E
sport: **10** basketball
team: **8** San Diego **14** Houston Rockets

Hayes, Helen
real name: **15** Helen Hayes Brown
nickname: **29** First Lady of the American Theater
son: **14** James MacArthur
roles: **7** Airport **9** Anastasia **22** The Sin of Madelon Claudet (Oscar)

Hayes, Rutherford B (Birchard) *see box*

hayseed 4 hick, rube **5** yokel **6** rustic **7** bumpkin, peasant **10** clodhopper

Hayward, Susan
real name: **14** Edythe Marrener
husband: **10** Jess Barker
born: **10** Brooklyn NY
roles: **11** I Want to Live (Oscar) **14** I'll Cry Tomorrow, My Foolish Heart **18** With a Song in My Heart **23** Smash Up The Story of a Woman

Hayworth, Rita
real name: **22** Margarita Carmen Cansino
husband: **7** Aly Khan **10** Dick Haymes **11** Orson Welles
born: **10** Brooklyn NY
roles: **5** Gilda **9** Cover Girl **14** Separate Tables **17** Miss Sadie Thompson, You'll Never Get Rich

hazan 18 cantor of a synagogue

Haydn, Franz Joseph
born: **6** Rohrau **7** Austria
composer of: **7** The Bird, The Joke **10** Gypsy Rondo, The Seasons **11** The Creation **12** Emperor's Hymn, Wild Band Mass **13** The Apothecary **14** Lord Nelson Mass, Theresienmesse **15** Mass in Time of War **16** Il Mondo della Luna, Mariazellermesse **17** The World of the Moon **38** The Seven Last Words of Our Savior on the Cross
quartet: **3** Sun **4** Bird, Frog, Lark, Tost **5** Dream, Razor, Witch **6** Fifths, Maiden **7** Emperor, Erdoedy, Russian, Sunrise, The Bell, The Hunt **8** Farmyard, Horseman, The Jokes **9** The Donkey **14** The House on Fire, The Row in Vienna
symphony: **4** Fire **5** Paris **6** Le Midi, Le Soir, Loudon, Merkur, Oxford, The Hen **7** Evening, Le Matin, Mercury, Morning, Salomon, The Bear, The Hunt **8** Abschied, Alleluia, Drum Roll, Farewell, Military, Mourning, Surprise, The Clock, The Queen, The Storm **9** Children's, Christmas **10** La Passione, La Tempesta, The Miracle, The Passion **11** The Imperial **12** Der Philosoph, Maria Theresa, The Afternoon **13** Auf dem Anstand **14** The Philosopher **15** The Schoolmaster, Trauersymphonie, With the Horn Call **17** At the Hunting Place **18** Mit dem Hornersignal

Hayes, Rutherford B (Birchard)
  nickname: **8** Rud Hayes
  presidential rank: **10** nineteenth
  party: **10** Republican
  state represented: **2** OH
  defeated: **5** (Green Clay) Smith **6** (James B) Walker, (Peter) Cooper, (Samuel Jones) Tilden
  vice president: **7** (William Almon) Wheeler
  cabinet:
    state: **6** (William Maxwell) Evarts
    treasury: **7** (John) Sherman
    war: **6** (Alexander) Ramsey **7** (George Washington) McCrary
    attorney general: **6** (Charles) Devens
    navy: **4** (Nathan) Goff (Jr) **8** (Richard Wigginton) Thompson
    postmaster general: **3** (David McKendree) Key **7** (Horace) Maynard
    interior: **6** (Carl) Schurz
  born: **10** Delaware OH
  died/buried: **9** Fremont OH
  education:
    preparatory school: **4** Webb
    College: **6** Kenyon
    Law School: **7** Harvard
  religion: **9** Methodist
  political career: **24** US House of Representatives
    city solicitor of: **10** Cincinnati
    governor of: **4** Ohio
  civilian career: **6** farmer, lawyer
  military service: **6** US Army **8** Civil War **12** Ohio infantry **18** brevet major general
  notable events of lifetime/term: **10** Depression (of 1873) **15** railroad strikes (of 1877) **18** civil service reform **24** specie payments resumption
    Act: **26** Bland-Allison Silver Purchase
  father: **10** Rutherford
  mother: **6** Sophia (Birchard)
  siblings: **7** Lorenzo **11** Sarah Sophia **13** Fanny Arabella
  wife: **4** Lucy (Ware Webb)
  children: **5** Fanny **9** James Webb (renamed Webb Cook) **11** George Crook **12** Manning Force, Scott Russell **14** Joseph Thompson, Sardis Birchard (renamed Birchard Austin) **15** Rutherford Platt

hazard 3 bet **4** dare, luck, risk **5** fluke, guess, offer, peril, stake, wager **6** chance, danger, expose, gamble, menace, mishap, submit, threat **7** advance, daresay, imperil, pitfall, presume, proffer, suppose, venture **8** accident, chance it, endanger, jeopardy, theorize, threaten, throw out **9** mischance, speculate, tempt fate, volunteer **10** conjecture, jeopardize, misfortune **11** coincidence, hypothesize, imperilment, take a chance, trust to luck **12** endangerment, happenstance, stroke of luck

Hazard of New Fortunes, A
  author: **18** William Dean Howells

hazardous 4 iffy **5** risky, shaky **6** chancy, unsafe, unsure **7** dubious, unsound

8 doubtful, insecure, perilous, unstable **9** dangerous, uncertain **10** precarious, unreliable **11** speculative, threatening **13** untrustworthy

haze 3 fog **4** daze, film, mist, pall, veil **5** cloak, cloud, smoke, vapor **6** mantle, muddle, screen **9** fogginess **12** befuddlement, bewilderment **16** state of confusion

hazel 3 nut **4** tree **5** brown, shrub, tawny **8** brownish **14** yellowish-brown
  varieties: **4** tree **5** Chile, witch **6** winter **7** Chinese, Turkish **8** American, European, Japanese **11** spike winter **12** Chinese witch **13** Japanese witch **15** buttercup winter

Hazel
  character: **12** George Baxter,

Harold Baxter **13** Dorothy Baxter
  cast: **9** Don DeFore **12** Shirley Booth, Whitney Blake **13** Bobby Buntrock
  creator: **6** Ted Key

hazelnut 7 Corylus
  varieties: **6** beaked **7** Chinese, Turkish **8** American, European, Japanese

Hazlitt, William
  author of: **17** The Spirit of the Age **32** The Characters of Shakespeare's Plays

hazy 3 dim **5** dusky, faint, filmy, foggy, misty, murky, smoky, vague **6** bleary, blurry, cloudy, smoggy, veiled **7** bleared, general, muddled, obscure, unclear **8** confused, nebulous, overcast **9** ambiguous, uncertain **10** ill-defined, indefinite

head *see box, p. 438*

head
  contains: **4** eyes **5** brain, mouth, skull **9** braincase **10** optic nerve **12** ocular muscle **13** cranial cavity, lacrimal organ, orbital cavity **14** buccaval cavity

headache 5 trial **6** strain, stress **7** problem, trouble **8** migraine, nuisance **10** affliction, difficulty **13** inconvenience, pain in the neck

headdress 3 cap, hat **6** bonnet **7** chapeau **12** headcovering

headland 4 bank, crag **5** bluff, cliff **8** palisade **9** precipice **10** promontory

headlong 6 abrupt **8** abruptly, heedless, pell-mell, reckless **9** headfirst, impetuous **10** heedlessly, recklessly **11** impetuously, precipitate, precipitous **13** head over heels, precipitously

Headlong Hall
  author: **17** Thomas Love Peacock

headman 5 chief **6** leader **7** foreman **8** alderman, princeps **9** commander **10** councilman, supervisor **14** public official, superintendent

head-on 6 direct **7** frontal **10** face-to-face

headshrinker 6 shrink **7** analyst **12** psychiatrist **13** psychoanalyst

headstrong 4 rash **6** dogged, mulish, unruly **7** defiant, froward, willful **8** contrary, obdurate, reckless, stubborn **9** hotheaded, imprudent, impulsive, obstinate, pigheaded

head 2 go, IQ **3** aim, CEO, end, hie, tip, top **4** acme, apex, bent, boss, czar, font, fore, gift, king, lead, main, mind, peak, rise, rule, turn, well **5** begin, brain, chief, crest, crown, drive, first, front, guide, pilot, prime, queen, ruler, start, steer **6** climax, crisis, direct, genius, govern, launch, leader, manage, origin, ruling, source, spring, summit, talent, vertex, zenith **7** ability, admiral, captain, command, conduct, control, foreman, general, go first, highest, leading, make for, manager, marshal, monarch, precede, premier, primary, proceed, ranking, supreme, topmost **8** aptitude, be head of, big wheel, capacity, chairman, dictator, director, dominant, foremost, fountain, fruition, headmost, initiate, judgment, managing, pinnacle, start off, superior, suzerain, upper end **9** acuteness, beginning, commander, commodore, extremity, forefront, front rank, governing, intellect, introduce, mentality, paramount, potentate, president, principal, sovereign, supervise, uppermost **10** administer, be master of, birthplace, cleverness, commandant, commanding, conclusion, first place, gray matter, inaugurate, lead the way, move toward, perception, preeminent, supervisor, wellspring **11** be at the helm, controlling, culmination, discernment, forward part, highest rank, officiate at, preside over, superintend, take the lead, termination **12** apprehension, field marshal, fountainhead, guiding light, place of honor, take charge of, take the reins, turning point, utmost extent **13** administrator, go at the head of, most prominent, prime minister, understanding **14** chief executive, highest ranking, superintendent **15** be in the vanguard, make a beeline for, quickness of mind **16** commander-in-chief, direct one's course, inevitable result **17** commanding general, have authority over **18** be in the driver's seat, chairman of the board, go in the direction of **21** chief executive officer

10 bullheaded, incautious, refractory **11** intractable **12** incorrigible, recalcitrant, ungovernable, unmanageable **14** uncontrollable **22** bent on having one's own way

heady 4 hard **6** potent, strong **8** alluring, exciting, inviting, stirring, tempting **9** seductive, thrilling **10** high-octane **11** high-voltage, tantalizing **12** exhilarating, intoxicating

heal 4 cure, knit, mend **5** right, salve, treat **6** heal up, remedy, settle, soothe **7** compose, get well, improve, recover, rectify, relieve **8** heal over, make well **9** alleviate, make whole, reconcile, conciliate, convalesce, recuperate **11** set to rights **14** make harmonious, return to health **20** restore good relations

healed 4 knit **5** cured **6** mended **7** got well **8** relieved

healing 6 curing **7** mending **8** knitting, soothing **9** emollient, improving, restoring **10** making well **11** restorative **13** strengthening
  god of: 6 Apollo **7** Phoebus, Pythius **9** Asclepius, Musagetes **11** Aesculapius
  goddess of: 4 Iaso

health 5 vigor **7** fitness, stamina **8** strength, vitality **9** hardihood, hardiness, well-being **10** robustness **16** general condition **17** physical condition
  goddess of: 6 Hygeia

healthful 7 healthy **8** hygienic, salutary **9** wholesome **10** beneficial, nourishing, nutritious, salubrious **12** healthgiving, invigorating

healthiness 6 health **9** good shape, soundness **10** good health, robustness **12** salutariness **13** good condition, healthfulness, wholesomeness **14** salubriousness

healthy 3 fit **4** hale **5** hardy, sound **6** hearty, robust, strong, sturdy **8** vigorous **9** in the pink **10** able-bodied **12** in fine fettle **18** sound of mind and limb

heap 3 gob, lot **4** fill, gobs, hunk, load, lots, lump, mass, mess, pack, pile, slew **5** amass, award, batch, bunch, flood, group, mound, ocean, slews, stack, store, world **6** accord, assign, bundle, deluge, engulf, gather, jumble, load up, oceans, oodles, pile up, plenty, worlds **7** barrels, cluster, collect, mete out, present **8** good

deal, inundate, pour upon **9** abundance, gathering, great deal, multitude, profusion **10** assemblage, collection, shower upon **11** aggregation, concentrate **12** accumulation **13** agglomeration

heap up 5 amass **6** pile up **7** stack up **10** accumulate

hear 4 heed **5** admit, favor, grant, judge, learn **6** attend, be told, gather, look on **7** approve, concede, examine, find out, receive, witness **8** accede to, appear at, discover, hear tell, hold with, listen to **9** acquiesce, ascertain, hearken to **10** understand **11** acknowledge

hear!
  French: 4 oyez
  cry used by: 10 court crier
  preceded: 12 proclamation

hearing 5 probe, sound **6** review **7** council, earshot, inquiry **8** audience **9** interview **10** conference **11** examination, questioning **12** consultation **13** interrogation, investigation

hearken to 4 heed, mark, mind **6** attend **8** listen to **11** take to heart **14** pay attention to

Hearns, Thomas
  nickname: 6 Hitman
  sport: 6 boxing
  class: 12 middleweight, welterweight

hearsay 4 talk **5** rumor **6** gossip, report **8** idle talk **9** grapevine **11** scuttlebutt

heart 3 hub, nub **4** base, core, crux, guts, love, meat, mood, pith, root, soul **5** humor, pluck, spunk, valor **6** center, daring, desire, kernel, middle, nature, source, spirit **7** bravery, charity, courage, emotion, essence, nucleus, stomach **8** audacity, backbone, boldness, clemency, feelings, firmness, fondness, gameness, interior, main part, sympathy **9** affection, fortitude, gallantry, inner part, rudiments, sentiment, tolerance **10** brass tacks, compassion, enthusiasm, essentials, foundation, gentleness, indulgence, manfulness, principles, resolution, tenderness, true nature **11** busiest part, central part, disposition, forgiveness, nitty-gritty, temperament **12** fearlessness, fundamentals, quintessence, resoluteness **13** audaciousness
  part: 5 aorta, valve **6** atrium **7** chamber **9** ventricle
  pumps: 5 blood

heartache 3 woe **4** pain

5 grief **6** misery, sorrow **7** anguish, sadness, torment, trouble **8** distress **9** suffering **11** tribulation, unhappiness

heartbreaker 4 vamp **5** flirt, tease **8** coquette

Heartbreak House
author: **17** George Bernard Shaw

hearten 4 abet **5** cheer **6** assure, solace **7** animate, cheer up, comfort, console, enliven, gladden **8** brighten, embolden, energize, inspirit, reassure **9** encourage **10** invigorate

heartening 7 hopeful **9** favorable **10** auspicious, reassuring **11** encouraging

heartfelt 4 deep, full **5** total **6** ardent, devout, entire, honest **7** earnest, fervent, genuine, intense, sincere **8** complete, profound, thorough **10** keenly felt **12** all-inclusive, wholehearted

hearth 4 home **5** abode, house **8** fireside **9** fireplace, household **10** family life **12** family circle **13** chimney corner
    goddess of: **4** Caca **5** Salus, Vesta **6** Hestia

Heart Is a Lonely Hunter, The
author: **15** Carson McCullers character: **8** Mr Singer **9** Mick Kelly **10** Dr Copeland, Jake Blount **11** Biff Brannon

heartless 4 cold, mean **5** cruel **6** brutal, savage, unkind **7** callous, inhuman, unmoved **8** pitiless, ruthless, uncaring **9** unfeeling, unpitying, unstirred **10** unmerciful **11** coldhearted, cold-blooded, hardhearted, insensitive **12** cruelhearted, unresponsive **13** unsympathetic

Heart of Darkness
author: **12** Joseph Conrad character: **5** Kurtz **7** Marlowe

Heart of Dixie
nickname of: **7** Alabama

Heart of Juliet Jones, The
creator: **9** Stan Drake character: **3** Eve

Heart of Midlothian, The
author: **14** Sir Walter Scott

Heart of the Matter, The
author: **12** Graham Greene character: **5** Yusef **6** Wilson **7** Mrs Rolt **9** Mrs Scobie **11** Major Scobie

heart-stopper 5 belle **6** beauty **7** charmer, stunner **8** knockout **10** good-looker

13 beautiful girl **14** beautiful woman

hearty 4 hale, warm, well **5** ample, hardy, sound **6** lively, robust, strong **7** cordial, genuine, healthy, profuse, sincere, zestful **8** complete, effusive, generous, thorough, vigorous **9** heartfelt, unbounded **10** unreserved **12** enthusiastic, unrestrained, wholehearted **13** physically fit

hearty appetite
French: **10** bon appetit

Heaslop, Ronald
character in: **15** A Passage to India author: **7** Forster

heat 3 fry **4** bake, boil, cook, sear, stew, warm, zeal **5** ardor, broil, roast, steam **6** braise, climax, fervor, height, simmer, stress, thrill, warmth, warm up **7** hotness, make hot, passion, rapture, swelter **8** fervency, hot spell, warmness **9** eagerness, intensity, transport **10** enthusiasm, excitement **12** bring to a boil

heated 3 hot **5** angry, fiery, irate **6** bitter, fierce, raging, stormy **7** excited, fervent, furious, intense, violent **8** frenzied, inflamed, vehement **9** emotional **10** infuriated, passionate **11** impassioned, tempestuous

heated discussion 7 dispute **8** argument **10** war of words **11** controversy **12** disagreement

heath 5 Erica
varieties: **4** Tree **5** Berry, Besom, Irish, Otago, Spike **6** Dorset, Scotch, Spring **7** Cornish, Fringed, Spanish, Twisted **9** Cranberry **11** Cross-leaved

Heathcliff
character in: **16** Wuthering Heights author: **6** Bronte

heathen 3 goy **4** boor **5** pagan **6** savage **7** atheist, gentile, infidel **8** agnostic, idolator **9** barbarian, ignoramus **10** polytheist, troglodyte, unbeliever **11** non-believer **17** uncivilized native

heather 7 Calluna
varieties: **3** Bog, Red **4** Bell, Snow **5** Beach, False, White **6** French, Golden, Scotch **8** Corsican, Mountain **9** Christmas **11** White winter **13** Mediterranean **18** Everblooming French

Heat of the Day, The
author: **14** Elizabeth Bowen

heat up 3 fan **4** goad, warm, whet **6** arouse **7** enhance, sharpen **8** increase **9** aggravate, intensify **10** strengthen

heave 3 peg, pry, sob **4** arch, blow, cast, emit, fire, hurl, lift, moan, pant, puff, puke, toss **5** boost, bulge, chuck, eject, fling, groan, hoist, lever, pitch, raise, retch, sling, surge, swell, throw, vomit **6** dilate, drag up, draw up, exhale, expand, haul up, launch, let fly, propel, pull up, tilt up, yank up **7** elevate **8** thrust up **9** discharge, palpitate **11** regurgitate

heaven, Heaven, the Heavens 3 wow **4** Zion **5** bliss, glory, mercy, space **6** my oh my, utopia **7** delight, ecstasy, Elysium, my stars, nirvana, Olympus, rapture **8** boy oh boy, goodness, land sake, paradise, Valhalla **9** afterlife, dreamland, next world, Shangri-la **10** afterworld, Beulah Land, life beyond, outer space, perfection, sheer bliss **11** enchantment, the Holy City, world beyond, world to come **12** eternal bliss, good gracious, New Jerusalem, the City of God, the firmament **13** Abraham's bosom, Elysian fields, seventh heaven **14** heavens to Betsy, our eternal home **15** life everlasting, our Father's house, the heavenly city **16** goodness gracious, Isle of the Blessed, supreme happiness, the abode of saints, the Celestial City, the vault of heaven **17** complete happiness, the wild blue yonder **18** Island of the Blessed, the celestial sphere, the heavenly kingdom, the kingdom of Heaven **19** the celestial expanse **21** the happy hunting ground
    god of: **2** An **3** Anu **4** Jove, Zeus **7** Jupiter

Heaven Can Wait (1943)
director: **13** Ernst Lubitsch cast: **10** Don Ameche **11** Gene Tierney **12** Marjorie Main **13** Charles Coburn

Heaven Can Wait (1978)
director: **9** Buck Henry **12** Warren Beatty cast: **10** Dyan Cannon, Jack Warden **12** Warren Beatty **13** Julie Christie remake of: **17** Here Comes Mr Jordan

heavenly 6 divine **7** angelic, blessed, saintly, sublime **8** beatific, blissful

Heavens and Earth
  author: **19** Stephen Vincent Benet

Heaven's My Destination
  author: **14** Thornton Wilder

heavy *see box*

heavy-handed 5 harsh
  6 clumsy **7** awkward **8** bungling **9** graceless, maladroit
  10 blundering, oppressive, ungraceful

heavyhearted 3 sad **4** glum
  6 dismal, gloomy, morose
  7 doleful, forlorn, joyless, unhappy **8** dejected, downcast
  9 cheerless, depressed, sorrowful **10** despondent, melancholy **11** downhearted
  14 down in the dumps, down in the mouth

Hebe
  goddess of: **5** youth **6** spring
  father: **4** Zeus
  mother: **4** Hera
  brother: **4** Ares
  husband: **8** Hercules
  handmaiden to: **4** gods
  corresponds to: **8** Juventas

Heber
  wife: **4** Jael

Hebrew alphabet
  or: **5** aleph
  b/v: **4** beth
  g: **5** gimel
  d: **6** daleth
  h: **2** he **5** cheth
  v/w: **3** vav
  z: **5** zayin
  y/j/i: **3** yod
  k/kh: **4** kaph

l: **5** lamed
m: **3** men
n: **3** nun
`: **4** ayin
p/f: **2** pe
k: **4** koph
r: **4** resh
sh/s: **4** shin
s: **3** sin **4** sadi **6** samekh
t: **3** tav **4** teth

Hebrew Judge 4 Ehud, Elon, Jair, Tola **5** Abdon, Ibzan
  6 Gideon, Samson, Samuel
  7 Deborah, Othniel, Shamgar
  8 Jephthah

Hebrew months
  first: **4** Ahib, Nisn **6** Ehanim, Tishri
  second: **3** Bul, Civ **4** Iyar **7** Heshvan
  third: **5** Sivan **6** Kislev
  fourth: **5** Tebet **6** Tammuz, Tebeth
  fifth: **2** Ab **7** Shelbat
  sixth: **4** Adar, Elul **6** Veadar
  seventh: **4** Abib **5** Nisan **6** Tishri **7** Ethanim
  eighth: **3** Zif **4** Iyer **11** Marcheshvan
  ninth: **5** Sivan **7** Chislev
  tenth: **6** Tabeth, Tammuz
  eleventh: **2** Ab **6** Shebat
  twelfth: **4** Adar, Elul

Hecabe *see* **6** Hecuba

Hecaleius
  epithet of: **4** Zeus

he carved it
  Latin: **8** sculpsit

Hecate
  also: **6** Hekate
  goddess of: **5** earth, Hades

associated with: **6** hounds **7** sorcery **10** crossroads
corresponds to: **5** Brimo

Hecatonchires
  also: **9** Centimani
  form: **5** giant
  names: **5** Gyges **6** Cottus **8** Briareus
  father: **6** Uranus
  mother: **4** Gaea
  number of heads: **5** fifty
  number of arms: **10** one hundred

heckle 3 boo **4** bait, hiss, hoot, mock, ride, twit **5** annoy, bully, chivy, harry, hound, taunt **6** badger, harass, harrow, hector, jeer at, molest, needle **7** provoke **9** shout down

hectare
  abbreviation of: **2** ha

hectic 3 mad **4** wild **6** stormy **7** chaotic, frantic, furious **8** feverish, frenetic, frenzied, headlong **9** breakneck, turbulent **10** tumultuous

hectoliter
  abbreviation of: **2** hl

hectometer
  abbreviation of: **2** hm

hector 4 bait, ride **5** bully, harry, hound, tease, worry **6** badger, harass, needle, plague **7** torment

Hector
  father: **5** Priam
  mother: **6** Hecuba
  brother: **5** Paris
  sister: **9** Cassandra
  wife: **10** Andromache
  son: **8** Astyanax
  hero of: **9** Trojan War
  killed by: **8** Achilles

Hecuba
  also: **5** Maera **6** Hecabe
  father: **5** Atlas
  husband: **5** Priam **8** Tegeates
  son: **5** Paris **6** Hector **7** Helenus, Polites, Troilus **9** Deiphobus, Polydorus
  daughter: **6** Creusa **7** Laodice **8** Polyxena **9** Cassandra
  changed into: **3** dog **5** bitch
  hound of: **7** Icarius

Hecuba
  author: **9** Euripides
  character: **8** Odysseus, Polyxena **9** Agamemnon, Polydorus **10** Polymestor

Hedda Gabler
  author: **11** Henrik Ibsen
  character: **10** Judge Brack **11** Hedda Tesman, Thea Elvsted **12** George Tesman **13** Eilert Lovberg **17** Miss Juliana Tesman

heder 12 Jewish school

---

heavy 3 big, fat, sad **4** deep, dull, full, hard, lazy, slow **5** broad, bulky, dense, grave, gross, harsh, hefty, large, obese, plump, rough, stout, thick **6** clumsy, coarse, deadly, dreary, fierce, gloomy, leaden, pained, portly, raging, rugged, savage, solemn, strong, sturdy, torpid, woeful **7** awesome, complex, copious, doleful, forlorn, furious, intense, joyless, languid, lumpish, massive, notable, onerous, profuse, roaring, ruinous, serious, tearful, tedious, violent, weighty **8** abundant, agonized, burdened, crushing, cumbrous, damaging, dejected, desolate, downcast, forceful, grieving, grievous, imposing, lifeless, listless, mournful, pedantic, profound, seething, sluggish, stricken, tiresome, unwieldy **9** apathetic, cheerless, corpulent, depressed, difficult, excessive, extensive, harrowing, important, injurious, laborious, lethargic, lumbering, miserable, momentous, ponderous, rampaging, sorrowful, turbulent, wearisome **10** burdensome, calamitous, cumbersome, distressed, full of care, immoderate, impressive, inordinate, melancholy, monotonous, noteworthy, oppressive, overweight, pernicious, phlegmatic, unbearable, unstinting **11** crestfallen, deleterious, destructive, detrimental, distressing, extravagant, intemperate, intolerable, significant, tempestuous, unendurable, unrelenting, unremitting **12** considerable, disconsolate, hard to endure, overwhelming, unrestrained **13** consequential, grief-stricken, of great import **16** laden with sorrows **18** of great consequence

hedge 3 hem **4** duck, edge, ring, wall **5** bound, dodge, evade, fence, guard, hem in, limit **6** border, margin, shut in, waffle **7** barrier, enclose, mark off, outline **8** encircle, hedgerow, surround **9** be evasive, delineate, demarcate, insurance, pussyfoot, temporize **10** equivocate, protection **11** delineation, row of bushes **12** compensation **13** circumference, fence of shrubs **14** beg the question, counterbalance **17** beat around the bush

he died
Latin: **5** obiit

he does not pursue
Latin: **14** non prosequitur

hedonist 8 Sybarite **9** debauchee, libertine **10** dissipater, profligate, sensualist, voluptuary **14** pleasure seeker

hedonistic 7 sensual **9** epicurean, libertine, sybaritic **10** voluptuous **11** intemperate **13** self-indulgent **15** pleasure-seeking

he drew this
Latin: **10** delineavit

Hedrick, Zelma Kathryn
real name of: **14** Kathryn Grayson

heed 4 care, mind, obey **5** bow to, pains, study **6** concur, follow, hold to, notice, regard **7** defer to, observe, perusal, respect, yield to **8** accede to, consider, listen to, prudence, scrutiny, submit to **9** attention, be ruled by, give ear to **10** bear in mind comply with, precaution, take note of **11** carefulness, examination, heedfulness, mindfulness, observation, take to heart **12** take notice of **13** attentiveness **14** fastidiousness, meticulousness, pay attention to, scrupulousness **17** conscientiousness

heedful 4 wary **5** alert, aware, cagey, chary **7** alive to, careful, mindful, prudent **8** cautious, discreet, vigilant, watchful **9** attentive, concerned, conscious

heedless 3 lax **4** rash **5** slack **6** remiss, unwary **7** foolish, unaware, witless **8** careless, mindless, reckless, uncaring **9** foolhardy, frivolous, impetuous, imprudent, negligent, oblivious, unheeding, unmindful **10** incautious, neglectful, unthinking, unwatchful **11** harebrained, improvident, inattentive, thoughtless, un-

concerned, unobservant, unobserving **12** happy-go-lucky **14** scatterbrained

heedlessly 5 blind **6** rashly **8** headlong **9** foolishly, witlessly **10** carelessly, mindlessly, recklessly **11** frivolously, impetuously, impulsively, negligently, unmindfully **12** neglectfully, unthinkingly **13** inattentively, thoughtlessly, unconcernedly **15** inconsiderately, uncooperatively

heedlessness 8 rashness **9** unconcern **10** negligence **11** inattention, unawareness **12** carelessness, indiscretion, mindlessness, recklessness **13** unmindfulness **15** thoughtlessness **16** irresponsibility

heel 3 cad, cur, end, rat **4** list, rind, tilt **5** churl, crust, louse **6** rotter **7** bounder, caitiff, dastard

he engraved it
Latin: **8** sculpsit

Heep, Uriah
character in: **16** David Copperfield
author: **7** Dickens

he flourished
Latin: **7** floruit

hefty 3 big **5** beefy, bulky, burly, heavy, husky, large, stout **6** brawny, hearty, mighty, robust, rugged, strong, sturdy **7** hulking, massive, sizable, weighty, well-fed **8** muscular, powerful, stalwart, thickset **9** corpulent, strapping **11** substantial

Hegeleos
father: **8** Tyrsenus

Hegemone
origin: **8** Athenian
member of: **6** Graces

hegemony 7 control **9** authority, dominance, influence, supremacy

Heggen, Thomas
author of: **9** Mr Roberts

hegira 6 exodus, flight **7** journey

Heh see **6** Ogdoad

he himself said it
Latin: **9** ipse dixit

Heidrun
origin: **12** Scandinavian
form: **4** goat
yields: **4** mead
feeds warriors in: **8** Valhalla

height 4 acme, apex, hill, peak, rise **5** bluff, cliff, crest, knoll, limit, mound, tower **6** apogee, heyday, summit, zenith **7** hilltop, maximum, pla-

teau **8** altitude, eminence, highland, highness, mountain, palisade, pinnacle, tallness, ultimate **9** elevation, extremity, flowering, high point, loftiness, supremacy **10** perfection, promontory **11** culmination **12** consummation, upward extent, utmost degree, vantage point

heighten 5 raise **7** elevate **8** increase **9** aggravate, intensify

heil 4 hail

Heimberger, Eddie Albert
real name of: **11** Eddie Albert

Heimdall
origin: **12** Scandinavian
god of: **4** dawn **5** light
number of mothers: **4** nine
guards: **7** bifrost **13** rainbow bridge
killed by: **4** Loki
noted for: **7** hearing **8** eyesight

Heine, Heinrich
author of: **9** Atta Troll **11** Book of Songs **19** Germany A Winter's Tale

Heinlein, Robert
author of: **10** Double Star **16** Starship Troopers **20** The Green Hills of Earth **22** Stranger in a Strange Land **23** The Moon Is a Harsh Mistress

heinous 4 evil, foul, vile **5** gross, nasty **6** grisly, horrid, odious, sinful, wicked **7** beastly, ghastly, hideous, inhuman, vicious **8** infamous, shocking, terrible **9** abhorrent, atrocious, loathsome, monstrous, nefarious, offensive, repugnant, repulsive, revolting, sickening **10** abominable, deplorable, despicable, detestable, disgusting, iniquitous, outrageous, scandalous, villainous **11** disgraceful, distasteful **12** contemptible **13** objectionable, reprehensible

heinousness 4 evil **7** outrage **8** atrocity, baseness, enormity, foulness, savagery, vileness, villainy **9** barbarity, depravity, malignity **12** inhumanity **13** loathsomeness, monstrousness **14** outrageousness

heir, heiress 7 legatee **9** inheritor **10** inheritrix **11** beneficiary, inheritress **12** heir apparent **15** heir presumptive

Heiress, The
director: **12** William Wyler
based on novel by: **10** Henry James

entitled: **16** Washington Square
cast: 13 Miriam Hopkins **15** Montgomery Clift, Ralph Richardson **17** Olivia de Havilland
score: 12 Aaron Copland
Oscar for: 7 actress (de Havilland)

Hekate *see* **6** Hecate

Hel
origin: 12 Scandinavian
goddess of: 5 death
rules: 8 Niflheim
father: 4 Loki
mother: 9 Angerboda, Angrbodha, Angurboda
brother: 6 Fenrir, Fenris **11** Iormungandr, Jormungandr **14** Midgard Serpent
color of body: 4 blue **5** flesh
home of: 4 dead

Helen
father: 4 Zeus
mother: 4 Leda
brother: 6 Castor, Pollux
sister: 8 Timandra **12** Clytemnestra
husband: 8 Menelaus
abducted by: 5 Paris
carried off to: 4 Troy
abduction caused: 9 Trojan War

Helena
character in: 20 All's Well That Ends Well **21** A Midsummer Night's Dream
author: 11 Shakespeare

Helenor
mentioned in: 6 Aeneid
position: 6 prince
home: 5 Lydia
accompanied: 6 Aeneas

Heliadae
sons of: 6 Helius, Rhodes

helicopter
invented by: 8 Sikorsky

Heliopolis
city of: 2 On

Helios
origin: 5 Greek
god of: 3 sun
father: 8 Hyperion
mother: 4 Thia
children: 5 Circe **6** Aeetes **8** Phaethon
corresponds to: 3 Sol

heliotrope 12 Heliotropium
varieties: 6 garden, winter, yellow **7** seaside

helium
chemical symbol: 2 He

hell, Hell 5 agony, grief, Hades, misery, the pit **7** Abaddon, anguish, despair, Gehenna, inferno, remorse, torment **8** Appolyons, hell fire, the abyss **9** martyrdom, perdi-
tion, suffering **10** lake of fire **12** hopelessness, wretchedness **13** bottomless pit, Satan's kingdom, the lower world, the underworld **14** place of the lost, the Devil's house, the nether world, the shades below **15** everlasting fire, home of lost souls, infernal regions **16** abode of the damned

Helle
father: 7 Athamas
mother: 7 Nephele
stepmother: 3 Ino
brother: 7 Phrixus
death by: 8 drowning

Hellen
king of: 8 Thessaly
father: 9 Deucalion
mother: 6 Pyrrha
wife: 6 Orseis
son: 5 Dorus **6** Aeolus, Xuthus
ancestor of: 8 Hellenes

Hellenic Republic *see* **6** Greece

Heller, Joseph
author of: 10 Good as Gold **14** Catch-Twenty-Two **17** Something Happened

hellion 5 devil, rogue, scamp **9** scoundrel **13** mischief-maker

hellish 4 foul, vile **5** awful **6** brutal **7** hateful **8** accursed, damnable, dreadful, horrible, infernal **9** atrocious, revolting **10** abominable, disgusting

Hellman, Lillian
author of: 5 Maybe **10** Pentimento **13** Scoundrel Time **14** The Little Foxes, Toys in the Attic **15** Watch on the Rhine **16** The Children's Hour **17** An Unfinished Woman **22** Another Part of the Forest

hello
French: 7 bonjour
German: 8 guten tag
Spanish: 10 buenos dias
Italian: 4 ciao **10** buon giorno
Latin: 5 salve

Hello-Central
character in: 36 A Connecticut Yankee in King Arthur's Court
author: 5 Twain

help *see* **box**

helper 3 aid **4** aide **5** angel **6** backer, deputy, patron, second **7** adjunct, partner, servant **8** adjutant, advocate, champion, confrere, co-worker, employee, retainer **9** assistant, associate, auxiliary, colleague, man Friday, right hand, supporter **10** accomplice, aide-de-camp, apprentice, benefactor, girl Friday **11** confederate, helping hand, subordinate **12** collaborator, right-hand man **13** good samaritan **14** fairy godmother

helpful 4 fine, good, kind, nice **6** usable, useful **8** obliging, splendid, valuable **9** excellent, favorable, practical **10** beneficial, profitable, supportive **11** considerate, cooperative, serviceable **12** advantageous, constructive **13** accommodating

helping hand 3 aid **4** aide, hand **5** boost **6** assist, hand up, helper, succor **7** abettor, support **9** assistant **10** assistance

helplessness 8 weakness **9** impotence, inability, infirmity **10** dependence, feebleness, ineptitude **12** incapability, incompetence, inefficiency **13** powerlessness, vulnerability

help 3 aid **4** back, balm, calm, care, crew, cure, ease, gift, lift, save **5** allay, emend, force, guide, hands, salve, serve, staff **6** advice, advise, assist, give to, menial, relief, remedy, rescue, soothe, succor, uphold **7** advance, backing, console, correct, endorse, further, helpers, improve, nurture, promote, rectify, relieve, servant, service, stand by, support, welfare, workers, workmen **8** advocate, befriend, champion, domestic, factotum, farmhand, guidance, laborers, maintain, mitigate, retainer, retrieve, side with **9** alleviate, chip in for, employees, encourage, extricate, lend a hand, make whole, promotion, put at ease, underling, workhands, work force **10** ameliorate, apprentice, assistance, assistants, bring round, corrective, friendship, go to bat for, hired hands, kind regard, minister to, preventive, protection, stick up for **11** advancement, benevolence, cooperation, endorsement, furtherance, good offices, helping hand, make healthy, restorative **12** bring through, contribute to, contribution, hired helpers, intercede for **13** collaboration, cooperate with, encouragement, take the part of

Helsinki
capital of: **7** Finland

hem 3 box, rim **4** bind, brim, edge, welt **5** bound, brink, skirt, verge **6** border, edging, fringe, impede, margin, turn up **7** confine, enclose, stammer, stutter, turning **8** compress, encircle, restrain, surround

he made it
Latin: **5** fecit

Hemera
father: **6** Erebus
mother: **3** Nyx
corresponds to: **3** Eos

Hemerasia
epithet of: **7** Artemis
means: **13** she who soothes

hem in 4 best **5** fence **7** besiege, confine, enclose **8** encircle, surround

Hemingway, Ernest
author of: **9** In Our Time **14** A Moveable Feast **15** A Farewell to Arms, The Sun Also Rises **16** To Have and Have Not **18** Islands in the Stream, The Old Man and the Sea **19** For Whom the Bell Tolls **21** The Snows of Kilimanjaro **34** The Short Happy Life of Francis Macomber

hemiptera
class: **8** hexapoda
phylum: **10** arthropoda
group: **3** bug

Hemithea
father: **6** Cycnus
mother: **7** Proclea
sister: **5** Tenes
pursued by: **8** Achilles
swallowed up by: **5** earth

hemlock 5 Tsuga **15** Conium maculatum
varieties: **5** Dwarf, Water **6** Canada, Ground, Poison **7** Siebold, Spotted, Western **8** Carolina, Japanese, Mountain

hemp 14 Cannabis sativa
varieties: **3** Bog **5** Cuban, Sisal **6** Deccan, Indian, Manila **7** African **8** Deckaner **9** Bowstring, Mauritius **10** New Zealand **13** Colorado River **15** Ceylon bowstring, Indian bowstring **16** African bowstring

hen
young: **6** pullet

Henchard, Michael
character in: **22** The Mayor of Casterbridge
author: **5** Hardy

henchman 4 goon, thug

6 flunky, lackey, minion, stooge, yes-man **7** gorilla **8** hanger-on, hireling, retainer **9** attendant, bodyguard **10** hatchet man, lieutenant **12** right-hand man, strong-arm man

Henderson, Marge
creator/artist of: **10** Little Lulu

Henioche
epithet of: **4** Hera
means: **10** charioteer

henna 3 dye **5** rinse **6** auburn, russet **8** cinnamon **11** rust-colored **12** reddish-brown **13** copper-colored

henpecked 4 meek **5** timid **6** docile **8** obedient **10** browbeaten, submissive, wife-ridden **11** unassertive

Henry, Frederic
character in: **15** A Farewell to Arms
author: **9** Hemingway

Henry Esmond
author: **16** William Thackeray
character: **5** Frank **7** Beatrix **9** Lord Mohun **10** Father Holt **11** James Stuart **12** Rachel Esmond **13** Francis Esmond

Henry IV
author: **18** William Shakespeare
character: **7** Hotspur **11** Prince Henry, Thomas Percy **14** Edmund Mortimer, Sir Walter Blunt **15** John of Lancaster, Mistress Quickly, Sir John Falstaff **18** Earl of Westmoreland, King Henry the Fourth

Henry V
author: **18** William Shakespeare
character: **7** Dauphin, Montjoy **15** Charles the Sixth (King of France) **17** Princess Katharine
director: **15** Laurence Olivier
cast: **11** Leslie Banks **12** Robert Newton **13** Renee Asherson **15** Laurence Olivier

Henry VI
author: **18** William Shakespeare
character: **6** Edward (Prince of Wales) **7** Charles (Dauphin of France), Eleanor, Louis XI (King of France) **8** Lady Bona, Lady Grey **9** Joan of Arc **10** Lord Talbot **11** Bolingbroke **12** John Beaufort, Lord Clifford, Lord Hastings **13** Henry Beaufort, Joan La Pucelle **15** Margaret of Anjou, Margery Jour-

dain **16** Bastard of Orleans, Cardinal Beaufort
duke: **4** York (Richard Plantagenet) **7** Bedford, Suffolk **8** Somerset **10** Gloucester
earl: **7** Suffolk, Warwick **9** Salisbury
Richard Plantagenet's son: **6** Edmund, Edward, George **7** Richard

Henry VIII
author: **18** William Shakespeare
character: **7** Cranmer **8** Gardiner **10** Anne Boleyn **12** Thomas Wolsey **14** Queen Katharine, Thomas Cromwell **16** Cardinal Campeius
duke: **7** Norfolk, Suffolk **10** Buckingham

Henze, Hans Werner
born: **7** Germany **10** Westphalia
composer of: **6** Ariosi, Ondine **8** King Stag **10** El Cimarron **11** Konig Hirsch **12** The Bassarids, The Young Lord **14** Being Beauteous **15** The Runaway Slave **17** Boulevard Solitude **18** Der Prinz von Homburg, The Raft of the Medusa **19** Elegy for Young Lovers **48** The Long and Weary Journey to the Flat of Natasha Ungeheur

Heorot
great hall in: **7** Beowulf
author: **7** unknown

he painted it
Latin: **6** pinxit

Hepburn, Audrey
real name: **19** Audrey Hepburn-Ruston
husband: **9** Mel Ferrer
born: **7** Belgium **8** Brussels
roles: **6** Ondine **7** Charade, Sabrina **9** Bloodline, Funny Face **10** My Fair Lady **11** War and Peace **12** Roman Holiday (Oscar), The Nun's Story **13** Green Mansions, Wait Until Dark **18** Love in the Afternoon **19** Breakfast at Tiffany's

Hepburn, Katharine
co-star: **12** Spencer Tracy
born: **10** Hartford CT
roles: **7** Desk Set, Holiday **8** Adam's Rib **10** Alice Adams, Pat and Mike, Summertime **12** Morning Glory (Oscar), On Golden Pond (Oscar), The Rainmaker **14** Woman of the Year **15** The African Queen, The Lion in Winter (Oscar) **18** Suddenly Last Summer **20** The Philadelphia Story

23 Guess Who's Coming to Dinner (Oscar) **24** Long Day's Journey into Night

Hephaestus
 also: **10** Hephaistos
 father: **4** Zeus
 mother: **4** Hera
 god of: **4** fire **11** handicrafts **12** metalworking
 vocation: **5** smith
 wife: **9** Aphrodite
 corresponds to: **6** Vulcan

Hephaistos *see* **10** Hephaestus

Hephzibah
 husband: **8** Hezekiah
 son: **8** Manasseh

Hepzibah *see* **9** Hephzibah

Hera
 also: **4** Here
 origin: **5** Greek
 queen of: **6** Heaven
 father: **6** Cronos, Cronus, Kronos
 mother: **4** Rhea
 brother: **4** Zeus
 husband: **4** Zeus
 son: **4** Ares
 daughter: **9** Eilithyia **10** Hephaestus
 birthplace: **5** Samos
 festival: **7** Daedala
 counterfeit: **7** Nephele
 corresponds to: **4** Juno
 epithet: **6** Anthea, Bunaea **8** Henioche **9** Prodromia

Heracles *see* **8** Hercules

Heracles, Children of
 author: **9** Euripides
 character: **6** Hyllus, Iolaus **7** Alcmene, Macaria **8** Demophon **10** Eurystheus

Heracles, Madness of
 author: **9** Euripides
 character: **4** Hera **5** Lycus **6** Megara **7** Theseus **8** Heracles **10** Amphitryon

Heraclid
 descendant of: **8** Hercules

Heraclidae
 children of: **8** Hercules

Heraea
 origin: **5** Greek
 form: **8** festival

Herakles *see* **8** Hercules

herald 4 clue, omen, sign **5** crier, envoy, token, usher **6** augury, inform, report, reveal, symbol **7** courier, divulge, portent, presage, publish, usher in, warning **8** announce, forecast, foregoer, foretell, proclaim **9** advertise, harbinger, indicator, make known, messenger, precursor, prefigure, publicize **10** forerunner, indication, proclaimer **11** bruit abroad, communicate,

give voice to, predecessor **13** give tidings of

heraldic emblem 4 arms **5** crest **8** blazonry, insignia **10** coat of arms

heraldry *see box*

herb 4 drug **5** plant, spice **6** annual, physic **7** herbage, perfume **8** aromatic, biennial, medicine **9** flavoring, perennial, seasoning, succulent
 kind: **3** bay, rue **4** corn, dill, hemp, mint, rose, sage **5** anise, basil, curry, chili, grass, onion, peony, thyme, wheat **6** catnip, celery, chives, clover, fennel, garlic, pepper, sesame **7** boneset, caraway, ginseng, lavender, mustard, oregano, parsley **8** camomile, licorice, rosemary, tarragon **9** buttercup, marijuana, spearmint **10** peppermint **11** wintergreen

Herbert, George
 author of: **9** The Temple

Herbert, Victor
 born: **6** Dublin **7** Ireland
 composer of: **14** Babes in Toyland, Hero and Leander **15** Naughty Marietta

herbivorous 10 vegetarian **11** plant-eating **14** noncarnivorous

Herceius
 epithet of: **4** Zeus
 means: **14** of the courtyard

herculean, Herculean 4 hard **5** burly, hefty, tough **6** brawny, mighty, robust, rugged, strong, sturdy **7** arduous, onerous **8** muscular, powerful, toilsome, wearying **9** difficult, fatiguing, laborious, strapping, strenuous **10** burdensome, exhausting, formidable, prodigious **12** backbreaking

Hercules
 also: **7** Alcides **8** Heracles, Herakles **9** Carnopian
 father: **4** Zeus
 mother: **7** Alcmene
 cousin: **10** Eurystheus
 wife: **4** Hebe **6** Megara **8** Deianira
 son: **5** Lamus **6** Hyllus **8** Telephus **11** Therimachus
 daughter: **7** Macaria
 teacher: **6** Chiron
 gift: **8** strength
 performed: **6** labors
 number of labors: **6** twelve
 epithet: **7** Charops **8** Buphagus **9** Ipoctonus
 corresponds to: **6** Sancus **10** Semo Sancus

Hercyna
 form: **5** nymph

heraldry
 also called: **4** arms **10** coat of arms
 black: **5** sable
 blue: **5** azure
 bottom: **4** base
 center: **5** fesse
 coat of arms of cities/ countries/colleges: **14** impersonal arms
 coat of arms on shield/ crest/helmet/motto: **19** armorial achievement
 colors: **8** tincture
 concerns family's: **8** heritage **9** genealogy
 described as: **9** blazoning
 divided diagonally: **7** per bend
 divided vertically and horizontally: **9** quartered
 for holding shield: **10** supporters
 fur: **4** vair **6** ermine
 gold/yellow: **2** or
 green: **4** vert
 helmet top: **5** crest
 horizontal band: **4** fess
 intrafamily distinctions: **12** differencing
  daughter: **7** lozenge
  eldest son: **5** label
  younger son: **7** cadency
 left part: **8** sinister
 main figure: **6** charge **8** ordinary **14** heraldic device
 metal: **2** or **6** argent
 motto in: **6** scroll
 orange: **5** tenne
 placed on lord's: **6** banner, shield **8** garments **14** horse trappings
 portrayed as: **6** emblem, symbol
 purple: **7** purpure
 red: **5** gules
 red-purple: **8** sanguine
 right part: **6** dexter
 shield: **10** escutcheon
 sunshade: **8** mantling
  held by: **5** wreath
  made of: **4** silk
 surface/background: **5** field
 top: **5** chief
 two or more colors: **16** lines of partition
 vertical band: **4** pale
 when worn by followers: **5** badge **6** livery
 white/silver: **6** argent

location: 8 fountain
playmate: 10 Persephone

herd 3 lot, mob 4 army, band,
body, gang, goad, host, lead,
mass, pack, spur 5 array,
bunch, crowd, drive, drove,
flock, force, group, guide,
horde, party, press, rally,
swarm, tribe, troop 6 gather,
huddle, legion, muster, number, throng 7 cluster, collect,
company, convene, round up
8 assemble, assembly, conclave 9 gathering, multitude
10 assemblage, collection
11 convocation
12 congregation

Herds
god of: 8 Silvanus, Sylvanus

herdsman 6 cowboy, driver,
drover 7 cowpoke 8 shepherd

Herdsman
constellation of: 6 Bootes

herd together 5 flock, group
6 gather 7 cluster, collect
10 congregate 12 band
together

Here see 4 Hera

hereafter 5 limbo 6 heaven
8 paradise 9 afterlife, from
now on, next world, Purgatory 10 afterworld, future life,
henceforth, life beyond, ultimately 11 in the future, world
to come 12 at a later date, at
a later time, henceforward,
subsequently 14 life after
death 15 heavenly kingdom

here and there 6 around
11 at intervals 18 in this place
and that
Latin: 6 passim

Here Comes Mr Jordan
director: 13 Alexander Hall
cast: 11 Claude Rains, Evelyn
Keyes, Rita Johnson
16 Robert Montgomery
remade as: 13 Heaven Can
Wait

hereditary 6 inborn, inbred
7 genetic 9 ancestral, heritable,
inherited 10 congenital,
handed-down 11 established,
inheritable, traditional

here lies
Latin: 8 hic jacet

heresy 7 dissent, fallacy
8 apostasy 10 dissension, het-
erodoxy, iconoclasm, irreligion 11 unorthodoxy
13 nonconformity 15 unsound
doctrine

heretic 7 skeptic 8 apostate,
recreant, recusant, renegade
9 dissenter 10 backslider
11 freethinker, misbeliever

12 deviationist
13 nonconformist

heretical 7 radical 9 dissident
10 unorthodox 12 iconoclastic
13 nonconforming, noncon-
formist 14 unconventional

heretofore
French: 8 ci-devant

Hereward the Wake
author: 15 Charles Kingsley

Hergesheimer, Joseph
author of: 8 Java Head
19 The Three Black Pennys

heritage 6 estate, legacy
7 portion 9 patrimony, tradition 10 birthright 11 inheritance 16 family possession

Hermaphroditus
father: 6 Hermes
mother: 9 Aphrodite
loved by: 8 Salmacis
joined with: 8 Salmacis
became: 8 bisexual

Hermes
origin: 5 Greek
occupation: 6 herald
messenger of: 4 gods
father: 4 Zeus
mother: 4 Maia
son: 3 Pan 6 Prylis
7 Daphnis
14 Hermaphroditus
birthplace: 7 Arcadia
god of: 4 luck 5 roads, sleep
6 dreams, wealth 7 cunning,
thieves 8 commerce 9 fertility, invention, merchants
invented: 4 lyre
sandals had: 5 wings
epithet: 6 Dolius 8 Agoraeus
9 Spelaites 10 Criophorus
11 Argiphontes 12 Argei-
phontes, Psychopompus
corresponds to: 5 Thoth
7 Mercury

hermetic 6 mystic, occult
7 obscure 8 abstruse, airtight,
esoteric, mystical 9 recondite

Hermia
character in: 21 A Midsummer Night's Dream
author: 11 Shakespeare

hermine, L'
author: 11 Jean Anouilh

Hermione
character in: 14 The Winter's
Tale
author: 11 Shakespeare

Hermione
father: 8 Menelaus
mother: 5 Helen
husband: 7 Orestes
son: 9 Tisamenus

hermit 7 eremite, recluse
8 cenobite, monastic, solitary
9 anchorite 11 desert saint

14 solitudinarian 16 religious
recluse

hermitage 5 abbey 6 friary,
priory 7 convent, retreat
8 cloister 9 monastery

Hermod
origin: 12 Scandinavian
father: 4 Odin 5 Othin
race: 4 Asar 5 Aesir
negotiates return of:
5 Baldr 6 Balder, Baldur

hero, heroine 4 idol, star
7 gallant 8 brave man, champion, great man, male lead,
male star, noble man 9 daredevil, daring man, main actor 10 adventurer, leading
man 11 protagonist, valorous
man 12 man of courage, man
of the hour 13 chivalrous
man, popular figure 15 fearless fighter, idealized person,
intrepid warrior, legendary
person

Hero
character in: 19 Much Ado
About Nothing
author: 11 Shakespeare

Hero
vocation: 9 priestess
priestess of: 9 Aphrodite
lover: 7 Leander
death by: 7 suicide
8 drowning

Herod Antipas
father: 13 Herod the great
mother: 8 Malthace
grandfather: 9 Antipater
wife: 8 Herodias
half brother: 6 Philip
beheaded: 14 John the
Baptist

Herodias
husband: 6 Philip 12 Herod
Antipas
daughter: 6 Salome

Herodotus
called: 15 Father of History
wrote history of: 11 Persian
Wars

Herod Philip
daughter: 6 Salome

heroic 4 bold, epic 5 brave,
grand, noble 6 daring 7 classic, exalted, gallant, Homeric,
valiant 8 elevated, fearless,
highbrow, inflated, intrepid,
mythical, resolute, valorous
9 bombastic, dauntless, dignified, grandiose, high-flown,
legendary, undaunted 10 chivalrous, courageous 11 exaggerated, extravagant,
lionhearted, pretentious, unflinching 12 mythological, ostentatious, stouthearted

heroic act 4 feat 7 exploit
9 brave deed

heroism 5 valor **6** daring **7** bravery, courage, prowess **8** boldness, chivalry, nobility **9** fortitude, gallantry **11** intrepidity **12** fearlessness **13** dauntlessness **14** courageousness **15** lionheartedness

Herophilus
field: **7** anatomy
nationality: **5** Greek
experimented with: **15** postmortem exams

Heros
author: **8** Menander

herpetophobia
fear of: **8** reptiles

Herrenvolk 10 master race

Herrick, Robert
author of: **10** Hesperides **20** Corinna's Going A Maying **26** Gather ye rosebuds while ye may

Herriman, George
creator/artist of: **8** Krazy Kat

Herschel, William
field: **9** astronomy
nationality: **7** British
discovered: **6** Uranus

Herse
father: **7** Cecrops
sister: **8** Aglauros, Aglaurus, Agraulos
lover: **6** Hermes
son: **5** Ceryx **8** Cephalus

Hersey, John
author of: **7** The Wall **9** Hiroshima **13** A Bell for Adano, The Conspiracy **22** My Petition for More Space

Hertz, Heinrich
field: **7** physics
nationality: **6** German
discovered: **13** electric waves **18** wireless telegraphy
named for him: **13** hertzian waves

Herzog
author: **10** Saul Bellow

he sculptured it
Latin: **8** sculpsit

Hesiod
author of: **8** Theogony **12** Works and Days

Hesione
father: **8** Laomedon
husband: **7** Telamon
son: **6** Teucer
rescued by: **8** Hercules

hesitancy 10 indecision, reluctance, unsureness **11** uncertainty, vacillation **12** irresolution

hesitant 5 loath **6** unsure **7** halting **8** doubtful, wavering **9** diffident, faltering, reluctant, tentative, uncertain, undecided **10** hesitating, indecisive, irresolute **11** half-hearted, hanging back, vacillating **15** shilly-shallying **17** lacking confidence, sitting on the fence

hesitate 4 balk, halt **5** delay, pause, shy at, waver **6** falter **7** scruple, stick at **8** be unsure, hang back **9** stickle at, vacillate **10** dillydally, shrink from, think twice **11** be reluctant, be uncertain, be undecided, be unwilling, stop briefly **12** be irresolute, shilly-shally **16** straddle the fence

hesitating 8 doubtful, hesitant **10** indecisive, irresolute, on the fence

he speaks
Latin: **8** loquitur

Hesperia
also: **5** Italy **16** Iberian Peninsula

Hesperides
author: **13** Robert Herrick

Hesperides
form: **6** nymphs
guarded: **12** golden apples
guarded with: **5** Ladon **6** dragon
names: **5** Aegle **6** Hestia **7** Erythea, Hespera **8** Arethusa **9** Hespereia, Hesperusa
islands of the: **7** blessed
form of: **6** heaven

Hesperis
mother: **8** Hesperus
mother of: **10** Hesperides

Hess, Victor Francis
field: **7** physics
discovered: **10** cosmic rays
awarded: **10** Nobel Prize

Hesse, Hermann
author of: **6** Demian **9** Rosshalde **10** Siddhartha **11** Steppenwolf **12** Magister Ludi **14** Peter Camenzind **15** Beneath the Wheel **16** Death and the Lover, Journey to the East, The Glass Bead Game

Hesselberg, Melvyn Edouard
real name of: **13** Melvyn Douglas

hessionite
species: **6** garnet

Hestia
origin: **5** Greek
goddess of the: **6** hearth
father: **6** Cronos, Cronus, Kronos
mother: **4** Rhea
corresponds to: **5** Vesta

Heston, Charlton
real name: **13** Charles Carter
born: **10** Evanston IL
roles: **5** El Cid, Moses **6** Ben-Hur (Oscar) **15** Planet of the Apes **18** The Ten Commandments **21** The Agony and the Ecstasy **22** The Greatest Show on Earth

Heterodontosaurus
type: **8** dinosaur **10** ornithopod
location: **6** Africa
period: **8** Triassic

heterogeneous 5 mixed **6** motley, unlike, varied **7** diverse, jumbled **8** assorted **9** composite, disparate, divergent, unrelated **10** dissimilar, variegated **11** diversified **13** miscellaneous

hew 2 ax **3** cut, lop **4** chop, form, hack, mold **5** carve, model, prune, sever, shape **6** chisel, cut out, devise **7** cut down, fashion, whittle **8** chop down **9** sculpture

He Who Gets Slapped
author: **14** Leonid Andreyev

he wrote it
Latin: **8** scripsit

hex 4 harm, jinx, sign **5** curse, spell, witch **6** hoodoo, voodoo, whammy **7** bewitch, evil eye, ill wind, possess **8** sorcerer **9** sorceress **11** malediction

Hexateuch 27 first six books of Old Testament
see also: **7** Books of **12** Old Testament

heyday 4 acme **5** bloom, crest, flush, prime, vigor **6** zenith **9** flowering, salad days

Heyerdahl, Thor
author of: **7** Kon-Tiki **16** The Ra Expeditions

Hezekiah
father: **4** Ahaz
wife: **9** Hephzibah
means: **18** Jehovah strengthens

Hi and Lois
creator: **9** Dik Browne **10** Mort Walker
character:
  brother: **12** Beetle Bailey
  children: **3** Dot **4** Chip **5** Ditto **6** Trixie
  dog: **4** Dawg
  friend: **7** Thirsty

hiatus 3 gap **4** void **5** blank, break, lapse, space **6** lacuna, vacuum **7** interim **8** interval **10** disruption **12** interruption

Hiawatha, The Song of
author: **24** Henry Wadsworth Longfellow

character: 5 Nahma **7** Kwasind, Nokomis, Wenonah **8** Mondamin **9** Chibiabos, Minnehaha **11** Mudjekeewis **12** Pau-Puk-Keewis, Pearl-Feather

hibernate 5 sleep **6** retire **8** withdraw **13** become dormant

hibernating 6 asleep **7** dormant **8** inactive, sleeping **9** quiescent

Hibernia *see* **7** Ireland

hibiscus
varieties: 7 Chinese **8** Hawaiian, Japanese

Hicetaon
father: 8 Laomedon
brother: 5 Priam

hic jacet 8 here lies

hickory 5 Carya
varieties: 4 Pale, Sand **5** Broom, Swamp, Water **6** Pignut **7** Chinese **8** Mountain, Shagbark **9** Mockernut, Shellbark **10** White-heart **12** Small-fruited

Hicks, Edward
born: 11 Attleboro PA
artwork: 19 The Peaceable Kingdom

Hidatsa (Minitari, Gros Ventre)
language family: 6 Siouan
location: 7 Montana **11** North Dakota
related to: 6 Mandan **7** Arikara

hidden away 6 buried, cached **7** stashed **8** closeted, pocketed, secluded, secreted **9** concealed **10** out of sight **11** stashed away **12** inaccessible, undiscovered

hidden meaning 6 enigma, puzzle, riddle, secret **7** mystery

hidden motive
French: 13 arriere pensee

hide 4 mask, pelt, skin, veil **5** cache, cloak, cloud, cover **6** lie low, screen, shroud **7** conceal, curtain, leather, obscure, repress, seclude, secrete **8** disguise, suppress

hideaway 7 hideout, retreat **11** hiding place, secret place

hideous 4 grim, ugly, vile **5** awful **6** horrid, odious **7** ghastly, macabre **8** dreadful, gruesome, horrible, shocking **9** abhorrent, appalling, frightful, grotesque, loathsome, monstrous, repellent, repugnant, repulsive, revolting, sickening **10** abominable,

detestable, disgusting, horrendous

hiding place 5 cache **8** hideaway **9** hidey hole **10** repository **11** secret place

Hieronimo
character in: 17 The Spanish Tragedy
author: 3 Kyd

hier wird Deutsch gesprochen 18 German is spoken here

Higgins, Henry
character in: 9 Pygmalion **10** My Fair Lady
author: 4 Shaw

Higgs
character in: 7 Erewhon
author: 6 Butler

high 3 gay, top **4** main, tall **5** aloft, chief, far up, grand, great, jolly, lofty, merry, noble, prime, sharp, undue, way up **6** alpine, august, elated, jovial, joyful, joyous, shrill **7** capital, eminent, exalted, excited, extreme, gleeful, leading, notable, playful, primary, serious, soaring, soprano **8** cheerful, elevated, exultant, foremost, imposing, jubilant, mirthful, peerless, piercing, strident, superior, towering, uncurbed **9** ascendant, excellent, excessive, exuberant, important, overjoyed, principal, prominent, unbridled, uppermost **10** exorbitant, immoderate, inordinate, preeminent **11** cloud-capped, exaggerated, exhilarated, extravagant, high-pitched, illustrious, intemperate, predominant, significant, sky-scraping **12** earsplitting, high-reaching, lighthearted, unreasonable, unrestrained **13** consequential, distinguished

high-and-mighty 5 lofty **6** lordly **7** haughty **8** arrogant **9** imperious **11** overbearing

highborn 5 noble **8** highbred, wellborn **9** patrician **10** of high rank, upper-class **12** aristocratic, of high degree, silk-stocking **13** of gentle blood

highbred 5 noble, regal **6** lordly **7** refined **8** highborn, wellborn **9** patrician **11** aristocracy, blue-blooded

highbrow 4 snob **5** brain **7** bookish, Brahmin, egghead, elitist, erudite, scholar, thinker **8** cultured, mandarin, snobbish **9** scholarly **10** cultivated, double-dome, mastermind **12** intellectual **13** knowledgeable

highest good
Latin: 11 summum bonum

highest point
Latin: 11 ne plus ultra

high fashion
French: 12 haute couture

high-flown 4 wild **5** lofty, proud **6** absurd, florid, lordly, turgid, unreal **7** flowery, orotund, pompous **8** elevated, fabulous, inflated **9** bombastic, excessive, fantastic, grandiose **10** flamboyant, immoderate, inordinate, outrageous **11** exaggerated, extravagant, highfalutin, pretentious, sententious **12** magniloquent, preposterous, presumptuous, unreasonable, unrestrained **13** grandiloquent, self-important

High-German
language family: 12 Indo-European
branch: 8 Germanic
group: 15 Western Germanic
subgroup: 11 German-Dutch
division: 6 German **7** Yiddish

high-hat 4 aloof **6** formal, la-di-da, snooty **7** haughty **8** snobbish **12** supercilious

highjinks, hijinks 6 antics, capers, pranks, stunts **11** shenanigans **12** monkeyshines

highland, Highlands 4 rise **7** heights, plateau, uplands **8** headland **9** tableland **10** promontory **11** hill country **17** mountainous region
refers especially to: 8 Scotland

highlight 4 peak **6** accent, climax, stress **7** feature, point up **9** emphasize, high point, underline **10** accentuate, focal point, make bright

highly qualified 3 fit **4** able **7** trained **8** eligible, prepared, skillful **9** practiced **10** proficient **11** experienced **12** accomplished

highly regarded 6 prized **7** admired, revered **8** esteemed **9** respected, treasured **13** well thought of

highly valued 4 dear **5** loved **6** adored **7** beloved, revered **8** esteemed, precious **9** cherished, treasured

highly visible 7 glaring, obvious **8** distinct **9** prominent **11** conspicuous, outstanding

high-minded 4 fair, just **5** lofty, moral, noble **6** honest, worthy **7** ethical, sincere, upright **8** truthful, virtuous **9** exemplary, honorable, reputable, righteous, uncorrupt **10** chivalrous, idealistic, principled, scrupulous **13** conscientious, square-dealing

High Noon
director: **13** Fred Zinnemann
cast: **10** Gary Cooper (Will Kane), Grace Kelly **12** Lloyd Bridges **14** Thomas Mitchell
score: **14** Dimitri Tiomkin
Oscar for: **5** actor (Cooper)

high old time 4 ball, lark **5** fling, revel, spree **8** escapade

high-pitched 5 acute, sharp **6** shrill **7** clarion, squeaky **8** piercing

high place 4 hill, peak, rise **5** bluff, cliff, knoll, ridge **6** height, summit, upland **7** hillock, hummock, plateau **8** eminence, mountain **9** elevation **10** prominence, promontory

high point, highest point 3 cap, top **4** acme, apex, peak **5** crest, crown **6** apogee, climax, height, heyday, summit, tiptop, vertex, zenith **8** eminence, pinnacle **9** flowering **10** prominence **11** culmination

high position 4 note **8** eminence, high rank, standing **9** supremacy **10** ascendancy, importance, notability, prominence **11** distinction, preeminence

high-powered 7 driving, dynamic **8** forceful **9** ambitious, assertive, energetic, go-getting **10** aggressive **11** hard-driving

high praise 5 kudos, paean **6** eulogy **7** hosanna, plaudit **8** encomium **9** laudation, panegyric **11** acclamation

high-priced 4 dear, high **6** costly, pricey **9** expensive **10** exorbitant, overpriced **11** extravagant

high-principled 5 moral, noble **6** chaste, honest, worthy **7** ethical, upright **9** honorable, reputable **10** idealistic **11** responsible, trustworthy **13** conscientious

high quality 5 merit **7** quality **9** greatness **10** excellence, perfection **11** distinction, superiority

high-ranking 3 top **5** grand, great, lofty, regal, royal **6** august **7** eminent, exalted, supreme **8** elevated, esteemed, imposing **9** important, paramount, venerable **10** preeminent **11** illustrious **13** distinguished

High Sierra
director: **10** Raoul Walsh
cast: **9** Ida Lupino **10** Alan Curtis, Joan Leslie **13** Arthur Kennedy **14** Humphrey Bogart (Mad Dog Earle)
remade as: **17** Colorado Territory **19** I Died a Thousand Times

high society 5 elite **9** haut monde, top drawer **11** aristocracy **14** creme de la creme
French: **9** haut monde

High Society
director: **14** Charles Walters
cast: **10** Bing Crosby, Grace Kelly **11** Celeste Holm **12** Frank Sinatra, Louis Calhern **14** Louis Armstrong
score: **10** Cole Porter
remake of: **20** The Philadelphia Story
song: **8** True Love **10** Did You Evah? **16** You're Sensational

high-speed 4 fast **5** quick, rapid, swift **6** speedy **7** express

high-spirited 5 vital **6** lively **8** animated **9** exuberant, vivacious **12** effervescent, enthusiastic

high spirits 5 vigor **6** gaiety **7** delight, elation **8** gladness, vitality, vivacity **9** animation **10** enthusiasm, exaltation, excitement, joyousness, liveliness **12** exhilaration **16** lightheartedness

high-strung 4 edgy **5** jumpy, moody, tense **6** uneasy **7** jittery, nervous, uptight **8** neurotic, restless, skittish **9** emotional, excitable, impatient, wrought-up **10** hysterical **13** oversensitive, temperamental **14** easily agitated, hypersensitive

High Tor
author: **15** Maxwell Anderson

highway 7 freeway, parkway, thruway **8** hard road, highroad, main road, speedway, turnpike **9** paved road **10** expressway, interstate, main artery **12** four-lane road, thoroughfare
British: **9** coach road, royal road **12** King's highway **13** Queen's highway

highwayman 5 crook, thief **6** bandit, outlaw, robber **7** brigand, footpad

hike 4 rise, roam, rove, trek, walk **5** leg it, march, raise, tramp **6** draw up, hoof it, jerk up, pull up, ramble, trudge, wander **7** hitch up, raise up **8** addition, increase **9** expansion **10** escalation **12** augmentation **13** journey on foot **14** go by shank's mare

Hilaira
vocation: **9** priestess
priestess of: **7** Artemis
father: **9** Leucippus
abducted by: **6** Castor

hilarious 3 gay **5** jolly, merry, noisy **6** jocund, jovial, joyful, joyous, lively **7** comical, gleeful, riotous **8** jubilant, mirthful **9** exuberant, laughable, very funny **10** boisterous, hysterical, rollicking, uproarious, vociferous **11** exhilarated **12** high-spirited **13** highly amusing **14** laugh-provoking

hilarity 3 fun, gig, joy **4** glee, riot **5** laugh, mirth, noisy **6** comedy, gaiety, giggle, levity **7** chortle, chuckle, jollity **8** hysteria, laughter **9** amusement, funniness, joviality, jubilance, merriment **10** exuberance **12** exhilaration, humorousness **14** uproariousness

Hilbert, David
field: **8** geometry **11** mathematics
nationality: **6** German
formulated: **12** modern axioms

Hilda Lessways
author: **13** Arnold Bennett

hill 4 bank, dune, heap, pile, ramp, rise **5** bluff, butte, cliff, climb, grade, knoll, mound, mount, slope **6** height **7** hillock, hilltop, hummock, incline, upgrade **8** eminence, foothill, highland, hillside **9** acclivity, declivity, downgrade, elevation **10** prominence, promontory

Hill, Arthur
born: **6** Canada **7** Melfort **12** Saskatchewan
roles: **13** All the Way Home **15** The Ugly American **17** Look Homeward Angel **25** Who's Afraid of Virginia Woolf?

Hill, George Roy
director of: **8** The Sting (Oscar) **23** The World According to Garp **29** Butch Cassidy and the Sundance Kid

Hiller, Arthur
director of: **25** The Americanization of Emily

hillock 4 hill, rise **5** knoll, mound **7** hummock **8** eminence

Hill Street Blues
character: **5** LaRue, Renko **9** Bobby Hill, Jablonski, Joe

Coffey, Lucy Bates **10** Fay Furillo, Mick Belker, Washington **11** (Lt) Norman Buntz **12** Howard Hunter, (Captain) Frank Furillo **13** Henry Goldblum **14** Joyce Davenport
cast: 8 Joe Spano **10** Bruce Weitz, Ed Marinaro, Kiel Martin **11** Betty Thomas, Charles Haid, Dennis Franz **12** Robert Prosky **13** James B Sikking, Michael Warren, Veronica Hamel **14** Taurean Blacque **15** Daniel J Travanti

Hilton, James
author of: **11** Lost Horizon **14** Good-Bye Mr Chips

Himeros
origin: **5** Greek
god of: **12** erotic desire
associated with: **4** Eros

Hind *see* **5** India

Hind and the Panther, The
author: **10** John Dryden

Hindarfjall *see* **8** Hindfell

Hindemith, Paul
born: **5** Hanau **7** Germany
composer of: **8** The Demon **9** Cardillac **10** Heriodiade **12** Ludus Tonalis, Neues vom Tage, News of the Day **13** Sancta Susanna **14** Cupid and Psyche, Mathis Der Maler **15** In Praise of Music **17** Murder Hope of Women **18** Die Harmonie der Welt, Nobilissima Visione **19** The Four Temperaments **23** Morder Hoffnung der Frauen

hinder 3 bar **4** curb, foil, stay, stop **5** block, check, delay, deter, spike, stall **6** arrest, detain, fetter, hamper, hobble, hog-tie, hold up, impede, retard, stifle, stymie, thwart **7** inhibit **8** encumber, handicap, hold back, obstruct, restrain, slow down **9** frustrate, hamstring **13** interfere with

Hindfell
also: **11** Hindarfjall
origin: **12** Scandinavian
mountain slept on by: **8** Brynhild

Hindi
language family: **12** Indo-European
branch: **11** Indo-Iranian
group: **5** Indic
official language of: **5** India

hindmost 4 last, rear **7** tail end **12** farthest back

hindpart 4 tail **6** far end **7** rear end **8** backside, buttocks, haunches **9** afterpart, posterior

hindquarters 4 rear, rump **7** rear end, tail end **8** back legs, backside, buttocks, haunches **9** posterior

hindrance 3 bar **4** clog, curb, snag **5** catch **6** fetter **7** barrier, shackle **8** blockade, blockage, handicap, obstacle **9** barricade, restraint, retardant **10** constraint, difficulty, impediment, limitation **11** encumbrance, obstruction, restriction **12** interference **14** stumbling block

hinge 4 hang, rest, turn **5** pivot, swing **6** depend **7** be due to **9** arise from **10** result from **11** be subject to, emanate from **13** revolve around

hint 3 bit, jot, tip **4** clue, idea, iota **5** grain, imply, pinch, tinge, touch, trace, whiff **6** little, notion, tip off **7** inkling, pointer, signify, soupcon, suggest, whisper **8** allusion, indicate, innuendo, intimate **9** insinuate, suspicion **10** impression, indication, intimation, smattering, suggestion **11** implication, indirection, insinuation **12** flea in the ear, slight amount **13** word to the wise

hinted 7 implied, oblique **8** implicit, indirect **9** suggested

hinterland 6 sticks **7** boonies, country **8** interior, midlands **9** backwater, backwoods, boondocks, rural area **11** countryside

Hiordis
also: **7** Hjordis
origin: **12** Scandinavian
mentioned in: **8** Volsunga
husband: **7** Sigmund
son: **6** Sigurd

Hippalectryon
form: **7** monster
head and forelegs of: **5** horse
legs, tail and body of: **4** cock

Hippocampus
form: **7** monster
body of: **5** horse
tail of: **4** fish

Hippocrene
form: **6** spring
location: **12** Mount Helicon

Hippocurius
epithet of: **8** Poseidon
means: **12** horse tending

Hippodamas
daugher: **8** Perimele
drowned: **8** Perimele

hippodrome 5 arena **6** circus **7** stadium **8** coliseum

Hippogriff
form: **7** monster
combined: **5** horse **7** griffin

Hippolochus
father: **11** Bellerophon
son: **7** Glaucus

Hippolyta *see* **9** Hippolyte

Hippolyte
also: **7** Antiope **9** Hippolyta
queen of: **7** Amazons
husband: **7** Theseus
son: **10** Hippolytus
Hercules stole her: **6** girdle

Hippolytus
author: **9** Euripides
character: **7** Artemis, Phaedra, Theseus **9** Aphrodite

Hippolytus
father: **7** Theseus
mother: **9** Hippolyta
stepmother: **7** Phaedra
loved by: **7** Phaedra
killed by: **8** Poseidon

Hippomedon
member of: **18** Seven against Thebes

Hippomenes
suitor of: **8** Atalanta
son: **13** Parthenopaeus

Hipponous
vocation: **7** warrior
home: **4** Troy
daughter: **8** Periboea
killed by: **8** Achilles

Hippothous
king of: **7** Arcadia
father: **8** Poseidon
mother: **5** Alope

hire 3 fee, get, let, pay **4** cost, gain, rent **5** lease, wages **6** charge, employ, engage, income, obtain, profit, retain, reward, salary, secure, take on **7** appoint, charter, payment, procure, stipend **8** earnings, receipts **9** emolument **10** recompense **12** compensation, remuneration

hireling 4 goon, thug **6** flunky, lackey, menial, minion, stooge **7** gorilla **8** henchman, retainer **9** strong-arm **10** hatchet man

Hiroshima
author: **10** John Hersey

hirsute 5 bushy, downy, hairy, nappy, wooly **6** shaggy, woolly **7** bearded, bristly, prickly, unshorn **8** bristled, unshaven **9** whiskered **11** bewhiskered

His Girl Friday
director: **11** Howard Hawks
cast: **9** Cary Grant **12** Gene Lockhart, Ralph Bellamy **15** Rosalind Russell

remake of: 12 The Front
Page

Hispania *see* **5** Spain

hiss 3 boo **4** mock, razz **6** deride, heckle, hoot at, jeer at,
revile **7** catcall, scoff at, sneer
at **9** shout down **10** Bronx
cheer **16** give the raspberry

histology
 study of: **6** tissue

historian
 American: 4 Webb
 5 Adams **6** Brooks, De
 Voto, Durant, Fisher,
 Miller, Nevins, Sparks,
 Turner **7** Morison,
 Parkman, Taussig
 8 Bancroft, Channing,
 Prescott, Robinson
 10 Hofstadter
 British: 4 Bede (the Venerable) **6** Gibbon,
 Turner **7** Toynbee
 8 Macaulay **9** Trevelyan
 Chinese: 10 Ssu-ma
 Ch'ien, Ssu-Ma Kuang
 French: 5 Bayle, Blanc,
 Bloch, Taine **7** Braudel
 8 Mabillon, Michelet,
 Voltaire **11** Tocqueville
 German: 5 Ranke
 7 Mommsen **8** Spengler **10** Burckhardt,
 Treitschke
 Greek: 8 Polybius **9** Herodotus **10** Thucydides
 Islamic: 8 al Tabari
 10 Ibn Khaldun
 Italian: 4 Polo, Vico
 5 Croce **11** Machiavelli
 12 Guicciardini
 Latin: 4 Livy **7** Sallust,
 Tacitus
 Scottish: 7 Carlyle

historic 5 famed **7** notable
8 renowned **9** memorable,
well-known **10** celebrated
11 outstanding

historical 4 past, real, true
6 actual, bygone, former **7** ancient, factual **8** attested, recorded **9** authentic
10 chronicled, documented

historical period 3 age, era
4 date, time **5** epoch, stage

history 4 epic, saga, tale
5 story **6** annals, change,
growth, record, resume, review **7** account, the past **8** old
times **9** chronicle, days of old,
narration, narrative, portrayal,
tradition, yesterday **10** bygone
days, days of yore, olden

times, the old days, yesteryear **11** bygone times, development, former times, local
events, major events, world
events **12** actual events **13** an
unusual past, human progress
14 military action, national
events, recapitulation **15** political change

**History of Colonel Jacque,
The**
 author: **11** Daniel Defoe

History of Henry VII
 author: **12** Francis Bacon

History of Mr Polly, The
 author: **7** H G Wells
 character: **6** Miriam **8** Uncle
 Jim **13** The Plump Woman

History of the English-Speaking Peoples, A
 author: **17** Winston S
 Churchill

**His Toy, His Dream, His
Rest**
 author: **12** John Berryman

histrionics 4 fuss **6** acting, tirade **7** bluster, bombast **8** outburst **9** dramatics, hamminess,
staginess, theatrics **10** dramaturgy, playacting **11** performance, rodomontade
13 melodramatics, temper tantrum, theatricality **16** ranting
and raving

hit *see* **box**

hit back 7 counter, get even,
pay back **9** fight back, retaliate **10** strike back

hitch 3 tie, tug **4** curb, draw,
halt, haul, hike, jerk, knot,
loop, pull, snag, stop, yank,
yoke **5** catch, check, clamp,
delay, raise, tying **6** attach,
couple, fasten, mishap, secure,
tether **7** bracket, connect, harness, joining, mistake, problem, trouble **8** coupling,
handicap, make fast, obstacle
9 attaching, fastening, hindrance, mischance, restraint
10 connection, difficulty, impediment, limitation **11** restriction **12** complication,
interruption, loop together,
put in harness **14** stumbling
block

Hitchcock, Alfred
 director of: **6** Frenzy, Marnie, Psycho **7** Rebecca, Vertigo **8** Lifeboat, The Birds
 9 Notorious, Suspicion
 10 Family Plot, Rear Window, Spellbound **13** To
 Catch a Thief **14** Dial M for
 Murder, Shadow of a
 Doubt **15** The Lady Vanishes **16** North by Northwest **17** Strangers on a
 Train **18** The Thirty-Nine

hit 3 bat, jab, lob, rap,
tap **4** bang, bash, beat,
belt, blow, boon, bump,
butt, clip, club, coup, cuff,
damn, drub, find, flog,
hurt, move, pelt, poke,
slam, slap, slug, sock, stir,
swat **5** abash, baste, clout,
crack, crush, flail, knock,
paste, pound, punch,
reach, rouse, smack,
smash, smite, thump,
touch, upset, whack **6** affect, arouse, assail, attack,
attain, batter, cudgel, effect, impact, incite, pommel, revile, strike, thrash,
thwack, wallop, winner
7 achieve, assault, censure,
clobber, condemn, execute,
godsend, impress, inflame,
provoke, quicken, realize,
shatter, success, triumph,
trounce, victory **8** arrive at,
bang into, blessing, bring
off, denounce, lambaste,
overcome, reproach **9** criticize, deal a blow, devastate, lash out at,
overwhelm, sensation,
smash into **11** collide with,
connect with, deal a
stroke, strike out at **12** go
straight to **13** make a
bull's-eye, send to the
mark **14** popular success,
strike together **16** mount
an offensive

Steps **19** The Trouble with
Harry **20** Foreign
Correspondent

hither 2 on **4** here, near
5 close **6** closer, nearby,
nearer, onward **7** close by,
forward **8** over here **11** to this
place **12** to the speaker

hitherto 6 ere now, hereto
7 thus far, till now, up to
now **8** until now **10** before
this, heretofore

Hitler, Adolf
 author of: **9** Mein Kampf

hit man 6 killer, slayer **8** assassin, hired gun, murderer
11 executioner
12 exterminator

Hitman
 nickname of: **12** Thomas
 Hearns

hit-or-miss 3 lax **6** casual, fitful **7** aimless, cursory **8** slapdash **9** haphazard
10 incomplete **11** purposeless,
superficial, unorganized
12 unsystematic **15** catch-as-catch-can

hive 3 hub 5 heart 6 center, colony 7 cluster 9 busy place 11 swarm of bees

Hjordis *see* 7 Hiordis

Hliod *see* 4 Liod

H M S Pinafore
subtitle: 23 The Lass That Loved a Sailor
operetta by: 18 Gilbert and Sullivan
character: 11 Dick Deadeye 14 Ralph Rackstraw 15 Captain Corcoran, Little Buttercup, Sir Joseph Porter 17 Josephine Corcoran

Hoagland, Edward
author of: 15 African Calliope 17 The Tugman's Passage

hoar 3 old 4 aged, rime 5 frost, moldy, mushy, passe, stale, white 6 old hat 7 ancient, antique, elderly, grayish 8 grizzled 9 out of date

hoard 4 fund, heap, mass, pile 5 amass, buy up, cache, lay up, store 6 save up, supply 7 acquire, collect, lay away, reserve 8 quantity 9 amassment, gathering, stockpile, store away 10 accumulate, collection 12 accumulation

hoarse 5 gruff, harsh, husky, raspy, rough 6 croaky 7 cracked, rasping, raucous, throaty 8 gravelly, guttural, scratchy

hoary 3 old 4 aged, gray, hoar 5 dated, passe, white 6 grayed, old hat 7 ancient, antique, grizzly 8 grizzled, whitened 9 out-of-date 11 gray with age 12 white with age

hoax 3 gyp 4 bilk, dupe, fake, fool, gull, yarn 5 bluff, cheat, cozen, fraud, prank, spoof, trick 6 canard, delude, humbug, take in 7 deceive, defraud, fiction, mislead, swindle 8 hoodwink 9 bamboozle, chicanery, deception, fish story, victimize 10 hocus-pocus

Hoban, James
architect of: 13 The White House, Great Hotel (Washington, DC)

Hobbes, Thomas
author of: 9 Leviathan

Hobbit, The
part of: 14 Lord of the Rings
author: 10 J R R Tolkien

hobble 4 bind, gimp, halt, limp 5 block, check, cramp 6 fetter, hamper, hinder, hog-tie, impede, lumber, stymie, thwart, toddle 7 inhibit, manacle, shackle, shamble, shuffle, stagger, stumble 8 encumber, handicap, hold back, lame gait, obstruct, restrain, restrict 9 constrain, frustrate, hamstring 10 uneven gait, walk lamely 13 interfere with

hobby 7 pastime, pursuit 8 sideline 9 amusement, avocation, diversion 10 relaxation 13 entertainment 14 divertissement

hobbyhorse 5 hobby 7 pastime 8 interest, toy horse 9 diversion 10 enthusiasm 11 distraction 12 rocking horse

hobgoblin 3 imp 5 bogey 6 goblin 7 bugaboo

hobnob 3 mix 4 club 6 mingle 7 consort, hang out 9 associate, rub elbows 10 fraternize

hobo 3 beg, bum 5 stiff, tramp 6 beggar, cadger, loafer 7 drifter, migrant, moocher, vagrant 9 derelict, vagabond, wanderer 9 scrounger 11 beachcomber

hoc est 6 this is

Ho Chi Minh City
formerly: 6 Saigon
river: 6 Saigon
delta: 6 Mekong
former capital of: 9 Indochina 11 Cochin China 12 South Vietnam

hockey
athlete: 8 Bobby Orr, Brad Park 9 Bobby Hull, Ken Dryden, Mike Bossy 10 Doug Harvey, Eddie Shore, Ed Giacomin, Gordie Howe, Guy Lafleur, Ray Bearque, Rod Gilbert, Stan Mikita 11 Bobby Clarke, Brian Leetch, Denis Potvin, Eric Lindros, Jean Ratelle, Mark Messier 12 Emile Francis, Jean Beliveau, Marcel Dionne, Mario Lemieux, Phil Esposito, Wayne Gretzky 13 Bernard Parent, Jacques Plante, Larry Robinson, Pat La Fontaine 14 Alex Delvecchio, Maurice Richard 15 Bernie Geoffrion

hockey team *see box*

hocus-pocus 4 bosh, bull, hoax, sham 5 chant, charm, cheat, magic, spell 6 bunkum, deceit, fakery, humbug 7 con game, hogwash, rubbish, swindle 8 delusion, flimflam, tommyrot, trickery 9 deception, moonshine, poppycock 10 dishonesty, flapdoodle, hankypanky, magic spell, magic words, mumbo jumbo, subterfuge 11 bewitchment, incantation, legerdemain, magic tricks

hockey team
Anaheim: 11 Mighty Ducks
Boston: 6 Bruins
Buffalo: 6 Sabres
Calgary: 6 Flames
Chicago: 10 Black Hawks
Colorado: 9 Avalanche
formerly: 15 Quebec Nordiques
Dallas: 5 Stars
Detroit: 8 Red Wings
Edmonton: 6 Oilers
Florida: 8 Panthers
Hartford: 7 Whalers
Los Angeles: 5 Kings
Montreal: 9 Canadiens
New Jersey: 6 Devils
New York: 7 Rangers 9 Islanders
Ottawa: 8 Senators
Philadelphia: 6 Flyers
Pittsburgh: 8 Penguins
St Louis: 5 Blues
San Jose: 6 Sharks
Tampa Bay: 9 Lightning
Toronto: 10 Maple Leafs
Vancouver: 7 Canucks
Washington: 8 Capitals
Winnipeg: 4 Jets

12 fiddle-faddle, magic formula 13 sleight of hand

Hoder
also: 5 Hodur
origin: 12 Scandinavian
brother: 5 Baldr 6 Balder, Baldur
father: 4 Odin 5 Othin
killed: 5 Baldr 6 Balder, Baldur

hodgepodge, hotchpotch 3 mix 4 hash, mess 6 jumble, medley, muddle 7 melange, mixture 8 mishmash 9 composite, confusion, patchwork, potpourri 10 miscellany

Hodur *see* 5 Hoder

Hoenir
origin: 12 Scandinavian
race: 5 Vanir
created: 3 Ask 5 Embla

Hoff, Jacobus Hendricus van't
field: 9 chemistry
nationality: 5 Dutch
researched: 7 gas laws 10 carbon atom 14 thermodynamics
awarded: 10 Nobel Prize

Hoffman, Dustin
born: 12 Los Angeles CA
roles: 5 Lenny 6 Ishtar 7 Tootsie 8 Papillon 10 Ratso Rizzo 11 The Graduate 12 Little Big Man 14 Kramer vs Kramer (Oscar), Midnight Cowboy 19 All the President's Men

Hofmann, Hans
born: **7** Germany
11 Weissenberg
artwork: **6** Spring **7** The
Gate **13** Effervescence
14 Fantasia in Blue, Magenta and Blue **16** Sanctum
Sanctorum

Hofstadter, Richard
author of: **14** The Age of
Reform

hog 3 pig, sow, **4** arch, boar,
trim **5** broom, sheep, swine
6 gorger, porker **7** baconer,
glutton, take all **9** razorback
10 locomotive

Hogan, Paul
country: **9** Australia
roles: **10** Mick Dundee
15 Crocodile Dundee

Hogan's Heroes
character: **7** (Peter) Newkirk
8 Lt Carter **10** Sgt (Hans)
Schultz **11** Louis LeBeau
14 Col Robert Hogan **15** Col
Wilhelm Klink
cast: **8** Bob Crane **10** John
Banner, Larry Hovis
11 Robert Clary **13** Richard
Dawson **15** Werner
Klemperer

Hogarth, William
born: **6** London **7** England
artwork: **12** Captain Coram
14 A Rake's Progress
15 Marriage a la Mode, The
Beggar's Opera **16** A Harlot's Progress **19** Garrick as
Richard III

hogshead 3 keg, tun, vat
4 butt, cask, drum **6** barrel

hogwash 3 rot **4** bull, bunk
5 hokum, hooey, stuff
6 bunkum, drivel, hot air,
humbug **7** baloney, blather,
spinach, twaddle **8** claptrap,
nonsense, tommyrot **9** poppycock **10** applesauce **11** foolishness **13** horsefeathers **16** stuff
and nonsense

hoi polloi 6 rabble, the mob
7 the herd **8** canaille, populace, riffraff, the crowd, the
plebs **9** the masses, the proles,
the vulgar **10** commonalty
12 the multitude **14** the lower
orders, the proletariat, the
rank and file **15** the common
people, the lower classes, the
working class

hoist 4 lift **5** heave, raise, run
up **6** bear up, pull up, take
up, uplift **7** elevate, raise up,
upraise **9** bear aloft

Hokan
language family: **17** Hokan-
Coahuiltecan
subgroup: **4** Pomo, Seri,
Yana **5** Karok, Washo, Yuman **7** Chontal, Chumash,
Esselen, Jicaque **8** Subtiaba
9 Chimariko **14** Shasta-
Achomawi
tribe: **8** Achomawi

Hokan-Coahuiltecan
language branch: **5** Hokan
12 Coahuiltecan **17** Subtiaba-Tlappanec

Hokusai, Katsushika
born: **3** Edo **5** Japan, Tokyo
artwork: **5** Crabs, Manga
10 Waterfalls **11** Chushingura **25** Thirty-six Views of
Mount Fuji

Holabird, William
partner: **11** Martin Roche
architect of: **12** Gage Building **13** Cable Building,
Crerar Library (City Hall,
Chicago) **14** Tacoma Building **15** McClurg Building
17 Marquette Building

Holbein, Hans (the Elder)
born: **7** Germany **8** Augsburg
son: **11** Hans Holbein (the
Younger)
artwork: **11** St Sebastian
14 Fountain of Life
18 Kaisheim Altarpiece
31 Presentation of Christ in
the Temple

**Holbein, Hans (the
Younger)**
born: **7** Germany **8** Augsburg
father: **11** Hans Holbein (the
Elder)
artwork: **7** Erasmus **9** Henry
VIII **11** Jane Seymour
12 Dance of Death **13** The
Dead Christ

hold *see* **box**

hold a candle to 5 equal,
match **6** be up to **7** compare

8 approach **10** be as good as
11 come close to, compete
with **12** be comparable
14 bear comparison

hold against 6 resent
8 begrudge

hold back 3 lag **4** curb, deny,
keep, slow **5** check, dally,
limit, stall **6** arrest, bridle, falter, refuse **7** contain, inhibit,
keep out, reserve, retrain
8 hesitate, keep back, maintain, restrain, withhold
9 constrain

hold close 3 hug **5** clasp
6 cuddle, harbor **7** cherish,
embrace, snuggle

Holden, William
real name: **23** William
Franklin Beedle Jr
nickname: **4** Bill
born: **9** O'Fallon IL
roles: **6** Picnic **7** Network, Sabrina **9** Golden Boy **13** Born
Yesterday **14** The Country
Girl **15** Stalag Seventeen
(Oscar), Sunset Boulevard
23 The Bridge on the River
Kwai

hold fast 4 fuse, hold **5** cling,
stick **6** adhere

hold firmly 4 grip **5** clasp,
grasp **6** clench, clinch, clutch
10 grab hold of

hold forth 7 expound **9** discourse, expatiate

hold in abeyance 5 table
6 recess, shelve **7** suspend
8 lay aside, postpone

hold in bondage 7 control,
enchain, enslave, entrall
8 dominate **9** subjugate
12 make a slave of

hold 4 bear, bind, bond, curb, deem, grip, halt, have, hilt,
keep, knob, lock, prop, rule, stay, sway, take, urge **5** block,
brace, carry, check, clasp, cling, count, defer, grasp, guard,
limit, offer, power, shaft, shore, stall, stand, stick, strap,
think, unite, watch **6** adhere, affirm, assert, assume, cleave,
clinch, clutch, deduct, detain, direct, enfold, handle, hinder,
hold up, join in, manage, occupy, reckon, regard, retain,
submit, take in, tender, thwart, uphold **7** advance, believe,
carry on, command, conduct, confine, contain, control, declare, embrace, enclose, enforce, execute, hold off, include,
inhibit, mastery, possess, present, presume, prevent, profess,
propose, protect, repress, reserve, support, suppose, surmise,
suspend, toehold, venture **8** advocate, conceive, conclude,
consider, engage in, foothold, handhold, hold back, hold
down, leverage, maintain, obligate, postpone, purchase, put
forth, restrain, restrict, set aside, suppress, withhold **9** advantage, anchorage, authority, be in force, dominance, forestall,
frustrate, influence, keep valid, ownership, stay fixed, stick
fast **10** ascendancy, attachment, desist from, domination, possession, put forward, understand **11** accommodate, preside
over

holdings 6 assets **8** property **10** securities **11** commodities

hold in high regard 5 honor, prize, value **6** admire, esteem, revere **7** cherish, respect **8** look up to, treasure, venerate **10** rate highly, set store by **13** think highly of **18** attach importance to

hold one's own 4 cope **6** manage **7** contend **11** be a match for **20** maintain one's position **22** keep one's head above water

hold rapt 5 charm **7** beguile, bewitch, enchant **8** enthrall, entrance **9** captivate, enrapture, fascinate, spellbind, transport

hold to 4 bind **8** obligate

hold together 4 bind, fuse, glue, hold, join **5** cling, stick, unite **6** cement, cohere **7** combine **11** consolidate

holdup 3 rob **4** bear, halt, stay, stop **5** delay, heist, steal, theft **6** hijack, retain, uphold **7** robbery, stickup, support, sustain **8** stoppage **9** hindrance **12** interruption

hold up 4 prop, slow **5** block, brace, check, delay **6** bear up, detain, endure, hinder, impede, manage **7** bolster, present, stand up, support, sustain **8** keep back, obstruct **13** rob at gunpoint

hold up under 4 bear **6** endure, manage **8** tolerate

hold warmly 3 hug **5** clasp **6** cuddle **7** embrace, snuggle

hole 3 den, gap, pit **4** brig, cage, cave, flaw, keep, lair, rent, slit, slot **5** break, crack, fault, shaft **6** breach, burrow, cavern, cavity, crater, defect, dugout, lockup, pocket, prison, tunnel **7** dungeon, fallacy, opening, orifice, slammer **8** aperture, dark cell, puncture **9** concavity, open space **10** depression, excavation **11** discrepancy, hollow place, indentation, perforation **13** inconsistency

Holgrave, Mr
  character in: 24 The House of the Seven Gables
  author: 9 Hawthorne

holiday *see box*

holiness 8 sanctity **9** godliness **10** sacredness **11** blessedness, saintliness

Holland *see* **11** Netherlands

Holle
  origin: 8 Germanic

---

holiday 3 gay **4** fete, gala **6** cheery, fiesta, joyful, joyous, junket, outing **7** festive, holy day, jubilee **8** cheerful, feast day, festival, vacation **11** celebrating, celebration, merrymaking
  American: 6 Easter **8** Arbor Day, Labor Day **9** Christmas (Dec 25), Halloween (Oct 31) **10** Father's Day, Good Friday, Mother's Day **11** Columbus Day, Election Day, Memorial Day, New Year's Day (Jan 1), Veterans' Day (Nov 11) **12** Children's Day, Thanksgiving **15** Independence Day (July 4), St Valentine's Day (Feb 14) **23** National Grandparents' Day
    birthday: **8** Lincoln's **11** Robert E Lee's (Jan 19), Washington's **17** Martin Luther King's (Jan 15)
    Hawaiian: **13** Kamehameha Day (June 11)
  British: 8 Hogmanay (Dec 31) **9** Boxing Day (Dec 26) **11** Harvest Home **12** Guy Fawkes Day (Nov 5), Twelfth Night (Jan 5) **14** Queen's Birthday (June) **15** Commonwealth Day (May 24), Mothering Sunday **19** Feast of Saint Swithin (July 15)
  Canadian: 11 Victoria Day **14** Queen's Birthday, Remembrance Day
  Chinese: 7 New Year **15** Lantern Festival **17** Confucius' Birthday (Sept 28) **18** Dragon Boat Festival
  French: 11 Bastille Day (May 14)
  German: 11 Oktoberfest
  Greek: 7 Genesia **11** Feast of Pots
  Indian: 4 Holi **6** Basant, Diwali (New Year) **17** Hindu fire festival **22** Mahatma Gandhi's Birthday (Oct 2)
  Irish: 16 Saint Patrick's Day (March 17)
  Italian: 13 Liberation Day (April 25)
  Japanese: 11 Hina-Matsuri **12** Children's Day (May 5), Feast of Dolls (March 3) **15** Constitution Day (May 3) **17** Girls' Doll Festival
  Jewish: 5 Purim **6** Sukkot **7** Shavuot, Sukkoth **8** Hanukkah, Passover **9** Yom Kippur **12** Rosh Hashanah **20** Hamishah Assar B'Shevat, The New Year of the Trees **21** Feast of the Tabernacles
  Korean: 6 Ch'usok
  Latin American: 12 Day of the Race
  Moslem: 7 Mouloud **8** Id-al-Adha, Id-al-Fitr **12** Maulid-an-Nabi **14** month of Ramadan
  religious: 6 Advent **7** Lady Day (Mar 25) **8** Epiphany, Shabuoth **9** Candlemas, Mardi Gras, Martinmas (Nov 11), Pentecost **10** Whitsunday **11** All Souls' Day (Nov 2) **12** Ascension Day, Ash Wednesday, Feast of Weeks **13** Shrove Tuesday, Trinity Sunday **15** Annunciation Day (Mar 25) **16** Feast of All Saints **20** Feast of Corpus Christi **23** Day of Our Lady of Guadalupe (Dec 12) **27** Purification of the Virgin Mary **30** Feast of the Immaculate Conception (Dec 8)
  Roman: 7 Feralia **10** Saturnalia
  Scottish: 8 Hogmanay **12** Candlemas Day **19** Festival of the Virgin
  South American: 21 Simon Bolivar's Birthday (July 24)
  Sri Lankan: 5 Wesak
  Soviet Union: 6 May Day (May 1) **14** Lenin's Birthday (April 22) **39** Day of the Great October Socialist Revolution (Nov 7)
  Swedish: 13 Santa Lucia Day (Dec 13)
  Thailand: 11 Visakha Puja

---

goddess of: 4 moon
corresponds to: 7 Berchta, Perchta
form: 5 witch

holler 4 bark, roar, yell **5** gripe, shout **6** bellow, cry out, grouse **8** complain **9** hue and cry

---

Holliday, Judy
  real name: 11 Judith Tuvim
  born: 9 New York NY
  roles: 8 Adam's Rib **13** Born Yesterday (Oscar) **15** Bells Are Ringing

Hollinshed, Raphael
  author of: 37 Chronicles of

hollow

England Scotland and Ireland

hollow 3 dip, low, rut 4 cave, dale, deep, dell, dent, dull, glen, hole, sink, vain, vale, void 5 ditch, empty, false, muted 6 cavern, cavity, crater, dig out, dimple, furrow, futile, groove, pocket, sunken, vacant, vacuum, valley 7 channel, concave, useless 8 crevasse, empty out, excavate, gouge out, indented, not solid, nugatory, rumbling, scoop out, specious, unfilled 9 cavernous, concavity, deceptive, depressed, fruitless, pointless, valueless, worthless 10 depression, profitless, sepulchral, unavailing, unresonant 11 indentation, meaningless, nonresonant 12 unprofitable 13 curving inward, disappointing, reverberating 14 expressionless, unsatisfactory 15 inconsequential

Holloway, Stanley
born: 6 London 7 England
roles: 10 My Fair Lady 15 Alfred Doolittle 18 The Lavender Hill Mob

Hollow Men
author: 7 T S Eliot

hollowness 4 void 6 vacuum 7 vacancy 9 emptiness

hollow out 4 bore 5 drill 6 dig out 8 carve out, gouge out, scoop out 9 chisel out 13 tunnel through

holly 4 Ilex
varieties: 3 box, sea 4 dune 5 Cuban, Dutch, dwarf, false, Furin, Kashi, swamp, Tsuru 6 desert, horned, Oregon, Sarvis, Soyogo, summer 7 African, Chinese, English, Georgia, Madeira 8 American, European, hedgehog, Japanese, Kurogane, mountain 9 box-leaved, Highclere, miniature, moonlight, porcupine, Singapore 10 Costa Rican, luster-leaf, West Indian 11 large-leaved, Puerto Rican, screw-leaved 12 Canary Island, gold hedgehog, myrtle-leaved, smooth-leaved 14 silver hedgehog

hollyhock 6 mallow 7 Antwerp, figleaf 8 biennial 9 ficifolia, Malvaceae 10 alcea rosea

Hollywood's Mermaid
nickname of: 14 Esther Williams

Hollywood Squares
host: 12 John Davidson 13 Peter Marshall
regular: 8 Wally Cox 10 Joan

Rivers 13 Charley Weaver, Shadoe Stevens

Holmes, Oliver Wendell
author of: 12 Old Ironsides 30 The Autocrat of the Breakfast Table

Holmes, Sherlock
address: 11 (221B) Baker Street
appears in: 13 The Sign of Four 14 The Naval Treaty 15 A Study in Scarlet, The Speckled Band 16 Scandal in Bohemia, The Blue Carbuncle, The Copper Beeches 18 The Red-Headed League, The Solitary Cyclist 22 Hound of the Baskervilles
assistants: 21 Baker Street Irregulars
author: 16 (Sir) Arthur Conan Doyle
brother: 7 Mycroft
foe: 17 Professor Moriarty
hat: 11 deerstalker
hobby: 6 violin
housekeeper/landlady: 9 Mrs Hudson
keeps tobacco in: 7 slipper 14 Turkish slipper
police: 17 Inspector Lestrade
sidekick: 12 Dr John Watson
vice: 7 cocaine 17 hypodermic syringe 20 seven-per-cent solution

Holmwood, Arthur
character in: 7 Dracula
author: 6 Stoker

holocaust 4 ruin 5 havoc 6 ravage 7 bonfire, carnage, inferno, killing 8 butchery, genocide, massacre 10 deadly fire, mass murder 11 devastation 12 annihilation 13 conflagration

Holofernes
character in: 16 Love's Labour's Lost
author: 11 Shakespeare

Holofernes
general of: 14 Nebuchadnezzar
killed by: 6 Judith

Holst, Gustav Theodore
born: 7 England 10 Cheltenham

composer of: 7 Savitri 10 Egdon Heath, Ode to Death, The Planets 11 Hammersmith 12 St Paul's Suite 13 Fugal Concerto 14 The Hymn of Jesus, The Perfect Fool 16 Somerset Rhapsody 17 The Cloud Messenger 19 Hymns from the Rig-Veda

holy 4 pure 5 godly, moral, pious 6 adored, devout, divine, sacred, solemn 7 angelic, blessed, from God, revered, saintly, sinless 8 faithful, hallowed, heavenly, reverent, virtuous 9 from above, guileless, religious, righteous, spiritual, undefiled, unspotted, unstained, unworldly, venerated, worshiped 10 heaven-sent, immaculate, inviolable, sacrosanct, sanctified, worshipped 11 consecrated, pure in heart, uncorrupted
Latin: 7 sanctus

Holy Ark
Hebrew: 10 Aron Kodesh

holy of holies
Latin: 16 sanctum sanctorum

Holy one see 5 Jesus

Holy Spirit, Holy Ghost
9 Paraclete 13 presence of God 23 third person of the Trinity
Latin: 15 Spiritus Sanctus
Greek: 12 Hagion Pneuma

holy war
Arabic: 5 jehad, jihad

Holy Willie's Prayer
author: 11 Robert Burns

Homadus
form: 7 centaur
killed by: 8 Hercules

homage 5 honor 6 esteem, praise, regard 7 respect, tribute, worship 8 devotion 9 adoration, adulation, deference, obeisance, reverence 10 exaltation, veneration 13 glorification

Homagyrius
epithet of: 4 Zeus
means: 9 assembler

hombre 3 man

home 5 abode, haunt, haven, house 6 asylum, cradle, refuge 7 habitat, hangout 8 domicile, dwelling, hospital 9 orphanage, poorhouse, residence 10 habitation, native land, sanatorium 11 institution 12 fountainhead 13 dwelling place, home sweet home 14 stamping ground 16 place of residence 18 natural environment 25 place where one hangs one's hat

Home Burial
author: **11** Robert Frost

homegrown 5 local **6** native
8 domestic **10** indigenous

Home Is the Sailor
author: **10** Jorge Amado

homelike 4 cozy **5** comfy,
homey **6** simple **8** cheerful,
domestic, familiar, informal,
inviting **11** comfortable

homely 4 cozy, drab, snug
5 comfy, homey, plain **6** modest, rustic, simple **7** artless,
natural **8** everyday, familiar,
homelike, homespun, ordinary,
uncomely **9** graceless **10** ill-
favored, provincial, unaffected,
unassuming, ungraceful, unhandsome **11** comfortable
12 plain-looking, unattractive
13 unpretentious

homer 15 Biblical measure

Homer
author of: **5** Iliad **7** Odyssey

Homer, Winslow
born: **8** Boston MA
artwork: **9** High Cliff
10 Breezing Up, Eight Bells
11 Marine Coast, Northeast-
er, The Life Line **13** The
Fog Warning, The Gulf
Stream **21** Inside the Bar
Tynemouth, Prisoners from
the Front

home rule 8 autonomy
11 sovereignty **12** independence **14** self-government

homespun 5 plain **6** folksy,
homely, modest, native, sim-
ple **7** artless, natural **8** down-
home, homemade **9** hand-
woven **10** hand-loomed,
unaffected **11** hand-crafted,
hand-wrought
13 unpretentious

homey 4 cozy **6** casual, folksy
8 down-home, homelike,
homespun, informal
15 unsophisticated

homicide 6 killer, murder,
slayer **7** slaying **8** foul play,
murderer, regicide, vaticide
9 bloodshed, man killer, man-
slayer, matricide, parricide,
patricide, uxoricide **10** fratricide **11** infanticide
12 manslaughter

homiletic 7 preachy **8** didactic
10 moralizing

homily 6 sermon **7** lecture
10 preachment **11** exhortation

homogeneous 4 akin, pure
7 kindred, similar, uniform,
unmixed **8** all alike, constant,
of a piece **9** identical, unvarying **10** consistent **13** of the
same kind, unadulterated

homology 7 analogy **8** likeness,
relation **10** similarity **12** relationship **14** correspondence

Honduras *see box*

hone 4 long, moan, pine, tool,
whet **5** stroke, strope, whine,
yearn **6** hanker, grumble, mutter, sharpen **9** whetstone

Honegger, Arthur
born: **5** Havre **6** France
nationality: **5** Swiss
member of: **6** Les Six, The
Six
composer of: **5** Rugby **6** Judith **7** L'Aiglon **8** Antigone
9 The Eaglet **10** Le Roi
David **13** Pastorale d'ete
18 Jeanne d'Arc au Bucher,
Liturgical Symphony **19** Pacific Two-Thirty-One

honest 4 fair, just, open, real,
true **5** blunt, frank, legal,
plain, solid, valid **6** candid, decent, lawful, proper, square
7 artless, ethical, genuine, sin-

cere, upright **8** bona fide,
clear-cut, faithful, innocent,
reliable, straight, true-blue,
truthful, virtuous **9** authentic,
blameless, guileless, honorable,
ingenuous, reputable, righteous **10** aboveboard, dependable, forthright, law-abiding,
legitimate, on the level, principled, reasonable, scrupulous,
unaffected, unreserved
11 plainspoken, trustworthy,
undisguised **12** on the up-and-
up, tried and true **13** conscientious, fair and square
15 straightforward, unsophisticated **16** as good as one's
word, straight-shooting
17 open and aboveboard

honesty 4 word **5** honor
7 probity **8** fairness, good
name, morality, scruples, veracity **9** innocence, integrity,
rectitude, sincerity **10** principles **11** just dealing, uprightness **12** faithfulness,

---

Honduras
name means: **6** depths
capital/largest city: **11** Tegucigalpa
others: **4** Tela, Yoro **5** Copan, Danli, Lapaz **6** Roatan
7 Gracias, La Ceiba **8** Trujillo, Yuscaran **9** Choluteca, Juti-
calpa **10** El Progreso **11** Comayaguela **12** Puerto Cortes,
San Pedro Sula
measure: **4** vara **5** milla **6** mecate **7** cajuela
monetary unit: **4** peso **7** centavo, lempira
island: **3** Bay **5** Bahia, Utila **6** Roatan **7** Bonacca, Guanaja
lake: **5** Criba, Yojoa **6** Brewer
mountain: **4** Pija **6** Agalta **7** Celaque **9** Esperanza
highest point: **8** Las Minas
river: **4** Coco, Sico, Ulua **5** Aguan, Lempa, Negro, Tinto,
Wanks **6** Patuca, Sulaco **7** Olancho, Paulaya, Segovia
8 Guiavope, Santiago **9** Choluteca **10** Chamelecon
sea: **7** Pacific **8** Atlantic **9** Caribbean
physical feature:
    coast: **5** North **8** Mosquito **10** Costa Norte
    gulf: **7** Fonseca **8** Honduras
    port: **7** Laceiba **8** Trujillo
people: **4** Maya, Paya, Sumo, Ulva **5** Carib, Lenca, Pipil
6 Tauira **7** Jicaque, mestizo, Miskito **8** Mosquito
    discoverer: **8** Columbus
    farmer: **9** campesino
language: **7** English, Spanish
religion: **13** Roman Catholic
place:
    ruins: **5** Copan **8** Tenampua
feature:
    bird: **9** zenzontle
    dance: **5** sique **7** mascaro
    estate: **10** latifundia
    farm: **6** milpas **10** minifundia
    musical instrument: **7** caramba, marimba
    tree: **8** cockspur
food:
    beans: **8** frijoles
    beef dish: **6** tapado
    corn: **5** maize
    stuffed corn cake: **10** naca tamale
    tripe stew: **8** mondongo

reputability, truthfulness
13 guiltlessness, square dealing **15** trustworthiness **16** incorruptibility, straight shooting

honeybee
    classification: 6 social
    live in: 4 hive **6** colony
    headed by: 5 queen
    male: 5 drone
    laborer: 6 worker
    food-gatherer: 7 forager
    gather: 6 nectar, pollen
    produce: 5 honey
    queen's food: 10 royal jelly

honeyed 4 kind **5** sweet **6** sugary **7** cloying, fawning **10** flattering, saccharine
12 ingratiating
13 complimentary

honeyed words 4 line **7** blarney **8** cajolery, flattery, soft
soap **9** sweet talk

Honey in the Horn
    author: 7 H L Davis

Honeymooners, The
    character: 8 Ed Norton
    12 Alice Kramden, Ralph
    Kramden, Trixie Norton
    cast: 8 Jane Kean **9** Art Car-
    ney **12** Sheila MacRae
    13 Audrey Meadows, Jackie
    Gleason, Joyce Randolph
    Ralph's job: 9 bus driver
    Ed's job: 5 sewer
    lodge: 8 Raccoons

---

honor 3 pay **4** cash, fame, laud, note, take **5** adore, exalt,
extol, favor, glory, grant, leave, power, right, truth, value
6 accept, admire, credit, esteem, homage, praise, redeem, regard, renown, repute, revere, virtue **7** acclaim, commend, decency, dignify, glorify, honesty, liberty, probity, respect,
tribute, worship **8** eminence, fairness, good name, goodness,
justness, look up to, make good, pleasure, prestige, sanction,
venerate, veracity **9** adoration, celebrity, constancy, deference, greatness, integrity, principle, privilege, rectitude, reverence, sincerity **10** admiration, compliment, exaltation, good
report, importance, notability, permission, prominence, veneration **11** acknowledge, approbation, distinction, pay homage to, recognition, think much of, uprightness
12 commendation, faithfulness, high standing, pay tribute to,
truthfulness **13** authorization, bow down before, glorification,
have regard for, honorableness, make payment on **14** high-
mindedness, scrupulousness **15** illustriousness, trustworthiness **17** a feather in one's cap, conscientiousness

---

honeysuckle 8 Lonicera
    19 Aquilegia canadensis, Justi-
    cia californica **24** Rhododen-
    dron prinophyllum
    varieties: 3 fly **4** bush, cape
    5 coral, giant, grape, hairy,
    swamp **6** desert, French,
    purple, yellow **7** Arizona,
    Jamaica, trumpet **8** Hima-
    laya, Japanese, swamp fly,
    Tatarian **9** chaparral, Tartar-
    ian **10** yellow cape **11** Eu-
    ropean fly **12** giant
    Burmese, long-flowered,

Hong Kong
    name means: 13 incense harbor **14** fragrant harbor
    capital: 8 Victoria
    largest city:
        section: 7 Kowloon **8** Hong Kong, Victoria
        others: 4 Tai O **5** Tai Po **8** Aberdeen, Pingshan, Yuenlong
        9 Shataukok **10** Sheungshui
    division: 7 Kowloon **8** Hong Kong **14** New Territories
    government: 18 British crown colony
    head of state: 14 British monarch **15** governor general
    island: 5 Lamma **6** Lan Tao, Lantau, Middle, Poi Toi
    8 Hong Kong **9** Ap Lei Chau **11** Stonecutter
    mountain: 6 Castle **8** Victoria
    highest point: 9 Tai Mo Shan
    river: 5 Pearl **6** Canton **8** Sham Chun
    sea: 10 South China
    physical feature:
        bay: 4 Mirs **6** Quarry **7** Kowloon, Repulse **9** Deep Water
        harbor: 4 Tolo **8** Aberdeen, Hong Kong, Victoria
        peak: 8 Victoria
        peninsula: 7 Kowloon
    people: 5 Hakka, Haklo, Punti, Tanka **7** British, Chinese
    8 American, Japanese **9** Cantonese **10** Portuguese
    language: 7 Chinese, English **9** Cantonese
    religion: 5 Hindu, Islam **6** Taoism **8** Buddhism
    12 Christianity
    feature:
        airport: 6 Kai Tak
        clothing: 6 samfoo **9** cheongsam
        houseboat: 6 sampan
        rock: 5 Amahs **6** Sha Tin
        temple: 18 Ten Thousand Buddhas

    South African **13** Hall's
    Japanese

Honeythunder, Mr
    character in: 22 The Mystery
    of Edwin Drood
    author: 7 Dickens

Hong Kong *see box*

Honiara
    capital of: 14 Solomon
    Islands

honi soit qui mal y pense
    31 shamed be the one who
    thinks evil of it
        motto of: 16 Order of the
        Garter

honk 4 toot **5** blare, blast
7 trumpet

honky-tonk 4 dive **7** gin mill
9 roadhouse, nightclub

honor *see box*

honorable 4 good **5** noble, title **6** decent, honest, lordly,
square **7** upright **9** elevated,
reputable, respected **10** creditable **11** distinctive, illustrious,
respectable, trustworthy
12 considerable
13 distinguished

hood 4 cowl, lout, punk
5 bully, rowdy, scarf, tough
6 vandal **7** hoodlum, ruffian
8 hooligan **9** barbarian, roughneck **10** delinquent
12 headcovering

Hood, Raymond
    architect of: 11 RCA Build-
    ing (Rockefeller Center)
    17 Daily News Building
    (NYC) **18** McGraw-Hill Build-
    ing (NYC) **22** Chicago Trib-
    une Building **24** American
    Radiator Building
    style: 13 International

hoodlum 4 hood, punk, thug
5 crook, rowdy, tough **6** gun-

man **7** bruiser, gorilla, mobster, ruffian **8** criminal, gangster, hooligan, plug-ugly **9** desperado, strong arm **10** delinquent

hoodwink 3 gyp **4** dupe, fool, gull, hoax, rook **5** cheat, cozen, trick **7** deceive, defraud, mislead, swindle **8** inveigle **9** bamboozle, victimize

hook 3 arc, bag, bow, nab, net **4** arch, bend, bill, curl, gaff, grab, loop, take, trap, wind **5** angle, catch, crook, curve, elbow, fluke, hitch, latch, seize, snare **6** buckle, collar, fasten, peavey, secure **7** capture, crampon, ensnare, grapnel, grapple, pothook **8** crescent, make fast **9** horseshoe

Hooke, Robert
  field: 7 physics **9** astronomy
  nationality: 7 British
  discovered: 9 Orion star
    15 Jupiter rotation
    20 moon's center of gravity
    21 earth's center of gravity
  invented: 10 microscope
  named for him: 15 law of elasticity

hooked 8 addicted **9** compelled, obsessive **10** compulsive, habituated **14** uncontrollable

hooked cross
  German: 10 Hakenkreuz

hook up 4 ally, dock, join **5** hinge **6** couple, link up **7** connect **8** assemble **10** articulate **11** fit together **14** fasten together

hooligan 4 hood, lout, punk **5** bully, rowdy, tough **6** vandal **7** hoodlum, ruffian **9** barbarian, roughneck **10** delinquent

hoopla 4 hype **8** ballyhoo **9** promotion, publicity **10** hullabaloo, propaganda **11** advertising **15** public relations

Hoosier Schoolmaster, The
  author: 15 Edward Eggleston

Hoosier State
  nickname of: 7 Indiana

hoot 3 boo, din **4** bawl, blow, hiss, honk, howl, jeer, moan, mock, razz, roar, wail, yelp, yowl **5** shout, sneer, taunt, whoop **6** bellow, chorus, cry out, deride, outcry, racket, scream, shriek, shrill, tumult, uproar **7** catcall, cry down, scoff at, screech, sing out, sneer at, snicker, ululate, wailing, whistle **8** proclaim, shouting **9** caterwaul, commotion, raspberry, screaming, snicker at **10** Bronx cheer, screeching

Hoover, Herbert Clark
  nickname: 13 Great Engineer **14** Great Secretary **17** Great Humanitarian **18** Great Public Servant
  presidential rank: 11 thirty-first
  party: 10 Republican
  state represented: 2 CA
  defeated: 5 (Alfred Emanuel) Smith **6** (George William) Norris, (Norman) Thomas, (William Frederick) Varney, (William Zebulon) Foster **8** (Verne L) Reynolds
  vice president: 6 (Charles) Curtis
  cabinet:
    state: **7** (Henry Lewis) Stimson
    treasury: **5** (Ogden Livingston) Mills **6** (Andrew William) Mellon
    war: **4** (James William) Good **6** (Patrick Jay) Hurley
    attorney general: **8** (William DeWitt) Mitchell
    navy: **5** (Charles Francis) Adams
    postmaster general: **5** (Walter Folger) Brown
    interior: **6** (Ray Lyman) Wilbur
    agriculture: **4** (Arthur Mastick) Hyde
    commerce: **6** (Robert Patterson) Lamont, (Roy Dikeman) Chapin
    labor: **4** (William Nuckles) Doak **5** (James John) Davis
  born: 12 West Branch IA
  died: 13 New York City NY
  buried: 12 West Branch IA
  education:
    University: **8** Stanford
  religion: 5 Quaker **16** Society of Friends
  interests: 7 fishing
  vacation spot: 10 Camp Hoover **11** Rapidan Camp **22** Shenandoah National Park
  author: 7 Memoirs **11** On Growing Up **14** An American Epic **16** Years of Adventure **18** Principles of Mining, The Great Depression **20** America's First Crusade **21** American Individualism, The Challenge to Liberty **24** The Ordeal of Woodrow Wilson **25** The Problems of Lasting Peace **26** The Cabinet and the Presidency **28** Addresses Upon the American Road **51** The State Papers and Other Public Writings of Herbert Hoover
  political career: 19 US Food Administrator
    head of: **23** American Relief Committee **28** Commission for Relief in Belgium
    director: **38** General Relief and Reconstruction of Europe
    member/chairman: **22** Supreme Economic Council
    secretary of: **8** Commerce
    chairman of: **17** Hoover Commissions
  civilian career: 6 author **14** mining engineer **18** consulting engineer
  notable events of lifetime/term: 15 Great Depression
    conference: **11** London Naval
    crash of: **11** stock market
    independence for: **11** Philippines
    Tariff: **11** Hawley-Smoot
  father: 10 Jesse Clark
  mother: 6 Huldah (Randall Minthorn)
  siblings: 3 May **13** Theodore Jesse
  wife: 3 Lou (Henry)
  children: 10 Allan Henry **12** Herbert Clark
  first lady:
    vice president of: **10** Girl Scouts

hop 3 bob **4** ball, jump, leap, prom, romp, skip, step, trip **5** bound, caper, dance, frisk, mixer, vault **6** bounce, gambol, prance, soiree, spring **7** Humulus
  varieties: 4 Wild **5** False **6** Common **8** European, Japanese

hope 3 yen **4** help, wish **5** crave, dream, faith, fancy, trust **6** aspire, belief, chance, desire, expect, hunger, rescue,

yen for 7 believe, count on, craving, dream of, longing, long for **8** ambition, daydream, feel sure, optimism, prospect, reckon on, reliance, yearn for, yearning **9** assurance, hankering, have faith, hunger for, salvation, take heart **10** anticipate, aspiration, assumption, be bent upon, confidence, conviction, expectancy **11** be confident, contemplate, expectation, have an eye to, possibility, presumption, reassurance, saving grace **12** anticipation, be optimistic, heart's desire **13** encouragement, have a fancy for, look forward to **14** have a hankering **17** great expectations **18** have one's heart set on **19** look on the bright side

Hope, Anthony
  real name: 21 Sir Anthony Hope Hawkins
  author of: 15 Rupert of Hentzau **18** The Prisoner of Zenda

Hope, Bob
  real name: 16 Leslie Townes Hope
  co-star: 10 Bing Crosby **13** Dorothy Lamour
  born: 6 Eltham **7** England
  roles:
    Road to: **3** Rio **4** Bali **6** Utopia **7** Morocco **8** Hong Kong, Zanzibar **9** Singapore

hopeful 7 assured, in hopes **8** cheering, sanguine, trusting **9** confident, expectant, favorable, fortunate, promising **10** auspicious, heartening, of good omen, optimistic, propitious, reassuring **11** encouraging **12** anticipative

hopeless 3 sad **4** lost, vain **6** abject, futile **7** forlorn, useless **8** dejected, downcast **9** depressed, incurable, pointless **10** beyond help, despairing, despondent, impossible, melancholy, past remedy **11** downhearted, heartbroken, irreparable, irrevocable, pessimistic, sick at heart **12** beyond recall, disconsolate, heavyhearted, irredeemable, irreversible **13** grief-stricken, irretrievable **14** down in the mouth, sorrow-stricken

hopelessness 7 despair **8** futility **9** pessimism **11** uselessness

Hopi (Hopitu, Moki)
  language family:
    10 Shoshonean
  location: 7 Arizona
  adapted culture of: 6 Pueblo
  ceremony: 10 snake dance

Hopkins, Anthony
  born: 5 Wales **10** Port Talbot
  roles: 10 Audrey Rose **11** A Doll's House **12** Young Winston **14** The Elephant Man **15** The Lion in Winter

Hoples
  father: 3 Ion

Hopper, Edward
  born: 7 Nyack NY
  artwork: 10 Nighthawks **18** Early Sunday Morning, House by the Railroad **19** Second Story Sunlight **20** Sunlight in a Cafeteria **21** Lighthouse at Two Lights

Horae
  also: 4 Hour
  goddesses of: 5 decay **6** growth **7** seasons **11** social order
  names: 4 Dice, Dike **5** Irene **7** Eunomia

Horatii
  form: 7 triplets **8** brothers
  sister: 7 Horatia
  champions of: 4 Rome
  fought: 8 Curiatii

Horatio
  character in: 6 Hamlet
  author: 11 Shakespeare

Horatio
  character in: 17 The Spanish Tragedy
  author: 3 Kyd

Horatius
  origin: 5 Roman
  defended: 6 bridge
    over: **5** Tiber
    against: **9** Etruscans

Horcus
  origin: 5 Greek
  god of: 5 oaths

horde 3 mob **4** band, gang, host, pack **5** bunch, crowd, crush, drove, party, swarm, tribe, troop **6** legion, throng **7** company **8** assembly **9** gathering, multitude **10** assemblage **12** congregation

Horgan, Paul
  author of: 10 Whitewater **13** Lamy of Santa Fe **18** The Thin Mountain Air

horizon 4 area **5** field, range, realm, scope, vista, world **6** bounds, domain, sphere **7** compass, expanse, outlook, purview, stretch **8** frontier, prospect **11** perspective

horizontal 4 even, flat **5** flush, level, plane, plumb, prone **6** supine **8** parallel (to something) **9** lying down, prostrate, reclining, recumbent **14** flat on one's back

horizontal support 3 tie

4 beam **5** brace, joist **6** girder, header, lintel **8** crossbar

hormone 5 auxin **6** cortin **7** estrone, insulin, steroid **8** endocrin, estrogen, galactin, lactogen, secretin **9** adrenalin, cortisone **12** progesterone, testosterone

horn 4 tusk **5** cornu, point, spike **6** antler **11** excrescence
  brass instrument: 4 oboe, tuba **5** bugle **6** cornet **7** bassoon, trumpet **8** alto horn, baritone, clarinet, trombone **9** euphonium, saxophone **10** French horn, mellophone, sousaphone **11** English horn

Horn of Africa *see* **7** Somalia

Hornung, Paul
  nickname: 9 Golden Boy
  sport: 8 football
  position: 6 runner **11** placekicker
  team: 15 Green Bay Packers

horny 4 hard **5** tough **7** callous **8** callused, hardened **12** thick-skinned **14** pachydermatous

horologe 5 clock **9** timepiece **11** chronometer

horrendous 4 gory **5** awful **6** horrid **7** ghastly, hideous **8** dreadful, horrible, shocking, terrible **9** appalling, frightful, repellent, repulsive, revolting **10** horrifying

horrible 3 bad **4** foul, rank, vile **5** awful, nasty **6** grisly, horrid, odious **7** ghastly, hideous **8** dreadful, gruesome, shocking, terrible, unsavory **9** abhorrent, appalling, atrocious, frightful, harrowing, loathsome, monstrous, obnoxious, repellent, repulsive, revolting, sickening **10** abominable, despicable, detestable, disgusting, forbidding, nauseating, unbearable, unpleasant **11** disquieting, distasteful, unspeakable **12** disagreeable, insufferable

horrid 3 bad **4** foul, grim, ugly **5** awful, nasty, rough **6** bratty, horror, shaggy, wicked **7** fearful, hideous **8** dreadful, gruesome, horrible, shocking, terrible **9** bristling, frightful, offensive, revolting, vexatious **10** abominable, detestable, unpleasant **11** troublesome **12** disagreeable

horrific 4 dire **5** awful **7** fearful, ghastly **8** dreadful, horrible, shocking, terrible **9** appalling

horrified 6 aghast **8** appalled

9 petrified, terrified **10** frightened **13** thunderstruck **14** terror-stricken

horrify 5 daunt, repel, shock **6** appall, dismay, revolt, sicken **7** disgust, petrify, terrify **8** affright, disquiet, frighten, nauseate **10** disconcert, dishearten **11** make one sick **15** make one turn pale **18** make one's flesh creep **22** make one's hair stand on end

horrifying 5 awful, dread **8** alarming, dreadful **10** terrifying **11** frightening, hairraising

horror 3 woe **4** fear **5** alarm, crime, dread, panic **6** dismay, hatred, misery, terror **7** anguish, cruelty, disgust, dislike, outrage, torment **8** atrocity, aversion, distaste, distress, hardship, loathing **9** antipathy, awfulness, privation, repulsion, revulsion, suffering **10** abhorrence, affliction, discomfort, inhumanity, repugnance **11** abomination, detestation, hideousness, trepidation **12** apprehension, terribleness, wretchedness

horror-struck 6 aghast **7** fearful **8** appalled **9** horrified, terrified **10** frightened **13** scared to death

hors de combat 8 disabled **13** out of the fight

hors d'oeuvre 3 dip **6** canape, relish, tidbit **9** antipasto, appetizer **10** finger food

horse *see box, p. 460*

horseback riding
athlete: **11** Frank Chapot **17** William Steinkraus

horse collar 3 zip **4** zero **5** aught, zilch **6** cipher, naught **8** goose egg

Horse Knows the Way, The
author: **9** John O'Hara

horseman 5 groom, rider **6** hussar, jockey, lancer, ostler **7** cossack, dragoon, hostler, trainer, trooper **9** postilion, stableboy, stableman **10** cavalryman, equestrian, roughrider **11** horse marine, stable owner **12** equestrienne, horse breeder, horse soldier, stable keeper **14** cavalry soldier, horseback rider, mounted trooper

horseplay 6 pranks **7** foolery **9** cutting up **10** buffoonery, tomfoolery **13** fooling around, horsing around

horse racing
jockey: **8** Del Insko **11** Bill Hartack, Eddie Arcaro **12** Angel Cordero, Bill Haughton, Laffit Pincay, Steve Cauthen **13** Johnny Longden, Stanley Dancer **15** Willie Shoemaker
god of: **6** Consus

Horseshoe Robinson
author: **12** John P Kennedy

horse soldier 6 hussar, lancer **7** dragoon, trooper **8** cavalier, horseman **10** cavalryman

horse trooper 6 hussar, lancer **7** dragoon, Mountie **8** cavalier, horseman **10** cavalryman **12** horse soldier **14** mounted soldier **16** mounted policeman

Horton, Edward Everett
sidekick of: **11** Fred Astaire
born: **10** Brooklyn NY
roles: **15** Cinderella Jones, Her Primitive Man **18** Springtime for Henry

Horus
origin: **8** Egyptian
god of: **3** sun
Greek name: **10** Harcorates
symbol: **6** falcon
mother: **4** Isis
father: **6** Osiris
enemy: **3** Set **4** Seth

hosannas 4 yeas **5** kudos **6** bravos, cheers, paeans **7** acclaim, hurrahs, huzzahs, yippees **8** applause **10** hallelujas **11** halleluiahs

hose 5 socks **7** hosiery **9** stockings

Hosea
father: **5** Beeri

hosiery 3 sox **4** hose **5** socks **6** nylons, tights **7** leotard **9** stockings

hospitable 4 open, warm **6** genial **7** cordial **8** amenable, amicable, friendly, gracious, sociable, tolerant **9** agreeable, convivial, receptive, welcoming **10** accessible, gregarious, neighborly, openhanded, openminded, responsive **12** approachable

hospital 4 home **6** asylum, clinic **7** sick bay **8** pavilion, rest home **9** infirmary **10** polyclinic, sanatorium **11** nursing home **13** medical center
French: **9** hotel Dieu

hospital, private
French: **13** maison de sante

hospitality 5 cheer **6** warmth **7** welcome **8** openness **9** geniality **10** cordiality, heartiness, kindliness **11** amicability,

sociability **12** congeniality, conviviality, friendliness **13** Gemutlichkeit **14** hospitableness, neighborliness **15** warmheartedness
god of: **6** Sancus **10** Dius Fidius, Semo Sancus

host, hostess 3 lot, mob **4** army, band, body, crew, gang, mess **5** array, crowd, drove, group, horde, party, swarm, troop **6** legion, throng **7** company, maitre d', meeting **8** conclave, congress, hosteler, hotelier, landlord, welcomer **9** gathering, innkeeper, multitude **10** confluence, convention, headwaiter, party giver, proprietor **11** convocation, hotel keeper **12** congregation, head waitress, hotel manager, proprietress, receptionist **17** restaurant manager **18** master of ceremonies **20** mistress of ceremonies

hostage 7 captive **8** prisoner

Hostage, The
author: **12** Brendan Behan

hostel 3 inn **4** hall **5** hotel, lodge **7** hospice, lodging, shelter **8** hospital, hostelry

hostile 3 icy **4** cold, mean, ugly **5** angry, at war, enemy, testy **6** at odds, at outs, bitter, chilly, cranky, malign, touchy, unkind **7** opposed, vicious, warring **8** battling, clashing, contrary, fighting, opposing, snappish, spiteful, venomous **9** bellicose, bristling, dissident, malicious, malignant, truculent **10** contending, ill-natured, malevolent, on bad terms, unfriendly **11** belligerent, contentious, disagreeing, ill-disposed, quarrelsome **12** antagonistic, cantankerous, disagreeable, disputatious, incompatible **13** argumentative, at loggerheads, unsympathetic

hostile act 4 raid **6** strike, threat **7** assault, offense **8** act of war, invasion **9** hostility, incursion **10** aggression

hostile nation 5 enemy **7** invader

hostility 3 war **4** duel, feud, fray, hate **5** anger, clash, fight, venom **6** battle, combat, enmity, fracas, hatred, malice, rancor, spleen **7** contest, dispute, ill will, scuffle, warfare, warring **8** act of war, argument, battling, conflict, fighting **9** animosity, antipathy, bickering **10** antagonism, bitterness, contention, dissidence, opposition, state of war **11** altercation, malevolence, vi-

horse 4 colt, foal, hack, jade, mare, plug, pony, sire, stud **5** bronc, filly, mount, pacer, pinto, steed **6** bronco, dobbin, equine **7** cavalry, charger, cow pony, gelding, hackney, hussars, lancers, mustang, palfrey, trotter **8** cossacks, dragoons, galloper, stallion, troopers, yearling **9** broodmare, racehorse **10** cavalrymen, draft horse **12** horse cavalry, horse marines, quarter horse, thoroughbred **13** horse soldiers, mounted troops **15** mounted troopers, mounted warriors
  Achilles': 7 Xanthus
  Alexander the Great's: 10 Bucephalus
  anatomy: 4 hock, hoof, loin, mane, tail **5** croup, flank, shank **6** cannon, gaskin, haunch, stifle **7** coronet, crupper, fetlock, gambrel, nostril, pastern, withers **11** throatlatch
  Australian: 5 dingo, myall **8** warragal, warrigal, yarraman
  breed: 6 Morgan, Nubian, Tarpan **7** Arabian, Belgian, mustang **8** Galloway, Shetland **9** Appaloosa, Percheron **10** Clydesdale, Lippizaner **12** Narragansett, Standardbred, Thoroughbred **15** Tennessee-Walker
  Caligula's: 9 Incitatus (made a senator)
  castrated: 7 gelding
  color: 3 bay, dun **4** gray, pied, roan, zain **5** morel, pinto **6** calico, dapple, sorrel **7** piebald **8** chestnut, palomino, schimmel (gray)
  combining form: 4 eque, equi **5** hippo
  Dick Turpin's: 9 Black Bess
  Don Quixote's: 9 Rosinante
  family: 7 Equidae **9** Miohippus, Orohippus
  female: 3 dam **4** mare **5** filly
  French: 6 cheval
  gear: 3 bit **4** rein, tack **6** saddle **7** blinder, harness, snaffle **9** surcingle **11** saddlecloth
  Gen Custer's: 8 Comanche
  Gen Grant's: 10 Cincinnati
  Gen Robert E Lee's: 9 Traveller
  Gen Sherman's: 6 Rienzi
  genus: 5 equus
  Gulliver's Travels: 9 Houyhnhnm
  kind: 3 cob **4** race **6** bronco, hunter, jumper **7** charger, mustang, palfrey, quarter, trotter **8** destrier
  legendary: 6 Trojan
  Lone Ranger's: 6 Silver
  male: 4 colt **8** stallion
  measure: 4 hand
  Mohammed's: 7 Alborak
  movie/story: 6 Flicka **8** Champion **11** Black Beauty **14** National Velvet **16** The Black Stallion
  Napoleon's: 7 Morengo
  Orlando's: 11 Vegliantino
  pace: 4 lope, trot **5** amble **6** canter, gallop
  pair of: 4 span, team **6** tandem
  race: 5 derby, plate **6** exacta **7** pick six **8** claiming, handicap **9** allowance **11** daily double, sweepstakes **12** steeplechase, weight-for-age
    Triple Crown: **7** Belmont **9** Preakness **13** Kentucky Derby
  riding show: 8 gymkhana
  Rinaldo's: 6 Bayard
  Roy Rogers': 7 Trigger
  Sigurd's: 5 Grani
  small: 4 pony
  Stonewall Jackson's: 12 Little Sorrel
  Tom Mix's: 4 Tony
  three: 6 randem, troika **7** unicorn
  Wellington's (at Waterloo): 10 Copenhagen
  wild: 5 fuzzy **6** bramby, kumrah, outlaw, tarpan **7** jughead **8** bangtail, fuzztail, warragal, warrigal
  Will Rogers': 8 Soapsuds **10** Bootlegger
  winged: 7 Pegasus
  young: 4 colt, foal **5** filly **8** yearling

ciousness **12** belligerence, contrariness, disagreement **14** unfriendliness, vindictiveness

hot 3 new, top **4** good, late, live, near, warm **5** fiery, fresh, nippy, sharp **6** ardent, baking, biting, fervid, fierce, heated, hectic, latest, molten, raging, recent, red-hot, stormy, sultry, torrid **7** boiling, burning, earnest, excited, furious, intense, melting, peppery, piquant, popular, pungent, searing, violent **8** agitated, animated, broiling, feverish, frenzied, roasting, scalding, sizzling, steaming, vehement, very warm **9** emotional, excellent, scorching, simmering, very close, wrought-up **10** attractive, blistering, passionate, smoldering, successful, sweltering **11** electrified, fast-selling, most popular, radioactive, sought after, tempestuous **12** incandescent **14** fast and furious, highly seasoned, in close pursuit

hot air 7 bombast 8 rhetoric 9 hyperbole 12 exaggeration 13 overstatement

hotel 3 inn 5 lodge, motel 6 hostel 7 hospice, lodging 8 hostelry, motor inn

Hotel, The
author: 14 Elizabeth Bowen

hotel de ville 9 a city hall
literally: 16 mansion of the city

hotel Dieu 9 a hospital 12 mansion of God

Hotel New Hampshire, The
author: 10 John Irving

hothouse 6 tender 7 fragile, nursery 8 delicate 10 glass-house, greenhouse 12 conservatory 13 over-protected

hot temper 4 fire 5 anger 6 pepper 8 acrimony 9 short fuse

hot-tempered 7 peppery 9 emotional, excitable 13 easily ruffled, quick-tempered

hot water 3 jam 4 mess 6 pickle 7 trouble 10 difficulty 11 predicament

Houghston, Walter
real name of: 12 Walter Huston

hound 3 dog, fan, nag, nut, pup 4 bait, buff, hunt, mutt, tail 5 annoy, chase, doggy, freak, harry, lover, pooch, puppy, stalk, track, trail, whelp, worry 6 addict, badger, canine, follow, harass, hector, keep at, needle, pester, pursue 7 bedevil, poochie 9 keep after 10 aficionado, hunting dog 11 afficionado
dog breed: 6 beagle, borzoi, saluki 7 basenji, harrier, whippet 9 dachshund, greyhound 10 bloodhound, otter hound 11 Afghan hound, basset hound, Ibizan hound 12 pharaoh hound 14 Irish wolfhound 15 English foxhound 16 American foxhound 17 Norwegian elkhound, Scottish deerhound 18 Rhodesian ridgeback 20 black and tan coonhound
group of: 3 cry 4 mute, pack

Hound of the Baskervilles, The
author: 19 Sir Arthur Conan Doyle
character: 8 Dr Watson 14 Sherlock Holmes 19 Sir Henry Baskerville

hour 3 day 4 span, time 5 space 6 period 8 interval
abbreviation: 2 hr

Hour see 5 Horae

house, House 4 clan, firm, hall, home, keep, line, shop 5 abode, board, lodge, put up, store 6 billet, church, family, garage, harbor, strain, temple 7 Commons, company, concern, contain, council, descent, dynasty, lineage, quarter, shelter, theater 8 ancestry, assembly, audience, building, business, congress, domicile, dwelling 9 ancestors, household, residence 10 auditorium, family tree, habitation, hippodrome, opera house, spectators 11 accommodate, concert hall, corporation, legislature, noble family, partnership, royal family 12 business firm, lower chamber, meeting place, organization 13 dwelling place, establishment
god of: 8 Silvanus, Sylvanus

housebreaker 5 thief 6 robber 7 burglar 8 pilferer 9 purloiner 10 cat burglar 14 second-story man

housebreaking 5 theft 7 break-in, robbery 8 burglary, stealing 12 burglarizing 19 breaking and entering

House Divided, A
author: 9 Pearl Buck

House for Mr Biswas, A
author: 9 V S Naipaul

household 4 home 5 house 6 family, hearth 8 of a house 9 for a house 10 for a family, for home use 12 family circle
goddess of: 6 Brigit

household help 4 cook, maid 7 footman, steward 8 domestic, gardener, handyman, houseboy 9 charwoman, chauffeur, domestics, majordomo, nursemaid 11 housekeeper

household of three
French: 12 menage a trois

House in Paris, The
author: 14 Elizabeth Bowen

House Made of Dawn
author: 13 N Scott Momaday

House of Atreus, The
author: 9 Aeschylus
character: 7 Electra, Orestes 9 Aegisthus, Agamemnon, Cassandra 12 Clytemnestra

house of health
French: 13 maison de sante

House of Mirth, The
author: 12 Edith Wharton
character: 8 Lily Bart, Mr Selden 9 Gus Trenor 10 Judy Trenor, Mr Rosedale, Percy Gryce 12 Bertha Dorset, George Dorset

House of the Seven Gables, The
author: 18 Nathaniel Hawthorne
character: 10 Mr Holgrave 14 Phoebe Pyncheon 16 Clifford Pyncheon 20 Judge Jaffrey Pyncheon, Miss Hepzibah Pyncheon

house of worship 6 chapel, church, mosque, temple 8 basilica 9 cathedral, synagogue 10 house of God, Lord's house, tabernacle

housewife 4 wife 9 homemaker 11 housekeeper

housing 4 case, home 5 abode, house 6 casing, jacket, sheath, shield 7 lodging, shelter 8 covering, domicile, dwelling, envelope, lodgment, quarters 9 enclosure, residence 10 habitation 14 accommodations

Housman, A E
author of: 14 A Shropshire Lad

Houston
baseball team: 6 Astros
basketball team: 7 Rockets
canal: 11 Houston Ship
channel: 12 Buffalo Bayou
football team: 6 Oilers 8 Gamblers
landmark: 4 NASA 12 Alley Theater 14 Jesse James Hall 22 Manned Spacecraft Center 29 San Jacinto Battlefield Monument
  battleship: 5 Texas
named after: 10 Sam Houston
planned by: 7 A C Allen, J K Allen
stadium: 9 Astrodome
street: 15 Old Spanish Trail
university: 4 Rice 12 Texas Medical 13 Texas Southern

Houston, Sam
position: 9 US Senator
governor of: 5 Texas 9 Tennessee
president of: 15 Republic of Texas
served in: 9 Creek Wars 15 Texas Revolution
battle: 10 San Jacinto
defeated: 9 Santa Anna

Houyhnhnms
fictional people in: 16 Gulliver's Travels
author: 5 Swift

hovel 3 hut 4 dump, hole 5 cabin, shack 6 shanty

hover 4 flit, hang 5 float, haunt, pause, poise, waver 6 attend, falter, seesaw 7 flitter, flutter 9 fluctuate, hang about, vacillate

Hovhaness, Alan
born: 12 Somerville MA
composer of: 10 Magnificat

how
Latin: 7 quo modo

Howard, Ron
born: 2 OK 6 Duncan
roles: 4 Opie 9 Happy Days
16 American Graffiti, Richie
Cunningham 19 The Andy
Griffith Show
director of: 6 Cocoon, Gung
Ho, Splash, Willow

Howard, Sidney
author of: 13 The Silver
Cord 22 They Knew What
They Wanted

Howard, Trevor
born: 7 England
12 Cliftonville
roles: 6 The Key 13 Ryan's
Daughter, Sons and Lovers
14 Brief Encounter 23 The
Invincible Mr Disraeli

Howard's End
author: 9 E M Forster
character: 9 Jacky Bast
10 Paul Wilcox, Ruth Wil-
cox 11 Henry Wilcox, Leonard Bast 13 Charles Wilcox,
Helen Schlegel 16 Margaret
Schlegel, Theobald Schlegel

how are you
German: 8 wie geht's 9 wie
geht es

Howe, Elias
nationality: 8 American
invented: 13 sewing machine

Howells, William Dean
author of: 12 Indian Sum-
mer 15 A Modern Instance
20 A Hazard of New For-
tunes, The Rise of Silas
Lapham

How Green Was My Valley
author: 16 Richard Llewellyn
director: 8 John Ford
character: 6 Marged 7 Bron-
wen 10 Beth Morgan
11 Iestyn Evans 12 Gwilym
Morgan
Morgan children: 4 Davy,
Huur, Ivor, Owen
5 Ianto 6 Gwilym
8 Angharad
cast: 7 Anna Lee 9 John
Loder 11 Donald Crisp
12 Maureen O'Hara
13 Roddy McDowall, Walter
Pidgeon
Oscar for: 7 picture 8 director 15 supporting actor
(Crisp)

howl 3 bay, cry 4 bark, hoot,
roar, wail, yell, yelp, yowl
5 groan, shout, cry out, outcry,
scream, shriek, uproar
7 ululate

howler 4 goof 5 error 6 boo-
boo 7 blooper, blunder,
mistake

**How To Win Friends and
Influence People**
author: 12 Dale Carnegie

hoyden 3 imp 4 brat, chit
6 tomboy

Hoyle, Fred
field: 9 astronomy
nationality: 7 British
developed: 17 steady-state
theory

Hoyt, Rosemary
character in: 16 Tender Is
the Night
author: 10 Fitzgerald

Hreidmar
origin: 12 Scandinavian
mentioned in: 8 Volsunga
son: 5 Otter, Regin 6 Fafnir
killed by: 6 Fafnir

Hsitsang *see* 5 Tibet

Hualapai
language family: 5 Yuman
location: 7 Arizona
related to: 7 Yavapai
9 Havasupai

hub 3 nub 4 axis, core 5 focus,
heart, pivot 6 center, middle
10 focal point

Hubble, Edwin Powell
field: 9 astronomy
studied: 15 galactic nebulae
named for him: 14 Hubble
constant

hubbub 3 din 4 fuss, stir, to-
do 5 noise 6 babble, bedlam,
bustle, clamor, pother, racket,
ruckus, tumult, uproar 7 ferment, turmoil 8 disorder 9 agitation, commotion, confusion,
hue and cry 10 hullabaloo,
hurly-burly 11 disturbance,
pandemonium 12 perturbation

Hubert
creator: 11 Dick Wingert

huckleberry 9 Vaccinium
11 Gaylussacia
varieties: 2 He 3 Box, Red
4 Blue, Shot 5 Black, Dwarf,
Hairy, Squaw, Sugar 6 Garden 8 Thin-leaf 9 Evergreen
10 California, Little-leaf

**Huckleberry Finn (The Ad-
ventures of)**
author: 9 Mark Twain
character: 3 Jim 9 Tom Sawyer 12 Widow Douglas
13 Judge Thatcher

huckster 5 adman 6 badger,
hawker, kidder, seller, vendor
7 haggler, peddler

Hud
director: 10 Martin Ritt
cast: 10 John Ashley, Paul

Newman 12 Patricia Neal
13 Melvyn Douglas
14 Brandon de Wilde
Oscar for: 7 actress (Neal)
15 supporting actor
(Douglas)

huddle 4 heap, herd, mass,
mess 5 bunch, crowd, group
6 cuddle, curl up, jumble,
medley, muddle, nestle,
throng 7 cluster, collect, meeting, snuggle 8 converge, disarray, disorder 9 confusion,
gathering 10 conference, discussion, hodge-podge 12 think
session

Hudibras
author: 12 Samuel Butler
character: 6 Ralpho 8 Crow-
ders 9 Sidrophel

Hudson, Rock
real name: 12 Roy Scherer Jr
co-star: 8 Doris Day
born: 10 Winnetka IL
roles: 5 Giant 10 Pillow
Talk 15 A Farewell to Arms,
McMillan and Wife
20 Magnificent Obsession

Hudson, W H
author of: 13 Green Man-
sions, The Purple Land
17 Far Away and Long Ago

hue 4 cast, tint, tone 5 color,
shade, tinge 8 tincture
10 coloration

hue and cry 4 call, howl,
roar, yell, yowl 5 alarm, alert,
shout, storm 6 bellow, clamor,
hubbub, outcry, shriek, uproar 7 thunder 10 cry of
alarm, hullabaloo

huff 3 pet 4 fury, rage, snit
7 bad mood, dudgeon, out-
rage 8 ill humor, vexation
9 annoyance, petulance 10 fit
of anger, fit of pique,
resentment

huffy 4 curt, hurt 5 angry,
cross, irate, moody, sulky,
surly, testy 6 cranky, grumpy,
moping, morose, shirty, sullen,
touchy 7 in a snit, peevish,
waspish, wounded 8 churlish,
offended, petulant, snappish
9 glowering, in a lather, in a
pucker, irritable, querulous,
rancorous, resentful, sensitive
10 ill-humored, out of sorts
11 disgruntled, quarrelsome,
thin-skinned 12 discontented
14 easily offended, hard to
live with, hypersensitive

hug 4 hold 5 clasp 6 clutch,
cuddle, nestle 7 cling to, embrace, snuggle, squeeze 9 hold
close, hover near 11 keep
close to 13 cling together, follow closely 15 parallel closely,
press to the bosom

huge 4 vast **5** giant, great, jumbo **6** mighty **7** immense, mammoth, massive, titanic **8** colossal, enormous, gigantic, imposing **9** cyclopean, extensive, herculean, leviathan, monstrous **10** gargantuan, monumental, prodigious, staggering, stupendous **11** elephantine, extravagant, spectacular **12** overwhelming **14** Brobdingnagian

hugeness 4 bulk **8** enormity, vastness **9** great size, immensity, largeness, magnitude **11** massiveness

Huggins, Charles Brenton
   field: **10** physiology
   researched: **6** cancer
      12 chemotherapy
   awarded: **10** Nobel Prize

Hughes, Langston
   author of: **9** The Big Sea
      12 One-Way Ticket **13** The
      Weary Blues **19** Shakespeare
      in Harlem **20** The Panther
      and the Lash

Hughes, Richard
   author of: **18** A High Wind
      in Jamaica

Hughes, Thomas
   author of: **19** Tom Brown's
      Schooldays

Hugh the Drover
   opera by: **15** Vaughan
      Williams
   character: **4** Mary **12** The
      Constable **14** John the
      Butcher

Hugin
   origin: **12** Scandinavian
   form: **5** raven
   owned by: **4** Odin **5** Othin
   personifies: **7** thought
   duty: **10** newsbearer
   other raven: **5** Munin

Hugo, Victor
   author of: **13** Les Miserables
      16 Notre Dame de Paris
      23 The Hunchback of Notre
      Dame
   character: **9** Esmeralda,
      Quasimodo

hulk 4 ship **5** giant, wreck **8** behemoth

hulking 3 big **5** bulky, heavy, husky **7** massive **8** powerful, unwieldy **9** oversized, ponderous **10** cumbersome

hull 3 pod **4** case, husk, peel, rind, skin **5** shell, shuck **7** coating **8** carapace **9** epidermis, tegmentum **10** integument

Hull, Isaac
   served in: **19** War of Eighteen-Twelve

sunk ship: 9 Guerriere (British)
   commander of ship:
      12 Constitution

hullabaloo 3 din **4** stir **5** babel **6** bedlam, clamor, hubbub, ruckus, tumult, uproar **9** confusion **11** pandemonium
   Yiddish: **7** tzimmes

hum 4 buzz, purr, whir **5** croon, drone, thrum **6** be busy, bustle, intone, murmur, thrive **7** buzzing, droning, purring, vibrate **8** be active, whirring **9** vibration **10** faint sound **13** be in full swing

human 3 man **5** of man, of men **6** gentle, humane, kindly, mortal, person **7** hominid, like man, manlike **8** merciful, personal **10** anthropoid, individual **11** Homo sapiens, sympathetic

Human Comedy, The
   author: **14** Honore de Balzac,
      William Saroyan

Human Condition, The
   author: **12** Hannah Arendt

humane 4 kind **5** human **6** kindly, tender **7** pitying **8** merciful **9** unselfish **10** benevolent, bighearted, charitable, goodwilled **11** magnanimous, sympathetic, warmhearted **12** humanitarian **13** compassionate, philanthropic

humaneness 8 kindness, sympathy **10** compassion, gentleness, kindliness **11** benevolence **12** mercifulness **15** warmheartedness

Human Factor, The
   author: **12** Graham Greene

humanitarian 4 kind **6** humane **8** generous **10** altruistic, benevolent, charitable **11** kindhearted **12** large-hearted **13** compassionate, philanthropic **14** philanthropist

humanity 3 man **4** love **5** mercy **6** people **7** charity, mankind, mortals **8** goodwill, kindness, sympathy **9** humankind, humanness, mortality **10** compassion, gentleness, humaneness, kindliness, tenderness **11** benevolence, Homo sapiens, human beings, human nature, magnanimity **12** the human race **13** brotherly love, fellow feeling **15** warmheartedness **16** fraternal feeling

humanum est errare 12 to err is human

Humbert Humbert
   character in: **6** Lolita
   author: **7** Nabokov

humble 3 low **4** meek, poor **5** abase, abash, crush, lower, lowly, plain, shame **6** common, debase, demean, demure, gentle, modest, shabby, simple, subdue **7** chasten, conquer, degrade, mortify, obscure, put down **8** bring low, derogate, disgrace, dishonor, inferior, ordinary, plebeian, pull down, wretched **9** bring down, embarrass, humiliate, make lowly, miserable **10** inglorious, lowranking, make humble, obsequious, put to shame, respectful, unassuming **11** deferential, subservient, unimportant, unpresuming **12** self-effacing, take down a peg **13** insignificant, unpretentious **14** unostentatious **15** inconsequential, undistinguished

humbled 5 cowed **7** abashed, debased, subdued **9** conquered, disgraced **10** brought low, humiliated

Humboldt, Alexander von
   nationality: **6** German
   originator of: **7** ecology
      10 geophysics

Humboldt's Gift
   author: **10** Saul Bellow

humbug 3 fib, gyp, lie **4** bull, bunk, dupe, fake, fool, gull, hoax, liar, lies, sham **5** cheat, cozen, dodge, faker, fraud, hokum, lying, quack, spoof, trick **6** bunkum, con man, deceit, fibber, phooey, take in **7** beguile, blather, cheater, deceive, falsify, fiction, forgery, mislead, rubbish, sharper, swindle **8** artifice, claptrap, flimflam, flummery, hoodwink, impostor, nonsense, perjurer, pretense, swindler, trickery **9** bamboozle, charlatan, deception, fabricate, falsehood, hypocrisy, hypocrite, imposture, mendacity, poppycock, trickster **10** balderdash, hocus-pocus, mountebank, pretension **11** counterfeit, make-believe **12** equivocation, misrepresent **13** confidence man, double-dealing, falsification **15** pretentiousness

humdinger 4 lulu **5** dandy, doozy **6** beauty, hummer, marvel **8** Jim dandy, superior **10** ripsnorter **12** lollapalooza **13** extraordinary

humdrum 4 blah, dull, dumb, flat **5** banal, trite **6** boring, common, dreary **7** insipid, mundane, routine, tedious, trivial **8** everyday, lifeless, mediocre, ordinary, tiresome, wearying **9** hackneyed, unvarying, wearisome **10** monotonous, pedestrian, uneventful, unexciting, uninspired **11** commonplace, indifferent, uninspiring **12** conventional, run-of-the-mill **13** unexceptional, uninteresting

humerus
  bone of: **8** upper arm

humid 4 damp, dank **5** moist, muggy, soppy **6** clammy, steamy, sticky, sultry

humidity 4 smog **8** dampness, moisture **9** mugginess **10** stickiness

humiliate 5 abash, crush, shame **6** debase, humble, subdue **7** chagrin, chasten, degrade, mortify, put down **8** belittle, bring low, disgrace, dishonor **9** discomfit, embarrass **11** make ashamed **13** bring down a peg

humiliated 7 abashed, crushed, debased, humbled **8** degraded **9** chagrined, disgraced, mortified

humiliation 5 shame **7** chagrin **8** disgrace, dishonor **9** abasement **10** debasement **11** degradation **12** discomfiture **13** embarrassment, mortification

humility 7 modesty, shyness **8** meekness, timidity **9** lowliness **10** demureness, diffidence, humbleness **11** bashfulness **13** self-abasement **17** unpretentiousness

hummock 4 hill, rise **5** knoll, mound **7** hillock, tussock

Humologumena 17 New Testament books

humor 3 wit **4** baby, gags, mood, puns **5** farce, jests, jokes, spoil **6** cajole, comedy, joking, pamper, parody, satire, soothe, suffer, temper, whimsy **7** appease, flatter, foolery, fooling, indulge, jesting, mollify, placate, spirits, waggery **8** drollery, give in to, jocosity, low humor, nonsense, raillery, ridicule, tolerate, travesty, wordplay **9** burlesque, funniness, low comedy, put up with, slapstick, wittiness **10** buffoonery, caricature, comicality, comply with, high comedy, jocoseness, jocularity, tomfoolery, wisecracks, witticisms **11** broad comedy, disposition, foolishness, frame of mind, go along with **12** monkeyshines **13** ludicrousness **14** ridiculousness

humorist 3 wag, wit **4** card **5** comic **8** comedian

humorous 5 comic, droll,

funny, witty **6** jocose **7** amusing, comical, jocular, waggish **8** farcical, mirthful, sportive **9** facetious, laughable, ludicrous, satirical, whimsical **10** ridiculous **11** nonsensical, rib-tickling **13** sidesplitting

hump 4 arch, bend, bump, knob, lift, lump, rise **5** bulge, hunch, knurl, mound, put up, tense **8** swelling **9** convexity **10** projection, prominence **11** excrescence

Humperdinck, Engelbert
  born: **4** Bonn **7** Germany
  composer of: **10** The Miracle **15** Hansel and Gretel

Humphry Clinker
  author: **19** Tobias George Smollet
  character: **10** Mr Dennison **12** Jerry Melford, Lydia Melford **14** George Dennison, Matthew Bramble **15** Winifred Jenkins **18** Miss Tabitha Bramble **26** Lieutenant Obadiah Lismahago

Humpty Dumpty
  character in: **22** Through the Looking Glass
  author: **7** Carroll

hunch 4 arch, bend, clue, hump, idea **5** tense **7** feeling, glimmer, inkling **8** good idea **9** intuition, suspicion **10** foreboding **11** premonition **12** presentiment

Hunchback of Notre Dame, The
  author: **10** Victor Hugo
  character: **9** Esmeralda, Gringoire, Quasimodo **12** Claude Frollo **20** Phoebus de Chateaupers

hunched 4 bent **7** crooked, slumped, stooped **9** contorted

hundredweight
  abbreviation: **3** cwt

Hungary see box

hunger 3 yen **4** itch, love, lust, want, wish **5** crave, greed **6** desire, famine, hanker, liking, relish, thirst **7** burn for, craving, itch for, long for, pant for **8** appetite, fondness, voracity, yearn for, yearning **9** hankering, lust after **10** greediness, starvation **11** have a yen for, thirst after **12** malnutrition, ravenousness

hungry 5 eager **6** greedy **7** starved **8** ravenous, starving **9** voracious

hunk 3 gob, wad **4** clod, glob, lump, mass **5** block, chunk, piece **6** gobbet **7** portion **8** quantity

hunt 4 seek **5** chase, probe, shoot, stalk, trace, track, trail **6** course, follow, pursue **7** explore, go after, look for **8** coursing, drive out **9** ferret out, search for, try to find **11** go in quest of, inquire into **14** riding to hounds **20** leave no stone unturned

Hunt, Richard Morris
  architect of: **8** Biltmore (Asheville NC) **11** Marble House (Newport RI), The Breakers (Newport RI) **12** Lenox Library (NYC) **14** Studio Building (NYC) **19** National Observatory (Washington DC) **22** William Vanderbilt House (NYC) **23** Metropolitan Museum of Art (NYC)

hunter
  constellation of: **5** Orion
  French: **8** chasseur

Hunter, Jim
  nickname: **7** Catfish
  sport: **8** baseball
  position: **7** pitcher
  team: **14** New York Yankees **16** Oakland Athletics

Hunter, Kim
  real name: **8** Jane Cole
  born: **9** Detroit MI
  roles: **16** Stairway to Heaven, The Seventh Victim **21** A Streetcar Named Desire

Hunters
  goddess of: **11** Britomartis

Hunting
  god of: **7** Verbius
  goddess of: **5** Diana **7** Artemis

Hunting Dogs
  constellation of: **13** Canes Venatici

hurdle 4 jump, leap, snag, wall **5** bound, clear, fence, hedge, vault **6** hazard **7** barrier **8** obstacle, surmount **9** hindrance, roadblock **10** difficulty, impediment, spring over **11** obstruction **12** interference **14** stumbling block

hurl 4 cast, toss **5** chuck, fling, heave, pitch, sling, throw **6** launch, let fly, propel **7** fire off, project **9** discharge

hurly-burly 4 stir **5** furor **6** action, bustle, hubbub, hustle, uproar **8** activity **9** commotion **10** hullabaloo

hurrah, hurray 4 fine, good **5** bravo, cheer, great, huzza **6** huzzah, salute **7** acclaim, hosanna **9** excellent, halleluia, wonderful **10** exaltation, hallelujah

Hungary
capital/largest city: 8 Budapest
others: 4 Gyor, Pecs **5** Harta **6** Mohacs, Sopron, Szeged **7** Komarom, Miskolc, Szentes **8** Dubrecen, Kaposuar, Szegedin **9** Kecskemet **10** Albertirsa **11** Nagykanizsa, Szombathely
measure: 3 ako **4** hold, yoke **5** itcze, marok, metze **7** huvelyk
monetary unit: 4 gara **5** balas, krone, pengo **6** filler, forint, gulden, korona, ongara, ungara
weight: 7 vamfont **8** vammazsa
island: 8 Margaret
lake: 5 Ferto **7** Balaton, Velence **9** Blatensee **10** Neusiedler, Plattensee
mountain: 4 Alps, Bukk **5** Matra, Tatra **6** Bakony, Mecsek, Vertes **7** Cserhat, Gerecse **8** Borzsony, Zempleni **9** Korishegy **10** Carpathian
highest point: 5 Kekes
river: 3 Mur, Sio **4** Duna, Raab, Raba, Sajo, Zala **5** Bodva, Drava, Drave, Ipoly, Kapos, Koros, Maros, Tarna, Tisza **6** Danube, Henrad, Poprad, Szamos, Theiss, Zagyva **7** Vistula **8** Berretyo
physical feature:
  canal: **3** Sio **6** Sarviz
  forest: **6** Bakony
  plain: **6** Puszta
  port: **5** Fiume
people: 3 Hun **4** Serb **5** Croat, Gypsy **6** Cigany, Magyar, Slovak, Ugrian
  composer: **5** Lehar, Liszt **6** Bartok, Kodaly
  national hero: **5** Arpad
  playwright: **6** Molnar
language: 6 German, Magyar, Slovak **8** Croatian **9** Hungarian **10** Finno-Ugric
religion: 8 Lutheran **9** Calvinism **13** Roman Catholic **16** Eastern Orthodoxy
place:
  church: **32** Gothic Coronation Church of Matthias
  ruins: **8** Aquincum
  square: **6** Heroes
  tomb: **14** Turbe of Gul Baba **16** Father of the Roses
feature:
  dance: **3** kos **7** czardas **10** varsoviana
  dog: **4** puli
  musical instrument: **8** taragata **9** czimbalom
food:
  dish: **6** gulyas **7** goulash **15** chicken paprikas
  pastry: **4** rete **5** torte
  wine: **5** Tokay **10** Bulls Blood

Hurt, John
born: 7 England **22** Chesterfield Derbyshire
roles: 5 Alien **8** Partners **14** The Elephant Man **15** Midnight Express

Hurt, William
roles: 8 Body Heat **9** Gorky Park **10** Eyewitness **11** The Big Chill **13** Broadcast News **20** Kiss of the Spider Woman, Children of a Lesser God

hurtful 5 cruel **6** deadly **7** abusive, baleful, harmful **8** crushing, improper, stinging, wounding **9** injurious

hurtle 3 fly, hie, run, zip **4** bolt, dart, dash, race, rush, tear, whiz **5** bound, lunge, scoot, shoot, speed, spurt, whisk **6** charge, gallop, plunge, scurry **7** scamper, scuttle **11** go like a shot **13** go like the wind **14** go lickety-split

husband 3 man **4** keep, mate, save **5** amass, groom, hoard, hubby, store **6** old man, retain, save up, spouse **7** consort **8** conserve, maintain, preserve, set aside **10** accumulate, bridegroom, married man

husbandry 7 farming **9** geoponics **11** agriculture, cropraising **12** conservation
god of: 9 Aristaeus

hush 4 calm **5** quell, quiet, shush, still **6** shut up, soothe **7** be quiet, be still, keep mum, mollify, silence **8** be silent, pipe down, quietude **9** quiet down, quietness, stillness **10** knock it off **11** tranquility **12** peacefulness, tranquillity

hushed 4 calm **5** quiet, still **6** calmed, gentle, lulled, silent **7** allayed, quieted, soothed, stifled **8** pacified, silenced, tranquil **12** tranquilized **13** tranquillized

hush money 5 bribe **6** payoff, payola **7** tribute **9** blackmail, extortion

huskiness 5 brawn **9** beefiness **10** hoarseness, robustness, ruggedness, sturdiness **11** muscularity

husky 3 big **5** beefy, burly, gruff, harsh, hefty, plump, rough, solid, stout, thick **6** brawny, coarse, hoarse, robust, stocky, strong, sturdy **7** cracked, grating, rasping, raucous, throaty **8** athletic, croaking, guttural, muscular, powerful, thickset **9** strapping **10** overweight **12** strong as an ox **15** broad-shouldered

hurricane 7 cyclone, monsoon, tempest, typhoon **9** windstorm

Hurricane, The
director: 8 John Ford
cast: 7 Jon Hall **9** Mary Astor **12** C Aubrey Smith **13** Dorothy Lamour, Raymond Massey
setting: 9 Manikoora

hurried 4 fast **5** hasty **6** hectic, rushed, speedy **7** cursory, frantic **8** careless, feverish, frenetic, headlong, slapdash, slipshod **9** breakneck, haphazard, impulsive **11** precipitate, superficial

hurry 3 ado, zip **4** bolt, dart, dash, fuss, goad, prod, rush, stew, whiz **5** egg on, haste, speed **6** flurry, hasten, hustle, push on, scurry, tumult, urge on **7** drive on, flutter, press on, scuttle, speed up, turmoil **8** make time, move fast, pressure, scramble, step on it **9** commotion, go quickly, make haste, step along **10** accelerate, get a move on, get hopping, lose no time, make tracks **11** come quickly, get cracking, go like a shot, go like sixty **12** step on the gas **13** go like the wind **14** cover the ground **15** hustle and bustle

hurt *see box, p. 466*

hurt 3 cut, mar **4** ache, balk, burn, foil, harm, lame, maim, mark, maul, pain, pang, scar **5** agony, block, check, grief, limit, lower, pique, smart, spike, sting, stung **6** aching, bruise, damage, deface, dismay, grieve, hamper, hinder, impair, impede, injure, lessen, mangle, marked, miffed, misery, morose, narrow, offend, oppose, pained, piqued, reduce, retard, thwart, weaken **7** agonize, bruised, chagrin, cripple, crushed, damaged, disable, exclude, inhibit, injured, mangled, painful, scarred, scratch, torment, torture, trouble, wounded **8** aggrieve, crippled, decrease, dejected, diminish, disabled, dismayed, distress, encumber, hold back, minimize, mutilate, obstruct, offended, preclude, restrain, smarting, soreness, wretched **9** aggrieved, annoyance, chagrined, dejection, disfigure, forestall, frustrate, heartsick, indignant, miserable, mortified, mutilated, resentful, scratched, suffering **10** discomfort, distressed, heartbreak, melancholy, resentment **11** aggravation, crestfallen, heartbroken **12** disheartened, wretchedness **13** cut to the quick, embarrassment, mortification

hussar 8 cavalier, horseman **10** cavalryman **12** horse soldier, horse trooper **14** mounted soldier

hussy 4 bawd, jade, minx, tart **5** wench, whore **6** harlot, wanton **7** baggage, trollop **8** strumpet **9** brash girl, lewd woman, saucy miss **10** adulteress, loose woman, prostitute **11** brazen woman, fallen woman **12** scarlet woman **17** woman of easy virtue

hustle 3 ado, fly **4** bolt, dart, dash, fuss, prod, push, rush, stir, toss **5** elbow, hurry, nudge, scoot, shove, throw **6** bounce, bustle, flurry, hasten, hubbub, jostle, scurry, tumult **7** flutter, scuttle, speed up, turmoil **8** make time, scramble, shoulder, step on it **9** commotion, make haste, step along **10** lose no time **11** hurry-scurry, move quickly **12** be aggressive

hustler 4 doer **6** con man, dynamo, hooker **8** go-getter, livewire, swindler **10** prostitute **12** streetwalker

Hustler, The
director: **12** Robert Rossen
cast: **10** Paul Newman **11** Piper Laurie **12** George C Scott **13** Jackie Gleason (Minnesota Fats)

Huston, John
director of: **8** Key Largo **10** The Misfits **11** Moulin Rouge **12** Prizzi's Honor **13** Asphalt Jungle **15** The African Queen **16** The Maltese Falcon **19** The Night of the Iguana **27** The Treasure of the Sierra Madre (Oscar)
father: **12** Walter Huston
wife: **11** Evelyn Keyes

born: **8** Nevada MO
roles: **9** Chinatown **11** Winter Kills

Huston, Walter
real name: **15** Walter Houghston
son: **10** John Huston
born: **6** Canada **7** Toronto
roles: **9** Dodsworth **18** All That Money Can Buy **27** The Treasure of the Sierra Madre

hut 4 shed **5** cabin, hutch, shack **6** lean-to, shanty **7** cottage, shelter

hutch 3 pen, sty **4** cage, coop, cote, crib, shed **5** stall **9** enclosure

Hutchinson, A S M
author of: **13** If Winter Comes

Hutton, Betty
real name: **18** Betty June Thornburg
born: **13** Battle Creek MI
roles: **15** Annie Get Your Gun **19** Greatest Show on Earth

Hutton, James
field: **7** geology
nationality: **8** Scottish
founder of: **7** geology

Hutton, Timothy
father: **9** Jim Hutton
roles: **4** Taps **6** Daniel **14** Ordinary People **22** The Falcon and the Snowman

Huxley, Aldous
author of: **11** Crome Yellow **13** Brave New World **17** Point Counter Point

Huxley, Julian
field: **7** biology
nationality: **7** British
promoted theory of: **9** evolution

Huygens, Christiaan
nationality: **5** Dutch
invented: **13** pendulum clock
discovered: **12** Saturn's rings
formulated: **17** wave theory of light

hyacinth 10 Hyacinthus **20** Hyacinthus orientalis
varieties: **4** musk, pine, star, wild, wood **5** Dutch, grape, Roman, water **6** common, garden, meadow, nutmeg, starry, summer, Tassel **7** feather, peacock **11** common grape

Hyacinthus
father: **7** Amyclas
daughter: **7** Orthaea
loved by: **6** Apollo **8** Zephyrus
killed by: **5** quoit **6** discus
from his blood sprang: **6** flower
  petals marked: **4** AI-AI
  means: **4** alas

Hyades
also: **5** Hyads **10** Palilicium
form: **6** nymphs
father: **5** Atlas **7** Oceanus
mother: **6** Tethys **7** Pleione
sisters: **8** Pleiades
nurtured: **8** Dionysus
placed among: **5** stars

Hyads see **6** Hyades

hybrid 5 cross **7** amalgam, mixture **9** composite, half-breed **10** crossbreed

hybridize 5 cross **14** cross-fertilize, cross-pollinate

Hydra
form: **12** water serpent
number of heads: **4** nine
killed by: **8** Hercules

hydrangea
varieties: **4** Wild **6** French, Peegee **8** Climbing

hydrogen
chemical symbol: **1** H

hydrophobia 6 rabies
fear of: **5** water

Hygeia
father: **9** Asclepius
goddess of: **6** health
corresponds to: **5** Salus

hygienic 4 pure **5** clean **7** aseptic, healthy, sterile **8** germ-free, harmless, salutary, sanitary **9** healthful, wholesome **10** salubrious, unpolluted **11** disease-free, disinfected, uninjurious **12** prophylactic **14** uncontaminated

Hylaeus
form: **7** centaur
born on: **5** cloud

Hylas
father: **9** Thiodamas
mother: **8** Menodice
companion of: **8** Hercules

Hyllus
father: **8** Hercules
mother: **6** Melite **8** Deianira
wife: **4** Iole
son: **9** Cleodaeus
grandson: **7** Temenus
built: **11** funeral pyre
for: **8** Hercules

Hymen
also: **9** Hymenaeus
god of: **8** marriage
holds: **5** torch
corresponds to: **8** Talassio

Hymenaeus *see* **5** Hymen

hymenoptera
class: **8** hexapoda
phylum: **10** arthropoda
group: **3** ant, bee **4** wasp
6 chacid, sawfly **12** ichneumon fly

hymn 5 paean, psalm **6** anthem **12** song of praise **14** devotional song **17** song in praise of God

Hymn to Proserpine
author: **24** Algernon Charles Swinburne

Hypatia
author: **15** Charles Kingsley

hyperbole 8 metaphor **11** enlargement **12** exaggeration **13** magnification, overstatement **14** figure of speech

hyperbolize 6 overdo **7** amplify, magnify, stretch **9** embroider, overstate **10** exaggerate

hyperborean 6 arctic **8** freezing, northern **13** septentrional

Hyperborean
inhabitant of: **8** Paradise

Hyperenor
mentioned in: **5** Iliad
brother: **9** Euphorbus, Polydamas
member of: **6** Sparti
killed by: **8** Menelaus

Hyperion
also: **6** Helios
form: **5** Titan
father: **6** Uranus
mother: **4** Gaea
sister: **5** Theia
son: **6** Helios

daughter: **3** Eos **6** Selene
corresponds to: **6** Apollo

Hyperion
author: **9** John Keats
24 Henry Wadsworth Longfellow

Hypermnestra
member of: **8** Danaides
husband: **7** Lynceus
son: **4** Abas

hypersensitive 6 touchy **9** emotional **13** temperamental

Hypnos
also: **6** Hypnus
god of: **5** sleep
father: **6** Erebus
mother: **3** Nyx
brother: **8** Thanatos
corresponds to: **6** Somnus

hypnotic 9 soporific **11** mesmerizing **12** spellbinding

hypnotize 7 control **9** mesmerize, spellbind

Hypnus *see* **6** Hypnos

hypocrisy 6 deceit, fakery **7** falsity **9** duplicity, mendacity, phoniness **10** dishonesty **11** dissembling, insincerity **12** two-facedness

hypocrite 5 phony **8** deceiver **9** pretender **10** dissembler

Hypocrite 15 whited sepulcher

hypocritical 5 false, phony **7** feigned **8** feigning, two-faced **9** deceitful, deceptive, dishonest, insincere, truthless **11** counterfeit

hyporchema
form: **9** choral ode
origin: **5** Greek
honored: **6** Apollo **8** Dionysus

hypothalamus
regulates: **15** body temperature
located in: **5** brain

hypothesis 6 theory, thesis **7** premise, theorem **8** proposal **9** assertion, postulate **10** assumption, conclusion, conjecture **11** explanation, guesstimate, presumption, proposition, speculation, supposition

hypothesize 5 infer **6** assume **7** imagine, presume, suppose **8** theorize **9** postulate, speculate **10** conjecture

hypothetical 7 assumed, dubious **8** possible, supposed **9** imaginary, uncertain **10** contingent, postulated **11** conditional, conjectural, presumptive, speculative, theoretical **12** questionable **13** suppositional

Hypselosaurus
type: **8** dinosaur, sauropod
location: **6** France **8** Mongolia
period: **10** Cretaceous

Hypseus
king of: **7** Lapiths
father: **6** Peneus
mother: **6** Creusa
daughter: **6** Cyrene **8** Themisto **9** Astyagyia

Hypsilophodon
type: **8** dinosaur **10** ornithopod
location: **7** England
period: **10** Cretaceous

Hyrie
transformed into: **4** swan

Hyrmina
grandfather: **8** Endymion
son: **5** Actor

Hyrnetho
father: **7** Temenus
grandfather: **12** Aristomachus
husband: **10** Deiphontes

Hyrtius
allied with: **7** Trojans

hyssop 8 Hyssopus **18** Hyssopus officialis
varieties: **5** anise, giant, water **9** blue giant **10** nettleleaf **11** fennel giant, purple giant, yellow giant **12** Mexican giant **13** fragrant giant, wrinkled giant

Hyssop 13 Biblical plant

hysteria 3 fit **5** panic **6** frenzy **8** delirium

hysterical 5 crazy, droll **6** absurd, crazed, raving **7** amusing, comical **8** farcical, frenzied, worked-up **9** laughable, ludicrous, wrought-up **10** distracted, distraught, ridiculous, uproarious **11** carried away, overwrought, wildly funny **13** beside oneself, out of one's wits **14** uncontrollable

hysterics 3 fit **12** emotionalism

I, Claudius
 author: **12** Robert Graves
 story of: **36** Tiberius Claudius
  Drusus Nero Germanicus
  (Emperor of Rome)

I, the Jury
 author: **14** Mickey Spillane

Iache
 form: **5** nymph
 companion of: **10** Persephone

**I Am a Fugitive from a
Chain Gang**
 director: **11** Mervyn LeRoy
 cast: **8** Paul Muni **11** Helen
  Vinson **13** Glenda Farrell,
  Preston Foster

Iambe
 occupation: **11** storyteller
 storyteller for: **7** Demeter

I am unwilling to contend
 Latin: **14** nolo contendere

Iamus
 father: **6** Apollo
 mother: **6** Evadne
 became: **7** prophet

Ianthe
 husband: **5** Iphis

Iapetus
 member of: **6** Titans
 father: **6** Uranus
 mother: **4** Gaea
 wife: **6** Themis
 son: **5** Atlas **9** Menoetius
  10 Epimetheus, Prometheus

Iapyx
 father: **8** Daedalus

Iardanus
 king of: **5** Lydia
 daughter: **7** Omphale

Iasion
 founder of: **7** Trojans
 twin brother: **8** Dardanus

Iaso
 goddess of: **7** healing
 father: **9** Asclepius

Iasus
 father: **8** Lycurgus

daughter: **8** Atalanta
abandoned: **8** Atalanta

Ibanez, Vicente Blasco
 author of: **30** The Four
  Horsemen of the Apocalypse

Iberian Peninsula
 also: **8** Hesperia

Ibsen, Henrik
 author of: **6** Ghosts **8** Peer
  Gynt **11** A Doll's House,
  Hedda Gabler, Rosmersholm,
  The Wild Duck **16** The Mas-
  ter Builder **18** An Enemy of
  the People, John Gabriel
  Borkman

Iceland
 other name: **15** Lydveldid Island
 capital/largest city: **9** Reykjavik
 others: **3** Hof **6** Geysir **7** Akranes, Husavik **8** Akureyri,
  Keflavik, Kopasker **9** Kopavogur **10** Hveragerdi, Isafjor-
  dur **12** Siglufjordur **13** Hafnarfjordur, Neskaupstadur,
  Seydisfjordur
 government:
   general assembly: **7** Althing
 measure: **3** set **4** alin **5** almud **6** almenn, ferfet, pattur
  7 fathmur, fermila, oltunna
 monetary unit: **5** aurar, eyrir, krona
 weight: **4** pund **5** pound, tunna **6** smjors
 island: **7** Heimaey, Surtsey, Westman
 lake: **6** Myvatn **10** Thorisvatn **14** Thingvallavatn
 mountain: **5** Jokul **10** Orafajokul
   volcano: **4** Laki **5** Askja, Hekla, Katla **7** Surtsey
 highest point: **17** Hvannadalshnjukur
 river: **5** Hvita **7** Fnjoska, Thjorsa **15** Jokulsa a Fjollum
 sea: **9** Greenland **13** North Atlantic
 physical feature:
   fjord: **4** Eyja
   geyser: **5** gryla **6** geysir **11** Great Gusher
   glacier: **6** Jokull **11** Orafajokull, Vatnajokull
   plain: **15** Skeidharasandur
   waterfall: **8** Godafoss, Gullfoss **9** Dettifoss
 people: **6** Celtic, Viking **8** Norseman **9** Norwegian
   first settler: **8** Arnarson
   hero: **4** Bele, Eric, Leif **10** Sigurdsson
 language: **5** Norse **9** Icelandic
 religion: **19** Evangelical Lutheran
 place:
   national shrine: **11** Thingvellir
 feature:
   airport: **9** Kopavogur
   bird: **4** gull **6** falcon **9** gyrfalcon
   literary genre: **4** saga
   wrestling: **5** glima
 food:
   dish: **4** skyr, svio **7** bloomor **8** harofisk

Ibzan 11 Hebrew judge

I came, I saw, I conquered
Latin: 12 veni vidi vici
author: 12 Julius Caesar

Icarius
son: 8 Perilaus
daughter: 7 Erigone
8 Penelope
hospitable to: 8 Dionysus
hound dog: 5 Maera

Icarus
father: 8 Daedalus
built: 5 wings
flew too near: 3 sun
death by: 8 drowning

ice 3 gem 4 berg, floe, gems,
rime 5 chill, frost, glace
6 freeze, icicle, jewels 7 crystal, dessert, glacier, jewelry,
sherbet 8 diamonds 11 refrigerant, refrigerate

ice-cold 3 icy 4 cold 5 gelid,
polar 6 arctic, bitter, frigid,
frosty, wintry 7 chilled,
frosted, glacial, subzero
8 chilling, freezing, Siberian,
unheated, unwarmed 9 stone-
cold, supercold 11 hyperborean, supercooled 12 bone-
chilling

ice cream 7 dessert, sherbet

Iceland *see box*

Icelus
origin: 5 Greek
god of: 6 dreams
assumed shapes of:
7 animals
epithet: 8 Phobetor
corresponds to: 8 Morpheus

Iceman
nickname of: 12 George
Gervin

Iceman Cometh, The
author: 12 Eugene O'Neill

Ice Palace
author: 10 Edna Ferber

ice skating
athlete: 9 Janet Lynn, John
Curry 10 Carol Heiss, Dick
Button, Eric Heiden, Sonja
Henie 11 Sheila Young
12 Peggy Fleming 13 Doro-
thy Hamill, Scott Hamilton
14 Linda Fratianne

ich dien 6 I serve
motto of: 13 Prince of Wales

I Ching 30 ancient Chinese
book of divination

ichor
form: 5 fluid
in veins of: 4 gods

Ichthyocentaur
form: 8 creature
location: 3 sea
head/torso: 5 human

legs: 5 horse
tail: 4 fish

iciness 4 cold 5 chill 9 frigidity 10 chilliness, frostiness,
wintriness 12 slipperiness

ici on parle francais
18 French is spoken here
19 here one speaks French

icky 5 gluey, gooey, gross,
gucky, gummy, mushy, nasty,
tacky, weepy 6 sticky, syrupy,
viscid 7 maudlin, viscous
8 bathetic 9 glutinous, offensive, repulsive, revolting
10 disgusting 12 mucilaginous

icon, ikon 4 idol 5 image 6 effigy, figure, statue 7 picture
8 likeness 11 sacred image

iconoclast 5 rebel 7 radical,
upstart 9 dissenter 13 nonconformist, revolutionary

icy 3 raw 4 cold, cool 5 aloof,
gelid 6 arctic, chilly, frigid,
frosty, frozen, glazed, sleety,
wintry 7 distant, glacial,
haughty, hostile 8 chilling,
freezing, slippery 9 impassive
10 forbidding, unfriendly
11 coldhearted, unemotional

Ida
form: 5 nymph
watched over: 4 Zeus

Idaea
form: 5 nymph
domain: 8 Mount Ida
husband: 7 Phineus
9 Scamander
son: 6 Teucer

Idaho *see box*

Idas
father: 8 Aphareus
mother: 5 Arene
brother: 7 Lynceus
wife: 8 Marpessa
daughter: 9 Cleopatra

idea 4 clue, hint, view 6 belief,
notion 7 concept, feeling, inkling, insight, opinion, outlook,
thought 8 approach, proposal,
solution 9 sentiment 10 conception, conclusion, conviction, impression, indication,
intimation, suggestion 12 apperception, appreciation
13 approximation, mental picture, understanding 14 interpretation, recommendation

ideal 3 aim 4 hero, idol

Idaho
abbreviation: 2 ID 3 Ida
nickname: 3 Gem
capital/largest city: 5 Boise
others: 4 Buhl 5 Malad, Nampa 6 Moscow 7 Orofino, Rex-
burg 8 Caldwell, Lewiston 9 Pocatello, Twin Falls
10 Idaho Falls 11 Coeur d'Alene
college: 17 Northwest Nazarene
explorer: 13 Lewis and Clark
feature: 9 Sun Valley 17 Continental Divide
dam: 5 Oxbow 8 Brownlee
national monument: 16 Craters of the Moon
tribe: 5 Banak, Shake 6 Cayuse, Paiute, Spokan 7 Bannock,
Kutenai, Spokane 8 Kalispel, Nez Perce, Sahaptin, Shoshone, Shoshoni 9 Shoshonee 11 Coeur d'Alene
people: 9 Ezra Pound, Sacagawea 11 Chief Joseph 17 William Edgar Borah
lake: 4 Bear 5 Grey's 6 Priest 11 Coeur d'Alene, Pend Oreille 22 American Falls Reservoir
land rank: 10 thirteenth
mountain: 4 Ryan 5 Rocky 6 Rhodes, Taylor, Tetons
7 Cabinet 8 Bannocks, Big Baldy, Bluenose, Sawtooth
9 Wasatches 10 Clearwater 11 Beaverheads, Bitterroots
13 Selkirk Ranges
highest point: 5 Borah
physical feature:
falls: 5 Moyie 8 Shoshone 9 Upper Mesa
springs: 4 Soda 6 Hooper 7 Lavahot
river: 4 Bear 5 Boise, Snake, St Joe 6 Locksa, Salmon
7 Payette, Spokane 8 Kootenai 11 Coeur d'Alene, Pend
Oreille
state admission: 10 forty-third
state bird: 16 mountain bluebird
state flower: 7 syringa
state motto: 13 It Is Perpetual 16 Let It Be Perpetual
state song: 15 Here We Have Idaho
state tree: 16 western white pine

5 dream, model **7** epitome, optimal, pattern, perfect **8** exemplar, last word, paradigm, standard, ultimate **9** archetype, criterion, excellent, exemplary, faultless, matchless, objective **10** impeccable **11** inspiration

idealism 8 optimism **9** meliorism **10** utopianism **11** romanticism

idealist 7 dreamer, utopian **8** romantic **9** Pollyanna, stargazer, visionary **11** romanticist **13** perfectionist

idealized 6 dreamy **7** utopian, wishful **8** fanciful, illusory, romantic **10** optimistic **11** pie-in-the-sky, unrealistic **13** insubstantial

idea man 7 advisor **8** inventor **9** innovator **10** consultant **12** entrepreneur

idee fixe 9 fixed idea
   music: 14 recurring motif

idem 24 the same as previously given **28** the same as previously mentioned

identical 4 twin **7** uniform **8** self-same, very same **9** duplicate **15** interchangeable **17** indistinguishable

identification 5 badge, label **8** passport **9** detection **10** connection, revelation **11** affiliation, association, credentials, pinpointing, recognition **12** confirmation, verification **13** ascertainment

identify 4 know **5** place **6** verify **7** combine, pick out, specify **9** associate, designate, determine, recognize, single out **11** distinguish

identifying device 4 logo, mark, sign **5** badge **6** emblem, ensign, symbol **8** insignia, logotype

identity 4 name, self **6** accord **7** harmony, oneness, rapport **9** unanimity **11** delineation, duplication, personality **13** individuality **15** differentiation, distinctiveness

ideology 5 dogma, ethos **6** ideals, theory **7** program **8** doctrine **9** rationale **10** principles

Ides of March, The
   author: 14 Thornton Wilder

id est 6 that is
   abbreviation: 2 ie

idiocy 5 folly **6** lunacy **7** fatuity, inanity, madness, suicide **8** insanity **9** absurdity, asininity, cretinism, mongolism, stupidity **11** foolishness **13** foolhardiness, senselessness

idiom 5 argot, lingo, slang **6** brogue, jargon, patois, phrase, speech **7** dialect **8** language, localism, parlance **10** vernacular **13** colloquialism

idiomatic 6 common **8** informal, ordinary **10** vernacular **14** conversational

idiosyncrasy 5 quirk **6** oddity **7** anomaly **9** mannerism **11** distinction, peculiarity **12** eccentricity

idiot 3 ass **4** boob, dolt, dope, fool, jerk **5** cluck, dummy, dunce, moron, ninny **6** cretin, dimwit, nitwit **7** halfwit **8** dumbbell, numskull **9** blockhead, numbskull, simpleton **10** nincompoop

Idiot, The
   author: 16 Fyodor Dostoevsky
   character: 7 Myshkin **11** Mme Epanchin **14** Aglaya Epanchin, Parfen Rogozhin **16** Natasya Filipovna **19** Ganya Ardalionovitch **22** Prince Lef Nicolaievitch

idiotic 5 crazy, dopey, nutty **6** absurd, addled, stupid **7** asinine, doltish, foolish, moronic **9** foolhardy, imbecilic, senseless **10** half-witted, irrational, ridiculous **12** feebleminded **13** rattlebrained

I direct
   Latin: 6 dirigo
   motto of: 5 Maine

idle 4 laze, lazy, loaf, vain **5** empty, inert, petty, vapid, waste, while **6** drowsy, fallow, futile, otiose, putter, torpid, unused **7** aimless, fritter, jobless, languid, trivial, useless, wait out **8** baseless, bootless, fool away, inactive, indolent, listless, slothful, sluggish, trifling **9** at leisure, enervated, fruitless, lethargic, out of work, pointless, somnolent, valueless, worthless **10** not working, unemployed, unoccupied **11** unimportant **12** unproductive **15** unsubstantiated

idleness 5 sloth **7** inertia **8** laziness, lethargy **9** indolence **10** inactivity **11** joblessness, languidness **12** sluggishness, unemployment
   French: 8 flanerie

idler 3 bum **6** loafer **7** drifter, vagrant **10** ne'er-do-well
   French: 7 flaneur

idol 4 hero, icon **5** relic **6** effigy, statue **7** darling **8** artifact **10** simulacrum, golden calf **11** graven image, inspiration

idolatry 5 mania **7** madness, passion, worship **8** devotion **9** adoration, obsession **10** veneration **11** idolization, infatuation **12** image worship **13** preoccupation

idolization 7 worship **9** adulation, reverence **10** exaltation, veneration

idolize 5 adore, deify, honor, prize **6** admire, revere **7** worship **8** treasure, venerate **9** reverence **11** apotheosize

Idomeneo, re di Creta
   also: 20 Idomeneus King of Crete
   opera by: 6 Mozart
   character: 4 Ilia **7** Electra **8** Idamante, Poseidon

Idomeneus
   king of: 5 Crete
   father: 9 Deucalion

I don't know what
   French: 12 je ne sais quoi

Idothea
   form: 5 nymph
   father: 7 Proteus

I Dream of Jeannie
   character: 7 Jeannie **9** Dr Bellows **10** (Captain) Tony Nelson **11** Gen Peterson, (Captain) Roger Healey **13** Amanda Bellows
   cast: 9 Bill Daily **11** Barbara Eden, Hayden Rorke, Larry Hagman **13** Barton MacLane, Emmaline Henry
   Tony's job: 9 astronaut

Idun, Iduna
   also: 5 Ithun **6** Ithunn
   origin: 12 Scandinavian
   goddess of: 6 spring
   husband: 5 Brage, Bragi
   kept: 11 youth apples

idyllic 6 rustic, sylvan **7** bucolic **8** arcadian, pastoral, peaceful, romantic **9** unspoiled

Idylls of the King, The
   author: 18 Alfred Lord Tennyson
   based on story of: 10 King Arthur

Ierne *see* **7** Ireland

if 2 an **6** though **7** whether **8** although, provided **9** condition, supposing **10** even though **11** stipulation, supposition

iffy 4 moot **5** risky **6** chancy, unsure **7** dubious, erratic **8** arguable, doubtful **9** debatable, uncertain, undecided, unsettled, whimsical **10** capricious, disputable, unresolved **11** conjectural, speculative **12** questionable **13** problematical, unpredictable

Ifriqiyah *see* **7** Tunisia

If Winter Comes
author: **13** A S M Hutchinson

if you please
French: **12** s'il vous plait

Iggdrasil *see* **9** Yggdrasil

ignitable 8 burnable **9** flammable **10** combustive, incendiary **11** combustible, inflammable **13** conflagrative

ignite 4 burn, fire **5** blaze, flame, light **6** blow up, kindle **7** explode, inflame **8** take fire, touch off **9** catch fire, set fire to, set on fire **11** catch on fire

ignoble 3 low **4** base, foul, mean, vile **6** craven **7** debased, heinous **8** cowardly, degraded, depraved, indecent, infamous, inferior, shameful, unworthy **9** dastardly, nefarious **10** degenerate, despicable **11** disgraceful **12** contemptible, dishonorable **13** discreditable, pusillanimous **14** unconscionable

ignominious 3 low **5** sorry **6** abject **8** grievous, shameful, wretched **9** degrading **10** despicable, inglorious, unbearable **11** disgraceful, humiliating **12** dishonorable, disreputable **13** discreditable

ignominy 5 shame **6** infamy **8** contempt, disgrace, dishonor **11** degradation, humiliation

ignoramus 4 fool **5** dunce **6** nitwit **7** low-brow **8** numskull **9** numbskull, simpleton **10** illiterate **11** know-nothing

ignorance 9 confusion **10** illiteracy **11** unawareness **12** backwardness **13** obliviousness, unfamiliarity **15** unenlightenment

ignorant 4 dumb **5** naive **6** stupid **7** asinine, blind to, fatuous, shallow, unaware **8** innocent, untaught **9** in the dark, unknowing, unlearned, untrained, untutored, unworldly **10** illiterate, uneducated, uninformed, unlettered, unschooled **11** insensitive, uncognizant **12** unperceptive **13** irresponsible, unenlightened, unintelligent **15** unknowledgeable

ignore 4 omit, skip, snub **5** scorn **6** eschew, slight **7** neglect **8** overlook, pass over **9** disregard

Igraine
character in: **16** Arthurian romance
son: **6** Arthur

Iguanodon
type: **8** dinosaur **10** ornithopod
means: **11** iguana tooth
found by: **13** Gideon Mantell
location: **6** Africa, Europe, Sussex **7** Belgium, England
period: **10** Cretaceous
characteristic: **10** duck-billed

ikebana
Japanese: **21** art of arranging flowers

Ile de France *see* **9** Mauritius

Ilha Formosa *see* **6** Taiwan

Iliad, The
author: **5** Homer
character: **5** Paris, Priam **6** Hector **8** Achilles, Menelaus **9** Agamemnon, Patroclus **11** Helen of Troy
subject: **9** Trojan War

Iliniwek *see* **8** Illinois

Ilion
Greek name for: **11** ancient Troy

Ilione
father: **5** Priam
mother: **6** Hecuba
husband: **11** Polymnestor
son: **8** Deipylus
raised: **9** Polydorus

Ilioneus
mentioned in: **6** Aeneid
home: **4** Troy
vocation: **7** warrior
fled: **4** Troy
fled with: **6** Aeneas
killed by: **8** Peneleus

Ilithyia *see* **10** Eileithyia

Ilium
Latin name for: **11** ancient Troy

ill, ills 3 woe **4** evil, foul, harm, sick, vile **5** abuse, cross, no way, surly, trial **6** ailing, damage, hardly, injury, laid up, malady, malice, nowise, plague, poorly, sickly, sorrow, unkind, unwell, wicked **7** ailment, cruelty, disease, failing, harmful, invalid, not well, ominous, outrage, peevish, trouble, unlucky, unsound **8** diseased, mischief, scarcely, sinister, vengeful **9** afflicted, complaint, infirmity, malicious, unhealthy **10** affliction, disturbing, foreboding, indisposed, misfortune, wickedness **11** abomination, acrimonious, malefaction, threatening, unfavorable **12** inauspicious, unpropitious **15** under the weather

ill-advised 4 dumb, rash **5** hasty, silly **6** myopic, stupid, unwise **7** foolish **9** foolhardy, ill-judged, impolitic, imprudent, misguided, senseless **10** indiscreet, unthinking **11** injudicious **12** shortsighted **13** ill-considered, irresponsible

ill-at-ease 3 shy **4** edgy **6** on edge, uneasy **7** abashed, fidgety, nervous **8** bothered, troubled **9** disturbed, nonplused, perturbed **10** disquieted, nonplussed **11** discomfited, discomposed, embarrassed **12** disconcerted **13** self-conscious, uncomfortable **15** discountenanced

ill-boding 4 dire **7** ominous **9** ill-omened **11** apocalyptic **12** inauspicious

ill-bred 4 rude **5** crude **7** boorish, uncivil, uncouth **8** churlish, impolite **10** unmannerly **11** ill-mannered **12** discourteous

ill-defined 3 dim **4** hazy **5** faint, murky **6** blurry **7** blurred, clouded, shadowy **8** nebulous, obscured **10** indistinct

illegal 5 wrong **6** banned **7** illicit **8** criminal, not legal, outlawed, unlawful **9** felonious, forbidden **10** actionable, prohibited, proscribed **12** illegitimate, unauthorized, unsanctioned **13** against the law

illegible 7 unclear **8** obscured **9** scribbled **10** unreadable **14** indecipherable, undecipherable, unintelligible

illegitimate 7 bastard, illegal, illicit, lawless, natural **8** baseborn, improper, unlawful **10** prohibited **11** misbegotten, unwarranted **12** unauthorized, unsanctioned

ill-fated 6 doomed, jinxed **7** hapless, unlucky **8** blighted, luckless **9** ill-omened **10** ill-starred

ill-favored 4 ugly **5** plain **6** homely **8** unlovely **9** repulsive, unsightly **12** disagreeable, unattractive

ill-fortune 6 mishap **7** bad luck **8** calamity, disaster, hardship **9** adversity **10** misfortune **11** catastrophe

ill health 6 malady **7** ailment, disease, illness **8** sickness **9** infirmity

ill-humored 5 sulky, testy **6** crabby, grumpy, sullen **7** grouchy **10** in a bad mood, unfriendly, unsociable illiberal 5 petty, small 6 biased, narrow 7 bigoted 9 hidebound 10 brassbound, intolerant, prejudiced, ungenerous 11 opinionated, small-minded 12 narrow-minded, shortsighted

illicit 7 illegal, lawless 8 criminal, improper, not legal, unlawful 9 felonious 10 prohibited 11 black-market, clandestine 12 illegitimate, not permitted, unauthorized 13 against the law, impermissible 15 under-the-counter

Illinois *see box*

Illinois (Iliniwek)
language family: 9 Algonkian 10 Algonquian
tribe: 6 Peoria 7 Cahokia, Tamaroa 9 Kaskaskia, Moingwena 10 Michigamea
location: 4 Iowa, Ohio 7 Indiana 8 Illinois, Michigan, Missouri 9 Wisconsin
built: 12 Cahokia Mound
murdered: 7 Pontiac

related to: 5 Miami 6 Ojibwa 7 Ojibway

illiterate 7 witless 8 childish, ignorant, unversed 9 unlearned, untutored 10 amateurish, incoherent, uneducated, uninformed, unlettered, unreliable, unschooled 11 not educated, uninitiated, unscholarly 12 uninstructed 13 unenlightened, ungrammatical 15 unknowledgeable

ill-made 6 shoddy 7 awkward 8 deformed, inferior 9 makeshift, malformed 10 jerry-built, jury-rigged 15 misproportioned

ill-mannered 4 rude 5 crude 6 coarse 7 boorish, ill-bred, loutish, uncivil 8 impolite 9 offensive, ungallant 10 ill-behaved, ungracious 12 discourteous 13 disrespectful

ill-natured 4 sour 5 cross, nasty, surly 6 bitter, cranky, malign 7 caustic, grouchy, peevish 8 captious, churlish, spiteful, venomous 9 crotchety, irascible, irritable, malignant, rancorous, splenetic 10 ill-humored, unfriendly 11 acrimonious, contentious, quarrelsome 12 antagonistic, cantankerous

illness 6 malady 7 ailment, disease 8 disorder, sickness 9 complaint, ill health, infirmity 10 affliction, disability, poor health 11 malfunction 13 indisposition

illness recovery
god of: 11 Telesphorus

illogical 4 wild 5 crazy, dopey, nutty, silly, wacky 6 absurd, far-out, screwy 7 asinine, offbeat, unsound 9 erroneous, senseless 10 fallacious, irrational, off-the-wall, ridiculous 11 incongruent, incongruous, nonsensical, unreasoning 12 inconsistent, preposterous, unreasonable 13 contradictory

ill-omened 4 dire 7 adverse, ominous 9 ill-boding 11 apocalyptic, unfavorable 12 inauspicious, unpropitious

ill-smelling 4 foul, high, olid, rank 5 fetid, fusty 6 putrid, rancid, smelly, stinky, strong 7 reeking 8 stinking 10 malodorous

ill-starred 4 dire 5 fatal 6 tragic 7 adverse 8 ill-fated 10 calamitous, disastrous 11 unfortunate 12 catastrophic, inauspicious

ill-suited 5 inapt 8 mismated, unsuited 9 misjoined, unfitting 10 ill-adapted, ill-matched, malapropos, mismatched, unbecoming, unsuitable 11 incongruous, unbefitting, uncongenial 12 incompatible, inconsistent 13 inappropriate

ill-tempered 4 mean, rude, sour 5 angry, cross, harsh, nasty, testy 6 bitter, cranky, shirty 7 acerbic, furious, grouchy, peevish, waspish 8 choleric, churlish, petulant 9 crotchety, irascible, irritable 10 bad-natured, ill-humored, ill-natured, in a bad mood, unpleasant 11 acrimonious 12 cantankerous

ill-treatment 4 harm 5 abuse 6 ill-use, injury, misuse 7 cruelty 13 mortification

illuminate 5 edify, light 7 clarify, enhance, explain, light up 8 brighten, illumine, instruct, spell out 9 elucidate, enlighten, exemplify, irradiate, make clear 12 throw light on 13 cast light upon

Illinois
abbreviation: 2 IL 3 Ill
nickname: 4 Tall 6 Sucker 7 Prairie 13 Land of Lincoln
capital: 11 Springfield
largest city: 7 Chicago
others: 4 Pana 5 Alton, Cairo, Elgin, Flora, Olney, Pekin 6 Albion, Berwyn, Canton, Herrin, Joliet, Peoria, Skokie 7 Batavia, Decatur, Genesco, Mendota, Nokomis 8 Evanston, Rockford, Waukegan 9 Centralia 10 Barrington 11 Bloomington
college: 4 Knox 5 Barat 6 Aurora, DePaul, Eureka, Loyola, Olivet, Quincy, Nimer 7 Bradley, Chicago, Wheaton 8 Millikin 9 Augustana 12 Northwestern 16 Illinois Wesleyan 23 Illinois Institute of Tech
explorer: 6 Joliet 7 Jolliet 9 Marquette
feature: 10 stockyards
  airport: 5 O'Hare
  museum: 18 Science and Industry
  seaway: 10 St Lawrence
  trail: 7 Lincoln
tribe: 3 Fox 4 Sauk 9 Kaskaskia
people: 9 Black Hawk, Jack Benny 10 Jane Addams, Walt Disney 12 Carl Sandburg 15 Ernest Hemingway 18 Engineer Casey Jones 20 William Jennings Bryan
lake: 3 Fox 5 Grass 7 Calumet 8 Michigan, Pistakee
land rank: 12 twenty-fourth
mountain: 6 Ozarks
  highest point: 12 Charles Mound
physical feature:
  hills: 7 Shawnee
president: 14 Abraham Lincoln
river: 4 Ohio, Rock 5 Spoon 6 Wabash 7 Chicago, Elkhorn 8 Big Muddy, Illinois, Mackinaw, Sangamon 9 Kaskaskia 10 Des Plaines 11 Mississippi
state admission: 11 twenty-first
state bird: 8 cardinal
state flower: 6 violet
state motto: 29 State Sovereignty—National Union
state song: 8 Illinois
state tree: 7 burl oak 8 white oak

illuminated 3 lit **5** lit up
6 bright **7** lighted **9** clarified,
decorated, illumined
10 brightened, elucidated,
irradiated

illumination 6 lights, wisdom
7 insight **8** lighting **9** education, knowledge **10** illumining,
lighting up, perception, revelation **11** edification, information, instruction, irradiation
13 comprehension,
enlightenment

Illuminations, Les
   author: **13** Arthur Rimbaud

illumined 3 lit **7** lighted **8** luminous **11** illuminated

ill-use 4 harm, hurt **5** abuse
6 injure, misuse **7** assault, cruelty, harming **8** maltreat, mistreat **10** bodily harm
12 maltreatment, mistreatment

illusion 5 error, fancy **6** mirage,
vagary, vision **7** caprice, chimera, fallacy **8** delusion, phantasm **9** deception, false idea,
misbelief, semblance, unreality **10** apparition, false image,
hocus-pocus, humbuggery,
impression **11** false belief
13 hallucination, misconception, misimpression
15 misapprehension

illusive 5 false **6** unreal
7 phantom, seeming **8** apparent, chimeric, fanciful, fantastic, illusory **9** deceptive
10 ostensible **11** illusionary

illusory 4 sham **5** false **6** unreal **7** seeming **8** apparent, delusive, fanciful, illusive,
spurious **9** deceptive, erroneous, imaginary **10** fallacious,
misleading, ostensible
11 counterfeit, unrealistic
13 hallucinatory

illustrate 4 show **6** define
7 clarify, explain, picture,
point up, portray **8** decorate,
ornament **9** bring home, delineate, elucidate, emphasize,
make clear, represent **10** illuminate **11** demonstrate **12** pic-
torialize, throw light on
16 make intelligible

illustration 5 image, plate
6 figure **7** drawing, example,
picture **8** instance, specimen
9 portrayal **10** photograph
14 representation
15 exemplification

illustrious 5 famed, great **6** famous **7** eminent, honored
8 glorious, lustrous, peerless,
renowned, splendid **9** acclaimed, brilliant, exemplary,
matchless, prominent **10** celebrated **11** magnificent
13 distinguished

illustriousness 8 grandeur
9 greatness **11** distinction
12 magnificence

ill will 4 gall **5** anger, spite
6 animus, enmity, hatred, malice, rancor, spleen **7** dislike
8 acrimony, aversion, bad
blood, loathing **9** animosity,
antipathy, hostility **10** abhorrence, antagonism, bitterness,
contention **11** malevolence
12 hard feelings,
spitefulness

ill wind 7 bad luck **8** bad
break, hard luck **9** adversity,
mischance **10** misfortune

Illyrius
   father: **6** Cadmus

Ilmarinen
   origin: **7** Finnish
   form: **10** blacksmith
   hero in: **8** Kalevala
   forged: **5** Sampo
   Sampo's owner: **5** Louhi

I Love Lucy
   character: **9** Fred Mertz
      10 Ethel Mertz **11** Little
      Ricky, Lucy Ricardo
      12 Ricky Ricardo
   cast: **9** Desi Arnaz **11** Lucille
      Ball, Vivian Vance **14** Wil-
      liam Frawley
   Ricky's club: **7** Babaloo
      9 Tropicana

Il Penseroso
   author: **10** John Milton
   companion piece: **8** L'Allegro

image 4 copy, icon, idea, idol
6 double, effigy, fetish, figure,
memory, simile, statue, symbol, visage **7** concept, picture,
replica **8** likeness, metaphor,
portrait **9** depiction, duplicate,
facsimile, mirroring, semblance **10** photograph, reflection, simulacrum
11 countenance, delineation,
incarnation **12** recollection, reproduction **13** mental picture
14 figure of speech,
representation

imaginable 8 feasible **9** thinkable **11** conceivable

imaginary 4 sham **5** fancy,
phony **6** made-up, unreal
7 fancied, fiction, figment
8 delusion, fabulous, fanciful,
illusion, illusory, invented,
mythical, romantic **9** fantastic,
figmental, legendary **10** factitious, fictitious **11** counterfeit,
make-believe

imagination 5 fancy **7** cunning,
thought **9** ingenuity, invention **10** astuteness, creativity,
enterprise **12** creativeness
13 inventiveness **14** thoughtfulness **15** creative thought,
resourcefulness

imaginative 6 clever **7** unusual **8** creative, inspired, original **9** ingenious, inventive
10 innovative **11** resourceful
12 enterprising **16** off the
beaten path, out of the
ordinary

imagine 5 fancy, guess, infer,
judge **6** assume, gather **7** believe, dream up, picture, presume, pretend, project,
suppose, surmise, suspect
8 conceive, envisage, envision
9 fantasize, visualize
10 conjecture

imbecile 3 ass **4** dolt, dope,
fool, jerk **5** dummy, dunce, idiot, moron, ninny **6** nitwit
7 dingbat **8** dumbbell **9** blockhead, simpleton
10 nincompoop

imbecilic 4 dumb **5** inane,
silly **6** absurd, stupid **7** asinine,
foolish **8** careless, mindless
11 thoughtless

imbecility 6 idiocy **8** dullness,
dumbness **9** asininity, stupidity, thickness
16 simplemindedness

imbibe 4 swig, tope **5** drink,
quaff **6** guzzle, ingest, tipple
7 consume, partake, swallow
8 chugalug, toss down, wash
down

imbiber 4 wino **5** drunk, toper
7 drinker, tippler **8** consumer,
drunkard, ingester

Imbrius
   mentioned in: **5** Iliad
   father: **6** Mentor
   killed by: **6** Teucer

imbroglio 3 row **4** fray
5 brawl, broil, clash, fight,
melee, scrap **6** fracas, ruckus,
rumpus, uproar **7** scuffle **8** argument **9** confusion **11** altercation, embroilment
12 entanglement
13 embarrassment

imbue 4 fill, fire, tint **5** bathe,
color, endow, steep, tinge
6 arouse, infuse **7** animate,
impress, ingrain, inspire, instill, pervade, suffuse **8** permeate, tincture **9** inculcate

Imhotep
   father: **4** Ptah
   mother: **7** Sekhmet
   position: **6** scribe, vizier,
      writer **9** architect, physician
   architect of pyramid:
      8 Sakkarah

imitate 3 ape **4** copy, mime
5 mimic **6** mirror, parody, parrot **7** emulate, pass for **8** look
like, simulate **9** duplicate, represent **10** caricature **11** counterfeit, impersonate

imitation 4 fake, mock, sham **5** aping, phony **6** ersatz, parody **7** man-made, mimicry, takeoff **8** travesty **9** burlesque, facsimile, semblance, simulated, synthetic **10** adaptation, artificial, caricature, impression, similarity, simulation **11** counterfeit, duplication, make-believe **12** reproduction **13** impersonation **14** representation

Imitation of Christ, The
   author: **13** Thomas a Kempis

immaculate 4 pure **5** clean, ideal **6** chaste, intact, virgin **7** perfect, saintly, sinless **8** flawless, innocent, spotless, unsoiled, virginal, virtuous **9** faultless, guiltless, shipshape, stainless, unstained, unsullied **11** spic and span, untarnished **13** above reproach, unimpeachable **14** irreproachable **15** unexceptionable

immanent 6 inborn, inbred, innate **7** natural **8** inherent **9** ingrained, intrinsic **10** congenital, deep-rooted, deep-seated, indigenous, indwelling **11** instinctive, instinctual

Immanuel 7 Messiah **11** Jesus Christ
   means: **9** God with us

immaterial 7 ghostly, shadowy, trivial **8** bodiless, ethereal, mystical, noumenal, spectral, trifling, unbodied **9** spiritual, unearthly **10** evanescent, extraneous, impalpable, intangible, irrelevant, of no moment **11** disembodied, incorporeal, not relevant, unimportant **12** extramundane, extrasensory **13** insignificant, insubstantial, unsubstantial **14** of no importance **15** inconsequential, of little account

immature 5 green, young **6** callow, unripe **7** babyish, kiddish, puerile **8** childish, juvenile, unformed, youthful **9** embryonic, half-grown, infantile, not mature, pubescent **10** unfinished, unmellowed **11** out of season, rudimentary, undeveloped **16** wet behind the ears

immeasurable 7 endless, immense **8** infinite **9** boundless, limitless, unbounded, unlimited **10** fathomless **11** illimitable, inestimable, measureless, never-ending **12** incalculable, interminable, unfathomable **13** inexhaustible

immediate 4 near, next, nigh **5** close, hasty, local, swift **6** abrupt, nearby, prompt, recent, speedy, sudden **7** express,

instant, nearest **8** adjacent, punctual **9** proximate, undelayed **10** contiguous **13** instantaneous

immediately 3 now **9** instantly, right away **10** this minute **12** without delay
   French: **11** tout de suite

immemorial 5 olden **7** ageless, ancient **8** dateless, hallowed, timeless **9** ancestral, legendary, venerable **11** time-honored **12** long-standing, mythological **15** long-established

immense 4 huge, vast **5** great **7** mammoth, massive **8** colossal, enormous, gigantic **9** extensive, monstrous **10** prodigious, stupendous, tremendous **11** measureless **14** Brobdingnagian

immensity 8 enormity, hugeness, vastness **9** largeness **12** enormousness

immerse 3 dip **4** duck, dunk, sink, soak **5** bathe, douse, lower, steep **6** absorb, drench, engage, occupy, plunge **7** engross **8** submerge

immerse briefly 3 dip **4** dunk

immersion 7 bathing, dunking **8** drowning **10** absorption, submersion **11** engrossment, involvement, submergence **13** concentration, preoccupation

immigrant 5 alien **7** migrant, settler **8** colonist, newcomer **9** foreigner, nonnative

immigrate 6 move to, settle **7** migrate **8** colonize

imminent 4 near **7** looming **8** menacing, perilous **9** immediate, impending **10** near at hand **11** approaching, close at hand, threatening

immobile 4 fast **5** fixed, quiet, rigid, stiff, still **6** at rest, laid up, rooted, secure, stable, static **7** riveted **9** immovable, not moving, quiescent, steadfast **10** motionless, stationary, stock-still **11** unbudgeable **13** incapacitated

immobilize 3 fix, set **4** stud **6** disarm, freeze, splint **7** disable **8** paralyze, transfix **12** incapacitate

immoderate 5 undue **7** extreme **8** whopping **9** excessive, unbridled **10** exorbitant, gargantuan, inordinate, prodigious **11** extravagant, intemperate, uncalled-for **12** unreasonable, unrestrained **14** unconscionable

immoderation 6 excess **10** de-

bauchery **11** dissipation, prodigality, unrestraint **12** extravagance, intemperance, recklessness **13** excessiveness **14** prodigiousness

immodest 4 lewd, vain **5** gross, loose **6** brazen, coarse, risque, wanton **7** pompous **8** boastful, braggart, indecent, inflated, unchaste **9** bombastic, conceited, shameless **10** indecorous, indelicate, peacockish, suggestive **11** exaggerated, pretentious **12** self-centered

immoral 4 evil, lewd **5** dirty, wrong **6** sinful, wicked **7** corrupt, heinous, obscene, raunchy, vicious **8** depraved, indecent, infamous, prurient **9** debauched, dissolute, nefarious, salacious, unethical **10** dissipated, iniquitous, licentious, profligate **12** pornographic, unprincipled

Immoralist, The
   author: **9** Andre Gide

immorality 3 sin **4** evil **9** decadence, depravity, indecency, obscenity, prurience **10** corruption, debasement, degeneracy, sinfulness **13** salaciousness

immortal 3 god **6** divine **7** abiding, eternal, undying **8** enduring **9** deathless **11** everlasting **12** imperishable

Immortals 6 giants, greats, titans **7** the gods **8** demigods **13** all-time greats
   Greek/Roman: **8** pantheon

immovable 3 icy, set **4** cold, fast **5** fixed **6** dogged, secure, steely, stolid **7** adamant, settled **8** detached, fastened, immobile, obdurate, resolute, stubborn **9** heartless, impassive, unfeeling **10** inexorable, inflexible, stationary, unbendable **11** coldhearted, unbudgeable **12** unchangeable **13** unimpressible, unsympathetic **16** unimpressionable

immune 4 free, safe **5** clear **6** exempt **9** protected, resistant **11** invulnerable **13** unsusceptible

immunity 7 freedom **9** exemption **10** resistance **16** unsusceptibility

immure 3 hem, pen **4** cage, coop, jail, wall **6** entomb, intern, wall in, wall up **7** confine, enclose, seclude **8** cloister, imprison **11** incarcerate

immutability 9 endurance, stability **14** changelessness

immutable 4 firm **5** fixed,

solid **6** stable **7** lasting **8** constant, enduring **9** permanent, unaltered, unvarying **10** changeless, inflexible, unchanging **11** unalterable **12** unchangeable, unmodifiable **14** intransmutable **16** incontrovertible

Imogen
character in: **9** Cymbeline
author: **11** Shakespeare

imp 3 elf **4** brat **5** demon, devil, gnome, pixie, scamp **6** goblin, hoyden, rascal, sprite, urchin **7** upstart **9** hobgoblin **10** evil spirit, leprechaun

impact 4 jolt **5** brunt, crash, force, shock, smash **6** burden, effect, thrust **7** contact **9** collision, influence **10** concussion **11** implication **12** repercussion

impair 3 mar **4** harm, hurt **6** damage, hinder, injure, lessen, reduce, weaken, worsen **7** cripple, subvert, vitiate **8** decrease, enervate, enfeeble, undercut **10** debilitate **11** detract from

impaired 6 broken, faulty, flawed **7** damaged **9** defective, deficient, imperfect

impairment 4 flaw, harm **5** fault **6** damage, defect, injury, malady **7** ailment, illness **8** debility, disorder, handicap, sickness, weakness **9** detriment, hindrance, infirmity **10** disability, impediment, inadequacy **12** debilitation

impale 3 fix, pin **4** tack **5** affix, stick **8** transfix **10** run through

impart 4 give, lend, tell **5** grant, offer, share **6** accord, afford, pass on, relate, render, report, reveal **7** confide, consign, deliver, divulge, mention **8** bestow on, confer on, disclose, dispense **9** make known **10** contribute **11** communicate

impartial 4 fair, just **7** neutral **8** detached, unbiased **9** equitable, objective **10** evenhanded, fair-minded, open-minded **11** nonpartisan **12** unprejudiced **13** disinterested, dispassionate

impartiality 7 justice **8** equality, fair play, fairness **10** detachment, neutrality **11** objectivity

impasse 4 snag **7** dead end, dilemma **8** cul-de-sac, deadlock, quandary, standoff **9** stalemate **10** blind alley, bottleneck, standstill **11** predicament

impassioned 5 eager, fiery **6** ardent, heated **7** earnest, excited, fervent, intense, rousing, zealous **8** animated, forceful, inspired, stirring

impassive 4 calm, cool **5** aloof, stony **6** sedate, stolid **7** stoical, unmoved **8** reserved **9** apathetic, untouched **10** impervious, insensible, phlegmatic **11** emotionless, indifferent, inscrutable, unemotional, unperturbed **13** dispassionate, imperturbable, unimpressible **16** unimpressionable

impassiveness 8 coldness **9** aloofness, stolidity **12** indifference **15** emotionlessness

impassivity 6 apathy **8** coolness, stoicism **9** aloofness, stolidity **10** dispassion **15** emotionlessness **16** imperturbability

impatient 4 edgy **5** fussy, hasty, itchy, rabid, tense, testy **6** ardent, touchy **7** annoyed, anxious, brusque, hurried, nervous, peevish, restive **8** agitated, feverish, restless **9** excitable, irascible, irritable, irritated **10** high-strung, intolerant, passionate **12** enthusiastic

impeach 4 slur **6** accuse, assail, attack, charge, impugn, indict **7** arraign, slander **8** badmouth, belittle, question **9** challenge, discredit, disparage, inculpate **11** incriminate **16** call into question

impeccable 7 perfect **8** flawless **9** blameless, excellent, faultless **10** immaculate **11** unblemished **12** irreprovable, unassailable **13** unimpeachable **14** irreproachable **15** unexceptionable

impecunious 4 poor **5** broke, needy **6** hard-up **7** pinched **8** bankrupt, indigent **9** destitute, insolvent, penniless **10** down-and-out, straitened **12** impoverished **15** poverty-stricken

impede 5 block, check, delay, deter, stall **6** arrest, halter, hamper, hinder, retard, stymie, thwart **7** disrupt, inhibit **8** hold back, obstruct, slow down **9** frustrate, interrupt, sidetrack **13** interfere with

impediment 4 flaw **5** block, delay **6** defect **7** barrier **8** blockage, drawback, handicap, obstacle **9** deformity, hindrance **10** detraction **11** obstruction **12** interference **14** stumbling block

impedimenta 4 gear **7** bag-

gage **9** equipment **13** accoutrements, paraphernalia

impel 4 goad, prod, push, spur, urge **5** drive, force **6** compel, incite, induce, prompt **7** require **8** motivate **9** constrain, stimulate **11** necessitate

impend 4 brew, hang, loom **5** hover, lower **6** menace **8** approach, draw near, overhang, threaten

impending 4 near **6** coming **7** brewing, looming **8** imminent, menacing, oncoming **9** immediate **11** approaching, forthcoming, threatening

impenetrable 5 dense, solid, thick **6** sealed **7** elusive, obscure **8** puzzling **9** insoluble **10** impassable, impervious, insensible, intangible, inviolable, mysterious, unpalpable **11** inscrutable, unenterable **12** inaccessible, inexplicable, invulnerable, unfathomable **16** incomprehensible

impenitent 4 lost **6** inured **7** callous, defiant **8** hardened, obdurate **9** unashamed **10** uncontrite **11** remorseless, unrepentant, unrepenting **12** incorrigible, unapologetic **13** irreclaimable

imperative 6 urgent **7** crucial, needful **8** critical, pressing **9** essential, mandatory, necessary, requisite **10** compulsory, obligatory **11** unavoidable

imperceptible 5 minor, scant, small **6** hidden, minute, slight, subtle **7** minimal **8** academic **10** indistinct **12** undetectable, unnoticeable **13** infinitesimal, insignificant, unappreciable, unperceivable **14** inconsiderable

imperceptive 5 blind **9** unfeeling **11** insensitive, unobservant **12** inpercipient, unperceptive **13** unsympathetic

imperfect 6 faulty, flawed **8** deformed, fallible, impaired **9** blemished, defective

imperfection 4 flaw **5** fault **6** defect **7** blemish **8** weakness **9** deformity **10** faultiness, impairment, inadequacy **11** fallibility, shortcoming **13** insufficiency **14** incompleteness

imperial 5 bossy **6** feudal, lordly **8** despotic **9** arbitrary, imperious **10** autocratic, high-handed, peremptory, repressive, tyrannical **11** dictatorial, domineering, magisterial, overbearing **13** authoritarian

Imperial Presidency, The
    author: 20 Arthur M Schlesinger Jr

imperil 4 risk 6 chance, expose, gamble, hazard 8 endanger 10 compromise, jeopardize 13 put in jeopardy

imperious 5 bossy, lofty 6 lordly 7 haughty 8 arrogant, despotic, imperial 10 autocratic, commanding, peremptory, tyrannical 11 dictatorial, domineering, overbearing 13 high-and-mighty

imperiousness 9 arrogance, loftiness 11 haughtiness

imperishable 6 stable 7 durable, lasting 14 indestructible

imperium 4 rule 5 realm 6 domain, empire 8 dominion 11 sovereignty

impermanent 7 passing 8 fleeting, fugitive, not fixed, unstable 9 ephemeral, temporary, transient 10 evanescent, transitory, unenduring

impermeable 5 dense, solid, tight 6 opaque 9 nonporous 10 impervious, waterproof

impersonal 4 dead 6 remote 7 general, inhuman, neutral 8 detached, lifeless, soulless 9 impartial, impassive, inanimate, inorganic, objective 10 spiritless 11 perfunctory 13 disinterested, dispassionate

impersonate 3 ape 4 copy, mime 5 mimic 6 pose as 7 imitate, portray 9 personify, represent 11 pretend to be 12 masquerade as

impertinence 4 sass 5 cheek, sauce 7 affront 8 audacity, boldness, rudeness 9 freshness, impudence, insolence, sauciness 10 cheekiness, disrespect, effrontery, incivility 11 irrelevance 17 disrespectfulness, inappropriateness

impertinent 4 rude 5 fresh, surly 6 brassy, brazen, smarty 7 uncivil 8 arrogant, impudent, insolent 9 extrinsic, insulting, unrelated 10 extraneous, immaterial, irrelevant, not germane, peremptory, unmannerly 11 unimportant 12 discourteous, presumptuous 13 disrespectful, inappropriate 14 beside the point

imperturbability 5 poise 6 aplomb 8 calmness, coolness 9 composure, sangfroid 10 equanimity, steadiness 11 self-control, tranquility 12 tranquillity 14 presence of mind, self-possession

imperturbable 4 calm, cool 6 sedate, serene 8 composed 9 collected, impassive, unanxious, unfazable, unruffled 10 impervious 11 levelheaded, undisturbed, unexcitable, unflappable, unflustered 13 dispassionate, unsusceptible

impervious 6 closed 8 immune to 11 impermeable 12 impenetrable, inaccessible, invulnerable 14 unapproachable

impetuosity 8 rashness 11 spontaneity, unrestraint 12 recklessness 13 impulsiveness 14 capriciousness

impetuous 4 rash 5 hasty 6 abrupt, stormy 7 rampant, violent 8 forcible, headlong, vehement 9 impulsive 10 capricious, inexorable, relentless, unexpected 11 precipitate 14 unpremeditated

impetus 4 prod, push, spur 5 boost, drive, force, start 6 motive 7 impulse 8 momentum, stimulus 9 impulsion, incentive 10 motivation, propulsion 11 moving force, stimulation

impiety 9 blasphemy, sacrilege 10 disrespect, irreligion 11 irreverence, ungodliness

impinge 7 intrude, obtrude, violate 8 encroach, infringe, trespass 10 transgress

impious 7 godless, immoral, profane, ungodly 8 apostate, renegade 9 perverted 10 iniquitous, irreverent 11 blasphemous, irreligious 12 iconoclastic, sacrilegious 13 disrespectful

impiousness 7 impiety 9 blasphemy, sacrilege 10 disrespect 11 irreverence, ungodliness

impish 5 elfin 7 implike, puckish, roguish 8 prankish, rascally, sportive 11 mischievous

implacable 10 inexorable, inflexible, relentless, unamenable 11 intractable, unrelenting 12 unappeasable, unpacifiable 14 irreconcilable, uncompromising

implant 3 fix, set, sow 4 root 5 embed, graft, imbed, inlay, teach 6 infuse, insert 7 impress, instill 8 entrench 9 establish, inculcate 10 impregnate

implausible 8 doubtful, unlikely 9 illogical, senseless 10 far-fetched, improbable, incredible, outrageous, ridiculous 12 preposterous, unbelievable, unreasonable 13 inconceivable

implement 4 tool 5 begin, enact, piece, start 6 device 7 achieve, article, fulfill, realize, utensil 8 activate, carry out 9 apparatus, appliance, equipment, materials 10 accomplish, bring about, instrument 11 set in motion 13 put into effect

implicate 7 connect, embroil, ensnare, involve 8 entangle 9 associate, inculpate 11 incriminate

implication 6 effect 7 outcome 8 innuendo, overtone 9 inference 10 connection, intimation, suggestion 11 association, connotation, consequence, insinuation, involvement 12 entanglement, ramification, significance

implicit 5 total 6 hinted, innate 7 certain, implied, staunch 8 absolute, complete, inferred, inherent, profound, resolute 9 deducible, steadfast, suggested 10 understood, unreserved, unshakable 13 unquestioning

implied 5 tacit 7 oblique 8 indirect 9 implicity, indicated

implode 11 burst inward 17 compress violently

implore 3 beg 4 urge 6 obtest 7 beseech, entreat 9 importune, plead with 10 supplicate

imply 4 hint, mean 6 denote 7 bespeak, betoken, connote, presume, signify, suggest 8 evidence, indicate, intimate 9 insinuate 10 presuppose

impolite 4 rude 7 ill-bred, uncivil 9 impolitic, unfitting, ungenteel, unrefined 10 undecorous, unmannerly 12 discourteous 13 disrespectful, inconsiderate

impoliteness 8 rudeness 10 bad manners, incivility 11 boorishness, discourtesy

import 6 burden, moment, thrust 7 meaning 9 overtones 10 importance 11 connotation, implication 12 ramification, significance

importance 4 rank 5 value, worth 6 esteem, import, moment, repute, weight 7 stature 8 eminence, position 9 influence, relevance 11 consequence, seriousness, weightiness 12 significance 13 essentialness, momentousness

Importance of Being Earnest, The
    author: 10 Oscar Wilde
    character: 12 Cecily Cardew,

Jack Worthing, Letitia Prism **16** Gwendolen Fairfax **17** Algernon Moncrieff (Algy) **20** Lady Augusta Bracknell **21** Reverend Canon Chasuble

important 5 great, major **7** leading, notable, seminal, serious, weighty **8** creative, esteemed, foremost, original **9** momentous, prominent **10** imperative, meaningful, preeminent, remarkable **11** distinctive, influential, significant **13** consequential

imported 5 alien **6** exotic **7** foreign **9** not native

importunate 7 begging **8** pleading **9** imploring **10** entreating, persistent **11** troublesome **12** supplicating

importune 3 beg, sue **4** pray **5** plead **6** adjure, exhort **7** beseech, entreat, implore **8** appeal to, petition **10** supplicate

importunity 4 plea **6** appeal **7** request **8** entreaty, petition **12** supplication

impose 3 set **4** levy **5** apply, enact, foist, force, lay on **6** peddle, slap on **7** command, dictate, inflict, palm off, place on **8** establish, institute, introduce, prescribe **10** thrust upon

impose upon 5 annoy **6** bother, ill-use **8** ill-treat, maltreat, mistreat **15** take advantage of

imposing 5 grand, lofty **7** massive, stately **8** majestic, striking, towering **10** commanding, impressive, monumental **11** outstanding **12** awe-inspiring

imposition 5 abuse **6** burden, ill use **8** foisting **10** obligation **15** taking advantage

impossible 8 stubborn **9** insoluble **10** unbearable, unsolvable, unyielding **11** intolerable, intractable, not possible **12** insufferable, intransigent, unachievable, unanswerable, unattainable, unimaginable, unmanageable **13** inconceivable **16** out of the question

impost 3 fee, tax **4** duty, fine, toll **6** charge, excise, tariff **10** assessment

impostor 4 sham **5** cheat, duper, fraud, phony, quack **6** con man **7** bluffer, shammer **8** deceiver **9** charlatan, defrauder, pretender, trickster **10** dissembler, mountebank **11** counterfeit, flimflam man, masquerader, pettifogger **12** impersonator

imposture 4 fake, hoax, play, ruse, sham **5** cheat, fraud, trick **6** deceit, humbug **7** forgery, swindle **8** artifice, delusion, pretense, quackery **9** deception, falsehood, imitation **10** pretension **11** charlatanry, counterfeit, fraudulence **12** charlatanism **13** impersonation, mountebankery

impotence 8 weakness **9** paralysis **10** disability, incapacity, inefficacy **12** helplessness **13** powerlessness **14** ineffectuality **15** ineffectiveness

impotent 4 weak **5** frail **6** feeble **7** hapless **8** disabled, feckless, helpless **9** paralyzed, powerless **11** ineffective

impound 3 pen **4** cage **5** pen in, seize **6** coop up, encage, lock up, shut in **7** confine **13** hold in custody

impoverish 4 bust, ruin **5** break, drain **6** beggar, pauper, reduce **7** deplete, exhaust **8** bankrupt, make poor **9** pauperize **18** send to the poorhouse

impoverished 4 poor **6** abject, barren, bereft, effete, used up **7** drained, sterile, wanting, worn out **8** depleted, indigent, wiped out **9** destitute, exhausted **10** down-and-out, pauperized **11** impecunious **12** unproductive, without means

impractical 6 sloppy, unwise **8** careless, quixotic, romantic **10** loose-ended, starry-eyed **11** unrealistic **12** disorganized **13** helter-skelter, unintelligent

imprecation 5 curse **8** anathema **11** malediction

impregnable 6 mighty, potent, strong, sturdy **8** powerful **10** invincible **12** invulnerable, unassailable, unattackable **13** unconquerable

impregnate 3 wet **4** soak **5** steep **6** dampen, drench, imbrue, infuse **7** moisten, suffuse **8** fructify, inundate, permeate, saturate **9** fecundate, fertilize **10** inseminate

impresario 7 manager, sponsor **8** director **9** conductor, organizer **12** entrepreneur

impress 4 grab, move, stir, sway **5** reach, touch **6** affect, excite, sink in, strike **8** bedazzle **9** electrify, influence, overpower, overwhelm

impression 4 idea, mark, mold, view **5** hunch, stamp, trace, track **6** belief, effect, impact, notion **7** contour, feeling, impress, imprint, opinion, outline, surmise **9** influence, reception, sensation **10** conviction **11** indentation **13** understanding

impressionable 8 gullible, passible, sentient **9** affective, receptive **10** vulnerable **11** suggestible

impressive 5 grand **6** august, moving **8** exciting, imposing, majestic, striking **9** memorable, thrilling **11** magnificent, outstanding **12** awe-inspiring, overpowering, soul-stirring **13** unforgettable

imprimis 15 in the first place

imprint 3 fix **4** etch, mark, sign **5** infix, press, stamp, title **6** indent **7** engrave, impress **8** inscribe **9** engraving **10** depression, impression **11** indentation

imprison 3 pen **4** jail **6** coop up, engage, entomb, immure, lock up **7** confine, fence in, impound, shackle **8** restrain **9** constrain **11** hold captive, incarcerate

improbable 8 doubtful, unlikely **9** illogical **11** implausible **12** unreasonable **13** unforeseeable

improbable solution in a play's plot
Latin: **13** deus ex machina

impromptu 6 sudden **7** offhand **9** impulsive, makeshift, on the spot **10** improvised, off the cuff, unexpected, unprepared **11** spontaneous, unrehearsed **14** extemporaneous, unpremeditated, without warning **15** spur-of-the-moment **16** extemporaneously, on a moment's notice **19** off the top of one's head

improper 4 lewd **5** inapt, unfit **8** indecent, off-color, unseemly **9** ill-suited, irregular **10** indecorous, malapropos, out of place, suggestive, unbecoming, unsuitable **12** inharmonious **13** inappropriate, unconformable
French: **5** outre

impropriety 5 gaffe **7** blunder, faux pas **9** gaucherie, indecorum, vulgarity **10** bad manners **11** boorishness **12** impoliteness, indiscretion

improve 4 help **5** rally **6** better, enrich, repair **7** correct, develop, enhance **9** cultivate **10** ameliorate, recuperate

improvement 4 gain **6** reform, repair **7** advance, upswing

8 additive, progress **9** amendment **10** betterment, emendation, refinement **11** advancement, enhancement, reclamation **12** amelioration **14** reconstruction

improvidence 10 imprudence **11** prodigality **12** extravagance, wastefulness **13** shiftlessness **16** shortsightedness

improvident 6 lavish **8** prodigal, reckless, wasteful **9** imprudent, negligent, unthrifty **10** thriftless **11** extravagant, spendthrift **12** shortsighted **14** unparsimonious

improvise 5 ad-lib **6** make up, wing it **11** extemporize

improvised 5 ad-lib **7** devised, offhand **8** invented **9** concocted, contrived, dreamed-up, extempore, hatched-up, impromptu, makeshift **10** off-the-cuff, originated, unprepared **11** extemporary, spontaneous, unrehearsed **12** extemporized **14** extemporaneous, unpremeditated **15** improvisational, spur-of-the-moment

imprudent 4 rash **5** crazy, dopey **6** unwise **7** foolish **8** heedless, mindless, untoward **9** foolhardy **10** ill-advised, incautious, indiscreet, unthinking **11** inadvisable, injudicious, thoughtless **13** ill-considered

impudence
   Yiddish: **7** chutzpa **8** chutzpah

impudent 4 bold, rude **5** brash, fresh, nervy, saucy **6** brazen, cheeky **7** forward, upstart **8** impolite, insolent **9** bumptious, shameless **11** impertinent, smart-alecky, wiseacreish **12** discourteous **13** disrespectful

impugn 4 deny **5** knock, libel **6** assail, attack, berate, negate, oppose **7** asperse, slander **8** denounce, question **9** challenge, criticize **10** contradict **14** call in question, cast aspersions **16** call into question

impugnment 7 slander **10** aspersions

impulse 4 bent, goad, push, spur, urge, whim **5** drive, fancy, force **6** desire, motive, notion, thrust, whimsy **7** caprice, impetus, whimsey **8** instinct, momentum, movement, stimulus, stirring **9** incentive **10** incitement, motivation **11** inclination, inspiration, instigation

impulsive 4 rash **7** driving, offhand **8** forceful, forcible, no-

tional **9** impelling, impetuous, impromptu, unplanned, whimsical **10** capricious, incautious, propellant, propelling **11** involuntary, spontaneous **12** devil-may-care **13** unpredictable **14** extemporaneous, unpremeditated **15** spur-of-the-moment

impulsiveness 8 rashness **11** impetuosity, spontaneity, unrestraint **12** recklessness, whimsicality **14** capriciousness

impunity 8 immunity **9** clearance, exemption, privilege **10** absolution **11** prerogative **12** dispensation

impure 4 foul, lewd **5** dirty **6** coarse, filthy, smutty **7** debased, defiled, immoral, lustful, noisome, noxious, obscene, sullied, tainted, unclean **8** degraded, devalued, immodest, improper, indecent, polluted, prurient, unchaste, vitiated **9** lecherous, salacious, unrefined **10** indecorous, indelicate, libidinous, licentious **11** adulterated, depreciated, unwholesome **12** contaminated

impurity 5 alloy, dross, filth, taint **8** foulness **9** dirtiness, pollutant, pollution **10** adulterant, corruption, defilement **11** contaminant, taintedness, uncleanness **12** adulteration **13** contamination, foreign matter **15** unwholesomeness

imputation 6 charge **10** accusation, allegation, ascription **11** attribution

impute 5 refer **6** assign, charge, credit, relate **7** ascribe **9** attribute

inability 10 inaptitude, incapacity, ineptitude **12** helplessness, incapability, incompetence **13** maladroitness, powerlessness

in absence
   Latin: **10** in absentia

in absentia 9 in absence

inaccessible 9 not at hand **11** unreachable **12** unattainable, unobtainable **14** unapproachable

in accord 9 agreeable, approving, in harmony, of one mind **10** concurring, consenting **11** in agreement
   French: **9** en rapport

inaccuracy 4 goof, slip **5** error, fault, wrong **6** boo-boo **7** blunder, erratum, fallacy, mistake **9** unclarity **10** faultiness **11** imprecision, inexactness **13** incorrectness, unreliability **14** fallaciousness

inaccurate 3 off **5** false, wrong **6** faulty **7** inexact **8** mistaken **9** erroneous, imprecise, incorrect, off target **10** fallacious, unreliable **11** not on target, off the track **13** wide of the mark

Inachus
   god of: 6 rivers
   king of: 5 Argos
   father: 7 Oceanus
   mother: 6 Tethys
   wife: 5 Melia
   son: 9 Aegialeus, Phoroneus
   daughter: 2 Io

inaction 8 abeyance, deferral, dormancy, dullness, idleness **9** cessation, indolence **10** inactivity, quiescence, somnolence, suspension **11** complacency

inactive 4 dull, idle, lazy **5** inert, quiet, still **6** low-key, otiose, static, torpid, unused **7** dormant, languid **8** indolent, slothful, sluggish **9** do-nothing, easygoing, leisurely, sedentary, somnolent **10** on the shelf **11** inoperative **12** out of service

inactivity 4 rest **5** quiet **6** disuse **7** inertia **8** dormancy, idleness, inaction **9** stillness **10** quiescence

in actuality
   Latin: **6** in esse

in addition 3 and, too **4** also, more, plus, then **5** above, added, again, extra **6** as well, beyond **7** besides, further **8** moreover **10** additional **12** additionally, supplemental

inadequacy 4 lack **7** failing **10** deficiency, impairment **11** shortcoming **13** insufficiency

inadequate 5 inept, short, unfit **6** meager, scanty, too raw **7** lacking, not up to, wanting **8** below par, unfitted **9** deficient, imperfect, incapable **11** incompetent, unqualified **12** insufficient

inadmissible 10 disallowed, extraneous **11** intolerable **12** not permitted, unacceptable **14** nonpermissible

in advance 6 before, in time, sooner **7** earlier **9** before now **10** beforehand **11** ahead of time **13** before the fact

inadvertent 7 unmeant **10** accidental, fortuitous, unintended, unthinking **11** involuntary **13** unintentional **14** unpremeditated

inadvisable 5 risky **6** chancy, unwise **9** impolitic, imprudent

10 ill-advised **11** inexpedient, injudicious, inopportune

in aeternum 7 forever

in agreement
French: **9** en rapport

inalienable 6 sacred **8** absolute, defended, inherent **9** protected **10** inviolable, sacrosanct **12** unassailable **13** unforfeitable, unimpeachable

in all
Latin: **6** in toto

in all places 10 every place, everywhere, far and near, far and wide

in a low voice
Latin: **9** sotto voce

inamorata 4 lady, love **5** lover **7** beloved, darling **8** ladylove, mistress, paramour, truelove **10** sweetheart

inane 4 dumb **5** dopey, empty, silly, vapid **6** absurd, jejune, stupid **7** asinine, fatuous, foolish, idiotic, insipid, shallow, vacuous **9** pointless, senseless **10** ridiculous, unthinking **11** meaningless, nonsensical **13** unintelligent

inanimate 4 cold, dead, dull **5** inert **6** asleep, stolid **8** lifeless, soulless **9** inorganic, insensate, nonliving, senseless, unfeeling **10** insensible, insentient **11** unconscious

inanity 6 drivel **7** hogwash, vacuity **8** nonsense, vapidity **9** absurdity, asininity, silliness **11** foolishness **13** pointlessness, senselessness **14** ridiculousness

Inanna
origin: **8** Sumerian
goddess of: **3** war **4** love
sister: **10** Ereshkigal
realm: **6** heaven
corresponds to: **6** Ishtar **7** Astarte, Mylitta **9** Ashtoreth

in any case 6 anyhow, anyway **9** at any rate **10** in any event

in any event 6 anyhow, anyway **9** at any rate, in any case

inapplicable 5 unfit **6** not apt **8** unsuited **10** inapposite, irrelevant, not germane, unsuitable **12** incompatible, not pertinent **13** inappropriate

inappropriate 5 inapt **8** ill-timed, improper, unsuited **9** unfitting **10** indecorous, in bad taste, out of place, unbecoming, unsuitable **11** incon-

gruous **12** incompatible, infelicitous
French: **10** mal a propos

inapt 8 improper, unseemly, unsuited **9** ill-suited, incorrect, unfitting **11** incongruous **13** inappropriate

inaptness 9 inability, ineptness **10** clumsiness, inaptitude, ineptitude **12** incompetence **13** maladroitness **14** unskillfulness

in arrears 4 late **7** overdue **10** delinquent

inarticulate 4 dumb, mute **7** babbled, blurred, garbled, mumbled **8** confused, wordless **9** paralyzed **10** incoherent, indistinct, speechless, tongue-tied **12** inexpressive **14** unintelligible **15** uncommunicative

inartistic 9 graceless, inelegant, tasteless **10** ungraceful **11** unaesthetic **12** unattractive

in a series
French: **7** en suite

in a set
French: **7** en suite

in attendance 4 here **7** present, serving **9** appearing, caring for, on the spot, waiting on **12** accompanying, looking after, taking care of

inattention 6 apathy **10** negligence **12** carelessness **14** lack of interest **16** absentmindedness, unresponsiveness

inattentive 7 unaware **8** careless, heedless **9** forgetful, negligent, unmindful **10** distracted **11** daydreaming, thoughtless, unobservant **12** absentminded

inaugurate 5 set up, start **6** induct, launch **7** instate, kick off, usher in **8** initiate **9** institute, undertake **10** embark upon **11** set in action

inauguration 5 start **9** beginning, induction **10** dedication **11** origination **12** commencement

inaugurator 6 author, father **7** creator, founder, starter **9** initiator, organizer **10** originator, prime mover

inauspicious 7 unlucky **9** ill-chosen, ill-omened **10** badly timed, disastrous **11** unfavorable, unfortunate, unpromising **12** infelicitous, unpropitious

in a vacuum
Latin: **7** in vacuo

in bad faith
Latin: **8** mala fide

in being
Latin: **6** in esse

in blazing crime
Latin: **18** in flagrante delicto

inborn 5 basic **6** inbred, innate, native **7** natural **8** inherent **9** inherited, intrinsic, intuitive **10** congenital **11** fundamental, instinctive **14** constitutional

inbred 6 inborn, innate, primal **7** natural **8** inherent **9** ingrained, inherited, intrinsic, intuitive **10** congenital, deep-rooted, deep-seated, hereditary, indwelling **11** instinctive, instinctual **12** deeply rooted **14** constitutional

Inca
language family: **7** Quechua
location: **4** Peru **5** Chili **7** Bolivia, Ecuador **9** Argentina **12** South America
leader: **7** Huascar **8** Topa Inca **9** Atahualpa, Pachacuti **10** Manco Capac **11** Huayna Capac
conquered by: **7** Pizarro
ruins: **11** Machu Picchu, Sacsahuaman, Tambo Machay

incalculable 7 dubious **8** infinite **9** countless, uncertain **11** inestimable, innumerable, measureless, uncountable **12** immeasurable, incomputable **13** unforeseeable, unpredictable

incandesce 4 burn, glow **5** flare, flash

incandescent 7 dynamic, glowing, radiant **8** electric, galvanic, magnetic, white-hot **9** brilliant **11** high-powered **12** electrifying **13** scintillating

incantation 3 hex **4** jinx **5** chant, charm, magic, spell **6** voodoo **7** sorcery **8** wizardry **10** black magic, hocus-pocus, invocation, mumbo-jumbo, necromancy, witchcraft **11** abracadabra, conjuration

incapable 5 inept, unfit **6** unable **8** helpless, impotent, inferior **9** powerless, unskilled, untrained **10** inadequate **11** incompetent, ineffective, inefficient, unqualified

incapacitate 4 maim, undo **5** lay up **7** cripple, disable **8** enfeeble, handicap, paralyze, sideline **9** make unfit **10** disqualify **13** make powerless **14** put out of action **15** render incapable

incapacitated 6 laid up **8** crippled, disabled, disarmed, helpless, stricken **9** hamstrung, paralyzed, sidelined **10** on the shelf, prostrated **11** immobilized, out of action **12** hors de combat **14** flat on one's back

incapacity 7 illness **8** sickness **9** crippling **10** deficiency, disability **12** incapability

incarcerate 3 pen **4** jail **6** commit, coop up, immure, intern, lock up **7** confine, impound **8** imprison, restrain

incarceration 9 detention **10** commitment, internment **11** confinement, durance vile **12** imprisonment **18** institutionalizing

incarnate 8 embodied, manifest **9** personify **10** actualized, in the flesh **11** objectified, personified

Incarnations
   author: **16** Robert Penn Warren

incautious 4 rash **5** brash **6** unwary **8** careless, heedless, reckless **9** hotheaded, impetuous, imprudent, impulsive, overhasty **10** headstrong, indiscreet, unthinking **11** injudicious, thoughtless

incendiary 8 agitator, arsonist **12** inflammatory

incense 5 anger **6** burn up, enrage, madden **7** inflame, provoke **9** infuriate, make angry **13** make indignant
   spice: **6** stacte

incensed 3 mad **5** angry, irate **6** fuming, raging **7** enraged, furious **8** burned up, inflamed, outraged, provoked **9** affronted, indignant **10** infuriated

incentive 4 lure, spur **6** come-on, motive **8** stimulus **10** enticement, inducement, motivation **11** inspiration **13** encouragement

inception 5 birth, debut, onset, start **6** origin, outset **7** arrival **9** beginning **12** commencement, inauguration

incessant 8 constant, unbroken, unending **9** ceaseless, continual, perpetual, unceasing **10** continuous, persistent **11** everlasting, unrelenting, unremitting **12** interminable **13** uninterrupted

inch
   abbreviation: **2** in

In Chancery
   author: **14** John Galsworthy
   part of trilogy: **11** Forsyte Saga

inchoate 7 budding, nascent **8** formless, unformed, unshaped **9** amorphous, begin-

ning, embryonic, incipient, shapeless **10** commencing, disjointed, uncohesive **11** unorganized **12** disconnected

incidence 4 rate **5** range, scope **6** extent **8** occasion **9** frequency, happening **10** commonness, occurrence, phenomenon **11** routineness

incident 5 clash, event, scene **6** affair **7** episode, related **8** occasion **9** happening **10** incidental, occurrence **11** contretemps, disturbance

incidental 5 minor **9** accessory, secondary **10** extraneous, unexpected **11** subordinate, unlooked-for

incidentally 7 apropos, by the by **8** by the way **9** in passing **14** speaking of that **15** parenthetically **21** while we're on the subject

incidentals 6 extras **8** minutiae **10** minor items **11** accessories, odds and ends **13** appurtenances

incinerate 4 burn **7** consume, cremate **9** carbonize **13** reduce to ashes

incineration 6 firing **7** burning, flaming **8** ignition, kindling **9** cremation **10** combustion **13** carbonization

incinerator 4 oven **6** burner **7** furnace

incipient 7 budding, nascent **8** inchoate **9** beginning, embryonic, fledgling, promising **10** developing, half-formed **11** rudimentary

in circulation 4 rife **6** abroad, around **7** at large **9** all around **11** going around **12** spread around **14** around and about **15** making the rounds

incise 4 etch **5** carve **7** cut into, engrave

incision 3 cut **4** scar, gash, nick, slit **5** cleft, notch, score, slash, slice, wound **6** furrow

incisive 4 curt, keen **5** acute, brisk, crisp, sharp **6** biting, shrewd **7** cutting, express, mordant, precise, probing, summary **8** analytic, piercing **9** trenchant, well-aimed **10** perceptive **11** intelligent, penetrating

incite 4 goad, prod, stir **5** drive, egg on, impel, rouse **6** arouse, excite, fire up, foment, induce, prompt, stir up, urge on **7** actuate, agitate, inflame, provoke **8** activate **9** instigate, stimulate

incitement 6 urging **7** arousal, driving, goading **8** egging on, exciting, firing up, stirring **9** agitating, fomenting, inflaming, prompting, provoking **10** activation, stirring up **11** provocation, stimulation

incivility 8 rudeness **9** barbarism, impudence, indecorum, surliness, vulgarity **10** bad manners, coarseness, disrespect **11** boorishness, discourtesy, misbehavior, uncouthness **12** impoliteness, tactlessness **14** unpleasantness

inclement 3 raw **4** foul **5** harsh, nasty, rough **6** bitter, severe, stormy **7** violent **11** tempestuous

inclination 3 bow, dip, nod **4** bend, bent, hill, rake, rise **5** grade, pitch, slant, slope **6** liking **7** bending, leaning, sloping **8** fondness, lowering, penchant, tendency **9** acclivity, inclining, proneness **10** preference, proclivity, propensity **11** disposition **12** predilection **14** predisposition

incline 3 bow **4** bend, cant, hill, lean, like, rake, seem, tend, tilt, wont **5** be apt, enjoy, pitch, slant, slope **6** prefer **7** decline **8** be likely, gradient **9** acclivity **10** lean toward **11** bend forward, have a mind to

inclined 3 apt **5** prove **6** liable, likely **7** given to **10** disposed to **11** predisposed

incline downward 3 dip, sag **4** sink **5** droop, slant, slope

inclined to delay 4 slow **5** tardy **6** remiss **8** dawdling, dilatory, sluggish **9** reluctant **12** foot-dragging **13** dillydallying **15** procrastinating

include 5 cover **6** enfold, entail, take in **7** contain, embrace, involve, subsume **8** comprise **9** encompass **10** comprehend **11** incorporate

inclusive 7 general, overall **8** sweeping, taking in **9** embracing, including **10** comprising, encircling **11** surrounding **12** encyclopedic **13** comprehending, comprehensive, incorporating **15** all-encompassing

incognito 7 unknown, unnamed **8** nameless **9** concealed, disguised, protected **10** in disguise, uncredited, undercover, unrevealed **11** undisclosed **12** unidentified **14** unacknowledged, unrecognizable

incognizant 6 obtuse **7** un-

aware **8** ignorant, unseeing
9 unknowing **13** unconscious
of **15** uncomprehending

incoherent 7 muddled, unclear **8** confused, rambling
9 illogical **13** disjointed, irrational **11** bewildering, nonsensical **12** inconsistent
14 unintelligible

In Cold Blood
 author: 12 Truman Capote
 director: 13 Richard Brooks
 cast: 11 Paul Stewart, Robert
 Blake, Scott Wilson **12** John
 Forsythe

income 5 means, wages
6 salary **7** revenue **8** earnings **9** emolument
10 livelihood

income, annual
 French: **5** rente

incomparable 8 peerless
9 matchless, unequaled, unrivaled **10** inimitable **11** superlative **12** transcendent
13 beyond compare
14 unapproachable

incompatible 6 at odds **7** jarring **8** clashing, contrary, unsuited **10** at variance,
discordant, mismatched
11 disagreeing, incongruous,
uncongenial **12** antagonistic,
inconsistent, inharmonious
13 contradictory,
inappropriate

incompatibility 6 strife **7** discord **8** friction, variance **9** disaccord, wrangling
10 antagonism **11** being at
odds, discordance **13** lack of
harmony

incompetency 9 inability, unfitness **10** ineptitude **11** lack
of skill **12** inefficiency
15 ineffectiveness

incompetent 5 inept, unfit
8 inexpert **9** incapable, unskilled, untrained **11** ineffective, ineffectual, inefficient,
unqualified **14** lacking ability

incomplete 6 broken **7** partial,
wanting **9** defective, deficient
10 unfinished **11** fragmentary

incompleteness 8 omission
10 deficiency **11** shortcoming
15 unfinished state

incomprehensible 7 obscure
8 abstruse, baffling **9** confusing **10** befuddling **11** bewildering, inscrutable,
ungraspable **12** impenetrable,
unfathomable **14** unintelligible **19** beyond comprehension,
beyond understanding

incomprehension 10 bafflement, puzzlement **12** bewil-

derment **19** failure to
understand

inconceivable 7 strange **8** unlikely **10** improbable, incredible **11** unthinkable **12** beyond
belief, unbelievable, unimaginable **14** highly unlikely

in conclusion
 French: **5** enfin

inconclusive 4 open **9** unsettled **10** indecisive, indefinite,
unresolved, up in the air
11 not definite **12** unconvincing, undetermined
13 indeterminate

incongruity 8 variance **9** disparity **10** aberration, disharmony, divergence
11 abnormality, discrepancy
13 dissimilarity, inconsistency,
unsuitability
17 inappropriateness

incongruous 3 odd **6** far-out
8 contrary **10** at variance, discrepant, out of place, outlandish, unsuitable **11** conflicting,
disagreeing **12** incompatible,
inconsistent, out of keeping
13 contradictory, inappropriate **14** irreconcilable

inconsequential 5 petty
6 slight **7** trivial **8** nugatory,
picayune, piddling, trifling
9 valueless **10** negligible, of
no moment **11** meaningless,
unimportant **13** insignificant
15 of no consequence

inconsiderable 5 light, minor,
petty, small **6** little, modest,
paltry, slight **7** minimal, trivial **8** picayune, trifling **9** no
big deal **10** negligible **11** unimportant **13** insignificant, no
great shakes
15 inconsequential

inconsiderate 4 rash, rude
6 remiss, unkind **7** uncivil
8 careless, impolite, tactless,
uncaring **9** negligent **10** ungracious, unthinking **11** insensitive, thoughtless
12 disregardful, uncharitable

inconsistency 8 variance
9 disparity **10** difference, divergence **11** discrepancy, incongruity **12** disagreement
13 dissimilarity

inconsistent 6 fickle **7** erratic,
wayward **8** contrary, notional,
unstable, variable **9** changeful,
dissonant **10** changeable, discrepant, inconstant, irresolute
11 inaccordant, incongruous,
inconsonant, vacillating **12** incompatible, inharmonious
13 contradictory, unpredictable **14** irreconcilable

inconsolable 7 crushed **8** de-

jected, desolate, wretched
9 miserable **10** despondent
12 disconsolate **13** brokenhearted

inconsonant 10 discordant
12 out of keeping,
unharmonious

inconspicuous 3 dim **5** faint,
muted **6** modest **9** unnoticed
10 unapparent, unassuming
11 unobtrusive **12** not egregious, unnoticeable
14 unostentatious

inconstancy 10 fickleness, infidelity **11** instability **14** capriciousness, changeableness,
unfaithfulness

inconstant 6 fickle, untrue
7 erratic **8** cavalier, disloyal,
unstable **9** mercurial **10** capricious, changeable, unfaithful
11 interrupted, uncommitted,
undedicated, unsteadfast

incontinence 8 rashness
12 recklessness **13** lack of control **16** irresponsibility

incontinent 8 unchaste
12 unrestrained

incontrovertibility 8 sureness
9 certainty **12** absoluteness,
definiteness **13** undeniability
14 irrefutability, conclusiveness **15** indisputability **16** in-
contestability
17 unquestionability

incontrovertible 9 apodictic
10 unarguable, undeniable
11 established, irrefutable
12 indisputable **14** beyond
question, unquestionable

inconvenience 6 bother, put
out **7** trouble **8** hardship,
headache, nuisance **9** annoyance, disoblige, put one out
10 discomfort **13** be a nuisance to, pain in the neck

inconvenient 7 awkward, unhandy **8** annoying, tiresome,
untimely **10** bothersome, burdensome **11** distressing, inopportune, troublesome

Incoronazione di Poppea, L'
 also: 22 The Coronation of
 Poppea
 opera by: 10 Monteverdi
 character: 4 Nero **6** Ottone
 7 Ottavia

incorporate 4 fuse **6** embody,
work in **7** include **10** amalgamate, assimilate **11** consolidate

incorporated 6 united **8** embodied, included **11** amalgamated, assimilated
12 consolidated

incorporeal 6 occult, unreal
7 ghostly, phantom **8** bodiless
9 spiritual, unearthly, un-

fleshly, unworldly **10** immaterial, intangible **11** disembodied **12** supernatural **13** insubstantial

incorrect 5 false, wrong **6** untrue **7** inexact **8** mistaken **9** erroneous **10** fallacious, inaccurate

incorrectness 5 error **9** wrongness **10** inaccuracy **12** carelessness, slovenliness

incorrigible 6 unruly **8** hardened, hard-core, hopeless **10** beyond help, delinquent **11** intractable **12** beyond saving, past changing, unmanageable **14** uncontrollable

incorrigible child French: **14** enfant terrible

incorruptible 4 pure **6** honest **7** upright **8** reliable **9** faultless, righteous **10** unbribable **11** trustworthy **14** irreproachable

increase 3 wax **4** grow **5** add to, swell **6** enrich, expand **7** advance, augment, burgeon, enhance, enlarge **8** multiply **12** become larger

increasing 7 growing **9** enlarging, expansion, extending, extension **10** drawing out **11** enlargement **12** augmentation

incredible 6 absurd **7** amazing, awesome **10** astounding, farfetched, remarkable **11** astonishing **12** preposterous, unbelievable, unimaginable **13** extraordinary, inconceivable

Incredible Hulk, The character: **9** Jack McGee **11** David Banner cast: **9** Bill Bixby **10** Jack Colvin **11** Lou Ferrigno

incredulous 7 dubious **8** doubtful **9** skeptical **10** suspicious **11** distrustful **12** disbelieving

increment 4 gain, rise **5** raise **6** growth, profit **7** benefit **8** addition, increase **9** accretion **10** supplement **11** enlargement **12** accumulation, appreciation, augmentation **13** proliferation

incriminate 5 blame **6** accuse, charge, indict

incrimination 5 blame **7** charges **10** accusation, indictment

incubate 3 set, sit **4** plot **5** breed, brood, clock, cover, hatch **6** scheme **7** develop, gestate, sit upon **8** generate

incubus 5 demon **8** bad dream **9** nightmare

inculcate 5 drill, imbue, infix, teach, train **6** impart, infuse **7** implant, impress, instill **8** instruct **7** brainwash, condition, enlighten **12** indoctrinate

inculpable 5 clear **8** innocent **9** blameless, guiltless, not guilty **10** not at fault, unblamable **14** not responsible

incur 6 arouse, assume, incite, stir up **7** acquire, bring on, involve, provoke **8** bring out, contract, fall into

incurable 8 cureless, hopeless **9** ceaseless **10** beyond cure, inveterate, relentless, unflagging **12** incorrigible, irremediable **13** dyed-in-the-wool, uncorrectable

incursion 4 push, raid **5** foray **6** attack, inroad, sortie **7** assault **8** invasion **11** advance into, impingement **12** encroachment, infiltration

indebted 5 bound **7** bounden **8** beholden, grateful, thankful **9** obligated **10** chargeable **11** accountable **15** under obligation

indebtedness 4 debt **5** debit **7** arrears **9** liability **10** balance due, obligation **11** liabilities

indecency 10 immorality **12** unseemliness **13** offensiveness, salaciousness **14** indecorousness

indecent 4 blue, lewd, rude **5** bawdy, dirty **6** filthy, smutty, vulgar **7** ignoble, ill-bred, immoral, obscene, uncivil **8** immodest, improper, prurient, unseemly **9** offensive, salacious **10** in bad taste, indecorous, indiscreet, licentious, unbecoming **11** unwholesome **12** pornographic

Indecent Obsession, An author: **17** Colleen McCullough

indecipherable 7 cryptic **9** enigmatic, illegible **10** unreadable **11** inscrutable

indecision 5 doubt **6** acrisy **7** dilemma, swither **8** wavering **10** hesitation **11** fluctuation, vacillating, vacillation, uncertainty **12** irresolution

indecisive 4 weak **7** dubious, unclear **8** doubtful, hesitant, wavering **9** confusing, debatable, mercurial, uncertain, unsettled **10** disputable, hesitating, irresolute, wishy-washy **11** halfhearted, vacillat-

ing **12** inconclusive **13** indeterminate **17** blowing hot and cold

indecorous 5 gross **6** sinful, wicked **7** ill-bred **8** immodest, improper, low-class, unseemly **9** unfitting **10** unbecoming, unsuitable **11** blameworthy **13** inappropriate, reprehensible

indecorum 8 bad taste **9** immodesty, indecency, vulgarity **11** impropriety **12** impoliteness, unseemliness

indeed 5 truly **6** in fact, really **7** for sure, in truth **8** actually, to be sure **9** certainly, in reality, veritably **10** positively, to be honest, undeniably **11** joking apart **13** in point of fact, with certainty **14** to tell the truth **15** as a matter of fact, without question **16** strictly speaking

indefatigable 6 dogged **7** staunch **8** diligent, sedulous, tireless, untiring **9** energetic **10** persistent, unflagging, unwearying **11** persevering, unfaltering **13** inexhaustible

indefensible 8 improper, vincible **9** pregnable, untenable **10** vulnerable **11** defenseless, inexcusable, unprotected, unspeakable **12** open to attack, unpardonable **13** unjustifiable

indefinite 3 dim **5** vague **6** unsure **7** inexact, obscure, unknown **8** doubtful **9** ambiguous, amorphous, limitless, tentative, uncertain, unsettled **10** ill-defined, indecisive, indistinct, inexplicit **11** illimitable, measureless, unspecified **12** undetermined **13** indeterminate

indefiniteness 6 vagary **9** ambiguity, vagueness **10** indecision **11** uncertainty **12** equivocation

indelible 4 fast **5** fixed, vivid **7** lasting **8** deep-dyed **9** ingrained, memorable, permanent **10** unerasable **11** unremovable **12** ineradicable **13** unforgettable

indelicate 4 lewd, rude **5** broad, crude, gross **6** clumsy, coarse, risque, vulgar **7** awkward, obscene **8** immodest, improper, indecent, off-color, unseemly **9** offensive, unrefined **10** indecorous, indiscreet, suggestive, unbecoming

in demand 7 popular **9** desirable **11** sought after

indemnification 7 payment **10** recompense, reparation **12** compensation

indemnify 3 pay **5** atone, cover, repay **6** insure, secure **7** pay back, protect, rectify, require, satisfy **8** make good **9** make right, make up for, reimburse **10** compensate, make amends, recompense, remunerate **15** make restitution

indemnity 7 redress **8** coverage, security **9** insurance, repayment **10** protection **11** restitution **12** compensation **15** indemnification

indent 5 notch, set in **6** recess **7** set back

indentation 3 bay, cut, pit **4** dent, nick **5** gouge, inset, niche, notch, score **6** cavity, furrow, pocket, recess **8** incision **9** concavity **10** depression

indented 6 hollow, sunken, zigzag **7** concave, notched **9** depressed

indenture 4 bind **8** contract **10** apprentice

indentured 5 bound **10** contracted **11** apprenticed

independence 7 freedom, liberty **8** autonomy **10** liberation **11** sovereignty **12** emancipation, self-reliance **14** self-government **17** self-determination

independent 4 free **7** solvent, well-off **8** affluent, separate, unallied, well-to-do **9** apart from, exclusive, on one's own, sovereign, uncoerced, well-fixed **10** autonomous, well-heeled **11** self-reliant, unconnected **12** unassociated, uncontrolled **13** self-directing, self-governing, unconstrained **15** individualistic, self-determining

indescribable 9 ineffable **11** beyond words, indefinable, unutterable **12** overwhelming **13** inexpressible **17** beyond description **20** beggaring description

indestructible 8 enduring **9** permanent **11** everlasting, infrangible, unbreakable **12** imperishable

indeterminate 5 vague **7** obscure, unclear **8** not clear **9** ambiguous, uncertain, undefined **10** indefinite, perplexing, unresolved **11** problematic, unspecified **12** undetermined, unstipulated

index 4 clue, mark, sign **5** proof, token **7** catalog, symptom **8** evidence, glossary, register **9** catalogue, indicator **10** indication **13** manifestation **16** alphabetical list

Index Librorum Prohibitorum 22 index of prohibited books

index of prohibited books Latin: **25** Index Librorum Prohibitorum

India *see box, p. 484*

Indian constellation: **5** Indus

Indiana *see box, p. 485*

Indiana basketball team: **6** Pacers

Indiana author: **10** George Sand character: **4** Noun **7** Delmare **13** Rodolphe Brown **15** Raymon de Ramiere

Indianapolis football team: **5** Colts

Indic language family: **12** Indo-European branch: **11** Indo-Iranian subgroup: **5** Hindi, Oriya **6** Nepali, Sindhi **7** Bengali, Marathi, Pakrits, Panjabi **8** Assamese, Gujarati, Kashmiri **9** Sinhalese

indicate 4 mean, show, tell **5** imply **6** denote, evince, record, reveal **7** bespeak, point to, signify, specify, suggest **8** point out, register, stand for **9** be a sign of, designate, establish, make known, represent, symbolize

indication 4 clue, hint, mark, omen, sign **5** token **6** augury, boding, signal **7** gesture, mention, portent, presage, showing, symptom, telling, warning **8** evidence, pointing **9** foretoken **10** foreboding, indicating, intimation, signifying, suggestion **11** designation, premonition **13** demonstration, manifestation

indicative 8 symbolic **10** denotative, emblematic, evidential, expressive, indicatory, suggestive **11** connotative, designative, significant, symptomatic **13** symptomatical **14** characteristic, representative

indicator 4 clue **5** guide **7** pointer **10** indication

indict 4 cite **6** accuse, charge, have up, impute, pull up **7** arraign, bring up, impeach **9** criminate, inculpate, prosecute **11** incriminate **13** prefer charges

indifference 6 apathy **7** disdain, neglect **8** coldness, no import **9** aloofness, unconcern **10** negligence, paltriness,

triviality **11** disinterest, impassivity, inattention, insouciance, nonchalance **12** carelessness, unimportance **13** impassiveness, insensibility, insensitivity **14** insignificance, lack of interest

indifferent 4 cool, fair, rote, so-so **5** aloof **6** medium, modest **7** average, unmoved **8** detached, mediocre, middling, moderate, ordinary, passable **9** apathetic, impassive, not caring, unmindful **10** impervious, insensible, insouciant, nonchalant, second-rate, uninspired **11** commonplace, perfunctory, unconcerned **12** uninterested **13** insusceptible **15** undistinguished **17** betwixt and between, neither good nor bad

indigence 4 need, want **6** penury **7** beggary, poverty **9** pauperism, privation **11** destitution, dire straits **13** pennilessness

indigenous 6 native **7** endemic **8** domestic, homebred **9** home-grown **10** aboriginal **13** autochthonous, originating in

indigent 4 poor **5** needy **6** hard-up, in need, in want **7** pinched **8** badly off **9** destitute, moneyless, penniless **12** impoverished **15** poverty-stricken

indiges title in: **4** Rome suggests: **11** deification *for service to:* **7** country

indigestible 4 rich **13** unassimilable

indignant 3 mad **4** sore **5** angry, huffy, irate, riled **6** fuming, miffed, peeved, piqued, put off, put out **8** incensed, offended, provoked, steaming, worked up, wrathful **9** resentful, wrought up **10** displeased, infuriated **15** on one's high horse

indignation 3 ire **4** fury, huff, rage **5** pique, wrath **6** animus, choler, dismay, uproar **7** umbrage **8** vexation **9** annoyance **10** irritation, resentment **11** displeasure

indignity 4 slur **5** abuse **6** insult, slight **7** affront, offense, outrage **8** dishonor, rudeness **9** injustice **11** discourtesy, humiliation **12** mistreatment **13** slap in the face

indigo 3 dye **4** blue **8** dark blue, deep blue, navy blue **10** Indigofera varieties: **4** wild **5** false

India

other name: 4 Hind 6 Bharat 12 Bharat Varsha
capital: 8 New Delhi
largest city: 8 Calcutta
others: 4 Agra, Gaya, Pune 5 Dacca, Poona, Surat 6 Bombay, Jaipur, Kanpur, Lahore, Madras, Madura, Mysore, Nagpur 7 Banaras 8 Kolhapur, Mandalay, Mirzapur, Shahpura, Srinagar 9 Ahmedabad, Bangalore, Hyderabad 10 Darjeeling
division: 3 Goa 5 Assam, Bihar, Jammu 6 Kerala, Orissa, Punjab, Sikkim 7 Gujarat, Haryana, Kashmir, Manipur, Tripura 8 Nagaland 9 Karnataka, Meghalaya, Rajasthan, Tamil Nadu 10 West Bengal 11 Daman and Diu, Maharashtra, Pondicherry 12 Uttar Pradesh 13 Andhra Pradesh, Madhya Pradesh 15 Himachal Pradesh
measure: 3 ady, gaz, gez, jow, lan 4 byee, coss, depa, doph, hath, koss, kunk, raik, rati, seit, taun, tola 5 bigha, covid, crosa, denda, depoh, drona, erosa, garce, hasta, krosa, parah, ratti, salay, yojan 6 adhaka, amunam, covido, cudava, dumbha, geerah, moolum, mushti, ouroub, palgat, parran, prasha, ropani, tipree, unglee, yojana 7 dhanush, gavyuti, khahoon, niranga, prastha 8 okthabah
monetary unit: 3 lac, pie 4 lakh, pice 5 abidi, rupee
weight: 3 mod, pai, vis 4 drum, hoen, kona, pala, pank, pice, ruay, tael, tali, tola, wang, yava 5 adpad, candy, hubba, maund, tical 6 karsha 8 mangelin
island: 6 Agatti, Chilka 7 Andaman, Minicoy, Nicobar 8 Amindivi 9 Laccadive 11 Lakshadweep
lake: 5 Jheel, Lonar, Wular 6 Chilka, Colair, Dhebar, Kolair 7 Kolleru, Pulicat, Pushkar, Sambahr
mountain: 8 Aravalli 9 Broad Peak, Distaghil, Himalayas, Karakoram, Nanda Devi, Rakaposhi 10 Gasherbrum, Masherbrum 11 Nanga Parbat 12 Eastern Ghats, Kanchenjunga, Western Ghats
  hills: 4 Chin, Naga 5 Khasi 6 Lushai 7 Nilgiri
highest point: 12 Godwin Austen
river: 3 Son 4 Beas, Kosi, Tapi 5 Gogra, Indus, Jumna, Tapti 6 Gandak, Ganges, Jhelum, Kaveri, Kistna, Sutlej, Yamuna 7 Cauveri, Cauvery, Chambal, Damodar, Hooghly, Krishna, Narbada, Narmada 8 Godavari, Mahanadi 10 Bhagirathi 11 Brahmaputra
sea: 6 Indian 7 Arabian
physical feature:
  bay: 6 Bengal
  cape: 7 Comorin
  desert: 4 Thar 9 Rajasthan
  forest: 3 Gir
  gulf: 5 Kutch 6 Cambay, Mannar
  pass: 9 Karakoram
  plain: 12 Indo-Gangetic
  plateau: 6 Deccan 7 Shillon 11 Chota Nagpur
  rains: 7 monsoon
  strait: 4 Palk
  swamp: 9 Sundarban 11 Rann of Kutch
  valley: 13 Vale of Kashmir
people: 2 Ao 3 Gor 4 Bhil 5 Aryan 6 Badaga, Pathan 7 Sherani 9 Dravidian 10 Andamanese
  caste: 3 Jat 5 Sudra 6 Rajput, Shudra 7 Brahman, Brahmin, Harijan, Maratha, Vaishya 9 Kshatriya 11 Untouchable
  dynasty: 5 Gupta, Mogul 6 Maurya, Rajput 8 Marathas 14 Delhi Sultanate
  god: 4 Kali, Rama, Siva 5 Durga, Laxmi, Shiva 6 Brahma, Kumara, Vishnu 7 Ganesha, Hanuman, Krishna, Lakshmi 9 Kartikeya 10 Subramanya
  ruler: 5 Akbar, Asoka, Babur, Timur 7 Humayun 8 Hyder Ali, Jahangir 9 Aurangzeb, Shah Jahan 11 Rajiv Gandhi, Tippu Sultan 12 Indira Gandhi 13 Queen Victoria 15 Jawaharlal Nehru, Mohandas K (Mahatma) Gandhi 18 Chandragupta Maurya
language: 4 Urdu 5 Hindi, Oriya, Tamil 6 Sindhi, Telugu 7 Bengali, English, Kannada, Malayam, Marathi, Punjabi 8 Assamese, Gujarati, Kashmiri, Sanskrit 9 Malayalam
religion: 4 Sikh 5 Hindu, Islam, Parsi 7 Jainist, Judaism 8 Buddhism 11 Zoroastrian 12 Christianity
place:
  cathedral: 10 Saint Thome
  fortress: 3 Red 11 Saint George
  mausoleum: 8 Taj Mahal
  minaret: 9 Qutb Minar
  mosque: 10 Jama Masjid
  park: 6 Maidan
  president's residence: 17 Rashtrapati Bhavan
  railway station: 8 Victoria
  shrine: 7 Raj Ghat
  street: 7 Raj Path 11 Chowringhee, Marine Drive 12 Chandni Chauk 14 Connaught Place
  temple: 5 Birla 6 Ellora, Golden 7 Kailasa 10 Ajanta Cave
feature:
  dance: 6 nautch 7 cantico
  religious text: 7 Rig Veda
  shrine: 5 stupa
food:
  beer: 5 apong
  bread: 7 chapati
  liquor: 4 soma, sura 5 shrab
  tea: 5 assam

Indiana
   abbreviation: 2 IN **3** Ind
   nickname: 7 Hoosier
   capital/largest city: 12 Indianapolis
   others: 4 Gary, Peru **6** Brazil, Goshen, Hobart, Jasper, Kokomo, Marion, Muncie, Wabash **7** Elkhart, Ft Wayne, Hammond, LaPorte, Whiting **8** Columbus, Richmond **9** Lafayette, Mishawaka, South Bend, Vincennes **10** Evansville, Huntington, Logansport, Terre Haute **11** Bloomington, East Chicago **12** Connorsville, Michigan City
   college: 4 Ball **6** Bethel, Butler, DePauw, Goshen, Marion, Purdue, Wabash **9** Notre Dame **10** Evansville, Valparaiso
   explorer: 7 La Salle
   feature: 10 New Harmony **12** Indian mounds
      national memorial: **14** Lincoln boyhood
   tribe: 3 Wea **5** Miami **7** Shawnee
   people: 7 Hoosier **10** Cole Porter, Eugene Debs, Gus Grissom, Red Skelton **12** Wilbur Wright **15** Booth Tarkington, Theodore Dreiser **18** James Whitcomb Riley
   lake: 5 Clear, James **6** Monroe **7** Manitou, Wawasee **8** Michigan **9** Mansfield **11** Maxinkuckee
   land rank: 12 thirty-eighth
   mountain: 13 Greensfort Top
   physical feature:
      cave: **9** Wyandotte
   river: 4 Ohio **5** White **6** Maumee, Wabash **8** Kankakee **10** Tippecanoe, Whitewater
   state admission: 10 nineteenth
   state bird: 8 cardinal
   state flower: 5 peony **6** zinnia
   state motto: 19 Crossroads of America
   state song: 28 On the Banks of the Wabash Far Away
   state tree: 5 tulip **11** tulip poplar

7 bastard **8** wild blue **9** blue false **10** plains wild, white false **12** prairie false **13** fragrant false

indirect 5 vague **6** remote, zigzag **7** crooked, devious, distant, evasive, hedging, oblique, winding **8** rambling, tortuous **9** ancillary, secondary **10** circuitous, derivative, digressive, discursive, incidental, meandering, roundabout, unintended **13** unintentional

indirection 8 rambling **10** digression, meandering, zigzagging **14** circuitousness, circumlocution, roundaboutness

indiscernible 6 hidden **9** invisible **10** indistinct **12** undetectable, unnoticeable **13** imperceptible

indiscreet 6 unwise **7** foolish **8** careless, tactless, unseemly **9** foolhardy, ill-judged, impolitic, imprudent, tasteless, untactful **10** incautious **11** improvident, injudicious, thoughtless, unbefitting, uncalled-for **12** undiplomatic **13** inconsiderate, uncircumspect

indiscretion 8 rashness **10** im-

prudence **12** carelessness, heedlessness, recklessness, tactlessness **13** foolhardiness, insensitivity **15** thoughtlessness **16** irresponsibility

indiscriminate 6 motley, random **7** aimless, chaotic, jumbled, mongrel **8** confused, slapdash, unchoosy **9** haphazard, hit-or-miss **10** hodgepodge **11** promiscuous, unselective **12** disorganized, unsystematic **16** higgledy-piggledy, undistinguishing

in disorder 5 messy **6** blowsy, frowsy, mussed, sloppy, untidy **7** ruffled, rumpled, tousled, unkempt **8** uncombed **10** disarrayed, disheveled, disordered, disorderly **11** disarranged

indispensable 5 basic, vital **6** needed **7** crucial, needful **8** required **9** essential, mandatory, necessary, requisite **10** compulsory, imperative, obligatory **11** fundamental

indispensable condition
   Latin: 10 sine qua non

indispensable element
   9 basic need, essential, necessity, requisite **10** sine qua non **11** requirement

indisposed 3 ill **5** loath **6** ailing, averse, laid up, sickly, unwell **8** opposed **8** hesitant, taken ill **9** bedridden, reluctant, unwilling **10** not oneself **11** disinclined **15** under the weather

indisposition 5 upset **6** malady **7** ailment, illness **8** sickness **9** complaint, ill health

indisputable 4 sure **7** assured, certain, decided, evident, obvious **8** absolute, apparent, clear-cut, definite, positive **10** conclusive, unarguable, undeniable **11** indubitable, irrefutable **12** unassailable, unmistakable **13** incontestable **14** unquestionable **16** incontrovertible **20** beyond a shadow of doubt

indissoluble 5 fixed **7** abiding, lasting **8** constant, enduring **9** immutable, indelible, permanent, perpetual **11** everlasting **12** imperishable, ineradicable

indistinct 3 dim **4** weak **5** faint, muddy, murky, vague **6** cloudy, hidden **7** blurred, clouded, muffled, obscure, shadowy, unclear **8** confused, nebulous, puzzling **9** ambiguous, enigmatic, illegible, inaudible, uncertain **10** ill-defined, incoherent, indefinite, mysterious, out of focus **11** not distinct **13** indeterminate **14** indecipherable, unintelligible **16** incomprehensible

indistinguishable 7 obscure, unclear **9** invisible **10** indistinct, unapparent **12** unnoticeable, unobservable **13** a carbon copy of, identical with, imperceptible, inconspicuous, indiscernible

individual 6 person, unique **7** one's own, private, special, unusual **8** distinct, especial, original, personal, separate, singular, somebody, specific, uncommon **9** different, exclusive **10** particular **11** distinctive, independent **12** personalized **14** characteristic, unconventional

individuality 6 cachet **10** uniqueness **11** distinction, singularity, specialness **13** particularity **15** distinctiveness

individually 4 each **5** apart **6** apiece, singly **8** a la carte, uniquely **10** one at a time, peculiarly, personally, separately **12** respectively **13** distinctively **18** characteristically

indoctrinate 5 brief, drill, teach, train, tutor **6** infuse, school **7** educate, implant, instill **8** initiate **9** brainwash, inculcate **12** propagandize

indoctrination 5 drill **8** drilling, teaching, training **9** education, schooling **10** initiation, instilling **11** inculcation, instruction

Indo-European
language branch: 5 Greek **6** Celtic, Italic **7** Romance **8** Albanian, Armenian, Germanic **9** Anatolian, Tocharian **11** Balto-Slavic, Indo-Iranian

Indo-Iranian
language family: 12 Indo-European
ancient: 7 Avestan **8** Sanskrit **10** Old Persian
modern Iranian: 5 Indic, Tajik **6** Pashto **7** Baluchi, Kurdish, Persian
modern Indic: 4 Pali **5** Hindi, Oriya **6** Nepali, Sindhi **7** Bengali, Marathi, Panjabi **8** Assamese, Gujarati, Kashmiri **9** Sinhalese

indolence 5 sloth **7** inertia, languor, laxness **8** idleness, laziness **10** inactivity

indolent 4 lazy **5** inert, slack **7** lumpish **8** dawdling, dilatory, inactive, listless, slothful, sluggish **9** do-nothing, easygoing, lethargic, shiftless **13** lackadaisical

indomitable 6 dogged **7** doughty, staunch, valiant **8** cast-iron, fearless, intrepid, resolute, stalwart, stubborn **9** dauntless, steadfast, undaunted **10** courageous, formidable, invincible, unwavering, unyielding **11** insuperable, persevering, unflinching, unshrinking **12** invulnerable, unassailable **13** indefatigable, irrepressible, unconquerable

Indonesia *see box*

indoors 6 at home, inside, shut in, shut up, within **10** in the house **11** sequestered

Indo-Pacific
language subgroup: 4 Kate **5** Kiwai **7** Andaman, Merauke **8** Highland, Tasmania **9** Ekari-Moni, Hollandia, Timor-Alor **10** New Britain **12** Astrolabe Bay, Bougainville **14** Vogelkop-Kamoro **16** Eastern New Guinea, Northern Salomons **17** Northern Halmahera

indorse *see* **7** endorse

In Dubious Battle
author: 13 John Steinbeck

indubitable 4 sure **7** certain **9** undoubted **10** conclusive **11** irrefutable, unequivocal **12** indisputable, unmistakable **14** unquestionable **16** incontrovertible

indubitably 6 surely **7** for sure **8** of course **9** certainly, doubtless **10** for certain **11** undoubtedly **12** without doubt **14** unquestionably, with no question

induce 3 get **4** coax, spur, sway **5** cause, impel **6** arouse, effect, incite, lead to, prompt **7** actuate, bring on, dispose, incline, inspire, produce, provoke, win over **8** activate, motivate, occasion, persuade **9** encourage, influence, instigate, prevail on **10** bring about, bring round, give rise to **11** prevail upon, set in motion

inducement 4 bait, goad, spur **5** cause **6** ground, motive, reason **8** stimulus **9** incentive **10** allurement, attraction, en-

---

Indonesia
other name: 9 Nusantara **12** Tanah Airkita **21** Netherlands East Indies
capital/largest city: 7 Jakarta **8** Djakarta
others: 5 Bogor, Medan **6** Malang, Manado **7** Bandung **8** Macassar, Semarang, Surabaya **9** Hollandia, Palembang, Surakarta **10** Jogjakarta, Yogyakarta **11** Banjarmasin
measure: 5 depah, depoh
monetary unit: 3 sen **6** rupiah
weight: 5 catty, ounce, thail **6** soekoe
island: 3 Aru **4** Bali, Buru, Java **5** Ambon, Ceram, Seram, Spice, Sumba, Timor **6** Bangka, Borneo, Flores, Lombok, Madura, Tidore **7** Belawan, Celebes, Morotai, Sumatra, Sumbawa, Ternate **8** Belitung, Moluccas, Sulawesi **9** Halmahera, New Guinea **10** Kalimantan **11** Lesser Sunda **12** Greater Sunda
lake: 4 Toba **5** Ranau **6** Towuti
river: 4 Hari, Musi, Solo **5** Rokan **6** Asahan, Barito, Kampar **7** Brantas, Kaptuas **9** Indrogiri, Mamberamo, Martapura
sea: 4 Java, Savu **5** Banda, Ceram, Timor **6** Flores, Indian **7** Arafura, Celebes, Molucca, Pacific **10** Philippine, South China
physical feature:
  strait: **5** Sunda **7** Makasar, Malacca **8** Makassar
  volcano: **6** Slamet **8** Krakatoa
people: 5 Batak, Dayak, Dyaks, Malay **6** Papuan, Toraja **7** Battaks, Chinese, Igorots **8** Acehnese, Achinese, Balinese, Javanese, Madurese, Sudanese **11** Minang Kabau
  leader: **7** Suharto, Sukarno
language: 5 Tetum **6** Bahasa, Igorot **7** English, Gyarung, Malayan **8** Balinese, Chamorro, Javanese, Madurese, Sudanese **10** Indonesian, Polynesian
religion: 5 Hindu, Islam **7** animism **8** Buddhism **12** Christianity, Confucianism
place:
  palace: **6** Kraton
  pyramid: **5** Stupa **9** Borobudur
  shrine: **6** Dagoba, Kraton
feature:
  cap: **5** pitji
  cloth: **5** batik
  jacket: **6** kebaja
  lizard: **12** Komodo dragon
  scarf: **9** selendang
  shadow play: **6** wajang, wayang
  skirt: **4** kain **6** sarong
  tree: **4** supa
food:
  ceremonial dinner: **9** selamatan

ticement, incitement, persuasion, temptation
11 inspiration, instigation, provocation

induct 5 crown, draft, frock **6** enlist, invest, lead in, ordain, sign up **7** bring in, install, instate, usher in **8** enthrone, initiate, register **9** conscript, establish, introduce **10** consecrate, inaugurate

in due course 4 then **6** thence **10** eventually **11** accordingly **15** at the proper time **19** in the fullness of time

indulge 4 baby **5** favor, humor, serve, spoil, treat **6** coddle, cosset, oblige **7** appease, cater to, gratify, yield to **8** pander to **9** give way to **11** accommodate, go along with, mollycoddle

indulgence 6 excess, luxury **8** kindness, lenience, patience **9** allowance, benignity, tolerance **10** compassion, debauchery, profligacy, sufferance **11** dissipation, forbearance, forgiveness **12** extravagance, graciousness, immoderation, intemperance **13** understanding **14** permissiveness

indulgent 4 kind **6** benign, tender **7** clement, lenient, patient, sparing **8** humoring, obliging, tolerant, yielding **9** easygoing, forgiving, pampering **10** forbearing, permissive **11** complaisant, forebearing **12** conciliatory **13** understanding

industrious 4 busy **6** active **7** zealous **8** diligent, occupied, sedulous, tireless **9** assiduous, energetic **10** productive, purposeful, unflagging **11** hardworking, painstaking, persevering, unremitting **12** businesslike, enterprising **13** indefatigable

industry 2 go **4** toil, zeal **5** field, labor, trade **6** bustle, energy, hustle **8** activity, business, commerce, hard work **9** assiduity, diligence **10** enterprise **11** application, manufacture **12** perseverance, sedulousness **13** assiduousness **15** industriousness **16** indefatigability

inebriate 3 sot **4** lush, soak, wino **5** drunk, rummy, souse, toper **6** barfly, boozer **7** tippler **8** drunkard **9** alcoholic **11** dipsomaniac

inebriated 4 high **5** drunk, oiled, tight, tipsy **6** bombed, loaded, potted, stoned, tanked, zonked **7** drunken, smashed, sozzled, wrecked **8** besotted **9** befuddled, plastered **10** in one's cups **11** intoxicated **12** transcendent **13** indescribable, inexpressible **14** incommunicable, transcendental

in effect 6 active **8** a reality **9** activated, effective, operative **11** in operation

ineffective 4 vain, weak **6** futile **7** useless **8** impotent **9** fruitless, incapable, powerless, worthless **10** inadequate **11** inefficient, inoperative, not much good, of little use **12** unproductive

ineffectual 4 lame, vain, weak **5** inept **6** feeble, futile **7** hapless, useless **8** impotent **10** inadequate, not up to par, profitless, unavailing **11** incompetent, ineffective, inefficient **12** unproductive, unprofitable, unsuccessful **13** inefficacious **14** unsatisfactory

inefficient 5 inept, slack **6** futile **8** slipshod **9** pointless, unskilled **10** inadequate **11** incompetent, indifferent, ineffective, ineffectual **12** not efficient, unproductive **13** inefficacious **14** good-for-nothing

inelegance 9 crudeness, grossness, roughness, vulgarity **10** coarseness **13** tastelessness

inelegant 4 ugly **6** coarse, common **8** inferior **9** tasteless, unrefined **10** ungraceful

ineligible 5 unfit **10** unentitled, unsuitable **11** not eligible, unqualified **12** disqualified, unacceptable

ineluctable 4 sure **5** fated **7** certain **10** ineludible, inevasible, inevitable, inexorable, sure as fate, unevadable **11** inescapable, irrevocable, unavoidable, unstoppable **13** unpreventable

inept 5 empty, inane, silly, unapt **6** clumsy **7** asinine, awk-

ward, fatuous, foolish **8** bungling **9** maladroit, pointless, senseless, unfitting, unskilled, untrained **10** out of place, unsuitable **11** incompetent, ineffective, ineffectual, inefficient, nonsensical, unqualified **13** inappropriate, inefficacious

ineptitude 9 inability **10** clumsiness, inadequacy **11** awkwardness **12** incompetence **14** ineffectuality **15** ineffectiveness

inequality 8 imparity, inequity **9** disparity, diversity, prejudice **10** difference, divergence, favoritism, unfairness, unlikeness **11** inconstancy, unequalness **12** irregularity, variableness **13** disproportion, dissimilarity, dissimilitude

inequity 4 bias **9** injustice, prejudice **10** favoritism, inequality, unfairness **14** discrimination

ineradicable 7 lasting **9** indelible, permanent **10** inerasable **12** ineffaceable **14** indestructible

inert 4 dull, numb **5** slack, still **6** leaden, static, supine, torpid **7** languid, passive **8** immobile, inactive, listless, sluggish **9** impassive, inanimate, quiescent **10** motionless, phlegmatic, stationary

inertia 6 apathy, stupor, torpor **7** languor **8** dullness, inaction, laziness, lethargy **9** indolence, inertness, lassitude, passivity, torpidity, weariness **10** inactivity, supineness **11** passiveness **12** listlessness, sluggishness

inertness 6 apathy **8** lethargy **9** passivity **10** quiescence **12** sluggishness **14** motionlessness

inescapable 4 sure **7** certain, evident **8** manifest, positive **10** inevitable **11** ineluctable, predestined, unavoidable

in esse 7 in being **11** in actuality **16** actually existing

inestimable 7 sumless **8** precious **9** priceless **10** invaluable **11** beyond price, measureless **12** immeasurable, incalculable, unmeasurable

inevitable 4 sure **5** fated **7** certain **8** destined **10** ineludible **11** ineluctable, inescapable, predestined, unavoidable **13** predetermined, unpreventable

inexact 3 off **6** faulty, sloppy **8** careless, slovenly **9** defective, imperfect, imprecise **10** inaccurate, unspecific **11** approximate

in exactly the same words
Latin: **19** verbatim et literatim

inexcusable 10 unbearable **11** intolerable, unallowable **12** indefensible, unforgivable, unpardonable **13** unjustifiable

inexhaustible 7 endless **8** infinite, tireless, unending **9** boundless **13** indefatigable **15** measurelessness

in existence 5 alive **6** extant, living **8** existent, existing **9** surviving, to be found

inexorable 4 firm **5** cruel, stiff **6** dogged **7** adamant **8** obdurate, pitiless, ruthless **9** immovable, merciless, unbending **10** adamantive, determined, inflexible, relentless, unyielding **11** inescapable, intractable **12** irresistible **14** uncompromising

inexpedient 6 futile, unwise **7** useless **11** detrimental, impractical, inadvisable, injudicious, undesirable **13** not worthwhile **15** disadvantageous

inexpensive 5 cheap **8** moderate **9** low-priced **10** economical, reasonable **13** nominal-priced, popular-priced

inexpensive table wine
French: **12** vin ordinaire

inexperienced 5 fresh, green, naive **6** callow **7** untried **8** inexpert, unversed **9** unfledged, unskilled, untrained, untutored **10** unfamiliar, unschooled, unseasoned **11** uninitiated, unpracticed **12** unaccustomed, unacquainted, unconversant **15** unsophisticated

inexpert 5 inept **6** clumsy, gauche **7** awkward **8** bungling **9** incapable, maladroit **10** amateurish, unpolished, unskillful **11** incompetent, ineffective, inefficient, unqualified **14** unaccomplished

inexplicable 8 abstruse, baffling, puzzling **9** insoluble **10** insolvable, mysterious, mystifying, perplexing **11** enigmatical, inscrutable **12** unfathomable **13** unaccountable, unexplainable **14** undecipherable **16** incomprehensible

inexpressive 5 blank, empty **6** vacant **14** expressionless

in extenso 12 at full length

in extremis 9 near death **11** in extremity **15** on the outer edges **19** at the uttermost limit

in extremity
Latin: **10** in extremis

in fact
Latin: **7** de facto

infallible 4 sure **7** assured, certain, perfect **8** flawless, inerrant, positive, reliable, surefire, unerring **9** apodictic, faultless, foolproof, unfailing **10** dependable, impeccable **11** irrefutable **13** unimpeachable **16** incontrovertible

infamous 3 low **4** base, evil, foul, vile **6** odious, sinful, sordid, wicked **7** corrupt, heinous, ignoble, immoral, knavish **8** damnable, recreant, shameful **9** abhorrent, monstrous, nefarious, notorious **10** abominable, detestable, iniquitous, of evil fame, outrageous, perfidious, profligate, scandalous, scurrilous, villainous **11** disgraceful, of ill repute, opprobrious, treacherous **12** dishonorable, disreputable

infamy 4 evil **5** odium, shame **7** scandal **8** contempt, disgrace, dishonor, ignominy, villainy **9** discredit, disesteem, disrepute, notoriety **10** corruption, opprobrium, wickedness **11** abomination **13** despicability, notoriousness

infancy 6 cradle, nonage **8** babyhood, minority **9** beginning, childhood, inception **10** immaturity

infant 3 kid **4** babe, baby **5** child **7** neonate, newborn, toddler **8** nursling, suckling

infantile 7 babyish **8** childish, juvenile **9** childlike, infantine **10** infantlike, sophomoric

infantryman 6 Zouave **7** dogface, dragoon **8** chasseur, doughboy, sorefoot **11** foot soldier

infatuated 7 charmed, smitten **8** beguiled, enamored, inflamed, obsessed **9** bewitched, enchanted, entranced **10** captivated, enraptured, enthralled, spellbound **11** carried away, intoxicated **12** having a crush

infatuation 4 rave **5** craze, crush, folly, mania **6** desire **7** passion **9** obsession, puppy love **10** enthusiasm **11** fascination, foolishness **12** passing fancy

infect 4 ruin **5** spoil, taint, touch **6** blight, damage, poison **7** afflict, corrupt **9** indispose, influence **11** contaminate

infected 6 impure, morbid, septic **7** corrupt, tainted **8** cankered, diseased, poisoned **12** contaminated

infection 6 blight **7** disease **9** contagion, virulence **11** suppuration

infectious 8 catching, epidemic, virulent **9** catchable, infective, spreading **10** compelling, contagious, inoculable **11** captivating **12** communicable, irresistible

infecund 6 barren, farrow **7** sterile **9** infertile **12** unproductive

infer 4 deem **5** glean, guess, judge, opine **6** deduce, gather, reason, reckon **7** presume, suppose, surmise **8** conclude **9** speculate **10** conjecture

inference 4 clue **10** intimation, suggestion **11** insinuation

inferior 4 poor **6** junior **8** low-grade, mediocre **9** secondary **10** low-quality, second-rate, subsidiary **11** indifferent, subordinate, subservient, substandard **12** not up to snuff

infernal 4 vile **5** awful, black, lower **6** cursed, Hadean, nether **7** heinous, hellish, Stygian, vicious **8** accursed, damnable, devilish, fiendish, horrible, terrible **9** atrocious, execrable, malicious, monstrous, nefarious, Plutonian **10** abominable, demoniacal, diabolical, flagitious, horrendous, iniquitous
also: **9** Tartarean
refers to: **10** underworld

inferno 4 hell, oven **5** abyss, Hades **6** hotbox, the pit, Tophet **7** furnace, roaster, sizzler **8** hellfire, hellhole, scorcher **9** perdition **10** lower world, underworld **11** netherworld **12** fiery furnace **13** nether regions **15** infernal regions **16** fire and brimstone, the bottomless pit

Inferno
part I of: **12** Divine Comedy
author: **14** Dante Alighieri

infertile 4 arid, bare **6** barren, effete, fallow **7** drained, sterile **8** depleted, desolate, impotent, infecund **9** exhausted, fruitless **10** unfruitful, unprolific **12** unproductive **13** nonproductive

infest 4 team **5** beset, crawl, creep, swarm **6** abound, infect, plague, ravage **7** overrun, torment **9** crawl with, swarm with

infestation 6 plague, ravage **9** lousiness, pervasion **11** overrunning **12** overswarming

in few words
Latin: **12** paucis verbis

infidel 5 pagan **6** savage **7** atheist, heathen, heretic, skeptic **8** agnostic, apostate, idolater **9** barbarian **10** unbeliever **11** nonbeliever

infidelity 6 breach **7** falsity, perfidy **8** adultery, betrayal **9** disregard, violation **10** disloyalty, infraction **12** nonadherence **13** nonobservance, transgression **14** unfaithfulness

infiltrate 4 leak, seep **5** imbue, steep **6** absorb, seep in **7** pervade **8** colonize, permeate **9** insinuate, penetrate

infinite 4 vast **5** great **7** endless, immense **8** enormous **9** boundless, limitless, unbounded, unlimited **10** tremendous, without end **11** illimitable, measureless **12** immeasurable, incalculable, interminable **13** inexhaustible **15** uncircumscribed

infinitesimal 3 wee **4** puny, tiny **6** minute **10** diminutive, negligible **11** microscopic **13** imperceptible, inappreciable, insignificant, undiscernible **14** extremely small, inconsiderable

infinity 7 forever **8** eternity **10** infinitude, perpetuity **11** endlessness, eternal time **12** sempiternity **13** boundlessness, limitlessness **14** illimitability **15** everlastingness, immeasurability, incalculability, measurelessness **16** inexhaustibility **19** incomprehensibility

Infiri
gods of: **10** underworld

infirm 3 ill **4** weak, worn **5** anile, frail, shaky **6** ailing, feeble, poorly, sickly **7** failing, fragile, unsound **8** decrepit, disabled, helpless, unstable, weakened **9** doddering, emaciated, enervated, enfeebled,

powerless **11** debilitated **12** strengthless

infirmary 6 clinic **7** sick bay **8** hospital

infirmity 4 flaw **5** fault **6** defect, malady **7** ailment, failing, frailty, illness **8** debility, disorder, handicap, sickness **9** fragility, frailness **10** deficiency, disability, infirmness **11** instability **12** debilitation, imperfection, unstableness **13** indisposition, vulnerability

in flagrante delicto 14 in blazing crime **22** in the heat of the evil deed

inflame 4 fire, rile **5** craze, rouse **6** arouse, enrage, excite, heat up, ignite, incite, kindle, madden, stir up, work up **7** agitate, incense, provoke **8** enkindle **9** electrify, stimulate **10** intoxicate

inflamed 3 mad **5** angry, irate, riled **6** crazed, fuming, roused **7** aroused, enraged, excited, fired up, furious, incited **8** agitated, incensed, provoked, reddened **9** steamed up, stirred up **10** infuriated **11** intensified

inflame with love 6 enamor **9** enrapture, impassion, infatuate

inflammable 5 fiery **8** choleric, volatile **9** excitable, flammable, ignitable, impetuous, overhasty, sensitive **10** high-strung, incendiary **11** combustible, precipitate **12** inflammatory

inflammation 4 acne, fire, gout, sore **6** canker, firing **7** arousal, chafing **8** bursitis, ignition, kindling, soreness, sore spot, swelling **9** agitation **10** incitement, irritation **13** conflagration, rabblerousing
suffix: **4** itis

inflammatory 5 fiery, rabid **8** arousing, enraging, inciting, mutinous, volcanic **9** demagogic, explosive, insurgent **10** incendiary, rebellious **11** combustible, fulminating, inflammable, intemperate, provocative **13** rabble-rousing, revolutionary

inflate 5 bloat, swell **6** blow up, dilate, expand, fill up, pump up **7** distend, improve, puff out **10** appreciate **11** rise in value

inflated 5 blown, gassy, tumid, wordy **6** blew up, turgid **7** bloated, blown up, dilated, flowery, pompous, swollen,

verbose **8** boastful, enlarged, expanded **9** bombastic, distended, overblown, swelled up **10** rhetorical, swelled out **11** exaggerated, pretentious

inflection 4 tone **5** tenor **6** accent **10** modulation **11** enunciation, tone of voice **12** articulation **13** pronunciation

inflexible 4 firm, hard, taut **5** fixed, rigid, solid, stiff **6** dogged, mulish **7** adamant **8** obdurate, resolute, stubborn **9** hidebound, immovable, immutable, ironbound, obstinate, pigheaded, stringent, tenacious, unbending, unplastic **10** adamantine, determined, headstrong, impervious, implacable, inexorable, unwavering, unyielding **11** hard and fast, intractable, not flexible, unmalleable **12** unchangeable **14** uncompromising

inflict 4 dump **5** lay on, wreak **6** impose, unload **7** put upon **9** visit upon **10** administer, perpetrate **11** bring to bear

inflorescence 5 bloom **6** flower **7** blossom, cluster **8** blooming **9** flowering **10** blossoming
type: **4** cyme **5** spike, umbel **6** corymb, raceme, spadix **7** panicle **9** capitulum **14** verticillaster

influence 4 hold, move, pull, stir, sway **5** clout, guide, impel, power **6** arouse, effect, incite, induce, prompt, weight **7** act upon, actuate, control, dispose, incline, inspire, mastery, potency, provoke **8** dominion, leverage, persuade, pressure, prestige **9** advantage, authority **10** ascendancy, domination, predispose

influential 6 moving, potent, strong **7** leading, weighty **8** forceful, powerful, puissant **9** effective, effectual, important, inspiring, momentous **10** activating **11** efficacious, significant **12** instrumental **13** consequential

influx 5 entry **6** inflow **7** arrival, indraft, ingress **9** flowing in, incursion, inpouring **10** converging, inundation **12** infiltration

in force 6 extant **7** en masse **8** in effect **9** effective, operative **11** in existence, in operation, operational **14** in large numbers

inform 3 rat **4** fink, tell **5** edify **6** advise, clue in, notify, snitch, squeal, tattle, tell on, tip off **7** apprise, let know **8** acquaint, denounce, forewarn, report to **9** declare to, enlighten **11** communicate, familiarize, serve notice **14** blow the whistle

inform against 5 rat on **6** betray, fink on, tell on **7** sell out **8** denounce, squeal on **11** double-cross **16** blow the whistle on

informal 4 easy **6** casual, simple **7** natural, offhand **8** familiar **9** easygoing, not formal **10** unofficial **11** spontaneous **12** come-as-you-are **13** unceremonious, unconstrained **14** unconventional

informal preliminary conference
French: **10** pourparler

informant 6 source **7** adviser, tipster **8** appriser, informer, notifier, reporter **9** announcer, spokesman **10** respondent **11** enlightener, horse's mouth, spokeswoman

information 4 data, news **5** facts, notes **6** notice, papers, report **7** account, tidings **8** briefing, bulletin, evidence, material **9** documents, knowledge, materials **10** communique **11** fact-finding **12** announcement, intelligence, notification **13** enlightenment

informed 4 told, up on, wise **5** aware, posted, talked, taught, warned **7** abreast, advised, knowing, learned, tattled **8** apprised, betrayed, educated, notified, reported, snitched, up to date **9** au courant, permeated **10** acquainted, instructed **11** enlightened, intelligent **13** knowledgeable

informer 3 rat **4** fink **5** Judas **6** canary **7** blabber, stoolie, tattler, traitor **8** betrayer, mouchard, snitcher, squealer **11** stool pigeon

Informer, The
author: **13** Liam O'Flaherty
director: **8** John Ford
cast: **10** Una O'Connor **11** Wallace Ford **12** Heather Angel **13** Margot Grahame, Preston Foster **14** Victor McLaglen
score: **10** Max Steiner
remade as: **7** Up Tight

infraction 6 breach **8** trespass **9** violation **10** peccadillo **11** lawbreaking **12** disobedience, encroachment, infringe-ment, unobservance **13** nonobservance, transgression

infrastructure 4 base, root **5** basis **6** bottom, fabric, ground **7** bedrock, footing, support **9** framework, substrate **10** foundation, groundwork, substratum **12** substructure, underpinning **14** understructure

infrequent 3 few **4** rare **6** fitful, seldom, unique **7** unusual **8** sporadic, uncommon **9** spasmodic **10** occasional **16** few and far between

infringe 5 break **6** butt in, invade **7** disobey, impinge, infract, intrude, violate **8** encroach, overstep, trespass **10** contravene, transgress

in front 5 ahead, first **6** before **7** forward

in full possession of one's faculties
Latin: **12** compos mentis

infuriate 3 vex **4** gall, rile **5** anger, chafe **6** enrage, madden, offend **7** incense, inflame, outrage, provoke **8** irritate **9** aggravate, burn one up, make angry **10** exasperate **15** raise one's dander

infuriating 7 irksome **8** annoying, enraging **9** maddening, provoking **10** irritating **11** aggravating **12** exasperating, inflammatory

infuse 5 imbue **7** fortify, implant, inspire, instill **8** impart to, pour into **9** inculcate, insinuate, introject

in futuro 11 in the future

Inge, William
author of: **6** Picnic **7** Bus Stop **19** Come Back Little Sheba **26** The Dark at the Top of the Stairs

in general 7 as a rule, usually **10** by and large, on the whole

ingenious 4 deft **6** adroit, artful, clever, crafty, expert, shrewd **7** cunning **8** masterly, original, skillful, stunning **9** brilliant, dexterous, inventive, masterful **11** resourceful

ingenuity 5 flair, skill **7** cunning, know-how, mastery **8** aptitude, deftness, facility **9** adeptness, dexterity, expertise, sharpness **10** adroitness, astuteness, brilliance, cleverness, shrewdness **11** imagination **12** good thinking, skillfulness **13** ingeniousness, inventiveness **15** imaginative-ness, quick-wittedness, resourcefulness

ingenuous 4 open **5** frank, naive **6** direct, honest **7** artless, genuine, natural, up front **8** trusting **9** guileless **10** unaffected **11** openhearted **13** simplehearted **15** straightforward, unsophisticated **16** straightshooting

ingenuousness 7 naivete **8** openness **9** frankness **11** artlessness

ingest 3 eat **4** gulp, take **5** drink **6** absorb, devour, imbibe, take in **7** consume, swallow **8** gulp down

inglorious 3 low **4** base, evil, mean, vile **6** odious **7** corrupt, heinous, ignoble **8** depraved, flagrant, infamous, shameful, shocking **9** atrocious, degrading, nefarious **10** despicable, detestable, outrageous, scandalous **11** disgraceful, ignominious, opprobrious **12** contemptible, dishonorable

in good condition
French: **10** embonpoint

in good health 2 OK **4** fine, hale, well **6** hearty, robust, tiptop **7** healthy **8** all right, blooming, vigorous **9** full of pep, in the pink **17** full of vim and vigor

in good time 5 early **7** betimes **11** ahead of time

ingot 3 bar **5** block

ingrained 4 deep, firm **5** fixed **6** inborn, inbred, innate, rooted **8** inherent, thorough **9** confirmed, implanted, indelible, intrinsic **10** deep-rooted, deep-seated, inveterate **14** constitutional

Ingram, Blanche
character in: **8** Jane Eyre
author: **6** Bronte

ingratiating 4 oily **5** sweet **6** genial, smarmy **7** affable, amiable, cordial, fulsome, gushing, likable, lovable, winning, winsome **8** charming, engaging, friendly, gracious, magnetic, pleasing, unctuous **9** appealing, congenial **10** attractive, enchanting, obsequious, oleaginous, personable, persuasive **11** captivating, good-humored, self-serving **12** presumptuous

ingratiation 7 blarney **8** flattery **9** sweet talk **12** inveiglement **13** blandishments

ingratitude 14 ungratefulness **18** lack of appreciation

ingredient 4 part **6** aspect, factor **7** element, feature **9** component, essential, principle **11** constituent, contributor **12** integral part

Ingres, Jean-Auguste-Dominique
born: **6** France **9** Montauban
artwork: **9** Odalisque, The Source **13** Mme Moitessier **14** The Turkish Bath **15** Valpincon Bather **16** Roger and Angelica **17** The Vow of Louis XIII **21** Comtesse d'Haussonville **25** The Ambassadors of Agamemnon **26** The Vow of Louis the Thirteenth

ingress 5 entry, way in **6** access **8** entrance

inhabit 5 lodge **6** live in, occupy, people, settle, tenant **7** dwell in **8** populate, reside in

inhabitant 6 inmate, lessee, lodger, native, renter, tenant **7** boarder, citizen, denizen, dweller, settler **8** occupant, occupier, resident, villager **9** inhabiter

inhalation 4 gasp **5** sniff **6** breath **11** breathing in

inhale 5 sniff, snuff **6** suck in **7** inspire, respire **9** breathe in, inbreathe

inherent 6 inborn, inbred, innate, native **7** natural **9** essential, ingrained, intrinsic **10** deep-rooted, hereditary, inveterate **11** inalienable, inseparable **14** constitutional

inherit 3 get **6** be left, come by **7** acquire **8** come into **9** come in for **10** fall heir to

inheritance 6 devise, estate, legacy **7** bequest **8** bestowal, heritage **9** endowment, patrimony **10** bequeathal, birthright

inherited 8 came into, heirloom, unearned **10** handed down

inheritor 4 heir **7** legatee **11** beneficiary

Inherit the Wind
director: **13** Stanley Kramer
based on play by: **10** Robert E Lee **14** Jerome Lawrence
cast: **8** Dick York **9** Gene Kelly **10** Elliot Reid **11** Harry Morgan **12** Spencer Tracy (Clarence Darrow) **13** Frederic March (William Jennings Bryan) **16** Florence Eldridge

inhibit 3 bar, gag **4** curb, stop **5** block, check **6** arrest, enjoin, forbid, hinder, impede, muzzle **7** control, harness, prevent, repress, smother **8** hold back, obstruct, prohibit, restrain, restrict, suppress **9** constrain **11** hold in leash

inhibited 4 cold **6** barred, curbed, frigid **7** bridled, checked, guarded **8** hindered, reserved **9** repressed **10** controlled, obstructed, restrained **11** constrained, discouraged, held in check **12** unresponsive **14** under restraint

inhibition, inhibitions 5 check **7** reserve **8** blockage **9** misgiving, restraint, stricture **10** constraint, impediment **11** guardedness, mental block, obstruction, restriction **12** constriction **17** self-consciousness

in high spirits 2 up **3** gay **5** happy, merry **6** elated, jaunty, joyful, joyous **7** buoyant **8** carefree, ecstatic, exultant, jubilant **9** overjoyed **11** exhilarated, on cloud nine **13** up in the clouds **15** on top of the world

in hoc signo vinces 26 in this sign shalt thou conquer
motto of: **19** Constantine the Great
from vision of: **5** cross

inhospitable 4 cold, cool, rude **5** aloof **6** unkind **7** distant, hostile **8** impolite **10** unfriendly, ungracious, unobliging, unsociable **11** standoffish, uncongenial, unreceptive, unwelcoming **12** discourteous, unneighborly **13** inconsiderate **14** unapproachable **15** unaccommodating

inhuman 5 cruel **6** brutal, savage **7** brutish, satanic, vicious **8** barbaric, demoniac, fiendish, pitiless, ruthless, venomous **9** barbarous, heartless, malignant, merciless, monstrous, unfeeling **10** diabolical, malevolent **11** coldhearted, coldblooded, hardhearted

inhumane 6 brutal, savage **7** inhuman **8** fiendish, pitiless, ruthless **9** barbarous, heartless, merciless, unfeeling, unpitying **10** unmerciful **11** coldblooded, hardhearted **12** bloodthirsty **13** unsympathetic

inhumanity 6 sadism **7** cruelty **8** atrocity, savagery **9** barbarism, barbarity, brutality **11** brutishness, heinousness, malevolence, viciousness **12** fiendishness, ruthlessness **13** heartlessness, mercilessness **15** cold-bloodedness **16** bloodthirstiness

inhumation 6 burial **9** interment **10** entombment

inimical 5 toxic **6** at odds **7** harmful, hateful, hostile, hurtful, ruinous **8** venomous, virulent **9** dangerous, ill-willed, injurious, on the outs, poisonous, rancorous **10** unfriendly **11** acrimonious, deleterious, destructive, detrimental, ill-disposed **12** antagonistic, antipathetic, disputatious **13** at loggerheads, at sword's point

inimitable 4 rare **6** unique **7** supreme **8** peerless **9** matchless, nonpareil, unequaled, unmatched, unrivaled **10** consummate, preeminent, unexcelled **11** superlative, unsurpassed **12** incomparable, unparalleled **13** beyond compare

iniquitous 4 base, evil, vile **6** sinful, wicked **7** corrupt, debased, immoral, vicious **8** depraved, infamous **9** nefarious **10** evil-minded **12** blackhearted **13** reprehensible

iniquity 3 sin **4** evil, vice **5** wrong **6** infamy **7** knavery, outrage, roguery **8** inequity, villainy **9** depravity, evildoing, flagrancy, turpitude **10** corruption, dishonesty, immorality, miscreancy, profligacy, sinfulness, unfairness, unjustness, wickedness, wrongdoing **11** abomination **13** transgression **14** gross injustice **15** unrighteousness

in isolation
Latin: **7** in vacuo

initial 5 first **6** maiden, primal **7** opening, primary **8** germinal, original, starting **9** beginning, inaugural, incipient **10** commencing, initiatory **12** introductory

initiate 4 haze, open **5** begin, found, set up, start **6** induct, invest, launch, take in **7** bring in, install, kick off, receive, usher in **8** be opened, commence, get going, set afoot, set going **9** enter upon, establish, institute, introduce, originate **10** inaugurate, lead the way **11** break ground, get under way, take the lead **12** acquaint with **13** blaze the trail **15** familiarize with **16** lay the first stone, lay the foundation **19** start the ball rolling

initiation 5 onset, start **6** outset **7** genesis, opening **8** entrance, guidance, outbreak, starting **9** beginning, inception, induction **10** admittance, initiating, ushering in **11** inculcation **12** commencement, inauguration, introduction **14** indoctrination **15** formal admission

initiative 4 lead **8** dynamism **9** first move, first step **10** creativity, enterprise, get-up-and-go, leadership **11** originality **12** forcefulness **14** aggressiveness

in its original place
Latin: **6** in situ

inject 3 put **4** pump **5** force, imbue, infix **6** infuse, insert **7** instill, throw in **8** intromit **9** interject, introduce **11** interpolate

injection 4 hypo, shot **7** booster, vaccine **9** antitoxin, insertion **10** hypodermic **11** inoculation, vaccination **12** shot in the arm

injudicious 4 dumb, wild **5** crazy **6** stupid, unwise **7** foolish, unsound **8** heedless, reckless **9** audacious, foolhardy, hotheaded, imprudent, senseless **10** self-willed, unsuitable **11** inadvisable

injunction 4 writ **5** edict, order **7** command **10** admonition, court order

Injun Joe
character in: **9** Tom Sawyer
author: **9** Mark Twain

injure 3 mar **4** harm, hurt, lame, maim **5** abuse, spoil, stain, sting, sully, wound, wrong **6** bruise, damage, debase, deface, deform, impair, malign, mangle, misuse, offend, scathe **7** afflict, affront, blemish, violate, vitiate **8** do harm to, ill-treat, lacerate, maltreat, mutilate **9** disfigure

injured 4 hurt, lame **6** abused, harmed, maimed, marred, piqued **7** bruised, damaged, defaced, grieved, scathed, wounded, wronged **8** crippled, deformed, impaired, insulted, offended **9** afflicted, affronted, aggrieved **10** disfigured

injurious 7 abusive, adverse, harmful, hurtful, noxious, ruinous **8** damaging, inimical **9** corrosive **10** calamitous, disastrous, pernicious **11** deleterious, destructive, detrimental

injury 3 cut **4** blow, gash, harm, hurt, stab **5** abuse, wound **6** bruise, damage, lesion **7** affront, outrage, scratch **9** aspersion, contusion, indignity, injustice **10** afflic-

tion, defamation, detraction, disservice, impairment, laceration, mutilation **12** vilification

injustice 3 sin **4** bias, evil **5** wrong **6** injury **7** bigotry, offense, tyranny **8** foul play, inequity, iniquity **9** prejudice, unjust act **10** disservice, favoritism, inequality, infraction, partiality, unfairness, unjustness, wrongdoing **11** malpractice, persecution **12** encroachment, infringement, partisanship **13** transgression

in keeping 6 normal **7** natural **8** becoming **9** congruous, consonant **10** consistent **11** appropriate, in agreement **12** in compliance, in conformity

inkling 3 cue, tip **4** clue, hint, idea **6** notion **7** glimmer, whisper **8** innuendo **9** suspicion, vague idea **10** conception, glimmering, indication, intimation, suggestion **11** insinuation, supposition

inky 3 jet **4** dark **5** black, raven, sable **7** stygian **9** coal-black

inlet 3 bay **4** cove, gulf **5** bight, fiord, firth, fjord **6** harbor, strait **7** estuary, narrows **8** waterway

in line 4 even **6** in a row **7** aligned, in order **8** queued up, straight **12** under control

in loco 7 in place **16** in the proper place

in loco parentis 16 replacing a parent **19** in the place of a parent

inmate 3 con **5** felon **6** lodger, tenant **7** convict, denizen **8** prisoner, resident **10** inhabitant

in medias res 19 in the middle of things **21** in the middle of the story

in memoriam 10 in memory of **13** as a memorial to, to the memory of

In Memoriam A H H
author: **18** Alfred Lord Tennyson

in memory of
Latin: **10** in memoriam

In Memory of W B Yeats
author: **7** W H Auden

inmost 5 inner **6** inside **7** central **8** interior **9** innermost

in motion 5 afoot, astir **6** active, moving **7** on the go, working **8** under way **9** on the

move, operating, operative **10** responsive

In My Father's Court
author: **19** Isaac Bashevis Singer

inn 5 hotel, lodge, motel **6** hostel, tavern **7** hospice, pension **8** hostelry **9** roadhouse **11** caravansary, public house
French: **7** auberge
Spanish: **6** posada

innards 4 guts **6** bowels, vitals **7** gizzard, insides, viscera **10** intestines **14** liver and lights

innate 6 inborn, inbred, native **7** natural **8** inherent **9** essential, ingrained, inherited, intrinsic, intuitive **10** congenital, hereditary, indigenous **11** instinctive **14** constitutional

inner 6 hidden, inside, inward, mental, middle **7** central, private, psychic **8** esoteric, interior, internal **9** concealed, emotional, spiritual, unobvious **10** more secret **12** more intimate **13** psychological

inner circle 4 core **5** bosom, heart **6** center **7** nucleus

inner city 8 core city, downtown **9** urban area **10** city limits, metropolis **11** central city **16** metropolitan area

Inner Mongolia
other name: **9** Neimenggu, Neimengku
capital: **6** Hohhot **7** Huhehot
desert: **4** Gobi
tent: **4** yurt

innermost 6 inmost, secret **7** deepest **10** deep-rooted, deep-seated **11** most private **12** most intimate, most personal

innermost part 4 core, crux, pith, soul **6** center, kernel **7** essence, nucleus

Inness, George
born: **10** Newburgh NY
artwork: **7** The Monk **14** Home of the Heron, Peace and Plenty **16** Delaware Water Gap **17** The Delaware Valley **19** The Lackawanna Valley

Innisfail see **7** Ireland

innkeeper 4 host **6** tapper, venter **7** padrone **8** boniface, hosteler, hotelier, landlord, publican **10** proprietor **12** maitre d'hotel, restaurateur

innocence 6 purity **7** naivete **8** chastity **9** freshness **10** clean hands, simplicity **11** artlessness, sinlessness **12** incorrup-

tion, spotlessness
13 blamelessness, guilelessness, guiltlessness, impeccability, inculpability, ingenuousness, stainlessness
14 immaculateness

innocent 3 tot **4** baby, naif, open, pure, tyro **5** clean, naive **6** chaste, honest, novice, simple **7** artless, ingenue, sinless, upright **8** harmless, pristine, spotless, virginal, virtuous **9** blameless, childlike, faultless, greenhorn, guileless, guiltless, ingenuous, innocuous, little one, stainless, uncorrupt, undefiled, unstained, unsullied, unworldly, well-meant **10** artless one, immaculate, impeccable, inculpable, tenderfoot, young child **11** inoffensive, unblemished, uncorrupted, unmalicious, unoffending **12** unsuspicious **13** meaning no harm, unimpeachable **14** above suspicion, irreproachable
15 unsophisticated
Latin: **12** integer vitae

Innocents, The
director: **11** Jack Clayton
based on story by: **10** Henry James (The Turn of the Screw)
cast: **11** Deborah Kerr, Megs Jenkins **13** Peter Wyngarde **15** Michael Redgrave
script: **12** Truman Capote **16** William Archibald

Innocents Abroad, The
author: **9** Mark Twain (Samuel Clemens)

innocuous 4 dull, mild **5** banal, empty, trite, vapid **6** barren **7** insipid **8** harmless, innocent, painless **9** pointless **11** commonplace, inoffensive, meaningless

innocuousness 6 safety **9** blandness, innocence **12** harmlessness **15** inoffensiveness

in no uncertain terms
7 clearly, plainly **9** expressly **10** definitely, distinctly **13** categorically, unequivocally

innovation 5 shift **7** novelty **8** updating **10** alteration, dernier cri, new measure, remodeling, renovation **11** institution, latest thing **12** commencement, inauguration, introduction, streamlining **13** modernization

innovator 7 deviser, planner **9** contriver **10** instigator, originator **11** inaugurator

Innu see **17** Montagnais-Naskapi

innuendo 4 hint **7** whisper **8** overtone **9** inference **10** imputation, intimation **11** implication, insinuation

innumerable 6 myriad **8** numerous **9** countless **10** numberless, unnumbered **12** incalculable **13** multitudinous

Ino
also: **9** Leucothea
goddess of: **3** sea
father: **6** Cadmus
mother: **8** Harmonia
sister: **5** Hgave **6** Semele **7** Autonoe
husband: **7** Athamas
son: **8** Learchus **10** Melicertes
stepson: **7** Phrixus
stepdaughter: **5** Helle
saved: **8** Odysseus
cared for infant: **8** Dionysus
changed into: **10** sea goddess

inoculate 5 imbue, shoot **6** infuse, inject, insert **7** implant, instill **8** immunize **9** inculcate, vaccinate

inoculation 4 shot **6** needle **7** booster **9** injection **10** hypodermic **11** vaccination **12** immunization

inoffensive 4 mild, safe **5** bland **7** neutral **8** harmless, innocent **9** endurable, innocuous, tolerable **10** sufferable **11** unoffending **15** unobjectionable

inoffensiveness 6 safety **9** innocence **10** neutrality **12** harmlessness **13** innocuousness

in one's debt 7 obliged **8** beholden, indebted **9** obligated **15** under obligation

in one's own person
Latin: **16** in propria persona

in one's own place
Latin: **7** suo loco

in one's own right
Latin: **7** suo jure

in one's rightful place
Latin: **7** suo loco

inoperable 6 broken **10** broken down, unworkable **11** ineffective

in operation 5 in use **7** in force, working **8** in effect **9** operating, operative

inoperative 4 dead, down **8** inactive **10** not working, out of order

inopportune 7 awkward **8** ill-timed, untimely **10** badly timed, ill-advised, unsuitable **11** troublesome, undesirable, unfavorable, unfortunate

12 inauspicious, incommodious, inconvenient, unpropitious, unseasonable **13** inappropriate **15** disadvantageous

in order 2 OK **4** neat, tidy **6** proper **7** correct, perfect **8** all right

inordinate 5 undue **6** lavish, wanton **7** extreme, profuse, surplus **8** needless, overmuch, shocking **9** excessive **10** deplorable, exorbitant, immoderate, irrational, outrageous, scandalous **11** disgraceful, extravagant, intemperate, overflowing, superfluous, uncalled-for, unnecessary **12** unreasonable, unrestrained **13** superabundant **14** supersaturated, unconscionable **16** disproportionate

inordinately 6 overly, unduly **9** extremely **11** excessively **12** immoderately, outrageously, prodigiously **13** extravagantly, intemperately, superfluously, unnecessarily

inorganic 4 dead **7** mineral **8** lifeless **9** inanimate, nonliving **10** artificial

in passing
French: **9** en passant

in perpetuum 7 forever

in petto 11 in the breast **12** not disclosed

in pieces 6 broken **7** asunder, smashed **8** in shreds, sundered **9** torn apart **13** in smithereens

in place
Latin: **6** in loco, in situ

in plain sight 7 exposed, obvious **10** in full view, noticeable **12** out in the open **17** in front of one's nose

in posse 11 potentially **13** in possibility

in possibility
Latin: **7** in posse

In Praise of Darkness
author: **15** Jorge Luis Borges

in propria persona 15 in one's own person

inquest 5 probe **7** autopsy, delving, hearing, inquiry, probing **8** necropsy **10** postmortem **11** inquisition **13** investigation

inquire 3 ask **5** probe, query, study **6** search **7** examine, explore, inspect **8** check out, look into, look over, question **9** track down **10** look deeper, scrutinize **11** investigate

inquirer 5 asker, snoop **6** seeker **7** auditor, querier, quizzer, student **8** pollster, searcher **9** catechist **10** inquisitor, questioner **12** interlocutor, interrogator, investigator

inquiry, enquiry 4 hunt, quiz **5** probe, query, quest, study **6** search, survey **7** inquest **8** analysis, question, research, scrutiny **9** interview **10** inspection **11** examination, exploration, inquisition, questioning **13** interrogation, investigation

inquisitive 4 nosy **6** prying, snoopy **8** meddling, snooping **9** inquiring, intrusive, searching **10** meddlesome, too curious **11** interfering, overcurious, questioning

in re 13 in the matter of

in reality
   Latin: **7** de facto

in rem 15 against the thing of a legal proceeding: **18** against the property

in rerum natura 19 in the nature of things

in retreat 10 backing off, retreating **11** withdrawing, backing away

in reverse 8 backward **9** backing up **22** in the opposite direction

insalubrious 7 harmful, noisome, noxious **8** inimical, virulent **9** injurious, unhealthy **10** pernicious **11** deleterious, detrimental, unhealthful, unwholesome

insane 3 mad **4** bats, daft, dumb, loco, nuts, wild, zany **5** balmy, batty, crazy, loony, manic, nutty, potty **6** absurd, crazed, raving **7** berserk, bizarre, bonkers, cracked, foolish, idiotic, lunatic, tetched, touched, unsound **8** demented, frenzied, maniacal, unhinged **9** eccentric, imbecilic, imprudent, insensate, paranoiac, psychotic, senseless **10** ridiculous, unbalanced **11** injudicious **12** mad as a hatter, off one's chump, round the bend, unreasonable **13** off one's rocker, out of one's head, out of one's mind, out of one's wits, schizophrenic **15** bats in the belfry, mad as a March hare, stark staring mad **17** nutty as a fruitcake

insanity 5 folly, mania **6** idiocy, lunacy, raving **7** madness **8** dementia, paranoia **9** aberrance, absurdity, craziness, monomania, psychosis, stupidity **10** aberration **11** derangement, foolishness, unsoundness **12** loss of reason **13** hallucination, mental illness, schizophrenia, senselessness

insatiable 8 ravenous **9** insatiate, limitless, voracious **10** bottomless, gluttonous, implacable, omnivorous **12** unappeasable, unquenchable

inscribe 3 pen **4** etch, mark, seal, sign **5** blaze, brand, carve, write **6** chisel, incise, letter, scrawl **7** engrave, impress, imprint **8** scribble **9** autograph

inscription 5 motto, title **6** legend, rubric **7** address, caption, epigram, epitaph, heading, titulus, writing **8** colophon, epigraph, graffiti **9** engraving, lettering **10** dedication

inscrutable 6 arcane, hidden, masked, veiled **7** deadpan, elusive **8** baffling, puzzling **9** concealed, enigmatic **10** mysterious, mystifying, perplexing, poker-faced, unknowable, unreadable, unrevealed **12** inexplicable, unfathomable, unsearchable **14** indecipherable, unintelligible **16** incomprehensible

In Search of Identity
   author: **12** Anwar el-Sadat

insect 3 ant, bee, bug, fly **4** flea, gnat, moth, pest, wasp **5** aphid, imago **6** bedbug, beetle, cicada, earwig, hornet, mantis, mayfly, vermin **7** chigger, cricket, firefly, katydid, ladybug, termite **8** horsefly, housefly, lacewing, mosquito **9** arthropod, butterfly, cockroach, dragonfly **10** silverfish **11** grasshopper
   study of: 10 entomology
   young: 4 grub, pupa **5** larva, nymph **6** larvae, maggot **9** chrysalis **11** caterpillar
   anatomy: 4 palp **5** cerci, notum **6** cercus, feeler, labium, labrum, ocelli, thorax **7** antenna, maxilla, ocellus **8** antennae, mandible, maxillae **9** proboscis, spiracles **10** ovipositor **11** exoskeleton

insectivore 4 mole **5** shrew **6** desman, tenrec **7** moon rat **8** alamiqui, anteater, hedgehog **9** solenodon

insecure 4 weak **5** frail, risky, shaky **6** infirm, unsafe, unsure, wobbly **7** dubious, exposed, not firm, not sure, rickety, unsound **8** critical, doubtful, in danger, perilous, unstable, unsteady **9** dangerous, diffident, hazardous, in a bad way, tottering, unassured, uncertain, under fire **10** endangered, precarious, ramshackle, unreliable, unshielded, vulnerable **11** defenseless, dilapidated, unprotected, unsheltered

insecurities 4 risk **5** peril **6** danger, hazard **7** pitfall **8** jeopardy **11** contingency

insecurity 5 doubt **9** self-doubt, shakiness **10** diffidence, unsafeness **11** dubiousness, incertitude, instability, uncertainty **12** doubtfulness, endangerment, insecureness, unsteadiness **13** vulnerability **14** precariousness **15** defenselessness, lack of assurance **16** apprehensiveness

insensate 4 cold **5** cruel **6** brutal **8** inhumane **9** heartless, unfeeling **11** unconscious

insensibility 4 coma **5** swoon **6** apathy, torpor, trance **8** blackout, dullness, lethargy, numbness, obduracy, oblivion, stoicism **9** analgesia, catalepsy **10** anesthesia, obtuseness **12** incognizance, indifference, mindlessness **13** insensitivity, unfeelingness **15** unconsciousness

insensible 4 cold **9** insensate, senseless **11** unconscious

insensitive 4 cold, dead, numb **5** blase **7** callous **8** hardened **9** apathetic, impassive, insensate, unaware of, unfeeling **10** impervious, insensible **11** indifferent, unconcerned **12** thick-skinned **15** uncompassionate

insensitiveness 8 rudeness **10** coarseness, indelicacy **12** tactlessness **13** insensibility, insensitivity **17** inconsiderateness

inseparable 8 attached **11** indivisible, unseverable **12** indissoluble

insert 3 add **5** embed, enter, imbed, infix, inlay, inset, pop in, put in, set in **6** infuse, inject, push in, tuck in **7** drive in, implant, intrude, place in, press in, slide in, stick in, stuff in, wedge in **8** thrust in **9** interject, interlard, interpose, introduce **10** put between **11** interpolate, intersperse

insertion 2 ad **5** entry, graft, inlay, inset **7** implant **11** insinuation, parenthesis **12** interjection **13** advertisement

inset 4 gore **5** embed, godet,

imbed, inlay, panel **6** insert
9 insertion

in seventh heaven 6 elated,
joyful, joyous **8** ecstatic, euphoric **9** exuberant, rapturous
11 on cloud nine **13** up in the
clouds

inside 2 in **5** inner **6** inmost,
inward, secret **7** private **8** cliquish, esoteric, interior, internal, intimate **9** inner part,
inner side, innermost
12 confidential

inside information 3 tip
10 inside dope

inside out 9 backwards **10** in
disorder, topsy turvy **11** wrong
side to

insides 4 guts **6** bowels, vitals
7 gizzard, innards, viscera
10 intestines

insidious 3 sly **4** foxy, wily
5 shady **6** artful, covert, crafty,
sneaky, subtle, tricky
7 crooked, cunning, devious,
furtive **8** guileful, slippery,
sneaking, stealthy **9** concealed,
deceitful, designing, disguised,
secretive, underhand **10** contriving, perfidious, pernicious,
undercover, undetected
11 clandestine, deleterious,
treacherous, underhanded
12 disingenuous, falsehearted
13 Machiavellian, surreptitious

insight 6 acumen **9** intuition
10 perception **11** discernment,
penetration **12** apprehension,
perceptivity, perspicacity
13 comprehension, intuitive-
ness **14** perceptiveness
  French: **6** apercu

insignia 3 bar **4** mark, sign,
star **5** badge, medal, patch
6 emblem, stripe, symbol
7 chevron, epaulet, oak leaf
10 decoration **13** badge of
office

insignificance 8 puniness
9 pettiness, smallness **10** meagerness, triviality **11** irrelevance **12** unimportance

insignificant 4 puny **5** petty,
small **6** flimsy, meager, minute, paltry **7** trivial **8** niggling, not vital, nugatory,
picayune, piddling, trifling
9 minuscule, worthless **10** immaterial, irrelevant, negligible,
of no moment, second-rate
11 indifferent, meaningless,
unimportant **12** nonessential
13 small potatoes **14** inconsiderable **15** inconsequential, of
little account, of no consequence **18** not worth
mentioning

insincere 5 false, lying **6** un-

true **7** devious, evasive
8 guileful, two-faced, uncan-
did **9** deceitful, dishonest,
equivocal **10** fraudulent, perfidious, untruthful **11** dissembling **12** disingenuous,
hypocritical, mealymouthed
13 dissimulating, double-
dealing

insincerity 4 sham **6** deceit
8 pretense, uncandor **9** deception, falseness, hypocrisy,
mendacity **11** affectation, shallowness, unfrankness **12** un-
candidness **13** artificiality
16 disingenuousness

insinuate 5 imply **6** inject, insert **7** asperse, let fall, suggest,
wheedle, whisper **8** intimate
10 ingratiate **11** worm one's
way

insinuation 4 hint **8** allusion,
infusion, innuendo **9** aspersion, insertion, intrusion
10 allegation, imputation, intimation, suggestion **11** implication, penetration
12 ingratiation, interjection

insipid 4 arid, blah, drab, dull,
flat, lean **5** banal, bland,
empty, inane, stale, trite,
vapid **6** barren, boring, jejune,
stupid **7** prosaic **8** lifeless, zest-
less **9** pointless, savorless,
tasteless, wearisome **10** monotonous, namby-pamby,
wishy-washy **11** commonplace **12** unappetizing
13 characterless,
uninteresting

insist 4 aver, hold, urge, warn
5 claim, vouch **6** assert, demand, exhort, repeat, stress
7 caution, command, contend,
persist, protest, require **8** admonish, maintain **9** reiterate
10 asseverate **13** lay down the
law **14** take a firm stand
15 stand one's ground

insistence 6 demand, urging
7 urgency **8** exigency, pressure **9** clamoring **11** persistence **12** perseverance
14 imperativeness

insistent 4 firm **7** adamant
8 emphatic, repeated, stubborn **9** assertive, demanding
10 determined, unyielding
11 unrelenting

in situ 7 in place **18** in its
original place

insolence 4 gall **7** disdain, hauteur **8** audacity **9** arrogance,
impudence **10** brazenness, disrespect, effrontery, incivility,
lordliness **11** haughtiness, presumption **12** disobedience, impertinence, impoliteness
13 bumptiousness, imperious-

ness **14** unmannerliness
16 superciliousness

insolent 4 rude **5** fresh, nervy
6 brazen, cheeky **7** defiant,
galling, haughty **8** arrogant,
impolite, impudent **9** audacious, bumptious, insulting
10 disdainful, outrageous, unmannerly **11** impertinent,
overbearing **12** contemptuous,
discourteous, presumptuous,
supercilious **13** disrespectful

insoluble 12 inexplicable, unanswerable **13** undissolvable,
unexplainable **14** undecipherable **16** incomprehensible

insolvent 5 broke **6** ruined
8 bankrupt, wiped out **9** destitute, moneyless, penniless
10 down-and-out, out of
money **11** impecunious
12 impoverished, overextended

insomnia 11 nuit blanche, per-
vigilium, wakefulness **12** in-
somnolence **13** sleeplessness

insouciant 4 airy **5** perky
6 breezy, casual, jaunty
7 buoyant, offhand **8** carefree,
debonair, flippant **9** easygoing,
mercurial, unruffled, sans
souci, whimsical **10** capricious,
nonchalant, untroubled **11** free
and easy, indifferent, unconcerned **12** devil-may-care,
happy-go-lucky, lighthearted

inspect 3 eye **4** scan **5** probe,
study **6** peer at, peruse, review, survey **7** examine, explore, observe **8** pore over
10 scrutinize **11** contemplate,
investigate, reconnoiter

inspection 4 scan **5** audit,
check, probe, study **6** review,
survey **7** perusal **8** checking,
scrutiny **9** appraisal, oversight
11 examination

inspector 7 analyst, auditor
8 analyzer, examiner, overseer,
reviewer **9** appraiser, detective **11** scrutinizer
12 investigator

Inspector-General, The
  author: **12** Nikolai Gogol
  character: **4** Anna, Osip
  5 Maria **26** Ivan Alexandro-
  vich Hlestakov **35** Anton
  Antonovich Skvoznik-
  Dmukhanovsky

inspiration 4 idea, spur
5 fancy, flash **6** motive **7** impulse **8** afflatus, stimulus **9** incentive, influence, prompting
10 compulsion, incitement,
motivation, revelation
13 encouragement

inspire 4 fire, stir **5** cause, exalt, impel, rouse **6** arouse, excite, induce, prompt, vivify

7 animate, enliven, hearten, produce, promote, provoke, quicken **8** embolden, engender, enkindle, illumine, inspirit, motivate, occasion **9** encourage, galvanize, influence, stimulate **10** give rise to, illuminate

inspired 3 apt **5** fired, moved **6** elated **7** elegant, exalted, excited, incited, touched, well-put **8** creative, original, prompted **9** impressed, ingenious, inventive, motivated **10** encouraged, felicitous, influenced, stimulated, well-chosen **11** exhilarated, imaginative **13** well-expressed

inspiring 5 grand **6** moving **7** awesome **8** eloquent, stirring **9** affecting, brilliant **10** impressive **11** encouraging, magnificent, stimulating

inspirit 5 boost, cheer, rouse **6** buoy up, uplift **7** animate, comfort, enliven, hearten, inspire **9** encourage, give a lift

in spite of himself
French: **9** malgre lui

instability 8 wavering, weakness **9** hesitancy **10** fitfulness, hesitation, indecision, insecurity **11** flightiness, fluctuation, inconstancy, vacillation **12** irresolution, unstableness, unsteadiness **13** changeability, inconsistency, mercurialness, vulnerability **14** capriciousness, changeableness

install, instal 3 lay **4** seat **5** crown, embed, imbed, lodge, plant **6** induct, invest, locate, move in, ordain **7** arrange, emplace, instate, receive, situate, station, usher in **8** coronate, initiate, position **9** establish **10** inaugurate, set in place

installation 5 plant **6** agency **8** facility **9** formation, induction **10** foundation, initiation, ordination **11** appointment, institution, investiture **12** inauguration, military base, organization **13** establishment

installment 4 part, unit **5** issue **6** laying **7** chapter, payment, section, segment **8** division, fragment, locating

instance 4 case, time **6** sample **7** example **8** occasion, specimen **9** precedent, prototype **10** antecedent **11** case in point **12** circumstance, illustration

instant 5 flash, jiffy, quick, trice **6** abrupt, minute, moment, prompt, second, sudden **8** premixed **9** immediate,

on the spot, precooked, twinkling **10** ready-to-use **11** split second **12** unhesitating

instantaneous 5 rapid, swift **6** abrupt, direct, prompt, speedy, sudden **9** immediate **13** quick as a flash

instantaneously 6 at once **7** quickly, rapidly **8** in a flash, in no time, instanter, right now **9** on the spot, right away **11** immediately **21** in the twinkling of an eye

instantly 6 at once **7** quickly **8** directly, in a flash, promptly, right now **9** instanter, on the spot **10** here and now **11** immediately **12** quick as a wink, without delay **15** instantaneously **17** without hesitation

instar
insect period between:
  5 molts **7** molting

in statu quo 17 in the state in which (something is or was)

Instauratio Magna
  author: **12** Francis Bacon

instead 6 in lieu, rather **10** in its place

instigate 4 goad, spur, urge **5** begin, rouse, start **6** foment, incite, kindle, prompt, stir up **7** provoke **8** initiate **9** stimulate **10** bring about **11** set in motion

instigator 6 shaper **7** inciter **9** architect, innovator **10** prime mover, ringleader

instill, instil 4 pour **5** mix in, teach **6** impart, induce **7** implant, inspire **8** engender **9** inculcate

instinct 4 gift **5** knack **6** genius, nature **7** faculty **8** aptitude, capacity, tendency **9** intuition, mother wit **10** proclivity

instinctive 6 inborn, inbred, innate, native **7** natural **8** inherent, inspired **9** automatic, impulsive, intuitive, unlearned **10** deep-seated, unacquired **11** instinctual, involuntary, spontaneous

institute 4 pass **5** begin, enact, found, set up, start **6** ordain, school **7** academy, college, society **8** commence, get going, initiate, organize **9** establish, introduce, originate, prescribe, undertake **10** constitute, foundation, inaugurate **11** association, get under way **13** put into effect **14** bring into being

institution 4 rite **5** habit,

usage **6** custom, prison, ritual, school **7** academy, college, company, fixture **8** bughouse, madhouse, nuthouse, seminary **9** institute **10** convention, crazy house, foundation, university **11** association **12** organization **13** establishment

institutionalize 6 commit, detain **7** confine, put away **8** imprison **11** incarcerate

in strict confidence 7 sub rosa **9** between us, entre nous, privately **14** confidentially **15** between you and me **16** between me and thee, between ourselves

instruct 3 bid **5** brief, coach, drill, guide, order, teach, train, tutor **6** advise, direct, inform, notify, school **7** apprise, command, educate **8** acquaint **9** catechize, enlighten **12** indoctrinate

instruction 8 coaching, guidance, pedagogy, teaching, training, tutelage, tutoring **9** education **11** instructing **14** indoctrination

instructions 4 rule **5** maxim, moral, motto **6** advice, homily, lesson **7** precept **9** direction, guideline **11** explanation, information **12** prescription **13** specification **14** recommendation

instructive 8 didactic, edifying **11** educational **12** enlightening

instructor 3 don **4** guru **5** coach, guide, tutor **6** mentor **7** counsel, maestro, teacher, trainer **8** educator, lecturer **9** governess, pedagogue, preceptor, professor **10** schoolmarm **12** schoolmaster **13** schoolteacher **14** schoolmistress

instrument 4 deed, tool **5** agent, grant, means, paper **6** agency, device, gadget, medium **7** charter, machine, utensil, vehicle **8** contract **9** apparatus, appliance, equipment, expedient, implement, mechanism **11** contrivance

Instrument, The
  author: **9** John O'Hara

instrumental 5 vital **6** active, useful **7** crucial, helpful **8** a means to, decisive, valuable **9** assisting, conducive, effective, effectual, essential **10** functional **12** contributory

instrumentality 5 force, means **6** agency, charge **9** in-

fluence, mediation
12 intervention

insubordinate 6 unruly **7** defiant **8** insolent, mutinous
9 fractious **10** disorderly, rebellious, refractory **11** disobedient, intractable, uncompliant
12 recalcitrant, ungovernable, unsubmissive

insubordination 6 mutiny, revolt **7** anarchy **8** sedition **9** rebellion **10** dissention, insurgence, unruliness **12** disobedience, insurrection
13 noncompliance
14 refractoriness

insubstantial 4 airy, weak
5 frail, shaky, small **6** flimsy, modest, paltry, slight, unreal
7 fragile, trivial, unsound
8 baseless, bodiless, delicate, ethereal, gossamer, piddling, trifling, unstable **9** imaginary, visionary **10** groundless, immaterial, impalpable, intangible **12** apparitional
14 inconsiderable

in succession
French: **7** en suite

insufferable 7 hateful **8** dreadful **10** abominable, detestable, disgusting, outrageous, unbearable **11** intolerable, unendurable, unspeakable
13 insupportable

insufficiency 4 lack, need, want **6** dearth **7** drought, paucity **8** scarcity, shortage
10 deficiency, inadequacy, meagerness, scantiness
11 undersupply

insufficient 6 scanty, skimpy, sparse **7** lacking, wanting
8 impotent **9** deficient, not enough **10** inadequate **11** incompetent **14** unsatisfactory

insular 5 petty **6** biased, narrow **7** bigoted, limited **8** isolated **9** illiberal, insulated, parochial **10** intolerant, prejudiced, provincial **12** narrowminded

insulate 5 cover **6** cut off, detach, enisle, shield **7** cushion, isolate, protect, seclude **8** separate **9** segregate, sequester
10 disconnect

insult 3 cut **4** slap **5** abuse, cheek, scorn **6** deride, offend, slight **7** affront, offense, outrage **8** be rude to, belittle, rudeness **9** disparage, impudence, indignity **11** discourtesy, lese majesty

insulting 4 rude **5** nasty **7** abusive, uncivil, vicious **8** impolite, insolent **9** invidious, offensive **10** defamatory, de-

rogatory **11** disparaging
12 discourteous
13 disrespectful

insuperable 8 crushing **9** defeating **10** impassable, impossible, invincible, unbeatable, unyielding **12** inexpugnable, overpowering, overwhelming
13 overmastering, unconquerable **14** insurmountable

insurance 6 policy **8** coverage, security, warranty **9** assurance, guarantee, indemnity

insure 6 secure **10** underwrite

insurgent 5 rebel **7** lawless
8 mutineer, mutinous, partisan, renegade, resister, revolter **9** breakaway, dissident, guerrilla **10** disorderly, rebellious **11** disobedient **13** insubordinate, revolutionary, revolutionist **15** insurrectionist

insurmountable 8 hopeless, too great **10** unbeatable
11 beyond reach, insuperable
13 unconquerable

insurrection 4 riot **6** mutiny, revolt, rising **8** outbreak, uprising **9** rebellion **10** insurgence, revolution

intact 4 safe **5** sound, whole
6 unhurt **7** perfect **8** complete, integral, unbroken, unharmed
9 undamaged, uninjured, untouched **10** in one piece, unimpaired **11** in good shape
15 without a scratch

intangible 5 vague **7** elusive, shadowy **8** abstract, ethereal, fleeting, fugitive **9** transient
10 accidental, evanescent, immaterial, impalpable **11** abstraction, untouchable
12 imponderable **13** imperceptible, insubstantial

integer 5 digit, whole **6** entity, figure, number **7** numeral
11 whole number

integer vitae 8 innocent
15 blameless in life

integral 4 full **5** basic, total, whole **6** entire, intact **7** perfect, rounded **8** complete, finished, inherent **9** component, essential, fulfilled, necessary, requisite **10** fulfilling **11** constituent, well-rounded
13 indispensable

integrate 3 mix **4** fuse **5** blend, merge, unify, unite **6** mingle
7 combine **8** intermix
10 amalgamate **11** desegregate **13** bring together

integrated 6 entire, joined, linked, united **7** blended, merged, unified, unitary
8 combined **9** composite, undi-

vided **10** harmonized, reconciled **11** coordinated, synthesized **12** desegregated, unsegregated

integration 5 union **6** fusion, mixing **8** blending **9** combining, synthesis **11** combination
12 assimilation
13 desegregation

integrity 5 unity **6** purity, virtue **7** decency, honesty, probity **8** cohesion, morality, strength **9** character, coherence, principle, rectitude, wholeness **11** reliability, selfrespect, uprightness
12 completeness

integument 4 coat, hide, husk, rind, skin **5** shell, **7** coating, cuticle, epiderm, exoderm
8 covering, envelope, membrane

integumentary system
    component: **4** hair, skin
    5 nails

intellect 3 wit **4** mind **5** brain, sense **6** brains, wisdom
7 thinker **9** cognition, mentality **10** perception **11** mental power, rationality **12** intellectual, intelligence **13** consciousness, understanding

intellectual 4 sage **5** brain
6 brainy, mental, pundit, savant **7** bookish, egghead, scholar, thinker **8** abstract, academic, cerebral, highbrow, longhair, mandarin, rational, studious **9** intellect, of the mind, reasoning, scholarly
10 thoughtful **11** intelligent
    French: **9** bel-esprit

intelligence 4 dope, news
6 acumen, advice, brains, notice, report, wisdom **7** tidings
8 sagacity **9** intellect, knowledge **10** advisement, shrewdness **11** information
12 notification, perspicacity
13 comprehension, understanding

intelligent 4 keen, sage, wise
5 alert, canny, quick, sharp, smart **6** astute, brainy, bright, clever, shrewd **7** knowing, prudent **8** informed, sensible, thinking **9** brilliant, sagacious
10 perceptive, thoughtful
11 clearheaded, quick-witted, sharp-witted **12** well-informed
13 perspicacious

intelligentsia 7 academe
8 thinkers **10** ivory tower
13 intellectuals

intelligible 5 clear, lucid **7** evident, obvious **8** apparent, clear-cut, coherent, definite, distinct **11** unambiguous, welldefined **12** unmistakable

14 comprehensible, understandable

intemperance 10 alcoholism, insobriety **11** dissipation, drunkenness, inebriation **12** immoderation, recklessness **13** excessiveness **16** irresponsibility

intemperate 5 harsh **6** brutal, rugged, severe **7** extreme, violent **8** bibulous, uncurbed **9** dissolute, excessive, inclement **10** dissipated, gluttonous, immoderate, inordinate **11** extravagant, inabstinent, incontinent **12** unrestrained **13** overindulgent

intend 3 aim **4** mean, plan, wish **6** aspire, design, expect **7** project, propose, resolve **9** calculate, determine **10** have in mind **11** contemplate

intended 5 meant **6** fiance, future **7** engaged, fiancee, implied, willful **8** proposed, purposed **9** affianced, betrothed, bride-to-be, groom-to-be, voluntary **10** calculated, deliberate **11** intentional

intense 4 deep, keen **5** acute, sharp **6** ardent, potent, strong **7** burning, earnest, extreme, fervent, violent **8** emphatic, forceful, forcible, powerful, vehement **10** passionate **12** concentrated, considerable

intensely 4 very **5** hotly **6** deeply, keenly **7** acutely, eagerly, vividly **8** ardently, heatedly, terribly **9** extremely, fervently, seriously, violently, zealously **10** forcefully, powerfully, profoundly, vehemently, vigorously **11** excessively, exquisitely, strenuously **12** considerably, passionately **13** energetically

intensify 5 boost **6** deepen, worsen **7** magnify, quicken, sharpen **8** escalate, heighten, increase, redouble **9** aggravate, reinforce **10** accelerate, strengthen

intensifying 9 worsening **10** increasing, magnifying, redoubling, sharpening **11** aggravating, heightening, reinforcing **12** exacerbating **13** strengthening

intensity 4 zeal **5** ardor, depth, force, power, vigor **6** energy, fervor **7** emotion, passion, potency **8** severity, strength **9** magnitude, vehemence **11** earnestness **12** forcefulness

intensive 6 all-out **7** growing, radical **8** complete, sweeping, thorough **10** exhaustive, increasing **11** comprehensive

12 concentrated **13** thoroughgoing

intent 3 aim, end, set **4** bent, gist, plan **5** drift, fixed **6** burden, design, import, steady **7** earnest, intense, meaning, purport, purpose **8** absorbed, piercing, resolved **9** engrossed, insistent, intention, steadfast, substance, tenacious, unbending **10** determined, unwavering **11** preoccupied **12** concentrated, significance, undistracted **13** determination, premeditation

intention 3 aim, end **4** goal, plan **6** design, intent, object, target **7** purpose, resolve **9** objective **10** resolution **13** determination

intentional 6 willed **7** planned **8** designed, intended **9** voluntary **10** calculated, deliberate, purposeful **12** contemplated, premeditated **13** done on purpose

intently 6 deeply, raptly **9** fervently, zealously **10** absorbedly **11** attentively **12** passionately **18** without distraction **22** with undivided attention

intentness 10 absorption **11** engrossment **13** concentration

inter 4 bury **5** inurn **6** entomb, inhume **7** inearth, lay away **9** lay to rest **11** ensepulcher

interact 4 join, mesh **5** coact, unite **6** engage **7** combine, conjoin **8** dovetail **9** cooperate, interlace, intermesh, interplay, interwork **10** coordinate, interreact

inter alia 16 among other things

inter alios 17 among other persons

interbreed 3 mix **5** cross **8** intermix **10** crossbreed

intercede 5 plead **6** step in **7** mediate, speak up **9** arbitrate, interpose, intervene, offer help **12** offer support **14** put in a good word **16** lend a helping hand

intercept 3 nab **4** grab, stay, stop, take **5** catch, seize **6** ambush, arrest, cut off, detain **7** deflect, reroute

intercessor 5 agent **6** bishop, broker **8** advocate, mediator **9** go-between, middleman **12** intermediary, spokesperson

interchange 5 shift **6** switch **7** trading **8** exchange, junction, swapping, transfer **9** alternate,

crossover **10** substitute **11** give and take, reciprocity

interchangeable 8 parallel, tradable **9** analogous **10** equivalent, switchable, synonymous **12** exchangeable, transposable **13** corresponding

interconnected 8 adjacent **10** contiguous, juxtaposed **12** conterminous, labyrinthine

intercourse 4 talk **5** trade **6** coitus, parley **7** pairing, traffic **8** colloquy, commerce, congress, coupling, dealings, exchange **9** communion, discourse, relations **10** connection, copulation **12** conversation **14** communications, correspondence

interdict 3 ban, bar **5** taboo **6** enjoin, forbid **7** barring, censure **8** prohibit, restrain, restrict **9** proscribe **11** forbiddance, prohibition **12** proscription

interdiction 3 ban **7** barring **11** forbiddance, prohibition **12** proscription

interest, interests 4 gain, good, part, weal **5** bonus, hobby, share, stake, touch, yield **6** absorb, affect, behalf, divert, engage, notice, profit, regard **7** attract, benefit, concern, holding, involve, pastime, portion, pursuit, service **8** dividend **9** advantage, attention, avocation, curiosity, preoccupy, suspicion **10** absorption, investment **11** engrossment **13** preoccupation

interested 6 active **7** engaged **8** diverted **9** committed, concerned **10** fascinated, responsive

interesting 7 curious **8** engaging, magnetic, pleasing, riveting, striking **9** absorbing, appealing, arresting **10** attractive, suspicious **11** fascinating, stimulating **12** entertaining

interfere 3 jar, mix **6** butt in, horn in, meddle, rush in, step in **7** counter, intrude **8** conflict **9** frustrate, intercede, interpose, intervene **11** get in the way **14** be a hindrance to, be an obstacle to, be inconsistent, stick in one's oar

interference 3 bar **6** static **8** clashing, conflict, friction, invasion, meddling **9** collision, hindrance, intrusion **12** interception, interruption, intervention

interfere with 6 hinder, impede, thwart **7** disrupt **9** interrupt

interim 7 stopgap 8 interval, meantime, temporal 9 interlude, temporary, tentative 10 pro tempore 11 provisional

interior 4 bush 5 inner 6 inmost, inside, inward 8 internal 9 backwoods, heartland, innermost, upcountry 10 hinterland

Interiors
director: 10 Woody Allen
cast: 10 E G Marshall 11 Diane Keaton 12 Marybeth Hurt 13 Geraldine Page 15 Kristin Griffith 16 Maureen Stapleton
screenplay: 10 Woody Allen

interject 5 put in 6 inject, insert, slip in 7 force in, sneak in, throw in 9 interpose, introduce 11 interpolate

interjection 2 ah, er, lo, oh, ow, um 3 aha, cry, fie, hey, huh, ugh, wow 4 ahem, alas, darn, dear, drat, egad, gosh, heck, jeez, oops, ouch, phew, rats 5 aside, golly, zowie 6 eureka, hooray, hurrah, hurray 7 gee-whiz, jeepers 9 insertion 11 ejaculation, exclamation 13 interpolation, interposition

interlace 3 mix 4 knit, link 5 braid, plait, twine, twist, weave 7 wreathe 9 alternate 10 intertwine, interweave 11 intersperse

interlaced 5 woven 6 linked, twined 7 braided, knitted, plaited, twisted 8 entwined, latticed, wreathed 9 interknit 10 interwoven 11 intertwined 12 interspersed

interlocutor 8 minstrel 9 converser, dialogist 12 interrogator 14 man in the middle

interlope 6 invade, meddle 7 intrude, obtrude 8 encroach, infringe, trespass 9 interfere

interloper 7 invader, meddler 8 intruder, outsider 10 interferer, trespasser 11 gatecrasher 15 persona non grata

interlude 5 break, event, letup, pause 6 recess 7 episode, respite 8 incident, interval 12 intermission 14 breathing spell

intermediary 6 midway, umpire 7 referee 8 bridging, mediator 9 go-between, inbetween, mediating, middleman 10 arbitrator 11 adjudicator, arbitrating

intermediate 3 mid 4 fair, mean, so-so 6 median, medium, middle, midway 7 average, halfway, mediate,

midmost 8 mediocre, middling, moderate 11 intervening

interment 6 burial 7 funeral 10 entombment, inhumation

Intermezzo
director: 13 Gregory Ratoff
cast: 8 Edna Best 12 Leslie Howard 13 Cecil Kellaway, Ingrid Bergman

interminable 6 prolix 7 endless 8 infinite, unending 9 boundless, ceaseless, incessant, limitless, perpetual, unlimited 10 continuous, long-winded 11 illimitable 12 long-drawn-out

intermingle 3 mix 4 fuse 5 blend, merge, mix up, unite 6 commix 7 combine 8 emulsify, intermix 9 commingle, interfuse, interlace 10 amalgamate, homogenize, interblend 12 conglomerate

intermission 3 gap 4 halt, rest, stop 5 break, pause 6 hiatus, recess 7 interim 8 interval, stoppage 9 interlude 10 suspension

intermittent 6 fitful 8 on and off, periodic, sporadic 9 irregular, recurrent, spasmodic 10 occasional 13 discontinuous 15 on-again-off-again

intermix 3 mix 5 blend, cross, mix in 6 mingle 10 crossbreed, interbreed 11 intermingle, intersperse

intern 6 commit, detain 7 confine, impound 8 imprison, restrain

internal 5 inner, state 6 inmost 8 domestic, interior 9 executive, political, sovereign 12 governmental 14 administrative

international 9 worldwide 12 cosmopolitan

international affairs
god of: 6 Sancus 10 Dius Fidius, Semo Sancus

internment 9 detention 10 commitment, impounding 11 confinement 12 imprisonment

inter nos 16 between ourselves

interpolate 3 add 5 put in 6 inject, insert, work in 7 implant, intrude, stick in, throw in, wedge in 8 sandwich 9 insinuate, interject, interlard, interline, intervene, introduce 11 intercalate, intersperse

interpose 6 butt in, impose, inject, insert, meddle, step in 7 intrude, mediate, obtrude

9 arbitrate, insinuate, intercede, interfere, interject, interrupt, intervene, negotiate 11 come between, interpolate

interpret 3 see 4 read, take 6 accept, define, render, reword 7 clarify, explain, make out, restate, unravel 8 construe, decipher 9 elucidate, explicate, figure out, make clear, puzzle out, translate 10 account for, paraphrase, understand

interpretation 7 reading, version 8 analysis 9 rendition 10 commentary 11 explanation 12 construction

interpreter 7 analyst 9 explainer 10 translator 11 commentator

interrelated 9 companion, connected 10 compatible, correlated 13 complementary, correspondent, corresponding

interrelation 10 connection 11 association, correlation 12 relationship

interrogate 3 ask 4 test 5 grill, probe, query 7 examine 8 question 9 catechize 11 investigate 12 cross-examine 18 give the third degree

interrogation 4 quiz 5 probe, query 7 inquiry 8 grilling, querying, question, quizzing 9 catechism, inquiring 11 examination, inquisition, questioning

interrupt 4 stop 5 sever 7 cut in on, disjoin, disturb 8 break off 9 break in on, intersect, punctuate 10 disconnect 11 discontinue 13 interfere with

interrupted 6 broken, cut off, halted 7 checked, stalled, stopped 8 arrested, broke off, deferred 9 broken off, disturbed, suspended 11 broke in upon, intercepted 12 discontinued

interruption 3 gap 4 halt, rift, stop 5 break, pause 6 hiatus, lacuna 9 hindrance, interlude 11 obstruction 12 interference, intermission 13 disconnection, discontinuity

inter se 15 among themselves 17 between themselves

intersect 4 meet 5 cross 6 bisect, divide 7 overlap 8 crosscut, transect, traverse 9 cut across 10 crisscross

intersection 6 corner 8 crossing, junction 10 crossroads 11 interchange

intersperse 3 dot, mix
5 strew **6** mingle, pepper
7 bestrew, scatter, wedge in
8 disperse, intermix, sprinkle
9 broadcast, interfuse, interject, interlard, interpose
11 intercalate, interpolate

interstice 4 slit, slot **5** crack,
space **7** opening, orifice **8** aperture, interval

intertwine 4 lace **5** braid,
plait, twine, twist, weave
7 entwine **8** entangle
9 interlace

interval 3 gap **4** gulf, rest, rift
5 break, cleft, pause, space,
spell **6** breach, hiatus, recess,
season **7** interim, opening
9 interlude **10** interspace, separation **12** intermission,
interruption

intervene 4 pass **6** befall, butt
in, step in **7** break in, intrude,
mediate **9** arbitrate, intercede,
interfere, interpose, interrupt,
take place **10** come to pass
11 come between

intervention 9 butting in, intrusion, mediation **10** breaking
in, stepping in **11** arbitration
12 intercession, interference
13 interposition
14 intermediation

interview 4 chat, talk **6** parley **7** meeting **8** audience
10 conference, evaluation,
round table **11** questioning
12 consultation,
conversation

interweave 3 mix **4** fuse, join,
knit, lace, link **5** blend, braid,
plait, twine, twist **6** splice
7 wreathe **9** interlace, interknit **10** intertwine
11 intersperse

intestinal 5 inner **7** enteric
8 internal, visceral

intestines 4 guts **6** bowels
7 insides, viscera **8** entrails

in the air 2 up **5** above, aloft
7 skyward **8** all about, in the
sky, overhead **10** everywhere
11 in the clouds

in the doghouse 9 in bad
odor **10** in disfavor, in disgrace, in ill favor **11** in
disrepute

in the end 6 one day **7** finally **8** sometime **10** eventually, ultimately **13** sooner or
later **17** in the course of time
French: **5** enfin

in the family
French: **9** en famille

in the first place
Latin: **8** imprimis

in the future
Latin: **8** in futuro
Spanish: **6** manana

In the Heat of the Night
director: **13** Norman Jewison
cast: **8** Lee Grant **10** Rod
Steiger **11** Warren Oates
13 Sidney Poitier (Virgil
Tibbs)
score: **11** Quincy Jones
Oscar for: **5** actor (Steiger)
7 picture **10** screenplay

in the know 9 cognizant
11 on the inside **13** fully informed, knowledgeable
23 having inside information

in the manner of
French: **3** a la **7** a la mode

in the matter of
Latin: **4** in re

in the meantime
Latin: **9** ad interim

in the middle of things
Latin: **11** in medias res

in the midst of 5 among
7 amongst **12** surrounded by
13 in the middle of

in the nature of things
Latin: **13** in rerum natura

in the neighborhood of
6 almost, around, nearly
7 close to **9** generally, just
about **10** more or less, not far
from **13** approximately **15** in
the vicinity of

in the place cited
Latin: **6** loc cit **10** loco citato

in the place of a parent
Latin: **14** in loco parentis

in the same manner that
Latin: **7** quo modo

in the same place
Latin: **4** ibid **6** ibidem

in the state in which
Latin: **10** in statu quo

in the style of
French: **7** a la mode

in the very act of committing the crime
Latin: **18** in flagrante delicto

in the vicinity of 4 near **6** almost, around, nearly **7** close
to **9** just about **10** more or
less, not far from **13** approximately **19** in the neighborhood of

in the way
French: **6** de trop

in the whole
Latin: **6** in toto

in the work cited
Latin: **5** op cit **11** opere
citato

in the year of the reign
Latin: **9** anno regni

in the year of the world
Latin: **9** anno mundi

In This House of Brede
author: **11** Rumer Godden

**in this sign shalt thou
conquer**
Latin: **16** in hoc signo vinces
motto of: **19** Constantine the
Great
from vision of: **5** cross

intimacy 5 amity **6** caring,
warmth **8** dearness, fondness
9 affection, closeness
10 chumminess, endearment,
fraternity, lovemaking, tenderness **11** brotherhood, camaraderie, familiarity
12 friendliness

intimate 3 pal **4** chum, dear,
deep, hint **5** bosom, buddy,
close, crony, imply, rumor
6 allude, direct **7** guarded, private, special, suggest **8** detailed, familiar, indicate,
personal, profound, thorough
9 cherished, confidant, firsthand, innermost, insinuate
12 confidential
French: **6** intime

intimately 7 closely **8** secretly,
very well **9** privately **10** familiarly, personally **11** essentially **13** intrinsically
14 confidentially

intimation 4 clue, hint, sign
5 rumor **7** inkling, portent
8 allusion, innuendo **10** indication, suggestion **11** insinuation **13** veiled comment

Intimations of Immortality
author: **17** William
Wordsworth

intime 4 cozy **8** intimate

in time 6 before, sooner **7** earlier **9** before now, in advance
10 beforehand, eventually
11 ahead of time **13** before
the fact, sooner or later

intimidate 3 cow **5** alarm,
bully, daunt, scare **6** coerce,
menace, subdue **7** buffalo, terrify **8** browbeat, frighten
9 terrorize

intimidated 5 cowed, fazed
6 scared **7** crushed, daunted,
subdued **10** browbeaten,
frightened, terrorized

intimidation 7 tyranny **8** bullying, coercion **9** despotism
11 browbeating, terrorizing,
tyrannizing **12** scare tactics

intimidator 5 bully **6** despot
7 coercer **9** oppressor, tormenter, tormentor **10** browbeater

into 2 in, to 5 among 6 inside, toward, within 7 against

intolerable 7 hateful, racking 9 abhorrent, agonizing, excessive, loathsome, torturous 10 abominable, outrageous, unbearable 11 unendurable 12 excruciating, insufferable, unreasonable 13 insupportable

intolerance 4 bias 6 racism 7 bigotry 8 weak spot 9 no stomach, prejudice 10 chauvinism, xenophobia 12 low tolerance 16 hypersensitivity, narrow-mindedness

Intolerance
   director: 10 D W Griffith
   cast: 8 Mae Marsh 11 Lillian Gish 12 Robert Harron 17 Constance Talmadge

intolerant 7 bigoted, hostile, jealous 9 fanatical, parochial, resentful, sectarian 10 prejudiced, xenophobic 11 mistrustful 12 chauvinistic, closed-minded, narrow-minded

intonation 4 tone 5 pitch 6 accent 8 chanting 10 modulation, inflection

intone 3 hum, say 4 song 5 chant, croon, drawl, mouth, speak, utter, voice 6 murmur, recite 8 intonate, modulate, singsong, vocalize 9 enunciate, pronounce 10 articulate

in toto 5 in all, uncut 6 entire, wholly 7 totally 8 as a whole, entirely, outright 10 completely, in the whole, unabridged 11 all together, uncondensed

intoxicant 3 gin, rum 4 beer, grog, wine 5 booze, drink 6 liquor, tipple, whisky 7 alcohol, spirits, whiskey 8 cocktail, highball 9 inebriant

intoxicated 4 high, rapt 5 drunk, oiled, tight, tipsy 6 bombed, elated, loaded, stewed, stinko, stoned, zonked 7 drunken, exalted, smashed, wrecked 9 delighted, enchanted, entranced, plastered 10 enthralled, inebriated, infatuated, in one's cups 11 exhilarated, transported

intoxicating 4 hard 5 heady 6 potent 7 elating 9 alcoholic, spiritous 11 inebriating 12 exhilarating

intoxication 3 joy 5 bliss 7 elation, rapture 8 euphoria 9 poisoning, tipsiness 10 excitement, insobriety 11 drunkenness, inebriation 12 befuddlement, stupefaction

intractable 6 mulish, ornery,

unruly 7 froward, willful 8 obdurate, perverse, stubborn 9 fractious, obstinate 10 headstrong, inflexible, refractory 11 unmalleable 12 contumacious, incorrigible, ungovernable, unmanageable 14 hard to cope with, uncontrollable

intransigent 7 diehard 8 obdurate, stubborn 9 steadfast, unmovable 10 inflexible, iron-willed, unyielding 11 intractable, unbudgeable 14 uncompromising

intrepid 4 bold 5 brave 6 daring, heroic 7 doughty, valiant 8 fearless, resolute, valorous 9 audacious, dauntless 10 courageous, undismayed 11 adventurous

intrepidity 4 guts 5 spunk, valor 6 mettle 7 bravery, courage 8 backbone 9 fortitude, sangfroid 12 fearlessness 13 dauntlessness

intricacy 10 complexity 11 involvement 12 complication, entanglement 15 complicatedness

intricate 6 knotty, tricky 7 complex, devious, tangled 8 involved 9 entangled 11 complicated

intrigue 3 spy 4 fire, plot 5 amour 6 absorb, arrest, scheme 7 attract, collude, knavery, romance 8 conspire, enthrall, scheming 9 fascinate, machinate, titillate 10 conspiracy, love affair 11 machination 13 double-dealing 15 interest greatly, tickle one's fancy

intriguer 7 cheater, plotter, schemer 8 conniver, finagler 9 trickster 10 machinator, wirepuller 11 conspirator, Machiavelli, manipulator

intriguing 8 engaging, exciting 9 absorbing, beguiling 11 captivating, enthralling, fascinating, interesting

intrinsic 5 basic, per se 6 inborn, inbred, innate, native 7 natural 8 inherent 9 essential, ingrained 10 indigenous, underlying 11 fundamental

introduce 3 add 4 show, urge 5 begin, offer, put in, start 6 create, expose, import, inform, infuse, insert 7 advance, bring in, kick off, lead off, present, propose, sponsor, throw in 8 acquaint, initiate, lead into 9 establish, institute, interject, interpose, make known, originate, recommend

10 put forward 11 familiarize, interpolate

introduction 6 change 7 novelty, opening, preface, prelude 8 foreword, preamble, prologue 9 insertion, precursor 10 bringing in, conducting, innovation, ushering in 11 instituting, institution

introductory 7 initial 9 beginning, prefatory 10 initiatory, precursory 11 acquainting, preliminary 13 get-acquainted

introspection 8 brooding 10 meditation, reflection, rumination 12 deliberation, self-analysis, self-scrutiny 13 contemplation, soul-searching 15 self-examination, self-observation, self-questioning

introspective 7 pensive 10 reflective 13 contemplative, lost in thought

introversion 7 reserve 8 brooding 10 constraint, diffidence, withdrawal 13 introspection

introvert 5 loner 7 brooder, thinker 13 contemplative, private person

introverted 3 shy 5 stiff 8 reserved 9 inhibited, repressed, withdrawn 10 antisocial, restrained 13 inner-directed, introspective

intrude 4 push 6 butt in, impose, meddle, thrust 7 obtrude 8 encroach, trespass 9 interfere, interlope, interpose, intervene

intruder 10 encroacher, interferer, interloper, intervener, trespasser 11 gate-crasher

Intruder in the Dust
   author: 15 William Faulkner

intrusive 4 nosy 5 pushy 6 prying, snoopy 8 in the way, invasive 9 hindering, obtrusive, officious, unwelcome 10 meddlesome 11 impertinent, interfering, interruptive

intuition 5 flash, hunch 7 insight, surmise 8 instinct 9 guesswork, telepathy 10 sixth sense 11 second sight 12 clairvoyance, precognition

intuitive 6 inborn, inbred, innate, native 7 natural, psychic 10 telepathic 11 clairvoyant, instinctive, intuitional, nonrational 12 extrasensory

Inuit see 6 Eskimo

inundate 4 glut 5 drown, flood, swamp 6 deluge, drench, engulf **8** load down, overcome, overflow, saturate, submerge **9** overwhelm **10** overburden, overspread

inundation 4 glut **5** flood **6** deluge **9** avalanche

in unison 5 as one **8** in chorus **9** all at once **11** all together

inure 5 adapt, steel, train **6** adjust, custom, harden, season, temper **7** toughen **8** accustom **9** acclimate, get used to, habituate **10** discipline, naturalize, strengthen **11** acclimatize, desensitize, familiarize **12** become used to **15** learn to live with **16** become hardened to

in use 8 employed **9** operating **11** functioning, operational

in vacuo 9 in a vacuum **11** in isolation

invade 5 flood, limit **6** assail, attack, engulf, infect, infest **7** assault, overrun, violate **8** permeate, restrict, strike at, trespass **9** intrude on, march into, penetrate

invader 6 raider **8** attacker, intruder, marauder **9** aggressor, assailant **10** trespasser

invalid 4 null, sick, void, weak **5** false **6** ailing, infirm, sickly, unwell **7** amputee, cripple, unsound, useless **8** disabled, not valid, nugatory, weakened **9** enfeebled, forceless, illogical, paralytic, powerless, worthless **10** dead letter, fallacious, paraplegic **11** debilitated, ineffective, inoperative, unsupported **12** unconvincing **13** incapacitated, unsupportable **14** good-for-nothing, valetudinarian

invalidate 5 annul **6** cancel, refute, repeal, weaken **7** nullify, vitiate **8** abrogate, make void, undercut **9** discredit, undermine **11** countermand

invalidation 7 voiding **9** annulment **10** abrogation **12** cancellation **13** nullification

invaluable 4 rare **6** choice **9** priceless **11** beyond price, inestimable

invariable 7 uniform **8** constant **9** immutable, unfailing, unvarying **10** changeless, consistent, unchanging, unwavering **11** unalterable, undeviating **12** unchangeable

invariably 4 ever **6** always **7** forever **9** every time, uniformly **10** all the time, constantly **11** perpetually,

universally **15** in every instance **16** without exception

invasion 4 raid **5** foray **6** attack, breach, inroad, sortie **7** assault **8** trespass **9** incursion, intrusion, onslaught **10** aggression, juggernaut, usurpation **11** penetration **12** encroachment, infiltration, infringement, overstepping

Invasion of the Body Snatchers
　director:
　　1956 version: **9** Don Siegel
　　1978 version: **13** Philip Kaufman
　cast:
　　1956 version: **10** Dana Wynter, Larry Gates **11** King Donovan **13** Kevin McCarthy
　　1978 version: **11** Brooke Adams **12** Jeff Goldblum, Leonard Nimoy **16** Donald Sutherland

invective 4 rant **5** venom **6** insult **7** censure, railing, sarcasm **8** diatribe **9** contumely **10** execration, harsh words, revilement **11** verbal abuse **12** billingsgate, denunciation, vilification, vituperation

inveigh 4 rail, slam **5** abuse, knock, scold **6** rebuke, revile **7** censure, put down, run down, upbraid **8** belittle, denounce, harangue, reproach **9** castigate, criticize, dress down **10** vituperate

inveigh against 5 abuse **6** defame, rail at, revile **7** protest **8** denounce **9** castigate

inveigle 4 coax, lure **5** tempt, trick **6** allure, cajole, entice, rope in, seduce, suck in **7** beguile, ensnare, flatter, mislead, wheedle **8** persuade, soft-soap **9** bamboozle, sweet-talk

inveiglement 7 coaxing **8** cajolery, flattery **9** wheedling **10** enticement, persuasion **13** blandishments

invent 4 coin **6** cook up, create, devise, make up **7** concoct, develop, fashion, think up, trump up **8** conceive, contrive **9** conjure up, fabricate, formulate, originate **10** come up with **11** put together

invented 6 fabled, made up **8** fabulous, fanciful, mythical **9** fantastic, imaginary, legendary **10** apocryphal, fictitious

Inventing America
　author: **10** Garry Wills

invention 3 lie **4** fake, sham **6** design, device, gadget **7** fic-

tion, forgery, machine **8** creation, trumpery **9** apparatus, discovery, fertility, implement, ingenuity, inventing **10** concoction, creativity, production **11** contraption, contrivance, development, fabrication, imagination, originality, origination **13** dissimulation, inventiveness, prevarication **15** resourcefulness

invention
　god of: **6** Hermes

inventive 6 bright, clever **9** ingenious **11** resourceful

inventiveness 9 ingenuity **10** cleverness, creativity **11** imagination, orginality **15** imaginativeness

inventor 5 maker **6** author **7** creator, deviser **8** engineer, producer, tinkerer **9** architect, generator, innovator **10** discoverer, originator
　of air brake: **12** Westinghouse
　of automobile: **7** Daimler
　of barometer: **10** Torricelli
　of camera: **7** Eastman
　of cotton gin: **7** Whitney
　of cylinder lock: **4** Yale
　of dynamite: **5** Nobel
　of elevator: **4** Otis
　of gyrocompass: **6** Sperry
　of helicopter: **8** Sikorsky
　of linotype: **12** Mergenthaler
　of machine gun: **7** Gatling
　of movable type: **9** Gutenberg
　of phonograph, incandescent lamp, mimeograph, dictating machine, fluoroscope: **6** Edison
　of photography: **6** Niepce, Talbot **8** Daguerre
　of reaper: **9** McCormick
　of radio: **7** Marconi
　of revolver: **4** Colt
　of rocket engine: **7** Goddard
　of sewing machine: **4** Howe
　of sleeping car: **7** Pullman
　of steamboat: **6** Fulton
　of steam engine: **4** Watt
　of steam locomotive: **10** Stephenson
　of telegraph: **5** Morse
　of telephone: **4** Bell
　of wireless telegraph: **7** Marconi
　of vulcanized rubber: **8** Goodyear

inventory 4 roll **5** goods, index, stock **6** roster, supply **7** catalog **8** register, schedule **9** stock list **10** accounting **11** merchandise, stock-taking

inverse 8 backward, contrary, converse, indirect, inverted, opposite, reversed **11** back to front, bottom-to-top, right-to-left

inversion 7 turning **8** reversal **9** ectropion, turnabout **10** transposal **12** resupination **13** transposition

inverted 7 inverse **8** bottom up **10** upside-down

invest 4 fill, garb, give **5** adorn, allot, array, color, cover, dress, endow, imbue **6** clothe, devote, enable, enrich, infuse, supply **7** appoint, license **8** set aside **9** apportion

investigate 4 sift **5** probe, query, study **6** survey **7** analyze, dissect, explore, inspect **8** ask about, look into, pore over, question, research **9** anatomize, delve into **10** scrutinize

investigation 5 probe, study **6** review, search, survey **7** anatomy, inquiry **8** analysis, research, scrutiny **10** dissection, inspection **11** fact-finding

investigator 6 shamus **7** analyst, gumshoe **8** examiner, inquirer, observer **9** detective **10** private eye, researcher

investment 4 ante, risk **5** share, stake **7** venture **8** offering

inveterate 6 inured **7** adamant, chronic, diehard **8** constant, habitual, hardened **9** confirmed, incurable, ingrained, recurrent, steadfast **10** continuous, deep-rooted, deep-seated **11** established **12** long-standing, unregenerate **15** unreconstructed

invidious 7 vicious **8** spiteful **9** insulting, malicious, offensive, rancorous, resentful, slighting **10** malevolent

invigorate 4 stir **5** brace, cheer, liven, pep up, renew, rouse, zip up **6** jazz up, vivify **7** animate, enliven, fortify, refresh, restore **8** energize, vitalize **9** stimulate **10** exhilarate, rejuvenate, strengthen

invigorated 6 braced **7** revived **8** animated, restored, vivified **9** energized, full of pep, quickened, refreshed **10** stimulated **11** rejuvenated **12** strengthened **17** full of vim and vigor

invigorating 7 bracing **9** animating, healthful **10** energizing, enlivening, quickening, refreshing, vitalizing **11** restorative, stimulating **12** rejuvenating **13** strengthening

invincible 10 unbeatable **11** impregnable, indomitable, insuperable **12** invulnerable, undefeatable **13** irrepressible,
unconquerable **14** insurmountable

in vino veritas 18 in wine there is truth

inviolable 4 holy, pure **6** chaste, divine, sacred, secret **7** blessed **8** hallowed **9** dedicated, inviolate, undefiled **10** sacrosanct **11** consecrated, impregnable, trustworthy **12** impenetrable, invulnerable, unassailable **13** incorruptible

inviolate 4 pure **6** intact, sacred, secret **8** hallowed **9** unaltered, unchanged, undefiled, unstained **10** inviolable, sacrosanct

invisible 6 covert, hidden, unseen, veiled **7** obscure **9** concealed, unseeable **10** unapparent **13** imperceptible, undiscernible

Invisible Man
    author: **12** Ralph Ellison

Invisible Man, The
    author: **7** H G Wells

invitation 3 bid **4** call, lure **5** offer **7** bidding, summons **8** open door **9** challenge **10** allurement, enticement, inducement, temptation **12** solicitation

invite 3 bid **4** call, lure, urge **5** tempt **6** entice, induce **7** attract, solicit, welcome **9** encourage

inviting 4 warm **8** alluring, charming, engaging, enticing, magnetic, tempting **9** appealing, welcoming **10** attractive, intriguing

invocation 4 plea **6** appeal, orison, prayer **8** petition **9** summoning **12** supplication

in vogue 2 in **6** modish **7** a la mode, current, in style, stylish **9** in fashion **11** fashionable **12** le dernier cri

invoke 3 beg, use **5** apply **6** ask for, employ **7** beseech, conjure, entreat, implore, pray for **8** call upon, petition, resort to **9** appeal for, call forth, implement, importune, introduce **10** supplicate

involuntary 6 forced, reflex **7** coerced **8** unchosen, unwilled **9** automatic, reluctant, unwilling **10** compulsory **11** inadvertent, instinctive, spontaneous, unconscious **13** unintentional **15** against one's will

involve 5 imply, mix up **6** commit, engage, entail, wrap up
7 contain, embroil, include **8** comprise, depend on, entangle **9** implicate, preoccupy

involved 7 complex, engaged, mixed up, wound up **8** absorbed, immersed **9** committed, elaborate, embroiled, engrossed, entangled, intricate, wrapped up **10** implicated **11** complicated, preoccupied

involve deeply 5 mix up **6** absorb, commit, wrap up **7** embroil, engross, immerse **8** entangle **9** implicate, preoccupy

invulnerable 10 formidable, invincible, unbeatable **11** impregnable, indomitable, insuperable **12** imperishable, inexpugnable, unassailable, undefeatable **13** unconquerable, undestroyable

inward, inwards 5 inner **6** mental, toward **7** going in, ingoing, private **8** incoming, interior, inwardly, personal **9** spiritual, the inside **10** interiorly

in what way
    Latin: **7** quo modo

in which case 4 then, when **6** thence **9** whereupon **11** accordingly **12** at which point

In Which We Serve
    director: **9** David Lean **10** Noel Coward
    script: **10** Noel Coward
    cast: **9** John Mills **10** Noel Coward **12** Bernard Miles, Celia Johnson

in wine there is truth
    Latin: **13** in vino veritas

Io
    father: **7** Inachus
    husband: **9** Telegonus
    loved by: **4** Zeus
    son: **7** Epaphus
    changed into: **6** heifer
    color of heifer: **5** white
    guarded by: **5** Argus
    pursecuted by: **6** gadfly
    sent by: **4** Hera
    corresponds to: **4** Isis

Iobates
    king of: **5** Lycia
    son-in-law: **7** Proteus
    commissioned to kill:
        11 Bellerophon

Iodama
    priestess of: **6** Athena

iodine
    chemical symbol: **1** I

Iolanthe
    author: **9** W S Gilbert

Iolaus
    father: **8** Iphicles

mother: 10 Automedusa
uncle: 8 Hercules
companion: 8 Hercules
charioteer of: 8 Hercules

Iole
father: 7 Eurytus
loved by: 8 Heracles
husband: 6 Hyllus

Ion
author: 9 Euripides
character: 6 Apollo, Athene,
Crensa, Xuthus

Iormungandr *see*
11 Jormungandr

iota 3 bit, jot **4** atom, spot,
whit **5** shred, spark, speck
7 smidgin **8** particle **9** scintilla
11 faint degree, small
amount **15** tiniest quantity

IOU 4 chit, debt, note **10** obligation **12** promise to pay
14 promissory note

Iowa *see box*

Iowa, Ioway
language family: 6 Siouan
location: 4 Iowa
related to: 3 Oto **8** Missouri

Ioxus
father: 10 Melanippus
grandfather: 7 Theseus
grandmother: 8 Perigune

Iphicles
father: 10 Amphitryon
mother: 7 Alcmene
half-brother: 8 Hercules
son: 6 Iolaus

Iphidamas
father: 7 Antenor
mother: 6 Theano
killed by: 9 Agamemnon

Iphigenia
father: 9 Agamemnon
mother: 12 Clytemnestra
brother: 7 Orestes
sister: 7 Electra
12 Chrysothemis
saved by: 7 Artemis

Iphigenia in Aulis
author: 9 Euripides
character: 8 Achilles, Menelaus **9** Agamemnon
12 Clytemnestra

Iphigenia in Tauris
author: 9 Euripides
character: 5 Thoas **6** Athena
7 Orestes, Pylades

Iphigenie en Aulide
also: 16 Iphigenia in Aulis
opera by: 5 Gluck
character: 7 Artemis, Calchas **8** Achilles **9** Agamemnon **12** Clytemnestra

Iphigenie en Tauride
also: 17 Iphigenia in Tauris
opera by: 5 Gluck
character: 5 Diana, Thoas
(King of Scythia) **7** Orestes,
Pylades **9** the Furies

Iphitus
father: 7 Eurytus
sister: 4 Iole

Ipoctonus
epithet of: 8 Hercules
means: 10 worm-killer

ipse dixit 15 he himself said
it **21** assertion without proof

ipsissima verba 8 verbatim
12 the very words

ipso facto 15 by the fact itself **24** by the very nature of
the deed

ipso jure 14 by the law itself
16 by operation of law

Iraklion
capital of: 5 Crete

Iran *see box*

Iraq *see box*

irascibility 8 acerbity **9** bad
temper, crossness, testiness
10 crabbiness, crankiness
11 peevishness, waspishness
12 irritability
16 cantankerousness

irascible 5 cross, testy
6 cranky, grumpy, ornery,
touchy **7** grouchy, peevish,
waspish **8** choleric **9** irritable,
splenetic **10** ill-humored
11 bad-tempered, hot-
tempered, intractable
12 cantankerous

irate 3 mad **5** angry, livid,
rabid, riled, vexed **6** galled
7 angered, annoyed, enraged,
furious **8** burned up **9** indignant, irritated **10** infuriated

ire 4 fury, rage **5** anger, wrath
6 choler **7** outrage, umbrage
8 vexation **10** resentment
11 indignation

Ireland *see box, p. 506*

Ireland forever
Gaelic: 11 Erin go bragh

I Remember Mama
director: 13 George Stevens
based on play by: 13 John
Van Druten

Iowa
abbreviation: 2 IA
nickname: 7 Hawkeye
capital/largest city: 9 Des Moines
others: 4 Ames **5** Amana, Mason, Perry **6** Algona, Keokuk,
Le Mars, Marion, Newton **7** Anamosa, Clinton, Dubuque,
Ft Dodge, Ottumwa **8** Waterloo **9** Davenport, Ft Madison,
Marquette, Mason City, Sioux City **10** Burlington, Cedar
Falls, West Branch **11** Cedar Rapids **12** Marshalltown
13 Council Bluffs
college: 3 Coe **5** Corot, Drake, Loras **7** Cornell, Parsons
8 Grinnell, Wartburg **12** Iowa Wesleyan
explorer: 6 Joliet **7** Jolliet **9** Marquette **13** Lewis and Clark
feature: 13 Amana Colonies **17** first apple orchard
  ***church:* 11** Little Brown
  ***national historical site:* 13** Herbert Hoover
  ***national monument:* 12** Effigy Mounds
  ***state fair:* 4** Iowa
tribe: 3 Fox **4** Sauc **5** Ioway, Omaha **9** Muscoutin,
Winnebago
people: 7 Hawkeye **9** Grant Wood **10** John L Lewis
11 Billy Sunday **15** Buffalo Bill Cody, Charles Ringling
lake: 5 Clear, Storm **6** Spirit **7** Rathbun **11** East Okoboji,
West Okoboji
land rank: 11 twenty-fifth
president: 13 Herbert Hoover
river: 4 Iowa **5** Cedar, Floyd, Skunk **8** Big Sioux, Missouri
9 Des Moines **11** Mississippi, Nishnabotna
12 Wapsipinicon
state admission: 11 twenty-ninth
state bird: 16 eastern goldfinch
state flower: 8 wild rose
state motto: 45 Our Liberties We Prize and Our Rights
We Will Maintain
state song: 13 The Song of Iowa
state tree: 3 oak

Iran
name means: 15 land of the Aryans
other name: 6 Persia
capital/largest city: 6 Tehran **7** Teheran
others: 3 Qum **4** Shah **5** Ahwaz, Urmia **6** Abadan, Bandar, Kashan, Meshed, Shiraz, Tabriz **7** Birjand, Hamadan, Isfahan, Mashhad, Zahidan **11** Bandar Abbas
supreme head of state: 5 faghi **17** religious guardian
measure: 3 gaz, zar, zer **4** cane **5** gareh, kafiz, makuk, qasab **6** charac, chebel, ghalva **7** capicha, chenica, farsakh, mansion, mishara **8** parasang, piamaneh, stathmos
monetary unit: 3 pul **4** asar, gran, rial **5** bisti, daric, dinar, larin, shahi, toman **6** stater **7** ashrafi, pahlavi
weight: 3 ser **4** dung, rotl, seer **5** abbas, artel, pinar, ratel **6** batman, dirhem, karwar, miscal, nimman **7** abbassi **8** tcheirek
lake: 5 Niris, Tasht, Tuzlu, Urmia **6** Sahweh, Sistan **7** Maharlu **8** Nemekser, Urumiyeh
mountain: 6 Elburz, Zagros
highest point: 8 Demavend
river: 4 Aras **5** Araks, Atrak, Atrek, Karun, Safid, Sefid **6** Gargan
sea: 7 Arabian, Caspian
physical feature:
   desert: **9** Dasht-i-Lut **11** Dasht-i-Kavir
   gulf: **4** Oman **7** Persian
   strait: **6** Hormuz
people: 3 Lur, Tat **4** Arab, Kurd, Turk **5** Medes **6** Galcha, Gilani, Jewish, Shugni **7** Baluchi, Persian **8** Armenian, Bactrian, Bartangi, Parthian, Scythian **9** Bakhtiari **11** Azerbaijani, Mazandarani
   dynasty: **5** Qajar **7** Arsacid, Pahlavi, Safavid **8** Parthian, Seleucid **9** Sassanian **10** Achaemenid
   poet: **11** Omar Khayyam
   ruler: **5** Abbas, Cyrus **6** Darius, Xerxes **10** Rafsanjani **23** Shah Mohammed Reza (Riza) Pahlavi **25** Ayatollah Ruhollah Khomeini
language: 4 Luri, Zend **5** Farsi, Turki **6** Arabic **7** Baluchi, Kurdish, Persian **8** Armenian **11** Azerbaijani
religion: 5 Baha'i, Islam **7** Judaism **9** Shia Islam **11** Zoroastrian **12** Christianity
place:
   dam: **5** Karaj
   mosque: **4** Shad **5** Royal **12** Masjidi-i-Shah **18** Madreseh Chahar Bagh
   ruins: **4** Susa **10** Persepolis
feature: 13 Peacock Throne
   head cloth: **6** chador **7** chawdar
   parliament: **6** majlis
   underground water channel: **5** qanat
food: 5 kabob
   soured milk: **4** mast
   stuffed vegetables/leaves: **5** dolma **6** dolmeh

Iraq
capital/largest city: 7 Baghdad
others: 2 Ur **3** Kut **5** Al Faw, Amara, Ashur, Basra, Erbil, Mosul, Najaf, Qurna **6** Hillah, Kirkuk, Tikrit **7** Karbala, Mandali, Samarra, Umm Qasr **8** Al Zubair
division:
   ancient: **5** Akkad, Sumer **7** Assyria **9** Babylonia **11** Mesopotamia
monetary unit: 4 fils **5** dinar
lake: 6 al-Milh **7** Sanniya **8** al-Hammar
mountain: 6 Qalate, Zagros **7** Qaarade **9** Kurdistan
highest point: 7 Halgurd
river: 6 Diyala, Hawran, Tigris **8** Great Zab **9** al-Ubayyid, Euphrates, Little Zab **11** Shatt-al-Arab
physical feature:
   desert: **6** Syrian **8** al-Hajava
   gulf: **7** Persian
people: 4 Arab, Kurd **7** Bedouin
   leader: **6** Faisal, Sargon **7** Abbasid, Hussein, Ottoman **9** Hammurabi **13** Harun al-Rashid, Saddam Hussein **14** Nebuchadnezzar **16** Abbasid Caliphate
language: 5 Farsi **6** Arabic **7** Kurdish, Persian, Turkish
religion: 5 Islam **12** Christianity
place:
   ancient: **14** Hanging Gardens
   arch: **9** Ctesiphon
   mosque: **5** Great **9** Kadhimain
   ruins: **2** Ur **7** Babylon, Nineveh, Samarra
   Sumerian temple tower: **8** Ziggurat
feature:
   marketplace: **4** souk
   war: **4** Gulf **11** Desert Storm **12** Desert Shield

cast: 10 Ellen Corby, Irene Dunne, Philip Dorn **12** Oscar Homolka **16** Barbara Bel Geddes
setting: 12 San Francisco

Irene
member of: 5 Horae
personifies: 5 peace
corresponds to: 3 Pax

iridescence 7 glitter **11** opalescence, pearliness **12** nacreousness, play of colors

iridescent 5 shiny **7** glowing **8** colorful, nacreous **9** prismatic **10** changeable, opalescent **11** rainbowlike

iris
varieties: 3 fan, red **4** roof, wall, wild **5** Dutch, dwarf, house **6** copper, German, orchid, Sierra, Spuria, violet, yellow **7** African, bearded, crested, English, Evansia, Lamance, peacock, Persian, Prairie, Spanish, walking **8** Japanese, mourning, Siberian, stinking **9** beachhead, beardless, butterfly, Palestine **10** snake's-head

Iris
goddess of: 7 rainbow
messenger of: 4 gods
father: 7 Thaumas
mother: 7 Electra
sisters: 7 Harpies
husband: 8 Zephyrus

Ireland
> **other name: 4** Eire, Erin **5** Ierne **8** Hibernia **9** Innisfail **11** Emerald Isle
> **capital/largest city: 6** Dublin
> **others: 4** Cobh, Cork, Erne, Suir, Tara **5** Adare, Ennis, Sligo **6** Bangor, Galway, Lurgan, Mallow, Tralee, Ulster **7** Athlone, Belfast, Donegal, Dundalk, Kildare, Wexford **8** Drogheda, Kilkenny, Limerick **9** Craigavon, Tipperary, Waterford **10** Queenstown **11** Londonderry
> **school: 7** Trinity
> **division: 4** Cork, Down, Mayo **5** Clare, Kerry, Meath **6** Antrim, Armagh, Galway, Tyrone, Ulster **7** Donegal, Kildare, Wexford, Wicklow **8** Kilkenny, Limerick **9** Fermanagh, Killarney, Tipperary, Waterford **11** Londonderry
> > *ancient:* **6** Ulster **7** Munster **8** Connacht, Leinster
> **head of government: 9** taoiseach (prime minister)
> **measure: 4** mile **6** bandle **8** crannock
> **monetary unit: 3** rap **4** real **5** pence, pound **6** turney **8** shilling
> **island: 3** Man **4** Aran, Bear, Holy, Tory **5** Clare, Clear, Magee **6** Achill, Saltee, Whiddy **7** Blasket, Gorumna, Rathlin **8** Aranmore, Inisheer **9** Inishmore **10** Inishbofin
> **lake: 3** Doo, Key, Ree, Tay **4** Conn, Derg, Erne, Mask **5** Allen, Barra, Capra, Gowna, Leane, Lough, Neagh **6** Boderg, Cooter, Corrib, Ennell **7** Dromore, Gougane, Oughter, Sheelin **9** Killarney
> **mountain: 5** Galty **6** Croagh, Mourne **7** Errigal, Muckish, Patrick, Wicklow **8** Comeragh **10** Benna Beola, Twelve Bens, Twelve Pins **13** Knockmealdown **19** Macgillycuddy's Reeks
> **highest point: 13** Carrantuohill
> **river: 3** Lee, May **4** Bann, Deel, Erne, Nore, Suir **5** Boyne, Clare, Feale, Flesk, Foyle, Laune **6** Bandon, Barrow, Corrib, Liffey, Slaney **7** Kenmare, Munster, Shannon **10** Blackwater
> **sea: 5** Irish **8** Atlantic
> **physical feature:**
> > *bay:* **4** Clew **5** Sligo **6** Bantry, Dingle, Galway, Tralee **7** Donegal, Dundalk
> > *cape:* **5** Clear
> > *channel:* **5** North **9** St George's
> > *cliffs:* **5** Moher
> > *point:* **6** Cahore **8** Carnsore
> **people: 4** Celt, Erse, Gael **6** Celtic **9** Hibernian
> > *author:* **4** Shaw **5** Behan, Burke, Joyce, Swift, Synge, Wilde, Yeats **6** O'Casey, Steele **7** Beckett, O'Connor **8** O'Faolain, Sheridan, Stephens **9** Goldsmith, O'Flaherty **13** St John Gogarty
> > *leader:* **4** Tone **6** Devlin, Valera **7** Grattan, Parnell, Redmond **8** O'Connell **9** Brian Boru **12** Saint Patrick
> > *legend:* **9** Cuchulain **11** Finn MacCool
> **language: 5** Irish **6** Gaelic **7** English
> **religion: 8** Anglican **13** Roman Catholic
> **feature:**
> > *airport:* **7** Shannon
> > *castle:* **4** Tara **7** Blarney
> > *crystal:* **9** Waterford
> > *dance:* **3** jig **4** reel
> > *game:* **7** hurling
> > *lottery:* **16** Irish Sweepstakes
> > *manuscript:* **11** Book of Kells
> > *museum:* **10** James Joyce
> > *political movement:* **8** Sinn Fein
> > *race:* **10** Irish Derby
> > *relic:* **13** Ardagh Chalice
> > *revolutionary society:* **6** Fenian
> > *stone:* **7** Blarney
> > *street:* **8** O'Connell
> > *theater:* **5** Abbey
> **food:**
> > *beer:* **5** stout

Irish 4 Erse **4** Celtic, dander, Gaelic, temper
> **accent: 6** brogue
> **death spirit: 7** banshee
> **flower: 8** shamrock
> **girl: 7** colleen
> **king: 9** Brian Boru
> **legislature: 4** Dail
> **saint: 7** Patrick
> **society: 8** Sinn Fein
> **theater: 5** Abbey

Irish gods 14 Tuatha De Danann

Irishman 4 Celt, Gael, Kelt, Mick **5** Paddy **7** Irisher **9** Hibernian, orangeman **10** bogtrotter

Irish Mist
> **origin: 7** Ireland
> **ingredient: 5** cream **12** Irish whiskey

Irish Mythology *see box*

irk 3 bug, vex **4** gall **5** annoy **6** bother, pester, ruffle **7** provoke **8** irritate

irksome 5 pesky **6** plaguy, vexing **7** plaguey, tedious **8** annoying, tiresome, wearying **9** difficult, provoking, vexatious, wearisome **10** bother-

Irish Mythology
cats: **8** Kilkenny
fairies: **4** Side
god of love/beauty/
  youth: **7** Angus Og
god of poetry/elo-
  quence: **4** Ogma
god of sea: **8** Manannan
gods: **14** Tuatha De
  Danann
hero: **10** Cuchulainn
invaders/ancestors:
  9 Milesians
king: **4** Bres **5** Ronan
  9 Conchobar
  10 Matholwych
king of gods: **4** Finn
  5 Fionn
pirate/demon:
  8 Fomorian
sea goddess: **3** Ler, Lir
spirit: **4** Puca **5** Pooka
  *corresponds to Brit-
  ish:* **4** Puck

some, irritating, nettlesome
11 troublesome

iron
  chemical symbol: **2** Fe

Iron Age
  period of: **4** time
  followed age of: **6** Bronze

ironclad 5 fixed **6** strict **9** immutable, permanent **10** inexorable, inflexible, rigoristic,
unchanging **11** irrevocable,
unalterable **12** irreversible, unchangeable, unmodifiable

Iron Horse
  nickname of: **9** Lou Gehrig

ironic, ironical 3 odd **5** funny,
weird **6** biting **7** abusive, caustic, curious, cutting, mocking,
strange **8** derisive, sardonic,
sneering, stinging **9** facetious,
insincere, pretended, sarcastic
10 surprising, unexpected
11 implausible, incongruous
12 inconsistent
13 contradictory

irons 5 bonds **6** chains **7** fetters, presses, smooths **8** manacles, shackles **9** golf clubs,
handcuffs **10** restraints

Ironside
  character: **7** (Det Sgt) Ed
  Brown **10** Mark Sanger
  11 Fran Belding **12** Eve
  Whitfield **14** Robert Ironside
  cast: **11** Don Galloway, Don
  Mitchell, Raymond Burr
  13 Elizabeth Baur **15** Barbara Anderson

irony 7 mockery, sarcasm **9** absurdity **11** incongruity, indirection **12** contrariness
13 facetiousness
14 implausibility

Iroquoian
  tribe: **6** Cayuga, Mohawk,
  Oneida, Seneca **8** Cherokee,
  Iroquois, Onandaga **9** Tuscarora **12** Kaniengehaga

Iroquois
  language family: **9** Iroquoian
  tribe: **6** Cayuga, Mohawk,
  Oneida, Seneca **8** Onondaga
  9 Tuscarora
  location: **6** Canada **7** New
  York **11** Connecticut
  13 Massachusetts
  leader: **11** Cornplanter, Joseph Brant
  formed: **10** Six Nations
  19 League of the Iroquois
  supernatural force: **6** Orenda
  prophet: **10** Ganiodaiyo

Irra
  origin: **8** Akkadian
  god of: **10** pestilence

irrational 6 absurd **7** foolish,
unsound **8** baseless **9** illogical,
unfounded **10** ill-advised, unthinking **11** nonsensical, unreasoning **12** unreasonable

irreclaimable 4 lost **6** wicked
7 corrupt, debased **9** abandoned, reprobate **12** disreputable, irredeemable,
irreformable **16** beyond
redemption

irreconcilable 7 opposed
12 incompatible, inconsistent,
intransigent, unadjustable, unappeasable, unbridgeable

irreformable 6 wicked **7** corrupt **9** abandoned, reprobate,
shameless **11** unrepentant
12 disreputable
13 irreclaimable

irrefutable 10 undeniable
12 indisputable, not refutable
13 proof positive **14** unquestionable **16** incontrovertible

irrefutably 6 surely **10** definitely, positively, undeniably
12 conclusively, indisputably
13 incontestably **14** unquestionably **16** incontrovertibly

irregular 3 odd **5** bumpy,
queer, rough **6** broken, uneven **7** crooked, unusual
8 aberrant, abnormal, improper, peculiar, singular
9 anomalous, desultory, eccentric, haphazard, not smooth,
out of line, unaligned, unfitting **10** indecorous, unex-

pected, unsuitable
12 asymmetrical, unmethodical, unsystematic **13** inappropriate, nonconforming
14 unconventional
16 uncharacteristic

irregularity 7 anomaly
9 asymmetry, deviation **10** aberration, divergence, unevenness **11** abnormality,
peculiarity **12** constipation,
eccentricity

irrelevant 5 inapt **7** foreign,
off base **9** unfitting, unrelated
10 extraneous, immaterial,
malapropos, not apropos, not
germane **11** impertinent, unconnected **12** nonpertinent
14 beside the point

irreligion 7 atheism **8** apostasy,
unbelief **9** disbelief
11 godlessness

irreligious 6 unholy **7** godless,
impious, profane, ungodly
8 agnostic **9** atheistic **10** irreverent **11** unbelieving **12** not
religious, sacrilegious

irremediable 8 hopeless **9** incurable **11** irreparable **12** beyond remedy

irreparable 9 unfixable
10 remediless **12** irremediable,
irreversible **13** beyond redress,
uncompensable, uncorrectable

irreplaceable 6 unique **9** essential **13** indispensable

irrepressible 7 vibrant **8** bubbling, galvanic, undamped
9 ebullient **10** boisterous, full
of life **11** tempestuous **12** unquenchable **13** unsquelchable
14 uncontrollable,
unrestrainable

irreproachable 8 flawless
9 blameless, faultless, stainless,
unspotted **10** impeccable, inculpable **11** unblemished
12 above reproof, without
fault **13** unimpeachable

irresistible 8 alluring, enticing **9** beckoning, seductive
10 enchanting, superhuman
11 tantalizing **12** overpowering, overwhelming

irresolute 4 weak **6** fickle, unsure **8** doubtful, hesitant, unsteady, wavering **9** faltering,
uncertain, undecided, unsettled **10** changeable, hesitating,
indecisive, unresolved
11 vacillating

irresolution 5 doubt **9** hesitancy **10** hesitation, indecision

irresponsibility 8 rashness
10 immaturity, imprudence

11 foolishness **12** carelessness, heedlessness, indifference, indiscretion, recklessness **13** unreliability **15** thoughtlessness, undependability **17** untrustworthiness

irresponsible 4 rash **7** foolish **8** careless, immature, reckless **9** imprudent, overhasty **10** capricious, incautious, unreliable **11** harebrained, indifferent, injudicious, thoughtless **12** undependable **13** ill-considered, untrustworthy **14** not responsible, scatterbrained

irresponsible person
  French: **14** enfant terrible

irreverence 7 impiety **9** blasphemy, sacrilege **10** irreligion

irreverent 5 saucy **6** brazen **7** impious, profane **8** critical, impudent, sneering **9** debunking, shameless, skeptical, slighting **11** blasphemous, disparaging, irreligious **12** nose-thumbing **13** disrespectful

irrevocable 5 final **10** conclusive **11** unalterable **12** irreversible, unchangeable

irritability 6 spleen **8** acerbity, edginess **9** crossness, huffiness, petulance, testiness **10** crabbiness, crankiness, impatience **11** fretfulness, peevishness, short temper, waspishness **12** irascibility

irritable 5 testy **6** grumpy, touchy **7** fretful, grouchy, peevish, pettish, waspish **8** snappish **9** impatient, irascible **10** ill-humored **11** easily vexed, ill-tempered

irritate 3 irk, vex **5** anger, annoy, chafe, peeve **6** nettle, worsen **7** inflame, provoke **8** make sore **9** aggravate, make angry **10** exasperate

irritated 3 mad, raw **4** sore **5** cross, irked, irate, testy, vexed **6** chafed, crabby, galled, miffed, peeved, piqued, put out **7** annoyed, burning, nettled, peevish **8** burned up, choleric, incensed, inflamed, provoked **9** impatient, irascible **10** aggravated **11** exasperated

irritating 5 acrid, harsh, rough **7** caustic, chafing, galling, irksome, rasping **8** abrasive, annoying **9** provoking, vexatious **10** bothersome **11** infuriating, troublesome **12** exasperating

irritation 6 bother **7** chafing **8** distress, vexation **9** annoy-ance **10** discomfort **11** irksomeness

irruption 4 raid **5** break, foray **6** inroad **7** upsurge **8** bursting, invasion **9** incursion, intrusion

Irus see **7** Arnaeus

Irving, John
  author of: **20** The Hotel New Hampshire **23** The World According to Garp

Irving, Washington
  author of: **10** Salmagundi **12** Rip Van Winkle **13** The Sketch Book **23** The Legend of Sleepy Hollow

Isaac
  father: **7** Abraham
  mother: **5** Sarah
  brother: **7** Ishmael
  wife: **7** Rebekah
  son: **4** Esau **5** Jacob
  birthplace: **5** Gerar
  burial place: **9** Machpelah
  blessed: **5** Jacob
  sacrificed at: **6** Moriah

Isaac of York
  character in: **7** Ivanhoe
  author: **5** Scott

Isabella
  character in: **17** Measure for Measure
  author: **11** Shakespeare

Isaiah
  means: **12** Jehovah saves
  father: **4** Amoz
  son: **11** Shearzashub **18** Maharshalalhashbaz

Iscariot see **5** Judas

Ischepolis
  father: **9** Alcathous

Ischys
  killed because of: **10** infidelity
  loved: **7** Coronis
    Coronis loved by: **6** Apollo

Isenstein
  origin: **12** Scandinavian
  home of: **8** Brunhild
  location: **8** Isenland

I serve
  German: **7** ich dien
  motto of: **13** Prince of Wales

Iseult, Isolde
  character in: **16** Arthurian romance

I shall rise again
  Latin: **8** resurgam

Ishbosheth
  father: **4** Saul
  killed by: **6** Baanah, Rechab
  burial place: **6** Hebron

Isherwood, Christopher
  author of: **13** Berlin Stories **17** Down There on a Visit
  character: **11** Sally Bowles

Ishmael
  character in: **8** Moby Dick
  author: **8** Melville

Ishmael
  father: **7** Abraham
  mother: **5** Hagar
  means: **11** God will hear
  brother: **5** Isaac
  son: **5** Kedar **7** Kedemah
  descendant of: **10** Ishmaelite

Ishtar
  also: **7** Mylitta
  origin: **8** Assyrian **10** Babylonian
  goddess of: **3** war **4** love
  queen of: **6** heaven
  corresponds to: **6** Inanna **7** Astarte **9** Ashtoreth

Ishum
  origin: **8** Akkadian
  god of: **4** fire
  companion: **4** Irra

Isis
  origin: **8** Egyptian
  goddess of: **9** fertility
  hieroglyphic symbol: **6** throne
  husband: **6** Osiris
  brother: **6** Osiris
  son: **5** Horus
  father: **3** Geb, Keb
  mother: **3** Nut
  horns of: **3** cow
  headdress: **9** solar disk
  corresponds to: **2** Io

Iskowitz, B Edward Israel
  real name of: **11** Eddie Cantor

Islam
  adherent: **4** Sufi **5** Shiah **6** Moslem, Muslim, Shiite, Wahabi **7** Sunnite **8** Islamite **9** Mussulman **10** Mohammedan
  crusade: **5** Jahad, Jihad
  deity: **5** Allah
  flight from Mecca: **6** hegira
  founder/prophet: **8** Mohammed, Muhammad
  holy city: **5** Mecca **6** Medina
  other names: **9** Moslemism **13** Mohammedanism
  pilgrimage to Mecca: **4** hadj
  priest: **4** imam
  scripture: **5** Koran

Islamabad
  capital of: **8** Pakistan

Islamic 6 Moslem, Muslim **10** Mohammedan

island 4 isle **5** atoll, haven, islet, oasis **6** refuge **7** enclave, retreat, shelter **9** sanctuary

Islands of the Blessed see **10** Hesperides

isle, islet 3 ait, cay, key **4** holm **5** islet **6** island

Isle of Cloves see **8** Tanzania

Isle of Spice see **7** Grenada

Isleta (Tuei)
language family: **6** Pueblo, Tanoan
location: **9** New Mexico, Rio Grande

Ismene
father: **7** Oedipus
mother: **7** Jocasta
uncle: **5** Creon
sister: **8** Antigone
brother: **9** Polynices

isn't that so?
French: **9** n'est-ce pas?
German: **9** nicht wahr?

isolate 6 banish, detach **7** seclude **8** insulate, separate, set apart **9** segregate, sequester **10** disconnect, place apart, quarantine

isolated 4 lone, solo **5** alone, apart **6** cut off, lonely, remote, unique **7** insular, removed **8** detached, secluded, set apart, solitary **9** separated, unrelated **10** segregated **11** out-of-the-way, quarantined, sequestered

isolation 7 privacy **8** solitude **9** aloneness, apartness, hermitism, seclusion **10** desolation, detachment, insularity, insulation, quarantine, separation **11** confinement, segregation **12** separateness

isoptera
class: **8** hexapoda
phylum: **10** arthropoda
group: **7** termite **8** white ant

Ispahan
also: **7** Isfahan **8** Aspadana
location: **4** Iran
capital of: **6** Persia
river: **8** Zayandeh

I Speak for Thaddeus Stevens
author: **15** Elsie Singmaster

I Spy
character: **13** Kelly Robinson **14** Alexander Scott
cast: **9** Bill Cosby **10** Robert Culp
Kelly's cover: **9** tennis pro

Israel
former name: **5** Jacob
means: **12** soldier of God
wrestled with: **5** angel

Israel *see box*

Israel, tribes of 3 Dan, Gad **4** Levi **5** Asher, Judah **6** Joseph, Reuben, Simeon **7** Zebulun **8** Benjamin, Issachar, Naphtali

Israel-born
Hebrew: **5** sabra

Israelite 3 Jew **6** Hebrew, Jewish, Semite **7** Judaist **8** Hebraist
descended from: **5** Jacob

Israel
other name: **4** Zion **6** Canaan, Yishuv **9** Palestine **12** Promised Land
capital: **9** Jerusalem
largest city: **12** Tel Aviv-Jaffa
others: **4** Acre, Elat, Gaza **5** Eilat, Elath, Haifa, Holon, Jaffa, Jenin **6** Ashdod, Bat Yam, Dimona, Hebron, Nablus **7** Netanya, Rehovot, Tel Aviv **8** Nazareth, Ramallah, Ramat Gan **9** Beersheba, Bene Beraq, Bethlehem
school: **6** Hebrew **14** Technion-Israel **26** Weizmann Institute of Science
division: **5** Judea, Negev, Sinai **7** Galilee **8** West Bank **9** Gaza Strip **12** Golan Heights
government:
  legislature: **7** Knesset
  political parties: **5** Labor, Likud, Mapam
measure: **3** cab, car, hin, kab, kor **4** bath, ezba, omer, reed **5** cubit, donum, dunam, ephah, ganeh, homer, kaneh
monetary unit: **3** mil **5** agora, agura, pound, pruta **6** agorot, shekel
lake: **5** Huleh **7** Dead Sea **8** Kinneret, Tiberias **12** Sea of Galilee
mountain: **4** Nafh, Sagi **5** Harif, Ramon, Tabor **6** Atzmon, Carmel, Hatira
highest point: **5** Meron **6** Meiron
river: **4** Qarn **5** Faria, Malik, Sareq **6** Hadera, Jordan, Kishon, Qishon, Sarida, Yarkon, Yarmuk **7** Lakhish
sea: **3** Red **4** Dead **7** Galilee **13** Mediterranean
physical feature:
  bay: **5** Haifa
  desert: **5** Negev, Sinai
  gulf: **5** Aqaba
  plain: **5** Judea **6** Sharon **7** Zebulun **9** Esdraelon
people: **3** Jew **4** Arab **5** Druze **10** Circassian
  ancient: **6** Hebrew
  immigrant: **4** olim
  Jew born in Israel: **5** sabra
  leader: **4** Eban, Meir **5** Begin, Dayan, Herzl, Peres, Rabin **6** Ben-Zvi, Eshkol **7** Sharett **8** Weizmann **9** Ben-Gurion
language: **6** Arabic, French, Hebrew **7** English, Yiddish
religion: **5** Baha'i, Islam **7** Judaism **12** Christianity
place:
  church: **13** Holy Sepulcher
  gates to Old Jerusalem: **3** New **4** Dung, Zion **5** Jaffa **6** Herod's **8** Damascus **10** St Stephen's
  mosque: **13** Dome of the Rock
  mount: **4** Zion **6** Olives, Scopus
  shrine: **3** Bab **4** Book **11** Wailing Wall, Western Wall **18** Garden of Gethsemane
  tomb: **9** Sanhedrin **10** King David's
  way of sorrows: **11** Via Dolorosa
feature: **14** Dead Sea Scrolls
  collective village: **7** kibbutz **9** kibbutzim
  cooperative village: **6** moshav **8** moshavim
  dance: **4** hora
  movement: **7** Zionism
  Palestinian uprising: **8** intifada
  peace agreement: **16** Camp David Accords
  tree: **5** judas
  wave of immigration: **5** aliya **6** aliyot
food:
  dish: **4** pita **6** hummus **7** falafel

king: 4 Ahab, Elah, Jehu, Omri, Saul 5 David, Hosea, Nadab, Zimri

Issachar
 father: 5 Jacob
 mother: 4 Leah
 brother: 3 Dan, Gad 4 Levi 5 Asher, Judah 6 Joseph, Reuben, Simeon 7 Zebulun 8 Benjamin, Naphtali
 sister: 5 Dinah
 descendant of:
  11 Issacharite

Is Sex Necessary?
 author: 7 E B White 12 James Thurber

issuance 8 emission 9 allotment, discharge, emanation 12 dispensation, distribution

issue 4 gush, rise, stem 5 allot, arise, ensue, erupt, go out, heirs, spout, yield 6 emerge, follow, number, result, spring 7 dispute, emanate, flow out, give out, outcome, outflow, pass out, problem, proceed, product, progeny 8 children, dispense, drainage, eruption, granting, heritors, issuance, question 9 circulate, discharge, effluence, grow out of, offspring, posterity, pour forth

10 distribute, outpouring 11 consequence, descendants, publication 12 dispensation, distributing

Istanbul
 area: 7 Beyoglu 8 Stamboul
 capital of: 6 Turkey
 formerly: 9 Byzantium 14 Constantinople
 landmark: 10 Hippodrome 11 Hagia Sophia 12 Galata Bridge 14 Bosporus Bridge 26 Palais de la Culture d'Istanbul
 mosque: 3 New 8 Mihrimah 9 Yeni Camii 11 Suleymaniye

Italy
 also: 8 Hesperia
 capital/largest city: 4 Roma, Rome
 others: 4 Pisa 5 Genoa, Milan, Padua, Turin, Udine 6 Amalfi, Ancona, Assisi, Naples, Rimini, Savona, Venice, Verona 7 Bologna, Bolzano, Brescia, Catania, Messina, Palermo, Ravenna, Taranto, Trieste 8 Florence
 division: 6 Apulia, Latium, Marche, Molise, Umbria, Veneto 7 Abruzzi, Liguria, Tuscany 8 Calabria, Campania, Lombardy, Piedmont 10 Basilicata 12 Valle d'Agosta 13 Emilia-Romagna 17 Trentino-Alto Adige 19 Friuli-Venezia Giulia
  independent enclave: 9 San Marino 11 Vatican City
 measure: 3 pie 4 orna 5 palma, palmo, punto, salma, stero 6 barile, miglie, moggio, rubbio, tomolo 7 braccio, secchio 8 giornata, quadrato
 monetary unit: 4 lira, lire, tara 5 grano, paolo, soldo 6 danaro, denaro, ducato 7 testone 8 zecchino 9 centesini
 weight: 5 carat, libra, oncia, pound 6 denaro, libbra
 island: 4 Elba 5 Capri, Egadi, Eolie 6 Ischia, Istria, Linosa, Lipari, Sicily, Ustica 7 Aeolian, Trieste, Vulcano 8 Lampione, Sardinia 9 Borromean, Lampedusa, Stromboli 10 Isola Bella 11 Pantelleria
 lake: 4 Como, Iseo, Nemi 5 Garda 6 Albano, Lesina, Lugano, Varano 7 Bolsena, Perugia 8 Maggiore 9 Bracciano, Trasimeno
 mountain: 4 Alps, Etna, Visa 5 Amaro, Blanc, Corno, Somma 6 Cimone, Ortles 9 Apennines, Dolomites, Maritimes 11 Gennargentu 12 Gran Paradiso 16 Abruzzi Apennines
  Alps: 6 Apuane, Carnic, Julian, Otztal 7 Bernina 8 Ligurian 9 Lepontine
  volcano: 7 Vulcano 8 Vesuvius 9 Stromboli
 highest point: 4 Rosa
 river: 2 Po 4 Adda, Agri, Arno, Liri, Nera, Reno, Sele, Taro 5 Adige, Crati, Mannu, Oglio, Parma, Piave, Salso, Stura, Tiber, Tirso 6 Aniene, Belice, Isonzo, Mincio, Ofanto, Panaro, Rapido, Sangro, Simeto, Tanaro, Tevere, Ticino 7 Biferno, Bradano, Chienti, Metauro, Montone, Ombrone, Pescara, Rubicon, Secchia, Trebbia 8 Volturno
 sea: 6 Ionian 8 Adriatic, Ligurian 10 Tyrrhenian 13 Mediterranean
 physical feature:
  bay: 6 Naples
  channel: 5 Malta
  grotto: 4 Blue
  gulf: 5 Gaeta, Genoa 6 Venice 7 Salerno, Taranto 11 Manfredonia
  hills of Rome: 7 Caelian, Viminal 8 Aventine, Palatine, Quirinal 9 Esquiline 10 Capitoline
  lagoon: 6 Venice
  pass: 5 Resia 6 Maloja 7 Bernina, Brenner, Simplon 9 Mont Cenis 13 Saint Gotthard 17 Great Saint Bernard
  resort: 14 Italian Riviera
  strait: 6 Sicily 7 Messina, Otranto 9 Bonifacio
 people: 7 Italian
  ancient: 5 Latin, Remus 6 Sabine 7 Lombard, plebian, Romulus 8 Etruscan 9 patrician
  architect: 5 Nervi, Ponti, Salvi 6 Vasari 7 Alberti, Guarini, Juvarra, Vignola 8 Ammanati, Bramante, Palladio 9 Borromini, De Sanctis 12 Brunelleschi, Michelangelo
  artist: 5 Balla, Carra 6 Batoni, Gaulli, Guardi, Titian 7 Bellini, Chirico, Cimabue, Cortona, Da Vinci, Raphael, Tiepolo, Uccello 8 Carracci, Mantegna, Masaccio, Severini 9 Benvenuti, Canoletto, Giorgione 10 Botticelli, Caravaggio, Modigliani, Tintoretto 11 Buoninsegna, Fra Angelico 12 Michelangelo 13 Giotto Bondone 14 della Francesca
  composer: 5 Verdi 7 Bellini, Cavalli, Corelli, Puccini, Rossini, Vivaldi 8 Mascagni, Piccinni 9 Donizetti, Scarlatti 10 Monteverdi, Palestrina 11 Leoncavallo

museum: 13 Topkapi Palace **14** Archaeological **20** Turkish and Islamic Art
rulers: 4 Rome **6** Athens, Darius, Rhodes, Sparta **8** Persians, Suleiman **9** Macedonia **11** Latin Empire **12** Ottoman Turks **15** Byzantine Empire, Turkish Republic **19** Constantine the Great
sea: 5 Black **7** Marmara **8** Bosporus **10** Golden Horn

isthmus 4 neck, spit **5** point, strip **6** narrow, strait, tongue **7** narrows

name: 4 Suez **6** Panama **7** Corinth

Isus
father: 5 Priam
killed by: 9 Agamemnon

I sustain the wings
Latin: 12 sustineo alas
motto of: 10 US Air Force

Italiano, Anna Maria Louise
real name of: 12 Anne Bancroft

Italic
language family: 12 Indo-European

branch: 5 Latin, Oscan **7** Umbrian

Italy *see box*

itch 3 yen **4** ache, long, pine **5** crave, crawl, creep, yearn **6** desire, hanker, hunger, thirst, tickle **7** craving, prickle **8** appetite, have a yen, pruritis, tingling, yearning **9** hankering

it does not follow
Latin: 11 non sequitur

item 4 unit **5** entry, piece, point, story, thing **6** detail, matter, notice, report **7** ac-

---

emperor: **4** Nero, Otho **5** Galba, Nerva, Titus **6** Trajan **7** Hadrian **8** Caligula, Claudius, Commodus, Domitian, Octavian, Tiberius **9** Caracalla, Vespasian, Vitellius **10** Diocletian **11** Constantine **13** Antoninus Dius **14** Caesar Augustus, Marcus Aurelius
film director: **6** de Sica **7** Fellini **8** Visconti **9** Antonioni **10** Bertolucci, Rossellini, Wertmuller, Zeffirelli
god: **4** Juno, Mars **5** Ceres, Diana, Janus, Lares, Venus **6** Apollo, Vulcan **7** Bacchus, Jupiter, Minerva, Neptune, Penates **8** Quirinus
Italian author: **4** Levi **5** Bembo, Bruno, Pulci, Tasso **6** Artino, Vasari **7** Ariosto, Bassani, Deledda, Moravia **8** Bandello, Petrarch **9** Boccaccio, D'Annunzio, Sannazaro **10** Cavalcanti, Guinicelli, Metastasio, Pirandello, Straparola **11** Castiglione, Machiavelli **12** Guicciardini, Michelangelo **14** Dante Alighieri
Latin author: **4** Cato, Livy, Ovid **5** Pliny, Varro **6** Cicero, Gallus, Horace, Seneca, Vergil, Virgil **7** Donatus, Juvenal, Martial, Plautus, Sallust, Tacitus, Terence **8** Boethius, Catullus, Lucilius, St Jerome **9** St Ambrose, Suetonius **11** St Augustine
ruler: **4** Moro **6** Cavour, Enrico **7** Mazzini **9** Mussolini **10** Berlinguer **14** Victor Emmanuel **15** Alcide de Gasperi
ruler/military leader: **5** Sulla **6** Brutus, Pompey, Seneca **7** Crassus, Lepidus **8** Gracchus **10** Mark Antony **12** Gaius Marious, Julius Caesar **15** Cassius Longinus, Scipio Africanus **18** Tarquinius Superbus
ruling family of city-state: **4** Este **6** Medici, Sforza **8** Visconti
sculptor: **6** Canova, Marini, Pisano **7** Bernini, Bologna, Cellini **8** Antelami, Boccioni, Ghiberti **9** Donatello, Sansovino **10** Giacometti, Pollaiuolo, Verrocchio **11** Della Robbia **12** Michelangelo
wife: **7** Poppaea **9** Agrippina, Messalina **13** Livia Drusilla
language: 5 Ladin, Latin **6** French, German **7** Italian, Slovene **8** Friulian **9** Sardinian
religion: 13 Roman Catholic
place:
  arch: **11** Constantine
  baths: **9** Caracalla
  bridge: **5** Sighs **12** Ponte Vecchio
  cathedral/church: **5** Siena **7** St Mark's, Vatican **8** San Marco, St Peter's **13** Sistine Chapel
  fountain: **5** Trevi
  museum: **5** Duomo **6** Uffizi **8** Bargello, National **10** Capitoline **11** Pitti Palace, Villa Giulia **16** Gallerio Borghese
  opera house: **7** La Scala
  palace: **5** Doges
  road: **9** Appian Way
  ruins: **5** Forum **7** Capitol, Pompeii **8** Pantheon **9** Catacombs, Colosseum **11** Herculaneum **13** Circus Maximus
  steps: **7** Spanish
  tower: **18** Leaning Tower of Pisa
feature:
  unification movement: **12** Risorgimento
food:
  cheese: **6** romano **7** fontina, ricotta **8** parmesan
  dish: **5** pizza **6** scampi **7** gnocchi, lasagna, lasagne, polenta, ravioli, risotto **9** antipasti, antipasto **17** chicken cacciatora, cacciatore
  ice cream: **6** gelato **7** spumoni
  meat: **6** salami **9** pepperoni **10** mortadella, prosciutto
  soup: **8** caciucco **10** minestrone
  wine: **7** Chianti

count, article, feature, subject
8 dispatch, notation **9** paragraph **10** particular **11** news article

itemization 4 list **7** listing
11 enumeration

itemize 6 detail **7** specify
8 spell out **9** enumerate

items of business 4 list
6 agenda, docket **7** program
8 schedule

iterate 6 repeat **7** restate
9 reiterate

It Girl
   nickname of: **8** Clara Bow

it grows as it goes
   Latin: **12** crescit eundo
   motto of: **9** New Mexico

It Happened One Night
   director: **10** Frank Capra
   cast: **8** Alan Hale, Ward
   Bond **10** Clark Gable
   11 Roscoe Karns **14** Walter
   Connolly **16** Claudette
   Colbert
   Oscar for: **5** actor (Gable)
   7 actress (Colbert), picture
   8 director
   remade as: **16** Eve Knew
   Her Apples **20** You Can't
   Run Away from It

I think therefore I am
   Latin: **13** cogito ergo sum
   said by: **9** Descartes

Ithomatas *see* **4** Zeus

Ithun, Ithunn *see* **4** Idun

itinerant 5 nomad, rover
6 roamer, roving **7** migrant,
nomadic, roaming, vagrant
8 vagabond, wanderer, wayfarer **9** footloose, transient,
traveling, wandering, wayfaring **11** peripatetic

itinerary 3 log **5** diary, route
6 course **7** account, circuit,
day book, journal **8** schedule
9 timetable **10** travel plan

**it is not clear; it is not
evident**
   Latin: **9** non liquet

**it is not lawful; it is not
permitted**
   Latin: **8** non licet

it is sweet to do nothing
   Italian: **14** dolce far niente

Itonia
   epithet of: **6** Athena

It's a Gift
   director: **13** Norman Z
   McLeod
   cast: **8** W C Fields **9** Baby
   LeRoy, Tommy Bupp **10** T
   Roy Barnes **13** Charles Sellon, Morgan Wallace
   14 Kathleen Howard

remake of: 17 It's the Old
Army Game

It's a Wonderful Life
   director: **10** Frank Capra
   cast: **9** Donna Reed **11** Beulah Bondi **12** Henry Travers,
   James Stewart **13** Gloria
   Grahame **15** Lionel
   Barrymore
   remade as: **22** It Happened
   One Christmas

itsy-bitsy 3 wee **4** tiny
5 dwarf, pygmy, small, teeny
6 bantam, little, minute, petite **9** miniature, miniscule
10 diminutive, teeny-weeny
11 microscopic, pocket-sized

It Takes a Thief
   character: **8** Noah Bain
   12 Alister Mundy, Wallie
   Powers **14** Alexander Mundy
   cast: **11** Edward Binns, Fred
   Astaire **12** Robert Wagner
   13 Malachi Throne

Itylus
   father: **6** Zethus
   mother: **5** Aedon
   killed by: **5** Aedon

Itys
   father: **6** Tereus
   mother: **6** Procne
   killed by: **6** Procne
   to revenge: **9** Philomela

Itza
   language family: **6** Toltec
   location: **6** Mexico **7** Chichen,
   Yucatan **14** Central America

Iulus *see* **8** Ascanius

Ivanhoe
   author: **14** Sir Walter Scott
   character: **7** Rebecca **8** Guilbert **9** Robin Hood **10** Lady
   Rowena **11** Isaac of York
   12 King Richard I **14** Cedric
   the Saxon, Sir Brian de
   Bois **16** Wilfred of Ivanhoe
   19 King Richard the First

Ivanhoe, Burle Icle
   real name of: **8** Burl Ives

I've Got a Secret
   host: **10** Bill Cullen, Garry
   Moore, Steve Allen

Ives, Burl
   real name: **16** Burle Icle
   Ivanhoe
   nickname: **17** Wayfaring
   Stranger
   born: **6** Hunt IL
   roles: **8** Big Daddy **10** East of
   Eden **13** The Big Country
   14 Our Man in Havana
   16 Cat on a Hot Tin Roof
   18 Desire Under the Elms

Ives, Charles
   born: **9** Danbury CT
   composer of: **11** Putnam's
   Camp **13** Concord Sonata
   19 Washington's Birthday

20 Central Park in the
Dark **21** The Unanswered
Question **23** Three Places in
New England

Ivory Coast
   capital/largest city:
   7 Abidjan
   new capital:
   12 Yamoussoukro
   others: **3** Man **4** Divo
   5 Daloa, Tabou **6** Adzobe, Bonoua, Bouake,
   Danane, Gagnoa **7** Korhogo, Odienne, Seguela **8** Dimbokro
   9 Agboville, Bondoukou, Sassandra
   10 Abengourou
   11 Grand Bassam
   14 Ferkessedougou
   monetary unit: **5** franc
   7 centime
   highest point: **5** Nimba
   river: **3** Bia **5** Comoe,
   Komoe **7** Bandama,
   Cavally **9** Sassandra
   ocean: **8** Atlantic
   physical feature:
     cape: **6** Palmas
     gulf: **6** Guinea
     lagoon: **3** Aby **5** Ebrie
     wind: **9** harmattan
   people: **3** Abe, Dan, Kru,
   Kwa **4** Akan, Bete,
   Dida, Guro, Koua, Lobi,
   Wobe **5** Abron, Abure,
   Attie, Baule, Guere,
   Mande, Mossi **6** Baoule,
   Lagoon, Senufo, Senufu **7** Dan Guro, Kroumen, Malinke, Voltaic
   10 Anyi-Baoule
   11 Lobi-Kulango
   12 Agnis-Ashanti
   language: **4** Akan
   6 Dioula, French
   religion: **5** Islam **7** animism **13** Roman
   Catholic
   place:
     canal: **5** Vridi
     dam: **7** Bandama
     game reserve:
     9 Sassandra
   feature: **7** kola nut

Ivory Coast *see* **11** Sierra
Leone

ivory-towered 6 remote **8** academic, romantic **11** conjectural, impractical, theoretical,
unrealistic **12** hypothetical

ivy 6 Cissus, Hedera **15** Kalmia
latifolia
   varieties: **3** fan, red **4** baby,
   tree **5** grape, Irish, Nepal,

water **6** aralia, Baltic, Boston, canary, devil's, German, ground, marine, parlor, poison, spider, switch **7** colchis, English, Italian, Madeira, Mexican, parsley, Persian, Swedish **8** Algerian, American, coliseum, fragrant, Japanese, red-flame **9** bird's-foot, ghost-tree, heart-leaf **10** five-leaved, Kenilworth, variegated **12** Hagenburger's **13** Solomon Island **14** miniature grape **15** Gloire-de-Marengo

Ivy League colleges 4 Yale **5** Brown **7** Cornell, Harvard **8** Columbia **9** Dartmouth, Princeton **12** Pennsylvania (Penn)

I Want to Live!
  director: 10 Robert Wise
  cast: 12 Simon Oakland, Susan Hayward (Barbara Graham) **13** Theodore Bikel **15** Virginia Vincent
  score: 12 Johnny Mandel
  Oscar for: 7 actress (Hayward)

I will defend
  Latin: 6 tuebor

IWW 8 Wobblies **10** labor union **27** Industrial Workers of the World
  leader: 4 Debs **6** DeLeon **7** Haywood
  members: 6 miners **9** lumbermen **16** migratory workers

Ixion
  king of: 8 Lapithae
  wife: 3 Dia
  son: 9 Pirithous
  children: 8 centaurs
  loved: 4 Hera
  punished by: 4 Zeus
  bound to: 5 wheel

Iyar 17 second Hebrew month

Iynx
  father: 3 Pan
  mother: 4 Echo

Izmir
  formerly: 6 Smyrna
  location: 6 Turkey **9** Aegean Sea **11** Gulf of Izmir
  settle by: 7 Ionians **8** Aeolians
  ruled by: 13 Ottoman Empire

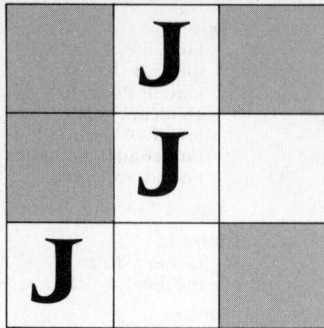

ja 3 yes

jab 3 cut, dig, hit, rap, tap **4** belt, blow, bump, clip, goad, lick, pelt, plug, poke, poke, prod, sock, stab, swat **5** elbow, nudge, paste, swing **6** strike, stroke

Jabal
   father: 6 Lamech
   mother: 4 Adah
   brother: 5 Jubal

jabber 3 gab, gas **4** blab **5** clack, prate **6** babble, cackle, drivel, gibber, gossip, hot air, patter, ramble, rattle, raving **7** blabber, blather, chatter, gushing, maunder, palaver, prating, prattle, ranting, twaddle, twattle **8** chitchat, idle talk, nonsense, talk idly **9** gibberish **10** maundering **14** chitterchatter

jack 4 flag **5** knave **6** ensign

jackass 3 ass **4** fool, mule **5** burro, dummy, idiot **6** donkey

Jack Benny Show, The
   cast: 8 Mel Blanc **9** Dennis Day, Don Wilson **11** Frank Nelson **13** Artie Auerbach, Eddie (Rochester) Anderson **14** Mary Livingston
   Jack's car: 7 Maxwell
   Jack played: 6 violin

jacket 4 case, coat **5** cover **6** blazer, casing, folder, sheath **7** wrapper **8** envelope, mackinaw, wrapping **9** container, enclosure, short coat, sport coat **10** dinner coat **11** windbreaker

Jack Sheppard
   author: 16 William Ainsworth

Jackson, Andrew *see box*

Jackson, Anne
   husband: 10 Eli Wallach
   born: 10 Millvale PA
   roles: 3 Luv **10** The Typists

Jackson, Charles
   author of: 14 The Lost Weekend

Jackson, Glenda
   born: 7 England **10** Birkenhead
   roles: 10 Elizabeth R **11** Women in Love (Oscar) **13** A Touch of Class (Oscar) **14** The Music Lovers **16** Mary Queen of Scots **18** Sunday Bloody Sunday
   politics: 11 Labour Party **18** Member of Parliament

Jackson, Jesse Louis
   party: 10 Democratic
   born: 12 Greenville SC
   education: 20 University of Illinois **26** Chicago Theological Seminary **49** North Carolina Agricultural and Technical State College
   religion: 7 Baptist
   political career: 17 Democratic primary
   civilian career: 4 SCLC **9** PUSH Excel **13** Operation PUSH **20** Operation Breadbasket **24** National Rainbow Coalition **37** Southern Christian Leadership Conference

Jackson, Michael
   born: 2 IN **4** Gary
   father: 6 Joseph
   mother: 9 Katherine
   siblings: 4 Tito **5** Janet, Randy **6** Jackie, La Toya, Marlon **7** Maureen **8** Jermaine
   wife: 16 Lisa Marie Presley
   trademark: 5 glove
   recordings: 3 Bad **7** Triumph, Victory **8** Thriller **9** Dangerous **10** Off the Wall
   film: 6 The Wiz
   group: 8 Jacksons **11** Jackson Five

Jackson, Reggie
   nickname: 13 Mister October
   sport: 8 baseball
   position: 8 outfield
   team: 9 Oakland A's **14** New

York Yankees **16** Los Angeles Angels

Jackson, Shirley
   author of: 10 The Lottery **28** We Have Always Lived in the Castle

Jackson, Stonewall (Thomas)
   served in: 8 Civil War **10** Mexican War
   side: 11 Confederate
   battle: 7 Bull Run **8** Antietam, Richmond **9** Seven Days **14** Fredericksburg **16** Chancellorsville, Shenandoah Valley

Jacksonville
   football team: 5 Bulls **7** Jaguars

Jacob
   father: 5 Isaac
   mother: 7 Rebekah
   brother: 4 Esau
   wives: 4 Leah **6** Rachel
   concubines: 5 Bilah **6** Zilpah
   son: 3 Dan, Gad **4** Levi **5** Asher, Judah **6** Joseph, Reuben, Simeon **7** Zebulun **8** Benjamin, Issachar, Naphtali
   daughter: 5 Dinah
   dream of: 6 ladder
   wrestled with: 5 angel
   name changed to: 6 Israel
   burial place: 9 Machpelah

Jacob, Francois
   field: 7 biology
   nationality: 6 French
   discovered: 3 RNA
   awarded: 10 Nobel Prize

Jacobs, Amos Muzyad
   real name of: 11 Danny Thomas

jade
   species: 7 jadeite **8** nephrite
   source: 5 Burma, China **6** Mexico **7** Mogaung **10** New Zealand **12** United States

jaded 5 blase, bored, sated, spent, stale, tired, weary

514

Jackson, Andrew
nickname: **10** Old Hickory
presidential rank: **7** seventh
party: **10** Democratic
state represented: **2** TN **9** Tennessee
defeated: **4** (Henry) Clay **5** (John Quincy) Adams
vice president: **7** (John Caldwell) Calhoun **8** (Martin) Van Buren
cabinet:
  state: **6** (Louis) McLane **7** (John) Forsyth **8** (Martin) Van Buren **10** (Edward) Livingston
  treasury: **5** (William John) Duane **6** (Louis) McLane, (Samuel Dulucenna) Ingham **8** (Levi) Woodbury
  war: **4** (Lewis) Cass **5** (John Henry) Eaton
  attorney general: **5** (Roger Brooke) Taney **6** (Benjamin Franklin) Butler **7** (John McPherson) Berrien
  navy: **6** (John) Branch **8** (Levi) Woodbury **9** (Mahlon) Dickerson
  postmaster general: **5** (William Taylor) Barry **7** (Amos) Kendall
born: **8** Waxhaw SC
died/buried: **11** Nashville TN
education:
  college: **4** none
  studied: **3** law
  admitted to: **3** bar
religion: **12** Presbyterian
political career: **8** US Senate **24** US House of Representatives
  judge: **22** Tennessee Superior Court
civilian career: **6** lawyer
military service: **12** major general **16** brigadier general
  defeated: **6** Creeks **9** Cherokees
  captured: **9** Pensacola
  military governor of: **7** Florida
notable events of lifetime/term:
  battle: **5** Alamo **10** New Orleans
  fought: **5** duels
  scandal/wife suspected of: **6** bigamy
  war: **8** Creek War **13** Revolutionary **16** First Seminole War **19** War of Eighteen Twelve
father: **6** Andrew
mother: **9** Elizabeth (Hutchinson)
siblings: **4** Hugh **6** Robert
wife: **6** Rachel (Donelson Robards)
children:
  adopted: **11** wife's nephew **15** Andrew Jackson Jr

6 cloyed, dulled, fagged **7** glutted, satiate, spoiled, wearied, worn-out **8** dog-tired, fatigued, overused, satiated, shopworn, tired out **9** exhausted, played out, surfeited **11** overwearied **12** overindulged

jadeite
variety: **4** jade

Jael
husband: **5** Heber
killed: **11** Sisera

jagged 5 jaggy, rough, spiny **6** barbed, broken, craggy, nicked, ridged, rugged, snaggy, spiked, thorny, uneven, zigzag **7** angular, bristly, cragged, notched, pointed, spinous, studded **8** indented, serrated **9** irregular, knifelike **10** crenulated, saw-toothed **12** sharptoothed

Jaggers, Mr
character in: **17** Great Expectations
author: **7** Dickens

jaguar 3 cat **5** tiger **6** feline **7** panther **8** uturuncu

jail 3 bag, can, jug, nab, pen **4** book, brig, bust, cell, keep, stir **5** clink, pinch, pound, run in, seize **6** arrest, collar, cooler, lockup, prison, take in **7** arraign, bring in, capture, confine, dungeon, slammer **8** bastille, big house, hoosegow, imprison, stockade **9** apprehend, black hole, calaboose, guardroom, workhouse **10** guardhouse **11** incarcerate, reformatory **12** halfway house, penitentiary, reform school, station house **13** hold in custody, police station **14** detention house **16** penal institution **17** house of correction

jailbird 3 con **5** felon **7** convict **8** prisoner

jailer 5 guard, screw **6** gaoler, keeper, warden **7** turnkey **9** custodian

Jair 11 Hebrew judge

Jakarta, Djakarta
capital of: **9** Indonesia

Jake's Thing
author: **12** Kingsley Amis

jalopy 3 car **4** auto, heap **5** motor **6** wheels **7** flivver, machine, vehicle **8** motorcar **9** tin lizzie **10** automobile

jam 3 fix, mob, ram, sea **4** army, cram, herd, host, mess, pack, push, stop **5** block, cease, crowd, crush, drove, flock, horde, pinch, press, shove, stall, stick, stuff, swarm, tie-up, wedge **6** arrest, edge in, pickle, plight, scrape, strait, throng, thrust, work in, worm in **7** congest, dilemma, foist in, force in, squeeze, suspend, trouble **8** hot water, obstruct, quandary, sandwich **9** interrupt, multitude, overcrowd **11** malfunction, predicament **13** agglomeration

Jamaica *see box, p. 516*

jamboree 2 do **4** bash, gala **5** party, revel, spree **6** fiesta, frolic **7** blowout, jubilee, shindig **8** carnival, carousal, festival **9** festivity **11** celebration
French: **4** fete **13** fete champetre

James 7 apostle
also called: **12** James the Less
father: **7** Zebedee **8** Alphaeus
brother: **4** John, Levi **5** Judas
disciple of: **5** Jesus
killed by: **12** Herod Agrippa
with John called: **13** sons of thunder

James, Henry
author of: **11** Daisy Miller, The American **13** The Bostonians, The Golden Bowl **14** Roderick Hudson, The Ambassadors **15** The Aspern Papers **16** Washington Square **17** The Turn of the Screw, The Wings of the Dove **18** The Portrait of a Lady **19** Princess Casamassima

Jamaica

name means: 18 land of wood and water
capital/largest city: 8 Kingston
others: 6 May Pen **8** Ocho Rios **9** Morant Bay, Port Maria, Port Royal **10** Mandeville, Montego Bay **11** Port Antonio, Spanish Town **12** Saint Ann's Bay, Savanna-la-Mar
head of state: 14 British monarch **15** governor general
monetary unit: 7 quattie
island: 4 Navy **15** Greater Antilles
mountain: 8 Sir John's
highest point: 4 Blue
river: 5 Black, Cobre, Great, Minho, White **9** Rio Grande
sea: 8 Atlantic **9** Caribbean
physical feature: 13 Portland Bight
  area: **14** Cockpit Country
  bay: **4** Buff, Hope, Long **6** Morant **9** Discovery **10** Black River, Bluefield's, Old Harbour
  point: **6** Galina **8** Portland **9** North East, North West, South East **11** North Negril, South Negril
people: 7 African, Chinese **10** East Indian
  ancient: **6** Arawak **7** Ciboney
  discoverer: **8** Columbus
  leader: **5** Seaga **6** Garvey, Manley **10** Bustamente
language: 6 Creole **7** English
religion: 7 Baptist **8** Anglican **9** Methodist **11** Church of God, Rastafarian **13** Roman Catholic
place:
  beach: **11** Doctor's Cave
  botanical garden: **4** Hope
  racetrack: **12** Caymanas Park
feature:
  evil spirits: **7** duppies
  guerrilla fighters: **7** Maroons
  tree: **4** poui **5** cedar, ceiba, mahoe, saman **6** cassia, guango **7** logwood **8** mahogany **9** casuarina, poinciana **10** silkcotton **11** lignum vitae
  witch doctor: **8** obeah man
food:
  coffee: **12** Blue Mountain
  drink: **3** rum **4** jake **8** tia maria
  fruit: **5** guava, mango **6** pawpaw
  spicy soup: **9** pepper pot

noy, chime, clang, clank, clash, crash, upset **6** jingle, racket, rattle **7** clangor, clatter, grate on **8** irritate **9** cacophony **11** reverberate **13** reverberation **14** tintinnabulate

janitor 5 super **6** porter **8** handyman **9** caretaker, custodian, janitress **11** cleaning man **12** cleaning lady **13** cleaning woman **14** maintenance man, superintendent

Janssen, David
  real name: 16 David Harold Meyer
  born: 9 Naponee NE
  roles: 6 Harry O **11** The Fugitive **14** Richard Diamond **15** Dr Richard Kimble

January

event: 15 Inauguration Day (every 4 years)
flower: 8 snowdrop **9** carnation
French: 7 Janvier
gem: 6 garnet
German: 6 Januar
holiday: 8 Epiphany (6) **11** New Year's Day (1) **12** Twelfth Night (5)
Italian: 7 Gennaio
number of days: 9 thirty-one
origin of name: 5 Janus
  Roman god of: **5** doors **8** doorways **10** beginnings
place in year:
  Gregorian: **5** first
  Julian/Roman: **8** eleventh
Spanish: 5 Enero
Zodiac sign: 8 Aquarius **9** Capricorn

James, P D
  author of: 12 Cover Her Face **13** Innocent Blood **15** Unnatural Causes **21** Shroud for a Nightingale **22** Death of an Expert Witness
  character: 13 Adam Dalgliesh

James the Less *see* **5** James

jammed 4 full **5** stuck **6** filled, loaded, massed, packed, rammed, wedged **7** blocked, crammed, crowded, crushed, pressed, stuffed **8** overfull, squeezed **10** obstructed, sandwiched **11** overcrowded

Janacek, Leos
  born: 8 Hukvaldy **14** Czechoslovakia
  composer of: 5 Mladi, Youth **6** Jenufa **9** In the Mist **10** Taras Bulba **13** Katya Kabanova **14** Glagolitic Mass **17** On an Overgrown Path **18** The Makropoulos

Case **21** From the House of the Dead, The Cunning Little Vixen **24** The Diary of One Who Vanished, The Excursions of Mr Broucek

Jane
  character in: 6 Tarzan
  author: 9 Burroughs

Jane Eyre
  author: 15 Charlotte Bronte
  character: 5 Mason **7** Mrs Reed **10** Grace Poole, Mary Rivers, Mrs Fairfax **11** Adele Varens, Bertha Mason, Diana Rivers **12** Bessie Leaven, St John Rivers **13** Blanche Ingram **15** Edward Rochester
  school: 6 Lowood
  house: 10 Thornfield
  director: 15 Robert Stevenson
  cast: 11 Orson Welles **12** Joan Fontaine **14** Margaret O'Brien

jangle 3 din, jar **4** ring **5** an-

Janus
  origin: 5 Roman
  god of: 8 doorways **9** rising sun **10** beginnings, setting sun

Japan *see box*

Japanese
  independent language of: 5 Japan **13** Ryukyu Islands

jape 4 gibe, joke **5** antic, caper, prank **7** mockery

Japheth
  father: 4 Noah
  brother: 3 Ham **4** Shem

Jaques
  character in: 11 As You Like It
  author: 11 Shakespeare

Japan
    other name: 5 Nihon 6 Nippon
    name means: 18 Land of the Rising Sun
    capital/largest city: 3 Edo 5 Tokyo
    others: 4 Kobe, Naha 5 Kyoto, Osaka 6 Nagoya, Sendai 7 Fukuoka, Niigata, Sapporo 8 Kanazawa, Kawasaki, Nagasaki, Yokohama 9 Hiroshima, Kagoshima 10 Kitakyushu
    school: 4 Chuo, Keio 5 Hosei, Kyoto, Nihon, Tokyo 6 Sophia, Waseda 7 Fukuoka 8 Doshisha
    head of state: 7 emperor
    measure: 2 go 3 boo, cho, djo, fun, inc, ken, kin, kon, rin, shi, sho, sun, tan 4 hiro, isse, kati, koku, niyo, shoo 5 carat, catty, issho, ittan, momme, picul, shaku 6 kwamme 8 hiyakkin 9 hiyak-hiro 11 komma-ichida, kujira-shaku
    monetary unit: 2 bu 3 mon, rin, rio, sen, shu, yen 4 cash, mibu, oban 5 koban, obang, tempo 6 cobang, ichebu, ichibu, itzebu, kobang 7 itzeboo, itziboo
    weight: 2 mo 3 fun, kon, rin 4 kati, kwan 5 carat, catty, momme 8 hiyakkin
    island: 3 Iki, Izu, Oki, Tsu 4 Oita, Sado, Yaku 5 Amami, Awaji, Bonin, Hondo, Kuril, Rebun, Sikok 6 Honshu, Kiushu, Kyushu, Loochu, Marcus, Riukiu, Tanega, Tyukyu 7 Cipango, Hachijo, Iwo Jima, Okinawa, Rishiri, Shikoko, Shikoku, Volcano 8 Hokkaido, Miyajima, Okigunto, Okushiri, Tsushima, Yakujima
    lake: 4 Biwa, Suwa, Toya 6 Towada 8 Kutchawa, Shikotsu
    mountain: 3 Uso, Zao 5 Asahi, Asama, Hondo, Yesso 6 Asosan, Enasan, Hiuchi, Kiusiu, Yariga 7 Hakusan, Kujusan, Tokachi 8 Fujiyama 9 Japan Alps
    highest point: 4 Fuji 7 Fujisan
    river: 4 Tone, Yalu 8 Ishikari, Tonegawa 11 Shinano-gawa
    sea: 3 Suo 5 Japan 6 Inland 7 Amakusa, Okhotsk, Pacific 8 Tsushima
    physical feature:
        bay: 3 Ise 4 Miku, Tosa, Yedo 5 Amort, Mutsu, Osaka, Otaru, Tokyo 6 Ariake, Atsumi, Sendai, Suruga, Toyama, Wakasa 7 Uchiura
        cape: 3 Iro, Oki, Oma, Toi 4 Daio, Esan, Jizo, Mela, Mino, Noma, Nomo, Sada, Sawa, Shio, Soya, Suzu 5 Erimo, Kyoga, Rurui 6 Todoga 7 Shiriya 8 Ashizuri, Shakotan 12 Muroto Nojima
        channel: 3 Kii 5 Bungo
        current: 5 Japan 7 Okhotsk 8 Kuro Shio
        divine wind: 8 kamikaze
        gulf: 6 Sagami
        plain: 4 Nobi 5 Kanto
        strait: 4 Soya 5 Korea, Osumi 6 Nemuro, Tanega, Tokara 7 Tsugaru 8 Tsushima 9 La Perouse
    people: 3 Eta 6 Korean 8 Japanese, Okinawan 10 Buramkumin
        ancient: 4 Ainu 5 Jomon, Yayoi
        artist: 4 Okyo 5 Buson, Jocho, Korin, Taiga, Unkei 6 Bun:ho, Eitoku, Kenzan, Koetsu, Reisai, Sesshu, Sesson, Shubun 7 Baiitsu, Choshun, Foujita, Gyokudo, Hokusai, Josetsu, Sanraku, Sharaku, Sotatsu, Utamaro 8 Harunobu, Kiyonaga, Motonobu 9 Hiroshige, Mitsunobu
        author: 5 Basho 7 Abe Kobo 8 Mori Ogai 11 Ueda Akinari 12 Ihara Saikaku, Mishima Yukio, Sakyo Komatsu 13 Natsume Soseki, Zeami Motokiyo 14 Shimazaki Toson, Tsubouchi Shoyo 15 Motoori Norinaga, Murasaki Shikibu 16 Fujiwara Nokisaki, Kawabata Yasunari 17 Tanizaki Junichiro 19 Chikamatsu Monzaemon
        dynasty: 5 Meiji, Taira 6 Yamato 8 Fujiwara, Minamoto
        leader: 4 Hojo 5 Kammu, Meiji 6 Go-Toba, Ieyasu 7 Akihito, Go-Daigo 8 Hirohito, Nobunaga, Yoritomo 9 Hideyoshi, Yoshimasa 10 Tojo Hideki, Yoshimitsu 11 Hara Takashi, Ito Hirobumi 12 Tanaka Kakuei 13 Konoe Fumimaro, Shotoku Taishi 14 Yoshida Shigeru 15 Ashikaga Takauji 18 Matsukata Mayayoshi
        legendary ruler: 5 Jimmu, Jingo 7 Izanagi
        shogunate: 8 Ashikaga, Kamakura, Tokugawa
    language: 8 Japanese
        alphabet/characters: 4 kana 5 kanji 8 hiragana, katakana
        dialect: 5 Kanto
    religion: 6 Tendai 7 Shingon 8 Buddhism 9 Shintoism 12 Confucianism
    place:
        castle: 4 Nijo
        hall: 5 Hoodo 7 Phoenix 12 Golden Buddha
        mausoleum: 4 Ojin 7 Nintoku
        palace: 7 Akasaka, Katsura
        shrine: 5 Heian 11 Itsukushima 16 Grand Shrine of Ise
        temple: 6 Kotoku 7 Byodoin, Horyuji, Ryoanji, Senso-ji, Todaiji 8 Enkakuji, Kenchoji, Kofukuji 9 Kinkakuji 13 Asakusa Kannon
    feature:
        abacus: 7 soroban
        bed: 5 futon
        clothing: 6 kimono
        festival: 13 Cherry Blossom

(continued)

Japan (*continued*)
- *firm:* **4** Sony **5** Honda **6** Mitsui, Nissan, Toyota, Yasuda **7** Iwasaki **8** Sumitomo **10** Mitsubishi
- *flower arranging:* **7** ikebana
- *painting style:* **4** kano, tosa **5** nanga, nisee, onnae, rarae, rimpa, shijo **6** chinso, otokoe, sesshu, ukiyoe **7** konpeki, nihonga, yamatoe
- *paper folding art:* **7** origami
- *poem:* **4** waka **5** haiku, tanka
- *puppet theater:* **7** bunraku
- *rush floor covering:* **6** tatami
- *sport:* **4** judo **6** karate **13** sumo wrestling
- *statue:* **8** Daibutsu **11** Great Buddha
- *tea ceremony:* **7** chanoyu
- *theater:* **2** no **3** noh **6** kabuki
- *the way of the warrior/code of honor:* **7** bushido
- *tree:* **6** bonsai
- *wood block print:* **6** ukiyoe
- **food:**
  - *beverage:* **4** sake **8** green tea
  - *dish:* **5** sushi **7** sashimi, tempura **8** sukiyaki, teriyaki, yakitori
  - *noodle:* **4** soba

---

jar 3 din, jug, pot, urn **4** bong, bray, buzz, daze, faze, jolt, rock, stir, stun **5** blare, blast, brawl, clang, clank, crash, crock, flask, floor, quake, shake, shock, throw, upset **6** beaker, bottle, impact, jangle, jiggle, joggle, racket, rattle, vessel **7** agitate, astound, clangor, clatter, confuse, disturb, fluster, perturb, shake up, startle, stupefy, trouble, upheave, vibrate **8** befuddle, bewilder, bleating, canister, clashing, convulse, decanter, demijohn, disquiet, distract, unsettle **9** agitation, cacophony, container **10** concussion, discompose, disconcert, receptacle **11** discordance
- **Spanish: 4** olla

jargon 4 bosh, bull, bunk, cant **5** argot, fudge, hooey, idiom, lingo, prate, usage **6** babble, brogue, drivel, patois, pidgin, piffle **7** baloney, blabber, blather, dialect, fustian, hogwash, prattle, rubbish, twaddle **8** folderol, malarkey, nonsense, parlance, tommyrot, verbiage **9** gibberish, moonshine, poppycock, rigmarole **10** balderdash, flapdoodle, hocus-pocus, rigamarole, vernacular, vocabulary **11** abracadabra, jabberwocky, phraseology, shibboleths **12** gobbledygook, lingua franca **14** grandiloquence

Jarley, Mrs
- character in: **19** The Old Curiosity Shop
- author: **7** Dickens

Jarndyce, John
- character in: **10** Bleak House
- author: **7** Dickens

jarring 4 rude **5** harsh, rough **6** jangly **7** grating, jolting, rasping, shaking **8** clashing, grinding, jangling, rattling, strident **9** dissonant, wrenching **10** discordant **12** nerve-racking **13** nerve-wracking

Jarry, Alfred
- author of: **7** King Ubu **11** Ubu in Chains **13** Ubu the Cuckold

jasmine 8 Jasminum
- varieties: **4** blue, cape, rock, star **5** crape, night, royal

---

Java
- other name: **5** Djawa
- capital/largest city: **7** Jakarta **8** Djakarta
- others: **5** Bogor, Dessa **6** Kediri, Malang **7** Bandung, Batavia **8** Semarang, Surabaja, Surabaya **9** Surakarta **11** Djokjakarta **13** Pelabuhanratu
- government: **17** island of Indonesia
- measure: **3** kan **4** paal, rand **5** palen
- weight: **4** amat, pond, tali **5** pound **6** soekel
- island: **4** Bali **5** Sunda **6** Lombok, Madura
- mountain: **4** Amat, Gede **5** Lawoe, Murjo, Prahu **6** Raoeng, Slamet **8** Soembing
- highest point: **6** Semuru **7** Semeroe
- river: **4** Solo **7** Brantas
- sea: **4** Java **6** Indian **7** Pacific
- physical feature:
  - *plateau:* **4** Ijen
  - *strait:* **5** Sunda
- people: **5** Krama, Kromo **6** Kalang **8** Javanese, Madurese **9** Sundanese
  - *dynasty:* **7** Mataram **9** Majapahit, Srivijaya
- language: **4** Kavi, Kawi **5** Malay **6** Sassak **8** Balinese, Madurese, Sudanese **16** Bahasa Indonesian
- religion: **5** Hindu, Islam **7** animism **8** Buddhism
- place:
  - *temple:* **6** Chandi, Thandi **9** Borobudur, Prambanan
- feature:
  - *cloth:* **3** kat **5** batik, kapok
  - *dance:* **7** seri mpi
  - *dancer:* **6** bedoyo
  - *fishing boat:* **4** prau
  - *ornamental dagger:* **4** kris
  - *puppet play:* **6** wajang, wayang
- food:
  - *fruit:* **6** durian, lomboy, nangca **7** gondang

6 orange, yellow **7** Arabian, Chilean, Italian, Spanish **8** Carolina, cinnamon, Japanese, Paraguay, pinwheel, primrose, windmill **9** angelwing **10** Catalonian, Madagascar **11** Confederate

Jason
  leader of: 9 Argonauts
  father: 5 Aeson
  mother: 8 Alcimede, Polymede
  half-brother: 6 Pelias
  son: 5 Thoas **6** Euneus, Pheres **7** Medeius **8** Mermerus, Tisander **9** Alcimenes, Thessalus
  daughter: 7 Eriopis
  teacher: 6 Chiron **7** centaur, Cheiron
  retrieved: 12 Golden Fleece
  ship: 4 Argo
  loved by: 5 Medea
  loved: 6 Glauce

Jasper, John
  character in: 22 The Mystery of Edwin Drood
  author: 7 Dickens

jaundiced 5 blase, bored **6** bitter **7** cynical, envious, hostile, jealous **8** covetous, doubting, satiated **9** green-eyed, resentful, skeptical **10** embittered, suspicious **11** mistrustful

jaunt 4 spin, tour, trip **6** airing, flight, junket, outing, ramble, stroll **9** adventure, excursion, promenade, short trip **10** expedition

jaunty 4 airy, neat, trim **5** natty, perky **6** blithe, bouncy, breezy, dapper, lively, sporty, spruce **7** buoyant **8** carefree, debonair **9** sprightly, vivacious **12** lighthearted, high-stepping, highspirited

Java *see box*

javelin 4 dart **5** lance, shaft, spear **10** projectile

jaw 3 gab, rap **4** chat, chin, talk **7** jawbone, palaver **8** chitchat, converse, mandible **10** chew the fat, chew the rag **11** confabulate

Jaws
  author: 13 Peter Benchley
  director: 15 Steven Spielberg
  cast: 10 Robert Shaw **11** Roy Scheider **12** Lorraine Gary **15** Richard Dreyfuss
  score: 12 John Williams
  Oscar for: 5 score

Jayhawker State
  nickname of: 6 Kansas

jazz musician 8 Art Tatum **10** Miles Davis **11** Lester

Young **12** Benny Goodman, John Coltrane **13** Charlie Parker, Duke Ellington **14** Dizzy Gillespie, Louis Armstrong, Ornette Coleman

jealous 4 wary **7** anxious, envious, mindful **8** covetous, grudging, watchful **9** concerned, green-eyed, regardful, resentful **10** possessive, protective, suspicious **11** mistrustful, mistrusting **12** apprehensive

jealousy 4 envy **8** distrust, jaundice, mistrust **9** suspicion **10** resentment **12** covetousness **14** possessiveness **16** green-eyed monster
  color: 5 green

Jebus
  city captured by: 5 David
  renamed: 9 Jerusalem
  inhabitant: 8 Jebusite

jeer 3 boo, bug, dig, rap **4** barb, hiss, hoot, mock, razz, slam, slur **5** abuse, flout, hound, knock, scoff, scorn,

sneer, taunt, whoop **6** deride, harass, heckle, hector, insult, revile **7** catcall, laugh at, mockery, obloquy **8** derision, ridicule, scoffing **9** aspersion, contumely, poke fun at, whistle at

Jeffers, Robinson
  author of: 5 Medea, Tamar **6** Cawdor **8** Solstice **9** Dear Judas **12** Roan Stallion **14** Thurso's Landing **18** The Women at Point Sur **21** The Tower Beyond Tragedy

Jefferson, Arthur Stanley
  real name of: 10 Stan Laurel

Jefferson, Thomas *see box*

Jeffersons, The
  character: 8 Florence **9** Tom Willis **11** Helen Willis **12** Harry Bentley **15** George Jefferson, Lionel Jefferson, Louise Jefferson, Ralph the Doorman **20** Jenny Willis Jefferson
  cast: 9 Mike Evans **10** Da-

Jefferson, Thomas
  nickname: 16 Sage of Monticello
  presidential rank: 5 third
  party: 20 Democratic-Republican
  state represented: 2 VA
  defeated: 5 (John) Adams **8** (Charles Cotesworth) Pinckney
  vice president: 4 (Aaron) Burr **7** (George) Clinton
  cabinet:
    state: **7** (James) Madison
    treasury: **6** (Samuel) Dexter **8** (Albert) Gallatin
    war: **8** (Henry) Dearborn
    attorney general: **6** (Caesar Augustus) Rodney **7** (Levi) Lincoln **12** (John) Breckenridge
    navy: **5** (Robert) Smith
  born: 2 VA **14** Shadwell estate **15** Goochland (Albemarle) County
  died/buried: 10 Monticello
  education: 14 William and Mary
  interests: 6 violin **7** writing **11** agriculture **12** architecture
  favorite foods: 10 French food **11** French wines
  vacation: 12 Poplar Forest
  author: 25 Declaration of Independence, Notes on the State of Virginia **39** A Summary View of the Rights of British America
  political career: 8 governor **16** House of Burgesses **19** Virginia legislature **25** Declaration of Independence, Second Continental Congress
    secretary of: **5** state
    minister to: **6** France
  civilian career: 6 farmer, lawyer
  notable events of lifetime/term:
    expedition: **13** Lewis and Clark
    prohibition of: **19** importation of slaves
    purchase: **9** Louisiana
  father: 5 Peter
  mother: 4 Jane (Randolph)
  siblings: 4 Jane, Lucy, Mary **6** Martha **8** Randolph **9** Anna Scott, Elizabeth **10** Peter Field
  wife: 6 Martha (Wayles Skelton)
  children: 4 Mary **6** Martha

mon Evans, Marla Gibbs,
Roxie Roker **11** Ned Werti-
mer **12** Paul Benedict
13 Franklin Cover, Isabel
Sanford **14** Sherman Hem-
sley **15** Berlinda Tolbert
George's business: 11 dry
cleaning
spinoff from: 14 All in the
Family

Jeffreys, Harold
  field: 7 physics **9** astronomy
  nationality: 7 British
  explained: 7 weather
  studied: 10 Earth's core
  11 solar system

Jeffries, James Jackson
  nickname: 14 The Boilermaker
  sport: 6 boxing
  class: 11 heavyweight

jehad, jihad 6 strife **7** holy
war **8** struggle

Jehioada
  father: 7 Paseach
  son: 7 Benaiah
  means: 12 Jehovah knows

Jehoshaphat
  father: 3 Asa **6** Ahitub, Nim-
shi, Parnah
  mother: 8 Jehorani
  means: 13 Jehovah judges

Jehova 3 god **5** diety

Jehu
  father: 6 Hanani
  11 Jehoshaphat

jejune 4 dull **5** banal, inane,
stale, trite, vapid **7** humdrum,
insipid, puerile **10** ordinary
9 hackneyed **10** pedestrian,
unexciting, unoriginal, wishy-
washy **11** commonplace
12 conventional
13 uninteresting

jell 3 gel, jam, set **4** clot, firm
5 jelly **7** congeal, thicken
9 coagulate **10** gelatinize

Jellyby, Mrs
  character in: 10 Bleak House
  author: 7 Dickens

jellyfish 5 hydra, polyp, softy
6 coward, medusa, nettle
7 sunfish **8** weakling **10** cten-
ophore, pantywaist **11** milquetoast, mollycoddle
12 coelenterate, invertebrate,
siphonophore **18** Portuguese
man-of-war

je ne sais quoi 13 I don't
know what **18** indefinable
quality

Jenkins, Richard Walter, Jr
  real name of: 13 Richard
Burton

Jenner, Bruce
  sport: 13 track and field
  known for: 9 decathlon
  won: 8 Olympics

Jenner, Edward
  nationality: 7 British
  discovered: 11 vaccination
  19 smallpox inoculation

Jenney, William Le Baron
  architect of: 21 Home Insurance Building (Chicago)

jeopardize 4 risk **6** expose,
hazard **7** imperil **8** endanger
10 compromise **11** put into
danger

jeopardy 4 risk **5** peril **6** danger, hazard **8** exposure, unsafety **9** liability **10** insecurity
11 imperilment **12** endangerment **13** vulnerability
14 precariousness

Jephthah 11 Hebrew judge
  father: 6 Gilead

Jeremiah
  father: 7 Hilkiah
  10 Habazaniah
  daughter: 7 Mamutal
  grandson: 7 Jehohaz
  friend, scribe: 6 Baruch

jerk 3 ass, tic, tug **4** dope,
dupe, fool, pull, snap, yank
5 dummy, dunce, idiot, klutz,
pluck, shake, spasm, start,
twist **6** quiver, reflex, thrust,
twitch, wrench **7** tremble
8 convulse **9** trembling

jerky 4 beef, meat **5** jolty,
jumpy **6** choppy, elboic,
jouncy **7** biltong, charqui, fidgety, twitchy **9** dried beef, spasmodic, twitching

Jeroboam
  father: 5 Joash, Nebat
  successor: 9 Zachariah

jerry-built 4 weak **5** frail, run-
up, shaky, tacky **6** faulty,
flimsy, shoddy, sleazy **7** rickety, unsound **8** gimcrack, slipshod, thrown-up, unstable
9 cheap-jack, defective
10 ramshackle **13** unsubstantial **14** thrown-together

jersey 3 cow **5** maillot, shirt
6 tricot **7** sweater **8** camisole,
guernsey, pullover
10 undershirt

Jersey Joe
  nickname of: 10 Joe Walcott

Jerubbaal see **6** Gideon

Jerusalem
  author: 12 William Blake

Jerusalem
  former name: 5 Jebus
  pool of: 6 Siloam **8** Bethesda

Jerusalem
  Arabic: 14 Bayt al-Muqaddas
  capital of: 6 Israel
  Hebrew: 12 Yerushalayim
  hills: 7 Judaean
  landmark: 6 al-Aqsa **11** Wail-

ing Wall, Western Wall
12 Israel Museum **13** Dome
of the Rock **14** Dead Sea
Scrolls **15** Shrine of the
Book **17** Rockefeller Museum **24** Church of the Holy
Sepulcher
  mount: 6 Olives, Scopus
  river: 6 Kidron
  ruler: 5 Arabs, David, Herod
6 Persia, Romans **7** British,
Saladin, Seljuks, Solomon
8 Ayyubids, Fatimids, Ptolemy I **9** Crusaders, Maccabees, Mamelukes **10** Ca-
naanites **12** Antiochus III
13 Pontius Pilate **15** Byzantine Empire **17** Alexander
the Great, Antiochus the
Third
  street: 11 Via Dolorosa

Jerusalem Delivered
  author: 13 Torquato Tasso

Jervis, Mrs
  character in: 6 Pamela
  author: 10 Richardson

jessamine 8 Jasminum
  varieties: 3 day **5** night,
poet's **6** orange, yellow
12 willow-leaved **13** night-
blooming **14** Carolina yellow

Jesse
  father: 4 Obed
  grandfather: 4 Boaz
  grandmother: 4 Ruth
  great-grandfather: 5 Rahab
  son: 5 David, Eliab **7** Shammah **8** Abinadab

jest 3 gag, pun **4** fool, game,
gibe, jape, joke, josh, quip
5 act up, crack, laugh, prank,
tease, trick **6** banter, bon mot
9 wisecrack, witticism **10** crack
jokes, pleasantry **11** horse
around

jester 3 wag, wit **4** card, fool,
mime, zany **5** clown, comic,
joker, mimer, mimic **6** madcap, mummer **7** buffoon **8** comedian, funnyman, humorist,
quipster **9** harlequin **10** motley
fool **11** merry-andrew, panto-
mimist, punchinello

jesting 6 joking **7** teasing
8 sportive **9** bantering, unserious **12** wisecracking

Jesus
  also called: 7 Holy One, Messiah **8** Nazarene, Son of
God **9** the Christ **12** Man of
Sorrows **13** Prince of Peace
14 Savior Anointed
  mother: 4 Mary
  stepfather: 6 Joseph
  birthplace: 9 Bethlehem
  lived in: 8 Nazareth
  death place: 9 Jerusalem
  buried by: 17 Joseph of
Arimathea
  disciples: 4 John, Jude

5 James, Peter, Simon
6 Andrew, Philip, Thomas
7 Matthew **12** James the
Less **13** Judas Iscariot
20 Bartholomew Nathanael
  secret follower: 9 Nicodemus
  famous discourse: 16 Sermon
  on the Mount

jet 4 gush **5** flush, issue, shoot,
spout, spray, spurt, surge,
swash **6** effuse, nozzle, rush
up, squirt, stream **7** sparger,
sprayer, Spritze, syringe **8** atomizer, fountain, shoot out,
Spritzer **9** discharge, sprinkler

Jethro
  daughter: 8 Zipporah
  son-in-law: 5 Moses

Jetsons, The
  character: 5 Astro **10** Jane
  Jetson, Judy Jetson **11** Elroy Jetson **12** George Jetson **13** Cosmo G Spacely
  voices: 8 Mel Blanc **10** Daws
  Butler, Don Messick, Janet
  Waldo **13** George O'Hanlon
  14 Penny Singleton

jettison 4 dump **5** eject, scrap
6 unload **7** cast off, discard
8 throw out **9** discharge, eliminate, pitch over, throw over
13 toss overboard

jetty 4 dike, dock, mole, pier,
quay, slip **5** black, ebony,
groin, levee, raven, sable,
wharf **6** bridge **7** sea wall
8 buttress **10** breakwater

jeu de mots 3 pun **11** play
on words

jeu d'esprit 9 witticism
17 witty literary work
  literally: 12 play of spirit

jeune fille 4 girl **9** young girl
13 unmarried girl

jeunesse doree 11 gilded
youth, golden youth

Jeven 3 God

Jew 6 Essene, Hebrew, Judean,
Semite **7** Edomite, Judaist,
Moabite **8** Hebraist, Sephardi
9 Israelite

jewel 3 ace, gem, pip **4** bead,
dear, find, ring, whiz **5** honey,
pearl, prize, stone, tiara
6 bangle, bauble, brooch,
locket, winner **7** earring, pendant, trinket **8** bracelet, knockout, necklace, ornament, pure
gold, treasure **9** humdinger,
lavaliere **10** topnotcher
11 crackerjack, masterpiece

jewelry 4 gems, gold **6** silver
7 bangles, gewgaws, regalia
8 trinkets **10** adornments
14 precious stones

Jewett, Sarah Orne
  author of: 26 The Country of
  the Pointed Firs

Jewish 6 Hebrew, Judaic
7 Hebraic, Semitic
  bread: 5 matzo **6** matzoh
  7 challah
  candelabrum: 7 menorah
  ceremonial robe: 5 kitel
    color: 5 white
  coming of age: 10 bar mitzvah, bat mitzvah
  dietary laws: 7 kashrut
  8 kashruth
  group: 8 Hadassah **9** B'nai
  B'rith
  holy day/festival: 5 Purim,
  seder **6** Sukkot **7** Shavuot
  8 Chanukah, Hanukkah,
  Passover **9** Yom Kippur
  12 Rosh Hashanah
  law/scripture: 5 Torah **6** Ge-
  mara, Talmud, Tanach
  7 Mishnah
  liturgical prayer: 6 Yigdal
  8 Kol Nidre
    recited on eve of: 9 Yom
    Kippur
  marriage canopy: 6 chupah
  prayerbook: 6 mahzor, siddur **7** machzor
  quarter: 6 ghetto, mellah
  school: 5 heder **6** cheder
  skullcap: 5 kipah **8** yarmulka
  **service to commemorate the
  dead: 6** Yizkor
  synagogue: 4 shul **5** schul
  toast: 8 mazel tov

Jewkes, Mrs
  character in: 6 Pamela
  author: 10 Richardson

Jew of Malta, The
  author: 18 Christopher
  Marlowe
  character: 7 Abigail, Barabas
  8 Ithamore **15** Governor of
  Malta

Jezebel
  director: 12 William Wyler
  cast: 10 Bette Davis, Fay
  Bainter, Henry Fonda
  11 Donald Crisp, George
  Brent **15** Margaret Lindsay
  Oscar for: 7 actress (Davis)
  17 supporting actress
  (Bainter)

Jezebel
  father: 7 Ethbaal
  husband: 4 Ahab
  daughter: 8 Athaliah
  opposed: 6 Elijah
  killed: 6 Naboth
  father-in-law: 4 Omri

jib 3 arm, shy **4** balk, boom,
sail, tack **5** demur, gigue,
stick **6** recoil **7** scruple

Jibaro see **6** Jivaro

jibe 2 go **3** fit **4** mesh, tack
5 agree, fit in, match, shift,
tally **6** accord, concur, square

7 conform **8** coincide, dovetail **9** harmonize **10** correspond, go together **11** fit
together

jiffy 4 jiff **5** flash, shake, trice
6 minute, moment, second
7 half a mo, instant **9** twinkling **10** nanosecond **11** microsecond, millisecond, split
second

jigger 4 dram, shot **5** glass
6 device, doodad, gadget, object **7** bicycle, gimmick, measure **9** doohickey, shot glass
10 boneshaker **11** contraption,
thingumabob

jiggle 4 jerk **5** shake **6** bounce,
fidget, joggle, jostle, twitch,
wiggle **7** agitate, wriggle

jihad see **5** jehad

jilt 5 leave **6** betray, desert
7 forsake, let down **12** break
off with **17** break an
engagement

Jim
  character in: 15 (The Adventures of) Huckleberry Finn
  author: 5 Twain

jimmy 3 bar, pry **5** force, lever **7** crowbar

jingle 4 ring **5** clang, clank,
clink, ditty **6** jangle, tinkle
7 clatter, ringing **8** doggerel,
facetiae, limerick **10** catchy
poem, catchy song **12** product
theme **13** reverberation
14 commercial tune
16 tintinnabulation

Jingle, Alfred
  character in: 14 Pickwick
  Papers
  author: 7 Dickens

jingoism 10 chauvinism, flagwaving, patriotics **11** nationalism **14** overpatriotism, spread-
eagleism **15** superpatriotism
16 ultranationalism

jinn 3 imp **5** afrit, demon, ge-
nie, jinni **6** afreet, spirit
8 jinniyeh

jinx 3 hex **5** curse **6** plague,
whammy **7** bugaboo, bugbear,
evil eye, ill wind, nemesis
9 evil spell
  French: 9 bete noire

jitterbug 5 dance, lindy **8** lindy
hop **12** boogie-woogie

jitters 6 shakes **7** anxiety, fidgets, jim-jams, shivers, willies
9 jumpiness, quivering, shakiness, tenseness, the creeps,
whim-whams **10** uneasiness
11 butterflies, fidgetiness, nervousness **12** skittishness
13 heebie-jeebies
16 screaming-meemies

jittery 5 jumpy **6** uneasy **7** anxious, nervous

Jivaro, Shuara, Jibaro
   tribe: 6 Achual, Antipa **8** Aguaruna, Huambiza
   location: 4 Peru **7** Ecuador **12** South America
   noted for: 7 tsantsa (shrunken heads)

Joab
   mother: 7 Zeruiah
   brother: 6 Asahel **7** Abishai
   commanded: 10 David's army
   killed: 5 Abner, Amasa **7** Absalom
   killed by: 7 Benaiah
   conspired to overthrow: 5 David

Joad family
   characters in: 16 The Grapes of Wrath
   members: 2 Ma, Pa **3** Tom **4** Noah **6** Connie **12** Rose of Sharon
   author: 9 Steinbeck

Joakim
   wife: 7 Susanna

Joash
   means: 15 Jehovah is strong
   father: 4 Ahab **7** Ahaziah, Jehohaz
   son: 6 Gideon, Shelah **7** Amaziah
   succeeded: 8 Athaliah

job 3 lot **4** care, duty, part, role, spot, task, work **5** chore, craft, field, place, quota, share, stint, trade, trust **6** affair, career, charge, errand, living, metier, office, output **7** calling, concern, mission, opening, portion, product, pursuit **8** activity, business, capacity, contract, exercise, function, position, province, vocation **9** allotment, piecework, situation **10** assignment, commission, engagement, enterprise, livelihood, occupation, profession **11** achievement, appointment, performance, undertaking **14** accomplishment, responsibility

Job
   father: 8 Issachar
   friend: 5 Elihu **6** Bildad, Zophar **7** Eliphaz

job holder 6 worker **8** employee, hireling

job seeker 7 hopeful **8** aspirant **9** applicant, candidate

Jocasta
   also: 8 Epicaste
   queen of: 6 Thebes
   father: 9 Menoeceus
   brother: 5 Creon

husband: 5 Laius **7** Oedipus
   son: 7 Oedipus **8** Eteocles **9** Polynices
   daughter: 6 Ismene **8** Antigone
   death by: 7 hanging, suicide

Jochebed
   father: 4 Levi
   husband: 5 Amram
   nephew: 5 Amram
   son: 5 Aaron, Moses

jockey 5 Baeza, Krone **6** Arcaro, Pincay **7** Cauthen, Cordero, Cruguet, Hartack **8** McCarron, McHargue, Turcotte **9** Shoemaker, Velasquez

jocose 3 fun **4** arch **5** comic, droll, funny, jolly, merry, witty **6** joking, jovial **7** amusing, comical, jesting, jocular, playful, roguish, teasing, waggish **8** humorous, mirthful, prankish, sportive **9** facetious

jocular 3 gay **5** droll, funny, jolly, merry, witty **6** jocose, jocund, joking, jovial **7** amusing, jesting, playful, roguish, rompish, waggish **8** humorous, mirthful, prankish, sportive **9** facetious **10** frolicsome **12** entertaining, lighthearted

jocund 5 jolly, merry **6** breezy, cheery, elated, jovial, lively **8** cheerful, debonair, pleasant **9** easygoing **10** untroubled **12** happy-go-lucky, lighthearted

Joel
   means: 12 Jehovah is God
   father: 4 Nebo **6** Samuel **7** Azariah, Pedaiah, Pethuel
   brother: 6 Nathan

Joe Palooka
   creator: 9 Ham Fisher **11** Tony DiPreta
   character:
      children: 3 Joe **5** Buddy **7** Joannie
      friend: 9 Little Max **10** Jerry Leemy
      manager: 11 Knobby Walsh
      valet: 6 Smokey
      wife: 8 Anne Howe
   profession: 5 boxer

jog 3 bob, jar, tug **4** jerk, pull, rock, stir, trot, yank **5** nudge, shake, twist **6** bounce, jiggle, jostle, jounce, prompt, twitch, wrench **7** actuate, animate **8** activate, energize **9** stimulate

jogger 4 memo **6** layboy, runner **7** trotter **8** reminder **10** memorandum

Johannesburg
   airport: 8 Jan Smuts
   area: 4 Rand **9** Transvaal
   capital of: 11 South Africa

landmark: 13 Carlton Centre **14** Africana Museum **16** Union Observatory **17** Zoological Gardens **20** Melrose Bird Sanctuary
   township: 6 Soweto **7** Lenasia **10** Nancefield
   university: 13 Rand Afrikaans, Witwatersrand

John
   father: 7 Zebedee
   brother: 5 James
   son: 5 Peter
   called, with brother: 9 Boanerges **13** sons of thunder
   pertaining to John or his writings: 9 Johannine

John Brown's Body
   author: 19 Stephen Vincent Benet

John Gabriel Borkman
   author: 11 Henrik Ibsen

John Mark see 4 Mark

Johnny Belinda
   director: 13 Jean Negulesco
   cast: 8 Lew Ayres **9** Jane Wyman **15** Charles Bickford
   Oscar for: 7 actress (Wyman)

Johnny Cash Show, The
   cast: 9 Jim Varney **10** Howard Mann **11** Carl Perkins, Steve Martin **14** June Carter Cash, Tennessee Three **15** Statler Brothers **32** Mother Maybelle and the Carter Family

Johnny-come-lately 8 newcomer **9** latecomer **10** new arrival **11** late arrival

Johnny U
   nickname of: 12 Johnny Unitas

Johns, Glynis
   born: 8 Pretoria **11** South Africa
   roles: 11 Mary Poppins **13** The Sundowners **17** A Little Night Music **26** Around the World in Eighty Days

Johns, Jasper
   born: 9 Augusta GA
   artwork: 4 Flag **6** Studio, Target **8** Watchman **10** Fool's House **12** Device Circle **13** Painted Bronze (Beer Cans) **14** The Barber's Tree **19** Target with Four Faces **22** Target with Plaster Casts

Johnson, Andrew see box

Johnson, Earvin
   nickname: 5 Magic
   sport: 10 basketball
   position: 5 guard
   team: 16 Los Angeles Lakers

Johnson, Andrew
  presidential rank: 11 seventeenth
  party: 8 Democrat
  state represented: 2 TN
  defeated: 5 no one
    succeeded upon death of: 7 Lincoln
  vice president: 4 none
  cabinet:
    state: 6 (William Henry) Seward
    treasury: 9 (Hugh) McCulloch
    war: 7 (Edwin McMasters) Stanton 9 (John McAllister)
      Schofield
    attorney general: 5 (James) Speed 6 (William Maxwell)
      Evarts 8 (Henry) Stanbery
    navy: 6 (Gideon) Welles
    postmaster general: 7 (Alexander Williams) Randall
      8 (William) Dennison
    interior: 5 (John Palmer) Usher 6 (James) Harlan 8 (Or-
      ville Hickman) Browning
  born: 9 Raleigh NC
  died: 16 Carter's Station TN
  buried: 13 Greeneville TN
  education: 9 no college 12 self-educated
  political career: 8 US Senate 13 vice president 22 House
    of Representatives
    only president to be: 9 impeached (1868)
    found: 9 not guilty
    mayor of: 11 Greeneville (TN)
    governor of: 9 Tennessee
  civilian career: 6 tailor
  military service: 8 Civil War 12 US Volunteers 16 briga-
    dier general
    military governor of: 9 Tennessee
  notable events of lifetime/term: 14 Reconstruction
    Purchase: 6 Alaska
  father: 5 Jacob
  mother: 4 Mary (McDonough)
    stepfather: 15 Turner Dougherty
  sibling: 7 William
  wife: 5 Eliza (McCardle)
  children: 4 Mary 6 Andrew, Martha, Robert 7 Charles

Johnson, Jack (John Arthur)
  nickname: 11 Little Artha
    14 Galveston Giant
  sport: 6 boxing
  class: 11 heavyweight

Johnson, Lyndon Baines
see box, p. 524

Johnson, Philip Cortelyou
  architect of: 10 Glass House
    (New Canaan CT), Wiley
    House (New Canaan CT)
    12 Hodgson House (New Ca-
    naan CT) 13 Pennzoil Place
    (Houston TX) 14 Bolssonas
    House (New Canaan CT)
    16 Amon Carter Museum
    (Ft Worth TX) 17 Sheldon
    Art Gallery (Lincoln NE)
    18 A T and T Headquarters
    (NYC), Kline Science Center
    (Yale) 19 New York State
    Theater (Lincoln Center)

Johnson, Samuel
  author of: 8 Rasselas, The
    Idler 18 The Lives of the
    Poets 22 The Vanity of Hu-
    man Wishes 30 Dictionary
    of the English Language

Johnson, Walter
  nickname: 8 Big Train
  sport: 8 baseball
  position: 7 pitcher
  team: 18 Washington
    Senators

John the Baptist
  father: 9 Zechariah
  mother: 9 Elizabeth
  descendant of: 5 Aaron
  precurser of: 5 Jesus 10 the
    Messiah

joie de vivre 11 joy of living
  19 delight in being alive

join 3 hug, mix 4 abut, ally,
  band, bind, fuse, glue, link,
  meet, pool 5 affix, brush,
chain, enter, graze, marry,
merge, paste, reach, skirt,
stick, touch, unify, unite
6 adjoin, attach, bridge, cement, cohere, couple, fasten,
scrape, solder, splice 7 combine, connect, verge on 8 border on, enlist in, enroll in,
federate, hold fast 9 associate,
cooperate, syndicate 10 amalgamate, fraternize 11 confederate, consolidate
12 conglomerate

joined 3 met, wed 4 tied
5 bound, fused, glued, mated,
yoked 6 allied, bonded, linked,
merged, paired, seamed,
united, welded 7 coupled, married, related, spliced 8 attached, cemented, combined,
enlisted, fastened 9 bracketed,
connected 10 associated, hand-
in-hand, integrated 11 hand-
in-glove

join forces 4 ally 5 merge,
unite 6 league, team up
7 combine 8 coalesce 9 affiliate, cooperate 11 consolidate
12 band together

joint 4 hock, knee, knot, link
5 elbow, hinge, nexus 6 allied,
common, mutual, shared,
united 7 knuckle, unified
8 combined, communal, coupling, junction, juncture 9 associate, community, conjoined,
corporate, unanimous 10 associated, collective, connection,
hand-in-hand, like-minded
11 coalitional, conjunctive, cooperative 12 articulation, consolidated 13 collaborative
  kind:
    ball and socket: 3 hip
      8 shoulder
    fused: 5 skull 11 base of
      spine
    hinged: 4 knee 5 elbow
    unfused: 3 hip, jaw
      4 knee 5 elbow 8 shoulder

joint action 7 concert 8 teamwork 11 cooperating, cooperation, give-and-take
13 collaboration, participation

joint effort 7 concert 8 teamwork 11 cooperation
13 collaboration

jointly 8 arm in arm, in common, in unison, mutually, together, unitedly 10 conjointly,
hand-in-hand, side by side
12 collectively 13 in association, in conjunction

join together 3 wed 4 fuse,
weld 5 marry, unify, unite
6 solder 9 integrate 10 amalgamate 11 consolidate,
incorporate

Johnson, Lyndon Baines
nickname: **3** LBJ **15** Landslide Lyndon
presidential rank: **11** thirty-sixth
party: **10** Democratic
state represented: **2** TX
succeeded upon death of: **7** Kennedy
defeated: **4** (Earle Harold) Munn, (Eric) Hass **6** (John) Kasper **7** (Clifton) DeBerry **9** (Barry Morris) Goldwater
vice president: **4** none (first term) **8** (Hubert Horatio) Humphrey
cabinet:
  state: **4** (David Dean) Rusk
  treasury: **4** (Joseph William) Barr **6** (Clarence Douglas) Dillon, (Henry Hamill) Fowler
  defense: **8** (Clark McAdams) Clifford, (Robert Strange) McNamara
  attorney general: **5** (William Ramsey) Clark **7** (Robert Francis) Kennedy **10** (Nicholas deBelleville) Katzenbach
  postmaster general: **6** (Lawrence Francis) O'Brien, (William Marvin) Watson **9** (John Austin) Gronouski
  interior: **5** (Stewart Lee) Udall
  agriculture: **7** (Orville Lothrop) Freeman
  commerce: **5** (Cyrus Rowlett) Smith **6** (John Thomas) Connor, (Luther Hartwell) Hodges **10** (Alexander Buel) Trowbridge
  labor: **5** (William Willard) Wirtz
  HEW: **5** (Wilbur Joseph) Cohen **7** (John William) Gardner **10** (Anthony Joseph) Celebrezze
  HUD: **4** (Robert Colwell) Wood **6** (Robert Clifton) Weaver
  transportation: **4** (Alan Stevenson) Boyd
born: **11** (near) Stonewall TX
died/buried: **13** (near) Johnson City TX
education:
  teachers' college: **19** Southwest Texas State
  law school: **10** Georgetown
religion: **17** Disciples of Christ
vacation spot: **8** LBJ Ranch
author: **15** The Vantage Point
political career: **8** US Senate **13** vice president **24** US House of Representatives
civilian career: **7** teacher
military service: **6** US Navy **10** World War II **11** World War Two
notable events of lifetime/term: **9** race riots **12** Great Society
  act: **11** Civil Rights **12** Voting Rights **19** Economic Opportunity
  assassination of: **14** Robert F Kennedy **18** Martin Luther King Jr
  capture of: **6** Pueblo
  Pueblo captured by: **10** North Korea
  treaty: **23** Nuclear Non-Proliferation
  war: **7** Vietnam **11** Arab-Israeli
father: **7** Sam Ealy
mother: **7** Rebekah (Baines)
siblings: **10** Sam Houston **12** Lucia Huffman **13** Josefa Hermine, Rebekah Luruth
wife: **7** Claudia (Alta Taylor)
  nickname: **8** Lady Bird
children: **9** Lynda Bird **10** Luci Baines
First Lady:
  responsible for: **24** Highway Beautification Act
  author: **16** A White House Diary

6 solder **9** integrate **10** amalgamate **11** consolidate, incorporate

join up 6 enlist, enroll, sign up **9** volunteer

joist 4 beam **5** brace **6** timber **7** support

joke 3 gag, pun, wit **4** butt, dupe, fool, gibe, goof, gull, jape, jest, josh, lark, mock, quip **5** antic, caper, cinch, clown, farce, prank, put-on, roast, tease, trick **6** banter, bon mot, deride, frolic, gambol, gibe at, jeer at, parody, satire, take in, target, trifle, whimsy **7** buffoon, bumpkin, chortle, lampoon, laugh at, nothing, scoff at, smile at, snicker **8** anecdote, badinage, pooh-pooh, pushover, repartee, ridicule, town fool, travesty **9** burlesque, diversion, horseplay, simpleton, wisecrack, witticism **10** pleasantry **11** horse around, monkeyshine **13** facetiousness, laughingstock

joker 3 wag, wit **4** snag, trap, zany **5** catch, clown, hitch, mimic, rider, snare, trick **6** jester, madcap **7** codicil, pitfall, punster **8** addendum, comedian, funnyman, humorist **10** subterfuge, supplement **11** wisecracker
  French: **7** farceur

jokester 3 wag **5** comic, cutup, joker **8** comedian **9** prankster

Joliba *see* **5** Niger

Joliot-Curie, Frederic
  field: **9** chemistry
  nationality: **6** French
  discovered: **23** artificial radioisotopes
  awarded: **10** Nobel Prize
  wife: **16** Irene Joliot-Curie

Joliot-Curie, Irene
  field: **7** physics
  nationality: **6** French
  discovered: **23** artificial radioisotopes
  awarded: **10** Nobel Prize
  husband: **14** Frederic Joliot
  father: **11** Pierre Curie
  mother: **10** Marie Curie

jollity 3 fun **4** glee, play, romp **5** cheer, mirth, revel, sport **6** frolic, gaiety **7** revelry, whoopee **8** hilarity **9** amusement, festivity, jocundity, joviality, merriment, pleasure **10** jocularity **11** merrymaking **12** conviviality

jolly 3 gay **5** droll, funny, happy, merry **6** jocund, jovial **7** gleeful, jocular, playful **8** cheerful, mirthful, sportive

9 fun-loving **10** delightful, rollicking **12** high-spirited

jolt 3 bob, jar, jog **4** bump, jerk, jump, stun **5** lurch, quake, shake, shock, start, throw, upset **6** bobble, bounce, jiggle, joggle, jostle, jounce, quiver, trauma, twitch **7** disturb, perturb, setback, shake up, shaking, startle **8** convulse, reversal **9** agitation, take aback **11** thunderbolt

Joltin' Joe
   nickname of: **11** Joe DiMaggio

Jonah
   father: **7** Amittai
   swallowed by: **9** large fish
   preached in: **7** Nineveh
   hometown: **10** Gathhepher

Jonathan
   means: **11** Jehovah gave
   father: **4** Jada, Saul **6** Joiada, Kereah **8** Abiathar
   friend: **5** David
   son: **9** Meribkaal **12** Mephibosheth

Jonathan Livingston Seagull
   author: **11** Richard Bach

Jonathan Wild
   author: **13** Henry Fielding

Jones, Carolyn
   born: **10** Amarillo TX
   roles: **8** Morticia **15** The Addams Family

Jones, Inigo
   architect of: **11** Queen's House (Greenwich) **14** Banqueting Hall (Whitehall Palace, London)
   restoration: **16** St Paul's Cathedral

Jones, James
   author of: **7** Whistle **14** The Thin Red Line **15** Some Came Running **18** From Here to Eternity

Jones, James Earl
   born: **11** Arkabutla MS
   roles: **6** The Man **7** Othello **8** Star Wars **15** The Emperor Jones **17** The Great White Hope
   voice of: **10** Darth Vader

Jones, John Paul
   served in: **11** Russian navy **16** Revolutionary War **21** British merchant marine
   commander of ship: **6** Ranger **10** Providence **15** Bonhomme Richard
   defeated ship: **7** Serapis
   saying: **23** "I have not yet begun to fight"

Jones, Shirley
   husband: **11** Jack Cassidy, Marty Ingels
   born: **10** Smithton PA

   roles: **8** Carousel, Oklahoma **11** Elmer Gantry, The Music Man **18** The Partridge Family

Jong, Erica
   author of: **5** Fanny **12** Fear of Flying **18** At the Edge of the Body **20** How to Save Your Own Life

jonquil 4 bulb, lily **8** daffodil **9** narcissus

Jonson, Ben
   author of: **6** The Fox **7** Sejanus, Volpone **11** A Tale of a Tub **12** The Alchemist **15** Bartholomew Fair **18** Every Man in His Humo(u)r **21** Every Man out of His Humo(u)r **23** Epicene or the Silent Woman

Jordan see box

Jordan, Robert
   character in: **19** For Whom the Bell Tolls
   author: **9** Hemingway

Jormungandr
   also: **10** Jormungand **11** Iormungandr **14** Midgard Serpent
   origin: **12** Scandinavian
   form: **7** serpent
   father: **4** Loki
   mother: **9** Angerboda, Angrbodha, Angurboda
   brother: **6** Fenrir, Fenris
   sister: **3** Hel
   wrapped around: **5** world
   killed by: **4** Thor
   death place: **6** Vigrid
   killed: **4** Thor

Jo's Boys
   author: **15** Louisa May Alcott

Jordan
   other name: **24** Hashemite Kingdom of Jordan
   capital/largest city: **5** Amman
      ancient name: **12** Philadelphia
   others: **4** Krak, Ma'an, Salt **5** Aqaba, Ariha, Irbid, Jenin, Karak, Kerak, Sarga, Zarga, Zerke **6** Bethel, Hebron, Jarash, Jerash, Madaba, Nablus, Ramtha **7** Al-Agaba, Bethany, El-Kerak, El Zerga, Jericho, Kirmoab, Nabulus, Samaria **8** Al-Khalil, Ram Allah **9** Bethlehem, Jerusalem
   school: **7** yarmouk
   division: **8** East Bank, West Bank **11** Transjordan
   ancient state: **4** Edom, Moab **5** Ammon, Judah **6** Gilead
   head of state: **4** king
   monetary unit: **4** fils **5** dinar
   mountain: **3** Hor **4** Nebo **5** Bukka, Dabab **6** Ataiba, Gilead, Mubrak
   highest point: **9** Jabal Ramm, Jebel Ramm
   river: **6** Jordan, Yarmuk **11** Nahr-az-Zarga
   sea: **3** Red **4** Dead **7** Galilee **13** Mediterranean
   physical feature:
      desert: **6** Syria
      gulf: **5** Aqaba
      plateau: **11** Transjordan
      valley: **4** Ghor **9** Great Rift
      wind: **7** Khamsin
   people: **4** Arab, Kurd **7** Bedouin, Checher **8** Armenian, Assyrian **10** Circassian **11** Palestinian
      ancient: **8** Armonite **9** Nabataean
      ruler: **5** Talal **6** Faisal, Greeks, Romans **7** Hussein **8** Abdullah, Selucidas **9** Crusaders **10** Ibn Hussein, Nabataeans **12** Ottoman Turks **18** Abdullah Ibn Hussein
      tribe: **5** Qaysi **6** Yamani
   language: **6** Arabic
   religion: **5** Islam **13** Greek Orthodox
   place:
      canal: **8** East Gher
      ruins: **5** Ajlun, Petra **6** Jarash **7** Al Karak
   feature:
      headdress: **8** kaffiyeh
      village headman: **7** mukhtar
      village square: **5** sahah
   food:
      dessert: **7** baklava
      pastry: **7** katayif

Joseph
father: **4** Bani **5** Aseph, Jacob **10** Mattathias
mother: **6** Rachel
brother: **3** Dan, Gad **4** Levi **5** Asher, Judah **6** Reuben, Simeon **7** Zebulun **8** Benjamin, Issachar, Naphtali
wife: **4** Mary **5** Asenath
stepson: **5** Jesus
also called: **20** Barsabbas of Arimathea **21** Barsabbas of Arimathaea
buried: **5** Jesus
slave of: **8** Potiphar

Joseph Andrews
author: **13** Henry Fielding
character: **5** Fanny **9** Lady Booby **11** Mrs Slipslop, Parson Adams, Peter Pounce **13** Pamela Andrews

josh 3 guy, kid, rag, rib **4** dish, haze, jape, jest, jive, joke, quiz, razz, ride, twit **5** chaff, jolly, put on, roast, tease **6** banter, needle **8** ridicule

Joshua
means: **18** Jehovah is salvation
father: **3** Nun
succeeded: **5** Moses
captured: **7** Jericho, Lachish
hid spies: **5** Rahab

Josiah
means: **12** Jehovah heals
father: **9** Zephaniah
succeeded: **4** Amon

jostle 3 jab **4** bump, butt, poke, prod, push **5** crowd, elbow, shove **7** collide **8** shoulder **10** hit against, run against **12** knock against

jot 3 bit, dot **4** list, mite, note, snip, whit **5** enter, speck, trace **6** record, trifle **7** modicum, one iota, put down, set down, smidgen, snippet **8** flyspeck, particle, register, scribble, take down **9** scintilla

Jotham
son: **4** Ahaz

Jo the crossing sweeper
character in: **10** Bleak House
author: **7** Dickens

jotting 4 memo, note **6** doodle **8** scribble **10** memorandum, scribbling

Jotun
origin: **12** Scandinavian
form: **5** giant
conflicts with: **4** gods
enemy: **4** Asar **5** Aesir

Jotunheim
origin: **12** Scandinavian
realm of: **6** giants

Joukahainen
origin: **7** Finnish
form: **8** magician

location: **7** Lapland
tried to kill: **11** Vainamoinen

Joule, James Prescott
field: **7** physics
nationality: **7** British
established law of: **20** conservation of energy
named for him: **10** unit of work

jounce 3 bob **6** bounce **7** rebound **8** ricochet

Jourdain, Monsieur
character in: **21** The Bourgeois Gentleman **22** Le Bourgeois Gentilhomme
author: **7** Moliere

Jourdan, Louis
real name: **11** Louis Gendre
born: **6** France **9** Marseille
roles: **4** Gigi **6** Can Can **9** Octopussy **15** The Paradine Case **23** Three Coins in the Fountain **24** Letter from an Unknown Woman

journal 3 log **5** album, daily, diary, paper, sheet **6** annual, ledger, memoir, record, weekly **7** almanac, daybook, gazette, history, logbook, monthly, tabloid **8** calendar, magazine, notebook, register, yearbook **9** chronicle, newspaper, quarterly, scrapbook **10** chronology, confession, memorandum, memory book, periodical, record book **11** account book, daily record, publication **13** autobiography

journalist 6 author, editor, writer **7** byliner, diarist, newsman **8** reporter **9** columnist, newswoman **12** newspaperman **13** correspondent **14** newspaperwoman

Journal of the Plague Year, A
author: **11** Daniel Defoe

journey 3 fly, way **4** roam, rove, sail, tour, trek, trip, wend **5** jaunt, quest, route, tramp **6** course, cruise, flight, junket, outing, ramble, roving, travel, voyage, wander **7** circuit, meander, odyssey, passage, transit **8** divagate, navigate, sightsee, vagabond **9** excursion, itinerary, take a trip, wandering **10** divagation, expedition, pilgrimage **11** peregrinate **13** peregrination

Journey Into Fear
author: **10** Eric Ambler

journey's end 4 goal **9** objective **11** destination

Journey to the End of the Night
author: **20** Louis-Ferdinand Celine

joust 4 tilt **5** combat, jostle **7** contend, contest, tourney **8** run a tilt **10** contention, tournament

Jove *see* **7** Jupiter

jovial 3 gay **5** jolly, merry, sunny **6** blithe, cheery, hearty, jocose, jocund **7** buoyant, gleeful, jocular, playful, zestful **8** cheerful, humorous, laughing, mirthful, sportive **9** convivial, fun-loving, hilarious **10** delightful, frolicsome, rollicking

joviality 3 fun **4** glee **5** cheer, gaity, mirth **7** delight, jollity, revelry **8** buoyancy **9** jocundity, merriment **10** joyfulness, liveliness **11** high spirits

jowl 3 jaw **5** cheek, chops **6** muzzle **8** mandible

joy 3 gem **4** glee **5** jewel, pride, prize **6** gaiety **7** delight, ecstasy, elation, rapture **8** gladness, pleasure, treasure **9** enjoyment, happiness **10** excitement, exultation, jubilation **11** contentment, delectation **12** cheerfulness, exhilaration, satisfaction
goddess of: **6** Hathor

Joyce, James
author of: **7** Ulysses **9** Dubliners **13** Finnegan's Wake **31** A Portrait of the Artist as a Young Man

joyful 4 glad, rosy **5** happy **6** bright, elated **7** blessed, pleased **8** cheerful, ecstatic, exultant, gladsome, jubilant, pleasing **9** delighted, full of joy, overjoyed **10** delightful, enraptured, gratifying, heartening **11** pleasurable, transported **12** heartwarming

joyless 3 sad **4** glum, grim **5** black **6** dismal, gloomy, morbid, woeful **7** doleful, forlorn, unhappy **8** dejected, desolate, dolorous, downcast, mournful **9** cheerless, depressed, sorrowful, woebegone **10** despondent, in the dumps, lugubrious, melancholy **11** downhearted, pessimistic **12** disconsolate, heavyhearted **14** down in the mouth

joy of living
French: **11** joie de vivre

Joy of Sex, The
author: **11** Alex Comfort

joyous 3 gay **4** glad **5** happy, merry **7** festive, gleeful **8** cheerful, gladsome, mirthful **9** rapturous, wonderful **10** delightful, gratifying, hearten-

ing **11** pleasurable
12 heartwarming, lighthearted

joyousness 4 glee **8** gladness
9 happiness, merriment
10 blitheness, exuberance
11 high spirits
16 lightheartedness

Jubal
father: **6** Lamech
mother: **4** Adah
brother: **5** Jabal

jubilant 3 gay **4** glad **5** happy,
jolly, merry **6** blithe, cheery,
elated, enrapt, joyful, joyous
7 buoyant, charmed, gleeful,
pleased, radiant, smiling
8 cheerful, ecstatic, exultant,
gladsome, laughing, mirthful
9 delighted, delirious, exuberant, gladdened, gratified, overjoyed, rapturous, rejoicing,
rhapsodic **10** blithesome, captivated, enraptured **11** exhilarated, intoxicated, tickled
pink **12** happy as a lark, lighthearted **13** in high spirits

jubilation 5 bliss **9** rejoicing
11 celebration **12** exhilaration

jubilee 2 do **4** bash, fete, gala
5 blast, party **6** frolic, revels
7 blowout, holiday, revelry,
shindig **8** festival, wingding
9 festivity **10** jubilation, observance **11** anniversary, celebration, merrymaking
12 conviviality
13 commemoration

Juda
father: **6** Joanna, Joseph
8 Hananiah

Judah
father: **5** Jacob
mother: **4** Leah
brother: **3** Dan, Gad **4** Levi
5 Asher, Judah **6** Joseph,
Reuben, Simeon **8** Benjamin,
Issachar, Naphtali
sister: **5** Dinah
wife: **5** Shuah
son: **2** Er **4** Onan **5** Perez,
Zerah **6** Baruch, Shelah
daughter-in-law: **5** Tamar
last king of: **8** Zedekiah
descendant of: **8** Judahite

Judah, tribes of see **14** Israel, tribes of

Judas
brother: **5** James
also called: **8** Thaddeus
disciple of: **5** Jesus

Judas Iscariot 8 betrayer
disciple of: **5** Jesus
betrayed: **5** Jesus
replaced by: **8** Matthias

Jude 7 apostle
brother: **5** James

Jude the Obscure
author: **11** Thomas Hardy

character: **10** Jude Fawley
12 Arabella Donn, Sue
Bridehead **14** Drusilla Fawley **16** Little Father Time
17 Richard Phillotson

judge 3 try **4** deem, find, hear,
rank, rate **5** fancy, gauge,
guess, infer, juror, value,
weigh **6** assess, assume, censor, critic, decide, deduce, expert, reckon, regard, review,
rule on, settle, size up, umpire **7** adjudge, analyze, arbiter, believe, conduct, discern,
imagine, justice, referee, resolve, suppose, surmise **8** appraise, assessor, conclude,
consider, estimate, official, reviewer **9** appraiser, arbitrate,
ascertain, authority, determine,
evaluator, moderator **10** adjudicate, arbitrator, conjecture,
magistrate **11** adjudicator, connoisseur, distinguish **12** pass
sentence

judgment, judgement
4 view **5** sense, taste **6** acumen, belief, decree, ruling
7 finding, opinion, verdict
8 decision, estimate, sentence
9 appraisal, deduction, valuation **10** assessment, conclusion, conviction, discretion,
perception, persuasion,
shrewdness **11** arbitration, discernment, percipience **14** discrimination, perceptiveness

Judgment at Nuremberg
director: **13** Stanley Kramer
cast: **11** Judy Garland
12 Spencer Tracy **13** Burt
Lancaster **14** Richard Widmark, William Shatner
15 Marlene Dietrich, Montgomery Clift **16** Maximilian
Schell
Oscar for: **5** actor (Schell)

Judgment Day 8 doomsday
13 end of the world **14** day of
reckoning **15** the Last
Judgment

Judgment Day
author: **13** James T Farrell

Judgment of Paris see
5 Paris

judicial 5 legal **8** imposing, juristic, majestic, official **9** mag-
istral **11** magisterial
13 distinguished

judiciary 5 bench, court
11 court system

judicious 4 just, sage, wise
5 acute, sober, sound **6** astute,
shrewd **7** knowing, politic,
prudent, tactful **8** sensible
9 sagacious **10** diplomatic, discerning, percipient, reasonable,
reflective, thoughtful **11** level-

headed **13** perspicacious
14 discriminating

judiciousness 4 tact **6** acumen,
wisdom **8** prudence, sagacity
9 good sense **10** discretion
11 discernment, percipience
12 perspicacity
14 discrimination

Judique, Mrs Tanis
character in: **7** Babbitt
author: **5** Lewis

Judith
husband: **4** Esau
killed: **10** Holofernes

Judith Paris
author: **11** Hugh Walpole

jug 3 jar, urn **4** ewer **5** crock,
stein **6** bottle, carafe, flagon,
vessel **7** pitcher, tankard **8** decanter, demijohn **9** container

juggle 4 redo **5** alter **6** modify
7 falsify **8** disguise, fool with
9 keep aloft **10** manipulate,
meddle with, reorganize,
tamper with, tinker with
12 misrepresent

juggler 5 cheat **6** jester **8** con-
juror, deceiver, jongleur, magician, shuffler **15** prestidigitator

Juice
nickname of: **9** O J Simpson

juicy 3 wet **4** lush, racy **5** fluid,
lurid, moist, pulpy, runny,
sappy, spicy, vivid **6** fluent,
liquid, risque, watery **7** flowing, graphic **8** colorful, dripping, exciting, luscious
9 succulent, thrilling **10** intriguing **11** captivating, fascinating, picturesque,
provocative, sensational,
tantalizing

Jules and Jim
director: **16** Francois Truffaut
cast: **10** Henri Serre
11 Marie Dubois, Oskar
Werner **12** Jeanne Moreau

Julia
character in: **20** Two Gentlemen of Verona
author: **11** Shakespeare

Julia
character: **10** Corey Baker,
Eddie Edson, Julia Baker
11 Hannah Yarby **14** Earl J
Waggedorn, Marie Wagge-
dorn **15** Dr Morton Chegley
cast: **10** Lloyd Nolan, Marc
Copage **11** Betty Beaird, Michael Link **12** Eddie Quillan,
Lurene Tuttle, Paul Win-
field **14** Diahann Carroll

Julia
director: **13** Fred Zinnemann
based on story by: **14** Lillian
Hellman (Pentimento)
cast: **9** Jane Fonda (Lillian

Hellman) **11** Hal Holbrook
12 Jason Robards (Dashiell
Hammett) **15** Vanessa Redgrave (Julia) **16** Maximilian
Schell
Oscar for: 12 screenwriter
15 supporting actor (Robards) **17** supporting actress
(Redgrave)

Julius Caesar
  author: 18 William
  Shakespeare
  character: 6 Brutus (Marcus
  Brutus), Portia **7** Cassius
  (Gaius Cassius) **9** Calpurnia
  10 Mark Antony (Marcus
  Antonius)
  director: 17 Joseph L
  Mankiewicz
  cast: 10 James Mason
  11 Deborah Kerr, Greer Garson, John Gielgud **12** Edmond O'Brien, Louis
  Calhern, Marlon Brando

July
  flower: 8 larkspur **9** water lily
  French: 7 Juillet
  holiday: 11 Bastille Day
  (14), Dominion Day
  (1) **15** Independence
  Day (4) **16** Saint Swithin's Day (15)
  gem: 4 ruby
  German: 4 Juli
  Italian: 6 Luglio
  number of days:
  9 thirty-one
  origin of name: 12 Julius Caesar
  place in year:
    Gregorian: **7** seventh
    Roman: **5** fifth
  Spanish: 5 Julio
  Zodiac sign: 3 Leo
  6 Cancer

jumble 3 mix **4** heap, mess,
olio, stew **5** bunch, chaos, mix
up, pitch, snarl **6** ball up,
medley, muddle, pile up, tangle, tumble **7** clutter, farrago,
melange, mixture, scatter
8 disarray, mishmash **9** aggregate, confusion, patchwork,
potpourri **10** hodgepodge, miscellany, salmagundi **11** gallimaufry **12** accumulation
14 conglomeration

jumbled 5 messy **7** chaotic,
mixed up, snarled, tangled
8 confused **9** cluttered, illogical **10** disjointed, incoherent
11 disarranged **12** disconnected, disorganized

jumbo 4 huge, vast **5** giant
6 mighty **7** immense, mam-

moth, titanic **8** colossal, enormous, gigantic, towering
9 cyclopean, monstrous, oversized **10** monumental, stupendous **11** elephantine,
mountainous

jump 3 hop **4** buck, leap, pass,
skip **5** boost, bound, pitch,
start, surge, vault, wince
6 ambush, attack, blench,
bounce, flinch, gambol, go
over, hurdle, prance, recoil,
spring, switch, upturn, zoom
up **7** advance, barrier, digress,
maunder, overrun, upsurge
8 fall upon, obstacle **9** barricade, increment, skyrocket
10 impediment **11** obstruction
12 augmentation

jumper 4 frog, sled, toad
5 dress, horse, shirt, smock
6 blouse, hopper, jacket,
leaper **7** overall **8** coverall,
kangaroo

jump for joy 5 exult **7** rejoice

jumpy 5 nervy, shaky **6** goosey,
uneasy **7** alarmed, anxious,
fidgety, fretful, jittery, nervous, panicky, twitchy, uptight **8** aflutter, agitated,
fluttery, skittish **9** trembling,
twitching **10** frightened
12 apprehensive

junction 6 linkup **7** conflux,
joining **10** confluence, crossroads **11** concurrence, convergence, interchange
12 intersection

juncture 4 pass, seam **5** joint
6 crisis, linkup, moment
7 closure, joining, meeting
8 interval, occasion **10** confluence, connection **11** convergence, point in time
12 intersection **13** critical point

June *see box*

jungle 4 bush, wild **5** woods
10 rain forest, wilderness
11 undergrowth **12** swampy
forest, virgin forest

Jungle, The
  author: 13 Upton Sinclair
  character: 3 Ona **5** Jonas
  6 Marija **8** Elzbieta **12** Jurgis
  Rudkus **13** Antanas Rudkus
  criticism of: 19 meat-packing
  industry

Jungle Books, The
  author: 14 Rudyard Kipling
  character: 3 Kaa **5** Akela,
  Baloo, Hathi **6** Buldeo, Mes-
  sau, Mowgli **8** Bagheera
  9 Shere Khan **11** Gray Brother

Jungle Jim
  creator: 11 Alex Raymond
  character: 4 Joan, Kolu

junior 5 later, lower, minor,
newer **6** lesser **7** younger

June
  characteristic:
  8 weddings
  event: 12 Midsummer
  Day (24), Midsummer
  Eve (23) **14** summer
  solstice (21)
  flower: 4 rose
  French: 4 Juin
  gem: 5 pearl **9** moonstone **11** alexandrite
  German: 4 Juni
  holiday: 7 Flag Day (14)
  10 Father's Day (third
  Sunday) **13** Kameha-
  meha Day (11) **22** Jefferson Davis' birthday (3)
  Italian: 6 Giugno
  number of days: 6 thirty
  origin of name: 4 Juno
  (Roman goddess)
  6 Junius (Roman clan)
  8 juniores (youths)
  place in year:
    Gregorian: **5** sixth
    Roman: **6** fourth
  saying: 24 What is so
  rare as a day in June
  Spanish: 5 Junio
  Zodiac sign: 6 Cancer,
  Gemini

8 inferior **9** secondary
11 subordinate

juniper 9 Juniperus
  varieties: 4 ashe, plum
  5 Greek, Irish, shore **6** common, ground, needle, Polish,
  Sierra, Syrian **7** African, incense, prickly, Sargent
  8 creeping, drooping, mountain, red-berry, Waukegan
  9 alligator, blue-spire, Himalayan, prostrate **10** California **11** cherrystone
  12 Canary Island, sweet-
  fruited **13** Rocky Mountain

junk 4 dump **5** scrap, trash,
waste **6** debris, litter, refuse
7 clutter, discard, garbage, rubbish, rummage **8** castoffs, oddments, throw out **9** dispose of,
throw away **11** odds and ends

junket 4 tour, trip **7** journey
9 excursion

Juno
  origin: 5 Roman
  queen of: 6 heaven
  father: 6 Saturn
  brother: 7 Jupiter
  husband: 7 Jupiter
  son: 4 Mars
  protectress of: 5 women
  8 marriage
  epithet: 6 Lucina, Moneta
  7 Curitis, Pronuba, Sospita
  festival: 10 Matronalia
  corresponds to: 4 Hera, Here

Juno and the Paycock
author: 10 Sean O'Casey

junta 5 cabal 7 council 9 committee 18 military government

Jupe, Sissy
character in: 9 Hard Times
author: 7 Dickens

Jupiter
also: 4 Jove
god of: 5 light 7 heavens, weather 9 lightning 11 thunderbolt
epithet: 5 Ultor 7 Elicius, Pluvius
corresponds to: 4 Zeus

Jupiter
position: 5 fifth
satellite: 2 Io 6 Europa 8 Amalthea, Callisto, Ganymede
characteristic: 7 red spot

Jurassic period
dinosaur from: 10 Diplodocus 11 Apatosaurus, Stegosaurus 12 Brontosaurus, Camarasaurus, Camptosaurus, Ceratosaurus, Megalosaurus 13 Brachiosaurus, Compsognathus, Ornitholestes

Jurgen
author: 17 James Branch Cabell

Jurgens, Curt
also: 11 Curd Jurgens
born: 6 Munich 7 Germany
roles: 12 The Blue Angel 16 The Spy Who Loved Me

jurisdiction 3 say 4 area, beat, rule, sway, zone 5 field, range, reach, scope 6 bounds, domain, sphere 7 circuit, command, compass, control, quarter 8 district, dominion, hegemony, latitude, precinct, province 9 authority, bailiwick 10 legal right 11 prerogative

jurist 5 judge 6 lawyer 7 counsel, justice 8 advocate, attorney 9 barrister, counselor, solicitor 10 magistrate 12 legal adviser 13 attorney-at-law

jury 5 panel, peers 6 assize, twelve 9 committee, makeshift, veniremen

jury-rigged 9 improvised, makeshift, temporary

jus 3 law 5 right

jus civile 8 civil law

jus gentium 12 law of nations

jus naturale 11 law of nature

jus sanguinis 12 right of blood
(law) citizenship of child is same as: 7 parents

jus soli 11 right of land, right of soil
(law) citizenship of child based on place of: 5 birth

just 3 but, due 4 fair, firm, good, only, sane 5 fully, moral, quite, solid, sound 6 at most, barely, decent, hardly, honest, lately, merely, proper, simply, strong, worthy 7 condign, ethical, exactly, fitting, logical, merited, only now, upright 8 adequate, balanced, deserved, entirely, narrowly, recently, scarcely, sensible, suitable, unbiased 9 befitting, blameless, equitable, honorable, impartial, justified, objective, perfectly, precisely, reputable, righteous, unbigoted, uncorrupt 10 aboveboard, absolutely, acceptable, fair-minded, high-minded, no more than, nothing but, not long ago, principled, reasonable, scrupulous, upstanding 11 appropriate, justifiable, trustworthy, well-founded 12 conscionable, open to reason, unprejudiced, well-grounded 13 conscientious, disinterested, dispassionate

just about 6 almost, around, barely, nearly 7 close to 10 not far from 12 on the point of 13 approximately

Just Above My Head
author: 12 James Baldwin

just a moment ago
French: 11 tout a l'heure

justice 5 honor, right, truth 6 amends, equity, the law, virtue 7 honesty, payment, penalty, probity, redress 8 fair play, fairness, goodness, legality 9 atonement, integrity, rightness 10 correction, lawfulness, legitimacy, reparation 11 just desserts, proper cause, uprightness 12 chastisement, compensation, equitability, remuneration, satisfaction 13 due punishment, equitableness, justification, righteousness 17 constitutionality
god of: 7 Forsete, Forseti
goddess of: 4 Dice, Dike 6 Astrea 7 Astraea

Justice
author: 14 John Galsworthy

Justice Clement
character in: 19 Every Man in His Humour
author: 6 Jonson

justice to all
Latin: 15 justitia omnibus
motto of: 18 District of Columbia

justifiable 9 excusable 10 defensible 11 explanatory, extenuating, supportable

justification 5 alibi 6 excuse 7 apology, defense, pretext, support 8 sanction 10 accounting, adjustment, validation 11 explanation, vindication 12 confirmation 13 rectification 14 reconciliation

justification for existence
French: 11 raison d'etre

justify 6 back up, defend, excuse, uphold 7 bear out, confirm, explain, support, sustain, warrant 8 sanction, validate 9 vindicate 10 account for, prove right

justitia omnibus 12 justice to all
motto of: 18 District of Columbia

just now
French: 11 tout a l'heure

just the same 6 anyhow, anyway 12 nevertheless

just the thing 7 apropos 8 suitable 11 appropriate 12 exactly right

Justus see 5 Titus

jut 5 bulge 6 beetle, extend 7 poke out, project 8 overhang, protrude, shoot out, stand out, stick out 13 thrust forward

jute 19 Corchorus capsularis
varieties: 5 Bimli, China, Tossa, white 7 bastard 10 Bimlipatum

Juturna
form: 5 nymph
goddess of: 5 lakes 7 streams
father: 6 Daunus
brother: 6 Turnus
loved by: 7 Jupiter

juvenile 5 child, minor, young, youth 6 boyish, callow, infant, junior 7 girlish 8 childish, immature, teenager, youthful 9 childlike, pubescent, stripling, youngster 10 adolescent, sophomoric 15 unsophisticated

Juventas
protectress of: 14 military age men

juxtaposed 6 next to 8 adjacent, touching 9 proximate 10 contiguous, side by side 12 conterminous

juxtaposition 5 touch 7 balance, contact 8 contrast, nearness 9 adjacency, proximity 10 apposition, contiguity

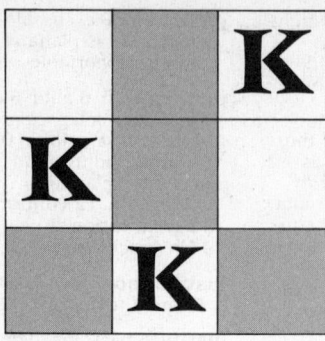

K
character in: **9** The Castle
author: **5** Kafka

Ka
origin: **8** Egyptian
form: **6** spirit
trait: **11** immortality

kabob 5 cabab, cabob, kabab, kebab, kebob **7** shaslik **8** shashlik **9** shashlick

Kabul
capital of: **11** Afghanistan

Kafka, Franz
author of: **7** Amerika **8** The Trial **9** The Castle **16** The Metamorphosis

kahlua
type: **6** brandy
origin: **6** Mexico
flavor: **6** coffee
with rum: **10** Black Maria
with tequila: **9** Brave Bull
with vodka: **12** Black Russian

Kahn, Albert
architect of: **15** River Rouge Plant **17** Highland Park Plant **20** Athletic Club Building (Detroit) **21** General Motors Building (Detroit)

Kahn, Louis Isadore
architect of: **16** Kimbell Art Museum (Ft Worth TX) **23** Yale Center for British Art **24** Yale University Art Gallery **28** Phillips Exeter Academy Library (NH) **31** Richards Medical Research Building (U of PA) **33** Salk Institute for Biological Studies (La Jolla CA)

Kahn, Madeline
born: **8** Boston MA
roles: **9** Paper Moon **10** What's Up Doc? **14** Blazing Saddles **17** Young Frankenstein

kaiser 5 ruler **7** emperor, Wilhelm **8** autocrat

kakemono 6 scroll **13** hanging object

kale 16 Brassica oleracea (Acephala Group)
varieties: **3** sea **4** Ruvo, tall, tree **6** Indian, Scotch **7** cabbage, Chinese, Italian, kitchen **8** Siberian **9** flowering, Tronchuda **10** decorative, ornamental, Portuguese **13** dwarf Siberian **16** ornamental-leaved

kaleidoscopic 6 mobile, motley **7** protean **8** shifting, unstable, variable **9** checkered **10** changeable, variegated **11** fluctuating, many colored, rainbowlike, vacillating **12** ever-changing

Kaleva 8 folk hero
origin: **7** Finnish **8** Estonian

Kalevala
origin: **7** Finnish
form: **4** epic

Kali
also: **3** Uma **5** Durga **7** Parvati
husband: **4** Siva **5** Shiva
festival: **6** dewali
goddess of: **5** death **7** disease

Kalidasa
author of: **9** Meghaduta, Sakuntala **10** Shakuntala **14** Cloud Messenger

Kalimantan *see* **6** Borneo

Kalki
author: **9** Gore Vidal

Kampala
capital of: **6** Uganda

Kampuchea *see* **8** Cambodia

Kandinsky, Wassily (Vasily)
born: **6** Moscow, Russia
artwork: **7** Striped **8** Twilight **10** Black Lines **11** Impressions **12** Blue Mountain (no 84), Compositions, Violet Orange **13** Black Relation **14** Improvisations **15** Capricious Forms **17** Bavarian Mountains, The Street in Murnau **23** Painting with White Border

Kanga
character in: **13** Winnie the Pooh
author: **5** Milne

kangaroo
young: **4** joey
group of: **3** mob **5** troop

Kaniengehaga *see* **6** Mohawk

Kansas *see box*

Kansas City
baseball team: **6** Royals
basketball team: **5** Kings
football team: **6** Chiefs
landmark: **12** Union Station **22** Nelson-Atkins Art Gallery
river: **6** Kansas **8** Missouri

Kant, Immanuel
author of: **20** Critique of Pure Reason

Kantor, MacKinlay
author of: **13** Andersonville

Karloff, Boris
real name: **17** William Henry Pratt
born: **7** Dulwich, England
roles: **12** Frankenstein

karma 3 act **4** aura, deed, duty, fate, rite **5** force, power **6** action, kismet, spirit **7** destiny **9** vibration

Kasdan, Lawrence
director of: **11** The Big Chill

Kashmiri
language family: **12** Indo-European
branch: **11** Indo-Iranian
group: **5** Indic
spoken in: **5** (northern) India

kashruth, kashrut 7 fitness **17** Jewish dietary laws

Kansas
abbreviation: 2 KS **4** Kans
nickname: 5 Wheat **9** Jayhawker, Sunflower **15** Garden of the West
capital: 6 Topeka
largest city: 7 Wichita
others: 4 Hays, Iola **5** Colby, Dodge **6** Salina **7** Abilene, Chanute, Emporia, Liberal **8** Atchison, Lawrence **9** Great Bend **10** Belleville, Hutchinson, Kansas City **11** Coffeeville, Leavenworth **12** Junction City
college: 5 Baker, Tabor **7** Bethany **8** Sterling, Washburn
explorer: 8 Coronado
feature: 16 Eisenhower Center
  fort: **5** Riley, Scott
  Indian training school: **16** Haskell Institute
  penitentiary: **11** Leavenworth
  reservoir: **11** Tuttle Creek
tribe: 3 Kaw **4** Pani **5** Kansa, Kiowa, Osage **6** Pawnee **7** Arapaho, Wichita **8** Cheyenne, Comanche, Kickapoo
people: 7 Jayhawk **11** Damon Runyon **13** Amelia Earhart, Karl Menninger **14** Walter Chrysler **15** Edgar Lee Masters
lake: 6 Cheney, Kerwin, Neosho **7** Milford
land rank: 10 fourteenth
mountain:
  highest point: **9** Sunflower
physical feature:
  plains: **5** Great, Osage
president: 17 Dwight D Eisenhower
river: 3 Kaw **6** Kansas **8** Arkansas, Cimarron, Missouri **9** Smoky Hill **10** Republican
state admission: 12 thirty-fourth
state bird: 17 western meadowlark
state flower: 9 sunflower
state motto: 29 To the Stars Through Difficulties
state song: 14 Home on the Range
state tree: 10 cottonwood

Katharina
character in: 19 The Taming of the Shrew
author: 11 Shakespeare

Katmandu, Kathmandu
capital of: 5 Nepal

Katzenjammer Kids
also: 17 Captain and the Kids
creator: 12 Rudolph Dirks
character: 4 Hans **5** Fritz, Momma **10** der Captain **12** der Inspector

Kaufman, George S
author of:
  with Edna Ferber: 9 Stage Door **13** Dinner at Eight **14** The Royal Family
  with Moss Hart: 15 Once in a Lifetime **20** You Can't Take It with You **21** The Man Who Came to Dinner

Kay (Sir Kay)
character in: 16 Arthurian romance
foster brother: 6 Arthur

Kaye, Danny
real name: 19 David Daniel Kaminski
born: 10 Brooklyn NY

roles: 19 The Inspector General **21** Hans Christian Andersen

Kaye, M M
author of: 9 Trade Wind **12** Death in Kenya **15** Death in Zanzibar, Shadow of the Moon, The Far Pavilions

Kazakhstan
capital/largest city: 7 Alma-Ata
others: 9 Karaganda **13** Petropavlovsk, Semipalatinsk
head of state: 9 president
government: 8 republic
monetary unit: 5 ruble
sea: 4 Aral **7** Caspian
physical feature: 7 steppes **12** Lake Balkhash
people: 6 Kazakh
language: 6 Kazakh

Kazan, Elia
director of: 10 East of Eden, Viva Zapata **15** On the Waterfront (Oscar) **18** Splendor in the Grass **19** Gentleman's Agreement (Oscar) **20** A Tree Grows in Brooklyn **21** A Streetcar Named Desire

Kazantzakis, Nikos
author of: 13 Zorba the Greek **14** Freedom or Death, The Greek Passion **25** The Last Temptation of Christ

kazoo
5 bazoo, zarah **6** hewgag **11** eunuch flute
French: 8 mirliton

Keach, Stacy
real name: 18 Walter Stacy Keach Jr
born: 10 Savannah GA
roles: 3 Doc **6** Luther **10** Mike Hammer **24** Twinkle Twinkle Killer Kane

Kearny, Stephen Watts
served in: 10 California, Mexican War
commander of: 13 Army of the West
occupied: 9 New Mexico
battle: 10 San Gabriel, San Pasqual

Keaton, Buster
real name: 19 Joseph Francis Keaton
born: 7 Piqua KS
roles: 6 Go West **7** College **10** The General **12** The Cameraman

Keaton, Diane
real name: 9 Diane Hall
born: 12 Los Angeles CA
roles: 4 Reds **7** Sleeper **8** Baby Boom **9** Annie Hall (Oscar) **12** Shoot the Moon, The Godfather **13** The Good Mother **14** Play It Again Sam **19** Looking for Mr Goodbar **20** The Little Drummer Girl

Keats, John
author of: 5 Lamia **8** Endymion, Hyperion, Isabella **11** Ode to Autumn, Ode to Psyche **14** Ode on Indolence **15** Ode on Melancholy, The Eve of St Agnes **16** Ode on a Grecian Urn **17** Ode to a Nightingale **20** La Belle Dame Sans Merci **31** On First Looking into Chapman's Homer

Kedemah
also called: 5 Kedar
father: 7 Ishmael
mother: 5 Hagar
descendant of: 8 Kedarite

Keel (of Argo)
constellation of: 6 Carina

Keel, Howard
real name: 17 Harry Clifford Leek
costar: 14 Kathryn Grayson
born: 11 Gillespie IL
roles: 6 Dallas, Kismet **8** Showboat **10** Kiss Me

Kate **13** Clayton Farlow
15 Annie Get Your Gun
27 Seven Brides for Seven
Brothers

Keeler, Ruby
husband: **8** Al Jolson
costar: **10** Dick Powell
born: **6** Canada **7** Halifax
roles: **15** Footlight Parade
17 Forty-Second Street
32 Gold Diggers of Nineteen
Thirty Three

keel over 5 faint, swoon, upset **7** capsize, tip over **8** collapse, fall down, fall flat, flip
over, overturn, turn over
10 turn turtle

keen 4 avid, fine **5** acute, alert,
eager, sharp **6** ardent, astute,
clever, fervid, fierce, shrewd
7 earnest, excited, fervent, intense, zealous **8** incisive **9** impatient, paper thin, razorlike
10 discerning **11** finely honed,
impassioned, penetrating,
quick-witted **12** enthusiastic
13 perspicacious
14 discriminating

keen-eyed 5 alert **8** vigilant,
watchful **9** attentive, eagle-
eyed, observant, sharp-eyed,
wide-awake

keen-minded 5 acute, sharp,
smart **6** astute, clever, shrewd
10 perceptive **11** penetrating

keenness 4 zeal, zest **5** ardor
6 acumen, fervor **7** passion
9 acuteness, eagerness, sharpness **10** astuteness, cleverness,
enthusiasm, excitement,
shrewdness **11** discernment
12 anticipation, intelligence,
perspicacity

keen-sighted 4 sage, wise
5 acute, sharp **6** astute,
shrewd **8** piercing **9** eagle-
eyed, judicious, sagacious,
sharp-eyed **10** discerning
11 intelligent, penetrating
12 clear-sighted, sharp-sighted
13 perspicacious

keep 3 bar **4** clog, fort, have,
heap, hold, mind, pile, stay
5 abide, block, carry, cramp,
delay, deter, guard, honor, lay
in, place, stack, stall, stand,
stick, stock, store, tie up,
tower **6** arrest, castle, detain,
donjon, endure, hamper,
hinder, hobble, hold up,
impede, living, pay for, remain, retain, retard **7** care for,
carry on, citadel, deposit, furnish, inhibit, observe, possess,
prevent, shackle, support, sustain **8** conserve, continue, encumber, fortress, hang on to,
hold back, maintain, obstruct,
preserve, restrain **9** celebrate,
constrain, hamstring, perse-

vere, persist in, ritualize, safeguard, solemnize, watch over
10 accumulate, daily bread,
livelihood, provide for, stronghold, sustenance **11** commemorate, maintenance,
memorialize, subsistence
12 room and board
13 fortification

keep an eye on 5 watch
7 oversee **9** chaperone, look
after, watch over

keep apart 7 isolate **8** separate **9** segregate

keep at bay 7 beat off, fend
off, ward off **8** stave off

keep back 5 check, delay
6 detain, hold up, retain
8 withhold

keep busy 3 use **6** employ, engage, occupy **7** utilize

keep clear of 4 shun **5** avoid,
dodge, elude, evade, skirt
6 escape

keep company 4 date **5** court
7 consort, hang out **8** go
around, go steady **9** accompany, associate **10** fraternize,
go together

keeper 5 guard, nurse
6 duenna, escort, jailer, sentry,
warden **7** curator **8** chaperon,
guardian, retainer, sentinel,
wet nurse **9** attendant, bodyguard, caretaker, chaperone,
custodian, governess, nursemaid, protecter, protector
11 conservator, nurserymaid
13 guardian angel

keep in mind 8 consider, remember **10** think about

keep mum 13 button one's lip

keep off 7 fend off, stay off,
ward off **8** stave off

keep one's counsel 12 remain silent **13** button one's
lip

keep open 8 hold open
16 leave unscheduled

keep out 6 reject **8** prohibit
9 blackball, blacklist

keep out of sight 4 hide
5 cover **6** lay low, lie low
7 conceal, cover up, secrete
10 camouflage

keep private 4 hide **7** conceal,
reserve **8** withhold

keepsake 5 relic, token **6** emblem, memory, symbol **7** memento **8** memorial, reminder,
souvenir **11** remembrance
18 token of remembrance

keep secret 4 hide **6** hush
up **7** conceal, cover up **8** suppress, withhold

keep silent 10 remain dumb
15 not breathe a word

keep steady 5 poise **7** balance **9** stabilize

keep to 5 cling, stick **6** adhere, be true, cleave, hold to
7 be loyal, stand by
8 maintain

keg 3 tub, tun, vat **4** butt,
cask, drum, tank **6** barrel
7 rundlet **8** hogshead, puncheon **9** container, kilderkin

Kellerman, Sally
born: **11** Long Beach CA
roles: **4** MASH **15** Hot Lips
Houlihan

Kelly, Gene
real name: **17** Eugene Curran
Kelly
born: **12** Pittsburgh PA
roles: **7** Pal Joey **9** Brigadoon, On the Town **13** Anchors Aweigh **15** Singin' in
the Rain **17** An American
in Paris **18** The Three
Musketeers

Kelly, Grace
husband: **21** Prince Rainier
Grimaldi
nickname: **11** Ice Princess
born: **14** Philadelphia PA
roles: **7** Mogambo **8** High
Noon **10** Rear Window
11 High Society **13** To Catch
a Thief **14** Dial M for Murder, The Country Girl
(Oscar)

Kelly, Walt
creator/artist of: **4** Pogo

kelp 3 ash **4** agar, alga, leag
5 varec, varic, wrack
7 seaweed
source of: **4** soda **6** iodine
9 potassium

Kelpie
origin: **8** Scottish
form: **5** horse **6** spirit
habitat: **4** lake **5** river
causes: **8** drowning
warns of: **8** drowning

Kelvin
abbreviation: **1** K

Kelvin, William Thomson
field: **7** physics
11 mathematics
nationality: **7** British
worked on: **4** heat
11 electricity
invented: **12** electrometer,
galvanometer **13** tide
predictor
named for him: **22** Kelvin
temperature scale

Kempis, Thomas a
author of: **20** The Imitation
of Christ

Kenaz
father: 7 Eliphaz
son: 5 Caleb 7 Othniel

Keneally, Thomas
author of: 12 Confederates
14 Schindler's List

Kenilworth
author: 14 Sir Walter Scott
character: 6 Alasco, Dudley
(Earl of Leicester) 10 Amy
Robsart 12 Wayland Smith
13 Richard Varney
14 Queen Elizabeth 15 Flibbertigibbet 16 Edmund
Tressilian

Kennedy, Arthur
real name: 17 John Arthur
Kennedy
born: 11 Worcester MA
roles: 6 Becket 9 All My
Sons 11 Peyton Place
12 Blind Victory 16 Death
of a Salesman

Kennedy, Frank
character in: 15 Gone With
the Wind
author: 8 Mitchell

Kennedy, John Fitzgerald
see box

**Kennicott, Dr Will and
Carol**
characters in: 10 Main Street
author: 5 Lewis

Kentucky see box, p. 534

Kenya see box, p. 535

Kepler, Johannes
nationality: 6 German
invented: 14 convex eye-
piece 21 astronomical
telescope
formulated:
*three laws of planetary
motion (Kepler's Laws):*
10 law of areas 11 har-
monic law 24 elliptical
orbit of planets
author of: 14 Astronomia
nova, Harmonice mundi
16 Rudolphine Tables
23 Mysterium cosmographi-
cum 30 Epitome astronom-
iae Copernicanae

Ker
form: 6 spirit
associated with: 5 death
corresponds to: 6 Furies

kerchief 5 cloth, scarf 7 muffler 8 babushka, neckwear
9 headpiece, neckcloth
11 neckerchief
12 handkerchief

Keres
origin: 5 Greek
spirits of: 4 evil 5 death
6 old age 7 disease

Keres-Siouan
language branch: 5 Keres

Kennedy, John Fitzgerald
nickname: 3 JFK 4 Jack
presidential rank: 11 thirty-fifth
party: 10 Democratic
state represented: 2 MA
defeated: 5 (Richard Milhous) Nixon
vice president: 7 (Lyndon Baines) Johnson
cabinet:
state: 4 (David Dean) Rusk
treasury: 6 (Clarence Douglas) Dillon
defense: 8 (Robert Strange) McNamara
attorney general: 7 (Robert Francis) Kennedy
postmaster general: 3 (James Edward) Day 9 (John
Austin) Gronouski
interior: 5 (Stewart Lee) Udall
agriculture: 7 (Orville Lothrop) Freeman
commerce: 6 (Luther Hartwell) Hodges
labor: 5 (William Willard) Wirtz 8 (Arthur J) Goldberg
HEW: 8 (Abraham Alexander) Ribicoff 10 (Anthony Joseph) Celebrezze
born: 11 Brookline MA
died: 8 Dallas TX
died by: 13 assassination
assassinated by: 6 (Lee Harvey) Oswald
buried: 25 Arlington National Cemetery
education:
prep school: 6 Choate
University: 7 Harvard 9 Princeton 23 London School of
Economics
religion: 13 Roman Catholic
interests: 7 sailing 8 football 13 touch football
vacation spot: 9 Cape Cod MA 13 Hyannis Port MA
author: 15 Strategy of Peace, Why England Slept 17 Profiles in Courage (Pulitzer Prize)
political career: 9 US Senator 24 US House of
Representatives
civilian career: 17 newspaper reporter
military service: 6 US Navy 10 lieutenant 11 World War
Two
commander of: 6 PT boat
notable events of lifetime/term: 9 Bay of Pigs 10 Berlin
Wall, Peace Corps 18 Cuban missile crisis
march: 11 Civil Rights
treaty: 14 Nuclear Test-Ban
quote: 17 Ich bin ein Berliner (I am a Berliner) 35 We
stand today on the edge of a New Frontier 61 Ask not
what your country can do for you ask what you can do
for your country
father: 13 Joseph Patrick
mother: 4 Rose (Fitzgerald)
siblings: 4 Jean 6 Eunice, Joseph 8 Kathleen, Patricia,
Rosemary 11 Edward Moore 13 Robert Francis
wife: 10 Jacqueline (Lee Bouvier)
nickname: 6 Jackie
second marriage to: 7 Onassis
children: 14 John Fitzgerald, Patrick Bouvier (died in infancy) 15 Caroline Bouvier

7 Caddoan 9 Iroquoian
11 Siouan-Yuchi

kernel 3 nub, nut, pip, pit
4 core, germ, gist, pith, seed
5 grain, stone 6 center, marrow 7 nucleus 12 quintessence

Kerouac, Jack
author of: 6 Big Sur 9 On
the Road 13 The Dharma
Bums 16 Lonesome Traveler

Kerr, Deborah
real name: 22 Deborah Jane
Kerr-Trimmer
born: 8 Scotland
11 Helensburgh
roles: 11 Edward My Son,
The King and I 12 The
Hucksters 13 The Sundown-
ers 14 Separate Tables, The
Chalk Garden 18 From Here
to Eternity 19 The Night of

Kentucky
abbreviation: 2 KY
nickname: 9 Bluegrass 11 Corncracker
capital: 9 Frankfort
largest city: 10 Louisville
others: 5 Berea 6 Corbin, Hazard 7 Ashland, Glasgow, Newport, Paducah, Shively 8 Danville 9 Covington, Henderson, Lexington, Owensboro 12 Bowling Green, Hopkinsville, Madisonville
college: 5 Berea 6 Centre 7 Ashbury, Brescia 8 Ursuline 12 Transylvania
explorer: 11 Daniel Boone
feature: 7 Obelisk
  birthplace: 14 Abraham Lincoln
  fort: 4 Knox
  national park: 11 Mammoth Cave
  race: 13 Kentucky Derby
  racetrack: 14 Churchill Downs
  trail: 10 Wilderness
tribe: 7 Shawnee 8 Cherokee, Iroquois
people: 11 corncracker, John M Harlan 13 Louis Brandeis 16 Frederick M Vinson, Robert Penn Warren
lake: 8 Kentucky 10 Cumberland
land rank: 13 thirty-seventh
mountain: 4 Pine 10 Cumberland
  highest point: 5 Black 8 Big Black
physical feature:
  basin: 9 Bluegrass
  cave: 7 Mammoth
  gap: 10 Cumberland
  plain: 7 Coastal
  plateau: 10 Cumberland
president: 14 Abraham Lincoln
  Confederate president: 14 Jefferson Davis
river: 3 Dix 4 Ohio, Salt 5 Green 6 Barren 7 Licking 8 Big Sandy, Kentucky 9 Tennessee 10 Cumberland 11 Mississippi
state admission: 9 fifteenth
state bird: 8 cardinal
state flower: 9 goldenrod
state motto: 26 United We Stand Divided We Fall
state song: 17 My Old Kentucky Home
state tree: 10 coffee tree 11 tulip poplar 12 yellow poplar

the Iguana 20 Heaven Knows Mr Allison

Kesey, Ken
  author of: 21 Sometimes a Great Notion 25 One Flew Over the Cuckoo's Nest

Ketcham, Hank
  creator/artist of: 15 Dennis the Menace

kettle 3 pan, pot, tub, vat 6 boiler, teapot, tureen 8 cauldron, crucible, saucepan

Ketubim 8 writings 11 Hagiographa

Keturah
  husband: 7 Abraham

key 3 cue, fit 4 clue, gear, mode, suit 5 adapt, light, point, scale 6 adjust, answer, direct, opener 7 address, finding, meaning, pointer 8 indicant, solution, tonality

9 indicator 10 exposition, indication, resolution 11 elucidation, explanation, explication, translation 14 interpretation

Key, Ted
  creator/artist of: 5 Hazel

keyboard instrument 5 organ, piano 6 spinet 8 psaltery, virginal 9 harmonium 10 clavichord, pianoforte 11 harpsichord

keyed up 5 tense 7 excited, nervous 8 volatile 9 emotional, explosive

key element 9 essential, vital part 18 primary constituent 20 indispensable element

Key Largo
  director: 10 John Huston
  based on story by: 15 Maxwell Anderson
  cast: 12 Claire Trevor, Lauren Bacall 14 Humphrey Bo-

gart 15 Edward G Robinson, Lionel Barrymore
  Oscar for: 17 supporting actress (Trevor)

Keynes, John Maynard
  author of: 44 The General Theory of Employment Interest and Money

keynote 3 nub 4 core, gist, pith 5 heart, theme 6 marrow 7 essence, nucleus, pattern 8 main idea, quiddity 9 substance 11 nitty-gritty, salient idea 12 central point

keystone 4 base, crux, root 5 basis 8 gravamen, linchpin 9 principle 10 foundation, mainspring

Keystone State
  nickname of:
    12 Pennsylvania

Key to Rebecca, The
  author: 10 Ken Follett

Khachaturian, Aram Ilich
  born: 6 Tiflis 7 (Soviet) Georgia
  composer of: 6 Gayane 9 Spartacus 12 Song of Stalin

khaki 5 cloth 6 fabric 7 uniform 9 olive-drab 14 yellowish-brown

khan, kahn 3 inn 4 lord 5 chief, ruler 6 prince 7 emperor 9 chieftain, sovereign 11 caravansary
  famous: 4 Yuan 6 Kublai 7 Genghis 8 Ghenghis

Khartoum
  capital of: 5 Sudan

Khartvelian
  language family: 9 Caucasian
  includes: 8 Georgian

Khayyam, Omar
  author of: 11 The Rubaiyat

Khnum
  origin: 8 Egyptian
  form: 3 ram
  created: 6 humans
  used: 4 clay

Khoisan
  language spoken by: 3 San 7 Bushmen 9 Khoikhoin 10 Hottentots
  includes: 5 Hatsa 7 Sandawe
  distinguishing sound: 5 click

kibitzer 3 pry 5 prier, snoop 6 butt-in 7 meddler, snooper, watcher 8 busybody 9 buttinsky

kick 3 fun, hit, out, pep, vim 4 beef, boot, dash, fret, fume, fuss, life, punt, snap, tang, zest 5 eject, force, gripe, growl, power, punch, verve, vigor 6 flavor, grouch, grouse,

Kenya
capital/largest city: 7 Nairobi
others: 5 Nyeri, Thika, Wajir **6** Kisumu, Kitale, Lodwar, Moyale, Nakuru, Webuye **7** Eldoret, Kericho, Malindi, Mandera, Mombasa, Nanyuki **9** Lokitaung
measure: 4 wari
monetary unit: 4 cent **5** pound **8** shilling
island: 5 Manda, Patta
lake: 6 Magadi, Nakuru, Natron, Rudolf **7** Turkana **8** Naivasha, Victoria
mountain: 5 Elgon, Kulai, Nyira, Nyiru **6** Matian **7** Logonot **8** Aberdare
highest point: 5 Kenya **6** Kinyaa **9** Kirinyaga
river: 3 Lak **4** Athi, Dawa, Kuja, Tana **5** Nzoia **6** Galana **8** Turkwell
sea: 6 Indian
physical feature:
  bay: **7** Formosa
  desert: **6** Chalbi
  escarpment: **3** Mau
  gulf: **9** Kavirondo
  highlands: **5** Kenya, Kisii, Luyla **7** Kericho
  plain: **4** Kano
  plateau: **5** Nandi, Yatta **6** Elgeyo
  valley: **9** Great Rift
people: 3 Luo **4** Arab, Meru **5** Bantu, Elgey, Galla, Kamba, Kisii, Luhya, Masai, Nandi, Tugen **6** Kikuyu, Ogaden, Somali **7** Baluhya, Hamitic, Hilotic, Kipsigi, Swahili, Turkana **8** Kalenjin, Marakwet
  god: **4** Ngai
  leader: **5** Mboya **12** Jomo Kenyatta **13** Daniel Arap Moi
language: 3 Luo **5** Bantu, Luhya, Masai **6** Kikuyu **7** English, Swahili **8** Guyerati **10** Hindustani
religion: 5 Islam **7** animism **8** Anglican **13** Roman Catholic
place:
  archeological excavation: **11** Gamble's Cave
  mosque: **5** Khoja
  museum: **9** Fort Jesus
  national park/wildlife preserve: **4** Meru **5** Nyeri, Tsavo **6** Arusha **7** Manyara, Nairobi, Samburu **8** Aberdare, Amboseli **10** Lake Nakuru, Mount Kenya, Rift Valley
  ruins: **4** Gedi
feature:
  garment: **5** kanga **7** kitenge
  round house: **6** shamba
  secret organization: **6** Mau Mau
  tree: **6** ayieke, baobab
food:
  fish: **7** tilapia
  wine: **5** tembo

object, recoil, remove, return, strike, stroke, thrill **7** boot out, cast out, grumble, fly back, protest, rebound, sparkle, turn out **8** backlash, complain, jump back, piquancy, pleasure, pungency, reaction, throw out, vitality **9** amusement, animation, complaint, enjoyment, find fault, grievance, intensity, make a fuss, objection **10** excitement, spring back **11** give the gate, remonstrate, send packing, show the door **12** protestation **13** gratification, remonstration

Kickapoo
language family: 9 Algonkian **10** Algonquian
location: 5 Texas **6** Kansas, Mexico **9** Chihuahua, Wisconsin
related to: 3 Fox, Sac **4** Sauk

kickback 3 cut **5** bribe, graft, share **6** boodle, payoff, payola **9** hush money **10** commission, percentage, protection, recompense **12** compensation, remuneration **15** protection money

kick downstairs 4 bust **6** demote **7** degrade

kickoff 5 start **7** opening **9** beginning, inception, launching **12** inauguration

kick out 4 oust **5** eject, evict, expel **8** throw out **9** discharge

kicks 3 fun **7** thrills **8** pleasure **10** excitement **11** stimulation

kick upstairs 5 boost **7** advance, elevate, promote

Kicva
origin: 5 Welsh
husband: 7 Pryderi

kid 3 rag, rib, tot **4** baby, fool, gull, jest, joke, josh, mock, ride, tyke **5** bluff, child, cozen, harry, put on, tease, trick, youth **6** delude, infant, moppet, plague, shaver, squirt **7** beguile, deceive, laugh at, mislead **8** goat hide, goatskin, hoodwink, juvenile, ridicule, teenager, yearling **9** bamboozle, billy goat, little one, make fun of, nanny goat, offspring, young goat, youngster **10** adolescent **11** goat leather, young person **12** little shaver

Kid, The
nickname of: 11 Ted Williams

kid around 5 clown, cut up **10** fool around, play around **11** clown around

Kidder, Margot
born: 6 Canada **11** Yellow Knife
roles: 7 Sisters **8** Lois Lane, Superman **14** Some Kind of Hero **19** The Amityville Horror

Kiddush 6 prayer **8** blessing **14** sanctification

kidnap 5 seize, steal **6** abduct, hijack, snatch **7** bear off, capture, impress, skyjack **8** bear away, carry off, shanghai **10** run off with **11** make off with **13** hold for ransom

Kidnapped
author: 20 Robert Louis Stevenson
character: 9 Alan Breck **10** Rankeillor **12** David Balfour **15** Ebenezer Balfour

Kigali
capital of: 6 Rwanda

Kiley, Richard
born: 9 Chicago IL
roles: 7 Redhead **13** Man of La Mancha **16** Advise and Consent

Kilkenny Cats
origin: 5 Irish
form: 4 cats
number: 3 two
left after fight: 5 tails

kill 4 beat, do in, halt, hang, ruin, slay, stay **5** break, check, drown, erase, lynch, quell, shoot, waste **6** behead, defeat, murder, poison, rub out, stifle **7** bump off, butcher, cut down, destroy, execute, garrote, silence, smother, squelch, wipe out **8** blow away, dispatch, get rid of, knock off, massacre, strangle, string up **9** dismember, finish off, shoot down, slaughter, suffocate **10** asphyxiate, decapitate, disembowel, extinguish, guillotine, put a stop to, put an end to, put to death **11** assassinate, burn to death, electrocute, exterminate **13** mortally wound

killer 6 hit man, slayer **7** butcher **8** assassin, murderer **11** executioner **12** exterminator

Killers, The
director: **13** Robert Siodmak
based on story by: **15** Ernest Hemingway
cast: **10** Ava Gardner **12** Edmond O'Brien **13** Burt Lancaster

killer whale 4 orca **7** grampus **11** Orcinus orca

killing 4 coup **5** fatal **6** big hit, deadly, lethal, mortal, murder **7** bonanza, cleanup, deathly, hanging, slaying, success, suicide **8** butchery, fatality, homicide, lynching, massacre, regicide, shooting, smash hit, stabbing, windfall **9** bloodshed, execution, garroting, martyrdom, matricide, murderous, patricide, poisoning, slaughter, uxoricide **10** cleaning up, decimation, fratricide, immolation, impalement, sororicide, strangling **11** crucifixion, devastating, elimination, infanticide **12** annihilation, death-dealing, decapitation, excruciating, guillotining, manslaughter, master stroke, stroke of luck, violent death **13** electrocution, extermination, strangulation **17** capital punishment

Killing Fields
director: **11** Roland Joffe
based on article by: **15** Sydney Schanberg (The Death and Life of Dith Pran)
cast: **10** Haing S Ngor **12** Sam Waterston
Oscar for: **15** supporting actor (Ngor)

Killing Time
author: **12** Thomas Berger

killjoy 6 grouch **8** grumbler, sourball, sourpuss **9** Cassandra, gloomy Gus, worrywart

10 complainer, malcontent, spoilsport, wet blanket **11** crapehanger, party-pooper

kill time 4 idle **6** dawdle **9** waste time **10** fool around

Kilmer, Joyce
author of: **5** Trees

kiln 3 ost **4** bake, burn, fire, oast, oven **5** drier, glaze, stove, tiler **7** furnace **8** calciner, limekiln **9** oasthouse

kiloliter
abbreviation: **2** kL

kilometer
abbreviation: **2** km

Kilwich
origin: **5** Welsh
form: **6** prince
performed: **6** labors
number of labors: **4** five
married: **5** Olwen

Kim
author: **14** Rudyard Kipling
character: **9** Mahbub Ali **11** Tibetan Lama **12** Kimball O'Hara **16** Colonel Creighton **22** Hurree Chunder Mookerjee

kin 4 akin, clan, kith, race **5** folks, tribe **6** family, people **7** kinfolk, kinsmen, related **8** clansmen, kinfolks **9** next of kin, relations, relatives, tribesmen **10** kith and kin **11** connections, consanguine, distaff side, spindle side **13** flesh and blood **14** kissing cousins

kind 3 ilk **4** cast, make, mold, sort, type **5** brand, breed, caste, civil, class, genre, genus, style **6** benign, gentle, kidney, kindly, nature, polite, strain, tender **7** amiable, cordial, variety **8** amicable, friendly, generous, gracious, merciful, obliging **9** courteous **10** bighearted, charitable, neighborly, thoughtful **11** considerate, description, designation, good-hearted, good-humored, good-natured, softhearted, sympathetic, warmhearted, well-meaning **12** affectionate, well-disposed **13** accommodating, compassionate, tenderhearted, understanding
French: **6** gentil

kindhearted 4 good, warm **6** benign, gentle, humane, kindly, loving **7** helpful **8** amicable, generous, gracious, merciful **10** altruistic, charitable, thoughtful **11** considerate, good-hearted, good-natured, softhearted, sympathetic, warmhearted, well-meaning **12** affectionate, humanitarian **13** accommodating, compas-

sionate, philanthropic, tenderhearted, understanding

kindheartedness 5 mercy **8** altruism, goodness, goodwill, humanity, sympathy **10** compassion, humaneness, tenderness **11** benefaction, benevolence, magnanimity **12** graciousness, philanthropy **13** consideration, understanding, unselfishness **14** charitableness **15** humanitarianism

kindle 4 fire, goad, prod, stir, urge, whet **5** awake, light, rouse, waken **6** arouse, excite, foment, ignite, incite, induce, stir up **7** agitate, animate, inflame, inspire, provoke, quicken, sharpen **8** enkindle **9** call forth, intensify, set fire to, set on fire, stimulate **10** invigorate

kindling 4 fuel **5** brush, paper, twigs **6** firing, tinder **7** burning, flaming **8** firewood, igniting, ignition, lighting, shavings **9** brushwood **10** combustion, enkindling

kindly 4 good, warm **6** benign, gentle, gently, humane, tender, warmly **7** amiable, amiably, civilly, cordial, devoted, patient **8** amicable, amicably, benignly, friendly, generous, gracious, humanely, merciful, tenderly **9** cordially, courteous **10** benevolent, bighearted, charitable, charitably, generously, graciously, mercifully, neighborly **11** considerate, good-humored, good-natured, magnanimous, softhearted, sympathetic, warmhearted, well-meaning **12** affectionate, benevolently, bigheartedly, humanitarian **13** compassionate, considerately, good-humoredly, good-naturedly, magnanimously, philanthropic, softheartedly, tenderhearted, understanding, warmheartedly, well-meaningly **14** affectionately, well-manneredly **15** compassionately, sympathetically, tenderheartedly, understandingly **17** philanthropically

kindness 3 aid **4** gift, help **5** favor, grace, mercy **6** bounty **7** charity **8** good deed, good turn, goodness, goodwill, humanity, patience, sympathy **9** tolerance **10** act of grace, assistance, compassion, generosity, humaneness, kind office, toleration **11** benefaction, beneficence, benevolence, magnanimity **12** act of charity, graciousness, philanthropy **13** consideration, understanding, unselfishness

14 charitableness
15 humanitarianism

Kind of Anger, A
author: **10** Eric Ambler

kindred 4 akin, like **5** alike
6 allied, united **7** related, similar **8** agreeing, familial, matching **9** accordant, analogous, congenial, simpatico **10** harmonious, resembling **11** consanguine, sympathetic
13 corresponding

kine 4 cows, oxen **6** cattle
9 livestock

kinfolk 3 kin **6** family **7** kinsmen **9** relations, relatives
10 kith and kin

king 3 HRH **5** liege, ruler
7 monarch **8** suzerain **9** potentate, protector, sovereign
10 His Majesty **11** crowned head, royal person, the anointed **18** defender of the faith
   Latin: **3** rex

king/emperor/dynasty *see box*

King, Frank
creator/artist of: **13** Gasoline Alley

King, Stephen
author of: **2** It **4** Cujo **6** Carrie, Misery **9** Christine, Salem's Lot, The Stand
10 Night Shift, The Shining
11 Firestarter, Pet Sematary, The Dead Zone **12** Skeleton Crew, The Dark Tower
16 Different Seasons, The Tommyknockers

King and I, The
director: **10** Walter Lang
cast: **10** Rita Moreno, Yul Brynner **11** Deborah Kerr
12 Martin Benson
score: **21** Rodgers and Hammerstein
remake of: **20** Anna and the King of Siam
song: **12** Shall We Dance?
16 Getting to Know You, Hello Young Lovers
18 Something Wonderful

King Arthur
opera by: **7** Purcell
character: **6** Merlin, Osmond, Oswald **8** Emmeline, Philadel **14** Duke of Cornwall

kingdom 4 land **5** duchy, field, realm, state **6** domain, empire, nation, sphere **7** country, dukedom **8** dominion, monarchy **9** territory **12** principality

King John
author: **18** William Shakespeare
character: **6** Elinor **9** Constance **11** Prince Henry
13 Hubert de Burgh
15 Blanch of Castile, Lewis the Dauphin
16 Arthur of Bretagne, Cardinal Pandulph, William Longsword, William Mareshall
19 Philip Faulconbridge, Robert Faulconbridge

King Kong
director: **13** Merian C Cooper **17** Ernest B Schoedsack
cast: **7** Fay Wray **10** Bruce Cabot **11** James Flavin
12 Noble Johnson **15** Robert Armstrong
setting (final scene): **19** Empire State Building
score: **10** Max Steiner

King Lear
author: **18** William Shakespeare
character: **5** Edgar, Regan
6 Edmund **7** Goneril **8** Cordelia **10** Earl of Kent
12 Duke of Albany, King of

---

king/emperor/dynasty
  of **Afghanistan: 8** Barakzai
  of **Albania: 3** Zog **9** Ahmet Zogu
  of **Algeria: 3** bey, dey **6** disawa **8** Jugurtha **9** bevlerbay, Masinissa
  of **Austria: 7** Charles, Francis **9** Ferdinand, Habsburgs **10** Franz Josef
  of **Bahrain: 9** al-Khalifa
  of **Belgium: 7** Leopold **8** Baudouin
  of **China: 3** Han, Sui **4** Chou, Ch'in, Ming, Sung, T'ang **5** Ch'ing, Shang **6** Manchu
  of **Crete: 5** Minos
  of **Denmark 4** Hans, Knud **6** Canute **8** Frederik **9** Christian **10** Gorm the Old **15** Harold Bluetooth
  of **Egypt: 5** Khufu, Menes, Zoser **6** Farouk, Khafre, Ptulol, Ramses **7** Saladin **8** Horemheb, Menkaure **9** Akhenaten, Amenemhet, Amenhotep **10** Mentuhotep **11** Tutankhamen
  of **England: 3** Hal **4** Cnut, John, Lear **5** Henry, James **6** Alfred, Arthur, Canute, Edmund, Edward, Egbert, George, Harold **7** Charles, Richard, Stephen, William **9** Cymbeline **18** Richard Coeur de Lion **19** Richard the Lionheart **21** Richard the Lionhearted
  of **France: 5** Henri, Louis **6** Clovis, Philip **7** Charles **8** Napoleon **9** Hugh Capet **11** Charlemagne **13** Louis Philippe **14** Henry of Navarre
  of **Germany: 6** Kaiser **7** Wilhelm **9** Frederick **10** Barbarossa
  of **Greece: 5** Creon **6** Atreus **7** Theseus **8** Menelaus **9** Agammemnon **11** Constantine
  of **India: 5** Akbar, Asoka, Babur, Gupta, Mogul, Timur **6** Maurya, Rajput **7** Humayun **8** Hyder Ali, Jahangir, Marathas **9** Aurangzeb, Shah Jahan **11** Tippu Sultan **14** Delhi Sultanate **18** Chandragupta Maurya
  of **Iran: 5** Abbas, Cyrus, Qajar **6** Darius, Xerxes **7** Arsacid, Pahlavi, Safavid **8** Parthian, Seleucid **9** Sassanian **10** Achaemenid **15** Shah Reza Pahlavi
  of **Iraq: 6** Faisal, Sargon **7** Hussein **9** Hammurabi **13** Harun al-Rashid **14** Nebuchadnezzar
  of **Ireland: 9** Brian Boru
  of **Italy/Rome: 4** Nero, Otho **5** Galba, Nerva, Titus **6** Trajan **7** Hadrian **8** Caligula, Claudius, Commodus, Domitian, Octavian, Tiberius **9** Caracalla, Vespasian, Vitellius **10** Diocletian **11** Constantine **13** Antoninus Dius **14** Caesar Augustus, Marcus Aurelius, Victor Emmanuel
  of **Japan: 5** Jimmu, Jingo, Meiji, Taira **6** Yamato **7** Akihito, Izanagi **8** Ashikaga, Fujiwara, Hirohito, Kamakura, Minamoto, Tokugawa
  of **Java: 7** Mataram **9** Majapahit, Srivijaya
  of **Jordan: 5** Talal **6** Faisal **7** Hussein **8** Abdullah, Selucidas **10** Ibn Hussein, Nabataeans

(continued)

king / emperor / dynasty (*continued*)
   of **Korea: 2** Yi **4** Choe **5** Ki-tse, Koryo **6** Chi-tsi, Chi-tzu, Tangun
   of **Kuwait: 5** Ahmad, Sabah, Salem **7** Mubarak **12** Jaber al-Ahmed, Sabah al-Salim
   15 Abdullah al-Salim
   of **Liechtenstein: 7** Florian **13** Francis Joseph **16** von Liechtenstein
   of **Luxembourg: 8** Sigefroi, Wencelas **12** Jean l'Aveugle **21** House of Nassau-Weilburg
   of **Madagascar: 6** Merina
   of **Malawi: 6** Maravi
   of **Maldives: 4** Didi
   of **Mexico: 10** Maximilian
   of **Monaco: 5** Louis **6** Albert, Honore **7** Antoine, Charles, Rainier **9** Florestan
   of **Mongolia: 8** Jahangir, Jehangir **10** Kublai Khan, Tsendenbal **11** Genghis Khan
   of **Morocco: 7** Alawite, Almohad **9** Almoravid
   of **Nepal: 8** Mahendra **9** Tribhuwan **10** Birenda Bir **12** Bikram Sha Dev **17** Prithwi Narayan
   Sha
   of the **Netherlands: 7** William
   of **Nigeria: 3** Ife, Nok, Oyo **5** Benin **6** Fulani **10** Kanem-Borno
   of **Norway: 4** Olaf, Olav **5** Olave, Oscar **6** Haakon, Harold, Magnus, Sverre
   of **Peru: 7** Huascar **9** Atahualpa **10** Manco Capac
   of **Poland: 5** Piast **7** Casimir, Jagello **8** Augustus
   of **Portugal: 6** Manuel, Philip, Sancho **7** Alfonso **9** Ferdinand, Sebastian **23** Prince Henry the
   Navigator
   of **Qatar: 18** Ahmad bin Ali al-Thani **22** Khalifa bin Hamad al-Thani
   of **Rumania: 5** Carol **7** Michael
   of **Russia: 4** Ivan, Paul **5** Peter **6** Alexis **7** Michael **8** Nicholas **9** Alexander **12** Boris Godunov
   of **Sardinia: 12** Charles Felix **13** Charles Albert **14** Victor Emmanuel
   of **Saudi Arabia: 4** Fahd, Saud **6** Faisal, Khalid **7** Ibn Saud **9** Abdul Aziz
   of **Scotland: 5** David, James **6** Duncan **7** Kenneth, Macbeth, Malcolm, Stuarts, William
   9 Alexander **14** Robert the Bruce **19** Bonnie Prince Charlie
   of **Sicily: 4** Eryx **5** Bomba, Henry, Peter, Roger **7** Charles, Cocalus, Leontes **9** Ferdinand,
   Frederick
   of **Spain: 6** Pelayo, Philip, Ramiro, Sancho, Witiza **7** Alfonso, Almohad, Charles, Umayyad
   8 al-Mansur, Reccared, Roderick **9** Almoravid, Ferdinand, Leovigild **10** Juan Carlos **11** Abd al-
   Rahman, Reccosvinth
   of **Swaziland: 3** Kbe **5** Nyama **6** Mswati, Sozisa **7** Sobhuza
   of **Sweden: 4** Vosa, Wasa **5** Oscar **6** Gustav **8** Gustavus **10** Carl Gustav **12** Gustav Adolph
   13 Charles Gustav **22** Jean Baptiste Bernadotte
   of **Syria: 5** Rezin **6** Faisal, Hazael **8** Benhadad **9** Antiochus
   of **Thailand: 4** Rama **7** Chakkri, Mongkut **10** Chao Phraya **12** Prahjadhipok **13** Chulalongkorn
   17 Bhumibol Adulyadej
   of **Tongo: 11** George Tupou **14** Taufaahau Tupou
   of **Tunisia: 6** Hafsid **7** Fatimid **8** Aghlabid, Almohade **10** Husseinite
   of **Turkey: 8** Mausolus
   of **Uganda: 6** Mutesa, Mwanga **8** Kabarega
   of **Upper Volta: 4** Naba **5** Mogho
   of **Zimbabwe: 9** Lobengula, Mzilikaze

France **14** Duke of Cornwall **16** Earl of Gloucester

kingly 5 grand, noble, regal, royal **6** august, lordly, mighty **7** queenly, stately **8** absolute, despotic, glorious, kinglike, imperial, majestic, princely, splendid **9** imperious, monarchal, patrician, sovereign **10** autocratic, commanding, tyrannical **11** magnificent **12** awe-inspiring

Kingman, Dave
  nickname: 4 Kong
  sport: 8 baseball
  position: 8 outfield **9** first base
  team: 11 Chicago Cubs, New York Mets **14** New York Yankees, San Diego Padres **16** California Angels **18** San Francisco Giants

king of gods 4 Amen, Amon, Finn, Zeus **5** Ammon, Enlil, Fionn, Wotan **6** Marduk **8** Merodach **12** Baal Merodach **13** Fionn MacCumal

King of Hearts
  character in: 28 Alice's Adventures in Wonderland
  author: 7 Carroll

King of Righteousness
  11 Melchizedek

Kingsley, Ben
  roles: 6 Gandhi (Oscar) **8** Betrayal

Kingsley, Charles
  author of: 7 Hypatia **10** Alton Locke **11** Westward Ho! **14** The Water Babies **15** Hereward the Wake

King Solomon's Mines
  author: 13 H Rider Haggard
  character: 5 Twala **6** Gagool, Umbopa **14** Sir Henry Curtis **15** Allan Quatermain, Captain John Good

King's Row
  author: 14 Henry Bellamann
  director: 7 Sam Wood
  cast: 10 Betty Field **11** Ann Sheridan, Claude Rains **12** Ronald Reagan **13** Charles Coburn **14** Judith Anderson, Robert Cummings
  score: 21 Erich Wolfgard Korngold
  character: 11 Drake McHugh, Elise Sandor **13** Randy Monaghan **14** Cassandra Tower, Parris Mitchell

Kingston
  capital of: 7 Jamaica

Kingu
origin: **8** Akkadian
father: **4** Apsu
mother: **6** Tiamet
blood used by: **2** Ea **6** Marduk **8** Merodach **12** Baal Merodach
blood used for: **8** creation

kink 4 coil, flaw, knot, pang **5** cramp, crick, crimp, frizz, gnarl, hitch, quirk, snarl, spasm, twist **6** defect, foible, glitch, oddity, tangle, twinge, vagary **7** crinkle, frizzle **8** crotchet **9** queerness, stiffness, weirdness **10** difficulty **11** peculiarity, singularity **12** charley horse, complication, eccentricity, freakishness, idiosyncrasy, imperfection

kinky 3 odd **4** sick, wiry **5** kooky, queer **6** frizzy, matted, quirky, twisty **7** bizarre, deviant, frizzly, knotted, strange, tangled, twisted, unusual **8** aberrant, abnormal, crinkled, freakish, frizzled, peculiar, perverse **9** eccentric, unnatural **10** unorthodox **13** idiosyncratic

Kinshasa
capital of: **5** Zaire

kinsman 3 sib, son **4** aunt, heir **5** child, uncle **6** cousin, father, mother, parent, sister **7** brother **8** daughter, landsman, relation, relative **9** offspring **10** countryman **11** grandfather, grandmother **13** blood relation, blood relative

Kiowa
language family: **6** Tanoan
location: **6** Plains **7** Montana **8** Colorado, Oklahoma
allied with: **7** Arapaho **8** Comanche **11** Kiowa Apache
deity: **5** Taime

Kiowa Apache
language family:
12 Shapwailutan
location: **6** Plains

Kipling, Rudyard
author of: **3** Kim **8** Gunga Din, Mandalay **11** Danny Deaver **12** The Seven Seas **13** Just So Stories, The Jungle Book **18** Barrack-Room Ballads, Captains Courageous

Kipps
author: **7** H G Wells

Kirchhoff, Gustav Robert
field: **7** physics
nationality: **6** German
discovered: **6** cesium **8** rubidium
developed: **12** spectroscope
named for him: **19** electric circuit laws

Kirchner, Ernst Ludwig
born: **7** Germany **13** Aschaffenburg
artwork: **11** Street Scene **12** Street Berlin **13** Moonlit Winter **21** Self-portrait with Model

Kiribati
other name: **14** Gilbert Islands
capital/largest city: **6** Tarawa
others: **5** Betio **7** Bairiki, Bonriki **9** Bikenibeu
school: **12** South Pacific
monetary unit: **4** cent **6** dollar
island: **5** Flint, Ocean **6** Banaba, Canton, Malden, Tarawa **7** Abemama, Fanning, Gilbert, Marakei, Nonouti, Phoenix, Vostock **8** Caroline, Starbuck **9** Christmas, Enderbury, Tabiteuea **10** Butaritari, Equatorial, Washington **12** Northern Line, Southern Line
sea: **7** Pacific
people: **8** Banabans **10** Polynesian **11** Micronesian
language: **6** Samoan **7** English **10** Gilbertese
religion: **5** Baha'i **8** Anglican **9** Methodist **11** Church of God **13** Roman Catholic **19** Seventh Day Adventist

kirsch, kirschwasser
type: **6** brandy **7** liqueur
origin: **6** France **7** Germany **11** Switzerland
flavor: **6** cherry
with gin: **7** Florida **10** Lady Finger
with vodka: **12** Volga Boatman

kismet 3 end, lot **4** doom, fate **5** moira **7** destiny, fortune, portion **8** God's will **10** Providence **11** will of Allah **12** circumstance **13** inevitability **14** predestination

kiss 4 buss, neck **6** smooch, salute **8** osculate

Kiss for Cinderella, A
author: **12** James M Barrie

kit 3 rig **4** gear **5** tools **6** outfit, tackle, things **7** devices **8** supplies, utensils **9** equipment, trappings **10** implements, provisions **11** furnishings, impedi-

ments, instruments, necessaries **13** accoutrements, paraphernalia

Kitasato, Shibasaburo
field: **12** bacteriology
nationality: **8** Japanese
isolated: **7** anthrax, tetanus **9** dysentery **13** bubonic plague
developed: **19** diphtheria antitoxin

kitchen 6 bakery, cocina, galley **7** cuisine **8** cookroom, scullery **9** bakehouse, cookhouse

Kitchener, Horatio Herbert
also: **18** first Earl Kitchener
nationality: **7** British
served in: **7** Boer War **15** South African War
battle: **8** Khartoum, Omdurman
governor of: **8** the Sudan
commander in chief of: **5** India **12** Egyptian army
consul general of: **5** Egypt

kitel 20 Jewish ceremonial robe
color: **5** white

Kitely
character in: **19** Every Man in His Humour
author: **6** Jonson

kittenish 3 coy **7** playful **10** coquettish

Klamath
language family: **8** Penutian
location: **6** Oregon **10** California
related to: **5** Modoc **6** Cayuse, Molala

Klee, Paul
born: **11** Switzerland **14** Munchenbuchsee
artwork: **9** Locksmith **11** Ad Parnassum **18** Barbarian Sacrifice, Demon above the Ships **20** The Twittering Machine **22** Revolution of the Viaduct **23** Dance-Play of the Red Skirts **24** Dance Monster to my Soft Song **35** The Vocal Fabric of the Singer Rosa Silber

Kleist, Heinrich von
author of: **11** Penthesilea **14** The Marquise of O **16** The Broken Pitcher **18** The Prince of Homburg

Kline, Kevin
roles: **11** The Big Chill **13** Sophie's Choice **17** Pirates of Penzance

Klugman, Jack
born: **14** Philadelphia PA
roles: **6** Quincy **12** Oscar Madison, The Odd Couple

klutz 5 dummy **9** blockhead **11** satchelfoot **13** fumblefingers

klutzy 4 dumb 6 clumsy, stupid 7 awkward 9 graceless

knack 4 bent, gift, turn 5 flair, forte, skill 6 genius, talent 7 ability, faculty, finesse 8 aptitude, capacity, facility 9 dexterity, expertise, ingenuity, quickness, readiness 10 adroitness, capability, cleverness, competence, efficiency, propensity 11 inclination, proficiency 13 dexterousness

knave 3 cad, cur, dog, rat 5 phony, rogue, scamp 6 con man, rascal, rotter, varlet, wretch 7 bounder, culprit 8 scalawag, swindler 9 charlatan, con artist, reprobate, scoundrel 10 blackguard 11 rapscallion 14 good for nothing

knee breeches 8 breeches, jodhpurs, knickers 9 plus fours

kneel 3 bow 6 curtsy, kowtow, salaam 7 bow down 9 genuflect 13 make obeisance 16 prostrate oneself

knell 4 peal, ring, toll 5 chime, sound 6 stroke 7 pealing, ringing, tolling

Knickerbocker Holiday
    author: 15 Maxwell Anderson

knickknack, nicknack 3 toy 6 bauble, gewgaw, trifle 7 bibelot, trinket 8 frippery, gimcrack 9 bagatelle, bric-a-brac, plaything 11 thingamajig

knife 3 cut 4 dirk, shiv, stab 5 blade, slash, wound 6 cutter, pierce 7 cut down, cutlery 8 cut apart, lacerate, mutilate
    type: 3 pen 4 jack 5 bowie, bread, putty, table 6 dagger, paring, pocket 7 butcher, carving, hunting, machete, palette, pruning, scalpel 8 skinning, stiletto, surgical 11 switchblade

knight 4 hero 7 fighter, gallant, paladin, soldier, Templar, warrior 8 cavalier, champion, defender, guardian, horseman, Lancelot 9 gentleman, man-at-arms, protecter, protector 10 equestrian, vindicator

Knight
    character in: 18 The Canterbury Tales
    author: 7 Chaucer

Knightley, George
    character in: 4 Emma
    author: 6 Austen

Knights, The
    author: 12 Aristophanes
    character: 5 Demus 6 Nicias 11 Demosthenes 20 Cleon the Paphlagonian

knit 3 tat 4 ally, bind, draw, join, knot, link 5 braid, plait, twist, unify, unite, weave 6 attach, crease, fasten, furrow, stitch 7 connect, crochet, wrinkle 10 intertwine, interweave 12 draw together

knob 3 nub 4 bulb, bump, grip, hold, hump, knot, knur, lump, node, snag 5 bulge, gnarl, knurl, latch, lever, swell 6 handle, nubbin 8 handhold, swelling, tubercle 9 convexity 10 projection, prominence, protrusion 12 protuberance, protuberancy

knock 3 bat, hit, pat, rap, tap 4 bang, beat, belt, blow, bomb, bump, clip, cuff, dash, kick, lick, push, slam, slap, sock, swat, thud 5 abuse, cavil, clout, crack, crash, decry, pound, punch, smack, smash, smite, thump, whack 6 batter, carp at, defeat, hammer, jostle, murder, peck at, pummel, strike, stroke, thwack, wallop 7 censure, condemn, failure, setback 8 belittle, lambaste 9 criticism, criticize, deprecate, disparage, reprehend 12 condemnation, faultfinding, reprehension

knock down 4 deck, down, drop, fell 5 floor 7 flatten 8 bowl over, discount 9 take apart 11 disassemble

knock off balance 6 rattle 7 shake up 8 unsettle 9 take aback 11 disorganize

knockout 2 KO 4 doll 5 beaut, Venus 6 beauty, eyeful 7 stunner

knock out of shape 4 maul 5 crush 6 batter, beat up, mangle

knoll 4 hill, rise 5 mound

knot 3 bun 4 bump, frog, heap, hump, loop, lump, mass, pack, pile, star, tuft 5 braid, bunch, clump, group, hitch, knurl, plait, twist 6 bundle, circle 7 cat's-paw, chignon, cluster, epaulet, rosette 8 ornament 9 gathering 10 assemblage, collection, intertwist 13 interlacement
    type: 3 bow, top 4 flat, slip 5 slide 6 double, single, square 7 running 8 hangman's, overhand, shoulder, surgeon's 9 half-hitch 11 figure-eight, midshipman's

Knots Landing
    character: 9 Abby Ewing, Gary Ewing 10 Greg Sumner 11 Valene Ewing 12 Mac Mackenzie 14 Karen Mackenzie, Paige Forrester
    cast: 10 Donna Mills, Joan Van Ark 11 Julie Harris, Kevin Dobson, Michelle Lee 13 William Devane 14 Douglas Sheehan, Ted Shackelford 17 Nicolette Sheridan

knotty 4 hard 5 bumpy, rough, tough 6 coarse, flawed, knobby, knurly, rugged, snaggy, thorny, tricky, uneven 7 complex, gnarled, knurled, nodular 8 baffling, involved, puzzling, ticklish, unsmooth 9 blemished, difficult, intricate 10 perplexing 11 complicated, troublesome 12 rough-grained 13 coarse-grained, problematical

know 3 see 6 be sure, be wise, notice 7 be smart, discern, make out, realize 8 identify, perceive 9 apprehend, be assured, be aware of, be certain, be close to, get wise to, recognize 10 be informed, be positive, understand 11 be confident, be sagacious, be thick with, distinguish, feel certain, have down pat, have no doubt 12 discriminate, have down cold, have the ear of 13 be cognizant of, be intelligent, have knowledge, rub elbows with 14 be familiar with

knowable 9 thinkable 11 conceivable, discernible, perceivable 14 understandable

Knowell, Edward
    character in: 19 Every Man in His Humour
    author: 6 Jonson

know for sure 9 be certain 10 be positive

know-how 3 art 4 bent, gift 5 craft, flair, knack, savvy, skill 6 talent 7 ability, mastery 8 aptitude, capacity, deftness 9 adeptness, expertise, knowledge, technique 10 adroitness, capability, competence, experience, expertness 11 proficiency 12 skillfulness 15 professionalism
    French: 11 savoir-faire

knowing 4 deep, wise 5 aware, canny, sharp, smart, sound 6 astute, brainy, bright, clever, shrewd 7 erudite, fraught, learned, sapient 8 academic, educated, eloquent, highbrow, literary, profound, schooled, sensible 9 conscious, judicious, revealing, sagacious 10 discerning, expressive, meaningful, perceptive, percipient, scholastic, widely read 11 enlightened, intelligent, significant **12** intellectual, well-informed **13** comprehending, knowledgeable, perspicacious, philosophical, sophisticated, understanding

knowing how to live
  French: **11** savoir-vivre

knowing just what to do
  French: **11** savoir-faire

know-it-all 5 brash **13** overconfident

knowledge 3 ken, tip **4** data, hint, news **5** sense **6** memory, notice, report, wisdom **7** inkling, mention, tidings **8** learning **9** awareness, education, erudition, schooling, statement **10** cognizance, intimation, perception **11** cultivation, declaration, familiarity, information, realization, recognition, revelation, scholarship **12** announcement, book learning, intelligence, notification **13** communication, comprehension, consciousness, enlightenment, pronouncement
  god of: **4** Odin **5** Othin

knowledgeable 3 hip **8** at home in, versed in **12** familiar with, well-informed **14** acquainted with, conversant with
  French: **9** au courant

knowledge of the world
  French: **11** savoir-vivre

known 5 noted, plain **6** common, famous, patent **7** evident, obvious, popular **8** apparent, definite, distinct, familiar, manifest, palpable **9** notorious, prominent **10** celebrated, recognized **11** self-evident

know thyself
  Greek: **13** gnothi seauton

knuckle under 5 yield **6** give in, submit **7** bow down **9** surrender **10** capitulate

knurled 5 bumpy, lumpy **6** gnarly, knobby, knotty, knurly, nubbly, ridged **7** bulging, gnarled, knotted, nodular

Koch, Robert
  field: **12** bacteriology
  nationality: **6** German
  isolated: **2** TB **12** tuberculosis
  awarded: **10** Nobel Prize

Kodaly, Zoltan
  born: **7** Hungary **9** Kecskemet
  composer of: **9** Hary Janos **11** Czinka Panna, Missa Brevis, Szekely Fono **14** Budavari Te Deum **15** Dances of Galanta **17** Dances of Marosszek, Peacock Varia-

tions, Psalmus Hungaricus **28** The Spinning Room of the Szekelys

Koestler, Arthur
  author of: **14** Darkness at Noon **15** The Sleepwalkers

Kojak
  character: **5** (Det) Rizzo **7** (Det) Stavros **9** (Lt) Theo Kojak **10** (Det) Saperstein **11** Frank McNeil **12** (Lt) Bobby Crocker
  cast: **9** Dan Frazer **10** Vince Conti **11** Kevin Dobson, Mark Russell **12** Telly Savalas **13** George Savalas (Demosthenes)
  trademark: **8** lollipop
  phrase: **14** Who loves ya baby?

Kollwitz, Kathe
  real name: **12** Kathe Schmidt
  born: **10** Konigsberg **11** East Prussia
  artwork: **3** War **5** Death, Pieta **11** Proletariat **13** Weavers' Revolt (Weaver's Rebellion) **14** Mother and Child, The Peasants' War **18** Death Seizing a Woman

Kol Nidre 4 vows **8** promises **22** Jewish liturgical prayer
  recited on eve of: **9** Yom Kippur

Kong
  nickname of: **11** Dave Kingman

Kon-Tiki
  author: **13** Thor Heyerdahl

kook 3 nut **5** crazy, flake, loony, wacko **6** cuckoo, weirdo **7** dingbat **8** crackpot **9** ding-a-ling, eccentric, fruitcake, harebrain, screwball **10** crackbrain

Korah
  father: **4** Esau **6** Hebron **7** Eliphaz
  conspired with: **6** Abiram, Dathan
  rebelled against: **5** Aaron, Moses

Korea *see box, p. 542*

Koridethianus 16 Greek unical codex

Korman, Harvey
  born: **9** Chicago IL
  roles: **11** High Anxiety **13** Danny Kaye Show **14** Blazing Saddles **16** Carol Burnett Show

Kornberg, Arthur
  field: **12** biochemistry
  sythesized: **3** DNA, RNA **15** ribonucleic acid **20** deoxyribonucleic acid
  awarded: **10** Nobel Prize

kosher 5 right **6** proper **7** ethical **10** aboveboard **12** on the up and up

Kosinski, Jerzy
  author of: **5** Steps **7** Cockpit **9** Blind Date **10** Being There **11** Passion Play **12** The Devil Tree **14** The Painted Bird

Kowalski, Stanley
  character in: **21** A Streetcar Named Desire
  author: **8** Williams

kowtow 4 bend, fawn **5** cower, stoop, toady **6** bow low, cringe, curtsy, grovel, salaam **7** truckle **8** bootlick, butter up, softsoap **9** genuflect **11** applepolish **12** bow and scrape **16** prostrate oneself

kowtowing 7 fawning, servile **8** toadying **9** groveling **10** obsequious

Kraken
  origin: **9** Norwegian
  form: **7** monster
  habitat: **3** sea
  caused: **10** whirlpools

Kramer, Stanley
  director of: **10** On the Beach **11** Ship of Fools **14** Inherit the Wind, The Defiant Ones **19** Judgment at Nuremberg

Kramer vs Kramer
  director: **12** Robert Benton
  based on novel by: **11** Avery Corman
  cast: **10** Howard Duff **11** Justin Henry, Meryl Streep **13** Dustin Hoffman, Jane Alexander
  Oscar for: **5** actor (Hoffman) **7** picture **8** director **10** screenplay **17** supporting actress (Streep)

Krantz, Judith
  author of: **8** Scruples **13** Princess Daisy **16** I'll Take Manhattan, Mistral's Daughter

Krazy Kat
  creator: **14** George Herriman
  character:
    cop: **12** Offissa B Pupp
    mouse: **6** Ignatz
  prop: **5** brick
  place: **4** jail **14** Coconino County **24** Kelly's Exclusive Brick Yard

Krebs, Hans Adolf
  field: **9** chemistry
  nationality: **6** German
  discovered: **15** citric acid cycle
  awarded: **10** Nobel Prize

Korea

other name: 6 Choson 17 land of morning calm

capital:
  North Korea: 9 Pyongyang
  South Korea: 5 Seoul

largest city: 5 Seoul

others: 5 Masan, Mokpo, Pusan, Sinpo, Suwon, Taegu, Wonju 6 Chonju, Inchon, Kangso, Kunsan, Taejon, Wonsan 7 Hanyang, Hungnam, Kaesong, Kangson, Kwangju 8 Chongjin, Chunchon, Kimchaek

school: 5 Busan 6 Yonsei 7 Hanyang 8 Kim Chaek, Kyung Hee 9 Kim Il Sung

division:
  ancient: 5 Silla 6 Choson 7 Koguryo, Paekche

monetary unit: 3 woh, won 4 chun, hwan, kwan

weight: 3 won

island: 4 Chin, Koje 5 Cheju, Sinmi 6 Anmyon, Huksan, Namhae 7 Tokchok 8 Quelpart 10 Paengnyong

mountain: 4 Wang 5 Chiri, Halla 6 Kwanmo, Sobaek 7 Diamond, Kyebang, Nangnim, Taebaek 8 Chang-pai, Hamgyong, Myohyang 9 Paektu-san 10 Kumgang-san

highest point: 6 Paektu 9 Paektu-san

river: 3 Han, Kin, Kum, Kun, Nam 4 Lobk, Yalu 5 Amnok, Imjin, Tumen 6 Namhan, Pukhan, Somjin, Soyang, Yesong 7 Naktong, Taedong 8 Changjin, Youngsan 9 Chongchon

sea: 5 Japan 6 Yellow 9 East China

physical feature:
  bay: 5 Korea 6 Yongil 7 Kanghwa, Kyonggi 9 Tongjoson
  cape: 4 Musu
  point: 7 Changgi 8 Changsan
  strait: 5 Korea
  valley: 7 Naktong

people: 6 Korean
  artist: 8 Chong Son 10 Kimtlong-do
  dynasty: 2 Yi 4 Choe 5 Koryo
  leader: 6 Sejong 8 Yi Sung-gy 9 Kim Il Sung 11 Chun Doo Hwan, Syngman Rhee 12 Park Chung Hee
  legendary leader: 5 Ki-tse 6 Chi-tse, Chi-tzu, Tangun
  poet: 10 Hwang Chini

language: 6 Korean
  alphabet: 6 hangul

religion: 6 Taoism 7 animism 8 Buddhism 9 Chondogyo 12 Christianity, Confucianism

place:
  palace: 8 Kyongbok
  temple: 7 Haein-sa 17 Hall of Eternal Life
  tomb: 14 Dancing Figures

feature:
  clothing: 5 chima
  game: 3 yut 5 akoan 6 ho-hpai 7 kol-ye-si 9 ryong-hpai, sang-ryouk 10 ke-pouk-hpai, sin-syo-tyen 12 tjak-matchi-ki 15 kko-ri-pouk-tchi-ki
  martial art: 9 tae-kwon-do
  musical instrument: 6 chaing 7 kayagum, komungo
  porcelain: 7 Celadon
  porch: 4 maru
  pottery: 8 pun-chong

food:
  bean curd: 4 tubu
  hot pickle: 6 kimchi
  meat-filled dumpling: 5 mandu
  noodle: 5 kuksu

Kreisler, Fritz
  born: 6 Vienna 7 Austria
  composer of: 7 Allegro 10 Praeludium 15 Caprice Viennois 16 Tambourin Chinois

Kreutzer, Rodolphe
  born: 6 France 10 Versailles
  composer of: 16 Etudes ou Caprices

Kreutzer Sonata, The
  author: 10 Leo Tolstoy
  character: 13 Mme Pozdnishef, Trukhashevsky 16 Vasyla Pozdnishef

Krieg 3 war

Kriemhild
  origin: 8 Germanic
  mentioned in: 14 Nibelungenlied
  brother: 7 Gunther
  husband: 9 Siegfried
  slew: 5 Hagan 7 Gunther
  avenged: 6 murder 9 Siegfried
  corresponds to: 6 Gudrun, Kudrun 7 Guthrun

Kristin Lavransdatter
  author: 12 Sigrid Undset

Kronos *see* 6 Cronus

Krook
  character in: 10 Bleak House
  author: 7 Dickens

Kropp, Albert
  character in: 25 All Quiet on the Western Front
  author: 8 Remarque

krypton
  chemical symbol: 2 Kr

Kuala Lumpur
  capital of: 8 Malaysia

Kubla Khan
  author: 15 Samuel Coleridge

Kubrick, Stanley
  director of: 6 Lolita 9 Spartacus 11 Barry Lyndon 12 Paths of Glory 13 Dr Strangelove (or How I Learned to Stop Worrying and Love the Bomb) 16 A Clockwork Orange 30 Two Thousand and One A Space Odyssey

kudo, kudos 4 fame 5 award, glory, honor, prize 6 esteem, praise, renown, repute 7 acclaim, plaudit 8 citation, prestige 9 celebrity, laudation 10 admiration, decoration 12 commendation 14 celebratedness

Kudrun *see* 6 Gudrun

Kukla, Fran & Ollie
  hostess: 11 Fran Allison
  puppet: 5 Kukla, Ollie (Oliver J Dragon) 8 Mercedes 9 Cecil Bill 10 Col Crackie 11 Beulah Witch 12 Olivia

Dragon **13** Delores Dragon
14 Fletcher Rabbit **18** Mme
Ophelia Oglepuss

Kulla
origin: **8** Egyptian, Sumerian
world of: **4** dead
god of: **6** bricks

Kullervo
origin: **7** Finnish
mentioned in: **8** Kalevala
form: **5** slave
death: **7** suicide

kummel
origin: **7** Germany
flavor: **7** caraway

kumquat 10 Fortunella
varieties: **4** oval **5** round
6 Marumi, Nagami **16** Australian desert

Kung Fu
character: **8** Master Po **9** Master Kan **14** Kwai Chang
Caine
cast: **8** Keye Luke **9** Philip
Ahn **11** Radames Pera **14** David Carradine
Caine raised in: **13** Shaolin
Temple

kunzite
species: **9** spodumene

Kupka, Frank (Frantisek)
born: **6** Opocno **7** Bohemia
14 Czechoslovakia
artwork: **12** Black Accents,
The Cathedral **16** Etude pour
la Fugue **17** Fugue in Red
and Blue **23** Fugue in Two
Colors Amorpha **25** Philosophical Architecture

Kuprin, Aleksandr
author of: **7** The Duel
10 Yama the Pit

Kurosawa, Akira
director of: **3** Ran **8** Rashomon
12 Seven Samurai

Kurtz
character in: **15** Heart of
Darkness
author: **6** Conrad

Kuwait *see box*

Kwa
language family: **16** Niger-
Kordofanian
group: **10** Niger-Congo
includes: **3** Ewe, Ibo, Twi
4 Bini, Nupe, Togo **6** Yoruba
7 Dahomey

Kwakiutl
language family: **8** Wakashan
location: **6** Canada **15** British
Columbia, Vancouver Island
20 Queen Charlotte Island
related to: **6** Nootka
10 Bellabella
noted for: **10** totem poles
15 Cannibal Society, wooden
sculpture
called: **14** potlatch people

Kyd, Thomas
author of: **17** The Spanish
Tragedy

Kyrgyzstan
other name: **9** Kirghizia
capital/largest city: **6** Frunze
7 Bishkek
head of state: **9** president
government: **8** republic
monetary unit: **3** som
mountain: **8** Tian Shan
people: **5** Uzbek **6** Kyrgyz
7 Kirghiz
language: **6** Turkic **7** Kirghiz
religion: **6** Muslim **10** Sunni
Islam

Kyrie eleison 13 Lord have
mercy

Kuwait
name means: **9** small fort
capital/largest city:
10 Kuwait City
others: **6** Ahmadi **7** Ha-
walli **8** Abdullah, al-Jah-
rah, Fahaheel,
Shuwaykh **9** al-Shuayba
12 Mena al-Ahmadi,
Mina Abd Allah, Mina
al-Ahmadi
head of state: **4** emir
monetary unit: **4** fils
5 dinar
island: **5** Warba **7** Bubi-
yan, Failaka
physical feature:
bay: **6** Kuwait **12** Khor
Abdullah
duststorm: **4** kaus
gulf: **7** Persian
oasis: **6** Jahrah
people: **4** Arab **5** Iraqi, Saudi **6** Indian **7** Bedouin
8 Egyptian **9** Pakistani
11 Palestinian
ruling family: **5** Sabah
sheikh (Sabah family):
5 Ahmad, Salem **7** Mubarak **12** Jaber al-Ah-
med, Sabah al-Salim
15 Abdullah al-Salim
religion: **5** Islam
war: **4** Gulf **11** Desert
Storm, Persian Gulf
12 Desert Shield
enemy: **4** Iraq **13** Saddam Hussein

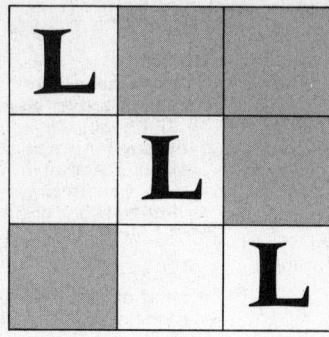

Laban
  father: 7 Bethuel
  grandfather: 5 Nahor
  daughter: 4 Leah **6** Rachel
  sister: 7 Rebekah
  son-in-law: 5 Jacob

Labdacus
  king of: 6 Thebes
  father: 9 Polydorus
  mother: 7 Nycteis
  grandfather: 7 Nycteus
  brother: 5 Lycus
  son: 5 Laius
  grandson: 7 Oedipus

label 3 tag **4** mark, name, note, seal, sign, slip **5** brand, stamp, tally, title **6** define, docket, ticket **7** earmark, mark off, sticker **8** classify, describe **9** designate **10** denominate, put a mark on **11** appellation, designation, inscription **12** characterize **13** specification **14** classification, identification **16** characterization

labor, labour 4 plod, toil, work **5** slave, sweat **6** drudge, effort, suffer **7** agonize, travail, workers, workmen **8** drudgery, exertion, laborers, manpower, plodding, plug away, struggle, struggle **9** employees, grind away, work force **10** birth pangs, childbirth, menial work, smart under **11** birth throes, manual labor, parturition **12** accouchement, be affected by, be burdened by, be troubled by **13** be the victim of **14** employ one's time, work like a slave

labored 5 heavy, stiff **6** clumsy, forced, wooden **7** awkward, cramped, halting, studied **8** drawnout, overdone, strained **9** contrived, difficult, laborious, maladroit, ponderous, unnatural **13** self-conscious, unspontaneous

laborer 4 hand **6** coolie,

drudge, menial, toiler, worker **7** plodder, workman **8** handyman, hired man, hireling, workhand **9** hired hand **10** roustabout, wage earner, workingman **11** proletarian **12** manual worker **16** blue-collar worker

laborious 4 hard **6** brutal, severe, uphill **7** arduous, irksome, labored, onerous, wearing **8** rigorous, tiresome, toilsome, wearying **9** demanding, difficult, effortful, fatiguing, herculean, strenuous, wearisome **10** burdensome, oppressive, struggling **11** troublesome

laboriously 4 hard **9** arduously **14** with difficulty **15** with great effort

laboriousness 5 trial **8** tough job **10** difficulty, rough going, uphill work **11** arduousness **12** hard sledding **15** troublesomeness

labor omnia vincit 15 work conquers all
  motto of: 8 Oklahoma

Labors of Hercules *see* **8** Hercules

labyrinth 3 web **4** knot, maze **5** snarl **6** jungle, morass, riddle, tangle **7** complex, network **9** intricacy, mare's nest **10** complexity, perplexity, wilderness **11** convolution

Labyrinth
  form: 4 maze
  location: 5 Crete
  built by: 8 Daedalus
  housed: 8 Minotaur

Lacaille, Nicholas Louis de
  field: 9 astronomy
  nationality: 6 French
  mapped: 14 constellations

lace 3 tie **4** beat, bind, cane, dope, lash, whip **5** braid, cinch, close, flail, spank,

spike, strap, tie up, truss **6** dope up, fasten, flavor, infuse, punish, secure, switch, tether, thrash **7** fortify, spice up, suffuse, tighten **8** chastise, make fast, make taut **10** strengthen **11** add liquor to **12** add spirits to, draw together, give a beating

Lacedaemon
  father: 4 Zeus
  mother: 8 Taygete
  wife: 6 Sparta
  son: 7 Amyclas
  daughter: 8 Eurydice
  founder of: 6 Sparta

lacerate 3 cut, rip **4** gash, hurt, pain, scar, stab, tear **5** lance, sever, slash, slice, wound **6** deface **7** agonize, scratch, torment, torture **8** distress, give pain, puncture **10** excruciate **11** inflict pain

lacerating 5 acute **6** fierce, severe **7** cutting, extreme, intense, violent **12** excruciating

laceration 3 cut, rip **4** tear **5** wound **10** mutilation

Lachaise, Gaston
  born: 5 Paris **6** France
  artwork: 12 Standing Nude
  13 Standing Woman
  14 Floating Figure

Lachesis
  form: 4 Fate
  holds: 12 thread of life
  determines: 6 length
  7 destiny

lachrymose 3 sad **5** teary, weepy **6** crying **7** maudlin, tearful, weeping **8** mournful **10** melancholy

lack 4 miss, need, want **6** dearth **7** absence **8** omission, scarcity, shortage **9** be missing, be short of, depletion, neediness, privation, scantness **10** deficiency, exhaustion **11** deprivation, fall short of **12** be inadequate **13** be

caught short, be deficient in
14 be found wanting, be
insufficient

lackadaisical 4 idle **7** languid,
loafing **8** lifeless, listless, mindless **9** apathetic, lethargic,
unexcited **10** inanimated,
phlegmatic, spiritless, unaspiring, uninspired **11** indifferent,
languishing, unambitious, unconcerned, unexcitable, unmo-
tivated **12** uninterested
13 dillydallying

lackey 4 page **5** slave, toady,
usher, valet **6** butler, flunky,
helper, menial, minion, squire,
waiter **7** servant, steward
8 employee, follower, hanger-
on, hireling, inferior, retainer
9 assistant, attendant, cupbearer, mercenary, underling

lacking 7 needing, wanting
9 deficient **10** inadequate
12 falling short, insufficient
French: 6 manque

lackluster 4 blah, dead, drab,
dull **5** bland, muted **6** boring,
dreary, leaden, pallid, somber
7 humdrum, nothing, prosaic,
subdued **8** lifeless, mediocre,
ordinary **9** colorless **10** lusterless **11** commonplace **12** run-
of-the-mill **13** uninteresting

lack of conviction 5 doubt
8 question **9** misgiving **10** hesitation, indecision
11 uncertainty

lack of faith 5 doubt **7** atheism **8** distrust, mistrust
9 disbelief, suspicion

lack of feeling 6 apathy
8 coldness, numbness **11** impassivity **15** emotionlessness,
hardheartedness,
passionlessness

lack of interest 5 ennui
6 apathy **7** boredom **9** unconcern **12** indifference

lack of respect 8 contempt,
rudeness **9** disregard **10** disrespect **11** discourtesy, irreverence **12** impoliteness

lack of skill 9 inability
10 clumsiness, ineptitude
11 awkwardness
12 incompetency

Laclos, Pierre Choderlos de
author of: 22 Les Liaisons
Dangereuses

Lacombe, Lucien
director: 10 Louis Malle
cast: 12 Pierre Blaise **13** Aurore Clement **16** Holger
Lowenadler

laconic 4 curt **5** blunt, brief,
pithy, short, terse **7** compact,
concise, pointed, summary

8 succinct **9** condensed **10** to
the point **12** concentrated
14 sparing of words

lacquer 4 coat **5** glaze **7** coating, shellac, varnish

lacrimoso
music: 7 tearful

lacrosse
Indian name: 9 bagataway
circle around goal: 6 crease
players/team: 3 ten
position: 6 goalie **9** attack-
man **10** defenseman,
midfielder
term: 6 riding **8** clearing

lacuna 3 gap, pit **4** gulf, hole,
void **5** blank, break, crack,
ditch, pause, space **6** breach,
cavity, hiatus **7** caesura, fissure, interim, opening, vacancy **8** interval, omission
10 interstice, suspension
12 interruption
13 discontinuity

lacustrine 7 aquatic **11** lake-
growing **12** lake-dwelling

lacy 4 fine **5** filmy, gauzy,
meshy, netty, sheer, webby
6 barred, frilly, netted, porous,
webbed **7** gridded, netlike
8 cobwebby, delicate, filigree,
gossamer, lacelike, retiform
9 filigreed **10** diaphanous, re-
ticulate **11** latticelike,
transparent

lad 3 boy, kid **5** sprig, youth
6 shaver, sprout **8** juvenile,
young man **9** schoolboy, stripling, young chap, youngster
11 young fellow

Ladd, Alan
son: 5 David **6** Alan Jr
co-star: 12 Veronica Lake
born: 12 Hot Springs AR
roles: 5 Shane **13** The Blue
Dahlia **14** The Great Gatsby,
This Gun for Hire

ladies' man 4 beau, stud
5 spark **7** playboy **8** cavalier,
gay blade

La Dolce Vita
director: 15 Federico
Fellini
cast: 9 Lex Barker, Nadia
Gray **10** Anouk Aimee
11 Anita Ekberg **19** Marcello Mastroianni

Ladon
form: 6 dragon
father: 6 Typhon
mother: 7 Echidna
number of heads: 7 hundred
guarded: 6 garden
garden owned by:
10 Hesperides
killed by: 8 Hercules

ladrone 5 thief **6** bandit,
outlaw

lady 4 wife **5** woman **6** female,
matron, spouse **7** duchess,
peeress **8** baroness, countess
10 aristocrat, noblewoman
11 gentlewoman, marchioness,
viscountess, woman of rank
13 well-bred woman
German: 4 frau
Italian: 5 donna
Spanish/Portuguese: 4 dona

Lady Chatterley's Lover
author: 10 D H Lawrence
character: 7 Mellors **19** Constance Chatterley

Lady Eve, The
director: 14 Preston Sturges
cast: 10 Henry Fonda
13 Charles Coburn **14** Eugene Pallette **15** Barbara
Stanwyck, William Demarest

Lady for a Day
director: 10 Frank Capra
based on story by: 11 Damon Runyon
cast: 9 Guy Kibbee, May
Robson **13** Warren William
remade as: 19 Pocketful of
Miracles

Lady from Dubuque, The
author: 11 Edward Albee

Lady from the Sea, The
author: 11 Henrik Ibsen

Lady in Chair
constellation of:
10 Cassiopeia

ladylike 5 civil **6** modest, polite, proper **7** courtly, elegant,
genteel, refined **8** cultured,
decorous, mannerly, polished,
well-bred **9** courteous, dignified **10** cultivated **11** respectable **12** well-mannered **13** well
brought up

Lady of the Camellias, The
see 7 Camille

Lady of the Lake, The
author: 14 Sir Walter Scott
character: 9 Allan Bane
11 Roderick Dhu **12** Ellen
Douglas **13** Malcolm
Graeme **14** James Fitz-
James, James of Douglas

Lady Oracle
author: 14 Margaret Atwood

lady's maid
French: 14 femme de
chambre

Lady's Not for Burning,
The
author: 14 Christopher Fry

lady's-slipper, Lady-slipper
11 Cypripedium **12** Paphiope-
dilum, Phragmipedium
varieties: 4 pink **5** showy
8 mountain, ram's-head
9 two-leaved **10** small

white **11** large yellow, small yellow

Lady Vanishes, The
director: **15** Alfred Hitchcock
cast: **9** Paul Lukas **13** Dame May Whitty **15** Michael Redgrave **16** Margaret Lockwood

Lady Windermere's Fan
author: **10** Oscar Wilde
character: **10** Mrs Erlynne **14** Lord Darlington, Lord Windermere **18** Lord Augustus Lorton

Laelaps
form: **5** hound
borrowed from: **8** Cephalus
borrowed by: **10** Amphitryon

Laertes
son: **8** Odysseus

Laertes
character in: **6** Hamlet
author: **11** Shakespeare

Laertiades
epithet of: **8** Odysseus
means: **12** son of Laertes

Laestrygones
form: **6** giants
characteristic: **9** cannibals

La Farge, John
born: **9** New York NY
artwork: **14** Maua Our Boatman **17** The Muse of Painting **18** Red and White Peonies

La Fayette, Comtesse de
author of: **19** La Princesse de Cleves

Lafayette, Marquis de
also: **38** Marie Joseph Paul Yves Roch Gilbert du Motier
nationality: **6** French
served in: **14** July Revolution **16** French Revolution **18** American Revolution
battle: **8** Yorktown **10** Brandywine

Lafcadio's Adventures (The Vatican Swindle)
author: **9** Andre Gide

La Fontaine, Jean de
author of: **6** Fables

lag 4 drag, halt, inch, limp, snag **5** dally, delay, hitch, tarry, trail **6** be idle, be late, be slow, dawdle, falter, hold up, linger, loiter, trudge **7** be tardy, setback, slacken, stagger **8** be behind, hang back, slowdown **9** be overdue, inch along **10** drag behind, slackening **11** slowing down **12** bide one's time, take one's time **13** falling behind, procrastinate

laggard 4 mope, poke, slow, slug **5** idler, snail, tardy

6 loafer, remiss **7** dallier, dawdler, lounger **8** lingerer, loiterer, potterer, putterer, slowfoot, slowpoke, sluggard, sluggish **9** do-nothing, straggler **12** dilly-dallier **13** stick-in-the-mud

lagniappe, lagnappe 3 tip **4** gift, perk **5** bonus, favor, prize **7** largess, memento, present **8** gratuity, largesse **9** pourboire

Lagos
former capital of: **7** Nigeria

Lahr, Bert
real name: **14** Irving Lahrheim
born: **9** New York NY
roles: **12** Cowardly Lion **13** The Wizard of Oz

laic 3 lay **5** civil **6** laical **7** amateur, popular, profane, secular, worldly **8** temporal **11** nonclerical, nonpastoral **12** secularistic **13** inexperienced **15** nonprofessional **17** nonecclesiastical

lair 3 den, lie, mew **4** hole, nest **5** cover, haunt **6** burrow, cavern, covert **7** hideout, retreat **8** hideaway **9** sanctuary **12** resting place

laissez-faire, laisser-faire 8 hands off **9** let them be, unconcern **12** indifference **14** let-alone policy, live and let live **15** noninterference, nonintervention

laissez-passer 4 pass **6** permit **11** allow to pass

Laius
king of: **6** Thebes
father: **8** Labdacus
great-grandfather: **6** Cadmus
wife: **7** Jocasta
son: **7** Oedipus
killed by: **7** Oedipus

Lajeunesse, Gabriel
character in: **10** Evangeline
author: **10** Longfellow

lake *see* **box**

Lake, Harriette
real name of: **10** Ann Sothern

Lake, Veronica
real name: **29** Constance Frances Marie Ockelman
co-star: **8** Alan Ladd
born: **10** Brooklyn NY
roles: **13** The Blue Dahlia **14** I Married a Witch, This Gun for Hire **16** Sullivan's Travels

Lake Isle of Innisfree, The
author: **7** W B Yeats

Lakes
goddess of: **7** Juturna

L'Allegro
author: **10** John Milton
companion piece: **11** Il Penseroso

Lalo, (Victor Antoine) Edouard
born: **5** Lille **6** France
composer of: **7** Namouna **8** Le Roi d'Ys **11** The King of Ys **15** Spanish Symphony **18** Symphonie Espagnole

Lamar, Ruby
character in: **9** Sanctuary
author: **8** Faulkner

Lamarck, Jean B
field: **7** biology
forerunner of theory of: **9** evolution
author of: **21** Philosophie Zoologique

La Mare, Walter de
author of: **16** Memoirs of a Midget

Lamarr, Hedy
real name: **21** Hedwig Eva Maria Kiesler
born: **6** Vienna **7** Austria
roles: **7** Ecstasy **16** Samson and Delilah

Lamas, Fernando
wife: **10** Arlene Dahl **14** Esther Williams
born: **9** Argentina **11** Buenos Aires
roles: **13** The Merry Widow **16** Dangerous When Wet **23** The Girl Who Had Everything

Lamb, Charles
author of: **12** Essays of Elia **13** Dream Children **25** A Dissertation upon Roast Pig **31** Specimens of English Dramatic Poets

lambaste 4 beat, drub, lick, pelt, whip **5** scold, smear **6** berate, defeat, pummel, rebuke, subdue, thrash, wallop **7** bawl out, censure, chew out, clobber, cuss out, shellac, trounce **8** bludgeon, denounce, vanquish **9** castigate, dress down, light into, overwhelm, reprimand

lambent 6 bright **7** radiant, shining **8** luminous, lustrous **10** flickering, shimmering

Lambeosaurus
type: **8** dinosaur **10** ornithopod
location: **6** Canada
period: **10** Cretaceous

Lambert, Constant
born: **6** London **7** England
composer of: **9** Horoscope, Rio Grande **14** Romeo and Juliet **17** Music for Orches-

lake
of Afghanistan: 7 Helmand **13** Hamud-i-Helmand
of Albania: 4 Ulze **5** Matia, Ohrid **6** Prespa **7** Ochrida, Scutari, Shkoder **8** Ohridsko
of Algeria: 5 Hodna **6** Sabkha **7** Cherqui, Fedjadj, Meirhir **10** Azzel Matti, Meherrhane
of Andorra: 11 Engolasters
of Argentina: 6 Viedma **7** Cardiel, Fagnano, Musters **11** Buenos Aires, Mar Chiquita, Nahuel
   Huapi
of Armenia: 3 Van **5** Sevan, Urmia **8** Urumiyah
of Australia: 4 Eyre **5** Carey, Cowan, Frome, Moore, Wells **6** Austin, Barlee, Bulloo, Dundas,
   Harris, Mackay **7** Amadeus, Blanche, Everard, Torrens **8** Carnegie, Gairdner **9** MacDonald
   10 Yammayamma **14** Disappointment
of Austria: 6 Almsee **7** Fertoto, Mondsee **8** Bodensee, Traunsee **9** Constance **10** Neusiedler
of Benin: 5 Aheme **6** Nokoue
of Bolivia: 5 Poopo **7** Allagas, Coipasa, Rogagua **8** Titicaca **10** Desaguader
of Botswana: 3 Dow, Xau **5** Ngami
of Brazil: 4 Aima, Feia **5** Mirim **13** Logo dos Platos
of Burma: 4 Inle
of Burundi: 7 Rugwero **8** Tshohoha **10** Tanganyika
of Cambodia/Kampuchea: 8 Tonle Sap
of Cameroon: 4 Chad
of Canada: 4 Cree, Erie, Gras, Seul **5** Garry, Huron, Rainy **6** Louise, St John **7** Abitibi, Dubawnt, Nipigon, Ontario, Testlin **8** Kootenay, Manitoba, Okanagan, Reindeer, Superior, Winnipeg **9** Athabaska, Great Bear, Nipissing **10** Great Slave, Mistassini **12** Winnipegosis
of Central African Republic: 4 Assa
of Chad: 4 Chad
of Chile: 5 Ranco **6** Yelcho **7** Puyehue, Rupanco **8** Cochrane **10** General Paz, Llanquihue
   11 Buenos Aires
of China: 3 Tai **4** Chao, Na-mu **5** Kaoyu, Oling, Telli **6** Bamtso, Bornor, Ebinor, Erhhai,
   Khanka, Lopnor, Namtso, Poyang **7** Chaling, Hungtse, Karanor, Kokonor **8** Hulunnor, Montcalm, Taroktso, Tellinor, Tienchih, Tsinghai, Tungting
of Colombia: 4 Tota
of the Congo: 5 Mweru, Tumba **6** Albert, Nyanza, Upemba **7** Leopold **11** Stanley Pool
of Costa Rica: 6 Arenal
of Denmark 6 Arreso
of Djibouti: 4 Abbe **5** Assal
of Dominican Republic: 10 Enriquillo
of Egypt: 4 Edku, Idku **5** Qarun, Maryut, Moeris, Nasser **7** Manzala **8** Burullus, Mareotis
of El Salvador: 5 Guiha, Guija **8** Ilopango **10** Coatepeque
of England: 8 Grasmere **9** Ennerdale, Ullswater, Wastwater **10** Buttermere, Windermere
   12 Derwentwater **13** Coniston Water
of Estonia: 5 Pskov **6** Peipus **9** Vortsjarv
of Ethiopia: 3 Abe **4** Tana **5** Abaya, Shola, Tanna, Tsana, Tzana, Zeway **6** Dambea, Dembea,
   Rudolf **8** Blue Nile, Stefanie
of Finland: 3 Juo, Muo **4** Kemi, Kiui, Nasi, Oulu, Puru, Pyha, Simo **5** Enara, Enare, Hauki,
   Inari, Kalla, Lappa, Lesti, Puula, Saima **6** Ladoya, Lentua, Saimaa, Sounne, Syvari **7** Koitere,
   Nilakka **8** Pielinen **9** Kallavesi, Pielavesi
of France: 6 Annecy, Cazaux, Geneva
of Gabon Republic: 7 Anengue, Azinguo
of Germany, East: 6 Muritz
of Germany, West: 9 Constance **11** Inner Alster, Outer Alster
of Ghana: 5 Volta **8** Bosumtwi
of Greece: 5 Karla, Volve **6** Copais, Kopais, Prespa, Voweis **8** Ioannina, Koroneia, Vistonis
   9 Trichonis, Vegoritis
of Grenada: 10 Grand Etang
of Guatemala: 5 Dulce, Guija, Peten **6** Izabal **7** Atitlan **9** Amatitlan, Peten Itza
of Haiti: 8 Saumatre
of Honduras: 5 Criba, Yojoa **6** Brewer
of Hungary: 5 Ferto **7** Balaton, Velence **9** Blatensee **10** Neusiedler, Plattensee
of Iceland: 6 Myvatn **10** Thorisvatn **14** Thingvallavatn
of India: 5 Jheel, Lonar, Wular **6** Chilka, Colair, Dhebar, Kolair **7** Kolleru, Pulicat, Pushkar,
   Sambahr
of Indonesia: 4 Toba **5** Ranau **6** Towuti
of Iran: 5 Niris, Tasht, Tuzlu, Urmia **6** Sahweh, Sistan **7** Maharlu **8** Nemekser, Urumiyeh
of Iraq: 6 al-Milh **7** Sanniya **8** al-Hammar
of Ireland: 3 Doo, Key, Ree, Tay **4** Conn, Derg, Erne, Mask **5** Allen, Barra, Carra, Gowna,
   Leane, Lough, Neagh **6** Boderg, Cooter, Corrib, Ennell **7** Dromore, Gougane, Oughter, Shee-
   lin **9** Killarney
of Israel: 5 Huleh **7** Dead Sea **8** Kinneret, Tiberias **12** Sea of Galilee
of Italy: 4 Como, Iseo, Nemi **5** Garda **6** Albano, Lesina, Lugano, Varano **7** Bolsena, Perugia
   8 Maggiore **9** Bracciano, Trasimeno

(continued)

lake (*continued*)

of Japan: 4 Biwa, Suwa, Toya **6** Towada **8** Kutchawa, Shikotsu
of Kazakhstan: 8 Balkhash
of Kenya: 6 Magadi, Nakuru, Natron, Rudolf **7** Turkana **8** Naivasha, Victoria
of Lebanon: 5 Quran **6** Qirawn
of Lithuania: 5 Dysna
of Luxembourg: 8 Haut Sure
of Madagascar: 5 Itasy **7** Alaotra, Kinkony
of Malawi: 5 Nyasa **6** Chilwa, Malawi
of Mali: 2 Do **4** Debo **5** Garou **7** Korarou **9** Faguibine
of Mexico: 7 Chapala, Texcoco **9** Patzcuaro
of Mongolia: 3 Uvs **5** Har Us **6** Bor Nor **7** Ghirgis, Ubsa Nor **8** Airik Nor, Durga Nor, Hobsogol, Khara Usu **9** Khubsugul, Khukhu-Nur **10** Khirgis Nor
of Montenegro: 7 Scutari, Shkoder
of Mozambique: 5 Nyasa **6** Chuali, Nyassa **8** Nhavarre
of Myanmar: 4 Inle
of Nauru: 11 Buada Lagoon
of the Netherlands: 7 Haarlem **10** Ijsselmeer **11** Grevelingen, Hazinguliet
of New Zealand: 3 Ada **4** Gunn, Ohau **5** Hawea, Taupo **6** Pukaki, Pupuke, Te Anau, Tekapo, Wanaka **7** Brunner, Diamond, Kanieri, Okareka, Rotorua **8** Okataina, Paradise, Rotoaira, Wakatipi **9** Manapouri
of Nicaragua: 7 Managua **9** Nicaragua
of Niger: 4 Chad
of Nigeria: 4 Chad
of the Nile: 4 Tana **5** Kyoga, Tsana **6** Albert, Edward, Nasser **8** Victoria
of Norway: 4 Alte **5** Ister, Mjosa, Snasa **6** Femund **7** Rostavn, Tunnsjo
of Panama: 5 Gatun
of Paraguay: 4 Vera, Ypoa **8** Ypacarai
of Peru: 8 Titicaca
of Poland: 5 Goplo, Mamry **8** Niegocin, Sniardwy **13** Stettin Lagoon
of Puerto Rico: 5 Loiza **6** Carite **8** Dos Bocas **9** Caonillas, Guatajaca
of Rumania: 5 Sinoe **6** Snagov
of Russia: 3 Seg **4** Azor, Kola, Neva **5** Byelo, Chany, Elton, Erara, Ilmen, Lacha, Onega, Vozhe **6** Baikal, Ladoga, Tengiz **10** Caspian Sea
of Rwanda: 4 Kivu **5** Ihema **6** Bufera, Bulera, Mohasi **7** Rugwero, Ruhnodo **8** Mugesera, Tshohoha
of Sardinia: 6 Omodeo
of Scotland: 3 Awe, Dee, Lin, Tay **4** Earn, Fyne, Gair, Gare, Linn, Ness, Oich, Ryan, Sloy **5** Duich, Leven, Lochy, Lough, Morar, Maree, Nevis **6** Laggan, Linnhe, Lomond **7** Katrine, Rannoch, St Marys
of Senegal: 6 Guiers
of Sicily: 7 Pergusa **8** Camarina
of Spain: 4 Lago **9** Albrifera
of the Sudan: 2 No **4** Chad, Toad **6** Nasser
of Sweden: 4 Ster **5** Asnen, Malar, Silja, Vaner **6** Vanern, Vatter, Wennen **7** Hielmar, Malaren, Vattern **8** Dalalven **9** Hjalmaren
of Switzerland: 3 Uri, Zug **4** Biel, Thon, Thun **5** Ageri, Leman, Morat **6** Bienne, Brienz, Geneva, Lugano, Sarnen, Wallen, Zurich **7** Hallwil, Lucerne, Lungern **8** Maggiore, Vierwald **9** Bielersee, Constance, Neuchatel, Sarnersee, Thunersee
of Syria: 5 Merom **7** Djeboid **8** Tiberias
of Tanzania: 5 Eyasi, Nyasa, Rukwa **6** Malawi, Natron, Nyassa **7** Manyara **8** Victoria **10** Tanganyika
of Thailand: 9 Nong Lahan
of Tibet: 3 Aru, Bam, Bum, Nam **4** Mema, Tosu **5** Jagok, Tabia **6** Dagtse, Garhur, Kashun, Nam Iso, Seling, Tangra, Yamdok **7** Kyaring, Terinam, Tsaring, Zilling **8** Jiggitai **9** Tengrinor **11** Manasarowar
of Tunisia: 6 Achkel, Djerid **7** Bizerte
of Turkey: 3 Tuz, Van **7** Egridir **8** Beysehir
of Uganda: 5 Kioga, Kyoga **6** Albert, Edward, George **8** Victoria
of the United States: 4 Erie, Mead **5** Huron, Tahoe **6** Cayuga, Finger, George, Itasca, Oneida, Seneca **7** Iliamma, Ontario **8** Michigan, Superior **9** Champlain, Great Salt, Salton Sea, Teshekpuk, Winnebago **10** Okeechobee **11** Yellowstone **13** Pontchartrain, Wallenpaupack, Winnipesaukee **14** Lake of the Woods
of Uruguay: 5 Merin, Mirim **18** Embalse del Rio Negro
of Venezuela: 9 Maracaibo, Tacarigua
of Wales: 4 Bala **6** Vyrnwy
of Yugoslavia: 4 Bled **5** Ohrid **6** Prespa **7** Ochrida, Scutari
of Zaire: 4 Kivu **5** Mweru, Tumba **6** Albert, Edward, Upemba **9** Mai-Ndombe **10** Tanganyika
of Zambia: 5 Mweru **6** Kariba **9** Bangweulu **10** Tanganyika
of Zimbabwe: 4 Kyle **6** Kariba

tra **27** Summer's Last Will and Testament

lame 4 game, halt, weak **5** sorry **6** clumsy, feeble, flimsy, infirm, maimed **7** failing, halting, hobbled, limping, unsound, wanting **8** crippled, deformed, disabled **9** deficient, faltering **10** inadequate **11** ineffectual **12** insufficient, unconvincing, unpersuasive **14** unsatisfactory

lamebrain 3 ass, sap **4** fool **5** booby, dunce, idiot, moron, ninny **6** dimwit, nitwit **7** fathead, half-wit **8** bonehead, dumb-dumb, imbecile, lunkhead, numskull **9** blockhead, numbskull **10** dunderhead, nincompoop **11** chowderhead

lamebrained 4 dumb **6** stupid **7** asinine, foolish, idiotic, moronic **8** crackpot **9** dimwitted, imbecilic **10** half-witted **12** feeble-minded, simpleminded

Lamech
 father: 9 Methusael **10** Methuselah
 wives: 4 Adah **6** Zillah
 son: 5 Jabal, Jubal **9** Tubalcain
 daughter: 6 Naamah

lament 3 cry, sob **4** moan, wail, weep **5** dirge, mourn **6** bewail, outcry, plaint, regret **7** deplore, keening, requiem, whimper **8** mourning **9** death song **11** condole with, lamentation **12** funeral music **13** complain about **14** express pity for, show concern for, sympathize with **15** commiserate with

lamentable 4 dire **6** woeful **7** piteous **8** dreadful, grievous, pathetic, pitiable, shameful, terrible, wretched **9** miserable **10** deplorable **11** distressing, regrettable, unfortunate **13** disheartening, heartbreaking

Lamia
 author: 9 John Keats

Lamia
 form: 7 monster
 characteristic: 12 bloodsucking

La Motta, Jake (Jacob)
 nickname: 9 Bronx Bull
 sport: 6 boxing
 class: 12 middleweight
 movie biography: 10 Raging Bull

Lamour, Dorothy
 real name: 23 Mary Leta Dorothy Kaumeyer
 trademark: 6 sarong

co-star: 7 Bob Hope **10** Bing Crosby
 born: 12 New Orleans LA
 roles:
  ***Road to: 3** Rio **4** Bali **6** Utopia **7** Morocco **8** Hong Kong, Zanzibar **9** Singapore*

L'Amour, Louis
 author of: 5 Hondo, Lando **7** Sackett, Shalako **8** Conagher **10** Key-Lock Man, Rivers West **14** The Californios, The Daybreakers **15** Westward the Tide **16** How the West Was Won, Over on the Dry Side **21** The Man from Broken Hills, To the Far Blue Mountains

lamp 4 bulb **5** light, torch **6** beacon **7** blinker, lantern **9** headlight, spotlight **10** chandelier, floodlight, klieg light, night light **11** searchlight **12** ceiling light, reading light **14** ceiling fixture
 invented by:
  ***arc: 6** Staite*
  ***incandescent: 6** Edison*
  ***incandescent frosted: 6** Pipkin*
  ***incandescent gas: 8** Langmuir*
  ***Kleig: 7** Kleigel*
  ***mercury vapor: 6** Hewitt*
  ***miner's safety: 4** Davy*
  ***neon: 6** Claude*

Lampedusa, Giuseppe di
 author of: 10 The Leopard

Lampetia
 father: 6 Helius
 mother: 6 Neaera

lampoon 5 farce, put-on, spoof, squib **6** parody, satire, send up **7** mockery, takeoff **8** diatribe, ridicule, satirize, travesty **9** broadside, burlesque **10** caricature, pasquinade **11** make light of

Lamus
 father: 8 Hercules
 mother: 7 Omphale
 attacked: 5 ships

Lamy of Santa Fe
 author: 10 Paul Horgan

lanai 7 veranda

Lancaster, Burt
 real name: 22 Burton Stephen Lancaster
 born: 9 New York NY
 roles: 5 Moses **9** All My Sons, Local Hero **11** Elmer Gantry (Oscar) **12** Atlantic City, The Rainmaker **13** The Rose Tattoo **14** Seven Days in May **16** Sorry Wrong Number **17** Birdman of Al-

catraz **18** From Here to Eternity **19** Come Back Little Sheba, Sweet Smell of Success

lance 4 gaff, pike **5** shaft, spear **7** assegai, halberd, harpoon, javelin

Lancelot, Launcelot
 character in: 16 Arthurian romance
 lover: 9 Guinevere
 home: 10 Joyous Gard

lancer 8 cavalier, horseman **10** cavalryman **12** horse soldier, horse trooper **14** mounted soldier

Lanchester, Elsa
 real name: 17 Elizabeth Sullivan
 husband: 15 Charles Laughton
 born: 7 England **8** Lewisham
 roles: 15 Come to the Stable **22** The Bride of Frankenstein **24** Witness for the Prosecution **25** The Private Life of Henry VIII **31** The Private Life of Henry the Eighth

land 3 get, lea, nab, net **4** area, dirt, dock, gain, grab, lawn, loam, moor, park, soil, take, ward, zone **5** acres, catch, earth, grass, green, humus, light, put in, realm, seize, shire, snare, state, tie up, tract **6** alight, anchor, canton, clinch, colony, county, debark, domain, empire, fields, ground, meadow, nation, parish, realty, region, secure **7** acreage, capture, country, descend, dry land, grounds, kingdom, pasture, section, set down, subsoil, terrain, win over **8** come down, district, dominion, farmland, homeland, location, mainland, make land, make port, precinct, property, province, republic, vicinity **9** cornfield, disembark, grassland, lay anchor, lay hold of, lead one to, reach land, territory **10** bring one to, carry one to, come to land, drop anchor, fatherland, motherland, native land, native soil, real estate, settle down, settlement, terra firma, wheat field **11** countryside, put into port **12** commonwealth, put into shore, real property, village green **13** the old country

Landau, Lev Davidovitch
 field: 7 physics
 nationality: 7 Russian
 discovered: 12 liquid helium **14** ferromagnetism
 awarded: 10 Nobel Prize

landed property 5 manor
6 estate 8 compound
12 countryplace

land force 4 army 6 legion,
troops 7 legions 8 infantry,
soldiers, soldiery 9 artillery

**Landless, Neville and
Helena**
  characters in: 22 The Mystery of Edwin Drood
  author: 7 Dickens

landlord 5 owner 6 holder,
squire 8 landlady 9 landowner,
possessor 10 freeholder, landholder, proprietor 13 property
owner 14 lord of the manor

landmark 8 keystone, monument, signpost 9 benchmark,
guidepost, highlight, high
point, milestone, watershed
11 cornerstone 12 turning
point 16 historic building

Landmarks
  god of: 8 Terminus

Land of Enchantment
  nickname of: 9 New Mexico

Land of Lincoln
  nickname of: 8 Illinois

Land of Opportunity
  nickname of: 8 Arkansas

Land of Sky-blue Waters
  nickname of: 9 Minnesota

Land of Steady Habits
  nickname of: 11 Connecticut

**Land of Ten Thousand
Lakes**
  nickname of: 9 Minnesota

Land of the Dakotas
  nickname of: 11 North
  Dakota

Land of the Midnight Sun
  nickname of: 6 Alaska

Landon, Michael
  real name: 20 Eugene Maurice Orowitz
  born: 13 Forest Hills NY
  roles: 7 Bonanza 15 Highway
  to Heaven 19 Little Joe
  Cartwright 20 I Was a
  Teenage Werewolf 23 Little
  House on the Prairie

landscape 4 view 5 scene,
sight, vista 6 aspect 7 scenery
8 panorama, prospect 9 spectacle 10 rural scene, scenic
view 14 natural scenery

landscape architect 7 Le
Notre, Olmsted

landsman 10 countryman
13 fellow citizen

Landsteiner, Karl
  field: 8 medicine 9 pathology
  distinguished: 10 blood types
  identified: 8 RH factor
  awarded: 10 Nobel Prize

lane 3 way 4 pass, path, road
5 alley, byway, drive, route,
track, trail 6 access, avenue,
bypath, course 7 passage,
roadway 8 alleyway, approach,
footpath 10 passageway

Lang, Walter
  director of: 7 Desk Set
  11 The King and I

Lange, Jessica
  born: 9 Cloquet MN
  roles: 7 Country, Frances,
  Tootsie 8 King Kong 11 All
  That Jazz 16 Crimes of the
  Heart 26 The Postman Always Rings Twice

Langella, Frank
  born: 9 Bayonne NJ
  roles: 7 Dracula 23 The Diary
  of a Mad Housewife

**Langhanke, Lucille
Vasconcellos**
  real name of: 9 Mary Astor

Langland, William
  author of: 12 Piers Plowman

Langmuir, Irving
  field: 9 chemistry
  invented: 15 atomic blowtorch 17 gas-tungsten lights
  awarded: 10 Nobel Prize

language *see box*

language, artificial
  of James Cooke Brown:
  6 Loglan
  of Hans Freudenthal: 6 Lincos 13 Lingua Cosmica
  of Alexander Gode:
  11 Interlingua
  of C K Ogden: 12 Basic
  English
  of J M Schleyer: 7 Volapuk
  of Jean Francois Sudre:
  8 Solresol
  of L L Zamehof: 9 Esperanto

language, extinct 6 Dacian,
Hattic, Lycian, Lydian, Palaic
7 Cornish, Elamite, Hittite,
Hurrian 8 Etruscan, Illyrian,
Phrygian, Sumerian, Thracian,
Urartian 9 Dalmatian 15 Cuneiform Luwian 18 Hieroglyphic Luwian

languid 4 dull, slow, weak
5 faint, heavy, inert, shaky,
spent, weary 6 feeble, infirm,
leaden, sickly, supine, torpid
7 rickety, unsound, worn-out
8 drooping, fatigued, inactive,
lifeless, listless, sluggish, unstable 9 apathetic, declining,
doddering, enervated, exhausted, inanimate, lethargic,
trembling, unhealthy 10 indisposed, spiritless 11 debilitated
12 on the decline
13 lackadaisical

languidness 6 apathy, torpor
7 inertia 8 lethargy 12 listlessness, sluggishness
13 indisposition

languish 3 ebb 4 fade, fail,
flag, wane, wilt 5 covet,
droop, faint 6 desire, hunger,
sicken, thirst, wither 7 dwindle, long for, pine for, sigh
for 8 diminish, give away,
take sick, yearn for 9 become
ill, break down, hanker for,
hunger for, thirst for, waste
away 10 go downhill 11 deteriorate, have a yen for, hunger after 12 be desirous of
13 go into decline

Languish, Lydia
  character in: 9 The Rivals
  author: 8 Sheridan

languor 5 ennui 6 torpor 7 inertia 8 dullness, hebetude,
lethargy 9 indolence, lassitude,
torpidity, weariness 10 dispassion, dreaminess 11 languidness, leisureness
12 lifelessness, listlessness,
sluggishness

lank 4 bony, lean, limp, thin
5 gaunt, spare 6 skinny,
slight 7 angular, scrawny
8 straight

lanky 4 bony, lean 5 gaunt,
gawky, rangy, spare, weedy
6 skinny 7 angular, scrawny
8 gangling, rawboned 11 tall
and thin

La Nouvelle Heloise
  author: 10 J J Rousseau

Lansbury, Angela
  born: 6 London 7 England
  roles: 4 Mame 8 Gaslight
  10 JB Fletcher 11 Sweeney
  Todd 14 Murder She Wrote
  15 Jessica Fletcher 22 The
  Manchurian Candidate

Laocoon
  vocation: 6 priest
  father: 5 Capys
  brother: 8 Anchises
  son: 10 Thymbraeus
  warned: 7 Trojans
  warned of: 11 Trojan horse
  killed by: 8 serpents

Laodamas
  father: 8 Eteocles
  defended: 6 Thebes
  killed: 9 Aegialeus
  killed by: 8 Alcmaeon

Laodamia
  father: 7 Acastus
  11 Bellerophon
  mother: 9 Astydamia
  husband: 11 Protesilaus
  lover: 4 Zeus
  son: 8 Sarpedon

Laodice
  father: 5 Priam
  mother: 6 Hecuba

language 4 cant, jive **5** argot, idiom, lingo, prose, slang, words **6** jargon, patois, speech, tongue **7** cursing, cussing, dialect, diction, wording **8** parlance, rhetoric, swearing, verbiage **9** discourse, elocution, profanity **10** expression, use of words, vernacular, vocabulary **11** imprecation, phraseology, profane talk **12** mother tongue, native tongue **13** colloquialism **14** public speaking, self-expression **16** manner of speaking, mode of expression **17** oral communication, reading and writing, verbal intercourse

 of Afghanistan: 4 Dari **5** Farsi **6** Afghan, Pashto, Pushtu **7** Balochi, Baluchi, Persian
 of Albania: 3 Geg **4** Cham, Gheg, Hish, Tosk **5** Greek **8** Albanian
 of Algeria: 6 Arabic, Berber, French, Zenata **7** Senhaja
 of Andorra: 6 French **7** Catalan, Spanish
 of Angola: 5 Bantu **8** Kimbundu, Oumbundu **9** Ovimbundu **10** Portuguese
 of Antigua and Barbuda: 7 English
 of Argentina: 7 Spanish
 of Armenia: 7 Russian **8** Armenian
 of Australia: 6 Yabber **7** English **9** aborigine (dialects)
 of Austria: 5 Czech **6** German, Magyar **8** Croatian **9** Slovenian
 of Azerbaijan: 6 Turkic
 of the Bahamas: 6 Creole **7** English
 of Bahrain: 4 Urdu **5** Farsi **6** Arabic **7** English, Persian
 of Bangladesh: 6 Bihari **7** Bengali, English
 of Barbados: 7 English
 of Belgium: 5 Dutch **6** French, German **7** Flemish
 of Benin: 3 Fon **5** Dendi **6** Bariba, French, Fulani, Yoruba
 of Bermuda: 7 English
 of Bhutan: 5 Hindi, Lhoke **7** Tibetan **8** Dzongkha, Nepalese
 of Bolivia: 6 Aymara **7** Quechua, Spanish
 of Borneo: 5 Malay **7** Chinese, English
 of Bosnia-Herzegovina: 13 Serbo Croatian
 of Botswana: 5 Bantu, Click **6** Tswana **7** English, Khoisan **8** Setswana
 of Brazil: 10 Portuguese
 of Brunei: 4 Iban **5** Malay **7** Chinese, English
 of Bulgaria: 9 Bulgarian
 of Burkina Faso: 4 Bobo, Lobi, More, Samo **5** Dyula, Mande, Mossi **6** French
 of Burundi: 6 French **7** Kirundi, Swahili
 of Cambodia/Kampuchea: 5 Khmer **6** French
 of Cameroon: 4 Bulu **5** Bantu, Bassa, Hausa **6** Douala, Ewondo, French, Fulani **7** English
  8 Bamileke, Fulfulde
 of Canada: 6 Eskimo, French **7** English
 of Canary Islands: 7 Spanish
 of Cape Verde: 7 Crioulo **10** Portuguese **13** Verdean Creole
 of Central African Republic: 5 Sango, Zande **6** French
 of Chad: 4 Sara **5** Turku **6** Arabic, French
 of Chile: 7 Spanish
 of China: 7 Chinese **8** Mandarin, Shanghai **9** Cantonese
 of Colombia: 7 Spanish
 of Comoros: 6 Arabic, French **7** Swahili **8** Malagasy
 of Congo: 4 Susu **5** Bantu, Fiote **6** French, Kituba **7** Bangala, Lingala
 of Costa Rica: 7 Spanish
 of Crete: 5 Greek **6** Minoan **7** Linear A, Linear B
 of Croatia: 8 Croatian **13** Serbo Croatian
 of Cuba: 7 Spanish
 of Cyprus: 5 Greek **7** Turkish **8** Armenian
 of Czechoslovakia/Czech Republic: 5 Czech **6** German, Magyar, Slovak **7** Russian **9** Hungarian
 of Denmark: 4 Odan **6** Danish **8** Faeroese **11** Greenlander
 of Djibouti: 4 Afar **6** Arabic, French, Somali
 of Dominican Republic: 6 French **7** English, Spanish
 of Ecuador: 6 Jibaro **7** Quechua, Spanish
 of Egypt: 6 Arabic, Coptic, French **7** English
 of El Salvador: 7 Spanish
 of England: 7 English
 of Equatorial Guinea: 4 Bubi, Fang **6** pidgin **7** Spanish
 of Eritrea: 7 Amharic
 of Estonia: 5 Tartu **10** Finno-Ugric
 of Ethiopia: 3 Giz **4** Afar, Agow, Geez, Saho **5** Geeze, Ghese, Smali, Tigre **6** Arabic, Harari
  7 Amharic, English, Italian, Russian **8** Gallinya, Irob-Saho, Tigrinya
 of Fiji: 5 Hindi **6** Fijian **7** English
 of Finland: 4 Avar, Lapp **5** Karen, Ugric, Vogul **6** Magyar, Ostyak, Tarast **7** Finnish, Olonets,
  Samoyed, Swedish **8** Estonian **10** Olenetsian
 of France: 6 French
 of Gabon Republic: 6 French
 of the Gambia: 4 Fula **5** Wolof **6** Fulani **7** English, Malinke **8** Mandingo
 of Georgia: 8 Georgian
 of Germany: 6 German **10** High German **11** Hochdeutsch
 of Ghana: 2 Ga **3** Ewe, Gur, Kwa, Twi **5** Fanti, Hausa **7** Dagomba, English

(continued)

language (*continued*)
  of Gibraltar: 7 English, Spanish
  of Greece: 5 Greek
  of Greenland: 6 Danish, Eskimo **11** Greenlandic
  of Grenada: 7 English
  of Guatemala: 6 Quiche **7** Spanish
  of Guinea: 5 Fulbe, Mande **6** Arabic, French, Fulani **7** English
  of Guinea-Bissau: 5 Fulah **7** Balante, Crioulo **8** Mandingo **10** Portuguese **21** Cape Verde-Guinea
    Creole
  of Guyana: 5 Hindi **7** English
  of Haiti: 6 Creole, French, patois
  of Honduras: 7 English, Spanish
  of Hong Kong: 7 Chinese, English **9** Cantonese
  of Hungary: 6 German, Magyar, Slovak **8** Croatian **9** Hungarian **10** Finno-Ugric
  of Iceland: 5 Norse **9** Icelandic
  of India: 4 Urdu **5** Hindi, Oriya, Tamil **6** Sindhi, Telugu **7** Bengali, English, Kannada, Malayam,
    Marathi, Punjabi **8** Assamese, Gujarati, Kashmiri, Sanskrit **9** Malayalam
  of Indonesia: 5 Tetum **6** Bahasa, Igorot **7** English, Gyarung, Malayan **8** Balinese, Chamorro,
    Javanese, Madurese, Sudanese **10** Indonesian, Polynesian
  of Iran: 4 Luri, Zend **5** Farsi, Turki **6** Arabic **7** Baluchi, Kurdish, Persian **8** Armenian
    11 Azerbaijani
  of Iraq: 5 Farsi **6** Arabic **7** Kurdish, Persian, Turkish
  of Ireland: 5 Irish **6** Gaelic **7** English
  of Israel: 6 Arabic, French, Hebrew **7** English
  of Italy: 5 Ladin, Latin **6** French, German **7** Italian, Slovene **8** Friulian **9** Sardinian
  of Ivory Coast: 4 Akan **6** Dioula, French
  of Jamaica: 6 Creole **7** English
  of Japan: 5 Kanto **8** Japanese
  of Java: 4 Kavi, Kawi **5** Malay **6** Sassak **8** Balinese, Madurese, Sudanese **16** Bahasa Indonesian
  of Jordan: 6 Arabic
  of Kazakhstan: 6 Kazakh
  of Kenya: 3 Luo **5** Bantu, Luhya, Masai **6** Kikuyu **7** English, Swahili **8** Buyerati **10** Hindustani
  of Kiribati: 6 Samoan **7** English **10** Gilbertese
  of Korea: 6 Korean
  of Kuwait: 6 Arabic
  of Kyrgyzstan: 6 Turkic **7** Kirghiz
  of Laos: 3 Lao, Man, Meo **6** French **7** English
  of Latvia: 7 Lettish
  of Lebanon: 6 Arabic, French, Syriac **7** English, Turkish **8** Armenian
  of Lesotho: 5 Sotho **7** English, Sesotho
  of Liberia: 3 Kru, Kwa **5** Mande **7** English
  of Libya: 6 Arabic, Berber **7** English, Italian
  of Liechtenstein: 6 German **10** Alemannish
  of Lithuania: 5 Zmudz **6** Baltic **10** Lithuanian
  of Luxembourg: 6 French, German **7** English **13** Letzeburgesch
  of Macao: 7 Chinese, English **9** Cantonese **10** Portuguese
  of Macedonia: 10 Macedonian
  of Madagascar/Malagasy Republic: 6 French **8** Malagasy, Malgache
  of Malawi: 3 Yao **4** Cewa **5** Bantu, Ngoni, Tonga **6** Nyanja **7** English, Tumbuka **8** Chichewa
    10 Chitumbuka
  of Malaysia: 4 Bugi, Dyak **5** Malay, Tamil **6** Battok, Rejang **7** Chinese, English, Lampong, Nias-
    ese **8** Achinese, Javanese, Makassar **14** Bahasa Malaysia
  of Maldives: 6 Arabic, Divehi
  of Mali: 5 Dogon, Dyula, Feulh, Mande, Marka **6** Berber, French, Fulani **7** Bambara, Malinke,
    Senoufo, Songhai
  of Malta: 7 English, Italian, Maltese
  of Mauritania: 4 Fula **5** Wolof **6** Arabic, French **7** Phoolor, Tukulor **8** Fulfulde, Mandingo **9** Sar-
    akolle **10** Hassaniyya
  of Mauritius: 4 Urdu **5** Hindi, Tamil **6** Creole, French **7** English
  of Mexico: 5 Mayan, Otomi **6** Mixtec **7** Mazahua, Mazatec, Nahuatl, Spanish, Totonac, Zapotec
    8 Tarascan
  of Moldova: 8 Romanian **9** Moldovian
  of Monaco: 6 French **7** English, Italian **10** Monegasque
  of Mongolia: 6 Kazakh **16** Khalkha Mongolian
  of Montenegro: 13 Serbo-Croatian
  of Morocco: 6 Arabic, Berber, French **7** Spanish
  of Mozambique: 3 Yao **5** Makua **6** Nyanji, Thonga **7** Swahili **10** Portuguese
  of Myanmar: 3 Lai **4** Chin, Kuki, Pegu, Shan **5** Karen **6** Kachin **7** Burmese
  of Namibia: 5 Bantu **6** German **7** English, Khoisan **9** Afrikaans
  of Nauru: 7 English, Nauruan
  of Nepal: 6 Nepali, Newari **7** English
  of the Netherlands: 5 Dutch **7** English, Frisian
  of New Guinea: 4 Motu **7** English **16** Melanesian Pidgin
  of New Zealand: 5 Maori **7** English
  of Nicaragua: 7 English, Spanish
  of Niger: 5 Hausa, Mande **6** Djerma, French, Fulani, Tuareg **8** Mandingo, Tamashek

(*continued*)

language (*continued*)

of **Nigeria: 3** Ibo **4** Efik, Igbo **5** Hausa **6** Yoruba **7** English
of **Norway: 4** Lapp **5** Norse **6** Bokmal **7** Nynorsk, Riksmal **8** Landsmal, Samnorsk **9** Landsmaal, Norwegian
of **Oman: 4** Urdu **5** Hindi **6** Arabic **7** Baluchi
of **Pakistan: 4** Urdu **6** Pushtu, Sindhi **7** Baluchi, Bengali, English, Punjabi
of **Panama: 7** English, Spanish
of **Paraguay: 6** German **7** Guarani, Spanish
of **Peru: 6** Aymara **7** English, Quechua, Spanish
of **the Philippines: 4** Moro **5** Bicol, Bikol **6** Ibanag **7** Cebuano, English, Ilocano, Spanish, Tagalog, Visayan **8** Filipino **9** Pampangan, Philipino **10** Samar-Leyte **13** Bamboo-English **14** Panay-Hiligayon
of **Poland: 6** Kaszub, Polish **10** Pomeranian
of **Polynesia: 4** Niue, Uvea **5** Maori **6** Samoan, Tongan **7** Austral, Tagalog, Tokelau **8** Hawaiian, Tahitian **9** Marquesan, Tuamatuan **10** Mangarevan
of **Portugal: 10** Portuguese
of **Qatar: 6** Arabic
of **Romania: 6** French, Magyar **7** Russian **8** Romanian, Rumanian **9** Hungarian
of **Russia: 5** Evenk **6** Buriat, Kalmyk **7** Finnish, Russian **8** Ossetian
of **Rwanda: 6** French **7** Swahili **11** Kinyarwanda
of **Samoa: 6** Samoan **7** English
of **San Marino: 7** Italian
of **Sao Tome and Principe: 10** Portuguese
of **Sardinia: 7** Italian
of **Saudi Arabia: 6** Arabic
of **Scotland: 4** Erse **6** Celtic, Gaelic, Keltic, Lallan **7** English, Lalland
of **Senegal: 5** Wolof **6** French
of **the Seychelles: 6** Creole, French **7** English
of **Sierra Leone: 4** Krio **5** Limba, Mende, Mendi, Temne **6** Creole **7** English
of **Singapore: 5** Malay, Tamil **7** Chinese, English **8** Mandarin
of **Slovakia: 6** Slavik, Slovak
of **Slovenia: 7** Slovene
of **the Solomon Islands: 7** English **13** Pidgin English **16** Melanesian Pidgin
of **Somalia: 6** Arabic, Somali **7** English, Italian
of **South Africa: 4** Taal, Zulu **5** Bantu, Hindi, Nguni, Sotho, Swazi, Tamil, Venda, Xhosa **6** Telegu, Thonga **7** English, Khoisan, Ndebele, Sesotho **8** Bujarati, Fanakalo **9** Afrikaans **13** Kitchen-Kaffir
of **Spain: 6** Basque **7** Catalan, Spanish **8** Balearic, Galician **9** Castilian, Valencian
of **Sri Lanka: 4** Pali **5** Tamil **7** English **9** Sinhalese
of **Sudan: 2** Ga **3** Efe, Ewe, Ibo, Kru, Vak, Vei **4** Efik, Mole, Tshi **6** Arabic, Nubian, Yoruba **7** English **8** Mandango, Mandingo **9** Ta Bedawie
of **Suriname: 5** Carib, Dutch, Hindi **6** Arawak **7** English **8** Javanese, Taki-Taki **10** Hindustani **11** Sranan Tongo **12** Sranang Tongo
of **Swaziland: 5** Ngumi **7** English, Siswati **9** Afrikaans **10** Portuguese
of **Sweden: 4** Lapp **7** Swedish
of **Switzerland: 5** Ladin **6** French, German **7** Italian **8** Romansch **14** Switzerdeutsch
of **Syria: 6** Arabic, French, Syriac **7** Aramaic, English, Kurdish, Turkish **8** Armenian
of **Taiwan: 4** Amon, Amoy **5** Hakka, Kuo Yu **6** Minnan **9** Taiwanese **15** Mandarin Chinese
of **Tajikistan: 5** Tajik **7** Tadzhik
of **Tanzania: 5** Bantu **6** Arabic **7** English, Khoisan, Nilotic, Swahili **8** Cushitic, Gujarati
of **Thailand: 3** Lao, Tai **4** Ahom, Shan, Thai **5** Kadai **7** Bangkok, English **9** Krung Thep **12** Chinese Malay
of **Tibet: 5** Balti **6** Ladkhi **7** Bhutani, Bodskad **8** Sanskrit **9** Bhutanese
of **Togo: 3** Ana, Ewe, Twi **4** Mina **5** Hausa **6** French, Kabrai, Kabrie **7** Bassari, Dagomba, Quatchi **8** Kotokoli, Lotocoli
of **Tonga: 6** Tongan **7** English
of **Trinidad and Tobago: 6** French **7** Chinese, English, Spanish **10** Portuguese **12** French Patois
of **Tunisia: 6** Arabic, Berber, French
of **Turkey: 6** Arabic **7** Kurdish, Turkish
of **Turkmenistan: 6** Turkic **10** West Turkic
of **Tuvalu: 6** Samoan **7** English **8** Tuvaluan **10** Polynesian
of **Uganda: 5** Ateso, Ganda **7** English, Luganda, Swahili
of **Ukraine: 9** Ukrainian
of **United Arab Emirates: 5** Farsi **6** Arabic **7** English, Persian
of **Uruguay: 7** Italian, Spanish
of **Uzbekistan: 5** Uzbek
of **Vanuatu: 6** French **7** Bislama, English **16** Melanesian Pidgin
of **Venezuela: 4** Pume **7** Spanish
of **Vietnam: 3** Yue **4** Cham **5** Khmer, Rhade **6** French **7** Chinese, English **9** Cantonese **10** Vietnamese
of **Wales: 5** Welsh **6** Celtic, Cymric, Keltic, Kymric **7** Cymraeg, English
of **Western Sahara: 16** Hassaniyya Arabic
of **Western Samoa: 6** Samoan **7** English
of **Yemen: 6** Arabic

(*continued*)

language (*continued*)
of Yugoslavia: **7** Bosnian, Slovene **8** Albanian, Croatian **9** Hungarian, Slovenian **10** Macedonian **11** Montenegrin **13** Herzegovinian, Serbo-Croatian
of Zaire: **5** Bantu **6** French **7** Chiluba, Kikongo, Lingala, Swahili **8** Sudanese, Tshiluba
of Zambia: **4** Lozi **5** Bemba, Lunda, Tonga **6** Luvale, Nyanja **7** English **9** Afrikaans
of Zimbabwe: **3** Ila **5** Bantu, Shona **7** English, Ndebele

husband: 8 Helicaon
son: 6 Pereus **7** Munitus

Laodocus
father: 6 Apollo
mother: 6 Phthia
killed by: 7 Aetolus

Laomedon
king of: 4 Troy
father: 4 Ilus
wife: 6 Strymo
son: 5 Priam **6** Lampus **7** Clytius **8** Hicetaon, Tithonus
daughter: 7 Hesione **8** Themiste

Laos *see box*

Laothoe
concubine of: 5 Priam
son: 6 Lycaon **9** Polydorus

Lao-tzu
author of: 10 Tao Te Ching

lap 3 sip **4** lick, wash **5** awash, drink, plash, slosh **6** babble, bubble, gurgle, lick up, murmur, ripple, splash, tongue

La Paz
administrative capital of: 7 Bolivia

lapis lazuli
species: 8 lazurite
source: 10 Badakhshan **11** Afghanistan

lapse 3 gap, sag **4** drop, fall, flaw, go by, loss, sink, slip, stop, wane **5** boner, break, cease, droop, error, fault, pause, slump **6** breach, elapse, expire, hiatus, laxity, pass by, period, recede, recess, run out, slip by, wither, worsen **7** blunder, decline, descent, failing, failure, faux pas, interim, passage, relapse, respite, subside **8** collapse, downfall, elapsing, interval, omission, slip away **9** backslide, disregard, interlude, oversight, slump down, terminate **10** degenerate, falling off, forfeiture, infraction, negligence, peccadillo, regression **11** backsliding, delinquency, dereliction, deteriorate, shortcoming **12** degeneration, intermission, interruption, lose validity **13** deterioration, process of time, slight mistake **14** become obsolete, fall into disuse

lapsus linguae 16 a slip of the tongue

lar *see* **5** lares

Lara
character in: 9 Dr Zhivago
author: 9 Pasternak

Laraia, Carol Maria
real name of: 13 Carol Lawrence

larceny 5 fraud, theft **7** bilking, forgery, looting, robbery, sacking **8** burglary, cheating, fleecing, stealing **9** extortion, pilferage, pilfering, swindling **10** absconding, peculation, plagiarism, purloining **11** defalcation, depredation **12** embezzlement, grand larceny, petit larceny, petty larceny, safecracking **13** appropriation, housebreaking **16** misappropriation

larder 5 cuddy **6** pantry, spence **7** buttery **8** food room **9** stillroom, storeroom **10** supply room **11** storage room

Lardner, Ring
author of: 11 The Love Nest, You Know Me Al **12** Treat Em Rough **16** Gullible's Travels

Larentalia
origin: 5 Roman
event: 8 festival

lares
form: 7 spirits
watched over: 5 house **6** hearth **9** community **10** crossroads
single member: 3 lar
companions: 7 penates
correspond to: 8 Dioscuri

large 3 big, fat **4** high, huge, vast, wide **5** ample, broad, grand, great, heavy, hulky, obese, plump, roomy **6** goodly, mighty, portly, rotund **7** copious, immense, liberal, massive, sizable **8** colossal, enormous, gigantic, imposing, man-sized, outsized, spacious, sweeping, towering **9** boundless, capacious, expansive, extensive, giantlike, kingsized, limitless, monstrous, overgrown, ponderous, strapping, unlimited, unstinted **10** exorbitant, gargantuan, stupendous **11** extravagant, far-reaching,

---

Laos
other name: 7 Lan Xang **23** land of a million elephants
capital/largest city: 9 Viengchan, Vientiane
others: 4 Nape **5** Pakse, Xieng **6** Paklay **7** Thakhek **11** Savannakhet, Xiang Khoang **12** Luang Prabang **14** Louangphrabang
school: 12 Sisavangvong
measure: 3 bak
monetary unit: 2 at **3** att, kip
mountain: 3 Lai, Loi, San **4** Copi, Khat **5** Atwat **6** Khoung, Tiubia **15** Annam Cordillera
highest point: 3 Bia **7** Phou Bia
river: 3 Noi **4** Done **5** Khong **6** Mekong, Sebang
physical feature:
  plain: **4** Jars
  plateau: **8** Bolovens
people: 2 Lu **3** Kha, Lao, Man, Meo, Tai, Yao, Yun **4** Miao, Thai **5** Hmong **8** Lao Teung **10** Phoutheung
  leader: **7** Fa Ngoun **13** Souphanouvong **14** Souligna Vongsa, Souvanna Phouma
language: 3 Lao, Man, Meo **6** French **7** English
religion: 7 animism **8** Buddhism **17** Theravada Buddhism
feature:
  Buddhist priest: **5** bonze
  Communist guerrilla group: **9** Pathet Lao
  musical instrument: **5** khene
  temple: **3** wat
  trail: **9** Ho Chi Minh

magnificent, substantial **12** considerable **13** comprehensive **14** Brobdingnagian

large-hearted 8 generous **10** altruistic, benevolent, charitable **12** humanitarian **13** philanthropic

largely 6 mainly, mostly, widely **7** chiefly, greatly **9** generally, primarily **10** on the whole **11** extensively, principally **12** considerably **13** predominantly, substantially **14** for the most part, to a great extent

largeness 7 bigness **8** enormity, hugeness **9** amplitude, greatness, immensity **11** massiveness **12** enormousness

large-scale 3 big **4** huge, vast, wide **5** broad, great **6** all-out, mighty **8** colossal, far-flung, gigantic **9** extensive, monstrous **10** gargantuan, stupendous, tremendous **11** far-reaching, wide-ranging **15** all-encompassing

largess, largesse 3 aid **4** boon, gift, help **5** favor, mercy **6** bounty, reward **7** charity, payment **8** bestowal, donation, gratuity, kindness, offering **9** benignity **10** assistance, generosity **11** benefaction, benevolence **12** philanthropy, remuneration

large store 8 emporium **11** supermarket **15** department store

largo
    music: 4 slow **14** dignified tempo

lark 3 gag **4** game, jape, romp, whim **5** antic, caper, fling, prank, spree, trick **6** frolic, gambol **7** caprice **8** escapade **11** high old time **12** sportiveness
    group of: 10 exaltation

larkspur 9 Consolida **10** Delphinium
    varieties: 4 Tall **5** Dwarf **6** Rocket

La Rochefoucauld, Francois
    author of: 6 Maxims **7** Maximes

larva
    insect stage after: 3 egg
    insect stage before: 4 pupa
    legless: 6 maggot

larvae
    form: 6 ghosts
    characteristic: 9 malignant

lascivious 4 foul, lewd **5** bawdy, dirty, gross, lurid **6** coarse, filthy, impure, ribald,

sordid, vulgar, wanton **7** immoral, lustful, obscene, ruttish, squalid **8** depraved, immodest, improper, indecent, prurient **9** lecherous, salacious, shameless **10** indelicate, licentious, unblushing **11** dirty-minded, unwholesome

lash 3 fix, hit, tie **4** beat, bind, blow, flog, moor, rope, whip **5** brace, curse, flail, hitch, knock, leash, pound, scold, smack, strap, thong, tie up, truss **6** attach, berate, buffet, fasten, hammer, pinion, revile, secure, strike, stroke, tether, thrash, whip up **7** lecture, scourge, upbraid **8** lambaste, make fast **9** castigate, horsewhip **10** take to task, tonguelash **11** rail against **13** cat-o'-nine-tails

lashed together 4 tied **5** bound **6** tied up **7** secured, trussed **8** fastened

lash out at 5 fly at **6** assail, attack, strike **8** fall upon

Las Palmas
    capital of: 13 Canary Islands

lass 4 girl, maid, miss **5** wench **6** damsel, female, lassie, lovely, maiden, pretty, virgin **7** colleen **10** schoolgirl, young woman

Lasser, Louise
    father: 8 S J Lasser
    husband: 10 Woody Allen
    born: 9 New York NY
    roles: 22 Mary Hartman Mary Hartman

lassie 4 girl, lass, maid **6** maiden **7** colleen **10** young woman

Lassie
    character: 5 Timmy **9** Doc Weaver **10** Jeff Miller, Paul Martin, Ruth Martin **11** Corey Stuart, Ellen Miller **12** Gramps Miller **17** Sylvester (Porky) Brockway
    cast: 10 Jan Clayton, Jon Provost, Jon Shepodd, Robert Bray **11** Arthur Space, Tommy Rettig **12** Donald Keeler, June Lockhart **14** Cloris Leachman, George Chandler **15** George Cleveland

lassitude 5 ennui **6** apathy, torpor **7** boredom, fatigue, inertia, languor, malaise **8** debility, doldrums, dullness, lethargy, weakness **9** faintness, indolence, tiredness, torpidity, wea-

riness **10** droopiness, drowsiness, enervation, exhaustion, feebleness, supineness **11** languidness, prostration **12** indifference, lack of energy, listlessness, sluggishness

lasso 4 lash, rope **5** catch, noose, reata, riata, thong **6** lariat

last 3 end **4** go on, keep, live, stay, wear **5** abide, after, exist, final, stand **6** behind, ending, endure, extend, finale, finish, hold on, hold up, remain, utmost **7** carry on, closing, extreme, finally, hold out, outlive, outwear, persist, stand up, subsist, survive, tailing **8** at the end, continue, doomsday, farthest, final one, furthest, hindmost, hold good, in back of, maintain, rearmost, terminal, terminus, trailing **9** in the rear, persevere **10** Armageddon, concluding, conclusion, conclusive, eventually, terminally, ultimately **11** crack of doom, crucial time **12** in conclusion, tagging along **13** Day of Judgment
    French: 7 dernier

Last Days of Pompeii, The
    author: 18 Edward Bulwer-Lytton
    character: 4 Ione **5** Nydia **7** Arbaces, Glaucus **9** Apaecides

Last Frontier
    nickname of: 6 Alaska

lasting 4 firm **5** fixed, solid **7** abiding, chronic, durable, eternal **8** constant, enduring, immortal, lifelong, long-term **9** incessant, lingering, long-lived, permanent, perpetual, steadfast, unceasing **10** continuing, deep-rooted, deep-seated, perdurable, persistent, protracted **11** established, never-ending **12** indissoluble **14** indestructible, of long duration **17** firmly established

lastly 6 at last **7** finally, to sum up **8** after all, in the end **10** on the whole **12** in conclusion **19** all things considered

Last of the Mohicans, The
    author: 19 James Fenimore Cooper
    character: 5 Magua, Uncas **9** Cora Munro **10** Alice Munro **11** Natty Bumppo

12 Chingachgook **18** Major Duncan Heyward

last part 3 end **6** ending, finale, finish **8** third act **10** denouement **12** final chapter

Last Picture Show, The
director: **16** Peter Bogdanovich
based on story by: **13** Larry McMurtry
cast: **10** Ben Johnson **11** Jeff Bridges **12** Ellen Burstyn **13** Eileen Brennan **14** Cloris Leachman, Cybill Shepherd, Timothy Bottoms
Oscar for: **15** supporting actor (Johnson) **17** supporting actress (Leachman)

Last Puritan, The
author: **15** George Santayana

La Strada
director: **15** Federico Fellini
cast: **11** Aldo Silvana **12** Anthony Quinn **15** Giulietta Masina, Richard Basehart
score: **8** Nino Rota
Oscar for: **11** foreign film

last resort
French: **8** pis aller

last resource
French: **8** pis aller

Last Tango in Paris
director: **18** Bernardo Bertolucci
cast: **12** Marlon Brando **14** Maria Schneider

Last Things
author: **6** C P Snow

Last Valley, The
author: **11** A B Guthrie Jr

Last Waltz, The
director: **14** Martin Scorsese
cast: **7** The Band **8** Bob Dylan **9** Neil Young **10** The Staples **11** Eric Clapton, Muddy Waters, Neil Diamond, Van Morrison **12** Joni Mitchell **13** Emmylou Harris

latch 3 bar **4** bolt, clip, hasp, hook, lock, loop, shut, snap **5** catch, clamp, close **6** buckle, button, clinch, fasten, secure **8** make fast **9** fastening

late 3 new **4** dead, gone, slow **5** fresh, tardy **6** held up, put off, recent **7** delayed, newborn, overdue, tardily **8** departed, detained, dilatory, passed on **9** after time, postponed **10** behindhand, behind time, dilatorily, unpunctual **16** recently deceased

late arrival 7 laggard **8** lateness, newcomer **9** immigrant, latecomer, tardiness **16** Johnny-come-lately

Late George Apley, The
author: **10** J P Marquand

lately 6 of late **7** just now **8** latterly, recently, right now **9** currently, presently, yesterday **10** not long ago **13** a short time ago

Late Mattia Pascal, The
author: **15** Luigi Pirandello

latency 8 abeyance, deferral, dormancy, inaction **10** quiescence, suspension

Late Night with David Letterman
feature: **11** Ask Mr Melman **15** Stupid Pet Tricks **18** Brush with Greatness, Stupid People Tricks
bandleader: **10** Paul Shafer
city: **7** New York

latent 6 covert, hidden **7** abeyant, dormant, lurking, passive **8** inactive, sleeping **9** concealed, potential, quiescent, suspended, unaroused, unexposed **10** in abeyance, intangible, unapparent, unrealized **11** not manifest, undeveloped, unexpressed **13** inconspicuous

later 4 next **5** since **6** behind, in time, mature **7** ensuing, tardily **8** in a while, in sequel **9** afterward, following, presently, thereupon **10** consequent, more recent, most recent, subsequent, succeeding, successive, thereafter **11** after a while, consecutive **12** subsequently, successively, toward the end

lateral 4 side **5** sided **7** flanked, oblique, sloping **8** edgeways, edgewise, flanking, sidelong, sideward, sideways, sidewise, skirting, slanting

latest cry
French: **10** dernier cri

latest fashion
French: **10** dernier cri

latest word
French: **10** dernier cri

lather 4 foam, head, scum, soap, suds **5** froth, spume, sweat **6** soap up **8** make foam, soapsuds **9** make froth **11** shaving foam

Latin
language family: **12** Indo-European
branch: **6** Italic
group: **7** Romance
subgroup: **6** French **7** Catalan, Italian, Romansh, Spanish **8** Romanian **9** Provencal **10** Portuguese **13** Rhaeto-Romanic

Latinus
king of: **6** Latium
father: **6** Faunus
mother: **6** Marica
wife: **5** Amata
daughter: **7** Lavinia

latitude 5 range, scope, sweep **6** leeway, margin **7** license **8** free play **9** amplitude, elbowroom, full swing **10** indulgence, liberality **11** opportunity, unrestraint **12** independence **15** freedom of action, freedom of choice **16** unrestrictedness

Latona see **4** Leto

La Tour, Georges de
born: **3** Vic **6** France **8** Lorraine
artwork: **7** Peasant **10** The New Born **12** Peasant's Wife, The Card Cheat **15** St Peter Penitent **16** The Fortune Teller **18** The Denial of St Peter **23** The Education of the Virgin **31** St Sebastian Tended by the Holy Women

Latrobe, Benjamin Henry
architect of: **9** US Capitol **15** Sedgeley Mansion (PA) **18** Baltimore Cathedral **22** Philadelphia Waterworks
style: **12** Greek Revival, Neoclassical **13** Gothic Revival

latter 3 end **4** last **5** final, later **6** ending, latest, modern **7** ensuing **8** terminal **10** most recent, subsequent, succeeding, successive **13** last-mentioned **15** second-mentioned

lattice 4 fret, grid **5** frame, grate **6** grille, screen **7** framing, grating, network, trellis, webwork **8** fretwork, openwork **9** framework, reticulum **11** trelliswork **12** reticulation

Latvia see box

laud 5 extol, honor **6** praise **7** acclaim, commend, glorify

laudable 5 model, noble **8** sterling **9** admirable, estimable, excellent, exemplary **10** creditable **11** commendable, meritorious **12** praiseworthy **13** unimpeachable **17** deserving of esteem **18** worthy of admiration

laudation 6 praise **7** acclaim **8** applause, approval **11** approbation **12** commendation

laudatory 8 admiring, honoring, praising **9** adulatory, approving, extolling, favorable **10** eulogistic, eulogizing, flattering, glorifying **11** acclamatory, approbatory, celebratory, encomiastic, panegyrical

Latvia
former name: **30** Latvian Soviet Socialist Republic
capital/largest city: **4** Riga
others: **5** Cesis, Libau **6** Dvinsk, Libava, Tukums **7** Jelgava,
Jurmala, Liepaja, Rezekne **8** Dunaberg, Dunaburg, Val-
miera **9** Ventspils **10** Daugavpils
government: **8** republic
measure: **3** let **4** stof **5** stoff, verst **6** arshin, kulmet **7** verchoc, verchok **8** krouchka, pourvete **9** deciatine, lofstelle,
pourvette **10** tonnseteel
monetary unit: **3** lat **4** latu **6** rublis, santim **7** kapeika,
santima
weight: **9** liespfund
lake: **7** Aluksne
river: **4** Ogre **5** Gauja, Venta **6** Salaca **7** Daugava, Lielupe
12 Western Dvina
sea: **6** Baltic
physical feature:
cape: **8** Domesnes
gulf: **4** Riga
strait: **4** Irbe
people: **3** Kur, Liv **4** Balt, Cour, Lett **7** Latgale, Latvian,
Russian, Zemgale
former ruler: **15** Teutonic Knights
language: **7** Lettish
religion: **8** Lutheran **13** Roman Catholic

12 commendatory
13 complimentary

Laudianus 16 Greek unical
codex

laugh 4 glee, ha-ha, ho-ho,
howl, roar **5** mirth **6** cackle,
giggle, guffaw, titter **7** break
up, chortle, chuckle, snicker,
snigger **10** bellylaugh, horse-
laugh **12** express mirth **14** roll
in the aisle, split one's sides

laughable 5 comic, dopey,
droll, funny, inane, merry,
silly, witty **6** absurd, stupid
7 amusing, asinine, comical,
foolish, risible **8** farcical, tickling **9** diverting, grotesque,
hilarious, ludicrous **10** outlandish, outrageous, ridiculous **11** rib-tickling
12 preposterous
13 sidesplitting

**Laugh-In, Rowan &
Martin's**
regular: **8** Dan Rowan **9** Gary
Owens, Judy Carne, Ruth
Buzzi **10** Dick Martin, Goldie Hawn, Larry Hovis, Lily
Tomlin **11** Arte Johnson,
Henry Gibson **12** Jo Anne
Worley **13** Eileen Brennan
saying: **10** Sock it to me
15 Here come de judge, You
bet your bippy **24** Beautiful
downtown Burbank **31** Look
that up in your Funk and
Wagnalls

laughingstock 3 ass **4** butt,
dupe, fool, joke **8** fair game
11 figure of fun

laugh off 6 deride **7** dismiss,
put down **8** belittle, ridicule
9 disparage

laughter 3 joy **4** glee **5** mirth
6 gaiety **7** jollity, revelry **8** hilarity **9** joviality, merriment
11 merrymaking **12** conviviality, exhilaration

Laughton, Charles
wife: **14** Elsa Lanchester
born: **7** England
11 Scarborough
roles: **9** Rembrandt **10** Jamaica Inn **13** Les Miserables **15** Ruggles of Red Gap,
The Paradine Case **16** Advise and Consent **17** Mutiny
on the Bounty **23** Barretts
of Wimpole Street, The
Hunchback of Notre Dame
24 Witness for the Prosecution **25** The Private Life of
Henry VIII (Oscar)

launch 4 fire, hurl **5** begin,
eject, float, found, impel,
shoot, start, throw **6** let fly,
propel, unveil **7** fire off, project, send off **8** catapult, initiate, premiere, put to sea
9 cast forth, discharge, establish, institute, introduce, set
afloat **10** embark upon, inaugurate, set forth on **11** set in
motion, venture upon
13 thrust forward **15** set into
the water

launder 4 soak, wash **5** clean,
rinse, scour, scrub **7** cleanse,
wash out **11** wash and
iron

Launfal
knight of: **10** roundtable

Laura
director: **13** Otto Preminger
cast: **11** Clifton Webb, Dana
Andrews, Gene Tierney
12 Vincent Price **14** Judith
Anderson

laurel 6 Kalmia, Laurus
13 Laurus nobilis **14** Ficus
benjamina **15** Cordia alliodora
varieties: **3** bog, pig **4** pale
5 black, dwarf, great, sheep
6 Alpine, cherry, ground,
Indian, purple, Sierra,
spurge, tropic **7** Chinese,
English, red-twig, weeping,
western **8** American, drooping, Himalaya, Japanese,
mountain, Portugal **9** Tasmanian **10** Australian, California, variegated
11 Alexandrian

Laurel, Stan
real name: **22** Arthur Stanley
Jefferson
partner: **11** Oliver Hardy
born: **7** England **9** Ulverston
roles: **8** Pardon Us **9** Saps at
Sea **10** Way Out West

laurels 4 fame **5** award, glory,
honor, kudos, prize **6** credit,
praise, renown, reward **7** acclaim, tribute **8** accolade, applause, citation **9** celebrity
10 decoration, popularity
11 acclamation, distinction,
recognition **12** commendation
15 illustriousness

Laurie
also: **16** Theodore Laurence
character in: **11** Little
Women
author: **6** Alcott

laus Deo 11 praise to God
13 praise be to God

Lautreamont, Comte de
author of: **19** Les Chants de
Maldoror

lavation 7 bathing, washing
8 ablution, cleaning
9 cleansing

lavender 4 herb, mint **5** aspic,
behen, lilac, spick, spike
6 purple **7** inkroot **8** amethyst,
stichado **9** lavendula
represents: **6** purity
uses: **6** sachet **7** perfume
8 medicine **9** cosmetics

laver 11 footed basin

Laverne and Shirley
character: **12** Frank De Fazio **13** Carmine Ragusa,
Lenny Kolowski, Mrs Edna
Babish, Shirley Feeney
14 Laverne De Fazio **15** Andrew (Squiggy) Squiggman
cast: **10** Eddie Mekka, Phil

Foster **12** Betty Garrett, David L Lander **13** Cindy Williams, Michael McKean, Penny Marshall
girls worked in: 12 Shotz Brewery
theme song: 23 Making Our Dreams Come True
spinoff from: 9 Happy Days

Lavinia
father: 7 Latinus
mother: 5 Amata
husband: 6 Aeneas

lavish 4 free, lush, wild **5** plush, waste **6** shower **7** copious, opulent, pour out, profuse **8** abundant, effusive, generous, prodigal, squander **9** bounteous, bountiful, dissipate, excessive, exuberant, impetuous, luxuriant, plenteous, plentiful, sumptuous, unsparing **10** immoderate, munificent, profligate, unstinting **11** extravagant, fritter away, intemperate, overindulge, overliberal, spend freely **12** give overmuch, greathearted, overwhelming, unrestrained, without limit

lavishness 6 bounty **8** lushness, opulence **9** profusion **10** luxuriance **11** munificence, prodigality **12** extravagance, immoderation **13** bountifulness, plenteousness, sumptuousness

Lavoisier, Antoine
field: 9 chemistry
nationality: 6 French
founder: 15 modern chemistry
named: 6 oxygen **8** hydrogen

law 3 act **4** bill, code, fuzz, rule, writ **5** axiom, bylaw, canon, dogma, edict, model, truth **6** decree, police **7** justice, mandate, precept, statute, theorem **8** absolute, legality, standard **9** criterion, enactment, gendarmes, legal form, ordinance, postulate, principle **10** civil peace, convention, due process, invariable, regulation **11** commandment, formulation, fundamental, orderliness, working rule **13** jurisprudence, standing order **14** generalization, rules of conduct **15** legal profession
Latin: 3 jus
goddess of: 4 Maat

law-abiding 6 honest **7** upright **9** honorable **10** aboveboard, principled

lawbreaker 3 con **4** hood, thug **5** crook, felon **6** outlaw **7** convict, culprit **8** criminal, jailbird, offender, scofflaw **9** miscreant, wrongdoer **10** delinquent, malefactor, recidivist **11** perpetrator **12** transgressor

lawful 3 due **5** legal, licit **6** proper, titled **7** allowed, granted **8** rightful **9** legalized, statutory, warranted **10** authorized, legitimate, prescribed **11** legitimized, permissible **15** legally entitled **16** legally permitted

lawless 6 unruly, wanton **7** chaotic, defiant, illegal, riotous, wayward **8** anarchic, mutinous, unlawful, wide open **9** insurgent, out of hand, unbridled **10** disorderly, licentious, rebellious, refractory, ungoverned **11** disobedient, lawbreaking, terroristic **12** disorganized, freewheeling, illegitimate, noncompliant, unrestrained **13** insubordinate, transgressive **14** uncontrollable

lawlessness 5 chaos **7** anarchy **8** disorder

lawn 4 park, turf, yard **5** glade, grass, sward **7** grounds, terrace **10** grassy plot, green field, greensward, meadowland **12** grassy ground

law of a place
Latin: 7 lex loci

Law of Moses 5 Torah **10** Pentateuch **15** Ten Commandments

law of nations
Latin: 10 jus gentium

law of nature
Latin: 11 jus naturale

Lawrence, Carol
real name: 16 Carol Maria Laraia
husband: 12 Robert Goulet
born: 13 Melrose Park IL
roles: 5 Maria **13** West Side Story

Lawrence, D H
author of: 10 The Rainbow **11** Women in Love **13** Sons and Lovers **20** Lady Chatterley's Lover

Lawrence, Ernest Orlando
field: 7 physics
invented: 9 cyclotron
awarded: 10 Nobel Prize

Lawrence, Gertrude
real name: 29 Alexandra Dagmar Lawrence Klasen
born: 6 London **7** England
roles: 9 Pygmalion **11** The King and I **17** The Glass Menagerie

Lawrence, T E
also: 16 Lawrence of Arabia
served in: 3 WWI **10** Arab Revolt

advisor to: 6 Faisal **12** Husayn Ibn Ali
fought against: 5 Turks **8** Ottomans
author of: 20 Seven Pillars of Wisdom

Lawrence of Arabia
director: 9 David Lean
cast: 10 Jose Ferrer, Omar Sharif **11** Claude Rains, Jack Hawkins, Peter O'Toole (T E Lawrence) **12** Alec Guinness, Anthony Quinn **13** Arthur Kennedy, Anthony Quayle
Oscar for: 7 picture **8** director **14** cinematography

Lawrence Welk Show, The
champagne lady: 8 Alice Lon **11** Norma Zimmer
cast: 7 Aladdin **11** Larry Hooper, Myron Floren **12** Bobby Burgess **13** Barbara Boylan, Lennon Sisters
Welk played: 9 accordion

lawyer 6 jurist, legist **7** counsel, shyster **8** advocate, attorney **9** barrister, counselor, solicitor **10** mouthpiece, prosecutor **11** pettifogger **12** legal advisor **14** special pleader **15** ambulance chaser

lax 4 hazy, limp, weak **5** agape, loose, slack, vague **6** casual, flabby, floppy, remiss **7** cryptic, flaccid, inexact, lenient, not firm, relaxed **8** careless, derelict, drooping, heedless, nebulous, slipshod, uncaring, yielding **9** confusing, imprecise, negligent, oblivious, undutiful, unheeding, unmindful **10** ill-defined, incoherent, neglectful, permissive **11** hanging open, indifferent, thoughtless, unconcerned **12** loose-muscled, unstructured **13** irresponsible **15** unconscientious

laxness 7 neglect **9** looseness, slackness **10** negligence **11** imprecision **12** carelessness, indifference

Laxness, Halldor Kiljan
author of: 12 Iceland's Bell **14** The Atom Station **17** Independent People **25** The Great Weaver from Kashmir

lay 3 air, bet, put, set **4** bear, fell, fine, form, give, laic, lend, levy, make, plan, poem, raze, rest, seat, song, tune **5** align, allot, apply, ditty, exact, floor, hatch, level, offer, place, stage, wager **6** assess, assign, ballad, charge, demand, depict, devise, gamble, ground, hazard, impose, impute, laical, layout, locate, melody, repose, strain **7** amateur, arrange, concoct, contour, deposit, dispose, forward, present, produce, profane, proffer, refrain, secular, set down, situate, station **8** allocate, assemble, beat down, give odds, inexpert, organize, oviposit, position **9** attribute, elucidate, enunciate, formulate, knock down, knock over, prostrate, roundelay, situation **10** cause to lie, topography **11** arrangement, disposition, nonclerical, orientation, put together **12** conformation **13** configuration, inexperienced, nonspecialist **14** partly informed, unprofessional **15** nonprofessional **17** nonecclesiastical

lay at the door of 6 assign **7** ascribe **8** charge to **9** attribute

lay bare 4 bare, show **6** expose, reveal, unmask, unveil, unwrap **7** divulge, exhibit, publish, uncover **8** disclose **9** broadcast, make known **10** make public **11** communicate

lay down arms 5 yield **6** give up **7** succumb **8** cry quits **9** surrender **10** capitulate **11** come to terms, sue for peace **13** declare a truce **17** acknowledge defeat

layer 3 bed, lap, ply **4** coat, fold, leaf, seam, slab, tier, zone **5** level, plate, scale, sheet, stage, story **6** lamina **7** stratum **9** thickness

layman 4 laic **6** sister **7** amateur, brother **8** outsider **9** churchman **10** catechumen **11** churchwoman, communicant, parishioner **15** nonprofessional **16** member of the flock

layoff 4 fire **6** firing, idling, ouster, the axe **7** dismiss, release, sacking, the boot, the gate, the sack **8** pink slip, shutdown **9** closedown, discharge, dismissal, hard times, the bounce **10** cashiering, depression, the heave-ho **11** furloughing, termination **12** unemployment **13** disemployment, walking papers **20** discharge temporarily

lay off 7 dismiss, forfeit, release, set free **8** get rid of, liberate **9** discharge, terminate **11** give the gate, send packing

Lay of the Last Minstrel, The
   author: 14 Sir Walter Scott
   character: 8 Margaret, The Dwarf **13** Lady Buccleuch, Lord Cranstoun **17** Master of Buccleuch **19** Ghost of Michael Scott **21** Sir William of Deloraine

lay on 6 bestow, confer, supply **7** present, provide

lay open 4 open **6** expose, open up **7** clarify **9** make plain **18** make understandable

layout 4 form, plan **5** chart, draft, dummy, model, motif, spend **6** design, expend, pay out, sketch, spread **7** diagram, drawing, fork out, outline, pattern **8** disburse, shell out **9** blueprint, delineate, placement, spread out, structure **11** arrangement, composition

lay waste 4 ruin **5** level, wreck **6** ravage **7** despoil, destroy, wipe out **8** demolish, desolate **9** devastate, eradicate **10** annihilate, obliterate

Lazarus 6 beggar
   means: 8 God helps
   sister: 4 Mary **6** Martha
   hometown: 7 Bethany
   resurrected by: 5 Jesus

Lazarus
   author: 14 Leonid Andreyev

Lazarus, Mell
   creator/artist: 5 Momma **9** Miss Peach

lazurite
   variety: 11 lapis lazuli

lazy 3 lax **4** idle, slow **5** inert, slack **6** drowsy, sleepy, torpid **7** laggard, languid **8** inactive, indolent, listless, slothful, sluggish **9** apathetic, easygoing, lethargic, shiftless **10** languorous, slow-moving **13** unindustrious **15** unwilling to work

lazy person 5 drone, idler **6** loafer **14** good-for-nothing

Leach, Archibald Alexander
   real name of: 9 Cary Grant

Leachman, Cloris
   born: 11 Des Moines IA
   roles: 7 Phyllis **11** High Anxiety **12** Kiss Me Deadly **17** Young Frankenstein **18** Mary Tyler Moore Show, The Last Picture Show

lead 2 go **3** aim, top **4** clue, draw, edge, have, head, hero, hint, live, lure, pass **5** charm, excel, guide, model, outdo, pilot, steer, tempt **6** allure, convey, direct, entice, extend, induce, manage, margin, pursue, seduce **7** advance, attract, bring on, command, conduct, control, example, go first, incline, issue in, marshal, pioneer, precede, proceed, produce, stretch, surpass, undergo **8** domineer, go before, guidance, moderate, outstrip, persuade, priority, result in, shepherd, star part **9** advan-

tage, come first, direction, go through, headliner, influence, plurality, rank first **10** branch into, experience, first place, indication, precedence, precedency, set the pace, show the way, tend toward **11** antecedence, be in advance, leading role, preside over, protagonist

lead
   chemical symbol: 2 Pb

lead astray 4 dupe, lure **6** delude **7** beguile, deceive, ensnare, mislead **19** lead up the garden path

leaden 4 dark, dull, glum, gray **5** inert, murky **6** dreary, gloomy, numbed, somber, torpid **7** grayish, languid **8** burdened, careworn, darkened, deadened, listless, sluggish, unwieldy **9** depressed, inanimate **10** cumbersome, hard to move

leader 4 boss, guru, head **5** chief, guide, mogul **6** bigwig, honcho, master, mentor, tycoon **7** captain, foreman, kingpin, magnate, manager, pioneer, prophet **8** director, superior **9** chieftain, commander, conductor, godfather, pacemaker, patriarch **10** forerunner, pacesetter, pathfinder, supervisor **11** frontrunner, torchbearer, trailblazer

leadership 4 helm, lead, sway **5** reins, wheel **7** command, primacy **8** charisma, guidance, headship, hegemony **9** captaincy, supremacy **10** domination, mastership **11** managership, preeminence, stewardship **12** directorship, governorship, guardianship, self-reliance **13** ability to lead, self-assurance **14** administration **15** managerial skill, superintendency **17** authoritativeness

leading 3 top **4** head, main **5** basic, chief, first, great, prime **6** ruling **7** advance, guiding, initial, leadoff, notable, primary, ranking, stellar, supreme, topmost **8** advanced, dominant, foremost **9** directing, essential, governing, nonpareil, paramount, principal, prominent, sovereign, unrivaled **10** motivating, preeminent, underlying **11** controlling, outstanding, pacesetting **12** unchallenged, unparalleled **13** most important **14** quintessential **15** most influential, most significant

lead on 4 goad **5** egg on **6** entice **7** mislead, support **9** en-

courage 19 lead up the garden path

lead the way 4 lead, show, take **5** guide **6** escort **7** conduct

leaf 4 flip, foil, page, skim **5** blade, bract, folio, frond, green, inset, petal, sheet, thumb **6** browse, glance, insert, needle **7** foliole, lamella, leaflet **9** cotyledon, extension, turn green **10** lamination **12** sheet of metal

leaflet 2 ad **4** bill **5** flier, flyer, tract **6** folder, notice **7** booklet, handout **8** brochure, bulletin, circular, handbill, pamphlet **9** broadside, throwaway **10** broadsheet **12** announcement **13** advertisement

league 4 ally, band **5** cabal, group, guild, merge, union **6** cartel **7** combine, compact, company, network, society **8** alliance **9** coalition **10** conspiracy, federation, fraternity, join forces **11** association, confederacy, confederate, consolidate, cooperative, partnership **13** collaboration, confederation, confraternity

Leah
means: 7 wild cow
father: 5 Laban
husband: 5 Jacob
sister: 6 Rachel
slave: 6 Zilpah
son: 4 Levi **5** Judah **6** Reuben, Simeon **7** Zebulun **8** Issachar
daughter: 5 Dinah
burial place: 9 Machpelah

leak 3 ebb, rip **4** blab, gash, hole, ooze, rent, rift, seep, vent **5** break, chink, cleft, crack, drain, exude, fault, spill **6** breach, efflux, escape, filter, let out, reveal, take in **7** confide, crevice, divulge, dribble, fissure, let slip, opening, outflow, rupture, seepage **8** aperture, disclose, draining, give away, puncture **9** discharge, percolate **10** interstice, make public **11** be permeable, perforation **12** admit leakage **16** let enter or escape

leakage 5 issue **7** outflow, seepage **9** discharge

Leakey, Louis S Bazett
field: 12 anthropology
discovered: 8 early man
worked at: 8 Tanzania **12** Olduvai Gorge
wife: 4 Mary
son: 7 Richard

lean 3 aim, bow, tip **4** bend, cant, lank, list, poor, rely, rest, slim, tend, thin, tilt

5 gaunt, lanky, lurch, scant, slant, slope, small, spare, weedy **6** barren, depend, meager, modest, nonfat, prefer, scanty, skinny, sparse, svelte **7** angular, count on, incline, recline, scraggy, scrawny, slender, spindly, trust in, willowy **8** exiguous, rawboned, resort to, skeletal **9** emaciated **10** inadequate, set store by **11** be partial to, have faith in, prop oneself **12** insufficient, seek solace in **14** rest one's weight, support oneself

Lean, David
director of: 10 Summertime **11** Oliver Twist **13** Doctor Zhivago, Ryan's Daughter **15** A Passage to India **16** Lawrence of Arabia (Oscar) **17** Great Expectations **23** The Bridge on the River Kwai (Oscar)

Leander
loved: 4 Hero
swam nightly: 10 Hellespont
death by: 8 drowning

leaning 4 bent, turn **5** slant **7** relying **8** affinity, tendency **9** proneness **10** dependence, partiality, preference, proclivity, propensity **11** inclination **14** predisposition

leap 3 hop **4** jete, jump, romp, rush, skip **5** bound, caper, frisk, vault **6** bounce, cavort, frolic, gambol, hasten, hurtle, prance, spring **7** hop over **8** jump over **9** bound over, saltation **10** hurtle over, jump across, spring over

Learchus
father: 7 Athamas
mother: 3 Ino
killed by: 7 Athamas

learn 3 con **4** hear **6** detect, master, pick up **7** find out, uncover, unearth **8** discover, memorize **9** ascertain, determine, ferret out **10** become able **12** find out about

learned 4 deep, wise **7** erudite **8** cultured, educated, informed, lettered, literate, profound, schooled, well-read **9** scholarly **10** cultivated **12** accomplished, intellectual, welleducated **13** knowledgeable

Learned, Michael
roles: 5 Nurse **10** The Waltons

learner 4 tyro **5** pupil **6** novice, rookie **7** draftee, recruit, scholar, student, trainee **8** beginner, disciple, enlistee, follower, freshman, neophyte **9** fledgling, greenhorn, novitiate, proselyte, schoolboy

10 apprentice, schoolgirl, tenderfoot **11** schoolchild

learning 5 study **6** wisdom **7** culture **8** teaching **9** education, erudition, knowledge, schooling **11** cultivation, edification, information, instruction, scholarship **13** comprehension, enlightenment, understanding

Learning
god of: 5 Thoth

leash 4 curb, lead, line, rein, ruin **5** strap, thong **6** bridle, choker, fasten, hold in, stifle, string, tether **7** contain, control, harness **8** restrain, suppress

Leather-Stocking Tales
author: 19 James Fenimore Cooper
includes: 10 The Prairie **11** The Pioneers **13** The Deerslayer, The Pathfinder **20** The Last of the Mohicans
hero of: 7 Hawkeye **10** Pathfinder, The Trapper **11** Natty Bumppo **13** The Deerslayer **15** Leather-stocking **16** Le Longue Carabine

leave 2 go **3** fly **4** cede, exit, flee, keep, quit, will **5** allot, be off, cause, endow, forgo, going, split, waive, yield **6** assign, bug out, commit, decamp, depart, desert, eschew, forego, give up, legate, move on, recess, resign, retain, set out **7** abandon, abscond, bequest, consent, consign, deposit, entrust, forsake, holiday, let stay, liberty, parting, produce, push off, release, respite, retreat, sustain, take off, time off **8** approval, bequeath, farewell, furlough, generate, give over, maintain, result in, sanction, shove off, vacation **9** allowance, apportion, departure, hotfoot it, let remain, surrender, tolerance **10** concession, depart from, embark from, go away from, indulgence, permission, relinquish, retire from, sabbatical, sufferance, withdrawal **11** bid farewell, endorsement **13** absent oneself, understanding

leave a ship 4 land **6** debark **8** go ashore **9** disembark **11** abandon ship

leave behind 6 desert, vacate **7** abandon, discard, forsake **8** evacuate **9** cast aside **10** relinquish **11** outdistance

leave cold 4 bore **12** leave unmoved **15** leave unaffected

Leave It To Beaver
character: **11** June Cleaver, Ward Cleaver **12** Eddie Haskell, Wally Cleaver **13** Beaver (Theodore) Cleaver
cast: **7** Tony Dow **9** Ken Osmond **12** Hugh Beaumont, Jerry Mathers **18** Barbara Billingsley

leave off 3 end **4** halt, quit, stop **5** cease **6** desist, finish **7** suspend **8** conclude **11** discontinue, refrain from

leave out 4 drop, omit **6** except, reject **7** exclude

Leaves of Grass
author: **11** Walt Whitman

leave suddenly 3 fly **4** flee **6** cut out, decamp, run off **7** abscond, make off, run away, rush off, take off **11** take a powder **15** be off and running

leave-taking 4 exit **5** adieu **7** good-bye, leaving, parting, send-off **8** au revoir, farewell **9** departure **10** withdrawal

leave undone 4 quit **6** give up **7** abandon, forsake, neglect **8** give up on

Lebanon *see box*

Le Bel, Joseph Achille
field: **9** chemistry
nationality: **6** French
founded: **15** stereochemistry

Le Bourgeois Gentilhomme
author: **7** Moliere
character: **7** Cleonte, Dorante **9** M Jourdain **16** Monsieur Jourdain

Le Carre, John
real name: **13** David Cornwell
author of: **11** A Perfect Spy **13** Smiley's People **18** The Looking Glass War **19** A Small Town in Germany **20** The Little Drummer Girl **21** The Honorable Schoolboy **22** Tinker Tailor Soldier Spy **26** The Spy Who Came in from the Cold

lechayim, lehayim 6 to life

Lecheates
epithet of: **4** Zeus
means: **10** in childbed

lecherous 4 lewd **5** randy **6** carnal **7** goatish, lustful, ruttish **8** prurient **9** salacious, satyrlike **10** lascivious, libidinous, licentious, lubricious

lechery 4 lust **8** lewdness **9** carnality, prurience **10** satyriasis **11** lustfulness, nymphomania **13** salaciousness **14** lasciviousness

Le Cid
author: **9** Corneille
composer: **13** Jules Massenet

Leconte de Lisle, Charles
author of: **14** Poemes Antiques, Poemes Barbares

Le Corbusier
real name: **23** Charles Edouard Jeanneret
architect of: **10** La Tourette (monastery) **15** Notre Dame du Haut (Ronchamp France) **16** Unite d'Habitation (Marseilles)
planned city of: **10** Chandigarh (capital of the Punjab)

style: **6** Purism **12** New Brutalism

lecture 4 talk **5** chide, scold, speak **6** homily, preach, rail at, rebuke, sermon, speech **7** address, censure, chiding, expound, oration, reading, reproof, reprove, upbraid, warning **8** admonish, call down, harangue, moralize, reproach **9** discourse, hold forth, reprimand, sermonize, talking-to **10** preachment, take to task **12** chastisement, disquisition, remonstrance

lecture hall 9 classroom

Lebanon
ancient name: **9** Phoenicia
capital/largest city: **6** Beirut **8** Beyrouth
others: **3** Sur **4** Arca, Tyre **5** Ehden, Halba, Hamat, Sahle, Saida, Sayda, Sidon, Sofar, Zahla, Zahle **6** Byblos, Ghazir, Juniye, Tibnin **7** Baalbek, Batroun, Bsherri, Rachaya, Tripoli, Zgharta **8** Djezzine, El Hermel, Hasbaiya, Merjuyun **9** Broummana, Marjayoun **10** Beited Dine, Heliopolis
ancient city:
  8 Carthage
school: **4** Arab **8** American, Lebanese **11** Saint Joseph
division:
  ancient: **4** Tyre **5** Arwad, Sidon **6** Byblos, Jubayl
monetary unit: **5** livre, pound **7** piastre
lake: **5** Quran **6** Qirawn
mountain: **4** Mzar **5** Aruba **6** Hermon **7** Lebanon, Sannine **8** Kadischa, Kenisseh **9** Kennisseh **10** al-Mukammal **11** Anti-Lebanon
highest point: **7** es Sauda **13** Qurnat al-Sawda
river: **3** Dog, Joz **5** Barid, Kebir, Lycos **6** Auwali, Barada, Damour, Litani **7** Hasbani, Leontes, Orontes **8** Kasemieh
sea: **13** Mediterranean
physical feature:
  cape: **10** Pigeon Rock **11** Ras esh Shiqa **12** Qadisha Gorge
  plain: **4** Bika **5** Bekaa
  valley: **5** Beqaa **6** al-Biqa **9** Great Rift
  wind: **7** khamsin
people: **4** Arab **11** Palestinian
  ancient: **9** Canaanite **10** Phoenician
  leader: **6** Bashir, Sarkis **7** Chamoun **8** Franjieh **9** al-Din Maan **11** Amin Gemayel **13** Bashir Gemayel
  poet: **11** Kahil Gibran
  rulers: **5** Arabs **6** French, Greeks, Romans **8** Hittites, Ottomans, Persians **9** Assyrians, Crusaders, Egyptians, Mamelukes **11** Babylonians
language: **6** Arabic, French, Syriac **7** English, Turkish **8** Armenian
religion: **5** Druse, Druze, Islam **8** Maronite, Melchite **10** Protestant **11** Monophysite **12** Christianity **13** Greek Catholic **14** Greek Orthodoxy **17** Armenian Orthodoxy
place:
  dam: **5** Qarun
  ruins: **7** Baalbek **15** Temple of Bacchus, Temple of Jupiter
feature:
  Christian group: **10** Phalangist
  dance: **6** dabkeh, dabkey
  tree: **5** cedar
food:
  dish: **6** kibbeh **8** tabouleh
  drink: **4** arak **6** arrack

10 auditorium 12 amphitheater, assembly hall

lecturelike 7 donnish, preachy 8 academic, didactic, pedantic 9 homiletic 10 moralizing

Leda
father: 8 Thestius
husband: 9 Tyndareus
lover: 4 swan, Zeus
son: 6 Castor, Pollux 8 Dioscuri 10 Polydeuces
daughter: 5 Helen 6 Phoebe 8 Philonoe, Timandra 12 Clytemnestra

Leda and the Swan
author: 7 W B Yeats

ledge 4 sill, step 5 ridge, shelf 6 mantel, offset 8 foothold, shoulder 10 projection 11 mantelpiece, mantelshelf, outcropping

Lee, Henry
nickname: 15 Light Horse Harry
served in: 16 Revolutionary War
member of: 10 US Congress 19 Continental Congress
governor of: 8 Virginia
suppressed: 16 Whiskey Rebellion
son: 7 Robert E

Lee, Robert E
father: 5 Henry 15 Light Horse Harry
born: 11 Stratford VA 18 Westmoreland County
wife: 21 Mary Ann Randolph Custis
served in: 8 Civil War 10 Mexican War
commander of: 22 Army of Northern Virginia
suppressed raid: 9 John Brown 12 Harper's Ferry
battle: 7 Bull Run 8 Antietam 10 Gettysburg 14 Fredericksburg 16 Chancellorsville, Seven Days' Battles
surrendered at: 20 Appomattox Court House
president of: 17 Washington College

Lee, Spike
original name: 17 Sheldon Jackson Lee
born: 2 GA 7 Atlanta
wife: 17 Tonya Linette Lewis
films: 8 Malcolm X 10 School Daze 11 Jungle Fever 15 Do the Right Thing, She's Gotta Have It 31 Joe's Bed-Stuy Barbership We Cut Heads
company: 18 Forty Acres and A Mule
ads for: 4 Nike

leek 18 Allium ampeloprasum

varieties: 4 lily, rose, sand, wild 5 lady's 6 meadow

leer 4 ogle 5 fleer, smirk 6 goggle

leery 4 wary 5 cagey, chary 6 unsure 7 guarded 8 cautious, doubtful, hesitant 9 skeptical, undecided 10 suspicious 11 circumspect, distrustful, mistrustful

Leeuwenhoek, Anton van
field: 10 microscopy
father of: 12 microbiology
discovered: 13 red blood cells

leeway 4 play 5 scope, slack 6 margin 7 cushion, headway, reserve 8 headroom, latitude 9 allowance, clearance, elbowroom, extra time, tolerance 11 flexibility 13 room for choice 14 margin for error 15 maneuverability

left behind 7 vacated 8 deserted, forsaken, forsook 9 abandoned, discarded, evacuated 12 relinquished

leftover 6 excess, legacy, unused 7 overage, residue, surplus, uneaten 8 leavings, oddments, residual, survivor 9 carry-over, remainder, remaining

left-wing 7 leftist, liberal, radical 9 socialist 11 progressive

left-winger 7 leftist, liberal, radical 9 socialist 11 progressive

Lefty
nickname of: 5 Gomez 12 Steve Carlton

leg 3 gam, lap, pin 4 limb, part, post, prop 5 brace, femur, shank, stage, stump, tibia 6 column, fibula, member, pillar 7 portion, section, segment, stretch, support, upright

legacy 4 gift 6 devise, estate 7 bequest, vestige 8 heirloom, heritage, leftover, survivor 9 carry-over, throwback, tradition 10 birthright, hand-me-down 11 inheritance

legal 4 fair 5 licit, of law, valid 6 kosher, lawful 7 cricket 8 forensic, judicial, juristic, rightful 9 courtroom, juridical 10 legitimate, sanctioned 11 permissible

legal advisor 6 lawyer 7 counsel 8 advocate, attorney 9 barrister, counselor, solicitor 13 attorney-at-law 14 counselor-at-law

legal form 4 writ 8 document 10 instrument

legality 8 validity 9 licitness

10 lawfulness, legitimacy 17 constitutionality

legalization 8 sanction 9 enactment 10 permission, validation 13 authorization 14 legitimization

legalize 5 enact 6 permit 8 sanction, validate 9 authorize 10 legitimize

legal residence 4 home 8 domicile, dwelling

legal tender 4 cash 5 money 8 currency

legate 5 agent, envoy 6 deputy 8 emissary 14 representative

legatee 4 heir 9 inheritor 11 beneficiary

legation 7 embassy, mission 8 ministry 9 consulate 10 delegation 11 chancellery

legend 3 key 4 edda, lore, myth, saga, tale 5 fable, motto, story, title 7 caption, fiction, proverb 8 folklore 11 inscription

legendary 5 famed 6 fabled, famous, mythic 7 storied 8 fabulous, fanciful, mythical 9 imaginary 10 apocryphal, celebrated, fictitious, proverbial

Legend of Good Women, The
author: 15 Geoffrey Chaucer
character: 4 Dido 5 Medea 6 Thisbe 7 Alceste, Ariadne, Lucrece, Phyllis 9 Cleopatra, Hypsipyle, Philomela 12 Hypermnestra

Legend of Sleepy Hollow, The
author: 16 Washington Irving
character: 12 Brom Van Brunt (Brom Bones), Ichabod Crane 16 Katrina Van Tassel

Leger, Fernand
born: 6 France 8 Argentan
artwork: 8 Bargeman 10 Adam and Eve, The Wedding, Three Women 11 The Builders, The Cyclists, The Mechanic, The Stairway 14 The Great Parade 15 Le Grand Dejeuner 16 Contrasting Forms, Nudes in the Forest 21 Butterflies and Flowers

legerdemain 7 cunning 8 deftness, jugglery, juggling, trickery 9 deception 10 adroitness, artfulness 11 maneuvering 13 sleight of hand 16 prestidigitation

legible 4 neat 5 clear, plain 7 visible 8 clear-cut, distinct, readable 12 decipherable

14 comprehensible, understandable

legion 3 mob, sea **4** army, host, mass **5** corps, drove, horde, spate, swarm **6** myriad, throng, troops **7** brigade **8** division **9** multitude

leg irons 5 bonds, irons **6** chains **7** fetters **8** shackles

legislation 3 act **4** bill **6** ruling **7** measure, statute **9** amendment, enactment, lawmaking, ordinance

legislator 7 senator **8** alderman, delegate, lawgiver, lawmaker **10** councilman **11** assemblyman, congressman **13** congresswoman **14** representative **15** parliamentarian

legislature 4 diet **5** house **6** senate **7** chamber, council **8** assembly, congress **10** parliament

legitimacy 8 legality, validity **10** lawfulness **11** correctness, genuineness **12** authenticity, rightfulness **15** appropriateness

legitimate 4 fair, just, true **5** legal, licit, sound, valid **6** lawful, proper **7** correct, genuine, logical, tenable **8** rightful **9** authentic, justified, plausible **10** believable, reasonable **11** appropriate, well-founded

leg-pull 4 hoax **9** deception **13** practical joke

Legree, Simon
  character in: 14 Uncle Tom's Cabin
  author: 5 Stowe

LeGuin, Ursula K
  author of: 13 Lathe of Heaven **14** Rocannon's World **15** The Dispossessed **16** Always Coming Home **21** The Left Hand of Darkness

Lehar, Franz (Ferencz)
  born: 7 Komarno (then Hungary, now Czechoslovakia)
  composer of: 9 Gipsy Love **13** The Merry Widow **20** The Count of Luxembourg

Lehmbruck, Wilhelm
  born: 7 Germany **9** Meiderich
  artwork: 11 Rising Youth **12** Man Flung Down, Praying Woman, Seating Youth **13** Kneeling Woman, Standing Woman, Standing Youth

Leigh, Janet
  husband: 10 Tony Curtis
  daughter: 14 Jamie Lee Curtis
  born: 8 Merced CA
  roles: 6 Psycho, The Fog **10** The Vikings **11** Little Women, Touch of Evil

Leigh, Vivien
  real name: 17 Vivian Mary Hartley
  husband: 15 Laurence Olivier
  born: 5 India **10** Darjeeling
  roles: 11 Ship of Fools **12** Anna Karenina **13** Blanche du Bois, Scarlett O'Hara **14** Waterloo Bridge **15** Gone With the Wind (Oscar) **17** That Hamilton Woman **21** A Streetcar Named Desire (Oscar), Roman Spring of Mrs Stone

Leighton, Margaret
  husband: 12 Max Reinhardt **14** Laurence Harvey, Michael Wilding
  born: 7 England **10** Barnt Green **14** Worcestershire
  roles: 12 The Go-Between **13** The Winslow Boy **14** Separate Tables **19** The Night of the Iguana

leisure 4 ease, rest **6** recess, repose **7** holiday, respite, time off **8** free time, vacation **9** diversion, idle hours, spare time **10** recreation, relaxation

leisurely 4 idle, slow **6** casual, slowly **7** languid, relaxed, restful **9** unhurried **10** slow-moving **11** lingeringly, unhurriedly **12** without haste **13** lackadaisical

Lemminkainen
  origin: 7 Finnish
  mentioned in: 8 Kalevala
  role: 4 hero

Lemmon, Jack
  real name: 18 Jack Uhler Lemmon III
  wife: 11 Felicia Farr
  born: 8 Boston MA
  roles: 7 Missing **10** April Fools **12** Save the Tiger (Oscar), The Apartment, The Great Race, The Odd Couple **13** China Syndrome, Mister Roberts, Some Like It Hot **18** Days of Wine and Roses, Under the Yum-Yum Tree **19** How to Murder Your Wife

lemon 11 Citrus limon
  varieties: 4 wild **5** dwarf, giant, Meyer, water **6** garden, wonder **9** wild water **12** Chinese dwarf **14** American wonder

Lemuralia
  origin: 5 Roman
  event: 8 festival
  to exorcise: 6 ghosts

lemures
  form: 6 ghosts
  characteristic: 10 maleficent **11** troublesome

Lenaea
  origin: 8 Athenian
  event: 8 festival

lend 4 give, loan **6** impart, invest, supply **7** advance, furnish **10** contribute

lend a hand 3 aid **6** assist **7** help out

lend assistance 3 aid **4** abet, help **6** succor **7** relieve **16** give a helping hand

lend one's name to 7 endorse, support **9** recommend

length 3 run **4** span, term, time **5** piece, range, reach **6** extent, period **7** compass, measure, portion, section, segment, stretch **8** distance, duration, end to end **9** longitude, magnitude **11** elapsed time, measurement

lengthen 3 pad **5** add to **6** expand, extend, let out, pad out **7** augment, drag out, draw out, fill out, prolong, spin out, stretch **8** elongate, flesh out, increase, protract **9** attenuate, string out

lengthened 8 drawn out, extended **9** augmented, elongated, prolonged, stretched **10** attenuated, grew longer

lengthening 8 full form **9** extending, extension **10** elongation, stretching **11** extenuation, protraction **12** prolongation

lengthy 5 windy, wordy **6** padded, prolix **7** endless **8** drawn out, extended, overlong, rambling **9** elongated, extensive, garrulous, long-drawn, prolonged **10** digressive, discursive, long-winded, protracted **12** interminable

leniency 5 mercy **7** charity **8** clemency **9** tolerance **10** compassion **11** forbearance, magnanimity **12** mercifulness **13** forgivingness

lenient 4 kind, mild, soft **6** gentle **7** clement, liberal, patient, sparing **8** merciful, moderate, tolerant **9** easygoing, forgiving, indulgent **10** benevolent, charitable, forbearing, permissive **11** kindhearted, soft-hearted, sympathetic **13** compassionate, tenderhearted

Lenni-Lenape *see* **8** Delaware

Lenny
  director: 8 Bob Fosse

cast: 8 Jan Miner 11 Stanley Beck 13 Dustin Hoffman (Lenny Bruce) 14 Valerie Perrine (Honey Harlowe)

Le Notre, Andre
landscape architect of: 6 Clagny 9 Tuileries 10 Versailles 12 Saint Germain 13 Fontainebleau 22 Chateau de Vaux-le-Vicomte

lens
invented by:
    achromatic: 7 Dollond
    bifocal: 8 Franklin
    fused bifocal: 6 Borsch

Lenya, Lotte
real name: 16 Karoline Blamauer
husband: 9 Kurt Weill
born: 7 Austria, Hitzing
roles: 5 Jenny 18 From Russia with Love, The Seven Deadly Sins, The Threepenny Opera

Leo
symbol: 4 lion
planet: 3 Sun
rules: 7 romance 10 creativity
born: 4 July 6 August

Leonard, Elmore
author of: 4 Swag 5 Glitz, Stick 6 Hombre 7 La Brava 9 Cat Chaser, Gold Coast, Gunsights, The Hunted 10 Mr Majestyk 12 The Big Bounce 14 Fifty-Two Pick-Up, Valdez Is Coming 16 Double Dutch Treat, The Bounty Hunters 18 Forty Lashes Less One

Leonardo da Vinci
born: 5 Italy, Vinci
artwork: 8 Mona Lisa 13 The Last Supper 15 The Annunciation 19 The Battle of Anghiari 21 The Adoration of the Magi

Leonato
character in: 19 Much Ado About Nothing
author: 11 Shakespeare

Leoncavallo, Ruggiero
born: 5 Italy 6 Naples
composer of: 8 Serafita 9 Pagliacci

Leontes
character in: 14 The Winter's Tale
author: 11 Shakespeare

Leonteus
leader of: 6 Greeks
leader at: 4 Troy
suitor of: 5 Helen

leopard 3 cat 7 panther 10 spotted cat
group of: 4 leap

Leos
occupation: 6 herald

father: 7 Orpheus
sacrificed: 9 daughters

Leo the Lip
nickname of: 11 Leo Durocher

lepidoptera
class: 8 hexapoda
phylum: 10 arthropoda
group: 4 moth 9 butterfly

leprechaun 3 elf, imp 5 dwarf, gnome 6 sprite 12 little person

Ler
also: 3 Lir
origin: 5 Irish
personifies: 3 sea
son: 8 Manannan
corresponds to: 4 Llyr

Lesage, Alain
author of: 7 Gil Blas 8 Turcaret

Lescaze, William
architect of: 18 Borg-Warner Building (Chicago) 38 Philadelphia Savings Fund Society Building

Lescot, Pierre
architect of: 10 Cour Carree 20 Fontaine des Innocents
rebuilding of: 6 Louvre

Lesotho *see box*

less 6 barely, little 7 smaller 8 meagerly, slighter 10 not as great 11 more limited

lessen 3 ebb 4 ease, sink, thin, wane 5 abate, lower 6 dilute, reduce, shrink 7 abridge, decline, dwindle, lighten, slacken, subside 8 contract, de-

crease, diminish, mitigate, wind down 9 alleviate 10 depreciate

lessening 6 waning 8 decrease, dilution 9 abatement, deduction, dwindling, reduction, shrinkage 10 diminution, lightening, mitigation, shortening, slackening 11 abridgement, alleviation, contraction, diminishing, slacking off 12 abbreviation, condensation, depreciation

lesser 4 less 5 minor 7 humbler, smaller 8 inferior, slighter 9 secondary 11 secondarily

Lesser Dionysia
also: 13 Rural Dionysia
event: 8 festival
origin: 6 Attica

Lessing, Doris
author of: 8 Shikasta 16 The Four-Gated City 17 The Golden Notebook 20 The Sirian Experiments 21 The Children of Violence 37 Marriages Between Zones Three Four and Five 42 The Making of the Representative for Planet Eight

lesson 5 class, drill, guide, model, moral, study 6 caveat, notice, rebuke 7 caution, example, message, reading, segment, warning 8 exemplar, exercise, homework 9 deterrent 10 admonition, advisement, assignment, punishment, recitation, Scrip-

---

Lesotho
other name: 10 Basutoland
capital/largest city: 6 Maseru
others: 4 Roma 5 Joels 6 Leribe, Morija 7 Quthing, Sekakes 8 Mafeteng, Matsieng 9 Marakabei, Qachas Nek, Semonkong 10 Butha Buthe, Mokhotlong, Thaba Bosiu 11 Mohales Hoek 12 Sehlabathebe, Teyateyaneng
head of state: 4 king
monetary unit: 4 cent, rand
mountain: 6 Maloti, Maluti 7 Central 8 Injasuti, Machache 10 Ben Macdhui 11 Drakensberg, Thaba Putsoa
highest point: 16 Thabana Ntlenyana
river: 5 Senqu 6 Orange, Tugela 7 Caledon 9 Makhaleng
physical feature:
    gorge: 5 Oxbow
people: 4 Zulu 5 Bantu, Tembu 6 Basuto 7 Basotho
    leader: 7 Moshesh 9 Mosheshwe 10 Moshoeshoe 14 Leabua Jonathan
language: 5 Sotho 7 English, Sesotho
religion: 7 animism 13 Roman Catholic 18 Lesotho Evangelical
feature:
    blanket: 4 kobo
    house: 8 rondavel
    water project: 11 Malibamatso

tures **11** instruction
12 remonstrance

Lestrade, Inspector
  character in: **14** (The Adventures of) Sherlock Holmes
  author: **10** Conan Doyle

Le Sueur, Lucille Fay
  real name of: **12** Joan Crawford

let 4 make, rent **5** admit, allow, cause, grant, lease, leave **6** enable, permit, sublet, suffer **7** approve, charter, concede, empower, endorse, hire out, license, warrant **8** sanction, sublease, tolerate **9** authorize

let down 4 drop **5** lower **6** betray **8** push down **10** disappoint **11** disillusion

letdown 3 rue **4** balk, blow **6** fizzle, regret **7** chagrin, setback **8** comedown **10** anticlimax, bafflement, bitter pill, dashed hope, discontent **11** frustration **12** blighted hope, discomfiture **13** mortification **14** disappointment, disenchantment, disgruntlement **15** disillusionment, dissatisfaction

let fall 4 drop **5** let go **7** release

let fly 4 cast, hurl **5** eject, fling, heave, sling, throw **6** launch, propel

let go 3 axe, can **4** fire, free, lose, oust, sack **6** bounce, give up

lethal 5 fatal, toxic **6** deadly, mortal **7** baneful, killing **8** venomous, virulent **9** dangerous, malignant, poisonous **11** destructive **13** mortally toxic

lethargic 4 dull, idle, lazy **5** inert **6** drowsy, sleepy, torpid **7** languid, passive **8** comatose, indolent, listless, slothful, sluggish **9** apathetic, enervated, somnolent, soporific **10** dispirited, lackluster, unspirited **11** debilitated, indifferent

lethargy 5 sloth **6** apathy, stupor, torpor **7** inertia, languor **8** dullness, laziness **9** indolence, lassitude, torpidity **10** drowsiness, inactivity **12** indifference, listlessness, slothfulness, sluggishness

Lethe
  form: **5** river
  location: **5** Hades
  caused: **13** forgetfulness

let in 5 admit **7** receive **12** allow to enter

let loose 4 free **5** let go **6** let

fly 7 release, set free, unleash **8** give vent, liberate **12** give free rein

Leto
  also: **6** Latona
  form: **7** goddess
  father: **5** Coeus
  mother: **6** Phoebe
  son: **6** Apollo
  daughter: **7** Artemis

let off 5 let go **6** acquit, excuse, exempt **7** release, set free **8** liberate **9** discharge

let slip 6 betray, expose, reveal **7** divulge, uncover **8** blurt out, disclose, give away

Let's Make a Deal
  host: **9** Monty Hall
  announcer: **10** Jay Stewart

letter 4 note **7** epistle, message, missive **8** dispatch, document **9** substance **10** billet-doux

Letter, The
  director: **12** William Wyler
  based on story by: **15** Somerset Maugham
  cast: **10** Bette Davis **14** Frieda Inescort **15** Gale Sondergaard, Herbert Marshall, James Stephenson
  setting: **6** Malaya

letter ordering imprisonment
  French: **14** lettre de cachet
  carried seal of: **4** king **9** sovereign

letters 8 learning **9** erudition **10** literature **13** belles lettres

Letters from the Underground
  author: **16** Fyodor Dostoevsky

Letter to Three Wives, A
  director: **17** Joseph L Mankiewicz
  cast: **10** Ann Sothern **11** Jeanne Crain, Jeffrey Lynn, Kirk Douglas; Paul Douglas **12** Linda Darnell, Thelma Ritter
  Oscar for: **6** script **8** director

let the buyer beware
  Latin: **12** caveat emptor

let the people rule
  Latin: **13** regnat populus
  motto of: **8** Arkansas

let there be light
  Latin: **7** fiat lux

lettre de cachet 26 letter ordering imprisonment **28** letter under the sovereign's seal

lettuce 7 Lactuca
  varieties: **3** cos **5** chalk, frog's, lamb's, water **6** Boston, garden, miner's **7** iceberg, prickly, romaine

8 escarole **9** asparagus **11** common lamb's

letup 4 lull **5** pause **6** relief **7** respite **8** decrease, interval, slowdown, stopping, surcease, vacation **9** abatement, cessation, interlude, lessening, remission **10** slackening **11** retardation

Let Us Now Praise Famous Men
  author: **9** James Agee

Let us therefore be joyful
  Latin: **15** Gaudeamus igitur

Leucaeus
  epithet of: **4** Zeus
  means: **16** of the white poplar

Leuce
  form: **5** nymph
  changed into: **6** poplar
  color of poplar: **5** white

Leucippe
  father: **6** Minyas **7** Thestor
  mother: **10** Orchomenus
  son: **8** Teuthras

Leucippides
  refers to: **6** Phoebe **7** Hilaira

Leucippus
  father: **8** Perieres
  mother: **10** Gorgophone
  brother: **8** Aphareus
  fathered: **11** Leucippides
  daughter: **6** Phoebe **7** Arsinoe, Hilaira
  pursued: **6** Daphne
    disguised as: **4** girl
  killed by: **6** nymphs

Leucophryne
  epithet of: **7** Artemis

Leucothea *see* **3** Ino

Leucus
  mentioned in: **5** Iliad
  companion of: **8** Odysseus
  usurped throne of: **9** Idomeneus
  killed by: **8** Antiphus

Le Vau, Louis
  architect of: **6** Louvre **10** Versailles **12** Hotel Lambert **22** Chateau de Vaux-le-Vicomte **24** College des Quatres Nations

levee 3 dam **4** bank, dike, pier, quay, wall **5** ditch, jetty, ridge, wharf **6** durbar **9** reception **10** embankment

level 3 aim, bed **4** even, flat, rank, raze, tied, vein, zone **5** align, floor, flush, grade, layer, plane, point, stage, story, wreck **6** direct, height, lay low, reduce, smooth, topple **7** aligned, even out, flatten, landing, on a line, station, stratum, uniform **8** equalize, make even, posi-

tion, tear down, together
9 devastate, elevation, knock
down **10** consistent, horizontal, on a par with, unwrinkled **11** achievement, neck
and neck **12** on an even keel

level-headed 4 sage **5** sound
6 poised, stable, steady **7** prudent **8** balanced, cautious,
composed, sensible **9** collected,
judicious, practical, unruffled
10 cool-headed, dependable,
thoughtful **11** circumspect
12 even-tempered **13** dispassionate **14** self-controlled

levelheadedness 6 aplomb
9 good sense, soundness, stability **10** equanimity **11** common sense **13** judiciousness

Levene, Sam
real name: **12** Samuel Levine
born: **6** Russia
roles: **12** Guys and Dolls
13 Nathan Detroit **15** The
Sunshine Boys

lever 3 bar, pry **5** jimmy,
raise **7** crowbar

Lever, Charles
author of: **14** Charles
O'Malley

**Leverrier, Urbain Jean
Joseph**
field: **9** astronomy
nationality: **6** French
co-discovered: **7** Neptune
worked with: **14** John Couch
Adams

Levi
father: **5** Jacob **6** Melchi,
Symeon
mother: **4** Leah
son: **6** Kohath, Merari
7 Gershom
brother: **3** Dan, Gad **5** Asher,
Judah **6** Joseph, Reuben,
Simeon **7** Zebulun **8** Benjamin, Issachar, Naphtali
sister: **5** Dinah
violated: **5** Dinah
also called: **7** Matthew
descendant of: **6** Levite

Leviathan 6 dragon **10** sea
monster
means: **13** spirally bound
represents: **14** terrible
powers

Leviathan
author: **12** Thomas Hobbes

Levin, Ira
author of: **13** Rosemary's
Baby

Levin, Konstantin
character in: **12** Anna
Karenina
author: **7** Tolstoy

Levi-Strauss, Claude
method: **13** structuralism
author of: **13** Mythologiques,

The Savage Mind **16** Tristes
Tropiques **22** Structural An-
thropology **29** Elementary
Structures of Kinship

Levitch, Joseph
real name of: **10** Jerry Lewis

levity 3 fun **5** mirth **6** joking,
whimsy **8** hilarity, trifling
9 flippancy, frivolity, lightness,
silliness **10** jocularity, pleasantry, triviality **11** flightiness,
foolishness **16** lightheartedness

levy 3 fee, tax **4** duty, make,
toll, wage **5** draft, exact, start
6 assess, call up, charge, demand, enlist, excise, impose,
muster, pursue, tariff **7** carry
on, collect **9** calling up, conscript, prosecute **10** assessment, imposition
12 conscription

Levy, Marion
real name of: **15** Paulette
Goddard

**Lew Archer, Private
Detective**
author: **13** Ross MacDonald

lewd 5 bawdy **6** ribald, risque,
vulgar, wanton **7** goatish, immoral, lustful, obscene **8** indecent, prurient **9** lecherous,
libertine, salacious **10** lascivious, libidinous, licentious, lubricious **11** Rabelaisian
12 pornographic

Lewis, C S
author of: **10** Perelandra
13 Prince Caspian, The Last
Battle **14** Surprised by Joy,
The Silver Chair, Til We
Have Faces **17** The Horse
and His Boy **18** The Magi-
cian's Nephew **19** The
Screwtape Letters **20** Out of
the Silent Planet **21** The
Chronicles of Narnia **25** The
Voyage of the Dawn
Treader **29** The Lion the
Witch and the Wardrobe

Lewis, Jerry
real name: **13** Joseph Levitch
partner: **10** Dean Martin
born: **8** Newark NJ
roles: **8** The Caddy **10** The
Bellboy, The Sad Sack
11 Cinderfella **12** The
Geisha Boy **16** Artists and
Models **17** The Nutty Professor **20** The Disorderly
Orderly

Lewis, Sinclair
author of: **7** Babbitt **9** Dodsworth **10** Arrowsmith, Main
Street **11** Elmer Gantry
14 Cass Timberlane

lexicon 5 gloss, index **8** code
book, glossary, synonymy,
wordbook, wordlist **9** thesaurus, wordstock **10** dictionary,

vocabulary **11** concordance,
onomasticon

lex loci 11 law of a place

lex non scripta 9 common
law **12** unwritten law

lex scripta 10 statute law,
written law

Leyden, Lucas (Lukas) van
born: **6** Leiden, Leyden
14 The Netherlands
artwork: **12** Last Judgment
14 The Card Players, The
Game of Chess **26** Mo-
hammed and the Murdered
Monk

Lhasa, Lassa
capital of: **5** Tibet

liability 4 debt, drag, duty,
onus **5** debit, minus **6** arrear,
burden **8** drawback, handicap,
obstacle **9** hindrance **10** impediment, obligation **11** encumbrance, shortcoming
12 disadvantage, indebtedness
13 inconvenience **14** responsibility, stumbling block

liable 3 apt **4** open **5** prone
6 likely **7** exposed, ripe for,
subject **8** disposed, inclined
9 obligated, sensitive **10** answerable, chargeable, vulnerable **11** accountable,
responsible, susceptible

liaison 4 bond, link **5** amour,
union **7** contact **8** alliance, intrigue, mediator **9** adventure,
dalliance, go-between **10** connection, flirtation, love affair
11 association, cooperation, interchange **12** coordination, entanglement **13** communication

liar 6 fibber **8** perjurer **9** falsi-
fier **10** fabricator **11** storyteller **12** prevaricator

libation 4 wine **5** drink, water
6 liquid **8** ambrosia, beverage,
offering, potation **9** sacrifice

Libation Bearers, The see
10 Choephoroe

libel 4 slur **5** smear **6** defame,
malign, revile, vilify **7** asperse,
blacken, calumny, obloquy,
slander **8** derogate **9** aspersion,
discredit, disparage **10** calumniate, defamation
12 vilification

Libeled Lady
director: **10** Jack Conway
cast: **8** Myrna Loy **10** Jean
Harlow **12** Spencer Tracy
13 William Powell **14** Walter Connolly
remade as: **9** Easy to Wed

Libera
origin: **7** Italian
goddess of: **4** wine **9** fertility,
vineyards

husband: 5 Liber
corresponds to:
10 Persephone

liberal 5 ample, broad **6** casual, lavish **7** leftist, lenient **8** abundant, advanced, flexible, generous, handsome, left-wing, prodigal, reformer, tolerant, unbiased **9** bounteous, bountiful, impartial, not strict, plenteous, reformist, unbigoted, unsparing **10** fair-minded, forbearing, left-winger, munificent, not literal, openhanded, open-minded, unrigorous, unstinting **11** broad-minded, enlightened, extravagant, libertarian, magnanimous, progressive **12** freethinking, humanitarian, open to reason, unprejudiced **14** latitudinarian

Liberalia
origin: 5 Roman
event: 8 festival

liberality 10 generosity **11** benevolence, munificence **12** philanthropy **13** bountifulness **14** openhandedness

liberate 5 let go **6** let out, redeem, rescue, spring **7** absolve, deliver, manumit, release, set free **8** let loose **9** discharge, disengage, extricate, unshackle **10** emancipate **11** disencumber

liberated 5 freed, let go **7** rescued, set free **8** let loose, released **10** discharged, extricated **11** emancipated

liberation 6 escape, rescue **7** freedom, freeing, release **8** delivery **9** letting go, releasing **11** manumission **12** emancipation

Liberia *see box*

Libertas
origin: 5 Roman
personifies: 7 liberty

liberte egalite fraternite 25 liberty equality fraternity
motto of: 16 French Revolution

liberties 6 misuse **7** license **9** violation **10** distortion **11** familiarity, impropriety **13** falsification

libertine 4 goat, lewd, rake, roue **5** loose, satyr **6** lecher, wanton **7** immoral, lustful, seducer **8** unchaste **9** debauchee, dissolute, lecherous, reprobate, womanizer **10** immoralist, lascivious, libidinous, licentious, profligate, sensualist, voluptuary

liberty 5 leave, right **7** freedom, license **8** autonomy, delivery, free time, furlough, sanction, vacation **9** privilege

10 liberation, permission, shore leave **11** citizenship, manumission **12** carte blanche, dispensation, emancipation, independence **15** enfranchisement **17** self-determination

liberty equality fraternity
French: 24 liberte egalite fraternite
motto of: 16 French Revolution

Libra
symbol: 6 scales **7** balance
planet: 5 Venus
rules: 8 marriage
born: 7 October **9** September

Libreville
capital of: 13 Gabon Republic

Libya *see box, p. 568*

lice
variety: 4 bird, crab **5** human, pubic, spiny **7** chewing, sucking **8** barklice, booklice **9** guinea pig **13** mammal chewing

license 3 let **4** pass, visa **5** allow, grant, leave, right **6** enable, laxity, permit **7** anarchy, approve, certify, charter, empower, endorse, freedom, liberty, warrant **8** accredit, audacity, disorder, latitude, passport, sanction, temerity **9** admission, allowance, authorize, franchise, looseness, privilege, slackness **10** brazenness, commission, debauchery, unruliness **11** certificate, free passage, lawlessness, libertinism, presumption, safeconduct **12** carte blanche, dispensation, recklessness

licentious 4 lewd **5** dirty, loose **6** amoral, sleazy, wanton **7** brutish, goatish, immoral, lawless, lustful, raunchy, ruttish **8** depraved, prodigal **9** abandoned, debauched, dissolute, excessive, lecherous, libertine, salacious **10** dissipated, lascivious, libidinous, lubricious, profligate, ungoverned **11** promiscuous **12** unprincipled, unrestrained, unscrupulous **13** irresponsible, unconstrained

licentiousness 7 abandon **8** lewdness **10** immorality, wantonness

licit 5 legal, legit, valid **6** kosher, lawful **9** allowable, statutory **10** acceptable, admissible, authorized, legitimate, sanctioned **11** permissible **12** authorizable, sanctionable **14** constitutional

lick 3 bit, dab, hit, jot, lap **4** beat, blow, drub, fire, hint, iota, rout, slap, snip, sock,

Liberia
capital/largest city: 8 Monrovia
others: 4 Sino **5** Gribo, Rebbo **6** Bopora, Gbanga, Harper, Kakata **7** Bgarnga, Kolahun, Nanakru, Tappita, Vonjama **8** Buchanan, Garraway, Marshall, Nanakaru, Sass Town **9** Grand Cess, River Cess, Roysville **10** Careysburg, Greenville, Sanoquelli **11** Robertsport **12** Sanniquellie
school: 7 Liberia **10** Cuttington **15** Our Lady of Fatima **16** Booker Washington
  religious school/secret society: 4 poro **5** sande
measure: 4 kuba
monetary unit: 4 cent **6** dollar
mountain: 3 Uni **4** Bong, Putu **5** Niete, Nimba **9** Bomi Hills
highest point: 6 Wutivi
river: 4 Cess, Lofa, Mano **5** Duobe, Lotta, Manna, Morro, Sinoe **6** Cestos, Douobe **7** Cavalla, Cavally **8** San Pedro **9** Saint John, Saint Paul, Sehnkwehn
sea: 8 Atlantic
physical feature:
  wind: 9 harmattan
people: 2 Gi **3** Gio, Kra, Kru, Kwa, Vai, Vei **4** Gola, Kroo, Krou, Loma, Mano, Toma **5** Bassa, Gibbi, Gissi, Grebo **6** Gbande, Kpelle, Kpuesi, Krooby, Kruman **7** Krooboy, Krooman **8** Mandingo **15** Americo-Liberian
  leader: 3 Doe **6** Tubman **7** Roberts, Tolbert
language: 3 Kru, Kwa **5** Mande **7** English
religion: 5 Islam **7** animism **10** Protestant **12** Christianity
feature:
  clothing: 5 lappa
  rubber plantation: 9 Firestone

Libya
   capital/largest city: **7** Tripoli
      summer capital: **8** Benghazi
   others: **4** Homs, Marj, Surt **5** Beida, Darna, Derna, Khums, Kufra, Sebha, Sidri, Zawia **6** Garian, Murzuq, Tobruk **7** Es Sidar, Gharyan, Misrata **8** Ajdabiya, Misurata, Rashanuf **12** Marsa el Brega
   school: **7** Alfateh **9** Garyounis
   division: **6** Fezzan **9** Cyrenaica **12** Tripolitania
   measure: **3** dra, pik, saa **4** kele **5** bozze, donum, jabia, teman, uckia **6** barile, gorraf, misura **7** mattaro, termino **8** kharouba
   weight: **4** kele **6** gorraf **8** kharouba
   monetary unit: **5** dinar
   mountain: **5** Green **13** Jabal al Akhdar, Tibesti Massif
   highest point: **9** Bette Peak
   sea: **13** Mediterranean
   physical feature:
      desert: **6** Libyan, Sahara **9** Calanscio
      gulf: **5** Bomba, Sidra, Sirte
      oasis: **4** Ghat **5** Kufra, Sebha **7** Tazerbo **8** Al-Kufrah, Ghudamis
      plain: **6** al Marj, Gefara **7** Jaffara
      plateau: **12** Gebel Nefuisa, Jabal Nafusah
      wind: **6** ghibli
   people: **4** Arab, Tebu **6** Berber, Tuareg **7** Gaetuli **8** Getulans, Harratin
      leader: **6** Battus **7** Jalloud, Qadhafi **8** Aegyptus **9** al-Qaddafi, Karamanli **13** Idris al-Senusi
      religious leader: **8** al-Senusi
      ruler: **4** Rome **5** Italy **6** Greece **9** Phoenicia **12** Ottoman Turks
   language: **6** Arabic, Berber **7** English, Italian
      alphabet: **8** tifinagh
   religion: **5** Islam
   feature: **14** Tropic of Cancer
      clothing: **5** lanaf **9** barracano
      festival: **3** Mez **7** Fantasi
      Islamic law: **6** sharia
      leader: **6** sheikh
      ruins: **11** Leptis Magna
   food:
      dish: **5** bazin **8** couscous
      red pepper: **6** filfil

Licymnius
   father: **9** Electryon
   mother: **5** Midea
   wife: **8** Perimede
   son: **5** Melas **6** Oeonus **7** Argeius
   nephew: **8** Hercules

lid **3** cap, top **4** cork, curb, plug **5** cover, limit **7** ceiling, maximum, stopper, stopple **9** operculum, restraint

lie **3** fib **4** loll, rest, stay

suck, whip **5** crack, punch, sally, shred, spank, speck, taste, touch, trace **6** defeat, ignite, kindle, master, sample, stroke, subdue, thrash, tongue, wallop **7** clobber, conquer, modicum, smidgen, trounce **8** outmatch, overcome, particle, vanquish **9** overpower, overthrow, scintilla, subjugate **10** smattering **12** denunciation

5 abide, exist, range, story **6** belong, deceit, extend, inhere, lounge, obtain, remain, repose, sprawl **7** falsify, fiction, perjury, recline, romance, untruth **8** misstate, tall tale **9** deception, embellish, embroider, fabricate, falsehood, invention **10** equivocate **11** fabrication, prevaricate **12** equivocation **13** falsification, prevarication **17** misrepresentation

Liechtenstein *see box*

lie down **6** retire **7** go to bed, recline **8** take a nap **11** take a snooze **15** catch forty winks

life **4** path, soul, zest **5** being, human, plant, story, verve, vigor **6** animal, career, course, energy, memoir, person, spirit **8** creature, duration, life span, lifetime, lifework, organ-

ism, survival, vitality, vivacity **9** animation, biography, existence, life story, longevity **11** subsistence **13** autobiography
French: **3** vie

Life at the Dakota
   author: **17** Stephen Birmingham

Life Before Man
   author: **14** Margaret Atwood

Lifeboat
   director: **15** Alfred Hitchcock
   cast: **10** John Hodiak **12** Mary Anderson **13** William Bendix **16** Tallulah Bankhead

life-giving **5** vital **9** vivifying **12** invigorating

lifeless **4** dead, dull, flat, late **5** inert, stiff, vapid **6** boring, hollow, static, torpid, wooden **7** defunct **8** deceased, departed, inactive, lifeless, sluggish **9** colorless, inanimate **10** lackluster, spiritless

Liechtenstein
   capital/largest city: **5** Vaduz
   others: **4** Haag **6** Balzer, Eschen, Iradug, Schaan **7** Balzers, Bendern, Nendeln, Planken, Triesen **12** Schellenberg
   division:
      ancient province: **6** Rhaeti **7** Rhaetia
   government:
      legislature: **7** Landtag
   monetary unit: **6** rappen **7** franken
   mountain: **4** Alps **8** Naafkopf, Rhatikon **12** Three Sisters
   highest point: **15** Vorder-Grauspitz
   river: **5** Rhine
   physical feature:
      valley: **6** Lavena, Samina
   people: **8** Alemanni
      leader: **7** Florian **15** Francis Joseph II **16** von Liechtenstein
   language: **6** German **10** Alemannish
   religion: **13** Roman Catholic
   place:
      castle: **9** Gutemburg, Gutenberg
   feature:
      legendary dwarf: **10** wildmannli
      wine: **7** Vaduzer

lifelessness 5 death 7 inertia 8 dullness, limpness, vapidity 9 blandness 10 flaccidity, inactivity 13 colorlessness

Life of Dante
author: 17 Giovanni Boccaccio

Life of Emile Zola
director: 15 William Dieterle
cast: 8 Paul Muni 11 Donald Crisp 12 Gloria Holden 15 Gale Sondergaard 17 Joseph Schildkraut (Dreyfus)
Oscar for: 7 picture

Life of Man, The
author: 14 Leonid Andreyev

Life of Riley, The
character: 4 Babs 6 Dangle, Junior 8 Peg Riley 9 Jim Gillis 10 Cunningham, Digby (Digger) O'Dell 11 Waldo Binney 13 Chester A Riley 14 Honeybee Gillis
cast: 9 John Brown, Lanny Rees, Sid Tomack 10 Tom D'Andrea 12 Emory Parnell, Wesley Morgan 13 Gloria Winters, Jackie Gleason, Lugene Sanders, Robert Sweeney, William Bendix 14 Gloria Blondell, Rosemary DeCamp 16 Douglas Dumbrille, Marjorie Reynolds, Sterling Holloway

Life of Samuel Johnson, The
author: 12 James Boswell

life of the party 7 show-off 9 extrovert 13 exhibitionist 17 hail-fellow-well-met

Life on the Mississippi
author: 9 Mark Twain

life span 4 life 8 lifetime 14 life expectancy

Life Studies
author: 12 Robert Lowell

Life With Father
author: 13 Clarence Day Jr
director: 13 Michael Curtiz
cast: 9 ZaSu Pitts 10 Irene Dunne 11 Edmund Gwenn 13 William Powell 15 Elizabeth Taylor
setting: 11 New York City

lifework 6 career 7 calling 8 vocation 10 livelihood, occupation, profession

lift 4 high, palm, pick, rear, rise, soar, take 5 boost, climb, exalt, filch, heave, hoist, pinch, raise, steal, swipe 6 ascend, ascent, banish, cancel, pilfer, pirate, pocket, remove, revoke, snatch, thieve, uplift, vanish 7 elation, elevate, purloin, raise up, raising, rescind, scatter, upraise 8 disperse 9 disappear, dissipate, float

away 10 ascendance, move upward, plagiarize, put an end to 11 appropriate, countermand, inspiration, make off with, reassurance 12 give a boost to, shot in the arm 13 encouragement, enheartenment

ligament
holds: 5 bones

Ligeia
author: 13 Edgar Allan Poe
character: 19 Lady Rowena Trevanion

Ligeti, Gyorgy
composer of: 7 Lontano 11 Atmospheres 13 Ramifications

light *see box*

light-colored 4 pale 5 beige, blond 6 blonde, flaxen, pastel 7 neutral, whitish 9 yellowish

light-complexioned 4 fair, pale 12 white-skinned

lighten 4 buoy, ease, lift 5 abate, allay, blaze, elate, flare, flash, gleam, shine 6 buoy up, lessen, reduce, revive, temper, unload, uplift 7 assuage, enliven, gladden, inspire, light up, relieve 8 brighten, mitigate, moderate, unburden 9 alleviate, coruscate, disburden, irradiate 10 illuminate, make bright 11 become light, disencumber, make lighter, scintillate

light-filled 5 sunny 6 bright 7 well-lit 11 illuminated

lighthearted 3 gay 4 airy, glad 5 jolly, merry, sunny 6 blithe, cheery, joyful, joyous, lively 7 buoyant, cheered, chipper 8 carefree, cheerful, sanguine 9 sprightly 10 insouciant, untroubled 11 free and easy 12 effervescent

lightheartedness 3 joy 4 glee 5 mirth 8 gladness 9 happiness, merriment 10 blitheness, exuberance, joyfulness, joyousness 11 high spirits

Light in August
author: 15 William Faulkner
character: 8 Doc Hines, Joe Brown 9 Lena Grove, McEachern 10 Byron Bunch 12 Joanna Burden, Joe Christmas

lightless 4 dark 5 black, murky 7 stygian 9 unlighted 13 unilluminated

lightly 6 airily, easily, gently, nimbly, softly, thinly, weakly 7 blandly, faintly, quickly, readily, swiftly, timidly 8 blithely, facilely, gingerly, meagerly, slightly, sparsely 9 buoyantly, sparingly 10 carelessly, flippantly, hesitantly, moderately 11 frivolously, slightingly 13 indifferently, thoughtlessly, unconcernedly, without effort 14 without concern

---

light 3 gay 4 airy, beam, easy, fair, fall, find, fire, glow, lamp, land, pale, puny, side, soft, stop 5 aglow, angle, blaze, blond, faint, flame, funny, glare, guide, happy, jolly, match, model, perch, petty, put on, roost, shine, slant, small, spare, spark, sunny, torch 6 alight, aspect, beacon, blithe, bright, candle, chance, frugal, gentle, get off, ignite, jaunty, kindle, luster, meager, paltry, scanty, settle, simple, slight, turn on 7 amusing, buoyant, chipper, clarify, come off, descend, get down, gleeful, insight, lantern, lighten, lighter, lucifer, not dark, not rich, paragon, radiant, radiate, sparkle, sunbeam, trivial 8 approach, attitude, bleached, blondish, brighten, carefree, cheerful, come upon, discover, dismount, ethereal, exemplar, gossamer, graceful, illumine, jubilant, luminous, meet with, moderate, moonbeam, not heavy, paradigm, radiance, sportive, step down, switch on, trifling, untaxing 9 brilliant, catch fire, direction, encounter, frivolous, irradiate, light-hued, set fire to, sprightly, stumble on, sylphlike, viewpoint 10 abstemious, brightness, brilliance, burdenless, come across, come to rest, effortless, effulgence, floodlight, happen upon, illuminate, light-toned, luminosity, manageable, restricted, set burning, weightless 11 conflagrate, elucidation, illuminated, information, make radiant, superficial, undemanding, underweight 15 inconsequential
god of: 6 Apollo 7 Mithras, Phoebus, Pythius 8 Heimdall 9 Musagetes
Latin: 3 lux
measurement: 7 candela 11 candlepower

lightness 8 airiness, radiance 10 brightness, fluffiness, luminosity 12 illumination, luminousness

lightning rod
  invented by: 8 Franklin

light of day 8 daylight, sunlight, sunshine

light sleep 3 nap 4 doze 6 catnap, snooze 10 forty winks

light wind 4 waft 6 breeze, zephyr 10 gentle wind 11 breath of air

Lightwood, Mortimer
  character in: 15 Our Mutual Friend
  author: 7 Dickens

lignum vitae 10 wood of life
  tree species: 8 Guaiacum

Ligure 8 gemstone

likable, likeable 4 nice 6 genial 7 amiable, lovable, winsome 8 charming, engaging, loveable, pleasant, pleasing 9 agreeable, appealing, simpatico 10 attractive 11 complaisant, sympathetic

like 4 akin, care, dote, same, wish 5 enjoy, equal, fancy, favor, savor 6 admire, allied, choose, esteem, relish 7 approve, cognate, endorse, matched, related, similar, support, uniform 8 be fond of, parallel, selfsame, think fit 9 analogous, congruent, have a mind, identical 10 comparable, equivalent, homologous, resembling 11 be partial to, much the same 12 feel inclined, have a crush on, take a shine to 13 corresponding, find agreeable 14 take pleasure in

Like a Bulwark
  author: 13 Marianne Moore

likelihood 8 prospect 10 good chance 11 possibility, probability 12 potentiality

likely 3 apt, fit 4 able 6 liable, proper 8 credible, destined, inclined, probable, probably, rational, reliable, suitable 9 befitting, plausible, promising, qualified 10 believable, presumably, reasonable 11 appropriate, verisimilar 16 in all probability

like-mindedness 6 accord 7 concord, harmony, rapport 8 affinity 9 agreement 12 congeniality 13 compatibility

likeness 5 image, model, study 6 effigy 7 analogy, picture, replica 8 affinity, portrait 9 agreement, depiction, facsimile, portrayal, rendition, semblance 10 similarity, similitude 11 delineation, resemblance 14 correspondence, representation

likes 9 favorites 10 prejudices 11 preferences 12 inclinations, partialities

likewise 3 and, eke, too 4 also 5 ditto 6 as well 7 besides, equally, the same 8 moreover 9 similarity 10 in addition

liking 4 bent 5 fancy, taste 7 leaning 8 affinity, appetite, fondness, penchant, soft spot, weakness 9 affection 10 partiality, preference, proclivity, propensity 11 inclination 12 predilection

Li'l Abner
  creator: 6 Al Capp
  character: 5 Pappy 7 Wolf Gal 10 Joe Btfsplk, Mammy Yokum, Marryin' Sam 11 Adam Lazonga, Hairless Joe 12 Tobacco Rhoda 13 Joanie Phoanie 14 Daisy Mae Scragg, Evil-Eye Fleegle, Stupefyin' Jones 15 Fearless Fosdick, Henry Cabbage Cod, Lonesome Polecat, Moonbeam McSwine 16 General Bullmoose, Sir Cecil Cesspool 17 Sen Jack S Phogbound 18 J Roaringham Fatback 21 Appassionata von Climax
  brewery: 23 Big Barnsmell's Skonk Works
  event: 15 Sadie Hawkins Day
  juice: 16 Kickapoo Joy Juice
  kingdom: 14 Lower Slobbovia
  mountain: 11 Onnecessary
  people: 7 Schmoos 8 Kingmies
  place: 8 Dogpatch
  railroad: 11 West Po'k Chop
  ruler: 14 King Nogoodnick

lilac 7 Syringa
  varieties: 4 late, vine, wild 6 common, Indian, summer 7 Chinese, cut-leaf, Persian 9 Himalayan, Hungarian 12 Japanese tree 16 Catalina mountain

Lili
  director: 14 Charles Walters
  cast: 9 Mel Ferrer 11 Leslie Caron, Zsa Zsa Gabor 16 Jean-Pierre Aumont

Lilies of the Field
  director: 11 Ralph Nelson
  cast: 8 Lisa Mann 10 Lilia Skala 13 Sidney Poitier
  Oscar for: 5 actor (Poitier)

Liliom
  author: 12 Ferenc Molnar

lillet
  type: 8 aperitif
  origin: 6 France
  flavor: 6 orange
  color: 3 red 5 white

Lilliput
  fictional land in: 16 Gulliver's Travels
  author: 5 Swift

lilliputian 3 wee 4 tiny 5 dwarf, short, small, teeny, weeny 6 little, midget, minute, petite 9 miniature 10 diminutive, teeny-weeny 11 pocket-sized

Lilongwe
  capital of: 6 Malawi

lily *see box*

lily-livered 6 afraid, craven, scared, yellow 7 chicken, fearful, gutless 8 cowardly 9 dastardly 12 fainthearted 13 pusillanimous, yellow-bellied 14 chicken-hearted, chicken-livered 22 showing the white feather

lily-white 4 good, pure 6 biased, decent, proper, racist 7 bigoted, upright 8 all-white, innocent, virtuous 9 blameless, exclusive, exemplary, faultless, guiltless, honorable, righteous 10 impeccable, inculpable, prejudiced, segregated, upstanding 11 uncorrupted 12 unintegrated 13 unimpeachable 14 discriminatory, irreproachable

Lima
  capital of: 4 Peru
  foothills of: 5 Andes
  founder: 7 Pizarro
  nickname: 11 city of kings
  ocean: 7 Pacific
  port: 6 Callao
  river: 5 Rimac
  square: 12 Plaza de Armas

limb 3 arm, gam, leg, pin 4 part, spur, twig, wing 5 bough, shoot, sprig 6 branch, member 9 appendage, extension, outgrowth 10 projection, prosthesis

limber 5 agile, lithe, relax 6 loosen, pliant, supple 7 bending, elastic, lissome, pliable 8 flexible 9 lithesome, malleable

lime 18 Citrus aurantifolia
  varieties: 3 key 4 wild 7 Mexican, Persian, Rangpur, Spanish 8 Mandarin 10 West Indian 14 Australian wild 15 Australian round 16 Australian desert, Australian finger

lily 6 Lilium
varieties: 3 Alp, cow, day, pig **4** Arum, bell, boat, corn, fawn, fire, flax, herb, palm, pine, pond, rain, roan, rock, sand, Sego, star, toad, wood **5** adobe, Aztec, blood, bugle, calla, coast, cobra, crane, Cuban, fairy, globe, glory, Gray's, Ifafa, lemon, magic, natal, queen, regal, royal, showy, snake, spear, swamp, sword, tiger, torch, trout, water, wheel **6** Alpine, Amazon, Canada, Crinum, desert, Easter, eureka, ginger, hidden, Kaffir, Marhan, meadow, one-day, orange, Oregon, shasta, Sierra, spider, sunset, tartar, turban, voodoo, yellow, Zephyr **7** African, Bermuda, chamise, checker, garland, leopard, madonna, Nankeen, panther, redwood, thimble, toad-cup, triplet, trumpet, western **8** Atamasco, Barbados, bluebead, Carolina, climbing, Columbia, flamingo, gloriosa, Guernsey, Humboldt, Jacobean, Japanese, long's red, Mariposa, Martagon, Michigan, mountain, paradise, Peruvian, plantain, Siberian, Solomon's, St Bruno's, St James's, turk's cap **9** alligator, avalanche, butterfly, caucasian, celestial, chaparral, checkered, Eucharist, Kamchatka, naked-lady, orange-cup, pineapple, pinewoods, pot-of-gold, red ginger, red spider, St Joseph's **10** belladonna, blackberry, blue funnel, fairy water, giant water, globe spear, gold-banded, Josephine's, orange-bell, pink Easter, pygmy water, royal water, small tiger, St Bernard's, Washington, white water, wild yellow, yellow-bell, yellow pond **11** African corn, Amazon water, blue African, candlestick, dwarf ginger, golden-rayed, milk-and-wine, Palmer spear, Scarborough, southern red, yellow water **12** African blood, Chinese white, golden spider, prickly water, resurrection, speckled wood, white trumpet **13** Bermuda Easter, cape blue water, Chinese sacred, Egyptian water, fragrant water, India red water, lavender globe, magnolia water, minor Turk's-cap, perfumed fairy, pink porcelain, scarlet ginger, showy Japanese, tuberous water, wild orange-red **14** Chinese-lantern, lesser Turk's cap, little Turk's-cap, Santa Cruz water, yellow Turk's-cap **15** Australian water, backhouse hybrid, golden hurricane, scarlet Turk's-cap **16** American Turk's cap, Bellingham hybrid, Cape Cod pink water, fragrant plantain, Japanese Turk's-cap, western orange-cup **17** midsummer plantain **18** European white water, seersucker plantain **20** narrow-leaved plantain

Limenia
epithet of: 9 Aphrodite
means: 11 of the harbor

limit 3 end **4** curb **8** boundary, end point, restrain, ultimate **13** breaking point

limitation 4 curb **5** quota **8** boundary, decrease **9** lessening, reduction, restraint **10** shortening **11** abridgement, restriction, shortcoming **13** qualification, specification

limited 5 fixed **6** finite, narrow **7** bounded, cramped, defined, minimal, special **8** confined **9** delimited, specified **10** controlled, restrained, restricted **13** circumscribed

limitless 7 endless, eternal, unbound **8** infinite, unending **9** boundless, unlimited **11** measureless **12** immeasurable

limits 3 rim, top **4** curb, edge **5** bound, check, quota **6** border, define, fringe, margin, narrow **7** ceiling, confine, delimit, inhibit, maximum, qualify **8** confines, frontier, restrain, restrict **9** perimeter, periphery, prescribe, restraint **10** boundaries **11** limitations **12** restrictions

limn 4 draw **6** sketch **7** picture **9** delineate

Limnaea
epithet of: 7 Artemis
means: 9 of the lake

Limnoria
member of: 7 Nereids

Limon
father: 8 Tegeates
mother: 5 Maera
brother: 8 Scephrus
killed: 8 Scephrus

limp 3 lax **4** gimp, halt, soft,

weak **5** crawl, loose, skulk, slack **6** droopy, falter, flabby, floppy, hobble **7** flaccid **8** drooping, lameness, yielding **9** dead tired, enervated, exhausted

limpid 4 pure **5** clear, lucid **8** clear-cut, pellucid, vitreous **11** crystalline, perspicuous, translucent, transparent, unambiguous **15** straightforward

Lincoln, Abraham *see box, p. 572*

Lind, James
field: 8 medicine
nationality: 8 Scottish
eliminated: 6 scurvy

Lindbergh, Anne Morrow
author of: 14 Gift from the Sea **15** Bring Me a Unicorn **16** North to the Orient **19** War Within and Without

linden 5 Tilia
varieties: 6 Indoor **7** Crimean **8** American, Japanese **9** Mongolian **10** Manchurian **11** Large-leaved **13** Pendent silver **19** Small-leaved European

lindy 5 dance **8** lindy hop **9** jitterbug

line, lines 4 card, cord, dash, draw, file, idea, mark, note, part, race, rank, rope, rule, tier, word **5** align, array, breed, cable, craft, front, house, model, queue, range, score, slash, stock, trade **6** belief, border, column, crease, family, furrow, letter, method, metier, policy, report, scheme, series, stance, strain, strand, streak, stripe, system, thread **7** calling, circuit, conduit, contour, cordage, example, lineage, marshal, outline, pattern, purpose, pursuit, queue up, routine, towline, wrinkle **8** ancestry, business, dialogue, doctrine, fishline, ideology, inscribe, position, postcard, trenches, vanguard, vocation **9** conductor, crow's foot, direction, frontline, genealogy, intention, principle **10** barricades, convention, firing line, livelihood, long stroke, occupation, procession, profession, underscore **11** demarcation

lineage 4 line **5** blood, stock **7** descent **8** ancestry, heredity, pedigree **9** genealogy, parentage **10** derivation, extraction

linen
fabric: 6 canvas, damask **7** butcher, cambric **8** birds-eye **9** huckaback
plant: 4 flax

Lincoln, Abraham
  nickname: **9** Honest Abe **20** Illinois Rail Splitter
  presidential rank: **9** sixteenth
  party: **4** Whig **10** Republican
  state represented: **2** IL
  defeated: **4** (John) Bell **7** (John Charles) Fremont, (Stephen Arnold) Douglas **9** (George Brinton) McClellan **12** (John Cabell) Breckinridge
  vice president: **6** (Hannibal) Hamlin **7** (Andrew) Johnson
  cabinet:
    state: **6** (William Henry) Seward
    treasury: **5** (Salmon Portland) Chase **9** (Hugh) McCulloch, (William Pitt) Fessenden
    war: **7** (Edwin McMasters) Stanton, (Simon) Cameron
    attorney general: **5** (Edward) Bates, (James) Speed
    navy: **6** (Gideon) Welles
    postmaster general: **5** (Montgomery) Blair **8** (William) Dennison
    interior: **5** (Caleb Blood) Smith, (John Palmer) Usher
  born: **2** KY **8** log cabin **11** Larue County **17** Sinking Spring farm
  died: **12** Washington DC, Fords Theater
    died by: **13** assassination
    assassinated by: **15** John Wilkes Booth
  buried: **13** Springfield IL
  education:
    educated by: **4** self
    studied: **3** law
  interests: **7** theater
    received patent for: **25** adjustable buoyant chambers (for lifting boats)
  political career: **16** state legislature **24** US House of Representatives
  civilian career: **6** lawyer **8** surveyor **10** postmaster
  military service:
    War: **9** Black Hawk
    US Army: **7** private
    captain of company of: **10** volunteers
  notable events of lifetime/term: **8** Civil War **24** Emancipation Proclamation
    Act: **9** Homestead, Income Tax, Judiciary **12** Conscription
    debates: **14** Lincoln-Douglas
    speech: **17** Gettysburg Address
  father: **6** Thomas
  mother: **5** Nancy (Hanks)
    stepmother: **5** Sarah (Bush Johnston)
  siblings: **5** Sarah **6** Thomas
    stepbrother: **4** John
    stepsister: **7** Matilda **9** Elizabeth
  wife: **4** Mary (Ann Todd)
  children: **6** Thomas **10** Robert Todd **11** Edward Baker **14** William Wallace

finest from: **7** Belgium, Ireland
processing term: **6** shives, sliver **7** carding, hackled, retting **8** beetling, breaking, rippling, spinning **9** scutching

line of march **4** path **5** route, track **11** parade route

line of reasoning **4** case **7** premise **8** argument **10** hypothesis

line up **4** book **5** align **6** engage, even up **7** arrange, pro-cure, program, queue up **8** schedule **9** form a line, put in a row **10** arrange for

line-up **5** slate **6** roster **8** schedule

linger **3** lag **4** idle, last, stay, wait **5** dally, delay, tarry, trail **6** dawdle, hang on, loiter, remain **7** persist, survive **9** die slowly **10** dillydally, hang around

lingering **4** slow **7** abiding, chronic, delayed, lagging, lasting, staying, waiting **8** daw-dling, delaying, dragging, drawn out, dwelling, enduring, hovering, tarrying **9** loitering, remaining **10** protracted, sauntering **15** procrastinating

lingo **4** cant, talk **5** argot, idiom, slang **6** jargon, patois, tongue **7** dialect **8** language, parlance **10** vernacular

linguist **8** polyglot **10** grammarian, translator **11** etymologist, interpreter, philologist, phonetician, phonologist, semanticist **12** morphologist **13** lexicographer

liniment **4** balm **5** salve **7** unguent **8** ointment **9** emollient

link **3** tie **4** bind, bond, fuse, loop, ring **5** group, joint, tie in, unite **6** couple, relate, splice **7** bracket, combine, conjoin, connect, involve, liaison **8** junction, relation **9** associate, implicate **10** connection, connective **11** association **12** interconnect, relationship

linkage **3** tie **4** bond **6** hookup **10** connection **11** affiliation, association, correlation

link up **4** dock, join **6** couple, hook up **7** connect **9** affiliate **14** fasten together

Linnaeus, Carolus
  field: **6** botany
  nationality: **7** Swedish
  developed: **8** taxonomy **18** nomenclature system

linotype
  invented by: **12** Mergenthaler

Linton, Edgar
  character in: **16** Wuthering Heights
  author: **6** Bronte

Linus
  vocation: **4** poet **8** musician
  father: **6** Apollo
  mother: **8** Psamathe
  inventor of: **6** melody, rhythm
  identified with: **5** crops **9** withering **10** harvesting
  student: **8** Hercules
  killed by: **8** Hercules

Liod
  also: **4** Ljod **5** Hliod
  origin: **12** Scandinavian
  mentioned in: **8** Volsunga
  husband: **7** Volsung
  daughter: **5** Signy
  son: **7** Sigmund

lion **3** cat **6** cougar **7** wildcat **9** celebrity **12** man of the hour **15** king of the jungle
  group of: **5** pride
  constellation of: **3** Leo

lionhearted **4** bold **5** brave

6 heroic 7 valiant 8 fearless, intrepid, stalwart, unafraid, valorous 9 audacious, dauntless 10 courageous 11 indomitable 12 stouthearted

Lion in Winter, The
  director: 13 Anthony Harvey
  cast: 10 Jane Merrow 11 Peter O'Toole (Henry II) 13 Timothy Dalton 14 Anthony Hopkins 16 Katharine Hepburn (Eleanor of Aquitaine)
  Oscar for: 7 actress (Hepburn)

lionize 5 deify, exalt 6 admire, praise, revere 7 acclaim, adulate, ennoble, flatter, glorify 8 enshrine, eulogize 9 celebrate, glamorize 10 aggrandize 11 immortalize

lion's share 4 bulk, most 8 majority 9 major part 11 greater part 13 preponderance

lip 3 lap, rim 4 brim, edge, kiss, lick, wash 5 apron, mouth, spout, utter 6 labial, labium, margin 8 backtalk, labellum 9 insincere 10 embouchure, mouthpiece 11 superficial

Lipchitz, Jacques
  real name: 17 Chaim Yakob Lipchiz
  born: 9 Lithuania 11 Druskieniki 12 Druskininkai
  artwork: 4 Head 6 Bather, Figure 7 Harpist 9 Sacrifice 10 Prometheus 11 Benediction, Joie de Vivre 12 Peace on Earth 14 Man with a Guitar 15 Acrobats on a Ball, Man with Mandolin, Song of the Vowels 17 Notre Dame de Liesse, Sailor with a Guitar 19 Pierrot with Clarinet, Return of the Prodigal 24 Virgin of the Inverted Heart

Lipmann, Fritz Albert
  field: 12 biochemistry
  discovered: 9 Coenzyme A
  awarded: 10 Nobel Prize

Lippi, Filippino
  born: 5 Italy, Prato
  father: 15 Fra Filippo Lippi
  artwork: 20 The Vision of St Bernard 24 The Life of St Thomas Aquinas 26 The Lives of Sts Philip and John

Lippi, Fra Filippo
  born: 5 Italy 8 Florence
  son: 9 Filippino
  artwork: 15 Madonna and Child, The Feast of Herod 19 The Tarquinia Madonna 21 Coronation of the Virgin 25 The Madonna Adoring Her Child

liqueur 3 ale 4 beer, grog 5 booze, drink, hooch 7 alcohol, potable, spirits 8 beverage, potation 9 aqua vitae, drinkable, inebriant, moonshine 10 intoxicant
  almond: 8 amaretto
  anise: 8 absinthe
  apple: 8 calvados
  apricot: 10 abricotine
  caraway: 6 kummel 7 aquavit
  chocolate: 12 creme de cacao
  citrus: 10 goldwasser, liquor d'or
  coffee: 6 Kahlua
  grape: 6 Metaxa
  herb: 6 pernod 7 raspail 10 vielle cure 11 fiori alpini
  honey: 8 Drambuie
  medicinal: 11 Benedictine
  mint: 13 creme de menthe
  orange: 6 strega 7 curacao 9 cointreau 12 Grand Marnier
  raspberry: 9 framboise

liquid 5 drink, fluid 6 melted, molten, thawed 7 potable 8 beverage, solution

liquidate 3 hit, pay 4 kill 5 clear, erase, waste 6 cancel, murder, pay off, rub out, settle, wind up 7 abolish, break up, destroy, wipe out 8 close out, conclude, demolish 9 discharge, dispose of, eradicate, put to rest, terminate 10 account for, do away with 11 assassinate

liquor 3 gin, rum, rye 5 booze, broth, hooch, juice, sauce, vodka 6 brandy, liquid, Scotch 7 bourbon, extract, spirits, whiskey 9 drippings 10 inebriants 11 intoxicants
  measure: 4 pint, pony, shot 5 fifth, quart 6 jigger, magnum

Lir *see* 3 Ler

Lisbon
  capital of: 8 Portugal
  landmark:
    castle: 11 Saint George
    monastery: 9 Jeronimos
    square: 10 Black Horse
    tower: 5 Belem
  Moorish name: 7 Lixbuna
  ocean: 8 Atlantic
  Portuguese: 6 Lisboa
  river: 5 Tagus
  Roman name: 14 Felicitas Julia
  rulers: 5 Moors 6 French, Romans 7 British, Germans, Spanish 11 Phoenicians

lissome 5 agile, lithe, quick 6 limber, lively, nimble, pliant, supple 7 slender 8 flexible, graceful 9 lithesome, sprightly 11 light-footed

list 3 tip 4 bend, heel, lean,

roll, tilt 5 index, slant, slate, slope, table 6 careen, muster, record, roster 7 catalog, incline, leaning 8 register, schedule, tabulate 9 catalogue, inventory

listen 4 hark, hear, heed, list 6 attend 7 give ear, hearken 8 give heed, listen in, overhear 9 be all ears, bend an ear, eavesdrop 10 take notice 12 pay attention

listener 3 ear 6 hearer 7 auditor 10 overhearer 12 eavesdropper

Lister, Joseph
  field: 7 surgeon 8 medicine
  nationality: 7 British
  pioneer of: 17 antiseptic surgery

listless 4 down, dull, lazy 6 dreamy, drowsy, leaden, mopish, torpid 7 languid 8 inactive, indolent, lifeless, sluggish 9 apathetic, enervated, lethargic, soporific 10 phlegmatic, spiritless 11 indifferent, unconcerned 12 uninterested 13 lackadaisical

Liston, Charles
  nickname: 5 Sonny
  sport: 6 boxing
  class: 11 heavyweight

Liszt, Franz (Ferencz)
  born: 7 Hungary, Raiding
  composer of: 5 Dante (symphony), Faust (symphony) 8 Christus 9 Psalm XIII 10 Nuages gris 13 Psalm Thirteen 17 Years of Pilgrimage 18 Annees de Pelerinage 19 Hungarian Rhapsodies 22 The Legend of St Elizabeth

Litae
  daughters of: 4 Zeus
  personify: 6 prayer

litany 4 list 7 account, catalog, recital 9 catalogue, narration, rendition 10 recitation, repetition 11 description, enumeration

lit de justice 32 formal sessions of French parliament
  literally: 12 bed of justice

literacy 7 culture 8 learning 9 erudition 11 edification, eruditeness, learnedness, scholarship 12 intelligence 13 enlightenment

literal 4 real, true 5 exact 6 actual, direct, honest, strict 7 correct, factual, precise, prosaic 8 accurate, faithful, reliable, truthful, verbatim 9 authentic 10 ad litteram, dependable, meticulous, scrupulous, undisputed

11 trustworthy, undeviating, word-for-word 12 matter-of-fact 13 authoritative, conscientious, unimaginative, unimpeachable

literary 6 poetic 7 bookish, of books 8 artistic, lettered, literate 12 intellectual

literate 7 learned 8 cultured, educated, lettered, literary, schooled, well-read 12 well-informed 13 knowledgeable

literati 9 highbrows 12 connoisseurs 13 intellectuals 14 intelligentsia

literature 4 lore 5 books, works 6 papers, theses 7 letters 8 classics, writings 9 treatises 11 scholarship 12 publications 13 belles lettres, dissertations

lithe 5 agile 6 limber, nimble, pliant, supple 7 lissome, pliable 8 bendable, flexible, graceful

Lithgow, John
  roles: 9 Footloose 17 Terms of Endearment 21 Harry and the Hendersons 23 The World According to Garp

lithium
  chemical symbol: 2 Li

Lithuania *see box*

litigation 4 suit 7 contest, dispute, lawsuit 10 contention, day in court 11 controversy, disputation, legal action, prosecution

litter 3 bed 4 heap, junk, lair, mess, nest, pile 5 issue, strew, trash, young 6 debris, jumble, pallet, refuse 7 bedding, clutter, kittens, progeny, puppies, rubbish, scatter 8 leavings 9 offspring, stretcher

little 3 bit, dot, jot, wee 4 dash, drop, hint, iota, mean, mild, tiny, whit 5 brief, crumb, elfin, faint, fleet, hasty, never, petty, pinch, pygmy, quick, scant, short, small, speck, trace 6 bantam, hardly, meager, minute, narrow, paltry, petite, rarely, seldom, skimpy, slight, trifle 7 minimum, modicum, not much, passing, stunted, trivial 8 dwarfish, fragment, inferior, mediocre, not at all, not often, particle, piddling, pittance, scarcely, slightly, somewhat, trifling, unworthy 9 by no means, deficient, hardly any, itsy-bitsy, itty-bitty, miniature, momentary, pint-sized, third-rate, worthless 10 diminutive, inflexible, negligible, short-lived, suggestion, under-sized 11 commonplace, Lilliputian, microscopic, of no account, opinionated, pocket-sized, scarcely any, small amount, unimportant 12 insufficient, run-of-the-mill, short-sighted 13 infinitesimal, insignificant, next to nothing

Little Annie Rooney
  creator: 14 Darrell McClure

Little Artha
  nickname of: 11 Jack Johnson

Little Big Man
  author: 12 Thomas Berger
  director: 10 Arthur Penn
  cast: 11 Faye Dunaway 12 Martin Balsam 13 Dustin Hoffman (Jack Crabb) 14 Chief Dan George 15 Richard Mulligan

Lithuania
  other / former name:
    5 Litva 7 Lietuva 33 Lithuanian Soviet Socialist Republic
  capital / largest city:
    5 Vilna 6 Kaunas 7 Vilnius
  others: 4 Balt, Lett 5 Aesti, Kouno, Memel 6 Kovnac 7 Jelgava, Palanga, Telsiai 8 Ignalina, Kapsukas, Klaipeda, Siauliai 9 Panevezys 10 Elektrenai
  government: 8 republic
  monetary unit: 3 lit 5 marka 6 centas 7 ostmark, skatiku 8 auksinas
  lake: 5 Dysna
  mountain: 15 Samogitian Hills
  highest point: 9 Juozapine
  river: 5 Neman, Neris, Rusne 6 Dubysa, Nieman, Viliya 7 Nemunas, Nevezis, Nevezys 8 Pregolya
  sea: 6 Baltic
  physical feature:
    lagoon: 8 Courland, Kuronian
  people: 4 Balt, Lett 5 Zhmud 6 Jewish, Litvak, Polish 7 Aistian, Russian, Yatvyag 10 Lithuanian, Samogitian 11 Belorussian
  language: 5 Zmudz 6 Baltic 10 Lithuanian
  religion: 8 Lutheran 13 Roman Catholic

little by little
  French: 7 peu a peu
  Spanish: 9 poco a poco

Little Caesar
  director: 11 Mervyn LeRoy
  cast: 13 Glenda Farrell 15 Edward G Robinson (Caesar Enrico Bandello) 18 Douglas Fairbanks Jr

Little Daedala
  origin: 7 Boeotia
  event: 8 festival
  honoring: 4 Hera, Zeus

Little Dorrit
  author: 14 Charles Dickens
  character: 3 Amy (Little Dorrit), Tip 4 Rugg 5 Casby, Fanny, Flora, Gowan 6 Affery, Merdle, Pancks, Rigaud (Blandois) 7 Meagles 8 Mr F's Aunt 9 Mrs Merdle 10 Flintwinch 13 Arthur Clennam, William Dorrit 16 Monsieur Blandois, Young John Chivery

Little Drummer Girl, The
  author: 11 John Le Carre

Little Emily, Little Em'ly
  character in: 16 David Copperfield
  author: 7 Dickens

Little Fox
  constellation of: 9 Vulpecula

Little Foxes, The
  author: 14 Lillian Hellman
  character: 13 Regina Giddens
  director: 12 William Wyler
  cast: 10 Bette Davis (Regina) 12 Teresa Wright 14 Richard Carlson 15 Herbert Marshall
  prequel: 22 Another Part of the Forest

Little Gidding
  author: 7 T S Eliot

Little Girls
  author: 14 Elizabeth Bowen

Little House on the Prairie
  author: 18 Laura Ingalls Wilder
  character: 6 Albert 7 Dr Baker 8 Rev Alden 9 Mr Edwards 10 Andy Garvey, Lars Hanson, Nels Oleson 11 Adam Kendall, Alice Garvey, Mary Ingalls 12 Grace Ingalls, Laura Ingalls, Nellie Oleson, Willie Oleson 13 Carrie Ingalls, Harriet Oleson 14 Charles Ingalls, Eva Beadle Simms, Jonathan Garvey 15 Caroline Ingalls
  cast: 10 Dabbs Greer, Kevin Hagen 11 Karl Swenson, Merlin Olsen, Richard Bull 12 Hersha Parady, Karen Grassle, Victor French 13 Alison Arngrim, Linwood Boomer, Michael Landon

14 Melissa Gilbert 15 Jonathon Gilbert, Sidney Greenbush, Wendy Turnbeaugh
16 Brenda Turnbeaugh, Charlotte Gilbert, Lindsay Greenbush 17 Katherine McGregor, Matthew Laborteaux, Patrick Laborteaux
18 Melissa Sue Anderson
setting: 6 Winoka 9 Minnesota, Plum Creek 11 Walnut Grove

Little John
character in: 9 Robin Hood

Little King, The
creator: 10 Otto Soglow
technique: 9 pantomine

little-known 6 unsung 7 obscure, unnoted 10 unrenowned

Little Learning, A
author: 11 Evelyn Waugh

Little Lord Fauntleroy
author: 15 Frances H Burnett

Little Lulu
creator: 14 Marge Henderson

Little Match Girl, The
author: 21 Hans Christian Andersen

Little Men
author: 15 Louisa May Alcott

Little Mermaid, The
author: 21 Hans Christian Andersen

Little Minister, The
author: 12 James M Barrie

Little Mo
nickname of: 15 Maureen Connolly

Little Nemo in Slumberland
creator: 11 Winsor McCay
character: 6 Dr Pill 8 cannibal, princess
    clown: 4 Flip
    dog: 6 Blutch

little one 3 tot 4 babe, baby, tyke 5 child 6 infant, wee one 7 toddler

Little Orphan Annie
creator: 10 Harold Gray
character:
    foster father: 13 Daddy Warbucks
    dog: 5 Sandy
saying: 13 Leapin' Lizards

Little Prince, The
author: 21 Antoine de Saint-Exupery

Little Rhody
nickname of: 11 Rhode Island

Little Tramp
nickname of: 14 Charlie Chaplin

Little Women
author: 15 Louisa May Alcott

character: 6 Laurie (Theodore Lawrence), Marmee 10 John Brooke 14 Professor Bhaer
    March sisters: 2 Jo 3 Amy, Meg 4 Beth
director:
    1933 version: 11 George Cukor
    1949 version: 11 Mervyn LeRoy
cast (1933): 9 Paul Lukas 10 Frances Dee, Jean Parker 11 Joan Bennett 16 Katharine Hepburn (Jo)
cast (1949): 9 Mary Astor 10 Janet Leigh 11 June Allyson 12 Peter Lawford 14 Margaret O'Brien 15 Elizabeth Taylor

liturgical 6 ritual 10 ceremonial 11 ceremonious, sacramental

liturgy 4 mass, rite 6 ritual 7 service, worship 8 ceremony, services 9 communion, sacrament

lituus
form: 5 staff
shape: 7 crooked

Lityerses
father: 9 King Midas
held: 15 reaping contests
killed: 6 losers

livable, liveable 4 cozy, snug 5 comfy, homey 8 bearable, passable, pleasant, suitable 9 agreeable, endurable, enjoyable, habitable, tolerable 10 acceptable, convenient, gratifying, satisfying, worthwhile 11 comfortable

live 2 be 3 hot 4 bunk, feed, stay 5 abide, afire, aglow, alive, dwell, exist, fiery, lodge, quick, stand, vital 6 ablaze, active, aflame, alight, at hand, billet, bodily, endure, hold on, living, obtain, occupy, red-hot, remain, reside, settle, thrive 7 animate, at issue, be alive, blazing, breathe, burning, current, flaming, fleshly, going on, ignited, persist, prevail, subsist, survive 8 existent, flourish, get ahead, get along, have life, increase, multiply, physical, pressing, take root, up-to-date, white-hot 9 breathing, corporeal 10 draw breath

live and keep well
Latin: 11 vive valeque

Live and Let Die
author: 10 Ian Fleming

live dissolutely 7 carouse, debauch 9 dissipate 11 overindulge

livelihood 3 job 5 trade 6 career, living, metier 7 calling,

support, venture 8 business, position, vocation 9 situation 10 enterprise, line of work, occupation, profession, sustenance 11 maintenance, subsistence, undertaking

liveliness 3 pep, zip 5 vigor 7 agility 8 alacrity, vitality, vivacity 9 animation, briskness, eagerness 10 ebullience, nimbleness 13 sprightliness

lively 5 alert, brisk, eager, peppy, perky, vivid 6 active, ardent, bouncy 7 buoyant, excited, fervent, intense 8 animated, spirited, vigorous 9 energetic, excitable, sprightly, vivacious 12 enthusiastic

liven 4 buoy 5 cheer, elate, pep up 6 perk up, vivify 7 animate, delight, enliven, fortify, gladden, hearten, punch up, quicken 8 brighten, embolden, energize, inspirit 10 exhilarate, invigorate, strengthen

liver
stores: 8 glycogen
color: 3 red 5 brown
produces: 4 bile 10 blood cells

Livermore Larruper
nickname of: 7 Max Baer

livery 4 garb, suit 5 dress 6 attire 7 costume, raiment, regalia, uniform 8 clothing 9 vestments

Lives of a Bengal Lancer
director: 13 Henry Hathaway
cast: 10 Gary Cooper 12 Franchot Tone 14 Sir Guy Standing 15 Richard Cromwell

Lives of the Poets, The
author: 13 Samuel Johnson

live through 4 know 7 survive, undergo 9 go through 10 experience

livid 3 mad 5 angry, irate, riled, vexed 6 fuming, galled, purple, raging 7 bruised, enraged, furious 8 contused, incensed, inflamed, outraged, provoked, wrathful 9 indignant, steamed up, ticked off 10 discolored, infuriated 11 exasperated

living 3 job 4 life, live, work 5 alive, being, quick, trade 6 active, bodily, career, extant, income 7 animate, calling, fleshly, going on, organic, venture 8 business, embodied, enduring, existent, existing, material, up-to-date, vocation 9 animation, breathing, corporeal, existence, incarnate, lifestyle, operative, permanent, remaining, surviving, way of life **10** employment, enterprise, having life, in the flesh, line of work, livelihood, occupation, persisting, prevailing, profession, subsisting, sustenance **11** maintenance, subsistence **13** drawing breath

living being 8 creature, organism

living conditions 10 atmosphere **11** environment **13** circumstances

living picture
French: **13** tableau vivant

living quarters 4 home **5** abode, house **6** billet **7** housing, lodging, shelter **8** domicile, dwelling, quarters **9** apartment, residence **10** habitation **13** dwelling place

Livy
also: **11** Titus Livius
author of: **13** Ab urbe condita **26** From the Foundation of the City

lizard 3 dab, eft, uma **4** adda, gila, newt, seps, tegu **5** agama, anole, anoli, gecko, idler, shrink **6** aguana, dragon, iguana, komodo, moloch **7** lounger, monitor, reptile, saurian **8** dinosaur, lacerata, scorpion **9** alligator, blindworm, chameleon, crocodile, galliwasp **10** chuckwalla, glass snake, horned toad, salamander **11** gila monster **12** Komodo dragon
characteristic: **6** scales **7** molting **9** oviparous **11** cold-blooded **12** regeneration
constellation of: **7** Lacerta

Ljod see **4** Liod

llama 6 alpaca, kechua, mammal, vicuna **7** guanaco **8** ungulate **13** Peruvian sheep

Llewellyn, Richard
author of: **19** How Green Was My Valley

Llew Llaw Gyffes
origin: **5** Welsh
father: **7** Gwydion
mother: **9** Arianhrod
wife: **10** Blodenwedd
curses bestowed by: **9** Arianhrod

Lloyd
origin: **5** Welsh
form: **8** magician
cast spells upon: **7** Pryderi

Lloyd, Harold
born: **10** Burchard NE
roles: **9** Feet First **10** Safety Last **11** The Freshman **13** The Kid Brother

Llud
also: **4** Ludd, Nudd
origin: **5** Welsh
king of: **7** Britain
rid kingdom of: **6** plague
famous for: **10** generosity

Llyr
origin: **5** Welsh
son: **10** Manawyddan
corresponds to: **3** Ler, Lir

load 3 try, vex **4** care, fill, haul, heap, lade, pack, pile **5** cargo, crush, stack, stuff, worry **6** burden, hamper, hinder, lading, misery, strain, weight **7** afflict, carload, freight, oppress, trouble **8** capacity, contents, encumber, handicap, pressure, shipload, shipment **9** overwhelm, planeload, truckload, wagonload, weigh down **10** affliction, deadweight, depression, misfortune, oppression **11** encumbrance

loads 4 lots, much **5** heaps, piles, scads **6** oodles, plenty **14** more than enough

loaf 4 idle, loll **5** dally **6** be lazy **7** goof off **8** kill time, malinger **9** do nothing, goldbrick, laze about, waste time **10** take it easy **12** lounge around

loafer 3 bum **4** shoe **5** idler **6** no-good **7** laggard, shirker, sponger, wastrel **8** deadbeat, loiterer, sluggard **9** goldbrick, lazybones **10** lazy person, malingerer, ne'er-do-well **11** couch potato **12** lounge lizard **15** drugstore cowboy
French: **7** flaneur

loan 4 lend **5** allow **6** credit **7** advance, lending **8** mortgage **9** advancing

loath 4 loth **6** averse **7** against, counter, hostile, opposed **8** inimical **9** reluctant, resisting, unwilling **10** indisposed, set against **11** disinclined

loathe 4 hate **5** abhor, scorn **6** detest, eschew **7** deplore, despise, disdain, dislike **9** abominate **10** blench from, flinch from, recoil from, shrink from **11** keep clear of, shy away from **14** draw back from, be unable to bear, find disgusting, view with horror **16** have no stomach for

loathing 4 hate **5** odium **6** hatred **7** disgust, dislike **8** aversion, distaste **9** antipathy, repulsion, revulsion **10** abhorrence, repugnance **11** abomination, detestation

loathsome 4 foul, mean, rank, vile **5** nasty **6** odious **7** hate-

ful **9** abhorrent, invidious, obnoxious, offensive, repugnant, repulsive, revolting, sickening **10** abominable, despicable, detestable, disgusting, nauseating, unbearable **11** distasteful

lobby 5 foyer **8** anteroom, politick **9** vestibule **11** antechamber, pull strings, waiting room **12** entrance hall

local 6 narrow, native, nearby **7** insular, limited **8** citywide, confined, regional **9** adjoining, homegrown, parochial, sectional **10** provincial **11** territorial **12** neighborhood **13** circumscribed

locale 4 area, site, spot, zone **6** region **7** quarter, section, setting **8** locality, location, precinct, province, vicinity **12** neighborhood

locality 4 area, site, spot, zone **5** place **6** locale, region **7** quarter, section **8** district, location, precinct, province, vicinity **9** territory **12** neighborhood

locate 3 fix, put **4** find, live, post, seat, stay **5** dwell, place **6** detect, move to, reside, settle **7** deposit, discern, hit upon, set down, situate, station, uncover, unearth **8** come upon, meet with, pinpoint **9** establish, ferret out, light upon, search out, stumble on, track down **10** settle down **12** put down roots

location 4 site, spot **5** place **6** locale **8** district, position **9** situation **11** whereabouts **12** neighborhood

Lochinvar
character in: **7** Marmion
author: **5** Scott

lock 3 bar, dam, pen **4** bang, bolt, cage, coil, curl, grab, grip, hank, hold, hook, jail, join, link, tuft **5** catch, clamp, clasp, grasp, latch, seize, skein, tress, unite **6** clinch, coop up, fasten, lock up, secure, shut in **7** confine, embrace, entwine, grapple, impound, padlock, ringlet **8** dock gate, imprison **9** canal gate, fastening, floodgate, interlink **10** intertwine, sluice gate **11** incarcerate

lock, cylinder
invented by: **4** Yale

Lockhart, Gene
daughter: **12** June Lockhart
granddaughter: **11** Ann Lockhart
born: **6** Canada, London **7** Ontario
roles: **12** Madame Bovary

16 Death of a Salesman
19 The Inspector General
20 Abe Lincoln in Illinois

lock horns 4 feud, tiff **5** argue, brawl, clash, fight **7** dispute, quarrel, wrangle **8** squabble **9** altercate

Lockit
character in: **12** Beggar's Opera
author: **3** Gay

lockup 3 jug, pen **4** jail, stir **5** clink, pokey **6** cooler, prison **7** slammer **8** big house, hoosegow **11** reformatory **12** penitentiary

lock up 3 pen **4** cage, jail **6** coop up, secure **7** confine, impound **8** imprison, restrain, restrict **11** incarcerate

Lockyer, Joseph Norman
field: **9** astronomy
nationality: **7** British
discovered: **6** helium

loco citato 15 in the place cited
abbreviation: **6** loc cit

locomotive
invented by:
  electric: **4** Vail
  experimental: **6** Fenton, Hedley **10** Stephenson, Trevithick
  first US: **6** Cooper
  practical: **10** Stephenson

Locrian Ajax *see* **4** Ajax

Locrus
king of: **8** Locrians

locust 7 Robinia
varieties: **4** moss **5** black, honey, mossy, swamp, sweet, water **6** clammy, yellow **7** African, bristly **8** shipmast **10** West Indian **13** Allegheny moss, South American

locution 4 term **5** idiom, trope, usage **6** phrase, saying **7** wording **8** idiolect, phrasing **9** set phrase, utterance, verbalism **10** expression **11** phraseology, regionalism **12** turn of phrase **14** figure of speech

lode 3 bed **4** seam **7** deposit

lodge 3 bed, hut **4** camp, file, room, stay **5** cabin, catch, hotel, house, motel, put up **6** billet, harbor, resort, submit **7** cottage, quarter, shelter, sojourn **8** register

lodging 4 room **8** quarters **13** accommodation

Lofn
origin: **12** Scandinavian
goddess of: **18** forbidden marriages

permission given by: 4 Odin **5** Othin

loft 3 lob **5** attic, pop up **6** belfry, garret **7** balcony, gallery, hit high, mansard **8** top floor **9** attic room, throw high **10** clerestory

loftiness 5 pride **9** arrogance **11** haughtiness **13** imperiousness **16** superciliousness

Lofting, Hugh
author of: **11** Dr Doolittle

lofty 4 cold, high, tall **5** aloof, grand, great, noble, proud **6** lordly, mighty, remote, snooty **7** distant, eminent, exalted, haughty, leading, soaring, stately, stuck-up, sublime **8** arrogant, elevated, glorious, imposing, insolent, majestic, puffed-up, scornful, snobbish, superior, towering **9** conceited, dignified, imperious, important **10** disdainful, hoity-toity, preeminent **11** high ranking, illustrious, patronizing **12** high-reaching **13** condescending, distinguished, high-and-mighty, self-important

lofty bearing 7 dignity, majesty **10** augustness **11** stateliness

log 5 block, diary, stump **6** docket, lumber, record, timber **7** account, daybook, journal, logbook **8** calendar, schedule

loges 5 boxes **7** balcony **9** mezzanine

loggia 5 lanai, porch **6** arcade, piazza **7** balcony, gallery

Logi
origin: **12** Scandinavian
form: **3** man
personifies: **4** fire
defeated: **4** Loki

logic 5 sense **6** reason **7** cogency **8** analysis, argument **9** coherence, deduction, good sense, induction **10** dialectics

logical 5 clear, sound, valid **6** cogent, likely **7** germane **8** coherent, rational, relevant, sensible **9** deducible, pertinent, plausible **10** analytical, consistent, most likely, reasonable **11** enlightened, intelligent **13** well-organized

logos 4 word **5** ratio **6** saying, speech **7** thought **9** discourse, reckoning **10** proportion

logy 4 dull **5** inert, tired, weary **6** drowsy, groggy, sleepy, torpid **8** comatose, lifeless, listless, sluggish **9** enervated, inanimate, lethargic **10** phlegmatic **12** hebetudinous

Lohengrin
opera by: **6** Wagner
character: **4** Elsa **6** Ortrud **9** Gottfried (Duke of Brabant) **25** Count Frederick of Telramund

Lohengrin
origin: **8** Germanic
knight of: **9** Holy Grail
father: **8** Parsifal, Parzival

loiter 4 idle, laze, loaf, loll, lurk **5** dally, skulk, slink, tarry **6** dawdle **10** dillydally, hang around **11** hover around **12** shilly-shally

Loki
origin: **12** Scandinavian
mentioned in: **9** Lokasenna
god of: **4** fire
son: **6** Fenrir, Fenris
daughter: **3** Hel
fathered: **10** Jormungand **11** Iormungandr, Jormungandr **14** Midgard Serpent
mother of his children: **9** Angerboda, Angrbodha, Angurboda
caused death of: **5** Baldr **6** Balder, Baldur
form: **5** giant
extorted treasure from: **7** Andvari
function: **4** evil **6** strife

Lolita
author: **15** Vladimir Nabokov
character: **14** Humbert Humbert
director: **14** Stanley Kubrick
based on novel by: **15** Vladimir Nabokov
cast: **7** Sue Lyon (Lolita) **10** James Mason (Humbert Humbert) **12** Peter Sellers **14** Shelley Winters

loll 3 sag **4** drag, drop, flap, flop, idle, lean, loaf **5** droop, relax, slump **6** dangle, dawdle, lounge, repose, slouch, sprawl **7** goof off, recline **8** flop over, languish

Lollobrigida, Gina
born: **5** Italy **7** Subiaco
roles: **7** Trapeze **14** Anne of Brooklyn, The Wayward Wife **15** Solomon and Sheba **20** Buona Sera Mrs Campbell **27** The World's Most Beautiful Woman

Loman, Willy
character in: **16** Death of a Salesman
author: **6** Miller

Lombard, Carole
real name: **15** Jane Alice Peters
husband: **10** Clark Gable
born: **11** Fort Wayne IN
roles: **12** My Man Godfrey **13** Nothing Sacred, To Be

Or Not To Be **16** Twentieth Century

Lome
capital of: **4** Togo

London *see box*

London, Jack
author of: **9** White Fang **10** The Sea Wolf **16** The Call of the Wild

lone 4 only, sole **5** alone **6** single, unique **8** isolated, singular, solitary, unpaired **9** unabetted **10** individual, unattended, unescorted **13** companionless, unaccompanied

loneliness 9 isolation, seclusion **12** lonesomeness, solitariness **14** friendlessness

Loneliness of the Long Distance Runner, The
director: **14** Tony Richardson
cast: **11** Avis Bunnage, Peter Madden **12** Tom Courtenay **15** Michael Redgrave

lonely 6 remote **7** forlorn **8** deserted, desolate, forsaken, hermitic, isolated, lonesome, secluded, solitary, unsocial **9** by oneself, reclusive, withdrawn **10** friendless, unattended **11** uninhabited, unpopulated **12** unfrequented **13** companionless, unaccompanied

Lone Ranger, The
character: **5** Tonto
cast: **8** John Hart **12** Clayton Moore **14** Jay Silverheels
horse: **5** Scout **6** Silver

Lone Ranger used: 13 silver bullets
theme: **19** William Tell Overture

lonesome 5 alone, aloof **6** lonely **7** forlorn, insular **8** desolate, detached, forsaken **9** alienated, withdrawn **10** friendless, unfriended **13** companionless

Lone Star State
nickname of: **5** Texas

long 4 hope, lust, pine, sigh, want, wish **5** covet, crave, yearn **6** aspire, hanker, hunger, thirst **7** lengthy, spun out **8** drawn-out, extended, have a yen, in length, unending **9** elongated, extensive, prolonged **10** be bent on, protracted **11** far-reaching, have a desire **12** from end to end, interminable, outstretched

Long, Crawford Williamson
field: **8** medicine
first used: **5** ether

Longaville
character in: **16** Love's Labour's Lost
author: **11** Shakespeare

Long Day's Journey into Night
author: **12** Eugene O'Neill
director: **11** Sidney Lumet
cast: **13** Dean Stockwell **14** Jason Robards Jr **15** Ralph Richardson **16** Katharine Hepburn

Longest Day, The
director: **10** Ken Annakin

12 Andrew Marton, Bernard Wicki
cast: **9** John Wayne, Mel Ferrer **10** Henry Fonda, Red Buttons, Robert Ryan, Rod Steiger **12** Peter Lawford
setting: **8** Normandy (Allied invasion)

Longevity
goddess of: **11** Anna Perenna

long-faced 4 glum **6** dismal, gloomy **7** doleful, unhappy **8** dejected, mournful **10** lugubrious **14** down in the mouth

Longfellow, Henry Wadsworth
author of: **8** Hyperion, (The Song of) Hiawatha **10** Evangeline **15** Paul Revere's Ride **18** Tales of a Wayside Inn **21** The Wreck of the Hesperus **27** The Courtship of Miles Standish

longing 3 yen **4** wish **6** ardent, pining, thirst **7** craving, wishful **8** desirous, yearning **9** hankering, hungering **10** aspiration **11** languishing

long-lasting 7 chronic, lengthy, tedious **8** enduring, extended **9** prolonged **10** continuing, protracted

long live
French: **4** vive

long past 3 old **5** olden **6** gone by, of yore **7** ancient, long ago **8** long gone

long-standing 4 long **5** hardy, hoary **6** rooted **7** abiding, ancient, chronic, durable, lasting **8** enduring, habitual, hallowed, unfading **9** confirmed, continual, long-lived, perennial, perpetual, venerable **10** continuous, deep-rooted, deep-seated, inveterate, persistent, persisting **11** long-lasting, time-honored **15** long-established

Longstreet, James
served in: **8** Civil War
side: **11** Confederate
battle: **7** Bull Run **10** Gettysburg **11** Chickamauga **14** Fredericksburg **18** Wilderness Campaign
after war joined: **11** Republicans
US minister to: **6** Turkey

Long Voyage Home, The
director: **8** John Ford
based on play by: **12** Eugene O'Neill
cast: **9** Ian Hunter, John Wayne **13** Wilfrid Lawson **14** Thomas Mitchell **15** Barry Fitzgerald

London
airport: **7** Gatwick **8** Heathrow, Stansted
architect: **4** Wren
area: **4** Soho **6** Camden **7** Brixton, Chelsea, Holborn, Pimlico **8** Vauxhall **9** Bayswater, Belgravia, Islington, Southwark **10** Bloomsbury, Kensington, Paddington, Shoreditch **11** Notting Hill, St John's Wood **13** Knightsbridge
capital of: **7** England **12** Great Britain **13** United Kingdom
landmark: **6** Big Ben **8** Hyde Park **9** Whitehall, Wimbledon **11** Regent's Park, Saint James's, Tate Gallery, Tower Bridge **12** Covent Garden, London Bridge **13** British Museum, Tower of London **14** British Library, Speaker's Corner **15** National Gallery, Trafalgar Square **16** Buckingham Palace, Piccadilly Circus, Westminster Abbey **17** Kensington Gardens, Royal Festival Hall, Westminster Palace **18** Houses of Parliament **19** Saint Paul's Cathedral **23** Victoria and Albert Museum
police: **7** bobbies
established by: **13** Sir Robert Peel
prime minister's residence: **16** Ten Downing Street
river: **6** Thames
Roman name: **9** Londinium
subway: **11** Underground

long-wearing 5 tough
6 strong, sturdy **7** durable,
lasting **8** enduring
11 substantial

long-winded 5 wordy **6** prolix
7 lengthy, tedious, verbose
8 rambling **9** garrulous **10** digressive, discursive

long-windedness 8 rambling
9 garrulity, prolixity, verbosity,
wordiness **14** discursiveness

Lonnrot, Elias
author of: **8** Kalevala

look 3 air, see **4** cast, face,
gape, gaze, mien, ogle, peek,
peep, scan, seem, show, view
5 front, glare, guise, sight,
stare, study, watch **6** appear,
behold, glance, regard, survey
7 bearing, examine, exhibit,
glimpse **8** demeanor, manifest,
once-over, presence, scrutiny
10 appearance, be directed,
cut a figure, expression, scrutinize **11** contemplate, countenance, observation

look after 4 help **6** assist, defend **7** help out, protect
10 minister to **11** watch out
for **17** take under one's wing

look askance at 7 condemn
8 object to **9** frown upon
10 disapprove **14** discountenance **15** take exception to
16 find unacceptable, view
with disfavor

look at 3 see **4** view **6** behold,
notice, regard **7** examine, inspect, witness **10** scrutinize

Look Back in Anger
director: **14** Tony Richardson
based on play by: **11** John
Osborne
cast: **7** Mary Ure **10** Edith
Evans **11** Claire Bloom
13 Richard Burton **15** Donald Pleasance

look down on 7 despise, disdain **9** frown upon, patronize
10 condescend **13** put on airs
with **14** hold in contempt

looker-on 6 viewer **7** watcher,
witness **8** beholder, observer,
onlooker **9** bystander, spectator

look for 4 seek **5** await **6** expect, pursue **7** hunt for
9 search for **10** anticipate

look for the woman
French: **15** cherchez la
femme

look forward to 5 await
6 expect **7** long for, wait for
9 pin hope on **10** anticipate
17 count the days until

Look Homeward, Angel
author: **11** Thomas Wolfe
character: **7** Ben Gant **9** Eliza

Gant **10** Eugene Gant, Laura
James, Oliver Gant **15** Margaret Leonard

Looking Backward
author: **13** Edward Bellamy

look in the eye 4 defy, face
5 brave **8** confront **9** challenge

look into 5 probe **7** examine,
explore **10** scrutinize **11** inquire into, investigate

lookout 4 heed **5** guard, scout,
vigil **6** patrol, sentry **7** spotter
8 observer, sentinel, watchdog,
watchman **9** alertness, attention, awareness, readiness, vigilance **10** precaution
11 guardedness, mindfulness,
watchkeeper **12** surveillance,
watchfulness

look out 4 mind **6** beware
8 take care, watch out **9** be
careful, be on guard **11** take
warning **12** be on the alert

look over 4 scan, skim
5 judge **6** assess, peruse, survey **7** dip into **8** appraise,
evaluate **13** browse through,
glance through

look through 4 scan, skim
6 browse, peruse **7** dip into
8 look over **9** check over
13 glance through

look toward 7 count on
10 anticipate **13** look forward
to

look upon 3 see **4** view **6** behold, gaze at, look at **7** observe, stare at

look upon as 4 deem, hold
5 count, judge, think **6** regard,
view as **7** account, believe
8 consider, take to be

look up to 5 honor **6** admire,
esteem, revere **7** respect
8 venerate

loom 4 hulk, rise, soar
5 tower **6** appear, ascend,
emerge **8** stand out **9** take
shape

loom, power
invented by: **10** Cartwright

loop 3 eye **4** bend, coil, curl,
furl, ring, roll, turn **5** braid,
curve, noose, plait, twirl,
twist, whorl **6** circle, eyelet,
spiral **7** opening, ringlet **8** aperture, encircle, loophole
10 wind around **11** convolution, curve around

Loos, Anita
author of: **22** Gentlemen Prefer Blondes

loose 4 fast, free, lewd, undo,
wild **5** freed, let go, slack, untie, vague **6** freely, loosen, unbind, undone, untied, wanton

7 immoral, inexact, loosely,
release, set free, slacken, unbound, uncaged, unchain, unleash, unloose, unyoked
8 careless, heedless, liberate,
not tight, rakehell, unbridle,
unchaste, unfasten, unjoined,
untether **9** abandoned, debauched, dissolute, imprecise,
liberated, libertine, unbridled,
unchained, unleashed, unman-
acle, unshackle **10** dissipated,
inaccurate, licentious, not
binding, profligate, unattached,
unexacting, unfastened, unfettered, unhandcuff, untethered
11 not fastened, unconnected
12 unimprisoned
13 unconstrained

loose-fitting 4 limp **5** baggy,
loose, slack **6** draped, droopy
7 sagging **9** overlarge,
oversized

loosely connected 5 jerky
6 fitful **8** episodic, rambling
9 spasmodic, wandering **10** digressive, discursive,
meandering

loosen 3 lax **4** ease, free,
undo **5** break, relax, untie
6 limber, unbend, unbind
7 release, relieve, slacken, unchain, unscrew **8** liberate, unbuckle, unfasten, work free
10 emancipate

looseness 8 fastness, lewdness,
wildness **9** slackness, vagueness **10** debauchery, immorality, inaccuracy, profligacy,
wantonness **11** dissipation, dissolution, imprecision **12** carelessness, heedlessness,
inexactitude **14** licentiousness

loot 3 rob **4** haul, raid, sack,
swag, take **5** booty, prize,
strip **6** boodle, fleece, pilfer,
ravage, spoils **7** pillage, plunder, ransack **11** stolen goods

looter 5 thief **6** robber, vandal
7 brigand **8** pillager **9** despoiler, plunderer

lop 3 cut **4** chip, chop, crop,
dock, flop, sned, snip, trim
5 droop, prune, sever **6** cut
off, deduct, detach, remove,
slouch **7** cut back **8** amputate,
truncate

Lopez, Nancy
sport: **4** golf
husband: **9** Ray Knight
plays: **8** baseball

lopsided 4 awry **5** askew
6 aslant, tipped, uneven
7 crooked, leaning, listing,
slanted, tilting, unequal
8 cockeyed, inclined, slanting
9 irregular **10** asymmetric, off-
balance, unbalanced **15** dis-

proportional
16 disproportionate

loquacious 5 gabby, talky, windy, wordy **6** blabby, chatty, prolix **7** prating, verbose, voluble **8** babbling, chattery **9** garrulous, prattling, talkative **10** chattering, long-winded

loquitur 8 he speaks **9** she speaks

lord 4 king **5** chief, crown, ruler **6** leader, master **7** monarch **8** overlord, seignior, superior **9** commander, landowner, sovereign **10** landholder, proprietor
   Japanese: 6 daimyo
   Turkish: 3 beg, bey

Lord
   Latin: 7 Dominus

Lord be with you, the
   Latin: 15 Dominus vobiscum

Lord have mercy
   Greek: 12 Kyrie eleison

Lord Jim
   author: 12 Joseph Conrad
   character: 5 Stein **6** Marlow **9** Dain Waris **14** Gentleman Brown

lordliness 7 disdain **8** contempt **9** arrogance, insolence, loftiness **11** haughtiness **13** imperiousness **16** superciliousness

lordly 4 cold **5** aloof, bossy, grand, lofty, noble, proud, regal **6** august, remote, snooty **7** distant, elegant, eminent, exalted, haughty, stately, stuck-up **8** arrogant, despotic, imposing, majestic, princely, puffed-up, scornful, snobbish **9** conceited, dignified, imperious, sumptuous **10** disdainful, hoity-toity, tyrannical **11** dictatorial, domineering, magisterial, magnificent, patronizing **13** condescending, high-and-mighty, self-important

Lord of the Flies
   author: 14 William Golding

Lord of the Rings, The
   author: 10 J R R Tolkien

Lord Raingo
   author: 13 Arnold Bennett

Lord Weary's Castle
   author: 12 Robert Lowell

lore 7 beliefs, legends **10** traditions

Lorelei
   also: 7 Lurelei
   origin: 8 Germanic
   form: 5 nymph
   dwelling place: 5 cliff, Rhine

lured: 7 boatmen
caused shipwrecks by: 7 singing

Loren, Sophia
   real name: 14 Sofia Scicolone
   husband: 10 Carlo Ponti
   born: 4 Rome **5** Italy
   roles: 5 El Cid **8** Two Women (Oscar) **9** Arabesque, Houseboat **13** Man of La Mancha **14** The Black Orchid **18** Desire Under the Elms **20** Marriage Italian Style **21** A Countess from Hong Kong, The Pride and the Passion

Lorentz, Hendrik Anton
   field: 7 physics
   nationality: 5 Dutch
   discovered: 17 special relativity
   named for him: 21 Lorentz transformation **34** Lorentz-Fitzgerald Length Contraction
   awarded: 10 Nobel Prize

Loring, Eugene
   choreographer of: 11 Billy the Kid

Lorna Doone
   author: 11 R D Blackmore
   character: 8 John Ridd **9** Tom Faggus **11** Carver Doone **13** Sir Ensor Doone **14** Jeremy Stickles **15** Reuben Huckaback

Lorre, Peter
   real name: 16 Laszlo Lowenstein

born: 7 Hungary **9** Rosenberg
   roles: 1 M **7** Mad Love **10** Casablanca, The Verdict **12** The Big Circus **14** Three Strangers **16** The Maltese Falcon **18** Crime and Punishment, The Mask of Dimitrios

Lorry, Jarvis
   character in: 16 A Tale of Two Cities
   author: 7 Dickens

Los Angeles *see box*

lose 4 fail, miss **6** forget, ignore, mislay **7** confuse, forfeit **8** misplace **9** fail to win, stray from **10** be the loser, fail to heed **11** be thrown off **12** be defeated in, be deprived of, suffer loss of, take a licking

lose control 5 break, crack **7** crack up **9** fall apart **10** go to pieces **15** go off the deep end

lose faith 6 give up **7** despair **9** lose heart **10** have no hope **18** become disenchanted

lose force 3 die **7** run down **9** lose power

lose heart 6 give up **7** despair **17** become discouraged

lose one's cool 12 fly into a rage **13** become enraged, throw a tantrum **14** lose one's temper **15** fly off the handle

loser 4 flop **7** failure **8** de-

Los Angeles
   airport: 3 LAX **7** Burbank **23** Los Angeles International
   area: 5 Watts **6** Bel Air, Downey, Venice **7** Anaheim, Compton, Norwalk **8** Mar Vista, Pasadena, Torrance, Westwood **9** Brentwood, Hollywood, Inglewood, Long Beach **10** Culver City **11** Century City, Garden Grove, Palos Verdes, Santa Monica **12** Beverly Hills, Marina del Rey **16** Pacific Palisades
      San Fernando Valley: **6** Encino **7** Tarzana, Van Nuys, Ventura **10** Northridge **11** Sherman Oaks
   baseball team: 7 Dodgers
   basketball team: 6 Lakers **8** Clippers
   football team: 4 Rams **7** Express, Raiders
   hockey team: 5 Kings
   landmark: 5 Forum **10** Disneyland **11** Civic Center, Getty Museum, Watts Towers **12** Griffith Park **13** Farmers' Market, Hollywood Bowl, Hollywood Park, La Brea Tar Pits, Magic Mountain **15** Knott's Berry Farm **16** Bonaventure Hotel **17** Norton Simon Museum **22** Grauman's Chinese Theater **23** Griffith Park Observatory
   mountains: 10 San Gabriel **11** Santa Monica
   nickname: 15 City of the Angels
   street: 4 Vine **10** Rodeo Drive **12** Olvera Street **15** Mulholland Drive **16** Van Nuys Boulevard **17** Wilshire Boulevard **18** Hollywood Boulevard **20** Santa Monica Boulevard
   university: 3 USC **4** UCLA **7** Caltech **10** Pepperdine **17** Occidental College **31** California Institute of Technology

feated **9** conquered
10 vanquished

lose track of 4 lose **9** let escape **11** lose sight of

lose vigor 4 flag **5** droop
6 sicken, weaken, wither
7 decline

Losing Battles
author: **11** Eudora Welty

loss 4 ruin **5** wreck **6** defeat, losing **7** licking, removal, undoing **8** overturn, riddance, wrecking **9** abolition, mislaying, privation **10** amount lost, demolition, extinction, forfeiture, misplacing, number lost **11** bereavement, deprivation, destruction, dissolution, eradication, expenditure, extirpation

loss of life 5 death **8** fatality
9 mortality

lost 5 stray **6** absent, astray, killed, ruined, wasted **7** lacking, mislaid, missing, misused, strayed, wrecked **8** absorbed, murdered, perished, vanished, wiped out **9** abolished, destroyed, engrossed, misplaced, off-course **10** demolished, eradicated, extirpated, gone astray, misapplied, squandered **11** annihilated, misdirected, obliterated, preoccupied
12 exterminated

Lost Honor of Katharina Blum, The
author: **12** Heinrich Boll

Lost Horizon
author: **11** James Hilton
character: **10** Hugh Conway, Rutherford **12** Henry Barnard, Miss Brinklow **14** Father Perrault **20** Captain Mallison Chang
director: **10** Frank Capra
cast: **5** Margo **8** H B Warner, Sam Jaffe **9** Jane Wyatt **10** John Howard **12** Isabel Jewell, Ronald Colman **14** Thomas Mitchell **19** Edward Everett Horton
setting: **5** Tibet

Lost Illusions
author: **14** Honore de Balzac

Lost in America
director: **12** Albert Brooks
cast: **12** Albert Brooks, Julie Hagerty

Lost in Space
character: **5** Robot **7** Don West **12** Judy Robinson, Will Robinson **13** Penny Robinson **14** Dr Zachary Smith **15** Maureen Robinson **16** Prof John Robinson
cast: **9** Billy Mumy **11** Guy Williams, Mark Goddard

12 June Lockhart, Marta Kristen **14** Jonathan Harris **16** Angela Cartwright
ship: **9** Jupiter II

Lost in the Funhouse
author: **9** John Barth

Lost in the Stars
author: **15** Maxwell Anderson

lost in thought 7 pensive **8** absorbed **9** engrossed, wrapped up **13** contemplative, in a brown study, introspective

Lost Lady, A
author: **11** Willa Cather

Lost Ones, The
author: **13** Samuel Beckett

Lost Patrol, The
director: **8** John Ford
cast: **8** Alan Hale **11** Wallace Ford **12** Boris Karloff **14** Victor McLaglen
score: **10** Max Steiner

Lost Weekend, The
author: **14** Charles Jackson
director: **11** Billy Wilder
cast: **9** Jane Wyman, Mary Young **10** Frank Falen, Ray Milland **11** Philip Terry **12** Doris Dowling **13** Howard da Silva
Oscar for: **5** actor (Milland) **7** picture **8** director **10** screenplay

lot 4 fate, lots, many, much, plot **5** field, patch, quota, share, straw, tract **6** oceans, oodles, ration **7** counter, measure **8** beaucoup, property **9** allotment, allowance, great deal

Lot
grandfather: **5** Terah
father: **5** Haran
uncle: **7** Abraham
son: **5** Ammon
hometown: **5** Sodom
rescued by: **6** angels
fled to: **4** Zoar

lothario 3 rip **4** rake, roue, wolf **5** lover, Romeo, sheik **6** lecher **7** Don Juan, seducer, swinger **8** Casanova, loverboy **9** debauchee, debaucher, libertine, womanizer **10** ladykiller, profligate, sensualist **11** philanderer, skirt-chaser

Lothario
character in: **15** The Fair Penitent
author: **4** Rowe

Loti, Piere
author of: **18** An Iceland Fisherman

lotion 4 balm, wash **5** salve **6** liquid **7** unction, unguent **8** cosmetic, liniment, ointment,

solution **9** demulcent, emollient, freshener, skin cream **10** after-shave, astringent **11** conditioner, embrocation, moisturizer

Lotis
form: **5** nymph
changed into: **4** tree **5** lotus

lotophagi
means: **11** lotus-eaters

lots 4 much **5** heaps, loads, plots, scads **10** quantities

lotus 7 Nelumbo **13** Nymphaea lotus
varieties: **4** blue **5** water, white **6** sacred **8** American, Egyptian **10** East Indian

lotus-eaters 9 lotophagi

loud 5 gaudy, noisy, showy, vivid **6** bright, flashy, garish **7** blatant, booming, intense, splashy **8** colorful, sonorous **9** clamorous, deafening **10** resounding, stentorian, thundering, vociferous **11** ear-piercing, loudmouthed **12** earsplitting, ostentatious

loud sound 4 bang, boom, clap, honk, howl, peal, roar, slam, toot **5** blare, blast, burst, crash **6** bellow, report, scream, shriek **7** clatter, thunder **9** explosion **10** detonation

Lou Grant
character: **6** Animal **8** Joe Rossi **10** Art Donovan **11** Charlie Hume **12** Billie Newman **15** Margaret Pynchon
cast: **10** Jack Bannon, Mason Adams **11** Edward Asner, Linda Kelsey **12** Robert Walden **13** Nancy Marchand **14** Darryl Anderson
paper: **17** Los Angeles Tribune
spinoff of: **18** Mary Tyler Moore Show

Louhi
origin: **7** Finnish
form: **9** sorceress
mistress of: **7** Pohjola
defeated by: **11** Vainamoinen
enemy of: **5** Finns

Louis, Joe
real name: **14** Joe Louis Barrow
nickname: **11** Brown Bomber
sport: **6** boxing
class: **11** heavyweight

Louis, Morris
born: **11** Baltimore MD
artwork: **4** Veil **5** Signa **7** Stripes **8** Unfurled **15** Mountains and Sea

Louise
opera by: **11** Charpentier
character: **6** Julian

Louisiana
  abbreviation: **2** LA
  nickname: **5** Bayou, Sugar **6** Creole **7** Pelican
  capital: **10** Baton Rouge
  largest city: **10** New Orleans
  others: **5** Houma **6** Bunkie, Gretna, Kenner, Minden, Monroe, Ruston **7** Bastrop **8** Bogalusa **9** Lafayette, Opelousas **10** Alexandria, Shreveport **11** Lake Charles
  college: **3** LSU **6** Loyola, Tulane **7** Dillard, Newcomb **9** Grambling
  explorer: **7** La Salle **9** Iberville **13** Pierre Lemoyne
  feature:
    area: **5** bayou **13** French Quarter
    festival: **9** Mardi Gras
    music: **4** jazz
    stadium: **9** Sugar Bowl
    street: **7** Bourbon
  tribe: **4** Adai, Ioni, Rees, Waco **5** Caddo, Haini, Washa **6** Eyeish, Pawnee **7** Andarko, Arikara, Atakapa **8** Ovachita **9** Bayogoula, Nachitoch
  people: **5** Cajun **6** Creole **7** Acadian, pelican **8** Huey Long **14** Lillian Hellman, Louis Armstrong
  island: **5** Avery
  lake: **3** Iat **4** Iatt **5** Caddo, Clear, Cross, Larto, White **6** Borgne, Saline **8** Darbonne, Maurepas **9** Bistineau, Calcasieu, Catahoula **10** False River **13** Pontchartrain
  land rank: **11** thirty-first
  mountain:
    highest point: **8** Driskill
  physical feature: **15** Head of the Passes **17** coastal marshlands
    delta: **11** Mississippi
    gulf: **6** Mexico
    salt domes: **11** Five Islands
  river: **3** Red **5** Amite, Bayou, Pearl **6** Tensas **8** Ouachita **11** Mississippi
  state admission: **10** eighteenth
  state bird: **19** eastern brown pelican
  state flower: **8** magnolia
  state motto: **5** Union **7** Justice **10** Confidence
  state song: **15** Give Me Louisiana **16** You Are My Sunshine
  state tree: **11** bald cypress

Louisiana Lightning
  nickname of: **9** Ron Guidry

lounge 4 flop, idle, laze, loaf, loll, rest, sofa **5** couch, dally, divan, lobby, relax, sleep, slump **6** dawdle, daybed, repose, slouch, sprawl **7** recline, slumber **8** kill time, languish **9** davenport, do nothing, lie around, vestibule **10** dillydally, stretch out, take it easy

lourd
  music: **5** heavy

Lourenco Marques
  capital of: **10** Mozambique

louse 3 cad, rat **4** heel **5** churl, knave **6** rascal, rotter, vermin **8** parasite **9** scoundrel

louse up 3 mar **4** goof, muff, ruin **5** botch, spoil **6** bungle, foul up, mess up **7** butcher, do badly, screw up **9** mismanage **11** make a mess of

lousiness 9 nastiness **10** crumminess, horridness, rottenness **11** inferiority, infestation **13** despicability, unsuitability **14** unpleasantness

lousy 3 bad **4** mean **5** awful, nasty **6** crummy, rotten, shabby, unkind **7** hateful, vicious **8** dreadful, inferior, infested, terrible **9** unethical, worthless **10** pediculous, second-rate, unpleasant **12** contemptible

lout 3 ape, oaf **4** boor, clod **5** booby, churl, clown, dummy, dunce, klutz, yokel **6** lummox, rustic **7** bumpkin, dullard

loutish 4 rude **5** crude **6** coarse, gauche, oafish, vulgar **7** boorish, uncouth **9** unrefined **10** unpolished **11** peasantlike

lovable, loveable 4 cute **5** sweet **6** cuddly, lovely, taking **7** darling, winning, winsome **8** adorable, charming, engaging, fetching **9** endearing **10** enchanting **11** captivating

Lovberg, Eilert
  character in: **11** Hedda Gabler
  author: **5** Ibsen

love 3 man **4** beau, bent, dear, girl, mind, turn **5** adore, amity, amour, angel, ardor, enjoy, fancy, flame, honey, lover, savor, taste, woman **6** admire, bask in, choice, esteem, fellow, relish **7** beloved, charity, cherish, concord, darling, dearest, emotion, leaning, passion, rapture, revel in, sweetie **8** affinity, be fond of, devotion, fondness, goodwill, hold dear, loved one, mistress, paramour, penchant, precious, sympathy, treasure, truelove, weakness **9** adoration, affection, boyfriend, delight in, inamorata, rejoice in, sentiment **10** admiration, appreciate, attachment, cordiality, friendship, girlfriend, partiality, proclivity, solicitude, sweetheart, sweetie pie, tenderness **11** amorousness, benevolence, brotherhood, inclination, infatuation **12** be enamored of, congeniality, predilection
  god of: **4** Amor, Eros **5** Cupid **7** Angus Og
  goddess of: **5** Freia, Freya **6** Hathor, Inanna, Ishtar **7** Mylitta **9** Aphrodite

Love, the Magician
  also: **11** El Amor Brujo
  ballet by: **5** Falla

love affair 5 amour **7** liaison, romance **14** affaire de coeur

Love Boat, The
  character: **3** Ace **10** (Cruise Director) Julie McCoy **11** (Dr) Adam Bricker, (Purser Burl) Gopher Smith **14** (Captain) Merrill Stubing **15** (Bartender) Isaac Washington
  cast: **8** Ted Lange **10** Fred Grandy **11** Lauren Tewes **12** Bernie Kopell, Gavin MacLeod
  ship: **15** Pacific Princess

love child 7 bastard **12** natural child **17** illegitimate child

love conquers all
  Latin: **15** omnia vincit amor

loved one 4 love, wife

5 lover **6** fiance, spouse **7** beloved, dearest, fiancee, husband **9** boyfriend **10** girlfriend, sweetheart **12** family member

Love for Three Oranges, The
opera by: **9** Prokofiev

Love in the Afternoon
director: **11** Billy Wilder
cast: **10** Gary Cooper **13** Audrey Hepburn **16** Maurice Chevalier
setting: **5** Paris

Lovelace, Richard
author of: **18** To Althea from Prison **23** To Lucasta Going to the Wars

loveliness 6 beauty **9** good looks **11** pulchritude **14** attractiveness

lovely 4 cute, fine, good **5** sweet **6** comely **7** elegant, lovable, winning, winsome **8** adorable, alluring, charming, engaging, fetching, handsome, pleasant, pleasing **9** agreeable, beautiful, endearing, enjoyable, exquisite **10** attractive, delightful, enchanting **11** captivating, fascinating **12** irresistible

Love Machine, The
author: **16** Jacqueline Susann

Love Me Tonight
director: **15** Rouben Mamoulian
cast: **8** Myrna Loy **14** Charlie Ruggles **16** Maurice Chevalier **17** Jeanette MacDonald
score: **14** Rodgers and Hart
song: **4** Mimi **5** Lover **14** Isn't It Romantic

love of country
Latin: **11** amor patriae

Love of One's Neighbor
author: **14** Leonid Andreyev

lover 3 fan, man, nut **4** beau, buff, dear, girl, love **5** freak, honey, swain, woman, wooer **6** fellow, suitor **7** admirer, beloved, darling, devotee, fanatic, sweetie **8** follower, loved one, lover boy, mistress, paramour, truelove **9** boyfriend, inamorata **10** aficionado, enthusiast, girlfriend, sweetheart **11** afficionado
French: **6** bon ami **9** bonne amie
Italian: **8** cicisbeo

Lovers and Other Strangers
director: **8** Cy Howard
cast: **8** Gig Young **9** Anne Meara, Bea Arthur **11** Anne Jackson **13** Bonnie Bedelia, Harry Guardino **14** Cloris Leachman, Michael Brandon **17** Richard Castellano

love seat 4 sofa **5** couch **6** settee **13** courting chair

lovesick 7 amorous **8** yearning **10** moonstruck

Love's Labour's Lost
author: **18** William Shakespeare
character: **4** Dull **5** Maria **7** Berowne, Costard, Dumaine **8** Rosaline **9** Ferdinand, Katherine **10** Holofernes, Jaquenetta, Longaville **16** Princess of France **18** Don Adriano de Armado

Love Song of J Alfred Prufrock, The
author: **7** T S Eliot

Love Story
author: **10** Erich Segal

Love-wit
character in: **12** The Alchemist
author: **6** Jonson

loving 4 fond, kind, warm **6** ardent, caring, doting, erotic, tender **7** amatory, amorous, devoted **8** enamored, friendly **10** benevolent, passionate, solicitous **11** sympathetic, warmhearted **12** affectionate

loving word 9 sweet talk **10** endearment **12** sweet nothing

low 4 base, blue, deep, down, evil, glum, mean, soft, vile **5** awful, cruel, dirty, dumpy, faint, gross, lower, lowly, muted, prone, quiet, short, small, squat **6** brutal, coarse, common, cruddy, crummy, feeble, gentle, gloomy, humble, hushed, little, paltry, scurvy, softly, sordid, stubby, stumpy, sunken, vulgar, wicked **7** coastal, concave, corrupt, doleful, heinous, muffled, obscene, quietly, snubbed, squalid, subdued, unhappy **8** cowardly, degraded, dejected, depraved, downcast, inferior, low-lying, low-slung, mediocre, murmured, sawed-off, soothing, terrible, trifling, undersea, unworthy **9** dastardly, depressed, lethargic, nefarious, prostrate, repugnant, repulsive, submarine, submerged, truncated, unethical, whispered **10** abominable, despicable, despondent, dispirited, melancholy, outrageous, scandalous **11** ignominious, scoundrelly, underground, unimportant **12** contemptible, disheartened, dishonorable **14** down in the mouth

lowbred 6 coarse, common, vulgar **7** lowbrow, peasant **10** lower-class, uncultured

low-down 4 base, mean **5** dirty **10** despicable **12** contemptible **13** reprehensible

Lowell, James Russell
author of: **12** The Cathedral **15** The Biglow Papers **16** A Fable for Critics **21** The Vision of Sir Launfal

Lowell, Robert
author of: **8** Day by Day **9** Skunk Hour **10** The Dolphin **11** Life Studies **15** For the Union Dead **16** Lord Weary's Castle

Lowenstein, Laszlo
real name of: **10** Peter Lorre

lower 3 cut, dim **4** damp, drop, duck, mute, pare, sink, sulk **5** frown, glare, pared, prune, scowl **6** deduct, glower, lop off, muffle, reduce, soften, subdue **7** curtail, depress, immerse, let down, put down, reduced, repress, shorten **8** decrease, diminish, grow dark, lessened, make less, pare down, pull down, submerge, take down, tone down **9** curtailed, decreased, make lower, pared down **10** abbreviate, diminished

lower-case letter 9 minuscule **11** small letter

lower-class 4 poor **6** common **7** lowbred, lowbrow, peasant **9** unrefined **10** blue-collar **12** working-class

lower classes 6 proles, rabble **8** canaille, riffraff **9** hoi polloi, peasantry **11** proletariat **13** the common herd, working people **16** the great unwashed

lower depths 4 pits, scum **5** dregs **6** rabble **8** canaille, riffraff **14** scum of the earth

Lower Depths, The
also called: **11** At the Bottom **14** A Night's Lodging
author: **10** Maxim Gorky

lower in rank 4 bust **6** demote **7** degrade

lower in spirits 6 deject, sadden **7** depress **8** dispirit **10** dishearten

low-key 4 soft **5** loose, muted **6** gentle, subtle **7** muffled, relaxed, subdued **8** laid-back, softened, soft-sell **9** modulated, toned-down **10** low-pitched, restrained **11** low-pressure, understated, unobtrusive **14** unostentatious

lowliness 8 baseness 9 obscurity 10 humbleness

lowly 3 low 6 humble, modest, simple, softly 7 ignoble, lowborn, lowbred, obscure 8 baseborn, plebeian 10 unassuming 11 proletarian 13 unpretentious

low-minded 4 lewd, vile 5 crude, gross 6 coarse, smutty, vulgar 7 obscene, uncouth 9 obnoxious, offensive 11 disgraceful 12 contemptible

low point, lowest point 4 base, foot, zero 5 depth, nadir, worst 6 bottom 7 perigee 10 rock bottom

low-priced 5 cheap, token 6 budget, modest 7 bargain, cut-rate, low-cost, nominal, reduced 8 closeout, moderate 9 dirt-cheap 10 discounted, economical, marked-down, reasonable 11 inexpensive 15 bargain-basement

low-ranking 5 minor, petty 11 subordinate, unimportant

low-spirited 3 low, sad 4 blue, down, glum 6 gloomy, morose, woeful 7 doleful, forlorn, unhappy 8 dejected, desolate, downcast 9 depressed, heartsore, sorrowful, woebegone 10 despondent, dispirited, melancholy 11 crestfallen, discouraged, downhearted 12 disconsolate, disheartened 14 down-in-the-mouth

low spirits 4 funk 5 gloom 6 dismay, sorrow 7 despair 8 dejected 9 pessimism 10 depression, desolation, melancholy, moroseness 11 despondency 12 hopelessness 14 discouragement 15 downheartedness

Loxias epithet of: 6 Apollo means: 9 ambiguous

Loy, Myrna real name: 13 Myrna Williams co-star: 13 William Powell born: 13 Raidersburg MT roles: 10 The Thin Man 11 Nora Charles 17 Cheaper by the Dozen 22 The Best Years of Our Lives

loyal 4 firm, true 6 trusty 7 devoted, dutiful, staunch 8 constant, faithful, reliable, resolute, true-blue 9 steadfast 10 dependable, scrupulous, unswerving, unwavering 11 trustworthy 12 tried and true

loyalist 4 tory 12 conservative

Loyalties author: 14 John Galsworthy

loyalty 6 fealty 8 devotion, fidelity, firmness 9 adherence, constancy 10 allegiance 11 reliability, staunchness 12 faithfulness 13 dependability, steadfastness 15 trustworthiness

lozenge 4 drop, pill 6 tablet, troche 8 pastille 9 cough drop

Luanda capital of: 6 Angola

Lubitsch, Ernst director of: 9 Ninotchka 13 Heaven Can Wait, To Be or Not To Be

Lucas, Charlotte character in: 17 Pride and Prejudice author: 6 Austen

Lucentio character in: 19 The Taming of the Shrew author: 11 Shakespeare

Lucerne German: 6 Luzern river: 5 Reuss landmark: 9 Hofkirche 11 Am Rhyn House 15 Mariahilf Church

Lucia di Lammermoor opera by: 9 Donizetti based on novel by: 14 Sir Walter Scott *called:* 20 The Bride of Lammermoor

Luciana character in: 17 The Comedy of Errors author: 11 Shakespeare

Luciani, Albino 13 Pope John Paul I 20 Pope John Paul the First

lucid 5 clear 6 bright, direct, normal 7 certain, precise, radiant, shining 8 accurate, apposite, dazzling, luminous, lustrous, pellucid, positive, rational, specific 9 brilliant, sparkling 10 articulate, perceptive, responsive, to the point 11 clearheaded, crystalline, illuminated, resplendent, transparent 12 crystal clear, intelligible 13 clear thinking, scintillating, well-organized 14 comprehensible, understandable 15 straightforward

Lucifer means: 5 Satan 11 fallen angel, light bearer

Lucina origin: 5 Roman goddess of: 10 childbirth corresponds to: 4 Juno 8 Ilithyia 10 Eileithyia

Lucio character in: 17 Measure for Measure author: 11 Shakespeare

luck 3 lot 4 fate 5 karma 6 chance, kismet 7 destiny, fortune, success, triumph, victory 8 accident, fortuity, good luck, Lady Luck 11 good fortune, piece of luck 12 happenstance god of: 12 Bonus Eventus

lucky 4 good 5 happy 6 in luck, timely 7 blessed, favored 9 favorable, fortunate, opportune, promising 10 auspicious, beneficial, felicitous, of good omen, propitious 12 providential

Lucky Jim author: 12 Kingsley Amis

lucky piece 5 charm 6 amulet 8 talisman 10 lucky charm

lucrative 7 gainful 8 fruitful 10 beneficial, high-income, high-paying, profitable 11 moneymaking 12 remunerative

Lucretia husband: 26 Lucius Tarquinius Collatinus raped by: 16 Sextus Tarquinius death by: 7 suicide

Lucretius author of: 13 De rerum natura 19 On the nature of things

Lucullan 4 rich 6 lavish 7 gourmet 9 epicurean, luxurious

Lucy Show, The also: 9 Here's Lucy character: 9 Kim Carter 10 Lucy Carter 11 Craig Carter 12 Harry Conners, Vivian Bagley 13 Mary Jane Lewis, Sherman Bagley 14 Lucy Carmichael 15 Chris Carmichael, Harrison Cheever, Jerry Carmichael, Theodore J Mooney 18 Harrison Otis Carter cast: 9 Ralph Hart 10 Candy Moore, Dick Martin, Gale Gordon, Lucie Arnaz, Roy Roberts 11 Desi Arnaz Jr, Lucille Ball, Vivian Vance 12 Jimmy Garrett 13 Mary Jane Croft

Ludd *see* 4 Llud

ludicrous 4 wild 5 comic, crazy, funny 6 absurd, far-out 7 amusing, comical 8 farcical 9 laughable 10 outlandish, ridiculous 11 nonsensical 12 preposterous

Ludlum, Robert
author of: **15** The Matlock Paper **17** The Bourne Identity, The Parsifal Mosaic, The Road to Gandolfo **18** The Osterman Weekend **19** The Gemini Contenders **20** The Rhinemann Exchange **23** The Chancellor Manuscript, The Scarlatti Inheritance

Luftwaffe 9 air weapon **18** German Nazi air force

lug 3 tow, tug **4** bear, drag, draw, haul, pull, tote **5** carry, heave **9** transport

Lug
origin: **5** Irish
habitat: **5** solar

luggage 4 bags, gear **6** trunks **7** baggage, effects, valises **9** suitcases **13** accouterments

Luggnagg
fictional land in: **16** Gulliver's Travels
author: **5** Swift

Lugnasad
origin: **5** Irish
feast date: **11** August first

Lugosi, Bela
real name: **10** Bela Blasko
born: **5** Lugos **7** Hungary
roles: **7** Dracula **21** Murders in the Rue Morgue

lugubrious 4 dour, glum **6** gloomy, morose, rueful, somber, woeful **7** doleful, elegiac **8** dolorous, downcast, funereal, mournful **9** miserable, sorrowful, woebegone **10** depressing, melancholy

Lukas, George
director of: **8** Star Wars **16** American Graffiti

Luke
birthplace: **7** Antioch
companion: **4** Paul
wrote: **6** Gospel

lukewarm 4 cool, mild, warm **5** aloof, tepid **8** detached, uncaring **9** apathetic, temperate **11** halfhearted, indifferent, perfunctory, unconcerned **12** uninterested **13** lackadaisical **14** unenthusiastic **15** body-temperature, room-temperature

lull 3 gap **4** calm, ease, halt, hush **5** break, pause, quell, quiet, still **6** hiatus, lacuna, pacify, recess, soothe, subdue **7** assuage, caesura, compose, mollify, respite **8** breather, calmness **9** interlude **12** brief silence, interruption

Lully, Jean-Baptiste
born: **5** Italy **8** Florence
composer of: **4** Atys, Isis **6** Persee, Psyche, Roland, Thesee **7** Alceste, Phaeton **10** Le Sicilien, Proserpine **11** Bellerophon **13** Acis et Galatee, Amadis de Gaule, L'Amour medecin **14** Acis and Galatea, Armide et Renaud, Le mariage force **16** Cadmus et Hermione **17** Achille et Polyxene, Cadmus and Hermione **19** Achilles and Polyxene **20** Les Amants magnifiques **22** Le Bourgeois Gentilhomme, Monsieur de Pourceaugnac

lulu 3 pip **5** dandy, doozy **8** Jim Dandy **9** allowance, humdinger, wonderful **10** remarkable

lumber 3 log **4** plod, wood **5** barge, clump, stamp **6** boards, planks, trudge, waddle **7** shamble, shuffle **8** flounder **9** fell trees

Lumber State
nickname of: **5** Maine

Lumet, Sidney
director of: **7** Network, Serpico **13** The Pawnbroker **14** Twelve Angry Men **15** Dog Day Afternoon **24** Long Day's Journey Into Night

luminary 3 VIP **5** light, wheel **6** bigwig **7** big shot, notable **8** somebody **9** celebrity, dignitary, personage **10** luminosity **11** illuminator

luminescent 5 aglow **7** glowing **8** gleaming, luminous **9** twinkling **10** flickering, glimmering, glistening, shimmering **11** fluorescent **14** phosphorescent

luminosity 4 glow **5** gleam, sheen, shine **6** luster **8** radiance **10** brightness, brilliance

luminous 6 bright **7** glowing, radiant, shining **8** lustrous **9** brilliant **10** irradiated **11** illuminated, luminescent **15** reflecting light

lump 3 gob, mix **4** bump, cake, clod, fuse, heap, hunk, knob, knot, mass, node, pile, pool **5** amass, batch, blend, bunch, chunk, clump, group, knurl, merge, tumor, unite **6** gather, growth, nodule **7** collect, combine, compile **8** assemble, swelling **9** aggregate **10** protrusion, tumescence **11** excrescence **12** protuberance

lumpish 4 dull, slow **5** bulky, dumpy, heavy, lumpy **6** clumsy **7** awkward **8** cloddish, ungainly, unwieldy **9** corpulent **10** cumbersome, overweight

Lumpkin, Tony
character in: **18** She Stoops to Conquer
author of: **9** Goldsmith

lump together 4 fuse, pool **7** combine **10** amalgamate **11** consolidate, incorporate

Luna
personifies: **4** moon

lunacy 5 folly, mania **6** idiocy **7** madness **8** dementia, insanity **9** absurdity, asininity, craziness, silliness, stupidity **10** imbecility, imprudence, insaneness **11** foolishness **13** foolhardiness, senselessness

lunatic 3 mad, nut **4** daft, loco **5** batty, crazy, loony, nutty, potty **6** cuckoo, insane, madman, maniac, screwy **7** bonkers, cracked, touched **8** crackers, demented, demoniac, deranged, maniacal, unhinged **9** psychotic, senseless **10** irrational, psychopath, reasonless, unbalanced **11** crazy person, mentally ill, not all there **12** crackbrained, insane person, psychopathic, round the bend **13** off one's rocker, of unsound mind, out of one's mind

lunch
French: **8** dejeuner

luncheonette 4 cafe **5** diner **7** beanery **8** snack bar **9** hash house, lunchroom **10** coffee shop **11** eating house **12** lunch counter, sandwich shop

lunchroom 4 cafe **5** diner, grill **8** snack bar **9** cafeteria **12** luncheonette

lunge 3 cut, jab **4** dash, dive, pass, rush, stab **5** hit at, lurch, swing, swipe **6** attack, charge, plunge, pounce, thrust **7** set upon **8** fall upon, strike at **9** make a pass

lunkhead 3 ass **4** dope, fool **5** booby, dunce, idiot, moron, ninny **6** dimwit, nitwit **7** fathead, halfwit **8** bonehead, dumb-dumb, imbecile, numskull **9** blockhead, lamebrain, numbskull **10** dunderhead, nincompoop **11** chowderhead

Lunt, Alfred
wife: **12** Lynn Fontanne
born: **11** Milwaukee WI
roles: **12** The Guardsman **13** The Ragged Edge

Lupercalia
origin: **5** Roman
event: **8** festival

Lupercus
honoring: **6** Faunus
8 Lupercus
to procure: **9** fertility

Lupercus
origin: **5** Roman
god of: **9** fertility
corresponds to: **3** Pan
6 Faunus

Lupino, Ida
husband: **10** Howard Duff
12 Collier Young, Louis
Hayward
born: **6** London **7** England
roles: **8** Devotion **10** The
Hard Way **12** Junior Bonner, Women's Prison **13** Escape Me Never **15** Strange
Intruder **17** On Dangerous
Ground **18** The Light That
Failed, While the City
Sleeps

lurch 4 cant, keel, list, reel,
roll, sway, tilt, toss **5** lunge,
pitch, slant **6** careen, plunge,
swerve, teeter, totter **7** incline,
stagger, stumble

lure 4 bait, coax, trap **5** bribe,
decoy, snare, tempt **6** allure,
cajole, come-on, entice, induce, seduce **7** attract, beguile **8** cajolery, persuade
9 fascinate, tantalize **10** allurement, attraction, enticement,
inducement, temptation
11 drawing card
12 blandishment

Lurelei *see* **7** Lorelei

lurid 4 gory, grim **5** eerie, fiery,
vivid **6** bloody **7** carmine,
flaming, ghastly, glaring,
glowing, graphic, scarlet, shining **8** dramatic, rubicund, sanguine, shocking **9** appalling,
bright-red **11** sensational
12 melodramatic
13 bloodcurdling

lurk 4 hide **5** prowl, skulk,
slink, sneak **9** lie in wait

Lusaka
capital of: **6** Zambia

luscious 5 tasty **6** savory
7 scented **8** aromatic, fragrant,
perfumed **9** delicious, flavorful,
succulent, toothsome **10** appetizing, delectable **13** mouth-
watering

lush 4 posh, rich **5** dense,
fancy, grand **6** ornate **7** elegant, profuse **8** abundant, prolific, splendid **9** elaborate,
luxuriant, luxurious, sumptuous **11** flourishing,
magnificent

Lusia
epithet of: **7** Demeter
means: **6** bather

lust 5 covet, crave **6** be lewd
7 craving, lechery, passion

8 lewdness **9** carnality, hunger
for, sexuality **10** satyriasis
14 lasciviousness,
libidinousness

lust after 4 want **5** covet,
crave **6** desire **11** have a yen
for, have an eye on, hunger
after, thirst after

luster 4 fame, glow **5** gleam,
glory, gloss, honor, merit,
sheen, shine **6** dazzle **7** burnish, glimmer, glitter, sparkle
8 prestige, radiance **9** radiation **10** brightness, brilliance,
luminosity, notability, refulgence **11** distinction **12** luminousness, resplendence
15 illustriousness

lusterless 3 dim, wan **4** dead,
drab, dull, flat **5** faded, matte,
muted **7** prosaic **9** colorless,
tarnished

Lust for Life
author: **11** Irving Stone
director: **16** Vincente
Minnelli
based on story by: **11** Irving
Stone
cast: **11** James Donald, Kirk
Douglas (Vincent Van
Gogh), Pamela Brown
12 Anthony Quinn (Gaugin)
Oscar for: **15** supporting actor (Quinn)

lustful 4 lewd **6** carnal **8** pru-

rient **9** lecherous, salacious
10 lascivious, libidinous

lustrous 6 bright, glossy
7 glowing, radiant, shining
8 dazzling, gleaming, luminous, polished **9** burnished, effulgent **10** glistening
11 coruscating, illuminated
12 incandescent

lusty 4 hale **5** husky, sound
6 brawny, hearty, robust, rugged, sturdy, virile **7** healthy
8 vigorous **9** exuberant, strapping **10** full of life **11** uninhibited **12** unrestrained,
wholehearted **13** irrepressible

Luther, Martin
born: **7** Germany **8** Eisleben
author: **16** Ninety-Five
Theses **27** On the Freedom
of a Christian Man **46** Address to the Christian Nobility of the German Nation
51 A Prelude Concerning
the Babylonian Captivity of
the Church
excommunicated by: **8** Pope
Leo X **15** Pope Leo the
Tenth
summoned before: **11** Diet of
Worms
founded: **11** Lutheranism,
Reformation
13 Protestantism

lux 5 light

Luxembourg *see box*

Luxembourg
other name: **9** Luxemburg **13** Lucilinburhuc
name means: **10** little fort
capital/largest city: **10** Luxembourg
others: **4** Hamm **5** Roodt, Wiltz **6** Mersch, Remich **7** Kop-
stal, Lintgen, Petange, Redange, Vianden **8** Capellen, Cler-
vaux, Diekirch, Frisange **9** Dudelange **10** Echternach,
Ettelbruck, Hesperange, Larochette **11** Differdange, Wor-
meldange **12** Grevenmacher, Troisvierges, Wasserbillig
14 Esch-sur-Alzette
division: **6** Esleck **7** Bon Pays, Gutland, Oesling
measure: **5** fuder
monetary unit: **5** franc **7** centime
lake: **8** Haut Sure
mountain: **8** Ardennes
highest point: **8** Huldange **9** Burgplatz **11** Wemperhardt
river: **3** Our **4** Sure, Syre **5** Alert, Clerf, Eisch, Mosel,
Sauer, Wiltz **6** Chiers **7** Alzette, Moselle **8** Petrusse
11 Ernz Blanche
physical feature:
  plateau: **4** Bock **8** Ardennes, Lorraine
  valley: **7** Moselle
people: **6** French, German **12** Luxembourger
  ruler: **8** Sigefroi, Wencelas **12** Jean l'Aveugle **21** House
  of Nassau-Weilburg
  saint: **10** Willibrord
language: **6** French, German **7** English **13** Letzeburgesch
religion: **13** Roman Catholic
food:
  pastry: **20** les pensees brouillees

luxuriant 4 lush, rank **5** dense, fancy, grand **6** florid, ornate **7** elegant, flowery, profuse, teeming **8** abundant, splendid **9** elaborate, exuberant, luxurious, overgrown, sumptuous **10** flamboyant **11** extravagant, flourishing, magnificent

luxuriate 4 bask **6** relish **7** delight **8** wallow in **9** indulge in

luxurious 4 rich **5** grand **6** costly, effete **7** elegant, wealthy **8** decadent, pampered **9** enjoyable, expensive, indulgent, sumptuous **10** gratifying **11** comfortable, pleasurable

luxuriousness 4 ease **6** luxury **7** comfort **8** richness **10** costliness **13** sumptuousness

luxury 5 bliss **6** heaven, riches, wealth **7** delight **8** paradise, pleasure **9** enjoyment **10** high living, indulgence **12** extravagance, nonessential, nonnecessity, satisfaction **13** gratification

LXX *see* **15** Septuagint

Lyaeus
  epithet of: **8** Dionysus
  means: **8** loosener

Lycaeus
  epithet of: **4** Zeus
  means: **7** wolfish

Lycaon
  king of: **7** Arcadia
  father: **8** Pelasgus
  son: **8** Maenalus, Tegeates
  tested: **4** Zeus
  turned into: **4** wolf

Lycidas
  author: **10** John Milton
  elegy for: **10** Edward King

Lycomedes
  king of: **6** Scyrus
  daughter: **8** Deidamia
  pushed over cliff: **7** Theseus

Lycon
  mentioned in: **5** Iliad
  vocation: **7** warrior

home: **4** Troy
killed by: **8** Peneleus

Lycophron
  origin: **5** Greek
  father: **9** Periander
  exiled to: **7** Corcyra
  killed by: **10** Corcyreans
  committed: **6** murder
  went to: **4** Troy
  killed by: **6** Hector

Lycotherses
  king of: **7** Illyria
  wife: **5** Agave
  killed by: **5** Agave

Lycurgas
  king of: **6** Edones, Thrace
  son: **5** Dryas
  persecuted: **8** Dionysus
  killed: **5** Dryas

Lycus
  king of: **6** Thebes **7** Cilicia
  father: **7** Pandion **9** Chthonius
  mother: **5** Pylia
  brother: **7** Nycteus
  wife: **5** Dirce
  niece: **7** Antiope
  son: **5** Lycus
  succeeded: **8** Sarpedon
  killed by: **6** Zethus **7** Amphion **12** Antiope's sons

Lygodesma
  epithet of: **7** Artemis
  means: **11** willow-bound

lying down 5 in bed, prone **6** supine **7** napping, resting **8** snoozing **9** reclining, recumbent **10** taking a nap **13** taking a snooze

Lyle, Albert Walter
  nickname: **6** Sparky
  sport: **8** baseball
  position: **7** pitcher
  team: **12** Boston Red Sox **14** New York Yankees
  author of: **11** The Bronx Zoo

Lyly, John
  author of: **20** Euphues and His England **22** Euphues the Anatomy of Wit

lynch 4 hang **6** gibbet **8** string up

Lynde, Paul
  born: **13** Mount Vernon OH
  roles: **12** Bye Bye Birdie **16** Hollywood Squares **17** Beach Blanket Bingo **18** Under the Yum-Yum Tree

Lyngi
  origin: **12** Scandinavian
  mentioned in: **8** Volsunga
  rival of: **7** Sigmund
  sought: **7** Hiordis, Hjordis
  killed: **7** Sigmund
  killed by: **6** Sigurd

lynx 3 cat **6** bobcat **7** wildcat

Lyonnesse
  place in: **16** Arthurian romance
  birthplace of: **8** Tristram

Lyre
  constellation of: **4** Lyra

lyric, lyrical 6 poetic **7** lilting, melodic, musical, singing, tuneful **8** songlike **9** melodious **10** euphonious **11** mellifluent, mellifluous **13** sweetsounding

Lyrical Ballads
  author: **17** William Wordsworth **21** Samuel Taylor Coleridge

lyrics 4 poem **5** words

Lyrus
  father: **8** Anchises
  mother: **9** Aphrodite

Lysander
  character in: **21** A Midsummer Night's Dream
  author: **11** Shakespeare

Lysippe
  father: **7** Proetus
  mother: **5** Antia

Lysistrata
  author: **12** Aristophanes
  character: **7** Lampito **8** Cinesias, Cleonice, Myrrhine **10** Magistrate **14** Old Men of Athens (Chorus)

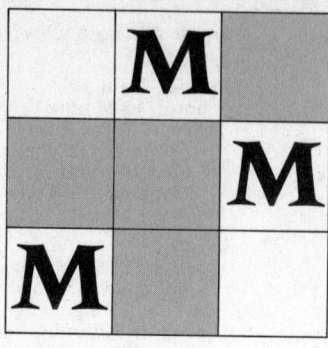

M

director: 9 Fritz Lang
cast: 10 Peter Lorre **11** Inge Landgut **12** Ellen Widmann **15** Gustav Grundgens
setting: 6 Berlin

Maat
origin: 8 Egyptian
goddess of: 3 law **13** righteousness
symbol: 7 feather

Mabinogian
origin: 5 Welsh
tales of: 7 romance

macabre 4 grim **5** eerie, weird **6** grisly, horrid **7** ghastly, ghostly **8** dreadful, gruesome, horrible, horrific **9** frightful, ghostlike, unearthly **11** frightening

Macao *see box*

Macareus
father: 6 Aeolus
mother: 7 Encrete
sister: 6 Canace

MacArthur, Douglas
served in: 3 WWI **4** WWII **9** Korean War, World War I **10** World War II **11** World War One, World War Two
commander of: 15 Rainbow (42nd) Division **19** United Nations forces **24** US army forces in the Pacific
rank: 15 five-star general **16** army chief of staff
battle: 5 Luzon, Pusan **6** Inchon **9** New Guinea **11** Leyte Island, Philippines **14** Bismark Islands, Solomon Islands **15** Bataan Peninsula **16** Admiralty Islands, Corregidor Island
accepted surrender of: 5 Japan
    surrender occurred aboard: **8** Missouri
chairman of: 13 Remington Rand
author of: 13 Reminiscences

smoked: 11 corncob pipe
saying: 12 "I shall return"

Macbeth
author: 18 William Shakespeare
character: 6 Banquo, Duncan (King of Scotland) **7** MacDuff, Malcolm **11** Lady Macbeth **12** Three Witches
director: 13 Roman Polanski
cast: 8 Jon Finch **10** Martin Shaw **13** Nicholas Selby **14** Francesca Annis

Maccabees
title of: 5 Judas
patriarch: 10 Mattathias
means: 8 hammerer

MacDonald, John D
author of: 11 Condominium
character: 11 Travis McGee

MacDonald, Ross
real name: 13 Kenneth Millar
author of: 8 The Chill **10** Black Money **13** The Blue

Macao
other name: 5 Ao-men, Macau
territory of: 8 Portugal
monetary unit: 3 avo **6** pataca, pataco
island: 5 Taipa **7** Coloane
highest point: 5 Hag-Sa
river: 5 Pearl **6** Canton
sea: 10 South China
people: 7 Chinese, Macaoan **10** Portuguese
language: 7 Chinese, English **9** Cantonese **10** Portuguese
religion: 6 Taoism **8** Buddhism **13** Roman Catholic
place:
    street: **11** Praia Grande
feature:
    houseboat: **6** sampan

Hammer **14** The Goodbye Look
character: 9 Lew Archer

MacDowell, Edward Alexander
born: 9 New York NY
composer of: 9 Sea Pieces **11** To a Wild Rose **13** Fireside Tales **15** Poems after Heine **16** Hamlet and Ophelia, New England Idylls, Woodland Sketches

MacDuff
character in: 7 Macbeth
author: 11 Shakespeare

mace
origin: 9 Indonesia
from same tree as: 6 nutmeg
tree: 17 Myristica fragrans
use: 4 fish **7** seafood **9** cherry pie, pound cake **16** chicken fricassee

Macedonia
capital/largest city: 6 Skopje
head of state: 9 president
government: 8 republic
monetary unit: 5 denar
river: 4 Crna **6** Vardar
people: 4 Turk **9** Albanian **10** Macedonian
language: 10 Macedonian
religion: 27 Macedonian Orthodox Christian

macerate 4 fade, mash, pulp, soak **5** souse, steep **6** shrink, soften, squash, wither **7** decline, liquefy, shrivel **8** dissolve, emaciate, fluidize, permeate, saturate **9** liquidize, waste away **10** lose weight

MacGraw, Ali
real name: 12 Alice MacGraw
husband: 8 Bob Evans **12** Steve McQueen
born: 12 Pound Ridge NY
roles: 7 Dynasty **9** Love Story **10** The Getaway

13 The Winds of War
15 Goodbye Columbus

Machaerus
killed: **11** Neoptolemus

Machaon
father: **9** Asclepius
brother: **10** Podalirius
wife: **8** Anticlea
son: **8** Alexanor, Gorgasus
10 Nicomachus
vocation: **9** physician
served in: **9** Trojan War

Macheath, Captain
character in: **12** Beggar's
Opera
author: **3** Gay

ma chere 6 my dear

Machiavelli, Niccolo
author of: **9** The Prince
11 The Art of War **16** Discourses on Livy

Machiavellian 6 amoral,
crafty **7** cunning, devious
8 scheming **9** deceitful,
designing **10** perfidious **11** self-
serving, treacherous, underhanded **12** falsehearted,
unscrupulous

machination 4 plot, rule, ruse
5 dodge **6** design, device,
scheme **8** artifice, intrigue,
maneuver **9** stratagem **10** conspiracy **11** contrivance

machine 3 set **4** army, body,
camp, club, gang, pool, ring
5 corps, crowd, force, group,
setup, trust, union **6** device,
system **7** combine, coterie, faction, society **9** apparatus, appliance, machinery,
mechanism, structure **11** association **12** organization
13 establishment

machine gun
invented by: **7** Gatling
improved by: **5** Maxim
9 Hotchkiss

machinery 4 gear **5** setup,
tools **6** agency, makeup, system, tackle, wheels **9** apparatus, mechanism, resources,
structure **12** contrivances,
organization

macho 5 he-man, manly
6 strong, virile

Machpelah
location: **6** Hebron
burial place of: **4** Leah
5 Isaac, Jacob, Sarah
7 Abraham, Rebekah

Macilente
character in: **22** Every Man
out of His Humour
author: **6** Jonson

MacInnes, Helen
author of: **13** North from
Rome **14** Above Suspicion

16 Decision at Delphi
17 The Venetian Affair
21 The Salzburg Connection

macintosh, mackintosh
7 slicker **8** raincoat
10 waterproof

Mack, Connie
real name: **30** Cornelius
Alexander McGillicuddy
sport: **8** baseball
position: **7** manager
team: **21** Philadelphia
Athletics

MacKellar
character in: **21** The Master
of Ballantrae
author: **9** Stevenson

mackerel
young: **5** spike **6** tinker
7 blinker

mackinaw 4 coat **6** jacket
8 overcoat

MacLaine, Shirley
real name: **19** Shirley Mac-
Lean Beaty
brother: **12** Warren Beatty
born: **10** Richmond VA
roles: **6** Can Can **10** Being
There **11** Irma La Douce
12 Sweet Charity, The
Apartment **15** Some Came
Running, The Turning
Point, Two for the Seesaw
16 The Children's Hour
17 Terms of Endearment
(Oscar) **19** The Trouble with
Harry **20** The Bliss of Mrs
Blossom

MacMurray, Fred
wife: **9** June Haver
born: **10** Kankakee IL
roles: **11** My Three Sons
12 The Apartment **14** Above
Suspicion, The Caine Mu-
tiny **15** Double Indemnity
20 The Miracle of the Bells

Macro-Chibchan
language branch: **6** Paezan
8 Chibchan

macrocosm 6 cosmos, nature
7 heavens **8** creation, universe **9** firmament

Macro-Ge
language family: **11** Ge-
Pano-Carib
group: **2** Ge **6** Bororo, Caraja

Macro-Panoan
language family: **11** Ge-
Pano-Carib
group: **6** Panoan
10 Guaycuruan

mad 4 avid, daft, loco, nuts,
wild **5** angry, balmy, crazy,
irate, nutty **6** ardent, crazed,
cuckoo, fuming, insane,
miffed, screwy, ticked
7 cracked, enraged, excited, fanatic, furious, in a huff, luna-

tic, riled up, teed off,
touched **8** crackers, demented,
deranged, frenzied, incensed,
maniacal, provoked, unhinged,
up in arms, worked up,
wrathful **9** devoted to, non
compos, seeing red, ticked off,
wrought up **10** distracted, distraught, infatuated, infuriated,
in love with, irrational, unbalanced **11** boiling over, exasperated, impassioned, not all
there **12** enthusiastic, round
the bend **13** beside oneself, in
high dudgeon, not quite right,
off one's rocker, out of one's
mind

Madagascar *see box, p. 590*

madam, madame 3 Mrs
4 dame, lady **6** matron **7** dow-
ager **8** mistress
German: **4** Frau
Spanish: **6** senora
Italian: **7** signora
Spanish/Portuguese: **4** dona
Italian: **5** donna

Madame Bovary
author: **15** Gustave Flaubert
character: **10** Emma Bovary,
Leon Dupuis **13** Charles
Bovary **17** Rodolphe
Boulanger

Madame Butterfly
also: **15** Madama Butterfly
opera by: **7** Puccini
character: **5** Bonze **6** Suzuki
9 Cho-Cho-San, Cio-Cio-San,
Sharpless **14** Prince Yama-
dori **19** Lieutenant
Pinkerton

mad as a hatter 3 mad
4 daft, nuts **5** crazy, nutty
6 insane **7** cracked, touched
8 demented, deranged, unhinged **10** unbalanced **13** off
one's rocker, out of one's
head **14** off one's trolley
15 mad as a March hare
17 nutty as a fruitcake

mad as a March hare
3 mad **4** daft, nuts **5** crazy,
nutty **6** insane **7** cracked,
touched **8** demented, deranged,
unhinged **10** unbalanced
12 mad as a hatter **13** out of
one's head **14** off one's trolley **17** nutty as a fruitcake

madcap 4 rash, wild, zany
5 brash, clown, giddy, joker
6 unruly **7** erratic, flighty,
foolish **8** reckless **9** hotheaded,
impetuous, impulsive, sense-
less **10** incautious **11** impractical, thoughtless
12 unconsidered **13** inconsiderate, undisciplined

madden 3 vex **4** gall **5** anger,
craze, pique, upset **6** enrage,
frenzy **7** derange, incense, inflame, outrage, provoke, tor-

Madagascar
other name: 16 Malagasy Republic
capital/largest city: 10 Tananarive 12 Antananarivo
others: 6 Tulear 7 Majanga, Nossibe, Toliary 8 Manakara, Tamatave 9 Faradofay, Mananjory, Toamasina 10 Antisirabe 11 Antsiranana, Diego-Suarez, Fort Dauphin
measure: 7 gantang
monetary unit: 5 franc 7 centime
island: 6 Barren, Radama 7 Nossi-Be 11 Sainte-Marie 12 Chesterfield
lake: 5 Itasy 7 Alaotra, Kinkony
mountain: 4 Boby 9 Ankaratra 12 High Plateaus, Tsiafajavona 17 Tsaratanana Massif
highest point: 11 Maromokotro
river: 5 Ikopa, Mania, Sofia 7 Mangoky, Mangoro, Onilahy 8 Ivoloina, Manambao, Mananara 9 Betsiboka, Manambolo 10 Manarandra 11 Tsiribihina
ocean: 6 Indian
physical feature:
　bay: 6 Radama 8 Antongil 9 Mahajamba 10 Sahamalaza
　cape: 5 Amber 10 Saint-Andre 11 Sainte-Marie 14 Saint-Sebastien
　channel: 10 Mozambique
　lagoon: 9 pangalane
　plateau: 9 Ankaizina
people: 4 Arab, Bara, Hova 5 Malay 6 Merina, Tanala 7 African 8 Betsileo, Mahafaly, Malagasy, Sakalava 9 Antaimoro, Antaisaka, Antandroy, Tsimihety 10 Indonesian, Polynesian 13 Betsimisaraka
　dynasty: 6 Merina
　leader: 9 Ratsiraka, Tsiranana 11 Ranamantsoa
language: 6 French 8 Malagasy, Malgache
religion: 5 Islam 7 animism 10 Protestant 13 Roman Catholic
place:
　market: 4 Zoma
　royal estate: 4 Rova
feature:
　animal: 4 zebu 5 lemur 6 foussa
　musical instrument: 11 jego vaotavo
　proverb: 8 hainteny
　shawl: 5 lamba
food:
　vegetable: 7 brettes

ment, unhinge 9 aggravate, infuriate, unbalance 10 exasperate

made 5 built 6 formed 7 created 8 composed, produced 9 assembled, developed 10 fabricated 11 constructed 12 manufactured

madeira
type: 4 wine 6 brandy 7 liqueur 8 aperitif
origin: 7 Madeira

Madeira Islands
capital: 7 Funchal
city: 5 Monte
island: 6 Grande 7 Dezerte, Madeira 8 Desertas 9 Selvagens 10 Porto Santo
ocean: 8 Atlantic
owned by: 8 Portugal
stone aqueduct: 7 levadas
wine: 4 Bual 5 Tinta, Tinto

6 Canary, Gomera 7 Malmsey, Marsala, Sercial 8 Verdelho

made-up 5 false 7 assumed, created 8 fanciful, invented 9 fictional, imaginary, pretended, thought-up 10 fictitious 11 make-believe, theoretical 12 hypothetical

Mad Hatter
character in: 28 Alice's Adventures in Wonderland
author: 7 Carroll

madhouse 6 asylum, bedlam, uproar 7 turmoil 8 loony bin, nuthouse

Madison, James *see box*

madman 3 nut 5 loony 6 maniac 7 lunatic 8 demoniac 9 psychotic 10 psychopath 11 crazy person

Mad Max
director: 12 George Miller
cast: 9 Mel Gibson
sequel: 14 The Road Warrior 17 Beyond Thunderdome (with Tina Turner)

madness 6 lunacy, oddity 8 delusion, dementia, illusion, insanity 9 craziness 11 derangement

Madonna
nickname: 15 The Material Girl
husband: 8 Sean Penn
recordings: 7 Madonna 8 True Blue 11 Like A Prayer, Like A Virgin
films: 9 Dick Tracy 11 Truth or Dare 12 Who's That Girl 14 Body of Evidence 16 Shanghai Surprise 17 A League of Their Own 23 Desperately Seeking Susan
tour: 6 Girlie 13 Blond Ambition
books: 3 Sex

Madrid
area: 9 Salamanca 19 Ciudad Universitaria
capital of: 5 Spain
landmark: 14 National Palace 18 Biblioteca Nacional
　bull ring: 22 Plaza de Toros Monumental
　museum: 5 Prado
mountain: 18 Sierra de Guadaramma
river: 10 Manzanares
square: 10 Plaza Mayor 11 Plaza del Sol 13 Plaza de Espana
street: 13 Paseo del Prado

Madwoman of Chaillot
author: 13 Jean Giraudoux

Mael
origin: 5 Irish
father: 5 Ronan
killed by: 5 Ronan

maelstrom 4 eddy 5 shoot, swirl 6 bedlam, rapids, tumult, uproar, vortex 7 riptide, torrent 8 disorder, madhouse, undertow, upheaval 9 confusion, whirlpool 10 white water 11 pandemonium

maenad, menad 5 lenae 7 bacchae, bassara 8 clodones, thyiades 9 bacchante 10 mimallones
companion of: 7 Bacchus 8 Dionysus

Maenalus
father: 6 Lycaon

Maeterlinck, Maurice
author of: 8 The Blind 11 The Blue Bird, The Intruder 19 Pelleas and Melisande

Madison, James
nickname: 23 Father of the Constitution
presidential rank: 6 fourth
party: 20 Democratic-Republican
state represented: 2 VA
defeated: 7 (DeWitt) Clinton 8 (Charles Cotesworth)
Pinckney
vice president: 5 (Elbridge) Gerry 7 (George) Clinton
cabinet:
  state: 5 (Robert) Smith 6 (James) Monroe
  treasury: 6 (Alexander James) Dallas 8 (Abraham Al-
  fonse Albert) Gallatin, (George Washington) Campbell,
  (William Harris) Crawford
  war: 6 (James) Monroe, (William) Eustis 8 (William Harris) Crawford 9 (John) Armstrong
  attorney general: 4 (Richard) Rush 6 (Caesar Augustus)
  Rodney 7 (William) Pinkney
  navy: 5 (William) Jones 8 (Paul) Hamilton 13 (Benjamin
  Williams) Crowninshield
born: 12 Port Conway VA 16 King George County
died/buried: 2 VA 12 Orange County 16 Montpelier estate
education:
  tutored at home by: 15 Rev Thomas Martin
  school: 15 Donald Robertson
  college of: 9 New Jersey (now Princeton University)
religion: 12 Episcopalian
interests: 3 law 11 agriculture 14 natural history
author: 16 Federalist Papers (with Hamilton and Jay)
  24 Memorial and Remonstrances 29 Journal of the Federal Convention
political career: 24 US House of Representatives 25 Second Continental Congress
  secretary of: 5 state
  signed: 12 Constitution
civilian career: 6 farmer 7 planter
military service:
  colonel of: 19 Orange County militia
notable events of lifetime/term: 19 War of Eighteen
Twelve
  battle of: 10 New Orleans
  treaty of: 5 Ghent
  Washington DC burned by: 7 British
father: 5 James
mother: 7 Eleanor (Rose Conway)
siblings: 5 Sarah 6 Reuben 7 Ambrose, Catlett, Francis,
William 9 Elizabeth 11 Nelly Conway 13 Frances Taylor
wife: 8 Dorothea (Payne Todd)
  nickname: 6 Dolley
first lady:
  saved: 11 state papers 25 George Washington's portrait

ma foi 6 my word, really 7 my
faith

magazine 6 weekly 7 arsenal,
journal, monthly 9 quarterly
10 periodical, powder room
13 military depot, munitions
room

Magdalene *see* 4 Mary

magenta 6 maroon 7 carmine,
crimson, fuchsia 9 vermilion
12 purplish rose 13 reddish
purple

Maggie
character in: 16 Cat on a
Hot Tin Roof
author: 8 Williams

**Maggie: A Girl of the
Streets**
author: 12 Stephen Crane

maggot 4 grub, worm 5 larva
8 mealworm

Magi
also called: 7 Wisemen
11 astrologers
followed: 15 Star of
Bethlehem
visited: 5 Jesus
gifts: 4 gold 5 myrrh
12 frankincense
singular: 5 magus

magic 4 lure 5 charm, spell
6 hoodoo, voodoo 7 sorcery

8 charisma, jugglery, witchery,
wizardry 9 occultism, voodooism 10 allurement, black
magic, demonology, divination, hocus-pocus, witchcraft
11 captivation, conjuration,
enchantment, fascination, legerdemain, the black art
12 entrancement 13 sleight of
hand 16 prestidigitation
god of: 5 Thoth

Magic
nickname of: 13 Earvin
Johnson

Magic Flute, The
also: 14 Die Zauberflote
opera: 6 Mozart
character: 6 Pamina, Tami-
no 8 Papagena, Papageno,
Sarastro 10 Monostatos
12 Queen of Night

magician 5 magus 6 shaman,
wizard 7 juggler, warlock
8 conjurer, sorcerer 9 alchemist 11 illusionist, medicine
man, necromancer, witch doctor 12 escape artist
15 prestidigitator

Magic Mountain, The
author: 10 Thomas Mann
character: 6 Naphta
7 Clavdia 11 Hans Castorp,
Settembrini 15 Joachim
Ziemssen

magisterial 9 imperious
10 autocratic, peremptory
11 dictatorial, domineering,
overbearing 13 condescending

**Magister Ludi: The Glass
Bead Game**
author: 12 Hermann Hesse

magistrate 2 JP 5 judge 7 pre-
fect 17 justice of the peace

magna cum laude 15 with
great praise

Magna Graecia 27 ancient
Greek colonies in Italy

Magna Mater 3 Ops 4 Rhea
6 Cybele

Magnani, Anna
nickname: 10 Nannerella
roles: 8 Open City 13 The
Rose Tattoo (Oscar) 15 The
Fugitive Kind 21 Secret of
Santa Vittoria

magnanimous 7 liberal 8 generous, princely 9 forgiving,
unselfish 10 altruistic, beneficent, charitable 12 large-
hearted 13 philanthropic

magnate 3 VIP 5 giant, mogul,
nabob 6 big gun, bigwig,
leader, tycoon 7 big shot, notable 8 big wheel, great man
9 celebrity 13 empire builder,
industrialist

magnesium
chemical symbol: 2 Mg

magnetic 8 alluring, charming, inviting 9 of a magnet, seductive 10 attractive, enchanting, entrancing, persuasive 11 captivating, charismatic, fascinating 12 irresistible

magnetism 4 lure 5 charm 6 allure 8 charisma 9 mesmerism, seduction 10 allurement, attraction, enticement 11 captivation, enchantment, fascination

magnification 5 honor 7 worship 9 adoration, blowing up, expansion, inflation, reverence 11 acclamation, enlargement, idolization 12 exaggeration 13 amplification, glorification, overstatement

magnificence 4 pomp 5 glory, state 6 luxury 7 glitter, majesty, royalty 8 grandeur, richness, splendor 10 brilliance 13 sumptuousness

magnificent 4 fine 5 grand, noble 6 august, superb 7 elegant, exalted, stately, sublime 8 glorious, imposing, majestic, splendid 9 brilliant, exquisite, wonderful 10 commanding, impressive 11 resplendent 12 transcendent 13 extraordinary

Magnificent Ambersons, The
director: 11 Orson Welles
based on novel by: 15 Booth Tarkington
cast: 7 Tim Holt 10 Anne Baxter 12 Joseph Cotten 14 Agnes Moorehead 15 Dolores Costello

Magnificent Obsession, The
author: 13 Lloyd C Douglas

Magnificent Seven, The
director: 11 John Sturges
cast: 10 Brad Dexter, Eli Wallach, Yul Brynner 11 James Coburn 12 Robert Vaughn, Steve McQueen 13 Horst Buchholz 14 Charles Bronson
setting: 6 Mexico
score: 14 Elmer Bernstein
remake of: 12 Seven Samurai
sequel: 16 Return of the Seven 20 Magnificent Seven Ride

magnify 4 laud 5 adore, boost, exalt, extol 6 blow up, double, expand, praise, puff up, revere 7 acclaim, amplify, enlarge, glorify, greaten, inflate, stretch, worship 8 heighten, maximize, overrate 9 embroi-der, overstate, reverence 10 exaggerate

magniloquence 7 bombast, fustian 8 euphuism, tumidity 9 pomposity, turgidity 10 orotundity 11 fanfaronade, grandiosity 14 grandiloquence 15 pretentiousness

magniloquent 5 tumid, windy, wordy 6 turgid 7 pompous, verbose 8 inflated 9 bombastic 13 grandiloquent

magnitude 4 bulk, fame, mass, size 6 extent, renown, repute, volume 7 bigness, expanse, measure 8 eminence, enormity, hugeness, vastness

magnolia
varieties: 4 ashe, star 6 saucer 7 Chinese 8 southern, umbrella 11 great-leaved

Magnum, P. I.
character: 2 TC 4 Rick 7 Higgins 12 Thomas Magnum
cast: 10 Tom Selleck 12 Roger E Mosley 13 John Hillerman
setting: 6 Hawaii

Magog
father: 7 Japheth

Magritte, Rene Francois Ghislain
born: 7 Belgium 8 Lessines
artwork: 14 La Belle Captive, The False Mirror, The Key of Dreams 15 Memory of a Voyage 18 L'Empire des Lumieres (The Empire of Light), The Menaced Assassin

Magua
character in: 20 The Last of the Mohicans
author: 6 Cooper

Magus see 4 Magi

Magwitch, Abel
character in: 17 Great Expectations
author: 7 Dickens

Magyar 9 Hungarian

Mahican see 7 Mohican

Mahler, Gustav
born: 7 Austria, Bohemia
composer of: 12 Resurrection (symphony No 2) 15 Das Klagenlied 16 Songs of a Wayfarer 17 Das Lied von der Erde, Kindertotenlieder, The Song of the Earth 19 Des Knaben Wunderhorn 28 Lieder eines fahrenden Gesellen

mahogany 4 tree, wood 5 brown 8 hardwood 9 Swietenia 12 reddish-brown
varieties: 3 red 5 swamp, white 7 African, big-leaf, Florida, Senegal, Spanish 8 Honduras, mountain 9 Nyasaland, Venezulan 10 West Indian

Mahon, Christopher
character in: 27 The Playboy of the Western World
author: 5 Synge

mahzor, machzor 16 Jewish prayer book

Maia
member of: 8 Pleiades
place in group: 6 eldest
father: 5 Atlas
mother: 7 Pleione
son: 6 Hermes

maid 6 tweeny 7 servant 8 domestic 9 hired girl, housemaid, lady's maid, nursemaid 10 parlor maid 11 maidservant 12 upstairs maid 13 female servant
French: 6 au pair

maiden, maidenly 4 girl, lass, maid, miss 5 chick, first 6 chaste, damsel, lassie, virgin 7 colleen, girlish, ingenue, initial, untried 8 original, virginal, youthful 9 inaugural, soubrette, unmarried 10 demoiselle, initiatory 12 introductory

Maid Marian
beloved of: 9 Robin Hood

maidservant 4 amah, ayah, char, lass, maid 5 bonne 6 au pair, tweeny 7 abigail 8 charlady, domestic 9 hired girl, lady's maid, tirewoman 10 handmaiden, parlormaid

Maidu
language family: 8 Penutian
location: 10 California
noted for: 8 basketry

mail 4 arms, post 5 armor 6 get out 7 airmail, harness, letters, panoply 8 dispatch, packages 9 postcards 10 send by mail, send by post, suit of mail 11 surface mail 12 mail delivery, put in the mail 13 postal service 14 defensive armor, drop in a mailbox 17 post-office service

Mailer, Norman
author of: 15 An American Dream 16 Armies of the Night 18 The Naked and the Dead 19 The Executioner's Song

Maillol, Aristide
born: 6 France 13 Banyuls-sur-mer

artwork: 5 Night, Torso **7** Le Desir (Desire) **11** Ile de France **12** Young Cyclist **14** Action in Chains, The Three Nymphs **16** The Mediterranean (Seated Woman) **17** Monument to Cezanne, Monument to Debussy **18** Venus with a Necklace

maim 3 cut, rip **4** gash, lame, maul, rend, tear **5** slash, wound **6** deface, hobble, injure, mangle, savage **7** cripple, disable **8** lacerate, mutilate **9** disfigure, dismember, hamstring **12** incapacitate

main 4 head **5** chief, prime, vital **6** urgent **7** capital, central, crucial, leading, primary, special, supreme **8** critical, foremost, pressing **9** essential, important, necessary, paramount, principal, requisite **10** particular, preeminent **11** outstanding, predominant **13** consequential, indispensable

Main, Marjorie
  real name: 13 Mary Tomlinson

partner: 12 Wallace Beery **13** Percy Kilbride
born: 7 Acton IN
roles: 7 Dead End **8** Ma Kettle

Maine *see box*

mainly 6 mostly **7** chiefly **8** above all **9** in the main, most of all, primarily **10** on the whole **11** principally **13** predominantly **14** for the most part, in great measure **16** first and foremost

main point 3 nut **4** core, crux, gist, meat **5** basis, heart, theme **6** kernel **7** essence **10** brass tacks **11** nitty-gritty **15** sum and substance

mainspring 5 agent, cause **6** motive **9** incentive **10** motivation

mainstay 4 prop **6** anchor, pillar **7** bulwark **8** backbone, buttress **16** pillar of strength

Main Street
  author: 13 Sinclair Lewis

character: 14 Carol Kennicott **15** Dr Will Kennicott

maintain 4 aver, avow, hold, keep **5** claim, state, swear **6** affirm, allege, assert, defend, insist, keep up, uphold **7** care for, contend, declare, finance, profess, stand by, support, sustain **8** conserve, continue, preserve **9** keep alive, keep going **10** provide for, take care of

maintenance 4 keep **6** living, repair, upkeep **7** keeping, support **10** livelihood, protection, sustenance **11** safekeeping, subsistence, sustainment **12** conservation, preservation, safeguarding

Main-Travelled Road
  author: 13 Hamlin Garland

maison de sante 10 sanitarium **13** house of health

maize 4 corn, milo **5** grain **6** cereal, silage, yellow **7** zea mays **10** Indian corn

majestic, majestical 5 grand, lofty, noble, regal, royal **6** august, famous, superb **7** elegant, eminent, stately, sublime **8** esteemed, glorious, imperial, imposing, princely, renowned, splendid **10** impressive **11** illustrious, magnificent **13** distinguished

majesty 4 pomp **5** glory **6** luster **7** dignity **8** elegance, eminence, grandeur, mobility, splendor **9** elevation, loftiness, solemnity, sublimity **10** augustness **11** distinction, stateliness **12** gloriousness, magnificence **14** impressiveness

major 4 main **5** chief, prime, vital **6** larger, urgent **7** capital, crucial, greater, leading, primary, ranking, serious, supreme **8** critical, foremost, pressing **9** essential, important, necessary, paramount, principal, requisite **10** preeminent **11** outstanding, predominant, significant **13** consequential, indispensable

Major Barbara
  director: 13 Gabriel Pascal
  based on play by: 17 George Bernard Shaw
  cast: 11 Deborah Kerr, Rex Harrison, Wendy Hiller **12** Robert Morley, Robert Newton **14** Sybil Thorndike

majority 4 bulk, mass **8** best part, legal age, maturity **9** adulthood, seniority, woman-

---

Maine
  abbreviation: 2 ME
  nickname: 6 Lumber **8** Pine Tree **10** Wonderland
  capital: 7 Augusta
  largest city: 8 Portland
  others: 4 Bath, Saco **5** Hiram, Orono **6** Auburn, Bangor **7** Kittery **8** Boothbay, Lewiston, Ogunquit **9** Bar Harbor, Biddeford, Brunswick, Skowhegan **10** Waterville **11** Millinocket, Presque Isle
  college: 5 Bates, Colby **7** Bowdoin
  explorer: 6 Cabots **8** Norsemen
  feature: 8 lobsters **19** West Quoddy Headlight
    beach: **10** Old Orchard
    national park: **6** Acadia
    waterway: **18** Allagash Wilderness
  tribe: 6 Abnaki **7** Wewenoc
  people: 10 downeaster **11** Dorothea Dix **19** Edna St Vincent Millay **24** Henry Wadsworth Longfellow
  island: 4 Orrs **8** Mt Desert **10** Campobello
  lake: 5 Sebec, Wyman **6** Sebago **8** Rangeley, Schoodic **9** Flagstaff, Moosehead **10** Chesuncook
  land rank: 11 thirty ninth
  mountain: 5 Kineo, White **7** Bigelow **8** Cadillac
    highest point: **8** Katahdin
  physical feature:
    bay: **5** Casco **9** Penobscot **12** Merrymeeting **13** Passamaquoddy
    sand dunes: **13** Desert of Maine
  river: 4 Saco **6** St John **7** St Croix **8** Allagash, Kennebec **9** Aroostook, Kennebago, Penobscot **12** Androscoggin
  state admission: 11 twenty third
  state bird: 9 chickadee
  state fish: 16 land-locked salmon
  state flower: 7 thistle **8** pine cone **22** white pine cone and tassel
  state motto: 7 I Direct
  state song: 16 State of Maine Song
  state tree: 16 eastern white pine

hood **10** lion's share
13 preponderance

major key (in music)
German: **3** dur

Major prophets *see*
8 prophets

majuscule 7 capital **11**
large letter **13** capital letter
15 upper-case letter

make 3 fix **4** form, kind, mark,
meet, pass **5** beget, brand,
build, catch, cause, enact,
erect, force, frame, impel,
press, reach, shape, speak, utter **6** attain, compel, create,
devise, draw up, effect, foment, makeup, oblige, render
7 appoint, compose, deliver,
dragoon, fashion, produce, require **8** arrive at, assemble,
engender **9** cause to be, constrain, construct, establish,
fabricate, formation, legislate,
pronounce, structure **10** bring
about, fashioning **11** composition, manufacture

make a bet 3 bet **4** risk
5 stake, wager **6** chance, gamble, hazard, plunge
7 venture

make a clean breast of
7 confess, lay bare, own up
to **8** blurt out **14** come clean
about

make a dash 3 fly, run
4 flee **6** escape **7** get away
8 make a run **10** make a
break, take flight **12** make a
getaway

make a deal 5 agree **6** settle
10 compromise **11** come to
terms, meet halfway **14** strike
a bargain

make advances 8 approach,
come on to, sound out
11 proposition **13** make overtures, put the moves on

make a fuss over 6 dote on
7 protest **8** crow over

make again 4 copy **6** remake,
repeat **9** duplicate
11 reconstruct

make a getaway 4 bolt, flee,
skip **6** escape **7** get away,
make off, run away **8** make a
run, slip away **9** break free,
cut and run, make a dash
10 break loose, fly the coop,
take flight

make a gift of 4 give **6** donate **7** present **8** bequeath
10 contribute

make allowance for 6 excuse, pardon **7** forgive, indulge **8** bear with, pass over

make amends 5 atone **6** make

up, square **7** expiate **9** do penance **10** compensate

make a mess of 3 mar
4 goof, muff, ruin **5** botch,
spoil **6** bungle, foul up, mess
up **7** butcher, do badly, louse
up, screw up **9** mismanage

make a mistake 3 err **4** goof
6 mess up, slip up
12 miscalculate

make an effort 3 try **5** essay
6 strive, work at **7** attempt
8 endeavor

make appear 5 evoke **6** elicit
7 produce **9** conjure up
10 bring forth

make a racket 3 cry **4** howl,
yell **5** shout **6** bellow, clamor,
holler, scream **7** bluster
8 make a din **10** vociferate
12 raise a rumpus

make a stab at 3 try **5** essay,
guess **6** reckon, take on **7** attempt, surmise, venture **8** estimate, give a try **9** undertake
10 conjecture **11** approximate
12 take a crack at, take a
fling at

make a stand 9 stand fast
13 refuse to yield **17** fight to
the last man

make a statement 6 remark
7 clarify, comment, discuss,
explain, expound **9** elucidate,
talk about

make aware 4 tell **5** edify
6 advise, inform, notify, reveal **7** apprise **8** acquaint, disclose **9** divulge to, enlighten,
introduce **11** familiarize
16 bring to (one's) attention

make away with 3 eat **4** kill,
take **5** spend, steal **6** kidnap,
murder **7** abolish, consume,
destroy **8** carry off, embezzle,
get rid of **9** dissipate

make-believe 4 fake, sham
5 false, phony **6** made-up,
make-up, unreal **7** assumed,
charade, fantasy, feigned, fiction **8** creation, imagined, invented, pretense, spurious
9 fantastic, imaginary, invention, pretended, simulated
10 artificial, fictitious
11 counterfeit, fabrication
13 falsification

make certain of 6 assure,
clinch, ensure **8** be sure of
10 make sure of

make damp 5 bedew
6 dampen **7** moisten **8** sprinkle

make dark 3 dim **6** darken
7 blacken, obscure

make different 4 vary **5** alter,
amend **6** change, modify, mu-

tate **7** convert, remodel
9 transform, transmute
12 metamorphose

make distinctive 8 set apart
9 single out **11** distinguish
12 characterize **13** differentiate

make easy 4 ease **6** smooth
7 explain, lighten **8** simplify
10 clear a path, facilitate

make eligible 5 allow **6** permit **7** entitle, qualify
9 authorize

make evident 4 show
5 prove **6** reveal **7** exhibit
8 manifest **9** establish, make
clear, make plain
11 demonstrate

make fast 3 fix **4** moor **5** affix,
tie up **6** attach, fasten, secure
7 connect

make feeble 6 weaken **7** wear
out **8** enervate **10** debilitate,
devitalize

make furious 5 anger **6** enrage, madden **7** incense, inflame **9** infuriate

make giddy 5 dizzy **12** make
unsteady **15** make lightheaded

make good 5 repay **6** arrive,
make it **7** fulfill, succeed
11 reach the top **15** make
restitution

make happy 5 amuse, cheer
6 please **7** delight, gratify
9 entertain

make haste slowly
Latin: **12** festina lente

make hostile 5 repel **6** offend
7 provoke **8** alienate
10 antagonize

make ill 5 repel **6** infect, revolt, sicken **7** afflict, disgust,
repulse **8** disagree, distress,
make sick, nauseate **9** discomfit **14** turn the stomach

make ill at ease 5 upset
6 rattle **7** fluster **8** distress
9 discomfit, embarrass
10 disconcert

make impure 4 foul, soil
5 dirty, spoil, taint **6** befoul,
blight, defile, infect, poison
7 corrupt, pollute **10** adulterate **11** contaminate

make inroads 6 invade **7** impinge, intrude **8** encroach, infringe, trespass **9** penetrate

make known 4 tell **6** advise,
impart, inform, notify, report,
reveal, unveil **7** apprise, divulge, lay bare, publish, uncover **8** disclose **9** broadcast
10 give notice, make public
11 communicate

make less forceful 6 soften,

weaken 9 undermine 10 devitalize, emasculate

make light of 8 belittle, minimize, pooh-pooh, sneeze at 9 deprecate, disparage, underrate 10 depreciate, undervalue 13 underestimate

make merry 5 revel 7 carouse, roister 9 celebrate, have a ball 15 paint the town red

make much of 5 honor 6 praise 7 acclaim, applaud, commend, flatter 8 fuss over

make nervous 5 annoy, upset 7 agitate, disturb, perturb, trouble, unnerve 10 disconcert

make off with 5 steal 6 abduct, kidnap, snatch 7 bear off 8 carry off 10 run off with 11 get away with

make one's blood boil 5 anger 6 enrage, madden 7 incense, inflame 9 infuriate

make one's eyes pop 4 stun 5 shock 6 dazzle 7 stagger, startle 8 astonish 9 electrify 11 flabbergast

make out 3 see 4 espy 6 behold, descry, detect, fill in, notice 7 discern, observe, pick out 8 get along, perceive, write out 12 catch sight of

make plain 7 clarify, clear up, explain, lay open 9 elucidate, explicate, make clear 10 illuminate 11 disentangle, shed light on 12 bring to light

make possible for 5 allow 6 enable, permit 7 empower, qualify 10 capacitate

make public 3 air 4 tell, vent 5 print, utter, voice 6 expose, inform, reveal, spread 7 declare, display, divulge, exhibit, express, give out, publish 8 announce, disclose, proclaim, televise 9 broadcast, circulate, publicize

maker, Maker 3 god 4 poet 5 smith 6 author, forger 7 builder, creator, founder 8 declarer, inventor, producer 9 architect, generator 10 originator 12 manufacturer

make ready 5 prime 7 arrange, forearm, prepare

make reparation for 5 atone, repay 6 pay for 10 compensate, recompense, remunerate

make restitution 5 repay 7 pay back 9 reimburse 10 compensate, recompense

make right 3 fix 5 amend, emend 6 remedy, repair 7 correct, improve, rectify

make self-conscious 5 abash 6 rattle 7 chagrin, fluster 9 discomfit, embarrass 10 disconcert

makeshift 6 make-do 7 standby, stopgap 8 slapdash 9 alternate, expedient, temporary, tentative 10 substitute 11 provisional

make sick 6 revolt 7 disgust 8 nauseate

make smaller 6 lessen, reduce, shrink, take in 8 decrease, diminish

make sure 5 cinch 6 assure, clinch, decide, ensure, secure, settle 9 ascertain 11 double-check

make thinner 4 thin 6 dilute 9 water down 10 adulterate

make tracks 2 go 4 scat, shoo 5 be off, leave, scram 6 beat it, cut out, depart, go away 8 withdraw 10 hit the road

make uncomfortable 3 try 7 agitate, perturb 8 disquiet, distress 9 discomfit, embarrass 10 discompose

make uneasy 7 disturb, perturb, trouble, unnerve 8 disquiet, distress 9 discomfit, embarrass 10 discomfort, discompose, disconcert

make uniform 4 even 5 equal 6 smooth 7 balance 8 equalize 10 straighten

makeup 5 frame 9 character, cosmetics, framework, structure 11 composition, personality 12 constitution, organization

make up 4 form 5 cover 6 invent 7 arrange, concoct 8 assemble 9 improvise, reconcile 10 compensate, constitute 11 put together

make up for 5 atone 7 expiate 8 make good 10 make amends 13 compensate for

make up one's mind 6 decide 7 resolve 9 determine

make use of 3 use 5 apply 6 employ, engage, occupy 7 exploit, utilize 8 keep busy, put to use 13 turn to account

make weary 4 do in, poop, tire 7 exhaust, wear out 8 enervate

makeweight 6 weight 7 ballast

make well 4 cure, heal

make wider 5 widen 6 dilate, expand 7 broaden, stretch 9 spread out

make worse 6 worsen 8 heighten, increase 9 aggravate, intensify 10 exacerbate

making excuses 8 alibiing 9 defending 10 justifying 11 apologizing

Making of the President, The (series) author: 14 Theodore H White

making the rounds 5 about 6 abroad 11 circulating, going around 13 going the route

Malachi means: 11 my messenger identified with: 4 Ezra 8 Mordecai, Nehemiah 10 Zerubbabel

maladroit 5 inept 6 clumsy, gauche 7 awkward, unhandy 8 bumbling, bungling, tactless 9 impolitic, unskilled 10 blundering, left-handed, ungraceful

maladroitness 9 gaucherie, inability 10 clumsiness, ineptitude 11 awkwardness, unhandiness 12 incompetence

malady 7 ailment, disease, illness 8 disorder, sickness 9 affection, complaint, infirmity 10 affliction, disability

mala fide 10 in bad faith, not genuine

malaise 4 pang 5 throb 6 twinge 7 anxiety 8 disquiet 9 lassitude 10 uneasiness, discomfort 12 nervousness

Malamud, Bernard author of: 8 The Fixer 9 God's Grace 10 The Natural, The Tenants 11 Dubin's Lives 12 The Assistant

Malaprop, Mrs character in: 9 The Rivals author: 8 Sheridan

Malawi see box, p. 596

Malaysia see box, p. 597

Malcolm character in: 7 Macbeth author: 11 Shakespeare

Malcolm X original name: 13 Malcolm Little born: 2 NE 5 Omaha religion: 5 Islam 11 Black Muslim 13 Nation of Islam assassinated in: 6 Harlem 11 New York City book about: 26 The Autobiography of Malcolm X author: 9 Alex Haley film about: 8 Malcolm X director: 8 Spike Lee

malcontent 4 glum, sour 5 rebel 6 grouch, grumpy, morose, sullen, uneasy 7 grouchy, growler, repiner, restive 8 de-

Malawi
  other name: 9 Nyasaland
  capital: 8 Lilongwe
  largest city: 8 Blantyre
  others: 4 Bana 5 Dedza, Limbe, Mzuzu, Zomba 6 Kasese,
    Mzimba, Salima 7 Chipoka, Chiromo, Deep Bay, Karonga,
    Katumbi 8 Chikwawa, Chilumbe, Kota Kota, Nkata Bay
    9 Monkey Bay 10 Port Herald 12 Fort Johnston,
    Livingstonia
  monetary unit: 6 kwacha 7 tambala
  lake: 5 Nyasa 6 Chilwa, Malawi
  mountain: 11 Livingstone
  highest point: 6 Mlanje 7 Mulanje
  river: 3 Bua 5 Shire 7 Dwangwa 11 South Rukuru
  physical feature:
    highlands: 5 Shire
    plateau: 5 Nyika
    valley: 5 Shire 9 Great Rift
  people: 3 Yao 4 Sena 5 Bantu, Lomwe, Ngoni 6 Cheiva,
    Maravi, Ngonde, Nyanja 7 Tumbuka
    dynasty: 6 Maravi
    explorer: 16 David Livingstone
    leader: 5 Banda
  language: 3 Yao 4 Cewa 5 Bantu, Ngoni, Tonga 6 Nyanja
    7 English, Tumbuka 8 Chichewa 10 Chitumbuka
  religion: 5 Islam 7 animism 10 Protestant 12 Presbyterian
    13 Roman Catholic
  feature:
    village: 5 mudzi

jected, downcast, grumbler, restless 9 insurgent, irritable 10 complainer, despondent 11 faultfinder 12 discontented, dissatisfied, faultfinding, hard to please

mal de mer 11 seasickness

Malden, Karl
  real name: 16 Mladen Sekulovich
  born: 6 Gary IL
  roles: 6 Patton 8 Baby Doll 15 On the Waterfront 21 A Streetcar Named Desire 24 The Streets of San Francisco

Maldives *see box*

male 3 boy, man, ram 4 bull 5 manly, youth 6 tomcat 7 manlike, rooster 8 stallion 9 billy goat, masculine

Male
  capital of: 8 Maldives

male bird 4 cock 5 drake 6 gander 7 rooster

maledict 4 damn 5 curse 8 denounce 9 proscribe 12 anathematize

malediction 5 curse 8 anathema, diatribe 9 damnation, evil spell 10 execration 11 fulmination, imprecation 12 denunciation, proscription

malefactor 5 felon, knave, rogue 6 sinner 7 culprit 8 criminal, evil-doer, offender 9 miscreant, scoundrel, wrong-doer 10 malfeasant

male hairdresser
  French: 8 coiffeur

malentendu 7 mistake 16 misunderstanding

male power
  god of: 7 Priapus

Malevich, Kasimir Severinovich
  born: 4 Kiev 6 Russia
  artwork: 11 Black Square 15 The Knife Grinder 18 Eight Red Rectangles 19 Woman with Water Pails 34 Suprematist Composition White on White

malevolence 4 evil, hate 5 spite 6 enmity, grudge, hatred, malice, rancor, spleen 7 despite, ill will 9 hostility, malignity 10 antagonism, malignance, malignancy 12 spitefulness 13 maliciousness

malevolent 5 surly 6 malign, sullen 7 baleful, vicious 8 sinister, spiteful, venomous 9 invidious, malicious, malignant, rancorous, resentful 10 ill-natured, pernicious, revengeful 11 acrimonious, ill-disposed 14 ill-intentioned

malfeasance 5 crime 8 mis-

deeds 10 misconduct, wrongdoing

malformation 9 deformity 10 aberration, distortion 11 abnormality, monstrosity, peculiarity 12 grotesquerie, irregularity 13 disfigurement

malformed 7 twisted 8 deformed 9 contorted, distorted, grotesque, irregular, misshapen

malfunction 6 glitch, malady 7 problem 9 complaint

malgre lui 16 in spite of himself

Mali *see box, p. 598*

malice 4 hate 5 spite, venom 6 enmity, grudge, hatred, rancor 7 ill will 8 acrimony 9 animosity, malignity 10 antagonism, bitterness, evil intent, resentment 11 malevolence 12 spitefulness

malice aforethought
  legal term: 51 planning to commit a crime without just cause or provocation

malicious 7 baleful, harmful, hateful, vicious 8 spiteful 9 invidious, malignant, rancorous, resentful 10 malevolent, revengeful, vindictive 11 acrimonious, ill-disposed

malign 3 bad 4 evil 5 abuse, black 6 defame, revile, vilify 7 baneful, harmful, hateful, noxious, ominous, put down, run down, slander 8 backbite, bad mouth, belittle, derogate, menacing, sinister 9 denigrate, deprecate, disparage, injurious, malicious, malignant 10 malevolent, pernicious, speak ill of 11 deleterious, detrimental, threatening 14 inveigh against

malignancy 5 spite, tumor 6 cancer, malice, rancor 7 ill will, sarcoma 8 acrimony, neoplasm, toxicity 9 carcinoma, hostility, virulence 10 bitterness 11 malevolence, viciousness 12 hard feelings, spitefulness, vengefulness 13 poisonousness

malignant 4 evil 5 fatal, toxic 6 bitter, deadly 7 hateful, hostile, vicious 8 fiendish, spiteful, venomous, virulent 9 invidious, malicious, poisonous, rancorous, resentful 10 diabolical, evil-minded, malevolent, pernicious, revengeful, vindictive 11 acrimonious, ill-disposed

malignant spirit 3 imp 5 demon, devil 7 gremlin

malignity 4 evil 5 spite, venom 6 animus, rancor,

Malaysia
  capital/largest city: 11 Kuala Lumpur
  others: 4 Ipoh, Sibu **5** Anson, Davao, Telok **6** Iloilo, Johore, Kupang, Manado, Penang, Pinang **7** Bintulu, Kuantan, Kuching, Melalap **8** Port Weld, Sandakan **10** Georgetown, Kota Baharu **11** Johor Baharu, Port Dickson **12** Kota Kinabulu **14** Port Swettenham
  division: 5 Sabah **6** Malaya **7** Malacca, Sarawak
  head of state:
    supreme head of state: 18 yang di-pertuan agong
  measure: 3 pau, tun **4** para, pipe, tael, wang **5** parah **6** chupak, parrah **7** gantang
  monetary unit: 3 sen, tra **4** taro, trah **7** ringgit, tampang
  weight: 4 chee, mace, tael, wang **7** tampang
  island: 6 Banggi, Borneo, Labuan, Penang, Pinang, Tioman **7** Pangkor, Sebatik **8** Langkawi **10** Perhentian **11** Balambangan
  mountain: 4 Bulu, Hose, Iban, Iran, Main, Mulu, Niut, Raja **5** Murjo, Niapa, Ophir **6** Blumut, Kapuas, Leuser, Slamet **7** Binaija, Brassey, Crocker **8** Rindjani **11** Gunong Korbu, Gunong Tahan
  highest point: 8 Kinabalu
  river: 5 Klang, Kutai, Perak **6** Barito, Pahang, Rajang, Rejang **7** Sarawak **12** Kinabatangan
  sea: 4 Sulu **7** Celebes **10** South China
  physical feature:
    bay: **5** Labuk
    cape: **5** Sirik
    highlands: **7** Cameron
    passage: **6** Sibutu
    peninsula: **5** Malay
    point: **13** Tanjong Gelang
    strait: **6** Johore **7** Balabac, Malacca
  people: 4 Iban **5** Dayak, Malay **6** Indian **7** Chinese, Kadazan **9** Pakistani, Sri Lankan **10** Bangladesh, Indonesian
  language: 4 Bugi, Dyak **5** Malay, Tamil **6** Battok, Rejang **7** Chinese, English, Lampong, Niasese **8** Achinese, Javanese, Makassar **14** Bahasa Malaysia
    alphabet: **5** tagal
  religion: 5 Hindu, Islam **6** Taoism **7** animism **8** Buddhism **12** Christianity, Confucianism
  place:
    mosque: **8** National
  feature:
    cap: **7** songkok
    cloth: **4** tapa **5** batik
    clothing: **4** baju, malo, sari **5** badju, pareu **6** cabaya, kebaya, sam-foo, sarong **9** cheongsam
    dance: **4** haka, hula **5** joget
    game: **9** sepakraga
    hamlet: **7** kampong
    parish: **5** mukim
    rice paddy: **4** padi
    scarf: **9** selendang
    self-defense: **5** silat
    shadow play: **6** menora
    spirit: **5** hantu
  food:
    drink: **4** kava
    fruit: **6** durian **8** rambutan **10** mangosteen

Maldives
  capital/largest city:
    4 Male
  government:
    legislature: **6** Majlis
  monetary unit: 5 laree, rupee
  island: 3 Ari, Gan **4** Addu, Male **5** Rasdu **6** Felidu, Hulele, Mulaku **7** Malcolm, Minicoy, Nilandu **8** Maldives, Suvadiva **9** Fadiffolu, Wilingili **10** Haddummati, Kolumadulu **11** Tiladummati **13** Ihavandiffulu, Miladummadulu **16** North Malosmadulu, South Malosmadulu
  sea: 6 Indian **7** Arabian **9** Laccadive
  physical feature:
    channel: **4** Wadu **7** Kardiva **8** Veimandu **10** Equatorial **11** Eight Degree **17** One and a Half Degree
  people: 4 Arab **6** Indian **9** Sinhalese **10** Singhalese
    ruling family/sultans: **4** Didi
  language: 6 Arabic, Divehi
  religion: 5 Islam
  feature:
    coconut fiber: **4** coir
    dried coconut: **5** copra

Malle, Louis
  director of: 10 Pretty Baby **12** Atlantic City **13** Lacombe Lucien **16** Murmur of the Heart

malleable 6 docile, pliant **7** ductile, plastic, pliable **8** flexible, moldable, workable **9** adaptable, compliant, teachable, tractable **10** governable, manageable **12** easily shaped **13** easily wrought **14** impressionable

mallet
  type: 6 rubber, wooden **12** plastic-faced

mallophaga
  class: 8 hexapoda
  phylum: 10 arthropoda
  group: 8 bird lice **10** biting lice

malnutrition 10 emaciation, starvation **16** undernourishment

malodorous 4 rank **5** acrid, fetid, musty **6** putrid, smelly

spleen **7** ill will **8** acrimony **9** animosity **12** hard feelings, spitefulness, venomousness

malinger 4 loaf **5** dodge, evade, shirk, slack **7** goof off **9** goldbrick

mall 4 yard **5** court, plaza **6** arcade, circus, piazza, square

8 cloister **9** colonnade, esplanade, promenade **10** quadrangle **12** parade ground

Mallarme, Stephane
  author of: 8 Herodias **18** L'Apres Midi d'un faune **19** The Afternoon of a Faun

Mali
other name: 11 French Sudan 12 French Soudan 16 Sudanese Republic
capital/largest city: 6 Bamako
others: 3 Gao 5 Kayes, Mopti, Segou 6 Djenne 7 Sikasso 8 Taoudeni, Timbuktu 10 Tombouctou
division: 5 Sahel 7 Azaouad
monetary unit: 5 franc 7 centime
lake: 2 Do 4 Debo 5 Garou 7 Korarou 9 Faguibine
mountain: 4 Mina 6 Iforas 7 Manding
highest point: 12 Hombori Tondo
river: 4 Bani 5 Bagoe, Bakoy, Diaka, Niger 6 Bafing, Bakoye, Baoule, Faleme 7 Azaouak, Senegal
physical feature:
   desert: 6 Sahara 8 Chech Erg 10 Sekkane Erg 13 Haricha Hamada
   plateau: 14 Adrar des Iforas
   valley: 5 Niger 7 Tilemsi
people: 3 Bwa 4 Fula, Kyan, Moor, Peul 5 Dogon, Dyula, Fulbe, Marka 6 Berber, Dognon, Fulani, Senufo, Tuareg 7 Bambara, Fellata, Malinke, Miniaka, Songhai, Soninke 8 Khasonke, Mandingo, Senoulfo
   leader: 4 Umar 5 Keita 6 Traore 9 Mansa Musa
language: 5 Dogon, Dyula, Feulh, Mande, Marka 6 Berber, French, Fulani 7 Bambara, Malinke, Senoufo, Songhai
religion: 5 Islam 7 animism
place:
   ruins: 8 Terhazza
feature:
   empire: 4 Mali 5 Ghana 7 Bambara, Songhai

7 noisome, reeking 8 stinking 12 foul-smelling

Malone, Dorothy
real name: 20 Dorothy Eloise Maloney
husband: 15 Jacques Bergerac
born: 9 Chicago IL
roles: 11 Peyton Place 14 Too Much Too Soon 16 Written on the Wind

Malory, Sir Thomas
author of: 14 Le Morte d'Arthur

Malpighi, Marcello
field: 10 physiology
nationality: 7 Italian
founded: 18 microscopic anatomy

malpractice 10 negligence

Malraux, Andre
author of: 8 Man's Fate 11 Anti-Memoirs, Days of Wrath, The Royal Way 13 The Conquerors 18 The Voices of Silence

Malta see box

Maltese Falcon, The
author: 15 Dashiell Hammett
director: 10 John Huston
cast: 9 Mary Astor (Bridget O'Shaughnessy) 10 Peter Lorre (Joel Cairo) 12 Elisha Cook Jr (Wilmer), Gladys George 14 Humphrey Bogart (Sam Spade) 17 Sydney Greenstreet (the Fat Man)
character: 6 Wilmer 8 Sam Spade 9 Joel Cairo 11 Miles Archer 12 Casper Gutman, Floyd Thursby 18 Brigid O'Shaughnessy

Malta
capital: 8 Valletta
largest city: 6 Sliema
others: 5 Marfa, Mdina, Mgarr, Mosta, Nadut, Paola, Rabat 6 Zejtun 7 Senglea, Zeibrun 8 Cospicua, Floriana, Mellieha, Victoria 10 Birkirkara, Birzebbuga, Vittoriosa
measure: 4 rotl 5 artal, canna, parto, ratel, salma 6 kantar 7 caffiso
monetary unit: 4 cent 5 grain, grano, pound
island: 4 Gozo 5 Malta 6 Comino, Filfla 7 Filfola 9 Cominotto 10 Comminotto
highest point: 12 Dingli Cliffs
sea: 13 Mediterranean
physical feature:
   bay: 7 St Paul's 8 Mellieha 10 Marsaxlokk
   channel: 11 North Comino, South Comino
   harbor: 5 Grand 10 Marsamxett
people: 7 Maltese
   leader: 7 Mintoff 9 Buttigieo 18 Parisot de La Valette
   ruler: 5 Arabs 6 Romans 7 British 8 Napoleon 10 Byzantines 11 Hospitalers, Phoenicians 13 Carthaginians 15 Holy Roman Empire, Knights of St John
language: 7 English, Italian, Maltese
religion: 13 Roman Catholic
feature:
   gondola boat: 7 dghaisa

remade as: 13 Satan Met a Lady

malt liquor 3 ale 4 beer, bock, brew 5 stout 6 porter

maltreat 4 harm, hurt 5 abuse 6 ill-use, injure 8 mistreat

maltreatment 5 abuse 6 ill-use, injury 7 assault, cruelty 10 bodily harm, oppression 11 manhandling, molestation, persecution 12 mistreatment

Malvolio
character in: 12 Twelfth Night
author: 11 Shakespeare

Mama
character: 4 Nels 6 Dagmar, Katrin, TR Ryan 9 Aunt Jenny 10 (Papa) Lars Hansen 11 (Mama) Marta Hansen
cast: 8 Iris Mann 9 Peggy Wood, Ruth Gates 11 Judson Laire, Robin Morgan 12 Rosemary Rice 13 Dick Van Patten, Kevin Coughlin
dog: 6 Willie
based on book: 16 Mama's Bank Account
setting: 12 San Francisco
theme: 12 Holverg Suite 13 The Last Spring

Mamers see 4 Mars

mamma, mama 2 ma 3 mam, mom, mum 4 wife 5 madre, mammy, mater, mommy,

mummy, mumsy, woman
6 mother, parent

mammal *see box*

mammon, Mammon 4 gain,
gold **5** money **6** profit, riches,
wealth **9** affluence **11** possessions **13** material goods, the
god of money

Mammon, Sir Epicure
character in: **12** The
Alchemist
author: **6** Jonson

mammoth 4 huge **5** great
6 mighty **7** immense, massive

8 colossal, enormous, gigantic,
whopping **9** cyclopean, herculean, monstrous, ponderous,
very large **10** gargantuan,
monumental, prodigious, stupendous, tremendous **11** elephantine, mountainous

Mammy
character in: **15** Gone With
the Wind
author: **8** Mitchell

Mamoulian, Rouben
director of: **13** Love Me Tonight, Silk Stockings
14 Queen Christina, The
Mark of Zorro

Mamurius
copied: **6** Ancile

man 3 boy, guy, one **4** chap,
gent, hand, male, soul
5 equip, hubby, human, staff
6 anyone, attend, butler, fellow, fit out, helper, outfit,
people, person, spouse, waiter,
worker **7** footman, husband,
laborer, mankind, someone,
subject, workman **8** employee,
garrison, handyman, henchman, humanity, liegeman,
somebody **9** assistant, gentleman, hired hand, humankind
11 Homo sapiens
Spanish: **6** hombre

Man, first 4 Adam
12 Alalcomeneus
Nordic: **3** Ask

Man, Woman and Child
author: **10** Erich Segal

man-about-town 5 blade
7 playboy **8** cavalier, gay
blade **12** boulevardier

manacle, manacles 3 ply,
run, use **4** cope, fare, head,
rule, work **5** bonds, get on,
guide, irons, order, pilot, shift,
steer, wield **6** chains, direct,
fetter, govern, handle, make
go **7** command, conduct, control, operate, oversee, shackle,
succeed, survive, work out
8 cope with, deal with, dominate, get along, handcuff, maneuver, shackles **9** bracelets,
handcuffs, look after, supervise, watch over **10** accomplish, administer, bring about,
manipulate, put in irons, take
care of **11** be at the helm,
hand-fetters, preside over, put
in chains, superintend **12** have
charge of, hold the reins

manage 4 care, rule **6** bosses,
charge, wheels **7** bigwigs,
command, conduct, control,
dealing, running, tactics **8** big
shots, guidance, handling, ordering, planning, strategy, top
brass **9** direction, directors, operation **10** conducting, executives, overseeing, regulation
11 generalship, negotiation,
supervision, supervisors, transaction **12** manipulation, organization **14** administration,
administrators
15 superintendence

manageable 4 easy **6** docile,
pliant, wieldy **8** amenable,
flexible **9** compliant, tractable
10 governable, submissive
12 controllable

management 4 boss, head
5 agent, chief **7** foreman, planner **8** overseer **9** budgeteer,
majordomo, organizer, tactician **10** impresario, negotiator,

---

mammal
  bat (chiroptera): 4 tomb **5** fruit, naked, smoky **7** mastiff,
  vampire **9** fisherman, horseshoe, leaf-nosed, sac-winged,
  slit-faced, thumbless **10** disk-winged, free-tailed, mous-
  tached **11** funnel-eared, hollow-faced, mouse-tailed
  12 false vampire, sheath-tailed, sucker-footed, yellow-
  winged **14** vespertilionid **21** New Zealand short-tailed
  carnivore: 3 cat, dog, fox **4** bear, lion, lynx, mink, puma,
  wolf **5** civet, dingo, fossa, hyena, otter, panda, skunk,
  tayra, tiger **6** badger, bobcat, coyote, ferret, grison,
  hyaena, jackal, jaguar, marten, olingo, weasel **7** polecat,
  raccoon **8** aardwolf, kinkajou, mongoose, suricate **9** wolverine **10** cacomistle, coatimundi
  cetacea: 4 gray **5** pilot, right, whale **6** beluga, killer **7** dolphin, rorqual **8** humpback, narwhale, porpoise **10** sperm
  whale **11** beaked whale **16** bottle-nosed whale
  edentata: 5 sloth **8** anteater **9** armadillo, tree sloth
  egg-laying: 7 echidna **13** spiny anteater **18** duck-billed
  platypus
  even-toed ungulate: 2 ox **3** elk, hog, pig **4** deer, goat,
  oxen **5** bison, camel, llama, moose, okapi, sheep **6** alpaca,
  cattle, duiker, vicuna **7** buffalo, caribou, gazelle, giraffe,
  guanaco, muntjak, peccary **8** antelope **9** mouse deer
  10 chevrotain **12** hippopotamus
  hyracoidea: 5 hyrax
  insect-eating: 4 mole **5** shrew **6** desman, tenrec **7** gym-
  nure, moon rat **8** hedgehog **9** shrew-mole, solenodon
  10 golden mole, otter shrew, water shrew **13** elephant
  shrew
  lagomorpha: 4 hare, pika **6** rabbit
  marsupials / pouched: 5 koala **6** cuscus, numbat, possum,
  wombat **7** opossum, wallaby **8** kangaroo **9** bandicoot,
  phalanger **14** Tasmanian devil
  odd-toed ungulate: 3 ass **5** horse, kiang, tapir, zebra **6** onager, quagga **10** rhinoceros
  pinnipedia: 4 seal **6** walrus **7** sea lion
  primate: 5 lemur, loris, potto **6** avahis, aye-aye, baboon,
  galago, gibbon, indris, monkey, people **7** gorilla, tamarin,
  tarsier **8** marmoset, simpoona **9** orangutan, tree shrew
  10 chimpanzee
  proboscidea: 8 elephant
  rodent: 4 cavy, vole **5** coypu, gundi, hutia, mouse
  6 agouti, beaver, coruro, gerbil, gopher, jerboa, nutria
  7 blesmol, cane rat, hamster, lemming, mole-rat, rock
  rat **8** capybara, chipmunk, dormouse, sewellel, spiny rat,
  squirrel, tucu-tuco, viscacha **9** chozchori, false paca, pa-
  caranas, porcupine, woodchuck **10** chinchilla, prairie dog,
  springhare **11** kangaroo rat, pocket mouse, viscacha rat
  13 kangaroo mouse **16** Speke's pectinator
  sirenia: 6 dugong, sea cow **7** manatee
  tubulidentata: 8 aardvark

supervisor **11** manipulator
13 administrator
14 superintendent

manager 4 boss, head **5** agent, chief **7** foreman, planner **8** overseer **9** budgeteer, major-domo, organizer, tactician **10** impresario, negotiator, supervisor **11** manipulator **13** administrator **14** superintendent

managerial 9 executive **10** management **11** supervisory **14** administrative, organizational

Managua
    capital of: **9** Nicaragua

Manala see **7** Tuonela

Manama
    capital of: **7** Bahrain

manana 6 future **8** tomorrow **11** in the future

Man and Superman
    author: **17** George Bernard Shaw

Manannan
    origin: **5** Irish
    god of: **3** sea
    father: **3** Ler, Lir

Manassa Mauler
    nickname of: **11** Jack Dempsey

Manasseh
    father: **6** Joseph
    mother: **7** Asenath
    great uncle: **4** Esau
    grandfather: **5** Jacob
    descendant of: **9** Manassite

man-at-arms 7 fighter, soldier, warrior **9** combatant **10** cavalryman

Manawyddan
    origin: **5** Welsh
    father: **4** Llyr
    sister: **7** Branwen
    brother: **4** Bran **9** Evnissyen
    wife: **8** Rhiannon
    rescued: **7** Pryderi

Manchester, William
    author of: **11** The Last Lion **14** American Caesar **15** Goodbye Darkness

Manchuria see box

Mandalay
    found in: **18** Barrack-Room Ballads
    author: **14** Rudyard Kipling

mandamus
    legal term: **48** writ from a superior court commanding that a thing be done
    literally: **9** we command

Mandan
    language family: **6** Siouan

Manchuria
    also: 7 Manchow
    city: 5 Aigun, Hulan, Kirin, Peian, Penki **6** Anshan, Antung, Dairen, Fu-Shun, Hailar, Harbin, Hokang, Mukden, Penchi, Yenchi **7** Hulutao, Ikuliho, Ssuping, Tantung **8** Chinchao, Paicheng, Shenyang **9** Changchun, Chiamussu, Manchouli, Miuchwang **10** Port Arthur **11** Chichihaerh, Mutanchiang
    peninsula: 8 Liaotung
    province: 5 Jehol, Jilin, Kirin **8** Liaoning **12** Heilongjiang, Heilungkiang
    river: 4 Amur, Liao, Yalu **5** Argun, Mutan, Nonni, Tumen **6** Ussuri **7** Sungari
    tribe: 5 Tungu **6** Manchu, Mongol

---

location: **11** North Dakota
ceremony: **5** Okipa

Mandarins, The
    author: **16** Simone de Beauvoir

Mandasuchus
    type: **8** dinosaur
    period: **8** Triassic

mandate 5 edict, order **6** behest, charge, decree **7** bidding, command, dictate **8** approval, sanction **9** authority, direction, directive **10** commission, dependency **11** instruction, requisition **12** protectorate **13** authorization

mandatory 7 binding, exigent, needful **8** required **9** called for, essential, necessary, requisite **10** compulsory, imperative, obligatory, peremptory

Mande
    language family: **16** Niger-Kordofanian
    group: **10** Niger-Congo
    includes: **3** Vai **5** Mende **7** Bambara, Malinke

Mandelbaum Gate, The
    author: **11** Muriel Spark

Manderly
    house in: **7** Rebecca
    author: **9** Du Maurier

mandible 3 jaw **4** beak, bill, jowl **7** maxilla **8** lower jaw
    part: **4** mala **5** angle, molar, ramus **6** corpus

Mandrake the Magician
    creator: **7** Lee Falk **9** Phil Davis
    character: **5** Narda **6** Lothar

Manes
    spirits or souls of: **4** dead

Manet, Edouard
    born: **5** Paris **6** France
    artwork: **7** Olympia **8** The Fifer **9** Emile Zola **10** Argenteuil **12** The Guitarist **19** Le Dejeuner sur l'Herbe (Luncheon on the Grass) **25** The Bar at the Folies-Bergeres **31** Execution of the Emperor Maximilian

Manette, Dr and Lucie
    characters in: **16** A Tale of Two Cities
    author: **7** Dickens

maneuver 4 move, plot, ploy **5** dodge, guide, pilot, steer, trick **6** deploy, device, gambit, scheme, tactic **7** finagle **8** artifice, contrive, intrigue **9** stratagem **10** manipulate **11** contrivance, machination, pull strings

Man for All Seasons, A
    director: **13** Fred Zinnemann
    based on play by: **10** Robert Bolt
    cast: **9** Leo McKern **10** Robert Shaw **11** Orson Welles, Wendy Hiller **12** Paul Scofield (Sir Thomas More), Susannah York **14** Nigel Davenport **15** Vanessa Redgrave
    Oscar for: **5** actor (Scofield) **7** picture **8** director

Manfred
    author: **21** George Gordon Lord Byron

man Friday 4 aide **8** adjutant, employee **9** assistant **10** aide de camp **12** right-hand man

Man from St Petersburg, The
    author: **10** Ken Follett

Man from UNCLE, The
    character: **9** Mr Waverly **12** Napoleon Solo **13** Illya Kuryakin
    cast: **11** Leo G Carroll **12** Robert Vaughn **13** David McCallum
    foe: **6** THRUSH

manful 5 brave **8** resolute **10** courageous

manganese
    chemical symbol: **2** Mn

mangle 3 cut **4** harm, hurt, lame, maim, maul, ruin, tear **5** crush, press, slash **6** damage, impair, injure **7** flatten **8** lacerate, mutilate **9** disfigure

manhandle 4 maul **5** abuse **6** batter **7** rough up **8** maltreat, mistreat **9** pull about, push about **10** knock about, slap around

Manhattan
director: **10** Woody Allen
cast: **9** Anne Byrne **10** Woody Allen **11** Diane Keaton, Meryl Streep **13** Michael Murphy **15** Mariel Hemingway

Manhattan Transfer
author: **13** John Dos Passos

manhood 5 prime **8** legal age, machismo, majority, maleness, maturity, virility **9** adulthood, manliness, mature age **10** manfulness **11** masculinity

mania 4 rage **5** craze **6** frenzy, lunacy, raving **7** craving, madness, passion **8** delirium, delusion, dementia, fixation, hysteria, insanity **9** monomania, obsession **10** aberration, compulsion, enthusiasm, fanaticism **11** fascination, infatuation

maniac 3 ass, nut **4** fool **5** loony **6** cuckoo, madman, nitwit **7** half-wit, lunatic **9** psychotic, screwball, simpleton **10** crackbrain, psychopath

manic 2 up **4** high **7** excited, frantic, hyped up **8** agitated, frenzied, worked up **9** wrought up **10** freaked out, switched on **11** hyperactive

manifest 4 bare, open, show **5** clear, frank, plain **6** candid, evince, expose, patent, reveal, unveil **7** display, divulge, evident, exhibit, express, obvious, uncover, visible **8** apparent, disclose, evidence, indicate, palpable **9** make known **10** noticeable **11** demonstrate, make visible, self-evident, transparent, unconcealed, undisguised

manifestation 4 show **7** display, example, symptom **8** evidence, instance **10** exhibition, expression, indication, revelation **12** illustration, presentation, proclamation, public notice **13** demonstration

manifesto 4 bull **5** edict, ukase **6** notice **9** broadside, statement **10** communique, encyclical **11** declaration **12** announcement, annunciation, notification, proclamation, public notice **13** position paper, pronouncement **14** pronunciamento

manifold 4 many **6** myriad, varied **7** complex, diverse

8 multiple, numerous **9** many-sided, multiform **10** variegated **11** diversified, innumerable **12** multifarious **13** multitudinous

Manila
capital of: **11** Philippines
former name: **8** Maynilad
island: **5** Luzon
landmark: **9** Rizal Park **16** San Agustin Church
river: **5** Pasig
section: **10** Quezon City
university: **10** Santo Tomas

Man in the Gray Flannel Suit, The
author: **11** Sloan Wilson

manipulate 3 pat, ply, use **4** feel, work **5** drive, pinch, wield **6** employ, finger, handle, manage, stroke **7** control, deceive, defraud, massage, operate, squeeze

Manitoba *see box*

Mankiewicz, Joseph L
director of: **6** Sleuth **9** Cleopatra **11** All About Eve (Oscar) **12** Guys and Dolls, Julius Caesar **18** The Ghost and Mrs Muir **19** A Letter to Three Wives (Oscar)

mankind 3 man **6** people **7** mortals, persons, society **8** humanity **9** humankind **11** Homo sapiens

manlike 5 macho, manly **6** virile **8** hominoid **9** masculine

manly 4 bold, male **5** brave, hardy, husky, noble **6** brawny,

daring, heroic, manful, plucky, robust, strong, sturdy, virile **7** gallant, staunch, valiant **8** athletic, fearless, malelike, muscular, powerful, resolute, stalwart, vigorous **9** masculine, strapping **10** chivalrous, courageous **11** gentlemanly, indomitable, self-reliant **12** stouthearted
Spanish: **5** macho

man-made 4 mock, sham **6** formed **7** crafted, created **8** produced **9** fashioned, readymade, simulated, synthetic **10** artificial, fabricated, factitious, originated **11** constructed, handcrafted **12** manufactured

Mann, Delbert
director of: **5** Marty (Oscar) **14** Separate Tables

Mann, Thomas
author of: **12** Buddenbrooks **13** Death in Venice, Doctor Faustus **16** The Magic Mountain

manna, Manna 4 boon **5** award **6** reward **7** bonanza **16** divine sustenance

mannequin 4 form **5** dummy, model **6** figure

manner 3 air, way **4** form, kind, make, mode, mold, race, rank, sort, type **5** brand, breed, caste, genre, grade, guise, habit, stamp, style **6** aspect, custom, method, strain **7** bearing, conduct, fashion, species, variety **8** behavior, carriage, category, demeanor,

Manitoba
bay: **6** Hudson
capital: **8** Winnipeg
city: **6** Carman, The Pas **7** Brandon, Caribou, Dauphin, Selkirk **8** Flin Flon, Lynn Lake, Wabowden, Winnipeg **9** Churchill, Killarney, Sherridon, Swan River **10** St Boniface **11** Norway House, York Factory **16** Portage La Prairie
flower: **11** windflower **13** prairie crocus
Indian tribe: **4** Cree **6** Eskimo, Ojibwa **8** Chippewa **10** Assiniboin
lake: **4** God's, Swan **5** Cedar, Moose **6** Island **7** Dauphin, Red Deer **8** Manitoba, Reindeer, St Martin, Waterhen, Winnipeg **9** Granville
mountain: **4** Hart **5** Baldy
name means: **16** lake of the prairies **18** Great Spirit's strait **19** Great Spirit's narrows
nickname: **15** Prairie Province **16** Keystone Province
province of: **6** Canada
river: **3** Red **4** Seal, Swan **5** Hayes **6** Nelson, Roseau, Souris **7** Pembina **8** Winnipeg **9** Churchill **11** Assiniboine **12** Saskatchewan
university: **7** Brandon **10** St Boniface

practice, presence **9** character
10 appearance, deportment
14 classification

mannered 6 formal **7** stilted,
studied **8** affected **9** contrived,
unnatural **10** artificial
11 ceremonious

mannerism 4 airs, pose
5 habit **8** pretense **10** pretension **11** affectation, singularity **12** eccentricity,
idiosyncrasy

mannerly 5 civil **6** polite
7 courtly, gallant, genteel, refined **8** well-bred **9** courteous
10 chivalrous **11** gentlemanly,
well-behaved

manner of living
Latin: **12** modus vivendi

**manner of looking at the
world**
German: **14** Weltanschauung

manner of speaking 7 diction **9** elocution **10** intonation **13** pronunciation

manners 6 polish **7** decorum
8 behavior, breeding, courtesy
9 amenities, deference, etiquette, gallantry, gentility, politesse, propriety
10 deportment, politeness, refinement **11** courtliness

Mannix
character: **9** Joe Mannix,
Peggy Fair **10** (Lt) Adam Tobias **13** Lou Wickersham
cast: **10** Gail Fisher, Robert
Reed **11** Mike Connors
16 Joseph Campanella

Mannon family
members: **4** Ezra, Orin
7 Lavinia **9** Christine
characters in: **22** Mourning
Becomes Electra
author: **6** O'Neill

Manoah
son: **6** Samson

mano a mano 5 alone **8** conflict **13** confrontation, in a
small group
literally: **10** hand to hand

Man of a Thousand Faces
nickname of: **9** Lon
Chaney

Man of Nazareth
author: **14** Anthony Burgess

Man of Property, The
author: **14** John Galsworthy

Man of Sorrows *see* **5** Jesus

Manolin
character in: **18** The Old
Man and the Sea
author: **9** Hemingway

Manon Lescaut
author: **11** Abbe Prevost

Manor, The
author: **19** Isaac Bashevis
Singer

manor house 6 estate, man-
oir **7** chateau, mansion
11 stately home

manpower 4 help **5** brawn, labor **9** work force, employees

manque 6 failed, missed
7 lacking **11** fallen short,
unfulfilled

Mansart, Francois
architect of: **14** Chateau de
Berny **18** Hotel de la Vril-
liere **33** Church of Sainte
Marie de la Visitation
feature: **11** mansard roof

manservant 5 groom, valet
6 butler **7** footman **8** factotum
9 chauffeur

Man's Fate
author: **12** Andre Malraux

Mansfield, Jayne
real name: **14** Vera Jane
Palmer
husband: **14** Mickey Hargitay
born: **10** Bryn Mawr PA
roles: **15** Hell on Frisco Bay
26 Will Success Spoil Rock
Hunter

Mansfield, Katherine
author of: **5** Bliss **12** The
Dove's Nest **14** The Garden
Party

Mansfield Park
author: **10** Jane Austen
character: **5** Yates **8** Mrs
Grant **9** Mrs Norris, Rush-
worth **10** Fanny Price
11 Lady Bertram **12** Mary
Crawford **13** Henry Crawford **16** Sir Thomas Bertram
Bertram children: **3** Tom
5 Julia, Maria **6** Edmund

mansion 5 manor, villa **6** castle, estate, palace **7** chateau
10 manor house

manslaughter 6 murder **7** killing **8** homicide

manta 3 ray **4** cape **5** cloak,
shawl **9** devilfish

Mantegna, Andrea
born: **5** Italy **14** Isola di
Carturo
artwork: **9** Parnassus
16 Camera degli Sposi
(Bridal Chamber) **18** The
Triumph of Caesar, The
Triumph of Virtue **20** Madonna della Vittoria

**Man That Corrupted Had-
leyburg, The**
author: **9** Mark Twain

Mantius
father: **8** Melampus
son: **6** Clitus

mantle 4 cape, film, mask,
pall, veil **5** cloak, cloud, cover,
scarf, tunic **6** canopy, screen,
shroud **7** blanket, curtain,
wrapper **8** covering, envelope,
mantilla

Mantle, Mickey (Charles)
sport: **8** baseball
position: **8** outfield
team: **14** New York
Yankees

manual 6 primer **8** handbook,
physical, textbook, workbook
9 guidebook **10** done by
hand **12** hand-operated, non-
automatic **15** instruction
book

manual skill 8 deftness **9** dexterity, handiness **10** adroitness **12** coordination

manufacture 4 form, make,
mold **5** build, frame **6** cook
up, create, devise, invent,
make up **7** concoct, fashion,
produce, think up, trump up
8 assemble **9** construct, fabricate **11** mass-produce, put
together

manufacturing 8 devising
9 inventing, producing **10** industrial **11** fabricating,
nonagrarian

manumission 7 freeing **10** liberation **11** setting free
12 emancipation

manumit 4 free **7** set free
8 liberate **10** emancipate

manure 4 dung **5** feces **6** ordure **7** compost, excreta
8 dressing **10** fertilizer

manuscript 6 script **10** typescript **14** shooting script
15 written document

Manvah
son: **6** Samson

**Man Who Came to Dinner,
The**
director: **15** William Keighley
based on play by: **8** Moss
Hart **14** George S Kaufman
cast: **10** Bette Davis **11** Ann
Sheridan, Billie Burke
12 Monty Woolley **13** Richard Travis

**Man Who Fell to Earth,
The**
director: **12** Nicholas Roeg
cast: **7** Rip Torn **9** Buck
Henry **10** Candy Clark,
David Bowie

**Man Who Shot Liberty Va-
lence, The**
director: **8** John Ford
cast: **9** John Wayne, Lee
Marvin, Vera Miles **12** Edmund O'Brien, James
Stewart

Man Who Was Thursday, The
author: 12 G K Chesterton

Man Without a Country, The
author: 17 Edward Everett Hale
character: 11 Philip Nolan

many 4 a lot, lots 5 a heap, heaps, piles 6 divers, dozens, myriad, scores, sundry 7 numbers, several, various 8 numerous 9 countless 10 a profusion, numberless 11 an abundance, innumerable 13 multitudinous

manzanita 14 Arctostaphylos
varieties: 4 dune, Ione, Otay 5 hairy, hoary, Morro, Parry, Pecho 6 island, Sonoma, woolly 7 Mexican, Pajarro, pine-mat 8 big-berry, Del Norte, Eastwood, Mariposa, Monterey, shagbark, Stanford 9 Fort Bragg, green-leaf, Florida, Persian, scarlet, striped 8 big-tooth, Drummond, full-moon, Hawthorn, Hornbeam, Japanese, mountain, Shantung, Sycamore, Tatarian 9 ash-leaved, eagle-claw, flowering, paperbark, Schwedler, Tartarian 11 Montpellier 12 Pennsylvania 13 Rocky Mountain, Southern sugar 18 Rocky Mountain sugar

map 4 plan, plot 5 chart, graph, ready 6 design, devise, lay out 7 arrange, diagram, prepare, project 8 contrive, organize 9 elevation 10 make a map of, projection 14 representation 18 topographical chart

maple 4 Acer
varieties: 3 red 4 Amur, hard, rock, soft, vine 5 black, chalk, field, hedge, Nikko, river, sugar, swamp, white 6 Balkan, canyon, Norway, Oregon, parlor, sierra, silver, Triden 7 big-leaf, Florida, Persian, scarlet, striped 8 big-tooth, Drummond, full-moon, Hawthorn, Hornbeam, Japanese, mountain, Shantung, Sycamore, Tatarian 9 ash-leaved, eagle-claw, flowering, paperbark, Schwedler, Tartarian 11 Montpellier 12 Pennsylvania 13 Rocky Mountain, Southern sugar 18 Rocky Mountain sugar

map out 3 map 5 chart, draft 6 devise, lay out 7 diagram, outline 8 block out 9 delineate, formulate

Maputo
capital of: 10 Mozambique

mar 4 hurt, maim, mark, nick, ruin, scar 5 botch, spoil, stain, taint 6 blight, damage, deface, defile, impair 7 blemish, destroy, scratch 8 diminish, mutilate 9 disfigure

Marabar Caves
setting in: 15 A Passage to India
author: 7 Forster

Maranatha
means: 9 O Lord come

maraschino
type: 7 liqueur
origin: 5 Italy
flavor: 6 cherry
color: 3 red 5 white

Marathi
language family: 12 Indo-European
branch: 11 Indo-Iranian
group: 5 Indic
spoken in: 5 (northern) India

Marathonian bull see 10 Cretan bull

marauder 6 looter, pirate, ranger 7 corsair, ravager, spoiler 8 pillager 9 buccaneer, despoiler, guerrilla, plunderer, privateer 10 depradator, freebooter

marble 3 jet 4 vein 5 agate 6 basalt, blotch, mottle, streak 7 calcite 8 dolomite 9 limestone 10 serpentine, travertine 12 anthraconite
quarry: 7 Carrara

Marble Faun, The
author: 18 Nathaniel Hawthorne
character: 5 Hilda 6 Kenyon, Miriam 9 Donatello

marbles
type: 3 mib, taw 4 aggy, duck, immy, migg 5 agate, monny, scrap 6 commie, glassy, hoodle, marine 7 cat's eye, rainbow, shooter 9 carnelian 16 peppermint stripe
term: 3 hit 4 shot 6 edgers, ringer 7 bowling, for fair, histing, lagging, lag line, lofting 8 circling, for keeps, hunching 9 pitch line 10 roundsters 11 knuckle down 13 knuckling down

Marc, Franz
born: 6 Munich 7 Germany
artwork: 10 Blue Horses 12 Yellow Horses 13 Fighting Forms

Marceline
character in: 19 The Marriage of Figaro
author: 12 Beaumarchais

march 2 go 4 hike, rise, step, trek, walk 5 tramp 6 file by, growth, parade 7 advance, proceed 8 progress 9 group walk 10 go directly, procession, walk in step 11 advancement, development, progression 12 martial music

March
event: 8 Passover 9 Mardi Gras 11 Ides of March (15) 12 Ash Wednesday 13 vernal equinox (21)
flower: 7 jonquil 8 daffodil
French: 4 Mars
gem: 10 aquamarine, bloodstone
German: 4 Marz
holiday: 6 Easter 12 St Joseph's Day (19) 13 St Patrick's Day (17)
Italian: 5 Marzo
number of days: 9 thirty-one
origin of name: 4 Mars
Roman god of: 3 war
place in year:
Gregorian: 5 third
Roman: 5 first
saying: 20 Beware the Ides of March 40 March comes in like a lion and goes out like a lamb
Spanish: 6 Marcha
Zodiac sign: 5 Aries 6 Pisces

March, Fredric
real name: 29 Ernest Frederick McIntyre Bickel
born: 8 Racine WI
roles: 11 A Star Is Born 12 Anna Karenina, The Buccaneer 13 Les Miserables 14 Anthony Adverse, Inherit the Wind, Mary of Scotland, Seven Days in May 16 Death of a Salesman 17 Alexander the Great, Dr Jekyll and Mr Hyde (Oscar), The Desperate Hours 18 Death Takes a Holiday 19 The Affairs of Cellini 22 The Best Years of Our Lives (Oscar) 23 Barretts of Wimpole Street

Marchen 8 folk tale 9 fairy tale

Marcheshvan 17 eighth Hebrew month

March family
members: 2 Jo 3 Amy, Meg 4 Beth 6 Marmee
characters in: 11 Little Women
author: 6 Alcott

March Hare
character in: 28 Alice's Adventures in Wonderland
author: 7 Carroll

Marchmain family
  characters in: **19** Brideshead
  Revisited
  author: **5** Waugh

Marciano, Rocky
  real name: **23** Rocco Francis
  Marchegiano
  nickname: **19** Brockton
  Blockbuster
  sport: **6** boxing
  class: **11** heavyweight

Marconi, Guglielmo
  nationality: **7** Italian
  nickname: **16** father of
  wireless
  invented/discovered: **5** radio **12** radio signals
  16 magnetic detector
  30 wireless high frequency
  telegraph
  shared (1919): **20** Nobel
  Prize for physics

Marcus Welby MD
  character: **11** (Dr) Steven
  Kiley **13** Consuelo Lopez
  cast: **11** James Brolin, Robert
  Young **12** Elena Verdugo

**Mardi (and a Voyage
Thither)**
  author: **14** Herman Melville
  character: **4** Alma, Jarl,
  Mohi, Taji **5** Media, Samoa,
  Yoomy **6** Yillah **7** Annatoo
  10 Babbalanja, Braidbeard
  11 Queen Hautia

Mardi Gras 7 holiday **8** carnival, festival, jamboree **10** fat
  Tuesday

Marduk
  also: **8** Merodach **12** Baal
  Merodach
  origin: **10** Babylonian
  chief of: **4** gods

mare 3 sea **9** brood-mare
  11 female horse

mare nostrum 6 our sea
  ancient Roman name for:
  13 Mediterranean

mares of Diomedes see
  8 Diomedes

margin 3 hem, rim **4** edge,
  side **5** bound, skirt, verge
  6 border, fringe, leeway
  7 confine **8** boundary **9** allowance, extra room, safeguard

marginal 9 on the edge **11** in
  the margin **12** barely useful

mariage de convenance
  21 marriage of convenience

Marica
  also: **9** Dea Marica
  origin: **5** Roman
  goddess of: **7** marshes

marigold 7 Tagetes
  varieties: **3** big, bur, fig, pot
  4 cape, corn, wild **5** Aztec,
  fetid, field, marsh, water

  6 desert, French, signet
  7 African **12** sweet-scented

marijuana, marihuana 3 boo,
  kif, pot, tea **4** hash, hemp,
  herb, weed **5** bhang, dagga,
  ganja, grass, joint **6** moocah,
  reefer **7** hashish **8** cannabis,
  locoweed, mary jane

Marin, John Cheri (3rd)
  born: **12** Rutherford NJ
  artwork: **8** Sea Piece
  12 Maine Islands **13** Tunk
  Mountains **16** Beach Flint
  Island **19** Movement Fifth
  Avenue **21** Seaside Interpretation **26** Camden Mountain
  across the Bay

marine 3 sea **5** naval **7** aquatic,
  oceanic, of ships, pelagic
  8 maritime, nautical, of the
  sea, seagoing **9** salt-water, seafaring **10** oceangoing
  13 oceanographic

mariner 3 gob, tar **4** salt **5** pilot **6** sailor, sea dog, seaman
  7 boatman **8** deck hand,
  helmsman, seafarer **9** navigator, yachtsman **10** bluejacket
  12 seafaring man **16** able-
  bodied seaman

Marion, Francis
  nickname: **8** Swamp Fox
  served in: **16** Revolutionary
  War
  type of warfare: **9** guerrilla
  area fought in: **13** South
  Carolina
  battle: **12** Eutaw Springs

marionette 6 puppet
  10 fantoccino

Maris
  companion of: **8** Sarpedon

marital 6 wedded, wifely
  7 married, nuptial, spousal
  8 conjugal **9** connubial, husbandly **10** of marriage
  11 matrimonial

maritime 5 naval **6** marine
  7 aquatic, coastal, oceanic, of
  ships **8** nautical, of the sea,
  seagoing **9** seafaring

marjoram
  botanical name: **8** Majorana,
  O vulgare, Origanum **16** M
  hortensis moench
  origin: **4** Asia
  13 Mediterranean
  family: **4** mint
  symbol of: **5** honor
  9 happiness
  charm against: **10** witchcraft
  used as: **12** air sweetener
  use: **4** eggs, fish, meat
  5 salad **8** stuffing **9** vegetable

Marjorie Morningstar
  author: **10** Herman Wouk

mark 3 cut, mar, pit **4** dent,
  goal, harm, heed, line, mind,

  nick, note, pock, rate, scar,
  show, sign, spot **5** badge,
  brand, grade, judge, label,
  notch, point, proof, score,
  stain, stamp, token, track
  6 attend, bruise, deface, denote, emblem, evince, injure,
  intent, rating, regard, reveal,
  streak, symbol, target, typify
  7 betoken, blemish, correct,
  imprint, measure, scratch, signify, suggest, symptom, write
  in, write on **8** bull's-eye, colophon, disclose, evidence, hallmark, indicate, manifest, point
  out, standard, stand for **9** be a
  sign of, criterion, designate,
  disfigure, objective, symbolize,
  yardstick **10** impression, indication, touchstone **11** distinguish **12** characterize
  13 differentiate

Mark
  also: **8** John Mark
  mother: **4** Mary
  cousin: **8** Barnabas
  wrote: **11** Gospel

Mark (King Mark)
  character in: **16** Arthurian
  romance

Mark Antony
  also: **14** Marcus Antonius
  character in: **12** Julius
  Caesar
  author: **11** Shakespeare

mark down 4 note **5** enter,
  lower **6** record, reduce **7** put
  down **9** write down

marked 5 clear, great, noted,
  plain **6** dotted, scored, severe,
  showed, spotty, tabbed,
  tagged, traced **7** branded, labeled, pointed, specked, spotted, stained, tracked
  8 destined, speckled, striking,
  targeted **9** indicated, prominent **10** emphasized, identified,
  made note of, noticeable, remarkable, singled out **11** conspicuous, distinctive,
  outstanding **12** considerable
  13 distinguished

marker 3 IOU, peg, run, tab
  4 chip, flag, sign **5** score
  6 etcher, scorer, tablet, ticket
  7 counter **8** bookmark, memorial, monument, recorder

market 4 hawk, sell, vend
  5 stand **6** bourse, peddle, retail **7** grocery **9** dispose of
  10 curb market, meat market
  11 butcher shop, grocer's
  shop, marketplace

marketplace 4 mart **5** agora,
  arena, plaza **6** bazaar, market,
  square **8** exchange

Mark of Zorro, The
  director: **15** Rouben
  Mamoulian

cast: 11 Tyrone Power
12 Linda Darnell **13** Basil
Rathbone **15** Gale
Sondergaard
score: 12 Alfred Newman

mark out 8 describe
9 delineate

marksman 8 dead shot, good
shot, sure shot **9** crack shot
12 sharpshooter

marksmanship 3 aim **5** skill
8 accuracy **13** sharpshooting

Marley's Ghost
character in: 15 A Christmas
Carol
author: 7 Dickens

Marlow
character in: 7 Lord Jim
author: 6 Conrad

Marlowe
character in: 15 Heart of
Darkness
author: 6 Conrad

Marlowe, Christopher
author of: 8 Edward II
13 Doctor Faustus, The Jew
of Malta **14** Hero and Leander **15** Edward the Second
19 Tamburlaine the Great

Marmax
suitor of: 10 Hippodamia
murdered by: 8 Oenomaus

Marmee
character in: 11 Little
Women
author: 6 Alcott

Marmion
author: 14 Sir Walter Scott
character: 11 Lord Marmion
13 Ralph de Wilton **14** Clare
Fitz-Clare **16** Archibald
Douglas **19** Constance de
Beverley

Marnie
director: 15 Alfred Hitchcock
cast: 10 Diane Baker **11** Sean
Connery, Tippi Hedren

maroon 4 plum, wine **6** desert,
strand **7** abandon, forsake, magenta **8** cast away, jettison
9 put ashore **10** cast ashore,
terra cotta **11** brownish-red,
leave behind **15** leave high
and dry

Marpessa
origin: 5 Greek
father: 6 Euenos
loved by: 4 Idas **6** Apollo
chose: 4 Idas

Marple, Miss Jane
detective created by:
14 Agatha Christie

Marquand, J P
author of: 13 Wickford

Point **18** The Late George
Apley
character: 6 Mr Moto

marquee 4 tent **6** awning, canopy **8** marquise

marred 6 ruined **7** damaged,
injured, spoiled **8** impaired
9 blemished, destroyed
10 disfigured

Marrener, Edythe
real name of: 12 Susan
Hayward

marriage 7 wedding, wedlock
8 nuptials **9** matrimony
god of: 4 Frey **5** Freyr, Hymen **9** Hymenaeus
goddess of: 3 Fri **5** Frigg,
Frija **6** Frigga, Tellus

Marriage a la Mode
author: 10 John Dryden

marriage broker
Yiddish: 8 shadchan
9 schatchen

marriage of convenience
French: 19 mariage de
convenance

Marriage of Figaro, The
also: 15 Le Nozze di Figaro
opera: 6 Mozart
character: 7 Susanna
8 Countess **9** Cherubino, Dr
Bartolo **10** Marcellina
13 Count Almaviva

Marriage of Figaro, The
author: 12 Beaumarchais
character: 6 Figaro **7** Suzanne **8** Cherubin **9** Marceline **10** Dr Bartholo
13 Count Almaviva
16 Countess Almaviva

**Marriages Between Zones
Three, Four and Five**
author: 12 Doris Lessing

married 3 wed **5** mated
6 joined, united, wedded
7 hitched, marital **8** combined,
espoused **9** connubial **11** matrimonial, tied the knot

married woman
German: 4 frau

marry 3 wed **7** espouse, make
one **10** get spliced, tie the
knot **13** join in wedlock
14 join in marriage, lead to
the altar, take in marriage

Marryat, Frederick
author of: 11 Peter Simple
16 Mr Midshipman Easy

Mars
also: 6 Mamers, Mavors
origin: 5 Roman
god of: 3 war
mother: 4 Juno
wife: 5 Nerio
epithet: 5 Ultor **8** Gradivus
corresponds to: 4 Ares

Mars
position: 6 fourth
nickname: 9 Red Planet
satellite: 6 Deimos, Phobos

Marseillaise 20 French national anthem

marsh 3 bog, fen **5** swamp
6 morass, slough **7** bottoms,
wetland **8** quagmire **9** everglade, marshland, quicksand

Marsh, Dame Ngaio
author of: 9 Dead Water
12 Final Curtain **13** Death
at the Bar **14** Enter a Murderer **19** Singing in the
Shrouds
character: 10 Troy Alleyn
14 Roderick Alleyn

Marsh, Reginald
born: 5 Paris **6** France
artwork: 9 The Bowery
10 Pip and Flip **14** Why Not
Use the El? **16** Tattoo and
Haircut **17** Twenty-Cent
Haircut

marshal 5 align, array, chief,
group, order **6** deploy, draw
up, gather, leader, line up,
muster **7** arrange, collect,
manager, sheriff **8** assemble,
director, marechal, mobilize,
organize **9** fire chief **10** law officer, supervisor **11** police
chief **12** chief officer, field
marshal **13** generalissimo

Marshall, George C
served in: 3 WWI **4** WWII
9 Korean War, World War
I **10** World War II
11 World War One, World
War Two
rank: 12 chief of staff
16 general of the army
author of: 12 Marshall Plan
secretary of: 5 state
7 defense
winner of: 15 Nobel Peace
Prize (1953)

Marshall, Penny
husband: 9 Rob Reiner
born: 7 Bronx NY
roles: 5 Myrna **12** The Odd
Couple **14** Laverne DeFazio
17 Laverne and Shirley
director: 3 Big

marshy 3 wet **4** miry **5** boggy,
fenny, muddy **6** swampy
7 paludal, paludic
11 waterlogged

marsupial 5 koala **6** numbat,
possum, wombat **7** cuscuse,
opossum, wallaby **8** kangaroo
9 bandicoot, phalanger
14 Tasmanian devil

Marsyas
form: 5 satyr
played: 5 flute

mart 4 show **6** market **8** exchange **9** trade fair, trade show **10** exposition

Martha
sister: **4** Mary
brother: **7** Lazarus
hometown: **7** Bethany

martial 7 hostile, Spartan, warlike **8** militant, military **9** bellicose, combative, soldierly **10** pugnacious **11** belligerent, contentious

Martian Chronicles, The
author: **11** Ray Bradbury

Martin, Dean
real name: **16** Dino Paul Crocetti
partner: **10** Jerry Lewis
born: **14** Steubenville OH
roles: **8** Matt Helm, Rio Bravo, The Caddy **9** The Stooge **10** Living It Up **12** Four for Texas, Sailor Beware **14** Toys in the Attic **15** Some Came Running **16** Artists and Models

Martin, Mary
son: **11** Larry Hagman
born: **13** Weatherford TX
roles: **6** I Do I Do **8** Peter Pan **12** Sound of Music, South Pacific

Martin, Steve
born: **6** Waco TX
roles: **7** The Jerk **17** Pennies From Heaven, Saturday Night Live **19** The Man with Two Brains **20** Dead Men Don't Wear Plaid **26** Planes Trains and Automobiles

Martin Chuzzlewit
author: **14** Charles Dickens
character: **5** Mercy **7** Charity **8** Tom Pinch **9** Pecksniff, Ruth Pinch, Sarah Gamp **10** Mark Tapley, Mary Graham **15** Jonas Chuzzlewit **17** Anthony Chuzzlewit

martinet 6 despot, tyrant **8** dictator **10** hard master, taskmaster **11** drillmaster, Simon Legree **12** little Caesar **13** authoritarian, drill-sergeant

Marty
director: **11** Delbert Mann
cast: **10** Betsy Blair **11** Joe De Santis **14** Ernest Borgnine **15** Esther Minciotti
Oscar for: **5** actor (Borgnine) **7** picture
script: **14** Paddy Chayefsky

martyr 5 saint **8** sufferer

martyrdom 5 agony **6** ordeal **7** anguish, torment, torture **9** bitter cup, suffering **10** affliction **11** cup of sorrow **13** crown of thorns

marvel 4 gape **6** be awed, rarity, wonder **7** miracle **8** be amazed **9** spectacle **10** phenomenon

Marvell, Andrew
author of: **9** The Garden **16** To His Coy Mistress

marvelous, marvellous 4 A-one, fine **5** grand, great, super **6** divine, lovely, superb **7** amazing **8** colossal, fabulous, heavenly, smashing, splendid **9** fantastic, first-rate, wonderful **10** phenomenal, remarkable, stupendous **11** astonishing, magnificent, outstanding, sensational **13** extraordinary

marvelous to relate
Latin: **13** mirabile dictu

Marwood, Mrs
character in: **16** The Way of the World
author: **8** Congreve

Marx, Bernard
character in: **13** Brave New World
author: **6** Huxley

Marx, Karl
author of: **10** Das Kapital **18** Communist Manifesto (with Friedrich Engels)

Marx Brothers 5 Chico (Leonard), Gummo (Milton), Harpo (Adolph, Arthur) Zeppo (Herbert) **7** Groucho (Julius)
costar: **14** Margaret Dumont
born: **9** New York NY
roles: **8** Coconuts, Duck Soup **11** The Big Store **13** Horse Feathers **14** A Day at the Races, Animal Crackers, Monkey Business **16** A Night at the Opera
Groucho's TV show: **14** You Bet Your Life

Mary 6 Virgin **7** Madonna **8** Holy Mary **9** Magdalene, of Cleopas **10** Virgin Mary **11** Mother of God, Regina Coeli **13** Queen of Heaven **15** Mother of Sorrows **17** Mother of the Church
mother: **4** Anna, Anne
husband: **6** Joseph **7** Alpheus, Cleopas
son: **4** Jude, Mark **5** Jesus, Moses, Simon **12** James the Less
sister: **6** Martha
brother: **7** Lazarus **8** Barnabas
cousin: **9** Elizabeth
hometown: **8** Nazareth
visitor: **7** Gabriel
flower: **4** lily **8** marigold

Mary
author: **10** Sholem Asch

Maryland *see box*

Mary Poppins
director: **15** Robert Stevenson
based on story by: **9** P L Travers
cast: **6** Ed Wynn **11** Dick Van Dyke (Bert), Glynis Johns **12** Julie Andrews **14** David Tomlinson **16** Hermione Baddeley
score: **13** Robert Sherman **14** Richard Sherman
Oscar for: **4** song **5** score **7** actress (Andrews) **13** visual effects
song: **14** Chim-chim-cheree

Mary Queen of Scots
director: **14** Charles Jarrott
cast: **12** Trevor Howard **13** Glenda Jackson (Elizabeth I), Timothy Dalton **14** Nigel Davenport **15** Patrick McGoohan, Vanessa Redgrave (Mary of Scotland)

Mary Tyler Moore Show, The
character: **8** Lou Grant **9** Ted Baxter **12** Gordon (Gordy) Howard, Mary Richards, Sue Ann Nivens **13** Bess Lindstrom **14** Marie Slaughter **15** Murray Slaughter **16** Phyllis Lindstrom, Rhoda Morgenstern **23** Georgette Franklin Baxter
cast: **8** John Amos **9** Ted Knight **10** Betty White **11** Edward Asner **12** Gavin MacLeod, Georgia Engel **13** Joyce Bulifant, Lisa Gerritsen, Valerie Harper **14** Cloris Leachman
setting: **11** Minneapolis

Mary Worth
creator: **8** Carey Orr **9** Dale Allen **10** Dale Connor **13** Allen Saunders
character: **4** Bill, Slim

Masaccio
real name: **26** Tommaso di Ser Giovanni di Mone
born: **5** Italy **27** Castel San Giovanni di Valdarno
artwork: **14** The Holy Trinity **15** The Tribute Money **24** The Expulsion from Paradise

Mascagni, Pietro
born: **5** Italy **7** Leghorn
composer of: **4** Iris **6** Nerone **7** Isabeau **10** Le Maschere **11** L'Amico Fritz **14** Il Piccolo Marat **19** Cavalleria Rusticana

masculine 4 bold, male **5** brave, hardy, husky, macho, manly **6** brawny, daring, manful, plucky, robust, strong, sturdy, virile **7** staunch, valiant **8** athletic, fearless, forceful, intrepid, muscular,

Maryland
abbreviation: 2 MD
nickname: 4 Free **7** Cockade **12** Old Line State
capital: 9 Annapolis
largest city: 9 Baltimore
others: 5 Essex **6** Easton, Laurel, Towson **8** Aberdeen, Bethesda, Pocomoke **9** Frederick, Ocean City, Rockville **10** Cumberland, Hagerstown, Pikesville **11** Catonsville, College Park
college: 4 Hood **7** Goucher, St John's **10** Washington **11** Towson State **12** Johns Hopkins **21** Annapolis Naval Academy
feature:
  fort: **7** McHenry
  national battlesite: **8** Antietam
  presidential retreat: **9** Camp David
  race: **9** Preakness **12** Steeplechase
  racetrack: **5** Bowie **6** Butler, Laurel **7** Pimlico
tribe: 5 Conoy **9** Nanticoke
people: 6 Wesort **8** Terrapin **10** Spiro Agnew **11** crawthumper **14** Sargent Shriver **15** Francis Scott Key
  explorer: **7** Calvert
lake: 8 Patapsco **9** Deep Creek, Loch Raven, Pretty Boy **10** Rocky Gorge **11** Triadelphia
land rank: 11 forty second
mountain: 4 Dans **8** Piedmont **9** Blue Ridge **11** Appalachian
  highest point: **8** Backbone
physical feature:
  bay: **10** Chesapeake
  sea: **8** Atlantic
  swamp: **7** Pocoson
  valley: **5** Great **10** Hagerstown
river: 3 Elk **7** Chester, Potomac **8** Choptank, Patapsco, Patuxent, Pocomoke **11** Susquehanna
state admission: 7 seventh
state bird: 15 Baltimore oriole
state fish: 11 striped bass
state flower: 14 black-eyed Susan
state motto: 22 Manly Deeds Womanly Words **43** Thou Hast Crowned Us With the Shield of Thy Good Will
state song: 18 Maryland My Maryland
state tree: 8 white oak

---

powerful, resolute, vigorous **9** strapping **10** courageous **11** indomitable, self-reliant **12** stouthearted

Masefield, John
author of: 7 Cargoes **8** Sea Fever **16** Salt Water Ballads

Maseru
capital of: 7 Lesotho

mash 4 mush **5** crush, paste, puree, smash **6** squash **8** mishmash **9** pulverize

M*A*S*H
character: 10 (Capt) BJ Hunnicut, (Lt Col) Henry Blake, (Maj) Frank Burns **12** (Corp) Radar O'Reilly **13** Father (John) Mulcahy, (Capt Benjamin Franklin) Hawkeye Pierce, (Col) Sherman Potter **14** (Corp) Maxwell Klinger **15** (Maj Margaret) Hot Lips Houlihan **19** (Capt

John) Trapper John McIntyre **24** (Maj) Charles Emerson Winchester
cast: 8 Alan Alda **9** Jamie Farr **11** Harry Morgan, Loretta Swit, Mike Farrell, Wayne Rogers **12** Gary Burghoff **13** Larry Linville **15** McLean Stevenson **16** David Ogden Stiers **18** William Christopher
war: 6 Korean
MASH stands for: 26 Mobile Army Surgical Hospital
tent: 5 Swamp
theme: 17 Suicide Is Painless

M*A*S*H
director: 12 Robert Altman
cast: 10 Jo Ann Pflug **11** Elliot Gould (Trapper John McIntyre), Tom Skerritt (B J Hunnicut) **12** Gary Burghoff (Radar O'Reilly), Robert Duvall (Frank Burns) **14** Sally Kellerman (Margaret Hot

---

Lips Houlihan) **16** Donald Sutherland (Hawkeye Pierce)

masjid 6 mosque

mask 4 hide, veil **5** blind, cloak, cover **6** domino, screen, shroud **7** conceal, cover-up, curtain, obscure **8** disguise **9** face guard, false face **10** camouflage, keep secret

Mask
director: 16 Peter Bogdanovich
cast: 4 Cher **10** Eric Stoltz (Rocky Dennis), Sam Elliott

masked 9 concealed, covered up, disguised **10** in disguise, masquerade

Masked Ball, A
also: 17 Un Ballo in Maschera
opera by: 5 Verdi
character:
  first version: **9** Count Horn **10** King Gustav **12** Count Ribbing
  second version: **3** Sam, Tom **13** Count Riccardo

masking 6 hiding **7** veiling **8** covering **9** eclipsing, obscuring **10** concealing, covering up

Mason, Bertha
character in: 8 Jane Eyre
author: 6 Bronte

Mason, James
wife: 6 Pamela
born: 7 England **12** Huddersfield
roles: 6 Lolita **7** Lord Jim **9** Bloodline **10** Georgy Girl **13** Heaven Can Wait **14** Humbert Humbert, Murder by Decree, The Seventh Veil **15** Prisoner of Zenda **16** North by Northwest **17** The Boys from Brazil

Mason, Marsha
husband: 9 Neil Simon
born: 9 St Louis MO
roles: 10 Chapter Two **11** Blume in Love **14** The Goodbye Girl **15** Max Dugan Returns **17** Cinderella Liberty

Masque of the Red Death, The
author: 13 Edgar Allan Poe

masquerade 4 mask, ruse, veil **5** cloak, cover, guise, trick **6** masque, pose as, screen, shroud **7** cover-up, pretext **8** artifice, pretense **9** bal masque **10** camouflage, masked ball, subterfuge **11** impersonate **12** harlequinade

Masquerade Party
host: 9 Bert Parks **10** Bud

Collier 11 Peter Donald
12 Eddie Bracken, Robert Q
Lewis 14 Douglas Edwards

mass, Mass 3 jam, lot, mob
4 body, bulk, cake, clot, heap,
host, hunk, knot, lump, pack,
pile 5 amass, batch, block,
bunch, chunk, clump, corps,
crowd, crush, group, horde,
press, stack, troop 6 bundle,
gather, matter, throng,
weight 7 collect, pyramid
8 assemble, best part, main
body, majority, material 9 aggregate, Eucharist, gathering,
plurality 10 accumulate, assemblage, assortment, collection, concretion, congregate,
cumulation, lion's share
11 aggregation, consolidate,
greater part 12 accumulation,
congregation 13 Holy Com-
munion, holy sacrament, preponderance 14 conglomeration

Massachusetts *see box*

massacre 7 butcher, carnage
8 butchery, decimate 9 bloodbath, slaughter 10 mass murder 12 bloodletting

massage 3 rub 4 flex 5 chafe,
knead 6 finger, handle, stroke
7 rubbing, rub down, stretch
8 kneading, stroking 10 manipulate 12 manipulation

Massasoit *see*
10 Wampanoags

Massenet, Jules Emile
Frederic
born: 6 France 9 St Etienne
composer of: 5 Le Cid,
Manon, Thais 7 Werther
9 Herodiade 11 David Riz-
zio 12 Don Quichotte 13 Le
Roi de Lahore 21 Le Jon-
gleur de Notre-Dame

masses 6 plebes, proles, rabble, the mob 7 the many
8 the crowd 9 hoi polloi, plebeians 11 the populace, the
riffraff 12 the multitude 13 the
common herd 14 the proletariat, the rank and file 15 the
common people, the lower
classes, the working class
16 the great unwashed

Masset *see* 10 Skidegatta

massive 4 huge, vast 5 ample,
bulky, great, heavy, hefty,
massy, solid 7 hulking, immense, mammoth, titanic,
weighty 8 colossal, enormous,
gigantic, imposing, towering,
whopping 9 cyclopean, extensive, monstrous, ponderous
10 gargantuan, impressive,
monumental, stupendous
11 elephantine, substantial

massiveness 4 bulk, size

Massachusetts
abbreviation: 2 MA 4 Mass
nickname: 3 Bay 7 Puritan 9 Baked Bean, Old Colony
capital/largest city: 6 Boston
others: 4 Ayer, Lynn, Otis 5 Athol, Barre, Lenox, Salem
6 Agawam, Dedham, Groton, Nahant, Natick, Revere,
Saugus, Woburn 7 Belmont, Beverly, Concord, Danvers,
Everett, Holyoke, Ipswich, Medford, Peabody, Taunton,
Waltham 8 Brockton, Chicopee, Cohasset, Plymouth, Scituate, Yarmouth 9 Arlington, Attleboro, Braintree, Brookline, Cambridge, Lexbridge, Lexington, Worcester
10 Gloucester, New Bedford, Pittsfield 11 Springfield
12 Provincetown, Williamstown
college: 3 MIT 5 Clark, Curry, Smith, Tufts 6 Babson
7 Amherst, Harvard, Simmons, Wheaton 8 Brandeis, Williams 9 Hampshire, Holy Cross, Merrimack, Radcliffe,
Wellesley 11 Springfield 12 Mount Holyoke, Northeast-
ern 13 Boston College
feature: 10 Walden Pond 12 Plymouth Rock
 national seashore: 7 Cape Cod
 village: 13 Old Sturbridge
tribe: 6 Nauset 8 Pocomtuc 10 Wampanoags
people: 8 Pilgrims 9 Amy Lowell, Elias Howe 10 Cyrus
Field, Eli Whitney 11 Clara Barton, John Hancock, Samuel Adams, Samuel Morse 12 Henry Thoreau, Robert
Lowell, Winslow Homer 13 James Whistler, Joseph Kennedy, Robert Kennedy 14 Emily Dickinson 15 Henry Cabot Lodge 16 Benjamin Franklin, Edward ''Ted''
Kennedy 17 Ralph Waldo Emerson 18 Bartholomew Gos-
nold, James Russell Lowell, Nathanial Hawthorne
19 Oliver Wendell Holmes, William Cullen Bryant
21 John Greenleaf Whittier
 explorer: 8 Norsemen
island: 5 Duke's 9 Nantucket 13 Chappaquidick 15 Martha's Vineyard
lake: 5 Onota 7 Quabbin, Rohunta, Webster 8 Long Pond
11 Watuppa Pond 16 Assawompsett Pond
17 Chaubunagungamaug
land rank: 10 forty-fifth
mountain: 3 Tom 6 Brodie, Potter 7 Alander, Everett, Taconic 10 Berkshires
 highest point: 8 Greylock
physical feature:
 bay: 8 Buzzard's
 cape: 3 Ann, Cod
 sea: 8 Atlantic
president: 9 John Adams 14 Calvin Coolidge 15 John
Quincy Adams 21 John Fitzgerald Kennedy
river: 6 Nashua 7 Charles, Concord, Quaboag, Taunton
8 Chicopee 9 Deerfield, Merrimack 10 Blackstone, Housatonic 11 Connecticut
state admission: 11 thirty-sixth
state bird: 9 chickadee
state flower: 9 mayflower 15 trailing arbutus
state motto: 37 With the Sword She Seeks Peace Under
Liberty 45 By the Sword We Seek Peace But Peace Only
Under Liberty
state song: 22 All Hail to Massachusetts
state tree: 11 American elm

8 enormity, hugeness, vastness 9 amplitude, bulkiness,
greatness, immensity, largeness, magnitude

mast 4 main, nuts, pole, post,
spar 5 spirit, staff, stick, stuff
6 acorns, pillar 9 beechnuts,
chestnuts

type: 4 fore, main 6 jigger,
mizzen
support: 4 bibb

master 3 ace 4 able, A-one,
best, boss, curb, deft, head,
lord, main, tame, whiz
5 check, chief, crack, grasp,
owner, prime, ruler 6 bridle,

choice, expert, genius, gifted, govern, leader, manage, subdue, wizard **7** conquer, control, excel at, head man, manager, primary, skilled, skipper, supreme **8** director, dominate, finished, governor, masterly, overcome, overlord, overseer, regulate, suppress, talented, virtuoso **9** authority, conqueror, craftsman, first-rate, paramount, practiced, principal **10** controller, proficient, supervisor **12** get the hang of, ship's captain

Master Builder, The
  author: **11** Henrik Ibsen

master craftsman 7 artisan **12** masterworker **13** skilled worker

masterful 4 able, deft **5** bossy **6** expert, superb **7** dynamic, skilled **8** finished, forceful, masterly, resolute, skillful, virtuoso **9** excellent **10** commanding **11** domineering, self-reliant **12** accomplished, strong-willed **13** authoritarian, self-confident

masterfulness 6 genius **10** capability, competence, excellence **11** proficiency

Master Melvin
  nickname of: **6** Mel Ott

mastermind 4 plan, sage **6** direct, expert, genius, master, pundit, wizard **7** old hand, planner **8** conceive, director, engineer, organize, virtuoso **9** authority, initiator, organizer **10** specialist **11** moving force

Master of Ballantrae, The
  author: **20** Robert Louis Stevenson
  character: **4** Chew **5** Teach **9** MacKellar **11** Henry Durrie, James Durrie **12** Alison Graeme, Francis Burke, Secundra Dass

master of the family
  Latin: **13** paterfamilias

masterpiece 5 jewel, prize **7** classic, paragon **8** monument, treasure **9** nonpareil **10** brainchild **11** chef d'oeuvre, ne plus ultra, prizewinner

Masterpiece Theater
  host: **13** Alistair Cooke

master race
  German: **10** Herrenvolk

Masters, Edgar Lee
  author of: **19** Spoon River Anthology

Mastersingers of Nuremberg, The
  also: **27** Die Meistersinger von Nurnberg
  opera by: **6** Wagner
  character: **9** Eva Pogner, Hans Sachs **10** Beckmesser **18** Walther von Stolzing

mastery 4 rule, sway **5** grasp **7** ability, command, control **8** deftness, whip hand **9** dominance, supremacy, upper hand **10** adroitness, attainment, domination, leadership **11** achievement, acquirement, proficiency, superiority **14** accomplishment

masticate 4 chew, gnaw **5** champ, munch **6** nibble

Mastroianni, Marcello
  born: **5** Italy **11** Fontana Liri
  roles: **13** Eight and a Half **7** La Notte **11** La Dolce Vita, The Stranger, White Nights **19** Divorce Italian Style

mat 3 dim, pad, rug **4** dead, dull, flat **5** doily, muted **6** carpet, matrix, tangle **7** bedding, bolster, coaster, cushion, support **8** entangle **10** lackluster, lusterless
  Japanese: **6** tatami

Mata Hari
  real name: **21** Gertrud Margarete Zelle
  worked as: **3** spy **6** dancer
  worked for: **7** Germans
  executed by: **6** French

match 3 fit **4** game, join, mate, meet, pair, peer, suit, twin, yoke **5** adapt, agree, equal, event, unite **6** couple, double, oppose **7** be alike, be equal, combine, connect, contend, contest, vie with **8** parallel **9** companion, duplicate, harmonize **10** correspond, equivalent, tournament **11** competition, counterpart

matched 5 equal **8** of a piece **9** identical **11** coordinated

matching 4 twin **5** equal **6** paired **10** equivalent **11** harmonizing **13** corresponding

matchless 4 rare **7** supreme **8** crowning, foremost, peerless, sterling, superior **9** exemplary, first rate, priceless, paramount, unequaled, unmatched, unrivaled **10** invaluable, preeminent, unbeatable, unexcelled **11** inestimable, superlative, unsurpassed **12** incomparable, unparalleled

matchmaker
  Yiddish: **8** shadchan **9** schatchen

mate 3 pal **4** chum, twin,

wife **5** buddy, crony, hubby, match **6** couple, friend, spouse **7** cohabit, comrade, consort, husband, pair off, partner **8** copulate, coworker, sidekick **9** associate, colleague, companion, duplicate **10** better half, equivalent **11** confederate, counterpart **12** fellow worker, ship's officer

materfamilias 15 mother of a family

material 5 stuff **6** matter **8** elements **9** substance **12** constituents

materialism 5 greed **12** covetousness **15** acquisitiveness

materialistic 6 greedy **8** covetous, grasping **11** acquisitive, unspiritual

materiality 9 existence **11** tangibility

materialization 5 ghost, shade **6** coming, wraith **7** phantom, specter **9** emergence **10** apparition, appearance **13** manifestation

materialize 4 loom, rise, show **5** bob up, issue, pop up **6** appear, crop up, emerge, turn up **9** come forth **10** burst forth **11** come to light, spring forth **12** come into view

materially 7 vitally **8** palpably, tangibly **9** in the main, seriously **10** monetarily **11** corporeally, essentially, financially, in substance **12** considerably, emphatically **13** significantly, substantially **14** for the most part

material possessions 6 assets, estate, wealth **7** fortune **8** property **10** belongings **12** worldly goods

material proof 8 evidence **13** documentation

materials 4 data **5** cloth, facts, notes, tools **6** stocks, stores, timber **7** fabrics, figures **8** concrete, dry goods, supplies, textiles **9** citations, equipment, machinery, yard goods **10** essentials, piece goods, quotations, references **11** impressions **12** observations **15** bricks and mortar

materiel 4 gear **6** stores **8** supplies **9** equipment, materials **10** provisions **16** military supplies

Mater Matuta *see* **6** Matuta

maternal 4 fond **6** doting **8** motherly **9** of a mother, shielding **10** motherlike, protective, sheltering

maternity 5 labor **8** delivery **9** pregnancy **10** childbirth, motherhood **11** parturition **12** accouchement, childbearing

Mater Turrita *see* **6** Cybele

mathematical, mathematic 5 exact, rigid **6** strict **7** precise **8** accurate, rigorous, unerring **10** meticulous, scientific, scrupulous **11** punctilious, well-defined **13** computational

mathematician
American: **5** Aiken **6** Wiener
British: **6** Newton **7** Babbage
French: **6** Fermat **9** D'Alembert, Descartes
German: **5** Frege, Gauss **6** Bessel **7** Hilbert
Greek: **6** Euclid, Thales **11** Anaximander
Norwegian: **4** Abel
Swiss: **5** Euler **9** Bernoulli

Mathewson, Christy
nickname: **5** Matty **6** Big Six
sport: **8** baseball
position: **7** pitcher
team: **13** New York Giants

Matholwych
king of: **7** Ireland
wife: **7** Branwen

matinee 9 early show **16** early performance **20** afternoon performance

Mating Season, The
author: **11** P G Wodehouse

Matisse, Henri Emile Benoit
born: **6** France **16** Chateau Cambresis (Le Cateau)
artwork: **5** Dance, Music **8** The Slave **10** Odalisques **11** Joie de Vivre **12** Harmony in Red, La Serpentine **13** Head with Tiara, The Open Window **15** Bathers by a River, Memory of Oceanie, Woman with the Hat **16** Heads of Jeannette **19** Torso with Arms Raised **20** Goldfish and Sculpture

Matralia
origin: **5** Roman
event: **8** festival

matriarch 7 dowager **10** female head, grande dame **11** female ruler **12** female leader **13** materfamilias

matriculate 4 join **5** enter **6** enlist, enroll, sign up **7** check in **8** register

matriculation 9 signing up **10** enrollment **12** registration

matrimonial 6 bridal, wedded, wifely **7** marital, married, nuptial, spousal **8** conjugal, hymeneal **9** affianced, connubial, husbandly **11** epithalamic

matrimony 7 wedlock **8** marriage **11** holy wedlock

matrix 3 die **4** cast, form, mold **5** frame, punch, stamp

matron 4 dame **5** madam **7** dowager **8** forelady, mistress, overseer **9** forewoman **10** directress **11** housekeeper **12** married woman **14** superintendent

Matronalia
origin: **5** Roman
event: **8** festival

matter 3 fix **4** gist, snag, text **5** count, drift, event, sense, stuff, theme, thing, topic **6** affair, crisis, import, moment, object, scrape, strait, thesis **7** content, dilemma, episode, essence, purport, signify, subject, trouble **8** argument, business, elements, exigency, material, obstacle, quandary **9** adventure, emergency, happening, situation, substance **10** difference, difficulty, experience, impediment, importance, occurrence, perplexity, proceeding **11** carry weight, consequence, predicament, transaction **12** circumstance, significance

matter-of-course 5 usual **6** common **7** routine **8** everyday, ordinary, standard **9** customary **11** commonplace, established

matter-of-fact 4 real **5** blunt, frank **6** candid, direct **7** factual, literal, mundane, natural, prosaic **8** ordinary, sensible **9** outspoken, practical, pragmatic, realistic **10** hardheaded, no-nonsense, unaffected, uninspired, unromantic **11** commonplace, common-sense, down-to-earth, straight-out **13** unimaginative, unsentimental **15** straightforward

matter-of-factness 10 detachment **11** impassivity **12** practicality **13** impassiveness **17** unimaginativeness

Matter of Time, A
author: **12** Jessamyn West

Matthau, Walter
real name: **13** Walter Matthow **23** Walter Matuschanskavasky
born: **9** New York NY
roles: **5** Kotch **8** A New Leaf **10** Plaza Suite **11** Pete n Tillie **12** Bad News Bears, Ensign Pulver, Oscar Madison, The Front Page, The Odd Couple **15** California Suite, The Sunshine Boys **16** The Fortune Cookie **22** A Guide for the Married Man

Matthew 7 apostle
father: **7** Alpheus
also called: **4** Levi
wrote: **6** Gospel

Matthiessen, Peter
author of: **10** Sand Rivers **14** The Snow Leopard

maturation 6 growth **8** fruition, ripening **9** growing up

mature 4 ripe **5** adult, bloom, grown, manly, of age, ready, ripen **6** flower, grow up, mellow, nubile, virile **7** blossom, develop, grown-up, matured, womanly **8** finished, maturate, seasoned **9** come of age, completed, full-blown, full-grown, perfected, practiced **10** middle-aged **11** become adult, experienced, full-fledged, in one's prime **12** marriageable

Mature, Victor
born: **12** Louisville KY
roles: **7** The Robe **11** After the Fox, Kiss of Death **12** Cry of the City, One Million BC **16** Samson and Delilah **19** Androcles and the Lion

matured 3 big **4** aged, ripe **5** adult, grown **6** formed **7** ripened **8** flowered, mellowed, seasoned **9** blossomed, developed, full-blown, full-grown **11** full-fledged

maturity 7 manhood **8** legal age, majority, practice, ripeness **9** adulthood, composure, full bloom, readiness, seasoning, womanhood **10** completion, experience, full growth, maturation, matureness, perfection **11** culmination, fulfillment **12** age of consent

Matuschanskavasky, Walter
real name of: **13** Walter Matthau

Matuta
origin: **5** Roman
goddess of: **3** sea **4** dawn **7** harbors **10** childbirth
called: **11** Mater Matuta

Maud
author: **18** Alfred Lord Tennyson

Maude
character: **5** Carol **7** Phillip **10** Henry Evans **12** Florida Evans, Maude Findlay, Mrs Naugatuck **13** Walter Findlay **14** Dr Arthur Harmon **20** Vivian Cavender Harmon
cast: **8** Bill Macy, John Amos **10** Conrad Bain **11** Esther Rolle **13** Brian Morrison, Rue McClanahan **14** Beatrice Arthur, Kraig Metzinger **15** Adrienne Barbeau **16** Hermione Baddeley

spinoff from: 14 All in the Family
spinoff: 9 Good Times

maudlin 5 gushy, mushy, teary **6** slushy **7** gushing, mawkish, tearful **8** bathetic **9** emotional **10** lachrymose **11** sentimental **13** overemotional

maudlinism 6 bathos **11** mawkishness **14** sentimentalism, sentimentality

Maugham, W Somerset
author of: 9 The Circle **10** Our Betters **11** Cakes and Ale **12** Miss Thompson **13** The Razor's Edge **14** Of Human Bondage **15** The Constant Wife **18** The Moon and Sixpence **21** Lady Frederick Ashenden

maul 4 beat **5** stomp **6** batter, beat up, bruise, mangle, pummel, thrash **7** rough up **9** manhandle **10** knock about

Mauldin, Bill
creator/artist of: 7 Up Front **12** Willie and Joe

maunder 4 loaf **5** drift, run on, stray **6** babble, dawdle, gabble, gibber, ramble, wander **7** blather, meander, prattle, saunter **8** flounder, ramble on, straggle **9** go on and on, hem and haw **10** dillydally

maundering 7 diffuse **8** rambling **9** wandering **10** digressive, disjointed, roundabout **14** drift, run on, stray **6** babble, dawdle, gabble, gibber, ramble, wander **7** blather, meander, prattle, saunter **8** flounder, ramble on, straggle **9** go on and on, hem and haw **10** dillydally

Maupassant, Guy de
author of: 6 Belami **9** Ball of Fat, Mont-Oriol **11** A Woman's Life, The Necklace **12** Ball of Tallow **16** Mademoiselle Fifi

Mauriac, Francois
author of: 8 Genitrix **10** The Egoists **12** Viper's Tangle **15** A Kiss to the Leper, The Desert of Love **20** A Woman of the Pharisees

Mauritania *see box*

Mauritius *see box*

mausoleum 10 family tomb **11** stately tomb **18** sepulchral monument

mauve 4 plum, puce **5** lilac **6** violet **8** lavender **11** light purple **12** bluish purple

maverick 5 loner **8** yearling **9** dissenter, dissident, eccentric **11** independent **13** individualist, noncomformist

Maverick
character: 12 Bart Maverick,

Mauritius
other name: 11 Ile de France
capital/largest city: 9 Port Louis
others: 6 Reduit **8** Curepipe **9** Mahebourg **13** Quartre Bornes **19** Grande Riviere Sud-Est
head of state: 14 British monarch **15** governor general
monetary unit: 4 cent **5** rupee
island: 3 Est **4** Flat **5** Ambre, Cerf's, Morne, Round **7** Agalega, Serpent **9** Mauritius, Rodrigues, Rodriguez, St Brandon **12** Gunner's Quoin **15** Cargados Carajos
highest point: 27 Piton de la Petite Riviere Noire
sea: 6 Indian
people: 6 Creole, French, Indian **7** African, Chinese **8** European **13** Indo-Mauritian
 leader: 8 Jugnauth **9** Ramgoolam
 ruler: 5 Dutch **6** French **7** English
language: 4 Urdu **5** Hindi, Tamil **6** Creole, French

Mauritania
capital/largest city: 10 Nouakchott
others: 4 Atar **5** Kaedi, Rosso **6** Fderik **7** Akjoujt **10** Nouadhibou
division: 5 Sahel **7** Chemama
monetary unit: 5 khoum **7** ouguiya
highest point: 11 Kediat Idjil
river: 7 Senegal
sea: 8 Atlantic
physical feature:
 desert: 6 Sahara
 valley: 7 Chemama **12** Senegal River
people: 4 Arab, Fula, Moor **5** Black, Fulbe, Wolof **6** Bafour, Berber, Fulani **7** African, Soninke, Tukulor **8** Sarakole **9** Sarakolle **10** Toucouleur **12** Halphoolaren
 leader: 4 Luly **5** Salek **6** Daddah **8** Haidalla
 ruler: 6 France **9** Almoravid **14** Kingdom of Ghana
language: 4 Fula **5** Wolof **6** Arabic, French **7** Phoolor, Tukulor **8** Fulfulde, Mandingo **9** Sarakolle, Hassaniya
religion: 5 Islam
place:
 mosque: 5 Grand
feature:
 beehive hut: 4 ruga
 priest-teacher: 8 marabout
 waterskin: 6 guerba
food:
 dish: 7 meshuri
 tea: 5 attay

Bret Maverick **13** Brent Maverick **16** Samantha Crawford **24** Cousin Beauregard Maverick
cast: 9 Jack Kelly **10** Roger Moore **11** James Garner **13** Diane Brewster, Robert Colbert

Mavors *see* **4** Mars

maw 4 craw, crop, jaws **5** mouth **6** gullet, muzzle, throat

mawkish 5 gushy, mushy, teary **7** maudlin, tearful **9** emotional, nostalgic, schmaltzy **10** lachrymose **11** sentimental **15** oversentimental

mawkishness 4 mush **5** slush **6** bathos **9** mushiness, soppiness **10** maudlinism, slushiness **14** sentimentalism, sentimentality

maxim 3 saw **4** rule **5** adage, axiom, motto **6** old saw, saying, truism **7** proverb **8** aphorism, apothegm **9** platitude

Maximes
author: 23 Francois La Rochefoucauld

Maxims of the Law
author: 12 Francis Bacon

maximum 3 top 4 most 6 utmost 7 highest, largest, maximal, optimum, supreme 8 foremost, greatest 9 paramount 11 unsurpassed

May
characteristic: 7 Maypole 13 queen of the May
flower: 8 hawthorn 15 lily of the valley
French: 3 Mai
gem: 7 emerald
German: 3 Mai
holiday: 6 May Day (1) 10 Mother's Day (2nd Sunday) 11 Memorial Day (last Monday) 14 Armed Forces Day (3rd Saturday)
Italian: 6 Maggio
number of days: 9 thirty-one
origin of name: 4 Maia
Roman goddess of: 6 spring
place in year:
Gregorian: 5 fifth
Roman: 5 third
saying: 27 April showers bring May flowers
Spanish: 4 Mayo
Zodiac sign: 6 Gemini, Taurus

May, Elaine
real name: 12 Elaine Berlin
partner: 11 Mike Nichols
born: 14 Philadelphia PA
roles: 8 A New Leaf 15 California Suite
director of: 16 The Heartbreak Kid
writer/director of: 8 A New Leaf

Maya
city: 4 Coba 5 Tulum, Uxmal 6 Akumal, Cuello, Izamal 8 Calakmul, Palenque 11 Chichen Itza
conqueror: 8 Alvarado
day: 5 uayeb
language family: 5 Mayan 10 Maya-Quiche
location: 5 Tikal 6 Belize, Mexico 7 Chiapas, Mayapan, Tabasco, Yucatan 8 Honduras 9 Guatemala 11 Chichen Itza 14 Central America
month: 5 uinal 6 uninal
noted for: 9 astronomy

12 architecture 19 hieroglyphic writing
rain god: 4 Chac 5 Chaac 7 Chac Mol 8 Chac Mool
ruins: 9 Yaxchilan 20 Temple of Inscriptions
underworld: 7 Xibalba
year: 4 haab

maybe 6 mayhap 7 perhaps 8 feasibly, possibly 9 perchance 10 God willing, imaginably 11 conceivably 12 peradventure

Maybe
author: 14 Lillian Hellman

Mayberry RFD
character: 5 Alice 7 Aunt Bee 8 Sam Jones 9 Mike Jones 10 Goober Pyle 11 Emmett Clark 13 Howard Sprague, Millie Swanson
cast: 8 Ken Berry 10 Jack Dodson 11 Buddy Foster, Paul Hartman 13 Alice Ghostley, Arlene Golonka, Frances Bavier, George Lindsey

mayfly
varieties: 5 small 6 stream 9 burrowing

mayhem 4 maim 6 felony 7 battery, cripple 8 mutilate, violence 9 crippling, dismember 10 mutilation 13 disfigurement

may he rest in peace
Latin: 16 requiescat in pace

may it do good
Latin: 6 prosit

Maylie, Mrs and Rose
characters in: 11 Oliver Twist
author: 7 Dickens

Mayo, Virginia
real name: 13 Virginia Jones
husband: 12 Michael O'Shea
born: 9 St Louis MO
roles: 17 The West Point Story 22 The Best Years of Our Lives 26 The Secret Life of Walter Mitty

Mayor of Casterbridge, The
author: 11 Thomas Hardy
character: 13 Donald Farfrae, Richard Newson 14 Lucetta Le Sueur 15 Michael Henchard 19 Elizabeth Jane Newson, Susan Henchard-Newson

Mays, Willie
nickname: 9 Say Hey Kid
sport: 8 baseball
position: 11 center field
team: 11 New York Mets 13 New York Giants 18 San Francisco Giants

may she live forever
Latin: 12 esto perpetua
motto of: 5 Idaho

may she rest in peace
Latin: 16 requiescat in pace

maze 5 snarl 6 jungle, tangle 7 complex, meander, network 9 labyrinth 11 convolution

mazel tov 8 good luck

Mbabane
capital of: 9 Swaziland

McCambridge, Mercedes
real name: 32 Carlotta Mercedes Agnes McCambridge
born: 8 Joliet IL
roles: 5 Giant 8 Cimarron 11 Touch of Evil 14 All the King's Men 15 A Farewell to Arms 18 Suddenly Last Summer

McCarey, Leo
director of: 8 Duck Soup 10 Going My Way (Oscar) 13 The Awful Truth (Oscar) 15 Ruggles of Red Gap 17 The Bells of St Mary's

McCarthy, Mary
author of: 8 The Group

McCay, Winsor
creator/artist of: 23 Little Nemo in Slumberland

McClellan, George B
nickname: 25 Little Mac the Young Napoleon
served in: 8 Civil War 10 Mexican War
side: 5 Union
commander of: 16 Army of the Potomac
battle: 8 Antietam 18 Peninsular campaign
governor of: 9 New Jersey

McCloud
character: 10 Sam McCloud 13 Chris Coughlin, (Sgt) Joe Broadhurst 14 Peter B Clifford
cast: 8 JD Cannon 11 Terry Carter 12 Dennis Weaver, Diana Muldaur

McClure, Darrell
creator/artist of: 17 Little Annie Rooney

McCrea, Joel
wife: 10 Frances Dee
born: 12 Los Angeles CA
roles: 11 Buffalo Bill 14 Palm Beach Story 16 Sullivan's Travels, The Great Man's Lady 17 Reaching for the Sun, The More the Merrier 20 Foreign Correspondent

McCreary, Fainy (Mac)
character in: 3 USA
author: 9 Dos Passos

McCullers, Carson
author of: 17 The Mortgaged Heart 18 Member of the Wedding 21 The Ballad of the Sad Cafe 23 Reflections

in a Golden Eye, The Heart Is a Lonely Hunter

McCullough, Colleen
author of: **13** The Thornbirds **19** An Indecent Obsession

McCutcheon, George Barr
author of: **9** Graustark

McEvoy, JP
creator/artist of: **10** Dixie Dugan

McFee, William
author of: **15** Casuals of the Sea

McGillicuddy, Cornelius Alexander
real name of: **10** Connie Mack

McGinley, Phyllis
author of: **12** Three Decades **15** A Pocketful of Wry **24** The Horse Who Lived Upstairs

McHale's Navy
character: **7** Christy **9** Willy Moss **11** Fuji Kobiaji, Happy Haines **12** Harrison (Tinker) Bell, Lester Gruber **13** Virgil Farrell, (Ensign) Charles Parker, (Lt Cdr) Quinton McHale **14** (Lt) Elroy Carpenter **18** (Capt) Wallace B Binghamton
cast: **8** Joe Flynn **9** Tim Conway **10** Billy Sands, Gary Vinson, John Wright, Yoshio Yoda **11** Bob Hastings, Edson Stroll **12** Gavin MacLeod **14** Carl Ballantine, Ernest Borgnine

McKenna, Siobhan
born: **7** Belfast, Ireland
roles: **11** King of Kings **13** Doctor Zhivago **14** Of Human Bondage **24** Playboy of the Western World

McKim, Charles M
architect of: **27** Lutheran Church of the Redeemer (Houston)

McKim, Mead, and White
partners: **13** Stanford White **18** Charles Follen McKim **21** William Rutherford Mead
architects of: **11** Century Club **14** University Club, Washington Arch **17** Vanderbilt Mansion **18** Columbia University (NYC) **19** Boston Public Library, Pennsylvania Station (NYC), (first) Madison Square Garden (NYC) **21** New York Herald Building, Pierpont Morgan Library (NYC) **31** Madison Square Presbyterian Church
style: **7** Shingle **18** Italian Renaissance

McKinley, William
nickname: **13** Major McKinley
presidential rank: **11** twenty-fifth
party: **10** Republican
state represented: **2** OH
defeated: **4** (Eugene Victor) Debs **5** (Seth Hockett) Ellis, (William Jennings) Bryan **6** (John McCauley) Palmer, (Wharton) Barker **7** (Charles Eugene) Bentley, (John Granville) Woolley, (Jonah Fitz Randolph) Leonard **8** (Charles Horatio) Matchett, (Joseph Francis) Malloney, (Joshua) Levering
vice president: **6** (Garret Augustus) Hobart **9** (Theodore) Roosevelt
cabinet:
state: **3** (John Milton) Hay, (William Rufus) Day **7** (John) Sherman
treasury: **4** (Lyman Judson) Gage
war: **4** (Elihu) Root **5** (Russell Alexander) Alger
attorney general: **4** (Philander Chase) Knox **6** (John William) Griggs **7** (Joseph) McKenna
navy: **4** (John Davis) Long
postmaster general: **4** (James Albert) Gary **5** (Charles Emory) Smith
interior: **5** (Cornelius Newton) Bliss **9** (Ethan Allen) Hitchcock
agriculture: **6** (James) Wilson
born: **7** Niles OH
died: **9** Buffalo NY
died by: **13** assassination
buried: **8** Canton OH
education:
college: **10** Allegheny
law school: **6** Albany
religion: **9** Methodist
author: **37** The Tariff in the Days of Henry Clay and Since
political career: **24** US House of Representatives
governor of: **4** Ohio
civilian career: **6** lawyer
military service: **7** captain **8** Civil War **11** brevet major
notable events of lifetime/term:
Act: **13** Dingley Tariff
Peace Conference: **5** Hague
Treaty of: **5** Paris
war with: **5** Spain
father: **7** William
mother: **5** Nancy (Campbell Allison)
siblings: **4** Anna, Mary **5** Abner, Helen, James **10** Abbie Celia **12** David Allison **14** Sarah Elizabeth
wife: **3** Ida (Saxton)
children: **3** Ida **9** Katherine

McManus, George
creator/artist of: **12** The Newlyweds **16** Bringing Up Father

McMath, Virginia Katherine
real name of: **12** Ginger Rogers

McMeekan, Wayne
real name of: **10** David Wayne

McMillan, Edwin Mattison
field: **7** physics **9** chemistry
developed:
16 synchrocyclotron
awarded: **10** Nobel Prize

McMillan and Wife
character: **7** Mildred **13** Sally McMillan **14** (Sgt) Charles Enright **15** (Commissioner) Stewart McMillan
cast: **10** John Schuck, Rock Hudson **11** Nancy Walker **15** Susan Saint James

McMurtry, Larry
author of: **10** Texasville **12** Lonesome Dove **14** Horseman Pass By **18** The Last Picture Show

McPhee, John
author of: **16** In Suspect Terrain **20** Coming into the

McQueen, Steve *(continued)*
Country **23** The Curve of Binding Energy **26** Encounters with the Archdruid

McQueen, Steve
real name: **21** Terrence Steven McQueen
wife: **10** Ali MacGraw
born: **8** Slater MO **14** Indianapolis IN
roles: **7** Bullitt, The Blob **8** Papillon **14** The Great Escape, The Sand Pebbles **16** The Cincinnati Kid **17** Thomas Crown Affair, Wanted Dead or Alive **19** The Magnificent Seven

McTeague
author: **11** Frank Norris

mea culpa 7 my fault **14** through my fault

Mead, Margaret
author of: **14** My Earlier Years **16** Blackberry Winter **18** Coming of Age in Samoa **20** Growing Up in New Guinea **42** Sex and Temperament in Three Primitive Societies
husband: **14** Gregory Bateson

Meade, Dr and Mrs
characters in: **15** Gone With the Wind
author: **8** Mitchell

Meade, George Gordon
served in: **8** Civil War **10** Mexican War
side: **5** Union
battle: **7** Bull Run **8** Antietam **10** Gettysburg **13** South Mountain **14** Fredericksburg **16** Chancellorsville **18** Peninsular campaign
commander of: **16** Army of the Potomac

meadow 3 lea **4** mead, park

meager 4 bare, lean, slim, thin **5** scant, short, spare, token **6** little, paltry, scanty, scarce, skimpy, slight, sparse **7** scrimpy, slender, stinted, wanting **9** deficient **10** inadequate **12** insufficient **13** insubstantial

meagerness 8 sparsity **9** smallness **10** inadequacy, measliness, scantiness, skimpiness, sparseness **13** insufficiency **14** insignificance

Meagles
character in: **12** Little Dorrit
author: **7** Dickens

meal 4 bran, chow, diet, eats, fare, food, grub, menu **5** feast, flour, grits **6** farina, groats, repast, spread **7** banquet, cooking, cuisine, oatmeal **8** cornmeal, victuals **10** bill of fare **11** nourishment, refreshment

mealymouthed 6 unsure **7** devious **8** hesitant **9** deceptive, insincere

mean *see box*

meander 4 loop, rove, wind **5** snake, stray, twist **6** circle, ramble, spiral, wander, zigzag **8** undulate **9** convolute, corkscrew

meandering 7 devious, sinuous, turning, winding **8** indirect, rambling, tortuous, twisting **9** wandering **10** circuitous, roundabout, serpentine

meaning 3 aim, end **4** gist, goal, hint, meat, pith, plan, view **5** drift, force, point, sense, value, worth **6** burden, design, intent, object, scheme, thrust, upshot **7** content, essence, pointer, purport, purpose **9** intention, substance **10** denotation, indication, intimation, suggestion **11** implication **12** significance **15** sum and substance

meaningful 4 deep **5** meaty, pithy **6** useful **7** pointed, serious **8** eloquent, explicit, pregnant **9** designing, important **10** expressive, gratifying, portentous, purposeful, suggestive, worthwhile **11** significant, substantial **13** consequential

meaningless 5 trite **6** absurd, paltry, stupid **7** aimless, fatuous, foolish, idiotic, shallow, trivial, useless **8** baffling, piddling, puzzling **9** enigmatic, facetious, frivolous, illegible, senseless, valueless, worthless **10** incoherent, mystifying, perplexing **11** bewildering, inscrutable, nonsensical, purposeless, unessential, unimportant **12** impenetrable, inexplicable, inexpressive, preposterous **13** insignificant, unsubstantial **14** undecipherable

Mean Joe
nickname of: **9** Joe Greene

means 3 way **4** jack, mode **5** bread, dough, funds, money **6** avenue, course, income, method, resort, riches, wealth **7** capital, dollars, measure, process, revenue **8** property **9** affluence, long green, resources, substance **11** alternative, wherewithal

mean-spirited 3 low **4** base, poor, vile **5** cheap, nasty, petty, small, snide, sorry, tight, venal **6** abject, measly, paltry, scurvy, shabby, sordid, stingy **7** ignoble, miserly, selfish, vicious **8** tightwad, wretched **9** miserable, penurious **10** ungenerous **12** parsimonious

Mean Streets
director: **14** Martin Scorsese
cast: **11** Amy Robinson, David Proval **12** Harvey Keitel, Robert DeNiro

meantime 7 interim **8** interval **9** meanwhile

meanwhile 8 meantime **12** concurrently, in the interim **13** at the same time **14** simultaneously

measurable 10 assessable, computable, mensurable, reckonable **11** appraisable **12** determinable

---

mean 3 low, par, say **4** base, evil, norm, plan, poor, rude, rule, vile, want, wish **5** aim at, cheap, close, cruel, imply, nasty, petty, small, tight, venal **6** denote, flimsy, greedy, hint at, intend, malign, medium, menial, normal, paltry, sleazy, sordid, stingy, tell off, trashy, unfair **7** average, balance, betoken, dream of, drive at, express, hoggish, inhuman, miserly, point to, propose, purpose, regular, resolve, selfish, signify, squalid, suggest, think of, trivial, vicious **8** aspire to, gimcrack, grasping, indicate, inferior, inhumane, intimate, low-grade, picayune, piddling, pitiless, rubbishy, say truly, shameful, standard, stand for, trifling, uncaring, wretched **9** illiberal, low-paying, malicious, mercenary, merciless, miserable, niggardly, penurious, symbolize, unfeeling **10** avaricious, compromise, despicable, have in mind, have in view, jerry-built, low-ranking, malevolent, pinchpenny, second-rate, ungenerous, villainous **11** closefisted, commonplace, disgraceful, happy medium, hardhearted, self-seeking, small-minded, tightfisted, unimportant **12** contemptible, disagreeable, dishonorable **13** insignificant, unsympathetic **15** inconsequential

measure 3 act, law **4** bill,
plan, rule, size, step, time
5 bound, clock, gauge, judge,
limit, means, plumb, quota,
range, scale, scope, share,
sound, value **6** amount, assess,
course, degree, design, extent,
method, resort, scheme, survey **7** portion, project **8** appraise, evaluate, proposal,
quantity **9** allotment, allowance, enactment, procedure,
restraint, yardstick **10** limitation, moderation, proceeding,
temperance

measure, unit of *see box,
p. 616*

measured 5 equal, exact
6 steady **7** precise, regular,
studied, uniform **8** verified
10 calculated, deliberate
11 cold-blooded, intentional,
well-planned **12** premeditated
13 predetermined

Measure for Measure
author: **18** William
Shakespeare
character: **5** Lucio **6** Angelo,
Juliet **7** Claudio, Escalus,
Mariana **8** Isabella
9 Vincentio

measureless 7 endless **8** infinite **9** boundless, unlimited
12 immeasurable

measurement *see box,
p. 618*

measure out 6 ration **7** dole
out, mete out **9** apportion

meat 3 nut **4** core, fare, food,
gist, grub **5** heart, point
6 kernel **7** edibles, essence, nucleus **8** victuals **9** provender,
substance **10** provisions, sustenance **11** comestibles,
nourishment

Mechaneus
epithet of: **4** Zeus
means: **9** contriver

mechanic 6 joiner **7** artisan
9 automatic, craftsman, ma-
chinist **11** uninspired
12 grease monkey

mechanical 4 cold **7** routine
9 automatic, unfeeling **10** impersonal, self-acting, unthinking **11** instinctive, involuntary,
machinelike, perfunctory, unconscious **13** machine-driven

mechanism 4 tool **5** motor,
works **7** machine, utensil
9 apparatus, appliance, implement, machinery **10** instrument **11** contrivance

Meda
husband: **9** Idomeneus
lover: **6** Leucus

medal 5 award, honor, prize

6 laurel, reward, ribbon, trophy **8** citation **9** medallion
10 decoration

Medawar, Peter Brian
field: **7** biology
nationality: **7** British
discovered: **23** acquired immune tolerance
awarded: **10** Nobel Prize

meddle 5 mix in **6** butt in,
horn in, kibitz **7** intrude, pry
into **9** interfere, interlope, intervene **10** tamper with

meddler 3 pry **5** snoop **7** Paul
Pry **8** busybody **10** interferer,
Nosy Parker

meddlesome 4 nosy **5** pushy
6 prying, snoopy **7** pushing
8 meddling, snooping **9** intrusive, obtrusive, officious
11 impertinent, interfering
12 presumptuous

Medea
author: **9** Euripides
character: **5** Creon, Jason
6 Aegeus, Glauce

Medea
form: **9** sorceress
father: **6** Aeetes
mother: **5** Idyia
aunt: **5** Circe
brother: **8** Apsyrtus
sister: **9** Chalciope
lover: **5** Jason
son: **6** Medeus, Pheres
8 Mermerus, Tisander **9** Alcimenes, Thessalus
killed: **7** her sons
escaped to: **6** Athens

Medeus
father: **6** Aegeus
mother: **5** Medea

media 5 press, radio **9** maga-
zines **10** billboards, journalism,
newspapers, television
11 journalists
singular: **6** medium

medial 4 mean **6** median
7 average

median 3 mid, par **4** mean,
norm **5** mesne **6** center, medial, medium, middle **7** average, central, halfway
8 middling, midpoint, moderate **12** intermediate

mediate 6 pacify, step in, umpire **7** referee **8** moderate
9 arbitrate, intercede, interpose, intervene, negotiate, reconcile **10** conciliate,
propitiate

mediation 6 parley **10** adjustment, compromise, discussion
11 arbitration, give-and-making,
negotiation, peacemaking
12 conciliation, intercession,
intervention, pacification
14 reconciliation

mediator 6 umpire **7** referee
9 go-between, moderator
10 arbitrator, negotiator,
peacemaker, reconciler
12 intermediary

medical 7 healing **8** curative,
remedial, salutary, sanative
9 medicinal **10** medicative
11 restorative, therapeutic

medical abbreviation *see
box, p. 618*

Medical Center
character: **9** (Dr) Joe Gan-
non **11** Nurse Wilcox, (Dr)
Paul Lochner **13** Nurse
Chambers **14** Nurse Court-
land, (Dr) Jeanne Bartlett
cast: **9** James Daly **11** Chad
Everett, Chris Hutson
12 Audrey Totter, Jayne
Meadows **14** Corinne
Camacho

medical practitioner 6 doctor,
medico **9** physician

medication 4 balm **5** tonic
6 elixir, remedy **7** nostrum,
panacea **8** medicine **10** medicament, palliative **11** restorative

Medici, Giovanni de' 8 Pope
Leo X **15** Pope Leo the Tenth

Medici, Giulio 14 Pope Clement VII **21** Pope Clement the
Seventh

medicine 4 balm, drug, pill
5 salve, tonic **6** remedy **7** nostrum **10** healing art, medication **11** restorative
12 therapeutics **13** materia
medica
god of: **9** Asclepius
11 Aesculapius

medieval 8 Dark Ages **10** antiquated, Middle-Ages **12** old-
fashioned **14** pre-Renaissance

mediocre 4 so-so **5** petty
6 common, meager, medium,
normal, paltry, slight **7** average **8** inferior, ordinary, passable, trifling **9** tolerable
10 negligible, pedestrian,
second-rate **11** commonplace,
indifferent, unimportant
12 run-of-the-mill **13** inappreciable, insignificant **14** fair-to-
middling, inconsiderable
15 inconsequential,
undistinguished

mediocrity 8 poorness **9** pettiness **10** low-quality, meagerness, paltriness, triviality
11 inferiority **12** indifference,
ordinariness, unimportance
14 insignificance
15 commonplaceness

meditate 4 muse, plan **5** aim
at, study, think **6** devise, ponder **7** concoct, dream of, propose, reflect **8** cogitate,

measure, unit of

of Afghanistan: 3 paw, sir **5** jerib, karoh **6** khurds **7** kharwar
of Algeria: 3 pik **5** rebis, tarri **6** termin
of Argentina: 4 sino **5** legua **6** cuadra, lastre **7** manzana
of Australia: 4 arna, naut, saum
of Austria: 4 fass, fuss, joch, mass, muth, yoke **5** halbe, linie, meile, metze, pfiff, punkt **6** achtel, becher, leipoa, seidel **7** klafter, viertel **8** dreiling **12** futtermassel
of Belgium: 3 vat **4** aune, pied **5** carat **6** perche **8** boisseau
of Bolivia: 6 league **7** celemin
of Borneo: 7 gantang
of Brazil: 2 pe **4** moio, sack, vara **5** braca, legoa, milha, tonel **6** canada, cuarto, quarto, tarefa **7** garrafa **8** alqueire
of Bulgaria: 3 oka, oke **5** krine, lekhe, likhe
of Canada: 3 ton **5** minot, perch, point **6** arpent **7** chainon
of the Canary Islands: 8 fanegada
of Chile: 4 vara **5** legua, linea **6** cuadra **7** fanega
of China: 3 cho, fan, fen, pau, tou, tun, yan, yin **4** chek, chih, fang, kish, papa, quei, shih, teke, tsan, tsun **5** catty, chang, ching, sheng, shing **6** chupak, gungli, kungho, kungmu, tching **7** kungfen, kungyin **8** kungchih, kungshih **9** kungching
of Colombia: 4 vara **7** azumbre, celemin
of Costa Rica: 4 vara **5** cafiz, cahiz **6** fanega, tercia **7** cajuela, cantaro, manzana **10** caballeria
of Cuba: 4 vara **5** bocoy, cocoy, tarea **6** cordel, fanega **10** caballeria
of Czechoslovakia: 3 lan **4** mira **5** korec, liket, stopa **6** merice, strych
of Denmark: 3 ell, fod, mil, pot **4** alen **5** album, anker, kande, linje, paegl **7** landmil, oltonde, ortonde, skieppe, viertel **8** fjerding **9** ottingkar **10** korntonde
of the Dominican Republic: 3 ona **5** tarea **6** fanega
of Ecuador: 5 libra **6** cuadra, fanega
of Egypt: 3 apt, dra, hen, rob **4** arab, dira, draa, khet, nief, ocha, roub, theb, wudu **5** abdat, ardab, cubit, farde, fedan, keleh, kerat, kilah, sahme **6** artaba, aurure, baladi, kantar, keddah, robhah, schene **7** choryos, daribah, malouah, roubouh, toumnah **8** kassabah, kharouba **10** diramimari, diribaladi
of El Salvador: 4 vara **5** cafiz, cahiz **6** fanega **7** batella, botella, cantara, manzana
of England: 3 cut, ell, lea, pin, rod, ton, tun, vat **4** acre, bind, butt, comb, coom, cran, foot, gill, goad, hand, hank, heer, hide, inch, last, line, mile, nail, pace, palm, peck, pint, pipe, pole, pool, rood, rope, sack, seam, span, trug, typp, wist, yard, yoke **5** bodge, chain, cubit, digit, float, floor, fluid, hutch, jugum, minim, ounce, perch, point, prime, quart, skein, stack, truss **6** barrel, bovate, bushel, cranne, fathom, firkin, gallon, hobbet, hobbit, league, manent, oxgang, pottle, runlet, square, strike, sulung, thread, tierce **7** auchlet, furlong, kenning, quarter, rundlet, seamile, spindle, tertian, virgate **8** carucate, chaldron, hogshead, landyard, puncheon, quadrant, standard
of Estonia: 3 tun **4** elle, liin, sund, toll, toop **5** verst **6** sagene, versta **7** kulimet **8** tonnland
of Ethiopia: 3 tat **4** cubi, kuba **5** derah, messe **6** cabaho, sinjer, sinzer, tanica **7** entelam, farsakh, farsang, ghebeta
of Finland: 5 kannu, verst **6** fathom, kannor **8** ottinger, skalpund, tunnland
of France: 3 pot, sac **4** aune, mine, pied, velt **5** arpen, carat, ligne, minot, pinte, point, pouce, velte **6** arpent, hemine, league, quarte, setier
of Greece: 3 pik **4** bema, piki, pous **5** baril, chous, cubit, diote, doron, maris, pekhe, podos, pygon, xylon **6** acaena, bacile, barile, cotula, dichas, gramme, hemina, koilon, lichas, milion, orgyia, palame, pechys, schene, xestes **7** bacvhel, chenica, choenix, cyathos, diaulos, metreta, stadium, stremma **8** condylos, daktylos, dekapode, dolichos, medimnos, medimnys, metretes, palaiste, plethron, plethrum, stathmos **9** hemiekton, oxybaphon
of Guatemala: 4 vara **6** cuarta, tercia **7** cajuela, manzana **10** caballeria
of Guinea: 7 jacktan
of Honduras: 4 vara **5** milla **6** mecate **7** cajuela
of Hungary: 3 ako **4** hold, yoke **5** itcze, marok, metze **7** huvelyk
of Iceland: 3 set **4** alin **5** almud **6** almenn, ferfet, pottur **7** fathmur, fermila, oltunna
of India: 3 ady, gaz, gez, jow, lan **4** byee, coss, depa, doph, hath, koss, kunk, raik, rati, seit, taun, tola **5** bigha, covid, crosa, danda, depoh, drona, erosa, garce, hasta, krosa, parah, ratti, salay, yojan **6** adhaka, amunam, covido, cudava, cumbha, geerah, moolum, mushti, ouroub, palgat, parran, prasha, ropani, tipree, unglee, yojana **7** dhanush, gavyuti, khahoon, niranga, prastha **8** okthabah
of Indonesia: 5 depah, depoh
of Iran: 3 gaz, zar, zer **4** cane **5** gareh, kafiz, makuk, qasab **6** charac, chebel, ghalva **7** capicha, chenica, farsakh, mansion, mishara **8** parasang, piamaneh, stathmos
of Ireland: 4 mile **6** bandle **8** crannock
of Israel: 3 cab, car, hin, kab, kor **4** bath, ezba, omer, reed **5** cubit, donum, dunam, ephah, ganeh, homer, kaneh
of Italy: 3 pie **4** orna **5** palma, palmo, punto, salma, stero **6** barile, miglie, moggio, rubbio, tomolo **7** braccio, secchio **8** giornata, quadrato

of Japan: 2 go 3 boo, cho, djo, fun, inc, ken, kin, kon, rin, shi, sho, sun, tan 4 hiro, isse, kati, koku, niyo, shoo 5 carat, catty, issho, ittan, momme, picul, shaku 6 kwamme 8 hiyak-kin 9 hiyak-hiro 11 komma-ichida, kujira-shaku
of Java: 3 kan 4 paal, rand 5 palen
of Kenya: 4 wari
of Laos: 3 bak
of Latvia: 3 let 4 stof 5 stoff, verst 6 arshin, kulmet 7 verchoc, verchok 8 krouchka, pourvete 9 deciatine, lofstelle, pourvette 10 tonnseteel
of Liberia: 4 kuba
of Libya: 3 dra, pik, saa 4 kele 5 bozze, donum, jabia, teman, uckia 6 barile, gorrah, misura 7 mattaro, termino 8 kharouba
of Luxembourg: 5 fuder
of Madagascar: 7 gantang
of Malaysia: 3 pau, tun 4 para, pipe, tael, wang 5 parah 6 chupak, parrah 7 gantang
of Malta: 4 rotl 5 artal, canna, parto, ratel, salma 6 kantar 7 caffiso
of Mexico: 3 bag, pie 4 alma, onza, vara 5 almud, baril, carga, jarra, labor, legua, libra, linea, marco, sitio 6 adarme, almude, arroba, carega, fanega, ochaua, terceo 7 pulgada, quintal 9 cuarteron, cuartillo 10 caballeria
of Morocco: 4 kala, muhd, rotl, saah, sahh, ueba 5 artal, cadee, gerbe, ratel 6 covado, dirhem, fanega, izenbi, kintar, tangin, tomini 8 quintral
of Myanmar: 2 ly 3 dha, gon, mau, sao, tao, tat 4 byee, phan, seit, taun, that 5 shita, thuoc 6 lamany, palgat 7 chaivai 8 okthabah
of the Netherlands: 2 el 3 aam, ahm, ell, kan, vat 4 duim, mijl, rood, rope 5 anker, roede, wisse 6 bunder, legger, maatje, mutsje, streep 7 schepel 8 mimgelen, steekkan
of Nicaragua: 4 vara 5 cahiz 6 suerte 7 cajuela, manzana 10 cabelleria
of Norway: 3 fot, mal 4 alen 5 kande 6 fathom 7 skieppe 9 korntonde
of Panama: 7 celemin
of Paraguay: 3 pie 4 lino, lira, lire, vara 5 legua 6 cuadra, fanega
of Peru: 4 topo 5 galon 7 celemin 8 fanegada
of the Philippines: 4 loan 5 braza, catty, cavan, chupa, fardo, ganta, picul, punto 6 apatan, balita, lachsa, quinon 7 quilate 8 chinanta
of Poland: 3 cal 4 mila, pret 5 morga, sazen, vloka, wloka 6 cwierc, cwierk, kwarta, lokiec 7 garniec 9 kwarterka
of Portugal: 2 pe 4 bota, moio, vara 5 almud, fanga, geira, linha, milha 6 almude, covado 7 alquier, ferrado, selamin 8 alqueire
of Puerto Rico: 6 cuerda 10 cabelleria
of Rumania: 7 faltche
of Russia: 3 fut, lof 4 duim, fass, loof, pood, quar, stof 5 duime, foute, korec, korek, ligne, osmin, pajak, stoff, stoof, vedro, verst 6 charka, liniya, osmina, paletz, sagene, stekar, tchast, tsarki, versta, verste 7 archine, arsheen, botchka, chkalik, garnetz, verchoc, verchok 8 boutylka, chetvert, krouchka, kroushka 9 chetverik 10 dessiatine 11 polugarnetz
of Scotland: 3 cop 4 boll, cran, fall, mile, peck, pint, rood, rope, span 5 crane, lippy 6 audlet, davach, firlot, lippie, noggin 7 chalder, choppin 8 mutchkin, stimpart, stimpert 9 particate, shaftment, shathmont
of Sicily: 5 salma 7 caffiso
of Sierra Leone: 4 load 6 kettle
of Somalia: 3 top 4 caba 5 chela, darat, tabla 6 cubito 8 parsalah
of South Africa: 4 vara
of Spain: 3 pie 4 codo, dedo, paso, vara 5 braza, cahiz, carga, legua, medio, palmo, sesma 6 cordel, cuarta, fanega, racion, yugada 7 azumbre, celemin, estadel, pulgada 8 fanegada
of Sri Lanka: 4 para, seer 5 parah 6 amunam, parrah
of Sudan: 2 ud
of Suriname: 7 ketting
of Sweden: 3 aln, fot, ref, tum 4 alar, amar, famn, kapp, last, stop 5 carat, foder, kanna, linje, nymil, spann 6 fathom, jumfru 7 oxhuvud, tunland 8 fjarding, koltunna, tunnland
of Switzerland: 3 imi, pot 4 aune, fuss, muid, pied, zoll 5 lieue, linie, maass, pouce, staab, toise 6 perche, strich 7 klafter, viertel 9 quarteron 10 holzlafter 11 holzklafter
of Syria: 5 makuk 6 garava
of Thailand: 2 wa 3 can, ken, niv, rai, sat, sok, wah 4 cohi, keup, niou, tang 5 kwien, leeng, sesti, vouah 6 kabiet, kanahn 7 chaimeu 8 changawn 9 anukabiet
of Tunisia: 3 saa 4 saah 5 cafiz 6 mettar 8 milerole
of Turkey: 3 dra, oka, pik 4 draa, khat, kile, zira 5 berri, kileh, zirai 6 arshin, chinik, fortin, halebi 7 nocktat
of Uruguay: 4 vara 6 cuadra, suerte
of Venezuela: 5 galon, milla 6 fanega 7 estadel
of Vietnam: 4 gang, phan, thon
of Wales: 5 cover 7 cantred, crannoc, listred
of Yugoslavia: 3 oka, rif 4 akov, ralo 5 donum, khvat, lanaz, płaze, stopa 6 motyka, ralico 9 danoranja

measurement 4 area, mass, size 5 depth, width 6 extent, height, length, volume, weight 7 breadth, content, gauging 8 capacity, plumbing, sounding 9 amplitude, appraisal, dimension, magnitude, measuring, reckoning, surveying 10 assessment, estimation, evaluation 11 mensuration
  Biblical: 4 omer 5 cubit, ephah 6 shekel
  champagne: 6 magnum 8 jeroboam, rehoboam 9 balthazar 10 methuselah, salmanazar 14 Nebuchadnezzar
  cloth: 4 bolt
  cotton: 4 bale
  electricity: 3 ohm 4 volt, watt 5 joule 6 ampere 10 horsepower
  energy: 3 BTU 5 joule 7 calorie 11 kilocalorie 18 British thermal unit
  firewood: 4 cord
  force: 4 dyne 6 newton 7 poundal
  gold/jewelry: 5 carat, karat, point
  Greek: 4 mina 5 cubit 6 obolos, talent 7 drachma, stadion
  gun: 5 gauge 7 caliber
  light: 7 candela 11 candlepower
  liquor/spirits: 4 pint, pony, shot 5 fifth, quart 6 jigger, magnum
  metric system: 5 liter, meter 9 deciliter, decimeter, dekaliter, dekameter, kiloliter, kilometer, nanometer 10 centiliter, centimeter, cubic meter, hectoliter, hectometer, milliliter, millimeter 11 square meter 14 cubic dekameter 15 cubic centimeter, cubic millimeter, square decimeter, square dekameter, square kilometer 16 square centimeter, square hectometer, square millimeter
  metric weight: 3 ton 4 gram 5 tonne 7 quintal 8 dekagram, kilogram 9 centigram, hectogram, microgram, milligram
  paper: 4 ream 5 quire
  pressure: 6 pascal 10 atmosphere
  Roman: 2 as 5 cubit, libra 6 pondus 7 stadium
  sound: 7 decibel
  temperature: 6 degree, Kelvin 7 Celsius 10 Fahrenheit
  time: 3 day 4 hour, week, year 5 month, score 6 decade, minute, second 7 century 10 millennium, nanosecond 11 microsecond, millisecond
  typography: 2 em, en 4 pica 5 point
  unit: 3 cup, rod 4 acre, dram, foot, gill, inch, link, mile, peck, pint, yard 5 chain, minim, ounce, quart 6 barrel, bushel, circle, degree, fathom, gallon 7 furlong, hectare 8 angstrom, hogshead, teaspoon 9 cubic foot, cubic inch, cubic yard, square rod 10 fluid ounce, right angle, square foot, square inch, square mile, square yard, tablespoon 25 international nautical mile
  weight: 3 ton 4 dram 5 grain, ounce, pound 7 scruple 8 short ton 9 ounce troy, pound troy 11 pennyweight 13 hundredweight

medical abbreviation
  a c: 11 before meals
  ad lib: 8 as needed 9 as desired
  agit: 5 shake
  aq: 5 water
  b i d: 9 twice a day
  cap: 4 take 7 capsule
  coch: 8 spoonful
  dil: 6 dilute 8 dissolve
  fldxt: 12 fluid extract
  ft: 4 make
  ft mist: 12 make a mixture
  ft pulv: 11 make a powder
  gr: 5 grain
  gt: 4 drop
  gtt: 5 drops
  h s: 9 at bedtime
  in d: 5 daily
  lot: 6 lotion
  mod praesc: 21 in the manner prescribed
  O: 4 pint
  O D: 8 right eye
  O S: 7 left eye
  O U: 9 in each eye
  ol: 3 oil
  p c: 9 after food 10 after meals
  p o: 7 by mouth
  p r n: 25 as circumstances may require
  pil: 3 pill
  pulv: 6 powder
  q i d: 14 four times daily
  rep: 6 repeat
  s o s: 11 if necessary
  ss: 7 one half
  tab: 6 tablet
  t i d: 15 three times daily
  ut dict: 10 as directed

consider, contrive, mull over, ruminate 9 dwell upon 10 deliberate 11 contemplate

meditation 4 yoga 5 study 6 musing, poring 7 mulling, reverie, thought 8 brooding 9 discourse, pondering 10 cogitation, reflection, rumination 12 deliberation 13 consideration, contemplation

Mediterranean
  called by ancient Romans: 11 mare nostrum
  coast: 7 Riviera
  gulf: 5 Lions, Sidra, Tunis 7 Antalya, Catania, Taranto 8 Hammamet 9 Iskenderon
  island: 4 Elba 5 Capri, Corfu, Crete, Ibiza, Malta 6 Cyprus, Euboea, Lesbos, Rhodes, Sicily 7 Corsica, Majorca, Minorca 8 Balearic, Sardinia
  resort: 4 Nice 5 Capri 6 Cannes 7 Riviera 9 Cote d'Azur 10 Costa Brava
  river into: 2 Po 4 Ebro, Nile 5 Rhone
  sea: 5 Black 6 Aegean, Ionian 8 Adriatric, Ligurian 10 Tyrrhenian
  strait: 8 Bosporus 9 Bosphorus, Gibraltar 11 Dardanelles
  wind: 7 mistral, sirocco

medium 3 way 4 form, mean, mode, tool 5 means, organ 6 agency, avenue, common, milieu, normal 7 average, balance, channel, diviner, psychic, setting, vehicle 8 middling, moderate, ordinary 9 go-between, middle way, mid-course 10 atmosphere, compromise, golden mean, instrument, moderation 11 clairvoyant, environment, happy medium 12 crystal-gazer, intermediary, intermediate, middle ground, spiritualist, surroundings 13 fortuneteller 15 instrumentality

medley 4 hash, mess, olio 6 jumble, mosaic 7 farrago, melange, mixture 8 mishmash, pastiche 9 patchwork, potpourri 10 assortment, hodgepodge, miscellany 11 gallimaufry

Medon
mentioned in: 5 Iliad
   7 Odyssey
father: 6 Oileus
mother: 5 Rhene
position: 6 herald
friend of: 8 Penelope
killed by: 6 Aeneas

medulla
part of: 5 brain
controls: 6 glands 7 muscles

Medusa
form: 6 Gorgon
father: 7 Phorcys
mother: 4 Ceto
sisters: 6 Graiae
loved by: 8 Poseidon
children: 7 Pegasus
   8 Chrysaor
sight of her caused people
   to turn to: 5 stone
killed by: 7 Perseus

meek 4 mild 6 docile, gentle,
humble, modest 8 lamblike,
retiring, tolerant, yielding
9 compliant, spineless, tractable, weak-kneed 10 spiritless,
submissive, unassuming 11 acquiescent, complaisant, deferential, unassertive,
unresisting 13 long-suffering,
tenderhearted, unpretentious

meekness 7 pliancy, shyness
8 docility, humility 9 passivity
10 diffidence, humbleness
11 bashfulness 13 nonresistance 14 self-effacement

meet 3 apt, fit 4 abut, face,
good, heed, obey 5 cross,
equal, greet, match, rally,
right 6 adjoin, answer, border,
follow, gather, muster, proper,
seemly 7 abide by, collect,
convene, execute, fitting, fulfill, observe, perform, respect,
run into, satisfy, welcome
8 assemble, becoming, bump
into, confront, converge, decorous, opposite, relevant, suitable 9 agreeable, allowable,
befitting, congruous, discharge,
encounter, intersect, permitted,
pertinent 10 admissable, comply with, congregate, felicitous 11 acknowledge,
appropriate, permissible
12 come together

meet eye to eye 4 face
8 confront, face up to 11 meet
vis-a-vis

meet halfway 6 settle 9 make
a deal 10 compromise
11 come to terms 14 strike a
bargain 18 split the difference

meet head on 4 face 5 crash
6 oppose 7 collide, crack up
8 confront, face up to 9 challenge, encounter

meeting 4 date 5 group, tryst

6 caucus 7 council 8 assembly,
conclave, congress 9 encounter, gathering 10 conference,
convention, engagement, rendezvous 11 assignation, convocation, get-together
12 introduction, presentation
13 confrontation

Meeting at Telgte
author: 11 Gunter Grass

meeting of the minds
7 concert, concord, harmony
9 agreement 11 concordance
13 understanding

meeting place 5 mecca 10 focal point, rendezvous

Meet Me in St Louis
director: 16 Vincente
   Minnelli
cast: 8 Leon Ames, Tom
   Drake 9 Mary Astor 11 Judy
   Garland 12 June Lockhart,
   Marjorie Main 13 Lucille
   Bremer 14 Margaret O'Brien
song: 11 Trolley Song 14 The
   Boy Next Door 33 Have
   Yourself a Merry Little
   Christmas

Meet the Press
moderator: 9 Ned Brooks
   10 Bill Monroe 11 Edwin
   Newman 14 Lawrence Spi-
   vak, Martha Rountree

meet with 4 meet 6 endure
7 undergo 8 come upon 9 encounter 10 come across,
experience

Mefitis
also: 8 Mephitis
prevented: 5 winds
kind of winds: 7 harmful

Megaera
member of: 6 Furies

Megalosaurus
type: 8 dinosaur
means: 11 great lizard
found by: 15 William
   Buckland
period: 8 Jurassic

Megamede
husband: 12 King Thespius
number of daughters: 5 fifty

Megapenthes
father: 7 Proetus 8 Menelaus
mother: 10 Stheneboea

Megara
father: 5 Creon
husband: 8 Hercules
son: 11 Therimachus

Mehuman 6 eunuch

Meilichius
epithet of: 4 Zeus
means: 8 gracious

Mein Kampf
author: 11 Adolf Hitler

means: 7 my fight 8 my
battle

Meitner, Lise
field: 7 physics
nationality: 8 Austrian
contributed to: 21 atomic
   bomb development
discovered: 12 protactinium
   16 fission of uranium

Melaenis
epithet of: 9 Aphrodite
means: 5 black

Melampus
father: 8 Amythaon
mother: 7 Idomene
brother: 4 Bias
wife: 7 Lysippe
son: 4 Abas 7 Mantius
   10 Antiphates
vocation: 4 seer 6 healer

melancholia 7 despair
10 depression, desolation, melancholy 11 despondency

melancholy 4 blue, glum
5 blues, dumps, gloom,
moody 6 dismal, dreary,
gloomy, mopish, morose, somber 7 despair, doleful, forlorn,
joyless, unhappy 8 dejected,
desolate, doldrums, dolorous,
downcast, funereal, mournful
9 cheerless, dejection, depressed, heartsick, moodiness,
plaintive 10 calamitous, depressing, depression, despondent, dispirited, gloominess,
low spirits 11 despondency,
discouraged, downhearted, forlornness, languishing, melancholia, sick at heart,
unfortunate 12 disconsolate,
heavyhearted 14 down in the
dumps, down in the mouth
16 disconsolateness
French: 6 triste 9 tristesse

melange 3 mix 6 jumble, medley 7 mixture 8 compound,
mishmash, pastiche 9 pasticcio,
patchwork, potpourri 10 assemblage, assortment, hodgepodge, miscellany
11 gallimaufry

Melanion
suitor of: 8 Atalanta

Melanippe
form: 4 foal
foal born to: 6 Euippe
transformed into: 4 Arne,
   girl
father: 4 Ares
queen of: 7 Amazons

Melanosaurus
type: 8 dinosaur
period: 8 Triassic

Melanthius
goatherd for: 8 Odysseus

Melantho
handmaiden for: 8 Penelope

Melas
father: **7** Phrixus
mother: **10** Chalciiope
brother: **5** Argus **8** Phrontis
10 Cytissorus

Melbourne
bay: **7** Hobson's **11** Port
Phillip
landmark: **20** Flemington
Racecourse
river: **5** Yarra **6** Plenty
9 Mary Creek, Patterson
11 Maribyrnong **12** Diamond
Creek **13** Kororoit Creek
14 Dandenong Creek, Gardiner's Creek **16** Moonee
Ponds Creek
state: **8** Victoria
university: **6** Monash **7** La
Trobe

Melchizedek
means: **19** king of
righteousness
hometown: **5** Salem
contemporary: **7** Abraham

meld 3 mix **4** fuse, join
5 blend, merge, unite **6** jumble, mingle **7** combine **8** coalesce, intermix, scramble
9 commingle **10** amalgamate,
intertwine, interweave
11 consolidate, incorporate,
intermingle

Meleager
father: **4** Ares **6** Oeneus
mother: **7** Althaea
uncle: **9** Plexippus
slew: **14** Calydonian boar
loved: **8** Atalanta
killed: **15** mother's brothers
sisters: **11** Meleagrides

Meleagrides
sisters of: **8** Meleager
transformed into: **10** guinea
hens
transformed by: **7** Artemis

melee 3 row **4** fray, riot
5 brawl, scrap, set-to **6** fracas,
rumpus, tussle **7** scuffle **8** disorder, dogfight **9** commotion,
fistfight **10** free-for-all **11** altercation, pandemonium

Melete
member of: **5** Muses
personifies: **10** meditation

Melia
form: **5** nymph
born from: **5** blood
blood of: **6** Uranus

Meliad
form: **5** nymph
nymph of: **6** flocks **10** fruit
trees

Meliae
nymphs of: **5** Melic

Meliboea
form: **6** maiden

Melicertes
father: **7** Athamas
mother: **3** Ino
changed into: **8** Palaemon

Melie
form: **5** nymph
son: **6** Amycus

Melissa
sister: **8** Amaethea
nourished: **4** Zeus

mellifluous 4 soft **5** sweet
6 dulcet, mellow, smooth
7 musical **8** resonant **9** full-
toned, melodious **10** euphonious, harmonious, sweet-
toned **13** sweet-sounding

Mellors
character in: **20** Lady Chatterley's Lover
author: **8** Lawrence

mellow 4 rich, ripe, soft
5 drunk, sweet **6** mature, season, soften **7** matured, relaxed **8** luscious, tolerant
9 delicious **10** full-bodied
11 sympathetic **12** full-
flavored **13** compassionate,
understanding

mellowness 8 full body, fullness, maturity, richness, ripeness, softness **9** tolerance
10 compassion, smoothness
12 lusciousness, pleasantness

melodic 5 lyric **7** tuneful

melodious 4 rich, soft **5** clear,
lyric, sweet **6** dulcet, mellow,
smooth **7** melodic, musical,
ringing, tuneful **8** resonant
9 full-toned **10** euphonious,
sweet-toned **11** mellifluent,
mellifluous

melodrama 9 theatrics
12 emotionalism
13 theatricality

melodramatic 5 corny,
hammy, hokey, stagy **7** maudlin, mawkish **8** cornball, frenzied **10** flamboyant, histrionic
11 exaggerated, overwrought,
sensational, sentimental, spectacular **13** overemotional

melody 3 air **4** aria, song,
tune **5** ditty, theme **6** ballad,
strain, timbre **7** concord, euphony **10** musicality **11** tunefulness **12** mellifluence
13 melodiousness **14** harmoni-
ousness **15** mellifluousness

melon
varieties: **4** pear **5** mango,
snake, stink **6** casaba, citron,
Dudaim, netted, nutmeg, orange, winter **7** Persian, serpent **8** honeydew
10 cantaloupe, preserving,
watermelon **11** pomegranate **16** Oriental pickling,

Queen Anne's pocket
17 Chinese preserving

Melpomene
member of: **5** Muses
personifies: **7** tragedy

melt 4 fade, fuse, pass, thaw
5 blend, merge, shade, touch
6 affect, disarm, dispel, soften,
vanish **7** appease, dwindle, liquefy, mollify, scatter **8** dissolve **9** disappear, dissipate,
evaporate, waste away
10 arouse pity, conciliate,
propitiate

melt away 5 dry up **8** vaporize **9** evaporate

Melus
father: **7** Cinyras
mother: **6** Cyprus
changed into: **9** apple tree

Melville, Herman
author of: **4** Omoo **5** Mardi,
Typee **7** Redburn **8** Moby
Dick **9** Billy Budd **12** Benito
Cereno **16** The Confidence
Man **20** Bartleby the
Scrivener

Melville, Julia
character in: **9** The Rivals
author: **8** Sheridan

Melvin and Howard
director: **13** Jonathan
Demme
cast: **9** Paul LeMat **12** Jason
Robards **15** Mary
Steenburgen
Oscar for: **6** script **17** sup-
porting actress
(Steenburgen)

member 3 arm, leg, toe **4** foot,
hand, limb, part, tail, wing
5 bough, digit, organ, piece,
shoot **6** branch, finger, pinion
7 element, portion, section,
segment **8** fragment **9** appendage, component, extremity
10 ingredient **11** constituent

member
of the bar: **4** beak **7** counsel
8 advocate, attorney **9** barrister, counselor **10** mouthpiece **12** legal advisor
13 attorney-at-law
of a crew: **4** hand, mate
6 ensign, ganger, gunner,
purser, yeoman **7** bowsman,
oarsman, steward, swabbie
8 cabin boy, coxswain, deckhand, helmsman **9** first
mate, navigator
of faculty: **3** don, PhD
4 prof **5** tutor **6** doctor, master **7** teacher **8** lecturer
9 professor **10** instructor
of family: **3** son **4** aunt
5 niece, uncle **6** cousin, father, mother, nephew, sis-
ter **7** brother **8** daughter,
grandson **11** grandfather,

grandmother
13 granddaughter
of legislature: 4 whip 6 deputy 7 senator, speaker 8 delegate, lawmaker
10 legislator, politician
11 congressman 12 congresswoman
14 representative
of religious order: 3 nun
4 dame, monk 5 Clare, friar, priest 6 father, hermit, Jesuit, sister 7 Alexian, ascetic, brother, Cluniac, Templar
8 Capuchin, cenobite, minister, Trappist 9 Carmelite, Dominican 10 Carthusian, Cistercian, Franciscan
11 Augustinian, Benedictine
14 mother superior

Member of the Wedding, The
author: 15 Carson McCullers
character: 6 Jarvis 11 Janice Evans 13 Frankie Addams, John Henry West 16 Honey Camden Brown 18 Berenice Sadie Brown

membership 4 club 6 league, roster 7 company, society
9 community, personnel
10 connection, fellowship, fraternity 11 affiliation, association, brotherhood

membrane 3 web 4 film, skin
6 lining, sheath 7 coating
8 envelope, pellicle 9 thin sheet 10 integument

memento 5 favor, relic, token
6 record, trophy 8 keepsake, memorial, reminder, souvenir
11 memorabilia, remembrance 12 remembrancer
13 commemoration

memento mori 23 remember that thou must die 31 object serving as a reminder of death

Memnon
origin: 8 Oriental 9 Ethiopian
father: 8 Tithonus
mother: 3 Eos 4 Dawn
brother: 8 Emathion
companions: 10 Memnonides
fought with: 7 Trojans
killed by: 8 Achilles

Memnonides see 6 Memnon

memo
French: 11 aide memoire

memoir 4 life 5 diary 7 journal 9 biography, life story
10 adventures 11 confessions, experiences, reflections 13 autobiography, recollections, reminiscences

Memoirs of a Dutiful Daughter
author: 16 Simone de Beauvoir

memorabilia 6 papers 7 records 8 archives 9 documents

memorable 6 famous 7 eminent, notable, salient 8 historic, stirring, striking
9 important, momentous, prominent, red-letter 10 celebrated, impressive, noteworthy, remarkable 11 illustrious, outstanding, significant 13 distinguished, extraordinary, unforgettable

memorandum 4 memo, note
5 brief 6 agenda, minute, record 7 jotting 8 reminder
11 brief report, list of items

memorial 6 homage 7 tribute
8 monument 10 monumental
11 testimonial
13 commemorative

memorialization 11 celebration 13 commemoration

memorialize 4 mark 5 honor
9 celebrate 11 commemorate, pay homage to 12 pay tribute to

memory 4 fame, mark, name, note 5 glory, honor, token
6 esteem, recall, regard, renown, repute 7 memento, respect 8 eminence, keepsake, memorial, prestige, reminder, souvenir 10 estimation, reputation 11 distinction, remembering, remembrance, testimonial 12 recollection, remembrancer, reminiscence
13 commemoration
goddess of: 9 Mnemosyne

Memphis
football team: 9 Showboats

menace 3 cow 4 risk 5 bully, daunt, peril 6 danger, hazard, threat 7 imperil, pitfall, portend, presage, terrify 8 browbeat, endanger, forebode, jeopardy, threaten 9 terrorize
10 intimidate, jeopardize 11 be a hazard to, imperilment
12 endangerment

menacing 7 hostile 9 dangerous 11 belligerent, threatening, treacherous
12 antagonistic

Menaechmi
author: 7 Plautus

menage a trois 9 threesome
16 household of three

Menander
author of: 5 Heros 13 Perikeiromene 14 The Arbitration, The Misanthrope
16 The Rape of the Lock

Men at Arms
author: 11 Evelyn Waugh

Mencken, H L
author of: 10 Prejudices
19 The American Language
editor of: 10 The Mercury
11 The Smart Set

mend 3 fix 4 cure, darn, heal, knit 5 amend, emend, patch
6 better, reform, remedy, repair, revise 7 correct, improve, rectify, restore, retouch, touch up 8 overhaul, renovate
9 meliorate 10 ameliorate
11 recondition

mendacious 5 false, lying
8 spurious 9 deceptive 10 misleading, untruthful

mendacity 5 fraud, lying 6 deceit 7 falsity, perfidy 9 chicanery, deception, duplicity, falsehood, hypocrisy 10 dishonesty 11 insincerity
13 double-dealing, falsification, prevarication 14 untruthfulness 17 misrepresentation

Mendel, Gregor Johann
field: 6 botany
nationality: 8 Austrian
discovered: 14 laws of heredity
founded: 8 genetics

Mendeleyev (Mendeleev), Dimitri Ivanovich
field: 9 chemistry
nationality: 7 Russian
devised: 11 periodic law
13 periodic table

Mendelssohn, (Jakob Ludwig) Felix
born: 7 Germany, Hamburg
composer of: 6 Elijah, St Paul 7 Athalie, Italian (symphony No 4), Lorelei, Ruy Blas 8 Antigone, Scottish (symphony No 3) 11 Reformation (symphony No 5), The Hebrides 12 Hymn of Praise (symphony No 2)
17 Songs without Words
21 A Midsummer Night's Dream

mendicant 6 beggar 10 almsseeker, panhandler

Mending Wall
author: 11 Robert Frost

Menelaus
king of: 6 Sparta
father: 6 Atreus
mother: 6 Aerope
brother: 9 Agamemnon
wife: 5 Helen
son: 11 Megapenthes, Nicostratus
daughter: 8 Hermione

mene mene tekel upharsin
30 numbered numbered weighed divided
foretells destruction of:
10 Belshazzar

from Biblical book of:
6 Daniel

Menestheus
regent of: 6 Athens
rejected by: 5 Helen
assisted: 8 Menelaus

Menesthius
father: 9 Areithous
fought with: 6 Greeks
killed by: 5 Paris

menhaden 4 pogy 5 pogie
6 bunker 7 alewife, bugfish,
ellfish, fatback, herring, old-
wife, sardine 8 bonyfish, hardhead, ladyfish 10 mossbunker

menial 3 low 4 mean 5 drone,
lowly, slave, toady 6 abject,
drudge, flunky, helper, humble, lackey 7 fawning, ignoble,
servant, servile, slavish
8 cringing, employee 9 degrading, groveling, sycophant,
truckling, underling 10 apprentice, obsequious 11 bootlicking, subordinate, subservient, sycophantic

menial labor 4 toil 5 grind
8 drudgery

Menjou, Adolphe
born: 12 Pittsburgh PA
roles: 9 Golden Boy, Pol-
lyanna 11 A Star Is Born
12 The Front Page 13 A
Woman of Paris 15 A Fare-
well to Arms, State of the
Union 16 Little Miss
Marker 18 A Bill of
Divorcement

meno
music: 4 less

Menodice
form: 5 nymph
son: 5 Hylas

Menoeceus
descendant of: 6 Sparti
father: 5 Creon
son: 5 Creon
daughter: 7 Jocasta
death by: 7 suicide

Menoetes
occupation: 7 cowherd

Menoetius
member of: 6 Titans
9 Argonauts
father: 7 Iapetus
mother: 7 Clymene
brother: 5 Atlas 10 Epimetheus, Prometheus
son: 9 Patroclus

**Menominee, Menomini,
Menomonie**
language family: 9 Algon-
kian 10 Algonquian
location: 4 Ohio 7 Indiana
8 Illinois, Michigan
9 Wisconsin

menorah 11 candelabrum, candlestick 12 candleholder
number of candles: 5 seven

Menotti, Gian-Carlo
born: 5 Italy 10 Cadigliano
composer of: 9 The Consul,
The Medium 12 The Island
God, The Telephone
19 Amelia Goes to the Ball
24 Amahl and the Night
Visitors

**mens sana in corpore
sano** 22 a sound mind in a
sound body

mental 5 crazy, nutty 6 insane,
psycho 7 cracked, lunatic,
psychic 8 abstract, cerebral,
neurotic, rational 9 disturbed,
in the mind, of the mind,
psychotic 10 disordered, subjective, unbalanced 11 intelligent, mentally ill
12 intellectual, metaphysical
13 psychological

mental application 9 diligence 10 absorption, intentness 11 deep thought,
engrossment, fixed regard
13 concentration 14 close
attention

mental disorder 5 quirk 6 lunacy, oddity 7 madness 8 delusion, insanity, neurosis
9 craziness, psychosis 10 aberration 11 abnormality, derangement, mental lapse,
peculiarity, strangeness 12 eccentricity, idiosyncrasy
13 schizophrenia 15 manic
depression

mental hospital 6 asylum
8 madhouse 11 institution

mental institution 6 asylum
8 madhouse 12 insane asylum

mentality 4 mind 6 acumen,
brains, wisdom 8 judgment,
sagacity 9 intellect 10 gray
matter, perception 11 discernment 12 intelligence,
perspicacity

mental lapse 5 quirk 6 lunacy, oddity 7 madness
8 rambling, straying 9 wandering 10 aberration 11 derangement, peculiarity
12 eccentricity 13 forgetfulness

mentally incapable
Latin: 15 non compos mentis

mentally sound
Latin: 12 compos mentis

Mentes
origin: 7 Taphian
rank: 7 captain

mention 3 say 4 cite, hint,
name, tell 5 imply, state
6 hint at, notice, remark, report, tell of 7 comment, di-

vulge, inkling, narrate,
observe, recount, refer to,
specify 8 allude to, allusion,
disclose, intimate 9 insinuate,
make known, reference, statement, touch upon, utterance
10 advisement, indication, suggestion 11 designation, insinuation, observation
12 acquaintance, announcement, notification 13 communication, enlightenment,
specification

mentor 4 guru 5 guide, tutor
6 master 7 adviser, monitor,
proctor, teacher 9 counselor,
preceptor, professor
10 instructor

Mentor
advisor of: 8 Odysseus
educated: 10 Telemachus

Mephibosheth
father: 4 Saul 8 Jonathan
also called: 9 Meribbaal
grandfather: 4 Saul
son: 5 Micha

Mephistopheles
character in: 5 Faust
author: 6 Goethe

Mephitis see 7 Mefitis

mer 3 sea

Merab
father: 4 Saul
sister: 6 Michal
brother-in-law: 5 David

mercantile 5 trade 8 business
10 commercial 16 buying-and-
selling

mercantilism 5 trade 8 business, commerce, exchange
13 commercialism

Mercedes
character in: 21 The Count
of Monte Cristo
author: 5 Dumas (pere)

mercenary 5 venal 6 for pay,
greedy 7 for gain, selfish
8 covetous, grasping, hireling,
monetary 10 avaricious 11 acquisitive, paid soldier 12 hired
soldier

merchandise 4 sell 5 goods,
stock, trade, wares 6 deal in,
market 7 effects, staples
8 huckster 9 advertise, publicize, traffic in 10 belongings,
buy and sell, distribute
11 commodities 12 stock in
trade

merchant 6 broker, dealer,
hawker, jobber, monger,
trader, vendor 7 peddler
8 chandler, retailer, salesman
9 purchaser, tradesman
10 saleswoman, shopkeeper,
wholesaler 11 storekeeper,
tradeswoman

Merchant of Venice, The
author: **18** William
Shakespeare
character: **6** Portia **7** Antonio, Jessica, Lorenzo, Nerissa, Shylock **8** Bassanio,
Gratiano

merci 8 thank you

merci beaucoup 16 thank
you very much

merciful 4 kind **6** benign, humane, tender **7** clement, feeling, lenient, pitying, sparing
8 gracious **9** forgiving **10** beneficent **11** kindhearted, softhearted, sympathetic **13** compassionate, understanding

mercifulness 8 clemency,
kindness, leniency, sympathy
9 benignity **10** compassion,
humaneness **11** beneficence,
forgiveness **13** understanding

merciless 4 fell **5** cruel, harsh
6 fierce, severe **7** callous, inhuman **8** inhumane, pitiless,
ruthless **9** ferocious, heartless,
unpitying, unsparing **10** relentless, unmerciful **11** cold-
blooded, hardhearted, remorseless, unrelenting

Mercouri, Melina
husband: **11** Jules Dassin
born: **6** Athens, Greece
roles: **7** Topkapi **10** Gaily
Gaily **13** Never on Sunday
15 Once Is Not Enough

mercurial 6 fickle, lively, mobile **7** erratic, flighty, kinetic,
protean **8** electric, spirited, unstable, variable, volatile **9** impetuous, impulsive
10 capricious, changeable, inconstant **11** fluctuating **13** irrepressible, unpredictable

mercury
chemical symbol: **2** Hg

Mercury
origin: **5** Roman
messenger of: **4** gods
god of: **7** science, thieves
8 commerce **9** eloquence
corresponds to: **6** Hermes,
Ogmios

Mercutio
character in: **14** Romeo and
Juliet
author: **11** Shakespeare

mercy 4 pity **5** grace **6** lenity
7 charity **8** blessing, clemency,
humanity, kindness, lenience,
leniency, sympathy **9** good
thing, tolerance **10** compassion, humaneness, lucky
break **11** benevolence, forbearance, forgiveness, piece of
luck **13** commiseration, fellow

feeling **15** softheartedness
17 tenderheartedness
Latin: **12** misericordia

Mercy seat *see* **16** Ark of the
Covenant

Merdle
character in: **12** Little Dorrit
author: **7** Dickens

mere 4 bald, bare, sole **5** plain,
scant, sheer, utter **6** common,
paltry **7** mundane **8** nugatory,
ordinary, trifling **10** negligible,
uneventful **11** commonplace,
unmitigated **13** insignificant,
unappreciable
14 inconsiderable

mere 6 mother

Meredith, Burgess
wife: **15** Paulette Goddard
born: **11** Cleveland OH
roles: **5** Magic, Rocky **6** Batman (the Penguin) **7** Madame X **8** Foul Play
12 Hurry Sundown, Of Mice
and Men **15** Magnificent
Doll, Such Good Friends
16 Advise and Consent

Meredith, George
author of: **9** The Egoist
10 Modern Love **14** Evan
Harrington **16** Beauchamp's
Career **19** Diana of the
Crossways **25** The Ordeal of
Richard Feverel

merely 3 but **4** just, only
5 quite **6** barely, in part,
purely, simply, solely **7** utterly **8** scarcely, wholly
10 absolutely

meretricious 4 mock, sham
5 bogus, false, phony
6 pseudo, shoddy, tawdry
8 delusive, specious, spurious
9 deceptive **10** fraudulent, misleading **11** counterfeit

merge 4 fuse, join, weld
5 blend, unify, unite **6** link
up **7** combine **8** coalesce, converge, intermix **9** associate, become one, integrate, interfuse,
interlock **10** amalgamate, synthesize **11** confederate, consolidate **12** band together,
interconnect

mergence 3 mix **5** blend
7 merging, mixture **8** mingling **10** concoction
11 combination

Mergenthaler, Ottmar
nationality: **8** American
invented: **8** linotype

merger 5 union **7** wedding
8 marriage **9** coalition
12 amalgamation **13** confederation, consolidation

Meribbaal *see*
12 Mephibosheth

meridian 3 tip, top **4** acme,
apex, brow, peak **5** crest,
crown, point, ridge **6** apogee,
climax, summit, vertex, zenith **7** heights **8** pinnacle
11 culmination

Merimee, Prosper
author of: **6** Carmen
7 Colomba

Meriones
mentioned in: **5** Iliad
vocation: **6** archer
father: **5** Molus

merit 4 earn, rate **5** value,
worth **6** credit, desert, invite,
prompt, talent, virtue **7** ability,
benefit, deserve, quality, stature, warrant **8** efficacy **9** advantage **10** be worthy of,
excellence, worthiness **11** distinction **12** be entitled to,
have a right to
13 justification

merited 3 due **5** rated
6 earned **8** deserved, rightful

meritorious 4 fine **6** worthy
8 laudable **9** admirable, estimable, excellent, exemplary
10 creditable, noteworthy
11 commendable, exceptional
12 praiseworthy

Mermaid Tycoon
nickname of: **14** Esther
Williams

Merman, Ethel
real name: **20** Ethel Agnes
Zimmermann
husband: **14** Ernest Borgnine
born: **9** Astoria NY
autobiography: **6** Merman
roles: **11** Call Me Madam
12 Anything Goes, Panama
Hattie **15** Annie Get Your
Gun **16** Stage Door Canteen **21** Alexander's Ragtime
Band

Mermerus
father: **5** Jason
mother: **5** Medea

Merodach *see* **6** Marduk

Merope
member of: **8** Pleiades
father: **5** Atlas **8** Oenopion
husband: **7** Polybus **8** Sisyphus **11** Cresphontes,
Polyphontes
son: **7** Aepytus
raped by: **5** Orion
raised: **7** Oedipus

merrily 5 gaily **6** gladly
7 briskly, happily, lightly, lus-
tick, quickly **8** blithely, jo-
cundly, jovially, joyfully,
joyously **9** festively, gleefully
10 cheerfully, laughingly,
mirthfully **11** hilariously, viva-
ciously **14** lightheartedly

Merrimac *see* **9** Pennacook

merriment 3 fun 4 glee
5 cheer, mirth 6 frolic, gaiety,
hoopla, levity 7 good fun, jollity, revelry, whoopee 8 hilarity, laughter 9 amusement,
festivity, good humor, jocundity, joviality 10 jocularity, jubilation, liveliness, skylarking
11 celebration, gleefulness,
good spirits, merrymaking
12 conviviality, exhilaration,
sportiveness
16 lightheartedness

Merriweather, Mrs
character in: 15 Gone With
the Wind
author: 8 Mitchell

merry 3 gay 5 happy, jolly
6 blithe, cheery, jocund, jovial,
joyous, lively 7 festive, gleeful,
jocular 8 animated, carefree,
cheerful, gladsome, laughing,
mirthful, partying, reveling,
sportive 9 convivial, fun-
loving, sprightly, vivacious
10 frolicsome, rollicking, skylarking 12 high-spirited,
lighthearted

merrymaking 5 sport 6 frolic,
gaiety, hoopla, revels 7 jollity,
revelry, whoopee 8 carousal
9 festivity, fun-making, high
jinks, merriment, rejoicing,
whoop-de-do 10 saturnalia
11 bacchanalia, celebration,
festivities 12 conviviality

**Merry Wives of Windsor,
The**
author: 18 William
Shakespeare
character: 4 Ford, Page
5 Caius 6 Doctor, Fenton
7 Slender 8 Anne Page
12 Mistress Ford, Mistress
Page 15 Mistress Quickly,
Sir John Falstaff

mesa 4 hill, peak 5 bench,
butte, table 7 plateau, terrace
9 cartouche, tableland

Mescalero
language family: 6 Apache
location: 6 Mexico 9 New
Mexico
related to: 5 Lipan
10 Chiricahua

**Meserve, Margaret
Hamilton**
real name of: 16 Margaret
Hamilton

Meservey, Robert Preston
real name of: 13 Robert
Preston

mesh 3 fib, net, web 4 grid,
jibe 5 agree, sieve, tally 6 engage, enmesh, grille, plexus,
screen 7 connect, engaged,
netting, network, webbing,
webwork 8 dovetail, interact,
lacework, meshwork, open-
work 9 grillwork, interlock,
intermesh 10 coordinate, correspond, interweave, wicker-
work 11 fit together,
latticework 12 reticulation

Meshach
former name: 7 Mishael
companion: 6 Daniel
friend: 8 Abednego, Shadrach

**Mesmer, Franz (Friedrich)
Anton**
nationality: 6 German
developed: 8 hypnosis

mesmerize 5 charm 7 bewitch 8 enthrall, entrance
9 fascinate, hypnotize, magnet-
ize, spellbind, transport

Mesopotamian mythology
god of agriculture/earth:
5 Dagan
*corresponds to Phoeni-
cian:* 5 Dagon

Mesquakie see 3 Fox

mess 3 fix 4 hash, stew 5 mix-
up, pinch 6 crisis, jumble, litter, muddle, pickle, plight,
scrape, strait 7 clutter, dilemma, trouble 8 disarray, disorder, hot water, mess hall,
mishmash, quandary 9 cafeteria, confusion, imbroglio, re-
fectory, situation
10 commissary, difficulty, dining hall, dining room, hodgepodge 11 predicament
14 conglomeration

message 4 news, note, word
5 moral, point, theme 6 letter,
notice, report 7 meaning, missive, purport, tidings 8 bulletin, dispatch 9 statement
10 communique, memoran-
dum 12 intelligence
13 communication

mess around with 4 test
6 try out 8 fool with, play
with 10 tinker with 14 experiment with

Messene
husband: 8 Polycaon

messenger 5 envoy 6 bearer,
runner 7 carrier, courier
8 delegate, emissary 9 deliverer, go-between 11 delivery
boy, delivery man
12 intermediary

messenger of gods 4 Iris
6 Hermes 7 Mercury

**Messiaen, Olivier Eugene
Prosper Charles**
born: 6 France 7 Avignon
composer of: 11 Exotic
Birds, Turangalila 13 Chron-
ochromie 20 Le Nativite du
Seigneur 22 Quartet for the
End of Time 27 Vingt Re-
gards sur l'Enfant Jesus
33 Et exspecto resurrecti-
onem mortuorum 41 Trans-
figuration de Notre Seigneur
Jesus Christ

Messiah
means: 11 anointed one
see also: 10 Jesus

Messick, Dale
creator/artist of: 19 Brenda
Starr Reporter

messiness 5 chaos, mix-up,
upset 6 jumble 7 clutter 8 disarray, disorder, scramble,
shambles 9 confusion 10 disharmony, sloppiness, untidiness 12 dishevelment
14 disarrangement
15 disorganization

mess up 3 mar 4 goof, muff,
ruin 5 botch, spoil 6 bungle,
foul up, jumble 7 blunder,
butcher, disturb, do badly,
louse up, screw up 9 mismanage 10 disarrange 11 disorganize, make a mess of, make
an error 12 make a mistake

messy 4 ugly 6 blowsy, frowsy,
grubby, sloppy, tricky, untidy
7 awkward, chaotic, jumbled,
tangled, unkempt 8 confused,
littered 9 cluttered, difficult
10 bedraggled, disheveled, disordered, slatternly, topsy-turvy,
unenviable, unpleasant 11 disarranged 12 embarrassing,
inextricable 13 uncomfortable

Mesthles
commander of army of:
5 Maeon

mesto
music: 8 mournful

Mestor
father: 7 Perseus
mother: 9 Andromeda
daughter: 9 Hippothoe

Metabus
daughter: 7 Camilla

metal see box

Metalious, Grace
author of: 11 Peyton Place

metalworking
god of: 6 Vulcan 10 He-
phaestus, Hephaistos

metamorphose 6 change, mutate 7 convert 9 transform
11 transfigure

Metamorphoses
author: 4 Ovid

metamorphosis 8 mutation
10 alteration, conversion
11 permutation 12 change of
form, modification 13 radical
change, transmutation
14 transformation 15 series of
changes, startling change,
transfiguration
18 transmogrification

metal
  alloy: 5 brass 6 bronze, nickel, pewter, solder
  bar: 3 gad 4 risp 5 ingot
  bolt: 5 rivet
  box: 8 canister
  casting: 3 peg
  classification: 5 light, noble 6 alkali, common 7 coinage 8 platinum, precious 9 rare earth 10 low-melting, refractory, transition 11 high-melting 14 semiconductors
  clippings: 7 scissel
  coarse: 5 matte
  corrosion: 4 rust
  crude: 3 ore 4 slug
  cymbals: 3 tal
  deposit: 4 lode, vein
  design: 7 chasing
  disk or plate: 4 shim 5 medal, paten 6 platen, sequin
  eyelet: 7 grommet
  filings: 5 lemel
  god of: 6 Vulcan 10 Hephaestus
  heaviest: 6 osmium
  kind: 3 tin 4 gold, iron, lead, zinc 6 barium, cerium, cesium, copper, erbium, nickel, osmium, radium, silver, sodium 7 arsenic, bismuth, calcium, holmium, iridium, lithium, rhodium, silicon, terbium, thulium 8 actinium, aluminum, antimony, europium, lutetium, platinum, rubidium, samarium, selenium, titanium, tungsten 9 beryllium, magnesium, palladium, potassium, ruthenium, strontium 10 molybdenum, phosphorus
  layer: 7 plating
  leaf: 4 foil
  lightest: 7 lithium
  liquid: 7 mercury
  mass: 3 pid 5 ingot 7 bullion
  piece: 4 jack, slug
  refuse: 4 slag 5 dross
  shaper: 5 swage
  suit: 4 mail 5 armor 6 armour
  thread: 4 lame, wire
  trademark: 5 monel
  ware: 4 tole 6 Revere
  worker: 5 smith 6 forger, welder 7 armorer, riveter 8 armourer 9 goldsmith, ironsmith 10 blacksmith 11 coppersmith, silversmith 12 metallurgist

Metamorphosis, The
  author: 10 Franz Kafka

Metanira
  husband: 6 Celeus
  son: 4 Abas 9 Demophoon 11 Triptolemus

metaphor 5 image, trope 6 simile 7 analogy 8 metonymy, parallel 11 equivalence 14 figure of speech, representation

metaphysical 5 basic, lofty, vague 6 far-out 7 eternal 8 abstract, abstruse, esoteric, mystical, ultimate 9 essential, high-flown, recondite, universal 10 impalpable, intangible, jesuitical, oversubtle 11 existential, fundamental, ontological, speculative 12 cosmological, intellectual, unanswerable 13 philosophical 15 epistemological

Metaphysics
  author: 9 Aristotle

metaxa
  type: 6 brandy 7 liqueur
  origin: 6 Greece

mete, mete out 5 allot 6 assign, divide 7 deal out, dole out 8 allocate, disburse, dispense 9 apportion, parcel out 10 administer, distribute, measure out

meteoric 4 fast 5 fiery, rapid, swift 6 speedy, sudden 7 blazing, flaming, instant 8 flashing, unabated 10 inexorable 11 ineluctable, unstoppable

meter
  abbreviation: 1 m

Meter
  epithet of: 6 Athena
  means: 6 mother

method 3 way 4 form, mode, plan, tack 5 means, order, style, usage 6 course, design, manner, scheme, system 7 fashion, formula, process, program, purpose, routine 8 approach, efficacy 9 procedure, technique, viability 13 modus operandi

methodical, methodic 4 neat, tidy 5 exact 7 careful, logical, orderly, precise, regular, uniform 10 analytical, deliberate, meticulous, systematic 12 businesslike 13 well-regulated

methodization 5 order 11 arrangement 12 organization 14 categorization, classification 15 systematization

methodize 5 order 7 arrange 8 classify, organize 11 systematize

Methuselah
  father: 5 Enoch
  son: 6 Lamech
  years lived: 23 nine hundred and sixty nine
  known as: 9 oldest man

meticulous 4 nice 5 exact, fussy 7 finical, finicky, precise 8 exacting, sedulous 10 fastidious, particular, scrupulous 11 painstaking, punctilious 13 conscientious, perfectionist

meticulousness 4 care 5 pains 12 sedulousness, thoroughness 14 fastidiousness, scrupulousness 17 conscientiousness

metier 3 job 4 area, line, work 5 craft, field, forte, trade 7 calling, pursuit 8 activity, business, lifework, province, vocation 9 specialty 10 employment, livelihood, occupation, profession

meting out 8 alloting 9 bestowing, doling out 10 allocating, conferring, consigning, dealing out, dispensing 11 designating 12 apportioning, distributing, measuring out

Metioche
  father: 5 Orion
  sister: 7 Menippe

Metion
  father: 10 Erechtheus
  mother: 9 Praxithea
  brother: 7 Cecrops

Metis
  member of: 6 Titans
  father: 7 Oceanus
  mother: 6 Tethys
  consort of: 4 Zeus
  daughter: 6 Athena

Metiscus
charioteer of: **6** Turnus

metrical narrative
French: **5** roman

Metropolis
director: **9** Fritz Lang
cast: **10** Alfred Abel **12** Brigitte Helm

metropolitan area 4 city
8 core city, downtown, environs **9** inner city, precincts,
urban area **10** city limits, metropolis **11** central city
16 business district

mettle 3 vim **4** grit, guts
5 nerve, pluck, spunk, valor,
vigor **6** spirit **7** bravery, courage, heroism **8** audacity, backbone, boldness, gameness,
temerity **9** derring-do, fortitude, gallantry, manliness
10 enthusiasm, resolution
11 intrepidity **12** fearlessness
13 determination

mettlesome 4 bold, edgy
5 brave, fiery **6** ardent, plucky,
spunky **7** gingery, peppery

8 restless, skittish, spirited
9 excitable, impatient **10** courageous, high-strung **12** high-
spirited

Mexica *see* **5** Aztec

Mexico *see box*

Mexico City
Aztec name: **12** Tenochtitlan
capital of: **6** Mexico
landmark: **13** Mercado
Merced **15** Chapultepec
Park **19** Basilica of
Guadalupe
bull ring: **11** Plaza Mexico
floating gardens:
10 Xochimilco
pyramids: **11** Teotihuacan
square: **6** Zocalo **22** Plaza de
las Tres Culturas
street: **16** Paseo de la
Reforma

Meyer, David Harold
real name of: **12** David
Janssen

Meyerbeer, Giacomo
real name: **17** Jacob Lieb-
mann Beer

born: **6** Berlin **7** Germany
composer of: **7** Dinorah
10 Le Prophete, The African, The Prophet **12** Les
Huguenots, The Huguenots,
The North Star **14** Robert le
Diable, Robert the Devil

Mezentius
king of: **7** Etruria
noted for: **7** cruelty
son: **6** Lausus
killed by: **6** Aeneas

mezza voce
music: **9** half voice **10** half
volume

mezzo
music: **4** half

Miami
bay: **8** Biscayne
county: **4** Dade
developer: **7** Flagler
football team: **8** Dolphins
museum: **4** Lowe **12** Villa
Viscaya
ocean: **8** Atlantic
people: **5** Cuban **8** Hispanic
section: **7** Hialeah **10** Bal
Harbour **11** Coral Gables

Mexico
other name: **8** New Spain
capital/largest city: **10** Mexico City
others: **4** Leon **5** La Paz, Taxco **6** Cancun, Celaya, Merida, Oaxaca, Puebla, Toluca **7** Durango,
Guaymas, Tampico, Tijuana, Torreon **8** Acapulco, Culiacan, Ensenada, Irapuato, Mazatlan,
Mexicali, Saltillo, Veracruz **9** Chihuahua, Matamoros, Monterrey, Queretaro, Salamanca, Zacatecas **10** Hermosillo **11** Guadalajara, Nuevo Laredo **12** Ciudad Juarez, Villahermosa **13** Coatzacoalcos, Piedras Negras, San Luis Potosi **14** Puerto Vallarta **15** Netzahualcoyotl
   ancient city: **4** Tula **7** Texcoco **8** Tlacopan **10** Monte Alban **11** Teotihuacan **12** Tenochtitlan
     13 Tula de Allende
division: **6** Colima, Oaxaca, Puebla, Sonora **7** Chiapas, Durango, Hidalgo, Jalisco, Sinaloa, Tabasco, Yucatan **8** Campeche, Coahuila, Tlaxcala, Veracruz **9** Chihuahua, Michoacan, Nuevo
Leon, Zacatecas **13** San Luis Potosi **14** Baja California
measure: **3** bag, pie **4** alma, onza, vara **5** almud, baril, carga, jarra, labor, legua, libra, linea,
marco, sitio **6** adarme, almude, arroba, carega, fanega, ochaua, terceo **7** pulgada, quintal
   9 cuarteron, cuartillo **10** caballeria
monetary unit: **4** onza, peso **5** adobe, claco, tlaco **6** azteca, cuarto, dinero **7** centavo, piaster
weight: **3** bag **4** onza **5** libra, marco **6** arroba, tercio **7** quintal
island: **6** Carmen, Cedros **7** San Jose, Tiburon **8** Cerralvo **10** Tres Marias **13** Espiritu Santo
   14 Santa Magdalena, Santa Margarita **15** Angel de la Guarda
lake: **7** Chapala, Texcoco **9** Patzcuaro
mountain: **6** Colima, Tacana, Toluca **9** Paricutin **11** Ixtacihuatl, Sierra Madre **12** Popocatepetl
   14 Sierra Zacateca **16** Chiapas Highlands **24** Transverse Volcanic Sierra
highest point: **7** Orizaba **12** Citlaltepetl
river: **4** Mayo **5** Yaqui **6** Balsas, Fuerte, Grande, Panuco **8** Colorado, Grijalva **10** Papaloapan,
Usumacinta **13** Bravo del Norte, Coatzacoalcos, Lerma-Santiago
sea: **7** Pacific **8** Atlantic **9** Caribbean
physical feature:
   bay: **8** Campeche **9** Olas Atlas
   cape: **10** Corrientes
   desert: **6** Sonora
   gulf: **6** Mexico **8** Campeche **10** California **11** Tehuantepec
   isthmus: **11** Tehuantepec
   peninsula: **7** Yucatan **14** Baja California
   plain: **7** Tabasco
   plateau: **7** Mexican
   valley: **7** Chiapas
people: **6** Indian **7** mestizo, Spanish
   architect: **7** O'Gorman

stadium: 10 Orange Bowl
tropical garden: 9 Fairchild
university: 5 Barry **8** St
Thomas
zoo: 11 Crandon Park

Miami (Twightwee)
language family: 9 Algonkian **10** Algonquian
tribe: 3 Wea **5** Miami
10 Piankashaw
location: 4 Ohio **7** Indiana
8 Illinois, Michigan
9 Wisconsin
leader: 12 Little Turtle
allied with: 6 Peoria

Miami Vice
character: 4 Gina **5** Trudy
8 (Capt) Castillo **13** Riccardo
Tubbs, Sonny Crockett
cast: 10 Don Johnson
11 Olivia Brown **15** Saundra
Santiago **16** Edward James
Olmos **20** Phillip Michael
Thomas

Micah Clarke
author: 19 Sir Arthur Conan
Doyle

Micawber, Mr
character in: 16 David
Copperfield
author: 7 Dickens

Micha
father: 9 Meribbaal
12 Mephibosheth
grandfather: 8 Jonathan
great-grandfather: 4 Saul

Michael
author: 17 William
Wordsworth

Michael
means: 12 Who is like God
father: 8 Izrahiah
11 Jehoshaphat
son: 4 Omri **8** Zabadiah
also: 9 archangel

Michel
father: 4 Saul
husband: 5 David, Palti
sister: 5 Merab

**Michelangelo di Buonarotti
(Simoni)**
architect of: 11 Campidoglio
(Capitoline Hill) **12** Medici
Chapel (Florence)

13 Farnese Palace **21** Palazzo Medici-Riccardi (Florence) **22** Palazzo dei
Conservatori (Capitoline
Hill) **24** Convent of San
Marco Library
born: 5 Italy **7** Caprese
patron: 12 Pope Julius II
14 Lorenzo d'Medici
19 Pope Julius the Second
21 Lorenzo the Magnificent
artwork: 5 David, Moses,
Pieta **6** Brutus, Slaves **7** Bacchus **9** The Victor **10** Holy
Family **12** Madonna Pitti
15 The Last Judgment
18 Conversion of St Paul
20 Madonna Seated on a
Step, Sistine Chapel Ceiling
21 The Flight of the Lapites,
The Martyrdom of St Peter

Michelozzo
architect of: 21 Palazzo
Medici-Riccardi (Florence)
24 Convent of San Marco
Library

Michelson, Albert A
field: 7 physics

Mexico (*continued*)
    composer: **6** Chavez
    emperor: **10** Maximilian
    explorer: **6** Cortes, Cortez **7** Cordoba **8** Alvarado, Grijalva
    god: **6** Tlaloc **12** Quetzalcoatl **14** Huitzilopochtl
    leader: **3** Gil **4** Diaz **5** Lopez, Rubio, Villa **6** Calles, Huerta, Juarez, Madero, Valdes, Zapata
       7 Obregon **8** Carranza, Iturbide, Portillo, Santa Ana **9** Diaz Ordaz, Montezuma, Rodriguez
       13 Madrid Hurtado **16** Salinas de Gortari
    revolutionary/priest: **13** Morelos y Pavon **16** Hidalgo y Costilla
    soldier/explorer: **12** conquistador
    viceroy: **7** Mendoza
    writer: **3** Paz **5** Nervo, Reyes, Yanez **6** Azuela, Guzman, Najera **7** Fuentes
   language: 5 Mayan, Otomi **6** Mixtec **7** Mazahua, Mazatec, Nahuatl, Spanish, Totonac, Zapotec
    8 Tarascan
   religion: 13 Roman Catholic
   place:
    cathedral: **10** Assumption
    center of Mexico City: **6** Zocalo **21** Plaza de la Constitucion
    floating gardens: **10** Xochimilco
    museum: **28** Shrine of the Virgin of Guadalupe
    park: **7** Alameda **11** Chapultepec
    ruins: **5** Mitla, Uxmal **8** Palenque **10** Monte Alban **11** Chichen Itza, Teotihuacan **20** Temple
      of Quetzalcoatl
    street: **13** Avenida Juarez **16** Paseo de la Reforma
    temple/pyramid: **7** Cholula **8** Castillo
   feature:
    agreement: **5** NAFTA
    Christmas tradition: **6** pinata
    coffee plantation: **5** finca
    empire: **4** Maya **5** Aztec, Olmec **6** Mixtec, Toltec **7** Zapotec
    large estate: **8** hacienda
    musician: **8** mariachi
    small farm/commune: **6** ejidos
    sport: **7** jai alai **12** bullfighting
    tree: **9** sapodilla **11** chicozapote
   food:
    corn cake: **8** tortilla
    dish: **4** mole, taco **5** huevo, pollo **6** tamale **7** burrito, chorizo, taquito, tostada **8** empanada
     9 enchilada, guacamole, sopadilla **10** chili verde, quesadilla **11** chimichanga **12** chili relleno
    drink: **6** pulque **7** tequila

established: 12 speed of light 15 velocity of Earth
awarded: 10 Nobel Prize

Michener, James A
author of: 5 Space 6 Alaska, Hawaii, Iberia, Legacy, Poland 8 Caravans, Sayonara 9 The Source 10 Centennial, Chesapeake 11 The Covenant, The Drifters 16 The Fires of Spring 18 The Bridges at Toko-ri 22 Tales of the South Pacific

Mickey Mouse
creator: 10 Walt Disney
character: 5 Morty 6 Ferdie 11 Minnie Mouse
cow: 10 Clarabelle

Micklewhite, Maurice Joseph
real name of: 12 Michael Caine

Micmac
language family: 9 Algonkian 10 Algonquian
location: 6 Canada 10 Nova Scotia 12 Newfoundland,

New Brunswick 14 Gaspe Peninsula 16 Cape Breton Island 18 Prince Edward Island

microbe 4 germ 5 virus 6 gamete, zygote 8 bacillus, parasite 9 bacterium 10 spirochete 13 microorganism, streptococcus 14 staphylococcus

microbiologist
American: 7 Waksman 9 Baltimore
Dutch: 11 (van) Leeuwenhoek

Micronesia
part of: 7 Oceania
island: 3 Nui 4 Guam, Rota, Truk, Wake 5 Makin, Nauru, Wotho 6 Bikini, Ellice, Majuro, Ponape 7 Gilbert, Mariana 8 Caroline, Kiribati, Marshall

microorganism 3 bug 4 germ 5 virus 7 microbe 8 bacillus, pathogen 9 bacterium

microphobia
fear of: 12 small objects

microscope
invented by:
  compound: 7 Janssen
  electronic: 5 Knoll, Ruska
  field ion: 7 Mueller
single lens model improved by: 11 (van) Leeuwenhoek
  first observed: 8 protozoa 13 red blood cells 19 single-celled animals

microscopic, microscopical 4 tiny 5 teeny 6 atomic, minute 9 invisible 10 diminutive, very little 13 imperceptible, infinitesimal

microscopy
founder: 11 Robert Hooke 13 Jan Swammerdam 16 Marcello Malpighi 19 Anton van Leeuwenhoek

Midas
king of: 7 Phrygia
father: 7 Gordius
gift: 11 golden touch
gift from: 7 Silenus
ears changed to those of: 3 ass
changed by: 6 Apollo

midday 4 noon 7 noonday 8 meridian, noontide, noontime

middle 3 act, gut, hub, mid 4 core, main 5 belly, heart, midst, waist 6 center, course, medial, median, midway, throes 7 central, halfway, midmost, midriff, nucleus, process, stomach 8 midpoint 9 heartland 10 midsection 12 intermediate

---

Michigan
abbreviation: 2 MI 4 Mich
nickname: 4 Lake 9 Wolverine 10 Automobile 15 Water Wonderland 16 Winter Wonderland
capital: 7 Lansing
largest city: 7 Detroit
others: 4 Caro, Troy 5 Flint, Niles, Wayne 6 Adrien, Alpena, Bad Axe, Monroe, Owosso, Warren, Wassar 7 Bay City, Holland, Jackson, Livonia, Midland, Pontiac, Saginaw, Trenton, Wyoming 8 Ann Arbor, Cadillac, Dearborn, Escanaba, Ironwood, Manistee, Muskegon, Petoskey, Royal Oak 9 Cheboygan, Hillsdale, Kalamazoo, Marquette, Port Huron, Roseville, Wyandotte 10 Birmingham, River Rouge 11 Battle Creek, Grand Rapids 12 Benton Harbor, Traverse City 13 Sault Ste Marie, St Clair Shores
college: 4 Alma, Hope 5 Wayne 6 Adrian, Albion, Calvin, Olivet, Owosso 7 Detroit, Oakland 9 Hillsdale, Kalamazoo, Marygrove
feature:
  bridge: 8 Mackinac
  canal: 3 Soo 12 Sault St Marie
  festival: 12 Holland Tulip
  national park: 10 Isle Royale
  village: 10 Greenfield
tribe: 6 Ojibwa, Ottawa 8 Chippewa 10 Potawatomi
people: 9 Henry Ford, wolverine 11 Bruce Catton, Edgar A Guest, Julie Harris, Ralph Bunche, Ring Lardner 16 Charles Lindburgh
  explorer: 6 Joliet 7 La Salle, Nicolet 9 Marquette 12 Etienne Brule, Sault St Marie
island: 8 Mackinaw
lake: 4 Burt, Erie 5 Clear, Huron, Round, Torch 6 Austin, Devils, Moline 7 Bawbees, St Clair 8 Houghton, Michigan, Superior
land rank: 11 twenty-third
mountain: 6 Copper 7 Gogebic 9 Menominee, Porcupine
  highest point: 12 Mount Curwood
physical feature:
  bay: 7 Saginaw, Thunder 8 Keweenaw, Sturgeon
  straits: 8 Mackinac
president: 10 Gerald Ford
river: 4 Cass 5 Grand, Huron 6 Raisin 7 Detroit, Saginaw, St Clair, St Mary's 8 Escanaba, Muskegon 9 Menominee
state admission: 11 twenty-sixth
state bird: 5 robin
state fish: 5 trout
state flower: 12 apple blossom
state motto: 11 I Will Defend 39 If You Seek a Pleasant Peninsula Look About You
state song: 18 Michigan My Michigan
state tree: 16 eastern white pine

Middle Ages
  French: **8** moyen age

middle-class 4 mass **8** ordinary **9** bourgeois **10** mainstream, middlebrow

middle Europe
  German: **12** Mitteleuropa

middle ground 4 mean **7** balance **8** midpoint **11** equilibrium **12** common ground

Middle Kingdom see **5** China

middleman 5 agent **6** broker, dealer, jobber **7** liaison **8** mediator **9** go-between **10** wholesaler **11** distributor, intercessor **12** entrepreneur, intermediary

Middlemarch
  author: **11** George Eliot
  character: **5** Celia **12** Will Ladislaw **13** Rosamond Viney **14** Dorothea Brooke, Edward Casaubon, Tertius Lydgate **15** Sir James Chettam

middlemost 4 mean **5** inner **6** inmost, median **7** central, midmost **8** interior

middle-of-the-road 8 moderate **10** mainstream

middle-of-the-roader 8 moderate **12** mainstreamer

middle way
  Latin: **8** via media

middling 4 fair, so-so **6** medium **7** average, fairish, minimal **8** mediocre, moderate, ordinary, passable **9** tolerable **10** pretty good, second-rate **11** indifferent **12** run-of-the-mill, unremarkable

Midea see **9** Licymnius

Midgard
  also: **10** Mithgarthr
  origin: **12** Scandinavian
  means: **10** abode of man
  located between: **8** Niflheim **10** Muspelheim
  connected to Asgard by: **7** bifrost **13** rainbow bridge
  formed from brow of: **4** Ymir

Midgard Serpent see **11** Jormungandr

midget 4 doll, runt **5** dwarf, pygmy **6** peewee, puppet, shrimp, squirt **7** manikin **8** half-pint, munchkin, small fry, Tom Thumb **9** pipsqueak **10** fingerling, homunculus **11** hop-o'-my-thumb, lilliputian

Midian
  father: **7** Abraham
  mother: **7** Keturah
  descendant of: **9** Midianite

midlands 8 interior **10** hinterland **13** central region

midmost 5 inner **6** inmost, middle **7** central, pivotal **8** interior **10** middlemost

Midnight Cowboy
  director: **15** John Schlesinger
  cast: **9** Jon Voight **11** John McGiver, Sylvia Miles **13** Brenda Vaccaro, Dustin Hoffman (Ratso Rizzo)
  Oscar for: **7** picture

Midnight Express
  director: **10** Alan Parker
  cast: **8** John Hurt **9** Bo Hopkins, Brad Davis (Billy Hayes) **10** Randy Quaid **12** Irene Miracle
  setting: **13** Turkish prison
  score: **14** Giorgio Moroder
  Oscar for: **5** score **6** script

midori
  type: **7** liqueur
  origin: **5** Japan
  flavor: **5** melon

midpoint 4 core, mean **5** focus **6** center, middle **15** point of no return

midriff 3 gut **4** guts **5** belly, tummy **6** paunch **7** abdomen, stomach **9** diaphragm **10** midsection **11** breadbasket

midst 3 eye, hub **4** core **5** bosom, heart, thick **6** center, depths, middle **7** nucleus **8** interior

Midsummer Night's Dream, A
  author: **18** William Shakespeare
  character: **4** Puck (Robin Goodfellow) **6** Bottom, Helena, Hermia, Oberon **7** Theseus, Titania **8** Lysander **9** Demetrius, Hippolyta

midterm 4 exam, test **6** review **11** examination

midwife
  French: **11** accoucheuse

mien 3 air **4** look **5** guise, style **6** aspect, manner, visage **7** bearing, feature **8** attitude, behavior, carriage, demeanor, presence **9** semblance **10** appearance, deportment, expression **11** countenance

Mies van der Rohe, Ludwig
  architect of: **14** German Pavilion (1929 International Exposition, Barcelona), Lake Shore Drive (apartment towers, Chicago), Tugendhat House (Brno Czechoslovakia) **15** National Gallery (West Berlin), Seagram Building (NYC)

style: **13** International
principle: **10** less is more

miff 3 irk, vex **4** rile **5** anger, annoy, chafe, pique **6** nettle, offend, rankle **7** affront, provoke **8** irritate **9** put one off **10** exasperate **11** make one sore **14** rub the wrong way **15** raise one's dander

Mifune, Toshiro
  born: **5** China **8** Tsingtao
  roles: **6** Midway, Shogun **8** Rashomon **12** Seven Samurai **13** Throne of Blood

Miggs, Miss
  character in: **12** Barnaby Rudge
  author: **7** Dickens

might 3 may **5** brawn, clout, force, power, vigor **6** energy, muscle **7** potency, prowess **8** strength **9** influence, lustihood, puissance, toughness **10** capability, competence, durability, robustness, sturdiness **11** capableness **12** forcefulness

mighty 4 able, bold, huge, vast, very **5** brave, hardy, husky, lusty, stout, truly **6** brawny, manful, potent, really, robust, strong, sturdy **7** immense, massive, titanic, valiant **8** colossal, enormous, forceful, gigantic, imposing, majestic, powerful, puissant, stalwart, towering, valorous, vigorous **9** monstrous, strapping **10** courageous, gargantuan, invincible, monolithic, monumental, prodigious, stupendous **11** elephantine, exceedingly, indomitable, of great size **12** overpowering, particularly **13** exceptionally **14** Brobdingnagian

Migonitis
  epithet of: **9** Aphrodite
  means: **6** uniter

migrate 4 move, trek **6** travel **7** journey **8** emigrate, relocate, resettle **9** immigrate

migration 4 trek **6** exodus, flight, moving **7** passage **8** diaspora, movement

mikado 5 ruler **7** emperor, monarch **9** sovereign **15** Japanese emperor

Mikado, The
  subtitle: **15** The Town of Titipu
  operetta by: **18** Gilbert and Sullivan
  character: **4** Ko-Ko **6** Peep-Bo, Yum-Yum **7** Katisha, Pooh-Bah **8** Nanki-Poo, Pish-Tush **9** Pitti-Sing

Mikkelsen, Dahl
also: 3 Mik
creator/artist of:
8 Ferd'nand

mikrophobia
fear of: 5 germs

mikvah 35 public establishment
for ritual bathing
used by: 12 Orthodox Jews

mild 4 calm, easy, soft, warm
5 balmy, bland 6 docile, gentle, placid, serene, smooth
7 pacific, summery 8 delicate,
moderate, not sharp, pleasant,
soothing, tranquil 9 easygoing,
emollient, not severe, not
strong, temperate 10 forbearing, not extreme, springlike
11 complaisant, uninjurious
12 good-tempered

mildew 4 mold 6 blight,
fungus

mildewed 5 fusty, moldy
10 discolored

mildness 8 calmness, delicacy,
serenity, softness 9 placidity
10 gentleness, good temper

Mildred Pierce
director: 13 Michael Curtiz
based on novel by: 10 James
M Cain
cast: 9 Ann Blyth, Eve Arden 10 Jack Carson
12 Bruce Bennett, Joan
Crawford, Zachary Scott
Oscar for: 7 actress
(Crawford)

mild-tempered 7 equable, patient 9 easygoing 11 good-
natured, unflappable

mile
abbreviation: 2 mi

Miles, Sarah
brother: 11 Christopher
husband: 10 Robert Bolt
born: 7 England
11 Ingatestone
roles: 6 Blow-Up 10 The Servant 11 The Hireling
13 Ryan's Daughter 16 Lady
Caroline Lamb

miles gloriosus 15 boastful
soldier

Miles Gloriosus
author: 7 Plautus

Milesian
origin: 5 Irish
invaders from: 5 Spain
invaded: 7 Ireland
defeated: 14 Tuatha De
Danann
ancestors of: 5 Irish

milestone 7 jubilee 8 milepost,
signpost 10 road marker
11 anniversary 12 red-letter
day, turning point

Milestone, Lewis
director of: 12 Of Mice and
Men, The Front Page 13 A
Walk in the Sun 17 Mutiny
on the Bounty 25 All Quiet
on the Western Front
(Oscar)

Milestones
author: 13 Arnold Bennett

Miletus
father: 6 Apollo
mother: 4 Aria
son: 6 Caunus
daughter: 6 Byblis

milieu 5 scene 7 culture, element, setting 8 ambience,
backdrop 10 background
11 environment, mise-en-
scene 12 surroundings

militant 7 defiant, extreme,
martial, warlike, warring
8 fighting, military 9 assertive,
bellicose, combatant, combative 10 aggressive, pugnacious
11 belligerent, contentious
12 disputatious, paramilitary,
warmongering
14 uncompromising

military 4 army 5 armed, crisp
6 strict, troops 7 martial, militia, Spartan, warlike 8 generals, soldiers 9 combative,
defensive, regulated, soldierly,
warmaking 10 regimented
11 armed forces, belligerent,
soldierlike

military force 4 army, navy
6 legion, troops 7 legions, militia 8 military, regiment, soldiers, soldiery 9 battalion
11 fighting men 13 fighting
force

military machine 4 army
6 legion, troops 11 armed
forces 13 fighting force

military rank abbreviation
see box

military storehouse 6 armory 7 arsenal 8 magazine
9 arms depot 13 ordnance depot 14 ammunition dump

military stores 7 arsenal,
weapons 8 ordnance 9 munitions 10 ammunition

military unit 4 army, crew,
unit 5 corps, force, squad
6 legion, outfit 7 brigade, company 8 regiment, squadron
9 battalion, task force 10 contingent, detachment

milksop 4 baby, wimp
5 mouse, pansy, sissy, softy
6 coward 7 crybaby, nebbish
8 mama's boy, poltroon, weakling 9 fraidy-cat 10 namby-
pamby, pantywaist, scaredy-
cat, weak sister
11 milquetoast, mollycoddle

**military rank
abbreviation**
admiral: 3 adm
brigadier general: 2 bg
7 brig gen
captain: 3 cpt 4 capt
chief petty officer:
3 CPO
colonel: 3 col
commander: 5 comdr
corporal: 3 cpl
ensign: 3 ens
general: 3 gen
lieutenant: 2 lt 5 lieut
lieutenant colonel: 3 ltc
5 lt col
lieutenant general: 5 lt
gen 8 lieut gen
major: 3 maj
master sergeant: 4 msgt
private: 3 pvt
private first class: 3 pfc
sergeant: 3 sgt
sergeant first class:
3 sfc
sergeant major: 4 smaj
6 sgt maj
specialist: 4 spec

mill 4 roam, teem 5 crush,
grind, shape, swarm, works
6 finish, groove 7 factory,
meander 8 converge 9 granulate, pulverize

Mill, John Stuart
author of: 9 On Liberty
14 Utilitarianism 20 The
Subjection of Women
28 Principles of Political
Economy

Millais, Sir John Everett
born: 7 England
12 Southhampton
artwork: 7 Bubbles 9 Blind
Girl 12 Autumn Leaves,
Chill October 13 My First
Sermon 18 Lorenzo and Isabella 25 Christ in the Carpenter's Shop 36 Young
Men of Benjamin Seizing
Their Brides

Millament, Mrs
character in: 16 The Way of
the World
author: 8 Congreve

Milland, Ray
real name: 21 Reginald
Truscott-Jones
born: 5 Neath, Wales
roles: 9 Beau Geste
11 Blonde Crazy 14 Dial M
for Murder, The Lost Weekend (Oscar) 22 Bulldog
Drummond Escapes

Millar, Kenneth
real name of: 13 Ross
MacDonald

Millay, Edna St Vincent
author of: **11** Second April
13 The Harp Weaver
19 Make Bright the Arrows
20 A Few Figs from Thistles

Mille, Agnes de
choreographer of: **5** Rodeo
15 Fall River Legend

millennium 13 thousand
years **9** age of gold **21** one-
thousandth anniversary

Miller
character in: **18** The Canterbury Tales
author: **7** Chaucer

Miller, Ann
real name: **17** Lucille Ann
Collier
autobiography: **15** Miller's
High Life
born: **9** Chireno TX
roles: **9** On the Town, Stage
Door **10** Hit the Deck, Kiss
Me Kate **11** Sugar Babies
16 The Kissing Bandit

Miller, Arthur
wife: **13** Marilyn Monroe
author of: **8** The Price
11 The Crucible **12** After
the Fall **16** Death of a
Salesman **18** A View from
the Bridge

Miller, Henry
author of: **5** Nexus, Sexus
6 Plexus **14** Tropic of Cancer **17** Tropic of Capricorn
18 The Rosy Crucifixion
21 The Colossus of Maroussi

Milles, Carl
real name: **23** Wilhelm Carl
Emil Anderson
born: **5** Lagga **6** Sweden
artwork: **5** Diana, Jonah
6 Europa **12** Man and Nature, Playing Bears **13** Peace
Monument **15** Orpheus
Fountain **18** Meeting of the
Waters, Saltsjobaden Church
(bronze doors)

millet 16 Panicum miliaceum
varieties: **3** hog **5** pearl,
Sanwa **6** finger, Indian
7 African, foxtail, Italian
8 barnyard, browntop, Japanese **16** Japanese barnyard

Millet, Jean-Francois
born: **6** France, Gruchy
artwork: **5** Sower **7** Angelus
11 The Gleaners, The Win-
nower **14** Potato Planters,
The Man with a Hoe
23 Oedipus Taken from the
Tree

Millett, Kate
author of: **6** Flying **14** Sexual
Politics

milligram
abbreviation: **2** mg

milliliter
abbreviation: **2** mL

millimeter
abbreviation: **2** mm

Millionaire, The
character: **14** Michael
Anthony
cast: **12** Marvin Miller

Mill on the Floss, The
author: **11** George Eliot
character: **8** Bob Jakin, Mrs
Glegg **9** Lucy Deane, Mrs
Pullet **11** Philip Wakem,
Tom Tulliver **12** Stephen
Guest **14** Maggie Tulliver

Mills, Hayley
real name: **15** Rose Vivian
Mills
father: **4** John
sister: **6** Juliet
husband: **11** Ray Boulting
born: **6** London **7** England
roles: **8** Tiger Bay **9** Pollyanna **11** Summer Magic
13 The Parent Trap **14** The
Chalk Garden **15** The Moon-
Spinners **19** In Search of
Castaways **20** The Trouble
with Angels

Mills, John
daughter: **6** Hayley, Juliet
born: **7** England
10 Felixstowe
roles: **12** Tunes of Glory
13 Ryan's Daughter **14** The
Chalk Garden **17** Great Expectations **19** Swiss Family
Robinson

Mills, Robert
architect of: **10** Post Office
(Washington DC) **12** Patent
Office (Washington DC)
14 Circular Church (Charleston) **15** Unitarian Church
(Philadelphia) **16** Treasury
Building (Washington DC)
18 Washington Monument
25 Sansom Street Baptist
Church (Philadelphia)
29 Egyptian Revival Monument Church (Richmond
VA)
style: **12** Greek Revival

millstream 3 run **4** race
5 brook, canal, creek, river
6 branch

Milne, A A
author of: **13** Winnie-the-
Pooh **20** The House at Pooh
Corner
character: **3** Roo **4** Pooh
5 Kanga **6** Eeyore, Piglet,
Tigger **16** Christopher Robin

Milosz, Czeslaw
author of: **11** Native Realm,
The Usurpers **13** Bells in
Winter **14** Seizure of Power,
The Captive Mind

milquetoast 4 wimp **7** milksop,
nebbish **11** mollycoddle

Milton
author: **12** William Blake

Milton, George
character in: **12** Of Mice and
Men
author: **9** Steinbeck

Milton, John
author of: **7** Lycidas **8** L'Allegro **11** Il Penseroso **12** Areopagitica, Paradise Lost
15 Samson Agonistes
16 Paradise Regained **29** On
the Morning of Christ's
Nativity

Milton Berle Show, The
host: **11** Milton Berle
regulars: **10** Fatso Marco
11 Arnold Stang, Jack Collins, Milton Frome, Ruth
Gilbert **12** Irving Benson
13 Bobby Sherwood
announcer: **8** Sid Stone
11 Jimmy Nelson **13** Jack
Lescoulie
orchestra: **8** Alan Roth, Billy
May **11** Victor Young
theme: **7** Near You
Milton Berle's nickname:
12 Mr Television
sponsor: **5** Buick **6** Texaco

Milwaukee
baseball team: **7** Brewers
basketball team: **5** Bucks
Indian name: **16** Mahn-a-
waukee Seepe
lake: **8** Michigan
river: **9** Milwaukee, Menomo-
nee, **12** Kinnickinnic
university: **9** Marquette

mimic 3 ape **4** aper, copy,
echo, mime **6** mirror, parrot
7 copycat, copyist, feigner, imitate, take off **8** imitator, simulate **9** reproduce
10 burlesquer **11** counterfeit,
impersonate **13** impressionist

Mimir
origin: **12** Scandinavian
god of: **3** sea
decapitated by: **5** Vanir
head sent to: **4** Odin **5** Othin
oracle for: **4** Asar **5** Aesir

mimosa 14 Acacia dealbata
18 Albizia Julibrissin
varieties: **5** Texas **6** golden
7 prairie **8** Egyptian

mince 4 dice, pose **5** grate,
shred **6** refine, soften **7** posture, qualify **8** chop fine, hold
back, mitigate, moderate, palliate **9** gloss over, put on airs,
whitewash **12** attitudinize
14 affect delicacy, affect primness **15** give oneself airs **16** affect daintiness, soften one's
speech **18** cut into small
pieces **19** be mealymouthed

about **20** cut into tiny particles

mince words 5 dodge, hedge, stall **10** equivocate **11** be ambiguous **13** avoid the issue **17** beat around the bush

mind 4 hate, heed, note, obey, tend, will, wits **5** abhor, bow to, brain, focus, sense, watch **6** brains, choice, detest, eschew, follow, intent, liking, memory, notice, notion, reason, recall, regard, resent, sanity **7** dislike, marbles, observe, opinion, outlook, thought **8** adhere to, attend to, be wary of, judgment, object to, reaction, response, submit to, take care, thinking **9** attention, awareness, be careful, cognition, faculties, intellect, intention, look after, sentiment **10** be cautious, comply with, conception, conclusion, gray matter, impression, perception, propensity, recoil from, reflection, shrink from, take care of **11** acquiesce to, be wary about, inclination, percipience, point of view, rationality, remembrance **12** apprehension, disapprove of, intelligence, recollection, reminiscence, take charge of, take notice of **13** be conscious of, comprehension, concentration, consciousness, consideration, contemplation, look askance at, preoccupation, ratiocination, retrospection, understanding **14** pay attention to
German: **5** Geist

mindful 4 wary **5** aware **7** alert to, alive to, careful, heedful **8** cautious, sensible, watchful **9** cognizant, conscious, observant, regardful **10** absorbed in, open-eyed to, thoughtful **11** attentive to, engrossed in, taken up with **12** occupied with **15** preoccupied with

mindfulness 9 alertness, awareness **10** perception **12** acquaintance **13** attentiveness, consciousness, understanding

mindless 6 insane, obtuse, stupid **7** asinine, doltish, idiotic, unaware, witless **8** careless, heedless **9** apathetic, cretinous, imbecilic, oblivious, unattuned, unheeding **10** neglectful, regardless, sophomoric, unthinking **11** inattentive, indifferent, nonsensical, thoughtless, unobservant, unreasoning **12** disregardful, simple-minded **13** inconsiderate, unintelligent **14** indiscriminate

mine 3 pit **4** fund **5** cache, hoard, shaft, stock, store **6** dig

for, quarry, supply, tunnel, wealth **7** extract, reserve **8** dig under, excavate, treasure **9** abundance, booby-trap **10** excavation **12** accumulation

Mineo, Sal
real name: **14** Salvatore Mineo
born: **7** Bronx NY
roles: **5** Giant, Tonka **6** Exodus **18** Rebel Without a Cause, Who Killed Teddy Bear?

mineral *see box*

Minerva
origin: **5** Roman
goddess of: **3** war **4** arts **6** wisdom **11** handicrafts
corresponds to: **6** Athena

mingle 3 mix **4** fuse, join **5** blend, merge, unite **6** hobnob **7** combine, consort **8** coalesce, intermix **9** associate, circulate, commingle, interfuse, interlard, socialize **10** amalgamate, fraternize, intertwine, interweave **11** intermingle, intersperse **12** rub shoulders

miniature 3 wee **4** tiny **5** elfin, pygmy **6** bantam, little, petite **9** minuscule **10** diminutive, pocket-size, small-scale **11** Lilliputian, microcosmic, microscopic

minim
abbreviation: **3** min

minimal 5 token **7** minimum, nominal **13** least possible, unappreciable

minimize 5 dwarf **6** reduce, shrink **8** belittle, mitigate **9** underrate **10** depreciate, undervalue

minimum 4 base **5** basic, least **7** modicum **8** smallest

minister 4 abbe, tend **5** padre, rabbi, serve, vicar **6** answer,

cleric, father, oblige, parson, pastor, priest **7** care for, cater to **8** attend to, chaplain, pander to, preacher, reverend **9** clergyman, secretary **10** evangelist, revivalist, take care of **11** accommodate **12** ecclesiastic **13** cabinet member

ministerial 6 cleric **8** churchly, clerical, pastoral, priestly **14** ecclesiastical

ministration 3 aid **4** care **6** charge **7** comfort **9** attention **10** protection **11** supervision

Ministry of Fear, The
author: **12** Graham Greene

Minitari *see* **7** Hidatsa

Minnehaha
character in: **8** Hiawatha
author: **10** Longfellow

Minnelli, Liza
father: **8** Vincente
mother: **11** Judy Garland
born: **12** Los Angeles CA
roles: **6** Arthur **7** Cabaret (Oscar) **14** New York New York **16** The Sterile Cuckoo **17** Flora the Red Menace

Minnelli, Vincente
director of: **4** Gigi (Oscar) **9** Brigadoon **11** Lust for Life **15** Bells Are Ringing, Meet Me in St Louis **16** Father of the Bride **17** An American in Paris

Minnesota *see box*

Minni *see* **7** Armenia

minor 5 child, light, petty, small, youth **6** infant, lesser, paltry, slight **7** trivial **8** nugatory, picayune, piddling, teenager, trifling **9** secondary, youngster **10** adolescent **11** subordinate, unimportant **13** insignificant **14** inconsiderable **15** inconsequential

---

mineral 3 jet, ore **4** coal, gold, iron, mica, opal, spar, talc **5** beryl, topaz **6** augite, barite, blende, cerine, copper, galena, garnet, iolite, pinite, rutile, sandix, silver, sphene, spinel, sulfur **7** amesite, apatite, azurite, biotite, bornite, calcite, citrine, coesite, crystal, cuprite, cyanite, element, gahnite, helvite, jadeite, kernite, kunzite, niobite, olivine, prasine, zeolite, zircon **8** asbestos, borocite, chlorite, cinnabar, corundum, dolomite, epsomite, fayalite, feldspar, fluorite, graphite, hematite, lazulite, siderite, sodalite, stibnite, triplite, wellsite **9** aragonite, argentite, carnelian, celestite, cerussite, danburite, fosterite, kaolinite, lawsonite, magnetite, malachite, muscovite, petroleum, phenakite, scapolite, tridymite, turquoise, wulfenite **10** calaverite, chalcedony, orthoclase, pyrrhotite, sphalerite, tourmaline, wolfachite **11** alexandrite, chrysoberyl, melanterite **12** brazilianite, chalcopyrite, fincalconite, fluorapatite **13** rhodochrosite

Minnesota
abbreviation: 2 MN 4 Minn
nickname: 6 Gopher 9 North Star 19 Land of Sky-blue Waters 22 Land of Ten Thousand Lakes
capital: 6 St Paul
largest city: 11 Minneapolis
others: 3 Ada, Ely 4 Mora 5 Edina 6 Austin, Duluth, Newulm, Winona 7 Babbitt, Bemidji, Fosston, Hibbing, Mankato, Red Wing, St Cloud 8 Brainerd, Moorhead 9 Albertlea, Blue Earth, Richfield, Rochester, Roseville 10 Minnetonka, Robinsdale 11 Bloomington, St Louis Park 14 Brooklyn Center 18 International Falls
college: 6 Bethel, St Olaf, Winona 7 Bemidji, Hamline 8 Adolphus, Augsburg, Carleton, St Thomas 10 Macalester
feature:
 monument: 10 Paul Bunyan
 national monument: 9 Pipestone 12 Grand Portage
 national park: 9 Voyageurs'
 Norse artifact: 19 Kensington Rune Stone
tribe: 5 Sioux 6 Dakota, Ojibwa, Santee 8 Chippewa 9 Menominee
people: 11 Judy Garland 12 Mayo brothers 13 Harold Stassen, Lauris Norstad, Sinclair Lewis 16 F Scott Fitzgerald
 explorer: 8 Hennepin, Norsemen, Radisson 9 Greysolon 12 Groseilliers 19 Sieur Duluth of du Lhut
lakes: 3 Red 5 Leech, Rainy 6 Itasca 7 Bemidji 8 Superior 9 Mille Lacs 10 Minnewaska 14 Lake of the Woods, Winnibigoshish
land rank: 7 twelfth
mountain: 6 Cuyuna, Mesabi 7 Misquah 9 Vermilion
 highest point: 5 Eagle
physical feature: 6 Big Bog 14 Northwest Angle
 falls: 9 Minnehaha
river: 3 Red 5 Rainy 6 Pigeon 7 St Croix, St Louis 9 Des Moines, Minnesota 10 St Lawrence 11 Mississippi
state admission: 12 thirty-second
state bird: 10 common loon
state fish: 7 walleye
state flower: 14 moccasin flower 24 pink and white lady's slipper
state motto: 17 The Star of the North
state song: 13 Hail Minnesota
state tree: 13 Norway red pine
baseball team: 5 Twins
football team: 7 Vikings
hockey team: 10 North Stars

minority 4 less 5 youth 6 lesser, nonage 7 boyhood, infancy 8 girlhood 9 childhood, juniority 10 immaturity 11 adolescence

minor-league 4 punk 5 dinky, seedy, tacky 6 cheesy, common, lesser, shabby 8 inferior, small-fry 9 secondary, small-time 10 bush-league, second-rate 13 insignificant

Minos
king of: 5 Crete
father: 4 Zeus
mother: 6 Europa
brother: 8 Sarpedon 12 Rhadamanthys
wife: 8 Pasiphae
daughter: 7 Ariadne, Phaedra
ordered: 9 Labryinth
became: 5 judge
 in: 5 Hades

Minotaur
form: 7 monster
combined: 3 man 4 bull
father: 10 Cretan bull
mother: 8 Pasiphae
home: 9 Labyrinth
ate flesh of: 6 humans
killed by: 7 Theseus

minstrel 4 bard, poet 6 dancer, end man, lyrist, player, singer 8 comedian, songster 9 blackface, poetaster, serenader, versifier 10 troubadour 11 entertainer 12 interlocutor, vaudevillian 15 song-and-dance man

mint
varieties: 3 dog, red 4 wood 5 apple, field, lemon, stone, water 6 coyote, dotted, orange, Scotch 7 Meehan's 8 bergamot, Corsican, creep-

ing, Japanese, mountain 9 pineapple
flavor: 7 menthol 9 spearmint 10 peppermint
liqueur: 13 creme de menthe
botanical name: 6 Mentha 8 Labiatae, M spicata 9 M piperita
origin: 13 Mediterranean
related herb: 7 oregano 8 marjoram, rosemary
symbol of: 11 hospitality
mythical nymph: 6 Mintha
 beloved of: 5 Pluto
 Mintha trod underfoot by: 10 Persephone
cure for: 7 hiccups
antidote for: 16 sea serpent stings
use: 4 lamb 5 salad 6 fruits

Minthe
form: 5 nymph
changed into: 9 mint plant
changed by: 10 Persephone

minuscule 3 wee 4 tiny 5 small 6 minute 10 teenyweeny 11 small letter 13 infinitesimal 15 lower-case letter

minute 3 wee 4 fine, puny, tiny, wink 5 close, exact, flash, jiffy, petty, scant, shake, teeny, trice 6 breath, little, moment, petite, second, slight, strict 7 careful, instant, minikin, precise 8 detailed, itemized, trifling 9 miniature, twinkling 10 a short time, diminutive, exhaustive, meticulous, negligible, scrupulous 11 Lilliputian, microscopic 12 sixty seconds 13 conscientious, imperceptible, inappreciable, infinitesimal, insignificant 14 extremely small, inconsiderable
abbreviation: 3 min

minute portion 3 bit, sip 4 bite 5 crumb, grain, scrap, shred, speck 6 morsel, sliver 7 swallow 8 fragment, mouthful, particle

minutiae 6 trivia 7 trifles 8 niceties 10 bagatelles, pedantries, subtleties 11 odds and ends, particulars 12 minor details, trivialities 15 particularities

minx 4 jade, slut 5 hussy, huzzy, wench 7 baggage 10 prostitute

Minyades
daughters of: 6 Minyas

Miolnir
hammer of: 4 Thor

mir 5 peace, world 21 Russian village commune

mirabile dictu 12 strange to say 17 marvelous to relate

miracle 4 omen, sign 6 marvel,

wonder **7** mystery, portent, prodigy **9** divine act, sensation, spectacle **10** phenomenon **11** masterpiece

Miracle of Morgan's Creek, The
director: **14** Preston Sturges
cast: **9** Diana Lynn **11** Betty Hutton **12** Brian Donlevy, Eddie Bracken **15** William Demarest

Miracle on 34th Street
director: **12** George Seaton
based on story by: **15** Valentine Davies
cast: **9** John Payne **11** Edmund Gwenn (Kris Kringle), Natalie Wood **12** Gene Lockhart, Maureen O'Hara, Thelma Ritter
Oscar for: **12** screenwriter **15** supporting actor (Gwenn)

Miracle Worker, The
director: **10** Arthur Penn
cast: **9** Patty Duke (Helen Keller) **10** Victor Jory **11** Inga Swenson **12** Anne Bancroft (Anne Sullivan)
Oscar for: **7** actress (Bancroft) **17** supporting actress (Duke)

miraculous 6 divine **7** amazing, magical **9** marvelous, visionary, wonderful **10** incredible, mysterious, phenomenal, prodigious, remarkable **11** astonishing, astounding, exceptional, spectacular, supernormal **13** extraordinary, preternatural, wonderworking **14** thaumaturgical

miraculous food 5 manna

Miraculous writing
also: **4** mene **5** perez, tekel **8** upharsin
means: **7** divided, weighed **8** numbered
interpreted by: **6** Daniel

mirage 5 fancy **7** fantasy **8** delusion, illusion, phantasm **9** unreality **12** will-o'-the-wisp **13** hallucinations, misconception **14** castle in the air **15** optical illusion

Miranda
character in: **10** The Tempest
author: **11** Shakespeare

Miranda, Carmen
real name: **26** Maria do Carmo Miranda da Cunha
nickname: **18** Brazilian Bombshell
born: **8** Portugal **16** Marco de Canavezes
roles: **10** Copacabana **14** That Night in Rio **15** Weekend in Havana **16** Down Argentine Way **22** Springtime in the Rockies

mire 3 bog, fen, mud **4** cake, muck, ooze, soil **5** marsh, muddy, slime, slush, smear **6** enmesh, sludge **7** begrime, bog down, ensnare, spatter **8** besmirch, entangle, quagmire

Miriam
father: **5** Amram
mother: **8** Jochebed
brother: **5** Aaron, Moses

Miro, Joan
born: **5** Spain **8** Montroig **9** Barcelona
artwork: **9** Help Spain, The Reaper **13** Dutch Interior **14** Constellations **16** Catalan Landscape **19** Dog Barking at the Moon **20** Still Life with Old Shoe **26** Woman and Bird in the Moonlight

mirror 4 copy, show **5** glass, image, model **7** epitome, example, paragon, reflect **8** exemplar, manifest, paradigm, standard **10** reflection **11** cheval glass **12** looking glass

mirth 4 glee **6** gaiety, levity **7** jollity **8** drollery, hilarity, laughter **9** amusement, festivity, happiness, jocundity, joviality, merriment **10** jocularity **11** good spirits, merrymaking, playfulness **12** cheerfulness

mirthful 3 gay **4** glad **5** happy, jolly, merry **6** blithe, jocose, jovial, joyful, joyous **7** gleeful, jocular, risible

mirthless 3 sad **4** dour, glum **6** gloomy, morose **7** joyless, unhappy **8** dejected **9** cheerless, sorrowful **10** in the dumps, melancholy **14** down in the mouth

miry 3 wet **4** oozy **5** boggy, mucky, muddy, slimy, slushy, soggy **6** claggy, swampy **7** sloughy

misadventure 3 ill **4** slip **6** mishap **7** debacle, failure, reverse, setback **8** bad break, calamity, casualty, disaster **9** adversity, mischance **10** infelicity, misfortune **11** catastrophe, contretemps

misanthrope 5 cynic **7** skeptic **9** pessimist **10** misogynist

Misanthrope, Le
author: **7** Moliere
character: **7** Alceste, Arsinoe, Eliante **8** Celimene, Philinte

misanthropic 4 cold **5** surly **6** morose **7** cynical, distant **10** antisocial, unfriendly, unsociable **11** distrustful **12** discourteous, inhospitable, unneighborly, unpersonable,

unresponsive **14** unapproachable **15** unaccommodating

misapplication 5 abuse **6** misuse **11** improper use **13** misemployment

misapply 5 abuse **6** misuse **9** misemploy **13** use improperly

misapprehension 5 mixup **7** mistake **11** misjudgment **13** misconception **14** miscalculation **15** false impression, misconstruction **16** misunderstanding **17** misinterpretation

misappropriate 4 bilk **5** abuse, cheat, mulct, steal **6** misuse **7** defraud, purloin, swindle **8** embezzle, misapply, peculate **9** defalcate, misemploy

misappropriation 6 misuse, taking **11** defalcation **12** embezzlement

misbehave 5 act up **7** disobey, do wrong **10** transgress **15** get into mischief

misbehavior 5 lapse **7** misdeed, offense **8** acting up, trespass **9** impudence **10** bad conduct, bad manners, disrespect, misconduct **11** delinquency, dereliction, impropriety, misdemeanor **12** indiscretion **13** transgression **16** obstreperousness, unmanageableness

misbelief 8 delusion, illusion **13** misconception

miscalculate 3 err **8** misjudge **10** guess wrong **11** misestimate

miscalculation 5 error **10** inaccuracy **13** misestimation

miscarriage 4 slip **5** botch **6** fizzle **7** default, failing, failure, misfire, undoing, washout **8** casualty, collapse

miscarry 4 fail **5** abort, botch **6** fizzle, go awry **9** terminate **12** come to naught

miscellanea 8 analects **9** anthology, gleanings, scrapbook **10** collection, miscellany, selections **11** collectanea

miscellaneous 5 mixed **6** divers, motley, sundry, varied **7** diverse, mingled, various **8** assorted, manifold **9** different **11** diversified **13** heterogeneous

miscellaneous collection
Latin/pseudo Latin: **14** omnium-gatherum

miscellany 5 blend **6** jumble, medley **7** melange, mixture, variety **8** analects, extracts, mishmash, pastiche **9** anthology, gleanings, potpourri

10 assortment, collection, hodgepodge, salmagundi, selections **11** collectanea, compilation, gallimaufry, miscellanea **14** conglomeration, omnium-gatherum

mischance 6 ill lot, mishap **7** bad luck, ill luck, ill wind **8** accident **9** adversity **10** infelicity, misfortune **12** misadventure

mischief 4 evil **5** wrong **6** injury, malice **7** devilry, knavery, roguery **8** deviltry, foul play, plotting, scheming, villainy **9** depravity, devilment, rascality **10** orneriness, wrongdoing **11** naughtiness, playfulness, roguishness, shenanigans, willfulness **12** prankishness, sportiveness **14** capriciousness

mischief-maker 3 imp **5** demon, devil, scamp **7** gremlin, hellion **9** scoundrel **10** hell-raiser

mischievous 3 sly **5** elfin **6** elfish, impish, malign, vexing, wicked **7** harmful, naughty, noxious, playful, roguish, teasing, vicious, waggish **8** annoying, devilish, prankish, spiteful, sportive **9** injurious, malicious, malignant, uninvited **10** frolicsome, gratuitous, pernicious **11** deleterious, destructive, detrimental, uncalled for **12** exacerbating

misconceive 3 err **4** lose, miss **8** misjudge **12** misinterpret **13** misunderstand

misconception 5 error **8** delusion **11** misjudgment **13** erroneous idea **15** misapprehension, misconstruction **16** misunderstanding **17** misinterpretation, misrepresentation

misconduct 7 misdeed, misstep **10** misprision, peccadillo, wrongdoing **11** delinquency, dereliction, impropriety, malefaction, malfeasance, misbehavior, misdemeanor **13** transgression

misconstrue 7 distort, mistake **8** misjudge **9** misreckon, misrender **12** misapprehend, miscalculate, misinterpret, mistranslate **13** misunderstand

miscreant 3 bum **4** heel **5** knave, scamp **6** bad egg, rascal, sinner, wretch **7** villain **8** evildoer, lost soul, scalawag **9** reprobate, scoundrel **10** blackguard, black sheep, malefactor

misdeed 3 sin **4** slip **5** crime, lapse, wrong **6** felony **7** faux

pas, offense, outrage **8** atrocity, trespass **9** violation **10** misconduct, peccadillo **11** malfeasance, misbehavior, misdemeanor **12** indiscretion, infringement **13** transgression

misdemeanor 3 sin **5** crime, fault **7** offense, misdeed **8** disorder **10** peccadillo **11** misbehavior **13** transgression

misdoer 5 crook **8** criminal **9** miscreant, wrongdoer **10** delinquent

mise en scene 6 milieu **7** setting **8** ambience **10** atmosphere, background **11** environment **12** stage setting, surroundings

misemployment 6 misuse **14** misapplication

Misenus
  father: **6** Aeolus

miser 5 piker **7** hoarder, niggard, Scrooge, skimper **8** tightwad **9** skinflint **10** cheapskate, pinchpenny **12** pennypincher, stingy person

Miser, The
  also: **6** L'Avare
  author: **7** Moliere
  character: **5** Elise **6** Valere **7** Anselme, Cleante, Mariane **8** Harpagon

miserable 3 sad **4** mean **5** inept, needy, sorry **6** abject, scurvy, shabby, sordid, woeful **7** abysmal, crushed, doleful, forlorn, grieved, hapless, unhappy **8** beggarly, degraded, dejected, desolate, dolorous, feckless, inferior, mournful, pathetic, pitiable, rubbishy, very poor, wretched **9** appalling, atrocious, cheerless, depressed, desperate, heartsick, sorrowful, woebegone **10** chapfallen, deplorable, despicable, despondent, heavy-laden, lamentable, second-rate, unbearable **11** crestfallen, heartbroken, unfortunate **12** contemptible, disconsolate, impoverished **13** broken-hearted **14** down in the mouth

Miserables, Les
  author: **10** Victor Hugo
  character: **6** Javert **7** Cosette, Fantine **10** Thenardier **11** Jean Valjean **15** Father Madeleine, Marius Pontmercy **17** Eponine Thenardier

misericordia 5 mercy **10** compassion

miserliness 6 penury **9** frugality, parsimony **10** stinginess

13 niggardliness, penny-pinching **15** tight-fistedness

miserly 4 mean, near **5** cheap, tight **6** frugal, greedy, meager, stingy **7** selfish **8** grasping, grudging, pinching **9** illiberal, niggardly, penurious, scrimping **10** avaricious, ungenerous **11** closefisted, closehanded, tight-fisted **12** parsimonious **13** penny-pinching

misery 3 woe **4** blow **5** agony, curse, grief, trial **6** ordeal, regret, sorrow **7** anguish, bad deal, bad news, chagrin, despair, sadness, torment, trouble **8** bad scene, calamity, disaster, distress, exaction, hardship **9** dejection, heartache, privation, suffering **10** affliction, bitter pill, depression, desolation, melancholy, misfortune **11** catastrophe, despondency, tribulation **12** wretchedness

Misfits, The
  director: **10** John Huston
  based on story by: **12** Arthur Miller
  cast: **10** Clark Gable, Eli Wallach **12** Thelma Ritter **13** Marilyn Monroe **15** Montgomery Clift

misfortune 4 blow, loss **6** misery, mishap **7** bad luck, reverse, setback, tragedy, trouble **8** calamity, casualty, disaster, downfall, hard luck, hardship **9** adversity, hard times, ruination **10** affliction, ill fortune **11** catastrophe, tribulation **12** misadventure

misgiving, misgivings 4 fear **5** alarm, doubt, dread, qualm, worry **7** anxiety, dubiety **8** disquiet, mistrust **9** suspicion **10** foreboding, skepticism **11** dubiousness, uncertainty **12** apprehension, doubtfulness, presentiment, reservations **14** second thoughts

misguided 5 at sea **6** adrift, faulty, misled, unwise **7** in error **8** mistaken **9** erroneous, imprudent, led astray, off course **10** ill-advised, indiscreet, misadvised **11** injudicious, misdirected, misinformed

Mishael see **7** Meshach

mishap 4 slip, snag **5** botch **6** fiasco, slipup **7** reverse, setback **8** casualty, disaster **9** mischance **10** difficulty, misfortune **11** miscarriage **12** misadventure

mishmash 3 mix **4** hash, stew **5** salad **6** jumble, medley, muddle 7 melange 8 mixed bag, pastiche, scramble 9 patchwork 10 assemblage, crazy quilt, hodgepodge, miscellany, salmagundi 14 conglomeration, omniumgatherum

misinform 7 deceive, mislead 8 misguide 9 misdirect 10 lead astray 12 misrepresent

misinterpret 11 misconstrue 12 misapprehend 13 misunderstand

misinterpretation 13 misconception 16 misunderstanding 17 misrepresentation

misjudge 3 err 7 mistake 10 exaggerate, understate 11 misconceive, misconstrue 12 misapprehend, miscalculate, misinterpret, overestimate 13 misunderstand, underestimate

mislay 4 lose, miss 8 displace, misplace

mislead 4 dupe, fool, gull 6 betray, delude, entice, seduce, take in 7 beguile, deceive 8 hoodwink, inveigle, misguide 9 bamboozle, misdirect, misinform, play false, victimize 10 lead astray 11 double-cross, string along

misleading 6 luring 8 deluding 9 deceiving 10 misguiding 11 hoodwinking

mismanage 3 mar 4 flub, muff, ruin 5 botch, spoil 6 bollix, bungle, foul up, mess up 7 louse up, screw up 9 mishandle 11 make a hash of, make a mess of

misnomer 8 misusage, solecism 9 barbarism, misnaming 11 malapropism

misogynic 7 cynical 11 woman-hating 12 misanthropic

misogynist 5 cynic 10 womanhater 11 misanthrope

misplace 4 lose 5 abuse 6 mislay 11 lose track of

misreckon 8 misjudge 10 guess wrong, miscompute 11 misestimate 12 miscalculate

misrepresent 7 falsify, mislead 8 disguise

misrepresentation 7 mockery 8 altering, travesty, twisting 9 burlesque, doctoring 10 caricature, distortion, falsifying 12 adulteration, exaggeration, misstatement 13 falsification

miss 4 blow, girl, lack, lady, lass, lose, loss, maid, muff,

skip, slip, want 5 avert, avoid, error, forgo, let go, woman 6 bypass, damsel, escape, forego, lassie, maiden, miscue, pass by 7 blunder, colleen, default, failure, fly wide, let pass, let slip, long for, mistake, neglect, old maid, overrun, pine for 8 leave out, omission, overlook, pass over, senorita, slip up on, spinster, yearn for 9 disregard, fall short, false step, gloss over, go without, overshoot, oversight, surrender, young lady 10 demoiselle, schoolgirl 12 be absent from 13 feel the loss of, mademoiselle

missal 10 prayer book

missed
  French: 6 manque

misshapen 7 twisted 8 deformed 9 contorted, distorted

missile 4 ball, dart 5 arrow, lance, shaft, shell, spear, stone 6 bullet, rocket 7 harpoon, javelin 10 projectile

missing 4 AWOL, gone, lost 6 absent 7 lacking, left out, not here 8 avoiding, skipping 10 longing for, not present 11 overlooking, yearning for 12 disregarding

Missing
  director: 22 Constantine Costa-Gavras
  cast: 8 John Shea 10 Jack Lemmon 11 Sissy Spacek 13 Melanie Mayron

Missing Persons and Other Essays
  author: 12 Heinrich Boll

mission 3 end, job 4 task 5 quest 6 charge 7 calling, mandate, pursuit 8 legation, ministry 9 objective 10 assignment, commission, delegation, enterprise 11 raison d'etre, undertaking

Mission
  tribe: 7 Chumash, Juaneno, Luiseno 8 Diegueno 9 Costanoan 10 Gabrielino 11 Fernandario
  location: 10 California

Mississippi
  abbreviation: 2 MS 4 Miss
  nickname: 5 Bayou 6 Mudcat 8 Magnolia
  capital/largest city: 7 Jackson
  others: 6 Biloxi, Helena, Laurel, Tupelo, Winona 7 Belzoni, Corinth, Grenada, Natchez 8 Bogalusa, Columbus, Gulfport, Meridian 9 Kosciusko, Vicksburg 10 Clarksdale, Pascagoula 11 Hattiesburg 13 Pass Christian
  college: 4 Rust 6 Alcorn 7 Jackson 8 Belhaven, Millsaps, Tougaloo 11 Mississippi 12 Blue Mountain, William Carey
  feature: 12 Natchez Trace
    national military park: 9 Vicksburg
    national seashore: 11 Gulf Islands
  tribe: 3 Sac 5 Tious 6 Biloxi, Mandan, Tunica 7 Choctaw, Natchez, Tonikan 8 Chicksaw
  people: 11 Eudora Welty 15 William Faulkner 17 Tennessee Williams
    explorer: 6 DeSoto, Joliet 9 Iberville, Marquette
  island: 3 Cat 4 Horn, Ship 9 Petit Bois
  lake: 4 Enid 6 Sardis 7 Barnett, Grenada 8 Pickwick 9 Arkabutla, Okatibbee
  land rank: 12 thirty-second
  highest point: 7 Woodall
  physical feature:
    delta: 10 Yazoo Basin
    hills: 8 Fall Line 9 Tennessee 11 Loess Bluffs
    prairie: 5 Black 7 Jackson
    sound: 11 Mississippi
  river: 4 Leaf 5 Pearl, Yazoo 8 Big Black 9 Tombigbee, Yalobusha 10 Homochitto, Pascagoula 11 Mississippi 12 Tallahatchie
  state admission: 9 twentieth
  state bird: 11 mockingbird
  state flower: 8 magnolia
  state motto: 14 By Valor and Arms
  state song: 13 Go Mississippi
  state tree: 8 magnolia

Mission: Impossible
character: 5 Casey, Paris
10 Rollin Hand 11 Dana
Lambert, James Phelps
12 Daniel Briggs 13 Barney
Collier 14 Cinnamon Carter,
Willie Armitage
cast: 10 Greg Morris, Peter
Lupus, Steven Hill 11 Bar-
bara Bain, Peter Graves
12 Leonard Nimoy, Martin
Landau 14 Lynda Day
George 15 Lesley Ann
Warren

Mississippi *see box*

missive 4 note 6 billet, letter
7 epistle, message 13 communication 14 correspondence

Miss Julie
author: 16 August Strindberg

Miss Lonelyhearts
author: 13 Nathanael West

Missouri *see box*

Miss Peach
creator: 11 Mell Lazarus
character: 3 Ira 6 Arthur,
Lester, Marcia 8 Francine
place: 9 Kamp Kelly 11 Kelly
School

misspend 5 waste 8 squander
9 dissipate, throw away
11 fritter away

misspent 6 wasted 8 depraved
9 debauched, dissolute, idled
away 10 misapplied, profitless,
squandered, thrown away

misstate 5 alter 6 bollix, garble 7 confuse, distort, falsify,
pervert 8 misquote 9 misre-
port 12 misrepresent

misstatement 3 fib, lie 4 tale
5 error 7 falsity, untruth
9 falsehood 13 prevarication
17 misrepresentation

misstep 3 sin 4 goof, slip,
vice 5 boner, error, fault,

gaffe, lapse 6 boo-boo, defect,
foul-up 7 blooper, faux pas, offense, screw-up 11 delin-
quency, dereliction,
shortcoming 12 indiscretion
13 transgression

miss the mark 4 fail 9 fall
short 11 come up short

miss the point 7 mistake
11 fail to catch, misconceive
12 misapprehend
13 misunderstand

mist 3 fog 4 haze, murk,
smog 5 steam, vapor 7 drizzle

mistake 4 slip 5 boner, error,
gaffe, mix-up 6 slipup
7 blooper, blunder, confuse,
faux pas, misstep 8 confound,
misjudge 9 misreckon, oversight 11 misconstrue, misiden-
tify 12 misapprehend,
miscalculate, misinterpret
13 misunderstand
14 miscalculation
French: 10 malentendu

mistaken 5 at sea, false,
wrong 6 faulty, untrue 7 at
fault, in error, unsound 8 deceived 9 erroneous, illogical,
incorrect, off course, unfounded 10 fallacious, groundless, inaccurate, ungrounded
11 unjustified

Mister
Yiddish: 3 Reb

Mister Roberts
author: 12 Thomas Heggen
director: 8 John Ford
11 Mervyn LeRoy
cast: 8 Ward Bond 10 Henry
Fonda, Jack Lemmon (En-
sign Pulver) 11 Betsy Palmer, James Cagney
13 William Powell
Oscar for: 15 supporting actor (Lemmon)

Mister Saturday Night
nickname of: 13 Jackie
Gleason

mistreat 4 harm 5 abuse,
bully, hound, wrong 6 harass,
ill-use, injure, misuse, molest
7 assault, oppress, outrage,
pervert, torment, violate 8 ill-
treat, maltreat 9 brutalize,
manhandle, mishandle,
persecute

mistreatment 5 abuse 6 ill-
use, injury 7 assault, cruelty,
harming 10 bodily harm,
oppression 11 manhandling,
molestation, persecution
12 maltreatment

mistress 3 Mrs 4 doxy, lady,
Miss 5 lover, Madam 6 ma-
tron 8 ladylove, paramour
9 concubine, headwoman,
housewife, inamorata, kept

Missouri
abbreviation: 2 MO
nickname: 5 Ozark 6 Show-Me 7 Bullion 15 Mother of the
West
capital: 13 Jefferson City
largest city: 7 St Louis
others: 5 Eldon, Hayti, Lamar, Macon, Rolla 6 Butler,
Joplin, Mexico 7 Bethany, Bolivar, Cameron, Clayton, Lebanon, Moberly, Sedalia 8 Berkeley, Columbia, Hannibal,
Kirkwood, Sikeston, St Joseph 10 Bonne Terre, Kansas
City 11 Springfield, Warrensburg 12 Independence
13 Cape Girardeau, Webster Groves
college: 5 Avila, Drury 6 Tarkio 7 Lincoln, St Louis, Webster 8 Stephens 10 Washington 11 Westminster
feature:
  dam: 5 Osage
tribe: 3 Fox, Sac 4 Sauk 5 Osage 7 Shawnee 8 Cherokee,
Missouri
people: 7 TS Eliot 9 Mark Twain 10 Jesse James 11 Omar
Bradley 12 Helen Traubel, Sara Teasdale 13 John J
Pershing, Marianne Moore, Samuel Clemens 15 Reinhold
Niebuhr 22 George Washington Carver
  explorer: 6 Joliet 7 La Salle 9 Marquette
lake: 7 Norfolk 9 Tablerock, Taneycomo 10 Bull Shoals
14 Kaysinger Bluff 15 Lake of the Ozarks
land rank: 10 nineteenth
mountain: 6 Ozarks 10 St Francois
  highest point: 8 Taumsauk
physical feature: 8 Bootheel 9 Big Spring
  plains: 4 Till 5 Osage
  plateau: 5 Ozark
president: 12 Harry S Truman
river: 4 Salt 5 Grand, Osage, White 6 Platte 7 Current,
Meramec 8 Big Muddy, Chariton, Missouri 9 Des Moines,
Gasconade, St Francis 11 Mississippi
state admission: 12 twenty-fourth
state bird: 8 bluebird
state flower: 8 hawthorn
state motto: 41 The Welfare of the People Shall Be the
Supreme Law
state song: 13 Missouri Waltz
state tree: 7 dogwood

woman **10** chatelaine, girl-friend, sweetheart

mistrust 5 doubt, qualm **7** anxiety, dubiety, suspect **8** distrust, question, wariness **9** challenge, chariness, leeri-ness, misgiving, suspicion **10** disbelieve, skepticism

misty 4 dewy, hazy **5** filmy, foggy, murky **6** cloudy, opaque, steamy **8** nebulous, overcast, vaporous **10** indistinct

misunderstand 7 confuse, mis-read, mistake **8** misjudge **9** misreckon **11** misconceive, misconstrue **12** misapprehend, miscalculate, misinterpret, miss the point

misunderstanding 4 rift, spat **5** set-to **7** discord, dispute, quarrel, wrangle **8** conflict, squabble **10** difference, dissen-sion, misreading **11** alterca-tion, contretemps, misjudgment **12** disagreement **13** misconception **15** false impression, misapprehension **16** miscomprehension **17** misinterpretation French: **10** malentendu

misuse 4 harm, hurt **5** abuse, waste, wrong **6** debase, injure **7** corrupt, exploit, outrage, pervert, profane **8** ill-treat, maltreat, misapply, mistreat, wrong use **9** misemploy **10** corruption, perversion, prostitute **11** desecration, prof-anation, squandering **12** ill treatment, maltreatment, mis-treatment, prostitution **13** misemployment **14** misap-plication **15** take advantage of

Mitchell, Billy (William Lendrum)
advocate of: **8** air power
court-martialed for: **15** insubordination
served in: **3** WWI
rank: **16** brigadier general
commander of: **15** US army air forces

Mitchell, Margaret
author of: **15** Gone With the Wind

Mitchell, Silas Weir
author of: **9** Hugh Wynne (Free Quaker) **11** Roland Blake

Mitchell, Thomas
born: **11** Elizabeth NJ
roles: **7** Our Town **8** Doc Boone **9** The Outlaw **10** Stagecoach **11** Gerald O'Hara, Lost Horizon **15** Gone With the Wind **19** Only Angels Have Wings

Mitchell, William
real name of: **10** Peter Finch

Mitchum, Robert
born: **12** Bridgeport CT
roles: **6** Midway **10** Winds of War **11** Thunder Road **13** Ryan's Daughter, The Longest Day, The Sundown-ers **15** The Story of G I Joe **16** Farewell My Lovely **20** Heaven Knows Mr Allison

mite 3 bit, jot **4** atom, iota, whit **5** scrap, speck **6** spider **7** smidgen **8** arachnid, particle

Mitford, Jessica
author of: **21** The American Way of Death **22** Kind and Usual Punishment

Mitford, Nancy
author of: **14** Noblesse Oblige **16** The Pursuit of Love **18** Love in a Cold Climate

Mithgarthr see **7** Midgard

Mithraeum
temple of: **7** Mithras

Mithras
origin: **7** Persian
god of: **5** light, truth
corresponds to: **3** Sol

mitigate 4 ease **5** allay, blunt **6** lessen, reduce, soften, soothe, temper, weaken **7** as-suage, lighten, mollify, pla-cate, relieve **8** diminish, moderate, palliate **9** alleviate, extenuate **10** ameliorate

mitigating 6 easing **8** allaying, blunting, reducing **9** assuaging, lessening, relieving, softening, tempering **10** lightening, mod-erating, palliating, palliative **11** diminishing, extenuating **12** ameliorating

Mitrephorus
epithet of: **8** Dionysus
means: **15** headband-bearing

Mitteleuropa 12 middle Europe

mitzvah, mitsvah 8 good deed **11** commandment

mix 3 add **4** beat, club, fold, fuse, join, stir, whip **5** admix, alloy, blend, merge, put in, unite **6** commix, fusion, hob-nob, mingle **7** combine, con-sort, include, mixture **8** assembly, coalesce, com-pound, intermix, mingling **9** associate, commingle, inter-fuse, interlard, introduce, so-cialize **10** amalgamate, fraternize, intertwine, inter-weave **11** incorporate, inter-mingle, intersperse, put together

mixed 4 coed **5** fused **6** hybrid, motley **7** alloyed, blended, in-mixed, mingled, mongrel, not pure **8** combined **9** composite, uncertain **10** ambivalent, inde-cisive, interwoven, variegated **11** adulterated, diversified, half and half, put together **12** con-glomerate, inconclusive **13** heterogeneous, male-and-female, miscellaneous

mixed-up 6 addled **7** chaotic, jumbled, muddled, tangled **8** confused, rambling **9** befud-dled, illogical, nonplused, per-plexed **10** bewildered, disjointed, incoherent, irra-tional, nonplussed **12** discon-nected, disorganized **13** disharmonious, heter-ogeneous

Mixtec
tribe: **7** Zapotec

mixture 3 mix **4** hash, stew **5** alloy, blend, union **6** fusion, jumble, medley **7** amalgam, melange **8** compound, mish-mash, pastiche **9** admixture, composite, potpourri **10** com-mixture, hodgepodge, salma-gundi **11** association, combination **12** adulteration, amalgamation, intermixture

mixup 4 mess, riot **5** fight, me-lee **6** fracas, muddle, tangle **7** mistake **8** disorder **9** confu-sion, imbroglio **11** misjudg-ment **14** miscalculation **16** miscomprehension, misunderstanding

mix up 5 addle **6** mess up, muddle **7** confuse, nonplus, perplex **8** befuddle, bewilder **10** disarrange

Mneme
member of: **5** Muses
personifies: **6** memory

Mnemosyne
origin: **5** Greek
member of: **6** Titans
goddess of: **6** memory
father: **6** Uranus
mother: **4** Gaea
daughters: **5** Muses

Moabite god 7 Chemosh

moan 3 sob **4** keen, wail **5** groan **6** bemoan, bewail, la-ment, plaint **7** grumble **11** lamentation

moan over 5 mourn **6** be-moan, bewail, lament **7** cry over **8** weep over **10** grieve over

moat 4 foss **5** ditch, fosse, graff **6** gutter, rundel, trench

mob 4 gang, herd **5** crowd, crush, horde, Mafia, swarm **6** masses, rabble, throng

7 flock to **8** assembly, populace, surround **9** gathering, hoi polloi, multitude, plebeians, syndicate **10** converge on **11** proletariat, rank and file **14** organized crime

mobile 6 active, motile **7** kinetic, movable, nomadic **8** portable, rootless **9** footloose, traveling, wandering **10** ambulatory, locomotive

mobilize 6 call up, muster, summon **7** marshal **8** activate, organize **10** call to arms **11** put in motion

mobster 4 hood **6** hitman **7** hoodlum, Mafioso **8** gangster **10** gang member

Moby Dick
    author: **14** Herman Melville
    character: **4** Ahab **5** Stubb **7** Ishmael **8** Fedallah, Queequeg, Starbuck

mock 3 ape **4** copy **5** belie, mimic, scorn, spurn, taunt **6** deride, insult, jeer at, parody, revile, show up **7** imitate, laugh at, let down, profane, scoff at, sneer at **8** ridicule **9** burlesque, frustrate, make fun of, poke fun at **10** caricature, disappoint, make game of **11** make sport of

mockery 4 joke, sham **5** farce, scorn **7** jeering, mimicry, sarcasm **8** derision, raillery, ridicule, scoffing, travesty **9** burlesque, contumely **10** disrespect, ridiculing **13** laughingstock

Mock Turtle
    character in: **28** Alice's Adventures in Wonderland
    author: **7** Carroll

mode 3 cut, fad, way **4** form, rage, rule **5** craze, means, style, taste, trend, vogue **6** course, custom, manner, method, system **7** fashion, process **8** approach, practice **9** condition, procedure, technique **10** appearance

model 4 cast, copy, form, mold, show, type **5** build, dummy, ideal, shape, sport, style **6** design, mirror, mockup **7** display, example, fashion, outline, paragon, pattern, perfect, replica, subject, variety, version **8** exemplar, paradigm, peerless, standard **9** archetype, criterion, exemplary, facsimile, mannequin, prototype, simulated **10** simulacrum **14** representation, representative

model on 6 base on **7** found on **10** derive from

mode of operating
    Latin: **2** mo **13** modus operandi

moderate 4 calm, cool, curb, fair, hush, mild, tame **5** abate, chair, sober **6** direct, gentle, lessen, manage, medium, modest, soften, subdue, temper **7** average, careful, conduct, control, oversee **8** diminish, measured, mediocre, middling, ordinary, passable, rational, regulate, restrain, tone down **9** judicious, peaceable, temperate, unruffled **10** not violent, reasonable **11** inexpensive, preside over **12** mainstreamer, medium-priced

moderation 7 abating, economy **8** allaying **9** abatement, frugality, lessening, remission, restraint **10** continence, diminution, mitigation, palliation, relaxation, temperance **11** alleviation, forbearance, self-control **12** moderateness **13** temperateness **14** abstemiousness **19** avoidance of extremes

moderator 8 chairman, mediator **10** chairwoman, negotiator

modern 3 new **6** modish, recent **7** current, in vogue **8** up-to-date **10** present-day **11** fashionable, streamlined **12** contemporary **15** contemporaneous **16** twentieth-century

Modern Comedy, A
    author: **14** John Galsworthy

modernistic 6 modern **7** moderne **10** new-fangled **12** contemporary

modernity 5 vogue **7** fashion, new look, novelty, the rage **8** last word **14** newfangledness **15** contemporaneity **16** new fashionedness

modernize 4 redo **5** renew **6** do over, revamp, update **7** restore **8** redesign, renovate **9** refurbish **10** regenerate, rejuvenate, streamline **11** recondition **13** bring up to date **16** move with the times

modern times 5 today **8** nowadays **10** the present **13** the here and now

Modern Times
    director: **14** Charles Chaplin
    cast: **12** Henry Bergman **14** Charlie Chaplin, Chester Conklin **15** Paulette Goddard **19** Stanley "Tiny" Sandford

modest 3 coy, shy **4** meek, prim **5** plain, quiet, timid

6 demure, humble, proper, simple **7** bashful, limited, nominal, prudish, unshowy **8** blushing, discreet, moderate, reserved, timorous **9** diffident, shrinking **10** unassuming **11** circumspect, constrained, inexpensive, puritanical, straitlaced, unassertive, unobtrusive **12** medium-priced, not excessive, self-effacing, unpretending **13** unpretentious **14** unostentatious

modesty 7 coyness, prudery, reserve, shyness **8** humility, plainess, timidity **9** propriety, restraint, reticence **10** constraint, demureness, diffidence, humbleness, simplicity **11** bashfulness, naturalness **12** timorousness **14** reasonableness, self-effacement **15** inexpensiveness

modicum 3 bit, dab, jot **4** atom, dash, drop, inch, iota, mite, whit **5** crumb, grain, pinch, scrap, speck, tinge, touch **6** morsel, sliver, snatch, trifle **7** handful, minimum, smidgen **8** fraction, fragment, particle **9** little bit **10** sprinkling **11** small amount **13** small quantity

modification 6 change **8** revision **9** variation **10** adjustment, alteration, conversion, emendation, regulation **14** transformation **15** differentiation

modify 4 redo, vary **5** adapt, alter, limit, lower, remit **6** adjust, change, narrow, reduce, remold, revise, rework, soften, temper **7** control, convert, qualify, remodel, reshape **8** moderate, modulate, restrain, restrict, tone down **9** condition, refashion, transform, transmute **10** reorganize **12** transmogrify

Modigliani, Amedeo
    born: **5** Italy **7** Leghorn, Livorno
    artwork: **10** Seated Nude **13** Reclining Nude, Yellow Sweater **15** Jeanne Hebuterne

modish 2 in **3** now **4** chic **5** natty, nifty, sharp, smart, today **6** dapper, snazzy, spiffy, trendy, with it **7** a la mode, current, faddish, in style, in vogue, stylish, voguish **9** highstyle **11** fashionable **13** up-to-the-minute

Modoc
    language family: **12** Shapwailutan
    division: **10** Lutuamnian
    location: **6** Oregon **10** California

leader: 14 Chief Kintpuash
(Captain Jack)
related to: 7 Klamath

Modred
character in: 16 Arthurian
romance

Mod Squad, The
character: 9 Linc Hayes,
(Capt) Adam Greer **11** Julie
Barnes, Pete Cochran
cast: 11 Michael Cole, Peggy
Lipton, Tige Andrews
19 Clarence Williams III

modulate 4 pass **5** lower **6** accord, attune, change, reduce,
soften, temper **8** moderate,
progress, regulate, tone down,
turn down **9** harmonize

modulation 4 tone **5** pitch **6** accent **9** reduction **10** expression,
regulation, transition

modus operandi 15 mode of
operating
abbreviation: 2 mo

modus vivendi 14 manner of
living

Moerae *see* **5** Fates

Mogadishu, Mogadiscio
capital of: 7 Somalia

mogul 3 VIP **4** czar, lord
5 baron, power, wheel **6** bigwig, tycoon **7** big shot, magnate, notable **8** big wheel
9 personage, potentate

Mohammed *see box*

Mohammedan 4 Sufi **6** Moslem, Muslim, Shiite **7** Islamic,
Moorish, Sunnite **10** Mahome-
tan, Muhammadan,
Muhammedan

Mohave, Mojave
language family: 5 Yuman
location: 7 Arizona
10 California

Mohawk (Kaniengehaga)
language family: 9 Iroquoian
location: 6 Canada, Quebec
7 New York **11** Lake Ontario
leader: 8 Hiawatha **11** Joseph
Brant
member of: 19 League of the
Iroquois

Mohegan, Mohican, Mahican
language family: 9 Algonkian
10 Algonquian
location: 7 New York **9** Wisconsin **11** Connecticut
12 Hudson Valley
leader: 5 Occom, Uncas
12 Chingachgook
allied with: 6 Pequot
with Delaware: 11 Loup Indians, Wolf Indians

Mohammed
also: 7 Mahomet, Prophet
8 Muhammad
born: 5 Mecca
clan: 6 Hashim
daughter: 6 Fatima
deity: 5 Allah
died: 6 Medina
father: 8 Abdallah,
Abdullah
father-in-law: 7 Abu Bakr,
Abubekr
flight: 4 hadj **6** hegira,
hejira
follower: 6 Moslem, Muslim, Wahbi
10 Mohammedan
grandfather: 13 Abd al-
Muttalib
horse: 5 Buraq **7** Alborrak
mother: 5 Amina
religion: 5 Islam
shrine: 5 Kaaba
son: 7 Ibrahim
 adopted: **3** Ali
successor: 4 imam **5** calif
6 caliph **7** Abu Bakr
tribe: 7 Koreish, Quraysh
uncle: 5 Abbas **8** Abu
Talib
wife: 5 Aisha **6** Ayesha,
Safiya **7** Khadija **8** Khad-
idja, Kadijah

subject of novel: 20 The Last
of the Mohicans
 author: **19** James Fenimore
Cooper

Moira
personifies: 4 fate

Moirai *see* **5** Fates

moist 3 wet **4** damp, dank,
dewy **5** humid, misty, muggy,
rainy **6** clammy, drippy, watery
7 aqueous, drizzly, tearful,
wettish, wet-eyed **8** dripping,
vaporous **10** lachrymose

moisten 3 dew, wet **4** damp,
hose, mist, soak **5** spray, water
6 dampen, douche, splash,
sponge **8** humidify, irrigate,
saturate, vaporize **10** moisturize

moisture 3 dew, wet **4** damp,
mist **5** sweat, vapor **7** drizzle,
exudate, wetness **8** dampness,
dankness, humidity **9** moistness, mugginess **10** wateriness
11 evaporation **12** perspiration

Mojave *see* **6** Mohave

Moki *see* **4** Hopi

mold 3 cut, die, ilk **4** cast,
form, kind, line, make, rust,
sort, turn, type **5** brand, frame,
knead, model, shape, stamp,
train **6** blight, create, figure,
fungus, kidney, lichen, matrix,
mildew, render, sculpt, shaper
7 contour, convert, develop,
fashion, outline, pattern, quality, remodel **9** character, construct, formation, structure,
transform

Moldova
other name: 8 Moldavia
capital/largest city: 8 Chisinau, Kishinev
head of state: 9 president
government: 8 republic
monetary unit: 5 ruble
river: 8 Dniester
people: 7 Gagauzi **8** Moldovan
9 Moldavian
language: 8 Romanian
9 Moldavian
religion: 15 Russian Orthodox

moldy 5 fusty, hoary, musty,
stale **7** spoiled **8** mildewed

molest 3 irk, vex **4** fret, harm,
hurt **5** abuse, annoy, beset,
harry, worry **6** attack, bother,
harass, hector, injure, pester,
plague **7** assault, disturb, torment, trouble **8** maltreat

**Moliere (Jean-Baptiste
Poquelin)**
author of: 6 Scapin **8** Tartuffe,
The Miser **10** Amphitryon
13 Le Misanthrope **17** The
School for Wives **19** The
Imaginary Invalid **20** The
School for Husbands **22** Le
Bourgeois Gentilhomme

Moll Flanders
author: 11 Daniel Defoe
character: 5 Robin
6 Jemmy E **10** Sea Captain

mollification 8 soothing **9** pla-
cation **11** appeasement, assuagement **12** conciliation

mollify 4 calm, curb, dull, ease,
lull **5** abate, allay, blunt, check,
quell, quiet, still **6** lessen, pacify, reduce, soften, soothe,
temper **7** appease, assuage,
lighten, placate **8** decrease,
mitigate, moderate, palliate,
tone down

mollusk 4 clam, slug **5** conch,
cowry, murex, snail, squid,
whelk **6** chiton, cockle, cowrie,
limpet, mussel, oyster, teredo,
triton **7** abalone, bivalve, geoduck, octopus, scallop **8** argo-
naut, nautilus, shipworm
9 shellfish **10** cuttlefish, nudi-
branch, periwinkle

mollycoddle 3 pet **4** baby,
wimp **5** sissy, spoil **6** cosset,
coward, pamper **7** cater to,
crybaby, indulge, milksop
8 give in to, mama's boy,

weakling **9** cream puff
11 milquetoast, overindulge

Molnar, Ferenc
author of: **6** Liliom **7** The
Swan **12** The Guardsman

Moloch 3 god **5** diety
also: **6** Molech
worshiped by: **9** Ammonites

Molorchus
form: **7** peasant

Molossus
father: **11** Neoptolemus
mother: **10** Andromache

molt 4 cast, shed, slip
6 change, slough **7** castoff, discard, ecdysis **8** exuviate

molten 6 melted, red-hot **7** fu-
sible, igneous, smelted **8** mag-
matic **9** liquefied

molto
music: **4** very

Molus
father: **4** Ares
mother: **8** Demonice
son: **8** Meriones

Moly
form: **4** herb
given to: **8** Odysseus
given by: **6** Hermes
to counteract spells of:
5 Circe

Momaday, N Scott
author of: **18** The House
Made of Dawn **21** The Way
to Rainy Mountain

moment 5 flash, jiffy, trice,
value, worth **6** import, minute,
second, weight **7** concern,
gravity, instant **8** interest,
juncture **9** twinkling **10** importance **11** consequence,
weightiness **12** significance

momentary 5 brief, hasty,
quick, short **6** sudden **7** instant, passing **8** flashing, fleeting, fugitive, imminent
9 ephemeral, immediate, temporary, transient **10** short-
lived, transitory
13 instantaneous

momentous 5 grave **7** crucial,
fateful, salient, serious,
weighty **8** critical, decisive,
eventful **9** essential, important,
ponderous **11** far-reaching, influential, significant, substantial **12** earthshaking
13 consequential

momentous occurrence
5 event **8** occasion **9** milestone **12** red-letter day, turning point

momentum 2 go **4** dash, push
5 drive, force, speed, vigor
6 energy, moment, thrust

7 headway, impetus, impulse
8 velocity **10** propulsion

Mommsen, Theodor
author of: **16** The History of
Rome

Momus
also: **5** Momos
god of: **7** censure **8** ridicule

Monaco *see box*

Monaco-Ville
capital of: **6** Monaco

monarch 3 HRH **4** czar, doge,
emir, khan, king, rani, shah
5 rajah, ruler, queen **6** kaiser,
prince **7** czarina, emperor, empress, majesty, pharaoh
8 kaiserin, princess **9** chieftain,
potentate

monarchical 9 czaristic **10** autocratic **11** dictatorial

monastery 5 abbey **6** friary,
priory **7** convent, nunnery, retreat **8** cloister

monastic 7 ascetic, monkish,
recluse **8** celibate, hermitic, secluded, solitary **9** cloistral, reclusive, unworldly
10 cloistered, hermitlike
11 sequestered
13 contemplative

mon cher 6 my dear

Moncrieff, Algernon (Algy)
character in: **27** The Importance of Being Earnest
author: **5** Wilde

Mond, Mustapha
character in: **13** Brave New
World
author: **6** Huxley

Monday
French: **5** lundi
German: **6** montag
heavenly body: **4** moon
Italian: **6** lunedi
means: **12** day of the moon
Spanish: **5** lunes

Mondrian, Piet
real name: **23** Pieter Cornelis
Mondriaan
born: **10** Amersfoort **14** The
Netherlands
artwork: **5** Trees **10** The Red
Tree **12** Ocean and Pier
17 Evening Landscapes
18 Landscape with a Mill
20 Broadway Boogie-
Woogie **29** Composition in
Red Yellow and Blue

Monet, Claude Oscar
born: **5** Paris **6** France
artwork: **7** Poplars **9** Hay-
stacks, The Thames **11** Water Lilies **14** Rouen
Cathedral **16** Women in the
Garden **17** Impression Sunrise **18** Mornings on the
Seine **21** The Bridge at
Argenteuil

Moneta
epithet of: **4** Juno
means: **7** advisor

monetary 6 fiscal **9** budgetary,

Monaco
capital: **11** Monaco-Ville
largest city: **10** Monte Carlo
others: **9** Fontville
division: **9** Fontville **10** Monte Carlo **11** La Condamine,
Monaco-Ville
head of government: **15** minister of state
head of state: **6** prince
monetary unit: **5** franc **7** centime
river: **7** Vesubie
sea: **13** Mediterranean
physical feature: **9** Cote d'Azur
people: **6** French **7** Italian **10** Monegasque
oceanographer: **15** Jacques Cousteau
prince: **5** Louis **6** Albert, Honore **7** Antoine, Charles,
Rainier **9** Florestan
princess: **10** Grace Kelly
ruler: **4** Rome **5** Genoa **6** Greece **8** Grimaldi, Saracens
9 Phoenicia
language: **6** French **7** English, Italian **10** Monegasque
religion: **13** Roman Catholic
place:
beach: **8** Larvotto
casino: **10** Monte Carlo
gardens: **6** Exotic
museum: **12** Oceanography
park: **18** Princess Antoinette
feature:
auto race: **15** Monaco Grand Prix

financial, pecuniary,
sumptuary

money 4 cash, coin 5 bread,
bucks, dough, funds 6 assets,
riches, specie, wealth 7 capital,
coinage, payment, revenue,
scratch 8 currency, hard cash,
proceeds 9 affluence, long
green 10 collateral, green-
backs 11 wherewithal

money-carrier
French: 12 porte-monnaie

moneyed, monied 4 rich
5 flush, swell 6 flashy, loaded
7 elegant, opulent, solvent,
wealthy 8 affluent
10 prosperous

money-grubbing 5 venal
6 greedy 8 covetous, grasping
9 mercenary 10 avaricious

money lender 6 banker,
lender, usurer 7 lombard, shylock 9 loanshark
10 pawnbroker

money saved 7 nest egg, savings 10 investment

money spent 6 outlay 7 payment 8 expenses
11 expenditure

Mongolia *see box*

Mongolian
language family: 6 Altaic
group: 6 Buryat 7 Khalkha

Mongoose, The
nickname of: 11 Archie
Moore

mongrel 3 cur 4 mutt 5 mixed
6 hybrid 7 bastard 8 offshoot
9 anomalous, crossbred
10 crossbreed

moniker 3 tag 4 name 5 label,
title 6 eponym, handle 7 epithet, surname 8 cognomen,
nickname, taxonomy 9 sobriquet 11 appellation, designation 12 denomination

monitor 2 TV 4 tend 5 guide,
teach 6 censor, direct, pickup,
police, screen, sensor 7 oversee, proctor, scanner 8 overseer, watchdog 9 supervise
14 disciplinarian

monk 4 abbe 5 abbot, friar
6 hermit 7 brother, holy man,
recluse 8 cenobite, monastic
9 anchorite
French: 5 frere

Monk, The
author: 19 Matthew Gregory
Lewis

Monkees, The
cast/musician: 9 Davy Jones,
Peter Tork 10 David Jones
11 Micky Dolenz, Mike
Nesmith

Mongolia
other name: 13 Outer Mongolia
capital/largest city: 9 Ulan Bator
others: 5 Kobdo 6 Darhan 10 Choibalsan, Sukhe Bator,
Tsetserlik, Uliassutai
ancient capital: 9 Karakoram
government:
legislature: 17 People's Great Hural 18 People's Great
Khural
monetary unit: 5 mongo, mungo 6 tugrik 7 tughrik
weight: 3 lan
lake: 3 Uvs 5 Har Us 6 Bor Nor 7 Ghirgis, Ubsa Nor
8 Airik Nor, Durga Nor, Hobsogol, Khara Usu 9 Khubsugul, Khukhu-Nur 10 Khirgis Nor
mountain: 4 Cast, Orog 5 Altai 6 Kentei, Sevrej 7 Ich
Ovoo, Khangai, Khentei 8 Tannu-Ola 9 Edrengijn 10 Cagaan Bogd 11 Munky Sardyk 14 Hangayn-Hentiyn,
Monch Chajrchan
highest point: 10 Tabun Bogdo
river: 3 Tes 4 Egin, Onon, Tuul, Uldz 5 Kobdo, Tesin
6 Orkhon 7 Kerulen, Selenga, Selenge 8 Dzabkhan,
Dzavchan
physical feature:
desert: 4 Gobi 5 Ordos, Shamo
plateau: 8 Mongolia
region: 10 Great Lakes
people: 5 Oirat, Tungu 6 Buryat, Darbet, Khoton, Mongol
7 Kazakhs, Khalkha 8 Tuvinian 9 Dariganga
leader: 8 Jahangir, Jehangir 10 Kublai Khan, Tsendenbal 11 Genghis Khan
ruler: 4 Huns 5 Ching 6 Manchu 7 Kirghiz, Uighurs
8 Hsiung-nu
spiritual/secular ruler: 12 Living Buddha 21 Jebtsun
Damba Khutu Khtu
language: 6 Kazakh 16 Khalkha Mongolian
religion: 7 Lamaism 9 Shamanism 15 Tibetan Buddhism
place:
monastery: 6 Gandun
feature:
felt tent: 4 yurt
nomadic herder: 4 arat
food:
fermented mare's milk: 5 airag

monkey 3 ape, ass, toy 4 butt,
dupe, fool, jerk 5 clown,
jimmy 6 baboon, fiddle, meddle, simian, tamper, tinker,
trifle 7 buffoon, primate
13 laughingstock
group of: 5 troop
god: 7 Hanuman
kind: 3 owl 4 saki, titi
5 aotus, lemur 6 baboon,
guenon, howler, langur,
rhesus, spider 7 colobus,
Goeldi's, guereza, macaque,
tamarin, tarsier, uakaris
8 capuchin, mandrill, marmoset, squirrel, talapoin
11 douroucouli

monkey business 6 capers
9 highjinks 11 shenanigans

monkeyshines 6 antics, capers, pranks 7 hijinks 10 buffoonery, tomfoolery
11 foolishness

Monks (Edward Leeford)
character in: 11 Oliver Twist
author: 7 Dickens

monocle 4 quiz 5 glass 7 lorg-
non 8 eyeglass

Monoclonius
type: 8 dinosaur
10 ceratopsid
location: 12 North America
characteristic: 6 horned

Monod, Jacques
field: 7 biology
nationality: 6 French
researched: 3 RNA 8 genetics
awarded: 10 Nobel Prize

monograph 8 tractate, treatise
9 discourse 12 disquisition,
dissertation

monolith 5 stone 6 column,
menhir, pillar, statue 7 obelisk 8 memorial, monument

monologue, monolog
6 screed, sermon, speech 7 address, lecture, oration 9 discourse, soliloquy
11 expatiation 12 disquisition

monopolize 3 own 6 absorb, corner, manage, take up
7 consume, control, preempt
8 arrogate, dominate, regulate, take over 9 cartelize
11 appropriate

monopoly 4 bloc 5 trust 6 cartel, corner 7 combine, control
8 dominion 9 copyright, ownership, syndicate 10 consortium, domination
11 sovereignty 12 jurisdiction
14 proprietorship

monotonous 3 dry 4 dull, flat
5 banal 6 boring, dreary, jejune, stodgy, torpid 7 droning, humdrum, insipid, mundane, prosaic, routine, tedious
8 plodding, singsong, tiresome, toneless, unvaried 9 colorless, soporific, wearisome 10 pedestrian 11 repetitious, somniferous 13 uninteresting

monotony 3 rut 5 ennui 6 tedium 7 boredom, humdrum
8 dullness, flatness, prosaism, sameness 9 iteration 10 dreariness, redundancy, uniformity
11 reiteration, tediousness
13 wearisomeness
14 predictability

Monroe, Earl
nickname: 12 Earl the Pearl
sport: 10 basketball
position: 5 guard
team: 16 Baltimore Bullets
　　21 New York
　　Knickerbockers

Monroe, James *see box*

Monroe, Marilyn
real name: 23 Norma Jean
　　Mortenson Baker
husband: 11 Joe DiMaggio
　　12 Arthur Miller
born: 12 Los Angeles CA
roles: 7 Bus Stop, Niagara
　　10 The Misfits 13 Some Like
　　It Hot 16 The Seven-Year
　　Itch 22 Gentlemen Prefer
　　Blondes, How To Marry a
　　Millionaire 23 The Prince
　　and the Showgirl

Monrovia
capital of: 7 Liberia

monseigneur 6 my lord

monsieur 2 Mr 3 sir 6 mister, my lord

Monsieur Beaucaire
author: 15 Booth Tarkington

Monsignor Quixote
author: 12 Graham Greene

Monroe, James
presidential rank: 5 fifth
party: 20 Democratic-Republican
state represented: 2 VA
defeated: 4 (Rufus) King 5 (John Quincy) Adams
vice president: 8 (Daniel D) Tompkins
cabinet:
　　state: 5 (John Quincy) Adams
　　treasury: 8 (William Harris) Crawford
　　war: 7 (John Caldwell) Calhoun
　　attorney general: 4 (Richard) Rush, (William) Wirt
　　navy: 8 (Samuel Lewis) Southard, (Smith) Thompson
　　　　13 (Benjamin Williams) Crowninshield
born: 2 VA 18 Westmoreland County
died: 13 New York City NY
buried: 10 Richmond VA
education: 14 William and Mary (did not graduate)
religion: 12 Episcopalian
author: 67 A View of the Conduct of the Executive in the
　　Foreign Affairs of the United States
political career: 8 US Senate
　　governor of: 8 Virginia
　　minister: 5 Spain 6 France 12 Great Britain
　　secretary of: 3 war 5 state
civilian career: 6 lawyer
military service: 5 major 7 captain 10 lieutenant 16 Revolutionary War 17 lieutenant colonel
　　wounded in Battle of: 7 Trenton
notable events of lifetime/term: 5 Panic (of 1819)
　　14 Monroe Doctrine
　　Agreement: 9 Rush-Bagot
　　Compromise: 8 Missouri
　　war: 8 Seminole
father: 6 Spence
mother: 9 Elizabeth (Jones)
siblings: 6 Andrew, Spence 9 Elizabeth 11 Joseph Jones
wife: 9 Elizabeth (Kortright)
　　nickname: 5 Eliza
children: 11 Maria Hester 14 Eliza Kortright

---

monster 4 Fury 5 beast, brute, demon, devil, fiend, freak, ghoul, giant, golem, harpy, hydra, satyr, titan 6 dragon, gorgon, marvel, oddity, savage, threat, wonder, wretch, zombie 7 anomaly, caitiff, centaur, chimera, deviant, incubus, mammoth, mermaid, vampire, variant, villain 8 bogeyman, colossus, gargoyle, succubus, werewolf 9 barbarian, curiosity, cutthroat, scoundrel 10 blackguard, phenomenon 11 abnormality, miscreation 12 Frankenstein, lusus naturae

monstrosity 5 freak 7 monster

monstrous 4 bald, evil, huge
5 cruel, giant 6 grisly, mighty, odious 7 ghastly, harried, heinous, hideous, hulking, immense, mammoth, obscene, obvious, satanic, titanic, vicious 8 colossal, enormous, fiendish, flagrant, gigantic, gruesome, horrible, outright, shocking 9 atrocious, egre-

gious, nefarious, revolting
10 diabolical, gargantuan, outrageous, prodigious, scandalous, stupendous, tremendous, villainous 14 Brobdingnagian

monstrousness 8 baseness, enormity, evilness, vileness, villainy 9 barbarity, depravity, malignity 10 inhumanity, wickedness 11 heinousness, viciousness 13 atrociousness, offensiveness 14 outrageousness

Montagnais-Naskapi (Innu)
language family: 9 Algonkian 10 Algonquian
　　tribe: 8 Nascapee 9 Mistassin
　　10 Bersiamite, Montagnais
　　11 Papinachois
location: 5 Maine 6 Canada, Quebec 17 Maritime
　　Provinces
occupation: 7 hunters 10 fur traders

Montague family
characters in: 14 Romeo and Juliet
author: 11 Shakespeare

Montaigne, Michel de
author of: 6 Essais, Essays

Montalban, Ricardo
born: 6 Mexico 10 Mexico
City
roles: 4 Khan 8 Mr Roarke
9 The Colbys 13 Fantasy Island 24 Star Trek II The
Wrath of Khan

Montalvo, Garcia de
author of: 12 Amadis of Gaul

Montana *see box*

Montana, Bob
creator/artist of: 6 Archie

Montand, Yves
real name: 7 Ivo Livi
wife: 14 Simone Signoret
born: 5 Italy 14 Monsum-
mano Alto
roles: 1 Z 12 Let's Make
Love 14 Is Paris Burning?

montani semper liberi
28 mountaineers are always
free men
motto of: 12 West Virginia

Montcalm, Louis Joseph
also: 17 Marquis de
Montcalm
nationality: 6 French
served in: 18 French and Indian War
battle: 6 Oswego, Quebec
(siege) 8 Carillon 11 Ticonderoga 16 Fort William
Henry
killed in battle at: 6 Quebec
15 Plains of Abraham

mont-de-piete 10 pawnbroker
literally: 10 bank of pity

Montenegro *see box*

Monteverdi, Claudio
born: 5 Italy 7 Cremona
composer of: 5 Adone, Or-
feo 7 Arianna 14 La Favola
d'Orfeo 17 The Fable of Orpheus 21 The Coronation of
Poppea 22 L'incoronazione
di Poppea 24 Il Ritorno
d'Ulisse in patria 34 Il Com-
battimento di Tancredi e
Clorinda

Montevideo
capital of: 7 Uruguay

Montana
abbreviation: 2 MT 4 Mont
nickname: 6 Big Sky 7 Bonanza, Stubtoe 8 Mountain,
Treasure
capital: 6 Helena
largest city: 8 Billings
others: 4 Kipp 5 Butte, Havre, Malta 6 Hardin 7 Bozeman,
Chinook, Choteau, Forsyth, Glasgow, Roundup 8 Anaconda, Missoula 9 Kalispell 10 Great Falls
college: 7 Carroll 10 Great Falls 13 Rocky Mountain
feature: 17 Continental Divide
  cemetery: 6 Custer
  national park: 7 Glacier 11 Yellowstone
tribe: 4 Cree, Crow, Hohe 5 Sioux 6 Atsima, Atsina, Salish 7 Arapaho, Bannock, Kutenai, Siksika 8 Cheyenne,
Chippewa, Flatfoot, Flathead, Shoshone 9 Blackfeet
11 Assiniboine
people: 8 Myrna Loy 9 Will James 10 Gary Cooper
14 Charles Russell 15 Jeannette Rankin
  explorer: 13 Lewis and Clark 16 Pierre Jean de Smet
lake: 5 Tiber 6 Hebgen 8 Flathead, Fort Peck, Medicine
10 Yellowtail 11 Canyon Ferry, Hungry Horse
land rank: 6 fourth
mountain: 4 Ajax 5 Baldy, Cowan, Crazy, Lewis 6 Sphinx,
Torrey 7 Bighorn, Big Belt, Hilgard, Purcell, Rockies,
Trapper 8 Absaroka, Gallatin, Pentagon, Snowshoe
  highest point: 11 Granite Peak
physical feature: 10 Great Falls
river: 3 Sun 4 Milk 5 Clark, Teton 6 Marias, Powder,
Tongue, Willow 7 Madison, Shields 8 Columbia,
Kootenai, Missouri 9 Blackfoot 10 Bitterroot 11 Mussel-
shell, Yellowstone
state admission: 10 forty-first
state bird: 17 western meadowlark
state fish: 26 black-spotted cutthroat trout
state flower: 10 bitterroot
state motto: 13 Gold and Silver
state song: 7 Montana
state tree: 13 Ponderosa pine

Montenegro
name means: 13 black
mountain
other name: 4 Zeta
8 Crna Gora
capital: 7 Cetinje 8 Titograd 9 Podgorica
cities: 3 Bar 5 Kotor, Ti-
vat 6 Niksic, Ulcinj
8 Antivari, Dulcigno,
Ivangrad, Pljevlja
10 Hercegnovi 11 Sveti
Stefan
division:
  Roman province:
  7 Illyria
governed by:
  10 Yugoslavia
monetary unit: 4 para
6 florin 7 perpera
lake: 7 Scutari, Shkoder
mountain: 8 Durmitor
11 Dinaric Alps
river: 3 Lim 4 Piva, Tara,
Zeta 6 Moraca
7 Ceotina
sea: 8 Adriatic
physical feature:
  gulf: 5 Kotor
people: 4 Serb, Slav
11 Montenegrin
  *former ruler (Ortho-
  dox bishop):* 7 vla-
  dike 8 vladlika
language: 13 Serbo-
Croatian
religion: 16 Serbian
Orthodoxy

Montgomery, Bernard Law
see box

Montgomery, Robert
real name: 17 Henry Mont-
gomery Jr
daughter: 9 Elizabeth
born: 8 Beacon NY
roles: 11 The Big House
13 Night Must Fall 17 Here
Comes Mr Jordan

month
abbreviation: 2 mo

Month in the Country, A
author: 12 Ivan Turgenev

months, Hebrew *see box*

Mont-Oriol
author: 15 Guy de
Maupassant

Montreal *see box*

Montresor
character in: 20 The Cask of
Amontillado
author: 3 Poe

**Mont Saint Michel and
Chartres**
author: 10 Henry Adams

Montgomery, Bernard Law
also: **27** (first) Viscount Montgomery of Alamein
author of: **7** Memoirs **17** A History of Warfare
battle: **9** El Alamein
chief: **19** British general staff
commander of: **17** British Eighth Army **32** British occupation forces in Germany
commando raid: **6** Dieppe
deputy supreme commander: **4** NATO
Eighth Army called: **10** Desert Rats
evacuation of: **7** Dunkirk
fought against: **6** Rommel **11** Africa Corps, Afrika Korps
invasion: **6** Sicily **8** Normandy
member: **12** House of Lords
nationality: **7** British
nickname: **5** Monty
served in: **3** WWI **4** WWII

months, Hebrew
first: **4** Ahib, Nisn **6** Ehanim, Tishri
second: **3** Bul, Civ **4** Iyar **7** Heshvan
third: **5** Sivan **6** Kislev
fourth: **5** Tebet **6** Tammuz, Tebeth
fifth: **2** Ab **7** Shelbat
sixth: **4** Adar, Elul **6** Veadar
seventh: **4** Abib **5** Nisan **6** Tishri **7** Ethanim
eighth: **3** Zif **4** Iyar **11** Marcheshvan
ninth: **5** Sivan **7** Chislev
tenth: **6** Tebeth, Tammuz
eleventh: **2** Ab **6** Shabat
twelfth: **4** Adar, Elul

Monty
nickname of: **15** Montgomery Clift **17** (General) Bernard Montgomery

monument 4 slab **5** token **6** shrine **7** memento, obelisk, witness **8** cenotaph, memorial, monolith, reminder **9** testament, tombstone **10** gravestone **11** remembrance, testimonial **13** commemoration

Montreal
airport: **6** Dorval **8** St Hubert **12** Cartierville
baseball team: **5** Expos
founder: **11** Maisonneuve
hill: **10** Mount Royal
hockey team: **9** Canadiens
island: **5** Jesus **6** Bizard, Perrot **8** Montreal **9** des Soeurs **14** de Boucherville
lake: **7** St Louis
landmark: **12** Place des Arts **13** Molson Stadium **16** Chateau de Ramezay **17** Church of Notre Dame, St Sulpice Seminary **21** Man and His World Exhibit
original name: **10** Ville-Marie
province: **6** Quebec
river: **6** Ottawa **10** St Lawrence **11** des Prairies **14** des Milles Isles
subway: **5** Metro
university: **6** McGill

monumental 4 huge **5** fatal, heavy **7** awesome, classic, epochal, immense, lasting, massive **8** colossal, decisive, enduring, gigantic, historic, immortal, statuary **9** cyclopean, egregious, memorable **10** horrendous, monolithic, shattering, stupendous **11** inestimable **12** catastrophic **13** unprecedented

mooch 3 beg, bum **5** cadge **6** hustle, sponge **7** solicit **8** freeload

mood 5 blues, dumps, humor **6** spirit, temper **7** feeling **8** doldrums, vexation **9** condition **10** depression, gloominess, melancholy **11** disposition, melancholia, temperament **14** predisposition **16** hypersensitivity

moody 4 mean **5** sulky, surly, testy **6** crabby, dismal, fickle, gloomy, mopish, morbid, morose, sullen **7** erratic, flighty, peevish, unhappy **8** brooding, dejected, notional, variable, volatile **9** impetuous, impulsive, irascible, irritable, mercurial, saturnine, whimsical **10** capricious, changeable, despondent, inconstant, lugubrious, melancholy **11** pessimistic **12** inconsistent **13** temperamental, unpredictable

Mookerjee, Hurree Chunder
character in: **3** Kim
author: **7** Kipling

moon 4 gape, lamp, luna, roam **5** dream, month, stare **6** dawdle, wander **8** daydream **9** satellite
god of: **3** Sin **5** Nanna **6** Meztli
goddess of: **4** Luna **5** Diana, Holle, Tanit **6** Hecate, Hekate, Phoebe, Selena, Selene, Tanith **7** Artemis, Astarte, Cynthia
full: **9** plenilune
new: **5** prime
waning: **7** waiand

Moon and Sixpence, The
author: **16** W Somerset Maugham

moonless 4 dark **5** black, murky **7** stygian **9** lightless, unlighted **13** unilluminated

Moonlighting
character: **11** Maddie Hayes **12** Agnes Dipesto, David Addison
cast: **11** Bruce Willis **13** Allyce Beasley **14** Cybill Shepherd
detective agency: **8** Blue Moon

Moon Mullins
creator: **12** Frank Willard
character: **4** Kayo **5** Mamie **9** Mushmouth **11** Uncle Willie **15** Lady Plushbottom, Lord Plushbottom **16** Moonshine Mullins

Moon of the Caribbees, The
author: **12** Eugene O'Neill

moonshine 5 hokum **6** bunkum, humbug **7** bootleg **8** clockade, homebrew, malarky, nonsense **10** balderdash, bathtub gin **11** mountain dew

moonstone
species: **8** feldspar
source: **5** Burma, Mogok

Moonstone, The
author: **13** Wilkie Collins
character: **7** Dr Candy **12** Lady Verinder, Sergeant Cuff **13** Franklin Blake **14** John Herncastle, Rachel Verinder **15** Rosanna Spearman **16** Godfrey Ablewhite

moor 3 fen **4** dock, down, fell, lash, wold **5** affix, berth, chain, heath, marsh, tie up **6** anchor, attach, fasten, secure, steppe, tether, tundra, upland **7** savanna, tie down **8** make fast **9** wasteland

Moore, Archie
nickname: **11** The Mongoose

real name: 18 Archibald Lee Wright
sport: 6 boxing
class: 16 light-heavyweight

Moore, Clement C
author of: 23 A Visit from Saint Nicholas

Moore, Dick
creator/artist of: 13 Gasoline Alley

Moore, Dudley
nickname: 12 Cuddly Dudley
wife: 11 Suzy Kendall, Tuesday Weld
born: 5 Essex **7** England **8** Dagenham
roles: 3 Ten **6** Arthur **8** Lovesick, Six Weeks **9** Bedazzled **13** Micki and Maude **16** Arthur on the Rocks **17** Like Father Like Son
plays: 5 piano

Moore, George
author of: 12 Esther Waters **15** Hail and Farewell

Moore, Henry
born: 7 England **10** Castleford
artwork: 4 Mask **8** Two Forms **9** North Wind **10** Bird Basket **11** Family Group, Head of a Girl **12** Locking Piece **13** Nuclear Energy **15** Reclining Figure **20** Four-Piece Composition

Moore, Marianne
author of: 12 Like a Bulwark, Nevertheless, O To Be a Dragon, Tell Me Tell Me

Moore, Mary Tyler
husband: 11 Grant Tinker
born: 10 Brooklyn NY
roles: 4 Mary **12** Mary Richards **14** Ordinary People **18** The Dick Van Dyke Show **21** The Mary Tyler Moore Show

Moore, Mrs
character in: 15 A Passage to India
author: 7 Forster

Moore, Roger
born: 6 London **7** England
roles: 8 The Saint **12** Simon Templar
as James Bond: **9** Moonraker, Octopussy **13** Live and Let Die **16** The Spy Who Loved Me **22** The Man with the Golden Gun

Moorehead, Agnes
born: 9 Clinton MA
roles: 6 Endora **9** Bewitched **11** Citizen Kane **13** Johnny Belinda **15** Dear Dead Delilah **20** Magnificent Obsession **23** The Magnificent Ambersons

mooring 4 hook, line, rope **5** cable, chain **6** anchor, hawser

moot 4 open **7** eristic **8** arguable, disputed **9** debatable, undecided, unsettled **10** disputable, unresolved **11** conjectural **12** questionable **13** controversial, problematical **14** controvertible

mope 4 fret, pine, pout, sulk **5** brood, worry **6** grieve, grouse, lament, repine **7** grumble **8** languish

Mopsus
occupation: 4 seer
mother: 5 Manto
grandfather: 8 Tiresias
member of: 9 Argonauts
founded: 6 oracle
location: 6 Mallus **7** Cilicia
cofounder: 11 Amphilochus
epithet: 9 Ampycides

moral 3 tag **4** fair, just, pure **5** adage, maxim, motto, noble, right **6** honest, lesson, proper, saying **7** epigram, ethical, message, proverb, saintly **8** aphorism, didactic, personal, virtuous **9** estimable, homiletic, honorable, preaching **10** aboveboard, high-minded, principled **11** meritorious, sermonizing, tendentious **12** conscionable

moral code 6 ethics **9** integrity, standards **10** principles

morale 4 mood **6** spirit, temper **10** confidence, resolution **11** disposition
French: 13 esprit de corps

morality 5 honor **6** ethics, habits, tastes, virtue **7** modesty, probity **8** fairness, goodness **9** integrity, rectitude **10** chasteness **11** uprightness **13** righteousness

moralize 6 preach **7** lecture

moralizing 7 preachy **8** didactic **9** homiletic

morally corrupt 6 effete **8** decadent, depraved **10** degenerate

moral sense 9 integrity **10** conscience

morass 3 bog, fen **4** mire **5** marsh, swamp **6** slough **8** quagmire, wetlands **9** quicksand

morbid 3 sad **4** dour, glum, grim **5** moody **6** gloomy, morose, somber **8** brooding **9** depressed, saturnine **10** despondent, lugubrious **11** melancholic, pessimistic, unwholesome

morbid condition 6 malady **7** ailment, disease, illness **8** sickness **9** infirmity

Morcerf, Comte de (Fernand)
character in: 21 The Count of Monte Cristo
author: 5 Dumas (pere)

mordant 6 biting, bitter **7** acerbic, caustic, cutting, waspish **8** incisive, piercing, scathing, scornful, stinging, venomous, virulent **9** acidulous, malicious, sarcastic, trenchant **11** acrimonious

Mordecai
cousin: 6 Esther
served: 15 Ahasuerus Xerxes
enemy: 5 Haman

more 5 added, extra, other, spare **6** longer **7** further, reserve **10** additional **12** additionally, supplemental **13** supplementary

More, Thomas
author of: 6 Utopia

Moreau, Frederic
character in: 21 A Sentimental Education
author: 8 Flaubert

Moreau, Gustave
born: 5 Paris **6** France
artwork: 7 Orpheus **13** Dance of Salome (Salome Dancing), The Apparition **16** Hesiod and the Muse **18** The Poet and the Siren **19** Oedipus and the Sphinx **27** Diomedes Devoured by His Horses

Morehouse, J Ward
character in: 3 USA
author: 9 Dos Passos

Morel, Paul
character in: 13 Sons and Lovers
author: 8 Lawrence

Moreno, Rita
real name: 20 Rosita Dolores Alverio
born: 7 Humacao **10** Puerto Rico
roles: 13 Pagan Love Song, The Deerslayer, West Side Story **15** Singin' in the Rain

more or less 5 about **6** around **8** somewhat **9** generally, just about **13** approximately

moreover 3 too **4** also **7** besides, further **11** furthermore **12** more than that

mores 4 code **5** ethos, forms, rules **7** customs, rituals **9** etiquette, practices, standards **10** traditions

11 conventions, observances, proprieties

more than enough 5 ample **6** excess, plenty **7** copious, profuse **8** plethora **9** abundance, amplitude, bountiful, excessive, profusion **10** oversupply

Morgan, Daniel
served in: **16** Revolutionary War
commander of: **8** riflemen **13** sharpshooters
battle: **7** Cowpens **8** Saratoga **12** Bemis Heights, Freeman's Farm
helped suppress: **16** Whiskey Rebellion

Morgan, Thomas Hunt
founder of: **8** genetics
awarded: **10** Nobel Prize

Morgan, William De
author of: **11** Joseph Vance

Morgan family
characters in: **19** How Green Was My Valley
members: **4** Beth, Davy, Huur, Ivor, Owen **5** Ianto **6** Gwilym **8** Angharad
author: **9** Llewellyn

morganite
color: **4** pink **5** peach

Morgan le Fay
character in: **16** Arthurian romance

Moriae Encomium (In Praise of Folly)
author: **7** Erasmus

Moriarty, Professor
character in: **14** (The Adventures of) Sherlock Holmes
author: **10** Conan Doyle

moribund 5 dying **6** doomed, waning **10** stagnating

Morier, James
author of: **18** Hajji Baba of Ispahan

morituri te salutamus 28 we who are about to die salute thee
said by: **15** Roman gladiators
said to: **13** Roman emperors

Mork & Mindy
character: **4** Mork **6** Eugene **10** Cora Hudson **13** Mindy McConnel **17** Frederick McConnel
cast: **9** Pam Dawber **11** Conrad Janis **13** Elizabeth Kerr, Robin Williams **14** Jeffrey Jacquet
Mork's planet: **3** Ork
phrase: **8** nanu nanu
spinoff from: **9** Happy Days

Morland, Catherine
character in: **15** Northanger Abbey
author: **6** Austen

Morley, Robert
born: **6** Semley **7** England
roles: **5** Melba **10** Oscar Wilde **11** Beau Brummel, Edward My Son **12** Major Barbara **15** Marie Antoinette, The African Queen **21** The Man Who Came to Dinner

Mormon State
nickname of: **4** Utah

morning 4 dawn **5** early, sunup **7** sunrise **8** daybreak, daylight, forenoon **9** matutinal

morning-glory 7 Ipomoea **10** Calystegia **11** Convolvulus
varieties: **3** red **4** wild **5** beach, dwarf **6** Ceylon, common, silver, woolly, yellow **9** Brazilian **16** Imperial Japanese

Morocco *see box*

moron 3 ass, nut, oaf, sap **4** boob, dolt, dope, fool **5** dummy, dunce, idiot, loony, ninny **6** dimwit, nitwit **7** halfwit, jackass **8** bonehead, dumbbell, dumbhead, imbecile,

---

Morocco
other name: **7** Barbary **8** Maroquin **9** Al Maghrib **13** Maghrib el Aksa **19** Mauretania Tingitana
capital: **5** Rabat **6** Rabbat
largest city: **10** Casablanca
others: **3** Fes, Fez, Sla **4** Ifni, Safi, Sale, Sali, Taza **5** Ceuta, Oujda, Porte, Saffi **6** Agadir, Meknes, Semara, Tetuan **7** Elarish, Kenitra, Larache, Mazagan, Mililla, Mogador, Tangier, Tetouan **8** Kouribga, Tinerhir **9** Marrakech, Marrakesh **10** Youssoufia **11** Port-Lyautey
division:
  disputed territory: **13** Western Sahara
head of state: **4** king
measure: **4** kala, muhd, rotl, saah, sahh, ueba **5** artal, cadee, gerbe, ratel **6** covado, dirhem, fanega, izenbi, kintar, tangin, tomini **8** quintral
monetary unit: **4** flue, okia, rial **5** floos, franc, okieh, ounce **6** dirham, miskal **8** mouzouna
weight: **4** rotl **5** artel, ratel **6** dirhem, kintar **7** quintal
island: **7** Madeira
mountain: **3** Rif **4** Bani **5** Abyla, Atlas, Sarro **8** Tidiguin **9** Anti-Atlas, High Atlas, Jebel-Musa **11** Middle Atlas
highest point: **12** Jebel Toubkal **13** Djebel Toubkal
river: **3** Dra, Ziz **4** Sous **5** Sebou **6** Gheris **7** Tensift **8** Moulouya **9** Oum er Rbia
sea: **8** Atlantic **13** Mediterranean
physical feature:
  cape: **3** Nun, Sim **4** Juby, Noun, Rhir **6** Cantin
  desert: **6** Sahara
  oasis: **8** Tafilelt
  plain: **5** Rharb
  strait: **9** Gibraltar
  valley: **7** Ouergha
  wind: **5** leste **7** charqui
people: **4** Arab, Moor **6** Berber, French **7** Spanish
  dynasty: **7** Alawite, Almohad **9** Almoravid
  leader: **5** Idris **7** Lyautey **8** Hassan II **9** Abd el-Krim
  philosopher: **8** Averroes
language: **6** Arabic, Berber, French **7** Spanish
religion: **5** Islam
place:
  ruins: **9** Volubilis
feature:
  clothing: **4** haik **7** jellaba
  hat: **3** fez
  Islamic holy war: **5** jehad, jihad
  shanty town: **10** bidonville
food:
  dish: **8** couscous

numskull 9 blockhead, numb-skull, simpleton **10** mutton-head, nincompoop

Moroni
capital of: **7** Comoros

Moros
mother: **3** Nyx
personifies: **4** fate

morose 3 low, sad **4** blue, dour, glum, sour **5** cross, moody, sulky, surly, testy **6** cranky, gloomy, grumpy, mopish, solemn, sullen **7** waspish **8** churlish, down-cast, mournful **9** depressed, irascible, saturnine **10** despon-dent, melancholy **11** crestfallen

moroseness 5 gloom **8** glum-ness **9** pessimism, sulkiness, surliness **10** sullenness

Morpheus
god of: **6** dreams
father: **6** Hypnos

morphology
study of: **9** structure

Morris, Dinah
character in: **8** Adam Bede
author: **5** Eliot

Morris, Willie
author of: **5** Yazoo **10** Good Old Boy **15** North Toward Home

Morris, Wright
author of: **8** Will's Boy **10** Plain's Song **13** Field of Vision, My Uncle Dudley

Morrison, Jeanette Helen
real name of: **10** Janet Leigh

Morrison, Marion Michael
real name of: **9** John Wayne

Morrison, Toni
real name: **19** Chloe An-thony Wofford
author of: **4** Sula, Jazz **7** Be-loved, Tar Baby **12** The Blu-est Eye **13** Song of Solomon
honor: **10** Nobel Price **13** Pu-litzer Prize

Morrow, Vic
born: **7** Bronx NY
roles: **6** Combat **8** Cimarron **14** God's Little Acre **15** The Twilight Zone **18** Portrait of a Mobster **19** The Black-board Jungle

Morse, Samuel F B
nationality: **8** American
invented: **9** Morse code **17** electric telegraph **24** electromagnetic telegraph

morsel 3 bit, nip, sip **4** bite, drop, iota, whit **5** crumb, grain, piece, scrap, snack, speck, taste, touch, trace **6** dollop, nibble, sliver, tidbit

7 modicum, segment, swallow **8** fraction, fragment, mouthful, particle **9** scintilla

mortal 4 deep, type **5** fatal, grave, human **6** deadly, lethal, living, person, severe **7** earthly, extreme, intense, mundane **8** creature, enor-mous, fleeting, temporal **9** character, corporeal, ephem-eral **10** individual, transitory **12** unimaginable

mortality 7 carnage **8** fatality **9** bloodshed, ephemeral, slaughter **10** transience **11** ev-anescence **12** impermanence **13** extermination **14** transitoriness

mortar 6 cannon, cement, ves-sel **7** plaster **8** adhesive

Morte d'Arthur, Le
author: **12** Thomas Malory

Mortgaged Heart, The
author: **15** Carson McCullers

mortification 3 rot **5** decay, shame **7** chagrin, penance **8** ignominy **11** humiliation **12** putrefaction **13** embarrassment

mortified 6 rotted **7** abashed, ashamed, debased **8** dismayed, festered, tortured **9** chagrined, putrefied **11** discomfited, embarrassed

mortify 3 rot **4** deny, fast **5** abash, decay, shame **6** ap-pall, fester **7** chagrin, horrify, putrefy **9** discomfit, embarrass **10** discipline, disconcert

Mosaic law 10 Pentateuch **15** Ten Commandments

Mosan
language family:
14 Algonkian-Mosan
subgroup: **6** Nootka **8** Che-makum, Kwakiutl, Quileute, Salishan, Wakashan **9** Chemakuan

Moscow
airport: **12** Sheremetyevo
canal: **11** Moscow-Volga
capital of: **4** USSR **6** Russia **11** Soviet Union
hills: **5** Lenin
landmark: **7** Kremlin **9** Gorky Park, Red Square **12** Lenin Library **13** Izmailovo Park, Sokolniki Park **14** Bolshoi Theater **16** Moscow Art Theater **21** Luzhniki Sports Complex
museum: **6** Armory **7** Push-kin **10** Historical **16** Tretya-kov Gallery **28** Central Museum of the Soviet Army
river: **5** Setun, Volga, Yauza **6** Moscow
Russian: **6** Moskva

Moses
father: **5** Amram
mother: **8** Jochebed
sister: **6** Miriam
brother: **5** Aaron
wife: **8** Zipporah
son: **7** Eliezar, Gershom
father-in-law: **6** Jethro
received: **15** Ten Commandments
patriarch of: **10** Israelites
saw: **11** burning bush
successor: **6** Joshua
pertaining to: **6** Mosaic

Moses, Grandma
real name: **17** Anna Mary Robertson, Mary Anne Robertson
born: **11** Greenwich NY
artwork: **23** Out for the Christmas Trees

mosey 4 poke **5** amble **6** stroll **7** saunter, shuffle

Moslem 4 Moor **5** Islam, Sunni **6** Muslim, Shiite **7** Is-lamic **10** Mohammadan, Muhammadan

mosque 6 temple
Arabic: **6** masjid, musjid

Mosquito Coast, The
author: **11** Paul Theroux

Mosquito State
nickname of: **9** New Jersey

moss
varieties: **4** ball, club, gold, rose **5** broom, bunch, coral, ditch, fairy, Irish, spike, wa-ter **6** Scotch, spring **7** cush-ion, haircap, peacock, Spanish **8** floating, fountain, Japanese, mat spike **9** dwarf club, flowering **10** little club, pincushion **11** basket spike, meadow spike, shin-ing club **12** treelet spike **13** Douglas's spike

Mossbauer, Rudolph Ludwig
field: **7** physics
nationality: **6** German
discovered: **15** Mossbauer ef-fect **28** recoil-free gamma ray absorption
awarded: **10** Nobel Prize

Mosses from an Old Manse
author: **18** Nathaniel Hawthorne

most 4 best, very **6** degree **7** maximum **9** extremely

most distant point 5 limit, reach **8** boundary **9** extremity

Mostel, Zero
real name: **16** Samuel Joel Mostel
born: **10** Brooklyn NY
roles: **8** The Front **10** Rhi-noceros **11** The Enforcer **12** The Producers **15** Du

Barry Was a Lady **16** Fiddler on the Roof **17** Panic in the Streets

most important 3 key, top **4** head, main **5** chief **7** central, highest, leading **8** cardinal, dominant, foremost, greatest **9** paramount, principal, uppermost **10** preeminent **11** outstanding, predominant

mostly 6 mainly **7** as a rule, chiefly, greatly, largely **8** above all **9** generally, primarily, specially **10** especially **11** principally **12** particularly **13** predominantly

most prominent 7 leading **8** dominant **10** preeminent **11** outstanding

most successful 6 banner, record **7** winning **10** triumphant **11** outstanding

mote 3 dot **4** iota **5** speck **8** particle **9** scintilla

moth
 varieties: **4** hawk, luna, tent **5** ghost, gypsy, plume, royal, swift, yucca **6** hornet, lappet, miller, urania **7** clothes, emperor, flannel, hook tip, leopard, tussock **8** army worm, forester, imperial, polka dot **9** carpenter, clearwing **10** forest tent **11** pseudosphex **12** African peach **13** American tiger, giant Hercules **14** tropical sphinx **15** Chinese silkworm, glover's silkworm **20** striped morning sphinx

moth-eaten 5 holey **6** old-hat **7** worn-out **8** outmoded **10** antiquated, threadbare **11** dilapidated

mother 3 mom, mum **4** bear, mama, mind, mums, rear, tend **5** beget, breed, mater, momma, mommy, mummy, nurse, raise **6** origin, source **7** care for, indulge, nurture, old lady, produce, protect **8** conceive, stimulus **10** wellspring **11** inspiration
 French: **4** mere
 Spanish: **5** madre
 of wind: **3** Eos
 of stars: **3** Eos
 of gods: **5** Nammu

mother country 8 homeland **10** fatherland, native land, native soil, old country **13** native country

Mother Goose in Prose
 author: **14** Lyman Frank Baum

motherly 4 kind **6** gentle, loving, tender **7** devoted **8** mater-

nal, parental **9** indulgent **10** protective, sheltering

mother of a family
 Latin: **13** materfamilias

Mother of the West
 nickname of: **8** Missouri

mother's helper
 French: **6** au pair

motif 4 form, idea **5** shape, style, theme, topic **6** design, figure, thread **7** pattern, refrain, subject **9** treatment

motion 3 cue, nod **4** flow, flux, move, sign, stir **5** drift **6** action, beckon, signal, stream **7** gesture, kinesis, passage, request **8** mobility, movement, progress **10** indication, suggestion **11** gesticulate, proposition **13** gesticulation **14** recommendation

motionless 4 calm, dead, idle **5** fixed, inert, still **6** at rest, frozen, stable, static **8** immobile, inactive, lifeless, tranquil, unmoving **9** immovable, quiescent **10** stationary, transfixed **11** immobilized **12** unresponsive

motion picture 3 pic **4** cine, film, show **5** flick, movie **6** cinema, talkie **8** flickers **10** photodrama **11** picture show **13** moving picture

motivate 4 goad, move, stir **5** egg on, impel **6** arouse, induce, prompt, stir up, turn on **7** actuate, provoke **8** activate, persuade **9** influence, stimulate

motivation 5 cause **6** reason **7** impetus, impulse **9** causation, impulsion **11** provocation

motive 3 aim, end **4** goal, spur **5** cause **6** design, object, reason **7** grounds, purpose **8** occasion, stimulus, thinking **9** incentive, intention, prompting, rationale **10** enticement, incitement, inducement **11** inspiration, instigation, provocation

motley 4 pied **5** mixed, tabby **6** hybrid, sundry, unlike, varied **7** dappled, piebald, watered **8** assorted, brindled, speckled **9** checkered, composite, different, disparate, divergent, harlequin, patchwork **10** dissimilar, iridescent, polychrome, variegated **11** diversified, incongruous, varicolored **12** multicolored **13** heterogeneous, kaleidoscopic, miscellaneous

motor 3 car **4** auto, ride, tour **5** drive, pilot, wheel **6** engine,

turbine **7** machine **8** efferent **10** automobile

motorcar 4 auto, heap **6** jalopy, wheels **7** flivver, machine, vehicle **9** tin lizzie **10** automobile

motor vehicle 3 bus, car, van **4** auto, heap, limo **5** motor, truck, wagon **6** jalopy, pickup, wheels **7** flivver, hardtop, machine, omnibus, town car, vehicle **8** limosine **9** tin lizzie **10** automobile **11** convertible

mottled 4 pied **5** tabby **7** blotchy, flecked, piebald, specked **8** brindled, speckled, stippled **10** iridescent, multicolor, variegated **11** varicolored **12** parti-colored **13** kaleidoscopic, polychromatic

motto 3 saw **4** rule **5** adage, axiom, maxim **6** byword, dictum, saying, slogan, truism **7** epigram, precept, proverb **8** aphorism **9** catchword, principle, watchword

moue 4 pout **7** grimace

Moulin Rouge
 director: **10** John Huston
 cast: **10** Jose Ferrer (Toulouse-Lautrec) **11** Suzanne Flon, Zsa Zsa Gabor **12** Eric Pohlmann
 setting: **5** Paris **10** Montmartre

mound 4 bump, dune, heap, hill, pile, rick **5** knoll, mogul, ridge, stack **7** bulwark, hillock, hummock, rampart **9** earthwork **10** embankment **12** entrenchment

Mound Builders
 location: **15** Ohio River Valley **22** Mississippi River Valley
 known for: **13** earthen mounds

mount 3 fit, fix, rig, set, wax **4** go up, grow, pony, rise, soar **5** affix, camel, climb, equip, frame, horse, scale, steed, surge, swell **6** ascend, fit out, outfit, set off **7** augment, charger, climb up, get over, get upon, install, set into **8** elephant, increase, multiply, straddle **9** intensify

mountain see box, p. 650

Mountain
 constellation of: **5** Mensa

mountaineers are always free men
 Latin: **19** montani semper liberi
 motto of: **12** West Virginia

mountain 3 alp 4 peak 5 bluff, butte, range, ridge 6 height, massif 7 volcano 8 eminence, high-land 9 elevation

of Afghanistan: 3 Koh 5 Safeo 6 Chagai, Pamirs 7 Nowshak 8 Koh-i-Baba, Safed Koh, Sulaiman 9 Himalayas, Hindu Kush, Istoro Nal 11 Khwaja Amran, Paropamisus

of Albania: 5 Shala 6 Pindus 8 Koritnjk 10 Mount Korab 12 Albanian Alps

of Algeria: 5 Aissa, Atlas, Aures, Dahra, Tahat 6 Chelia 7 Ahaggar, Kabylia, Mouydir 8 Djurjura 9 Djurdjura, Tell Atlas 12 Saharan Atlas

of Andorra: 6 d'Etats 8 l'Estanyo 8 Pyrenees 10 Cataperdis 11 Como Pedrosa

of Angola: 4 Moco 5 Chela 6 Loviti 16 Humpata Highlands

of Antigua and Barbuda: 9 Boggy Peak

of Argentina: 4 Toro 5 Andes, Chato, Laudo, Potro 6 Conico, Pissis, Rincon 8 Famatina, Mural-lon, Olivares, Tronador, Zapaleri 9 Aconcagua, Tupungato 10 Cordillera 13 Ojos del Salado 15 Cerro Mercedario, Sierra de Cordoba

of Armenia: 6 Ararat, Taurus 8 Karabekh 7 Aladagh 12 Mount Aragats

of Australia: 3 Ise 4 Blue, Olga, Ossa, Zeil 5 Bruce, Snowy 6 Cradle, Doreen, Garnet, Gawler, Magnet, Morgan 7 Bongong, Gregory 8 Augustus, Brockman, Cuthbert, Herbert, Jusgrave, Mulligan, Surprise 9 Murchison, Kosciusko, Woodroffe 14 Australian Alps 15 New England Range 18 Great Dividing Range

of Austria: 4 Alps 6 Tirols, Tyrols, Stubai 8 Eisenerz, Rhatikon 9 Dolomites, Kitzbuhel 10 Hohe Tauern 13 Grossglockner 14 Silvretta Group

of Azerbaijan: 8 Caucasus

of Bangladesh: 10 Keokradong 15 Chittagong Hills

of Barbados: 6 Chalky 7 Hillaby

of Belgium: 8 Ardennes 16 Signal de Botrange

of Benin: 7 Atakora

of Bhutan: 5 Black 9 Himalayas 10 Chomo Lhari, Kula Kangri

of Bolivia: 4 Jara 5 Andes, Cusco, Cuzco 6 Sajama, Sorata, Sunsas 7 Illampu 8 Ancohuma, Illi-mani, Mururata, Sansimon, Santiago, Zapaleri 12 Eastern Range, Western Range 18 Cordillera Oriental 20 Cordillera Occidental

of Borneo: 4 Iran, Raja 5 Saran 6 Kapuas, Muller, Nijaan, Tebang 8 Kinabalu, Kinibalu, Schwaner

of Bosnia-Herzegovina: 11 Dinaric Alps

of Brazil: 3 Mar 5 Geral, Organ, Piaui 6 Acarai, Gurupi, Parima, Urucum 7 Amambai, Carajas, Gradaus, Neblina, Oragaos, Roraima 8 Bandeira, Itatiaia, Roncador, Tombador 9 Pacaraima, Sugar Loaf 10 Tumuc-Humac

of Brunei: 6 Teraja 9 Ulu Tutong 10 Pagon Priok

of Bulgaria: 3 Kom 5 Botev, Pirin, Sapka 6 Balkan, Musala, Sredna 7 Vikhren 8 Musallah 11 Rila-Rhodope

of Burkina Faso: 4 Tema 8 Nakourou 10 Tenakourou, Tenekourou

of Burundi: 8 Nyarwana 9 Nyamisana

of Cambodia: 3 Pan 7 Dangrek, Dong Rek 8 Cardamom, Elephant 10 Phnom Aoral, Phnom Aural

of Cameroon: 5 Mbabo 7 Bambuto, Kapsiki, Mandara 8 Batandji, Cameroon 9 Atlantika

of Canada: 5 Coast, Logan, Royal 6 Robson, Skeena 7 Cariboo, Cascade, Purcell, Rockies, Sel-kirk, Stelias, St Elias 8 Columbia, Hazelton, Monashee 9 Mackenzie, Notre Dame, Tremblant 10 Laurentian, Richardson, Shickshock 14 Jacques Cartier

of Canary Islands: 5 Teide, Teyde 6 La Cruz 8 El Cumbre, Tenerife

of Cape Verde: 4 Cano, Fogo 10 Pico de Cano

of Central African Republic: 5 Karre, Tinga 6 Mongos 9 Dar Challa 11 Kayagangiri

of Chad: 7 Tibesti, Touside 9 Emi Koussi

of Chile: 4 Maca, Toro 5 Chato, Maipo, Maipu, Paine, Potro, Pular, Torre, Yogan 6 Apiwan, Burney, Conico, Jervis, Poquis, Rincon 7 Chaltel, Copiapo, Fitzroy, Palpana, Velluda 8 Coch-rane, Tronador, Yanteles 9 Tupungato 13 Ojos del Salado

of Colombia: 5 Abibe, Andes, Baudo, Chita, Cocuy, Huila, Pasto 6 Ayapel, Perija, Purace, To-lima, Tunahi 7 Chamusa, del Ruiz 8 Oriengal 10 Santa Marta 14 Cristobal Colon 17 Central Cordillera, Eastern Cordillera, Western Cordillera

of Costa Rica: 4 Poas 5 Barba, Irazu 6 Blanco 7 Central, Gongora 9 Talamanca, Turrialba 10 Guanacaste 14 Chirripo Grande

of Crete: 3 Ida 5 Dikte, Phino 6 Juktas 7 Lasithi, Madaras 8 Leuka Ori, Theodore, Thriphte 9 Psiloriti

of Croatia: 10 Julian Alps 11 Styrian Alps

of Cuba: 6 Copper 7 Cristal, Maestra, Organos 8 Camaguey, Trinidad, Turquino 9 Las Villas 11 Pinar del Rio 12 Guaniguanico 14 Sancti-Spiritus

of Czechoslovakia/Czech Republic: 3 Ore 5 Grant, Tatra 6 Sumava 7 Gerlach, Sudeten 8 Krko-nose 9 High Tatra 10 Carpathian 11 Gerlachovka

of Denmark: 12 Ejer Bavnehoj, Yding Skovhoj 14 Himmelbjaerget

of Djibouti: 5 Gouda 9 Moussa Ali

of Dominican Republic: 4 Tina 5 Gallo, Neiba 6 Duarte 7 Baoruco, Central 8 Bahoruco, Oriental 13 Septentrional

of Ecuador: 5 Andes **6** Condor, Sangay **7** Cayambe **8** Antisana, Cotopaxi **9** Cotacachi, Pichincha **10** Chimborazo
of Egypt: 5 Sinai, Uekia **6** Gharib **8** Katerina **9** Katherina **13** Shayib al-Banat
of El Salvador: 6 Izalco **8** Santa Ana
of England: 5 Black **7** Pennine, Snowdon **8** Cambrian, Cumbrian **11** Scafell Pike
of Ethiopia: 4 Amba, Batu, Guge, Guna, Talo **5** Ahmar, Choke **9** Rasdashan, Ras Deshen
of Finland: 6 Haltia **7** Laltiva **10** Saari Selka **11** Haldetsokka
of France: 4 Alps, Jura **5** Blanc, Pelat **6** Vosges **8** Ardennes, Pyrenees **9** Mont Blanc **10** French Alps **11** Pic Montcalm
of Gabon Republic: 5 Mpele **7** Chaillu, Cristal, Mikongo **8** Balaquri, Birougou, Iboundji
of Georgia: 8 Caucasus
of Germany: 3 Ore **4** Harz **8** Feldberg **9** Zugspitze **10** Erzgebirge **11** Black Forest, Fichtelberg **12** Bavarian Alps
of Ghana: 8 Afadjato **12** Akwapim Hills
of Gibraltar: 6 Misery
of Greece: 3 Ida **4** Idhi, Oeta, Oite, Ossa **5** Athos **6** Ithome, Peleon, Pelion, Pindus **7** Grammos, Helicon, Olympus, Rhodope **8** Hymettos, Smolikas, Targetos, Taygetus **9** Parnassus **10** Hagion Oros, Lycabettus, Pentelicus
of Greenland: 5 Forel, Payer **7** Khardyu **8** Peterman **9** Gunnbjorn **15** Petermannsbjerg
of Guatemala: 4 Agua, Mico **5** Fuego, Madre **6** Pacaya, Tacana **7** Atitlan, Toliman **8** La Candon, Las Minas, Tajumuko **9** Tajamulco **10** Acatenango, Santa Maria **12** Cuchumatanes
of Guinea: 4 Loma **5** Nimba **6** Tamgue **11** Fouta Djalon
of Guyana: 5 Amuku, Ariwa, Kamoa **6** Akarai, Kanuku **7** Caburai **9** Pacaraima
of Haiti: 4 Nord **5** Cahos **6** Macaya, Noires **7** Lahotte, Laselle **8** Troudeau
of Honduras: 4 Pija **6** Agalta **7** Celaque **8** Las Minas **9** Esperanza **25** Central American Cordillera
of Hong Kong: 6 Castle **8** Victoria **9** Tai Mo Shan
of Hungary: 4 Alps, Bukk **5** Kekes, Matra, Tatra, Vetes **6** Bakony, Mecsek **7** Cserhat, Gerecse **8** Borzsony, Zempleni **9** Korishegy **10** Carpathian
of Iceland: 4 Laki **5** Askja, Hekla, Jokul, Katla **7** Surtsey **10** Orafajokul **16** Hvannadalshnukur
of India: 8 Aravalli **9** Broad Peak, Distaghil, Himalayas, Karakoram, Nanda Devi, Rakaposhi **10** Gasherbrum, Masherbrum **11** Nanga Parbat **12** Eastern Ghats, Godwin Austen, Kanchenjunga, Western Ghats
of Iran: 6 Elburz, Zagros **8** Demavend
of Iraq: 6 Qalate, Zagros **7** Halgurd, Qaarade **9** Kurdistan
of Ireland: 5 Galty **6** Croagh, Mourne **7** Errigal, Muckish, Patrick, Wicklow **8** Comeragh **10** Benna Beola, Twelve Bens, Twelve Pins **13** Carrantuohill, Knockmealdown **19** Macgillycuddy's Reeks
of Israel: 4 Nafh, Sagi **5** Harif, Meron, Ramon, Tabor **6** Atzmon, Carmel, Hatira, Meiron
of Italy: 4 Alps, Etna, Rosa, Viso **5** Amaro, Blanc, Corno, Somma **6** Cimone, Ortles **7** Vulcano **8** Vesuvius **9** Apennines, Dolomites, Maritimes, Stromboli **10** Apuane Alps, Carnic Alps, Julian Alps, Otztal Alps **11** Bernina Alps, Gennargentu **12** Gran Paradiso, Ligurian Alps **13** Lepontine Alps **16** Abruzzi Apennines
of Jamaica: 4 Blue **8** Sir Johns
of Japan: 3 Uso, Zao **4** Fuji **5** Asahi, Asama, Hondo, Yesso **6** Asosan, Enasan, Hiuchi, Kiusiu, Yariga **7** Fujisan, Hakusan, Kujusan, Tokachi **8** Fujiyama **9** Japan Alps
of Java: 4 Amat, Gede **5** Lawoe, Murjo, Prahu **6** Raoeng, Semuru, Slamet **7** Semeroe **8** Soembing
of Jordan: 9 Jabal Ramm, Jebel Ramm
of Kenya: 5 Elgon, Kenya, Kulai, Nyira, Nyiru **6** Kinyaa, Matian **7** Logonot **8** Aberdare **9** Kirinyaga
of Korea: 4 Wang **5** Chiri, Halla **6** Kwanmo, Paektu, Sobaek **7** Diamond, Kyebang, Nangnim, Taebaek **8** Chang-pai, Hamgyong, Myohyang **9** Paektu-san **10** Kumgang-san
of Kyrgyzstan: 8 Tian Shan
of Laos: 3 Bia, Lai, Loi, San **4** Copi, Khat **5** Atwat **6** Khoung, Tiubia **7** Phou Bia **15** Annam Cordillera
of Lebanon: 4 Mzar **5** Aruba **6** Hermon **7** es Sauda, Lebanon, Sannine **8** Kadischa, Kenisseh **9** Kennisseh **10** al-Mukammal **11** Anti-Lebanon **13** Qurnat al-Sawda
of Lesotho: 6 Maloti, Maluti **7** Central **8** Injasuti, Machache **10** Ben Macdhui **11** Drakensberg, Thaba Putsoa **16** Thabana Ntlenyana
of Liberia: 3 Uni **4** Bong, Putu **5** Niete, Nimba **6** Wutivi **9** Bomi Hills
of Libya: 5 Green **9** Bette Peak **13** Jabal al Akhdar, Tibesti Massif
of Liechtenstein: 4 Alps **8** Naafkopf, Rhatikon **12** Three Sisters **15** Vorder-Grauspitz
of Lithuania: 9 Juozapine **15** Samogitian Hills
of Luxembourg: 8 Ardennes, Huldange **9** Burgplatz **11** Wemperhardt
of Madagascar: 4 Boby **9** Ankaratra **11** Maromokotro **12** High Plateaus, Tsiafajavona **17** Tsaratanana Massif
of Malawi: 6 Mlanje **7** Mulanje **11** Livingstone
of Malaysia: 4 Bulu, Hose, Iban, Iran, Main, Mulu, Niut, Raja **5** Murjo, Niapa, Ophir **6** Blumut, Kapuas, Leuser, Slamet **7** Binaija, Brassey, Crocker **8** Kinabalu, Rindjani **11** Gunong Korbu, Gunong Tahan

(continued)

mountain (*continued*)

of Mali: 4 Mina **6** Iforas **7** Manding **12** Hombori Tondo

of Mexico: 6 Colima, Tacana, Toluca **7** Orizaba **9** Paricutin **11** Ixtacihuatl, Sierra Madre **12** Citlaltepetl, Popocatepetl **14** Sierra Zacateca **16** Chiapas Highlands **24** Transverse Volcanic Sierra

of Mongolia: 4 Cast, Orog **5** Altai **6** Kentei, Sevrej **7** Ich Ovoo, Khangai, Khentei **8** Tannu-Ola **9** Edrengijn **10** Cagaan Bogd, Tabun Bogdo **11** Munky Sardyk **14** Hangayn-Hentiyn, Monch Chajrchan

of Montenegro: 8 Durmitor **11** Dinaric Alps

of Morocco: 3 Rif **4** Bani **5** Abyla, Atlas, Sarro **8** Tidiguin **9** Anti-Atlas, High Atlas, Jebel-Musa **11** Middle Atlas **12** Jebel Toubkal **13** Djebel Toubkal

of Mozambique: 5 Binga **7** Lebombo

of Myanmar: 4 Chin, Naga, Pegu, Popa **5** Dawna **6** Arakan, Kachin, Lushai, Patkai **7** Karenni **8** Nattaung, Peguyona, Saramati, Victoria **10** Tenasserim **11** Hkakabo Razi, Manipur Hill **12** Tanen Taunggi

of Namibia: 9 Brandberg **14** Khomas Highland, Koakoveld Hills

of Nepal: 6 Cho Oyu, Churia, Makalu **7** Everest, Lhotse I, Manaslu, Siwalik **8** Lhotse II **9** Annapurna, Himalayas **10** Dhaulagiri, Gosainthan, Himalchuli **11** Ganesh Himal **12** Kanchenjunga **14** Mahabharat Lekh

of New Guinea: 4 Snow **6** Orange **7** Bismark, Wilhelm **8** Victoria **9** Carstensz **10** Puncak Jaya **11** Owen Stanley **12** Albert Edward

of New Zealand: 4 Cook, Eden, Flat, Owen **5** Allen, Chope, Lyall, Mitre, Ohope, Otari, Young **6** Egmont, Stokes, Tasman **7** Aorangi, Cameron, Coronet, Ernslaw, Huiarau, Pihanga, Ruahine, Ruapehu, Tauhera, Tutamee, Tyndall **8** Aspiring, Richmond, Tauranga **9** Messenger, Murchison, Ngauruhoe, Raukumara, Tongariro **11** Remarkables **12** Southern Alps

of Nicaragua: 4 Leon **5** Negro, Viejo **6** Madera, Telica **7** Managua, Mogoton, Saslaya **9** Momotombo

of Norway: 5 Sogne **6** Kjolen **7** Numedal **8** Blodfjel, Snohetta, Telemark, Ustetind **9** Harteigen, Jotunheim, Langfjell, Ramnanosi **10** Dovrefjell, Galdhoepig, Glitretind, Vibmesnosi **11** Myrdalfjell **12** Galdhopiggen **13** Glittertinden **14** Aardangerjokul, Hallingskarvet, Skagastolstind

of Pakistan: 3 Pab, Pub **4** Salt **6** Makran **7** Kirthar **8** Himalaya, Safed Koh, Sulaiman **9** Hindu Kush, Karakoram, Tirich Mir **11** Makran Coast **12** Godwin Austin **13** Central Makran **14** Takht-i-Sulaiman

of Panama: 4 Baru, Maje **5** Chico, Gandi **6** Darien **7** Columan, San Blas, Veragua **8** Chiriqui, Santiago, Tabasara **10** Costa Rican **14** Serrania de Sapo **15** Aspave Highlands **17** Cordillera Central

of Peru: 5 Andes **7** El Misti, Huamina **8** Coropuna **9** Huascaran

of Philippines: 3 Apo, Iba **4** Mayo, Taal **5** Albay, Askja, Hibok, Mayon, Pulog **6** Pagsan **7** Banahao, Canlaon

of Poland: 4 Rysy **5** Tatra **6** Beskid **7** Pieniny, Sudeten **9** Beshchady, High Tatra, Holy Cross **10** Carpathian

of Portugal: 4 Acor, Lapa **5** Gerez, Marao, Mousa **6** Bornes, Peneda **7** Larouco **8** Caramulo **9** Caldeirao, Monchique **11** Pico da Serra **14** Serra da Estrela

of Puerto Rico: 4 Toro **5** Cayey, Punta **6** Yunque **8** Guilarte, Luquilla **10** Torrecilla **17** Cordillera Central

of Rumania: 5 Banat, Bihor, Negoi **6** Codrul, Rodnei **7** Apuseni, Balkans, Caliman, Fagaras **8** Pietrosu **9** Moldavian **10** Carpathian, Moldoveanu **17** Transylvanian Alps

of Russia: 5 Altai, Lenin, Sayan, Urals **6** Anadyr, Elbrus, Koryak, Pamirs, Pobedy **7** Belukha, Crimean, Khibiny, Stanovi, Zhiguli **8** Caucasus, Dzhughur, Stanavoi, Tien Shan **9** Kopet Dagh, Narodnaya, Pamir-Alai, Yablonovy **10** Carpathian **11** Sikhote-Alin, Verkhoyansk

of Rwanda: 7 Mitumba, Virunga **8** Muhavura **9** Karisimbi

of Samoa: 4 Fito, Vaea **5** Alava **6** Savaii **7** Matafao **8** Silisili **9** Rainmaker

of San Marino: 6 Titano **9** Apennines

of Sardinia: 4 Rasu **5** Ferry, Linas **7** Gallura, Limbara **8** Marghine, Serpeddi, Vittoria **11** Gennargentu

of Saudi Arabia: 5 Razih **6** Tuwayq **10** Jebal Sawda

of Scotland: 5 Attow, Ochil **6** Sidlaw **7** Cheviot **8** Ben Nevis, Grampian **9** Ben Lomond, Highlands, Trossachs

of Senegal: 6 Gounou **12** Fouta Djallon

of Sicily: 4 Erei, Etna, Moro, Sori **5** Aetna, Atlas, Erici, Hybla, Iblei, Ibrei **7** Nebrodi, Vulcano **9** Apennines, Le Madonie, Stromboli **10** Peloritani

of Sierra Leone: 4 Loma **9** Bintimani **10** Tingi Hills

of Sikkim: 7 Dongkya, Donkhya **9** Himalayas, Singalili **10** Darjeeling **12** Kanchenjunga

of Singapore: 6 Mandai **7** Panjang **10** Bukit Timah

of Slovakia: 7 Sudetes **8** Low Tatra **9** High Tatra, Slovak Ore **10** Carpathian, Nizke Tatry **11** Visoke Tatry **15** White Carpathian

of the Solomon Islands: 5 Balbi **11** Popomanasiu

of Somalia: 5 Guban **7** Surud Ad **11** Migiurtinia, Ogo Highland

of South Africa: 3 Aux, Kop **5** Table **7** Kathkin **8** Injasuti **9** Stormberg **10** Devil's Peak, Sneeuwberg **11** Drakensberg **12** Giant's Castle **13** Witwatersrand **14** Mont-aux-Sources **15** Great Escarpment

of Spain: 4 Gata 5 Aneto, Rouch, Teide 6 Cuenca, Estats, Europa, Gredos, Magina, Morena, Nethou, Nevada, Teleno, Toledo 7 Alcaraz, Banuelo, Catalan, Cerredo, Demanda, Iberian, La Sagra, Moncayo, Perdido 8 Almanzor, Asturias, Galician, Maladeta, Monegros, Montseny, Mulhacen, Penalara, Pyrenees 10 Albarracin, Cantabrian, Guadarrama, Torrecilla

of Sudan: 4 Nuba 6 Red Sea 7 Imatong, Kinyeti 9 Dongotona 10 Jabal Marra, Jebel Marra 18 Ethiopian Highlands

of Suriname: 4 Emma 6 Kayser, Oranje 10 Julianatop, Tumuc-Humac, Wilhelmina 13 Eilert's Il Haan, Van Ach Van Wyck 15 Guiana Highlands

of Swaziland: 7 Emlembe 8 Highveld 11 Drakensberg

of Sweden: 4 Sarv 5 Ammar, Kebne 6 Helags, Kjolen, Ovniks, Sarjek 7 Kjollen 10 Kebnekaise

of Switzerland: 3 Dom 4 Alps, Jura, Rigi, Rosa, Todi 5 Adula, Blanc, Cenis, Eiger, Genis, Karpf, Righi 6 Linard, Pizela, Sentis 7 Bernina, Beverin, Grimsel, Pilatus, Rotondo 8 Balmhorn, Jungfrau 9 Weisshorn 10 Diablerets, Matterhorn, St Gotthard, Wetterhorn 11 Burgenstock 12 Dufourspitze 13 Rheinwaldhorn 14 Finsteraarhorn

of Syria: 6 Carmel, Hermon 7 Alawite, Libanus 10 Nusairiyya 11 Anti-Lebanon

of Taiwan: 5 Tatun 6 Tzukao, Yu Shan 7 Taitung 8 Morrison 10 Sinkao Shan 11 Hsin-Kao Shan 15 Chungyang Shanmo

of Tajikistan: 13 Communism Peak

of Tanzania: 4 Kibo, Mero 8 Usambara 11 Kilimanjaro

of Thailand: 5 Dawna, Khieo 6 Phanom 8 Dang Raek, Inthanon, Kao Prawa, Maelamun 9 Khao Luang 11 Bilauktaung, Doi Inthanon

of Tibet: 5 Kamet, Sajum 6 Kailas, Kunlun 7 Bandala, Everest 9 Himalayas, Karakoram

of Tunisia: 5 Atlas 6 Chambi, Mrhila 7 Tebessa 8 High Tell, Zaghouan 12 Northern Tell 18 Dorsale Tunnisienne

of Turkey: 2 Ak 3 Ala 4 Alai, Dagh, Kara 5 Hasan, Hinis, Honaz, Murat, Murit 6 Ala Dag, Ararat, Bingol, Bolgar, Pontic, Suphan, Taurus 7 Aladagh, Erciyas 8 Karacali 10 Kackar Dagi

of Uganda: 4 Oboa 5 Elgon 7 Virunga 9 Mufumbiro, Ruwenzori 10 Margherita 18 Mountains of the Moon

of Ukraine: 7 Crimean 10 Carpathian

of United States: 4 Hood 5 Coast, Green, Kenai, Ozark, Rocky, White 6 Alaska, Brooks, De-Long, Elbert, Helena, Mesabi, Pocono, Shasta 7 Cascade, Chugach, Foraker, Harvard, Kilauea, Massive, Olympic, Olympus, Rainier, St Elias, Whitney 8 Catskill, Davidson, Endicott, Katahdin, Mauna Loa, McKinley, Mitchell, Ouachita, St Helens, Wrangell 9 Allegheny, Blue Ridge, Kuskokwim, North Peak, Pike's Peak 10 Black Hills, Blanca Peak, Grand Teton, Washington, Williamson 11 Appalachian, Santa Monica 12 Sierra Nevada 14 Berkshire Hills

of Uruguay: 6 Animas 10 Grand Hills 14 Cuchilla Grande 15 Mirador Nacional

of Venezuela: 3 Pao 4 Pava, Yair 5 Andes, Duida, Icutu 6 Concha, Cuneva, Merida, Parima, Sierra, Yumari 7 Bolivar, Imutaca, Masaiti, Roraima 8 Gurupira 9 Pacaraima 10 Auyan-Tepui 11 Turimiquire 18 Cordillera del Norte

of Vietnam: 6 Badinh, Badink 7 Nindhoa, Ninhhoa 8 Fansipan, Knontran, Ngoklinh, Ngoklink, Tchepone, Tclepore 18 Annamese Cordillera

of Wales: 6 Berwyn 7 Snowdon 8 Cambrian 9 Prescelly 13 Brecon Beacons

of Western Samoa: 4 Fito, Vaea 13 Mauga Silisili

of Yemen: 6 Shuayb, Thamir 7 Djehaff

of Yugoslavia: 5 Karst 6 Balkan 7 Rhodope, Triglav 8 Crna Gora, Durmitor 9 Sar-Pindus 10 Carnic Alps, Julian Alps, Karawanken 11 Dinaric Alps 13 Slovenian Alps 20 Northern Albanian Alps

of Zaire: 7 Crystal, Mitumba, Virunga 9 Ruwenzori 10 Margherita, Nyaragongo 18 Mountains of the Moon

of Zambia: 8 Muchinga 12 Mafinga Hills

of Zimbabwe: 5 Vumba 6 Manica 7 Inyanga 9 Inyangani 11 Chimanimani, Matopo Hills

---

humbug 7 hustler, sharper 8 huckster, operator, swindler 9 charlatan, con artist 11 quacksalver

mounted soldier 6 hussar, lancer 7 dragoon 8 cavalier, horseman 10 cavalryman

mourn 3 cry, rue, sob 4 keen, pine, wail, weep 6 bemoan, bewail, grieve, lament, regret, sorrow 7 deplore, despair 8 languish, weep over

mournful 3 sad 5 black, sorry, weepy 6 dismal, rueful, som-ber, triste, woeful 7 doleful, joyless, unhappy 8 dejected, dirgeful, dolorous, funereal, grievous, saddened 9 depressed, plaintive, sorrowful 10 depressing, dispirited, lamentable, lugubrious, melancholy 11 distressing, melancholic **12** heavy hearted

mourning 3 woe **5** black, crape, dolor, grief, weeds **6** sorrow **7** anguish, despair **8** grieving **9** lamenting, sorrowing **11** bereavement, lamentation

Mourning Becomes Electra
author: **12** Eugene O'Neill
character: **4** Seth **10** Hazel Niles, Peter Niles **16** Captain Adam Brant
Mannon family: **4** Ezra, Orin **7** Lavinia **9** Christine

mourning period
Hebrew: **6** shibah, shivah

mouser 3 cat **4** puss **5** kitty, pussy **6** feline **8** pussycat

Mousetrap, The
author: **14** Agatha Christie

mousseline 6 muslin

mousy 3 shy **4** drab, dull **5** timid, wimpy **7** bashful, fearful **8** timorous **9** colorless, unnoticed, withdrawn **11** unobtrusive **13** inconspicuous

mouth 3 bay, say **4** bell, jaws, lips **5** inlet, speak, voice **6** outlet, portal **7** declare, estuary, opening **8** aperture, propound **9** pronounce

mouthful 3 dab **4** bite **5** taste **6** morsel, nibble

mouthpiece 4 reed **6** lawyer **7** counsel **8** advocate, attorney **9** counselor

mouth-watering 8 inviting, tempting **9** appealing **10** appetizing **11** tantalizing

movable, moveable 4 free **5** loose **6** mobile, motile, moving **8** portable **10** changeable

movables 4 gear **5** goods **7** baggage, effects, luggage **9** equipment **10** belongings **11** impedimenta, possessions **13** accoutrements, paraphernalia

move 2 go **3** act, ask, get **4** bear, deed, fire, lead, pass, ploy, step, stir, sway, turn, urge **5** begin, budge, carry, cause, drive, impel, plead, rouse, shift, touch **6** action, affect, arouse, attack, convey, excite, exhort, incite, induce, motion, prompt, strike, stroke, switch **7** advance, budging, gesture, go ahead, impress, inspire, measure, operate, proceed, propose, provoke, request, suggest **8** function, interest, locomote, maneuver, motivate, persuade, relocate, start off, stirring, transfer,

transmit **9** impassion, influence, recommend, stimulate, transport, transpose **10** transplant **11** opportunity

move downward 3 dip **4** dive, drop, fall, sink **6** plunge, tumble **7** decline, descend, plummet **8** decrease

movement 4 part **5** drive, steps, works **6** action, effort, motion **7** crusade, measure, program, section **8** activity, division, gestures, maneuver, progress, stirring **9** agitation, execution, mechanism, operation **10** locomotion **11** undertaking

move out 5 leave **6** depart, vacate **8** evacuate

move quickly 3 fly, run **4** bolt, dash, race, rush, tear **5** hurry **6** hasten, sprint

move sideways 4 edge **5** sidle **8** sidestep

move slyly 4 edge, lurk **5** sidle, skulk, slink, sneak, steal

move up 5 boost, climb, heave, hoist, raise, scale **6** ascend, uplift **7** advance, elevate, promote, upraise

move upward 4 rise, soar **5** climb, mount **6** ascend **7** take off

movie 4 film, show **5** flick **6** cinema **7** feature, picture, showing **9** screening
invented by:
machine: **7** Jenkins
panoramic: **6** Waller
projector: **6** Edison
talking: **14** Warner Brothers

moving 5 motor **6** mobile, motile **8** exciting, poignant, spurring, stirring, touching **9** affecting, inspiring **10** impressive, locomotive, motivating **11** interacting, stimulating

moving about 5 astir **6** active **7** on the go

Moving Target, A
author: **14** William Golding

Mowgli
character in: **14** The Jungle Books
author: **7** Kipling

moxie 4 grit, guts, sand **5** nerve, pluck, spunk **6** mettle, spirit **7** courage, stamina **8** audacity, backbone **9** hardihood,

Mozambique
capital/largest city: **6** Maputo **15** Lourenco Marques
others: **4** Tete **5** Beira, Pemba, Zumbo **6** Chemba, Nacala, Pafuri, Sofala **7** Nampula **8** Mutarara **9** Inhambane, Quelimane **11** Porto Amelia
school: **15** Eduardo Mondlane
monetary unit: **6** escudo **7** centavo, metical
island: **6** Inhaca **7** Angoche **8** Bazanuto **9** Benguerua
lake: **5** Nyasa **6** Chuali, Nyassa **8** Nhavarre
mountain: **7** Lebombo
highlands: **6** Namuli **9** Gorongosa
highest point: **5** Binga
river: **4** Buzi, Save **5** Lurio, Msalu **6** Rovuma, Ruvuma **7** Ligonha, Limpopo, Lugenda, Messaio, Zambezi **8** Changane
ocean: **6** Indian
physical feature:
cape: **7** Delgado
channel: **10** Mozambique
people: **3** Yao **5** Bantu, Chopi, Lomue, Lomwe, Macua, Makua, Ngoni, Nguni, Shona **6** Maravi, Thouga **7** Maconde, Makonde **10** Portuguese
explorer: **11** Vasco de Gama
leader: **8** Chissano **9** Dos Santos **12** Samora Machel **15** Eduardo Mondlane
language: **3** Yao **5** Makua **6** Nyanji, Thonga **7** Swahili **10** Portuguese
religion: **5** Islam **7** animism **13** Roman Catholic
place:
game reserve: **8** Marromeu **9** Gorongosa, Gorongoza **18** Maputo Elephant Park
reservoir: **11** Cabora Bassa
feature:
bride price: **6** lobolo

toughness **10** pluckiness
13 dauntlessness

moyen age 10 Middle Ages

Mozambique *see box*

Mozart, Wolfgang Amadeus
see box

Mr, Mister
Russian: **8** gospodin
French: **8** monsieur
Yiddish: **3** Reb

Mr B
character in: **6** Pamela
author: **10** Richardson

Mr Basketball
nickname of: **8** Bob Cousy

**Mr Britling Sees It
Through**
author: **7** H G Wells

Mr Cub
nickname of: **10** Ernie Banks

Mr Deeds Goes to Town
director: **10** Frank Capra
cast: **10** Gary Cooper (Longfellow Deeds), Jean Arthur
14 George Bancroft

Mr Ed
character: **9** Carol Post
10 Kay Addison, Wilbur
Post **12** Roger Addison
14 Gordon Kirkwood, Winnie Kirkwood
cast: **8** Leon Ames **9** Alan
Young **11** Connie Hines,
Edna Skinner **12** Larry Keating **18** Florence MacMichael
Mr Ed was: **12** talking horse

Mr Flood's Party
author: **22** Edwin Arlington
Robinson

Mr Midnight
nickname of: **10** Steve Allen

Mr Peepers
character: **9** Mrs Gurney
11 Marge Weskit, Mr Remington **12** Harvey Weskit
14 Nancy Remington
15 Robinson Peepers **20** Superintendent Bascom
cast: **8** Wally Cox **9** Gage
Clark **11** Ernest Truex, Marion Lorne, Tony Randall
14 Patricia Benoit **16** Geor-
giann Johnson
Mr Peepers taught: **7** science
school: **13** Jefferson High

Mr Sammler's Planet
author: **10** Saul Bellow

Mrs Dalloway
author: **13** Virginia Woolf
character: **10** Miss Kilman,
Peter Walsh, Sally Seton
15 Richard Dalloway
16 Clarissa Dalloway
17 Elizabeth Dalloway

Mrs Miniver
director: **12** William Wyler
cast: **11** Greer Garson
12 Teresa Wright **13** Dame
May Whitty, Walter Pidgeon
Oscar for: **7** actress (Garson),
picture **8** director **17** supporting actress (Wright)

**Mr Smith Goes to
Washington**
director: **10** Frank Capra
cast: **9** Guy Kibbee **10** Jean
Arthur **11** Claude Rains
12 Edward Arnold, James
Stewart **14** Thomas Mitchell

Mrs Parkington
author: **14** Louis Bromfield

**Mrs Stevens Hears the
Mermaids Singing**
author: **9** May Sarton

Mrs Warren's Profession
author: **17** George Bernard
Shaw

Mr Television
nickname of: **11** Milton
Berle

much 3 far **4** a lot, lots
5 about, ample, heaps, loads,
often **6** almost, indeed, nearly,
overly, rather, scores **7** copious, greatly **8** abundant, good
deal, plenty of, quantity,
somewhat, striking **9** decidedly, important, plenteous,
plentiful, regularly **10** frequently, impressive, noteworthy, oftentimes, satisfying,
sufficient, worthwhile **11** appreciable, exceedingly, excessively, sufficiency
12 considerable **13** approximately, consequential

Much Ado About Nothing
author: **18** William
Shakespeare
character: **4** Hero **7** Claudio,
Don John, Leonato **8** Beatrice, Benedick, Dogberry,
Don Pedro

much in little
Latin: **13** multum in parvo

much loved 4 dear **7** beloved,
darling, dearest **8** precious
9 cherished, treasured

mucilage 3 gum **4** glue
5 paste **6** cement **8** adhesive

mucilaginous 5 gluey, gummy,
gunky **6** gloppy, sticky
8 adhesive

muck 3 mud **4** dirt, dung,
gunk, mire, ooze, slop **5** filth,
slime **6** sewage, sludge **7** compost, garbage

muck up 4 soil **5** dirty,
muddy **7** pollute

mud 4 dirt, muck, soil, wire

Mudcat State
nickname of: **11** Mississippi

muddied 5 dirty, grimy
6 grubby, soiled **7** stained
8 begrimed, confused

muddle 3 fog **4** blow, daze,
haze, mess, muff, ruin
5 botch, chaos, mix up, spoil,
throw **6** boggle, bungle, fumble, goof up, jumble, mess up,
pother, rattle **7** blunder, clutter, confuse, nonplus, stupefy
8 bewilder, confound, disarray,
disorder **13** disconcertion
14 disarrangement

muddlebrained 5 inept **7** witless **8** confused
11 lamebrained

muddled 5 fuzzy **7** bemused
8 confused **10** bewildered

Mozart, Wolfgang Amadeus
born: **7** Austria **8** Salzburg
composer of: **4** Linz (symphony No 36) **5** Paris (symphony
No 31) **6** Prague (symphony No 38) **7** Don Juan, Haffner
(symphony No 35), Jupiter (symphony No 41), Requiem,
Turkish (concerto) **8** Idomeneo **9** Credo Mass, Mitridate
10 Lucio Silla **11** Don Giovanni, Hunt Quartet, Il Re Pas-
tore, Sparrow Mass **12** A Musical Joke, Cosi Fan Tutte
(So Do They All or Women Are Like That), Haydn Quar-
tet, Spatzenmesse **13** The Magic Flute, Trumpet Sonata,
Turkish Sonata **14** Coronation Mass, Stadler Quintet, Die
Zauberflote **15** Haffner Serenade, La Finta Semplice, Prus-
sian Quartet **16** Dissonant Quartet, La Clemenza di Tito,
Posthorn Serenade, Serenata Notturna **17** A Little Night
Music **18** Jeunehomme Concerto, La Finta Giardiniera,
The Clemency of Titus **19** Bastien und Bastienne, The
Marriage of Figaro **20** Eine Kleine Nachtmusik, The Pre-
tender Gardener **21** Der Schauspieldirektor, Ein Musikal-
ischer Spass **22** The Pretending Simpleton **25** Die
Entfuhrung aus dem Serail **27** The Abduction from the
Seraglio

muddy 4 dull **5** dirty, grimy, vague **6** filthy, grubby **7** obscure **8** begrimed, confused

muff 5 botch, spoil **6** bungle **10** handwarmer

muffle 3 gag **4** dull, hush, mask, mute, veil, wrap **5** cloak, cover, quell, quiet, still **6** dampen, deaden, shroud, soften, stifle, swathe **7** conceal, enclose, envelop, silence, swaddle

muffled 3 low **4** dull, soft **5** faint, muted **6** dulled, feeble, hushed, veiled **7** cloaked, covered, quelled, quieted, stilled, subdued, swathed, wrapped **8** deadened, shrouded, silenced, softened, swaddled **9** concealed, enveloped, inaudible **10** indistinct, suppressed

mug 3 cup **4** face, puss, toby **5** stein, stoup **6** beaker, flagon, goblet, kisser, visage **7** chalice, tankard, toby jug, tumbler **11** countenance

mugger 8 assailer, attacker **9** assailant, assaulter

mugginess 4 damp **8** dampness, dankness, humidity **9** humidness **10** sultriness **14** oppressiveness

muggy 5 close, humid **6** clammy, steamy, sticky, stuffy, sultry, sweaty **8** steaming, vaporous **10** oppressive, sweltering

Muisca *see* **7** Chibcha

mulberry 5 Morus
varieties: **3** red **4** Aino **5** black, paper, white **6** French, Indian **7** Russian **8** American, silkworm

Mulciber
epithet of: **6** Vulcan
means: **6** melter

mulct 4 bilk **6** extort **7** defraud, swindle

mule 3 ass **5** burro **6** donkey **7** jackass
group of: **4** span

mulish 5 balky **6** ornery **8** perverse, stubborn **9** fractious, obstinate **10** refractory **11** intractable **12** recalcitrant

Mulius
wife: **7** Agamede
father-in-law: **6** Augeas
position: **8** spearman
killed by: **6** Nestor

mull, mull over 5 study, weigh **6** ponder **8** consider, meditate, pore over, ruminate **10** deliberate

Muller
character in: **25** All Quiet on the Western Front
author: **8** Remarque

Muller, Hermann Joseph
field: **8** genetics
researched: **5** X-rays **8** mutation
awarded: **10** Nobel Prize

Muller, Paul
field: **9** chemistry
nationality: **5** Swiss
established: **16** DDT as insecticide
awarded: **10** Nobel Prize

Mulligan, Buck
character in: **7** Ulysses
author: **5** Joyce

multicolored 10 variegated

multifarious 4 many **5** mixed **6** divers, motley, sundry, varied **7** diverse, protean, several, various **8** manifold, numerous **9** different, multiplex **10** variegated **11** diversified **13** heterogeneous, miscellaneous

multiple 4 many **7** various **8** manifold

multiply 5 add to, beget, breed, raise **6** extend, spread **7** augment, enhance, enlarge, magnify **8** generate, heighten, increase **9** intensify, procreate, propagate, reproduce **11** proliferate

multitude 3 mob **4** army, herd, host, mass, pack, slew **5** array, crowd, crush, drove, flock, flood, horde, troop **6** legion, myriad, scores, throng **7** conflux

multum in parvo 12 much in little **23** a great deal in a small space

mum 4 mute **5** quiet, still, tacit **6** silent **8** taciturn, wordless **9** secretive **12** closemouthed **15** uncommunicative

mumble 5 growl, grunt, mouth **6** murmur, mutter, rumble **7** stammer **9** hem and haw

mumbo jumbo 3 rot **4** blah, bosh, cant, tosh **5** bilge, hokum, hooey, tripe **6** hot air, humbug **7** baloney **8** flummery **9** gibberish, sophistry **10** double talk, hocus pocus **11** doublespeak, jabberwocky, obfuscation **12** fiddle-faddle, gobbledygook, obscurantism

Mummy, The
director: **10** Karl Freund
cast: **10** Zita Johann **12** Boris Karloff, David Manners **16** Bramwell Fletcher

munch 4 chew, gnaw **5** champ, chomp, crush, grind **9** masticate

Munch, Edvard
born: **5** Loten **6** Norway **10** Hedemarken
artwork: **6** The Cry **7** Puberty, The Kiss **9** The Scream **11** Dance of Life **12** Frieze of Life **21** Death in the Sick Chamber

Munchkins
characters in: **13** The Wizard of Oz
author: **4** Baum

mundane 5 petty **7** earthly, humdrum, prosaic, routine, worldly **8** day-to-day, everyday, ordinary **9** practical **10** pedestrian **11** commonplace, down-to-earth, terrestrial

Muni, Paul
real name: **16** Muni Weisenfreund
born: **7** Austria, Lemberg (now Lvov USSR)
roles: **6** Juarez **8** Scarface **10** The Valiant **12** The Good Earth **14** Clarence Darrow, Inherit the Wind **15** The Last Angry Man **18** The Life of Emile Zola **22** The Story of Louis Pasteur (Oscar) **26** I Am a Fugitive from a Chain Gang

municipal 4 city **5** civic **6** public **9** community **14** administrative

municipality 4 city, town **6** parish **7** village **8** township **9** bailiwick

munificence 6 bounty **7** charity **8** largesse **9** patronage **10** generosity, liberality **11** benefaction, beneficence, benevolence **12** philanthropy **13** bounteousness, bountifulness **14** charitableness **15** humanitarianism

munificent 4 free **6** kindly, lavish **7** liberal, profuse **8** generous, princely **9** bounteous, bountiful **10** altruistic, beneficent, benevolent, charitable, freehanded, open-handed **11** extravagant, magnanimous **12** eleemosynary, humanitarian **13** philanthropic

Munin
origin: **12** Scandinavian
form: **5** raven
owned by: **4** Odin **5** Othin
personifies: **6** memory
duty: **10** newsbearer
other raven: **5** Hugin

Munitus
father: **6** Acamas
mother: **7** Laodice

Muppet Show, The
character: **4** Rolf **5** Gonzo
6 Animal, Beaker **7** Scooter
9 Miss Piggy **10** Fozzie Bear
13 Kermit the Frog (Kermie)

Murasaki, Lady
author of: **14** The Tale of
Genji

murder 4 kill, slay **5** abuse,
waste **6** mangle, misuse
7 butcher, corrupt, cut down,
killing **8** homicide, knock off
9 agonizing, slaughter **10** bastardize, formidable, impossible,
oppressive, unbearable **11** assassinate, intolerable **12** manslaughter **13** assassination, very
difficult **14** commit homicide,
use incorrectly

murderer 4 Cain **6** killer, slayer
7 butcher **8** assassin, Barabbas,
homicide **9** cutthroat

Murder in the Cathedral
author: **7** T S Eliot

**Murder of Roger Ackroyd,
The**
author: **14** Agatha Christie

**Murder on the Orient
Express**
author: **14** Agatha Christie

murderous 4 gory **5** cruel,
rough **6** bloody, brutal, deadly,
savage, trying **7** killing **9** dangerous, difficult, ferocious
11 devastating **12** bloodthirsty,
disaggreeable

Murdoch, Iris
author of: **7** The Bell **11** Under the Net **12** A Severed
Head, The Sea the Sea
14 The Black Prince **15** Nuns
and Soldiers **17** The Good
Apprentice, The Nice and
the Good

**Murillo, Bartolome (Bartolo-
meo) Esteban**
born: **5** Spain **7** Seville
artwork: **13** Angels' Kitchen
14 Death of St Clare **15** The
Two Trinities **17** Vision of St
Anthony **23** The Immaculate
Conception **24** Dream of the
Roman Patrician

murk 3 fog **4** haze, mist
5 gloom **6** miasma **8** darkness

murky 3 dim **4** dark, gray, hazy
5 dusky, foggy, misty **6** cloudy,
dismal, dreary, gloomy, somber
7 obscure, sunless **8** lowering,
overcast, vaporous **9** cheerless

murmur 3 hum **4** buzz, purl,
purr, sigh **5** drone, sough,
swish **6** lament, mumble, mutter, rumble, rustle **7** grumble,
lapping, whimper, whisper
8 low sound, susurrus **9** complaint, undertone

murophobia
fear of: **4** mice

Murphy, Eddie
roles: **3** Raw **13** Trading Places
14 The Golden Child
15 Coming to America,
Forty-Eight Hours **16** Beverly
Hills Cop **17** Saturday Night
Live **19** Beverly Hills Cop
Two

Murray, Bill
roles: **7** Stripes **9** Meatballs
10 Caddyshack **12** Ghostbusters **13** The Razor's Edge
17 Saturday Night Live
27 Not Ready for Prime Time
Players

Muscat, Masqat
capital of: **4** Oman

muscle *see box*

muscular 3 fit **5** burly, husky,
tough **6** brawny, sinewy,
strong **8** athletic, powerful
9 strapping

muscular contraction
5 cramp, crick, spasm **6** stitch
12 charley horse

---

muscle 4 grit, thew **5** bi-
cep, brawn, force, might,
power, sinew, vigor **6** energy, flexor, tendon **7** potency, prowess, stamina
8 virility **9** puissance
10 sturdiness **16** muscular
strength
kind: **4** limb **5** axial
6 smooth **7** dynamic,
flexors, special, striped
8 postural, striated **9** ab-
ductors, extensors, vol-
untary **11** involuntary
fuel: **4** food
action: **4** pull
specific: **6** rectus **7** deltoid,
oblique **8** omohyoid **9** ab-
dominal, abdominis, sar-
torius **10** pectoralis
11 intercostal, sternohy-
oid **13** biceps brachii,
rectus femoris **14** vastus
medialis **15** brachioradi-
alis, vastus lateralis
16 serratus anterior, ten-
sor fascia lata **17** quadri-
ceps femoris
18 transverse thoracic
19 sternocleidomastoid
20 transversus abdominis
supplementary structure:
6 sheath **10** deep fascia,
retinacula **14** synovial
bursae, synovial sheath

---

musculoskeletal system
component: **4** bone **6** muscle,
tendon **8** ligament

muse 4 mull **6** ponder, review
7 reflect **8** cogitate, consider,
meditate, ruminate **9** speculate
10 deliberate **11** contemplate

Muses
also: **7** the Nine **8** Pierides
10 Castalides
form: **9** goddesses
names: **4** Clio **5** Aoede, Erato,
Mneme **6** Melete, Thalia,
Urania **7** Euterpe **8** Calliope
9 Melpomene **10** Polyhymnia
11 Terpsichore
father: **4** Zeus
mother: **9** Mnemosyne
corresponds to: **7** Camenae

mush 5 slush **6** drivel **8** porridge **14** sentimentalism,
sentimentality

mushiness 5 slush **6** bathos
10 sponginess **11** mawkishness
14 sentimentalism,
sentimentality

---

mushroom 4 grow
5 burst, fungi **6** blow up,
expand, fungus, spread,
sprout **7** burgeon, explode,
shoot up **8** flourish, increase, spring up **9** toadstool **11** proliferate
part: **3** cap **4** veil **5** gills,
stalk, tubes, volva **6** button, hyphae, spores
7 annulus, basidia
10 rhizomorph
non-poisonous: **5** field,
honey, morel, table
6 oyster **7** inky cap, parasol **8** puffball, shiitake
9 fairy-ring, morchella,
shaggy cap, stinkhorn
10 champignon **11** chan-
terelle **12** edible bolete,
slippery jack **16** old man
of the woods
poisonous: **7** amanita
8 death cap, sickener
9 fly agaric **12** jack-o-lan-
tern **13** devil's boletus
15 destroying angel
study of: **8** mycology

---

mushy 4 soft **5** foggy, misty,
pappy, pulpy, vague **6** cloudy,
quaggy, spongy **7** maudlin,
mawkish, squashy, squishy
8 effusive, romantic, squelchy
10 lovey-dovey **11** sentimental,
tear-jerking **12** affectionate

Musial, Stan
nickname: **10** Stan the Man

sport: 8 baseball
team: 16 St Louis Cardinals

music 4 song, tune **5** score
6 melody **7** euphony, harmony
8 lyricism **10** minstrelsy
11 tunefulness
13 melodiousness
  god of: 5 Brage, Bragi
  6 Apollo **7** Phoebus, Pythius
  9 Musagetes

musical 5 lyric, sweet **6** dulcet
7 lilting, lyrical, melodic, tuneful **9** melodious **10** euphonious, harmonious **11** mellifluent

musical instrument *see box*

musical terms *see box*

musician 4 bard **5** piper **6** artist, player, singer, violer **7** bandman, cellist, drummer, pianist, twanger **8** minstrel, organist, virtuoso **9** performer, trumpeter, violinist **11** saxophonist

Music Man, The
  director: 13 Morton Da Costa
  cast: 12 Buddy Hackett, Shirley Jones (Marian the librarian) **13** Robert Preston (Professor Harold Hill)
  15 Hermione Gingold
  setting: 9 River City
  score: 15 Meredith Willson
  song: 15 Till There Was You
  19 Seventy-six Trombones

music school 12 conservatory
  French: 13 conservatoire

musing 6 absent, dreamy
7 mulling **8** absorbed **9** pondering **10** meditating, meditative, reflecting, reflective

musjid 6 mosque

Muskogean, Muskhogean
  tribe: 4 Cree **7** Alabama, Alibamu, Choctaw, Natchez
  8 Seminole **9** Chickasaw

Muslim *see* **6** Moslem

muslin
  French: 10 mousseline

muss 4 mess foul up, jumble, ruffle, rumple, tangle, tousle **7** crumple, disturb **8** dishevel, disorder **9** bedraggle
10 disarrange

mussed 5 messy **6** frowzy, untidy **7** ruffled, rumpled, tousled, unkempt **8** uncombed
10 disarrayed, disheveled, disordered, disorderly
11 disarranged

Mussorgsky (Moussorgsky), Modest Petrovich
  born: 5 Pskov **6** Russia
  member of: 7 The Five
  composer of: 7 Sunless **10** The Nursery **12** Boris Godunov
  13 Khovanshchina **19** Night on Bald Mountain

mustard
  botanical name: 5 B alba **6** B hirta, B nigra **7** B juncea
  8 Brassica
  also called: 7 sinapis
  origin: 4 Asia **5** China
  use: 6 hotdog, sauces **7** egg roll **9** hamburger **13** salad dressing

muster 4 call **5** amass, raise, rally **6** gather, line up, summon **7** collect, company, convene, convoke, marshal, meeting, round up, turnout
8 assemble, assembly, mobilize
9 convocate, gathering **10** assemblage, confluence, congregate, inspection **11** aggregation
12 accumulation
13 agglomeration

musty 3 old **4** damp, dank, worn **5** banal, dirty, dusty, moldy, stale, tired, trite

musical terms
  agitated: 7 agitato
  all players/singers together: 5 tutti
  becoming quicker:
    11 accelerando
  continue without a break:
    5 segue
  disconnected/each note separate: 8 staccato
  end: 4 fine
  expressively: 10 espressivo
    abbreviation: 4 espr
  fast: 6 veloce **7** allegro
  gentle: 5 soave
  gently: 9 doucement
  getting slower:
    10 allargando
  getting weaker and slower: 7 calando
  gradually getting louder:
    9 crescendo
    abbreviation: 5 cresc
  gradually getting softer:
    10 diminuendo
    11 decrescendo
    abbreviation: 3 dim
    4 decr
  gradually slowing:
    11 rallentando
    abbreviation: 4 rall
  half: 5 mezzo
  half voice/half volume:
    9 mezza voce
  heavy: 5 lourd
  in an undertone/in a low voice: 9 sotto voce
  leisurely: 6 comodo
  less: 4 meno
  light: 8 leggiero
  little: 4 poco
  lively: 3 vif
  loud: 5 forte
    abbreviation: 1 f
  moderately slow and even: 7 andante
  more: 3 piu
  mournful: 5 mesto

musical instrument 3 lur, sax, saz **4** bass, bell, drum, fife, gong, harp, horn, lute, lyre, oboe, outi, pipe, tuba, viol **5** argul, banjo, bugle, cello, cobza, flute, kazoo, organ, piano, guena, rabob, sansa, shawm, sheng, sitar, viola **6** bagana, chimes, cornet, cymbal, fiddle, guitar, spinet, treble, violin, zither **7** bagpipe, bassoon, cittern, clavier, kithara, marimba, panpipe, pibcorn, piccolo, samisen, strings, tambura, theorbo, timpani, trumpet, ukulele **8** autoharp, bass drum, calliope, clarinet, dulcimer, Jew's harp, mandolin, psaltery, recorder, talharpa, triangle, trombone, virginal **9** accordion, balalaika, castanets, harmonica, harmonium, krummhorn, rommelpot, saxophone, snare drum, xylophone **10** bongo drums, clavichord, concertina, flugelhorn, French horn, kettledrum, sousaphone, tambourine, vibraphone **11** English horn, harpsichord **12** jouhikantele
  classification: 4 horn, reed, wind **5** brass **6** string **8** keyboard, woodwind **10** electronic, percussion

6 frousy, frouzy, frowsy, frowzy, old hat, stuffy **7** worn-out **8** familiar, mildewed **9** hackneyed **10** antiquated, threadbare **11** commonplace

mutable 6 fickle **7** pliable **8** flexible, variable **9** adaptable, alterable, mercurial, versatile **10** adjustable, changeable, inconstant, modifiable, permutable **11** convertible, metamorphic **13** transformable

mutate 4 turn **5** alter **6** change **7** convert **9** transform

mutation 6 change **7** anomaly **9** deviation, variation **10** alteration **12** modification **13** metamorphosis **14** transformation

not too much: 9 non troppo
plucked instead of bowed: 9 pizzicato
   abbreviation: **4** pizz
quick/vivacious: 6 vivace
repeat from beginning: 6 da capo
   abbreviation: **2** D C
shaking and quavering/ rapid alternation of notes: 5 trill
silent: 4 tace
singing/songlike/flowing: 9 cantabile
sliding: 9 glissando
slow: 5 lento **6** adagio
slow dignified tempo: 5 largo
slow down: 5 cedez
smooth/connected: 6 legato
soft: 5 piano
   abbreviation: **1** p
solemn/serious: 5 grave
sorrowful: 7 dolente
strict time: 10 tempo gusto
sudden accent: 9 sforzando
   abbreviation: **2** sf
sweetly: 5 dolce
tearful: 9 lacrimoso
tenderly: 10 affettuoso
trembling vibrating effect/ rapid reiteration of a single pitch: 7 tremolo
very: 5 molto
very loud: 10 fortissimo
   abbreviation: **2** ff
very soft: 10 pianissimo
   abbreviation: **2** pp
with fire: 8 con fuoco
with spirit/vigor: 7 con brio
with style/taste: 8 con gusto
with the mute: 10 con sordino

---

15 transfiguration
18 transmogrification

mutatis mutandis 30 necessary changes having been made

mute 3 mum **4** dumb **5** quiet, tacit **6** silent **8** aphasiac, nonvocal, reserved, reticent **9** unsounded, unuttered, voiceless **10** speechless **12** inarticulate, noncommittal, unpronounced **13** unarticulated **15** uncommunicative

muted 3 dim, low **4** dull, soft, weak **5** quiet **6** dulled, feeble **7** muffled **8** deadened, softened **10** indistinct, lackluster

mutilate 4 lame, maim **6** cut off, deform, excise, mangle **7** butcher, cripple **8** amputate, lacerate, truncate **9** disfigure, dismember

mutineer 5 rebel **9** dissident, insurgent **10** malcontent **15** insurrectionist

mutinous 6 unruly **10** dissenting, rebellious **13** revolutionary

Mutinus
   origin: 5 Roman **7** Italian
   god of: 9 fertility
   fertility in: 8 marriage
   corresponds to: 7 Priapus

mutiny 4 coup **5** rebel **6** revolt, rise up **8** takeover, upheaval, uprising **9** overthrow, rebellion **10** insurgency **12** insurrection

Mutiny on the Bounty
   author: 15 Charles Nordhoff, James Norman Hall
   character: 6 Tehani **9** Roger Byam **12** William Bligh (Captain Bligh) **13** George Stewart **17** Fletcher Christian
   director: 10 Frank Lloyd
   cast: 10 Clark Gable (Fletcher Christian) **12** Eddie Quillan, Franchot Tone **13** Herbert Mundin **15** Charles Laughton (Captain Bligh)
   Oscar for: 7 picture

mutt 3 cur, dog, pup **5** puppy **7** mongrel

mutter 4 carp **5** gripe, growl, grunt **6** grouch, grouse, kvetch, mumble, murmur, rumble **7** grumble, whisper **8** complain

mutual 5 joint **6** common, shared **7** related **8** communal, returned **10** coincident, reciprocal **11** correlative, interactive

mutual understanding 6 accord **9** agreement

muzzle 3 gag **4** bind, curb **5** check, quiet, still **6** bridle, rein in, stifle **7** harness, silence **8** strangle, suppress, throttle

Myanmar *see box*

My Antonia
   author: 11 Willa Cather

My Darling Clementine
   director: 8 John Ford
   cast: 7 Tim Holt **8** Ward Bond **10** Henry Fonda (Wyatt Earp) **12** Linda Darnell, Victor Mature (Doc Holliday) **13** Walter Brennan

my dear
   French: 7 ma chere, mon cher

My Fair Lady
   director: 11 George Cukor
   based on play by: 17 George Bernard Shaw (Pygmalion)
   cast: 11 Rex Harrison (Professor Henry Higgins) **13** Audrey Hepburn (Eliza Doolittle) **15** Stanley Holloway **16** Wilfrid Hyde-White
   score: 14 Lerner and Loewe
   Oscar for: 7 picture
   song: 14 The Rain in Spain **24** I Could Have Danced All Night

my faith
   French: 5 ma foi

my fault
   Latin: 8 mea culpa

Mygdon
   king of: 8 Bebryces
   killed by: 8 Hercules

Myles
   king of: 7 Laconia
   invented: 9 grain mill

Mylitta *see* **6** Ishtar

My Little Margie
   character: 7 Charlie **9** Mrs Odetts **11** Mr Honeywell **13** Freddie Wilson **14** Margie Albright, Vernon Albright **15** Roberta Townsend

my lord
   French: 8 monsieur **11** monseigneur
   Italian: 9 monsignor **10** monsignore

My Man Godfrey
   director: 13 Gregory La Cava
   cast: 10 Alice Brady, Mischa Auer **11** Gail Patrick **13** Carole Lombard, William Powell

Mynes
   king of: 9 Lyrnessus
   wife: 7 Briseis
   killed by: 8 Achilles

myriad 6 untold **7** endless **8** infinite, manifold **9** boundless, countless, limitless, uncounted **11** innumerable, measureless **12** immeasurable, incalculable **13** multitudinous

myrmidon 6 cohort **8** follower, henchman

Myrmidons
   people of: 6 Aegina **8** Thessaly
   created by: 4 Zeus
   created from: 4 ants
   characteristic: 7 warlike
   leader: 6 Peleus **8** Achilles

Myrrha
   also: 6 Smyrna
   father: 11 King Cinyras
   loved: 7 Cinyras

Myanmar
former name: 5 Burma
other name: 16 Land of the Pagodas
capital: 6 Yangon **7** Rangoon
   ancient capital: **3** Ava **4** Pegu **8** Mandalay
largest city: 7 Rangoon
others: 2 Ye **3** Ava **4** Pegu **5** Akyab, Bhamo, Katha, Minbu, Namtu, Papun, Prome, Tavoy **6** Hsenwi, Hsipaw, Lashio, Maymyo, Monywa, Shwebo **7** Bassein, Henzada, Pakokku, Toungoo **8** Moulmein, Myingyan
measure: 2 ly **3** dha, gon, mau, sao, tao, tat **4** byee, phan, seit, taun, that **5** shita, thuoc **6** lamany, palgat **7** chaivai **8** okthabah
monetary unit: 3 pya **4** kyat
weight: 2 ta **3** can, pai, vis **4** binh, kyat, ruay, viss **5** behar, candy, ticul **6** abucco **7** pciktha
lake: 4 Inle
mountain: 4 Chin, Naga, Pegu, Popa **5** Dawna **6** Arakan, Kachin, Lushai, Patkai **7** Karenni **8** Nattaung, Peguyoma, Saramati, Victoria **10** Tenasserim **11** Manipur Hill **12** Ta-nen Taunggi
highest point: 11 Hkakabo Razi
river: 3 Hka **4** Salwin, Sutang **7** Irawadi, Kaladan, Myitnge, Salween, Schweli, Sittang **8** Chindwin, Indawgyi **9** Irrawaddy
sea: 7 Andaman
physical feature:
   bay: **4** Siam **6** Bengal, Hunter **7** Heanzay **8** Thailand
   gulf: **8** Martaban
   plateau: **4** Shan
   port: **5** Akyab **7** Bassein, Henzada **8** Moulmein
people: 2 Ao, Vu, Wa **3** Kaw, Lai, Lao, Mon, Pyu, Tai, Was **4** Akha, Chin, Juki, Kadu, Laos, Lolo, Miao, Naga, Sema, Shan, Thai, Tsin **5** Karen, Lhota **6** Birman, Burman, Kachin, Peguan, Rengma **7** Akhlame, Burmese, Kakhyen, Palauna, Palaung, Siamese **8** Mon-Khmer **9** Arakanese **12** Tibeto-Berman
language: 3 Lai **4** Chin, Kuki, Pegu, Shan **5** Karen **6** Kachin **7** Burmese, English
religion: 5 Hindu, Islam **8** Buddhism **12** Christianity
place:
   mines: **6** Mawchi **7** Bawdwin
   pagoda: **9** Shwe Dagon
   road: **4** Ledo **5** Burma **9** Stillwell
feature:
   ball game: **7** chin-lon
   festival: **5** Water **6** Lights **10** Thadin-gyut
   silk headband: **10** gaungbaung
   skirt: **6** longyi
   traveling theatrical group: **4** Pwes

crime: 6 incest
son: 6 Adonis
changed into: 6 myrtle **9** myrrh tree

myrtle 6 Myrtus **10** Vinca minor **14** Myrtus communis **18** Cyrilla racemiflora **23** Umbellularia californica
varieties: 3 bog, gum, sea, wax **4** cape, Jew's, sand **5** crape, crepe, downy, dwarf, Greek, honey, scent **6** German, Oregon, Polish, willow **7** box sand, classic, running, Swedish **10** Western tea **11** candleberry, Queen's crape, sandverbena **13** Allegheny sand, bracelet honey, California wax **16** Australian willow

mysophobia
fear of: 4 dirt

mysterious 4 dark **6** cloudy, covert, hidden, secret **7** cryptic, obscure, strange, unknown **8** baffling, puzzling **9** enigmatic, secretive **10** perplexing, sphinx-like, undercover **11** clandestine, inscrutable **12** impenetrable, inexplicable, supernatural, unfathomable **13** surreptitious **14** undecipherable

Mysterious Stranger, The
author: 9 Mark Twain

mystery 6 enigma, occult, puzzle, riddle, secret **7** problem, secrecy **9** conundrum, obscurity, symbolism, vagueness **11** ambivalence, elusiveness **12** ineffability, quizzicality **13** ineffableness, mystification

mystical, mystic 5 inner **6** hidden, occult **7** cryptic, obscure **8** abstruse, esoteric, ethereal, symbolic **9** enigmatic, secretive **10** cabalistic, symbolical, unknowable **11** inscrutable, nonrational **12** metaphysical, otherworldly **14** transcendental

mystification 9 confusion **10** bafflement, perplexity, puzzlement **12** bewilderment

mystify 4 fool **5** elude **6** baffle, puzzle **7** confuse, deceive, mislead, perplex **8** bewilder, confound **9** bamboozle

myth 3 fib, lie **4** tale, yarn **5** error, fable, story **6** canard, legend **7** fantasy, fiction, hearsay, parable **8** allegory, delusion, illusion, tall tale **9** fairy tale, falsehood **10** shibboleth **13** prevarication

mythical, mythic 6 fabled, unreal **8** illusory **9** imaginary, legendary, pretended **10** conjured-up, fabricated, fantasized, fictitious **13** unsubstantial

mythological, mythologic 6 unreal **8** fabulous, illusory, imagined **9** fantastic, imaginary, legendary, unfactual **10** fictitious

My Three Sons
character: 11 Chip Douglas, Mike Douglas **12** Steve Douglas **13** Robbie Douglas **18** Katie Miller Douglas, Uncle Charley O'Casey **20** Ernie Thompson Douglas, Michael Francis (Bub) O'Casey
cast: 8 Don Grady, Tina Cole **12** Tim Considine **13** Fred MacMurray **14** William Frawley **15** Barry Livingston, William Demarest **17** Stanley Livingston
dog: 5 Tramp

my word
French: 5 ma foi

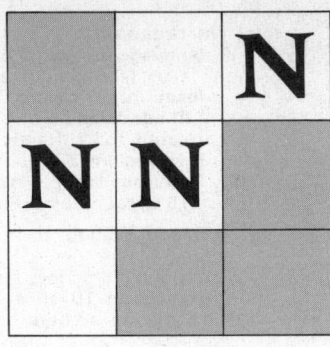

nab 4 bust, grab, nail, snag
5 catch, pinch, seize, snare
6 arrest, collar, detain, haul
in, pick up, pull in, snatch
7 capture 9 apprehend

nabob 4 lord 5 mogul, nawab
6 deputy, tycoon 7 magnate
8 governor 9 plutocrat 10 capitalist 11 billionaire,
millionaire

Nabokov, Vladimir
author of: 3 Ada 6 Lolita
8 Pale Fire

Nabonidus
son: 10 Belshazzar

Nadab
father: 5 Aaron 6 Gibeon
7 Shammai 8 Jeroboam
mother: 8 Elisheba
brother: 5 Abihu 7 Eleazar,
Ithamar

nadir 4 base, zero 5 floor 6 apogee, bottom 7 nothing 8 low
point 10 rock bottom 11 lowest point

Nadja
author: 11 Andre Breton

nag 4 fury, goad, harp 5 annoy, devil, harpy, scold,
shrew, vixen 6 badger, bicker,
harass, hassle, heckle, hector,
nettle, peck at, pester, pick at,
pick on, plague, rail at, tartar,
virago 7 bedevil, upbraid
8 battle-ax, irritate 9 importune, termagant, Xanthippe

Nahua *see* 5 Aztec

Nahuatl *see* 10 Uto-Aztecan

Naiad
form: 5 nymph
location: 5 water

nail 3 fix, pin 4 claw 5 talon
6 fasten, hammer, secure
part: 3 bed 4 root

Naipaul, V S
author of: 10 Guerrillas 15 A
Bend in the River 17 A
House for Mr Biswas

19 The Return of Eva Pe-
ron, The Suffrage of Elvira

Nairobi
capital of: 5 Kenya

naive 4 open 5 green, plain
6 candid, simple, unwary, unwise 7 artless, foolish, natural,
unjaded 8 gullible, immature,
innocent 9 childlike, credulous, guileless, ingenuous, unspoiled, unworldly
10 unaffected, unassuming
11 susceptible 12 unsuspecting,
unsuspicious
15 unsophisticated

naivete, naiveté 6 candor
7 modesty 8 openness 9 cre-
dulity, frankness, greenness,
innocence, sincerity 10 cal-
lowness, simplicity 11 artlessness, foolishness, naturalness
12 childishness, inexperience
13 ingenuousness 14 unaffectedness 16 simplemindedness

naked 4 bald, bare, nude,
pure 5 bared, frank, plain,
sheer 6 patent, simple, unclad
7 blatant, exposed 8 disrobed,
laid bare, manifest, palpable,
undraped, wide-open 9 in the
buff, unclothed, uncovered,
undressed 11 perceptible, un-
appareled, unqualified, unvarnished 15 in the altogether

Naked and the Dead, The
author: 12 Norman Mailer

Naked City
character: 5 Libby 9 (Det)
Adam Flint 10 (Det Lt) Dan
Muldoon, (Lt) Mike Parker
11 (Det) Jim Halloran,
(Ptlm/Sgt) Frank Arcaro
13 Janet Halloran
cast: 9 Paul Burke 11 Nancy
Malone 12 John McIntire
13 Harry Bellaver, Horace
McMahon, Suzanne Storrs
15 James Franciscus
setting: 11 New York City
theme: 19 Somewhere in the
Night

**Namath, Joe (Joseph
William)**
nickname: 11 Broadway Joe
sport: 8 football
position: 11 quarterback
team: 11 New York Jets

namby-pamby 3 coy 4 dull,
prim, weak 5 banal, inane,
vapid 6 prissy 7 insipid, mincing, sapless 9 colorless, innocuous, simpering 10 indecisive,
wishy-washy 13 characterless

name 3 tag 4 call, term 5 label,
title 6 choose, ordain, select
7 appoint, baptize, epithet,
specify 8 christen, cognomen,
delegate, deputize, nominate,
taxonomy 9 authorize, designate, signature, sobriquet
10 commission 11 appellation,
designation 12 denomination,
nomenclature

nameless 5 minor 7 obscure,
unknown, unnamed 8 unti-
tled 9 anonymous, unheard-of,
unhonored 12 undesignated

namely
Latin: 3 viz 9 videlicet

Name of the Game
character: 8 Andy Hill 9 Joe
Sample, Ross Craig 10 Dan
Farrell, Jeff Dillon 11 Glenn
Howard 12 Peggy Maxwell
cast: 9 Ben Murphy, Gene
Barry 10 Mark Miller
11 Cliff Potter, Robert
Stack 13 Tony Franciosa
15 Susan Saint James
business: 8 magazine
10 publishing

Name of the Rose, The
author: 10 Umberto Eco

Name That Tune
host: 9 Red Benson 10 Bill
Cullen 12 George de Witt
orchestra: 11 Harry Salter

Namibia *see box, p. 662*

Nammu
origin: 8 Sumerian

Namibia
other name: 15 South
West Africa
capital/largest city:
8 Windhoek
others: 6 Tsumeb 8 Lu-
deritz 9 Walvis Bay
10 Oranjemund, Swak-
opmund
12 Keetmanshoop
monetary unit: 4 cent,
rand
mountain: 14 Khomas
Highland, Koakoveld
Hills
highest point:
9 Brandberg
river: 4 Fish 6 Cunene,
Orange 7 Zambezi
8 Okavango
sea: 8 Atlantic
physical feature:
  bay: 6 Walvis
  desert: 5 Namib
    8 Kalahari
  region: 12 Caprivi
    Strip
people: 4 Nama
5 Bantu 6 Damara, Her-
ero, Ovambo, Tswara
7 Bushman, colored
8 Okavango 9 Hottentot
language: 5 Bantu
6 German 7 English,
Khoisan 9 Afrikaans
religion: 7 animism
8 Lutheran
feature:
  homeland: 9 bantustan

mother of: 4 gods
personifies: 3 sea

Namtar
origin: 8 Akkadian, Sumerian
form: 5 demon
personifies: 5 death

Nana
author: 9 Emile Zola

Nana (Nurse)
character in: 8 Peter Pan
author: 6 Barrie

Nancy
character in: 11 Oliver Twist
author: 7 Dickens

Nancy
creator: 15 Ernie Bushmiller
character: 6 Sluggo 10 Aunt
Fritzi

Nanna
origin: 12 Scandinavian
husband: 5 Baldr 6 Balder,
Baldur
habitat: 4 moon

Nannerella
nickname of: 11 Anna
Magnani

nanometer
abbreviation: 2 nm

Naoise
origin: 5 Irish
wife: 7 Deirdre
uncle: 9 Conchobar
killed by: 9 Conchobar
father: 6 Usnach, Usnech

Naomi
husband: 9 Elimelech
daughter-in-law: 4 Ruth
son: 6 Mahlon 7 Chilion

nap 3 nod 4 doze, rest 6 catnap, drowse, siesta, snooze
7 doze off, drop off, goof off,
shut-eye, slumber 8 drift off
10 forty winks

Napaeae
form: 6 nymphs
location: 4 dell

napery 5 doily 6 linens, nap-
kin 10 tablecloth

Naphtali
father: 5 Jacob
mother: 6 Bilkah
brother: 3 Dan, Gad 4 Levi
5 Asher, Judah 6 Joseph,
Reuben, Simeon 7 Zebulun
8 Benjamin, Issachar
sister: 5 Dinah
descendant of: 10 Naphtalite

Napoleon Bonaparte *see
box*

**Napoleon of Notting Hill,
The**
author: 12 G K Chesterton

Narcaeus
father: 8 Dionysus
mother: 7 Physcoa

narcissism 6 egoism, vanity
7 conceit 8 self-love 11 egocentrism 16 self-centeredness

narcissist 6 egoist 7 egotist
11 egocentrist 12 self-absorbed,
self-admiring

narcissistic 4 smug, vain
6 vanity 7 conceit, selfish
8 egotistic, puffed-up 9 conceited 10 egocentric, egoistical 11 egomaniacal, egotistical

narcissus
varieties: 5 poet's 6 poetaz
7 leedsii, trumpet 10 paper-
white, polyanthus 16 primrose peerless

Narcissus
father: 8 Cephisus
mother: 8 Leiriope
loved: 7 himself
loved by: 4 Echo
punished by: 9 Aphrodite
changed into: 6 flower

narcotic 4 drug 6 opiate
8 medicine, sedative 9 soporific 10 medicament, medication,
painkiller 12 tranquilizer
14 pharmaceutical

Narragansett
language family: 9 Algon-
kian 10 Algonquian
location: 11 Connecticut,
Rhode Island
related to: 7 Niantic
involved in: 9 Pequot War
14 King Philip's War
15 Great Swamp Fight

narrate 6 detail, recite, relate,
render, repeat, retell 7 portray,
recount 8 describe, set forth
9 chronicle 10 tell a story
15 give an account of

narration 7 recital, telling
8 relating, speaking 9 voice-
over 10 recitation, recounting
11 chronicling, description
12 storytelling

narrative 4 tale 5 story 6 report 7 account, recital 8 dialogue, episodic 9 anecdotal,
chronicle, statement 10 historical 12 storytelling

**Narrative of Arthur Gordon
Pym, The**
author: 13 Edgar Allan Poe

Napoleon Bonaparte
also: 9 Napoleon I
18 Emperor of the
French
battle: 3 Ulm 5 Eylau
6 Lutzen, Moscow, Tou-
lon (siege), Wagram
7 Bautzen, Dresden,
Leipzig, Marengo, Mon-
dovi 8 Borodino, Water-
loo 9 Friedland
10 Austerlitz 13 Aspern-
Essling, Jena-Auerstadt,
Peninsular War 22 War
of the Fifth Coalition
born: 7 Corsica
exile to: 4 Elba 11 Saint
Helena
fought against: 7 Kutu-
zov 10 von Blucher,
Wellington 14 Barclay
de Tolly
French fleet destroyed
at: 9 Trafalgar
  destroyed by:
    6 Nelson
laws: 14 Napoleonic
Code
marshal/general under:
3 Ney 5 Murat 7 Mas-
sena 10 Bernadotte
position: 7 emperor
11 first consul 13 con-
sul for life
tomb: 5 Paris 9 Invalides
wife: 9 Josephine
20 Marie-Louise of
Austria

narrow 3 set **4** fine, slim
5 close, scant, small, tight
6 biased, scanty **7** bigoted,
cramped, pinched, shallow,
slender, tapered **8** confined,
dogmatic, isolated, squeezed
9 hidebound, illiberal, parochial **10** attenuated, compressed, intolerant, provincial,
restricted **11** constricted, inca-
pacious, opinionated, reactionary **12** conservative

narrowing 5 taper **8** tapering
9 squeezing **11** compressing
12 constricting

narrow-minded 5 petty **7** bigoted, prudish **8** one-sided
9 hidebound, parochial, unworldly **10** provincial **11** opinionated, reactionary,
straitlaced **12** conservative
15 unsophisticated

narrow-mindedness 4 bias
7 bigotry **9** prejudice **10** unfairness **11** intolerance

narrows 4 neck, pass **5** canal
6 ravine, strait **7** channel, isthmus, passage

Nasca see **5** Nazca

**Nascimento, Edson Arantes
do**
    real name of: 4 Pele

Nash, Ogden
    author of: 6 Versus **9** Hard
    Lines **20** The Private Dining
    Room **21** I'm a Stranger
    Here Myself

Nashville
    director: 12 Robert Altman
    cast: 10 Karen Black, Lily
    Tomlin **11** Henry Gibson
    12 Ronee Blakley **13** Bar-
    bara Harris, Michael Mur-
    phy **14** Keith Carradine
    16 Geraldine Chaplin
    Oscar for: 4 song
    song: 6 I'm Easy

Nassau
    capital of: 7 Bahamas

nasty 4 foul, mean, vile **5** awful **6** odious **7** beastly, hateful,
vicious **8** horrible **9** repellent,
revolting **10** abominable, disgusting, nauseating, unpleasant **11** distasteful
12 disagreeable

Natchez
    language family:
    10 Muskhogean
    tribe: 6 Avoyel, Taensa
    location: 11 Mississippi
    13 South Carolina
    allied with: 7 Choctaw
    practiced: 14 head flattening

nates 4 buns, rear, rump, seat
7 rear end **8** buttocks,
haunches **9** fundament, posterior **12** hindquarters

Nathan
    father: 5 Attai
    served: 5 David **7** Solomon

Nathanael see **5** Jesus **8** Apostles **11** Bartholomew

nation 4 host, race **5** realm,
state, tribe **6** empire, people
7 country, kingdom **8** republic **9** community **11** sovereignty **12** commonwealth

national park see box

National Velvet
    director: 13 Clarence Brown
    cast: 10 Anne Revere
    11 Donald Crisp **12** Mickey
    Rooney **14** Angela Lans-
    bury **15** Elizabeth Taylor
    Oscar for: 17 supporting ac-
    tress (Revere)
    sequel: 19 International
    Velvet

native 4 home **5** basic, local,
natal **6** inborn, inbred, innate,
savage **7** citizen, endemic, natural **8** domestic, inherent, national, paternal **9** aborigine,
elemental, homegrown, in-
grained, inherited, intrinsic,
primitive **10** congenital, countryman, hereditary, indigenous **11** instinctive
12 countrywoman
13 autochthonous

native country 7 country
8 homeland **10** fatherland
13 mother country

native-grown 5 local **8** domestic **9** homegrown
10 indigenous

native land 8 homeland
10 birthplace, fatherland, native soil **13** mother country,
native country

native of Israel
    Hebrew: 5 sabra

native soil 8 homeland **10** fatherland, native land
13 mother country, native
country

Native Son
    author: 13 Richard Wright

natty 4 chic, neat, posh, tidy,
trim **5** smart **6** dapper,
jaunty, snappy, spruce **7** dashing, modish, stylish
11 fashionable

Natty Bumppo
    also: 7 Hawkeye **10** Pathfind-
    er, The Trapper **13** The
    Deerslayer **15** Leatherstock-
    ing **16** Le Longue Carabine
    character in: 23 The Leather-
    stocking Tales
    friend: 5 Uncas
    12 Chingachgook
    author: 6 Cooper

---

national park
    Alaska: 13 Mount McKinley
    Arizona: 11 Grand Canyon **15** Petrified Forest
    Arkansas: 10 Hot Springs
    California: 7 Redwood, Sequoia **8** Yosemite **11** Kings Can-
    yon **14** Channel Islands, Lassen Volcanic
    Canada: 4 Yoho **5** Banff, Fundy **6** Jasper, Kluane **8** Koo-
    tenay **9** Auyuittuq **13** Waterton Lakes
    Colorado: 5 Estes **9** Mesa Verde **13** Rocky Mountain
    Florida: 10 Everglades
    Hawaii: 9 Haleakala **15** Hawaii Volcanoes
    Kentucky: 11 Mammoth Cave
    Maine: 6 Acadia
    Michigan: 10 Isle Royale
    Minnesota: 9 Voyageurs
    Montana: 7 Glacier **11** Yellowstone
    New Mexico: 15 Carlsbad Caverns
    North Carolina: 19 Great Smoky Mountains (with
    Tennessee)
    North Dakota: 17 Theodore Roosevelt
    Oklahoma: 6 Platte
    Oregon: 10 Crater Lake
    South Dakota: 8 Badlands, Wind Cave
    Tennessee: 6 Shiloh **13** Cumberland Gap **19** Great Smoky
    Mountains (with North Carolina)
    Texas: 7 Big Bend **18** Guadalupe Mountains
    Utah: 4 Zion **6** Arches **11** Bryce Canyon, Canyonlands,
    Capital Reef
    Virginia: 10 Shenandoah **26** Colonial National Historical
    Washington: 7 Olympic **12** Mount Rainier **13** North
    Cascades
    Wyoming: 10 Grand Teton **11** Yellowstone

natural 5 plain **6** inborn, native, normal **7** earthly, genuine, regular **8** God-given, inherent **9** essential, intuitive, unstudied **10** unaffected, unmannered **11** instinctive, spontaneous, terrestrial **13** unpretentious **14** characteristic **15** straightforward

Natural, The
director: **13** Barry Levinson
based on story by: **14** Bernard Malamud
cast: **10** Glenn Close **12** Robert Duvall **13** Robert Redford

natural child 7 bastard **9** love child **17** illegitimate child

natural gift 5 flair **6** talent **7** ability, faculty **8** aptitude **9** attribute, endowment

natural habitat 5 range **6** domain, milieu **7** element **9** territory **11** environment

naturalize 5 adapt, adopt **6** adjust **8** accustom **9** acclimate **11** domesticate, familiarize

naturalness 4 ease **9** sincerity **10** simplicity **11** artlessness, genuineness **12** unconstraint **14** unaffectedness

nature 4 bent, kind, mood, sort, type **5** birth, earth, globe, humor, stamp, style, trait **6** cosmos, spirit **7** essence, feature, variety **8** category, creation, instinct, property, universe **9** character **11** disposition, peculiarity **12** constitution **13** particularity **14** characteristic
goddess of: **6** Cybele **9** Dindymene **10** Berecyntia

Nature
author: **17** Ralph Waldo Emerson

naught 3 nil **4** zero **5** nihil, zilch **6** cipher **7** nothing, useless **9** worthless

naughty 3 bad **4** blue **5** bawdy, dirty **6** ribald, risque, vulgar **7** wayward, willful **8** devilish, off-color, perverse **9** fractious, obstinate **11** disobedient, misbehaving, mischievous **12** pornographic, recalcitrant, unmanageable **13** disrespectful

Naum
son: **4** Amos

Nauru *see* box

nausea 7 disgust, heaving **8** contempt, loathing, retching, sickness, vomiting **9** repulsion, revulsion **10** queasiness **11** airsickness, biliousness, car sickness, seasickness **12** upset stomach **14** motion sickness, travel sickness

Nauru
other name: **14** Pleasant Island
capital: **13** Yaren District
cities: **3** Boe, Ewa **4** Aiwo, Ijuw **5** Baiti, Buada, Nibok, Uaboe, Yaren **6** Anabar, Anetan, Meneng **7** Anibare **10** Denigomodu
monetary unit: **4** cent **6** dollar
lake: **11** Buada Lagoon
sea: **7** Pacific
physical feature:
bay: **7** Anibare
lagoon: **5** Buada
point: **4** Anna **6** Meneng
people: **7** Chinese **10** Melanesian, Polynesian **11** Micronesian
explorer: **9** John Fearn
language: **7** English, Nauruan
religion: **10** Protestant **13** Roman Catholic
feature: **9** phosphate

Nausea
author: **14** Jean-Paul Sartre

nauseate 5 repel, upset **6** offend, revolt, sicken **7** disgust, repulse **8** make sick **15** turn one's stomach

nauseated 3 ill **4** sick **5** upset **6** queasy **8** repelled, revolted **9** disgusted

nauseating 9 offensive, repellent, repulsive, revolting, sickening **10** disgusting

nauseous 4 sick **5** upset **6** queasy **9** abhorrent, nauseated, offensive, repellent, repulsive, revolting, sickening, upsetting **10** disgusting, nauseating **12** unappetizing

Nausicaa
father: **8** Alcinous
position: **8** princess
aided: **8** Odysseus

Nausithous
father: **8** Poseidon
mother: **8** Periboea
occupation: **8** helmsman
employer: **7** Theseus
became: **4** king
realm: **8** Phaeacia

Nautes
advisor to: **6** Aeneas

nautical 5 naval **6** marine **7** aquatic, boating, oceanic **8** maritime, of the sea, seagoing, yachting

nautical mile
abbreviation: **3** nmi

Nautilus
submarine in: **32** Twenty Thousand Leagues Under the Sea
author: **5** Verne

Navajo, Navaho (Dine)
language family: **10** Athapascan, Athapaskan
location: **4** Utah **7** Arizona **9** New Mexico
noted for: **7** weaving **14** silversmithing
dwelling: **5** hogan

navigate 3 fly **4** ride, sail, ship **5** cross, steer **6** cruise, voyage **8** maneuver, sail over **11** plot a course **12** chart a course

navigation 7 boating, sailing **8** cruising, piloting, voyaging **9** traveling **10** seamanship
god of: **5** Niord, Njord

Navigators Islands *see* **12** Western Samoa

navy 5 fleet **6** armada, convoy **8** flotilla, warships

navy-blue 6 indigo **8** dark blue, deep blue

nay 4 also, deny, vote **5** never **6** denial, refuse **7** against, but also, refusal **8** negative

Nazarene *see* **5** Jesus

Nazarene, The
author: **10** Sholem Asch

Nazca, Nasca
location: **4** Peru **12** South America
noted for: **8** ceramics, textiles **10** Nazca lines (sketches on plain)

Nazi air force
German: **9** Luftwaffe

Nazi swastika
German: **10** Hakenkreuz

N'Djamena
capital of: **4** Chad

Neaera
mentioned in: **7** Odyssey
form: **5** nymph
father: **6** Pereus
cousin: **9** King Aleus
husband: **9** King Aleus
son: **7** Cepheus
daughter: **4** Auge **6** Evadne **8** Lampetia

Neal, Patricia
husband: **9** Roald Dahl
born: **9** Packard KY
roles: **3** Hud (Oscar) **15** A Face in the Crowd, The Fountainhead **18** The Subject Was Roses

near 4 nigh **5** about, close **6** all but, almost **7** close by, close to, looming **8** approach, come up to, imminent, next door **9** alongside, close with, impending **10** hereabouts **11** approaching, practically, proximately, threatening **13** approximately

nearby 5 close, handy **6** at hand **7** close by **8** next door **9** adjoining **10** accessible, hereabouts

near death
    Latin: **10** in extremis

near home 5 close **7** close by **10** hereabouts

nearly 4 nigh **5** about **6** all but, almost **7** close to, roughly **11** practically **13** approximately

nearly equal 5 close **7** similar **10** nip-and-tuck **11** approaching

nearly even 5 close **10** head to head, nip-and-tuck **11** neck and neck

nearness 8 intimacy, vicinity **9** adjacency, closeness, handiness, immediacy, proximity **10** contiguity **11** propinquity **12** availability, neighborhood **13** accessibility, approximation

neat 4 tidy **5** clean, great **6** groovy **7** concise, correct, orderly **8** accurate, exciting, original, straight, striking, succinct **9** competent, dexterous, efficient, ingenious, organized, purposive, shipshape **10** controlled, immaculate, methodical, systematic **11** imaginative, intelligent, uncluttered

neatness 5 order **8** tidiness **11** orderliness **12** organization

Nebraska *see box*

nebris
    skin of: **4** fawn

Nebrophonus *see* **5** Thoon

Nebuchadnezzar
    father: **12** Nabopolassar
    son: **12** Evilmerodach

nebula 4 Crab, Ring, Veil **5** Great **6** Lagoon **7** Rosette **9** Horsehead

nebulous 3 dim **4** dark, hazy **5** murky, vague **6** cloudy **7** obscure, unclear **8** confused **9** ambiguous, uncertain **10** impalpable, indefinite, indistinct, intangible **13** indeterminate

necessarily 8 perforce **9** naturally **10** inevitably, inexorably **11** accordingly **12** compulso-

rily **13** automatically, axiomatically, unqualifiedly **16** incontrovertibly

necessary 6 needed, urgent, wanted **7** crucial, desired, exigent, fitting, needful **8** required **9** called for, essential, requisite **10** compulsory, imperative, obligatory **13** indispensable

necessary changes having been made
    Latin: **15** mutatis mutandis

necessitate 5 cause, force, impel **6** compel, demand, oblige **7** call for, enforce, require **9** constrain, prescribe

necessitation 5 cause, force **6** demand, duress **8** coercion, pressure **10** compulsion, constraint, obligation **11** enforcement, requirement

necessity, necessities 4 must, need **6** demand, needed **7** urgency **8** exigency, pressure **9** essential, requisite **10** sine qua non **11** requirement **13** indispensable
    Latin: **10** sine qua non

neck 3 pet **4** kiss, nape, pass **6** caress, cervix, cuddle, fondle, smooth, strait **7** channel, isthmus, make out **9** narrowing

neckerchief 5 scarf **8** bandanna, kerchief

necklace 3 tie **5** beads, chain, noose **6** choker, collar, locket, pearls, string **7** jewelry, pendant **8** ornament **9** lavaliere

necktie 3 bow **4** band **5** ascot, black, scarf **6** cravat, string **7** Windsor **10** four in hand **11** half Windsor **12** hangman's rope

necromancer 5 hexer, magus, witch **6** wizard **7** charmer, warlock **8** conjurer, exorcist, magician, sorcerer **9** enchanter, occultist, voodooist **10** soothsayer **13** black magician, thaumaturgist

necromancy 5 magic, spell **7** sorcery **8** black art **10** witchcraft **11** enchantment, foretelling

necrophobia
    fear of: **5** death **10** dead bodies

necropolis 8 cemetery **9** graveyard **12** burial ground **13** burying ground

Nectar
    drink of: **4** gods
    gives: **4** life

Neda
    form: **5** nymph, river
    location: **11** mountaintop

Nebraska
    abbreviation: **2** NE **4** Nebr
    nickname: **4** Beef **8** Antelope **10** Blackwater, Cornhusker **12** Treeplanter's
    capital: **7** Lincoln
    largest city: **5** Omaha
    others: **5** Cozad **6** Gering **7** Kearney **8** Beatrice, Hastings **9** Broken Bow **11** Grand Island, North Platte, Scottsbluff
    college: **4** Dana **5** Doane **8** Duchesne, Hastings **9** Creighton **15** Midland Lutheran
    feature: **8** Boys' Town
        national monument: **11** Scott's Bluff **15** Agate Fossil Beds
    tribe: **3** Oto **4** Otoe **5** Kiowa, Omaha, Ponca, Sioux **6** Pawnee
    people: **10** Henry Fonda **11** Fred Astaire, Roscoe Pound
    lake: **7** Merritt, Sherman, Swanson **10** McConaughy **13** Lewis and Clark
    land rank: **9** fifteenth
    physical feature: **8** Badlands
        hills: **4** Sand **5** Drift, Loess
        plains: **5** Great
    river: **4** Loup **5** Logan **6** Dismal, Nemaha, Platte **7** Big Blue, Elkhorn **8** Missouri, Niobrara **10** Little Blue, Republican **12** Harlan County
    state admission: **13** thirty-seventh
    state bird: **17** western meadowlark
    state flower: **9** goldenrod
    state motto: **20** Equality Before the Law
    state song: **17** Beautiful Nebraska
    state tree: **3** elm **10** cottonwood

need 4 lack, want, wish
5 crave, exact 6 demand, penury 7 call for, longing, poverty, require, straits 8 distress, exigency, yearn for 9 essential, extremity, indigence, necessity, requisite 10 bankruptcy, insolvency 11 desideratum, destitution, necessitate, requirement 13 impecuniosity, pennilessness

needed 5 vital 7 crucial 9 essential, necessary, requisite 13 indispensable

needful 7 wishful 8 required 9 essential, necessary, requisite 10 imperative 13 indispensable

needle 3 vex 4 josh, leaf, ride, twit 5 annoy, chaff, harry, taunt, tease 6 badger, harass, hector 7 torment 9 indicator

needle-shaped 5 sharp 6 peaked, spiked 7 pointed 8 piercing 10 bodkin-like

needless 7 useless 9 excessive, pointless, redundant 10 gratuitous, pleonastic, unavailing 11 dispensable, purposeless, superfluous, uncalled-for, unessential, unnecessary 12 overabundant

needlework 6 sewing 7 basting, brocade, darning, tacking, tatting 8 applique, knitting, quilting 9 stitching 10 embroidery 11 cross stitch, needle point

needy 4 poor 5 broke 6 hardup, in want 8 indigent, strapped 9 destitute, moneyless, penniless 10 down-and-out 12 impoverished 15 poverty-stricken

ne'er-do-well 3 bum 5 idler, loser 6 loafer, no-good 7 goofoff, sad sack, wastrel 8 layabout 9 do-nothing, no-account 10 black sheep 14 good-for-nothing

nefarious 3 bad, low 4 base, evil, foul, vile 6 odious, wicked 7 beastly, ghastly, heinous, hellish, ungodly, vicious 8 depraved, devilish, infamous, infernal, shameful 9 atrocious, execrable 10 abominable, despicable, detestable, iniquitous, scandalous, villainous 11 disgraceful, opprobrious, unspeakable 12 dishonorable 13 unmentionable

Nefertem
origin: 8 Egyptian
personifies: 5 lotus
true identity: 4 Ptah

negate 4 deny, veto, void

5 quash, quell, rebut 6 defeat, disown, refute, repeal, revoke, squash 7 blot out, destroy, disavow, gainsay, nullify, retract, reverse, squelch, wipe out 8 abrogate, disallow, disclaim, set aside, vanquish 9 overthrow, overwhelm, repudiate 10 contradict, invalidate

negating 7 denying, voiding 8 refuting, revoking 9 reversing 10 cancelling, nullifying 11 disallowing 12 invalidating, setting aside 13 contradicting

negation 6 denial 7 counter 8 reversal 9 rejection 10 abrogation, disclaimer, refutation 11 confutation, repudiation 12 invalidation 13 contradiction, nullification

negative 4 blue, dark 5 bleak 6 at odds, gloomy 7 dubious, opposed 8 contrary, doubtful, downbeat, inimical, opposing, refusing 9 declining, demurring, dissident, jaundiced, objecting, rejecting, reluctant, skeptical, unwilling 10 dissenting, fatalistic 11 disagreeing, pessimistic 12 antagonistic, disapproving 13 uncooperative 14 unenthusiastic

neglect 4 fail, omit 5 let go, shirk 6 forget, ignore, laxity, pass by, pass up, slight 7 abandon, default, laxness, let pass, let ride, let slip 8 be remiss, idleness, let slide, omission, overlook, pass over, shake off 9 disregard, oversight, passivity, slackness 10 inaccuracy, negligence, remissness 11 dereliction, inattention, inexactness 12 carelessness, fecklessness, indifference, slovenliness 13 noncompliance, unfulfillment 14 nonpreparation 16 underachievement

neglected 7 dropped, ignored, omitted, shirked, unkempt 8 forsaken, untended 9 abandoned, cast aside, forgotten 10 overlooked, uncared for 11 disregarded

neglectful 4 lazy 5 slack 6 remiss, untrue 8 careless, derelict, heedless 9 forgetful, negligent, oblivious, unheeding, unmindful 10 inconstant, thriftless, unfaithful, unthinking, unwatchful 11 improvident, inattentive, indifferent, respectless, thoughtless, unobservant 12 devil-may-care, disregardant, disregardful, happygo-lucky 15 procrastinating

negligee, neglige 4 robe 6 kimono 7 wrapper 8 bathrobe,

peignoir 9 housecoat 12 dressing gown

negligence 6 laxity 7 neglect 11 disregarded 12 carelessness

negligent 3 lax 5 slack 6 remiss, untidy 8 careless, heedless, slovenly 9 forgetful, unheeding, unmindful 10 neglectful, unthinking, unwatchful 11 inattentive, indifferent, thoughtless, unobservant 13 inconsiderate

negligible 5 minor, petty, small 6 minute, paltry, slight 7 trivial 8 piddling, trifling 11 unimportant 13 insignificant 15 inconsequential

negotiate 4 cash, make, pass 6 barter, cash in, convey, dicker, haggle, handle, manage, redeem, settle 7 arrange, consign, deliver, discuss, get over 8 contract, cope with, deal with, hand over, make over, pass over, sign over, transact, transfer, transmit, turn over 10 bargain for 11 come to terms, meet halfway

negotiation 4 deal 6 treaty 8 argument, haggling 9 dickering 10 bargaining 11 arbitration, arrangement 12 compromising

negotiator 7 arbiter 8 mediator 9 go-between 10 arbitrator 12 intermediary

Negrette, Lolita Dolores
real name of: 13 Dolores Del Rio

Nehemiah
father: 5 Azbuk 14 Hachaliah

neigh 5 hinny 6 nicker, whinny

neighbor 4 abut, meet 5 touch 6 adjoin, be near, border, friend 7 conjoin 8 borderer, border on 9 associate 12 acquaintance

neighborhood 4 area, part, side, ward 5 place, range 6 locale, parish, region, sphere 7 quarter, section 8 confines, district, environs, precinct, purlieus, vicinity 9 community

neighboring 4 near, next 5 close 6 at hand, nearby 7 close by 8 abutting, adjacent 9 adjoining, bordering 10 contiguous 11 surrounding 12 circumjacent

neighborly 4 kind 5 civil 6 chummy, kindly, polite 7 affable, amiable, cordial, helpful 8 amicable, friendly, gracious, obliging 9 courteous 10 hospitable 11 considerate, warmhearted 12 well-disposed

Neighbors
author: **12** Thomas Berger

Neith
origin: **8** Egyptian
personifies: **10** femininity
son: **2** Ra
corresponds to: **6** Athena

Nekhbet
origin: **8** Egyptian
form: **7** vulture
guardian of: **5** Egypt **10** Upper Egypt

Neleus
king of: **5** Pylos, Pylus
father: **8** Poseidon
mother: **4** Tyro
twin brother: **6** Pelias
wife: **7** Chloris
son: **6** Nestor
12 Periclymenus
daughter: **4** Pero
refused purification to:
8 Hercules
killed by: **8** Hercules

Nelides
epithet of: **6** Nestor

Nelson, Harriet Hilliard
real name: **14** Peggy Lou Snyder
husband: **5** Ozzie
son: **4** Rick **5** David
born: **11** Des Moines IA
roles: **30** The Adventures of Ozzie and Harriet

Nelson, Horatio
also: **14** Viscount Nelson
nationality: **7** British
battle: **9** Trafalgar **11** Bay of Abukir **15** Battle of the Nile **16** Cape Saint Vincent **18** Battle of Copenhagen
defeated: **5** Danes **6** French **7** Spanish
flagship: **7** Victory
killed at: **9** Trafalgar
lover: **16** Emma Lady Hamilton

Nelson, Ozzie
real name: **18** Oswald George Nelson
wife: **15** Harriet Hilliard
son: **4** Rick **5** David
born: **12** Jersey City NJ
roles: **30** The Adventures of Ozzie and Harriet

Nemean
epithet of: **4** Zeus

Nemean lion
strangled by: **8** Hercules

nemesis 4 ruin **5** match, rival **7** avenger, justice, revenge, undoing **8** downfall, punisher, Waterloo **9** overthrow, vengeance **10** punishment **11** destruction, retaliation, retribution **16** instrument of fate

Nemesis *see* **8** Adrastea

nemine contradicente
11 unanimously **18** no one contradicting

nemine dissentiente
11 unanimously **15** no one dissenting

Nemo
character in: **10** Bleak House
author: **7** Dickens

Nemo, Captain
character in: **32** Twenty Thousand Leagues Under the Sea
author: **5** Verne

neologism, neology 7 coinage **9** nonce word

neon
chemical symbol: **2** Ne

neonate 4 baby **6** infant **7** newborn

neophyte 4 tyro **5** pupil **6** novice, rookie **7** convert, entrant, learner, recruit, student, trainee **8** beginner, disciple, newcomer **9** greenhorn, novitiate, proselyte **10** apprentice, tenderfoot **11** probationer

neoplasm 5 tumor **6** cancer, growth **7** sarcoma **9** carcinoma **10** malignancy **14** carcinosarcoma

Nepal *see box*

Nepali
language family: **12** Indo-European
branch: **11** Indo-Iranian
group: **5** Indic
spoken in: **5** Nepal

nepenthe 4 drug **5** drink, opium **6** heroin, opiate **7** hashish **8** narcotic

Nephele
counterfeit of: **4** Hera
formed by: **4** Zeus
husband: **7** Athamas
children: **8** centaurs
son: **7** Phrixus
daughter: **5** Helle

nephrite
variety: **4** jade

ne plus ultra 4 acme **12** highest point

Neptune
origin: **5** Roman

Nepal
other name: **9** Shangri-La
capital/largest city: **8** Katmandu **9** Kathmandu
others: **5** Patan, Patna **6** Gurkha **7** Birganj **8** Bhadgaon, Lalitpur **9** Bhaktapur **10** Biratnagar
university: **9** Tribhuvan
division: **5** Terai **13** High Himalayas
monetary unit: **4** anna, pice **5** mohar, paisa, rupee
mountain: **6** Cho Oyu, Churia, Lhotse, Makalu **7** Manaslu, Siwalik **9** Annapurna, Himalayas **10** Dhaulagiri, Gosainthan, Himalchuli **11** Ganesh Himal **12** Kanchenjunga **14** Mahabharat hekh
highest point: **9** Mt Everest
river: **4** Kali, Kosi, Mugu, Seti **5** Babai, Bheri, Rapti, Sarda, Tamur **6** Gandak **7** Karnali **8** Narayani
physical feature:
  plain: **5** Terai
  valley: **5** Nepal **8** Katmandu
people: **3** Rai **4** Aoul **5** Bhote, Limbu, Magar, Murmi, Newar, Tharu **6** Bhutia, Gurkha, Gurung, Nepali, Sherpa, Tamang **7** Kiranti, Tibetan **8** Gorkhali, Nepalese
  birthplace of: **6** Buddha **13** Gautama Buddha **17** Siddhartha Gautama
  king: **8** Mahendra **9** Tribhuwan **18** Prithwi Narayan Shah **23** Birenda Bir Bikram Shah Dev
  ruler: **4** Rana **5** Malla **6** Rajput
language: **6** Nepali, Newari
religion: **8** Buddhism, Hinduism
place:
  dam: **6** Gandak
  shrine: **9** Swayambhu **10** Gorakhnath
feature:
  animal: **3** dzo, yak **7** dzopkyo
  arch: **6** Juddha
  god/goddess: **5** Indra **6** Kumari
  legend: **4** Yeti **17** abominable snowman
  soldiers: **6** Gurkha

Neptune
- god of: 3 sea
- corresponds to: 8 Poseidon

Neptune
- position: 6 eighth
- satellite: 6 Nereid, Triton
- color: 5 green

Nereid
- form: 5 nymph
- location: 3 sea
- father: 6 Nereus

Nereus
- god of: 3 sea
- father: 6 Pontus
- mother: 4 Gaea
- father of: 7 Nereids
- number of Nereids: 5 fifty
- son: 7 Nerites

Nergal
- origin: 8 Akkadian
- ruler of: 4 dead
- consort of: 10 Ereshkigal

Nerissa
- character in: 19 The Merchant of Venice
- author: 11 Shakespeare

Nerites
- father: 6 Nereus
- mother: 5 Doris
- transformed into: 6 mussel
- transformed by: 9 Aphrodite

neritic 7 aquatic, coastal 8 offshore

Nero
- name: 18 Nero Claudius Caesar
- emperor of: 4 Rome
- mother: 9 Agrippina
- father: 19 Domitius Ahenobarbus
- stepfather: 8 Claudius
- tutor: 6 Seneca
- son: 11 Britannicus
- wife: 7 Octavia 13 Poppaea Sabina

nerve 4 dash, gall, grit, guts, sass 5 brass, cheek, crust, pluck, spunk, valor 6 mettle, spirit 7 bravery, courage 8 backbone, boldness, coolness, gameness, strength, tenacity 9 arrogance, assurance, derring-do, endurance, flippancy, fortitude, gallantry, hardihood, hardiness, impudence, insolence, sauciness 10 assumption, brazenness, confidence, effrontery, steadiness 11 intrepidity, presumption 12 fearlessness, impertinence, resoluteness 13 determination 16 stouteartedness

nerveless 4 calm, dead, weak 5 brave, frail, inert 6 feeble, flabby 7 flaccid 8 cowardly 9 powerless 10 courageous 12 fainthearted

nervous 4 wild 5 jumpy, shaky, tense 6 touchy, uneasy 7 alarmed, anxious, excited, fearful, fidgety, jittery, peevish, ruffled 8 feverish, neurotic, skittish, startled, timorous, unstrung 9 delirious, disturbed, excitable, impatient, irritable, sensitive, trembling, tremulous, unsettled 10 highstrung, hysterical 12 apprehensive

nervousness 6 tremor 7 anxiety, flutter, shaking, tension 8 hysteria, timidity 9 agitation, quivering, the creeps, the shakes, trembling, twitching 10 the fidgets, touchiness 11 disturbance, fidgetiness, stage fright 12 apprehension, excitability, irascibility, irritability, perturbation, timorousness 16 hypersensitivity

nervous system
- component: 4 ears, eyes 5 brain, taste, touch 7 ganglia 8 nerve end 10 nerve fiber, spinal cord

nervy 4 bold, firm, rude 5 brash, gutty, gutsy, sassy 6 brassy, brazen, cheeky, gritty, plucky, strong 7 assured, nervous 10 courageous, determined 12 stouthearted

Nesbitt, Cathleen
- born: 7 England 8 Cheshire
- roles: 10 My Fair Lady 18 Upstairs Downstairs 23 Three Coins in the Fountain

Nessus
- form: 7 centaur
- shot by: 8 Hercules
- caused death of: 8 Hercules

n'est-ce pas? 10 isn't that so?

nestle 3 lie, pet 4 live, snug, stay 5 clasp, dwell, lodge 6 bundle, caress, coddle, cosset, cuddle, enfold, fondle, huddle, nuzzle, occupy, remain, settle 7 embrace, inhabit, lie snug, snuggle 8 lie close 10 settle down

Nest of Gentlefolk
- author: 23 Ivan Sergeyevich Turgenev

Nest of Simple Folk, A
- author: 12 Sean O'Faolain

Nestor
- origin: 5 Greek
- attributes: 6 oldest, wisest
- father: 6 Neleus
- son: 10 Thasymedes 11 Pisistratus
- epithet: 7 Nelides

net 3 web 4 earn, gain, grab, grid, grip, mesh, snag, take, trap 5 catch, clasp, grate, seize, snare 6 clutch, enmesh, gather, grille, obtain, pick up, screen, snap up, take in 7 acquire, bring in, capture, collect, ensnare, grating, lattice 8 entangle, gather in, gridiron, meshwork 9 apprehend, grillwork, lay hold of, screening 10 accumulate 11 latticework
- constellation of: 9 Reticulum

nether 5 basal, below, lower, under 6 bottom, lowest 8 downward, inferior 9 subjacent 10 bottommost

Netherlands *see box*

Netherlands East Indies *see* 9 Indonesia

netherworld 4 hell 5 Hades 10 underworld 14 infernal region

nettle 3 vex 4 bait, gall, miff, rile 5 annoy, beset, chafe, harry, pique, sting 6 bother, harass, ruffle 7 perturb, prickle, provoke 8 irritate 9 displease 10 exasperate

nettle 6 Urtica
- varieties: 4 dead, dumb, hemp, rock 5 false, flame, hedge, horse, Roman 6 spurge 7 painted 8 stinging 9 white dead 11 spotted dead 12 western horse

network 3 web 4 grid, mesh, trap 5 grate, group, snare 6 grille, scheme, system 7 complex, netting, station

Network
- director: 11 Sidney Lumet
- based on story by: 14 Paddy Chayefsky
- cast: 9 Ned Beatty 10 Peter Finch, Wesley Addy 11 Faye Dunaway 12 Robert Duvall 13 William Holden 16 Beatrice Straight
- Oscar for: 5 actor (Finch) 7 actress (Dunaway) 17 supporting actress (Straight)

neuroptera
- class: 8 hexapoda
- phylum: 10 arthropoda
- group: 7 ant lion, fishfly 8 alderfly, lacewing, snakefly

neurotic 4 sick 7 anxious, intense, nervous 8 abnormal, unstable 9 disturbed, obsessive, unhealthy 10 distraught, immoderate 11 overwrought

neuter 5 fixed 6 barren, fallow, gelded, spayed 7 asexual, sexless, sterile 8 impotent 9 infertile

Neutra, Richard J
- architect of: 15 Mathematics Park (Princeton) 16 Lovell Heath House (Los Angeles

Netherlands
  other name: 7 Holland 12 Low Countries
  capital/largest city: 9 Amsterdam
  others: 3 Urk 5 Delft, Lisse 6 Almelo, Arnhem, Leiden, Velsen 7 Haarlem, Helmond, Hengelo, Limburg, Tilberg, Tilburg, Utrecht 8 Aalsmeer, Enschede, Ijmuiden, Nijmegen, The Hague 9 Apeldoorn, Dordrecht, Eindhoven, Groningen, Rotterdam 12 Scheveningen
  division: 6 Twente 7 Drenthe, Limburg, Utrecht, Zeeland 9 Friesland, Groningen 10 Gelderland, Overijssel 12 North Brabant, North Holland, South Holland 19 Netherlands Antilles
  government:
    legislature: 4 Raad 11 Eerste Kamer, Tweede Kamer
  head of state: 5 queen
  measure: 2 el 3 aam, ahm, ell, kan, vat 4 duim, mijl, rood, rope 5 anker, roede, wisse 6 bunder, legger, maatje, mutsje, streep 7 schepel 8 mimgelen, steekkan
  monetary unit: 4 doit, oord, raps 5 crown, daler, rider, ryder 6 florin, gulden, stiver, suskin 7 daalder, ducaton, escalan, escalin, guilder, stooter, stuiver 8 albertin, ducatoon 9 dubbeltje 12 rijksdaalder 13 albertustaler
  weight: 3 ons 4 last, pond 5 bahar 6 korrel 7 wichtje
  island: 5 Texel 7 Ameland, Frisian 8 Antilles, Vlieland
  lake: 7 Haarlem 10 Ijsselmeer 11 Grevelingen, Havingvliet
  highest point: 11 Vaalserberg
  river: 3 Eem, Lek 4 Leck, Maas, Waal, Ysel 5 Donge, Hunse, Meuse, Rhine, Schie, Yssel 6 Dintel, Dommel, Ijssel, Kromme 7 Scheldt
  sea: 5 North
  physical feature:
    canal: 6 Oranje 7 Juliana, Merwede 8 Drentsch, North Sea 10 Wilhelmina 11 New Waterway
    former bay: 9 Zuider Zee
    port: 9 Europoort
  people: 5 Dutch 7 Frisian 9 Hollander 10 Surinamese 12 Netherlander 13 South Moluccan
    artist: 4 Eyck, Hals 5 Appel, Bosch 7 Van Gogh, Vermeer 8 Mondrian, Ruisdael 9 Rembrandt
    author: 6 Vondel 7 Erasmus, Grotius, Spinoza 8 Vestdijk 9 Anne Frank
    explorer: 6 Tasman
    king: 7 William
    queen: 7 Beatrix, Juliana 10 Wilhelmina
    ruler: 5 Spain 13 House of Orange 15 Holy Roman Empire
    scientist: 7 Huygens 11 Leeuwenhoek
  language: 5 Dutch 7 English, Frisian
  religion: 13 Dutch Reformed, Protestantism 16 Roman Catholicism
  place:
    airport: 8 Schiphol
    bird sanctuary: 9 Waddenzee
    miniature town: 9 Madurodam
    museum: 9 Frans Hals, Stedelijk 11 Mauritshuis, Rijksmuseum 14 Vincent Van Gogh 19 Boymans-van Beuningen
    seat of government: 7 Den Haag 8 The Hague 11 'sGravenhage
    tower: 14 Schreierstoren
  feature:
    cheese market: 9 kaasmarkt
    earth mounds: 6 terpen
    flower: 5 tulip
    flower parade: 12 Bloemencorso
    pottery: 5 Delft
    reclaimed land: 6 polder
    wooden shoes: 7 klompen
  food:
    cheese: 4 Edam 5 Gouda 6 Leyden 7 cottage
    dish: 10 nasi goreng, rijsttafel
    drink: 3 gin 8 anisette, schmapps
    pea soup: 10 erwtensoep

CA) 17 von Sternberg House (Northridge CA) 22 Orange County Courthouse (Santa Ana CA)

neutral 4 mean 5 aloof 6 medium, middle, normal, remote 7 average 8 pacifist, peaceful, unbiased 9 impartial, in-between, peaceable, withdrawn 10 achromatic, indefinite, of two minds, unaffected, uninvolved 11 half-and-half, indifferent, nonpartisan, unconcerned 12 fence sitting, intermediate, noncombatant 13 disinterested, dispassionate 14 nonbelligerent, noninterfering 16 nonparticipating 18 noninterventionist

neutralize 4 halt, stop 5 annul, block, check 6 cancel, defeat, impede, negate, offset, stymie 7 balance, disable, nullify, prevent 8 overcome, suppress 9 frustrate, overpower

Nevada
  abbreviation: **2** NV **3** Nev
  nickname: **6** Silver **9** Sagebrush
  capital: **10** Carson City
  largest city: **8** Las Vegas
  others: **3** Ely, Nye **4** Elko, Reno **6** Fallon, Nellis, Sparks, Storey, Washoe **7** Boulder, Gerlach **9** Hawthorne, Henderson **11** Weed Heights **12** Virginia City
  explorer: **7** Fremont **13** Jedediah Smith
  feature: **12** Comstock Lode
    dam: **5** Davis **6** Hoover
    hot springs: **4** Tule **9** Punch Bowl, Steam Boat
    national monument: **11** Death Valley
  tribe: **5** Modoc, Washo **6** Digger, Mohave, Paiute **7** Klamath **8** Achomawi, Atsugewi, Shoshone
  lake: **4** Mead, Ruby **5** Tahoe, Weber **6** Mohave, Walker **7** Pyramid **8** Lahontan, Rye Patch **9** Wild Horse
  land rank: **7** seventh
  mountain: **4** East, Pine, Ruby **5** White **7** Rockies, Toiyabe, Wasatch **13** Sierra Nevadas
    highest point: **12** Boundary Peak
  physical feature: **7** geysers **10** hot springs
    basin: **5** Great
    cave: **6** Gypsum
    desert: **7** Sonoran
    plateau: **8** Columbia
  river: **5** Reese **6** Carson, Walker **7** Truckee **8** Colorado, Humboldt
  state admission: **11** thirty-sixth
  state bird: **7** sagehen **16** mountain bluebird
  state flower: **9** sagebrush
  state motto: **16** All for Our Country
  state song: **15** Home Means Nevada
  state tree: **9** pinon pine **15** single-leaf pinon

10 counteract **12** counterpoise, incapacitate **14** counterbalance

neutralizer 7 blocker **9** nullifier **12** counteractor, counteragent **15** counterbalancer

Neuvillette, Christian de
  character in: **16** Cyrano de Bergerac
  author: **7** Rostand

Nevada *see box*

never 4 ne'er **7** not ever **8** at no time, not at all

never-ending 6 steady **7** abiding, eternal, lasting, nonstop **8** constant, enduring, immortal, infinite, repeated, unbroken **9** ceaseless, continual, incessant, perennial, perpetual,

New Brunswick
  abbreviation: **2** NB
  bay: **5** Fundy, Maces **7** Shepody **9** Chignecto, Miramichi **13** Passamaquoddy
  channel: **5** Minas **10** Grand Manan
  city: **7** Moncton **8** Bathurst **9** Riverview **10** Edmundston, Saint John **11** Fredericton
  island: **4** Deer **6** Miscou **7** Machias **10** Campobello, Grand Manan
  known as: **16** Atlantic province, maritime province
  lake: **5** Grand **8** Oromocto **12** Magaguadavic **14** Chiputneticook
  people: **5** Irish **6** French **7** Acadian, English **8** American, Scottish **9** Algonkian **10** Anglo Saxon
  religion: **6** Canaan **7** Baptist **8** Anglican **10** Protestant **12** Presbyterian, United Church **13** Roman Catholic
  river: **5** Cains, Green **6** Renous, Salmon **7** Tobique **8** Kedgwick, Nashwak, Oromocto **9** Miramichi, Patapedia, Saint John **10** Nepisiguit, Richibucto, Saint Croix **11** Petitcodiac, Restigouche, Upsalguitch **12** Kennebecasis

recurring, unceasing **10** continuous, persistent, relentless **11** everlasting, unremitting **12** interminable, undiminished **13** uninterrupted

never-failing 4 firm, sure **6** proven, trusty **7** abiding **8** enduring, reliable **9** steadfast **10** dependable **11** trustworthy, undeviating, unfaltering **12** unhesitating, tried-and-true

nevermore 6 no more **10** never again

Never on Sunday
  director: **11** Jules Dassin
  cast: **11** Jules Dassin, Titos Vandis **14** Georges Foundas, Melina Mercouri
  setting: **6** Greece

nevertheless 3 but, yet **6** anyhow, anyway, even so, though **7** however **8** after all, although **10** contrarily, in any event, regardless **12** contrariwise **15** notwithstanding

Neville, Constance
  character in: **18** She Stoops to Conquer
  author: **9** Goldsmith

new 4 late **5** fixed, fresh, green, novel **6** modern, reborn, recent, remote, unused **7** altered, changed, current, just out, rebuilt, resumed, untried **8** original, reopened, repaired, restored, up-to-date **9** recreated, refreshed, remodeled, renovated, uncharted, unessayed, untouched **10** revivified, unexplored, unfamiliar, ungathered, unseasoned, unventured **11** regenerated, uncollected, unexercised **12** unaccustomed **13** reconstructed, reinvigorated

New Atlantis
  author: **12** Francis Bacon

New Brunswick *see box*

New Centurions, The
  author: **14** Joseph Wambaugh

newcomer 4 tyro **5** alien **6** novice **7** entrant **8** intruder, neophyte, outsider, stranger **9** foreigner, immigrant, outlander **10** interloper, trespasser

Newcomes, The
  author: **25** William Makepeace Thackeray

New Deal Agency 3 AAA, CCC, CWA, FCA, FHA, FSA, NRA, NYA, PWA, REA, SEC, SSB, TVA, WPA **4** FCIC, FDIC, FERA, HOLC, NLRD, USHA

New Delhi
    capital of: 5 India
    designed by: 7 Lutyens
    earlier city: 5 Dilli
    8 Dhillika, Din Panah,
    Kilookai **9** Firozabad
    11 Tughlukabad **12** In-
    draprastha **13** Shah
    Jahanabad
    invader: 5 Timur **6** Ab-
    dali **7** British, Rohilas
    8 Marathas **9** Nadir
    Shah
    landmark: 7 Red Fort
    9 India Gate, Qutb
    Minar **10** Iron Pillar,
    Jama Masjid **12** Huma-
    yun's Tomb **14** Con-
    naught Place
    15 Rajghat Memorial
    17 Rashtrapati Bhavan
    (Presidential Palace)
    23 Jantar Mantar Ob-
    servatory **30** Gandhi
    National Museum and
    Library
    river: 6 Yamuna
    street: 7 Raj Path
    (Kingsway)
    university: 15 Jawaharlal
    Nehru

New England *see box*

newfangled 5 novel **6** modern,
modish **7** stylish

new-fashioned 6 modern,
modish **7** stylish
8 up-to-date

Newfoundland
    abbreviation: 4 Nfld
    capital: 10 Saint Johns
    city: 19 Happy Valley Goose
    Bay
    lake: 7 Jeddore, Melville
    8 Meelpaeg
    10 Michikamau
    mountain: 9 Long Range
    river: 5 Eagle **6** Fraser, Gan-
    der **8** Exploits, Naskaupi
    9 Churchill
    section: 8 Labrador

New Granada *see*
    8 Colombia

New Guinea *see box*

New Hampshire *see box,*
p. 672

Newhart
    character: 4 Dick **6** Joanna
    7 Michael **9** Stephanie
    cast: 9 Mary Frann **10** Bob
    Newhart, Julia Duffy **12** Pe-
    ter Scolari

New England
    capital: 6 Boston **7** Augusta, Concord **8** Hartford **10** Mont-
    pelier, Providence
    city: 4 Lynn **5** Barre **6** Bangor, Lowell, Nashua **7** Hyannis,
    Rutland, Warwick **8** Brockton, Cranston, Lawrence, Lew-
    iston, New Haven, Portland, Stamford **9** Cambridge, Fall
    River, New London, Pawtucket, Waterbury, Worcester
    10 Bridgeport, Burlington, Manchester, Pittsfield, Ports-
    mouth, Woonsocket **11** Brattleboro, Springfield
    football team: 8 Patriots
    Indians: 6 Abnaki, Pequot **7** Mahican, Mohegan, Niantic,
    Nipmuck, Wangunk **8** Algonkin, Iroquois **9** Algonquin,
    Pennacook **10** Quinnipiac **12** Narragansett
    lake: 6 Sebago, Tiogue **7** Sunapee **9** Champlain, Moose-
    head **10** Candlewood **11** Pemaduncook **13** Winnipesaukee
    mountain: 5 Green, White **8** Greylock, Katahdin **9** Berk-
    shire, Mansfield **10** Washington **11** Appalachian
    river: 5 Otter **6** Thames **7** Charles **8** Kennebec, Pawtucket,
    Winooski **9** Merrimack, Missiquoi, Naugatuck, Pawcatuck,
    Penobscot, Saint John **10** Housatonic, Providence, Quinni-
    piac **11** Connecticut **12** Androscoggin
    state: 5 Maine **7** Vermont **11** Connecticut, Rhode Island
    12 New Hampshire **13** Massachusetts

New Guinea
    other name: 14 Papua New Guinea
    capital/largest city: 11 Port Moresby
    others: 3 Lae, Wau **4** Daru **5** Soron, Wewak **6** Aitape, Ki-
    kori, Medang, Rabaul **7** Gorolka, Kitbadi
    division:
        eastern half of island: **9** Indonesia, Irian Jaya
        western half of island: **14** Papua New Guinea
    government: 22 constitutional monarchy
    head of state: 14 British monarch **15** governor-general
    monetary unit: 4 kina, toea
    island: 3 Aru **4** Aroe, Buka **5** Arroe, Ceram, Japen, Jobie,
    Manus **6** Cretin, Mussau, Ninigo, Waigeu **7** Sainson, Solo-
    mon **8** Bismarck, Kiriwina, Schouten, Woodlark **9** Admi-
    ralty, Trobriant **10** Louisiande, New Britain, New Ireland
    12 Bougainville **14** D'Entrecasteaux
    mountain: 4 Snow **6** Orange **8** Bismarck, Victoria **9** Car-
    stensz **11** Owen Stanley **12** Albert Edward
    highest point:
        Irian Jaya: **9** Carstensz **10** Puncak Jaya
        Papua New Guinea: **7** Wilhelm
    river: 3 Fly **4** Hamu, Hany, Ramu **5** Degul, Sepik **6** Kikori,
    Purari **7** Amberno, Markham
    sea: 5 Ceram, Coral, Sepik **6** Indian **7** Arafura, Pacific, Sol-
    omon **8** Bismarck
    physical feature:
        bay: **3** Oro **5** Milne **8** Geelvink
        gulf: **4** Huon **5** Papua
        strait: **6** Torres, Vitiaz
    people: 5 Pygmy **6** Papuan **7** Negrito **10** Melanesian
        explorer: **15** Jorge de Menesses
        ruler: **7** Germany **9** Australia **12** Great Britain
    language: 4 Motu **7** English **16** Melanesian Pidjin
    religion: 7 animism **10** Protestant **13** Roman Catholic
    feature:
        bird: **7** mudlark **9** cassoway
    food:
        dried coconut meat: **5** copra

Newhart, Bob
    born: 9 Chicago IL
    roles: 7 Newhart **10** Cold
    Turkey **17** The Bob Newhart
    Show

New Hebrides *see*
    7 Vanuatu

New Jersey *see box,*
p. 672

New Hampshire
abbreviation: 2 NH
nickname: 7 Granite
capital: 7 Concord
largest city: 10 Manchester
others: 5 Dover, Keene 6 Berlin, Durham, Exeter, Nashua 7 Hanover, Laconia 8 Sandwich
  9 Claremont, Rochester 10 Portsmouth 12 Bretton Woods
college: 5 Keene 6 Rivier 9 Dartmouth, St Anselms 10 New England
feature: 14 Great Stone Face
  notch: 7 Kinsman, Pinkham 8 Crawford 9 Franconia
tribe: 6 Abnaki 9 Pennacook
people: 11 Robert Frost 12 Daniel French 13 Daniel Webster, Horace Greeley, Mary Baker
  Eddy
  explorer: 9 Champlain 16 Captain John Smith
island: 4 Star 5 White 6 Shoals 7 Lunging
lake: 5 Squam 7 Ossipee, Sunapee, Umbagog 8 Newfound 10 Winnisquam 13 Winnipesaukee
land rank: 11 forty-fourth
mountain: 5 Flume, White 6 Moriah, Paugus 7 Waumbek 8 Chocorua, Sandwich 9 Franconia,
  Monadnock 11 Profile Peak 12 Presidential
  highest point: 10 Washington
physical feature:
  bay: 5 Great
president: 14 Franklin Pierce
river: 4 Saco 6 Israel 7 Bellamy 8 Souhegan 9 Merrimack 10 Piscataqua 11 Connecticut,
  Salmon Falls 12 Androscoggin
state admission: 5 ninth
state bird: 11 purple finch
state flower: 11 purple lilac
state motto: 13 Live Free Or Die
state song: 15 Old New Hampshire 26 New Hampshire My New Hampshire
state tree: 10 paper birch, white birch

New Jersey
abbreviation: 2 NJ
nickname: 6 Garden 8 Mosquito
capital: 7 Trenton
largest city: 6 Newark
others: 4 Lodi 5 Ewing, Ft Lee 6 Camden, Dumont, Haddon, Kearny, Linden, Nutley, Orange,
  Rahway, Totowa 7 Bayonne, Cape May, Clifton, Hoboken, Hohokus, Keyport, Madison, Mat-
  awan, Netcong, Oradell, Paramus, Passaic, Raritan, Teaneck, Tenafly, Wyckoff 8 Carteret,
  Cranford, Freehold, Garfield, Hillside, Metuchen, Paterson, Secaucus, Watchung 9 Bridgeton,
  Elizabeth, Englewood, Hawthorne, Irvington, Maplewood, Montclair, Ocean City, Princeton
  10 Asbury Park, Belleville, Ft Monmouth, Hackensack, Jersey City, Livingston, Long Branch,
  Morristown, Perth Amboy 11 Bergenfield 12 Atlantic City, Collingswood, New Brunswick
colleges: 4 Drew 6 Upsala 7 Rutgers 8 Caldwell, Monmouth, St Peter's 9 Princeton, Seton
  Hall 10 Bloomfield 18 Fairleigh-Dickinson
feature: 9 Boardwalk 16 Delaware Water Gap
tribe: 8 Delaware 11 Lenni-Lanape
people: 9 Aaron Burr 11 Joyce Kilmer, Paul Robeson 12 Stephen Crane, Thomas Edison
  13 James Lawrence 19 James Fenimore Cooper
  explorer: 6 Hudson 9 Verrazano
lake: 6 Mohawk 9 Greenwood, Hopatcong
land rank: 10 forty-sixth
mountain: 8 Piedmont 10 Kittatinny 13 First Watchung 14 Second Watchung
  highest point: 9 High Point
physical feature: 9 Palisades, Sandy Hook
  bay: 8 Delaware
  cape: 3 May
  sea: 8 Atlantic
president: 15 Grover Cleveland
river: 4 Toms 6 Dennis, Haynes, Hudson, Mantua, Ramapo 7 Mullica, Passaic, Raritan 8 Co-
  hansey, Delaware, Tuckahoe 10 Hackensack
state admission: 5 third
state bird: 16 eastern goldfinch
state flower: 6 violet
state motto: 20 Liberty and Prosperity
state tree: 6 red oak
basketball team: 4 Nets
football team: 8 Generals
hockey team: 6 Devils

New Mexico
abbreviation: 2 NM 4 N Mex
nickname: 8 Sunshine 17 Land of Enchantment
capital: 7 Santa Fe
largest city: 11 Albuquerque
others: 3 Jal 4 Taos 5 Aztec, Belen, Hobbs, Raton 6 Clovis, Deming, Gallup, Grants 7 Artesia, Bananea, Roswell, Socorro, Torreon 8 Carlsbad 9 Las Cruces, Los Alamos 10 Alamogordo 13 Piedras Negras
college: 7 Sante Fe 11 Albuquerque
feature: 11 Four Corners
  dam: 5 Butte 8 Elephant
  labs: 6 Sandia 17 Los Alamos National
  national monument: 10 Aztec Ruins, White Sands 11 Chaco Canyon 17 Gila Cliff Dwelling
  national park: 15 Carlsbad Caverns
  observatory: 14 Sacramento Peak
tribe: 3 Sia 4 Hano, Piro, Tano, Taos, Tewa, Tiwa, Zuni 5 Acoma, Jemez, Kares, Manso, Pecos, Tiqua, Tonoa 6 Apache, Isleta, Laguna, Navaho, Navajo, Pueblo 7 Anasazi, Picuris 8 Santa Ana 9 Mescalero 12 Santo Domingo
people: 9 Kit Carson, Peter Hurd 11 Bill Mauldin
  explorer: 5 Onate 6 de Niza, de Vaca 8 Coronado
lake: 6 El Vado, Navajo, Sumner 7 Conchas 8 McMillan 10 Alamogordo 13 Elephant Butte
land rank: 5 fifth
mountain: 5 Jemez 6 Sandia 7 Manzano, Mimbres, Rockies, Truchas 8 Mogollon 9 Guadalupe, San Andres 10 Nacimiento, Sacramento 11 Mount Taylor 15 Sangre de Christo
  highest point: 11 Wheeler Peak
physical feature:
  basin: 8 Tularosa
  desert: 15 Jornada de Muerto
  plains: 5 Great
river: 3 Ute 4 Gila 5 Pecos 7 San Jose, San Juan 8 Canadian 9 Rio Grande
state admission: 12 forty-seventh
state bird: 10 roadrunner
state fish: 14 cutthroat trout
state flower: 5 yucca
state motto: 15 It Grows as It Goes
state song: 14 O Fair New Mexico 16 Asi es Nuevo Mexico
state tree: 5 pinon 8 tarantah 15 velvet ash pinyon

Malice, The Color of Money 16 Cat on a Hot Tin Roof, The Left-Handed Gun, The Long Hot Summer, The Silver Chalice 29 Butch Cassidy and the Sundance Kid

New Mexico *see box*

New Orleans
basketball team: Jazz
event: 9 Mardi Gras, Sugar Bowl 25 International Jazz Festival
football team: 6 Saints
landmark: 7 Cabildo 9 Old Square, Superdome 10 Vieux Carre 12 Pirate's Alley 13 French Quarter
noted for: 4 jazz
people: 5 Cajun 6 Creole 7 Acadian
river: 11 Mississippi
street: 5 Royal 7 Bourbon
university: 6 Loyola, Tulane

news 4 dirt, dope, talk, word 5 flash, libel, piece, rumor, story 6 babble, expose, gossip, report 7 account, article, chatter, hearsay, lowdown, mention, message, release, scandal, slander, tidings 8 bulletin, dispatch, exposure 9 statement 10 communique, disclosure, divulgence, revelation 11 information 12 announcement, intelligence

news account 4 item 5 story 6 report 7 release 8 bulletin, dispatch 10 communique

newsmonger 6 gossip 8 busybody, reporter

News of the Day
also: 12 Neues vom Tage
opera by: 9 Hindemith
character: 5 Laura 7 Eduoard

Newsome, Chadwick
character in: 14 The Ambassadors
author: 5 James

New Spain *see* 6 Mexico

newspaper 3 rag 5 daily, paper, sheet 6 herald, weekly 7 courant, gazette, journal, tabloid, tribune 10 periodical 11 publication

New Testament
books of: 4 Acts, John, Jude, Luke, Mark 5 James, Peter, Titus 6 Romans 7 Hebrews, Matthew, Timothy 8 Philemon 9 Ephesians, Galatians 10 Colossians, Revelation 11 Corinthians, Philippians 13 Thessalonians
books: 12 Humologumena

Newton, Isaac
field: 11 mathematics
nationality: 7 British

Newley, Anthony
wife: 11 Joan Collins
born: 6 London 7 England
roles: 11 Oliver Twist 25 Stop the World I Want to Get Off 41 The Roar of the Greasepaint The Smell of the Crowd

newly 4 anew 6 afresh, lately, of late 7 freshly, just now 8 recently

newly rich person
French: 12 nouveau riche

Newlywed Game, The
host: 10 Bob Eubanks
executive producer: 11 Chuck Barris

Newlyweds, The
creator: 13 George McManus
character: 12 Baby Snookums

Newman, Barnett
born: 9 New York NY
artwork: 7 Abraham, The Wild 8 Onement I 18 Stations of the Cross 19 Vir Heroicus Sublimis

Newman, Christopher
character in: 11 The American
author: 5 James

Newman, John Henry (Cardinal)
author of: 18 Apologia pro Vita Sua

Newman, Paul
wife: 14 Joanne Woodward
born: 11 Cleveland OH
roles: 3 Hud 6 Harper, Picnic 8 The Sting 10 The Hustler, The Verdict 12 Cool Hand Luke 15 Absence of

New York
   abbreviation: 2 NY
   nickname: 6 Empire 9 Excelsior
   capital: 6 Albany
   largest city: 7 New York
   others: 3 Rye 4 Rome, Troy 5 Ilion, Islip, Nyack, Olean, Owego, Utica 6 Attica, Auburn, Co-
     hoes, Elmira, Goshen, Ithaca, Oneida, Oswego, Tappan 7 Ardsley, Babylon, Batavia, Buffalo,
     Congers, Endwell, Geneseo, Hewlett, Mahopac, Merrick, Messena, Mineola, Montauk,
     Oneonta, Pennyan, Suffern, Syosset, Wantagh, Yaphank, Yonkers 8 Bethpage, Catskill, Endi-
     cott, Herkimer, Kingston, Ossining, Pottsdam, Saratoga, Tuckahoe 9 Rochester, Scarsdale
     10 Binghamton, Bronxville, Mamaroneck 11 Cooperstown, New Rochelle, Schenectady, White
     Plains 12 Poughkeepsie
   college: 4 Bard, CUNY, Iona, Pace, SUNY 5 Finch, Keuka 6 Hobart, Hunter, Vassar 7 Adelphi,
     Barnard, Colgate, Cornell, Fordham, St John's 8 Columbia, Skidmore, Syracuse 9 Juilliard,
     Rochester, West Point 13 Sarah Lawrence 30 Rensselaer Polytechnic Institute
   feature:
       building: 11 Empire State
       hall of fame: 8 baseball
       park: 7 Central
       prison: 6 Attica 8 SingSing
       square: 5 Times 6 Herald
       statue: 7 Liberty
       street/avenue: 4 Park, Wall 5 Fifth 7 Madison 8 Broadway
       tomb: 6 Grant's
   tribe: 4 Erie 6 Cayuga, Mohawk, Oneida, Seneca 7 Mohican, Montauk 8 Iroquois, Onondaga
     9 Manhattan, **people:** 7 John Jay 8 Walloons 9 Jonas Salk 10 Henry James 11 Rockefeller,
     Walt Whitman 12 Eugene O'Neill 13 DeWitt Clinton, John Burroughs 14 Herman Melville
     15 Peter Stuyvesant 16 Eleanor Roosevelt, Washington Irving 17 Fiorello La Guardia
       explorer: 6 Hudson 9 Champlain, Verrazano 16 Dutch West India Co
   island: 4 Fire, Long 5 Ellis 6 Staten 7 Bedloe's, Fisher's, Liberty, Shelter, Welfare 8 Thousand
     9 Governors, Manhattan
   lake: 4 Erie 6 Cayuga, Finger, George, Oneida, Otisco, Otsego, Owasco, Placid, Seneca 7 Co-
     nesus, Ontario, Saranac, Schroon 8 Saratoga 9 Champlain
   land rank: 9 thirtieth
   mountain: 4 Bear 5 Slide 7 Taconic 9 Catskills 11 Adirondacks
       highest point: 5 Marcy
   physical feature:
       bay: 7 Jamaica, Peconic 8 Moriches
       canal: 4 Erie 7 Gowanus
       falls: 7 Niagara
       valley: 6 Mohawk
   president: 14 Martin Van Buren 14 Teddy Roosevelt 15 Millard Fillmore 17 Theodore Roose-
     velt 23 Franklin Delano Roosevelt
   river: 4 East 5 Black, Tioga 6 Harlem, Hoosic, Hudson, Mohawk, Oswego 7 Ausable, Genesee,
     Niagara 10 St Lawrence 11 Susquehanna
   state bird: 8 bluebird
   state fish: 10 brook trout
   state flower: 4 rose
   state motto: 9 Excelsior (Ever upward, Still higher)
   state tree: 10 sugar maple

discovered laws of: 6 motion 7 gravity 8 calculus
discovered: 13 color spectrum 15 binomial theorem
   16 method of fluxions
invented: 21 infinitesimal
   calculus

New York *see box*

New York City *see box*

New Zealand *see box,*
p. 676

next-door 8 adjacent 9 adjoining 10 connecting, contiguous,
   juxtaposed, side-by-side,
   12 conterminous

next to 6 beside 8 abutting,
   adjacent 9 adjoining, bordering 10 contiguous, juxtaposed
   12 conterminous

next world, the 6 Heaven
   8 eternity, paradise 12 the
   hereafter 14 the world to
   come

Nez Perce (Numipu)
   language family:
       10 Shahaptian
   location: 5 Idaho 6 Oregon
       10 Washington
   leader: 11 Chief Joseph

Niamey
   capital of: 5 Niger

nib 3 end, tip, top 4 apex,
   peak 5 point 6 height, tiptop,
   vertex 7 extreme 8 pinnacle
   9 extremity

nibble 3 nip 4 bite, chew,
   gnaw, peck 5 crumb, munch,
   speck, taste 6 crunch, morsel,
   peck at, tidbit 8 fragment,
   particle

Nibelung, ring of
   origin: 8 Germanic
   mentioned in:
       14 Nibelungenlied
   stolen by: 8 Alberich

Nibelungenlied
   origin: 8 Germanic
   form: 4 epic

New York City

airport: 3 JFK 6 Newark 9 La Guardia 12 John F Kennedy

area: 4 Soho 6 Harlem 7 Chelsea, Midtown, Tribeca 9 Chinatown, Manhattan 10 Stuyvesant 11 Brownsville, Little Italy 13 Spanish Harlem 16 Greenwich Village 17 Bedford-Stuyvesant

baseball team: 4 Mets 7 Yankees

basketball team: 6 Knicks 14 Knickerbockers

borough: 5 Bronx 6 Queens 8 Brooklyn, Richmond 9 Manhattan

early governor: 10 Stuyvesant

football team: 4 Jets 6 Giants

former name: 12 New Amsterdam

hockey team: 7 Rangers 9 Islanders

island: 4 City, Long 5 Ellis, Ward's 6 Riker's, Staten 7 Liberty 8 Randall's 9 Governor's, Manhattan, Roosevelt

landmark: 5 Macy's 8 Bronx Zoo 11 Battery Park, Central Park, Penn Station, Shea Stadium, Times Square 12 Carnegie Hall 13 Gracie Mansion, Lincoln Center, Port Authority, Trinity Church, United Nations, Yankee Stadium 14 Waldorf-Astoria 15 NY Public Library, NY Stock Exchange, Seagram Building, Statue of Liberty 16 Bellevue Hospital, Chrysler Building, World Trade Center 17 Hayden Planetarium, Rockefeller Center, Woolworth Building 18 Radio City Music Hall 19 Empire State Building, Grand Central Station, Madison Square Garden, St Patrick's Cathedral 22 Metropolitan Opera House 26 Sloan-Kettering Cancer Center 29 Cathedral of Saint John the Divine

mayor: 4 Koch 6 Walker 9 La Guardia

museum: 6 Jewish 7 Whitney 9 Cloisters 10 Guggenheim 12 Cooper-Hewitt, Metropolitan 15 Frick Collection 17 Museum of Modern Art (MOMA) 30 American Museum of Natural History

river: 4 East 6 Harlem, Hudson

street: 6 Bowery 8 Broadway 9 Lexington 10 Park Avenue, Wall Street 11 Central Park, Fifth Avenue, Sutton Place 13 Madison Avenue 17 Forty-Second Street

university: 3 NYU 6 Queens 7 Barnard, Fordham, Yeshiva 8 Brooklyn, Columbia 13 Hunter College 22 Juilliard School of Music 23 City University of New York

---

date written: 17 thirteenth century
related to: 8 Volsunga
author: 7 unknown
character: 5 Etzel (Attila), Hagen 6 Gernot 7 Gunther 8 Brunhild, Dankwart, Giselher 9 Kriemhild, Siegfried

Nibelungs, Niblungs
origin: 8 Germanic, Teutonic
followers of: 9 Siegfried
race: 6 dwarfs
possessed by: 8 treasure
captured by: 9 Siegfried
family of: 7 Gunther

Nicaragua *see box, p. 677*

nice 4 deft, fine, good, kind 5 dandy, exact, fussy, great, swell 6 divine, genial, lovely, proper, seemly, strict, subtle 7 amiable, amusing, careful, cordial, correct, finicky, genteel, likable, precise, refined, winning 8 accurate, charming, cheerful, delicate, friendly, gracious, jim-dandy, ladylike, pleasant, pleasing, rigorous, skillful, unerring, virtuous, well-bred 9 agreeable, congenial, excellent, fantastic, marvelous, sensitive, wonderful 10 attractive, delightful, enchanting, entrancing, fastidious, methodical, meticulous, scrupulous 11 interesting, painstaking, pleasurable, punctilious, respectable, sympathetic, warmhearted 13 compassionate, understanding, well brought up 17 overconscientious

Nice and the Good, The
author: 11 Iris Murdoch

nicely 6 neatly 7 exactly, fussily, happily 9 carefully, precisely 10 accurately, critically, pleasantly, unerringly 11 faultlessly, fortunately, opportunely 12 attractively, fastidiously

nicety 4 care, tact 5 flair, grace 6 acumen, polish 7 culture, finesse, insight 8 accuracy, delicacy, elegance, subtlety 9 attention, exactness, precision 10 refinement 11 cultivation, penetration, preciseness, sensitivity 12 perspicacity, subtle detail, tastefulness 13 elaborateness, particularity 14 discrimination, fastidiousness, meticulousness

niche 4 cove, nook, slot 5 berth, trade 6 alcove, cavity, corner, cranny, dugout, hollow, metier, recess 7 calling 8 position, vocation 9 cubbyhole 10 depression, pigeonhole 11 proper place 13 hole in the wall

Nicholas Nickleby
author: 14 Charles Dickens
character: 5 Smike 11 Arthur Gride, Newman Noggs 12 Kate Nickleby, Madeline Bray 13 Lord Verisopht, Ralph Nickleby 14 Frank Cheeryble 15 Sir Mulberry Hawk, Vincent Crummles, Wackford Squeers 17 Cheeryble Brothers

Nichols, Mike
director of: 7 Catch-22 11 The Graduate (Oscar) 15 Carnal Knowledge 25 Who's Afraid of Virginia Woolf?

Nicholson, Ben
born: 6 Denham 7 England
artwork: 9 Fireworks 11 White Relief 12 Tuscan Relief 13 Painted Relief 14 At the Chat Botte

Nicholson, Jack
born: 9 Neptune NJ
roles: 8 Ironweed 9 Chinatown, Easy Rider 10 The Shining 12 Prizzi's Honor, The Passenger 13 The Last Detail 14 Five Easy Pieces 15 Carnal Knowledge 17 Terms of Endearment 20 The Witches of Eastwick 22 The King of Marvin Gardens 25 One Flew Over the Cuckoo's Nest (Oscar) 26 The Postman Always Rings Twice

nicht wahr? 10 isn't that so?

Nicippe
father: 6 Pelops
son: 10 Eurystheus

nick 3 cut, jag, mar 4 chip, dent, gash, mark, scar 5 cleft, gouge, notch, score, wound 6 damage, deface, indent, injure, injury 7 marking, scarify, scoring, scratch 8 incision, lacerate 10 depression 11 indentation

nickel
chemical symbol: 2 Ni

New Zealand
  other name: 8 Aotearoa **12** Nieuw Zeeland **23** Land of the Long White Cloud
  capital: 10 Wellington
  largest city: 8 Auckland
  others: 5 Leuin, Oreti, Otaki, Taupo **6** Clutha, Foxton, Oamaru, Picton, Timaru **7** Dunedin,
    Manu Kau, Raetihi, Rotorua **8** Hamilton, Kawakawa, Touranga **9** Lyttelton **10** Queenstown
    12 Christchurch, Invercargill, Port Chalmers **13** Port Nicholson **14** Napier-Hastings **15** Pal-
    merston North
  school: 5 Otago **6** Massey **7** Waikato **8** Auckland, Victoria **10** Canterbury
  division: 11 North Island, South Island
  head of state: 14 British monarch **15** governor general
  monetary unit: 4 cent **6** dollar
  island: 4 Cook, Niue, Otea **5** North, South **6** Bounty, Chatam, Snares **7** Stewart, Tokelau
    8 Auckland, Campbell, Kermadec, Puketutu **9** Antipodes **10** Resolution, Three Kings **12** Great
    Barrier
  lake: 3 Ada **4** Gunn, Ohau **5** Hawea, Taupo **6** Pukaki, Pupuke, Te Anau, Tekapo, Wanaka
    7 Brunner, Diamond, Kanieri, Okareka, Rotorua **8** Okataina, Paradise, Rotoaira, Wakatipu
    9 Manapouri
  mountain: 4 Eden, Flat, Owen **5** Allen, Chope, Lyall, Mitre, Ohope, Otari, Young **6** Egmont,
    Stokes, Tasman **7** Cameron, Coronet, Ernslaw, Huiarau, Pihanga, Ruahine, Ruapehu, Tau-
    hera, Tutamoe, Tyndall **8** Aspiring, Richmond, Tauranga **9** Messenger, Murchison, Ngauru-
    hoe, Raukumara, Tongariro **11** Remarkables **12** Southern Alps
  highest point: 4 Cook **7** Aorangi
  river: 4 Avon **5** Mokau, Waipa **6** Clutha, Rakaia, Tamaki, Waihou, Wairau, Wairoa **7** Waikato,
    Waitaki **8** Clarence, Manawatu, Wanganui **10** Rangitikei
  sea: 6 Tasman **12** South Pacific
  physical feature:
    bay: **4** Ohua **5** Evans, Hawke, Lyall **6** Awarua, Cloudy, Golden, Plenty, Tasman **7** Fitzroy,
      Pegasus, Poverty **8** Halfmoon, Rangaunu
    bight: **7** Karamea **10** Canterbury **13** North Taranaki, South Taranaki
    cape: **4** East, West **5** North **6** Egmont **8** Farewell, Foulwind, Palliser **9** Southwest
    channel: **8** Colville
    falls: **10** Sutherland
    glacier: **3** Fox **6** Tasman **11** Franz Joseph
    gulf: **7** Hauraki
    harbor: **7** Kaipara, Manukau **9** Waitemata
    peninsula: **5** Mahia, Otago
    plains: **10** Canterbury
    sound: **8** Doubtful
    strait: **4** Cook **7** Foveaux
  people: 3 Ati **5** Arawa, Dutch, Maori **7** British, Ringatu **10** Polynesian
    author: **5** Frame **9** Mansfield **10** Ngaio Marsh **12** Ashton-Warner
    explorer: **4** Cook **6** Tasman
    mountain climber: **7** Hillary
  language: 5 Maori **7** English
  religion: 8 Anglican **9** Methodist **10** Protestant **12** Presbyterian **13** Roman Catholic
  place:
    national park: **9** Fiordland, Fjordland, Tongariro
  feature:
    animal: **7** tuatara
    bird: **3** kea, tui **4** kiwi, weka **6** takahe **7** apteryx **8** bellbird
    tree: **4** rimu, tawa **5** kauri, matai **6** totara
  food:
    fish: **4** mako
    fruit: **4** kiwi **9** tamarillo **17** Chinese gooseberry

---

Nickel Mountain
  author: 11 John Gardner

nickname 6 handle **7** agno-
men, epithet, moniker, pet
name **8** baby name, cognomen **9** pseudonym, sobriquet
10 diminutive **11** appellation,
designation

Nicomachean Ethics
  author: **9** Aristotle

Nidhogg
  origin: 12 Scandinavian

form: 7 serpent
domain: 8 Niflheim
gnaws on lowest root of:
  9 Iggdrasil, Yggdrasil

Nielsen, Carl August
  born: 6 Odense **7** Denmark
  composer of: 9 Maskarade
    12 Saul and David **16** Inex-
    tinguishable (symphony No
    4)

Nietzsche, Friedrich
  author of: 14 The Will to
    Power **17** Beyond Good and
    Evil, The Birth of Tragedy
    20 Thus Spake Zarathustra

Niflheim
  origin: 12 Scandinavian
  ruler of: 3 Hel
  purpose: 10 punish dead
  climate: 3 fog **4** cold

nifty 4 chic, fine, neat, posh
5 natty, smart **6** clever, dapper **7** dashing, stylish **8** splendid **10** attractive
11 fashionable

Niger *see box*

Nicaragua
  capital/largest city: 7 Managua
  others: 4 Leon, Rama **6** Masaya **7** Corinto, Granada **8** Jinotega **9** Matagalpa **10** Bluefields, Chinandega
  division: 13 Mosquito Coast
  measure: 4 vara **5** cahiz **6** suerte **7** cajuela, manzana **10** cabelleria
  monetary unit: 4 peso **7** centavo, cordoba
  weight: 3 bag **4** caha, caja **8** tonelada
  island: 7 Ometepe
  lake: 7 Managua **9** Nicaragua
  mountain: 4 Leon **5** Negro, Viejo **6** Madera, Telica **7** Managua, Saslaya **9** Momotombo
  highest point: 7 Mogoton
  river: 4 Coco, Tuma **5** Wanks **6** Grande, Poteca **7** San Juan **8** Tipitapa **9** Escondido
  sea: 7 Pacific **9** Caribbean
  physical feature:
    gulf: **7** Fonseca
  people: 4 Mico, Mixe, Rama, Smoo, Ulva **5** Cukra, Diria, Lenca, Sambo, Toaca **6** Mangue **7** mestizo, Miskito **8** Mosquito **9** Matagalpa
    author: **5** Dario
    explorer: **6** Davila **7** Cordoba **8** Columbus
    group: **6** Contra **10** Sandinista
    leader: **6** Somoza, Walker, Zelaya **7** Nicardo **8** Chamorro
  language: 7 English, Spanish
  religion: 13 Roman Catholic
  place:
    cathedral: **12** Metropolitan
  feature:
    dance: **5** sones **10** zapateados, zarabandas
  food:
    beans: **8** frijoles
    dish: **10** naca tamale
    drink: **5** tiste **9** pinolillo
    fruit: **6** zapote

Niger
  other name: 6 Joliba, Kworra, Ramtil
  capital/largest city: 6 Niamey
  others: 5 Goure **6** Agadex, Agadez, Maradi, Tahoua, Zinder
  division:
    region: **3** Air **5** Arlit, Sahel
  monetary unit: 5 franc **7** centime
  lake: 4 Chad
  mountain: 7 Bagzane **9** Air Massif
  highest point: 7 Greboun
  river: 5 Niger **6** Dillia
  physical feature:
    desert: **6** Sahara
    oasis: **6** Kaouar
    plateau: **5** Djado **6** Tegama **7** Tchigai **8** Mengueni **11** Adar Doutchi, Djerma Ganda
  people: 4 Daza, Idjo, Idyo, Idzo, Peul, Teda **5** Hausa, Warri **6** Djerma, Fulani, Kanuri, Songha, Toubou, Tuareg **13** Djerma-Songhai
    conqueror: **13** Usman Dan Fodio
    leader: **5** Diori **6** Saibou **7** Ousmane **8** Kountche
  language: 5 Hausa, Mande **6** Djerma, French, Fulani, Tuareg **8** Mandingo, Tamashek
  religion: 5 Islam **7** animism **12** Christianity
  place:
    ruins: **6** Agadez
  feature:
    cavalry: **5** Dosso
    empire: **4** Mali **6** Fulani **7** Songhai **10** Kanem-Borno
    tree: **6** acacia, baobab

Nigeria *see box, p. 678*

niggard 4 mean **5** cheap, miser, tight **6** stingy **7** miserly **8** scrimper **9** skinflint **10** ungenerous **12** parsimonious

niggardliness 6 penury **8** meanness **9** closeness, parsimony **10** stinginess **11** miserliness **13** penny-pinching **15** tight-fistedness

niggardly 4 mean, poor **5** cheap, close, sorry, tight **6** flimsy, frugal, meager, measly, paltry, saving, scanty, shabby, stingy, tawdry **7** miserly, scrubby, sparing, thrifty **8** beggarly, grubbing, grudging, stinting, wretched **9** illiberal, mercenary, miserable, penurious **10** hardfisted, second-rate, ungenerous **11** closefisted **12** contemptible, insufficient, parsimonious

Nigger of the Narcissus, The
  author: 12 Joseph Conrad
  character: 5 Baker **6** Donkin **9** James Wait **12** Old Singleton

niggling 5 fussy, minor, petty, small **7** finicky **8** caviling, nugatory, picayune, piddling, trifling **9** quibbling **10** negligible, nit-picking **12** pettifogging **13** insignificant **15** inconsequential

nigh 4 near **5** close, handy **6** almost, at hand, nearly **7** close by **8** adjacent **9** bordering **11** neighboring, practically

night 4 dark, dusk **7** bedtime, evening, sundown **8** darkness, eventide **9** murkiness, obscurity **13** tenebrousness
  goddess of: 3 Nox

nightclub
  French: 5 boite **11** boite de nuit

nightfall 4 dark, dusk **6** sunset **7** evening, sundown **8** darkness, eventide, gloaming, moonrise, twilight
  French: 10 crepuscule

Night Gallery
  host: 10 Rod Serling

nightingale
  group of: 5 watch

Nightline
  host: 9 Ted Koppel

nightly 4 dark **7** evening, obscure **9** nocturnal **11** nocturnally

nightmare 7 incubus **8** bad dream, succubus **13** hallucination

Nigeria
  capital: **5** Abuja
  largest city: **5** Lagos
  others: **3** Aba, Ado, Ede, Isa, Iwo, Jos, Oyo **4** Bida, Bidi, Buea, Kano, Offa, Yola **5** Benin, Bonny, Enugu, Warri, Zaria **6** Burutu, Ibadan, Ilesha, Ilorin, Kachia, Kaduna, Kadune, Kokoto, Mushin, Takoba **7** Calabar, Onitsha, Oshogbo **8** Abeokuta **9** Maiduguri, Ogbomosho **12** Port Harcourt
  division: **3** Air, Isa, Oyo **4** Kano, Nupe, Ondo **5** Asben, Benin, Bornu, Ijebu, Ogoja, Warri **6** Biafra, Degema, Owerri, Sokoto **7** Adamawa
  monetary unit: **4** kobo **5** naira
  lake: **4** Chad
  highest point: **7** Dimlang
  river: **3** Oli **4** Gana, Yobe **5** Benin, Benue, Cross, Niger **6** Kaduna, Sokoto **7** Calabar, Gongola **8** Komadugu **9** Sambreiro
  sea: **8** Atlantic
  physical feature:
    bight: **5** Benin, Bonny **6** Biafra
    delta: **5** Niger
    gulf: **6** Guinea
    plains: **5** Bornu **9** Hausaland
    plateau: **3** Jos, Udi **6** Bauchi
    port: **5** Lagos **7** Calabar **8** Harcourt
  people: **3** Abo, Aro, Djo, Ebo, Edo, Ibo, Ijo, Tiv, Vai **4** Beni, Bini, Eboe, Efik, Egba, Ejam, Ekoi, Idyo, Igbo, Ijaw, Nupe **5** Angas, Benin, Gwari, Hausa **6** Chamba, Fulani, Ibibio, Kanuri, Yoruba **11** Hausa-Fulani
    author: **6** Achebe
    British colonial ruler: **6** Goldie, Lugard
    kingdom: **3** Ife, Nok, Oyo **5** Benin **6** Fulani **10** Kanem-Borno
    leader: **5** Gowon **6** Balewa, Ojukwu, Schick **7** Awolowo, Azikine, Azikiwe, Shagari **8** Obasanjo **9** Babangida **13** Usman dan Fodio
  language: **3** Ibo **4** Efik, Igbo **5** Hausa **6** Yoruba **7** English
  religion: **5** Islam **7** animism **12** Christianity
  place:
    dam: **6** Kainji
    mosque/walled city: **4** Kano
  feature:
    dress: **4** riga **7** agbados
    tree: **5** abura, afara **6** obeche **10** terminalia
    war: **7** Biafran

Nile
  boat: **5** baris **6** cangia, nuggar, sandal **7** felucca, gaiassa **8** dahabeah
  cities: **3** Qus **4** Abri, Argo, Idfu, Isna, Juba, Qina **5** Aswan, Asyut, Cairo, Kokka, Kusti, Luxor, Meroe, Minya, Rejaf, Saite, Tanis, Tanta **6** Atbara, Faiyum **7** Malakel, Mansura, Rosetta **8** Khartoum, Omdurman, Rusayris **9** Was Madani **10** Alexandria
  dam: **6** Sannar **9** Aswan High, White Nile
  desert bordering: **6** Libyan, Nubian **7** Arabian
  falls: **5** Ripon **8** Kabalega **9** Murchison
  feature: **6** Sphinx
    pyramid: **4** Giza
    temple: **8** Ramses II **9** Abu Simbel **11** Deir el-Bahri, Medinet Habu
  flows into:
    13 Mediterranean
  flows through: **5** Egypt, Kenya, Sudan, Zaire **6** Rwanda, Uganda **7** Burundi **8** Ethiopia, Tanzania
  island: **4** Roda **6** Philae
  lake: **4** Tana **5** Kyoga, Tsana **6** Albert, Edward, Nasser **8** Victoria
  other name: **4** Hapi **20** The Father of the Rivers
  people: **3** Jur, Luo, Lwo, Nuo, Suk **4** Bari, Beja, Golo, Luoh, Madi **5** Nilot **7** Shilluk
  plain: **6** Gezira
  plant: **4** sudd **5** lotus
  starting point: **5** Tsana **8** Victoria
  swamp: **4** Sudd
  tributary: **4** Arab **5** Rahad, Sobat **6** Atbara, Ghazai, Kagera **7** Rosetta **8** Blue Nile, Damietta **9** Bahr Jebel, White Nile

Night of the Iguana, The
  director: **10** John Huston
  based on play by: **17** Tennessee Williams
  cast: **7** Sue Lyon **8** Skip Ward **10** Ava Gardner **11** Deborah Kerr **13** Richard Burton
  setting: **6** Mexico

nightshade 16 Solanum dulcamara
  varieties: **4** ball **5** black **6** common, deadly, sticky **7** Malabar **8** stinking **9** melon-leaf, poisonous, soda-apple **10** enchanter's

Nights of Cabiria
  director: **15** Federico Fellini
  cast: **13** Amedeo Nazzari **14** Francois Perier **15** Giulietta Masina
  remade as: **12** Sweet Charity

nightstick 3 rod **4** mace, wand **5** baton, staff **6** cudgel **7** scepter **8** bludgeon **9** billy club, truncheon **10** shillelagh

nighttime 4 late **5** night **9** latenight, nighttide, nocturnal

Night to Remember, A
  director: **8** Roy Baker
  based on story by: **10** Walter Lord
  cast: **9** Jill Dixon **11** Kenneth More **13** David McCallum **16** Laurence Naismith
  setting: **7** Titanic

nihil 7 nothing

nihilism 5 chaos **6** anomie **7** license **9** amorality, anarchism, emptiness, terrorism **10** alienation, iconoclasm, radicalism, skepticism **11** agnosticism, lawlessness, nothingness **12** nonexistence **16** irresponsibility

nihilist 5 rebel **9** anarchist, terrorist **13** revolutionary

Nihon *see* **5** Japan

Nike
  origin: **5** Greek
  goddess of: **7** victory
  father: **11** Titan Pallas
  mother: **4** Styx

brother: **5** Zelos
corresponds to: **6** Athena
  8 Victoria

nil 4 none, null, zero **6** cipher,
naught **7** nothing, nullity
11 nonexistent

Nile *see box, p. 678*

Niles, Hazel and Peter
  characters in: **22** Mourning
    Becomes Electra
  author: **6** O'Neill

nil nisi bonum 21 nothing unless it is good

nil sine numine 27 nothing
without the divine will
  motto of: **8** Colorado

nimble 4 deft, spry **5** agile,
fleet, light, quick, rapid, ready,
swift **6** active, expert, lively,
prompt, speedy, supple **8** animated, skillful, spirited **9** dexterous, mercurial, sprightly
10 proficient

nimbleness 7 agility **8** alacrity,
spryness **9** dexterity, quickness **10** limberness, suppleness

nimble-witted 5 droll, witty
6 clever **11** resourceful

nimbus 4 aura, disk, halo
5 cloud, vapor **7** aureole
8 radiance

Nimitz, Chester
  served in: **3** WWI **4** WWII
  commander of: **12** Pacific
    fleet
  rank: **12** fleet (five-star) admi-
    ral **22** chief of naval
    operations
  battle: **6** Midway **9** Leyte
    Gulf **13** Philippine Sea

Nimoy, Leonard
  born: **8** Boston MA
  roles: **7** Mr Spock **8** Star
    Trek **17** Mission Impossible
    21 Star Trek: The Voyage
    Home **22** Star Trek: The
    Wrath of Khan **25** Star
    Trek: The Search for Spock

Nimrod
  father: **4** Cush
  grandfather: **3** Ham
  great grandfather: **4** Noah
  founded: **5** Calah, Resen
    7 Nineveh **8** Rehoboth

nincompoop 4 boob, dolt,
dope, fool, jerk **5** dummy,
dunce, idiot, klutz, moron,
ninny **6** dimwit, lummox, nitwit **7** half-wit, jackass **8** bonehead, dummkopf, imbecile,
lunkhead, numskull **9** blockhead, dumb bunny, harebrain,
numbskull, simpleton **10** dunderhead, dunderpate, muddlehead, noodlehead
11 knucklehead, rattlebrain
12 featherbrain, scatterbrain

Nine, the *see* **5** Muses

Nineteen Eighty-Four
  author: **12** George Orwell
  character: **5** Julia **6** O'Brien
    11 Charrington **12** Winston
    Smith

1919
  author: **13** John Dos Passos

Ninety-Five Theses
  author: **12** Martin Luther

Nineveh
  founder: **6** Nimrod

Nine worthies
  mentioned in: **16** medieval
    romances
  three each of: **4** Jews **6** Pa-
    gans **10** Christians
  names: **5** David **6** Arthur,
    Hector, Joshua **11** Charle-
    magne **12** Julius Caesar
    15 Judas Maccabaeus
    17 Alexander the Great
    18 Godefroy de Bouillon

Ningal
  origin: **8** Sumerian
  son: **3** Utu
  consort of: **5** Nanna

Ninib *see* **7** Ninurta

Ninlil
  origin: **8** Sumerian
  goddess of: **3** air

ninny 3 ass, sap **4** fool, simp
5 booby, dunce, idiot, moron
6 dimwit, nitwit **7** fathead,
half-wit **8** bonehead, dumb-
dumb, imbecile, lunkhead,
numskull **9** blockhead, dumb
bunny, lamebrain, numbskull
10 dunderhead, nincompoop
11 chowderhead

Ninotchka
  director: **13** Ernst Lubitsch
  cast: **9** Ina Claire **10** Bela Lu-
    gosi, Greta Garbo **13** Mel-
    vyn Douglas
  setting: **5** Paris
  remade as: **13** Silk Stockings

Ninurta
  also: **5** Ninib
  origin: **8** Sumerian
    10 Babylonian
  type of god: **4** hero
  personifies: **4** wind **9** south
    wind
  father: **5** Enlil
  avenger of: **5** Enlil

Ninus
  wife: **9** Semiramis
  founder of: **7** Nineveh

Niobe
  father: **8** Tantalus
  mother: **5** Dione
  brother: **6** Pelops
  husband: **7** Amphion
  children: **9** seven sons
    14 seven daughters
  children called: **6** Niobid

taunted: **4** Leto
children killed by: **6** Apollo
  7 Artemis
changed into: **5** stone
changed by: **4** Zeus

Niord
  also: **5** Njord
  origin: **12** Scandinavian
  god of: **4** wind **10** navigation,
    prosperity
  king of: **5** Vanir
  son: **4** Frey **5** Freyr
  daughter: **5** Freia, Freya

nip 3 cut, lop **4** bite, clip, crop,
dock, grab, grip, ruin, snag,
snap, snip **5** blast, check, chill,
clamp, clasp, crack, crush,
frost, grasp, pinch, quash,
seize, sever, shear, snare,
tweak **6** benumb, clutch, cut
off, freeze, pierce, snatch, sunder, thwart **7** curtail, destroy,
shorten, squeeze **8** compress,
cut short, demolish **9** frustrate **10** abbreviate

nip-and-tuck 5 close

nip in the bud 7 prevent
8 preclude **9** forestall, frustrate

Nipper, Susan
  character in: **12** Dombey and
    Son
  author: **7** Dickens

Nippon *see* **5** Japan

nippy 3 raw **5** brisk, chill,
crisp, sharp **6** biting, chilly
7 cutting

Nisn 16 first Hebrew month

nit-pick 4 carp, pick **5** cavil
9 criticize

nitrate 4 salt **5** ester **6** sodium
9 potassium **10** fertilizer

nitrogen
  chemical symbol: **1** N

nitty-gritty 4 core, crux, gist,
meat, pith **5** heart **7** essence
9 substance

nitwit 3 ass **4** clod, dolt, fool
5 booby, dummy, dunce, idiot,
klutz, moron, ninny **7** fathead,
pinhead **8** bonehead, dumb-
dumb, imbecile, lunkhead,
meathead, numskull, peabrain
9 birdbrain, blockhead, lamebrain, numbskull **10** dunderhead, nincompoop,
noodlehead **11** chowderhead

Niven, David
  real name: **21** James David
    Graham Niven
  autobiography: **16** The
    Moon's a Balloon **21** Bring
    on the Empty Horses
  born: **8** Scotland
    10 Kirriemuir
  roles: **11** Phileas Fogg **12** Ca-
    sino Royale, My Man God-
    frey **14** The Pink Panther,

Nixon, Richard Milhous
presidential rank: 13 thirty-seventh
party: 10 Republican
state represented: 2 NY
defeated: 7 (George Corley) Wallace **8** (Hubert Horatio) Humphrey
vice president: 4 (Gerald Rudolph) Ford **5** (Spiro Theodore) Agnew
cabinet:
  state: **6** (William Pierce) Rogers **9** (Henry A) Kissinger
  treasury: **5** (William E) Simon **6** (George P) Shultz **7** (David Matthew) Kennedy **8** (John
    Bowden) Connally
  defense: **5** (Melvin Robert) Laird **10** (Elliot L) Richardson **11** (James R) Schlesinger
  attorney general: **5** (William B) Saxbe **8** (John Newton) Mitchell **10** (Elliot L) Richardson
    11 (Richard G) Kleindienst
  postmaster general: **6** (Winton Malcolm) Blount
  interior: **6** (Rogers Clark Ballard) Morton, (Walter Joseph) Hinkel
  agriculture: **4** (Earl Lauer) Butz **6** (Clifford Morris) Hardin
  commerce: **4** (Frederick B) Dent **5** (Maurice Hubert) Stans
  labor: **6** (George Pratt) Shultz **7** (James Day) Hodgson, (Peter J) Brennan
  HEW: **5** (Robert Hutchinson) Finch **10** (Caspar W) Weinberger, (Elliot Lee) Richardson
  HUD: **4** (James T) Lynn **6** (George Wilcken) Romney
  transportation: **5** (John Anthony) Volpe **8** (Claude S) Brinegar
born: 2 CA **10** Yorba Linda
died: 7 New York **11** New York City
education:
  college: **8** Whittier
  law school: **14** Duke University
religion: 6 Quaker **16** Society of Friends
interests: 8 football
vacation spot: 11 Key Biscayne (FL), San Clemente (CA)
dog: 8 Checkers **11** King Timahoe
author: 9 Six Crises **10** The Real War **11** Beyond Peace **27** RN: The Memoirs of Richard Nixon
political career: 8 US Senate **13** Vice President **24** US House of Representatives
civilian career: 6 lawyer
military service: 6 US Navy **10** lieutenant, World War II
notable events of lifetime/term:
  Calley court martialed for: **13** Mylai Massacre
  court martial of: **6** Calley
  creation of: **10** Bangladesh
  crisis: **3** oil **6** energy
  embargo on: **3** oil
  first men on: **4** moon
  incident: **11** Wounded Knee
  pardon of Nixon by: **4** Ford
  publication of: **14** Pentagon Papers
  resignation of: **5** Agnew, Nixon
  scandal: **9** Watergate
  student deaths at: **9** Kent State
  treaty: **10** Seabed Arms **32** Nonproliferation of Nuclear Weapons
  trip to: **5** China
  war: **7** Vietnam **10** Middle East **12** East Pakistan
quotes: 31 A respectable Republican cloth coat **35** You won't have Nixon to kick around any
  more
father: 14 Francis Anthony
mother: 6 Hannah (Milhous)
siblings: 11 Arthur Burdg **12** Harold Samuel **13** Edward Calvert, Francis Donald
wife: 8 (Thelma Catherine) Patricia (Ryan)
  nickname: **3** Pat
children: 5 Julie **8** Patricia
  Julie married: **15** David Eisenhower
  Patricia married: **9** Edward Cox
  Patricia's nickname: **6** Tricia

Separate Tables (Oscar)
16 Stairway to Heaven,
Wuthering Heights **18** The
Prisoner of Zenda
26 Around the World in
Eighty Days

Nix
  origin: 8 Germanic
  form: 6 spirit
  habitat: 5 water

Njord *see* **5** Niord

no 3 nay, nix, not **4** none, veto

Noah
  father: 6 Lamech
  grandfather: 10 Methuselah
  son: 3 Ham **4** Shem **7** Japheth
  grandson: 3 Put **4** Cush **6** Ca-
    naan **7** Misraim
  great grandson: 6 Nimrod
  built: 3 ark

collected: 7 animals
survived: 5 flood
pertaining to: 8 Noachian

Noah's Ark
made of: 10 gopherwood

nob 4 peer, toff **5** swell **9** patrician **10** aristocrat

Nobel, Alfred
nationality: 7 Swedish
invented: 8 dynamite
originated: 10 Nobel Prize

Nobel Prizes *see box,*
p. 682

nobility 5 elite, lords **7** dignity, majesty, peerage, primacy, royalty **8** breeding, eminence, grandeur, high rank, prestige, splendor **9** gentility, grandness, greatness, loftiness, sublimity, supremacy **10** blue bloods, mightiness, patricians, patriciate, upper crust **11** aristocracy, distinction, exaltedness, preeminence, stateliness, superiority **12** magnificence

nobility obliges
French: 14 noblesse oblige

noble 3 don **4** high, just, lord, peer **5** famed, grand, great, lofty, moral, regal, royal **6** famous, gentle, honest, knight, lordly, squire, superb, worthy **7** awesome, courtly, eminent, ethical, exalted, grandee, stately, sublime, supreme, upright **8** baronial, cavalier, elevated, glorious, handsome, highborn, imperial, imposing, lordlike, majestic, princely, renowned, selfless, splendid, superior, virtuous **9** chevalier, dignified, estimable, excellent, exemplary, gentleman, honorable, patrician, personage, reputable **10** aristocrat, impressive, preeminent **11** magnanimous, magnificent, meritorious, pureblooded, trustworthy **12** aristocratic, thoroughbred **13** distinguished, incorruptible
French: 6 gentil

Noble House
author: 12 James Clavell

nobleman 4 lord, peer **7** grandee **9** patrician **10** aristocrat

noblesse oblige 15 nobility obliges

noblewoman 4 dame, lady, rani **5** begum, queen **6** milady **7** czarina, duchess, empress, peeress, sultana **8** baroness, contessa, countess, maharani, princess **11** marchioness

Nobody Knows My Name
author: 12 James Baldwin

nocturnal 4 dark **5** night **7** nightly, obscure **8** darkling **9** nighttime

Nocturne
author: 15 Frank Swinnerton

nod 3 bob **4** doze, hail, show, sign **5** agree, greet, lapse, let up **6** assent, beckon, concur, drowse, motion, reveal, salute, signal **7** consent, drop off, fall off, gesture, signify **9** recognize

node 3 bud **4** bump, burl, hump, knob, knot, lump **5** bulge, joint **6** button **8** swelling **10** prominence, tumescence **11** excrescence **12** protuberance

Nodosaurus
type: 8 dinosaur
10 ornithopod
location: 12 North America

nodule 3 sac, wen **4** bump, cyst, knob, knot, lump, stud **5** bulge **6** growth **8** swelling **9** outgrowth **10** projection, prominence, protrusion, tumescence **11** excrescence **12** protuberance

noel, Noel 4 yule **5** carol **8** yuletide **9** Christmas **13** Christmastide

Noemon
mentioned in: 7 Odyssey
supplied: 4 ship
supplied ship to:
10 Telemachus

No Exit
author: 14 Jean-Paul Sartre

noggin 3 cup, mug **4** bean, head, pate **5** gourd **6** noodle

Noggs, Newman
character in: 16 Nicholas Nickleby
author: 7 Dickens

Noguchi, Hideyo
field: 12 bacteriology
nationality: 8 Japanese
isolated: 8 syphilis

noise 3 ado, din **4** bang, blab, boom, echo, pass, roar, stir, wail **5** babel, blare, blast, bruit, rumor, sound, voice **6** bedlam, clamor, hubbub, racket, repeat, report, rumble, tumult, uproar **7** barrage, bluster, clatter, thunder **8** brawling, gabbling, rumbling, shouting **9** cacophony, cannonade, circulate, commotion, discharge **10** dissonance, hullabaloo **11** pandemonium **12** caterwauling, vociferation **13** reverberation

noiseless 5 quiet, still, tacit **6** hushed, silent **9** soundless, voiceless

noisemaker 4 bell, horn **5** siren **6** rattle **7** clacker, clapper, snapper, whistle

noisome 4 foul, rank **5** acrid, fetid, toxic **6** putrid, rotten, smelly **7** baneful, harmful, hurtful, noxious, reeking **8** mephitic, stinking **9** injurious, offensive, poisonous, unhealthy **10** malodorous, nauseating, pernicious **11** deleterious, detrimental **12** evil-smelling

noisy 4 loud **5** alive **6** lively, raging, shrill, stormy **7** blaring, blatant, furious, grating, jarring, rackety **8** animated, piercing, strident **9** clamorous, deafening, dissonant, turbulent **10** boisterous, clangorous, discordant, rampageous, resounding, thundering, thunderous, tumultuous, uproarious **11** cacophonous, tempestuous **12** earsplitting

Nolan, George Brendan
real name of: 11 George Brent

Nolan, Lloyd
born: 14 San Francisco CA
roles: 22 Lieutenant Colonel Queeg **26** The Caine Mutiny Court Martial

Nolde, Emil
real name: 10 Emil Hansen
born: 5 Nolde **7** Germany
artwork: 7 Prophet **10** Papua Youth **11** Tropical Sun **12** The Magicians, The Pentecost **13** The Last Supper, Three Russians **14** Doubting Thomas **20** Life of Maria Aegyptica **22** Christ Among the Children, Christ and the Adulteress

nolens volens 10 willy-nilly **19** whether willing or not

noli me tangere 10 touch me not

nolle prosequi 14 do not prosecute **19** be unwilling to pursue

nolo contendere 21 I am unwilling to contend

no longer able to fight
French: 12 hors de combat

no longer in existence
4 dead, gone, lost **7** defunct, died out, extinct **8** vanished

Nolte, Nick
born: 7 Omaha NE
roles: 5 Weeds **7** The Deep **10** Cannery Row **12** I Love Trouble **13** Prince of Tides **14** Rich Man Poor Man **15** Forty-Eight Hours **16** North Dallas Forty, Jefferson in Paris

Nobel Prizes

Literature:

1901: **20** Rene F A Sully-Prudhomme
1902: **14** Theodor Mommsen
1903: **20** Bjornstjerne Bjornson
1904: **13** Jose Echegaray
15 Frederic Mistral
1905: **17** Henryk Sienkiewicz
1906: **14** Giosue Carducci
1907: **14** Rudyard Kipling
1908: **13** Rudolf C Eucken
1909: **13** Selma Lagerlof
1910: **12** Paul von Heyse
1911: **18** Maurice Maeterlinck
1912: **16** Gerhart Hauptmann
1913: **21** Sir Rabindranath Tagore
1915: **13** Romain Rolland
1916: **19** Verner von Heidenstam
1917: **11** K A Gjellerup
17 Henrik Pontoppidan
1919: **15** Carl F G Spitteler
1920: **10** Knut Hamsun
1921: **13** Anatole France
1922: **25** Jacinto Benavente y Martinez
1923: **18** William Butler Yeats
1924: **17** Wladyslaw S Reymont
1925: **17** George Bernard Shaw
1926: **13** Grazia Deledda
1927: **12** Henri Bergson
1928: **12** Sigrid Undset
1929: **10** Thomas Mann
1930: **13** Sinclair Lewis
1931: **14** Erik A Karlfeldt
1932: **14** John Galsworthy
1933: **10** Ivan A Bunin
1934: **15** Luigi Pirandello
1936: **12** Eugene O'Neill
1937: **17** Roger Martin du Gard
1938: **10** Pearl S Buck
1939: **15** Frans E Sillanpaa
1944: **15** Johannes V Jensen
1945: **15** Gabriela Mistral
1946: **12** Hermann Hesse
1947: **9** Andre Gide
1948: **7** T S Eliot
1949: **15** William Faulkner
1950: **15** Bertrand Russell (Earl Russell)
1951: **14** Par F Lagerkvist
1952: **15** Francois Mauriac
1953: **21** Sir Winston L S Churchill
1954: **15** Ernest Hemingway
1955: **15** Halldor K Laxness
1956: **16** Juan Ramon Jimenez

1957: **11** Albert Camus
1958: **15** Boris L Pasternak
1959: **18** Salvatore Quasimodo
1960: **14** Saint-John Perse
1961: **9** Ivo Andric
1962: **13** John Steinbeck
1963: **13** George Seferis
1964: **14** Jean Paul Sartre
1965: **17** Mikhail A Sholokhov
1966: **10** Nelly Sachs
17 Samuel Joseph (Shmuel Y) Agnon
1967: **19** Miguel Angel Asturias
1968: **16** Yasunari Kawabata
1969: **13** Samuel Beckett
1970: **22** Aleksandr I Solzhenitsyn
1971: **11** Pablo Neruda
1972: **12** Heinrich Boll
1973: **12** Patrick White
1974: **13** Eyvind Johnson
14 Harry Martinson
1975: **14** Eugenio Montale
1976: **10** Saul Bellow
1977: **17** Vicente Aleixandre
1978: **19** Isaac Bashevis Singer
1979: **14** Odysseus Elytis
1980: **13** Czeslaw Milosz
1981: **12** Elias Canetti
1982: **20** Gabriel Garcia Marquez
1983: **14** William Golding
1984: **15** Jaroslav Seifert
1985: **11** Claude Simon
1986: **11** Wole Soyinka
1987: **13** Joseph Brodsky
1988: **13** Naguib Mahfouz
1989: **10** Camilo Cela
1990: **10** Octavio Paz
1991: **14** Nadine Gordimer
1992: **12** Derek Walcott
1993: **12** Toni Morrison
1994: **11** Kenzaburo Oe
1995: **12** Seamus Heaney
1996: **17** Wislawa Szymborska

Physiology/Medicine:

1901: **15** Emil A von Behring
1902: **13** Sir Ronald Ross
1903: **12** Niels R Finsen
1904: **11** Ivan P Pavlov
1905: **10** Robert Koch
1906: **12** Camillo Golgi
19 Santiago Ramon y Cajal
1907: **16** Charles L A Laveran
1908: **11** Paul Ehrlich
15 Elie Metchnikoff
1909: **11** Emil T Kocher
1910: **14** Albrecht Kossel
1911: **16** Allvar Gullstrand
1912: **12** Alexis Carrel
1913: **14** Charles R Richet

1914: **12** Robert Barany
1919: **11** Jules Bordet
1920: **12** Shack A S Krogh
1922: **12** Otto Meyerhof
14 Archibald V Hill
1923: **13** John J R Macleod
20 Sir Frederick G Banting
1924: **15** Willem Einthoven
1926: **15** Johannes Fibiger
1927: **19** Julius Wagner-Jauregg
1928: **16** Charles J H Nicolle
1929: **17** Christiaan Eijkman
20 Sir Frederick G Hopkins
1930: **15** Karl Landsteiner
1931: **12** Otto H Warburg
1932: **12** Edgar D Adrian
21 Sir Charles Sherrington
1933: **13** Thomas H Morgan
1934: **12** George R Minot
14 George H Whipple, William P Murphy
1935: **11** Hans Spemann
1936: **9** Otto Loewi **13** Sir Henry H Dale
1937: **31** Albert Szent-Gyorgyi von Nagyrapolt
1938: **16** Corneille Heymans
1939: **13** Gerhard Domagk
1943: **9** Henrik Dam **12** Edward A Doisy
1944: **14** Herbert S Gasser, Joseph Erlanger
1945: **11** Ernst B Chain
16 Sir Howard W Florey
19 Sir Alexander Fleming
1946: **14** Hermann J Muller
1947: **9** Carl F Cori
10 Gerty T Cori **16** Bernardo A Houssay
1948: **11** Paul H Muller
1949: **11** Walter R Hess
21 Antonio C de A F Egas Moniz
1950: **12** Philip S Hench
14 Edward C Kendall
16 Tadeus Reichstein
1951: **10** Max Theiler
1952: **14** Selman A Waksman
1953: **13** Fritz A Lipmann, Sir Hans A Krebs
1954: **11** John F Enders
13 Thomas H Weller
17 Frederick C Robbins
1955: **14** Axel H T Theorell
1956: **13** Andre Cournand
15 Werner Forssmann
20 Dickenson W Richards Jr
1957: **11** Daniel Bovet
1958: **12** Edward L Tatum
13 George W Beadle
15 Joshua Lederberg
1959: **11** Severo Ochoa
14 Arthur Kornberg
1960: **13** Peter B Medawar
15 Sir Frank M Burnet

1961: **14** Georg von Bekesy
1962: **12** James D Watson **14** Francis H C Crick **16** Maurice H F Wilkins
1963: **16** Alan Lloyd Hodgkin **18** Sir John Carew Eccles **20** Andrew Fielding Huxley
1964: **11** Feodor Lynen **12** Konrad E Bloch
1965: **10** Andre Lwoff **12** Jacques Monod **13** Francois Jacob
1966: **17** Francis Peyton Rous **21** Charles Brenton Huggins
1967: **10** George Wald **12** Ragnar Granit **20** Haldan Keffer Hartline
1968: **13** Robert W Holley **14** H Gobind Khorana **18** Marshall W Nirenberg
1969: **11** Max Delbruck **14** Alfred D Hershey, Salvador E Luria
1970: **11** Ulf von Euler **13** Julius Axelrod **14** Sir Bernard Katz
1971: **17** Earl W Sutherland Jr
1972: **13** Rodney R Porter **14** Gerald M Edelman
1973: **12** Konrad Lorenz **13** Karl von Frisch **17** Nikolaas Tinbergen
1974: **12** Albert Claude **15** Christian de Duve **16** George EmilPalade
1975: **12** Howard M Temin **14** David Baltimore, Renato Dulbecco
1976: **15** Baruch S Blumberg **22** Daniel Carleton Gajdusek
1977: **13** Andrew Schally, Rosalyn S Yalow **14** Roger Guillemin
1978: **11** Werner Arber **13** Daniel Nathans, Hamilton Smith
1979: **13** Allan M Cormack **17** Godfrey Hounsfield
1980: **11** Jean Dausset **12** George D Snell **15** Baruj Benacerraf
1981: **11** David H Hubel **12** Roger W Sperry **14** Torsten N Wiesel
1982: **9** John R Vane **15** Bengt Samuelsson **17** Sune Karl Bergstrom
1983: **17** Barbara McClintock
1984: **11** Niels K Jerne **13** Cesar Milstein **16** Georges J F Koehler
1985: **13** Michael S Brown **16** Joseph L Goldstein

1986: **12** Stanley Cohen **18** Rita Levi-Montalcini
1987: **14** Susumu Tonegawa
1988: **10** James Black **14** Gertrube B Elion **16** George H Hitchings
1989: **12** Harold Varmas **14** J Michael Bishop
1990: **12** Joseph Murray **14** E Donnall Thomas
1991: **10** Edwin Neher **11** Bert Sakmann
1992: **10** Edwin Krebs **12** Edmond Fisher
1993: **12** Phillip Sharp **14** Richard Roberts
1994: **12** Alfred Gilman **13** Martin Rodbell
1995: **12** Edward B Lewis **14** Eric F Wieschaus **26** Christiane Nuesslein-Volhard
1996: **13** Peter C Doherty **16** Rolf M Ziwkernagel

Chemistry:
1901: **16** Jacobus H van't Hoff
1902: **11** Emil Fischer
1903: **16** Svante A Arrhenius
1904: **16** Sir William Ramsay
1905: **17** J F W Adolf von Baeyer
1906: **12** Henri Moissan
1907: **13** Eduard Buchner
1908: **19** Sir Ernest Rutherford
1909: **14** Wilhelm Ostwald
1910: **11** Otto Wallach
1911: **11** Marie S Curie
1912: **12** Paul Sabatier **14** Victor Grignard
1913: **12** Alfred Werner
1914: **17** Theodore W Richards
1915: **18** Richard Willstatter
1918: **10** Fritz Haber
1920: **13** Walther Nernst
1921: **14** Frederick Soddy
1922: **13** Francis W Aston
1923: **10** Fritz Pregl
1925: **16** Richard Zsigmondy
1926: **15** Theodor Svedberg
1927: **15** Heinrich Wieland
1928: **12** Adolf Windaus
1929: **15** Sir Arthur Harden **19** Hans von Euler-Chelpin
1930: **11** Hans Fischer
1931: **9** Carl Bosch **16** Friedrich Bergius
1932: **14** Irving Langmuir
1934: **11** Harold C Urey
1935: **16** Irene Joliot-Curie **19** Frederic Joliot-Curie
1936: **12** Peter J W Debye
1937: **10** Paul Karrer **17** Sir Walter N Haworth

1938: **11** Richard Kuhn
1939: **14** Adolf Butenandt, Leopold Ruzicka
1943: **14** Georg von Hevesy
1944: **8** Otto Hahn
1945: **16** Artturi I Virtanen
1946: **12** James B Sumner **13** John H Northrop **15** Wendell M Stanley
1947: **17** Sir Robert Robinson
1948: **12** Arne Tiselius
1949: **15** William F Giauque
1950: **9** Kurt Alder, Otto Diels
1951: **13** Glenn T Seaborg **14** Edwin M McMillan
1952: **14** Archer J P Martin, Richard L M Synge
1953: **17** Hermann Staudinger
1954: **13** Linus C Pauling
1955: **17** Vincent du Vigneaud
1956: **15** Nikolai N Semenov **20** Sir Cyril N Hinshelwood
1957: **17** Sir Alexander R Todd (Baron Todd)
1958: **15** Frederick Sanger
1959: **17** Jaroslav Heyrovsky
1960: **13** Willard F Libby
1961: **12** Melvin Calvin
1962: **10** Max F Perutz **12** John C Kendrew
1963: **11** Giulio Natta, Karl Ziegler
1964: **26** Dorothy Mary Crowfoot Hodgkin
1965: **19** Robert Burns Woodward
1966: **15** Robert S Mulliken
1967: **12** Manfred Eigen **15** Sir George Porter **27** Ronald George Wreyford Norrish
1968: **11** Lars Onsager
1969: **9** Odd Hassel **13** Derek H R Barton
1970: **18** Luis Federico Leloir
1971: **15** Gerhard Herzberg
1972: **13** Stanford Moore **18** Christian B Anfinsen, William Howard Stein
1973: **16** Ernst Otto Fischer **17** Geoffrey Wilkinson
1974: **10** Paul J Flory
1975: **14** John W Cornforth, Vladimir Prelog
1976: **16** William N Lipscomb
1977: **13** Ilya Prigogine
1978: **13** Peter Mitchell
1979: **11** Georg Wittig **13** Herbert C Brown
1980: **8** Paul Berg **13** Walter Gilbert **15** Frederick Sanger

(continued)

Nobel Prizes (*continued*)
1981: **12** Kenichi Fukui **13** Roald Hoffmann
1982: **9** Aaron Klug
1983: **10** Henry Taube
1984: **21** Robert Bruce Merrifield
1985: **11** Jerome Karle **16** Herbert A Hauptman
1986: **8** Yuan T Lee **12** John C Polanyi **16** Dudley Herschbach
1987: **11** Donald J Cram **16** Charles J Pederson
1988: **11** Robert Huber **13** Hartmut Michel **17** Johann Deisenhofer
1989: **10** Thomas Cich **12** Sidney Altman
1990: **10** Elias Corey
1991: **12** Richard Ernst
1992: **13** Rudolph Marcus
1993: **10** Kary Mullis **Michael Smith**
1994: **10** George Olah
1995: **11** Paul Crutzen, Mario Molina **16** F Sherwood Rowland
1996: **11** Robert F Curl **15** Richard E Smalley, Sir Harold W Kroto

Physics:
1901: **16** Wilhelm K Roentgen
1902: **12** Pieter Zeeman **15** Hendrik A Lorentz
1903: **11** Marie S Curie, Pierre Curie **15** A Henri Becquerel
1904: **11** John W Strutt (Lord Rayleigh)
1905: **13** Philipp Lenard
1906: **16** Sir Joseph Thomson
1907: **16** Albert A Michelson
1908: **15** Gabriel Lippmann
1909: **10** Karl F Braun **16** Guglielmo Marconi
1910: **20** Johannes D van der Waals
1911: **11** Wilhelm Wien
1912: **10** Nils G Dalen
1913: **20** Heike Kamerlingh Onnes
1914: **10** Max von Laue
1915: **16** Sir William H Bragg, Sir William L Bragg
1917: **14** Charles B Barkla
1918: **9** Max Planck
1919: **13** Johannes Stark
1920: **17** Charles E Guillaume
1921: **14** Albert Einstein
1922: **10** Nils H D Bohr
1923: **15** Robert A Millikan
1924: **14** Karl M G Siegbahn

1925: **11** Gustav Hertz, James Franck
1926: **11** Jean B Perrin
1927: **14** Arthur H Compton **15** Charles T R Wilson
1928: **18** Sir Owen W Richardson
1929: **15** Louis V de Broglie
1930: **23** Sir Chandrasekhara V Raman
1932: **16** Werner Heisenberg
1933: **11** Paul A M Dirac **16** Erwin Schrodinger
1935: **16** Sir James Chadwick
1936: **11** Victor F Hess **13** Carl D Anderson
1937: **16** Clinton J Davisson **17** Sir George P Thomson
1938: **11** Enrico Fermi
1939: **11** Ernest O Lawrence
1943: **9** Otto Stern
1944: **11** Isidor I Rabi
1945: **13** Wolfgang Pauli
1946: **14** Percy W Bridgman
1947: **18** Sir Edward V Appleton
1948: **17** Patrick M S Blackett
1949: **12** Hideki Yukawa
1950: **12** Cecil F Powell
1951: **14** Ernest T S Walton **17** Sir John D Cockcroft
1952: **10** Felix Bloch **14** Edward M Purcell
1953: **12** Frits Zernike
1954: **7** Max Born **12** Walther Bothe
1955: **13** Polykarp Kusch, Willis E Lamb Jr
1956: **11** John Bardeen **15** Walter H Brattain **16** William B Shockley
1957: **11** Tsung Dao Lee **12** Chen Ning Yang
1958: **9** Igor Y Tamm **10** Ilya M Frank **15** Pavel A Cherenkov
1959: **11** Emilio Segre **15** Owen Chamberlain
1960: **13** Donald A Glaser
1961: **16** Robert Hofstadter, Rudolf L Mossbauer
1962: **10** Lev D Landau
1963: **11** J Hans Jensen **16** Eugene Paul Wigner **18** Maria Goeppert Mayer
1964: **17** Charles Hard Townes **25** Nikolai Gennadiyevich Basov **30** Aleksandr Mikhailovich Prokhorov
1965: **18** Shinichiro Tomonaga **22** Julian Seymour Schwinger, Richard Phillips Feynman
1966: **13** Alfred Kastler

1967: **17** Hans Albrecht Bethe
1968: **12** Luis W Alvarez
1969: **14** Murray Gell-Mann
1970: **12** Hannes Alfven **15** Louis Eugene Neel
1971: **11** Dennis Gabor
1972: **11** John Bardeen, Leon N Cooper **20** John Robert Schreiffer
1973: **8** Leo Esaki **11** Ivar Giaever **15** Brian D Josephson
1974: **12** Antony Hewish **13** Sir Martin Ryle
1975: **8** Aage Bohr **13** Ben R Mottelson **15** L James Rainwater
1976: **12** Samuel C C Ting **13** Burton Richter
1977: **13** John H Van Vleck, Sir Nevill Mott **15** Philip W Anderson
1978: **12** Arno A Penzias, Peter Kapitza (Pyotr Kapitsa) **13** Robert W Wilson
1979: **10** Abdus Salam **14** Sheldon Glashow, Steven Weinberg
1980: **9** Val L Fitch **12** James W Cronin
1981: **12** Kai M Siegbahn **14** Arthur Schawlow **19** Nicolaas Bloembergen
1982: **14** Kenneth G Wilson
1983: **14** William A Fowler **25** Subrahmanyan Chandrasekhar
1984: **11** Carlo Rubbia **15** Simon van der Meer
1985: **16** Klaus von Klitzing
1986: **10** Ernst Ruska, Gerd Binner **14** Heinrich Rohrer
1987: **12** K Alex Mueller **13** J Georg Bednorz
1988: **13** Leon M Lederman **14** Melvin Schwartz **15** Jack Steinberger
1989: **11** Hans Dehmelt **12** Norman Ramsey, Wolfgang Paul
1990: **12** Henry Kendall **13** Richard Taylor **14** Jerome Friedman
1991: **12** Pierre Gennes
1992: **13** George Charpak
1993: **12** Joseph Taylor, Russell Hulse
1994: **13** Clifford Shull **17** Bertram Brockhouse
1995: **11** Martin L Perl **15** Frederick Reines
1966: **9** David M Lee **16** Douglas D Osheroff **17** Robert C Richardson

Peace:
1901: **13** Frederic Passy **15** Jean Henri Dunant

1902: **12** Elie Ducommun **18** Charles Albert Gobat
1903: **17** Sir William R Cremer
1904: **27** Institute of International Law
1905: **24** Baroness Bertha von Suttner
1906: **17** Theodore Roosevelt
1907: **12** Louis Renault **14** Ernesto T Moneta
1908: **12** Fredrik Bajer **14** Klas P Arnoldson
1909: **16** Auguste Beernaert **35** Paul H Balluat d'Estournelles de Constant
1910: **24** International Peace Bureau
1911: **12** Alfred H Fried **13** Tobias M C Asser
1912: **9** Elihu Root
1913: **15** Henri La Fontaine
1917: **30** International Red Cross Committee
1919: **13** Woodrow Wilson
1920: **13** Leon Bourgeois
1921: **15** Christian L Lange **19** Karl Hjalmar Branting
1922: **14** Fridtjof Nansen
1925: **13** Charles G Dawes **26** Sir Joseph Austen Chamberlain
1926: **14** Aristide Briand **16** Gustav Stresemann
1927: **12** Ludwig Quidde **17** Ferdinand E Buisson
1929: **13** Frank B Kellogg
1930: **15** (Lars Olof Jonathan) Nathan Soderblom
1931: **10** Jane Addams **20** Nicholas Murray Butler
1933: **15** Sir Norman Angell
1934: **15** Arthur Henderson
1935: **16** Carl von Ossietzky
1936: **19** Carlos Saavedra Lamas
1937: **13** E A Robert Cecil (Viscount Cecil)
1938: **36** Nansen International Office for Refugees
1944: **30** International Red Cross Committee
1945: **11** Cordell Hull
1946: **9** John R Mott **11** Emily G Balch
1947: **21** Friends Service Council **31** American Friends Service Committee

1949: **11** John Boyd Orr (Baron Orr)
1950: **12** Ralph J Bunche
1951: **11** Leon Jouhaux
1952: **16** Albert Schweitzer
1953: **15** George C Marshall
1954: **51** Office of the United Nations High Commissioner for Refugees
1957: **14** Lester B Pearson
1958: **28** Rev Dominique Georges Henri Pire
1959: **16** Philip J Noel-Baker
1960: **14** Albert J Luthuli
1961: **15** Dag Hammarskjold
1962: **13** Linus C Pauling
1963: **25** League of Red Cross Societies **30** International Red Cross Committee
1964: **18** Martin Luther King Jr
1965: **26** United Nations Children's Fund (UNICEF)
1968: **10** Rene Cassin
1969: **30** International Labor Organization (ILO)
1970: **14** Norman E Borlaug
1971: **11** Willy Brandt
1973: **8** Le Duc Tho **15** Henry A Kissinger
1974: **10** Eisaku Sato **12** Sean MacBride
1975: **15** Andrei D Sakharov
1976: **13** Betty Williams **15** Mairead Corrigan
1977: **20** Amnesty International
1978: **10** Anwar Sadat **13** Menachem Begin
1979: **12** Mother Teresa
1980: **19** Adolfo Perez Esquivel
1981: **51** Office of the United Nations High Commissioner for Refugees
1982: **10** Alva Myrdal **19** Alfonso Garcia Robles
1983: **10** Lech Walesa
1984: **17** Bishop Desmond Tutu
1985: **51** International Physicians for the Prevention of Nuclear War
1986: **10** Elie Wiesel
1987: **17** Oscar Arias Sanchez

1988: **31** United Nations peacekeeping troops
1989: **9** Dalai Lama
1990: **16** Mikhail Gorbachev
1991: **13** Aung San Suu Kyi
1992: **15** Rigoberta Menchu
1993: **9** F W de Klerk **13** Nelson Mandela
1994: **11** Yasir Arafat, Shimon Peres **12** Yitzhak Rabin
1995: **13** Joseph Rotblat
1996: **14** Jose Ramos Horta **23** Carlos Filepe, Ximenes Belo

Economics:
1969: **12** Jan Tinbergen, Ragnar Frisch
1970: **14** Paul A Samuelson
1971: **13** Simon S Kuznets
1972: **13** Kenneth J Arrow, Sir John R Hicks
1973: **15** Wassily Leontief
1974: **12** Gunnar Myrdal **18** Friedrich A von Hayek
1975: **17** Tjalling C Koopmans **18** Leonid V Kantorovich
1976: **14** Milton Friedman
1977: **11** Bertil Ohlin, James E Meade
1978: **13** Herbert A Simon
1979: **14** Sir Arthur Lewis **15** Theodore Schultz
1980: **14** Lawrence R Klein
1981: **10** James Tobin
1982: **14** George J Stigler
1983: **12** Gerard Debreu
1984: **15** Sir Richard Stone
1985: **16** Franco Modigliani
1986: **19** James McGill Buchanan
1987: **12** Robert M Solow
1988: **13** Maurice Allais
1989: **14** Trygve Haavelmo
1990: **12** Merton Miller **13** William Sharpe **14** Harry Mrkowitz
1991: **11** Ronald Coase
1992: **10** Gary Becker
1993: **11** Robert Fogel **12** Douglas North
1994: **8** John Nash **12** John Harsanyi **14** Reinhard Selten
1995: **14** Robert E Lucas Jr
1996: **14** James A Mirrlees **15** William S Vickrey

nomad 4 hobo 5 gypsy, mover, rover, stray, tramp 6 roamer 7 migrant, rambler, refugee, runaway, strayer, vagrant 8 bohemian, emigrant, migrator, renegade, traveler, vagabond, wanderer 9 immigrant, itinerant, straggler

nomadic 6 roving 7 migrant, roaming, vagrant 8 drifting, vagabond 9 footloose, itinerant, migratory, strolling, traveling, wandering

nom de guerre 5 alias 7 war name 9 pseudonym 11 assumed name

nom de plume 5 alias 7 pen name 9 false name, pseudonym 11 assumed name, writing name

nomenclature 5 lingo, terms 6 jargon, naming 8 language, taxonomy 10 nomination, vocabulary

nominal 3 low 5 cheap, small 6 puppet 7 minimum, titular 8 baseless, moderate, official, so-called 9 pretended, professed, purported, suggested 10 groundless, ostensible, reasonable

nominate 3 tag 4 call, name, pick, term 5 elect, label, style 6 choose, invest, select 7 elevate, install, propose, suggest 9 authorize, recommend

nomination 8 election 9 accession, selection 10 suggestion

nominee 7 hopeful 8 aspirant, eligible 9 applicant, candidate 10 competitor, contestant

nonadjustable 5 fixed, rigid 9 immovable 10 inflexible

nonalcoholic 4 soft 15 nonintoxicating

nonattendance 3 cut 7 absence, truancy 11 absenteeism

nonbeliever 5 cynic, pagan 7 atheist, doubter, heathen, infidel, skeptic 8 agnostic, apostate 10 backslider, empiricist, questioner, unbeliever 11 disbeliever, freethinker 14 doubting Thomas

nonbinding 8 optional 9 voluntary 12 unimperative 13 discretionary

nonchalance 9 composure, unconcern 13 offhandedness French: 11 insouciance

nonchalant 3 lax 4 cool, idle, lazy 5 blase, slack 6 casual 7 languid, offhand, unmoved 8 careless, heedless, indolent, listless 9 apathetic, collected, easygoing, lethargic, unexcited,

unheeding, unmindful, unruffled, unstirred, withdrawn 10 insensible, insouciant, phlegmatic, unaffected

noncombatant 7 neutral 8 civilian

noncommittal 3 mum 4 cool, mute, safe, wary 5 vague 7 careful, evasive, guarded, neutral, politic, prudent 8 cautious, discreet, reserved 9 ambiguous, equivocal, tentative 10 indecisive, indefinite, unspeaking 11 circumspect, temporizing

noncompliance 6 breach 7 failure, neglect 9 disregard 10 resistance 11 dereliction

noncompliant 6 unruly 7 defiant, froward, naughty, wayward 8 contrary, mutinous, perverse, stubborn 9 differing, dissident, fractious, objecting, obstinate, resistant, resistive, undutiful 10 disorderly, dissenting, rebellious, refractory, unorthodox, unyielding

non compos mentis 14 not of sound mind 17 mentally incapable

nonconfirming 7 denying 8 negating, refuting 9 rejecting 10 disavowing 11 disclaiming, repudiating

nonconformist 3 nut 4 beat, card 5 freak, hippy, loner, rebel 6 oddity, weirdo 7 heretic, oddball, radical 8 bohemian, crackpot, deserter, maverick, original, reformer, renegade, vagabond 9 character, dissenter, dissident, eccentric, exception, insurgent, protester, screwball 10 dissenting, iconoclast, rebellious, schismatic 13 individualist, revolutionary

nonconformity 5 quirk 6 oddity 7 anomaly 9 deviation, rebellion 10 aberration, divergence, resistance

noncongenial 6 unlike 8 opposite 9 different, disparate, ill-suited, unrelated 10 dissimilar 11 disagreeing 12 disagreeable, incompatible 13 unsympathetic

nondescript 5 usual, vague 8 ordinary 9 amorphous, colorless 11 stereotyped 12 unimpressive 13 characterless, undistinctive, unexceptional 15 undistinguished

nonentity 4 zero 6 cipher, nobody 7 nothing, no-count, nullity 8 small-fry, unperson 10 mediocrity

nonessential 6 luxury, trivia 7 trivial 9 extrinsic, secondary,

trimmings 10 accidental, extraneous, incidental, irrelevant, peripheral, subsidiary

nonexclusive 4 open 6 public, shared 7 divided 12 unrestricted

nonexistence 4 lack, void 7 absence 8 oblivion 11 nothingness

nonexistent 4 gone 5 short 6 absent 7 lacking, missing, wanting 11 unavailable 12 insufficient

nonirritating 4 calm 5 bland 6 benign 7 calming 8 soothing, tranquil 9 temperate

nonmaterialistic 9 spiritual 10 idealistic 12 intellectual

nonmember 5 guest 7 outcast, visitor 8 outsider

nonnatural 7 manmade 9 synthetic 10 artificial, fabricated, factitious 12 manufactured

nonobservance 6 breach 7 failure, neglect 9 disregard 11 dereliction 13 noncompliance

non obstante 15 notwithstanding

no-nonsense 4 grim, hard 5 grave, harsh, rigid, sober, stern 6 ardent, intent, severe, solemn, strict 7 earnest, serious 8 critical, diligent, exacting, resolute 9 committed, dedicated, demanding, hardnosed, practical, pragmatic, unbending, unsparing 10 determined, hard headed, purposeful, sobersided 12 businesslike

nonpareil 5 elite, ideal, model, super 6 symbol, unique 7 epitome, paragon, pattern, supreme 8 exemplar 9 unequaled, unmatched, unrivaled 10 apotheosis 11 exceptional, unsurpassed 13 extraordinary 14 representative French: 11 ne plus ultra 14 creme de la creme

nonparticipation 7 refusal 8 eschewal, forgoing 9 avoidance, eschewing 10 abstaining, abstention, refraining, sitting out 11 forbearance

nonpartisan 4 fair, just 8 unbiased, unswayed 9 equitable, impartial, objective, unbigoted 10 impersonal, uninvolved 12 freethinking, unaffiliated, unimplicated, uninfluenced, unprejudiced 13 disinterested

nonpermissible 9 forbidden 10 disallowed 11 intolerable 12 inadmissible, unacceptable

nonplus 4 balk, faze, foil, halt, stop 5 abash, stump, upset

6 baffle, bother, dismay, muddle, puzzle, stymie **7** astound, confuse, disturb, mystify, perplex **8** astonish, bewilder, confound, deadlock **9** dumbfound, embarrass **10** disconcert **11** flabbergast **14** discountenance

nonplussed, nonplused 5 at sea, fazed **7** at a loss, baffled, floored, mixed-up, muddled, puzzled, stumped **8** confused **9** befuddled, mystified, unsettled **10** bewildered, confounded **12** disconcerted

nonpoisonous 4 safe **8** nontoxic **11** nonvenomous, nonvirulent

nonpresence 3 cut **7** absence, truancy **11** absenteeism

nonprofessional 3 lay **4** laic **7** dabbler
  French: 7 amateur **10** dilettante

nonresident 7 tourist, visitor **9** transient **11** out-of-towner

nonresistance 6 assent **7** pliancy **8** docility, giving in, meekness, yielding **9** deference, obedience, passivity **10** compliance, conforming, conformity, pliability, submission **12** acquiescence, complaisance

nonresistant 4 meek **6** docile, pliant **7** passive, pliable **8** deferent, obedient, yielding **9** compliant **10** conforming, submissive **11** acquiescent, complaisant, deferential

nonscholarly 8 untaught **9** unlearned **10** uneducated, unlettered, unpedantic, unschooled

nonsectarian 10 ecumenical **11** interchurch **16** undenominational **17** nondenominational **19** interdenominational

nonsense 3 rot **4** bosh, bunk **5** folly, trash **6** antics, babble, drivel, joking, piffle **7** baloney, blather, bombast, chatter, fooling, garbage, hogwash, inanity, prattle, rubbish, trifles, twaddle **8** claptrap, flummery **9** absurdity, frivolity, gibberish, high jinks, horseplay, moonshine, silliness, stupidity **10** balderdash, flapdoodle, tomfoolery, triviality **11** foolishness, shenanigans **12** childishness, extravagance **13** facetiousness, ludicrousness, senselessness **14** ridiculousness **15** meaninglessness

nonsensical 4 wild **5** crazy, funny, inane, silly **6** absurd, stupid **7** asinine, comical, foolish **8** farcical **9** facetious,

laughable, ludicrous **10** irrational, ridiculous

non sequitur 15 it does not follow

nonspecialized 11 generalized

nonspecific 4 hazy **5** vague **7** general, inexact **9** imprecise, uncertain **10** indefinite, undetailed **11** approximate, generalized

nonspiritual 7 earthly, profane, secular, worldly **8** material, temporal **13** materialistic

nonstop 7 endless, express **8** constant, unbroken **9** incessant **10** continuous, unrelieved **11** unremitting **12** interminable

nonstudious 9 unlearned **10** uneducated, unlettered, unpedantic, unschooled

nontaxable 9 sheltered **10** deductible

nontechnical 6 simple **8** academic **13** uncomplicated

nontypical 7 unusual **8** abnormal, uncommon **9** anomalous, irregular **16** unrepresentative

nonuniform 5 mixed **6** unlike **7** altered, changed, erratic, unalike **8** changing, variable **9** deviating, different, irregular, multiform **10** dissimilar **11** fluctuating, nonstandard **12** inconsistent

nonvital 9 accessory, extrinsic **10** disposable, expendable, incidental **11** dispensable, superfluous, unessential, unimportant, unnecessary

nonvocational 8 academic

nonvolitional 6 reflex **8** unwilled **9** automatic **11** instinctive, involuntary, spontaneous **12** uncontrolled

noodle 4 bean, head, pate **5** gourd, pasta **6** noggin **8** practice **9** improvise

nook 3 den **4** cove, lair **5** haven, niche **6** alcove, cavity, corner, cranny, dugout, recess, refuge **7** retreat, shelter **8** hideaway **9** cubbyhole **10** depression **11** hiding place

noon 6 midday, zenith **8** high noon, meridian

noose 3 tie **4** bond, hang, loop **5** catch, hitch, lasso, snare **6** choker, entrap, halter, lariat, tether

Nootka
  language family: 8 Wakashan
  tribe: 5 Makah **6** Hoiath, Ozette **7** Ahosath, Nitinat

8 Machlath, Otsosath, Tokwaath **9** Ihatisath, Mowachath, Nochalath, Qayokwath, Tsishaath, Yoloilath **10** Hishkwiath, Hochoqtlis, Manohisath, Tlaokwiath **11** Chiqtlisath, Hopachasath, Qiltsamaath
  location: 10 Washington **15** Vancouver Island
  leader: 8 Maquinna **10** Wikaninish
  related to: 5 Makah
  noted for: 7 whaling

Nordhoff, Charles
  author of: 17 Mutiny on the Bounty (with James Norman Hall)

Nordic Mythology *see* **21** Scandinavian Mythology

norm 3 par **4** rule, type **5** gauge, model **7** average, measure, pattern **8** standard **9** barometer, criterion, yardstick **12** measuring rod

norm, the norm 7 the mean, the rule **9** the median **10** the average **14** the common thing

normal 3 fit, par **4** sane **5** sound, usual **6** steady **7** average, healthy, natural, regular, typical, uniform **8** constant, expected, mediocre, middling, ordinary, rational, reliable, standard **9** incessant, steadfast, unceasing **10** conforming, consistent, continuous, dependable, reasonable, unchanging **11** conformable, right-minded, unremitting **12** conventional **13** uninterrupted **14** representative

Normandy, Normandie
  beach: 4 Gold, Juno, Utah **5** Omaha, Sword
  borders: 7 Picardy **8** Brittany **14** English Channel
  church/shrine: 12 Saint Etienne **15** Mont Saint Michel
  city: 4 Caen **5** Rouen **7** Le Havre **9** Cherbourg
  event: 4 D Day **17** Operation Overlord
  region of: 6 France
  river: 5 Seine

Norn
  origin: 12 Scandinavian
  form: 6 virgin **7** goddess
  personifies: 4 fate
  original Norn: 5 Urdar
  the three: 3 Urd **5** Skuld **8** Verdandi
  known as: 12 weird sisters

Norris, Frank
  author of: 6 The Pit **8** McTeague **10** The Octopus

Norse Mythology *see* **21** Scandinavian Mythology

north 5 polar, upper 6 arctic

North America *see box*

Northanger Abbey
author: 10 Jane Austen
character: 8 Mrs Allen
10 John Thorpe 12 James
Morland 14 Isabella Thorpe
16 Catherine Morland
Tilney family: 5 Henry
7 Captain, Eleanor, General

North by Northwest
director: 15 Alfred Hitchcock
cast: 9 Cary Grant 10 James
Mason 11 Leo G Carroll
12 Martin Landau 13 Eva
Marie Saint 17 Jessie Royce
Landis
setting (climax): 13 Mount
Rushmore
score: 15 Bernard Herrmann

North Carolina *see box*

North Dakota *see box,
p. 690*

North Dallas Forty
director: 11 Ted Kotcheff

based on story by: 9 Peter
Gent
cast: 8 Mac Davis 9 Nick
Nolte 11 Dayle Haddon
14 Charles Durning

Northern Crown
constellation of: 14 Corona
Borealis

Northern Rhodesia *see*
6 Zambia

North Korea *see* 5 Korea

North Star State
nickname of: 9 Minnesota

North Toward Home
author: 12 Willie Morris

North Vietnam *see* 7 Vietnam

Northwest Passage
director: 9 King Vidor
author: 14 Kenneth Roberts
cast: 10 Ruth Hussey
11 Robert Young 12 Spencer
Tracy 13 Walter Brennan

Northwest Territories *see
box, p. 690*

North wind
associated with: 6 Boreas

Norton, Thomas
author of: 8 Gorboduc (with
Thomas Sackville)

Norway *see box, p. 691*

Norwegian Mythology *see*
21 Scandinavian Mythology

nose
sense of: 5 smell
part: 7 nostril 14 olfactory
patch

nosegay 4 posy 7 bouquet
10 tussy-mussy

nosiness 6 prying 9 curiosity
15 inquisitiveness

nostalgia 6 pining, regret 7 remorse 11 languishing, remembrance 12 homesickness
13 regretfulness

Nostradamus
name: 7 Michael 17 Michelde
Notredame
occupation: 7 prophet 9 physician 10 astrologer
13 metaphysicist
wrote: 9 Centuries

Nostromo
author: 12 Joseph Conrad

nostrum 4 balm, cure, dose,
drug 5 draft 6 elixir, physic,
potion, remedy 7 cure-all, formula, panacea 8 medicine
9 treatment 10 medicament
12 prescription

nosy, nosey 6 prying, snoopy
7 all ears, curious 8 snooping
9 intrusive 11 inquisitive, overcurious 13 eavesdropping

nota bene 8 note well 10 take
notice

notability 4 fame 6 import,
moment, renown 8 eminence
9 celebrity 10 importance,
prominence 11 consequence,
distinction, preeminence
12 significance

notable 3 VIP 4 name 5 famed,
wheel 6 biggie, bigwig, famous, marked 7 eminent, salient 8 luminary, renowned,
striking 9 celebrity, dignitary,
personage, prominent, reputable 10 celebrated, pronounced,
remarkable 11 conspicuous,
outstanding, personality
13 distinguished

notably 7 visibly 8 markedly
10 distinctly, strikingly
11 prominently 12 unmistakably 13 conspicuously,
outstandingly

not alike 8 distinct 9 different,
differing, disparate, divergent
10 dissimilar 11 contrasting

North America
nation: 4 Cuba 5 Haiti 6 Belize, Canada, Mexico, Panama
7 Bahamas, Jamaica 8 Barbados, Honduras 9 Costa Rica,
Guatemala, Nicaragua 10 El Salvador, Puerto Rico, Saint
Lucia 12 Saint Vincent, United States 17 Dominican Republic, Trinidad and Tobago 28 Saint Vincent and the
Grenadines
desert: 7 Sonoran
island: 4 Long 6 Baffin, Cayman, Kodiak 7 Antigua, Bermuda, Iceland 8 Aleutian, Catalina, Thousand 9 Antilles,
Greenland, Nantucket, Vancouver 10 Cape Breton
12 Newfoundland, Prince Edward 14 Queen Charlotte
ocean/sea/bay: 6 Arctic, Baffin, Bering, Hudson, Mexico
7 Chukchi, Lincoln, Pacific 8 Amundsen, Atlantic, Beaufort, Labrador 9 Caribbean, Greenland 10 California,
Chesapeake, St Lawrence
river: 3 Red 4 Ohio 5 Peace, Snake, Yukon 6 Hudson
8 Arkansas, Colorado, Columbia, Missouri 9 Churchill,
Mackenzie, Rio Grande 10 St Lawrence 11 Mississippi
12 Saskatchewan
lake: 4 Erie 5 Huron 7 Ontario 8 Michigan, Superior, Winnipeg 9 Great Bear, Nicaragua 10 Great Lakes, Great
Slave
mountain range: 5 Ozark, Rocky 6 Alaska 7 Cascade
9 Blue Ridge 10 Laurentian 11 Appalachian, Sierra
Madre 12 Sierra Nevada
highest point: 13 Mount McKinley
lowest point: 11 Death Valley
city: 4 Nome 5 Miami 6 Boston, Dallas, Denver, Havana,
Ottawa, Quebec 7 Atlanta, Calgary, Chicago, Detroit,
Houston, Memphis, New York, Phoenix, Seattle, Toronto
8 Montreal, Portland, San Diego 9 Anchorage, Milwaukee, Reykjavik, Vancouver 10 Kansas City, Los Angeles,
Mexico City, New Orleans, Washington 11 Philadelphia,
San Antonio, San Francisco
mineral: 3 oil, tin 4 coal, gold, lead, salt, zinc 6 cobalt,
copper, nickel, quartz, silver 7 iron ore, mercury, sulphur, uranium 8 aluminum, antimony, asbestos, chromium, platinum, titanium, tungsten 9 magnesium,
manganese, petroleum 10 molybdenum, natural gas

North Carolina
abbreviation: **2** NC **4** N Car
nickname: **7** Tar Heel **8** Old North **10** Turpentine
capital: **7** Raleigh
largest city: **9** Charlotte
others: **4** Bath **6** Durham, Lenoir, Shelby, Wilson **7** Edenton, Hickory, Kinston, New Bern, Roxboro, Tarboro **8** Gastonia **9** Albemarle, Asheville, Goldsboro, Henderson, Kitty Hawk, Lumberton **10** Chapel Hill, Greensboro, Greenville, Kannapolis, Wilmington **11** Statesville, Thomasville, Williamston **12** Fayetteville, Jacksonville, Winston-Salem
college: **4** Duke, Elon **7** Catawba **8** Davidson **10** Wake Forest
feature:
  battle site: **18** Guilford Courthouse
  national park: **19** Great Smoky Mountains (with Tennessee)
  national seashore: **11** Cape Lookout **12** Cape Hatteras
tribe: **3** Eno **5** Coree **6** Cheraw **7** Buffalo, Moratok, Pamlico **8** Chowanoc, Hatteras **9** Tuscarora
people: **6** O Henry (William Sidney Porter) **7** tarheel **11** Billy Graham, Thomas Wolfe **13** Dolley (Dolly) Madison, Edward R Murrow **14** Richard Gatling
  explorer: **6** de Soto **8** de Ayllon **9** Verrazano
island: **7** Roanoke
lake: **6** Norman, Phelps **7** Fontana **8** Waccamaw **12** Mattamuskeet
land rank: **12** twenty-eighth
mountain: **5** Black, Unaka **6** Harris **9** Blue Ridge **10** Great Smoky **13** Clingman's Dome
  highest point: **8** Mitchell
physical feature: **10** Outer Banks **11** French Broad **15** Little Tennessee
  cape: **4** Fear **7** Lookout **8** Hatteras
  plateau: **8** Piedmont
  sea: **8** Atlantic
  sound: **4** Core **5** Bogue **7** Croatan, Pamlico
  swamp: **6** Dismal
president: **9** James Polk **13** Andrew Johnson
river: **3** Haw, Tar **4** Fear **5** Neuse **6** Chowan, Lumber, Peedee, Yadkin **7** Roanoke, Wateree
state admission: **7** twelfth
state bird: **8** cardinal
state fish: **11** channel bass
state flower: **7** dogwood **9** goldenrod
state motto: **20** To Be Rather Than To Seem
state song: **16** The Old North State
state tree: **4** pine
state dance: **4** shag

notation **5** entry **10** memorandum

not bright **3** dim **4** dark, dull **5** dense, dusky, murky **6** cloudy, stupid **7** clouded **8** obscured **13** unilluminated

notch **3** cut **4** dent, mark, nick **5** grade, level, score **6** degree **7** scoring, scratch **11** indentation

not disclosed
Italian: **7** in petto

note **4** bill, fame, line, mark **5** bread, draft, enter, green, money, write **6** regard, renown **7** epistle, jot down, lettuce, message, missive, put down, scratch, set down, voucher **8** currency, dispatch, eminence, mark down, perceive **9** bank draft, celebrity, greenback **10** communique, importance, memorandum, prominence, reputation **11** certificate, consequence, distinction

notebook **3** log **5** diary **6** record **7** journal **9** looseleaf
French: **6** cahier

noted **6** famous **7** eminent **8** renowned **9** prominent, reputable **10** celebrated, remarkable **11** illustrious, outstanding **13** distinguished

Notes from the Underground
author: **16** Fyodor Dostoevsky

note well
Latin: **8** nota bene

noteworthy **7** unusual **8** singular **9** important **10** remarkable **11** outstanding, significant, substantial **12** considerable **13** distinguished, exceptional

not far from **4** near **6** all but, almost, nearly **7** close to **8** not quite **13** approximately

not genuine **4** fake, sham **5** bogus, false, phony **6** ersatz, unreal **7** feigned **8** spurious **9** imitation, insincere, pretended, synthetic **10** artificial, fraudulent **11** counterfeit **12** hypocritical
Latin: **8** mala fide

not germane **9** extrinsic, unrelated **10** extraneous, immaterial, irrelevant **11** incongruous, inconsonant, unconnected **12** incompatible, nonessential **13** inappropriate

not guilty **5** clear **8** innocent **9** blameless **10** inculpable, unblamable

nothing **3** air, nix, zip **4** none, zero **5** stuff, trash, zilch **6** bauble, bubble, cipher, gewgaw, naught, trifle, trivia **7** duck egg, nullity, rubbish, trinket **8** goose egg **9** bagatelle, obscurity **14** insignificance **16** inconsequentials
Latin: **5** nihil

nothing is created from nothing
Latin: **16** ex nihilo nihil fit

nothingness **4** void **5** death **8** oblivion **9** emptiness **10** triviality **12** nonexistence **14** insignificance

Nothing Sacred
director: **14** William Wellman
cast: **13** Carole Lombard, Frederic March **14** Walter Connolly
score: **11** Oscar Levant
remade as: **10** Living It Up
script: **8** Ben Hecht

nothing unless it is good
Latin: **12** nil nisi bonum

nothing without the divine will
Latin: **13** nil sine numine
motto of: **8** Colorado

notice **3** eye, see **4** dope, heed, info, mark **5** goods **6** poster, rating, regard, review, take in **7** leaflet, mention, observe, warning **8** brochure, circular, critique, handbill, pamphlet

North Dakota
abbreviation: **2** ND **4** N Dak
nickname: **5** Sioux **11** Flickertail **16** Land of the Dakotas
capital: **8** Bismarck
largest city: **5** Fargo
others: **5** Minot **9** Bottineau, Jamestown, Williston **10** Grand Forks
college: **4** Mary **9** Jamestown
feature:
  dam: **4** Oahe **8** Garrison
  garden: **18** International Peace
  national park: **17** Theodore Roosevelt
tribe: **5** Sioux **6** Mandan **7** Arikara, Hidatsa **8** Chippewa
people: **12** Eric Sevareid
  explorer: **6** Carver **8** Thompson, Varennes **13** Lewis and Clark
lake: **5** Stump **6** Devils **9** Sakakawea
land rank: **11** seventeenth
mountain: **6** Turtle **8** Killdeer **10** Black Butte
  highest point: **10** White Butte
physical feature:
  basin: **9** Williston
  plain: **8** The Slope
  valley: **8** Red River
river: **3** Red **4** Park, Rush **5** Cedar, Goose, Heart, James, Knife, Mouse **6** Souris **7** Deslacs, Pembina **8** Missouri, Cheyenne, Wild Rice **9** Otter Tail **10** Cannonball **11** Yellowstone **12** Boise de Sioux **14** Little Missouri **18** Red River of the North
state admission: **8** fortieth **11** thirty-ninth (with South Dakota)
state bird: **17** western meadowlark
state fish: **12** northern pike
state flower: **15** wild prairie rose
state motto: **45** Liberty and Union Now and Forever One and Inseparable
state song: **15** North Dakota Hymn
state tree: **11** American elm

Notorious
director: **15** Alfred Hitchcock
cast: **9** Cary Grant **11** Claude Rains **12** Louis Calhern **13** Ingrid Bergman

not pertinent 9 unrelated **10** extraneous, immaterial, irrelevant **11** incongruous, unconnected **13** inappropriate

not quite 6 all but, almost, nearly

not required 8 elective, optional **9** voluntary

not too seriously
Latin: **13** cum grano salis

Notus
origin: **5** Greek
personifies: **9** south wind

not wanted
French: **6** de trop

notwithstanding
Latin: **11** non obstante

not working 4 dead **8** inactive **10** unemployed **11** inoperative **12** unresponsive

Nouakchott
capital of: **10** Mauritania

nourish 4 feed **5** nurse **6** suckle **7** nurture, sustain

nourishing 4 rich **6** hearty **7** healthy **9** fostering, nurturing, wholesome **10** nutritious, sustaining **11** maintaining

9 appraisal, attention, knowledge, statement **10** advisement, cognizance, disclosure **11** declaration, information **12** announcement, intelligence **13** advertisement, communication, specification

noticeable 5 clear, plain **7** evident, obvious **8** definite, distinct, manifest, palpable, striking **10** observable **11** appreciable, conspicuous, perceivable, perceptible **12** unmistakable

notification 4 news, word **6** advice, report **7** message, release **8** bulletin, dispatch **9** statement **10** communique **11** information **12** announcement, intelligence **13** communication

notify 4 tell, warn **6** advise, inform **7** apprise, let know **8** acquaint, send word **9** enlighten

not indigenous 5 alien **6** exotic **7** foreign **8** imported **9** nonnative **10** extraneous **11** naturalized

notion 4 idea, view, whim **5** fancy, humor, quirk **6** belief, vagary, whimsy **7** caprice, conceit, concept, opinion **8** crotchet **9** suspicion **10** conception, intimation **12** eccentricity

not native 5 alien **6** exotic **7** foreign **8** imported **10** extraneous **11** naturalized

not of sound mind
Latin: **15** non compos mentis

not ordinary 4 rare **6** exotic, unique **7** bizarre, foreign, strange, unusual **8** peculiar, singular, uncommon **9** anomalous, different, fantastic **11** distinctive, outstanding **14** unconventional

notoriety 4 blot **5** shame, stain **6** infamy, stigma **7** scandal **8** disgrace, dishonor, ignominy **9** discredit, disrepute **11** degradation

notorious 6 arrant **7** blatant, glaring **8** infamous, renowned **9** egregious **10** celebrated, outrageous **11** outstanding

Northwest Territories
abbreviation: **3** NWT
borders: **7** Alberta **8** Manitoba **9** Baffin Bay, Hudson Bay **11** Arctic Ocean, Beaufort Sea, Labrador Sea **12** Saskatchewan **15** British Columbia
city: **6** Inuvik **8** Hay River **9** Fort Smith **11** Yellowknife **12** Frobisher Bay
country: **6** Canada
Inuit land: **7** Nunavut
island: **5** Banks, Devon **6** Baffin **7** Melville **8** Bathurst, Somerset, Victoria **9** Ellesmere **11** King William **13** Prince of Wales, Prince Patrick **14** Queen Elizabeth
mineral: **3** oil **4** gold, lead, zinc **6** silver **8** tungsten **9** petroleum
mountain: **21** Mount Sir James Mac Brien
native: **5** Inuit **6** Eskimo
territory: **8** Franklin, Keewatin **9** Mackenzie

Norway

other name: 5 Norge 20 Land of the Midnight Sun
capital: 4 Oslo 11 Christiania
largest city: 4 Oslo
others: 3 Gol, Nes 4 Bodo, Moss, Odda, Rena, Voss 5 Bjort, Floro, Hamar, Molde, Skien, Skjak, Vadso 6 Bergen, Horton, Larvik, Narvik, Tromso 7 Alesund, Arendal, Drammen, Harstad, Sandnes 8 Aalesund, Kirkenes 9 Stavanger, Trondheim 10 Hammerfest 12 Kristiansand
division: 3 Amt 4 Oslo 5 Fylke, Troms 6 Bergen, Opland, Tromso 7 Finmark, Hedmark, Ostfold 8 Letemark, Nordland, Rogaland, Vestfold 9 Ostlandet
   former: 11 Kalmar Union
   province called: 6 fylker
government:
   legislature: 8 Storting
head of state: 4 king
measure: 3 fot, mal 4 alen 5 kande 6 fathom 7 skieppe 9 korntonde
monetary unit: 3 ore 5 krone
weight: 3 lod 4 mark, pund 10 bismerpund
island: 4 Vega 5 Bomlo, Donna, Froya, Hitra, Hopen, Senja, Smola, Soroy 6 Alsten, Averoy, Bouvet, Hinnoy, Karmoy, Kvaloy, Solund, Vannoy 7 Gurskoy, Lofoten, Mageroy, Seiland 8 Jan Mayen, Svalbard
lake: 4 Alte 5 Ister, Mjosa, Snasa 6 Femund 7 Rostavn, Tunnsjo
mountain: 5 Sogne 6 Kjolen 7 Numedal 8 Blodfjel, Snohetta, Telemark, Ustetind 9 Harteigen, Jotunheim, Langfjell, Ramnanosi 10 Dovrefjell, Galdhoepig, Glitretind, Vibmesnosi 11 Myrdalfjell 14 Aardangerjokul, Hallingskarvet, Skagastolstind
highest point: 12 Galdhopiggen 13 Glittertinden
river: 3 Ena 4 Alta, Klar, Otra, Rana, Tana, Teno 5 Bardu, Begna, Glama, Lagen, Orkla, Otter, Rauma, Reisa 6 Glomma, Lougen, Namsen, Pasvik
sea: 5 North 6 Arctic 7 Barents 8 Atlantic 9 Norwegian, Skagerrak
physical feature:
   cape: 4 Naze 7 Nordkyn 8 Nordkapp 9 Lindesnes
   fjord: 4 Oslo 5 Sogne
   glacier: 12 Jostedalsbre
   inlet: 2 Is 3 Kob, Ran 4 Alst, Ands, Bokn, Nord, Ofot, Salt, Sunn, Tyri, Vest 5 fiord, fjord, Folda, Lakse, Sogne 6 Bjorna, Hadsel 7 Hortens 9 Trondheim
   plateau: 5 Doure, Dovre, Fjeld 9 Hardanger
people: 4 Lapp 5 Samme 6 Nordic, Viking
   artist: 5 Munch
   author: 5 Ibsen 6 Hamsun, Undset 7 Holberg 8 Bjornson 9 Wergeland
   composer: 5 Grieg 7 Sinding 8 Svendsen
   explorer: 4 Eric, Leif, Mohn, Sars 6 Nansen 8 Amundsen
   explorer/statesman: 6 Nansen 8 Amundsen 9 Heyerdahl
   king: 4 Olaf, Olav 5 Olave, Oscar 6 Haakon, Harold, Magnus, Sverre
   Nazi collaborator: 8 Quisling
   Norse god/goddess: 3 Sif, Tyr 4 Frey, Idun, Loki, Odin, Thor 5 Bragi, Freya, Hoder, Woden 6 Balder, Eostre, Frigga, Hermod
   sculptor: 8 Vigeland
language: 4 Lapp 5 Norse 6 Bokmal 7 Nynorsk, Riksmal 8 Landsmal, Samnorsk 9 Landsmaal, Norwegian
religion: 19 Evangelical Lutheran 22 National Church of Norway
place:
   castle: 8 Akershus
   cathedral: 7 Nidaras
   museum: 7 Kon Tiki 10 Viking Ship 15 Polar Expedition
   park: 7 Frogner
former colony: 7 Vinland
feature:
   dance: 6 gangar 7 halling 8 springar 9 spingleik
   literature form: 4 edda, saga
food:
   bread: 8 flat brod
   cheese: 3 Ost 7 gjetost 9 gammelost, Jarlsberg
   drink: 7 aquavit

12 invigorating
13 strengthening

nourishment 4 chow, eats, food, grub, meat 5 bread 6 viands 8 victuals 9 nutriment, nutrition 10 sustenance 11 comestibles

nouveau riche 9 newly rich (person)

Novak, Kim
   real name: 19 Marilyn Pauline Novak
   born: 9 Chicago IL
   roles: 6 Picnic 7 Pal Joey, Vertigo 14 Of Human Bondage 17 Bell Book and Candle 20 The Jeanne Eagels Story 22 The Man with the Golden Arm 31 Amorous Adventures of Moll Flanders

Nova Scotia *see box, p. 692*

Nova Scotia
  borders: 10 Bay of
    Fundy **12** New Bruns-
    wick **13** Atlantic
    Ocean **16** Gulf of St
    Lawrence **20** Northum-
    berland Strait
  city: 5 Truro **6** Sydney
    7 Amherst, Halifax
    8 Glace Bay, Yarmouth
    9 Dartmouth **10** New
    Glasgow
  country: 6 Canada
  island: 10 Cape Breton
  means: 11 New Scotland
  mineral: 3 oil **4** lead,
    salt, sand, zinc **6** barite,
    gravel, gypsum, silver
    9 celestite, petroleum
    10 natural gas
  mountain: 5 North
    8 Cobequid
  part of: 12 Appalachi-
    ans **17** Maritime Prov-
    inces **18** Atlantic
    Provinces
  river: 4 Avon **5** Clyde
    6 LaHave, Medway,
    Mersey **7** St Mary's
    12 Shubenacadie

novel 3 new **6** unique **7** unusual **8** original, singular, uncommon **9** different
10 innovative, unorthodox
14 unconventional
  French: 5 roman

novelty 5 token **6** bauble,
change, gewgaw **7** memento,
newness, trinket **8** gimcrack,
souvenir, surprise **9** bagatelle,
variation **10** innovation, knickknack, uniqueness
11 originality

November *see box*

novice 4 tyro **5** pupil **7** amateur, learner, student **8** beginner, disciple, newcomer
9 greenhorn **10** apprentice,
tenderfoot

Novum Organum
  author: 12 Francis Bacon

novus ordo seclorum 24 a
new order of the ages is born
  author: 6 Vergil, Virgil
  work: 8 Eclogues
  motto of: 11 US Great Seal

Now, Voyager
  director: 12 Irving Rapper
  cast: 10 Bette Davis
    11 Claude Rains, Janis Wil-
    son, Paul Henreid **12** Gladys
    Cooper
  score: 10 Max Steiner

now and then 8 on-and-off,
periodic, sometime, sporadic
9 irregular, sometimes, temporary **10** infrequent, occasional
11 irregularly **12** infrequently,
occasionally, periodically,
sporadically

Now Playing at Canterbury
  author: 14 Vance Bourjaily

Nox
  goddess of: 5 night

noxious 4 foul **6** deadly, lethal,
putrid **7** baneful, beastly,
harmful, hurtful, noisome
8 damaging, virulent **9** injurious, loathsome, poisonous,
revolting **10** abominable, disgusting, pernicious, putrescent **11** deleterious **12** foul-
smelling

nth degree 5 limit **6** utmost
7 extreme

nuance 5 shade, touch
6 nicety **7** finesse **8** delicacy,
fineness, keenness, subtlety
9 sharpness, variation
10 modulation, refinement
11 discernment

nub 4 core, crux, gist, hump,
knob, knot, lump, node
5 bulge, heart **6** kernel **7** essence **8** swelling **10** projection,
prominence, tumescence
11 nitty-gritty
12 protuberance

nubbin 3 ear **4** corn, lump,
stub **5** bulge, fruit, piece,
stump **10** diminutive

Nubbles, Kit
  character in: 19 The Old Cu-
    riosity Shop
  author: 7 Dickens

nubbly 5 lumpy, rough
6 coarse, knobby, pebbly

nucleus 3 nub **4** core, pith,
seed **5** heart **6** center,
kernel

Nudd *see* **4** Llud

nude 3 raw **4** bare **5** bared, naked **6** unclad **7** exposed **8** in
the raw, stripped **9** unadorned,
unarrayed, unclothed, uncovered, undressed
  French: 9 au naturel

nudge 3 jab, jog, nod **4** bump,
jolt, poke, prod, push **5** elbow,
press, punch, shove, touch
6 jostle, motion, signal
8 indicate

nugatory 4 idle **5** empty **6** hollow, otiose, paltry **7** trivial,
useless **8** piddling, trifling
9 meritless, valueless, worthless **10** profitless **11** ineffec-

tual **12** functionless
15 inconsequential

nugget 4 hunk, lump **5** chunk,
piece

nuisance 4 bore, fret, hurt,
pain, pest **5** curse, thorn,
worry **6** blight, bother, burden, plague **7** scourge, torment, trouble **8** handicap,
vexation **9** annoyance, grievance **10** affliction, irritation,
misfortune, pestilence **11** aggravation, botheration
13 inconvenience

Nuk
  capital of: 9 Greenland

Nukualofa
  capital of: 5 Tonga

null 2 NG **4** void **6** no good
7 invalid **9** valueless, worthless **10** immaterial **11** inoperative, nonexistent,
unimportant **13** insignificant

nullification 6 repeal **7** voiding **8** recision **9** abolition, annulment **10** abrogation,
rescinding **11** abolishment
12 cancellation,
invalidation

nullify 4 veto, void **5** annul
6 cancel, repeal, revoke
7 abolish, rescind, retract
8 abrogate, make void, override, set aside **10** invalidate

nullity 6 cipher, naught
7 nothing **9** nonentity

Numanus
  brother-in-law: 6 Turnus

numb 4 dead **6** frozen **8** dead-

November
  event: 11 Election Day
  flower:
    13 chrysanthemum
  French: 8 Novembre
  gem: 5 topaz
  German: 8 November
  holiday: 11 All Souls'
    Day (2), Veterans Day
    (11) **12** All Saints' Day
    (1), Guy Fawkes Day
    (5), Thanksgiving (4th
    Thursday)
  Italian: 8 Novembre
  number of days: 6 thirty
  origin of name: 5 novem
    (Latin meaning nine)
  place in year:
    Gregorian: **8** eleventh
    Roman: **5** ninth
  Spanish: 9 Noviembre
  Zodiac sign: 7 Scorpio
    11 Sagittarius

ened **9** insensate, unfeeling
10 insensible, narcotized
12 anesthetized

number 3 mob, sum, tot
4 army, bevy, book, herd,
host, mass, part **5** array,
bunch, count, crowd, digit,
group, issue, swarm, tally, total **6** amount, cipher, figure,
reckon, scores, symbol
7 chapter, company, compute,
edition, foliate, integer, numeral, passage, section **8** division, estimate, magazine,
numerate, paginate, quantity
9 abundance, aggregate, calculate, character, enumerate,
multitude, paragraph, quarterly **10** assemblage, quantities **13** preponderance

**numbered numbered
weighed divided**
Aramaic: 21 mene mene
tekel upharsin
foretells destruction of:
10 Belshazzar
Biblical book of: 6 Daniel

numberless 6 myriad **7** copious, umpteen **8** unending, zil-
lions **9** countless, plenteous,
unbounded, uncounted **11** illimitable, uncountable **12** immeasurable
13 multitudinous

numbness 8 deadness
11 insentience

numeral 5 digit **6** cipher, figure, letter, number, symbol
7 integer **9** character

numerate 3 add **5** count, tally,
total **6** number, reckon
7 compute, tick off
9 calculate

numerophobia
fear of: 7 numbers

numerous 4 many **6** myriad
7 copious, profuse **8** abundant
9 plentiful **13** multitudinous

Numidia see **7** Algeria

Numipu see **8** Nez Perce

Numitor
king of: 9 Alba Longa
father: 5 Proca
brother: 7 Amulius
daughter: 10 Rhea Silvia
grandson: 5 Remus
7 Romulus

numskull, numbskull 3 sap
4 dolt, dope, fool, jerk
5 dummy, dunce, idiot, klutz,
ninny **6** dimwit, nitwit **7** dullard, half-wit **8** bonehead,
dummkopf, imbecile, lunk-
head, silly ass **9** blockhead,
simpleton **10** dunderhead,
muttonhead, nincompoop,

noodlehead **11** chowderhead,
knucklehead **12** scatterbrain

Nun see **4** Nunu

nuncio 5 envoy **6** legate **8** diplomat, minister **9** messenger
10 ambassador **11** papallegate
14 representative

nunnery 5 abbey, order
6 priory **7** cenacle, convent
8 cloister **9** hermitage, monastery **10** sisterhood

Nun's Story, The
director: 12 Fred Zinneman
based on story by: 12 Kathryn Hulme
cast: 10 Dean Jagger, Edith
Evans, Peter Finch **13** Audrey Hepburn, Peggy Ash-
croft **15** Colleen Dewhurst

Nunu
also: 3 Nun
origin: 8 Egyptian
god of: 5 ocean
personifies: 5 chaos

nuptial 7 marital **8** conjugal,
hymeneal **9** connubial
11 matrimonial

nuptials 7 wedding **8** marriage
9 espousals, hymeneals
12 matrimonials

Nurmi, Paavo
nickname: 13 The Flying
Finn
sport: 5 track
won: 8 Olympics

nurse 4 feed **5** nanny, treat
6 attend, doctor, foster, harbor, remedy, sister, succor,
suckle **7** care for, nourish,
nurture, promote, sustain **8** attend to,
guardian **9** attendant, cultivate,
encourage, governess
Hindi/Indian: 4 ayah

nursery 6 hotbed **9** incubator,
preschool **10** greenhouse,
schoolroom **12** conservatory,
kindergarten

nurture 4 feed, mess, rear,
tend **5** breed, raise, teach,
train, tutor **6** foster, school
7 bring up, develop, educate,
nourish, prepare, sustain, vic-
tual **8** instruct, maintain
9 cultivate, provision **10** discipline, strengthen

Nusantara see **9** Indonesia

Nusku
origin: 8 Sumerian
10 Babylonian
visier of: 5 Enlil

nut 3 fan, pit **4** buff, seed
5 freak, idiot, loony, stone
6 madman, maniac, zealot
7 devotee, fanatic, lunatic,

oddball **8** crackpot **9** eccentric,
screwball **10** aficionado,
enthusiast, psychopath
11 afficionado

Nut
origin: 8 Egyptian
goddess of: 3 sky

nut-brown 5 tawny **6** auburn,
brunet **8** brunette, cinnamon

Nutcracker, The
also: 13 Shchelkunchik
ballet by: 11 Tchaikovsky
based on fairy tale by:
11 E T A Hoffmann
contains: 17 Waltz of the
Flowers **24** Dance of the
Sugar-Plum Fairy

nutmeg
botanical name: 17 Myristica
fragrans
from same plant as: 4 mace
origin: 9 Indonesia
use: 5 punch **6** eggnog **8** desserts **10** vegetables **11** baked
dishes

Nutmeg State
nickname of: 11 Connecticut

nutriment 4 chow, eats, fare,
feed, food, meat, mess
5 board **6** fodder, forage **7** aliment, edibles **8** eatables, victuals **9** foodstuff, groceries,
provender **10** provisions, sustenance **11** nourishment,
subsistence

nutrition 4 chow, feed, food,
grub **6** fodder, forage, silage
7 edibles, rations **8** eatables
9 groceries, pasturage, provender **10** foodstuffs, provisions,
sustenance **11** nourishment,
subsistence

nutritious 9 wholesome
10 nourishing, sustaining

nuts 3 mad **4** bats, daft
5 balmy, crazy, dotty, loony,
potty, wacko, wacky **6** insane
7 bananas, bonkers, cracked,
touched **8** demented, deranged,
unhinged **10** unbalanced

nutty 3 mad **4** daft **5** balmy,
crazy, dippy, dotty, goofy, inane, loony, silly, wacko,
wacky **6** cuckoo, insane,
screwy, weirdo **7** bonkers,
cracked, foolish, lunatic, me-
shuga, touched **8** bughouse,
demented **9** senseless **10** ad-
dlepated, squirrelly **11** harebrained **12** crackbrained

nuzzle 3 pat, pet **4** buss, kiss
5 smack **6** caress, coddle, cosset, cuddle, fondle, nestle
7 embrace, snuggle

Nyasaland see **6** Malawi

Nycteus 694

Nycteus
father: 9 Chthonios
brother: 5 Lycus
daughter: 7 Antiope, Nycteis

Nyctimus
father: 6 Lycaon

nyctophobia
fear of: 8 darkness 14 the
dark of night

nymph 5 belle, dryad, naiad,
sylph 6 beauty 7 charmer

Nymphaea
epithet of: 9 Aphrodite
means: 6 bridal

Nyx
form: 7 goddess
personifies: 5 night
originated from: 5 Chaos

children: 3 Ker 4 Eris 5 Fates,
Geras, Momus, Moros,
Oizys 6 Aether, Hemera,
Hypnos, Somnus 7 Nemesis,
Oneiroi 8 Thanatos

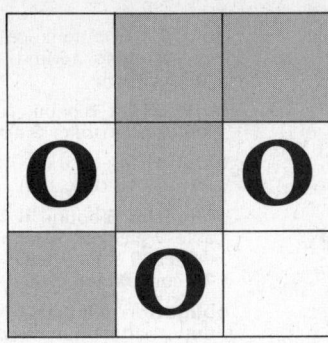

oaf **3** sap **4** boob, boor, clod, dolt, dope, fool, jerk, lout **5** booby, dummy, dunce, idiot, klutz, moron, ninny **6** lummox, nitwit **7** dullard, halfwit **8** bonehead, imbecile, numskull **9** blockhead, ignoramus, numbskull, simpleton **10** dunderhead, nincompoop

oafish **4** rude **5** crude **6** coarse, gauche, vulgar **7** boorish, doltish, loutish, uncouth **9** unrefined **10** unpolished

oak *see box*

Oak, Gabriel
   character in: **22** Far From the Madding Crowd
   author: **5** Hardy

Oakie, Jack
   real name: **19** Lewis Delaney Offield
   born: **9** Sedalia (Sadalia) MO
   roles: **16** The Great Dictator **17** Alice in Wonderland

Oakland
   baseball team: **2** As **9** Athletics
   football team: **8** Invaders

oar **3** row **4** pole **5** blade, rower, scull **6** paddle, propel **9** propeller
   blade: **4** palm, peel
   fulcrum: **5** thole **7** oarlock, rowlock
   part: **4** loom **5** shaft **6** collar

oarsman **5** pilot, rower **6** bowman **7** mariner, sculler **8** helmsman **9** gondolier, propeller

oasis **5** haven **6** asylum, harbor, refuge **7** retreat, sanctum, shelter **9** green spot, sanctuary, water hole **11** fertile area **13** watering place

oast **4** kiln, oven

oat, oats **5** Avena **11** Avena sativa
   varieties: **3** sea **4** wild **6** po-

tato **8** animated **9** Tartarian **11** slender wild

Oates, Joyce Carol
   author of: **4** Them **9** Childwold **10** Bellefleur, Wonderland **11** Unholy Loves, Wheel of Love **15** Son of the Morning **18** A Bloodsmoor Romance **19** Do With Me What You Will

oath **3** vow **5** curse **6** avowal, pledge **8** cuss word, swearing **9** affidavit, blasphemy, expletive, obscenity, profanity **10** adjuration, deposition **11** affirmation, attestation, declaration, imprecation, malediction

oaths
   god of: **6** Horcus, Sancus **10** Dius Fidius, Semo Sancus

oatmeal **6** cereal **7** pottage **8** drammock, porridge

Obadiah **4** Obad **7** prophet **12** minor prophet
   father: **4** Azel **6** Jehiel **8** Izrahiah, Shemaiah
   son: **8** Ishmaiah
   predicted fall of: **4** Edom

Obata, Gyo
   architect of: **20** Dallas-Ft Worth Airport **25** National Air and Space Museum (Smithsonian Institute)

obdurate **5** cruel, harsh **6** mulish **7** adamant, callous, unmoved, willful **8** hardened, pitiless, stubborn, uncaring **9** immovable, merciless, obstinate, pigheaded, unfeeling, unpitying, unsparing, untouched **10** bullheaded, headstrong, inflexible, unmerciful, unyielding **11** cold-blooded, hardhearted, intractable **12** ungovernable, unmanageable **13** unsympathetic **14** uncontrollable **15** uncompassionate

---

oak 7 Quercus
   varieties: **3** bur, cow, pin, red, she **4** bear, blue, cork, deer, Holm, jack, live, maul, post, silk **5** black, Emory, holly, scrub, ubame, water, white **6** basket, Belote, canyon, Ceylon, Daimyo, gambel, gander, Havard, Indian, island, Kermes, Konara, laurel, Oregon, poison, possum, Turkey, Turner, valley, willow, yellow **7** Ballota, Bartram, Belloot, Catesby, Durmast, English, Georgia, Italian, Kellogg, leather, Lebanon, overcup, scarlet, shingle, Spanish, tanbark, truffle, western **8** Arkansas, bluejack, chestnut, McDonald, mossy-cup, shinnery, Texas red **9** blackjack, Engelmann, flowering, Jerusalem, Mongolian, pubescent, swamp post **10** Chinquapin, Darlington, ring-cupped, Spanish red, swamp white **11** huckleberry, Japanese red, northern pin, northern red, Shumard's red **12** interior live, laurel-leaved, rock chestnut, southern live, yellowbarked **13** dwarf chestnut, oriental white, swamp chestnut **14** Austrian turkey, California live, yellow chestnut **15** California black, California field, California scrub, California white **16** high-ground willow **17** Japanese evergreen **18** Rocky Mountain scrub

obedience 8 docility, yielding **9** deference, ductility, obeisance **10** accordance, allegiance, compliance, subjection, submission **11** conformance, dutifulness, willingness **12** acquiescence, subservience, tractability **14** conformability, submissiveness

obedient 5 loyal **6** docile **7** devoted, dutiful **8** amenable, faithful, obeisant, yielding **9** compliant, tractable **10** governable, law-abiding, respectful, submissive **11** acquiescent, deferential, subservient

obeisance 3 bow **5** honor **6** curtsy, esteem, fealty, homage, regard **7** loyalty, respect **8** courtesy, fidelity, humility, kneeling **9** deference, obedience, reverence **10** allegiance, humbleness, subjection, submission, veneration **11** prostration **12** genuflection **13** self-abasement

obelisk 5 pylon, shaft, tower **6** column, dagger, needle, pillar **8** memorial, monolith, monument

Oberon
character in: **21** A Midsummer Night's Dream
author: **11** Shakespeare

Oberon
opera by: **5** Weber
character: **5** Reiza
setting: **18** court of Charlemagne **21** court of Haroun al Rashid

Oberon, Merle
real name: **26** Estelle Merle O'Brien Thompson
husband: **14** Alexander Korda
born: **8** Tasmania
roles: **5** Hotel **7** Desiree **15** A Song to Remember **16** Wuthering Heights **19** The Scarlet Pimpernel **25** The Private Life of Henry VIII **30** The Private Life of Henry the Eighth

obese 3 fat **5** gross, heavy, plump, porky, pudgy, stout, tubby **6** chubby, fleshy, portly, rotund **7** paunchy **9** corpulent **10** overweight, potbellied

obesity 3 fat **7** fatness, liposis **8** adiposis, enormity **9** heaviness, plumpness, stoutness **10** corpulence, overweight

obey 4 heed, mind **5** bow to, serve **6** assent, concur **7** abide by, observe, respect, yield to **8** accede to, submit to **9** acquiesce, conform to, succumb to **10** comply with, toe the line **12** follow orders

obfuscate 4 blur **5** befog **6** garble, mess up, muddle **7** becloud, confuse, distort, fluster, obscure, stupefy **8** confound, scramble **10** complicate

obfuscation 8 flummery **9** confusion **10** doubletalk, mumbo jumbo

obi 4 sash **5** obeah **6** girdle

obiit 6 he died **7** she died

obiter dictum 9 diversion **10** digression, divagation, side remark

object 3 aim, end, use **4** body, butt, dupe, form, gist, goal, pith, prey **5** abhor, basis, cause, knock, point, sense, thing **6** balk at, carp at, design, device, dingus, gadget, intent, loathe, motive, oppose, quarry, reason, target, victim **7** article, cavil at, condemn, dislike, essence, frown on, meaning, mission, protest, purpose, subject **8** be averse, cynosure, denounce **9** abominate, criticize, doohickey, incentive, intention, objective, principle, recipient, substance **10** inducement, phenomenon **11** contrivance, explanation, thingamabob, thingamajig **12** be at odds with, disapprove of, significance **13** find fault with, take exception **18** remonstrate against

objection 4 beef, kick **5** cavil **7** protest **8** demurral, rebuttal **9** challenge, complaint, criticism, exception **10** dissension, opposition **11** disapproval, reservation **12** disagreement **13** contradiction **14** disapprobation, opposing reason **15** counter argument

objectionable 4 foul, vile **5** nasty **6** odious **8** unseemly **9** abhorrent, loathsome, obnoxious, offensive, revolting **10** abominable, despicable, disgusting, unbearable, unpleasant **11** displeasing, distasteful, intolerable, unendurable **12** disagreeable, unacceptable **13** inappropriate

objective 3 aim, end **4** fair, goal, just, mark, real **6** actual, design, intent, target **7** mission, purpose **8** detached, unbiased, unswayed **9** impartial, intention, uncolored **10** impersonal, open-minded **11** destination **12** uninfluenced, unprejudiced **13** disinterested, dispassionate

objectivity 8 fairness **10** detachment, neutrality **12** impartiality

object to 7 condemn, dislike **9** frown upon **12** disapprove of **14** discountenance **15** take exception to **16** find unacceptable

objet d'art 5 bijou, curio **7** bibelot, trinket **9** art object

oblation 4 gift **8** offering **9** offertory **10** collection

obligated 5 bound **6** forced, liable **7** pledged **8** beholden, indebted **9** committed **11** constrained

obligation 4 bond, care, debt, duty, oath, onus, word **6** charge, pledge **7** compact, promise **8** contract, guaranty, warranty **9** agreement, guarantee, liability **10** a favor owed, commitment, constraint **12** indebtedness **13** answerability, understanding **14** accountability, responsibility

obligatory 7 binding **8** coercive, enforced, required **9** mandatory, necessary, requisite **10** compulsory, imperative, peremptory **11** unavoidable

oblige 3 aid **4** bind, help, make **5** favor, force, impel, serve **6** assist, coerce, compel **7** require, support **8** obligate **9** constrain **11** accommodate, do a favor for, necessitate **13** do a service for, to be duty bound

obliged 5 bound **7** favored, pleased **8** assisted, beholden, indebted, required, thankful **9** compelled **12** accommodated

obliging 4 kind **6** polite **7** amiable, helpful **8** cheerful, friendly, gracious **9** agreeable, courteous **10** solicitous **11** complaisant, considerate, cooperative, good-natured, sympathetic **12** well-disposed **13** accommodating

oblique 3 sly **4** awry **5** askew **6** aslant, covert, hinted, masked, tilted, veiled **7** cloaked, devious, furtive, implied, slanted, sloping **8** allusive, diagonal, inclined, indirect, slanting, sneaking **9** suggested, underhand

obliterate 4 raze **5** erase, level **6** cancel, delete, efface, remove, rub out **7** abolish, blot out, destroy, expunge, wipe out **9** eradicate, write over **10** annihilate, strike over

obliteration 8 deletion **9** abolition, expunging, wiping out **11** blotting out, destruction, eradication **12** annihilation

oblivion 5 limbo **7** the void **9** blankness, disregard, obscurity, unconcern **11** blotting out, nothingness **12** nonexistence **13** forgetfulness, insensibility, obliviousness **14** insignificance **15** unconsciousness

oblivious 8 careless **9** forgetful, unaware of, unmindful **10** heedless of, insensible **11** inattentive, unconcerned, unobservant **12** disregardful, undiscerning **13** unconscious of

Oblonsky, Prince Stepan
  character in: 12 Anna Karenina
  author: 7 Tolstoy

obloquy 5 abuse, odium, shame **6** infamy, rebuke **7** calumny, censure, railing **8** contempt, disfavor, disgrace, ignominy, reviling **9** discredit, invective **10** defamation, opprobrium, scurrility **11** degradation, humiliation, verbal abuse **12** billingsgate, condemnation, denunciation, dressing-down, vilification

obnoxious 4 foul, vile **5** nasty **6** odious **7** hateful **8** unseemly **9** abhorrent, loathsome, offensive, repellent, repugnant, revolting **10** abominable, despicable, detestable, disgusting, nauseating, unbearable, unpleasant **11** displeasing, intolerable, unendurable **12** disagreeable, insufferable **13** inappropriate, objectionable

oboe family
  instruments: 5 shawm **6** curtal, pommer, racket **7** bassoon, bombard, curtall, hautboy **8** crumhorn, schalmey, tenoroon **10** Cor Anglais, oboe d'Amore **11** English horn, heckelphone, sarusophone **12** oboe da caccia, sarrusophone **13** contra bassoon, double bassoon

O'Brian, Hugh
  real name: 11 Hugh J Krampe
  born: 11 Rochester NY
  roles: 9 Wyatt Earp **27** The Life and Legend of Wyatt Earp

O'Brien, Edna
  author of: 5 Night **11** A Pagan Place **13** The Lonely Girl **14** The Country Girl **20** August Is a Wicked Month **24** Girls in Their Married Bliss

O'Brien, Margaret
  real name: 18 Angela Maxine O'Brien
  born: 12 Los Angeles CA
  roles: 8 Jane Eyre **11** Little Women **15** Meet Me in St

Louis **24** Our Vines Have Tender Grapes

O'Brien, Pat
  real name: 26 William Joseph Patrick O'Brien
  born: 11 Milwaukee WI
  roles: 12 Hildy Johnson, The Front Page **13** Some Like It Hot, The Last Hurrah **20** Angels with Dirty Faces **22** Knute Rockne All American
  autobiography: 12 Wind on My Back

obscene 4 blue, foul, lewd **5** dirty **6** filthy, smutty, vulgar **8** indecent, prurient **9** salacious **10** lascivious, lubricious **12** pornographic, scatological **16** morally offensive

obscenity 8 cuss word, lewdness **9** dirtiness, indecency, profanity, prurience, swear word, taboo word, vulgarity **10** filthiness, smuttiness **11** pornography **13** salaciousness **14** four-letter word, lasciviousness

obscuration 7 eclipse, masking, veiling **8** cloaking, clouding, covering **9** darkening, shadowing **10** concealing **11** concealment

obscure 3 dim, fog **4** blur, dark, hide, mask, veil **5** bedim, befog, block, cloak, cloud, cover, dingy, dusky, faint, murky, vague **6** cloudy, darken, hidden, muddle, screen, shadow, shroud, somber, unsung **7** becloud, conceal, confuse, cryptic, curtain, eclipse, shadowy, unclear, unknown, unnoted **8** befuddle, confused, disguise, nameless, puzzling **9** confusing, enigmatic, forgotten, lightless, obfuscate, uncertain, unheard of, unlighted **10** indefinite, indistinct, overshadow, perplexing, unrenowned **11** indefinable, inscrutable, little known, out-of-the-way, unimportant **12** unfathomable **13** inconspicuous, insignificant, unilluminated **15** inconsequential

obscurity 3 fog **4** mist **5** cloud, shade **6** shadow **7** dimness, mystery, opacity, privacy **8** darkness **9** ambiguity, seclusion, vagueness **10** cloudiness

obsequies 5 rites **6** burial **7** funeral **15** memorial service

obsequious 6 menial **7** fawning, servile, slavish **8** cowering, cringing, toadying **9** kowtowing, truckling **11** bootlicking, deferential,

subservient, sycophantic **12** ingratiating, mealy-mouthed **14** apple-polishing

observance 4 rite **6** custom, regard, ritual **7** heeding, keeping, obeying **8** ceremony, practice **9** adherence, attending, attention, following, formality, solemnity **10** ceremonial, compliance **11** celebration, observation **13** commemoration **15** memorialization

observant 5 alert, awake, aware **7** careful, heedful, mindful **8** vigilant, watchful **9** attentive, conscious, regardful, wide-awake **10** perceptive **12** on the lookout

observation 4 heed, idea, view **5** probe **6** eyeing, notice, remark, search, seeing, survey, theory **7** comment, finding, opinion, viewing **8** interest, judgment, scrutiny, spotting, watching **9** assertion, attention, beholding, detection, diagnosis, discovery, glimpsing, observing, statement **10** cognizance, commentary, inspection, reflection **11** description, examination, heedfulness **12** surveillance, watchfulness **13** pronouncement **20** first-hand information

observatory 5 tower **7** lookout **9** satellite **11** planetarium
  name: 4 Hale, Lick **6** Yerkes **7** Palomar, Whipple **8** Kitt Peak, Mt Wilson **11** Las Campanas, Mount Wilson **12** Big Bear Solar **14** Royal Greenwich

observe 3 eye, say, see **4** espy, heed, keep, mark, note, obey, ogle, spot, view **5** honor, opine, state, watch **6** assert, behold, detect, follow, notice, peer at, regard, remark, size up, survey **7** abide by, comment, declare, defer to, execute, fulfill, glimpse, inspect, make out, mention, perform, reflect, respect, stare at **8** adhere to, announce, carry out, discover, perceive, sanctify, theorize **9** celebrate, recognize, solemnize **10** be guided by, comply with, consecrate **11** acknowledge, acquiesce to, commemorate, take stock of **12** catch sight of **14** pay attention to

observer 6 viewer **7** watcher **8** onlooker **12** investigator

obsessed 5 beset **7** haunted **8** hung up on, maniacal **9** dominated, possessed **10** controlled **15** having a fixation

obsession 5 craze, mania, quirk **6** phobia **8** fixation **9** fixed idea, monomania **11** infatuation **13** preoccupation **16** overwhelming fear **18** neurotic conviction

obsolescent 8 dying out **9** declining **11** on the way out **12** disappearing **16** becoming obsolete **17** becoming out-of-date

obsolete 3 out **5** dated, passe **6** bygone **7** antique, archaic, extinct **8** outdated, out of use, outmoded **9** out-of-date **10** antiquated **12** old-fashioned, out of fashion

obstacle 3 bar **4** curb, snag **5** block, catch, check **6** hurdle **7** barrier, problem **8** blockade, stoppage **9** barricade, hindrance, roadblock **10** difficulty, impediment, limitation **11** obstruction, restriction **12** interference **14** stumbling block

obstetrician
French: **10** accoucheur

obstinacy 8 rigidity **10** mulishness, resistance **11** willfulness **12** stubbornness **13** inflexibility, intransigence, pigheadedness

obstinate 6 dogged, mulish **7** staunch, willful **8** obdurate, resolute, stubborn **9** pigheaded, steadfast, tenacious, unbending **10** headstrong, inflexible, refractory, self-willed, unyielding **11** intractable **12** recalcitrant, ungovernable, unmanageable **14** uncontrollable **20** unreasonably stubborn

obstreperous 4 loud **5** noisy **6** unruly **8** perverse **9** clamorous, rampaging **10** boisterous, disorderly, refractory, roistering, uproarious, vociferous **11** disobedient **12** uncontrolled, ungovernable, unmanageable, unrestrained **14** uncontrollable

obstruct 3 bar **4** curb, halt, hide, mask, stop **5** block, check, cloak, close, cover, dam up, debar, delay, limit, stall **6** arrest, hinder, hobble, impede, plug up, retard, shroud, stifle, thwart **7** eclipse, inhibit, shut off **8** blockade, choke off, close off, restrict, suppress, throttle **9** barricade, frustrate **18** bring to a standstill

obstruction 3 bar **4** curb, snag, stop **5** block, check, hitch **6** hurdle **7** barrier **8** blockage, obstacle, stoppage **9** barricade, hindrance **10** bottleneck, impediment **11** encumbrance

obtain 3 get **4** earn, gain, hold, take **5** exist, glean, stand **6** attain, come by, gather, pick up, secure **7** achieve, acquire, prevail, procure, receive **9** get hold of **14** get one's hands on **16** gain possession of

obtainment 11 achievement, acquirement, acquisition, procurement

obtrude 5 eject, expel, force **6** butt in, impose, meddle, thrust **7** presume, project **9** interfere

obtrusive 4 nosy **5** brash **6** prying, snoopy **7** bulging, forward, salient **8** familiar, meddling **9** intruding, intrusive, prominent **10** aggressive, jutting out, meddlesome, projecting, protruding **11** conspicuous, impertinent, interfering, outstanding, protuberant, sticking out, trespassing **12** interrupting, presumptuous

obtuse 4 dull, slow **5** blunt, dense, thick **6** simple, stupid **7** blunted **8** ignorant, not sharp **9** unpointed **10** insensible, not pointed, slow-witted **11** insensitive, unsharpened **12** imperceptive, thick-skinned **15** uncomprehending

obtuseness 8 dullness **9** denseness, ignorance, stupidity **13** insensitivity **14** slow-wittedness **15** thick-headedness **16** lack of perception, simplemindedness **19** lack of comprehension

obverse 4 face **5** front **10** complement **11** counterpart of coin: **4** head

obviate 5 avert, avoid, parry **6** divert, remove **7** fend off, prevent, ward off **8** preclude, stave off **9** forestall, sidetrack, turn aside **10** circumvent, do away with **11** nip in the bud

obvious 5 clear, plain **6** patent **7** evident, glaring, visible **8** apparent, distinct, manifest, palpable, striking, unhidden, unmasked, unveiled **10** undeniable **11** conspicuous, discernible, perceptible, self-evident, unconcealed, undisguised **12** in plain sight, unmistakable **24** plain as the nose on your face

O'Casey, Sean
author of: **10** Purple Dust **12** The Green Crow **17** Juno and the Paycock **18** The Shadow of a Gunman **20** The Plough and the Stars

occasion 4 base, time **5** basis, cause, event **6** advent, affair, chance, elicit, ground, lead to, motive, prompt, reason **7** episode, grounds, inspire, opening, provoke, venture **8** incident, instance **9** adventure, happening, rationale, situation **10** bring about, experience, motivation, occurrence **11** celebration, explanation, opportunity, provocation **12** circumstance, special event, suitable time **13** justification, opportune time **14** convenient time, important event, particular time

occasional 4 rare **6** fitful, random **8** sporadic, uncommon **9** irregular, recurring, scattered, spasmodic, uncertain **10** incidental, infrequent, now and then, unreliable **12** intermittent

occasionally 6 rarely, seldom **7** at times **8** fitfully **9** sometimes **10** now and then **11** irregularly **12** infrequently, once in a while, periodically, sporadically **14** from time to time, intermittently **15** every now and then, once in a blue moon

occidental 7 Western **8** American, European **9** Hesperian, Westerner

occlude 4 clog, plug **5** block, choke, close **6** shut up, stop up **7** congest, shut off, stopper **8** choke off, obstruct **9** barricade, constrict **11** strangulate

occult 4 dark **5** magic **6** arcane, hidden, mystic, secret, veiled **7** obscure, private **8** esoteric, mystical, shrouded **9** concealed **10** cabalistic, mysterious, unrevealed **11** undisclosed **12** supernatural

occupancy 3 use **6** tenure **7** tenancy **8** lodgment **9** enjoyment, habitancy **10** engagement, habitation, occupation, possession **11** inhabitancy

occupant 5 owner **6** lessee, lodger, native, renter, roomer, tenant **7** dweller, settler **8** colonist, occupier, resident **9** addressee **10** inhabitant **11** householder

occupation 3 job **4** line, work **5** craft, forte, trade **6** career, living, metier, sphere **7** calling, control, pursuit, seizure **8** activity, business, capacity, conquest, lifework, vocation **9** specialty **10** employment, line of work, livelihood, possession, profession, subjection **11** foreign rule, subjugation **14** specialization **15** military control **18** military occupation

occupied 5 in use **6** amused, took up, used up **7** dwelt in, engaged, lived in, overran, overrun, taken up **8** absorbed, tenanted **9** concerned, conquered, inhabited, resided in **12** had control of, held in thrall **13** was situated in **16** took possession of

occupy 3 use **4** be in, be on, busy, fill, hold **5** amuse, sit in **6** absorb, employ, engage, fill up, room in, take up **7** concern, conquer, dwell in, engross, enslave, inhabit, lodge in, overrun, pervade, possess **8** permeate, reside in, saturate **9** entertain, subjugate **10** monopolize **11** have control **12** be situated in, hold in thrall **14** be the tenants of **16** take possession of

occur 3 hit **4** rise **5** arise, ensue **6** appear, befall, crop up, emerge, happen, result, strike, turn up **7** be found, come off, develop **8** spring up **9** come about, eventuate, take place, transpire **10** come to pass **11** materialize **13** cross one's mind, enter one's mind

occurrence 5 event **6** affair **7** episode, venture **8** business, incident, instance, occasion **9** adventure, emergence, happening, situation, unfolding **10** appearance, experience, proceeding **11** development, transaction **12** circumstance **13** manifestation **15** materialization

ocean 3 sea **4** deep, main, pond **5** flood, water **7** big pond, high sea **9** briny deep
  god of: 3 Nun **4** Nanu **7** Neptune, Oceanus **8** Poseidon

Oceania, Oceanica 9 Melanesia, Polynesia **10** Micronesia **11** Australia
  ocean: 12 South Pacific
  island: 4 Cook, Guam, Fiji, Maui, Niue, Wake **5** Aunuu, Bonin, Kauai, Lanai, Tonga **6** Bikini, Futuna, Hawaii, Marcus, Midway, Rurutu, Tahiti, Tubuai, Tuvalu, Wallis **7** Gambier, Gilbert, Iwo Jima, Leeward, Mariana, Molokai, Phoenix, Solomon, Tokelau, Tuamotu, Tutuila, Vanuatu, Volcano **8** Aitutaki, Bismarck, Bora-Bora, Johnston, Kiribati, Marshall, Pitcairn, Windward **9** Australia, Christmas, Marquesas, Trobriand **10** New Zealand **12** New Caledonia, Western Samoa **14** Papua New Guinea **15** French Polynesia

oceanic 6 marine **7** aquatic, pelagic **8** seagoing **9** thalassic

Oceanid
  form: 5 nymph
  location: 3 sea
  father: 7 Oceanus
  mother: 6 Tethys

Oceanus
  member of: 6 Titans
  father: 6 Uranus
  mother: 4 Gaea
  consort of: 6 Tethys
  father of: 8 Oceanids **9** river gods
  son: 7 Proteus
  daughter: 5 Doris, Persa **7** Philyra
  form: 6 stream

ocelot 3 cat **7** wildcat

Ochimus
  king of: 6 Rhodes
  father: 6 Helius
  wife: 9 Hegetoria
  daughter: 7 Cydippe

ochlophobia
  fear of: 6 crowds

Ockelman, Constance Frances Marie
  real name of: 12 Veronica Lake

Ocnus
  origin: 6 Tuscan
  father: 8 river god
  mother: 5 Manto
  founded: 6 Mantua
  personifies: 16 unavailing effort

O'Connor, Carroll
  born: 7 Bronx NY
  roles: 12 Archie Bunker, Archie's Place **14** All in the Family
  restaurant: 12 The Ginger Man

O'Connor, Donald
  born: 9 Chicago IL
  roles: 9 Beau Geste **15** Singin' in the Rain **18** Tom Sawyer Detective **21** Francis the Talking Mule

O'Connor, Flannery
  author of: 9 Wise Blood **15** The Habit of Being **17** Mystery and Manners **20** A Good Man Is Hard to Find, The Violent Bear It Away

Ocrisia
  position: 5 slave
  slave to: 7 Tarquin **8** Tanaquil
  son: 14 Servius Tullius

Octavia
  brother: 8 Augustus
  husband: 4 Nero **10** Mark Antony
  grandson: 8 Caligula

October
  flower: 6 cosmos **9** calendula
  French: 7 Octobre
  gem: 4 opal **10** tourmaline
  German: 7 Oktober
  holiday: 9 Halloween (31), Yom Kippur **11** Columbus Day (12) **12** Rosh Hashanah **16** United Nations Day (24)
  Italian: 7 Ottobre
  number of days: 9 thirty-one
  origin of name: 4 octo (Latin meaning eight)
  place in year:
    Gregorian: 5 tenth
    Roman: 6 eighth
  Spanish: 7 Octubre
  Zodiac sign: 5 Libra **7** Scorpio

October Light
  author: 11 John Gardner

Octopus, The
  author: 11 Frank Norris

odd 4 rare **5** extra, funny, queer, spare, weird **6** casual, far-out, quaint, single, sundry, unique **7** bizarre, curious, not even, strange, surplus, unusual, various **8** freakish, leftover, peculiar, periodic, singular, sporadic, uncommon **9** irregular, remaining, spasmodic, unmatched **10** occasional, outlandish **13** miscellaneous **15** being one of a pair **16** out of the ordinary **17** not divisible by two

oddball 3 nut **4** kook **5** freak **6** weirdo **8** crackpot, original **9** character, eccentric, screwball **10** one-of-a-kind

Odd Couple, The
  character: 3 Roy **5** Myrna, Roger, Speed **6** Miriam, Murray, Vinnie **10** Felix Unger **11** Gloria Unger **12** Cecily Pigeon, Oscar Madison **14** Blanche Madison **15** Gwendolyn Pigeon, (Dr) Nancy Cunningham
  cast: 10 Al Molinaro, Archie Hahn **11** Brett Somers, Carol Shelly, Jack Klugman, Larry Gelman, Monica Evans, Tony Randall **12** Garry Walberg, Janice Hansen, Ryan McDonald **13** Elinor Donahue, Joan Hotchkiss, Penny Marshall
  setting: 11 New York City
  Felix's job: 12 photographer
  Oscar's job: 12 sportswriter

based on play by: 9 Neil Simon

Odd Couple, The
director: 8 Gene Saks
based on play by: 9 Neil Simon
cast: 10 Jack Lemmon (Felix Unger) 11 Herb Edelman, John Fiedler 13 Walter Matthau (Oscar Madison)

oddity 5 freak, sight 6 marvel, rarity, wonder 9 curiosity, queerness 10 phenomenon, uniqueness 11 abnormality, bizarreness, peculiarity, singularity, strangeness, unusualness 12 eccentricity, freakishness 13 individuality, unnaturalness 14 outlandishness
Latin: 8 rara avis

oddly amusing 5 droll, kooky 9 laughable, whimsical 10 ridiculous

odd person 3 nut 4 kook 5 flake, freak 6 looney, weirdo 7 oddball 8 crackpot 9 character, eccentric, screwball

odds and ends 4 olio 6 scraps 8 remnants 9 leftovers 10 hodgepodge, miscellany 11 this and that 13 bits and pieces 18 miscellaneous items

ode 4 epic, hymn, poem 5 lyric, paean, psalm, verse 6 ballad 8 canticle
type: 8 Horatian, Pindaric

Ode on a Grecian Urn
author: 9 John Keats

Ode on Indolence
author: 9 John Keats

Ode on Melancholy
author: 9 John Keats

Ode to a Nightingale
author: 9 John Keats

Ode to Autumn
author: 9 John Keats

Ode to Duty
author: 17 William Wordsworth

Ode to Psyche
author: 9 John Keats

Ode to the West Wind
author: 18 Percy Bysshe Shelley

Odets, Clifford
author of: 9 Golden Boy 12 Awake and Sing 14 The Country Girl 15 Waiting for Lefty 17 The Flowering Peach

Odin *see box*

odious 4 evil, foul, vile 5 hated, nasty 6 rotten 7 hate-

ful, heinous, hideous 8 infamous 9 invidious, loathsome, monstrous, obnoxious, offensive, repugnant, repulsive, revolting, sickening 10 abominable, despicable, detestable, disgusting, nauseating, unbearable 11 intolerable, unendurable 12 contemptible 13 objectionable

odium 5 shame 6 hatred, infamy 7 disgust 8 contempt, disfavor, disgrace, dishonor, ignominy 9 antipathy, discredit, disesteem, disrepute 10 abhorrence, disrespect, opprobrium, repugnance 11 detestation, disapproval 14 disapprobation

odonata
class: 8 hexapoda
phylum: 10 arthropoda
group: 9 damselfly, dragonfly

odor 4 aura 5 aroma, scent, smell, stink 6 flavor, stench 7 bouquet, essence, perfume 9 effluvium, fragrance 10 atmosphere

odoriferous 4 rank 5 acrid, fetid 6 putrid, smelly 7 noisome, odorous, pungent, reeking, scented 8 aromatic, fragrant, perfumed, stinking 10 malodorous

odorous 4 rank 5 acrid, fetid 6 smelly 7 noisome, pungent, reeking, scented 8 aromatic, fragrant, perfumed, stinking

Odysseus
also: 7 Ulysses
king of: 6 Ithaca

Odin
also: 5 Othin
brother: 2 Ve 4 Vili
children: 4 Hodr, Thor 5 Baldr 6 Balder, Baldur
corresponds to: 5 Wotan
counterpart: 5 Wotan
court: 8 Valhalla
father: 3 Bor
god of: 3 war 6 poetry, wisdom 9 knowledge
grandson: 7 Volsung
home: 9 Gladsheim
horse: 8 Sleipnir
magic ring: 8 Draupnir
origin: 12 Scandinavian
raven: 5 Hugin, Munin
remaining eye: 3 sun
ruler of: 5 Aexir
spear: 7 Gungnir
throne: 10 Hlidskjalf
wife: 3 Fri 5 Frigg, Frija 6 Frigga
wolf: 4 Geri 5 Freki

---

father: 7 Laertes
mother: 8 Anticlea
hero of: 5 Iliad 7 Odyssey
wife: 8 Penelope 9 Callidice
son: 9 Telegonus 10 Polypoetes, Telemachus 11 Polyporthis
seduced by: 5 Circe
killed by: 9 Telegonus
epithet: 10 Laertiades

Odyssey
author: 5 Homer
character: 4 Zeus 5 Arete, Circe, Helen 6 Athene, Nestor, Scylla, Sirens 7 Calypso, Cyclops 8 Alcinous, Menelaus, Nausicaa, Odysseus, Penelope, Poseidon, Tiresias 9 Charybdis 10 Telemachus 11 Lotus-eaters

Oedipus
king of: 6 Thebes
father: 5 Laius
mother: 7 Jocasta
foster father: 7 Polybus
foster mother: 6 Merope 8 Periboea
wife: 7 Jocasta
son: 8 Eteocles 9 Polynices
daughter: 6 Ismene 8 Antigone
killed: 5 Laius
defeated: 5 Sphinx

Oedipus at Colonus
author: 9 Sophocles
character: 5 Creon 6 Elders, Ismene 7 Theseus 8 Antigone 9 Polynices

Oedipus Rex (Oedipus Tyrannus)
author: 9 Sophocles
character: 5 Creon, Laius 7 Jocasta 8 Tiresias

oeil-de-boeuf 16 small round window
literally: 8 bull's eye

Oeneus
king of: 7 Calydon
wife: 7 Althaea
son: 8 Meleager

Oenomaus
king of: 4 Elis, Pisa
father: 4 Ares
mother: 7 Sterope
daughter: 10 Hippodamia
murdered: 6 Marmax

Oenone
form: 5 nymph
father: 6 Cebren
husband: 5 Paris

Oenopion
king of: 5 Chios
father: 8 Dionysus
mother: 7 Ariadne
daughter: 6 Merope
blinded: 5 Orion

Oersted, Hans Christian
field: 7 physics
nationality: 6 Danish

founded: 16 electromagnetism
isolated: 16 metallic aluminum
named for him: 11 oersted unit

oeuvre 4 work **5** works **13** artist's output

O'Faolain, Sean
author of: 15 The Heat of the Sun **17** A Nest of Simple Folk **22** Midsummer Night's Madness

of a piece 5 alike, equal **7** matched, the same **8** all in one **9** analogous, identical **10** equivalent, homogenous, synonymous **13** evenly matched, one and the same

of bad character 5 shady **8** unsavory **11** of ill repute **12** disreputable, unprincipled

off 2 by **3** bad, far, ill, odd **4** afar, away, down, from, kill, poor, stop **5** amiss, apart, aside, crazy, wrong **6** absent, begone, lessen, remote **7** distant, further, in error, stopped, tainted **8** abnormal, canceled, inferior, mistaken **9** imperfect

offal 4 junk, slag **5** dregs, trash, waste **6** debris, refuse **7** carcass, carrion, garbage, grounds, remains, residue, rubbish **8** leavings

off base 5 amiss, wrong **8** improper, mistaken **10** out of order, unsuitable **13** inappropriate

offbeat 3 odd **7** strange **8** peculiar **9** different, eccentric **14** unconventional

off-center 6 askew **7** strange **9** eccentric **10** imbalanced, nonaligned, unbalanced **12** unreasonable **14** unconventional

off-color 4 blue, lewd, racy, sexy **5** bawdy, dirty, salty, spicy **6** earthy, risque, smutty, wicked **7** naughty, obscene, raunchy **8** improper, indecent, scabrous **9** offensive **10** indelicate, indiscreet, suggestive

off duty 8 inactive **9** at leisure **10** unoccupied **13** on one's own time

Offenbach, Jacques
born: 7 Cologne, Germany
composer of: 13 La Belle Helene **15** Tales of Hoffmann, La Vie Parisienne **22** Orpheus in the Underworld

offend 3 err, sin, vex **4** fret, gall, miff, rile **5** anger, annoy, chafe, lapse, pique, wound **6** insult, madden, nettle, ran-

kle **7** affront, disgust, incense, inflame **8** irritate **9** aggravate, displease, misbehave **10** antagonize, disgruntle, exasperate, transgress **13** fall from grace

offender 5 crook, felon **6** sinner **7** culprit **8** criminal, violator **9** wrong doer **10** malefactor, trespasser

offense 3 sin **4** gibe, harm, slap, slip, snub, twit **5** abuse, crime, lapse, taunt **6** attack, charge, felony, insult **7** affront, assault, misdeed, outrage, umbrage **8** atrocity, enormity, evil deed, rudeness **9** impudence, indignity, insolence, offensive, violation **10** aggression, disrespect, infraction, peccadillo, wickedness **11** delinquency, humiliation, malfeasance, misdemeanor, shortcoming **13** embarrassment, transgression **15** breach of conduct

offensive 4 foul, rank, rude, ugly **5** nasty, onset **6** attack, horrid **7** abusive, assault, hideous, offense, uncivil **8** charging, impudent, insolent, storming **9** abhorrent, assailing, attacking, insulting, loathsome, obnoxious, onslaught, repugnant, repulsive, revolting, sickening, ungallant **10** abominable, aggression, aggressive, assaulting, bombarding, detestable, disgusting, nauseating, unmannerly, unpleasant **11** belligerent, distasteful, intolerable **12** disagreeable, embarrassing, insufferable **13** disrespectful, objectionable

offensiveness 8 rudeness **9** impudence, insolence, nastiness **10** disrespect, horridness, incivility **13** repulsiveness **14** unpleasantness **15** distastefulness

offer 3 bid **5** put up **6** bestow, extend, render, submit, tender **7** advance, hold out, present, proffer, propose, suggest **8** bestow on, offering, overture, proposal, propound, put forth **9** be willing, volunteer **10** invitation, put forward, submission, suggestion **11** make a motion, proposition **12** bring forward **14** put on the market **19** place at one's disposal

offer hospitality 4 host **7** welcome **8** play host **9** entertain **10** give a party, have guests **13** keep open house

offering 3 bid **4** alms, gift **5** goods, wares **6** course **7** charity, present, tribute **8** anathema, bestowal, donation, oblation **9** sacrifice

11 beneficence **12** contribution
to God: 6 corban **7** deodate
to household deities: 4 bali

offertory 4 gift **8** oblation, offering **10** collection

offhand, offhanded 5 ad-lib, hasty **6** casual, chance, random **7** relaxed **8** careless, cavalier, heedless **9** facetious, haphazard, impromptu, unplanned, unstudied **10** improvised, nonchalant, off-the-cuff, unprepared **11** spontaneous, thoughtless, unconcerned, unrehearsed **12** off-the-record **14** extemporaneous, unpremeditated

office 3 job **4** post, role **8** capacity, function, position **10** commission, occupation **11** appointment

officer 3 cop **4** head **7** manager **8** director, gendarme, governor **9** constable, detective, executive, patrolman, policeman, president, secretary, treasurer **10** bureaucrat **12** commissioner **13** administrator, vice-president

officers 8 managers **10** executives, management **14** administration

Officers and Gentlemen
author: 11 Evelyn Waugh

offices 4 duty, help, task **5** favor, trust **6** charge **7** service **8** function, province **10** assistance

office seeker 7 hopeful, nominee **8** aspirant **9** candidate

office worker 5 clerk, steno **6** typist **9** file clerk, secretary **10** bookkeeper, keypuncher **13** data processor **14** clerical worker

official 5 agent **6** formal, vested **7** manager, officer **8** approved, chairman, director, licensed **9** authentic, certified, dignitary, executive, warranted **10** accredited, authorized, sanctioned, supervisor **11** functionary **13** administrator, authoritative **14** administrative **18** administrative head

official communication 5 edict, order, ukase **6** report **7** release **8** bulletin **10** communique **12** proclamation

officialdom 10 government **11** authorities, bureaucracy **14** administration

official paper 4 writ **5** order **8** document **10** instrument

officiate 3 run **4** head, lead **5** chair, emcee **6** direct, handle, manage **7** oversee, pre-

side **8** moderate, regulate
9 supervise **10** administer
11 superintend **12** be in
charge of

officious 6 prying **7** pompous
8 meddling **9** intrusive, kibitz-
ing, obtrusive **10** high-handed,
meddlesome **11** domineering,
interfering, overbearing, patronizing **13** high and mighty,
self-assertive, self-important
16 poking one's nose in

Offield, Lewis Delaney
real name of: **9** Jack Oakie

offset 6 redeem **7** balance, nullify **8** equalize, knock out
9 cancel out, make up for
10 counteract, neutralize
11 countervail **13** compensate
for, counterweight
14 counterbalance

offshoot 4 limb **5** scion, shoot
6 branch **7** adjunct **9** aftermath, by-product, outgrowth
10 descendant

offspring 3 fry **4** heir, seed
5 brood, child, issue, scion,
spawn, young **6** family, litter
7 progeny **8** children, increase
9 posterity **10** descendant,
succession **11** descendants

off the mark 5 amiss **6** afield,
astray **9** off target **16** off the
right track

off-the-record 5 privy **6** secret **7** private **11** undisclosed
12 confidential **16** not to be
disclosed **17** not for
publication

off the top of one's head
5 ad-lib **7** offhand **9** extempore, impromptu **10** improvised, unprepared
11 extemporary, unrehearsed
14 extemporaneous,
unpremeditated

of good quality 4 good
6 worthy **8** superior **9** excellent **10** creditable

of high rank 5 noble, regal,
royal **6** lordly, titled **7** courtly
11 blue-blooded **12** aristocratic

Of Human Bondage
author: **16** W Somerset
Maugham
director: **12** John Cromwell
character: **5** Weeks **7** Hayward **11** Louisa Carey,
Philip Carey **12** Sally
Athelny, William Carey
13 Mildred Rogers, Miss
Wilkinson, Thorpe Athelny
cast: **10** Bette Davis, Frances
Dee, Kay Johnson **12** Leslie
Howard

of its own kind
Latin: **10** sui generis

Of Mice and Men
author: **13** John Steinbeck
director: **14** Lewis Milestone
character: **4** Slim **5** Candy
6 Crooks, Curley **11** Lennie
Small **12** George Milton
cast: **10** Betty Field **11** Lon
Chaney Jr (Lenny) **15** Burgess Meredith, Charles
Bickford
score: **12** Aaron Copland

of one's own right
Latin: **8** sui juris

of poor quality 5 junky
6 flimsy, shoddy, sleazy,
trashy **8** inferior
11 substandard

of secondary importance
8 nonvital **9** accessory, extrinsic **10** incidental **11** dispensable, unnecessary
12 nonessential

often 3 oft **4** much **7** usually
8 commonly, ofttimes **9** generally, regularly **10** constantly,
frequently, habitually, oftentimes, repeatedly **11** continually, customarily, over and
over, recurrently **12** periodically, time and again

**of the dead say nothing
but good**
Latin: **21** de mortuis nil nisi
bonum

of the faith
Latin: **6** de fide

of their own kind
Latin: **10** sui generis

of the old school 5 passe
8 outdated, outmoded
9 out-of-date **12** conservative,
old-fashioned **18** establish-
mentarian

Of Time and the River
author: **11** Thomas Wolfe
character: **10** Eugene Gant

oft-repeated 5 trite **7** popular
8 constant, familiar, frequent,
habitual, well-worn **9** continual, recurring, well-known
10 persistent **11** widely-known

of what good
Latin: **7** cui bono

Ogdoad
also: **3** Heh
origin: **8** Egyptian
number of gods: **5** eight

ogle 3 eye **6** gape at, gawk at,
goggle, leer at **7** stare at
8 goggle at **10** give the eye,
scrutinize **15** give the once-
over, stare at greedily **16** cast
sheep's eyes at, gaze at with
desire

Ogma
origin: **5** Irish

god of: **6** poetry **9** eloquence
inventor of: **12** Ogham letters

Ogmios
origin: **6** Gaelic
god of: **9** eloquence
corresponds to: **7** Mercury

ogre, ogress 5 brute, demon,
fiend, ghoul, harpy **6** despot,
tyrant **7** bugbear, monster
8 bogeyman, dictator, martinet **11** slave driver

Ogygia
island of: **7** Calypso

Ogygus
king of: **7** Boeotia
father: **8** Poseidon

O'Hara, John
author of: **7** Pal Joey **11** A
Rage to Live **13** The Instrument **14** From the Terrace,
The Hat on the Bed
16 Butterfield Eight **17** Ten
North Frederick **19** The
Horse Knows the Way
20 Appointment in Samarra

O'Hara, Maureen
real name: **18** Maureen
Fitzsimmons
nickname: **18** Queen of
Technicolor
born: **7** Ireland **8** Milltown
roles: **10** Lady Godiva **11** The
Quiet Man **13** North to
Alaska, The Parent Trap
16 The Foxes of Harrow
19 How Green Was My Valley **20** Hunchback of Notre
Dame **27** Miracle on Thirty-
fourth Street

O'Hara, Scarlett
character in: **15** Gone With
the Wind
family: **6** Gerald **7** Carreen,
Suellen
author: **8** Mitchell

O Henry
real name: **19** William Sidney Porter
author of: **11** The Last Leaf
16 Cabbages and Kings, The
Gift of the Magi **18** The
Cop and the Anthem
19 The Ransom of Red
Chief

Ohio *see* box

Ohm, Georg Simon
field: **7** physics
nationality: **6** German
discovered: **20** electrical
resistance
named for him: **7** ohm unit

oil 4 balm, lard **5** cream, salve
6 anoint, grease, pomade
7 unguent **8** liniment, ointment **9** lubricant, lubricate,
melted fat, petroleum
12 melted grease
type: **4** corn, fuel, hair

Ohio
abbreviation: 2 OH
nickname: 7 Buckeye
capital: 8 Columbus
largest city: 9 Cleveland
others: 3 Ada **4** Kent, Lima **5** Akron, Berea, Cadiz, Niles, Parma, Piqua, Xenia **6** Athens, Canton, Dayton, Elyria, Lorain, Marion, Newark, Tiffin, Toledo, Warren **7** Ashland, Findlay, Fremont, Norwood, Wooster **8** Alliance, Bluffton, Fostoria, Lakewood, Marietta, Sandusky **9** Ashtabula, Kettering, Lancaster, Massillon, Struthers, Vermilion, Willowick **10** Cincinnati, Huntington, Portsmouth, Rocky River, Willoughby, Youngstown, Zanesville **11** Painesville, Springfield **12** Steubenville
college: 4 Kent **5** Akron, Hiram, Miami **6** Dayton, Kenyon, Xavier **7** Antioch, Oberlin, Wooster **8** Defiance, Dennison, Marietta, Ursuline **10** Wittenberg **11** Case Western **12** Bowling Green, Ohio Wesleyan
feature:
  hall of fame: **11** Pro Football
  race: **12** Soap Box Derby
tribe: 4 Erie **7** Wyandot **13** Mound Builders
people: 7 buckeye, Cy Young **8** Zane Grey **10** Clark Gable, T Hart Crane **11** Annie Oakley, Lillian Gish **12** James Thurber, Lowell Thomas, Norman Thomas **13** Neil Armstrong, Orville Wright, Thomas A Edison **14** Barney Oldfield, Clarence Darrow **15** William T Sherman **16** Sherwood Anderson **18** Norman Vincent Peale
  explorer: **7** La Salle
lake: 4 Erie **5** Grand **6** Berlin, Dillon, Hoover, Indian **8** Delaware **13** Mosquito Creek
land rank: 35 thirty-fifth
mountain:
  highest point: **12** Campbell Hill
physical feature:
  caverns: **4** Ohio, Zane **6** Seneca
  spring: **8** Blue Hole
president: 13 Ulysses S Grant **14** James A Garfield, Warren G Harding **15** William McKinley **16** Rutherford B Hayes **17** William Howard Taft **20** William Henry Harrison
river: 5 Grand, Miami **6** Maumee, Scioto, Wabash **7** Hocking **8** Cuyahoga, Sandusky **9** Muskingum, Tennessee **10** Cumberland **11** Monongahela
state admission: 11 seventeenth
state bird: 8 cardinal
state flower: 16 scarlet carnation
state motto: 27 With God All Things Are Possible
state song: 13 Beautiful Ohio
state tree: 7 buckeye

5 crude, motor, olive, whale **7** cooking, mineral **9** safflower, vegetable

Oilean Ajax *see* **4** Ajax

Oileus
king of: 6 Locris
member of: 9 Argonauts
father: 10 Hodoedocus
mother: 9 Agrianome
son: 5 Medon **13** Ajax the Lesser

oily 5 fatty, lardy, slick **6** greasy, smarmy **7** buttery, fawning, servile **8** slippery, slithery, toadying, unctuous **9** groveling, sebaceous **10** lubricious, oleaginous **11** boot-licking, subservient **12** ingratiating

ointment 4 balm **5** salve **6** lotion, pomade **7** pomatum, unguent **8** liniment **9** emollient, spikenard

Oizys
mother: 3 Nyx
personifies: 4 pain

Ojibwa, Ojibway *see* **8** Chippawa

OK 4 fine, good **7** approve, endorse **8** all right, approval **9** authorize **11** endorsement **13** authorization
  French: 7 d'accord

O'Keeffe, Georgia
born: 12 Sun Prairie WI
artwork: 7 Stables **9** Black Iris **14** Patio with Cloud **15** Lake George Barns **22** Light Coming on the Plains **26** Black Flower and Blue Larkspur

Oklahoma *see box, p. 704*

Oklahoma!
director: 13 Fred Zinnemann
cast: 10 Rod Steiger **11** Eddie Albert **12** Gordon MacRae, Shirley Jones **13** Gloria Grahame, James Whitmore **18** Charlotte Greenwood
score: 21 Rodgers and Hammerstein
song: 23 People Will Say We're in Love **24** Surrey with the Fringe on Top

Olbers, Heinrich Wilhelm Matthaus
field: 9 astronomy
nationality: 6 German
discovered: 5 Vesta **6** comets, Pellas **9** asteroids

old 4 aged, used **5** hoary, of age **6** beat-up, bygone, of yore **7** ancient, antique, archaic, elderly, outworn, rundown, vintage, wornout **8** battered, decrepit, familiar, grizzled, much-used, obsolete, outdated, timeworn **9** crumbling, hackneyed, out-of-date, venerable, weathered **10** antiquated, broken-down, grayheaded, ramshackle, tumbledown **11** dilapidated, from the past, gray with age, obsolescent, time-honored, traditional **12** deteriorated, oldfashioned, white with age **13** weather-beaten **14** of long standing **15** long established

Old Aches and Pains
nickname of: 11 Luke Appling

old age 6 dotage **7** ripe age **8** maturity, senility **11** advanced age **15** second childhood

Old and the Young, The
author: 15 Luigi Pirandello

Old Bay State
nickname of:
13 Massachusetts

Old Bulgarian
also: 15 Old Church Slavic
language family: 12 Indo-European
group: 11 Balto-Slavic
status: 7 archaic
used in: 14 Orthodox church

Old Chinook
nickname of: 10 Washington

Oklahoma
  abbreviation: **2** OK **4** Okla
  nickname: **6** Boomer, Sooner
  capital/largest city: **12** Oklahoma City
  others: **3** Ada **4** Alva, Enid, Hugo **5** Altus, Miami, Ponca,
    Tulsa **6** Duncan, El Reno, Guymon, Idabel, Lawton
    7 Ardmore, Guthrie, Sapulpa, Shawnee **8** Anadarko, Fort
    Sill, Muskogee **9** Blackwell, Claremore, McAlester
    10 Stillwater **12** Bartlesville
  college: **5** Tulsa **6** Norman **7** Cameron **8** Langston, Phillips
    10 Stillwater **11** Oral Roberts **12** Oklahoma City **15** Beth-
    any Nazarene **17** American Christian
  feature:
    hall of fame: **14** American Indian
    national park: **6** Platte
  tribe: **3** Kaw, Oto **4** Iowa, Loup, Otoe, Waco **5** Caddo,
    Kansa, Osage, Ponca **6** Apache, Ottawa, Pawnee, Qua-
    paw **7** Shawnee, Wichita **8** Arapahoe, Tawakoni
    Five Civilized Tribes: **5** Creek **7** Choctaw **8** Cherokee,
      Seminole **9** Chickasaw
  people: **4** Okie **6** sooner **9** Jim Thorpe **10** Will Rogers
    12 Mickey Mantle **14** Maria Tallchief
    explorer: **8** Coronado
  lake: **5** Atoka, Grand, Hulah **6** Texoma, Wister **7** Eufaula,
    Heyburn, Oologah **8** Keystone **9** Pensacola, Tenkiller
    10 Fort Gibson **11** Thunderbird **12** Markham Ferry
    17 Lake O' The Cherokees
  land rank: **10** eighteenth
  mountain: **6** Ozarks **8** Ouachita
    highest point: **9** Black Mesa
  physical feature: **9** Panhandle
    plains: **5** Great
  river: **3** Red **5** Grand **6** Little, Neosho **7** Washita **8** Arkan-
    sas, Canadian, Cimarron **9** Verdigris **15** Muddy Boggy
    Creek
  state admission: **10** forty-sixth
  state bird: **23** scissor-tailed flycatcher
  state fish: **9** white bass
  state flower: **9** mistletoe
  state motto: **22** Labor Conquers All Things
  state song: **8** Oklahoma
  state tree: **6** redbud

Old Colony State
  nickname of:
  13 Massachusetts

Old Curiosity Shop, The
  author: **14** Charles Dickens
  character: **5** Quilp **9** Fred
  Trent, Mrs Jarley **10** Kit
  Nubbles, Sally Brass
  11 Grandfather **12** Sampson
  Brass **13** Dick Swiveller
  15 Little Nell Trent **18** The
  Single Gentleman

Old Dominion
  nickname of: **8** Virginia

olden 4 past **6** bygone, former,
  of yore **7** ancient, long-ago
  8 departed

Oldest Man 10 Methuselah

old-fashioned 5 corny, dated,
  passe **7** antique, archaic **8** obsolete, outdated, outmoded
  9 out-of-date **10** antiquated,
  out of style **11** obsolescent,

traditional **12** long-standing,
out of fashion **13** unfashionable **14** behind the times

Old-Fashioned Girl, An
  author: **15** Louisa May Alcott

Old Franklin State
  nickname of: **9** Tennessee

old hand 3 pro **6** expert, master **8** virtuoso **9** authority
  12 professional

old hat 5 passe, stale **6** demode **7** archaic, outworn
  8 obsolete, outdated, outmoded **9** out-of-date **10** antiquated, superseded
  11 obsolescent **12** old-
  fashioned **13** unfashionable
  14 behind the times

old-line 11 established, traditional **12** conservative

Old Line State
  nickname of: **8** Maryland

Old Love
  author: **19** Isaac Bashevis
  Singer

Old Maid, The
  author: **12** Edith Wharton

Old Man and the Sea, The
  author: **15** Ernest Hemingway
  character: **7** Manolin
  8 Santiago

Old Mortality
  author: **14** Sir Walter Scott
  character: **5** Edith **11** Henry
  Morton **12** Basil Olifant,
  Lord Evandale **19** John Balfour of Burley **21** Lady Margaret Bellenden **27** Colonel
  Grahame of Claverhouse

Old Mortality
  author: **19** Katherine Anne
  Porter

Old North
  nickname of: **13** North
  Carolina

**Old Patagonian Express,
The**
  author: **11** Paul Theroux

old saw 5 adage, maxim
  6 cliche, saying, truism **7** bromide, proverb **9** old saying
  10 expression **11** old chestnut

oldster 5 elder **6** codger, old
  man **7** ancient **8** old woman
  13 senior citizen

Old Testament
  first five books:
  10 Pentateuch
  first six books: **9** Hexateuch
  first seven books:
  10 Heptateuch
  books of: **3** Job **4** Amos,
  Ezra, Joel, Ruth **5** Hosea,
  Jonah, Kings, Micah, Nahum, Songs, Tobit **6** Baruch,
  Daniel, Esther, Exodus, Haggai, Isaiah, Joshua, Judges,
  Judith, Psalms, Samuel, Sir-
  ach, Wisdom **7** Ezekiel, Genesis, Malachi, Numbers,
  Obadiah **8** Habakkuk, Jeremiah, Macabees, Nehemiah,
  Proverbs **9** Leviticus, Zechariah, Zephaniah **10** Chronicles **11** Deuteronomy
  12 Ecclesiastes **13** Song of
  Solomon **14** Ecclesiasticus

Oldtown Folks
  author: **19** Harriet Beecher
  Stowe

Old Wives' Tale, The
  author: **13** Arnold Bennett

old-world 6 formal **7** courtly,
  gallant, old-line **8** European,
  orthodox **10** ceremonial, chivalrous, prescribed **11** ceremonious, continental, established,
  traditional **12** conservative,
  conventional, old-fashioned

Ole
  character in: 16 Giants of
    the Earth
  author: 7 Rolvaag

Olen
  occupation: 4 poet
  location: 5 Lycia

Olenska, Ellen
  character in: 17 The Age of
    Innocence
  author: 7 Wharton

oleoresin 3 gum 5 anime,
  apiol, elemi 6 balsam 7 solvent 10 turpentine

olio 4 stew 6 jumble, medley
  7 melange, mixture 8 mishmash 9 potpourri 10 assortment, collection, hodgepodge,
  hotchpotch, miscellany

olive 12 Olea europaea
  varieties: 3 tea 4 wild
    5 black, false, holly, sweet
    6 common, desert, spurge
    7 Russian 8 American, fra-
    grant 11 Californian

olive-drab 5 khaki
  13 greenish-brown

Oliver
  character in: 11 As You Like
    It
  author: 11 Shakespeare

Oliver!
  director: 9 Carol Reed
  based on story by:
    14 Charles Dickens (Oliver
    Twist)
  cast: 8 Jack Wild, Ron
    Moody (Fagin) 10 Mark Les-
    ter (Oliver), Oliver Reed
    11 Shani Wallis
  Oscar for: 7 picture
    8 director
  remake of: 11 Oliver Twist
  song: 16 Consider Yourself,
    Food Glorious Food 17 As
    Long As He Needs Me

Oliver Twist
  author: 14 Charles Dickens
  character: 5 Fagin, Monks
    (Edward Leeford), Nancy
    6 Bumble 9 Bill Sikes, Mrs
    Maylie 10 Mr Brownlow,
    Rose Maylie
  director: 9 David Lean
  cast: 8 Kay Walsh 12 Alec
    Guinness (Fagin), Robert
    Newton 13 Anthony Newley
    (Artful Dodger) 16 Francis L
    Sullivan, John Howard
    Davies
  remade as: 7 Oliver!

Olivia
  character in: 12 Twelfth
    Night
  author: 11 Shakespeare

Olivier, Sir Laurence
  born: 7 Dorking, England

  wife: 11 Vivien Leigh
    13 Joan Plowright
  roles: 6 Becket, Hamlet (Os-
    car), Henry V, Sleuth 7 Re-
    becca 11 Marathon Man
    16 Wuthering Heights
    17 Pride and Prejudice, The
    Boys from Brazil, The Dev-
    il's Disciple 19 Shoes of the
    Fisherman 23 The Prince
    and the Showgirl

olivine
  variety: 7 peridot

olla 3 jar, pot 10 earthen pot

Olmsted, Frederick Law
  landscape architect of:
    11 Central Park (NYC, with
    Calvert Vaux) 12 Prospect
    Park (Brooklyn NY) 13 Fair-
    mount Park (Philadelphia)
    14 Biltmore Estate (Asheville
    NC), Mount Royal Park
    (Montreal)

Olsen, Merlin (Jay)
  sport: 8 football
  team: 14 Los Angeles Rams
  TV roles: 12 Father Murphy
    15 Highway to Heaven
    23 Little House on the
    Prairie

Olsson, Ann-Margret
  real name of: 10 Ann-
    Margret

O Lucky Man
  director: 15 Lindsay
    Anderson
  cast: 9 Alan Price 13 Rachel
    Roberts 15 Malcolm Mc-
    Dowell, Ralph Richardson
  score: 9 Alan Price

Olwen
  origin: 5 Welsh
  form: 8 princess
  father: 16 Yspadaden
    Penkawr

Olympic Games *see box*

Omaha
  language family: 6 Siouan
    7 Dhegiha
  location: 4 Iowa 8 Nebraska,
    Oklahoma

Oman *see box, p. 706*

omega 3 end 4 last 5 final
  6 ending 8 terminus
  opposite: 5 alpha

omen 4 sign 5 token 6 augury,
  herald 7 auspice, portent, presage, warning 9 foretaste, harbinger, precursor
  10 foreboding, indication

Omet 15 Biblical measure

ominous 7 unlucky 8 menacing, minatory, monitory, sinister 9 dismaying, ill-omened
  10 foreboding, ill-starred,
  portentous

Olympic Games
  site:
    1896: 6 Athens
    1900: 5 Paris
    1904: 7 St Louis
    1906: 6 Athens
    1908: 6 London
    1912: 9 Stockholm
    1920: 7 Antwerp
    1924: 5 Paris
      8 Chamonix
    1928: 8 St Moritz
      9 Amsterdam
    1932: 10 Lake Placid,
      Los Angeles
    1936: 6 Berlin
      21 Garmisch-
      Partenkirchen
    1948: 6 London 8 St
      Moritz
    1952: 4 Oslo
      8 Helsinki
    1956: 9 Melbourne
      15 Cortina d'Ampezzo
    1960: 5 Tokyo
      11 Squaw Valley
    1968: 8 Grenoble
      10 Mexico City
    1972: 6 Munich
      7 Sapporo
    1976: 8 Montreal
      9 Innsbruck
    1980: 6 Moscow
      10 Lake Placid
    1984: 8 Sarajevo
      10 Los Angeles
    1988: 5 Seoul
      7 Calgary
    1992: 9 Barcelona
      11 Albertville
    1994: 11 Lillehammer
    1996: 7 Atlanta

omission 3 gap 4 hole 7 neglect 9 exception, exclusion,
  oversight 10 leaving out, negligence 11 delinquency, elimination 12 noninclusion
  13 neglected item 16 something omitted

omit 3 cut 4 drop, fail, jump,
  miss, shun, skip 5 avoid,
  elide 6 bypass, delete, except,
  forget, ignore, slight 7 excerpt,
  exclude, let slip, neglect
  8 leave out, overlook, pass
  over, preclude, set aside
  11 forget about

omnia vincit amor 15 love
  conquers all

Omnibus
  host: 13 Alistair Cooke

omnipotent 6 mighty 7 supreme 8 almighty, powerful,
  puissant 11 all-powerful

omniscient 7 all-wise, su-

Oman
other name: **13** Muscat and Oman
capital: **6** Masqat, Muscat
largest city: **5** Matra **6** Matrah
others: **3** Sur **4** Fida **5** Dubai, Nazwa, Nigwa, Sohar, Wazit **6** Khasab, Marbat, Murbat, Suwaih, Tinouf **7** Khabura, Salalah **8** Ashkhara
government: **9** Sultanate
head of state/government: **6** sultan
monetary unit: **3** gaj, gaz **4** rial **5** baiza, ghazi **7** mahmudi
island: **6** Masera, Masira **7** Masirah **10** Kuria Muria
mountain: **4** Qara **5** Hafit, Harim, Nakhl, Tayin **8** el-Akhdar **11** Jabal Akhdar **13** Green Mountain
highest point: **6** al-Sham
sea: **6** Indian **7** Arabian
physical feature:
   cape: **7** Madraka **9** Ras Al Hadd **13** Ras Dharbat 'Ali
   gulf: **4** Oman
   peninsula: **7** Arabian **8** Musandam
   plain: **6** Dhofar **7** Batinah
   strait: **6** Hormuz
people: **4** Arab
   ruler: **12** Qabus Bin Said **13** Said Bin Taimur
language: **4** Urdu **5** Hindi **6** Arabic **7** Baluchi
religion: **5** Islam
war: **4** Gulf **11** Desert Storm

preme **8** infinite **9** all-seeing **10** all-knowing, preeminent

omnium gatherum 23 miscellaneous collection

omnivorous 7 hoggish **8** edacious, ravenous **9** crapulous, rapacious, voracious **10** gluttonous, polyphagic, predacious **12** pantophagous

Omoo
author: **14** Herman Melville
character: **10** Captain Bob **15** Doctor Long Ghost

Omphale
queen of: **5** Lydia
father: **8** Iardanus
husband: **6** Tmolus
son: **5** Lamus
served by: **8** Hercules

Omri
father: **6** Becher **7** Michael
son: **4** Ahab
daughter-in-law: **7** Jezebel

on 2 at **4** atop, near, over, upon **5** about, above, ahead, along, anent **7** against, forward, planned **8** abutting, adjacent, attached, intended, touching **9** occurring **10** concerning, juxtaposed

On
father: **6** Peleth
city of: **10** Heliopolis

on-and-off 6 spotty **8** episodic **9** irregular, spasmodic, temporary **10** now-and-then, occasional

On Beginning and Perishing
author: **9** Aristotle

once **7** ages ago, long ago, one time **8** formerly, hitherto, years ago **9** at one time **10** heretofore, previously **11** a single time, for the nonce, in times past, some time ago **12** in the old days, some time back **13** once upon a time, on one occasion

once-in-a-lifetime 6 unique **7** special **8** singular **11** one-time-only

once more 4 anew **5** again **9** once again, over again **11** one more time

on cloud nine 6 elated, joyful, joyous **8** ecstatic, euphoric **9** exuberant, rapturous **15** in seventh heaven

oncoming 5 close **7** looming, nearing **8** imminent **9** advancing, impending, onrushing **11** approaching, bearing down

on course 8 on target **15** on the right track

Ondine
author: **13** Jean Giraudoux

one **2** an **3** you **4** a man, lone, only, sole **5** a body, a soul, whole **6** a thing, entire, single, unique **7** a person, someone **8** complete, singular, solitary, somebody **10** individual, unrepeated

One, Two, Three
director: **11** Billy Wilder
cast: **11** James Cagney **12** Pamela Tiffin **13** Arlene Francis, Horst Buchholz

setting: **10** West Berlin
score: **11** Andre Previn

O'Neal, Ryan
real name: **16** Patrick Ryan O'Neal
born: **12** Los Angeles CA
daughter: **10** Tatum O'Neal
roles: **9** Love Story, Paper Moon **10** What's Up Doc **11** Barry Lyndon, Peyton Place **16** Rodney Harrington

O'Neal, Tatum
born: **12** Los Angeles CA
father: **9** Ryan O'Neal
roles: **9** Paper Moon **12** Bad News Bears **14** Little Darlings **19** International Velvet
husband: **11** John McEnroe

one and the same 5 equal **7** matched **9** identical

one by one 6 singly **10** one at a time, separately, single file **12** individually

One Day at a Time
character: **9** Ann Romano **11** Julie Cooper **13** Barbara Cooper **15** Dwayne Schneider
cast: **14** Bonnie Franklin **15** Pat Harrington Jr **17** Mackenzie Phillips, Valerie Bertinelli

One Day in the Life of Ivan Denisovich
author: **23** Aleksandr Solzhenitsyn Jr

One Fat Englishman
author: **12** Kingsley Amis

One Flew Over the Cuckoo's Nest
director: **11** Milos Forman
based on story by: **8** Ken Kesey
cast: **13** Jack Nicholson **14** Louise Fletcher, Michael Beryman **15** William Redfield
Oscar for: **5** actor (Nicholson) **7** actress (Fletcher), picture **8** director **10** screenplay

One Hour with You
director: **11** George Cukor **13** Ernst Lubitsch
cast: **14** Genevieve Tobin **16** Maurice Chevalier **17** Jeanette MacDonald
remake of: **17** The Marriage Circle
song: **14** What Would You Do

one-hundred percent 5 sheer, total, utter, whole **7** supreme **8** absolute, complete **10** consummate **17** through-and-through

O'Neill, Eugene
author of: **8** The Straw **11** The Hairy Ape **12** Ah

Wilderness, Anna Christie
13 Marco Millions **14** Glencairn Cycle **15** The Emperor Jones, The Iceman Cometh **16** Beyond the Horizon, Strange Interlude, The Great God Brown **18** Desire Under the Elms **20** The Moon of the Caribees **22** A Moon for the Misbegotten, All God's Chillun Got Wings, Mourning Becomes Electra **24** Long Day's Journey into Night

Oneiros
also: **6** Oniros
origin: **5** Greek
god of: **6** dreams

oneness 5 union, unity **7** concord, harmony **8** entirety, identity, sameness, totality **9** agreement, aloneness, integrity, wholeness **10** uniformity, uniqueness **11** singularity **12** completeness **13** individuality

one-of-a-kind 4 rare **6** unique **7** strange, unusual **8** original **9** eccentric

onerous 5 heavy **6** taxing **7** arduous, painful, weighty **8** crushing, grievous **9** demanding, wearisome **10** burdensome, exhausting, oppressive **11** distressing **12** hard to endure

one thing in return for another
Latin: **10** quid pro quo

one-time 3 old **4** past **5** early, prior **6** former, recent **7** earlier, quondam **8** previous **9** erstwhile
French: **8** ci-devant

one voice 4 solo **6** unison **7** concert

one who has a fixed income
French: **7** rentier

On First Looking Into Chapman's Homer
author: **9** John Keats

on foot
French: **5** a pied

ongoing 7 endless, lasting **8** enduring, unbroken, unending **10** continuing, proceeding **11** never-ending, unremitting **13** uninterrupted

On Golden Pond
director: **10** Mark Rydell
based on play by: **14** Ernest Thompson
cast: **9** Jane Fonda **10** Doug McKeon, Henry Fonda (Norman Thayer Jr) **16** Katharine Hepburn
setting: **5** Maine

Oscar for: 5 actor (Fonda) **7** actress (Hepburn)

on guard 4 wary **5** alert **7** careful, heedful **8** cautious, vigilant, watchful

on hand 5 handy, on tap **6** at hand **9** available **10** accessible, convenient **14** at one's disposal

on horseback
French: **7** a cheval

onion 6 Allium **10** Allium cepa
varieties: **3** red, sea, top **4** leek, tree, wild **5** green, gypsy, pearl, swamp, Welsh, white **6** German, potato, yellow **7** Bermuda, Danvers, nodding, prairie, shallot, Spanish **8** climbing, Egyptian, false sea, scallion, Valencia **9** Catawissa, ever-ready, flowering, two-bladed **10** multiplier, red-skinned **16** Japanese bunching
origin: **9** Asia Minor
called by Robert Louis Stevenson: **14** rose among roots

Onion Field, The
author: **14** Joseph Wambaugh

Oniros see **7** Oneiros

On Liberty
author: **14** John Stuart Mill

onlooker 5 gazer, ogler **6** viewer **7** watcher, witness **8** beholder, kibitzer, observer **9** bystander, spectator **10** eyewitness, rubberneck

only 4 just, lone, sole **5** alone **6** barely, merely, purely, simply, single, singly, solely, unique **7** at least **8** by itself, singular, solitary **9** by oneself, exclusive, unmatched **10** individual, no more than, nothing but, one and only, unrepeated **11** exclusively **12** individually, unparalleled

on one's uppers 5 broke **9** destitute **10** down and out

On Plants
author: **9** Aristotle

On Revolution
author: **12** Hannah Arendt

onrush 4 flow, flux, gush, tide, wave **5** flood, onset, storm, surge **6** attack, charge, deluge, spring, stream **7** assault, cascade, current, torrent **9** avalanche

onset 4 push, raid **5** birth, sally, start **6** attack, charge, onrush, outset, thrust **7** assault, genesis, infancy, offense **8** founding, invasion, outbreak, storming **9** beginning, inception, incursion, offensive, onslaught **10** incipience, initiation **12** commencement, inauguration

onslaught 4 coup, push, raid **5** blitz, foray, onset, sally **6** attack, charge, putsch, thrust **7** assault, offense **8** invasion **9** incursion, offensive **10** aggression, blitzkrieg

on tap 5 handy **6** at hand, on hand **9** available **10** accessible, convenient

Ontario
bay: **6** Hudson
canal: **5** Trent **6** Rideau
capital: **7** Toronto
city: **3** Emo **4** Galt **6** London, Ottawa **7** Windsor **8** Hamilton, Kingston **9** Kitchener
explored by: **5** French **6** British
industry: **6** mining **11** agriculture **13** manufacturing
lake: **6** Simcoe
province of: **6** Canada
river: **6** Ottawa, Thames **7** Niagara **10** St Lawrence
settled by: **9** Loyalists
university: **4** York **5** Brock, Trent **8** McMaster

on the alert 4 wary **7** careful, mindful, on guard **8** cautious, watchful **9** wide awake **12** on the lookout

On the Beach
author: **10** Nevil Shute
director: **13** Stanley Kramer
cast: **10** Ava Gardner **11** Fred Astaire, Gregory Peck **13** Donna Anderson **14** Anthony Perkins

on the contrary
French: **11** au contraire

on the dot 7 exactly **8** promptly **9** on the nose, precisely **10** punctually

on the face
Latin: **7** ex facie

on the go 4 busy **6** active, mobile **8** in motion **9** energetic, on the move **13** indefatigable

On the Heavens
author: **9** Aristotle

On the Morning of Christ's Nativity
author: **10** John Milton

on the move 5 astir **6** active, mobile **7** on the go **8** in motion

on the nose 5 exact **7** exactly, precise **8** accurate, on target **9** precisely **10** accurately, on the money

on the outer edges
Latin: **10** in extremis

on the right track 8 on
course, on target

On the Soul
author: **9** Aristotle

On the Town
director: **9** Gene Kelly
12 Stanley Donen
cast: **9** Ann Miller, Gene
Kelly, Vera-Ellen **12** Betty
Garrett, Frank Sinatra
setting: **11** New York City
score: **11** Adolph Green,
Betty Comden **16** Leonard
Bernstein
song: **14** New York New
York

On the Waterfront
director: **9** Elia Kazan
cast: **8** Lee J Cobb **10** Karl
Malden, Pat Henning, Rod
Steiger **12** Leif Erickson,
Marlon Brando **13** Eva
Marie Saint
Oscar for: **5** actor (Brando)
7 picture **8** director
10 screenplay **17** supporting
actress (Saint)

on the whole 9 in general
10 by and large **27** considering the circumstances

onto 4 atop, upon **5** aware,
privy **6** aboard

onus 4 duty, load **5** cross
6 burden, strain, weight **9** liability **10** obligation **11** encumbrance **13** burden of proof
14 responsibility

onus probandi 13 burden of
proof

onward, onwards 5 ahead,
along **7** forward, ongoing
9 advancing, frontward
11 moving ahead, progressive
French: **7** en avant, en route

On Wings of Eagles
author: **10** Ken Follett

oodles 4 gobs, lots, many
5 heaps, loads, scads **6** plenty

ooze 4 drip, leak, mire, muck,
seep, silt **5** bleed, drain, exude, slime, sweat **6** filter,
sludge **7** dribble, leakage, seepage, soft mud, trickle **8** allu-
vium **9** discharge, exudation,
percolate, secretion, transpire

oozing 5 leaky, weepy
6 sweaty **7** exuding, seepage,
seeping **8** bleeding, sweating

opal
color: **3** red **5** black, white
6 orange **11** transparent
source: **6** Mexico **9** Australia
14 Lightning Ridge
variety: **8** fire opal

opalescent 5 milky **6** pearly
8 irisated, luminous
10 iridescent

opaque 4 dark, dull, hazy
5 muddy, murky **7** clouded,
muddied, obscure, unclear
8 abstruse **9** difficult
12 impenetrable, unfathomable **14** nontranslucent,
nontransparent, unintelligible
16 incomprehensible

opaqueness 7 opacity **8** dullness **9** denseness, muddiness,
murkiness, obscurity **10** cloudiness **11** unclearness
15 impenetrability **17** unintelligibility
19 incomprehensibility

open 4 ajar, fair, just,
wide **5** agape, begin, clear,
crack, found, frank, plain,
unbar **6** candid, create, direct, expand, gaping, honest, launch, unfold, unlock,
unseal, unshut **7** artless,
exposed, lay open, natural,
not shut, sincere, unblock,
unclose, yawning **8** commence, extended, outgoing,
unbiased, unclosed, unfasten, unfenced, unfolded,
unlocked, unsealed **9** available, coverless, establish,
expansive, impartial, institute, not closed, objective,
originate, receptive, unbigoted, unbounded, uncov-
ered, uncrowded,
undertake, welcoming
10 accessible, forthright,
impersonal, inaugurate, responsive, unenclosed, un-
fastened **11** extroverted,
uncluttered, uninhabited
12 permit access, unobstructed, unprejudiced
13 disinterested, doing
business **15** straightforward

open-air 7 outdoor, outside
10 unconfined
Italian: **8** al fresco

open and aboveboard 6 candid, honest **7** ethical **10** forthright **12** on the up and up
15 straightforward

Open Boat, The
author: **12** Stephen Crane

Open City
director: **17** Roberto
Rossellini
cast: **11** Aldo Fabrizi, Anna
Magnani **16** Marcello
Pagliero
setting: **4** Rome

open-eyed 5 alert, awake,
aware **7** heedful, mindful
8 vigilant, watchful, wide-
eyed **9** attentive,
wide-awake

open-handed 6 lavish **7** liberal **8** generous, prodigal
9 bounteous, bountiful **10** altruistic, beneficent, benevolent,
ungrudging, unstinting
11 magnanimous

openhandedness 10 generosity, liberality **11** benevolence,
generousity, munificence
12 extravagance

openhearted 7 artless, sincere
8 trusting **9** ingenuous

opening 3 gap, job **4** gash,
hole, rent, rift, slit, slot, spot,
tear, vent **5** break, chink,
cleft, crack, place, space, start
6 breach, chance **7** fissure,
kickoff, preface, prelude, send-
off, vacancy **8** aperture, occasion, overture, position **9** beginning, first part, launching,
situation **10** initiation **11** opportunity, possibility **12** commencement, inauguration,
installation, introduction

openly 6 freely **7** frankly **8** directly, honestly, publicly
9 obviously

open-minded 4 fair **7** liberal
8 amenable, flexible, tolerant,
unbiased **9** adaptable, impartial, objective, receptive **10** responsive, undogmatic
11 broad-minded **12** unprejudiced **13** disinterested,
nonjudgmental

openmouthed 4 agog, awed
5 agape **6** aghast, amazed
8 wide-eyed **9** awestruck, bewitched, marveling, staggered,
stupefied, surprised **10** astonished, confounded **10** dumbstruck, enthralled, spellbound
11 dumbfounded **12** wonderstruck **13** flabbergasted,
thunderstruck

openness 6 candor **7** honesty
8 daylight **9** frankness, sincerity **11** artlessness **13** guilelessness **14** forthrightness
19 straightforwardness

open sanction 8 free hand,
free rein **13** full authority
French: **12** catre blanche

open the eyes of 8 disabuse
11 set straight

open to choice 8 elective, optional **9** voluntary

openwork 3 net **4** lace **6** eyelet **7** lattice, Madeira, tracery
8 filigree

opera 5 score **7** musical **8** libretto **11** composition
  by Bizet: 6 Carmen
  by Delibes: 5 Lakme
  by Gounod: 5 Faust
  by Leoncavallo: 10 I Pagliacci
  by Mozart: 8 Idomeneo **10** Magic Flute **11** Don Giovanni
    12 Cosi fan tutte **16** Marriage of Figaro
  by Offenbach: 15 Tales of Hoffmann
  by Ponchielli: 10 La Gioconda
  by Puccini: 5 Tosca **8** La Boheme **12** Manon Lescaut
    15 Madame Butterfly
  by Rossini: 8 Tancredi **11** William Tell **15** The Barber of
    Seville
  by Smetana: 13 The Bartered Bride
  by Strauss: 6 Salome **7** Elektra **15** Ariadne auf Naxos
    16 Der Rosenkavalier
  by Tchaikovsky: 12 Eugene Onegin
  by Verdi: 4 Aida **6** Otello **8** Falstaff **9** Rigoletto **10** La Tra-
    viata **11** Il Trovatore
  by Wagner: 8 Parsifal **9** Lohengrin **10** Tannhauser **16** Tris-
    tan and Isolde **17** The Flying Dutchman **21** The Ring of
    the Nibelungs
  comic: 5 buffa **7** comique
  glass: 9 lorgnette
  hat: 5 crush, gibus
  house: 3 Met **6** Sydney **7** La Scala **12** Covent Garden,
    Metropolitan
  singer: 4 bass, diva **5** buffa, buffo, tenor **7** soprano **10** co-
    loratura, prima donna
  singular: 4 opus
  solo: 4 aria
  text: 8 libretto

operate 2 go **3** run **4** go in, work **6** behave, manage, open up **7** oversee, perform **8** function **11** superintend **14** perform surgery **18** perform an operation

operating 6 active **7** working **8** in motion **9** operative **10** responsive

operation 5 force **6** action, agency, effect **7** conduct, pursuit, running, surgery, working **8** activity, exertion **9** influence, procedure **10** management, overseeing **11** exploratory, performance, supervision **15** instrumentality, superintendence

operative 3 spy **4** dick **5** agent, in use **6** acting, active, shamus, worker **7** in force, working **8** in effect, in motion, workable **9** activated, detective, effective, effectual, operating **10** functional, private eye, responsive **11** efficacious, secret agent

operator 4 doer, user **5** agent, pilot **6** driver, worker **7** manager **9** performer

opere citato 14 in the work cited
  abbreviation: 5 op cit

Ophelia
  character in: 6 Hamlet
  author: 11 Shakespeare

Opheltes
  also: 10 Archemorus

ophidiophobia
  fear of: 6 snakes

Ophion
  form: 7 serpent
  created from: 9 north wind
  created by: 8 Eurynome

Ophir
  father: 6 Joktan
  source of: 4 gold

opiate 4 dope **6** downer **7** anodyne **8** hypnotic, narcotic, nepenthe, sedative **9** analgesic, calmative, soporific, stupefier **10** depressant, painkiller, palliative **12** somnifacient, stupefacient, tranquilizer

opine 3 say **4** deem **5** allow, guess, offer, state, think **6** assume, reckon **7** believe, imagine, presume, suggest, surmise **8** conclude, consider, estimate **9** speculate, volunteer **10** conjecture, have a hunch

opinion 4 idea, view **6** belief, notion, theory **7** surmise **8** estimate, judgment, thinking **9** sentiment, suspicion **10** assessment, assumption, conception, conclusion, conjecture, conviction, estimation, evaluation, impression, persuasion **11** speculation

opinionated 8 dogmatic, obdurate, stubborn **9** obstinate, pigheaded, unbending **10** bullheaded, headstrong, inflexible, unyielding **12** closedminded **14** uncompromising

O Pioneers!
  author: 11 Willa Cather

Opis
  companion of: 7 Artemis

Opobalsammum 12 Biblical tree

Oppenheimer, Julius Robert
  field: 7 physics
  directed development of:
    10 atomic bomb
      location: 9 Los Alamos,
        New Mexico
  chaired: 3 AEC **22** Atomic
    Energy Commission

Opper, Frederick
  creator/artist of: 13 Happy
    Hooligan **17** Alphonse and
    Gaston, And Her Name Was
    Maud

opponent 3 foe **5** enemy, rival **8** resister **9** adversary, assailant, contender, disputant **10** antagonist, challenger, competitor, opposition

opportune 3 apt **5** happy, lucky **6** proper, timely **7** fitting **8** suitable **9** expedient, favorable, fortunate, well-timed **10** auspicious, convenient, felicitous, profitable, propitious, seasonable **11** appropriate **12** advantageous

opportunity 4 time, turn **5** means **6** chance, moment **7** opening **8** occasion **9** situation **10** good chance **11** contingency

oppose 4 buck, defy **5** fight **6** battle, combat, resist, thwart **7** contest **8** obstruct **9** withstand **12** be set against, speak against

opposed 3 con **4** anti **6** averse, pitted **7** adverse, against, counter, hostile **8** contrary, disputed, objected, resisted **9** contested, countered **10** confronted, contrasted, reciprocal **12** contradicted

opposer 5 rival **8** opponent **9** adversary **10** antagonist, competitor

opposite 5 other **6** facing **7** adverse, counter, reverse **8** contrary, converse, opposing **9** differing **11** conflicting **12** antagonistic, antithetical **13** contradictory, counteractive

opposite number 5 equal **8** parallel **10** equivalent **11** correlative, counterpart

opposition 3 foe **5** enemy, rival **6** enmity **8** aversion, defiance, opponent **9** adversary, contender, hostility, other side, rejection **10** antagonism, antagonist, competitor, negativism, resistance **11** contrariety, disapproval **12** disagreement

oppress 3 tax, try, vex **4** pain **5** abuse, worry **6** burden, deject, grieve, sadden, sorrow **7** depress, trouble **8** cast down, dispirit, maltreat **9** despotize, persecute, tyrannize, weigh down **10** discourage, dishearten

oppressed 7 crushed **9** exploited **10** tyrannized **11** downtrodden, subservient

oppressive 5 cruel, harsh **6** brutal, severe, trying, vexing **7** onerous, painful, wearing **8** despotic, grievous, pressing **9** worrisome **10** burdensome, depressing, repressive, tyrannical, wearing **11** distressing, hardhearted, troublesome **12** discouraging **13** uncomfortable

oppressor 6 despot, tyrant **8** autocrat, dictator

opprobrious 4 base **6** wicked **7** abusive, corrupt, damning **8** infamous, reviling, shameful, shocking **9** malicious, maligning, nefarious, vilifying, vitriolic **10** censorious, deplorable, despicable, malevolent, outrageous, scandalous, scurrilous, unbecoming **11** acrimonious, disgraceful, fulminating **12** condemnatory, denunciatory, dishonorable, disreputable, faultfinding **13** hypercritical, objectionable, reprehensible

opprobrium 5 shame **6** infamy **8** disgrace, dishonor **9** disrepute **12** denunciation

Ops
origin: **5** Roman
goddess of: **6** plenty
husband: **6** Saturn
son: **7** Jupiter
called: **10** Magna Mater
corresponds to: **4** Rhea
6 Cybele **9** Dindymene
10 Berecyntia

opt 4 pick, take **5** elect, fix on, go for **6** choose, prefer, select **7** vote for **8** decide on, settle on

opt for 4 pick, take **5** adopt **6** choose, select, take up **7** embrace, espouse, fix upon, pick out **8** decide on, settle on

optimism 10 confidence **11** hopefulness **12** cheerfulness, sanguineness **13** bright outlook, encouragement

optimistic 6 bright **7** hopeful, roseate **8** buoyed up, cheerful, sanguine **9** confident, favorable, heartened, promising **10** auspicious, encouraged, heartening, propitious **11** encouraging, rose-colored **12** enthusiastic

Optimist's Daughter, The
author: **11** Eudora Welty

optimum 4 acme, A-one, best, peak **5** crest, ideal, prime **6** choice, height, select, zenith **7** capital, perfect, supreme **8** flawless **9** faultless, first-rate **10** perfection, unexcelled **11** superlative **12** quintessence

option 4 will **5** voice **6** choice, liking **8** decision, election, free will, pleasure **9** franchise, privilege, selection **10** discretion, partiality, preference **11** alternative **12** predilection

optional 4 open **8** elective, unforced **9** allowable, openended, voluntary **10** volitional **11** not required **12** discretional **13** discretionary, nonobligatory

opulence 6 bounty, plenty, riches, wealth **7** fortune **8** elegance, luxuries, richness **9** abundance, affluence, amplitude, profusion **10** cornucopia, lavishness, plentitude, prosperity **11** copiousness, great wealth **13** sumptuousness

opus 4 work **5** piece **6** effort **7** attempt, product **8** creation **9** handiwork, invention **10** brainchild, production **11** composition

oracle, Oracle 4 sage, seer **5** augur, sibyl **6** wizard **7** adviser, diviner, prophet **9** predictor, Scripture **10** forecaster, soothsayer **11** clairvoyant

oral 5 vocal **6** spoken, verbal, voiced **7** uttered **8** ingested **9** swallowed **10** of the mouth, verbalized **11** articulated, using speech
Latin: **8** viva voce

orange
varieties: **4** king, mock, sour, wild **5** blood, hardy, natal, navel, Osage, sweet **6** bitter, common, Panama, Temple **7** Florida, Mexican, Satsuma,

Seville, Spanish **8** Bergamot, Mandarin, Otaheite, Valencia **9** Tachibana, vegetable **10** Chinese box, trifoliate **13** African cherry, Mediterranean **15** Jamaica mandarin **17** house-blooming mock
liqueur: **7** Curacao

orangutan, orang-outang
3 ape **4** mias **5** satyr **6** primate **10** anthropoid
characteristic: **8** arboreal
11 herbivorous
native land: **6** Borneo
7 Sumatra
species: **13** Pongo pygmaeus

ora pro nobis 9 pray for us

orate 6 recite, speak **7** declaim **11** make a speech

oration 4 talk **5** spiel **6** eulogy, sermon, speech **7** address, lecture, recital **9** discourse, monologue, panegyric **10** peroration **11** declamation **12** disquisition, formal speech

orator 6 talker **7** speaker **8** lecturer, preacher **9** declaimer **10** sermonizer **11** rhetorician, speechmaker, spellbinder **12** elocutionist **13** public speaker

oratory 6 speech **7** bombast **8** delivery, rhetoric **9** elocution, eloquence, preaching **11** declamation **12** speechifying, speechmaking **14** grandiloquence

orb 4 ball, moon **5** globe **6** sphere **7** globule **8** spheroid

orbit 3 way **4** path **5** cycle, route, track **6** circle, course **7** channel, circuit, pathway **10** trajectory **13** revolve around **14** circumnavigate

orchards
god of: **9** Vertumnus

orchestra 3 pit **4** band **6** stalls **7** parquet **8** ensemble, parterre **12** Philharmonic

orchestrate 5 adapt, score **7** arrange, compose

orchestration 5 score **10** adaptation **11** arrangement **12** organization

orchid *see box*

Orcus
god of: **10** underworld
punishes: **7** perjury
corresponds to: **3** Dis
5 Hades, Pluto **8** Dis Pater

ordain 4 name, rule, will **5** elect, enact, frock **6** decree, invest **7** adjudge, appoint, command, dictate **8** delegate, deputize, instruct **9** determine,

orchid
  varieties: 3 bat, bee, fen, fly, nun, nut 4 baby, blue, dove, moth, nun's, rein, swan 5 black, chain, cigar, cobra, coral, giant, jewel, pansy, Salep, showy, snowy, spice, tiger, water, widow 6 bamboo, bottle, cradle, dollar, Easter, helmet, mirror, monkey, pigeon, ragged, sawfly, shower, spider, stream, virgin 7 Alaskan, cow-horn, fringed, hooker's, jumping, peacock, rainbow, rosebud, scarlet, soldier 8 bee-swarm, Cooktown, cranefly, fried-egg, gold-lace, green-fly, hyacinth, nun's-hood, poor-man's, Savannah, scorpion, white nun, windmill, woodland 9 blunt-leaf, butterfly, chocolate, Christmas, clam-shell, green rein, green swan, white rein 10 buttonhole, five-leaved, golden swan, hay-scented, late spider, leafy white, Sierra rein, slender bog 11 cockle-shell, crested rein, dancing-doll, dancing-lady, early spider, golden chain, green-winged, one-leaf rein, pink slipper, purple-spire, rattlesnake, round-leaved 12 green fringed, pink scorpion, purple-hooded, Southern rein, tall white bog, white fringed 13 crested yellow, golden fringed, green woodland, Northern green, ragged fringed, yellow fringed 14 crested fringed, large butterfly, little club-spur, white butterfly 15 lesser butterfly, lily-of-the-valley 16 downy rattlesnake, Florida butterfly, Northern small bog, purple fringeless, small round-leaved, white-flowered bog 18 large purple fringed, leafy Northern green, small purple fringed, Southern small white 19 lesser purple fringed 20 greater purple fringed

legislate, prescribe, pronounce 10 commission, consecrate

ordeal 4 care, pain 5 agony, grief, trial, worry 6 burden, misery, sorrow, strain, stress 7 anguish, concern, torment, tragedy, trouble 8 calamity, distress, pressure, vexation 9 heartache, nightmare, suffering 10 affliction, oppression 11 tribulation, unhappiness 12 wretchedness 16 trying experience

Ordeal of Richard Feverel, The
  author: 14 George Meredith

order 3 bid, law 4 body, book, calm, club, fiat, form, kind, rank, rule, sort, type 5 breed, caste, class, grade, group, guild, house, lodge, quiet, ukase 6 adjure, ask for, charge, decree, degree, demand, dictum, direct, engage, enjoin, family, status, stripe, system 7 agree to, bidding, caliber, call for, command, company, control, dictate, harmony, pattern, quality, request, reserve, silence, society, species, station 8 alliance, category, division, grouping, instruct, neatness, position, purchase, sorority, standing, tidiness 9 framework, structure, ultimatum 10 discipline, federation, fraternity, imperative, sisterhood, tabulation 11 arrangement, association, broth-

erhood, commandment, confederacy, designation, instruction, tranquility 12 codification, organization, peacefulness, tranquillity 13 pronouncement 14 categorization, classification

ordered 4 bade, neat, trim 7 regular, uniform 8 arranged 9 shipshape 10 systematic

orderliness 8 neatness, tidiness 10 discipline 12 organization

orderly 4 neat, tidy 5 civil, quiet 6 proper, spruce 8 peaceful 9 organized, peaceable, shipshape, tractable 10 classified, controlled, methodical, restrained, systematic 11 disciplined, uncluttered, well-behaved

ordinance 3 act, law 4 bull, fiat, rule, writ 5 canon, edict, order 6 decree, dictum, ruling 7 command, mandate, statute 9 enactment 10 regulation 11 commandment

ordinarily 7 as a rule, usually 8 commonly, normally 9 generally, regularly, routinely 10 habitually 11 customarily 12 on the average 14 conventionally

ordinary 4 dull, so-so 5 usual 6 common, normal 7 average, humdrum, routine, trivial, typical 8 everyday, familiar, habitual, mediocre, standard

9 customary 10 pedestrian, uninspired 11 commonplace, indifferent, stereotyped, traditional, unimportant 12 conventional, run-of-the-mill, unimpressive 13 insignificant, unexceptional, unimaginative, uninteresting 15 inconsequential, undistinguished

Ordinary People
  director: 13 Robert Redford
  author: 11 Judith Guest
  cast: 10 Judd Hirsch 13 Timothy Hutton 14 Mary Tyler Moore 16 Donald Sutherland
  Oscar for: 7 picture 8 director 12 screenwriter 15 supporting actor (Hutton)

ordinary wine
  French: 12 vin ordinaire

ordnance 4 arms 6 cannon 9 armaments, artillery, munitions

ordnance depot 6 armory 7 arsenal 18 military storehouse

ore 3 tin 4 gold, iron, lead, paco, rock, zinc 5 metal 6 bronze, copper, galena, sulfur 7 halvans, mineral 8 aluminum, cinnabar, hematite 9 melachite
  byproduct: 6 gangue
  deposit: 3 bed 4 lode, mine, vein 7 bonanza
  layer: 4 seam 5 stope
  trough: 6 strake
  worthless: 4 slag 5 dross, matte

Oread
  form: 5 nymph
  location: 8 mountain
  companion of: 7 Artemis

oregano
  name means: 16 joy of the mountain
  botanical name: 8 O vulgare, Origanum
  also: 6 organy, origan 8 marjoram 9 pizza herb 11 Mexican sage, winter sweet
  origin: 13 Mediterranean
  family: 4 mint
  cure for: 11 indigestion 14 loss of appetite
  first aid for: 12 spider stings 14 scorpion stings
  use: 5 pizza 6 broths 8 stuffing 12 tomato dishes 13 Italian dishes

Oregon *see box, p. 712*

Oregon Trail, The
  author: 14 Francis Parkman

Oresteia
  author: 9 Aeschylus
  trilogy includes: 9 Agamemnon, Eumenides 10 Choephoroe

Oregon
abbreviation: 2 OR 4 Oreg
nickname: 6 Beaver, Sunset 7 Webfoot 13 Sawdust Empire
capital: 5 Salem
largest city: 8 Portland
others: 5 Nyssa 6 Albany, Eugene 7 Ashland, Astoria, Medford 8 Portland, Roseburg 9 Corvallis, Pendleton 10 Grant's Pass, Willamette 12 Klamath Falls
college: 4 Reed 7 Pacific 8 Linfield, Portland 10 Willamette 13 Lewis and Clark
feature:
   fort: 5 Boise 6 Casper 7 Kearney, Laramie
   national park: 10 Crater Lake
tribe: 4 Coos 5 Alsea, Kusan, Modoc, Wasco, Yanan, Yunca 6 Cayuse, Chetco, Chinoo, Kuitsh, Molala, Siletz, Tenino, Umpqua 7 Bannock, Clatsop, Klamath, Sastean, Shastan, Takelma, Walpapi, Yaquina 8 Clackama, Klikitat, Nez Perce, Sahaptin, Umatilla 9 Kalapuyan, Tillamook 10 Kalapooian, Wallawalla
people: 10 Wayne Morse 12 Linus Pauling 15 Phyllis McGinley
   explorer: 13 Lewis and Clark
lake: 5 Abert, Waldo 6 Harney, McNary 7 John Day, Klamath, Malheur
   deepest in US: 6 Crater
land rank: 5 tenth
mountain: 6 Mazama, Tacoma, Walker, Wilson 7 Elkhorn, Grizzly, Jackass, Rainier, Tidbits, Wallowa 8 Cascades 9 Blue Coast, Marys Peak 10 Strawberry
   highest point: 4 Hood
physical feature:
   bay: 4 Coos
   caves: 11 Marble Halls
   wind: 7 Chinook
river: 5 Rogue, Snake 6 Imnaha, Owyhee, Powder, Umpqua 7 Blitzen, John Day, Klamath, Silvie's 8 Columbia 9 Deschutes 10 Willamette
state admission: 11 thirty-third
state bird: 17 western meadowlark
state fish: 13 chinook salmon
state flower: 7 mahonia 11 Oregon grape
state motto: 8 The Union
state song: 14 Oregon My Oregon
state tree: 10 Douglas fir

Orestes
author: 9 Euripides
character: 5 Helen 6 Apollo, Furies 7 Electra, Pylades 8 Menelaus

Orestes
father: 9 Agamemnon
mother: 12 Clytemnestra
sister: 7 Electra 9 Iphigenia
wife: 8 Hermione
son: 9 Tisamenus
killed: 9 Aegisthus 12 Clytemnestra
pursued by: 6 Furies

Orfeo, L'
also: 17 The Story of Orpheus
opera by: 10 Monteverdi

Orfeo ed Euridice
also: 18 Orpheus and Eurydice
opera by: 5 Gluck

character: 4 Amor, Zeus 6 Furies

Orff, Carl
born: 6 Munich 7 Germany
composer of: 7 Der Mond, The Moon 8 Antigone, Die Kluge 9 Schulwerk 10 Prometheus 13 Carmina Burana, The Clever Girl 14 Catulli Carmina 16 Oedipus der Tyrann, Oedipus the Tyrant

organ 6 agency 7 journal, vehicle 9 harmonium 10 hurdygurdy, instrument 11 publication

organic 5 alive, quick 6 living 7 animate, natural, ordered, planned, unified 8 designed, physical 9 patterned 10 anatomical, harmonious, methodical, systematic

12 nonsynthetic 13 physiological 14 constitutional

organism 4 cell 5 plant, whole 6 animal, entity, system 7 complex, network, society 8 creature 9 bacterium 10 federation 11 association, corporation, institution, living thing 13 microorganism

organization 4 club, firm, sect 5 corps, group, order, party, union 6 design, league, making, outfit 7 company, forming, harmony, pattern, society 8 alliance, assembly, business, grouping, ordering 9 arranging, formation 10 federation, fellowship, fraternity 11 arrangement, association, composition, corporation, formulation, structuring 12 constitution, coordination 13 establishment, incorporation

organizational 10 managerial 13 developmental 14 administrative

organize 4 file, form, tidy 5 found, group, index, order, set up 6 codify, create, neaten, tidy up 7 arrange, catalog, develop 8 classify, tabulate 9 establish, formulate, originate 10 categorize, coordinate 11 make orderly, systematize

organized 4 neat, tidy 7 logical, orderly 8 coherent 10 methodical, systematic

orgiastic 4 wild 6 wanton 7 drunken, riotous 9 abandoned, debauched, Dionysian, dissolute, libertine 10 dissipated, licentious 12 bacchanalian, unrestrained 13 overindulgent, undisciplined

orgy 7 debauch, wassail 8 carousal 9 bacchanal 10 saturnalia 11 bacchanalia

orient, the Orient 3 fix, set 4 Asia, find 6 locate, relate, square 7 situate 8 accustom 9 acclimate, reconcile 10 the Far East 11 Eastern Asia, familiarize

oriental 4 Arab, fine, Thai, Turk 5 Asian 6 bright, Indian, Korean 7 Asiatic, Chinese, Eastern, Iranian, shining 8 Japanese, lustrous, precious, superior 10 Vietnamese
animal: 4 zebu 5 rasse
building: 6 pagoda
dish: 5 pilau, pilaw 6 pilaff
drum: 6 tomtom
food fish: 3 tai
garment: 3 aba 6 sarong
inn: 4 Khan 5 serai 6 imaret 11 caravansary

laborer: 6 coolie
market: 3 suk, sug **4** souk
  6 bazaar
nurse: 4 amah, ayah
prince: 4 amir, haja
sail: 6 lateen
sash: 3 obi
shrub: 3 tea **5** henna
  8 oleander
wagon: 5 araba
weight: 2 mo **4** rotl, tael
  5 catty, liang **6** cantar

orientation 8 location **9** alignment, direction, situation
  10 adjustment **11** acclimation
  15 acclimatization,
  familiarization

orifice 3 gap, pit **4** hole, slit,
  slot, vent **5** cleft, inlet,
  mouth **6** cavity, cranny, hollow, lacuna, pocket, socket
  7 crevice, fissure, opening,
  passage **8** alveolus, aperture,
  entrance

origin 4 base, line, race, rise,
  root **5** agent, basis, birth,
  breed, cause, house, stock
  6 author, family, father,
  ground, growth, mother, reason, source, spring, strain
  7 creator, descent, genesis, lineage, taproot **8** ancestry, nativity, producer **9** beginning,
  emergence, evolution, generator, inception, parentage, principle **10** derivation, extraction,
  foundation **12** commencement,
  fountainhead

Origin, The
  author: 11 Irving Stone

original 3 new **4** bold **5** basic,
  basis, first, fresh, novel **6** daring, primal, unique **7** example,
  initial, pattern, primary, seminal, strange, unusual **8** atypical, creative, earliest,
  germinal, primeval, singular,
  uncommon **9** different, essential, first copy, formative, inaugural, ingenious, inventive,
  prototype **10** aboriginal, newfangled, primordial, underlying, unfamiliar, unorthodox
  11 fundamental, imaginative
  12 introductory **13** extraordinary **14** unconventional

**Original Amateur Hour,
  The**
  host: 7 Ted Mack

originality 6 daring **7** newness,
  novelty **8** boldness **9** freshness,
  ingenuity **10** cleverness, creativity, uniqueness **11** imagination, singularity, unorthodoxy
  13 individuality, inventiveness
  17 unconventionality

originally 7 at first, by birth
  8 uniquely **9** initially, unusually **10** creatively **11** differ-

ently, inventively
  13 imaginatively

originate 4 come, flow, rise,
  stem **5** arise, begin, draft,
  found, issue, start **6** create,
  crop up, derive, design, devise,
  emerge, evolve, father, invent,
  sprout **7** develop, emanate,
  proceed **8** commence, conceive, envision, initiate, organize, spring up **9** establish,
  fabricate, formulate, germinate **10** inaugurate

origination 5 birth **7** genesis
  9 inception, invention **10** conception, initiation **11** germination **12** commencement
  13 establishment

Origin of Species, The
  author: 13 Charles Darwin

**Origins of Totalitarianism,
  The**
  author: 12 Hannah Arendt

Orion
  form: 5 giant
  vocation: 6 hunter
  pursued: 8 Pleiades
  killed by: 7 Artemis
  became: 13 constellation

Orithyia
  father: 10 Erechtheus
  mother: 9 Praxithea
  abducted by: 6 Boreas
  son: 5 Zetes **6** Calais
  daughter: 6 Chione
    9 Cleopatra

Oriya
  language family: 12 Indo-
    European
  branch: 11 Indo-Iranian
  group: 5 Indic
  spoken in: 5 (northern) India

Orkney Islands
  county seat: 8 Kirkwall
  country: 8 Scotland
  firth: 8 Pentland
  island: 3 Hay **6** Rousay, San-
    day **7** Westray **8** Stronsay
    14 South Ronaldsay
  largest city: 6 Pomona

Orlando
  author: 13 Virginia Woolf
  character: 5 Sasha **14** Nicho-
    las Greene **28** Archduchess
    Harriet of Roumania, Mar-
    maduke Bonthrop
    Shelmerdine

Orlando
  character in: 11 As You Like
    It
  author: 11 Shakespeare

Orlando Furioso
  author: 7 Ariosto
  character: 6 Rogero **7** Rin-
    aldo **8** Agramant, Angelica,
    Rodomont **9** Bradamant
    11 Charlemagne

Orley Farm
  author: 15 Anthony Trollope

ormolu 5 alloy, brass, paste
  6 bronze **7** gilding **8** ornament
  imitation of: 4 gold
  used to decorate: 5 clock
    9 furniture

ornament 4 deck, gild, trim
  5 adorn **6** bedeck, enrich, finery, frills **7** festoon, furbish,
  garnish **8** beautify, decorate,
  furbelow, trick out, trimming
  9 accessory, adornment, embellish **10** decoration, enrichment **11** elaboration
  13 embellishment
  14 beautification

ornamental 4 gilt **5** fancy
  6 chichi, rococo **10** decorative
  ball: 4 bead **6** pompom
  button: 4 stud
  grass: 4 neti
  loop: 5 picot
  metal: 5 niello

ornamentation 7 garnish
  8 trimming **9** adornment
  10 decoration
  13 embellishment

ornate 5 fancy, showy **6** flashy,
  florid, lavish, rococo
  7 adorned, baroque, flowery
  9 decorated, elaborate, sumptuous **10** flamboyant **11** embellished, pretentious
  12 ostentatious

ornery 4 curt, mean **5** surly,
  testy **6** crabby, grumpy, shirty
  7 grouchy, peevish, waspish
  8 snappish **9** dyspeptic, irascible, irritable **10** ill-natured
  11 ill-tempered, quarrelsome
  12 cantankerous

Orneus
  father: 10 Erechtheus
  brother: 6 Metion **7** Cecrops
  son: 6 Peteos

Ornitholestes
  type: 8 dinosaur
  period: 8 Jurassic

Ornithomimus
  type: 8 dinosaur
  period: 10 Cretaceous

ornithophobia
  fear of: 5 birds

ornithopod
  type of: 8 dinosaur
  member: 9 Iguanodon **10** Ed-
    montonia, Nodosaurus
    11 Anatosaurus, Polacan-
    thus, Saurolophus, Scolosau-
    rus, Stegosaurus
    12 Ankylosaurus, Campto-
    saurus, Lambeosaurus, Pisa-
    nosaurus **13** Acanthopholis,
    Corythosaurus, Hypsilopho-
    don, Palaeoscincus **14** Thes-
    celosaurus

15 Parasaurolophus, Procheneosaurus **17** Heterodontosaurus

Ornytus *see* **7** Teuthis

orotund 4 full, rich **5** clear **6** strong **7** pompous, ringing, vibrant **8** resonant, sonorous **9** bombastic **10** resounding, rhetorical, stentorian
Latin: **10** ore rotundo

Orowitz, Eugene Maurice
real name of: **13** Michael Landon

oro y plata 13 gold and silver
motto of: **7** Montana

Orozco, Jose Clemente
born: **6** Mexico **7** Jalisco (Zapotlan) **12** Ciudad Guzman
artwork: **5** Grief **9** Catharsis **11** Omniscience **12** House of Tears **16** National Allegory, Social Revolution **18** Hidalgo and Castillo

Orphans of the Storm
director: **10** D W Griffith
cast: **11** Dorothy Gish, Lillian Gish **17** Joseph Schildkraut

Orpheus
vocation: **4** poet **8** musician
mother: **8** Calliope
wife: **8** Eurydice
member of: **9** Argonauts
went into: **5** Hades
killed by: **7** Maenads

Orpheus in the Underworld
also: **15** Orphee aux Enfers
operetta by: **9** Offenbach

Orsino
character in: **12** Twelfth Night
author: **11** Shakespeare

ort 3 bit **5** crumb, dregs, scrap **6** morsel, refuse, trifle **7** remnant **8** leavings, leftover

Orthaea
father: **10** Hyacinthus

Orthia
epithet of: **7** Artemis
means: **7** upright

orthodox 5 fixed, pious, usual **6** devout, narrow **7** limited, regular, routine **8** accepted, approved, official, ordinary, standard **9** customary, religious **11** commonplace, conformable, established, traditional **12** conventional **13** authoritative, circumscribed

orthoptera
class: **8** hexapoda
phylum: **10** arthropoda
group: **4** leaf **5** stick **6** locust, mantid **7** cricket **9** cockroach **11** grasshopper

Orwell, George
real name: **15** Eric Arthur Blair
author of: **4** 1984 **10** Animal Farm **18** Nineteen Eighty Four **29** Politics and the English Language

oryx 5 beisa **6** pickax **7** gazelle, gemsbok **8** antelope, leucoryx

Osage (Wazhazhe)
language family: **6** Siouan
location: **6** Kansas **8** Arkansas, Missouri, Oklahoma

Oscan
language family: **12** Indo-European
branch: **6** Italic

Oschophoria
origin: **8** Athenian
event: **8** festival
honoring: **7** vintage **8** Dionysus

oscillate 4 vary **5** pulse, swing, waver **6** change, seesaw **7** librate, pulsate, vibrate **8** hesitate **9** alternate, come and go, fluctuate, hem and haw, vacillate **10** ebb and flow, equivocate **12** shilly-shally **16** move back and forth

O'Shaughnessy, Brigid
character in: **16** The Maltese Falcon
author: **7** Hammett

osier 3 rod **4** wand **5** salix, withe **6** willow **7** dogwood, wilgers **9** twigwithy
species: **14** Salix viminalis
use: **6** wicker **8** basketry

Osiris
origin: **8** Egyptian
god of: **4** dead, Nile
judge of: **4** dead
king of: **4** dead
wife: **4** Isis
sister: **4** Isis
son: **5** Horus
brother: **3** Set **4** Seth **5** Horus
killed by: **3** Set **4** Seth

Oskar Matzerath
character in: **7** Tin Drum
author: **5** Grass

Oslo
capital of: **6** Norway
former name: **11** Christiania
landmark: **8** Storting (Parliament) **11** Royal Palace
mountain: **12** Holmenkollen
park: **7** Frogner
peninsula: **8** Akershus
street: **14** Karl Johansgate

Osmond, Gilbert
character in: **18** The Portrait of a Lady
author: **5** James

Ossian
character in: **12** Gaelic poetry

ossify 6 harden **7** stiffen **9** fossilize

ossuary 8 boneyard **10** depository, receptacle

ostensible 6 avowed **7** alleged, assumed, feigned, implied, nominal, outward, seeming, surface, titular, visible **8** apparent, declared, illusory, manifest, specious **9** pretended, professed **10** presumable **11** perceivable

ostentation 4 airs, dash, fuss, pomp, ritz, show **5** glitz, gloss, swank **6** splash **7** display, glitter **8** flourish, pretense **9** pageantry, pomposity, showiness, spectacle
French: **7** etalage

ostentatious 4 loud **5** gaudy, showy **6** flashy, florid, garish **7** pompous **8** affected, immodest, overdone **9** grandiose, obtrusive **10** flamboyant, showing off **11** conspicuous, exaggerated, pretentious **15** flaunting wealth

Osterreich *see* **7** Austria

ostracize 3 cut **4** oust, shun, snub **5** avoid, expel **6** banish, disown, reject **7** exclude, shut out **9** blackball, blacklist

Ostwald, Wilhelm
field: **9** chemistry
nationality: **6** German
founded: **17** physical chemistry

O'Sullivan, Maureen
born: **5** Boyle **7** Ireland **15** County Roscommon
daughter: **9** Mia Farrow
roles: **4** Jane (Tarzan movies) **16** David Copperfield **17** Pride and Prejudice **19** Hannah and her Sisters

Otello
also: **7** Othello
opera by: **5** Verdi **7** Rossini

O tempora! O mores! 14 O times! O customs!

Othello
director: **11** Stuart Burge
author: **18** William Shakespeare
character: **4** Iago **6** Cassio, Emilia **9** Desdemona
cast: **11** Frank Finlay, Joyce Redman, Maggie Smith **15** Laurence Olivier

other 4 more **5** added, extra, spare **6** unlike **7** further, reverse **8** contrary, opposite **9** alternate, auxiliary, different, remaining **10** additional, contrasted, dissimilar **11** contrasting **13** contradictory, supplementary **14** differentiated

Other Gods
author: **9** Pearl Buck

Other Side of Midnight, The
author: **13** Sidney Sheldon

other than 3 but **4** save **6** except, saving **7** barring, besides **9** excepting, excluding

otherwise 5 if not **6** or else **9** inversely **10** contrarily **11** differently **12** contrariwise

otherworldly 7 sublime **8** heavenly **9** celestial **14** transcendental

Othin *see* **4** Odin

Othniel 11 Hebrew judge
father: **5** Kenaz
brother: **5** Caleb
wife: **6** Achsah

O times! O customs!
Latin: **14** O tempora! O mores!

Otionia
father: **10** Erechtheus
sister: **10** Protogonia
death by: **9** sacrifice
for victory of: **9** Athenians
over: **11** Eleusinians

otiose 4 idle, lazy **6** futile **7** laggard, resting, useless, worn-out **8** abortive, impotent, inactive, indolent, listless, slothful, sluggish **9** fruitless, lethargic, powerless, somnolent **10** unavailing **11** incompetent, ineffective, inoperative, unrewarding **12** unproductive

Otomi
tribe: **7** Capotec

O'Toole, Peter
born: **7** Ireland **9** Connemara
roles: **6** Becket **7** Creator, Lord Jim **13** Man of La Mancha **14** Goodbye Mr Chips, My Favorite Year, The Last Emperor **15** The Lion in Winter **16** Lawrence of Arabia, What's New Pussycat **18** How to Steal a Millon

O'Trigger, Sir Lucius
character in: **9** The Rivals
author: **8** Sheridan

Ott, Mel
nickname: **9** Boy Wonder **12** Master Melvin
sport: **8** baseball
position: **8** outfield
team: **13** New York Giants

Ottawa
capital of: **6** Canada
early name: **6** Bytown
falls: **6** Rideau **9** Chaudiere
landmark: **18** National Arts Centre **19** Dominion Observatory, Parliament Buildings

river: **6** Ottawa, Rideau **8** Gatineau
university: **8** Carleton

Ottawa
language family: **9** Algonkian **10** Algonquian
location: **4** Ohio **6** Canada, Kansas **7** Ontario **12** Lake Michigan
leader: **7** Pontiac

Otter
origin: **12** Scandinavian
mentioned in: **8** Volsunga
form: **5** otter
father: **8** Hreidmar
killed by: **4** Loki

ottoman, Ottoman 4 seat, Turk **5** couch, divan, stool **7** sultane, Turkish **9** footstool
color: **3** red **9** vermilion
governor: **3** bey, dey **5** pasha
ruler: **5** Osman **8** Suleiman
standard: **4** ale

Otus
form: **5** giant
member of: **7** Aloidae
father: **8** Poseidon
mother: **9** Iphimedia
brother: **9** Ephialtes

Ouagadougou
capital of: **10** Upper Volta **11** Burkina Faso

oui 3 yes

ounce
abbreviation of: **2** oz

ounce troy
abbreviation of: **3** oz t

Our Bill
creator: **14** Harry Haenigsen
character: **6** Walter

Our Crowd
author: **17** Stephen Birmingham

Our Miss Brooks
character: **8** Mrs Davis **12** Connie Brooks, Walter Denton **13** Osgood Conklin, Philip Boynton **14** Harriet Conklin
cast: **8** Eve Arden **10** Dick Crenna, Gale Gordon, Jane Morgan **14** Gloria McMillan, Robert Rockwell
Miss Brooks taught: **7** English
school: **11** Madison High

Our Mutual Friend
author: **14** Charles Dickens
character: **4** Wegg **5** Venus **6** Boffin **11** Bella Wilfer **17** Mortimer Lightwood, Young John Harmon (Handford, Rokesmith)

our sea
Latin: **11** mare nostrum
ancient Roman name for: **13** Mediterranean

Our Town
author: **14** Thornton Wilder
character: **12** Simon Stimson
Gibbs family: **2** Dr **3** Mrs **6** George **7** Rebecca
Webb family: **2** Mr **3** Mrs **5** Emily, Wally
director: **7** Sam Wood
cast: **10** Fay Bainter **11** Martha Scott **13** William Holden

oust 4 fire, sack **5** eject, evict, expel **6** banish, bounce, put out, remove, unseat **7** boot out, cashier, cast out, dismiss, kick out **8** throw out **9** discharge, give the ax **11** give the gate, send packing

ouster 6 firing **7** removal, sacking **8** bouncing, ejection, eviction **9** discharge, dismissal, expelling, expulsion, overthrow **10** banishment, cashiering **11** dislodgment, drumming out, throwing out **13** dispossession

out 2 ex **4** away **5** aloud, eject, forth, not in, passe **6** absent, begone, excuse, public **7** outside **8** exterior, external, revealed **9** in society, in the open, published **10** extinguish

out-and-out 4 pure, sure **5** sheer, total, utter **6** arrant **7** perfect **8** absolute, complete, hardened, outright, positive, thorough **9** confirmed, downright, unlimited **10** inveterate **11** straight out, unequivocal, unmitigated, unqualified **12** unregenerate, unrestricted **13** dyed-in-the-wool, thoroughgoing, unadulterated, unconditional **14** unquestionable

outbrazen 4 dare, defy, face **8** confront **9** challenge, stand up to

outbreak 5 burst **7** display **8** epidemic, eruption, invasion, outburst **9** explosion **10** outpouring **13** demonstration

outbuilding 4 barn, shed **5** privy **6** garage, stable **7** latrine **8** outhouse, woodshed

outburst 5 blast, burst **7** display, thunder **8** eruption, outbreak **9** explosion **10** outpouring **11** fulmination **13** demonstration

outcast 5 exile, rover **6** ousted, outlaw, pariah, roamer **7** refugee, runaway **8** banished, castaway, deportee, derelict, expelled, fugitive, rejected, vagabond **9** discarded **10** expatriate

Outcast of the Islands, The
author: **12** Joseph Conrad

Outcault, R F
creator/artist of: **11** Buster Brown **12** The Yellow Kid

outcome 3 end **5** fruit, issue **6** effect, payoff, result, upshot **9** aftermath, outgrowth **11** aftereffect, consequence

outcry 3 cry **4** howl, roar, yell, yelp, yowl **5** noise, shout, whoop **6** bellow, clamor, hubbub, scream, shriek, uproar **7** clangor, protest, screech **9** commotion, complaint, crying out, hue and cry, objection **10** cry of alarm, hullabaloo **12** caterwauling, remonstrance

outdated 5 passe **7** antique **8** outmoded **9** out-of-date **10** antiquated **12** old-fashioned

outdo 3 top **4** beat, best **5** excel, worst **6** better, defeat, exceed, outfox, outwit **7** eclipse, outplay, outrank, surpass **8** outclass, outshine, outstrip, overcome **9** transcend

outdoor festival
French: **13** fete champetre

outdoor market 5 agora **6** bazaar **10** flea market **11** marketplace

outer 6 distal, remote **7** extreme, farther, outside, outward, without **8** exterior, external, outlying **9** outermost **10** farther out, peripheral

outer edge 3 lip, rim, tip **5** bound **6** margin **8** boundary **9** extremity

Outer Mongolia
also: **24** Mongolian People's Republic
border: **5** China **6** Russia **11** Soviet Union
capital: **4** Urga **5** Kulun **9** Ulan Bator
currency: **5** mongo **6** tugrik
desert: **4** Gobi **5** Shamo
language: **7** Khalka
mountain range: **5** Altai, Altay **7** Khangai

outermost 5 outer **6** utmost **7** extreme, outside, outward, surface **8** exterior, external **11** farthest out, most distant, superficial

outfit 3 fit, rig **4** gear **5** array, dress, equip, getup, habit, rig up **6** clothe, supply **7** appoint, costume, furnish **8** accouter, ensemble, wardrobe **9** equipment, provision, trappings **13** accoutrements, paraphernalia

outflow 5 issue **7** leakage, seepage **8** drainage **9** discharge

outgo 4 beat, cost, exit, pass

5 excel, issue, outdo **6** efflux, egress, outlay, outlet **7** outflow, surpass **8** outstrip **9** departure **11** expenditure

outgoing 4 warm **6** genial, social **7** amiable, cordial, exiting, leaving **8** friendly, going out, outbound, sociable **9** convivial, departing **10** gregarious **11** extroverted, sympathetic, warmhearted

outgoing person 9 extrovert **17** hail-fellow-well-met

outgrowth 3 end **4** knob, knot, node **5** bulge, fruit, issue, shoot **6** result, sequel, sprout, upshot **7** product **8** offshoot **9** aftermath **10** conclusion, projection **11** aftereffect, consequence, culmination, excrescence, outcropping **12** protuberance

outing 4 hike, ride, spin, tour, trip, walk **5** drive, jaunt, tramp **6** airing, junket, ramble **7** holiday **9** excursion **10** expedition

outlander 5 alien, exile **6** emigre **7** invader, settler **8** intruder, newcomer, stranger, wanderer **9** Auslander, barbarian, foreigner, immigrant **10** tramontane **12** ultramontane

outlandish 3 odd **5** kooky, queer, weird **6** far-out **7** bizarre, curious, strange, unusual **8** freakish, peculiar **9** eccentric, fantastic, grotesque, unheard-of **10** incredible, outrageous, ridiculous **12** preposterous, unbelievable, unimaginable, unparalleled **13** inconceivable **14** unconventional

outlast 6 endure, hold on, keep on, remain, stay on **7** carry on, hold out, outstay, outwear, perdure, persist, prevail, survive **8** continue

outlaw 3 ban, bar **4** deny, stop **5** felon **6** bandit, forbid, pariah **7** exclude, outcast **8** criminal, disallow, fugitive, prohibit, suppress **9** desperado, interdict, miscreant, proscribe **10** highwayman

outlay 3 fee **4** cost **5** outgo, price **6** charge **7** expense, payment **8** spending **11** amount spent, expenditure **12** disbursement

outlet 3 way **4** door, duct, exit, gate, path, vent **5** means **6** avenue, egress, escape, portal **7** channel, conduit, gateway, opening, passage

outline 4 plot **5** brief, trace

6 digest, limits, resume, review **7** contour, diagram, profile, summary, tracing **8** abstract, synopsis **9** blueprint, delineate, lineation, perimeter, periphery, sketch out **10** abridgment, silhouette **11** delineation **12** condensation
French: **6** apercu

outlook 4 view **5** scene, sight, vista **6** aspect, chance **7** picture, promise **8** attitude, forecast, panorama, prospect **9** spectacle, viewpoint **10** assumption **11** expectation, frame of mind, perspective, point of view, presumption, probability **12** anticipation

outlying 5 outer, rural **6** far-off, remote **7** distant, exurban **8** exterior, suburban **10** peripheral

outmoded 5 corny, dated, passe, tired **6** demode, old hat **7** antique, archaic, vintage **8** obsolete, old-timey, outdated **9** out-of-date **10** antiquated **12** old-fashioned, out-of-fashion **14** behind the times
French: **6** demode

Out of Africa
director: **13** Sydney Pollack
cast: **11** Meryl Streep (Baroness Karen Blixen, Isak Dinesen) **13** Robert Redford (Denys Finch Hatton) **19** Klaus Maria Brandauer (Baron Bror von Blixen)

out of bed 2 up **5** astir **9** up and at 'em **10** on one's feet, up and about **12** rise and shine

out-of-date 5 dated, passe **8** outmoded **10** antiquated **12** old-fashioned
French: **6** demode

out of doors 3 out **5** forth **6** abroad **7** outside **8** alfresco **12** in the open air

out-of-fashion 5 passe **8** obsolete, outmoded **9** out-of-date **12** old-fashioned
French: **6** demode

out of hand 4 wild **5** rowdy **6** unruly **10** disorderly **12** obstreperous, out of control, unmanageable, unrestrained **14** uncontrollable

out of keeping 8 atypical, peculiar, unseemly **9** anomalous, irregular **11** incongruous **12** inconsistent **13** inappropriate

out of kilter 4 awry **5** askew **6** uneven **7** crooked, oblique

out of line 6 unruly **9** excessive **10** exorbitant **12** presumptuous, unreasonable

out of many one
  Latin: **13** e pluribus unum
  motto of: 12 United States

out of one's head 3 mad
  4 daft, nuts **5** crazy, nutty
  6 insane **7** cracked, touched
  8 demented, deranged, unhinged **10** unbalanced **12** mad
  as a hatter, off his rocker
  15 mad as a March hare
  17 nutty as a fruitcake

out of operation 4 dead,
  down **8** inactive **10** not working, out of order
  11 inoperative

out of order 5 amiss **6** faulty
  10 not working **11** inoperative, uncalled-for
  13 inappropriate

out of place 3 odd **8** unseemly **10** unsuitable **11** incongruous, inconsonant
  13 inappropriate

out of shape 4 bent **5** unfit
  6 flabby, warped **7** crooked
  8 deformed **9** distorted,
  untrained

out of sorts 5 cross, huffy,
  testy **6** crabby, cranky,
  touchy **7** bearish, grouchy,
  peevish **8** petulant, snappish
  9 crotchety, irritable **10** ill-humored **11** ill-tempered
  12 cantankerous **13** short-tempered

out of the books of
  Latin: **8** ex libris

out of the fight
  French: **12** hors de combat

out of the ordinary 4 rare
  6 unique **7** notable, unusual
  8 singular, uncommon
  10 phenomenal, remarkable
  11 exceptional
  13 extraordinary

Out of the Past
  director: **15** Jacques
  Tourneur
  based on novel by: **13** Geoffrey Homes (Daniel Mainwaring) (Build My Gallows
  High)
  cast: **9** Jane Greer **11** Kirk
  Douglas, Richard Webb
  13 Rhonda Fleming, Robert
  Mitchum

out of touch 7 mixed-up
  8 unstable **11** disoriented
  12 out of contact
  13 incommunicado

out-of-towner 7 tourist, visitor **9** sojourner, transient
  11 nonresident

outpace 4 pass **5** outdo **6** exceed, outrun **8** outstrip

outpouring 6 deluge **7** barrage,
  gushing, outflow **8** effusion

output 4 crop, gain, take
  5 yield **6** profit **7** harvest, produce, product, reaping, turnout **8** gleaning, proceeds
  9 gathering **10** production
  11 achievement **12** productivity **14** accomplishment

outrage 4 evil, gall, rile **5** anger, shock, wrong **6** arouse,
  enrage, insult, madden, offend,
  ruffle **7** affront, incense, provoke, steam up **8** atrocity, disquiet, enormity, iniquity
  9 barbarity, indignity, infuriate **10** discompose, disrespect,
  exasperate, gross crime, scandalize **11** desecration, monstrosity, profanation
  13 barbarousness, get one's
  back up, make one see red,
  slap in the face, transgression
  17 make one's blood boil

outraged 3 mad **5** angry, irate,
  riled **6** fuming, raging **7** enraged, furious **8** incensed, inflamed, offended **9** affronted,
  indignant **10** displeased,
  infuriated

outrageous 4 base, foul, rank,
  rude, vile **5** gross **6** brutal,
  odious, wicked **7** abusive, extreme, galling, heinous, immense, inhuman **8** enormous,
  flagrant, inhumane, insolent,
  scornful, shocking **9** atrocious,
  barbarous, excessive, insulting,
  maddening, monstrous, nefarious, offensive, shameless
  10 despicable, exorbitant, horrifying, immoderate, iniquitous, scandalous
  11 disgraceful, infuriating, unspeakable, unwarranted
  12 contemptible, contemptuous, exasperating, preposterous, unreasonable
  13 disrespectful, reprehensible
  14 unconscionable

outrageousness 8 enormity
  9 immensity **10** wickedness
  13 atrociousness, monstrousness, offensiveness
  16 preposterousness

outre 8 improper

outreach 6 exceed **7** surpass

outright 4 full **5** sheer, total,
  utter **6** at once, entire,
  openly **7** utterly, visibly **8** absolute, complete, entirely, patently, promptly, thorough
  9 downright, forthwith, instantly, on the spot, out-and-out **10** absolutely, altogether,
  completely, manifestly, thoroughly, unreserved **11** immediately, unmitigated,
  unqualified **12** demonstrably,

undiminished **13** thoroughgoing, unconditional

outrival 3 dim **5** excel, outdo
  6 exceed **7** eclipse, surpass
  8 outshine **9** transcend
  10 overshadow, tower above

outrush 4 gust **8** overflow

outset 4 dawn **5** birth, start
  7 dawning **9** beginning, departure, threshold
  12 commencement

outshine 3 dim **5** excel, outdo
  6 exceed **7** eclipse, surpass
  9 transcend **10** overshadow

outside 4 case, face, skin
  5 alien, faint, outer **6** facade,
  remote, sheath, slight **7** coating, distant, foreign, obscure,
  outdoor, outward, strange, surface **8** covering, exterior, external, outdoors **9** nonnative,
  outer side, outermost **10** extraneous, out-of-doors,
  unfamiliar

outsider 5 alien **7** outcast
  8 onlooker, stranger **9** bystander, foreigner, nonmember **14** nonparticipant

outskirts 3 rim **4** edge **6** limits,
  verges **7** borders, fringes, margins, suburbs **8** environs **9** periphery, precincts
  10 perimeters **11** extremities

outspoken 5 blunt, frank
  6 candid, direct, honest **7** artless **9** guileless, ingenuous, unsparing **10** forthright,
  unreserved **11** opinionated,
  plainspoken **13** undissembling
  15 straightforward,
  undissimulating

outspread 5 broad **6** opened,
  spread **7** laid out **8** expanded,
  extended, unfolded, unfurled,
  unrolled **9** spread out,
  stretched **12** outstretched

outstanding 3 due **5** famed,
  great, owing **6** famous, unpaid **7** eminent, notable, payable **8** foremost, renowned,
  striking **9** best known, exemplary, in arrears, marvelous,
  memorable, prominent, unsettled **10** celebrated, noteworthy,
  phenomenal, remarkable
  11 exceptional, magnificent,
  uncollected **13** distinguished,
  extraordinary, unforgettable

outstrip 4 pass **6** exceed, outrun **7** outpace, surpass
  11 leave behind

outward 5 outer **7** evident,
  outside, surface, visible **8** apparent, exterior, external,
  manifest **10** observable, ostensible **11** perceivable, perceptible, superficial

outward appearance 4 mien 6 aspect, facade, manner 7 bearing 8 demeanor, exterior

Outward Bound
author: 10 Sutton Vane

outwardly 7 clearly, visibly 9 evidently, seemingly 10 apparently, manifestly, ostensibly 13 on the face of it 16 to all appearances

outwards 3 out 4 away

outweigh 6 exceed 7 eclipse, surpass 8 override 9 rise above 10 overshadow 11 predominate, prevail over 13 be heavier than, weigh more than

outwit 4 dupe, foil, fool, trap 5 trick 6 baffle, outfox, take in, thwart 7 ensnare 8 outsmart 9 get around 10 circumvent 11 outmaneuver

outworn 5 dated, passe 6 bygone 7 defunct, disused, extinct 8 obsolete, rejected 9 abandoned, discarded, forgotten, out-of-date 10 antiquated, superseded 12 old-fashioned 13 unfashionable

ouzo
type: 7 liqueur
origin: 6 Greece
flavor: 5 anise
substitute for: 8 absinthe

oval 5 ovate, ovoid 6 curved, ovular 7 obovate, oviform, rounded 9 egg-shaped 10 elliptical 11 ellipsoidal

ovation 6 cheers, homage, hurrah, hurray, huzzah 7 acclaim, fanfare, tribute 8 applause, cheering 9 adulation 11 acclamation

oven 3 umu 4 kiln, oast 5 baker, range, stove 6 hearth 7 broiler, chamber, kitchen, roaster
clay: 7 tandoor
fork: 7 fruggan, fruggin
mop: 6 scovel

over 3 too 4 also, anew, done, else, gone, past 5 above, again, ended, extra, often 6 afresh, bygone, lapsed, no more, to boot 7 at an end, elapsed, expired, settled, surplus 8 finished, in excess, once more, too great 9 completed, concluded, excessive, remaining 10 additional, all through, in addition, passed away, repeatedly, terminated 11 a second time, superfluous

overabundance 4 glut 6 excess 7 surfeit, surplus 8 plethora 9 abundance, profusion 10 oversupply 11 superfluity 14 superabundance 15 super-

saturation 21 embarrassment of riches
French: 19 embarras de richesses

over again 4 anew 5 again 7 all over 8 once more 9 once again

overall 5 total 6 entire 7 general 8 complete, long-term, sweeping 9 extensive, long-range, panoramic 10 exhaustive, widespread 12 all-embracing, all-inclusive 13 comprehensive, thoroughgoing

over-and-above 5 added, extra 7 added on, besides 10 additional, in addition 13 supplementary

overawe 6 dazzle 9 overpower, overwhelm 10 intimidate

overbalance 5 upset 6 topple 8 outweigh

overbearing 5 cocky 6 lordly, snooty 7 haughty, high-hat, pompous, stuck-up 8 arrogant, despotic, egoistic 9 conceited, imperious, know-it-all 10 autocratic, disdainful, egoistical, high-handed, tyrannical 11 dictatorial, domineering, egotistical 13 high-and-mighty, self-assertive, self-important

overburden 3 tax 4 load, task, tire 5 whelm 7 exhaust, wear out 8 encumber, overwork, surcharge 9 overwhelm

overcast 4 dark, dull, gray, hazy 5 foggy, misty, murky 6 cloudy, dreary, gloomy, leaden 7 sunless 8 lowering 11 overclouded, threatening

overcharge 3 gyp, pad 4 rook, skin, soak 5 bleed, cheat, gouge, stick, sting, usury 6 extort, fleece 7 exploit 10 exaggerate

overcoat 3 mac 5 parka 6 duster, poncho, raglan, tabard, ulster 7 oilskin, paletot, topcoat 8 burberry, mackinaw 9 greatcoat, inverness, pea jacket 10 mackintosh, trenchcoat 12 chesterfield, Prince Albert

Overcoat, The
author: 12 Nikolai Gogol
character: 9 Petrovich 26 A Certain Important Personage 28 Akakii Akakiievich Bashmachkin

overcome 4 beat, best, lick 5 crush, quell 6 defeat, master, subdue 7 conquer, put down, survive, win over 8 suppress, surmount, vanquish 9 overpower, overthrow, overwhelm, transcend 11 prevail over,

triumph over 14 get the better of

overconfident 5 brash 6 cheeky 8 arrogant, cocksure, egoistic, immodest, impudent 9 conceited 10 egoistical 11 egotistical, self-assured 12 presumptuous

overcrowd 3 jam 4 cram, fill, pack 5 stuff 7 congest

overcrowded 6 filled, jammed, packed 7 crammed, stuffed 9 congested, jampacked

overdecorated 5 gaudy, showy 6 flashy, garish 9 unsightly 12 ostentatious

overdelicacy 11 genteelness, prudishness 12 priggishness 14 overrefinement

overdo 4 gild 6 expand 7 amplify, ham it up, magnify, overact 8 overplay 9 embroider, overstate 10 do to excess, exaggerate 11 carry too far, hyperbolize 12 lay it on thick 13 stretch a point

overdue 4 late, slow 5 tardy 7 belated, delayed, past due 8 dilatory 10 behindhand, behind time, unpunctual 11 long delayed

overdue debt 7 arrears 10 balance due 18 balance outstanding

overflow 4 glut 5 flood 6 excess 7 run over, surplus 8 flow over, inundate, plethora, slop over 9 overspill, profusion 10 overspread, oversupply 11 copiousness, superfluity 13 overabundance 14 superabundance

overflowing 4 full 5 flush 7 replete, swamped 8 abundant, flooding 9 abounding, inundated 11 running over

overgarment 4 cape, coat, robe 5 cloak, habit, parka, shawl, smock 6 blazer, blouse, duster, jacket, kimono, mantle, poncho 7 sweater, topcoat, wrapper 8 cardigan, raincoat 9 gaberdine, housecoat

overgrown 4 rank 5 giant 7 blown-up 8 colossal, enlarged, forested, gigantic 9 luxuriant, oversized

overhang 3 jut 4 eave 5 bulge, drape, eaves, jetty 6 beetle, impend, sadden, shelve 7 project, suspend 8 protrude, threaten 9 projection

overhaul 4 beat, pass 5 catch 6 revamp 7 rebuild, remodel, restore, service 8 overtake, renovate 11 catch up with, recondition, reconstruct

overhead 3 nut **4** atop, roof
5 above, aloft, on top, upper
6 upward **7** ceiling, topmost,
up above **8** superior **9** overly-
ing, uppermost
11 overhanging

overindulge 4 baby **5** spoil,
stuff **6** overdo, pamper, pig
out **7** carouse, overeat **9** dissipate **11** mollycoddle

overjoyed 6 elated, joyous
8 ecstatic, euphoric, exultant,
jubilant, thrilled **9** delighted,
enchanted, exuberant, gratified **10** enraptured, enthralled
11 carried away, tickled pink,
transported **12** happy as a lark

overlay 4 coat **5** cover, layer
6 carpet, veneer **7** blanket,
coating **8** covering
11 superimpose

overload 3 tax **4** glut **5** flood,
whelm **6** deluge, excess
7 burnout, surfeit **8** encumber
9 innundate, surcharge

overlook 4 miss, omit, skip
6 excuse, forget, give on, ignore, pass up, slight, survey,
wink at **7** blink at, command,
forgive, let ride, neglect
8 leave out, look over, pass
over, shrug off **9** disregard,
look out on **10** tower above
11 forget about, have a view
of, leave undone

overlord 4 czar, tsar **7** emperor, monarch **8** autocrat
12 supreme ruler **13** absolute
ruler

overly 3 too **4** very **6** highly,
unduly **7** acutely, too much
8 overmuch, severely, to a
fault, unfairly **9** extremely, intensely **10** needlessly **11** exceedingly, excessively
12 exorbitantly, immoderately,
inordinately, unreasonably
18 disproportionately

overly trusting 5 naive **8** gullible **9** credulous
12 unsuspicious

overmodest 3 coy **4** prim
7 prudish **8** priggish
11 puritanical

overmuch 3 too **6** excess
7 surplus **8** plethora
9 profusion

overpass 4 span **6** bridge
9 crossover

overpower 4 beat, best, move,
sway **5** crush, quell, worst
6 defeat, master, subdue
7 conquer **8** overcome, vanquish **9** influence, overwhelm

overpowering 6 mighty,
strong **8** crushing **10** astounding **12** overwhelming

overpraise 4 line **7** blarney,
fawning **8** flattery
11 fulsomeness

overpriced 6 costly **7** too
high **9** expensive **10** exorbitant

overproud 4 vain **8** arrogant,
egoistic **9** conceited **10** egoistical **11** egotistical, swell-
headed **13** self-important

overrate 9 overprize, over-
value **10** overesteem, overpraise **12** overestimate
13 make too much of

overrefined 7 genteel, prudish **8** priggish **12** overdelicate

override 5 crush, quash **7** reverse **8** set aside **10** commission **11** countermand

overrule 4 deny, veto **5** annul,
eject, repel, waive **6** cancel,
refuse, reject, revoke **7** dismiss, nullify, outvote **8** disallow, outweigh, override,
overturn, preclude, set aside,
throw out **9** repudiate **10** invalidate **11** countermand

overrun 4 loot, raid, sack
5 choke **6** deluge, engulf, infest, invade **7** despoil, pillage,
plunder, surplus **8** inundate,
overgrow, pour in on, rove
over **9** overwhelm, surge over,
swarm over

overseas, oversea 5 alien
6 abroad, exotic **7** foreign
8 external **11** ultramarine
12 transoceanic **14** in foreign
lands

oversee 3 run **4** boss, rule
5 guide, pilot, see to, steer,
watch **6** direct, govern, handle, manage **7** carry on, command **8** attend to, overlook,
regulate **9** supervise **10** administer **11** keep an eye on, preside over, superintend **12** have
charge of

overseeing 7 bossing, guiding,
running **8** guidance, handling,
managing **10** leadership, management **11** attending to, supervising, supervision
13 administering **14** administrating, administration, superintending **15** superintendence

overseer 4 boss, head **5** chief
7 captain, foreman, manager
8 director, governor **10** supervisor, taskmaster **11** slave
driver **13** administrator
14 superintendent

overshadow 3 fog **4** hide,
mask, veil **5** cover, dwarf,
shade **6** darken, screen,
shroud **7** conceal, eclipse,
obscure **8** outshine
9 tower over

overshadowing 7 eclipse,
masking, shading, veiling
8 cloaking **9** darkening, eclipsing, obscuring **10** concealing,
surpassing **11** concealment, obscuration **12** towering over

overshoe 3 gum **4** boot **6** arctic, gaiter, galosh, patten, rubber **7** galoshe

overshoot 4 pass **6** exceed, go
over **8** go beyond

oversight 6 laxity, slight
7 blunder, mistake, neglect
8 omission **9** disregard **10** negligence **11** inattention
12 carelessness, heedlessness,
inadvertence **13** careless error
14 neglectfulness
15 thoughtlessness

oversized 4 huge, vast **7** immense, mammoth **8** colossal,
enormous, gigantic **10** monumental **14** Brobdingnagian

overspending 12 extravagance,
throwing away

overspread 3 fog **4** coat, fill,
pave **5** bathe, cloud, cover,
paint, plate, smear **6** clothe,
infest **7** blanket, diffuse, overlay, overrun, pervade, suffuse
8 disperse **9** whitewash

overstate 6 overdo, play up
7 enlarge, inflate, lay it on,
magnify, stretch, touch up
8 increase, overdraw, oversell
9 embellish, embroider, enlarge on, overpaint **10** exaggerate, overstress **15** spread it
on thick

overstep 6 exceed **7** violate
10 transgress

oversupply 4 glut **6** excess
7 surfeit, surplus, too much
8 plethora **11** undue amount
13 overabundance
14 superabundance

overt 4 open **5** plain **6** public
7 evident, obvious, visible
8 apparent, manifest, palpable,
revealed **10** easily seen, noticeable, observable, ostensible **11** perceivable, perceptible,
unconcealed, undisguised

overtake 4 go by, pass
5 catch, reach **6** befall, gain
on **7** run down **8** approach,
overhaul **11** catch up with

overtax 4 tire **5** abuse, hoist
6 burden, exceed, strain,
stress **7** exhaust **8** overload,
overwork **9** misemploy
10 overburden

over the hill 3 old **4** aged
5 aging **7** elderly **11** past the
peak **13** past one's prime

overthrow 4 undo **5** crush
6 defeat, mutiny, topple

7 abolish, undoing **8** downfall, overcome, overturn, toppling **9** abolition, bring down, overpower, rebellion **10** do away with, revolution

overtire 3 fag **4** bush, do in, poop **5** drain **7** exhaust, fatigue, wear out **8** enervate

overtone 3 hue **4** hint **5** drift **8** coloring, innuendo **10** intimation, suggestion **11** connotation, implication, insinuation

overtrustful 8 gullible **9** credulous **12** unsuspecting, unsuspicious **13** unquestioning

overture 3 bid **6** motion, signal, tender **7** advance, gesture, preface, prelude **8** approach, foreword, offering, preamble, prologue, proposal **9** beginning **10** invitation, suggestion **11** opening move, proposition **12** introduction

overturn 4 beat, oust **5** crush, upend, upset **6** defeat, depose, thrash, topple **7** capsize, conquer, turn out **8** overcome, push over, vanquish **9** knock down, knock over, overpower, overthrow, overwhelm **14** turn topsy-turvy, turn upside down

overturning
French: **14** bouleversement

overweening 5 bossy, cocky, pushy **6** brassy **7** haughty, pompous **8** arrogant, egoistic **9** bigheaded, imperious **10** disdainful, egoistical, highhanded, immoderate **11** domineering, egotistical, overbearing, patronizing **12** presumptuous **13** high-and-mighty, overconfident, self-important

overweight 3 fat **5** dumpy, fatty, gross, hefty, obese, piggy, plump, pudgy, stout, tubby **6** chubby, chunky, fleshy, portly, rotund **7** fattish, well-fed **8** roly-poly **9** corpulent **10** potbellied, well-padded **11** beer-bellied, overstuffed **15** well-upholstered

overwhelm 4 beat, bury **5** crush, quash, quell, swamp **6** defeat, engulf **7** conquer, overrun, stagger **8** bowl over, confound, inundate, overcome, vanquish **9** devastate, overpower, overthrow, subjugate

overwhelming 8 crushing **10** staggering **11** astonishing, devastating **12** overpowering

overwork 3 tax **4** task, tire, toil **5** labor **6** burden, strain **7** exhaust, overtax, wear out **9** misemploy **10** overburden

overwrought 4 wild **5** riled **6** touchy, uneasy **7** excited, nervous, ruffled **8** agitated, frenzied, inflamed, wild-eyed, worked up **9** perturbed, wrought up **10** distracted, high-strung **11** carried away, overexcited

Ovid
author of: **6** Amores **7** Tristia **8** Heroides **11** Ars Amatoria **12** The Art of Love **13** Metamorphoses

ovule 3 egg, nit **4** germ, ovum **6** embryo **7** seedlet

ovum 3 egg **4** cell, germ, seed **5** spore **6** gamete **8** oosphere

owe 8 be in debt **11** be obligated **12** be beholden to, be indebted to

owed 3 due **5** owing **6** unpaid **9** in arrears **11** outstanding

Owen Marshall, Counselor at Law
character: **11** Jess Brandon **12** Frieda Krause **15** Melissa Marshall
cast: **9** Lee Majors **10** Arthur Hill **11** Joan Darling **17** Christine Matchett

owing 3 due **4** owed **6** unpaid **9** in arrears **11** outstanding

own 4 avow, have, hold, keep, tell **5** admit, allow, grant, yield **6** assent, concur, retain **7** concede, possess, private **8** disclose, maintain, personal **9** acquiesce, confess to, consent to, recognize **10** individual, particular **11** acknowledge

owner 6 holder, master **7** partner **8** landlady, landlord, mistress **9** copartner, landowner, possessor **10** landholder, proprietor **11** householder, titleholder **12** proprietress

own up to 5 admit **6** accept **7** confess **8** blurt out **9** recognize **11** acknowledge **14** come clean about

ox 3 oaf **4** bull, clod, musk, urus, zebu **5** aiver, beast, bison, gayal, steer **6** auroch, bantin, bovine **7** banteng, buffalo **10** clodhopper
Cambodian: **7** Kouprey, Kouproh
Celebesian: **3** goa, noa **4** anoa
extinct: **4** urus **7** aurochs
family: **7** bovidae
genus: **3** bos
horned: **4** reem
hornless: **4** moil
Indian: **4** gaur
Paul Bunyan's: **4** Babe
  color: **4** blue

stall: **4** crib
team: **4** yoke
Tibetan: **3** yak
wild: **3** ure **4** anoa
young: **4** stot **5** stirk

Ox-Bow Incident, The
author: **21** Walter Van Tilburg Clark
character: **5** Canby, Croft **6** Davies, Gerald, Martin, Tetley **9** Gil Carter
director: **14** William Wellman
cast: **10** Henry Fonda **11** Dana Andrews **12** Anthony Quinn **13** William Blythe **14** Mary Beth Hughes

oxen
group of: **4** yoke

oxide 8 compound
afterburn: **4** calx
calcium: **4** calx, lime
cobalt: **6** zaffer, zaffre
element: **6** oxygen
iron: **4** rust **8** hematite, limonite **9** colcothar, magnetite
make by heat: **7** calcine
sodium: **4** soda
zinc: **6** cadmia

oxidize 4 burn, char, rust **7** corrode

Oxyderces
epithet of: **6** Athena
means: **10** bright-eyed

oxygen
chemical symbol: **1** O

Oxylus
origin: **8** Aetolian
punishment: **5** exile
chosen leader of: **10** Heraclidae
led invasion of: **12** Peloponnesus

oyez 4 hear **6** attend
cry used by: **10** court crier
preceded: **12** proclamation

Ozark Jubilee
host: **8** Red Foley **10** Webb Pierce
theme: **12** Sugarfoot Rag

Ozark State
nickname of: **8** Missouri

Ozick, Cynthia
author of: **10** Levitation **17** The Cannibal Galaxy **21** The Messiah of Stockholm

Ozzie and Harriet, The Adventures of
cast: **11** David Nelson, Ozzie Nelson, Ricky (Eric) Nelson **13** Harriet Nelson

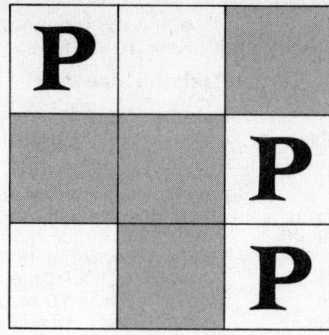

pa **3** dad, paw, pop **4** papa
5 daddy **6** father
mate: 2 ma

pace 4 clip, flow, gait, rate,
step, walk **5** amble, speed,
tread **6** motion, stride, stroll
7 saunter **8** momentum, slow
gait, velocity

**Pacelli, Eugenio Maria Giu-
seppe Giovanni 11** Pope
Pius XII

pachyderm 5 hippo, rhino
8 elephant, ungulate **10** rhinoceros **12** hippopotamus
characteristic: 4 tusk **5** ivory,
trunk **12** thick-skinned
prehistoric: 7 mammoth
8 mastodon

pachydermatous 4 hard
5 horny, tough **7** callous
8 callused, hardened, leathery
12 thick-skinned **13** elephant-
hided

pacific 4 calm **5** quiet, still
6 gentle, placid, serene,
smooth **7** halcyon, restful
8 dovelike, peaceful, tranquil
9 pacifying, peaceable, reposeful, unruffled **10** harmonious,
untroubled **11** inoffensive, undisturbed **12** conciliatory

pacification 8 soothing **11** appeasement, peacemaking
12 conciliation, nonagression
14 reconciliation

pacify 4 calm **5** allay, quiet
6 soothe **7** appease, assuage,
compose, mollify, placate
9 reconcile **10** conciliate,
propitiate

Pacino, Al
real name: 13 Alberto Pacino
born: 9 New York NY
roles: 7 Serpico **8** Scarface
12 Author Author, The Godfather **15** Dog Day Afternoon, Michael Corleone
16 And Justice for All

pack 3 box, jam, kit, lot, mob,

set, tie **4** bevy, bind, cram,
fill, heap, herd, load, mass
5 batch, bunch, clump, covey,
crowd, drove, flock, group,
horde, stuff, swarm, truss
6 bundle, gaggle, gather,
packet, parcel, passel, throng
7 cluster, package **8** assemble
9 container, multitude **10** assortment, collection, miscellany **12** accumulation

package 3 box, kit **4** case,
pack, wrap **6** bundle, carton,
encase, packet, parcel, wrap
up **9** container, wrappings

packed 4 full **6** filled, jammed,
loaded, massed, rammed,
wedged **7** crammed, crowded,
crushed, pressed, stuffed
8 overfull, squeezed **10** sandwiched **11** overcrowded

packet 3 bag, box **4** bale, pack,
roll **5** pouch, sheaf **6** bundle,
parcel, quiver **7** package

pack closely 4 cram, pack
5 press, stuff **7** compact
8 compress

pact 4 bond **6** treaty **7** compact **8** alliance, contract, covenant **9** agreement, concordat
10 convention **11** concordance **13** understanding

pad 3 mat **4** fill **5** stuff **6** blow
up, fatten, tablet **7** bolster,
cushion, inflate, protect, puff
out **8** mattress, notebook
9 upholster **10** cushioning,
stretch out

padding 6 filler, lining **7** filling,
packing, surfeit, surplus, wad-
ding **8** stuffing, verbiage,
wrapping **9** prolixity, verbosity,
wordiness **10** redundancy
11 verboseness **12** extravagance **14** superabundance

**Paderewski, Ignace (Ignacy
Jan)**
born: 6 Poland **9** Kurilowka
composer of: 5 Manru
9 Minuet in G

pad out 5 add to **6** expand, extend **7** amplify, augment, enlarge, stretch **8** elongate,
increase, lengthen

padre 6 cleric, father, priest
8 chaplain **9** clergyman

paean 6 anthem, eulogy **7** hosanna **9** laudation, panegyric
10 hallelujah **11** acclamation
12 hymn of praise
form: 4 hymn, song
characteristic: 6 joyful
12 thanksgiving

Paeon
form: 3 god
position: 9 physician
served gods of: 7 Olympia
corresponds to: 6 Apollo

Paeonia
epithet of: 6 Athena
means: 6 healer

Paezan
language family: 13 Macro-
Chibchan
group: 4 Paez **5** Choco
6 Warrau **8** Colorado

pagan 7 atheist, heathen, infidel **8** idolator **9** barbarian
10 heathenish, idolatrous,
polytheist, unbeliever **11** nonbeliever **12** polytheistic

Paganini, Niccolo
born: 5 Genoa, Italy
played: 6 violin
composer of: 19 The Carnival of Venice

page 3 boy, lad **4** beep, call,
girl, leaf **5** folio, groom, sheet,
youth **6** knight, number, summon **7** callboy, contact **8** announce **9** attendant,
messenger **10** apprentice,
manservant
blank: 7 flyleaf
left-hand: 5 verso
right-hand: 5 recto

Page, Geraldine
born: 12 Kirksville MO
husband: 7 Rip Torn

roles: **5** Hondo **9** Interiors
11 Pete-n-Tillie **14** Summer
and Smoke **16** A Trip to
Bountiful (Oscar), Sweet
Bird of Youth

Page and Mistress Page
characters in: **22** The Merry
Wives of Windsor
author: **11** Shakespeare

pageant 4 pomp, rite, show
6 parade, ritual **7** display
8 ceremony **9** spectacle **10** exhibition, procession
12 extravaganza

pageantry 4 pomp, rite, show
5 drama, flair **6** ritual, splash
7 display, glitter, pageant
8 ceremony, grandeur, splendor **9** showiness, spectacle,
theatrics **10** flashiness **11** ostentation **12** extravagance,
magnificence

Paget, James
field: **7** surgery **8** medicine
nationality: **7** British
founder of: **9** pathology

Pagliacci, I
also: **9** The Clowns
opera by: **11** Leoncavallo
character: **5** Canio, Nedda,
Tonio **6** Silvio

Pagnol, Marcel
author of: **5** Cesar, Fanny
6 Marius, Topaze

Pago Pago
capital of: **13** American
Samoa

Paige, Leroy
nickname: **7** Satchel
sport: **8** baseball
position: **7** pitcher

pain 3 vex, woe **4** ache, gall,
hell, hurt, pang, rile **5** agony,
annoy, chafe, grief, pinch,
pique, smart, sting, throb,
worry **6** aching, grieve, harass,
misery, ordeal, sadden, sorrow, stitch, twinge **7** agonize,
anguish, disturb, hurting, malaise, sadness, torment, torture, trouble **8** distress,
smarting, soreness **9** displease,
heartache, suffering **10** affliction, discomfort, exasperate,
heartbreak **11** unhappiness
12 wretchedness

Paine, Thomas
author of: **9** The Crisis
11 Common Sense **14** The
Rights of Man

painful 3 sad **4** dire **5** sharp
6 aching, dismal, dreary,
trying **7** arduous, hurtful, racking **8** grievous, grueling, pathetic, piercing, smarting,
stinging, very sore **9** agonizing, difficult, sorrowful, throbbing, torturous **10** afflictive,

disturbing, lamentable, unpleasant **11** disquieting, distasteful, distressful, distressing
12 disagreeable, excruciating

pain in the neck 4 bane
6 bother **7** torment **8** headache, nuisance **9** annoyance
10 affliction

painstaking 5 fussy **7** careful,
earnest, finicky, precise **8** diligent, exacting, thorough **9** assiduous, energetic, strenuous
10 meticulous, scrupulous
11 industrious, persevering,
punctilious **13** conscientious,
thoroughgoing

paint 4 coat, daub, draw, limn,
swab, tint **5** adorn, brush,
color, cover, horse, rouge,
shade, stain **6** depict, enamel,
makeup, opaque, sketch **7** pigment, portray, stipple, touch
up **8** cosmetic, decorate, describe, variegate **9** delineate,
represent

Painted Bird, The
author: **13** Jerzy Kosinski

painter 6 artist, drawer
8 sketcher **9** old master **10** delineator **11** illustrator, landscapist, miniaturist
13 watercolorist

Painter, Painter's Easel
constellation of: **6** Pictor

painting 3 art, oil **5** draft, mural, piece **6** canvas, design,
tablet **7** cartoon, daubing,
drawing, graphic, picture, tableau **8** panorama, portrait,
seascape **9** depiction, landscape, still life **10** cerography,
watercolor **11** perspective
12 illustration
colloidal: **7** tempera
method: **9** encaustic
on plaster: **5** secco **6** fresco
one-color: **8** monotint
10 monochrome
opaque: **7** gouache
religious: **5** Pieta
style: **5** genre
tool: **5** brush, easel, knife
6 canvas, roller, sponge
7 palette **8** spraygun

pair 3 duo **4** dyad, mate, span,
team, yoke **5** brace, match,
unite **6** couple **7** combine,
doublet, match up, pair off,
twosome

pair off 10 go two by two
11 form couples

Paiute
language family:
10 Shoshonean
tribe: **12** Mono-Paviosto,
Snake Indians **13** Digger Indians **14** Northern Paiute,
Southern Paiute
location: **4** Utah **5** Idaho

6 Nevada, Oregon **7** Arizona **10** California

Pakistan *see box*

Pakula, Alan
director of: **19** All the President's Men

pal 4 chum, mate, pard
5 buddy, crony **6** cohort,
friend **7** comrade, partner
8 alter ego, intimate, sidekick
9 associate, colleague, companion, confidant **10** accomplice,
bosom buddy **13** boon
companion

palace 5 villa **6** castle **7** chateau, mansion **8** hacienda
French: **6** palais
Italian: **7** palazzo

Palaeoscincus
type: **8** dinosaur
10 ornithopod
location: **12** North America
period: **10** Cretaceous

palais 6 palace **17** municipal
building **18** government
building

Palamedes
lieutenant of: **9** Agamemnon

pal around 7 consort, hang
out **9** associate, be friends, run
around **10** fraternize

palatable 5 tasty **6** savory
8 pleasant **9** agreeable, toothsome **10** appetizing

palatial 4 posh, rich **5** grand,
noble, plush, regal, ritzy,
showy **6** swanky **7** elegant, opulent, stately **8** imposing,
splendid **9** grandiose, luxurious, sumptuous **10** monumental **11** magnificent

palaver 3 gab **4** chat, talk
5 prate **6** confer, gossip, parley **7** consult, discuss, prattle
8 chitchat, idle talk **10** chew
the fat, chew the rag, conference, discussion

palazzo 6 palace

pale 3 pen, wan **4** fold, post
5 ashen, close, light, pasty,
stake, white **6** anemic, blanch,
paling, pallid, picket, sallow,
whiten **7** closure, confine,
deathly, ghastly, upright, whitish **8** bleached, palisade
9 bloodless, colorless, deathlike, enclosure, ghostlike
10 ash-colored, cadaverous,
light-toned

Pale Horse, Pale Rider
author: **19** Katherine Anne
Porter

paleness 6 pallor **7** wanness
8 dullness **9** whiteness
13 colorlessness

Pakistan
name means: 13 Land of the Holy, Land of the Pure
capital: 9 Islamabad
largest city: 7 Karachi
others: 3 Dir, Sui **4** Mari, Sidi **5** Dacca, Qasim, Ralat **6** Chalna, Khulna, Lahore, Multan, Quetta **7** Larkana, Sialkot **8** Jamalpur, Lyallpur, Peshawar, Sargodha **9** Hyderabad **10** Gujranwala, Rawalpindi
school: 9 U of Punjab **10** U of Karachi **12** U of Hyderabad **16** Allama Iqbal Open U **22** Pakistan U of Agriculture **39** Pakistan Institute of International Affairs
division: 3 Dir **4** Sind, Swat **5** Hunza, Kalat **6** Bengal, Kharan, Punjab **7** Chitral **8** Khairpur, Peshawar **10** Bahawalpur, Waziristan **11** Baluchistan
  empire: **5** Gupta, Mogul **6** Kushan, Maurya **7** British, Magadha
  seceded state: **10** Bangladesh
monetary unit: 4 anna, pice **5** paisa, rupee
weight: 4 seer, tola **5** maund
mountain: 3 Pab, Pub **4** Salt **6** Makran **7** Kirthar **8** Himalaya, Safed Koh, Sulaiman **9** Hindu Kush, Karakoram **11** Makran Coast **13** Central Makran **14** Takht-i-Sulaiman
highest point: 9 Tirich Mir **12** Godwin Austin
river: 3 Nal **4** Bado, Beas, Ravi, Swat, Zhob **5** Dasht, Indus, Kabul **6** Chenab, Ganges, Jamuna, Jhelum, Kundar, Porali, Sutlej **7** Jamunna
sea: 7 Arabian
physical feature:
  bay: **8** Soymiani
  canal: **4** Nara **5** Rohri
  cape: **5** Fasta, Jaddi **6** Jiwani
  delta: **6** Ganges **11** Char-Manpura
  desert: **4** Sind, Thal, Thar
  mountain pass: **5** Bolan **6** Khyber
  plateau: **11** Baluchistan
  valley: **5** Kohat
people: 5 Sindi, Wazir **6** Afridi, Bengal, Mahsud, Pathan, Sindhi **7** Baluchi, Brahuis, Puktuns, Punjabi, Sherani **8** Khattack, Pushtuns, Shinwari, Yusefazi **11** Mohammedzai
  leader: **6** Jinnah **7** Aly Khan **8** Ayub Khan, Zia Ul-Haq **9** Ali Bhutto, Yahya Khan **13** Benazir Bhutto, Mujibur Rahman **15** Mahmud of Ghaznbi
  poet: **5** Igbal, Iqbal
language: 4 Urdu **6** Pushtu, Sindhi **7** Baluchi, Bengali, English, Punjabi
religion: 5 Hindu, Islam **8** Buddhism **12** Christianity
place:
  dam: **6** Mangla **7** Tarbela
  gardens: **8** Shalamar
  mosque: **8** Badshahi
  tomb: **15** Emperor Jahangir
feature:
  clothing: **5** kurta, pugri, qamis **6** jinnah **7** dupatta, shalwar **8** sherwani **9** churidars
food:
  bread: **8** chappati
  dish: **5** kebab, pilaf **6** qormas, salans, sautes **10** vermicelli
  yogurt: **4** dahi

paleontology
  study of: 18 correlation of parts
  founder: 13 Georges Cuvier

Palermo
  capital of: 6 Sicily

Pales
  origin: 5 Roman
  protector of: 6 flocks **9** shepherds
  festival: 7 Parilia

Palestine *see* **6** Israel

Palestrina, Giovanni Pierluigi da
  born: 5 Italy **10** Palestrina
  composer of: 11 Stabat Mater **18** Missa Papae Marcelli

Paley, Grace
  author of: 26 The Little Disturbances of Man **30** Enormous Changes at the Last Minute

Palici
  origin: 5 Roman
  form: 4 gods **5** twins
  gods of: 14 sulphur springs

Palilicium *see* **6** Hyades

paling 4 pale, rail **5** fence, stake **6** picket

Palinurus
  steersman of: 6 Aeneas

palisade 5 close, fence **7** bulwark, rampart **8** stockade **9** enclosure

palisades 4 crag **5** ledge **6** bluffs, cliffs **10** escarpment, promontory

pall 4 cloy, haze, sate **5** gloom, weary **6** shadow, sicken **7** dimness, satiate **8** darkness **10** become dull, be tiresome, depression, desolation, melancholy, moroseness, oppression

Palladio, Andrea
  real name: 26 Andrea di Pietro della Gondola
  architect of: 12 Villa Rotunda (Vicenza Italy) **14** Teatro Olimpico (Vicenza) **19** Church of Il Redentore (Venice) **26** Church of San Giorgio Maggiore (Venice)
  style: 9 Palladian

Pallas *see* **6** Athena

Pallas Athena *see* **6** Athena

pallet 3 bed, cot **4** bunk, tick **5** berth **8** mattress, platform

palliate 4 calm, curb, ease, hush, lull, tame **5** abate, allay, check, quiet, sooth, still **6** lessen, modify, reduce, soften, subdue, temper **7** assuage, comfort, cushion, lighten, relieve **8** decrease, diminish, minimize, mitigate, moderate **9** alleviate **10** ameliorate

palliative 4 balm **6** solace **7** anodyne, comfort **10** comforting

pallid 3 wan **4** ashy, blah, dull, pale **5** ashen, bland, pasty, vapid, waxen **6** boring, chalky, peaked, sallow **7** ghostly, humdrum, insipid, tedious **8** blanched, lifeless **9** bloodless, colorless **10** monotonous **13** anemic looking, unimaginative, uninteresting

pallor 7 wanness **8** paleness

9 pastiness, whiteness
10 ashen color, pallidness
11 ghostliness 13 bloodlessness, colorlessness

palm *see box*

Palm Beach Story, The
director: 14 Preston Sturges
cast: 9 Mary Astor 10 Joel
McCrea, Rudy Vallee
15 William Demarest
16 Claudette Colbert

Palmer, Arnold
sport: 4 golf
noted for: 10 Arnie's Army

Palmer, Lilli
real name: 17 Lillie Marie
(Maria Lilli) Peiser
born: 5 Posen 7 Germany
husband: 11 Rex Harrison
14 Carlos Thompson
roles: 11 Body and Soul
autobiography: 22 Change
Lobsters and Dance

Palmer, Vera Jane
real name of: 14 Jayne
Mansfield

Palmetto State
nickname of: 13 South
Carolina

Palm Sunday
author: 12 Kurt Vonnegut

palmy 4 rosy 5 balmy, sunny
6 golden 7 booming, halcyon
8 blooming, pleasant, thriving
9 agreeable, bounteous, congenial 10 prosperous, successful 11 flourishing,
pleasurable

Palmyra
Biblical name: 6 Tadmor

palpable 5 clear, plain 7 evident, obvious, tactile, visible
8 apparent, definite, distinct,
feelable, manifest, tangible
9 touchable 10 noticeable
11 discernible, perceivable,
perceptible 12 recognizable,
unmistakable

palpitate 4 beat 5 pound,
shake, throb 6 quaver, quiver,
shiver 7 flutter, tremble, vibrate 9 go pit-a-pat

palsied 7 quaking, shaking,
spastic 9 trembling

palsy-walsy 5 close, palsy,
thick 6 chummy 8 friendly, intimate 10 buddy-buddy
14 thick as thieves

paltriness 10 triviality 12 unimportance 14 insignificance
18 inconsequentiality

paltry 4 poor, puny 5 petty,
sorry 6 measly, shabby
7 scrubby, trivial 8 inferior,
picayune, piddling, trifling,
wretched 11 unimportant
13 insignificant, of little
value 14 inconsiderable
15 inconsequential

Pama-Nyungan
language spoken by:
10 aborigines
spoken in: 9 Australia

Pamela
author: 16 Samuel
Richardson
character: 3 Mr B 9 Mrs Jervis, Mrs Jewkes 10 Lady
Davers 13 Pamela Andrews

pamper 5 humor, spoil 6 coddle, cosset 7 cater to, indulge
8 give in to 11 mollycoddle

pampered 7 coddled, humored 8 indulged 9 catered-to,
cosseted

pamphlet 5 tract 6 folder
7 booklet, leaflet 8 brochure,
bulletin, circular 9 monograph,
throwaway

pan 3 boo, map, mug, pot
4 face, hiss 6 kisser 8 ridicule,
saucepot 9 criticize

Pan
also: 7 Sinoeis
origin: 5 Greek
form combined: 3 man
4 goat
god of: 6 flocks 7 forests
8 pastures 9 shepherds
father: 4 Zeus 6 Hermes
loved: 4 Echo 5 Pitys
6 Syrinx
invented: 5 pipes 6 syrinx
corresponds to: 6 Faunus

panacea 6 elixir 7 cure-all,
nostrum 13 universal cure

panache 4 dash, tuft 5 flair,
plume, style, verve
11 flamboyance

Panama *see box*

Panama City
capital of: 6 Panama

pancake 4 blin 5 blini, crepe,
kisra, latke, lefse 6 blintz,
makeup 7 fritter, hotcake
8 flapjack, slapjack 11 griddlecake 12 silver dollar
day: 13 Shrove Tuesday

---

palm
varieties: 3 Fan, Ita, Key, Nut, Oil, Wax 4 Cane, Date,
Doom, Doub, Doum, Fern, Hair, Hemp, King, Lady, Nipa,
Nypa, Rock, Sago, Step, Tala, Wine 5 Areca, Areng, Assai, Betel, Black, Bread, Broom, Curly, Grass, Honey, Inaga, Ivory, Jelly, Latan, Manac, Nikau, Peach, Queen,
Royal, Snake, Spine, Sugar, Syrup, Toddy, Yatay, Zombi
6 Bamboo, Barbel, Barrel, Bottle, Cherry, Cohune, Coyoli,
Gebang, Gomuti, Gru-gru, Hesper, Kentia, Licuri, Manila,
Mazari, Needle, Nibung, Parlor, Pignut, Raffia, Rattan,
Ruffle, Sagisi, Sentry, Silver, Thatch, Thread, Yellow
7 Arikury, Cabbage, Calappa, Coconut, Coquito, Feather,
Fiji fan, Funeral, Jaggery, Leopard, Mexican, Moriche,
Overtop, Palmyra, Prickly, Spindle, Talipot, Weddell
8 Betel nut, Carnauba, Cucurite, Dwarf fan, Fishtail,
Good luck, Ivory-nut, Mangrove, Pandanus, Peaberry,
Princess, Roebelin, Umbrella, Wild date, Windmill
9 Alexander, Alexandra, Butterfly, Christmas, Desert fan,
Gippsland, Guadalupe, Hurricane, India date, Macarthur,
Ouricouri, Panama-hat, Petticoat, Piccabeen, Porcupine,
Pygmy date, Silver saw, Solitaire, Spiny-club, Traveler's
10 African oil, Black-fiber, Canary date, Chinese fan, Cuban belly, Cuban royal, Everglades, Franceschi, Saw cabbage, Sealing-wax, Thatch-leaf, Washington 11 American
oil, Chilean wine, European fan, Gingerbread, Mexican
blue, Morass royal, Senegal date, Slender lady, Woolly
butia 12 Caribee royal, Egyptian doum, Florida royal,
Miniature fan, Walking-stick 13 Australian fan, Australian ivy, Australian nut, Belmore sentry, Feather-duster,
Florida silver, Florida thatch, Forster sentry, Golden
feather, Miniature date, San Jose hesper 14 Common
princess, East Indian wine, Puerto Rican hat, Tufted fishtail, Yellow princess 15 Burmese fishtail, Chinese fountain, Chinese windmill, Yellow butterfly 16 Hispaniolan
royal, Northern bangalow, Puerto Rican royal 17 Australian cabbage, Clustered fishtail, Mexican Washington, Piccabeen bangalow 18 South American royal

Panama
  capital/largest city: 10 Panama City
  others: 4 Daid **5** Ancon, Colon **6** Azuero, Balboa, Gamboa **8** Dos Bocas, Penonome, Santiago **9** Cristobal **10** Portobello
  division: 5 Cocle, Colon **6** Darien, Panama **7** Herrera **8** Chiriqui, Veraguas **9** Los Santos **12** Bocas del Toro
  measure: 7 celemin
  monetary unit: 4 cent **6** balboa **10** centesimos
  island: 5 Coiba, Pearl **6** Cebaco, Multas, Taboga **7** San Blas **10** Isla Del Rey **12** Bocas del Toro, Juan Gallegos **13** Barro Colorado
  lake: 5 Gatun
  mountain: 4 Baru, Maje **5** Chico, Gandi **6** Darien **7** Columan, San Blas, Veragua **8** Santiago, Tabasara **10** Costa Rican **14** Serrania de Sapo **15** Aspave Highlands **17** Cordillera Central
  highest point: 8 Chiriqui
  river: 5 Chepo, Sambu, Tuira **6** Bayano, Panugo **7** Chagres
  sea: 7 Pacific **9** Caribbean
  physical feature:
    bay: **5** Limon **6** Panama
    dam: **5** Gatun
    gulf: **6** Darien, Panama, Parita **7** Montijo, San Blas **8** Chiriqui **9** Mosquitos, San Miguel
    isthmus: **6** Darien, Panama **7** San Blas
    lagoon: **8** Chiriqui
    peninsula: **6** Azuero **8** Valjente
  people: 4 Cuna **5** Choco **6** Guaymi **7** mestizo
    canal builder: **7** Lesseps
    explorer: **6** Balboa **8** Bastidas, Columbus
    leader: **4** Royo **5** Arias **7** Noriega **8** Guerrero, Torrijos **9** Espriella **12** Simon Bolivar
    poet: **4** Miro **5** Korsi, Sinan
  language: 7 English, Spanish
  religion: 13 Roman Catholic
  place:
    church: **7** San Jose **15** Virgen del Carmen
    plaza: **13** Independencia
    ruins: **9** Old Panama
  feature:
    clothing: **7** montuno, pollera
    dance: **4** caja **7** pujador **9** tamborito
    tree: **4** yaya **5** maria, quira **6** alfaje, cativo
    US operation: **9** Just Cause
  food:
    meat: **6** tazajo
    soup: **8** sancocho

Pancks
  character in: 12 Little Dorrit
  author: 7 Dickens

pancreas
  produces: 7 insulin

Pandareus
  father: 6 Lycaon, Merops
  daughter: 5 Aedon **6** Merope **9** Cleothera
  wounded: 8 Menelaus
  stole: 9 golden dog
  turned to: 5 stone
  killed by: 8 Diomedes

Pandarus
  character in: 18 Troilus and Cressida, Troilus and Criseyde
  author: 7 Chaucer **11** Shakespeare

Pandarus
  son: 7 Alcanor
  companion of: 6 Aeneas

pandemic 4 rife **7** rampant **8** epidemic **10** prevailing, widespread **21** dangerously contagious

pandemonium 3 din **5** chaos **6** bedlam, clamor, hubbub, racket, rumpus, tumult, uproar **7** turmoil **8** disorder **9** commotion **10** hullabaloo **11** disturbance

Pandemos
  epithet of: 9 Aphrodite

pander, panderer 4 mack, pimp **5** cadet **7** hustler **8** procurer **9** maquereau, souteneur **12** flesh-peddler

Pandion the Younger
  king of: 6 Athens
  later reigned in: 6 Megara

Pandora
  form: 10 first woman
  created by: 10 Hephaestus
  presented to: 10 Epimetheus
  daughter: 6 Pyrrha
  given by gods: 3 box
    box contained: **4** hope **5** evils

Pandrosos
  position: 9 priestess
  first priestess of: 6 Athena
  father: 7 Cecrops
  mother: 8 Agraulos

panegyric 6 eulogy, homage, praise **7** tribute **8** citation, encomium, good word **9** extolment, laudation **10** compliment **11** testimonial **12** commendation

panegyrize 4 laud **5** extol **6** praise **8** eulogize

panel 4 jury, pane **5** board, group, piece **6** insert **7** divider **8** bulkhead **9** committee, partition **10** round table **11** compartment, expert group, select group **13** advisory group

pang 4 ache, pain **5** agony, pinch, smart, stick, sting, throb **6** stitch, twinge **7** anguish **8** distress **9** suffering **10** discomfort

Pangloss
  character in: 7 Candide
  author: 8 Voltaire

pang of conscience 5 demur, qualm **6** unease **7** remorse, scruple **9** misgiving **10** uneasiness **11** compunction

panhandle 3 beg, bum **5** cadge, mooch **6** hustle **7** solicit **9** importune

Panhandle State
  nickname of: 12 West Virginia

Panhellenius
  epithet of: 4 Zeus
  means: 14 god of all Greeks

panic 5 alarm, dread, go ape, scare **6** fright, horror, terror **7** anxiety **8** affright, hysteria **9** cold sweat, confusion, fall apart **10** go to pieces **11** nervousness, trepidation **12** apprehension, perturbation **13** consternation

panicky 6 scared **7** alarmed, anxious **9** terrified **10** frightened **13** panic-stricken, scared to death **14** terror-stricken

panic-stricken 6 afraid, scared **7** alarmed, anxious, fearful, panicky **9** terrified

13 scared to death 14 terror-stricken

Panjabi
language family: 12 Indo-European
branch: 11 Indo-Iranian
group: 5 Indic
spoken in: 5 (northern) India

Pankrits
language family: 12 Indo-European
branch: 11 Indo-Iranian
form of: 5 Indic
followed use of: 8 Sanskrit

pannier 3 bag 4 hoop 6 basket, dossel, pantry 7 corbeil, drapery 9 framework, overskirt
literally: 11 breadbasket

Panomphaeus see 4 Zeus

Panopeus
father: 6 Phocus
mother: 7 Asteria
twin brother: 6 Crisus

Panoptes
epithet of: 5 Argus
means: 7 all eyes

panorama 5 scene, vista 6 survey 7 diorama, picture, scenery, tableau 8 long view, overview, prospect 10 scenic view 11 perspective 12 bird's-eye view

panoramic 3 ide 7 overall 8 bird's-eye, extended, sweeping 9 extensive 10 far-ranging 11 far-reaching 12 all-embracing, all-inclusive 15 all-encompassing

pansy 5 Viola
varieties: 4 Wild 5 Field 6 Garden, Orchid 8 Japanese 9 Miniature 11 Monkey-faced 12 European wild

pant 4 blow, gasp, huff, puff 6 wheeze

pant after 4 seek 5 covet, crave 6 desire, pursue 7 hope for, long for, lust for, wish for 8 yearn for 9 hanker for, hunger for, lust after 11 thirst after, have a yen for 14 set one's heart on

Pantagruel see 22 Gargantua and Pantagruel

panther 3 cat 6 cougar 7 leopard

Panthous
priest of: 6 Apollo
counselor of: 5 Priam
father: 6 Othrys
son: 9 Euphorbus, Hyperenor, Polydamas

Pantomime Quiz
host: 10 Mike Stokey 15 Pat Harrington Jr

pantry 5 ambry, store 6 closet, galley, larder 7 butlery, buttery, pannier, spicery 8 cupboard, scullery

pants 5 jeans 6 denims, shorts, slacks 7 drawers, panties 8 breeches, britches, knickers, trousers 9 bluejeans, dungarees 10 underpants 11 undershorts 12 underdrawers

pantywaist 4 wimp 5 sissy, softy 7 crybaby, milksop 8 mama's boy, weakling 10 namby-pamby, sissy-pants, weak sister 11 Milquetoast, mollycoddle 13 sissy-britches

Panurge
character in: 22 Gargantua and Pantagruel
author: 8 Rabelais

Panza, Sancho
character in: 10 Don Quixote
author: 9 Cervantes

pap 3 rot 4 bosh, junk, mash, mush, pulp, tosh 5 gruel, paste 6 cereal, drivel, Pablum, trivia 7 rubbish, twaddle 8 soft food 10 balderdash, flapdoodle, triviality

papa 2 pa 3 dad, doc, paw, pop 5 daddy, poppy 6 father, priest 9 Hemingway
mate: 4 mama

Papa Bear
nickname of: 11 George Halas

Papago
language family: 5 Piman 10 Uto-Aztecan
location: 6 Mexico 7 Arizona
related to: 4 Pima

papal 9 apostolic, of the pope 10 pontifical

Papaleo, Anthony
real name of: 16 Anthony Franciosa

paper 4 bond, deed, news, opus, pulp, work 5 daily, draft, essay, stock, theme 6 record, report, tissue, weekly 7 article, gazette, journal, monthly, tabloid, writing 8 document, gift wrap 9 cardboard, chronicle, newspaper, newsprint, onionskin 10 instrument, manuscript, paperboard, periodical, stationery, typescript 11 certificate, composition, publication

Paper Chase, The
character: 10 James T Hart, Willis Bell 13 Asheley Brooks 14 Elizabeth Logan, Jonathan Brooks 15 Franklin Ford III 19 Thomas Craig Anderson 29 Professor Charles W Kingsfield Jr
cast: 10 James Keane 11 Robert Ginty 12 Deka

Beaudine, John Houseman 13 James Stephens, Jonathan Segal 14 Francine Tacker, Tom Fitzsimmons
subject: 9 law school
Kingsfield's specialty: 11 contract law

paper measure 4 ream 5 quire

Paper Moon
director: 16 Peter Bogdanovich
cast: 9 Ryan O'Neal 10 Tatum O'Neal 12 Madeline Kahn (Trixie Delight) 13 John Hillerman
Oscar for: 17 supporting actress (O'Neal)

Paphian see 9 Aphrodite

Paphos
also: 6 Paphus
father: 9 Pygmalion
mother: 7 Galatea

Paphus see 6 Paphos

Papua New Guinea
formerly: 16 British New Guinea
capital: 11 Port Moresby
town: 3 Thu, Lae 4 Ioma 6 Kikori, Madang
province of: 9 Indonesia
province: 9 West Irian
monetary unit: 4 kina
island: 6 Misima 10 New Britain
archipelago: 8 Bismarck
lake: 6 Murray
river: 3 Fly 4 Ramu
sea: 5 Coral 7 Solomon
strait: 6 Torres
people: 4 Hula, Kate 5 Kiwai, Kwoma 6 Banaro 7 Arapesh 10 Melanesian
language: 7 English

papyrus 4 pith, reed 5 paper, sedge 6 scroll 7 bulrush 8 document 10 manuscript
accordion pleated: 6 orihon
genus: 7 Cyperus
origin: 5 Egypt 9 Nile delta 10 Nile valley
use: 3 mat 4 rope, shoe, sail 5 paper

par 5 level, usual 6 normal, parity 7 average, balance, the norm 8 equality, evenness, identity, sameness, standard 9 stability 11 equilibrium, equivalency 12 equal footing 13 identicalness

parable 4 myth, tale 5 fable, story 6 homily, legend 8 alle-

gory, apologue, folk tale
9 folk story **12** morality tale

Paracelsus
  author: **14** Robert Browning

parade 4 line, pomp, show
5 array, march, strut, train,
vaunt **6** column, defile, flaunt,
review, string **7** caravan, cortege, display, show off
8 vaunting **9** cavalcade, flaunting, march past, motorcade,
pageantry, put on airs, spectacle **10** exposition, grandstand,
procession **11** progression
13 demonstration

paradigm 5 ideal, model **6** matrix, sample **7** example, paragon, pattern **8** exemplar,
original, standard **9** archetype,
criterion, prototype, yardstick

paradise 3 joy **4** Eden **5** bliss
6 heaven, utopia **7** delight, ecstasy, nirvana, rapture
8 pleasure **9** enjoyment, happiness, Shangri-la, transport
11 happy valley **12** Garden of
Eden, satisfaction **13** gratification, seventh heaven **15** Land
of Cockaigne

Paradise 5 Annwn **6** Annfwn

Paradise
  also: **9** Paradisio
  part three of: **12** Divine
    Comedy
  author: **14** Dante Alighieri

Paradise Lost
  author: **10** John Milton
  character: **3** Eve, God
    4 Adam **5** Satan **6** Christ
    7 Lucifer

Paradise of the Pacific
  nickname of: **6** Hawaii

Paradise Regained
  author: **10** John Milton

paradisiacal 7 elysian, sublime **8** blissful, empyreal, empyrean, ethereal, heavenly
9 celestial, unearthly
12 otherworldly

paradox 5 poser **6** enigma,
oddity, puzzle, riddle **7** anomaly **11** incongruity
13 inconsistency

paradoxical 9 ambiguous,
enigmatic, equivocal
13 contradictory

paragon 4 norm **5** ideal,
model **6** symbol **7** example,
pattern **8** exemplar, paradigm,
standard **9** archetype, criterion,
prototype, yardstick
10 apotheosis

Paraguay *see box*

parallel 4 akin, like, same,
twin **5** alike, equal, match
6 follow **7** abreast, analogy, be

alike, similar **8** analogue, likeness, relation **9** alongside,
analogous, corollary, duplicate **10** collateral, comparable,
comparison, concurrent, connection, equivalent, similarity
11 coextensive, coincidence,
comparative, compare with,
correlation, correlative, counterpart, equidistant, resemblance **12** correspond to
13 corresponding
14 correspondence

parallelism 8 affinity, likeness,
sameness **9** agreement
10 comparison, similarity, similitude **11** resemblance
14 correspondence

parallelogram 5 rhomb
6 square **7** diamond, rhombus
8 rhomboid **9** rectangle
11 plane figure
13 quadrilateral

paralyze 4 stun **6** benumb,
deaden, disarm, freeze,

Paraguay
  capital/largest city: **8** Asuncion
  others: **3** Ita **4** Rica, Yuty **5** Belen, Luque, Pilar, Villa
    7 Caacupe **8** Trinidad **9** Paraguari **10** Concepcion, Villar-
    rica **11** Encarnacion **26** Puerto Presidente Stroessner
  division: **6** Guaira, Itapua, Olimpo **7** Caazapa **8** Boqueron
    10 Concepcion
  measure: **3** pie **4** lino, lira, lire, vara **5** legua **6** cuadra,
    fanega
  monetary unit: **4** peso **7** guarani, centimo
  weight: **7** quintal
  island:
    floating island: **8** camalote
  lake: **4** Vera, Ypoa **8** Ypacarai
  river: **3** Apa **5** Guazu, Negro, Plata, Verde, Ypane
    6 Acaray, Parana **7** Aguaray, Confuso **8** Paraguay
    9 Aquidaban, Pilcomayo, Tebicuary, Tibiquare **10** Monte
    Lindo **14** Riacho Gonzales **15** Riacho Mosquitos
  physical feature:
    falls: **6** Guaira
    plains: **5** Chaco
    plateau: **6** Parana
  people: **6** Abipon, Moskoi **7** Guarani, mestizo **8** Guayaqui
    artist: **7** Bestard
    author: **3** Pla **4** Baez **6** Alcala, Bastos, Correa, O'Leary
      7 Cervera **8** Casaccia
    composer: **8** Asuncion
    leader: **5** Lopez **7** Francia **10** Stroessner **16** Antequera y
      Castro
    sculptor: **8** Guggiari
  language: **6** German **7** Guarani, Spanish
  religion: **9** Mennonite **13** Roman Catholic
  place:
    church: **10** Villarrica **11** Incarnation
    dam: **6** Itaipu
    memorial: **16** Pantheon of Heroes
    museum: **5** Godoi
    palace: **10** Government
  feature:
    animal: **4** puma **5** tapir **6** iguana, jaguar **7** peccary
    bird: **6** toucan
    clothing: **5** fajas, typoi **6** poncho **7** rebozos **9** bombachas
      10 alpargatas
    communes: **11** reducciones
    dance: **7** Sante Fe **15** Paraguayan polka
    fish: **7** piranha
    lace: **7** nanduti
    music: **8** quarania
    townspeople: **9** comuneros
    tree: **5** ceiba **7** lapacho **9** quebracho
  food:
    bread: **5** chipa, mbeyu
    dish: **12** sopa paraguay
    tea: **9** yerba mate
    vegetable: **8** mandioca

weaken **7** cripple, destroy, disable, petrify, stupefy, wipe out **8** demolish, enfeeble **10** debilitate, immobilize, neutralize **12** incapacitate

Paramaribo
capital of: **8** Suriname

paramount 4 main **5** chief **6** utmost **7** capital, highest, leading, premier, supreme **8** cardinal, dominant, foremost, greatest, peerless, superior **9** essential, principal, unmatched **10** preeminent **11** outstanding, predominant **12** incomparable, preponderant, transcendent

paramour 3 man **4** doxy **5** lover, Romeo **6** gigolo **7** Don Juan **8** Casanova, fancy man, lothario, lover boy, mistress **9** boyfriend, concubine, courtesan, inamorata, inamorato, kept woman **10** girl friend, lady friend, sugar daddy

paranoid 4 wary **7** deluded **9** paranoiac **11** distrustful **14** oversuspicious

parapet 7 bulwark, rampart **8** abutment, palisade **9** barricade, earthwork **10** battlement, breastwork

paraphernalia 3 rig **4** gear **5** stuff **6** outfit, tackle, things **7** effects, harness, regalia **8** fittings, material, supplies, utensils **9** apparatus, equipment, trappings **10** belongings, implements, properties, provisions **11** accessories, furnishings **13** accoutrements

paraphrase 5 recap **6** rehash, reword **7** restate **8** rephrase **12** recapitulate

Parasaurolophus
type: **8** dinosaur **10** ornithopod
location: **6** Canada
period: **10** Cretaceous

parasite 5 leech **6** beggar, cadger, loafer **7** moocher, shirker, slacker, sponger **8** deadbeat **9** goldbrick, scrounger **10** freeloader **11** bloodsucker
inside host: **12** endoparasite
outside host: **12** ectoparasite

parasol 5 shade **6** shadow **7** roundel **8** sunshade, umbrella
mushroom: **7** lepiota

par avion 5 by air

parboil 4 boil **5** scald **6** blanch **7** precook

Parca
origin: **5** Roman
member of: **6** Parcae

goddess of: 7 destiny **10** childbirth

Parcae see **5** Fates

parcel 3 lot **4** bale, pack, part, plot **5** allot, piece, tract **6** bundle, divide, packet **7** carve up, deal out, dole out, package, portion, section, segment, split up **8** allocate, dispense, disperse, division, fraction, fragment, property **9** allotment, allowance, apportion, partition **10** distribute **11** piece of land

parceling out 9 allotment, doling out, meting out **10** allocation, assignment, dealing out **12** distribution **13** apportionment

parcel out 5 allot **7** dole out, give out, mete out **8** allocate, dispense, divide up **9** apportion **10** distribute, portion out

parch 4 bake, burn, char, sear **5** dry up, singe **6** dry out, scorch, sun-dry, wither **7** blister, shrivel **9** dehydrate, dessicate, evaporate

parched 3 dry **4** arid **6** barren **8** withered **9** shriveled **10** dehydrated, desiccated

parchment 6 scroll, vellum **7** papyrus **8** goatskin **9** sheepskin

pardon 5 grace, mercy **6** excuse, wink at **7** absolve, amnesty, blink at, forbear, forgive, indulge, release, set free **8** overlook, reprieve, shrug off **9** discharge, disregard, exculpate, exonerate, remission, vindicate **10** absolution, indulgence **11** deliverance, exculpation, forbearance, forgiveness **12** grant amnesty **16** forgive and forget

Pardoner
character in: **18** The Canterbury Tales
author: **7** Chaucer

pare 3 cut, lop **4** clip, crop, dock, hull, husk, peel, skin, trim **5** lower, prune, shave, shear, shell, shuck, slash, strip **6** lessen, reduce, shrink **7** curtail, cut back **8** decrease, diminish **11** decorticate

pare down 3 cut **4** trim **5** shave **6** reduce **7** abridge, curtail, cut down, shorten **8** condense, cut short, diminish **10** abbreviate

parent 3 dam **4** sire **5** model **6** father, mother **7** creator **8** ancestor, begetter, exemplar, original, producer **9** precursor, prototype **10** antecedent, fore-

runner, originator, procreator, progenitor **11** predecessor

parentage 5 birth, roots, stock **6** family, origin, strain **7** descent, lineage **8** ancestry, forbears, heredity, pedigree **9** ancestors, genealogy **10** background, derivation, extraction, family tree **11** antecedents

Parentalia
origin: **5** Roman
event: **8** festival

parenthetical 5 aside **6** braced, casual **8** inserted **9** bracketed **10** extraneous, immaterial, incidental, interposed, irrelevant **11** impertinent, intervening, superfluous

par excellence 8 superior **10** preeminent

parfait d'amour
type: **7** liqueur
flavor: **7** violets
color: **6** purple

Paria
form: **5** nymph
loved by: **5** Minos
children: **7** Chryses **9** Eurymedon, Nephalion, Philolaus

pariah 5 exile, rover, stray **6** outlaw, roamer **7** outcast **8** vagabond, wanderer **10** expatriate **11** undesirable, untouchable

paring 4 chip, snip **5** scrap, shred, slice **6** sliver **7** cutting, peeling, shaving **8** fragment

pari passu 6 fairly **7** equably **10** side by side **13** equal progress **17** without partiality

Paris see **box**

Paris
character in: **14** Romeo and Juliet
author: **11** Shakespeare

Paris
postion: **6** prince
father: **5** Priam
mother: **5** Hecuba
brother: **6** Hector **9** Polydorus
sister: **9** Cassandra
wife: **6** Oenone
abducted: **5** Helen
judgment of: **14** apple of discord
awarded apple to: **9** Aphrodite
killed by: **11** Philoctetes

parish 4 fold **5** flock, shire **6** canton, county **7** diocese, section **8** brethren, district, precinct, province **9** community, pastorate **10** department **11** archdiocese **12** congregation, neighborhood

parity 7 balance **8** equality,

Paris
  airport: **4** Orly **9** Le Bourget **15** Charles de Gaulle
  area: **5** Passy **6** Clichy, Marais, Ternes, Wagram **7** Auteuil
  8 Chaillot, Gobelins, Left Bank, St Honore **9** Les Halles,
  Right Bank, St Germain **10** Montmartre, Rive Droite,
  Rive Gauche, Val de Grace **11** Ile de la Cite **12** Hotel de
  Ville, Latin Quarter, Montparnasse
  capital of: **6** France
  city planner: **9** Haussmann
  island: **10** Ile St Louis **11** Ile de la Cite
  landmark: **8** Pantheon **9** Notre Dame **10** Paris Opera, Sacre
  Coeur **11** Eiffel Tower, La Madeleine, Palais Royal
  12 Elysee Palace, Hotel de Ville, Place Vendome **13** Arc
  de Triomphe, Palais Bourbon **14** Bois de Boulogne, Place
  de l'Etoile, Pompidou Center, Sainte Chapelle, Tomb of
  Napoleon **15** Bois de Vincennes **16** Luxembourg Palace
  17 Hotel des Invalides, Place de la Bastille, Place de la
  Concorde **18** Jardin des Tuileries **20** Place Charles de
  Gaulle
  nickname: **11** city of light
  river: **5** Seine
  street: **9** Haussmann, Invalides **10** Grand Armee **11** Saint
  Michel **12** Montparnasse, Saint Germain **13** Champs Elys-
  ees **15** Charles de Gaulle
  subway: **5** Metro
  university: **8** Sorbonne

sameness **10** coequality, uniformity **11** equivalence, equivalency **14** correspondence

park 4 lawn **5** field, green,
grove, woods **6** common,
meadow, square **7** grounds, reserve **8** parkland, preserve,
woodland **9** grassland, sanctuary **10** public park,
quadrangle

Parker, Dorothy
  author of: **9** Big Blonde
  10 Enough Rope **13** Death
  and Taxes **18** After Such
  Pleasures **19** Laments for
  the Living

Parkman, Francis
  author of: **30** France and
  England in North America

parkway 6 avenue **9** boulevard **12** thoroughfare

parlance 4 talk **5** idiom, lingo
6 speech **16** manner of
speaking

Parlement of Fowles, The
  author: **15** Geoffrey Chaucer

parley 4 talk **6** confab,
powwow, summit **7** council,
meeting, palaver **8** conclave
9 discourse, mediation, peace
talk **10** conference, discussion
11 arbitration, negotiation
12 conversation

parliament 4 diet **5** court,
house, junta **6** fan-tan, senate,
sevens **7** cabinet, council **8** assembly, congress **9** high court
11 legislature **12** three
estates

Communist: **6** Soviet **9** polit-
buro, presidium
estate: **12** House of Lords
14 House of Commons
Germanic: **9** Bundesrat, Bun-
destag, Bolksraad
11 Volkshammer
Greek: **5** Boule
Icelandic: **7** Althing
Israeli: **7** Knesset **8** Knesseth
Scandinavian: **7** Lagting,
Riksdag **8** Lagthing, Stort-
ing **9** Odelsting, Storthing
Spanish: **6** Cortes

parlor 5 salon **6** saloon **8** best
room **9** front room **10** living
room **11** drawing room, sitting
room

Parnopius
  epithet of: **6** Apollo
  means: **9** locust god

parochial 5 local, petty, small
6 church, little, narrow, parish **7** insular, limited **8** regional **9** hidebound, illiberal,
religious, sectional, small-
town **10** provincial, restricted
11 countrified **12** narrow-
minded

parodos
  from Greek drama: **9** choral
  ode

parody 5 mimic **6** satire **7** lampoon, takeoff **8** satirize, travesty **9** burlesque, take off on
10 caricature

Parolles
  character in: **20** All's Well
  That Ends Well
  author: **11** Shakespeare

paroxysm 3 fit **5** spasm, spell
7 seizure **10** convulsion

parrot 3 ape **4** bird, echo,
lory **5** macaw, mimer, mimic
6 chorus, monkey **7** copycat,
imitate **8** cockatoo, imitator,
parakeet **9** reiterate

parry 4 duck, shun **5** avert,
avoid, dodge, elude, repel
7 beat off, fend off, repulse,
ward off **8** sidestep, stave off
10 circumvent, fight shy of

Parsifal
  opera by: **6** Wagner
  character: **6** Kundry **8** Amfortas, Klingsor
  9 Gurnemanz

Parsifal Mosaic, The
  author: **12** Robert Ludlum

parsimonious 5 close, tight
6 frugal, saving, stingy **7** miserly, sparing, thrifty **9** niggardly, penurious
10 economical, ungenerous
11 closefisted, tightfisted
13 money-grubbing, penny-
pinching

parsimony 6 thrift **7** economy
8 meanness **10** stinginess
13 niggardliness
15 tightfistedness

parsley 19 Petroselinum
crispum
  varieties: **5** Horse **7** Chinese,
  Italian **12** Turnip-rooted
  related herb: **4** dill **5** cumin
  6 fennel
  garland worn by: **8** Hercules
  gives speed to: **6** horses
  use in: **11** fines herbes
  12 bouquet garni

parson 5 clerk, padre **6** cleric,
divine, father, pastor, priest,
rector **7** dominie **8** minister,
preacher, reverend, shepherd,
sky pilot **9** clergyman
  French: **4** abbe, cure

parsonage 5 glebe, manse
7 deanery, rectory, Vatican
8 vicarage **9** pastorate

part 2 go **3** bit, job **4** care,
chip, duty, hunk, item, open,
rend, role, slit, task, tear,
unit **5** break, chore, crumb,
guise, leave, piece, place,
scrap, sever, shard, share,
sherd, shred, slice, split
6 branch, charge, cleave, depart, detach, detail, divide, go
away, member, morsel, region,
sector, set out, sliver, sunder
7 concern, cutting, disjoin, element, portion, push off, section, segment, snippet **8** break
off, business, capacity, disguise, disunite, division, fraction, fragment, function,
separate, set forth, start out
9 character, component, disen-

gage, go one's way **10** assignment, break apart, department, disconnect, get up and go, ingredient, mosey along, say good-bye **11** be on one's way, call it quits, constituent, subdivision

partake 5 enjoy, savor, share **6** join in, sample **7** share in **8** engage in **11** participate

part from 5 leave **9** break with **12** separate from

Parthenia
epithet of: **6** Athena
means: **6** virgin

Parthenius see **9** Plexippus

Parthenopaeus
father: **10** Hippomenes
mother: **8** Atalanta
member of: **18** Seven against Thebes

Parthenope
form: **5** siren

Parthenos
means: **6** virgin

partial 6 biased, unfair, unjust **7** limited, slanted **8** one-sided, partisan **9** factional **10** fractional, incomplete, interested, prejudiced, subjective, unbalanced, unfinished **11** fragmentary, inequitable, predisposed, uncompleted **12** inconclusive, prepossessed

partiality 4 bent, bias, love, tilt **5** fancy, slant, taste **6** choice, liking **7** leaning **8** affinity, fondness, penchant, tendency, weakness **9** prejudice **10** attraction, favoritism, preference, proclivity, propensity **11** inclination **12** one-sidedness, partisanship, predilection **14** predisposition

partially 6 in part, partly **7** partway **8** somewhat **9** piecemeal **12** fractionally, incompletely

participant 4 ally **5** party **6** cohort, fellow, helper, member, player, sharer, worker **7** partner **8** confrere, partaker **9** accessory, associate, colleague, performer **10** accomplice **11** contributor, shareholder **12** collaborator, participator

participate 5 share **6** join in **7** partake, perform **8** engage in, take part **9** play a part

particle 3 bit, jot **4** atom, iota, mite, snip, whit **5** crumb, grain, scrap, shred, speck, trace **6** morsel, tittle, trifle **7** granule, modicum, smidgen, snippet **9** scintilla

parti-colored 4 pied **5** plaid

6 motley **7** checked, dappled, mottled **8** colorful **9** checkered **10** variegated **11** many-colored **12** multicolored

particular 4 sole **5** exact, fixed, fussy, picky **6** single, strict **7** express, finicky, special **8** concrete, critical, definite, detailed, distinct, especial, exacting, explicit, itemized, personal, separate, specific **9** demanding **10** fastidious, individual, meticulous, scrupulous **11** painstaking, persnickety, punctilious, well-defined **12** hard to please

particularize 6 detail **7** itemize, specify **9** enumerate

particularly 6 mainly **7** notably **8** markedly **9** eminently, expressly, specially, supremely, unusually **10** definitely, distinctly, especially, explicitly, strikingly **11** principally, prominently **13** exceptionally **15** extraordinarily

particulars 5 facts, items **6** events **7** details **9** specifics **13** circumstances

parti pris 15 position decided **20** preconceived attitude

partisan 3 fan **4** ally **6** backer, biased, rooter, zealot **7** booster, devotee, partial, slanted **8** adherent, advocate, champion, follower, one-sided, upholder **9** guerrilla, insurgent, irregular, jayhawker, supporter **10** bushwacker, enthusiast, prejudiced, subjective, unbalanced **11** sympathizer

partition 4 wall **5** allot, fence, panel **6** assign, divide, screen **7** barrier, deal out, divider, mete out, parting, split up **8** allocate, bulkhead, dispense, disperse, dividing, division, separate **9** allotment, apportion, parcel out, separator, severance, splitting, subdivide **10** allocation, assignment, distribute, separation **11** demarcation, segregation **12** distribution, dividing wall **13** apportionment

partly 6 in part **7** part way **8** somewhat **9** not wholly, partially, to a degree **10** relatively **12** fractionally, incompletely **13** after a fashion, comparatively

partly open 4 ajar **5** agape **6** gaping **7** cracked **8** half-open, unclosed **9** squinting **10** half-closed

partner 3 aid, pal **4** ally, chum, mate, wife **5** aider, buddy **6** fellow, friend, helper, sharer, spouse **7** comrade, co-

owner, husband **8** confrere, helpmate, partaker, sidekick, teammate **9** accessory, assistant, associate, colleague, companion, co-partner **10** accomplice, better half, joint owner **11** confederate, participant **12** collaborator

Partners, The
author: **16** Louis Auchincloss

Parton, Dolly
roles: **10** Nine to Five, Rhinestone **30** The Best Little Whorehouse in Texas

partridge
group of: **5** covey

Partridge
character in: **8** Tom Jones
author: **8** Fielding

Partridge Family, The
character: **13** Reuben Kinkaid **14** Danny Partridge, Keith Partridge, Tracy Partridge **15** Connie Partridge, Laurie Partridge **20** Christopher Partridge
cast: **8** Susan Dey **11** David Madden **12** Brian Forster, David Cassidy, Shirley Jones **13** Danny Bonaduce, Suzanne Crough **14** Jeremy Gelbwaks
song: **14** I Think I Love You

Parts of Animals
author: **9** Aristotle

parturition 5 birth **8** delivery **10** childbirth **11** giving birth **12** childbearing

party 2 do **4** band, bash, body, crew, fete, gang, team, unit, wing **5** corps, force, group, squad **6** affair, at-home, league, soiree **7** accused, blowout, company, coterie, faction **8** alliance, claimant, conclave, litigant, winging **9** appellant, coalition, defendant, festivity, gathering, plaintiff, reception **10** contestant, federation, petitioner, respondent **11** celebration, confederacy, get-together, participant, paticipator, perpetrator

party-pooper 4 drag **10** spoilsport, wet blanket

parvenu 4 snob **6** nobody **7** upstart **8** arrivist, mushroom **9** arriviste **12** nouveau riche

Pascal, Blaise
nationality: **6** French
invented: **7** syringe **13** adding machine **14** hydraulic press
author of: **7** Pensees **19** Lettres provinciales **20** Essay pour les coniques

Pascin, Julius
real name: **6** Pincas

born: 5 Vidin 8 Bulgaria
artwork: 6 Femmes 12 Les
 Deux Amies 17 Ginette et
 Mireille

Pasiphae
 father: 6 Helios
 mother: 7 Perseis
 husband: 5 Minos
 daughter: 7 Ariadne, Phaedra 9 Acacallis
 became enamored of:
  10 Cretan bull
 mother of: 8 Minotaur

Pasithea
 member of: 6 Graces

Pasolini, Pier Paolo
 director of: 13 Arabian
  Nights

pass 2 go 3 cap, die, end, gap,
 hit, top, use, way 4 best,
 busy, fill, flow, give, go by,
 go on, hand, kick, lane, meet,
 toss 5 canal, exact, excel,
 gorge, gulch, leave, outdo,
 route, spend, throw, trail
 6 accept, affirm, avenue, be
 over, canyon, convey, course,
 decree, depart, devote, elapse,
 employ, engage, exceed, expend, expire, finish, go away,
 go past, occupy, ordain, permit, pickle, plight, ratify, ravine, slip by, strait, take up,
 vanish 7 achieve, advance, approve, channel, confirm, consume, deliver, die away,
 eclipse, freebie, glide by, go
 ahead, let have, narrows,
 pathway, present, proceed,
 qualify, satisfy, slide by, surpass 8 blow over, dissolve, exigency, fade away, furlough,
 go beyond, go onward, hand
 over, juncture, legalize, melt
 away, outshine, outstrip, pass
 away, peter out, progress,
 quandary, sanction, transfer,
 transmit, turn over 9 authorize, disappear, evaporate, extremity, hand along, legislate,
 situation, terminate 10 accomplish, difficulty, free ticket, get
 through, move onward, overshadow, passageway 11 predicament, proposition
 12 complication, run its
 course, solicitation, stand the
 test 13 authorization 15 amorous overture
 French: 13 laissez passer

passable 4 fair, open, so-so
 5 clear 6 not bad 8 adequate,
 fordable, mediocre, middling
 9 allowable, crossable, naviga-
 ble, tolerable 10 acceptable,
 admissible, pretty good
 11 presentable, respectable,
 traversable 12 unobstructed

passage 3 way 4 hall, pass,
 path, road, tour, trek, trip
 5 aisle, canal, piece, route,

verse 6 access, clause, column,
 course, junket, tunnel, voyage 7 channel, chapter, hallway, journey, passing, portion,
 section, transit 8 approach, approval, corridor, movement,
 sanction, sentence 9 enactment, excursion, paragraph,
 selection, ship's fare 10 acceptance, expedition, ordain-
 ment 11 affirmation,
 endorsement, legislation, progression 12 confirmation, legalization, ratification
 13 authorization

passage out 4 exit 6 egress,
 outlet

Passages
 author: 10 Gail Sheehy

Passage to India, A
 author: 9 E M Forster
 character: 6 Dr Aziz 8 Mrs
  Moore 12 Adela Quested
  13 Cecil Fielding, Ronald
  Heaslop 16 Professor
  Godbole
 setting: 11 Chandrapore
  12 Marabar Caves
 director: 9 David Lean
 cast: 9 Judy Davis 12 Alec
  Guinness 13 Peggy Ash-
  croft 15 Victor Bannerjee
 Oscar for: 17 supporting actress (Ashcroft)

passageway 4 exit, hall, lane,
 path, walk 5 aisle 6 access, arcade, tunnel 7 doorway, gang-
 way, gateway, hallway,
 passage 8 corridor, entrance,
 entryway, sidewalk
 12 companionway

pass away 3 die 6 depart, expire, pass on, perish 7 decease 8 pass over 13 go to
 one's glory 14 give up the
 ghost

pass by 4 go by, pass 5 lapse
 6 elapse, roll by, slip by
 7 glide by, slide by 8 slip
 away

passe 4 past 5 faded, hoary,
 stale 6 demode, lapsed,
 quaint 7 ancient, antique, archaic, disused, outworn, retired 8 obsolete, outdated,
 outmoded 9 out-of-date 10 antiquated 11 prehistoric 12 antediluvian, old-fashioned, out
 of fashion 13 superannuated

passenger 4 fare 5 rider
 8 commuter, stowaway, traveler, wayfarer

Passepartout
 character in: 26 Around the
  World in Eighty Days
 author: 5 Verne

pas seul
 ballet: 9 solo dance
 literally: 8 solo step

passim 12 here and there, repeated item

passing 5 brief, death, dying
 6 demise, fickle 7 decease, passage 8 adequate, fleeting 9 enactment, ephemeral, momentary, temporary, transient
 10 evanescent, expiration, not
 failing, short-lived, transitory
 11 impermanent, legislating

**passing the bounds of
 propriety**
 French: 5 outre

passion 4 fire, idol, love, lust,
 rage, urge 5 ardor, craze,
 fancy, flame, gusto, heart,
 mania 6 desire, fervor, hunger,
 thirst, warmth 7 beloved, craving, ecstasy, emotion, feeling,
 rapture 8 loved one 9 carnality, eagerness, inamorata, intensity, obsession, sentiment,
 transport, vehemence 10 carnal love, enthusiasm 11 amorousness, earnestness,
 infatuation

passionate 3 hot 4 sexy
 5 fiery 6 ardent, carnal, erotic,
 fervid, fierce, heated, loving,
 raging 7 amorous, earnest, excited, feeling, fervent, furious,
 intense, lustful 8 desirous, ecstatic, inflamed, sensuous, vehement 9 emotional, heartfelt,
 wrought-up 11 tempestuous
 12 enthusiastic, intoxicating

passionfruit
 type: 7 liqueur
 origin: 6 Hawaii
 flavor: 5 peach

passionless 4 calm, cold
 6 placid, serene 7 passive
 8 tranquil 9 apathetic, unfeeling 10 spiritless 11 emotionless, indifferent, unemotional

Passion Play
 author: 13 Jerzy Kosinski

passive 5 inert 6 docile 7 dormant, patient, pliable 8 enduring, inactive, lifeless, listless,
 resigned, yielding 9 apathetic,
 compliant, impassive, quiescent, tractable 10 spiritless,
 submissive 11 acquiescent, unassertive, unresisting
 12 nonresistant

passiveness 6 apathy 7 inertia 8 docility 10 quiescence
 11 resignation 12 acquiescence, lifelessness 14 submissiveness 16 unresponsiveness

passivity 6 apathy 7 inertia
 8 docility, meekness 11 resignation 12 complaisance, lifelessness 13 nonresistance
 14 submissiveness

pass muster 2 do 5 serve
 6 answer 8 be enough 10 be

adequate **12** be sufficient **14** be satisfactory

pass on 3 die **6** depart, expire **7** decease **8** pass away **13** go to one's glory **14** give up the ghost, leave this world **15** breathe one's last

pass over 6 ignore, slight **7** neglect **8** overlook **10** brush aside

pass up 4 miss **6** ignore, refuse

password 3 key **4** word **6** byword, slogan **7** keyword, tessera **9** catchword, watchword **10** open sesame, secret word, shibboleth **11** countersign, passe-parole

Password
 host: **11** Allen Ludden

past 2 by **4** gone **5** ended, prior **6** beyond, bygone, former, gone by **7** ancient, earlier, elapsed, expired, history, long ago, through **8** departed, finished, previous **9** antiquity, days of old **10** days gone by, days of yore, historical, olden times, passed away, yesteryear **11** dead and gone, former times, times gone by **12** ancient times

pasta 4 orzo, ziti **6** elbows, shells **7** gnocchi, lasagna, pastina, ravioli, rotelli **8** ditalini, linguini, macaroni, rigatoni, tortelli **9** canelloni, cavatelli, fettucine, manicotti, spaghetti **10** tortellini, vermicelli
 ingredient: **3** egg **5** flour

past due 4 late **5** tardy **7** belated, overdue **9** in arrears **10** behindhand

paste 3 gum, hit **4** glue, seal, sock **5** affix, punch, stick **6** attach, cement **7** stickum **8** adhesive, mucilage

pastel 3 dim **4** pale, soft **5** chalk, faded, faint, light, muted **6** crayon **13** washed-out **13** coloring stick **14** coloring pencil

Pasternak, Boris
 author of: **9** Dr Zhivago

Pasteur, Louis
 field: **9** chemistry
 nationality: **6** French
 originated: **14** anti-rabies shot, pasteurization
 founded: **12** microbiology
 disproved: **21** spontaneous generation

pastime 3 fun **4** game, play **5** hobby, sport **9** amusement, avocation, diversion **10** relaxation **11** distraction **13** entertainment **14** divertissement

pastis
 type: **7** liqueur
 flavor: **8** licorice
 substitute for: **8** absinthe

past one's prime 3 old **4** aged **5** aging **7** elderly **9** venerable **11** over the hill **12** in one's dotage

pastor 4 cure, dean **5** padre, vicar **6** cleric, father, parson, priest, rector **8** chaplain, minister, preacher **9** clergyman

pastoral 5 rural **6** rustic **7** bucolic, idyllic **8** arcadian, clerical, priestly **9** episcopal **10** sacerdotal **11** ministerial **14** ecclesiastical

Pastoral Symphony, The
 author: **9** Andre Gide

pastorate 6 clergy **8** ministry, the cloth **10** priesthood

pastures
 god of: **3** Pan **6** Dumuzi

pasty 3 wan **4** ashy, gray, pale **5** ashen, gluey, gooey, gummy, white **6** anemic, chalky, doughy, pallid, peaked, sallow, sticky **7** deathly, starchy **9** bloodless, colorless, ghostlike, glutinous, like paste **12** mucilaginous

pat 3 apt, dab, hit, pet, rap, tap **4** cake, daub, easy, glib, slap **5** exact, ideal, ready, slick, thump **6** caress, facile, fondle, simple, smooth, stroke, thwack **7** apropos, fitting, perfect, precise, reliant **8** flippant, suitable **9** contrived, pertinent, rehearsed

patch 3 fix, lot **4** area, darn, mend, plot, spot, zone **5** field, sew up, tract **6** garden, repair, stitch **7** expanse, stretch **8** clearing, insignia **9** reinforce **13** reinforcement

patchwork 4 hash, mess **6** jumble, medley, muddle, tangle **7** grab bag, melange, mixture **8** mishmash, mixed bag, pastiche, scramble **9** confusion, potpourri **10** hodgepodge, miscellany, salmagundi **11** gallimaufry **14** conglomeration, omniumgatherum

pate 3 pie **4** brow, head **5** brain, crown, paste, pastry, patty, skull **6** noddle, noggin, noodle **9** meat paste

patella
 bone of: **7** kneecap

patent 4 bald, bold, open, rank **5** clear, gross, overt, plain **6** permit **7** decided, evident, express, glaring, license, obvious **8** apparent, distinct,

flagrant, manifest, palpable, registry, striking **9** copyright, downright, prominent **10** pronounced, unreserved **11** conspicuous, copyrighted, indubitable, self-evident, trademarked, transparent, unconcealed, undisguised **12** unmistakable **15** nonprescription

paterfamilias 6 father **17** father of the family, master of the family **20** master of the household

paternal 4 kind **6** tender **8** fatherly, parental, vigilant, watchful **9** concerned, indulgent **10** benevolent, fatherlike, interested, solicitous **11** patriarchal

Pater Patriae 18 father of his country

path 3 way **4** lane, plan, road, walk **5** byway, means, orbit, route, track, trail **6** access, bypath, course **7** pathway, process, walkway **8** approach, footpath

pathetic 3 sad **6** moving, rueful, woeful **7** doleful, piteous, pitiful **8** dolorous, grievous, pitiable, poignant, touching, wretched **9** affecting, miserable, plaintive, sorrowful **10** deplorable, lamentable, to be pitied **11** distressing

Pathfinder, The
 author: **19** James Fenimore Cooper
 character: **9** Arrowhead, Dew-of-June **10** Charles Cap **11** Mabel Dunham, Natty Bumppo **12** Chingachgook **13** Jasper Western **14** Sergeant Dunham **18** Lieutenant Davy Muir

Pathfinders, The
 author: **10** Gail Sheehy

pathogen 3 bug **4** germ **5** virus **7** microbe **8** bacillus **9** bacterium **13** microorganism

pathophobia
 fear of: **7** disease

pathos 3 woe **5** agony **6** misery **7** anguish, feeling, sadness **8** distress **9** heartache, poignancy, sentiment **10** desolation **12** pitiableness **13** plaintiveness

Paths of Glory
 director: **14** Stanley Kubrick
 cast: **11** Kirk Douglas, Ralph Meeker **13** Adolphe Menjou

pathway 4 lane, path, road **5** alley, route, track **6** course **7** passage, walkway **8** footpath **10** passageway

patience 5 poise 7 stamina
8 industry, tenacity 9 composure, diligence, fortitude, restraint, tolerance 10 equanimity, resolution, sufferance
11 application, forbearance,
longanimity, persistence, self-
control 12 perseverance,
tirelessness

Patience
author: 9 W S Gilbert

patient 4 case 6 dogged, serene 8 composed, diligent, enduring, resolute, tireless
9 dauntless, tenacious, undaunted 10 determined, forbearing, persistent, sick
person, unflagging, unswerving, unwavering 11 indus-
trious, persevering,
unfaltering, unperturbed
13 indefatigable, long-suffering, uncomplaining

patio 4 deck 5 lanai, porch
6 piazza 7 terrace, veranda

patois 5 argot, idiom, lingo
6 jargon 7 dialect
10 vernacular

Paton, Alan
author of: 19 Too Late the
Phalarope 20 Cry the Be-
loved Country 24 Ah but
Your Land Is Beautiful

pat on the back 6 praise
7 plaudit 10 compliment
12 commendation

patriarch 5 elder, ruler 6 father, leader, old man 8 male
head 9 chieftain
13 paterfamilias

patrician 4 lord, peer 5 noble
6 lordly 7 genteel, stately
8 highborn, imposing, nobleman, princely, well-bred
9 blueblood, dignified, gentleman 10 aristocrat, upper-class
12 aristocratic, silk-stocking

patrimony 3 lot 5 dower,
share 6 devise, estate, legacy
7 portion 8 bestowal, heritage,
jointure 9 endowment 10 bequeathal, birthright 11 inheritance 12 hereditament

patriotism
Latin: 11 amor patriae

Patroclus
father: 9 Menoetius
mother: 8 Periapis
friend: 8 Achilles
killed by: 6 Hector

patrol 5 guard, scout, watch
6 ranger, sentry, warden
7 protect 8 sentinel 9 safeguard, walk a beat, watchman, watch over 10 stand
watch

patron 5 angel, buyer 6 backer,

client, friend, helper 7 habitue, shopper, sponsor, visitor
8 advocate, attender, champion, customer, defender, financer, promoter, upholder
9 protector, spectator, supporter 10 benefactor, encourager, frequenter, well-wisher
11 sympathizer 12 benefac-
tress 14 philanthropist

patronage 3 aid 4 help 5 favor, plums, trade 6 buying,
custom, spoils 7 backing, charity, clients, dealing, support
8 advocacy, auspices, business,
commerce 9 clientele, customers, fosterage 10 assistance,
friendship, pork barrel, protection, purchasing 11 benefaction, sponsorship 12 philanthropy 13 encouragement

patronize 5 humor 6 shop at
7 buy from 8 deal with, frequent 9 trade with
10 condescend

patsy 4 dupe, pawn, tool
7 cat's-paw, fall guy

patter 3 pad, pat, rap, tap
4 beat, drum 5 pound, thrum
6 tattoo 7 rat-a-tat, spatter,
tapping 8 drumming, sprinkle

pattern 4 copy, form, mold,
plan 5 draft, guide, ideal,
mimic, model, motif, shape
6 design, follow, sample 7 emulate, example, fashion, imitate, paragon 8 exemplar,
original, paradigm, parallel,
simulate, specimen, standard
9 archetype, criterion, duplicate, prototype 10 apotheosis,
stereotype 12 illustration

Patton
director: 17 Franklin
Schaffner
cast: 10 Karl Malden (Omar
Bradley) 12 George C Scott
(George Patton), Stephen
Young 13 Michael Strong
Oscar for: 5 actor (Scott),
story 7 picture 8 director
10 screenplay (Francis Ford
Coppola and Edmund H
North)

Patton, George S
nickname: 15 Old Blood and
Guts
served in: 3 WWI 4 WWII
11 World War One, World
War Two
commander of: 9 Third Army
invasion of: 8 Normandy
11 North Africa
capture of: 6 Sicily
battle: 5 Bulge
wore: 21 ivory-handled
revolvers
memoirs: 12 War As I Knew
It

Patty Duke Show, The
character: 7 Richard 8 Ross
Lane 9 Cathy Lane, Patty
Lane 10 Martin Lane
14 Natalie Masters
cast: 9 Jean Byron, Patty
Duke 10 Paul O'Keefe
14 Eddie Applegate 16 William Schallert

paucis verbis 10 by few
words, in few words 12 with
few words

paucity 4 lack 6 dearth 7 fewness, poverty 8 exiguity, poorness, puniness, scarcity,
shortage, sparsity, thinness
10 deficiency, meagerness,
scantiness, scarceness
13 insufficiency

Paul
former name: 4 Saul
hometown: 6 Tarsus
teacher: 8 Gamaliel
companion: 5 Silas 7 Timothy 8 Barnabas, John Mark
9 Trophimus
cities visited: 4 Rome
5 Derbe, Perga, Troas 6 Lys-
tra, Paphos 7 Antioch, Corinth, Ephesus, Iconium,
Miletus, Salamis 8 Caesarea,
Damascus, Neapolis, Phi-
lippi 9 Macedonia
12 Thessalonica
conversion place: 14 road to
Damascus
wrote: 8 epistles

Paul Bunyan
author: 12 James Stevens
character: 9 Shanty Boy
10 Hels Helson 11 King
Bourbon 12 Sourdough
Sam 13 Babe the Blue Ox
14 Hot Biscuit Slim
16 Johnny Inkslinger

Pauli, Wolfgang
field: 7 physics
researched: 13 quantum
theory
established: 14 Pauli principle 18 exclusion principle
awarded: 10 Nobel Prize

Paulina
character in: 14 The Winter's
Tale
author: 11 Shakespeare

Pauling, Linus Carl
field: 12 biochemistry
worked on: 8 proteins
18 molecular structure
advocated: 8 Vitamin C
awarded: 10 Nobel Prize
awarded for: 5 peace
9 chemistry

paunch 3 gut, pot 5 belly,
tummy 7 abdomen, stomach
8 potbelly 9 bay window, beer
belly, spare tire 10 midsection 11 breadbasket,
corporation

pauper 6 beggar 7 almsman
8 bankrupt, indigent 9 insolvent, mendicant 10 poor person, starveling 11 charity
case 12 down-and-outer

pause 3 gap 4 halt, rest, stop,
wait 5 break, cease, delay, let
up 6 hiatus 7 interim, time
out 8 break off, hesitate, interval 9 cessation, interlude
10 deliberate, suspension
12 intermission,
interruption

pave 3 tar 4 face 6 cement
7 asphalt, surface 8 black top
9 resurface 10 macadamize

pavement 4 slab 5 brick 6 cement, hearth, street, tarmac
7 asphalt, cobbles, macadam
8 concrete, driveway, flagging,
sidewalk 9 flagstone

pavilion 4 tent, ward, wing
5 arbor, kiosk 6 gazebo 7 pergola 9 bandshell
11 summerhouse

Pavlov, Ivan Petrovich
   nationality: 7 Russian
   researched: 9 digestion
   studied: 20 behavior conditioning 21 Pavlovian
   conditioning
   awarded: 10 Nobel Prize

paw 2 pa 3 dad, pop, toe
4 feel, foot, grab, hand, maul,
mitt, papa 5 daddy, flail,
touch 6 caress, clutch, father,
handle, scrape, strike 7 rough
up 8 forefoot 9 mishandle
   mate: 3 maw

pawn 4 bond, dupe, hock,
tool 5 agent, patsy 6 flunky,
lackey, pledge, puppet 7 cat's
paw 8 borrow on, creature,
guaranty, henchman, hireling,
security 9 assurance, guarantee, underling 10 instrument
12 raise money on 14 give as
security

pawnbroker
   French: 11 mont-de-piete

Pawnbroker, The
   director: 11 Sidney Lumet
   cast: 10 Rod Steiger (Sol Na-
   zerman) 11 Brock Peters
   12 Jaime Sanchez 19 Geraldine Fitzgerald
   setting: 6 Harlem

Pawnee (Chahiksichhiks)
   language family: 7 Caddoan
   location: 5 Texas 8 Nebraska,
   Oklahoma 9 New Mexico
   related to: 7 Arikara
   god: 6 Tirawa

Pawtuxet
   location: 13 Massachusetts
   leader: 7 Squanto

Pax
   origin: 5 Roman

   goddess of: 5 peace
   corresponds to: 5 Irene

pax vobiscum 14 peace be
with you

pay 3 fee 4 foot, give, meet
5 grant, honor, remit, repay,
serve, wages, yield 6 ante up,
chip in, extend, income,
profit, render, return, salary,
settle 7 benefit, bring in,
cough up, payment, present,
proffer, stipend 8 be useful,
earnings, paycheck, shell out
9 bear fruit, liquidate, reimburse 10 come across, compensate, make good on,
recompense 12 compensation
13 reimbursement

payable 3 due 4 owed 5 owing 6 mature, unpaid 8 to be
paid 9 in arrears, spendable
10 demandable, expendable,
receivable 11 outstanding

pay attention 4 heed, note
6 attend, notice 7 observe

Payaya
   language family:
   12 Coahuiltecan
   location: 5 Texas

pay back 5 repay 7 counter,
get even 9 reimburse, retaliate 10 recompense, remunerate 15 make restitution

pay for 6 redeem 7 expiate
8 atone for 9 answer for, suffer for 10 compensate, recompense, remunerate 13 make
amends for 17 make reparation for

pay heed 6 notice 8 consider
11 concentrate 12 pay attention 13 put one's mind to

pay homage 5 defer, honor
7 acclaim 10 pay tribute

paying back 9 repayment
11 getting even 12 making
good on 13 reimbursement

paymaster 6 bursar, purser
7 cashier 10 cashkeeper

payment 3 fee, pay 4 debt
6 outlay, paying, salary 7 premium 8 defrayal, spending
9 allowance, discharge 10 recompense, remittance, settlement 11 expenditure,
installment, liquidation
12 compensation, contribution,
disbursement, remuneration
13 reimbursement

pay no heed to 4 defy 6 ignore, slight 7 disobey, neglect,
violate 8 overlook, pass over
9 disregard 10 brush aside, infringe on 14 shut one's eyes
to 16 pay no attention to
17 transgress against

payoff 3 end 4 soap 5 bribe,

graft 6 climax, crunch, finale,
finish, grease, payola, result,
upshot, windup 7 outcome
8 clincher 9 hush money
10 bottom line, conclusion,
denouement, protection, resolution 11 culmination

pay off 5 bribe 6 buy off, suborn 13 grease the palm

payola 5 bribe, graft 6 grease,
payoff

pay out 5 spend 6 expend, lay
out 7 fork out 8 allocate, disburse, dispense, shell out
10 distribute

pay suit 3 woo 5 court 8 pay
court

Payton, Walter
   nickname: 9 Sweetness
   sport: 8 football
   position: 11 running back
   team: 12 Chicago Bears

pay tribute to 4 laud, tout
5 boost, toast 6 praise, salute
7 applaud, commend 8 eulogize 10 compliment 16 sing
the praises of

Payuga
   tribe: 4 Agaz 6 Magach 7 Ca-
   digue, Payagua, Sarigue, Sia-
   cuas, Tacumbu
   location: 8 Paraguay 12 South
   America

pea 5 Pisum 12 Pisum sativum
   varieties: 4 Flat, Love, Snow,
   Wild 5 Beach, Caley, Chick,
   Congo, Coral, Field, Glory,
   Green, Heart, Heath, Hoary,
   No-eye, Rough, Sugar,
   Sweet 6 Angola, Canada,
   Desert, Garden, Marble, Pi-
   geon, Rosary, Scurfy,
   Winged, Winter 7 Catjang,
   Darling, English, Rabbit's,
   Seaside 8 Earthnut, Egyp-
   tian, Princess, Shamrock
   9 Asparagus, Black-eyed,
   Butterfly, Chaparral, Jerusa-
   lem, Partridge, Perennial
   10 Australian, Singletary,
   Wild winter 11 Everlasting,
   Sturt desert, Two-flowered,
   Winter sweet 12 Edible-pod-
   ded 14 Austrian winter
   15 Australian flame

peace 4 calm, ease 5 amity,
truce 6 accord, repose 7 concord, content, entente, harmony 8 serenity 9 agreement,
armistice, composure, placidity 12 pacification, tranquillity 14 reconciliation
   god of: 4 Frey 5 Freyr
   goddess of: 3 Pax
   9 Concordia
   Hebrew: 6 shalom
   Russian: 3 mir

Peace
   author: 12 Aristophanes

peace be with you
Latin: **11** pax vobiscum

peaceful 4 calm **5** quiet, still
6 placid, serene, silent **7** pacific, restful **8** amicable,
friendly, tranquil **9** agreeable,
peaceable, peacetime **10** harmonious, nonviolent, nonwar-
ring, pacifistic, untroubled
11 undisturbed

peacefulness 4 calm **7** concord, harmony **8** calmness, serenity **9** placidity
11 tranquility

peacemaker 8 diplomat, mediator, placater **9** go-between
10 ambassador, arbitrator, negotiator **11** adjudicator, concil-
iator, pacificator, peacekeeper,
peacemonger **12** intermediary

peacemaking 9 pacifying, placating, placatory **11** reconciling **12** conciliating,
conciliatory, pacification

peace offering 6 amends
11 appeasement
12 conciliation

peace of mind 8 security, serenity **11** tranquility **16** freedom from worry

peace to you
Hebrew: **14** shalom aleichem

peach 13 Prunus persica
varieties: **4** Muir, Peak, Sims,
Vine, Wild **5** Gaume, Hiley,
Pavie **6** Carmen, Crosby,
Desert, Foster, J H Hale,
Lovell, Orejon, Paloro, Peen-
to, Salwey **7** Dixigem, Dix-
ired, Elberta, Persian, Qua-
dong **8** Champion, Crawford,
Isabella, Redhaven, Russelet
9 Alexander, Freestone,
Halehaven, Rochester,
Southland **10** Clingstone,
Goldeneast, Heath Cling,
Summer Snow **12** Chinese
Cling, Iron Mountain,
Mountain Rose, Oldmixon
Free **13** Golden Jubilee, Old-
mixon Cling, Phillips Cling
14 Belle of Georgia
peach-like: **7** apricot
9 nectarine

Peach State
nickname of: **7** Georgia

Peachum, Polly
character in: **12** Beggar's
Opera
author: **3** Gay

peachy 4 fine, keen **5** dandy,
super, swell **9** excellent, marvelous, wonderful

peacock
group of: **6** muster

Peacock
constellation of: **4** Pavo

Peacock, Thomas Love
author of: **12** Headlong Hall
14 Crotchet Castle, Nightmare Abbey

Peacock Spring, The
author: **11** Rumer Godden

peak 3 tip, top **4** acme, apex
5 crest, crown, flood, prime
6 apogee, climax, summit, zenith **8** pinnacle **9** culminate
11 culmination

peaked 3 ill, wan **4** lean, pale,
thin, weak **5** ashen, drawn,
gaunt, spare, spiked, spiny,
white **6** ailing, infirm, pallid,
pointy, sallow, sickly, skinny,
spiked **7** haggard, pinched,
pointed, scrawny, tapered,
wizened **9** emaciated, shriveled **11** debilitated

peal 3 din **4** boom, clap, ring,
roar, roll, toll **5** blare, blast,
clang, crack, crash, knell
6 rumble **7** clangor, resound,
ringing **10** resounding **11** reverberate **13** reverberation
14 tintinnabulate
16 tintinnabulation

Peale, Charles Willson
born: **17** Queen Anne County
MD
son: **9** Raphaelle, Rembrandt
12 Titian Ramsay
artwork: **26** The Exhumation
of the Mastodon
portrait: **8** Franklin **9** Jefferson, John Adams
10 Washington

Peale, Raphaelle
born: **13** Bucks County PA
father: **14** Charles Willson
brother: **9** Rembrandt **12** Titian Ramsay
artwork: **12** After the
Bath

Peale, Rembrandt
born: **13** Bucks County PA
father: **14** Charles Willson
brother: **9** Raphaelle **12** Titian Ramsay
artwork: **15** The Court of
Death
portrait: **9** Jefferson
10 Washington

peal of bells 7 clangor, ringing **16** tintinnabulation

peanut 3 pod, tot **4** puny,
seed **5** petty, small **6** goober,
legume, measly, paltry
8 earthpea **9** little one
species: **15** Arachis hypogaea

Peanuts
creator: **13** Charles Schulz
character: **4** Lucy **5** Linus
6 Marcie, Snoopy **9** Schroe-
der **12** Charlie Brown
15 Peppermint Patty
Halloween figure: **12** Great
Pumpkin

Snoopy's plane: 12 Sopwith
Camel
Snoopy's foe: 8 Red Baron
saying: **9** Good Grief

pear 5 Pyrus **13** Pyrus
communis
varieties: **4** Bosc, Sand **5** Anjou, Asian, Blind, Melon,
Smith **6** Balsam, Burrel, Butter, Comice, Common, Gar-
ber, Garlic, Orient, Seckel,
Warden **7** Chinese, Kieffer,
Prickly, Vinegar **8** Bartlett,
Japanese, Oriental **9** Alligator, Evergreen, Muscadine
10 Beurre Bosc, Brandywine,
Chaumontel **11** Birch-leaved,
Bon Chretien, Paper-spined,
Winter Nelis **12** Beurre
d'Anjou, Easter Beurre, Sacred garlic, Willow-leaved
13 Flemish Beauty, Waite
Bergamot **15** Doyenne du
Comice **18** Duchesse
d'Angouleme

pearl
grows in: **6** oyster
genus: **8** Pinctada
source: **6** Red Sea **9** Caribbean **11** Persian Gulf
12 South Pacific **16** Gulf of
California
composed of: **5** nacre **9** aragonite **10** conchiolin
13 mother-of-pearl
quality: **6** luster
11 iridescence
color: **4** blue, rose **5** black,
brown, cream, green, white
6 yellow
shape: **5** round **7** baroque
type: **8** cultured, Oriental
(saltwater) **9** simulated
10 freshwater

Pearl-Fishers, The
also: **19** Les Pecheurs de
Perles
opera by: **5** Bizet
setting: **6** Ceylon

Pearl of the Antilles *see*
4 Cuba

peasant 4 boor, esne, peon,
serf **5** churl, knave, yokel
6 farmer, rustic, worker **7** la-
borer, lowlife, villein
10 countryman, dirt farmer
Arabic: **6** fellah
Indian: **4** ryot **5** kisan **6** raiyat
Irish: **4** kern
Russian: **5** kulak **6** muzhik
Scottish: **6** cotter

peasantlike 5 crude, rough
6 coarse, oafish, rustic, vulgar
7 boorish, loutish, uncouth
9 unrefined **10** unpolished

peccadillo 4 slip **5** lapse **6** boo-
boo **7** blunder, faux pas, misdeed, misstep **8** petty sin, trespass **9** false move, wrong
step **10** misconduct, wrongdo-

ing **11** misdemeanor **13** transgression

peck 3 pat, rap, tap **4** buss, gobs, lots, mess **5** a slew, batch, bunch, heaps, scads, smack, snack, stack, thump **6** nibble, oodles, pick at, strike, stroke, worlds **8** light jab **9** abundance, light kiss **11** eight quarts
  abbreviation of: 2 pk

Peck, Gregory
  real name: 17 Eldred Gregory Peck
  born: 9 La Jolla CA
  roles: 8 Moby Dick **10** On the Beach, Spellbound **11** The Yearling **12** Duel in the Sun, Roman Holiday **15** The Paradine Case **16** Twelve O'Clock High **17** The Boys from Brazil, The Guns of Navarone **18** To Kill a Mockingbird (Oscar) **19** Gentleman's Agreement, The Keys of the Kingdom **21** The Snows of Kilimanjaro **26** The Man in the Gray Flannel Suit
  autobiography: 12 An Actor's Life

Peckinpah, Sam
  director of: 9 Straw Dogs **12** The Wild Bunch

Pecksniff
  character in: 16 Martin Chuzzlewit
  author: 7 Dickens

peculiar 3 odd **5** queer, weird **6** far-out, quaint, unique **7** bizarre, curious, erratic, private, special, strange, typical, unusual **8** abnormal, distinct, freakish, personal, singular, specific **9** eccentric, exclusive, whimsical **10** capricious, individual, outlandish, particular **11** distinctive **13** idiosyncratic **14** characteristic, distinguishing, representative, unconventional

peculiarity 4 mark **5** badge, stamp, trait **6** oddity **7** feature, quality **8** odd trait **9** attribute, queerness, weirdness **10** eraticism, uniqueness **11** abnormality, bizarreness, distinction, singularity, strangeness **12** eccentricity, freakishness, idiosyncrasy **13** particularity, unnaturalness **14** characteristic **21** distinguishing quality

pecuniary 6 fiscal **8** economic, monetary **9** budgetary, financial

pedagogic 7 bookish, donnish **8** academic, didactic, pedantic, tutorial **9** scholarly **11** educational **12** professorial **13** instructional

pedagogue, pedagog 5 tutor **7** teacher **8** academic, educator **9** professor **10** instructor, schoolmarm **12** educationist, schoolmaster **13** schoolteacher **14** schoolmistress

pedant 6 purist **8** bookworm **9** dogmatist **13** methodologist

pedantic 5 fussy **7** bookish, finicky, pompous, stilted **8** academic, didactic, dogmatic **10** nitpicking, scholastic **11** doctrinaire, punctilious **13** hairsplitting **14** overparticular

Pedasus
  mentioned in: 5 Iliad
  twin brother: 7 Aesepus
  killed by: 8 Euryalus

peddle 4 hawk, sell, vend **6** retail **7** deal out **8** dispense

Peder Victorious
  character in: 16 Giants of the Earth
  author: 7 Rolvaag

pedestal 4 base, foot **6** bottom, plinth **10** foundation

pedestrian 6 walker **7** mundane, prosaic, tedious, trekker **8** mediocre, ordinary, stroller **9** itinerant **10** ambulatory, for walking, unexciting **11** commonplace, peripatetic, unimportant **12** foot-traveler, run-of-the-mill **13** insignificant, perambulating, perambulatory, unimaginative **15** inconsequential

pedigree 4 line **6** family, strain **7** descent, lineage **8** ancestry **9** bloodline, parentage **10** derivation, extraction, family tree **13** line of descent

peek 3 pry **4** peep, peer **5** watch **6** glance **7** glimpse

peel 4 bark, hull, husk, pare, rind, skin, tear, zest **5** flake, scale, shuck, spade, strip **6** remove **7** undress **11** decorticate

peel off 6 remove **7** veer off **8** strip off

peep 4 peek, peer, skim, word **5** cheep, chirp, tweet **6** emerge, glance, murmur, mutter, squeak **7** chirrup, glimpse, peeping, peer out, twitter, whimper, whisper **9** come forth, quick look

peeper 3 eye **4** frog **6** voyeur **10** peeping Tom

peer 4 gape, gaze, look, lord, peek, peep **5** equal, noble, stare **6** appear, emerge, squint **7** compeer **8** nobleman **9** blue blood, gentleman, patrician **10** aristocrat

peerage 8 nobility **10** blue bloods, patricians **11** aristocracy

Peer Gynt
  author: 11 Henrik Ibsen
  character: 3 Ase **7** Solveig **12** The Great Boyg **16** The Button Moulder

peerless 7 supreme **8** flawless **9** faultless, matchless, unequaled, unmatched, unrivaled **10** consummate, inimitable, preeminent, surpassing, unexcelled **11** superlative, unsurpassed **12** incomparable, transcendent

peeve 3 bug, eat, irk, vex **4** fret, gall, rile **5** annoy, chafe, eat at, frost, gripe **6** gnaw at, nettle **7** dislike, perturb, provoke **8** irritate, vexation **9** aggravate, annoyance, complaint, grievance **10** exasperate, irritation **11** aggravation, provocation **12** exasperation, give one a pain **13** pain in the neck **14** thorn in the side

peevish 4 mean **5** cross, huffy, sulky, surly, testy **6** crabby, cranky, grumpy **7** grouchy, pettish **8** churlish, petulant, snappish **9** fractious, irritable, querulous, splenetic **10** ill-humored, ill-natured **11** bad-tempered, ill-tempered, quarrelsome **12** cantankerous

peewee 4 tiny **5** dwarf, small, teeny **6** little, midget, minute **9** itsy-bitsy, itty-bitty, minuscule **10** diminutive, teeny-weeny **11** Lilliputian

Pee Wee
  nickname of: 11 Harold Reese

peg 3 pin **4** nail **5** cleat, dowel, spike, thole **6** skewer, toggle **8** fastener, tholepin

Pegae
  form: 6 spring
  spring of: 6 Dryope

Pegasus
  form: 5 horse
  characteristic: 6 winged
  mother: 6 Medusa
  ridden by: 11 Bellerophon

Peggotty, Clara
  character in: 16 David Copperfield
  author: 7 Dickens

Pei, I M (Ieoh Ming)
  architect of: 12 East Building (National Gallery of Art), L'Enfant Plaza (Washington DC) **14** East-West Center (U of Hawaii), Mile High Center (Denver) **15** Place Ville Marie (Montreal) **16** John

Hancock Tower (Boston)
18 Everson Museum of Art
(Syracuse NY) **22** Kips Bay
Plaza Apartments (NYC)
36 National Center for Atmospheric Research (Boulder
CO)

peignoir 4 gown **6** kimono
8 negligee **9** nightgown
12 dressing gown

Peiser, Lillie Marie
real name of: 11 Lilli Palmer

pejorative 7 mocking **8** debas-
ing, negative, scornful **9** degrading, demeaning, slighting
10 belittling, derogatory, detracting, disdainful, ridiculing,
unpleasant **11** deprecatory, disparaging, downgrading
12 contemptuous, depreciatory,
disapproving
15 uncomplimentary

Peking
also: 7 Beijing
means: 15 northern capital
capital of: 5 China
landmark: 9 Bell Tower,
Drum Tower, Ming Tombs
10 Pei-hai Park **12** Palace
Museum **13** Forbidden City
14 Hall of Classics, Temple
of Heaven **15** Marco Polo
Bridge **17** Temple of Confucius **18** Old Legation Quarter **19** Temple of
Agriculture **20** Great Hall of
the People, Hall of Supreme
Harmony **21** Mausoleum of
Mao Tse-tung **22** Palace of
Heavenly Purity **26** Monument to the People's He-
roes **32** Revolutionary and
Historical Museum
mountain: 7 Taihang
river: 3 Hai **7** Ch'ao-pai
8 Yungting
square: 9 T'ien-an Men
university: 8 Tsinghua
walled city: 5 Inner, Outer,
Tatar **7** Chinese

pelagic 6 marine **7** aquatic,
oceanic **9** thalassic **11** sea-
dwelling

Pelagon
mentioned in: 5 Iliad
ally of: 8 Sarpedon

Pelasgus
also: 9 Corynetes
son: 6 Lycaon **7** Temenus
first: 3 man
founder of: 10 Pelasgians

Pele
real name: 24 Edson Arantes
do Nascimento
sport: 6 soccer
team: 13 New York Cosmos
nationality: 9 Brazilian

Pelegon
mentioned in: 5 Iliad

god of: 5 river
mother: 8 Periboea
son: 11 Asteropaeus

Peleus
king of: 6 Phthia
9 Myrmidons
father: 6 Aeacus
mother: 6 Endeis
brother: 7 Telamon
half-brother: 6 Phocus
wife: 6 Thetis **8** Antigone
son: 8 Achilles
daughter: 8 Polydora

pelf 4 gain **5** booty, lucre,
money **6** mammon, riches,
spoils

Pelias
father: 8 Poseidon
mother: 4 Tyro
twin brother: 6 Neleus
wife: 8 Anaxibia
son: 7 Acastus
nephew: 5 Jason

Pelican State
nickname of: 9 Louisiana

Pelides
descendant of: 6 Peleus

pelisse 4 cape, coat **5** cloak
6 mantle

Pelleas (King Pelleas)
character in: 16 Arthurian
romance
daughter: 6 Elaine

Pelleas and Melisande
also: 18 Pelleas et Melisande
opera by: 7 Debussy
character: 6 Golaud, Yniold
author: 18 Maurice
Maeterlinck

pellet 3 pea **4** ball, bead, drop,
pill **5** pearl, stone **6** marble,
pebble, sphere **7** globule

pell-mell 6 rashly **7** hastily
8 slapdash **9** hurriedly, posthaste **10** at half cock, carelessly, heedlessly, recklessly
11 hurry-scurry, impetuously,
imprudently **12** incautiously
13 helter-skelter, precipitately,
thoughtlessly

pellucid 5 clear, lucid **10** articulate **11** crystalline, translucent, transparent
12 intelligible
14 understandable

Pelopia
father: 8 Thyestes
raped by: 8 Thyestes
son: 9 Aegisthus

Pelops
father: 8 Tantalus
sister: 5 Niobe
son: 6 Atreus, Sciron **7** Le-
treus **8** Pittheus, Thyestes
9 Alcathous **10** Chrysippus

daughter: 7 Nicippe **8** Lysid-
ice **9** Astydamia
resurrected by: 6 Hermes

pelt 3 fur, hit, rap **4** belt, coat,
hide, skin, sock **5** pound,
punch, whack **6** batter, buffet,
fleece, pepper, pummel, strike,
thrash, thwack **7** clobber

Pemphredo
member of: 6 Graeae, Graiae

pen 3 sty **4** cage, coop, crib,
fold **5** draft, hutch, pound,
quill, stall, write **6** corral, pencil, scrawl **7** compose, pad-
dock **8** compound, scribble,
stockade **9** ballpoint, enclosure

penal 7 of jails **8** punitive
9 punishing **10** corrective, penalizing **11** castigatory, retrib-
utive **12** disciplinary

penalty 4 fine **7** forfeit
8 handicap **9** suffering **10** assessment, forfeiture, infliction,
punishment **11** retribution
12 disadvantage

penance 9 atonement, expiation, hair shirt, penitence
10 contrition, repentance
12 propitiation
13 mortification

Penates
protectors of: 4 home
companions: 5 lares

penchant 4 bent, bias, gift,
turn **5** fancy, flair, knack,
taste **6** liking, relish **7** leaning
8 affinity, fondness, tendency
9 prejudice, proneness, readiness **10** attraction, partiality,
preference, proclivity, propensity **11** disposition, inclination **12** predilection
14 predisposition

pendant 3 fob **6** locket
15 hanging ornament

Pendennis
author: 25 William Makepeace Thackeray
character: 9 Laura Bell
10 Henry Foker **12** Blanche
Amory **13** Emily Costigan
14 Helen Pendennis, Major
Pendennis **15** Arthur
Pendennis

pendent, pendant 7 hanging,
jutting, pensile **8** dangling,
swinging **9** extending, pendulous, suspended **10** projecting,
protruding **11** overhanging,
protuberant

pendente lite 16 during litigation **19** with a lawsuit
pending

pending 8 imminent **9** undecided, unsettled **10** in suspense, unfinished, unresolved,

up in the air **11** in the offing **12** undetermined

pendulous 7 hanging, pendent, pensile, sagging **8** dangling, drooping, swinging **9** suspended

pendulum
invented by: **7** Galileo

Penelope
father: **7** Icarius
mother: **8** Periboea
husband: **8** Odysseus **9** Telegonus
son: **6** Ifalus **10** Telemachus **11** Polyporthis
fended off: **7** suitors

penetrate 3 get **4** bore **5** catch, enter, prick **6** decode, fathom, invade, pierce, seep in **7** cut into, discern, pervade, unravel **8** decipher, perceive, permeate, puncture, saturate, traverse **9** figure out, perforate **10** comprehend, cut through, impregnate, infiltrate, see through, understand **11** pass through

penetrating 4 keen **5** acrid, alert, alive, aware, harsh, heady, sharp, smart **6** astute, biting, clever, shrewd, strong **7** caustic, pungent, reeking **8** piercing, redolent, stinging **9** pervading, pervasive, trenchant **10** discerning, perceptive, percipient, permeating, saturating, thoughtful **11** intelligent, sharp-witted **13** perspicacious

penetration 5 foray, grasp **6** access, boring **7** insight, passage **8** infusion, invasion, keenness, piercing **9** intrusion, quickness, sharpness **10** astuteness, cleverness, perception, puncturing, shrewdness **11** discernment, perforation **12** intelligence, perspicacity

Peneus
god of: **5** river
river: **6** Peneus
son: **7** Hypseus
daughter: **6** Daphne

Penguin Island
author: **13** Anatole France

peninsula 4 cape **5** point **8** headland **10** promontory

Peninsular State
nickname of: **7** Florida

penitence 6 regret, sorrow **7** penance, remorse **9** atonement, attrition, expiation **10** contrition, repentance **11** compunction, humiliation

penitent 5 sorry **6** rueful **7** atoning, devotee, pilgrim **8** contrite **9** regretful, repentant **10** remorseful

penitentiary 3 pen **4** jail, stir **5** joint **6** prison **7** slammer **8** big house

Penn, Arthur
director of: **12** Little Big Man **14** Bonnie and Clyde **16** The Miracle Worker

Penn, Sean
wife: **7** Madonna
roles: **7** Bad Boys **15** Shanghai Express **22** The Falcon and the Snowman **24** Fast Times at Ridgemont High

Pennacook (Merrimac)
language family: **9** Algonkian **10** Algonquian
location: **5** Maine **6** Quebec **7** New York, Vermont **10** New England **12** New Hampshire **13** Massachusetts
leader: **11** Wannalancet **12** Passaconaway
related to: **6** Abnaki

pen name
French: **10** nom de plume

pennant 4 flag, jack **6** banner, burgee, colors, ensign, pennon **7** bunting **8** ensignia, standard, streamer **9** banderole, oriflamme

penniless 4 poor **5** broke, needy **6** busted, ruined **8** bankrupt, indigent, strapped, wiped out **9** destitute, flat broke, insolvent, moneyless **10** down-and-out, pauperized **12** impoverished **15** poverty-stricken

pennon 4 flag, jack **6** banner, colors, ensign **7** pennant **8** standard, streamer

Pennsylvania *see box*

penny 3 sum **4** cent **5** cheap, pence **6** copper, stiver **7** trivial

penny-pinching 5 close, tight **6** stingy **7** miserly **8** grudging **9** niggardly, penurious **10** ungenerous **11** tight-fisted **12** parsimonious

Penny Serenade
director: **13** George Stevens
cast: **9** Cary Grant **10** Irene Dunne **11** Beulah Bondi **13** Edgar Buchanan

pennyweight
abbreviation of: **3** dwt

Penobscot
language family: **9** Algonkian **10** Algonquian
location: **5** Maine **13** Old Town Island
members of: **17** Abnaki Confederacy

Penrod
author: **15** Booth Tarkington
sequel: **12** Penrod and Sam **13** Penrod Jashber

character: **6** Herman, Verman **9** Sarah Crim **11** Rupe Collins **13** Marjorie Jones **15** Penrod Schofield
dog: **4** Duke

pensee 7 thought **10** reflection

Pensees
author: **12** Blaise Pascal

pension 5 grant **6** income, retire **7** annuity, stipend, subsidy **9** allowance **13** boardinghouse **14** retirement fund

pensive 3 sad **5** grave **6** dreamy, musing, solemn, somber **7** serious, wistful **8** dreaming **10** meditative, melancholy, reflective **11** daydreaming **13** contemplative, introspective **15** sadly thoughtful

Pentateuch 10 Law of Moses **28** first five books of Old Testament
see also: **7** books of **12** Old Testament

Penthesilea
queen of: **7** Amazons
father: **4** Ares
mother: **6** Otrere
sister: **9** Hippolyta
killed by: **8** Achilles

Pentheus
king of: **6** Thebes
father: **6** Echion
mother: **5** Agave
grandfather: **6** Cadmus

pent-up 7 boxed-up, checked, stifled **8** hedged-in, held back, penned-in, penned-up, reined in, stored-up **9** bottled-up, repressed **10** restrained, suppressed

penurious 5 close **6** frugal, stingy **7** miserly, sparing **8** stinting **9** niggardly **12** parsimonious **13** penny-pinching

penury 4 need, want **7** poverty **9** indigence, privation **10** bankruptcy, insolvency **11** destitution **14** impoverishment

Penutian
language branch: **4** Coos **5** Huave, Maidu, Mayan, Miwok **6** Wintun, Yokuts **7** Chinook, Klamath, Takelma, Totonac **8** Sahaptin **9** Mixe-Zoque, Tsimshian
tribe: **5** Maidu **7** Klamath

peon 4 pawn, serf **5** slave **6** drudge, menial, worker **7** footman, laborer, orderly, peasant, servant

peony 7 Paeonia
varieties: **4** Tree **7** Chinese,

Pennsylvania
abbreviation: 2 PA **5** Penna
nickname: 8 Keystone
capital: 10 Harrisburg
largest city: 12 Philadelphia
others: 4 Erie, Etna, Plum, York **5** Avoca, Baden **6** Beaver,
Bethel, Butler, Easton, Emmaus, Radnor, Ridley, Sharon
7 Altoona, Baldwin, Bristol, Chester, Ephrata, Hanover,
Hershey, Lebanon, Reading **8** Abington, Braddock, Bradford, Bryn Mawr, Carlisle, Clairton, Harrison, Hazelton,
Monessen, Scranton, Shamokin **9** Aliquippa, Allentown,
Bethlehem, Charleroi, Haverford, Jeannette, Johnstown,
Lancaster, Meadville, Mill Creek, Newcastle, Swissvale,
Uniontown, Whitehall **10** Carbondale, Gettysburg, Mc-
Keesport, Norristown, Pittsburgh **11** Springfield, Wilkes
Barre **12** State College, Williamsport
college: 3 PSU **4** Penn, Pitt **5** Gratz, Thiel **6** Drexel, Lehigh, Temple **7** Juniata, LaSalle, Ursinus **8** Alliance, Bryn
Mawr, Bucknell, Duquesne, Lycoming **9** Dickinson, Lafayette, Penn State, St Josephs, Villanova **10** Pittsburgh,
Swarthmore **12** Carnegie Tech **17** Pennsylvania State
feature:
  battle site: **10** Gettysburg
  bell: **7** Liberty
  hall: **12** Independence
  historical site: **11** Valley Forge
tribe: 6 Seneca **7** Shawnee **8** Delaware **11** Lenni-Lanape
13 Susquehannock
people: 5 Amish, Dutch **10** Stan Musial **11** Andrew Wyeth,
Ethel Waters, Mary Cassatt, Stuart Davis **12** Andrew Mellon, Anthony Wayne, Margaret Mead, Martha Graham,
Samuel Barber, Thomas Eakins **13** Clifford Odets, Gertrude Stein **14** George S Kaufman **15** Maxwell Anderson
19 Stephen Vincent Benet
  explorer: **5** Brule **6** Hudson **11** Hendrickson
lake: 4 Erie **7** Harveys **8** Conneaut **10** Pymatuning
13 Wallenpaupack
land rank: 11 thirty-third
mountain: 5 South **6** Pocono **11** Alleghenies
  highest point: **5** Davis
physical feature:
  peninsula: **11** Presque Isle
  valley: **5** Great
president: 13 James Buchanan
river: 4 Ohio **6** Lehigh **7** Clarion, Genesee, Juniata, Licking, Towanda **8** Caldwell, Delaware, Schrader **9** Allegheny **10** Schuylkill **11** Monongahela, Susquehanna
state admission: 6 second
state bird: 12 ruffed grouse
state fish: 10 brook trout
state flower: 14 mountain laurel
state motto: 28 Virtue Liberty and Independence
state tree: 7 hemlock

Tibetan **8** Majorcan
11 Chinese tree **12** Common
garden

people 3 kin **5** folks **6** family,
humans, the mob **7** kinfolk,
mankind, mortals, the herd
8 citizens, humanity, populace,
the crowd **9** ancestors, citizenry, commoners, human-
kind, relatives, the masses, the
public, the rabble **10** population **11** homo sapiens, human
beings, individuals, inhabitants, John Q Public, men and
women, the millions

People Are Funny
  host: 13 Art Linkletter

pep 3 vim, zip **4** dash, life,
snap **5** gusto, verve, vigor
6 energy, ginger, spirit **8** vitality, vivacity **9** animation
10 enthusiasm, get-up-and-go,
liveliness

Pepe Le Moko
  director: 14 Julien Duvivier
  cast: 9 Jean Gabin **13** Gabriel
  Gabrio, Mireille Balin
  remade as: 6 Casbah
  7 Algiers

peperomia
  varieties: 3 Ivy **6** Prayer, Vin-
  ing **7** Ivy-leaf, Leather, Red-
  edge **8** Coin-leaf, Platinum
  9 Flowering **10** Silver-edge,
  Silver-leaf, Watermelon
  11 Green-ripple **13** Emerald-
  ripple, Little fantasy

Pepita
  character in: 21 The Bridge
  of San Luis Rey
  author: 6 Wilder

Peppard, George
  born: 9 Detroit MI
  wife: 15 Elizabeth Ashley
  roles: 6 Tobruk **7** Banacek
  8 The A-Team **16** The Carpetbaggers **19** Breakfast at
  Tiffany's

pepper 3 dot **6** shower, strafe
7 bombard **8** sprinkle **9** condiment, vegetable

pepper, peppercorn
  botanical name: 5 Piper **7** P
  nigrum **8** Capsicum **10** Pi-
  peraceae **11** C frutescens
  color: 3 red **5** black, green,
  white
  origin: 5 India **6** Brazil, Ceylon **7** Malabar, Sarawak, Sumatra **8** Alleppey, Pandjang,
  Sri Lanka **11** Tellicherry
  varieties: 3 Red **4** Baby, Bell,
  Bird, Cone, Long, Wild
  5 Betle, Black, Chili, Cubeb,
  Green, Japan, Sweet,
  White **6** Cherry **7** Cayenne,
  Celebes, Cluster, Tabasco
  8 Capsicum **9** Mild water
  10 Australian, Red cluster
  12 Mountain long, Tabasco-
  sauce
  French: 6 poivre
  German: 7 pfeffer
  Italian: 4 pepe
  Latin: 5 piper
  Persian: 5 biber **6** pilpil
  Spanish: 8 pimienta
  Swedish: 6 peppar
  Sanskrit: 7 pippali

peppermint 6 Mentha
  varieties: 4 Gray **5** Black,
  River, White **6** Silver, Sydney **9** Blackbutt **10** Robertson's **11** Broad-leaved
  15 Mount Wellington
  17 Narrow-leaved black
  19 Nichol's willow-leaved

peppermint schnapps
  type: 7 liqueur
  flavor: 4 mint

peppery 3 hot **5** fiery, sharp,
spicy **7** burning, piquant, pungent **14** highly seasoned

peppy 4 spry **5** brisk, perky
6 active, bouncy, frisky, lively,
snappy **7** dynamic **8** animated,
spirited, vigorous **9** energetic,
full of pep, sparkling,

sprightly, vivacious
12 enthusiastic

pep up 4 fire **6** excite, vivify,
wake up **7** animate, enliven,
quicken **8** vitalize

Pepys, Samuel
author of: **10** Pepys' Diary

Pepys' Diary
author: **11** Samuel Pepys

Pequot
language family: **9** Algonkian **10** Algonquian
location: **11** Connecticut,
Rhode Island

perambulate 4 pace, tour,
walk **5** amble, mosey **6** ramble, stroll **7** meander, saunter
9 promenade

perceivable 7 visible **8** apparent, distinct **10** detectable, noticeable, observable
11 discernible, perceptible
13 ascertainable

perceive 3 get, see **4** feel,
hear, know, note **5** grasp,
savvy, sense, smell, taste **6** deduce, detect, gather, notice
7 discern, make out, observe,
realize **8** conclude, discover
9 apprehend, be aware of, recognize **10** comprehend, understand **11** distinguish

perceptible 5 clear, plain
7 evident, notable, obvious,
visible **8** apparent, distinct,
manifest, palpable, tangible,
unhidden **9** prominent **10** detectable, noticeable, observable **11** conspicuous,
discernible, perceivable, unconcealed, well-defined **12** dis-
coverable, unmistakable
13 ascertainable

perception 5 grasp, sense
7 faculty **8** judgment **9** awareness, detection **10** cognizance,
conception **11** discernment,
recognition **12** apprehension
13 comprehension, consciousness, understanding
14 discrimination

perceptive 4 keen **5** acute,
aware, quick, sharp **6** astute,
shrewd **8** sensible **9** sensitive
10 discerning, insightful, responsive **11** intelligent, penetrating, quick-witted
13 understanding

perch 3 sit **4** land, rest, seat
5 eyrie, light, roost **6** alight,
settle

Perchta
also: **7** Berchta
origin: **8** Germanic
goddess of: **5** death **9** fertility
corresponds to: **5** Holle

Percival, Perceval
character in: **16** Arthurian
romance

percolate 4 boil, brew **6** bubble, seethe

percussion instrument
4 gong **5** anvil, bells, tabor
6 chimes, rattle **7** celesta, cymbals, marimba, taboret, tim-
pani **8** bass drum, side drum,
triangle **9** castanets, dulcitone,
snare drum, tenor drum, typo-
phone, xylophone **10** kettledrum, tambourine
12 Glockenspiel, tubular bells

Percy, Walker
author of: **8** Lancelot **12** The
Moviegoer **14** Love in the
Ruins **15** The Second Coming **16** The Last Gentleman

Perdita
character in: **14** The Winter's
Tale
author: **11** Shakespeare

perdition 4 Hell, ruin **8** hellfire **9** damnation, ruination
11 destruction
12 condemnation

Perdix
also: **9** Polycaste
brother: **8** Daedalus
son: **5** Talus
changed into: **9** partridge

pere 6 father, senior

Pere Goriot
author: **14** Honore de Balzac
character: **15** Monsieur Vau-
trin **17** Eugene de Rastig-
nac, Madame de Beauseant
18 Victorine Taillefer
26 Countess Anastasie de
Restaud, Baroness Delphine
de Nucingen

peregrination 4 trip **5** jaunt,
sally **6** hiking, junket, roving,
travel **7** journey, roaming
8 rambling, trekking **9** excursion, wandering **10** expedition

Peregrine Pickle
author: **14** Tobias Smollett

Pereira, William
architect of: **13** Cape Canaveral **20** Transamerica Building (San Francisco)

Perelman, S J
author of: **10** Eastward Ha
15 One Touch of Venus
(with Ogden Nash and Kurt
Weill) **16** The Road to Mil-
town **18** Strictly from Hunger **24** Under the Spreading
Atrophy

peremptory 5 final **6** biased,
lordly **8** absolute, decisive,
dogmatic **9** assertive, imperious **10** aggressive, high-
handed, imperative, obligatory,

undeniable **11** dictatorial,
domineering, irrevocable,
opinionated, overbearing, unavoidable, unequivocal
12 closed-minded, irreversible
13 authoritative **14** unquestionable **16** incontrovertible

perennial 5 fixed **7** durable,
lasting, undying **8** constant,
enduring, timeless **9** ceaseless,
continual, immutable, incessant, long-lived, permanent,
perpetual, unceasing, unfailing **10** changeless, continuous,
persistent, unchanging **11** everlasting, long-lasting, unremitting **12** imperishable
14 indestructible

Pereus
father: **6** Elatus
mother: **7** Laodice

Perez, Manuel Benitez
nickname: **10** El Cordobes

perfect 4 pure, true **5** exact,
ideal, whole **6** effect, entire,
evolve, strict **7** achieve, develop, fulfill, precise, realize,
sublime, supreme **8** absolute,
accurate, complete, faithful,
finished, flawless, peerless,
thorough, unbroken, unerring
9 blameless, faultless, matchless, undamaged, unequaled,
unrivaled, untainted **10** accomplish, consummate, im-
maculate, impeccable,
scrupulous, unimpaired **11** superlative, unblemished, unmitigated, unqualified

perfection 6 purity **9** achiev-
ing, evolution, exactness, precision, sublimity
10 completion, excellence,
ideal state **11** development,
fulfillment, perfectness, realization, superiority **12** accurateness, consummation,
flawlessness **13** faultlessness,
impeccability
14 accomplishment

perfectly 5 fully, quite
6 purely, wholly **7** totally, utterly **8** entirely, superbly
9 downright, supremely
10 absolutely, altogether, completely, flawlessly, impeccably,
infinitely, positively, thoroughly **11** faultlessly, wonderfully **12** consummately,
preeminently, to perfection,
without fault **13** without defect **14** to the nth degree,
without blemish

perfidious 5 false, lying
6 shifty, sneaky **7** corrupt
8 cheating, disloyal, two-faced
9 deceitful, dishonest, faithless **10** traitorous, treasonous,
unfaithful, untruthful
11 treacherous, treasonable

12 dishonorable, undependable, unscrupulous **13** double-dealing, untrustworthy

perfidy 6 deceit **7** treason **8** bad faith, betrayal **9** falseness, recreancy, treachery, two-timing **10** disloyalty, infidelity **11** double-cross, inconstancy **13** breach of faith, deceitfulness, double-dealing, faithlessness **14** unfaithfulness

perforate 4 bore, gash, hole, slit, stab **5** drill, prick, punch, slash, split, stick **6** pierce **8** puncture **9** lancinate, penetrate

perform 2 do **3** act **4** meet, play **5** enact **6** attain, depict, effect, finish, render, troupe **7** achieve, execute, fulfill, portray, present, pull off, realize **8** carry out, knock off **9** discharge, dispose of, polish off, represent **10** accomplish, bring about, consummate, perpetrate, take part in

performance 4 play, show **5** doing, opera **6** ballet **7** concert, conduct, recital **8** ceremony, dispatch, exercise **9** acquittal, discharge, execution, rendering, spectacle **10** attainment, completion, exhibition, performing, production **11** achievement, fulfillment, realization, transaction **12** consummation, effectuation, perpetration, presentation **13** entertainment **14** accomplishment

perfume 4 odor **5** aroma, scent, smell **7** bouquet, cologne, essence, extract, sweeten **9** aromatize, fragrance

perfumed 7 odorous, scented **8** aromatic, fragrant **11** odoriferous **12** sweet-scented **13** sweet-smelling

perfunctory 3 lax **5** hasty **6** casual **7** cursory, offhand, routine **8** careless, listless, lukewarm **9** apathetic, negligent **10** mechanical, spiritless, unthinking **11** halfhearted, inattentive, indifferent, passionless, superficial, unconcerned **13** disinterested

Pergamus
father: **11** Neoptolemus
mother: **10** Andromache

pergola 5 arbor, bower **6** ramada **7** balcony, trellis

Per Hanea
character in: **16** Giants of the Earth
author: **7** Rolvaag

perhaps 5 maybe **6** mayhap **8** peut-etre, possibly **9** per-

chance **10** God willing, imaginably **11** conceivably **12** peradventure

Perialla
form: **9** priestess
priestess of: **6** Delphi

Periapis
also: **8** Periopis
father: **6** Pheres
son: **9** Patrocles

Periboea
father: **9** Alcathous, Hipponous
husband: **6** Oeneus **7** Polybus
son: **6** Tydeus **7** Olenias, Pelegon **14** Telamonian Ajax
foster son: **7** Oedipus

Perichole, La
character in: **21** The Bridge of San Luis Rey
author: **6** Wilder

Pericles, Prince of Tyre
author: **18** William Shakespeare
character: **5** Cleon **6** Marina, Thaisa **7** Dionyza **9** Antiochus **10** Lysimachus

Periclymenus
father: **6** Neleus **8** Poseidon
grandfather: **8** Poseidon
gift: **13** shape-changing
killed by: **8** Hercules

periderm 4 bark **8** covering **9** sheathing

peridot
species: **7** olivine
source: **5** Burma, Mogok **8** Zebirget
color: **11** yellow-green

perigee 5 depth, nadir **8** low point

Perikeiromene (The Rape of the Ringlets)
author: **8** Menander

peril 4 risk **6** danger, hazard, menace, threat **7** pitfall **8** jeopardy, unsafety **10** insecurity **11** uncertainty **13** cause for alarm, vulnerability

Perilaus
father: **7** Icarius
cousin: **12** Clytemnestra

perilous 5 risky, shaky **6** chancy, unsafe, unsure **7** ominous **8** insecure, slippery, ticklish **9** dangerous, hazardous, uncertain **10** precarious, vulnerable **11** threatening, venturesome

Perimedes
mentioned in: **7** Odyssey
companion of: **8** Odysseus
father: **10** Eurystheus

Perimele
father: **10** Hippodamas

ravished by: **8** Achelous
changed into: **6** island

perimeter 4 edge **6** border, bounds, margin **8** confines **9** periphery **10** borderline **13** circumference

period 3 age, end, eon, era **4** halt, stop, term, time **5** close, epoch, limit **6** finale, finish, season **7** curtain **8** duration, interval **9** cessation, interlude
French: **6** siecle

periodic, periodical 6 cyclic **7** regular, routine **8** frequent, repeated, seasonal **9** recurrent, recurring **12** intermittent

periodical 5 daily, paper **6** annual, review, weekly **7** journal, monthly **8** bulletin, magazine **9** newspaper, quarterly **10** newsletter **11** publication **12** newsmagazine

periodically 5 often **9** regularly, routinely **10** frequently, repeatedly **12** occasionally

Periopis see **8** Periapis

peripatetic 6 roving **7** migrant, nomadic, roaming, walking **8** rambling, tramping **9** itinerant, migratory, traveling, wandering **10** ambulating, ambulatory **12** Aristotelian, gallivanting **13** peregrinating

Periphas
mentioned in: **5** Iliad
king of: **6** Attica
father: **6** Epytus
vocation: **6** herald **7** warrior
changed into: **5** eagle
changed by: **4** Zeus

periphery 4 edge **5** bound **6** border **7** fringes **8** boundary **9** outskirts, perimeter **13** circumference

Periphetes
form: **5** giant
father: **7** Copreus
ally of: **7** Trojans
killed by: **7** Theseus

perish 3 die **5** decay **6** expire, vanish **7** crumble **8** pass away **9** disappear **10** come to ruin, wither away **11** be destroyed

perishable 8 fleeting, unstable **9** ephemeral **10** evanescent, short-lived, transitory **12** decomposable

perished 4 dead, died **7** expired **8** lifeless **10** passed away

periwinkle 5 Vinca **12** Catharanthus
varieties: **4** Rose **6** Common, Lesser **7** Greater **10** Madagascar

perjury 13 false swearing **14** lying under oath **20** giving false testimony

Perkins, Anthony
 born: **9** New York NY
 roles: **6** Psycho **11** Norman Bates **14** Catch Twenty-Two **17** Look Homeward Angel **18** Desire Under the Elms, Friendly Persuasion

perk up 4 lift **5** cheer, rally, renew **6** buoy up, lift up, revive **7** animate, enliven, gladden **8** brighten, vitalize **9** stimulate **10** rejuvenate

perky 3 gay **4** pert **5** alert, brisk, happy, saucy, sunny **6** jaunty, lively **7** smiling **8** animated, cheerful, spirited **9** sprightly, vivacious **11** free and easy **12** full of spirit, lighthearted

permanent 3 set **4** perm, wave **6** stable **7** abiding, durable, endless, eternal, lasting, undying **8** constant, enduring, immortal, infinite, unending, unfading **9** deathless, immutable, long-lived, perpetual, unfailing **10** changeless, unyielding **11** everlasting, long-lasting, never-ending, unalterable **12** imperishable

permeate 4 fill **5** imbue **6** infuse **7** pervade **8** saturate **9** penetrate **11** pass through, seep through, soak through

per mensem 10 by the month

permissible 5 legal, licit **6** lawful **7** allowed, granted **8** licensed **9** allowable, permitted, tolerated **10** admissible, authorized, legitimate, sanctioned **12** unprohibited

permission 5 grant, leave **6** assent, permit **7** consent, license **8** approval, sanction **9** agreement, allowance **10** compliance, concession, indulgence **11** approbation, endorsement **12** acquiescence, dispensation **13** authorization

permissive 3 lax **7** lenient **8** allowing, granting, tolerant **9** assenting, easygoing, indulgent **10** consenting, forbearing, permitting **11** acquiescent **13** unprohibitive **14** unproscriptive

permit 2 OK **3** let **5** allow **6** endure, suffer **7** agree to, approve, condone, endorse, let pass, license, warrant **8** bear with, sanction, tolerate **9** authority, authorize, consent to, put up with **11** give leave to **12** give assent to **13** authorization
 French: **13** laissez passer

permit to leave 4 free **5** let go **6** excuse **7** dismiss, release, set free **8** liberate **9** allow to go, discharge, send forth

pernicious 5 fatal, toxic **6** deadly, lethal, mortal **7** baneful, harmful, noxious, serious **8** damaging, venomous **9** dangerous, injurious, malignant, poisonous **10** disastrous **11** deleterious, destructive, detrimental

pernod
 type: **8** aperitif
 flavor: **5** anise
 substitute for: **8** absinthe
 with gin: **7** Dubarry
 with orange juice: **9** Tiger Tail
 with rum: **8** Shanghai
 with rye: **3** TNT

Pero
 father: **6** Neleus
 mother: **7** Chloris
 husband: **4** Bias

peroration 6 sermon, speech, tirade **7** address, lecture, oration **8** diatribe, harangue, jeremiad **9** discourse, philippic **10** filibuster **11** declamation, exhortation

perpendicular 4 sine **5** erect, plumb, sheer, steep **7** upright **8** vertical **10** right angle

perpetrate 2 do **5** enact **6** commit, pursue **7** execute, inflict, perform, pull off **8** carry out, transact

perpetration 5 doing **9** committal **10** commission, committing, performing **11** carrying out, performance

perpetrator 9 performer **11** participant

perpetual 7 abiding, endless, eternal, lasting **8** constant, enduring, repeated, unending **9** ceaseless, continual, incessant, permanent, sustained, unceasing **10** continuous **11** everlasting, never ending, unremitting **12** interminable **13** inexhaustible, uninterrupted

perpetuate 4 save **7** sustain **8** continue, maintain, make last, preserve **10** eternalize **11** immortalize, memorialize

perpetuity 7 all time, forever **8** eternity, infinity **9** end of time **10** permanence **11** endlessness **12** perpetuation, timelessness **13** perdurability, perennialness

perplex 5 mix up, stump **6** baffle, boggle, muddle, puzzle, rattle **7** confuse, mystify, nonplus **8** befuddle, bewilder, confound **9** dumbfound

perplexed 7 anxious, amazed, baffled, bemused, muddled, puzzled **8** confused, doubtful, involved **9** befuddled, intricate, mystified **10** astonished, bewildered, nonplussed

perplexing 4 hard, mazy **6** thorny **7** complex **10** mysterious
 riddle: **9** conundrum

perplexity 9 confusion **10** bafflement, puzzlement **12** bewilderment **13** mystification

perquisite 3 due **4** gift, perk **5** right **6** reward **7** benefit, present **9** advantage, emolument, privilege **10** honorarium, inducement, recompense **13** fringe benefit

Perry, Matthew Calbraith
 served in: **10** Mexican War **19** War of Eighteen Twelve
 rank: **9** commodore
 helped establish: **7** Liberia
 commander of: **17** US African Squadron
 gained treaty with: **5** Japan

Perry, Oliver Hazard
 nickname: **14** Hero of Lake Erie
 served in: **13** Tripolitan War **19** War of Eighteen-Twelve
 battle: **8** Lake Erie
 commander of ship: **7** Niagara **8** Lawrence
 defeated: **7** British
 saying: **31** We have met the enemy and they are ours

Perry, William
 nickname: **12** Refrigerator
 sport: **8** football
 team: **12** Chicago Bears

Perry Como Show, The
 regulars: **8** Don Adams **9** Jack Duffy, Paul Lynde **10** Pierre Olaf **11** Kaye Ballard **12** Sandy Stewart **14** Fontane Sisters **17** Ray Charles Singers **18** Louis Da Pron Dancers **19** Peter Gennaro Dancers
 orchestra: **13** Mitchell Ayres
 theme: **16** Dream Along with Me

Perry Mason
 character: **6** Lt Drum **7** Lt Tragg **9** Paul Drake **10** Lt Anderson **11** Della Street **14** Hamilton Burger
 cast: **9** Wesley Lau **10** Ray Collins **11** Barbara Hale, Raymond Burr **13** William Hopper, William Talman **15** Richard Anderson

Persa
 father: **7** Oceanus
 mother: **6** Tethys

persecute 3 vex **4** bait **5** abuse, annoy, bully, harry, hound **6** badger, harass, harrow, hector, plague **7** oppress, torment **8** maltreat **9** tyrannize, victimize

Persephone
  also: 4 Cora, Kore **10** Proserpina, Proserpine
  queen of: 5 Hades
  father: 4 Zeus
  mother: 7 Demeter
  husband: 5 Hades
  abducted by: 5 Pluto
  ate seeds of: 11 pomegranate
  epithet: 11 Carpophorus
  corresponds to: 5 Brimo **6** Libera **8** Despoena

Perseus
  father: 4 Zeus
  mother: 5 Danae
  grandfather: 8 Acrisius
  wife: 9 Andromeda
  son: 6 Mestor, Perses **7** Alcaeus, Heleius **9** Electryon, Sthenelus
  daughter: 10 Gorgophone
  saved: 9 Andromeda
  killed: 6 Gorgon, Medusa

perseverance 8 tenacity **10** doggedness, resolution **11** persistence **12** resoluteness **13** determination, steadfastness

persevere 6 hang on, keep on **7** persist **8** keep at it, plug away, work hard **9** not give up, stick to it **10** be resolute, be resolved, hammer away **11** be obstinate, be steadfast, hang in there

persevering 6 dogged **8** constant, diligent, resolute, sedulous **9** keeping on, steadfast, tenacious **10** determined, persistent, unflagging **11** hardworking, industrious, unremitting

Pershing, John J
  nickname: 9 Black Jack
  served in: 3 WWI **11** Philippines, World War One **18** Spanish-American War
  commander of: 21 Mexican border campaign
  trained: 27 American Expeditionary Forces
  battle: 10 Kettle Hill **11** San Juan Hill
  fought against: 5 Moros **11** Pancho Villa
  rank: 16 brigadier general **18** general of the armies
  memoirs: 26 My Experiences in the World War
    won: 13 Pulitzer Prize (for history)

Persia see **4** Iran

Persian Gulf War
  caused by: 4 Iraq **13** Saddam Hussein **14** Kuwait invasion

  took place in: 4 Iraq **6** Kuwait **10** Middle East **11** Saudi Arabia
  leaders:
  Allies: 11 Colin Powell **15** Khalid bin Sultan **18** H Norman Schwarzkopf
  Iraq: 13 Saddam Hussein
  operations: 11 Desert Storm **12** Desert Shield
  weapons: 4 Scud **5** AWACS **6** Abrams, Apache **7** Bradley, Patriot, Stealth **8** Tomahawk
  battle: 6 Khafji **18** mother of all battles

Persian Mythology
  god of light/truth: 7 Mithras

Persians, The
  author: 9 Aeschylus
  character: 6 Atossa, Xerxes **13** Ghost of Darius

persist 4 go on, last, stay **6** endure, hang on, hold on, remain **7** hold out, survive **8** continue, keep at it, not yield **9** not give up, persevere, stand fast, stick to it **10** be resolute **11** be obstinate, be tenacious, hang in there, never say die

persistence 8 tenacity **9** diligence **11** application **12** perseverance **13** determination

persistent 6 dogged **7** abiding, endless, eternal, lasting **8** constant, enduring, obdurate, resolute, stubborn **9** continual, incessant, obstinate, perpetual, steadfast, sustained, tenacious, unceasing, unfailing **10** continuous, determined, persisting, relentless, unshakable, unswerving **11** persevering, unrelenting, unremitting **12** interminable **13** inexhaustible

Perske, Betty Joan
  real name of: 12 Lauren Bacall

persnickety 5 fussy **6** choosy **7** finical, finicky **8** picayune **10** fastidious, fuddy-duddy, meticulous, nitpicking, particular, pernickety **11** overprecise, punctilious **13** overdemanding

person 4 body, soul **5** being, human **6** mortal **8** creature **9** earthling **10** human being, individual, living body, living soul

persona 5 being **6** facade **9** character

personable 4 warm **7** affable, amiable, cordial, likable, tactful **8** amicable, charming, friendly, outgoing, pleasant, sociable **9** agreeable **10** attractive, diplomatic **11** complaisant, sympathetic **12** well-disposed, well-mannered

personage 3 VIP **5** nabob **6** bigwig **7** big name, big shot, notable **8** big wheel, luminary, somebody **9** celebrity, dignitary **11** heavyweight **12** leading light, public figure **13** highmuck-a-muck

persona grata 16 acceptable person **34** acceptable diplomatic representative

personal 3 own **5** privy **6** bodily, inward, secret **7** private, special **8** intimate, physical **9** corporeal, exclusive **10** individual, particular, subjective **12** confidential

personality 5 charm **6** makeup, nature **8** charisma, identity **9** magnetism **10** affability, amiability **11** disposition, temperament **12** friendliness **13** agreeableness, individuality **15** distinctiveness

persona non grata 15 unwelcome person **18** unacceptable person **33** unwelcome diplomatic representative

personification of see box, p. 744

personify 6 embody **7** express **9** exemplify, incarnate, represent, symbolize **11** externalize, incorporate, personalize **12** characterize

personnel 4 crew **5** staff **7** members, workers **8** manpower **9** employees, work force **10** associates

Person to Person
  host: 13 Edward R Murrow **18** Charles Collingwood

perspective 4 view **5** scape, scene, vista **7** outlook **8** overview, prospect **9** broad view, viewpoint **12** bird's-eye view

perspicacious 4 keen **5** acute, alert, awake, sharp **6** astute, shrewd **9** clear-eyed, sagacious **10** discerning, perceptive **11** clearheaded, keen-sighted, penetrating, sharp-witted **12** clear-sighted

perspicacity 6 acumen **8** keenness, sagacity **9** acuteness, alertness, sharpness **10** astuteness, perception, shrewdness **11** discernment **14** discrimination

persuadable 7 willing **8** amenable, obliging **9** malleable, tractable **10** open-minded **16** open to suggestion

persuade 3 get **4** coax, lure, move, sway **5** tempt **6** cajole, entice, induce, prompt

Personification of

aging: 4 Elli
air: 4 Amen, Amon
5 Ammon **6** Aether
astronomy: 6 Urania
breath: 4 Amen, Amon
5 Ammon
chaos: 4 Nunu
choral song:
11 Terpsichore
comedy: 6 Thalia
confusion: 5 Chaos
conscience: 5 Aidos
courage: 5 Arete **6** Virtus
dance: 8 Polymnia
10 Polyhymnia
11 Terpsichore
death: 4 Mors **6** Namtar
8 Thanatos
desert: 3 Set **4** Seth
desire: 6 Pothos
divine punishment:
3 Ate **7** Nemesis
east wind: 5 Eurus
9 Volturnus
echo: 4 Echo
emulation: 5 Zelos
familial affection:
6 Pietas
fate: 4 Norn **5** Moira,
Moras
fear: 6 Deimos
femininity: 5 Neith
fire: 4 Logi
force: 3 Bia
good faith: 5 Fides
grain blight: 7 Robigus
heaven: 6 Uranus
hostile nature:
8 Fomorian
idyllic poetry: 6 Thalia
liberty: 8 Libertas
longing: 6 Pothos

lotus: 8 Nefertem
meditation: 6 Melete
memory: 5 Mneme,
Munin
moon: 4 Luna
nature: 7 Eriking
night: 3 Nox
north wind: 6 Boreas
order: 7 Eunomia
pain: 5 Oizys
past: 3 Urd
peace: 5 Irene
prayer: 5 Litae
present: 8 Verdandi
punishment: 5 Poena,
Poine
recklessness: 3 Ate
revenge: 5 Poena, Poine
Roman nation:
8 Quirinus
sacred music: 8 Polymnia **10** Polyhymnia
sea: 3 Ler, Lir
5 Nammu **6** Pontus
8 Thalassa
sky: 6 Aether, Hathor
soul: 6 Psyche
southeast wind: 5 Eu-
rus **9** Volturnus
south wind: 5 Notus
7 Ninurta
strength: 6 Cratus
sun: 3 Sol
thought: 5 Hugin
tragedy: 9 Melpomene
truth: 7 Alethia
unavailing effort:
5 Ocnus
wealth: 6 Plutus
west wind: 8 Favonius,
Zephyrus
wind: 7 Ninurta
zeal: 5 Zelos

7 wheedle, win over **8** convince, inveigle, motivate, talk
into **9** influence

Persuasion
author: 10 Jane Austen
character: 7 Mrs Clay **8** Mrs
Croft **11** Lady Russell
12 Admiral Croft **25** Captain
Frederick Wentworth
Elliot family: 4 Anne
7 William **9** Elizabeth, Sir
Walter
Musgrove family: 4 Mary
6 Louisa **7** Charles
9 Henrietta

persuasive 6 cogent **7** coaxing,
logical, winning **8** alluring,
credible, forceful, inviting **9** effective, plausible, seductive
10 believable, compelling, convincing **11** influential

pert 4 flip, spry **5** alert, brash,
brisk, fresh, nervy, perky,
quick, saucy **6** brassy, brazen,

cheeky, lively, nimble **7** chipper **8** flippant, impolite, impudent, insolent **9** audacious,
energetic, insulting, sprightly,
wide-awake **11** impertinent,
smart-alecky **12** discourteous

pertain 2 be **5** apply, touch
6 befall, belong, relate **7** concern, connect

pertinacious 6 dogged **8** stubborn **9** obstinate, tenacious
10 persistent, unyielding
11 persevering

pertinacity 9 obstinacy
10 mulishness **11** persistence,
willfulness **12** contrariness, ob-
durateness, perverseness, stubbornness **13** determination,
inflexibility, intransigence, pigheadedness **14** bullheadedness,
intractability

pertinence 9 relevance **11** germaneness **12** appositeness
13 applicability

pertinent 3 apt **4** meet **7** apropos, fitting, germane, related
8 apposite, material, relevant,
suitable **9** befitting, concerned,
congruent, connected **10** applicable, consistent, to the
point
 Latin: 5 ad rem

perturb 5 upset, worry
6 bother **7** disturb, fluster,
trouble **8** disquiet, distress
10 discompose, disconcert

perturbation 5 alarm, upset,
worry **6** dismay **7** anxiety,
concern, turmoil **8** distress
9 agitation, commotion **10** excitement **11** disquietude, trepidation **12** apprehension,
discomposure **13** consternation

perturbed 5 upset **7** annoyed,
worried **8** agitated, troubled
9 disturbed **12** disconcerted

perturbing 6 vexing **7** irksome **8** annoying **9** vexatious
10 bothersome, irritating, unsettling **11** disquieting, distressing, troublesome
13 disconcerting

Peru *see box*

Perugino, Pietro
real name: 14 Pietro
Vannucci
also called: 10 Il Perugino
14 Pier della Pieve
born: 5 Italy **15** Citta della
Pieve
artwork: 24 The Crucifixion
with Saints **26** Delivery of
the Keys to St Peter **27** The
Giving of the Keys to St Peter **32** Apparition of the Virgin to St Bernard, Christ
Delivering the Keys to St
Peter

perusal 5 study **6** review
7 reading **8** scanning, scrutiny
10 inspection, run-through
11 examination, look-through
12 scrutinizing
13 contemplation

peruse 3 con **4** read, scan
5 study **6** search, survey **7** examine, inspect **10** scrutinize

pervade 4 fill **5** imbue **6** infuse **7** suffuse **8** permeate, saturate **9** penetrate **13** spread
through **17** diffuse throughout

pervasive 4 rife **7** rampant
8 dominant **9** prevalent
10 ubiquitous **11** omnipresent,
predominant

perverse 5 balky **6** dogged,
mulish, ornery **7** wayward,
willful **8** contrary, obdurate,
stubborn **9** obstinate, pigheaded **10** hardheaded, headstrong, inflexible, rebellious

Peru

capital/largest city: 4 Lima
  Inca capital: **5** Cuzco

others: 3 Ica **4** Puno **5** Cuzco, Paita, Pisco, Tacna **6** Callao, Talara **7** Huanuco, Iquitos **8** Arequipa, Castilla, Chiclayo, Chimbote, Mollendo, Pucallpa, Trujillo **9** Cajamarca **10** Yurimaguas

school: 8 Trujillo **9** San Marcos

division: 3 Ica **4** Lima, Puno **5** Cusco, Cuzco, Junin, Piura, Tacna **6** Ancash, Loreto, Tumbes
  Inca empire: **13** Tahuantinsuyo

measure: 4 topo **5** galon **7** celemin

monetary unit: 3 sol **5** libra **6** dinero, reseta **7** centavo

weight: 5 libra **7** quintal

island: 6 Chinca **7** Chincha

lake: 8 Titicaca

mountain: 5 Andes **7** El Misti, Huamina **8** Coropuna

highest point: 9 Huascaran

river: 3 Ene, Ica, Ilo **4** Napo, Napu **5** Piura, Rimac **6** Amazon, Oroton, Pampas, Yaguas, Yavari **7** Curaray, Mantaro, Maranon, Pastaza, Tapiche, Ucayali **8** Apurimac, Huallaga, Urubamba **11** Madre de Dios, Paucartambo

sea: 7 Pacific

physical feature:
  current: **6** el nino
  desert: **5** Nazca **7** Atacama, Sechura
  drizzling rain: **8** ilovizna
  fog: **5** garua
  gulf: **9** Guayaquil
  plateau: **7** Tablazo

people: 4 Ande, Boro, Cana, Inca, Inka, Lama, Pano, Peba, Piro, Yutu **5** Campa, Carib, Chana, Colan, Colla, Jwaro, Moche, Nasca, Senci, Yagua, Yunca **6** Atalan, Aymara, Canchi, Chanca, Chanka, Chimer, Cholos, Cocama, Jibaro, Kechua, Omagua, Quiche, Quolla, Setibo, Sipibo **7** Changos, Chincha, Chuncho, Mestizo, Mochica **8** Amahuaca, Criollos, Mayoruma, Quechuia **9** Callawaya **10** Tiahuanaca, Tiatinagua **11** Chumpivilca
  artist: **4** Lazo **7** Montero, Sabogal, Szyszlo **8** Codesido
  author: **4** Vega **5** Palma, Prada **8** Caviedes **10** Mariategui
  explorer: **7** Pizarro
  Inca leader: **7** Huascar **9** Atahualpa **10** Manco Capac
  leader: **5** Balta, Pardo, Prado, Torre **7** Bolivar **8** Castilla, Fujimori **9** Santa Cruz **13** Belaunde Terry **15** Leguiay y Salcedo, Morales Bermudez

language: 6 Aymara **7** English, Quechua, Spanish

religion: 13 Roman Catholic

place:
  bullring: **11** Plaza de Acho
  center of Lima: **12** Plaza de Armas
  church: **10** La Compania
  open market/street: **9** Calle Real
  ruins: **5** Huaco **8** Chan-Chan **9** Cajamarca **11** Machu-Picchu **22** Fortress of Sacsayhuaman

feature:
  animal: **5** llama **6** alpaca, vicuna **7** guanaco
  commune: **6** ayllus
  dance: **5** cueca, kaswa **6** cachua
  farmers: **10** campesinos
  priest: **6** villac
  slums: **9** barriadas
  tree: **8** cinchona

food:
  dish: **3** aji, cuy **7** ceviche **10** anticuchos
  drink: **5** pisco **6** chicha **11** aguardiente

11 disobedient, intractable, wrongheaded

perversion 9 depravity **10** corruption, degeneracy, immorality **11** dissipation, dissolution

pervert 4 warp **5** abuse **6** debase, misuse **7** contort, corrupt, degrade, deprave, distort, falsify, subvert **8** misapply **9** desecrate **12** misrepresent

perverted 5 false **6** faulty, untrue, warped **7** corrupt, debased, deviant, twisted, unsound **8** aberrant, abnormal, degraded, depraved **9** contorted, distorted, erroneous, imperfect, unnatural **10** fallacious, unbalanced **12** misconceived, misconstrued **13** misunderstood

Peschkowsky, Michael Igor
  real name of: 11 Mike Nichols

pesky 7 chafing, galling, irksome **8** annoying **9** maddening, obnoxious, offensive, vexatious **10** bothersome, disturbing, nettlesome **11** aggravating, distasteful, infuriating, pestiferous, troublesome **12** disagreeable, exasperating **13** objectionable

pessimism 5 gloom **7** despair **10** gloominess **12** hopelessness **13** gloomy outlook **14** discouragement **15** downheartedness

pessimist 7 kill-joy **8** sourpuss **9** Cassandra, defeatist, gloomy Gus **10** spoilsport, wet blanket **11** crepehanger **13** prophet of doom

pessimistic 6 gloomy **8** hopeless **10** despairing, dispirited **11** discouraged, downhearted

pest 4 bane **5** curse **6** blight, bother **7** scourge **8** nuisance, vexation **9** annoyance **10** irritation **13** pain in the neck

pester 3 irk, nag, vex **4** bait, fret **5** annoy, harry, taunt, worry **6** badger, bother, harass, hector, nettle, plague **7** disturb, provoke, torment, trouble **8** irritate

pesticide 3 DDT **7** biocide **8** fumigant **9** fungicide, germacide, vermicide **11** insecticide
  user: 12 exterminator

pestilence 6 blight, plague **7** disease **8** epidemic
  god of: 4 Irra

pet 3 pat **4** baby, dear **6** caress, choice, fondle, stroke **7** beloved, darling, dearest, favored **8** favorite **9** cherished,

preferred **10** sweetheart
14 apple of one's eye

pet activity 5 hobby **7** passion **8** interest **10** enthusiasm, hobbyhorse

Peter 7 apostle
means: 4 rock
also called: 5 Simon
6 Cephas
father: 4 John **5** Jonas
brother: 6 Andrew
birthplace: 9 Bethsaida
hometown: 9 Capernaum
disciple of: 5 Jesus
companion: 4 John **5** James
rebuked: 7 Ananias
8 Sapphira
secretary: 8 Silvanus
pertaining to: 7 Petrine

Peter and the Wolf
composed by: 9 Prokofiev

Peter Grimes
opera by: 7 Britten
character: 11 Ellen Orford

Peter Heering, Cherry Heering
type: 6 brandy **7** liqueur
origin: 7 Denmark
flavor: 6 cherry
color: 3 red

Peter Ibbetson
author: 15 George Du Maurier

peter out 3 ebb **7** decline, dwindle, fall off, give out
8 diminish

Peter Pan
author: 11 James Barrie
character: 9 Nurse Nana
10 Tinker Bell **11** Captain Hook **12** Wendy Darling

Peter Quince at the Clavier
author: 14 Wallace Stevens

Peters, Jane Alice
real name of: 13 Carole Lombard

petiole 4 stem **5** spine, stalk, stipe **8** peduncle **9** leafstalk

petite 3 wee **4** tiny **5** small **6** little **9** miniature
10 diminutive

petition 3 ask, beg, sue **4** plea, pray, seek, suit, urge **5** press **6** appeal, invoke, orison, prayer **7** apply to, beseech, entreat **8** appeal to, call upon, entreaty, proposal **9** imploring, plead with, request of **10** invocation, supplicate **11** application, beseechment, requisition **12** solicitation, supplication

petitioner 6 suitor **8** claimant **9** solicitor, suppliant **10** supplicant

pet name 8 nickname **9** sobri-

quet **10** diminutive, endearment

pet phrase 5 maxim, motto **6** saying, slogan **9** catchword

Petre (Lord)
character in: 16 The Rape of the Lock
author: 4 Pope

petrified 4 hard **5** dense, solid, stony **6** frozen **8** hardened, rocklike **9** paralyzed **10** solidified **11** hard as a rock, scared stiff **13** turned to stone

Petrified Forest, The
director: 10 Archie Mayo
based on play by: 14 Robert Sherwood
cast: 9 Dick Foran **10** Bette Davis **12** Leslie Howard **14** Humphrey Bogart (Duke Mantee)
setting: 7 Arizona

Petronius
author of: 9 Satyricon

Petruchio
character in: 19 The Taming of the Shrew
author: 11 Shakespeare

Petticoat Junction
character: 10 Floyd Smoot, Sam Drucker **11** Homer Bedloe, Kate Bradley **12** Charlie Pratt, Dr Janet Craig, Steve Elliott, Wendell Gibbs **14** Betty Jo Bradley, Uncle Joe Carson **15** Billie Jo Bradley, Bobbie Jo Bradley
cast: 9 Frank Cady, Linda Kaye, Mike Minor, Rufe Davis **10** Pat Woodell **11** Charles Lane **12** Bea Benaderet, Byron Foulger, June Lockhart, Lori Saunders **13** Edgar Buchanan, Gunilla Hutton, Jeannine Riley **14** Meredith MacRae, Smiley Burnette
setting: 11 Hooterville **14** Shady Rest Hotel
train: 10 Cannonball

petto 5 chest **6** breast

petty 4 mean **5** minor, small **6** flimsy, paltry, shabby, slight **7** ignoble, trivial **8** niggling, picayune, piddling, trifling **10** ungenerous **11** small-minded, unimportant **12** narrow-minded **13** insignificant **14** inconsiderable **15** inconsequential

petulance 9 poutiness, sulkiness **11** fretfulness, peevishness **12** irritability

petulant 4 sour **5** cross, gruff, huffy, sulky, surly, testy **6** grumpy, sullen, tetchy, touchy **7** bearish, crabbed, fretful, grouchy, peevish, pet-

tish, uncivil **8** snappish **9** crotchety, fractious, irascible, irritable **10** ill-natured, out of sorts, ungracious **11** complaining, contentious, ill-tempered, quarrelsome, thin-skinned **12** cantankerous, faultfinding

Petulia
director: 13 Richard Lester
cast: 10 Arthur Hill, Pippa Scott **12** George C Scott, Joseph Cotten **13** Julie Christie, Shirley Knight **18** Richard Chamberlain
setting: 12 San Francisco

petunia
varieties: 4 Wild **7** Mexican, Seaside **10** Large white **12** Common garden **14** Violet-flowered

peu a peu 14 little by little

peu de chose 14 trifling matter **17** unimportant matter

pew 4 seat **5** bench **6** settle

Peychaud Bitters
type: 8 aperitif
origin: 10 New Orleans

Peyton Place
author: 14 Grace Metalious
character: 9 Rita Jacks (Harrington) **10** Hannah Cord, Steven Cord **12** Matthew Swain **13** Betty Anderson (Harrington Cord Harrington), Elliott Carson, Julie Anderson **14** Dr Michael Rossi, Dr Robert Morton, George Anderson **16** Allison Mackenzie (Harrington), Leslie Harrington, Norman Harrington, Rodney Harrington **18** Constance Mackenzie (Carson)
cast (television): 8 Ed Nelson **9** Kent Smith, Mia Farrow, Ryan O'Neal **10** Tim O'Connor **11** Kasey Rogers, Paul Langton, Ruth Warrick **12** Henry Beckman, James Douglas **13** Dorothy Malone **14** Barbara Parkins, Patricia Morrow, Warner Anderson **19** Christopher Connelly
director (movie): 10 Mark Robson
cast (movie): 9 Hope Lange **10** Lana Turner, Lloyd Nolan **13** Arthur Kennedy
score: 11 Franz Waxman

Phaeax
father: 8 Poseidon
mother: 7 Corcyra
ancestor of: 10 Phaeacians

Phaedo
author: 5 Plato

Phaedra
father: 5 Minos
mother: 8 Pasiphae

sister: 7 Ariadne
husband: 7 Theseus
son: 6 Acamas 8 Demophon
stepson: 10 Hippolytus
loved: 10 Hippolytus
death by: 7 hanging, suicide

Phaenna
origin: 5 Greek 7 Spartan
member of: 6 Graces

Phaethon
father: 6 Helios
mother: 7 Clymene

phalanx 6 column, parade
9 formation 13 ranks and files

Phallus
image of: 9 male organ
symbol of: 9 fertility
carried in: 6 comedy
9 festivals
associated with: 3 Pan
6 Hermes 7 Demeter
8 Dionysus

phantasm 5 ghost, shade,
spook 6 mirage, spirit, vision
7 fantasy, figment, incubus,
phantom, specter 8 delusion,
illusion, succubus
10 apparition

Phantasus
origin: 5 Greek
god of: 6 dreams

phantom 5 dream, ghost 6 mirage, spirit, vision, wraith
7 chimera, specter 8 illusion,
phantasm 10 apparition
13 hallucination

Phantom, The
creator: 7 Lee Falk 8 Ray
Moore
nickname: 16 The Ghost
Who Walks
mask: 5 black
costume: 6 purple

Phantom of the Opera, The
director:
1925 version: 12 Rupert
Julian
1943 version: 11 Arthur
Lubin
cast:
1925 version: 9 Lon Chaney 11 Mary Philbin, Nor-
man Kerry
1943 version: 10 Hume
Cronyn, Jane Farrar, Nelson
Eddy 11 Claude Rains
12 Edgar Barrier 13 Susanna
Foster
setting: 10 Paris Opera

Phaon
occupation: 7 boatman
location: 8 Mitylene
given: 5 youth 6 beauty
given by: 9 Aphrodite

pharos 5 light 6 beacon, signal 7 seamark 10 lighthouse,
watchtower

phase 4 side, step, view 5 angle, facet, guise, level, slant,
stage 6 aspect, degree, period
7 feature 8 attitude, juncture
9 condition, viewpoint 10 appearance 11 development
12 circumstance

pheasant
group of: 4 nest, nide

Phedre, Phaedra
author: 6 Racine
character: 6 Aricia 7 Theseus 10 Hippolytus

Phegeus
king of: 7 Psophis
son: 5 Axion 7 Temenus
daughter: 7 Arsinoe
purified: 8 Alcmaeon
ordered death of:
8 Alcmaeon

Phenix *see* 7 Phoenix

phenomenal 5 super 6 unique
7 amazing, unusual 8 singular,
superior, uncommon 9 fantastic, marvelous, unheard-of
10 incredible, miraculous, prodigious, remarkable, stupendous, surpassing
11 astonishing, exceptional,
outstanding, sensational, spectacular 12 overwhelming, unparalleled 13 extraordinary,
unprecedented

phenomenon 5 thing 6 marvel, rarity, wonder 7 episode,
miracle 8 incident, occasion
9 actuality, curiosity, exception, happening, nonpareil,
sensation 10 fact of life, occurrence, proceeding
11 contingency

Phereclus
also: 10 Harmonides
father: 6 Tecton
built: 5 ships

Pheres
king of: 6 Pherae
father: 8 Cretheus
mother: 4 Tyro
son: 7 Admetus, Idomene
daughter: 8 Periapis

Periphetes
epithet: 9 Corynetes

phial 4 vial 6 bottle, vessel
9 container

Phidias
born: 6 Athens, Greece
artwork: 4 Zeus 6 Amazon
13 Lemnian Athene (Athena
Lemnia) 15 Apollo Parno-
pios, Athena Parthenos,
Athena Promachos

Philadelphia
baseball team: 8 Phillies
basketball team: 13 Seventy-
sixers
bay: 8 Delaware
football team: 5 Stars
6 Eagles

founded/planned by: 4 Penn
hockey team: 6 Flyers
landmark: 6 US Mint 8 City
Hall 11 Liberty Bell
12 Christ Church, Congress
Hall 13 Franklin Field, Roosevelt Park 14 Betsy Ross
House, Carpenter's Hall
15 Gloria Dei Church, Veterans Stadium 16 Indepen-
dence Hall
means: 19 city of brotherly
love
museum: 5 Rodin 15 Fels
Planetarium 16 Barnes
Foundation 17 Franklin
Institute
river: 8 Delaware
10 Schuylkill
university: 4 Penn 6 Drexel,
Temple 9 Jefferson, St Joseph's 22 Curtis Institute of
Music

Philadelphia Story, The
director: 11 George Cukor
based on play by: 11 Philip
Barry
cast: 9 Cary Grant 10 Ruth
Hussey 12 James Stewart
16 Katharine Hepburn
Oscar for: 5 actor (Stewart)
remade as: 11 High Society

Philammon
father: 6 Apollo
mother: 6 Chione
half-brother: 9 Autolycus
son: 8 Thamyris
vocation: 8 musician

philanderer 3 rip 4 rake, wolf
5 flirt 6 lecher, tomcat, wanton 7 dallier, Don Juan, gallant, swinger, trifler 8 lothario,
lover boy, rakehell 9 adulterer,
libertine, womanizer 10 lady-
killer 11 woman-chaser

**philanthropic, philanthropi-
cal** 7 liberal 8 generous
9 bounteous 10 almsgiving, beneficent, benevolent, charitable, munificent
11 magnanimous 12 eleemosynary, humanitarian

philanthropist 5 donor, giver
8 do-gooder 9 almsgiver
11 contributor 12 humanitarian 13 Good Samaritan

philanthropy 6 bounty 7 charity 8 goodness 10 almsgiving,
generosity, liberality 11 beneficence, benevolence, munificence 13 unselfishness
14 charitableness, openhandedness 15 humanitarianism
16 largeheartedness 18 public-
spiritedness

Philaster
author: 30 Francis Beaumont
and John Fletcher

Philemon
friend: 4 Paul

Philippines

named for: 15 Philip II of Spain

capital/largest city: 6 Manila

others: 3 Iba **4** Agoa, Bogo, Cebu, Debu, Naga, Palo **5** Albay, Davao, Gapan, Iriga, Lanao, Laoag, Pasay, Vigan **6** Aparri, Baguio, Cavite, Ilagan, Iloilo, Tarlac **7** Bacolod, Basilan, Calapan, Dagupan, Legaspi **8** Batangas, Caloocan, Cotabato, Tacloban **9** Zamboanga **10** Cabanutuan, Dumaguette, Quezon City

school: 10 Santo Tomas **14** Ateneo de Manila

division: 4 Abra, Cebu **5** Aklan, Albay, Bohol, Capiz, Davao, Lanao, Leyte, Rizal, Samar **6** Agusan, Bataan, Cavite, Iloilo, Laguna, Quezon, Tarlac **7** Isabela, Lepanto, Surigao

measure: 4 loan **5** braza, catty, cavan, chupa, fardo, ganta, picul, punto **6** apatan, balita, lachsa, quinon **7** quilate **8** chinanta

monetary unit: 4 peso **6** conant, peseta **7** centavo

weight: 5 catty, picul **6** lachsa **7** quilate **8** chinanta

island: 4 Cebu, Cuyo, Jolo, Poro, Sulu **5** Batan, Bohol, Leyte, Luzon, Panay, Samar, Ticao **6** Culion, Lubang, Negros **7** Babuyan, Batanes, Bisayan, Masbate, Mindoro, Palawan, Paragua, Polillo, Visoyan **8** Mindanao **10** Corregidor, Marinduque

lake: 4 Taal **5** Lanao

mountain: 3 Iba **4** Mayo, Taal **5** Albay, Askja, Hibok, Mayon, Pulog **6** Pagsan **7** Banahao, Canlaon

highest point: 3 Apo

river: 4 Abra, Agno **5** Magat, Pasig **6** Agusan, Laoang **7** Cagayan **8** Mindanao, Pampanga

sea: 4 Sulu **5** Samar **7** Celebes, Pacific, Visayan **10** Philippine, South China

physical feature:
  bay: **6** Manila
  falls: **9** Pagsanjan **14** Maria Christina
  gulf: **4** Moro **5** Albay, Davao, Leyte, Ragay **8** Lingayen
  hot springs: **8** Los Banos
  national park: **12** Mayon Volcano
  ocean trench: **8** Mindanao
  peninsula: **6** Bataan
  storm: **6** bagyos **7** monsoon, typhoon
  volcano: **8** Pinatubo

people: 3 Ati, Eta, Ita, Tao **4** Aeta, Ifil, Moro, Sulu, Tino **5** Abaca, Aripa, Batak, Batan, Bicol, Bikol, Busao, Lutao, Mundo, Sinay, Tagal, Vicol, Yakan **6** Apayao, Baluga, Bilaan, Biscol, Bontoc, Bontok, Busaos, Ibanag, Ibilao, Ifugao, Igalot, Igorot, Illano, Isinai, Lutayo, Manabo, Manobo, Montes, Sambal, Tagala, Timaua, Timawa, Zambal **7** Bagoboo, Bisayan, Cagayan, Ilocano, Itanega, Malanoa, Mangyan, Naboloi, Negrito, Tagalog, Tirurai, Visayan **8** Arupaata, Babaylan, Bukidono, Filipino, Igorotte, Manguian, Pampanga **9** Arupaatta, Dulangane, Macajambo, Pampangao, Tinguiane **10** Magindanao, Pangasinan **11** Calalangane
  author: **5** Rizal
  explorer: **7** Legazpe **8** Magellan **10** Villalobos
  leader: **5** Ramos **6** Aquino, Marcos, Osmena, Quezon **9** Aguinaldo, Bonifacio, Macapagal, Magsaysay **11** Roxas y Acuna

language: 4 Moro **5** Bicol, Bikol **6** Ibanag **7** Cebuano, English, Ilocano, Spanish, Tagalog, Visayan **8** Filipino, Pilipino **9** Pampangan **10** Samar-Leyte **13** Bamboo-English

religion: 7 animism **9** Aglipayan **10** Protestant **13** Roman Catholic **15** Iglesia ni Kristo

place:
  church: **14** Saint Augustine
  esplanade: **6** Luneta
  fort: **4** Cota, Gota, Kota **5** Lotta **10** Corregidor
  president's palace: **10** Malacanang
  street: **7** Escolta
  US bases: **5** Clark **8** Subic Bay
  walled city: **10** Intramuros

feature:
  animal: **7** carabao, tamarau, tarsier **9** mouse deer
  bird: **7** creeper
  clothing: **4** saya **6** camisa **10** balintawak **12** mestiza terno **13** barong tagalog
  dance: **9** tinikling
  drama: **8** moro-moro
  guerrilla fighter: **3** huk
  musicians: **12** musikongbuho
  naval base: **6** Cavite
  song: **8** kundiman
  village: **8** barangay

food:
  dish: **3** poi **4** baha, sabu, taro **5** balut
  drink: **4** beno, vino **5** bubud **6** tampoy **7** pangasi

slave: 8 Onesimus
wife: 6 Baucis
entertained: 4 Hera, Zeus
became: 12 temple priest

Philip
hometown: 9 Bethsaida
disciple of: 5 Jesus

Philippines *see box*

philistine 5 yahoo **6** savage
7 Babbitt, lowbrow, prosaic
8 ignorant **9** barbarian, bourgeois, unrefined, untutored
10 conformist, uncultured, uneducated, uninformed, unlettered **11** commonplace
12 conventional, uncultivated
13 unenlightened **15** conven-
tionalist **16** anti-intellectual

Philistine city 4 Gath

Philius
epithet of: 4 Zeus
means: 8 friendly

Phillotson, Richard
character in: 14 Jude the
Obscure
author: 5 Hardy

Philoctetes
author: 9 Sophocles
character: 8 Heracles, Odysseus **11** Neoptolemus
inherits arms of: 8 Hercules
father: 5 Poeas, Poias
killed: 5 Paris

philodendron
varieties: 5 Dubia, giant
6 common **7** cut-leaf, red-
leaf **8** blushing **9** black-gold,
heart-leaf, horsehead, spade-
leaf, split-leaf **10** fiddle-leaf,
variegated, velvet-leaf
11 leather-leaf

Philoetius
cowherd of: 8 Odysseus

Philomela
position: 8 princess
realm: 6 Athens
father: 7 Pandion
sister: 6 Procne
brother-in-law: 6 Tereus
raped by: 6 Tereus
transformed into: 7 swallow
11 nightingale

Philomelides
king of: 6 Lesbos
defeated by: 8 Odysseus

Philonome *see* **9** Phylonome

philosopher/theologian *see box*

Philosopher's Pupil, The
author: 11 Iris Murdoch

philosophic, philosophical
4 calm **5** quiet, stoic **6** serene
7 erudite, learned, logical, patient, stoical **8** abstract, composed, rational, resigned,

tranquil **9** impassive, judicious,
sagacious, unexcited, unruffled **10** complacent, fatalistic,
reasonable, theorizing,
thoughtful **11** imperturbed,
theoretical, unemotional
14 self-restrained

philosophy 4 calm, view
5 ideas, logic **6** reason **7** beliefs, opinion, thought **8** doctrine, fatalism, patience,
serenity, stoicism, thinking
9 basic idea, composure, es-
thetics, principle, reasoning,
restraint, viewpoint **10** conception, theorizing **11** complacency, convictions,
forbearance, impassivity, metaphysics, rationalism,
resignation
means: 12 love of wisdom
branch: 6 ethics **8** ontology
10 aesthetics **11** metaphysics **12** epistemology

term: 8 noumenon **9** causal-
ity, dialectic, solipsism
school of: 7 Sophism **8** idealism, Milesian, Stoicism
9 Epicurean, pantheism, Pla-
tonism **10** empiricism, prag-
matism, Skepticism
11 rationalism **12** Aristotelian, neoplatonism **13** Phe-
nomenology, scholasticism
14 existentialism **17** logical
positivism

Phil Silvers Show, The
character: 6 Fender **7** Col
Hall, Henshaw **8** Doberman
9 Sgt Ritzik **12** Sgt Joan Hogan **13** Rocco Barbella, Sgt
Ernie Bilko
cast: 8 Joe E Ross, Paul
Ford **10** Alan Melvin, Her-
bie Faye **13** Harvey Lembeck **15** Elisabeth Fraser,
Maurice Gosfield

---

philosopher/theologian 4 sage **6** savant **7** thinker, wise
man **8** logician, reasoner **9** theorizer **11** rationalist, truth
seeker **12** dialectician **13** metaphysician
  Alsatian: 10 Schweitzer
  American: 4 Eddy **5** Dewey, James, Royce, Smith, Young
  6 Mather, Peirce **7** Edwards, Niebuhr, Russell, Tillich
  8 Williams **9** McPherson **14** Elijah Muhammad
  Austrian: 12 Wittgenstein
  British: 3 Fox **4** Hume, Inge, Knox, More, Owen **5** Bacon,
  Burke, Locke, Moore **6** Biddle, Cotton, Hobbes, Huxley,
  Newman, Wesley **7** Bentham, Bradley, Carlyle, Cranmer,
  Russell, Spencer **8** Berkeley, Wycliffe **9** Whitehead
  13 Thomas a Becket **14** William of Occam
  Chinese: 6 Lao-tzu **9** Confucius
  Christian: 6 Calvin, Luther, Origen, St Paul **7** Abelard **8** St
  Anselm **9** St Patrick **10** Duns Scotus, St Benedict **11** St
  Augustine **14** William of Occam **15** St Thomas Aquinas
  16 St Albertus Magnus
  Czech: 3 Hus
  Danish: 11 Kierkegaard
  Dutch: 7 Erasmus, Spinoza
  El Salvadorian: 9 Masferrer
  French: 5 Comte **6** Calvin, Pascal, Sartre **7** Abelard, Berg-
  son, Diderot **8** Maritain, Rousseau, Voltaire **9** Descartes,
  Levy-Bruhl, Montaigne **11** Montesquieu
  German: 4 Kant, Marx **5** Buber, Hegel **6** Boehme, Fichte,
  Herder, Luther **7** Husserl, Jaspers, Leibniz **9** Heidegger,
  Nietzsche, Schelling **10** Muhlenberg **11** Melanchthon
  12 Schopenhauer **13** Thomas a Kempis **14** Schleiermacher
  Greek: 5 Plato **6** St Paul, Thales **8** Socrates **9** Aristotle
  10 Anaxagoras, Anaximenes, Heraclitus, Parmenides, Py-
  thagoras **11** Anaximander
  Indian: 6 Buddha **16** Siddharta Gautama
  Islamic: 7 al Kindi **8** al-Farabi, Averroes, Avicenna **9** al
  Ghazali **10** Ibn Khaldun
  Italian: 5 Bruno **7** Aquinas, Mazzini **10** St Benedict, Zeno
  of Elea **17** St Francis of Assisi
  Japanese: 6 Suzuki
  Jewish: 7 Spinoza **10** Maimonides
  Latin: 8 Plotinus **11** St Augustine
  Spanish: 8 Averroes **10** Maimonides **13** Ortega y Gasset
  16 Ignatius of Loyola
  Swedish: 10 Swedenborg
  Swiss: 7 Zwingli

setting: **6** Kansas **10** Fort Baxter

Philyra
father: **7** Oceanus
mother: **6** Tethys
mother of: **6** Chiron
changed into: **10** linden tree

Phlegethon
also: **14** Pyriphlegethon
form: **5** river
location: **10** underworld

phlegmatic 4 calm, cool, dull **6** serene **7** languid, passive, stoical **8** listless, sluggish, tranquil **9** apathetic, impassive, lethargic, unfeeling **10** nonchalant, spiritless **11** indifferent, insensitive, unconcerned, unemotional, unexcitable **12** unresponsive **13** imperturbable, unimpassioned **15** undemonstrative

Phlegyas
king of: **8** Lapithae
condemned: **6** Apollo

Phlias
father: **8** Dionysus
member of: **9** Argonauts

phlox
varieties: **4** blue, fall, moss, sand, star **6** annual, smooth **7** prickly **8** creeping, drummond, mountain, trailing **9** perennial, sword-leaf, thick-leaf **15** summer perennial

Phnom-Penh
airport: **10** Pochentong
also: **8** Pnom Penh
capital of: **8** Cambodia **9** Kampuchea
pagoda: **12** Preah Morokot
river: **6** Mekong **8** Tonle Sap

Phobetor
epithet of: **6** Icelus
means: **9** terrifier

phobia *see box*

Phobos
also: **6** Phobus
father: **4** Ares

Phocus
father: **6** Aeacus **8** Ornytion
mother: **8** Psamathe
half-brother: **6** Peleus **7** Telamon
wife: **7** Antiope
killed by: **7** Telamon
burial place: **8** Tithorea

Phoebe
member of: **6** Titans
father: **6** Uranus
mother: **4** Gaea
sister: **6** Themis
daughter: **4** Leto **7** Asteria
identified with: **4** moon
corresponds to: **5** Diana **7** Artemis

Phoebus *see* **6** Apollo

Phoenicia *see* **7** Lebanon

Phoenician Mythology
god of agriculture/earth: **5** Dagon
corresponds to Mesopotamian: **5** Dagan
bird: **6** Phenix **7** Phoenix **8** Phoeonix
goddess of fertility/reproduction: **7** Astarte

Phoenissae (The Phoenician Maidens)
author: **9** Euripides
character: **5** Creon **7** Jocasta, Oedipus **8** Adrastus, Antigone, Eteocles, Tiresias **9** Polynices **10** Menoikieus

Phoenix
basketball team: **4** Suns
capital of: **7** Arizona
event: **5** rodeo
feature: **10** Papago Park **22** Desert Botanical Gardens
football team: **9** Wranglers
river: **4** Salt

Phoenix, Phoeonix
also: **6** Phenix
origin: **10** Phoenician
form: **4** bird
gift: **11** immortality
king of: **9** Dolopians
father: **7** Amyntor
mother: **8** Cleobule
brother: **6** Cadmus
sister: **6** Europa
foster son: **8** Achilles
ancestor of: **11** Phoenicians

Pholus
form: **7** centaur
guarded: **4** wine
wine a gift from: **8** Dionysus

phonograph 4 hi-fi **5** phono **6** stereo **8** Victrola **9** turntable **10** gramophone **12** record player

phonophobia
fear of: **13** speaking aloud

phony, phoney 4 fake, hoax, mock, sham **5** bogus, false, fraud, trick **6** forged, pseudo, unreal, untrue **7** forgery **8** specious, spurious **9** decep-

---

phobia 5 dread **6** horror, terror **7** bugaboo, bugbear **8** aversion, loathing **12** apprehension **16** unreasonable fear **19** overwhelming anxiety
fear of animals: **9** zoophobia
fear of birds: **13** ornithophobia
fear of blushing: **13** erythrophobia
fear of bridges: **13** gephyrophobia
fear of cats: **10** gatophobia **12** aelurophobia, ailurophobia
fear of closed/confined spaces: **14** claustrophobia
fear of crowds: **11** ochlophobia
fear of darkness/the dark of night: **11** nyctophobia
fear of death: **13** thanatophobia
fear of death/dead bodies: **11** necrophobia
fear of dirt: **10** mysophobia
fear of disease: **11** pathophobia
fear of fire: **10** pyrophobia
fear of flowers: **11** anthophobia
fear of flying: **10** aerophobia
fear of germs: **11** mikrophobia
fear of hair: **12** trichophobia
fear of heights: **10** acrophobia
fear of insanity: **13** dementophobia
fear of lightning: **11** astraphobia
fear of men: **11** androphobia
fear of mice: **10** murophobia
fear of numbers: **12** numerophobia
fear of open spaces: **11** agoraphobia
fear of pain: **10** algophobia
fear of people: **12** anthrophobia
fear of reptiles: **13** herpetophobia
fear of snakes: **13** ophidiophobia
fear of speaking aloud: **11** phonophobia
fear of spiders: **13** arachnophobia
fear of strangers: **10** xenophobia
fear of thunder: **12** brontophobia
fear of the number thirteen: **17** triskaidekaphobia
fear of vehicles/driving: **11** amaxophobia
fear of water: **10** aquaphobia **11** hydrophobia
fear of women: **10** gynophobia

tive, imitation, pretended, synthetic **10** artificial, fraudulent, not genuine **11** counterfeit, make-believe, unauthentic

Phorbas
  son of: **8** Lapithes
  dispelled: **6** plague
    plague of: **8** serpents
  leader of: **4** Troy
    allies of: **9** Phygians
    killed by: **4** Ajax
  form: **5** boxer
    killed: **8** pilgrims
    killed by: **6** Apollo

Phorcids
  father: **7** Phorcys
  mother: **4** Ceto

Phorcys
  god of: **3** sea
  sister: **4** Ceto
  children: **5** Ladon **6** Graiae
  7 Echidna, Gorgons
  8 Phorcids
  harbor in: **6** Ithaca

Phormio
  author: **7** Terence

phosphorus
  chemical symbol: **1** P

photograph **3** pic **4** film, snap **5** image, print, shoot, still **6** candid, glossy **7** mugshot, picture, tintype **8** likeness, portrait, snapshot **12** daguerrotype
  bath: **5** fixer, toner **7** reducer **9** developer
  book: **5** album

photographer
  American: **4** Haas, Hine, Penn, Riis, Rose, Tice **5** (Ansel) Adams, Annan, Arbus, Brady, Evans, Hawes, Lange, Lynes, Smith, White **6** Avedon, Coburn, Eakins, Man Ray, Strand, Turner, Weston **7** Burrows, Eastman, Gardner, Jackson, Watkins **8** Bogardus, Davidson, Steichen **9** Muybridge, O'Sullivan, Rothstein, Stieglitz **10** Cunningham, Southworth **11** Bourke-White, Eisenstaedt, Turberville **13** Watson-Schutze
  British: **5** Evans, Frith **6** Bailey, Beaton, Fenton, Mayall, Talbot **7** Cameron **8** Brewster, Robinson **9** Rejlander **10** MacPherson
  French: **5** Marey, Nadar **6** Baldus, DuCamp, Le Secq, Newton, Niepce **7** Lumiere **8** Daguerre **12** Sabatier-Blot **14** Cartier-Bresson
  German: **4** Hoch **5** Ernst **7** Hausman **8** Stelzner **13** Renger-Patzsch
  Hungarian: **7** Kertesz **10** Moholy-Nagy
  Japanese: **4** Ikko

  Scottish: **4** Hill **7** Adamson
  Spanish: **7** Picabia

photostat **4** copy **7** replica **9** duplicate, facsimile **12** reproduction

phrase **3** put, say **4** word **5** couch, idiom, maxim, state, utter, voice, words **6** cliche, dictum, impart, remark, saying, truism **7** declare, express, proverb **8** aphorism, banality, locution **9** enunciate, find words, platitude, utterance, verbalize, word group **10** articulate, expression **11** communicate

phraseology **5** style **7** diction, wording **13** choice of words **18** manner of expression

Phrixus
  father: **7** Athamas
  mother: **7** Nephele
  stepmother: **3** Ino
  sister: **5** Helle
  wife: **9** Chalciope
  son: **5** Argus, Melas **8** Phrontis **10** Cytissorus

Phrontis
  father: **7** Phrixus
  mother: **9** Chalciope
  brother: **5** Argus, Melus **10** Cytissorus
  husband: **8** Panthous

Phthia
  mentioned in: **5** Iliad
  concubine of: **7** Amyntor
  seduced by: **7** Phoenix
  son: **5** Dorus **8** Laodocus **10** Polypoetes

Phyleus
  king of: **6** Ephyra
  father: **6** Auglas
  wife: **8** Timandra
  children: **5** Meges **10** Astyocheia

Phyllis
  father: **8** Phylleus
  husband: **8** Demophon
  loved: **6** Acamas

Phylomache
  son: **7** Acastus
  daughter: **8** Alcestis

Phylonome
  also: **9** Philonome
  husband: **6** Cycnus
  stepson: **5** Tenes

physical **4** real **5** human, solid **6** actual, animal, bodily, carnal, living **7** fleshly, natural, sensual **8** apparent, concrete, corporal, existent, existing, external, material, palpable, tangible **9** corporeal, essential, of the body **11** substantive

physical checkup **4** exam **8** physical **11** examination **19** physical examination

physical condition **5** shape **7** fitness, stamina **12** constitution

physical disorder **6** malady **7** ailment, disease, illness **8** sickness **9** ill health, infirmity

physical training **3** gym **6** sports **8** exercise **9** athletics, shaping up **10** gymnastics, working out **12** conditioning

physician **2** GP, MD **3** doc **5** medic **6** doctor, medico **7** surgeon **8** sawbones **10** specialist **11** medicine man, pill peddler **13** medical doctor
  Alsatian: **10** Schweitzer
  American: **4** Long, Rush, Salk **5** Sabin **6** Dooley, Gorgas **7** Huggins, Whipple **8** Williams **9** Blackwell **11** Landsteiner
  British: **5** Paget **6** Adrian, Harvey, Jenner, Lister
  Canadian: **4** Best **7** Banting
  Dutch: **7** Eijkman
  French: **7** Charcot
  German: **6** Mesmer **7** Fechner, Virchow **10** Blumenbach
  Greek: **10** Herophilus **11** Hippocrates **12** Erasistratus
  Italian: **8** Malpighi
  Russian: **6** Pavlov
  Scottish: **4** Lind
  South African: **7** Barnard

Physician to Olympian gods **5** Paeon **6** Apollo

physicist
  American: **4** Hess, Rabi **5** Bethe, Gamow, Pauli, Yalow **6** Bekesy, Teller, Townes, Watson **7** Richter, Seaborg **8** Einstein, Lawrence, Van Allen **9** Michelson **11** Chamberlain, Oppenheimer
  Austrian: **7** Doppler, Meitner
  British: **4** Born **5** Bragg, Hooke, Joule **6** Kelvin **7** Gilbert, Thomson **8** Chadwick, Rayleigh **9** Cockcroft **10** Rutherford
  Danish: **4** Bohr **7** Oersted
  Dutch: **6** Zeeman **7** Lorentz
  French: **6** Ampere **7** Broglie, Coulomb, Fresnel **8** Foucault **9** Becquerel **11** Joliot-Curie
  German: **3** Ohm **5** Hertz, Stark **6** Planck **7** Rontgen, Wegener **8** Humboldt, Roentgen **9** Kirchhoff, Mossbauer **10** Fahrenheit, Fraunhofer
  Indian: **5** Raman
  Irish: **7** Tyndall **10** Fitzgerald
  Italian: **5** Fermi

Russian: 6 Landau **8** Cerenkov, Sakharov
Scottish: 7 Rankine

Physics
author: **9** Aristotle

physiognomy 4 face **5** shape **6** facade, visage **7** contour, outline, profile **8** features **10** silhouette **11** countenance

physiology
founder: **13** William Harvey
study of: **8** function
study of nervous sytem: **15** neurophysiology

Phytalus
hospitable to: **7** Demeter
given: **7** fig tree

Phyteus
epithet of: **6** Apollo

pianissimo
music: **8** very soft
abbreviation: **2** pp

pianist 4 Hess **5** Liszt, Watts **6** Busoni, Chopin, Gilels, Serkin **7** Cliburn, Hofmann, Richter **8** Backhaus, Horowitz, Schnabel, Schumann, Thalberg, von Bulow **9** Barenboim, Casadesus, Gieseking **10** Gottschalk, Rubinstein **12** Rachmaninoff

piano
invented by: **10** Cristofori
player piano: **9** Fourneaux

piano
music: **4** soft
abbreviation: **1** p

piazza 5 patio, porch **6** square **7** gallery, portico, veranda

Piazzi, Giuseppe
field: **9** astronomy
nationality: **7** Italian
discovered: **5** Ceres
catalogued: **5** stars

picaresque 6 daring **7** raffish, roguish, waggish **8** devilish, prankish, rascally, scampish **9** foolhardy **10** roistering **13** adventuresome **14** mischiefloving

Picasso, Pablo
born: **5** Spain **6** Malaga
artwork: **4** Dove **6** Guitar, Jester **7** Ma Jolie, Rooster, She-Goat **8** Guernica **9** Bull's Head, Notre Dame **11** Seated Woman, Woman Diving **12** Head of a Woman **13** Seated Bathers **14** Minotauromachy, Mother and Child, Women of Algiers **15** Ambroise Vollard, Man Holding a Lamb, The Charnel-House, The Large Profile, The Three Dancers **16** Nude in an Armchair **17** Girl Before a Mirror, The Glass of Absinth, The Three Musicians **20** Still Life with a Candle **22** Les Demoiselles d'Avignon **23** Portrait of Gertrude Stein

picayune, picayunish 5 dinky, petty, small **6** flimsy, little, measly, paltry, slight **7** trivial **8** niggling, nugatory, piddling, trifling **11** unimportant **13** insignificant **14** inconsiderable **15** inconsequential

Piccini, Nicola (Piccinni, Niccola)
born: **4** Bari **5** Italy
composer of: **5** Didon **6** Roland **11** The Good Girl **15** La buona figliola **18** Iphigenie en Tauride

pick 3 cut **4** crop **5** cream, elect, elite, pluck, prize **6** choice, choose, detach, flower, gather, opt for, select **7** collect, fix upon, harvest, pull off, pull out, the best **9** single out **10** decide upon, favored one, preference, settle upon

picket 4 pale, post **5** fence, go out, guard, hem in, pen in, stake, watch **6** corral, paling, patrol, sentry, shut in, strike, tether, wall in **7** boycott, enclose, hedge in, lookout, striker, upright, walk out **8** blockade, palisade, restrain, restrict, sentinel **9** blockader, boycotter, protester, restraint, stanchion

picketing 5 march **7** protest **8** marching, on strike, striking **10** protesting **12** protest march **13** demonstrating, demonstration

Pickett, George E
served in: **8** Civil War **10** Mexican War
side: **11** Confederate
battle: **10** Gettysburg
famous for: **6** charge

Pickford, Mary
real name: **15** Gladys Mary Smith
nickname: **18** America's Sweetheart
born: **6** Canada **7** Toronto
husband: **16** Douglas Fairbanks **18** Charles Buddy Rogers
roles: **4** Rags **8** Coquette (Oscar) **9** Pollyanna **19** The Taming of the Shrew **21** The Poor Little Rich Girl **23** Rebecca of Sunnybrook Farm
home: **8** Pickfair
memoirs: **17** Sunshine and Shadow
formed: **13** United Artists
partners: **10** D W Griffith **14** Charlie Chaplin **16** Douglas Fairbanks

pickings 4 loot **5** booty **6** scraps, spoils **7** plunder, takings **9** leftovers

pickle 3 fix, jam **4** corn, dill, mess, sour **6** crisis, plight, scrape **7** dilemma, gherkin, mustard **8** cucumber, hot water, quandary **9** emergency, extremity, tight spot **10** difficulty, kosher dill, pretty pass **11** predicament **14** bread-and-butter

pickled 5 drunk **6** soused **8** powdered

pick on 5 annoy, bully **6** harass, jibe at **7** torment **8** browbeat

pick out 3 see **4** espy **6** choose, descry, detect, notice, select **7** discern, make out **8** perceive **12** catch sight of

pickup 4 rise **5** boost, truck **7** advance **9** impromptu **11** improvement **12** acceleration

pick up 3 buy, get **6** gather, lift up, look up, obtain, secure **7** acquire, develop, improve, procure **8** contract, retrieve **9** cultivate, get better

Pickwick Papers
author: **14** Charles Dickens
character: **6** Perker, Tupman, Wardle, Winkle **9** Sam Weller, Snodgrass **10** Mrs Bardell **11** Emily Wardle **12** Alfred Jingle, Rachel Wardle **13** Arabella Allen

picky 5 fussy **6** choosy **7** finicky **10** fastidious, particular **11** persnickety **14** discriminating

Picrochole
character in: **22** Gargantua and Pantagruel
author: **8** Rabelais

picture 3 see **4** copy, draw, film **5** fancy, flick, image, model, movie, paint, photo, study **6** cinema, depict, double, mirror, sketch **7** believe, drawing, essence, etching, feature, imagine, paragon, portray, tintype **8** envision, likeness, painting, snapshot **9** delineate, duplicate, facsimile, portrayal, represent **10** call to mind, carbon copy, conceive of, dead ringer, embodiment, illustrate, photograph **11** delineation **12** illustration, see in the mind **13** daguerreotype, motion picture, moving picture, spitting image **14** representation **15** exemplification, personification

Picture of Dorian Gray, The
   author: **10** Oscar Wilde
   character: **9** James Vane, Sibyl Vane **13** Basil Hallward **15** Lord Henry Wotton

picturesque 6 exotic, quaint **7** unusual **8** artistic, charming, colorful, striking **9** beautiful, pictorial **10** attractive **11** distinctive, imaginative, interesting

Picumnus
   also: **8** Pilumnus
   origin: **5** Roman
   god of: **9** fertility **11** agriculture

Picus
   origin: **5** Roman **7** Italian
   god of: **11** agriculture
   father: **6** Saturn
   associated with: **10** woodpecker
   loved by: **5** Circe
   changed into: **10** woodpecker
   son: **6** Faunus

piddling 4 puny **5** petty, small **6** flimsy, little, measly, modest, paltry, skimpy, slight **7** trivial **8** picayune, trifling **9** niggardly **11** unimportant **13** insignificant **15** inconsequential

pie 4 tart **6** pastry, quiche **7** cobbler, dessert **8** turnover
   liner: **5** crust, shell
   top: **7** lattice **8** meringue

piebald 6 motley **7** dappled, flecked, mottled, spotted **8** many-hued, speckled **10** variegated **11** many-colored, varicolored **12** multicolored, parti-colored

piece 3 bit, cut, fix, pat **4** blob, case, hunk, item, lump, mend, part, play, unit, work **5** chunk, drama, essay, patch, scrap, shard, share, shred, slice, story, study, thing **6** amount, entity, length, member, paring, repair, review, sample, sketch, sliver, swatch **7** article, cutting, example, patch up, portion, restore, section, segment **8** creation, division, fraction, fragment, instance, quantity, specimen **9** component, selection **11** composition

piece de resistance 13 principal dish **14** principal event

piece goods 5 cloth, goods **6** fabric **8** dry goods, material **9** yard goods

piecemeal 9 gradually **10** fragmented, one at a time **14** little by little

piece of the action 3 cut, fee **5** piece **7** portion, rake-off **10** commission, percentage

pied 6 motley **7** checked, dappled, mottled, piebald **8** colorful **9** checkered **10** variegated **11** many-colored **12** parti-colored

pied-a-terre 17 temporary dwelling
   literally: **12** foot on ground

Pied Piper of Hamlin, The
   author: **14** Robert Browning

Pielus
   father: **11** Neoptolemus
   mother: **10** Andromache

pier 4 anta, dock, mole, quay, slip **5** jetty, levee, wharf **6** pillar **7** landing, support **10** breakwater

pierce 3 cut **4** hurt, pain, stab **5** drill, lance, prick, spear, spike, stick, sting, wound **6** grieve, impale **7** affront **8** distress, puncture **9** penetrate, perforate **10** cut through, run through

Pierce, Franklin *see box*

piercing 3 raw **4** keen, loud **5** angry, cruel, sharp **6** biting, bitter, fierce, shrill **7** caustic, cutting, furious, grating, hurtful, intense, painful, probing **8** strident **9** agonizing, deafening, searching, shrieking, torturous **10** screeching **11** penetrating **12** earsplitting, excruciating **13** ear-shattering

Pierian
   pertains to: **5** Muses

Pierian Spring
   form: **8** fountain

Pierides *see* **5** Muses

Pierce, Franklin
   nickname: **29** Young Hickory of the Granite Hills
   presidential rank: **10** fourteenth
   party: **8** Democrat
   state represented: **2** NH
   defeated: **4** (John Parker) Hale **5** (Winfield) Scott
   vice president: **4** (William Rufus Devane) King (died in office)
   cabinet:
      state: **5** (William Learned) Marcy
      treasury: **7** (James) Guthrie
      war: **5** (Jefferson) Davis
      attorney general: **7** (Caleb) Cushing
      navy: **6** (James Cochran) Dobbin
      postmaster general: **8** (James) Campbell
      interior: **10** (Robert) McClelland
   born: **14** Hillsborough (Hillsboro) NH
   died/buried: **9** Concord NH
   education:
      Academy: **7** Hancock **11** Francestown
      College: **7** Bowdoin
      studied: **3** law
   religion: **12** Episcopalian
   political career: **8** US Senate **16** state legislature **24** US House of Representatives
   civilian career: **6** lawyer
   military service: **6** US Army **10** Mexican War **16** brigadier general
   notable events of lifetime/term:
      Act: **6** Tariff (of 1857)
      bill: **14** Kansas-Nebraska
      civil war in: **6** Kansas
      first US: **10** World's Fair
      Manifesto: **6** Ostend
      Purchase: **7** Gadsden
      treaty of: **8** Kanagawa
   father: **8** Benjamin
   mother: **4** Anna (Kendrick)
   siblings: **5** Henry, Nancy **7** Charles, Harriet **9** Charlotte **12** John Sullivan **16** Benjamin Kendrick
      half sister: **9** Elizabeth
   wife: **4** Jane (Means Appleton)
   children: **8** Benjamin, Franklin **11** Frank Robert

Piero della Francesca (Piero dei Franceschi)
  born: 5 Italy 16 Borgo San Sepolcro
  artwork: 12 Duke of Urbino 15 The Resurrection 18 Federigo and His Wife 19 St John the Evangelist 20 Flagellation of Christ 23 The Compassionate Madonna, The Legend of the True Cross, The Old Age and Death of Adam 24 The History of the True Cross 45 The Madonna and Saints with Frederigo da Montefeltro

Pierre
  author: 14 Herman Melville

Piers Plowman
  author: 15 William Langland

Pietas
  personifies: 17 familial affection

piety 7 loyalty, respect 8 devotion, humility 9 godliness, piousness, reverence 10 devoutness 11 dutifulness, religiosity 13 religiousness

pig 3 hog 5 piggy, porky, swine 6 porker 7 glutton, guzzler 8 gourmand 9 chowhound 11 gormandizer
  male: 4 boar
  female: 3 sow
  young: 5 shoat 6 piglet 11 suckling pig

pigeon
  young: 5 squab 8 squeaker

pigeonhole 4 rank, rate, type 5 brand, cubby, group, label, niche 8 category, classify 9 cubbyhole 10 categorize 11 compartment

pigheaded 6 dogged, mulish 7 willful 8 contrary, obdurate, perverse, stubborn 9 insistent, obstinate, unbending 10 bullheaded, inflexible, refractory, unyielding 11 opinionated, wrongheaded

Piglet
  character in: 13 Winnie-the-Pooh
  author: 5 Milne

pigment 3 dye 4 tint 5 color 8 coloring, dyestuff 14 coloring matter

pigmentation 5 color 9 skin color 10 coloration

pigtail 5 braid, plait, queue 8 ponytail

pike 4 bill 5 lance, spear, spike 6 poleax 7 assegai, freeway, halberd, harpoon, highway, javelin, parkway, thruway 8 autobahn, hard road, speedway, toll road, turnpike 10 expressway, interstate, throughway 12 superhighway
  British: 12 King's Highway 13 Queen's highway
  German: 8 autobahn

piker 5 miser 7 niggard, trifler 8 tightwad 9 skinflint 10 cheapskate, pinchpenny 12 penny pincher

Pilar
  character in: 19 For Whom the Bell Tolls
  author: 9 Hemingway

pilaster 4 pier 6 column, pillar 7 support, upright 8 baluster

pile 3 nap 4 heap, mass, pier, post, shag, warp 5 amass, batch, fluff, grain, hoard, mound, plush, stack, store 6 fleece, gather, piling, pillar 7 collect, pyramid, support, surface, upright 8 assemble, quantity 9 abundance, amassment, profusion, stanchion 10 accumulate, assortment, collection, foundation 11 agglomerate, aggregation, fibrousness 12 accumulation

pile up 4 bank, heap 5 amass, hoard, mound, stack 7 collect 10 accumulate

pile-up 3 jam, mob 4 mass 5 snarl 8 crowding, gridlock 10 bottleneck, congestion 11 obstruction 12 overcrowding

pilfer 3 cop, rob 4 hook, lift 5 boost, filch, heist, pinch, steal, swipe 6 finger, pirate, snitch, thieve 7 purloin 8 shoplift 10 plagiarize

pilferer 5 thief 6 robber 7 burglar 10 shoplifter, sneak thief

pilgrim, Pilgrim 4 haji 5 exile, hadji 6 palmer 7 pioneer, Puritan, settler 8 newcomer, traveler, wanderer, wayfarer 9 foreigner
  father: 5 Alden
  founder: 10 Separatist
  interpreter: 7 Squanto
  leader: 8 Standish
  protector: 7 Templar
  ship: 9 Mayflower, Speedwell

Pilgrim, Billy
  character in: 18 Slaughterhouse Five
  author: 8 Vonnegut

pilgrimage 4 hadj, trek 6 ramble, roving, voyage 7 journey, roaming, sojourn 8 long trip 9 excursion, wandering 13 peregrination

Pilgrim's Progress, The
  author: 10 John Bunyan

  character: 7 Despair, Hopeful 8 Apollyon, Faithful 9 Christian, Ignorance 10 Evangelist 14 Worldly Wiseman

pill 3 rob 4 ball, pell 5 bolus 6 bullet, pellet, tablet, pilule 7 capsule 8 medicine 9 cigarette

pillage 3 rob 4 loot, raid, sack 5 booty, rifle, strip 6 fleece, maraud, piracy, ravage, spoils 7 despoil, looting, plunder, robbery 9 filchings 10 plundering

pillager 6 looter, vandal 7 brigand 9 despoiler, plunderer

pillar 3 VIP 4 pile, post, rock 5 shaft, wheel 6 column, piling 7 obelisk, support, upright 8 champion, mainstay, pilaster, somebody 9 colonnade, stanchion

Pillars of Society, The
  author: 11 Henrik Ibsen

pillow 3 pad 7 bolster, cushion 8 headrest

pilot 4 lead 5 flyer, guide, steer 6 airman, direct, escort, fly-boy, handle, leader, manage 7 aviator, birdman, conduct, control 8 aeronaut, coxswain, helmsman, navigate, wheelman 9 accompany, sky jockey, steersman

Pilot, The
  author: 19 James Fenimore Cooper

Pima (Aatam, Pima Alto)
  language family: 10 Uto-Aztekan
  location: 7 Arizona
  related to: 6 Papago
  descendants of: 7 Hohokam

Pima Alto *see* 4 Pima

Piman
  tribe: 6 Papago

pin 4 bind, clip, tine 5 affix, badge, clasp, dowel, medal, prong 6 brooch, fasten, pinion, secure, skewer 8 hold down, hold fast, restrain 10 decoration
  type: 3 hat 4 push 5 stick, thole 6 breast, common, diaper, safety 8 straight

pincer 4 claw 5 chela

pinch 3 bit, cop, jam, jot, nab, nip 4 bust, crib, grab, iota, lift, mite, pain, snip, spot 5 catch, cramp, crimp, crush, filch, run in, speck, steal, swipe, trace, trial, tweak 6 arrest, clutch, collar, crisis, misery, ordeal, pickle, plight, snatch, snitch, strait, tittle

7 capture, purloin, squeeze, tighten **8** compress, exigency, hardship **9** apprehend, emergency **10** affliction, difficulty, discomfort **11** predicament

Pinch, Tom
   character in: 16 Martin Chuzzlewit
   author: 7 Dickens

pinch hitter 5 proxy **7** stand-in **9** alternate **10** substitute

pinchpenny 5 miser **6** frugal, stingy **7** niggard, prudent, thrifty
   Dickensian: 7 Scrooge

Pindar
   author of: 4 Odes **8** Epinicea

pine 3 die, ebb **4** flag, long, sigh, wilt **5** covet, crave, droop, yearn **6** desire, expire, hanker, weaken, wither **7** decline, dwindle, pant for **8** languish **9** hunger for, waste away **11** have a yen for, thirst after **12** fail in health

pine *see* **box**

Pine Tree State
   nickname of: 5 Maine

pin hope on 6 bank on **7** count on, long for, wish for **8** aspire to, yearn for **10** anticipate

pink 8 Dianthus
   varieties: 3 Sea **4** fire, moss, pine, rose, wild **5** cameo, clove, dairy, grass, marsh,

swamp **6** button, ground, indian, Kirtle, maiden **7** cheddar, cottage, cushion, Mullein, rainbow **8** Childing, Deptford, election **11** clusterhead **13** fringed indian, spottle kirtle **16** California indian

pinnacle 3 cap, top **4** acme, apex, peak **5** crest, crown, spire, tower **6** belfry, height, summit, tiptop, vertex, zenith **7** steeple **9** bell tower, campanile

pinochle
   also known as: 7 binocle, pinocle **8** penuchle
   derived from: 7 bezique
   points/game: 11 one thousand

pinpoint 3 dot, jot **4** iota, spot **5** speck **6** detail **8** home in on, localize, zero in on **12** characterize

pint
   abbreviation of: 2 pt

pinxit 11 he painted it **12** she painted it

pioneer 5 found, start **6** create, father, herald, invent, leader **7** develop, founder **8** colonist, discover, explorer **9** be a leader, developer, establish, harbinger, innovator, precursor **10** antecedent, forerunner, lead the way, pathfinder, show the way **11** establisher, predecessor, trailblazer **12** first

settler, frontiersman **13** blaze the trail **14** early immigrant, founding father
   Hebrew: 6 halutz
   7 chalutz

Pioneers, The
   author: 19 James Fenimore Cooper
   character: 10 Indian John **11** Judge Temple, Natty Bumppo **13** Oliver Edwards **14** Hiram Doolittle **15** Elizabeth Temple

pious 4 holy **5** godly **6** devout, divine **7** sainted, saintly **8** faithful, reverent, unctuous **9** dedicated, insincere, pietistic, religious, spiritual **10** worshipful **11** reverential **12** hypocritical **13** rationalizing, sanctimonious, self-righteous **14** holier-than-thou

Pip
   character in: 17 Great Expectations
   author: 7 Dickens

pipe 4 duct, main, peep, sing, tube **5** cheep, chirp, trill, tweet **6** warble **7** conduit, twitter, whistle **8** conveyor **9** conductor **10** play a flute **12** play a bagpipe

Pippa Passes
   author: 14 Robert Browning

piquant 3 hot **4** acid, racy **5** peppy, salty, sharp, spicy, tangy, zesty **6** biting, bitter, bright, clever, lively, savory **7** mordant, peppery, pungent, rousing **8** animated, incisive, piercing, spirited, stinging, vigorous **9** sparkling, trenchant **11** interesting, provacative, stimulating **13** scintillating **14** highly seasoned, strong-flavored

pique 3 ire, irk, vex **4** gall, goad, miff, snit, spur, stir **5** annoy, peeve, rouse, spite **6** arouse, excite, grudge, kindle, malice, nettle, offend **7** affront, incense, perturb, provoke, quicken, umbrage **8** disquiet, irritate, vexation **9** annoyance, displease, stimulate **10** discomfort, exasperate, irritation, resentment **11** displeasure, humiliation, ill feelings, indignation **12** exasperation, hurt feelings **13** embarrassment, mortification, put one's back up **14** vindictiveness

piqued 5 angry, riled, vexed **6** galled, miffed, peeved **7** annoyed, aroused, excited, kindled, nettled, stirred **9** affronted, irritated **10** displeased, stimulated

---

pine 5 Pinus
   varieties: 3 air, nut, red **4** blue, chir, gray, hoop, Huon, Imou, Jack **5** beach, cedar, Cuban, Emodi, giant, house, Kauri, pitch, Scots, screw, scrub, shore, slash, stone, sugar, white **6** Aleppo, Apache, Bhutan, Bishop, celery, Dammar, digger, ground, Jersey, Korean, limber, Mallee, Norway, Parana, Pinyon, Scotch, spruce, Torrey, Totara, yellow **7** Amboina, Benguet, big-cone, Chilean, Chinese, cluster, Cypress, Formosa, Georgia, Gerard's, hickory, jointed, long-tag, prickly, prince's, running, Soledad **8** Austrian, Buddhist, cow's-tail, knob-cone, lace-bark, Loblolly, longleaf, mahogany, Monterey, mountain, Nepal nut, old-field, princess, umbrella **9** Brazilian, Calabrian, Chilghoza, Jerusalem, lodgepole, Oyster Bay, shortleaf, white-bark **10** Australian, Bunya-bunya, dwarf stone, Macedonian, Moreton Bay, red cypress, Swiss stone, Tenasserim **11** African fern, bristlecone, common screw, Japanese red, Parry pinyon, Port Jackson, thatch screw, twisted-leaf, Veitch screw **12** black cypress, Canary Island, Chinese water, eastern white, frankincense, Italian stone, Mexican stone, Mexican white, two-leaved nut, western white **13** dwarf Siberian, Japanese black, Japanese white, Mexican yellow, New Caledonian, Norfolk Island, Swiss mountain, table mountain **14** Himalayan white, Rottnest Island, southern yellow **15** Mueller's cypress **16** Japanese umbrella, single-leaf pinyon **18** Rough-barked Mexican **19** Rocky Mountain yellow

Pirandello, Luigi
author of: 17 The Old and
the Young 18 Tonight We
Improvise 19 The Late Mattia Pascal 31 Six Characters
in Search of an Author

pirate 3 rob 5 steal 6 raider,
robber, sea dog 7 brigand, corsair, plunder 8 marauder
9 buccaneer, privateer
10 freebooter
flag: 9 blackjack 10 Jolly
Roger
name: 4 Kidd 6 Morgan
7 Lafitte 10 Blackbeard

Pirate Coast see 18 United
Arab Emirates

Pirates of Penzance, The
author: 9 W S Gilbert
comic opera by: 18 Gilbert
and Sullivan
character: 4 Kate, Ruth
5 Edith, Mabel 6 Isabel
8 Frederic, Sergeant 10 Pirate King 14 General
Stanley

Pirithous
prince of: 8 Lapithae
father: 4 Zeus
mother: 3 Dia
son: 10 Polypoetes
friend of: 7 Theseus

Pirous
led allies of: 6 Thrace

pis aller 10 last resort 12 last
resource

Pisan Cantos
author: 9 Ezra Pound

Pisander
rank: 7 captain
member of: 9 Myrmidons

Pisanio
character in: 9 Cymbeline
author: 11 Shakespeare

Pisanosaurus
type: 8 dinosaur
10 ornithopod
location: 12 South America
period: 8 Triassic

Pisces
symbol: 4 fish
planet: 7 Jupiter, Neptune
rules: 7 secrets
born: 13 February-March

Pisistratidae
sons of: 11 Pisistratus
names: 7 Hippias
10 Hipparchus

Pisistratus
tyrant of: 6 Athens
father: 11 Hippocrates
son: 7 Hippias 10 Hipparchus

Pissarro, Camille
born: 8 St Thomas 16 Danish
West Indies
artwork: 8 Red Roofs
15 Morning Sunlight

21 Lower Norwood Snow
Scene 28 Peasant Woman
with a Wheelbarrow

pistol (revolver)
invented by: 4 Colt

pit 3 dip, nut 4 dent, hole,
nick, pock, scar, seed 5 gouge,
gully, match, notch, stone
6 cavity, crater, dimple, furrow, hollow, indent, kernel,
oppose, trough 7 scratch
8 contrast, pockmark 9 concavity, juxtapose 10 depression, set against
11 indentation

Pit, The
author: 11 Frank Norris

Pitana
form: 5 nymph
daughter: 6 Evadne

Pit and the Pendulum, The
author: 13 Edgar Allan Poe

pitch 3 bob, dip, fix, lob, set,
shy, top 4 apex, cant, cast,
fall, fire, hurl, jerk, jolt, peak,
rock, tone, toss 5 angle,
chuck, crown, erect, fling,
grade, heave, level, lurch,
place, plant, point, raise, set
up, shake, slant, sling, slope,
sound, throw 6 degree, height,
let fly, locate, plunge, propel,
settle, summit, topple, tumble,
zenith 7 bobbing, incline,
rocking, station 8 delivery,
harmonic, lurching, pinnacle,
undulate 9 declivity, establish,
oscillate 10 undulation 11 oscillation 12 fall headlong
speed of: 9 vibration

pitcher 3 jar, jug 4 ewer
6 carafe 8 decanter 9 container 10 spitballer
and catcher: 7 battery
award: 7 Cy Young
brother duo: 4 Dean 5 Perry
6 Niekro
Hall of Famer: 4 Ford,
Wynn 6 Koufax 8 Drysdale
left-hander: 8 southpaw
relief staff: 7 bullpen
reliever: 7 fireman

pitch in 5 begin 7 share in
8 take part 9 cooperate, get to
work, join hands 10 act
jointly, contribute, get started
11 collaborate, participate
12 make an effort, pull together, work together

pitch into 5 fly at 6 assail,
have at 7 assault, set upon

piteous 3 sad 6 moving, woeful 7 pitiful 8 pathetic, pitiable, poignant, touching
9 affecting 10 deplorable
11 distressing 12 heart-rending 13 heartbreaking

pitfall 4 risk, trap 5 peril,

snare 6 ambush, danger, hazard 7 springe 8 quagmire
9 booby trap, quicksand
14 stumbling block

pith 4 core, gist, meat 5 heart,
point 7 essence, meaning
12 significance

pithy 5 terse 6 cogent 7 concise 8 forceful, succinct 9 effective, trenchant
10 expressive, meaningful, to
the point 12 concentrated

pitiful 3 sad 4 poor 5 sorry
6 abject, measly, moving, paltry, shabby 7 doleful, forlorn,
piteous 8 dreadful, god-awful,
mournful, pathetic, pitiable,
poignant, touching, wretched
9 miserable, plaintive, worthless 10 abominable, despicable,
lamentable 11 distressing
12 arousing pity, contemptible,
heartrending

pitiless 5 cruel 6 brutal 7 inhuman, unmoved 8 ruthless,
uncaring 9 heartless, merciless,
unpitying, unsparing, un-
touched 10 implacable,
relentless, unmerciful
11 cold-blooded, hardhearted,
indifferent, insensitive,
unrelenting

pittance 4 mite 5 crumb 6 little, trifle 7 minimum, modicum, smidgen

Pittheus
father: 6 Pelops
mother: 10 Hippodamia
brother: 7 Troezen
daughter: 6 Aethra

Pittsburgh
baseball team: 7 Pirates
feature: 14 Fort Pitt Mu-
seum 15 Buhl
Planetarium
football team: 8 Steelers
formerly: 8 Fort Pitt 12 Fort
Duquesne
hockey team: 8 Penguins
noted for: 5 steel
river: 4 Ohio 9 Allegheny
11 Monongahela
university: 8 Duquesne
14 Carnegie-Mellon

Pittypat, Aunt
character in: 15 Gone With
the Wind
author: 8 Mitchell

pituitary
located in: 5 brain
known as: 11 master gland

pity 5 mercy, shame 6 lament,
lenity, regret 7 charity, feel
for, weep for 8 bleed for,
clemency, humanity, leniency,
sad thing, sympathy 10 compassion, condolence, indulgence, kindliness, tenderness
11 crying shame, forbearance,

magnanimity **12** feel sorry for **13** commiseration

Pityocamptes
epithet of: **5** Sinis
means: **10** pine-bender

Pitys
form: **5** nymph
loved by: **3** Pan
changed into: **8** pine tree

piu
music: **4** more

pivot 4 axis, axle, hang, rely, spin, turn **5** focus, hinge, twirl, wheel, whirl **6** center, circle, depend, rotate, swivel **7** fulcrum, hinge on, revolve **9** pirouette

pivotal 5 vital **7** crucial **8** critical, decisive **9** climactic **11** determining

pivotal point 4 axis **12** turning point **13** crucial moment

pixy 3 elf **5** fairy **6** sprite **10** leprechaun

pizzicato
music: **21** plucked instead of bowed
abbreviation: **4** pizz

placable 7 lenient **8** flexible, tolerant, yielding **9** indulgent, relenting **10** appeasable, forbearing **12** reconcilable

placard 4 bill, sign **6** notice, poster **8** bulletin **13** advertisement

placate 4 calm, lull **5** quiet **6** pacify, soothe **7** appease, assuage, mollify, win over **9** alleviate **10** conciliate, propitiate

placatory 9 appeasing, pacifying **10** mollifying **12** conciliatory **13** accommodative

place 3 fix, job, put, set **4** area, city, digs, duty, farm, firm, home, land, plot, post, rank, rest, shop, site, spot, town, zone **5** abode, affix, array, berth, house, lodge, niche, plant, point, ranch, space, stand, state, store, venue **6** assign, attach, county, harbor, invest, locale, locate, office, region, settle **7** appoint, borough, company, concern, country, deposit, install, quarter, shelter, situate, station, village **8** building, business, classify, district, domicile, dwelling, ensconce, find hire, function, identify, locality, location, lodgings, position, premises, property, province, quarters, remember, standing, township, vicinity **9** recognize, residence, situation, territory **10** commission, get a job for, habitation **11** appointment,

find work for, whereabouts **12** neighborhood **13** establishment
Latin: **4** situ

Place in the Sun, A
director: **13** George Stevens
based on novel by: **15** Theodore Dreiser (An American Tragedy)
cast: **14** Keefe Brasselle, Shelley Winters **15** Elizabeth Taylor, Montgomery Clift
Oscar for: **5** score **9** direction **10** screenplay

placement 8 grouping, location **10** assignment, employment **11** arrangement, disposition, positioning

place of residence 4 home **5** abode, house **7** address, lodging **8** domicile, dwelling **9** residence **10** habitation **14** living quarters

place to stand on
Greek: **6** pou sto

place upright 5 erect, raise **7** stand up

placid 4 calm, mild **5** quiet **6** gentle, poised, serene, smooth **7** pacific, restful **8** composed, peaceful, tranquil **9** collected, unexcited, unruffled **10** untroubled **11** undisturbed, unexcitable **13** imperturbable, self-possessed **15** undemonstrative

plague 3 irk, vex, woe **4** bane, evil, fret, gall, pain, pest **5** agony, chafe, curse, harry, haunt, peeve, worry **6** badger, blight, bother, burden, cancer, harass, misery, nettle **7** afflict, disturb, perturb, scourge, torment, trouble **8** aggrieve, calamity, disquiet, distress, hardship, pandemic **9** embarrass, persecute, suffering **10** affliction, Black Death, pestilence, visitation
French: **5** peste

Plague, The
author: **11** Albert Camus
character: **7** Rambert **10** Jean Tarrou **11** Joseph Grand **14** Father Paneloux, Raymond Cottard **15** Dr Bernard R Rieux

Plague Dogs, The
author: **12** Richard Adams

plain 4 bald, bare, open **5** blunt, clear, frank, naked, vivid **6** candid, common, direct, homely, honest, modest, simple **7** average, glaring, legible, obscure, obvious, plateau, prairie, sincere, visible **8** apparent, clear-cut, distinct, everyday, explicit, manifest, ordinary, palpable, specific,

straight, striking, uncomely, unlovely **9** grassland, outspoken, prominent, tableland, unadorned, undiluted **10** forthright, pronounced, unaffected, unassuming, unhandsome, unreserved, well-marked **11** commonplace, conspicuous, discernible, not striking, open country, outstanding, plain-spoken, unambiguous, undecorated, undisguised, unequivocal, ungarnished, unvarnished, well-defined **12** matter-of-fact, not beautiful, unattractive, unmistakable, unornamented **13** unembellished, unpretentious, without frills **14** comprehensible, understandable **15** straightforward, undistinguished

Plain Dealer, The
author: **16** William Wycherley

plainly 6 baldly, openly, simply **7** bluntly, clearly, frankly, visibly, vividly **8** candidly, directly, honestly, markedly, modestly **9** doubtless, obviously **10** apparently, definitely, distinctly, explicitly, manifestly, ordinarily, positively, strikingly, undeniably **11** beyond doubt, discernibly, prominently, undoubtedly **12** unaffectedly, unassumingly, unmistakably, without doubt **13** conspicuously, unambiguously, unequivocably **14** comprehensibly, unquestionably

plainness 10 homeliness, simplicity **12** ordinariness

plainspoken 4 open **5** bluff, blunt, frank, plain **6** candid, direct, honest **7** genuine, sincere **8** explicit, straight **9** openfaced, outspoken, unsparing **10** above board, forthright, point-blank **11** straight-out **15** straightforward

plaint 3 cry, sob **4** beef, moan, wail **5** gripe **6** charge, grouse, grudge, lament, regret, squawk **7** grumble, reproof **8** reproach **9** complaint, grievance, objection **10** accusation, resentment **12** remonstrance

plaintive 3 sad **6** rueful **7** doleful, moaning, piteous, pitiful, tearful **8** dolorous, grievous, mournful, pathetic, wretched **9** lamenting, sorrowful, woebegone **10** lugubrious, melancholy **12** heartrending

plait 5 braid, queue, twine, twist, weave **7** pigtail **10** intertwine

plan 3 aim, map, way **4** form, idea, plot **5** frame, shape

6 design, devise, intend, lay out, map out, method, scheme, sketch 7 diagram, outline, prepare, program, project, propose, purpose 8 block out, conceive, contrive, organize, proposal, strategy, think out 9 blueprint, fabricate, procedure, stratagem 10 conception, suggestion 11 proposition
French: 8 demarche

Planchet
character in: 18 The Three Musketeers
author: 5 Dumas (pere)

Planck, Max
field: 7 physics
nationality: 6 German
developed: 13 quantum theory 15 Planck's constant
awarded: 10 Nobel Prize

Planctae
form: 5 rocks
characteristic: 8 shifting

plane 3 jet 4 bird, flat 5 level, plumb 6 degree, status 7 regular, station 8 aircraft, airplane, position, standing 9 condition, elevation
type: 4 jack 5 block

planet, planets 13 celestial body
first: 7 Mercury
second: 5 Venus
third: 5 Earth
  satellite: 4 Moon
fourth: 4 Mars
  satellite: 6 Deimos, Phobos
  nickname: 9 Red Planet
fifth: 7 Jupiter
  satellite: 2 Io 6 Europa 8 Amalthea, Callisto, Ganymede
  characteristic: 7 red spot
sixth: 6 Saturn
  satellite: 4 Rhea 5 Dione, Janus, Mimas, Titan 6 Phoebe, Tethys 7 Iapetus 8 Hyperion 9 Enceladus
  characteristic: 5 rings
seventh: 6 Uranus
  satellite: 5 Ariel 6 Oberon 7 Miranda, Titania, Umbriel
  color: 9 blue-green
  characteristic: 5 rings
eighth: 7 Neptune
  satellite: 6 Nereid, Triton
  color: 5 green
ninth: 5 Pluto
  satellite: 6 Charon
asteroid/minor planet/planetoid: 4 Eros, Juno 5 Ceres, Vesta 6 Chiron, Hermes, Icarus, Pallas 7 Astraea, Hidalgo

planetary 6 astral 7 earthly 9 celestial 11 terrestrial 12 astronomical

Planet of the Apes
director: 18 Franklin J Schaffner
based on novel by: 12 Pierre Boulle
cast: 9 Kim Hunter 12 Maurice Evans 13 Roddy McDowall 14 Charlton Heston
script: 10 Rod Serling

plank 4 deal, deck, slab 5 board, shole, stone 8 platform

planned 7 devised, schemed 8 designed, expected, foreseen, intended, prepared 9 mapped out, organized, projected, rehearsed 10 calculated, purposeful, thought out 11 intentional, prearranged, prepared for 12 premeditated

planner 6 author, framer 7 creator, deviser 8 arranger, designer 9 architect, organizer

plant 4 bush, herb, mill, moss, shop, slip, tree, vine, weed, wort, yard 5 algae, flora, fungi, grass, set in, shrub, works 6 flower, foster, infuse, set out 7 factory, foundry, herbage, implant, inspire, instill, scatter, sow seed 8 business, engender, seedling 9 broadcast, cultivate, establish, inculcate, propagate, vegetable 10 transplant, vegetation 13 establishment, sow the seeds of 14 put in the ground

plaster 4 coat, daub, sand 5 grout, smear 6 bedaub, gypsum, lather, stucco 7 overlay, spackle
mixture of: 4 lime 5 water 6 gypsum

plastered 5 drunk 6 coated, daubed, soused 7 covered, crocked, smeared, swacked 8 mortared, polluted, stuccoed 10 inebriated 11 intoxicated

plastic 4 soft 6 pliant, supple 7 ductile, elastic, pliable 8 flexible, formable, moldable, shapable, yielding 9 malleable, tractable

Platanistius
epithet of: 6 Apollo
means: 22 god of the plane-tree grove

plate 4 dish 6 saucer 7 helping, platter, portion, serving 10 platterful 11 serving dish

plateau 4 mesa 5 table 6 upland 8 highland 9 tableland

Plateosaurus
type: 8 dinosaur, sauropod
location: 6 Europe 7 Germany
period: 8 Triassic

platform 4 dais, goal, plan

5 creed, plank, stage, stand 6 podium, policy, pulpit, tenets 7 program, rostrum

Plath, Sylvia
author of: 5 Ariel 10 The Bell Jar

platinum
chemical symbol: 2 Pt

platitude 3 saw 6 cliche, old saw, truism 7 bromide 8 banality, chestnut 11 commonplace

platitudinous 5 banal, corny, stale, tired, trite, vapid 6 jejune 8 bromidic, ordinary 9 hackneyed 10 pedestrian, unexciting, unoriginal 12 cliche-ridden, conventional 13 unimaginative

Plato
author of: 4 Laws 5 Crito 6 Phaedo 7 Apology, Gorgias, Sophist, Timaeus 8 Philebus, Republic 9 Symposium 10 Parmenides

platoon 4 band, body, crew, team, unit 5 corps, force, group 10 detachment

platter 4 dish, disk, lanx 6 salver 7 record 8 trencher 9 recording

plaudit, plaudits 4 rave 5 cheer, kudos 6 hurrah, huzzah, praise 7 acclaim, bouquet, ovation 8 applause, approval, cheering 10 compliment, hallelujah 11 approbation 12 commendation

plauditory 8 admiring, praising 9 extolling, laudatory, praiseful 12 commendatory 13 complimentary

plausible 5 sound, valid 6 likely 7 logical, tenable 8 credible, feasible, possible, probable, rational, sensible 10 acceptable, believable, convincing, persuasive, reasonable 11 conceivable, justifiable

Plautus
author of: 7 Stichus 8 Mercator 9 Amphitruo, Menaechmi, Pseudolus 10 Amphitryon 14 Miles Gloriosus

play 3 act, fun, toy 4 jest, lark, romp, room, show 5 antic, caper, drama, enact, farce, frisk, revel, space, sport, sweep, swing 6 act out, cavort, comedy, frolic, gambol, leeway, trifle 7 disport, have fun, pageant, perform, skylark, tragedy, vie with 8 pleasure, take part 9 amusement, diversion, elbowroom, enjoyment, make merry, melodrama, perform on, personify, represent, spectacle **10** recreation **11** impersonate, merrymaking

playboy 4 rake, wolf **5** Romeo, sheik **6** lecher **7** Don Juan, swinger **8** Casanova, hedonist, Lothario, party boy **9** jet-setter, ladies' man, partygoer, womanizer **10** lady-killer, profligate **14** pleasure seeker **15** good-time Charlie

Playboy of the Western World, The
    author: 19 John Millington Synge
    character: 8 Old Mahon **9** Widow Quin **10** Shawn Keogh **16** Christopher Mahon, Margaret Flaherty (Pegeen)

play down 9 underplay **11** de-emphasize

played out 4 beat **5** all in, spent, weary **6** bushed, done in, pooped **7** drained, wearied, worn out **8** depleted, dog tired, fatigued, tired out, unreeled **9** dead tired, exhausted

player 4 jock, mime **5** actor **6** mummer **7** actress, athlete, trouper **8** gamester, opponent, thespian **9** adversary, contender, performer **10** antagonist, competitor, contestant, team member **11** entertainer, participant

play false 4 dupe **5** trick **6** betray **7** deceive, two-time **10** be disloyal **12** be unfaithful **13** be treacherous

playfellow 3 pal **4** chum **5** buddy **6** friend **8** playmate

playful 6 frisky, impish, lively **7** amusing, coltish, jesting, waggish **8** humorous, mirthful, prankish, sportive **9** fun-loving, sprightly **10** capricious, frolicsome, rollicking **12** lighthearted
    French: **8** espiegle

playful trick
    French: **11** espieglerie

play host 4 host **9** entertain **10** give a party, have guests **13** keep open house

playing field 4 bowl **5** arena **7** diamond, stadium **8** gridiron **10** playground **12** amphitheater

playing piece 3 man **4** disk **5** piece **7** counter

play in water 3 dip **4** swim **6** dabble, paddle, splash

play Judas 6 betray **7** sell out, two-time **9** play false **11** double-cross

playmate 3 pal **4** chum

5 buddy **6** friend **10** playfellow

play of spirit
    French: **10** jeu d'esprit

play on words
    French: **9** jeu de mots

plaything 3 toy **4** dupe **5** patsy, sport **6** bauble, trifle **9** diversion

play truant 3 cut **4** skip **8** be absent **9** play hooky

play with 5 bandy **7** torment, toy with **11** have fun with

playwright 6 author, writer **9** dramatist, scenarist **10** dramatizer, dramaturge, librettist, play doctor **12** dramatic poet, dramaturgist, scriptwriter **13** melodramatist

plea 4 suit **5** alibi **6** appeal, excuse, prayer **7** apology, begging, defense, pretext, request **8** argument, entreaty, petition **10** adjuration, beseeching **11** explanation, extenuation, vindication **12** solicitation, supplication **13** justification

plead 3 ask, beg **6** adjure, enjoin **7** beseech, entreat, implore, request, solicit **8** appeal to, petition **9** importune **10** supplicate

pleader 6 beggar **8** advocate, defender, implorer **9** apologist, beseecher **10** importuner, supplicant

plead with 3 beg **4** pray **6** adjure **7** beseech, implore **10** supplicate

Pleasance, Donald
    born: 7 England, Worksop
    roles: 12 The Caretaker **14** The Great Escape **16** You Only Live Twice **17** The Eagle Has Landed **24** The Greatest Story Ever Told

pleasant 4 fine, good, mild, nice, soft, warm **6** genial, gentle, lovely, polite **7** affable, amiable, cordial, likable, tactful **8** amicable, charming, cheerful, friendly, inviting, pleasing, sociable **9** agreeable, congenial, enjoyable **10** attractive, felicitous, gratifying, gregarious, satisfying **11** good-humored, good-natured, pleasurable **13** companionable

Pleasant Island see **5** Nauru

pleasantry 4 jape, jest, joke, quip **5** sally **6** bon mot **8** greeting **9** wisecrack, witticism **10** salutation

pleasant-tasting 4 mild **5** sweet, tasty **6** savory **8** luscious **9** delicious, palatable,

succulent **10** appetizing, delectable **11** scrumptious **13** mouth-watering

please 3 opt **4** like, suit, want, will, wish **5** amuse, charm, elate, elect **6** choose, desire, divert, prefer, thrill, tickle **7** content, delight, gladden, gratify, satisfy **8** enthrall, entrance **9** enrapture, entertain, fascinate, make happy **10** be inclined **14** give pleasure to
    French: **12** s'il vous plait
    German: **5** bitte
    Spanish: **8** por favor

pleased 4 glad **5** happy, proud **6** elated **8** thrilled **9** delighted, gratified

please reply
    French: **4** rsvp **20** repondez s'il vous plait

pleasing 6 genial, polite **7** affable, amiable, amusing, likable, winning **8** charming, cheerful, friendly, inviting, mannerly **9** agreeable, congenial, diverting, enjoyable **10** attractive, delightful, gladdening, gratifying, satisfying **11** captivating, fascinating, good-humored, good-natured, pleasurable **12** entertaining, well-mannered

pleasing inactivity
    Italian: **14** dolce far niente

pleasurable 8 pleasing **9** agreeable, enjoyable **10** delightful

pleasure 3 fun, joy **4** like, will, wish **5** bliss, cheer, mirth **6** choice, desire, gaiety, option **7** delight, elation, rapture **9** amusement, diversion, enjoyment, festivity, happiness, merriment, selection **10** exultation, jubilation, preference, recreation **11** high spirits, inclination **13** entertainment, gratification **15** beer and skittles **16** lightheartedness
    goddess of: 8 Voluptas

pleasure-giving 7 amusing **8** pleasing **9** agreeable, enjoyable **10** delightful **11** pleasurable **12** entertaining

Pleasure of His Company, The
    author: 19 Cornelia Otis Skinner

pleasure trip 4 tour **5** jaunt **6** outing **8** vacation **9** excursion

pleat 4 fold **5** crimp, frill **6** crease

pleated 6 fluted, folded **7** creased, crimped **10** corrugated

plebeian 3 low 4 base, mean
5 banal 6 coarse, common,
vulgar 7 lowborn, lowbrow,
popular 8 commoner, everyman, low-class, ordinary
9 bourgeois, common man,
unrefined 10 average man, uncultured 11 bourgeoisie, commonplace, proletarian
12 uncultivated

plebs 5 demos 6 masses
7 commons 8 populace 9 commoners, hoi polloi, plebeians
11 bourgeoisie 12 common
people

plecoptera
   class: 8 hexapoda
   phylum: 10 arthropoda
   group: 8 stone fly

pledge 3 vow 4 bail, bond,
oath, pact, pawn, word
5 swear, troth 6 assert,
avowal, surety 7 compact,
promise, warrant 8 contract,
covenant, guaranty, security,
warranty 9 agreement, assurance, guarantee 10 adjuration,
collateral

Pleiades
   father: 5 Atlas
   mother: 7 Pleione
   half-sisters: 6 Hyades
   names: 4 Maia 6 Merope
      7 Alcyone, Celaeno, Electra,
      Sterope, Taygete
   number of daughters:
      5 seven

plenary 4 full 6 entire 7 perfect 8 absolute, complete

plenitude 4 glut, heap, mass
5 flood 6 bounty, plenty,
wealth 7 quality, surfeit, surplus 8 fullness, plethora, totality 9 abundance, amplitude,
profusion, repletion, wholeness 10 cornucopia, entireness,
quantities 11 ample supply,
copiousness, full measure, sufficiency 12 completeness
14 more than enough

plenteous 6 lavish 7 copious,
profuse 8 abundant 9 bountiful, plentiful

plentiful 4 lush 5 ample, large
6 lavish 7 copious, liberal, profuse 8 abundant, generous, infinite, prolific 9 abounding,
bounteous, bountiful, plenteous, unsparing, unstinted
11 overflowing
13 inexhaustible

plenty 4 gobs, lots, slew
5 scads 6 luxury, oceans, oodles, riches, wealth, worlds
8 opulence 9 abundance, affluence, good times, great deal,
plenitude, profusion, well-
being 10 prosperity 11 ample

amount, good fortune, sufficiency 12 a full measure
   goddess of: 3 Ops

plethora 4 glut 5 flood 6 excess, wealth 7 overage, surfeit,
surplus 8 fullness 9 abundance,
amplitude, plenitude, profusion 10 oversupply, redundancy, surplusage
11 superfluity 13 overabundance 14 more than enough,
superabundance

Plexippus
   also: 10 Parthenius
   father: 7 Phineus 8 Thestius
   brother: 7 Pandion
   sister: 7 Althaea
   nephew: 8 Meleager
   killed by: 8 Meleager

pliable 5 lithe 6 limber, pliant,
supple 7 elastic, plastic,
springy, willing 8 flexible,
yielding 9 adaptable, compliant, receptive, resilient,
tractable 10 manageable, responsive, submissive 11 acquiescent 13 accommodating
14 easily bendable,
impressionable

pliancy 8 docility, meekness,
yielding 9 passivity 10 compliance, pliability, submission,
suppleness 11 flexibility
12 complaisance

pliant 4 meek 6 supple 7 pliable 8 flexible, yielding 9 compliant 10 submissive
11 deferential

pliers
   type: 10 fixed-joint 11 com-
      bination, needle-nosed, side-
      cutting 17 offset
      combination

plight 3 fix, jam 5 pinch, state,
trial 6 crisis, muddle, pickle,
scrape 7 dilemma, impasse,
straits, trouble 8 distress, exigency 9 condition, emergency,
extremity, situation 10 difficulty 11 predicament, tribulation, vicissitude
12 circumstance

Plisthenes
   brother/half-brother: 8 Men-
      elaus 9 Agamemnon
   father: 6 Atreus
   mother: 6 Cleola
   sister/half-sister: 8 Anaxibia
   sister-in-law: 12 Clytemnestra
   uncle: 8 Thyestes

plod 4 drag, grub, moil, plug,
slog, toil 5 grind, sweat,
tramp 6 drudge, lumber,
trudge, waddle 7 peg away,
shuffle 8 struggle
9 persevere

plodding 4 dull 6 clumsy
8 trudging 9 laborious
10 pedestrian

plot 3 lot, map 4 area, draw,
mark, plan, tale, yarn 5 chart,
draft, field, patch, space, story,
tract 6 action, design, scheme,
sketch 7 collude, compute, diagram, outline, section 8 clearing, conspire, contrive, evil
plan, intrigue, maneuver
9 blueprint, calculate, determine, incidents, narrative,
story line, stratagem 10 conspiracy, secret plan
11 machination

plotting 4 wily 6 artful, crafty
7 cunning 8 scheming 9 conniving, designing 10 intriguing

Plough and the Stars, The
   author: 10 Sean O'Casey

plover
   group of: 4 wing
      12 congregation

plow, plough 3 cut, dig
4 push, till, work 5 break, dig
up, drive, forge, press, shove,
spade 6 furrow, harrow,
loosen, plunge, turn up
7 break up 8 bulldoze
9 cultivate
   invented by:
      cast iron: 7 Ransome
      disc: 5 Hardy

plowable 6 arable 7 friable
8 farmable, tillable
10 cultivable

Plowright, Joan
   born: 5 Brigg 7 England
   husband: 15 Laurence Olivier
   roles: 13 A Taste of Honey
      15 The Entertainers

ploy 4 game, ruse, wile 5 trick
6 design, gambit, scheme, tactic 7 gimmick 8 artifice, maneuver, strategy 9 stratagem
10 subterfuge

pluck 4 draw, grab, grit, guts,
jerk, pick, sand, yank 5 spunk,
valor 6 daring, mettle, pull at,
snatch, spirit, uproot 7 bravery, courage, pull off, pull
out, resolve 8 boldness, temerity, tenacity 9 extirpate, fortitude 10 doggedness,
resolution 11 persistence
12 perseverance
13 determination

pluck out 7 extract, pick out,
pull out

plucky 4 bold, game 5 brave,
gutsy 6 daring, spunky
7 doughty, valiant 8 fearless,
intrepid, spirited, unafraid,
valorous 9 audacious, dauntless, undaunted 10 courageous,
mettlesome 11 lionhearted,
unflinching 12 stouthearted

plug 4 bung, cork 5 close,
stuff 6 fill up, stanch, stop up
7 shut off, stopper, stopple

plug up 3 dam 4 clog, plug
5 block, choke, dam up, stuff
6 stop up 7 congest 8 obstruct

plum
varieties: 3 hog 4 Coco, date,
Duhr, gage, Java, sand, sloe,
wild 5 beach, black, goose,
Islay, Jaman, Lansa, Moxie,
nanny, Natal, shore, Simon
6 August, Batoko, Canada,
Cheney, cherry, common,
Damson, ground, Indian,
Jambul, Kaffir, Kelsey, Lomboy, Pigeon, Sapote, Sierra,
Sisson 7 apricot, Burbank,
Cheston, Jambosa, Malabar,
Orleans, Pacific, Spanish,
Wickson 8 American, Assyrian, Burdekin, European,
Hortulan, Jambolan, Japa-
nese, Oklahoma, Prunello,
Victoria 9 Allegheny, Chickasaw, Governor's, greengage,
marmalade, Myrobalan,
wild-goose 10 Madagascar
13 Queensland hog

plumb 4 lead, test, true
5 gauge, level, probe, sheer,
sound 6 fathom 7 examine,
measure, plummet 8 plumb
bob, straight, vertical
9 penetrate

plume 3 pen 4 down 5 egret,
pique, preen, pride, prize,
quill 7 feather
military: 7 panache

Plumed Serpent, The
author: 10 D H Lawrence

Plummer, Christopher
real name: 28 Arthur Christopher Orme Plummer
born: 6 Canada 7 Toronto
wife: 11 Tammy Grimes
12 Elaine Taylor
roles: 14 Murder by Decree
15 The Sound of Music
18 Baron Georg von Trapp
20 The Man Who Would Be
King 25 The Return of the
Pink Panther

plummet 4 dive, fall 6 plunge,
tumble 8 nosedive 12 fall
headlong

plump 4 drop, firm, flop, plop,
sink 5 blunt, buxom, obese,
plunk, pudgy, solid, spill,
stout 6 abrupt, chubby, direct,
fleshy, portly, rotund, sprawl,
stocky, tumble 7 rounded
8 collapse, outright 9 corpulent

plumpness
French: 10 embonpoint

plunder 3 rob 4 haul, loot,
raid, sack, swag, take 5 booty,
rifle, prize, strip 6 fleece, maraud, pilfer, ravage, spoils
7 despoil, pillage, ransack, takings 9 filchings 10 pilferings

plunderer 6 looter, vandal

7 brigand 8 pillager
9 despoiler

plunge 3 dip, fly, run 4 bolt,
cast, dart, dash, dive, drop,
duck, fall, jerk, roll, jump,
leap, push, reel, rock, rush,
sink, sway, tear, toss 5 douse,
drive, heave, lunge, lurch,
pitch, press, shoot, speed,
surge, swarm, whisk 6 charge,
hasten, hurtle, hustle, scurry,
sprint, streak, thrust, tumble
7 descend, immerse, scuttle
8 scramble, submerge, submerse 12 fall headlong

plunk 4 pick, thud 5 pluck,
plumb, strum, twang 6 dollar
7 exactly 8 squarely
9 precisely

plurality 4 bulk, most 8 majority 13 preponderance

plus 5 added, extra, other,
spare 6 useful 7 helpful 9 auxiliary, desirable 10 additional,
beneficial 12 advantageous,
supplemental
13 supplementary

plush 4 lush, posh, rich
5 fancy, grand, ritzy, swank,
thick 6 classy, deluxe, lavish,
snazzy, swanky 7 elegant, opulent 8 palatial 9 luxurious,
sumptuous 11 extravagant

plushy 4 soft 5 cushy, swank
7 opulent, velvety 9 luxurious,
sumptuous

Plutarch
author of: 13 Parallel Lives

Plutarch's Lives
author: 8 Plutarch

Pluto
also: 5 Hades
god of: 10 underworld
corresponds to: 3 Dis 5 Orcus 8 Dis Pater

Pluto
position: 5 ninth
satellite: 6 Charon

plutocrat 5 mogul 6 fat cat,
tycoon 9 financier 10 capitalist

plutonic 7 abyssal, igneous
9 cimmerian, intrusive,
vulcanian

plutonium
chemical symbol: 2 Pu

Plutus
author: 12 Aristophanes
character: 5 Cario 9 Chremy-
lus 11 Blepsidemus
god of: 6 wealth

Plutus
personifies: 6 wealth
father: 6 Iasion
mother: 7 Demeter

Pluvius
epithet of: 7 Jupiter

ply 3 fly, run 4 leaf, sail, work
5 layer, offer, plait, plate,
press, sheet, slice, twist,
wield 6 employ, follow, handle, lamina, pursue, sheath,
strand, supply 7 besiege, carry
on, labor at, operate, stratum,
utilize 8 exercise, navigate,
practice, put to use, urge
upon 9 thickness
10 manipulate

poach 3 rob 4 cook 5 shirr,
steal 6 plunge, simmer
7 trample 8 encroach, trespass

pocket 3 bag, get, pit 4 gain,
lode, sack, vein 5 pouch,
purse, pygmy, small, steal,
strip, usurp 6 attain, bantam,
cavity, come by, hollow, little,
obtain, pilfer, strain, streak
7 chamber, compact, handbag,
placket, receive 8 arrogate, envelope, portable 9 miniature
10 diminutive, receptacle
11 appropriate, compartment

Pocket, Herbert
character in: 17 Great
Expectations
author: 7 Dickens

pocketbook 3 bag 5 pouch,
purse 6 clutch, wallet 7 handbag, satchel 8 moneybag,
notecase 9 coin purse
10 money purse 11 shoulder
bag
French: 12 porte-monnaie

pocket flask 5 flask 6 bottle
7 canteen

pocket-sized 3 wee 4 tiny
5 dwarf, pygmy, small 6 bantam, little, midget, minute, petite 7 compact 9 miniature
10 diminutive, vest-pocket

poco
music: 6 little

Pocock, Mamie
character in: 14 The
Ambassadors
author: 5 James

pod 4 case, hull, husk 5 shell
6 jacket, sheath 8 pericarp,
seed case 10 seed vessel

Podarces
mentioned in: 5 Iliad
father: 8 Iphiclus
brother: 11 Protesilaus
commanded: 8 Pythians

Podes
home: 4 Troy
occupation: 7 warrior
killed by: 8 Menelaus

Podgorica
capital of: 10 Montenegro

podium 4 dais, foot, wall
5 stipe 7 lectern 8 pedestal,
platform 9 footstalk

Poe, Edgar Allan
   author of: 6 Ligeia 7 Israfel,
   To Helen 8 The Bells, The
   Raven 10 Annabel Lee, The
   Gold Bug 18 The Purloined
   Letter 20 The Cask of
   Amontillado, The Pit and
   the Pendulum 22 The
   Masque of the Red Death
   24 The Fall of the House of
   Usher, The Murders in the
   Rue Morgue 29 The Narra-
   tive of Arthur Gordon Pym

Poeas
   also: 5 Poias
   lit: 11 funeral pyre
   pyre of: 8 Hercules
   son: 11 Philoctetes

poem 3 lay, ode 4 epic, song
   5 elegy, idyll, lyric, rhyme,
   verse 6 ballad, jingle, sonnet
   8 doggerel, limerick,
   madrigal

Poema del Cid *see* 6 The Cid

**Poems Chiefly in the Scot-
tish Dialect**
   author: 11 Robert Burns

Poena
   also: 5 Poine
   personifies: 7 revenge
   10 punishment

poet 4 bard 5 maker 6 lyrist,
   rhymer, singer 7 reciter 8 lyri-
   cist, minstrel, verseman 9 bal-
   ladeer, balladist, poetaster,
   rhymester, sonneteer, versifier
   10 improviser, librettist,
   songwriter

poetaster 4 bard, poet
   6 rhymer, writer 8 poetizer,
   rimester 9 rhymester, versifier

poetic, poetical 5 lyric 7 lilting, lyrical, melodic, musical
   8 metrical, rhythmic, songlike
   9 melodious 11 imaginative

Poetics
   author: 9 Aristotle

poetizer 4 bard, poet 6 rhymer, writer 8 rhymster 9 poetaster, versifier

poetry 5 poesy, rhyme, verse
   13 versification
   god of: 4 Odin, Ogma
   5 Brage, Bragi, Othin
   6 Apollo 7 Phoebus, Pythius 9 Musagetes

Pogo
   creator: 9 Walt Kelly
   character: 9 Porkypine, Wiley
   Catt 10 Boll Weevil 12 PT
   Bridgeport 13 Deacon Mush-
   rat, Mole MacCarony
   alligator: 6 Albert
   fox: 11 Seminole Sam
   frog: 15 Moonshine Sonata
   hound: 18 Beauregard
   Bugleboy
   possum: 4 Pogo

skunk: 16 Ma'm'selle
   Hepzibah
snake: 7 Snavely
sorcerer: 10 Howland Owl
turtle/pirate captain:
   14 Churchy La Femme
place: 15 Okefenokee Swamp

Pohjola
   origin: 7 Finnish
   identified with: 7 Lapland
   location: 12 North Finland

poignant 3 sad 5 sharp 6 biting, moving, rueful, woeful
   7 cutting, doleful, piquant, piteous, pitiful, pungent, tearful
   8 grievous, pathetic, piercing,
   pitiable, touching 9 affecting,
   sorrowful, trenchant 10 lamentable 11 distressing, penetrating 12 heartrending

Poine *see* 5 Poena

point 3 aim, end, hit, nib, run,
   tip, use 4 apex, bend, bode,
   core, game, gist, goal, item,
   mark, meat, pike, pith, spur,
   time, turn, unit 5 argue,
   cause, guide, heart, imply,
   level, limit, place, prong,
   prove, score, sense, slant,
   spike, stage, steer, tally, train,
   value 6 aspect, basket, degree,
   detail, direct, hint at, kernel,
   marrow, moment, number, object, reason 7 essence, feature,
   instant, portend, presage, purpose, quality, signify, suggest,
   testify 8 indicate, intimate,
   juncture, main idea, manifest,
   offshoot, position, sharp end
   9 condition, extension, intention, objective, outgrowth
   10 foreshadow, particular, projection, prominence, promontory 11 demonstrate
   12 protuberance

point-blank 5 blunt 6 direct
   10 forthright 11 plainspoken

Point Counter Point
   author: 12 Aldous Huxley

point d'appui 4 prop, stay
   24 point of battle line support

pointed 5 acute, blunt, sharp
   6 biting, direct, peaked,
   pointy 7 cutting, fitting, hint-
   ing, telling 8 accurate, incisive, piercing 9 aciculate,
   acuminate, cuspidate, pertinent, trenchant 10 emphasized, forthright
   11 appropriate, conspicuous,
   insinuating, penetrating

pointer 3 arm, tip 4 hand,
   hint 5 arrow, guide, stick
   6 needle 7 caution, warning
   9 indicator 10 admonition, advisement, suggestion 13 piece
   of advice 14 recommendation
   dog breed: 16 German wirehaired 17 German short-

haired 25 wirehaired
   pointing griffon

pointless 4 dull 5 blunt 6 absurd, futile, obtuse, stupid
   7 aimless, invalid, rounded,
   unedged, useless 8 bootless,
   worn down 9 fruitless, illogical, senseless, unpointed,
   worthless 10 irrational, irrelevant, ridiculous, unavailing
   11 ineffectual, meaningless,
   purposeless, unsharpened
   12 inapplicable, preposterous,
   unproductive, unprofitable,
   unreasonable

point of view 4 side 5 angle,
   slant 6 aspect 7 outlook 8 attitude 9 viewpoint 10 standpoint 11 frame of mind,
   perspective

point the way 5 guide, pilot,
   usher 6 direct 8 indicate, navigate 14 give directions

point to 5 argue, imply 6 denote 7 express 8 indicate

point up 6 stress 9 emphasize,
   underline 10 accentuate,
   underscore

Poirot, Hercule
   detective created by:
   14 Agatha Christie
   nationality: 7 Belgian
   famed for: 10 moustaches
   phrase: 15 little grey cells
   played by: 12 Peter Sellers

poise 4 calm 5 raise 6 aplomb
   7 balance, elevate 8 presence
   9 assurance, composure, hold
   aloft, sangfroid 10 equanimity
   11 savoir faire, self-command,
   self-control 13 self-assurance
   14 presence of mind, self-confidence 15 be in equilibrium

poised 7 assured 8 composed
   9 confident 10 controlled
   11 self-assured 13 self-
   possessed

poison 4 bane, evil, harm
   5 curse, taint, toxin, venom
   6 cancer, canker, debase, defile, impair, infect, plague,
   weaken 7 corrode, corrupt, degrade, disease, outrage, pollute 8 enormity, make sick
   9 malignity 10 adulterate, corruption, debilitate, malignancy,
   pestilence 11 abomination,
   contaminate

poisonous 5 fatal, toxic
   6 deadly, lethal, mortal
   7 baneful, noxious 8 venomous, virulent 10 pernicious
   11 deleterious 12 pestilential

Poitier, Sidney
   born: 7 Miami FL
   wife: 13 Joanna Shimkus
   roles: 11 Virgil Tibbs 12 A
   Patch of Blue, For Love of

Ivy, Porgy and Bess **13** To Sir with Love **14** The Defiant Ones **15** A Raisin in the Sun **16** Lilies of the Field (Oscar) **17** They Call Me Mr Tibbs **19** In the Heat of the Night, The Blackboard Jungle, Uptown Saturday Night **23** Guess Who's Coming to Dinner?

Pokanoket *see*
10 Wampanoags

poke 3 dig, hit, jab **4** butt, drag, gore, idle, jolt, prod, push, stab **5** crawl, dally, delay, mosey, nudge, punch, stick, thump **6** dawdle, fiddle, potter, thrust **7** meander, saunter, shamble, shuffle **8** hang back **10** dillydally **12** shilly-shally

poker
  derived from: 5 as nas, gilet **6** brelan **7** primero **11** brouillotte
  cards/hand: 4 five **5** seven
  bets: 4 ante **5** chips
  hand: 4 pair **5** flush **8** straight, two pairs **9** full house **10** royal flush **11** four of a kind **12** three of a kind **13** straight flush
  term: 4 call, fold **5** check, raise **6** ante up **7** reraise
  variation: 4 draw, stud **5** jacks **8** jackpots **12** five-card draw **13** seven-card stud

poky, pokey 4 dull, jail, slow **5** dowdy, small **6** dreary, shabby, stodgy, stuffy **7** cramped **8** confined, dawdling, dilatory, frumpish **9** puttering **10** monotonous
  creature: 5 sloth, snail **6** turtle **8** slowpoke, tortoise

Polacanthus
  type: 8 dinosaur **10** ornithopod

Poland *see box, p. 764*

Polanski, Roman
  director of: 4 Tess **7** Macbeth **9** Chinatown **13** Rosemary's Baby

polar 3 icy **6** arctic, frigid, wintry **7** glacial, ice-cold **8** freezing **9** antarctic **11** nothernmost **12** southernmost

pole 3 rod **4** mast, spar **5** shaft, staff, stick **6** tongue **9** pikestaff
  flax holder: 7 distaff
  pertaining to: 5 nodal
  sacred: 7 Asherah
  Scottish: 5 caber
  tribal: 5 totem
  vehicular: 4 neap

Polias, Poliatas
  epithet of: 6 Athena

police, police officer 4 cops, dick, fuzz, tidy **5** clean, guard **6** neaten, patrol, tidy up **7** clean up, control, marshal, officer, protect, sheriff **8** bluecoat, flatfoot, gendarme, regulate, spruce up, troopers **9** gendarmes, men in blue, patrolmen **10** traffic cop **11** arm of the law, keep in order **12** constabulary, cop on the beat
  French: 8 gendarme
  Italian: 11 carabiniere

Police Woman
  character: 9 (Det) Joe Styles, (Lt) Paul Marsh **11** (Det) Pete Royster, (Lt) Bill Crowley **12** (Sgt Suzanne) Pepper Martin
  cast: 9 Ed Bernard **11** Val Bisoglio **12** Earl Holliman **14** Angie Dickinson, Charles Dierkop

policy 3 way **4** plan, rule **5** habit, style **6** custom, design, method, scheme, system **7** program, routine, tactics **8** behavior, platform, practice, strategy **9** principle, procedure

Polieus
  epithet of: 4 Zeus
  means: 5 urban

polish 3 oil, wax **4** buff, sand **5** class, emend, glaze, gloss, grace, rouge, rub up, shine **6** pumice, refine, smooth **7** burnish, correct, culture, enhance, finesse, improve, perfect, sauvity, touch up **8** varnish **8** abrasive, courtesy, elegance, round out, urbanity **9** gentility, politesse, sandpaper **10** politeness, refinement **11** cultivation, good manners

polished 4 able, deft, fine, oily **5** oiled, suave, waxed **6** buffed, expert, glassy, glazed, glossy, polite, rubbed, sanded, shined, urbane **7** capable, elegant, genteel, refined, skilled **8** cultured, finished, mannerly, masterly, skillful, smoothed **9** brilliant, burnished, courteous, masterful, practiced, varnished **10** cultivated, proficient **11** experienced **12** accomplished

polish off 6 finish **8** complete, get rid of **9** dispose of

polite 4 high **5** civil, elite **6** proper **7** courtly, elegant, gallant, genteel, refined **8** cultured, mannerly, polished, well-bred **9** civilized, courteous, diffident, patrician **10** cultivated, respectful **11** ceremonious, fashionable, gentlemanly, well-behaved **12** well-mannered

politeness 7 decorum **8** courtesy **9** gentility, propriety **10** refinement **11** good manners

Polites
  character in: 7 Odyssey
  brother: 5 Paris **6** Hector
  companion: 8 Odysseus
  father: 5 Priam
  mother: 6 Hecuba
  sister: 9 Cassandra
  transformed by: 5 Aeaea, Circe
  transformed into: 3 hog, pig **5** swine

politic 4 wily, wise **5** chary, suave **6** artful, astute, shrewd, subtle **7** mindful, prudent, tactful **8** cautious, discreet, scheming **9** designing, expedient, judicious, opportune **10** contriving, diplomatic **11** calculating, circumspect, machinating **13** Machiavellian

political party 3 GOP **4** Tory, Whig **5** Labor **7** faction **9** Communist, Greenback, Socialist **10** Democratic, Republican **11** Know-Nothing

political refugee 2 DP **5** exile **6** emigre **10** expatriate **15** displaced person

politician 8 politico **9** incumbent, statesman **10** campaigner, legislator **12** officeholder, office seeker **13** public servant

politics 10 government, statecraft **11** party policy **13** statesmanship **14** affairs of state

Politics
  author: 9 Aristotle

Politic Would-Be, Lord and Lady
  characters in: 7 Volpone
  author: 6 Jonson

Poliuchus
  epithet of: 6 Athena
  means: 14 city-protecting

Polixenes
  character in: 14 The Winter's Tale
  author: 11 Shakespeare

Polk, James Knox *see box, p. 765*

polka 5 dance **10** round dance **13** Bohemian dance

poll 4 head, vote **5** count, tally **6** census, survey, voting **7** canvass, figures, returns **8** register, sampling **9** interview, nose count **10** count noses, voting list **11** voting place

Pollack, Sydney
  director of: 11 Out of Africa (Oscar) **12** The Way We

Poland
  other name: 6 Polska **17** the land of the plain
  capital/largest city: 6 Warsaw
    medieval capital: **6** Cracow, Krakow
  others: 3 Lwo **4** Kodz, Kolo, Lida, Lodz, Lvov, Lyck, Nysa, Oels, Pila **5** Brest, Bytom, Chelm,
    Dukla, Narev, Opole, Posen, Radom, Sroda, Torun, Vilna **6** Danzig, Elblag, Gdansk, Gdynia,
    Gnesen, Grodno, Kalisz, Kielce, Kracow, Lublin, Poznan, Tarnow, Zabrze **7** Beuthen, Breslau,
    Chorzow, Garocin, Gliwice, Litousk, Litovsk, Lyublin, Oleztyn, Stettin, Wroclaw **8** Frombork,
    Gleiwitz, Katowice, Lidzbark, Liegnitz, Oswiecim, Przemysl, Szczecin, Tarnopol **9** Auschwitz,
    Bialogard, Bialystok, Bydgoszcz, Sosnowiec, Szcezecin, Walbrzych **11** Czestochowa
  school: 6 Warsaw **12** Jagiellonian
  division: 7 Galicia, Silesia **8** Podlesia, Volhynia **9** Lithuania, Pomerania
  measure: 3 cal **4** mila, pret **5** morga, sazen, vloka, wloka **6** cwierc, cwierk, kwarta, lokiec
    7 garniec **9** kwarterka
  monetary unit: 4 abia **5** dalar, ducat, grosz, marka, zloty **6** fennig, groszy, gulden, halerz, ko-
    rona **8** groschen
  weight: 3 lut **4** funt **6** kamian **7** skrupul
  island: 5 Wolin
  lake: 5 Goplo, Mamry **8** Niegocin, Sniardwy **13** Stettin Lagoon
  mountain: 5 Tatra **6** Beskid **7** Pieniny, Sudeten **9** Beshchady, High Tatra, Holy Cross
    10 Carpathian
  highest point: 4 Rysy
  river: 3 Bug, San **4** Alle, Brda, Gwda, Lyna, Nysa, Oder, Styr **5** Biala, Drana, Dwina, Narev,
    Narew, Notec, Podra, Seret, Warta, Wista **6** Neisse, Niemen, Nyeman, Pilica, Pripet, Prosna,
    Styrpa, Wieprz **7** Nemunas, Vistula, Wistoka **8** Dniester
  sea: 6 Baltic
  physical feature:
    forest: **10** Bialowieza
    gulf: **6** Danzig, Gdansk
    lagoon: **7** Stettin **12** Frischeshaff
    plain: **7** Silesia
    plateau: **6** Lublin
  people: 4 Pole, Slav **5** Mazur **8** Silesian
    astronomer: **10** Copernicus
    author: **7** Reymont **8** Zeromski **10** Mickiewicz, Wyspianski **11** Sienkiewicz
    composer: **6** Chopin **10** Paderewski
    dynasty: **5** Piast **7** Jagello
    king: **7** Casimir **8** Augustus
    leader: **5** Kania **6** Gierek **7** Gomulka, Mieszko **8** Boleslaw **9** Pilsudski, Stanislaw **10** Jaruzel-
      ski, Kosciuszko, Lech Walesa
    pope: **10** John Paul II **20** Cardinal Carol Wojtyla
    queen: **7** Jadwiga
  language: 6 Kaszub, Polish **10** Pomeranian
  religion: 13 Roman Catholic
  place:
    castle: **5** Wawel
    church: **6** St John **10** Panna Maria
    monastery: **9** Jasna Gora
    monument: **17** Heroes of the Ghetto
    national park: **5** Ojcow **10** Bialowieza
    palace: **7** Casimir
  feature:
    folk dance: **5** polka **7** mazurka **9** krakowiak, polonaise
    union: **10** Solidarity
  food:
    dish: **5** bigos **7** kolduny
    drink: **5** vodka **7** Krupnik
    sausage: **8** kielbasa
    soup: **7** barszca

Were **15** Absence of Malice **23** They Shoot Horses Don't They?

Pollock, Jackson
  born: 6 Cody WY
  artwork: 5 Scent **9** Blue Poles **10** The She-Wolf **11** Convergence **12** Autumn Rhythm **13** Eyes in the Heat **17** Easter and the Totem **20** Guardians of the Secret

pollutant 5 fumes, smoke, waste **7** exhaust **8** emission, impurity

pollute 4 foul, soil **5** dirty, sully **6** befoul, debase, defile **7** deprave, profane **9** desecrate **10** adulterate, make filthy **11** contaminate

polluted 4 foul **5** dirty, drunk **6** impure, soiled **7** corrupt, profane, smashed, unclean **9** poisonous **12** contaminated

Polk, James Knox
  presidential rank: **8** eleventh
  party: **8** Democrat
  state represented: **2** TN
  defeated: **4** (Henry) Clay **6** (James Gillespie) Birney
  vice president: **6** (George Mifflin) Dallas
  cabinet:
    state: **8** (James) Buchanan
    treasury: **6** (Robert John) Walker
    war: **5** (William Learned) Marcy
    attorney general: **5** (John Young) Mason **6** (Isaac)
      Toucey **8** (Nathan) Clifford
    navy: **5** (John Young) Mason **8** (George) Bancroft
    postmaster general: **7** (Cave) Johnson
  born: **2** NC **17** Mecklenburg County
  died/buried: **2** TN **9** Nashville
  education: **11** prep schools **16** tutored privately
    University: **13** North Carolina
  religion: **9** Methodist
  political career: **16** state legislature **17** Speaker of the
    House **24** US House of Representatives
    governor of: **9** Tennessee
  civilian career: **6** lawyer
  notable events of lifetime/term:
    boundary dispute: **9** Northwest
    discovery in California of: **4** gold
    Proviso: **6** Wilmot
    treaty of: **16** Guadalupe Hidalgo
    war: **7** Mexican
  father: **6** Samuel
  mother: **4** Jane
  siblings: **7** John Lee **9** Jane Maria, Naomi Tate **10** Lydia
    Eliza **12** Marshall Tate, Samuel Wilson **14** William Hawk-
    ins **15** Franklin Ezekiel, Ophelia Clarissa
  wife: **5** Sarah (Childress)
  children: **4** none

pollution 7 fouling, soiling **8** defiling, dirtying, foulness, impurity **9** befouling, pollutant **11** uncleanness **12** adulteration **13** contaminating, contamination

Pollux *see* **15** Castor and Pollux

Pollyanna
  director: **10** David Swift
  based on story by:
    13 Eleanor Porter
  cast: **9** Jane Wyman **10** Karl Malden **11** Hayley Mills, Richard Egan

polo
  equipment: **6** mallet
  period of play: **7** chukker
  championship: **10** Camacho Cup **13** Coronation Cup **16** Cup of the Americas

Polonius
  character in: **6** Hamlet
  author: **11** Shakespeare

Polska *see* **6** Poland

poltergeist 5 ghost **6** spirit
  literally: **10** noise-ghost
  manifestation: **5** knock, noise, prank

Poltergeist
  director: **10** Tobe Hooper
  cast: **12** Craig T Nelson **14** Jobeth Williams **16** Beatrice Straight
  co-writer/producer: **15** Steven Spielberg

poltroon 6 coward, craven **7** caitiff, chicken, dastard **11** yellow-belly

Polybates
  member of: **8** Gigantes

Polycaste *see* **6** Perdix

Polydora
  father: **6** Peleus
  mother: **8** Antigone
  husband: **5** Borus
  son: **10** Menestheus

Polydorus
  mentioned in: **5** Iliad
  father: **5** Priam **10** Hippomedon
  mother: **6** Hecuba
  killed by: **10** Polymestor **11** Polymnestor
  avenged by: **6** Hecuba
  member of: **7** Epigoni
    descendant of: **18** Seven against Thebes

polygon 10 multiangle
  11 plane figure
  eight-sided: **7** octagon
  equal angled: **6** isogon
  five-sided: **8** pentagon
  four-sided: **6** square **7** rhombus **8** tetragon **9** rectangle, trapezoid
  nine-sided: **7** nonagon
  seven-sided: **8** heptagon
  six-sided: **7** hexagon
  ten-sided: **7** decagon
  three-sided: **8** triangle
  twelve-sided: **9** dodecagon

Polyhymnia
  also: **8** Polymnia
  member of: **5** Muses
  personifies: **5** dance **11** sacred music
  mother: **9** Mnemosyne

Polyidus
  revived: **7** Glaucus

Polymastus
  epithet of: **7** Artemis
  means: **12** many-breasted

polymer 5 dimer, nylon **6** hydrol **7** hexamer **8** oligomer

Polymnestor
  king of: **6** Thrace
  killed: **9** Polydorus

Polymnia *see* **10** Polyhymnia

Polyneices *see* **9** Polynices

Polynesia *see box, p. 766*

Polynices
  also: **10** Polyneices
  father: **7** Oedipus
  mother: **7** Jocasta
  uncle: **5** Creon
  brother: **7** Oedipus **8** Eteocles
  sister: **6** Ismene **8** Antigone
  killed by: **8** Eteocles

polyp 5 coral, hydra, tumor **6** growth, isopod **7** octopod **10** sea anemone

Polypemon *see* **10** Procrustes

Polyphemus
  form: **7** Cyclops **12** one-eyed giant
  father: **6** Elatus **8** Poseidon
  mother: **6** Thoosa
  joined: **9** Argonauts
  killed: **4** Acis
  blinded by: **8** Odysseus
  loved: **7** Galatea

Polyphides
  king of: **6** Sicyon
  vocation: **4** seer
  protected: **8** Menelaus **9** Agamemnon

Polyphontes
  brother: **11** Cresphontes
  killed: **11** Cresphontes

polyphony 7 organum **8** faburden **11** fauxbourdon **12** counterpoint

Polynesia
  name means: **11** many islands
  cities: **4** Apia **7** Papeete **8** Auckland, Pago Pago
    9 Nukualofa
  island: **4** Cook, Line **5** Samoa, Tonga **6** Easter, Ellice, Hawaii, Midway, Tahiti, Tubuai, Tuvalu **7** Austral, Maupiti, Phoenix, Society, Tokelau, Tuamotu **8** Pitcairn **9** Marquesas **10** New Zealand **15** French Polynesia
  sea: **7** Pacific
  people: **3** Ati **5** Maori **6** Kanaka, Nivean, Samoan, Tongan **9** Nesogaean **10** Polynesian
    explorer: **4** Cook **6** Tasman, Wallis **8** Magellan **9** Roggeveen **12** Bougainville
  language: **4** Niue, Uvea **5** Maori **6** Samoan, Tongan **7** Austral, Tagalog, Tokelau **8** Hawaiian, Tahitian **9** Marquesan, Tuamatuan **10** Mangarevan
  religion: **12** Christianity
  place:
    legendary origin: **8** Hawaiiki
  feature:
    chief: **5** matai
    clothing: **5** pareu **6** sarong **8** lavalava
    dance: **4** hula, siva
    dwelling: **4** fale
    family social unit: **4** aiga
    priest: **7** kahunas
    supernatural power: **4** mana
  food:
    dish: **3** kai, poi **4** taro **8** palusami
    drink: **3** ava **4** kava, kawa

Polypoetes
  king of: **10** Thesprotia
  father: **6** Apollo **8** Odysseus
    9 Pirithous
  mother: **6** Phthia **9** Callidice
    10 Hippodamia
  leader of: **6** Greeks

Polyporthis
  father: **8** Odysseus
  mother: **8** Penelope

polysaccharide **6** insulin,
  starch **7** dextrin **8** galactin,
  lichenin **9** cellulose
  12 carbohydrate

Polytechnus
  wife: **5** Aedon

Polyxena
  father: **5** Priam
  mother: **6** Hecuba
  loved by: **8** Achilles

Polyxenus
  grandfather: **6** Augeas

Polyxo
  advisor to: **9** Hypsipyle

Pomaria *see* **7** Algeria

Pomerania
  capital: **7** Stettin
  city: **5** Thorn, Torun
    6 Anklam
  country: **6** Poland **7** Germany
  island: **5** Rugen **6** Usedom
  province: **7** Pomorze

pommel, pummel 4 beat, hilt,

horn, knob, pake **6** finial,
strike **9** saddlebow

Pomona
  origin: **5** Roman
  goddess of: **10** fruit trees

pomp 4 show **5** front, glory,
style **7** display **8** ceremony,
flourish, grandeur, splendor
9 pageantry, showiness, solemnity, spectacle **10** brilliance
11 affectation, grandiosity, ostentation, pompousness
12 magnificence **14** stately display **15** pretentiousness

pompous 4 vain **5** proud
6 lordly, uppish **7** haughty
8 affected, arrogant, mannered,
overdone, puffed-up, snobbish
9 conceited, egotistic, grandiose, imperious **10** blustering,
swaggering **11** overbearing,
patronizing, pretentious **12** ostentatious, presumptuous, supercilious, vainglorious
13 condescending, high and
mighty, self-important

Ponchielli, Amilcare
  born: **5** Italy **7** Cremona
  composer of: **10** La Gioconda **15** Dance of the
    Hours

poncho 4 cape **5** cloak, shawl
6 mantle, serape

pond 4 pool, tarn **5** basin **6** lagoon **9** small lake, water hole

ponder 4 muse **5** study **6** wonder **7** examine, reflect **8** cogitate, consider, mull over,
ruminate **9** brood over, cerebrate, reflect on, speculate,
think over **10** deliberate, meditate on, puzzle over
11 contemplate

ponderous 3 big **4** dull
5 bulky, heavy, hefty, large,
wordy **6** boring, bovine,
dreary **7** awkward, droning,
hulking, labored, lumpish,
massive, tedious, weighty
8 cumbrous, enormous, sluggish, unlively, unwieldy **9** corpulent, graceless, lumbering,
wearisome **10** burdensome,
cumbersome, long-winded,
lusterless, monotonous,
unexciting, ungraceful
11 heavy-handed

pontiff 4 pope **6** bishop, priest
8 pontifex

pontifical 7 pompous
8 churchly, clerical, dogmatic,
priestly **9** apostolic, episcopal,
imperious **11** opinionated,
overbearing, patronizing, pretentious **13** authoritarian, condescending **14** ecclesiastical

Pontus
  personifies: **3** sea
  father: **2** Ge
  son: **6** Nereus **7** Phorcys

pony 3 nag **4** crib, trot **5** glass,
horse, pinto **7** mustang
9 racehorse
  breed: **6** Exmoor **8** Shetland

pooh-pooh 5 knock **7** disdain,
put down, run down, sneer
at **8** belittle **9** disparage

Pooka *see* **4** Puca

pool 3 pot **4** ally, bank, lake,
mere, pond, tarn **5** group,
kitty, merge, share, union,
unite **6** puddle, splash, stakes
7 combine **8** alliance, fishpond,
millpool **9** coalition **10** amalgamate, collective **11** association, consolidate, cooperative
13 confederation

Poole, Grace
  character in: **8** Jane Eyre
  author: **6** Bronte

poop 3 fag **4** bush, deck, do in,
tire **7** exhaust, fatigue, wear
out **8** enervate

pooped 4 beat **5** all in, spent,
tired, weary **6** bushed, done
in **7** drained, wearied, worn
out **8** fatigued, tired out
9 dead tired, exhausted, played
out

poor 3 sad **4** bare, dead, vain,
worn **5** broke, empty, needy,
sorry **6** barren, fallow, faulty,
futile, hard up, in need, in

want, meager, paltry, wasted
7 forlorn, sterile, unhappy, unlucky, wanting **8** badly off,
bankrupt, beggarly, depleted,
desolate, devoid of, grieving,
indigent, inferior, pathetic,
pitiable, strapped, unworthy,
wretched **9** defective, deficient,
destitute, exhausted, fruitless,
imperfect, infertile, insolvent,
in straits, miserable, moneyless, penniless, unfertile,
worthless **10** distressed, inadequate, pauperized **11** impecunious, unfortunate
12 impoverished, uncultivable,
unproductive, unprofitable
15 poverty-stricken

Poor People
   author: **16** Fyodor Dostoevsky

Poor Richard's Almanac
   author: **16** Benjamin Franklin

Poor White
   author: **16** Sherwood
   Anderson

pop 4 bang, boom, come, shot,
snap, soda **5** arise, blast, burst,
crack **6** appear, report **7** explode **8** detonate **9** discharge,
explosion, soft drink
10 detonation

pope *see box*

Pope, Alexander
   author of: **10** The Dunciad
   12 An Essay on Man
   15 Eloisa to Abelard **16** The
   Rape of the Lock **18** An Essay on Criticism **20** Epistle
   to Dr Arbuthnot

Pope, John Russell
   architect of: **17** Jefferson
   Memorial **20** National Gallery of Art **23** Temple of
   the Scottish Rite **24** National Archives Building

Popeye
   character in: **9** Sanctuary
   author: **8** Faulkner

popinjay 3 fop **4** beau
5 dandy **7** coxcomb

poplar 7 Populus **22** Lirioden-
dron tulipifera
   varieties: **4** gray **5** black,
   downy, tulip, white **6** balsam, Eugene, yellow **8** Carolina, Lombardy, necklace
   10 Queensland **12** Chinese
   white, silver-leaved
   13 Western balsam

poppy 7 Papaver
   varieties: **3** sea **4** blue, bush,
   corn, snow, tree, wind,
   wood **5** field, opium, plume,
   satin, tulip, water, Welsh
   6 arctic, desert, horned
   7 Asiatic, flaming, Iceland,
   Mexican, prickly, Shirley,
   Western **8** Flanders, hare-

bell, Matilija, oriental **9** Celandine **10** California, island
tree **12** Mexican tulip
13 yellow Chinese **14** California tree
   drug: **5** opium **6** heroin
   8 morphine

poppycock 3 rot **4** bosh, bunk,
jive, tosh **5** froth, fudge,
hooey, stuff, trash **6** drivel,
humbug **7** baloney, blabber,
blather, eyewash, fustian, garbage, hogwash, inanity, prattle, rubbish, twaddle
8 falderal, flummery, nonsense, tommyrot, wish-wash
9 absurdity, gibberish, moonshine, rigmarole **10** applesauce, balderdash, flapdoodle,
hocus-pocus, mumbo-jumbo,
rigamarole **11** abracadabra,
jabberwocky **12** fiddlefaddle,
gobbledygook

poppy seed
   botanical name: **7** Papaver
   11 P somniferum (sleep-
   bearing poppy)
   color: **4** blue **5** white
   origin: **4** Asia **6** Europe
   guards against: **9** creditors
   use: **5** bread, cakes, rolls
   6 sweets **10** vegetables
   11 butter sauce

populace 4 folk **6** people, public **7** society **9** citizenry, community **10** population

popular 5 cheap, civic, civil,
stock **6** famous, public, social
7 admired, current, general, in
favor **8** accepted, approved,
communal, familiar, favorite,
in demand, national, orthodox **9** community, preferred,
prevalent, well-known, well-
liked **10** affordable, celebrated,

pope 3 Leo **4** John, Paul, Pius **5** Peter, Urban **6** Adrian, Eugene, Julius, Martin, Sixtus **7** Clement, Gregory **8** Benedict,
Innocent, John Paul, Nicholas **9** Alexander, Callistus
   also: **12** Bishop of Rome **13** Vicar of Christ **14** Primate of
   Italy, Supreme Pontiff **16** Archbishop of Rome **18** Metropolitan of Rome, Patriarch of the West **25** Servant of the
   Servants of God
   office: **6** Papacy **7** Holy See **11** Seat of Peter
   elected by: **18** College of Cardinals
   elected in: **8** conclave
   signal that election is concluded: **10** white smoke
   resides: **4** Rome **10** the Vatican **11** Vatican City
   former residence: **13** Lateran Palace
   summer residence: **14** Castel Gondolfo
   papal land holding: **9** patrimony **21** patrimony of Saint
   Peter
   first pope: **10** Saint Peter
   pope who crowned Charlemagne: **6** Leo III
   pope who excommunicated Luther: **4** Leo X
   pope who authorized Michelangelo to paint Sistine
   Chapel: **8** Julius II
   "September Pope": **9** John Paul I
   real name of pope:
      Alexander VI: **15** Rodrigo de Borgia
      Callistus III: **15** Alfonso de Borgia
      Clement VII: **14** Giulio de' Medici
      John XXIII: **22** Angelo Giuseppe Roncalli
      John Paul I: **13** Albino Luciani
      John Paul II: **12** Karol Wojtyla **18** Archbishop of
      Krakow
      Leo X: **16** Giovanni de' Medici
      Pius XI: **12** Achille Ratti
      Pius XII: **35** Eugenio Maria Giuseppe Giovanni Pacelli
   popes of Avignon papacy: **6** Urban V **8** Clement V, John
   XXII **9** Clement VI, Gregory XI, Nicholas V **10** Innocent
   VI **11** Benedict XII
   popes during Great Western Schism:
      Avignon: **10** Clement VII **12** Benedict XIII
      Pisa: **9** John XXIII **10** Alexander V
      Rome: **7** Urban VI **10** Boniface IX, Gregory XII **11** In-
      nocent VII
   papal bull/encylical: **11** Unam sanctam **12** Humanae vitae,
   Rerum novarum, Vox in excelso **13** Pacem in terris
   15 Mater et magistra **19** Populorum progressio **22** Sacer-
   dotalis caelibatus

democratic **11** established, fashionable, inexpensive, of the people, sought-after

popularity 4 fame, note **5** favor, glory, kudos, vogue **6** esteem, regard, renown, repute **7** acclaim, fashion **8** approval **9** celebrity, notoriety **10** acceptance, admiration, notability, reputation **11** acclamation

popular opinion
  Latin: **9** vox populi

popular whim 3 fad **4** rage **5** craze, mania **7** passion **11** infatuation

populate 6 occupy, people, settle **7** inhabit

populated 5 urban **7** peopled, settled **8** citified, occupied **9** inhabited

population 4 folk **6** people, public **8** citizens, populace **9** citizenry, habitancy, residents **11** body politic, commonality, inhabitants

populous 5 dense **6** jammed **7** crowded, peopled, teeming **8** swarming, thronged

porcelain 5 china **11** ceramic ware

porch 4 stoa **5** lanai, plaza, stoop **7** balcony, narthex, portico, veranda **8** solarium, verandah **9** colonnade, vestibule

pore 4 hole, read, scan **5** probe, study **6** outlet, peruse, ponder, review, search, survey **7** dig into, examine, explore, inspect, orifice **8** aperture, consider **9** delve into

Porfiry
  character in: **18** Crime and Punishment
  author: **10** Dostoevsky

Porgy
  author: **13** DuBose Heyward

Porgy and Bess
  opera by: **14** George Gershwin
  character: **4** Bess **5** Porgy **11** Sportin' Life

pornographic 4 blue, lewd **5** bawdy, dirty, gross **6** coarse, filthy, smutty, vulgar **7** obscene **8** indecent, off-color, prurient **9** salacious **10** lascivious, licentious

porous 4 lacy **6** spongy **7** riddled **8** cellular, pervious **9** absorbent, permeable, sievelike **10** penetrable **11** honeycombed

Porphyrion
  member of: **8** Gigantes

porpoise 4 leap **5** whale **6** pal-

ach, puffer, seahog **7** cowfish, dolphin, surface **8** cetacean
  genus: 8 Phocaena **9** Delphinus

porridge 4 pobs, samp **5** atole, brose, brout, gruel **6** cereal **7** crowdie, oatmeal, polenta **8** flummery

Porrima see **9** Antevorta

porringer 4 bowl, dish **6** vessel **9** container **10** receptacle

port 4 dock, pier, quay **5** haven, wharf **6** harbor, refuge **7** dry dock, landing, mooring, seaport, shelter **9** anchorage, harborage **11** destination

port
  type: **4** wine **6** brandy
  origin: **8** Portugal
  variety: **4** ruby **5** tawny **7** vintage
  with brandy: **9** Betsy Ross
  with vermouth: **10** Broken Spur

portable 5 handy, light, small **6** bantam, pocket **7** compact, folding, movable **8** cartable, haulable, liftable **9** ready-to-go **10** convenient, conveyable, manageable, vest-pocket **11** pocket-sized

portal, portals 4 adit, arch, door, gate **5** entry **6** wicket **7** doorway, gateway, portico **8** approach, entrance **9** threshold, vestibule **10** portcullis **11** entranceway

Port-au-Prince
  capital of: **5** Haiti

porte-monnaie 5 purse **10** pocketbook **12** money-carrier

portend 4 bode **5** augur **6** denote, herald, warn of **7** bespeak, betoken, point to, predict, presage, signify, suggest **8** forebode, forecast, foretell, forewarn, prophesy **9** foretoken, prefigure **10** foreshadow

portent 4 omen, sign **5** token **6** augury, boding, threat **7** presage, warning **9** harbinger **10** foreboding **11** forewarning

portentous 6 superb **7** amazing, fateful, ominous, pompous **8** alarming, menacing **9** bombastic, grandiose, prophetic **10** foreboding, incredible, prodigious, remarkable, stupendous, surprising **11** astonishing, exceptional, frightening, pretentious, significant, superlative, threatening **12** inauspicious, intimidating, unpropitious

porter 4 brew **5** stout **6** bearer, coolie, redcap, skycap **7** carrier **8** conveyer **9** conductor

Porter, Katherine Anne
  author of: **11** Ship of Fools **12** Old Mortality **14** Flowering Judas **15** The Leaning Tower **18** Pale Horse Pale Rider

Porter, William Sidney
  real name of: **6** O Henry

portfolio 4 case, file **5** album **6** binder, folder **7** dossier **8** envelope **9** scrapbook **10** securities

Porthos
  character in: **18** The Three Musketeers
  author: **5** Dumas (pere)

Portia
  character in: **12** Julius Caesar **19** The Merchant of Venice
  author: **11** Shakespeare

portico 4 stoa **5** lanai **6** piazza **7** balcony, veranda, walkway

portion 3 cut, lot, sum **4** dole, doom, fate, luck, part **5** carve, cut up, moira, piece, sever, share, slice, split **6** amount, divide, kismet, parcel, ration, sector **7** break up, deal out, destiny, fortune, helping, measure, section, segment, serving **8** allocate, disperse, division, fraction, fragment, quantity, separate **9** allotment, allowance, demarcate, partition **10** allocation, distribute, percentage

portion out 5 allot **6** ration **7** dole out, mete out, prorate **8** allocate, dispense, divide up **9** apportion, parcel out **10** distribute, measure out

Portland
  basketball team: **12** Trailblazers
  football team: **8** Breakers
  river: **8** Columbia **10** Willamette
  university: **4** Reed

Port Louis
  capital of: **9** Mauritius

portly 3 big, fat **4** full **5** beefy, burly, heavy, large, obese, plump, pudgy, round, stout, tubby **6** brawny, chubby, fleshy, rotund, stocky **9** corpulent

Portman, John
  architect of: **15** Peachtree Center (Atlanta)

portmanteau 3 bag **4** grip **5** cloak **6** mantle, valise **8** suitcase **9** gladstone

Port Moresby
capital of: **9** New Guinea

Portnoy's Complaint
author: **10** Philip Roth

Port of Spain
capital of: **17** Trinidad and Tobago

Porto-Novo
capital of: **5** Benin

portrait 5 cameo **6** sketch **7** drawing, picture **8** likeness, painting, vignette **9** depiction **10** impression, photograph **11** description

Portrait of a Lady, The
author: **10** Henry James
character: **11** Madame Merle, Pansy Osmond **12** Isabel Archer **13** Gilbert Osmond, Lord Warburton, Ralph Touchett **14** Caspar Goodwood **18** Henrietta Stackpole

Portrait of the Artist as a Young Man
author: **10** James Joyce
character: **4** Emma **12** Simon Dedalus **14** Stephen Dedalus

portray 3 ape **4** draw, play **5** carve, enact, mimic, model, paint **6** depict, detail, figure, pose as, sketch **7** imitate, narrate, picture **8** describe, set forth, simulate **9** delineate, represent, sculpture **10** illustrate, photograph **11** impersonate **12** characterize

portrayal 7 picture **8** portrait **9** picturing **11** delineation, description **14** representation **16** characterization

ports
god of: **8** Portunus

Portugal *see box, p. 770*

Portuguese Guinea *see* **12** Guinea-Bissau

Portuguese West Africa *see* **6** Angola

Portunus
origin: **5** Roman
god of: **5** ports **7** harbors

posada 3 inn **12** halting place

pose 3 air, set **4** cast, mien **5** group, order, state, style **6** line up, stance, submit **7** advance, arrange, bearing, bring up, posture, present, propose, show off, suggest **8** attitude, carriage, position, propound, set forth, throw out **9** mannerism, postulate **10** put forward

Poseidon
also: **9** Asphalius
origin: **5** Greek
god of: **3** sea
caused: **11** earthquakes
father: **6** Cronos
mother: **4** Rhea
brother: **4** Zeus
wife: **10** Amphitrite
lover: **2** Ge **6** Aethra, Medusa, Thoosa **7** Demeter
child: **5** Arion **6** Triton **7** Antaeus, Pegasus, Theseus **8** Chrysaor **10** Polyphemus
symbol: **5** horse **7** trident
epithet: **11** Ennosigaeus, Hippocurius **12** Prosclystius
corresponds to: **7** Neptune

poser 5 facer **6** puzzle **7** problem **8** examiner, stickler

posh 4 chic **5** fancy, ritzy, smart, swell **6** chi-chi, classy, deluxe, lavish, swanky **7** elegant, opulent, refined, stylish **9** high-class, luxurious **11** extravagant

position 3 fix, job, put, set **4** duty, pose, post, role, site **5** array, caste, class, locus, lodge, order, place, stand, state **6** career, charge, ground, locate, office, plight, stance, status **7** arrange, deposit, opinion, outlook, posture, situate, station, vantage **8** attitude, capacity, eminence, function, locality, location, prestige, standing **9** condition, elevation, establish, placement, situation, viewpoint **10** assignment, commission, importance, notability, prominence **11** appointment, consequence, disposition, distinction, frame of mind, point of view

position decided upon
French: **9** parti pris

positive 4 firm, good, real, sure **5** total **6** narrow, useful **7** assured, certain, gainful, helpful **8** absolute, cocksure, complete, decisive, definite, dogmatic, explicit, obdurate, salutary **9** assertive, confident, convinced, effective, immovable, practical, satisfied, veritable **10** applicable, autocratic, beneficial, conclusive, definitive, optimistic, undisputed, undoubting **11** affirmative, cooperative, dead certain, dictatorial, irrefutable, opinionated, overbearing, practicable, progressive, self-assured, serviceable, unequivocal, unqualified **12** confirmatory, constructive, contributory, unchangeable **13** corroborative, thoroughgoing **16** incontrovertible

positively 9 assuredly, certainly, decidedly, literally **10** absolutely, definitely **11** confidently, indubitably **12** emphatically, indisputably, unmistakably, without doubt **13** affirmatively, categorically, unqualifiedly **14** beyond question, unhesitatingly, unquestionably

possess 3 own **4** grab, have, hold **5** boast, enjoy **6** absorb, fixate, obsess, occupy **7** acquire, bedevil, bewitch, command, conquer, consume, control, enchant, overrun **8** dominate, dominate, maintain, take over, vanquish **9** fascinate, hypnotize, influence, mesmerize

Possessed, The
author: **16** Fyodor Dostoevsky
character: **5** Marya, Pyotr **6** Shatov **7** Nikolay **16** Varvara Stavrogin **17** Stepan Verhovensky

possession 4 hold **5** asset, poise, title **6** effect, owning **7** command, control, control, custody, tenancy **8** calmness, coolness, dominion, province, resource **9** belonging, composure, occupancy, ownership, placidity, sangfroid, territory **10** equanimity, even temper, occupation, possessing **11** equilibrium, self-control **12** accoutrement, protectorate

possibility 4 hope, odds, risk **6** chance, gamble, hazard **7** promise **8** prospect **9** prospects **10** likelihood **11** contingency, eventuality, feasibility, probability, workability **12** potentiality **14** practicability

possible 8 credible, feasible, workable **9** potential, thinkable **10** achievable, admissible, attainable, cognizable, compatible, contingent, imaginable, manageable, obtainable, reasonable **11** conceivable, performable, practicable **12** hypothetical

possibly 5 at all, maybe **6** mayhap **7** could be, perhaps **8** in any way, normally **9** at the most, perchance **10** by any means, God willing **11** conceivably

post 2 PX **3** fix, job, put, set **4** base, beat, camp, pale, part, pile, pole, role, seat, send, spot, work **5** brace, house, lodge, place, put up, round, shaft, stake **6** advise, column, inform, locate, notify, office, picket, report, settle, splint, tack up **7** apprise, declare, install, mission, publish, quarter, routine, situate, station, support, upright **8** acquaint, announce, capacity, disclose, exchange, fasten up, function, instruct, mainstay, position, proclaim **9** advertise, broad-

Portugal
  capital/largest city: 6 Lisbon
  others: 4 Beja, Faro, Ovar **5** Braga, Evora, Olhao, Porto, Viseu **6** Aveiro, Guarda, Leiria,
    Oporto, Sintra **7** Algarve, Amadora, Bragama, Cascoes, Coimbra, Covilha, Estoril, Funchal,
    Granada, Setubal **8** Barreiro, Portimao **9** Lusitania **10** Portalegre **14** Vila Nova de Gaia
    Roman city: **10** Portus Cale
  school: 5 Minho **6** Aveiro, Lisbon, Oporto **7** Coimbra
  division: 3 Goa **4** Tejo, Tete **5** Beira, Evora, Macao, Minho, Timor **6** Azores, Loanda **7** Algarve,
    Madeira **8** Alemteho, Rebatejo **9** Cape Verde **10** Mozambique **11** Estremadura
    Roman district: **9** Lusitania
  measure: 2 pe **4** bota, moio, vara **5** almud, fanga, geira, linha, milha **6** almude, covado
    7 alquier, ferrado, selamin **8** alqueire
  monetary unit: 3 avo, rei **4** peca, real **5** conto, crown, dobra, indio, justo, rupia **6** escudo, ma-
    cuta, octave, pataca, testad, tostao, vintem **7** angalar, centavo, crusado, miereis, testone
    8 equipaga, johannes
  weight: 4 onca, once **5** libra, marco **6** arroba **7** arratel **9** excropulo
  island: 6 Azores **7** Madeira **8** Terceira
  mountain: 4 Acor, Lapa **5** Gerez, Marao, Mousa **6** Bornes, Peneda **7** Larouco **8** Caramulo
    9 Caldeirao, Monchique **14** Serra da Estrela
  highest point: 11 Pico da Serra
  river: 3 Sor, Tua **4** Lima, Mino, Mira, Sado, Seda, Tago, Tajo, Tejo, Vara **5** Douro, Duero, Le-
    goa, Micha, Minho, Sabar, Tagus, Vouga, Zatas **6** Cavado, Chanca, Quarto, Tamega, Zezere
    7 Mondego, Selamin, Sorraia **8** Quadiana, Tonelada
  ocean: 8 Atlantic
  physical feature:
    bay: **7** Setubal
    cape: **4** Roca **7** Mondego **8** Espichel **9** St Vincent
    peninsula: **7** Iberian
    port: **4** Faro **6** Aveiro, Lisbon, Oporto **7** Leixoes
  people: 4 Celt, Moor **7** Iberian **10** Portuguese
    artist: **7** Pereira **9** Goncalves **13** Soares dos Reis
    author: **5** Dinis **6** Camoes, Vieiva **7** Garrett, Vicente **9** Deus-Ramos
    explorer: **3** Cam, Cao **4** Dias, Diaz **6** Cabral, Da Gama **7** Almeida **8** Magellan **11** Albuquer-
      que **23** Prince Henry the Navigator
    king: **6** Manuel, Philip, Sancho **7** Alfonso **9** Ferdinand, Sebastian
    leader: **5** Eanes **6** Dombal, Soares **7** Caetano, Carmona, Salazar, Spinola
    queen: **5** Maria **9** Elizabeth
  language: 10 Portuguese
  religion: 13 Roman Catholic
  place:
    church: **5** Jesus **6** Christ **11** Os Jeronimos, Sao Lourenco **12** Old Cathedral **13** Santa Engra-
      cia **16** Sao Vicente de Fora
    city square: **15** Praca do Comercio
    dam: **6** Belver, Idanha **13** Castelo do Bode
    fortress-church: **12** Leco do Bailio
    monastery: **8** Alcobaca **12** Hieronymites **20** Santa Maria da Victoira
    monument: **11** Discoveries
    museum: **13** Soares dos Reis
    palace: **6** Cintra
    shrine: **6** Fatima
  colony: 5 Macad, Macao
    former colony: **3** Goa **5** Timor **6** Angola **7** Sao Tome **8** Principe, St Thomas **9** Cape Verde
      10 Mozambique **12** Guinea Bissau
  feature:
    song: **4** fado
  food:
    dish: **8** bacalhau, bucellas **10** calcavella **11** carcavellos
    sausage: **8** linguica
    wine: **4** port **7** madeira

cast, circulate, enlighten, establish, make known,
situation **10** assignment,
settlement

postdate 6 follow **7** succeed
9 come after

poster 4 bill, sign **6** notice

7 placard **8** bulletin
13 advertisement

posterior 3 bum, can **4** back,
butt, prat, rear, rump, seat,
tail, tush **5** fanny, stern,
tushy **6** behind, bottom, caudal, dorsal, hinder **7** keister
8 backside, buttocks, derriere,

hindmost, rearward
9 aftermost

Posterior Analytics
  author: 9 Aristotle

posterity 5 heirs, issue,
young **6** family **7** descent, history, lineage, progeny **8** chil-

dren **9** offspring **10** succession, successors **11** descendants

post hoc, ergo propter hoc 29 after this therefore because of it
describes: **14** logical fallacy

Posthumus, Leonatus
character in: **9** Cymbeline
author: **11** Shakespeare

Postman Always Rings Twice, The
director: **10** Tay Garnett
based on story by: **10** James M Cain
cast: **10** Hume Cronym, Lana Turner **12** John Garfield **13** Cecil Kellaway

postpone 4 stay **5** defer, delay, table, waive **6** put off, remand, shelve **7** adjourn, lay over, reserve, suspend

postponement 4 stay **5** delay **6** recess **7** tabling **8** abeyance, deferral **9** deferment, extension **10** suspension

postscript 2 ps **5** rider **7** codicil **8** addendum **10** attachment

postulate 5 axiom, guess **6** assume, hazard, submit, theory **7** premise, presume, propose, surmise, theorem **8** put forth, theorize **9** speculate **10** assumption, conjecture, hypothesis, presuppose **11** hypothesize, presumption

posture 3 air, set **4** case, mien, mood, pose, post, tone **5** phase, place, shape, state, tenor **6** aspect, stance, status **7** bearing, contour, station **8** attitude, carriage, position, standing **9** condition, situation **11** predicament **12** circumstance

Postvorta
form: **5** nymph
member of: **7** Camenae
knowledge of: **4** past

posy 5 bloom, motto **6** flower, phrase **7** blossom, bouquet, corsage, garland, nosegay

pot 3 pan **4** ruin **5** crock, kitty **6** vessel **9** container, marijuana **11** rack and ruin
Spanish: **4** olla

potable 3 ale **5** clean, drink, water **6** liquor **8** beverage, quencher **9** drinkable

potage 4 soup **9** thick soup

potassium
chemical symbol: **1** K

potato 16 Solanum tuberosum
varieties: **3** air, yam **4** duck, swan, wild, Zulu **5** Idaho, Irish, Maine, rural, swamp, sweet, white **6** Russet

7 Burbank, epicure, prairie, Telinga
dish: **4** chip **5** baked, salad **6** mashed **8** au gratin **9** lyonnaise, scalloped **11** french fries **12** baked stuffed

Potawatomi
language family: **9** Algonkian **10** Algonquian
location: **4** Ohio **6** Kansas **7** Indiana **8** Illinois, Michigan, Oklahoma **9** Wisconsin
leader: **7** Pontiac
united with: **6** Ojibwa, Ottawa **7** Ojibway

Potemkin
director: **17** Sergei Eisenstein
cast: **14** Vladimir Barsky **16** Alexander Antonov **17** Grigori Alexandrov
famous segment: **11** Odessa Steps

potency 3 vis **5** force, power **6** energy **8** efficacy, strength, virility, vitality

potent 5 solid, tough **6** mighty, strong **7** dynamic **8** forceful, forcible, powerful, vigorous **9** effective, operative **10** compelling, convincing, formidable, impressive, persuasive **11** efficacious, influential **12** overpowering

potentate 4 lord **5** chief, mogul, ruler **6** prince, satrap, sultan **7** emperor, monarch **8** overlord, suzerain **9** chieftain, sovereign

potential 6 covert, hidden, latent **7** dormant, lurking, passive **8** implicit, possible **9** concealed, quiescent, unexerted **10** unapparent, unrealized **11** conceivable, undisclosed, unexpressed

potentiality 7 ability **10** capability **13** possibilities

potentially
Latin: **7** in posse

pother 3 ado **4** fuss, stir, todo **6** bustle, flurry, hustle, tumult **8** activity **9** agitation, commotion

Pothos
companion of: **9** Aphrodite
personifies: **6** desire **7** longing

potion 4 brew, dram **5** draft, tonic **6** elixir **7** mixture, philter **8** libation, potation **10** concoction

Pot of Gold, The
author: **7** Plautus

Potok, Chaim
author of: **9** The Chosen

10 Wanderings **15** The Book of Lights

potpourri 4 hash, mess, olio, stew **6** jumble, medley, mosaic, motley **7** farrago, goulash, melange, mixture **8** mishmash, pastiche **9** patchwork **10** hodgepodge, miscellany, salmagundi **11** gallimaufry, olla podrida

pottage 4 soup, stew **6** brewis **8** porridge

Potter, Beatrix
author of: **11** (The Tale of) Peter Rabbit **21** The Tailor of Gloucester

Potter, Muff
character in: **9** Tom Sawyer
author: **9** Twain

potter's field 8 boneyard, cemetery **9** graveyard **12** burial ground **13** burying ground

pottery 5 china **8** clayware, crockery **11** ceramic ware, earthenware

pouch 3 bag, kit, sac **4** sack **5** purse **6** pocket, wallet **7** handbag, satchel **8** carryall, ditty bag, reticule, rucksack **9** container **10** pocketbook, receptacle

Poulenc, Francis
born: **5** Paris **6** France
member of: **6** Les Six, The Six
composer of: **9** Les Biches **13** The Carmelites **22** Dialogues des Carmelites

poultice 7 plaster **8** dressing **10** medicament

poultry 3 hen **4** cock, duck, fowl, swan **5** capon, geese, goose, quail **6** grouse, layers, pigeon, turkey **7** chicken, peacock, rooster **8** pheasant **9** partridge **10** guinea fowl
breed: **6** Ancona, Bantam **7** Cornish, Dorking, Leghorn **9** Wyandotte **12** Plymouth Rock **14** Rhode Island Red
disease: **3** pip **4** roup, tick
farm: **7** hennery
house: **4** coop

pounce 4 jump, leap **5** fly at, swoop **6** ambush, dash at, jump at, plunge, snatch, spring **8** downrush, fall upon, surprise

Pounce, Peter
character in: **13** Joseph Andrews
author: **8** Fielding

pound 4 bang, beat, drub, drum, maul **5** clomp, clout, crush, grind, march, paste, smack, stomp, throb, thump,

tramp 6 batter, bruise, cudgel, hammer, pummel, strike, thrash, thwack, wallop 7 clobber, crumble, pulsate, thunder, trounce 8 lambaste 9 fustigate, palpitate, pulverize 13 sixteen ounces
abbreviation: 2 lb

Pound, Ezra
author of: 6 Cantos 8 Personae 11 Exultations, Pisan Cantos

pound troy
abbreviation: 3 lb t

pour 3 tap 4 drip, drop, flow, gush, ooze, rain, seep, slop 5 drain, flood, issue, spill, spout 6 decant, deluge, drench, effuse, squirt, stream 7 cascade, draw off, dribble, lade out 15 rain cats and dogs 16 come down in sheets 17 come down in buckets

pourboire 3 tip 8 gratuity
literally: 11 for drinking

pourparler 29 informal preliminary conference
literally: 10 for talking

Poussin, Nicholas
born: 6 France 10 Les Andelys
artwork: 10 The Seasons 14 Birth of Bacchus, St John on Patmos 17 Bacchanalian Revel 18 The Burial of Phocion 19 The Poet's Inspiration 20 The Arcadian Shepherds 23 Landscape with Polyphemus, The Holy Family on the Steps 27 The Adoration of the Golden Calf

pou sto 14 place to stand on, where I may stand 16 base of operations

pout 4 crab, fret, fume, mope, sulk 5 brood, frown, lower, scowl 6 glower
French: 4 moue

poverty 4 lack, need, want 6 dearth, penury 7 beggary, deficit, paucity 8 scarcity, shortage 9 indigence, neediness, pauperism, privation 10 bankruptcy, deficiency, insolvency, meagerness, mendicancy 11 destitution 13 insufficiency, pennilessness 14 impoverishment

poverty-stricken 4 poor 5 broke, needy 8 indigent 9 destitute, penniless 10 down and out

powder 4 dust, talc 5 emery 6 pollen, talcum 7 crumble 9 pulverize
antiseptic: 6 formin 7 aristol
applier: 4 puff

cookery: 4 soda
cosmetic: 5 blush, rouge 7 compact
poisonous: 5 robin

powder-blue 5 azure 6 pastel 7 sky-blue 8 pale-blue 9 light-blue, robin's egg

powdery 5 dusty, mealy 6 chalky, floury, grated, ground, milled 7 crushed, pestled 8 shredded 10 comminuted, pulverized, triturated

Powell, Dick
real name: 14 Richard E Powell
born: 14 Mountain View AR
wife: 11 June Allyson 12 Joan Blondell
costar: 10 Ruby Keeler
roles: 7 Mrs Mike 8 Cornered 12 Johnny O'Clock 13 Murder My Sweet 15 Footlight Parade 17 Forty-second Street 32 Gold Diggers of Nineteen Thirty-three

Powell, Jane
real name: 12 Suzanne Burce
born: 10 Portland OR
roles: 5 Irene 12 Royal Wedding 13 A Date with Judy 27 Seven Brides for Seven Brothers

Powell, John
nickname: 4 Boog
sport: 8 baseball
team: 16 Baltimore Orioles

Powell, Michael
codirector: 17 Emeric Pressburger
director of: 11 The Red Shoes 14 Black Narcissus 16 Stairway to Heaven

Powell, SR
creator/artist of: 22 Sheena Queen of the Jungle

Powell, William
born: 12 Pittsburgh PA
wife: 13 Carole Lombard
costar: 8 Myrna Loy
roles: 10 Philo Vance, The Thin Man 11 Nick Charles 12 My Man Godfrey 13 Mister Roberts 14 Life with Father 16 The Great Ziegfeld 22 How to Marry a Millionaire

power 4 gift, sway 5 brawn, force, might, right, ruler, skill, vigor 6 energy, genius, muscle, status, talent 7 faculty, license, operate, potency, quality 8 activate, aptitude, capacity, energize, iron grip, pressure, prestige, property, strength, vitality 9 attribute, authority, endowment, influ-

ence, puissance 10 capability, competence
Latin: 3 vis

Power, Tyrone
born: 12 Cincinnati OH
wife: 9 Annabella 14 Linda Christian
roles: 10 Jesse James 12 Blood and Sand 13 The Razor's Edge 14 Nightmare Alley, The Mark of Zorro 15 The Sun Also Rises 18 Captain from Castile

Power and the Glory, The
author: 12 Graham Greene

powerful 5 hardy, husky, stout 6 brawny, cogent, mighty, moving, potent, robust, sturdy 7 intense, rousing 8 athletic, emphatic, exciting, forceful, incisive, muscular, stalwart, vigorous 9 effective, energetic, herculean, strapping 10 able-bodied, commanding, invincible

powerhouse 9 strongman 10 power plant 15 generating plant

powerless 4 weak 6 feeble, infirm 7 unarmed 8 crippled, disabled, feckless, helpless, impotent 9 incapable, pregnable, prostrate 10 impuissant, vulnerable, weaponless 11 debilitated, defenseless, immobilized 13 incapacitated

powerlessness 8 debility, weakness 9 impotence, inability, infirmity 10 enervation, feebleness, inadequacy, incapacity 12 helplessness, incapability, inefficiency 13 vulnerability

Power Politics
author: 14 Margaret Atwood

powers that be 9 higher-ups 10 government 11 authorities 13 establishment 14 administration

Powhatan
language family: 9 Algonkian 10 Algonquian
tribe: 11 Confederacy
location: 8 Atlantic, Maryland, Virginia
leader: 8 Powhatan 11 Opechancano 13 Wahunsonacock
member: 10 Pocahontas

powwow 4 meet, talk 5 forum 6 caucus, confer, huddle, parley 7 consult, convene, council, discuss, meeting, palaver 8 assembly, colloquy, conclave, congress 9 discourse, interview 10 colloquium, conference, convention, discussion, round table 12 consultation

Poyser, Martin
    character in: 8 Adam Bede
    author: 5 Eliot

practicable 6 doable, viable
8 feasible, possible, workable
9 practical 10 achievable, attainable, functional

practical 4 able 5 solid, sound
6 expert, useful, versed
7 skilled, trained, veteran,
working 8 seasoned, sensible,
skillful 9 efficient, judicious,
practiced, pragmatic, qualified,
realistic 10 functional, hardheaded, instructed, proficient,
systematic, unromantic
11 down-to-earth, experienced,
pragmatical, serviceable, utilitarian 12 accomplished, businesslike, matter-of-fact
13 unsentimental

practical joke 4 jape 5 caper,
prank, stunt, trick

practically 6 all but, almost,
nearly 8 actually, in effect
9 basically, in the main, just
about, virtually 11 essentially
13 fundamentally, substantially

practice 2 do 3 use, way
4 deed, mode, play, rule, ruse,
ways, wont 5 apply, dodge,
drill, habit, train, trick, usage
6 action, custom, device, effect, follow, manner, method,
pursue, ritual, work at 7 conduct, fashion, perform, process, qualify, routine, utilize
8 carry out, engage in, exercise, live up to, maneuver, rehearse, tendency, training
9 execution, operation, perform in, procedure, rehearsal,
seasoning, set to work, turn
to use 10 discipline, observance, prepare for, repetition
11 application, be engaged in,
performance, preparation

practiced 4 able, fine 5 adept
6 adroit, expert 7 capable,
drilled, pursued, skilled,
trained 8 masterly, polished,
seasoned, skillful, worked at
9 competent, engaged in, masterful, qualified, rehearsed
10 cultivated, proficient 11 experienced, prepared for
12 accomplished

practice sorcery 5 charm
7 bewitch, conjure, enchant
9 work magic 10 cast a spell

Practicing History
    author: 15 Barbara W
    Tuchman

practitioner 6 doctor 7 dentist
9 performer 12 professional

pragmatic 5 sober 8 sensible
9 hard-nosed, practical, realistic 10 hardheaded, hard-
boiled 11 down-to-earth,

utilitarian 12 businesslike,
matter-of-fact, unidealistic
13 materialistic, unsentimental

Praia
    capital of: 9 Cape Verde

prairie 3 bay 5 llano, pampa,
plain 6 camass, meadow,
steppe 7 quamash 9 grassland
    apple: 9 breadroot
    berry: 9 trampillo
    chicken: 6 grouse
    dog: 6 gopher, marmot
    schooner: 12 covered wagon
    state: 8 Illinois
    wolf: 6 coyote

Prairie, The
    author: 19 James Fenimore
    Cooper
    character: 4 Inez 9 Dr Bat-
    tius, Ellen Wade, Hard-
    Heart, Paul Hover 10 Esther
    Bush 11 Abiram White, Ish-
    mael Bush, Natty Bumppo
    16 Captain Middleton

Prairie State
    nickname of: 8 Illinois

praise 4 laud, tout 5 cheer, exalt, extol, honor 6 esteem, eulogy, hurrah, regard, revere
7 acclaim, applaud, approve,
build up, commend, glorify,
plaudit, respect, root for, tribute, worship 8 accolade, applause, approval, encomium,
eulogize, venerate 9 adoration,
celebrate, good words, laudation, panegyric 10 admiration,
compliment, panegyrize
11 approbation, compliments,
testimonial 12 appreciation,
commendation, congratulate
14 congratulation
    Hebrew: 6 hallel

praise be to God
    Latin: 7 laus Deo

praiseful 8 praising 9 extolling,
laudatory 10 plauditory
12 commendatory
13 complimentary

praiseworthiness 5 merit
10 excellence 12 admirability,
desirability 14 commendability

praiseworthy 4 fine 6 worthy
8 laudable 9 admirable, estimable, excellent, exemplary
11 commendable, meritorious

pram, praam, prahm 4 boat
5 buggy 6 vessel 7 rowboat
8 carriage, stroller
12 perambulator

prance 4 jump, leap, romp,
skip 5 bound, caper, dance,
frisk, strut, vault 6 bounce, cavort, frolic, gambol, spring
7 swagger

prank 4 joke, lark 5 antic, caper, spoof, stunt, trick 6 gambol 8 escapade, mischief

9 horseplay 10 shenanigan,
tomfoolery

prate 3 gab, yak 4 blab, brag,
chat, crow, talk 5 boast
6 babble, gabble, jabber
7 blabber, chatter, prattle,
twaddle, twattle

Prathet Thai *see* 8 Thailand

Pratt, William Henry
    real name of: 12 Boris
    Karloff

prattle 3 gab, yak 4 blab
5 prate 6 babble, gabble, hot
air, jabber 7 blather, chatter,
twaddle 8 cackling, chitchat,
gabbling 9 gibbering, jabbering

Pravda 16 Russian newspaper
    literally: 5 truth

Praxithea
    husband: 10 Erechtheus
    daughters: 8 Orithyia
    10 Protogonia

pray 3 beg, bid, sue 4 urge
5 cry to, plead 7 beseech, entreat, implore, request, solicit
8 call upon, invocate, petition
9 importune 10 supplicate

prayer 6 litany, orison, praise
7 worship 9 adoration
12 thanksgiving
13 glorification

prayerful 4 holy 5 godly,
pious 6 devout, solemn 8 reverent 9 pietistic, religious, spiritual 10 worshipful
11 reverential

prayers 4 hope, plea, suit
5 dream 6 appeal 7 request
8 entreaty, petition 10 aspiration, invocation 11 beseechment 12 solicitation,
supplication

prayer service 9 devotions
13 prayer meeting 14 worship
service

pray for us
    Latin: 11 ora pro nobis

pray to 3 beg 5 plead 7 address, entreat, worship 8 call
upon, petition, venerate
10 supplicate

preach 4 urge 6 advise, exhort 7 counsel, declare, expound, profess 8 admonish,
advocate, homilize, proclaim,
stand for 9 discourse, hold
forth, preachify, prescribe,
pronounce, propagate, sermonize 10 evangelize, promulgate

preacher 5 vicar 6 curate, parson, pastor 8 chaplain, homi-
list, minister, reverend, sky
pilot 9 churchman, clergyman
10 evangelist, prebendary, sermonizer 12 ecclesiastic
13 man of the cloth

preachy 8 didactic, pedantic
10 moralistic, moralizing

prearranged 7 planned 10 calculated, deliberate, purposeful
11 intentional 12 premeditated

pre-Cambrian 5 Azoic
6 Eozoic 7 primary 10 Archeozoic 11 Proterozoic

precarious 5 risky, shaky
6 chancy, unsafe 7 dubious
8 alarming, critical, doubtful,
insecure, perilous, sinister,
ticklish, unstable, unsteady
9 hazardous, uncertain
10 touch-and-go, unreliable,
vulnerable 12 questionable,
uncontrolled, undependable
13 problematical

precaution 4 care 7 caution,
defense 8 prudence, security,
wariness 9 foresight, provision,
safeguard 10 protection
11 carefulness, forethought,
heedfulness 12 anticipation
14 circumspection

precede 8 antecede, antedate,
go before 9 go ahead of
10 come before

precedence, precedency
8 priority 10 importance, preference, prevalence 11 antecedence, preeminence
12 predominance, preexistence

precedent 5 model 7 example,
pattern 8 standard 9 criterion,
guideline

preceding 5 prior 6 former
7 earlier 8 anterior, previous
9 aforesaid, foregoing 10 antecedent, first-named, precursory 11 preexistent,
preliminary 14 abovementioned, aforementioned, first-
mentioned

precept 3 law 4 bull, code,
rule 5 axiom, canon, edict,
maxim, motto, tenet, truth,
ukase 6 byword, decree, dictum 7 dictate, mandate, statute 8 standard, teaching
9 ordinance, principle, yardstick 10 regulation 11 commandment, declaration

preceptor 5 coach, tutor
6 mentor 7 advisor, teacher
8 director 9 admonitor, counselor, principal 10 headmaster
12 headmistress

precincts 7 suburbs 8 environs 9 districts, outskirts
10 boundaries 12 subdivisions
15 surrounding area

precious 4 dear, rare 5 fussy,
sweet 6 adored, choice, costly,
dainty, prissy, prized, valued
7 beloved, darling, finical, finicky, lovable 8 adorable, affected, uncommon, valuable

9 cherished, expensive, exquisite, priceless, treasured
10 fastidious, high-priced, invaluable, meticulous, particular 11 beyond price,
inestimable, overrefined,
pretentious

Precious Bane
author: 8 Mary Webb

precipice 4 crag 5 bluff, cliff,
ledge 8 headland, palisade
9 cliff edge, declivity
10 escarpment

precipitate 4 cast, hurl, rash,
spur 5 drive, fling, hasty,
throw 6 abrupt, hasten,
launch, let fly, propel, rushed,
speedy, thrust 7 advance,
bring on, hurried, quicken,
speed up 8 catapult, expedite,
headlong, reckless 9 discharge,
foolhardy, impetuous, imprudent, impulsive 10 accelerate,
incautious 11 thoughtless

precipitation 4 hail, rain,
rush, snow 5 haste, sleet
8 rainfall, rashness 9 hastiness 11 impetuously

precipitous 5 hasty, sharp,
sheer, steep 6 abrupt
9 impetuous

precis 5 brief 6 apercu, digest,
resume, sketch 7 epitome, outline, rundown, summary 8 abstract, synopsis 10 abridgment,
compendium 12 condensation
14 recapitulation

precise 4 true 5 exact, fussy,
rigid 6 strict 7 careful, express,
finicky, literal 8 accurate,
clear-cut, definite, distinct, explicit, incisive, specific 9 unbending 10 fastidious,
inflexible, meticulous, particular, to the point 11 painstaking, unequivocal

precision 5 rigor 8 accuracy,
fidelity 9 attention, exactness
11 factualness, preciseness
12 authenticity, truthfulness
14 meticulousness

preclude 3 bar, dam 4 balk,
curb, foil, stop 5 avert, avoid,
block, check, debar, deter
6 arrest, hamper, hinder,
thwart 7 head off, inhibit, prevent 8 stave off 9 forestall,
frustrate 11 nip in the bud

preclusion 9 exclusion, restraint 10 prevention

precocious 3 apt 5 quick,
smart 6 bright, clever, gifted,
mature 8 advanced
9 brilliant

preconception 4 bias 6 notion 9 fixed idea, prejudice
11 prejudgment, presumption
14 predisposition

precursor 4 mark, omen, sign
5 token, usher 6 herald 7 portent, symptom, warning
8 vanguard 9 harbinger, messenger 10 antecedent, forerunner 11 predecessor

precursory 5 prior 8 anterior,
previous 9 precedent 10 antecedent 11 preexistent

predaceous, predacious
9 predatory, rapacious
10 meat-eating 11 carnivorous,
flesh-eating

predate 7 precede 8 antecede,
antedate, go before

predatory 8 thievish 9 larcenous, marauding, pillaging, piratical, rapacious, raptorial,
vulturine 10 plunderous,
predacious

predecessor 7 forbear
8 ancestor, forebear, foregoer
10 antecedent, forefather,
forerunner

predestination 4 fate 6 kismet 7 destiny, fortune 8 God's
will 10 providence 13 inevitability, preordination
16 predetermination

predetermined 5 fated 7 decided, planned 8 destined
10 calculated, deliberate, preplanned 11 intentional, prearranged, predestined
12 foreordained, premeditated

predicament 3 fix, jam 4 bind,
mess 5 pinch 6 corner, crisis,
pickle, plight, scrape, strait
7 dilemma, trouble 8 hot water, quandary 9 imbroglio, sad
plight 10 difficulty,
perplexity

predicate 4 base, real, rest,
true 5 found, imply 6 affirm,
assert 7 commend, connote,
declare 8 proclaim

predict 4 omen 5 augur 6 divine 7 betoken, foresee, presage 8 envision, forecast,
foretell, prophesy 10 anticipate 13 prognosticate

prediction 6 augury 7 portent
8 forecast, prophecy 10 divination 11 declaration, foretelling, soothsaying
12 announcement, anticipation, proclamation 13 crystal
gazing 15 prognostication

predilection 4 bent, bias, love
5 fancy, favor, taste 6 desire,
hunger, liking, relish 7 leaning 8 appetite, fondness, penchant, tendency 9 prejudice,
proneness 10 attraction, partiality, preference, proclivity,
propensity 11 inclination
13 prepossession
14 predisposition

predispose 4 bias, lure, sway, urge 5 tempt 6 entice, induce, prompt, seduce 7 dispose, incline, win over 8 persuade 9 encourage, influence, prejudice

predisposed 3 apt 5 given, prone 8 inclined

predisposition 7 leaning 8 tendency 11 inclination

predominance 7 command, control 8 currency 9 dominance, supremacy 10 ascendancy, importance, prevalence 11 preeminence, superiority 12 universality

predominant 4 main 5 chief, major 6 potent, ruling, strong 7 leading, supreme 8 dominant, forceful, powerful, reigning, vigorous 9 ascendant, important, paramount, sovereign 11 controlling, influential 13 authoritative

predominate 4 lead 7 prevail 8 dominate

predominating 5 chief 6 ruling 8 dominant, superior 9 principal 10 commanding, prevailing 11 controlling, predominant 13 authoritative

preeminence 9 greatness, supremacy 10 ascendancy, importance, leadership, notability, prominence 11 distinction, superiority 12 predominance

preeminent 4 best 5 famed 6 famous 7 eminent, honored, supreme 8 dominant, foremost, greatest, peerless, renowned, superior 9 matchless, paramount, unequaled, unrivaled 10 celebrated, consummate 11 illustrious, predominant, unsurpassed 12 incomparable, second to none, unparalleled 13 distinguished
  French: 13 par excellence

preempt 4 take 5 seize, usurp 8 arrogate, take over 10 commandeer, confiscate 11 appropriate, expropriate

preen 3 pin 4 perk, trim 5 adorn, dress, groom, plume, pride, primp, prink 6 brooch, smooth
  wings: 4 whet

preexistent 5 prior 8 anterior, previous 9 precedent 10 antecedent, precursory

preface 4 open 5 begin, proem, start 6 launch 7 prelude 8 commence, foreword, initiate, lead into, overture, preamble, prologue 9 introduce 12 introduction

prefer 3 opt 4 file 5 adopt, elect, exalt, fancy, favor, lodge, offer 6 select, take to, tender 7 dignify, elevate, ennoble, fix upon, pick out, present, proffer, promote 8 graduate, set forth 9 single out

preference 4 bent, bias, pick 5 fancy 6 liking, option 7 leaning 8 favoring, priority 9 advantage, prejudice, proneness, selection, supremacy 10 ascendancy, partiality, precedence, proclivity, propensity 11 first choice, inclination 12 predilection 13 predomination 14 predisposition
  French: 4 gout

prefigure 4 hint, type 6 shadow, typify 7 foresee, imagine, presage, suggest 9 adumbrate 10 foreshadow

pregnant 4 full, rich 6 fecund, filled, gravid 7 copious, fertile, fraught, replete, seminal, teeming, weighty 8 forceful, fruitful, prolific 9 abounding, expecting, gestating, important, luxuriant, momentous, plenteous, potential, with child, with young 10 impressive, life-giving, meaningful, parturient, productive, suggestive 11 having a baby, proliferous, provocative, significant 12 fructiferous, in a family way
  French: 8 enceinte

prehistoric 3 old 7 ancient 10 immemorial
  continent: 8 Atlantis
  epoch: 6 Eocene 7 Miocene 8 Pliocene 9 Oligocene, Paleocene 11 Pleistocene
  era: 8 Cenozoic, Mesozoic 9 Paleozoic 10 Archeozoic 11 Proterozoic
  implement: 4 celt 6 eolith
  period: 7 Neogene, Permian 8 Cambrian, Devonian, Jurassic, Silurian, Triassic 9 Paleogene 10 Cretaceous, Ordovician, Quaternary
  reptile: 8 dinosaur

prehistoric era 6 Ice Age 8 Cenozoic, Jurassic, Mesozoic, Triassic 9 Paleozoic 10 Cenomanian, Cretaceous 11 Precambrian 15 Upper Cretaceous 16 Pleistocene Epoch

prehistoric man see 8 early man

prejudice 3 ill, mar 4 bias, harm, hurt, loss, sway 5 slant, spoil, taint 6 damage, impair, infect, injure, injury, poison 7 bigotry 8 jaundice 9 detriment 10 favoritism, impair-

ment, partiality, predispose, unfairness 11 contaminate, intolerance, prejudgment 12 disadvantage, one-sidedness, predilection 13 preconception 14 discrimination, predisposition

prejudiced 6 biased, unfair, unjust 7 bigoted, slanted 9 arbitrary 10 intolerant 11 close-minded, opinionated 12 narrow-minded

prejudicial 3 bad 6 biased 7 harmful, hurtful 8 damaging, inimical, sinister 9 injurious 11 deleterious, detrimental

prelate 5 abbot 6 bishop, cleric 9 churchman, clergyman 12 ecclesiastic

preliminary 9 prelusive, prelusory 10 initiatory, precursory, prefatory 11 preparative, preparatory 12 introductory

prelude 7 opening, preface 8 overture, preamble, prologue 9 beginning 11 preliminary, preparation 12 introduction

Prelude, The
  author: 17 William Wordsworth

premature 3 raw 5 green, hasty 6 callow, unripe 7 too soon, unready 8 abortive, ill-timed, immature, previous, too early, untimely 9 embryonic, overhasty, unfledged, unhatched, vestigial 10 incomplete, unprepared 11 inopportune, precipitate, rudimentary, undeveloped 12 unseasonable

premeditated 7 planned, plotted, studied, willful 8 intended 9 conscious, contrived, voluntary 10 calculated, considered, deliberate, predevised, purposeful 11 in cold blood, intentional, prearranged, predesigned 13 predetermined 22 with malice aforethought

premeditation 4 plan 6 design 7 purpose 11 calculation, forethought, preplanning 12 deliberation

premier 3 bet 4 head 5 chief, first 6 oldest 7 leading, supreme 8 earliest, foremost 9 principal 13 prime minister

Preminger, Otto
  director of: 5 Laura 11 Carmen Jones 16 Anatomy of a Murder

premise 6 theory 8 argument 9 postulate, principle 10 assumption, hypothesis 11 presumption, proposition, supposition 14 presupposition

premises 4 site 8 environs, property, vicinity 9 precincts

premium 4 gain, gift 5 award, bonus, prize 6 bounty, return, reward 7 benefit, payment 8 priority 9 high value, incentive 10 great stock, recompense, reparation 11 overpayment 12 appreciation, compensation, inflated rate, remuneration 13 consideration, encouragement

premonition 4 omen, sign 5 hunch, token 6 augury 7 auspice, feeling, inkling, portent, presage 9 foretoken 10 foreboding, indication, prediction 11 forewarning 12 presentiment

preoccupation 9 immersion, obsession 10 absorption, detachment, dreaminess, employment 11 abstraction, involvement 16 absent-mindedness

preoccupied 6 absent, dreamy 8 absorbed, immersed, involved, obsessed 9 engrossed, wrapped up 10 abstracted, distracted 12 absent-minded

preoccupy 6 absorb, arrest, obsess, take up, wrap up 7 engross, immerse 9 fascinate

preparation 8 prudence, readying 9 foresight, preparing, provision, safeguard 10 precaution 11 expectation, forethought 12 anticipation

preparations 5 plans 7 elixirs 8 guidance, measures, mixtures, training, tutelage 9 dressings, educaiton, seasoning, tinctures 11 concoctions, confections 12 arrangements 13 preliminaries, prepared foods, prescriptions

prepare 3 fix 5 adapt, prime, ready 7 arrange, be ready, provide 8 get ready 9 make ready, rearrange, take steps

prepared 4 done 5 fixed, ready 6 cooked, primed 7 planned 8 arranged, finished 9 made ready, rehearsed 11 provided for

prepayment 6 credit 7 advance 9 allowance 11 downpayment

preponderance, preponderancy 4 bulk, glut, mass 6 excess 7 surfeit, surplus 8 majority, plethora 9 dominance, plurality, profusion 10 domination, lion's share, oversupply, prevalence, redundance 12 predominance

preponderant 3 key 4 main 5 chief, first, major, prime 7 highest, leading, primary, supreme 8 dominant, foremost, greatest 9 paramount, principal, uppermost 10 prevailing 11 outstanding, predominant

prepossessing 4 nice 7 winsome 8 alluring, charming, engaging, inviting, pleasant, striking 9 beguiling 10 attractive, bewitching, enchanting, entrancing, personable 11 captivating, fascinating, tantalizing

preposterous 5 inane, outre, silly 6 absurd, stupid 7 asinine, bizarre, fatuous, foolish, idiotic 9 imbecilic, laughable, ludicrous 10 irrational, outrageous, ridiculous 11 nonsensical, unthinkable 12 unreasonable

prerequisite 4 need 6 demand 8 demanded, exigency, required 9 called for, condition, de rigueur, essential, mandatory, necessary, necessity, postulate, requisite 10 imperative, sine qua non 11 requirement, stipulation 13 indispensable, qualification

prerogative 3 due 5 claim, grant, right 6 choice, option 7 freedom, liberty, license, warrant 9 advantage, exemption, franchise, privilege 10 birthright

presage 4 bode, omen, osse, sign 5 augur, token 6 augury, herald 7 betoken, portend, portent, predict 8 forecast, foreshow, foretell, indicate 9 foresight 10 foreboding, foreshadow, indication, prediction, prescience, prognostic 11 premonition 12 presentiment

presbyter 5 elder 13 church officer

prescience 7 presage 9 foresight, prevision 13 foreknowledge

prescribe 3 fix, set 4 rule, urge 5 enact, order 6 assign, decree, demand, direct, enjoin, impose, ordain, settle 7 appoint, command, dictate, require, specify 8 advocate, proclaim 9 authorize, establish, institute, legislate, recommend, stipulate

prescribed 3 set 5 fixed 6 thetic 9 formulary

prescript 3 law 4 rule 5 order 7 precept, statute 10 regulation

prescriptive 7 binding 8 demanded, dictated, didactic, required 9 customary,

mandatory, requisite 10 compulsory, imperative, obligatory

presence 3 air 4 life, look, mien 5 being, curse, favor, ghost, group, midst 6 aspect, entity, figure, manner, shadow, spirit, vision, wraith 7 bearing, company, eidolon, phantom, specter 8 carriage, charisma, demeanor, features, phantasm, revenant, vitality 9 character, existence 10 apparition, attendance, deportment, expression, lineaments 11 reification, subsistence 12 neighborhood 13 manifestation

presence of mind 6 aplomb 8 calmness, coolness 9 composure, sangfroid 10 equanimity, steadiness 14 self-possession

present 2 in 3 fee, now, tip 4 alms, aver, boon, cite, gift, give, here, near, nigh, read, show, tell 5 about, award, frame, grant, offer, state, today 6 accord, allege, assert, at hand, bestow, bounty, call up, chip in, coeval, confer, donate, hand in, impart, legacy, nearby, on hand, recite, relate, render, rooted, submit, summon, supply, tender, turn in 7 advance, bequest, bring on, current, declare, deliver, display, dole out, exhibit, expound, give out, instant, largess, mete out, not away, produce, profess, proffer, propose, provide, recount, vicinal 8 donation, embedded, existent, existing, give away, give over, gratuity, hand over, nowadays, oblation, offering, propound, put forth 9 apprise of, attending, draw forth, endowment, ensconced, hold forth, immediate, implanted, in the room, introduce, make known, not absent, on-the-spot, prevalent, pronounce, surrender, the moment, unremoved 10 asseverate, come up with, contribute, here and now, liberality, perquisite, put forward 11 benefaction, communicate 12 accounted for, bring forward, contemporary, in attendance

presentable 4 chic, so-so 6 decent, modish, not bad, proper 7 stylish 8 becoming, passable, suitable 9 tolerable 10 acceptable, good enough 11 appropriate, fashionable, fit to be seen, respectable

presentation 3 fee, tip 4 boon, gift, show 5 favor, grant, offer 6 bounty 7 advance, display, exhibit, largess, present, proffer **8** bestowal, exposure, gratuity, oblation, offering, overture, proposal **9** unfolding **10** appearance, compliment, disclosure, exhibition, exposition, liberality, production, proffering, submission, unfoldment **11** benefaction, performance, proposition **13** demonstration

presentiment 7 feeling **10** foreboding **11** forewarning, premonition **12** apprehension

presently 3 now **4** anon, soon **7** shortly **8** directly, in a while, this week, this year **9** at present, currently, forthwith **10** any time now, before long, pretty soon **11** after a while, at the moment **12** in a short time **French: 11** tout a l'heure

preservation 6 saving **7** defense **9** salvation **10** protection **11** maintenance, safekeeping **12** conservation, safeguarding

preservative 4 salt **5** brine, spice **8** marinade **12** formaldehyde

preserve, preserves 3 can, dry, jam **4** corn, cure, park, salt, save, seal **5** guard, haven, jelly, nurse, put up, smoke, sweet **6** comfit, defend, embalm, foster, freeze, pickle, refuge, season, secure, shield **7** care for, compote, mummify, protect, reserve, shelter **8** conserve, insulate, keep safe, maintain, marinate **9** dehydrate, keep sound, marmalade, safeguard, sanctuary, sweetmeat, watch over **10** confection, keep intact, perpetuate **11** refrigerate, reservation

preside 4 boss, host, rule **5** chair, watch **6** direct, govern, manage **7** command, conduct, control, hostess, oversee **8** chairman, overlook, regulate **9** keep order, supervise **10** administer **11** superintend **12** administrate, take the chair

president, President 4 head **5** ruler **8** chairman **12** chief officer, chief of state, first citizen **14** chief executive **16** commander in chief, executive officer, head of government

president of US *see box*

preside over 5 chair, guide **6** direct, govern, manage **7** con-

---

president of US
  first: 16 George Washington
  second: 9 John Adams
  third: 15 Thomas Jefferson
  fourth: 12 James Madison
  fifth: 11 James Monroe
  sixth: 15 John Quincy Adams
  seventh: 13 Andrew Jackson
  eighth: 14 Martin Van Buren
  ninth: 20 William Henry Harrison
  tenth: 9 John Tyler
  eleventh: 10 James K Polk
  twelfth: 13 Zachary Taylor
  thirteenth: 15 Millard Fillmore
  fourteenth: 14 Franklin Pierce
  fifteenth: 13 James Buchanan
  sixteenth: 14 Abraham Lincoln
  seventeenth: 13 Andrew Johnson
  eighteenth: 13 Ulysses S Grant
  nineteenth: 16 Rutherford B Hayes
  twentieth: 14 James A Garfield
  twenty-first: 17 Chester Alan Arthur
  twenty-second: 15 Grover Cleveland
  twenty-third: 16 Benjamin Harrison
  twenty-fourth: 15 Grover Cleveland
  twenty-fifth: 15 William McKinley
  twenty-sixth: 17 Theodore Roosevelt
  twenty-seventh: 17 William Howard Taft
  twenty-eighth: 13 Woodrow Wilson
  twenty-ninth: 14 Warren G Harding
  thirtieth: 14 Calvin Coolidge
  thirty-first: 13 Herbert Hoover
  thirty-second: 18 Franklin D Roosevelt
  thirty-third: 12 Harry S Truman
  thirty-fourth: 17 Dwight D Eisenhower
  thirty-fifth: 12 John F Kennedy
  thirty-sixth: 14 Lyndon B Johnson
  thirty-seventh: 13 Richard M Nixon
  thirty-eighth: 11 Gerald R Ford
  thirty-ninth: 11 (James E) Jimmy Carter (Jr)
  fortieth: 12 Ronald Reagan
  forty-first: 10 George Bush
  forty-second: 11 (William Jefferson) Bill Clinton

---

duct **8** dominate **9** supervise **10** administer **11** superintend

Presley, Elvis Aron
  nickname: 14 Elvis the Pelvis **15** King of Rock n Roll
  born: 6 Tupelo **11** Mississippi
  wife: 9 Priscilla
  daughter: 9 Lisa Marie
  father: 6 Vernon
  mother: 6 Gladys
  twin brother: 11 Jessie Garon
  manager: 16 Colonel Tom Parker
  home: 9 Graceland
  location: 7 Memphis **9** Tennessee
  song: 8 Hound Dog **10** All Shook Up **11** Don't Be Cruel **12** Love Me Tender **13** Jailhouse Rock **14** Blue Suede Shoes **15** Heartbreak Hotel **17** That's All Right Mama
  film: 7 G I Blues **9** Loving You **10** Blue Hawaii, King Creole **12** Love Me Tender, Viva Las Vegas **13** Jailhouse Rock

press 2 TV **3** beg, bug, dun, hit, hug, jam, mob, pet, tap, tax **4** army, body, cram, duty, heap, herd, host, iron, mash, mill, pack, prod, push, rush **5** beset, bunch, clasp, crowd, crush, drove, exact, flick, force, horde, hound, hurry, media, plead, radio, set on, steam, stuff, surge, swarm **6** appeal, bother, burden, caress, compel, duress, enjoin, exhort, extort, fondle, gather, huddle, legion, mangle, push in, reduce, smooth, strain, stress, throng **7** cluster, collect, depress, embrace, entreat, flatten, implore, newsmen, oppress, snuggle, squeeze, trouble **8** assemble, bear down, bear upon, calender, compress, condense, hot-press, insist on, pressure, printing, push down **9** annoyance, be hard put, constrain, constrict, final form, force down, force from, importune, multitude, reporters **10** compulsion, congregate, newspapers, obligation, supplicate, television, thrust down **11** journalists, periodicals, publication **12** bear down upon, broadcasting, come together, news services, newspapermen **14** Fourth Estate

Pressburger, Emeric *see* **13** Michael Powell

press down 7 compact, depress **8** push down

press forward 5 drive **6** push on **7** advance **10** forge ahead

press home 6 stress **9** emphasize, underline **10** accentuate, underscore

pressing 5 vital **6** crying, needed, urgent **7** crucial, exigent, needful **8** critical **9** clamoring, demanding, essential, important, insistent, necessary **10** imperative **11** importunate **13** indispensable

pressing necessity 6 crisis **7** urgency **8** exigency **9** emergency

press on 9 move ahead, persevere **10** accelerate, forge ahead **11** move forward

pressure 4 bias, care, load, need, pull, sway, want **5** force, hurry, pinch, power, press, trial **6** burden, demand, strain, stress, weight **7** anxiety, density, gravity, potency, squeeze, straits, tension, trouble, urgency **8** coercion, distress, exigency, interest **9** adversity, grievance, heaviness, influence, necessity **10** affliction, compaction, compulsion, difficulty, oppression

pressure measurement 6 pascal **10** atmosphere

prestige 4 fame, mark, note **5** glory, honor **6** esteem, import, regard, renown, report, repute **7** account, respect **8** eminence **9** authority, celebrity **10** importance, notability, prominence, reputation **11** consequence, distinction, preeminence **12** significance

prestigious 5 famed **6** famous **7** eminent, honored, notable **8** esteemed, renowned **9** acclaimed, important, prominent, reputable, respected, well-known **10** celebrated **11** illustrious, outstanding **13** distinguished

Preston, Robert
real name: **21** Robert Preston Meservey

born: **17** Newton Highlands MA
roles: **4** Mame **9** Semi-Tough **11** The Music Man **12** Junior Bonner **14** Victor Victoria **16** How the West Was Won

presumable 6 likely **8** apparent, probable **10** ostensible

presumably 6 likely **8** probably **9** assumably, doubtless **10** apparently, ostensibly **13** presumptively **14** unquestionably **15** in all likelihood **16** in all probability

presume 4 dare **5** fancy, guess, posit **6** assume, deduce, gather, have it, impose, take it **7** believe, imagine, suppose, surmise, suspect, venture **8** be so bold, conceive, make bold, make free **9** postulate, take leave **11** hypothesize, rely too much, think likely **12** take a liberty

presumed 7 assumed, deduced, posited **8** believed, imagined, supposed, surmised **9** suspected **10** postulated **13** took advantage **15** taken for granted

presumption 3 lip **4** gall **5** brass, cheek, guess, nerve, pride **6** belief, daring **7** egotism, premise, surmise **8** audacity, boldness, chutzpah, rudeness **9** arrogance, flippancy, impudence, insolence, postulate **10** assumption, conjecture, effrontery **11** forwardness, haughtiness, prejudgment, speculation, supposition **12** impertinence **13** preconception **14** presupposition

presumptuous 4 bold **5** brash, cocky, fresh, lofty, nervy, proud **6** brassy, brazen, daring, lordly **7** forward, haughty, pompous **8** arrogant, assuming, snobbish **9** audacious, imperious, shameless **10** disdainful **11** dictatorial, domineering, overbearing, patronizing **12** contemptuous, overfamiliar **13** overconfident

presuppose 6 assume **7** presume, suppose **9** speculate **10** conjecture **11** hypothesize

presupposed 7 assumed **8** presumed, supposed **10** speculated **11** conjectured

presupposition 7 premise **10** assumption **11** postulation, presumption

pretend 4 fake, sham **5** claim, fancy, feign, mimic, put on **6** affect, assume **7** imagine, imitate, playact, purport, suppose **8** simulate **9** dissemble **10** masquerade **11** counterfeit, dissimulate, impersonate, make believe

pretended
French: **9** soi-disant

pretender 5 faker, fraud, phony **8** claimant, imposter

pretense 4 airs, fake, hoax, mask, sham, show **5** cloak, cover, feint, guile, trick, vaunt **6** deceit **7** bluster, bombast, display, pretext **8** boasting, bragging, disguise, trickery **9** deception, false show, imposture, invention, pomposity **10** camouflage, pretension, showing off, subterfuge **11** affectation, counterfeit, fabrication, fanfaronade, make-believe, ostentation **12** affectedness

pretension 4 airs, pomp, show **5** claim, right, title **7** bombast, display **8** ambition, pretense, snobbery **9** hypocrisy, pomposity, showiness **10** aspiration, showing off **11** affectation, ostentation **13** grandioseness **14** self-importance **16** ostentatiousness

pretentious 4 airy, smug **5** gaudy, lofty, showy, stagy **6** flashy, florid, garish, ornate, tawdry **7** blown-up, fatuous, pompous, stuck-up **8** affected, assuming, boastful, inflated, overdone, pedantic, puffed-up, snobbish **9** bombastic, flaunting, insincere, presuming, unnatural **10** hoity-toity, theatrical **11** exaggerated, extravagant, overbearing **12** ostentatious, self-praising **13** high-and-mighty, self-important

pretentiousness 4 cant **6** humbug **9** hypocrisy **11** insincerity **17** sanctimoniousness

preternatural 5 eerie, weird **6** arcane, occult **7** bizarre, strange, uncanny **8** esoteric, mystical **9** unearthly, unworldly **10** miraculous, mysterious, superhuman **11** hypernormal, preterhuman, supernormal **12** extramundane, metaphysical, supernatural, supranatural **14** transcendental

pretext 5 basis, bluff, feint **6** excuse, ground **8** pretense **9** semblance **10** pretension, subterfuge **11** vindication

pretty 4 fair **5** bonny **6** comely, dainty, fairly, goodly, lovely, rather **7** shapely, sightly, well-set **8** alluring, charming, delicate, engaging, fetching, graceful, handsome, somewhat, well-made **9** beauteous, beautiful **10** adequately, attractive, moderately, reasonably **11** captivating, good-looking, symmetrical, well-favored

pretty child 4 doll **5** cutie **10** living doll

prevail 3 win **4** rule **5** exist, reign **6** abound, obtain, win out **7** conquer, succeed, triumph **8** have sway, hold sway, overcome **9** be a winner, be current **11** be prevalent, be the victor, carry the day, gain the palm, predominate **12** be victorious, be widespread, preponderate

prevailing 3 set **4** main **5** fixed, usual **6** normal **7** current, general, in style, popular **8** definite, dominant **9** customary, prevalent, principal **10** accustomed, widespread **11** established, predominant **12** conventional, preponderant

prevail over 4 beat **5** outdo **6** defeat **7** eclipse, surpass **8** overcome

prevail upon 4 sway **8** convince, persuade **9** influence

prevalent 4 rife **5** usual **6** common, normal **7** general, popular, rampant **8** abundant, everyday, familiar, frequent, habitual, numerous **9** customary, extensive, pervasive, universal **10** prevailing, ubiquitous, widespread **11** commonplace **12** conventional

prevaricate 3 fib, lie **4** fake **6** palter **7** deceive, distort, falsify, mislead, perjure **8** hoodwink, misstate **9** be evasive, dissemble **10** equivocate, tell a story **11** counterfeit **12** be untruthful, misrepresent

prevarication 3 fib, lie **5** fable **7** fiction, untruth, whopper **9** fairy tale, falsehood, fish story, invention **11** fabrication **12** equivocation **16** cock-and-bull story **17** misrepresentation

prevent 3 bar, dam **4** balk, foil, halt, stop, veto **5** avert, avoid, block, deter **6** arrest, forbid, thwart **7** deflect, draw off, fend off, obviate, rule out, ward off **8** hold back, preclude, prohibit, stave off, turn away **9** forestall, frustrate, intercept, sidetrack, turn aside **10** anticipate, counteract **11** nip in the bud

prevention 6 defeat **8** stoppage **9** avoidance, hindrance, obviation, restraint, thwarting **10** deterrence, inhibition, pre-

clusion **11** elimination, frustration **12** interception **13** forestallment

preview 5 sneak **6** sample, survey **8** futurama **9** foretaste **10** inspection

previous 5 early, prior **6** before, former **7** earlier **8** foregone **9** aforesaid, erstwhile, foregoing, preceding **10** antecedent **14** aforementioned

previously 4 once **6** before **7** earlier, long ago **8** back when, formerly **9** at one time, a while ago, earlier on **10** a while back, heretofore **11** in times past **12** sometime back

Prevost, Abbe
    author of: **12** Manon Lescaut

prey 3 eat **4** dupe, food, game, gull, kill **5** patsy, prize, quest **6** devour, infest, pigeon, quarry, sucker, target, victim **7** cat's-paw, consume, fall guy, live off **8** feed upon **9** feast upon **10** fasten upon, fatten upon, parasitize

Priam
    king of: **4** Troy
    father: **8** Laomedon
    brother: **8** Tithonus
    wife: **6** Hecuba
    son: **5** Paris **6** Hector **9** Polydorus
    daughter: **8** Polyxena **9** Cassandra
    number of sons: **5** fifty
    number of daughters: **5** fifty
    killed by: **11** Neoptolemus

Priamid
    father: **5** Priam

Priapus
    god of: **5** herds **7** gardens **9** fertility, male power **11** procreation
    father: **8** Dionysus
    mother: **9** Aphrodite
    corresponds to: **7** Mutinus

price 3 fee **4** cost, fine, rate **5** value, worth **6** amount, assess, charge, outlay **7** expense, penalty **8** appraise, evaluate, par value **9** face value, list price **10** forfeiture, punishment

Price, Fanny
    character in: **13** Mansfield Park
    author: **6** Austen

Price, Vincent
    born: **9** St Louis MO
    wife: **11** Coral Browne **12** Edith Barrett
    roles: **6** The Fly **8** The Raven **10** House of Wax **13** Tower of London **15** The House of Usher **20** The Pit and the Pendulum **22** The

Masque of the Red Death
    expert in: **3** art

Price Is Right, The
    host: **9** Bob Barker **10** Bill Cullen

priceless 4 dear, rare **6** costly, prized, valued **8** peerless, precious, valuable **9** cherished, expensive, treasured **10** high-priced, invaluable **11** beyond price **12** incomparable, without price **13** irreplaceable **17** worth a king's ransom

prick 5 stick **6** pierce **8** puncture

prickle 4 barb, itch **5** point, quill, smart, sting, thorn **6** tingle **7** barbule, bristle, spicule

prickly 5 itchy **6** coarse, thorny **8** scratchy, stinging **9** vexatious

pride 3 joy **4** airs, pomp, show **5** honor **6** egoism, parade, vanity **7** comfort, conceit, delight, dignity, display, egotism, swagger **8** pleasure, self-love, smugness **9** arrogance, be proud of, enjoyment, happiness, immodesty, pomposity, vainglory **10** pretension, self-esteem **11** haughtiness, ostentation, self-respect **14** self-importance

Pride and Prejudice
    author: **10** Jane Austen
    character: **7** Mr Darcy **9** Mr Bingley, Mr Collins, Mr Wickham **14** Charlotte Lucas **15** Caroline Bingley **21** Lady Catherine de Bourgh
        Bennet daughters: **4** Jane, Mary **5** Kitty, Lydia **9** Elizabeth
    director: **14** Robert Z Leonard
    cast: **10** Mary Boland **11** Edmund Gwenn, Greer Garson, Karen Morley **13** Ann Rutherford, Edna May Oliver **15** Laurence Olivier **16** Maureen O'Sullivan

Pride of the Yankees, The
    director: **7** Sam Wood
    cast: **8** Babe Ruth **9** Dan Duryea **10** Gary Cooper (Lou Gehrig) **12** Teresa Wright **13** Walter Brennan

priest 5 padre **6** cleric **8** minister, preacher **9** churchman **13** man of the cloth

priesthood 5 cloth **6** clergy **8** ministry, the cloth **9** pastorage

Priestley, J B
    author of: **9** Bright Day

11 Lost Empires **13** Angel Pavement **17** The Good Companions

Priestley, Joseph
field: 9 chemistry
nationality: 7 British
discovered: 6 oxygen **7** ammonia **13** nitrogen oxide
invented: 11 carbonation

priestly 8 churchly, clerical **10** sacerdotal **14** ecclesiastical

prig 5 bigot, prude **6** pedant **7** puritan **8** bluenose **9** formalist, hypocrite, nitpicker, pretender **10** fuddy-duddy **11** faultfinder **12** bluestocking, precisionist, stuffed shirt **14** attitudinarian

priggish 4 prim, smug **6** stuffy **7** prudish **9** blue-nosed **10** tight-laced **11** puritanical, strait laced **13** self-righteous, self-satisfied

prim 4 smug, tidy **5** fussy **6** prissy, proper, strict, stuffy **7** haughty, prudish **8** priggish, starched **9** squeamish, unbending **10** fastidious, fuddy-duddy, inflexible, no-nonsense, particular **11** overprecise, puritanical, stiff-necked, straitlaced

prima donna 4 diva, lead, star **6** singer **9** principal
literally: 9 first lady

primarily 6 mainly, mostly **7** chiefly, largely **9** basically, generally, in the main **11** essentially, principally **13** fundamentally, predominantly **14** for the most part **16** first and foremost

primary 3 key **4** main, star **5** basal, basic, chief, first, prime, vital **6** innate, native, oldest, primal, ruling, utmost **7** highest, initial, leading, nascent, natural **8** cardinal, dominant, earliest, greatest, inherent, original, primeval **9** beginning, elemental, essential, important, necessary, primitive, principal, prominent **10** aboriginal, elementary, indigenous, primordial, rudimental **11** fundamental, predominant, preparatory, rudimentary **12** introductory

primary constituent 5 basic **9** basic need, essential, necessity, requisite **10** sine qua non

primate 3 ape, man **5** avahi, indri, lemur, loris, potto **6** aye-aye, baboon, bishop, galago, gibbon, mammal, monkey **7** gorilla, tamarin, tarsier **8** marmoset, simpoona **9** orangutan, tree shrew **10** archbishop, chimpanzee

prime 2 A1 **3** ace, fit **4** best, main, peak, pink **5** adapt, basal, basic, bloom, breed, brief, chief, coach, early, first, groom, guide, lucky, raise, ready, train, tutor, vital **6** adjust, choice, fill in, flower, Grade A, height, heyday, inform, innate, native, oldest, primal, prompt, ruling, school, seemly, select, timely, utmost, zenith **7** educate, fitting, highest, leading, maximal, natural, prepare, primary, quality, supreme, top-hole **8** best days, cardinal, crowning, earliest, get ready, greatest, inherent, instruct, maturity, original, peerless, suitable, superior **9** befitting, elemental, essential, expedient, important, intrinsic, make ready, matchless, necessary, opportune, paramount, preferred, principal, provident, top-drawer, topflight, unmatched, well-timed **11** superlative, unsurpassed, without peer **12** unparalleled

prime example 5 model **7** classic **8** exemplar **9** archetype

prime mover 6 author **9** initiator, organizer **10** originator
Latin: 12 primum mobile

Prime of Miss Jean Brodie, The
author: 11 Muriel Spark

primer 3 cap **4** book **5** paint **6** manual, reader **8** hornbook, textbook **9** undercoat

primeval 5 early **6** oldest, primal **7** ancient, archaic **8** earliest, original **9** ancestral, legendary, primitive **10** aboriginal, indigenous, primordial **11** fundamental, prehistoric **12** antediluvian, mythological

primitive 4 bare **5** crude, early, first **6** native, simple **7** antique, archaic, artless, ascetic, austere, primary, Spartan **8** backward, earliest, original **9** beginning, unlearned, unrefined, unskilled **10** aboriginal, elementary **11** rudimentary, uncivilized, undeveloped

primordial 5 first **6** primal **7** initial **8** original, primeval **9** beginning, primitive **10** elementary **11** fundamental, prehistoric

primp 5 groom, plume, preen **6** doll up, make up **7** gussy up **8** prettify, spruce up

primrose 7 Primula **15** Primula vulgaris
varieties: 4 baby, cape, star

5 fairy **6** German, poison **7** Chinese, English, evening **8** bird's-eye **9** buttercup **12** beach evening, white evening **13** desert evening **14** Mexican evening

primum mobile 10 prime mover **16** first moving thing

primus inter pares 16 first among equals

prince
Italian: 8 principe
Turkish: 3 beg, bey

Prince
original name: 18 Prince Rogers Nelson
nickname: 12 Royal Badness
born: 2 MN **11** Minneapolis
recording: 6 For You, Parade, Prince **9** Dirty Mind **10** Purple Rain **11** Controversy **20** Around the World in a Day
film: 10 Purple Rain **13** Sign o' the Times **14** Graffiti Bridge **18** Under the Cherry Moon

Prince, The
author: 18 Niccolo Machiavelli

Prince and the Pauper, The
author: 9 Mark Twain
character: 4 Hugo **8** Tom Canty **9** John Canty **10** Hugh Hendon **11** Miles Hendon **19** Edward Prince of Wales

Prince Edward Island
abbreviation: 3 PEI
bay: 5 Rollo **6** Egmont **7** Bedeque **8** Cardigan, Malpeque **9** Cascumpec **12** Hillsborough
capital: 13 Charlottetown
gulf: 10 St Lawrence
people: 4 Scot **5** Irish, Scots **6** French **7** English
discoverer: 7 Cartier
province of: 6 Canada
river: 4 Dunk **5** Eliot, Yorke **12** Hillsborough
strait: 14 Northumberland

Prince Igor
also: 9 Kniaz Igor
opera by: 7 Borodin
character: 11 Khan Konchak
contains: 17 Polovetsian dances

princely 3 big **5** noble, royal **8** generous **11** magnificent

prince of darkness 5 Satan **7** Lucifer **8** the Devil **9** Beelzebub

Prince of Peace 5 Jesus **6** Christ

Princess and the Pea, The
author: 21 Hans Christian Andersen

Princess Casamassima
author: 10 Henry James

Princess Daisy
author: 12 Judith Krantz

Princesse de Cleves, La
author: 14 Mme de LaFayette

Princess Flavia
character in: 15 Prisoner of Zenda
author: 4 Hope

Prince Valiant
creator: 12 Harold Foster
character: 5 Ilene 9 Prince Arn 10 King Arthur
wife: 5 Aleta
nickname: 3 Val

principal 4 dean, fund, main, star 5 basic, chief, first, money, prime 6 master 7 capital, leading, primary, supreme 8 cardinal, dominant, foremost, greatest, superior, ultimate 9 essential, paramount, preceptor, prominent 10 capital sum, headmaster, leading man, preeminent 11 fundamental, predominant, protagonist 13 most important

principal constituent 4 base 12 chief feature 14 main ingredient

principal dish of a meal
French: 17 piece de resistance

principal event
French: 17 piece de resistance

principality 5 angel 9 princedom 14 celestial being, heavenly spirit

principally 6 mainly, mostly 7 chiefly, largely 8 above all 9 basically, primarily 10 especially 12 particularly 13 fundamentally, predominantly 14 for the most part 16 first and foremost

principe 6 prince

principle 3 law 4 code, fact, rule, view 5 axiom, basis, canon, credo, creed, dogma, honor, maxim, tenet, truth 6 belief, dictum, ethics, morals, maxim, theory, virtue 7 element, formula, honesty, precept, probity, scruple, theorem 8 attitude, doctrine, goodness, morality, position, rudiment, scruples, teaching 9 direction, integrity, rectitude, standards 10 assumption, regulation 11 fundamental, proposition, uprightness

principled 6 honest 7 upright 9 honorable 10 aboveboard, forthright

Pringle, John
real name of: 11 John Gilbert

prink 4 deck, fuss 5 adorn, preen, primp 6 spruce

print 3 die 4 copy, text, type 5 issue, plate, press, stamp, write 7 compose, edition, engrave, etching, gravure, impress, picture, publish, woodcut 10 lithograph, silkscreen 11 letterpress

printing press
invented by:
rotary: 3 Hoe
web: 7 Bullock

prior 6 former 7 earlier 8 anterior, previous 9 aforesaid, erstwhile, foregoing, prefatory 10 antecedent, precursory 11 going before, preexistent, preexisting, preparatory 14 aforementioned

Prior Analytics
author: 9 Aristotle

Prioress
character in: 18 The Canterbury Tales
author: 7 Chaucer

priority 7 urgency 9 immediacy, seniority 10 ascendancy, precedence, precedency, preference 11 antecedence, preeminence, superiority

priory 5 abbey 6 friary 7 convent, nunnery 8 cloister 9 hermitage, monastery

Prism, Letitia
character in: 27 The Importance of Being Earnest
author: 5 Wilde

prison 3 can, jug, pen 4 brig, gaol, jail, stir, tank 5 clink, joint, pokey, tower 6 cooler 7 dungeon, slammer 8 bastille, big house 9 calaboose, jailhouse

Prisoner of Zenda
author: 11 Anthony Hope
character: 14 Princess Flavia 17 Lady Rose Burlesdon, Rudolph Rassendyll 18 Antoinette de Mauban, Fritz von Tarlenhein 21 Michael Duke of Strelsau 22 Rudolph King of Ruritania
director: 12 John Cromwell
cast: 9 Mary Astor 10 David Niven 12 C Aubrey Smith, Ronald Colman (Rudolf Rassendyll) 16 Madeleine Carroll 18 Douglas Fairbanks Jr (Rupert of Hentzau)
setting: 9 Ruritania

prissy 4 prim 5 fussy 6 proper, stuffy 7 finicky, prudish 8 overnice 9 sissified 10 effeminate 11 strait-laced

Prissy
character in: 15 Gone With the Wind
author: 8 Mitchell

pristine 4 pure 8 unmarred, virginal 9 undefiled, unspoiled, unsullied, untouched 10 unpolluted 11 untarnished 14 uncontaminated

Pritchett, V S
author of: 11 Midnight Oil 16 Collected Stories, The Spanish Temper 19 On the Edge of the Cliff

privacy 6 secret 7 privity, retreat, secrecy 8 security, solitude 9 integrity, isolation, seclusion 10 retirement, withdrawal 11 privateness 12 dissociation, solitariness 13 sequestration

private 4 dark 5 fixed, privy 6 buried, closed, covert, hidden, lonely, remote, secret 7 cryptic, express, limited, obscure, special 8 confined, desolate, esoteric, hush-hush, isolated, lonesome, personal, secluded, solitary 9 concealed, exclusive, inviolate, invisible, nonpublic, not public, reclusive 10 classified, indistinct, mysterious, restricted, undercover, under wraps, unofficial, unrevealed 11 clandestine, nonofficial, sequestered, underground, undisclosed 12 confidential, off-the-record, unfrequented

privateer 6 pirate 7 brigand, corsair 9 buccaneer

private eye 4 dick 6 shamus 7 gumshoe 9 detective 12 investigator

Private Life of Henry VIII, The
director: 14 Alexander Korda
cast: 11 Merle Oberon, Robert Donat 12 Binnie Barnes 14 Elsa Lanchester (Anne of Cleves) 15 Charles Laughton (Henry VIII)

Private Life of the Master Race, The
author: 13 Bertold Brecht

Private Lives
author: 10 Noel Coward
character: 10 Elyot Chase, Sibyl Chase 12 Amanda Prynne, Victor Prynne

Private Lives of Elizabeth and Essex, The
director: 13 Michael Curtiz
cast: 10 Bette Davis (Elizabeth I), Errol Flynn (Essex) 11 Donald Crisp 12 Vincent Price 13 Nanette Fabray 17 Olivia de Havilland

also known as: 17 Elizabeth the Queen

privately 7 sub rosa **8** in secret, secretly **9** between us, entre nous, in private **12** in confidence **14** confidentially **15** between you and me **16** between ourselves **17** behind closed doors

privation 4 lack, need, want **5** pinch **6** misery, penury **7** beggary, poverty, straits **8** distress, exigency, hardship **9** indigence, neediness, pauperism **10** bankruptcy, mendicancy **11** destitution **14** impoverishment **15** impecuniousness

privilege 3 due **4** boon **5** allow, favor, grant, honor, power, right, title **6** patent, permit **7** benefit, charter, empower, entitle, freedom, liberty, license **8** pleasure **9** advantage, authority, franchise **10** birthright **11** entitlement, prerogative **12** prerequisite

privileged 4 free **6** exempt, immune **7** allowed, excused, granted, limited, special **8** entitled, licensed **9** empowered, not liable, permitted, warranted **10** authorized, sanctioned **13** unaccountable

prize 3 cup, gem, pip **4** like, lulu **5** award, catch, crown, dandy, honey, honor, jewel, medal, peach, pearl, value **6** admire, esteem, honors, regard, reward, ribbon, trophy **7** cherish, diamond, guerdon, honored, laurels, premium, respect, winning **8** accolade, champion, citation, hold dear, look up to, pure gold, treasure **9** humdinger, medallion **10** appreciate, blue ribbon, decoration, set store by **11** crackerjack, masterpiece

prized 4 dear **8** esteemed, precious **9** cherished, treasured

prizefight 2 go **4** bout **5** match **6** boxing **7** contest **10** fisticuffs

prizefighter 3 pug **5** boxer **7** slugger **8** pugilist **9** flyweight **11** heavyweight, lightweight **12** bantamweight, middleweight, welterweight **13** featherweight **16** light heavyweight

pro 3 for **5** forth **6** before, expert, master **8** favoring **9** authority **11** affirmative
opposite: 3 con **7** amateur

probability 4 odds **6** chance **10** likelihood

probable 6 likely **7** logical, seeming, tenable **8** apparent, assuring, credible, expected, possible, presumed, supposed **9** plausible, promising, thinkable **10** believable, in the cards, ostensible, presumable, reasonable **11** conceivable, encouraging, presumptive

probably 6 likely **10** most likely, presumably, supposedly **11** as like as not **15** in all likelihood

probe 4 hunt, quiz, seek, test **5** query, study, trial **6** pursue, review, search, survey **7** examine, fish for, inquest, inquire, inquiry, inspect, pry into, rummage **8** analysis, look into, question, research **9** penetrate **10** inspection, scrutinize **11** examination, exploration, interrogate, investigate **13** investigation

probity 5 honor **6** virtue **7** decency, honesty **8** goodness, morality **9** character, integrity, principle **11** uprightness **12** straightness **13** righteousness **14** high-mindedness **15** trustworthiness **16** incorruptibility

problem 5 poser, query **6** puzzle, riddle, unruly **8** question, stubborn **9** conundrum, difficult **10** difficulty **11** intractable **12** disagreement, hard to manage, incorrigible, unmanageable

problematic 7 dubious, unknown **8** doubtful, puzzling **9** difficult, enigmatic, uncertain, unsettled, worrisome **10** perplexing **11** paradoxical, troublesome **12** questionable, undetermined

pro bono publico 16 for the public good

proboscis 4 beak, nose **5** snoot, snout, trunk **6** siphon, sucker, syphon **7** rostrum
monkey: 4 kaha **5** kahua

procedure 2 MO **3** way **4** mode **6** course, manner, method **7** process, routine **8** approach, strategy **9** technique **11** methodology **13** modus operandi

proceed 2 go **3** act **4** come, flow, go on, grow, move, stem, work **5** arise, begin, ensue, issue, start **6** derive, follow, move on, push on, result, set out, spring **7** advance, carry on, emanate, go ahead, operate, press on, succeed **8** be caused, commence, continue, function, progress, take rise **9** be derived, go forward, move ahead, originate, undertake

proceedings 4 case, suit **5** cause, trial **6** doings, events, report **7** account, actions, affairs, lawsuit, matters, minutes, records, returns **8** activity, archives, goings on **9** incidents, memoranda **10** happenings, litigation, operations **11** occurrences **12** transactions

proceeds 3 net **4** gain, gate, pelf, take **5** gross, lucre, money, yield **6** assets, income, profit, reward **7** returns, revenue **8** earnings, pickings, receipts, winnings **9** box office

process 3 can, dry **4** fill, flow, flux, mode, plan, ship, step, writ **5** alter, candy, smoke, treat, usage **6** change, course, freeze, handle, manner, method, motion, policy, scheme, system **7** convert, measure, passage, prepare, project, summons **8** deal with, function, movement, practice, preserve, progress, subpoena **9** dehydrate, dispose of, freeze-dry, procedure, transform, unfolding **10** court order, proceeding

procession 4 file, line, rank **5** array, march, train **6** column, course, parade **7** caravan, cortege, pageant, passage **8** progress, sequence **9** cavalcade, motorcade **10** succession **11** progression

Procheneosaurus
type: 8 dinosaur **10** ornithopod
location: 6 Canada
period: 10 Cretaceous

proclaim 3 cry **4** tell **5** blare, state, voice **6** affirm, assert, blazon, herald, report, reveal **7** call out, declare, divulge, give out, profess, publish, release, sing out, trumpet **8** announce, disclose, set forth **9** advertise, broadcast, circulate, enunciate, hawk about, make known, publicize **10** make public, promulgate

proclamation 5 edict, ukase **6** decree **12** announcement **13** pronouncement

Proclea
husband: 6 Cycnus
son: 5 Tenes

Procles
twin of: 11 Eurysthenes

proclivity 3 yen **4** bent, bias **5** taste **6** desire, liking **7** impulse, leaning **8** affinity, appetite, penchant, soft spot, tendency **9** affection, prejudice, proneness 10 partiality, propensity 11 disposition, inclination 12 predilection 14 predisposition

Procne
sister: 9 Philomela
husband: 6 Tereus
changed into: 7 swallow

procrastinate 3 lag 5 dally, defer, delay, stall, tarry 6 dawdle, linger, loiter 7 adjourn 8 hang back, hesitate, hold back, kill time, postpone, put on ice 9 temporize, waste time 10 be dilatory, dillydally 11 play for time 12 drag one's feet

procrastinating 4 slow 5 tardy 6 remiss 8 dilatory 9 reluctant 12 foot-dragging 13 dillydallying

procreate 3 get 4 bear, sire 5 beget, breed, spawn 6 create, father, mother 7 produce 8 conceive, engender, generate, multiply 9 propagate, reproduce 10 bring forth 11 give birth to, proliferate

procreation
god of: 7 Priapus

procreator 4 sire 6 father 8 begetter

Procris
father: 8 Thespius
10 Erechtheus
husband: 8 Cephalus

Procrustes
also: 8 Damastes
9 Polypemon
robber who: 6 maimed
killed by: 7 Theseus

procure 3 buy, get, win 4 earn, gain, take 5 evoke, seize 6 attain, come by, effect, elicit, gather, incite, induce, obtain, pick up, secure 7 achieve, acquire, receive 8 contrive, purchase 10 accumulate, bring about, commandeer, lay hands on 11 appropriate

procurement 4 gain 7 seizure 8 purchase 10 attainment, purchasing 11 achievement, acquirement, acquisition 12 accumulation 13 appropriation

prod 3 jab, nag 4 flog, goad, lash, move, poke, push, spur, stir, urge, whip 5 egg on, impel, prick, rouse, shove, speed 6 excite, exhort, incite, needle, prompt, propel, stir up 7 actuate, animate, provoke, quicken 8 motivate, pressure 9 encourage, instigate, stimulate

prodigal 4 lush 5 ample 6 lavish, myriad, wanton 7 copious, profuse, replete, spender, teeming, wastrel 8 abundant, generous, numerous, reckless, swarming, wasteful 9 abounding, bounteous, bountiful, countless, excessive, exuberant, impetuous, luxuriant, plentiful, unthrifty 10 exorbitant, gluttonous, immoderate, inordinate, numberless, profligate, squanderer, thriftless 11 dissipating, extravagant, improvident, innumerable, intemperate, overliberal, precipitate, spendthrift 13 multitudinous

prodigality 10 imprudence, lavishness 12 extravagance, improvidence, overspending, wastefulness

prodigious 3 big 4 huge, rare, vast 5 grand, great, large 6 mighty, unique 7 amazing, immense 8 colossal, enormous, gigantic, renowned, singular, striking, terrific, uncommon, unwonted, wondrous 9 marvelous, monstrous, startling, wonderful 10 astounding, impressive, miraculous, monumental, noteworthy, remarkable, stupendous, surprising, tremendous 11 astonishing, exceptional, far-reaching, uncustomary, unthinkable 12 dumbfounding, overwhelming, unimaginable 13 extraordinary, inconceivable, unprecedented

prodigiously 10 enormously, incredibly, remarkably 12 inordinately, tremendously 13 astonishingly, exceptionally, extravagantly, outstandingly, spectacularly 14 overwhelmingly

prodigiousness 6 rarity 8 enormity, hugeness, vastness 10 uniqueness 11 singularity 12 extravagance

prodigy 4 whiz 6 expert, genius, marvel, master, rarity, wizard, wonder 7 stunner, whiz kid 8 rara avis 9 sensation 10 mastermind, phenomenon, wunderkind 11 wonder child

Prodromia
epithet of: 4 Hera
means: 7 pioneer

produce 4 bear, form, give, make, show 5 beget, bloom, cause, found, frame, hatch, set up, shape, yield 6 adduce, afford, create, devise, effect, evince, evolve, flower, fruits, greens, invent, reveal, sprout, supply, unmask, unveil 7 achieve, advance, bring in, compose, concoct, develop, display, divulge, exhibit, fashion, furnish, present, provide, staples, turn out, uncover 8 bring off, bring out, conceive, disclose, discover, generate, manifest, set forth 9 bear fruit, construct, fabricate, institute, make plain, originate, procreate, put on view, show forth 10 accomplish, bring about, come up with, effectuate, foodstuffs, give life to, give rise to, put in force, vegetables 11 bring to pass, give birth to, manufacture, materialize 14 bring into being

Producers, The
director: 9 Mel Brooks
cast: 9 Dick Shawn 10 Gene Wilder, Zero Mostel
11 Kenneth Mars

production 4 film, play, show 5 drama, movie 6 cinema, circus, making 7 display, exhibit, musical, showing 8 building, carnival, creation 9 execution, formation, producing, stage show 10 appearance, disclosure, revelation 11 fabrication, fulfillment, manufacture, origination, performance 12 construction, effectuation, introduction, presentation 13 demonstration, entertainment, manifestation, manufacturing, motion picture 15 materialization

productive 4 busy, rich 6 active, fecund, paying, useful 7 causing, copious, dynamic, fertile, gainful, teeming 8 creating, creative, fruitful, prolific, valuable, vigorous, yielding 9 effectual, luxuriant, plenteous, plentiful, producing 10 invaluable, profitable, worthwhile 11 efficacious, moneymaking, proliferous 12 contributing, fructiferous, remunerative

Proetus
father: 4 Abas
mother: 6 Aglaia
twin brother: 8 Acrisius
wife: 5 Antia 10 Stheneboea
son: 11 Megapenthes
daughter: 7 Iphinoe, Lysippe
10 Iphianassa
invented: 6 shield
enemy: 8 Acrisius

profanation 9 sacrilege 10 defilement 11 desecration

profane 3 lay 4 evil, foul, lewd, mock, vile 5 abuse, bawdy, crude, nasty, scorn, waste 6 coarse, debase, filthy, ill-use, impure, misuse, offend, revile, ribald, sinful, unholy, vulgar, wicked 7 abusive, earthly, godless, impious, obscene, outrage, pervert, pollute, satanic, secular, ungodly, violate, worldly **8** agnostic, diabolic, off-color, temporal, unchaste, undevout, unseemly **9** atheistic, blaspheme, desecrate, hellbound, heretical, misemploy, shameless, unsaintly **10** irreverent, prostitute **11** blasphemous, contaminate, irreligious, terrestrial, unbelieving **12** nonreligious, sacrilegious

profanity 5 filth, oaths **7** cursing, cussing, impiety **8** swearing **9** blasphemy, obscenity, scatology **10** dirty words, execration, expletives, scurrility, swearwords **11** irreverence, obscenities, ungodliness **12** billingsgate **15** four-letter words

profess 3 act, own, say **4** aver, avow, fake, sham, tell **5** admit, claim, feign, offer, put on, state, vouch **6** affirm, allege, assert, assume, depose **7** advance, certify, confess, confirm, contend, declare, embrace, pretend, purport **8** announce, lay claim, maintain, practice, proclaim, propound, simulate **9** believe in, dissemble, enunciate, hold forth **10** asseverate, put forward **11** acknowledge, counterfeit, dissimulate

professed 6 avowed **7** alleged **8** admitted **9** confessed, purported **12** acknowledged, self-declared **14** self-proclaimed

profession 3 job, law, vow **4** line, post, word, work **5** claim, craft, field, trade, troth **6** avowal, career, metier, office, pledge, plight, sphere **7** calling, promise, pursuit, service **8** averment, business, endeavor, industry, medicine, position, practice, teaching, vocation **9** assertion, assurance, guarantee, situation, specialty, statement, testimony **10** allegation, confession, deposition, employment, line of work, occupation, walk of life **11** affirmation, attestation, declaration, undertaking, word of honor **12** announcement, confirmation **13** pronouncement **15** acknowledgement

professional 4 paid **5** adept **6** expert **9** authority, competent, practiced **10** specialist **11** experienced

professionalism 5 savvy, skill **7** know-how **9** expertise **10** expertness

professor 3 don **6** regent

7 adjoint, teacher **8** lecturer **10** instructor
retired: 8 emeritus

Professor, The
author: **15** Charlotte Bronte

professorial 6 teachy **7** bookish, donnish, preachy **8** academic, didactic, pedantic, teachery **11** pedagoguish **13** schoolmarmish **15** schoolmasterish **16** schoolteacherish

Professor's House, The
author: **11** Willa Cather

proffer 5 offer **6** extend, tender **7** advance, hold out, present

proficiency 5 knack, skill **6** acumen **7** ability, knowhow **8** aptitude, capacity, deftness, facility **9** adeptness, dexterity, expertise, handiness **10** adroitness, capability, competence **13** qualification **14** accomplishment

proficient 3 apt **4** able, deft, good **5** adept, handy, quick, ready, sharp **6** adroit, clever, expert, gifted **7** capable, skilled, trained **8** masterly, polished, skillful, talented **9** competent, dexterous, effective, efficient, masterful, practiced, qualified, versatile **11** experienced **12** accomplished, professional

profile 4 form, side, tale **5** shape **6** figure, sketch **7** contour, drawing, outline, picture, skyline **8** half face, portrait, side view, vignette **9** biography **10** lineaments, silhouette **11** delineation **13** configuration

Profiles in Courage
author: **12** John F Kennedy

profit 3 pay, use **4** boon, earn, gain, good, help **5** avail, favor, money, serve, value **6** income, return **7** account, benefit, revenue, service, utility, utilize **8** earnings, interest, proceeds, receipts **9** advantage, make money **11** advancement

profitable 6 paying, useful **7** gainful **8** fruitful, salutary, valuable **9** favorable, lucrative, rewarding **10** beneficial, invaluable, productive, well-paying, worthwhile **11** moneymaking, serviceable **12** advantageous, remunerative

profitmaking 8 business **11** moneymaking **13** noncharitable

profits 4 gate, take **5** gains, yield **6** assets, income **7** returns, revenue **8** earnings, receipts

profligacy 10 lavishness **11** dissipation, dissolution, prodigality, unrestraint **12** extravagance, immoderation, improvidence, recklessness, wastefulness **13** excessiveness

profligate 4 evil, fast, rake, roue, wild **5** loose, satyr **6** erotic, lavish, sinful, sinner, wanton, wicked **7** corrupt, immoral, pervert, satyric, wastrel **8** degraded, depraved, prodigal, reckless, wasteful **9** abandoned, debauched, debauchee, dissolute, libertine, reprobate, sybaritic, unbridled, unthrifty, wrongdoer **10** degenerate, dissipated, dissipater, iniquitous, lascivious, licentious **11** extravagant, improvident, promiscuous, spendthrift **12** unprincipled, unrestrained

pro forma 15 according to form, as a matter of form

profound 4 deep, keen, sage, wise **5** acute, sober, utter **6** abject, hearty, moving, severe **7** decided, erudite, extreme, intense, knowing, learned, radical, serious, sincere **8** complete, educated, informed, piercing, positive, thorough **9** heartfelt, out-and-out, recondite, sagacious, scholarly **10** all-knowing, consummate, deep-seated, omniscient, pronounced, reflective, thoughtful **11** enlightened, far-reaching, penetrating **12** intellectual, soul-stirring **13** comprehensive, knowledgeable, philosophical, thoroughgoing

profundity 5 abyss, depth **6** wisdom **8** deepness, sagacity, sapience **9** erudition **11** learnedness, penetration **12** abstractness, abstruseness, profoundness **13** reconditeness, sagaciousness **16** impenetrableness

profuse 4 rich **5** ample, wordy **6** lavish, prolix **7** copious, diffuse, verbose **8** abundant, generous, prodigal, rambling, wasteful **9** bounteous, bountiful, excessive, garrulous, unthrifty **10** digressive, discursive, immoderate, inordinate, long-winded, loquacious, munificent **11** extravagant, improvident, intemperate, spendthrift

profuseness 9 abundance, diffusion, profusion, prolixity, verbosity, wordiness **10** lavishness **11** copiousness, diffuseness

profusion 4 glut **5** waste **6** excess **7** surfeit, surplus **8** pleth-

ora **9** abundance, multitude
10 oversupply **11** superfluity
12 extravagance, multiplicity

progenitor 8 ancestor, forebear **10** forefather

progeny 3 kin, son **4** clan,
heir, line, race, seed **5** blood,
breed, child, heirs, issue,
scion, stock, young **6** family
7 kindred, lineage **8** children,
offshoot **9** offspring, posterity
10 descendant

prognosticate 7 predict, presage **8** forecast, foretell, prophesy **9** foretoken

prognostication 6 augury
8 forecast, prophecy **10** divination, prediction

prognosticator 4 seer **5** augur **7** prophet **9** predictor
10 forecaster

program 4 bill, book, card,
list, plan, show **5** slate
6 agenda, design, docket, expect, intend, line up, notice,
series, sketch **7** arrange, outline **8** bulletin, calendar, play-
bill, register, schedule,
syllabus **9** timetable **10** curriculum, production, prospectus
12 presentation

progress 4 gain, grow, rise
5 climb, get on, mount, ripen
6 action, course, grow up,
growth, mature, stride **7** advance, develop, headway, improve, proceed, process,
success **8** get ahead, increase,
movement **9** get better, go forward, move ahead, promotion,
unfolding **10** betterment, enrichment, gain ground
11 achievement, advancement,
development, enhancement,
furtherance, improvement,
make headway, make
strides

progression 3 run **5** chain,
climb, order **6** ascent, course,
series, strain, string **7** advance **8** progress, sequence
10 succession **11** advancement,
continuance, furtherance
12 continuation **14** continu-
ousness **15** consecutiveness

progressive 7 dynamic, gradual, liberal, ongoing **8** activist,
advanced, populist, up-to-date
9 advancing, enlarging, reformist, spreading, traveling
10 ameliorist **11** incremental
12 enterprising

prohibit 3 ban, bar **4** curb,
deny, stay, stop, veto **5** block,
check, delay, limit **6** enjoin,
forbid, hamper, hinder,
impede, negate **7** inhibit, obviate, prevent, repress **8** disallow, obstruct, preclude,

restrain, restrict, suppress,
withhold **9** proscribe

prohibited
German: **8** verboten

prohibition 3 ban **4** veto
5 edict **7** embargo, sanction
10 temperance **11** forbiddance
12 interdiction

prohibitive, prohibitory
9 enjoining, hindering **10** forbidding, inhibitive, injunction,
preventative, repressive **11** disallowing, obstructive, restraining, restrictive, suppressive
12 inadmissible, unacceptable
13 disqualifying
15 circumscriptive

project 3 aim, job **4** cast, emit,
fire, goal, plan, send, task,
work **5** draft, eject, expel,
fling, frame, shoot, throw
6 beetle, design, devise, extend, hurtle, invent, jut out,
launch, map out, propel,
scheme **7** concoct, outline,
propose **8** activity, ambition,
bend over, contrive, forecast,
overhang, protrude, stand out,
stick out, throw out, transmit
9 calculate, discharge, ejaculate, intention, objective, plan
ahead **10** assignment **11** extrapolate, undertaking
12 predetermine

projected 6 hurled **7** hurtled,
planned **8** extended, forecast,
launched, overhung, proposed,
stood out, stuck out **9** mapped
out, propelled, protruded
10 catapulted **11** conjectural

projectile 4 dart **5** arrow,
spear **6** rocket **7** javelin,
missile

projecting part 3 arm, ell,
leg **4** eave, limb, tail **6** branch,
feeler, member **7** antenna
8 tentacle **9** appendage

projection 4 brow, bump,
eave **5** bulge, guess, jetty,
jutty, ledge, ridge, shelf **8** estimate, forecast, overhang
9 extension, extrusion **10** estimation, prediction, prospectus,
protrusion **11** guesstimate
12 protuberance **13** approximation, extrapolation

Prokofiev, Serge
born: **6** Russia **9** Sontsovka
composer of: **6** Lt Kije
10 Cinderella, The Gambler
11 War and Peace
13 Scythian Suite, The Fiery
Angel **14** Lieutenant Kije,
Romeo and Juliet, The
Prodigal Son **15** Alexander
Nevsky, Peter and the Wolf
17 Classical Symphony
22 The Love for Three Oranges **57** Cantata for the

Twentieth Anniversary of
the October Revolution

proletarian 6 worker **7** laborer **10** working man

proletariat 5 plebs **6** rabble,
the mob **7** populus **8** canaille,
laborers, populace **9** common-
age, commoners, hoi polloi,
the masses **10** commonalty
11 lower orders, rank and file,
wage earners **12** lower classes,
vulgus mobile, working class
15 the common people **16** the
great unwashed

proliferate 4 teem **5** breed,
hatch, spawn, swarm **8** increase, multiply **9** procreate,
propagate, pullulate **10** regenerate **11** overproduce

prolific 4 lush **6** fecund **7** copious, fertile, profuse **8** abundant, breeding, creative,
fruitful, yielding **9** luxuriant
11 germinative, multiplying,
procreative, progenitive, proliferous, propagating
12 reproductive

prolix 5 wordy **7** verbose
10 long-winded

prolixity 9 verbosity, wordiness **11** profuseness **14** long-
windedness

prologue 7 opening, preface,
prelude **8** foreword, overture,
preamble **9** beginning
12 introduction

prolong 5 delay **6** extend, retard **7** drag out, draw out,
spin out, stretch, sustain
8 continue, elongate, lengthen,
maintain, protract **9** attenuate
10 perpetuate

prolongation 5 delay **9** extending, extension **10** drawing
out **11** attenuation, dragging
out, lengthening, protraction,
retardation **12** perpetuation
13 streching out

prolonged 7 lengthy **8** drawn-
out, extended **9** continued,
long-lived **10** continuing,
lengthened, persistent, protracted **11** long-lasting

prom 3 hop **4** ball **5** dance
9 cotillion, promenade

Promachorma
epithet of: **6** Athena
means: **25** protectress of the
anchorage

Promachus
member of: **7** Epigoni
leader of: **9** Boeotians
epithet of: **6** Athena
means: **8** defender **9** protector

promenade 3 hop **4** ball,
prom, walk **5** dance **6** soiree,
stroll **9** cotillion

Prometheus
  member of: **6** Titans
  father: **7** Iapetus
  mother: **6** Themis **7** Clymene
  brother: **5** Atlas
    10 Epimetheus
  son: **9** Deucalion
  created mankind from:
    4 clay
  stole: **4** fire
  punished by: **4** Zeus
  chained to: **4** rock
  released by: **8** Hercules

Prometheus Bound
  author: **9** Aeschylus
  character: **2** Io **3** Bia
    6 Hermes, Kratos
    7 Oceanus **10** Hephaestus

Prometheus Unbound
  author: **18** Percy Bysshe
    Shelley
  character: **4** Asia, Ione
    5 Earth **7** Jupiter, Mercury,
    Panthea **8** Hercules
    9 Demogoron

prominence 3 tor **4** bump,
  dune, fame, hill, hump, knob,
  lump, mark, mesa, name,
  node, peak, rise, spur **5** bluff,
  bulge, cliff, crest, honor, jetty,
  jutty, knoll, knurl, might,
  mound **6** credit, height, renown, rising, summit, weight
  7 dignity, hillock, majesty,
  process **8** eminence, grandeur,
  mountain, nobility, outshoot,
  overhang, pinnacle, prestige,
  salience, splendor, swelling
  9 celebrity, convexity, elevation, extension, extrusion,
  greatness, influence, notoriety,
  precipice **10** brilliance, importance, notability, popularity,
  projection, promontory, protrusion, reputation, tumescence **11** distinction,
  excrescence, excurvature,
  preeminence, superiority
  12 protuberance, significance

prominent 6 convex, famous
  7 bulging, eminent, evident,
  glaring, honored, jutting, leading, notable, obvious, salient,
  staring, swollen **8** apparent,
  definite, excurved, extended,
  renowned, striking, swelling
  9 arresting, important, respected, well-known **10** celebrated, easily seen, jutting
  out, noticeable, preeminent,
  projecting, pronounced, protruding, protrusive, remarkable **11** conspicuous,
  discernible, illustrious, outstanding, prestigious, protuberant **12** recognizable
  13 distinguished

promiscuous 3 lax **4** fast,
  lewd, wild **5** loose, mixed
  6 casual, impure, medley, motley, rakish, wanton **7** aimless,

chaotic, diverse, immoral,
jumbled, mingled, mixed-up,
satyric **8** careless, confused,
immodest, sweeping, un-
chaste **9** composite, desultory,
dissolute, haphazard, perplexed, scrambled, wholesale
10 commingled, disordered,
disorderly, dissipated, intermixed, lascivious, licentious,
uncritical, undirected, unvir-
tuous, variegated **11** disarranged, incontinent,
indifferent, intemperate, unselective **12** disorganized, of
easy virtue, undiscerning
13 helter-skelter, heterogeneous, miscellaneous
14 indiscriminate

promise 3 vow **4** aver, avow,
  oath, word **5** agree, augur, imply, swear, troth, vouch **6** assure, avowal, hint of, parole,
  pledge, plight **7** be bound, betoken, suggest, warrant **8** covenant, indicate, warranty
  9 agreement, assurance, guarantee, potential, undertake
  11 declaration, stipulation,
  swear an oath, word of honor

Promised Land 6 Canaan
  nickname of: **10** California
    6 Israel

Promises
  author: **16** Robert Penn
    Warren

promising 4 rosy **5** happy,
  lucky **6** bright, rising **7** hopeful **8** assuring, cheerful, cheering **9** advancing, favorable,
  fortunate, looking up **10** auspicious, of good omen, optimistic, propitious, reassuring
  11 encouraging, inspiriting,
  up-and-coming

promissory note 3 IOU
  4 bond, chit **6** pledge **7** promise **9** agreement **10** obligation
  11 certificate

promontory 4 cape, hill, ness,
  spur **5** bluff, cliff, jetty, jutty,
  point **6** height **8** headland,
  overhang **9** peninsula, precipice **10** embankment,
  projection

promote 3 aid **4** abet, ease,
  help, plug, push **5** raise **6** assist, foster, prefer, refine **7** advance, develop, elevate,
  enhance, forward, further,
  support, upgrade, work for
  8 advocate, expedite, graduate
  9 advertise, cultivate, encourage, publicize

promoter 6 backer **8** advocate,
  champion **9** proponent,
  supporter

promotion 4 hype **5** raise
  7 advance, fanfare, puffery

8 ballyhoo, boosting, progress
  9 elevation, publicity, upgrad-
  ing **10** preferment **11** advancement, advertising,
  furtherance **12** promulgation
  13 advertisement,
  encouragement

promotive 7 helpful **9** conducive **10** beneficial **12** contributive, contributory, instrumental

prompt 3 cue **4** goad, keen,
  move, prod, push, spur, stir
  5 alert, alive, cause, drive, eager, force, impel, press, quick,
  ready, sharp **6** active, assist,
  bright, excite, incite, induce,
  intent, lively, on time, propel,
  remind, thrust, timely **7** actuate, animate, dispose, help
  out, incline, inspire, instant,
  on guard, provoke, zealous
  8 activate, inspirit, motivate,
  occasion, open-eyed, persuade,
  punctual, vigilant, watchful
  9 attentive, determine, efficient, immediate, influence,
  instigate, observant, open-
  eared, stimulate, wide-awake
  10 on one's toes **12** jog the
  memory, unhesitating
  13 instantaneous

prompting 6 cueing, urging
  7 goading **8** egging on **10** motivation **11** exhortation

promptly 3 pat **4** anon, soon,
  tite **6** pronto **7** quickly,
  swiftly **10** punctually
  11 immediately

promptness 5 haste **8** alacrity,
  celerity, dispatch **9** quickness,
  readiness, swiftness **11** punc-
  tuality **15** expeditiousness

promulgate 6 foster **7** explain,
  expound, present, promote,
  sponsor **8** instruct, set forth
  9 elucidate, enunciate, interpret **11** communicate

promulgation 9 fostering, promotion **11** circulation, instruction, sponsorship
  12 distribution, presentation,
  transmission **13** communication **14** interpretation

Pronaus
  epithet of: **6** Athena
  means: **12** of the pronaos
    pronaos: **15** before the
      temple

prone 3 apt **4** flat **5** level **6** liable, likely **7** subject, tending
  8 disposed, face-down, inclined **9** prostrate, reclining,
  recumbent **10** accustomed, habituated, horizontal **11** predisposed, susceptible

proneness 4 bent, bias, turn
  7 leaning **8** penchant, tendency **9** prejudice **10** proclivity, propensity **11** inclination

12 predilection
14 predisposition

prong 4 barb, hook, horn, spur, tine **5** point, spike, tooth **6** branch **10** projection

Pronoea
epithet of: 6 Athena
means: 11 forethought

pronoun 2 he, it, me, my, us, we, ye **3** all, any, few, her, his, one, she, thy, who, you **4** hers, mine, ours, some, thee, them, they, that, this, thou, what, whom **5** no one, their, these, thine, those, which, whose, yours **6** anyone, itself, myself, nobody **7** anybody, herself, himself, nothing, someone, whoever **8** somebody, whomever **9** everybody, something, whosoever **10** everything, themselves
French: 2 il, je, tu **3** lui, mes, moi **4** elle, vous
German: 2 er, es, du **3** ich, mir, sie **4** mein, mich
Italian: 2 io, me, mi, ti, tu, vi **3** cio, lei, lui, mio, tei, voi **4** egli, ella, essa, esse, essi, loro
Spanish: 2 el, la, lo, me, mi, tu, yo **4** ella, ello, suyo, tuyo **5** usted

pronounce 3 say **4** emit, form, rule **5** frame, judge, orate, sound, speak, state, utter, voice **6** decree **7** declare, enounce **8** announce, proclaim, vocalize **9** enunciate **10** articulate

pronounced 4 bold **5** broad, clear, plain, vivid **6** patent **7** decided, evident, obvious, visible **8** apparent, clear-cut, definite, distinct, manifest, positive, unhidden **9** arresting **10** noticeable **11** conspicuous, outstanding, undisguised, well-defined **12** recognizable, unmistakable **14** unquestionable

pronouncement 6 decree **11** declaration **12** announcement, proclamation

pronto 3 now **4** asap, fast, stat **5** quick **7** quickly **8** promptly **11** immediately

Pronuba
epithet of: 4 Juno

pronunciamento 5 edict **12** proclamation **13** pronouncement

pronunciation 6 accent **10** inflection **11** enunciation **12** articulation **16** manner of speaking

proof 4 test **5** essay, proof, sheet, trial **6** galley, ordeal **8** scrutiny, weighing **9** probation **10** assessment **11** attestation, examination **12** confirmation, ratification, verification **13** certification, corroboration, documentation **14** substantiation

proofreader's mark 3 cap, rom **4** dele, ital, stet **5** caret, space

prop 3 set **4** lean, rest, stay **5** brace, stand **6** hold up, pillar **7** bolster, shore up, support **8** buttress, mainstay, shoulder, underpin **9** stanchion, supporter, sustainer **13** reinforcement
French: 11 point d'appui

propaganda 6 hoopla **8** ballyhoo **9** party line, promotion, publicity **10** persuasion **11** advertising

propagandist 6 zealot **8** activist, exponent **9** apologist, proponent, publicist **12** spokesperson

propagate 3 air, sow **4** bear, tell **5** beget, breed, hatch, issue, rumor, spawn, spray **6** blazon, herald, impart, notify, preach, purvey, repeat, report, spread **7** bestrew, give out, implant, instill, publish, scatter, trumpet **8** disperse, engender, generate, increase, multiply, proclaim, put forth **9** broadcast, circulate, enunciate, give birth, inculcate, make known, procreate, publicize, reproduce

propagation 6 laying, siring **7** bearing **8** breeding, hatching, issuance, spawning, yielding **9** begetting, diffusion, gestation, pregnancy, spreading **10** dispersion, generation **11** circulation, engendering, giving birth, procreation, publication **12** distribution, reproduction, transmission **13** dissemination

pro patria 14 for one's country

propel 4 cast, goad, hurl, poke, prod, push, send, toss **5** drive, eject, force, heave, impel, pitch, shoot, shove, sling, start **6** launch, thrust **7** project **8** catapult **9** discharge **11** precipitate, set in motion

propeller, screw
invented by: 7 Stevens **8** Ericsson

propensity 4 bent, bias, turn **5** fancy, favor, taste **6** liking **7** leaning **8** affinity, penchant, pleasure, sympathy, tendency, weakness **9** prejudice **10** attraction, partiality, preference, proclivity **11** disposition, inclination **12** predilection **14** predisposition

proper 3 apt, fit, own **4** meet, nice, true **5** per se, right **6** decent, marked, modest, polite, seemly **7** apropos, correct, express, fitting, germane, precise, typical **8** assigned, becoming, decorous, orthodox, peculiar, relevant, specific, suitable **9** befitting, courteous, pertinent **10** acceptable, applicable, individual, particular, respective **11** appropriate, conformable, distinctive **12** conventional **14** characteristic, distinguishing, representative
French: 11 comme il faut

properly 5 aptly, right **7** exactly **8** decently, politely, suitably **9** correctly, perfectly, precisely **10** acceptably, accurately, decorously, tastefully **12** without error **13** appropriately **14** conventionally

property 4 hold, land, mark **5** acres, badge, funds, goods, means, point, stock, title, trait **6** aspect, assets, estate, moneys, realty, wealth **7** acreage, capital, earmark, effects, estates, feature, grounds, quality **8** chattels, holdings, treasure **9** attribute, ownership, resources, territory **10** belongings, real estate **11** investments, peculiarity, possessions, singularity **12** appointments, idiosyncrasy **13** individuality, particularity **14** characteristic, proprietorship

prophecy 6 augury **7** portent **8** forecast **10** divination, prediction, revelation **15** prognostication
god of: 6 Apollo **7** Phoebus, Pythius **9** Musagetes

prophesy 4 warn **5** augur **6** divine **7** forbode, foresee, portend, predict, presage **8** forecast, foretell, forewarn, soothsay **9** apprehend, premonish **13** prognosticate

prophet 4 seer **5** augur, guide, sibyl **6** oracle **7** diviner, palmist, seeress **8** preacher, sorcerer **9** Cassandra, divinator, geomancer, predictor, sorceress **10** evangelist, forecaster, foreteller, prophesier, prophetess, soothsayer **11** clairvoyant, intercessor, interpreter **12** crystal gazer **13** fortuneteller **14** prognosticator

Prophet, major 6 Baruch, Daniel, Elijah, Isaiah **7** Ezekiel **8** Jeremiah

Prophet, minor 3 Gad **4** Amos, Joel **5** Hosea, Jonah, Micah, Nahum **6** Haggai, Nathan **7** Malachi, Obadiah **8** Habakkuk **9** Zechariah, Zephaniah

Prophetess 4 Anna **6** Miriam **7** Deborah

prophetic, prophetical 5 vatic **6** mantic **7** fateful, ominous **8** oracular **10** portentous, predictive, presageful

Prophetic Books
author: **12** William Blake

Prophet of famine 11 Agabus

prophylactic 8 hygienic **10** preventive **13** contraceptive

propinquity 7 kinship **8** affinity, nearness, vicinity **9** closeness, proximity **10** similarity

propitiate 4 calm **5** allay **6** pacify, soothe **7** appease, assuage, mollify, placate **10** conciliate **11** accommodate

propitiation 8 soothing **11** appeasement **12** conciliation, pacification

propitious 3 fit **5** bonny, happy, lucky **6** benign, golden **8** suitable **9** agreeable, favorable, fortunate, opportune, promising, well-timed **10** auspicious, beneficial, felicitous **12** advantageous, providential

Propoetides
form: **7** maidens
home: **6** Cypria
changed into: **5** stone
angered: **9** Aphrodite
denied her: **8** divinity

proponent 6 backer, friend, patron, votary **7** booster **8** advocate, champion, defender, endorser, espouser, exponent, partisan, upholder **9** apologist, spokesman, supporter **10** enthusiast, vindicator **14** representative

proportion 5 ratio **7** balance, harmony **8** evenness, symmetry **9** agreement **11** consistency, correlation, perspective **12** distribution, relationship **14** commensuration, correspondence

proportionate 5 equal **8** balanced **10** comparable, equivalent **12** commensurate **13** commensurable, corresponding

proportions 3 fit, lot **4** area, bulk, form, gear, mass, part, size, span **5** adapt, gauge, grade, match, order, poise, quota, range, ratio, scope, shape, share, width **6** amount, degree, equate, extent, spread, volume **7** balance, breadth, conform, correct, expanse, measure, portion, rectify, segment **8** capacity, division, equalize, fraction, graduate, modulate, regulate **9** amplitude, apportion, greatness, harmonize, magnitude **10** dimensions **12** measurements

proposal 3 bid **4** idea, plan, plot, suit **5** draft, offer **6** appeal, course, design, motion, scheme, sketch, theory **7** outline, proffer, program, project **8** overture, prospect **9** stratagem **10** conception, invitation, nomination, prospectus, resolution, suggestion **11** proposition **12** presentation **14** recommendation

propose 3 aim, woo **4** hope, mean, plan, plot **6** aspire, design, expect, intend, scheme, submit, tender **7** advance, present, proffer, purpose, suggest, venture **8** affiance, propound, put forth, set about, set forth **9** determine, have a mind, introduce, recommend, undertake **10** come up with, have in mind, have in view, put forward **11** contemplate **14** pop the question **21** offer for consideration

proposition 4 deal, pass, plan **5** issue, offer, point, topic **6** matter, scheme **7** advance, bargain, solicit, subject **8** contract, proposal, question **9** agreement, assurance, guarantee **10** resolution, suggestion **11** make a pass at, negotiation, stipulation, undertaking **14** recommendation

propound 4 pose **5** boost **6** assert **7** advance, profess, propose **8** put forth, set forth

proprieties 7 decorum, manners **8** protocol **9** amenities, etiquette **10** civilities **11** conventions

proprietor 5 owner **6** holder, master **7** manager **8** landlord **9** landowner, possessor **10** landholder **11** titleholder **12** proprietress

propriety 7 aptness, decorum, dignity, fitness **8** courtesy **9** etiquette, formality, rightness **10** seemliness **11** correctness, good manners, savoir faire **12** becomingness, decorousness, good behavior, suit-

ableness **13** applicability **14** respectability **15** appropriateness

propulsion 6 launch, thrust **9** launching **10** propelling

prop up 5 brace **7** bolster, support **8** buttress

prorate 6 divide **9** apportion **10** distribute

Prorsa *see* **9** Antevorta

prosaic 3 dry **4** blah, dull, flat **5** prosy, stale, trite, vapid, wordy **6** common, jejune **7** humdrum, tedious **8** ordinary, plebeian, tiresome **9** hackneyed **10** monotonous, pedestrian, spiritless, unpoetical **12** matter-of-fact **13** platitudinous, unimaginative, uninteresting

Prosclystius
epithet of: **8** Poseidon
means: **7** flooder

proscribe 3 ban **4** damn **5** curse, exile **6** banish, forbid, outlaw **7** boycott, censure, condemn **8** denounce, prohibit **9** interdict, repudiate **10** disapprove **12** anathematize **13** excommunicate

proscription 3 ban **7** barring, censure **8** anathema **9** interdict **11** forbiddance, prohibition **12** condemnation, denunciation, interdiction **15** excommunication

prose 3 dry **4** dull **5** novel **7** fiction, quality, tedious, writing **8** sequence **9** discourse **10** expression **11** commonplace **13** unimaginative

prosecute 3 sue, try **4** wage **6** direct, go with, handle, indict, manage, pursue **7** arraign, carry on, conduct, execute, go to law, perform, prolong, stick to, sustain **8** continue, deal with, follow up, maintain **9** discharge, persist in **10** administer, put on trial, see through **11** take to court **12** bring to trial **14** bring to justice

prosecution 4 suit **6** action **7** conduct, pursuit **11** performance **14** administration

Proserpina *see* **10** Persephone

prosit 11 may it do good
used as: **5** toast

prospect, prospects 4 hope, plan, seek, view **5** scene, vista **6** aspect, design, search, vision **7** chances, explore, go after, look for, outlook, picture, promise, scenery **8** ambition, panorama, proposal

9 candidate, foretaste, intention, landscape, work a mine **10** expectancy, likelihood **11** expectation, possibility, probability **12** anticipation **13** contemplation

prospective 4 to be **6** coming, future, in view, likely, to come **7** looming **8** destined, eventual, expected, foreseen, hoped-for, intended, possible **9** about to be, impending, in the wind, looked-for, potential, promising **10** in prospect **11** approaching, forthcoming, threatening

prosper 4 gain **5** get on **6** flower, thrive **7** advance, succeed **8** fare well, flourish, fructify, get ahead, grow rich, increase, make good, progress **9** bear fruit **15** make one's fortune

prosperity 4 ease, gain **6** luxury, plenty, profit, wealth **7** advance, success, welfare **8** good luck, progress **9** abundance, advantage, affluence, blessings, golden age, good times, palmy days, run of luck, well-being **11** advancement, good fortune
   god of: 4 Frey **5** Freyr, Niord, Njord **12** Bonus Eventus
   goddess of: 5 Salus

Prospero
   character in: 10 The Tempest
   author: 11 Shakespeare

prosperous 4 fair, good, rich, rosy **5** happy, lucky, sunny **6** bright, golden, timely **7** hopeful, moneyed, opulent, smiling, wealthy, well-off **8** affluent, cheering, pleasing, thriving, well-to-do **9** favorable, fortunate, opportune, promising **10** auspicious, heartening, of good omen, propitious, reassuring, successful **11** comfortable, encouraging, flourishing **12** on easy street

Pross, Miss
   character in: 16 A Tale of Two Cities
   author: 7 Dickens

prostitute 4 bawd, jade, slut, tart **5** abuse, hussy, lower, spoil, whore **6** chippy, debase, defile, demean, floozy, harlot, hooker, misuse **7** cheapen, corrupt, debauch, degrade, hustler, pervert, profane, sell out, trollop **8** call girl, misapply, strumpet **9** courtesan, desecrate, misdirect, misemploy **12** streetwalker **14** lady of the night

prostrate 4 deck, flat **5** abase,

floor, prone, spent **6** fagged, kowtow **7** bow down, flatten, laid out, worn out **8** bowed low, overcome **9** bone weary, crouching, dead tired, exhausted, kneel down, lying flat, overthrow, recumbent **10** beseeching, horizontal **11** on one's knees **12** on bended knee, stretched out, supplicating **13** lying face down **15** fall to one's knees

prostration 3 bow, woe **5** grief **6** misery, sorrow **7** anguish, despair **8** distress, kneeling, weakness **9** abasement, dejection, heartache, impotence, lowliness, paralysis, weariness **10** depression, desolation, enervation, exhaustion, subjection, submission **11** desperation, despondency **12** genuflection, helplessness, wretchedness **13** depth of misery

prosy 4 dull, flat **5** banal, inane **6** stupid **7** humdrum, prosaic, tedious **9** wearisome **11** commonplace **13** uninteresting

protagonist 4 diva, hero, lead, star **7** heroine **9** headliner, principal, superstar, title role **10** leading man, prima donna **11** leading lady **12** danseur noble, jeune premier **13** jeune premiere, main character **14** prima ballerina **16** central character

protect 4 hide, keep, save, tend, veil **5** cover, guard **6** defend, harbor, screen, secure, shield **7** care for, shelter, sustain **8** conserve, maintain, preserve **9** look after, safeguard, watch over **10** take care of

protected 4 safe **5** saved **6** immune, secure **7** guarded, secured **8** anchored, defended, shielded **9** sheltered **10** inviolable **12** invulnerable

protection 3 aid **4** care, keep, wall **5** cover, fence, guard, haven, shade **6** asylum, buffer, charge, harbor, refuge, safety, saving, screen, shield **7** barrier, custody, defense, shelter, support **8** guarding, immunity, preserve, security **9** preserver, safeguard, sanctuary **10** assistance **11** safekeeping **12** championship, conservation, guardianship, preservation

protective 7 careful, heedful **8** fatherly, guarding, maternal, motherly, paternal, sisterly, vigilant, watchful **9** avuncular, brotherly, defensive, shielding

10 preventive, sheltering, solicitous **11** safekeeping **12** big-brotherly, safeguarding

protective covering 4 coat, hust, mail **5** armor, shell **6** shield **7** coating, plating **8** carapace **10** coat of mail **11** suit of armor **12** armor plating

protectorate 6 colony **7** mandate **8** province, dominion **9** satellite, territory **10** dependency, possession, settlement

protege 4 ward **5** pupil **6** charge **7** student, trainee **9** dependent

pro tempore 9 temporary **11** temporarily **15** for the time being

Protesilaus
   father: 8 Iphiclus
   brother: 8 Podarces
   wife: 8 Laodamia

protest 3 vow **4** aver, avow, beef, deny, kick **5** gripe, march, offer, sit-in, speak, state **6** affirm, allege, assert, assure, attest, avouch, cry out, insist, object, oppose, strike **7** boycott, contend, declare, dispute, dissent, hold out, profess, testify **8** announce, complain, demurral, disagree, maintain, propound, put forth, set forth **9** enunciate, objection, picketing, pronounce **10** asseverate, contradict, controvert, disapprove, disclaimer, dissidence, opposition, put forward, resistance **11** beg to differ, deprecation **12** disaffection, disagreement, remonstrance, renunciation **13** contradiction, demonstration, remonstration, take exception **14** discountenance

Protestant 5 Amish **6** Mormon, Quaker, Shaker **7** Baptist, Puritan **8** Anglican, Huguenot, Lutheran **9** Adventist, Calvinist, Methodist, Unitarian **12** Episcopalian, Presbyterian **17** Congregationalist **18** Christian Scientist

protest meeting 5 rally **13** demonstration

Proteus
   character in: 20 Two Gentlemen of Verona
   author: 11 Shakespeare

Proteus
   god of: 3 sea
   king of: 5 Egypt
   father: 7 Oceanus
   mother: 6 Tethys
   wife: 8 Psamathe
   son: 12 Theoclymenus
   daughter: 7 Theonoe

gift: 8 prophesy **12** form-changing **13** shape-changing

Prothoenor
leader of: 9 Boeotians

Protoceratops
type: 8 dinosaur **10** ceratopsid
period: 10 Cretaceous
location: 8 Mongolia **10** Gobi Desert
characteristic: 6 horned **7** armored

protocol 5 usage **7** customs, decorum, manners **8** good form **9** amenities, etiquette, formality, standards **11** conventions, proprieties **14** code of behavior, court etiquette, diplomatic code **17** dictates of society

Protogonia
father: 10 Erechtheus
mother: 9 Praxithea
sister: 7 Otionia

prototypal 5 model **7** classic **9** exemplary **10** archetypal, definitive **12** prototypical

prototype 5 model **7** example **8** original **9** archetype

protozoan 4 cell **5** ameba, cilia **6** amoeba **7** euglena **8** flagella, protista **9** eukaryote, pseudopod **10** paramecium, plasmodium **11** microscopic, unicellular **17** nonphotosynthetic

protract 6 extend, keep up **7** drag out, draw out, prolong, spin out **8** lengthen **9** keep going **10** stretch out

protracted 4 long **7** lengthy **8** drawn-out, extended **9** continued, long-lived, prolonged **10** lengthened, persistent **11** long-lasting

protraction 4 stay **7** lasting **9** extension **10** continuing, drawing out **11** continuance, dragging out, persistence **12** perseverance, prolongation

protrude 5 belly, bulge, swell **6** jut out **7** project **8** stand out, stick out **11** push forward

protrusion 4 bump, hump **6** hernia **8** swelling **9** extension **10** projection **12** prolongation, protuberance

protuberance 3 bow **4** bump, hump, knob, knot, lump, node, weal, welt **5** bulge, gnarl, ridge **6** rising **8** swelling **9** convexity, elevation, roundness **10** projection, prominence **11** excrescence, excurvature

protura
class: 8 hexapoda

phylum: 10 arthropoda
characteristic: 5 small **6** minute **7** eyeless **8** wingless

proud 4 fine, smug, vain **5** aloof, cocky, grand, great, happy, lofty, noble **6** august, lordly, snooty, snotty, strict, uppish, uppity **7** bloated, exalted, haughty, high-hat, pleased, pompous, revered, stately, storied, stuck-up, swollen **8** affected, arrogant, assuming, boastful, braggart, bragging, elevated, euphoric, glorious, inflated, insolent, majestic, prideful, puffed up, reserved, snobbish **9** admirable, cherished, conceited, contented, delighted, dignified, flaunting, gratified, honorable, imperious, know-it-all, satisfied, venerable **10** complacent, disdainful, high-minded, intolerant, principled, scrupulous **11** egotistical, independent, magnificent, overbearing, patronizing, punctilious **12** contemptuous, self-praising, supercilious, vainglorious **13** condescending, distinguished, high-and-mighty, self-important, self-satisfied **14** self-respecting, self-sufficient

Proudie, Dr
character in: 16 Barchester Towers
author: 8 Trollope

Proust, Marcel
author of: 23 Remembrance of Things Past **24** A la Recherche du Temps Perdu

prove 3 try **4** test **5** check, end up, probe **6** affirm, attest, result, try out, uphold, verify, wind up **7** analyze, bear out, certify, confirm, examine, justify, support, sustain, warrant, witness **8** document, evidence, look into, make good, manifest, result in, validate **9** ascertain, establish, eventuate, testify to **11** corroborate, demonstrate **12** authenticate, substantiate

proved 5 known **6** proven, upheld **8** affirmed, attested, borne out, verified **9** certified, confirmed, supported, sustained, warranted, witnessed **10** documented **11** established **12** corroborated, demonstrable **13** authenticated, substantiated

prove false 5 belie **6** refute, reject **7** explode **8** disprove **9** discredit **10** invalidate

proven 5 known **6** proved, upheld **8** accepted, affirmed, attested, borne out, verified

9 certified, confirmed, supported, sustained, warranted, witnessed **10** documented, verifiable **11** established **12** corroborated, demonstrable **13** authenticated, substantiated

provender 3 hay **4** chow, corn, eats, feed, food, grub, oats **5** grain **6** fodder, forage, ration, viands **7** nurture **10** provisions **11** subsistence

proverb 3 mot, saw **5** adage, axiom, maxim, moral, motto **6** byword, cliche, dictum, saying, truism **7** bromide, epigram, precept **8** aphorism, apothegm **9** platitude **11** commonplace **13** accepted truth, popular saying

prove wrong 5 belie **6** expose, refute **7** explode **8** disprove **9** discredit

provide 3 arm, fit, pay **4** give, plan **5** allow, award, cater, equip, grant, offer, state, yield **6** accord, afford, bestow, confer, donate, impart, outfit, render, save up, submit, supply, tender **7** arrange, deliver, furnish, prepare, present, produce, require, specify **8** dispense, get ready **9** make plans, postulate, stipulate **10** accumulate, contribute

provide for 7 care for **8** attend to, wait upon **9** look after **10** minister to, take care of

providence 8 prudence **9** foresight, husbandry, provision **11** forethought **14** circumspection, farsightedness, forehandedness

provident 4 wary **5** chary, ready **6** frugal, saving **7** careful, prudent, thrifty **8** cautious, discreet, equipped, vigilant **9** farseeing, judicious **10** discerning, economical, farsighted, forehanded, foreseeing, thoughtful **11** circumspect, foresighted, precautious **12** parsimonious, well-prepared

province 3 job **4** area, duty, part, role, zone **5** field, place, state **6** canton, charge, county, domain, office, region, sphere **7** section, station **8** business, capacity, function **9** authority, bailiwick, territory **10** assignment, department **11** subdivision **12** jurisdiction **13** scope of duties **14** arrondissement, responsibility

provincial 4 rude **5** crude, gawky, local, rough, rural **6** clumsy, gauche, homely, narrow, oafish, rustic **7** awkward, boorish, bucolic, country, hayseed, insular, loutish **8** cloddish, clownish, downhome, homespun, regional, yokelish **9** backwoods, parochial, small-town, unrefined **10** unpolished **11** clodhopping, countrified, territorial **15** unsophisticated

provision 6 giving **8** donation **9** endowment, providing, supplying **10** furnishing

provisional 6 acting, pro tem **7** interim **9** surrogate, temporary, tentative **10** substitute **11** conditional **12** probationary **15** for the time being

provisions 4 feed, food, term **6** clause, fodder, forage, stores, string, viands **7** article, commons, edibles, proviso **8** eatables, supplies, victuals **9** condition, groceries, provender, readiness, requisite **10** limitation, obligation, precaution, sustenance **11** arrangement, comestibles, forethought, preparation, requirement, reservation, restriction, stipulation, wherewithal **12** anticipation, modification **13** qualification **14** forehandedness, prearrangement

proviso 5 rider **6** clause, string **8** addition **9** amendment, condition **10** limitation **11** requirement, restriction, stipulation **12** modification **13** qualification

provocation 4 goad, spur **5** cause, pique **6** insult, slight **7** affront, offense **8** prodding, stimulus, vexation **9** actuation, annoyance **10** excitation, incitement, irritation, motivation **11** aggravation, fomentation, instigation, stimulation **12** perturbation

provocative 4 sexy **6** vexing **7** irksome **8** alluring, annoying, arousing, exciting, inviting, tempting **9** beguiling, provoking, ravishing, seductive, thrilling, vexatious **10** attractive, bewitching, enchanting, entrancing, intriguing, irritating **11** aggravating, captivating, fascinating, stimulating, tantalizing **12** intoxicating, irresistible

provoke 3 irk, vex **4** fire, gall, move, rile, stir **5** anger, annoy, cause, chafe, evoke, grate, impel, pique, rouse **6** arouse, awaken, compel, create, effect, elicit, enrage, excite, foment, incite, induce, kindle, madden, prompt, put out, stir up **7** actuate, agitate,

animate, bring on, incense, inflame, inspire, outrage, produce, quicken **8** generate, get to one, irritate, motivate **9** aggravate, call forth, establish, galvanize, infuriate, instigate, stimulate **10** bring about, exasperate, give rise to **11** get one's goat, put in motion **15** try one's patience **16** get under one's skin

prow 3 bow **4** stem **5** front **10** forward end

prowess 4 grit, guts **5** knack, might, nerve, power, skill, spunk, valor, vigor **6** daring, genius, mettle, spirit, talent **7** ability, bravery, courage, faculty, heroism, know-how, stamina **8** aptitude, boldness, strength **9** adeptness, derring-do, endurance, fortitude, gallantry, hardihood **10** competence, expertness **11** intrepidity, proficiency **12** fearlessness, skillfulness **13** dauntlessness **14** accomplishment

prowl 4 hunt, lurk, roam **5** creep, range, skulk, slink, snack, stalk, steal **6** ramble **8** scavenge

prowler 7 burglar **10** peeping Tom **16** suspicious person

proximate 4 near **5** close **6** beside, nearby, next to **8** adjacent, imminent, next-door **11** forthcoming

proximity 7 presence **8** locality, nearness, vicinity **9** closeness **10** contiguity **11** propinquity **12** togetherness

proxy 3 sub **4** vote **5** agent **6** ballot, deputy **7** stand-in **9** alternate **10** substitute

prude 4 prig **6** modest **7** puritan **9** hypocrite **10** goody-goody **13** prim and proper

prudence 4 care, tact **6** thrift, wisdom **7** caution, economy **9** austerity, foresight, frugality, parsimony **10** discretion, precaution **11** calculation, thriftiness **14** thoughtfulness

prudent 4 sage, sane, wary, wise **5** chary **6** frugal, saving, shrewd **7** careful, guarded, heedful, politic, sapient, sparing, thrifty **8** cautious, discreet, prepared, rational, sensible, vigilant **9** expedient, judicious, provident, sagacious, wideawake **10** discerning, economical, farsighted, prudential, reflecting, thoughtful **11** circumspect, considerate, foresighted, levelheaded,

precautious, well-advised **13** self-possessed

Prud'hon, Pierre-Paul
    born: **5** Cluny **6** France
    artwork: **14** Venus and Adonis **15** The Rape of Psyche **16** Empress Josephine **33** Crime Pursued by Vengeance and Justice **38** Justice and Divine Vengeance Pursuing Crime

prudish 3 shy **4** prim, smug **5** timid **6** demure, modest, prissy, queasy, stuffy **7** finical, mincing, precise, stilted **8** pedantic, priggish, skittish, starched **9** squeamish, Victorian **10** fastidious, old-maidish, overmodest, particular **11** punctilious, puritanical, straitlaced **13** sanctimonious, self-righteous

prudishness 8 primness **10** prissiness, puritanism **11** overmodesty **12** overdelicacy, priggishness ·**14** overrefinement

prudish phrase 9 euphemism **10** bowdlerism

prune 3 cut, lop **4** clip, crop, pull, snip, thin, trim **5** shear **6** reduce **7** abridge, clarify, curtail, shorten, thin out **8** condense, simplify **10** abbreviate

prunelle
    type: **7** liqueur
    origin: **6** France
    flavor: **4** plum

pruning 6 digest **8** clipping, snipping, synopsis, trimming **10** shortening **11** abridgement, cutting back, cut-down form **12** abbreviation, condensation

prurient 4 lewd, sexy **6** carnal **7** fleshy, goatish, immoral, lustful, obscene, priapic, satyric **9** lecherous, salacious **10** hot-blooded, lascivious, libidinous, licentious, lubricious, passionate **12** concupiscent

pry 4 butt, nose, peek, peer, poke, tear, work, worm **5** break, crack, delve, force, jimmy, lever, mix in, prize, probe, smoke, sniff, snoop, wrest, wring **6** butt in, ferret, horn in, meddle, search, winkle, wrench **7** explore, extract, inquire, intrude, squeeze **9** interfere, intervene **15** stick one's nose in

Pryderi
    origin: **5** Welsh
    father: **5** Pwyll
    mother: **8** Rhiannon
    stolen by: **5** Gwawl
    wife: **5** Kicva

prying 4 busy, nosy **7** peering, raising, seeking **8** levering, snooping **9** searching **10** intrusive, meddling **11** inquisitive

Prylis
father: **6** Hermes

Prynne, Hester
character in: **16** The Scarlet Letter
author: **9** Hawthorne

Pryor, Richard
born: **8** Peoria IL
roles: **6** The Wiz **9** Stir Crazy **12** Silver Streak **17** Lady Sings the Blues **19** Uptown Saturday Night

Prytanis
ally of: **8** Sarpedon
killed by: **8** Odysseus

psalm 3 ode **4** hymn, poem, song **5** canon, chant, verse **6** praise **7** cantata, glorify, introit **8** canticle

Psalter 12 Book of Psalms

Psamathe
member of: **6** Nereid
form: **8** princess
husband: **7** Proteus
son: **5** Linus **6** Phocus **12** Theoclymenus
daughter: **7** Theonoe

pseudo 4 fake, mock, sham **5** bogus, false, phony **6** forged **7** feigned **8** spurious **9** pretended, simulated, soi-disant **10** fictitious, fraudulent, self-styled **11** counterfeit, make-believe **13** self-described

pseudonym 5 alias **6** anonym **7** pen name **8** cognomen, nickname **9** false name, sobriquet, stage name **11** assumed name **16** professional name
French: **10** nom de plume **11** nom de guerre **12** nom de theatre

pseudonymic 7 assumed **10** fictitious **12** pseudonymous

pseudonymous 7 assumed **10** fictitious **11** pseudonymic

Psittacosaurus
type: **8** dinosaur **10** ceratopsid
period: **10** Cretaceous

psocoptera
class: **8** hexapoda
phylum: **10** arthropoda
group: **8** booklice

psyche 2 id **3** ego **4** mind, self, soul **5** anima **6** bowels, make up, spirit **8** superego **10** penetralia **11** personality, unconscious **12** subconscious

Psyche
personifies: **4** soul

loved by: **4** Eros **5** Cupid
daughter: **8** Voluptas

psychic 5 augur **6** medium, mental, mystic, occult, voyant **7** diviner, prophet, voyante **8** cerebral **9** paragnost, sensitive, spiritual **10** soothsayer, telepathic **11** clairvoyant, telekinetic, telepathist **12** extrasensory, intellectual, spiritualist, supernatural, supersensory **13** preternatural

Psycho
director: **15** Alfred Hitchcock
cast: **9** John Gavin, Vera Miles **10** Janet Leigh **12** Martin Balsam **14** Anthony Perkins
score: **15** Bernard Herrmann

psychoanalysis 7 therapy **8** analysis **14** physchotherapy

psychoanalyst 6 shrink **7** analyst **12** headshrinker

psychologist/psychiatrist
American: **4** Hall, Hull **5** Dewey, James, Lewin **6** Harlow, Horney, Miller, Rogers, Terman, Tolman, Watson, Witmer **7** Cattell, Chomsky, Erikson, Goddard, Guthrie, Johnson, Masters, Skinner **8** Brothers, Wechsler **9** Thorndike **10** Westheimer
Austrian: **5** Adler, Freud, Reich
British: **5** Ellis **7** Eysenck **9** Titchener
French: **5** Binet
German: **5** Wundt **6** Koffka, Kohler **7** Fechner **9** Helmholtz, Kraepelin **10** Ebbinghaus, Wertheimer **11** Krafft-Ebing
Russian: **6** Pavlov
Swiss: **4** Jung **6** Piaget

psychology *see box*

psychopomp
conductor of spirits to: **5** Hades **10** otherworld
epithet: **12** psychopompus
epithet of: **6** Charon, Hermes

psychosis 8 dementia, insanity, neurosis, paranoia **9** paranomia, unreality **10** pathomania **12** hallucinosis **13** schizophrenia **14** mental disorder

psychotherapy 7 therapy **8** analysis **14** psychoanalysis

psychotic 3 mad, nut **4** kook, loon **5** crazy, kooky, loony, nutty **6** insane, madman, maniac **7** lunatic **8** demented, deranged **9** disturbed **10** psychopath **12** insane person, psychopathic **15** non compos mentis

psychology 4 head, mind **6** makeup **7** feeling **8** attitude **15** mental processes
problem/illness: **6** phobia **7** obesity, smoking **8** hysteria, neuroses, paranoia, schizoid **9** drug abuse, obsession, psychoses **10** alcoholism, compulsion, depression **11** sociopathic **13** schizophrenia **14** sexual deviance **15** anxiety reaction **17** passive-aggressive
term: **2** id **3** ego **6** libido **7** empathy **8** neuroses, superego **9** catatonic, cognition, psychoses **10** inhibition, repression **11** behaviorism, unconscious **12** conditioning, transference **13** actualization, Rorschach test **14** identification, Oedipus complex **19** operant conditioning **20** behavior modification
type: **6** social **7** Gestalt **8** abnormal, clinical **9** cognitive **10** industrial **11** educational **12** experimental **13** developmental, physiological, psychometrics, psychophysics

Ptah
origin: **8** Egyptian
diety of: **17** universal creation
worshiped at: **7** Memphis

Pterelaus
descendant of: **8** Poseidon
mother: **9** Hippothoe
daughter: **8** Comaetho

Ptolemy
author of: **8** Almagest **9** Geography

Ptous
father: **7** Athamas
mother: **8** Themisto

pub 3 bar, inn **5** local **6** bistro, saloon, lounge, tavern **7** barroom, ginmill, rummery, rumshop, taproom **8** alehouse, grogshop, pothouse **9** roadhouse, speakeasy **10** beer parlor **11** public house

pubescent 7 teenage **8** immature, juvenile **10** adolescent

public *see box*

publication 4 book, news **5** is-

public 3 mob **4** folk, open **5** civic, civil, frank, overt, plain, state, trade **6** buyers, common, in view, masses, nation, patent, people, shared, social **7** evident, exposed, general, in sight, obvious, outward, patrons, popular, society, visible **8** apparent, audience, communal, divulged, everyone, manifest, national, passable, populace, revealed, societal, unbarred, unfenced **9** available, citizenry, clientele, community, disclosed, followers, following, free to all, hoi polloi, multitude, notorious, political, statewide, unabashed, unashamed, unbounded, used by all **10** accessible, attendance, nationwide, not private, observable, population, purchasers, recognized, supporters, unenclosed **11** body politic, bourgeoisie, commonality, conspicuous, countrywide, discernible, perceivable, proletariat, rank and file, unconcealed, undisguised **12** acknowledged, constituency, unobstructed, unrestricted **14** community-owned

sue, paper **6** digest, report **7** edition, gazette, journal, tabloid **8** bulletin, magazine, pamphlet **9** broadcast, newspaper **10** periodical **11** circulation, information **12** announcement, notification

public disturbance 4 riot **6** fracas, ruckus, uproar **7** turmoil **9** commotion

public house 3 bar, pub **5** local **6** saloon, tavern **7** gin mill, taproom **8** alehouse **9** roadhouse

publicity 4 hype, plug, puff **5** blurb, flack **7** build-up, puffery, write-up **8** ballyhoo, currency **9** attention, notoriety, promotion **10** propaganda, publicness **11** advertising, circulation, information **12** promulgation, public notice, salesmanship

publicize 4 hype, plug, puff, push, sell **6** herald **7** acclaim, promote **8** announce, ballyhoo, emblazon, proclaim **9** advertise, broadcast, make known,

propagate **10** make public, promulgate **11** circularize **12** propagandize

publicly
    Latin: **11** coram populo

public matter
    Latin: **10** res publica

public notice 5 edict, ukase **6** decree **8** bulletin **9** manifesto **12** proclamation **13** pronouncement **14** pronunciamento
    French: **7** affiche

public speaking 7 oratory **9** lecturing **12** speechmaking

public-spirited 8 generous **10** altruistic, benevolent **12** humanitarian

publish 3 air **4** tell, vent **5** issue, print, utter **6** herald, impart, put out, spread **7** declare, diffuse, divulge, give out, placard, promote, release, trumpet **8** announce, bring out, disclose, proclaim **9** advertise, broadcast, circulate, make known, propagate, publicize **10** make public, promulgate, put to press **11** communicate, disseminate

Puca
    also: **5** Pooka
    origin: **5** Irish
    form: **6** spirit
    corresponds to: **4** Puck

Puccini, Giacomo
    born: **5** Italy, Lucca
    composer of: **5** Tosca **8** La Boheme, Turandot **12** Manon Lescaut **14** Madam Butterfly **15** Madama Butterfly **18** La Fanciulla del West **22** The Girl of the Golden West

puce 3 red **7** dark red **13** purplish-brown

Puck
    also: **15** Robin Goodfellow
    character in: **21** A Midsummer Night's Dream
    author: **11** Shakespeare
    form: **6** spirit
    characteristic:
    11 mischievous
    corresponds to: **4** Puca **5** Pooka

pucker 4 fold, tuck **5** pinch, pleat, purse **6** crease, gather, ruffle, rumple, shrink **7** crinkle, crumble, squeeze, wrinkle **8** compress, contract **12** draw together

puckered 6 pursed, rucked, tucked **7** creased, crinkly, pinched, pleated **8** crinkled, gathered, wrinkled **10** compressed, corrugated

puckish 5 elfin **6** impish **7** playful **8** annoying **9** whimsical **11** mischievous

pudding 5 jello **6** junket **7** custard, dessert, tapioca **8** pandowdy **9** charlotte, yorkshire **14** floating island

pudgy, podgy 3 fat **5** buxom, dumpy, obese, plump, squat, stout, tubby **6** chubby, chunky, fleshy, rotund, stocky, stubby **7** paunchy **8** roly-poly, thickset

Pueblo (Cliff Dwellers)
    language family: **4** Tewa, Zuni **6** Queres, Tanoan **10** Shoshonean
    tribe: **4** Hopi, Tiwa, Towa, Tuei **5** Acoma, Kiowa **6** Isleta
    location: **4** Utah **7** Arizona **8** Colorado **9** New Mexico
    noted for: **5** adobe **12** architecture
    spirit: **7** Kachina **8** Katchina

puerile 3 raw **5** green, inane, petty, silly, vapid **6** callow, simple **7** babyish, foolish, trivial **8** childish, immature, juvenile, piddling **9** childlike, frivolous, infantile, senseless, worthless **10** irrational, ridiculous, sophomoric **11** harebrained, nonsensical

Puerto Rico *see box, p. 794*

puff 3 bow **4** blow, draw, emit, gasp, hump, node, pant, plug, suck, wisp **5** bloat, blurb, bulge, heave, smoke, swell, whiff **6** blow up, breath, dilate, exhale, expand, extend, flurry, inhale, rising, wheeze **7** bluster, bombast, distend, inflate, puffery, stretch **8** ballyhoo, be winded, dilation, encomium, flattery, flummery, swelling **9** convexity, discharge, elevation, euphemism, extension, inflation, panegyric, publicity, sales talk **10** be inflated, distention, exhalation, overpraise, protrusion, tuberosity **11** be distended, breathe hard, excrescence, excurvature **12** exaggeration, inflammation, protuberance, protuberancy **13** overlaudation **16** overcommendation **17** misrepresentation

puffed 5 baggy **7** bulbous, swollen **9** ballooned

puffed up 4 vain **5** proud, puffy **7** swollen **8** inflated **9** conceited **11** swell-headed **12** vainglorious **13** self-important

puffery 4 hype **7** big talk, blus-

Puerto Rico
  name means: 8 rich port
  other name: 9 Borinquen 15 San Juan Bautista
  capital/largest city: 7 San Juan
  others: 5 Cayey, Coamo, Lares, Ponce 6 Caguas, Dorado, Manati, Utuado 7 Arecibo, Bayamon, Fajardo, Guanica, Guayama, Humacao 8 Adjuntas, Cabo Rojo, Mayaguez 9 Aquadilla 11 Santa Isabel
  government: 32 self-governing commonwealth of the U S
  measure: 6 cuerda 10 caballeria
  island: 4 Mona 7 Culebra, Vieques 13 Caja de Muertos 15 Greater Antilles
  lake: 5 Loiza 6 Carite 8 Dos Bocas 9 Caonillas, Guatajaca
  mountain: 4 Toro 5 Cayey 6 Yunque 8 Guilarte, Luquilla 10 Torrecilla 17 Cordillera Central
  highest point: 5 Punta
  river: 5 Camuy, Canas, Loiza, Yauco 6 Anasco, Manati, Tanama 7 Arecibo, Fajardo, La Plata 9 Caonillas
  sea: 8 Atlantic 9 Caribbean
  physical feature:
    bay: 5 Sucia 6 Rincon 8 Boqueron 9 Aquadilla 14 Phosphorescent
    sound: 7 Vieques
  people: 6 gibaro 10 borinqueno
    explorer: 8 Columbus 11 Ponce de Leon
    leader: 10 Munoz Marin
  language: 7 English, Spanish
  religion: 10 Protestant 13 Roman Catholic
  place:
    area of San Juan: 7 Hato Rey 10 Rio Piedras
    beach: 7 Condado
    cathedral: 15 San Juan Bautista
    fortress: 7 El Morro 11 San Jeronimo 12 San Cristobal
    governor's residence: 11 La Fortaleza
    museum: 14 El Museo de Ponce
    reservoir: 5 Loiza
    tomb: 11 Ponce de Leon
  feature:
    bird: 4 rola 7 yeguita
    festival: 6 Casals
    housing development: 14 urbanizaciones
    song: 9 aguinaldo
    strolling musicians: 9 parrandas
    tree: 4 mora 5 yafua, yaray 8 emajagua, guayrote 10 guaranguao
  food:
    dish: 4 sama, sisi 9 moreillas 11 lechon asado
    drink: 3 rum 10 anis-golila

ter, bombast 9 hyperbole 11 braggadocio

puff out 5 bloat, bulge, swell 6 billow, expand 7 balloon, distend, enlarge, inflate

puffy 3 fat 5 round 6 fleshy 7 bloated, bulging, swollen 8 enlarged, expanded, inflamed, inflated, puffed up 9 corpulent, distended

pugilist 3 pug 5 boxer 7 battler, bruiser, fighter 12 prizefighter

pugnacious 7 defiant, hostile, warlike 8 menacing, militant 9 bellicose, combative, fractious 10 aggressive, un-friendly 11 belligerent, contentious, quarrelsome, threatening 12 antagonistic, disputatious 13 argumentative

pugnacity 9 hostility 10 antagonism 12 belligerence 13 combativeness 14 aggressiveness, fighting spirit 15 contentiousness

puissance 5 force, might, power 6 energy 7 potency, prowess 8 strength

pulchritude 6 beauty 8 fairness 9 bonniness, good looks 10 comeliness, loveliness, prettiness 12 gorgeousness, handsomeness 13 beauteousness, exquisiteness 14 attractiveness, personableness

pulchritudinous 4 fair, fine 5 bonny 6 comely, lovely, pretty 8 gorgeous, handsome 9 beauteous, beautiful, ravishing 10 attractive 11 good-looking

Pulitzer
  author: 10 W A Swanberg

Pulitzer Prize
  originator: 14 Joseph Pulitzer
  administered by: 18 Columbia University
  awarded for: 4 play 5 drama, music, novel 6 poetry 7 cartoon, feature, fiction, letters 9 biography, criticism, editorial, reporting 10 commentary, journalism, literature, nonfiction 11 photography 13 autobiography

pull 2 go 3 lug, rip, tow, tug 4 drag, draw, grab, haul, jerk, lure, move, rend, rive, tear, yank 5 drive, sever, shake, split, trawl, troll, twist, wrest, wring 6 allure, appeal, detach, dig out, entice, remove, sprain, strain, uproot, wrench 7 attract, draw out, extract, gravity, stretch, weed out 8 withdraw 9 extirpate, influence, magnetism, take in tow 10 allurement, attraction, enticement 11 fascination 14 attractiveness

pull apart 3 rip, tug 4 drag, rend, tear 6 detach, wrench 7 extract 8 separate 9 criticize, disengage 10 disconnect

pull away 5 wrest 7 remove 8 drawback, withdraw

pull back 7 back off, retreat 8 fall back, withdraw

Pullman, George Mortimer
  nationality: 8 American
  developed: 9 (railroad) dining car 11 (railroad) sleeping car

pull off 4 pull 6 commit, effect 7 execute, perform 8 carry out 10 perpetuate 13 participate in

pull on 3 don 5 put on 7 get into

pull one's leg 3 kid 4 fool, hoax 5 tease, trick 7 deceive 9 make fun of

pull out 5 leave 7 draw out, extract 8 withdraw

pull over, pullover 4 cite, stop 5 shirt 6 arrest, jersey, slip on, ticket, t-shirt 7 maillot, sweater 8 slip over

pull together 4 join 5 unite

7 pitch in, share in **8** take part **9** cooperate, join hands **10** act jointly, join forces **11** collaborate, participate

pull to pieces 5 shred **6** tear up **7** destroy **9** tear apart

pull up 4 halt, rein, stop, weed **5** check, hoist **6** arrest, uplift, uproot **7** extract, reprove

pulp 4 curd, mash, mush, pith **5** crush, flesh, paste, puree, slush, smash **6** squash, tissue **7** journal **8** magazine **9** masticate

pulsate 4 beat, tick, wave **5** pound, pulse, shake, throb, thump, waver **6** quaver, quiver, shiver **7** flutter, shudder, tremble, vibrate **8** undulate **9** alternate, come and go, oscillate, palpitate **10** ebb and flow **11** reverberate

pulse 4 beat **5** throb, thump **6** quiver, rhythm, stroke **7** cadence, pulsate, shudder, tremble, vibrate **9** oscillate, palpitate, pulsation, vibration **10** recurrence, undulation **11** oscillation, palpitation

pulverize 4 mash, mill **5** crumb, crush, grind, mince, pound **6** powder **7** atomize, crumble **9** comminate, granulate, triturate **12** reduce to dust

pulverized 6 ground, milled **7** crumbed, crushed, pounded **8** atomized, crumbled, crunched, powdered **10** granulated **12** ground to dust

pummel 4 beat, maul **5** pound **6** batter, thrash **7** trounce

pump 4 quiz, shoe, well **5** grill **7** inflate, slipper **8** question **9** draw water

Pump
    constellation of: **6** Antlia

Pump House Gang, The
    author: **8** Tom Wolfe

pumpkin 5 fruit, gourd, melon **6** squash **9** vegetable **12** jack o'lantern

pun
    French: **9** jeu de mots

punch 3 box, hit, jab **4** beat, blow, chop, clip, conk, cuff, pelt, plug, poke, slam, sock, swat **5** baste, clout, knock, paste, pound, smite, thump, whack **6** pummel, strike, stroke, thrust, thwack, wallop **7** clobber **9** haymaker **10** roundhouse

punchy 3 fat **5** dazed **6** stubby

8 confused, forceful **9** befuddled

punctilious 5 exact, fussy, picky, rigid **6** proper, strict **7** correct, finicky, precise **8** exacting, rigorous **9** demanding **10** meticulous, particular, scrupulous **11** painstaking

punctual 5 early, quick, ready **6** on time, prompt, steady, timely **7** instant, not late, regular **8** constant, on the dot **9** immediate, well-timed **10** in good time, seasonable **11** expeditious **13** instantaneous

punctuate 4 lace **5** break **6** pepper **7** scatter **8** separate, sprinkle **9** interrupt **11** intersperse

punctuation mark 4 dash **5** colon, comma, pause, point, slash **6** accent, ending, hyphen, parens, period, quotes **7** bracket **8** ellipsis **9** semicolon **10** apostrophe **11** parenthesis **12** question mark **13** quotation mark **16** exclamation point

puncture 3 cut **4** bite, hole, nick, pink **5** break, prick, stick, sting, wound **6** pierce **7** deflate, let down, opening, rupture **9** knock down, shoot down **10** depreciate **11** perforation

pundit 4 guru, sage **5** guide **6** critic, expert, master, mentor, savant, wizard **7** thinker **9** authority **13** learned person

pungent 3 hot **4** acid, keen, racy, sour, tart **5** acrid, acute, nippy, salty, sharp, smart, spicy, tangy, tasty, witty **6** biting, bitter, clever, savory, snappy, strong **7** acetous, caustic, cutting, mordent, peppery, piquant, pointed **8** incisive, piercing, poignant, smarting, stinging, stirring, vinegary, wounding **9** brilliant, flavorful, invidious, palatable, sarcastic, sparkling, trenchant **10** astringent, flavorsome, keen-witted **11** acrimonious, penetrating, provocative, stimulating, tantalizing **12** sharp-tasting **13** scintillating, sharp-smelling **14** highly flavored, highly seasoned

punish 4 beat, fine, flog, whip **6** avenge, rebuke **7** chasten, correct, reprove **8** admonish, chastise, imprison, penalize, sentence **9** castigate, dress down, retaliate **10** discipline, take to task **11** get even with, take revenge **14** bring to account **15** take vengeance on

punishing 5 harsh, penal **6** brutal, severe **7** abusive **8** scolding **9** torturing **10** chastizing, tormenting **11** castigating

punishment 4 fine **5** price **7** damages, deserts, flaying, forfeit, hanging, payment, penalty, penance, redress **8** flogging, punition, spanking, whipping **10** chastening, correction, crucifying, discipline, reparation **11** castigation, retribution **12** chastisement, penalization

punk 4 hood, lout, poor **5** bully, lousy, rowdy, tough **6** crummy, rotten **7** hoodlum, ruffian **8** hooligan **9** barbarian, roughneck **10** delinquent

Punt see **7** Somalia

Puntarvolo
    character in: **22** Every Man Out of His Humour
    author: **6** Jonson

punt e mes
    type: **8** aperitif
    origin: **5** Italy
    flavor: **6** orange
    color: **12** reddish-brown

puny 4 poor, thin, tiny, weak **5** frail, light, petty, runty, small **6** bantam, feeble, flimsy, infirm, little, meager, measly, paltry, sickly, slight, weakly **7** fragile, shallow, tenuous, trivial **8** delicate, impotent, picayune, piddling, runtlike, sawed-off, trifling **9** emaciated, miniature, mite-sized, pint-sized, worthless **10** diminutive, inadequate, picayunish, undersized **11** unimportant **12** insufficient **13** insignificant **14** inconsiderable, underdeveloped

pupa 3 egg **5** larva, nymph **6** cocoon **7** wiggler **9** chrysalis **14** transformation

pupil 4 coed, tyro **6** novice **7** learner, scholar, student, trainee **8** beginner, disciple, initiate **9** schoolboy **10** apprentice, schoolgirl **11** probationer **13** undergraduate

puppet 3 toy **4** doll, dupe, pawn, tool **6** flunky, lackey **7** cat's paw, manikin, servant **8** creature, henchman, hireling **9** jackstraw, lay figure, underling **10** figurehead, instrument, man of straw, marionette **11** subordinate

puppy 3 dog, pet, pup **6** canine

Purcell, Henry
    born: **6** London **7** England
    composer of: **9** Fantasias

10 Bell Anthem, Dioclesian, King Arthur (The British Worthy), The Tempest **12** Golden Sonata **13** Dido and Aeneas **14** The Indian Queen

purchase 3 buy **4** edge, hold **6** buying, pay for, pick up **7** footing, support, toehold **8** foothold, leverage **9** advantage, influence **11** acquirement, acquisition

pure 4 full, mere, neat, true **5** basic, clean, fresh, moral, sheer, stark, utter, whole **6** chaste, decent, entire, higher, virgin **7** angelic, ethical, perfect, sincere, sinless, sterile, unmixed, upright **8** absolute, abstract, complete, flawless, germfree, innocent, positive, purebred, sanitary, spotless, straight, thorough, unmarred, virginal, virtuous **9** blameless, downright, faultless, guileless, guiltless, healthful, inviolate, out-and-out, pedigreed, righteous, unalloyed, undefiled, unmingled, unspoiled, unsullied, untainted, wholesome **10** antiseptic, immaculate, inviolable, sterilized, uninfected, unmodified, unpolluted **11** conjectural, disinfected, fundamental, pure-blooded, speculative, theoretical, unblemished, uncorrupted, unqualified, untarnished **12** full-strength, hypothetical, thoroughbred **13** unadulterated, unimpeachable **14** above suspicion, uncontaminated

puree 4 bisk, pulp, soup **5** paste **6** bisque

purely 4 only **5** fully **6** merely, simply, solely, wholly **7** cleanly, morally, piously, totally **8** chastely, devoutly, entirely, worthily **9** admirably **10** absolutely, completely, flawlessly, in all honor, innocently, virginally, virtuously **11** essentially, faultlessly **13** incorruptibly

Purgatory, Purgatorio part II of: **12** Divine Comedy author: **14** Dante Alighieri

purge 4 kill, oust **5** crush, ex-pel **6** banish, emetic, pardon, physic, purify, remove, uproot **7** clean up, cleanse, cleanup, clyster, dismiss, expiate, purging, rout out, shake up **8** aperient, atone for, clean out, get rid of, laxative, sweep out, wash away **9** cathartic, discharge, eliminate, eradicate, liquidate, purgation, purgative **10** do away with **11** exterminate **12** obtain pardon (from), purification **15** obtain remission (from) **16** obtain absolution (from) **17** obtain forgiveness

purification 7 baptism **9** cleansing **13** sterilization

purify 4 boil **5** clear **6** filter **7** clarify, distill **8** make pure, sanitize **9** disinfect, sterilize **10** chlorinate, pasteurize **13** decontaminate

Puritani, I
also: **11** The Puritans
opera by: **7** Bellini
character: **14** Oliver Cromwell, Queen Henrietta **16** Lord Arthur Talbot

puritanical 4 prim **5** rigid, stiff **6** narrow, prissy, severe, strict, stuffy **7** ascetic, austere, bigoted, prudish, puritan, stilted **8** dogmatic, priggish **9** bluenosed, fanatical **11** stiff-necked, straitlaced **13** sanctimonious

Puritan State
nickname of:
13 Massachusetts

purity 5 honor, piety **6** virtue **7** clarity, decency, honesty, modesty **8** chastity, fineness, holiness, lucidity, morality, pureness, sanctity **9** cleanness, clearness, innocence, integrity, limpidity, plainness, rectitude, virginity **10** brilliance, chasteness, directness, excellence, immaculacy, simplicity, temperance, uniformity **11** cleanliness, homogeneity, saintliness, uprightness **12** virtuousness **13** guilelessness, guiltlessness **14** immaculateness **15** clear conscience **16** incorruptibility

purlieu 4 area **5** haunt, limit **6** border, locale, region, resort **7** district, environ **8** outskirt **11** surrounding **12** neighborhood

purloin 3 rob **5** steal **6** pilfer **11** appropriate, make off with

Purloined Letter, The
author: **13** Edgar Allan Poe

purloiner 5 thief **6** robber **7** burglar **8** pilferer

purple 4 plum, puce, racy **5** color, grape, lilac, lurid, mauve, royal **6** florid, orchid, turgid, violet **7** crimson, flowery, furious, fuchsia, magenta **8** amethyst, burgundy, imperial, lavender **9** gastropod

Purple Land see **7** Uruguay

Purple Rose of Cairo, The
director: **10** Woody Allen
cast: **9** Mia Farrow **11** Danny Aiello, Jeff Daniels

purport 3 aim, end **4** gist **5** claim, drift, point, sense, tenor, trend **6** allege, burden, design, import, intent, object, reason **7** bearing, meaning, profess, purpose **9** intention, objective, rationale, substance **11** implication **12** significance **13** signification

purpose 3 aim **4** goal, hope, mean, plan, will, wish **5** elect, point, sense **6** aspire, choose, decide, design, desire, intend, intent, motive, object, reason, scheme, target **7** drive at, meaning, mission, persist, project, propose, resolve, think to **8** ambition, conclude, endeavor, function, proposal, set about **9** determine, intention, objective, persevere, rationale, undertake **10** aspiration, motivation, resolution **11** contemplate, disposition, expectation, fixed intent, have a mind to, raison d'etre **13** commit oneself, determination

purposeful 7 decided, studied **8** resolute, resolved **9** committed, conscious **10** calculated, considered, deliberate, determined **11** intentional **12** premeditated, strong-willed

purposefulness 7 purpose, resolve **10** resolution **11** decidedness **12** decisiveness, resoluteness **13** determination

purposeless 6 random **7** aimless, useless **8** needless, plotless **9** desultory, driftless, haphazard, irregular, senseless, unplanned **11** meaningless **12** functionless, undetermined, unprofitable

purposely 8 by design **9** advisedly, expressly, knowingly, on purpose, willfully, wittingly **10** designedly, with intent **11** consciously, voluntarily **12** calculatedly, deliberately **13** intentionally

purse 3 bag **4** fold, fund, knit **5** award, bunch, pinch, pleat, pouch, prize, stake **6** clutch, coffer, gather, pucker, wallet **7** handbag, sporran, wrinkle

8 contract, moneybag, proceeds, treasury, winnings **10** pocketbook **11** shoulder bag
French: **12** porte-monnaie

purser 6 bursar **7** cashier **9** paymaster **10** cashkeeper

pursue 4 seek **5** aim at, chase, track, trail **6** aim for, follow, try for **7** be after, carry on, go after, perform **8** aspire to, engage in, labor for, run after **9** race after, strive for **10** chase after, push toward

pursuer 5 pupil **6** seeker **7** devotee, student **8** disciple, follower, searcher **10** aficionado

pursuit 4 hunt **5** chase **6** search **7** pastime **8** activity **9** following **10** occupation

purvey 3 get **4** give, hand **5** cater, equip, yield **6** obtain, outfit, supply **7** deliver, furnish, procure, provide

purveyor 4 pimp **6** seller **8** procurer, provider, supplier

purview 3 ken **4** area **5** field, range, reach, realm, savvy, scope, sweep **6** domain, extent **7** compass, horizon, outlook **8** dominion, overview **9** territory, viewpoint **10** commission, experience **11** mental grasp **13** comprehension, understanding **14** responsibility

push 2 go **3** dun, ram **4** butt, goad, jolt, move, plug, prod, spur, sway, urge, work, worm **5** boost, drive, egg on, elbow, fight, foray, force, forge, harry, hound, impel, nudge, press, rouse, shove, stick, stuff, vigor, wedge **6** arouse, badger, coerce, compel, energy, exhort, harass, heckle, hustle, incite, induce, inroad, jostle, plunge, prompt, propel, thrust, wiggle **7** advance, animate, buffalo, inspire, promote, provoke, squeeze **8** ambition, browbeat, motivate, persuade, shoulder, struggle, vitality **9** advertise, constrain, encourage, importune, incursion, instigate, make known, publicize, stimulate, strong-arm **10** get-up-and-go **11** make one's way, prevail upon, vim and vigor **12** force one's way, propagandize **13** determination

pushcart 5 wagon **6** barrow **8** handcart **10** handbarrow **11** wheelbarrow

push forward 4 goad, prod, spur **5** drive, impel, press **9** urge along

Pushkin, Alexander (Aleksandr)
author of: **12** Boris Godunov, Eugene Onegin **16** The Queen of Spades **17** The Bronze Horseman **19** The Captain's Daughter

push through 6 hasten **7** advance, forward **8** dispatch, expedite **10** accelerate, facilitate

pushy 8 forceful **9** assertive, insistent **10** aggressive **11** domineering **12** strong-willed **13** self-assertive

pusillanimous 7 fearful **8** cowardly, timorous **10** spiritless **11** lily-livered **12** apprehensive, fainthearted, mean-spirited

pusillanimousness 8 timidity **9** cowardice **12** yellow streak **13** yellow feather **16** faintheartedness **18** chickenheartedness

puss 3 cat, mug, pan **4** face **5** kitty **6** feline, kisser, kitten

pussyfoot 5 dodge, evade, hedge, sneak **6** tiptoe, weasel **8** sidestep **13** evade the issue **14** beg the question **15** walk on eggshells **16** straddle the fence

put 3 fix, lay, set **4** cast, pose, rest, word **5** bring, drive, force, heave, offer, pitch, place, state, throw **6** assign, employ, impute, phrase, submit **7** ascribe, deposit, express, present, propose **8** position **9** attribute, enunciate **10** articulate

put a damper on 4 cool, dull **7** depress, squelch **10** discourage, dishearten

put an edge on 4 hone, whet **6** excite **7** sharpen **9** stimulate

put an end to 4 halt, stop **5** annul, quash **6** cancel, finish, repeal, revoke **7** abolish, blot out, rescind, squelch, wipe out **8** abrogate, demolish, dispatch, stamp out **9** eliminate, eradicate, finish off **10** discourage, do away with, put a stop to **12** write finis to

put aside 5 table **6** forget **7** discard, lay away **10** relinquish

put away 3 eat **4** down, stow **5** stash **6** commit **7** confine, consume **9** drink down

put back 4 rout **5** delay **6** defeat, demote, impair, reject, return **7** replace, restore **9** reinstate

put down 4 note, post **5** crush,

enter, knock, quash, quell **6** dispel, enlist, record, subdue **7** deposit, disdain, sneer at, squelch **8** belittle, derogate, laugh off, pooh-pooh, suppress **9** denigrate, disparage, humiliate, write down **10** depreciate

put forth 5 offer **6** extend, put out **7** proffer, send out

put forward 4 pose **6** assert **7** advance, profess, propose **8** propound

put in irons 5 chain **6** fetter **7** manacle, shackle **8** handcuff

put in motion 4 move **5** begin, start **6** arouse, launch **8** activate, carry out, commence, initiate **9** instigate, undertake

put in order 5 array **6** neaten, tidy up **7** arrange **8** organize **10** straighten

put in plain sight 4 show **6** set out **7** display, exhibit

put in shackles 6 fetter, hobble **7** enchain, enslave, manacle **8** handcuff, imprison

put into circulation 4 move **5** issue, print **7** publish **10** pass around

put into effect 6 effect **7** achieve, enforce, execute, fulfill, realize **8** carry out, complete **10** accomplish, administer, consummate, effectuate, perpetrate **12** carry through

put into words 5 voice **7** express **8** describe **9** verbalize **10** articulate **11** communicate

Putnam, Abbie
character in: **18** Desire Under the Elms
author: **6** O'Neill

put off 5 delay, repel, stall **6** offend, rebuff, recess **7** adjourn, repulse, set sail, suspend **8** hold back, launched, offended, postpone, rebuffed, repelled, repulsed **9** interrupt **11** discontinue **13** procrastinate

put off guard 4 lull **6** disarm **10** make unwary

put on 3 don **5** affix **6** attach **7** dress in, get into, stick on **8** fasten to

put-on 8 pretense **11** affectation

put on guard 4 warn **5** alert **6** advise, tip off **7** caution **8** forewarn **9** make ready **10** precaution

put out 3 irk **5** annoy, issue

6 quench, retire 7 produce, publish 8 irritate 9 strike out 10 extinguish 11 manufacture 13 leave the shore

put out of order 5 mix up, upset 6 jumble, mess up, muddle 7 confuse, scatter 8 disarray, disorder, displace, put askew, scramble 10 disarrange 11 disorganize

putrefaction 3 rot 5 decay 7 rotting 8 spoilage, spoiling 10 rottenness 12 decompostion

putrefy 3 rot 4 turn 5 decay, spoil, taint 6 molder 8 putresce, stagnate 9 decompose 10 biodegrade 11 deteriorate 12 disintegrate

putrescent 4 foul, rank 5 fetid 6 smelly 7 rotting 8 decaying, spoiling, stinking 9 offensive 10 malodorous, putrefying 11 decomposing

putrid 3 bad 4 foul, rank 5 fetid 6 rancid, rotten, spoiled 7 tainted 8 decaying, polluted, purulent, stinking 9 putrefied 10 putrescent 11 decomposing 12 contaminated, putrefactive

putridity 5 decay, filth, taint 8 foulness, impurity 9 dirtiness, pollution, purulence, rancidity 10 rottenness 11 putrescence, uncleanness 13 contamination, decomposition

putsch 6 revolt 8 uprising

putter 4 fool, idle, laze, loaf, loll 5 dally, drift 6 dawdle, diddle, fiddle, loiter, lounge, piddle, potter, tinker 8 golf club, lallygag 10 dillydally

put to death 4 do in, hang, kill, slay 5 slain 6 done in, hanged, killed, murder, poison, rub out 7 bump off, butcher, execute 8 dispatch, executed, massacre, murdered, poisoned, strangle 9 bumped off, butchered, finish off, massacred, strangled, suffocate 11 assassinate, electrocute, exterminate 12 assassinated, electrocuted, exterminated

put to flight 4 rout, shoo 5 chase 6 dispel 7 cast out, scatter 8 drive off, send away 11 send packing

put together 4 join 5 unite 7 combine 8 assemble

put to shame 6 ashame 7 chagrin, mortify 9 discomfit, embarrass, humiliate

put to sleep 4 lull 5 quiet 6 sedate 8 knock out 9 narcotize 11 anesthetize

put to use 3 use 5 apply 6 employ, engage, occupy 7 exploit, utilize 9 make use of

put under a spell 5 charm 7 bewitch, enchant 8 entrance 9 fascinate, mesmerize, spellbind

put up 3 can 4 hang 5 erect, house, lodge, raise, store 6 billet 7 shelter 8 preserve 11 accommodate 14 furnish room for

put up with 4 bear, take 5 abide, brave, brook, stand 6 endure, suffer 7 stomach, sustain, undergo 8 stand for, submit to, tolerate 9 withstand 11 countenance

Puvis de Chavannes, Pierre Cecile
born: 5 Lyons 6 France
artwork: 6 Summer 13 Shepherd's Song 14 Ludus pro patria 16 The Poor Fisherman 17 Life of St Genevieve, The Inspiring Muses 21 Science Arts and Letters

Puyallop
language family: 8 Salishan, Wakashan 9 Algonkian 10 Algonquian
location: 10 Washington

Puzo, Mario
author of: 12 The Godfather

puzzle 4 foil, mull 5 brood, stump 6 baffle, enigma, outwit, ponder, riddle, wonder 7 confuse, dilemma, mystery, mystify, nonplus, perplex, problem 8 bewilder, confound, hoodwink 9 conundrum 10 bafflement, difficulty, perplexity 12 bewilderment, complication 13 mystification

puzzled 6 amazed 7 baffled 8 befogged, confused, troubled 9 astounded, befuddled, mystified, perplexed 10 bewildered, confounded, nonplussed

puzzling 7 elusive 8 baffling 9 confusing, enigmatic 10 mysterious, mystifying, perplexing 11 bewildering, confounding, enigmatical 12 unfathomable 16 hard to understand, incomprehensible

Pwyll
origin: 5 Welsh
form: 6 prince
steals: 8 Rhiannon
wife: 8 Rhiannon
son: 7 Pryderi

Pyanepsia
origin: 5 Greek 8 Athenian

event: 8 festival
honoring: 6 Apollo 7 harvest

Pygmalion
author: 17 George Bernard Shaw
character: 12 Henry Higgins 14 Eliza Doolittle
basis for: 10 My Fair Lady
director: 14 Anthony Asquith
cast: 11 Wendy Hiller (Eliza Doolittle) 12 Leslie Howard (Professor Henry Higgins) 13 Wilfrid Lawson

Pygmalion
king of: 6 Cyprus
avocation: 8 sculptor
statue named: 7 Galatea
loved: 7 Galatea
statue changed to: 5 woman
wife: 7 Galatea
daughter: 6 Paphos 8 Metharme

pygmy 3 elf, toy, wee 4 mite, runt, tiny 5 dwarf, elfin, short, small 6 bantam, midget, peewee, shrimp 7 manikin 8 dwarfish, half-pint, Tom Thumb 9 miniature, pipsqueak 10 diminutive, homunculus, undersized 11 Lilliputian

Pylades
father: 9 Strophius
mother: 8 Anaxibia
cousin: 7 Orestes
wife: 7 Electra
son: 5 Medon 9 Strophius
friend: 7 Orestes

Pylaemenes
king of: 13 Paphlagonians
killed by: 8 Menelaus

Pylaeus
mentioned in: 5 Iliad
rank: 7 captain

Pylas
king of: 6 Megara
uncle: 4 Bias
gave throne to: 17 Pandion the Younger

Pyncheon family
character in: 24 The House of the Seven Gables
members: 6 Phoebe 8 Clifford, Hepzibah 12 Judge Jaffrey
author: 9 Hawthorne

Pynchon, Thomas
author of: 1 V 15 Gravity's Rainbow 23 The Crying of Lot Forty-Nine

Pyongyang
capital of: 10 North Korea

Pyramus
form: 5 youth
location: 7 Babylon
loved: 6 Thisbe
died at tomb of: 5 Ninus

Pyrigenes
    epithet of: **8** Dionysus
    means: **10** born of fire

Pyriphlegethon *see*
    10 Phlegethon

pyromaniac 7 firebug **8** arsonist **10** incendiary **11** firestarter

Pyronia
    epithet of: **7** Artemis
    means: **11** fire goddess

pyrope
    species: **6** garnet
    color: **3** red

pyrophobia
    fear of: **4** fire

pyrotechnics 9 fireworks
    16 brilliant display **19** dazzling
    performance

Pyrrha
    father: **10** Epimetheus

    mother: **7** Pandora
    husband: **9** Deucalion

Pythia
    priestess of: **6** Apollo
    location: **6** Delphi
    delivered: **7** oracles

Pythias
    friend: **5** Damon

Pythius *see* **6** Apollo

Python *see* **8** Delphyne

quack 4 fake, sham **5** phony
6 pseudo **9** charlatan, pretender **10** fake doctor, fraudulent **11** counterfeit,
quacksalver **15** medical
impostor

quackery 5 bluff, guile **6** deceit **7** cunning **9** deception,
duplicity **12** charlatanism

quaff 4 down, gulp, swig
5 drink, lap up, swill **6** guzzle,
imbibe, tipple **7** swallow, toss
off **8** belt down, chug-a-lug
9 knock back **11** drink deeply

quagmire 3 bog, fen, fix, jam
4 mess, mire, ooze, quag,
sump **5** marsh, pinch, swamp
6 crisis, morass, muddle,
pickle, plight, scrape, slough,
sludge, strait **7** dilemma **8** hot
water, quandary **9** imbroglio,
intricacy, quicksand **10** difficulty, perplexity **11** Gordian
knot, involvement, predicament **12** entanglement

quail 3 shy **5** cower, quake,
shake **6** blanch, flinch, recoil,
shrink **7** run away, shudder,
tremble **8** fight shy, turn tail
9 lose heart **10** be cowardly,
lose spirit, take fright **11** lose
courage **12** have cold feet
16 shake in one's boots
17 shiver in one's shoes, show
a yellow streak

quail
  group of: 4 bevy **5** covey

quaint 3 odd **4** rare **5** droll,
queer **6** unique **7** antique, bizarre, curious, strange, unusual **8** charming, fanciful,
old-timey, original, peculiar,
singular, uncommon **9** eccentric, whimsical **10** antiquated,
outlandish **11** out-of-the-way,
picturesque **12** old-fashioned
13 extraordinary
14 unconventional

quake 4 wave **5** quail, shake,
spasm, throb **6** blanch, quaver,
quiver, ripple, shiver, thrill,
tremor **7** shudder, tremble
9 trembling **10** earthquake
18 seismic disturbance

qualification 4 gift **5** forte,
skill **6** talent **7** ability, faculty,
fitness, proviso **8** aptitude,
bona fide, capacity, property,
standard **9** attribute, condition,
endowment, exception, exemption, objection, postulate, provision, requisite **10** capability,
competency, credential, limitation **11** achievement, arrangement, eligibility, requirement,

reservation, restriction, stipulation **12** escape clause, modification, prerequisite,
suitableness **13** certification
14 accomplishment

qualified 3 fit **4** able, meet
5 adept, equal **6** expert, fitted,
suited, versed **7** capable,
guarded, hedging, knowing,
limited, skilled, trained **8** eligible, equipped, licensed, reserved, skillful, talented
9 ambiguous, certified, competent, efficient, equivocal, practiced **10** authorized, indefinite,
proficient, restricted **11** conditional, efficacious, experienced,
provisional **12** accomplished

qualify 3 fit **4** ease **5** abate,
adapt, alter, endow, equip,
limit, ready, train **6** adjust, enable, ground, modify, narrow,
permit, reduce, soften, temper **7** assuage, certify, empower, entitle, license, make
fit, prepare **8** describe, diminish, mitigate, moderate, restrain, restrict, sanction
9 authorize, condition, give
power, measure up **10** be accepted, be eligible, commission, legitimate
11 accommodate **12** characterize, circumscribe, make
eligible

qualifying 9 tempering **10** mitigating **11** eligibility, extenuating, preparatory

quality 4 mark, rank **5** blood,
class, grade, merit, trait, value,
worth **6** aspect, family, nature **7** caliber, dignity, faculty,
feature **8** capacity, eminence,
position, property, standing
9 attribute, character **11** disposition, distinction, high station, temperament
12 constitution, social status
13 qualification **14** characteristic

Quality Street
  author: 12 James M Barrie

qualm 4 turn **6** nausea **7** scruple, vertigo **9** faintness, giddiness, misgiving **10** dizzy spell, hesitation, queasiness, reluctance, uneasiness **11** compunction, reservation, sick feeling **13** indisposition, unwillingness **14** disinclination **18** twinge of conscience

quandary 3 fix, jam **4** mire **5** pinch **6** crisis, morass, pickle, plight, scrape, strait **7** dilemma, impasse **8** hot water, quagmire **9** imbroglio **10** difficulty **11** involvement, predicament **12** entanglement, kettle of fish

quantities 4 lots, much **5** heaps, loads **7** amounts

quantity 3 sum **4** area, bulk, dose, mass, size **5** quota, share **6** amount, dosage, extent, length, number, volume **7** expanse, measure, portion **8** vastness **9** abundance, aggregate, allotment, amplitude, extension, greatness, magnitude, multitude **10** proportion **11** measurement **13** apportionment

quarantine 7 confine, isolate **9** isolation, segregate, sequester **13** sequestration **15** cordon sanitaire **18** medical segregation

Quare Fellow, The
author: **12** Brendan Behan

quarrel 3 jar, nag, row **4** carp, feud, fuss, spat, tiff **5** argue, brawl, cavil, clash, fight, scrap **6** bicker, differ, strife **7** contend, discord, dispute, dissent, fall out, wrangle **8** argument, be at odds, conflict, squabble **9** altercate, bickering, complaint, find fault, have words, objection **10** contention, difference, dissension, dissidence, falling out **11** controversy **12** disagreement **13** breach of peace, contradiction, misunderstand **14** apple of discord **15** be at loggerheads **16** bone of contention, misunderstanding

quarreling 6 strife **7** discord **8** clashing, conflict, disunity, friction **9** bickering, disputing, scrapping, wrangling **10** contention, dissension, dissidence, squabbling **11** discordance **12** disagreement

quarrelsome 7 peevish **8** captious, churlish, contrary, militant, petulant **9** bellicose, combative, fractious, irascible, querulous, truculent **10** pugnacious **11** belligerent, contentious **12** antagonistic,

cantankerous, disagreeable, disputatious **13** argumentative

quarry 3 bed, dig, pit **4** game, lode, mine, prey **5** catch, stone **6** source, victim **8** excavate

quart
abbreviation: **2** qt

quarter, quarters 4 area, part, pity, post, side, spot, zone **5** board, house, lodge, mercy, place, put up, realm, rooms **6** billet, domain, fourth, locale, region, sphere **7** housing, install, lodging, shelter, station, terrain **8** clemency, district, humanity, leniency, locality, location, lodgings, position, precinct, province, sympathy **9** percent, direction, one-fourth, situation, territory **10** compassion, fourth part, indulgence, quadrisect **11** place to live, place to stay, three months **13** quarter dollar, specific place **14** accommodations **15** twenty-five cents

quarterstaff 4 pole **5** staff **6** cudgel

quartz
varieties: **4** sard **5** agate, topaz **8** amethyst **9** carnelian, tiger's-eye **11** rock crystal

quash 4 ruin, stop, undo, void **5** annul, crush, erase, quell, smash, wreck **6** cancel, delete, dispel, efface, quench, recall, revoke, squash, subdue, vacate **7** blot out, destroy, expunge, nullify, put down, repress, rescind, retract, reverse, squelch **8** abrogate, dissolve, override, overrule, overturn, set aside, suppress **9** devastate, eradicate, extirpate, overthrow, overwhelm, repudiate, strike out **10** annihilate, extinguish, invalidate, obliterate, put an end to **11** countermand, exterminate

quasi 4 near, part, semi **6** almost, ersatz **7** halfway, seeming, virtual **8** apparent, somewhat, so-called **9** imitation, synthetic **10** resembling

Quasimodo
character in: **23** The Hunchback of Notre Dame
author: **4** Hugo

Quatermain, Allan
character in: **17** King Solomon's Mines
author: **7** Haggard

quaver 4 beat, sway, wave **5** quake, shake, throb, trill, waver **6** falter, quiver, shiver, teeter, totter, tremor, wobble, writhe **7** pulsate, shudder, tremble, tremolo, vibrate, vi-

brato, wriggle **9** oscillate, trembling, vibration **14** tremulous shake

quay 4 dock, mole, pier **5** basin, jetty, levee, wharf **6** marina **7** landing **10** waterfront

queasy 5 giddy, upset **6** uneasy **7** bilious, sickish **8** nauseous, qualmish, troubled **9** nauseated, sickening, uncertain **10** nauseating **13** uncomfortable **16** sick to the stomach

---

Quebec
borders: **7** Ontario **8** Labrador **9** Hudson Bay **12** Newfoundland, United States **13** Atlantic Ocean **16** Gulf of St Lawrence
cape: **5** Gaspe
city: **6** Quebec **8** Montreal **10** Chicoutimi, Sherbrooke **13** Trois Rivieres
highest point: **18** Mont Jacques Cartier
hockey team: **9** Canadiens, Nordiques
island: **9** Anticosti
lake: **5** Gouin **9** Bienville, Eau Claire, Saint Jean **10** Mistassini **11** Manicouagan
mineral: **4** gold, zinc **6** copper **7** iron ore **8** asbestos **9** limestone
mountain: **5** Otish **10** Laurentian, Shickshock **11** Appalachian **12** Monteregians
province of: **6** Canada

Quechua
tribe: **4** Inca

Quedens, Eunice
real name of: **8** Eve Arden

queen 5 ranee **7** czarina, empress **8** princess **13** female monarch
French: **5** reine
German: **7** Konigin
Latin: **6** regina
Spanish: **5** reina

queen/empress/princess
of Egypt: **9** Cleopatra, Nefertari, Nefertiti **10** Hatshepsut, Hetepheres
of England: **3** Mab **4** Anne, Bess, Jane, Mary **7** Eleanor **8** Boadicea, Victoria **9** Catherine, Charlotte, Elizabeth, Guinevere **10** Bloody Mary, Elizabeth I **11** Elizabeth II, Jane Seymour

of France: 7 Eugenie 9 Josephine 11 Marie Louise
14 Marie de Medicis
15 Marie Antoinette
of Italy/Rome: 7 Poppaea
9 Agrippina, Messalina
13 Livia Drusilla
of Monaco: 8 Caroline
9 Stephanie 10 Grace Kelly
of the Netherlands: 7 Beatrix, Juliana 10 Wilhelmina
of Poland: 7 Jadwiga
of Portugal: 5 Maria
9 Elizabeth
of Russia: 9 Alexandra, Catherine 17 Catherine the Great
of Scotland: 4 Mary 13 Saint
Margaret 16 Mary Queen of Scots
of Spain: 8 Isabella 16 Elizabeth Farnese
of Sweden: 9 Christina
of Syria: 7 Zenobia

Queen Christina
director: 15 Rouben Mamoulian
cast: 8 Ian Keith 10 Greta Garbo, Lewis Stone 11 John Gilbert 12 C Aubrey Smith

Queen Mab
author: 18 Percy Bysshe Shelley

Queen of Amazons 9 Hippolyta, Hippolyte

Queen of Hearts
character in: 28 Alice's Adventures in Wonderland
author: 7 Carroll

Queen of Heaven 4 Hera, Mary 6 Ishtar 7 Mylitta

Queen of Spades, The
also: 12 Pikovaya Dama
opera by: 11 Tchaikovsky
character: 4 Lisa 6 Herman
8 Countess

Queen of Spades, The
author: 16 Alexander Pushkin

Queen of Technicolor
nickname of: 12 Maureen O'Hara

Queen of the Surf
nickname of: 14 Esther Williams

Queen's Necklace, The
author: 14 Alexandre Dumas (pere)
character: 5 Oliva 13 Count de Charny 15 Cardinal de Rohan, Count Cagliostro, Marie Antoinette 16 Andree de Taverney 18 Philippe de Taverney 21 Jeanne de la Motte Valois

Queequeg
character in: 8 Moby Dick
author: 8 Melville

queer 3 odd 4 daft, harm, hurt,

rare, ruin 5 crazy, dizzy, droll, faint, fishy, funny, giddy, shady, spoil, weird, woozy, wreck 6 absurd, damage, exotic, impair, injure, quaint, qualmy, queasy, thwart, unique 7 bizarre, comical, curious, disrupt, erratic, reeling, strange, touched, unusual
8 abnormal, bohemian, doubtful, fanciful, freakish, original, peculiar, uncommon, unhinged 9 eccentric, fantastic, grotesque, irregular, laughable, ludicrous, unnatural 10 capricious, compromise, farfetched, irrational, outlandish, remarkable, ridiculous, suspicious, unbalanced, unexampled, unorthodox 11 astonishing, exceptional, light-headed, out of the way, slightly ill, vertiginous 12 preposterous, questionable, unparalleled
13 extraordinary, nonconforming, unprecedented
14 unconventional
French: 5 outre

quell 4 calm, dull, ease, hush, lull, rout, ruin, stay, stem
5 abate, allay, blunt, crush, quash, quiet, still, worst, wreck 6 becalm, deaden, defeat, pacify, quench, reduce, soften, soothe, subdue 7 appease, assuage, compose, conquer, destroy, mollify, put down, scatter, silence, squelch 8 beat down, disperse, mitigate, overcome, palliate, stamp out, suppress, vanquish
9 alleviate, overpower, overthrow, overwhelm, subjugate
10 extinguish 11 tranquilize

quench 4 cool, sate 5 allay, crush, douse, quell, slake
6 dampen, put out, stifle 7 appease, blow out, put down, satiate, satisfy, smother
8 stamp out, suppress 10 annihilate, extinguish

Quentin Durward
author: 14 Sir Walter Scott
character: 8 Isabelle 9 Le Balafre 10 Jacqueline
11 King Louis XI 12 Lady Hameline 13 Ludovic Lesley 15 Countess of Croye
16 William de la Marck
18 Hayraddin Maugrabin
20 King Louis the Eleventh
21 Charles Duke of Burgundy 23 Count Philip de Crevecoeur

querulous 4 sour 5 cross, fussy, testy, whiny 6 cranky, touchy 7 crabbed, finical, finicky, fretful, grouchy, peevish, pettish, waspish, whining
8 captious, exacting, petulant, shrewish 9 difficult, grumbling, irascible, irritable, long-faced,

obstinate, resentful, splenetic
10 nettlesome 11 complaining, quarrelsome 12 disagreeable, discontented, disputatious, dissatisfied, faultfinding

query 3 ask 4 quiz 5 doubt, issue, quest 6 demand, impugn, search 7 dispute, examine, impeach, inquest, inquiry, inspect, problem, request, suspect 8 distrust, look into, mistrust, question, sound out
9 catechize, challenge, inquire of 10 controvert 11 examination, inquisition, interrogate, investigate, make inquiry
13 interrogation, investigation

quest 4 hunt, seek 6 pursue, search, voyage 7 crusade, journey, mission, pursuit, seeking
9 adventure 10 enterprise, pilgrimage 11 exploration

Quested, Adela
character in: 15 A Passage to India
author: 7 Forster

Quest for Fire
director: 17 Jean-Jacques Annaud
cast: 10 Ron Perlman 12 Rae Dawn Chong 13 Everett McGill

question 3 ask, rub 4 pump, quiz, test 5 doubt, drill, grill, issue, query 6 impugn, matter, motion, oppose 7 dispute, dubiety, examine, problem, subject, suspect 8 distrust, look into, mistrust, proposal, sound out 9 catechize, challenge, inquire of, misgiving, moot point, objection 10 difficulty, disbelieve 11 controversy, interrogate, investigate, proposition, uncertainty 12 crossexamine 13 consideration

questionable 4 moot 5 fishy, shady 6 unsure 7 dubious, in doubt, suspect 8 arguable, doubtful, puzzling, unproven
9 ambiguous, confusing, debatable, enigmatic, equivocal, in dispute, uncertain, undecided
10 apocryphal, disputable, indefinite, mysterious, mystifying, perplexing, suspicious
12 hypothetical 13 controversial, problematical

queue 3 row 4 file, line, rank
5 chain, train 6 column, string

quibble 3 nag 4 carp, spar
5 argue, cavil, dodge, fence, fudge, shift 6 bicker, haggle, hassle, nicety, niggle, waffle
7 evasion, nitpick, shuffle
8 artifice, pretense, squabble, subtlety, white lie 9 be evasive, duplicity 10 equivocate, pick a fight, subterfuge
11 distraction 12 equivocation

13 dodge the issue, prevarication

Quiche
language family: **5** Mayan
location: **9** Guatemala
12 South America **14** Central America

quick 3 apt **4** able, deft, fast, keen, spry **5** acute, adept, agile, alert, brief, brisk, eager, fiery, fleet, hasty, rapid, sharp, smart, swift, testy **6** abrupt, active, adroit, astute, brainy, bright, clever, expert, facile, flying, frisky, lively, nimble, prompt, shrewd, speedy, sudden, touchy, winged **7** hurried, peppery, waspish **8** animated, choleric, headlong, petulant, skillful, snappish, spirited, vigilant, vigorous **9** dexterous, energetic, excitable, impatient, impetuous, impulsive, irascible, irritable, sagacious, splenetic, sprightly, vivacious, whirlwind, wide-awake **10** discerning, high-strung, hot-blooded **11** accelerated, expeditious, hot-tempered, intelligent, lightfooted, penetrating, precipitate **12** nimble-footed **13** perspicacious, temperamental

quicken 4 fire, goad, move, rush, spur, stir, urge **5** drive, egg on, hurry, impel, pique, press, rouse, speed **6** affect, arouse, excite, hasten, hustle, incite, kindle, propel, revive, vivify **7** actuate, advance, animate, enliven, further, hurry on, inspire, provoke, refresh, sharpen **8** activate, dispatch, energize, enkindle, expedite, inspirit, vitalize **9** galvanize, instigate, stimulate **10** accelerate, invigorate **11** precipitate

quick glance
French: **9** coup d'oeil

quickly 4 anon, fast, soon **6** keenly, presto, pronto **7** briefly, hastily, rapidly, swiftly **8** promptly, speedily **9** instantly **11** immediately **12** lickety-split

Quickly, Mistress
character in: **22** The Merry Wives of Windsor
author: **11** Shakespeare

quickness 5 haste, speed **6** acuity **8** alacrity, celerity, keenness, rapidity **9** acuteness, alertness, dexterity, sharpness **10** cleverness, nimbleness, promptness **15** expeditiousness

quick-tempered 5 cross, testy **6** cranky, shirty, touchy **7** grouchy, peevish, waspish **8** choleric, churlish, shrewish, snappish **9** emotional, excitable, irascible, irritable **10** ill-

humored **11** bad-tempered, hot-tempered, quarrelsome **12** cantankerous **13** temperamental

quick-witted 4 keen **5** acute, alert, aware, quick, ready, sharp, smart, witty **6** astute, bright, clever, shrewd **8** incisive **9** brilliant, wide-awake **10** discerning, perceptive **11** clear-headed, intelligent, penetrating **13** perspicacious

quid pro quo 4 swap **5** trade **8** exchange **9** tit for tat **21** something for something

¿quien sabe 8 who knows?

quiescence 7 latency **8** dormancy, inaction **10** inactivity

quiescent 6 latent **7** dormant **8** inactive **10** in abeyance

quiet see box

quietly 5 coyly **6** calmly, humbly, meekly, mildly, mutely, softly, tamely **8** demurely, modestly, placidly, serenely, silently **9** bashfully, inaudibly, patiently **10** composedly, moderately, peacefully, tranquilly **11** collectedly, contentedly, diffidently, noiselessly, pacifically, soundlessly, temperately, unexcitedly **12** speechlessly, unassumingly, unboastfully **13** unobtrusively, unperturbedly **15** dispassionately, unpretentiously, without ceremony **16** unostentatiously **17** undemonstratively

Quiet Man, The
director: **8** John Ford
author: **13** Liam O'Flaherty
cast: **9** John Wayne **12** Maureen O'Hara **14** Mildred Natwick, Victor McLaglen **15** Barry Fitzgerald
setting: **7** Ireland
score: **11** Victor Young
Oscar for: **8** director

quietness 5 peace, quiet **7** silence **8** softness **9** stillness **12** peacefulness

quietude 4 calm, rest **6** repose **8** easiness **9** composure

Quigley, Jane
real name of: **13** Jane Alexander

quill 3 pen **4** fold, hair, pick, seta, stem, tube **5** pluck, plume, spike, spine, spool **6** bobbin, needle **7** bristle, feather, spindle **9** toothpick

Quilp
character in: **19** The Old Curiosity Shop
author: **7** Dickens

quilt 5 cover **6** spread **7** blanket **8** coverlet **9** bedspread, comforter

Quin, Widow
character in: **24** Playboy of the Western World
author: **5** Synge

Quincy, M. E.
character: **3** Lee **5** Danny, (Sgt) Brill **11** Sam Fujiyama, (Dr) Robert Astin **12** (Lt) Frank Monahan

quiet 3 low, mum **4** calm, curb, dull, ease, hush, lull, meek, mild, mute, rest, soft, stay, stop **5** abate, allay, blunt, check, fixed, inert, peace, plain, quell, still **6** arrest, at rest, deaden, docile, dozing, gentle, humble, hushed, lessen, mellow, modest, muffle, pacify, placid, repose, sedate, serene, settle, silent, simple, soften, soothe, stable, steady, stifle, subdue, weaken **7** assuage, clement, comfort, compose, dormant, halcyon, mollify, not busy, pacific, passive, patient, relieve, restful, silence, smother, subdued, suspend, unmoved **8** becalmed, calmness, comatose, composed, decrease, immobile, inactive, mitigate, moderate, muteness, not rough, not showy, palliate, peaceful, quietude, reserved, reticent, retiring, serenity, sleeping, stagnant, taciturn, tranquil **9** alleviate, collected, contented, easygoing, immovable, lethargic, make quiet, noiseless, not bright, peaceable, placidity, quietness, set at ease, soundless, stillness, temperate, terminate, unruffled, voiceless **10** coolheaded, gentleness, motionless, phlegmatic, put a stop to, relaxation, slumbering, speechless, stationary, stock-still, unassuming, untroubled **11** discontinue, tranquility, tranquilize, undisturbed, unexcitable, unobtrusive, unperturbed **12** bring to an end, even-tempered, inarticulate, peacefulness, tranquillity **13** at a standstill, dispassionate, imperturbable, noiselessness, soundlessness, unimpassioned, unpretentious **14** unostentatious, unpresumptuous **15** uncommunicative, undemonstrative

cast: 9 Robert Ito **10** John S Ragin **11** Jack Klugman, Joseph Roman, Val Bisoglio **12** Garry Walberg **13** Lynette Mettey
setting: 10 Los Angeles **11** Danny's Place

Quinn, Anthony
born: 6 Mexico **9** Chihuahua
wife: 16 Katherine DeMille
roles: 8 La Strada **10** Viva Zapata **11** Lust for Life **13** Zorba the Greek **17** The Guns of Navarone **22** Requiem for a Heavyweight, The Shoes of the Fisherman
autobiography: 14 The Original Sin

Quintana and Friends
author: 16 John Gregory Dunne

quintessence 4 core, gist, pith, soul **5** heart **6** elixir, marrow, nature **7** essence **8** exemplar, quiddity, sum total **9** substance **10** embodiment **12** distillation **15** personification, sum and substance

quip 3 gag, pun **4** barb, gibe, jape, jeer, jest, joke **5** crack, sally, spoof, taunt **6** banter, retort **7** epigram, putdown, riposte, sarcasm **8** badinage, raillery, repartee, wordplay **9** wisecrack, witticism
French: 6 bon mot **14** double entendre

Quirinus
origin: 5 Roman
god of: 3 war
personifies: 11 Roman nation
identified with: 7 Romulus

quirk 4 kink, turn, whim **6** fetish, foible, oddity, vagary, whimsy **7** caprice **8** crotchet, odd fancy **9** mannerism **10** aberration **11** abnormality, affectation, peculiarity, sudden twist **12** eccentricity, idiosyncrasy

quisling 6 puppet **7** traitor **12** collaborator **16** collaborationist

quit 3 end, rid **4** free, stop **5** cease, clear, forgo, leave, let go, waive, yield **6** depart, desist, disown, exempt, forego, give up, reject, resign, retire **7** abandon, disavow, drop out, forsake, take off **8** abdicate, absolved, forswear, renounce, withdraw **9** acquitted, foreswear, leave a job, surrender,

terminate **10** discharged, exculpated, exonerated, relinquish **11** discontinue

quite 4 very **5** fully, truly **6** highly, hugely, indeed, in fact, in toto, really, surely, vastly, verily, wholly **7** exactly, in truth, totally, utterly **8** actually, entirely, outright **9** assuredly, certainly, extremely, in reality, out-and-out, perfectly, precisely, unusually, veritably **10** absolutely, altogether, completely, enormously, positively, remarkably, throughout **11** exceedingly, excessively **12** considerably **13** exceptionally

Quito
capital of: 7 Ecuador

quiver 3 tic **4** jerk, jolt, jump, pant **5** quake, shake, spasm, throb **6** quaver, shiver, totter, tremor, twitch, wobble **7** flicker, flutter, pulsate, seizure, shudder, tremble, vibrate, wriggle **8** convulse **9** fluctuate, oscillate, palpitate, pulsation, quivering, twitching, vibration **10** convulsion **11** palpitation

Quiverful, Mr
character in: 16 Barchester Towers
author: 8 Trollope

quivering 7 shaking **9** agitating, quavering, shimmying, shivering, trembling, vibrating **10** flittering, fluttering, shuddering, twittering **11** palpitating

qui vive? 12 who goes there?

quixotic 4 wild **6** absurd, dreamy, madcap, poetic **7** utopian **8** fanciful, romantic **9** fantastic, impulsive, visionary, whimsical **10** chimerical, idealistic, ridiculous, starryeyed **11** impractical, ineffective, sentimental, unrealistic **12** preposterous **13** inefficacious

quiz 3 ask, rib **4** exam, joke, mock, pump, test **5** prank, query, taunt, tease **6** banter **7** examine, inquest, inquiry **8** question, ridicule, sound out **9** catechism, eccentric, inquire of **11** examination, inquisition, interrogate, investigate, questioning **12** cross-examine **13** interrogation, investigation **16** cross-examination

Quiz Kids
host: 8 Joe Kelly **14** Clifton Fadiman

quizzical 3 coy **4** arch **6** joking **7** baffled, curious, mocking, puzzled, teasing **8** derisive, impudent, insolent **9** bantering, inquiring, perplexed, searching **11** inquisitive, questioning

quoad hoc 12 as much as this, to this extent

quod erat demonstrandum 17 which was to be shown **24** which was to be demonstrated
abbreviation: 3 QED

quod erat faciendum 16 which was to be done

quod vide 8 which see
abbreviation: 2 qv

quo jure? 11 by what right?

quo modo 3 how **9** in what way **19** in the same manner that

quondam 4 erst, late, once, past **6** bygone, former **8** formerly, sometime **9** erstwhile

quota 4 part **5** share **6** ration **7** measure, minimum, portion **8** quantity **9** allotment **10** allocation, assignment, percentage, proportion **12** distribution **13** apportionment

quotation 5 quote **7** cutting, excerpt, extract, passage **8** citation, clipping **9** reference, selection **12** illustration

quote 4 cite, name **6** adduce, recall, repeat, retell **7** excerpt, extract, refer to **8** instance **9** exemplify, recollect, reproduce **10** paraphrase

quoted passage 7 excerpt, extract **9** quotation

quotidian 5 daily **6** common **8** everyday, ordinary **11** commonplace

Quo Vadis?
author: 17 Henryk Sienkiewicz
character: 4 Nero **5** Chilo, Lygia, Peter **8** Vinitius **9** Petronius, Tigellius
director: 11 Mervyn LeRoy
cast: 7 Leo Genn **11** Deborah Kerr **12** Peter Ustinov, Robert Taylor
setting: 11 ancient Rome

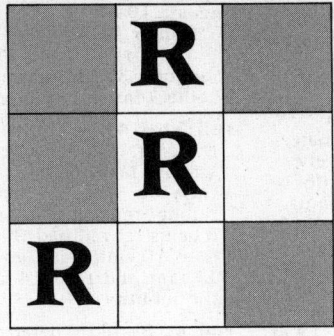

Ra
also: **2** Re
origin: **5** Greek **10** Heliopolis
god of: **3** sun
also worshipped by:
9 Egyptians

Rabat, Rabbat
capital of: **7** Morocco

rabbi 6 master, rabbin
7 scholar, teacher **9** clergyman **15** spiritual leader

rabbinical, rabbinic 8 clerical

rabbit 4 cony, hare, jack, lure
5 bunny, coney, lapin **6** novice, rodent **8** beginner **10** cot-
tontail, pacesetter

Rabbit Is Rich
author: **10** John Updike

Rabbit Redux
author: **10** John Updike

rabble 3 mob **5** swarm **7** the
herd **8** populace, riffraff
9 commoners, hoi polloi, the
masses **11** proletariat, rank
and file **12** lower classes
15 disorderly crowd **16** the
great unwashed
French: **8** canaille
German:
17 Lumpenproletariat

Rabelais, Francois
author of: **22** Gargantua and
Pantagruel

rabid 4 wild **6** ardent, crazed,
raging **7** berserk, fervent, frantic, violent, zealous **8** deranged, frenzied, maniacal,
wild-eyed **9** fanatical **11** hy-
drophobic **17** foaming at the
mouth

race 3 fly, run **4** dart, dash,
heat, rush **5** hurry **6** hasten,
hustle **7** contest, operate
8 campaign **11** competition

racecourse 4 turf **5** track
6 course **9** racetrack

Rachel
father: **5** Laban
husband: **5** Jacob
sister: **4** Leah
son: **6** Joseph **8** Benjamin
slave: **6** Bilhah

**Rachmaninov (Rachmani-
noff, Rakhmaninov),
Sergei**
born: **6** Russia **8** Novgorod
composer of: **15** Symphonic
Dances **16** The Isle of the
Dead **19** Second Piano Concerto **26** Rhapsody on a
Theme by (of) Paganini

Racine, Jean Baptiste
author of: **6** Phedre
7 Athalie **8** Berenice **10** Andromache **11** Britannicus

racism 7 bigotry **8** color bar
9 color line **10** race hatred, racial bias **11** segregation **15** racial prejudice **20** racial
discrimination

rack 4 buck, gait, hurt, neck,
pace, pain, path **5** agony,
cloud, exert, frame, raise,
track, trail, worry, wreck,
wring **6** canter, holder, strain
7 afflict, agonize, draw off, oppress, stretch, torment, torture **8** distress **9** suffering
10 destruction, excruciate, iron
maiden

racked 4 torn **5** paced
6 framed, pained, traced,
walked **7** annoyed, tracked,
trotted, wronged, worried
8 cantered, suffered, tortured
9 afflicted, anguished, destroyed, oppressed, tormented
10 persecuted

racket 3 din **4** game, line,
roar, stir **5** babel **6** clamor,
hubbub, rumpus, tumult, uproar **7** clangor, clatter, turmoil **8** business, shouting
9 commotion, loud noise
10 hullabaloo, hurly-burly, occupation, turbulence **11** dis-

turbance, pandemonium
12 caterwauling, vociferation

racketeer 4 hood **5** crook
6 bagman, bandit, extort
7 hoodlum, mafioso, mobster
8 criminal, gangster
12 extortionist

racking 7 painful **9** agonizing,
torturous **10** tormenting, unbearable **11** intolerable, unendurable **12** excruciating,
insufferable

raconteur 8 fabulist, narrator,
romancer **10** anecdotist
11 storyteller **13** teller of
tales **14** spinner of yarns

racy 4 keen **5** bawdy, crude,
heady, lurid, zesty **6** erotic,
lively, ribald, risque, smutty,
vulgar **7** buoyant, glowing, obscene, zestful **8** animated, exciting, immodest, indecent,
off-color, prurient, spirited,
vigorous **9** energetic, fast-
paced, salacious, sparkling
10 suggestive **11** stimulating
12 exhilarating, pornographic

radar
invented by: **4** Watt
6 Watson

Radcliffe, Mrs Ann
author of: **10** The Italian
21 The Mysteries of Udolpho

raddle 3 rod **4** reed, scar, twig
5 fence, hedge, rouge, stick,
weave **6** branch, ruddle **8** hematite, red ocher, red ochre
10 interweave

radiance, radiancy 3 joy
5 gleam, gleem, sheen **6** dazzle, luster **7** glitter, rapture,
sparkle **8** lambency, splendor
9 animation, happiness
10 brightness, brilliance, brilliancy, effulgence, luminosity,
refulgence **11** coruscation, iridescence **12** luminousness, resplendence **13** incandescence
god of: **5** Baldr **6** Balder,
Baldur

radiant 5 aglow, happy, sunny 6 bright, elated, joyous 7 beaming, glowing, pleased, shining 8 blissful, dazzling, ecstatic, flashing, gladsome, gleaming, luminous, lustrous 9 brilliant, delighted, effulgent, overjoyed, rapturous, refulgent, sparkling 10 glittering 12 incandescent 13 scintillating

radiate 4 beam, pour, shed 5 carry 6 spread 7 diffuse, diverge, give off, give out, scatter 8 disperse, emit heat, transmit 9 branch out, circulate, emit light, spread out 11 disseminate

radical 4 rash 5 basic, rebel 6 severe 7 drastic, extreme 8 left-wing, militant 9 extremist, firebrand 10 immoderate, inordinate 11 freethinker, fundamental, precipitate 13 revolutionary 22 antiestablishmentarian

radio
   invented by: 7 Donovan, Fleming, Marconi 8 De Forest, Nicolson 9 Armstrong, Fessenden 12 Alexanderson

radium
   chemical symbol: 2 Ra

radon
   chemical symbol: 2 Rn

raffish 3 low 4 fast, wild 5 cheap, rowdy, showy 6 common, flashy, rakish, tawdry, vulgar 7 boorish 8 rakehell 9 worthless 10 dissipated 12 devil-may-care, disreputable

raft 3 lot 4 mass 5 barge, float 6 plenty 7 carrier, pontoon 8 flatboat, platform, quantity 9 abundance, multitude

Raft, George
   real name: 11 George Ranft
   born: 9 New York NY
   roles: 8 Scarface 11 Johnny Angel 12 Guido Rinaldo 13 Some Like It Hot

rag 3 kid, rib 4 scap, song, tune, twit 5 cloth, taunt, taunt, tease 6 harass 7 torment 8 magazine 9 newspaper 11 ragtime tune 14 worn-out garment

ragamuffin 3 bum 4 hobo, waif 5 gamin, tramp 6 beggar, gamine, hoyden, sloven, urchin, wretch 7 vagrant 8 derelict, vagabond 9 itinerant, ragpicker 10 panhandler, street arab 11 guttersnipe 14 tatterdemalion

rage 3 fad, ire 4 boil, fume, fury, mode, rant, rave, roar 5 craze, furor, mania, pique, storm, vogue, wrath 6 blow up, choler, frenzy, seethe, spleen, temper 7 explode, fashion, ferment, flare up, madness, passion, rampage, umbrage 8 paroxysm, the thing 9 animosity, fulminate, raise cain, throw a fit, vehemence 10 bitterness, excitement, irritation, resentment, the "in" thing 11 displeasure, high dudgeon, indignation, the last word 12 current style, le dernier cri, perturbation, violent anger 13 temper tantrum 14 the latest thing 15 fly off the handle, froth at the mouth

Rage of Angels
   author: 13 Sidney Sheldon

ragged 4 rent, torn, worn 5 seedy, tacky 6 beat up, frayed, shabby, shaggy, shoddy 7 patched, run down, worn-out 8 battered, shredded, strained, tattered 9 overtaxed 10 aggravated, threadbare, worn to rags 11 exacerbated

ragging 5 chaff 6 banter 7 kidding, ribbing, teasing 8 chaffing, needling, raillery, taunting, twitting

raging 3 mad 4 wild 5 angry, livid, rabid, rough 6 fierce, raving, stormy 7 fervent, frantic, furious, rampant, violent 8 frenzied, incensed, storming 9 turbulent 10 blustering, ferocious, infuriated 11 tempestuous

Raging Bull
   director: 14 Martin Scorsese
   cast: 8 Joe Pesci 12 Frank Vincent, Robert De Niro (Jake La Motta) 13 Cathy Moriarty
   Oscar for: 5 actor (De Niro)

Ragnarok
   also: 15 Gotterdammerung 17 Twilight of the Gods
   origin: 12 Scandinavian
   event: 11 final battle
   battlefield: 6 Vigrid

ragout 4 hash, stew 7 borscht, goulash 9 fricassee

Ragtime
   author: 10 E L Doctorow

Rahab
   hometown: 7 Jericho
   husband: 6 Solmon
   hid: 12 Joshua's spies

raid 4 bust 5 foray, onset, sally, storm 6 attack, inroad, invade, razzia, sortie 7 assault, round-up 8 invasion 10 pounce upon 14 surprise attack

Raiders of the Lost Ark
   director: 15 Steven Spielberg
   cast: 10 Karen Allen, Wolf Kahler 11 Paul Freeman 12 Harrison Ford
   sequel: 30 Indiana Jones and the Temple of Doom

rail 3 bar 4 rage, rant 5 scold, fence, train 6 blow up, scream, take on 7 barrier, carry on, declaim, inveigh, railing, railway, the cars 8 banister, railroad 9 fulminate 10 vituperate, vociferate 11 rant and rave 14 foam at the mouth

rail at 5 scold 6 berate 7 chew out 9 castigate 14 inveigh against

railing 3 bar 5 fence, grate, rails 6 fender 7 barrier, parapet, support 8 banister 9 enclosing 10 balustrade

raillery 5 chaff, sport 6 banter, japing, joking, satire 7 fooling, jesting, joshing, kidding, ragging, razzing, ribbing, teasing 8 badinage, chaffing, roasting, twitting 10 lampoonery, persiflage, pleasantry

railroad sleeping car
   French: 8 wagon-lit

railroad station 5 depot 8 terminal, terminus

railway 4 tube 5 track, train 6 cogway, subway 7 cogroad, trolley 8 elevated, monorail, railroad 9 streetcar

raiment 4 duds, togs 5 dress 6 attire 7 apparel, clothes, costume, threads 8 clothing, garments 11 habiliments

rain, rains 4 down, drop, mist, pour 5 spate 6 deluge, lavish, shower, squall 7 drizzle, monsoon, torrent 8 downpour, drencher, plethora, rainfall, send down, sprinkle 9 hurricane, rainstorm 10 cloudburst 13 precipitation, thundershower 15 rain cats and dogs 16 come down in sheets 17 come down in buckets
   god of: 4 Thor

Rainbow
   goddess of: 4 Iris

Rainbow, The
   author: 10 D H Lawrence
   character: 10 Anna Lensky 11 Lydia Lensky, Tom Brangwen 12 Will Brangwen 14 Ursula Brangwen 15 Anton Skrebensky

Rainbow Bridge see 7 bifrost

raincoat 3 mac 4 mack 6 poncho, ulster 7 oilskin, slicker 8 burberry 9 tarpaulin 10 mackintosh, trenchcoat, waterproof

rainless 3 dry **4** arid, sere
10 desertlike

Rains, Claude
born: 6 London **7** England
wife: 11 Isabel Jeans
roles: 9 Notorious **10** Casablanca, Now Voyager **13** Mr Skeffington **14** Anthony Adverse **15** The Invisible Man **16** Lawrence of Arabia **17** Here Comes Mr Jordan **20** The Phantom of the Opera **23** Mr Smith Goes to Washington **24** The Adventures of Robin Hood

rain shower 6 shower **7** drizzle **8** sprinkle **12** thunderstorm

rainstorm 6 deluge, shower
8 downfall, downpour
10 cloudburst **12** thunderstorm

rainy 3 wet **4** damp **7** drizzly, showery **11** pouring rain
18 raining cats and dogs

raise 3 end **4** grow, hike, lift, rear, spur, urge **5** amass, boost, breed, build, erect, nurse, pique, put up, rouse, set up, spark **6** arouse, awaken, excite, foster, hike up, jack up, kindle, obtain, stir up **7** advance, bring in, bring up, canvass, collect, develop, elevate, inflame, inflate, inspire, nurture, procure, produce, sharpen, solicit **8** increase, summon up
9 construct, cultivate, elevation, promotion, stimulate, terminate **10** make higher, put forward **11** advancement

raise aloft 5 boost, hoist **6** lift up, uplift **7** elevate, upraise

raised 4 bred, grew **5** anted, built, grown **6** anteed, convex, jacked, lifted, reared, roused **7** aroused, erected, exalted, hoisted, honored, incited **8** elevated, embossed, leavened, mustered **9** brought up, collected **10** cultivated
11 resurrected

Raisin in the Sun, A
director: 12 Daniel Petrie
based on play by: 17 Lorraine Hansberry
cast: 7 Ruby Dee **9** Ivan Dixon **10** Diana Sands **13** Claudia McNeil, Sidney Poitier
setting: 7 Chicago

rake 4 comb, goat, roue
5 rogue, satyr, scour, sport **6** lecher, pepper, rascal **7** Don Juan, playboy, ransack, seducer, swinger **8** Casanova, Lothario, enfilade, prodigal, rakehell **9** debauchee, libertine, womanizer
10 immoralist,

profligate, sensualist, voluptuary

rake-off 3 cut, fee **5** piece
10 percentage **16** piece of the action

Rake's Progress, The
opera by: 10 Stravinsky
character: 10 Ann Trulove, Nick Shadow **11** Baba the Turk, Mother Goose, Tom Rakewell

rakish 4 airy **6** breezy, dapper, jaunty, sporty **7** dashing, gallant, immoral, lustful **8** cavalier, debonair, depraved, sporting **9** bumptious, debauched, dissolute, lecherous, libertine **10** dissipated, lascivious, profligate, sauntering, swaggering

rally 4 meet, rush **5** score, unite **6** caucus, gather, muster, pick up, powwow, revive **7** catch up, collect, get well, improve, recruit, reunite, revival **8** assemble, assembly, recovery **9** come round, gathering, get better, reconvene **10** assemblage, convalesce, convention, reassemble, recuperate **11** convocation, improvement, mass meeting, pull through, restoration **12** call together, congregation, recuperation **13** convalescence

ram 3 hit, jam **4** beat, bump, butt, dash, goat, slam **5** crash, drive, force, smash **6** batter, hammer, hurtle, strike, thrust **7** run into

Ram
constellation of: 5 Aries

ramble 3 gad **4** hike, roam, rove, wind **5** amble, drift, range, snake, twist **6** stroll, wander, zigzag **7** meander, saunter, traipse **8** gad about, idle walk **9** gallivant **11** perambulate, peregrinate

rambling 6 prolix, uneven
7 diffuse **10** circuitous, digressive, discursive, disjointed

rambunctious 4 wild **5** noisy, rowdy **6** active, unruly **7** raucous, untamed, violent **9** irascible **10** boisterous, pugnacious **11** quarrelsome **14** uncontrollable

Rameau, Jean-Philippe
born: 5 Dijon **6** France
composer of: 6 Platee **8** Dardanus **13** Les Fetes d'Hebe **14** Castor et Pollux **15** Castor and Pollux **16** Les Indes Galantes, The Indigo Suitors **17** Hippolyte et Aricie **20** La Princesse de Navarre

ramification 3 arm **4** part, spur **5** prong **6** branch **8** division, offshoot **9** branching, outgrowth **10** divergence, separation **11** consequence, subdivision

rampage 4 rage **5** storm **7** run amok, run riot

rampant 4 rife **5** erect **6** raging **8** epidemic, pandemic **9** prevalent, unchecked, universal **10** on hind legs, standing up, widespread **12** ungovernable, unrestrained **14** uncontrollable

rampart 7 barrier, bastion, bulwark, parapet **9** barricade, earthwork **10** breastwork **13** defensive wall, fortification **14** protective wall

Ramsay, William
field: 9 chemistry
nationality: 7 British
discovered: 4 neon **5** argon (in air) **6** helium **7** krypton
awarded: 10 Nobel Prize

ramshackle 5 shaky **6** flimsy, shabby **7** rickety, run-down **8** decrepit, unstable, unsteady **9** crumbling, tottering **10** tumbledown **11** dilapidated **13** deteriorating

Ramtil *see* **5** Niger

Ran
origin: 12 Scandinavian
goddess of: 3 sea
husband: 5 Aegir

ranch 4 farm **5** range **6** grange, spread **7** acreage, station **8** hacienda **10** plantation

rancher 6 cowboy, farmer, gaucho **7** cowhand, cowpoke **8** herdsman, sheepman, stockman **9** cattleman **10** cowpuncher

rancid 3 old **4** foul, gamy, high, rank **6** putrid, strong **8** mephitic, stinking **10** malodorous

rancor 4 hate **5** spite **6** animus, enmity, hatred, malice, spleen **7** ill will **8** acrimony **9** animosity, antipathy, hostility **10** antagonism, bitterness, ill feeling, resentment **11** malevolence **12** spitefulness

rancorous 5 nasty **6** bitter **7** hostile **8** churlish, spiteful, vengeful, venomous **9** splenetic **10** ill-natured **11** acrimonious **12** antagonistic

Rand, Ayn
author of: 13 Atlas Shrugged **15** The Fountainhead **17** Romantic Manifesto

Randall, Tony
real name: 16 Leonard Rosenberg
born: 7 Tulsa OK
roles: 9 Mr Peepers 10 Felix Unger, Pillow Talk 12 Harvey Weskit, The Odd Couple 13 The Mating Game 20 The Seven Faces of Dr Lao

random 5 stray 6 casual, chance 7 aimless, offhand 9 haphazard, hit-or-miss, unplanned 10 accidental, fortuitous, occasional, undesigned, unexpected, unintended 12 adventitious 13 unintentional 14 unpremeditated

Ranft, George
real name of: 10 George Raft

range 3 run 4 roam, rove 5 field, gamut, limit, orbit, reach, ridge, scope 6 bounds, domain, extend, massif, plains, radius, sierra, sphere, wander 7 explore, pasture, purview, stretch, variety 8 province 9 selection 11 grazing land 16 chain of mountains

Rangoon
capital of: 5 Burma
former name: 5 Dagon 6 Yangon
founder: 10 Alaungpaya
landmark: 10 Sule Pagoda 15 Shwe Dagon Pagoda
name means: 11 end of strife
river: 7 Rangoon
square: 12 Independence

rangy 4 tall 5 broad, lanky 9 expansive, extensive

rank 3 row 4 bald, file, foul, line, lush, rate, sort, tall, type, wild 5 class, crass, dense, grade, gross, level, nasty, order, sheer, stale, stand, total, utter 6 arrant, coarse, column, estate, filthy, jungly, lavish, rancid, status 7 come out, echelon, glaring, profuse, quality, rampart 8 absolute, complete, flagrant, position, standing, tropical 9 atrocious, be classed, come first, downright, have place, luxuriant, monstrous, overgrown 10 outrageous, scurrilous 11 highgrowing, ill smelling, unmitigated 12 overabundant 14 classification, social standing, strong smelling

rank and file 6 troops 17 enlisted personnel, general membership

Rankine, William John Macquorn
field: 7 physics
nationality: 8 Scottish
devised: 12 Rankine Cycle, Rankine Scale 26 Fahrenheit temperature scale
author of: 22 Manual of the Steam Engine

rankle 4 gall, rile 5 chafe, gripe, pique 6 fester 8 irritate 10 not sit well

ransack 3 gut 4 comb, loot, raid, rake, sack 5 rifle, scour, strip 6 ravage, search 7 despoil, pillage, plunder 8 lay waste 9 devastate, vandalize 14 rummage through, turn upside down

ransom 3 buy 4 free, save 5 atone, price 6 redeem, rescue 7 deliver, expiate, reclaim, recover, release 8 liberate, retrieve 10 liberation, redemption

Ransom, John Crowe
member of: 12 the Fugitives
author of: 14 I'll Take My Stand 16 Captain Carpenter 30 Bells for John Whiteside's Daughter

rant 4 fume, rage, rave, yell 5 orate, scold, spout, storm 6 bellow 7 bluster, bombast, bravado, explode 8 harangue 11 declamation 12 exaggeration

rap 3 jaw, pan, tap 4 bang, chat, drum, talk 5 blame, knock, roast, speak, thump 6 dump on 7 clobber 8 converse 9 criticize 10 come down on 11 communicate 14 responsibility, shoot the breeze

rapacious 6 greedy 7 looting, wolfish 8 covetous, grasping, ravenous, thievish 9 marauding, mercenary, pillaging, predatory, voracious 10 avaricious, insatiable, plundering, ransacking

rapacity 5 greed 7 avarice 10 greediness 12 covetousness, graspingness 13 mercenariness

Rape of Lucrece
author: 18 William Shakespeare
character: 7 Tarquin 9 Collatine

Rape of the Lock, The
author: 13 Alexander Pope
character: 5 Ariel 7 Belinda, Umbriel 9 Lord Petre 10 Thalestris

Raphael 9 archangel

Raphael
real name: 14 Raffaello Santi 15 Raffaello Sanzio
born: 5 Italy 6 Urbino
artwork: 7 Disputa 8 Julius II 10 Entombment 14 Sistine Madonna 17 The
School of Athens, The Virgin and Child 18 Madonna di Casa Tempi, The Transfiguration 19 The Triumph of Galatea 21 Baldassare Castiglione 22 The Marriage of the Virgin 24 The Expulsion of Heliodorus 28 The Madonna and Child with St John (La Belle Jardiniere)
architect of: 11 Villa Madama (Rome) 16 Pandolfini Palace (Florence) 22 Vidoni-Caffarelli Palace (Rome)

rapid 4 fast 5 brisk, fleet, hasty, quick, swift 6 active, flying, prompt, speedy 7 express, hurried, instant, rushing 8 agitated, feverish 9 galloping, unchecked 11 accelerated, expeditious, precipitate

rapidity 5 haste, speed 8 celerity, velocity 9 fleetness, quickness, swiftness 10 promptness

rapidly 4 fast 5 apace 7 briskly, hastily, quickly, swiftly 8 pellmell, speedily 9 hurriedly, like a shot, overnight 10 in high gear 11 at full speed 13 expeditiously, helter-skelter

rapids 5 chute 7 current 10 white water

rapport 3 tie 4 link 10 connection, fellowship 11 affiliation, camaraderie 12 relationship 13 understanding 17 interrelationship

rapprochement 6 accord 7 detente, entente 9 agreement 10 adjustment, compromise, settlement 11 appeasement, arrangement 12 conciliation, pacification 13 accommodation, harmonization, reconcilement, understanding 14 reconciliation 16 mutual concession

rapscallion 5 knave, rogue, scamp 6 rascal 7 low-life, villain 8 scalawag 9 scoundrel 10 blackguard, ne'er-do-well, rascallion 14 good-for-nothing

rapt 6 dreamy, enrapt, intent 7 bemused, charmed 8 absorbed, ecstatic 9 attentive, bewitched, delighted, enchanted, engrossed, entranced, rapturous 10 captivated, enraptured, enthralled, fascinated, interested, moonstruck, spellbound 11 transported

rapture 3 joy 5 bliss 6 thrill 7 delight, ecstasy, elation 8 euphoria, felicity 9 beatitude

rapturous 4 rapt 8 beatific, blissful, ecstatic 9 enthralled 10 enraptured

rare 3 few 6 scarce, unique 7 unusual 8 uncommon 10 hard to find, infrequent 11 exceptional, seldom found 16 few and far between

rarefied 4 thin 6 dilute, purify, rarify, reduce, refine, subtle 7 inflate 8 diminish 9 attenuate, extenuate

rarely 6 hardly, seldom 8 not often 10 hardly ever, uncommonly 12 infrequently, scarcely ever 15 once in a blue moon, on rare occasions 17 once in a great while

raring 4 agog, avid, keen 5 eager 8 desirous 9 impatient 12 enthusiastic

rarity 6 oddity 7 anomaly 8 scarcity 11 unusualness 12 uncommonness 14 remarkableness

rascal 3 cad, imp 4 rake 5 devil, knave, rogue, scamp 7 villain 8 rakehell, scalawag 9 prankster, reprobate, scoundrel, trickster 10 blackguard, delinquent 11 rapscallion

rash 5 brash, hasty 6 abrupt 7 foolish 8 careless, headlong, heedless, reckless 9 foolhardy, impetuous, imprudent, impulsive, premature, unadvised, unchecked 10 incautious, indiscreet, ungoverned, unthinking 11 adventurous, harebrained, injudicious, precipitate, thoughtless 12 devil-may-care, uncontrolled 13 irresponsible

rashness 8 audacity, boldness 9 riskiness 12 heedlessness, indiscretion, recklessness 13 foolhardiness, impulsiveness 15 precipitousness, thoughtlessness

Rashomon
  author: 18 Ryunosuke Akutagawa
  director: 13 Akira Kurosawa

Raskolnikov
  character in: 18 Crime and Punishment
  author: 10 Dostoevsky

rasp 3 irk, nag, rub, vex 4 fiie 5 chafe, grate, worry 6 abrade, scrape, wheeze 7 grating, scraper, scratch 8 abrasive, irritate 9 huskiness 10 hoarseness

raspberry 11 Rubus idaeus
  varieties: 3 red 4 hill 5 black, dwarf 6 Mysore, purple 8 European 9 flowering, Mauritius 11 American red 13 Rocky Mountain

15 Purple-flowering 22 Rocky Mountain flowering
  brandy: 9 Framboise

rasping 5 harsh, raspy, rough 6 hoarse 7 chafing, grating, nagging 8 abrading, scraping, worrying 9 offensive 10 irritating

Rasselas
  author: 13 Samuel Johnson
  character: 5 Imlac 6 Pekuah 7 Nekayah
  Rasselas's title: 17 Prince of Abyssinia

Rassendyll, Rudolph
  character in: 15 Prisoner of Zenda
  author: 4 Hope

rat 3 cad, cur 4 fink, heel 5 churl, knave, louse 6 betray, rascal, rotter, squeal, vermin 7 bounder, villain 8 informer, inform on 9 scoundrel 10 blackguard 11 stool pigeon

rate 3 fee 4 cost, deem, dues, levy, pace, rank, toll 5 class, count, price, speed, tempo 6 charge, figure, look on, regard, tariff 7 expense, measure 8 classify 10 assessment

rate highly 5 prize, value 6 admire, esteem 7 cherish, respect 8 treasure

Rathbone, Basil
  real name: 25 Philip St John Basil Rathbone
  born: 11 South Africa 12 Johannesburg
  roles: 6 Tybalt 7 Karenin 10 Dawn Patrol 11 Mr Murdstone 12 Anna Karenina 14 Romeo and Juliet, Sherlock Holmes, The Mark of Zorro 16 A Tale of Two Cities, David Copperfield 20 The Last Days of Pompeii 24 The Adventures of Robin Hood 25 The Hound of the Baskervilles

rather 4 a bit, very 5 quite 6 fairly, kind of, pretty, sort of 8 slightly, somewhat 10 moderately, more or less, relatively 13 comparatively

ratification 2 OK 4 okay 7 consent 8 approval, sanction 10 validation 11 affirmation, endorsement 12 confirmation 13 authorization, corroboration 14 seal of approval

ratify 2 OK 4 okay 6 affirm, uphold 7 agree to, approve, certify, confirm, endorse, support 8 accede to, make good, sanction, validate 9 authorize, consent to, make valid 11 acknowledge 12 authenticate

rating 4 mark, rank 5 class, grade, ratio, value 6 degree, rebuke, sailor, seaman 7 ranking 8 standing 9 appraisal 10 assessment, evaluation, percentage 14 classification

ratio 8 equation 10 proportion 11 arrangement 12 distribution 13 apportionment, fixed relation 15 proportionality 17 interrelationship 20 proportional relation

ration, rations 3 due 4 dole, food 5 allot 6 stores 7 measure, mete out 8 allocate 9 allotment, apportion, food share, provender, provision 10 provisions 13 apportionment

rational 4 sage, sane, wise 5 lucid, solid, sound 6 normal 7 logical 8 all there, balanced, credible, feasible 9 advisable, judicious, plausible, sagacious 10 reasonable 11 clearheaded, responsible 12 compos mentis 13 perspicacious 15 in one's right mind

rationale 5 basis, logic 6 excuse, reason 7 grounds 9 reasoning 10 key concept, philosophy 11 explanation, foundations 16 underlying reason

rationalize 6 excuse 7 explain, justify 8 palliate 9 whitewash 10 account for 11 explain away 13 put a gloss upon 14 make excuses for 16 make allowance for

rattan, ratan 4 cane, lash, palm, whip 5 thong 6 switch, wicker

Ratti, Achille 10 Pope Pius XI

rattle 3 gab, jar 4 faze 5 clang, clank, clink, prate, shake, throw, upset 6 bounce, flurry, jangle 7 agitate, blather, chatter, clatter, confuse, disturb, fluster, maunder, nonplus, perturb 8 bewilder, clacking, distract 9 discomfit 10 discompose, disconcert 11 roll loosely

rattlebrained 4 dumb 5 silly 6 stupid 7 asinine, doltish, foolish, idiotic, moronic, witless 9 brainless, imbecilic 10 fool-headed, half-witted 11 harebrained, lamebrained

rattled 5 fazed, upset 7 annoyed 9 disturbed, flustered, perturbed, thrown off 10 distracted 11 discomposed 12 disconcerted

rattle on 3 gab 4 blab 5 prate, run on 6 babble, gabble

7 blabber, chatter, prattle **16** run off at the mouth

ratty 4 poor, worn **5** angry, cross, nasty, testy **6** cranky, shabby, touchy **7** tangled, unkempt **9** wretched **9** irascible, motheaten **11** dilapidated

raucous 4 loud **5** harsh, raspy, rough **6** hoarse, shrill **7** blaring, grating, jarring **8** grinding, jangling, piercing, strident **9** dissonant **10** discordant, stertorous **11** cacophonous **12** earsplitting, inharmonious

raunchy 4 lewd **5** dirty, gross **6** coarse, smutty, vulgar **8** off-color

Rauschenberg, Robert
born: **12** Port Arthur TX
artwork: **3** Bed **5** Barge **7** Jammers **8** Monogram **11** Retroactive

ravage 3 gut **4** loot, raid, rape, raze, ruin, sack **5** strip, waste, wreck **6** maraud **7** despoil, destroy, overrun, pillage, plunder, ransack, shatter **8** demolish, desolate, lay waste, spoliate **9** devastate **10** lay in ruins

rave 3 wax **4** fume, go on, gush, rage, rant **5** be mad, kudos, storm **6** babble, bubble, ramble **7** be angry, bluster, carry on, explode, flare up, run amok, sputter, thunder **8** flattery **9** be furious, expatiate, go on and on, good press, laudatory **10** effervesce, high praise, rhapsodize **11** blow one's top, compliments

ravel 4 undo **6** unknit **7** unravel, untwine, untwist

Ravel, Maurice
born: **6** France **7** Ciboure
composer of: **6** Bolero **7** La Valse, Mirrors **8** Jeux d'eau **9** Fountains **11** Mother Goose, Sheherazade **14** Daphnis et Chloe **15** Gaspard de la Nuit, L'Heure Espagnole **17** Rapsodie Espagnole, The Tomb of Couperin **20** Pavane for a Dead Infant **21** Don Quichotte a Dulcinee **22** L'Enfant et les Sortileges, Pavane for a Dead Princess **27** Pavane pour une infante defunte, Valses nobles et sentimentales

raven 3 jet **4** crow, dark, inky, rook **5** black, ebony, sable **6** devour **9** coal-black

Raven, The
author: **13** Edgar Allan Poe

ravenous 6 greedy, hungry **7** piggish, starved **8** covetous, famished, grasping, ravening, starving **9** insatiate, predatory, rapacious, voracious **10** avaricious, gluttonous, insatiable

Ravenshoe
author: **13** Henry Kingsley

ravine 3 gap **4** pass, rift, wadi **5** abyss, break, chasm, cleft, crack, gorge, gulch, gully, split **6** arroyo, breach, canyon, clough, divide, valley **7** fissure **8** crevasse

raving 3 mad **4** wild **6** insane **7** ranting **8** frenzied **9** delirious

ravish 4 rape **5** abuse, charm, cheer **6** defile, snatch, tickle **7** delight, enchant, gladden, outrage, overjoy, violate **8** deflower, enthrall, entrance, knock out **9** captivate, enrapture, fascinate, transport

ravishing 8 alluring, charming, gorgeous, smashing, splendid, striking **9** beautiful **10** bewitching, delightful, enchanting, entrancing **11** captivating, fascinating, sensational

raw 4 bare, cold, damp, rare **5** basic, bleak, crude, frank, fresh, green, harsh, plain, rough, young **6** biting, bitter, brutal, callow, chilly, rookie, unripe **7** cutting, natural, nipping, numbing, unbaked, untried **8** blustery, freezing, ignorant, immature, inexpert, piercing, pinching, uncooked, untaught, untested **9** inclement, underdone, undrilled, unfledged, unrefined, unskilled, untrained, windswept **10** amateurish, unprepared, unseasoned **11** not finished, undercooked, undeveloped, unexercised, uninitiated, unpracticed, unprocessed, unvarnished **13** inexperienced, undisciplined, unembellished **15** not manufactured

rawboned 4 lean **5** gaunt, lanky, spare **7** angular

Rawdon, Captain
character in: **10** Bleak House
author: **7** Dickens

Rawhide
character: **5** Mushy **8** Gil Favor, Ian Cabot, Wishbone **9** Jim Quince, Pete Nolan **10** Rowdy Yates **11** Joe Scarlett, Solomon King **13** Clay Forrester **14** Hey Soos Patines
cast: **10** Sheb Wooley **11** Charles Gray, David Watson, Eric Fleming, Robert Cabal, Rocky Shahan, Steve

Raines **12** James Murdock, Paul Brinegar **13** Clint Eastwood **16** Raymond St Jacques

Rawlings, Marjorie Kinnan
author of: **11** The Yearling

rawness 3 nip **4** bite **5** chill **8** rudeness **9** crudeness, greenness, roughness, sharpness, vulgarity **10** chilliness **12** inexperience

ray 3 arm **4** beam, fish, line **5** gleam, light, shaft, shine, skate, trace **6** branch, streak, stream, stripe **7** radiate **8** particle, plowfish, radiance **9** emanation, radiation

Ray, Man
born: **14** Philadelphia PA
artwork: **4** Gift (Le Cadeau) **7** Manikin **9** The Lovers **13** Observing Time **45** The Rope Dancer Accompanies Herself with Her Shadows

Rayleigh, John William Strutt
field: **7** physics
nationality: **7** British
discovered: **5** argon
awarded: **10** Nobel Prize

rayon
invented by: **4** Swan

raze 4 fell, ruin **5** level, smash, wreck **6** reduce, remove, topple **7** destroy, flatten, wipe out **8** demolish, pull down, tear down **9** break down, dismantle, knock down **10** obliterate

razor
invented by: **6** Schick **8** Gillette

Razorback State
nickname of: **8** Arkansas

Re see **2** Ra

reach 3 get, hit **4** find, go to, grab, make, move **5** climb, enter, get to, grasp, seize, touch **6** attain, clutch, come to, extend, grab at, land at, secure, spread **7** contact, stretch **8** amount to, approach, arrive at **9** get hold of, set foot in **10** get as far as, outstretch, stretch out

reachable 6 at hand **8** possible **10** accessible, achievable, attainable, obtainable, procurable

reach the top 6 arrive **7** prosper, succeed **8** make good **13** hit the big time

react 4 work **6** answer, behave, resist, return **7** respond **11** reverberate

reaction 5 reply 6 answer, reflex 8 backlash, response 11 restoration 13 counteraction 14 chemical change 17 counterrevolution, right-wing comeback

reactionary 7 diehard 8 mossback, rightist 9 right-wing 10 regressive 11 right-winger 12 reversionary 17 ultraconservative 20 counterrevolutionary

react to 5 reply 6 answer 7 respond 11 acknowledge

read 2 go 3 say 4 note, scan, show 5 study, utter 6 adduce, peruse, recite 7 analyze, deliver, discern, explain, present 8 construe, decipher, indicate, perceive, pore over 9 apprehend, interpret, translate 10 comprehend, glance over, understand 11 extrapolate

Read, Piers Paul
  author of: 5 Alive 9 Polonaise 10 Monk Dawson, The Junkers, The Upstart 18 Professor's Daughter

Reade, Charles
  author of: 13 Peg Woffington 23 The Cloister and the Hearth

readily 6 at once, easily, freely, pronto 7 quickly 8 in no time, promptly, smoothly, speedily 9 expressly, hands down, instantly, willingly 10 graciously 11 immediately, straightway 12 effortlessly, ungrudgingly

readiness 8 alacrity, dispatch 9 alertness 10 promptness 12 preparedness

Reading on the Statute of Uses
  author: 12 Francis Bacon

read the riot act 5 chide, scold 6 berate, rebuke 7 censure, chasten, correct, lecture, reprove 8 admonish 9 dress down, reprimand 10 take to task

ready 3 apt, fit, set 4 deft, keen, ripe, up to 5 acute, alert, eager, equip, handy, on tap, prone, sharp 6 adroit, all set, artful, astute, at hand, bright, clever, expert, facile, fit out, liable, mature, on hand, primed, prompt, shrewd, speedy 7 cunning, equal to, prepare, present, tending, willing 8 disposed, inclined, masterly, punctual, skillful 9 attentive, dexterous, fitted out, furnished, ingenious, in harness, versatile, wide-awake 10 accessible, discerning, per-

ceptive, put in order 11 acquisitive, expeditious, predisposed, quick-witted, resourceful, serviceable

ready for use 5 handy, on tap 6 at hand, on hand 9 available 10 accessible, convenient 11 at one's elbow 14 at one's disposal

ready-made 10 off-the-rack 11 ready-to-wear, store-bought 17 store manufactured

ready money 4 cash 8 currency 10 cash on hand

ready to go 5 peppy 9 full of pep 10 raring to go 17 full of vim and vigor 24 bright-eyed and bushy-tailed

Reagan, Ronald Wilson *see box, p. 812*

real 4 pure, true 5 solid, valid 6 actual, honest 7 certain, factual, genuine, sincere 8 absolute, bona fide, positive, rightful, tangible, truthful 9 authentic, unalloyed, unfeigned, veracious, veritable 10 legitimate, unaffected 11 not affected, substantial, substantive, unvarnished 12 well-grounded 13 unadulterated 14 unquestionable

realistic 4 real 7 genuine, graphic, natural, precise 8 faithful, lifelike, truthful 9 authentic, depictive, objective, pragmatic 10 true-to-life 11 descriptive, down-to-earth 12 naturalistic 16 representational

reality 4 fact 5 truth 6 verity 9 actuality 11 materiality, tangibility 12 corporeality 14 substantiality 17 physical existence

realization 7 success 8 grasping 10 attainment, perception 11 achievement, culmination, fulfillment 12 appreciation, consummation 13 comprehension, understanding 14 accomplishment

realize 2 do 3 get, net 4 gain 5 clear, grasp 6 absorb, attain, fathom, gather, profit 7 achieve, acquire, cognize, discern, execute, fulfill, imagine, make out, perform, produce 8 carry out, complete, conceive, make good, perceive 9 actualize, apprehend, discharge, make money, penetrate, recognize 10 accomplish, appreciate, bring about, comprehend, consummate, effectuate, understand 11 bring to pass 12 carry through

realized 3 got 6 gained, netted,

proved, proven 7 cleared, grasped, made out, saw into 8 absorbed, accepted, effected, executed, existing, fathomed, gathered, imagined, made good, profited 9 completed, conceived, discerned, fulfilled, perceived, performed 10 actualized, penetrated, recognized, understood 11 appreciated, apprehended, consummated, established 12 accomplished, comprehended

really 5 truly 6 indeed, in fact, surely, verily 8 actually 9 certainly, genuinely, literally, veritably 10 absolutely, positively, truthfully 13 categorically 14 unquestionably

realm 4 land 5 field, orbit, state 6 domain, empire, nation, region, sphere 7 country, demesne, kingdom 8 dominion, monarchy, province 11 royal domain

real McCoy, the 4 real 7 genuine 9 authentic 12 the real thing

reap 3 get, win 4 earn, gain 5 glean, score 6 derive, gather, obtain, profit, secure, take in 7 acquire, bring in, harvest, procure, realize

rear 3 aft, end 4 back, heel 5 after, nurse, raise, stern, train 6 dorsal, foster 7 bring up, care for, cherish, develop, educate, nurture, postern, tail end 8 back part, hind part, hindmost 9 aftermost, after part, at the back, cultivate, in the back, posterior

Rear Window
  director: 15 Alfred Hitchcock
  based on story by: 15 Cornell Woolrich
  cast: 10 Grace Kelly 11 Raymond Burr 12 James Stewart, Thelma Ritter, Wendell Corey

Rea Silvia
  also: 4 Ilia 10 Rhea Silvia
  form: 12 vestal virgin
  lover: 4 Mars
  son: 5 Remus 7 Romulus

reason 4 wit 5 cause, logic, sense, solve 6 acumen, brains, figure, motive, sanity 7 grounds, insight 8 lucidity, occasion 9 awareness, faculties, intellect, normality, rationale, reasoning 10 perception 11 common sense, discernment, exhortation, explanation, penetration, rationality 12 apprehension, intelligence, perspicacity, think through 13 argumentation, comprehension, justification, mental bal-

Reagan, Ronald Wilson
  nickname: 5 Dutch **6** Ronnie
  presidential rank: 8 fortieth
  party:
    current: **10** Republican
    former: **10** Democratic
  state represented: 2 CA
  defeated: 6 (James Earl) Carter (Jr) **7** (Walter Frederick "Fritz") Mondale **8** (John Bayard) Anderson
  vice president: 4 (George Herbert Walker) Bush
  cabinet:
    state: **4** (Alexander M) Haig (Jr) **6** (George P) Shultz
    treasury: **5** (Donald T) Regan
    defense: **10** (Caspar W) Weinberger
    attorney general: **5** (William French) Smith
    interior: **4** (James) Watt **5** (William P) Clark
    agriculture: **5** (John R) Block
    commerce: **8** (Malcolm) Baldrige
    labor: **7** (Raymond J) Donovan
    health and human services: **7** (Margaret M) Heckler **9** (Richard S) Schweiker
    education: **4** (Terrel H) Bell
    HUD: **6** (Samuel R) Pierce (Jr)
    transportation: **4** (Elizabeth H) Dole **5** (Andrew L) Lewis (Jr)
    energy: **5** (Donald P) Hodel **7** (James B) Edwards
  born: 9 Tampico IL
  education:
    College: **6** Eureka
  religion: 17 Disciples of Christ
  interests: 2 TV **5** track **6** movies **8** football **9** chops wood **10** basketball, jelly beans **13** weightlifting **15** horseback riding
  vacation spot: 14 Rancho del Cielo (Santa Barbara CA)
  dog: 5 Lucky
  author: 18 Where Is the Rest of Me?
  political career:
    governor of: **10** California
  civilian career: 5 actor **17** radio sportscaster
    host: **15** Death Valley Days **22** General Electric Theater
    president of: **17** Screen Actors Guild
    roles: **8** King's Row **10** Brother Rat **13** John Loves Mary, The Hasty Heart **15** Bedtime for Bonzo **19** The Voice of the Turtle **20** Cattle Queen of Montana **21** The Girl from Jones Beach **22** Knute Rockne All American
  military service: 6 US Army **7** captain **10** World War II
  notable events of lifetime/term:
    approval of: **10** MX missiles
    assassination attempt on: **6** Reagan **14** Pope John Paul II
    attempted assassination on Reagan by: **15** John W Hinckley Jr
    bombing of: **5** Libya
    hostages freed in: **4** Iran
    invasion of: **7** Grenada
    marines sent to: **7** Lebanon
    nuclear disaster at: **9** Chernobyl
    Russians shot down: **14** Korean airliner
    scandal: **8** Irangate
  father: 10 John Edward
    nickname: **4** Jack
  mother: 5 Nelle (Wilson)
  siblings: 4 (John) Neil
  wife: 4 Jane (Wyman) **5** Nancy (Davis)
    Nancy Davis born: **18** Anne Frances Robbins
  children: 6 Ronald **7** Maureen, Michael (adopted) **8** Patricia
    Patricia also actress known as: **10** Patti Davis
  first lady:
    program: **9** Drug abuse, Just Say No **12** Alcohol abuse **18** Foster Grandparents

ance, understanding **15** clearheadedness

reasonable 4 fair, just, sage, sane, wise **5** sound **6** likely, proper **7** fitting, knowing, le-nient, logical, natural, patient, prudent **8** credible, moderate, possible, probable, rational, sensible, suitable, thinking **9** equitable, impartial, judicious, objective, plausible, temperate, tolerable **10** admissible, coolheaded, legitimate, not extreme, reflective, thoughtful **11** circumspect, intelligent, justifiable, levelheaded, not unlikely, of good sense, predictable, well-founded **12** not excessive, well-grounded **13** understanding **14** understandable **15** of sound judgment

reasonableness 5 logic **6** sanity, wisdom **8** fairness, prudence **9** good sense **10** moderation **11** credibility, objectivity, rationality **12** good judgment, impartiality, intelligence **13** judiciousness **14** circumspection, thoughtfulness **15** clearheadedness

reasonably 6 almost, fairly **8** passably, somewhat **10** moderately, more or less **13** approximately

reasoning 5 basis, logic **6** ground **7** thought **8** analysis, argument, thinking **9** deduction, inference, rationale **10** cogitation, reflection **11** penetration **13** ratiocination **14** interpretation

reason out 8 mull over **10** deliberate **12** think through

reassure 5 cheer **6** buoy up, uplift **7** bolster, comfort **8** inspirit **9** encourage **13** inspire hope in

reassured 6 buoyed **9** bolstered, comforted, heartened **10** emboldened, encouraged, inspirited

reassuring 7 hopeful **10** auspicious, comforting, heartening **11** encouraging

Reb 2 Mr **5** Rabbi **6** Mister

rebate 6 refund **8** discount **9** abatement

Rebecca
  author: 15 Daphne du Maurier
  character: 10 Jack Favell, Mrs Danvers (Danny) **12** Frank Crawley **13** Colonel Julyan, Maxim de Winter
  house: 9 Manderley
  director: 15 Alfred Hitchcock
  cast: 10 Nigel Bruce **12** Joan Fontaine **13** George Sanders **14** Judith Anderson (Mrs Danvers) **15** Laurence Olivier (Maxim de Winter)
  Oscar for: 7 picture

Rebecca
  character in: 7 Ivanhoe
  author: 5 Scott

Rebecca *see* **7** Rebekah

Rebecca of Sunnybrook Farm
  author: 17 Kate Douglas Wiggin
  character: 4 Cobb **8** Adam Ladd **11** Aunt Miranda

14 Rebecca Randall
15 Emma Jane Perkins

Rebekah
  also: 7 Rebecca
  father: 7 Bethuel
  husband: 5 Isaac
  brother: 5 Laban
  son: 4 Esau **5** Isaac, Jacob

rebel 3 shy **4** riot **5** avoid, quail, react, wince **6** flinch, mutiny, recoil, revolt, rise up, shrink **7** seceder, traitor, upstart **8** deserter, maverick, resister, turncoat **9** anarchist, dissenter, insurgent **10** iconoclast, malcontent, separatist **12** secessionist **13** nonconformist, revolutionary, revolutionist **15** insurrectionist

rebellion 6 mutiny, putsch, revolt **7** defiance, sedition, upheaval, uprising **9** coup d'etat **10** insurgency, revolution **12** insurrection

rebellious 6 unruly **7** defiant **8** contrary, mutinous, up in arms **9** alienated, fractious, insurgent, seditious, truculent, turbulent **10** disorderly, pugnacious, refractory **11** disobedient, intractable, quarrelsome **12** contumacious, recalcitrant, ungovernable, unmanageable **13** insubordinate, revolutionary **14** uncontrollable **15** insurrectionary

rebelliousness 8 defiance **9** rebellion **12** disobedience

Rebel Without a Cause
  director: 11 Nicholas Ray
  cast: 8 Sal Mineo **9** James Dean, Jim Backus **11** Natalie Wood

Rebirth
  god of: 4 Gwyn

rebound 3 bob **6** bounce, recoil, re-echo **7** flounce **8** recovery, ricochet **10** spring back

rebounding 7 rubbery, springy **9** resilient **11** ricocheting **12** bouncing back

rebuff 4 deny, snub **5** check, repel, spurn **6** ignore, put off, refuse, reject, slight **7** decline, put-down, refusal, repulse **8** turn down **9** disregard, rejection **10** putting off **12** cold shoulder **13** slap in the face **15** keep at a distance

rebuke 5 blame, chide, scold, score **6** berate **7** censure, chew out, chiding, lecture, reproof, reprove, upbraid **8** admonish, berating, call down, reproach, reproval, scolding **9** dress down, reprimand **10** admonition, chewing out, take to

task, upbraiding **11** castigation, disapproval **12** admonishment, dressing down, remonstrance, reprehension, take down a peg **13** find fault with, tongue-lashing **15** remonstrate with

rebuttal 5 reply **6** answer, denial, retort **7** defense, riposte **8** disproof, negation, response **9** disproval, rejoinder **10** refutation **11** confutation **12** counterreply, disagreement, surrejoinder **13** contradiction **15** counterargument

recalcitrant 5 balky **6** mulish, unruly **7** willful **8** contrary, stubborn **9** obstinate, pigheaded, unwilling **10** bullheaded, headstrong, refractory **11** disobedient, intractable **12** unsubmissive

recall 5 place **6** memory, revive **8** call back, remember **9** reanimate, recognize, recollect **10** reactivate, remobilize **11** reinstitute, remembrance **12** recollection **17** ability to remember

recant 4 deny **5** unsay **6** abjure, disown, recall, renege, repeal, revoke **7** disavow, rescind, retract **8** disclaim, forswear, renounce, take back, withdraw **9** foreswear, repudiate **10** apostatize **12** eat one's words **14** change one's mind

recantation 6 denial **9** disavowal **10** refutation, retraction, revocation **11** repudiation **12** renunciation

recapitulate 5 recap, sum up **6** relate, repeat, reword **7** recount, restate **8** rephrase **9** epitomize, reiterate, summarize **15** repeat in essence

recapture 6 retake **7** reprise **15** experience again

recede 3 ebb **5** abate **6** back up, go back, retire **7** regress, retreat, subside **10** retrogress

receipt 7 arrival, release, voucher **9** admission, discharge, receiving, reception **10** acceptance, admittance, possession, recipience **11** acquisition, transferral

receipts 3 pay **4** gain, gate, take **5** share, split, wages **6** income, recipe, return **7** formula, payment, profits, returns, revenue **8** earnings, proceeds **9** emolument **10** net profits **12** remuneration **13** reimbursement

receive 3 get **4** meet **5** admit, greet, put up **6** accept, come by, obtain, regard, secure, suffer, take in **7** acquire, adjudge, approve, be given, react to, sustain, undergo, welcome **8** meet with, submit to **9** encounter, entertain **10** experience **11** accommodate

receive willingly 6 accept **10** take gladly **16** accept with thanks **18** accept with open arms

receive with favor 6 praise **7** approve **10** appreciate

receive with open arms 6 invite **7** embrace, welcome **13** accept eagerly **19** roll out the red carpet

recent 3 new **4** late **5** fresh, novel **6** modern **8** up-to-date **9** latter-day **12** contemporary **13** up-to-the-minute

receptacle 3 bag, bin, box, can, jar **4** file, tray **6** basket, bottle, hamper, holder, hopper, vessel **7** carrier **8** receiver **9** container **10** depository, repository **11** compartment

reception 2 do **4** fete **5** party **6** affair, soiree **7** welcome **8** greeting **11** recognition **15** social gathering

receptive 8 amenable, friendly **10** accessible, hospitable, interested, open-minded, responsive **11** susceptible **12** approachable **17** favorably disposed

recess 3 bay, gap **4** bend, cell, cove, fold, gulf, lull, nook, pass, rest, slot **5** break, cleft, gorge, inlet, letup, niche, pause **6** alcove, corner, harbor, hiatus, hollow **7** holiday, interim, respite, time out **8** interval, vacation **9** interlude **10** pigeonhole **11** coffee break, indentation **12** intermission **14** breathing spell

recessed 4 sunk **6** paused, sunken **7** delayed **8** deferred, extended, indented **9** adjourned, dissolved, postponed, prolonged, withdrawn **10** terminated
church wall: **5** ambry
wall: **6** alcove

recesses 6 depths **10** inmost part, penetralia

recession 10 depression **11** recessional **16** economic downturn

recherche 4 rare **5** prize **6** choice, exotic, scarce, select, unique **7** special, unusual **8** original, superior, uncommon, valuable **9** different, priceless **10** one of a kind **11** exceptional

recipe 2 Rx **4** cure, rule **5** axiom **6** elixir, remedy **7** formula, receipt **12** instructions, prescription

recipient 4 heir **5** donee, taker **6** getter **7** legatee **8** accepter, acquirer, obtainer, receiver **9** presentee **11** beneficiary

reciprocal 6 common, linked, mutual, shared **8** returned **9** bilateral, exchanged, one for one **10** equivalent **11** give-and-take **12** interchanged, interrelated **13** complementary, corresponding, given in return **14** interdependent **15** interchangeable

reciprocate 4 feel **6** return **7** requite, respond **9** retaliate **10** make return **11** act likewise, give and take, interchange **12** give in return **19** return the compliment

reciprocity 8 exchange **11** give and take, interchange

recital 4 talk **6** report **7** concert, telling **8** delivery, reciting **9** discourse, narration, narrative, rendition **10** recitation **11** description, particulars, performance **12** dissertation, oral exercise **13** public reading **14** graphic account, recapitulation

recite 4 tell **5** quote, speak **6** relate, repeat **7** declaim, deliver, narrate, perform, recount **10** say by heart **11** communicate

reckless 4 rash, wild **5** giddy, hasty **6** daring, fickle, madcap, unwary **7** flighty, foolish, unaware **8** careless, cavalier, heedless, mindless, unsteady, volatile **9** daredevil, desperate, foolhardy, imprudent, impulsive, negligent, oblivious, unheeding, unmindful **10** incautious, indiscreet, insensible, neglectful, regardless, unthinking, unwatchful **11** harebrained, inattentive, precipitate, thoughtless, unconcerned **12** devil-may-care, unsolicitous **13** inconsiderate, irresponsible, uncircumspect **14** scatterbrained

recklessly 4 fast **5** blind **6** rashly, wildly **7** hastily **8** headlong **9** headfirst **10** carelessly, heedlessly **11** audaciously, desperately, impetuously, impulsively **12** unmindfully **13** irresponsibly, unconcernedly

recklessness 7 abandon **8** rashness **9** disregard, unconcern **10** imprudence, profli-

gacy **11** impetuosity **12** heedlessness, immoderation **13** foolhardiness **15** thoughtlessness **16** irresponsibility

reckon 3 add **4** bank, cope, deal, deem, plan, rank, rate **5** add up, class, count, fancy, guess, judge, tally, think, total, value **6** assess, decide, esteem, expect, figure, handle, regard **7** account, adjudge, balance, bargain, compute, imagine, presume, suppose, surmise **8** appraise, consider, estimate **9** calculate, determine, speculate

reckoning 3 tab **4** bill, doom **5** count, tally, total **6** adding, charge **7** account **8** estimate, judgment **9** appraisal, summation **10** estimation, evaluation **11** calculation, computation **13** final judgment **19** settling of an account

reclaim 6 reform, rescue **7** correct, recover, rectify, restore

recline 4 lean, loll, rest **6** lounge, repose, sprawl **7** lie back, lie down **12** take one's ease

reclining 7 lolling, resting **8** lounging, reposing **9** lying down, recumbent

recluse 3 nun **4** monk **5** crank, loner **6** hermit, hidden, secret **7** ascetic, eremite, erratic, oddball **8** cenobite, crackpot **9** eccentric **10** cloistered **11** sequestered **13** nonconformist

recognition 6 notice **9** discovery **10** acceptance, validation **13** comprehension, understanding **14** acknowledgment, identification **19** diplomatic relations

recognizable 5 clear, plain **8** distinct **10** detectable **11** discernable, perceivable, perceptible **12** identifiable, intelligible **13** ascertainable **14** comprehensible, understandable **15** distinguishable

recognizance 4 bond **6** pledge **10** obligation **11** recognition **15** acknowledgement

recognize 3 see **4** know, spot **5** admit, place, sight **7** discern, make out, pick out, realize, respect, yield to **8** identify, submit to **9** be aware of, concede to **10** appreciate, comprehend, understand **11** acknowledge **14** give the floor to

recognized 5 known **8** accepted, admitted, approved, familiar, realized **9** customary **10** accredited **11** traditional **12** acknowledged, conventional

recoil 4 fail, kick **5** blink, cower, demur, quail, shirk, start, wince **6** blench, cringe, falter, flinch, revolt **7** fly back, rebound, retreat **8** draw back, hang back, jump back **9** bound back **10** shrink back, spring back

recoil at 4 hate **5** abhor **6** detest, eschew, loathe **7** despise **9** abominate, shudder at **10** shrink from **12** be revolted by **14** view with horror **18** feel aversion toward

recoiling 7 wincing **9** flinching **10** rebounding **11** drawing back **13** shrinking back, springing back

recollect 5 place **6** recall **8** remember **10** call to mind

recollection 4 mind **6** memoir, memory, recall, record **11** remembrance **12** reminiscence **13** retrospection
  French: **8** souvenir

recommend 4 urge **5** favor, order **6** advise **7** counsel, endorse, propose, suggest **8** advocate, vouch for **9** encourage, prescribe **10** put forward **11** speak well of

recommendable 9 advisable, favorable **10** worthwhile

recommendation 4 plug **6** behest, praise **8** approval, good word **9** reference **11** endorsement **12** commendation

recompense 3 pay **5** repay **6** return, reward **7** payment **9** reimburse, repayment **10** compensate, remunerate, reparation **12** compensation, remuneration **15** indemnification

reconcile 5 fix up **6** adjust, make up, resign, settle, square **7** correct, patch up, rectify, reunite, win over **8** persuade **9** harmonize **10** conciliate, propitiate **11** set straight

reconcile oneself 6 submit **9** acquiesce **13** resign oneself

reconciliation 8 fixing up, making up, settling, squaring **10** adjustment, correction, patching up, rectifying **11** resignation, winning over **12** conciliation **13** justification, rectification **15** setting straight

recondite 4 deep **6** arcane, hidden **7** obscure, abstruse, esoteric **9** concealed **10** mysterious **16** incomprehensible

reconnaissance 6 survey **7** viewing **8** scouting, scrutiny **10** inspection **11** exploration, observation **12** surveillance **13** investigation **14** reconnoitering

reconnoiter 4 look **5** probe, scout **6** patrol, picket, survey **7** examine **8** remember, traverse

reconsider 5 amend **6** modify, ponder, review, revise **7** correct, rethink, sleep on **8** mull over, reassess **9** reexamine, think over **10** reevaluate **13** think better of **15** think twice about

reconstitute 7 restore **9** recompose **10** add water to **11** reconstruct

reconstruct 7 rebuild **8** make over, recreate **10** reassemble **11** reestablish **12** reconstitute

record 3 log **4** copy, file, list, memo, note, post, show, tape **5** admit, enter **6** annals, career, docket, enroll, report **7** account, archive, catalog, conduct, history, jot down, jotting, journal **8** document, indicate, register, take down **9** chronicle, introduce, write down **10** adventures, background, memorandum, transcribe **11** experiences, make an entry, performance, proceedings **12** unbeaten mark **14** top performance
  French: **11** compte rendu

record
  invented by: **4** Bell **6** Edison **7** Tainter **8** Berliner **10** Goldenmark

recount 4 tell **6** detail, recite, relate **7** explain, narrate **8** describe **9** count over

recoup 5 atone **6** redeem, regain **7** recover, replace **8** make good, retrieve **9** make up for, reacquire **13** make amends for

recourse 6 choice, option, resort **11** alternative, other choice

recover 4 heal, mend **5** rally **6** offset, pick up, recoup, redeem, regain, retake, revive **7** balance, get back, get well, improve, reclaim, restore, win back **8** make good, retrieve, revivify **9** make up for, reacquire, recapture, reconquer, repossess **10** come around, compensate, convalesce, recuperate, rejuvenate **11** pull through, resuscitate

recovery 4 cure **5** rally **6** recoup, rescue, upturn **7** revival, salvage **8** comeback **9** retrieval **10** betterment, regain-

ment **11** improvement, reclamation, reformation, restoration **12** recuperation **13** business cycle, convalescence

recreancy 8 apostasy **9** cowardice, desertion **10** cravenness, disloyalty, infidelity **13** faithlessness, pusillanimity **14** unfaithfulness

recreant 6 coward, craven, yellow **8** apostate, cowardly, deserter, disloyal, renegade **9** undutiful **10** unfaithful **11** lily-livered **12** dishonorable **13** pusillanimous, yellow-bellied

recreation 4 play **5** hobby, sport **7** pastime **9** amusement, avocation, diversion **10** relaxation **13** entertainment **15** leisure activity

recrimination 5 blame **6** charge **10** accusation **13** countercharge

recruit 4 hire **5** raise, renew **6** employ, enlist, enroll, muster, novice, recoup, revive, rookie **7** draftee, provide, recover, restore **8** beginner, newcomer **9** conscript **10** recuperate

rectangle 3 box **6** oblong, square **7** polygon **10** quadrangle **13** parallelogram, quadrilateral

rectangular 4 long **6** square **7** boxlike **11** right-angled **12** quadrangular **13** quadrilateral

rectification 6 fixing, reform **7** redress **8** righting, squaring **9** remedying, repairing **10** adjustment, correction, regulation **12** setting right **15** putting straight, putting to rights **16** straightening out

rectify 3 fix **4** cure, mend **5** amend, emend, focus, right **6** adjust, attune, reform, remedy, repair, revise, square **7** correct, redress **8** put right, regulate, set right **9** make right **10** straighten

rectitude 5 honor **7** decency, probity **8** morality **9** integrity, principle **11** uprightness **12** virtuousness **13** righteousness **14** high-mindedness **15** trustworthiness **16** incorruptibility **17** irreproachability

rector 6 cleric, parson, pastor, priest **8** minister, preacher **9** churchman, clergyman **12** ecclesiastic

recumbent 4 flat **5** prone **6** supine **7** leaning **8** couchant **9** lying down, prostrate, reclining **10** horizontal **12** stretched out

recuperate 4 heal, mend **7** get well, improve, recover **8** come back **9** get better **10** come around, convalesce **11** be on the mend, pull through **14** return to health **16** regain one's health

recuperation 8 recovery **11** restoration **13** convalescence

recuperative 11 restorative **15** health-restoring

recur 6 repeat, resume, return **7** persist **8** come back, continue, reappear **9** come again **10** occur again

recurrence 5 cycle, round **6** repeat, return **7** relapse, renewal, reprise, routine **8** iterance, rotation **10** continuity, repetition **11** periodicity **12** reappearance

recurrent 7 regular **8** frequent, periodic **9** recurring, repeating **10** repetitive **11** reappearing **12** intermittent **14** appearing again

red 4 pink, rose, rosy, ruby, wine **5** aglow, coral, flame, ruddy **6** auburn, cherry, florid, maroon **7** burning, crimson, flaming, flushed, glowing, scarlet **8** blooming, blushing, cardinal, inflamed, reddened, rubicund **9** rubescent, vermilion **12** blood-colored

Red and the Black, The (Le Rouge et le Noir)
    author: **8** Stendhal
    character: **6** Fouque **8** M de Renal **11** Julien Sorel **16** Mathilde de la Mole

Red Badge of Courage, The
    author: **12** Stephen Crane
    character: **6** Wilson **10** Jim Conklin **12** Henry Fleming

red-blooded 5 lusty, peppy, vital **6** ardent, robust, strong, sturdy **7** dynamic, intense **8** forceful, powerful, spirited, vigorous **9** energetic **10** hot-blooded, passionate

Red Branch
    origin: **5** Irish
    warriors of: **9** Conchobar

Redburn
    author: **14** Herman Melville

red-cheeked 4 rosy **5** ruddy **6** robust **8** blushing **12** apple-cheeked

Red Cross Knight
    character in: **15** The Faerie Queene
    author: **7** Spenser

redden 4 burn, glow **5** blush, color, flame, flush **9** go crimson **12** become florid

reddish 4 rosy, ruby **5** ruddy, rufus **6** flushy, rufous **7** roseate **8** rubicund

reddish-brown 4 rust **5** henna **6** auburn, copper, russet, sienna **8** chestnut, cinnamon

Red Earth People *see* **3** Fox

redeem 4 keep, save **5** cover **6** defray, ransom, recoup, reform, regain, rescue, settle **7** buy back, convert, fulfill, reclaim, recover, satisfy **8** atone for, make good, retrieve **9** discharge, make up for, repossess **10** evangelize, repurchase

redeemed 5 saved **7** claimed, rescued **8** made good, ransomed, reformed **9** atoned for, delivered, fulfilled, recovered **10** carried out, regenerate **11** repossessed

redemption 6 excuse, pardon, ransom, reform, rescue **7** salvage **8** recovery **9** amendment, atonement, exemption, expiation, salvation **10** conversion **11** deliverance, reformation

Redford, Robert
    real name: **20** Charles Robert Redford
    born: **13** Santa Monica CA
    roles: **8** The Sting **10** The Natural **11** Legal Eagles **12** The Candidate, The Way We Were **13** Downhill Racer **14** The Great Gatsby **15** Jeremiah Johnson **17** Barefoot in the Park **19** All the President's Men **20** Three Days of the Condor **29** Butch Cassidy and the Sundance Kid
    director: **14** Ordinary People (Oscar)

Redgrave, Lynn
    born: **6** London **7** England
    father: **18** Sir Michael Redgrave
    sister: **15** Vanessa Redgrave
    roles: **10** Georgy Girl **14** The Happy Hooker

Redgrave, Sir Michael
    born: **7** Bristol, England
    daughter: **4** Lynn **7** Vanessa
    roles: **11** Dan Peggotty **15** The Lady Vanishes **16** David Copperfield **22** Mourning Becomes Electra **27** The Importance of Being Earnest

Redgrave, Vanessa
    born: **6** London **7** England
    father: **18** Sir Michael Redgrave
    sister: **12** Lynn Redgrave

husband: **14** Tony Richardson
    roles: **5** Julia, Yanks **6** Agatha, Blow-Up, Morgan **7** Camelot, Isadora **9** Guinevere **16** Mary Queen of Scots **17** The Lady from the Sea

red-hot 5 aglow, fiery **6** heated, raging **7** blazing, burning, glowing, intense **12** all-consuming

red-letter 5 happy, lucky **6** banner **10** auspicious, felicitous

redness 4 glow **5** blush, flush **8** rosiness **9** ruddiness **10** floridness

redolence 5 aroma, savor **7** bouquet **9** fragrance, good smell **12** pleasant odor

redolent 5 balmy, spicy **6** savory, smelly **7** mindful, odorous, reeking, scented **8** aromatic, fragrant, perfumed, stinking **9** evocative, odiferous **10** expressive, indicative, suggestive **11** odoriferous, reminiscent **13** sweet-smelling

Redon, Odilon
    born: **6** France **8** Bordeaux
    artwork: **10** In the Dream, The Cyclops **11** Le Vieil Ange **13** Flowers of Evil **15** Violette Heymann

redouble 7 augment, magnify **8** heighten, multiply **9** intensify

redoubtable 7 awesome **8** alarming, imposing **10** formidable **11** illustrious **12** awe-inspiring

redound 4 lead, tend **5** cause, surge **6** abound **7** conduce, incline **8** overflow **10** contribute **11** reverberate

redress 4 ease **5** amend, right **6** amends, reform, relief, remedy **7** correct, payment, rectify, relieve **8** easement, set right **9** make up for **10** recompense, reparation **11** restitution **12** compensation, satisfaction **13** compensate for, rectification **15** indemnification **18** make retribution for

Red River
    director: **11** Howard Hawks
    cast: **9** Joanne Dru, John Wayne **11** John Ireland **13** Walter Brennan **15** Montgomery Clift

Red Rover, The
    author: **19** James Fenimore Cooper

Reds
    director: **12** Warren Beatty
    cast: **11** Diane Keaton

(Louise Bryant), Paul Sorvino **12** Warren Beatty (John Reed) **13** Jack Nicholson, Jerzy Kosinski **14** Edward Herrmann **16** Maureen Stapleton
Oscar for: 8 director **17** supporting actress (Stapleton)

Red Shoes, The
  author: 21 Hans Christian Andersen
  director: 13 Michael Powell **17** Emeric Pressburger
  cast: 12 Marius Goring, Moira Shearer **13** Anton Walbrook **14** Robert Helpmann

Red Skelton Show, The
  character: 8 Gertrude **10** Heathcliff **13** Mean Widdle Kid **14** San Fernando Red, Sheriff Deadeye, Willie Lump-Lump **16** Bolivar Shagnasty **17** Cauliflower McPugg **18** Clem Kadiddlehopper **20** Freddie the Freeloader
  saying: 7 I dood it
  closing line: 8 God bless

Red Sky at Morning
  author: 15 Richard Bradford

reduce 3 cut **4** bust, curb, diet, dull, ease, thin **5** abate, blunt, break, check, force, lower, slash, water **6** damage, demote, dilute, lessen, retard, soften, temper, weaken **7** assuage, atrophy, cripple, cut down, leave in **8** diminish, discount, enfeeble, mark down, minimize, mitigate, moderate, modulate, slim down, slow down, tone down, trim down **9** bring down, checkmate, undermine **10** debilitate, devitalize, slenderize **11** lower in rank **12** incapacitate

reduced form 6 digest **7** summary **9** short form **11** abridgement, contraction **12** abbreviation, condensation

reduce speed 4 slow **5** brake **6** rein in **8** slow down **10** decelerate

reduce to nothing 5 erase **7** abolish, destroy, wipe out **8** lay waste **9** eradicate, liquidate **10** annihilate **11** exterminate

reductio ad absurdum 22 reduction to an absurdity

reduction 3 cut **5** break **8** decrease, discount **9** abatement, lessening **10** concession **11** abridgement, subtraction

reduction to an absurdity
  Latin: 18 reductio ad absurdum

redundancy 6 excess **7** surplus **8** verbiage **9** tautology **10** repetition **11** diffuseness, superfluity **13** overabundance **14** circumlocution, repetitiveness

redundant 5 extra **6** excess **7** surplus **10** pleonastic **11** dispensable, inessential, overflowing, repetitious, superfluous, unnecessary **12** tautological **13** superabundant

redwood 19 Adenanthera pavonina, Sequoia sempervirens
  varieties: 4 dawn **5** coast, giant **7** Madeira

reed
  varieties: 3 bur **4** vine **5** Burma, giant **6** common **14** Mauritania vine

reed 9 six cubits

Reed, Sir Carol
  director of: 6 Oliver (Oscar) **11** The Third Man

Reed, Walter S
  field: 12 bacteriology
  discovered cause of: 11 yellow fever

reef 3 bar **4** bank, flat, spit **5** shelf, shoal **7** sandbar, shallow

reek 4 fume **5** smell, smoke, steam, stink **7** stench **7** give off **9** effluvium, emanation

reel 4 rock, roll, spin, sway **5** lurch, pitch, swirl, waver, whirl **6** rotate, teeter, totter, wobble **7** revolve, stagger, stumble

reeling 5 dizzy, giddy, shaky **6** whirly **8** spinning, unsteady **10** staggering **11** vertiginous

Reese, Harold
  nickname: 6 Pee Wee
  sport: 8 baseball
  position: 9 shortstop
  team: 15 Brooklyn Dodgers

Reeve
  character in: 18 The Canterbury Tales
  author: 7 Chaucer

Reeve, Christopher
  born: 9 New York NY
  roles: 8 Superman **9** Deathtrap **13** The Bostonians **15** Somewhere in Time

refer 2 go **4** cite, send, turn **6** advert, allude, direct, submit **7** consult, deliver, mention **8** hand over, transfer, transmit **9** pass along

referee 5 judge **6** decree, settle, umpire **7** arbiter, mediate **8** judgment, mediator, moderate **9** arbitrate, determine, intercede, intervene, moderator,

pronounce **10** adjudicate, arbitrator **11** adjudicator, intercessor **12** intermediary

reference 4 hint **7** inkling, mention **8** allusion, good word, innuendo **10** deposition, intimation, suggestion **11** affirmation, credentials, endorsement, implication, testimonial **13** certification **14** recommendation

reference book 5 atlas, bible **6** manual **9** guidebook **10** dictionary **12** encyclopedia

refine 6 filter, purify, strain **7** cleanse, develop, improve, perfect, process **9** cultivate

refined 5 clean, suave **6** gentle, polite, urbane **7** courtly, elegant, genteel **8** cleansed, cultured, delicate, finished, graceful, ladylike, mannerly, polished, purified, well-bred **9** civilized, clarified, courteous **10** cultivated, fastidious **11** gentlemanly **14** discriminating

refinement 5 grace **6** finish, nicety, polish, step up **7** advance, culture, dignity, finesse, suavity **8** breeding, civility, cleaning, courtesy, delicacy, elegance, fineness, revision, urbanity **9** amendment, cleansing, gentility, propriety **10** betterment, filtration, gentleness, politeness **11** advancement, cultivation, development, discernment, enhancement, good manners, improvement, progression, savoir faire, step forward **12** amelioration, distillation, graciousness, purification, tastefulness **13** courteousness, rectification **14** discrimination, fastidiousness

refitting 8 adapting **10** adaptation, remodeling **11** reequipping, resupplying

reflect 4 cast, copy, muse, show, undo **5** image, study, think, throw **6** betray, evince, expose, mirror, ponder, reason, return, reveal **7** condemn, display, exhibit, express, imitate, present, rebound, uncover **8** cogitate, consider, disclose, give back, indicate, manifest, meditate, mull over, register, ruminate, send back, set forth **9** bring upon, cerebrate, dwell upon, represent, reproduce, speculate, throw back, undermine **10** deliberate **11** concentrate, contemplate, demonstrate

reflection 4 blot, idea, slur, view **5** image, study **6** insult, musing, notion **7** opinion, re-

proof, thought **8** reproach, thinking **9** attention, pondering, sentiment **10** cogitation, conviction, derogation, impression, imputation, meditation, rumination **11** cerebration, insinuation, mirror image, pensiveness **12** deliberation **13** concentration, consideration, disparagement
French: **6** pensee

reflective 7 pensive **8** thinking **9** judicious, pondering **10** meditative, ruminative, thoughtful **11** speculative **13** contemplative

Reflex
author: **11** Dick Francis

reform 4 mend **5** amend, atone, emend **6** better, remedy, repair, repent, revise **7** convert, correct, improve, rebuild, rectify, remodel, restore **8** progress **9** amendment **10** correction **12** mend one's ways, rehabilitate **13** rectification **16** set straight again, turn over a new leaf

reformation 6 change, reform **9** amendment, reforming **10** alteration, conversion **11** improvement **12** modification **14** reorganization

refractory 5 balky **6** mulish, unruly **7** restive, wayward, willful **8** contrary, stubborn **9** fractious, obstinate, pigheaded **10** rebellious **11** disobedient, intractable **12** unmanageable

refrain 5 avoid, forgo **6** desist, eschew, forego, refuse, resist **7** abstain, forbear, hold off **8** leave off, renounce **11** curb oneself, keep oneself **12** stay one's hand **15** restrain oneself

refrain from 5 avoid, forgo **6** desist, eschew, forego **7** abstain, forbear **8** leave off, renounce

refresh 3 jog **4** prod **5** brace, renew, rouse **6** arouse, awaken, prompt, revive, stir up, vivify **7** cool off, freshen, quicken, recruit, restore **8** activate, energize, recreate **9** reanimate, stimulate **10** invigorate, rejuvenate, strengthen

refreshed 7 revived **8** animated, restored, vivified **9** enlivened, freshened **11** invigorated

refreshing 7 bracing **11** revivifying **12** invigorating **13** strengthening **15** thirstquenching

refreshment 4 bite, eats

5 drink, snack **6** bracer **7** potable **8** beverage, cocktail, pick-me-up, potation **9** appetizer, drinkable, refresher **10** recreation, relaxation **11** hors d'oeuvre, nourishment, restoration, restorative **12** food and drink, invigoration, rejuvenation **14** reinvigoration, thirst quencher

refrigerate 4 cool **5** chill **6** freeze **7** congeal **8** keep cold, keep cool, put on ice **9** keep on ice

Refrigerator, The
nickname of: **12** William Perry

refuge 4 home **5** haven **6** asylum, harbor, resort **7** hideout, retreat, shelter **8** safehold **9** anchorage, harborage, sanctuary **10** protection **12** port in a storm **14** help in distress, place of shelter

refugee 2 DP **5** exile **6** bolter, eloper, emigre **7** escapee, evacuee, runaway **8** emigrant, fugitive **9** absconder **10** expatriate **15** displaced person

refulgent 6 bright, lucent **7** glowing, lambent, radiant, shining **8** luminous, relucent **9** brilliant

refund 5 remit, repay **6** rebate, return **7** pay back **9** reimburse, repayment **10** recompense, remittance, remunerate **12** amount repaid **13** give back money, reimbursement **18** make restitution for **19** make compensation for

refurbish 4 mend, redo **5** clean, fix up, renew **6** repair, tidy up **7** freshen, improve, remodel, restore **8** overhaul, renovate, spruce up **11** recondition

refusal 2 no **3** nay **4** veto **6** denial **7** regrets **8** turndown **9** declining, rejection **10** nonconsent **11** declination, disapproval **13** nonacceptance, noncompliance, unwillingness

refuse 2 no **4** deny, junk, veto **5** spurn, trash, waste **6** forbid, litter, reject **7** decline, garbage, rubbish, say no to **8** disallow, prohibit, turn down, withhold

refuse pile 4 dump **6** midden **11** rubbish heap

refuse to submit 4 defy **5** rebel **6** resist **7** disobey, hold out, violate **10** transgress **12** fail to comply

refutation 4 veto **6** denial **7** counter **8** negation, rebuttal

9 disavowal **11** confutation, repudiation **12** invalidation **13** contradiction

refutatory 8 contrary, opposing **10** discrepant **11** conflicting, disagreeing **12** antithetical, inconsistent **13** contradictory **14** countervailing, irreconcilable

refute 4 deny **5** rebut **6** answer **7** confute, counter **8** disprove **9** challenge **10** contradict, invalidate **12** give the lie to

regain 6 recoup, redeem, retake **7** get back, reclaim, recover, win back **8** gain anew, get again, retrieve **9** recapture, repossess

regal 5 grand, noble, proud, royal **6** august, kingly, lordly **7** queenly, stately **8** imposing, kinglike, majestic, princely, splendid **9** queenlike **10** princelike **11** magnificent **13** splendiferous

regale 3 ply **4** fete **5** amuse, feast **6** divert, please **7** banquet, delight, lionize **8** enthrall **9** entertain **10** serve nobly **11** wine and dine **15** feed sumptuously

Regan
character in: **8** King Lear
author: **11** Shakespeare

regard 3 eye, see **4** care, heed, hold, mind, note, rate, scan, view **5** judge, point, think, value, watch **6** accept, admire, aspect, behold, detail, esteem, follow, gaze at, look at, matter, notice, reckon, survey, take in **7** account, believe, concern, put down, respect, set down, subject, thought **8** consider, estimate, listen to, look upon, look up to, note well, relation **9** attention, hearken to, reference **10** admiration, connection, estimation, meditation, reflection, scrutinize **11** contemplate, observation, think well of **12** appreciation **13** cast the eyes on, consideration, think highly of **14** pay attention to

regardful 5 civil **6** polite **7** mindful **8** reverent **9** courteous, observant **10** respectful **11** deferential, reverential

regard highly 6 admire, esteem **7** respect **10** appreciate

regarding 4 in re **5** about, anent **7** apropos **10** concerning, respecting

regardless 6 anyhow, anyway **10** for all that **11** nonetheless **12** nevertheless **15** notwithstanding **19** in spite of everything

regard with repugnance
4 hate **5** abhor **6** detest, loathe **7** despise **8** execrate **9** abominate, can't stand, shudder at **10** recoil from, shrink from **11** can't stomach **12** be revolted by **13** be nauseated by, find repulsive **18** feel aversion toward

regard with suspicion
5 doubt **7** suspect **8** distrust, mistrust, question

regenerate 5 renew **6** redeem, reform, revive, uplift **7** restore **8** inspirit, reawaken, retrieve, revivify **9** enlighten, resurrect **10** rejuvenate **11** resuscitate **12** generate anew **13** give new life to, make a new man of

regent 4 king **5** queen, ruler **8** governor **9** protecter, protector

regime 4 rule **5** power, reign **7** command, control, dynasty **8** dominion **9** direction **10** government, leadership, management **12** jurisdiction **14** administration

regimen 4 diet, rule **6** system **10** government

regimentation 5 order, rigor **6** method, system **7** control, regimen **9** orthodoxy **10** discipline, regulation, uniformity **12** rigorousness **13** methodization **19** doctrinaire approach

Regiment of Women
author: **12** Thomas Berger

Regin
origin: **12** Scandinavian
mentioned in: **8** Volsunga
brother: **6** Fafnir
raised: **6** Sigurd

region 4 area, land, zone **5** field, range, realm, space, tract **6** domain, sphere **7** country, expanse **8** district, locality, province, vicinity **9** territory **12** neighborhood

regional 5 areal, local, zonal **7** dialect **10** locational, provincial **11** territorial **12** geographical

register 3 log **4** dial, mark, roll, show **5** diary, gauge, meter, range, scale **6** betray, enlist, enroll, heater, ledger, record, sign up **7** betoken, check in, compass, counter, daybook, exhibit, express, logbook, point to, portray, set down **8** disclose, heat duct, heat vent, indicate, manifest, note down, radiator, recorder, registry, take down **9** indica-

tor, write down **10** calculator, heat outlet, hot-air vent, record book **12** put in writing

Regius 16 Greek unical codex

regnat populus 16 let the people rule
motto of: **8** Arkansas

regress 3 ebb **4** back, exit, fall **6** go back, recede, return, revert **7** relapse, retreat, reverse **8** fall back, pass back, withdraw **9** backslide **10** lose ground, retrogress **11** deteriorate **12** move backward

regressive 8 backward **9** declining, worsening **10** retrograde **13** retrogressive

regret 3 rue, woe **4** moan **5** grief, mourn, qualm **6** bemoan, bewail, lament, repent, sorrow, twinge **7** anguish, apology, deplore, eat crow, remorse, scruple **8** be rueful, grieve, weep over **9** apologies, grievance, heartache, rue the day **10** be sorry for, contrition, repentance, ruefulness **11** be ashamed of, compunction, lamentation, reservation **12** be remorseful, eat humble pie, eat one's words, self-reproach **13** feel sorrow for, regretfulness, second thought **14** disappointment, feel remorse for, remorsefulness **15** dissatisfaction **16** feel distress over, pang of conscience, self-condemnation

regretful 6 rueful **8** contrite **9** sorrowful **10** apologetic, remorseful **15** self-reproachful

regrettable 6 woeful **7** unhappy **8** grievous, pitiable **10** calamitous, deplorable, lamentable **11** unfortunate

regular 3 set **4** even, fine, real **5** daily, fixed, plain, usual **6** common, normal, proper, smooth, steady, trusty **7** classic, correct, genuine, habitue, natural, typical, uniform **8** absolute, accepted, complete, constant, everyday, faithful, familiar, frequent, habitual, loyalist, ordinary, orthodox, periodic, stalwart, standard, thorough, true blue **9** customary, recurrent, recurring, unvarying **10** consistent, dependable, invariable, periodical, unchanging **11** commonplace, down-to-earth, established, old reliable, symmetrical, undeviating **12** well-balanced **16** well-proportioned

regulate 3 fix **5** guide **6** adjust, direct, govern, handle, manage **7** balance, control, monitor, oversee, rectify

8 moderate, modulate, organize **9** supervise **10** regularize **11** superintend

regulation 4 rule **5** edict, order **6** decree **7** command, control, dictate, statute **8** handling **9** adjusting, direction, ordinance **10** adjustment **11** commandment **13** standing order

regulator 5 guide **7** manager **8** director, governor, overseer **9** moderator, modulator **10** adjustment, supervisor **14** superintendent **15** adjusting device

regurgitate 4 barf **5** vomit **7** throw up **8** disgorge

rehabilitate 3 fix **4** save **6** redeem, remake **7** restore, salvage **8** make over, readjust, renovate **9** reeducate **10** refurbish, reinstate **11** recondition, reconstruct, resocialize, set straight **13** straighten out **16** restore to society

rehash 6 repeat, retell, reword **7** restate **8** rephrase **9** iteration, rechauffe

rehearsal 5 drill, recap **6** tryout **7** hearing, reading, test run **8** audition, exercise, practice, trial run **9** polishing **10** perfecting, repetition, runthrough **11** preparation, reiteration, walk-through **14** recapitulation

rehearse 5 drill, ready, train **6** go over, polish, recite, relate, repeat, retell **7** narrate, prepare, recount **8** practice **9** reiterate **10** run through **13** read one's lines **14** give a recital of, study one's lines

Rehoboam
father: **7** Solomon
mother: **6** Naamah
son: **6** Abijah

Rehoboth
founder: **6** Nimrod

Reich, Charles
author of: **20** The Greening of America

Reichsfuhrer 11 Reich leader
chief of: **8** SS troops

reign 4 rule **6** govern, regime, regnum, tenure **7** command **8** dominion, hold sway, regnancy, tutelage **9** dominance, influence **10** government, incumbency **11** sovereignty, supervision **12** wear the crown **13** hold authority **14** have royal power, sit on the throne **15** occupy the throne **17** exercise authority **19** exercise sovereignty
Hindu: **3** raj

reign over 4 rule 6 govern 7 command, control 8 dominate

reimburse 5 pay up, remit, repay 6 rebate, refund 7 pay back 8 square up 9 indemnify 10 compensate, recompense, remunerate 15 make restitution

reimbursement 6 refund 9 indemnity, repayment 12 compensation, remuneration

rein, reins 4 curb, hold 5 check, limit, watch 6 bridle 7 control, harness 8 hold back, restrict, suppress 9 restraint 11 keep an eye on

Reiner, Carl
  born: 7 Bronx NY
  son: 9 Rob Reiner
  roles: 15 Your Show of Shows 21 It's a Mad Mad Mad Mad World
  created: 15 Dick Van Dyke Show
  director: 5 Oh God 7 The Jerk 8 The Comic 11 Where's Poppa?
  novel: 13 Enter Laughing

Reiner, Rob
  father: 10 Carl Reiner
  roles: 8 Meathead 10 Mike Stivik 14 All in the Family

reinforce 4 prop 5 steel 7 bolster, brace up, fortify, support 8 buttress 10 strengthen 12 make stronger

reinforcement 4 stay 5 brace, strut 7 bracing, support 10 assistance 11 buttressing 13 strengthening

reinstate 5 renew 6 revive 7 readmit, restore 11 reestablish, reinstitute, reintroduce

reinstatement 7 renewal, revival 11 restoration 13 reinstitution 14 reintroduction 15 reestablishment

reintroduce 6 revive 8 recreate 9 reinstate 11 reestablish, reinstitute

reintroduction 7 revival 10 recreation 11 restoration 13 reinstatement 15 reestablishment

reiterate 5 resay 6 hammer, rehash, repeat, retell, reword, stress 7 iterate, reprise, restate 8 rephrase 11 pound away at 12 recapitulate 13 go over and over

reject 4 deny 5 repel, spurn 6 rebuff, refuse 7 castoff, decline, discard, disdain, dismiss, flotsam, repulse, say no to 8 castaway, disallow, shrug

off, turn down, turn from 9 repudiate

rejected 6 denied, dumped, jilted 7 cast off, outcast, refused, spurned, unloved 8 disowned, forsaken, lovelorn 9 abandoned, discarded, disproved 10 unaccepted, repudiated 11 invalidated

rejection 6 rebuff 7 disdain, refusal 8 scorning, spurning 9 declining, dismissal, rebuffing, rejecting, ruling out

rejoice 5 exult, glory, revel 6 be glad 7 be happy, delight 8 be elated, jubilate 9 be pleased, celebrate, make merry 10 exhilarate, sing for joy 11 be delighted, be overjoyed 13 be transported

rejoice in 5 eat up, enjoy, savor 6 relish 7 revel in 9 delight in 13 be pleased with, get a kick out of 14 take pleasure in

rejoicing 5 mirth 6 gaiety 7 delight, ecstasy, elation, jollity, jubilee, revelry, triumph 8 cheering, gladness, pleasure, reveling 9 festivity, good cheer, happiness, jubilance, merriment 10 exultation, joyfulness, jubilation, liveliness 11 celebration, merrymaking

rejoin 6 answer, retort 7 respond

rejoinder 5 reply 6 answer, retort, return 7 riposte 8 backtalk, comeback, rebuttal, repartee, response 10 refutation 11 surrebuttal 12 counterblast, remonstrance, surrejoinder 13 countercharge 16 counterstatement

rejuvenate 6 revive 7 restore 8 revivify 9 reanimate 10 revitalize 12 reinvigorate 14 put new life into 17 make youthful again

relapse 4 fall 5 lapse 6 revert, worsen 7 decline, regress, reverse 8 fall back, sink back, slip back, turn back 9 backslide, reversion, worsening 10 degenerate, recurrence, regression, retrogress 11 backsliding, falling back 13 deterioration, retrogression 15 return to illness, turn for the worse

relate 3 say 4 link, tell 5 apply, refer, speak, state, utter 6 attach, belong, convey, detail, impart, recite, report, reveal 7 concern, connect, divulge, narrate, pertain, recount 8 describe, disclose 9 appertain, associate, feel close, make known 10 be rele-

vant 11 communicate, have rapport 12 be responsive, interact well, recapitulate 13 be sympathetic, have reference, particularize 15 feel empathy with, give an account of

related 3 kin 4 akin, said, told 7 kindred, recited 8 narrated, reported 9 recounted 15 of the same family

related by blood 3 kin 4 akin 7 kindred 14 consanguineous, of the same stock 21 having a common ancestor

relation 3 kin, tie 4 bond, link 5 tie-in 6 regard, report 7 account, bearing, concern, kinsman, recital, telling, version 8 relative 9 narrating, narration, narrative, reference, relevance, retelling 10 connection, pertinence, recitation 11 affiliation, application, association, correlation, description 13 applicability, communication 17 interrelationship

relationship 3 kin 5 blood, union 6 affair 7 kindred, kinship, liaison, sibship, society 8 affinity, alliance 10 connection 11 affiliation, association, correlation 13 consanguinity

relative 3 kin 4 clan, kith 5 blood, folks, tribe 6 allied, cousin, family, people 7 cognate, germane, kinfolk, kinsman, related 8 relation, relevant 9 connected, dependent, kinswoman, pertinent, referable 10 affiliated, applicable, associated, comparable, connection, connective, correlated, kith and kin, pertaining, relational, respective 11 appropriate, comparative, correlative, not absolute 12 interrelated 13 flesh and blood 14 interconnected

relax 4 bend, calm, ease, idle, laze, loaf, rest 5 let up, slack 6 be idle, be lazy, ease up, loosen, soften, soothe, unbend, unwind 7 cool off, holiday, make lax, slacken 8 decrease, loosen up, vacation 9 lie around 10 take it easy 12 enjoy oneself 13 make less tense 14 make less severe, make less strict

relaxation 3 fun 5 games, hobby, sport 6 repose 7 bending, leisure, pastime 8 pleasure 9 abatement, amusement, avocation, diversion, enjoyment, loosening, remission 10 recreation, slackening 11 refreshment 12 rest from work 13 entertainment

relaxed 3 lax 4 calm, cool,

easy, slow, soft **5** loose, slack **6** at ease, casual, gentle, remiss **7** flaccid, lenient **8** informal, laid back, unstrict **9** easygoing, leisurely, negligent, nerveless, unnervous **10** unstrained **11** free and easy, thoughtless
French: **6** degage

relaxed manner 4 ease **5** poise **6** aplomb **9** composure **10** confidence **11** naturalness **12** unconstraint **14** unaffectedness

relay 3 leg **4** race, tour **5** shift **6** length **8** transfer, transmit **9** conductor, regulator, satellite **10** retransmit
cylinder: **5** baton
part: **8** armature, receiver **11** transmitter **13** electromagnet
race: **6** medley **10** track event

release 4 free **5** let go, loose, untie **6** detach, let out, unbind **7** freeing, present, relieve, set free, unloose **8** liberate, set loose, unfasten **9** circulate, discharge, disengage, dismissal, extricate, letting go, releasing **10** distribute, liberating, liberation **11** circulation, communicate, extrication, publication, setting free **12** distribution, emancipation, set at liberty, setting loose

relegate 3 bar **5** eject, expel **6** assign, banish, charge, commit, demote, reject **7** cast out, consign, discard, dismiss, exclude, keep out, shut out **8** delegate **9** ostracize

relent 4 bend, melt **5** let up, relax, yield **6** give in, soften, unbend, weaken **7** give way **8** have pity **10** be merciful, capitulate, come around **11** give quarter, grow lenient **12** become milder **14** grow less severe

relentless 4 hard **5** harsh, rigid, stern, stiff **6** severe **7** adamant **8** pitiless, rigorous, ruthless **9** merciless **10** implacable, inexorable, inflexible, unyielding **11** remorseless, undeviating, unrelenting **14** uncompromising

relevance 7 aptness, fitness, meaning **9** propriety **10** pertinence **11** materiality, relatedness, suitability **12** significance **13** applicability **15** appropriateness

relevant 3 apt, fit **6** allied, suited, tied in **7** apropos, bearing, cognate, fitting, germane, related **8** apposite, material, suitable **9** connected, intrinsic,

pertinent, referring **10** applicable, associated, concerning, to the point **11** appropriate, significant **12** on the subject, to the purpose

reliable 4 true **5** solid, sound **6** trusty **8** faithful **9** unfailing **10** dependable **11** responsible, trustworthy **12** tried and true **13** conscientious

reliance 5 faith, trust **6** belief, credit **8** credence **9** assurance **10** confidence, dependence

relic 5 scrap, token, trace **7** antique, memento, records, remnant, vestige **8** artifact, fragment, heirloom, keepsake, reminder, souvenir **11** remembrance

relief 4 balm, cure, dole, rest **5** break, cheer **6** remedy **7** anodyne, elation, panacea, respite, welfare **8** antidote, easement, lenitive **9** abatement, reduction **10** mitigation, palliation, palliative **11** alleviation, assuagement, peace of mind **12** amelioration **13** encouragement **16** public assistance **17** welfare assistance
Italian: **7** rilievo

relieve 3 aid **4** calm, ease, free, help, mark **5** abate, allay, cheer, spell **6** assist, let out, pacify, remove, set off, solace, soothe, subdue, succor, temper **7** appease, assuage, break up, comfort, console, lighten, mollify, release, replace, support, take out **8** contrast, mitigate, palliate, reassure **9** alleviate, encourage, interrupt, punctuate **12** free from fear

relieved 5 freed **6** calmed, exempt **7** cheered, excused, solaced **8** consoled **9** comforted, reassured **10** encouraged

Religio Medici
author: **15** Sir Thomas Browne

religion 4 cult, sect **5** canon, creed, dogma, faith, piety **6** belief, church, homage **7** worship **8** devotion, theology **9** adoration, godliness, reverence **10** devoutness, persuasion, veneration **11** affiliation, belief in God **12** belief in gods, denomination, spirituality **13** system of faith **15** system of worship

religionist 8 believer **16** Godfearing person

religiosity 5 piety **8** devotion **10** fanaticism **15** religious fervor

religious 3 nun **4** holy, monk

5 exact, friar, godly, rigid **6** ardent, devout, divine, priest, sacred **7** devoted, staunch **8** constant, faithful, unerring **9** spiritual, steadfast **10** devotional, fastidious, Godfearing, meticulous, scrupulous, unswerving **11** punctilious, theological, undeviating **12** wholehearted **13** conscientious **14** denominational **15** spiritual-minded

religious belief 5 canon, credo, creed, dogma, tenet **8** doctrine

religious fervor 5 piety **7** ecstasy **8** holiness **9** godliness **10** devoutness **12** religiousity, spirituality

religious group 4 sect **12** denomination

religious orders
Christian: **6** Jesuit **7** Cluniac, Templar **8** Capuchin, Theatine, Trappist, Ursuline **9** Carmelite, Dominican **10** Carthusian, Cistercian, Franciscan **11** Augustinian, Benedictine, Camaldolite **16** Sisters of Charity **20** Order of the Visitation
non-Christian: **4** Sufi **7** Jainism **8** Dasanami

relinquish 4 cede, deny, drop, quit, shed **5** forgo, leave, let go, waive, yield **6** forego, give up, resign, vacate **7** abandon, cast off, discard, dismiss, forbear, forsake, release **8** abdicate, break off, disclaim, hand over, lay aside, put aside, renounce, sign away **9** deliver up, repudiate, surrender

relinquishable 9 forgoable **10** expendable, foregoable **11** dispensable **12** renounceable

relinquished 5 ceded, let go **6** gave up **7** forgone, given up, yielded **8** cast away, foregone, forsaken **9** abandoned, given away, renounced **10** left behind

relinquishment 7 cession **8** giving up, yielding **9** letting go, rejection, surrender **10** abnegation **11** repudiation **12** renunciation

relish 3 dig **4** like, love, tang, want, wish, zest **5** enjoy, fancy, gusto, savor, spice, taste **6** accent, desire, dote on, flavor, liking, palate **7** delight, longing, stomach **8** appetite, fondness, groove on, penchant, piquancy, pleasure **9** condiment, delight in, enjoyment, hankering, rejoice in **10** appreciate, ebullience, en-

thusiasm, exuberance, partiality, propensity **11** luxuriate
in **12** appreciation, be crazy
about, predilection, satisfaction **13** gratification
  type: 4 beef, corn **5** sweet
  7 chutney **6** pickle, tomato
  10 chili sauce, piccalilli
  11 horseradish

reluctance 10 hesitation
13 unwillingness
14 disinclination

reluctant 3 shy **4** slow **5** loath
6 averse **7** laggard **8** hesitant
9 diffident, unwilling **10** indisposed **11** disinclined

rely 3 bet **4** bank, lean, rest
5 count, swear, trust **6** credit,
depend, reckon **7** believe
10 feel sure of **11** be dependent **12** give credence

remain 4 go on, last, stay,
wait **5** abide, stand **6** be left,
endure, hang on, hold up, linger **7** not move, not stir, persist, prevail, stay put, subsist,
survive **8** continue, stand pat
10 be left over, stay behind

remainder 4 rest **5** waste **6** excess, refuse **7** balance, overage,
remains, remnant, residue,
surplus, wastage **8** leavings, residual, residuum **9** leftovers,
scourings **10** surplusage
11 superfluity

remains 4 body **5** stiff **6** corpse,
scraps **7** cadaver **8** dead body
9 leftovers

remark 3 say, see **4** espy,
mark, mind, note, view,
word **6** behold, look at, notice, regard, survey **7** comment, mention, observe, pay
heed **8** perceive **9** attention
10 commentary, give heed to,
make note of, reflection, take
note of **11** contemplate, observation **12** fix the mind on,
say in passing, take notice of
13 consideration **14** pay attention to

remarkable 6 signal **7** notable,
unusual **8** singular, striking
9 memorable **10** impressive,
noteworthy, phenomenal
11 conspicuous, exceptional,
outstanding **13** distinguished,
extraordinary, unforgettable

Remarque, Erich Maria
  author of: 25 All Quiet on
  the Western Front

**Rembrandt (Harmensz) van
Rijn**
  born: 6 Leiden, Leyden
  14 The Netherlands
  artwork: 6 Balaam **9** Bathsheba **13** The Night Watch
  (The Sortie of the Company
  of Captain Banning Cocq)

14 The Jewish Bride **15** Old
Woman Reading, The Bridal
Couple **19** The Blinding of
Samson **20** Christ Healing
the Sick **21** The Stoning of
St Stephen **22** Man with the
Golden Helmet, Self-Portrait
with Saskia, The Descent
from the Cross **24** The
Anatomy Lesson of Dr Tulp,
The Syndics of the Cloth
Hall **36** Aristotle Contem-
plating the Bust of Homer

remedial 7 healing, helpful,
mending **8** curative, salutary,
sanative **10** beneficial, corrective **11** meliorative, reforma-
tive, restorative, therapeutic
12 advantageous, correctional,
prophylactic

remedy 3 aid, fix **4** calm, cure,
ease, heal, help, mend
5 amend, emend, right **6** relief, repair, soothe **7** assuage,
correct, cure-all, improve, mollify, nostrum, panacea, rectify,
redress, relieve, restore **8** make
easy, medicine, mitigate, palliate, regulate, set right **9** alleviate, make sound, treatment
10 ameliorate, assistance, corrective, make better, medicament, medication, preventive
13 rectification **15** restore to
health

remember 3 tip **6** recall, reward **9** not forget, recognize,
recollect **10** appreciate, bear in
mind, call to mind, have in
mind, keep in mind, take care
of, take note of **11** bring to
mind **12** bear in memory

**remember that thou must
die**
  Latin: 11 memento mori

remembrance 5 favor, relic,
token **6** memory, recall **7** memento **8** keepsake, memorial,
reminder, souvenir **9** nostalgia **11** recognition, remembering **12** recognizance,
recollection, reminiscence
13 commemoration

**Remembrance of Things
Past**
  author: 12 Marcel Proust

Remembrance Rock
  author: 12 Carl Sandburg

Remick, Lee
  born: 8 Quincy MA
  roles: 16 Anatomy of a Murder, The Long Hot Summer
  18 Days of Wine and Roses

remind 9 put in mind, suggest
to **11** bring back to, bring to
mind, put in memory
16 awaken memories of

reminder of death
  Latin: 11 memento mori

**Remington, Frederic
Sackrider**
  born: 8 Canton NY
  artwork: 12 Bronco Buster
  23 Roping Horses in the
  Corral **32** Cavalry Charge on
  the Southern Plains

reminisce 4 mull, muse
6 ponder **7** reflect **8** hark back,
look back, remember **9** recollect, think back **12** tell old
tales **16** exchange memories,
swap remembrances

reminiscent 9 nostalgic, remindful, similar to **11** analogous to, remembering
12 recollecting **13** retrospective

remiss 3 lax **4** idle, lazy, slow
5 loose, slack **6** sloppy **7** laggard, loafing **8** careless, derelict, dilatory, inactive,
indolent, slipshod, slothful,
uncaring **9** do-nothing, forgetful, negligent, oblivious, shiftless, undutiful, unmindful
10 delinquent, neglectful, unthinking, unwatchful **11** inattentive, indifferent, thoughtless

remission 4 cure **5** lapse,
pause **6** hiatus, pardon **7** respite, retreat **8** decrease
9 abatement, acquittal, cessation, reduction, shrinkage
10 absolution, diminution,
hesitation, moderation, modulation, subsidence **11** exoneration, forgiveness, vindication

remit 3 pay **4** free, send, ship
5 clear, let go, relax, slack
6 excuse, let out, pardon, reduce **7** absolve, forgive, forward, release, set free,
slacken **8** decrease, diminish,
dispatch, liberate, make good,
moderate, overlook, pass over,
transmit **9** discharge, reimburse **10** compensate **11** put to
rights **13** send in payment

remnant 3 bit **5** piece, relic,
scrap, shred, token, trace
7 discard, remains, residue,
vestige **8** fragment, leavings,
leftover, monument, residuum,
survival **9** remainder **11** odds
and ends

remodel 4 redo **5** adapt, alter,
fix up **6** change, modify
7 convert, reshape **8** overhaul,
renovate **9** refashion, transform **11** recondition

remodeling 6 change **10** alteration, conversion **12** modification **13** transmutation
14 transformation

remonstrance 6 rebuke **7** censure **8** reproach, scolding
9 criticism, reprimand
10 admonition

remonstrate 5 argue, chide,

demur, scold **6** differ, object, rebuke **7** censure, chasten, contend, dispute, dissent, protest, reprove, upbraid **8** admonish, complain, reproach **9** criticize **10** take to task **11** expostulate **13** call to account

remorse 3 rue **4** pang **5** grief, guilt, qualm **6** regret, sorrow **7** anguish **9** penitence **10** contrition, repentance, ruefulness **11** compunction, lamentation, self-reproof **12** self-reproach **13** regretfulness **14** second thoughts

remorseful 8 contrite, penitent **9** chastened, regretful, repentant, sorrowful **10** apologetic **13** grief-stricken **18** conscience-stricken

remote 3 far **4** slim **5** alien, alone, aloof, faint, quiet **6** exotic, far-off, lonely, meager, slight **7** distant, dubious, faraway, foreign, removed, strange **8** detached, doubtful, isolated, secluded, separate, set apart, solitary, unlikely **9** withdrawn **10** far-removed, segregated **11** God-forsaken, implausible, out of the way, sequestered, standoffish

removal 6 moving, ouster **7** doffing **8** deletion, ejection **9** discharge, dismissal, expulsion, taking off, taking out **10** amputation, carting off, cutting away, dislodging, evacuation, lopping off **11** carrying off, chopping off, elimination, transferral **12** cancellation, displacement **14** transportation **15** transplantation

remove 4 doff, drop, fire, move, oust, quit **5** eject, erase, expel, leave, shift **6** cancel, change, cut off, delete, depart, go away, lop off, retire, unseat, vacate **7** blot out, boot out, cart off, chop off, cut away, dismiss, extract, kick out, retreat, take off, take out, wipe out **8** amputate, carry off, dislodge, displace, evacuate, get rid of, sweep out, take away, transfer, withdraw **9** discharge, eliminate, take leave, transport **10** make an exit, transplant

removed 3 off **4** away, took **5** alone, aloof, apart **6** remote **7** distant, faraway **8** abstract, detached, isolated, reticent, secluded **9** alienated, separate, unrelated, withdrawn **10** segregated, unsociable **11** interspaced, standoffish

remove from office 4 oust **6** depose, unseat **9** discharge

remunerate 3 pay **5** award, grant, repay **6** reward **7** requite, satisfy **9** indemnify, reimburse, vouchsafe **10** compensate, recompense **15** make restitution

remuneration 7 payment **9** repayment **10** recompense, reparation **12** compensation **13** reimbursement **15** indemnification

Remus
  father: **4** Mars
  mother: **4** Ilia **9** Rea Silvia **10** Rhea Silvia
  twin brother: **7** Romulus
  raised by: **7** she-wolf

renaissance 7 rebirth, renewal, revival **10** rekindling, renascence, resurgence **11** reawakening, reemergence, restoration **12** regeneration, rejuvenation, resurrection, risorgimento **14** revitalization, revivification **15** reestablishment

rend 3 cut, rip **4** hurt, pain, rive, sear, tear **5** break, crack, sever, split, wound **6** cleave, divide, pierce, sunder **7** afflict, rupture, shatter **8** dissever, fracture, lacerate, polarize, splinter **12** disintegrate, fall to pieces **15** break into pieces

render 2 do **4** cede, give, make, play **5** allot, grant, remit, yield **6** accord, donate, give up, supply, tender **7** deal out, dole out, execute, hand out, pay back, perform, present, requite **8** construe, dispense, fork over, hand over, pay as due, shell out, turn over **9** cause to be, interpret, surrender, translate **10** relinquish **12** give in return, make requital **13** cause to become, make available, make payment of

render impotent 6 defuse, weaken **7** disable, unnerve **8** paralyze **9** undermine **10** devitalize, emasculate

render inoperable 6 damage, impair **7** cripple, disable **12** incapacitate

render null and void 4 void **5** annul **6** cancel, repeal, revoke **7** abolish, nullify, rescind, retract, reverse **8** abrogate, dissolve **10** invalidate

rendezvous 4 date **5** focus, haunt, mecca, tryst **6** gather, muster **7** retreat **8** assemble **9** encounter, tete-a-tete **10** engagement, focal point **11** appointment, assignation, get together **12** meeting place,

watering hole **14** gathering place, stamping ground **15** agreement to meet **17** meet by appointment **18** prearranged meeting

rendition 7 edition, reading, version **9** depiction, portrayal, rendering **11** arrangement, performance, translation **14** interpretation

rend the air 3 cry **4** bawl, howl, wail **6** clamor, scream, shriek, squeal **7** screech **9** caterwaul

Renee Mauperin
  author: **24** Edmond and Jules de Goncourt

renegade 5 rebel **6** outlaw **7** heretic, runaway, slacker, traitor **8** apostate, betrayer, defector, deserter, forsaker, fugitive, mutineer, mutinous, quisling, recreant, turncoat **9** dissenter, insurgent **10** backslider, traitorous, treasonist, unfaithful

renege 7 back out, fink out, pull out **8** back down, fall back, withdraw **9** repudiate, weasel out **11** get cold feet **12** turn one's back **13** break a promise, break one's word **16** go back on one's word

renew 4 save **6** extend, pick up, redeem, resume, retain, revive **7** prolong, refresh, restore, salvage **8** continue, maintain **9** make sound, reinstate, sign again **10** begin again, offer again, regenerate, rejuvenate, revitalize **11** reestablish, take up again **12** reinvigorate **16** put back into shape

renewal 7 revival **9** extension **10** redemption **11** restoration **12** regeneration **13** reinstatement **14** revitalization

Renoir, Pierre-Auguste
  born: **6** France **7** Limoges
  artwork: **4** Lise **6** La Loge **10** The Bathers **12** Margot Berard, The Umbrellas **14** La Grenouillere **19** Le Moulin de la Galette **28** Mme Charpentier and Her Children, The Luncheon of the Boating Party

renounce 4 cede, deny, quit **5** forgo, waive **6** abjure, disown, eschew, forego, give up, recant, reject, resign **7** abandon, cast off, disavow, discard, dismiss **8** abdicate, abnegate, abrogate, disclaim, forswear, lay aside, part with, put aside, turn from, write off **9** cast aside, foreswear, repudiate

10 relinquish 13 give up claim to 15 wash one's hands of

renovate 3 fix 4 mend 6 remake, repair, revamp 7 improve, remodel, restore 8 make over 9 modernize, refurbish 10 redecorate

renown 4 fame, mark, note 6 repute, status 7 acclaim 8 eminence 9 celebrity, notoriety 10 popularity, prominence, reputation 11 distinction

renowned 5 famed, noted 6 famous 7 eminent, notable, popular 9 acclaimed, prominent, well-known 10 celebrated, noteworthy 11 outstanding 13 distinguished

rent 3 fee, gap, let, rip 4 dues, gash, hire, hole, rift, slit, tear 5 break, chasm, chink, cleft, crack, lease, split 6 breach, hiatus, rental, schism, tatter, wrench 7 charter, fissure, opening, payment, rent out, rupture 8 cleavage, crevasse, division, fracture 11 buy the use of 12 sell the use of

rente 6 income 7 revenue 12 annual income

rentier 21 one who has a fixed income

renunciation 6 denial 7 refusal 8 forgoing, spurning 9 disavowal, eschewing, foregoing, rejection, repulsion 10 abjuration, renouncing 11 abandonment, disclaiming, forswearing, repudiation 12 foreswearing 14 relinquishment

Renwick, James, Jr
architect of: 8 Main Hall (Vassar College) 11 Grace Church (NYC) 15 Corcoran Gallery (now Renwick Gallery, Washington, DC) 19 St Patrick's Cathedral (NYC) 22 Smithsonian Institution (Washington DC)
style: 13 Gothic Revival

reopen 7 restart 9 begin anew, reconvene, start anew 10 recommence, reinitiate 11 reestablish, reinstitute 12 reinaugurate

repair 2 go 3 fix 4 mend, move 5 amend, emend, patch, renew, shape, state 6 fixing, remedy, remove, retire 7 correct, mending, patch up, rebuild, rectify, redress, restore 8 make good, overhaul, patching, set right, withdraw 9 condition, make up for, refurbish, repairing 10 rebuilding 11 recondition

12 refurbishing 14 reconditioning

reparation 6 amends, return 7 damages, redress 8 requital 9 quittance 10 recompense 11 restitution 12 compensation, satisfaction 13 peace offering

repartee 6 banter, bon mot 7 riposte 8 badinage, chit chat, word play 10 persiflage, witty reply 11 witty retort 12 pleasantries 14 snappy comeback

repast 4 food, meal 5 board, feast, snack, table 6 spread 7 banquet 8 victuals 9 provision 11 nourishment, refreshment

repay 5 match 6 refund, return, reward 7 pay back, requite 9 get back at, indemnify, pay in kind, reimburse 10 recompense, remunerate 11 get even with, reciprocate 12 make requital 14 give in exchange, make a return for 15 make restitution, make retribution 19 return the compliment

repayment 10 paying back, recompense 12 compensation 13 reimbursement 17 making restitution

repeal 4 void 5 annul 6 cancel, revoke 7 abolish, nullify, rescind, voiding 8 abrogate, set aside 9 abolition, annulment 10 abrogation, invalidate, revocation 11 termination 12 cancellation, invalidation 13 nullification 18 declare null and void

repeat 4 echo, redo, tell 5 mimic, quote, rerun 6 pass on, recite, relate, retell 7 imitate, recount, restate, retread, say over 8 say again 9 duplicate, reiterate, reproduce 10 repetition 11 duplication, reiteration 12 perform again

repeated exercises 4 rote 5 drill 8 practice, training

repel 4 foil, rout 5 check 6 dispel, offend, oppose, put off, rebuff, resist, revolt, sicken 7 deflect, disgust, fend off, forfend, hold off, keep off, keep out, repulse, scatter, turn off, ward off 8 alienate, beat back, disperse, nauseate, push back, stave off, throw off 9 chase away, drive away, drive back, force back, frustrate, keep at bay, withstand

repellent 5 proof 9 abhorrent, loathsome, offensive, repelling, repugnant, repulsive, resisting, revolting, sickening 10 dis-

gusting, nauseating 11 distasteful, impermeable

repent 3 rue 6 bemoan, bewail, lament, regret, repine 7 deplore 8 mea culpa, weep over 9 be ashamed 10 be contrite, be penitent 11 be regretful, feel remorse

repentance 5 grief, guilt 6 regret, sorrow 7 remorse 9 penitence 10 contrition 11 compunction 12 self-reproach 16 self-condemnation 17 pangs of conscience

repercussion 4 echo 6 effect, result 8 backlash, reaction 10 concussion, side effect 11 aftereffect, consequence 13 reverberation 15 boomerang effect

repetition 6 repeat 9 iteration, retelling 11 reiteration, restatement 14 recapitulation

repetitious 5 wordy 6 prolix 8 repeated 9 redundant 10 repetitive

Repin, Ilya Efimovich
born: 6 Russia 8 Chugeyev
artwork: 15 The Volga Boatmen 18 Zaporozhye Cossacks 19 They Did Not Expect Him 26 Ivan the Terrible Kills His Son

replace 5 spell 6 return 7 put back, restore, succeed 8 supplant 9 supersede

replaceable 10 disposable, expendable 11 dispensable

replenish 5 renew 6 refill, reload 7 refresh, reorder, replace, restock, restore

replenished 7 renewed 8 refilled, replaced, restored 9 restocked

replenishment 7 renewal 9 refilling 10 restocking 11 replacement, restoration

replete 4 full 5 sated 6 gorged, loaded 7 crammed, fraught, stuffed, teeming 8 brimming, satiated 9 abounding, jam-packed, surfeited 11 well-stocked

repletion 4 glut 6 excess 7 surfeit, surplus 9 abundance, plenitude, profusion, satiation 11 sufficiency

replica 4 copy 5 model 6 double 8 likeness 9 duplicate, facsimile, imitation 12 reproduction

reply 5 react 6 answer, rejoin, retort 7 counter, respond 8 reaction, response 9 rejoinder 14 acknowledgment

reply if you please
French: **4** rsvp **20** repondez
s'il vous plait

reply to 6 answer **7** counter,
react to **8** retort to **9** respond
to **11** acknowledge

repondez s'il vous plait
11 please reply **16** reply if you
please
abbreviation: **4** rsvp

report 4 bang, boom, note,
talk, tell, word **5** crack, noise,
rumor, sound, state, story
6 appear, detail, expose, gossip, recite, record, relate, reveal, show up, tell on
7 account, article, check in,
divulge, hearsay, message,
missive, recount, summary,
version, write-up **8** announce,
denounce, describe, disclose,
dispatch, relation **9** discharge,
narration **10** communique,
detonation, memorandum
11 communicate, description,
information
French: **11** compte rendu

reporter 7 newshen, newsman **8** newshawk **9** anchor-
man, announcer, columnist,
newshound, newswoman
10 journalist, newscaster
11 commentator **12** newspaperman **13** correspondent
14 newspaperwoman

repose 3 lie **4** calm, ease, rest
5 quiet, relax **6** be calm, settle **7** leisure, recline, respite
8 quietude **10** inactivity, quiescence, relaxation **11** tranquility **12** peacefulness,
tranquillity

repository 5 depot **8** magazine **9** warehouse
10 storehouse

reprehend 5 decry **7** censure,
condemn, reprove **8** denounce,
reproach **9** criticize
10 disapprove

reprehensible 3 bad **4** base,
evil, foul, vile **6** guilty,
wicked **7** heinous, ignoble
8 blamable, culpable, infamous, shameful, unworthy
9 nefarious **10** censurable, despicable, villainous **11** blameworthy, condemnable,
disgraceful, inexcusable, opprobrious **12** unpardonable
13 objectionable, unjustifiable

reprehension 6 rebuke **7** censure, reproof **8** reproach
9 criticism **11** disapproval
12 condemnation, denunciation **14** disapprobation

represent 2 be **4** mean, show
5 enact, equal, state **6** denote,
depict, pose as, sketch, typify
7 betoken, express, outline,

picture, portray, present, serve
as **8** appear as, describe, indicate, stand for **9** delineate,
designate, symbolize **10** illustrate **11** emblematize, impersonate **12** characterize

representation 5 image **6** effigy, emblem, symbol **7** epitome, essence, picture
8 likeness **9** depiction, portrayal **10** embodiment **12** illustration **15** exemplification
16 characterization

representative 2 MP **3** rep
5 agent, envoy, proxy **6** deputy, varied **7** deputed, elected,
proctor, typical **8** balanced,
delegate, elective, emissary,
symbolic **9** delegated, exemplary, spokesman, surrogate,
typifying **10** delegatory, democratic, denotative, emblematic,
legislator, mouthpiece, republican, substitute, symbolical
11 assemblyman, congressman,
delineative, descriptive **12** ex-
emplifying, illustrative **13** as-
semblywoman,
congresswoman **14** characteristic, cross-sectional

repress 4 curb, hide, mask,
veil **5** box up, check, cloak,
cover, crush, pen up, quash,
quell **6** hold in, muffle, shut
up, squash, stifle, subdue
7 conceal, control, inhibit, put
down, silence, smother,
squelch **8** bottle up, hold back,
keep down, restrain, strangle,
suppress

repression 8 muffling **9** holding in, restraint, retention
10 inhibition, throttling
11 concealment, holding back,
suppression

reprieve 4 lull, stay **5** delay,
pause **6** pardon, parole **7** amnesty, respite **8** breather **9** remission **10** moratorium,
suspension **11** adjournment
12 postponement **14** breathing
spell

reprimand 4 trim **5** chide,
scold **6** berate, rail at, rebuff,
rebuke, revile **7** censure, chew
out, chiding, lecture, obloquy,
tell off, upbraid **8** admonish,
berating, chastise, denounce,
reproach, reproval, scolding,
take down, trimming **9** castigate, criticism, criticize, disparage, dispraise, dress down,
reprehend, reprobate **10** admonition, chewing out, opprobrium, take to task,
upbraiding **11** castigation
12 admonishment, denunciation, dressing down, remonstrance **13** disparagement
16 rap on the knuckles

reprisal 7 redress, revenge
8 requital **9** tit for tat, vengeance **11** counterblow, retaliation, retribution
13 counterattack
16 counteroffensive
Latin: **10** quid pro quo

reproach 4 blot, slur, spot
5 blame, chide, scold, shame,
stain, taint **6** charge, insult,
malign, rail at, rebuke, revile,
stigma, tirade, vilify **7** asperse,
blemish, censure, condemn, offense, reproof, reprove, scandal, tarnish, upbraid
8 admonish, denounce, diatribe, disgrace, dishonor, scolding **9** castigate, criticism,
criticize, discredit, disparage,
indignity, reprimand **10** stigmatize, take to task, tongue-
lash, upbraiding **11** degradation, humiliation
12 remonstrance **13** call to account, embarrassment

reprobate 3 bad, low **4** base,
evil, rake, roue, vile **5** scamp
6 pariah, rascal, rotter, sinner,
wanton, wicked **7** corrupt, outcast **8** castaway, depraved, derelict, evildoer, prodigal,
rakehell **9** abandoned, dissolute, miscreant, shameless,
wrongdoer **10** black sheep, degenerate, immoralist, profligate, voluptuary
11 rapscallion, untouchable
12 incorrigible, transgressor,
wicked person

reproduce 4 copy, redo, sire
5 beget, breed, match, spawn
6 mirror, repeat, re-echo
7 imitate, reflect **8** generate,
multiply **9** duplicate, procreate,
propagate, replicate, represent
11 counterfeit, proliferate

reproduction 4 copy **7** replica
8 breeding, likeness **9** duplicate, facsimile, imitation
10 carbon copy, generation,
simulation **11** procreation,
propagation **13** progeneration,
proliferation **14** multiplication,
representation
goddess of: **7** Astarte

reproductive system
component: **5** penis **6** testes,
uterus, vagina **7** ovaries

reproof 5 blame **6** rebuke
7 censure, chiding **8** reproach,
scolding **9** criticism, reprimand **10** admonition **12** condemnation, dressing-down,
remonstrance

reprovable 7 at fault **8** blamable, culpable **10** censurable
11 blameworthy
12 reproachable

reprove 5 chide, scold **6** rebuke **7** censure, chasten **8** ad-

monish, reproach **9** castigate, reprimand

reptile 3 asp, eft **4** newt, teju **5** agama, anole, gecko, skink, snake, viper **6** dragon, iguana, lizard, mugger, turtle **7** crawler, creeper, serpent, tuatara **8** basilisk, dinosaur, groveler, terrapin, tortoise **9** alligator, chameleon, crocodile, pterosaur **10** salamander, vertebrate **11** Gila monster, pterodactyl

republic 9 democracy
 Latin: 10 res publica

Republic
 author: 5 Plato

Republican Party
 also called: 3 GOP **13** Grand Old Party
 president belonging to:
 4 Bush, Ford, Taft **5** Grant, Hayes, Nixon **6** Arthur, Hoover, Reagan **7** Harding, Lincoln, (Andrew) Johnson **8** Coolidge, Garfield, Harrison, McKinley **9** (Theodore) Roosevelt **10** Eisenhower
 symbol: 8 elephant

Republic of China see **6** Taiwan

repudiate 4 deny, void **5** annul **6** cancel, desert, disown, reject, repeal, revoke **7** abandon, abolish, cast off, disavow, discard, forsake, nullify, protest, rescind, retract, reverse **8** abrogate, disclaim, dissolve, renounce

repudiation 6 denial **9** disavowal, rejection **10** abrogation, disclaimer, retraction

repugnance 4 hate **5** odium **6** hatred **7** disgust **8** aversion, loathing **9** antipathy, revulsion **10** abhorrence **11** abomination, detestation

repugnant 4 foul, vile **5** nasty **6** odious **7** adverse, counter, hateful, opposed **8** contrary, unsavory **9** abhorrent, loathsome, obnoxious, offensive, repellent, repulsive, revolting, sickening **10** abominable, detestable, disgusting, nauseating, unpleasant **11** distasteful, uncongenial, undesirable, unpalatable **12** antipathetic, disagreeable, insufferable, unacceptable, unappetizing **13** objectionable

repulse 4 shun **5** avoid, repel, spurn **6** ignore, rebuff, refuse, reject **7** refusal **8** shunning, spurning **9** rejection

repulsion 6 hatred **7** disgust, dislike **8** aversion, distaste, loathing **9** antipathy **10** ab-

horrence, repugnance **11** abomination, detestation **13** indisposition **14** disinclination

repulsive 4 vile **5** nasty **6** odious **7** hateful **9** abhorrent, loathsome, obnoxious, offensive, repellent, repugnant, revolting **10** abominable, detestable, disgusting, nauseating **11** distasteful **12** disagreeable **13** objectionable

repulsiveness 8 ugliness **13** loathsomeness, offensiveness **14** disgustingness, unpleasantness **16** disagreeableness

reputable 7 honored **8** esteemed, reliable **9** respected **10** creditable **11** respectable, trustworthy

reputation 4 name **7** stature **8** standing

repute 3 say **4** deem, fame, hold, view **5** judge, think **6** esteem, reckon, regard, renown **7** account, believe, suppose **8** consider, estimate, standing **9** celebrity, notoriety **10** prominence **14** respectability

request 3 ask **4** seek **6** ask for, bid for, desire, sue for **7** call for, entreat, solicit **8** petition **9** importune **11** application **12** solicitation

requiem 5 dirge **6** lament **8** threnody

requiescat in pace 11 rest in peace **16** may he rest in peace **17** may she rest in peace

require 3 bid **4** lack, miss, need, want **5** crave, imply, order **6** charge, compel, desire, direct, enjoin, entail, oblige **7** command, dictate **9** constrain **11** necessitate

required 6 forced, needed **7** obliged **9** compelled, essential, necessary **10** compulsory, imperative, obligatory

requirement 4 must **8** standard **9** criterion, essential, guideline, requisite **12** prerequisite **13** specification
 Latin: 10 sine qua non **11** desideratum

requisite 4 must, need **6** needed **8** required **9** essential, mandatory, necessary, necessity **10** compulsory, imperative, obligatory **11** requirement **12** prerequisite **13** indispensable
 Latin: 10 sine qua non **11** desideratum

requisition 4 form **7** request **11** application

requital 7 redress **9** repayment **11** retaliation **12** compensation **15** indemnification

rescind 4 void **5** annul, quash **6** cancel, recall, repeal, revoke **7** abolish, discard, nullify, retract, reverse **8** abrogate, dissolve, override, overrule **10** invalidate **11** countermand **12** counterorder

rescinding 6 recall **7** voiding **8** recision **9** abolition **10** abrogation, retraction, revocation **11** abolishment, dissolution **12** cancellation, invalidation **13** nullification

rescue 4 save **6** ransom, saving **7** deliver, freeing, recover, release, salvage **8** liberate, recovery **9** extricate **10** liberation **11** deliverance, extrication

research 5 probe, study **7** delving, inquiry **8** analysis, scrutiny **10** inspection **11** examination, exploration, factfinding, investigate, scholarship **13** investigation

resemblance 7 analogy **8** affinity, likeness, parallel **10** congruence, similarity, similitude **14** correspondence

resemble 5 favor **6** be like **8** be akin to, look like, parallel **9** take after

Resen
 founder: 6 Nimrod

resent 7 dislike

resentful 5 angry **6** bitter **7** annoyed **8** grudging, offended, provoked **10** displeased **12** dissatisfied

resentfulness 5 anger, spite **10** bitterness **15** dissatisfaction

resentment 3 ire **4** huff **5** anger, pique, spite **6** animus, malice, rancor **7** dudgeon, ill will, offense, umbrage **8** acerbity, acrimony, asperity, jealousy, soreness, sourness **9** animosity, crossness **10** bitterness, irritation **11** displeasure, indignation **12** irritability, vengefulness **14** vindictiveness

reservation 4 date **5** doubt **7** booking, proviso, scruple, strings **8** preserve **9** condition, hesitancy, provision **10** encampment, reluctance, settlement **11** appointment, compunction, stipulation, uncertainty **12** installation **13** accommodation, establishment, qualification **14** prearrangement

reserve 4 book, hold, keep, save **5** amass, delay, extra, hoard, lay up, spare, stock, table **6** backup, engage, retain, shelve, unused **7** husband, nest egg, savings **8** conserve, keep back, postpone, preserve, salt away, schedule, withhold **9** aloofness, reticence, stockpile **10** additional, prearrange

reserved 5 aloof, taken **6** booked, formal **7** distant, engaged **8** bespoken, retained, reticent, strained, unsocial **9** inhibited, spoken for **10** restrained, unsociable **11** ceremonious, constrained, standoffish **12** unresponsive **15** uncommunicative, undemonstrative

reservoir 4 fund, pool, tank, well **5** basin, fount, hoard, stock, store **6** supply **7** backlog, cistern **8** millpond **9** container, stockpile **10** depository, receptacle, repository **12** accumulation

res gestae 5 deeds **10** things done **15** accomplishments

reshape 4 redo **5** adapt, alter, block **6** change, modify, reform, remold, rework **7** convert, reframe, remodel **9** refashion, transform

reside 3 lie **4** live, rest, room **5** dwell, exist, lodge **6** belong, occupy **7** inhabit, sojourn **8** domicile

residence 3 pad **4** digs, flat, home, room, stay **5** abode, house, place **7** address, lodging, sojourn **8** domicile, dwelling, quarters **9** apartment, homestead, household **10** habitation
French: 10 pied a terre

resident 5 local **6** lodger, tenant **7** citizen, denizen, dweller **8** occupant, townsman **9** sojourner **10** inhabitant **11** housekeeper

residual 5 extra **7** abiding, lasting, surplus **8** enduring, leftover **9** lingering, remaining **10** continuing **13** supplementary

residue 4 rest **5** dregs **6** scraps **7** balance, remains, remnant **8** leavings **9** remainder
Latin: 8 residuum

resign 4 quit **5** leave **6** give up, submit **8** abdicate, disclaim, renounce **10** relinquish

resignation 8 fatalism, patience, quitting, stoicism **9** departure **10** equanimity, retirement, submission, withdrawal **11** passiveness **12** ac-

quiescence **13** nonresistance **14** submissiveness

resign oneself 5 yield **6** submit **9** acquiesce

resilience 6 recoil **7** rebound **8** buoyancy **10** elasticity **11** flexibility **12** adaptability **13** changeability, nonuniformity **16** lightheartedness

resilient 5 hardy **6** supple **7** buoyant, elastic, rubbery, springy **8** flexible **9** adaptable, expansive, resistant, tenacious **10** rebounding, responsive **13** irrepressible

resist 4 balk, foil, stem, stop **5** fight, repel **6** baffle, combat, oppose, refuse, reject, thwart **7** contest, counter, weather **8** beat back, turn down **9** frustrate, withstand **10** counteract

resistance 6 mutiny, rebuff **7** refusal **8** defiance, struggle **9** obstinacy, rebellion, rejection **10** contention, insurgency, opposition **11** obstruction **12** insurrection **13** intransigence, noncompliance, recalcitrance

resolute 5 stern **6** dogged, steady **7** earnest, staunch, zealous **8** decisive, diligent, intrepid, stubborn, untiring, vigorous **9** assiduous, obstinate, purposive, steadfast, tenacious, unbending **10** deliberate, determined, inflexible, persistent, relentless, unflagging, unswerving, unwavering, unyielding **11** industrious, persevering, undeviating, unfaltering, unflinching **12** pertinacious, strong-minded, strong-willed **13** indefatigable **14** uncompromising

resoluteness 7 purpose, resolve **8** decision, tenacity **11** decidedness, persistence **12** decisiveness, perseverance **13** determination, steadfastness **14** purposefulness

resolution 3 aim **4** goal, plan, zeal **5** design, energy, intent, mettle, motion, object, spirit **7** promise, purpose, resolve **8** ambition, proposal, solution, tenacity **9** constancy, intention, objective, resolving, stability **10** resilience, steadiness **11** earnestness, persistence **12** perseverance, resoluteness **13** determination, steadfastness **14** aggressiveness **16** indefatigability

resolve 4 plan **6** answer, decide, design, intend, set out, settle, vote on **7** adjudge, clear

up, explain, purpose **8** decision **9** determine, elucidate **10** commitment, resolution **12** resoluteness **13** determination **14** make up one's mind

resonant 4 full, rich **7** booming, orotund, ringing, vibrant **8** sonorous **9** bellowing **10** resounding, stentorian, thunderous **11** reverberant

resort 3 use **4** hope **5** apply, avail **6** chance, employ, take up **7** utilize **8** exercise, recourse **9** expedient

resound 4 echo, peal, ring **5** clang **6** re-echo **7** vibrate **11** reverberate **14** tintinnabulate

resounding 7 echoing, ringing **9** re-echoing **10** thundering, thunderous **13** reverberating

resource 8 recourse **9** expedient **11** wherewithal

resourceful 4 able **5** ready, sharp, smart **6** adroit, artful, bright, shrewd **7** capable, cunning **8** creative, original, skillful, talented **9** competent, effectual, ingenious, inventive **10** innovative, proficient **11** imaginative **12** enterprising

resourcefulness 9 ingenuity **10** creativity, enterprise **13** inventiveness

resources 5 funds, means, money **6** assets, income **7** capital, effects, revenue **10** belongings, collateral **11** possessions, wherewithal

respect 5 honor, point, sense **6** detail, esteem, matter, notice, praise, regard **7** bearing, feature, viewing **8** approval, courtesy, relation **9** affection, attention, deference, laudation, reference, relevance, reverence **10** admiration, connection, particular, veneration **11** point of view, recognition **12** appreciation, circumstance **13** consideration

respectability 7 decency, decorum **9** gentility, propriety **11** correctness, genteelness

respectable 4 fair **5** ample, civil, noble **6** decent, honest, polite, proper, worthy **7** correct, courtly, passing, refined, upright **8** becoming, decorous, moderate, polished **9** admirable, dignified, estimable, honorable, reputable **10** aboveboard, admissible, sufficient **11** presentable **12** considerable, praiseworthy, satisfactory

respected 6 valued, worthy
7 admired, honored, revered
8 esteemed **9** admirable,
venerated

respectful 5 civil **6** formal,
genial, polite **7** amiable, winning **8** admiring, decorous,
gracious, mannerly, obliging,
reverent **9** attentive, courteous,
regardful **10** personable, solicitous **11** ceremonious, deferential, reverential
13 accommodating

respects 4 heed, obey
5 honor, prize, value **6** admire,
esteem, fealty, follow, regard,
revere **7** abide by, cherish, defer to, observe, regards, tribute **8** adhere to, consider,
venerate **9** greetings **10** appreciate, understand **11** acknowledge, compliments
12 remembrances
13 consideration

Respighi, Ottorino
born: 5 Italy **7** Bologna
composer of: 8 La Fiamma,
The Birds **14** The Pines of
Rome **18** The Fountains of
Rome **19** La Boutique Fan-
tasque, The Fantastic Toy-
shop **27** Ancient Airs and
Dances for Lute

respiration 9 breathing

respiratory system
component: 4 lung, nose
6 larynx **7** pharynx, trachea
8 voice box, windpipe
9 bronchius, diaphragm
action: 9 breathing

respire 7 breathe

respite 4 lull **5** break, delay,
letup, pause **6** recess **8** reprieve **9** extension
12 intermission

resplendence 6 dazzle, luster
7 glitter **8** lambency, radiance
10 brilliance, luminosity, refulgence **12** circumstance,
magnificence

resplendent 6 bright **7** beaming, blazing, glowing, lambent,
radiant **8** dazzling, gleaming,
luminous, lustrous, splendid
9 brilliant, refulgent, sparkling **10** glittering
11 coruscating

respond 5 react, reply **6** answer, rejoin **7** speak up **9** recognize **11** acknowledge

respond to 6 answer **7** act
upon, react to, reply to
8 thank for **11** acknowledge

response 5 reply **6** answer, retort, return **7** riposte **8** comeback, feedback, reaction,
rebuttal **9** rejoinder **10** impression **13** countercharge

14 acknowledgment
16 counterstatement

responsibility 4 duty, task
5 blame, order, trust **6** burden,
charge **8** function **9** liability
10 obligation **11** culpability,
reliability **13** answerability, dependability **14** accountability
15 trustworthiness

responsible 5 adult, of age
6 guilty, liable, mature **7** at
fault, capable **8** culpable, reliable **9** demanding, executive,
important **10** answerable, creditable, dependable **11** accountable, challenging, trustworthy
13 conscientious
14 administrative

responsive 5 alive, awake,
sharp **8** reactive **9** receptive,
sensitive **11** retaliative, retaliatory, susceptible, sympathetic
13 compassionate, understanding **14** impressionable

responsiveness 6 action
7 concern **8** interest **9** attention, awareness **11** sensitivity
13 understanding

res publica 8 republic, the
state **12** commonwealth, public matter

rest 2 be **3** end, lay, lie, nap,
set **4** base, ease, halt, hang,
keep, laze, lean, loaf, loll, lull,
prop, rely, stay, stop **5** break,
death, exist, hinge, let up,
pause, peace, place, quiet, relax, sleep, stand **6** demise, depend, holder, lounge, others,
recess, remain, repose, reside,
scraps, snooze, trivet **7** balance, be based, be found, be
quiet, decease, deposit, holiday, leisure, lie down, recline,
remains, remnant, residue, respite, set down, slumber, support **8** breather, platform,
vacation **9** cessation, departure, leftovers, remainder, stillness **10** complement, quiet
spell, relaxation, standstill,
suspension **11** hibernation,
take time out **12** intermission,
interruption **13** take a
breather
Spanish: 6 siesta
Latin: 8 residuum

restaurant 5 diner **6** eatery
7 beanery, tearoom **9** cafeteria,
chop house, grillroom, hash-
house, lunchroom **11** coffeehouse **12** luncheonette
French: 4 cafe **6** bistro
9 brasserie
German: 11 rathskeller

restful 4 calm **5** quiet **6** placid,
serene **7** pacific, relaxed
8 peaceful, soothing, tranquil
10 unagitated **11** comfortable,
undisturbed

restfulness 4 ease **5** quiet
6 repose **8** serenity, softness
10 relaxation **11** tranquility
12 tranquillity

rest in peace
Latin: 16 requiescat in pace

restitution 6 amends **7** redress,
replevy **8** replevin, requital,
restoral **9** atonement, indemnity, repayment **10** recompense, reparation
11 restoration **12** compensation, remuneration, satisfaction **13** reimbursement,
reinstatement
15 indemnification

restive 5 balky **6** mulish, ornery, unruly **7** fidgety, wayward, willful **8** contrary,
stubborn **9** fractious, pigheaded **10** rebellious, refractory **11** disobedient,
intractable **12** recalcitrant,
unmanageable

restless 5 awake, jumpy **6** fitful, uneasy **7** anxious, fidgety,
fretful, jittery, nervous, on the
go, unquiet, wakeful, worried
8 agitated **9** excitable, impatient, incessant, insomniac, on
the move, sleepless, transient,
unsettled **10** disquieted, high-
strung **11** hyperactive
13 uncomfortable

restoration 7 revival **8** recovery **12** recuperation **13** convalescence, reinstatement
14 rehabilitation, reintroduction, reinvigoration
15 reestablishment

restorative 5 tonic **6** elixir
7 bracing, healing **8** curative
10 beneficial, energizing, fortifying **11** revivifying **12** invigorating, revitalizing
13 strengthening

restore 3 fix **4** cure, dose,
heal, mend **5** rally, renew,
treat **6** do over, recoup, remedy, repair, rescue, return, revive **7** convert, get back, patch
up, put back, rebuild, reclaim,
recover, refresh, remodel, retouch, touch up **8** energize,
give back, make over, make
well, medicate, renovate, retrieve, revivify, recreate
9 reanimate, refurbish, reinstall, reinstate, stimulate
10 exhilarate, revitalize,
strengthen **11** recondition, reconstruct, reestablish, reinstitute, resuscitate
12 rehabilitate, reinvigorate

restored 4 kept **5** saved **7** revived **8** replaced **9** conserved,
pressured **11** replenished
13 rehabilitated

restrain 3 gag **4** bind, curb,

hold, stop **5** check, leash, limit **6** arrest, bridle, fetter, muzzle, pinion, temper, tether **7** chasten, contain, curtail, harness, inhibit, prevent, shackle, trammel **8** handicap, hold back, restrict, suppress, withhold

restrained 4 cool **5** aloof **6** curbed **7** checked, distant **8** held back, reined in, reserved **10** controlled, unfriendly

restraint 4 curb **5** check **7** control **10** limitation

restrict 4 curb, hold **5** check, cramp, crimp, hem in, limit **6** hamper, impede, narrow, thwart **7** confine, inhibit, prevent, squelch **8** hold back, obstruct, straiten, suppress **9** constrain, frustrate **12** circumscribe

restricted 7 cramped, limited **8** confined, hampered, held back **9** exclusive **10** suppressed **13** circumscribed

restriction 4 rule **7** control, curbing, proviso **9** condition, provision **10** limitation, regulation **11** requirement, reservation, stipulation **13** consideration, qualification

restrictive 8 limiting **9** confining, exclusive **12** constraining

result 4 stem **5** arise, end up, ensue, fruit, issue, owe to **6** derive, effect, happen, pan out, report, sequel, spring, upshot, wind up **7** finding, opinion, outcome, product, turn out, verdict **8** decision, judgment, reaction, solution **9** aftermath, culminate, eventuate, originate, outgrowth **10** resolution **11** aftereffect, consequence, development, eventuality **13** determination

resume 2 CV **3** bio **4** go on **5** brief **6** digest **7** epitome, proceed, summary **8** abstract, continue, reembark, synopsis **9** biography, summation **10** abridgment, recommence **11** reestablish **13** condensation **Latin: 15** curriculum vitae **French: 6** precis

resumption 11 recommenced, restoration **12** continuation

resurgam 15 I shall rise again

resurgence 6 return **7** rebirth, renewal, revival **10** renascence **11** reemergence, renaissance **12** rejuvenation **13** recrudescence

retailer 5 store **6** dealer, seller, trader **8** merchant, provider, supplier **9** tradesman

10 wholesaler **11** distributor, storekeeper, tradeswoman **12** merchandiser **French: 9** vivandier **10** vivandiere

retain 4 hold, keep **5** grasp **6** absorb, recall **7** possess **8** hang on to, hold on to, maintain, memorize, remember **9** recollect

retainer 7 servant **8** employee **9** attendant

retainership 4 hire **6** employ **7** service **10** employment

retaliate 5 repay **6** avenge, pay off, return **7** counter, pay back, requite, revenge **11** reciprocate

retaliation 6 talion **7** deserts, revenge **8** reprisal, requital **9** vengeance **10** recompense **11** comeuppance, eye for an eye, interchange, just deserts, lex talionis, retribution **12** compensation **13** reciprocation **14** tooth for a tooth

retard 4 clog, drag **5** block, brake, check, delay **6** arrest, baffle, detain, fetter, hamper, hinder, hold up, impede, slow up **7** draw out, inhibit, prevent, prolong, slacken **8** hold back, obstruct, slow down **10** decelerate

retarded 4 dull, slow **6** simple **7** idiotic, moronic, unsound **8** backward, disabled **9** imbecilic, mongoloid, subnormal **10** slow-witted **11** handicapped **12** simpleminded

reticent 3 shy **5** quiet **6** closed, silent **7** subdued **8** reserved, retiring, taciturn **9** diffident, withdrawn **10** restrained **11** tight-lipped **12** closemouthed **15** uncommunicative

retinue 5 court, staff, suite, train **6** convoy **9** courtiers, employees, entourage, followers, following, personnel, retainers **10** associates, attendance, attendants

retire 6 depart, go away, remove, resign, resort, secede, turn in **7** drop out, retreat **8** abdicate, flake out, withdraw

retired French: 8 ci-devant

retiring 3 shy **4** meek **5** quiet, timid **6** demure, humble, modest **7** bashful **8** reserved, reticent, sheepish, timorous, unsocial **9** diffident, shrinking, withdrawn **10** unassuming **11** unassertive **12** self-effacing **13** inconspicuous, unpretentious **15** uncommunicative

retort 3 say **4** quip **5** rebut, reply **6** answer, rejoin, return **7** counter, respond, riposte **8** fire back, rebuttal **9** rejoinder

retract 4 deny **6** abjure, disown, draw in, recall, recant, recede, recoil, reel in, repeal, revoke **7** disavow, rescind, retreat, reverse **8** abnegate, abrogate, disclaim, draw back, forswear, peel back, pull back, renounce, take back, withdraw **9** foreswear, repudiate

retraction 6 recall **8** recision **9** disavowal **10** disclaimer, refutation, withdrawal

retreat 2 go **3** den **4** bolt, flee, port **5** haunt, haven, leave **6** asylum, depart, escape, flight, harbor, recoil, refuge, resort, retire, shrink **7** abscond, getaway, privacy, sanctum, shelter, shy away **8** back away, draw back, fall back, hideaway, move back, solitude, turn tail, withdraw **9** departure, isolation, reclusion, sanctuary, seclusion **10** evacuation, immurement, retirement, withdrawal **11** hibernation, rustication

retrench 5 slash **6** reduce, scrape, scrimp **7** curtail, cut back, cut down **8** conserve, cut costs **9** economize **15** tighten one's belt

retribution 6 amends, return, reward **7** justice, penalty, redress, revenge **8** reprisal, requital **9** vengeance **10** punishment, recompense, reparation **11** just deserts, restitution, retaliation, vindication **12** satisfaction **13** reciprocation, recrimination

retrieve 4 snag **5** fetch **6** ransom, recoup, redeem, regain, rescue **7** get back, reclaim, recover, salvage **9** recapture, repossess

retriever dog breed: 5 Irish **6** golden, Gordon **7** English **8** Labrador **10** flat-coated **11** curly-coated **13** Chesapeake Bay

retrograde 5 worse **6** worsen **7** inverse, retreat, reverse **8** backward **10** regressive **13** retrogressive

retrogress 6 worsen **9** backslide

retrogression 7 decline, setback **9** worsening **11** backsliding

retrogressive 8 backward **9** declining, worsening **11** backsliding

retrospect 6 review **9** flashback, hindsight **11** remembrance **12** afterthought, reminiscence **15** reconsideration

return 3 net **4** earn, gain **5** gross, recur, repay, yield **6** advent, come to, go back, income, profit, render, reseat, reward **7** arrival, benefit, produce, provide, put back, requite, restore, revenue **8** announce, come back, earnings, give back, hand down, interest, proceeds, reappear, recovery, restoral, send back **9** advantage, reinstall, reinstate, retrieval, reversion **10** homecoming, recurrence **11** reciprocate, reestablish, restoration **12** compensation, reappearance **13** reinstatement **15** reestablishment

Return, The
author: **14** Walter de la Mare

Return of the Native
author: **11** Thomas Hardy
character: **11** Diggory Venn, Eustacia Vye **12** Damon Wildeve **13** Clym Yeobright **17** Thomasin Yeobright

Return to Thebes
author: **10** Allan Drury

Reuben
father: **5** Jacob
mother: **4** Leah
brother: **3** Dan, Gad **4** Levi **5** Asher, Judah **6** Joseph, Simeon **7** Zebulun **8** Benjamin, Issachar, Naphtali
sister: **5** Dinah
descendant of: **9** Reubenite

reunite 5 rewed **7** remarry **9** reconcile

reveal 4 bare, show **6** betray, expose, impart, let out, unfold, unmask, unveil **7** display, divulge, exhibit, give out, lay bare, publish, uncover, unearth **8** disclose, evidence, manifest, point out

revealed 4 open **5** clear, known **7** evident, obvious **8** manifest

revel 4 romp **5** caper, enjoy **6** bask in, frolic, gambol, relish **7** carouse, delight, indulge, rejoice, roister, skylark **8** wallow in **9** celebrate

revelation 6 expose, vision **7** shocker **8** exposure, prophecy **9** admission, bombshell, discovery, eyeopener, unveiling **10** apocalypse, confession, disclosure, divulgence **11** divulgation, divulgement

revelatory 10 expressive

11 informative
13 communicative

reveler 6 barfly, ranter, player **7** drinker **8** bacchant, carouser, drunkard **9** roisterer, rollicker, skylarker **10** merrymaker

revelry 5 spree **7** jollity **8** carnival, carousal, festival, jamboree **9** high jinks, merriment, rejoicing **10** exultation, roistering **11** celebrating, celebration, merrymaking **12** conviviality **13** jollification **14** boisterousness
god of: **5** Comus

revenge 5 repay **7** pay back, requite **8** reprisal, requital **9** repayment, retaliate, vengeance, vindicate **10** recompense **11** eye for an eye, reciprocate, retaliation, retribution **12** satisfaction

revenue 3 pay **4** take **5** gains, wages, yield **6** income, profit, return, salary **7** annuity, pension, subsidy **8** earnings, interest, pickings, proceeds, receipts **9** allowance, emolument **12** compensation, remuneration

revenue, annual
French: **5** rente

reverberate 4 boom, echo, ring **5** carry **6** rumble **7** resound, thunder, vibrate

reverberation 4 boom, echo **6** rumble **7** ringing, thunder **8** rumbling **9** vibration **10** resounding, thundering

revere 5 honor **6** esteem **7** defer to, respect **8** venerate

revered 6 adored **7** admired, honored **9** estimable, respected, venerated, worshiped **10** worshipped

reverence 3 awe **4** fear **5** honor, piety **6** esteem, homage, regard **7** respect, worship **8** devotion **9** adoration, deference **10** admiration, devoutness, observance, veneration **11** prostration, religiosity **12** genuflection

reverent 4 pure **5** pious **6** devout, humble, solemn **7** adoring, awesome, devoted **8** faithful **9** religious, spiritual **10** respectful, worshipful

reverential 4 awed **10** respectful, worshipful **11** deferential

reverie 5 dream, fancy **6** musing **7** fantasy **8** daydream **9** dreamland, quixotism **10** brown study, meditation **12** extravagance **13** woolgathering **14** fantasticality

reverse 4 back, rear, tail, undo, void **5** annul, upend, upset **6** cancel, change, defeat, invert, mishap, negate, recall, recant, repeal, revoke, unmake, upturn **7** counter, failure, nullify, rescind, retract, setback, trouble **8** abrogate, backward, contrary, converse, hardship, inverted, opposite, override, overrule, set aside, turn over, withdraw **9** adversity, mischance, posterior, transpose **10** antithesis, invalidate, misfortune **11** countermand, counterpart, frustration **14** disappointment

revert 5 lapse **6** go back, repeat, return **7** regress, relapse **9** backslide **10** recidivate, retrogress

review 4 show **5** study, sum up **6** notice, parade, rehash, survey **7** analyze, journal, retrace, run over **8** critique, evaluate, hash over, magazine, reassess, report on, scrutiny **9** criticism, criticize, reexamine, reiterate, summarize **10** commentary, evaluation, exhibition, exposition, procession, reconsider, reevaluate, reflection, scrutinize **11** examination **12** presentation, reassessment, recapitulate, reevaluation **13** demonstration, retrospection **14** recapitulation **15** reconsideration
French: **11** compte rendu

revile 4 slur **5** abuse, curse, scold, scorn **6** berate, defame, deride, malign, rebuke, vilify **7** bawl out, chew out, slander, upbraid **8** belittle, denounce, execrate, reproach, sail into **9** blaspheme, castigate, denigrate, disparage **10** vituperate

reviler 6 critic, curser **8** vilifier **9** backbiter, slanderer **10** blasphemer

revise 4 edit, redo **5** alter, amend, emend, fix up **6** change, doctor, modify, recast, redact, revamp, review, update **7** correct, rectify, rewrite **8** emendate, overhaul

revision 6 change **7** edition **9** amendment, recension **10** alteration, correction, emendation **11** improvement **12** modification

revival 7 renewal **11** restoration **13** reinstatement, reinstitution, resuscitation

revive 5 dig up, renew **6** drag up, repeat **7** freshen, refresh, restage **8** reawaken **9** reanimate, reproduce, resurrect **11** resuscitate

revived 7 renewed **8** animated, repeated, restaged **9** enlivened, freshened, refreshed **10** reanimated, reawakened, reproduced **11** invigorated, resurrected **12** resuscitated

revocation 6 repeal **8** recision **9** abolition, annulment **10** abrogation, retraction **11** abolishment, elimination, repudiation **12** cancellation **13** nullification

revoke 4 void **5** annul, erase, quash **6** abjure, cancel, negate, recall, repeal, vacate **7** abolish, dismiss, expunge, nullify, rescind, retract, reverse **8** abrogate, call back, disallow, disclaim, override, overrule, renounce, set aside, take back, withdraw **9** repudiate **10** invalidate **11** countermand

revolt 4 coup, rise **5** rebel, repel, shock **6** appall, mutiny, offend, rise up, sicken **7** disgust, dissent, horrify, repulse **8** disorder, distress, nauseate, sedition, uprising **9** rebellion **10** insurgency, opposition, **12** factiousness, insurrection
German: **6** Putsch

revolting 4 foul, grim, vile **5** nasty **6** horrid, odious **7** hateful, noisome, noxious **8** dreadful, horrible, horrific, shocking, stinking **9** abhorrent, appalling, frightful, invidious, loathsome, obnoxious, offensive, repellent, repugnant, repulsive, sickening **10** abominable, disgusting, malodorous, nauseating **11** distasteful **12** disagreeable **13** objectionable

Revolt of the Angels, The
author: **13** Anatole France

revolution 6 mutiny, revolt, rising **8** circling, gyration, rotation, uprising **9** rebellion **12** insurrection **14** circumrotation, circumvolution
French: **4** coup **9** coup d'etat
German: **6** Putsch

revolutionary 7 radical **8** mutinous **9** extremist, insurgent, seditious **10** dissenting, rebellious, subversive **13** superadvanced, unprecedented **15** insurrectionary

revolve 4 spin, turn **5** twist, wheel **6** circle, gyrate, rotate **12** circumrotate

revolver 3 gat, gun, rod **4** colt **6** pistol, weapon **7** firearm, handgun, rotator, sidearm **10** six-shooter **20** Saturday night special

revulsion 8 aversion, distaste,

loathing **10** abhorrence, repugnance **11** detestation

reward 3 due **5** bonus, prize, repay, wages **6** bounty **7** deserts, guerdon, payment, premium, requite **9** reckoning **10** compensate, recompense, remunerate **12** compensation, remuneration **13** consideration
Latin: **10** quid pro quo

rewarding 8 pleasant, valuable **9** enjoyable **10** delightful, gratifying, satisfying **11** pleasurable

rework 4 redo **5** adapt, alter **6** modify **7** remodel, reshape **9** refashion, transform

rex 4 king

Reykjavik
capital of: **7** Iceland

Reynolds, Burt
born: **10** Waycross GA
wife: **9** Judy Carne **12** Loni Anderson
roles: **6** Shamus **9** Dan August, Semi-Tough **11** Deliverance **14** The Longest Yard **18** Smokey and the Bandit

Reynolds, Debbie
real name: **19** Mary Frances Reynolds
born: **8** El Paso TX
husband: **11** Eddie Fisher
roles: **13** The Singing Nun, The Tender Trap **15** Singin' in the Rain **19** Tammy and the Bachelor **23** The Unsinkable Molly Brown

Reynolds, Sir Joshua
born: **7** England **8** Plympton
artwork: **14** Lord Heathfield, Miss Jane Bowles **15** Commodore Keppel **18** Mrs Francis Beckford **21** Mrs Abington as Miss Prue **25** Mrs Siddons as the Tragic Muse **38** Lady Sarah Bunbury Sacrificing to the Graces

Rhadamanthus, Rhadamanthys
father: **4** Zeus
mother: **6** Europa
brother: **5** Minos **6** Aeacus **8** Sarpedon
became a judge in: **5** Hades

rhapsodic 6 elated **7** beaming, excited **8** blissful, ecstatic, thrilled **9** delirious, overjoyed, rapturous **11** exhilarated, transported

Rhea
member of: **6** Titans
father: **6** Uranus
mother: **4** Gaea
brother: **6** Cronos, Cronus, Kronos

husband: **6** Cronos, Cronus, Kronos
son: **4** Zeus **5** Hades **8** Poseidon
daughter: **4** Hera **6** Hestia **7** Demeter
called: **10** Magna Mater
corresponds to: **3** Ops **6** Cybele **9** Dindymene **10** Berecyntia
epithet: **6** Antaea

Rhea Silvia see **9** Rea Silvia

Rhene
mistress of: **6** Oileus
son: **5** Medon

Rhesus
owned: **6** horses
horses captured by: **8** Diomedes, Odysseus

rhetoric 4 bunk, wind **5** hokum, hooey **6** bunkum, hot air **7** fustian, oratory **8** euphuism **9** discourse, elocution, eloquence, hyperbole **10** hocus-pocus **11** flamboyance **13** magniloquence **14** grandiloquence

Rhetoric
author: **9** Aristotle

rhetorical 5 showy, windy **6** florid, ornate, purple, verbal **7** aureate, flowery **8** eloquent, inflated **9** bombastic, grandiose, highflown, stylistic **10** decorative, discursive, euphuistic, expressive, flamboyant, linguistic, oratorical, ornamental **11** disputative, embellished, extravagant **12** disputatious, elocutionary, magniloquent **13** argumentative, grandiloquent

Rhiannon
origin: **5** Welsh
husband: **5** Pwyll **10** Manawyddan
son: **7** Pryderi
accused of devouring: **7** Pryderi

Rhigmus
origin: **8** Thracian
ally of: **7** Trojans
killed by: **8** Achilles

rhinoceros
group of: **5** crash

Rhoda
character: **8** Gary Levy **9** Joe Gerard **12** Benny Goodwin **14** Ida Morgenstern, Sally Gallagher **17** Brenda Morgenstern, Martin Morgenstern **22** Rhoda Morgenstern Gerard
cast: **9** Anne Meara, David Groh, Ron Silver **11** Julie Kavner, Nancy Walker **12** Harold J Gould, Ray Buktenica **13** Valerie Harper

Rhode Island
  abbreviation: 2 RI
  nickname: 11 Little Rhody
  capital/largest city: 10 Providence
  others: 7 Bristol, Newport 8 Cranston, Kingston, Westerly
    9 Pawtucket, Wakefield 10 Woonsocket
  college: 5 Brown 6 Bryant 8 Pembroke 10 Barrington,
    Providence 11 Salve Regina 13 Mount St Joseph, Roger
    Williams 15 Johnson and Wales, Naval War College
  feature: 7 Newport
  tribe: 7 Niantic 9 Wampanoag 12 Narragansett
  people: 8 Puritans 12 George M Cohan 13 Gilbert Stuart,
    Matthew C Perry, Roger Williams 15 Ambrose Burnside,
    Nathanael Greene 17 Oliver Hazard Perry
  island: 5 Block, Rhode 8 Prudence 9 Aquidneck, Conanicut
  lake: 8 Scituate
    pond: 7 Wordens 8 Stafford, Watchaug
  land rank: 8 fiftieth
  mountain: 10 Durfee Hill
    highest point: 12 Jerimoth Hill
  physical feature:
    bay: 12 Narragansett
    sea: 8 Atlantic
    sound: 11 Block Island
  river: 7 Seekonk 8 Pawtuxet 9 Pawcatuck, Pawtucket, Poto-
    womut 10 Blackstone, Providence
  state admission: 10 thirteenth
  state bird: 14 Rhode Island Red
  state flower: 6 violet
  state motto: 4 Hope
  state song: 11 Rhode Island
  state tree: 8 red maple

Rhodesia see 8 Zimbabwe

rhodium
  chemical symbol: 2 Rh

rhododendron
  varieties: 4 tree 5 Bluet 6 Indian, Yunnan 7 catawba,
    fringed, Lapland, silvery, Smirnow 8 Carolina, Chapman's, Fortune's, Fujiyama,
    piedmont 9 Caucasian, honey-bell, West Coast
    11 leather-leaf 12 willow-leaved

rhodolite
  species: 6 garnet

Rhodope
  companion of: 7 Artemis
  skill: 7 hunting

Rhodopis
  also: 7 Rhodope
  form: 9 courtesan
  origin: 5 Greek 8 Thracian
  slave in: 5 Egypt
  lost: 7 slipper
  slipper found by:
    12 Psammetichus
  husband: 12 Psammetichus

Rhodus
  father: 8 Poseidon
  mother: 9 Aphrodite

Rhoeo
  father: 9 Staphylus
  mother: 12 Chrysothemis
  seduced by: 6 Apollo

Rhoetus
  member of: 8 Gigantes

rhubarb 5 Rheum 16 Rheum rhabarbarum
  varieties: 4 wild 5 monk's 6 garden, Sikkim 7 spinach
    8 mountain

rhyme 3 pun 4 poem, rune, song 5 chime, clink, meter,
  poesy, verse 6 jingle, poetry, rhythm 7 measure, poetize,
  versify 8 assonate, doggerel 10 consonance 12 alliteration
  game: 6 crambo

rhymer, rhymester 4 bard, poet 6 writer 8 minstrel, poetizer 9 poetaster, versifier 10 troubadour

Rhys, Jean
  author of: 7 Quartet 15 Voyage in the Dark, Wide Sargasso Sea

rhythm 4 beat, lilt, time 5 meter, pulse, swing, throb 6 accent, number, stress 7 cadence, measure 8 emphasis, movement 9 pulsation 10 recurrence 11 fluctuation,
  syncopation 12 accentuation

riant 3 gay 4 airy 5 jolly, merry 6 blithe, bright, jocund,
  jovial 7 smiling 8 cheerful, laughing, mirthful

ribald 4 lewd, racy, rude

5 bawdy, crude, gross 6 coarse, earthy, rakish, risque, vulgar,
  wanton 7 raffish, uncouth 8 improper, indecent, off-color,
  prurient, shocking 9 salacious, unrefined 10 lascivious, libidinous, licentious, suggestive

ribbon 3 bow, ray 4 band, sash 5 award, braid, prize,
  reins, strip 6 cordon, riband 7 binding, rosette 8 memorial,
  streamer 10 decoration

rice 5 Oryza 11 Oryza sativa
  varieties: 4 wild 6 Indian, pampas 8 mountain 9 Ten-
    nessee 10 annual wild
  dish: 5 grits, pilaf 7 pudding, risotto 8 porridge
    9 jambalaya
  liquor: 4 sake

Rice, Elmer
  author of: 11 Street Scene 16 The Adding Machine

Riceyman Steps
  author: 13 Arnold Bennett

rich 4 dark, deep, fine, lush 5 flush, heavy, loamy, sweet,
  vivid 6 bright, costly, fecund, lavish, mellow 7 fertile, filling,
  intense, moneyed, opulent, wealthy, well-off 8 abundant,
  affluent, fruitful, in clover, precious, prodigal, resonant,
  sonorous, splendid, valuable, well-to-do 9 abounding, estimable, expensive, luxuriant, luxurious, priceless, sumptuous 10 euphonious, produc-
  tive, propertied, prosperous 11 mellifluous 12 on easy
  street

Rich, Adrienne
  author of: 18 Diving into the Wreck

Richard, Maurice
  nickname: 6 Rocket
  sport: 6 hockey
  position: 7 forward
  team: 17 Montreal Canadiens

Richard Cory
  author: 22 Edwin Arlington Robinson

Richard Diamond, Private Detective
  character: 3 Sam 6 Lt Kile 9 Lt McGough 10 Karen
    Wells
  cast: 10 Russ Conway 11 Barbara Bain, Regis
    Toomey 12 David Janssen 13 Roxanne Brooks 14 Mary
    Tyler Moore
  viewers saw only Sam's: 4 legs

Richard II
  author: 18 William Shakespeare
  character: 11 John of Gaunt 13 Edmund Langley,

Thomas Mowbray **16** Henry
Bolingbroke **20** Earl of
Northumberland
  Duke of: **4** York **7** Au-
  merle, Norfolk **8** Here-
  ford **9** Lancaster

Richard III
  author: **18** William
  Shakespeare
  character: **6** George **7** Richard **8** Edward IV, Lady
  Anne **10** Henry Tudor (Earl
  of Richmond) **11** Lord Stanley **12** Lord Hastings
  13 Queen Margaret
  14 Queen Elizabeth **15** Edward the Fourth **17** Sir William Catesby **19** Edward
  Prince of Wales
    Duke of: **4** York **8** Clar-
    ence **10** Buckingham,
    Gloucester

Richardson, Henry Hobson
  architect of: **9** Sever Hall
  (Harvard) **11** Grace Church
  (West Medford MA)
  13 Trinity Church (Boston)
  23 State Asylum for the Insane (Buffalo NY) **27** Marshall Field Wholesale Store
  (Chicago)

Richardson, Samuel
  author of: **6** Pamela (or Virtue Rewarded) **8** Clarissa
  (Harlowe) **19** Sir Charles
  Grandison

Richardson, Sir Ralph
  born: **7** England
  10 Cheltenham
  roles: **6** Exodus **10** Oscar
  Wilde, Richard III, The
  Heiress **11** A Doll's House
  12 Anna Karenina **13** Doctor Zhivago **15** Richard the
  Third **20** Little Lord Fauntleroy **24** Long Day's Journey
  into Night **26** Greystoke The
  Legend of Tarzan

Richardson, Tony
  director of: **8** Tom Jones (Oscar) **15** Look Back in Anger **36** The Loneliness of
  the Long Distance Runner

riches 4 pelf **5** lucre, means
  6 assets, mammon, wealth
  7 fortune **8** opulence, treasure
  9 resources **10** prosperity
  11 possessions

richness 6 wealth **8** fullness,
  lushness, opulence **9** amplitude, intensity **10** lavishness,
  mellowness **12** completeness
  13 luxuriousness

Richter, Charles Francis
  field: **10** geophysics,
  seismology
  developed: **12** Richter scale
  24 measurement of
  earthquakes

rickety 4 weak **5** frail, shaky
  6 feeble, flimsy, infirm,
  wasted, weakly, wobbly
  7 fragile **8** decrepit, unsteady,
  withered **9** tottering **10** bro-
  kendown, tumbledown **11** debilitated, dilapidated,
  weakjointed **12** deteriorated

rid 4 free **5** clear, purge **6** remove **8** disabuse, liberate, unburden **9** disburden, eliminate
  11 disencumber

Ridd, John
  character in: **10** Lorna
  Doone
  author: **9** Blackmore

riddance 6 ouster, relief
  7 freeing, removal **8** ejection
  9 clearance, expulsion **11** deliverance, dislodgment

riddle 5 poser, rebus **6** enigma,
  puzzle, secret **7** mystery, problem, puzzler, stumper
  9 conundrum

ride 4 move **5** annoy, carry,
  drive, harry, hound **6** badger,
  handle, harass, hector, manage, needle, travel **7** control,
  journey, support **8** progress
  9 transport

rider 5 affix **6** suffix **7** adjunct,
  codicil **8** addendum, addition,
  appendix **9** amendment, appendage **10** attachment,
  supplement

Riders to the Sea
  author: **19** John Millington
  Synge

ridge 3 bar, rib, rim **4** bank,
  fret, hill, hump, rise, wale,
  weal, welt **5** bluff, crest,
  crimp, knoll, mound, spine
  6 ripple **7** crinkle, hillock,
  wrinkle **10** promontory
  11 corrugation

ridicule 3 guy, rib **4** gibe, jeer,
  josh, mock, razz, ride, twit
  5 mimic, scorn, taunt, tease
  6 deride, gibe at, parody
  7 lampoon, laugh at, mockery,
  ribbing, sarcasm, scoff at,
  sneer at, snicker, teasing
  8 belittle, derision, sneering,
  travesty **9** aspersion, burlesque,
  disparage, humiliate, make fun
  of, poke fun at **10** caricature,
  derogation, lampoonery
  13 disparagement
  god of: **5** Momos, Momus

ridiculous 3 odd **5** crazy, droll,
  funny, inane, nutty, queer,
  silly **6** absurd, screwy **7** amusing, asinine, bizarre, comical,
  fatuous, foolish, idiotic **8** farcical **9** fantastic, frivolous, grotesque, laughable, ludicrous,
  screwball, senseless **10** hysterical, incredible, irrational, out-

landish **11** astonishing,
nonsensical **12** preposterous,
unreasonable

Rienzi
  author: **18** Edward Bulwer-
  Lytton

Riesling, Paul
  character in: **7** Babbitt
  author: **5** Lewis

rife 5 close, dense, solid, thick
  6 common, packed **7** crowded,
  general, studded, teeming
  8 epidemic, pandemic, populous, swarming **9** chock-full,
  extensive, plumbfull, prevalent, universal **10** prevailing,
  widespread **11** predominant

riffraff 3 mob **4** herd, scum
  5 crowd, dregs, trash **6** masses,
  proles, rabble, vermin **9** peasantry **10** commonalty
  11 proletariat
  French: **8** canaille

rifle 3 rob **4** loot, sack **6** ravage **7** despoil, pillage, plunder,
  ransack **8** spoliate
  10 burglarize

rifle, repeating
  invented by: **7** Spencer

Rifleman, The
  character: **10** Lou Mallory,
  Mark McCain **11** Lucas
  McCain **14** Miss Milly
  Scott **20** Marshal Micah
  Torrance
  cast: **7** Paul Fix **10** Joan Tay-
  lor **12** Chuck Connors
  13 Patricia Blair **14** Johnny
  Crawford
  setting: **9** New Mexico, North
  Fork

rift 3 cut, gap **4** gash, gulf,
  rent, slit **5** abyss, break,
  chasm, chink, cleft, crack,
  fault, gorge, gulch, gully,
  split **6** breach, cranny, ravine
  7 breakup, crevice, fissure,
  quarrel, rupture **8** aperture,
  crevasse, division, fracture
  12 disagreement
  16 misunderstanding

rig 4 gear **5** equip **6** fit out,
  outfit **8** carriage **9** apparatus,
  equipment, machinery

Rigaud
  character in: **12** Little Dorrit
  author: **7** Dickens

Rigg, Diana
  born: **7** England **9** Doncaster
  roles: **6** Helena **8** Emma
  Peel **10** Bleak House
  11 Lady Dedlock, The
  Avengers **12** Julius Caesar
  21 A Midsummer Night's
  Dream **26** On Her Majesty's
  Secret Service

right 2 OK **3** due **4** deed, fair, good, just, meet, nice, real, sane, true, well **5** amend, emend, exact, grant, honor, ideal, legal, licit, moral, power, solve, sound, valid **6** actual, at once, decent, honest, lawful, morals, normal, proper, remedy, seemly, square, virtue **7** certain, correct, ethical, exactly, factual, fitting, freedom, genuine, liberty, license, perfect, precise, probity, redress, regular, standup, warrant **8** accurate, becoming, clear-cut, definite, directly, goodness, morality, promptly, properly, rational, sanction, straight, suitable, suitably, truthful, virtuous **9** allowable, authentic, authority, correctly, desirable, equitable, exemplary, favorable, favorably, honorable, integrity, nobleness, opportune, ownership, perfectly, precisely, presently, privilege, propriety, rectitude, veracious, veridical, vindicate **10** aboveboard, accurately, admissible, completely, convenient, infallible, legitimate, permission, preferable, reasonable, recompense, scrupulous, undisputed, unmistaken **11** inheritance, immediately, irrefutable, prerogative, punctilious **12** advantageous, jurisdiction, satisfactory **13** appropriately, authorization, incontestable, justification, unimpeachable **14** proprietorship, satisfactorily, unquestionable
Latin: **3** jus

right beside 6 next to **8** abutting, adjacent, touching

righteous 4 fair, good, holy, just **5** godly, moral, pious **6** chaste, devout, honest **7** ethical **8** elevated, innocent, reverent, virtuous **9** blameless, equitable, honorable, incorrupt, religious, spiritual, unsullied

righteousness
goddess of: **4** Maat

righteous person
Hebrew: **6** zaddik

rightful 3 due **4** just, true **5** legal, valid **6** lawful, proper **7** allowed, condign, correct, fitting, merited **8** deserved **9** deserving, equitable **10** authorized, designated, legitimate, prescribed, sanctioned **11** appropriate, inalienable **14** constitutional

right hand 4 aide, ally **6** helper **7** partner **8** adjutant **9** assistant
French: **10** aide-de-camp

right of blood
Latin: **12** jus sanguinis

right of soil/land
Latin: **7** jus soli

Right People, The
author: **17** Stephen Birmingham

right side up 7 upright **10** on one's feet

Right Stuff, The
director: **13** Philip Kaufman
author: **8** Tom Wolfe
cast: **8** Ed Harris **10** Sam Shepard
Oscar for: **5** score

right-wing 7 old-line **10** nonliberal **11** reactionary **12** conservative **14** nonprogressive

right-winger 8 rightist **11** reactionary **12** conservative

rigid 3 set **4** firm, hard, taut **5** fixed, harsh, sharp, stern, stiff, tense **6** formal, severe, strict, strong, wooden **7** austere **8** exacting, obdurate, rigorous, stubborn, unpliant **9** inelastic, stringent, unbending **10** inflexible, unyielding **11** puritanical, unrelenting **14** uncompromising

Rigoletto
opera by: **5** Verdi
character: **5** Gilda **9** Maddalena **11** Sparafucile **12** Duke of Mantua **15** Countess Ceprano **16** Count of Monterone

rigorous 5 exact, harsh, stern, tough **6** severe, strict, trying **7** austere, correct, precise **8** accurate, exacting **9** demanding, stringent **10** meticulous, scrupulous **11** challenging, punctilious

rig out 4 garb **5** array, dress **6** attire, clothe

rile 3 irk, vex **4** gall, miff, roil **5** anger, annoy, chafe, gripe, peeve, pique **6** bother, enrage, nettle, offend, plague **7** incense, inflame, provoke **8** irritate **9** aggravate, infuriate

Riley, James Whitcomb
author of: **18** Little Orphant Annie **25** When the Frost Is on the Punkin

rilievo 6 relief

Rilke, Rainer Maria
author of: **11** Book of Hours **12** Duino Elegies, Life and Songs **13** Divine Elegies **16** Sonnets to Orpheus **19** Letters to a Young Poet

rill 5 brook, cleft, creek **6** furrow, groove, runnel, stream **7** channel, rivulet **9** streamlet

rim 3 lip **4** edge, side **5** brink, ledge, verge **6** border, margin **9** outer edge

Rima
character in: **13** Green Mansions
author: **6** Hudson

Rimbaud, Arthur
author of: **12** Le Bateau Ivre **13** A Season in Hell **14** The Drunken Boat **16** Les Illuminations **17** Sonnet of the Vowels

rime 3 ice **4** hoar **5** chink, cleft, crack, crust, frost **7** crevice, fissure **9** hoarfrost

Rime of the Ancient Mariner, The
author: **21** Samuel Taylor Coleridge
character: **6** Hermit **9** Albatross **12** Wedding Guest **14** Ancient Mariner

Rimsky-Korsakov, Nikolai (Nicholas)
born: **6** Russia **8** Novgorod
member of: **7** The Five
composer of: **5** Mlada, Sadko **6** Kitezh **10** Night in May, Snow Maiden, Tzar Saltan **11** Sheherazade **12** Christmas Eve, Scheherezade **16** Spanish Capriccio **17** Capriccio Espagnol, The Golden Cockerel **21** Russian Easter Overture **29** Russian Easter Festival Overture

rind 4 bark, hull, husk, peel, skin **5** crust, shell **6** cortex, fringe **7** epicarp, surface **8** exterior
pork: **9** crackling

ring 4 aura, band, bloc, buzz, call, echo, gang, hoop, loop, peal, toll, tone **5** cabal, chime, clang, knell, party, sound **6** cartel, circle, cordon, herald, jangle, jingle, league, signal, strike, summon, tinkle **7** besiege, circuit, combine, enclose, quality, resound, seal off, vibrate **8** announce, blockade, encircle, proclaim, striking, surround **9** broadcast, encompass, perimeter, resonance, syndicate, ting-a-ling, vibration **10** federation **11** reverberate **12** circumscribe **13** circumference, reverbera-

tion **14** tintinnabulate
16 tintinnabulation

Ring and the Book, The
 author: **14** Robert Browning

Ring des Nibelungen, Der
 also: **12** The Ring Cycle
 20 The Ring of the
 Nibelung(s)
 opera by: **6** Wagner
 part one: **12** Das Rheingold,
 The Rhine Gold
 part two: **10** Die Walkure
 11 The Valkyrie
 part three: **9** Siegfried
 part four: **15** Gotterdammerung **17** Twilight of the
 Gods
 character: **4** Erda, Mime
 5 Freia, Hagen, Wotan
 6 Fafner, Fasolt **7** Gunther,
 Gutrune, Hunding **8** Alberich, Siegmund **9** Siegfried,
 Sieglinde, Valkyries
 10 Brunnhilde

ring down the curtain
 3 end **4** halt **6** finish **8** conclude **9** terminate

ringleader 5 chief **6** master
 10 mastermind

ringlet 4 curl **6** circle

ring-shaped 5 round **8** circular

**Rin Tin Tin, The Adven-
 tures of**
 character: **5** Rusty, (Cpl)
 Boone **9** (Sgt) Biff O'Hara
 10 (Lt) Rip Masters
 cast: **8** Lee Aaker **9** Joe Sawyer **10** James Brown, Rand
 Brooks

Rio Bravo
 director: **11** Howard Hawks
 cast: **8** Ward Bond **9** John
 Wayne **10** Dean Martin
 11 Ricky Nelson **13** Walter
 Brennan **14** Angie Dickinson

Rio de Janeiro see box

riot 4 rage **5** act up, arise, melee, rebel **6** fracas, mutiny, resist, revolt, rumpus, strife,
 tumult, uproar **7** rampage, run
 amok, trouble, turmoil **8** disorder, outburst, uprising, violence **9** commotion, confusion,
 rebellion **10** Donnybrook, turbulence **11** lawlessness, pandemonium **12** insurrection

rioting 6 tumult, uproar **7** turmoil **8** disorder, outbreak, violence **9** commotion
 11 disturbance

riotous 4 loud, wild **5** arroar,
 noisy, randy **6** stormy, unruly,
 wanton **7** bacchic, rampant,
 violent **8** bacchian **9** debauched, dissolute, insurgent,
 plentiful, tumultuous, turbulent **10** boisterous, dissipated,
 licentious, rebellious **11** in-

Rio de Janeiro
 airport: **6** Galeao
 architect: **5** Costa,
 Reidy **8** Niemeyer
 area: **4** Caju, Lapa **6** Ca-
 tete, Gamboa, Gloria,
 Grajau, Tijuca **7** Ca-
 tumbi, Ipanema **8** Bo-
 tafogo **10** Copacabana,
 Vila Isabel **12** Sao
 Cristovao
 bay: **8** Botafogo, Juru-
 juba **9** Guanabara
 bridge: **11** Costa e Silva
 celebration: **8** Carnival
 9 Mardi Gras
 discovered by: **6** Coelho
 former capital of:
 6 Brazil
 island: **10** Governador
 lake: **16** Rodrigo de
 Freitas
 landmark: **10** Candelaria
 14 Mount Corcovado
 15 Maracana Stadium
 17 Sugarloaf Mountain:
 statue of: **17** Christ
 the Redeemer
 means: **14** river of
 January
 ocean: **8** Atlantic
 people: **8** Cariocas
 replaced as capital by:
 8 Brasilia
 slums: **7** favelas
 suburb: **7** Niteroi

---

temperate, overcopious **12** unrestrained **13** superabundant
15 insurrectionary
 party: **4** orgy

rip 3 cut, gap **4** rend, rent, rift,
 rive, slit, tear **5** burst, sever,
 shred, slash, split **6** cleave
 7 fissure, rupture **8** cleavage,
 cut apart, fracture, incision,
 tear open **10** laceration

ripe 3 due, fit **4** come **5** ideal,
 ready **6** mature, mellow,
 primed, timely **7** perfect
 8 complete, finished, seasoned
 9 maturated **10** consummate
 12 accomplished

ripen 3 age **4** grow **5** bloom,
 fruit **6** flower, mature, mellow **7** develop

Rip Kirby
 creator: **11** Alex Raymond
 12 John Prentice

Ripley, Robert L
 author of: **14** Believe It or
 Not

Rip Van Winkle
 author: **16** Washington Irving

rise 4 bank, defy, dune, face,
 gain, go up, grow, hill, lift,

---

meet, soar **5** climb, get up,
knoll, march, mount, rebel,
ridge, spire, stand, surge,
swell, tower **6** ascend, growth,
mutiny, resist, revolt, rocket,
strike, thrive **7** advance, balloon, burgeon, disobey, elevate, headway, improve,
prosper, stand up, succeed, upswing **8** addition, flourish, increase, progress **9** expansion,
extension **10** embankment
11 advancement, enlargement

**Rise and Fall of the Third
 Reich, The**
 author: **14** William L Shirer

Rise of Silas Lapham, The
 author: **18** William Dean
 Howells
 character: **5** Irene **8** Mr Rogers, Penelope, Tom Corey
 9 Mrs Lapham

risible 4 rich **5** comic, droll,
 funny, merry, silly, witty
 6 absurd, jocose, jovial
 7 amusing, comical, jocular
 8 farcical, humorous, mirthful
 9 facetious, laughable, ludicrous, whimsical **10** ridiculous **11** nonsensical

rising sun
 god of: **5** Janus

risk 4 dare **5** peril **6** chance,
 danger, gamble, hazard **7** imperil, venture **8** endanger,
 jeopardy **9** speculate **10** jeopardize **11** imperilment, speculation, uncertainty
 12 endangerment

risky 6 chancy, daring, unsafe
 8 insecure, perilous, ticklish
 9 dangerous, daredevil, haphazard, hazardous, hit or miss,
 uncertain **10** precarious **11** adventurous, unprotected,
 venturesome

risque 4 blue, lewd, racy
 5 bawdy, dirty, gross, spicy
 6 coarse, daring, ribald,
 smutty, vulgar **7** immoral, obscene **8** immodest, improper,
 indecent, off-color **9** offensive,
 salacious **10** indecorous, indelicate, lascivious, licentious,
 suggestive **12** pornographic

rite 6 ritual **7** liturgy, service
 8 ceremony **9** formality, solemnity **10** ceremonial, observance

rite of passage 6 ritual
 7 baptism **8** ceremony, marriage **10** bar mitzvah, bat
 mitzvah, initiation **11** christening **12** confirmation

Rites of Passage
 author: **14** William Golding

Ritt, Martin
 director of: **3** Hud
 7 Sounder **8** Norma Rae,

The Front **26** The Spy Who Came in From the Cold

Ritter, John
  born: 9 Burbank CA
  father: 9 Tex Ritter
  roles: 9 Hooperman
  11 Americathon, Jack Tripper **13** Three's Company
  14 Captain Avenger

Ritter, Thelma
  born: 10 Brooklyn NY
  roles: 10 Pillow Talk, Rear Window, The Misfits **11** All About Eve **15** The Mating Season **17** Birdman of Alcatraz **18** With a Song in My Heart **19** A Letter to Three Wives, Pickup on South Street **21** The Proud and the Profane **27** Miracle on Thirty-Fourth Street

ritual 4 rite **7** service **8** ceremony **10** observance

ritual bathing place
  Jewish Orthodox: 6 mikvah

ritualistic 6 formal, solemn **10** ceremonial **11** ceremonious

ritualize 7 observe **9** celebrate, solemnize **13** ceremonialize

ritzy 4 chic, posh, tony **5** sharp, swank **6** classy, snazzy, spiffy **7** elegant, stylish **9** high-class, high-toned, luxurious, sumptuous

rival 3 foe **5** enemy, equal, excel, fight, match, outdo, touch **6** strive **7** eclipse, surpass **8** approach, opponent, opposing, outshine **9** adversary, competing, contender, disputant **10** antagonist, competitor, contending, contestant

Rivals, The
  author: 23 Richard Brinsley Sheridan
  character: 8 Bob Acres **9** Faulkland **11** Mrs Malaprop **13** Julia Melville, Lydia Languish **17** Sir Lucius O'Trigger **18** Sir Anthony Absolute **19** Captain Jack Absolute (Ensign Beverley)

rive 4 rend **5** crack, split **6** cleave, detach, divide, sunder **7** shatter **8** fracture

riven 4 rent, torn **5** split **7** cleaved, cracked **8** sundered **9** fractured, shattered

River, The
  director: 10 Jean Renoir
  based on novel by: 11 Rumer Godden
  cast: 5 Radha **13** Adrienne Corri, Arthur Shields, Nora Swinburne **15** Patricia Walters
  setting: 5 India **6** Bengal

Rivera, Diego
  born: 6 Mexico **10** Guanajuato
  artwork: 5 Sleep **8** Creation **11** Mother Earth **14** The Fecund Earth **15** Detroit Industry **18** Man at the Crossroads **21** Carnival of Mexican Life **23** Life in Pre-Hispanic Mexico

river mouth 5 delta, firth **7** estuary

rivers
  god of: 6 Peneus, Simois **7** Inachus

Rivers, Reba
  character in: 9 Sanctuary
  author: 8 Faulkner

rivet 3 fix, pin **6** absorb, clinch, engage, fasten, occupy **7** engross **8** fastener **9** fascinate

Rivieres du Sud *see* **6** Guinea

rivulet 3 run **4** rill **5** brook, creek **6** stream **9** streamlet

Riyadh
  capital of: 11 Saudi Arabia

Rizzuto, Phil
  nickname: 7 Scooter
  position: 9 shortstop
  sport: 8 baseball
  team: 14 New York Yankees

road 3 way **4** lane, path **5** byway, route, trail **6** avenue, street **7** freeway, highway, parkway **8** turnpike **9** boulevard **10** expressway, throughway **12** thoroughfare

Road Not Taken, The
  author: 11 Robert Frost

roads
  god of: 6 Hermes

road safety
  god of: 6 Sancus **10** Semo Sancus

Road to Gandolfo, The
  author: 12 Robert Ludlum

roam 3 gad **4** rove **5** drift, jaunt, prowl, range, stray, tramp **6** ramble, stroll, travel, wander **7** meander, traipse **8** divagate **9** gallivant **11** peregrinate

roan 5 horse **7** grayish, reddish, tannish **8** blackish, brownish

Roan Stallion
  author: 15 Robinson Jeffers

roar 3 bay, cry, din **4** bawl, boom, howl, roll, yell **5** blare, growl, grunt, noise, shout, snort **6** bellow, clamor, guffaw, outcry, racket, rumble, scream, shriek **7** bluster, resound, thunder **8** outburst **10** vociferate

roast 3 pan **4** bake **6** berate **7** scourge **8** barbecue **9** criticize

rob 4 bilk, lift, loot, raid, sack, skin **5** cheat, filch, heist, rifle, seize, steal **6** burgle, fleece, forage, hold up, pilfer, thieve **7** despoil, pillage, plunder, purloin, ransack, stick up, swindle **8** carry off, embezzle **9** bamboozle **10** burglarize **11** appropriate

Robards, Jason
  born: 9 Chicago IL
  wife: 12 Lauren Bacall
  roles: 5 Julia **7** Isadora **9** Dick Diver **10** Ben Bradlee **11** Jamie Tyrone **12** Hour of the Gun **15** A Thousand Clowns, Dashiell Hammett, Melvin and Howard, The Disenchanted **16** Tender Is the Night **19** All the President's Men **24** Long Day's Journey into Night

Robbe-Grillet, Alain
  author of: 8 Jealousy **9** The Voyeur **10** The Erasers **14** In the Labyrinth **19** Last Year at Marienbad

robber, Robber 4 yegg **5** crook, thief **6** bandit, con man, outlaw, pirate, raider **7** brigand, burglar, forager, rustler, sharper **8** Barabbas, marauder, swindler **9** buccaneer, despoiler, embezzler, larcenist, plunderer **10** highwayman, pickpocket

Robbins, Harold
  author of: 8 The Betsy **13** The Inheritors **14** Dreams Die First, The Adventurers **16** The Carpetbaggers **17** The Dream Merchants **18** Never Love a Stranger **20** A Stone for Danny Fisher **21** Seventy-Nine Park Avenue

Robbins, Jerome
  choreographer of: 8 Les Noces **9** Fancy Free, Interplay
  director of: 13 West Side Story (with Robert Wise, Oscar)

robe 4 gown **5** dress, habit, smock **6** duster **7** costume, garment **8** bathrobe, vestment **9** housecoat
  French: 8 negligee
  Japanese: 6 kimono

Robe, The
  author: 13 Lloyd C Douglas

robe-de-chambre 12 dressing-gown

Robert Kennedy and His Times
author: 20 Arthur M Schlesinger Jr

Roberts, Kenneth
author of: 16 Northwest Passage

Roberts, Rachel
born: 5 Wales 8 Llanelly
husband: 11 Rex Harrison
roles: 8 Foul Play 10 Oh Lucky Man 16 This Sporting Life 24 Murder on the Orient Express 29 Saturday Night and Sunday Morning

Robertson, Cliff
real name: 23 Clifford Parker Robertson
born: 9 La Jolla CA
wife: 11 Dina Merrill
roles: 5 PT-109 6 Charly (Oscar) 9 Obsession 11 Falcon Crest

Robertson, Oscar
nickname: 7 The Big O
sport: 10 basketball
position: 5 guard
team: 14 Milwaukee Bucks 16 Cincinnati Royals

Robeson, Paul
born: 11 Princeton NJ
roles: 7 Othello 8 Show Boat 11 Brutus Jones 15 The Emperor Jones 17 King Solomon's Mines 22 All God's Chillun Got Wings

Robigo
goddess of: 5 grain

Robigus
spirit of: 9 red mildew 11 grain blight

Robin, Christopher
character in: 13 Winnie-the-Pooh
author: 5 Milne

Robin Hood's Adventures
author: 7 unknown
character: 9 Friar Tuck 10 Little John 11 Will Scarlet 14 Band of Merry Men 18 Sir Richard of the Lea 19 Sheriff of Nottingham

robin's-egg-blue 4 aqua 5 azure 7 sky-blue 8 cerulean 9 light blue 10 aquamarine, powder-blue

Robinson, Edward G
real name: 18 Emmanuel Goldenberg
born: 7 Romania 9 Bucharest
roles: 8 Key Largo 12 Little Caesar, Rico Bandello 13 Scarlet Street 15 Double Indemnity, Flesh and Fantasy 16 House of Strangers 19 The Woman in the Window 20 A Dispatch from Reuters 21 Dr Ehrlich's Magic Bullet

Robinson, Edwin Arlington
author of: 6 Merlin 8 Amaranth, Tristram 10 King Jasper 11 Richard Cory 12 Captain Craig 13 Miniver Cheevy, Mr Flood's Party

Robinson, Jackie
sport: 8 baseball
team: 15 Brooklyn Dodgers
first black in: 12 major leagues

Robinson, Sugar Ray
real name: 19 Walker Smith Robinson
sport. 6 boxing
class: 12 middleweight, welterweight

Robinson Crusoe
author: 11 Daniel Defoe
character: 6 Friday

Rob Roy
author: 14 Sir Walter Scott
character: 11 Diana Vernon 18 Sir Frederick Vernon 23 Rob Roy MacGregor Campbell
Osbaldistone family:
5 Frank 7 William 9 Rashleigh 13 Sir Hildebrand

robust 3 fit 4 firm, hale, well, wiry 5 hardy, husky, lusty, sound, stout, tough 6 active, brawny, hearty, mighty, potent, rugged, sinewy, strong, sturdy, virile 7 healthy, staunch 8 athletic, forceful, muscular, powerful, stalwart, vigorous 9 energetic, healthful, strapping, wholesome 10 able-bodied 12 in fine fettle
French: 8 puissant

robustness 5 vigor 8 strength 10 good health, ruggedness, sturdiness 11 healthiness

Roche, Kevin
architect of: 13 Oakland Museum (CA) 14 Fine Arts Center (U of MA), Ford Foundation (NYC) 17 Knights of Columbus (New Haven CT) 21 One United Nations Plaza (NYC) 24 Union Carbide Headquarters (Danbury CT) 31 Power Center for the Performing Arts (U of Michigan)

Rochester
football team: 8 Panthers

Rochester, Edward
character in: 8 Jane Eyre
author: 6 Bronte

rock 3 bob, jar 4 crag, reef, roll, stun, sway, toss 5 cliff, flint, pitch, quake, shake, stone, swing, upset 6 gravel, marble, pebble, totter, wobble 7 agitate, bobbing, boulder, disturb, shaking 8 convulse, flounder, undulate, wobbling 9 limestone, oscillate, tottering 10 convulsion, undulation

Rock & Rye
type: 7 liqueur
flavor: 6 citrus
ingredient: 3 rye 9 rock candy

rock crystal
species: 6 quartz
color: 9 colorless

Rocket
nickname of: 14 Maurice Richard

rocket engine
invented by: 7 Goddard

Rockford Files, The
character: 10 John Cooper 11 Angel Martin, Jim Rockford 12 (Det) Dennis Becker 13 Beth Davenport, (Joseph) Rocky Rockford
cast: 9 Bo Hopkins, Joe Santos, Noah Beery 11 James Garner 14 Stuart Margolin 15 Gretchen Corbett

rock of Tarik see 9 Gibraltar

Rockwell, Norman
born: 9 New York NY
artwork:
covers: 19 Saturday Evening Post
mural: 15 Freedom of Speech

Rocky
director: 13 John G Avildsen
cast: 9 Burt Young 10 Talia Shire 11 Thayer David 12 Carl Weathers 15 Burgess Meredith 17 Sylvester Stallone (Rocky Balboa, the Italian Stallion)
setting: 12 Philadelphia
Oscar for: 7 editing, picture 8 director
sequel: 7 Rocky II, Rocky IV 8 Rocky III, Rocky Two 9 Rocky Four 10 Rocky Three

rod 4 cane, lash, mace, pale, pole, wand, whip 5 baton, birch, crook, staff, stake, stick 6 cudgel, rattan, switch 7 penalty, scepter, scourge 8 caduceus 9 stanchion 10 alpenstock, punishment 11 retribution 12 swagger stick
abbreviation: 2 rd

rod, Aaron's see 9 Aaron's rod

rodent 4 cavy, vole 5 coypu, gundi, hutia, mouse 6 agouti, beaver, cururo, gerbil, gopher, jerboa, nutria 7 blesmol, cane rat, hamster, lemming, mole-rat, rock rat 8 capybara, chipmunk, dormouse, pacarana, sewellel, spiny rat, squirrel, tucu-tuco, viscacha **9** chozchori, false paca, porcupine, woodchuck **10** chinchilla, prairie dog, springhare **11** kangaroo rat, pocket mouse, viscacha rat **13** kangaroo mouse **16** Speke's pectinator

Roderick Hudson
   author: **10** Henry James

Roderick Random
   author: **14** Tobias Smollett
   character: **5** Strap **8** Narcissa **10** Tom Bowling **12** Miss Williams

Rodin, (Francois) Auguste Rene
   born: **5** Paris **6** France
   artwork: **7** The Kiss **10** Head of Iris, The Thinker, Victor Hugo, Walking Man **14** John the Baptist, The Age of Bronze, The Gates of Hell **16** Monument to Balzac **19** The Burghers of Calais **23** The Man with the Broken Nose

rodomontade 4 rant **5** boast **6** hot air **7** blather, bluster, bombast, fustian **8** bragging, folderol, nonsense, rhetoric **10** balderdash, doubletalk **11** braggadocio **12** boastfulness

roe 3 doe, elk, hen **4** buck, deer, eggs, fawn, fish, hart, hind, milt **5** spawn, sperm **6** caviar **8** fish eggs
   of lobster: **5** coral

Roentgen, Rontgen, Wilhelm Konrad
   field: **7** physics
   nationality: **6** German
   discovered: **5** X-rays
   awarded: **10** Nobel Prize

Roethke, Theodore
   author of: **9** Open House, The Waking **11** The Far Field **15** Straw for the Fire, Words for the Wind

Rogers, Ginger
   real name: **23** Virginia Katherine McMath
   born: **14** Independence MO
   husband: **8** Lew Ayres **15** Jacques Bergerac, William Marshall
   partner: **11** Fred Astaire
   roles: **6** Top Hat **9** Stage Door **10** Hello Dolly, Kitty Foyle (Oscar) **12** Shall We Dance? **14** The Gay Divorcee **15** Flying Down to Rio, Tom Dick and Harry **17** Forty-Second Street **19** The Major and the Minor **21** The Barkleys of Broadway **30** The Story of Vernon and Irene Castle

Rogers, James Gamble
   architect of: **22** Northwestern University (Chicago) **33** Columbia-Presbyterian Medical Center (NYC)

Rogers, Roy
   real name: **11** Leonard Slye
   born: **12** Cincinnati OH
   wife: **9** Dale Evans
   sidekick: **10** Gabby Hayes
   singing group: **17** Sons of the Pioneers
   horse: **7** Trigger
   roles: **10** Apache Rose **11** Song of Texas **12** My Pal Trigger **13** Song of Arizona, Son of Paleface **17** Heart of the Rockies, Under Western Stars **18** Billy the Kid Returns **19** Tumbling Tumbleweeds **20** The Yellow Rose of Texas **22** Springtime in the Sierras

rogue 3 cur **5** devil, fraud, knave, scamp **6** bad man, rascal, rotter, varlet, wretch **7** bounder, hellion, villain **8** deceiver, evildoer, scalawag **9** miscreant, reprobate, scoundrel **10** blackguard, malefactor, mountebank, scapegrace **11** rapscallion **13** mischiefmaker **14** good-for-nothing **15** snake in the grass

Rogue Herries
   author: **11** Hugh Walpole

roguish 3 sly **4** arch **5** saucy **8** devilish, rascally **11** mischievous

Rohe, Vera-Ellen
   real name of: **9** Vera-Ellen

roil 3 irk, vex **4** mill, rile, stir **5** annoy, muddy **6** ruffle, seethe **7** agitate, disturb, perturb, provoke, turmoil **8** irritate **9** aggravate **10** exasperate

role 3 job **4** duty, part, pose, post, task, work **5** chore, guise **7** posture, service **8** capacity, function **9** character, portrayal **10** assignment **13** impersonation **14** representation **15** personification **16** characterization
   Latin: **7** persona

roll 4 boom, coil, curl, echo, flip, flow, furl, knot, list, loop, reel, roar, rock, spin, sway, toss, tube, turn, wind **5** coast, crack, lurch, pitch, sound, spool, surge, swell, swing, swirl, throw, twirl, twist, wheel, whirl **6** billow, gyrate, muster, roster, rotate, rumble, scroll, tumble **7** booming, catalog, entwine, resound, revolve, rocking, thunder, tossing, turning **8** cylinder, drumbeat, drumming, rumbling, sched-

ule, tumbling, undulate **9** inventory **10** undulation **11** reverberate **13** reverberation **15** turn over and over

Rolland, Romain
   author of: **14** Jean-Christophe **16** The Soul Enchanted

rollicking 3 gay **5** happy, jolly, merry, sunny **6** bright, hearty, jocund, jovial, joyous, lively **7** gleeful, jocular, playful, romping **8** cheerful, mirthful, spirited **9** exuberant, gamboling, sparkling, sprightly **10** frolicking, frolicsome, hysterical, rip-roaring **12** lighthearted

Rolvaag, Ole Edvart
   author of: **15** Peder Victorious, Their Father's God **16** Giants in the Earth

roly-poly 3 fat **5** obese, plump, pudgy, round **6** chubby, rotund **9** corpulent

Roma
   father: **7** Evander

roman 5 novel **17** metrical narrative

Roman Catholic church
   council/synod: **4** Pisa **5** Basel, Trent **6** Nicaea, Vienne, Whitby **7** Ephesus, Pistoia, Sardica **9** Chalcedon, Constance **12** First Vatican **13** Fourth Lateran, Second Vatican **14** Constantinople **15** Ferrara-Florence
   official Vatican yearbook: **18** Annuario Pontificio
   first Christian emperor: **11** Constantine
   gifts of territory/sovereignty to papacy: **15** Donation of Pepin **21** Donation of Constantine

romance 4 bosh, call, pull **5** amour, idyll, novel **6** affair, allure **7** fantasy, fiction **8** illusion **9** courtship, exoticism, fairy tale, fish story, invention, love story, melodrama, moonshine, tall story **10** attachment, concoction, flirtation, love affair **11** fabrication, fascination, imagination **12** exaggeration, relationship, self-delusion **13** flight of fancy, tender passion **16** affair of the heart

Romance language see **5** Latin

Romance of the Forest
   author: **12** Ann Radcliffe

Romances sans paroles
   author: **12** Paul Verlaine

Romancing the Stone
   director: **14** Robert Zemeckis

cast: 11 Danny De Vito
14 Kathleen Turner, Michael
Douglas
sequel: 17 The Jewel of the
Nile

Roman Holiday
director: **12** William Wyler
cast: **11** Eddie Albert, Gregory Peck **13** Audrey
Hepburn
Oscar for: **7** actress (Hepburn)

Romania *see* **7** Rumania

Roman measure 2 as **5** cubit,
libra **6** pondus **7** stadium

Roman Mythology *see box*

romantic 4 fond **5** mushy,
soppy **6** ardent, dreamy, loving, tender, unreal **7** amorous,
devoted, fervent, flighty, idyllic, utopian **8** enamored, fanciful, quixotic **9** fantastic,
idealized, imaginary, sensitive,
visionary, whimsical **10** idealistic, improbable, passionate
11 extravagant, impassioned,
impractical, rhapsodical, sentimental, unrealistic, warmhearted **12** melodramatic,
preposterous

Romantic Comedians, The
author: **12** Ellen Glasgow

romanticize 8 idealize
9 embroider

Romantic Manifesto
author: **7** Ayn Rand

Romany Rye, The
author: **17** George Henry
Borrow

Rome, ancient *see box,*
p. 841

Rome, Roma *see box,*
p. 841

Rome Haul
author: **14** Walter D
Edmonds

Romeo 4 beau **5** lover, sheik,
swain, wooer **7** Don Juan, gallant **8** Casanova, cavalier, Lothario **9** boyfriend, Lochinvar
French: **8** paramour
Latin: **9** inamorato

Romeo and Juliet
author: **18** William
Shakespeare
character: **5** Nurse, Paris
6 Tybalt **8** Benvolio, Mercutio **13** Friar Laurence
family: **7** Capulet
8 Montague
setting: **6** Verona

Romeo and Juliet
director:
1936 version: **11** George
Cukor
1968 version: **16** Franco
Zeffirelli

Roman Mythology
collective name for gods: **6** Superi
goddess of anguish: **8** Angerona
goddess of agriculture: **5** Ceres **6** Dea Dia, Vacuna
13 Acca Laurentia
Ceres corresponds to Greek: **7** Demeter
goddess of the arts: **7** Minerva
corresponds to Greek: **6** Athena
goddess of baking: **6** Fornax
goddess of chastity: **5** Fauna **7** Bona Dea
goddess of childbirth: **5** Parca **6** Lucina, Matuta, Parcae
11 Mater Matuta
goddess of the dawn: **6** Aurora, Matuta **11** Mater Matuta
Aurora corresponds to Greek: **3** Eos
goddess of destiny: **5** Parca **6** Parcae
goddess of discord: **9** Discordia
goddess of door hinges: **6** Cardea
goddess of the earth: **6** Tellus
corresponds to Greek: **4** Gaea
goddess of the family: **6** Cardea
goddess of fertility: **5** Fauna **6** Libera, Tellus
7 Bona Dea
Libera corresponds to Greek: **10** Persephone
Tellus corresponds to Greek: **4** Gaea
goddess of flowers: **5** Flora
goddess of fortune: **7** Fortuna
corresponds to Greek: **5** Tyche
goddess of fruit trees: **6** Pomona
goddess of gardens: **5** Venus
corresponds to Greek: **9** Aphrodite
goddess of grain/protectress against grain blight:
6 Robigo
goddess of harbors: **6** Matuta **11** Mater Matuta
goddess of harmony: **9** Concordia
goddess of the hearth: **4** Caca **5** Salus, Vesta
Salus corresponds to Greek: **6** Hygeia
goddess of heaven: **4** Juno
corresponds to Greek: **4** Hera
goddess of hunting: **5** Diana
corresponds to Greek: **6** Phoebe **7** Artemis
goddess of longevity: **11** Anna Perenna
goddess of love: **5** Venus
corresponds to Greek: **9** Aphrodite
goddess of marriage: **4** Juno **6** Tellus
corresponds to Greek: **4** Gaea, Hera
goddess of marshes: **6** Marica **9** Dea Marica
goddess of the moon: **5** Diana
corresponds to Greek: **6** Phoebe **7** Artemis
goddess of peace: **3** Pax **9** Concordia
Pax corresponds to Greek: **5** Irene
goddess of pleasure: **8** Voluptas
goddess of plenty: **3** Ops **10** Magna Mater
goddess of prosperity: **5** Salus
corresponds to Greek: **6** Hygeia
goddess of the sea: **6** Matuta **11** Mater Matuta
goddess of sleeping infants: **6** Cunina
goddess of the spring: **5** Venus
corresponds to Greek: **9** Aphrodite
goddess of storms: **11** Tempestates
goddess of victory: **8** Victoria
corresponds to Greek: **4** Nike
goddess of vineyards: **6** Libera
corresponds to Greek: **10** Persephone
goddess of war: **7** Bellona
corresponds to Greek: **5** Enyon
goddess of wine: **6** Libera
corresponds to Greek: **10** Persephone
goddess of wisdom: **7** Minerva
corresponds to Greek: **6** Athena

(continued)

Roman Mythology (*continued*)
god of agriculture: **5** Picus **6** Saturn **7** Eventus **12** Bonus Eventus
  corresponds to Greek: **6** Cronos, Cronus, Kronos
god of beginnings: **5** Janus
god of boundaries: **8** Terminus
god of commerce: **7** Mercury
  corresponds to Greek: **6** Hermes
god of the dead: **7** Veiovis
god of doorways: **5** Janus
god of drinking/revelry: **5** Comus
god of eloquence: **7** Mercury
  corresponds to Greek: **6** Hermes
god of farm boundaries: **8** Silvanus, Sylvanus
god of fertility: **7** Mutinus, Priapus **8** Lupercus, Picumnus
god of fire/metalworking: **6** Vulcan
  corresponds to Greek: **10** Hephaestus, Hephaistos
god of forest: **7** Virbius
god of gardens: **9** Vertumnus
god of good counsel: **3** Ops **6** Consus
god of grain/protector against grain blight: **7** Robigus
god of healing: **11** Aesculapius
  corresponds to Greek: **9** Asclepius
god of heavens: **4** Jove **7** Jupiter
  corresponds to Greek: **4** Zeus
god of herds: **8** Silvanus, Sylvanus
god of horse racing: **3** Ops **6** Consus
god of hospitality: **6** Sancus **10** Dius Fidius, Semo Sancus
god of the house: **8** Silvanus, Sylvanus
god of hunting: **7** Virbius
god of international affairs: **6** Sancus **10** Dius Fidius, Semo Sancus
god of landmarks: **8** Terminus
god of light: **6** Apollo
god of love: **4** Amor **5** Cupid
  corresponds to Greek: **4** Eros
god of luck: **7** Eventus **12** Bonus Eventus
god of medicine: **11** Aesculapius
  corresponds to Greek: **9** Asclepius
god of music: **6** Apollo
god of oaths: **6** Sancus **10** Dius Fidius, Semo Sancus
god of orchards: **9** Vertumnus
god of ports/harbors: **8** Portunus
god of prosperity: **7** Eventus **12** Bonus Eventus
god of the rising sun: **5** Janus

god of science: **7** Mercury
  corresponds to Greek: **6** Hermes
god of sea: **7** Neptune
  corresponds to Greek: **8** Poseidon
god of seasons: **9** Vertumnus
god of the setting sun: **5** Janus
god of sleep: **6** Somnus
  corresponds to Greek: **6** Hypnos, Hypnus
god of springs: **4** Fons
gods of sulphur springs (twins): **6** Palici
god of the sun: **3** Sol
  corresponds to Greek: **6** Helios **8** Hyperion
god of thievery: **7** Mercury
  corresponds to Greek: **6** Hermes
god of thunder: **7** Taranis
god of thunderstorms: **8** Summanus
god of the Tiber: **9** Tiberinus
god of uncultivated land: **8** Silvanus, Sylvanus
god of underworld: **3** Dis **5** Orcus **8** Dis Pater
  corresponds to Greek: **5** Pluto
god of war: **4** Mars **6** Mamers, Mavors **8** Quirinus
  corresponds to Greek: **4** Ares
god of weather: **4** Jove **7** Jupiter
god of weddings: **8** Talassio
  corresponds to Greek: **5** Hymen **9** Hymenaeus
god of the woods: **6** Faunus **8** Silvanus, Sylvanus
house spirits: **5** lares **7** penates
nymphs/deities with gift of prophecy: **7** Camenae
  names: **6** Egeria **8** Carmenta **9** Antevorta, Postvorta
  correspond to Greek: **5** Muses
protectress of childbirth: **8** Carmenta
protectress of cows/oxen: **6** Bubona
protector of flocks/shepherds: **5** Pales
protectress of military age men: **8** Juventas
  corresponds to Greek: **4** Hebe
protectress of women: **5** Diana
  corresponds to Greek: **6** Phoebe **7** Artemis
protectress of women/marriage: **4** Juno
queen of heaven: **4** Juno
  corresponds to Greek: **4** Hera, Here
staff of Mercury: **8** Caduceus
troublesome ghosts: **7** lemures

based on play by: **18** William Shakespeare
cast:
  1936 version: **12** Leslie Howard, Norma Shearer **13** Basil Rathbone, Edna May Oliver, John Barrymore
  1968 version: **9** Milo O'Shea **11** John McEnery, Michael York **12** Olivia Hussey **14** Leonard Whiting
score: **8** Nino Rota

Romeo and Juliet
symphony by: **7** Berlioz

opera by: **6** Gounod
orchestral piece by: **11** Tchaikovsky
ballet by: **9** Prokofiev

Romney, George
born: **7** England **15** Dalton-in-Furness
artwork: **5** Circe **9** Joan of Arc **11** Mrs Robinson, Sensibility **12** Mrs Davenport, Saint Cecilia **19** Mrs Carwardine and Son **22** The Death of General Wolfe **24** The Levenson-Gower Children **26** Sir Christopher and Lady Sykes

Romola
author: **11** George Eliot
character: **5** Bardo, Tessa **10** Tito Melema **15** Baldasarre Calvo

romp **3** hop **4** skip **5** caper, cut up, frisk, sport **6** frolic, gambol **7** disport, rollick

Romulus
father: **4** Mars
mother: **4** Ilia **9** Rea Silvia **10** Rhea Silvia
twin brother: **5** Remus
raised by: **7** she-wolf **9** Faustulus **12** Acca Larentia

Rome, ancient
  emperor: 4 Nero, Otho **5** Galba, Nerva, Titus **6** Trajan **7** Hadrian **8** Augustus, Caligula, Claudius, Commodus, Domitian, Tiberius **9** Caracalla, Vespasian, Vitellius **10** Diocletian **11** Constantine, Lucius Verus **13** Antoninus Pius **14** Marcus Aurelius
  emperor's bodyguard: 15 Praetorian Guard
  first citizen title: 8 princeps
  first triumvirate: 6 Caesar, Pompey **7** Crassus
  foe: 4 Gaul **5** Spain **6** Cimbri **7** Perseus, Philip V, Pyrrhus, Teutons **8** Carthage, Hannibal, Iberians, Jugurtha, Samnites, Tarentum, Umbrians **9** Etruscans, Macedonia, Seleucids **11** Latin League **12** Antiochus III **13** Achaean League, Hamilcar Barca
  general: 5 Sulla **6** Brutus, Marius, Pompey **7** Crassus **8** Octavian **10** Flamininus, Mark Antony **12** Julius Caesar **14** Caesar Augustus **20** Quintus Fabius Maximus, Scipio Africanus Major, Scipio Africanus Minor
  king: 12 Ancus Marcius **13** Numa Pompilius **16** Sextus Tarquinius **17** Tarquinius Priscus (Tarquin the Elder) **18** Tarquinius Superbus (Tarquin the Proud)
  reformer: 8 Gracchus
  republican ruler: 6 consul **7** senator, tribune **8** plebeian **9** optimates, patrician, populares **10** magistrate
  Roman peace: 9 Pax Romana
  second triumvirate: 6 Antony **7** Lepidus **8** Octavian (Caesar Augustus)

Rome, Roma
  airport: 8 Ciampino **15** Leonardo da Vinci
  area: 9 Cinecitta (Cinema City) **10** Trastevere **11** Vatican City
  capital of: 5 Italy **6** Latium **11** Papal States, Roman Empire
  church: 8 St Peter's **11** San Giovanni **18** Santa Maria Maggiore **19** San Paolo Fuori le Mura
  Italian: 4 Roma
  landmark: 5 Forum **7** Capitol **8** Pantheon **9** catacombs, Colosseum **12** Palazzo Doria **13** Circus Maximus, Lateran Palace, Sistine Chapel, Vatican Palace, Villa Borghese **14** Palazzo Corsini, Villa Farnesina **16** Baths of Caracalla, Castel Sant'Angelo, Palazzo Barberini **17** Arch of Constantine **19** Saint Peter's Basilica
  legendary founders: 5 Remus **6** Aeneas **7** Romulus
  nickname: 11 Eternal City
  mountain: 8 Apennine
  museum: 5 Doria **7** Colonna, Corsini, Vatican **8** Borghese, National **10** Capitoline
  river: 5 Tiber
  school: 33 Conservatorio di Musica Santa Cecilia
  sea: 10 Tyrrhenian
  seven hills: 7 Caelian, Viminal **8** Aventine, Palatine, Quirinal **9** Esquiline **10** Capitoline
  square/piazza: 6 Popolo, Spagna **7** Colonna, Venezia **9** Quirinale **11** Campidoglio
  state within: 11 Vatican City
  street: 9 Appian Way, Emmanuele **11** Via del Corso **13** Corso Vittorio
  subway: 13 Metropolitana

first king of: 4 Rome
founder of: 4 Rome

Romus
  father: 6 Aeneas **8** Ascanius
  possible founder of: 4 Rome

Ronan
  origin: 5 Irish
  form: 4 king
  son: 4 Mael
  killed: 4 Mael
  killed by: 13 grandchildren

Roncalli, Angelo Giuseppe
  13 Pope John XXIII **22** Pope John the Twenty-Third

Ronsard, Pierre de
  author of: 17 Sonnets pour Helene
  member of: 7 Pleiade

roofing 4 tile, turf **5** slate, terne **6** thatch **7** asphalt, ceiling, pantile, shingle **8** housetop

Roof of the World *see* **5** Tibet

rook 3 gyp **4** bilk, crow, dupe, gull **5** cheat, cozen, raven, trick **6** castle, fleece **7** deceive, defraud, swindle **8** chessman **9** bamboozle, victimize

rookie 4 tyro **6** novice **8** beginner **9** fledgling, greenhorn **10** apprentice, tenderfoot

Rookies, The
  character: 9 Jill Danko, (Officer) Mike Danko **10** (Lt) Eddie Ryker, (Officer) Chris Owens **12** (Officer) Terry Webster, (Officer) Willie Gillis
  cast: 11 Kate Jackson, Sam Melville **14** Bruce Fairbairn, Michael Ontkean **16** Gerald S O'Loughlin **18** Georg Stanford Brown

room 4 area **5** range, scope, space **6** chance, extent, leeway, margin, volume **7** chamber, cubicle, expanse, lodging **9** allowance, provision, territory **11** compartment
  French: 5 salle
  Spanish: 4 sala

Room at the Top
  director: 11 Jack Clayton
  based on novel by: 10 John Braine
  cast: 12 Heather Sears **14** Laurence Harvey, Simone Signoret **16** Hermione Baddeley
  Oscar for: 7 actress (Signoret)
  sequel: 11 Man at the Top **12** Life at the Top

Room 222
  character: 6 Bernie **9** Pete Dixon **11** Liz McIntyre **12** Alice Johnson **14** Seymour Kaufman
  cast: 11 Lloyd Haynes **13** David Jolliffe **14** Denise Nicholas, Karen Valentine **18** Michael Constantine
  school: 15 Walt Whitman High

roomy 3 big **4** huge, long, vast, wide **5** ample, broad, large **7** immense, lengthy, sizable **8** generous, spacious **9** boundless, capacious, expansive, ex-

Roosevelt, Franklin Delano
  presidential rank: 12 thirty-second
  party: 10 Democratic
  state represented: 2 NY
  defeated: 5 (Jacob Sechler) Coxey, (John W) Aiken, (Thomas Edmund) Dewey, (William) Lemke **6** (Alfred Mossman) Landon, (Claude A) Watson, (David Leigh) Colvin, (Herbert Clark) Hoover, (Norman) Thomas, (Roger Ward) Babson, (William David) Upshaw, (William Hope) Harvey, (William Zebulon) Foster **7** (Earl Russell) Browder, (Wendell Lewis) Willkie **8** (Edward A) Teichert, (Verne L) Reynolds
  vice president: 6 (Harry S) Truman, (John Nance) Garner **7** (Henry Agard) Wallace
  cabinet:
    state: **4** (Cordell) Hull **10** (Edward Reilly) Stettinius (Jr)
    treasury: **6** (William Hartman) Woodin **10** (Henry) Morgenthau (Jr)
    war: **4** (George Henry) Dern **7** (Henry Lewis) Stimson **8** (Harry Hines) Woodring
    attorney general: **6** (Francis) Biddle, (Frank) Murphy **7** (Robert Houghwout) Jackson **8** (Homer Stille) Cummings
    navy: **4** (Frank) Knox **6** (Charles) Edison **7** (Claude Augustus) Swanson **9** (James Vincent) Forrestal
    postmaster general: **6** (Frank Comerford) Walker, (James Aloysius) Farley
    interior: **5** (Harold LeClaire) Ickes
    agriculture: **7** (Claude Raymond) Wickard, (Henry Agard) Wallace
    commerce: **5** (Daniel Calhoun) Roper, (Jesse Holman) Jones **7** (Henry Agard) Wallace, (Henry Lloyd) Hopkins
    labor: **7** (Frances) Perkins (Wilson)
  born: 10 Hyde Park NY
  died: 13 Warm Springs GA **16** Little White House
  buried: 10 Hyde Park NY
  education:
    prep school: **6** Groton
    university: **7** Harvard
    law school: **8** Columbia
  religion: 12 Episcopalian
  interests: 3 art **4** polo **6** tennis, travel **7** fishing, hunting **8** shooting
  vacation spot: 13 Warm Springs GA **16** Campobello Island (Canada)
  dog: 4 Fala
  author: 27 The Happy Warrior: Alfred E Smith
  political career: 12 state senator
    assistant secretary of: **4** Navy
    governor of: **7** New York
  civilian career: 6 lawyer **11** bank officer
  notable events of lifetime/term: 4 D-Day, WWII **7** New Deal **10** atomic bomb, Depression, World War II **11** World War Two **13** United Nations **15** Atlantic Charter
    act: **9** Lend-Lease
    attack on: **11** Pearl Harbor
    conference: **5** Cairo, Yalta **7** Arcadia, Crimean, Teheran
    scandal: **11** Tammany Hall
  quote: 24 A day that will live in infamy **31** Meet every day's troubles as they come **36** The only thing we have to fear is fear itself **50** This generation of Americans has a rendezvous with destiny **53** I pledge you I pledge myself to a new deal for the American people
  father: 5 James
  mother: 4 Sara (Delano)
  siblings:
    half-brother: **5** James
  wife: 7 (Anna) Eleanor (Roosevelt)
  children: 5 James **7** Elliott **11** Anna Eleanor **13** John Aspinwell **14** Franklin Delano
  first lady:
    author: **7** On My Own **13** This I Remember, This Is My Story **34** The Autobiography of Eleanor Roosevelt
    chairwoman: **25** UN Commission on Human Rights
    codirector: **23** Office of Civilian Defense
    member: **35** Democratic National Campaign Committee
    newspaper column: **5** My Day
    US delegate to: **2** UN

tensive, unlimited **10** commodious

Rooney, Mickey
  real name: 9 Joe Yule Jr
  born: 10 Brooklyn NY
  wife: 10 Ava Gardner **13** Martha Vickers
  co-star: 11 Judy Garland
  roles: 4 Puck **8** Boys' Town **9** Andy Hardy **11** Sugar Babies **13** Mickey McGuire **14** Baby Face Nelson, National Velvet, The Human Comedy **21** A Midsummer Night's Dream **30** The Adventures of Huckleberry Finn

Roosevelt, Theodore
nickname: 5 Teddy
presidential rank: 11 twenty-sixth
party: 10 Republican
state represented: 2 NY
succeeded: 8 McKinley
defeated (second term): 4 (Eugene Victor) Debs **6** (Alton Brooks) Parker, (Thomas Edward)
Watson **7** (Austin) Holcomb, (Silas Comfort) Swallow **8** (Charles Hunter) Corregan
vice president: 4 none (1st term) **9** (Charles Warren) Fairbanks
cabinet:
  state: **3** (John Milton) Hay **4** (Elihu) Root **5** (Robert) Bacon
  treasury: **4** (Leslie Mortier) Shaw, (Lyman Judson) Gage **9** (George Bruce) Cortelyou
  war: **4** (Elihu) Root, (William Howard) Taft **6** (Luke Edward) Wright
  attorney general: **4** (Philander Chase) Knox **5** (William Henry) Moody **9** (Charles Joseph)
    Bonaparte
  navy: **4** (John Davis) Long **5** (William Henry) Moody **6** (Paul) Morton **7** (Victor Howard)
    Metcalf **8** (Truman Handy) Newberry **9** (Charles Joseph) Bonaparte
  postmaster general: **5** (Charles Emory) Smith, (George von Lengerke) Meyer, (Henry Clay)
    Payne, (Robert John) Wynne **9** (George Bruce) Cortelyou
  interior: **8** (James Rudolph) Garfield **9** (Ethan Allen) Hitchcock
  agriculture: **6** (James) Wilson
  commerce and labor: **6** (Oscar Solomon) Straus **7** (Victor Howard) Metcalf **9** (George Bruce)
    Cortelyou
born: 13 New York City NY
died/buried: 2 NY **9** Oyster Bay **10** Long Island
education:
  university: **7** Harvard
  law school: **8** Columbia (did not graduate)
religion: 13 Dutch Reformed
interests: 7 hunting (African game), writing **9** exploring (South America) **14** natural history
author: 11 Rough Riders **14** Oliver Cromwell **16** Gouverneur Morris, Thomas Hart Benton
17 African Game Trails, The New Nationalism **19** The Winning of the West **20** Letters to
His Children **21** America and the World War **24** The Foes of Our Own Household **25** Fear
God and Take Your Own Part **27** A Booklover's Holiday in the Open, Ranch Life and the
Hunting Trail, The Naval War of Eighteen-Twelve **28** Hero Tales from American History
29 Through the Brazilian Wilderness **33** Life Histories of African Game Animals
political career: 13 Vice President **15** NY State Assembly **24** US Civil Service Commission
  assistant secretary: **4** Navy
  governor of: **7** New York
  organized party: **9** Bull Moose **11** Progressive
civilian career: 6 author **7** rancher **14** public lecturer
military service: 15 NY National Guard **18** Spanish-American War
  organized cavalry regiment: **11** Rough Riders
  led charge up: **11** San Juan Hill
notable events of lifetime/term: 5 Panic (of 1907) **10** Square Deal **15** Nobel Peace Prize
22 San Francisco earthquake
  Act: **11** Reclamation **14** Meat Inspection **15** Hepburn Railroad, Pure Food and Drug
  bureau of: **12** Corporations **28** Immigration and Naturalization
  first flight by: **14** Wright Brothers
  revolution: **6** Panama
  treaty: **13** Hay-Pauncefote **15** Hay-Bunau-Varilla
quotes: 25 Hasten forward quickly there **28** Speak softly and carry a big stick
father: 8 Theodore
mother: 6 Martha (Bulloch)
siblings: 4 Anna **7** Corinne, Elliott
wife: 5 Alice (Hathaway Lee), Edith (Kermit Carow)
children: 6 Kermit **7** Quentin **8** Alice Lee, Theodore **10** Ethel Carow **16** Archibald Bulloch

Roosevelt, Franklin Delano
see box, p. 842

Roosevelt, Theodore *see box*

rooster
  young: 8 cockerel

root 3 fix, set **4** back, base,
bind, bulb, clap, hail, nail,
rise, stem **5** basis, boost,
cheer, fount, radix, start, stick,
tubes **6** bottom, fasten,
ground, motive, origin, reason,
second, source, spring **7** acclaim, applaud, bolster, cheer
on, pull for, radicle, support
8 fountain, occasion, shout
for **9** beginning, encourage,
establish, inception, rationale
10 derivation, foundation,
mainspring **11** fundamental
12 commencement,
fountainhead

Root, John Wellborn
  partner: 14 Daniel H
  Burnham
  architect of: 10 The Rookery **12** Hotel Statler (Washington DC), Montauk Block
  13 Hotel Tamanaco (Caracas) **17** Monadnock Build-

Roots
author: 9 Alex Haley
character: 3 Tom **4** Ames, Bell, Noah **5** Binta, Fanta, Grill, Irene, Kizzy, Lewis, Mingo, Omoro **6** Justin, Martha, Ordell **7** Fiddler, Gardner, Nyo Boto **8** Kintango, Mathilda, Mrs Moore, Tom Moore **9** Evan Brent, Missy Anne **10** Brima Cesay, Capt Davies, Carrington, Jemmy Brent, Kadi Touray, Kunta Kinte, Sam Bennett, Sister Sara **11** Mrs Reynolds, Squire James **12** John Reynolds **13** Chicken George **14** Sir Eric Russell, Stephen Bennett **15** Ol' George Johnson, Third Mate Slater **17** Dr William Reynolds
cast: 8 Burl Ives, John Amos, Ren Woods **9** Ben Vereen, Brad Davis, Moses Gunn, O J Simpson, Vic Morrow **10** Billy Hicks, Ian McShane, John Schuck, Lynne Moody, Olivia Cole, Paul Shenar, Ralph Waite, Robert Reed **11** Beverly Todd, Cicely Tyson, Doug McClure, Edward Asner, Gary Collins, Harry Rhodes, Lane Binkley, LeVar Burton, Lorne Greene, Maya Angelou, Sandy Duncan **12** Carolyn Jones, Chuck Connors, Leslie Uggams, Lloyd Bridges **13** Louis Gosset Jr, Madge Sinclair, William Watson **14** George Hamilton, Lynda Day George, Macdonald Carey **15** Lillian Randolph, Scatman Crothers, Thalmus Rasulala **16** Raymond St Jacques, Richard Roundtree **18** Georg Stanford Brown **20** Lawrence Hilton-Jacobs

---

ing, Palmolive Building (Chicago) **19** Rand-McNally Building

root for 5 boost **6** urge on **7** cheer on, pull for

root out 5 dig up **6** remove **7** extract, pull out, uncover, unearth **8** discover **9** extirpate, ferret out **12** bring to light

Roots *see box*

rope 3 gad, guy, tie, tow **4** bind, cord, fast, guss, hemp, line, lure, snag, trap, wire, yarn **5** cable, catch, chord, lasso, noose, riata, shank, strap, twine **6** corral, entice, hawser, lariat, seduce, string, tether **7** bobstay, cordage, halyard, lanyard, lashing, painter **8** dragline, restrain
fiber: 5 sisal

Rosaline
character in: 16 Love's Labour's Lost
author: 11 Shakespeare

rose 4 Rosa
varieties: 3 bog, dog, sun, tea, wax **4** baby, gold, moss, musk, rock, rush, sand, wood **5** briar, brier, China, fairy, field, malva, Ophir, pygmy, swamp **6** Alpine, Burnet, copper, cotton, damask, desert, French, ground, Karroo, Lenten, mallow, Nootka, Scotch, velvet **7** baby sun, Banksia, Bourbon, cabbage, cluster, Guelder, Manetti, pasture, prairie, rambler **8** Burgundy, Champney, Cherokee, chestnut, cinnamon, climbing, Japanese, Memorial, mountain, Noisette **9** Christmas, evergreen, hybrid tea, McCartney, Polyantha, Remontant, Turkestan **10** California, Chinquapin, shaggy-rock, underwater **11** confederate, giant velvet, hairy alpine **12** green Mexican, Hawaiian wood, Seven-sisters, white Mexican **13** Himalayan musk, Hybrid Bourbon, Persian yellow, Stuart's desert **15** hybrid perpetual **16** York-and-Lancaster

Rose, Pete (Peter Edward)
nickname: 13 Charlie Hustle
sport: 8 baseball
position: 7 baseman **8** outfield
team: 14 Cincinnati Reds **20** Philadelphia Phillies

Rosedale, Mr
character in: 15 The House of Mirth
author: 7 Wharton

Rosemary's Baby
director: 13 Roman Polanski
based on novel by: 8 Ira Levin
cast: 9 Mia Farrow **10** Ruth Gordon **14** John Cassavetes, Sidney Blackmer
Oscar for: 17 supporting actress (Gordon)

Rosenbloom, Maxie
nickname: 12 Slapsie Maxie
sport: 6 boxing
class: 16 light heavyweight

Rosencrantz
character in: 6 Hamlet
author: 11 Shakespeare

Rosenkavalier, Der
also: 18 The Knight of the Rose
opera by: 7 (Richard) Strauss
character: 6 Sophie **8** Octavian **9** Baron Ochs **11** Marschallin (Princess von Werderberg)

Rose of Sharon
character in: 16 The Grapes of Wrath
author: 9 Steinbeck

Rose Tattoo, The
director: 10 Daniel Mann
based on play by: 17 Tennessee Williams
cast: 11 Anna Magnani **13** Burt Lancaster
Oscar for: 7 actress (Magnani)

Roseanne
former name: 4 Barr **6** Arnold
husband: 3 Tom **6** Thomas
television:
  show: 8 Roseanne
  family:
    husband: 3 Dan
    children: 2 DJ **5** Becky **7** Darlene
    sister: Jackie
    town: Lanford

rosiness 5 bloom, blush, flush **7** redness **8** pinkness

Rosofsky, Barnet
real name of: 10 Barney Ross

Ross, Barney
real name: 14 Barnet Rosofsky
sport: 6 boxing
class: 12 welterweight

Ross, Katharine
born: 12 Los Angeles CA
aunt: 16 Katharine Hepburn
roles: 9 The Colbys **11** The Graduate **13** Stepford Wives **29** Butch Cassidy and the Sundance Kid

Rossellini, Roberto
director of: 6 Paisan **8** Open City **9** Stromboli **10** The Miracle
wife: 13 Ingrid Bergman

Rossen, Robert
director of: 11 Body and Soul **14** All the King's Men

Rossetti, Dante Gabriel
author of: 17 The Blessed Damozel
born: 6 London **7** England

group: 14 Pre-Raphaelites
artwork: 12 Beata Beatrix
15 The Annunciation
17 Ecce Ancilla Domini

Rossini, Gioacchino Antonio
born: 5 Italy **6** Pesaro
composer of: 5 Moise
6 Otello **8** Tancredi **10** Le Comte Ory, Semiramide
11 William Tell **12** Mose in Egitto **13** Guillaume Tell, La Cenerentola **15** Barber of Seville **20** Il Barbiere di Siviglia **22** La Cambiale di Matrimonio

Rossner, Judith
author of: 11 Attachments
14 Ordinary People
19 Looking for Mr Goodbar

Rostand, Edmond
author of: 7 L'Aiglon
10 Chantecler **12** The Romancers **16** Cyrano de Bergerac

roster 4 list, roll **5** cadre, panel, slate **6** agenda, docket, muster, record **7** catalog, listing, posting **8** register, schedule **9** catalogue, directory

rostrum 4 dais **5** stage, stand, stump **6** podium, pulpit **7** lectern, soapbox **8** platform

rosy 4 pink **5** ruddy **6** bright, florid **7** flushed, glowing, hopeful, reddish **8** blooming, blushing, cheerful, cheering, flushing, inflamed, rubicund **9** confident, favorable, promising, reddening, rubescent **10** auspicious, felicitous, optimistic, propitious, reassuring **11** encouraging, high-colored, inspiriting **13** full of promise

Roszak, Theodore
born: 6 Poland, Poznan
artwork: 5 Raven, Surge **7** Anguish **9** Chrysalis, Scavenger, Sea Quarry **11** Sea Sentinel **12** Amorphic Form, Thorn Blossom **18** Specter of Kitty Hawk **20** The Whaler of Nantucket **27** Recollections of the Southwest

rot 3 mar **4** bosh, bull, bunk, harm, hurt, warp **5** decay, go bad, spoil, stain, taint, trash **6** damage, debase, defile, drivel, impair, infect, injure, jabber, molder, poison **7** blather, corrupt, crumble, deprave, inanity, pervert, pollute, putrefy, rubbish, twaddle **8** flummery, folderol, nonsense, putresce **9** absurdity, decompose, gibberish, moonshine, poppycock, purulence, putridity **10** balderdash, corruption, degenerate, flapdoodle **11** contaminate, deteriorate, putrescence **12** disintegrate, fiddle-faddle, gobbledygook, putrefaction **13** contamination, decomposition, deterioration **14** disintegration **16** stuff and nonsense

rotate 4 eddy, reel, roll, spin, turn **5** pivot, swirl, twirl, twist, wheel, whirl **6** change, circle, gyrate, swivel **7** revolve **9** alternate, circulate, pirouette **11** interchange

Roth, Philip
author of: 8 The Facts
15 Goodbye Columbus
16 The Anatomy Lesson, Zuckerman Unbound
17 Portnoy's Complaint

Rothko, Mark
born: 6 Dvinsk, Latvia, Russia **16** Daugavpils Latvia
artwork: 5 Light **12** Central Green, Earth and Blue **14** Four Darks in Red

rotten 3 bad **4** base, foul, rank **5** dirty, fetid, nasty, reeky, venal **6** filthy, putrid, rancid, scurvy **7** corrupt, crooked, decayed, devious, immoral, tainted, very bad, vicious **8** criminal, decaying, indecent, purulent, two-faced **9** deceitful, dishonest, dissolute, faithless, insincere, mercenary, moldering, putrefied, worm-eaten **10** decomposed, iniquitous, putrescent, scurrilous, unpleasant, villainous **11** decomposing, disgraceful, treacherous **12** contemptible, dishonorable, unforgivable, unscrupulous **13** double-dealing, untrustworthy

rotter 3 cad, cur, rat **4** heel **5** knave, louse, rogue **6** no-good, rascal **7** bounder, caitiff, villain **9** scoundrel

rotund 3 fat **5** obese, ovate, ovoid, plump, pudgy, round, stout, tubby **6** chubby, curved, fleshy, portly **7** bulbous, lumpish, rounded **8** circular, globular **9** corpulent, egg-shaped, spherical **10** potbellied **11** full-fleshed

Rouault, Georges
born: 5 Paris **6** France
artwork: 3 Mr X **5** Clown **8** Le Chahut, Miserere, Twilight **9** The Mirror **10** The Old King **11** Fleurs du mal, The Holy Face **12** Head of a Clown **13** Little Olympia **14** The Three Judges **19** Small Family of Clowns **22** Christ Mocked by Soldiers **26** Les Reincarnations du Pere Ubu **28** The Child Jesus among the Doctors

roue 3 cad, rip **4** rake, wolf **6** lecher, wanton **7** bounder, dallier, Don Juan, playboy, seducer, trifler **8** Casanova, debauche, Lothario, rakehell **9** libertine, womanizer **10** profligate **11** philanderer, skirt-chaser

rough *see box*

rough going 8 struggle **10** difficulty **11** arduousness **13** laboriousness

Roughing It
author: 9 Mark Twain
character: 12 Brigham Young, Hank Erickson **16** Slade the Terrible

---

rough 3 raw **4** beat, hard, rude, wild **5** bluff, blunt, bumpy, crude, cruel, draft, green, gruff, harsh, hasty, husky, quick, raspy, rocky, scaly, sharp, surly, tough, vague **6** abrupt, beat on, broken, brutal, callow, choppy, clumsy, coarse, craggy, crusty, gauche, hoarse, jagged, knotty, ragged, raging, roiled, rugged, savage, severe, stormy, thrash, turbid, uneven, vulgar **7** austere, awkward, bearish, boorish, brusque, chapped, coarsen, drastic, extreme, general, gnarled, grating, ill-bred, inexact, jarring, loutish, outline, rasping, raucous, scraggy, sketchy, stubbly, uncouth, unlevel, untamed, violent **8** agitated, churlish, rigorous, scabrous, scratchy, strident, ungentle, unsmooth **9** brutalize, difficult, ferocious, imperfect, imprecise, inelegant, irregular, manhandle, sketch out, stringent, turbulent, uncourtly, unfeeling, ungenteel, unmusical, unrefined **10** discordant, incomplete, indelicate, push around, tumultuous, unfinished, ungracious, unmannerly, unpleasant, unpolished **11** approximate, cacophonous, ill-mannered, preliminary, rudimentary, tempestuous, unluxurious **12** inharmonious **13** inconsiderate, uncomfortable, ungentlemanly

rough it 4 camp 7 camp out

roughneck 4 hood, lout, punk
5 bully, rowdy, tough 6 vandal 7 hoodlum, ruffian 8 hooligan 9 barbarian 10 delinquent

roughness 7 crudity 8 acrimony, aviation, pungency, violence 9 gruffness, harshness, vulgarity 10 coarseness, inelegance, unevenness, unkindness 11 raucousness
12 irregularity, unsmoothness, unrefinement
13 undevelopment

rough sketch 5 draft 7 cartoon, outline

rough-textured 5 harsh
6 coarse, nubbly, shaggy, tweedy 7 bristly, prickly
8 scratchy 9 bristling
10 sandpapery

round 3 fat 4 full, oval 5 cycle, obese, orbed, ovate, ovoid, plump, pudgy, stout, total, tubby, whole 6 chubby, circle, curved, entire, fluent, intact, portly, rotund, series, smooth
7 flowing, globoid, perfect, rounded 8 circular, complete, globular, resonant, sonorous, spheroid, thorough, unbroken
9 corpulent, egg-shaped, spherical, undivided 10 ball-shaped, elliptical, harmonious, pearshaped, procession, succession
11 cylindrical, full-fleshed, mellifluent, progression

roundabout 5 wordy 6 random, zigzag 7 devious, erratic, oblique, sinuous, winding
8 indirect, rambling, tortuous, twisting 9 desultory 10 circuitous, discursive, meandering, serpentine 12 labyrinthine
14 circumlocutory

roundaboutness 9 wandering
10 digression, meandering
11 indirection 14 circuitousness, circumlocution

rounded 6 convex 7 curving
11 protuberant

rounding out 10 developing
12 augmentation
13 amplification

rounding-out 10 complement, completion, perfecting
12 consummation

rounds 4 beat 5 route, skirt, watch 7 circuit

roundup 6 muster, resume
7 meeting, summary 8 assembly 9 gathering 11 convocation

round up 6 gather, muster, summon 7 collect, convene, convoke, marshal 8 assemble
10 accumulate 12 call together

rouse 4 call, goad, move, prod,

spur, stir, wake 5 arise, awake, get up, pique, rally, waken 6 awaken, excite, foment, kindle, incite, stir up, summon, turn on, wake up
7 animate, inflame, inspire, provoke, shake up 8 activate
9 galvanize, instigate, stimulate

roused 2 up 5 astir, awake
7 excited, incited, kindled, rallied, shook up 8 awakened, inflamed, inspired, out of bed, shaken up 9 stirred up 10 up and about

rousing 5 brisk, peppy 6 active, lively 8 animated, exciting, stirring, vigorous 9 awakening, inspiring 10 energizing, refreshing, remarkable 11 provocative, stimulating
12 exhilarating, intoxicating
13 extraordinary

Rousseau, Henri Julien Felix
nickname: 10 Le Douanier
born: 5 Laval 6 France
artwork: 3 War 8 The Dream 12 Child on Rocks, The Waterfall 13 The Hungry Lion 15 Carnival Evening, The Snake Charmer
16 Bouquet of Flowers, The Sleeping Gypsy 17 The Poet and his Muse

Rousseau, Jean Jacques
author of: 5 Emile
11 Confessions 17 La Nouvelle Heloise, The Social Contract

Rousseau, (Pierre Etienne) Theodore
born: 5 Paris 6 France
artwork: 7 Evening 12 After the Rain 15 Edge of the Forest, Under the Birches
18 Descent of the Cattle, Oak Trees at Apremont
19 The Marsh in the Landes 20 The Valley of Tiffauges 21 Meadow Bordered by Trees

roust 4 bust 5 rouse 6 arrest, hassle 7 capture, seizure
12 apprehension

rout 4 beat, drub, lick, ruin, trim 5 chaos, cream, crush, panic, quell, repel, worst
6 defeat, subdue, thrash
7 beating, clobber, conquer, licking, repulse, scatter 8 drive off, drubbing, lambaste, overcome, vanquish 9 chase away, drive away, overpower, overthrow 11 put to flight 15 disorganization 18 throw into confusion

route 3 run 4 beat, pass, path, road, ship, tack 5 remit, round, track 6 artery, course,

detour, direct 7 circuit, highway, parkway, passage, roadway 8 dispatch, transmit, turnpike 9 boulevard, itinerary 10 throughway
12 thoroughfare

Route 66
character: 8 Linc Case 9 Tod Stiles 10 Buz Murdock
cast: 12 Glenn Corbett, Martin Milner 13 George Maharis
car: 8 Corvette

routine 4 dull 5 order, usual
6 boring, custom, method, normal, system 7 formula, regular, tedious, typical 8 habitual, ordinary, periodic, practice 9 customary, operation, technique 11 arrangement, predictable
12 conventional, run-of-the-mill 13 unexceptional

rove 4 roam 5 drift, prowl, range 6 ramble, stroll, travel, wander 7 meander, traipse
9 gallivant

roving 6 errant 7 aimless, gadding, migrant, nomadic, roaming, vagrant 8 errantry, rambling, restless 9 desultory, itinerant, traveling, uncertain, wandering 10 changeable, discursive, meandering, inconstant 11 peripatetic
14 discursiveness

row 4 file, line, rank, spat, tier, tiff 5 brawl, chain, melee, queue, range, scrap, set-to, train, words 6 column, fracas, scrape, series, string 7 echelon, quarrel, wrangle 8 argument, disorder, sequence, squabble
9 imbroglio, wrangling 10 difference, succession 11 altercation, contretemps

rowboat 3 gig 4 bark, dory
5 barge, canoe, dingy, scull, skiff 6 barque, caique, dinghy, wherry
seat: 4 taft

rowdy 6 unruly 7 lawless, raffish 9 roughneck 10 boisterous, disorderly
11 mischievous 12 obstreperous

Rowena, Lady
character in: 7 Ivanhoe
author: 5 Scott

rowing
athlete: 10 James Dietz
14 Anthony Johnson

Rowlands, Gena
real name: 23 Virginia Cathryn Rowlands
born: 9 Cambria WI
husband: 14 John Cassavetes
roles: 5 Faces 12 Opening Night 23 A Woman Under the Influence

Roxana
  subtitle: **20** The Fortunate
    Mistress
  author: **11** Daniel Defoe

royal 5 grand, regal **6** august,
  lavish, superb **7** stately **8** imposing, majestic, splendid
  9 monarchal, sovereign
  10 munificent **11** fit for a
  king, magnificent, resplendent

royalty 4 sway **7** command,
  majesty **8** dominion, hegemony, kingship, regality
  9 queenship, supremacy **11** divine right, sovereignty

Royaume de Belgique *see*
  7 Belgium

Roy Rogers
  ingredient: **9** ginger ale,
    grenadine
  also called: **13** Shirley
    Temple

Roy Rogers Show, The
  regular: **8** Pat Brady **9** Dale
    Evans
  theme: **16** Happy Trails to
    You
  horse: **7** Trigger
  dog: **6** Bullet
  jeep: **10** Nellybelle
  ranch: **10** Double R Bar

Ruanda *see* **6** Rwanda

rub 4 buff, swab, wipe **5** annoy, braze, catch, chafe,
  clean, hitch, knead, pinch,
  scour, scrub, smear, thing,
  touch, trick **6** abrade, finger,
  handle, polish, secret, smooth,
  spread, strait, stroke **7** burnish,
  dilemma, massage, problem,
  rubdown, setback, slather,
  trouble **8** handling, hardship,
  kneading, obstacle, stroking
  10 difficulty, impediment, manipulate **12** manipulation

**Rubaiyat of Omar
Khayyam, The**
  author: **11** Omar Khayyam
  translator: **16** Edward
    FitzGerald

rubber, vulcanized
  invented by: **8** Goodyear

rubber plant 13 Ficus elastica
  varieties: **4** baby **5** dwarf
    7 Chinese **8** American,
    creeping, Japanese **9** mistle-
    toe **11** small-leaved
    16 broad-leaved India

rubberstamp 6 affirm **7** approve, endorse

rubber tree 10 Schefflera
  varieties: **4** Para **5** India
    8 Castilla **11** West African

rubbery 5 tough **6** supple
  7 elastic **8** flexible **9** resilient
  11 stretchable

rubbing 7 chafing **8** abrading,
  scraping **12** manipulation

rubbish 3 rot **4** bosh, junk
  5 dross, offal, trash, waste
  6 babble, debris, drivel, idiocy,
  jetsam, litter, refuse, rubble
  7 blather, garbage, inanity,
  twaddle **8** folderol, nonsense
  9 gibberish, rigmarole, silliness **10** balderdash, flapdoodle,
  rigamarole

rubbish heap 4 dump **6** midden **10** refuse pile

rubble 4 junk, rock **5** brash,
  chalk, stent, stone, talus,
  trash **6** debris, refuse **7** rubbish **8** nonsense **9** fragments
  11 foolishness

rube 3 oaf **4** boor, clod, hick
  5 yokel **6** rustic **7** bumpkin,
  hayseed, peasant
  10 clodhopper

rub elbows 3 mix **4** club
  6 hobnob, mingle **7** consort,
  hang out **9** associate
  10 fraternize

Rubens, Peter Paul
  born: **6** Siegen **10** Westphalia
  artwork: **8** Lion Hunt **10** The
    Rainbow **15** The Garden of
    Love **17** Laocoon and his
    Sons **18** Battle of the Ama-
    zons **20** The Raising of the
    Cross **21** Landscape with
    Het Steen **22** The Descent
    from the Cross **23** Altarpiece
    of St Aldefonso **26** The Ado-
    ration of the Shepherds
    27 Marchesa Brigida
    Spinola-Doria, Mystic Mar-
    riage of St Catherine
    29 Rape of the Daughters of
    Leucippus **34** Helene Four-
    ment with Two of her
    Children

rubicund 3 red **4** rosy **5** ruddy
  6 florid **7** flushed, reddish

rubidium
  chemical symbol: **2** Rb

rub out 4 do in, kill, slay
  5 erase **6** efface, murder
  7 bump off, destroy, execute,
  expunge **8** massacre **10** obliterate, put to death **11** assassinate, exterminate

ruby
  species: **8** corundum
  source: **5** Burma, India, Mo-
    gok **7** Bangkok, Kashmir
    8 Sri Lanka, Thailand
  kind: **4** star
  color: **3** red

ruckus 3 row **4** fray, to-do
  5 brawl, broil, clash, fight,
  melee **6** battle, fracas, rumpus,
  uproar **7** scuffle **8** imbroglio
  10 donnybrook, free-for-all
  11 embroilment

ruddy 3 red **4** rosy **6** florid
  7 flushed, reddish, roseate,
  scarlet **8** blushing, rubicund,
  sanguine **11** rosy-cheeked

rude 3 raw **4** wild **5** blunt,
  crude, fresh, green, gross,
  gruff, rough, saucy, sulky,
  surly **6** abrupt, callow, clumsy,
  coarse, crusty, gauche,
  homely, rugged, rustic, sullen,
  uneven, vulgar **7** abusive, artless, awkward, boorish,
  brusque, brutish, ill-bred, loutish, profane, scraggy, uncivil,
  uncouth **8** churlish, homebred,
  ignorant, impolite, impudent,
  indecent, insolent, slapdash,
  untaught **9** inelegant, insulting, makeshift, primitive,
  roughhewn, uncourtly, ungallant, unlearned, unrefined, untrained, untutored **10** illiterate,
  indecorous, indelicate, peremptory, provincial, uncultured,
  uneducated, ungraceful, ungracious, unladylike, unmannerly,
  unpolished **11** bad-mannered,
  countrified, impertinent, uncivilized, uncourteous, undignified **12** discourteous, roughly
  built **13** disrespectful, inconsiderate, ungentlemanly

rudeness 9 bluntness, impudence, insolence, sauciness
  10 bad manners, coarseness,
  disrespect, incivility **11** boorishness, discourtesy **12** impertinence, impoliteness
  14 ungraciousness
  17 inconsiderateness

rudimentary 5 basic **6** simple
  7 initial, primary **8** immature
  9 elemental, formative, imperfect, premature, primitive, vestigial **10** elementary,
  incomplete, prototypal
  11 undeveloped

rudiments 6 basics **7** essence
  8 elements **9** beginning
  10 principles **12** fundamentals

**Rudkus, Jurgis and
Antanas**
  characters in: **9** The Jungle
  author: **8** Sinclair

Rudolph, Paul
  architect of: **16** Jewett Arts
    Center (Wellesley College)
    24 Government Services
    Center (Boston) **28** School of
    Architecture Building (Yale)

rue 4 Ruta
  varieties: **4** bush, lady, wall
    5 goat's **6** common,
    meadow **10** tall meadow
    11 early meadow **12** Alpine
    meadow

rue 5 mourn **6** bemoan, lament, regret, repent, repine
  7 deplore

rueful 3 sad 5 sorry 6 woeful 7 doleful 8 contrite, mournful, dolorous, penitent, repining 9 depressed, plaintive, regretful, sorrowful, sorrowing 10 deplorable, lamentable, melancholy, remorseful, unpleasant

ruffian 4 hood, thug 5 brute, bully, crook, knave, rogue, rough, rowdy, tough 6 mugger 7 hoodlum, villain 8 gangster, hooligan 9 cutthroat, roisterer, roughneck, scoundrel 10 blackguard

ruffle 4 fold, muss, wave 5 frill, plait, pleat, ruche, upset 6 edging, excite, muss up, pucker, rimple, ripple, rumple 7 agitate, confuse, crinkle, disturb, flounce, perturb, roughen, trouble, wrinkle 8 dishevel, disorder, disquiet, furbelow, unsettle 9 aggravate, agitation, commotion, corrugate 10 disarrange, discompose, disconcert 11 disturbance

ruffled 5 upset, vexed 7 annoyed, frilled, nettled, pleated 8 agitated, flounced, troubled 9 nonplused, unsettled 10 nonplussed

ruffle one's feathers 3 vex 5 anger, annoy, pique 6 enrage, madden, nettle 7 incense, outrage, provoke 9 displease, infuriate

Rugg
character in: 12 Little Dorrit
author: 7 Dickens

rugged 4 hale, hard, rude, wiry, worn 5 bumpy, hardy, harsh, husky, lined, rocky, rough, stern, tough 6 brawny, coarse, craggy, jagged, ridged, robust, severe, sinewy, sturdy, taxing, trying, uneven, virile 7 arduous, cragged, onerous, scraggy, uncouth 8 athletic, furrowed, muscular, stalwart, vigorous, wrinkled 9 difficult, graceless, irregular, laborious, masculine, roughhewn, strenuous, unrefined, weathered 12 uncultivated 13 weatherbeaten

Ruggles of Red Gap
director: 10 Leo McCarey
cast: 9 ZaSu Pitts 10 Mary Boland 14 Charlie Ruggles 15 Charles Laughton
remade as: 10 Fancy Pants

ruin, ruins 3 gut, pot 4 doom, fall, fell, harm, raze, seed 5 break, crush, decay, level, quash, quell, shell, spoil, upset, wreck 6 beggar, defeat, ravage, squash 7 destroy, failure, remains, shatter, undoing 8 bankrupt, demolish, downfall, lay waste, make poor, overturn, remnants, wreckage 9 breakdown, devastate, disrepair, overthrow, pauperize 10 impoverish 11 destruction, devastation, dissolution 14 disintegration

ruination 4 ruin 5 wreck 6 fiasco 7 trouble 8 disaster 9 adversity, cataclysm 11 destruction, devastation 12 misadventure

ruinous 4 dire 5 fatal 6 deadly 7 adverse, baneful 8 damaging, ravaging 10 calamitous, disastrous, pernicious 11 cataclysmic, deleterious, destructive, devastating 12 catastrophic

Ruisdael, Jacob (Jakob) van
born: 7 Haarlem 14 The Netherlands
uncle: 18 Salomon van Ruysdael
artwork: 5 Dunes 12 The Waterfall 13 View of Haarlem 14 Bentheim Castle 15 Winter Landscape 17 The Jewish Cemetery 28 View on the Amstel near Amsterdam

rule *see box*

rule out 4 omit 6 delete, except 7 exclude 9 eliminate

ruler 4 boss, czar, emir, head, khan, king, lord, shah, tsar, tzar 5 chief, judge, queen, rajah, sheik 6 dynast, leader, prince, satrap, shogun, sultan 7 arbiter, emperor, manager, measure, monarch, pharaoh, referee, viceroy 8 chairman, director, governor, suzerain 9 chieftain, commander, potentate, president, sovereign, yardstick 10 controller, supervisor 11 coordinator, crowned head, head of state, tape measure 12 straightedge 13 administrator

rules of conduct 6 ethics 9 moral code 10 principles 12 code of ethics

Rules of the Game
director: 10 Jean Renoir
cast: 10 Jean Renoir, Mila Parely, Nora Gregor 11 Marcel Dalio

ruling 6 decree 7 regnant 8 decision, dominant, reigning 9 enactment, governing, prescript 10 commanding, widespread 11 controlling, predominant 13 authoritative, predominating

ruling class 11 aristocracy 13 Establishment

Ruling Class, The
director: 10 Peter Medak

rule 3 law, run 4 find, form, head, lead, sway 5 adage, axiom, canon, guide, judge, maxim, model, order, reign 6 custom, decide, decree, direct, empire, govern, manage, method, policy, regime, settle, system 7 adjudge, command, control, declare, formula, precept, prevail, resolve, routine 8 conclude, doctrine, dominate, domineer, dominion, pass upon, practice, regnancy, regulate, standard 9 authority, criterion, determine, direction, establish, guideline, influence, ordinance, precedent, principle, pronounce, supremacy 10 adjudicate, administer, convention, domination, government, leadership, regulation, suzerainty 11 predominate, preside over, sovereignty 12 jurisdiction, prescription 14 administration
type: 5 bench 7 folding 9 steel tape
constellation of: 5 Norma

cast: 10 Arthur Lowe 11 Alastair Sim, Peter O'Toole 12 Harry Andrews

rum *see box*

Rumania *see box, p. 850*

rumble 4 bang, boom, clap, roar, roll 7 booming, resound, thunder 8 drumming 9 resonance 11 reverberate 13 reverberation

Rumford, Benjamin Thomson
invented: 10 photometer 11 calorimeter

Rumina
protectress of: 14 nursing mothers

ruminant 3 cow, elk, yak 4 deer, oxen 5 bison, camel, llama, moose, sheep 6 alpaca, cattle, vicuna 7 buffalo, giraffe, pensive 8 antelope 10 chevrotain, meditative, thoughtful 13 contemplative

ruminate 4 mull, muse 5 brood, study, think, weigh 6 ponder 7 reflect 8 cogitate, consider, meditate, mull over 9 speculate, think over 10 deliberate, think about 11 contemplate

ruminating 6 musing 7 pensive 8 thinking 10 meditating,

rum
  drink: 4 Bolo, Grog **6** Mojito **7** Gauguin **8** Daiquiri, Navy Grog, Pina Fria **9** Borinquen, Hurricane **10** Pina Colada **12** Boston Cooler **13** Planter's Punch **14** Fish House Punch **15** Bacardi Cocktail **18** Barbados Rum Swizzle
  ingredient: 8 molasses **9** sugar cane
  origin: 10 West Indies
  type: 4 dark **5** light
  with apple brandy: 6 Bolero **8** Apple Pie
  with apricot brandy: 11 Apricot Lady
  with black coffee: 9 Black Rose
  with bouillon: 6 Creole
  with bourbon: 14 Artillery Punch
  with brandy: 15 Quaker's Cocktail
  with Cointreau: 8 Acapulco **10** Casa Blanca **11** Beachcomber **12** Blue Hawaiian
  with cola: 9 Cuba Libre
  with creme de cacao: 6 Panama
  with curacao: 6 Mai-Tai **8** Blue Lady **12** Blue Hawaiian
  with Dubonnet: 3 BVD **10** Bushranger
  with Galliano: 9 Bossa Nova
  with gin: 3 BVD
  with guava: 8 Ocho Rios
  with kahlua: 10 Black Maria
  with milk: 6 Rum Cow **11** Tom-and-Jerry
  with Pernod: 8 Shanghai
  with sloe gin: 11 Shark's Tooth
  with Tia Maria: 10 Black Maria
  with vermouth: 6 Bolero **8** Apple Pie **10** Black Devil **11** Shark's Tooth

meditative, reflecting, reflective, thoughtful **11** chewing over, mulling over, speculative **13** contemplating, contemplative, introspective

rumination 5 study **6** musing **7** mulling, reverie, thought **8** brooding, thinking **9** pondering **10** cogitation, meditation, reflection **11** speculation **12** deliberation **13** consideration, contemplation **15** reconsideration

rummage 4 root **5** probe **7** examine, explore, ransack **10** disarrange, poke around **11** look through

rummy 3 sot **4** lush, soak **5** drunk, souse, toper **6** barfly, boozer **7** tippler **8** card game, drunkard **9** alcoholic **11** dipsomaniac
  also known as: 3 gin, rum **4** rhum **5** romme **8** gin rummy
  derived from: 8 conquien

rumor 4 talk **5** story **6** babble, gossip, report **7** hearsay, whisper **8** innuendo, intimate **9** circulate, insinuate **11** insinuation, scuttlebutt, supposition

rump 4 rear, seat **5** croup, stern **6** behind, bottom, breech, dorsum **7** rear end **8** backside, buttocks, derriere, haunches **9** posterior **12** hindquarters

Rumpelstiltskin
  origin: 8 Germanic
  form: 5 dwarf
  spun: 4 flax
  made: 4 gold

rumple 4 fold, muss **5** crimp, crush **6** crease, pucker, rimple, ruffle, tousle **7** crinkle, crumple, wrinkle **8** dishevel, disorder **9** corrugate **10** disarrange

rumpus 3 ado, row **4** fray, fuss, stir, to-do **5** brawl, melee, noise **6** affray, fracas, hubbub, pother, racket, ruckus, tumult, uproar **7** rhubarb, scuffle, tempest **8** brouhaha, upheaval **9** agitation, commotion, confusion, imbroglio **10** hullabaloo **11** disturbance, embroilment

run *see box, p. 851*

run aground 7 founder **8** collapse

runaround 4 slip **5** dodge **6** bypass **7** evasion **8** shunning, sidestep **9** avoidance **11** elusiveness, evasiveness **12** equivocation

run around 7 consort, hang out **9** associate, pal around **10** fraternize

runaway 4 pure **6** bolter **7** escapee, perfect, refugee **8** absolute, complete, deserter, fugitive **9** out-and-out, unalloyed **10** skedaddler **11** unmitigated, unqualified

run away 3 fly **4** flee **5** elope **6** decamp, escape, run off **7** abscond, make off **8** sneak off **10** fly the coop, make a break, take flight **12** make a getaway

rundown 5 brief **6** digest, precis, resume, review, sketch **7** outline, summary **8** abstract, synopsis **12** capitulation, condensation

run-down 5 frail, seedy, tacky, tired, weary **6** ailing, beat-up, feeble, shabby, sickly **7** rickety, worn out **8** fatigued, tattered **9** crumbling, exhausted **10** broken-down, tumbledown **11** dilapidated **12** deteriorated

run down 4 scan **5** knock **6** slight **7** detract, put down, run over **8** belittle, derogate, ridicule **9** denigrate, deprecate, discredit, disparage, downgrade, enumerate, underrate **10** depreciate, undervalue

run-in 5 brush, set-to **6** battle, fracas **7** scuffle **8** skirmish **9** encounter **10** engagement

run into 4 meet **8** flow into **9** encounter **10** chance upon, meet up with **11** collide with

run off 3 fly **4** flee **5** elope **6** escape **7** abscond, make off, runaway **9** steal away **10** take flight **15** head for the hills

run off at the mouth 3 gab **5** prate **6** babble, gabble **8** rattle on **11** talk too much

run off with 5 seize **6** abduct, kidnap **7** bear off **8** carry off **9** elope with **11** abscond with, make off with

run-of-the-mill 4 dull, so-so **5** banal, stock, usual **6** common, modest **7** average, humdrum, mundane, routine, typical **8** everyday, mediocre, middling, ordinary, passable, standard **10** second-rate **11** commonplace, indifferent, nondescript **12** unimpressive **13** unimaginative **15** undistinguished

runt 3 elf **4** chit **5** dwarf, pygmy **6** midget, peewee, shrimp **8** half-pint, Tom Thumb **11** Lilliputian
  Latin: 10 homunculus

Rumania
  other name: 7 Romania
  capital/largest city: 9 Bucharest
  others: 4 Aiud, Arad, Cluj, Deva, Iasi 5 Bacau, Balta, Cerna, Jassy, Neamt, Sibiu, Turnu, Yassy 6 Braila, Brasov, Brasso, Eforie, Galatz, Galeti, Lupeni, Mamaia, Oradea, Sighet 7 Bendery, Craiova, Focsani, Giurgiu, Ploesti, Severin 8 Bloiesti, Cernavti, Chisinau, Irongate, Kishenef, Satu-Mare, Temesvar 9 Constanta, Kolozsvar, Timisoara 10 Czernowitz 11 Klausenburg
  school: 4 Cuza
  division: 4 Alba, Iasi 5 Banat, Bihor, Jassy 6 Ardeal 7 Dobruja 8 Bucovina, Bukovina, Dobrogea, Moldavia, Walachia 9 Maramures 10 Bessarabia 12 Transylvania
    Roman province: 5 Dacia
  measure: 7 faltche
  monetary unit: 3 ban, lei, leu, lev, ley 4 bani 5 uncia 6 triens
  lake: 5 Sinoe 6 Snagov
  mountain: 5 Banat, Bihor 6 Codrul, Rodnei 7 Apuseni, Balkans, Caliman, Fagaras 8 Pietrosu 9 Moldavian 10 Carpathian, Moldoveanu 17 Transylvanian Alps
  highest point: 11 Moldoveanul
  river: 3 Alt, Jui, Olt 4 Prut 5 Aluta, Arges, Buzdu, Moros, Mures, Oltul, Schyl, Siret, Somes, Timis, Vedea 6 Crasna, Danube 7 Argesul 8 Bistrita, Ialomita, Iniester 9 Dimbovita, Jiul Mures
  sea: 5 Black
  physical feature:
    canal: 4 Bega
    forest: 6 Snagov 7 Baneasa
    gorge: 8 Iron Gate
    peninsula: 6 Balkan
    plain: 5 Banat 9 Moldavian, Walachian 13 Prahova Valley
    plateau: 7 Dobruja
    wind: 6 crivat
  people: 6 Dacian 8 Romanian, Rumanian
    artist: 8 Brancusi
    author: 7 Ionesco
    composer: 6 Enesco
    leader: 6 Carol I 7 Michael, Iliescu 8 Ioan Cuza 9 Ceausescu 12 Gheorghiu-Dej, Ion Antonescu
  language: 6 French, Magyar 7 Russian 8 Romanian, Rumanian 9 Hungarian
  religion: 7 Judaism 8 Lutheran 9 Calvinism, Unitarian 10 Protestant 13 Roman Catholic 16 Rumanian Orthodox
  place:
    castle: 4 Bran 7 Huniady
    church: 5 Golia 9 Mihaivoda 10 Cretulescu, Patriarchy 11 Curtea Veche, Stavropdeos, Trei Ierarhi
    monastery: 5 Humor 6 Arbore 7 Voronet 8 Sucerita 9 Moldovita
    museum: 11 Peles Castle
    palace: 9 mogosoaia
    park: 7 Baneasa
    resort: 5 Venus 6 Eforie, Mamaia, Neptun 7 Jupiter 10 Costinesti
  feature:
    community gathering: 9 sezatoare
    game: 4 oina
  food:
    dish: 6 ciorba 7 mititei, sarmala 8 mamaliga 11 imam bayildi
    plum brandy: 5 tuica

run through 5 spend, waste 6 expend, pierce 7 deplete, exhaust 8 rehearse, squander

runty 5 short 6 bantam 7 dwarfed, squatty, stunted 9 pint-sized

Runyon, Damon
  author of: 12 Guys and Dolls 16 Blue Plate Special

rupture 3 pop 4 part, rent, rift, snap 5 break, burst, clash, cleft, crack, split 6 breach, divide, schism, sunder 7 discord, disrupt, fissure 8 breaking, bursting, cleavage, dissever, disunion, disunite, fracture, friction, puncture 9 severance 10 dissension, falling out, separation 12 disagreement

R U R
  author: 10 Karel Capek

rural 4 hick 6 rustic 7 bucolic, country 8 pastoral 10 provincial 11 countrified

rural area 6 sticks 7 boonies, country 8 farmland 9 backwater, backwoods, boondocks 10 hinterland 11 countryside

Rural Dionysia *see* 14 Lesser Dionysia

ruse 4 hoax 5 blind, dodge, feint, shift, trick 6 deceit, device, scheme 8 artifice, maneuver 9 deception, stratagem 10 subterfuge 11 contrivance, machination

rush 3 hie, run 4 dart, dash, goad, leap, push, race, spur, tear, urge, whip 5 drive, haste, hurry, press, speed, storm 6 charge, hasten, hustle, plunge, scurry, sprint, urgent 7 scamper, urgency 8 dispatch, expedite, pressure, scramble 9 emergency 10 accelerate 11 top priority

rush 6 Juncus
  varieties: 3 bog 4 salt, soft, wood 5 spike 6 grassy 8 scouring 9 field wood, flowering 10 common wood, least spike 11 chair-maker's, greater wood, Japanese-mat 12 slender spike 13 dwarf scouring 14 common scouring 18 variegated scouring

Rush, Benjamin
  field: 8 medicine
  established first: 21 free medical dispensary
  signer of: 25 Declaration of Independence

rush light 3 dip 5 torch 6 candle, tallow

run 2 be, go **3** fly, get, hie, jog, pen, ply **4** bolt, boss, cost, dart, dash, defy, flee, flow, go by, head, kind, last, meet, melt, pass, pour, push, race, roll, rush, sort, tear, tour, trip, trot, type, vary **5** bleed, bound, class, court, drift, drive, genre, glide, hurry, impel, incur, issue, leave, pilot, print, speed, spell, split, stand, surge, total, while **6** become, canter, course, decamp, direct, elapse, endure, escape, extend, gallop, hasten, hustle, invite, ladder, manage, motion, move on, outing, period, pierce, propel, scurry, series, sprint, streak, stream, thrust, vanish, voyage, wander **7** abscond, add up to, advance, bring on, compete, current, display, freedom, get past, journey, liquefy, meander, operate, oversee, passage, proceed, publish, running, scamper, stretch, take off, vamoose **8** amount to, campaign, continue, dissolve, duration, evanesce, maneuver, meet with, navigate, progress, scramble, separate, tendency **9** direction, disappear, enclosure, encounter, excursion, go quickly, lose color, penetrate, skedaddle, supervise **10** coordinate, pilgrimage **11** continuance **12** beat a retreat, continuation, perpetuation
baseball: 5 point, score, tally **17** circuit of the bases

Rushworth
character in: 13 Mansfield Park
author: 6 Austen

Ruskin, John
author of: 13 Fors Clavigera **14** Modern Painters **17** The Stones of Venice **27** The Seven Lamps of Architecture

Russell, Bertrand
author of: 19 Why I Am Not a Christian **20** Principia Mathematica (with Alfred North)

Russell, Jane
real name: 29 Ernestine Jane Geraldine Russell
born: 9 Bemidji MN
discovered by: 12 Howard Hughes
roles: 4 Waco **9** The Outlaw **13** The French Line **22** Gentlemen Prefer Blondes, The Revolt of Mamie Stover

Russell, Rosalind
born: 11 Waterbury CT
roles: 5 Gypsy **6** Picnic **8** The Women **9** Hired Wife **10** Auntie Mame **11** Sister Kenny **13** His Girl Friday **14** My Sister Eileen **22** Mourning Becomes Electra

russet 5 apple, umber **6** auburn, copper **10** terra-cotta **11** rust-colored **12** reddish-brown

Russia *see box, p. 852*

Russian Hide-and-Seek
author: 12 Kingsley Amis

Russian village commune
3 mir

rust 3 rot **5** decay, stain **6** auburn, blight, russet **7** corrode, crumble, decline, oxidize **9** corrosion, oxidation **11** deteriorate **12** reddish-brown **13** reddish-yellow

rust-colored 5 henna **6** auburn, russet **8** cinnamon **12** reddish-brown

rustic 4 rube, rude **5** crude, plain, rough, rural, yokel **6** coarse, gauche, simple **7** awkward, boorish, bucolic, bumpkin, country, hayseed, loutish, peasant, uncouth **8** agrarian, churlish, cloddish, pastoral **9** inelegant, unrefined **10** clodhopper, countryman, provincial, uncultured, unpolished **11** countrified **13** country person **15** unsophisticated

rustle 3 rub **4** hiss, stir **5** swish, whish **6** riffle

rustler 5 thief **6** bandit, outlaw **7** brigand **9** desperado

rusty 5 moldy, stiff **6** rotten, rusted **7** reddish, tainted **8** corroded, sluggish **11** rust-colored **13** out of practice

rut 3 cut **4** mark **5** ditch, habit, score, tread **6** furrow, groove, gutter, hollow, trench, trough **7** channel, depress, dig into, pattern **8** monotony **9** deep track **10** depression **11** dull routine

Ruth
husband: 4 Boaz **6** Mahlon
son: 4 Obed
father-in-law: 9 Elimelech
mother-in-law: 5 Naomi
brother-in-law: 7 Chilion

Ruth, George Herman
nickname: 4 Babe **12** Sultan of Swat
sport: 8 baseball
position: 8 outfield
team: 14 New York Yankees

Rutherford, Dame Margaret
born: 6 London **7** England
roles: 7 The VIPs **10** Jane Marple **12** Blithe Spirit **27** The Importance of Being Earnest

Rutherford, Ernest
field: 7 physics
nationality: 7 British
discovered: 6 proton **13** atomic nucleus, beta radiation **14** alpha radiation, gamma radiation
awarded: 10 Nobel Prize

ruthless 5 cruel, harsh **6** brutal, deadly, savage **7** bestial, brutish, callous, inhuman, vicious **8** pitiless **9** barbarous, ferocious, heartless, merciless, murderous, unfeeling, unpitying, unsparing **10** relentless, sanguinary, unmerciful **11** cold-blooded, hardhearted, remorseless, unforgiving, unrelenting **12** bloodthirsty

ruthlessness 7 cruelty **9** barbarity, brutality, harshness **10** inhumanity, savageness **11** viciousness

Ruysdael, Salomon van
born: 7 Naarden **14** The Netherlands
nephew: 16 Jacob van Ruisdael
artwork: 9 River Bank **10** River Scene **14** River Landscape **18** River with Ferry Boat

Rwanda *see box, p. 853*

Ryan, Cornelius
author of: 13 A Bridge Too Far, The Last Battle, The Longest Day

Ryan, Robert
born: 9 Chicago IL
roles: 6 Caught **8** The Set-Up **9** Billy Budd, Crossfire **12** Clash by Night, The Wild Bunch **13** Act of Vio-

Russia (includes constituent republics of the former USSR)
other name: 17 Russian Federation
former name: 4 USSR **11** Soviet Union **31** Union of Soviet Socialist Republics
member of: 3 CIS **31** Commonwealth of Independent States
capital/largest city: 6 Moscow
others: 4 Baku, Eisk, Kiev, Okha, Omsk, Poti, Riga **5** Anapa, Batum, Gorki, Gorky, Memel,
Minsk, Sochi, Vilna, Yeisk **6** Batumi, Erevan, Frunze, Odessa, Rostov, Samara, Tiflis **7** Alma-
Ata, Derbent, Donetsk, Kharkov, Liepaja, Petsamo, Pivonia, Saratov, Tallinn, Tbilisi, Yerevan
8 Dushanbe, Kishinev, Murmansk, Pechenga, Taganrog, Tashkent **9** Ashkhabad, Astrakhan,
Balaklava, Kronstadt, Kuibyshev, Leningrad, Nikolayev, Petrograd, Ulyanovsk, Volgograd, Ya-
roslavl **10** Kronshtadt, Sevastopol, Stalingrad, Sverdlovsk **11** Chelyabinsk, Kaliningrad, Ma-
khachkala, Novorossisk, Novosibirsk, Vladivostok **12** St Petersburg **14** Dnepropetrovsk
division/country: 6 Latvia **7** Armenia, Belarus, Estonia, Georgia, Moldova, Siberia, Ukraine
8 Moldavia **9** Kirghizia, Lithuania, Turkmenia **10** Azerbaijan, Belorussia, Kazakhstan, Kyrgyzstan, Tajikistan, Uzbekistan **12** Tadzhikistan, Turkmenistan
   former: **4** Kiev **8** Novgorod
government:
   legislature: **4** Duma, Rada **7** Zemstvo **8** Congress
measure: 3 fut, lof **4** duim, fass, loof, pood, quar, stof **5** duime, foute, korec, korek, ligne, osmin, pajak, stoff, stoof, vedro, verst **6** charka, liniya, osmina, paletz, sagene, stekar, tchast,
tsarki, versta, verste **7** archine, arsheen, botchka, chkalik, garnetz, verchoc, verchok **8** boutylka, chetvert, krouchka, kroushka **9** chetverik **10** dessiatine **11** polugarnetz
monetary unit: 5 altin, bisti, copec, denga, grosh, kopek, ruble, shaur **6** abassi, copeck,
grivna, kopeck, piatak, rouble **7** poltina, valiuta **8** auksinas, deneshka, imperial, polushka
9 poltinnik **10** altininink, chervonets
weight: 3 lof, lot **4** dola, funt, lana, last, loof, loth, once, pood, poud **5** dolia
island: 5 Kuril **7** Hiiumaa, Karagin, Shantar, Vaygach, Wrangel **8** Kolguyev, Saaremaa, Sakhalin **9** Andreanof **12** Novaya Zemlya **13** Komandorskiye **14** Franz Josef Land, Novosibirskiye
15 Severnaya Zemlya
lake: 3 Seg **4** Aral, Azov, Kola, Sego, Topo, Vigo **5** Chany, Elton, Erara, Ilmen, Lacha, Onega,
Pskov, Vozhe **6** Baikal, Byeloe, Ladoga, Peipus, Selety, Taymyr, Tengiz, Zaysan **8** Balkhash
10 Caspian Sea
mountain: 5 Altai, Lenin, Sayan, Urals **6** Anadyr, Elbrus, Koryak, Pamirs, Pobedy **7** Belukha,
Crimean, Khibiny, Stanovi, Zhiguli **8** Caucasus, Dzhughur, Stanavoi, Tien Shan **9** Kopet
Dagh, Narodnaya, Pamir-Alai, Yablonovy **10** Carpathian **11** Sikhote-Alin, Verkhoyansk
highest point: 9 Communism
river: 3 Don, Ili **4** Amur, Lena, Neva, Ural **5** Dvina, Kuban, Neman, Volga **6** Kolyma, Moskva **7** Dnieper, Pechora, Yenisei **8** Amu Darya, Dniester, Ob-Irtysh, Syr Darya **9** Indigirka
sea: 4 Aral, Azov, Kara **5** Black, Japan, White **6** Arctic, Baltic, Bering, Laptev **7** Barents, Caspian, Chukchi, Okhotsk, Pacific
physical feature:
   gulf: **4** Azov **5** Mezen **9** Kara-Bogaz, Shelikhov
   peninsula: **4** Kola **5** Yamal **6** Crimea, Taymyr **7** Chukchi, Karelia **9** Kamchatka
   10 Mangyshlak
   strait: **5** Tatar **6** Bering **8** Bosporus **11** Dardanelles
people: 3 Jew **4** Slav **5** Ersar, Kulak, Tatar, Uzbec **6** Kazakh, Soviet, Velika **7** Chukchi, Cossack, Kirghiz, Latvian, Russian, Tadzhik, Turkmen **8** Armenian, Estonian, Georgian, Siberian
9 Moldavian, Ukrainian **10** Lithuanian **11** Azerbaijani, Belorussian
   actor: **12** Stanislavsky
   author: **5** Gogol **7** Nabokov, Pushkin, Tolstoy **8** Turgenev **9** Ehrenburg, Pasternak, Sholokhov **10** Dostoevsky **12** Solzhenitsyn
   composer: **6** Glinka **7** Borodin **9** Prokofiev **10** Mussorgsky, Stravinsky **11** Tchaikovsky
   12 Rachmaninoff, Shostakovich **14** Rimsky-Korsakov
   cosmonaut: **11** Yuri Gagarin
   czar/tsar/tzar: **4** Ivan, Paul **5** Peter **6** Alexis **7** Michael **8** Nicholas **9** Alexander **12** Boris
Godunov
   dancer: **7** Nureyev, Pavlova **8** Danilova, Nijinsky **11** Baryshnikov
   dynasty: **7** Romanov
   early people: **3** Hun **4** Goth **5** Tatar **6** Khazar, Mongol, Tartar **8** Norsemen, Scythian **9** Cimmerian, Sarmatian, Varangian
   empress: **9** Alexandra, Catherine
   hereditary noble: **5** boyar
   leader: **5** Beria, Lenin **6** Stalin, Suslov **7** Gromyko, Kosygin, Molotov, Trotsky, Yeltsin **8** An-
dropov, Brezhnev, Bukharin, Bulganin, Kerensky, Malenkov, Podgorny **9** Chernenko, Gorbachev **10** Khrushchev
   monk: **8** Rasputin
   prince: **4** Oleg **5** Rurik **8** Vladimir
   revolutionary: **9** bolshevik **10** Decembrist
   ruler: **5** Tatar **6** Mongol **8** Batu Khan
   scientist: **6** Pavlov **9** Mendeleev **11** Tsiolkovsky

Russia (*continued*)
   language: **5** Evenk, Tatar, Uzbek **6** Buriat, Kalmyk, Kazakh **7** Finnish, Kirghiz, Latvian, Russian, Tadzhik, Turkmen **8** Armenian, Estonian, Georgian, Ossetian **9** Moldavian, Ukrainian **10** Lithuanian **11** Belorussian
    alphabet: **8** cyrillic
   religion: **5** Islam **7** Judaism **8** Buddhism, Lutheran **10** Protestant **13** Roman Catholic **15** Russian Orthodox **16** Armenian Orthodox, Georgian Orthodox
   place: **7** Kremlin **9** Red Square
    art gallery: **9** Tretyakov
    castle: **8** Starosty
    cathedral: **5** Sobor **7** Zagorsk **8** St Basils
    cemetery: **11** Piskarevsky
    museum: **9** Hermitage **12** Petrodvorets **18** Cathedral of St Isaac
    palace: **6** Winter
    park: **5** Gorky
    ruins: **7** Bukhara **10** Echmiadzin **15** Gediminas Castle
    prison: **8** Lubyanka
    street: **11** Kreshchatik **14** Nevski Prospekt
    theater: **7** Bolshoi
   feature:
    collective farm: **7** kolkhoz
    country house: **5** dacha
    dance: **4** kolo **5** gopac, hopak, saber **6** cossac, trepak **7** cosaque, ziganka **8** kozachok **9** tzazatski
    dance company: **5** Kirov **7** Bolshoi
    labor camp: **5** gulag
    musical instrument: **9** balalaika
    secret police: **3** KGB, MGB **4** NKVD, OGPU **5** Cheka
    state farm: **7** sovkhoz
   food:
    caviar: **13** ikra zernistia
    cereal: **5** kasha
    sour cream: **7** smetana
    dessert: **8** vareniki
    dish: **4** plov **5** pirau **6** pelemo **8** osetrina, shashlyk **16** kotleta po kievski
    drink: **4** kvas **5** kvass, vodka **6** chacha, kumiss
    filled pastries: **8** piroshki, pirozhki
    soup: **5** shchi **6** borsch **7** borscht, borshch

Rwanda
   other name: **6** Ruanda
   capital/largest city: **6** Kigali
   others: **6** Biumba, Butare, Kibuye, Nyanza **7** Astrida, Gisenyi, Kibungu **8** Cyangugu **9** Ruhengeri
   division:
    colonial: **12** Ruanda-Urundi
   monetary unit: **5** franc **7** centime
   lake: **4** Kivu **5** Ihema **6** Bufera, Bulera, Mohasi **7** Rugwero, Ruhnodo **8** Mugesera, Tshohoha
   mountain: **7** Mitumba, Virunga **8** Muhavura
   highest point: **9** Karisimbi
   river: **6** Kagera, Ruzizi **7** Akagera **8** Akanyaru **9** Luvironza **10** Nyawarongo
   physical feature:
    forest: **7** Nyungwe
    valley: **11** Western Rift
   people: **3** Twa **4** Hutu **5** Batwa, Pygmy, Tutsi **6** Bahutu, Watusi **7** Batutsi
    explorer: **5** Speke **6** Gotzen
    leader: **9** Kayibanda **11** Habyarimana
   language: **6** French **7** Swahili **11** Kinyarwanda
   religion: **7** animism **13** Roman Catholic
   place:
    game reserve: **6** Gabiro
    park: **6** Albert, Kagera **16** Virunga Volcanoes
   feature:
    clothing: **5** pagne
    king: **5** mwami

lence, The Longest Day **14** About Mrs Leslie, God's Little Acre **17** Bad Day at Black Rock **18** The Woman on the Beach

Ryder, Albert Pinkham
   born: **12** New Bedford MA
   artwork: **12** The Race Track (Death on a Pale Horse) **15** Toilers of the Sea **27** Siegfried and the Rhine Maidens

rye 6 Secale
   varieties: **4** wild **5** giant **6** common **8** Aral wild, blue wild **9** Altai wild, giant wild, Volga wild **10** Canada wild **11** Chinese wild, Russian wild **12** Siberian wild, Virginia wild
   type: **6** liquor **7** whiskey
   origin: **7** Ireland **8** Scotland
   ingredient: **10** mash grains
   drink: **9** Cablegram **11** John Collins, Whiskey Sour
   with Cointreau:
    10 Temptation
   with Pernod: **3** TNT
   with vermouth: **8** Brooklyn **9** Algonquin

Saarinen, Eero
  father: 5 Eliel
  architect of: 11 St Louis
  Arch **20** Gateway to the
  West Arch (St Louis)
  26 Trans World Airlines Terminal (NYC) **28** General Motors Technical Center
  (Warren MI) **39** Columbia
  Broadcasting Company
  Headquarters (NYC)
  style: 13 International

Saarinen, Eliel
  son: 4 Eero
  architect of: 16 Cranbrook
  Academy (Bloomfield Hills
  MI) **18** Kleinhaus Music
  Hall (Buffalo) **19** Tanglewood Music Shed (MA)
  20 Christ Lutheran Church
  (Minneapolis MN), First
  Christian Church (Columbus
  IN)

Saba *see* **5** Sheba

Sabaoth 6 armies

Sabbath 8 Lord's Day **9** day of
rest

Sabbatical: A Romance
  author: 9 John Barth

saber, sabre 3 cut **4** kill,
stab **5** blade, sword, wound
6 cutlass, rapier, strike **7** cutlass, soldier **8** scimitar
10 broadsword

Sabin, Albert Bruce
  field: 8 medicine
  developed: 16 oral polio
  vaccine

sable 3 fur, jet **4** dark, inky
5 black, ebony, raven

sabotage 3 sap **6** retard **7** cripple, destroy, disable, disrupt,
subvert **8** paralyze **9** undermine, vandalize **10** subversion **12** incapacitate

sabra 11 Israeli-born **14** native
of Israel

Sabra
  type: 7 liqueur
  origin: 6 Israel
  flavor: 6 orange **9** chocolate

Sac *see* **4** Sauk

saccharine 5 gooey, mushy,
soppy, sweet **6** sugary, syrupy
7 candied, cloying, honeyed,
maudlin, mawkish, sugared
9 offensive, oversweet, revolting, sickening **10** disgusting,
nauseating **11** sentimental

sacerdotal 5 papal **8** clerical,
pastoral, priestly **9** apostolic,
canonical, episcopal **10** pontifical **11** ministerial **12** hierarchical **14** ecclesiastical

sack 3 bag, rob **4** loot, pack,
raid **5** pouch, spoil, store,
waste **6** duffel, maraud, rapine,
ravage, tear up **7** despoil, pillage, plunder, ransack **8** spoliate **9** depredate, duffel bag,
gunnysack, haversack, marauding **10** plundering, ravishment **11** depredation,
devastation **12** despoliation

Sackbut 18 Biblical instrument

Sackville, Thomas
  author of: 8 Gorboduc (with
  Thomas Norton)

sacrament 3 vow **4** rite
5 troth **6** pledge, plight, ritual
7 liturgy, promise, service
8 ceremony, contract, covenant **9** solemnity **10** ceremonial, obligation, observance
11 affirmation **12** ministration

sacramental 4 holy **6** ritual
7 blessed **10** ceremonial,
liturgical

Sacraments, Seven 7 Baptism, Penance **9** Eucharist,
Last Rites, Matrimony **10** Holy
Orders **12** Confirmation
13 Holy Communion **14** Extreme Unction, Reconciliation
18 Anointing of the Sick

sacred 4 holy **6** church

7 blessed, revered **8** Biblical,
hallowed, hieratic **9** religious,
venerable **10** sanctified, scriptural **11** consecrated
14 ecclesiastical

Sacred and Profane Love
Machine, The
  author: 11 Iris Murdoch

Sacred writings 5 Bible
11 Bibliotheca

sacrifice 4 cede, loss **5** forgo,
waive **6** forego, give up, homage **7** cession, forfeit, offer
up **8** immolate, oblation, offering, renounce **9** surrender
10 concession, immolation,
lustration, relinquish **12** renunciation **14** relinquishment

sacrilege 3 sin **7** impiety,
mockery, outrage **8** iniquity
9 blasphemy, profanity, violation **10** irreligion, sinfulness,
wickedness **11** desecration, impiousness, irreverence, profanation, profaneness

sacrilegious 7 impious, profane **10** irreverent **11** blasphemous, irreligious

sacrosanct 4 holy **5** godly
6 divine, solemn **8** hallowed,
heavenly **9** celestial, inviolate,
religious, spiritual **10** inviolable, unexamined **11** consecrated **12** unquestioned

sacrum
  bone of: 11 base of spine

sad 3 low **4** blue, grim, hard,
hurt **5** grave **6** dismal, solemn,
taxing, tragic, trying, woeful
7 adverse, crushed, doleful,
forlorn, grieved, joyless, maudlin, pitiful, serious, unhappy
8 dejected, desolate, downcast,
grievous, mournful, pathetic,
touching, troubled, wretched
9 cheerless, depressed, difficult,
miserable, sorrowful **10** calamitous, chapfallen, despairing, despondent, dispirited,
distressed, lachrymose, lament-

able, melancholy **11** crestfallen, distressing, pessimistic, troublesome, unfortunate **12** disconsolate, heartrending, heavyhearted, inconsolable **13** brokenhearted, griefstricken, heartbreaking **14** down in the dumps, down in the mouth
French: 6 triste

Sadat, Anwar el-
president of: 5 Egypt
awarded: 15 Nobel Peace Prize
author of: 18 In Search of Identity

sadden 4 damp, dash **5** crush **6** burden, deject, grieve, sorrow, subdue **7** depress **8** aggrieve, dispirit **10** discourage, dishearten

saddle with 9 stick with **10** burden with **12** encumber with **18** make responsible for

Sade, Marquis de
author of: 7 Justine **8** Juliette

sadistic 6 brutal **7** vicious **8** fiendish, perverse **9** perverted **12** bloodthirsty

Sadness
author: 15 Donald Barthelme

sadness
French: 9 tristesse

sad poem 5 elegy **6** lament

Sad Sack
creator: 11 George Baker

Saehrimnir
origin: 12 Scandinavian
form: 4 boar
served in: 8 Valhalla
feat: 12 regeneration

safe 4 firm, sure, wary **5** sound, vault, whole **6** intact, modest, secure, stable, steady, unhurt **7** certain, guarded, prudent **8** cautious, defended, discreet, harmless, reliable, unbroken, unharmed **9** innocuous, protected, undamaged, unexposed, unscathed **10** dependable, protecting **11** circumspect, impregnable, out of danger, trustworthy, unscratched **12** conservative, invulnerable, noncommittal

safeguard 4 ward **5** armor, charm **6** amulet, buffer, defend, harbor, screen, secure, shield **7** bulwark, defense, fortify, protect, shelter **8** conserve, garrison, preserve, security, talisman **10** precaution, protection

safekeeping 4 care **6** charge **7** custody **8** security **9** husbandry **10** protection **12** con-servation, guardianship, preservation

Safety Net, The
author: 12 Heinrich Boll

saffron
botanical name: 13 Crocus sativus
also called: 6 Krokus
Moorish: **6** Zafran
of all spices most: 6 costly
color: 6 orange, yellow **12** yellow-orange
used as: 8 coloring, cosmetic, medicine **9** fabric dye
origin: 5 Egypt, Syria **8** Holy Land **9** Palestine
use: 4 rice **5** bread, rolls

sag 3 bow, dip **4** drop, fail, flag, flap, flop, keel, lean, list, sink, sway, tilt, tire **5** droop, pitch, slump, weary **6** billow, plunge, settle, weaken **7** decline, descend, give way **8** diminish

saga 4 epic, myth, tale, yarn **6** legend **7** history, romance **9** adventure, chronicle, narrative
French: 11 roman-fleuve

sagacious 4 foxy, wise **5** acute, canny, sharp, smart, sound **6** astute, brainy, clever, shrewd **7** cunning, knowing, prudent, sapient, tactful **8** discreet, rational, sensible **9** judicious, practical **10** diplomatic, discerning, perceptive **11** calculating, intelligent **13** perspicacious **14** discriminating

sagacity 6 acumen, brains, smarts, wisdom **8** sapience **9** canniness, smartness **10** astuteness, braininess, cleverness, shrewdness **11** discernment **12** intelligence, perspicacity **13** judiciousness **14** discrimination

Sagan, Carl
author of: 6 Cosmos **7** Contact **16** The Dragons of Eden

Sagan, Francoise
real name: 16 Francoise Quoirez
author of: 13 A Certain Smile **15** Aimez-vous Brahms **16** Bonjour Tristesse

sage 4 guru, wise **5** sound **6** astute, pundit, savant, shrewd **7** egghead, knowing, prudent, sapient, scholar, wise man **8** mandarin, sensible **11** intelligent, philosopher
French: 6 savant
Latin: 5 magus, solon

sage 6 Salvia **12** S officinalis
varieties: 3 bog **4** baby, blue, gray, rose, sand, wood **5** black, lilac, Texas, white **6** autumn, common, desert, garden, purple, silver, yellow **7** bladder, gentian, scarlet, Spanish, thistle, Vervain **8** creeping, gray ball, mealy-cup, rose-leaf **9** Bethlehem, Jerusalem **11** Mexican bush **16** pineapple-scented
means: 6 to heal, to save
strengthens: 6 memory, wisdom **8** prudence
makes men: 8 immortal
origin: 7 Albania **10** Yugoslavia **13** Mediterranean
use: 4 pork **6** breads, cheese **7** chicken, poultry, seafood **8** stuffing

Sage of Concord
nickname of: 17 Ralph Waldo Emerson

Sagittarius
symbol: 6 archer **7** centaur
planet: 7 Jupiter
rules: 10 philosophy **15** higher education
born: 8 December, November

Sagittary
form: 7 centaur
carried: 3 bow

said 5 above, quoth **6** quoted, spoken, stated **7** related, uttered **8** repeated

Saigon
capital of: 7 Vietnam

sail 3 fly **4** boat, scud, skim, soar **5** drift, float, glide, steam **6** course, cruise, voyage **8** navigate **9** excursion

sailboat 4 saic, yawl **5** craft, ketch, sloop, yacht **6** vessel **7** sunfish **8** schooner **9** catamaran
part: 4 boom, mast **6** canvas **7** rigging **9** mainsheet

sailcloth 4 duck **6** canvas

Sailing to Byzantium
author: 7 W B Yeats

sailor 3 gob, tar **4** salt **6** sea dog, seaman **7** mariner, voyager **8** deckhand, seafarer **9** navigator, yachtsman

sailors
goddess of: 5 Brizo **11** Britomartis

Sails (of Argo)
constellation of: 4 Vela

saint 6 martyr
Buddhist: 5 arhat **11** bodhisattva
Chinese: 8 immortal
Islamic: 3 pir
lives of the saints: 8 menology **9** hagiology **11** hagiography **13** acta sanctorum
process of becoming: 12 canonization

relic box: 6 chasse
remains: 5 relic
symbol: 4 halo

Saint, Eva Marie
born: 8 Newark NJ
roles: 6 Exodus **15** On the
Waterfront **16** North by
Northwest

saint, patron *see box*

Saint, The
author: 16 Antonio Fogazzaro

Saint, The
author: 15 Leslie Charteris
character: 12 Simon Templar **26** Inspector Claude
Eustace Teal
cast: 10 Roger Moore

Saint Anthony's fire
6 herpes **8** ergotism, shingles
10 erysipelas

Sainte-Beuve, Charles
Augustin
author of: 19 Monday
Conversations

Saint Elmo's fire 5 flame,
hermo **6** castor, corona, furole,
helena **9** corposant
12 luminescence

Saint Esprit 9 Holy Ghost
10 Holy Spirit

Saint-Exupery, Antoine de
author of: 11 Night Flight
12 Southern Mail **15** The
Little Prince **16** Wind Sand
and Stars

Saint Francis
born: 6 Assisi
called: 9 Poverello

Saint-Gaudens, Augustus
born: 6 Dublin **7** Ireland
artwork: 7 Puritan **13** Mrs
Henry Adams (Grief)
14 General Sherman **15** Admiral Farragut **16** President
Lincoln

Saint Jack
author: 11 Paul Theroux

Saint Joan
author: 17 George Bernard
Shaw

Saint John's bread 5 carob

Saint John's wort 5 amber
6 tutsan **7** ascyrum, cammock
9 androseme, hypericum,
rosin-rose **10** broombrush
11 Aaron's-beard

saintliness 6 purity **8** goodness, holiness **9** beatitude, godliness **11** blessedness
12 spirituality

Saint Lucia, St Lucia
capital: 8 Castries
highest point: 5 Gimie
island group: 8 Windward
14 Lesser Antilles

saint, patron
acolytes: 13 John Berchmans
actors: 8 Genesius
artists: 4 Luke
astronomers: 7 Dominic
athletes: 9 Sebastian
authors: 14 Francis de Sales
aviators: 15 Our Lady of Loreto **16** Therese of Lisieux
17 Joseph of Cupertino
bakers: 8 Nicholas **18** Elizabeth of Hungary
bankers: 7 Matthew
barbers: 5 Louis **6** Cosmas, Damian
barren women: 9 Felicitas **14** Anthony of Padua
beggars/cripples: 5 Giles
blind: 6 Odilia **7** Raphael
bodily ills: 16 Our Lady of Lourdes
boy scouts: 6 George
brides: 14 Nicholas of Myra
builders: 13 Vincent Ferrer
butchers: 4 Luke **7** Hadrian **14** Anthony of Egypt
carpenters: 6 Joseph
cancer patients: 9 Peregrine
children: 10 Santa Claus **14** Nicholas of Myra
comedians: 5 Vitus
cooks: 6 Martha **8** Lawrence
deaf: 14 Francis de Sales
dying: 6 Joseph **7** Barbara
emigrants: 14 Frances Cabrini
England: 6 George
eye sufferers: 4 Lucy
falsely accused: 15 Raymond Nonnatus
farmers: 6 George **7** Isidore
fishermen: 5 Peter **6** Andrew
foreign missions: 13 Francis Xavier **16** Therese of Lisieux
foundlings: 13 Holy Innocents
France: 5 Denis
gardeners: 6 Fiacre, Phocas **7** Adelard, Dorothy, Tryphon
heart patients: 9 John of God
hospitals: 9 John of God **12** Jude Thaddeus **16** Camillus
de Lellis
housewives: 4 Anne
hunters: 6 Hubert **10** Eustachius
invalids: 4 Roch
Ireland: 7 Patrick
Italy: 7 Anthony
laborers: 5 James **7** Isidore **9** John Bosco
lawyers: 3 Ivo **4** Ives **8** Genesius **10** Thomas More
librarians: 6 Jerome
lovers: 9 Valentine
mariners: 7 Michael **19** Nicholas of Tolentino
mentally ill: 6 Dympna

language: 6 patois
location: 9 Caribbean

saintly 4 good, holy **5** godly,
moral, pious **6** devout **7** angelic, blessed, exalted, sinless,
upright **8** beatific, faithful, reverent, virtuous **9** believing, religious, righteous, spiritual
10 benevolent

Saint Paul
born: 6 Tarsus
companion: 4 Luke
epistle: 5 Titus **6** Romans
7 Hebrews, Timothy **8** Philemon **9** Ephesians, Galatians
10 Colossians **11** Corinthians, Philippians
13 Thessalonians

Saint Paul's Cathedral
(London)
architect: 4 Wren

Saint Peter
called: 4 Rock **5** Simon
6 Cephas
brother: 6 Andrew

Saint-Saens, (Charles)
Camille
born: 5 Paris **6** France
composer of: 12 Danse Macabre **14** Samson et Dalila
16 Samson and Delilah

merchants: 14 Nicholas of Myra **15** Francis of Assisi
metalworkers: 7 Eligius
miners: 7 Barbara
mothers: 6 Monica
musicians: 7 Cecilia, Dunstan **15** Gregory the Great
Norway: 4 Olaf
nurses: 6 Agatha **7** Alexius, Raphael **9** John of God
  16 Camillus de Lellis
painters: 4 Luke
philosophers: 6 Justin **21** Catherine of Alexandria
physicians: 4 Luke **6** Cosmas, Damian **7** Raphael
  9 Pantaleon
pilgrims: 5 James **7** Alexius
poets: 5 David **7** Cecilia
policemen: 7 Michael
poor souls: 19 Nicholas of Tolentino
postal workers: 7 Gabriel
priests: 19 Jean-Baptiste Vianney
printers: 8 Genesius **9** John of God **16** Augustine of Hippo
prisoners: 6 Dismas **7** Barbara **13** Joseph Cafasso
rheumatism: 15 James the Greater
sailors: 4 Elmo **7** Brendan, Erasmus, Eulalia **8** Cuthbert,
  Nicholas **11** Christopher **13** Peter Gonzales
scholars: 6 Brigid
scientists: 6 Albert
Scotland: 6 Andrew
sculptors: 6 Claude
seamen: 14 Francis of Paolo
sick: 7 Michael **9** John of God **16** Camillus de Lellis
singers: 7 Cecilia, Gregory
skiers: 7 Bernard
shoemakers: 7 Crispin
soldiers: 6 George **7** Hadrian **8** Ignatius **9** Joan of Arc, Sebastian **13** Martin of Tours
Spain: 5 James **8** Santiago
students: 13 Thomas Aquinas **21** Catherine of Alexandria
surgeons: 6 Cosmas, Damian
tailors: 9 Homobonus
tax collectors: 7 Matthew
teachers: 15 Gregory the Great **21** Catherine of Alexandria, Jean Baptiste de la Salle
theologians: 9 Augustine **16** Alphonsus Liguori
throat sufferers: 6 Blaise
travelers: 7 Raphael **11** Christopher **14** Anthony of Padua,
  Nicholas of Myra
Wales: 5 David
winegrowers: 7 Vincent
workingmen: 6 Joseph
writers: 14 Francis de Sales
youth: 13 John Berchmans **15** Aloysius Gonzaga, Gabriel
  Possenti

---

18 La Jeunesse d'Hercule
20 Carnival of the Animals

Saints' lives
  writer of: 12 hagiographer

Saint Vincent, St Vincent
  capital: 9 Kingstown
  highest point: 9 Soufriere
  Indian: 5 Carib **6** Arawak
  island group: 8 Windward
    14 Lesser Antilles
  islands: 10 Grenadines
  language: 6 patois
  location: 9 Caribbean
  volcano: 9 Soufriere

Saint Vitus' dance 6 chorea

Saitis *see* **6** Athena

sake 3 end **4** care, gain, good
  5 cause **6** behalf, object, profit,
  regard **7** account, benefit, concern, purpose, respect, welfare **8** interest **9** advantage
  11 enhancement
  13 consideration

sake
  type: 4 wine **6** spirit
  origin: 5 Japan
  ingredient: 4 rice

Sakharov, Andrei
  Dimitrievich
  field: 7 physics

nationality: 7 Russian
researched: 14 nuclear
  fission
defended: 12 civil liberty
exiled to: 5 Gorky
awarded: 10 Nobel Prize

Saki
  real name: 7 H H Munro
  author of: 8 Reginald
    20 Beasts and Super-Beasts
    21 The Chronicles of Clovis
    23 The Unbearable
    Bassington

salaam 3 bow **6** homage
  9 obeisance

Salacia
  partner of: 7 Neptune

salacious 4 lewd, sexy **7** lustful, obscene **8** indecent **9** lecherous **10** lascivious, libidinous
  12 pornographic

salad days 5 prime, youth
  6 heyday **9** flowering

salamander 3 eft **4** newt
  5 giant, siren, tiger **6** lizard,
  red eft **7** axolotl, urodela
  8 congo eel, mudpuppy **9** amphibian, fire-eater, proteidae
  10 hellbender, necturidae
  14 red-spotted newt

Salamis
  father: 6 Asopus
  mother: 6 Metope
  son: 8 Cychreus

Salammbo
  author: 15 Gustave Flaubert
  character: 5 Matho **8** Hamil-
    car, Spendius **9** Narr Havas
  setting: 8 Carthage

salary 3 pay **5** wages **6** income **7** stipend **8** earnings
  9 allowance, emolument
  10 recompense
  12 remuneration

sale 3 cut **7** bargain, selling,
  special **8** discount, exchange,
  markdown, transfer
  9 reduction

Salem
  home of: 11 Melchizedek

salesperson 5 agent, clerk
  6 vendor **8** huckster

salient 6 arrant, marked
  7 glaring, notable, obvious
  8 flagrant, manifest, palpable,
  striking **9** egregious, important, prominent **10** noteworthy, noticeable, pronounced, protruding, remarkable **11** conspicuous,
  outstanding, substantial
  12 considerable

Salii
  also: 6 Salian
  form: 7 priests
  priests of: 4 Mars

guarded: 7 ancilia **13** sacred shields

saline 4 salt **5** briny, salty **8** brackish

Salinger, J D
author of: 14 Franny and Zooey **18** The Catcher in the Rye

Salisbury
capital of: 8 Zimbabwe

Salisbury, Harrison E
author of: 16 American in Russia **19** A Journey for Our Times, Black Night White Snow

Salish (Flatheads)
language family: 8 Salishan
location: 5 Idaho **6** Oregon **7** Montana **10** Washington **15** British Columbia

Salishan
tribe: 6 Salish **8** Puyallop **9** Flatheads

Salk, Jonas Edward
field: 8 medicine
developed: 12 (inactivated) polio vaccine

salle a manger 10 dining room
literally: 13 hall for eating

sallow 3 wan **4** gray, pale **5** ashen, livid **6** anemic, pallid, sickly, yellow **7** bilious **9** jaundiced, washed-out, yellowish

sallowness 6 pallor **7** wanness **8** paleness **10** sickliness **11** biliousness **13** colorlessness, yellowishness

Sallust
author of: 9 Histories **13** War of Jugurtha **20** Conspiracy of Catiline

sally 3 mot **4** flow, pour, quip, raid, trip **5** erupt, foray, surge **6** attack, banter, charge, outing, retort, sortie, spring, thrust **7** debouch, journey **8** badinage, repartee **9** excursion, wisecrack, witticism **10** expedition **13** counterattack

Salmacis
form: 5 nymph
loved: 14 Hermaphroditus
joined with:
14 Hermaphroditus
became: 13 hermaphrodite **14** bisexual person

Salmagundi
author: 16 Washington Irving

salmon 4 fish, king **5** cohoe **6** silver **7** chinook, Pacific, quinnat, sockeye, spawner **8** Atlantic, humpback
enclosure: 4 yair
female: 4 raun **6** baggit

genus: 12 Oncorhynchus
hatchling: 4 pink **6** alevin
male: 3 gib **4** buck, cock
post-spawning: 4 kelt **7** shedder
pre-spawning: 7 gilling, girling
young: 4 parr **7** essling

Salmoneus
father: 6 Aeolus
mother: 7 Enarete
brother: 8 Sisyphus
wife: 6 Sidero **8** Alcidice
daughter: 4 Tyro
struck by: 9 lightning

Salome
father: 11 Herod Philip
mother: 8 Herodias
husband: 7 Zebedee
opera by: 7 (Richard) Strauss
character: 5 Herod (the Tetrarch) **8** Herodias, Jokanaan (John the Baptist) **9** Narraboth

salon 4 hall **7** gallery **11** drawing room **13** establishment

saloon 3 bar, inn, pub **6** bistro, tavern **7** barroom, ginmill, taproom **8** alehouse **9** roadhouse, speakeasy

salt 3 wit **4** best, corn, cure, pick, save **5** brine, briny, cream, elect, humor, savor, smack, souse, spice **6** choice, flavor, pickle, saline, season, select **8** brackish, marinate, piquancy, pungency **9** seasoning **12** quintessence

Salten, Felix
author of: 5 Bambi

salt water 3 sea **5** brine, ocean

salty 4 racy **5** briny, funny, spicy, terse, witty **6** corned, ribald, risque, saline **7** pungent, zestful **8** brackish, improper

salubrious 7 bracing, healthy **9** healthful, wholesome **10** beneficial, lifegiving **11** therapeutic **12** invigorating

salubriousness 11 healthiness **13** healthfulness, wholesomeness

Salus
origin: 5 Roman
goddess of: 6 health **10** prosperity
corresponds to: 6 Hygeia

salutary 4 good **5** tonic **6** useful **7** healing, healthy **8** curative, sanitary **9** healthful, wholesome **10** beneficial, profitable **12** advantageous

salutation 3 bow **5** hello, howdy, toast **6** curtsy **7** address, welcome **8** greeting **9** reception

Hawaiian: 5 aloha
Italian: 4 ciao
Latin: 3 ave

salute 3 ave **4** hail, kiss **5** bow to, cheer, greet, honor, nod to, salvo **6** accost, homage, praise, wave to **7** address, applaud, respect, welcome **8** accolade, applause, greeting **9** laudation, reverence **11** acclamation, recognition **12** congratulate

Salvador
author: 10 Joan Didion

salvage 4 junk, save **5** scrap **6** debris, rescue **7** recover, remains, restore **8** recovery, retrieve **9** retrieval **11** reclamation **12** rehabilitate

salvation 4 rock **5** grace **6** rescue, saving **8** election, lifeline, mainstay, recovery, survival **9** retrieval **10** protection, redemption **11** deliverance, reclamation **12** preservation

salve 4 balm, calm, ease, hail **5** hello **6** lessen, lotion, pacify, reduce, soothe, temper **7** anodyne, assuage, mollify, relieve, unguent **8** dressing, liniment, mitigate, moderate, ointment **9** alleviate, emollient, greetings **11** alleviative

salver 4 bowl, dish, tray **6** waiter **7** coaster

salvia 4 herb, mint, sage **5** shrub **8** mejorana **9** artemisia

salvo 5 burst **6** volley **7** barrage, battery **8** shelling **9** cannonade, fusillade **11** bombardment

sambuca
type: 7 liqueur
origin: 5 Italy
flavor: 5 anise **10** elderberry

same 4 like, twin, very **5** alike, equal **6** on a par **7** similar, uniform **8** parallel **9** identical, unchanged **10** consistent, equivalent, invariable **13** corresponding

same as previously given
Latin: 4 idem

sameness 6 parity **8** equality, evenness, likeness, monotony **10** similarity, uniformity **11** homogeneity **14** homogenousness

Samoa *see box*

Samoyed
language family: 6 Uralic
spoken in: 7 Siberia

sample 3 try **4** test **5** model, taste **7** dip into, examine, example, pattern, portion, segment **8** instance, paradigm,

Samoa
capital:
American Samoa: **8** Pago Pago
Western Samoa: **4** Apia
cities: **6** Utulei **7** Palauli **8** Fagatogo
division: **12** Western Samoa **13** American Samoa
monetary unit: **4** tala
island: **3** Ofu, Tau **4** Rose **5** Aunuu, Manua, Namua, Upolu **6** Manono, Nuulua, Savaii, Swains **7** Apolima, Nuutele, Olosega, Tutuila **8** Nuusafee
mountain: **4** Vaea **5** Alava **6** Savaii **7** Matafao **9** Rainmaker
highest point: **4** Fito **8** Silisili
sea: **12** South Pacific
physical feature:
bay: **5** Afono, Leone **6** Fagasa, Falefa, Safata **7** Lafanga, Masefau, Matautu **8** Massacre, Salealua **9** Saluofata
people: **6** Samoan **10** Polynesian
explorer: **9** Roggeveen **12** Bougainville
language: **6** Samoan **7** English
religion: **6** Mormon **9** Methodist **13** Roman Catholic **15** Latter Day Saints **19** Seventh-Day Adventist **26** Congregational Christianity
feature:
bird: **3** iao **4** lulu, lupe **6** manuao, manuma, maomao **7** manuali **8** manusina, manutagi
chief: **5** matai
chief's daughter: **5** taupo
cloth: **4** para, tapa
clothing: **5** pareu **8** lavalava, puletasi
dance: **4** siva
dwelling: **4** fale
food:
drink: **3** ava

specimen **10** experience **12** cross section, illustration **14** representative **15** exemplification

Sampo
origin: **7** Finnish
stolen by: **9** Ilmarinen **11** Vainamoinen **12** Lemminkainen
stolen from: **5** Louhi

Samson 11 Hebrew judge
father: **6** Manoah
mistress/betrayer: **7** Delilah
hometown: **5** Zorah

Samson Agonistes
author: **10** John Milton

Samuel 11 Hebrew judge
father: **7** Elkanah
mother: **6** Hannah
hometown: **5** Ramah
anointed: **4** Saul **5** David

Sana, Sanaa
capital of: **10** North Yemen

San Antonio
basketball team: **5** Spurs
football team: **11** Gunslingers
landmark: **8** The Alamo **9** River Walk

sanctification 8 blessing **9** hallowing **12** consecration
Hebrew: **7** Kiddush

sanctified 4 holy **6** sacred **7** blessed **8** hallowed **11** consecrated

sanctify 5 bless, exalt **6** anoint, hallow, purify, uphold **7** absolve, beatify, cleanse **8** dedicate, enshrine, make holy **10** consecrate, legitimate, legitimize **12** legitimatize

sanctimonious 6 solemn **7** canting, pompous, preachy **8** unctuous **9** overblown, pietistic **11** pharisaical, pretentious **14** holier-than-thou

sanctimoniousness 4 cant, sham **6** humbug **9** hypocrisy **11** insincerity **15** pretentiousness

sanction 5 allow, favor, leave **6** accept, assent, permit, ratify **7** agree to, approve, consent, endorse, liberty, license, penalty, support **8** approval, coercion, pressure **9** authority, authorize **10** legitimate, permission **11** countenance, endorsement **12** commendation, confirmation, ratification **13** authorization

sanctuary 4 park **5** cover, haven **6** asylum, chapel, church, refuge, safety, shrine, temple **7** reserve, retreat, shelter **8** preserve **10** protection

Sanctuary
author: **15** William Faulkner
character: **5** Tommy **6** Popeye **9** Ruby Lamar **10** Lee Goodwin, Reba Rivers **11** Temple Drake **12** Gowan Stevens, Horace Benbow

sanctum sanctorum 12 holy of holies

sanctus 4 holy

Sancus
also: **10** Semo Sancus
origin: **5** Roman
god of: **5** oaths **10** road safety **11** hospitality **20** international affairs
corresponds to: **8** Hercules **10** Dius Fidius

sand 4 grit, guts **5** pluck, spunk **6** mettle **7** bravery, courage, resolve **8** backbone **9** fortitude **10** resolution **12** resoluteness

Sand, George
real name: **14** Aurore Dudevant
author of: **5** Lelia **7** Indiana **8** Consuelo **9** Valentine **13** Story of My Life **14** The Country Waif, The Haunted Pool **17** Fanchon the Cricket **18** Les Maitres Sonneurs **23** The Countess of Rudolstadt

sandal 4 clog, flat, shoe, zori **5** scuff, thong **6** loafer **7** slipper **8** flipflop, huarache, moccasin, overshoe **10** espadrille

sandalwood 5 Algum, Almug

sand bank 4 dune, reef **5** shelf, shoal **7** shallow

sandbar 4 bank, flat, reef, spit **5** shelf, shoal **7** shallow

Sandbox, The
author: **11** Edward Albee

Sandburg, Carl
author of: **3** Fog **7** Chicago **12** Harvest Poems **13** Smoke and Steel **14** Abraham Lincoln, The Cornhuskers **15** Remembrance Rock

Sanders, George
born: **6** Russia **12** St Petersburg
wife: **10** Benita Hume, Magda Gabor **11** Zsa Zsa Gabor
roles: **6** The Fan **7** Ivanhoe, Rebecca **8** The Saint **9** The Falcon **11** All About Eve **12** Forever Amber, The Gay Falcon **18** The Moon and Sixpence **20** Foreign Correspondent **22** The Picture of

Dorian Gray **24** The House of the Seven Gables
autobiography: 25 Memoirs of a Professional Cad

San Diego
airport: 14 Lindbergh Field
area: 7 La Jolla, Old Town **8** Coronado **9** Point Loma **10** Balboa Park, Mission Bay **13** Mission Valley **14** Gaslamp Quarter
baseball team: 6 Padres
football team: 8 Chargers
founder: 13 Junipero Serra
landmark: 11 San Diego Zoo **14** Wild Animal Park **30** Scripps Institute of Oceanography

sandpiper 3 ree **4** bird, ruff **5** reeve, stint, wader **6** common, oxbird, plover **7** fiddler, haybird, spotted, tipbird **8** graybird, sandpeep, shadbird **10** beachrobin

Sands of Iwo Jima
director: 9 Allan Dwan
cast: 8 John Agar **9** Adele Mara, John Wayne **13** Forrest Tucker

sandwich 3 sub **4** club, deli, hero **5** hogie **6** burger, hoagie, insert **7** grinder, western **8** laminate **9** interpose, submarine **10** lamination **11** combination

sane 5 lucid, sober **7** logical **8** all there, balanced, credible, rational, sensible **9** judicious, plausible, sagacious **10** farsighted, reasonable **11** clearheaded, responsible
Latin: 12 compos mentis

Sanford and Son
character: 5 Bubba **6** Melvin **10** Aunt Esther **11** Donna Harris, Fred Sanford, Grady Wilson, Rollo Larson **12** Julio Fuentes, Officer Smith (Smitty) **13** Lamont Sanford
cast: 8 Redd Foxx **9** Don Bexley **11** Hal Williams, LaWanda Page, Slappy White, Whitman Mayo **12** Demond Wilson, Lynn Hamilton **13** Gregory Sierra **15** Nathaniel Taylor

San Francisco
baseball team: 6 Giants
bay: 12 San Francisco
county: 5 Marin **8** San Mateo **12** San Francisco
football team: 11 Forty-Niners
known as: 12 City by the Bay **19** City by the Golden Gate
landmark: 8 Alcatraz **16** Golden Gate Bridge
noted for: 8 cable car **9** earthquake (1906)

26 crookedest street in the world
street/section: 6 Market **7** Lombard, Nob Hill **8** Presidio **9** Chinatown **10** Montgomery **11** Embarcadero, Russian Hill

Sangallensis 16 Greek uncial codex

sangaree, sangria
flavor: 5 fruit, spice

sangfroid 5 poise **6** aplomb **7** balance **8** coolness **9** composure **10** confidence, equanimity **11** tranquility **12** tranquillity **16** imperturbability

sanguine 3 red **4** rosy **5** happy, ruddy, sunny **6** bright, elated, florid **7** buoyant, crimson, flushed, glowing, hopeful, reddish, scarlet **8** blooming, cheerful, inflamed, rubicund **9** confident **10** optimistic **12** lighthearted

Sanhedrin 7 council

sanitarium, sanitorium
8 hospital **11** institution
French: 13 maison de sante

sanitary 5 clean **7** aseptic, healthy, sterile **8** germ-free, hygienic **9** healthful, wholesome **10** salubrious, sterilized, uninfected, unpolluted **11** disinfected **12** prophylactic

sanitorium *see* **10** sanitarium

sanity 5 sense **6** reason **8** lucidity, saneness **9** coherence, normality **11** rationality **12** sensibleness **14** reasonableness **15** clearheadedness

San Jose
capital of: 9 Costa Rica

San Juan
capital of: 10 Puerto Rico

San Juan Bautista *see* **10** Puerto Rico

San Marino *see box*

San Salvador
capital of: 10 El Salvador

sans doute 12 without doubt

Sansovino, Andrea
real name: 14 Andrea Contucci
born: 8 Italy **14** Monte San Savino
artwork: 15 Baptism of Christ **20** Virgin Child and St Anne

Sansovino, Il
real name: 11 Jacopo Tatti
born: 5 Italy **7** Caprese
artwork: 4 Mars **7** Bacchus, Logetta, Neptune **10** Old Li-

San Marino
capital/largest city: 9 San Marino
others: 10 Serravalle **13** Borgo Maggiore
division: 8 Castelli
government:
legislature: 22 Great and General Council
monetary unit: 4 lira, lire **9** centesimi
mountain: 9 Apennines
highest point: 6 Titano
people: 7 Italian **11** San Marinese
founder: 7 Marinus
language: 7 Italian
religion: 13 Roman Catholic
place: 13 Valloni Palace **17** Palazzo del Governo **19** Basilica of San Marino
church: 5 Pieve **9** St Francis

brary **15** Madonna del Parto **16** St John the Baptist

sans pareil 12 without equal

sans peur et sans reproche 29 without fear and without reproach

sans souci 8 carefree **11** without care

Santa Cruz de Tenerife
capital of: 13 Canary Islands

Santayana, George
author of: 14 The Last Puritan **16** The Realms of Being, The Sense of Beauty **24** Skepticism and Animal Faith

Santiago
capital of: 5 Chile

Santiago
character in: 18 The Old Man and the Sea
author: 9 Hemingway

Santo Domingo
capital of: 17 Dominican Republic

Santo Domingo *see* **5** Haiti

Sao Tome
capital of: 18 Sao Tome and Principe

Sao Tome and Principe *see box*

sap 3 rob, tax **4** ruin, wear **5** bleed, drain **6** impair, reduce, weaken **7** afflict, cripple, deplete, destroy, disable, exhaust, subvert **8** enervate, enfeeble **9** devastate, undermine **10** debilitate, devitalize

---

Sao Tome and Principe
  capital/largest city:
    7 Sao Tome
  others: 8 Trindade
    11 Porto Alegre
    12 Santo Antonio
  monetary unit: 5 dobra
    6 escudo 7 centavo
  highest point: 7 Sao
    Tome
  sea: 8 Atlantic
  physical feature:
    bay: 11 Ana de
      Chaves
    gulf: 6 Guinea
  people: 7 African
    10 Portuguese 11 Cape
    Verdean
    explorer: 7 Escobar
      8 Santarem
  language: 10 Portuguese
  religion: 7 animism
    13 Roman Catholic
    19 Seventh Day Ad-
    ventist 21 Evangelical
    Protestant

---

sapient 4 wise 7 knowing
  8 profound 9 sagacious 10 discerning, perceptive 11 intelligent 13 knowledgeable

sap one's energy 3 fag
  4 bush, poop, tire 5 drain,
  weary 6 tucker, weaken 7 deplete, exhaust, fatigue, wash
  out 8 enervate, enfeeble
  10 debilitate, devitalize

Sapphira
  husband: 7 Ananias
  lied to: 5 Peter

sapphire 3 gem 4 blue 5 azure,
  jewel 6 indigo
  species: 8 corundum
  source: 5 Burma, Mogok
    6 Ceylon 7 Kashmir 8 Sri
    Lanka, Thailand 9 Australia
  kind: 4 star

Sappho
  author: 14 Alphonse Daudet

Sarah, Sarai
  father: 5 Asher
  former name: 5 Sarai
  husband: 7 Abraham
  son: 5 Isaac
  slave: 5 Hagar
  burial place: 9 Machpelah

sarcasm 3 rub 4 gibe, jeer,
  jest 5 irony, scorn, sneer,
  taunt 7 mockery 8 contempt,
  derision, ridicule, scoffing
  13 disparagement

sarcastic 5 acerb 6 biting, bitter, ironic 7 caustic, cutting,
  mocking, mordant 8 derisive,
  piercing, sardonic, scornful,
  sneering, stinging, taunting

  11 disparaging
  12 contemptuous

sarcoma 5 tumor 6 cancer,
  growth 8 neoplasm
  10 malignancy

sarcophagus 4 pall 6 coffin

sard
  species: 6 quartz

sardine 4 bang, cram, fish, lile,
  lour, pack 5 crowd 7 alewife,
  anchovy, herring 8 pilchard

Sardinia *see box*

Sardius 8 gemstone

sardonic 6 biting 7 caustic,
  cynical, jeering, mocking,
  mordant, satiric 8 derisive,
  scornful, sneering, taunting
  9 sarcastic 11 disparaging
  12 contemptuous

Sardonyx 8 gemstone

Sargent, John Singer
  born: 5 Italy 8 Florence
  artwork: 6 Madam X (Ma-
    dame Gautreau) 7 El Jaleo
    17 The Wyndham Sisters
    20 Robert Louis Stevenson
    21 Carnation Lily Lily Rose
    22 Daughters of Edward D
    Boit 24 Oyster Gatherers of
    Cancale

Sargom
  captured: 5 Accad
  successor: 11 Sennacherib

Saron
  king of: 7 Troezen

Saroyan, William
  author of: 12 My Name Is
    Aram 14 The Human Com-
    edy 17 The Time of Your
    Life 22 My Heart's in the
    Highlands

Sarpedon
  prince of: 5 Lycia
  father: 4 Zeus
  mother: 6 Europa 8 Laodamia
  uncle: 5 Cilix
  brother: 5 Minos
    12 Rhadamanthys
  ally of: 4 Troy
  friend: 7 Glaucus
  killed by: 9 Patroclus

Sarton, May
  author of: 5 Anger 11 Kinds
    of Love 17 Plant Dreaming
    Deep 20 Faithful Are the
    Wounds 33 Mrs Stevens
    Hears the Mermaids Singing

Sartor Resartus
  author: 13 Thomas Carlyle

Sartre, Jean-Paul
  author of: 6 Nausea, No
    Exit 8 The Words 17 The
    Roads to Freedom 19 Being
    and Nothingness
  philosophy: 14 Existentialism
  quote: 17 Hell is other
    people

sash 3 tie 4 band, belt 5 frame,

Sardinia
  other name: 8 Sardegna
  capital: 8 Cagliari
  cities: 4 Bono, Bosa 5 Nuoro, Olbia 7 Alghero, Bonorva,
    Sassari, Thatari 8 Iglesias, Oristano 11 Porto Torres
  division: 5 Nuoro 7 Arborea, Gallura, Sassari 8 Cagliari,
    Logudoro
  government: 13 region of Italy
  monetary unit: 7 carline
  island: 7 Caprera 8 Tavolara 9 Maddalena
  lake: 6 Omodeo
  mountain: 4 Rasu 5 Ferry, Linas 7 Gallura, Limbara
    8 Marghine, Serpeddi, Vittoria 11 Gennargentu
  river: 5 Mannu, Tirso 6 Lascia 8 Coghinas 10 Flumendosa
  sea: 13 Mediterranean
  physical feature:
    gulf: 6 Orosei, Palmas 7 Asinara 8 Cagliari, Oristano
    plain: 7 Sassari 9 Campidano
    strait: 9 Bonifacio
  people:
    king: 12 Charles Felix 13 Charles Albert 14 Victor
      Emmanuel
    leader: 6 Cavour
    ruler: 4 Pisa 5 Genoa, Spain 7 Austria, Vandals 9 Byzan-
      tium, Phoenicia 12 House of Savoy
  language: 7 Italian
  religion: 13 Roman Catholic
  feature:
    towers: 7 nuraghi
  food:
    cheese: 6 romano 8 pecorino

scarf, strip **6** casing, corset,
girdle, ribbon, window **7** baldric **8** casement **9** doorframe,
waistband **10** cummerbund
11 windowframe
  Japanese: 3 obi
  pulley weight: 5 mouse
  window: 5 chess

sashay 4 move, skip **5** glide,
mince **6** chasse, travel

Saskatchewan 5 river
8 province
  boundary: 7 Alberta, Montana **8** Manitoba **11** North
Dakota **12** Old Northwest
20 Northwest Territories
  capital: 6 Regina
  city: 8 Moose Jaw **9** Saskatoon **12** Prince Albert, Swift
Current
  country: 6 Canada
  Indian: 4 Cree **9** Chipewyan
10 Assiniboin
  lake: 8 Reindeer **9** Athabasca,
Wollaston
  mountain: 7 Cypress, Pasquia
9 Porcupine **14** Missouri
Coteau
  river: 9 Churchill, Frenchman
  river mouth: 12 Lake
Winnipeg

Sassoon, Siegfried
  author of: 26 The Memoirs
of a Fox-Hunting Man
26 The Memoirs of George
Sherston **29** The Memoirs of
an Infantry Officer

sassy 4 bark, bold, flip, rude,
tree **5** brash, fresh, saucy
6 mouthy, snippy **7** forward
8 impolite, impudent, insolent
12 discourteous
13 disrespectful

Satan 6 Belial, Moloch **7** Lucifer, Old Nick **8** Apollyon, the
Devil **9** Beelzebub **10** Old
Scratch, the Evil One, the
Tempter **11** fallen angel
12 the Foul Fiend **13** the Old
Serpent **14** Mephistopheles
19 the Prince of Darkness

satanic 3 bad **4** evil, vile
5 cruel **6** wicked **7** demonic,
heinous, hellish, inhuman, vicious **8** devilish, fiendish, infamous, infernal, sadistic
9 malicious, malignant **10** demoniacal, diabolical,
malevolent

satchel, Satchel 3 bag **4** case,
grip, sack **5** purse **6** valise
7 handbag **8** reticule, suitcase
9 carpetbag, Gladstone,
schoolbag
  pitcher, Hall of Famer:
5 Paige

sate 4 cloy, fill, glut **5** gorge,
stuff **7** surfeit

satellite 4 moon **5** crony,

toady **6** menial, puppet, vassal **7** servant **8** disciple, follower, hanger-on, parasite,
retainer **9** assistant, attendant,
companion, sycophant, tributary, underling

satellite state 6 colony **8** dominion **10** possession
12 protectorate

satiate 4 bore, cloy, fill, glut,
jade **5** slake, stuff, weary
6 overdo, quench, sicken
7 content, disgust, gratify, suffice, surfeit **8** nauseate, overfill, saturate

Satie, Erik
  born: 6 France **8** Honfleur
  composer of: 6 Parade
13 Pieces froides **16** The
Three Gymnasts **19** Limp
Preludes for a Dog **20** Pieces
en forme de poire **23** Pieces
in the Shape of a Pear

satiny 4 fine **5** shiny, silky
6 smooth

satire 5 irony **6** banter, parody,
send up **7** lampoon, mockery,
sarcasm, takeoff **8** acrimony,
derision, raillery, ridicule,
travesty **9** burlesque **10** caricature, persiflage

satirical 5 comic **6** biting, bitter **7** caustic, mocking, mordant **8** derisive, humorous,
ironical, sardonic, scornful,
sneering **9** malicious,
sarcastic

satirize 4 mock **6** parody
7 lampoon **9** burlesque
10 caricature

satisfaction 5 pride **6** amends
7 comfort, content, damages,
deserts, justice, payment, redress **8** pleasure, requital
9 answering, atonement, happiness, quittance, reckoning,
repayment **10** correction, recompense, remittance, settlement **11** contentment,
fulfillment, restitution
12 compensation, remuneration **13** gratification, rectification, reimbursement

satisfactory 2 OK **4** okay
8 adequate, all right, passable,
suitable **9** competent **10** acceptable, sufficient

satisfied 5 happy **7** content,
pleased **9** gratified **10** complacent **11** comfortable

satisfy 3 pay **4** fill, meet **5** annul, clear, remit, repay, serve,
slake **6** answer, assure, pacify,
pay off, please, quench, remove, settle **7** appease, content, delight, fulfill, gratify,
mollify, requite, suffice **8** convince, persuade, reassure

9 discharge, reimburse
10 compensate, recompense

satisfying 8 pleasant, pleasing
9 agreeable, enjoyable, rewarding **10** delightful, fulfilling,
gratifying **11** pleasurable

saturate 4 fill **5** cover, douse,
imbue, souse **6** drench, infuse
7 immerse, pervade, suffuse
8 permeate, submerge **10** impregnate, infiltrate

saturated 3 wet **4** full **5** drunk,
soggy, soppy **6** soaked, sodden **8** bursting

Saturday
  day of: 15 Biblical Sabbath
  French: 6 samedi
  from: 8 Saturnus
  German: 7 samstag
  heavenly body: 6 Saturn
  Italian: 6 sabato
  observance: 13 Jewish Sabbath **20** Seventh Day
Adventists
  Spanish: 6 sabado

Saturday Night Fever
  director: 10 John Badham
  cast: 11 Barry Miller
12 John Travolta **15** Karen
Lynn Gorney
  setting: 8 Brooklyn
  score: 7 Bee Gees
  sequel: 12 Staying Alive

Saturday Night Live, NBC's
  regular: 10 Bill Murray,
Chevy Chase, Dan Aykroyd,
Jane Curtin **11** Eddie Murphy, Gilda Radner, John Belushi **13** Garrett Morris,
Laraine Newman
  group: 27 Not Ready For
Prime Time Players
  bits: 4 Bees **7** Samurai
9 Coneheads **10** Church
Lady **13** Blues Brothers,
Weekend Update **16** Pathological Liar **18** Rosanne Rosanna-Dana

Saturn
  origin: 5 Roman
  god of: 11 agriculture
  consort of: 3 Ops
  son: 5 Picus
  corresponds to: 6 Cronos,
Cronus, Kronos

Saturn
  position: 5 sixth
  satellite: 4 Rhea **5** Dione,
Janus, Mimas, Titan
6 Phoebe, Tethys **7** Iapetus
8 Hyperion **9** Enceladus
  characteristic: 5 rings

saturnalia, Saturnalia
4 orgy **5** revel, spree **7** carouse, debauch, revelry **8** carousal **9** bacchanal
10 debauchery
  origin: 5 Roman
  event: 8 festival

honoring: 6 Saturn **13** sowing of crops

saturnine 4 dour, glum, grim **5** grave, staid, stern, sulky **6** gloomy, moping, morose, solemn, somber, sullen **7** austere, serious **8** dejected, downcast, reserved, sardonic, taciturn **9** apathetic, cheerless, withdrawn **11** downhearted **15** uncommunicative

satyr
  form: 5 deity
  location: 8 woodland

Satyricon
  author: 9 Petronius
  character: 4 Gito **8** Ascyltus, Eumolpus **9** Encolpius **10** Trimalchio

sauce 3 dip **4** sass **5** booze, gravy **6** fillip, flavor **7** alcohol **8** dressing, pertness **9** condiment, flippancy **12** impertinence
  basil: 5 pesto
  fish: 4 alec

hot: 7 Tabasco
Indian: 5 curry
salty: 3 soy

saucy 4 bold, pert, rude, trim **5** brash, cocky, fresh, natty, smart **6** brazen, cheeky, jaunty, lively, spruce **7** forward **8** flippant, impolite, impudent, insolent **9** audacious, barefaced, unabashed **11** impertinent, smart-alecky **12** discourteous **13** disrespectful

Saudi Arabia *see box*

Sauguet, Henri
  born: 6 France **8** Bordeaux
  composer of: 6 La Nuit **10** Les Forains, Les Mirages

Sauk, Sac
  family: 9 Algonkian **10** Algonquian
  tribe: 3 Fox, Sac **8** Kickapoo
  location: 4 Iowa, Ohio **6** Kansas **7** Indiana **8** Illinois, Michigan, Oklahoma **9** Wisconsin
  leader: 9 Blackhawk

related to: 8 Kickapoo **9** Mesquakie **11** Potawatomie
involved in: 12 Black Hawk War

Saul
  king of: 4 Edom **6** Israel
  father: 4 Kish
  daughter: 5 Merab **6** Michal
  son: 7 Abinoam **8** Jonathan **10** Ishbosheth
  succeeded: 6 Samlah
  anointed by: 6 Samuel
  hometown: 6 Gibeah **8** Rehoboth
  successor: 5 David
  former name: 4 Paul

Saunders, Allen
  creator/artist of: 9 Mary Worth

saunter 4 roam **5** amble, mosey, stray **6** loiter, ramble, stroll, wander **7** meander, traipse **8** straggle **9** promenade

Saurolophus
  type: 8 dinosaur **10** ornithopod
  location: 6 Canada **7** Alberta

sauropod
  type of: 8 dinosaur
  member: 9 Euhelopus **10** Diplodocus **11** Apatosaurus **12** Brontosaurus, Camarasaurus, Plateosaurus **13** Brachiosaurus, Hypselosaurus

sausage 5 frank, gigot, wurst **6** hot-dog, salami, weenie, wiener **7** baloney, bologna **8** kielbasa **9** bratwurst, pepperoni **10** liverwurst **11** frankfurter
  British: 6 banger

sauve qui peut 4 rout **8** stampede **18** every man for himself **23** let him save himself who can

savage 4 boor, wild **5** brute, cruel, feral, fiend, harsh, rough, yahoo **6** animal, bloody, brutal, fierce, maniac, native, rugged, unkind **7** brutish, hoodlum, ruffian, untamed, violent **8** barbaric, hooligan, pitiless, ruthless, sadistic **9** aborigine, barbarian, barbarous, ferocious, merciless, murderous, primitive **10** aboriginal, heathenish, relentless, uncultured, unmerciful **11** uncivilized **12** uncultivated **14** undomesticated

savagery 7 cruelty **8** ferocity **9** barbarism, barbarity, brutality **10** fierceness, inhumanity **12** pitilessness, ruthlessness

savanna, savannah 5 campo, plain **9** grassland

savant 6 genius **7** scholar **13** learned person

Saudi Arabia
  capital/largest city: 6 Riyadh
  others: 4 Abha, Hail, Taif **5** Hofuf, Hufuf, Jedda, Jidda, Yanbu, Yenbo **6** Anaiza, Dammam, Jiddah, Jubail **7** Alhofuf, Buraido, Dhahran **9** Ras Tanura
  holy city: **5** Mecca **6** Medina
  school: 5 Islam **13** King Abd al-Aziz **19** Imam Muhammad bin Saud **20** Petroleum and Minerals
  division: 4 Asir, Nejd **5** Hejaz **6** El Hasa
  government: 8 monarchy
  head of state/government: 4 king
  monetary unit: 5 girsh, gursh, pound, riyal
  weight: 3 oke
  mountain: 6 Tuwayq
  highlands: **4** Asir **5** Hejaz
  highest point: 5 Razih **10** Jebal Sawda
  sea: 3 Red
  physical feature:
    desert: **3** Red **5** Dahna, Nafud, Nefud, Nufud **6** al-Dahy, Dahana **10** Rub al Khali
    gulf: **5** Aqaba **7** Persian
    peninsula: **7** Arabian
    plain: **6** Tihama
    plateau: **4** Nejd
  people: 4 Arab **7** Bedouin
    king: **4** Fahd, Saud **6** Faisal, Khalid **7** Ibn Saud **9** Abdul Aziz
    religious leader: **8** Mohammed, Muhammad
  language: 6 Arabic
  religion: 5 Islam
    sect: **5** Sunni **6** Shiite **7** Wahhabi
  place:
    shrine: **5** Kaaba **10** Black Stone
  feature:
    annual pilgrimage: **4** hadj, hajj
    clothing: **3** aba **4** agal **5** thobe **6** ghutra
    kingdom: **5** Hejaz **7** Minaean, Ottoman, Sabaean **9** Himyarite
    laws of Islam: **6** sharia
    village school: **6** kuttab
    war: **4** Gulf **11** Desert Storm **12** Desert Shield

save 3 but **4** bank, free, help, hold, keep **5** amass, guard, hoard, lay by, lay up, put by, spare, stock, store **6** defend, except, garner, heap up, redeem, rescue, shield **7** deliver, deposit, husband, protect, put away, recover, reserve, salvage **8** conserve, preserve, retrench, withhold **9** economize, safeguard **10** accumulate

save up 5 amass, hoard **7** collect, put away **8** salt away, sock away **10** accumulate **12** squirrel away

saving 5 close, tight **6** frugal, stingy **7** careful, miserly, prudent, sparing, thrifty **8** markdown, stinting **9** illiberal, niggardly, provident, redeeming, restoring **10** economical, reclaiming, redemptory, reparative **12** compensating, conservative

savings 5 hoard **7** nest egg, reserve

savior 5 freer **7** rescuer **8** champion, defender, guardian, redeemer **9** deliverer, liberator, preserver, protecter, protector, salvation **11** emancipator

Savior 5 Jesus **6** Christ **8** Redeemer **10** the Messiah **11** Jesus Christ, the Son of God **13** Prince of Peace

Savior anointed 5 Jesus

savoir-faire 4 tact **5** poise **6** aplomb, polish **7** finesse, know-how, suavity **8** presence, urbanity **9** assurance, composure **10** adroitness, discretion, smoothness **11** worldliness **12** complaisance, graciousness **14** self-possession

savoir-vivre 16 knowing how to live **19** knowledge of the world

savor 3 try **4** aura, gist, like, odor, soul, tang, zest **5** aroma, enjoy, scent, smack, smell, spice, taste, trait **6** flavor, nature, relish, sample, season, spirit **7** essence, quality **8** piquancy, property, pungency **9** character, fragrance, substance **10** appreciate, experience **11** peculiarity **13** particularity **14** characteristic

savory 5 tangy, tasty, yummy **6** honest **7** odorous, piquant, pungent **8** alluring, aromatic, charming, edifying, fragrant, luscious, tasteful **9** delicious, flavorous, palatable, reputable, toothsome **10** appetizing, attractive, delectable **11** inoffen-sive, respectable, scrumptious **13** mouth-watering

savory
  botanical name: 8 Satureia, S montana **10** S hortensis
  origin: 13 Mediterranean
  varieties: 6 summer, winter
  use: 4 eggs, meat **5** beans, salad **6** sauces **8** dressing **11** chicken soup

savvy 5 catch, get it **7** know-how **10** comprehend, understand **13** understanding

saw 3 cut **4** tool **5** adage, maxim, slash **6** saying **7** proverb **8** aphorism
  type: 3 jig, rip **4** back, band, hack **5** miter **6** coping **7** keyhole **8** circular, crosscut

sawfly
  varieties: 4 stem, wood **5** cedar **6** pergid **7** conifer **8** horntail **11** web spinning

say 2 do **4** hint, hold, read, tell, vote, word **5** bruit, claim, guess, imply, judge, mouth, rumor, speak, state, utter, voice **6** allege, assert, assume, chance, convey, phrase, reason, recite, remark, render, repeat, report, reveal, spread **7** comment, contend, declare, deliver, divulge, express, imagine, mention, perform, suggest, suppose, surmise **8** announce, disclose, intimate, maintain, rehearse, vocalize **9** circulate, franchise, insinuate, pronounce, verbalize **10** articulate, conjecture **11** communicate

Sayers, Dorothy L
  author of: 9 Whose Body **12** Strong Poison **14** Have His Carcase, The Nine Tailors, Unnatural Death **15** Clouds of Witness, Five Red Herrings **16** Busman's

Scandinavian Mythology
  abode of man: 7 Midgard **10** Mithgarthr
  afterworld: 6 Manala **7** Tuonela
  began race of giants: 4 Ymir
  blacksmith/hero: 9 Ilmarinen
  boar: 10 Saehrimnir
  bridge of gods: 7 Bifrost
  dragon: 6 Fafnir
  dwarf: 5 Skuld **7** Andvari
  earth is made from: 4 Ymir
  elf: 4 Norn **8** Verdandi
  epic: 8 Kaleva
  final battle: 15 Gotterdammerung **17** Twilight of the Gods
  first god: 4 Buri **7** Forsete, Forseti
  first man: 3 Ask
  first woman: 5 Embla
  folk hero: 8 Kalevala
  giant: 4 Loki **5** Jotun, Thrym **6** Thiazi, Thjazi **7** Skrymir
  giantess: 3 Urd **5** Thokk **9** Angerboda, Angrbodha, Angurboda
  giant's realm: 9 Jotunheim
  goat: 7 Heidrun
  goddesses: 7 Asynjur
  goddess of death: 3 Hel
  goddess of forbidden marriages: 4 Lofn
  goddess of marriage: 4 Frey **5** Freyr
  goddess of peace: 4 Frey **5** Freyr
  goddess of prosperity: 4 Frey **5** Freyr
  goddess of spring: 4 Idun **5** Iduna, Ithun **6** Ithunn
  goddess of the sea: 3 Ran
  god of beauty/radiance: 5 Baldr **6** Balder, Baldur
  god of dawn: 8 Heimdall
  god of farming: 4 Thor
  god of fire: 4 Loki
  god of knowledge: 4 Odin **5** Othin
    corresponds to Germanic: **5** Wotan
  god of justice: 7 Forseti
  god of light: 8 Heimdall
  god of music: 5 Bragi
  god of navigation: 5 Niord, Njord
  god of poetry: 4 Odin **5** Bragi, Othin
    corresponds to Germanic: **5** Wotan
  god of prosperity: 5 Niord, Njord

Honeymoon **19** Murder
Must Advertise **30** Unpleasantness at the Bellona Club
character: 6 Bunter **11** Harriet Vane **15** Lord Peter
Wimsey

Say Hey Kid
nickname of: 10 Willie Mays

saying 3 saw **5** adage, maxim,
moral, motto **6** byword, dictum, truism **7** epigram, precept, proverb **8** aphorism,
apothegm **10** expression

Sayonara
director: 11 Joshua Logan
author: 13 James Michener
cast: 9 Miiko Taka **10** Red
Buttons **11** James Garner,
Martha Scott **12** Marlon
Brando, Miyoshi Umeki
16 Ricardo Montalban
score: 12 Irving Berlin
Oscar for: 15 supporting ac-

tor (Buttons) **17** supporting
actress (Umeki)

scabrous 5 dirty, rough, scaly
7 immoral, leprous **8** indecent,
off-color **9** salacious
10 suggestive **12** pornographic

scalding 3 hot **5** harsh **7** boiling, caustic **8** seething, steaming **9** sarcastic

scale, scales 3 key, set
4 chip, film, husk, peel, rise,
rule, skin **5** crust, flake, layer,
mount, order, plate, range, ratio, scour, shave, shell, weigh
6 adjust, ascend, goupen, ladder, lamina, octave, rub off,
scrape, series, spread **7** balance, chip off, clamber, climb
up, coating, lamella, measure
8 escalade, membrane, register,
regulate, spectrum, surmount
9 continuum, gradation **10** de-
laminate, graduation, propor-

tion **11** calibration,
progression **14** classification

scale down 4 trim **6** reduce
7 abridge, curtail, shorten
8 compress, condense, decrease, diminish, downsize,
moderate **10** abbreviate

scale insects
varieties: 3 lac, pit, wax
5 giant **6** ensign **7** armored
8 mealybug, tortoise
12 ground pearls

Scamandrius *see* **8** Astyanax

scamp 3 imp, rip **5** cut-up,
knave, rogue, tease **6** rascal,
rotter **7** bounder, villain
8 blighter, scalawag **9** miscreant, prankster, scoundrel
10 scapegrace **11** rapscallion
13 mischief-maker

scamper 3 fly, run, zip **4** dart,
dash, flit, race, romp, rush,
scud **5** frisk, hurry, scoot
6 frolic, gambol, hasten,
scurry, sprint **7** scuttle **9** skedaddle **21** running about
playfully

scan 4 skim **5** check, probe,
scour, study, sweep **6** peruse,
search, size up, survey **7** analyze, examine, explore, inspect **10** scrutinize

scandal 4 blot **5** abuse, libel,
odium, shame, stain **6** expose,
smirch, stigma **7** calumny, obloquy, outrage, slander **8** disgrace, dishonor, ignominy
9 aspersion, discredit, disesteem, sensation **10** debasement, detraction, opprobrium,
revilement **12** vituperation
13 disparagement,
embarrassment

scandalize 5 shock **6** appall,
defame, insult, offend **7** horrify, outrage **10** calumniate

scandalmonger 6 gossip
8 busybody **10** talebearer,
tattletale

scandalous 8 libelous, shameful, shocking **9** gossiping, offensive **10** defamatory,
outrageous, scurrilous, slanderous **11** disgraceful **12** disreputable **13** reprehensible

Scandinavian
language family: 12 Indo-
European
branch: 8 Germanic
group: 15 Western Germanic
language: 6 Danish **7** Swedish **9** Icelandic, Norwegian

Scandinavian Mythology
see box

scant 3 cut **4** bare **5** limit,
short, small, stint **6** in need,
meager, paltry, reduce, sparse

---

god of rain: 4 Thor
god of sea: 5 Aegir, Mimir
god of thunder: 4 Thor
god of underworld: 8 Niflheim
god of victory: 3 Tyr
god of war: 4 Odin **5** Othin
  corresponds to Germanic: **5** Wotan
god of wind: 5 Niord, Njord
god of wisdom: 4 Odin **5** Othin
  corresponds to Germanic: **5** Wotan
hero: 11 Vainamoinen **12** Lemminkainen
home of dead: 3 Hel
king: 5 Gjuki
magician: 11 Joukahainen
magic necklace: 11 Brisingamen
misty void: 11 Ginnungagap
mountain: 11 Hindarfjall
nature spirit: 7 Eriking
oak tree: 9 Barnstock, Branstock
Odin's court/hall: 8 Valhalla
Odin's father: 3 Bor
Odin's horse: 8 Sleipnir
Odin's magic ring: 8 Draupnir
Odin's palace: 9 Gladsheim
Odin's raven: 5 Hugin, Munin
Odin's spear: 6 Gungni
Odin's throne: 10 Hlidskjalf
Odin's wolf: 4 Geri **5** Freki
race of gods: 5 Vanir
saga: 8 Vulsunga
sea monster: 6 Kraken
serpent: 7 Nidhogg **11** Jormungandr
Sigmund's sword: 4 Gram
slave: 8 Kullervo
sorceress: 5 Louhi **8** Grimhild
Thor's hammer: 7 Miolnir
Thor's servant: 7 Thialfi
tree with three roots: 9 Iggdrasil, Yggdrasil
Valkyrie: 8 Brynhild **9** Brunhilde, Sigrdrifa **11** Brunnehilde
virgin goddess: 3 Urd **4** Norn **5** Skuld, Urdar **8** Verdandi
warrior: 8 Baresark **9** Berserker
watchdog: 4 Garm
wolf monster: 6 Fenrir, Fenris

7 limited **8** exiguous, hold back **9** deficient **10** inadequate, incomplete **12** insufficient

scantiness 10 deficiency, inadequacy, meagerness, skimpiness **13** insufficiency

scanty 4 thin **5** short, small **6** meager, modest, paltry, skimpy, sparse **7** slender, stunted **9** deficient **10** inadequate, undersized **12** insufficient

scapegoat, Scapegoat 4 butt, dupe, gull **5** patsy **6** Azazel, victim **7** fall guy **11** whipping boy **13** laughingstock

scapolite
 source: **5** Burma, Mogok

scapula
 bone of: **13** shoulder blade

scar 3 cut, pit **4** dent, flaw, gash, hurt, mark, pock, seam **5** brand, wound **6** affect, bruise, damage, deface, defect, impair, mangle **7** blemish, scratch **8** cicatrix, lacerate, mutilate **9** disfigure, influence

scarce 4 rare **6** scanty, sparse **7** unusual, wanting **8** uncommon **9** deficient

scarcely 4 just **6** at most, barely, hardly **7** but just, faintly **8** slightly

scarcity 4 lack, want **5** stint **6** dearth, rarity **7** fewness, paucity **8** rareness, shortage, sparsity, thinness **10** deficiency, scantiness, sparseness **12** uncommonness **13** insufficiency

scare 4 turn **5** alarm, daunt, panic, shake, shock, start **6** harrow, shiver **7** horrify, jitters, startle, terrify **8** disquiet, frighten **9** terrorize **10** disconcert, dishearten, intimidate **11** nervousness, palpitation **13** consternation

scarecrow 6 effigy **8** straw man

Scarecrow
 character in: **13** The Wizard of Oz
 author: **4** Baum

scared 5 shaky, timid, upset **6** afraid **7** alarmed, fearful, nervous, spooked **8** startled, timorous **9** diffident, terrified, tremulous **10** frightened **12** apprehensive, fainthearted **13** panic-stricken

scarf 3 boa **4** sash, veil, wrap **5** ascot, shawl, stole **6** choker, cravat, tippet **7** foulard, muffler, overlay **8** babushka, bandanna, mantilla **11** neckerchief

Scarface
 director: **11** Howard Hawks
 cast: **8** Paul Muni **9** Ann Dvorak **10** George Raft **12** Boris Karloff

scarify 3 cut **6** incise, loosen **7** break up, scratch **8** lacerate **9** cultivate

Scarlatti, Alessandro
 born: **6** Sicily **7** Palermo
 composer of: **11** Stabat Mater **17** Mitridate Eupatore, The Triumph of Honor **18** Il Trionfo dell Onore **23** Gli equivoci nel sembiante

Scarlatti, Domenico
 born: **5** Italy **6** Naples
 composer of: **7** Sonatas **9** Cat's Fugue, Essercizi **18** Le Donne di Buon Umore **20** The Good-Humored Ladies **23** Ottavia risituita al trono

scarlet 3 red **6** cherry, claret **7** carmine **8** cardinal

Scarlet Letter, The
 author: **18** Nathaniel Hawthorne
 character: **5** Pearl **12** Hester Prynne **16** Arthur Dimmesdale **18** Roger Chillingworth

scary 3 bad **5** awful, hairy **6** creepy **7** fearful **8** alarming, menacing, shocking **9** difficult **10** disturbing, terrifying **11** frightening, goosepimply, hair-raising, threatening **12** discomfiting

scat 3 off, out **4** away, shoo **5** be off, leave, scram **6** beat it, be gone, depart, get out, go away **7** get lost, vamoose

scathing 4 keen, tart **5** sharp **6** biting, brutal, savage **7** caustic, cutting, hostile, mordant, pointed, searing **8** incisive, stinging, virulent **9** ferocious, rancorous, scorching, trenchant, vitriolic, withering **10** lacerating **11** acrimonious, excoriating

scatter 3 sow **4** cast, flee, rout **5** strew, throw **6** dispel **8** disperse, sprinkle **9** broadcast, circulate, dissipate **10** distribute **11** disseminate

scatterbrained 4 rash, wild, zany **5** crazy, dizzy, giddy, nutty, silly **6** madcap, stupid **7** flighty, foolish **8** careless, heedless, reckless, unstable, unsteady **9** foolhardy, forgetful, frivolous, imprudent **11** birdbrained, empty-headed, harebrained **12** absent-minded, muddleheaded **13** irresponsible

scattered 6 random, spotty

7 diffuse **9** irregular **10** infrequent, occasional

scattering 6 sowing **7** casting **8** strewing **9** dispersal **10** dispersing, sprinkling **12** broadcasting, distribution **13** dissemination

scavenger 6 magpie **8** salvager **9** collector

scenario 4 book, idea, plan **6** scheme **7** concept, outline, summary **8** abstract, game plan, synopsis, teleplay **10** conception, manuscript, screenplay
 French: **6** precis

scene 3 act **4** fuss, part, show, site, spot, to-do, view **5** place, sight, vista **6** locale, region, survey, vision **7** display, episode, picture, scenery, setting **8** backdrop, division, locality, location, panorama, position, prospect, sequence **9** commotion, spectacle **10** background **11** whereabouts

scenery 4 sets, view **5** vista **7** terrain **9** backdrops, landscape, spectacle **11** backgrounds

Scenes from a Marriage
 director: **13** Ingmar Bergman
 cast: **10** Liv Ullmann **13** Bibi Andersson **15** Erland Josephson

scent 4 odor, path, wake, wind **5** aroma, smell, sniff, spoor, trace, track, trail **6** course, detect, inhale **7** bouquet, breathe, discern, essence, perfume, pursuit, suspect **9** aromatize, fragrance, get wind of, recognize **11** distinguish

scented 5 spicy **7** odorous, piquant, pungent **8** aromatic, fragrant, perfumed **9** odiferous **13** sweet-smelling

Scephrus
 father: **8** Tegeates
 brother: **5** Limon
 killed by: **5** Limon

Schaffner, Franklin
 director of: **6** Patton (Oscar) **15** Planet of the Apes

Schedius
 father: **7** Iphitus
 mother: **9** Hippolyte
 suitor of: **5** Helen

schedule 3 fix **4** book, list, plan, roll **5** fit in, slate, table **6** agenda **7** appoint, program, put down, set down **8** calendar **9** inventory, timetable

Scheele, Karl Wilhelm
 field: **9** chemistry
 nationality: **7** Swedish

discovered: 6 oxygen **8** chlorine **9** glycerine

Scheider, Roy
born: **8** Orange NJ
roles: **4** Jaws **11** All That Jazz, Blue Thunder, The Seven-Ups **14** Fifty-two Pickup **19** The French Connection

Schell, Maria
real name: **15** Margarete Schell
born: **6** Vienna **7** Austria
brother: **16** Maximilian Schell
roles: **8** Cimarron, Gervaise **11** End of Desire, White Nights **13** The Last Bridge **20** The Brothers Karamazov

Schell, Maximilian
born: **6** Vienna **7** Austria
sister: **11** Maria Schell
roles: **5** Julia **13** The Young Lions **19** Judgment at Nuremberg (Oscar) **21** The Man in the Glass Booth

scheme 3 map, way **4** plan, plot, ruse **5** cabal, chart, frame, means, shift, study **6** course, design, device, devise, layout, method, policy, sketch, system **7** complot, concoct, connive, drawing, network, outline, program, project, tactics **8** conspire, contrive, grouping, intrigue, maneuver, organize, strategy **9** machinate, procedure, stratagem **10** connivance, conspiracy **11** arrangement, contrivance, delineation, disposition, machination **12** organization

scheming 3 sly **4** arch, wily **6** artful, crafty, shrewd, tricky **7** cunning **8** slippery **9** conniving, designing, insidious **10** contriving, intriguing **11** calculating **13** Machiavellian

Schiller, (Johann) Friedrich von
author of: **8** Ode to Joy **9** Don Carlos **11** Maria Stuart, William Tell **17** The Bride of Messina **18** The Maiden of Orleans

schism 5 break, split **8** division **10** separation **14** disassociation

Schlegel family
characters in: **10** Howard's End
members: **5** Helen **8** Margaret, Theobald
author: **7** Forster

schlepp 3 lug **4** cart, haul, tote **5** carry **6** convey **9** transport

Schlesinger, Arthur M, Jr
author of: **13** A Thousand Days **15** The Age of Jackson **21** The Imperial Presidency **24** Robert Kennedy and His Times

Schlesinger, John
director of: **7** Darling **14** Midnight Cowboy (Oscar) **22** The Falcon and the Snowman

Schlesinger, Leon
creator/artist of: **9** Bugs Bunny

schmaltz 4 corn **14** sentimentalism, sentimentality

Schmeling, Max (Maxmillian Adolph Otto Siegfried)
nickname: **10** Black Uhlan
sport: **6** boxing
class: **11** heavyweight

Schneider, Romy
real name: **20** Rosemarie Albach-Retty
born: **6** Vienna **7** Austria
roles: **8** The Trial **11** The Cardinal **16** Boccaccio Seventy

Schoenberg, Arnold
born: **6** Vienna **7** Austria
composer of: **9** Erwartung **11** De Profundis, Expectation, Gurrelieder **12** The Lucky Hand **13** Moses and Aaron, Ode to Napoleon **14** Verklarte Nacht **16** Die Glucklich Hand, Resplendent Night **17** Transfigured Night **19** A Survivor from Warsaw, Pelleas and Melisande **26** The Book of the Hanging Gardens

Schoenius
father: **7** Athamas
mother: **8** Themisto
wife: **7** Clymene
daughter: **8** Atalanta

scholar 4 coed, sage **5** brain, grind, pupil **6** pundit, savant **7** egghead, learner, student, studier, wise man **8** bookworm, humanist, mandarin **9** collegian, schoolboy **10** schoolgirl **11** matriculant **12** intellectual **13** undergraduate

Scholar Gypsy, The
author: **13** Matthew Arnold

scholarly 6 humane **7** erudite, learned, liberal **8** academic, educated, informed, lettered, literate, well-read **12** intellectual

scholarship 5 grant **7** stipend **8** learning **9** education, endowment, erudition **12** intelligence, thoroughness **13** enlightenment

scholastic 8 academic, pedantic **9** pedagogic **11** educational **12** professorial **13** instructional

school 3 ism **4** view **5** bunch, crowd, faith, order, style, teach, train **6** belief, lyceum, method, system, theory **7** academy, college, educate, faction, thought **8** doctrine, instruct, seminary **9** institute **10** persuasion, university **12** denomination, kindergarten

schoolbook 3 abc **4** text **5** atlas **6** manual, primer, reader **7** grammar, lessons, speller

School for Scandal, The
author: **23** Richard Brinsley Sheridan
character: **5** Maria **6** Rowley **10** Lady Teazle **13** Joseph Surface, Lady Sneerwell **14** Charles Surface, Sir Peter Teazle **16** Sir Oliver Surface

School for Wives, The
author: **7** Moliere
character: **5** Agnes **6** Horace, Oronte **7** Enrique **8** Arnolphe **9** Chrysalde

schooling 5 drill **8** drilling, training **9** education **11** instruction, preparation **14** indoctrination

schoolmaster 4 head **5** tutor **7** dominie, pedagog, scholar, teacher **9** pedagogue, principal, professor **10** headmaster, instructor **12** disciplinarian
fish: **7** snapper
genus: **8** Lutianus
species: **6** apodus

Schubert, Franz Peter
born: **6** Vienna **7** Austria
composer of: **6** Little (symphony), Tragic (symphony No 4) **8** Sad Waltz **9** Rosamunde **11** Winterreise **12** Trout Quintet **13** Mourning Waltz **17** Die Schone Mullerin **18** Unfinished Symphony (No 8) **24** Death and the Maiden Quartet, Symphony of Heavenly Length

Schulz, Charles
creator/artist of: **7** Peanuts

Schuman, William
born: **9** New York NY
composer of: **8** Undertow **9** Credendum **14** The Mighty Casey **16** American Festival **18** New England Triptych

Schumann, Robert Alexander
born: **7** Germany, Zwickau
composer of: **6** Myrten, Spring (symphony No 1) **7** Rhenish (symphony No 3) **8** Arabeske, Carnival **9** Papillons **10** Novelettes

11 Blumenstuck, Butterflies, Nachtstucke, Nightpieces, Novelletten **12** Bunte Blatter, Dichterliebe, Flower Pieces, Kinderscenen, Kreisleriana, Motley Leaves **14** Fantasiestucke **16** David's Band Dances, Symphonic Studies **18** Davidsbundlertanze **19** Frauenliebe und Leben

Schwann, Theodor
field: **7** biology
nationality: **6** German
established: **10** cell theory

Schwarzenegger, Arnold
roles: **5** Twins **7** Red Heat **8** Commando, Predator, Red Sonja **11** Total Recall **13** The Terminator **15** Kindergarten Cop **17** Conan the Barbarian, Conan the Destroyer
wife: **12** Maria Shriver

Schweitzer, Albert
field: **8** medicine
worked in: **5** Gabon **6** Africa
founded: **17** Lambarene Hospital
awarded: **15** Nobel Peace Prize

Schwitters, Kurt
born: **7** Germany **8** Hannover
artwork: **7** Merzbau
collages called: **10** Merzbilden

science 3 art **5** skill **6** method **7** finesse **8** aptitude, facility **9** technique **10** discipline **11** acquirement
god of: **7** Mercury

scintilla 3 dot **4** atom, iota **5** shred, spark, speck, trace **7** glimmer **10** smithereen

scintillate 4 joke, snap **5** amuse, charm, flash, gleam, glint, shine, spark **7** glimmer, glisten, glitter, shimmer, sparkle, twinkle **9** coruscate **10** effervesce

scintillating 5 witty **6** bright, lively **8** animated, charming, dazzling **9** brilliant, ebullient, exuberant, sparkling **10** glittering **11** stimulating **12** effervescent

scion 3 son **4** heir, seed **5** child, issue **7** heiress, progeny **8** daughter, offshoot **9** offspring, posterity, successor **10** descendant **11** progeniture

Sciron
vocation: **6** robber
killed by: **7** Theseus

Scirophoria
also: **11** Skirophoria
origin: **5** Greek

event: **8** festival
honoring: **6** Athena

scissors 5 snips **6** blades, cutter, shears **7** clipper, snipper, trimmer
French: **8** secateur

scoff 4 jeer, mock, razz **5** flout, knock, taunt **6** deride, rail at, revile **7** condemn, laugh at, put down, run down **8** belittle, ridicule

Scofield, Paul
real name: **13** David Scofield
born: **7** England **14** Hurstpierpoint
roles: **8** King Lear **13** Sir Thomas More **17** A Man for All Seasons (Oscar)

scold 3 nag **5** chide, shrew **6** berate, carp at, nagger, rail at, rebuke, virago **7** censure, reprove, upbraid **9** castigate, criticize, dress down, reprehend, reprimand, termagant **10** complainer
Yiddish: **6** kvetch

scolding 7 chiding, reproof **8** berating, rebuking **9** reprimand, talking-to **10** admonition, upbraiding **11** castigation **12** admonishment **13** tongue-lashing

Scolosaurus
type: **8** dinosaur **10** ornithopod
location: **12** North America

sconce 11 candlestick **12** candleholder

scoop 4 bail, beat **5** clean, clear, gouge, ladle, spoon **6** burrow, dig out, dipper, hollow, shovel, trowel **7** dish out, lade out, lift out **8** excavate

scoop out 3 dig **5** gouge **8** excavate

scoot 3 run **4** dash, rush **6** scurry, sprint

Scooter
nickname of: **11** Phil Rizzuto

scope 3 aim **4** area, goal, rein, room, span, vent **5** field, force, grasp, range, reach **6** bounds, effect, margin, motive, spread, vision **7** bearing, compass, freedom, liberty, purpose, stretch **8** ambition, confines, latitude **9** extension, influence, intention **10** competence **11** application, destination **13** determination

scorch 3 dry **4** char, sear **5** parch, singe **6** dry out, scathe, wither **7** blacken **8** discolor **9** dehydrate

score, scores 3 cut, mar, run, tab, win **4** bill, debt, gain,

gash, goal, lots, make, mark, nick, slit **5** amass, count, facts, grade, hosts, judge, notch, point, slash, tally, truth **6** basket, charge, damage, deface, droves, groove, grudge, masses, pile up, strike, swarms, twenty **7** account, achieve, arrange, legions, reality, scratch, throngs **8** evaluate, incision, register **9** grievance **10** amount owed, difference, multitudes, obligation **11** orchestrate

scoria 4 slag **5** dross **6** cinder, refuse

scorn 5 spurn **6** ignore, rebuff, refuse, reject, slight **7** condemn, despise, disdain, mockery, repulse, sarcasm **8** contempt, derision, ridicule, scoffing, spit upon **9** arrogance, contumely, disregard, ostracize **10** look down on, opprobrium **11** haughtiness

scorned 7 derided, refused **8** despised, rebuffed, rejected, repulsed **9** disdained **10** deprecated, disparaged

scornful 6 lordly **7** cynical **8** arrogant, derisive, insolent, sardonic, scoffing, sneering **9** sarcastic **10** disdainful, ridiculing **11** disparaging **12** contemptuous, supercilious

Scorpio
symbol: **8** scorpion
planet: **4** Mars **5** Pluto
rules: **5** death **7** passion
born: **7** October **8** November

Scorpion 4 whip **7** scourge
constellation of: **8** Scorpius

Scorsese, Martin
director of: **10** After Hours, Raging Bull, Taxi Driver **11** Mean Streets **12** The Last Waltz

scotch 4 foil, kill, stop **5** crush, quash **6** thwart **7** destroy **8** confound, obstruct, sabotage, suppress **9** undermine **11** nip in the bud

scotch
type: **6** whisky **7** whiskey
origin: **8** Scotland
ingredient: **12** cereal grains
drink: **10** Scotch Mist **14** Highland Cooler
with amaretto: **9** Godfather
with cherry brandy: **12** Blood and Sand
with Drambuie: **9** Rusty Nail
with gin: **12** Barbary Coast
with vermouth: **6** Rob Roy **8** Affinity **10** Bobby Burns

Scotia
epithet of: **9** Aphrodite
means: **7** dark one

Scotland
  Roman name: 9 Caledonia
  capital: 9 Edinburgh
  largest city: 7 Glasgow
  others: 3 Ayr **4** Duns, Oban **5** Alloa, Banff, Brora, Burgh, Cupar, Ellon, Leith, Perth, Salen,
    Troon **6** Dundee, Girvan, Hawick **7** Airdrie, Alloway, Dunkeld, Falkirk, Frunock, Mallaig,
    Paisley, Renfrew **8** Aberdeen, Dumfries, Greenock, Hamilton, Kirkwall, Rothesay, Stirling
    9 Clydebank, Dumbarton, Greenlock, Inverness, Kirkcaldy, Peterhead, St Andrews **10** Coat-
    bridge, Kilmarnock, Motherwell **11** Dunfermline, Grangemouth
  school: 7 Glasgow **8** Aberdeen **9** Edinburgh **12** Saint Andrew's
  division: 3 Ayr **4** Bute, Fife, Ross **5** Angus, Banff, Moray, Nairn, Perth **6** Argyll, Lanark, Ork-
    ney **7** Berwick, Kinross, Lothian, Peebles, Renfrew, Selkirk, Wigtown **8** Aberdeen, Ayrshire,
    Cromarty, Dumfries, Roxburgh, Shetland, Stirling **9** Buteshire, Caithness, Dumbarton **10** Kin-
    cardine, Midlothian, Sutherland **11** Clackmannan, Kincudbight **12** Renfrewshire
    13 Stirlingshire
    kingdom: **8** Dalriada **11** Northumbria, Strathclyde
  government: 13 United Kingdom
  measure: 3 cop **4** boll, cran, fall, mile, peck, pint, rood, rope, span **5** crane, lippy **6** audlet,
    davach, firlot, lippie, noggin **7** chalder, choppin **8** mutchkin, stimpart, stimpert **9** particate,
    shaftment, shathmont
  monetary unit: 3 ecu **4** demy, doit, lion, mark, rial, ryal **5** bodle, broad, groat, plack, rider,
    turne **6** bawbee, folles **7** unicorn **8** atchison, hardhead **9** halfpenny **11** bonnetpiece
  weight: 4 boll, drop **5** trone **6** bushel
  island: 3 Rum **4** Aran, Bute, Eigg, Fair, Inch, Iona, Jura, Lona, Muck, Mull, Rhum, Skye
    5 Arran, Barra, Islay, Lewis **6** Harris, Orkney, Staffa **7** St Kilda **8** Berneray, Cumbraes, Hebri-
    des, Shetland **9** North Uist, South Uist
  lake/loch: 3 Awe, Dee, Lin, Tay **4** Earn, Fyne, Gair, Gare, Linn, Ness, Oich, Ryan, Sloy
    5 Duich, Leven, Lochy, Lough, Morar, Maree, Nevis **6** Laggan, Linnhe, Lomond **7** Katrine,
    Rannoch, St Mary's
  mountain: 4 Hope **5** Attow, Dearg, Nevis, Tinto, Wyvis **7** Cheviot, Macdhui, Merrick **8** Gram-
    pian **9** Ben Lomond, Cairngorm, Highlands, Trossachs
    hills: **5** Ochil **6** Calton, Sidlaw **7** Cheviot
  highest point: 8 Ben Nevis
  river: 3 Ayr, Dee, Don, Esk, Tay **4** Doon, Glen, Nith, Norn, Spey **5** Afton, Annan, Clyde,
    Forth, Garry, North, Tweed, Ythan **6** Affric, Teviot, Tummel **7** Deveron **8** Findhorn
  sea: 5 Irish, North **8** Atlantic, Hebrides
  physical feature:
    bay: **5** Scapa
    canal: **10** Caledonian
    channel: **5** Minch, North
    firth: **3** Tay **4** Kyle, Lorn **5** Clyde, Forth, Lorne, Moray **6** Linnhe, Solway **7** Comarty, Dor-
      noch **8** Pentland
    glen: **8** Glen More **9** Great Glen
    moor: **7** Rannoch
    valley: **8** Trossach
  people: 4 Gael, Pict, Scot **5** Norse
    artist: **7** Raeburn
    author: **5** Burns, Scott **6** Dunbar **7** Barbour, Douglas **8** Henryson **9** Stevenson **10** Conan-
      Doyle, MacDiarmid, Macpherson
    economist: **5** Smith
    historian: **7** Carlyle
    inventor: **4** Bell
    king: **5** David, James **6** Duncan **7** Kenneth, Macbeth, Malcolm, Stuarts, William **9** Alex-
      ander **14** Robert the Bruce
    philosopher: **4** Hume
    prime minister: **9** Macdonald, MacMillan **11** Douglas-Home
    prince: **19** Bonnie Prince Charlie
    queen: **4** Mary **13** Saint Margaret
    religious leader: **8** John Knox
    scientist: **7** Fleming
  language: 4 Erse **6** Celtic, Gaelic, Keltic, Lallan **7** English, Lalland
  religion: 12 Episcopalian, Presbyterian **13** Roman Catholic
  place:
    abbey: **5** Kelso **7** Melrose **8** Dryburgh, Jedburgh
    castle: **8** Stirling **9** Edinburgh **11** Eilean Donan
    church/kirk: **7** St Giles **11** St Cuthbert's
    royal residence: **8** Balmoral
    Scott's home: **10** Abbotsford
    street: **7** Prince's **9** Royal Mile **11** Sauchiehall

(*continued*)

Scotland (*continued*)
  feature:
    bird: **3** bae, cae **4** hern, muir, smeu **6** grouse, smeuth, snabby **7** jackdaw **8** throstle **9** swinepipe
    clothing: **4** kilt **6** tartan **12** Harris tweeds **13** Shetland knits **15** Fair Isle sweater
    dance: **3** bob **4** reel **7** walloch **9** ecossaise **10** petronella **11** strathsprey **12** gilliecallum **13** Highland fling
    game: **4** golf
    monster: **6** Nessie **8** Loch Ness
    musical instrument: **7** bagpipe
    symbol: **7** thistle
  food:
    bread: **5** scone
    cheese: **7** crowdie
    dish: **6** haggis **12** finnan haddie **15** kippered herring
    drink: **12** Scotch whisky
    soup: **11** cock-a-leekie

Scott, George C
  born: **6** Wise VA
  wife: **14** Trish Van Devere **15** Colleen Dewhurst
  roles: **4** Rage **6** Patton (Oscar, refused) **8** Jane Eyre **16** The New Centurions **18** The Day of the Dolphin

Scott, Sir Walter
  author of: **6** Rob Roy **7** Ivanhoe, Marmion **8** The Abbot, Waverley **10** Kenilworth **11** The Talisman **12** Guy Mannering, Old Mortality, The Antiquary **14** Quentin Durward **16** The Lady of the Lake **20** The Bride of Lammermoor, The Heart of Midlothian **23** The Lay of the Last Minstrel

Scottish Mythology
  spirit/horse: **6** kelpie

scoundrel 3 cad, cur **5** crook, knave, rogue, scamp, thief **6** rascal, rotter, varlet, weasel **7** bounder, ruffian, sharper, varmint, villain **8** scalawag, swindler, turncoat **9** miscreant, trickster **10** blackguard, copperhead, mountebank, ne'er-do-well **11** fourflusher, rapscallion **12** carpetbagger

scoundrelly 3 low **4** mean **7** debased **8** rascally **10** degenerate, despicable, villainous **12** contemptible, disreputable **13** reprehensible

Scoundrel Time
  author: **14** Lillian Hellman

scour 4 buff, comb, rake, scan **5** scrub, shine **6** abrade, polish, scrape **7** burnish, cleanse, ransack, rummage **8** brighten, traverse

scourge, Scourge 3 rod **4** bane, beat, cane, flog, lash, whip **5** birch, blast, curse, flail, strap **6** punish, switch, terror, thrash **7** censure, chasten **8** chastise, scorpion, vexation **9** castigate, excoriate **10** affliction, discipline, flagellate **11** troublement **13** cat-o'-nine-tails

scout 3 spy **4** case **5** guide, pilot **6** escort, spy out, survey **7** lookout, observe **8** outrider, point man, vanguard **9** recruiter **11** reconnoiter **13** reconnoiterer

scowl 4 pout **5** frown, glare, lower **6** glower **7** grimace

scrabble 3 paw **4** claw, rake **5** climb **6** drudge, jostle, scrape, scrawl **7** clamber, grapple, scratch **8** struggle

scram 3 out **4** scat, shoo **5** be off, leave **6** beat it, begone, depart, get out, go away **7** get lost, vamoose **10** make tracks

scramble 3 run, vie **4** race, rush **5** clash, fight, mix up, scrap, upset **6** battle, combat, engage, garble, jostle, jumble, mess up, scurry, strive, tussle **7** collide, confuse, disturb, scatter, scuffle, shuffle **8** disorder, struggle, unsettle **9** scrimmage **10** disarrange, free-for-all **11** competition, disorganize

scramble up 5 climb, mount, scale **7** clamber

scrap 3 bit, dab, jot, row **4** atom, drop, iota, junk, spat **5** brawl, crumb, fight, grain, melee, speck, trace, trash **6** fracas, morsel, refuse, ruckus, sliver **7** abandon, glimmer, minimum, modicum, quarrel, snippet **8** brouhaha, fraction, fragment, jettison, molecule, particle, squabble **10** free-for-all, smattering, sprinkling

scrapbook 5 album **9** portfolio **11** memorabilia, miscellanea

scrape 3 dig **4** buff, gash, mark, rasp, save, skin **5** amass, clean, fight, glean, gouge, grate, graze, grind, plane, run-in, score, scour, scuff, stint **6** abrade, bruise, forage, gather, groove, obtain, pick up, plight, scrimp, secure, smooth, tussle **7** acquire, burnish, dilemma, procure, rub hard, scratch, scuffle, straits **8** abrasion **9** economize, tight spot **10** difficulty **11** predicament **13** confrontation

scratch 3 cut, mar, rub **4** claw, etch, gash, nick, omit, rasp **5** dig at, erase, grate, graze, grind, score **6** cancel, delete, incise, remove, rub out, scrape, scrawl, streak, strike **7** blemish, blot out, exclude, expunge, rule out **8** abrasion, cross out, lacerate, scribble, withdraw **9** eliminate **10** laceration

scratchy 5 rough **6** coarse **7** bristly, prickly **9** irritated **10** irritating

scrawl 4 draw **5** write **6** doodle **7** scratch, writing **8** scrabble, scribble, squiggle **10** penmanship **11** handwriting

scrawniness 8 lankness, leanness, slimness, thinness **10** skinniness, slightness **11** slenderness

scrawny 4 bony, lank, lean, puny **5** drawn, gaunt, lanky, runty, spare **6** sinewy, skinny, wasted **7** angular, scraggy, spindly, stunted **8** rawboned, skeletal **9** emaciated, fleshless **10** attenuated, undersized **11** underweight

screak 4 rasp **5** grate, grind **6** shriek, squeak **7** screech

scream 4 howl, loud, roar, wail, yell, yelp, yowl **5** shout, whine **6** bellow, cry out, holler, outcry, shriek, squawk, squeal **7** screech **11** lamentation

screech 3 cry **4** howl, rasp **6** screak, scream, shriek **9** caterwaul

screen 3 see, web **4** cull, mask, mesh, rate, show, sift, sort, veil, view **5** class, cloak, cover, eject, films, grade, grate, group, guard, order, shade, sieve **6** buffer, cinema, defend, filter, mantle, movies, secure, shield, shroud, sifter, size up, strain, winnow **7** arrange, conceal, curtain, defense, discard, lattice, present, preview, project, protect, secrete, shelter, shutter, weed out **8** colander, coverage, evaluate, jalousie, separate, strainer, withhold **9** eliminate, partition, safeguard **10** protection **11** concealment

screw 4 bolt, join, knot, turn, warp **5** clamp, exact, force, gnarl, rivet, twist, wrest, wring **6** adjust, attach, deform, driver, extort, fasten, garble, wrench **7** contort, distort, pervert, squeeze, tighten **8** fastener, misshape **9** propeller

screwball 3 nut **4** kook **5** flake, freak **6** looney **7** lunatic **8** crackpot **9** character, eccentric

screwdriver
   type: 6 rachet **11** spiral-drive **12** Phillips-head

screwy 3 odd **4** daft **5** batty, dotty, flaky, funny, kinky, kooky, nutty, queer, wacky, weird **6** weirdo **7** oddball **8** peculiar **9** eccentric **10** unbalanced

Scriabin, Aleksandr (Scriabine, Skryabin)
   born: 6 Moscow, Russia
   composer of: 7 Mystery **10** Prometheus **12** Vers la flamme **13** Poem of Ecstasy, The Divine Poem, The Poem of Fire

scribble 4 tear **5** squib **6** doodle, scrawl **7** scratch **8** squiggle **9** pull apart
   fiber: 4 wool
   procedure: 7 carding

scribe, Scribe 3 cut **4** mark, tool **5** clerk, score **6** author, copier, penman, writer **7** copyist, teacher **8** recorder **9** archivist, scrivener, secretary **10** amanuensis, translator **12** newspaperman, stenographer **13** calligraphist

Biblical: 4 Ezra **6** Esdras
French dramatist: 8 Augustin
Palestinian: 5 sofer **6** sopher

scribe of gods 5 Thoth

scrimp 4 save **5** hoard, pinch, skimp, stint **8** begrudge **9** be sparing **12** pinch pennies

scrimping 6 frugal **7** sparing **10** economical **11** economizing **12** cheeseparing **15** pinching pennies

scrip 5 paper **8** document **11** certificate

scripsit 7 he wrote **8** she wrote

script 4 book, hand **5** lines, score **6** dialog **7** cursive **8** dialogue, libretto, longhand, scenario **10** manuscript, penmanship **11** calligraphy, chirography, handwriting

Scriptures, the 5 Bible **6** the Law, oracle **8** holy writ, the Bible, the Torah **10** the Gospels **11** The Good Book **12** New Testament, Old Testament, the Word of God **13** the Pentateuch, the Septuagint **14** sacred writings

scroll of the Torah
   Hebrew: 11 Sepher Torah

Scrooge, Ebenezer
   character in: 15 A Christmas Carol
   author: 7 Dickens

scrub 4 swab **5** brush, scour **8** scouring **9** brushwood, scrubbing

scrubby 4 base **6** brushy **7** stunted **8** inferior **10** undersized

scrumptious 5 juicy, tasty **6** savory, tender **8** luscious, pleasant, pleasing **9** agreeable, delicious, enjoyable, flavorful, succulent, toothsome **10** appetizing, delectable, delightful, flavorsome **13** mouth-watering

scruple 3 shy **4** balk, care, halt **5** demur, pause, qualm, waver **6** blench, ethics, falter **7** anxiety, concern, refrain **8** hesitate **9** fluctuate, misgiving, principle **10** conscience, hesitation **11** compunction, fearfulness, uncertainty **12** apprehension, doubtfulness, protestation **13** squeamishness **17** conscientiousness

Scruples
   author: 12 Judith Krantz

scrupulous 5 exact **6** honest **7** careful, dutiful, precise, upright **8** cautious, exacting, sedulous **9** honorable **10** deliberate, fastidious, metic-

ulous, principled **11** painstaking, punctilious **13** conscientious

scrupulousness 4 care **5** pains **9** exactness **14** meticulousness **17** conscientiousness

scrutinize 4 scan **5** probe, study **6** peruse, search, survey **7** explore, inspect, observe **11** investigate

scrutiny 5 study, watch **7** inquiry, perusal **9** attention **10** inspection **11** examination **12** surveillance **13** investigation

scuffle 3 row **4** spar **5** brawl, clash, fight, melee, scrap **6** fracas, jostle, rumpus, tussle **8** squabble, struggle **9** commotion, imbroglio **10** donnybrook, free-for-all

sculpsit 10 he carved it **11** she carved it **12** he engraved it **13** she engraved it **14** he sculptured it **15** she sculptured it

sculptor 6 artist, carver, caster, imager, molder **7** marbler, modeler **8** chiseler, engraver
   constellation: 19 Apparatus Sculptoris
   French: 5 Rodin
   Greek: 7 Phidias **10** Praxiteles
   Irish-American: 12 Saint-Gaudens
   Italian: 7 Cellini **12** Michelangelo
   tool: 6 chisel, graver **7** spatula **9** ebauchoir

sculpture 3 cut **4** bust, cast, head, work **5** cameo, carve, erode, model, mould **6** chisel, relief, statue **7** carving, erosion, faience **8** intaglio, statuary **9** cloissone, medallion, statuette
   medium: 4 clay **5** china, stone **6** bronze, enamel, marble **7** ceramic **9** porcelain **10** terra cotta **11** earthenware

scum 4 film, slag **5** crust, dregs, dross, trash **6** rabble, refuse **7** deposit, rubbish, surface **8** riffraff

scurrility 5 abuse **8** rudeness **9** indecency, obscenity, profanity **13** offensiveness, salaciousness

scurrilous 3 low **5** gross **6** coarse, vulgar **7** obscene **8** churlish, derisive, indecent, reviling **9** insulting, offensive, shameless **10** derogatory, detracting, indelicate, slanderous **11** disparaging, foulmouthed **12** contemptuous

scurry 3 hie **4** race, rush,

skim **5** haste, hurry, scoot, speed **6** bustle, hasten, hustle, spring **7** rushing, scamper, scuttle **8** hurrying, scooting, scramble **9** confusion, dispersal **10** scattering

scurvy 3 low **4** base, mean, vile **6** shabby **7** ignoble **9** worthless **10** despicable **12** contemptible, dishonorable

scuttle 4 sink **5** abort, hurry, scrap, speed, wreck **6** hasten, scurry **7** destroy, discard, scamper **8** dispatch, scramble

scuttlebutt 4 talk **5** rumor **6** gossip **7** hearsay, prattle, scandal **8** chitchat

Scylaceus
origin: **6** Lycian
ally of: **7** Trojans
death by: **7** stoning

Scylla
form: **5** nymph **7** monster
location: **3** sea **16** Straits of Messina **20** Whirlpool of Charybdis
father: **7** Phorcys
mother: **6** Hecate
loved by: **8** Poseidon
rival: **10** Amphitrite

Scyphius
first: **5** horse
created by: **8** Poseidon

sea 3 bay, ton **4** deep, gulf, host, lake, leap, lots, main, mass, slew, wave **5** bight, flock, flood, ocean, scads, spate, surge, swarm, swell, waves **6** legion, roller, scores, waters **7** breaker **9** abundance, multitude, profusion
French: **3** mer
god of: **5** Aegir, Memir **6** Nereus, Triton **7** Glaucus, Neptune, Phorcys, Proteus **8** Poseidon **9** Asphalius
goddess of: **3** Ino, Ran **6** Graeae, Graiae, Matuta **8** Dictynna, Menannan **9** Leucothea **10** Amphitrite

Sea, the Sea, The
author: **11** Iris Murdoch

Sea Around Us, The
author: **13** Rachel L Carson

seaboard 5 coast **9** shoreline

Seaborg, Glen Theodore
field: **7** physics
worked with: **14** actinide series **19** transuranic elements
headed: **3** AEC **22** Atomic Energy Commission
awarded: **10** Nobel Prize

seacoast 5 beach, coast, shore **7** seaside **8** littoral **9** coastland, coastline, shoreline, waterside
French: **4** cote
Italian: **4** lido **7** riviera

seafarers 5 salts **7** sailors, seadogs **8** mariners

Seagull, The
author: **12** Anton Chekhov
character: **5** Masha **6** Polina **10** Pyotr Sorin **11** Yevgeny Dorn **12** Ilya Shamraev, Irina Arkadin **13** Boris Trigorin, Nina Zaretchyn **16** Semyon Medvedenko **17** Konstantin Treplev

Seah 15 Biblical measure

Sea Hawk, The
director: **13** Michael Curtiz
cast: **10** Errol Flynn **11** Claude Rains, Donald Crisp **14** Brenda Marshall
score: **21** Erich Wolfgang Korngold

seal 2 OK **3** dam, fix **4** cork, lock, mark, plug, shut, stop **5** brand, close, stamp **6** accept, affirm, emblem, fasten, figure, ratify, secure, settle, shut up, signet, stop up, symbol, verify **7** approve, certify, confirm, endorse, imprint **8** colophon, conclude, fastener, hallmark, insignia, sanction, validate **9** determine, establish, trademark **10** impression **12** authenticate
Latin: **10** imprimatur

seal
young: **3** pup
group of: **3** pod

sea lion
young: **3** pup

seam 3 gap **4** line, lode, mark, scar, vein **5** break, chink, cleft, crack, joint, layer, notch **6** breach, furrow, incise, suture **7** crevice, fissure, joining, opening, rupture, stratum, wrinkle **8** junction, juncture **9** interface

seaman 3 gob, tar **4** hand, mate, salt **5** bosun, middy **6** lubber, merman, sailor, seadog **7** mariner **9** boatswain **10** bluejacket, midshipman

seamark 5 light **6** beacon, pharos, signal **10** lighthouse, watchtower

sea monster 6 dragon **9** Leviathan

seamstress 10 dressmaker
French: **9** midinette **10** couturiere

seamy 3 raw **4** dark **5** dirty, nasty, rough **6** coarse, sordid **7** squalid, unclean **10** unpleasant **11** unwholesome **12** disagreeable

Sea of Grass, The
author: **13** Conrad Richter

sear 4 burn, char, scar **5** blast,

singe, steel **6** harden, scorch **7** blister **9** cauterize **10** caseharden

search 4 comb, drag, fish, hunt, look, seek, sift **5** check, frisk, probe, quest, rifle, scour, snoop, study **6** survey, tracer **7** dragnet, examine, explore, inquiry, inspect, pry into, pursuit, ransack, rummage **8** overhaul, scrutiny **10** inspection, scrutinize **11** examination, exploration **13** investigation

Search, The
director: **13** Fred Zinnemann
cast: **9** Ivan Jandl **13** Aline MacMahon **14** Jarmila Novotna **15** Montgomery Clift
setting: **6** Berlin

Searchers, The
director: **8** John Ford
cast: **8** Ward Bond **9** John Wayne, Vera Miles **11** Natalie Wood **13** Jeffrey Hunter

searching 4 dour, keen, nosy **5** sharp **6** prying, shrewd, snoopy **7** curious, groping **8** exacting, piercing, rigorous, thorough **9** observant, quizzical, unsparing **11** inquisitive, penetrating **13** investigative

Seascape
author: **11** Edward Albee

seashore 5 beach, coast

seasick 3 ill **5** barfy, dizzy, faint, giddy, woozy **6** queasy **8** qualmish, vomitous **9** nauseated, squeamish **11** vertiginous

seasickness
French: **8** mal de mer

seaside 5 beach, coast, shore **9** shoreline

season 3 age, dry **4** fall, lace, tame, term **5** adapt, color, drill, inure, prime, ripen, shape, spell, spice, stage, train **6** accent, autumn, finish, flavor, inform, leaven, mature, mellow, period, refine, soften, spring, summer, temper, winter **7** enhance, enliven, prepare, quarter, stretch **8** accustom, duration, heighten, interval, ornament, practice **9** condition, cultivate, embellish **10** discipline

seasoned 6 herbed, inured, salted, spiced **7** veteran **8** flavored, hardened, peppered **9** competent, qualified **10** acclimated, accustomed, habituated **11** experienced **12** familiarized

seasoning 4 dill, herb, mace, sage, salt, zest **5** aging, basil, clove, gusto, onion, spice, thyme **6** drying, garlic, ginger, nutmeg, pepper, relish **7** oregano, paprika, parsley **8** allspice, cinnamon, marjoram, practice, ripening, rosemary, training **9** condiment, flavoring **10** maturation **11** orientation, preparation **15** familiarization

Season in Hell, A
   author: **13** Arthur Rimbaud

seasons
   god of: **9** Vertumnus
   goddess of: **4** Hour **5** Horae

seat 3 box, hub **4** axis, core, home, rump, site, sofa **5** abode, bench, chair, couch, croup, divan, fanny, heart, house, locus, place **6** behind, bottom, center, locale, settle **7** address, capital, cushion, habitat, housing, nucleus, rear end, situate **8** backside, buttocks, derriere, domicile, dwelling, haunches, location, quarters **9** posterior, residence **10** incumbency, membership **12** hindquarters

seat of justice 5 bench, court **8** tribunal **9** judiciary **10** courthouse

Seattle
   baseball team: **8** Mariners
   basketball team:
      11 Supersonics
   bay: **7** Elliott
   football team: **8** Seahawks
   lake: **10** Washington
   landmark: **11** Space Needle
   site of: **10** World's Fair
   sound: **5** Puget

Sea Wolf, The
   author: **10** Jack London

Sebastian
   character in: **12** Twelfth
      Night
   author: **11** Shakespeare

Seberg, Jean
   born: **14** Marshalltown IA
   husband: **10** Romain Gary
   roles: **6** Lilith **7** Airport
      9 Saint Joan **8** Breathless
      16 Bonjour Tristesse

Secchi, Angelo
   field: **9** astronomy
   nationality: **7** Italian
   classified: **5** stars

secede 4 quit **5** leave **6** resign, retire **7** forsake **8** withdraw **12** disaffiliate

secession 10 separation, withdrawal **14** disaffiliation

seclude 4 hide **6** retire **7** isolate **8** separate **9** sequester **10** dissociate

secluded 6 covert, cut off, lonely, remote, shut in **7** private **8** closeted, confined, isolated, shut away, solitary **9** reclusive, sheltered, unvisited, withdrawn **10** cloistered **11** out-of-the-way, sequestered **12** unfrequented

seclusion 5 exile **6** asylum, hiding **7** retreat **8** cloister, hideaway, solitude **9** hermitage, isolation, reclusion, sanctuary **10** quarantine, retirement, withdrawal **11** concealment **13** sequestration

second 3 aid **4** abet, back, help, wink **5** agent, favor, flash, jiffy, other, proxy, trice **6** assist, back up, deputy, fill-in, helper, minute, moment, uphold **7** advance, another, endorse, further, instant, one more, outdone, promote, stand by, stand-in, support **8** advocate, delegate, exceeded, inferior **9** alternate, assistant, attendant, encourage, surpassed, twinkling **10** additional, lieutenant, substitute, understudy **11** alternating, subordinate **14** representative
   abbreviation: **1** s **3** sec

secondary 5 lower, minor, other **6** backup, lesser **7** smaller **8** inferior, mediocre, middling **9** alternate, ancillary, auxiliary, following, resultant **10** consequent, subsequent, subsidiary **11** subordinate

second childhood 6 dotage **8** senility

secondhand 4 used **8** indirect **10** derivative

second-in-command 6 deputy **8** adjutant **9** assistant **10** lieutenant **13** vice president

second-rate 3 bad **4** poor, so-so **5** cheap, tacky **6** shabby **7** average **8** everyday, inferior, mediocre, middling **9** imperfect **10** inadequate, outclassed, pedestrian **11** commonplace, substandard **15** undistinguished

Second Sex, The
   author: **16** Simone de
      Beauvoir

second-story man 5 thief **6** robber **7** burglar **9** cracksman **10** cat burglar

second string 4 subs **5** bench **11** substitutes

second team 5 bench **11** substitutes

secrecy 6 hiding **7** mystery, privacy, private, silence, stealth **8** muteness, solitude **9** closeness, seclusion **10** covertness **11** concealment, furtiveness **13** sequestration

15 clandestineness, confidentiality, underhandedness **17** surreptitiousness **19** uncommunicativeness

secret 3 key, mum **4** dark **6** arcane, covert, enigma, hidden, mystic, occult, puzzle, recipe, unseen **7** formula, furtive, mystery, private, unknown **8** discreet, esoteric, hush-hush, secluded, stealthy **9** concealed, disguised, invisible, secretive **10** confidence, mysterious, undercover, unrevealed **11** camouflaged, clandestine, undisclosed, unpublished **12** confidential, unrevealable **13** surreptitious

Secret Agent
   character: **9** John Drake
   cast: **15** Patrick McGoohan
   theme: **14** Secret Agent Man

secretary 4 aide, desk **5** clerk **6** scribe **7** officer **8** recorder **10** amanuensis **12** stenographer
   French: **10** escritoire

secret council 8 conclave

secrete 4 hide, veil **5** cache, cloak, cover, stash **6** screen, shroud **7** conceal, curtain **8** disguise

secretive 3 mum, sly **4** mute **6** covert, silent **7** cryptic, evasive, furtive, laconic, private **8** discreet, reserved, reticent, stealthy, taciturn **9** enigmatic, withdrawn **10** mysterious **11** tight-lipped, underhanded, unrevealing **13** surreptitious **15** uncommunicative

secretiveness 7 mystery, stealth **9** reticence **11** furtiveness **14** inscrutability, mysteriousness **19** uncommunicativeness

Secret Life of Walter Mitty, The
   author: **12** James Thurber

sect 4 camp, cult **7** faction **8** division **10** persuasion **11** affiliation **12** denomination

sectarian 6 narrow **7** limited **8** clannish **9** exclusive, parochial **10** provincial, restricted

section 4 area, part, side, unit, ward, zone **5** piece, range, share, slice **6** region, sample, sphere **7** chapter, cutting, measure, passage, portion, segment, terrain **8** district, division, province, specimen, vicinity **9** allotment, increment, territory **10** department, proportion **11** installment **12** neighborhood

sector 4 area, zone **7** theater **8** district

secular 3 lay 4 laic 6 carnal 7 earthly, fleshly, mundane, profane, sensual, worldly 8 material, temporal 9 nonsacred 11 nonclerical 12 nonreligious, nonspiritual 17 nonecclesiastical

secundum 11 according to

secure 3 get, set 4 bind, easy, safe, sure 5 fixed, tight 6 at ease, defend, ensure, fasten, immune, insure, obtain 7 acquire, assured, certain, protect, shelter, tie down 8 absolute, carefree, composed, defended, definite, in the bag, positive, surefire 9 confident, guarantee, protected, reassured, safeguard, sheltered 10 guaranteed 11 impregnable 12 invulnerable, unassailable, unattackable, unthreatened

securities 5 bonds, title 6 stocks 12 certificates

security 4 bond, care, hope, keep 5 faith, trust 6 guards, pledge, police, safety, surety, troops 7 defense, deposit, promise, support 8 reliance, sureness, warranty 9 assurance, certainty, guarantee 10 collateral, confidence, conviction, protection, safeguards 11 maintenance, safekeeping 12 absoluteness, decisiveness, definiteness, positiveness, preservation

sedate 4 calm, cool 5 grave, quiet, sober, staid, still 6 poised, serene, solemn, steady 7 serious, subdued 8 composed, decorous, reserved 9 collected, dignified, impassive, unexcited, unruffled 10 cool-headed 11 levelheaded 13 imperturbable 15 undemonstrative

sedateness 7 decorum, dignity, gravity, reserve 8 calmness 9 composure, soberness, solemnity 11 impassivity, seriousness

sedative 6 easing, opiate 7 anodyne, calming 8 allaying, lenitive, narcotic, relaxing, soothing 9 analgesic, assuasive, calmative, composing, mitigator, soporific 10 comforting, palliative 11 alleviative 12 tranquilizer 13 tranquilizing

sedentary 5 fixed, inert, still 6 seated 7 resting, sitting 8 inactive, unmoving 9 quiescent 10 stationary, unstirring

sedge 4 reed 5 grass 10 marsh grass

sediment 4 lees, scum, slag 5 dregs, dross, waste 6 debris,

sludge 7 grounds, remains, residue 8 leavings 9 settlings

sedition 6 mutiny, revolt 7 treason 8 defiance, uprising 9 rebellion 10 disloyalty, insurgency, subversion, unruliness 11 lawlessness 12 disobedience, insurrection 14 rebelliousness, subversiveness

Sedley, Amelia and Joseph characters in: 10 Vanity Fair author: 9 Thackeray

seduce 4 lure, ruin 5 abuse, charm, tempt 6 allure, defile, entice, ravish 7 attract, conquer, corrupt, debauch, deprave, pervert, violate, win over 8 deflower, disgrace, dishonor, persuade 9 captivate

seducer 3 cad 4 wolf 5 letch, Romeo 7 defiler, Don Juan, playboy 8 Casanova, Lothario, lover-boy, ravisher, violater 9 corrupter, debaucher, womanizer 10 deflowerer 11 philanderer 12 heartbreaker **French:** 4 roue

seductive 4 sexy 8 alluring, charming, enticing, tempting 9 beguiling, disarming 10 attractive, bewitching, come-hither, enchanting, voluptuous 11 captivating, provocative

seductress 4 vamp 5 siren 7 charmer, Jezebel, Lorelei, mantrap 9 temptress 11 adventuress, enchantress **French:** 7 cocotte 11 femme fatale

sedulous 6 dogged 8 diligent, thorough 9 assiduous, steadfast 10 determined, persistent 11 industrious, painstaking, persevering 13 conscientious, indefatigable

sedulousness 4 zeal 8 industry, tenacity 9 assiduity, diligence 11 persistence 12 perseverance

see 3 dig, eye, spy, woo 4 date, espy, know, meet, mind, spot, view 5 court, grasp, sight, visit, watch 6 attend, behold, descry, escort, fathom, notice, regard, survey 7 consult, discern, glimpse, observe, picture, realize, receive, undergo, witness 8 conceive, consider, discover, envision, meditate, perceive, register, ruminate 9 accompany, apprehend, ascertain, determine, encounter, entertain, interview, recognize, visualize 10 appreciate, comprehend, experience, understand 11 contemplate, distinguish **Latin:** 4 vide

see above **Latin:** 9 vide supra

see after **Latin:** 8 vide post

see as above, see as stated above **Latin:** 11 vide ut supra

see before **Latin:** 8 vide ante

see below **Latin:** 9 vide infra

seed 3 pit, sow 4 germ 5 basis, grain, heirs, issue, ovule, plant, stone 6 embryo, origin, source 7 progeny 8 children 9 beginning, offspring, posterity 11 descendants

seedy 4 worn 5 dingy, faded, lousy, mangy, ratty, spent, tacky 6 scuffy, shabby 7 haggard, sickish, squalid 8 slovenly 10 threadbare 11 debilitated

see eye to eye 5 agree 6 concur 11 be of one mind

see fit 5 deign 6 choose, please

see further **Latin:** 8 vide post

seek 3 try 4 hunt 5 court, essay, trace 6 demand, invite, pursue 7 attempt, examine, explore, inspect, request, solicit, venture 8 endeavor 9 undertake 10 scrutinize 11 investigate

seek out 4 find 6 pursue 7 embrace, look for, solicit

seek proof 4 test 6 try out 7 analyze, examine 8 research 10 experiment 11 investigate

seem 4 look 6 appear

seeming 7 evident, obvious, surface 8 apparent, presumed, putative, supposed 10 ostensible 11 superficial

seemly 3 due 5 right 6 decent, polite, proper 7 correct, fitting, prudent, refined 8 becoming, decorous, suitable, tasteful, well-bred 9 befitting, courteous 10 acceptable, felicitous 11 appropriate 12 conventional **French:** 11 comme il faut

seep 4 drip, leak, ooze, soak 7 diffuse, dribble, suffuse, trickle 8 permeate 9 penetrate

seepage 4 ooze 5 flour, issue 7 leakage, outflow 9 discharge, dribbling, secretion, trickling

seer 4 sage 5 augur 6 medium, oracle 7 diviner, prophet, psychic 8 conjurer, sorcerer 9 sorceress, stargazer 10 astrologer, soothsayer 11 clair-

voyant, necromancer
13 fortuneteller
14 prognosticator

seesaw 5 waver **6** teeter **9** alternate, fluctuate, up-and-down, vacillate **12** teeter-totter

seethe 4 boil, brew, cook, fume, rage, rant, rave, roil, stew **5** churn, storm **6** blow up, bubble, simmer **7** bluster, smolder

seething 3 mad **7** boiling **8** agitated, bubbling, frenzied **10** distraught

see through 3 get **6** detect, effect, finish **7** achieve, execute, perform **8** carry out, complete, conclude **9** catch onto, figure out, penetrate **10** comprehend, understand

Segal, Erich
    author of: **9** Love Story **12** Oliver's Story **16** Man Woman and Child

Segal, George
    born: **9** New York NY
    roles: **11** Blume in Love, Where's Poppa? **13** A Touch of Class **18** Fun with Dick and Jane **25** Who's Afraid of Virginia Woolf?

segment 3 leg **4** part **5** cut up, piece, stage **6** cleave **7** disjoin, portion, section, split up **8** disunite, division, separate **9** increment **11** installment

segmented 5 cut up **7** split up **9** sectioned, separated

segregate 6 cut off, detach, divide **7** divorce, isolate, seclude, sort out **8** disunite, insulate, separate **9** sequester **10** disconnect, quarantine

segue
    music: **21** continue without a break

seine 3 net **4** drag, fish **5** trawl **7** dragnet

seism 5 quake, shock **6** tremor **8** tremblor, upheaval **10** earthquake

seize 3 bag, nab **4** grab, read **5** catch, glean, grasp, pinch, pluck, usurp **6** arrest, clutch, collar, gather, snatch **7** capture, embrace, impound, possess, utilize **8** arrogate **9** apprehend, overpower, overwhelm **10** commandeer, comprehend, confiscate, understand **11** appropriate

seize the day
    Latin: **9** carpe diem

seizure 3 fit **5** onset, spell, throe **6** access, arrest, attack, crisis, stroke, taking **7** capture,

episode **8** grasping, paroxysm **9** abduction, snatching **10** convulsion, kidnapping, possession, usurpation, visitation **11** impressment **12** apprehension, confiscation **13** appropriation, commandeering

Sejanus
    author: **9** Ben Jonson

Sekhmet
    origin: **8** Egyptian
    goddess of: **4** evil

Selden, Mr
    character in: **15** The House of Mirth
    author: **7** Wharton

seldom 6 rarely **8** scarcely **10** uncommonly **12** infrequently, occasionally, sporadically

select 3 tap **4** A-one, pick, posh **5** elect, elite, fancy **6** choice, choose, chosen, opt for, picked, prefer **8** four-star, superior, top-notch **9** exclusive, first-rate, preferred **10** first-class, privileged

selection 4 pick **5** range **6** choice, medley, option **7** program, variety **8** choosing, decision **9** potpourri **10** collection, miscellany, preference

selective 5 fussy, picky **6** choosy **7** careful, finicky **8** cautious **10** discerning, fastidious, meticulous, particular **14** discriminating

Selemnus
    vocation: **8** shepherd
    loved: **6** Argyra
    changed into: **5** river
    changed by: **9** Aphrodite

Selene
    goddess of: **4** moon
    father: **8** Hyperion
    mother: **5** Theia
    brother: **6** Helios
    sister: **3** Eos
    loved: **8** Endymion
    daughter: **5** Herse **6** Pandia
    corresponds to: **5** Diana **7** Artemis

self 3 ego **6** person, psyche **8** identity **10** individual **11** homogeneity, personality
    inner: **5** anima **6** animus
    Universal: **5** Atman

self-abnegation 7 modesty **8** humility **10** diffidence **11** bashfulness

self-absorbed 4 vain **8** egoistic **9** egotistical **10** egocentric **11** egotistical **12** narcissistic

self-absorption 6 egoism, vanity **7** conceit **11** egocentrism, selfishness **16** self-centeredness

self-admiration 6 vanity **7** conceit, egotism **8** smugness **9** immodesty, vainglory

self-assertive 4 bold **7** dynamic **8** forceful **9** ambitious, confident **10** aggressive

self-assuming 4 vain **8** arrogant, egoistic **9** conceited **10** egoistical **11** egotistical

self-assurance 6 aplomb **9** brashness **12** cocksureness
    French: **9** sangfroid

self-assured 5 brash, cocky **8** cocksure **9** confident

self-centered 4 vain **8** egoistic, immodest **9** conceited, egotistic **10** egocentric **11** egotistical, swellheaded **12** narcissistic

self-centeredness 6 egoism, vanity **7** conceit **10** narcissism **11** egocentrism

self-composure 5 poise **6** aplomb **8** calmness **10** equanimity

self-confidence 5 nerve, pluck **6** mettle, spirit **8** boldness, gameness **9** cockiness **10** resolution **12** cocksureness

self-conscious 7 awkward **8** affected **9** chagrined, ill at ease, unnatural **11** discomposed, embarrassed **12** disconcerted

self-consciousness 7 modesty, reserve, shyness **8** timidity **9** abashment, hesitancy, reticence **10** constraint, demureness, diffidence **11** bashfulness, fearfulness **12** apprehension, sheepishness

self-control 5 poise **6** aplomb **8** firmness, patience, sobriety **9** composure, soberness, soundness, stability, willpower **10** temperance **11** forbearance **14** cool-headedness, unexcitability **15** levelheadedness **16** imperturbability
    French: **9** sangfroid **11** savoir faire

self-critical 6 humble, modest **9** diffident **13** perfectionist

self-criticism 7 modesty **8** humility **10** diffidence **13** perfectionism

self-deception 7 fantasy **8** delusion, illusion **13** hallucination

self-declared 5 sworn **6** avowed **8** admitted **9** confessed, professed **12** acknowledged

self-denial 8 eschewal **10** abnegation, abstention, abstinence, continence

11 forbearance 12 renunciation 14 abstemiousness

self-deprecation
also: 16 self-depreciation
7 modesty 8 humility, meekness 10 humbleness

self-doubt 11 uncertainty

self-effacement 7 modesty, shyness 8 humility, meekness 10 diffidence 11 bashfulness

self-esteem 5 pride 10 confidence

self-evident 5 plain 6 patent 7 glaring, obvious 8 apparent, distinct, explicit, manifest, palpable 10 unarguable, undeniable 11 unambiguous, unequivocal 12 unmistakable 16 incontrovertible

self-explanatory 5 clear, lucid, plain 7 obvious 8 manifest 12 intelligible 15 straightforward

self-governing 4 free 9 sovereign 10 autonomous 11 independent

self-government 8 autonomy, home rule 11 sovereignty 12 independence

self-gratifying 11 intemperate

self-importance 6 egoism, vanity 8 smugness 9 arrogance, immodesty, pomposity, vainglory 11 egocentrism

self-important 4 smug, vain 7 pompous 8 egoistic, immodest 10 egocentric 11 egotistical 12 vainglorious

self-indulgence 12 extravagance, incontinence, intemperance

self-indulgent 9 libertine, sybaritic 10 hedonistic, voluptuous 11 extravagant, incontinent, intemperate

selfish 4 mean 5 tight, venal 6 greedy, stingy 7 miserly 8 covetous, egoistic grasping, grudging 9 egotistic, illiberal, mercenary, rapacious 10 avaricious, egocentric, ungenerous 11 egotistical 12 parsimonious, uncharitable

self-love 6 egoism, vanity 7 conceit, egotism 9 vainglory 10 narcissism 11 complacency, egocentrism, haughtiness 13 conceitedness 15 swellheadedness
French: 11 amour propre

self-possessed 4 calm, cool 6 poised 7 assured, courtly, refined 8 balanced, composed, polished, resolute 9 collected, confident 12 aristocratic 13 distinguished

self-possession 5 poise 6 aplomb 7 dignity 8 calmness, coolness 9 composure 10 confidence, equanimity, steadiness 16 imperturbability
French: 9 sangfroid

self-praise 6 vanity 7 conceit, egotism 8 bragging, smugness 9 arrogance, immodesty, vainglory 12 boastfulness
Italian: 11 braggadocio

self-propelling 9 automatic

self-questioning 10 uneasiness 13 soul-searching

self-reliance 8 sureness 9 assurance 12 independence

Self-Reliance
author: 17 Ralph Waldo Emerson

self-reliant 5 hardy 6 plucky 7 assured 8 resolute, spirited 10 mettlesome 11 independent 12 enterprising

self-reproachful 8 contrite 9 regretful 10 apologetic, remorseful

self-respecting 5 proud 7 upright 8 decorous 9 dignified, honorable 10 upstanding 11 circumspect 13 distinguished

self-restraint 9 willpower 10 continence 11 forbearance

self-righteous 4 smug 5 pious 7 pompous 9 insincere, pietistic 10 complacent, moralizing 11 pharisaical, pretentious 12 hypocritical, mealymouthed 13 sanctimonious 14 holier-than-thou

self-sacrificing 6 heroic 7 gallant 9 unselfish 10 altruistic, martyrlike

self-satisfaction 5 pride 6 vanity 8 smugness 11 complacency

self-satisfied 4 smug, vain 8 cocksure, priggish 9 overproud 10 complacent 11 egotistical 12 narcissistic, vainglorious 13 overconfident

self-secure 4 smug 7 content 9 contented 10 complacent

self-seeking 6 greedy 8 covetous

self-styled
French: 9 soi-disant

self-willed 8 obdurate, stubborn 9 obstinate, pigheaded 10 headstrong, refractory 11 intractable 12 ungovernable, unmanageable

sell 4 dump, hawk, vend 6 barter, betray, deal in, enlist, handle, market, peddle, unload 7 deceive, trade in, win over 8 convince, dispense

Selleck, Tom
roles: 8 Lassiter, Magnum PI 12 Thomas Magnum 15 High Road to China 16 Three Men and A Baby

seller 6 dealer, jobber, monger, trader, vendor 7 peddler 8 merchant, retailer, salesman 9 middleman, salesgirl, saleslady, tradesman 10 saleswoman, shopkeeper, wholesaler 11 salesperson, storekeeper

Sellers, Peter
real name: 19 Richard Henry Sellers
born: 7 England 8 Southsea
wife: 11 Britt Ekland
roles: 10 Being There 12 Casino Royale 13 Dr Strangelove, Murder by Death 14 A Shot in the Dark, The Pink Panther 16 What's New Pussycat? 17 Inspector Clouseau 18 The Mouse that Roared 21 The World of Henry Orient

Selli
priests of: 4 Zeus

sell out 6 betray 11 doublecross

semblance 3 air 4 cast, copy, look, show 5 image 6 aspect 7 bearing, replica 8 likeness, pretense 9 duplicate, facsimile 10 simulacrum 11 counterpart 12 reproduction 14 representation
French: 4 mien

Semele
also: 6 Thyone
father: 6 Cadmus
mother: 8 Harmonia
loved by: 4 Zeus
son: 8 Dionysus
sister: 3 Ino 5 Agave 7 Autonoe

seminal 7 primary 8 creative, fruitful, germinal, original 9 formative 10 generative, productive 11 germinative, originating

Seminole
language family: 9 Muskogean
tribe: 8 Cow Creek, Mikasaki
location: 6 Mexico 7 Florida, Georgia 10 Everglades
leader: 7 Osceola, Wild Cat 10 Coacoochie

Semiramis
queen of: 7 Assyria
husband: 5 Ninus
founder of: 7 Babylon

Semitic
language family: 11 Afro-Asiatic **13** Hamito-Semitic
eastern branch: 8 Akkadian, Assyrian **10** Babylonian
western branch: 4 Geez **5** Tigre **6** Arabic, Gurage, Harari, Hebrew, Minean, Sabean, Syriac **7** Amharic, Aramaic, Argobba, Moabite **8** Ethiopic, Tigrinya, Ugaritic **9** Canaanite **10** Himyaritic, Phoenician, Qatabanian
southwest branch: 6 Minean, Sabean **7** Amharic **10** Himyaritic, Qatabanian **11** North Arabic **19** South Arabic-Ethiopic

Semo Sancus *see* **6** Sancus

senatus consultum 17 Roman senate decree

send 4 cast, emit, head, hurl, lead, show, toss **5** drive, fling, guide, refer, relay, shoot, throw **6** convey, direct, launch, propel **7** conduct, deliver, forward, give off, project **8** dispatch, transmit **9** broadcast, cause to go, discharge **11** disseminate

send away 4 oust, rout, shoo **5** chase, evict

send forth 4 emit, gush **5** erupt, expel, issue, let go **7** dismiss, release **8** disgorge, dispatch **9** discharge

send off 4 post **7** forward **8** dispatch, disperse, transmit

send out 4 beam, emit **8** dispatch, transmit **9** discharge

send packing 3 axe, can **4** fire, oust, rout, sack, shoo **5** evict **6** bounce **7** cast out, dismiss

send to Coventry 3 cut **5** eject, expel **6** banish, ignore **7** cast out, exclude **9** ostracize

Seneca
language family: 9 Iroquoian
location: 7 New York **15** Canandaigua Lake
leader: 9 John Abeel, John O'Bail **11** Cornplanter
member: 19 League of the Iroquois

Senegal *see box*

senile 6 doting, infirm **7** foolish **8** decrepit **9** doddering, senescent **13** superannuated

senior, Senior 4 head, over **5** above, chief, doyen, elder, older **6** better **7** veteran **8** superior

seniority 6 tenure **9** longevity **10** precedence
French: 4 pere

Senegal
capital/largest city: 5 Dakar
others: 5 Bakel, Matam, Thies **7** Bignona, Kaolack, Kaollak **8** Diourbel, Kedougou, Linguere, Rufisque **10** Saint-Louis, Ziguinchor **11** Richard-Toll, Tambacounda
division: 7 Sudanic **8** Sahelian **9** Casamance
   empire: **4** Mali **5** Jolof **6** Tekrur
monetary unit: 5 franc **7** centime
island: 5 Goree
lake: 6 Guiers
mountain: 6 Gounou
highest point: 12 Fouta Djallon
river: 4 Sine **6** Faleme, Gambia, Saloum **7** Senegal **9** Casamance
sea: 8 Atlantic
physical feature:
   desert: **5** Ferlo
   peninsula: **9** Cape Verde
people: 4 Lebu, Peul, Soce **5** Diola, Dyola, Foula, Laobe, Peulh, Serer, Wolof **6** Fulani, Serere **7** Bambara, Malinke, Tukuler, Tukulor **8** Mandingo
   leader: **7** Senghor
language: 5 Wolof **6** French
religion: 5 Islam **7** animism **13** Roman Catholic
feature:
   musical instrument: **4** kora
   tree: **6** acacia, baobab **7** juniper, oil palm **10** raffia palm

---

senor 2 Mr **3** don **5** title **6** mister **8** Spaniard

senora 3 Mrs **4** lady, wife **5** madam, woman **8** mistress

senorita 4 lass, miss
abbreviation: 4 srta

senorita: 6 wrasse
genus: 8 Oxyjulis
species: 11 californica

sensation 3 hit **4** stir, to-do **6** thrill, uproar **7** feeling, scandal **9** agitation, awareness, commotion, detection **10** impression, perception

sensational 5 cheap, lurid **6** superb **8** dramatic, exciting, galvanic, shocking, striking **9** emotional, excellent, thrilling **10** electrical, scandalous **11** exaggerated, exceptional, extravagant, outstanding, spectacular **12** meretricious **13** extraordinary **14** heartthrobbing

sensationalism 7 scandal **9** luridness, melodrama **13** grandstanding **15** blood and thunder **16** yellow journalism

sense 3 see, use **4** aura, espy, feel, good, mind, note **5** grasp, guess, point, sight, smell, taste, touch, value, worth **6** descry, detect, divine, reason, regard, take in, wisdom **7** benefit, discern, faculty, feeling, hearing, meaning, purpose, realize, suspect **8** efficacy, function, judgment, perceive, sagacity **9** apprehend,

awareness, intuition, recognize **10** atmosphere, comprehend, definition, denotation, impression, understand **11** connotation, premonition, realization, recognition **12** appreciation, intelligence, perspicacity, practicality, presentiment **13** consciousness, signification, understanding **14** reasonableness

Sense and Sensibility
author: 10 Jane Austen
character: 10 Lucy Steele **13** Edward Ferrars, Robert Ferrars **14** Colonel Brandon, John Willoughby **16** Sir John Middleton
   Dashwood family: **4** John **5** Fanny **6** Elinor **8** Marianne

senseless 4 dumb, idle, numb **5** crazy, inane, nutty, silly **6** stupid, unwise **7** aimless, foolish, stunned, useless, witless **8** comatose, deadened **9** brainless, foolhardy, illogical, insensate, pointless **10** groundless, ill-advised, insensible, irrational, ridiculous **11** harebrained, meaningless, purposeless, unconscious **12** unreasonable **13** irresponsible

sense of duty 15 moral obligation **21** sense of responsibility

sensibilities 8 feelings, sore spot, thin skin **12** Achilles' heel **14** susceptibility

sensibility 7 feeling 10 perception 11 temperament 14 responsiveness

sensible 4 just, sage, sane, wise 5 aware, plain, sound 7 evident, knowing, logical, obvious, prudent, visible 8 apparent, apprised, credible, discreet, informed, palpable, possible, rational, tangible 9 cognitive, cognizant, conscious, judicious, plausible, sagacious 10 detectable, discerning, farsighted, noticeable, perceiving, perceptive, reasonable, responsive, thoughtful 11 discernible, enlightened, intelligent, perceptible, susceptible 13 perspicacious 14 discriminating

sensitive 4 fine, keen, sore 5 acute, exact 6 tender, touchy 7 painful, precise 8 accurate, delicate, faithful, sentient 10 perceptive, responsive 11 susceptible, thin-skinned 14 impressionable

sensitiveness 8 delicacy 10 touchiness

sensual 4 lewd, sexy 6 carnal, earthy, erotic 7 fleshly, lustful 9 lecherous 10 hedonistic, licentious, voluptuous

sensualist 8 hedonist, sybarite 9 libertine 10 voluptuary

sensuous 9 delicious, exquisite 10 delightful

sententious 7 orotund, pompous, preachy, stilted 8 didactic, pedantic 9 grandiose, high-flown, pietistic 10 judgmental, moralistic 13 sanctimonious

sentient 5 aware 7 alert to, alive to, awake to, mindful 8 sensible 9 conscious

sentiment, sentiments 4 idea 5 heart 6 notion 7 emotion, feeling, opinion, romance, thought 8 attitude 9 nostalgia, viewpoint 10 tenderness 11 romanticism 12 emotionalism 15 softheartedness

sentimental 5 mushy, weepy 7 maudlin, mawkish, tearful 8 pathetic, romantic 9 emotional, nostalgic 10 lachrymose 12 melodramatic, romanticized

Sentimental Education, A author: 15 Gustave Flaubert character: 6 Arnoux 9 Dambreuse, Rosanette 11 Des Lauriers, Louise Roque 14 Frederic Moreau

sentimentalism 4 corn, mush 5 slush 6 bathos, pathos

8 schmaltz 9 mushiness, soppiness 10 maudlinism, slushiness 11 mawkishness

sentimentality 4 mush 5 heart 6 bathos, pathos 10 sloppiness 11 mawkishness, temperament 12 emotionalism Yiddish: 6 kitsch

Sentimental Journey, A author: 14 Laurence Sterne character: 5 Maria 6 Yorick 7 La Fleur

sentinel 4 ward 5 guard, scout, watch 6 patrol, picket, ranger 7 lookout 8 guardian, watchman 9 guardsman

sentry 5 guard, watch 7 lookout, vedette, vidette 8 sentinel, watchman greeting: 4 halt

Seoul capital of: 10 South Korea

separate 3 cut 4 cull, fork, part, sift 5 break, crack, sever, split 6 bisect, detach, divide, ramify, remove, single, spread, sunder 7 crumble, disjoin, diverge, diverse, divorce, isolate, radiate 8 detached, discrete, distinct, disunite 9 bifurcate, break away, come apart, different, disunited, partition, segregate, subdivide 10 autonomous, disconnect, dissimilar, divaricate, individual 11 distinguish, independent

separated 6 cut off 7 severed 8 detached 10 disengaged 12 disconnected, disentangled

separate from 5 apart, leave

separately 5 apart 6 singly 7 asunder 9 severally 12 individually

Separate Tables director: 11 Delbert Mann based on play by: 15 Terence Rattigan cast: 10 David Niven 11 Deborah Kerr, Wendy Hiller 12 Rita Hayworth 13 Burt Lancaster Oscar for: 5 actor (Niven) 17 supporting actress (Hiller)

separation 3 gap 4 fork 5 break, space, split 6 breach, divide, schism 7 divider, divorce, good-bye, opening, parting, removal, sorting 8 boundary, distance, disunion, division, farewell, interval 9 branching, isolation, partition, severance 10 detachment, divergence 11 bifurcation, disjunction, segregation 12 estrangement 13 disconnection, disengagement 14 disassociation

Sepharvite god 10 Anammelech 11 Adrammelech

Sepharvites residents of: 6 Sippar

Sepher Torah 16 scroll of the Torah literally: 9 book of law

September characteristic: 11 harvest moon event: 14 aurora borealis, Northern lights 15 autumnal equinox flower: 5 aster 12 morning glory French: 9 Septembre gem: 8 sapphire 12 star sapphire German: 9 September holiday: 8 Labor Day (1st Monday) 9 Yom Kippur 10 Michaelmas (29) 12 Rosh Hashanah 15 Grandparents' Day Italian: 9 Settembre number of days: 6 thirty origin of name: 6 septum (Latin meaning seven) place in year: *Gregorian:* 5 ninth *Roman:* 7 seventh Spanish: 10 Septiembre Zodiac sign: 5 Libra, Virgo

septentrional 6 arctic 8 northern 11 hyperborean

Septuagint abbreviation: 3 LXX author: 10 the Seventy

sepulcher 4 tomb 5 crypt, grave, vault 7 ossuary 8 cenotaph 9 mausoleum, reliquary 10 necropolis

sepulchral 6 hollow 7 charnel 8 funereal, mournful, tomblike 10 lugubrious

sequel 3 end 6 finish, result, upshot 7 outcome, product 8 addendum, epilogue, followup, offshoot 9 aftermath, corollary, outgrowth 10 conclusion, postscript 11 consequence, culmination 12 continuation French: 10 denouement

sequence 3 run 4 flow 5 chain, cycle, order, round, train 6 course, parade, series, string 7 routine 8 schedule 9 cavalcade 10 procession, succession 11 arrangement, progression 14 successiveness 15 consecutiveness

sequester 6 banish, lock up, retire **7** confine, isolate, seclude **8** separate, withdraw **9** segregate **10** quarantine

sequestered 8 closeted, confined, isolated, secluded **9** insulated, sheltered, withdrawn **10** cloistered **11** dissociated

sequin 4 coin, disk **5** ducat **7** spangle **8** ornament
French: **9** paillette

seraglio 3 oda **5** harem, serai **6** zenana **9** gynaeceum

Seraiah
son: **4** Ezra

serape 4 cape **5** shawl **6** mantle, poncho

seraph 5 angel

seraphic 7 angelic **8** beatific, ethereal, heavenly **9** celestial

Seraphim 6 angels

Serapis
origin: **5** Greek **8** Egyptian
form: **5** deity
combination of: **4** Apis, Hapi **6** Osiris

Serbia see Yugoslavia

sere 3 dry **4** arid **6** barren **7** parched, wizened **8** droughty, scorched, withered **9** shriveled, unwatered, waterless **10** dehydrated, desiccated **12** dehumidified, moistureless

serene 4 calm, cool, fair **5** clear, quiet, still **6** bright, limpid, placid, poised, sedate, smooth **7** halcyon **8** composed, peaceful, pellucid, tranquil **9** dignified, unruffled **10** nonchalant, unobscured, untroubled **11** undisturbed, unexcitable, unperturbed **13** unimpassioned

serenity 7 dignity **8** calmness, coolness, quietude **9** composure, placidity **10** equanimity, quiescence **11** complacence, nonchalance, tranquility **12** peacefulness, tranquillity **13** collectedness
French: **9** sangfroid

serf 6 cotter, thrall, vassal **7** bondman, peasant, villein

serfdom 4 yoke **6** thrall **7** bondage, slavery **9** servitude, thralldom, vassalage **11** enslavement, subjugation

Sergeant York
director: **11** Howard Hawks
cast: **10** Gary Cooper, Joan Leslie **12** George Tobias **13** Walter Brennan
Oscar for: **5** actor (Cooper)

Sergestus
origin: **6** Trojan
companion to: **6** Aeneas

serial 7 regular **9** continued, piecemeal, recurring **10** continuous, sequential, successive **11** consecutive, incremental

series 3 set **5** chain, cycle, group, order **6** course, number, parade, string **8** sequence **10** procession, succession **11** progression

serious 3 bad, sad **4** grim **5** grave, heavy, sober, staid **6** rueful, sedate, severe, solemn, somber **7** crucial, decided, earnest, fateful, harmful, pensive, sincere, weighty **8** alarming, critical, dejected, downcast, frowning, perilous, resolute, resolved **9** crippling, dangerous, important, momentous, saturnine **10** determined, portentous, purposeful, thoughtful **13** consequential **14** incapacitating

seriousness 7 gravity **8** severity **9** sincerity, soberness, solemnity **10** importance **11** earnestness

sermon 6 homily, rebuke, tirade **7** lecture, reproof **8** diatribe, harangue **9** preaching **10** admonition, preachment **11** exhortation

serpent, Serpent 3 asp **5** cheat, devil, rogue, Satan, snake, viper **7** reptile, traitor **8** deceiver **9** trickster
constellation of: **7** Serpens

Serpent Holder
constellation of: **9** Ophiuchus

serpentine 4 mazy **6** spiral, zigzag **7** coiling, crooked, devious, sinuous, snaking, winding **8** flexuous, tortuous, twisting **10** circuitous, convoluted, meandering, roundabout, undulating **12** labyrinthine

Serpico
director: **11** Sidney Lumet
based on story by: **9** Peter Maas
cast: **8** Al Pacino **9** Jack Kehoe **12** John Randolph
setting: **11** New York City

serrate 5 notch **6** jagged, pinked, ridged **7** dentate, grooved, notched, toothed **10** sawtoothed

serration 5 notch, ridge, teeth, tooth **8** notching, sawtooth

servant 3 man **4** cook, girl, help, maid **5** valet **6** butler, flunky, helper, lackey, menial, minion, slavey **7** footman **8** domestic, employee, facto-

tum, henchman, hired man, retainer, scullion **9** attendant, chauffeur, hired girl, hired help, man Friday, underling **10** girl Friday **11** housekeeper

serve 2 do **3** act, aid **4** help, pass, suit, tend, work **5** avail, spend, treat **6** assist, attend, be used, do duty, oblige, supply, wait on **7** content, deliver, further, perform, present, promote, satisfy, suffice, work for **8** carry out, complete, function, hand over, minister **9** officiate **11** fill the bill

service, services 3 aid, use **4** help, mend, rite **5** avail, labor **6** adjust, agency, bureau, effort, employ, profit, repair, ritual, system **7** benefit, support, utility, waiting **8** ceremony, facility, maintain, military **9** advantage, provision, treatment **10** assistance, attendance, ceremonial, department, employment, observance, usefulness **11** celebration, convenience, maintenance **12** ministration **13** accommodation

serviceable 5 tough **6** rugged, strong, sturdy, usable, useful **7** durable, lasting **8** workable **9** effective, operative, practical **10** functional **11** utilitarian

serviceman 6 marine, sailor **7** soldier **9** repairman

servile 4 oily **6** abject, humble, menial **7** fawning, in bonds, slavish **8** cringing, scraping, toadying, unctuous **9** groveling, truckling **10** obsequious, submissive **11** bootlicking, subservient, sycophantic

serving 6 acting **7** dishful, helping, portion, waiting **8** plateful **9** assisting, attending, sufficing **11** ministering

serving counter 3 bar **6** buffet **9** sideboard

servitude 5 bonds **6** chains **7** bondage, fetters, serfdom, slavery **8** shackles **9** thralldom, vassalage **10** oppression **11** enslavement, subjugation **12** enthrallment, imprisonment

Servius Tullius
also: **7** Tullius
king of: **4** Rome
daughter: **6** Tullia
son-in-law: **7** Tarquin
killed by: **6** Tullia **7** Tarquin

sesame
also called: **10** benne seeds
botanical name: **14** Sesamum indicum
fairy tale: **10** "open sesame" **25** Ali Baba and the Forty Thieves

high in: 7 protein
former/mythical use: 3 oil
8 medicine **10** opens locks
11 lighting oil **16** discovers
secrets **21** discovers secret
places
use: 5 bread **6** salads
10 casseroles
use like: 8 nutmeats
11 chopped nuts

Sesame Street
character: 4 Bert, Elmo **5** Ernie, Herry, Oscar **6** Snuffy
7 Barkley, Big Bird, Mup-
pets **8** the Count **12** Telly
Monster **13** Cookie Monster **15** Mr Snuffleupagus

Sesostris
king of: 5 Egypt

session 4 bout, term **5** round,
synod **6** course, period
7 meeting, quarter, sitting
8 assembly, conclave, semester **10** conference, convention

set *see* **box**

Set
also: 4 Seth
origin: 8 Egyptian
form: 6 animal
personifies: 6 desert
brother: 6 Osiris
killed: 6 Osiris

set about 5 begin **6** assume
9 undertake **10** surrounded

set against 8 alienate,
estrange

set apart 5 allot **6** detach, divide **7** earmark, isolate **8** allocate, separate **9** apportion,
segregate **11** appropriate

set aside 4 kill **5** allot, annul
6 abjure, cancel, repeal, revoke **7** abandon, abolish, call
off, destroy, discard, earmark,
nullify, put away, rescind, retract, reverse **8** abrogate, allo-

cate, override, overturn
9 designate, repudiate **10** invalidate **11** discontinue

set at ease 5 cheer **6** please
7 appease, comfort, content,
gratify

set at liberty 4 free **5** let go
6 parole **7** manumit, release,
unchain **8** liberate, unfetter
9 unshackle **10** emancipate

setback 4 flop, loss, snag
5 hitch, slump **6** defeat, mishap, rebuff **7** failure, relapse,
reverse, undoing **8** reversal
9 adversity, mischance, worsening **10** misfortune, regression **13** retrogression
14 disappointment

set down 6 record **7** deposit

set forth 2 go **5** be off, leave
6 assert, avouch, depart **7** advance **8** advocate, propound
10 sally forth

set free 5 let go, loose, untie
6 acquit, loosen, pardon, parole, unbind, uncage, unlock
7 deliver, release **8** liberate,
unfetter **9** discharge, disengage, extricate
10 emancipate

Seth *see* **3** Set

Seth
means: 12 compensation
father: 4 Adam
mother: 3 Eve
son: 4 Enos

set in 5 arise, ensue, occur
6 arrive

set in motion 5 begin, start
6 launch **8** initiate **9** instigate,
originate **10** inaugurate

set in order 4 rank, sort
5 align **6** line up **7** arrange,
marshal **8** classify, organize
9 methodize **11** systematize

set of beliefs 5 credo, creed,
dogma, ethos **6** ethnic, tenets
8 doctrine **10** philosophy, principles **11** convictions

set off 6 depart **7** explode, go
forth **8** detonate, start out
10 sally forth

set on fire 4 burn **5** light
6 ignite, kindle

set out 4 pose **5** array, begin,
be off, place, range **6** deploy,
embark, intend **7** arrange, display **9** undertake

set right 7 correct **8** disabuse

set store by 5 prize, value
6 esteem **7** respect **8** treasure

set straight 5 edify **6** advise,
inform **7** educate **8** disabuse
9 enlighten

settee 4 seat, sofa **5** bench

setting 5 scene **6** fixing, locale **7** jelling **8** aligning, ambiance, locating, location,
mounting **9** adjusting, arranging, decreeing, hardening, or-
daining **10** congealing,
regulating, thickening **11** arrangement, determining, environment, prescribing,
solidifying **12** establishing,
surroundings
French: 6 milieu **11** mise-
en-scene

setting sun
god of: 5 Janus

settle 3 fix, pay, sag **4** calm,
drop, land, sink **5** agree, allay,
clear, droop, light, lodge,
perch, quiet **6** alight, choose,
decide, locate, move to, pacify, people, soothe **7** arrange,
clarify, clear up, compose, inhabit, rectify, resolve, satisfy,
sit down, situate **8** colonize,
make good, populate, take
root **9** determine, discharge,
establish, reconcile
11 precipitate

settled 4 sure **7** certain,
decided

settlement 3 sum **4** camp,
post **6** amount, colony, hamlet **7** bequest, outpost, payment, village **8** clearing,
peopling **9** clearance, discharge **10** adjustment, coloniz-
ing, encampment, resolution
11 acquittance, arrangement,
liquidation **12** amortization,
colonization, compensation,
satisfaction **14** reconciliation

settler 7 pioneer **8** colonist,
squatter **9** colonizer, immigrant **11** homesteader
12 frontiersman

settle upon 6 bestow **7** consign **8** bequeath

set 3 cut, fit, fix, gel, kit, lay, put, sic **4** club, drop, firm,
line, make, plop, post, rate, sink, stud, suit **5** adapt, align,
array, banal, bunch, crowd, embed, fixed, group, imbed, order, place, plunk, ready, rigid, scene, stale, stiff, stock, style,
trite, usual **6** adjust, assess, assign, attach, common, confer,
create, decree, frozen, harden, line up, locale, locate, ordain,
outfit, studio **7** arrange, bearing, complex, congeal, decided,
faction, install, jellify, machine, prepare, profile, regular, release, routine, scenery, service, setting, situate, station,
thicken, unleash **8** arranged, assembly, backdrop, carriage,
definite, estimate, everyday, familiar, firmness, habitual,
hardened, location, ornament, position, prepared, regulate,
rigidity, solidify, stubborn **9** apparatus, calibrate, customary,
determine, establish, hackneyed, immovable, obstinate, prescribe, represent, steadfast **10** accustomed, assortment, collection, inflexible **11** anticipated, commonplace, consolidate,
established, prearranged **12** conventional
French: 6 clique **7** coterie

settlings 4 lees **5** dregs **7** deposit, grounds, remains, residue **8** leavings

set-to 4 spat **5** brush, clash, run-in **6** battle, fracas **7** dispute, quarrel, scuffle **8** argument, skirmish, squabble **10** engagement, falling out **12** disagreement **13** confrontation
French: **11** contretemps

setup 4 plan **6** scheme, system **8** practice **9** apparatus **11** arrangement **12** organization

set up 3 rig **5** erect, found **7** arrange, install **9** construct, establish, institute **10** inaugurate, prearrange

set upon 3 mug **5** beset, fly at **6** assail, attack **7** besiege, lunge at **9** pitch into

Seurat, Georges Pierre
born: **5** Paris **6** France
artwork: **9** The Chahut, The Circus, The Models, The Parade, The Uproar **10** The Bathers **12** Le Grand Jatte, The Yoked Cart **19** Une Baignade Asnieres **23** A Bathing Scene at Asnieres, The Bec du Hoc at Grandchamp **40** Sunday Afternoon on the Island of La Grand Jatte

Seuss, Dr
real name: **19** Theodore Seuss Geisel
author of: **12** If I Ran the Zoo **14** The Cat in the Hat **15** Green Eggs and Ham, Horton Hears a Who, If I Ran the Circus **19** Horton Hatches the Egg **23** Mister Brown Can Moo Can You? **26** Thidwick The Big-Hearted Moose, How the Grinch Stole Christmas

Seve
nickname of: **20** Severiano Ballesteros

Seven Against Thebes
author: **9** Aeschylus
character: **6** Ismene **8** Antigone, Eteocles **9** Polynices **11** Theban Women
seven heroes: **6** Tydeus **8** Adrastus, Capaneus **9** Polynices **10** Amphiaraus, Hippomedon **13** Parthenopaeus

Seven Beauties
director: **14** Lina Wertmuller
cast: **11** Fernando Rey **13** Shirley Stoler **17** Giancarlo Giannini

Seven Brides for Seven Brothers
director: **12** Stanley Donen
cast: **9** Tammy Rall **10** Howard Keel, Jane Powell **11** Julie Newmar (Newmeyer), Russ Tamblyn **12** Jeff Richards **14** Virginia Gibson
score: **11** Saul Chaplin **12** Johnny Mercer
choreography: **11** Michael Kidd

Seven Pillars of Wisdom
author: **10** T E Lawrence

Seven Samurai
director: **13** Akira Kurosawa
cast: **11** Yoshio Inaba **13** Toshiro Mifune **14** Takashi Shimura
remade as: **19** The Magnificent Seven

seven seas 6 Arctic, Indian **9** Antarctic **12** North Pacific, South Pacific **13** North Atlantic, South Atlantic

Seven Sisters colleges 5 Smith **6** Vassar **7** Barnard **8** Bryn Mawr **9** Radcliffe, Wellesley **12** Mount Holyoke

Seventeen
author: **15** Booth Tarkington
character: **7** Genesis **9** Miss Pratt, Mrs Baxter **10** Jane Baxter, May Parcher **21** William Sylvanus Baxter

Seventh Seal, The
director: **13** Ingmar Bergman
cast: **9** Nils Poppe **11** Max von Sydow **13** Bibi Andersson **17** Gunnar Bjornstrand

77 Sunset Strip
character: **6** J R Hale, Kookie (Gerald Lloyd Kookson III), Roscoe **7** Suzanne **11** Jeff Spencer, Rex Randolph **12** Stuart Bailey
cast: **9** Edd Byrnes **10** Louis Quinn, Roger Smith **11** Richard Long, Robert Logan **14** Jacqueline Beer **16** Efrem Zimbalist Jr
Kookie's sayings: **10** a dark seven **12** the ginchiest **13** piling up the Z's **14** lend me your comb **15** play like a pigeon **17** headache grapplers **22** keep the eyeballs rolling

seven wonders of the world 8 pyramids (Egypt) **12** Olympian Zeus (sculpted by Phidias) **15** Temple of Artemis (at Ephesus) **16** Colossus of Rhodes **22** Lighthouse at Alexandria **23** hanging gardens of Babylon (of Semiramis) **24** Mausoleum at Halicarnassus

Seven Year Itch, The
director: **11** Billy Wilder
cast: **8** Tom Ewell **10** Sonny Tufts **11** Evelyn Keyes, Victor Moore **13** Marilyn Monroe
setting: **11** New York City

sever 3 saw **4** part, rend, rive, tear **5** slice, split **6** bisect, cleave, cut off, lop off **7** disjoin, rupture, split up **8** amputate, break off, cut in two, dissolve, disunite, separate, truncate **9** dismember, terminate **10** disconnect **11** discontinue

several 3 own **4** a few, some **6** divers, single, sundry **7** certain, diverse, express, private, special **8** assorted, distinct, peculiar, personal, separate, specific **9** different, exclusive **10** individual, particular, respective **11** distinctive, independent

severe 4 cold, dour, grim, wild **5** cruel, grave, harsh, plain, rough, sober, stern, stiff **6** biting, bitter, brutal, chaste, fierce, fuming, raging, savage, sedate, simple, somber, strict, taxing **7** austere, cutting, drastic, extreme, furious, intense, painful, serious, uniform, violent **8** piercing, rigorous, ruthless, stinging, vigorous **9** dangerous, demanding, difficult, draconian, merciless, saturnine, turbulent, unadorned, unsparing **10** forbidding, restrained, tumultuous **11** distressing, undecorated, unrelenting **12** conservative

severed 6 cut off **8** detached **9** uncoupled, unhitched **10** unfastened **11** unconnected **12** disconnected

Severini, Gino
born: **5** Italy **7** Cortona
artwork: **9** Harlequin **15** The Armored Train **25** Dancer Sea and Vase of Flowers **32** Dynamic Hieroglyph of the Bal Tabarin

severity 5 rigor **7** cruelty **8** acrimony, violence **9** austerity, gruffness, harshness, sternness **10** asceticism, difficulty, strictness, stringency **11** seriousness **12** grievousness

Seville
former name: **8** Hispalis
landmark: **7** Alcazar, Giralda
plain: **9** Andalusia
river: **12** Guadalquivir
ruler: **5** Moors **6** Romans **7** Vandals **8** Abbasids, Almohads, Iberians **9** Visigoths **10** Almoravids
Spanish: **7** Sevilla

sew 3 hem **4** mend, seam,

tack **5** unite **6** fasten, ground, stitch, suture **10** run aground loosely: **5** baste

sewage 5 waste **6** efflux, refuse **8** effluent **9** effluence

Seward, Dr
character in: **7** Dracula
author: **6** Stoker

sewing machine
invented by: **4** Howe

sex 4 Eros, love **6** coitus, gender, libido **7** coition **8** maleness **10** copulation, femaleness, femininity, generation, lovemaking **11** masculinity, procreation **12** reproduction

Sexton, Anne
author of: **15** All My Pretty Ones **22** To Bedlam and Part Way Back **23** The Awful Rowing Toward God

sexual 6 coital, erotic **7** amatory, genital, marital, sensual **8** conjugal, intimate, venereal **10** copulatory, generative, libidinous **11** procreative **12** reproductive

sexually stimulating 4 sexy **6** erotic, risque **9** salacious **10** suggestive **12** pornographic

sexy 4 lewd **5** bawdy **6** erotic **8** prurient **9** seductive **10** come-hither, coquettish, suggestive, voluptuous **11** flirtatious, provocative

---

---

sforzando
music: **12** sudden accent

Shabbas 7 Sabbath

shabby 3 low **4** mean, poor, torn, worn **5** cheap, dirty, mangy, raggy, ratty, seedy, sorry, tatty, tight **6** frayed, meager, ragged, sordid, unfair **7** ignoble, rundown, scruffy **8** beggarly, decaying, inferior, slovenly, unworthy, wretched **9** illiberal, miserable, neglected **10** ramshackle, threadbare, tumbledown, ungenerous **11** dilapidated **12** contemptible, deteriorated, dishonorable, impoverished

shabby bar 4 dive **5** joint **7** gin mill **9** honky-tonk

shack 3 hut **5** cabin **6** lean-to, shanty

shackle 3 bar, tie **4** balk, bind, cuff, curb, foil, rein **5** block, bonds, chain, check, cramp, cuffs, deter, irons, limit, stall **6** chains, fetter, hamper, hinder, hobble, hogtie, impede, pinion, retard, secure, tether, thwart **7** inhibit, manacle, prevent **8** encumber, handcuff, restrict **9** forestall, frustrate, hamstring, handcuffs **12** circumscribe

shackled 7 chained, in irons **8** in chains, manacled **10** handcuffed

shadchan, schatchen
10 matchmaker **14** marriage broker

Shaddai 3 God

shade 3 bit, dim, hue, jot **4** atom, cast, hint, hood, iota, tint, tone, veil, whit **5** blind, color, drape, tinge, touch, trace **6** awning, canopy, darken, screen, shadow, shield **7** curtain, modicum, shadows, shutter **8** darkness, particle, semidark **9** scintilla **10** suggestion
French: **7** soupcon
form: **6** spirit
location: **5** Hades

shadow, shadows 3 bit, dog **4** blot, hint, tail **5** cloud, ghost, hound, shade, smear, stain, stalk, taint, tinge, touch, trace, track, trail **6** blight, follow, pursue, smirch, smudge, threat **7** blemish, specter, whisper **8** penumbra **10** reflection, silhouette, suggestion

Shadow of a Doubt
director: **15** Alfred Hitchcock
cast: **10** Hume Cronyn **12** Joseph Cotten, Teresa Wright **14** Macdonald Carey **16** Patricia Collinge
remade as: **16** Step Down to Terror

Shadow of the Moon
author: **6** M M Kaye

Shadows on the Rock
author: **11** Willa Cather

shadowy 3 dim **5** shady **6** gloomy, unreal **7** obscure **8** illusory **9** tenebrous **10** indistinct **13** insubstantial

Shadrach
former name: **8** Hananiah
friend: **6** Daniel
companion: **7** Meshach **8** Abednego

shady 5 fishy **7** crooked, devious, dubious, shadowy **9** dishonest, unethical **10** suspicious **11** underhanded **12** disreputable, questionable **13** untrustworthy

shady dealings 5 fraud, graft **7** bribery **10** corruption, dishonesty

shaft 3 cut, pit, ray **4** barb, beam, dart, duct, flue, gibe, hilt, stem, vent, well **5** abyss, arrow, chasm, gleam, lance, patch, pylon, quill, shank, spear, spire, stalk, tower, trunk **6** cavity, column, funnel, handle, insult, pillar, streak, stream **7** affront, chimney, conduit, minaret, obelisk, spindle, steeple **8** brickbat, monolith, pilaster **9** aspersion **10** excavation

shaggy 5 bushy, downy, fuzzy, hairy, nappy, piled, wooly **6** tufted, woolly **7** bearded, hirsute, shagged, unshorn **9** whiskered **11** bewhiskered

shah 3 king **5** ruler **7** emperor, monarch **8** autocrat **9** sovereign

Shahaptian
tribe: **6** Numipu **8** Nez Perce

Shahn, Ben
born: **6** Kaunas **9** Lithuania
artwork: **5** Epoch **8** Handball **12** Seurat's Lunch, The Physicist **16** Pacific Landscape **18** Willis Avenue Bridge **28** The Passion of Sacco and Vanzetti

shake 3 jar, jog, mix **4** jerk, jolt, move, stir, stun, sway, wave **5** elude, quake, swing, touch **6** affect, bounce, jiggle, joggle, jostle, jounce, quaver, quiver, rattle, ruffle, shimmy, shiver, slough, totter, twitch, wobble **7** agitate, disturb, flicker, flutter, perturb, quaking, shudder, stagger, startle, tremble, unnerve, vibrate **8** brandish, disquiet, distress, flourish, frighten, throw off, unsettle, unstring **9** quivering, shivering, trembling **10** discompose, flickering, fluttering

shakedown 6 extort, payoff, search, tryout **7** testing **8** thorough **9** blackmail, extortion, hush money

Shakespeare, William *see box*

shakeup 5 purge **7** cleanup **8** turnover **10** clean sweep **11** realignment **13** rearrangement, redisposition, restructuring **14** redistribution, reorganization

shake up 3 mix **4** stir **5** churn **7** agitate, disturb

shakiness 6 tremor **10** insecurity **11** instability, uncertainty **12** unsteadiness

shaky 4 weak **5** frail, jumpy **6** flimsy, unsafe, unsure, wobbly **7** dubious, fidgety, fragile, halting, jittery, nervous, teetery **8** hesitant, insecure, unstable, unsteady, wavering **9** faltering, hazardous, quivering, teetering, tottering, trembling, tremulous, uncertain, undecided **10** inconstant, irresolute, precarious, unreliable, unresolved **11** vacillating **12** undependable

shallow 5 shoal **6** frothy, slight **7** surface, trivial **8** knee-deep, skin-deep, trifling **9** frivolous **11** meaningless, superficial, unimportant **13** insubstantial **15** inconsequential

shalom 5 peace

shalom aleichem 10 peace to you

sham 3 act **4** copy, fake **5** bogus, false, feign, fraud, phony, put on, trick **6** affect, assume, forged **7** feigned, forgery, imitate, pretend **8** pretense, simulate, spurious **9** imitation, pretended, simulated, synthetic **10** artificial, fraudulent **11** counterfeit, make-believe

Shamash
   origin: 8 Akkadian
   god of: 3 sun

shamble, shambles 4 limp **5** hitch, lurch, stall **6** hobble **7** shuffle **8** butchery **14** slaughterhouse

shame 5 guilt, odium **6** humble, stigma **7** chagrin, mortify, remorse, scandal **8** contempt, disgrace, dishonor, ignominy **9** disrepute, embarrass, humiliate **10** debasement, disrespect **11** degradation, humiliation, self-disgust **12** unworthiness **13** embarrassment, mortification **14** disappointment

shamed be the one who thinks evil of it
   Latin: 20 honi soit qui mal y pense

shamefaced 5 sorry **7** abashed, crushed, humbled, put-down **8** blushing, sheepish **9** chagrined, disgraced, mortified **10** humiliated, remorseful **11** embarrassed

shameful 3 low **4** base, mean, vile **6** odious **7** heinous, ignoble **8** shocking, unworthy **9** dastardly, degrading **10** deplorable, despicable, inglorious, iniquitous, outrageous, villainous **11** disgraceful, ignominious, opprobrious **12** contemptible, dishonorable **13** reprehensible

shameless 4 pert **5** brash, saucy **6** brazen, wanton **7** forward, immoral **8** degraded, flagrant, immodest, impudent, indecent **9** abandoned, audacious, barefaced, boldfaced, dissolute, unabashed **10** indecorous, unblushing, unreserved **11** disgraceful **12** dishonorable

shamelessness 4 gall ·**5** brass, cheek **8** audacity **10** brazenness, effrontery **11** forwardness, presumption

Shamgar 11 Hebrew judge

shamus 7 gumshoe **9** detective **10** private eye **12** investigator

Shane
   director: 13 George Stevens
   cast: 8 Alan Ladd **9** Van Heflin **10** Jean Arthur **11** Jack Palance **12** Elisha Cook Jr **13** Edgar Buchanan **14** Brandon de Wilde

Shanghai
   area: 23 International Settlement
   landmark: 13 Long Hua Temple **17** People's Opera House **28** Shanghai Industrial Exhibition
   river: 6 Wusung **7** Huang-P'u, Yangtze

Shangri-La *see* **5** Nepal

shanty 3 hut **5** cabin, hovel, shack **6** lean-to

shape 4 form, make, mold, trim **5** array, build, frame, guide, model, order **6** create, fettle, figure, health **7** contour, develop, fashion, outline, profile **8** physique **9** condition, construct, determine **10** silhouette **12** conformation **13** configuration

shapeless 5 baggy **8** formless **9** amorphous, irregular

shapely 3 fit **4** neat, trim **6** comely, gainly **11** symmetrical

shaper 9 architect, innovator **10** instigator, prime mover

Shapley, Howard
   field: 9 astronomy
   studied: 6 galaxy

Shapwailutan
   tribe: 5 Modoc **11** Kiowa Apache

Shardik
   author: 12 Richard Adams

share 3 cut **4** dole, part **5** allot, cut up, quota, split **6** ration **7** deal out, divvy up, mete out, percent, portion **8** allocate **9** allotment, allowance, apportion **10** percentage **13** apportionment

shared 5 joint **6** common, public **7** general **8** communal **10** collective

---

Shakespeare, William
   also: 10 bard of Avon **12** immortal bard
   author of: 6 Hamlet, Henry V **7** Henry IV, Henry VI, Macbeth, Othello **8** King John, King Lear, Pericles (Prince of Tyre) **9** Cymbeline, Henry VIII, Richard II **10** Coriolanus, Richard III, The Tempest **11** As You Like It **12** Julius Caesar, Twelfth Night **13** Rape of Lucrece, Timon of Athens **14** Romeo and Juliet, The Winter's Tale, Venus and Adonis **15** Titus Andronicus **16** Love's Labour's Lost **17** Measure for Measure, The Comedy of Errors **18** Antony and Cleopatra, Troilus and Cressida **19** Much Ado About Nothing, The Merchant of Venice, The Taming of the Shrew **20** All's Well That Ends Well **21** A Midsummer Night's Dream **22** The Merry Wives of Windsor **23** The Two Gentlemen of Verona
   birthplace: 15 Stratford-on-Avon
   theater: 4 Swan **5** Globe
   wife: 12 Anne Hathaway

share one's sorrow 7 condole **10** sympathize **11** commiserate

Sharif, Omar
real name: **15** Michael Shalhoub
born: **5** Egypt **10** Alexandria
roles: **3** Che **9** Dr Zhivago, Funny Girl, Funny Lady **11** Genghis Khan **12** Nick Arnstein **16** Lawrence of Arabia
expert on: **6** bridge

shark 3 ace **4** fish **5** cheat **6** expert, usurer, wizard **8** predator **9** trickster **12** extortionist

sharp *see box*

Sharp, Becky
character in: **10** Vanity Fair
author: **9** Thackeray

sharp-cornered 6 jagged **7** angular

sharp dresser 3 fop **4** dude **5** dandy **12** Beau Brummell, clotheshorse, fashion plate

sharpen 4 edge, hone, whet **5** grind, strop

sharply pointed 4 keen **5** acute **6** spiked **7** tapered **8** piercing **10** rapierlike **11** needle-nosed

sharpness 3 nip, wit **4** edge, tang **6** acuity, acumen **7** acidity, insight **8** acerbity, acridity, acrimony, keenness, pungency, saliency, tartness **9** acuteness, alertness, quickness **10** causticity, craftiness **12** perspicacity

sharp pain 4 pang, stab **5** cramp **6** twinge

sharpshooter
French: **10** tirailleur

sharp-sighted 5 acute **6** shrewd **8** piercing **9** farseeing **10** discerning, perceptive **11** penetrating **13** perspicacious

sharp-witted 4 keen **5** acute, alert, canny, quick, smart **6** astute, brainy, clever

Shatner, William
born: **6** Canada **8** Montreal
roles: **8** Star Trek, T J Hooker **17** Captain James T Kirk

shatter 4 rive, ruin **5** break, burst, crack, crash, crush, quash, smash, split, spoil, upset, wreck **6** squash, sunder, topple **7** crumble, destroy, explode, scuttle **8** demolish, fracture, overturn, splinter **9** devastate, pulverize

shattered 6 broken, dashed **7** crushed, smashed **8** crumbled, decrepit **9** flustered **10** demolished, fragmented, splintered, tumbledown **11** crestfallen, demoralized **13** disillusioned, disintegrated

shave 3 cut, lop, mow **4** clip, crop, dock, pare, skin, snip, trim **5** brush, graze, prune, shear **6** barber, cut off, fleece, glance, scrape **7** scissor

Shaw, George Bernard
author of: **7** Candida **9** Pygmalion, Saint Joan **12** Major Barbara **13** Arms and the Man **14** Man and Superman **15** Heartbreak House **16** Back to Methuselah **17** The Devil's Disciple, The Doctor's Dilemma **18** Caesar and Cleopatra **19** Androcles and the Lion **20** Mrs Warren's Profession
member of: **13** Fabian Society

Shaw, Irwin
author of: **12** Top of the Hill **13** The Young Lions **14** Beggarman Thief, Rich Man Poor Man

Shaw, Robert
born: **7** England **12** Westhoughton
wife: **7** Mary Ure
roles: **4** Jaws **7** The Deep **8** The Sting **12** Swashbuckler **13** The Caretakers **17** A Man for All Seasons **20** Force Ten from Navarone **28** The Taking of Pelham One-Two-Three
author of: **14** The Hiding Place **21** The Man in the Glass Booth

Shawabti
origin: **8** Egyptian
form: **8** figurine
where used: **6** burial

shawl 4 wrap **5** scarf **6** mantle **7** paisley **10** fascinator
Mexican: **6** serape
Spanish: **8** mantilla

Shawnee
language family: **9** Algonkian **10** Algonquian
location: **4** Ohio **6** Kansas **8** Missouri, Oklahoma **9** Tennessee **12** Pennsylvania **13** South Carolina
leader: **8** Tecumseh **11** Tenskwatawa
related to: **8** Delaware

She
author: **13** H Rider Haggard

shear 3 cut, lop **4** clip, crop, snip, trim **5** prune, shave **6** fleece, remove **7** deprive, relieve, scissor

Shearer, Norma
real name: **17** Edith Norma Shearer
born: **6** Canada **8** Montreal
husband: **14** Irving Thalberg
roles: **8** The Women **9** A Free Soul **11** The Divorcee (Oscar) **14** Romeo and Juliet, Their Own Desire **15** Marie Antoinette **26** The Barretts of Wimpole Street

shears 5 clips, trims **6** prunes **7** pruners **8** clippers, scissors, trimmers

sheath 3 pod **4** case, coat, skin **6** casing, jacket **7** capsule, coating, wrapper **8** covering, envelope, membrane, scabbard, slipcase, wrapping **9** container **10** receptacle

sheathing 6 casing, siding **8** covering

Sheba
father: **6** Bichri, Joktan, Raamah **7** Jokshan

---

sharp 3 sly **4** acid, curt, fine, foxy, high, keen, sour, tart, wily **5** acrid, acute, alert, angry, awake, blunt, clear, cruel, edged, gruff, harsh, nippy, piked, quick, rapid, salty, sheer, spiny, steep **6** abrupt, artful, astute, barbed, biting, bitter, clever, crafty, crusty, fierce, keenly, marked, pointy, severe, shrewd, shrill, strong, sudden, thorny, tricky, unkind **7** acutely, alertly, angular, bearish, bristly, brusque, caustic, closely, crabbed, cunning, cutting, drastic, exactly, extreme, galling, intense, nipping, piquant, pointed, prickly, quickly, raucous, toothed, violent **8** abruptly, distinct, on the dot, piercing, promptly, scathing, serrated, spiteful, stinging, strident, suddenly, venomous, vertical, vigilant, vinegary **9** conniving, deceptive, excessive, on the nose, precisely, rancorous, unethical, vitriolic **10** contriving, discerning, immoderate, inordinate, perceptive, punctually **11** attentively, calculating, on the button, penetrating, precipitous **12** unprincipled, unscrupulous **13** precipitously
French: **5** juste
Spanish: **7** en punto

grandfather: 4 Cush
7 Keturah
people of: 7 Sabeans

Shebat 19 eleventh Hebrew month

she carved it
Latin: **8** sculpsit

shed 3 hut **4** cast, doff, drop, emit, molt **5** exude, hovel, shack, spill, strew, throw **6** lean-to, shanty, shower, slough, spread **7** cast off, discard, let fall, let flow, radiate, scatter **8** disperse, lose hair, toolshed **9** broadcast, discharge, tool house **10** distribute **11** disseminate, outbuilding

she died
Latin: **5** obiit

shed light on 7 clarify, explain **9** elucidate, explicate, make clear, make plain **10** illuminate

She Done Him Wrong
director: 13 Lowell Sherman
cast: 7 Mae West (Diamond Lil) **9** Cary Grant, Noah Beery **13** Gilbert Roland

shed tears 3 cry, sob **4** bawl, weep **6** boohoo **7** blubber

Sheehy, Gail
author of: 8 Passages **14** The Pathfinders

Sheeler, Charles
born: 14 Philadelphia PA
artwork: 9 Landscape, Upper Deck **11** Incantation **12** City Interior, Rolling Power **15** Bucks County Barn, River Rouge Plant **31** American Landscape Nineteen Thirty

sheen 4 glow **5** glaze, gleam, glint, gloss, shine **6** luster, patina, polish **7** burnish, glister, glitter, shimmer **8** radiance **9** shininess **10** brightness, brilliance, effulgence, glossiness, luminosity, refulgence **12** luminousness, resplendence

Sheen, Martin
real name: 12 Ramon Estevez
born: 8 Dayton OH
son: 12 Charlie Sheen **13** Emilio Estevez
roles: 8 Badlands **12** The Believers **13** Apocalypse Now **14** Catch Twenty-two **18** The Subject Was Roses **27** The Execution of Private Slovik

Sheena, Queen of the Jungle
creator: 8 SR Powell **13** W Morgan Thomas
character: 3 Bob **4** Chim

she engraved it
Latin: **8** sculpsit

sheep
breed: 5 Iraqi **6** Hirrik, Merino, Panama, Romney, Somali **7** Cheviot, Karakul, Lincoln, Suffolk, Targhee **8** Columbia, Cotswold, Tatarian **9** Montadale, Romeldale, Southdown **10** Corriedale, Dorset Down, Dorset Horn, Shropshire, Sikkim Bera **11** Rambouillet **13** Hampshire Down **15** Border Leicester
female: 3 ewe
family: 7 Bovidae
genus: 4 Ovis
group of: 5 drove, flock **6** cosset
meat: 4 lamb **6** mutton
oil from: 7 lanolin
wild: 5 urial **6** argali **7** bighorn, mouflon
young: 4 lamb **7** lambkin **8** yearling

sheepish 3 shy **4** meek **5** timid **6** docile, guilty, humble **7** abashed, ashamed, bashful, fearful, hangdog, passive, servile **8** blushing, obedient, obeisant, timorous, yielding **9** chagrined, chastened, diffident, mortified, shrinking, tractable **10** shamefaced, submissive **11** embarrassed, subservient, unassertive, unresisting

sheepishness 7 chagrin **8** docility, meekness **10** diffidence **11** bashfulness **12** tractability **13** embarrassment **14** submissiveness **15** unassertiveness

Sheep Well, The
also: 13 Fuente Ovejuna
author: 10 Lope de Vega

sheer 4 fine, pure, thin **5** bluff, filmy, gauzy, plumb, sharp, steep, total, utter **6** abrupt **7** perfect, unmixed **8** absolute, complete, gossamer, vertical **9** out and out, unalloyed, unbounded, unlimited **10** consummate, diaphanous **11** precipitous, transparent, unmitigated, unqualified **12** unrestrained **13** perpendicular, unadulterated, unconditional

sheet 3 top **4** coat, film, leaf, pane, slab **5** layer, panel, piece, plate **6** sheath, square **7** blanket, coating, overlay **8** bed sheet, covering, membrane **9** rectangle

shegetz 12 non-Jewish boy, non-Jewish man

Sheldon, Sidney
author of: 9 Bloodline **12** Rage of Angels, The Na-

ked Face **15** If Tomorrow Comes **20** A Stranger in the Mirror **22** The Other Side of Midnight

shelf 4 bank, prop, reef, slab **5** ledge, shoal **6** mantel, mantle **7** bedrock, bracket, stratum **9** supporter **11** mantelpiece, mantelpiece

shell 3 pod **4** bomb, case, hulk, hull, husk, shot **5** pound, round, shuck **6** bullet, fire on, pepper, rocket **7** barrage, bombard, grenade, missile **8** carapace, skeleton **9** cartridge, framework **10** projectile

shellac 4 beat, drub, lick, whip **7** clobber, lacquer, trounce, varnish

Shelley, Mary Wollstonecraft
father: 13 William Godwin
husband: 18 Percy Bysshe Shelley
author of: 12 Frankenstein

Shelley, Percy Bysshe
author of: 7 Adonais, Alastor **8** Queen Mab, The Cenci **16** A Defence of Poetry, Ode to the West Wind **17** Prometheus Unbound

shellfish 4 clam, crab **5** prawn **6** cockle, mussel, oyster, shrimp **7** abalone, lobster, mollusk, scallop **8** barnacle, crawfish, crayfish **9** trunkfish **10** crustacean **13** softshell crab
spawn: 4 spat

shell out 3 pay **6** expend **8** allocate, disburse, dispense **10** contribute

shelter 5 cover, guard, haven, house, lodge **6** asylum, defend, harbor, refuge, safety, shield, take in **7** care for, housing, lodging, protect **8** quarters, security **9** safeguard, sanctuary **10** protection

Sheltered Life
author: 12 Ellen Glasgow

shelve 5 defer, table **6** put off **7** suspend **8** lay aside, postpone, put aside, put on ice, set aside **10** pigeonhole

Shem
father: 4 Noah
brother: 3 Ham **7** Japheth
son: 8 Arphazed
descendant of: 6 Semite

shenanigans 5 sport **6** antics, capers, hijinx, pranks, stunts, tricks **8** deviltry, mischief, nonsense **9** highjinks, horseplay, silliness **10** buffoonery, tomfoolery **11** roguishness **12** monkeyshines, sportive-

ness **14** monkey business
15 mischievousness

she painted it
Latin: **6** pinxit

shepherd 4 herd, lead, show,
tend **5** guard, guide, pilot
6 direct, escort, herder, keeper,
patron, shield **7** protect, shelter **8** champion, defender,
guardian, herdsman, provider
9 custodian, protector, safeguard **10** benefactor

**Shepherdess and the
Sweep, The**
author: **21** Hans Christian
Andersen

shepherds
god of: **3** Pan **6** Tammuz

sherbet 3 ade, ice **6** sorbet
7 dessert

Shere Khan
character in: **14** The Jungle
Books
author: **7** Kipling

Sheridan, Ann
real name: **16** Clara Lou
Sheridan
nickname: **9** Oomph Girl
born: **8** Denton TX
husband: **10** Scott McKay
11 George Brent **12** Edward
Norris
roles: **8** King's Row **11** Silver
River **12** Nora Prentiss
16 Wings for the Eagle
20 Angels with Dirty Faces

Sheridan, Philip H
served in: **8** Civil War **10** Indian Wars
side: **5** Union
commander of: **19** Army of
the Shenandoah
rank: **22** general in chief of
US army
battle: **9** Five Forks **10** Cedar
Creek, Winchester **11** Chattanooga, Chickamauga, Fisher's Hill **12** Sayler's Creek
18 Wilderness Campaign

Sheridan, Richard Brinsley
author of: **9** The Critic, The
Duenna, The Rivals **18** A
Trip to Scarborough **19** The
School for Scandal

sheriff 7 officer **9** constable

Sheriff of Nottingham
character in: **9** Robin Hood

**Sherman, William
Tecumseh**
nickname: **4** Cump
served in: **8** Civil War
10 Mexican War
side: **5** Union
battle: **6** Shiloh **7** Atlanta,
Bull Run **8** Savannah
9 Vicksburg **11** Chattanooga
15 Kenesaw Mountain
fought against: **8** Johnston

rank: **20** general in chief of
army
famous for: **13** march to the
sea (Georgia)
established: **29** Command
and General Staff College
saying: **9** War is hell

sherry
type: **4** wine **6** brandy
origin: **5** Spain
varieties: **4** fino (dry) **7** amo-
roso (sweet), oloroso (me-
dium dry)
drink: **6** Adonis, Bamboo
9 Andalusia
with gin: **11** Renaissance
with vermouth: **6** Brazil

Sherwood, Robert E
author of: **13** Idiot's Delight
15 Reunion in Vienna
18 The Petrified Forest
19 Roosevelt and Hopkins,
There Shall Be No Night
20 Abe Lincoln in Illinois
screenplay: **22** The Best
Years of Our Lives

she sculptured it
Latin: **8** sculpsit

she speaks
Latin: **8** loquitur

She Stoops to Conquer
author: **15** Oliver Goldsmith
character: **6** Marlow **8** Hastings **10** Sir Charles **11** Tony
Lumpkin **12** Mr Hardcastle
13 Mrs Hardcastle **14** Kate
Hardcastle **16** Constance
Neville

she wrote (it)
Latin: **8** scripsit

shibah, shivah 14 mourning
period
literally: **9** seven days

shibboleth 6 byword, saying,
slogan **8** apothegm
9 catchword

Shibboleth 17 Gileadite
password

shield 4 keep, star **5** aegis,
badge, cover, guard, house,
shade **6** buffer, button, emblem, ensign, fender, harbor,
screen, secure **7** buckler, defense, protect, shelter **8** insignia, keep safe, preserve
9 medallion, protecter, protector, safeguard **10** escutcheon,
protection

Shield (of Sobieski)
constellation of: **6** Scutum

shielded 6 hidden **7** guarded
9 concealed, protected,
sheltered

Shields, Brooke
real name: **20** Christa Brooke
Shields
born: **9** New York NY

roles: **10** Pretty Baby
11 Endless Love **13** The
Blue Lagoon

shift 2 go **4** move, slip, vary,
veer **5** hitch, stint **6** change,
swerve, switch **7** chemise,
turning, veering **8** exchange,
straight, transfer **9** deviation,
transpose, variation **10** alteration, assignment, reposition
11 alternating, fluctuation, interchange **12** modification
French: **8** camisole

shiftless 3 lax **4** idle, lazy
8 careless, inactive, indolent,
slothful **10** ne'er-do-well
13 lackadaisical **14** good-for-
nothing **15** unconscientious

shifty 4 foxy, wily **6** crafty,
sneaky, tricky **7** cunning, evasive **8** scheming, slippery
9 conniving, deceitful, dishonest **10** contriving, unreliable
11 maneuvering, treacherous
13 untrustworthy

Shikasta
author: **12** Doris Lessing

shiksa 13 non-Jewish girl
14 non-Jewish woman

shillelagh 4 club **5** stick **6** cudgel **9** truncheon

shilly-shally 5 stall, waver
6 dawdle, dither, falter, seesaw **8** hesitate **9** fluctuate,
hem and haw, oscillate,
vacillate

shilly-shallying 8 dawdling,
wavering **9** uncertain, undecided **10** indecision, indecisive,
irresolute **11** vacillation

Shimazaki Toson
author of: **5** Hakai **20** The
Broken Commandment

shimmer 4 beam, glow
5 blink, dance, flash, gleam,
quake, shine, waver **6** quiver,
shiver **7** flicker, flutter, glisten,
sparkle, tremble, twinkle, vibrate **8** blinking **9** coruscate
11 scintillate **12** phosphoresce

shindig 3 hop **4** ball, bash,
prom **5** dance, party **6** affair,
shindy **7** blowout, revelry
9 barn dance, festivity, record
hop **10** masked ball, the
dansant
French: **4** fete, gala **6** soiree
9 bal masque **10** bal
costume

shine 3 wax **4** beam, buff,
glow **5** blink, flash, glare,
gleam, glint, gloss, light, rub
up, sheen **6** dazzle, luster, polish, waxing **7** buffing, burnish,
flicker, glimmer, glisten, glister, glitter, radiate, shimmer,
sparkle, twinkle **8** brighten, radiance **9** coruscate, irradiate,

polishing **10** brightness, brilliance, burnishing, luminosity **11** scintillate **12** illumination, luminousness **13** incandescence

shininess 5 gleam, glint, gloss, sheen **6** luster, polish **7** shimmer

shining 5 aglow **6** glossy **7** glowing, radiant **8** gleaming, luminous, lustrous **9** brilliant, effulgent **11** illustrious **12** incandescent

Shining, The
author: **11** Stephen King

shiny 6 bright, glossy **7** glaring, glowing, radiant **8** gleaming, luminous, lustrous, polished **9** brilliant, burnished, effulgent, sparkling **10** glistening, glittering, shimmering **12** incandescent **13** scintillating

ship 4 crew, send **5** craft, liner, route, tramp, yacht **6** packet, tanker, vessel **7** carrier, cruiser, forward, steamer **8** dispatch **9** destroyer, freighter, steamship, transport **10** ocean liner

Ship of Fools
author: **19** Katherine Anne Porter
director: **13** Stanley Kramer
cast: **9** Jose Greco, Lee Marvin **10** Jose Ferrer **11** George Segal, Oscar Werner, Vivien Leigh **14** Simone Signoret **15** Elizabeth Ashley

shipshape 4 neat, snug, taut, tidy, trip, trim **5** tight **6** spruce **7** orderly

Shirer, William L
author of: **28** The Collapse of the Third Republic **29** The Rise and Fall of the Third Reich

shirk 4 duck, shun **5** avoid, dodge, elude, evade **6** escape, eschew, ignore **7** goof off, neglect **8** malinger, sidestep **9** goldbrick

shirker 5 piker **6** dodger, evader, loafer, rotter, truant **7** deserter, quitter, slacker **9** goldbrick **10** backslider, malingerer

Shirley Temple
ingredient: **9** ginger ale, grenadine
also called: **9** Roy Rogers

shirr 5 crimp, smock **6** gather, pucker **8** bake eggs

shirt 3 top **4** sark **5** frock, waist **6** blouse, bodice **10** underwaist

shirty 5 angry, irked, testy, vexed **7** annoyed **9** irritated **11** disgruntled

Shittimwood 12 Biblical tree

shiver 5 quake, shake **6** quaver, shimmy **7** shudder, tremble

shivers 3 bit **5** piece, shard **6** sliver **8** fragment

shivery 3 icy, raw **4** cold, cool **5** brisk, chill, crisp, nippy **6** arctic, biting, bitter, chilly, frigid, frosty, wintry **7** quaking, trembly **8** chilling **9** quivering **11** penetrating

shoal 3 bar **4** bank, flat **5** crowd, shelf **6** school **7** sand bar, shallow **8** sand bank

shock 3 jar, mat, mop **4** blow, bush, cock, crop, daze, jolt, mane, mass, pile, rick, rock, stun, turn **5** scare, shake, sheaf, stack, start, upset **6** appall, bundle, dismay, impact, offend, revolt, thatch, trauma **7** astound, disgust, disturb, horrify, outrage, perturb, stagger, startle, stupefy **8** astonish, bowl over, disquiet, distress, paralyze, surprise, unsettle **9** collision, overwhelm **10** concussion, discompose, disconcert **11** disturbance **13** consternation

shocking 4 foul **5** awful **6** grisly, horrid, odious **7** ghastly, hideous, jarring, jolting **8** gruesome, horrible, indecent, terrible, wretched **9** abhorrent, appalling, frightful, monstrous, offensive, repellent, repugnant, revolting, startling, upsetting **10** abominable, astounding, detestable, disgusting, disturbing, horrifying, outrageous, perturbing, scandalous, staggering, stupefying, surprising, unsettling **11** astonishing, disgraceful, disquieting **12** insufferable, overwhelming **13** disconcerting, reprehensible

shoddy 3 low **4** base, mean, poor **5** dirty, nasty, tacky **6** shabby, sloppy, stingy **7** lowdown, miserly **8** careless, inferior, slipshod **9** haphazard, negligent, niggardly **10** second-rate, ungenerous **11** inefficient **12** contemptible **13** inconsiderate, reprehensible

shoe
French: **9** chaussure

shoemaker 7 cobbler **9** bootmaker

Shoemaker's Holiday, The
author: **12** Thomas Dekker

Shoes of the Fisherman, The
author: **11** Morris L West

Shogun
author: **12** James Clavell

Sholokhov, Mikhail
author of: **19** And Quiet Flows the Don **21** The Virgin Soul Upturned

shoo 3 out **4** away, oust, rout, scat **5** be off, chase, leave, scram **6** beat it, be gone, depart, get out, go away **7** cast out, get lost, vamoose

shoot 3 bud, fly, hit **4** bolt, cast, dart, dash, drop, fell, fire, hurl, jump, kill, leap, nick, pelt, plug, race, rain, rush, stem, tear, toss, twig, wing **5** eject, fling, go off, hurry, shell, sling, speed, spray, sprig, spurt, sweep, throw, waste **6** charge, launch, let fly, pepper, propel, riddle, shower, spring, sprout **7** bombard, explode, pick off, tendril **8** catapult, detonate, open fire **9** discharge

Shootist, The
director: **9** Don Siegal
cast: **9** John Wayne, Ron Howard **10** Hugh O'Brien **11** Harry Morgan, Sheree North **12** James Stewart, Lauren Bacall, Richard Boone **13** John Carradine **15** Scatman Crothers

Shoot the Piano Player
director: **16** Francois Truffaut
cast: **11** Marie Dubois **12** Nicole Berger **14** Michele Mercier **15** Charles Aznavour
setting: **5** Paris

shoot up 4 rise, soar **6** rocket

shop 3 buy **4** hunt, look, mart, mill **5** plant, store, works **6** browse, market, studio **7** factory **8** emporium, purchase, workshop **9** patronize **10** windowshop **13** establishment
French: **7** atelier **8** boutique

shopkeeper 6 dealer, monger, trader, vendor **8** merchant, purveyor, retailer **9** tradesman

shopworn 5 banal, corny, faded, stale, tired, trite, vapid **6** jejune **10** threadbare

shore 4 bank, hold, land, prop **5** beach, brace, brink, coast **6** hold up, margin, strand **7** bolster, bulwark, seaside, support, sustain **8** buttress, mainstay, seaboard, seacoast, underpin **9** reinforce, riverbank, waterside **10** strengthen
Latin: **10** terra firma

shorebird 3 auk **4** rail, sora **5** snipe, stilt, wader **6** avocet, curlew, plover, puffin **7** lapwing **8** woodcock **9** guillemot, sandpiper **13** oyster catcher

shore up 4 prop **5** brace
6 prop up **7** bolster, support
8 buttress **9** reinforce

short 3 low **4** curt, lean, slim,
thin **5** brief, cross, elfin, fleet,
gruff, hasty, pygmy, quick,
runty, scant, sharp, small,
squat, terse, testy, tight
6 abrupt, bantam, little, meager, scanty, scarce, skimpy,
slight, sparse, stubby
7 brusque, compact, concise,
cursory, lacking, limited, not
long, not tall, slender, stunted,
summary, wanting **8** abridged,
abruptly, dwarfish, fleeting,
impolite, snappish, succinct,
suddenly, unawares **9** condensed, curtailed, deficient,
impatient, momentary, niggardly, pint-sized, truncated
10 by surprise, diminutive,
short-lived **11** abbreviated, ill-
tempered, Lilliputian, pocket-
sized **12** insufficient **13** precipitously **14** without warning

shortage 4 lack, want
6 dearth **7** deficit **8** leanness,
scarcity, sparsity **9** shortfall
10 deficiency, inadequacy,
scantiness, sparseness
13 insufficiency

shortcoming 4 flaw **5** fault
6 defect, foible **7** blemish, failing, failure, frailty **8** drawback, handicap, weakness
10 deficiency, inadequacy
12 imperfection

shorten 3 cut **4** clip, pare,
trim **5** prune, shave, shear
6 lessen, reduce **7** abridge, curtail, cut down **8** condense,
contract, cut short, decrease,
diminish **10** abbreviate

shortening 3 fat, oil **4** lard,
oleo **6** butter, digest **7** cutting,
summary **8** abstract, synopsis,
trimming **9** hemming up, mar-
garine, reduction **11** abridgement, compression,
contraction, curtailment
12 abbreviation, condensation

short form 6 digest, precis
7 summary **8** abstract, synopsis **11** abridgement, contraction **12** abbreviation,
condensation

**Short Happy Life of Francis
Macomber, The**
 author: **15** Ernest Hemingway

short journey 5 jaunt **6** outing **7** day trip **9** excursion

short-lived 5 brief **7** passing
8 fleeting **9** ephemeral, momentary, temporary, transient
10 evanescent, transitory,
unenduring **11** impermanent
24 here today and gone
tomorrow

shortly 4 anon, soon **7** by and
by **8** directly, in a trice,
promptly **9** forthwith, presently **10** before long
11 immediately

short narrative 5 essay,
story **6** sketch **8** anecdote
10 short story

shortsighted 4 rash **6** myopic
7 foolish **8** careless, heedless,
purblind, reckless, weak-eyed
9 amblyopic, imprudent **10** ill-
advised, incautious, unthinking **11** improvident, injudicious, nearsighted,
thoughtless **12** undiscerning
13 uncircumspect

short-tempered 4 curt **5** cross,
huffy, sharp, testy **6** abrupt,
cranky, crusty, grumpy, shirty,
touchy **7** bearish, grouchy,
peevish, waspish **8** choleric,
snappish **9** irascible, irritable,
splenetic **10** ill-humored, out
of sorts, short-fused **11** hot-
tempered, ill-tempered
12 cantankerous

Shosha
 author: **19** Isaac Bashevis
 Singer

Shoshone (Snake)
 language family:
  10 Shoshonean
 location: **4** Utah **5** Idaho
  6 Nevada **7** Wyoming
 translator: **9** Sacagawea

Shoshonean
 tribe: **4** Hopi, Moki **5** Snake
  6 Hopitu, Paiute **7** Bannock
  8 Comanche, Shoshoni

**Shostakovich, Dmitri
(Dimitri)**
 born: **6** Russia **12** St
 Petersburg
 composer of: **7** The Nose
  9 Leningrad (symphony No
  7) **11** May the First **12** The
  Golden Age **17** Katerina Is-
  mailova **19** Lady Macbeth of
  Mzensk

shot 2 go **3** hit, try **4** dose,
move, play, toss **5** balls, blast,
crack, drive, essay, guess,
salvo, slugs, throw **6** beat-up,
archer, bowman, chance, report, ruined, shabby, stroke,
volley **7** attempt, bullets, gun-
fire, shooter, surmise, worn-
out **8** decrepit, marksman, rifleman **9** discharge, explosion,
fusillade, injection **10** ammunition, conjecture, detonation
11 dilapidated, projectiles
12 falling apart, sharpshooter

shot in the arm 4 lift
5 boost **6** uplift **8** stimulus
13 encouragement

shot in the dark 5 guess
6 notion, theory **9** guesswork,

suspicion **10** assumption, conjecture, hypothesis

shoulder 3 rim **4** bank, bear,
brow, bump, edge, push, side,
take **5** brink, carry, crest, elbow, lunge, shove, skirt,
verge **6** assume, border, jostle,
margin, take on, thrust, uphold **7** scapula, support, sustain **8** clavicle **9** undertake

shoulder blade 7 scapula
8 omoplate **9** bladebone

shout 3 cry **4** bawl, call, hoot,
howl, roar, yell, yelp **5** burst,
cheer, hollo, whoop **6** bellow,
chorus, clamor, cry out, holler, hurrah, huzzah, outcry,
scream, shriek **7** call out, exclaim, screech, thunder **8** outburst **9** hue and cry
10 hullabaloo

shout down 3 boo **4** hiss
6 hoot at, revile **7** catcall, condemn **8** denounce, drown
out

shove 4 bump, butt, jolt, prod,
push **5** boost, crowd, drive, elbow, force, impel, nudge
6 joggle, jostle, propel, thrust
8 shoulder

show *see box*

Showboat
 author: **10** Edna Ferber

showcase 7 cabinet, counter,
display, exhibit, vitrine

showdown 3 war **6** battle, climax, combat, crisis **7** face-off
8 clashing, conflict **9** collision,
encounter **13** confrontation

shower 3 wet **4** fall, pour,
rain, rush **5** flood, salvo,
spray, surge **6** deluge, lavish,
splash, stream, volley, wealth
7 barrage, bombard, drizzle,
torrent **8** downpour, plethora,
sprinkle **9** profusion **10** cloudburst, inundation
11 bombardment

showiness 7 glitter **8** splendor
9 jazziness **10** flashiness **11** ostentation **14** grandiloquence

Show-me State
 nickname of: **8** Missouri

show-off 6 egoist **7** boaster,
egotist, windbag **8** braggart,
fanfaron, flaunter, strutter
9 extrovert, swaggerer
11 braggadocio **13** cock of the
walk, exhibitionist **14** life of
the party

showpiece 3 gem **5** jewel,
pearl, pride, prize **6** rarity,
wonder **7** classic, paragon
8 treasure **10** masterwork
11 chef d'oeuvre, masterpiece,
prizewinner **17** piece de
resistance

show 4 bare, bill, fair, give, lead, mark, play, pomp, pose, sham, sign **5** argue, coach, drama, endow, favor, front, grant, guide, movie, opera, prove, teach, token, tutor, usher **6** appear, attest, ballet, bestow, comedy, direct, effect, evince, expose, hint at, impart, inform, lavish, reveal, school, tender, unveil **7** bear out, bespeak, certify, conduct, confirm, display, exhibit, explain, lay bare, musical, picture, pretext, proffer, program, suggest, uncover **8** ceremony, delusion, disclose, dispense, evidence, illusion, indicate, instruct, intimate, manifest, operetta, point out, pretense, vaunting **9** establish, make clear, make known, represent, spectacle **10** appearance, disclosure, distribute, exhibition, exposition, expression, impression, indication, pretension, production, revelation **11** affectation, attestation, corroborate, counterfeit, demonstrate, performance, testimonial **12** bring to light, substantiate **13** demonstration, entertainment, manifestation, motion picture

show up 4 come **5** outdo **6** appear, arrive, attend, crop up, expose, loom up, reveal, turn up **9** be present **11** come to light, make a fool of **12** come into view **13** become visible

showy 4 loud **5** gaudy, vivid **6** flashy, florid, garish, ornate **7** pompous **8** colorful, gorgeous, imposing, splendid, striking **9** brilliant **11** magnificent, pretentious **12** ostentatious

Shqyptare, Shqiprija, Shqiperi *see* **7** Albania

shred 3 bit, ion, jot, rag **4** atom, band, hair, iota, spot, whit **5** grain, piece, scrap, speck, strip, trace **6** morsel, ribbon, sliver, tatter **7** snippet **8** fragment, molecule, particle **9** scintilla

shrew 3 hag, nag **5** harpy, scold, vixen, yenta **6** kvetch, virago **7** she-wolf **8** battle-ax, fishwife, harridan, spitfire **9** termagant, Xanthippe

shrewd 3 sly **4** foxy, keen, wily, wise **5** acute, cagey, canny, quick, sharp, slick, smart **6** artful, astute, clever, crafty, shifty, smooth, tricky **7** careful, cunning, knowing, probing, prudent **8** cautious, piercing, scheming, sensible, slippery **9** designing, farseeing, sagacious **10** contriving, discerning, farsighted, perceptive **11** calculating, circumspect, intelligent, penetrating, quickwitted, self-serving, sharpwitted **12** disingenuous **13** Machiavellian, perspicacious

shrewdness 6 acumen **7** cunning, slyness **8** foxiness, keenness, wiliness **9** acuteness, cageyness, sharpness, slickness, smartness **10** artfulness, astuteness, cleverness, craftiness, smoothness, trickiness **11** carefulness, discernment **12** slipperiness **16** disingenuousness

shriek 3 cry **4** call, hoot, howl, peal, yell, yelp **5** shout, whoop **6** cry out, holler, outcry, scream, squawk, squeak, squeal **7** screech

shrift 7 penance **9** atonement, expiation **10** confession

shrill 4 high, loud **6** piping **7** blaring, raucous **8** piercing, strident **9** clamorous **10** screeching **11** high-pitched, penetrating

shrine 5 altar **6** chapel, church, temple **7** sanctum **8** monument **9** sanctuary

shrink 3 ebb, shy **4** balk, duck, wane **5** cower, demur, dry up, quail, stick, wince **6** blench, bridle, cringe, flinch, lessen, pucker, recoil, reduce, refuse, retire **7** curtail, decline, deflate, dwindle, retreat, shorten, shrivel, shudder **8** compress, condense, contract, decrease, diminish, draw back, hang back, make less, withdraw **9** constrict **11** make smaller **12** draw together **13** become smaller

shrink from 4 hate, shun **5** abhor, evade **6** balk at, detest, eschew, loathe, resist **7** despise **8** recoil at **9** abominate, shudder at **12** be revolted by **13** find repulsive

shrinking 3 shy **5** timid **6** ebbing, waning **7** bashful **8** reticent, retiring, timorous **9** declining, dwindling **10** decreasing, shriveling **11** contraction, diminishing

shrive 6 pardon **7** absolve, forgive

shrivel 5 dry up, parch, wizen **6** pucker, scorch, shrink, wither **7** wrinkle

Shropshire Lad, A author: **9** A E Housman

shroud 4 hide, pall, veil, wrap **5** cloak, cloud, cover, sheet **6** clothe, mantle, screen, swathe **7** blanket, conceal, envelop **8** covering **9** cerecloth, cerements **11** burial cloth **12** graveclothes, winding sheet

shrub 4 bush **5** brush **8** beverage **10** fruit drink

shrubbery 4 bush **5** brush **6** bushes, shrubs **9** brushwood **10** underbrush **11** undergrowth

Shuara *see* **6** Jivaro

shuck 4 husk, peel, shed **5** chaff, shell, strip

shudder 4 jerk, pang **5** quake, shake, spasm, throb **6** quaver, quiver, shimmy, shiver, tremor, twitch **7** flutter, tremble **8** paroxysm **9** pulsation, trembling **10** convulsion

shudder at 4 hate **5** abhor **6** detest, loathe **8** recoil at **9** abominate, can't stand **10** recoil from, shrink from

shuffle 3 mix **4** drag, gimp, limp, step **5** scuff, slide **6** clumsy, jumble, scrape **7** shamble **8** scramble **9** rearrange **10** disarrange **11** interchange

shul, schul 9 synagogue

shun 5 avoid, dodge, elude, evade, forgo **6** eschew, forego, ignore, refuse, reject **7** boycott, disdain **10** circumvent, fight shy of, shrink from **11** keep clear of, shy away from **12** have no part of, keep away from, steer clear of, turn away from

shut 3 box **4** cage, coop, draw, fold, lock, snap **5** clasp, close, drawn, latch **6** closed, closet, corral, draw to, fasten, intern, locked, lock in, secure **7** confine, drawn to, enclose, fence in, impound, latched, secured **8** cloister, closed up, fastened, imprison **9** barricade, constrain **11** incarcerate

shut down 4 halt, stop **5** cease **7** suspend **9** close down, interrupt **11** discontinue

Shute, Nevil author of: **10** On the Beach

shut in 4 cage **5** caged, pen in **6** coop up, encage, lock up **7** confine, encaged, enclose **8** confined, cooped up, enclosed, locked up, restrain, restrict **10** restrained, restricted

shut one's eyes to 5 allow **6** ignore, wink at **8** overlook **9** connive in, disregard **11** pay no heed to **14** turn one's back on

shut out 3 bar **5** debar **6** defeat **7** exclude **8** obstruct, prohibit

shutter 5 blind, close, shade **6** screen **7** curtain

shut the door on 3 ban, bar **6** forbid, refuse, reject **7** exclude, keep out, shut out **8** prohibit

shut up 4 cage, coop, hush, lock, pent **5** close, pen in **6** immure **7** be quiet, confine, silence **8** imprison **11** incarcerate

shy 4 balk, meek, wary **5** chary, cower, dodge, leery, minus, scant, short, timid, under, wince **6** blench, demure, flinch, in need, modest, shrink, swerve **7** anxious, bashful, careful, fearful, lacking, needing, nervous, wanting **8** cautious, draw back, jump back, reserved, reticent, skittish, timorous **9** deficient, diffident, shrinking, tremulous **10** suspicious **11** distrustful **12** apprehensive **13** self-conscious

shy away from 4 duck, shun **5** avoid, dodge, spurn **6** balk at, refuse, reject **10** shrink from **12** steer clear of

Shylock
　character in: **19** The Merchant of Venice
　author: **11** Shakespeare

shyness 8 meekness, timidity **9** reticence **10** diffidence, insecurity **11** bashfulness **12** sheepishness, timorousness **14** self-effacement **15** unassertiveness

shyster 5 rogue **6** lawyer **8** attorney **10** mouthpiece **11** pettifogger **15** ambulance chaser

si 3 yes

Siam *see* **8** Thailand

Sibelius, Jean
　born: **7** Finland **10** Tavastehus
　composer of: **6** En Saga **7** Karelia, Legends, Tapiola, The Band **8** Kalevala **9** Finlandia **10** The Tempest **12** The Oceanides, Voces Intimae **14** Ride and Sunrise

Siberia, Siber 8 disfavor **10** punishment **14** undesirability
　city: **4** Omsk **5** Chita, Tomsk **6** Kurgan **7** Irkutsk, Yakutsk
　conqueror: **9** Timafeyev **11** Genghis Khan
　continent: **4** Asia
　gulf: **2** Ob
　inhabitant: **4** Yaku **5** Sagai, Tatar **6** Tartar **7** Yukagir **8** prisoner **17** political prisoner
　mountain range: **4** Ural **5** Altai, Altay
　river: **2** Ob **3** Ket, Ili, Taz **4** Amga, Amur, Lena, Onon **5** Ishim, Tobol **6** Olekma
　sea: **4** Kara **6** Laptev **7** Okhotsk

sibyl 4 seer **5** augur **6** oracle **7** diviner **9** predictor, sorcer-

ess **10** forecaster, prophetess, soothsayer **13** fortune teller **14** prognosticator

Sibyls
　form: **10** prophetess
　inspired by: **5** deity **6** Apollo
　names: **6** Libyan **7** Cumaean **10** Erythraean
　prophecies: **14** Sibylline Books

sic 2 so **4** thus

Sicilian Vespers, The
　also: **20** Les Vepres Siciliennes
　opera by: **5** Verdi
　character: **5** Elena **6** Arrigo **7** Procida **8** Monforte

Sicily *see box*

sick 3 ill **4** weak **5** frail, tired, weary **6** ailing, infirm, laid up, poorly, queasy, sickly, uneasy,

---

Sicily
　other name: **7** Sicilia **9** Trinacria, Triquetra
　capital/largest city: **7** Palermo
　others: **3** Aci **4** Enna, Noto **6** Ragusa **7** Augusta, Catania, Marsala, Messina, Trapani **8** Syracuse **10** Montelepre
　division: **4** Enna **6** Ragusa **7** Catania, Messina, Palermo, Trapani **8** Siracusa, Syracuse **9** Agrigento **13** Caltanissetta
　government: **13** region of Italy
　measure: **5** salma **7** caffiso
　monetary unit: **5** litra, oncia, uncia **6** carlin **7** carline, oncetta
　island: **5** Egadi **6** Lipari, Ustica **7** Pelagie **11** Pantelleria
　lake: **7** Pergusa **8** Camarina
　mountain: **4** Erei, Moro, Sori **5** Atlas, Erici, Hybla, Iblei, Ibrei **7** Nebrodi, Vulcano **9** Apennines, Le Madonie, Stromboli **10** Peloritani
　highest point: **4** Etna **5** Aetna
　river: **4** Acis **5** Salso, Torto **6** Belice, Simeto **7** Mazzaro, Platani
　sea: **6** Ionian **10** Tyrrhenian **13** Mediterranean
　physical feature:
　　cape: **4** Boeo, Faro **7** Lilibeo, Passaro, Passero, Pelorus
　　gulf: **4** Noto **7** Catania
　　strait: **7** Messina
　　wind: **7** sirocco
　people: **5** Elymi, Sican, Sicel **6** Sicani, Siculi
　　author: **9** Lampedusa **10** Pirandello
　　composer: **7** Bellini
　　king: **4** Eryx **5** Bomba, Henry, Peter, Roger **7** Charles, Cocalus, Leontes **9** Ferdinand, Frederick
　　ruler: **4** Rome **5** Arabs, Goths, Spain **6** Greeks **7** Germans, Normans, Vandals, Vikings **8** Carthage, Saracens **9** Aragonese, Byzantium, Egyptians, Phoenicia **15** Holy Roman Empire
　language: **7** Italian
　religion: **13** Roman Catholic
　place:
　　cathedral: **8** Monreale
　　resort: **4** Enna **8** Taormina
　　ruins: **14** Villa Imperiale **15** Temple of Concord **18** Valley of the Temples
　feature:
　　brigands: **5** Mafia
　　evening stroll: **11** passeggiata

unwell **7** crushed, grieved, invalid, unsound **8** delicate, stricken, troubled, wretched **9** afflicted, bored with, disturbed, miserable, nauseated, perturbed, suffering, unhealthy **10** disquieted, distressed, indisposed **11** discomposed, heartbroken **15** under the weather

sicken 5 repel, shock, upset **6** offend, revolt **7** disgust, horrify, make ill, repulse **8** nauseate **14** turn the stomach

sickening 4 foul, vile **5** nasty **7** noisome **8** horrible, unsavory **9** abhorrent, loathsome, offensive, repellent, repugnant, repulsive, revolting **10** disgusting, nauseating **11** distasteful

sickly 3 ill, wan **4** drab, flat, lame, pale, sick, weak **5** ashen, faint, frail, silly **6** ailing, feeble, flimsy, guilty, infirm, leaden, peaked, poorly, sneaky, torpid, unwell **7** insipid, invalid, unsound **8** delicate, smirking **9** afflicted, apathetic, bloodless, simpering, unhealthy **10** cadaverous, lackluster, namby-pamby, snickering, spiritless, uninspired, wishy-washy **11** ineffective **12** unconvincing **13** self-conscious

sickness 6 malady, nausea **7** ailment, disease, illness **8** debility, disorder, vomiting **9** complaint, frailness, ill health, infirmity **10** affliction, disability, invalidism, poor health, queasiness **11** unsoundness **12** qualmishness **13** indisposition

sic passim 12 so throughout

sic semper tyrannis 19 thus always to tyrants
    motto of: 8 Virginia

sic transit gloria mundi 33 thus passes away the glory of this world

Siddhartha
    author: 12 Hermann Hesse
    story of: 6 Buddha

siddur 16 Jewish prayer book
    literally: 5 order

side 3 hem, rim **4** area, body, brim, edge, half, hand, part, sect, team, view **5** angle, bound, cause, facet, flank, group, house, light, limit, minor, party, phase, skirt, slant, stand, stock **6** allied, aspect, behalf, belief, border, circle, clique, fringe, lesser, margin, region, sector, strain **7** askance, coterie, faction, lateral, lineage, oblique, opinion, postern, quarter, related, section, segment, surface **8** alliance, attitude, boundary, division, indirect, marginal, position, skirting **9** accessory, bloodline, coalition, on one side, perimeter, periphery, secondary, territory, viewpoint **10** collateral, contingent, federation, incidental, standpoint, subsidiary **11** affiliation, association, unimportant **13** insignificant

Side
    origin: 5 Irish
    form: 7 fairies
    owner: 14 Tuatha De Danann

sideboard 6 buffet **8** credenza

side by side 7 abreast **8** abutting, together **9** adjoining **11** cheek by jowl, in proximity
    Latin: 9 pari passu

Side Effects
    author: 10 Woody Allen

sidekick 3 pal **4** aide **5** buddy **6** deputy, friend **9** assistant **10** lieutenant

sideline 5 bench, hobby **8** boundary **9** avocation **14** put out of action

sidestep 4 duck **5** avert, avoid, dodge, elude, evade, skirt **6** bypass, escape **10** circumvent, fight shy of **12** steer clear of

sidestepping 7 dodging, ducking, eluding, evasion **8** skirting **9** avoidance **13** circumvention

sidewalk 4 curb **8** footpath, pavement **9** promenade

sideways, sideway 6 aslant **7** askance, lateral, oblique **8** crabwise, edgeways, edgewise, sidelong, sideward, sidewise **9** cross wise, laterally, obliquely, to the side **11** from one side

side with 5 agree **7** stand by, stick by, support **8** champion **12** take one's part

sidle 4 cant, edge, skew, veer **10** lateralize

Sidney, Sir Philip
    author of: 7 Arcadia **15** Defence of Poesie, Defence of Poetry **18** Apologie for Poetrie, Astrophel and Stella

Sidney, Sylvia
    real name: 11 Sophia Kosow
    born: 7 Bronx NY
    husband: 11 Luther Adler **12** Bennett A Cerf
    roles: 4 Fury **7** Dead End **11** Street Scene **13** Les Mise-rables **15** Madame Butterfly **17** An American Tragedy **24** Summer Wishes Winter Dreams

Sidrophel
    character in: 8 Hudibras
    author: 6 Butler

siecle 3 age **6** period **7** century

Siegel, Jerry
    creator/artist of: 8 Superman

Siegfried
    origin: 8 Germanic
    mentioned in: 14 Nibelungenlied
    father: 7 Sigmund
    mother: 9 Sieglinde
    wife: 9 Kriemhild
    killed by: 5 Hagen
    same as: 6 Sigurd
    killed: 6 Fafnir
    won for Gunther: 10 Brunnhilde
    stole: 9 Tarnkappe

Sieg Heil 13 hail to victory
    salute used by: 5 Nazis

Sieglinde
    origin: 8 Germanic
    mentioned in: 14 Nibelungenlied
    husband: 7 Sigmund
    son: 9 Siegfried

Sienkiewicz, Henryk
    author of: 8 Quo Vadis?

Sierra Leone *see box, p. 892*

siesta 3 nap **4** rest **5** break, sleep **6** cat nap, snooze **10** forty winks

sieve 4 sift **6** filter, riddle, screen, sorter, strain **7** tattler **8** colander, strainer **9** separator **12** blabbermouth

sift 4 sort **5** drift, probe, study **6** filter, review, screen, search, winnow **7** analyze, inspect, scatter, sort out **8** separate **10** scrutinize **11** distinguish, investigate **12** discriminate

Siggeir
    origin: 12 Scandinavian
    king of: 5 Goths
    wife: 5 Signy
    causes death of: 7 Volsung

sigh 3 sob **4** hiss, long, moan, pine, weep **5** brood, groan, mourn, whine, yearn **6** grieve, lament, sorrow

sight 3 ken, see, spy **4** bead, espy, gaze, spot, view **5** image, scene, vista **6** behold, seeing, survey, vision **7** display, exhibit, eyeshot, glimpse, observe, pageant, scenery, viewing, prospect **8** eyesight, perceive, prospect, scrutiny **9** peepsight,

Sierra Leone
  name means: 12 lion mountain
  other name: 9 Gold Coast **10** Grain Coast, Ivory Coast
  capital/largest city: 8 Freetown
  others: 2 Bo **5** Hepel, Kissi, Lungi, Pepel **6** Bonthe, Kenema, Makeni, Shenge, Sulima
  school: 6 Njaia U **9** Fourah Bay
  measure: 4 load **6** kettle
  monetary unit: 4 cent **5** leone
  island: 4 York **6** Banana, Turtle **7** Sherbro
  mountain: 4 Loma **10** Tingi Hills
  highest point: 9 Bintimani
  river: 3 Moa **4** Jong, Mano, Meli, Ribi, Sewa, Taia **5** Bagbe, Mongo, Morro, Rokel **6** Mabole, Rokkel, Scarcy, Waanje **13** Great Scarcies **14** Little Scarcies
  sea: 8 Atlantic
  physical feature:
    bay: **5** Yawri **7** Sherbro
    cape: **8** Shilling **11** Sierra Leone
    peninsula: **7** Turners **11** Sierra Leone
    wind: **9** harmattan
  people: 3 Vai **4** Kono, Loko, Susu **5** Bulom, Kissi, Limba, Mende, Mendi, Temne **6** Creole, Fulani, Syrian **7** Gallina, Koranko, Kuranko, Sherbro, Yalunka **8** Lebanese, Mandingo
    explorer: **6** Cintra
    leader: **6** Margai **7** Stevens
  language: 4 Krio **5** Limba, Mende, Mendi, Temne **6** Creole **7** English
  religion: 5 Islam **7** animism **12** Christianity
  place:
    wharf: **10** King Jimmys
  feature:
    cloth: **5** garra
    clothing: **5** lappa **6** caftan
    secret society: **4** poro
  food:
    dish: **4** fufu **7** cassava
    sauce: **7** palaver

sighthole, spectacle **10** appearance, visibility

sighted 3 saw **4** seen **6** seeing **8** not blind, observed

sightless 5 blind **8** unseeing **9** unsighted

sightly 4 fair **6** lovely, pretty **8** handsome, pleasing **9** appealing, beautiful **10** attractive

Sigmund
  origin: 8 Germanic **12** Scandinavian
  mentioned in: 8 Volsunga **14** Nibelungenlied
  king of: 11 Netherlands
  father: 7 Volsung
  mother: 4 Liod, Ljod **5** Hliod
  wife: 7 Hiordis, Hjordis **8** Borghild **9** Sieglinde
  sister: 5 Signy
  lover: 5 Signy
  son: 6 Sigurd **9** Siegfried, Sinfiotli

sign 3 nod **4** clue, hint, mark, note, omen, wave **5** badge, brand, index, stamp, token, trait **6** emblem, ensign, figure, herald, motion, signal, symbol **7** earmark, endorse, feature, gesture, go-ahead, placard, portent, presage, symptom, warning **8** evidence, forecast, inscribe, neon sign, road sign, signpost **9** autograph, billboard, guidepost, harbinger, indicator, nameplate, trademark **10** indication, intimation, prognostic, suggestion, underwrite **11** forewarning **13** manifestation **14** characteristic

signal 3 cue, nod **4** sign **6** beckon, famous, motion, unique **7** command, eminent, gesture, guiding, honored, notable, warning **8** high sign, password, pointing, renowned, singular, striking **9** arresting, directing, direction, important, indicator, memorable, momentous, prominent, watchword **10** commanding, impressive, indicating, indication, noteworthy, one-of-a-kind, remarkable **11** conspicuous, distinctive, exceptional, illus-

trious, outstanding, significant **12** considerable **13** consequential, distinguished, extraordinary, unforgettable

significance 3 aim **4** note **5** drift, force, merit, sense, value, worth **6** import, intent, moment, object, virtue, weight **7** concern, gravity, meaning, portent, purpose **8** eminence, interest, priority **9** authority, direction, influence, intention, relevance **10** excellence, importance, notability, prominence **11** consequence, distinction, implication

significant 4 main **5** chief, grave, great, major, prime, vital **6** cogent, signal **7** eminent, knowing, notable, serious, telling, weighty **8** critical, distinct, eloquent, eventful, material, pregnant, symbolic **9** important, momentous, paramount, principal, prominent **10** emblematic, expressive, indicative, meaningful, noteworthy, portentous, remarkable, suggestive **11** exceptional, influential, outstanding, substantial, symptomatic **12** considerable **13** consequential, demonstrative **14** representative

signify 4 mean, omen, show, tell **5** argue, augur, imply **6** convey, denote, evince, herald, hint at, import, reveal, typify **7** bespeak, betoken, connote, declare, exhibit, express, portend, predict, presage, promise, suggest **8** announce, disclose, evidence, forebode, foretell, indicate, intimate, manifest, proclaim, set forth, stand for **9** be a sign of, designate, represent, symbolize **10** foreshadow **11** communicate, demonstrate

signing up 7 joining **9** enlisting, enrolling **10** enlistment, enrollment **11** registering **12** registration **13** matriculating, matriculation

Sign of Four, The
  author: 19 Sir Arthur Conan Doyle
  character: 11 Mary Morstan **12** Dr John Watson **13** Jonathan Small **14** Sherlock Holmes, Thaddeus Sholto

Signoret, Simone
  real name: 32 Simone-Henriette-Charlotte Kaminker
  born: 7 Germany **9** Wiesbaden
  husband: 11 Yves Montand **12** Yves Allegret

roles: 10 Madame Rosa **11** Ship of Fools **12** Room at the Top (Oscar) **14** Is Paris Burning?
autobiography: 27 Nostalgia Isn't What It Used to Be

sign up 4 join **6** enlist, enroll, join up **8** register **9** volunteer **11** matriculate

Signy
origin: 12 Scandinavian
mentioned in: 8 Volsunga
father: 7 Volsung
brother: 7 Sigmund
son: 9 Sinfiotli
husband: 7 Siggeir

Sigrdrifa
also: 18 Brynhildr Sigrdrifa
origin: 9 Icelandic
mentioned in: 9 Elder Edda
member of: 9 Valkyries
disobeyed: 4 Odin **5** Othin
sleeps in circle of: 4 fire
awakened by: 6 Sigurd

Sigurd
origin: 12 Scandinavian
mentioned in: 8 Volsunga
father: 7 Sigmund
mother: 7 Hiordis, Hjordis
wife: 6 Gudrun, Kudrun **7** Guthrun
killed: 6 Fafnir
acquired treasure of: 8 Andavari
won for Gunnar: 8 Brynhild

Sigyn
origin: 12 Scandinavian
husband: 4 Loki

Sikes, Bill
character in: 11 Oliver Twist
author: 7 Dickens

Sikkim *see box*

Sikorsky, Igor
nationality: 7 Russian **8** American
invented: 10 helicopter

Silas Marner
author: 11 George Eliot
character: 5 Eppie **11** Dunstan Cass, Godfrey Cass **13** Aaron Winthrop, Nancy Lammeter

silence 3 gag **4** calm, curb, halt, hush, kill, rout, stop **5** allay, check, crush, peace, quash, quell, quiet, still **6** banish, deaden, defeat, muffle, muzzle, repose, squash, stifle, subdue **7** conquer, nullify, put down, quieten, repress, reserve, squelch **8** choke off, dumbness, muteness, overcome, serenity, suppress, vanquish **9** lay to rest, placidity, quietness, reticence, stillness, tongue-tie **10** extinguish, placidness, put an end to, strike dumb **11** taciturnity, tranquility **12** tranquillity **13** noise-

lessness, secretiveness, soundlessness **14** speechlessness **16** closemouthedness **19** uncommunicativeness

silent 3 mum **4** calm, dumb, idle, mute **5** inert, muted, quiet, still, tacit **6** covert, hidden, hushed, placid, serene, unsaid **7** dormant, implied, muffled **8** discreet, implicit, inactive, inferred, lifeless, peaceful, reserved, reticent, taciturn, tranquil, unspoken, wordless **9** concealed, intimated, noiseless, quiescent, secretive, soundless, suggested, unsounded, unwritten **10** insinuated, mysterious, speechless, tongue-tied, undeclared, understood, unrevealed, unstirring, untalked-of **11** close-lipped, tight-lipped, unexpressed, unmentioned, unpublished, untalkative, unvocalized **12** closemouthed, unpronounced **15** uncommunicative

Silent Spring
author: 13 Rachel L Carson

Silenus
god of: 6 forest
oldest: 5 satyr
father: 3 Pan **6** Hermes
foster father of: 8 Dionysus
teacher of: 8 Dionysus
companion of: 8 Dionysus
sons: 6 Sileni

silicon
chemical symbol: 2 Si

Sikkim
capital/largest city: 7 Gangtok
others: 6 Dikchu, Lachen, Namchi, Rangpo, Rumtek **7** Lachung **9** Chungtang
government: 12 state of India
mountain: 7 Dongkya, Donkhya **9** Himalayas, Singalili **10** Darjeeling **12** Kanchenjunga
river: 5 Tista **6** Ranjit **9** Lachen Chu **10** Lachung Chu
physical feature:
mountain pass: **6** Natu La **7** Jelep La
storm: **7** monsoon
people: 4 Rong **5** Bhote **6** Bhotia, Bhutia, Indian, Lepcha **7** Tibetan **8** Nepalese **9** Mongoloid
king: **7** chogyal
religion: 5 Hindu **7** Lamaism **15** Tibetan Buddhism

silk
fabric: 4 crin **5** crepe, ninon, satin, surah, tulle **6** faille, pongee, sendal, tussah **7** chiffon, foulard, organza, raw silk, taffeta **8** organzie, paduasoy **10** peau de soie **12** crepe de chine
lining: 7 sarsnet **8** sarcenet
measure: 6 denier
raw silk: 5 grege **6** greige **8** marabout
source: 6 cocoon **9** silkworms
waste: 4 noil **5** floss
watered: 5 moire
yarn/thread: 4 tram **5** floss

silk-stocking 6 uptown **8** highborn, highbred, wellborn **9** patrician **10** upperclass **11** blue-blooded **12** aristocratic

Silk Stockings
director: 15 Rouben Mamoulian
cast: 10 Janis Paige, Peter Lorre **11** Cyd Charisse, Fred Astaire
setting: 5 Paris
score: 10 Cole Porter
remake of: 9 Ninotchka

silky 4 fine, soft **6** satiny, smooth **11** fine-grained

silliness 5 folly **6** drivel, idiocy **7** inanity **9** absurdity, asininity, frivolity **10** buffoonery, tomfoolery **11** foolishness **13** pointlessness **14** playing the fool, ridiculousness

Sillitoe, Alan
author of: 10 Her Victory **29** Saturday Night and Sunday Morning **36** The Loneliness of the Long-Distance Runner

silly 3 mad **4** dumb **5** crazy, giddy, inane **6** absurd, frothy, insane, stupid, unwary, unwise **7** aimless, asinine, fatuous, foolish, idiotic, shallow, witless **8** childish, farcical **9** brainless, foolhardy, frivolous, laughable, ludicrous, pointless, senseless **10** illadvised, irrational, ridiculous **11** empty-headed, harebrained, meaningless, nonsensical, purposeless **12** muddleheaded, preposterous, simpleminded, unreasonable **13** inappropriate, irresponsible, muddlebrained, rattlebrained **14** featherbrained **15** inconsequential

Silmarillion, The
author: 10 J R R Tolkien

Silone, Ignazio
real name: 17 Secondo Tranquilli
author of: 9 Fontamara **12** Bread and Wine **26** The Story of a Humble Christian

Silvanus
also: **8** Sylvanus
god of: **5** herds, house,
woods **12** farm boundary
16 uncultivated land

silver 5 coins, plate **6** argent,
change **7** jewelry **8** argentum,
platinum **9** argentine
10 silverware
chemical symbol: **2** Ag

Silver, Long John
character in: **14** Treasure
Island
author: **9** Stevenson

Silver, Mattie
character in: **10** Ethan
Frome
author: **7** Wharton

Silvers, Phil
real name: **17** Philip
Silversmith
born: **10** Brooklyn NY
roles: **9** Top Banana **13** Ser-
geant Bilko **15** High Button
Shoes **22** A Guide for the
Married Man **37** A Funny
Thing Happened on the
Way to the Forum
autobiography: **14** The Laugh
Is on Me

Silvius
father: **6** Aeneas

s'il vous plait 6 please **11** if
you please

Simenon, Georges
author of: **8** The Train
12 Act of Passion **14** The
Little Saint **15** Maigret's
Memoirs **28** The Strange
Case of Peter the Lett
character: **21** Inspector Jules
Maigret

Simeon
father: **5** Jacob
mother: **4** Leah
brother: **3** Dan, Gad **4** Levi
5 Asher, Judah **6** Joseph,
Reuben **7** Zebulun **8** Benjamin, Issachar, Naphtali
sister: **5** Dinah
canticle: **12** nunc dimittis
descendant of: **9** Simeonite

similar 4 akin, like, twin
5 close **6** allied **7** cognate,
kindred **8** agreeing, matching,
parallel **9** analogous, duplicate **10** comparable, equivalent, resembling
11 approximate, correlative,
much the same, nearly alike
13 correspondent,
corresponding

similarity 7 harmony, kinship,
oneness **8** affinity, likeness,
nearness, sameness **9** agreement, closeness, congruity,
semblance **10** congruence, similitude **11** concordance, conformance, equivalence,

parallelism, reciprocity, resemblance **13** comparability
14 conformability,
correspondence

similarly 4 thus **5** alike
7 equally **8** likewise **11** furthermore, identically
15 correspondingly

similitude 7 analogy **8** likeness,
sameness **10** similarity **11** parallelism, resemblance

simmer 4 boil, burn, foam,
fume, stew **5** chafe, smart
6 bubble, burble, gurgle,
seethe, sizzle

simmer down 7 cool off
8 calm down **14** collect oneself, compose oneself

Simmons, Jean
born: **6** London **7** England
husband: **13** Richard Brooks
14 Stewart Granger
roles: **4** Trio **6** Hamlet **7** Desiree, Ophelia, The Robe
9 Spartacus, Young Bess
11 Elmer Gantry **12** Guys
and Dolls **14** The Happy
Ending **17** Great Expectations **19** Androcles and the
Lion

Simois
god of: **5** river

Simoisius
killed by: **14** Telamonian
Ajax

Simon
also known as: **5** Peter
son: **13** Judas Iscariot
disciple of: **5** Jesus

Simon, Neil
author of: **10** Chapter Two,
Plaza Suite **11** Biloxi Blues
12 The Odd Couple **15** The
Sunshine Boys **16** Come
Blow Your Horn **17** Barefoot
in the Park **21** Last of the
Red Hot Lovers **25** The Prisoner of Second Avenue

Simon & Simon
character: **7** AJ Simon **9** Rick
Simon **12** Cecilia Simon
13 Downtown Brown
cast: **7** Tim Reid **10** Mary
Carver **13** Gerald McRaney,
Jameson Parker
setting: **8** San Diego

Simon Boccanegra
opera by: **5** Verdi
setting: **5** Genoa
character: **5** Maria, Paolo
6 Andrea, Fiesco, Pietro
14 Amelia Grimaldi, Gabriele Adorno

Simonov, Konstantin
author of: **13** Days and
Nights

simpatico 7 likable **9** agreeable, congenial, gemutlich

simper 5 smirk **6** giggle, tee-
hee, titter **7** snicker, snigger

simple 4 bare, dull, dumb,
easy, open, slow, soft, true
5 basic, blunt, dense, frank,
green, homey, naive, naked,
plain, quiet, sheer, stark,
thick **6** callow, candid, common, direct, honest, modest,
obtuse, rustic, stupid **7** artless,
foolish, natural, sincere **8** absolute, innocent, not fancy,
ordinary, peaceful, straight,
workaday **9** downright, elemental, guileless, ingenuous,
out-and-out, unadorned, unfeigned, untrimmed, un-
worldly **10** elementary,
manageable, not complex, unaffected, uninvolved **11** commonplace, fundamental, plain-
spoken, rudimentary,
thick-witted, undecorated, unvarnished **12** not difficult, not
elaborate, uncompounded
13 inexperienced, uncomplicated, unembellished, unpretentious **15** straightforward,
unsophisticated

simple house 3 cot, hut
5 shack **6** chalet **7** cottage
8 bungalow

simpleminded 4 dull, dumb,
slow **5** dense, silly, thick
6 stupid **7** asinine, fatuous,
foolish, idiotic, moronic, witless **8** retarded **9** brainless,
dim-witted, imbecilic **10** dull-
witted, half-witted **11** empty-
headed, harebrained, lamebrained **12** feeble-minded

simpleton 3 ass, oaf **4** dolt,
dope, fool, hick, jerk, rube
5 booby, dummy, dunce,
goose, idiot, ninny, stupe
6 donkey, rustic **7** dullard,
jackass **8** dumbbell, imbecile,
numskull **9** blockhead, greenhorn, ignoramus, numbskull
10 nincompoop

simplicity 6 candor, purity
7 clarity, honesty, naivete
8 easiness, openness, serenity
9 austerity, clearness, innocence, plainness, restraint, sincerity **10** directness
11 artlessness, cleanliness, naturalness, obviousness
12 truthfulness **13** guilelessness, unworldliness
19 straightforwardness

simply 7 clearly, lucidly,
plainly, starkly **8** directly,
modestly **9** naturally **10** explicitly **11** ingenuously **12** in-
telligibly, unaffectedly
15 uncomplicatedly, unpretentiously **17** straightforwardly

Simpson, O J (Orenthal James)
nickname: **5** Juice
sport: **8** football
position: **11** running back
team: **10** USC Trojans **12** Buffalo Bills **23** San Francisco Forty-Niners

simulate 3 act, ape **4** copy, fake, play, pose, sham **5** feign, mimic, put on **6** affect, assume, invent **7** imitate, playact, pretend **9** dissemble, fabricate **11** counterfeit, make believe

simulated 4 fake, sham **5** phony **6** forged **7** manmade, pretend **9** imitation, synthetic **10** artificial, fabricated **11** counterfeit, make-believe

simultaneous 6 coeval **10** coexistent, coexisting, coincident, concurrent, synchronal, synchronic **11** concomitant, synchronous **12** accompanying, contemporary **15** contemporaneous

sin 3 err **4** evil, fall, slip, vice **5** crime, error, lapse, shame, stray, wrong **6** breach, do evil, offend **7** do wrong, misdeed, offense, scandal **8** disgrace, evil deed, iniquity, trespass, villainy **9** violation **10** infraction, transgress, wrongdoing **13** transgression

Sin
origin: **8** Akkadian
god of: **4** moon

Sinaiticus 16 Greek uncial codex

Sinatra, Frank
real name: **20** Francis Albert Sinatra
nickname: **8** The Voice **11** Old Blue Eyes
born: **9** Hoboken NJ
wife: **9** Mia Farrow **10** Ava Gardner
daughter: **12** Nancy Sinatra
son: **14** Frank Sinatra Jr
leader of: **7** Rat Pack
roles: **8** Tony Rome **12** Angelo Maggio, Guys and Dolls, The Detective **14** The Joker Is Wild **17** The First Deadly Sin **18** From Here to Eternity **22** The Man with the Golden Arm

Sinbad the Sailor
character in: **27** Arabian Nights' Entertainments

since 2 as **3** ago, for, yet **4** ergo, from **5** after, hence, later **6** thence, whence **7** because, whereas **8** in as much **9** therefore **10** afterwards **11** accordingly, considering **12** subsequently

archaic: **4** sith
prefix: **3** cis
Scottish: **4** syne

sincere 4 real **5** frank **6** candid, honest **7** artless, earnest, genuine, natural, serious **8** truthful **9** authentic, guileless, heartfelt, ingenuous, unfeigned **10** forthright, unaffected **11** in good faith, undeceitful **12** wholehearted **15** straightforward

sincerely 5 truly **6** really **8** honestly **9** earnestly, genuinely, seriously **10** truthfully **14** wholeheartedly

sincerity 6 candor **7** honesty, probity **8** openness **9** frankness, good faith **11** artlessness, earnestness, genuineness, seriousness **12** truthfulness **13** guilelessness, ingenuousness **14** forthrightness, unaffectedness **16** wholeheartedness **19** straightforwardness

Sinclair, Upton
author of: **9** The Jungle, World's End **12** Dragon's Teeth
character: **9** Lanny Budd

Sindhi
language family: **12** Indo-European
branch: **11** Indo-Iranian
group: **5** Indic
spoken in: **13** Northern India

sine die 17 without fixing a day (for future action or a future meeting)
literally: **13** without the day

sine prole 14 without progeny **16** without offspring

sine qua non 15 without which not **18** something essential **22** indispensable condition

sinew, sinews 4 grit, thew **5** fiber, nerve, power, vigor **6** muscle, tendon **7** stamina **8** ligament, strength, virility, vitality **10** resilience, strengthen

sinewy 4 wiry **5** beefy, nervy, thewy, tough **6** brawny, robust, strong **7** fibrose, stringy **8** muscular, powerful, vigorous

Sinfiotli
origin: **12** Scandinavian
mentioned in: **8** Volsunga
mother: **5** Signy
father: **7** Sigmund

sinful 3 bad **4** evil, vile **5** wrong **6** errant, unholy, wicked **7** corrupt, heinous, immoral, impious, ungodly, wayward **8** criminal, depraved, shameful **9** miscreant **10** de-

generate, despicable, iniquitous, profligate, villainous **11** disgraceful, irreligious, unrighteous

sing 3 hum **4** lilt, pipe **5** carol, chant, chirp, croon, trill, tweet **6** chirp, warble **7** chirrup, whistle **8** melodize

Sing Along with Mitch
regulars: **10** Diana Trask **11** Mitch Miller **12** Leslie Uggams, Louise O'Brien, Sandy Stewart **13** Gloria Lambert, Sing Along Gang, Sing Along Kids

Singapore *see box, p. 896*

singe 4 burn, char, sear **5** brand **6** scorch

singer 4 alto, bard, bass, diva, lark **5** tenor **7** crooner, soprano **8** baritone, minstrel, songbird, songster, vocalist **9** chanteuse, chantress, contralto **10** songstress, troubadour **11** nightingale **12** countertenor, mezzo-soprano

singer, female
French: **9** chanteuse

Singer, Isaac Bashevis
author of: **6** Shosha **7** Old Love **8** The Manor **9** The Estate **13** Gimpel the Fool **15** The Family Moskat **16** In My Father's Court **24** The Spinoza of Market Street

singer, professional
French, Italian: **10** cantatrice

singing group 4 trio **5** choir **6** chorus **7** quartet **8** glee club **13** choral society **17** barbershop quartet

Singin' in the Rain
director: **9** Gene Kelly **12** Stanley Donen
cast: **9** Gene Kelly, Jean Hagen **11** Cyd Charisse **13** Donald O'Connor **14** Debbie Reynolds
song: **11** Make 'em Laugh

single 3 one **4** lone, sole **5** unwed **6** maiden **7** only one **8** bachelor, singular, solitary, spinster, wifeless **9** unmarried **10** individual, spouseless **11** husbandless

single file 8 one by one **10** Indian file, one at a time **13** in a single line **16** one behind another

single-handedly 5 alone **7** unaided **9** by oneself, on one's own **10** unassisted **11** without help

single-minded 4 firm **6** dogged **7** devoted, intense,

Singapore
other name: 8 Singa Pur
name means: 13 city of the lion
capital/largest city: 9 Singapore
others: 4 Tuas 6 Changi, Jurong 7 Nee Soon 9 Paya Lebar, Woodlands 10 Bukit Timah, Queenstown 12 Bukit Panjang 15 Toa Payoh New Town
  medieval town: 7 Temasek
school: 7 Nanyang 8 National 9 Singapore
monetary unit: 4 cent 6 dollar
island: 4 Ubin 5 Brani, Bukum, Pesek 7 Semakau 8 Merlimau, Southern 10 Ayer Chawan, Ayer Merbau 11 Blakang Mati, Tekong Besar 12 Tekong Kechil
mountain: 6 Mandai 7 Panjang
highest point: 10 Bukit Timah
river: 6 Jurong, Sungei 7 Kallang, Seletar 9 Singapore
sea: 6 Indian 10 South China
physical feature:
  harbor: 6 Keppel 9 Serangoon
  strait: 6 Johore, Pandan 8 Sembilan 9 Singapore
people: 5 Malay 6 Indian 7 Chinese 9 Malaysian, Pakistani, Sri Lankan
  founder: 7 Raffles
  leader: 10 Lee Kwan Yew
language: 5 Malay, Tamil 7 Chinese, English 8 Mandarin
religion: 4 Sikh 5 Hindu, Islam 6 Taoism 8 Buddhism 12 Christianity, Confucianism
place:
  amusement park: 8 New World 10 Great World, Happy World
  aquarium: 8 Van Kleef
  cathedral: 9 St Andrews
  gardens: 7 Botanic
  hall: 16 Victoria Memorial
  industrial park: 6 Jurong
  mosque: 6 Sultan
  park: 6 Farber 7 Merlion 12 Raffles Place
  street: 16 Raffles Boulevard
  temple: 17 One Thousand Lights
feature:
  boat: 4 junk 6 sampan
  clothing: 4 sari

staunch, zealous 8 resolved, tireless, untiring 9 dedicated, steadfast, tenacious 10 determined, inflexible, persistent, relentless, unswerving, unwavering 11 persevering, unflinching

singleness 12 bachelorhood, spinsterhood 14 unmarried state 17 single blessedness

single out 4 pick, take 6 choose, opt for, select 7 call out, extract, fix upon, pick out 8 decide on, set apart, settle on 11 distinguish

sing the praises of 4 hail, laud, tout 5 boost, cheer, exalt, extol, honor 6 praise 7 acclaim, applaud, approve, commend 8 eulogize 9 celebrate 10 compliment

singular 3 odd 4 rare 5 queer 6 choice, quaint, select, unique 7 bizarre, curious, strange, unusual 8 aberrant, abnormal, atypical, freakish, peculiar, peerless, superior, uncommon, unwonted 9 anomalous, different, eccentric, fantastic, marvelous, matchless, unequaled, unnatural, wonderful 10 noteworthy, outlandish, prodigious, remarkable, surpassing, unfamiliar 11 exceptional, uncustomary 12 unparalleled 13 extraordinary, unaccountable, unprecedented 14 unconventional 16 out-of-the-ordinary

Sinhalese
language family: 12 Indo-European
branch: 11 Indo-Iranian
group: 5 Indic
spoken in: 6 Ceylon 8 Sri Lanka

sinister 4 dark, dire, evil, foul, rank, vile 5 black 6 cursed, malign, wicked 7 adverse, fearful, hellish, ominous, unlucky 8 accursed, alarming, damnable, devilish, infernal, menacing, rascally 9 dismaying, insidious, malignant 10 despicable, detestable, diabolical, disturbing, malevolent, perfidious, villainous 11 disquieting, frightening, threatening, treacherous, unfavorable, unpromising 12 blackhearted, inauspicious, unpropitious 13 Machiavellian, reprehensible

sink 3 dig, dip, ebb, lay, sag, set 4 bore, bowl, bury, drop, fall, seep, slip, soak, tilt, wane 5 basin, drill, drive, droop, drown, gouge, lower, slant, slope, slump, stoop, yield 6 engulf, go down, lessen, plunge, reduce, shrink, worsen 7 decline, descend, give way, go to pot, go under, put down, regress, subside, succumb 8 diminish, excavate, languish, lavatory, scoop out, submerge, submerse, washbowl 9 hollow out, wash basin 10 degenerate, depreciate, go downhill, retrogress 11 deteriorate, go to the dogs

sinless 4 good, holy, pure 6 chaste 7 upright 8 innocent, spotless, virtuous 9 reputable, righteous

sinner 8 apostate, evildoer, offender 9 miscreant, misfeasor, reprobate, wrongdoer 10 backslider, malefactor, malfeasant, recidivist, trespasser 12 transgressor

Sinnis *see* 5 Sinis

Sinoeis *see* 3 Pan

Sinon
pretended to be: 13 Greek deserter
told Trojans of: 11 Trojan Horse

Sino-Tibetan
language branch: 7 Sinitic 12 Tibeto-Burman
includes: 4 Naga 5 Karen 7 Burmese, Chinese 8 Kuki-Chin, Mandarin

Sins, Seven 4 envy, lust 5 anger, pride, sloth 8 gluttony 12 covetousness

sinuosity 10 slinkiness 11 convolution, sinuousness 12 tortuousness

sinuous 6 curved, folded, volute, zigzag 7 bending, coiling, curving, twisted, winding 8 indirect, mazelike, rambling, tortuous, twisting 9 wandering 10 circuitous, convoluted, meandering, roundabout, serpentine, undulating 12 labyrinthine

sinuousness 9 sinuosity
10 slinkiness **11** convolution
12 tortuousness

Sinus
also: **6** Sinnis
vocation: **6** robber
daughter: **8** Perigune
killed by: **7** Theseus
epithet: **12** Pityocamptes

Siouan
tribe: **4** Crow, Iowa **5** Ioway,
Omaha, C age, Sioux **6** Dakota, Mandan **7** Hidatsa
8 Minitari, Wazhazhe
10 Assiniboin, Gros Ventre
11 Assiniboine

Sioux *see* **6** Dakota

Sioux State
nickname of: **11** North
Dakota

sip 3 lap, nip, sup **4** dram,
drop **5** drink, savor, taste
6 sample **7** soupcon, swallow
10 thimbleful

siphon 4 tube **5** drain **7** draw
off

siphonaptera
class: **8** hexapoda
phylum: **10** arthropoda
group: **4** flea

Sippar residents
11 Sepharvites

Siqueiros, David Alfaro
born: **6** Mexico **9** Chihuahua
artwork: **12** New Democracy
13 Echo of a Scream
14 Trial of Fascism **15** Ascent of Culture, Burial of a
Worker **16** Towards the Cosmos **17** Death to the Invader **18** Polyforum
Siqueiros **22** March of Humanity on Earth
24 Cuauhtemoc Against the
Myth

sir
French: **8** monsieur

sire 4 king, lord **5** beget,
breed **6** create, father **7** creator **9** originate **10** originator,
progenitor

siren, Siren 4 horn, vamp
5 alarm, nymph, witch **6** sex-
pot **7** charmer, whistle **8** deceiver, sea nymph
9 temptress **10** seductress
11 enchantress **13** warning
signal **15** bewitching woman
French: **11** femme fatale
form: **5** nymph
location: **3** sea
lured sailors by: **7** singing

**Sir Gawain and the Green
Knight**
author: **7** unknown
character: **10** King Arthur

22 Sir Bernlak de
Hautdesert
horse: **9** Gringalet

Sirian Experiments, The
author: **12** Doris Lessing

Sisera
commander for: **5** Jabin
defeated by: **5** Barak

sissified 6 prissy **7** unmanly
8 womanish **10** effeminate

sissy 6 coward **8** weakling
9 fraidy-cat **10** scaredy-cat

sister 3 nun, kin, sib **5** nurse
6 female **7** sibling **8** feminist,
relation, relative
nautically: **6** secure
10 strengthen
society: **8** sorority

Sister Carrie
author: **15** Theodore Dreiser
character: **11** G W Hurst-
wood **12** Carrie Meeber
13 Charles Drouet

Sister Woman
character in: **16** Cat on a
Hot Tin Roof
author: **8** Williams

Sisyphean 4 hard **5** tough
6 uphill **7** arduous, onerous
8 toilsome **9** demanding, difficult, strenuous, wearisome
10 exhausting

Sisyphus
king of: **7** Corinth
father: **6** Aeolus
mother: **7** Enarete
brother: **9** Salmoneus
wife: **6** Merope
son: **5** Almus **7** Glaucus
8 Ornytion **10** Thersander
founded: **6** Ephyra **7** Corinth
rolled: **5** stone

sit 3 lie **4** loll, meet, mind,
rest, rule, stay **5** abide, chair,
nurse, perch, reign, roost,
squat, stand, teach, watch
6 attend, endure, gather, govern, linger, remain, reside, settle, sprawl **7** baby-sit, care for,
convene, preside **8** assemble,
be placed, be seated, chaperon **9** have a seat, officiate
10 deliberate **11** be in session

site 4 area, post, spot, zone
5 field, locus, place, point,
scene **6** ground, locale, region,
sector **7** section, setting, station **8** district, locality, location, position, province
9 territory **11** whereabouts

sit in judgment 5 judge **6** decide, settle **7** adjudge, mediate **9** arbitrate, reconcile
10 adjudicate **12** bring to
terms

situ 5 place

situate 3 put, set **4** post

5 build, house, lodge, place,
plant, stand **6** billet, locate,
settle **7** install, station **8** ensconce, position **9** construct,
establish

situation 3 fix, job **4** case,
duty, post, role, seat, site,
spot, work **5** berth, place,
state **6** locale, office, plight,
status **7** dilemma, posture, station **8** capacity, function, locality, location, position,
quandary **9** condition **10** assignment, livelihood **11** predicament **13** circumstances
14 state of affairs

sit upon 5 brood, cover,
hatch **8** incubate

Sivan 16 third Hebrew month

**Six Characters in Search
of an Author**
author: **15** Luigi Pirandello

six cubits 4 reed

Six Million Dollar Man
character: **11** Dr Rudy Wells,
(Col) Steve Austin **12** Oscar
Goldman
cast: **9** Lee Majors **13** Martin
E Brooks **15** Alan Oppenheimer, Richard Anderson
spinoff: **11** Bionic Woman

Sixty Minutes
correspondent: **9** Dan
Rather **10** Andy Rooney
11 Diane Sawyer, Mike Wallace, Morley Safer **13** Harry
Reasoner

sizable 5 ample, broad, large,
roomy **7** immense **8** spacious
9 capacious, good-sized

size 3 sum **4** area, bulk, mass,
sort **5** array, grade, group,
scope, total **6** amount, extent,
spread, volume **7** arrange, bigness, content, expanse,
stretch **8** capacity, classify,
quantity, totality **9** aggregate,
amplitude, greatness, largeness, magnitude **10** dimensions **11** measurement,
proportions

sizzle 3 fry **4** hiss, spit
7 crackle, frizzle, hissing, sputter **8** splutter **10** sputtering

skate 3 nag, ray **4** skid, skim,
slip **5** blade, coast, glide,
horse, slide **6** rotter
female: **4** maid
genus: **4** Raja
mark: **4** cusp

skein 4 coil, hank, reel, yarn
5 twist, tangle, thread **9** filaments, twistings
members: **4** fowl **5** ducks,
flock, geese **6** flyers

skeletal 4 bony, thin **5** gaunt

6 wasted **9** emaciated **10** cadaverous

skeleton 4 hulk **5** bones, frame, shell **9** framework
purpose: 7 support **8** protects **9** framework

Skelton, Red
real name: 21 Richard Bernard Skelton
born: 11 Vincennes IN
roles: 7 I Dood It **8** Ship Ahoy **12** Panama Hattie **16** Neptune's Daughter **17** The Fuller Brush Man **18** Clem Kadiddlehopper, Whistling in the Dark **20** Freddie the Freeloader

skeptic, sceptic 7 atheist, doubter, scoffer **8** agnostic **10** questioner, unbeliever **14** doubting Thomas

skeptical, sceptical 6 unsure **7** cynical, dubious **8** doubtful, doubting, scoffing **9** uncertain **11** incredulous, questioning, unbelieving, unconvinced **12** disbelieving **13** hypercritical

skepticism 5 doubt **7** dubiety **8** distrust, mistrust, unbelief **9** disbelief, suspicion **11** agnosticism, incredulity **12** doubtfulness **13** faithlessness

sketch 3 map **4** draw, plot, skit **5** chart, draft, graph, scene **6** depict, digest, precis, satire **7** drawing, lampoon, mark out, outline, picture, portray, summary, takeoff **8** abstract, rough out, synopsis, vignette **9** blueprint, burlesque, delineate, short play, summarize **11** preliminary **16** characterization

Sketch Book, The
author: 16 Washington Irving

sketchy 4 bare, hazy **5** brief, crude, light, rough, short, vague **6** meager, skimpy, slight **7** cursory, outline, shallow, slender **9** essential, rough-hewn, unrefined **10** incomplete, undetailed, unfinished, unpolished **11** preliminary, preparatory, provisional, superficial

skewed 5 slued **6** veered, warped **7** oblique, sheered, slanted, swerved, twisted **9** distorted

skewer 3 pin, rod **4** spit, stab **5** truss **6** pierce, skiver **7** impale **9** brochette **10** run through

skid 3 ski **4** drag, dray, skim, skip, sled, slip **5** coast, glide, skate, slide **6** runner, sledge

7 skitter **8** glissade, platform, sideslip

Skidbladnir
origin: 12 Scandinavian
ship of: 4 Frey **5** Freyr
feature: 11 collapsible

Skidegatta
tribe: 5 Haida

Skidmore, Owings, and Merrill
partners: 13 John Merrill Sr, Louis Skidmore **15** Nathaniel Owings
architects of: 10 Lever House (NYC) **11** AEC town site (Oak Ridge TN) **13** Banque Lambert (Brussels) **16** John Hancock Tower (Chicago) **17** Terrace Plaza Hotel (Cincinnati), US Air Force Academy (CO) **18** Mauna Kea Beach Hotel (Kamuela HI) **19** Istanbul Hilton Hotel (Turkey) **23** Beinecke Rare Book Library (Yale) **26** Chase Manhattan Bank Building (NYC) **33** American Republic Insurance Building (Des Moines IA)
world's tallest building:
10 Sears Tower (Chicago)

skiff 4 boat **6** dinghy **7** rowboat

skiing
athlete: 9 Phil Mahre **11** Bill Johnson, Cindy Nelson **13** Gustavo Thoeni, Robert Cochran **14** Marilyn Cochran, Martha Rockwell **15** Debbie Armstrong, Ingemar Stenmark, Jean Claude Killy **16** Michael Gallagher **17** Barbara Ann Cochran **20** Annemarie Proell Moser

Skikne, Larushka Misch
real name of: 14 Laurence Harvey

skill 4 gift **5** craft, knack **6** acumen, talent **7** ability, cunning, faculty, knowhow, mastery, prowess **8** artistry, capacity, deftness, facility **9** adeptness, dexterity, expertise, handiness, ingenuity **10** adroitness, cleverness, competence, experience, expertness **11** proficiency **12** skillfulness **13** inventiveness

skilled 6 adroit, expert **7** trained **8** skillful **9** competent, masterful, practiced **10** proficient **12** accomplished

skilled worker 7 artisan **9** craftsman **10** technician **15** master craftsman

skillful 3 apt **4** able, deft, keen **5** adept, handy, sharp, slick **6** adroit, clever, expert, facile, gifted **7** capable, cunning, skilled, trained, veteran

8 masterly, talented **9** competent, dexterous, ingenious, masterful, practiced, qualified **10** proficient, well-versed **11** experienced **12** accomplished, professional

skim 3 fly **4** flip, ream, sail, scan, scud, skid, skip **5** coast, float, glide, skate, sweep **6** bounce, scrape **7** dip into **8** glissade **10** glance over **11** leaf through, move lightly **12** thumb through

skimp 5 pinch, stint **6** scrimp, slight **8** be frugal, be stingy, hold back, withhold **9** economize **11** cut expenses, scrape along

Skimpole, Harold
character in: 10 Bleak House
author: 7 Dickens

skimpy 5 close, scant, small, spare, tight **6** frugal, meager, modest, scanty, slight, sparse, stingy **7** miserly, scrimpy, sparing, wanting **8** exiguous, grudging, smallish, stinting **9** illiberal, niggardly, penurious, scrimping **10** inadequate, incomplete, too thrifty **11** close fisted, tightfisted **12** insufficient, parsimonious **13** pennypinching **14** inconsiderable

skin 3 fur, pod **4** bark, case, coat, flay, hide, hull, husk, peel, pelt, rind, shell, abrade, casing, fleece, jacket, scrape, sheath, lay bare, epidermis, complexion, integument, body covering, outer coating
outer layer: 9 epidermis
contains: 3 fat **4** hair, pore, root **5** nerve **6** vessel **8** oil gland **10** sweat gland
body's largest: 5 organ
sense of: 4 cold, heat, pain **5** touch **8** pressure, tickling

skinflint 5 miser **7** hoarder, niggard, scrooge **8** tightwad **10** pinchpenny **12** penny pincher

Skinner, Cornelia Otis
author of: 23 The Pleasure of His Company (with Samuel Taylor) **24** Our Hearts Were Young and Gay (with Emily Kimbrough)

skinny 4 lank, lean, thin, wiry **5** gaunt, skid, lanky, spare **6** slight **7** angular, scraggy, scrawny, slender, spindly **8** gangling, rawboned, shrunken, skeletal **9** emaciated

Skin of Our Teeth, The
author: 14 Thornton Wilder

skip 3 bob, cut, hop **4** flee, flit, jump, leap, miss, omit, romp, shun, trip **5** bound, caper, dodge, elude, evade **6** bounce, escape, eschew, gambol, ignore, prance, spring **7** abscond, make off, neglect **8** leap over, leave out, overlook, pass over **9** disappear, disregard, do without, play hooky, skedaddle **10** fly the coop **12** be absent from

skirmish 4 fray, tilt **5** brush, clash, joust, run-in, scrap, set-to **6** action, affray, battle, fracas, tussle **7** scuffle **8** struggle **9** encounter, firefight, scrimmage **10** engagement

skirmisher
  French: **10** tirailleur

Skirnir
  origin: **12** Scandinavian
  servant of: **4** Frey **5** Freyr

Skirophoria *see* **11** Scirophoria

skirt 3 hem, rim **4** edge, gird, kilt, maxi, mini, ring, shun **5** avoid, evade, flank, hem in, verge **6** border, bounds, circle, dirndl, fringe, girdle, margin **7** enclose, envelop **8** boundary, encircle, go around, lie along **9** crinoline, outer area, perimeter, periphery **10** circumvent, fight shy of **12** circumscribe, detour around

skittish 3 shy **4** wary **5** chary, jumpy, leery, shaky, timid **6** fitful, unsure **7** bashful, fearful, fidgety, flighty, guarded, jittery, nervous, restive **8** cautious, restless, unstable, unsteady, volatile **9** demurring, excitable, impulsive, mercurial, reluctant **10** suspicious **11** distrustful

skittles
  equipment: **4** pins **6** cheese
  also called: **5** closh **6** cloddy
    8 roly-poly **10** Dutch bowls
  tabletop version: **15** Enfield
    skittles

Skrymir
  also: **10** Utgardloki
  origin: **12** Scandinavian
  form: **5** giant
  took to Jotunheim: **4** Loki,
    Thor **7** Thialfi

Skuld 4 Norn
  origin: **12** Scandinavian
  form: **5** dwarf
  personifies: **6** future
  developed from: **5** Urdar
  companions: **3** Urd
    8 Verdandi

skulduggery, skullduggery
  7 knavery **8** trickery **9** chicanery, deception **10** dirty trick **12** pettifoggery

skulk 4 hide, lurk **5** cower, creep, prowl, slink, sneak **9** pussyfoot

skull
  contains: **5** brain

Skull place 7 Calvary
  8 Golgotha

sky 5 space **9** firmament **10** atmosphere, outer space, the heavens **12** arch of heaven
  goddess of: **3** Fri, Nut
    5 Frigg, Frija **6** Frigga

sky blue 5 azure **8** cerulean, pale blue **9** clear blue, light blue

Sky King
  character: **5** Penny **7** Clipper
  cast: **10** Kirby Grant **11** Ron
    Haggerty **13** Gloria Winters
  ranch: **11** Flying Crown
  plane: **8** Songbird

skylarking 5 sport **6** antics **7** hijinks, romping **10** frolicking

skypilot 5 padre, rabbi **6** cleric, parson, priest **8** chaplain, minister **9** clergyman

skyward 2 up **6** upward **8** to the sky **10** heavenward **12** to the heavens

slab 3 wad **4** hunk, slat **5** block, board, chunk, plank, slice, wedge **10** thick slice

slack 3 lax **4** dull, easy, free, lazy, limp, slow, soft **5** baggy, loose, quiet, relax **6** easily, flabby, freely, limply, loosen, pliant, remiss, slowly, untied **7** flaccid, let up on, loosely, not busy, not firm, not taut, offhand, relaxed, slacken **8** careless, dilatory, flexible, heedless, inactive, indolent, listless, not tight, slapdash, slipshod, slothful, sluggish **9** leisurely, lethargic, negligent, slow-paced, unmindful, untighten **10** neglectful, nonchalant, permissive, slow-moving, sluggishly, unexacting, unfastened, unthinking **11** inattentive, indifferent, thoughtless, unconcerned, undemanding

slacken 4 curb, ease, flag, free, slow **5** abate, check, let go, let up, limit, loose, relax, slack **6** arrest, go limp, lessen, loosen, reduce, retard, soften, temper, weaken **7** dwindle, inhibit, release **8** decrease, diminish, keep back, mitigate, moderate, restrain, slow down, taper off **9** untighten

slacker 5 idler **6** dodger, loafer, truant **7** dallier, dawdler, goof-off, laggard, quitter, shirker **9** do-nothing, goldbrick **10** malingerer **14** good-for-nothing, procrastinator

slag 5 dross **6** cinder, scoria **8** clinkers

slake 4 calm, cool, curb, ease, hush, sate **5** allay, quell, quiet, still **6** modify, quench, soothe, subdue, temper **7** appease, assuage, compose, gratify, mollify, relieve, satiate, satisfy **8** decrease, mitigate, moderate **9** alleviate **11** tranquilize **14** take the edge off

slake off 4 wane **5** abate **6** lessen, reduce, weaken **7** decline, subside **8** diminish, fade away, slack off

slam 3 hit **4** bang, bump, slap **5** crash, smack, smash, throw

slammer 3 jug, pen **4** jail, stir **5** clink **6** cooler, lockup, prison **8** big house, hoosegow **9** calaboose, jailhouse **12** penitentiary

Slammin' Sammy
  nickname of: **8** Sam Snead

slander 4 soil **5** libel, smear, sully **6** defame, malign, revile, vilify **7** calumny **8** besmirch **9** falsehood **10** defamation, distortion **12** vilification **14** false statement **17** misrepresentation

Slaney, Mary *see* **10** Mary Decker

slang 4 cant, jive **5** argot, idiom, lingo **6** jargon **7** dialect

slant 4 bias, lean, list, rake, tilt, view **5** angle, color, pitch, slope **7** distort, incline, leaning **8** attitude **9** prejudice, viewpoint

slanted 4 awry **6** biased, tilted **7** colored, crooked, leaning, pitched, sloping **8** inclined **9** on an angle, on the bias **10** prejudiced

slanting 4 bias **5** alean, atilt **7** oblique, sloping **8** diagonal, glancing, inclined **10** distorting

slap 3 cut, hit **4** blow, clap, cuff, snub, swat **5** smack, whack **6** insult, rebuff, strike, wallop **9** rejection

slapdash 6 casual, sloppy **8** careless, slipshod, slovenly **9** haphazard

Slapsie Maxie
  nickname of: **15** Maxie Rosenbloom

slash 3 cut, rip **4** drop, gash, mark, pare, rend, rent, slit, tear **5** lower, slice **6** reduce, stroke **8** decrease, lacerate, lowering **9** reduction **10** laceration

slate 4 list **6** ballot, tablet, ticket **10** blackboard, chalkboard

slattern 4 drab, slob, slut 5 bitch, frump 6 harlot, sloven 7 trollop

slatternly 6 frowsy, frumpy, sloppy, untidy 7 unkempt 8 slipshod, slovenly

slaughter 4 kill, slay 6 pogrom 7 butcher, destroy, killing, wipe out 8 decimate, massacre 9 bloodbath 10 annihilate, butchering, mass murder 11 exterminate

Slaughterhouse Five
author: 12 Kurt Vonnegut
character: 12 Billy Pilgrim
setting: 7 Dresden

Slav 4 Pole, Serb, Sorb, Wend 5 Croat, Czech 6 Bulgar, Slovak 7 Russian, Serbian, Slovene, Sorbian 8 Bohemian, Croatian, Moravian 9 Bulgarian, Ruthenian, Slavonian, Slovadian, Ukrainian

slave 4 prey, serf, toil 6 addict, drudge, menial, thrall, toiler, vassal, victim 7 chattel, plodder 8 bondsman 9 workhorse 11 bond servant

slaver 5 drool 6 drivel 7 slobber

slavery 4 toil 5 grind, labor, sweat 6 strain 7 bondage, serfdom, travail 8 drudgery, struggle 9 captivity, treadmill, vassalage 11 enslavement, impressment, subjugation 12 enthrallment

Slavic
language family: 12 Indo-European
group: 11 Balto-Slavic
subgroup: 12 Old Bulgarian 13 Eastern Slavic, Western Slavic 14 Southern Slavic 15 Old Church Slavic

slavish 5 exact 6 strict 7 literal, servile 9 imitative, slavelike 10 derivative, obsequious, submissive, unoriginal 11 subservient 13 unimaginative

slay 4 do in, kill 6 murder 7 destroy, execute 8 massacre 9 slaughter 10 annihilate

slayer 6 hit man, killer 7 butcher 8 assassin, murderer 11 executioner 12 exterminator

slaying 6 murder 7 killing 8 homicide 9 execution

sleazy 5 cheap, tacky 6 flimsy, shabby, shoddy, trashy, vulgar 7 schlock 13 insubstantial

sleek 4 oily 5 shiny, silky, slick, suave 6 glossy, satiny, smooth 7 fawning, velvety 8 lustrous, unctuous 12 ingratiating

sleep 3 nap 4 doze, rest 5 death, peace 6 repose, snooze 7 slumber
god of: 6 Hypnos, Hypnus, Somnus

sleeping 6 asleep, dozing 7 dormant, napping, resting 8 snoozing 9 quiescent, somnolent 11 hibernating 19 in the arms of Morpheus

Sleeping Beauty, The
composer: 11 Tchaikovsky

sleeping car (railroad)
invented by: 7 Pullman

sleeping infants
goddess of: 6 Cunina

sleeping place 3 bed, cot 4 bunk 5 berth 6 pallet 7 bedroom 9 dormitory 10 bedchamber

sleepless 5 alert 7 wakeful 8 restless, watchful 9 insomniac, wide awake 11 industrious

sleeplessness 8 insomnia 9 alertness, attention 11 wakefulness 12 restlessness

sleep lightly 3 nap, nod 4 doze 6 catnap, snooze 15 catch forty winks

sleepy 4 dull 5 quiet, tired, weary 6 drowsy 8 fatigued, inactive 9 exhausted

sleigh 4 dray, sled 6 cutter, sledge, troika 8 transport

Sleipnir
origin: 12 Scandinavian
horse of: 4 Odin 5 Othin
legs: 5 eight

slender 4 lean, poor, slim, thin, weak 5 faint, scant, small, spare 6 feeble, little, meager, narrow, remote, skinny, slight 7 willowy 8 delicate

Slender
character in: 22 The Merry Wives of Windsor
author: 11 Shakespeare

Sleuth
director: 17 Joseph L Mankiewicz
based on play by: 14 Anthony Shaffer
cast: 12 Michael Caine 15 Laurence Olivier

slew 3 lot, ton 4 gang, heap, load, lots, peck, pile, raft 5 batch, did in 6 killed 8 murdered 12 assassinated

Slezak, Walter
born: 6 Vienna 7 Austria
father: 9 Leo Slezak
roles: 5 Fanny 8 Lifeboat 11 Dr Coppelius

slice 3 cut 4 pare 5 carve, piece, sever, shave 6 cut off, divide 7 portion, section, segment, whittle 8 separate 9 dismember

slick 3 sly 4 coat, film, foxy, oily, scum, waxy, wily 5 sharp, shiny, sleek 6 clever, glassy, glossy, greasy, satiny, smooth, tricky 7 coating, cunning 8 slippery 10 make glossy 11 fast-talking 13 smooth-talking

slicker 8 raincoat 9 sou'wester 10 mackintosh, waterproof

slide 4 fall, pass, ramp, skid, slip, veer 5 chute, coast, glide, lapse, slope 7 slither 8 sideslip 11 diapositive 12 transparency

slide by 4 go by 5 lapse 6 elapse, roll by, slip by 7 glide by 8 slip away

slight 3 cut 4 lean, slap, slim, snub, thin, tiny 5 frail, small, spare 6 insult, little, modest, rebuff 7 fragile, limited, slender 8 moderate 10 incivility, negligible, restricted 11 unimportant 13 imperceptible, inappreciable, infinitesimal

slight amount 3 bit 4 dash, drop 5 pinch, touch, trace 6 little 7 smidgen, smidgin, soupcon 8 smidgeon 9 little bit 10 smattering

slightly 6 feebly, rarely 8 meagerly, scantily, scarcely, somewhat 10 negligibly 13 superficially 15 insignificantly

slim 4 lean, thin 5 faint, small 6 meager, remote, skinny, slight, svelte 7 distant, slender, thready, willowy 10 negligible

slime 3 mud 4 mire, muck, ooze 6 sludge

slimy 4 foul, vile 5 gummy, mucky, nasty 6 creepy, putrid, sticky 7 viscous 9 glutinous, loathsome, obnoxious, offensive, repulsive

sling 3 net 4 cast 5 fling, throw 9 slingshot 10 arm support

Slingin' Sammy
nickname of: 10 Sammy Baugh

slingshot 5 sling 8 catapult

slink 4 slip 5 creep, prowl, skulk, sneak, steal 6 tiptoe

slip 3 put 4 dock, drop, fail, fall, leak, pass, sink, skid 5 berth, error, glide, lapse, scrap, shoot, shred, slide, sneak, sprig, steal, strip 6 es-

cape, sprout, ticket, worsen
7 blunder, chemise, cutting,
decline, faux pas, receipt, sapling, voucher **9** petticoat,
stripling, youngling, youngster **10** be revealed, get clear
of, imprudence, underdress
12 indiscretion

slip away 4 go by **5** lapse
6 elapse, escape **7** run away,
slide by **8** creep off **9** tiptoe off

slip by 4 go by, pass **5** lapse
6 elapse, pass by, roll by
7 glide by, slide by

slip of the tongue, a
    Latin: **13** lapsus linguae

slipper 4 mule, shoe **5** scuff
6 sandal

slippery 4 foxy, oily, waxy,
wily **5** slick, soapy **6** crafty,
glassy, greasy, shifty, smooth,
sneaky, tricky **7** devious **9** deceitful **10** contriving, unreliable
11 treacherous
13 untrustworthy

slipshod 3 lax **5** loose, messy
6 casual, sloppy, untidy **7** offhand **8** careless, slovenly
11 thoughtless

slip-up 4 flub, goof **5** botch, error, gaffe, lapse **6** boo-boo,
bungle, foul-up, mess-up, miscue **7** blooper, blunder, clinker,
faux pas, mistake, screw-up
9 oversight

slit 3 cut **4** gash **5** crack, slash
7 crevice, fissure **8** incision

slither 5 glide, slide **25** move
with a side-to-side motion

sliver 5 crumb, shred, slice,
snick **6** morsel **8** splinter

slivovitz
    type: **6** brandy **7** liqueur
    origin: **10** Yugoslavia
    flavor: **4** plum

slob 6 sloven **8** slattern

slobber 4 slop **5** drool **6** drivel,
slaver **7** dribble, sputter **8** salivate, splutter

sloe gin
    type: **7** liqueur
    flavor: **9** sloe berry **15** black-
        thorn berry
    drink: **11** Sloe Gin Fizz
    with bourbon: **9** Black Hawk
    with rum: **11** Shark's Tooth
    with vermouth: **10** Blackthorn

slogan 5 motto **6** byword **9** battle cry, catchword, watchword

sloop 4 boat, brig, ship **5** smack
8 sailboat, schooner

slop 3 mud **4** mire, muck, ooze
5 filth, slosh, slush, spill,
swash, swill, waste **6** refuse,
sludge, splash **7** garbage, spatter **8** splatter

slope 3 tip **4** bank, bend, lean,
tilt **5** angle, pitch, slant **7** descent, incline **9** downgrade
11 inclination

sloping 5 alean, steep **6** aslant
7 leaning, oblique, tilting **8** diagonal, inclined, on a slant,
slanting **9** slantways
11 declivitous

sloppiness 5 chaos, mix-up,
upset **6** jumble **7** clutter **8** disarray, disorder, shambles
9 messiness **10** disharmony,
untidiness **12** dishevelment
14 disarrangement
15 disorganization

sloppy 3 wet **5** dirty, messy,
muddy **6** marshy, sloshy,
slushy, sodden, soiled,
swampy, untidy, watery **7** unclean **10** disorderly

sloppy person 4 slob **6** sloven

slosh 3 lap **4** drop, mire, stir
5 slush, spill, swash **6** splash
8 flounder

slot 3 gap **4** slit **5** crack, niche,
notch
    machine: **14** one-armed bandit

sloth 6 phlegm, torpor **7** languor **8** idleness, laziness, lethargy **9** indolence, lassitude,
torpidity **12** listlessness, sluggishness **13** do-nothingness,
shiftlessness

slothful 3 lax **4** idle, lazy **5** inert **6** drowsy, otiose, supine,
torpid **8** indolent, listless, sluggish **9** do-nothing, lethargic,
negligent, shiftless **10** slug-
gardly **11** unambitious

slouch 4 bend **5** droop, hunch,
idler, slump, stoop **6** loafer
7 laggard, shirker, slacker
8 sluggard **9** goldbrick,
lazybones

Slovakia
    formerly part of:
        14 Czechoslovakia
    capital/largest city:
        10 Bratislava
    others: **6** Kosice
    head of state: **9** president
    government: **8** republic
    monetary unit: **5** crown
        6 koruna
    mountain: **7** Sudetes **8** Low
        Tatra **9** High Tatra, Slovak
        Ore **10** Carpathian, Nizke Ta-
        try **11** Visoke Tatry **15** White
        Carpathian

    river: **2** Uh **3** Vah **4** Hron **5** Ni-
        tra, Slana **6** Danube, Hornad,
        Ondava, Poprad **7** Laborec
        8 Latorica
    people: **5** Czech **6** Slavik, Slo-
        vak **9** Hungarian
    language: **6** Slavik, Slovak
    religion: **9** Christian **13** Roman
        Catholic

Slovenia
    capital/largest city: **9** Ljubljana
    others: **5** Celje, Koper, Kranj
        7 Maribor
    head of state: **9** president
    government: **8** republic
    monetary unit: **5** tolar
    river: **4** Sava **5** Drava
    sea: **8** Adriatic
    people: **8** Slovenes
    language: **7** Slovene
    religion: **13** Roman Catholic

slovenly 5 dirty, dowdy, messy
6 frowzy, sloppy, untidy **7** unclean, unkempt **8** careless,
slapdash, slipshod **10** disorderly, slatternly **11** indifferent,
unconcerned

slow 3 dim, off **4** curb, dull,
dumb, flag, late, long **5** brake,
check, dense, heavy, loath,
quiet **6** averse, boring, falter,
hinder, hold up, impede, obtuse, retard, stupid, torpid
7 belated, delayed, laggard,
lumpish, not busy, overdue,
tedious, unhasty **8** backward,
cautious, dawdling, dilatory,
dragging, drawn out, extended,
hesitant, inactive, obstruct,
sluggish, tarrying **9** dim-witted,
leisurely, lingering, ponderous,
prolonged, reluctant, snail-like,
unhurried **10** behind time, decelerate, deliberate, dull-witted,
indisposed, protracted, unexciting, unpunctual **11** disinclined,
halfhearted, reduce speed
12 impercipient, lose momentum, tortoiselike, unperceptive

slowdown 4 curb, flag **5** brake,
delay, letup, slump **6** ease-up,
falter, hinder, impede, lessen,
retard, slow-up **7** decline, fall-
off, letdown, setback, slowing,
subside **8** diminish, downturn,
flagging **9** grind down **10** decelerate, slackening, stagnation
11 reduce speed, retardation
12 deceleration

slow-moving 4 poky **5** pokey
6 idling **8** crawling, creeping,
dawdling, sluggish **9** leisurely,
snaillike **10** turtlelike
12 tortoiselike
    creature: **4** slug **5** loris, sloth,
        snail **6** turtle **8** tortoise

slowness 6 tedium **8** dullness
9 torpidity **10** snail's pace
12 backwardness, sluggishness

slow-paced 4 easy **7** gradual, laggard **8** sluggish **9** leisurely, lethargic, unhurried **10** deliberate

slowpoke 4 slug **5** idler, snail **7** dallier, dawdler, laggard, lie-abed, plodder **8** lingerer, slug-abed, tortoise **9** saunterer, straggler **11** foot-dragger

slow to learn 4 dull **5** dense, inapt **6** stupid **8** retarded **10** slow-witted

slow up 4 stem **5** delay **6** detain, hinder, impede, retard **8** slow down

slow-witted 4 dull **5** dense **7** doltish, idiotic, moronic **8** backward, retarded **9** imbecilic

sludge 3 mud **4** mire, muck, ooze, slop **5** dregs, slime, slush **8** sediment

slug 3 bat, hit **4** bash, belt, sock **5** baste, clout, pound, punch, smite, thump, whack, whale **6** batter, strike, wallop **7** clobber **8** lambaste

sluggard 4 lazy **5** drone, idler, sloth, snail **6** loafer, truant, turtle **7** dawdler, laggard **8** loiterer, slothful, slowpoke, tortoise **9** do-nothing, lazybones **11** couch potato **12** lounge lizard **13** stick-in-the-mud

sluggish 4 lazy, slow **5** inert **6** torpid **7** languid **8** inactive, indolent, lifeless, listless, slothful **9** leisurely, lethargic, soporific, unhurried **10** phlegmatic, protracted, spiritless

sluggishness 6 torpor **7** inertia **8** lethargy, slowness **9** lassitude **10** inactivity **12** listlessness

slum
Portuguese: **6** favela

slumber 3 nap **4** doze **5** sleep **6** snooze **8** vegetate **9** hibernate **10** be inactive, lie dormant

slump 3 dip, sag **4** drop, fall, slip **5** droop, lapse **6** plunge, slouch, tumble **7** decline, give way, reverse, setback **8** collapse

slur 3 cut, dig **4** mark, skip, spot **5** smear, stain, sully, taint **6** defame, ignore, insult, malign, mumble, mutter, slight **7** affront, blacken, blemish, let pass **8** mumbling, overlook, pass over **9** disregard, gloss over, muttering **11** run together

slush 4 slop **6** bathos **9** soppiness **11** mawkishness, melting snow **14** sentimentalism, sentimentality

slushiness 5 slush **10** sponginess **11** mawkishness **14** sentimentalism, sentimentality

slut 4 doxy, jade **5** bimbo, frump, hussy, tramp, wench, whore **6** floozy, harlot, sloven, wanton **7** jezebel, trollop **8** slattern, strumpet **10** prostitute

sly 4 foxy, wily **6** artful, covert, crafty, secret, shrewd, sneaky, tricky **7** cunning, furtive, playful, private **8** stealthy **9** conniving **11** dissembling, mischievous **12** confidential

Slye, Leonard
real name of: **9** Roy Rogers

slyness 5 craft **7** cunning, stealth **8** archness, foxiness, subtlety, wiliness **10** artfulness, craftiness, shrewdness, trickiness **11** furtiveness

smack 3 bit, hit, rap **4** blow, buss, clap, cuff, dash, hint, kiss, slap **5** savor, smell, smite, spank, taste, tinge, touch, trace, whack **6** buffet, flavor **7** suggest

small 4 mean, tiny, weak **5** faint, minor, petty, scant **6** feeble, lesser, little, meager, modest, narrow, petite, slight **7** bigoted, fragile, ignoble, trivial **8** not great, trifling **10** diminutive, provincial, undersized **11** of no account, opinionated, superficial, unimportant **13** insignificant

small details
Latin: **8** minutiae

smaller 4 less **5** lower **6** lesser, tinier **7** dinkier, littler, pettier, reduced, shorter **8** inferior

smallest 5 least **6** lowest **7** tiniest **8** dinkiest, pettiest, shortest **9** slightest

small intestine
part of: **15** digestive system
lined with: **5** villi

small-minded 4 mean **5** petty **6** narrow **7** bigoted **9** parochial **10** prejudiced **12** mean-spirited

smallness 8 meanness, tininess **9** pettiness **10** meagerness, triviality **12** dwarfishness **14** insignificance **18** inconsequentiality

small piece 3 bit, dab **4** chip, drop, snip **5** crumb, grain, piece, pinch, scrap, shred, speck **6** dollop, morsel **7** granule, smidgen, smidgin **8** fragment, particle, smidgeon

small quantity 3 bit, dab, few **5** touch **7** smidgen, smidgin, soupcon **8** smidgeon **9** little bit

small round window
French: **11** oeil-de-boeuf

small spot 3 dab, dot **5** fleck, speck

small talk 6 banter, gossip **7** chatter, prattle **8** chitchat, idle talk, repartee **9** bavardage, prattling **12** tittle-tattle

smart 4 ache, burn, chic, hurt, keen, neat, trim **5** brash, brisk, quick, sassy, sharp, sting, wince, witty **6** astute, blench, brainy, bright, clever, flinch, modish, shrewd, suffer **7** elegant, stylish **8** feel pain, vigorous **9** be painful, energetic **10** smart-aleck **11** fashionable, intelligent

smart aleck 6 smarty **7** showoff, windbag, wiseass, wise guy **8** blowhard, braggart, saucebox, wiseacre **9** know-it-all **11** smarty-pants **12** grandstander **13** exhibitionist

smarten up 7 dress up, improve **8** beautify, spruce up

smartness 6 acumen, wisdom **8** keenness, sagacity **9** acuteness **10** astuteness, cleverness, perception, shrewdness **12** intelligence, perspicacity

smash 3 hit **4** bang, bash, beat, blow **5** break, clout, crack, crash, crush **6** batter, strike, winner **7** clobber, crack-up, destroy, shatter, success, triumph **8** accident, demolish, splinter **9** collision, sensation **12** disintegrate

smash against 4 beat, lash **5** crash, pound, smite **6** batter, buffet **7** break on

smashed 5 drunk **6** soused, wasted, zapped, zonked **7** crashed, crushed **8** squashed **9** plastered, shattered **10** inebriated **11** intoxicated **17** under the influence **20** three sheets to the wind

smashing 5 great, super **6** superb **8** fabulous, terrific **9** fantastic, marvelous, wonderful **10** stupendous **11** magnificent, sensational **13** extraordinary

smashup 5 crash, wreck **7** crackup **8** accident **9** collision **12** fender bender

smattering 3 bit, dab **4** dash, drop **5** scrap **7** smidgen, smidgin, snippet **8** smidgeon **10** sprinkling

smear 3 mar, rub **4** blur, coat, daub, soil **5** cover, lay on, libel, stain **6** blotch, injure, malign, smirch, smudge, spread, streak **7** blacken, blemish, degrade, slander, splotch, tarnish **8** besmirch, besmudge **9** denigrate **10** accusation, obliterate

smell 4 feel, nose, odor, reek **5** aroma, fetor, scent, sense, sniff, stink **6** detect, stench **7** bouquet, perfume, suspect **8** perceive **9** emanation, fragrance, get wind of

smelly 4 rank **5** fetid **6** putrid **7** noisome, odorous, reeking **8** stinking **10** malodorous

Smerdyakov character in: **20** The Brothers Karamazov author: **10** Dostoevsky

Smetana, Bedrich born: **7** Bohemia **8** Litomysl **11** Leitomischl **14** Czechoslovakia composer of: **7** Ma Vlast **9** My Country **10** From My Life **11** Czech Dances **12** The Two Widows **16** The Bartered Bride

smidgen, smidgin, smidgeon 3 bit, dab **4** mite, snip **5** crumb, pinch, scrap, shred, speck, trace **6** dollop, morsel

Smike character in: **16** Nicholas Nickleby author: **7** Dickens

smile 4 beam, grin **5** favor, shine, smirk **6** simper

Smiles of a Summer Night director: **13** Ingmar Bergman cast: **11** Eva Dahlbeck **13** Ulla Jacobsson **15** Margit Carlquist **16** Harriet Andersson remade as: **17** A Little Night Music

Smiley's People author: **11** John Le Carre

Smintheus epithet of: **6** Apollo

smirch 4 blot, mark, soil, spot **5** dirty, smear, stain, sully, taint **6** blotch, damage, smudge, stigma **7** begrime, blacken, blemish, slander, tarnish **8** besmirch, besmudge, dishonor **9** discredit

smirk 4 grin, leer **5** sneer **6** simper **7** grimace

Smirke, Sir Robert architect of: **12** King's College (U of London) **13** British Museum (London) **19** Covent Garden Theater (London) style: **12** Greek Revival

smite 3 hit **4** swat **5** knock, smack, whack **6** enamor, strike, wallop **7** clobber

Smith, Adam author of: **18** The Wealth of Nations

Smith, Al creator/artist of: **11** Mutt and Jeff

Smith, Betty author of: **20** A Tree Grows in Brooklyn

Smith, Charles Aaron nickname: **5** Bubba sport: **8** football team: **14** Baltimore Colts

Smith, David born: **8** Decatur IN artwork: **3** Zig **4** Cubi **6** Oculus **8** Agricola, Main View, Sentinel, Star Cage **9** Australia, Royal Bird, Tank Totem **10** The Banquet **12** Detroit Queen **15** Lectern Sentinel **17** Medals for Dishonor **20** Hudson River Landscape **23** Song of an Irish Blacksmith

Smith, Gladys Mary real name of: **12** Mary Pickford

Smith, Harriet character in: **4** Emma author: **6** Austen

Smith, Lillian author of: **12** Strange Fruit

Smith, Maggie born: **6** Ilford **7** England husband: **14** Robert Stephens roles: **7** Othello **15** California Suite, The Pumpkin Eater **17** Travels with My Aunt **24** The Prime of Miss Jean Brodie (Oscar)

Smith, Winston character in: **18** Nineteen Eighty-Four author: **6** Orwell

smithereen 3 bit **4** atom **5** crumb, shard **8** fragment, particle **9** scintilla

Smithson, James field: **9** chemistry nationality: **7** British discovered: **11** smithsonite **13** zinc carbonite funded: **22** Smithsonian Institution

smitten 8 enamored **9** bewitched **10** enraptured, infatuated

smoke 4 draw, fume, pipe, puff, reek, suck **5** cigar, fumes **6** billow, inhale **7** light up, smolder **9** cigarette, have a drag

Smoke author: **12** Ivan Turgenev character: **5** Irina **7** Potugin **13** Tanya Shestoff **16** Gen-

eral Ratmiroff, Grigory Litvinoff **18** Kapitolina Shestoff

smoke screen 4 ruse **5** cover, dodge, front **6** screen **9** deception **10** camouflage, subterfuge

smoky 5 dingy, grimy, sooty **6** fuming, smudgy **7** reeking **10** smoldering

smolder 4 burn, fume, rage **5** smoke **6** seethe

Smollett, Tobias George author of: **14** (The Expedition of) Humphry Clinker, Roderick Random **15** Peregrine Pickle

smooch 3 pet **4** buss, kiss, neck **5** smack, spoon **7** make out

smooth 4 calm, ease, easy, even, flat, glib, help, mild, open, pave **5** allay, level, silky, sleek, suave **6** facile, mellow, placid, polish, refine, serene, soften, soothe, steady **7** appease, assuage, flatten, mollify, orderly, perfect, prepare, velvety **8** civilize, composed, make even, mitigate, peaceful, pleasant **9** collected, cultivate, easygoing, make level **10** facilitate, flattering, harmonious, methodical, uneventful **11** well-ordered **12** ingratiating **13** self-possessed, well-regulated

smoothness 8 evenness, fineness, flatness **9** silkiness, sleekness

smooth the feathers 4 calm **6** pacify, soothe **7** appease, assuage, mollify, placate **10** conciliate

smooth-tongued 4 glib **5** suave **6** fluent **8** unctuous **10** flattering **11** fast-talking **12** hypocritical, ingratiating

smother 4 hide, mask, wrap **5** choke, quash, snuff **6** deaden, quench, shower **7** conceal **8** keep down, strangle, suppress, surround **9** choke back, envelop in, suffocate **10** asphyxiate, extinguish

Smothers Brothers Comedy Hour, The regulars: **10** Don Novello, Pat Paulsen **11** Bob Einstein, Leigh French, Steve Martin, Tom Smothers **12** Betty Aberlin, Dick Smothers, John Hartford, Nino Senporty, Spencer Quinn **13** Mason Williams **14** Jennifer Warren, Sally Struthers **16** Anita Kerr Singers **17** Jimmy Joyce Singers **18** Louis DaPron Dancers

19 Marty Paich Orchestra
20 Denny Vaughn Orchestra, Ron Poindexter Dancers **21** Nelson Riddle Orchestra

smudge 4 blot, mark, soil, spot **5** dirty, smear, stain **6** smutch

smudgy 5 dirty, messy **6** filthy, grubby, smeary **7** sullied **8** befouled, unwashed **9** besmeared

smug 8 superior, virtuous **10** complacent **13** self-righteous, self-satisfied

smuggle 5 sneak **15** export illegally, import illegally

smuggled goods 10 contraband **14** illegal exports, illegal imports **18** prohibited articles

smuggler 6 runner **9** gunrunner, rumrunner **10** bootlegger **13** contrabandist

smugness 7 egotism **9** immodesty **11** superiority **12** virtuousness **16** self-satisfaction **17** self-righteousness

smut 4 dirt, porn, soot **5** filth, grime **6** smudge **9** obscenity, scatology **11** pornography

smutty 4 lewd **5** dirty, grimy, sooty **6** filthy, soiled, vulgar **7** obscene **8** indecent **12** pornographic

Smyrna *see* **6** Myrrha

Smythe, Reginald
  creator/artist of: **8** Andy Capp

snack 3 eat, tea **4** bite, nosh **5** munch **6** nibble, tidbit **7** take tea **8** lap lunch, munchies, nibblies, pick-me-up, snackies **9** collation, crunchies, elevenses **10** finger food, light lunch **11** cassecroute, coffee break, light repast, refreshment

snag 3 bar, rip **4** grab, stub, tear **5** block, catch, hitch, stump **7** barrier **8** obstacle **9** hindrance **10** difficulty, impediment, projection, protrusion **11** encumbrance, obstruction **14** stumbling block

Snagsby
  character in: **10** Bleak House
  author: **7** Dickens

snail
  French: **8** escargot

snake *see* **box**

Snake *see* **8** Shoshoni

snake, poisonous 9 Coactrice

Snake, the
  nickname of: **10** Ken Stabler

---

snake 5 sneak, viper **7** reptile, serpent, traitor **8** ophidian **9** reptilian
  combining form: 4 ophi **5** ophio, ophis **6** herpes **7** herpeto
  expert: 13 herpetologist
  fear of:
  13 herpetophobia
  genus: 7 Ophidia
  kind: 3 asp, boa, sea **4** file, habu, wart, whip **5** aboma, adder, cobra, coral, krait, mamba, tiger, viper **6** bongar, elapid, garter, gopher, python, taipan **7** rattler, sunbeam **8** anaconda, cerastes, moccasin, pit viper, ringhals **9** boomslang, colubrina, mole viper, puff adder **10** black mamba, bushmaster, copperhead, fer-de-lance, sidewinder **11** cottonmouth, diamond back, Gaboon viper, rattlesnake **12** slender blind **13** elephant-trunk, water moccasin **14** boa constrictor
  shedding: 7 ecdysis **8** moulting
  skin: 6 exuvia
  snake killer: 8 mongoose

Snake Pit, The
  author: **12** Sigrid Undset

snap 3 nip, pop **4** bark, bite, grab, lock, yelp **5** break, catch, cinch, clasp, click, close, crack, growl, hasty, latch, quick, snarl, spell **6** breeze, period, secure, snatch, sudden **8** careless, fastener, fracture **9** impulsive **11** thoughtless

snapdragon 11 Antirrhinum
  varieties: **4** wild **5** dwarf **6** common, garden, lesser **7** spurred **8** withered

snappish 4 edgy **5** cross, huffy, surly, testy **6** crabby, cranky, shirty, touchy **7** grouchy, huffish, peevish, waspish **8** captious, petulant **9** irascible, irritable, querulous **10** ill-humored, ill-natured, out of sorts **11** hot-tempered **12** cantankerous **13** quick-tempered, short-tempered

snappy 4 fast, tony **5** hasty, quick, rapid, ritzy, sharp, smart, swank, swift, swish **6** classy, dapper, jaunty, speedy, spiffy **7** stylish **12** lickety-split

---

snare 3 net **4** bait, hook, lure, ruse, trap **5** catch, decoy, noose, seize, trick **6** entrap **7** capture, ensnare, pitfall **9** deception **12** entanglement

snarl 3 mat **4** bark, clog, kink, knot, mess, snap **5** chaos, growl, ravel, twist **6** hinder, impede, jumble, muddle, tangle **7** confuse, lash out **8** disorder, entangle **9** confusion

snatch 3 bit, nab **4** grab, part, pull, take **5** catch, grasp, piece, pluck, seize, wrest **7** snippet **8** fragment

Snead, Sam
  nickname: **12** Slammin' Sammy
  sport: **4** golf
  won: **7** Masters

sneak 3 sly **4** slip **5** creep, knave, rogue, scamp, steal **6** lurker, rascal, secret, spirit **7** bounder, furtive, skulker, slinker, smuggle **8** scalawag, surprise **9** miscreant, scoundrel, secretive, underhand **11** rapscallion **13** surreptitious

sneak attack 4 raid **6** ambush **7** assault **9** ambuscade, incursion

sneak off 5 elope **6** decamp **7** abscond **9** steal away

sneaky 3 sly **4** mean **7** devious, furtive, vicious **9** malicious, secretive, underhand **10** traitorous **11** treacherous

sneer 4 jeer, leer, mock **5** scoff, scorn, smirk **6** deride, rebuff **7** disdain **8** belittle, ridicule

sneer at 5 knock, scorn **6** deride, malign **7** disdain, put down, run down **8** pooh-pooh **16** cast aspersions on

Sneerwell, Lady
  character in: **19** The School for Scandal
  author: **8** Sheridan

snicker 5 snort **6** cackle, giggle, simper, titter **7** snigger

snide 5 nasty **7** mocking **8** scoffing **9** malicious, sarcastic **11** insinuating **12** contemptuous

Snider, Edwin
  nickname: **4** Duke
  sport: **8** baseball
  position: **7** fielder
  team: **15** Brooklyn Dodgers

sniff 4 jeer, mock, odor **5** aroma, scoff, smell, snort, snuff, whiff **6** snivel **7** disdain, sniffle, snuffle **9** disparage

snip 3 bit, bob, cut, lop **4** brat, clip, crop, punk, snap, trim

5 clack, click, piece, prune, scrap, shear, twerp **6** sample, shrimp, swatch **7** cutting **8** fragment

snippy 4 curt, rude **5** sassy, saucy, short **6** cheeky, snotty **7** brusque **8** flippant, impudent, insolent, snippety **11** ill-mannered, impertinent, smart-alecky

snivel 3 cry **5** sniff, whine **6** boohoo **7** sniffle **8** complain

sniveler 6 coward, whiner **7** crybaby **10** complainer

snob 7 elitist **13** social climber

snobbish 4 vain **6** snooty, snotty **7** haughty, high-hat, stuck-up **8** arrogant, superior **10** disdainful **11** overbearing, patronizing, pretentious **13** condescending

Snodgrass
  character in: **14** Pickwick Papers
  author: **7** Dickens

snoop 3 pry **7** meddler, Paul Pry **8** busybody **10** Nosy Parker **12** eavesdropper

snoopy, Snoopy 4 nosy **6** beagle, prying **7** curious **8** meddling **10** meddlesome **11** inquisitive
  brother: **5** Spike
  creator: **6** Schulz
  friend: **9** Woodstock
  master: **12** Charlie Brown

snooze 3 nap **4** doze **5** sleep **6** cat nap, drowse, siesta **7** slumber **10** forty winks

Snopes family
  characters in: **9** The Hamlet
  members: **2** Ab **4** Flem, Mink **5** Isaac
  author: **8** Faulkner

snort 4 blow, gasp, huff, jeer, pant, puff, rage **5** blast, grunt, scoff, sneer, storm

snout 3 neb **4** beak, bill, nose **5** snoot, spout **6** muzzle, nozzle **9** proboscis

Snow, C P (Charles Percy Snow, Lord Snow)
  author of: **9** The New Men **10** Last Things, The Masters **14** A Coat of Varnish **16** Corridors of Power **20** Strangers and Brothers

Snow-Bound
  author: **21** John Greenleaf Whittier

snowfall 4 firn, neve **6** flurry **8** blizzard
  Scottish: **6** onding

Snow Leopard, The
  author: **16** Peter Matthiessen

Snow Queen, The
  author: **21** Hans Christian Andersen

Snows of Kilimanjaro, The
  author: **15** Ernest Hemingway

snow-white 4 pure **5** snowy **9** lily-white, pure white **11** white as snow

Snow White
  author: **15** Donald Barthelme

snowy 4 pure **5** white **7** nievous **8** pristine, spotless **9** blizzardy

snub 3 cut **5** blunt, check, scorn, short **6** ignore, rebuff, slight, stubby **7** disdain **9** retrousse **11** repudiation **12** cold shoulder **16** turn up one's nose at **19** give the cold shoulder

snuff 5 scent, smell, sniff, whiff **7** sniffle, snuffle

snuff out 5 crush **8** suppress **10** extinguish, put an end to

snug 4 cozy, neat, safe **5** close, tight **6** secure **7** compact **8** tranquil **9** sheltered, skin-tight **11** comfortable **12** close-fitting, tight-fitting **13** well-organized

snuggle 3 hug **4** nest **6** cuddle, curl up, enfold, nestle, nuzzle

Snyder, Peggy Lou
  real name of: **21** Harriet Hilliard Nelson

so
  Latin: **3** sic

soak 3 wet **4** seep **5** bathe, enter, steep **6** absorb, drench, sink in, take in, take up **7** immerse, pervade **8** permeate, saturate **9** penetrate

soaked 5 soggy **6** sodden, soused **7** sopping **8** drenched **9** saturated **11** waterlogged, wringing wet

soak up 4 blot **6** absorb, take up **8** sponge up

soak up warmth 4 bask **11** warm oneself **12** toast oneself

Soames Forsyte
  character in: **14** The Forsyte Saga
  author: **10** Galsworthy

Soap
  character: **5** Major **6** Benson **9** Billy Tate **10** Eunice Tate **11** Chester Tate, Corrine Tate, Danny Dallas, Jessica Tate, Jodie Dallas **12** Burt Campbell **18** Mary Dallas Campbell
  cast: **7** Ted Wass **9** Jimmy Baio **11** Diana Canova

12 Billy Crystal, Cathryn Damon, Jennifer Salt, Robert Mandan **14** Arthur Peterson **15** Richard Mulligan, Robert Guillaume **16** Katherine Helmond

soar 3 fly **4** rise, wing **5** climb, float, glide, mount, tower **8** take wing

soave
  music: **6** gentle

sob 3 cry **4** howl, wail, weep **6** lament, plaint, snivel **7** blubber, whimper

so be it 4 amen **7** let it be **9** let it be so

sober 3 dry, sad **4** cool, drab, dull, grim, sane **5** grave, sound, staid **6** dreary, sedate, solemn, somber, steady **7** joyless, prudent, serious, subdued **8** moderate, not drunk, rational **9** judicious, realistic, sorrowful, temperate **10** abstemious **11** levelheaded **13** dispassionate

So Big
  author: **10** Edna Ferber

sobriety 10 abstention, abstinence, continence, temperance **13** nonindulgence **14** abstemiousness

sobriquet 7 epithet, pet name **8** nickname **11** appellation

so-called
  French: **9** soi-disant

soccer
  athlete: **4** Pele **11** Johan Cruyff
  players/team: **6** eleven
  position: **6** goalie **7** forward **8** fullback, halfback **10** goalkeeper
  championship: **8** World Cup **11** European Cup, National Cup **13** Cup Winner's Cup
  violation: **5** hands **7** hacking, offside **11** obstructing
  gaining control of ball: **4** trap

sociable 6 social **7** affable, cordial **8** friendly, gracious, outgoing **9** agreeable, congenial, convivial **10** gregarious, neighborly **11** extroverted **13** companionable

social 2 in **5** smart **7** stylish **8** friendly, pleasant, sociable **9** agreeable **10** gregarious, neighborly **11** cooperative, fashionable **14** interdependent

Social Contract, The
  author: **19** Jean-Jacques Rousseau

social order
  goddess of: **4** Hour **5** Horae

society 4 body, club 5 elite, group 6 circle, gentry, league 7 mankind 8 alliance, humanity, nobility 9 community, humankind 10 blue bloods 11 aristocracy, association, high society, social order 12 organization 14 the four hundred 16 the general public

sociologist
American: 4 Mead, Park, Ward 5 Coser, Gerth, Mills, Small, Wirth 6 Bendix, Cooley, Merton, Speier, Sumner, Thomas 7 Parsons, Sorokin 8 Eberhard 10 Lazarsfeld
British: 4 Webb 8 Hobhouse, Mannheim 12 Carr-Saunders
Danish: 6 Geiger
French: 4 Aron 5 Comte 8 Durkheim, Gurvitch 9 Friedmann
German: 5 Konig, Weber, Wiese 6 Simmel 8 Habermas, Luckmann 10 Dahrendorf, Horkheimer
Hungarian: 6 Lukacs 8 Mannheim
Israeli: 5 Buber 10 Eisenstadt
Norwegian: 6 Aubert 7 Galtung
Swedish: 8 Carlsson

sociopathic 9 alienated 10 antisocial, rebellious

sock 3 box, hit, sox 4 belt, blow, slap 5 punch, smack, smash 6 strike, wallop 7 clobber 8 knee sock 9 ankle sock 13 short stocking

sod 4 soil, turf 5 divot, earth, grass, sward 10 greensward

soda 3 pop 4 base, cola 5 tonic 6 bicarb, sodium 7 barilla, seltzer 8 beverage, root beer 9 ginger ale, soft drink 11 bicarbonate 12 sarsaparilla
ash: 6 alkali
in faro: 9 first card
maker: 4 jerk

sodden 4 dull 5 heavy, lumpy, mushy, pasty, soggy, soppy 6 doughy, soaked 7 sopping 8 besotted, drenched, dripping, listless 9 saturated 10 wet through 14 expressionless

Soddy, Frederick
field: 9 chemistry
nationality: 7 British
discovered: 8 isotopes
worked with: 13 William Ramsay 16 Ernest Rutherford
awarded: 10 Nobel Prize

sodium
chemical symbol: 2 Na

Sodom
destroyed with: 5 Admah 6 Zeboim 8 Gomorrah

sofa 5 couch, divan 6 canape, lounge, settee 8 love seat 9 davenport 12 chesterfield

Sofia
Roman name: 12 Ulpia Serdica
Byzantine name: 9 Triaditsa
capital of: 8 Bulgaria
landmark: 13 Buyuk Dzhamiya 16 Saint Sofia Church 17 Saint George Church 24 Alexander Nevsky Cathedral 32 Cyril and Methodius National Library

soft 4 easy, kind, mild, pale, weak 5 downy, faint, furry, muted, quiet, silky, sleek 6 feeble, gentle, hushed, pliant, satiny, shaded, silken, smooth, supple, tender 7 lenient, not hard, pitying, pliable, restful, subdued, velvety 8 delicate, not sharp, shadowed, tolerant, tranquil, twilight 9 malleable, not strong 10 harmonious 11 sentimental, sympathetic 12 easily molded, low intensity 13 compassionate, pleasantly low 16 easily penetrated 19 having a breathy sound 21 requiring little effort 25 incapable of great endurance

soften 5 lower 6 lessen, subdue, temper 7 cushion, mollify 8 make soft, mitigate, moderate, palliate, tone down, turn down 10 ameliorate, make softer

softhearted 4 kind, soft, warm 6 benign, gentle, humane, kindly, tender 8 generous 9 forgiving, indulgent 10 benevolent 11 considerate, kindhearted, sympathetic, warmhearted 13 compassionate, tenderhearted

softly 6 easily, gently, mildly, weakly 7 quietly

softness 8 mildness 9 downiness, silkiness 10 fluffiness, gentleness, smoothness, tenderness 11 tranquility 12 tranquillity

soft soap 7 blarney 8 cajolery, flattery 10 persuasion

sogginess 7 wetness 8 dampness 9 mushiness 10 soddenness

soggy 5 heavy, mushy, pasty, soppy 6 doughy, soaked, sodden 7 sopping 8 drenched, dripping 9 saturated

Sogliardo
character in: 22 Every Man out of His Humour
author: 6 Jonson

Soglow, Otto
creator/artist of: 13 The Little King

Sohrab and Rustum
author: 13 Matthew Arnold

soi-disant 8 so-called 9 pretended 10 self-styled 18 calling oneself thus

soigne, soignee 4 chic, neat, tidy 5 sleek, smart 6 classy, modish 7 elegant 11 well-groomed

soil 4 dirt, foul, land, loam, ruin, soot, spot 5 dirty, earth, grime, humus, muddy, smear, stain, sully 6 debase, defile, ground, region, smudge 7 blacken, country, tarnish 8 disgrace

soiled 5 dirty, grimy, messy 6 filthy, grubby, smudgy 7 muddied, sullied, unclean 8 begrimed, unwashed 9 besmeared

soiree 4 ball, prom 5 dance, party 9 cotillion, promenade

sojourn 4 stay 5 abide, pause, visit 6 stay at 7 holiday, layover 8 stay over, stopover, vacation

sojourner 6 lodger, tenant 7 pilgrim, tourist, visitor 8 traveler 9 transient, weekender 10 daytripper, vacationer

Sol
origin: 5 Roman
form: 3 god
personifies: 3 sun
corresponds to: 6 Helios 7 Mithras 8 Hyperion

sola, solus 5 alone 9 by oneself

solace 4 calm 5 cheer 6 soothe 7 assuage, comfort, console 8 reassure 10 help in need 11 consolation, reassurance 18 relief in affliction

solder 4 fuse, join, weld 5 braze, stick

soldier 2 GI 3 PFC 5 major 6 worker, zealot 7 colonel, general, private, servant, trooper, veteran, warrior 8 follower, partisan, sergeant 10 lieutenant, serviceman 11 enlisted man, military man 14 militant leader 16 brigadier general

Soldier of Orange
director: 13 Paul Verhoeven

based on novel by: 13 Erik Hazelhoff
cast: 10 Peter Faber **11** Derek De Lint, Eddy Habbema, Rutger Hauer **12** Jeroen Krabbe **15** Susan Penhaligon
setting: 14 The Netherlands

Soldier's Embrace, A
author: 14 Nadine Gordimer

soldiery 4 army **6** legion, troops **7** legions, militia **8** military, soldiers **11** fighting men

sole 4 lone, only **6** single **8** solitary **9** exclusive

solely 5 alone **6** merely, purely, singly **8** uniquely **11** exclusively **14** single-handedly

solemn 4 dark, drab, grim, holy **5** grave, sober, staid **6** formal, gloomy, sacred, sedate, somber **7** earnest, serious, sincere **8** absolute **9** dignified, religious, spiritual, steadfast **10** ceremonial, depressing, determined **11** ceremonious **12** awe-inspiring

solemnity 3 awe **7** dignity **8** ceremony **9** formality, reverence **11** seriousness **12** circumstance

solemnize 4 mark **5** honor **6** hallow **7** observe **9** celebrate **10** consecrate **11** commemorate

solicit 3 ask **4** seek **5** plead **7** entreat, request **9** appeal for, importune

solicitation 6 appeal **7** request **8** entreaty **11** importuning

solicitor 6 beggar, lawyer **7** counsel **8** salesman **10** supplicant

solicitous 4 avid, keen **5** eager **6** ardent, intent **7** anxious, intense, longing, mindful, zealous **8** desirous **9** attentive, concerned, regardful **10** thoughtful **12** enthusiastic

solicitude 4 care, zeal **5** worry **7** anxiety, avidity, concern **9** attention **10** enthusiasm, inquietude, uneasiness **11** disquietude, fearfulness, overconcern **12** apprehension

solid 4 firm, hard, pure, real **5** dense, massy, sober, sound, tough **6** rugged, stable, steady, strong, sturdy **7** durable, genuine, lasting, unmixed **8** complete, concrete, constant, rational, reliable, sensible, tangible, thorough, unbroken **9** not hollow, unalloyed, unanimous, undivided, well-built **10** continuous, dependable, solidified **11** impermeable,

levelheaded, substantial, trustworthy **12** impenetrable **13** uninterrupted **15** well-constructed

solidarity 5 union, unity **7** harmony **9** closeness **11** cooperation, unification

solidify 3 fix, gel, set **4** cake, jell **6** cement, harden **7** congeal, stiffen, thicken **9** coagulate **11** crystallize **12** agglomerate

soliloquy 9 monologue **10** solo speech

Solinus
character in: 17 The Comedy of Errors
author: 11 Shakespeare

solitariness 8 solitude **9** aloneness, seclusion **13** reclusiveness

solitary 4 lone **6** hidden, lonely, remote, single **8** desolate, isolated, lonesome, secluded **9** concealed **10** cloistered **11** out-of-the-way, uninhabited **13** companionless

solitude 9 aloneness, isolation, seclusion, wasteland **10** desolation, loneliness, remoteness, wilderness

solo 5 alone **8** solitary **9** by oneself **10** unattended **12** singlehanded **13** unaccompanied
operatic: 4 aria

solo dance
ballet: 7 pas seul

Solomon
father: 5 David
mother: 9 Bathsheba
wife: 6 Naamah
son: 8 Rehoboam
brother: 5 Amnon **7** Absalom, Chileab **8** Adonijah
sister: 5 Tamar
visitor: 5 Sheba
wrote: 8 Proverbs **12** Ecclesiastes **13** Song of Solomon
built: 6 temple

Solomon Islands *see box*

so long
Spanish: 12 hasta la vista

solution 3 key **5** blend **6** answer, cipher **7** mixture, solving **8** emulsion **9** resolving **10** resolution, suspension, unraveling **11** explanation

solve 7 resolve, unravel, work out **8** decipher, unriddle, untangle **9** figure out **10** find the key **13** find the answer

solvent 7 diluent, soluble **9** dilutable **10** dissoluble, dissolvent **11** dissolvable **16** financially sound

Solymi
origin: 9 Asia Minor
occupation: 8 warriors

Solzhenitsyn, Aleksandr
author of: 13 The Cancer Ward **14** The First Circle **19** The Gulag Archipelago **22** August Nineteen-Fourteen **31** One Day in the Life of Ivan Denisovich

Somalia *see box, p. 908*

Solomon Islands
capital/largest city: 7 Honiara
others: 4 Auki, Bina, Gizo, Luti **5** Kieta, Munda **6** Tulagi **7** Yandina **8** Kira Kira **9** Tangarare **10** Sasamungga
head of state: 14 British monarch **15** governor-general
member of: 14 Spearhead Group
monetary unit: 4 cent **6** dollar
island: 4 Buka, Gizo, Savo **5** Ndeni, Ulawa **6** Tulagi **7** Malaita, Rennell, Solomon, Vangunu **8** Choiseul, Sikaiana, Vanikoro **9** Santa Cruz **10** New Georgia, Ontong Java **11** Guadalcanal, Santa Isabel **12** Bougainville, San Cristobal
mountain: 5 Balbi
highest point: 11 Popomanasiu
ocean: 7 Pacific
physical feature:
   gulf: **4** Huon, Kula
   sound: **10** New Georgia
   strait: **13** Indispensable
people: 7 Chinese **8** European **10** Melanesian, Polynesian
   explorer: **14** Mendana de Neyra
   leader: **8** Mamaloni **9** Kenilorea
language: 7 English **13** Pidgin English **16** Melanesian pidgin
religion: 8 Anglican **13** Roman Catholic

Somalia
  other name: 4 Punt **10** Somaliland **12** Horn of Africa
  capital/largest city: 9 Mogadishu **10** Mogadiscio
  others: 5 Burao, Merca **6** Mereka **7** Berbera, Galkayu, Kismayu **8** Belet Uen, Hargeisa **9** Chisimaio
  division: 6 Hawiya **9** Mijirtein **10** Midjertein
    colonial: **17** British Somaliland, Italian Somaliland
  measure: 3 top **4** caba **5** chela, darat, tabla **6** cubito **8** parsalah
  monetary unit: 4 besa **6** somalo **8** shilling **9** centesimi
  weight: 8 parsalah
  mountain: 5 Guban **11** Migiurtinia, Ogo Highland
  highest point: 7 Surud Ad
  river: 4 Juba **5** Daror, Nogal **9** Nugaaleed **11** Webi Shebeli **13** Webi Shabeelle
  sea: 6 Indian
  physical feature:
    bay: **5** Negro
    cape: **9** Guardafui
    desert: **4** Aror
    gulf: **4** Aden
    plateau: **3** Ogo **4** Haud
  people: 3 Sab **4** Asha **5** Galla **6** Hawiya, Isbaak, Somali **7** Danakil, Hamitic, Marehan, Samaale, Shuhali **8** Rahanwin
    leader: **9** Siad Barre **12** Ali Shermarke
  language: 6 Arabic, Somali **7** English, Italian
  religion: 5 Islam
  feature:
    boat: **4** dhow
    cloth: **7** banadir
    clothing: **4** futa, toga **6** sarong
    tree: **6** acacia, baobab **7** incense

5 robin, veery, vireo **6** canary, singer, thrush **7** warbler **11** nightingale

Song of Bernadette, The
  author: 11 Franz Werfel
  character: 13 Dean Peyramale **18** Sister Marie Therese **19** Bernadette Soubirous
  director: 9 Henry King
  cast: 8 Lee J Cobb **12** Vincent Price, William Eythe **13** Jennifer Jones **15** Charles Bickford
  Oscar for: 7 actress (Jones)

Song of Hiawatha *see* **8** Hiawatha

Song of Roland, The *see* **15** Chanson de Roland

Song of Solomon
  author: 12 Toni Morrison

Song of Solomon
  bride: 9 Shulamite

Song of Songs, The
  author: 16 Hermann Sudermann

Song of the Lark, The
  author: 11 Willa Cather

Songs of Experience
  author: 12 William Blake

Songs of Innocence
  author: 12 William Blake

Sonnets from the Portuguese
  author: 24 Elizabeth Barrett Browning

Sonnets to Orpheus
  author: 16 Rainer Maria Rilke

Sonny
  nickname of: 13 Charles Liston

Son of the Morning
  author: 15 Joyce Carol Oates

sonorous 4 deep, rich **6** florid **7** ringing, vibrant **8** eloquent, resonant **9** full-toned, grandiose **10** flamboyant, impressive, resounding **13** reverberating

Sons and Lovers
  author: 10 D H Lawrence
  character: 10 Clara Dawes **11** Baxter Dawes **13** Miriam Leivers
    Morel family: **4** Paul **5** Annie **6** Arthur, Walter **7** William **8** Gertrude

Sons of thunder 4 John **5** James
  also: 9 Boanerges

Somaliland *see* **7** Somalia

somber 4 dark, drab, gray, grim **5** grave, sober **6** dreary, gloomy, solemn **7** serious **8** funeral, mournful, toneless **9** cheerless **10** depressing, melancholy

Sombrero Fallout
  author: 16 Richard Brautigan

Some Like It Hot
  director: 11 Billy Wilder
  cast: 9 Joe E Brown, Pat O'Brien **10** George Raft, Jack Lemmon, Tony Curtis **13** Marilyn Monroe

Somers Islands *see* **7** Bermuda

something essential
  Latin: 10 sine qua non

something for something
  Latin: 10 quid pro quo

Something Happened
  author: 12 Joseph Heller

sometime 4 late, once **5** later **6** former **7** quondam **8** formerly, previous **9** erstwhile **10** occasional

sometimes 7 at times **10** now

and then, on occasion **12** occasionally, once in a while

somewhat 6 fairly, kind of, partly, sort of **8** passably **9** tolerably **10** moderately, more or less, reasonably **13** approximately

somnolent 4 dozy, dull **5** dopey **6** drowsy, groggy, sleepy, torpid **7** languid, nodding, out of it, yawning **8** hypnotic, sluggish **9** half-awake, lethargic, sopoforic **10** half-asleep, slumberous **11** heavy-lidded **13** semiconscious

Somnus
  origin: 5 Roman
  god of: 5 sleep
  mother: 3 Nyx
  brother: 4 Mors
  corresponds to: 6 Hypnos, Hypnus

son
  French: 4 fils

song 4 call, poem, tune **5** ditty, lyric, verse **6** ballad, melody, number, piping
  French: 7 chanson

songbird 4 chat, lark, wren

soon 4 anon **6** pronto **7** betimes, by and by, early on, ere long, quickly, shortly **8** directly **9** any minute, forthwith, instantly, presently, right away **10** before long **12** without delay **14** in a little while

sooner 6 before, in time **7** earlier **9** before now, in advance **10** beforehand **11** ahead of time

sooner or later 6 one day **7** finally, someday **8** in the end, sometime **10** eventually, ultimately **17** in the course of time, sometime or another

Sooner State
nickname of: **8** Oklahoma

soot 4 dirt, smut **5** crock, grime **6** carbon, smudge, smutch **7** residue **9** lampblack

soothe 4 calm, ease **6** lessen, pacify **7** appease, comfort, console, mollify, placate, relieve **8** mitigate, moderate **9** alleviate **11** tranquilize

soothing 4 mild **7** calming, healing, salving **9** appeasing, consoling, emollient, pacifying, placating **10** comforting, mitigating **13** tranquilizing

soothsayer 4 seer **5** sibyl **7** diviner, prophet **10** forecaster **13** fortune-teller

soothsaying 6 augury **8** divining, prophecy **10** divination, predicting, prediction **11** foretelling, prophesying

sooty 4 inky **5** black, dingy, dirty, grimy **6** smudgy, smutty **9** coal-black

sop 3 dip, tip, wet **4** dunk, soak **5** bribe **6** absorb, drench, payoff, payola, take up **8** gratuity, saturate **9** baksheesh, become wet, hush money

Sophie's Choice
author: **13** William Styron

Sophisms
author: **9** Aristotle

sophisticate 8 civilize **11** cosmopolite, disillusion, make worldly **12** cosmopolitan

sophisticated 6 subtle **7** complex, studied, worldly **8** advanced, cultured, highbrow, mannered, precious, seasoned **9** difficult **10** artificial, cultivated **11** complicated, experienced, worldly-wise **12** cosmopolitan, intellectual

sophistry 6 deceit **7** fallacy **8** subtlety **9** casuistry, chicanery, deception **10** distortion **12** speciousness

Sophocles
author of: **4** Ajax **7** Electra, Oedipus **8** Antigone **10** Oedipus Rex, Trachiniae

11 Philoctetes **16** Oedipus at Colonus **18** The Trachinian Women

sophomoric 6 callow **7** foolish, puerile **8** childish, immature, juvenile **9** infantile **10** adolescent **12** schoolboyish

soporific 4 lazy **5** balmy, heavy **6** drowsy, sleepy **8** hypnotic, sedative, sluggish **9** lethargic, somnolent **10** slumberous **11** somniferous **12** sleep-inducer **13** sleep-inducing

soppiness 4 corn, mush **5** slush **6** bathos **7** wetness **9** mushiness **10** slushiness **11** mawkishness **14** sentimentalism, sentimentality

sopping 3 wet **5** soggy, soppy **6** soaked, sodden **8** drenched, dripping **9** saturated **10** bedraggled, soaking wet

sorcerer 5 witch **6** shaman, wizard **7** warlock **8** magician **11** medicine man

sorceress 5 siren, witch **11** enchantress

sorcery 8 witchery, wizardry **9** shamanism **10** black magic, necromancy, witchcraft **11** enchantment

Sordello
author: **14** Robert Browning

sordid 3 low **4** base, rank, vile **5** dirty, gross **6** filthy, putrid, rotten, vulgar, wicked **7** corrupt, ignoble, squalid, unclean **8** degraded, depraved **9** debauched **12** disreputable

Sordido
character in: **22** Every Man out of His Humour
author: **6** Jonson

sordino, con
music: **11** with the mute

sore 4 hurt **5** acute, angry, great, harsh, irked, sharp, upset, wound **6** aching, pained, severe, tender **7** bruised, extreme, grieved, hurting, painful **8** agonized, critical, grievous, smarting, sore spot, wounding **9** agonizing, desperate, indignant, irritated, sensitive **10** distressed, unbearable **11** distressing **12** inflammation

So Red the Rose
author: **10** Stark Young

Sorel, Julien
character in: **17** The Red and the Black
author: **8** Stendhal

sorely 5 badly **7** greatly **8** se-

verely **9** extremely **10** critically **11** desperately

soreness 4 ache, pain **10** discomfort, irritation, tenderness

sorrel 3 bay **4** herb, roan, weed **5** brown, plant, Rumex **8** chestnut **12** reddish-brown
varieties: **3** red **4** dock, tree, wood **5** lady's, sheep **6** common, French, garden, Indian **7** redwood **8** Jamaican, mountain **10** violet wood **12** European wood

Sorrel, Hetty
character in: **8** Adam Bede
author: **5** Eliot

sorrow 3 woe **4** loss, weep **5** be sad, mourn, trial **6** grieve, lament **7** despair, sadness, travail, trouble **8** disaster, hardship **10** affliction, bad fortune, misfortune **11** catastrophe, unhappiness
French: **9** tristesse

sorrowful 3 sad **6** woeful **7** unhappy **8** affected, grieving, mournful **9** lamenting

Sorrows of Young Werther, The
author: **6** Goethe
character: **6** Albert **9** Charlotte (Lotte)

sorry 3 sad **6** woeful **7** grieved, pitiful, unhappy **8** contrite, pathetic, pitiable, wretched **9** miserable, regretful, repentant, sorrowful **10** deplorable, melancholy, remorseful, ridiculous **11** crestfallen **13** brokenhearted

sort 4 kind, list, make, sift, type **5** brand, class, grade, group, index, order **6** divide, person **7** arrange, catalog, species, variety **8** classify, organize, separate, take from **9** segregate **10** categorize, individual **11** systematize **14** classification

sortie 4 rush **5** onset **6** attack, charge **7** assault **8** storming **9** onslaught

sortilege 6 augury **7** auspice, sorcery **9** divination, witchcraft

sorting 8 dividing, grouping **9** arranging **10** organizing **11** classifying **12** categorizing

so-so 4 blah, fair **5** ho-hum **6** casual, modest **7** average, humdrum **8** adequate, bearable, mediocre, middling, ordinary, passable **9** tolerable **10** second-rate **11** commonplace, indifferent **12** run-of-the-mill **13** unexceptional **15** undistinguished

Sospita
epithet of: **4** Juno

sot 4 lush, soak **5** drunk,
rummy, souse, toper **8** drunkard, rumhound **9** alcoholic,
inebriate **11** dipsomaniac

Soter
epithet of: **4** Zeus
means: **6** savior

Sothern, Ann
real name: **13** Harriette Lake
born: **12** Valley City ND
husband: **10** Roger Pryor
14 Robert Sterling
roles: **6** Maisie **8** Cry Havoc
10 Lady Be Good **16** Private
Secretary **19** A Letter to
Three Wives

so throughout
Latin: **9** sic passim

sotto voce
music: **11** in a low voice
13 in an undertone, under
the voice

sought 6 hunted **7** pursued,
quested **9** attempted, looked
for **10** endeavored

soul 5 being, force **6** person,
spirit **7** essence **8** creature, vitality **9** inner core **10** embodiment, individual, vital force
11 inspiration **12** quintessence

soul-searching 10 discontent,
insecurity, uneasiness **15** dissatisfaction, self-questioning

soul-stirring 7 rousing **8** electric, exciting, stirring **9** inspiring, thrilling **11** galvanizing

sound 3 fit **4** deep, firm, good,
seem, tone, wise **5** drift,
hardy, noise, range, sober,
solid, tenor, utter, voice **6** intact, robust, severe, signal, stable, strong, sturdy **7** durable,
earshot, healthy, lasting, perfect, solvent **8** announce, rational, reliable, sensible,
thorough, unmarred **9** come
off as, competent, enunciate,
pronounce, undamaged, well-
built **10** articulate, dependable,
make a noise, reasonable, suggestion, untroubled **11** implication, penetrating,
responsible, substantial
13 thoroughgoing **15** hearing
distance, well-constructed

Sound and the Fury, The
author: **15** William Faulkner
character: **6** Dilsey **17** Sydney
Herbert Head
Compson family: **5** Jason
7 Candace (Caddy), Quentin **8** Benjamin (Benjy)

Sounder
director: **10** Martin Ritt
cast: **8** Taj Mahal **10** Kevin
Hooks **11** Cicely Tyson

12 Paul Winfield **13** Carmen
Mathews
sequel: **13** Sounder Part II

sound measure 7 decibel

**sound mind in a sound
body**
Latin: **21** mens sana in corpore sano

soundness of mind 6 reason,
sanity **9** normality **12** mental
health

Sound of Music, The
director: **10** Robert Wise
cast: **9** Peggy Wood **12** Julie
Andrews (Maria Von
Trapp) **13** Eleanor Parker
18 Christopher Plummer
setting: **7** Austria
score: **21** Rodgers and
Hammerstein
Oscar for: **7** picture
8 director
song: **5** Maria **6** Do-Re-Mi
9 Edelweiss **16** My Favorite
Things

sound out 3 ask **8** approach
15 make a proposal to, make
overtures to, put out feelers to

soup
French: **6** potage

soupcon 3 bit, dab, jot, tad
4 clue, dash, drop, hint
5 pinch, shade, taint, taste,
tinge, touch, trace, whiff **6** little, trifle **7** smidgen, smidgin,
vestige **8** smidgeon **9** little bit,
suspicion **10** smattering, sprinkling, suggestion **12** slight
amount

Soupy Sales
character: **9** White Fang
10 Black Tooth **13** Herman
the Flea, Hippy the Hippo,
Pookie the Lion, Willie the
Worm **14** Marilyn Monwolf

sour 3 bad **4** acid, dour, keen,
tart, turn **5** nasty, sharp, spoil,
surly, tangy, testy **6** crabby,
cranky, curdle, rancid, sullen,
turned **7** acerbic, bilious,
crabbed, curdled, ferment,
grouchy, peevish, spoiled, turn
off, uncivil, waspish **8** alienate,
choleric, embitter, jaundice,
petulant, unsavory, vinegary
9 acidulous, clabbered, fermented, irritable, jaundiced, of-

South Africa
capital: **8** Cape Town, Pretoria **12** Bloemfontein
largest city: **12** Johannesburg
others: **3** Aus **4** Mara, Stad **6** Benoni, Bononi, Braker, Dur-
ban, Garies, Severn, Soweto, Umtata, Untata **7** Brakpan,
Kokstad **8** Kaapstad, Mafeking, Modjadji **9** Germiston,
Kimberley **10** East London, Oudtshoorn **11** Krugersdorp,
Vereeniging **13** Port Elizabeth **16** Pietermaritzburg
school: **5** Natal **8** Capetown **13** Witwatersrand **15** Orange
Free State
division: **5** Natal **8** Backveld **9** Transvaal **10** Basutoland
12 Cape Province **14** Cape of Good Hope **15** Orange Free
State
independent homelands: **5** Venda **6** Ciskei **8** Transkei
10 bantustans **14** Bophuthatswana
goverment:
legislature: **4** Raad
measure: **4** vara
monetary unit: **4** cent, pond, rand **5** pound **6** florin
7 daalder **9** krugerand
mountain: **3** Aux, Kop **5** Table **7** Kathkin **9** Stormberg
10 Devil's Peak, Sneeuwberg **11** Drakensberg **12** Giant's
Castle **13** Witwatersrand **14** Mont-aux-Sources **15** Great
Escarpment
highest point: **8** Injasuti
river: **3** Hex **4** Vaal **5** Nosob **6** Modder, Molopo, Orange,
Tugela **7** Caledon, Kurumam, Limpopo **8** Olifants **9** Crocodile, Great Fish
ocean: **6** Indian **8** Atlantic
physical feature:
bay: **5** Algoa, False, Table **6** Mossel, Walvis **7** Walfish
8 Richard's, Saldanha **11** Saint Helena
cape: **7** Agulhas **8** Good Hope
current: **8** Benguela
desert: **5** Namib **8** Kalahari
plateau: **6** Karroo
region: **8** Highveld, Zululand **9** Kaffraria **11** Great Karroo **12** Little Karroo

fensive, prejudice, repugnant **10** astringent, ill-dispose, ill-humored, unpleasant **11** bad-tempered, distasteful, ill-tempered **12** disagreeable

sourball 4 crab **5** crank, grump **6** grouch **9** hard candy **10** curmudgeon

source 4 font, head, root **5** basis, cause, fount **6** author, father, origin, rising, spring **8** begetter, fountain **9** authority, beginning, headwater **10** antecedent, derivation, foundation, prime mover, wellspring

source and origin
Latin: **11** fons et origo

Sourdough State
nickname of: **6** Alaska

sourness 7 acidity, vinegar **8** acerbity, acrimony, ill humor, pungency, tartness **9** acridness, greenness **10** bitterness

sourpuss 4 bear, crab **5** crank, grump **6** griper, grouch **7** grouser, killjoy **8** grumbler, sorehead **10** bellyacher, complainer, crosspatch, curmudgeon, spoilsport

Sousa, John Philip
born: **12** Washington DC
composer of: **9** El Capitan **14** Washington Post **25** The Stars and Stripes Forever

souse 3 dip, sot **4** duck, dunk, lush, soak **5** douse, drunk, rummy, steep, toper **6** barfly, boozer, drench, pickle **7** immerse, tippler **8** drunkard, inundate, marinate, saturate, submerge **9** alcoholic, inebriate **11** dipsomaniac

soused 5 drunk **6** dunked, potted, zapped, zonked **7** pickled, sloshed, smashed **8** immersed **9** plastered **10** inebriated **11** intoxicated **17** under the influence **20** three sheets to the wind

South Africa *see box*

South America *see box*

South Carolina *see box, p. 912*

South Dakota *see box, p. 913*

southeast wind
associated with: **5** Eurus **9** Volturnus

South Africa *(continued)*
people: **3** San **4** Boer, Yosa, Zulu **5** Asian, Bantu, Namas, Nguni, Pondo, Sotho, Swazi, Tembu, Venda, Xhosa **6** Damara, Kaffir **7** African, British, Bushmen, English, Swahili **8** Bechuana, Coloured, Khoikhoi **9** Afrikaner, Hottentot
   author: **5** Paton **7** Luthuli **8** Gordimer
   civil rights advocate: **6** Gandhi
   explorer: **8** Riebeeck
   leader: **4** Biko, Tutu **5** Botha, Malan, Smuts, Tomba **6** Kruger, Rhodes **7** de Klerk, Hertzog, Mandela, Vorster **8** Verwoerd **9** Buthelezi, Pretorius
language: **4** Taal, Zulu **5** Bantu, Hindi, Nguni, Sotho, Swazi, Tamil, Venda, Xhosa **6** Telegu, Thonga **7** English, Khoisan, Ndebele, Sesotho **8** Bujarati, Fanakalo **9** Afrikaans
religion: **5** Hindu, Islam **7** animism, Judaism **8** Anglican **9** Methodist **12** Episcopalian, Presbyterian **13** Dutch Reformed, Roman Catholic
place:
   Cecil Rhodes' estate: **11** Groote Shuur
   game reserve: **5** Mkuze **6** Kruger **8** Hluhluwe
   monument: **11** Voortrekker
feature:
   bird: **4** taha
   bride price: **6** lobolo
   flower: **5** coral **6** clivia, protea **7** cowslip, fuchsia **9** phygelius **10** lachenalia
   organization: **3** ANC **7** Inkatha **23** African National Congress
   segregation: **9** apartheid
   tree: **7** assagai **9** jacaranda
food:
   corn: **6** mealie
   drink: **9** sundowner
   meat: **7** biltong **8** sosaties **9** boerewors

South America
bird: **5** macaw **7** seriema, tinamou **8** caracara
cape: **4** Horn
country: **4** Peru **5** Chile **6** Brazil, Guyana **7** Bolivia, Ecuador, Surinam, Uruguay **8** Colombia, Paraguay **9** Argentina, Venezuela **12** French Guiana
desert: **7** Atacama
explorer: **16** Francisco Pizarro **18** Pedro Alvares Cabral
hero: **12** Simon Bolivar **15** Jose de San Martin **16** Bernardo O'Higgins **18** Antonio Jose de Sucre
highest mountain: **9** Aconcagua
islands: **8** Falkland **9** Galapagos
lake: **8** Titicaca **9** Maracaibo
mountain range: **5** Andes
native: **2** Ge **3** Ona **4** Inca **5** Carib, Mayan **7** Quechua **10** Araucanian
plain: **5** llano, pampa
region: **9** Patagonia
river: **3** Apa **5** Plata **6** Amazon **7** Orinoco

Southern Comfort
type: **7** liqueur
origin: **10** New Orleans
flavor: **5** peach
base: **7** bourbon
drink: **13** Scarlett O'Hara **15** Plantation Punch
with bourbon: **14** Blended Comfort

Southern Cross
constellation of: **4** Crux

Southern Crown
constellation of: **15** Corona Australis

Southerner, The
director: **10** Jean Renoir
cast: **10** Betty Field **11** Beulah Bondi **12** Zachary Scott **13** Bunny Sunshine

Southern Fish
constellation of: **15** Piscis Austrinus

Southern Fly
constellation of: **5** Musca

Southern Rhodesia *see* **8** Zimbabwe

Southern Slavic
language family: **12** Indo-European

South Carolina
  abbreviation: 2 SC
  nickname: 7 Calinky **8** Palmetto
  capital/largest city: 8 Columbia
  others: 5 Aiken, Greer, Union **6** Belton, Camden, Cheraw, Conway, Dillon, Seneca, Sumter **7** Bamberg, Laurens, Manning **8** Beaufort, Florence, Newberry, Rock Hill, Walhalla **9** Greenwood **10** Charleston, Greenville, Orangeburg **11** Spartanburg
  college: 5 Allen, Coker **6** Furman, Lander **7** Claffin, Clemson, Erskine, Wofford **8** Benedict, Bob Jones, Columbia, Winthrop **13** Francis Marion **15** Citadel Military
  explorer: 6 Ayllon, Ribaut
  feature:
    beach: **6** Myrtle
    dam: **6** Saluda
    fort: **6** Sumter
    gardens: **7** Cypress
  tribe: 5 Pedee, Sewee **6** Cusabo, Santee, Waxhaw, Yamasi **7** Catawba, Shawnee, Sugeree, Wateree **8** Congaree
  people: 11 James Byrnes **12** Althea Gibson, John C Calhoun **13** Bernard Baruch, Francis Marion **14** Dizzy Gillespie
  island: 3 Sea **6** Parris **10** Hilton Head
  lake: 6 Marion, Murray **7** Catawba, Wateree **8** Hartwell, Moultrie **9** Clark Hill
  land rank: 8 fortieth
  mountain: 5 Kings **6** Little **9** Blue Ridge, Sassafras
  physical feature:
    bay: **8** Carolina
    plateau: **8** Piedmont
  president: 13 Andrew Jackson
  river: 5 Broad **6** Edisto, Pee Dee, Saluda, Santee **7** Ashepoo **8** Savannah
  state admission: 6 eighth
  state bird: 12 Carolina wren
  state flower: 13 yellow jasmine **17** Carolina jessamine
  state motto: 18 While I Breathe I Hope **26** Prepared in Mind and Resources
  state song: 8 Carolina
  state tree: 8 palmetto

sow 4 cast, seed **5** lodge, plant, set in, strew **6** inject, spread **7** implant, instill, scatter **8** disperse, sprinkle **9** broadcast, establish, introduce **11** disseminate

space 3 gap, sky **4** area, part, rank, room, seat, span, spot, term, time **5** berth, blank, break, chasm, ether, field, order, place, range, reach, scope, sweep, swing, width **6** hiatus, lacuna, line up, margin, period, set out, spread **7** arrange, breadth, compass, expanse, mark out, the void **8** distance, duration, infinity, interval, latitude, omission, organize, schedule, separate **9** amplitude, emptiness, keep apart, territory **10** distribute, interspace, interstice, outer space, separation, the heavens **11** nothingness, reservation, the universe **12** interruption, the firmament **13** accommodation

Space
  author: 13 James Michener

spacecraft 4 ship **6** rocket **7** orbiter, shuttle **9** satellite **10** rocketship

space flight
  US mission: 6 Apollo, Gemini, Skylab **7** Mercury
  US rocket: 5 Atlas, Titan **6** Saturn **8** Redstone
  US space shuttle: 8 Columbia **9** Discovery **10** Challenger
  Soviet mission: 5 Soyuz **6** Salyut, Vostok **7** Voskhod
  Soviet astronaut:
    first man in space: **11** Yuri Gagarin
    first woman in space: **19** Valentina Tereshkova
    first space walk by: **13** Aleksei Leonov
  American astronaut: 9 John Glenn, John Young **11** Alan Shepard, Edward White, Edwin Aldrin, Frank Borman, James Lovell **12** Roger Chaffee, Wally (Walter) Schirra **13** Charles Conrad, L Gordon Cooper, Virgil Grissom **14** Scott Carpenter, Thomas Stafford
    first man on moon: **13** Neil Armstrong
    Challenger seven: **12** Michael Smith, Ronald McNair **13** Francis Scobee, Gregory Jarvis, Judith Resnick **14** Ellison Onizuka **16** Christa McAuliffe

Spacek, Sissy
  real name: 19 Mary Elizabeth Spacek
  born: 9 Quitman TX

group: 11 Balto-Slavic
branch: 6 Slavic
language: 7 Slovene **9** Bulgarian **10** Macedonian **13** Serbo-Croatian

Southern Triangle
  constellation of: 18 Triangulum Australe

South Korea *see* **5** Korea

South Vietnam *see* **7** Vietnam

South West Africa *see* **7** Namibia

south wind
  associated with: 5 Notus

South Wind
  author: 13 Norman Douglas

South Yemen *see* **5** Yemen

souvenir 4 scar **5** relic, token **6** emblem, memory, trophy **7** memento **8** keepsake, reminder **11** remembrance

sovereign 4 czar, free, king, lord, main, tsar **5** chief, major, prime, queen, regal, royal **6** kingly, potent, prince, ruling, utmost **7** emperor, highest, leading, monarch, queenly, supreme **8** absolute, autocrat, dominant, foremost, imperial, overlord, powerful, princely, reigning **9** chieftain, governing, paramount, potentate, prepotent, principal, uppermost **10** autonomous, self-ruling **11** all-powerful, crowned head, independent, monarchical **12** supreme ruler **13** self-directing, self-governing

sovereignty 4 sway **5** crown, power **6** throne **7** command, control, freedom, primacy, scepter **8** autonomy, dominion, home rule, kingship, lordship, self-rule **9** authority, supremacy **10** ascendancy **11** paramountcy **12** independence, jurisdiction, predominance **14** self-government **17** self-determination

Soviet Union *see* **6** Russia

South Dakota

abbreviation: 2 SD **4** S Dak
nickname: 6 Coyote **8** Blizzard, Sunshine
capital: 6 Pierre
largest city: 10 Sioux Falls
others: 4 Lead, Leap **5** Huron **6** Custer, Eureka, Lemmon, Miller, Winner **7** Sturgis, Webster, Yankton **8** Aberdeen, Deadwood, Sisseton **9** Brookings, Rapid City **10** Vermillion
college: 5 Huron **7** Yankton **9** Augustana **10** Mount Marty, Sioux Falls **14** Dakota Wesleyan
explorer: 8 Varennes **13** Lewis and Clark
feature: 8 Deadwood
  battlefield: **11** Wounded Knee
  dam: **4** Oahe
  mine: **9** Homestake
  monument: **13** Mount Rushmore
  national park: **8** Badlands, Wind Cave
tribe: 5 Brule, Sioux **6** Dakota, Sutaio **8** Cheyenne
people: 10 Crazy Horse **11** Sitting Bull **14** George McGovern, Hubert Humphrey
lake: 4 Oahe **5** Sharp **8** Big Stone, Traverse **11** Francis Case **13** Lewis and Clark
land rank: 9 sixteenth
mountain: 4 Bear **5** Sheep, Table **6** Crook's, Moreau
  highest point: **6** Harney
  hills: **5** Black **7** Prairie
physical feature:
  butte: **7** Thunder **9** Deer's Ears **10** Castle Rock
  cave: **5** Jewel
river: 3 Bad **5** Grand, James, White **6** Moreau **8** Big Sioux, Cheyenne, Missouri **10** Vermillion
state admission: 8 fortieth **11** thirty-ninth (with North Dakota)
state bird: 18 ring-necked pheasant
state flower: 12 pasqueflower
state animal: 6 coyote
state motto: 21 Under God the People Rule
state song: 15 Hail South Dakota
state tree: 11 white spruce **16** Black Hills spruce

roles: 6 Carrie **7** Missing **8** Badlands, The River **10** Raggedy Man **16** Crimes of the Heart **18** Coal Miner's Daughter (Oscar)

spacious 4 vast, wide **5** ample, broad, large, roomy **7** immense, sizable **8** enormous **9** capacious, expansive, extensive, uncrowded **10** commodious

spaciousness 9 amplitude, largeness, roominess **13** capaciousness **14** commodiousness

Spade, Sam
  character in: 16 The Maltese Falcon
  author: 7 Hammett

Spain *see box, p. 914*

span 4 arch, area, last, term, wing **5** cover, cross, range, reach, scope, spell, sweep, vault **6** bridge, endure, extent, length, period **7** archway, breadth, measure, stretch, survive, trestle **8** distance, duration, interval **9** extension, reach over, territory **10** bridge over, dimensions **11** proportions, reach across, stretch over **12** extend across

spangle 4 star **5** bedew **6** sequin **7** glisten, glitter, shimmer, twinkle **9** bugle bead, coruscate, paillette

spaniel
  dog breed: 5 field **6** cocker, Sussex **7** clumber, Tibetan **10** Irish water **13** American water, English cocker, Welsh springer **15** English springer

Spanish (language, person) 7 espanol

Spanish Guinea *see* **16** Equatorial Guinea

Spanish Sahara *see* **13** Western Sahara

Spanish Tragedy, The
  author: 9 Thomas Kyd
  character: 7 Horatio, Lorenzo, Villupo **9** Alexandro, Balthazar, Hieronimo **10** Bel-Imperia **16** Ghost of Don Andrea

spank 3 hit, tan **4** beat, belt, blow, cane, flog, hide, lick, slap, whip, whop **5** birch, strap, whale **6** paddle, strike, switch, thrash, wallop **8** paddling **10** flagellate

spanking 4 very **5** brisk, fresh **7** beating **8** paddling, whipping **9** extremely, thrashing **10** punishment **12** chastisement

spanking new 5 fresh **6** unused **8** brand new **9** untouched

spar 4 boom, mast, pole **5** argue, fight, sprit **6** bicker **7** dispute, quarrel, wrangle **8** crossbar **10** crosspiece

spare 3 odd **4** bony, cede, free, give, keep, lank, lean, save, thin **5** amass, extra, forgo, gaunt, grant, guard, hoard, lanky, lay up, limit, pinch, rangy, scant, stint, weedy **6** acquit, afford, defend, donate, excess, exempt, forego, let off, meager, not use, pardon, scanty, shield, skimpy, skinny, slight, unused **7** forgive, haggard, husband, let go of, protect, release, relieve, reserve, scraggy, scrawny, shelter, skimp on, slender, surplus **8** conserve, hold back, leftover, liberate, part with, reprieve, set aside, skeletal, withhold **9** auxiliary, emaciated, exonerate, fleshless, safeguard, show mercy **10** additional, extraneous, relinquish, substitute, unconsumed **11** economize on, have mercy on, superfluous, unnecessary, use frugally **12** be merciful to, dispense with, supplemental **13** supernumerary, supplementary

spared 5 freed **6** exempt, immune **7** excused **8** absolved, excepted, relieved

sparing 4 near **5** close, scant **6** frugal, meager, saving, scanty, stingy **7** careful, miserly, thrifty **8** grudging, stinting **9** niggardly, penurious **10** economical, ungenerous **11** closefisted, tightfisted **12** parsimonious

spark 3 bit, jot **4** atom, beam, fire, iota, life **5** brand, ember, flash, gleam, pique, trace **6** arouse, excite, incite, spirit **7** flicker, glimmer, glitter, inspire, provoke, sparkle **8** vitality **9** animation, instigate, stimulate **10** get-up-and-go

Spain
  other name: 6 Iberia **8** Hispania
  capital/largest city: 6 Madrid
  others: 4 Adra, Aspe, Baza, Elda, Horo, Irun, Jaen, Leon, Noya, Olot, Reus, Rota, Sama,
  Vigo **5** Baena, Bejar, Cadiz, Cieza, Cueta, Ecija, Eibar, Elche, Gades, Gadir, Gijon, Ibiza,
  Jerez, Jodar, Liego, Lorca, Oliva, Palma, Palos, Ronda, Siero, Ubeda, Xeres, Yecla, Zafra
  6 Abdera, Aviles, Azuaga, Bilbao, Burgos, Coruna, Duenca, Gandia, Gerona, Getafe, Guadix,
  Hellin, Huelva, Huesca, Jativa, Lerida, Lucena, Malaga, Mataro, Merida, Murcia, Orense,
  Oviedo, Termel, Toledo, Utrera, Zamora **7** Almeria, Badajos, Cordoba, Daimiel, Granada,
  Jumilla, Linares, Logrono, Manresa, Segovia, Sevilla, Seville, Tarrasa, Vitoria **8** Alicante, Bad-
  alona, Figueras, Pamplona, Sabadell, Santiago, Torrente, Valencia, Zaragoza **9** Barcelona, Las
  Palmas, Saragossa
  school: 6 Ciudad, Madrid
  division: 4 Jaen, Leon, Lugo **5** Alava, Avila, Cadiz, Soria **6** Basque, Burgos, Coruna, Cuenca,
  Gerona, Huelva, Huesca, Lerida, Madrid, Malaga, Murcia, Orense, Oviedo, Teruel, Toledo,
  Zamora **7** Almeria, Caceres, Cordoba, Granada, Logrono, Navarra, Segovia, Sevilla, Vizcaya,
  Zadajoz **8** Albacete, Alicante, Baleares, Palencia, Valencia, Zaragoza **9** Catalonia
    kingdom: **4** Leon **6** Aragon **7** Castile, Galicia, Granada, Navarre **8** Asturias **9** al-Andalus, Cat-
    alonia **12** Spanish March
  government: 8 monarchy
    legislature: **6** Cortes
  head of state: 4 king
  measure: 3 pie **4** codo, dedo, paso, vara **5** braza, cahiz, carga, legua, medio, palmo, sesma
    6 cordel, cuarta, fanega, racion, yugada **7** azumbre, celemin, estadel, pulgada **8** fanegada
  monetary unit: 3 cob **4** duro, peso **5** dobla **6** cuarto, dinero, escudo **7** alfonso, centimo, pis-
    tole **8** doubloon
  weight: 4 onza **5** frail, libra, marco, tomin **6** arroba, dinero, dracma **7** arienzo, quilate, quin-
    tal **8** tonelada
  island: 5 Ceuta, Ibiza, Iviza, Palma **6** Canary, Gomera, Hierro **7** Alboran, Majorca, Melilla, Mi-
    norca **8** Balearic, Mallorca, Tagomago, Tenerife **9** Lanzarote **13** Fuerteventura
  lake: 4 lago **8** Albufera
  mountain: 4 Gata **5** Aneto, Rouch **6** Cuenca, Estats, Europa, Gredos, Magina, Morena, Nethou,
    Nevada, Teleno, Toledo **7** Alcaraz, Banuelo, Catalan, Cerredo, Demanda, Iberian, La Sagra,
    Moncayo, Perdido **8** Almanzor, Asturias, Galician, Maladeta, Monegros, Montseny, Penalara,
    Pyrenees **10** Albarracin, Cantabrian, Guadarrama, Torrecilla
  highest point: 5 Teide **8** Mulhacen
  river: 3 Sil, Ter **4** Cega, Ebro, Esla, Lima, Mino, Muga, Tajo, Ulla **5** Adaja, Cinca, Douro,
    Duero, Genil, Jalon, Jucar, Navia, Odiel, Riaza, Segie, Tagus, Tinto, Turia **6** Alagon, Aragon,
    Eresma, Huerva, Jarama, Orbigo, Segura, Torote **7** Almeria, Almonte, Arlanza, Barbate, Ca-
    briel, Gallego, Henares, Mijares, Perales **8** Duration, Guadiana **12** Guadalquivir
  sea: 8 Atlantic, Balearic **13** Mediterranean
  physical feature:
    bay: **5** Bahia **6** Biscay
    cape: **9** Trafalgar
    gulf: **5** Cadiz **8** San Jorge, Valencia
    peninsula: **7** Iberian
    plateau: **6** meseta
    strait: **9** Gibraltar
  people: 5 Diego, Gente, Latin **6** Basque, Espana **7** Catalan, Espanol, Iberian **8** Galician, Galle-
    gos, Maragato
    architect: **5** Gaudi
    artist: **4** Dali, Goya, Gris, Miro **6** Ribera **7** El Greco, Murillo, Picasso **8** Zurbaran
    9 Velazquez

Spark, Muriel
  author of: 11 Memento
  Mori **14** The Driver's Seat,
  The Only Problem **17** The
  Mandelbaum Gate, Territo-
  rial Rights **19** Loitering with
  Intent **21** A Far Cry from
  Kensington **24** The Prime of
  Miss Jean Brodie

sparkle 3 pep, pop, vim
  4 dash, elan, fizz, foam, glow,
  life **5** be gay, brand, cheer,
  ember, flash, froth, gleam,
  glint, light, shine, verve
  6 bubble, dazzle, fizzle, gaiety,
  spirit **7** be witty, flicker, glimmer, glisten, glitter, jollity, rejoice, shimmer, twinkle
  8 radiance, vitality, vivacity
  9 alertness, animation, briskness, coruscate, quickness
  10 be cheerful, brilliance,
  ebullience, effervesce, effulgence, exuberance, liveliness,
  luminosity **11** be vivacious,
  scintillate **12** cheerfulness, exhilaration, luminousness **13** effervescence, scintillation

sparkling 5 fizzy **6** bubbly
  7 fizzing, twinkly **8** bubbling,
  dazzling, glittery **9** twinkling
  10 glistening, glittering
  11 coruscating **12** effervescent
  13 scintillating

Sparky Lyle
  nickname of: 16 Albert Walter Lyle

sparse 3 few **4** thin **5** scant,
  spare **6** meager, scanty, scarce,
  skimpy, spotty, strewn **7** diffuse **8** exiguous, sporadic
  9 dispersed, scattered, spaced-
  out, uncrowded **10** infrequent
  16 few and far between

author: **4** Cela, Vega **5** Barea, Cueva, Rojas **6** Aleman, Alonso, Azorin, Baroja, Castro, Encina, Felipe, Ibanez, Miguel **7** Alarcon, Becquer, Cernuda, Ercilla, Gongora, Guillen, Jimenez, Machado, Unamuno **8** Montalvo, Zorrilla **9** Benavente, Cervantes, Goytisola **10** Aleixandre, Espronceda, Lope de Vega, Pardo Bazan **11** Garcia Lorca **12** Lopez de Ayala **13** Tirso de Molina **17** Calderon de la Barca
composer: **7** Albeniz **8** Granados, Victoria **13** Manuel de Falla
converted Moslem: **7** morisco
dynasty: **7** Almohad, Umayyad **9** Almoravid
explorer: **6** Balboa, Cortes **7** Pizarro **8** Columbus
Jesuit founder: **14** Ignatius Loyola
king: **6** Pelayo, Philip, Ramiro, Sancho, Witiza **7** Alfonso, Charles **8** al-Mansur, Reccared, Roderick **9** Ferdinand, Leovigild **10** Juan Carlos **11** Abd al-Rahman, Reccosvinth
leader: **4** Prim **5** Godoy **6** Franco **7** Canovas **11** Calvo Sotelo **13** Primo de Rivera **14** Suarez-Gonzalez
queen: **8** Isabella **16** Elizabeth Farnese
ruler: **4** Rome **5** Celts, Moors **6** Greece **7** Almeria, Vandals **8** Carthage **9** Phoenicia, Visigoths
scholar: **8** Averroes
warrior: **14** El Cid Campeador
language: **6** Basque **7** Catalan, Spanish **8** Balearic, Galician **9** Castilian, Valencian
religion: **7** Judaism **10** Protestant **13** Roman Catholic
place:
  aqueduct: **7** Segovia
  bridge: **7** Cordoba
  castle: **7** Alcazar **12** Santa Barbara
  cathedral bell tower: **7** Giralda
  center of Madrid: **12** Puerto del Sol
  church/cathedral: **4** Leon **6** Burgos, Gerona, Toledo **7** Seville **9** Barcelona, San Isidro **10** Santa Maria **14** Sagrada Familia
  fountain: **6** Cibele
  library: **8** Columbus
  minaret: **7** Seville
  mosque: **11** Great Mosque **19** Santo Cristo de la Cruz
  museum: **5** Prado **15** Museo de Pinturas
  palace: **7** Granada, Naranco **8** Alhambra, Escorial **9** Real Mayor
  park: **6** Retiro
  resort: **8** Marbella **10** Costa Brava **12** Torremolinos
  shrine: **32** Saint James at Santiago de Compostela
  street: **7** Ramblas **13** Paseo del Prado **16** Plaza de la Cibeles **19** Paseo de la Castellana
  synagogue: **10** El Transito
  theater: **6** Merida
  wall paintings/caves: **8** Altamira
possession: **5** Ceuta **6** Melill
feature:
  bar: **6** tascas
  dance: **5** tango **8** fandango, flamenco
  estate: **10** latifundia
  matador's suit: **12** traje de luces
  political party: **7** Falange
· food:
  dish: **6** cocido, paella **8** zarzuela
  soup: **8** gazpacho

---

sparseness 7 paucity **8** sparsity, thinness **10** meagerness, scantiness

Sparsit, Mrs
  character in: **9** Hard Times
  author: **7** Dickens

Spartacus
  director: **14** Stanley Kubrick
  cast: **8** Nina Foch **9** John Gavin **10** Tony Curtis **11** Jean Simmons, Kirk Douglas **12** Peter Ustinov **15** Charles Laughton, Laurence Olivier
  setting: **4** Rome
  score: **9** Alex North

spartan 4 hard **5** plain, stark, stern, stiff **6** frugal, severe, simple, strict **7** ascetic, austere **8** exacting, rigorous **9** stringent **10** abstemious, inexorable, inflexible, restrained, restricted **11** disciplined, self-denying **15** self-disciplined

Sparti
  occupation: **8** warriors

spasm 3 fit, tic **4** grip, jerk, pang **5** burst, cramp, crick, flash, onset, spell, spurt, start, storm, throe **6** access, attack, frenzy, twitch **7** seizure, shudder, tempest **8** eruption, paroxysm **9** explosion **10** convulsion

spasmodic 6 fitful **7** erratic, flighty **8** fleeting, periodic, sporadic **9** desultory, irregular, mercurial, transient **10** capricious, inconstant, occasional **12** intermittent **13** discontinuous

spat 4 tiff **5** argue, fight, scrap,

set-to 6 bicker, differ **7** contend, dispute, dissent, quarrel, wrangle **8** disagree, squabble **10** difference **11** altercation **12** disagreement **16** misunderstanding

spatter 4 slop, soil, spot **5** fleck, plash, spray, spurt, stain, swash **6** mottle, shower, splash **7** speckle, stipple **8** splatter, sprinkle

spawn 4 eggs, seed, teem **5** beget, breed, brood, fruit, yield **7** lay eggs, produce, product **8** engender, generate, multiply **9** offspring, propagate, reproduce **10** bring forth, give rise to **11** deposit eggs, give birth to, proliferate

speak 3 air, say **4** call, chat, deal, talk, tell **5** imply, orate, refer, shout, sound, state, treat, voice **6** advise, confer, convey, cry out, dilate, impart, mumble, murmur, mutter, preach, recite, relate, remark, report, reveal **7** bespeak, comment, consult, declaim, declare, discuss, divulge, expound, express, lecture, mention, suggest, whisper **8** announce, converse, disclose, harangue, indicate, proclaim, vocalize **9** discourse, enunciate, expatiate, hold forth, make known, pronounce, sermonize **10** articulate **11** communicate, give a speech

speakeasy 3 bar **6** saloon, tavern **7** gin mill **14** cocktail lounge

speaker 5 voice **6** orator, reader, talker **7** reciter **8** advocate, lecturer, preacher **9** declaimer, spokesman **10** discourser, monologist, mouthpiece, sermonizer **11** rhetorician, speechmaker, spokeswoman **13** valedictorian

speak highly of 4 laud **5** exalt, extol **6** praise **7** commend **8** eulogize **10** compliment **16** sing the praises of

speak ill of 4 slur **5** curse, knock, libel **6** defame, insult, malign, vilify **7** slander **8** badmouth **9** criticize, denigrate, discredit, disparage **13** find fault with **14** inveigh against

speak loudly 3 cry **4** bawl, call, hail, roar, yell **5** shout **6** bellow, clamor, cry out, halloo, holler **7** call out, speak up

speak of 7 mention, refer to **8** allude to **9** talk about, touch upon

speak to 6 talk to **7** address, lecture

speak together 3 gab, jaw, rap **4** chat, chin, talk **6** confer **7** chatter, palaver **8** chitchat, converse **10** chew the fat, chew the rag **11** communicate, confabulate

speak well of 4 laud **5** boost, extol **6** praise **7** acclaim, approve, commend, flatter, root for **8** eulogize **9** sweet talk **10** compliment, stick up for **13** speak highly of **16** sing the praises of **17** put in a good word for

spear 4 bolt, dart, gaff, gore, pike, spit, stab **5** lance, prick, shaft, spike, stick **6** impale, pierce **7** harpoon, javelin **8** puncture, transfix **9** penetrate **10** run through

spearhead 4 iron, lead **5** begin, found, start **6** launch, leader **7** creator, develop, founder, pioneer **8** begetter, conceive, initiate **9** establish, initiator, institute, originate, spokesman **10** inaugurate, instituter, prime mover **11** establisher, inaugurator, spokeswoman **12** avant-gardist

special 4 fast, good, rare **5** close, great, novel **6** ardent, proper, select, signal, unique **7** bargain, certain, devoted, endemic, feature, staunch, typical, unusual **8** distinct, especial, intimate, peculiar, personal, sale item, singular, specific, uncommon **9** headliner, high point, highlight, important, momentous, specialty, steadfast **10** attraction, individual, noteworthy, particular, remarkable **11** distinctive, exceptional, outstanding, specialized **12** extravaganza **13** distinguished, extraordinary **14** representative, unconventional **16** out of the ordinary **17** piece de resistance

specialist 4 buff **5** adept, maven **6** expert, master **9** authority **10** past master **11** connoisseur

specialization 5 focus, forte, major **6** metier **8** province **10** speciality **13** concentration

specialize 5 adapt, focus, major **6** pursue **10** narrow down **11** concentrate

specialty 4 bent, mark, turn **5** badge, focus, forte, hobby, major, stamp **6** genius, talent **7** earmark, faculty, feature, pursuit, special **8** aptitude **9** endowment, trademark **10** competence, profession **11** claim to fame, distinction

species 4 form, kind, make,

sort, type **5** breed, class, genre, group, order **6** kidney, nature, stripe **7** variety **8** category, division **11** designation, subdivision **14** classification

specific 5 exact, fixed **6** minute, stated, unique **7** bounded, certain, endemic, limited, pointed, precise, special, typical **8** clear-cut, concrete, confined, definite, detailed, especial, peculiar, personal, relevant, singular, tied-down **9** intrinsic, pertinent, specified **10** individual, particular, pinned-down, restricted **11** categorical, determinate, distinctive, unequivocal **13** circumscribed **14** characteristic

specification 6 detail **7** clarity **9** condition, precision, substance **11** enumeration, itemization, requirement, stipulation **12** concreteness **13** particularity, qualification **17** particularization

specifics 4 cure, fact, item **5** datum **6** detail, physic **10** medication, particular **12** circumstance

specify 4 cite, name **5** order **6** adduce, define, denote, detail **7** call for, focus on, itemize **8** describe, indicate, set forth **9** designate, enumerate, stipulate **13** particularize

specimen 4 case, type **5** model **6** sample **7** example **8** exemplar, instance **9** prototype **14** representative **15** exemplification

specious 5 false **6** faulty, tricky, untrue **7** dubious, invalid, unsound **8** slippery, spurious **9** casuistic, deceptive, illogical, incorrect, unfounded **10** fallacious, inaccurate, misleading **11** sophistical **12** questionable **15** unsubstantiated

speck 3 bit, dot, jot, pin **4** drop, hair, iota, mark, mite, mote, spot, whit **5** fleck, grain, pinch, trace **6** shadow, trifle **7** glimmer, modicum, speckle **8** farthing, flyspeck, particle **9** scintilla

speckled 4 pied **6** dotted **7** flecked, spotted, studded **8** freckled, peppered **9** sprinkled

spectacle 5 scene, sight **6** marvel, parade, rarity, wonder **7** display, exhibit, pageant **9** curiosity, rare sight **10** exhibition, exposition, phenomenon, production **12** extravaganza, presentation **13** demonstration

spectacles 6 lenses, shades
7 glasses 8 bifocals, pince-nez
10 eyeglasses

spectacular 4 gala, rich
5 grand, showy 6 daring
7 jeweled, opulent, stately
8 dramatic, fabulous, glorious,
gorgeous, splendid, striking
9 daredevil, elaborate, marvelous, spectacle, sumptuous,
thrilling 10 astounding, bespangled, eye-filling, impressive, theatrical
11 ceremonious, hair-raising,
magnificent, sensational
12 extravaganza, overwhelming 16 ostentatious show
19 elaborate production

spectator 3 fan 5 house
6 viewer 7 gallery, witness
8 audience, beholder, kibitzer,
observer, onlooker 9 by-
stander, sightseer 10 aficionado, eyewitness 11 afficionado,
theatergoer 12 rubbernecker

Spectator, The
author: 13 Joseph Addison,
Richard Steele

specter 5 demon, ghost, ghoul,
shade, spook 6 spirit, sprite,
vision, wraith 7 banshee, fantasy, phantom 8 phantasm,
presence, revenant 9 hobgoblin 10 apparition

spectral 4 airy 5 eerie, weird
6 creepy, spooky, unreal
7 ghastly, ghostly, phantom,
shadowy, uncanny 8 ethereal,
gossamer, vaporous
9 unearthly 10 chimerical,
phantasmal, wraithlike 11 incorporeal 12 otherworldly, supernatural 13 insubstantial

speculate 4 muse 5 brood,
dream, fancy, guess, study,
think, wager 6 chance, gamble, hazard, ponder, reason,
wonder 7 imagine, reflect, suppose, surmise, venture 8 cogitate, consider, meditate,
ruminate, theorize 10 conjecture, deliberate, excogitate,
play a hunch 11 contemplate,
hypothesize, take a chance
13 play the market

speculation 4 risk 7 venture
8 gambling 9 guesswork
10 conjecture, estimation
11 supposition

speculative 4 iffy 5 dicey,
risky 6 chancy 8 academic
11 conjectural, theoretical
12 experimental, hypothetical
13 suppositional

speculator 7 gambler, plunger
8 investor, operator, theorist
10 adventurer, arbitrager
11 arbitrageur

speech 4 talk 5 idiom, lingo,
slang, voice 6 appeal, gossip,
homily, jargon, sermon, tirade,
tongue 7 address, chatter,
comment, dialect, diction, lecture, oration, palaver, prattle,
remarks, talking 8 chitchat,
colloquy, converse, dialogue,
diatribe, harangue, language,
parlance, rhetoric, speaking
9 discourse, elocution, monologue, soliloquy, statement, utterance 10 discussion,
expression, recitation, salutation 11 declamation, declaration, enunciation, exhortation,
observation, valedictory 12 articulation, conversation, dissertation, vocalization
13 colloquialism, confabulation, pronouncement, pronunciation, verbalization

speechless 3 mum 4 dumb,
mute 6 silent 7 aphonic
8 wordless 9 stupefied
10 tongue-tied

speed 3 aid, hie, run, zip
4 dart, dash, help, race, rate,
rush, tear, zoom 5 boost, favor, gun it, haste, hurry, impel, speed, tempo 6 assist,
barrel, gallop, hasten, hurtle,
hustle, pick up, plunge, propel, scurry, step on it 7 advance,
further, hurry up, promote,
quicken, tear off 8 alacrity, celerity, dispatch, expedite, high-
tail, make time, momentum,
rapidity, step on it, velocity
9 bowl along, briskness, fleetness, give a lift, hastiness,
make haste, move along,
quickness, rapidness, swiftness 10 accelerate, expedition,
get a move on, go hell-bent,
lose no time, promptness,
spurt ahead 11 push forward
12 acceleration 13 burn up
the road

speedily 4 fast 5 apace, quick
6 pronto 7 hastily, rapidly,
swiftly 8 in no time,
promptly 9 post haste, right
away, summarily 11 on the
double 12 lickety-split

speed up 4 rush 5 hurry
6 hasten, step up 7 hop to it,
quicken 8 expedite, multiply,
step on it 9 encourage, intensify 10 accelerate, facilitate,
get a move on 12 step on the
gas

speedy 4 fast 5 brisk, early,
fleet, hasty, quick, rapid,
ready, swift 6 abrupt, lively,
sudden 7 express, hurried, running, summary 8 headlong
9 quick-fire, rapid-fire 10 not
delayed 11 precipitate

Spelaites
epithet of: 6 Hermes
means: 9 of the cave

spell 2 go 3 bit, hex 4 bout,
free, lull, mean, omen, snap,
term, time, tour, turn, wave
5 augur, break, charm, hitch,
imply, magic, pause, round,
stint, trick, while 6 allure,
course, denote, herald, hoodoo, make up, period, recess,
tenure, typify, voodoo 7 bespeak, betoken, connote,
glamour, portend, presage,
promise, purport, rapture, release, relieve, respite, signify,
sorcery, stretch, suggest
8 amount to, cover for, duration, forebode, forecast, foretell, indicate, interval, stand
for, witchery 9 form a word,
influence, interlude, represent,
symbolize 10 assignment, invocation, mumbo jumbo,
open-sesame 11 abracadabra,
bewitchment, enchantment,
fascination, incantation, pinchhit for, take over for
12 magic formula

spellbind 5 charm 7 bewitch,
enchant 8 enthrall, entrance,
intrigue, transfix 9 enrapture,
fascinate, hypnotize, mesmerize, transport

spellbound 4 rapt 5 agape
7 charmed 8 wordless 9 awestruck, bewitched, enchanted,
entranced, possessed
10 breathless, dumbstruck, enraptured, enthralled, fascinated, hypnotized,
mesmerized, speechless,
tongue-tied, transfixed
11 openmouthed, transported

Spellbound
director: 15 Alfred Hitchcock
cast: 9 John Emery 11 Gregory Peck, Leo G Carroll
13 Ingrid Bergman 14 Mi-
chael Chekhov
score: 11 Miklos Rosza
Oscar for: 5 score
dream sequences by:
12 Salvador Dali

spell out 6 define, detail
7 clarify, clear up, explain, expound, specify 8 describe
9 delineate, designate, elucidate, explicate, interpret, make
plain 10 illustrate

Spemann, Hans
field: 7 zoology
nationality: 6 German
worked in: 20 embryonic
development
awarded: 10 Nobel Prize

Spencer, Sir Stanley
born: 7 Cookham, England
9 Berkshire
artwork: 22 Resurrection of
Soldiers, The Resurrection
Cookham 31 Christ Preach-
ing at Cookham Regatta
43 Double Nude Portrait—

spend 918

the Artist and his Second
Wife

spend 3 pay, use 4 dole, fill,
give, pass 5 drain, empty, use
up, waste 6 devote, employ,
expend, invest, occupy, outlay,
pay out, take up 7 burn out,
consume, deplete, destroy, exhaust, fork out, scatter, wear
out 8 allocate, disburse, dispense, shell out, squander
9 dissipate, while away
10 impoverish

spendable 9 available 10 expendable 13 discretionary

spend foolishly 5 waste
8 misspend, squander 9 dissipate, throw away 11 fritter
away

spendthrift 6 lavish, waster
7 wastrel 8 prodigal, spend-all,
wasteful 10 big spender, profligate, squanderer 11 extravagant, improvident
12 overgenerous

Spengler, Oswald
author of: 19 The Decline of
the West

Spenlow, Dora
character in: 16 David
Copperfield
author: 7 Dickens

Spenser, Edmund
author of: 8 Amoretti 12 Epithalamion 15 The Faerie
Queene 22 The Shephearde's
Calendar

spent 4 beat, done, weak
5 faint, weary 6 bushed, done
in, used up 7 laid low, wearied, worn out 8 drooping, fatigued, tired out 9 enfeebled,
exhausted, fagged out, played
out, powerless, prostrate
11 debilitated, ready to drop
12 strengthless 14 on one's
last legs

Sperry, Elmer Ambrose
invented: 11 gyrocompass
22 airplane automatic pilot

spew 5 eject, expel, heave,
vomit 6 cast up 7 spit out
8 disgorge, throw out
11 regurgitate

spew up 4 spew 5 eject, expel,
spout, vomit 6 cast up
7 cough up, throw up 8 disgorge 11 regurgitate

sphere 3 orb 4 area, ball, beat,
pale 5 globe, orbit, range,
realm, scope 6 domain 7 compass, globule 8 province,
spheroid 9 bailiwick, round
body, territory 10 experience

spherical 5 orbic, round
6 global, rotund 7 globate, glo-

bose, orbical 8 globular 9 or-
bicular 11 globe-shaped
nearly: 8 obrotund

spheroid 3 orb 4 ball 5 globe
6 sphere 7 globule

spherule 4 ball, bead, drop
6 pellet 7 droplet, globule

Sphinx
form: 7 monster
bust of: 5 woman
body of: 4 lion
father: 6 Typhon 7 Orthrus
mother: 7 Echidna
8 Chimaera
proposed: 7 riddles
location: 6 Thebes
answered by: 7 Oedipus

spice 3 zip 4 herb, kick, snap,
tang, zest 5 savor 6 accent,
flavor, relish, stacte 7 pizzazz
8 piquancy, pungency 9 condiment, flavoring, seasoning
10 excitement

spicule 4 barb 5 point, spine
7 prickle

spicy 3 hot 4 keen, racy
5 acute, bawdy, fiery, nippy,
pithy, salty, sharp, tangy,
witty, zippy 6 clever, ribald,
risque, snappy, strong 7 gingery, peppery, piquant, pungent 8 aromatic, improper,
incisive, indecent, off-color,
piercing, redolent, spirited
9 sparkling, trenchant 10 indelicate, scandalous, suggestive 11 provocative
12 questionable 13 scintillating

spider
black widow marking:
9 hourglass
class: 9 Arachnida
combining form: 6 arachn
7 arachno
family: 7 Attidae 9 Drassidae
10 Citigradae, Pisauridae
famous: 9 Charlotte
fear of: 13 arachnophobia
kind: 4 crab, wolf 5 taint
7 jumping 8 trap-door 9 orb
weaver, solpugida, taran-
tula 10 black widow
13 daddy longlegs
mythology: 7 Arachne
nest: 5 nidus
order: 7 Araneae
part: 4 claw, coxa 5 femur,
tibia 6 tarsus 7 abdomen,
mammula, patella, pedicel,
scopula 9 chelicera, protar-
sis, spinneret 10 pedipalpus,
trochanter 11 calamistrum
13 cephalothorax
study of: 10 araneology
11 arachnology
young: 11 spiderlings

Spielberg, Steven
director of: 4 Jaws 14 The
Color Purple 19 Raiders of
the Lost Ark 21 ET The Ex-

tra Terrestrial (in his adven-
tures on earth) 29 Close
Encounters of the Third
Kind

spike 3 peg, pin 4 barb, nail,
spur, tine 5 briar, point,
prong, rivet, spine, stake,
thorn 6 needle, skewer
7 bramble, bristle, hobnail
8 spikelet

spill 3 run 4 blab, drip, drop,
dump, fall, flow, shed, slop,
tell, toss 5 slosh, throw,
waste 6 reveal, splash 7 let
flow, pour out 8 disclose,
overflow, overturn

Spillane, Mickey
real name: 13 Frank
Morrison
author of: 8 I the Jury
12 Kiss Me Deadly 14 The
Girl Hunters 15 The Death
Dealers
character: 10 Mike Hammer

spin 4 roll, tell, turn 5 swirl,
twirl, wheel, whirl 6 gyrate,
invent, relate, render, rotate,
unfold 7 concoct, narrate, recount, revolve 8 rotation, spinning 9 fabricate, pirouette

spinach 3 rot 4 bull, bunk
5 hokum, hooey, stuff
6 bunkum, hot air, humbug
7 baloney, blather, hogwash,
potherb 8 claptrap, nonsense,
tommyrot 9 poppycock, vegetable 10 applesauce 11 foolishness 16 stuff and nonsense

spinach 16 Spinacia oleracea
varieties: 4 wild 5 Cuban
6 Indian 7 Malabar 8 mountain 10 New Zealand
11 round-seeded 13 prickly-
seeded

spinal column 4 back 5 spine
8 backbone

spindly 4 puny 5 frail, leggy
6 skinny 7 scraggy 8 skeletal

spine 4 barb, horn, spur
5 briar, point, prong, quill,
spike, thorn 6 needle 7 bramble, bristle, prickle 8 backbone 9 vertebrae 12 spinal
column

spinel
source: 5 Burma, Mogok
color: 3 red 5 mauve

spineless 4 weak 5 timid
7 fearful 8 cowardly, cowering,
cringing, timorous, wavering
10 indecisive, irresolute, spiritless, weak-willed 11 lily-
livered, vacillating 12 fainthearted 13 pusillanimous
14 chickenhearted

spinelessness 8 timidity,
weakness 9 cowardice 10 indecision 11 fearfulness

12 cowardliness, irresolution **13** pusillanimity

spine-tingling 7 rousing **8** exciting **9** thrilling **11** hair-raising, sensational **12** breathtaking, electrifying

spinning jenny
  invented by: 10 Hargreaves

spinoff 5 issue **6** result **7** adjunct, outcome **8** offshoot **9** byproduct, outgrowth **10** descendant, side effect, supplement **11** aftereffect, consequence

spin out 4 skid **7** draw out **8** lengthen **9** attenuate

spinster 6 virgin **7** old maid **14** unmarried woman

spinsterhood 8 celibacy **9** virginity **11** old maidhood

spiral 4 coil, curl, gyre **5** helix, screw, whirl, whorl **6** coiled, curled **7** helical, ringlet, spiroid, whorled, winding **8** curlicue, twisting **9** corkscrew **11** screw-shaped

Spiral Staircase, The
  director: 13 Robert Siodmak
  based on story by: 14 Ethel Lina White (Some Must Watch)
  cast: 9 Kent Smith **11** George Brent **13** Rhonda Fleming **14** Dorothy McGuire, Ethel Barrymore

spire 3 cap, tip **4** apex, cone, peak **5** crest, point, shaft, tower **6** belfry, summit, turret, vertex **7** minaret, obelisk, steeple **8** pinnacle **9** bell tower, campanile

spirit 3 elf **4** mind, soul, urge, will **5** fairy, ghost, ghoul, heart, shade, spook **6** animus, dybbuk, goblin, psyche, sprite, wraith **7** banshee, bugaboo, bugbear, impulse, phantom, resolve, specter **8** phantasm, presence **9** hobgoblin, intellect **10** apparition, motivation, resolution
  German: 5 Geist

spirited 4 bold **5** fiery, nervy **6** frisky, lively, plucky **8** fearless, intrepid **10** courageous, mettlesome

spiritless 4 dull, limp, tame **6** abject **8** cowardly, lifeless, listless **9** apathetic, spineless **10** unanimated, world-weary **11** passionless

spirit of the time
  German: 9 Zeitgeist

spirits 3 aim, vim **4** bond, elan, fire, gist, glow, grit, guts, mood, sand, tone, vein, zeal, zest **5** ardor, drive, hu-

mor, pluck, sense, spunk, tenor, valor, verve, vigor **6** daring, effect, elixir, energy, fervor, intent, liquor, mettle, morale, stripe, temper, warmth **7** alcohol, avidity, bravery, courage, essence, extract, feeling, loyalty, meaning, purport, purpose, sparkle **8** attitude, audacity, backbone, boldness, devotion, emotions, feelings, tincture, vitality, vivacity **9** animation, eagerness, fortitude, intention, sentiment, stoutness, substance **10** allegiance, attachment, enterprise, enthusiasm, liveliness **11** disposition, doughtiness, staunchness **12** fearlessness, significance **13** dauntlessness, sprightliness **16** stouthearted-ness **17** alcoholic solution

spiritual 4 holy **5** godly, inner, moral, pious **6** divine, mental **7** blessed, churchy, ghostly, phantom, psychic **8** cerebral, hallowed, heavenly, platonic, priestly, spectral, supernal **9** celestial, Christian, innermost, of the soul, religious, unearthly, unfleshly, unworldly **10** devotional, immaterial, intangible, sacrosanct, sanctified **11** consecrated, incorporeal **12** metaphysical, otherworldly, supernatural **13** insubstantial, psychological **14** ecclesiastical

spirituality 5 piety **8** devotion, holiness **9** godliness, reverence **10** devoutness

spirituous 4 hard **6** strong **9** alcoholic, distilled **12** intoxicating

spit 3 bar, pop, rod **4** foam, hiss, reef, spew **5** atoll, drool, eject, fling, froth, shoal, throw **6** saliva, shower, shriek, skewer, slaver, sputum **7** dribble, scatter, slobber, spatter, spittle, sputter **8** headland, sandbank, turnspit **9** brochette, peninsula **10** promontory **11** expectorate

spite 3 irk, vex **4** gall, hate, hurt, pain **5** annoy, odium, sting, venom, wound **6** animus, enmity, grudge, harass, hatred, injure, malice, misuse, nettle, put out, rancor **7** ill will, mortify, provoke **8** bad blood, ill-treat, irritate, loathing, meanness **9** animosity, antipathy, hostility, humiliate, malignity, nastiness, vengeance **10** bitterness, resentment **11** detestation, malevolence **12** vengefulness **13** maliciousness, slap in the face **14** revengefulness, vindictiveness

spiteful 4 evil **5** nasty **6** bitter, malign, wicked **7** caustic, envious, hateful, hostile, vicious **8** grudging, vengeful, venomous **9** malicious, merciless, rancorous, resentful, sarcastic, splenetic **10** ill-natured, malevolent, vindictive **11** acrimonious, unforgiving **12** antagonistic

spitting image (the) 4 copy, mate, twin **6** double **9** duplicate **15** perfect likeness

splash 3 ado, hit **4** cast, dash, daub, soil, stir, toss, wash **5** bathe, break, fling, plash, slosh, smack, smear, stain, strew, surge, swash **6** batter, blazon, buffet, effect, impact, paddle, plunge, shower, spread, streak, strike, uproar, wallow, welter **7** bestrew, scatter, spatter, splotch **8** besmirch, discolor, disperse, splatter, sprinkle **9** bespatter, broadcast, commotion, sensation **10** spattering **11** splattering

splashy 5 jazzy, showy **6** flashy **10** glittering **11** spectacular **12** ostentatious

splatter 4 dash **6** splash **7** spatter

splay 4 awry **5** askew, broad **6** aslant, clumsy, extend, tilted, warped **7** awkward, crooked, fanlike, slanted, sloping, turn out **8** inclined, slanting **9** distorted, fan-shaped, irregular, outspread, spread out **10** stretch out

spleen 4 bile, gall **5** anger, spite, venom **6** animus, enmity, hatred, malice, rancor **7** ill will **8** acrimony, ill humor, vexation **9** animosity, bad temper, hostility **10** bitterness, resentment **11** malevolence, peevishness **12** irritability, spitefulness

splendid 4 fine, high, rare, rich **5** grand, lofty, noble, regal, royal **6** august, costly, ornate, superb **7** elegant, eminent, exalted, stately **8** dazzling, elevated, flashing, gleaming, glorious, gorgeous, imposing, majestic, palatial, peerless, terrific **9** admirable, beautiful, brilliant, effulgent, estimable, excellent, marvelous, sumptuous, wonderful **10** glittering, preeminent, remarkable, surpassing **11** exceptional, illustrious, magnificent, outstanding, resplendent, splendorous **12** transcendent **13** distinguished, splendiferous

Splendid Splinter
nickname of: **11** Ted
Williams

splendor 4 fire, pomp **5** gleam,
glory, light, sheen, shine
6 beauty, dazzle, luster, renown **7** burnish, glitter
8 grandeur, nobility, opulence,
radiance **9** intensity, sublimity **10** augustness, brilliance,
effulgence, irradiance, luminosity **11** preeminence, stateliness **12** gorgeousness,
luminousness, magnificence,
resplendence **13** incandescence

Splendor in the Grass
director: **9** Elia Kazan
based on story by: **11** William Inge
cast: **9** Pat Hingle **11** Natalie
Wood **12** Sean Garrison,
Warren Beatty **14** Audrey
Christie

splenetic 5 cross, nasty, surly,
testy **6** cranky, malign **7** bilious, hostile, peevish **8** choleric, spiteful, venomous
9 irascible, rancorous **11** acrimonious, ill-tempered **12** cantankerous, disagreeable

splice 3 wed **4** join, knit
5 graft, merge, plait, unite
7 connect **8** dovetail **9** interlace **10** intertwine, interweave **12** interconnect

splinter 4 chip **5** smash, split
6 needle, shiver, sliver **7** break
up, crumble, explode, shatter
8 fly apart, fracture, fragment
9 pulverize **12** disintegrate

split 3 hew **4** deal, dole, dual,
mete, part, rent, rift, rive,
snap, tear, torn **5** allot, break,
burst, cleft, crack, halve,
mixed, riven, sever, share
6 bisect, breach, broken,
cleave, differ, divide, ripped,
schism, shiver, sunder, varied
7 be riven, cracked, diverge,
divided, divorce, divvy up, fissure, give way, opening, portion, quarrel, rupture, severed,
twofold **8** alienate, allocate,
cleavage, disagree, dispense,
disperse, dissever, disunion,
disunite, division, fracture,
ruptured, splinter **9** apportion,
fractured, parcel out, partition,
segmented, segregate, separated, set at odds, subdivide,
undecided **10** alienation, ambivalent, break apart, difference, dissension, dissevered,
distribute, divergence, falling
out, separation, splintered
11 come between, part company, tear asunder **12** disagreement, estrangement

split off 7 deviate, diverge
8 separate **9** draw apart

split the difference 5 agree
6 settle **9** make a deal
10 compromise **11** come to
terms, meet halfway **14** strike
a bargain

splitting off 9 diverging
10 separating **12** drawing
apart

splitting up 8 dividing **9** di-
vorcing **10** breaking up, separating **11** subdividing
12 partitioning

splotch 4 blot, daub, mark,
spot **5** smear, stain **6** blotch,
smudge **13** discoloration

splurge 5 binge, spree
6 bender **8** live it up **10** indulgence, showing off
12 showy display **13** be extravagant, shoot the works
14 indulge oneself, self-
indulgence **22** throw caution
to the winds

splutter 4 hiss, spew, spit
5 burst, spray **6** gibber, jabber,
mumble, seethe **7** bluster,
slobber, spatter, sputter, stammer, stumble, stutter **9** hem
and haw **11** expectorate

Spodius
epithet of: **6** Apollo
means: **10** god of ashes

spodumene
variety: **7** kunzite

spoil 3 mar, rot **4** baby, flaw,
harm, mold, ruin, sour, turn
5 addle, botch, decay, go bad,
humor, taint **6** blight, bungle,
coddle, damage, deface, foul
up, impair, injure, mess up,
mildew, muddle, pamper
7 blemish, destroy, disrupt,
putrefy **8** mutilate **9** decompose, disfigure **11** deteriorate,
mollycoddle, overgratify,
overindulge

spoiled 3 bad, off **6** putrid, rotten, ruined **7** coddled, corrupt,
decayed, gone bad, went bad
8 indulged, overripe, pampered **9** putrefied **10** decomposed, frustrated
12 deteriorated **15** rotten to
the core

spoiler 6 vandal **8** underdog
9 deflector

Spoilers, The
author: **8** Rex Beach

spoils 4 haul, loot, swag, take
5 booty **6** bounty, prizes,
quarry **7** plunder, profits
8 benefits, comforts, pickings
9 amenities, patronage **11** per-
quisites **12** acquisitions

spoilsport 4 drag **10** wet blanket **11** party-pooper

spoken 4 oral, said **5** parol

6 verbal, voiced **7** uttered
9 expressed **10** pronounced
11 articulated

spokesman 5 agent, PR man,
proxy **6** backer, deputy
7 speaker **8** delegate, promoter **9** middleman, proponent, supporter, surrogate
10 mouthpiece, negotiator,
press agent **11** protagonist

sponge 3 bum, dry, mop, rub
4 blot, swab, wash **5** cadge,
clean, leech, mooch, towel
6 borrow, live on **7** cleanse,
moisten **8** freeload, impose on,
scrounge **9** panhandle

sponger 5 leech **6** cadger,
sponge **7** moocher **8** barnacle,
borrower, deadbeat
9 scrounger **10** freeloader
11 bloodsucker

sponsor 4 back **5** angel, set
up **6** backer, patron, uphold
7 finance, promote, support
8 advocate, champion, defender, financer, guardian,
partisan, promoter, start out,
upholder, vouch for, war-
ranty **9** guarantee, financier,
guarantor, proponent, protecter, protector, supporter
10 advertiser, stand up for,
underwrite

sponsorship 5 aegis **7** support
8 advocacy, auspices **9** patronage **12** championship

spontaneity 7 freedom **11** impetuosity, naturalness **12** unconstraint **13** impulsiveness,
offhandedness
18 extemporaneousness

spontaneous 4 free **5** ad lib
7 natural, offhand, willing
8 unbidden **9** automatic, extempore, impetuous, im-
promptu, impulsive,
ingenuous, unplanned, unstudied, voluntary **10** gratuitous,
improvised, off the cuff, unprompted **11** independent, instinctive, uncontrived
12 unhesitating **13** unconstrained **14** extemporaneous,
unpremeditated

spoof 3 kid **4** joke, josh, twit
6 parody, satire, sendup
7 joshing, kidding, lampoon,
mockery, ribbing, takeoff
8 satirize, travesty **9** burlesque,
take off on **10** caricature

spook 5 alarm, bogey, ghost,
haunt, scare, shade **6** goblin,
shadow, spirit **7** disturb, phantom, specter, startle, terrify,
unnerve **8** disquiet, frighten,
unsettle **9** hobgoblin, terrorize
10 apparition, intimidate

spooky 5 eerie, jumpy, scary,
weird **6** creepy **7** ghostly,

nervous **8** skittish
10 mysterious

sporadic 3 few **4** rare, thin
6 fitful, meager, random,
scarce, sparse, spotty **8** isolated, periodic, uncommon
9 haphazard, irregular, scattered, spasmodic **10** infrequent, now and then,
occasional **11** fragmentary
12 intermittent, widely
spaced **13** discontinuous
16 few and far between

sport 3 fun, toy **4** bear, butt,
game, goat, jest, joke, lark,
play, romp, trip **5** abuse, caper, carry, chaff, dally, frisk,
hobby, mirth, revel **6** antics,
cavort, frolic, gaiety, gambol,
misuse, monkey, take in, trifle **7** buffoon, contest, display,
disport, exhibit, gambler, jesting, jollity, kidding, mockery,
rollick, show off, skylark
8 badinage, derision, fair
game, flourish, hilarity, ill-
treat, raillery, ridicule, scoffing, trifling **9** amusement, athletics, daredevil, diversion,
festivity, joviality, make
merry, play games, scapegoat
10 persiflage, pleasantry, recreation, relaxation, skylarking
11 competition, distraction,
merrymaking **12** depreciation
13 entertainment, laughingstock **14** divertissement

sporting house 4 stew
5 house **6** bagnio, bordel
7 brothel **8** bordello, cathouse
10 bawdy house, fancy house,
whorehouse **14** house of ill
fame **16** house of ill repute
19 house of prostitution

sportive 6 blithe, frisky
7 playful **8** animated
10 frolicsome

sportsman 6 hunter
9 fisherman

Sportsman's Notebook, A
author: **12** Ivan Turgenev

sporty 6 casual, flashy, jaunty
8 informal

spot 3 dot, fix, see, spy **4** area,
bind, blot, daub, espy, flaw,
mark, part, seat, site, slur,
soil **5** brand, fleck, grime, locus, patch, place, point,
smear, space, speck, stain,
sully, taint, tract **6** blotch, defect, detect, locale, locate,
plight, region, sector, smirch,
smudge, splash, stigma
7 blemish, dilemma, discern,
light on, pick out, quarter,
section, spatter, speckle,
splotch, station **8** discolor, discover, disgrace, district, flyspeck, locality, location,
position, premises, reproach,

sprinkle **9** aspersion, discredit,
recognize, situation, territory
10 difficulty, imputation
11 predicament **12** bad situation, neighborhood
13 discoloration

spotless 4 pure **5** clean,
snowy **7** perfect, shining
8 flawless, gleaming, pristine,
unflawed, unmarred, unsoiled
9 faultless, stainless, unspotted,
unstained, unsullied, un-
tainted **10** immaculate, impeccable **11** unblemished,
untarnished **14** irreproachable
15 unexceptionable

spotted 3 saw **6** dotted, espied,
soiled **7** dappled, located, mottled, stained **8** detected, speckled **9** blemished, discerned,
spattered **10** discovered
13 caught sight of

spotty 6 fitful, pimply, random, uneven **7** blotchy, dappled, erratic, flecked, mottled,
spotted **8** episodic, freckled,
splotchy, sporadic, unsteady,
variable, wavering **9** broken
out, desultory, irregular, spasmodic, uncertain **10** capricious, inconstant, unreliable,
variegated **11** full of spots
12 disorganized, intermittent,
undependable, unmethodical,
unsystematic

spouse 4 mate, wife **7** consort,
husband, partner **8** helpmate
10 better half

spout 3 jet, lip **4** beak, flow,
go on, gush, nose, pipe, rant,
spew, tube, vent, well **5** eject,
erupt, expel, exude, issue,
mouth, shoot, snout, spray,
spurt, surge, vomit **6** nozzle,
outlet, sluice, squirt, stream,
trough **7** bluster, carry on,
channel, conduit, pour out
8 disgorge, fountain, harangue **9** discharge, hold
forth **10** waterspout **11** pontificate **12** emit forcibly **14** speak
pompously

sprawl 4 flop, lean, loll, wind
5 slump **6** branch, extend,
lounge, slouch **7** gush out,
meander, recline **8** languish,
reach out, straggle **9** spread
out **10** stretch out **11** spread-
eagle

spray 4 coat, mist, posy, twig
5 bough, burst, shoot, sprig,
treat, vapor **6** dampen, nozzle,
shower, splash, switch, volley
7 atomize, barrage, blossom,
bouquet, drizzle, moisten,
nosegay, scatter, spatter,
sprayer, syringe **8** atomizer,
disperse, droplets, moisture,
sprinkle **9** discharge, fusillade,
sprinkler, vaporizer

spread 3 air, lay **4** area, cast,
coat, open, pave, shed, span,
vent **5** apply, bruit, cloak,
cover, feast, field, issue, range,
reach, scope, smear, spray,
story, strew, sweep, table,
tract, width **6** bedaub, be
shed, blazon, extend, extent,
herald, length, notice, repeat,
report, unfold, unfurl, unroll
7 account, advance, article,
banquet, besmear, bestrew,
breadth, circuit, compass, declare, diffuse, divulge, expanse,
overlay, overrun, pervade,
plaster, publish, radiate, scatter, spatter, stretch, suffuse,
trumpet, untwine, write-up
8 announce, coverage, disperse, distance, increase, permeate, proclaim, sprinkle
9 broadcast, circulate, diffusion, expansion, extension,
make known, penetrate, pervasion, propagate, publicize,
radiation, spreading, suffusion,
ventilate **10** dispersion, distribute, make public, permeation,
promulgate, stretch out
11 communicate, disseminate,
noise abroad, proliferate
13 amplification, dissemination, proliferation

spread out 5 broad, widen
6 expand, extend **7** broaden,
diffuse, enlarge, radiate,
stretch **8** expanded, extended,
open wide **9** dispersed, outspread, scattered **10** distribute,
unhampered **11** unconfirmed
12 unrestricted
14 unconcentrated

spree 4 bout, orgy, toot
5 binge, drunk, fling, revel
6 bender **7** carouse, debauch,
revelry, splurge, wassail **8** carousal **9** bacchanal
10 saturnalia

sprightliness 8 buoyancy,
spryness, vivacity **9** animation,
briskness **10** breeziness, liveliness **16** lightheartedness

sprightly 3 gay **4** keen, spry
5 agile, alive, brisk, jolly,
merry **6** active, blithe, breezy,
cheery, jaunty, jovial, lively,
nimble **7** buoyant, chipper,
dashing, dynamic, playful
8 animated, cheerful, spirited,
sportive **9** energetic, vivacious
10 blithesome, frolicsome
12 lighthearted

spring 3 hop, jet, pop, spa
4 come, dart, flow, gush,
jump, kick, leap, loom, pool,
pour, rise, rush, stem, well
5 arise, baths, begin, bound,
caper, ensue, fount, issue,
lunge, shoot, spout, spurt,
start, surge, vault **6** appear,
bounce, derive, gambol, recoil,

reflex, result, sprout, stream
7 burgeon, crop out, descend,
emanate, proceed, release,
shoot up, start up, stretch,
trigger **8** buoyancy, commence, fountain, mushroom
9 come forth, entrechat, germinate, originate, saltation,
waterhole **10** break forth,
burst forth, elasticity, resiliency **11** flexibility
  goddess of: **4** Hebe **5** Venus

spring back 6 bounce, recoil
7 rebound **8** ricochet

spring flowers
  goddess of: **6** Thallo

Springhaven
  author: **11** R D Blackmore

springlike 4 mild, soft, warm
5 balmy

springs
  god of: **4** Fons **6** Palici
  goddess of: **4** Idun **5** Idura,
  Ithun **6** Ithunn

spring up 4 grow, rise **5** arise,
occur, pop up **6** crop up,
emerge, happen, sprout
9 originate **10** burst forth

springy 6 bouncy, spongy, supple **7** elastic **9** resilient
10 rebounding

sprinkle 4 dash, dust, rain
5 spray, strew, water **6** powder, shower, splash, spread,
squirt **7** bestrew, diffuse, drizzle, moisten, scatter, spatter
8 splatter

sprinkling 4 dash, drop, hint
5 pinch, touch **7** droplet, minimum, modicum, soupcon
8 sprinkle **10** smattering

sprint 3 run **4** dart, dash, kick,
race, rush, tear, whiz **5** burst,
shoot, spurt, whisk **7** scamper

sprit 3 bar **4** spar **8** crossbar
10 crosspiece

sprite 3 elf **5** fairy, pixie
10 leprechaun

sprout 3 bud, wax **4** grow
5 bloom, shoot, sprig **6** come
up, flower, spread, thrive
7 blossom, burgeon **8** multiply,
offshoot, put forth, spring up
9 germinate, outgrowth

spruce 4 chic, neat, tidy, trim
5 kempt, natty, sharp, smart
6 dapper **7** conifer, elegant
9 evergreen, shipshape
11 well-groomed **12** spick-and-
span
  French: **6** soigne

spruce 5 Picea
  varieties: **3** bog, cat, red
  4 blue **5** black, Hondo,
  Sitka, snake, white, Yeddo
  6 double, Norway **7** Alberta,

big-cone, Finnish, hemlock
8 Colorado, Sakhalin, Siberian **9** Himalayan, tiger-tail
10 Black Hills **12** Colorado
blue, Japanese bush

spry 4 deft, hale **5** agile, brisk,
quick **6** active, frisky, hearty,
jaunty, lively, nimble, supple
7 buoyant, chipper, playful
8 animated, spirited, sportive,
vigorous **9** energetic, sprightly,
vivacious **11** lightfooted

spunk 4 fire, grit, guts, salt,
sand **5** heart, nerve, pluck
6 daring, ginger, mettle, pepper, spirit **7** bravery, courage
8 backbone, boldness, gumption **10** feistiness

spur 3 arm, leg **4** fork, goad,
prod, whet, whip, wing
5 prick **6** branch, feeder, fillip,
hasten, motive, siding **7** impetus, impulse **8** excitant, stimulus **9** boot spike, encourage,
incentive, stimulant, stimulate,
tributary **10** incitement, inducement **11** instigation, provocation, stimulation
13 encouragement

spurge 9 Euphorbia
11 Pachysandra
  varieties: **5** caper, leafy,
  melon **6** ipecac, myrtle,
  tramp's **7** cypress, mottled,
  seaside, slipper **8** fiddler's,
  Japanese **9** Allegheny, flowering **10** Indian tree

spurious 4 fake, mock, sham
5 bogus, false, phony **6** faulty,
forged, hollow **7** feigned, unsound **8** specious **9** imitation,
simulated **10** fallacious, fraudulent, not genuine **11** counterfeit, make-believe,
unauthentic **12** illegitimate

spurn 4 mock, snub **5** flout, repel, scorn **6** rebuff, refuse, reject, slight **7** condemn, decline,
disdain, dismiss, repulse, scoff
at, sneer at **8** turn down
9 cast aside, disparage, repudiate **12** coldshoulder, look
down upon **16** turn up one's
nose at

spur-of-the-moment 5 ad-lib
7 offhand **9** extempore, impromptu **10** improvised, unprepared **11** extemporary,
spontaneous, unrehearsed
14 extemporaneous,
unpremeditated

spurt 3 jet **4** dart, dash, emit,
flow, gush, gust, rush, tear,
whiz **5** burst, flash, issue,
lunge, scoot, shoot, speed,
spout, spray, surge **6** access,
spring, sprint, squirt, stream
7 pour out **8** disgorge, ejection, eruption, fountain, outbreak, outburst **9** discharge,

explosion, spring out
10 outpouring

spy 3 pry, see **4** find, peep,
spot, view **5** scout, sight,
snoop **6** behold, descry, detect,
notice, shadow **7** discern,
glimpse, make out, observe
8 discover, informer, Mata
Hari, perceive, saboteur **9** keep
watch, operative, recognize
11 reconnoiter, secret agent
12 catch sight of **13** undercover man, watch secretly
14 espionage agent, fifth columnist **16** agent provocateur
17 intelligence agent

Spy 5 Caleb

Spy, The
  author: **19** James Fenimore
  Cooper

**Spy Who Came In from
the Cold, The**
  director: **10** Martin Ritt
  based on novel by: **11** John
  LeCarre
  cast: **11** Claire Bloom, Oskar
  Werner **12** Peter Van Eyck
  13 Richard Burton

Spy Who Loved Me, The
  author: **10** Ian Fleming
  director: **12** Lewis Gilbert
  cast: **10** Bernard Lee (M),
  Roger Moore (James Bond)
  11 Barbara Bach, Curt Jurgens (Stromberg), Richard
  Kiel (Jaws)

squabble 3 row, war **4** spat,
tiff **5** argue, brawl, clash,
fight, run-in, scrap, set-to,
words **6** battle, bicker, differ
7 contend, contest, dispute,
quarrel, wrangle **8** argument
9 have words, lock horns
10 bandy words, contention,
difference, dissension **11** altercation, controversy
12 disagreement

squadron 5 fleet **6** armada
8 flotilla **9** naval unit **10** escadrille **11** cavalry unit
12 military unit

squalid 4 foul, mean **5** dirty,
nasty **6** abject, filthy, horrid,
rotten, shabby, sloppy, sordid
7 decayed, reeking, run-down,
unclean **8** battered, degraded,
slovenly, wretched **9** miserable **10** broken-down, disheveled, ramshackle, slatternly,
tumbledown **11** dilapidated
12 deteriorated

squalidness 4 dirt **5** filth
7 squalor **8** foulness, meanness, vileness **9** dirtiness
10 sordidness **11** degradation,
uncleanness

squalor 4 dirt **5** filth **6** misery
7 neglect, poverty **8** foulness,
meanness, ugliness **9** dingi-

ness, dirtiness, nastiness, seediness **10** abjectness, grubbiness, sordidness **11** squalidness, uncleanness **12** wretchedness **13** uncleanliness

squander 4 blow **5** spend, waste **6** lavish, misuse **7** consume, deplete, exhaust **8** misspend **9** dissipate, throw away **10** run through **11** fritter away **14** spend like water

squanderer 6 waster **7** wastrel **8** prodigal **10** dissipater, profligate **11** spendthrift

squandering 7 wasting **8** prodigal, wasteful **9** imprudent **10** profligate **11** dissipating, extravagant, improvident, spendthrift **12** overspending, throwing away **14** frittering away **17** spending like water

square 3 box, fit **4** even, fogy, heal, hick, jerk, jibe, just, mend, park, prig **5** agree, align, blend, block, close, equal, green, match, place, plane, plaza, prude, tally **6** accord, adjust, candid, circus, cohere, common, concur, even up, fall in, honest, pay off, settle, smooth **7** arrange, balance, clear up, compose, conform, even out, flatten, mediate, patch up, rectify, resolve **8** block out, cornball, make even, quadrate, set right, settle up, truthful **9** arbitrate, discharge, equitable, harmonize, liquidate, make level, reconcile **10** clodhopper, correspond, quadrangle, straighten **11** marketplace **12** apple knocker, conservative **13** quadrilateral, stick-in-the-mud **15** straightforward
type: 1 T **3** try
11 combination

Square
character in: **8** Tom Jones
author: **8** Fielding

Square
constellation of: **5** Norma

square centimeter
abbreviation: **4** sq cm

square decimeter
abbreviation: **4** sq dm

square dekameter
abbreviation: **5** sq dam

square foot
abbreviation: **4** sq ft

square hectometer
abbreviation: **4** sq hm

square inch
abbreviation: **4** sq in

square kilometer
abbreviation: **4** sq km

square meter
abbreviation: **3** sq m

square mile
abbreviation: **4** sq mi

square millimeter
abbreviation: **4** sq mm

square rod
abbreviation: **4** sq rd

square yard
abbreviation: **4** sq yd

squash 3 jam **4** cram, mash, pulp **5** crowd, crush, level, quash, quell, smash, upset **6** dispel, squish **7** compact, destroy, flatten, put down, ram down, repress, squeeze, squelch, trample **8** compress, suppress **9** dissipate, overthrow, prostrate, undermine **10** annihilate, obliterate **11** concentrate

squash 9 Cucurbita
varieties: **4** bush **5** acorn **6** autumn, banana, summer, turban, winter **7** Hubbard, scallop **8** pattypan, zucchini **9** cocozelle, crookneck **12** Boston marrow **13** sweet dumpling **15** Canada crookneck, summer crookneck, winter crookneck

squat 5 cower, dumpy, dwell, kneel, pudgy **6** chunky, cringe, crouch, encamp, hunker, lie low, locate, move in, shrink, square, stocky, stubby, stumpy **8** thickset

squawk 5 blare, croak, gripe **6** scream, squall **7** grumble, protest, screech **8** complain

squeak 3 cry **4** peep, yelp **5** cheep, chirp, creak, grate **6** shriek, shrill, squeal **7** screech

squeal 3 cry **4** bawl, blab, fink, peep, sing, wail, yell, yelp **5** cheep, whine **6** inform, scream, shriek, shrill, squeak **7** screech

squealer 3 pig, rat **4** fink **6** canary, piglet, snitch **7** stoolie, tattler, traitor **8** informer **10** tattletale **11** stool pigeon **12** blabbermouth

squeamish 3 coy **4** prim, sick **5** fussy **6** demure, modest, proper, queasy **7** finical, finicky, mincing, prudish, sickish **8** delicate, nauseous, priggish, qualmish **9** finicking **10** fastidious **11** puritanical, straitlaced **13** sanctimonious

Squeers, Wackford
character in: **16** Nicholas Nickleby
author: **7** Dickens

squeeze 3 hug, jam, pry, ram

4 butt, cram, edge, grip, hold, pack, push **5** clasp, cramp, crowd, drive, elbow, grasp, press, shove, stuff, wedge, wrest, wring **6** clutch, coerce, compel, defile, elicit, extort, jostle, thrust, wrench **7** compact, draw out, embrace, extract, passage, pull out, tear out **8** compress, crowding, crushing, force out, pinching, press out, pressure, shoulder, withdraw **9** extricate, narrowing, stricture **10** bottleneck **11** compression, concentrate, consolidate **12** constriction

squelch 4 hush **5** abort, crush, quash, quell, quiet, smash **6** retort, squash **7** put down, riposte, silence **8** silencer, suppress

squire 4 date, take **5** court **6** attend, escort **7** consort, gallant, planter **8** cavalier, chaperon **9** accompany, attendant, boyfriend, chauffeur, companion, landowner **14** lord of the manor **16** country gentleman

Squire
character in: **18** The Canterbury Tales
author: **7** Chaucer

squirm 4 bend, jerk, toss, turn **5** pitch, shift, smart, sweat, twist, wince **6** blench, fidget, flinch, shrink, twitch, wiggle, writhe **7** agonize, contort, wriggle **8** flounder

squirt 3 jet **4** dash, gush, punk, runt **5** piker, shoot, spout, spray, spurt **6** shower, splash, stream **7** spatter **8** sprinkle **9** discharge, pipsqueak **10** besprinkle

Sri Lanka *see box, p. 924*

SS-GB
author: **11** Len Deighton

SS troops, chief of
12 Reichsfuhrer

stab 2 go **3** cut, jab, try **4** ache, bite, gash, gore, hurt, pain, pang, pass, shot, spit **5** essay, gouge, knife, lance, lunge, prick, qualm, slash, spear, spike, stick, sting, trial, wound **6** cleave, dagger, effort, impale, pierce, shiver, stroke, thrill, thrust, twinge **7** attempt, bayonet **8** endeavor, lacerate, transfix **10** laceration, run through

stability 5 poise **6** aplomb, fixity **7** balance **8** evenness, firmness, security, solidity **9** constancy, fixedness, solidness, soundness **10** continuity, durability, permanence, stableness, steadiness, sturdiness **11** abidingness, equilibrium,

Sri Lanka
other name: **6** Ceylon **8** Serendib **9** Taprobane
capital/largest city: **7** Colombo
  ancient capital: **11** Polonnaruwa **12** Anuradhapura
others: **3** Uva **5** Galle, Kandy **6** Jaffna, Mannar, Matale,
  Matara **7** Badulla, Kegalle, Negombo **8** Kalutara, Manku-
  lem, Moratuwa, Puttalam **9** Ratnapura **10** Batticaloa, Mul-
  laitivu **11** Ambalangoda, Trincomalee
division: **8** Dambulla, Sri Lanka **9** Taprobane
measure: **4** para, seer **5** parah **6** amunam, parrah
monetary unit: **4** cent **5** rupee
island: **5** Delft **6** Mannar **8** Sri Lanka
mountain: **5** Pedro **7** Sri Pada **9** Adam's Peak
highest point: **14** Pidurutalagala
river: **4** Kala **6** Deduru, Gal Ova **8** Aruvi Aru **9** Deburu
  Ova **11** Kelani Ganga **13** Mahaweli Ganga
sea: **6** Indian
physical feature:
  bay: **6** Bengal **8** Koddiyar
  falls: **8** Lazapana
  gulf: **6** Mannar
  peninsula: **6** Jaffna
  plateau: **6** Hatton
  strait: **4** Palk
people: **5** Malay, Tamil, Vedda **6** Veddah, Weddah
  7 Burgher, Mahinda, Malabar **8** Eurasian **9** Cingalese,
  Dravidian, Sinhalese **10** Singhalese
  leader: **11** Jayawardene **12** Bandaranaike
  ruler: **5** Dutch **7** British, Chinese **10** Portuguese
language: **4** Pali **5** Tamil **7** English **9** Sinhalese
religion: **5** Hindu, Islam **8** Buddhism
place:
  fortress: **8** Sigiriya
  gardens: **8** Hakgalle **10** Peradiniya
  national park: **6** Ruhuna **8** Wilpattu
  temple: **5** Tooth **6** Gal Oya **7** Kelanya **8** Runaweli
    9 Ruanvelli **10** Dankahlaka **12** Asokharamaya
feature:
  animal: **5** loris **12** wild elephant
  clothing: **4** sari **5** camba **6** sarong **7** cambaya **8** sherwani
  dancer: **7** Kandyan
  drama: **5** kolam **7** nadagam
  festival: **8** Perahera
  shrine: **6** dagoba
  tree: **4** doon, hora, palu, tala **5** domba, ebony **7** talipot
    8 halmilla, ironwood **9** satinwood **11** allaeanthus
    12 shimohabodhi

11 aggregation
12 accumulation

Stack, Robert
born: **12** Los Angeles CA
roles: **9** Eliot Ness **13** Name
  of the Game **15** The Untouchables **16** Written on
  the Wind **19** The High and
  the Mighty **24** The Bull-
  fighter and the Lady

Stackpole, Henrietta
character in: **18** The Portrait
  of a Lady
author: **5** James

Stacte 5 spice

stadium 4 bowl, park **5** arena,
field, stade **6** circus **8** ballpark,
coliseum **9** palaestra **10** hippodrome **12** amphitheater

Stael, Madame de
author of: **7** Corinne **8** Delphine **9** On Germany
  35 The Influence of Literature upon Society

staff 3 bat, man, rod **4** cane,
crew, help, pole, team, tend,
wand, work **5** cadre, force,
group, stave, stick **6** crutch,
cudgel, manage **7** retinue,
scepter, service, support **8** advisors, bludgeon, flagpole
9 billy club, employees, flagstaff, personnel **10** alpenstock,
assistants, shillelagh **12** walking stick

staff member 4 aide
6 worker **8** employee

stage 3 act **4** dais, play, spot,
step **5** arena, drama, grade,
level, phase, put on, sight,
stump **6** acting, locale, period,
podium, pulpit **7** perform,
present, produce, rostrum, setting, show biz, soapbox, theater **8** bearings, locality,
location, position, scaffold
9 dramatize, the boards

Stagecoach
director: **8** John Ford
cast: **9** John Wayne **10** Andy
  Devine **11** Louise Platt
  12 Claire Trevor **13** John
  Carradine **14** George Bancroft, Thomas Mitchell
Oscar for: **15** supporting actor (Mitchell)

stagecraft 5 drama **7** theater
9 theatrics **10** dramaturgy
11 thespianism **12** dramatic
arts

Stage Door
author: **10** Edna Ferber
  14 George S Kaufman
director: **13** Gregory La Cava
cast: **11** Andrea Leeds, Gail
  Patrick **12** Ginger Rogers
  13 Adolphe Menjou
  16 Katharine Hepburn

reliability **13** steadfastness
14 changelessness
16 unchangeableness

stabilize 7 balance **8** hold firm,
make firm **10** hold steady,
make steady

stabilizer 7 balance, ballast
8 additive **9** equipoise, gyro-
scope **10** ballasting **12** airplane
part **14** counterbalance

stable 4 barn, byre, even, firm,
mews, safe, true **5** fixed, loyal,
solid, sound **6** moored, secure,
steady, sturdy **7** abiding, durable, staunch, uniform **8** anchored, constant, cowhouse,
cowshed, enduring, faithful,
reliable, resolute, stalwart
9 immovable, steadfast **10** dependable, persisting, station-

ary, unchanging, unwavering
11 established, unfaltering
12 indissoluble,
unchangeable

Stabler, Ken
nickname: **8** the Snake
sport: **8** football
position: **11** quarterback
team: **13** Houston Oilers
  14 Oakland Raiders

staccato
music: **12** disconnected
  16 each note separate

stack 4 bank, flue, heap, load,
lump, mass, pile, rick **5** amass,
batch, bunch, clump, hoard,
mound, sheaf **6** bundle, funnel, gather **7** chimney **8** assemble, mountain
9 amassment **10** accumulate

stage setting
French: **11** mise en scene

stagger 3 jar **4** jolt, reel, stun, sway **5** amaze, lurch, shake, shock, waver **6** hobble, totter, wobble **7** astound, blunder, nonplus, overlap, shamble, startle, stumble, stupefy **8** astonish, bewilder, bowl over, confound, flounder, unsettle **9** alternate, dumbfound, give a turn, overwhelm, spread out **10** disconcert, knock silly, strike dumb **11** cause to reel, cause to sway, consternate, flabbergast, take in turns **12** make unsteady **15** throw off balance

staggering 7 amazing **8** shocking, stunning **9** startling **10** astounding **11** astonishing **12** breathtaking

stagnant 4 dead, dull, foul, lazy, slow **5** close, inert, quiet, slimy, stale, still **6** filthy, leaden, putrid, static, supine, torpid **7** dormant, dronish, languid, tainted **8** inactive, lifeless, listless, polluted, sluggish, standing **9** lethargic, ponderous, putrefied, quiescent **10** monotonous, motionless, not flowing, not running, stationary, unstirring, vegetative **13** uncirculating

stagnate 7 go to pot, lie idle, putrefy **8** go to seed, lie still, vegetate **10** stand still **11** cease to flow, deteriorate, stop growing **14** become inactive, become polluted, become sluggish

stagy 5 phony **8** affected, mannered **9** unnatural **10** artificial, factitious, theatrical

staid 5 grave, quiet, sober, stiff **6** decent, demure, proper, sedate, seemly, solemn, somber **7** earnest, prudish, serious, settled, subdued **8** decorous, priggish, reserved **9** dignified **10** complacent **15** undemonstrative

stain 3 dye, mar **4** blot, daub, flaw, foul, mark, ruin, slur, soil, spot, tint **5** brand, color, dirty, grime, libel, patch, shame, smear, speck, spoil, sully, taint **6** befoul, blotch, debase, defile, impair, malign, smirch, smudge, stigma, vilify **7** blacken, blemish, pigment, slander, splotch, subvert, tarnish **8** besmirch, coloring, discolor, disgrace, dishonor, dyestuff, tincture **9** denigrate, discredit, disparage, undermine **10** imputation, stigmatize **13** discoloration

stainless 5 clean, moral

6 chaste, decent **8** spotless, unsoiled **9** exemplary, unspotted, unsullied, untainted **11** unblemished

Stairway to Heaven
director: **13** Michael Powell **17** Emeric Pressburger
cast: **9** Kim Hunter **10** David Niven **12** Roger Livesey **13** Raymond Massey
original title: **21** A Matter of Life and Death

stake 3 bar, bet, peg, pot, rod **4** ante, back, grab, haul, lash, loot, moor, pale, pawn, pile, play, pole, post, prop, risk, stay, take **5** booty, brace, hitch, kitty, prize, purse, share, spike, stand, stick, treat, wager **6** chance, column, define, fasten, fetter, hazard, hold up, marker, picket, pillar, reward, secure, spoils, tether **7** delimit, finance, jackpot, mark off, mark out, outline, peg down, returns, sponsor, support, trammel, venture **8** interest, make fast, pickings, standard, winnings **9** delineate, demarcate, speculate, subsidize **10** investment, jeopardize, underwrite **11** involvement, speculation

Stalag 17
director: **11** Billy Wilder
cast: **9** Don Taylor **11** Peter Graves **12** Neville Brand **13** Harvey Lembeck, Otto Preminger, Richard Erdman, Robert Strauss, William Holden
Oscar for: **5** actor (Holden)

stale 4 dull, flat **5** banal, close, fusty, musty, trite, vapid **6** common **7** humdrum, insipid, prosaic, tedious, worn-out **8** mediocre, not fresh, ordinary, stagnant, unvaried **9** hackneyed, savorless, tasteless **10** monotonous, pedestrian, threadbare **11** commonplace **13** unimaginative, uninteresting

stalemate 3 tie **4** draw, halt **7** dead end, impasse **8** blockage, cul-de-sac, dead heat, deadlock, standoff **10** standstill

stalk 4 hunt, lurk, stem **5** haunt, march, prowl, shaft, spire, stamp, steal, stomp, strut, track, tramp, trunk **6** column, menance, stride **7** pedicel, pervade, swagger **8** hang over, threaten **9** creep up on, go through, sneak up on

stall 3 box, pen **4** cell, coop, halt, shed, shop, stop **5** block, booth, check, delay, kiosk, stand **6** arcade, arrest, hobble,

impede, pull up, put off **7** bed down, confine, cubicle, disable, trammel **8** obstruct, paralyze, postpone **9** be evasive, interrupt, stop short, temporize **10** equivocate **11** compartment, play for time, stop running **12** incapacitate **13** orchestra seat

Stallone, Sylvester
born: **9** New York NY
nickname: **3** Sly
roles: **4** FIST **5** Rambo, Rocky **9** John Rambo **10** First Blood, Rhinestone **11** Rocky Balboa **18** The Lords of Flatbush

stalwart 4 bold, firm, hale **5** beefy, brave, hardy, hefty, husky, manly, sound **6** brawny, gritty, heroic, mighty, plucky, robust, rugged, spunky, stable, strong, sturdy **7** gallant, staunch, valiant **8** constant, intrepid, muscular, powerful, resolute, valorous, vigorous **9** steadfast, strapping, unbending, undaunted **10** able-bodied, courageous, persistent, unflagging, unshakable, unswerving, unwavering, unyielding **11** indomitable, lionhearted, undeviating, unfaltering, unflinching, unshrinking **12** intransigent, stouthearted, strong-willed **14** uncompromising

stamina 4 pith **5** vigor **6** energy **8** vitality **9** endurance, hardiness, stoutness **10** ruggedness, sturdiness **12** perseverance, staying power

stammer 6 falter, fumble, mumble **7** sputter, stumble, stutter **8** splutter **9** hem and haw

stamp
collecting: **9** philately
first: **10** Penny Black
issued by: **12** Great Britain
inscribed with: **8** One Penny
picture of: **13** Queen Victoria
first-day hand stamper: **6** cachet
hole measurer: **16** perforation gauge
mounting paper: **5** hinge
not perforated: **11** imperforate
paper design: **9** watermark
rolls: **4** coil
tear holes: **12** perforations
tear slit: **8** roulette
unseparated group: **5** block
used mark: **8** postmark **12** cancellation
value suspended: **11** demonetized

stamp, stamp out 2 OK
3 die, tag **4** cast, kind, make, mark, mint, mold, seal, sort, type **5** brand, breed, clump, crush, erase, genre, label, march, order, print, pound, punch, quash, smash, stalk, stomp, strut, thump, tramp **6** banish, betray, emblem, expose, matrix, nature, put out, reveal, rub out, signet, step on, strain, stride, trudge **7** abolish, blot out, display, engrave, exhibit, impress, imprint, put down, squelch, trample, variety, voucher **8** get rid of, hallmark, identify, inscribe, intaglio, manifest, suppress, typecast **9** character, eliminate, engraving, eradicate, personify, signature, trademark **10** annihilate, do away with, extinguish, imprimatur, stigmatize, validation **11** attestation, certificate, demonstrate, distinguish, endorsement, exterminate, **12** characterize, official mark, ratification **13** certification **14** authentication, characteristic, identification

stampede 4 bolt, dash, flee, race, rout, rush **5** chaos, flood, panic **6** engulf **7** overrun, retreat, scatter **8** inundate **10** take flight **11** crowd around, pandemonium **12** beat a retreat
   French: 12 sauve qui peut

stanchion 4 post, prop, stay **5** brace, strut **7** support, upright

stand 2 be **3** put, set **4** draw, face, hold, last, move, rank, rear, rest, rise, stay, step, take, tent **5** abide, argue, booth, brook, erect, exist, get up, hoist, honor, kiosk, mount, place, put up, raise, shift, stall, treat **6** bear up, effort, endure, obtain, pay for, policy, remain, remove, stance, suffer, uphold **7** carry on, commend, counter, defense, endorse, finance, hold out, opinion, persist, posture, prevail, provide, stick up, stomach, support, survive, sustain, undergo, weather **8** advocate, be placed, champion, continue, pavilion, position, sanction, submit to, tolerate **9** be located, be present, be upright, persevere, put up with, sentiment, undertake, viewpoint **10** resistance, set upright **11** be permanent, countenance, disposition, point of view **13** remain in force, take a position
Stand, The
   author: 11 Stephen King

standard 3 leg **4** base, flag, foot, jack, post **5** basic, canon, guide, ideal, stock, usual **6** banner, column, common, ensign, normal, pillar **7** measure, pennant, regular, support, typical, upright **8** accepted, ordinary, streamer **9** criterion, customary, guideline, principle, prototype, stanchion, universal, yardstick **10** foundation, touchstone **11** requirement **13** specification

stand behind 4 back **7** endorse, support **8** champion, vouch for **9** recommend

standby 6 backup **9** alternate, available **10** substitute, understudy **11** old reliable **12** tried-and-true

stand by 4 keep **5** cling **6** adhere, be true, defend, hold to, keep to **7** be loyal, stick by **8** cleave to, maintain **10** be constant, be faithful, stick up for

stand fast 4 hold **6** resist **8** stand pat

stand for 4 bear **5** abide, favor, stand **6** embody **7** signify **8** advocate, submit to, tolerate **9** personify, put up with, represent, symbolize

stand-in 3 sub **5** agent, proxy **6** backup, deputy, double, fill-in, second **9** alternate, assistant, surrogate **10** substitute, understudy **11** pinch hitter, replacement

standing 3 age **4** life, rank, term, time **5** erect, fixed, grade, inert, order, place, still **6** at rest, static, status, tenure **7** dormant, footing, lasting, station, upended, upright **8** duration, inactive, position, stagnant, vertical **9** immovable, permanent, perpetual, quiescent, renewable **10** continuing, importance, motionless, reputation, stationary, unstirring **11** continuance **13** perpendicular

standoff 7 impasse **8** deadlock

standoffish 4 cool **5** aloof **6** formal, remote **7** distant, haughty **8** detached, reserved, solitary, taciturn **9** reclusive, withdrawn **10** antisocial, restrained, unfriendly, unsociable **12** inaccessible, misanthropic, unresponsive **14** unapproachable **15** uncommunicative, uncompanionable

standpoint 4 side **5** angle, slant **6** aspect **9** viewpoint **11** point of view

standstill 3 end **4** halt, stop **5** pause **6** hiatus **7** dead end, impasse **8** abeyance, deadlock, dead stop, full stop **9** breakdown, cessation, stalemate **10** suspension **11** termination **14** discontinuance

stand up for 4 back **5** boost **6** defend **7** further, promote, support **8** advocate, champion

stand up to 4 defy, face **5** brave **6** resist **8** confront **9** challenge

Stant, Charlotte
   character in: 13 The Golden Bowl
   author: 5 James

Stan the Man
   nickname of: 10 Stan Musial

Stanton, Adam
   character in: 14 All the King's Men
   author: 6 Warren

Stanwyck, Barbara
   real name: 11 Ruby Stevens
   born: 10 Brooklyn NY
   husband: 8 Frank Fay **12** Robert Taylor
   roles: 9 Big Valley, The Colbys **10** Ball of Fire, The Lady Eve **11** Meet John Doe **12** Stella Dallas **15** Double Indemnity **16** Sorry Wrong Number **20** Cattle Queen of Montana **22** Christmas in Connecticut

staple 3 key **4** main **5** basic, chief, major, prime, vital **6** leader **7** feature, primary, product **8** resource, vendible **9** commodity, essential, necessary **11** fundamental, raw material **13** indispensable

Stapleton, Jean
   real name: 12 Jeanne Murray
   born: 9 New York NY
   roles: 7 Dingbat **11** Edith Bunker **14** All in the Family

Stapleton, Maureen
   born: 6 Troy NY
   roles: 7 Airport **9** Interiors **12** Lonelyhearts **13** The Rose Tattoo **18** A View from the Bridge

star, stars *see box*

Starbuck
   character in: 8 Moby Dick
   author: 8 Melville

starch 5 vigor **6** sizing **8** backbone, gumption **10** stiffening

starched 5 crisp, sized, stiff **7** starchy **9** stiffened

starchy 5 rigid, stiff **6** formal, proper **7** correct **10** meticulous

star, stars 3 god, sun, VIP **4** diva, fate, hero, idol, lead, lion, name **5** comet, excel, giant, great, omens, shine **6** bigwig, do well, galaxy, meteor, nebula, planet **7** destiny, feature, fortune, goddess, heroine, notable, soloist, starlet, succeed, top draw **8** asteroid, cynosure, eminence, immortal, luminary, mainstay, Milky Way, portents, showcase, stand out, virtuoso **9** celebrity, headliner, meteoroid, principal, satellite, top banana **10** prima donna **11** All-American, drawing card, play the lead, protagonist **12** famous person, gain approval, heavenly body **13** celestial body, constellation **14** main attraction, predestination, prima ballerina
  brightest: 6 Sirius
  brightness measure: 9 magnitude **10** luminosity
  color: 3 red **4** blue **5** black, white **6** orange, yellow
  distance measure: 6 parsec **9** light year
  double star: 6 binary
  exploding star: 4 nova **9** supernova
  French: 6 etoile
  name: 4 Mira, Ross, Vega, Wolf **5** Cygni, Deneb, Rigel, Spica **6** Altair, Luyten, Pollux **7** Antares, Canopus, Capella, Lalande, Polaris, Procyon, Regulus, Tau Ceti **8** Achernar, Arcturus, Barnard's, Lacaille, Pleiades **9** Aldebaran, Fomalhaut **10** Beta Crucis, Betelgeuse **11** Delta Cephei, Epsilon Indi, Groombridge **12** Beta Centauri **14** Epsilon Eridani
  nearest: 13 Alpha Centauri
  position/motion: 7 azimuth **8** parallax **11** declination
  type: 5 dwarf, giant **6** pulsar **7** cluster, neutron **8** variable **9** black hole, collapsed

stare 3 eye **4** gape, gawk, gaze, ogle, peep, peer **5** glare, lower, watch **6** gaping, glower, goggle, ogling, regard **7** staring **8** once-over, scrutiny **9** fixed look **10** inspection, rubberneck

stare at 3 eye **4** ogle **5** watch **6** behold, gaze at, look at, regard **7** inspect, observe **10** scrutinize **11** contemplate

Star Is Born, A
  director:
    1937 version: **14** William Wellman
    1954 version: **11** George Cukor
    1976 version: **12** Frank Pierson
  cast:
    1937 version: **11** Janet Gaynor **13** Adolphe Menjou, Frederic March
    1954 version: **10** Jack Carson, James Mason **11** Judy Garland **15** Charles Bickford
    1976 version: **9** Gary Busey **11** Oliver Clark **15** Barbra Streisand **17** Kris Kristofferson
  Oscar for:
    1937 version: **5** story
  song:
    1954 version: **17** The Man That Got Away

stark 4 bare, bold, cold, grim, pure **5** bleak, blunt, clean, empty, fully, gross, harsh, naked, plain, plumb, quite, sheer, total, utter **6** arrant, barren, chaste, patent, severe, simple, vacant, wholly **7** austere, evident, forlorn, glaring, obvious, staring, utterly **8** absolute, complete, deserted, desolate, entirely, flagrant, forsaken, outright, palpable **9** abandoned, downright, out-and-out, unadorned, unalloyed, veritable **10** absolutely, altogether, completely, consummate **11** conspicuous, unmitigated **12** unmistakable

Stark, Johannes
  field: 7 physics
  nationality: 6 German
  described: 11 Stark Effect **14** dispersed light
  awarded: 10 Nobel Prize

Stark, Willie
  character in: 14 All the King's Men
  author: 6 Warren

starlet 7 actress, ingenue **9** bit player, pinup girl

Starsky and Hutch
  character: 5 Hutch (Ken Hutchinson) **7** (Dave) Starsky **9** Huggy Bear **11** (Capt) Harold Dobey
  cast: 9 David Soul **13** Antonio Fargas **14** Bernie Hamilton **17** Paul Michael Glaser
  car: 10 Ford Torino

start 3 aid, shy **4** dawn, drop, edge, form, gush, jerk, jolt, jump, lead, leap, odds, rush, turn **5** beget, begin, birth, blink, bound, eject, erupt, evict, flush, forge, found, issue, leave, leg up, onset, rouse, set up, shoot, spasm, spurt, wince **6** blench, broach, chance, create, depart, embark, emerge, fall to, father, flinch, ignite, kindle, launch, origin, outset, pop out, propel, recoil, set off, set out, spring, take up, twitch **7** advance, backing, disturb, genesis, make off, opening, push off, scatter, set sail, support, take off, turn out, usher in **8** advocacy, commence, creation, displace, embark on, engender, generate, get going, initiate, organize, priority, set about, set going, touch off **9** advantage, beginning, establish, fabricate, first step, inception, institute, introduce, originate, propagate, undertake, venture on **10** assistance, break forth, bring about, buckle down, burst forth, give rise to, inaugurate, initiation, plunge into, sally forth, venture out **11** break ground, put in motion, set in action **12** commencement, inauguration, introduction **14** set in operation

starting point 5 onset, start **8** zero hour **9** beginning
  Latin: 12 terminus a quo

startle 3 jar **4** faze **5** alarm, scare, shake, shock, upset **7** perturb, unnerve **8** disquiet, frighten, surprise, unsettle **9** give a turn **10** discompose, disconcert, intimidate

Star Trek
  character: 4 Sulu **5** Uhura **6** Scotty (Engineer Montgomery Scott), (Ensign) Chekov **7** Mr Spock **10** (Captain) James T Kirk, (Yeoman) Janice Rand **12** (Dr) Leonard McCoy **15** (Nurse) Christine Chapel
  cast: 11 George Takei, James Doohan **12** Leonard Nimoy, Majel Barrett, Walter Koenig **13** DeForest Kelly **14** William Shatner **15** Grace Lee Whitney, Nichelle Nichols
  ship: 10 (USS) Enterprise
  aliens: 8 Klingons, Romulans
  Spock's planet: 6 Vulcan
  pet: 7 tribble

starve 3 yen **4** burn, deny, fast, gasp, long, lust, pine **5** crave, raven, yearn **6** aspire, cut off, famish, hunger, refuse, thirst **7** deprive **8** be hungry, go hungry, languish

Star Wars
director: **11** George Lucas
cast: **10** Kenny Baker, Mark Hamill (Luke Skywalker) **12** Alec Guinness, Carrie Fisher (Princess Leia), Harrison Ford (Han Solo), Peter Cushing **14** Anthony Daniels
voice of Darth Vader: **14** James Earl Jones
score: **12** John Williams
Oscar for: **5** score
sequel: **15** Return of the Jedi **20** The Empire Strikes Back

stasimon 9 choral ode
literally: **8** standing

state 3 put **4** form, land, mind, mode, mood, pass, pomp **5** guise, offer, phase, realm, shape, stage **6** aspect, luxury, morale, nation, people, plight, recite, relate, report, ritual, status **7** comfort, country, declare, explain, expound, express, kingdom, narrate, posture, present, recount, spirits **8** attitude, ceremony, describe, dominion, monarchy, official, position, propound, republic, set forth **9** condition, elucidate, formality, full dress, high style, situation, structure **10** ceremonial, government **11** body politic, frame of mind, predicament, state of mind **12** commonwealth, constitution, governmental, principality **13** circumstances

state abbreviations *see box*

state admittance *see box*

state capitals *see box*

State Fair
author: **9** Phil Stong

state in detail 7 explain, expound **8** describe, spell out **9** explicate **16** give a full account

stateliness 7 dignity, majesty **10** augustness

stately 5 grand, lofty, noble, proud, regal, royal **6** august, formal, lordly **7** awesome, elegant, eminent **8** glorious, imperial, imposing, majestic **9** dignified, grandiose **10** ceremonial, impressive **11** magnificent

statement 3 tab **4** bill **5** check, claim, count, tally **6** avowal, charge, record, remark, report, speech **7** account, comment, invoice, mention, recital **8** relation, sentence **9** assertion, manifesto, reckoning, testimony, utterance, valuation

---

state abbreviations
Alabama: **2** AL **3** Ala
Alaska: **2** AK **4** Alas
Arizona: **2** AZ **4** Ariz
Arkansas: **2** AR **3** Ark
California: **2** CA **3** Cal **5** Calif
Colorado: **2** CO **4** Colo
Connecticut: **2** CT **4** Conn
Delaware: **2** DE **3** Del
Florida: **2** FL **3** Fla
Georgia: **2** GA
Hawaii: **2** HI
Idaho: **2** ID **3** Ida
Illinois: **2** IL **3** Ill
Indiana: **2** IN **3** Ind
Iowa: **2** IA
Kansas: **2** KS **4** Kans
Kentucky: **2** KY
Louisiana: **2** LA
Maine: **2** ME
Maryland: **2** MD
Massachusetts: **2** MA **4** Mass
Michigan: **2** MI **4** Mich
Minnesota: **2** MN **4** Minn
Mississippi: **2** MS **4** Miss
Missouri: **2** MO
Montana: **2** MT
Nebraska: **2** NE **4** Nebr
Nevada: **2** NV **3** Nev
New Hampshire: **2** NH
New Jersey: **2** NJ
New Mexico: **2** NM **4** N Mex
New York: **2** NY
North Carolina: **2** NC **4** N Car
North Dakota: **2** ND **4** N Dak
Ohio: **2** OH
Oklahoma: **2** OK **4** Okla
Oregon: **2** OR **4** Oreg
Pennsylvania: **2** PA **4** Penn **5** Penna
Rhode Island: **2** RI
South Carolina: **2** SC
South Dakota: **2** SD **4** S Dak
Tennessee: **2** TN **4** Tenn
Texas: **2** TX **3** Tex
Utah: **2** UT
Vermont: **2** VT
Virginia: **2** VA
Washington: **2** WA **4** Wash
West Virginia: **2** WV **3** W Va
Wisconsin: **2** WI **3** Wis
Wyoming: **2** WY **3** Wyo

---

10 accounting, allegation, communique, exposition, profession, recitation **11** declaration, delineation, explanation, observation **12** announcement, balance sheet **13** pronouncement, specification

---

state admittance
first: **8** Delaware
second: **12** Pennsylvania
third: **9** New Jersey
fourth: **7** Georgia
fifth: **11** Connecticut
sixth: **13** Massachusetts
seventh: **8** Maryland
eighth: **13** South Carolina
ninth: **12** New Hampshire
tenth: **8** Virginia
eleventh: **7** New York
twelfth: **13** North Carolina
thirteenth: **11** Rhode Island
fourteenth: **7** Vermont
fifteenth: **8** Kentucky
sixteenth: **9** Tennessee
seventeenth: **4** Ohio
eighteenth: **9** Louisiana
nineteenth: **7** Indiana
twentieth: **11** Mississippi
twenty-first: **8** Illinois
twenty-second: **7** Alabama
twenty-third: **5** Maine
twenty-fourth: **8** Missouri
twenty-fifth: **8** Arkansas
twenty-sixth: **8** Michigan
twenty-seventh: **7** Florida
twenty-eighth: **5** Texas
twenty-ninth: **4** Iowa
thirtieth: **9** Wisconsin
thirty-first: **10** California
thirty-second: **9** Minnesota
thirty-third: **6** Oregon
thirty-fourth: **6** Kansas
thirty-fifth: **12** West Virginia
thirty-sixth: **6** Nevada
thirty-seventh: **8** Nebraska
thirty-eighth: **8** Colorado
thirty-ninth/fortieth: **11** North Dakota, South Dakota
forty-first: **7** Montana
forty-second: **10** Washington
forty-third: **5** Idaho
forty-fourth: **7** Wyoming
forty-fifth: **4** Utah
forty-sixth: **8** Oklahoma
forty-seventh: **9** New Mexico
forty-eighth: **7** Arizona
forty-ninth: **6** Alaska
fiftieth: **6** Hawaii

state capitals
Alabama: 10 Montgomery
Alaska: 6 Juneau
Arizona: 7 Phoenix
Arkansas: 10 Little Rock
California: 10 Sacramento
Colorado: 6 Denver
Connecticut: 8 Hartford
Delaware: 5 Dover
Florida: 11 Tallahassee
Georgia: 7 Atlanta
Hawaii: 8 Honolulu
Idaho: 5 Boise
Illinois: 11 Springfield
Indiana: 12 Indianapolis
Iowa: 9 Des Moines
Kansas: 6 Topeka
Kentucky: 9 Frankfort
Louisiana: 10 Baton Rouge
Maine: 7 Augusta
Maryland: 9 Annapolis
Massachusetts: 6 Boston
Michigan: 7 Lansing
Minnesota: 6 St Paul
Mississippi: 7 Jackson
Missouri: 13 Jefferson City
Montana: 6 Helena
Nebraska: 7 Lincoln
Nevada: 10 Carson City

New Hampshire:
7 Concord
New Jersey: 7 Trenton
New Mexico: 7 Santa Fe
New York: 6 Albany
North Carolina: 7 Raleigh
North Dakota: 8 Bismarck
Ohio: 8 Columbus
Oklahoma: 12 Oklahoma City
Oregon: 5 Salem
Pennsylvania:
10 Harrisburg
Rhode Island:
10 Providence
South Carolina:
8 Columbia
South Dakota: 6 Pierre
Tennessee: 9 Nashville
Texas: 6 Austin
Utah: 12 Salt Lake City
Vermont: 10 Montpelier
Virginia: 8 Richmond
Washington: 7 Olympia
West Virginia:
10 Charleston
Wisconsin: 7 Madison
Wyoming: 8 Cheyenne

6 impede, rugged, steady, strong, sturdy **7** contain, zealous **8** constant, faithful, hold back, obstruct, resolute, stalwart **9** steadfast, well-built **10** watertight **11** substantial

stave off 7 beat off, fend off, keep off, ward off **9** keep at bay

stay 3 aim, guy, rib, rod **4** bunk, curb, foil, halt, live, pole, prop, rest, room, stem, stop **5** abide, block, brace, check, delay, dwell, lodge, quell, shore, stick, tarry, visit **6** endure, keep in, linger, rein in, remain, reside, splint, stifle, thwart **7** carry on, hold out, holiday, last out, persist, sojourn, support, ward off **8** abeyance, buttress, continue, hold back, mainstay, postpone, reprieve, restrain, standard, stopover, suppress, vacation, withhold **9** deferment, frustrate, persevere, staunchion **10** hang around, see through, suspension **12** postponement, reinforcement

stay put 4 stay **6** remain **8** stand pat

St Clare, Eva
character in: 14 Uncle Tom's Cabin
author: 5 Stowe

steadfast 4 keen, rapt **5** fixed **6** direct, intent, steady **8** resolute **9** attentive, obstinate, tenacious, undaunted **10** deep-rooted, deep-seated, inflexible, unchanging, unflagging, unwavering, unyielding **11** indomitable, persevering, unalterable, undeviating, unfaltering, unflinching **12** intransigent, single-minded, unchangeable, undistracted **14** uncompromising

steadfastness 8 tenacity **10** resolution **11** persistence **12** perseverance, resoluteness **13** determination

Steadfast Tin Soldier, The
author: 21 Hans Christian Andersen

steadiness 4 care **5** poise **6** aplomb **8** calmness, coolness, evenness, firmness **9** composure, sangfroid, stability **10** equanimity, resolution **11** carefulness, persistence, self-control, tranquility **12** resoluteness, tranquillity **13** dependability, steadfastness **14** presence of mind, self-possession **16** imperturbability

steady 4 even, firm, sure **5** sober **6** secure, stable **7** balance, careful, devoted, regular,

state of affairs 5 state **6** status **9** condition, situation **13** circumstances

State of the Union
director: 10 Frank Capra
cast: 10 Van Johnson **12** Spencer Tracy **13** Adolphe Menjou **14** Angela Lansbury **16** Katharine Hepburn

stateroom 5 cabin **8** quarters **11** compartment

statesman 8 diplomat **15** political leader

statesmanship 9 diplomacy **19** political leadership

static 5 fixed, inert, still **8** immobile, inactive, stagnant, unmoving **9** crackling, suspended **10** changeless, motionless, stationary, unchanging **12** interference

station 4 post, rank, site, spot, stop **5** caste, class, depot, grade, level, place **6** assign, degree, locate, sphere, status **7** footing, install **8** ensconce, facility, location, position, prestige, terminal, terminus **9** condition, firehouse, placement **10** dispensary, guardhouse, importance **11** emplacement, whistle-stop **12** headquarters

stationary 4 even, firm **5** fixed, inert **6** intact, moored, stable,

steady **7** riveted, uniform **8** constant, immobile, standing **9** dead-still, immovable, immutable, unchanged, unvarying **10** motionless, stock-still, transfixed **11** not changing, undeviating **12** unchangeable **13** standing still

Statius
author of: 6 Silvae **10** The Thebaid **12** The Achilleid

statue 8 monument **9** sculpture **14** representation

statuesque 5 regal **7** stately **8** majestic **9** dignified

stature 4 rank, size **5** place **6** height, regard **8** eminence, position, prestige, standing, tallness **9** elevation **10** importance, prominence, reputation **11** distinction

status 4 rank **5** caste, class, grade, place, state **6** degree **7** caliber, footing, station **8** eminence, position, prestige, standing **9** condition, situation **10** estimation **11** distinction

statute 3 law **7** precept **9** prescript

statute law
Latin: 10 lex scripta

staunch, stanch 3 dam **4** firm, stem, true **5** check, loyal, solid, sound, stout

serious, staunch **8** constant, faithful, frequent, habitual, hold fast, reliable, resolute, unending, untiring **9** ceaseless, confirmed, dedicated, immovable, incessant, stabilize, steadfast, tenacious, unceasing **10** continuing, continuous, coolheaded, deliberate, dependable, methodical, persistent, unflagging, unwavering **11** levelheaded, persevering, substantial, undeviating, unfaltering, unremitting **12** single-minded **13** conscientious

steal 3 buy, cop **4** copy, crib, flit, flow, lift, slip, take **5** creep, drift, filch, glide, pinch, skulk, slide, slink, sneak, swipe, usurp **6** borrow, elapse, escape, extort, filter, pilfer, pocket, rip off, snatch, snitch, thieve **7** bargain, defraud, diffuse, good buy, imitate, purloin, swindle **8** abstract, embezzle, good deal, liberate **10** burglarize, plagiarize **11** abscond with, appropriate, make off with **14** misappropriate

steal away 3 fly **4** bolt, flee, skip **5** elope **6** escape **7** get away, make off, slip out **8** creep off, slip away, sneak off **9** break free, tiptoe out **10** break loose, fly the coop **12** make a getaway

stealth 7 secrecy, slyness **10** covertness, sneakiness, subterfuge **11** furtiveness **12** stealthiness **13** secretiveness **15** unobtrusiveness **17** surreptitiousness

stealthy 3 sly **5** shady **6** covert, shifty, sneaky **7** devious, furtive **8** slippery, sneaking **9** secretive, underhand **11** clandestine, underhanded **12** hugger-mugger **13** surreptitious

steamboat
    invented by: **6** Fulton **9** Symington

steamed up 5 angry, het up, irate **6** raging **7** enraged, furious, riled up **8** heated up, inflamed **10** infuriated **12** mad as a wet hen **14** hot and bothered **17** hot under the collar

steamer 4 boat, clam, ship **5** liner, trunk **10** paddleboat **11** side-wheeler **12** stern-wheeler **13** paddle-wheeler

steel 4 dirk, foil, gird **5** blade, brace, knife, nerve, saber, sword **6** dagger, rapier **7** bayonet, cutlass, fortify, machete **8** falchion, scimitar **10** broadsword

process invented by: **8** Bessemer

Steele, Sir Richard
    pseudonym: **16** Isaac Bickerstaff
    author of: **9** The Tatler (with Joseph Addison) **10** The Funeral **12** The Spectator (with Joseph Addison) **13** The Lying Lover **16** The Tender Husband **18** The Conscious Lovers

steely 4 hard **5** stony **6** flinty **9** heartless, unfeeling **10** forbidding **11** cold-hearted

Steen, Jan
    born: **6** Leiden, Leyden **14** The Netherlands
    artwork: **7** Cabaret **11** The Egg Dance **12** Merry Company **14** Garden of the Inn **15** The Doctor's Visit, The Rhetoricians **16** The Morning Toilet **17** The Skittle Players **18** The World Topsy-Turvy, Young Woman Dressing

Steenburgen, Mary
    roles: **10** Cross Creek **13** Time After Time

steep 4 brew, bury, fill, soak **5** imbue, sharp, sheer, souse **6** abrupt, drench, engulf, infuse, plunge **7** immerse, pervade, suffuse **8** marinate, saturate, submerge **10** impregnate **11** precipitous

steeple 5 spire, tower **6** belfry **9** campanile

steer 3 aim, lay, run **4** bear, head, lead, make, sail **5** coach, guide, pilot **6** direct, govern, manage **7** conduct, proceed **8** navigate **9** supervise

steer clear of 4 shun **5** avert, avoid, dodge, evade, forgo, skirt **6** escape, eschew, forego **8** sidestep **9** keep shy of **11** abstain from, refrain from **16** give a wide berth to

Steerforth
    character in: **16** David Copperfield
    author: **7** Dickens

Steffens, Lincoln
    author of: **19** The Shame of the Cities

Stegosaurus
    type: **8** dinosaur **10** ornithopod
    location: **12** North America
    period: **8** Jurassic
    characteristic: **6** plated

Steiger, Rod
    real name: **20** Rodney Stephen Steiger
    born: **13** Westhampton NY
    wife: **11** Claire Bloom

roles: **8** Waterloo **13** The Longest Day, The Pawnbroker, W C Fields and Me **15** On the Waterfront **19** In the Heat of the Night (Oscar)

Stein, Clarence S
    architect of: **13** Temple Emanu-El (NYC)

Stein, Gertrude
    author of: **10** Three Lives **13** Tender Buttons **20** The Making of Americans **27** Autobiography of Alice B Toklas
    coined phrase: **14** lost generation

Steinbeck, John
    author of: **8** The Pearl **10** Cannery Row, East of Eden, The Red Pony **12** Of Mice and Men, Tortilla Flat **15** In Dubious Battle **16** The Grapes of Wrath **18** Travels with Charley **24** The Winter of Our Discontent

Steinmetz, Charles P
    field: **11** engineering
    developed: **2** AC **18** alternating current

Stella, Frank
    born: **8** Malden MA
    artwork: **4** Jill **5** Itata **14** Jasper's Dilemma **15** Guadalupe Island

Stella, Joseph
    born: **5** Italy **6** Naples
    artwork: **8** Full Moon (Barbados) **9** Sunflower, The Bridge **14** Brooklyn Bridge **16** Pittsburgh Winter **18** New York Interpreted **28** Battle of the Lights Coney Island

Stella Dallas
    director: **9** King Vidor
    cast: **9** John Boles **11** Anne Shirley **12** Barbara O'Neil **15** Barbara Stanwyck

stellar 6 astral, starry **7** leading **8** starring **9** brilliant, celestial, principal **11** outstanding

stem 3 dam **4** buck, cane, come, curb, grow, halt, rise, stay, stop **5** arise, block, check, deter, ensue, issue, quell, shank, shoot, speak, spire, stalk, stall, stock, trunk **6** arrest, derive, hinder, impede, oppose, resist, result, retard, spring, stanch, thwart **7** counter, pedicel, petiole, prevent, proceed, tendril **8** hold back, obstruct, peduncle, restrain, surmount **9** leafstalk, originate, withstand

stem from 5 arise, begin, start **6** derive **9** originate

stench 4 odor, reek **5** fetor, stink **8** bad smell **9** fetidness

Stendhal (Henri Marie Beyle)
author of: **17** The Red and the Black **18** Memoirs of an Egotist **22** The Charterhouse of Parma

Stengel, Charles Dillon
nickname: **5** Casey
sport: **8** baseball
position: **7** manager
team: **11** New York Mets **14** New York Yankees **15** Brooklyn Dodgers

Stentor
vocation: **6** herald
characteristic: **10** loud-voiced
voice as loud as: **8** fifty men

step 3 act **4** clip, gait, move, pace, rank, rung, span, walk **5** notch, phase, point, riser, stage, stair, strut, track, tramp, tread **6** action, degree, hobble, period, remove, stride **7** footing, measure, process, shamble, shuffle, swagger, trample **8** footfall, foothold, maneuver, purchase **9** footprint, gradation, procedure **10** proceeding

step down 4 quit **5** leave **6** resign, retire

Stephens, James
author of: **7** Deirdre **14** The Crock of Gold **21** The Charwoman's Daughter

Stephenson, George and Robert
nationality: **7** English
developed: **15** steam locomotive

Steppenwolf
author: **12** Hermann Hesse
character: **5** Maria, Pablo **7** Hermine **11** Harry Haller

Steps
author: **13** Jerzy Kosinski

step up 4 spur **6** come up **7** quicken, speed up **8** approach, escalate, expedite, increase **9** intensify **10** accelerate

stereotype 4 type **6** cliche **7** formula **8** typecast **10** categorize, pigeonhole **13** preconception

stereotyped 5 stale, trite **9** hackneyed **11** commonplace **13** unimaginative

sterile 4 bare, pure, vain **5** empty **6** barren, fallow, futile **7** aseptic, useless **8** abortive, bootless, impotent, infecund, sanitary **9** childless, fruitless, infertile, worthless **10** antiseptic, profitless, sterilized, unavailing, unfruitful, uninfected **11** disinfected, ineffective, ineffectual, unrewarding **12** unproductive, unprofitable **13** free from germs **14** uncontaminated

sterilize 6 purify **9** autoclave, disinfect **13** decontaminate

sterling 4 pure, true **5** noble **6** silver, superb, worthy **7** genuine, perfect **8** flawless, superior **9** admirable, estimable, first-rate, honorable **10** invaluable **11** meritorious, superlative

stern 4 cold, grim, hard **5** cruel, grave, harsh, rigid, sharp, stiff **6** brutal, gloomy, severe, somber, strict, unkind **7** austere, serious **8** coercive, despotic, frowning, pitiless, rigorous, ruthless, ungentle **9** reproving, stringent, unfeeling **10** forbidding, implacable, ironfisted, ironhanded, tyrannical, unmerciful **11** admonishing, cold-blooded, reproachful **12** unreasonable **13** unsympathetic **14** unapproachable

Stern (of Argo)
constellation of: **6** Puppis

Sterne, Laurence
author of: **14** Tristram Shandy **19** A Sentimental Journey
character: **9** Uncle Toby **12** Parson Yorick, Walter Shandy

sternum
bone of: **6** breast

Sterope
also: **8** Asterope
member of: **8** Pleiades
son: **8** Oenomaus

Steve Canyon
creator: **12** Milton Caniff
character: **7** Cheetah **9** Madam Lynx **10** Doe Redwood, Miss Mizzou **11** Savannah Gay **13** Copper Calhoun **14** Herself Muldoon **17** Princess Sun Flower
wife: **6** Summer
ward/cousin: **12** Poteet Canyon
Summer's son: **13** Leighton Olson

Stevens, George
director of: **5** Giant (Oscar), Shane **8** Gunga Din **9** Swing Time **13** I Remember Mama, Penny Serenade **14** A Place in the Sun (Oscar), Woman of the Year **16** The Talk of the Town **19** The Diary of Anne Frank

Stevens, Gowan
character in: **9** Sanctuary
author: **8** Faulkner

Stevens, James
author of: **10** Paul Bunyan

Stevens, Ruby
real name of: **15** Barbara Stanwyck

Stevens, Wallace
author of: **7** The Rock **9** Harmonium **13** Sunday Morning **17** Transport to Summer **23** Peter Quince at the Clavier, The Idea of Order at Key West, The Man with the Blue Guitar

Stevenson, Robert
director of: **8** Jane Eyre **10** Back Street **11** Mary Poppins

Stevenson, Robert Louis
author of: **9** Kidnapped **13** The Black Arrow **14** Treasure Island **18** Travels with a Donkey **21** A Child's Garden of Verses, Doctor Jekyll and Mr Hyde, The Master of Ballantrae

St Evremond, Marquis
character in: **16** A Tale of Two Cities
author: **7** Dickens

stew 4 fret, fume, fuss **5** chafe, gripe, steep, tizzy, worry **6** grouse, ragout, seethe, simmer **7** agonize, fluster, flutter, grumble, mixture **10** miscellany

steward 5 agent, proxy **6** deputy, factor, waiter **7** bailiff, manager, trustee **8** executor, overseer **10** controller, supervisor **11** comptroller **13** administrator **14** representative, ship's attendant **15** flight attendant

Stewart, James
born: **9** Indiana PA
roles: **4** Rope **6** Harvey **7** Vertigo **10** Rear Window, Shenandoah **11** Elwood P Dowd **14** Cheyenne Autumn **16** Anatomy of a Murder, Destry Rides Again, The Stratton Story **17** Bell Book and Candle, It's a Wonderful Life **18** It's a Wonderful World, The Spirit of St Louis **19** The Glenn Miller Story **20** The Philadelphia Story (Oscar), You Can't Take It with You **22** The Greatest Show on Earth **23** Mr Smith Goes to Washington

Stewart, Mary
real name: **22** Florence Rainbow Stewart
author of: **11** Crystal Cave **14** The Hollow Hills **15** The Moon-Spinners **16** My Brother Michael, The Ga-

briel Hounds **18** Airs Above the Ground, The Last Enchantment

St George's
capital of: **7** Grenada

Sthenelaus
vocation: **7** warrior
killed by: **9** Patroclus

Sthenele
father: **7** Acastus
son: **9** Patroclus

Sthenelus
king of: **7** Mycenae
father: **5** Actor **7** Perseus
mother: **9** Andromeda
brother: **6** Mestor **9** Electryon
son: **10** Eurystheus
daughter: **6** Medusa **7** Alcyone
member of: **7** Epigoni
companion of: **8** Hercules

Sthenius
epithet of: **4** Zeus
means: **6** strong

Stheno
member of: **7** Gorgons

Stichius
origin: **8** Athenian
rank: **7** captain
killed by: **6** Hector

stick 3 bar, bat, cue, dig, fix, jab, pin, put, rod, set **4** balk, bind, cane, club, curb, fuse, glue, hold, join, last, mire, nail, pink, poke, pole, seal, snag, stab, stop, tack, twig, wand, weld **5** abide, affix, baton, billy, block, catch, check, fagot, leave, lodge, paste, place, plant, prick, punch, shift, snarl, spear, spike, staff, stall, stake, stand, stave, stump **6** adhere, attach, boggle, branch, burden, cement, cudgel, detain, endure, fasten, hamper, hinder, hog-tie, impede, insert, pierce, puzzle, scotch, skewer, stymie, switch, thrust, thwart **7** confuse, crosier, inhibit, perplex, shackle, trammel **8** bewilder, bludgeon, caduceus, continue, obstruct, puncture **9** checkmate, constrain, perforate, truncheon, victimize **10** immobilize, shillelagh

stick fast 4 hold **5** cling, stick **6** adhere, cleave

stickler 3 bug, nut **5** crank, poser **6** enigma, purist, puzzle, riddle, zealot **7** devotee, dilemma, fanatic, mystery, stumper **8** martinet **10** enthusiast, monomaniac

sticks 4 skis **5** bonds, glues, twigs **6** pastes, Podunk **7** adheres, boonies, catches, cements, country **8** kindling

9 backwoods, boondocks, golf clubs, provinces **10** hicksville, hinterland **11** countryside, hinterlands

stick together 4 bind, fuse, glue, hold, join **5** cling, stick, unite **6** cement, cohere

stick-to-itiveness 8 tenacity **9** endurance **10** resolution **11** persistence **12** perseverance, resoluteness **13** determination, tenaciousness

stickum 3 gum **4** glue **5** paste **6** cement **8** adhesive, mucilage **12** rubber cement

stick up for 5 boost **6** defend **7** root for **11** speak well of **17** put in a good word for

stick with 4 stay **5** abide **6** keep at **7** stand by **9** accompany, persevere

sticky 3 wet **4** damp, dank **5** gluey, gooey, gummy, humid, moist, muggy, pasty, tacky **6** clammy, clingy, steamy, sultry, viscid **7** viscous **8** adherent, adhesive, clinging, cohesive, sticking **9** glutinous, tenacious **10** gelatinous **12** mucilaginous

stiff *see box*

stiff-necked 6 mulish **7** willful **8** contrary, obdurate, stubborn **9** obstinate, pigheaded, unbending **10** bullheaded, refractory, self-willed, unshakable, unyielding **11** intractable **12** intransigent, pertinacious

stiffness 7 tension **8** firmness, rigidity **9** aloofness, formality, tenseness, tightness **10** constraint **11** starchiness

stifle 3 gag **4** curb **5** check, choke **6** muffle, subdue **7** garrote, inhibit, repress, smother, squelch, swelter **8** keep back, restrain, strangle, suppress, throttle **9** suffocate **10** asphyxiate

stifling 3 hot **6** stuffy **7** airless **10** overheated

stigma 4 blot, flaw, mark, scar **5** brand, odium, shame, stain, taint **6** smirch, smudge **7** blemish, tarnish **8** disgrace, dishonor **11** mark of shame **12** besmirchment

stigmatize 5 brand, smear **6** debase, defame, smirch **7** villify **9** discredit, disparage

still 4 calm, hush **5** inert, quiet **6** at rest, hushed, pacify, settle, silent **7** appease, assuage, gratify, put down, repress, silence, turn off **8** immobile, overcome, restrain, suppress, unmoving **9** noiseless, soundless **10** motionless, put an end to, stationary, unstirring

stillness 4 calm, hush **5** quiet **6** repose **7** silence **8** calmness, inaction, quietude **9** composure **10** immobility, inactivity, quiescence **11** tranquility **12** tranquillity

Stillness at Appomattox, A
author: **11** Bruce Catton

stilted 4 cold, prim **5** rigid, stiff **6** forced, formal, stuffy, wooden **7** awkward, labored, pompous, starchy, studied, uptight **8** mannered, priggish, starched **9** graceless, unnatural **10** artificial **11** ceremonious, constrained

---

stiff 4 body, cold, cool, firm, grim, hard, high, iron, keen, prim, sore, taut **5** aloof, awful, brave, brisk, crisp, cruel, dense, fixed, gusty, harsh, heavy, rigid, sharp, smart, solid, steep, stern, tense, thick, tight, tough, undue **6** bitter, brutal, chilly, clumsy, corpse, dogged, forced, formal, raging, severe, steady, steely, strong, uneasy, viscid, wooden **7** austere, awkward, cadaver, clotted, decided, distant, drastic, extreme, fearful, intense, jellied, labored, precise, remains, settled, starchy, stately, staunch, steeled, stilted, uptight, valiant, violent, viscous **8** affected, constant, dead body, exacting, forceful, grievous, mannered, pitiless, pounding, powerful, resolute, resolved, rigorous, ruthless, spanking, stubborn, ungainly, unlimber, unshaken, vigorous **9** difficult, draconian, excessive, graceless, inelastic, inelegant, laborious, merciless, obstinate, resistant, steadfast, stringent, tenacious, unnatural **10** artificial, courageous, determined, exorbitant, formidable, gelatinous, immoderate, inflexible, inordinate, persistent, solidified, unswerving, unyielding **11** ceremonious, constrained, extravagant, indomitable, straitlaced, unfaltering, unflinching, unwarranted **12** strong-willed, unreasonable **14** uncompromising

Stilwell, Joseph W
  nickname: **10** Vinegar Joe
  served in: **3** WWI **4** WWII
  chief of staff for: **13** Chiang
    Kai-shek
  driven out of: **5** Burma

stimulant 5 tonic, upper **6** bracer **8** excitant **9** energizer

stimulate 3 fan **4** spur, stir, wake **5** alert, rouse **6** arouse, awaken, excite, incite, prompt, vivify **7** actuate, animate, inflame, inspire, quicken, sharpen **8** activate, enkindle, initiate, inspirit

stimulating 5 tonic **7** piquing **8** arousing, exciting, spurring, stirring, whetting **9** animating, provoking **10** energizing, refreshing **11** interesting, provocative

stimulus 4 goad, spur, whet **5** tonic **6** bracer, fillip, motive **7** impetus **8** excitant **9** activator, energizer, incentive, quickener, stimulant **10** incitement, inducement **11** provocation **13** encouragement

sting 3 cut, nip, rub, vex **4** ache, barb, bite, blow, burn, fire, gall, gnaw, goad, grip, hurt, itch, lash, move, pain, prod, rack, rasp, rile, sore, spur, stab, whip **5** anger, chafe, cross, egg on, grate, impel, pinch, pique, prick, shake, shock, smart, venom, wince, wound **6** arouse, awaken, excite, harrow, incite, insult, kindle, madden, nettle, offend, pierce, prompt, propel, stir up, tingle, twinge **7** actuate, agonize, disturb, incense, inflame, prickle, provoke, quicken, scourge, stinger, torment, torture **8** irritate, motivate, vexation **9** infuriate, instigate, penetrate **10** affliction, irritation

Sting, The
  director: **13** George Roy Hill
  cast: **10** Paul Newman, Ray
    Walston, Robert Shaw
    13 Eileen Brennan, Robert
    Redford **14** Charles Durning
  score: **11** Scott Joplin
  Oscar for: **7** picture
    8 director

stinginess 6 penury **9** parsimony **11** miserliness **13** niggardliness, penny-pinching **15** tight-fistedness

stinging 4 acid **5** harsh, sharp **6** biting, bitter **7** burning, caustic, cutting, pungent **8** piercing **9** sarcastic, satirical **10** astringent

stingy 4 lean, mean, thin **5** close, scant, small, tight **6** frugal, meager, modest, paltry, scanty, skimpy, sparse **7** miserly, scrimpy, slender, sparing **8** piddling, stinting **9** illiberal, niggardly, penurious **10** inadequate, ungenerous **11** closefisted, tightfisted **12** cheeseparing, insufficient, parsimonious **13** pennypinching

stink 4 odor, reek **5** fetor **6** stench **8** bad smell **17** smell to high heaven

stint 3 job **4** curb, duty, part, save, task, term, turn **5** check, chore, limit, quota, shift **6** reduce, scrimp **8** hold back, restrain, restrict, withhold **9** constrain, cut down on, economize **10** assignment, engagement **12** circumscribe, pinch pennies

stipend 5 grant, wages **6** income, salary **7** pension **8** fixed pay **9** allowance, emolument **10** honorarium, recompense **11** scholarship **12** compensation, remuneration

stipulate 4 cite, name **5** agree, allow, grant, state **6** assure, insure, pledge **7** promise, provide, specify, warrant **8** indicate, set forth **9** designate, guarantee

stipulation 4 term **7** proviso **9** condition **10** limitation **11** requirement, restriction

stipulative 7 limited **9** qualified, tentative **10** contingent, restricted **11** conditional, provisional **16** with reservations

stir 3 act, mix **4** beat, fire, goad, jolt, move, prod, rush, spur, to-do, whip **5** blend, rouse, shake, sough, start **6** arouse, awaken, bustle, commix, excite, flurry, hasten, hustle, kindle, mingle, mixing, moving, pother, quiver, rustle, shiver, tumult, twitch, uproar, vivify, work up **7** agitate, animate, enflame, flutter, inspire, provoke, quicken, scamper **8** energize, inspirit, intermix, mingling, movement, prodding, rustling, scramble, stirring **9** agitation, commingle, commotion, electrify, stimulate **10** get a move on, step lively **11** set in motion **12** exert oneself, make an effort

Stiria
  also: **8** Stiritis
  epithet of: **7** Demeter

Stiritis see **6** Stiria

stirred up 5 riled, upset **7** aroused, excited, kindled, ruffled **8** agitated, inflamed **9** disturbed **10** stimulated

stirring 5 astir, awake **6** moving **7** rousing **8** electric, exalting, exciting, in motion, spirited **9** inspiring, thrilling **10** up and about **11** galvanizing, stimulating **12** electrifying

stir up 5 upset **6** arouse, awaken, excite, kindle, ruffle **7** agitate, disturb **9** call forth, stimulate **10** antagonize

stir vigorously 3 mix **4** beat, whip **7** agitate

stitch 3 bit, jot, sew **4** ache, iota, kink, mend, pain, pang, seam, tack **5** baste, cramp, crick, piece, scrap, shoot, shred **6** suture, tingle, twinge, twitch **7** article, garment **8** particle **9** embroider **12** charley horse

St John's
  capital of: **17** Antigua and
    Barbuda

St Louis
  baseball team: **9** Cardinals
  football team: **9** Cardinals
  founded by: **13** Pierre
    Laclede
  hockey team: **5** Blues
  landmark: **11** Gateway Arch
  newspaper: **12** Post-Dispatch
  river: **11** Mississippi
  site of: **10** Exposition (1904)
  university: **10** Washington

stock 4 butt, clan, form, fund, haft, herd, hold, kind, line, pull, race, root, type **5** array, basic, birth, blood, breed, broth, cache, caste, equip, goods, grasp, hoard, house, offer, shaft, store, tribe, wares **6** cattle, family, fit out, formal, handle, origin, people, shares, source, staple, strain, supply **7** appoint, capital, descent, dynasty, furnish, lineage, provide, regular, reserve, routine **8** accoutre, ancestry, bouillon, heredity, pedigree, pro forma, quantity, standard **9** forebears, genealogy, inventory, livestock, ownership, parentage, provision, reservoir, selection **10** assortment, background, extraction, family tree, investment **11** merchandise, nationality, progeniture **12** accumulation **13** capital shares

Stockhausen, Karlheinz
  born: **7** Germany, Modrath
  composer of: **5** Cycle,
    Tempi **6** Groups, Hymnen,
    Mantra, Zyklus **7** Anthems,
    Gruppen, Momente **8** Attuning, Gold Dust, Kontakte,
    Stimmung **9** Goldstaub, Zeitmasze **10** Procession, Prozession **12** Kontrapunkte
    13 Klavierstucke **16** From

the Seven Days **17** Aus den Sieben Tagen

Stockholm
nickname: 16 Venice of the North
capital of: 6 Sweden
sea: 6 Baltic
lake: 7 Malaren
section: 8 Norrmalm **9** Sodermalm **11** Gamla Staden
landmark: 7 Skansen **8** City Hall **11** Great Church
site of: 10 Nobel Prize

stockpile 5 cache, hoard, stock, store **10** accumulate

stocky 5 dumpy, husky, pudgy, solid, squat, stout **6** blocky, chunky, stubby, stumpy, sturdy **8** thickset

stodgy 4 dull, flat **5** dated, heavy, lumpy, passe, staid, thick **6** boring, clumsy, dreary, narrow, prolix, stuffy **7** humdrum, pompous, prosaic, serious, starchy, tedious **8** lifeless, pedantic, tiresome **9** laborious, lumbering, wearisome **10** antiquated, inflexible, monotonous **12** indigestible, oldfashioned **13** uninteresting

stoic 4 calm **8** detached, fatalist, quietist, tranquil **9** impassive, unruffled **11** philosophic **13** dispassionate, imperturbable, unimpassioned

stoicism 8 fatalism **9** fortitude **11** impassivity, tranquility **12** tranquillity **16** imperturbability

stole 3 fur **4** cape, robe, took, wrap **5** crept, orary, scarf **6** swiped **7** filched, pinched, sneaked, tiptoed **8** mantilla, pilfered, snatched, vestment **9** embezzled, purloined

stolen 3 hot **5** taken **6** swiped **7** filched, pinched **8** pilfered, snatched **9** embezzled, illgotten, purloined

stolid 4 dull **5** dense **6** bovine, obtuse **7** lumpish **8** sluggish **9** apathetic, impassive, lethargic **10** phlegmatic **11** insensitive, unemotional

stolidity 6 apathy **8** lethargy **9** inertness **11** impassivity **12** sluggishness

stomach 3 maw, pot **4** bear, bent, bias, craw, crop, guts, mind, take **5** abide, belly, brook, fancy, humor, stand, taste, tummy **6** desire, endure, hunger, liking, middle, paunch, relish, retain, suffer, temper, thirst **7** abdomen, gizzard, leaning, midriff, swallow **8** affinity, appetite, bear with, keenness, overlook, pass

over, pleasure, potbelly, sympathy, tolerate **9** put up with **10** attraction, midsection, partiality, proclivity, propensity **11** breadbasket, countenance, disposition, inclination **12** predilection

stone 3 gem, nut, pip, pit **4** rock, seed **5** bijou, jewel **6** kernel, pebble **9** brilliant **10** throw rocks

Stone, Edward Durell
architect of: 9 US Embassy **17** Museum of Modern Art **33** Kennedy Center for the Performing Arts

Stone, Irving
author of: 9 The Origin **11** Lust for Life **12** Those Who Love **17** Sailor on Horseback, The President's Lady **19** Adversary in the House **21** The Agony and the Ecstasy

Stone, Oliver
born: 9 New York NY
profession: 6 writer **8** director
films: 3 JFK **7** Platoon **10** Wall Street **14** Heaven and Earth **15** Midnight Express **21** Born on the Fourth of July

stoned to death 5 Achan

stonefly
varieties: 5 giant, green **6** spring, winter **8** perlodid **9** roachlike **11** greenwinged **12** rolled-winged

stoneware 5 china **7** ceramic, pottery **8** crockery

stony 3 icy **4** cold **5** blank, bumpy, chill, rocky, rough, stern **6** coarse, craggy, flinty, frigid, jagged, marble, pebbly, rugged, severe, steely, stolid, uneven **7** austere, callous, granite, lithoid, stoical **8** concrete, deadened, gravelly, hardened, indurate, obdurate, ossified, pitiless, rocklike, soulless, uncaring **9** bloodless, heartless, merciless, petrified, unfeeling, untouched **10** adamantine, forbidding, fossilized, hard-boiled, inexorable, insensible, unaffected, unyielding

stool 5 bench **7** cricket, hassock, ottoman

stool pigeon 3 rat, spy **4** fink **5** decoy, patsy **6** snitch **7** peacher, stoolie, tattler **8** informer, squealer **10** talebearer, tattletale

stoop 3 bow, sag **4** bend, fall, sink **5** deign, droop, porch, slump, steps, yield **6** resort,

slouch, submit **7** concede, descend, succumb **8** doorstep **9** acquiesce **10** condescend **11** entranceway **19** roundshoulderedness

stooped 4 bent **5** bowed **7** deigned, hunched **9** contorted **12** condescended

stop 3 ban, bar, end **4** curb, fill, halt, hold, idle, plug, quit, rest, seal, stay, stem, wait **5** abide, block, brake, break, caulk, cease, check, close, depot, deter, dwell, lapse, lodge, pause, put up, spell, stall, stand, tarry, visit **6** alight, arrest, cut off, desist, draw up, expire, falter, finish, hamper, hiatus, hinder, pull up, recess, rein in, repose, run out, stanch, stop up, thwart **7** close up, halting, layover, occlude, prevent, respite, sojourn, station, suspend **8** abeyance, break off, conclude, cut short, hold back, intermit, interval, leave off, obstruct, pass away, peter out, postpone, preclude, restrain, suppress, surcease, terminal, terminus, wind down **9** cessation, frustrate, interlude, stand fast, terminate **10** desistance, drop anchor, put an end to, standstill, suspension **11** come to a halt, come to an end, destination, discontinue, prohibition, termination **12** intermission, interruption **17** come to a standstill **18** bring to a standstill

stopgap 7 stand-by **9** contrived, emergency, expedient, impromptu, makeshift, temporary, tentative **10** improvised, substitute **11** provisional
Latin: 5 ad hoc **6** pro tem

stop in 4 call **5** visit **6** drop in, look in

stop off 4 call **5** visit **6** drop in, look in, stop by

stoppage 4 halt **5** check, tieup **6** arrest **7** barrier, embargo, staying **8** blockage, checking, clogging, gridlock, obstacle **9** checkmate, hindrance, restraint, stricture **10** disruption, impediment **11** curtailment, obstruction **12** interruption

Stoppard, Tom
author of: 10 Travesties **33** Rosencrantz and Guildenstern Are Dead

stopper 3 lid **4** bung, cock, cork, plug **5** spile

Stopping by Woods on a Snowy Evening
author: 11 Robert Frost

Stop the Music
  host: **9** Bert Parks
  orchestra: **11** Harry Salter
  vocalist: **9** June Valli **11** Jaye
    P Morgan, Jimmy Blaine
    12 Marion Morgan **13** Betty
    Ann Grove, Estelle Loring

stop up 3 jam **4** clog **5** block,
choke **8** obstruct

Storax 12 Biblical tree

store 3 lot **4** fund, hold, host,
keep, mart, pack, pile, save,
shop **5** amass, array, cache,
faith, hoard, lay by, lay in,
lay up, stash, stock, trust,
value, wares **6** credit, esteem,
gather, heap up, legion, market, plenty, regard, riches,
scores, supply, volume,
wealth **7** deposit, effects, husband, put away, reserve, satiety **8** emporium, lay aside,
overflow, plethora, quantity,
reliance, richness, salt away,
sock away, stow away
9 abundance, inventory, multitude, profusion, provision, reservoir, stockpile
10 accumulate, confidence,
cornucopia, dependence, estimation, exuberance, luxuriance **11** copiousness, full
measure, prodigality, supermarket **12** accumulation
13 establishment

storehouse 4 bank, silo **5** depot, vault **7** arsenal, granary
8 elevator, magazine, treasury
9 stockroom, warehouse
10 depository, repository

storied 4 epic **6** fabled **8** fabulous **9** legendary

**Stories and Texts for
Nothing**
  author: **13** Samuel Beckett

storm 3 ado, row **4** blow,
fume, fuss, gale, rage, rant,
rave, roar, rush, stir, tear, to-
do **5** burst, furor, snarl, stalk,
stamp, stomp, tramp **6** assail,
attack, charge, clamor, deluge,
flurry, hubbub, pother, ruckus,
squall, strike, tumult, uproar
7 assault, besiege, bluster,
carry on, cyclone, rampage,
tempest, tornado, torrent, turmoil, twister, typhoon **8** blizzard, brouhaha, downpour,
eruption, fall upon, outbreak,
outburst, upheaval **9** agitation,
commotion, explosion, fulminate, hurricane, raise hell
10 cloudburst, hullabaloo
11 blow one's top, disturbance **12** blow one's cool, vent
one's rage

storm and stress
  German: **13** Sturm und Drang
  name of 18th century:
    16 literary movement

storms
  goddess of: **11** Tempestates

storm troopers
  German: **14** Sturmabteilung

stormy 4 foul, wild **5** rainy,
rough, snowy, windy **6** raging,
rugged **7** howling, roaring,
squally, violent **8** blustery
9 inclement, turbulent
10 blustering **11** tempestuous

story 3 fib, lie **4** news, plot,
tale, word, yarn **5** alibi, fable,
piece **6** excuse, legend, report,
sketch **7** account, article, parable, romance, tidings, version
8 allegory, anecdote, argument, dispatch, news item,
white lie **9** falsehood, narrative, statement, testimony
10 allegation **11** fabrication,
information **13** prevarication

Story of a Bad Boy, The
  author: **19** Thomas Bailey
    Aldrich

Story of G I Joe, The
  director: **14** William
    Wellman
  cast: **13** Freddie Steele, Rob-
    ert Mitchum **15** Burgess
    Meredith (Ernie Pyle)

**Story of Louis Pasteur,
The**
  director: **15** William Dieterle
  cast: **8** Paul Muni (Pasteur)
    11 Anita Louise **19** Jose-
    phine Hutchinson
  Oscar for: **5** actor (Muni)

stout 3 big, fat, fit **4** able,
bold, firm, true **5** brave,
bulky, burly, hardy, heavy,
hefty, husky, large, obese,
plump, pudgy, round, solid,
tough, tubby **6** brawny,
chubby, daring, fleshy, heroic,
mighty, plucky, portly, robust,
rotund, rugged, spunky,
steady, stocky, strong, sturdy
7 doughty, gallant, staunch,
valiant **8** athletic, constant, enduring, faithful, fearless, intrepid, leathery, muscular,
resolute, resolved, stalwart,
thickset, untiring, valorous,
vigorous **9** confident, corpulent, dauntless, steadfast, strapping **10** able-bodied,
courageous, determined, inflexible, unshakable, unswerving,
unwavering **11** indomitable,
lionhearted, unfaltering, unflinching, unshrinking

Stout, Rex
  author of: **10** Fer-de-Lance
    12 Too Many Cooks **16** If
    Death Ever Slept
  character: **5** Fritz **9** Nero
    Wolfe **13** Archie Goodwin

stouthearted 4 bold **5** brave,
gutsy, hardy **6** heroic, plucky,

spunky **7** valiant **8** fearless, intrepid, resolute, spirited, stalwart, unafraid, valorous
9 dauntless, undaunted
10 courageous **11** indomitable,
lionhearted, unblenching,
unflinching

stoutheartedness 4 grit, guts,
sand **5** nerve, pluck, spunk,
valor **6** daring, mettle **7** bravery, courage **8** boldness
12 fearlessness
13 dauntlessness

stoutness
  French: **10** embonpoint

stow 3 jam, put, set **4** cram,
load, pack, tuck **5** cache,
crowd, place, stash, store,
stuff, wedge **7** deposit,
squeeze **8** ensconce, salt away

Stowe, Harriet Beecher
  author of: **12** Oldtown Folks
    14 Uncle Tom's Cabin

Strachey, Lytton
  author of: **13** Queen Victo-
    ria **17** Elizabeth and Essex,
    Eminent Victorians
  member of: **15** Bloomsbury
    Group

strafe 7 bombard **8** fire upon
10 machine-gun

straggle 4 rove **5** drift, stray
6 sprawl, wander **7** deviate,
meander **8** divagate

straight 4 even, neat, tidy,
true **5** clear, frank, right,
solid, sound **6** candid, direct,
evenly, honest, square, unbent **7** aligned, erectly, in order, orderly, upright
8 accurate, adjusted, arranged,
directly, on a level, reliable,
squarely, truthful, unbroken
9 ceaseless, forthwith, incessant, instantly, not curved,
shipshape, sorted out, sustained, veracious **10** aboveboard, continuous, forthright,
four-square, methodical, persistent, straightly, successive,
unrelieved, unswerving, unwavering **11** consecutive, coordinated, immediately,
trustworthy, undeviating
13 uninterrupted

straighten 4 tidy **5** align **6** adjust, neaten, unbend **7** even
out **8** level out, square up
9 put in line **10** put in order,
stand erect

straightening 7 tidying **9** adjusting, alignment, evening
up, unbending **10** evening
out **11** leveling out **13** putting
in line **14** putting in order

straighten out 6 unbend **7** re-
align **8** redirect **10** discipline

straighten up 4 tidy **5** align,

clean, order **6** neaten, tidy up
7 arrange, stand up **8** organize

straightforward 4 open
5 blunt, frank **6** candid, direct,
honest, square **7** ethical, upright **8** straight **9** guileless,
honorable **10** aboveboard,
creditable, forthright, scrupulous **11** plainspoken,
trustworthy

straightforwardness 6 candor **7** honesty **12** truthfulness
14 forthrightness

straight from the shoulder
4 open **5** frank **6** candid, direct, openly **7** bluntly, frankly,
sincere **8** candidly, directly
9 downright

straightness 7 honesty
8 evenness **10** directness
11 uprightness

strain 3 air, tax, tug **4** kind,
line, pull, sift, song, sort, toil,
tune, type, vein **5** blood,
breed, drain, force, grain,
grind, group, heave, labor,
people, press, sieve, streak,
stock, trait, twist **6** burden,
drudge, effort, extend, family,
filter, genius, injure, injury,
melody, overdo, purify, refine,
screen, sprain, stress, weaken,
winnow, wrench **7** descent,
distend, exhaust, fatigue, lineage, overtax, species, stretch,
tension, tighten, try hard, variety, wear out **8** ancestry,
bear down, elongate, exertion,
hardship, heredity, make taut,
overwork, pressure, protract,
struggle, tendency **9** draw
tight, make tense, overexert,
parentage **10** buckle down,
derivation, extraction, overburden **11** disposition, huff and
puff, inclination **12** do double
duty, drive oneself, exert oneself **14** predisposition, work
like a horse, work like a slave

strained 5 tense **6** touchy
8 volatile **9** explosive
10 precarious

strait 7 channel, narrows,
passage

straitened 5 broke, needy
6 hard-up **7** pinched **8** bankrupt, indigent, strapped,
wiped-out **9** destitute, penniless, penurious **10** distressed,
pauperized, restricted **11** embarrassed **12** impoverished
15 poverty-stricken

Strait Is the Gate
author: **9** Andre Gide

straitlaced 4 prim **5** rigid,
stiff **6** formal, narrow, proper,
severe, strict **7** austere, prudish, uptight **8** reserved **9** inhibited **11** puritanical

14 overscrupulous
15 undemonstrative

straits 3 fix **4** hole **6** pickle,
plight **8** distress **9** extremity
10 difficulty **11** predicament
13 embarrassment

strand 4 bank, cord, lock,
rope **5** beach, braid, coast, fiber, leave, shore, tress, twist
6 desert, ground, maroon,
string, thread **8** filament, necklace, seacoast, seashore
9 component, go aground, riv-
erside, shipwreck **10** ingredient, run aground **15** leave
high and dry, leave in the
lurch

stranded 5 stuck **6** ashore
7 aground, beached
8 grounded **9** foundered
11 shipwrecked **14** left high
and dry, left in the lurch

strange 3 new, odd **4** lost
5 alien, queer **6** uneasy, unused **7** awkward, bizarre, curious, erratic, foreign,
unknown, unusual **8** aberrant,
abnormal, freakish, peculiar,
singular, uncommon **9** alienated, anomalous, eccentric, estranged, fantastic, ill at ease,
irregular, unnatural **10** bewildered, farfetched, out of place,
outlandish, unexplored, unfamiliar **11** discomposed, disoriented, out-of-the-way
12 unaccustomed, undiscovered, unhabituated **13** extraordinary, unaccountable,
uncomfortable
14 unconventional

Strange Fruit
author: **12** Lillian Smith

Strange Interlude
author: **12** Eugene O'Neill

strangeness 7 anomaly, oddness **9** queerness **10** aberration **11** abnormality,
peculiarity **12** eccentricity, idiosyncrasy, irregularity, unconformity **13** nonconformity

stranger 5 alien **8** newcomer,
outsider **9** auslander, foreigner,
immigrant, outlander

Stranger, The
author: **11** Albert Camus

Strangers on a Train
director: **15** Alfred Hitchcock
cast: **9** Ruth Roman **11** Leo
G Carroll, Marion Lorne
12 Robert Walker **13** Farley
Granger **17** Patricia
Hitchcock
remade as: **20** Once You
Kiss a Stranger

strange to say
Latin: **13** mirabile dictu

strangle 3 gag **4** stop **5** burke,

check, choke, crush, quell
6 muzzle, stifle **7** garrote, put
down, repress, smother,
squelch **8** choke off, snuff out,
suppress, throttle **9** suffocate
10 asphyxiate, extinguish

strangulate 8 choke off, compress, strangle **9** constrict

strap 3 tie **4** band, beat, belt,
bind, cord, flog, lash, whip
5 flail, leash, thong, truss
6 tether, thrash **7** scourge

strapped 8 bankrupt, wiped
out **9** insolvent, penniless
12 impoverished; without
funds

strapping 5 burly, hardy,
husky, stout **6** brawny, robust,
strong, sturdy **8** muscular,
powerful, stalwart

stratagem 4 game, plan, plot,
ploy, ruse, wile **5** blind,
dodge, feint, trick **6** deceit, device, scheme, tactic **8** artifice,
intrigue, maneuver, trickery
9 deception **10** subterfuge
11 contrivance, machination

strategic 3 key **4** wary **5** vital
6 clever **7** careful, crucial, cunning, guarded, planned, poli-
tic, prudent, turning
8 cautious, critical, decisive,
military, tactical, vigilant
9 important, momentous, principal **10** calculated, deliberate,
diplomatic **11** significant
13 consequential,
precautionary

strategy 4 game **5** craft, wiles
6 policy, scheme **7** cunning,
devices, tactics **8** artifice, art
of war, game plan, plotting
9 war policy **10** artfulness,
craftiness **11** grand design,
machination, maneuvering
12 military plan **15** military
science

stratosphere 3 sky **5** ozone
7 heavens **8** upper air **12** high
altitude **14** wild blue yonder

stratum 4 band, belt, seam,
zone **5** layer

Strauss, Johann (the Elder)
composer of: **13** Radetzky
March

**Strauss, Johann (the
Younger)**
composer of: **6** The Bat
13 Die Fledermaus, The
Gipsy Baron **16** Der
Zigeunerbaron
waltz: **12** Emperor Waltz
13 The Blue Danube
23 Tales from the Vienna
Woods

Strauss, Joseph
composer of: **17** Music of

the Spheres **27** The Village Swallows in Austria

Strauss, Richard
 born: **6** Munich **7** Germany
 composer of: **6** Salome
 7 Don Juan, Elektra **8** Arabella **9** Capriccio **10** Don Quixote **14** Ein Heldenleben **15** Ariadne auf Naxos **16** Der Rosenkavalier, Domestic Symphony, Till Eulenspiegel **19** Die Frau ohne Schatten **20** Die Aegyptische Helena, Thus Spake Zarathustra **21** Also Sprach Zarathustra **23** Death and Transfiguration

Stravinsky, Igor Feodorovich
 born: **6** Russia
 11 Oranienbaum
 composer of: **4** Agon
 6 Threni **7** Orpheus **8** The Flood **9** Card Party, Fireworks **10** Oedipus Rex, Petrouchka, Petruschka, Pulcinella **11** Jeu de Cartes, The Firebird **13** Dumbarton Oaks, Psalm Symphony **14** The Nightingale **15** Abraham and Isaac, The Rite of Spring **16** Requiem Canticles, The Rake's Progress **18** Le Sacre du Printemps

straw 3 hay **4** tube **5** chaff **7** pipette

strawberry 8 Fragaria
 varieties: **4** mock **5** beach **6** barren, Dunlap, garden, Indian **7** sow-teat **8** Klondike, Rosacean, Virginia, woodland
 liqueur: **13** creme de fraise

Straw Dogs
 director: **12** Sam Peckinpah
 cast: **9** T P McKenna **11** Susan George **12** Peter Vaughan **13** Dustin Hoffman

straw man 6 effigy **9** scapegoat, scarecrow

stray 4 lost, roam, rove, waif **5** drift **6** random, wander **7** digress, drifter **8** go astray, separate, set apart, straggle, straying, vagabond, wanderer **9** itinerant, misplaced, scattered, straggler **10** lost animal, lost person **11** lose one's way

straying 5 lapse **8** drifting, rambling **9** departure, deviation, wandering **10** abberation, digression, divergence

streak 3 bar, bed, fly **4** band, blot, blur, cast, dart, dash, daub, line, lode, race, rush, seam, tear, vein, whiz, zoom **5** layer, level, plane, smear, speed, strip, touch **6** blotch,

hurtle, smirch, smudge, strain, stripe **7** portion, splotch, stratum

stream 3 jet, run **4** blow, file, flow, flux, gush, pour, race, rill, rush, teem, tide, waft, wave **5** brook, burst, creek, float, flood, issue, river, shoot, spate, spill, spout, spurt, surge **6** abound, branch, course, deluge, extend, feeder, onrush, sluice **7** current, flutter, freshet, rivulet, torrent **8** effusion, fountain, overflow **9** profusion, tributary **11** watercourse

streamer 4 flag **6** banner, burgee **7** pennant

streamlet 3 run **4** rill **5** brook, creek **7** rivulet

streamlined 4 racy **5** clean, sleek **7** compact **8** up-to-date **9** organized **10** futuristic, modernized, simplified **11** aerodynamic

stream of abuse 6 tirade **8** diatribe, harangue **9** contumely, invective **12** vituperation

streams
 goddess of: **7** Juturna

Streep, Meryl
 real name: **16** Mary Louise Streep
 born: **14** Basking Ridge NJ
 roles: **8** Ironweed, Silkwood **11** Out of Africa **13** Falling in Love, Sophie's Choice (Oscar), The Deer Hunter **14** Kramer vs Kramer **25** The French Lieutenant's Woman

street 3 way **4** lane, mews, road **5** alley, block, route **6** avenue **7** highway, roadway, terrace, thruway **8** turnpike **9** boulevard **10** expressway **12** thoroughfare

Streetcar Named Desire, A
 author: **17** Tennessee Williams
 director: **9** Elia Kazan
 cast: **9** Kim Hunter (Stella Dubois Kowalski) **10** Karl Malden **11** Vivien Leigh (Blanche Dubois) **12** Marlon Brando (Stanley Kowalski)
 setting: **10** New Orleans
 score: **9** Alex North
 Oscar for: **7** actress (Leigh) **15** supporting actor (Malden) **17** supporting actress (Hunter)

Streets of San Francisco, The
 character: **9** (Det Lt) Mike Stone **10** (Inspector) Dan Robbins **11** (Inspector) Steve Keller

cast: **10** Karl Malden **12** Richard Hatch **14** Michael Douglas

strega
 type: **7** liqueur
 origin: **5** Italy
 flavor: **6** spices **10** orange peel
 with brandy: **10** Strega Flip

Streisand, Barbra
 real name: **20** Barbara Joan Streisand
 born: **10** Brooklyn NY
 husband: **11** Elliot Gould
 roles: **5** Yentl **9** Funny Girl (Oscar), Funny Lady **10** Fanny Brice, Hello Dolly, What's Up Doc? **11** A Star Is Born **12** The Main Event, The Way We Were

strength 4 beef, grit, kick, pith, sand, size **5** brawn, force, forte, might, pluck, power, sinew, spice, vigor **6** anchor, mettle, number, purity, spirit, succor, virtue **7** bravery, muscles, potency, stamina, support **8** backbone, buttress, efficacy, firmness, mainstay, security, solidity, tenacity, vitality **9** endurance, fortitude, hardiness, intensity, lustiness, puissance, stoutness, toughness, viability **10** robustness, sturdiness, sustenance **13** concentration, effectiveness **16** stouteartedness
 Latin: **3** vis

strengthen 4 prop **5** brace, renew, steel **6** harden **7** build up, enhance, fortify, improve, restore, shore up, support, sustain **8** buttress **9** reinforce

strength of character 4 grit, guts **5** pluck, spunk **6** mettle **7** resolve **8** backbone **9** fortitude **10** resolution **12** resoluteness **13** steadfastness

Strength of Fields
 author: **11** James Dickey

strenuous 4 hard **5** eager **6** active, ardent, dogged, taxing, uphill **7** arduous, dynamic, earnest, intense, zealous **8** animated, diligent, sedulous, spirited, untiring, vigorous **9** assiduous, difficult, energetic, laborious, punishing **10** exhausting, on one's toes **11** hardworking, industrious, painstaking **12** enterprising **13** indefatigable

stress 4 beat, mark **5** force, value, worth **6** accent, affirm, assert, burden, moment, repeat, strain, weight **7** anxiety, concern, feature, gravity, meaning, sawdust, tension, urgency **8** emphasis, pressure **9** emphasize, necessity, underline **10** accentuate, importance, insist upon, oppression, prominence, underscore **11** consequence, seriousness **12** accentuation, significance **13** consideration

stretch 4 span, term, tire **5** cover, reach, spell, stint, tract, while, widen **6** burden, deepen, expand, extend, period, sprawl, spread, spring, strain **7** distend, draw out, expanse, fatigue, lie over, overtax, pull out **8** distance, draw taut, duration, elongate, interval, lengthen, overtask, overwork, protract, put forth, reach out, tautness, traverse **9** be elastic, draw tight, make tense, make tight, overexert **10** elasticity, exaggerate, overburden, overcharge, overstrain, push too far, resiliency **11** carry too far **12** be expandable, be extendable **14** push to the limit

stretchable 7 elastic, rubbery **8** flexible **9** resilient

stretching 9 extending, extension **10** drawing out, elongation **11** attenuation, enlargement, lengthening, protraction **12** prolongation **13** amplification

stretching out 8 outreach **9** expansion, extending, extension **10** elongation **11** attenuation, lengthening **12** prolongation

stretch out 6 expand, extend **7** amplify, augment, draw out **8** elongate, lengthen, protract

Strether
character in: **14** The Ambassadors
author: **5** James

strew 3 sow **6** litter **7** scatter **8** disperse **9** broadcast **11** disseminate

stricken 3 ill **4** hurt, sick **7** injured, smitten, wounded **8** blighted, diseased **9** afflicted, taken sick **13** incapacitated

strict 4 nice **5** exact, rigid, stern **6** severe **7** austere, perfect **8** absolute, complete, exacting, rigorous, unerring **9** stringent **10** fastidious, inflexible, meticulous, scrupulous, unyielding **13** authoritarian, conscientious **14** uncompromising

strictly required
French: **9** de rigueur

stride 4 gait, lope, pace, step **5** march, stalk **7** advance, headway **8** long step, prog-

ress **11** advancement, improvement **13** take long steps

strident 5 harsh **6** shrill **7** grating, jarring, rasping, raucous **8** clashing, grinding, jangling, piercing, twanging **9** dissonant **10** discordant, screeching **11** cacophonous, high-pitched

Striebel, John H
creator/artist of: **10** Dixie Dugan

strife 6 unrest **7** discord, trouble, turmoil, warfare **8** conflict, disquiet, fighting, struggle, upheaval, violence **10** contention, convulsion, disharmony, dissension **11** altercation, disturbance

Strife
author: **14** John Galsworthy

strike 3 bat, box, hit, run, tap **4** bang, beat, belt, bump, clap, clip, club, come, cuff, drub, find, flog, lash, make, meet, pelt, ring, slam, slap, slug, sock, toll, whip, wipe **5** chime, clout, erase, flail, knell, knock, light, pound, punch, reach, smash, smite, sound, thump, tie-up, whack, whale **6** affect, arrive, assail, attack, batter, buffet, cancel, chance, charge, cudgel, delete, effect, fold up, hammer, pommel, remove, seem to, thrash, wallop **7** achieve, arrange, assault, boycott, impress, occur to, protest, put away, ram into, run into, scourge, scratch, stumble, unearth, walk out **8** appear to, bump into, come upon, cross out, dawn upon, discover, fall upon, lambaste, pull down, take down **9** burst upon, devastate, eliminate, encounter, eradicate, knock into, take apart **10** come across, flagellate, meet head-on **11** beat against, collide with, dash against **12** labor dispute, work stoppage

strike a bargain 5 agree **6** settle **9** make a deal **10** compromise **11** come to terms, meet halfway **18** split the difference **20** reach an understanding

strike back 7 counter, get even, hit back, pay back, riposte **9** fight back, retaliate **13** counterattack

strike dumb 4 daze, stun **5** amaze, shock **7** astound, stagger, stupefy **8** astonish, dumfound **9** dumbfound, electrify **11** flabbergast

strike noisily 4 bang, beat, clap, slam **5** thump

strike out 6 delete, fan out, set off, set out **7** take out **10** sally forth

strike sharply 3 rap **4** slap **5** crack

striking 6 marked **7** notable **9** prominent **10** astounding, impressive, noteworthy, noticeable, remarkable, surprising **11** conspicuous, outstanding **13** extraordinary

Strindberg, August
author of: **9** Miss Julie, The Father **10** A Dream Play **12** The Creditors **14** The Ghost Sonata **15** The Dance of Death

string 3 row **4** cord, file, line, rope **5** chain, queue, train, twine **6** column, extend, parade, series, spread, strand, thread **7** binding, stretch **8** necklace, sequence **10** procession, succession

stringent 5 close, harsh, spare, stern, stiff, tight **6** cogent, frugal, severe, strict **7** sparing **8** exacting, forceful, rigorous **9** demanding, effectual, unbending **10** inflexible, unyielding **14** uncompromising

strip 3 rob **4** band, flay, loot, peel, raid, sack, skin, slip, tear **5** field, flake, rifle, shave **6** denude, divest, length, ravage, remove, ribbon, stripe, unwrap **7** deprive, despoil, disrobe, draw off, lay bare, measure, plunder, pull off, ransack, uncover, undrape, undress **8** airstrip, desolate, lay waste, spoliate, unclothe **9** steal from **11** disencumber

stripe 3 bar **4** band, line, tape **5** braid, strip, swath **6** ribbon, streak **7** chevron **8** insignia **9** striation

stripling 3 boy, lad **5** minor, youth **8** teenager, young man **9** schoolboy, youngster **10** adolescent

stripped 4 bare, nude **5** naked **6** peeled, unclad **7** denuded, exposed, unrobed **8** disrobed, divested **9** unclothed, uncovered, undressed

strive 3 vie **4** push **5** essay, fight, labor **6** battle, strain **7** contend, try hard **8** endeavor, struggle **9** take pains, undertake **10** do one's best **12** apply oneself, do one's utmost, exert oneself, spare no pains **15** work like a Trojan **18** move heaven and earth **20** leave no stone unturned

striving 4 toil **5** exert, labor **6** effort, strain **7** toiling, travail **8** exertion, struggle **9** straining **10** struggling

stroke 3 bat, hit, pat, pet, tap **4** blow, chop, coup, deed, feat, poke, slap, sock, swat **5** brush, chime, fluke, punch, whack **6** caress, chance, wallop **7** massage, ringing, seizure, tolling **8** accident, apoplexy, flourish, movement, sounding, striking **11** achievement, coincidence, piece of luck, transaction **15** brain hemorrhage

stroll 4 tour, turn, walk **5** amble, mosey **6** ramble, wander **7** meander, saunter **9** poke along, promenade **14** constitutional

stroller 4 pram **5** buggy **6** ambler, walker **7** rambler **8** carriage **9** itinerant, pushchair, saunterer **10** promenader **12** perambulator

strong 3 hot **4** able, bold, deep, keen, tart **5** burly, clear, close, fiery, hardy, nippy, sharp, solid, sound, stout, tangy, tough, vivid **6** ardent, biting, brawny, bright, cogent, fervid, fierce, gritty, hearty, mighty, moving, plucky, potent, robust, savory, severe, sinewy, sturdy **7** buoyant, capable, devoted, earnest, fervent, healthy, intense, piquant, pungent, skilled, violent, zealous **8** animated, athletic, definite, diligent, distinct, emphatic, faithful, forceful, muscular, powerful, puissant, sedulous, spirited, stalwart, tireless, vehement, vigorous **9** assiduous, competent, confirmed, effective, energetic, herculean, resilient, tenacious, undiluted **10** compelling, convincing, courageous, deep-seated, persistent, proficient **11** impassioned, persevering, resourceful **12** advantageous, concentrated, highly spiced, high-spirited, unmistakable **13** indefatigable, well-qualified **14** highly flavored, highly seasoned
  Spanish: 5 macho

Strong
  character in: 7 Erewhon
  author: 6 Butler

strong-arm 3 cow **5** bully, force **6** coerce, compel **8** browbeat, threaten **10** intimidate

strong feeling 4 fear, hate, heat, love, zeal **5** anger, ardor **6** fervor, sorrow, warmth **7** despair, emotion, passion,

sadness **8** jealousy **9** happiness, vehemence **12** satisfaction

stronghold 4 fort, hold, home, keep **6** bunker, center, locale, refuge **7** bastion, bulwark, citadel, rampart, redoubt **8** fastness, fortress, safehold, stockade **10** battlement, blockhouse **13** fortification

strongly committed 4 true **5** loyal **6** ardent **7** devoted, staunch, zealous **8** adhering, faithful **9** dedicated, steadfast **10** passionate, unwavering

strong point 5 forte **6** anchor **8** mainstay, strength

strong-willed 5 pushy **8** forceful, positive **9** assertive **10** aggressive **11** domineering, self-assured **13** self-assertive

Strophius
  king of: 6 Phocis
  reared by: 7 Orestes

structural support 3 bar **4** beam, prop, stud **5** brace, joist **6** girder, rafter, timber **7** trestle **12** underpinning

structure 4 form, plan **6** design, makeup **7** arrange, edifice, pattern **8** assemble, building, conceive, organize **9** construct, formation **11** arrangement, composition, put together **12** conformation, construction, organization **13** configuration

struggle 3 vie, war **4** duel, feud, pull, push, spar, tilt **5** argue, brawl, brush, clash, fight, grind, joust, labor, match, scrap, trial **6** action, battle, combat, differ, effort, engage, jostle, oppose, resist, strain, stress, strife, strive, tussle **7** compete, contend, contest, grapple, quarrel, scuffle **8** conflict, endeavor, exertion, long haul, skirmish, work hard **9** encounter, lock horns, take pains **10** engagement **11** altercation, cross swords **15** work like a Trojan **18** move heaven and earth **20** leave no stone unturned

strut 4 sail **6** parade, sashay **7** peacock, swagger **9** promenade

Struthiomimus
  type: 8 dinosaur, theropod
  known as: 15 ostrich dinosaur
  period: 10 Cretaceous
  characteristic: 9 toothless

Stryver
  character in: 16 A Tale of Two Cities
  author: 7 Dickens

Stuart, Gilbert
  born: 15 North Kingston RI
  artwork: 16 George Washington

Stuart, J E B
  served in: 8 Civil War
  side: 11 Confederate
  commander of: 7 cavalry
  battle: 7 Bull Run **8** Antietam **10** Gettysburg **14** Fredericksburg **16** Chancellorsville **18** Peninsular campaign

Stuart Little
  author: 7 E B White

stub 3 end **4** bump, butt, dock, tail **5** crush, knock, snuff, stump **6** fag end, scrape **7** receipt, remains, tamp out, voucher **10** extinguish, torn ticket **11** counterfoil

stubble 5 beard **6** stumps **8** bristles, whiskers **9** cut stalks **16** five-o'clock shadow

stubborn 6 dogged, mulish, strong, sturdy **7** willful **8** forceful, obdurate, perverse, resolute **9** concerted, immovable, obstinate, pigheaded, resistant, tenacious, unbending, unmovable **10** bullheaded, headstrong, inflexible, persistent, purposeful, refractory, self-willed, unshakable, unyielding **11** indomitable, intractable, opinionated, uncompliant **12** hard to handle, recalcitrant, ungovernable, wholehearted

stubbornness 10 mulishness, obstinacy, resistance **11** willfulness **13** intransigence, pigheadedness

stubby 5 dumpy, pudgy, squab, squat, tubby **6** chubby, chunky, stocky, stodgy, stumpy **7** squatty **8** thickset

Stubtoe State
  nickname of: 7 Montana

stuck 3 dug, put **4** held **5** bound, fixed, fused, glued, mired, poked **6** balked, curbed, jabbed, joined, nailed, pasted, pinned, placed, sealed, spiked, tacked, thrust, welded **7** adhered, affixed, boggled, impeded, planted, pricked, punched, saddled, snarled, speared, stabbed, stalled, stumped, stymied **8** attached, burdened, cemented, fastened, inserted **9** punctured **10** obstructed, perforated **11** immobilized

stuck-up 4 vain **5** cocky **6** snooty, uppish, uppity **7** haughty, high-hat **8** arrogant, snobbish **9** bigheaded, conceited **10** disdainful, ego-centric, hoity-toity **11** over-bearing, swellheaded **13** self-important, self-satisfied

stud 3 dot **4** beam, buck, dude, sire **5** board, rivet **6** button **7** upright **8** fastener, macho man, nailhead

student 4 coed **5** pupil **6** reader **7** analyst, learner, scholar, watcher **8** disciple, examiner, follower, observer, reviewer **9** collegian, schoolboy, spectator **10** schoolgirl **11** commentator, interpreter, matriculant **13** undergraduate

studied 8 measured **10** calculated, deliberate, purposeful **11** intentional **12** premeditated

studious 6 brainy, intent **7** bookish, earnest, erudite **8** academic, cerebral, diligent, literate, well-read **9** laborious, scholarly **10** determined, purposeful, scholastic **11** painstaking **12** intellectual

Studs Lonigan
  series includes: **11** Judgment Day **12** Young Lonigan **29** The Young Manhood of Studs Lonigan
  author: **13** James T Farrell

study 3 den **4** cram, read **5** grind, probe **6** office, peruse, review, search, studio, survey **7** examine, explore, inquiry, library, observe, reading **8** analysis, consider, learning, pore over, read up on, research, scrutiny **9** delve into, education **10** glance over, inspection, scrutinize **11** examination, exploration, hit the books, inquire into, instruction, investigate, read closely, reading room, scholarship **13** consideration, investigation, school oneself, search through

Study in Scarlet, A
  author: **19** Sir Arthur Conan Doyle
  character: **12** Dr John Watson **13** Jefferson Hope, Tobias Gregson **14** Sherlock Holmes **17** Inspector Lestrade

Study of History, A
  author: **14** Arnold J Toynbee

stuff 3 act, bit, jam, pad, wad **4** best, bosh, bunk, cram, fill, gear, heap, load, pack, pile, sate, stow **5** cache, crowd, gorge, hokum, hooey, stash, store, thing, trash, wedge **6** burden, fill up, humbug, matter, staple, tackle, things, thrust, tricks, utmost **7** effects, essence, hogwash, overeat, rubbish, satiate, spinach, twaddle **8** darndest, falderal, material, nonsense **9** component, empty talk, substance **10** balderdash, belongings, gluttonize, ingredient, make a pig of **11** constituent, foolishness, overindulge, performance, possessions, raw material **12** quintessence **13** paraphernalia

stuff-and-nonsense 3 rot **4** bosh, bull, bunk **5** hokum, hooey, trash **6** bunkum, drivel, humbug **7** baloney, hogwash, spinach, twaddle **8** buncombe, claptrap, nonsense, tommyrot **9** poppycock **10** applesauce, balderdash, tomfoolery **11** foolishness **12** fiddlesticks **13** horsefeathers

stuffed 4 full **6** filled, jammed, loaded, packed, rammed, wadded **7** crammed, crushed, replete **8** overfull, satiated, squeezed **10** sandwiched

stuff in 4 cram, pack **6** devour **8** bolt down, compress, gobble up, wolf down

stuffing 5 farce **7** filling, packing, padding, wadding **8** dressing **9** forcemeat

stuffy 4 cold, smug **5** close, fusty, heavy, muggy, musty, staid **6** stodgy, sultry **7** airless, pompous **8** reserved, stagnant, stifling **9** clogged-up, congested, high-flown, stopped-up, stuffed-up **10** old-fogyish, oppressive, sweltering **11** pretentious, straitlaced, suffocating **12** supercilious, unventilated **13** ill-ventilated, self-satisfied, stale-smelling

stultify 4 balk **6** hinder, impair, impede, thwart **7** cripple, inhibit, nullify, vitiate **8** suppress **9** frustrate, hamstring **11** make useless

stumble 3 hit **4** fall, reel, roll, sway, trip **5** botch, lurch, pitch, spill **6** bungle, falter, happen, hash up, hobble, mess up, slip up, sprawl, topple, totter **7** blunder, misstep, shamble, stagger **8** flounder **10** take a spill **12** come by chance, make mistakes, pitch forward

stumble upon 4 find **7** learn of **8** come upon, discover **10** chance upon, happen upon **14** find by accident

stumbling block 3 bar, rub **4** snag **5** block, catch, hitch **6** hamper, hurdle **7** barrier, problem **8** drawback, obstacle **9** detriment, hindrance **10** difficulty, impediment **11** ob-struction **12** complication, interference

stump 3 end **4** butt, foil, stub, thud **5** befog, clomp, clonk, clump, clunk, stamp, stomp, tramp **6** baffle, nubbin, stymie **7** confuse, mystify, nonplus, perplex **8** bewilder, confound, dumfound, footfall, stomping, tramping **9** bamboozle, dumbfound

stun 4 daze, numb **5** amaze, shock **7** astound, stagger, startle, stupefy **8** astonish, dumfound **9** dumbfound **11** flabbergast

stunner 4 doll **5** beaut, Venus **6** beauty, eyeful **8** knockout **9** dreamboat **10** good-looker

stunning 6 dazing, lovely **7** amazing, numbing **8** shocking, striking **9** beautiful, exquisite, startling **10** astounding, staggering, stupefying **11** astonishing, dumfounding **12** dumbfounding, electrifying **14** flabbergasting

stunt 3 act **4** curb, feat **5** abort, check, cramp, dwarf, limit, stint, trick **6** impede, number, stifle **7** curtail, delimit **8** restrain, restrict, suppress

stunted 5 dumpy, runty **6** bantam **7** dwarfed, squatty, wizened **9** pint-sized **13** foreshortened

Stunt Man, The
  director: **11** Richard Rush
  cast: **9** Alex Rocco **11** Peter O'Toole (Eli Cross) **13** Allen Goorwitz, Sharon Farrell **14** Barbara Hershey, Steve Railsback

stupefaction 5 shock **8** numbness, surprise **9** amazement **12** astonishment

stupefied 5 dazed **6** amazed **7** shocked, stunned **8** benumbed **10** dumbstruck, dumfounded **11** dumbfounded **13** flabbergasted, thunderstruck

stupefy 4 daze, stun **5** amaze, shock **7** astound, nonplus, stagger **8** astonish, confound, dumfound, surprise **9** dumbfound, overwhelm **11** flabbergast

stupefying 8 shocking, stunning **11** dumfounding **12** dumbfounding, electrifying, overwhelming **14** flabbergasting

stupendous 3 big **4** huge, vast **5** giant, great, jumbo **6** mighty **7** amazing, immense, mammoth, massive, titanic, unusual **8** colossal, enormous, fabulous, gigantic, imposing, stunning, terrific **9** cyclopean, herculean, marvelous, monstrous, very great, very large, wonderful **10** astounding, gargantuan, incredible, monumental, phenomenal, prodigious, remarkable, surprising, tremendous, unexpected **11** astonishing, elephantine **13** extraordinary

stupid 4 dull, dumb **5** dense, inane, inept, silly **6** absurd, oafish, obtuse, simple, unwise **7** aimless, asinine, boorish, doltish, fatuous, foolish, idiotic, moronic, witless **8** backward, childish, heedless, mistaken, reckless, tactless **9** brainless, cretinous, dimwitted, duncelike, foolhardy, illjudged, imbecilic, imprudent, pointless, senseless **10** halfwitted, ill-advised, indiscreet, irrelevant, weak-minded **11** empty-headed, meaningless, nonsensical, purposeless, thoughtless **12** absentminded, muddleheaded, preposterous, simpleminded, slow-learning, unreasonable **13** ill-considered, inappropriate, irresponsible, rattlebrained, unintelligent

stupor 4 daze **5** faint **6** apathy, torpor **7** inertia **8** blackout, lethargy, numbness **9** inertness **10** somnolence **12** stupefaction **13** insensibility

sturdy 4 able, firm **5** brave, burly, gutsy, hardy, heavy, solid, sound, stout, tough **6** daring, dogged, gritty, heroic, mighty, plucky, robust, rugged, secure, sinewy, spunky, strong **7** defiant, doughty, durable, gallant, lasting, valiant **8** enduring, fearless, forceful, intrepid, muscular, powerful, resolute, spirited, stalwart, stubborn, vigorous, well-made **9** dauntless, strapping, unabashed, undaunted, well-built **10** courageous, determined, invincible **11** indomitable, substantial, unshrinking **12** highspirited, stouthearted **15** well-constructed

Sturges, John
director of: **14** The Great Escape **19** The Magnificent Seven

Sturges, Preston
director of: **10** The Lady Eve **16** Sullivan's Travels **17** The Palm Beach Story, Unfaithfully Yours **21** Hail the Conquering Hero **24** The Miracle of Morgan's Creek

Sturmabteilung 13 storm troopers

Sturm und Drang 22 German literary movement (18th century)
literally: **14** storm and stress

stygian 3 dim **4** dark **5** black, murky **6** dreary, gloomy, somber **7** hellish **8** funereal, infernal, starless **9** tenebrous, unlighted

style 3 fad **4** call, elan, kind, mode, name, pomp, rage, sort, type **5** charm, class, craze, favor, flair, grace, model, taste, trend, vogue **6** design, luxury, manner, polish **7** arrange, comfort, fashion, pattern **8** currency, elegance **9** affluence, designate **10** smoothness **11** savoir faire
French: **4** gout

stylish 3 hip, new **4** chic **5** natty, smart, swank **6** dapper, latest, modern, modish, with-it **7** a la mode, elegant, in vogue, voguish **8** up-todate **9** in fashion **11** fashionable **13** sophisticated, up-to-theminute

stymie 4 balk **5** block, check, stump **6** baffle, hinder, puzzle, thwart **7** confuse, mystify **8** confound, obstruct **9** frustrate

Stymphalides
origin: **8** Arcadian
form: **5** birds
attribute: **9** dangerous

Stymphalus
king of: **7** Arcadia
killed by: **6** Pelops
form: **4** lake
home of: **12** Stymphalides

Styracosaurus
type: **8** dinosaur **10** ceratopsid
location: **12** North America
period: **10** Cretaceous
characteristic: **6** horned

Styron, William
author of: **12** The Long March **13** Sophie's Choice **17** Lie Down in Darkness **18** Set This House on Fire **25** The Confessions of Nat Turner

Styx
form: **5** river
location: **5** Hades **10** underworld
father: **7** Oceanus
ferryman: **6** Charon

suave 6 silken, smooth, urbane **7** affable, elegant, politic **8** charming, gracious, mannerly, polished, unctuous **9** civilized **10** diplomatic, flattering **12** ingratiating **13** smooth-tongued

sub 5 below, proxy, under

6 backup, deputy, second **7** beneath, standby, stand-in **9** alternate, submarine, surrogate **10** substitute, understudy **11** pinch-hitter

subaltern 4 aide **6** helper **9** assistant **10** lieutenant **11** subordinate

subconscious 3 dim **7** dawning **9** intuitive **10** subliminal **11** instinctive

subdivide 6 divide **7** split up **8** separate **9** partition

subdivision 3 arm **4** wing **6** branch **7** chapter, section **8** offshoot **11** development **12** neighborhood

subdue 3 bow **4** calm, curb, down, drub, ease, foil, mute, rout, trim, whip **5** allay, break, check, crush, floor, quell, salve, smash, still **6** deaden, defeat, master, mellow, muffle, reduce, soften, soothe, temper, thrash **7** appease, assuage, conquer, mollify, oppress, overrun, put down, relieve, slacken, subject, trample **8** mitigate, moderate, overcome, palliate, surmount, tone down, vanquish **9** meliorate, overpower, overwhelm, quiet down, soft-pedal, subjugate **10** ameliorate **11** triumph over **12** tranquillize

subdued 4 dull **5** cowed, muted, quiet **7** abashed, crushed, humbled, muffled, quelled **8** deadened, overcame **10** humiliated, indistinct, lackluster **11** intimidated, overpowered

subduer 6 victor, winner **9** conqueror, overcomer **10** subjugator, vanquisher **11** intimidator

subject 4 bare, case, gist, open, pith, text **5** field, issue, liege, motif, prone, study, theme, topic **6** affair, expose, liable, matter, submit, thesis, vassal **7** bound by, citizen, concern, exposed, lay open **8** business, disposed, follower, obedient, question **9** dependent, subjected, substance **10** answerable, discipline, in danger of, make liable, put through, vulnerable **11** stipulatory, subordinate, subservient, susceptible

subjection 11 subjugation **12** subservience **13** regimentation, subordination

subjective 5 inner **6** biased **7** partial **8** partisan, personal **9** emotional **10** individual, prejudiced **12** nonobjective

subjoin 5 add on, affix, annex
6 append, attach, tack on

subjugate 4 tame 5 crush,
quell 6 subdue 7 conquer, put
down 8 dominate, suppress,
vanquish 10 overmaster

subjugation 6 chains, thrall
7 bondage, slavery 9 dominance, mastering, servitude,
thralldom 10 conquering, domination 11 enslavement,
vanquishing

subjugator 6 master, victor
7 subduer 9 conqueror, domi-
nator 10 vanquisher
11 slavemaster

sublimate 4 turn 5 exalt, shift
6 divert, purify 7 channel,
convert, elevate, ennoble 8 redirect, transfer 9 transform,
transmute 12 spiritualize

sublime 4 high 5 grand, great,
lofty, noble 6 superb 7 exalted,
stately 8 elevated, imposing,
majestic, splendid, terrific,
very good 9 estimable, excellent, marvelous, wonderful
12 awe-inspiring, praiseworthy

submarine
invented by: 7 Holland
even keel: 4 Lake
torpedo: 8 Bushnell

submerge 4 dive, sink 5 douse,
drown, flood, souse 6 deluge,
engulf, go down, plunge 7 go
under, immerse 8 inundate,
pour over, submerse

submerse 5 drown 6 engulf
7 immerse 8 inundate,
submerge

submersion 7 sinking
8 drowning 9 immersion
10 inundation 11 submergence

submission 8 giving in, meekness, tameness, yielding
9 handing in, obedience, passivity, surrender, tendering
10 compliance, remittance,
submitting 11 passiveness
12 acquiescence, capitulation,
presentation, subservience,
tractability 13 nonresistance
14 submissiveness

submissive 4 meek, mild
6 docile, humble, pliant 7 dutiful, fawning, passive, servile,
slavish 8 crawling, obedient,
toadying, yielding 9 compliant,
malleable, tractable, truckling
10 obsequious 11 acquiescent,
bootlicking, complaisant, deferential, subservient, unassertive 12 capitulating,
ingratiating, nonresisting
13 accommodating

submissiveness 8 docility,
meekness 9 passivity 10 com-

pliance 11 resignation
12 complaisance, tractability

submit 3 bow 4 bend, cede
5 agree, argue, claim, defer,
kneel, offer, stoop, yield
6 accede, assert, commit, comply, give in, give up, resort,
tender 7 contend, hold out,
present, proffer, propose, succumb, suggest 8 back down,
put forth 9 acquiesce, surrender, volunteer 10 capitulate,
put forward 12 knuckle under

submit an offer 3 bid
6 tender 7 proffer, propose

submit to 4 bear, take 5 abide,
brave, brook, stand 6 endure,
suffer 7 stomach, undergo
8 stand for, tolerate 9 put up
with

subnormal 3 bad, low 5 seedy,
sorry 6 crummy, dismal,
shabby, sleazy, subpar 7 abysmal 8 below par, inferior, mediocre, wretched 9 defective,
deficient 10 inadequate, second-rate 11 below normal,
substandard 12 insufficient

subordinate 4 help 5 lower
6 junior, lackey, lesser, menial, worker 7 servant, subject 8 hireling, inferior
9 ancillary, assistant, attendant, auxiliary, dependent, of
low rank, outranked, secondary, subaltern, underling
10 subsidiary 11 subservient

subordination 10 subjection
11 inferiority, subjugation
12 subservience
13 regimentation

suborn 5 bribe 6 buy off, pay
off

sub rosa 8 covertly, in secret,
on the sly, secretly 9 in private, privately 12 off-the-
record 14 confidentially
15 behind-the-scenes 17 behind closed doors

subscribe 4 help, sign 6 assent, chip in, donate 7 consent, endorse, support 8 hold
with 9 undersign 10 contribute

subsequent 4 next 7 ensuing
9 following, proximate
10 consequent, succeeding,
successive

subsequently 2 so 5 after,
later, since 9 afterward, following 10 succeeding
12 consequently

subservient 6 docile, menial
7 fawning, servile, slavish,
subject 8 cringing, toadying
9 accessory, ancillary, auxiliary, prostrate, truckling
10 obsequious, subsidiary

11 bootlicking, subordinate,
sycophantic 12 contributory,
ingratiating

subside 3 ebb, sag 4 calm,
drop, ease, sink, wane
5 abate, let up 6 cave in,
lessen, recede, settle, shrink
7 descend, dwindle 8 decrease,
diminish, level off, melt away,
moderate

subsidence 5 letup 6 easing,
ebbing, waning 7 calming
9 abatement, dwindling, lessening, recession, shrinking
10 decreasing, inactivity, moderation 12 diminishment

subsidiary 5 extra, lower, minor 6 branch, junior, lesser
7 adjunct 8 addition, division,
inferior 9 accessory, affiliate,
auxiliary, secondary 10 additional, supplement 11 subordinate 12 supplemental
13 supplementary

subsidy 3 aid 4 gift 5 award,
grant 7 backing, support 9 allotment, provision 10 fellowship, grant-in-aid, honorarium,
subvention 11 scholarship,
sponsorship 13 appropriation,
assistantship

subsist 4 live 5 exist 7 survive
9 stay alive 11 feed oneself,
support life 12 make ends
meet 23 keep body and soul
together

subsistence 6 living, upkeep
7 support 8 survival 10 livelihood, sustenance 11 maintenance, nourishment

substance 4 body, core, germ,
gist, pith, soul 5 force, heart,
means, money, sense, stuff
6 burden, import, intent, marrow, matter, riches, thrust,
wealth 7 element, essence,
keynote, purport, reality
8 backbone, material, property,
solidity 9 actuality, affluence,
basic idea, main point 10 ingredient 11 connotation, constituent, corporality
12 corporeality, quintessence
13 corporealness

substandard 3 bad 4 poor
5 awful, lousy 6 crummy,
shoddy 8 below par, inferior,
terrible 9 imperfect 10 second-
rate 11 second-class 12 below
average

substantial 3 big 4 firm, full
5 ample, bulky, large, massy,
solid, sound 7 massive, sizable 8 abundant 9 plenteous,
plentiful 10 monumental
12 considerable

substantiate 5 prove 6 verify
7 confirm, support, sustain

11 corroborate, demonstrate **12** authenticate

substantiated 6 proved, proven **7** factual **8** verified **9** supported **11** well-founded **12** corroborated, demonstrated, well-grounded **13** authenticated

substantiation 5 proof **8** evidence **11** affirmation **12** verification **13** corroboration, demonstration, documentation **14** authentication

substitute 3 act **6** backup, change, ersatz, fill in, switch **7** standby, stand in, stopgap **8** deputize, exchange, pinchhit, take over **9** alternate, makeshift, surrogate, temporary **10** understudy **11** alternative, pinch hitter, replacement

substitution 5 shift **6** change, switch **8** exchange, swapping **9** variation **10** alteration **11** replacement

substructure 4 base **6** ground **10** foundation, groundwork **12** underpinning

subsume 5 cover **6** assume, deduce **7** explain, include, involve **8** consider **13** subcategorize

subterfuge 4 ruse, sham, wile **5** blind, dodge, guile, shift, trick **6** scheme **7** evasion **8** artifice, intrigue, pretense, scheming **9** casuistry, chicanery, deception, duplicity, imposture, sophistry, stratagem **10** camouflage, sneakiness **11** deviousness, evasiveness, game-playing, machination, make-believe, smoke screen

subtle, subtile 3 sly **4** cagy, deft, fine, foxy, keen, wily **5** light, quick, sharp, slick **6** artful, astute, clever, crafty, expert, shifty, shrewd, tricky **7** cunning, devious, elusive, refined **8** delicate, indirect, masterly, skillful **9** deceptive, designing, ingenious, underhand **10** discerning **11** understated **13** perspicacious, sophisticated **14** discriminating

Subtle
  character in: **12** The Alchemist
  author: **6** Jonson

subtleties 7 nuances **10** fine points **11** refinements **12** distinctions

subtract 6 deduct, detach, lessen, reduce, remove **8** decrease, diminish, take away, withdraw

subtraction 7 removal **8** decrease **9** deduction, lessening, reduction **10** diminution, taking away, withdrawal **11** diminishing

suburbs 8 environs, vicinity **9** outskirts, periphery, precincts

sub verbo 12 under the word **15** under the heading

subversion 4 fall, ruin **6** defeat, mutiny **8** disorder, sabotage **9** overthrow, rebellion **10** corruption, disruption **11** destruction

subversive 7 traitor **8** quisling **9** insurgent, seditious **10** incendiary, traitorous, treasonous **11** seditionary **12** collaborator **13** revolutionary **14** fifth columnist **15** insurrectionary **16** collaborationist

subvert 3 mar **4** ruin, undo **5** smash, spoil, upset, wreck **6** defile, poison, ravage **7** despoil, destroy, disrupt, shatter **8** demolish, overturn **9** devastate, overthrow, undermine **11** contaminate

sub voce 21 under the specified word
  literally: **13** under the voice

succeed 3 hit, win **5** avail, catch, click **6** accede, do well, follow, move up **7** inherit, prevail, prosper, replace, triumph **8** make a hit, make good, supplant, take over **9** bear fruit, strike oil

succeed at 2 do **6** attain **7** execute, fulfill, perform, realize **8** carry out **9** make a go of **10** accomplish

succeeding 5 later **6** coming, future **7** ensuing **8** oncoming **9** following, impending, posterior **10** consequent, subsequent, successive

succeed to 6 follow **7** inherit **15** ascend the throne

succes d'estime 15 critical success

success 3 hit **4** fame **5** smash **7** triumph, victory **8** conquest **9** affluence **10** ascendancy, attainment, prosperity **11** achievement, advancement, fulfillment, good fortune

successful 4 rich **6** proven **7** perfect, wealthy, well-off **8** achieved, affluent, complete, fruitful, thriving **9** effective **10** prosperous, triumphant **11** efficacious, flourishing **12** accomplished, acknowledged

successful completion 7 success, victory, winning **9** execution **10** making good **11** achievement, culmination, fulfillment, realization **12** consummation **14** accomplishment

succession 3 run **5** chain, cycle, round, train **6** course, series **8** sequence **9** accession **10** assumption, procession, stepping-up, taking over **11** inheritance, progression

successive 7 ensuing **10** continuous, succeeding **11** consecutive

successor 4 heir **5** donee **7** devisee, heiress, heritor, legatee **8** follower, parcener **9** heritress, joint heir **10** coparcener, substitute **11** beneficiary, replacement, reversioner **12** heir apparent

succinct 4 neat **5** brief, crisp, pithy, short, terse, tight **6** direct, gnomic **7** clipped, compact, concise, summary **9** condensed **10** aphoristic, to the point **12** epigrammatic

succinctness 7 brevity **9** crispness, terseness **11** compactness, conciseness **12** condensation

succor 3 aid **4** help **5** nurse **6** assist, back up, relief, shield, wait on **7** comfort, nurture, protect, relieve, support, sustain **8** befriend **10** assistance, minister to, sustenance, take care of **11** give a lift to, helping hand, lend a hand to, maintenance **13** accommodation

succulent 5 juicy **6** fleshy **9** toothsome **10** appetizing

succumb 3 die **5** yield **6** accede, expire, give in, submit **7** defer to, give way, go under **8** pass away **9** surrender **10** capitulate, comply with **12** fall victim to

such as
  Latin: **2** eg **13** exempli gratia

such is life
  French: **9** c'est la vie

sucker 3 sap **4** boob, butt, dupe, fool, goat, gull, jerk, mark **5** chump, patsy **6** pigeon, victim **7** cat's-paw, fall guy **8** easy mark, fair game, pushover **9** schlemiel, soft touch **11** sitting duck

Sucker State
  nickname of: **8** Illinois

suck up 6 absorb, soak up **7** drink in **8** sponge up **9** swallow up

Sucre
legal capital of: **7** Bolivia

Sudan *see box*

Sudanese Republic *see*
4 Mali

sudden 4 rash **5** hasty, quick,
rapid **6** abrupt, speedy **7** instant **9** immediate, impetuous
10 surprising, unexpected, unforeseen **11** precipitate, unlooked-for **13** instantaneous,
unanticipated, unforeseeable

sudden development
French: **10** coup de main

suddenly 7 quickly **8** abruptly,
in no time **9** all at once, instantly, on the spot **11** in an
instant **12** all of a sudden, un-

expectedly **13** at short notice
14 without warning **20** on the
spur-of-the-moment **21** in the
twinkling of an eye

sudden movement 4 dart,
jolt **5** flash, spurt

sudden noise 3 pop **4** bang,
clap, slam **5** burst, crash **6** report **9** explosion

Sudermann, Hermann
author of: **5** Honor **8** Dame
Care **14** The Song of Songs

suds 3 ale **4** beer, brew, foam
5 draft, froth, lager **10** malt
liquor

sue 3 beg **4** pray **5** plead **6** appeal **7** beseech, entreat, im-

plore **8** petition **9** importune
10 supplicate

Sue, Eugene (Marie-Joseph)
author of: **15** The Wandering
Jew **19** The Mysteries of
Paris

suffer 4 ache, bear, hurt, pine
5 stand **6** endure, grieve, lament **7** agonize, despair, drop
off, fall off, stomach, sustain,
undergo **8** bear with, feel
pain, tolerate **9** go through,
put up with, withstand **10** be
impaired **11** deteriorate

suffer for 6 pay for **8** atone
for **9** answer for

suffering 3 woe **4** ache, care,
hurt, pain, pang **5** agony, dolor, grief, throe, trial **6** misery,
sorrow, twinge **7** anguish,
anxiety, torment, torture, travail **8** distress, soreness
9 heartache **10** affliction, discomfort, heavy heart, irritation **11** tribulation

suffice 2 do **4** last, meet, pass
5 avail, get by, serve **6** answer, make do **7** fulfill, qualify, satisfy

sufficiency 6 enough, plenty
7 surfeit **8** adequacy **9** abundance, ampleness, profusion

sufficient 5 ample **6** enough,
plenty **7** copious, minimal
8 abundant, adequate **9** plenteous, plentiful **11** up to the
mark **12** satisfactory

suffocate 3 gag **5** choke
6 quench, stifle **7** garrote,
smother **8** snuff out, strangle,
throttle **10** asphyxiate,
extinguish

suffuse 4 fill, soak **5** cover,
steep **6** infuse **7** diffuse, overrun, pervade **8** overflow, permeate, saturate **9** transfuse
10 impregnate, infiltrate,
overspread

Sugar State
nickname of: **9** Louisiana

sugary 5 mushy, sweet **6** syrupy **7** cloying, fulsome, gushing, honeyed, mawkish
8 cajoling, unctuous **10** flattering, saccharine

suggest 3 bid **4** move, urge
5 imply, posit **6** advise, hint
at, submit **7** advance, counsel,
propose **8** advocate, indicate,
intimate, propound **9** give a
clue, recommend **16** lead one
to believe

suggested 6 hinted **7** implied,
oblique **8** implicit, indirect,
possible, proposed

suggestion 3 dab, tip **4** dash,
hint, tint **5** grain, shade, taste,

Sudan
capital/largest city: **8** Khartoum
others: **3** Waw, Yei **4** Juba **5** Kosti, Meroe, Nyala, Obeid,
Opari, Segon **6** Atbara, Suakin **7** Aluboyd, Elobeid, Ge-
neina, Kassala, Malakal **8** Elfasher, Omdurman **9** al-
Ubayyid, Elgeneina, Port Sudan, Wad Medani
division: **7** Jonglei **9** Upper Nile **12** Bahr el Ghazal
16 Eastern Equatoria, Western Equatoria
ancient kingdom: **4** Alwa, Funj, Kush **7** Maqurra
measure: **2** ud
monetary unit: **5** pound **8** piastres
weight: **5** habba
lake: **2** No **4** Chad, Toad **6** Nasser
mountain: **4** Nuba **7** Imatong **9** Dongotona **10** Jabal Marra,
Jebel Marra **18** Ethiopian Highlands
highest point: **7** Kinyeti
river: **4** Nile **5** Sobat **6** Atbara **8** Blue Nile **9** White Nile
10 Bahr el-Arab **11** Bahr el-Jebel **12** Bahr el-Ghazal
sea: **3** Red
physical feature:
desert: **6** Libyan, Nubian
gum forest: **8** Kordofan
plain: **6** Gezira
sandstorm: **6** haboob
plateau: **8** Kordufan
swamp: **4** Sudd
people: **3** Bor, Dor, Fur **4** Arab, Bari, Beri, Bobo, Daza,
Egba, Fula, Golo, Nuba, Nuer, Poul, Sere **5** Anuak,
Bongo, Dinka, Fulah, Hausa, Joluo, Junje, Mosgu, Mossi,
Negro, Tibbu, Volta **6** Acholi, Azande, Gurusi, Hamite,
Lotuho, Makari, Nilote, Nubian, Senufo, Surhai, Tuareg
7 Balante, Baqqara, Gubayna, Jaaliin, Nilotes, Shilluk,
Songhai, Songhay, Songhoi, Sourhai **8** Kababish, Mandingo, Menkiera **9** Sarakille **10** Gurmantshi, Shaiquiyya
leader: **5** Mahdi **9** al-Nimeiry **10** Mehemet Ali **22** Jaafar
Mohammed al-Nemery
language: **2** Ga **3** Efe, Ewe, Ibo, Kru, Vak, Vei **4** Efik,
Mole, Tshi **6** Arabic, Nubian, Yoruba **7** English **8** Mandango, Mandingo **9** Ta Bedawie
religion: **5** Islam **7** animism **12** Christianity
place:
canal: **7** Jonglei
dam: **6** Sennar **8** Roseires **10** Jebel Aulia
temple: **4** Lion
tomb: **5** Mahdi
feature:
boat: **6** murkab
food: **4** dura **5** dukhn, kisra

tinge, touch, trace **6** advice, urging **7** counsel, feeling, pointer, soupcon **9** prompting, suspicion **10** intimation, sprinkling **11** exhortation **14** recommendation

suggestive 4 lewd, racy **5** bawdy, loose **6** risque, sexual, wanton **8** allusive, improper, indecent, off-color, prurient, unseemly **9** evocative, remindful, seductive, shameless **10** expressive, indelicate, licentious **11** provocative, reminiscent, stimulating

sui generis 6 unique **12** of her own kind, of his own kind, of its own kind **14** of their own kind

sui juris 14 of one's own right **31** capable of managing one's own affairs **36** capable of assuming legal responsibility

suit 3 fit **4** duds, garb, plea, togs **5** befit, court, getup, habit, match **6** appeal, attire, become, beseem, follow, livery, oblige, outfit, please, prayer, wooing **7** apparel, begging, clothes, content, costume, delight, gladden, gratify, raiment, satisfy, uniform **8** clothing, entreaty, jell with, make glad, petition **9** addresses, agree with, conform to, courtship, do one good, overtures, tally with, trappings **10** accord with, attentions, comply with, fall in with, habiliment, lovemaking, square with **11** accommodate, go along with **12** be becoming to, blandishment, correspond to, dovetail with, solicitation, supplication **13** accoutrements, be agreeable to, harmonize with **14** be acceptable to, be convenient to **15** be appropriate to **16** be appropriate for

suitable 3 apt, fit **4** meet **5** right **6** proper, seemly, worthy **7** apropos, fitting, germane **8** adequate, becoming, relevant **9** befitting, congruous, cut out for, pertinent, qualified **10** applicable, seasonable **11** appropriate **12** commensurate

suitcase 3 bag **4** grip **6** valise **7** satchel **8** knapsack, rucksack **9** duffel bag, gladstone, two-suiter **11** portmanteau **12** overnight bag, traveling bag

suite 3 set **4** flat **5** chain, court, group, rooms, round **6** convoy, series **7** company, cortege, retinue **8** servants **9** apartment,

followers, following **10** attendants **11** progression

suited 3 fit **7** adapted, attired, clothed, dressed, good for, matched **8** adjusted, agreeing, becoming **9** agreeable **11** appropriate, harmonizing

suit of armor 4 mail **5** armor **9** chain mail **10** coat of mail

suitor 4 beau, love **5** flame, lover, swain, wooer **6** fellow **7** admirer, gallant **8** young man **9** boyfriend **10** sweetheart

sulfur
chemical symbol: 1 S

sulk 4 crab, fret, fume, mope, pout **5** brood, chafe, frown, grump, scowl **6** glower, grouch **7** grumble **8** be in a pet, be miffed, be put out, be sullen, look glum **9** be in a huff **11** be resentful **12** be out of humor

sulky 6 morose, sullen **7** pouting **8** petulant

sullen 4 blue, dark, glum, grim, sore, sour **5** cross, heavy, moody, sulky, surly **6** crabby, dismal, dreary, gloomy, grumpy, morose, somber, touchy **7** crabbed, doleful, forlorn, grouchy, peevish **8** brooding, desolate, dolorous, funereal, mournful, petulant, scowling **9** cheerless, glowering, resentful, saturnine, splenetic, unamiable **10** depressing, foreboding, ill-humored, ill-natured, melancholy, out of humor, out of sorts, unsociable **11** ill-tempered **13** temperamental
French: 8 farouche

sullied 5 dirty **6** impure, soiled **7** defiled, stained, unclean **9** tarnished

Sullivan, Elizabeth
real name of: 14 Elsa Lanchester

Sullivan, John Florence
real name of: 9 Fred Allen

Sullivan, John L (Lawrence)
nickname: 15 Boston Strong Boy
sport: 6 boxing
class: 11 heavyweight
fought: 12 bareknuckled

Sullivan, Louis H
architect of: 16 Guaranty (now Prudential) Building (Buffalo NY) **18** Auditorium Building (Chicago), Wainwright Building (St Louis MO) **21** Carson Pirie Scott Store (Chicago), Stock Exchange Building (Chicago), Merchants' National Bank (Grinnell, IA), National

Farmers' Bank (Owatonna, MN)
principle: 21 "form follows function"
student: 16 Frank Lloyd Wright

Sullivan, Pat
creator/artist of: 11 Felix the Cat

Sullivan's Travels
director: 14 Preston Sturges
cast: 10 Joel McCrea **12** Veronica Lake **13** Robert Warwick **15** William Demarest

sully 4 ruin, soil, spot **5** dirty, spoil, stain **6** befoul, defame, defile, smudge **7** begrime, besmear, blemish, corrupt, pollute, tarnish **8** disgrace, dishonor **10** adulterate **11** contaminate

Sully, Thomas
born: 7 England **10** Horncastle
artwork: 13 Queen Victoria **23** The Passage of the Delaware **28** Colonel Thomas Handasyd Perkins **29** Washington Crossing the Delaware

sultan 4 king **5** ruler **7** emperor, monarch **9** sovereign

sultana 5 grape **6** raisin **7** empress **11** sultan's wife

sultry 3 hot **4** sexy **5** close, humid, muggy **6** erotic, stuffy, sweaty **7** sensual **8** stifling **10** oppressive, sweltering, voluptuous **11** provocative, suffocating

sum 4 cash, coin, jack **5** bread, bucks, dough, funds, score, tally, whole **6** amount, moolah **7** lettuce, measure **8** currency, entirety, quantity, sum total, totality **9** aggregate, summation **12** entire amount **13** amount of money

sumac 4 Rhus
varieties: 5 dwarf, lemon, scrub, sugar, swamp **6** desert, laurel, poison, smooth, velvet **7** scarlet, shining, tanner's, tobacco, wing-rib **8** fragrant, lemonade, Sicilian, staghorn, Venetian **9** elm-leaved, evergreen, Virginian **11** small-leaved **12** sweet-scented

sum and substance 4 core, crux, gist, guts, meat **5** heart **7** essence **10** brass tacks **11** nitty-gritty

Sumatra
chevrotain: 4 napu
city: 5 Medan **6** Padang **9** Palembang
country: 9 Indonesia

crop: 3 tea **6** coffee, rubber
currency: 6 rupiah
empire: 9 Srivijaya
highest point: 10 Mt Kerintji
inhabitant: 5 Batak, Malay
11 Minangkabau
mountain range: 7 Barisan
river: 4 Musi, Siak **6** Asahan
squirrel shrew: 4 tana
strait: 5 Sunda **7** Malacca

Sumerian Mythology *see*
19 Babylonian Mythology

**Summa Catholicae Fidei
Contra Gentiles**
author: 13 Thomas Aquinas

summa cum laude 17 with
highest praise

Summanus
origin: 5 Roman
god of: 13 thunderstorms

summarily 6 at once
7 quickly **8** directly, promptly,
speedily **9** forthwith, on the
spot **11** arbitrarily, immediately, straightway **12** straightaway, with dispatch, without
delay **13** at short notice, precipitately **14** unhesitatingly
20 on the spur of the
moment

summarize 5 sum up **6** digest
7 abridge, outline **8** abstract,
compress, condense **9** capsul-
ize, epitomize, synopsize
10 abbreviate **11** concentrate
12 recapitulate

summary 4 curt **5** brief, hasty,
rapid, short, terse, token
6 apercu, digest, precis, resume, sketch, sudden, survey
7 concise, cursory, epitome,
hurried, rundown **8** abridged,
abstract, analysis, succinct, syllabus, synopsis **9** breakdown,
condensed **10** abridgment, peremptory **11** perfunctory
12 abbreviation, condensation,
short version **13** instantaneous

Summa Theologiae
author: 13 Thomas Aquinas

summation 5 total **6** review
7 summary **8** addition **9** reckoning **19** concluding
statement

Summer and Smoke
author: 17 Tennessee
Williams
director: 14 Peter Glenville
cast: 9 Una Merkel **10** Rita
Moreno **12** Earl Holliman
13 Geraldine Page **14** Laurence Harvey

summer fruit
goddess of: 5 Carpo

summerhouse 5 arbor, cabin,
kiosk **6** cabana, gazebo, pagoda **7** cottage

Summerson, Esther
character in: 10 Bleak House
author: 7 Dickens

Summertime
director: 9 David Lean
based on story by: 14 Arthur Laurents (The Time of
the Cuckoo)
cast: 10 Isa Miranda **13** Darren McGavin, Rossano
Brazzi **16** Katharine
Hepburn
setting: 6 Venice

summery 3 hot **4** warm
5 balmy, close, humid, muggy,
sunny **6** stuffy, sultry, torrid,
vernal **8** aestival, roasting, stifling, sunshiny **9** scorching,
temperate **10** oppressive,
summerlike

summit 3 tip, top **4** acme,
apex, peak **5** crest, crown
6 apogee, climax, height, vertex, zenith **8** pinnacle **11** culmination **12** highest point
13 crowning point

summon 4 call **5** rouse
6 beckon, call on, draw on,
gather, invoke, muster, strain
7 call for, call out, command,
send for **8** activate, subpoena
9 call forth **12** call together
14 call into action, serve with
a writ

summons 4 call **8** citation,
subpoena **12** notification

summon up 4 stir **5** evoke
6 arouse, excite **7** collect, marshal, provoke **8** assemble **9** call
forth, stimulate

summum bonum 9 chief
good **11** highest good

sumptuous 4 dear, posh, rich
5 grand, plush, regal **6** costly,
deluxe, lavish, superb **7** elegant **8** splendid **9** elaborate,
expensive, luxurious **10** exorbitant, munificent **11** extravagant, magnificent, spectacular

sumptuousness 4 luxe **6** luxury **8** elegance, grandeur, richness, splendor
12 magnificence **13** expensive-
ness, luxuriousness

sum total 6 amount **8** totality
9 aggregate **11** final result

sum up 3 add **5** tally, total, tot
up **6** reckon **7** compute, count
up **9** calculate, enumerate,
summarize

sun
god of: 2 Ra, Re **3** Sol, Utu
5 Horus **6** Apollo, Helios
7 Shamesh **8** Hyperion

Sun Also Rises, The
author: 15 Ernest Hemingway

character: 10 Bill Gorton,
Jake Barnes, Robert Cohn
11 Pedro Romero **15** Lady
Brett Ashley, Michael (Mike)
Campbell

sunbathe 3 tan **4** bask **12** soak
up the sun **13** catch some
rays

Sunday
means: 11 day of the sun
heavenly body: 3 sun
day of: 4 rest **7** worship
8 blue laws
observance: 16 Christian
Sabbath
French: 8 dimanche
Italian: 8 domenica
Spanish: 7 domingo
German: 7 sonntag

Sunday best 6 finery **8** glad
rags **11** fine clothes **16** best
bib and tucker

Sunday Morning
author: 14 Wallace Stevens

sunder 4 rend, rive **5** crack,
sever **6** cleave, divide **8** separate **9** tear apart **10** break in
two **11** break in half

sundown 4 dusk **6** sunset
7 evening **8** eventide, twilight
9 nightfall

Sundowners, The
director: 13 Fred Zinnemann
cast: 11 Deborah Kerr, Dina
Merrill, Glynis Johns **12** Peter Ustinov **13** Robert
Mitchum
setting: 9 Australia

sundry 4 many **5** mixed **6** divers, motley, myriad, varied
7 diverse, several, various
8 assorted, manifold, numerous **9** different **10** dissimilar
12 multifarious **13** heterogeneous, miscellaneous

sun-filled 4 fair **5** clear, sunny
6 bright, cheery **8** cheerful
9 cloudless

sunfish 5 dwarf, perch, pigmy,
sunny **6** redear **7** lepomis,
longear, teleost **8** bluegill, sailboat **9** blackband **10** Sacramento **11** bluespotted,
centrarchid, pumpkinseed,
yellowbelly

sunflower 10 Helianthus
12 Balsamorhiza
varieties: 4 ashy **5** giant,
showy, stiff, swamp **6** common, desert, Oregon **7** dark-
eye, Mexican **8** thin-leaf
10 Maximilian **12** cucumber-
leaf

Sunflower State
nickname of: 6 Kansas

sunless 4 dark, dull, gray,

hazy **5** bleak, foggy, misty, murky, rainy **6** cloudy, dismal, dreary, gloomy, leaden, somber **8** overcast **9** cheerless **10** depressing

sunny 4 fair, fine **5** clear, happy, jolly, merry **6** blithe, breezy, bright, cheery, genial, jovial, joyful, joyous, sunlit **7** affable, amiable, buoyant, shining, smiling **8** cheerful, sunshiny **9** brilliant, cloudless, sparkling, unclouded **10** optimistic **12** lighthearted

sunrise 4 dawn **5** sunup **6** aurora **7** dawning **8** cockcrow, daybreak, daylight **10** break of day, crepuscule, newborn day **15** dawn's early light **16** rosy-fingered dawn

sunset 4 dusk **7** sundown **8** blue hour, eventide, gloaming, twilight **9** nightfall **10** close of day, crepuscule

Sunset Boulevard
  director: **11** Billy Wilder
  cast: **8** Jack Webb **9** Fred Clark **11** Hedda Hopper **12** Buster Keaton **13** Cecil B DeMille, Gloria Swanson (Norma Desmond), William Holden **16** Erich von Stroheim

Sunset State
  nickname of: **6** Oregon

sunshade 3 hat **5** visor **6** awning **7** parasol, roundel **8** sombrero, umbrella **9** sunscreen

Sunshine State
  nickname of: **7** Florida **9** New Mexico

sunstone
  species: **8** feldspar

suntan 3 tan **5** brown **6** bronze **7** sunburn

suo jure 14 in one's own right

suo loco 14 in one's own place **19** in one's rightful place

Suomen Tasavalta *see* **7** Finland

Suomi *see* **7** Finland

sup 3 eat, sip **4** dine, feed **5** drink, feast, supra **6** absorb, supper, supply **7** consume **8** superior **10** supplement **11** superlative **13** supplementary

Supai *see* **9** Havasupai

super 4 A-one, fine **5** grand, great, prime, prize, swell **6** grade-A, superb, tip-top **7** capital **8** peerless, superior, terrific, top-notch **9** excellent, fantastic, first-rate, marvelous,

matchless, non pareil, superfine, wonderful **10** first-class, tremendous, unexcelled, world-class **11** outstanding, superlative **12** incomparable **13** extraordinary

superabound 4 teem **5** swarm **6** thrive **7** burgeon **8** be rich in, flourish, overflow

superabundance 4 glut, riot **5** flood, spate **6** deluge, excess, plenty **7** surfeit, surplus **8** overdose, overflow, pleonasm, plethora **9** avalanche **10** inundation, oversupply, redundance **11** superfluity **12** extravagance **13** overabundance **14** more than enough
  French: 19 embarras de richesses

superabundant 4 lush **6** lavish **7** copious, profuse, teeming **8** swarming, thriving **9** exuberant, luxuriant **10** burgeoning **11** flourishing, overflowing

superb 4 A-one, rare, rich **5** elect, grand, regal **6** choice, costly, deluxe, golden, lordly, select, tip-top **7** elegant, stately **8** gorgeous, imposing, laudable, majestic, peerless, precious, princely, splendid, top-notch, very fine **9** admirable, excellent, expensive, exquisite, first-rate, luxurious, marvelous, matchless, priceless, sumptuous, top-drawer **10** first-class **11** crackerjack, magnificent **12** breathtaking, praiseworthy **15** of the first water

Super Bowl *see box, p. 948*

supercilious 5 proud **6** lordly, snooty, uppity **7** haughty, pompous, stuck-up **8** arrogant, prideful, snobbish **10** disdainful **11** egotistical, magisterial, overbearing, patronizing **12** vainglorious **13** condescending, high-and-mighty, self-important

superciliousness 4 airs **7** hauteur **8** snobbery **9** arrogance, pomposity **10** lordliness, snootiness **11** haughtiness **12** snobbishness **14** disdainfulness

superficial 4 slim **5** faint, outer, silly, trite **6** flimsy, hollow, myopic, slight **7** cursory, minimal, nodding, partial, passing, shallow, summary, surface **8** exterior, mindless, skin-deep **9** desultory, frivolous **10** incomplete **11** empty-headed, perfunctory **12** lacking depth, narrow-minded, on the surface, shortsighted

superficiality 6 myopia **9** frivolity **11** cursoriness, shallowness **13** desultoriness **16** narrow-mindedness, shortsightedness

superfine 4 A-one **6** choice, grade-A, superb, tip-top **8** superior, top-notch **9** excellent, extra fine, first-rate **10** first-class **11** outstanding, overrefined, superlative **13** extraordinary

superfluity 3 fat **5** extra, frill **6** excess, luxury **7** greater, surfeit, surplus **8** overflow, overmuch, plethora **11** gingerbread **12** extravagance **13** embellishment **14** superabundance

superfluous 5 extra, spare **6** excess **7** surplus **8** needless **9** excessive, redundant **10** extraneous, gratuitous, pleonastic **11** inessential, unnecessary **12** nonessential, overgenerous **13** superabundant, supernumerary **14** supererogatory

superhuman 4 epic **5** great **6** divine, heroic **7** godlike, supreme **8** superior **9** herculean, unearthly **10** miraculous, omnipotent **12** otherworldly, supermundane, supernatural, supranatural, transcendent **13** preternatural

Superi
  origin: **5** Roman
  collective name for: **4** gods

superintend 3 run **4** boss **6** direct, govern, manage **7** oversee **9** supervise, watch over **10** administer **12** administrate, have charge of

superintendence 6 charge **7** bossing, running **9** direction, governing **10** leadership, management, overseeing **12** jurisdiction **14** administration

superintendent 4 boss, head **5** chief **6** warden **7** foreman, headman, manager, proctor, steward **8** director, guardian, overseer **9** custodian **10** supervisor

superior 4 boss, fine **5** chief **6** better, choice, deluxe, leader, lordly, senior **7** greater, haughty, notable **8** arrogant, foremost, higher-up, peerless, snobbish **9** commander, excellent, first-rate, imperious, matchless, nonpareil, unrivaled **10** inimitable, noteworthy, preeminent, supervisor **11** exceptional, illustrious, patronizing **12** incomparable, more advanced, vainglorious

Super Bowl

1967:
winner: **15** Green Bay Packers
loser: **16** Kansas City Chiefs
site: **8** Coliseum **10** Los Angeles

1968:
winner: **15** Green Bay Packers
loser: **14** Oakland Raiders
site: **5** Miami **10** Orange Bowl

1969:
winner: **11** New York Jets
loser: **14** Baltimore Colts
site: **5** Miami **10** Orange Bowl

1970:
winner: **16** Kansas City Chiefs
loser: **16** Minnesota Vikings
site: **10** New Orleans **13** Tulane Stadium

1971:
winner: **14** Baltimore Colts
loser: **13** Dallas Cowboys
site: **5** Miami **10** Orange Bowl

1972:
winner: **13** Dallas Cowboys
loser: **13** Miami Dolphins
site: **10** New Orleans **13** Tulane Stadium

1973:
winner: **13** Miami Dolphins
loser: **18** Washington Redskins
site: **8** Coliseum **10** Los Angeles

1974:
winner: **13** Miami Dolphins
loser: **16** Minnesota Vikings
site: **7** Houston **11** Rice Stadium

1975:
winner: **18** Pittsburgh Steelers
loser: **16** Minnesota Vikings
site: **10** New Orleans **13** Tulane Stadium

1976:
winner: **18** Pittsburgh Steelers
loser: **13** Dallas Cowboys
site: **5** Miami **10** Orange Bowl

1977:
winner: **14** Oakland Raiders
loser: **16** Minnesota Vikings
site: **8** Pasadena, Rose Bowl

1978:
winner: **13** Dallas Cowboys
loser: **13** Denver Broncos
site: **9** Superdome **10** New Orleans

1979:
winner: **18** Pittsburgh Steelers
loser: **13** Dallas Cowboys
site: **5** Miami **10** Orange Bowl

1980:
winner: **18** Pittsburgh Steelers
loser: **14** Los Angeles Rams
site: **8** Pasadena, Rose Bowl

1981:
winner: **14** Oakland Raiders
loser: **18** Philadelphia Eagles
site: **9** Superdome **10** New Orleans

1982:
winner: **23** San Francisco Forty-Niners
loser: **17** Cincinnati Bengals
site: **7** Pontiac **10** Silverdome

1983:
winner: **18** Washington Redskins
loser: **13** Miami Dolphins
site: **8** Pasadena, Rose Bowl

1984:
winner: **17** Los Angeles Raiders
loser: **18** Washington Redskins
site: **12** Tampa Stadium

1985:
winner: **23** San Francisco Forty-Niners
loser: **13** Miami Dolphins
site: **8** Palo Alto **15** Stanford Stadium

1986:
winner: **12** Chicago Bears
loser: **18** New England Patriots
site: **9** Superdome **10** New Orleans

1987:
winner: **13** New York Giants
loser: **13** Denver Broncos
site: **8** Pasadena, Rose Bowl

1988:
winner: **18** Washington Redskins
loser: **13** Denver Broncos
site: **8** San Diego **17** Jack Murphy Stadium

1989:
winner: **23** San Francisco Forty-Niners
loser: **17** Cincinnati Bengals
site: **5** Miami **16** Joe Robbie Stadium

1990:
winner: **23** San Francisco Forty-Niners
loser: **13** Denver Broncos
site: **9** Superdome **10** New Orleans

1991:
winner: **13** New York Giants
loser: **12** Buffalo Bills
site: **5** Tampa **12** Tampa Stadium

1992:
winner: **18** Washington Redskins
loser: **12** Buffalo Bills
site: **9** Metrodome **11** Minneapolis

1993:
winner: **13** Dallas Cowboys
loser: **12** Buffalo Bills
site: **8** Pasadena, Rose Bowl

1994:
winner: **13** Dallas Cowboys
loser: **12** Buffalo Bills
site: **7** Atlanta **11** Georgia Dome

1995:
winner: **23** San Francisco Forty-Niners
loser: **16** San Diego Chargers
site: **5** Miami **16** Joe Robbie Stadium

1996:
winner: **13** Dallas Cowboys
loser: **18** Pittsburgh Steelers
site: **5** Tempe **7** Arizona **15** Sun Devil Stadium

13 condescending, distinguished, high-and-mighty
French: 13 par excellence

superlative 4 best **5** crack, prime **6** expert **7** supreme **8** foremost, greatest, peerless, superior **9** exquisite, first-rate, matchless, nonpareil, paramount, unequaled, unmatched, unrivaled **10** consummate, preeminent, surpassing **11** magnificent, unsurpassed **12** incomparable, transcendent, unparalleled **15** of the first water **17** of the highest order

superman
German: 10 Ubermensch

Superman
creator: 11 Jerry Siegel
character: 4 Lara **5** Jor-el, Kal-el **8** Eben Kent, Lois Lane, Sy Horton **9** Clark Kent **10** Jimmy Olsen, Martha Kent, Perry White
place: 7 Krypton **10** Metropolis, Smallville
nickname: 10 Man of Steel

supernatural 6 mystic, occult **7** psychic **9** spiritual, unearthly **10** miraculous, paranormal

superpatriotism 8 jingoism **10** chauvinism **11** nationalism

supersede 7 discard, replace, succeed **8** displace, set aside, supplant

supervise 4 boss, head **5** guide **6** direct, govern, handle, manage, survey **7** conduct, control, oversee **8** regulate **9** look after, watch over **10** administer

supervision 6 orders **7** control **8** guidance **9** direction **10** governance, government, management, regulation **12** surveillance **15** superintendence

supervisor 4 boss, head **5** chief **7** foreman, manager, steward **8** director, overseer **9** commander **13** administrator **14** superintendent

supper club 4 cafe **6** bistro **7** cabaret **9** nightclub, night spot

supplant 6 depose **7** replace **8** displace **9** supersede **14** take the place of

supple 5 lithe **6** limber, pliant **7** elastic, lissome, plastic, pliable **8** amenable, bendable, flexible, graceful, yielding **9** adaptable, compliant, malleable, tractable **10** submissive

supplement 5 add to, annex, extra, rider **6** extend, insert **7** adjunct, augment, codicil, section **8** addendum, addition,

appendix, increase **9** added part, corollary, extension **10** attachment, complement, postscript **12** augmentation

supplementary 5 added, extra **6** backup **7** added on, reserve **8** appended, attached, expanded, extended **9** ancillary, auxiliary, enlarging, secondary **10** additional, amplifying, augmenting **11** subordinate

suppliant 5 asker **6** beggar, cadger, seeker, suitor **7** almsman **8** claimant **9** almswoman, appellant, beseecher, entreater, mendicant **10** petitioner, supplicant **11** supplicator

supplicate 3 ask, beg **4** pray **5** plead **6** ask for **7** entreat **8** appeal to, call upon, petition

supplication 3 cry **4** plea, suit **6** appeal, orison, prayer **7** bumming, cadging, request **8** entreaty, mooching, petition **10** invocation **11** application, beseechment, imploration, imprecation, panhandling

supplies 4 gear **5** goods, items **8** material **9** equipment, foodstuff, trappings **10** provisions

supply 4 fund, give **5** cache, equip, grant, quota, stock, store, yield **6** bestow, outfit, render **7** deal out, deliver, furnish, present, provide, reserve **9** providing, provision, reservoir **10** allocation, come up with, contribute, furnishing

support 3 aid **4** base, bear, help, hold, keep, lift, pile, post, prop, stay **5** abide, boost, brace, brook, carry, favor, means, shore, stand **6** assist, back up, bear up, clinch, column, defend, endure, foster, hold up, pay for, pillar, ratify, second, succor, suffer, uphold, upkeep, verify **7** backing, bear out, bolster, comfort, confirm, defense, endorse, espouse, finance, further, keeping, nurture, shore up, sustain, warrant **8** abutment, accredit, advocacy, advocate, buttress, champion, espousal, maintain, pedestal, pilaster, sanction, strength, tolerate, vouch for **9** establish, guarantee, patronage, patronize, promotion, put up with, reinforce, stanchion, subsidize **10** assistance, livelihood, provide for, stand up for, stick up for, strengthen, sustenance, underwrite

supportable 9 endurable **10** defensible, verifiable **11** sustainable **12** demonstrable, maintainable

supporter 4 ally **6** backer, helper, patron **8** adherent, advocate, champion, defender, disciple, follower, partisan, upholder **10** benefactor, wellwisher **11** sympathizer

supposable 8 credible **9** thinkable **10** believable, imaginable **11** conceivable, perceivable

suppose 5 fancy, guess, judge, posit **6** assume, divine, gather, reckon **7** believe, imagine, presume, surmise, suspect **8** conceive, consider **9** predicate **11** hypothesize **14** take for granted

supposed 5 given **7** alleged, assumed **8** probable, putative **9** imaginary **11** conjectural, speculative, theoretical **12** hypothetical

supposition 4 idea, view **5** given, guess **6** belief, notion, theory, thesis **7** opinion, surmise **9** guesswork, postulate, suspicion **10** assumption, conjecture, hypothesis **11** predication, presumption, proposition, speculation

suppress 4 bury, curb, hide **5** check, crush, quash, quell, still **6** keep in, muffle, quench, squash, stifle, subdue **7** conceal, control, cover up, inhibit, put down, repress, silence, smother, squelch **8** hold back, keep back, overcome, restrain, restrict, snuff out, withhold **9** overpower **10** extinguish, keep secret, put an end to

suppressant 4 curb **5** brake **7** control **9** restraint

supremacy 5 power **7** mastery, primacy **10** ascendancy, domination, precedence **11** omnipotence, paramountcy, preeminence, sovereignty, superiority **13** transcendency

supreme 4 tops **5** chief, first, prime **6** ruling **7** extreme, highest, leading, perfect, topmost **8** absolute, dominant, foremost, peerless **9** matchless, nonpareil, paramount, principal, sovereign, unequaled, unlimited, unmatched, unrivaled, uppermost **10** commanding, consummate, unexcelled **11** all-powerful, superlative, unqualified, unsurpassed

Supreme Court
Chief Justices: 3 Jay (John) **4** Taft (William Howard) **5** Chase (Salmon), Stone (Harlan Fiske), Taney (Roger Brooke), Waite (Morrison), White (Edward) **6** Burger (Warren), Fuller (Melville), Hughes (Charles Evans),

Vinson (Frederick), Warren (Earl) **8** Marshall (John), Rutledge (John) **9** Ellsworth (Oliver), Rehnquist (William)
Associate Justices: 5 Black (Hugo), Story (Joseph), White (Byron) **6** Breyer (Stephen), Fortas (Abe), Holmes (Oliver Wendell), Powell (Lewis), Scalia (Antonin), Souter (David), Thomas (Clarence) **7** Brennan (William), Cardozo (Benjamin), Douglas (William O), Kennedy (Anthony), O'Connor (Sandra Day), Stevens (John), Stewart (Potter) **8** Blackmun (Harry), Brandeis (Louis), Ginsburg (Ruth Bader), Goldberg (Arthur), Marshall (Thurgood) **11** Frankfurter (Felix)
Cases: 15 Marbury v Madison **17** Gideon v Wainwright **18** McCulloch v Maryland **20** Griswold v Connecticut
abortion: **8** Roe v Wade
antitrust: **8** E C Knight **11** Standard Oil **15** Swift and Company **22** American Tobacco Company
civil rights: **9** Bakke Case **15** Plessy v Ferguson **30** Brown v Board of Education of Topeka
Japanese internment: **22** Korematsu v United States **24** Hirabayashi v United States
rights of accused: **15** Miranda v Arizona **17** Escobedo v Illinois
slavery: **13** Dred Scott Case **14** Scott v Sandford

surcease 4 quit, rest, stop **5** abate, cease, pause **7** die away, respite **8** conclude, leave off **11** come to an end, discontinue **17** come to a standstill

surcharge 3 tax **4** levy **6** excise, impost

surcingle 4 band, belt **5** girth **6** girdle **8** cincture

sure 4 fast, firm, true **5** solid, sound **6** stable, steady **7** assured, certain **8** accurate, failsafe, faithful, flawless, positive, reliable, surefire, unerring **9** confident, convinced, unfailing **10** dependable, infallible, undoubting **11** trustworthy **12** never-failing

surely 7 no doubt **8** of course, to be sure **9** assuredly, certainly, doubtless **10** by all means, definitely, for certain, infallibly, positively

sureness 6 surety **9** assurance, certainty, certitude **10** confidence **11** assuredness **12** positiveness **13** self-assurance

---

Suriname
other name: 7 Surinam **11** Dutch Guiana
capital/largest city: 10 Paramaribo
others: 6 Albina **7** Totness **9** Groningen **10** Brokopondo, Onverwacht **13** Nieuw Nickerie **14** Nieuw Amsterdam
measure: 7 ketting
monetary unit: 4 cent **7** guilder
lake: 14 Van Blommestein
mountain: 4 Emma **6** Kayser, Oranje **10** Tumuc-Humac, Wilhelmina **13** Eilerts Il Haan, Van Ach Van Wyck **15** Guiana Highlands
highest point: 10 Julianatop
river: 6 Maroni **7** Surinam **8** Nickerie, Suriname **9** Coppename **10** Courantijn, Courantyne, Tapanahoni
ocean: 8 Atlantic
physical feature:
  falls: **7** Kaiteur
people: 4 Boni, Bush, Trio **5** Djuka, Dutch **6** Creole, Wayana **7** African, Chinese **10** Amerindian, Boschneger, West Indian **11** Asian Indian
  settler: **22** Lord Willoughby of Parham
language: 5 Carib, Dutch, Hindi **6** Arawak **7** English **8** Javanese, Taki-Taki **10** Hindustani **11** Sranan Tongo **12** Sranang Tongo
religion: 5 Hindu, Islam **10** Protestant **13** Roman Catholic
feature:
  canoe: **6** corial
  clothing: **4** sari **5** dhoti **6** kamisa, sarong **10** koto-missie
  hat: **3** fez
  hut: **5** benab
  scarf: **9** selendong
  tree: **4** dali, lana, mora **5** dalli, genip, icica **7** acuyari, quassia **9** bethabara
food:
  drink: **7** paiwari

---

sure thing 4 fact **5** cinch **7** reality, sure bet **9** actuality, certainty **13** inevitability

surety 4 bail, bond **8** sureness **9** certainty, certitude, guarantee **10** confidence **12** positiveness

surface 3 top **4** coat, face, skin **5** crust, shell **6** facade, finish, veneer **7** coating, outside **8** covering, exterior **11** superficies

surfeit 4 cloy, glut, sate **5** gorge, stuff **6** excess **7** satiate, satisfy, surplus **8** overmuch, plethora **9** plenitude, profusion, repletion, satiation **10** oversupply, surplusage

surfeited 4 full **5** sated **6** gorged **7** glutted, replete, stuffed **8** overfull, satiated **9** satisfied

surge 4 rush, wave **5** flood, swell **7** torrent

Suriname *see box*

surliness 8 ill humor, rudeness **9** bad temper **11** discourtesy, grouchiness **12** irascibility

surly 4 rude, sour **5** cross, gruff, harsh, testy **6** abrupt, crusty, grumpy, sullen, touchy **7** bearish, crabbed, grouchy, hostile, peevish, uncivil, waspish **8** choleric, churlish, insolent, petulant, snappish, snarling **9** irascible, splenetic, unamiable **10** ill-humored, ill-natured, unfriendly **11** bad-tempered **12** discourteous

surmise 4 deem, idea **5** guess, infer, judge, opine, posit, think **6** belief, notion **7** believe, imagine, opinion, presume, suppose, suspect, thought **8** conclude, consider, theorize **9** suspicion **10** assumption, conjecture, hypothesis, presuppose **11** hypothesize, presumption, speculation, supposition **13** shot in the dark

surmount 3 top **4** best **5** clear, climb, scale, worst **6** defeat, master **7** conquer, get over **8** overcome, vanquish **11** prevail over, triumph over

surpass 3 top **4** beat, best **5** excel, outdo **6** exceed, outrun

7 eclipse **8** go beyond, outclass, outshine, outstrip, override **9** rise above, transcend **10** overshadow **11** go one better, leave behind, outdistance, triumph over **12** be better than, be superior to

surplus 4 glut **5** extra **6** excess **7** overage, surfeit **8** leftover, overflow, plethora, residual **10** oversupply, surplusage **11** superfluity, superfluous

surprise 4 stun **5** amaze, shock **6** ambush, wonder **7** astound, nonplus, set upon, stagger, startle, stupefy **8** astonish, confound, discover, dumfound, fall upon **9** amazement, bombshell, burst in on, dumbfound, take aback **10** defy belief, pounce upon, revelation, wonderment

surprise attack
   French: 10 coup de main

surrender 4 cede **5** forgo, let go, waive, yield **6** accede, forego, give up, render, submit, vacate **7** abandon, concede, forsake **8** delivery, forgoing, give over, giving up, hand over, part with, renounce, turn over, yielding **9** deliver up, foregoing **10** capitulate, relinquish, submission **11** lay down arms

surreptitious 6 covert, hidden, secret, veiled **7** furtive **8** hush-hush, stealthy **9** concealed, secretive **10** undercover **11** clandestine

surrogate 6 acting, deputy **7** interim, stand-in **9** temporary **10** substitute **11** provisional

surround 4 belt, ring **5** hedge, hem in **6** circle, enfold, engird, girdle, shut in **7** close in, compass, enclose, envelop, fence in, hedge in **8** encircle **9** encompass **12** circumscribe

surrounding area 7 suburbs **8** environs, vicinity **9** outskirts, precincts

surroundings 5 scene **6** milieu **7** habitat, setting **8** ambience, environs **10** atmosphere, conditions **11** environment **13** circumstances
   French: 11 mise en scene

Surt
   origin: 12 Scandinavian
   ruler of: 10 Muspelheim

surveillance 5 vigil, watch **8** scrutiny, trailing **11** observation **13** eavesdropping

survey 4 plot, poll, scan **5** gauge, graph, plumb, probe, scout, study **6** fathom, review **7** canvass, delimit, examine, inspect, measure, observe

8 analysis, block out, consider, look over, overview **10** scrutinize **11** contemplate, reconnoiter **12** pass in review **13** investigation

survival 5 relic **6** living **7** atavism, vestige **8** hangover **9** carry-over, throwback **11** subsistence **12** continuation, keeping alive

survive 4 last **5** abide, exist **6** endure, hang on, live on **7** hold out, outlast, outlive, persist, prevail, subsist **8** be extant, continue **9** keep alive **11** live through

surviving 6 extant **7** abiding, lasting **8** enduring, existent, existing, living on **9** hanging on, outliving, to be found **10** continuing, holding out, outlasting, persistent, persisting, subsisting **11** in existence **13** living through

Susanna
   husband: 6 Joakim
   accused of: 8 adultery
   saved by: 6 Daniel

susceptible 4 open **5** prone **7** alive to, subject **8** liable to, sensible **9** sensitive **10** disposed to, responsive, vulnerable **11** conducive to, receptive to, sensitive to, sympathetic

suspect 5 doubt, fancy, guess, judge, opine, posit, think **7** believe, imagine, presume, suppose, surmise **8** distrust, misdoubt, mistrust, question, theorize **9** speculate **10** conjecture **11** hypothesize, wonder about **14** alleged culprit, be suspicious of **19** have one's doubts about

suspend 4 halt, hang, quit, stay, stop **5** cease, check, defer, delay, sling, swing, table **6** append, arrest, dangle, put off, shelve **7** reserve **8** break off, cut short, leave off, postpone, withhold **9** interrupt, stop short **10** put an end to **11** discontinue **12** bring to a stop **18** bring to a standstill

suspenders 6 braces, straps **7** gallows, garters, hangers **8** elastics, galluses **10** supporters

suspense 7 anxiety, tension **8** edginess **9** curiosity **10** indecision **11** expectation, incertitude, uncertainty **12** anticipation **15** indetermination

suspenseful 7 anxious **8** dramatic, exciting **9** climactic, uncertain

suspension 4 stay **5** pause **6** hiatus, recess **7** tabling **8** abey-

ance, deferral **12** postponement **14** discontinuance

suspicion 4 idea **5** guess, hunch **6** notion **7** feeling, surmise **8** distrust, mistrust **10** conjecture, hypothesis **11** supposition

suspicious 4 wary **5** shady **7** dubious, suspect **8** doubtful, doubting, slippery **9** ambiguous **10** untrusting **11** distrustful, incredulous, mistrustful, open to doubt **12** disbelieving, questionable **13** untrustworthy

sustain 4 bear, feed, prop **5** abide, brave, brook, stand **6** bear up, endure, hold up, keep up, suffer, uphold **7** nourish, nurture, prolong, support, undergo **8** maintain, protract, tolerate, underpin **9** keep alive, withstand **10** experience

sustenance 4 food, gear **5** bread, means **6** living **7** aliment, support **9** provender **10** provisions **11** maintenance, nourishment, subsistence
   heaven-sent: 5 manna

sustineo alas 16 I sustain the wings
   motto of: 10 US Air Force

Suva
   capital of: 4 Fiji

svelte 4 fine, lean, neat, slim, thin, trim **5** lithe, spare **7** elegant, lissome, shapely, slender, willowy **8** graceful **9** sylphlike

Svengali
   character in: 6 Trilby
   author: 9 Du Maurier

swab 3 dab, mop **4** daub, lout, wipe **5** clean, cloth, patch, scrub **6** cotton, sponge **7** cleanse **8** specimen
   brand name: 4 Q-tip

swagger 5 strut, sweep **6** parade, sashay, stride **7** saunter **11** swashbuckle

swaggerer 6 gascon **7** boaster, bragger **8** blowhard, braggart, strutter **11** braggadocio

swain 4 beau **6** fellow, suitor **7** admirer, gallant **8** cavalier, young man **9** boyfriend **10** sweetheart

swallow 3 bit, nip, sip **4** down, gulp, swig **5** drink, quaff, swill, taste **6** credit, devour, gobble, guzzle, hold in, imbibe, ingest, tipple **7** believe, fall for, repress **8** gulp down, hold back, keep back, mouthful, suppress, withhold

swallow up 5 drown, eat up, swamp **6** absorb, engulf **7** consume, envelop **8** inundate **9** overwhelm **10** assimilate

swallow words 6 mumble, mutter

swamp 3 bog, fen **4** fill, mire, moor, ooze, quag, sink, slew, slue **5** bayou, beset, flood, marsh, swale **6** deluge, engulf, morass, slough **7** besiege, bottoms, envelop **8** inundate, quagmire, submerge, wash over **9** everglade, marshland, overwhelm, snow under, swallow up

swamped 7 deluged, flooded, glutted, overrun **9** inundated **11** overwhelmed

Swan
constellation of: **6** Cygnus

swan
young: **6** cygnet
group of: **4** bevy

swank 4 airs **5** ritzy **6** la-di-da, snooty, swanky **9** high-class, top-drawer **11** pretensions, pretentious **12** affectations, ostentatious **15** pretentiousness **16** superciliousness

swanky 4 chic, posh, rich **5** fancy, grand, jazzy, plush, ritzy, sharp, showy, smart, swank **6** flashy, snazzy, spiffy, sporty **7** dashing, elegant, splashy, stylish **9** sumptuous **11** fashionable

Swan Lake
composer: **11** Tchaikovsky

Swanson, Gloria
real name: **25** Gloria Josephine Mae Swenson
born: **9** Chicago IL
husband: **12** Wallace Beery
roles: **13** Sadie Thompson, The Trespasser **15** Sunset Boulevard

swap 5 trade **6** barter, dicker, switch **7** bargain **8** exchange **11** give and take

sward 3 sod **4** lawn, rind, skin, turf **5** grass

swarm 4 herd, host, mass, rush, teem **5** cloud, crowd, drove, flock, horde, press, surge **6** abound, legion, myriad, stream, throng **7** cluster, overrun **8** stampede **9** multitude

swarthy 4 dark **5** dusky, swart, tawny **6** brunet **8** brunette **11** dark-skinned **12** brown-colored, brown-skinned, olive-skinned **14** dark-complected **16** dark-complexioned

swashbuckler 9 buccaneer, daredevil **10** adventurer

swashbuckling 4 bold **7** dash-

ing **8** boasting **9** audacious, daredevil

swat 3 hit, tap **4** bash, belt, slam, slap, slug, sock **5** clout, knock, smack, smite, whack **6** buffet, strike, thwack, wallop **7** clobber

swathe 4 bind, wrap **5** cloak, cover **6** encase, enfold, enwrap **7** envelop, sheathe, swaddle

sway 4 bend, grip, hold, lead, list, move, reel, rock, roll, rule, spur, vary, wave **5** alter, clout, impel, power, reign, rouse, shift, swing, waver **6** change, domain, incite, induce, prompt, swerve, totter, waving, wobble **7** command, control, dispose, mastery, stagger, swaying **8** hesitate, iron hand, motivate, persuade, swinging, to-and-fro, undulate **9** authority, direction, encourage, fluctuate, influence, oscillate, pendulate, pulsation, stimulate, vacillate **10** domination, government, predispose, suzerainty, undulation **11** fluctuation, oscillation **12** back and forth, dictatorship, jurisdiction, manipulation

Swaziland *see box*

swear 3 vow **4** aver, avow, cuss **5** curse, vouch **6** adjure, assert, attest, pledge **7** certify, promise, warrant **9** blaspheme **10** take an oath, utter oaths **11** bear witness

swear by 7 believe, count on **9** believe in **10** put faith in

sweat 4 ooze, toil **5** exude, worry **6** effort **7** agonize **8** drudgery, hard work, perspire **9** exudation **12** perspiration

sweaty 3 wet **6** clammy, sticky **10** perspiring

Sweden *see box*

Swedish Punch
type: **7** liqueur
origin: **6** Sweden
base: **3** rum
with gin: **5** Biffy
with vermouth: **9** Grand Slam

Sweeney Among the Nightingales
author: **7** T S Eliot

sweep 3 arc, fly **4** dart, dash, race, rush, scud, tear, zoom **5** hurry, spell, swing, swish, swoop, whisk **6** charge, gather, scurry, stroke **7** stretch **8** distance

sweeping 5 broad **7** blanket, radical **9** extensive, out-and-out, wholesale **10** exhaustive, large-scale, widespread **11** far-reaching, wide-ranging **12** all-inclusive **13** comprehensive, thoroughgoing

sweepings 4 dirt, dust **6** refuse

sweep off one's feet 7 enchant **8** bedazzle **9** captivate, overpower, overwhelm

Swaziland
capital/largest city: **7** Mbabane
others: **5** Bunya, Hluti, Mpaka, Nsoko, Stegi **6** Gollel, Mhlume **7** Big Bend, Lobamba, Manzini **8** Havelock, Malkerns **9** Geodgegun, Hlatikulu, Mankaiana, Mankayana, Nhlangano, Pigg's Peak, Rocklands
government: **22** constitutional monarchy
head of state: **4** king
monetary unit: **4** rand **9** lilangeni
mountain: **8** Highveld **11** Drakensberg
highest point: **7** Emlembe
river: **5** Usutu **6** Komati, Lomati **8** Mhlatuze, Ngwavuma, Umbeluzi, Umbuluzi
physical feature:
  forest: **5** Usutu
  plateau: **7** Lebombo, Lubombo
people: **5** Asian, Bantu, Swazi **11** Eurafricans
  king: **3** Kbe **5** Nyama **6** Mswati **7** Sobhuza
  prince: **6** Sozisa
language: **5** Ngumi **7** English, Siswati **9** Afrikaans **10** Portuguese
religion: **7** animism **10** Protestant **13** Roman Catholic
feature:
  bride payment: **6** lobolo
  god: **14** Mkhulumngcandi
  ritual dance: **7** Incwala

Sweden

other name: 7 Sverige

capital/largest city: 9 Stockholm

others: 4 Lund, Umea **5** Boden, Boras, Edane, Falun, Gavle, Lulea, Malmo, Pitea, Visby **6** Arvika, Kiruna, Orebro **7** Uppsala **8** Goteborg, Jokkmokk, Vasteras **9** Jonkoping, Linkoping, Sundsvall **10** Eskilstuna, Gottenburg, Norrkoping, Skelleftea **11** Halsingborg

school: 4 Lund **7** Uppsala **8** Goteborg **9** Stockholm

division: 3 Lan **4** Laen **5** Skane **6** Kalmar, Orebro **7** Dalarna, Gotland, Lapland **8** Alvsborg, Blekinge, Elfsborg, Gotaland, Jamtland, Malmohus, Norrland, Svealand

government: 22 constitutional monarchy
  legislature: **7** Riksdag

head of state: 4 king

measure: 3 aln, fot, ref **4** alar, amar, famn, kapp, last, stop **5** carat, foder, kanna, linje, nymil, spann **6** fathom, jumfru **7** oxhuvud, tunland **8** fjarding, koltunna, tunnland

monetary unit: 3 ore **5** krona, krone **7** carolin **8** skilling **9** rigsdaler

weight: 3 ass, lod **4** last, mark, sten **5** carat **6** nylast **7** centner, lispund **8** skalpund, skeppund **9** shippound

island: 5 Oland **7** Gotland

lake: 4 Ster **5** Asnen, Malar, Silja, Vaner **6** Vanern, Vetter, Wenner **7** Hielmar, Malaren, Vattern **8** Dalalven **9** Hjalmaren

mountain: 4 Sarv **5** Ammar **6** Helags, Kjolen, Ovniks, Sarjek **7** Kjollen

highest point: 5 Kebne **10** Kebnekaise

river: 3 Dal **4** Gota, Klar, Lule, Pite, Umea **5** Indal, Kalix, Lulea, Pitea, Ranea, Torne **6** Lainio, Muonio **7** Ljusnan **8** Angerman

sea: 6 Baltic **8** Atlantic

physical feature:
  canal: **4** Gota
  gulf: **7** Bothnia
  sound: **6** Kalmar
  strait: **7** Oresund **8** Kattegat **9** Skagerrak

people: 4 Lapp **5** Norse, Swede **6** Viking
  actress: **9** Liv Ullman **10** Greta Garbo **13** Ingrid Bergman
  astronomer: **7** Celsius **8** Angstrom
  author: **8** Lagerlof **10** Lagerkvist, Strindberg
  diplomat: **12** Hammarskjold
  director: **13** Ingmar Bergman **14** Arne Sucksdorff
  inventor: **5** Nobel
  king: **4** Vosa, Wasa **5** Oscar **6** Gustav **8** Gustavus **10** Carl Gustav **12** Gustav Adolph **13** Charles Gustav **22** Jean Baptiste Bernadotte
  philosopher/scientist: **10** Swedenborg
  queen: **9** Christina
  scientist: **8** Linnaeus

language: 4 Lapp **7** Swedish

religion: 19 Evangelical Lutheran

place:
  castle: **9** Gripsholm
  center of Stockholm: **11** Gamla Staden
  park: **7** Skansen **12** Millesgarden
  theater: **18** Drottningholm Court
  walled city: **5** Visby

food: 11 smorgasbord
  cheese: **7** fontina **8** jarlberg **9** jarlsberg
  dish: **10** kottbullar
  drink: **5** glogg **7** aquavit

---

sweet 4 dear, kind, nice **5** candy, fresh **6** dulcet, mellow, smooth, sugary **7** amiable, cloying, darling, dessert, lovable, nonsalt, not salt, tuneful **8** fragrant, pleasant, pleasing **9** agreeable, melodious, sweetmeat, wholesome **10** attractive, confection, euphonious, saccharine **11** goodnatured, mellifluous, silvertoned, sympathetic **12** nonfermented

Sweet Bird of Youth
  director: 13 Richard Brooks
  based on play by: 17 Tennessee Williams
  cast: 8 Ed Begley **10** Paul Newman **13** Geraldine Page, Shirley Knight **17** Madeleine Sherwood
  Oscar for: 15 supporting actor (Begley)

sweetheart 4 beau, dear, love **5** flame, honey, lover, swain **6** fiance, old man, steady, suitor **7** beloved, darling, fiancee, old lady **8** ladylove, mistress, true love **9** boyfriend, inamorata, valentine **10** girlfriend, lady friend **15** gentleman friend
  French: 6 cherie

sweet life
  Italian: 9 dolce vita

Sweet Mama Stringbean
  nickname of: 11 Ethel Waters

sweetmeats 5 candy **6** sweets **7** bonbons **10** sugar candy **11** confections **13** confectionery

sweet-natured 5 sweet **6** benign, gentle, kindly **7** likable, lovable **8** pleasant **13** compassionate

sweetness
  French: 7 douceur

sweet roll 3 bun **6** Danish **7** cruller **8** doughnut **10** coffee cake **11** cinnamon bun

sweets 5 candy **7** goodies **8** desserts **10** sugar candy, sweetmeats **11** confections **13** confectionery

sweet-scented 8 aromatic, fragrant, perfumed, redolent

sweet-smelling 5 spicy **7** scented **8** aromatic, fragrant, perfumed, redolent **9** odiferous

sweet talk 6 cajole, praise **7** blarney, flatter **8** cajolery, flattery, soft soap **10** compliment **11** endearments, loving words **13** blandishments **14** fond utterances

Sweetwater
nickname of: 16 Nathaniel Clifton

sweet words 7 blarney 8 flattery, soft soap 9 sweet talk 12 honeyed words

swell 3 fop, wax 4 A-one, fine, good, grow, okay, puff, rise, wave 5 bloat, bulge, dandy, great, heave, mount, super, surge, throb, widen 6 billow, blow up, comber, expand, extend, fatten, puff up 7 amplify, breaker, burgeon, distend, inflate, stretch, thicken 8 fabulous, heighten, increase, lengthen, splendid, terrific 9 excellent, first-rate, intensify, marvelous, spread out 10 delightful, first-class, tremendous, undulation 11 pleasurable 12 clotheshorse, fashion plate, smart dresser

swell-headed 8 egoistic, puffed up 9 conceited 10 egoistical 11 egotistical 12 vainglorious 13 self-important

swelling 4 bump, lump 5 bulge, swell 8 dilation 9 puffiness 10 distension 11 enlargement 12 protuberance

swell out 5 bloat, bulge 6 billow, expand 7 distend, inflate, puff out

swelter 3 fry 4 boil, cook 5 be hot, broil, sweat 8 languish, perspire

sweltering 3 hot 5 humid, muggy 6 sultry, torrid 7 burning 8 sweating 10 oppressive, perspiring

sweltry 3 hot 4 dank 5 humid, muggy 6 baking, clammy, steamy, sticky, sultry, torrid 7 boiling 8 broiling, roasting, sizzling, stifling 9 scorching 10 blistering 11 suffocating

Swenson, Gloria Josephine Mae
real name of: 13 Gloria Swanson

Swept Away
subtitle: 38 by an unusual destiny in the blue sea of August
director: 14 Lina Wertmuller
cast: 16 Mariangela Melato 17 Giancarlo Giannini

swerve 3 shy, yaw 4 tack, turn, veer 5 avert, dodge, sheer, shift, stray 6 careen, change 7 deviate, digress, diverge 9 turn aside

swift 4 fast 5 brisk, fleet, hasty, quick, rapid 6 abrupt, flying, prompt, speedy 8 headlong 9 immediate 11 expeditious, precipitate

Swift, Jonathan
author of: 11 A Tale of a Tub 15 A Modest Proposal 16 Battle of the Books, Gulliver's Travels
fictional places: 6 Laputa 8 Lilliput 11 Brobdingnag
character: 6 Yahoos 10 Houyhnhnms 14 Lemuel Gulliver

swiftness 5 haste, speed 8 alacrity, celerity, dispatch, rapidity 9 quickness

swill 4 mash, slop, swig 5 quaff, waste 6 guzzle, refuse, scraps, soak up, tipple 7 garbage 8 chugalug, gulp down, leavings

swimming
athlete: 9 Diana Nyad, John Naber, Mark Spitz 10 Dawn Fraser, Kim Linehan, Linda Jezek 11 Claudia Kolb, Debbie Meyer, John Hencken 12 Brian Goodell, Bruce Furniss, Greg Louganis, John Kinsella 13 Jim Montgomery, Kornelia Ender, Michael Burton, Tracy Caulkens 14 Charles Hickcox, Duke Kahanamoku, Esther Williams, Gertrude Ederle 15 Cynthia Woodhead 16 Shirley Babashoff 17 Johnny Weissmuller

Swinburne, Algernon Charles
author of: 16 Hymn to Perserpine 17 Atalanta in Calydon 18 Songs Before Sunrise

swindle 2 do 3 con, gyp 4 bilk, dupe, gull, hoax, rook 5 cheat, cozen, fraud, mulct, steal, trick 6 delude, fleece, racket, rip-off 7 con game, deceive, defraud 8 embezzle, hoodwink 9 bamboozle, defalcate 12 embezzlement 14 confidence game

swindler 3 gyp 5 cheat, crook, faker, fraud 6 con man 7 sharper 8 chiseler, deceiver 9 charlatan, embezzler 10 mountebank 12 rip-off artist

swine 3 cad, cur, rat 4 pigs 5 beast, brute 6 animal
group of: 5 drift 7 sounder

Swineherd, The
author: 21 Hans Christian Andersen

swing 4 drop, hang, loop, move, rein, rock, sway, turn 5 pivot, rally, scope, sweep, whirl 6 dangle, decide, handle, manage, rotate, seesaw, stroke, wangle 7 compass, extract, freedom, inveigh, liberty, license, listing, pull off, rocking, rolling, suspend, swaying 8 maneuver, pitching, undulate 9 determine, influence, oscillate 10 accomplish, manipulate 11 be suspended, oscillation

Swing Time
director: 13 George Stevens
cast: 9 Eric Blore 11 Fred Astaire, Victor Moore 12 Betty Furness, Ginger Rogers 14 Helen Broderick
score: 10 Jerome Kern 13 Dorothy Fields
Oscar for: 4 song
song: 12 A Fine Romance 14 Pick Yourself Up 20 The Way You Look Tonight

swirl 4 bowl, eddy, reel, roll, spin, swim, turn 5 churn, twirl, twist, wheel, whirl 6 gyrate, rotate 7 revolve

Swiss Family Robinson
director: 10 Ken Annakin
cast: 9 John Mills 10 Janet Munro 14 Dorothy McGuire, James MacArthur, Sessue Hayakawa
author: 16 Johann Rudolf Wyss
character: 13 Emily Montrose
Robinson family: 4 Jack 5 Fritz 6 Ernest 7 Francis

switch 3 box, rod, tan 4 cane, jerk, lash, move, whip 5 birch, lever, shift, shunt, stick, swing, trade, whisk 6 button, change, handle 8 exchange 9 sidetrack 11 alternation

Switzerland *see* box

Swiveller, Dick
character in: 19 The Old Curiosity Shop
author: 7 Dickens

swollen 5 puffy 7 bloated, bulging, swelled 8 inflated, puffed-up 9 distended

swoon 5 faint 8 collapse, keel over 13 fall prostrate 17 become unconscious

swoop 4 dive, drop, rush 5 pitch, sweep 6 plunge, pounce, spring 7 descend, plummet 8 nose-dive, swooping 9 sweep down 12 rush headlong

sword 4 epee, foil 5 blade, saber, steel 6 rapier 7 cutlass 8 scimitar 10 broadsword

sybarite 8 hedonist 10 sensualist, voluptuary

sybaritic 4 rich 6 lavish 7 sensual 9 dissolute, epicurean, luxurious 10 dissipated, hedonistic, voluptuous 12 luxury-loving, pleasure-bent 13 self-

Switzerland
capital: **4** Bern
largest city: **6** Zurich
others: **3** Zug **4** Bale, Bern, Biel, Brig, Chur, Nyon, Sion, Thun **5** Basel, Basle, Berne, Coire, Surat, Vevey **6** Geneva, Geneve, Glarus, Lugano, Sarnen, Schwyz **7** Altdorf, Fyzabad, Herisau, Locarno, Lucerne, Luzerne, Zermatt **8** Lausanne, Montreux, St Moritz **9** Neuchatel, Solothurn **10** Bellinzona, Interlaken, Winterthur **12** Schaffhausen
school: **4** Bern **5** Basel **8** Catholic, Lausanne **28** Federal Institute of Technology
division: **3** Uri, Zug **4** Bern, Chur, Nyon, Vaud **5** Aarau, Basel, Basle, Berne, Sankt, Waadt **6** Aargau, canton, Gallen, Geneva, Geneve, Glaris, Glarus, Luzern, Obwald, Schwyz, St Gall, Tessin, Ticino, Valais, Wallis, Zurich **7** Atldorf, Grisons, Lucerne, Nidwald, Thurgau **8** Fribourg, Obwalden, St Gallen **9** Appenzell, Neuchatel, Neuenberg, Solothurn **10** Graubunden **11** Unterwalden **12** Schaffhausen
measure: **3** imi, pot **4** aune, fuss, muid, pied, zoll **5** lieue, linie, maass, pouce, staab, toise **6** perche, strich **7** klafter, viertel **9** quarteron **10** holzlafter **11** holzklafter
monetary unit: **5** franc, rappe **6** hallar, rappen **7** centime, duplone **8** baetzner
weight: **4** fund **5** pfund **7** centner, quintal **12** zugthierlast
lake: **3** Uri, Zug **4** Biel, Thon, Thun **5** Ageri, Leman, Morat **6** Bienne, Brienz, Geneva, Lugano, Sarnen, Wallen, Zurich **7** Hallwil, Lucerne, Lungern **8** Maggiore, Viervald **9** Bielersee, Constance, Neuchatel, Sarnersee, Thunersee
mountain: **3** Dom **4** Alps, Jura, Rigi, Rosa, Todi **5** Adula, Blanc, Cenis, Eiger, Genis, Karpf, Righi **6** Linard, Pizela, Sentis **7** Bernina, Beverin, Grimsel, Pilatus, Rotondo **8** Balmhorn, Jungfrau **9** Weisshorn **10** Diablerets, Matterhorn, St Gotthard, Wetterhorn **11** Burgenstock **12** Dufourspitze **13** Rheinwaldhorn **14** Finsteraarhorn
   mountain pass: **5** Cenis, Furka, Gemmi **6** Albula, Kinzig, Maloja, Usteri **7** Bernina, Brenner, Grimsel, Simplon, Splugen **8** Lotschen **10** St Gotthard
highest point: **12** Dufourspitze
river: **2** Po **3** Aar, Inn **4** Aare, Arve, Thur, Toss **5** Broye, Doubs, Linth, Reuss, Rhine, Rhone, Saane **6** Limmat, Maggia, Safane, Sarine, Ticino **8** Engadine, Pratigau
physical feature:
   glacier: **5** Rhone
   plateau: **5** Swiss
people: **5** Swiss
   artist: **4** Klee
   author: **5** Hesse, Spyri **6** Keller **8** Gotthelf, Rousseau **10** Durrenmatt
   educational reformer: **10** Pestalozzi
   hero: **4** Tell
   psychologist: **4** Jung **6** Piaget
   religious leader: **6** Calvin **7** Zwingli
   scientist: **9** Bernoulli
language: **5** Ladin **6** French, German **7** Italian **8** Romansch **14** Switzerdeutsch
religion: **9** Calvinism **10** Protestant **13** Roman Catholic
place:
   castle: **7** Chillon
   fountain: **7** Jet d'Eau
   playhouse: **6** Zurich
   resort: **5** Arosa, Davos **6** Gstaad **7** Zermatt **8** St Moritz **9** Schwagalp **10** Interlaken
   street: **14** Bahnhofstrasse
   tower: **5** Clock
feature:
   animal: **4** ibex **7** chamois
   flower: **9** edelweiss
   pageant: **9** Alpenfest
food:
   cheese: **6** bagnes, sbrinz **7** Gruyere **10** Emmentaler **11** Appenzeller
   dish: **5** rosti **6** fondue **8** raclette **11** grisons beef **14** bundnerfleisch
   drink: **11** cheri-suisse **14** marmot-chocolat

indulgent **14** pleasure-loving **15** pleasure-seeking

Sycamire 12 Biblical tree

sycamore 8 Platanus **18** Acer pseudoplatanus
varieties: **7** eastern **8** Egyptian

Sychaeus
also: **7** Acerbas
priest of: **8** Hercules

wife: **4** Dido
brother-in-law: **9** Pygmalion
murdered by: **9** Pygmalion

sycophant 4 tool **5** slave, toady **6** fawner, flunky, jackal, lackey, puppet, stooge, yes-man **7** cat's-paw **8** hanger-on, parasite, truckler **9** flatterer **10** bootlicker **11** lickspittle, rubber stamp **13** apple-polisher

Sydney
bay: **5** Walsh **11** Rushcutter's **13** Woolloomooloo
capital of: **13** New South Wales
cove: **4** Farm
founder: **7** Phillip
harbor: **7** Darling **11** Port Jackson
island: **4** Goat **6** Garden
landmark: **10** Opera House **11** Wynyard Park **13** Har-

bour Bridge **14** Fitzroy Gardens **15** Mitchell Library **16** Australian Museum, Hyde Park Barracks, Saint James Church **18** Rushcutter's Bay Park **21** Royal Botanical Gardens
river: 10 Parramatta
university: 9 Macquarie **13** New South Wales

Syleus
position: 4 king
killed by: 8 Hercules

sylvan 5 bushy, leafy, woody **6** wooded, woodsy **8** arcadian, forested, timbered, woodland **9** luxuriant, overgrown **10** forestlike

Sylvanus *see* **8** Silvanus

Sylvia
character in: 20 Two Gentlemen of Verona
author: 11 Shakespeare

Symaethis
form: 5 nymph
location: 3 sea
mother of: 4 Aeis

symbol 4 mark, sign **5** badge, token **6** emblem, figure, signal **10** indication **14** representation **15** exemplification

symbolize 4 mean **5** imply **6** denote, embody, symbol **7** betoken, connote, express, signify **8** stand for **9** emblemize, exemplify, personify, represent, signalize **10** allegorize **11** emblematize

symmetrical 7 orderly, regular **8** balanced **9** congruent **12** well-balanced **16** well-proportioned

symmetry 4 form **5** order **7** balance, harmony **9** congruity **10** conformity, regularity **11** equilibrium, orderliness, parallelism, shapeliness **15** proportionality

sympathetic 6 benign, humane, kindly **7** feeling, pitying **8** friendly, merciful **9** agreeable, approving, benignant, sensitive **10** benevolent, comforting **11** softhearted, warmhearted **12** sympathizing, well-disposed **13** commiserative, compassionate, tenderhearted, understanding

sympathize 4 back, pity, side **5** agree, favor **7** approve, feel for, go along, support **8** sanction **9** empathize **10** appreciate, be in accord, be sorry for **11** condole with, have pity for, stand behind

sympathy 4 pity **5** amity, favor, grief **6** accord, regard, sorrow **7** concern, concert,

concord, empathy, feeling, harmony, rapport, support **8** advocacy, affinity, approval, sanction **9** agreement, communion, patronage, unanimity **10** compassion, consonance, fellowship, friendship, tenderness **11** well-wishing **12** congeniality, partisanship **13** commiseration, consanguinity, fellow feeling, understanding

Symplegades
form: 5 rocks
location: 8 Bosporus **9** Euxine Sea
characteristic: 8 clashing, dark-blue

symposium 5 forum, synod **6** debate, parley, powwow **7** meeting **8** colloquy, con-

gress **10** conference, discussion, round table **12** deliberation **15** panel discussion

Symposium
author: 5 Plato
character: 7 Agathon **8** Phaedrus, Socrates **9** Pausanias **10** Alcibiades **11** Aristodemus **12** Aristophanes

symptom 4 mark, sign **5** token **6** signal **7** earmark, warning **8** evidence, giveaway **10** indication **15** prognostication

synagogue
Yiddish: 4 shul **5** schul

synchronal 11 concomitant, synchronous **12** contemporary, simultaneous

---

Syria
other name: 4 Aram
capital/largest city: 8 Damascus
others: 4 Hama, Homs, Nawa **5** Busra, Calno, Derra, Emesa, Halab, Hamah, Idlib, Jerud, Raqqa **6** Aleppo, Calneh, Dumeir, Fajami, Tadmor, Ugarit **7** Antioch, Latakia, Palmyra **8** Seleucia **9** Ghabaghib
school: 6 Aleppo, Syrian **11** Arab Academy
measure: 5 makuk **6** garava
monetary unit: 4 lira **5** pound **6** talent **7** piaster
weight: 4 cola **5** artal, ratel **6** talent
lake: 5 Merom **7** Djeboid **8** Tiberias
mountain: 6 Carmel **7** Alawite, Libanus **10** Nusairiyya **11** Anti-Lebanon
highest point: 6 Hermon
river: 3 Asi **6** Balikh, Barada, Jordan, Khabur, Yarmuk **7** Orontes **9** Asi Knabur, Euphrates
sea: 13 Mediterranean
physical feature:
  desert: **5** Hamad **6** Hauran, Syrian
  heights: **5** Golan
people: 4 Arab, Kurd, Turk **5** Alawi, Aptal, Druse, Druze **6** Afshar, Aissor, Aushar, Avshar, Awshar **7** Amorite, Ansarie, Bedouin, Nosaris, Saracen, Shemite **8** Ansarieh, Armenian **9** Ansariyah **10** Circassian **12** Khachaturian
  king: **5** Rezin **6** Faisal, Hazael **8** Benhadad **9** Antiochus
  leader: **10** T E Lawrence **12** Hafiz al-Assad **16** Lawrence of Arabia
  queen: **7** Zenobia
  ruler: **4** Rome **5** Arabs **6** France, Greeks, Persia **7** Mongols **8** Abbasids **9** Mamelukes, Phoenicia, Seleucids **11** Seljuk Turks **12** Ottoman Turks
language: 6 Arabic, French, Syriac **7** Aramaic, English, Kurdish, Turkish **8** Armenian
religion: 5 Druze, Islam **7** Alawite **12** Christianity **13** Greek Orthodox **23** Eastern Rite Christianity
place:
  dam: **5** Tabqa **9** Euphrates
  ruins: **7** Palmyra
  square: **7** Martyrs'
feature:
  animal: **9** dromedary
  clothing: **3** aba **4** abah **7** abayyah **8** kafiyyah
  marketplace: **4** souk
  tent: **8** bayt shar
  village common: **6** maidan

synchronous 10 synchronal 11 concomitant 12 contemporary, simultaneous

syndicalist 5 rebel 9 anarchist, insurgent 13 revolutionary

syndicate 5 group, trust, union 6 cartel, league, merger 7 combine 8 alliance 9 coalition 10 consortium, federation 11 association

Synge, John Millington
author of: 14 Riders to the Sea 19 Deirdre of the Sorrows 20 In the Shadow of the Glen 27 The Playboy of the Western World

synod 4 diet 13 governing body 15 advisory council 21 ecclesiastical council

synonym 8 analogue 10 equivalent 11 another name

synonymous 4 like, same 5 alike, equal 7 coequal 10 equivalent

synopsis 5 brief 6 apercu, digest, precis, resume 7 epitome, outline, rundown, summary

8 abstract, argument 11 abridgement

synopsize 6 digest 7 abridge, outline 8 abstract, condense 9 summarize

Synoptist 12 Gospel writer

synthesize 3 mix 4 fuse 5 blend 7 combine 8 compound 10 amalgamate

synthetic 4 fake, sham 5 phony 6 ersatz 7 man-made 9 unnatural 10 artificial 11 counterfeit 12 manufactured

Syri 16 Greek uncial codex

Syria *see box*

Syrinx
form: 5 nymph
location: 8 mountain
transformed into: 4 reed
transformed by: 3 Pan
made into: 7 panpipe
pipes called: 6 syrinx

system 4 body, unit 5 setup 6 method, scheme, theory

7 program, regimen, routine 8 organism 9 procedure, structure 10 hypothesis 11 arrangement 12 constitution, organization 13 modus operandi 15 mode of operation

systematic 4 neat, tidy 7 ordered, orderly, planned, precise, regular 8 constant 9 organized 10 methodical 12 businesslike, systematized 13 well-organized, well-regulated

systematization 5 order 8 ordering 9 gradation 10 organizing 11 arrangement 12 categorizing, codification, organization 13 methodization 14 categorization, classification

systematize 5 order 7 arrange 8 classify, organize 9 methodize

systematized 7 ordered 8 arranged, codified 9 organized 10 classified, methodized, systematic

tab 3 lip **4** bill, cost, flap, loop **5** check, price, strip, tally **6** tongue **7** eyehole **10** projection

tabard 4 cape, coat **5** cloak, tunic

Tabard Inn
    starting point in: 18 The Canterbury Tales

tabernacle 6 church, temple **14** house of worship

Tabeth 16 tenth Hebrew month

Tabitha
    also called: 6 Dorcas
    revived by: 5 Peter
    hometown: 5 Joppa

table 4 fare, list, roll **5** board, chart, index **6** record, roster, shelve, spread **7** catalog **8** lay aside, postpone, put aside, register, schedule, syllabus, synopsis **9** inventory **10** tabulation

Table
    constellation of: 5 Mensa

tableau 4 view **5** scene **7** pageant, picture, setting **8** grouping **9** depiction, spectacle, still life **11** arrangement, delineation **12** illustration **13** picturization

tableau vivant 13 living picture

tablespoon
    abbreviation: 4 tbsp

tablet 3 pad **4** leaf **5** bolus, panel, sheet, wafer **6** pellet, plaque, troche **7** lozenge, memo pad, surface **8** flat cake, thin slab **9** tablature **10** pad of paper, writing pad

tableware 5 china **6** dishes, plates **7** cutlery **8** crockery, utensils **9** chinaware, glassware **10** dinnerware, silverware **14** cups and saucers

taboo, tabu 3 ban **4** no-no **6** banned **8** anathema, outlawed, verboten **9** forbidden, social ban **10** in bad taste, prohibited, proscribed **11** disapproved, prohibition, unthinkable **12** interdiction, proscription, religious ban, unacceptable **13** unmentionable

tabulate 4 file, list, rank, rate, sort **5** chart, grade, group, index, order, range **6** codify **7** arrange, catalog, compute, diagram, sort out **8** classify, organize **9** methodize **10** categorize, make a table **11** systematize

tace
    music: 6 silent

tacit 7 assumed, implied **8** implicit, inferred, unspoken, unstated, wordless **10** undeclared, understood **11** unexpressed **15** taken for granted

taciturn 5 aloof, quiet **6** silent **7** laconic **8** reserved, reticent **9** secretive **11** tight-lipped **12** close-mouthed **15** uncommunicative

tack 3 add, peg, pin, way **4** clap, nail, slap, veer **5** affix, sheer, shift, spike, thole **6** append, attach, change, fasten, method, swerve, switch, zigzag **7** go about **8** approach, tholepin **9** short nail **12** change course **14** course of action

tackle 3 try **4** gear, lift **5** assay, begin, crane, hoist, jenny, throw, tools, winch **6** accept, assume, attack, take on, take up **7** attempt, capstan, derrick, embrace, go about, halyard, rigging **8** endeavor, engage in, material, set about, windlass **9** apparatus, enter upon, equipment, trappings, undertake **10** appliances, embark upon, implements **11** instruments **12** appointments **13** accoutrements, paraphernalia

tack on 3 add **5** annex **6** adjoin, append, attach **7** stick on, subjoin **8** fasten to

tacky 5 dowdy, gluey, gooey, gucky, gummy, messy, ratty, seedy, tatty **6** grubby, shabby, shoddy, sloppy, sticky, untidy, viscid **7** stringy, unkempt, viscous **8** adhesive, frazzled, slipshod, slovenly **10** disordered

tact 7 finesse, suavity **8** delicacy **9** diplomacy, suaveness **10** discretion **11** savoir faire, sensibility **13** consideration **14** circumspection
    French: 11 savoir-faire

tactful 5 suave **6** polite, smooth, subtle **7** politic **8** decorous, delicate, discreet, mannerly **9** sensitive **10** diplomatic, thoughtful **11** considerate

tactic 3 way **4** line, plan, tack **6** method, policy, scheme **8** approach **9** stratagem **14** course of action

tactics 9 maneuvers **18** battle arrangements, military operations

tactless 4 curt, rude **5** blunt, brash, rough **6** abrupt, clumsy, gauche, stupid **7** boorish **8** impolite **9** ham-handed, impolitic, imprudent, untactful **10** blundering, indelicate, indiscreet **11** insensitive, thoughtless **12** undiplomatic **13** ill-considered, inconsiderate
    French: 6 gauche

tactlessness 8 curtness **9** bluntness, gaucherie **10** abruptness, clumsiness, indelicacy **13** insensitivity, tastelessness

taedium vitae 5 ennui **12** tedium of life **22** feeling life is wearisome

Taft, William Howard *see box*

Taft, William Howard
  presidential rank: 13 twenty-seventh
  party: 10 Republican
  state represented: 2 OH
  defeated: 4 (Eugene Victor) Debs **5** (William Jennings) Bryan **6** (Daniel Braxton) Turney, (Eugene Wilder) Chafin, (Thomas Edward) Watson, (Thomas Louis) Hisgen **8** (August) Gillhaus
  vice president: 7 (James Schoolcraft) Sherman
  cabinet:
    state: **4** (Philander Chase) Knox
    treasury: **8** (Franklin) MacVeagh
    war: **7** (Henry Lewis) Stimson **9** (Jacob McGavock) Dickinson
    attorney general: **10** (George Woodward) Wickersham
    navy: **5** (George von Lengerke) Meyer
    postmaster general: **9** (Frank Harris) Hitchcock
    interior: **6** (Walter Lowrie) Fisher **9** (Richard Achilles) Ballinger
    agriculture: **6** (James) Wilson
    commerce and labor: **5** (Charles) Nagel
  born: 12 Cincinnati OH
  died: 12 Washington DC
  buried: 25 Arlington National Cemetery
  education:
    university: **4** Yale
    law school: **10** Cincinnati
  religion: 9 Unitarian
  interests: 4 golf
  author: 22 Four Aspects of Civic Duty **23** The United States and Peace **30** Our Chief Magistrate and His Powers **33** The Anti-Trust Act and the Supreme Court **65** The Presidency: Its Duties Its Powers Its Opportunities and Its Limitation
  political career: 18 US Solicitor General
    judge: **19** Federal Circuit Court
    president of: **21** Philippines Commission
    civil governor of: **11** Philippines
    secretary of: **3** War
    US Supreme Court: **12** Chief Justice
  civilian career:
    law professor: **4** Yale
    president: **22** American Bar Association
  notable events of lifetime/term: 19 Postal Savings System
    Act: **10** Webb-Kenyon **11** Mann-Elkinst **12** Payne-Aldrich
    sinking of: **7** Titanic
  father: 8 Alphonso
  mother: 6 Louisa (Maria Torrey)
  siblings: 5 Fanny **11** Henry Waters **12** Horace Dutton **15** Samuel Davenport
    half-brothers: **11** Peter Rawson **13** Charles Phelps
  wife: 5 Helen (Herron)
    nickname: **6** Nellie
  children: 11 Helen Herron **13** Charles Phelps **14** Robert Alphonso
  first lady:
    author: **24** Recollections of Full Years

tag 3 add, dog, tab **4** card, heel, mark, name, slip, stub, tail, term **5** add on, affix, annex, hound, label, title, trail **6** append, attach, attend, fasten, follow, handle, join to, marker, shadow, tack on, ticket **7** earmark, moniker, pendant **8** cognomen, identify, nickname **9** accompany, appendage, sobriquet

Tahiti
  artist: 7 Gauguin
  author: 9 Stevenson
  capital: 7 Papeete
  formerly: 8 Otaheite
  island group: 7 Society
  isthmus: 7 Taravao
  ocean: 7 Pacific
  volcano: 5 Roniu **7** Orohena
tail 3 dog **4** butt, seat **5** fanny, stalk, track, trail **6** follow,

shadow **7** back end, rear end **8** buttocks

tail end, tail-end 4 back, butt, rear, rump, tail **6** caudal **7** hind end, rear end **8** backside, buttocks, last part **9** posterior

tailor 3 fit, sew **4** make, redo **5** adapt, alter, build, shape **6** change, create, design, devise, modify **7** convert, fashion, produce **8** clothier, costumer **9** construct, couturier, fabricate, transform **10** dressmaker, seamstress

taint 3 mar, rot **4** blot, flaw, ruin, soil, spot, turn **5** dirty, fault, go bad, smear, spoil, stain, sully **6** damage, debase, defect, defile, smudge, stigma **7** blemish, putrefy, tarnish **8** besmirch **12** imperfection

tainted 5 dirty **6** impure, rotten **7** spoiled, stained, unclean **9** blemished, tarnished **10** besmirched

Taipei
  capital of: 6 Taiwan

Taiwan *see box, p. 960*

Tajikistan
  other name: 12 Tadzhikistan
  capital/largest city: **8** Dushanbe
  head of state: 9 president
  government: 8 republic
  monetary unit: 5 ruble
  mountain: 13 Communism Peak
  people: 5 Tajok, Uzbek **7** Tadzhik
  language: 7 Tadzhik
  religion: 11 Sunni Muslim

take *see box, p. 961*

take aback 5 amaze **7** astound **8** astonish, surprise **9** overwhelm

take a crack at 3 try **5** essay **6** hazard, tackle, take on **7** attempt, venture **9** have a go at, undertake **11** make a stab at

take advantage of 3 use **5** avail **7** exploit, utilize **10** profit from

take after 4 copy, echo **6** follow, repeat **7** imitate **8** resemble, simulate **9** duplicate, reproduce

take apart 7 destroy **8** demolish **9** dismantle, knock down

take a powder 4 blow, exit **5** go out, leave, scram, split **6** cut out, depart, escape **8** withdraw

take away 5 seize **6** lessen, reduce **7** abridge, bear off, curtail, detract **8** carry off,

Taiwan
   name means: 11 terraced bay
   other name: 7 Formosa **11** Ilha Formosa **15** Republic of China
   capital/largest city: 6 Taipei
   others: 4 Suao **5** Shoka, Takao **6** Tainan **7** Chilung, Hualien, Keelong, Keelung, Taoyuan **8** Fengshan, Kaohsiung, Taichung **9** Kaohsiung
   school: 7 Soochow, Tunghai **14** National Taiwan
   monetary unit: 4 yuan **6** dollar
   island: 5 Matsu **6** Lan Hsu, Penghu, Quemoy, Taiwan **7** Hungtou, Huoshao **10** Pescadores
   mountain: 5 Tatun **6** Tzukao **7** Taitung **15** Chungyang Shanmo
   highest point: 6 Yu Shan **8** Morrison **10** Sinkao Shan **11** Hsin-Kao Shan
   river: 5 Wuchi **6** Tachia **7** Choshui, Hualien, Tanshui
   sea: 7 Pacific **9** East China **10** Philippine, South China
   physical feature:
      cape: **7** Olwanpi
      channel: **5** Bashi
      gorge: **6** Taroko
      storm: **7** monsoon, typhoon
      strait: **6** Taiwan **7** Formosa
   people: 4 Yami **5** Hakka, Hoklo **7** Chinese, Malayan **9** Fukienese, Taiwanese **10** Indonesian, Polynesian **12** Kwangtungese
      goddess: **5** Matsu
      leader: **7** Koxinga **9** Sun Yat-sen **10** Yen Chia-Kan **13** Chiang Kai-shek **14** Cheng Cheng-Kung, Chiang Ching-kuo
   language: 4 Amon, Amoy **5** Hakka, Kuo Yu **6** Minnan **9** Taiwanese **15** Mandarin Chinese
   religion: 6 Taoism **7** animism **8** Buddhism **12** Christianity, Confucianism
   place:
      museum: **14** National Palace
      square: **12** Presidential
   feature:
      festival: **5** Ghost
      political party: **10** Kuomintang
   food:
      feast: **6** pai-pai

decrease, subtract **9** deprive of **11** make off with

take a whack at 3 try **5** essay **6** hazard, tackle **7** attempt, venture **8** give a try **9** have a go at **10** give a whirl **12** take a crack at

take back 6 abjure, recall, recant, renege **7** disavow, retract, reverse **8** forswear, withdraw

take captive 3 bag **4** snag, take, trap **5** catch, seize, snare **7** capture, ensnare **9** apprehend, lay hold of **12** take prisoner

take care 6 beware, be wary **9** be careful **10** be cautious **17** look before you leap

take care of 4 tend **6** assume **7** nurture **8** attend to, shoulder **10** minister to

take exception 5 demur

6 object, resent **11** look askance

take flight 3 fly **4** flee **6** escape, run off **7** abscond, fly away, run away, run free, take off **9** make a dash **10** fly the coop **12** make a getaway

take for granted 6 assume **10** undervalue

take heed 4 mind **6** beware **7** look out **8** take care, watch out **11** take warning

take hold 4 bite, grab, grip **5** grasp **6** clutch **7** catch on

take in stride 12 not skip a beat **13** be unperturbed

take into custody 3 bag, nab **4** book, bust, hold **5** catch, pinch, seize **6** arrest, collar, detain, secure **7** capture **9** apprehend **12** take prisoner

take into service 4 hire **6** employ, engage, retain, secure, take on

take issue 5 demur **6** differ **8** disagree **12** be at variance, stand opposed

take no notice of 6 ignore **9** disregard **11** pay no heed to **15** fail to recognize **16** pay no attention to **17** fail to acknowledge

take notice
   Latin: **8** nota bene

take notice of 3 see **4** heed, mark, note **6** call on, regard **7** observe **8** call upon **9** recognize **10** get a load of **11** acknowledge **14** pay attention to

take nourishment 3 eat **4** feed **10** break bread **14** take sustenance

takeoff 5 spoof **6** parody, satire **7** lampoon **9** burlesque **10** caricature

take off 4 doff, lift **5** leave **6** decamp, depart, detach, remove **7** lift off, peel off, run away **8** strip off **14** leave the ground

take off guard 5 catch **8** surprise **14** take by surprise

take on 4 bear, hire **6** accept, assume, engage **8** shoulder **9** undertake

take one's breath away 4 daze, stun **5** shock **7** stupefy **8** astonish, dumfound **9** dumbfound, electrify **11** flabbergast **15** make one's eyes pop

take out 4 date **5** court **6** delete, escort, remove **7** extract, isolate **8** abstract, separate, take home, withdraw **9** strike out

take over 4 take **5** seize **6** assume, take on, take up **8** shoulder **10** commandeer, confiscate **11** appropriate, expropriate, gain control

take pains 6 strive **7** attempt, try hard **8** endeavor, go all out **10** do one's best **11** give one's all **12** make an effort **15** knock oneself out **16** give one's best shot

take pleasure in 4 like, love **5** adore, eat up, enjoy, fancy, savor **6** dote on, relish, relish **7** revel in **9** rejoice in **10** appreciate **13** be pleased with, get a kick out of

take possession of 5 claim **10** confiscate **11** appropriate, expropriate

take prisoner 3 bag, nab

4 book, bust **5** catch, pinch, seize **6** arrest, collar **7** capture **9** apprehend **11** take captive **15** take into custody

take sick 3 ail **6** sicken **8** collapse **9** become ill **10** be stricken

take stock of 5 audit, check **6** assess, review, survey **7** examine, inspect **8** look over **9** inventory

take sustenance 3 eat **4** feed **10** break bread **15** take nourishment

take the cake 5 excel **7** beat all, surpass **12** beat the devil, win hands down

take the edge off 6 lessen, pacify, soothe, temper **7** appease, assuage, lighten, mollify **8** tone down

take the first step 5 begin, start **6** launch, set out **8** commence, embark on, initiate **9** undertake **10** inaugurate

take the place of 7 replace **8** displace, supplant **9** supersede

take to be 4 deem, hold **5** count, judge, think **6** assume, regard, view as **7** account, believe **8** consider **10** look upon as

take to heart 4 heed, mind **6** attend **8** consider **9** hearken to **13** give thought to **14** pay attention to

take to one's heels 3 fly **4** flee **6** escape **7** get away, run away **10** fly the coop, make a break, take flight **12** make a getaway **15** head for the hills

take to task 5 chide, scold **6** accuse, berate, charge, rail at, rebuke **7** bawl out, censure, chasten, chew out, reprove, upbraid **8** admonish, chastise, reproach **9** castigate, criticize, dress down, reprimand **10** tongue-lash **11** remonstrate **13** call to account

take turns 5 share **6** rotate **9** alternate

take under one's wing 6 assist, defend **7** protect **8** befriend **9** look after

take unfair advantage of 5 abuse **6** misuse **7** exploit

take up 4 lift **6** absorb, accept, assume, occupy, pick up, resume, soak up, suck up **7** discuss, drink in **8** consider, continue, sponge up, talk over **9** cultivate, swallow up

taking a siesta 6 dozing **7** napping **8** snoozing **10** taking a nap **18** catching forty winks

takings 4 loot **5** booty **6** spoils **7** plunder **8** pickings

Talamancan
tribe: 7 Cabecar

Talaria
form: 7 sandals
owner: 6 Hermes **7** Mercury
characteristic: 6 winged

Talassio
origin: 5 Roman
form: 3 god
invoked at: 8 weddings
corresponds to: 5 Hymen **9** Hymenaeus

tale 3 fib, lie **4** epic, myth, saga, yarn **5** fable, novel, rumor, story **6** legend, report

7 account, fiction, hearsay, recital, romance, scandal, untruth **8** anecdote **9** falsehood, fish story, narration, narrative, tall story **10** short story **11** fabrication, scuttlebutt **12** tittle-tattle **13** falsification, piece of gossip **16** cock-and-bull story

talebearer 6 gossip **7** blabber, reciter, tattler **8** busybody, informer, reporter, telltale **10** newsmonger, tattletale **11** storyteller **12** blabbermouth **13** scandalmonger

talent 4 bent, gift, turn **5** flair, forte, knack, skill **6** genius **7** faculty **8** aptitude, capacity, facility, strength **9** endowment **10** capability **11** proficiency

Talent 14 Biblical weight

talented 4 able **5** adept **6** expert, gifted **7** born for, capable, endowed, skilled **8** artistic, polished **9** brilliant, competent **10** proficient **11** well-endowed **12** accomplished

Tale of a Tub, A
author: 9 Ben Jonson **13** Jonathan Swift

Tale of Genji
author: 19 Lady Murasaki Shikibu

Tale of Two Cities, A
author: 14 Charles Dickens
character: 7 Gaspard, Stryver **9** Dr Manette, Miss Pross **11** Jarvis Lorry, John Barstad **12** Lucie Manette, Sydney Carton **13** Charles Darnay, Jerry Cruncher, Madame Defarge **18** Marquis St Evremonde
director: 10 Jack Conway
cast: 12 Blanche Yurka, Isabel Jewell, Reginald Owen, Ronald Colman (Sydney Carton) **13** Basil Rathbone, Edna May Oliver **14** Elizabeth Allan
setting: 16 French Revolution

Tales Before Midnight
author: 19 Stephen Vincent Benet

Talese, Gay
author of: 14 Honor Thy Father **16** Thy Neighbor's Wife

Tales of a Fourth Grade Nothing
author: 9 Judy Blume

Tales of a Wayside Inn
author: 24 Henry Wadsworth Longfellow

Tales of Hoffmann, The
also: 18 Les Contes d'Hoffmann
opera by: 9 Offenbach

take 3 buy, get, lug, nab, net, see, use **4** bear, bilk, deem, draw, feel, gain, grab, grip, haul, have, heed, hire, hold, know, lead, loot, mark, mind, move, need, obey, read, rent, sack, tote, work **5** bring, brook, carry, catch, cheat, claim, clasp, filch, grasp, gross, guide, infer, lease, seize, stand, steal, use up, usher, usurp **6** accept, assume, attain, clutch, convey, deduce, deduct, demand, derive, divest, employ, endure, escort, fleece, follow, look on, obtain, pilfer, pocket, profit, regard, remove, secure, snatch, suffer **7** acquire, agree to, believe, call for, capture, conduct, consume, deliver, make out, observe, pillage, plunder, purloin, receive, require, respect, stomach, succeed, suppose, undergo **8** accede to, assent to, conceive, conclude, consider, listen to, perceive, proceeds, purchase, shoulder, submit to, subtract, take away, tolerate, transfer **9** ascertain, be ruled by, consent to, deprive of, eliminate, get hold of, interpret, lay hold of, put up with, respond to, transport, undertake **10** commandeer, comply with, comprehend, confiscate, experience, lay hands on, take effect, understand **11** appropriate, begin to work, go along with, necessitate **13** help oneself to **14** avail oneself of, misappropriate

character: 6 Stella **7** Antonia, Olympia **9** Dr Miracle, Giulietta **11** E T A Hoffmann

Tales of Manhattan
author: **16** Louis Auchincloss

talisman 5 charm **6** amulet, fetish **10** lucky piece

Talisman, The
author: **14** Sir Walter Scott
character: **7** Conrade, El Hakim **10** Sir Kenneth **15** Queen Berengaria **19** Theodorick of Engaddi **20** Lady Edith Plantagenet **21** Richard the Lion-Hearted **31** Grand Master of the Knights Templars

talk 3 gab, jaw, rap, say **4** cant, chat, word **5** argot, idiom, lingo, noise, prate, rumor, slang, speak, state, utter **6** babble, bunkum, confab, confer, gossip, hot air, intone, jargon, parley, patois, powwow, preach, report, sermon, speech, take up, tirade **7** address, blarney, blather, chatter, consult, declare, deliver, dialect, discuss, express, hearsay, lecture, oration, palaver, prattle, twaddle **8** chitchat, colloquy, converse, dialogue, harangue, language, proclaim, rattle on, verbiage **9** discourse, enunciate, negotiate, pronounce, tete-a-tete, utterance **10** bandy words, conference, discussion, rap session, recitation, speak about **11** declamation, exhortation, pontificate, scuttlebutt **12** blatherskite, consultation, conversation, tittle-tattle **13** confabulation

talkative 5 gabby, talky, windy, wordy **6** babbly, chatty, prolix **7** gossipy, verbose, voluble **8** effusive **9** garrulous **10** long-winded, loquacious

talk big 4 brag, crow **5** boast, vaunt **7** puff oneself up **15** blow one's own horn **19** pat oneself on the back

talk down to 9 patronize **10** condescend

talker 6 gabber, gossip, magpie, orator **7** babbler, speaker, windbag **8** lecturer, prattler **9** chatterer, converser **10** chatterbox, mouthpiece **11** rumormonger, speechifier, speechmaker **12** blatherskite, spokesperson **13** scandalmonger **17** conversationalist

talk nonsense 6 babble, drivel, ramble

Talk of the Town, The
director: **13** George Stevens

cast: **9** Cary Grant **10** Jean Arthur **12** Ronald Colman **13** Edgar Buchanan, Glenda Farrell

talk out of 4 balk **6** thwart **8** dissuade **10** discourage

talk over 6 confer, review **7** consult, discuss, hash out

talk to 7 address, lecture, speak to **12** converse with

talk together 4 talk **6** confer **7** discuss **8** converse **9** discourse

tall 3 big **4** high **5** lanky, lofty, rangy **6** absurd **7** soaring, stringy **8** elevated, gangling, towering **10** incredible, long-limbed **11** embellished, exaggerated, implausible **12** preposterous, unbelievable **13** hard to believe, hard to swallow

tallow 3 fat, tip **5** taper **6** bougie, candle, cierge **9** rushlight

Tall State
nickname of: **8** Illinois

tall story 3 fib, lie **4** yarn **5** fable **7** fiction, untruth, whopper **9** fairy tale, falsehood, fish story, invention **11** fabrication **16** cock-and-bull story

tally 3 add, sum **4** jibe, list, mark, poll, post **5** agree, count, match, score, sum up, total **6** accord, census, concur, muster, reckon, record, square **7** catalog, compute, conform **8** coincide, mark down, register, scorepad, tabulate **9** calculate, harmonize, reckoning, scorecard **10** correspond **11** enumeration

talon 4 claw, nail, spur

Talos
form: **5** youth **7** monster
made of: **5** brass **6** bronze
made by: **10** Hephaestus
guarded: **5** Crete
destroyed by: **5** Medea
uncle: **8** Daedalus
killed by: **8** Daedalus

Talthybius
occupation: **6** herald
employer: **9** Agamemnon

Tamar
author: **15** Robinson Jeffers

Tamar
father: **5** David **7** Absalom
mother: **6** Maacah
husband: **2** Er **4** Onan **5** Judah, Uriah
brother: **5** Amnon **7** Absalom, Chileab, Solomon **8** Adonijah
son: **5** Zarah **6** Pharez

daughter: **8** Maachiah
father-in-law: **5** Judah

Tamburlaine the Great
author: **18** Christopher Marlowe
character: **6** Cosroe **7** Mycetes, Orcanes **8** Bajazeth **9** Callepine, Techelles, Zenocrate **10** Theridamas, Usumcasane

tame 4 curb, damp, dull, flat, meek, mild, rein **5** break, check, quiet, timid, train **6** boring, bridle, broken, docile, gentle, govern, manage, master, placid, pliant, serene, subdue **7** conquer, control, pliable, prosaic, repress, subdued, tedious **8** amenable, domestic, dominate, lifeless, overcome, regulate, restrain, suppress, timorous, tranquil **9** tractable **10** make docile, submissive, unexciting **11** complaisant, domesticate, unresisting **12** domesticated **13** uninteresting

tameness 8 docility **9** placidity **10** gentleness, insipidity **12** complaisance, tractability **13** domestication **14** submissiveness

Taming of the Shrew, The
author: **18** William Shakespeare
character: **6** Bianca, Gremio, Tranio **8** Baptista, Lucentio **9** Hortensio, Katharina, Petruchio, Vincentio
director: **16** Franco Zeffirelli
cast: **11** Michael York, Natasha Pyne **13** Richard Burton (Petruchio) **14** Michael Hordern **15** Elizabeth Taylor (Katharina), Vernon Dobtcheff
score: **8** Nino Rota

Tammuz
origin: **8** Sumerian
god of: **9** shepherds
Hebrew month: **6** fourth

Tam O'Shanter
author: **11** Robert Burns

Tampa Bay
football team: **7** Bandits **10** Buccaneers

tamper 3 mix **4** muck **6** butt in, fiddle, horn in, meddle, tinker **7** intrude, obtrude **9** interfere, intervene **10** fool around, mess around **12** monkey around

tamper with 5 alter **6** change, doctor **7** falsify

tan 4 roan **5** beige, brown, khaki, sandy, tawny **6** bronze, sorrel, suntan **7** bronzed

8 brownish, cinnamon, sunburnt **9** sunburned, suntanned **10** light brown **11** yellowbrown

Tanah Airkita see **9** Indonesia

Tananarive, Antananarivo
capital of: **10** Madagascar

Tanaquil
origin: **5** Roman
form: **5** queen
husband: **7** Tarquin **17** Tarquinius Priscus

Tandy, Jessica
born: **6** London **7** England
husband: **10** Hume Cronyn **11** Jack Hawkins
roles: **8** The Birds **10** The Gin Game **12** Forever Amber **21** A Streetcar Named Desire

tang 3 bit **4** bite, hint, odor, reek **5** aroma, punch, savor, scent, smack, smell, sting, tinge, touch, trace **6** flavor **8** acridity, piquancy, pungency, tartness **9** acridness, sharpness, spiciness **10** suggestion

Tange, Kenzo
architect of: **11** Press Center (Kofu) **16** Shizuoka Building (Tokyo) **19** Olympic Sports Stadia (Tokyo) **24** Kagawa Prefectural Offices (Takamatsu) **30** Imabara Municipal Office Building

tangibility 11 materiality, palpability **12** touchability

tangible 4 real **5** solid **6** actual **7** obvious **8** clear-cut, concrete, manifest, material, palpable, physical, positive **9** corporeal, touchable **10** verifiable **11** indubitable, substantial

tangle 3 fix, net, web **4** knot, maze, mesh, muss **5** ravel, skein, snarl, twist **6** jumble, jungle, ruffle, rumple, tousle **7** impasse, network **8** dishevel, disorder **9** labyrinth **10** disarrange

tangled 6 knotty **7** chaotic, complex, jumbled, mixed-up, snarled **11** complicated, intertwined

Tanguy, Yves
born: **5** Paris **6** France
artwork: **4** Fear **17** Mama Papa is Wounded, Untitled Landscape **18** Rose of the Four Winds **20** Slowly Toward the North **22** Four O'Clock in Summer Hope, Indefinite Divisibility **23** Multiplication of the Arcs **25** Extinction of Useless Lights

tank 3 vat **6** boiler **7** cistern **8** aquarium, fish tank **9** container, reservoir **10** armored car, receptacle **11** storage tank

Tannhauser and the Tournament of Song at Wartburg
opera by: **6** Wagner
also: **41** Tannhauser und der Sangerkrieg auf dem Wartburg
character: **5** Venus **7** Wolfram **9** Elizabeth

Tanoan
tribe: **4** Tuei **5** Kiowa **6** Isleta

tantalize 4 bait **5** charm, taunt, tease, tempt **6** entice, lead on **7** bewitch, provoke, torment **8** intrigue **9** captivate, fascinate, titillate **15** whet the appetite **18** make one's mouth water

tantalizing 7 teasing **8** inviting, tempting **9** appealing, leading on **10** intriguing **11** fascinating

Tantalus
king of: **4** Pisa **7** Phrygia
father: **8** Thyestes
wife: **12** Clytemnestra
son: **6** Pelops
daughter: **5** Niobe
punishment in Hades: **6** hunger, thirst

tantamount 4 like **5** equal **9** analogous **10** comparable, equivalent, on a par with **12** commensurate **13** commensurable

tantrum 3 fit **5** storm **7** flareup, rampage **8** outburst, paroxysm **9** explosion **12** fit of passion **13** burst of temper, conniption fit

Tanystropheous
type: **8** dinosaur
period: **8** Triassic

Tanzania see box, p. 964

Tao Te Ching
author: **6** Lao-tzu

Taotieh
origin: **7** Chinese
form: **6** animal

tap 3 pat, rap, use **4** cock, drum, peck, thud **5** spout, touch, valve **6** broach, employ, faucet, hammer, spigot, stroke, uncork, unplug **7** draw off, exploit, utilize **8** draw upon, stopcock **9** put to work, unstopper

taper 3 dip, wax **4** wick **5** light **6** candle, cierge, narrow **8** decrease **9** narrowing **10** diminution **12** come to a point

taper off 4 wane **5** abate **6** weaken **7** slacken, subside **8** decrease, diminish, fade away, slack off

tapestry 3 rug **5** arras, tapis **6** Bruges, fabric, mosaic **7** Gobelin, hanging, montage, weaving **8** Aubusson **12** wallcovering

Tapley, Mark
character in: **16** Martin Chuzzlewit
author: **7** Dickens

Tappertit, Simon
character in: **12** Barnaby Rudge
author: **7** Dickens

Taprobane see **8** Sri Lanka

taproom 3 bar, pub **6** lounge, saloon, tavern **8** alehouse **11** bar and grill, public house **14** cocktail lounge

Taranis
god of: **7** thunder

Taras Bulba
author: **12** Nikolai Gogol
character: **5** Ostap **6** Andrii, Yankel **26** Daughter of the Polish Waiwode

Tarascans, Tarascos
location: **6** Mexico **9** Michoacan **14** Central America
leader: **8** Zincicha **9** Tangaxoan, Tariacuri

Tarawa
capital of: **8** Kiribati

Tar Baby
author: **12** Toni Morrison

Tarchetius
king of: **9** Alba Longa

tardy 4 late, slow **5** slack **6** remiss **7** belated, languid, overdue **8** crawling, creeping, dilatory, slowpoke, sluggish **9** leisurely, not on time, reluctant, slow-paced, snail-like **10** behindhand, behind time, unpunctual **14** slow as molasses **15** procrastinating

tare 12 Biblical weed

target 3 aim, end **4** butt, dupe, goal, goat, gull, mark, plan, prey **5** patsy **6** design, intent, object, pigeon, victim **7** purpose **8** ambition **9** intention, objective **13** laughingstock

Targitaus
father: **4** Zeus
first inhabitant of: **7** Scythia

Tar Heel State
nickname of: **13** North Carolina

tariff 3 fee **4** cost, duty, fare, levy, rate, rent **5** price **6** charge, excise, impost **7** expense **8** input tax **9** excise tax, export tax **10** assessment, commission, freightage

Tarkington, Booth
author of: **6** Penrod **9** Seven-

Tanzania
other name: 12 isle of cloves
capital/largest city: 11 Dar es Salaam
new capital: 6 Dodoma
others: 4 Wete, 5 Kilwa, Lindi, Moshi, Tanga, Ujiji 6 Arusha, Kigoma, Mwadui, Mwanza, Tabora 7 Korogwe, Mtawara 8 Morogoro, Zanzibar 12 Kwasemangube, Zanzibar Town
division: 8 Zanzibar 17 union of Tanganyika
monetary unit: 4 cent 8 shilling
weight: 8 farsalah
island: 6 Mafia, Pemba 6 Latham 8 Zanzibar
lake: 5 Eyasi, Nyasa, Rukwa 6 Malawi, Natron, Nyassa 7 Manyara 8 Victoria 10 Tanganyika
mountain: 4 Kibo, Mero 8 Usambara
highest point: 11 Kilimanjaro
river: 4 Lupa, Ruvu, Wami 5 Ruaha 6 Kagera, Luwegu, Mbaesa, Rufiji, Rungwa, Ruvuma 7 Nkululu, Pangani 8 Mbenkuru 11 Mbarangandu
sea: 6 Indian
physical feature:
  crater: 10 Ngorongoro
  gorge: 7 Olduvai
  national park: 9 Serengeti
  plains: 9 Serengeti
  steppe: 5 Masai 8 Iwembere
  valley: 9 Great Rift
people: 2 Ha 4 Arab, Gogo, Goma, Haya, Hehe 5 Asian, Bantu, Masai 6 Arusha, Chagga, Sukuma, Wagogo, Wagoma 7 African, Makonde, Sambara, Sandawe, Shirazi, Swahili, Wabunga, Zongora 8 Nyakyusa, Nyamwezi
  early man: 13 zinjanthropus
  explorer: 6 Da Gama 7 Rebmann 11 Livingstone
  leader: 5 Sayid 6 Karume 7 Nyerere 16 Sultan of Zanzibar
language: 5 Bantu 6 Arabic 7 English, Khoisan, Nilotic, Swahili 8 Cushitic, Gujarati
religion: 5 Islam 7 animism 12 Christianity
feature:
  animal: 6 dik-dik
  cattle barn: 4 byre
  clothing: 4 sari 6 bui bui
  fly: 6 tsetse
  holiday: 8 Saba Saba
  homestead: 8 manyatta
food:
  dish: 5 ugali

minor arcana 12 lesser arcana 13 greater arcana
suit: 3 cup 4 coin, wand 5 baton, money, sword 6 cudgel 8 pentacle
face card: 4 king, page 5 knave, queen, valet 6 knight
major arcana: 4 Fool, Moon 5 Death 7 Justice 8 Judgment 9 Hanged Man 14 Wheel of Fortune

tarpaulin 4 tarp 6 canvas 9 dropcloth 15 waterproof cover

Tarpeia
form: 12 vestal virgin
father: 15 Spurius Tarpeius
betrayed: 4 Rome
betrayed to: 7 Sabines
killed by: 7 Sabines

Tarquin
king of: 4 Rome
origin: 8 Etruscan
also called: 17 Tarquinius Priscus 18 Tarquinius Superbus
wife: 8 Tanaquil

tarragon
botanical name: 20 Artemisia dracunculus
means: 6 dragon 12 little dragon
Arab: 7 tarkhum
French: 8 estragon
origin: 7 Siberia
used as: 8 purifier
flavor: 8 licorice
use: 4 fish 5 salad, sauce 10 mayonnaise 14 Bearnaise sauce

tarry 3 lag 4 bide, rest, stay, wait 5 abide, dally, delay, pause, stall 6 dawdle, linger, put off, remain 7 be tardy 8 hang back, postpone, stave off, take time 9 temporize 10 hang around 13 cool one's heels, procrastinate

tarsal
bone of: 5 ankle

Tarshish
father: 5 Javan 6 Bilhan

tart 3 pie 4 acid, sour 5 acerb, acrid, sharp, spicy, tangy 6 acetic, barbed, biting, bitter, crusty 7 caustic, cutting, piquant, pungent, sourish 8 vinegary 10 astringent 11 pastry shell

Tartarean *see* 8 infernal

Tartarin of Tarascon
author: 14 Alphonse Daudet

Tartarus
form: 5 abyss
below: 5 Hades
imprisoned: 6 Titans

teen 10 Alice Adams 13 Kate Fennigate 14 The Man from Home 17 Monsieur Beaucaire 19 The World Does Not Move 23 The Magnificent Ambersons

Tarleton, Stuart and Brent
characters in: 15 Gone With the Wind
author: 8 Mitchell

tarnish 3 dim 4 blot, dull, foul, soil, spot 5 dirty, erode, stain, sully, taint 6 befoul, darken, defame, defile, smirch, vilify 7 blacken, blemish, corrode, degrade, oxidize 8 besmirch, discolor, disgrace, dishonor 9 denigrate, discredit 10 lose luster, stigmatize 17 drag through the mud

tarnished 5 dirty 6 soiled 7 stained, sullied 8 oxidized 10 discolored

Tarnkappe
origin: 8 Germanic
mentioned in: 14 Nibelungenlied
form: 5 cloak
gives wearer: 8 strength 12 invisibility
stolen by: 9 Siegfried
stolen from: 8 Niblungs 9 Nibelungs

tarot
Italian: 6 naibes 7 attutti 8 tarocchi
German: 5 tarok
French: 5 tarau, tarot
cards/deck: 12 seventy-eight
division: 11 major arcana,

tartness 7 acidity, sarcasm

8 acerbity **9** sharpness **11** astringency

Tartuffe
  author: **7** Moliere
  character: **5** Damis, Orgon **6** Dorine, Elmire, Valere **7** Cleante, Mariane **14** Madame Pernelle

Tarzan
  author: **18** Edgar Rice Burroughs
  character: **3** Boy **4** Jane **7** Cheetah
  Tarzan also called: **15** Lord of Greystoke, Lord of the Jungle
  comic strip creator: **9** Hal Foster **12** Burme Hogarth

task 3 job **4** duty, work **5** chore, labor, stint **6** charge, errand **7** mission **8** business **10** assignment **11** undertaking **14** responsibility

Task, The
  author: **13** William Cowper

taskmaster 4 boss **6** despot, master, tyrant **7** foreman, headman, manager **8** director, martinet, overseer, stickler **10** supervisor **11** Simon Legree, slave driver **14** disciplinarian, superintendent

Tasmania
  bay: **5** Storm **6** Oyster
  capital: **6** Hobart
  city: **10** Launceston
  country: **9** Australia
  formerly: **14** Van Diemen's Land
  island: **4** Echo **6** Sorell
  mountain: **4** Ossa **6** Cradle
  river: **3** Esk
  strait: **4** Bass

Tasso, Torquato
  author of: **6** Aminta **7** Rinaldo **18** Jerusalem Delivered

taste 3 bit, nip, sip, try, yen **4** bent, bite, feel, meet, tang, test, whim **5** crumb, enjoy, fancy, savor, smack **6** desire, flavor, hunger, liking, morsel, relish, sample, thirst **7** craving, decorum, discern, forkful, insight, leaning, longing, savor of, smack of, swallow, undergo **8** appetite, delicacy, fondness, judgment, mouthful, penchant, piquancy, spoonful, yearning **9** encounter, hankering, partake of, propriety **10** experience, partiality, propensity, take a sip of **11** correctness, discernment, disposition, inclination, take a bite of **12** eat a little of, predilection **14** discrimination, drink a little of
  French: **4** gout

tasteful 7 elegant, refined

8 artistic, becoming, cultured, esthetic, handsome, suitable **9** beautiful, exquisite **10** attractive, well-chosen

tasteless 3 low **4** flat, mild, rude, weak **5** bland, cheap, crass, crude, gaudy, gross, tacky **6** coarse, common, flashy, garish, ribald, watery **7** insipid, uncouth **8** improper, indecent, unseemly **9** inelegant, offensive, unrefined **10** disgusting, flavorless, indecorous, indelicate, uncultured, unesthetic, unflavored, unsuitable **11** distasteful, insensitive

tastemakers 7 leaders **10** avant-garde, innovators **12** stylesetters, trendsetters

tasty 3 hot **5** spicy, tangy, yummy **6** savory **7** piquant, zestful **8** luscious **9** delicious, flavorful, palatable, toothsome **10** appetizing, delectable, flavorsome **11** good-tasting, scrumptious **12** full-flavored, well-seasoned

Tatar, Mr
  character in: **22** The Mystery of Edwin Drood
  author: **7** Dickens

Tatius
  also: **5** Titus
  co-ruler with: **7** Romulus

Tatler, The
  author: **13** Joseph Addison, Richard Steele

tattered 4 torn **6** broken, ragged, ripped, shabby, shaggy **10** disheveled **11** dilapidated

tatters 4 rags **6** shreds **7** patches

tattle 3 rat **4** blab **5** prate **6** gabble, gossip, snitch, squeal, tell on **7** blather, chatter, hearsay, prattle, twaddle **8** inform on **9** loose talk **11** mudslinging **12** tittle-tattle **13** tongue-wagging

tattletale 3 rat **4** fink **5** sneak **6** gossip, snitch **7** ratfink, stoolie, tattler **8** betrayer, busybody, informer, squealer, telltale **8** informer **10** newsmonger, talebearer **11** rumormonger, stool pigeon **12** blabbermouth, troublemaker **13** scandalmonger

Tatum, Edward Lawrie
  field: **8** genetics **12** biochemistry
  discovered: **19** gene characteristics
  awarded: **10** Nobel Prize

taunt 3 guy, rag **4** gibe, jeer, jive, mock, slur, twit **5** scoff, sneer, tease **6** deride, harass, insult, jeer at **7** provoke, rag-

ging, sneer at, snigger, torment **8** chaffing, derision, ridicule **9** make fun of, poke fun at, snigger at **10** harassment, make game of, tormenting **11** provocation

Taura
  form: **3** cow
  attribute: **6** sacred

taurobolium
  rite of: **7** baptism

Taurog, Norman
  director of: **6** Skippy (Oscar) **8** Boys' Town

Taurus
  symbol: **4** bull
  planet: **5** Venus
  rules: **5** money **9** resources
  born: **3** May **5** April

taut 4 neat, snug, tidy, trig, trim **5** rigid, smart, tense, tight **6** spruce **7** orderly **8** not loose, not slack **9** shipshape, unbending, unrelaxed **10** drawn tight, inflexible, nononsense **11** under strain **12** businesslike **13** well-regulated **15** well-disciplined

tavern 3 bar, pub **4** dive **6** bistro, saloon **7** barroom, gin mill, taproom **8** alehouse, drinkery, grogshop **9** beer joint, brasserie, honky-tonk, roadhouse **10** restaurant **11** public house **12** watering hole **14** cocktail lounge
  French: **7** auberge
  German: **8** Brauhaus

tawdry 4 loud **5** cheap, crass, gaudy, showy, tacky **6** flashy, garish, tinsel, vulgar **7** raffish **8** gimcrack **9** inelegant, obtrusive, tasteless **10** flamboyant **11** conspicuous, pretentious **12** meretricious, ostentatious

tawny 3 tan **4** fawn **5** beige, dusky, olive, sandy **6** bronze **7** swarthy **8** brownish **10** light brown **14** yellowish-brown

tax 3 sap, try **4** duty, lade, levy, load, tire, toll **5** drain, weigh **6** assess, burden, charge, custom, excise, impost, saddle, strain, tariff, weight **7** deplete, exhaust, stretch, wear out **8** exertion, overwork **10** assessment, obligation, overburden
  kind: **4** city **5** sales, state **6** county, excise, income, luxury **8** property **11** inheritance **12** excess profit

Taxi
  character: **9** John Burns, Tony Banta **10** Alex Rieger **11** Elaine Nardo, Latka Gravas **12** Bobby Wheeler, Louie De Palma
  cast: **9** Tony Danza **10** Judd

Hirsch **11** Andy Kaufman, Danny DeVito, Jeff Conaway **12** Marilu Henner **13** Randall Carver
company: 11 Sunshine Cab

taxicab 4 hack **6** jitney **7** droshky, hackney **8** hired car, rickshaw **10** automobile **11** jinrickshaw

Taxi Driver
  director: 14 Martin Scorsese
  cast: 10 Peter Boyle **11** Jodie Foster **12** Albert Brooks, Harvey Keitel, Robert De Niro **13** Leonard Harris **14** Cybill Shepherd
  setting: 11 New York City
  score: 15 Bernard Herrmann
  script: 12 Paul Schrader

taxonomy
  study of: 17 structure contrast **19** structure comparison

Taygete
  member of: 8 Pleiades
  father: 5 Atlas
  son: 10 Lacedaemon

Taylor, Elizabeth
  born: 6 London **7** England
  husband: 8 Mike Todd **10** John Warner **11** Eddie

Fisher, Nicky Hilton **13** Richard Burton **14** Michael Wilding
  roles: 5 Giant **7** Ivanhoe **9** Cleopatra **11** Little Women **12** The Sandpiper **14** A Place in the Sun, National Velvet, Raintree County **16** Butterfield Eight (Oscar), Cat on a Hot Tin Roof, Father of the Bride **18** Suddenly Last Summer **19** The Taming of the Shrew **25** Who's Afraid of Virginia Woolf (Oscar)

Taylor, Robert
  real name: 22 Spangler Arlington Brugh
  wife: 12 Ursula Thiess **15** Barbara Stanwyck
  roles: 7 Camille, Ivanhoe **8** Quo Vadis **11** Billy the Kid **14** Waterloo Bridge **20** Magnificent Obsession

Taylor, Zachary *see box*

Tchad *see* **4** Chad

Tchaikovsky, Peter (Piotr Ilyich Chaikovsky)
  born: 6 Russia **8** Votkinsk
  composer of: 7 Manfred, Mazeppa **8** Iolanthe, Pathetic (symphony No 6), Swan

Lake **9** Joan of Arc **10** Nutcracker **12** Eugene Onegin, Winter Dreams **14** Italian Caprice, Romeo and Juliet, The Enchantress **16** The Queen of Spades **17** Francesca da Rimini, The Sleeping Beauty **22** Eighteen-Twelve Overture

Tchile *see* **5** Chile

tea 16 Camellia sinensis
  varieties: 5 Assam, Bohea, China, green, pekoe, Yerba **6** Ceylon, Oolong, Oswego, Tisane **7** African, Arabian, cambric, crystal, Lapsang, Mexican, redroot, Spanish **8** bergamot, camomile, Earl Grey, Labrador, mountain, Paraguay, Siberian, Souchong, Woodruff **9** gunpowder, lemon balm, New Jersey, sassafras **10** Darjeeling, Philippine **11** Appalachian, Orange Pekoe **14** Irish breakfast **16** English breakfast

teach 5 coach, drill, edify, prime, tutor **6** inform, school **7** educate, implant, prepare **8** exercise, instruct **9** enlighten, inculcate **10** discipline **12** indoctrinate

Teach
  character in: 21 The Master of Ballantrae
  author: 9 Stevenson

teacher 3 don **5** coach, tutor **6** master, mentor **7** maestro, trainer **8** educator **9** preceptor, professor **10** instructor, schoolmarm **12** schoolmaster **13** schoolteacher **14** schoolmistress

teaching 5 dogma, tenet **6** belief **7** nurture, precept **8** doctrine, pedagogy, training, tutelage, tutoring **9** education, principle, schooling **10** conviction, philosophy **11** inculcation, instructing, instruction, preparation **14** indoctrination

tea dance
  French: 10 the dansant

teal
  group of: 5 ducks
  color: 4 blue **5** green

team 3 rig, set **4** ally, band, crew, five, gang, join, nine, pair, side, unit, yoke **5** force, group, merge, party, squad, staff, unify, unite **6** circle, clique, couple, eleven, league, tandem **7** combine, company, coterie, faction **8** alliance, federate **9** coalition, cooperate **10** amalgamate, federation, sports team, yoked group **11** association, consolidate, get

---

Taylor, Zachary
  nickname: 16 Old Rough and Ready
  presidential rank: 7 twelfth
  party: 4 Whig
  state represented: 2 LA
  defeated: 4 (Lewis) Cass **8** (Martin) Van Buren
  vice president: 8 (Millard) Fillmore
  cabinet:
    state: **7** (John Middleton) Clayton
    treasury: **8** (William Morris) Meredith
    war: **8** (George Walker) Crawford
    attorney general: **7** (Reverdy) Johnson
    navy: **7** (William Ballard) Preston
    postmaster general: **8** (Jacob) Collamer
    interior: **5** (Thomas) Ewing
  born: 12 Montebello VA **12** Orange County
  died: 12 Washington DC
  buried: 12 Louisville KY
  education: 9 no college **16** privately tutored
  religion: 12 Episcopalian
  political career: 21 none prior to presidency
  civilian career: 7 planter, soldier
  military service: 6 US Army **12** major general
    War: **7** Mexican **9** Black Hawk **19** War of Eighteen-Twelve **14** Second Seminole
  notable events of lifetime/presidency:
    treaty: **13** Clayton-Bulwer
  father: 7 Richard
  mother: 5 Sarah (Dabney Strother)
  siblings: 6 George **7** Hancock **11** Sarah Bailey **12** Elizabeth Lee, Emily Richard **13** Joseph Pannill **21** William Dabney Strother
  wife: 8 Margaret (Mackall Smith)
  children: 7 Richard **9** Sarah Knox **10** Ann Mackall **13** Margaret Smith, Mary Elizabeth, Octavia Panill

together, incorporate **12** band together, join together **13** confederation

teammate 4 ally **7** partner **8** co-player, coworker **9** associate, colleague, co-partner **11** confederate **12** collaborator

team spirit 10 group pride, solidarity **13** esprit de corps

team up 4 ally **5** unite **9** cooperate **10** join forces **11** collaborate

tear 3 fly, gap, hie, rip, run **4** bolt, dart, dash, grab, hole, mist, pull, race, rend, rent, rift, rive, rush, scud, slit, snag, swim, whiz, yank **5** abuse, break, crack, fault, pluck, scoot, seize, sever, shoot, shred, speed, split, spurt, sweep, whisk **6** breach, cleave, damage, divide, gallop, hasten, hustle, injury, plunge, ravage, scurry, snatch, sprint, sunder, wrench **7** disrupt, fissure, hard use, opening, rupture, scamper, scuttle **8** disunite, teardrop, scramble, splinter **9** come apart, hotfoot it, pull apart, skedaddle **10** impairment, make tracks **11** destruction **12** pull to pieces

tear down 4 raze **5** level, smash, wreck **7** destroy, flatten **8** demolish **9** dismantle, take apart

tearful 5 teary, weepy **6** crying **7** bawling, crushed, sobbing, wailing, weeping **8** mournful **9** lamenting, sniveling **10** blubbering, lachrymose, whimpering **11** heartbroken **12** inconsolable **13** brokenhearted

tear off 5 sever **6** detach, rip off **7** pull off **8** break off, separate **10** wrench away

Teasdale, Sara author of: **8** Love Song **11** Helen of Troy **13** Dark of the Moon **14** Flame and Shadow, Rivers to the Sea, Strange Victory

tease 3 guy, irk, nag, rag, vex **4** bait, gall, gibe, goad, haze, jeer, josh, mock, pest, rile, twit **5** annoy, chafe, harry, mimic, pique, scoff, sneer, taunt, worry **6** badger, bother, harass, hazing, heckle, hector, mocker, needle, pester, plague, teaser **7** bedevil, chafing, laugh at, needler, provoke, razzing, snigger, taunter, torment, worrier **8** derision, heckling, irritate, needling, ridicule **9** aggravate, make fun of, mimicking, persecute, tantalize, tormentor **10** harassment, tantalizer **11** persecution

teaspoon abbreviation: **3** tsp

Teazle, Sir Peter and Lady characters in: **19** The School for Scandal author: **8** Sheridan

technical 5 trade **10** mechanical, vocational **11** complicated, nonacademic **13** technological

technique 3 art, way **4** form **5** craft, knack, style **6** manner, method, system **7** formula, know-how **8** approach, facility **9** procedure **10** adroitness, expertness, technology **11** proficiency **12** skillfulness

Tecmessa father: **8** Teuthras son: **9** Eurysaces carried off by: **14** Telamonian Ajax

tedious 3 dry **4** drab, dull, long, slow **5** vapid **6** boring, dismal, dreary, jejune, tiring **7** humdrum, insipid, irksome, onerous, prosaic **8** drawn-out, lifeless, tiresome, wearying **9** fatiguing, laborious, wearisome **10** burdensome, exhausting, monotonous, oppressive, unexciting **13** time-consuming, unimaginative, uninteresting

tediousness 5 ennui **7** boredom **8** dullness, monotony

tedium 3 rut **5** ennui **7** boredom **8** drabness, dullness, monotony, sameness **10** dreariness **11** routineness **12** tiresomeness

tedium of life Latin: **12** taedium vitae

teem 4 brim, gush **5** swarm **6** abound **8** be full of, overflow **9** be overrun **15** burst at the seams

teeming 4 full **7** crowded **8** swarming **9** abounding, bounteous **11** overflowing

teeny-weeny 3 wee **4** tiny **5** dwarf **6** little, minute, petite **9** miniature, minuscule **10** diminutive, pocket-size **11** lilliputian, microscopic, pocket-sized

teeter 4 reel, sway **5** lurch, waver **6** seesaw, totter, wobble **7** stagger **8** hesitate **9** vacillate

teetotaler 3 dry **9** abstainer **10** nondrinker **14** prohibitionist

Tegeates father: **6** Lycaon

Tegucigalpa capital of: **8** Honduras

Tegyrius king of: **6** Thrace

Tehani character in: **17** Mutiny on the Bounty authors: **4** Hall **8** Nordhoff

Tehran, Teheran capital of: **4** Iran landmark: **10** Melaat Park **12** Marble Palace, Marmar Palace **14** Azadai Monument, Gulestan Palace, Saadabad Palace **15** Freedom Monument, Hosseineh Mosque, Shahyad Monument **23** Center for Islamic Studies means: **9** warm place mountain: **6** Elburz **8** Demavend ruler: **8** Khomeini **23** Muhammad Reza Shah Pahlavi

te igitur 13 thee therefore

Teiresias see **8** Tiresias

Telamon king of: **7** Salamis member of: **9** Argonauts father: **6** Aeacus mother: **6** Endeis brother: **6** Peleus half-brother: **6** Phocus wife: **6** Glauce **7** Eriboea son: **4** Ajax **6** Teucer friend: **8** Hercules

Telchines form: **6** beings characteristic: **9** malicious

Telegonus father: **7** Proteus **8** Odysseus mother: **5** Circe wife: **2** Io **8** Penelope killed: **8** Odysseus killed by: **8** Hercules

telegraph invented by: **5** Morse, Woods **6** Edison **7** Marconi

Telemachus father: **8** Odysseus mother: **8** Penelope son: **7** Latinus

Telemann, Georg Philipp born: **7** Germany **9** Magdeburg composer of: **9** Fantasias **10** Times of Day **12** Don Quichotte **14** Die Tageszeiten, Musique de Table

Telemus vocation: **4** seer father: **7** Eurymus warned: **10** Polyphemus

telepathy 3 ESP **10** sixth sense **11** second sight **12** clairvoyance **19** spirit communication, thought transference **22** extrasensory perception

Telephassa
husband: **6** Agenor

telephone
invented by: **4** Bell

Telephus
king of: **5** Mysia
father: **8** Hercules
mother: **4** Auge

telescope
invented by: **7** Galileo
10 Lippershey
astronomical: **6** Kepler

Telesphorus
god of: **15** illness recovery

telesterion
form: **8** building
purpose: **8** religion
11 celebration

television
invented by: **5** Baird **8** Zworykin **10** Farnsworth

tell 3 ask, bid, own, say, see **4** blab **5** bruit, count, order, speak, spout, state, utter, weigh, write **6** advise, babble, betray, blazon, depict, detail, direct, figure, impart, inform, number, recite, reckon, relate, report, reveal, sketch, unfold **7** apprise, command, compute, confess, declare, discern, divulge, express, find out, mention, narrate, portray, predict, publish, recount, request **8** acquaint, count off, describe, disclose, estimate, forecast, foretell, identify, instruct, perceive, register, set forth **9** apprehend, ascertain, broadcast, calculate, chronicle, enumerate, enunciate, influence, make known, pronounce, recognize **10** take effect **11** communicate, distinguish **12** discriminate **17** breathe a word about

Teller, Edward
field: **7** physics
developed: **8** atom bomb
12 hydrogen bomb

telling 5 solid, valid **6** cogent, potent **7** decided, weighty **8** decisive, definite, forceful, material, positive, powerful, striking **9** effective, effectual, important, momentous, trenchant **10** conclusive, definitive, impressive **11** efficacious, influential, significant **13** consequential

telltale 6 gossip **7** tattler **8** busybody, giveaway, informer, squealer **9** affirming, betraying, divulging, revealing, verifying **10** confirming, disclosing, newsbearer, talebearer, tattletale **11** informative **12** blabber-

mouth, enlightening **13** scandalmonger

Tellus
called: **10** Terra Mater
origin: **5** Roman
goddess of: **5** earth **8** marriage **9** fertility **11** agriculture
corresponds to: **4** Gaea

Telphusa
form: **5** nymph
location: **6** spring
characteristic: **7** cunning

Temenus
father: **8** Pelasgus **12** Aristomachus
brother: **11** Aristodemus, Cresphontes
reared: **4** Hera

temerity 4 gall **5** brass, cheek, nerve **8** audacity, boldness, chutzpah, rashness **9** brashness, freshness, impudence, insolence, pushiness, sauciness **10** brazenness, effrontery **11** forwardness **12** impertinence, indiscretion **13** foolhardiness, intrusiveness

Temin, Howard Martin
field: **8** genetics, oncology
discovered: **20** reverse transcriptase
awarded: **10** Nobel Prize

temper 3 ire **4** bile, calm, fury, gall, mood, rage **5** allay, anger, humor, pique, quiet, still, wrath **6** animus, anneal, choler, dander, harden, pacify, soften, soothe, spleen **7** appease, balance, compose, dudgeon, emotion, ferment, passion, toughen, umbrage **8** acrimony, bad humor, calmness, mitigate, moderate, palliate, vexation **9** annoyance, composure, huffiness **10** irritation, strengthen **11** displeasure, disposition, equilibrium, frame of mind, indignation, peevishness, tranquilize **12** churlishness, irascibility, irritability

temperament 4 bent, cast, mood, soul, tone **5** humor, tenor **6** makeup, nature, spirit, temper **7** leaning, quality **8** tendency **9** character **10** complexion **11** disposition, frame of mind, personality

temperamental 5 fiery, moody **6** fickle **7** erratic, peppery, willful **8** unstable, volatile **9** emotional, excitable, explosive, hotheaded, mercurial, sensitive, turbulent **10** capricious, headstrong, high-strung, hysterical, mettlesome, passionate, unreliable **11** tempestuous, thin-skinned

12 undependable **13** unpredictable

temperance 8 prudence, sobriety **9** restraint **10** abstention, abstinence, discretion, moderation, self-denial **11** forbearance, prohibition, self-control, teetotalism **14** abstemiousness, self-discipline

temperate 4 calm, cool, even, mild, sane, soft, warm **5** balmy, sober, sunny **6** gentle, mellow, sedate, steady **7** clement, patient, sparing **8** composed, moderate, pleasant, rational, tranquil **9** collected, easygoing, unruffled **10** coolheaded, reasonable **11** levelheaded **13** dispassionate, self-possessed, unextravagant, unimpassioned **14** self-controlled, self-restrained

temperature measurement
6 degree, Kelvin **7** Celsius **10** Fahrenheit

tempest 5 chaos, furor, storm **6** hubbub, tumult, uproar **8** brouhaha, outbreak, upheaval **9** agitation, cataclysm, commotion **10** hurly-burly, turbulence **11** disturbance

Tempest, The
author: **18** William Shakespeare
character: **5** Ariel **6** Alonso **7** Antonio, Caliban, Gonzalo, Miranda **8** Prospero **9** Ferdinand, Sebastian

Tempestates
origin: **5** Roman
goddesses of: **6** storms

tempestuous 3 hot **5** fiery **6** raging, stormy **7** excited, frantic, furious, violent **8** agitated, feverish, frenzied **9** emotional, explosive, turbulent, wrought-up **10** hysterical, passionate, tumultuous **11** impassioned, overwrought

Templar, Simon
character in: **8** The Saint
author: **9** Charteris

temple 4 fane, kirk **6** chapel, church, mosque, pagoda, priory, shrine **7** convent **8** basilica, pantheon **9** cathedral, joss house, monastery, sanctuary, synagogue **10** house of God, tabernacle **12** meetinghouse

Temple, Shirley
married name: **18** Shirley Temple Black
born: **13** Santa Monica CA
roles: **5** Heidi **10** Bright Eyes **15** Wee Willie Winkie **16** Little Miss Marker, The Little Colonel, The Littlest Rebel **18** Poor Little Rich

Girl **21** Susannah of the Mounties **23** Rebecca of Sunnybrook Farm

Temple, The
   author: **13** George Herbert

Temple Beau, The
   author: **13** Henry Fielding

tempo 4 clip, gait, pace, rate, time **5** meter, speed **6** pacing, stride, timing **8** momentum, velocity

tempo giusto
   music: **10** strict time

temporal 3 lay **5** civil **6** mortal **7** mundane, passing, profane, secular, worldly **8** day-to-day, fleeting, fugitive **9** ephemeral, temporary, transient **10** evanescent, noneternal **11** impermanent, nonclerical **12** nonspiritual **17** nonecclesiastical

temporary, temporarily 5 brief, fleet **7** interim, passing, stopgap **8** fleeting, fugitive **9** ephemeral, momentary, provisory, transient **10** evanescent, short-lived, transitory **11** impermanent, provisional **13** flash-in-the-pan
   Latin: **10** pro tempore

temporary dwelling
   French: **10** pied-a-terre

temporize 5 delay, hedge, stall, tarry, waver **8** hang back, maneuver **9** hem and haw, vacillate **10** equivocate **11** play for time **12** drag one's feet, tergiversate **13** procrastinate

tempt 3 try, woo **4** bait, draw, goad, lure, pull, risk **5** charm, decoy, prick, rouse **6** allure, arouse, entice, incite, invite, seduce **7** attract, bewitch, provoke **8** appeal to, intrigue, inveigle **9** captivate, tantalize **12** put to the test **13** take one's fancy **14** fly in the face of **15** whet the appetite

temptation 4 bait, draw, lure, pull, urge **5** charm, snare, spell **8** stimulus, tempting **9** incentive, seduction **10** allurement, attraction, enticement, incitement, inducement **11** captivation, fascination, provocation

tempter 5 Satan **7** enticer, seducer **8** the Devil

temptress 4 vamp **5** Circe, flirt, siren **7** charmer, Delilah, Jezebel, Lorelei, vampire **8** coquette **9** odalisque, sorceress **10** seductress **11** enchantress, femme fatale

tempus fugit 9 time flies

Ten (10)
   director: **12** Blake Edwards
   cast: **7** Bo Derek **11** Dudley Moore **12** Julie Andrews

tenable 6 viable **8** arguable, rational, sensible, workable **9** excusable **10** condonable, defendable, defensible, vindicable **11** justifiable, warrantable **12** maintainable

tenacious 3 set **4** fast, firm, hard, iron **6** dogged, mulish **7** adamant, staunch **8** clinging, constant, obdurate, resolute, stalwart, stubborn **9** immovable, obstinate, pigheaded, steadfast, unbending **10** determined, inexorable, inflexible, persistent, relentless, unswerving, unwavering, unyielding **11** persevering, undeviating, unfaltering, unremitting **12** intransigent, unchangeable **14** uncompromising

tenaciousness 8 tenacity **9** endurance **10** resolution **11** persistence **12** perseverance, resoluteness **13** determination **16** stick-to-itiveness

tenacity 8 strength **9** toughness **10** resolution **11** persistence **12** cohesiveness, perseverance, resoluteness **13** determination, tenaciousness **16** stick-to-itiveness

tenant 6 lessee, lodger, renter, roomer **7** boarder, denizen, dweller **8** occupant, resident **10** inhabitant **11** householder, leaseholder, paying guest

Tenant of Wildfell Hall, The
   author: **10** Anne Bronte

Tenants, The
   author: **14** Bernard Malamud

Ten Commandments *see box*

Ten Commandments, The
   director: **13** Cecil B DeMille
   cast: **8** Nina Foch **9** John Derek **10** Anne Baxter, Debra Paget, Yul Brynner **11** Martha Scott **12** Vincent Price **13** John Carradine, Yvonne De Carlo **14** Charlton Heston (Moses), Judith Anderson **15** Cedric Hardwicke, Edward G Robinson

tend 3 aim **4** bear, head, lead, lean, mind, move **5** be apt, guide, nurse, point, watch **6** extend, foster, manage, wait on **7** care for, nurture **8** attend to, be liable, be likely **9** bid fair to, gravitate, look after, supervise, watch over **10** minister to, predispose, take care of **11** keep an eye on

Ten Commandments
   also: **9** Decalogue
   given to: **5** Moses
   where given: **10** Mount Sinai
   inscribed on: **12** stone tablets
   first: **32** Thou shalt have no other Gods before me
   second: **37** Thou shalt not bow down before graven images
   third: **44** Thou shalt not take the name of the Lord thy God in vain
   fourth: **34** Remember the Sabbath Day and keep it holy
   fifth: **26** Honor thy father and thy mother
   sixth: **16** Thou shalt not kill
   seventh: **26** Thou shalt not commit adultery
   eighth: **17** Thou shalt not steal
   ninth: **46** Thou shalt not bear false witness against thy neighbor
   tenth: **17** Thou shalt not covet

tendency 3 aim, set **4** bent **5** drift, drive, habit, trend **6** course **7** heading, impulse, leaning, turning **8** penchant **9** direction, proneness, readiness **10** proclivity, propensity **11** disposition, gravitation, inclination **14** predisposition

tender 3 raw **4** fond, give, good, kind, soft, sore, weak **5** frail, green, place, young **6** aching, benign, callow, caring, dainty, extend, feeble, gentle, hand in, loving, prefer, submit, weakly **7** advance, fragile, hold out, painful, present, proffer, propose, suggest, swollen **8** delicate, generous, immature, inflamed, juvenile, merciful, propound, underage, youthful **9** lay before, sensitive, volunteer **10** benevolent, put forward, thoughtful, vulnerable **11** considerate, sentimental, softhearted, sympathetic, warmhearted **12** affectionate **13** compassionate, inexperienced, understanding **14** impressionable **15** unsophisticated

tenderfoot 4 tyro **6** novice, rookie **8** beginner, neophyte **9** fledgling, greenhorn **10** apprentice

tenderhearted 4 mild **6** benign, gentle, humane **8** generous, merciful **10** altruistic, benevolent, responsive, thoughtful **11** considerate, kindhearted, softhearted, sympathetic, warmhearted **13** compassionate, understanding

tenderheartedness 4 pity **5** heart **7** empathy **8** sympathy **10** compassion

tendering 6 giving **8** offering **9** advancing, extending, proposing **10** holding out, preferring, proffering, submitting, suggesting **11** propounding **12** volunteering

Tender Is the Night
author: 16 F Scott Fitzgerald
character: 8 Abe North
9 Dick Diver **11** Nicole Diver, Tommy Barban
12 Rosemary Hoyt

tenderness 4 love **6** aching, warmth **7** rawness **8** delicacy, fondness, goodness, humanity, kindness, mildness, smarting, softness, soreness, sympathy **9** affection **10** compassion, gentleness, humaneness, kindliness, lovingness **11** beneficence, benevolence, painfulness, sensitivity **12** mercifulness **14** loving kindness

tendon
part of: 21 musculoskeletal system

tendril 4 coil, curl **5** crook, shoot, sprig, twist **6** winder **7** climber, ringlet

tenebrous 3 dim **4** dark **5** murky **6** gloomy **7** obscure, shadowy **8** darkened, obscured **13** unilluminated

Tenes
father: 6 Cycnus
mother: 7 Proclea
stepmother: 9 Phylonome
sister: 8 Hemithea

tenet 4 rule, view **5** canon, credo, creed, dogma, maxim **6** belief, thesis **7** opinion **8** doctrine, ideology, position, teaching **9** principle **10** conviction, persuasion

Tennessee *see box*

tennis
athlete: 8 Don Budge, Jan Kodes, Rod Laver, Tom Okker **9** Bjorn Borg, Ivan Lendl, Stan Smith **10** Arthur Ashe, Bill Tilden, Jack Kramer, Maria Bueno, Pam Shriver, Roy Emerson, Steffi Graf **11** Alice Marble, Andre Agassi, Edward Dibbs, Ilie Nastase, John McEnroe,

Ken Rosewall, Tracy Austin **12** Althea Gibson, Darren Cahill, Francois Durr, Jimmy Connors, John Newcombe, Mats Wilander, Roscoe Tanner, Virginia Wade **13** Dennis Ralston, Harold Solomon, Manuel Orantes, Manuel Santana, Martin Riessen, Wendy Turnbull **14** Brian Gottfried, Guillermo Vilas, Hana Mandlikova, Pancho Gonzalez, Rosemary Casals **15** Charles Pasarell, Chris Evert Lloyd, Maureen Connolly, Richard

Stockton, Vitas Gerulaitis **17** Donald Schollander, Nancy Richey Gunter **18** Margaret Smith Court, Martina Navratilova **20** Helen Wills Moody Roark **21** Billie Jean Moffitt King, Evonne Goolagong Cawley

Tennyson, Alfred, Lord
author of: 4 Maud **7** Mariana, Ulysses **10** Enoch Arden, In Memoriam (A A H) **12** Locksley Hall, Morte d'Arthur **16** The Lady of Shalott **18** The Idylls of the

Tennessee
abbreviation: 2 TN **4** Tenn
nickname: 7 Big Bend **9** Volunteer **11** Old Franklin
capital: 9 Nashville
largest city: 7 Memphis
others: 5 Alcoa, Paris **6** Camden, Sparta **7** Bristol, Dickson, Pulaski **8** Franklin, Gallatin, Oak Ridge **9** Cedar Hill, Cleveland, Inglewood, Kingsport, Knoxville, Lexington **10** Greenbrier, Morristown, Old Hickory **11** Chattanooga, Clarksville, Springfield **12** Fayetteville, Murfreesboro **14** Hendersonville
college: 4 Fisk, Lane **5** Bryan, Siena **6** Bethel **7** Belmont, Lambuth, Lemoyne **8** Milligan, Tusculum **10** Vanderbilt **12** Southwestern **13** David Lipscomb **14** Meharry Medical **17** Tennessee Wesleyan
feature: 12 The Hermitage
  dam: **6** Norris, Wilson **7** Douglas
  fort: **5** Henry **8** Donalson, Nashboro
  national park: **6** Shiloh **13** Cumberland Gap **19** Great Smoky Mountains (with North Carolina)
  national parkway: **12** Natchez Trace
tribe: 7 Shawnee **8** Cherokee **9** Chickasaw
people: 7 Sequoya **8** John Bell **9** James Agee **10** Grace Moore **11** Bessie Smith, Cordell Hull **12** Davy Crockett **18** Carey Estes Kefauver **23** Alvin Cullum "Sergeant" York **32** Ernest Jennings "Tennessee Ernie" Ford
  explorer: **6** Arthur, De Soto **7** Jolliet, La Salle, Needham **9** Marquette
lake: 7 Douglas **8** Barkeley, Cherokee, Reelfoot, Watts Bar **10** Center Hill **11** Chickamauga
land rank: 12 thirty-fourth
mountain: 5 Guyot **7** Lookout, Smokies **9** Blue Ridge **10** Cumberland, Great Smoky
  highest point: **13** Clingman's Dome
physical feature:
  basin: **9** Nashville
  highlands: **11** Appalachian
  plain: **7** Coastal
  plateau: **10** Cumberland
president: 10 James K Polk **13** Andrew Jackson, Andrew Johnson
river: 3 Elk **4** Duck **5** Caney, Obion, Stone **6** Clinch **7** Hatchie, Holston **8** Hiwassee **9** Tennessee **10** Cumberland **11** French Broad, Mississippi **15** Little Tennessee
state admission: 9 sixteenth
state bird: 11 mockingbird
state flower: 4 flag, iris **6** maypop **13** passion flower
state motto: 16 America at Its Best **22** Agriculture and Commerce
state song: 11 My Tennessee **17** The Tennessee Waltz **19** My Homeland Tennessee **26** When It's Iris Time in Tennessee
state tree: 11 tulip poplar **12** yellow poplar

King **26** The Charge of the Light Brigade

tenor 4 gist **5** drift, sense, trend **6** course, import, intent, nature, object **7** content, essence, meaning, purport, purpose **8** argument, tendency **9** direction, intention, substance **11** connotation, implication **12** significance

tense 4 taut **5** brace, drawn, rigid, shaky, stiff, tight **6** braced, draw up, on edge, uneasy **7** anxious, excited, fearful, fidgety, jittery, nervous, restive, stiffen, uptight **8** agitated, make taut, restless, strained, timorous **9** tighten up, tremulous, wrought-up **10** high-strung, inflexible, unyielding **12** apprehensive

tension 5 dread **6** spring, strain, stress **7** anxiety, pulling, tugging **8** bad vibes, exertion, pressure, rigidity, tautness, traction **9** hostility, misgiving, stiffness, straining, tightness **10** stretching **11** fearfulness, nervousness, restiveness, trepidation **12** apprehension, elastic force, perturbation **13** bad vibrations, combativeness

tent 3 pup **4** care, hard **5** gauze, probe, tepee **6** bigtop, canvas, search, teepee, wigwam **7** shelter **8** pavilion **10** tabernacle

tentacle 3 arm **6** feeler **9** appendage

tentative 4 iffy **5** trial **6** acting **8** not final, proposed **9** ad interim, temporary, undecided, unsettled **10** contingent, indefinite, not settled **11** conditional, probational, provisional, speculative, unconfirmed **12** experimental, probationary **15** subject to change **18** under consideration

tentative procedure 4 test **5** flier, trail **6** feeler, tryout **7** venture **10** experiment **12** trial balloon

tenuous 4 slim, thin, weak **5** frail, shaky **6** flimsy, paltry, slight **7** fragile, shallow, slender **8** delicate, gossamer **9** uncertain **10** indefinite **11** halfhearted, unsupported **12** unconvincing **13** unsubstantial

tenure 4 rule, term, time **5** reign **7** tenancy **9** occupancy, retention **10** incumbency, occupation, permanency, possession **11** entitlement, job security **14** administration

tepee, teepee 4 chum, tent **5** lodge **6** wigwam **7** wickiup

tepid 4 cool, mild **7** languid, warmish **8** lukewarm, moderate **9** apathetic, impassive, temperate **10** nonchalant, phlegmatic **11** halfhearted, indifferent, unemotional **13** lackadaisical **14** unenthusiastic

tequila
  type: 6 spirit
  origin: 6 Mexico
  made from: 5 agave
    6 maguey
  used with: 4 lime, salt
    5 lemon
  drink: 7 Chapala **8** El Diablo
  with creme de cacao:
    8 Toreador
  with kahlua: 9 Brave Bull
  with orange juice: 7 Sunrise
  with Tia Maria: 9 Brave Bull
  with triple sec: 9 Margarita

Terah
  son: 5 Abram, Haran, Nahor

Teraphim
  origin: 6 Hebrew
  form: 4 idol

Ter Borch, Gerard (Terburg)
  born: 6 Zwolle **14** The Netherlands
  artwork: 8 Flea Hunt **10** The Concert **14** Peace of Munster **21** The Parental Admonition

Terbrugghen, Hendrick
  born: 8 Deventer **14** The Netherlands
  artwork: 14 The Flute Player **19** Liberation of St Peter **21** The Calling of St Matthew

terefah, trefah 9 not kosher

Tereus
  prince of: 6 Thrace
  father: 4 Ares
  wife: 6 Procne
  sister-in-law: 9 Philomela
  raped: 9 Philomela
  son: 4 Itys

tergal 4 back **6** dorsal

Terkel, Studs
  author of: 7 Working **9** Hard Times **14** American Dreams

term, terms 3 age, dub, era, tag **4** call, cite, item, name, span, time, word **5** catch, cycle, epoch, idiom, reign, spell, stage, state, style, while **6** clause, course, detail, period, phrase, status, string **7** dynasty, footing, proviso **8** duration, interval, position, standing **9** condition, designate, provision, relations, requisite **10** expression, span of

time 11 appellation, designation, requirement, stipulation **12** characterize, circumstance, prerequisite **14** administration

termagant 3 nag **4** fury **5** scold, shrew, vixen **6** ogress, virago **7** hellcat, hellion, she-wolf, tigress **8** battle-ax, fishwife, harridan, spitfire **9** Xanthippe

Termagant
  character in: 21 medieval morality plays

terminal 3 end **4** last **5** depot, fatal, final, stand **6** deadly, lethal, mortal **7** station **8** terminus **10** concluding

terminate 3 end **4** stop **5** cease, close, lapse **6** expire, finish, run out, wind up **8** complete, conclude **11** come to an end, discontinue **12** bring to an end

termination 3 end **4** halt **5** close, finis, lapse **6** ending, finale, finish, windup **7** closing **8** stoppage **9** cessation **10** completion, concluding, conclusion, expiration **15** discontinuation

terminus 3 end **4** stop **5** depot, limit **6** ending **7** extreme, station **8** boundary, last stop, terminal **9** extremity **10** conclusion

Terminus
  origin: 5 Roman
  god of: 9 landmarks **10** boundaries

terminus ad quem 10 end to which, final limit **11** ending point

terminus a quo 9 beginning **12** end from which **13** starting point

termite
  variety: 6 desert **7** dry wood **8** damp wood **10** powderpost, rotten wood **11** soldierless **12** subterranean

Terms of Endearment
  director: 12 James L Brooks
  based on novel by: 13 Larry McMurtry
  cast: 11 Debra Winger **13** Jack Nicholson **15** Shirley MacLaine
  Oscar for: 7 actress (MacLaine), picture **8** director **15** supporting actor (Nicholson)

Terpsichore
  member of: 5 Muses
  personifies: 7 dancing **10** choral song

Terra
  goddess of: 5 Earth

Greek: 4 Gaea
mother: 5 Chaos
offspring: 6 Pontus, Titans,
Uranus **7** Erinyes, Oceanus
8 Cyclopes **9** mountains
13 Hecatonchires

terrace 4 roof **5** level, patio,
plane, porch **6** street **7** balcony, plateau **9** esplanade,
promenade **10** embankment

Terraced Bay *see* **6** Taiwan

terra-cotta 4 clay **6** russet
8 brownish **12** reddish-brown
14 brownish-orange

terrain 4 area, zone **5** tract
6 ground, milieu, region **7** setting **8** district **9** territory
10 topography **11** countryside,
environment **12** surroundings

terra incognita 11 unknown
land **14** unexplored land, unknown subject **16** unknown
territory

Terra Mater *see* **6** Tellus

terrapin 3 box **4** emyd, emys
6 slider, turpin, turtle **8** tortoise **11** diamond back
family: 8 Emydidae
female: 6 heifer
male: 4 bull

terrestrial 4 land **6** earth's,
global, ground **7** earthly, mundane, worldly **8** riparian
10 earthbound

terrible 3 bad **4** dire, huge
5 awful, great, harsh, rough,
scary **6** brutal, fierce, horrid,
odious, severe, strong
7 beastly, extreme, fearful,
ghastly, hateful, heinous, hideous, intense **8** alarming,
dreadful, enormous, fearsome,
horrible, shocking, terrific
9 appalling, excessive, harrowing, monstrous, obnoxious, offensive, repulsive, revolting,
upsetting **10** disturbing, formidable, horrifying, immoderate,
inordinate, terrifying, tremendous, unpleasant **11** distasteful,
distressing, frightening, intolerable **12** insufferable
13 objectionable

terrier
dog breed: 3 fox **4** bull,
Skye **5** Cairn, Irish, Welsh
6 border, Boston **7** Norfolk,
Tibetan, wire fox **8** Airedale,
Lakeland, Scottish, Sealy-
ham **9** Kerry Blue **10** Australian, Bedlington,
Manchester **13** Dandie Dinmont **17** soft-coated wheat-
en, Staffordshire bull, West
Highland white **18** miniature schnauzer **21** American
Staffordshire

terrific 3 fab **4** fine, good,
huge **5** awful, great, harsh,
marvy, scary, super **6** bang-up,
fierce, severe, superb **7** extreme, fearful, intense, sen-
sash **8** alarming, dreadful,
enormous, fabulous, fearsome,
smashing, splendid, terrible
9 excellent, excessive, fantastic, harrowing, marvelous,
monstrous, upsetting, wonderful **10** disturbing, horrifying,
immoderate, inordinate, remarkable, stupendous, super-
duper, terrifying, tremendous
11 distressing, exceptional,
frightening, sensational **13** extraordinary **14** out of this
world

terrified 6 afraid, scared
7 alarmed, panicky **9** petrified
10 frightened **11** scared stiff
13 panic-stricken **14** terror-
stricken **17** frightened to death

terrify 3 cow **5** abash, alarm,
daunt, panic, scare, unman,
upset **6** appall, dismay **7** agitate, disturb, horrify, overawe,
petrify **8** disquiet, frighten
10 intimidate **17** make one's
skin crawl **20** make one's
blood run cold **22** make one's
hair stand on end

terrifying 5 awful, dread
7 fearful **8** alarming, dreadful
9 frightful **11** frightening, hair-
raising

territory 4 area, land, pale,
zone **5** clime, realm, state,
tract **6** bounds, colony, domain, empire, limits, locale,
nation, region, sector
7 acreage, kingdom, mandate,
terrain **8** confines, district, dominion, province **9** bailiwick
10 dependency **11** countryside
12 commonwealth, principality, protectorate

terror 3 awe **4** fear **5** alarm,
dread, panic **6** dismay, fright,
horror **7** anxiety **8** affright,
disquiet **9** agitation **11** disquietude, trepidation **12** apprehension, perturbation
13 consternation **16** fear and
trembling

terrorize 3 cow **5** abash, force
6 menace **7** terrify **8** browbeat,
bulldoze, threaten
10 intimidate

terror-stricken 6 afraid,
scared **7** alarmed, panicky
9 horrified, petrified, terrified
11 scared green, scared stiff
13 panic-stricken, scared to
death

Terry and the Pirates
creator: 12 Milton Caniff
character: 7 Pat Ryan **8** Terry
Lee **10** Dragon Lady

terse 4 curt, neat **5** brief, clear,
crisp, pithy, short **6** abrupt
7 clipped, compact, concise, laconic, pointed, summary
8 clearcut, incisive, succinct
9 axiomatic, condensed,
trenchant **10** compressed
11 unambiguous **12** epigrammatic **18** brief and to the
point

terseness 7 brevity **8** curtness
9 crispness **10** abruptness
11 compactness, conciseness
12 succinctness

Tesman family
characters in: 11 Hedda
Gabler
members: 5 Hedda **6** George
7 Juliana
author: 5 Ibsen

Tess (of the D'Urbervilles)
author: 11 Thomas Hardy
director: 13 Roman Polanski
cast: 8 John Bett **10** Peter
Firth, Tom Chadbon
14 Rosemary Martin
15 Nastassia Kinski (Tess)

test 4 exam, quiz **5** check, final, flyer, probe, proof, prove,
trial **6** dry run, feeler, try out,
verify **7** analyze, confirm, examine, midterm **8** analysis,
validate **9** catechism **11** corroborate, examination, investigate, questioning
12 confirmation, substantiate,
verification **13** comprehensive,
corroboration, investigation,
questionnaire

Testament 5 Bible **7** the
Book **10** Scriptures **12** New
Testament, Old Testament

testament 6 legacy **7** bequest
10 settlement

tester 6 canopy **8** examiner
10 questioner

testify 4 show **5** prove, swear
6 affirm, attest, evince **7** declare, signify **8** evidence, indicate, manifest **11** bear witness,
demonstrate **12** give evidence

testimonial 5 medal **6** ribbon,
trophy **7** tribute **8** citation,
memorial, monument **9** affidavit, reference **10** deposition
11 certificate, endorsement
12 commendation
14 recommendation

testimony 5 proof **6** avowal
7 witness **8** averment, evidence **9** affidavit, statement
10 deposition, indication,
profession **11** affirmation, attestation, endorsement
12 confirmation, verification
13 certification, corroboration,
demonstration, documentation,
manifestation
14 acknowledgment

testy 5 cross, moody **6** crabby, cranky, crusty, filthy, grumpy, snappy, sullen, touchy **7** fretful, peevish, waspish **8** captious, caviling, choleric, churlish, perverse, petulant, snappish, snarling **9** fractious, impatient, irascible, irritable, splenetic **10** ill-humored **11** acrimonious, contentious **12** cantankerous, faultfinding, sharp-tongued **13** quick-tempered, temperamental

tete-a-tete 4 chat, talk **6** parley **9** interview **12** conversation **13** confabulation

tether 3 tie **4** cord, rein, rope **5** chain, leash **6** fasten, halter, hobble, secure

Tethys
member of: 6 Titans
father: 6 Uranus
mother: 4 Gaea
husband: 7 Oceanus
mother of: 8 Oceanids **9** river gods
daughters: 13 three thousand
foster child: 4 Hera

Teucer
king of: 4 Troy
father: 7 Telamon **9** Scamander
mother: 5 Idaea **7** Hesione
half-brother: 9 Great Ajax **14** Telemonian Ajax
daughter: 5 Batia
skilled in: 7 archery
founded: 7 Salamis

Teuthis
also: 7 Ornytus
rank: 7 general
wounded: 6 Athena

Teuthras
mentioned in: 5 Iliad
king of: 5 Mysia **7** Phrygia
mother: 8 Leucippe
daughter: 8 Tecmessa
killed: 4 boar
  boar sacred to: 7 Artemis
killed by: 6 Hector

Teutonic 5 Dutch **6** German, Gothic, Nordic **7** British, English **8** Germanic **12** Scandinavian
alphabet character: 4 rune
demon: 3 alp
goddess of death: 3 Hel, Ran
goddess of peace: 7 Nerthus
god of peace: 6 Balder
god of thunder: 4 Thor
god of war: 3 Tiu, Tyr
god of wisdom: 4 Odin

Teutonic Mythology *see* **17** Germanic Mythology

Texas *see box*

text 5 motif, theme, topic, verse, words **6** manual, primer, sermon, thesis **7** content, passage, subject, word-ing **8** argument, sentence, textbook, workbook **9** paragraph, quotation **10** schoolbook **13** subject matter

textile 4 yarn **5** cloth, fiber **6** fabric **8** filament, material **9** yard goods **10** piece goods

texture 3 nap **4** feel, look **5** grain, touch, weave **6** makeup **7** quality, surface **8** fineness **9** character, structure **10** coarseness **11** composition

Tey, Josephine
real name: 19 Elizabeth MacKintosh
author of: 10 Brat Farrar **15** Miss Pym Disposes, The Singing Sands **17** The Daughter of Time **19** A Shilling for Candles
character: 9 Alan Grant

Thackeray, William Makepeace
author of: 9 Pendennis **10** Vanity Fair **11** Barry Lyndon, Henry Esmond, The Newcomes **13** The Virginians

Thaddeus of Arimathea
see **5** Judas

Thaddeus of Warsaw
author: 10 Jane Porter

Thai-Austronesian
language branch: 9 Thai-Kadai **12** Austronesian
includes: 5 Batak, Malay **6** Fijian, Samoan **7** Tagalog **8** Hawaiian, Javanese **15** Bahasa Indonesia
spoken in: 4 Fiji, Java **5** China, Samoa **6** Hawaii, Taiwan **7** Sumatra **9** Indonesia, Polynesia **10** Madagas-

Texas
abbreviation: 2 TX **3** Tex
nickname: 8 Lone Star
capital: 6 Austin
largest city: 7 Houston
others: 4 Gail, Rice, Vega, Waco **5** Bryan, Marfa, Ozona, Pampa, Tyler, Wiley **6** Baylor, Borger, Dallas, Denton, El Paso, Kileen, Laredo, Odessa, Quanah, Sonora **7** Abilene, Denison, Lubbock **8** Amarillo, Beaumont, Floydada **9** Fort Worth, Galveston **10** San Antonio **13** Corpus Christi
college: 3 SMU, TCU **4** Rice **5** Lamar, Wiley **6** Austin, Baylor **7** St Mary's, Trinity **10** Texas A and M **12** Southwestern **14** Texas Christian **16** Abilene Christian **17** Southern Methodist
feature:
  fort: 5 Alamo
  national park: 7 Big Bend **18** Guadalupe Mountains
  national seashore: 11 Padre Island
  state park: 10 San Jacinto
tribe: 4 Adar, Waco **5** Caddo, Lipan **6** Apache, Biloxi, Jumano, Kichai, Shuman, Tejano **7** Alabama, Hasinai, Tonkawa **8** Comanche, Querecho **9** Coushatta, Karankawa
people: 10 James S Hogg **12** Edward M House, Thomas C Clark **13** John B Connally, Samuel Houston **14** Chester W Nimitz, Mirabeau B Lamar, Samuel T Rayburn, Stephen F Austin, William B Travis **15** John Nance Garner, Thomas T Connally **19** Katherine Anne Porter
  explorer: 4 Vaca **7** La Salle
island: 5 Padre
lake: 6 Falcon, Sabine, Texoma **7** Amistad
river: 3 Red **5** Pecos **6** Brazos, Neches, Nueces, Sabine **7** Trinity **8** Colorado **9** Rio Grande **10** San Jacinto
land rank: 12 second
physical feature:
  bay: 13 Corpus Christi
  port: 7 Houston **9** Galveston **13** Corpus Christi
president: 14 Lyndon B Johnson **17** Dwight D Eisenhower
  Republic of Texas: 10 Sam Houston
state admission: 12 twenty-eighth
state bird: 11 mockingbird
state flower: 10 bluebonnet, yellow rose
state motto: 10 Friendship
state song: 13 Texas Our Texas
state tree: 5 pecan
baseball team: 7 Rangers

Thailand
  name means: 13 land of the free
  other name: 4 Siam **11** Prathet Thai
  capital/largest city: 6 Bankok **7** Bangkok
    old capital: **8** Thonburi **9** Ayutthaya
  others: 4 Ubon **5** Puket **6** Nakhon, Ranong **7** Ayudhya, Ayuthea, Lampang, Lamphur, Lopburi,
    Rahaeng, Singora, Songkla **8** Khonkaen, Kiangmai, Songkhla, Sukhotai, Thonburi **9** Ayut-
    thaya, Chiangmai, Chiengmai **10** Ratchasima **11** Phitsanulok **14** Ubonratchthani
  kingdom: 5 Funan **6** Khymer **8** Thonburi **9** Ayutthaya, Chiang Mai, Dvaravati, Sukhothai
    12 Subarnabhumi
  school: 9 Thammasat **13** Chulalongkorn
  head of state: 4 king
  measure: 2 wa **3** can, ken, niv, rai, sat, sok, wah **4** cohi, keup, niou, tang **5** kwien, leeng,
    sesti, vouah **6** kabiet, kanahn **7** chaimeu **8** changawn **9** anukabiet
  monetary unit: 2 at **3** att **4** baht **5** cutty, fuang **6** pynung, salung **11** bullet money
  weight: 3 bat, hap, pay, sen, sok **4** baht, haph, kati, klam **5** catty, chang, fuang, picul, pilul,
    tical **6** fluang, graini, salung, **7** tamlung
  island: 2 Ko **3** Kut, Tao **4** Chan, Rawi **5** Chang, Lanta, Samui, Thalu **6** Libong, Phuket
    7 Phangan, Terutao
  lake: 9 Nong Lahan
  mountain: 5 Dawna, Khieo **6** Phanom **8** Dang Raek, Kao Prawa, Maelamun **9** Khao Luang
    11 Bilauktaung
  highest point: 8 Inthanon **11** Doi Inthanon
  river: 3 Chi, Mun, Nan, Yom **4** Ping **5** Menam **6** Mekong, Meping **7** Salween **10** Chaophraya
  sea: 7 Andaman
  physical feature:
    gulf: **4** Siam **8** Thailand
    isthmus: **3** Kra
    pass: **12** Three Pagodas
    peninsula: **5** Malay
    plateau: **5** Korat **6** Khorat
  people: 3 Lao, Mon **4** Lawa, Shan, Thai **5** Malay **6** Indian, Khymer **7** Chinese, Siamese
    9 Cambodian **10** Vietnamese
    king: **4** Rama **7** Chakkri, Mongkut **10** Chao Phraya **12** Prahjadhipok **13** Chulalongkorn
      17 Bhumibol Adulyadej
    leader: **9** Phraruang **12** Kukrit-Pramoj
  language: 3 Lao, Tai **4** Ahom, Shan, Thai **5** Kadai, Malay **7** Bangkok, Chinese, English
    9 Krung Thep
  religion: 5 Islam **8** Buddhism **12** Christianity, Confucianism **17** Theravada Buddhism
  place:
    dam: **8** Bhumibol
    palace: **5** Grand
    ruins: **7** Ayuthia **9** Ayutthaya
    street: **7** Yawarai
    temple: **4** Dawn **7** Trimitr **10** Wat Phra Keo **11** Royal Chapel **13** Emerald Buddha
  feature:
    canal: **5** klong
    clothing: **6** panung, sarong **12** saffron robes
    festival: **12** Surin Round Up
    houseboat: **6** sampan
    temple: **3** wat
    tree: **4** teak
  food:
    fruit: **5** camut **6** durian, litchi, pomelo **8** rambutan **10** mangosteen

car **11** Philippines **12** Easter
Island

Thailand *see box*

Thais
  author: **13** Anatole France
  character: **8** Athanael
  composer: **8** Massenet

Thalassa
  personifies: **3** sea

thalassic 6 marine **7** aquatic,
deep-sea, neritic, oceanic,
pelagic

Thales
  field: **11** mathematics
  nationality: **5** Greek
  discovered: **18** geometry
    principles
  predicted: **11** sun's eclipse

Thalestris
  character in: **16** The Rape of
    the Lock
  author: **4** Pope

Thalia
  member of: **5** Muses **6** Graces

personifies: **6** comedy
  13 idyllic poetry
lover: **4** Zeus
killed by: **5** Erato

Thallo
  member of: **5** Horae
  goddess of: **13** spring flowers

Thamyris
  vocation: **4** poet **8** musician
  father: **9** Philammon
  mother: **7** Argiope
  punished for: **9** arrogance
  punished by: **5** Muses

punishment: **7** maiming
8 blinding

thanatophobia
fear of: **5** death

Thanatos
personifies: **5** death

thank 5 bless **12** be grateful
to **13** be much obliged **18** express gratitude to

thankful 7 obliged **8** beholden,
grateful **10** indebted to **12** appreciative, full of thanks
16 feeling gratitude **22** expressing appreciation

thankfulness 6 thanks **9** gratitude **12** appreciation,
gratefulness

thankless 4 vain **7** ingrate,
useless **8** bootless, caviling,
critical, heedless **9** fruitless,
unmindful, unwelcome
10 profitless, ungracious, ungrateful, uninviting, unpleasant, unrewarded, unthankful
11 distasteful, thoughtless, undesirable, unrewarding **12** disagreeable, faultfinding
13 inconsiderate, unappreciated **14** unacknowledged,
unappreciative

thanks 5 grace **8** blessing
9 gratitude **11** benediction
12 appreciation, gratefulness

thanks be to God
Latin: **10** Deo gratias

thanksgiving 6 thanks
8 blessing

Thanksgiving
started by: **8** Bradford,
Pilgrims
traditional food: **4** corn,
yams **6** turkey **10** pumpkin
pie **13** sweet potatoes
1.4 cranberry sauce
symbol: **9** ear of corn
12 horn of plenty

thank you
French: **5** merci
German: **5** danke
Spanish: **7** gracias
Italian: **6** grazie
Japanese: **4** domo

Thank You, Fog
author: **7** W H Auden

Thank You, Jeeves
author: **11** P G Wodehouse

thank you very much
French: **9** merci bien
13 merci beaucoup
German: **10** danke schon
Japanese: **11** domo arigato
Spanish: **13** muchas gracias

That Certain Feeling
author: **12** Kingsley Amis

Thatcher, Becky
character in: **9** Tom Sawyer
author: **5** Twain

Thatcher, Judge
character in: **15** (The Adventures of) Huckleberry Finn
author: **5** Twain

That Girl
character: **8** Ann Marie, Lou
Marie **10** Helen Marie, Ruth
Bauman **11** Jerry Bauman
12 Don Hollinger, Judy Bessemer **14** Dr Leon Bessemer
cast: **9** Lew Parker **10** Ted
Bessell **11** Alice Borden,
Bonnie Scott, Marlo
Thomas **12** Bernie Kopell
13 Dabney Coleman **14** Carolyn Daniels, Rosemary
DeCamp

that is
Latin: **2** ie **5** id est

that is to say
Latin: **3** viz **9** videlicet

that's life
French: **9** c'est la vie

thaw 4 melt, warm **5** relax
6 soften, unbend, warm up
7 liquefy, melting, thawing
8 dissolve **11** break the ice

Thea
companion of: **7** Artemis
ravished by: **6** Aeolus
changed into: **4** mare
mare named: **6** Euippe

Theale, Milly
character in: **17** The Wings
of the Dove
author: **5** James

theater 4 site **5** arena, drama,
house, movie, odeum, place,
scene, stage **6** cinema, lyceum **7** gallery, setting **8** assembly, audience, coliseum
9 colosseum, music hall, playhouse **10** assemblage, auditorium, movie house, spectators
11 histrionics, lecture hall,
theatricals **12** amphitheater,
show business

theatrical 4 film **5** hammy,
movie, showy, stage, stagy
6 flashy **7** fustian, show-biz,
stilted **8** affected, dramatic,
mannered, thespian **9** grandiose, unnatural **10** artificial,
histrionic **11** exaggerated, extravagant, pretentious, spectacular **12** magniloquent,
ostentatious, show-business
13 entertainment, grandiloquent **14** larger-than-life

theatrical trick
French: **13** coup de theatre

Thebaid
author: **7** Statius
character: **4** Atys **5** Creon
6 Ismene, Tydeus **7** Jocasta,

Theseus **8** Antigone, Capaneus, Eteocles, Opheltes, Tiresias **9** Menoeceus,
Polynices **10** Amphiaraus,
Hippomedon, Melanippus

the bottle 5 booze, drink,
sauce **6** liquor **7** alcohol **8** demon rum

the dansant 8 tea dance

thee therefore
Latin: **8** te igitur

theft 5 fraud **7** larceny, looting,
robbery **8** burglary, filching,
rustling, stealing, thievery
9 hijacking, pilfering, swindling **10** purloining **11** shoplifting **12** embezzlement
god of: **6** Hermes **7** Mercury

Theia
also: **4** Thia
member of: **6** Titans
father: **6** Uranus
mother: **4** Gaea
brother: **8** Hyperion
mother of: **8** Cercopes
son: **6** Helios
daughter: **3** Eos **6** Selene

**the life of the land is
maintained by
righteousness**
Hawaiian: **52** ua mau ke ea
o ka aina i ka pono
motto of: **6** Hawaii

Them
author: **15** Joyce Carol Oates

theme 3 air **4** song, text, tune
5 essay, focus, motif, point,
topic, tract **6** melody, report,
review, strain, thesis **7** keynote, premise, subject **8** argument, critique, question,
treatise **9** discourse, leitmotif,
monograph **10** commentary
11 composition, proposition
12 dissertation

Themis
member of: **6** Titans
father: **6** Uranus
mother: **4** Gaea
sister: **6** Phoebe
consort of: **4** Zeus
husband: **7** Iapetus
mother of: **5** Fates, Horae
6 Moerae **9** Seasons
son: **10** Prometheus
personifies: **7** justice

Themiste
father: **8** Laomedon
mother: **8** Eurydice
son: **8** Anchises

**Then Again, Maybe I
Won't**
author: **9** Judy Blume

thence 6 whence **9** from there,
therefore **11** accordingly, in
due course **13** from that place

the next world 6 Heaven

8 eternity, paradise **12** the hereafter **14** the world to come

the norm 7 the mean, the rule **9** the median **10** the average **14** the common thing

the Occident 7 the West **20** the western hemisphere

Theoclymenus
king of: **5** Egypt
father: **7** Proteus
mother: **8** Psamathe
vocation: **4** seer

theologian *see* **22** philosopher/ theologian

theological 4 holy **6** sacred **8** Biblical, dogmatic **9** apostolic, canonical, doctrinal, religious, spiritual **10** scriptural **14** ecclesiastical

theology 5 dogma **8** divinity, doctrine, religion

Theonoe
father: **7** Proteus, Thestor

Theophane
bore: **3** ram
fleece of ram: **6** golden

theoretical 8 abstract, academic, putative **11** conjectural, postulatory, speculative **12** hypothetical, nonpractical **13** suppositional

theorize 5 infer, posit, think **6** assume **7** imagine, presume, propose, suppose, surmise **8** propound **9** formulate, postulate, predicate, speculate **10** conjecture **11** hypothecate, hypothesize

theory 3 law **4** idea, view **5** guess **6** belief, notion, thesis **7** concept, opinion, science, surmise, thought **8** doctrine, ideology, judgment **9** deduction, postulate, principle **10** conclusion, conjecture, hypothesis, persuasion, philosophy **11** presumption, speculation, supposition

therapeutic, therapeutical 7 healing **8** curative, remedial, salutary, sanative **11** restorative **12** ameliorative

Therapne
means: **12** burial ground

therapy 7 healing **9** treatment **14** rehabilitation

thereafter 5 later **9** after that, afterward **10** afterwards, from then on **11** thenceforth **12** subsequently **14** from that time on

therefore 2 so **4** ergo, thus **5** hence **11** accordingly **12** consequently, on that ground **13** for that reason, in

consequence, on that account **14** for which reason

there is no disputing about tastes
Latin: **27** de gustibus non est disputandum

there it is
French: **5** voila

Therese Raquin
author: **9** Emile Zola
character: **7** Camille, Laurent

There Shall Be No Night
author: **15** Robert E Sherwood

thereupon 4 then **6** at once **7** thereon **8** directly, suddenly, upon that **9** forthwith, in a moment, upon which **11** immediately **12** straightaway, without delay

Therimachus
father: **8** Hercules
mother: **6** Megary
killed by: **8** Hercules

Theritas *see* **4** Ares

Thermasia
epithet of: **7** Demeter
means: **6** warmth

thermometer
invented by: **7** Galileo, Reaumur
mercury: **10** Fahrenheit

Thero
nurse of: **4** Ares

theropod
type of: **8** dinosaur
member: **10** Allosaurus, Antrodemus **11** Coelophysis, Gorgosaurus **13** Albertosaurus, Compsognathus, Struthiomimus, Tyrannosaurus

Theroux, Paul
author of: **9** Saint Jack **16** The Mosquito Coast **20** Riding the Iron Rooster **21** The Great Railway Bazaar **23** The Old Patagonian Express

Thersander
member of: **7** Epigoni

Thersilochus
mentioned in: **5** Iliad
killed by: **8** Achilles

Thersites
mentioned in: **5** Iliad
origin: **5** Greek
characteristics: **4** ugly **8** deformed **11** quarrelsome
accused Agamemnon of: **5** greed
accused Achilles of: **9** cowardice
fought in: **9** Trojan War
killed by: **8** Achilles

the same as 4 like **7** equal to **9** a match for **12** comparable to, equivalent to, tanta-

mount to **16** commensurate with

thesaurus 8 synonymy **10** word finder **11** synonymicon **12** word treasury **13** synonym finder **17** synonym dictionary **18** semantic dictionary

Thescelosaurus
type: **8** dinosaur **10** ornithopod
location: **6** Canada **12** United States
period: **10** Cretaceous

These Three
director: **12** William Wyler
based on play by: **14** Lillian Hellman (The Children's Hour)
cast: **10** Alma Kruger, Joel McCrea **11** Merle Oberon **13** Miriam Hopkins **15** Bonita Granville, Catherine Doucet

These Twain
author: **13** Arnold Bennett

Theseus
king of: **6** Athens
father: **6** Aegeus **8** Poseidon
mother: **6** Aethra
wife: **7** Phaedra
consort: **9** Hippolyta
lover: **7** Ariadne
son: **6** Acamas **8** Demophon **10** Hippolytus, Melanippus
helmsman: **10** Nausithous
killed: **5** Sinis **6** Sciron **8** Minotaur **10** Cretan bull, Procrustes

thesis 5 essay, paper, tract **6** notion, theory **7** article, concept, surmise **8** argument, critique, proposal, treatise **9** discourse, monograph, postulate, term paper **10** commentary, conjecture, hypothesis **11** composition, proposition, speculation, supposition **12** disquisition, dissertation

Thesmia
epithet of: **7** Demeter
means: **12** goddess of law

Thesmophorus
epithet of: **7** Demeter
means: **8** lawgiver

Thesophoria
origin: **5** Greek
event: **8** festival

thespian 3 ham **4** star **5** actor, extra **6** co-star, player, walk-on **7** actress, ingenue, trouper **8** juvenile **9** bit-player, guest star, performer, tragedian **10** leading man **11** leading lady, stage player

Thespian Lion
attacked: **6** flocks
flock owner: **10** Amphitryon
killed by: **8** Hercules

Thespius
founded city of: **8** Thespiae
wife: **8** Megamede
daughters: **5** fifty

Thessalus
king of: **8** Thessaly
father: **5** Jason **8** Hercules
mother: **5** Medea **9** Chalciope

the state
Latin: **10** res publica

Thestius
king of: **7** Aetolia
father: **4** Ares
mother: **8** Demonice

Thestor
son: **7** Calchas
daughter: **7** Theonoe
8 Leucippe

Thetis
member of: **7** Nereids
husband: **6** Peleus
sister: **8** Eurynome
son: **8** Achilles

the very words
Latin: **14** ipsissima verba

the world over 10 every
place, everywhere, far and
wide, near and far **11** in all
places

**They Shoot Horses, Don't
They?**
director: **13** Sydney Pollack
cast: **8** Gig Young **9** Bruce
Dern, Jane Fonda **10** Red
Buttons **12** Susannah York
13 Bonnie Bedelia **15** Michael Sarrazin
Oscar for: **15** supporting actor (Young)

They Won't Forget
director: **11** Mervyn LeRoy
cast: **10** Lana Turner, Otto
Kruger **11** Allyn Joslyn,
Claude Rains **12** Elisha Cook
Jr **13** Gloria Dickson

Thia see **5** Theia

Thialfi
origin: **12** Scandinavian
servant of: **4** Thor
talent: **8** fastness

Thiasos see **7** Thiasus

thiasus
also: **7** thiasos
group worshipping: **11** patron deity
followers of: **8** Dionysus
followers called: **6** satyrs
7 maenads

Thiazi
also: **6** Thjazi
origin: **12** Scandinavian
form: **5** giant
carried away: **4** Iden **6** apples

thick 3 big, fat **4** deep, dull,
dumb, slow, wide **5** broad,
bulky, close, dense, fuzzy,
great, heavy, husky, piled,
solid **6** chummy, heaped,
hoarse, lavish, obtuse, packed,
strong, stupid, viscid, wooden
7 blurred, clotted, compact, copious, crowded, decided, devoted, doltish, extreme,
intense, liberal, muffled, profuse, teeming, throaty, viscous **8** abundant, familiar,
friendly, generous, guttural,
intimate, profound, sisterly,
swarming **9** brotherly, condensed, fatheaded, glutinous,
plenteous, unstinted **10** coagulated, dull-witted, gelatinous,
indistinct, munificent, pronounced, slow-witted **11** inseparable, overflowing
12 concentrated, impenetrable,
inarticulate

thicken 3 set **4** cake, clot, jell
5 muddy **6** darken, deepen,
muddle **7** compact, congeal,
jellify **8** condense **9** coagulate,
intensify **10** gelatinize

thicket 4 bush, wood **5** brake,
brush, copse, grove, scrub
6 bushes, covert, forest,
shrubs **7** bracken **9** shrubbery
10 underbrush **11** undergrowth

thickheaded 4 dull, dumb,
slow **5** blank, dense, dopey,
thick **6** obtuse, stupid **8** ignorant **9** dim-witted, fatheaded
10 boneheaded, dull-witted,
half-witted, slow-witted
11 blockheaded, thick-witted
12 dunderheaded, thickskulled **13** chuckleheaded,
knuckleheaded

thickset 5 bulky, close, dense,
dumpy, husky, solid, squat,
stout, tubby **6** chunky, packed,
stocky, stubby, stumpy,
sturdy **8** close-set, heavyset,
roly-poly

thickskinned 4 hard **5** horny,
tough **6** inured **7** callous
8 callused, hardened **9** unfeeling, unmovable **10** impervious,
insensible **11** insensitive, unconcerned **13** imperturbable,
unsusceptible
14 pachydermatous

thick-skulled 4 dull **5** dense
6 stupid **11** thickheaded
12 dunderheaded

thick-witted 4 dull, slow
5 dense **6** stupid **7** idiotic, moronic **9** dim-witted, imbecilic
11 thickheaded **12** dunderheaded, simple-minded

thief 5 crook **6** bandit, mugger,
robber **7** burglar, filcher, rustler **8** hijacker, pilferer, swindler **9** defrauder, embezzler,
holdup man, larcenist, purloiner, racketeer **10** highwayman,
pickpocket, shoplifter

12 housebreaker, kleptomaniac **13** confidence man, pursesnatcher **14** second-story man

Thief of Bagdad, The
director: **9** Tim Whelan
12 Ludwig Berger **13** Michael Powell
cast: **4** Sabu **9** Rex Ingram
10 John Justin, June Duprez **11** Conrad Veidt

Thieves' Carnival
also: **15** Le Bal des Voleurs
author: **11** Jean Anouilh

thievish 3 sly **6** sneaky **7** furtive **8** stealthy, thieving **9** dishonest, larcenous, secretive,
thieflike **13** light-fingered, surreptitious **14** sticky-fingered

thigh 3 ham, leg **4** hock **5** femur, flank, ilium **6** gammon
pain: **8** meralgia

Thimbu, Thimphu
capital of: **6** Bhutan

thin 4 fine, lank, lean, slim,
weak **5** faint, gaunt, lanky,
prune, runny, scant, sheer,
spare, water **6** dilute, feeble,
narrow, not fat, reduce,
skinny, slight, sparse, watery
7 curtail, diluted, fragile,
scrawny, slender, spindly
8 delicate, diminish, finespun
9 emaciated, water down
10 inadequate, threadlike
11 transparent **12** insufficient
13 unsubstantial

thin-blooded 3 wan **4** pale,
weak **6** anemic, sickly

thing, things 3 act **4** deed,
feat, gear, item **5** event,
gizmo, goods, point **6** action,
affair, aspect, detail, dingus,
entity, gadget, matter, object,
person **7** article, clothes, concern, effects, feature, thought
8 business, clothing, creature,
movables **9** doohickey, equipment, happening, statement
10 belongings, human being,
occurrence, particular, proceeding **11** eventuality, living
being, possessions, thingamabob, thingamajig, transaction
12 circumstance
13 paraphernalia

thing already done
French: **12** fait accompli

thingamajig 5 gizmo **6** doodad,
gadget **11** contraption, contrivance, thingamabob
15 whatchamacallit

thing of no value
Latin: **5** nihil

things done
Latin: **9** res gestae

think 4 deem, mean, plan
5 brood, fancy, guess, judge

6 design, expect, intend, ponder, reason, recall, reckon 7 believe, dwell on, imagine, presume, propose, purpose, reflect, suppose, surmise 8 cogitate, conceive, conclude, contrive, meditate, mull over, remember, ruminate 9 recollect, speculate 10 anticipate, deliberate, have in mind, keep in mind 11 contemplate, use one's mind, use one's wits 13 rack one's brain

thinkable 8 knowable 10 imaginable 11 conceivable, perceivable

think about 4 mull 6 debate, ponder 7 reflect 8 consider, mull over 10 deliberate

think alike 5 agree 11 be of one mind, see eye to eye

thinker 4 sage 6 savant, wizard 7 egghead, scholar 9 intellect 10 mastermind 11 mental giant, philosopher 13 metaphysician

think fit 4 deem 5 deign, stoop 7 consent 10 condescend

think highly of 5 favor, honor, value 6 admire, esteem, revere 7 approve, respect 8 look up to, venerate 10 set store by

think ill of 4 hate 5 decry 6 detest 7 condemn, deplore, despise, dislike 8 object to 9 abominate, disparage, frown upon 10 disapprove 13 look askance at 14 discountenance 15 take exception to 16 find unacceptable, view with disfavor

thinking 4 view 5 smart, stand, study 6 belief, bright 7 concept, surmise, thought 8 cultured, educated, judgment, position, rational, studious 9 brainwork, deduction, inference, reasoning 10 conclusion, cultivated, impression, meditation, meditative, reflection, reflective, rumination, thoughtful 11 intelligent, speculation 12 deliberation 13 consideration, contemplation, contemplative, philosophical, sophisticated, using one's head 15 paying attention

Thinking Reed, The
author: 15 Dame Rebecca West

think over 5 study, weigh 8 cogitate, consider, mull over 11 reflect upon 12 deliberate on

think through 5 weigh 6 ponder 7 analyze 8 appraise, consider, evaluate

think up 5 frame, hatch 6 create, invent 7 concoct, dream up 8 conceive, contrive

think well of 4 like 6 admire 8 look up to 10 appreciate

Thin Man, The
author: 15 Dashiell Hammett
character: 7 Morelli 11 Nick Charles, Nora Charles 13 Arthur Nunheim, Mimi Jorgensen 15 Herbert Macaulay 18 Christian Jorgensen
  Wynant family: 5 Clyde 7 Dorothy, Gilbert
director: 11 W S Van Dyke II
cast: 4 Asta 8 Myrna Loy (Nora Charles) 13 William Powell (Nick Charles)
sequel (film): 14 Another Thin Man 15 After the Thin Man 16 Song of the Thin Man 18 The Thin Man Goes Home

Thin Mountain Air, The
author: 10 Paul Horgan

thin out 5 prune 6 dilute, reduce, weaken 7 weed out 9 water down 10 adulterate

thinskinned 5 cross, huffy, sulky, testy 6 grumpy, sullen, touchy 7 crabbed, peevish 8 petulant, snappish 9 irascible, irritable, sensitive, squeamish 11 ill-tempered, quarrelsome, susceptible 12 cantankerous 13 oversensitive 14 hypersensitive

third estate
French: 9 tiers etat

Third Man, The
director: 9 Carol Reed
based on story by: 12 Graham Greene
cast: 10 Alida Valli 11 Orson Welles (Harry Lime) 12 Joseph Cotten, Trevor Howard 16 Wilfrid Hyde-White
setting: 6 Vienna

Third Wave, The
author: 12 Alvin Toffler

thirst 3 yen 4 itch, lust, pant 5 ardor, covet, crave, yearn 6 desire, fervor, hunger, relish 7 craving, passion, stomach 8 appetite, keenness, voracity, yearning 9 hanker for, hankering 11 thirstiness

thirsty 3 dry 4 avid 5 eager 7 parched 9 thirsting

Thirteen O'Clock
author: 19 Stephen Vincent Benet

Thirty-Nine Steps, The (The 39 Steps)
author: 10 John Buchan
director: 15 Alfred Hitchcock

cast: 11 Robert Donat 13 Godfrey Tearle, Lucie Mannheim, Peggy Ashcroft 16 Madeleine Carroll

This Above All
author: 10 Eric Knight

Thisbe
loved: 7 Pyramus
location: 7 Babylon
death by: 7 suicide
death at tomb of: 5 Ninus

this is
Latin: 6 hoc est

This Is Your Life
host: 12 Ralph Edwards
announcer: 9 Bob Warren

Thisoa
form: 5 nymph
tended: 4 Zeus

thistle 7 Cirsium
varieties: 3 Oat 4 Bull, Holy, Milk, Star 5 Glove, Plume, White 6 Canada, Cotton, Golden, Scotch, Silver 7 Blessed, St Mary's 8 Fishbone, Mountain, Plumless 9 Argentine, Thornless 10 Great globe, Small globe 11 Mountain sow 14 Acanthus-leaved

Thjazi see 6 Thiazi

Thoas see 5 Thoon

Thokk
origin: 12 Scandinavian
form: 8 giantess
refused to weep for: 5 Baldr 6 Balder, Baldur
possible disguise of: 4 Loki

Thomas 7 apostle
means: 4 twin
also called: 7 Didymus, Doubter 8 Doubting

Thomas, Ambroise
born: 4 Metz 6 France
composer of: 6 Mignon

Thomas, Danny
real name: 16 Amos Muzyad Jacobs
born: 11 Deerfield MI
daughter: 11 Marlo Thomas
roles: 13 The Jazz Singer 16 Make Room for Daddy 19 I'll See You in My Dreams

Thomas, Dylan
author of: 8 Fern Hill 13 Under Milk Wood 23 A Child's Christmas in Wales

Thomas, George H
nickname: 20 The Rock of Chickamauga
served in: 8 Civil War 10 Mexican War
side: 5 Union
commander of: 19 Army of the Cumberland

battle: **9** Nashville **11** Chattanooga, Chickamauga

Thomas, Marlo
real name: **14** Margaret
Thomas
born: **9** Detroit MI
father: **11** Danny Thomas
husband: **11** Phil Donahue
roles: **8** That Girl

Thomas, W Morgan
creator/artist of: **22** Sheena
Queen of the Jungle

Thomas a Kempis
author of: **20** The Imitation
of Christ

**Thompson, Estelle Merle
O'Brien**
real name of: **11** Merle
Oberon

Thomson, Joseph John
field: **7** physics
nationality: **7** British
discovered: **8** electron
awarded: **10** Nobel Prize

Thomson, Thomas John
born: **6** Canada **9** Claremont
artwork: **9** Spring Ice **11** The
Jack Pine **12** Northern
Lake **13** Northern River

Thomson, Virgil
born: **12** Kansas City MO
composer of: **9** Portraits
16 The Mother of Us All
21 Four Saints in Three
Acts

thong 4 band **5** strap, strip
6 sandal **7** binding

Thoon
also: **5** Thoas
11 Nebrophonus
member of: **8** Gigantes
attacked wall of: **6** Greeks
killed by: **8** Hercules
10 Antilochus

Thor
origin: **12** Scandinavian
god of: **4** rain **7** farming,
thunder
rode: **7** chariot
chariot pulled by: **5** goats
wielded: **6** hammer **7** Miolnir
father: **4** Odin **5** Othin

thorax 5 chest, trunk **6** breast,
cavity **8** forebody

Thoreau, Henry David
author of: **6** Walden (Life in
the Woods) **17** Civil
Disobedience

thorium
chemical symbol: **2** Th

thorn 3 woe **4** bane, barb,
care, gall, spur **5** cross, curse,
spike, spine, sting **6** plague
7 prickle, scourge, torment,
trouble **8** nuisance, vexation
9 annoyance, sore point **10** af-

fliction, bitter pill, infliction,
irritation

thorn 9 Crataegus
varieties: **3** Box **4** Lily, Pear
5 Camel, Hedge, White
6 Christ, Karroo, Mysore,
Sallow, Sickle, Winter
7 Thirsty **8** Cockspur, Egyptian, Kangaroo, Quick-set
9 Jerusalem, Paper-bark
10 Washington **11** Crucifixion **13** Yellow-fruited

Thornbirds, The
author: **17** Colleen
McCullough

Thornburg, Betty June
real name of: **11** Betty
Hutton

Thornfield
house in: **8** Jane Eyre
author: **6** Bronte

Thornhill, Squire
character in: **19** The Vicar of
Wakefield
author: **9** Goldsmith

thorn in the side 4 bane
7 torment **9** annoyance
10 irritation

thorny 4 dire, hard **5** spiny,
tough **6** barbed, spiked, sticky,
trying **7** arduous, brambly,
complex, crucial, irksome,
prickly **8** annoying, critical, involved, ticklish **9** bristling,
dangerous, difficult, vexatious
10 formidable, nettlesome, perplexing **11** complicated,
troublesome

thorough 4 full, pure **5** sheer,
total, utter **6** entire **7** careful,
perfect, uniform **8** absolute,
complete, of a piece **9** downright, out-and-out **10** consistent, definitive, exhaustive,
meticulous **11** painstaking, unmitigated, unqualified **12** all-
embracing, all-inclusive

**thoroughbred, Thorough-
bred 7** unmixed **8** purebred
9 blueblood, pedigreed, racehorse **10** aristocrat **11** full-
blooded, pure-blooded
12 silkstocking

thoroughfare 4 road **6** avenue,
street **7** freeway, highway,
parkway, roadway, thruway
8 main road, turnpike
9 boulevard, concourse
10 expressway, interstate
12 superhighway **13** through
street

thoroughgoing 5 utter **6** arrant **7** extreme **8** outright
9 confirmed, notorious, out-
and-out **11** undisguised,
unmitigated

thoroughly 5 fully **7** totally,
utterly **8** entirely **9** carefully,

downright, out-and-out, perfectly, uniformly **10** absolutely,
completely, throughout **11** in-
clusively **12** consistently, ex-
haustively, meticulously **13** in
all respects **15** from top to
bottom **17** through and
through **18** from beginning to
end

Thorpe, Isabella
character in: **15** Northanger
Abbey
author: **6** Austen

**Thorpe, Jim (James
Francis)**
sport: **8** football **13** track and
field
won: **8** Olympics
named: **11** All-American

Thorvaldsen, Albert Bertel
born: **7** Denmark
10 Copenhagen
artwork: **4** Hope **9** Lord Byron **14** Cupid and Psyche
16 The Lion of Lucerne
22 Cupid and the Three
Graces **24** Jason with the
Golden Fleece

Thoth
origin: **8** Egyptian
god of: **5** magic **6** wisdom
8 learning
scribe of: **4** gods
inventor of: **6** letter
7 numbers
corresponds to: **6** Hermes
head of: **4** ibis **6** baboon

though 3 tho, yet **4** even, that
5 still **6** albeit, even if
7 granted **8** although, granting **9** admitting **12** nevertheless **15** notwithstanding

thought 3 aim, end **4** goal,
idea, plan, view **5** credo,
dogma, fancy, tenet **6** belief,
caring, design, intent, musing,
notion, object, regard,
scheme **7** concept, concern,
opinion, purpose, reverie, surmise **8** doctrine, judgment,
kindness, thinking **9** attention,
intention, objective, sentiment **10** brown study, cogitation, conception, conclusion,
meditation, reflection, rumination **11** expectation, imagination, speculation, supposition
12 anticipation, deliberation
13 consideration, contemplation, introspection
French: **6** pensee

thoughtful 4 kind **6** caring,
loving, musing **7** pensive,
probing, serious, wistful
8 thinking **9** attentive **10** meditative, neighborly, reflective,
solicitous **11** considerate, kindhearted **13** contemplative,
introspective

thoughtfulness 7 probing,

thought **8** kindness, thinking **10** meditation, reflection **11** questioning **13** attentiveness, consideration, contemplation **14** solicitousness **15** kindheartedness

thoughtless **4** dumb, rash, rude **5** silly **6** stupid, unkind **7** foolish **8** careless, heedless, impolite, reckless **9** imprudent **10** ill-advised, indiscreet, neglectful, unthinking **11** harebrained, improvident, inadvertent, inattentive, insensitive **12** absent-minded, unreflecting **13** ill-considered, inconsiderate, rattlebrained **14** scatterbrained

thoughtlessness **7** neglect **8** rashness, rudeness **9** oversight, unconcern **10** imprudence, negligence, unkindness **11** inattention **12** carelessness, heedlessness, impoliteness, recklessness **13** insensitivity **15** inattentiveness **16** absentmindedness

Thousand Clowns, A
director: **7** Fred Coe
based on play by: **11** Herb Gardner
cast: **11** Barry Gordon **12** Jason Robards, Martin Balsam **13** Barbara Harris
setting: **11** New York City
Oscar for: **15** supporting actor (Balsam)

Thousand Days, A
author: **20** Arthur M Schlesinger Jr

thou too
Latin: **8** tu quoque

thrall **4** serf **5** slave **6** chains **7** bondage, serfdom, servant, slavery **9** servitude **11** enslavement, subjugation

thralldom **6** chains **7** bondage, serfdom, slavery **9** servitude **11** enslavement, subjugation

thrash **4** beat, cane, drub, flog, jerk, lash, maul, toss, whip **5** birch, flail, heave, solve, spank, strap **6** jiggle, joggle, plunge, pommel, squirm, switch, thresh, tumble, wiggle, writhe **7** flounce, resolve, scourge, trounce **8** argue out, lambaste **9** thresh out **10** flagellate

Thrasydemus
also: **11** Thrasymelus
squire of: **8** Sarpedon
killed by: **9** Patroclus

Thrasymedes
father: **6** Nestor
brother: **10** Antilochus

Thrasymelus see **11** Thrasydemus

threadbare **4** dull, worn **5** banal, stale, stock, tacky, trite **6** boring, frayed, jejune, ragged, shabby **7** cliched, humdrum, napless, prosaic, raveled, routine, worn-out **8** bromidic, everyday, pileworn **9** hackneyed, well-known **11** commonplace, stereotyped **12** conventional, overfamiliar **15** the worse for wear

threads **4** duds, togs **6** attire **7** apparel, clothes, strands, strings **8** clothing, garments **9** filaments

threat **4** omen, risk **5** peril **6** danger, hazard, menace **7** ill omen, portent, warning **8** jeopardy **10** foreboding **11** commination, premonition **12** intimidation

threaten **3** cow **4** warn **6** impend, menace **7** imperil **8** endanger, forewarn, hang over **9** terrorize **10** be imminent, intimidate, jeopardize

threatening **4** grim **7** baleful, ominous, warning **8** alarming, imminent, menacing, sinister **9** ill-omened, impending **10** forbidding, foreboding **11** approaching, forewarning, terrorizing **12** inauspicious, intimidating, unpropitious

three
French: **5** trois

Three-Cornered Hat, The
author: **21** Pedro Antonio de Alarcon

Three Faces of Eve, The
director: **15** Nunnally Johnson
cast: **8** Lee J Cobb **9** Nancy Kulp **10** David Wayne **12** Vince Edwards **14** Joanne Woodward
narration by: **13** Alistair Cooke
Oscar for: **7** actress (Woodward)

Three Lives
includes: **9** Melanctha **11** The Good Anna **13** The Gentle Lena
author: **13** Gertrude Stein

Three Men in a Boat
author: **13** Jerome K Jerome

Three Musketeers, The
author: **14** Alexandre Dumas (pere)
director: **13** Richard Lester
character: **5** Athos **6** Aramis **7** Porthos **8** Planchet **9** D'Artagnan **12** Lady de Winter **17** Cardinal Richelieu **18** Constance Bonacieux
cast: **10** Oliver Reed **11** Faye Dunaway (Milady), Michael York (D'Artagnan), Raquel

Welch **12** Frank Findlay **14** Charlton Heston, Christopher Lee **16** Geraldine Chaplin **18** Richard Chamberlain
sequel: **17** The Four Musketeers

Three's Company
character: **5** Larry **9** Janet Wood **10** Helen Roper **11** Chrissy Snow, Jack Tripper **12** Stanley Roper
cast: **10** John Ritter, Norman Fell **11** Joyce DeWitt **12** Audra Lindley, Richard Kline **13** Suzanne Somers

Three Sisters
director: **10** John Sichel **15** Laurence Olivier
author: **12** Anton Chekhov
character: **13** Fyodor Kuligin **14** Baron Tusenbach, Vassily Solyony **17** Alexandr Vershinin
Prozorov family: **4** Olga **5** Irina, Masha **6** Andrey **7** Natasha
cast: **9** Alan Bates **11** Derek Jacobi, Jeanne Watts **13** Joan Plowright, Louise Purnell **15** Laurence Olivier

Three Soldiers
author: **13** John Dos Passos

threnody **5** dirge, elegy **6** lament **7** requiem

threshold **4** dawn, door, edge, sill **5** brink, limen, onset, start, verge **6** portal **7** doorway, gateway, opening, prelude **8** doorsill, entrance **9** beginning, groundsel, inception **10** groundsill **11** entranceway **12** commencement **13** starting point

Thriae
form: **6** nymphs
nursed: **6** Apollo
taught: **6** Hermes

Thriambus
epithet of: **8** Dionysus

thrift **7** economy **8** prudence **9** frugality, husbandry, parsimony **10** moderation **11** sparingness, thriftiness **14** reasonableness **15** closefistedness **16** parsimoniousness

thriftiness **5** tight **6** thrift **7** economy **8** prudence **9** frugality, parsimony **13** pennypinching **15** closefistedness, tightfistedness **16** parsimoniousness

thriftless **6** lavish **8** feckless, prodigal, wasteful **11** extravagant, improvident

thrifty **6** frugal, saving, stingy **7** sparing **9** niggardly, pennywise **10** economical **11** closefisted, economizing, tight-

fisted **12** parsimonious
13 penny-pinching

thrill 4 fire, glow, kick, stir
5 flush, rouse, throb **6** arouse,
excite, quiver, tickle, tingle,
tremor **7** delight, impress, inspire, tremble **9** adventure,
electrify, enrapture, galvanize,
stimulate, transport
12 satisfaction

thrilled 4 agog **7** excited **9** delighted, overjoyed
11 transported

thrilling 7 awesome **8** engaging, exciting, riveting, stirring **9** absorbing, exquisite
10 delightful **11** fascinating,
pleasurable, provocative, sensational, tantalizing, titillating
12 electrifying

thrip
variety: **6** banded **10** tube
tailed **11** heterothrip,
merothripid

thrive 3 wax **4** boom **5** bloom,
get on **6** fatten **7** burgeon,
prosper, succeed **8** flourish, get
ahead, grow rich

thriving 4 busy, lush, rank,
rich **7** wealthy, well-off
8 blooming, in clover, vigorous, well-to-do **9** flowering,
luxuriant **10** blossoming, prospering, prosperous, succeeding,
successful **11** flourishing

throat 3 maw **4** craw, gula,
neck **5** gorge **6** gullet **7** chamber, jugulum, passage,
pharynx
lozenge: **6** pastil
nautical: **3** jaw **4** jaws, nock
part: **6** fauces, larynx, tonsil
7 glottis, trachea
pertaining to: **5** gular
seizing: **4** knot **5** hitch
12 cuckold's knot
swelling: **6** goiter

throaty 3 dry, low **4** base,
deep **5** gruff, husky, thick
6 hoarse **7** cracked, grating,
rasping **8** croaking, guttural,
resonant, sonorous **9** full-toned

throb 4 beat, jerk, pant
5 heave, pulse, shake **6** quiver,
tremor, twitch **7** beating, flutter, pulsate, shaking, tremble,
vibrate **9** palpitate, pulsation,
quivering, throbbing, trembling, vibration **10** fluttering
11 oscillation, palpitation
13 reverberation

throes 5 agony, chaos, pangs
6 ordeal, spasms, tumult **7** anguish, turmoil **8** disorder, paroxysm, upheaval **9** confusion,
paroxysms **10** convulsion,
disruption

thrombus 4 clot **9** blood clot
11 coagulation

throng 3 jam **4** army, cram,
herd, host, mass, mill, pack,
rush **5** bunch, crowd, crush,
flock, flood, horde, press,
surge, swarm **6** deluge, gather,
huddle, stream **7** cluster, collect **8** assemble, converge
9 multitude **10** assemblage,
congregate

thronged 4 full **6** jammed,
mobbed, packed **7** crammed,
crowded, flocked, swarmed,
teeming **8** swarming **9** congested, jampacked
11 overflowing

throttle 3 gag, gas **4** stop
5 block, burke, check, choke
6 stifle **7** garrote, seal off, shut
off, silence, smother **8** choke
off, gas pedal, strangle **9** fuel
lever, fuel valve **11** strangulate

through, thru 4 done, past
5 ended **6** direct **7** express
8 finished, from A to Z, to
the end **9** all the way, completed, concluded **10** terminated **12** long-distance
15 from first to last **18** from
beginning to end **20** from one
end to the other

through and through 5 total
6 wholly **7** totally, utterly
8 complete **10** completely,
thoroughly **15** from top to
bottom **18** from beginning to
end **20** from one end to the
other

through my fault
Latin: **8** mea culpa

throughout 7 all over **10** all
the time, everywhere **11** in
every part **16** all the way
through **18** from beginning to
end

Through the Looking Glass
sequel to: **17** Alice in
Wonderland
author: **12** Lewis Carroll
character: **4** Gnat, Lion **5** Alice, Dinah **7** Red King, Unicorn **8** Red Queen **9** Red
Knight, White King
10 Tweedledee, Tweedledum,
White Queen **11** Black Kitten, White Kitten, White
Knight **12** Humpty Dumpty

throw 3 lob, pit, put, shy
4 cast, hurl, shot, toss
5 chuck, fling, floor, heave,
impel, pitch, place, put in, put
on, sling **6** hurtle, launch, let
fly, propel, unseat **7** project
8 delivery **9** knock down, put
around

throw away 7 cast off, discard **8** get rid of

throw down 5 let go **8** drop
hard, hurl down, toss down
9 fling down

throw into disorder 5 upset
7 agitate, disrupt **10** disarrange

throw off 4 emit, gush **5** exude **7** abandon, cast off, mislead **8** get rid of, shake off,
shrug off **9** cast aside, discharge, give forth, pour forth

throw off the scent 7 confuse, mislead **8** confound
19 throw out a red herring

throw out 4 beam, emit, oust
5 eject, evict, expel, exude
6 banish, bounce, remove
7 discard, dismiss, toss out
8 get rid of, jettison **9** cast
aside, throw away

throw overboard 4 dump
7 cast off, discard **8** jettison,
toss over

throw suspicion upon
11 cast doubt on **17** bring
into question

throw up 4 barf, spew **5** eject,
expel, spout, vomit **6** cast up,
spew up **7** cough up **8** disgorge **9** discharge
11 regurgitate

thrust 3 jab, jam, ram **4** butt,
pass, poke, prod, push, raid,
stab **5** boost, drive, foray,
force, impel, lunge, press,
sally, shove, swipe **6** attack,
charge, pierce, plunge, propel,
sortie, strike, stroke **7** assault,
impetus, impulse, riposte
8 momentum **9** incursion
10 aggression

thrust aside 4 dump **6** shelve
7 discard **8** get rid of, throw
off, throw out **9** cast aside,
dispose of, throw away

thrust at 6 assail, attack
7 lunge at **8** strike at

thrust out 4 spew, spit **5** eject,
expel, vomit **6** extend, propel
7 protrude

Thrym
origin: **12** Scandinavian
form: **5** giant
killed by: **4** Thor
demanded return of: **5** Freia,
Freya

Thucydides
author of: **28** History of the
Peloponnesian War

thud 4 bang **5** clunk, knock,
smack, thump

thug 4 hood **6** bandit, gunman,
hit man, killer, mugger, robber **7** hoodlum, mobster, ruffian **8** assassin, gangster,
murderer **9** cutthroat

thumb 5 hitch **6** finger, handle **9** hitchhike **10** catch a
ride, hitch a ride **11** flip
through, leaf through

Thumbelina
author: 21 Hans Christian
Andersen

thumbnail 5 brief, short
7 compact, concise

thump 3 hit, jab, rap 4 bang,
beat, clip, cuff, poke, slam,
slap, swat, thud 5 clout, clunk,
knock, pound, punch, smack,
whack 6 batter, bounce, buffet, pommel, strike, thwack
8 collapse, lambaste

thunder 4 boom, clap, echo,
peal, roar, roll 5 crack, crash
6 rumble 7 explode, resound
8 rumbling 9 discharge, explosion 11 reverberate, thunderbolt, thunderclap
god of: 4 Thor 5 Donar
7 Taranis

thunderbolt 4 dart 5 flash,
shaft 6 stroke

Thunderstorms, god of
8 Summanus

thunderstruck 4 agog, awed
5 agape 6 aghast, amazed
8 confused, overcome 9 astounded, awestruck, perplexed,
surprised 10 astonished, bewildered 11 dumbfounded
13 flabbergasted

Thunder-ten-Tronckh
character in: 7 Candide
author: 8 Voltaire

Thurber, James
author of: 12 The New
Yorker 14 Is Sex Necessary
(with E B White), The Catbird Seat 16 The Owl in the
Attic 18 My Life and Hard
Times, The Thurber Carni-
val 26 The Secret Life of
Walter Mitty

Thurber Carnival, The
author: 12 James Thurber

Thurio
character in: 20 Two Gentlemen of Verona
author: 11 Shakespeare

Thursday
French: 5 jeudi
from: 4 Thor
German: 10 donnerstag
heavenly body: 4 Jove
7 Jupiter
Italian: 7 giovedi
Latin: 9 Dies Jovis
observance: 12 Holy Thurs-
day, Thanksgiving 13 Corpus
Christi 14 Maundy Thurs-
day 17 Ascension Thursday
Scandinavian: 7 torsdag
Spanish: 6 jueves

Thurso's Landing
author: 15 Robinson Jeffers

thus 2 so 4 ergo 5 hence 6 like
so 8 like this 9 as follows, in
this way, therefore, wherefore 11 accordingly 12 consequently, in this manner 13 for
this reason
Latin: 3 sic

thus always to tyrants
Latin: 17 sic semper tyrannis
motto of: 8 Virginia

**thus passes away the glory
of this world**
Latin: 21 sic transit gloria
mundi

Thus Spake Zarathustra
also: 21 Also Sprach
Zarathustra
author: 18 Friedrich
Nietzsche

thwack 3 box, hit, rap 4 bang,
blow, slam, slap 5 baste, clout,
knock, smack, thump, whack
6 buffet, paddle, strike, wallop

Thwackum
character in: 8 Tom Jones
author: 8 Fielding

thwart 3 bar 4 balk, foil, stop
5 check, cross 6 baffle, hinder,
oppose 7 inhibit, prevent,
ward off 8 obstruct, stave off
9 frustrate 10 contravene

Thyestean banquet
meal of: 10 human flesh

Thyestes
author: 6 Seneca

Thyestes
father: 6 Pelops
mother: 10 Hippodamia
brother: 6 Atreus
half-brother: 10 Chrysippus
sister-in-law: 6 Aerope
son: 9 Aegisthus
daughter: 7 Pelopia

Thyiad see 9 bacchante

Thymbraeus
father: 7 Laocoon

thyme
botanical name: 6 Thymus
9 T vulgaris
varieties: 4 Wild 5 Basil,
Lemon, Water 6 Common,
Garden, Golden 7 Caraway,
Spanish
symbol of: 8 activity
attracts: 4 bees
conjures: 9 fairy folk
use: 4 fish 7 poultry 8 stuffing 10 Creole food 21 New
England clam chowder

Thymoetes
king of: 6 Athens
elder of: 7 Trojans

Thyone see 6 Semele

Thyoneus
epithet of: 8 Dionysus
means: 11 son of Thyone

Thyrsis
author: 13 Matthew Arnold

Thyrus
staff of: 8 Dionysus
tipped with: 8 pine cone
twined with: 3 ivy 5 vines

thysanoptera
class: 8 hexapoda
phylum: 10 arthropoda
group: 5 thrip

thysanura
class: 8 hexapoda
phylum: 10 arthropoda
group: 8 firebrat 10 silverfish
11 bristletail

Tia Maria
type: 6 brandy 7 liqueur
origin: 7 Jamaica
flavor: 6 coffee
with rum: 10 Black Maria
with tequila: 9 Brave Bull
with vodka: 12 Black Russian

Tiamat
origin: 8 Akkadian
consort of: 4 Apsu
children: 4 gods

tiara 4 band 5 crown, miter
6 diadem 7 coronet 8 frontlet,
ornament 9 headdress

Tiaxcaltec
language family: 5 Nahua
location: 6 Mexico 14 Central
America

Tiber
god of: 9 Tiberinus

Tiberinus
origin: 5 Roman
god of: 5 Tiber

Tibet see box

tibia
bone of: 4 shin

tic 6 twitch 12 facial twitch
13 tic douloureux 19 trigemi-
nal neuralgia

tick 3 dot, tap 4 beat, line, list,
mark, nick, note 5 blaze,
check, clack, click, enter,
notch, swing, throb 6 record,
slight, stroke 7 scratch, vibrate 8 mark down, register,
ticktock 9 checkmark, chronicle, oscillate, pulsation,
vibration

ticket 3 tag 4 card, mark, pass,
slip, stub 5 label, slate 6 ballot, coupon, marker, roster
7 sticker, voucher 14 list of
nominees, traffic summons
type: 4 trip 7 parking,
traffic 9 admission

tickle 4 itch 5 amuse, cheer,
prick, sting, throb 6 divert,
please, regale, stroke, thrill,
tingle, twitch 7 delight, enchant, enliven, gladden, gratify, prickle, rejoice 8 enthrall,
entrance 9 captivate, fascinate,
titillate 12 scratchiness 15 do
one's heart good

Tibet
  other name: 3 Bod 4 Bhot 5 Tobet 8 Hsitsang 10 Land of Snow 14 Roof of the World
  capital: 5 Lassa, Lhasa
  city: 3 Noh 5 Karak 6 Chamdo, Gartok 7 Changtu, Totling 8 Gyangtse, Jihkatse, Shigatse 9 Chiangtzu
  government: 23 autonomous region of China
  monetary unit: 5 tanga
  lake: 3 Aru, Bam, Bun, Nam 4 Mema, Tosu 5 Jagok, Tabia 6 Dagtse, Garhur, Kashun, Nam Iso, Seling, Tangra, Yamdok 7 Kyaring, Teriman, Tsaring, Zilling 8 Jiggitai 9 Tengrinor 11 Manasarowar
  mountain: 5 Kamet, Sajum 6 Kailas, Kunlun 7 Bandala 8 Himalaya 9 Karakoram
  highest point: 7 Everest
  river: 3 Nak, Nau, Sak 4 Song 5 Hwang, Indus 6 Mekong, Sutlej, Yellow 7 Hwang Ho, Matsang, Melsang, Salween, Tsangpo, Yangtze 11 Brahmaputra
  physical feature:
    plain: 4 Kham 9 Chang Tang
    valley: 7 Tsangpo
  people: 5 Asian, Balti, Bodpa, Drupa 6 Bhotia, Champa, Drokpa, Khamba, Khambu, Panaka, Sherpa, Tangut 7 Bhotiya, Bhutani, Gyarung, Taghlik, Tibetan 9 Mongoloid
    patron god: 14 Avalokitesvara
    ruler: 4 Yuan 6 Mongol 9 dalai lama 13 Songtsan Gampo
  language: 5 Balti 6 Ladkhi 7 Bhutani, Bodskad 8 Sanskrit 9 Bhutanese
  religion: 5 Bonko 7 Lamaism
  place:
    Indian border: 11 McMahon Line
    palace: 7 Potalaf
    temple: 7 Jokhang 10 Tashi Lumpo 11 Tashi Lhunpo
  feature:
    animal: 3 dzo, yak 5 kiang 7 mastiff 8 musk deer 10 giant panda
    clothing: 5 chuba
    dance: 4 cham 9 achelhamo
    dog: 9 lhasa apso
    leader: 9 dalai lama
    legend: 4 yeti 17 abominable snowman
    monastery: 8 lamasery
    monk: 4 lama
  food:
    dish: 6 tsamba, tsampa
    drink: 5 chang

ticklish 4 hard 5 itchy, tough 6 knotty, thorny, tickly, touchy, tricky 7 awkward, prickly 8 critical, delicate, scratchy, tingling 9 difficult, intricate, sensitive, uncertain 11 complicated

tidal basin 3 bay 5 inlet, sound 6 lagoon 7 estuary 11 arm of the sea

tidbit 3 bit 4 item 5 treat 6 morsel 8 delicacy, mouthful 9 choice bit

tide 4 flow, neap, wave 5 drift, state 7 current 8 movement, tendency, undertow 9 direction 10 ebb and flow, wax and wane 11 rise and fall

tidings 4 news, word 6 advice, notice, report 8 good word 11 declaration, information 12 announcement, intelligence, notification

tidy 4 neat, trig, trim 5 ample, array, clean 6 goodly, neaten, tidy up 7 arrange, careful, clean up, orderly, precise, regular, sizable 8 neaten up, spotless, spruce up 9 organized, regulated, shipshape 10 immaculate, methodical, meticulous, put in order, straighten 11 substantial 12 businesslike, considerable, straighten up 15 in apple-pie order

tidy up 5 clean 6 neaten 9 freshen up 10 put in order, straighten

tie 3 rod 4 ally, band, beam, belt, bind, bond, cord, draw, duty, join, knot, lash, line, link, rope, sash, yoke 5 brace, cable, cinch, limit, marry, match, truss, unite 6 attach, bow tie, clinch, couple, cravat, engage, fasten, girdle, hamper, hinder, ribbon, secure, string, tether 7 confine, connect, kinship, necktie, support 8 affinity, cincture, dead heat, make a bow, make fast, relation, restrain, restrict, tied vote 9 constrain, crossbeam, fastening 10 allegiance, connection, cummerbund, obligation 11 affiliation, come out even 12 relationship 13 connecting rod 15 divide the honors

Tiepolo, Giovanni Battista (Giambattista)
  born: 5 Italy 6 Venice
  artwork: 10 Kaisersaal (salon) 11 Treppenhaus (staircase) 14 The Crucifixion 16 Ronaldo and Armida 20 Madonna of Mount Carmel 21 The Communion of St Lucia, The Triumph of Aphrodite 24 St Thekla and the Pestilence 28 Apotheosis of Francesco Barbaro 28 The Worship of the Bronze Serpent

tier 3 row 4 bank, file, line, rank, step 5 layer, level, range, story 7 stratum 14 stratification

Tierney, Gene
  born: 10 Brooklyn NY
  husband: 11 Oleg Cassini
  roles: 5 Laura 10 Belle Starr 11 Tobacco Road 13 A Bell for Adano 16 Leave Her to Heaven 18 The Ghost and Mrs Muir

tiers etat 11 third estate
  in French politics: 7 commons

tie-up 3 jam 4 snag 5 block, hitch, snarl 6 slow-up 7 failure 8 blockage, gridlock, stoppage 9 breakdown 10 bottleneck, disruption 11 malfunction 13 embouteillage

tie up 3 tie 4 bind, gird, lash, rope 5 hitch, snarl, strap, truss 6 engage, fasten, hinder, impede, occupy, secure, tangle 8 entangle

tiff 4 huff, miff, rage, snit, spat 5 clash, run-in, scrap, tizzy, words 6 hassle 7 dispute, quarrel, rhubarb, wrangle 8 argument, ill humor, squabble 10 difference 11 altercation 12 disagreement 16 misunderstanding

tiger 3 cat 6 cougar, jaguar 7 fighter, wildcat
young: 5 whelp

Tiger Joy
author: 19 Stephen Vincent Benet

tiger's-eye
species: 6 quartz

Tigger
character in: 13 Winnie-the-Pooh
author: 5 Milne

tight 4 busy, firm, full, hard, high, snug, taut 5 blind, close, dense, drunk, exact, happy, harsh, lit up, rigid, scant, solid, stern, stiff, tense, tipsy, tough 6 firmly, frugal, gorged, hard-up, jammed, juiced, loaded, scarce, secure, severe, skimpy, sloppy, soused, stewed, stingy, stoned, strict, trying, zonked 7 austere, closely, compact, crammed, crowded, drunken, miserly, onerous, pickled, pie-eyed, smashed, solidly, sparing, stuffed 8 grudging, rigorous, securely, too small 9 deficient, difficult, illiberal, jam-packed, niggardly, penurious, plastered, skintight, stringent, worrisome 10 burdensome, compressed, glassy-eyed, impassable, inadequate, inebriated, inflexible, in one's cups, nip-and-tuck, nose-to-nose, tyrannical, ungenerous, unyielding 11 closefisted, constricted, dictatorial, impermeable, intoxicated, troublesome, well-matched 12 close-fitting, impenetrable, insufficient, parsimonious 13 closely fitted, feeling no pain 14 fitting closely, uncompromising 20 three sheets to the wind

tighten 5 pinch 6 anchor, fasten, narrow, secure 7 squeeze 8 contract, make fast, make taut 9 constrict 14 take up the slack

tighten one's belt 4 save 5 skimp, stint 6 scrimp 8 conserve, cut costs 9 economize 11 cut expenses 12 pinch pennies

tightfisted 5 cheap, mingy, tight 6 greedy, stingy 7 miserly 9 illiberal, niggardly, penurious 10 avaricious 11 closefisted 12 cheeseparing, parsimonious 13 penny-pinching

tightfistedness 6 penury 9 parsimony 10 stinginess 11 miserliness 13 niggardliness, penny-pinching

tight-fitting 4 snug 5 tight

8 too small 9 skintight 11 constricted 12 constricting 15 like a second skin

tight-laced 4 prim 6 prissy, stuffy 7 prudish 8 priggish 9 inhibited, repressed, Victorian 11 puritanical, standoffish, straitlaced 13 self-righteous

tight-lipped 3 mum 4 curt 5 brief, quiet, short, terse 8 discreet, reserved, reticent, taciturn 10 unsociable 11 untalkative 12 close-mouthed 15 uncommunicative

tightly packed 5 dense 6 jammed 7 compact, crammed, stuffed 10 compressed 12 concentrated

tightwad 5 miser, piker 7 niggard, Scrooge 9 lickpenny, skinflint 10 cheapskate, pinchpenny 12 moneygrubber

till 3 sow 4 even, farm, plow, seed, tray, unto up to 6 before, coffer, drawer, harrow, plough 7 as far as, develop, prepare 8 moneybox, treasury 9 cultivate 12 cash register
geological: 5 drift

tillable 6 arable 8 farmable, plowable 10 cultivable

tillage 7 farming, plowing 11 agriculture, cultivation

Till Eulenspiegel
also: 16 Tyll Eulenspiegel
origin: 8 Germanic
means: 14 practical joker

Tillie the Toiler
creator: 12 Russ Westover
character: 3 Mac 7 Mr Chase

Tilney, Henry
character in: 15 Northanger Abbey
author: 6 Austen

tilt 3 row, tip 4 cant, lean, list, rake, spar, tiff 5 brawl, fence, fight, grade, joust, pitch, slant, slope 6 affray, battle, combat, oppose 7 contest, dispute, incline, quarrel 8 argument, skirmish, squabble 9 encounter 10 tournament 11 altercation

Timaeus
author: 5 Plato

Timandra
father: 9 Tyndareus
mother: 4 Leda
brother: 6 Castor, Pollux
sister: 5 Helen
12 Clytemnestra
husband: 7 Echemus, Phyleus
son: 5 Meges
cursed by: 9 Aphrodite

timber 4 bush, logs, wood 5 copse, trees, woods 6 boards, forest, lumber 7 thicket

timberland 5 woods 6 forest, sticks 8 woodland

timbre 4 tone 5 pitch 9 resonance

time, times 3 age, day, eon, era 4 beat, days, hour, term, week, year 5 clock, cycle, epoch, event, match, month, phase, spell, stage, tempo, while, years 6 adjust, chance, decade, moment, period, rhythm, season 7 century, episode, freedom, instant, liberty, measure, stretch 8 duration, incident, interval, occasion 10 experience, generation 11 opportunity, synchronize

time flies
Latin: 11 tempus fugit

time-honored 6 common, normal 7 regular, revered 8 accepted, standard 9 customary, respected, universal

timeless 7 abiding, durable, endless, eternal, lasting, undying 8 enduring, immortal, infinite, unending 9 boundless, ceaseless, deathless, immutable, incessant, permanent, perpetual 10 continuous, persistent 11 everlasting, never-ending 12 interminable, unchangeable 13 never-stopping 14 indestructible

timely 6 prompt 8 punctual 9 opportune, well-timed 10 convenient, felicitous, seasonable 12 providential

Time Machine, The
author: 7 H G Wells
character: 4 Eloi 5 Weena 8 Morlocks 12 Time Traveler

Time of Your Life, The
author: 14 William Saroyan
director: 8 H C Potter
cast: 8 Ward Bond 11 James Cagney, Wayne Morris 12 Jeanne Cagney 13 William Bendix 17 Broderick Crawford

timepiece 5 clock, watch 8 horologe 11 chronometer

Time Remembered
author: 11 Jean Anouilh

Timerman, Jacobo
author of: 38 Prisoner Without a Name Cell Without a Number

timesaving 5 quick 6 speedy 9 efficient 11 expeditious

time without end 7 forever 8 eternity, infinity

timeworn 3 old 4 aged, worn 5 dated, hoary, passe, stale, trite 6 age-old, beat-up, oldhat, shabby 7 ancient, antique 8 battered, dog-eared, obsolete, overused **9** hackneyed, out of date, venerable, weathered **10** antiquated **12** antediluvian

timid 3 coy, shy **6** afraid, humble, modest, scared **7** bashful, fearful **8** cowardly, retiring, sheepish, timorous **9** diffident, shrinking, spineless, weak-kneed **10** unassuming **12** apprehensive, fainthearted **13** pusillanimous

timidity 7 modesty, shyness **8** cold feet, humility **9** cowardice, timidness **10** diffidence **11** bashfulness, fearfulness, trepidation **12** sheepishness, timorousness **13** spinelessness **16** faint-heartedness

timidness 7 shyness **8** meekness, timidity **10** diffidence, insecurity **11** bashfulness **12** timorousness **14** submissiveness **15** unassertiveness **16** faintheartedness

Timon of Athens
author: **18** William Shakespeare
character: **6** Lucius **7** Flavius **8** Lucullus **9** Apemantus, Ventidius **10** Alcibiades, Sempronius

Timor
capital: **4** Dili
country: **8** Portugal **9** Indonesia
islands: **5** Sunda **11** Lesser Sunda
strait: **5** Ombai

timorous 3 shy **4** meek **5** timid **6** afraid **7** anxious, bashful, fearful **8** retiring **9** shrinking **10** submissive **12** fainthearted

timorousness 7 shyness **8** cold feet, meekness, timidity **9** cowardice **11** fearfulness, trepidation **16** faintheartedness

Timothy
mother: **6** Eunice
grandmother: **4** Lois
companion: **4** Paul **8** Silvanus

tin
chemical symbol: **2** Sn

tincture 6 elixir **7** essence, extract, spirits **8** solution **11** concentrate

Tinder Box, The
author: **21** Hans Christian Andersen

Tin Drum, The
author: **11** Gunter Grass
director: **17** Volker Schlondorff
character: **14** Oskar Matzerath
cast: **10** Mario Adorf **12** David Bennent (Oskar)

13 Angela Winkler **16** Daniel Olbrychski **17** Katharina Tahlbach
Oscar for: **11** foreign film

tine 3 die, tip **4** barb, lose, tyne **5** point, prong, spike **6** bodkin, branch, perish, skewer **7** destroy, forfeit

tinge 3 dye **4** cast, dash, hint, lace, tint, tone, vein **5** color, imbue, shade, smack, stain, taste, touch, trace **6** flavor, infuse, nuance, season **7** instill, soupcon **9** suspicion

tingle 5 sting, throb **6** thrill, tickle, tremor **7** flutter, prickle **9** prickling, pulsation **11** palpitation

Tinia
origin: **8** Etruscan
chief: **3** god

Tinker, Tailor, Soldier, Spy
author: **11** John Le Carre

Tinker Bell
character in: **8** Peter Pan
author: **6** Barrie

tinkle 4 ding, peal, ping, ring **5** chime, chink, clank, clink, plink **6** jingle **9** ting-a-ling

tin lizzie 3 car **4** auto, heap **5** motor **6** jalopy, wheels **7** flivver, machine, motocar, vehicle **10** automobile **12** motor vehicle

Tin Man, Tin Woodsman
character in: **13** The Wizard of Oz
author: **4** Baum

tinsel 4 sham, show **5** gloss **6** sequin **7** glitter, spangle **8** pretense **9** gaudiness **10** camouflage, decoration, masquerade **11** affectation, false colors, make-believe, ostentation

tint 3 dye, hue **4** hint, tone, wash **5** color, frost, shade, stain, tinge, touch, trace **6** nuance **7** pigment **8** coloring, tincture **10** suggestion

Tintern Abbey
author: **17** William Wordsworth

tintinnabulate 4 peal, ring, toll **5** chime, clang, knell, sound **6** jingle, tinkle

tintinnabulation 4 gong, peal, ring, toll **5** chime, knell **6** jingle **7** clangor, pealing, ringing **8** clanging, ding-dong, jingling, tinkling **11** peal of bells

Tintoretto, Jacopo
real name: **13** Jacopo Robusti
born: **5** Italy **6** Venice
artwork: **8** Paradise **13** The

Last Supper **14** The Crucifixion **16** The Road to Calvary **17** Bacchus and Ariadne **18** Apotheosis of St Roch, The Flight into Egypt **20** Susannah and the Elders **21** The Temptation of Christ **26** St Mark Frees a Christian Slave **27** The Finding of the Body of St Mark **32** The Miracle of St Mark Rescuing a Slave

tiny 3 wee **5** pygmy, runty, small, teeny **6** bantam, little, midget, minute, petite **8** dwarfish **9** itsy-bitsy, miniature, minuscule, pint-sized **10** diminutive, teeny-weeny, undersized **11** Lilliputian, microscopic, pocket-sized **12** teensy-weensy

Tiny Alice
author: **11** Edward Albee

Tiny Tim
character in: **15** A Christmas Carol
author: **7** Dickens

tip 3 cap, pat, tap, top **4** acme, apex, barb, brow, cant, clue, head, hint, hook, lean, list, peak, rake, tilt **5** crest, crown, pitch, point, prong, slant, slope, spike, upend, upset **6** advice, reward, stroke, summit, tip-off, topple, upturn, vertex, zenith **7** capsize, incline, leaning, lowdown, pointer, sharpen, tilting, tipping, warning **8** gratuity, overturn, pinnacle, slanting **9** baksheesh, lagniappe **10** admonition, inside dope, perquisite, suggestion, turn turtle **11** forewarning **13** word to the wise
French: **7** douceur

tipcart 4 cart **8** dumpcart, pushcart

Tiphys
member of: **9** Argonauts
occupation: **9** steersman

tip off 3 tip **4** warn **5** alert **6** caveat **7** caution, warning **8** forewarn **11** forewarning

tip over 5 upend, upset **7** capsize **8** flip over, keel over, overturn, turn over **10** turn turtle

Tippett, Michael Kemp
born: **6** London **7** England
composer of: **9** King Priam **13** The Knot Garden **15** A Child of Our Time **20** The Midsummer Marriage **22** The Vision of St Augustine **32** Concerto for Double String Orchestra

tipple 5 drink, quaff **6** guzzle, imbibe, liquor **8** beverage

tippler 3 sot 4 lush, soak, wino 5 drunk, rummy, souse, toper 6 bibber, boozer, sponge 7 guzzler, imbiber, swiller, tosspot 8 drunkard 9 alcoholic, inebriate 10 booze hound 11 dipsomaniac

tipsy 4 high 5 awash, blind, drunk, happy, lit-up, stiff, tight 6 juiced, loaded, sloppy, sodden, soused, stewed, stoned 7 drunken, pickled, pie-eyed, smashed 9 inebriate, plastered 10 glassy-eyed, inebriated, in one's cups 11 intoxicated 12 half seas over 13 feeling no pain 20 three sheets to the wind

tip-top 4 A-one 5 elite, super 7 supreme 8 very fine 10 consummate 11 exceptional, superlative 13 extraordinary

tirade 5 curse 6 screed 7 lecture 8 diatribe, harangue, jeremiad, scolding 9 invective, reprimand 11 castigation, fulmination 12 condemnation, denunciation, dressing-down, vilification, vituperation

tirailleur 10 skirmisher 12 sharpshooter

Tirane, Tirana
  capital of: 7 Albania

tire 3 fag, irk 4 bore 5 annoy, weary 6 bother, tucker 7 disgust, exhaust, fatigue, wear out 8 be sick of 10 make sleepy 11 be fed up with 12 lose interest, lose patience

tire
  invented by: 6 Dunlop 7 Thomson

tired 4 beat 5 all in, weary 6 bushed, drowsy, fagged, pooped, sleepy 7 wearied, worn out 8 dog-tired, fatigued, tuckered 9 enervated, exhausted, played out

tireless 6 steady 7 devoted, staunch 8 constant, faithful, resolute, untiring 9 steadfast, unceasing, unwearied 10 determined, unflagging, unswerving 11 hard-working, industrious, never-tiring, persevering, unfaltering, unremitting 13 indefatigable

Tiresias
  also: 9 Teiresias
  vocation: 7 prophet
  father: 6 Everes
  mother: 8 Chariclo
  grandfather: 6 Udaeus
  home: 6 Thebes
  struck: 5 blind
  character in: 7 Odyssey 10 Oedipus Rex
  characteristic: 9 blind seer

tiresome 4 drab, dull, hard 6 boring, deadly, dismal, tiring, trying, vexing 7 arduous, fagging, humdrum, irksome, tedious, wearing 8 annoying, wearying 9 difficult, fatiguing, laborious, wearisome 10 bothersome, exhausting, monotonous 13 uninteresting

Tisamenus
  leader of: 9 Boeotians
  father: 7 Orestes
  mother: 8 Hermione
  vocation: 4 seer
  killed by: 10 Heraclidae

Tishri 18 seventh Hebrew month

Tisiphone
  member of: 6 Furies

'Tis Pity She's a Whore
  author: 8 John Ford
  character: 6 Donado, Florio, Putana 7 Soranzo, Vasques 8 Bergetto, Giovanni, Grimaldi 9 Annabella, Hippolita 11 Richardetto 16 Friar Bonaventura

tissue
  kind: 4 bone, skin 5 nerve 6 muscle

titan 5 giant, great, mogul 7 magnate

Titan
  race of: 4 gods
  father: 6 Uranus
  mother: 2 Ge 4 Gaea
  names: 5 Coeus, Crius 6 Cronus 7 Iapetus, Oceanus 8 Hyperion
  sisters: 8 Titaness
    names of sisters: 4 Rhea 5 Theia 6 Phoebe, Tethys, Themis 9 Mnemosyne

Titan, The
  sequel to: 12 The Financier
  author: 15 Theodore Dreiser
  character: 13 Peter Laughlin 15 Berenice Fleming, Stephanie Platow 16 Aileen Cowperwood 23 Frank Algernon Cowperwood

Titan, the see 6 Helios

Titaness see 5 Titan

Titania
  character in: 21 A Midsummer Night's Dream
  author: 11 Shakespeare

titanic 4 huge, vast 5 giant, great, stout 6 mighty, strong 7 immense, mammoth 8 colossal, enormous, gigantic, whopping 9 herculean, humongous, monstrous 10 gargantuan, monumental, prodigious, stupendous

titanium
  chemical symbol: 2 Ti

Titanomachy
  revolt of: 7 Iapetus

tit for tat 8 exchange 10 quid pro quo 13 an eye for an eye

Tithonus
  father: 8 Laomedon
  brother: 5 Priam
  loved by: 3 Eos
  son: 6 Memnon 8 Emathion

Titian
  real name: 15 Tiziano Vecellio
  born: 5 Italy 13 Pieve di Cadore
  artwork: 5 Pieta 12 The Bacchanal, Tribute Money 13 Noli Me Tangere 15 Diana and Actaeon, The Rape of Europa 16 The Pesaro Madonna, The Venus of Urbino 17 Bacchus and Ariadne, The Death of Actaeon, The Girl in a Fur Wrap, The Three Ages of Man 18 Charles V at Muhlberg, The Adrian Bacchanal, The Young Englishman 19 Francis I Roi de France 20 Sacred and Profane Love 21 Venus and the Lute Player 23 The Madonna of the Cherries 24 Pope Paul III and his Nephews, The Assumption of the Virgin

titillate 5 charm, rouse, tease, tempt 6 allure, arouse, excite, seduce, tickle, turn on 7 attract, provoke 8 entrance 9 captivate, fascinate, stimulate 15 whet the appetite

titillating 8 alluring, exciting, tempting 9 seductive 10 suggestive 11 provocative

title 3 dub 4 deed, name, rank, term 5 claim, crown, grade, label, place, right 6 status, tenure 7 entitle, epithet, station 8 christen, nobility, position 9 condition, designate, ownership 10 legal right, lordly rank, noble birth, possession 11 appellation, designation 12 championship

titled 5 named, noble, regal, royal 6 called, lordly 7 courtly 8 entitled 10 designated 11 blue-blooded 12 aristocratic

Titograd
  capital of: 10 Montenegro

titter 5 chirp, smirk 6 cackle, giggle, simper, teehee 7 chuckle, snicker, snigger

tittle 3 bit, dot, jot 4 atom, iota, mite 5 speck 8 particle

Tittle, Y A (Yelberton Abraham)
  sport: 8 football

position: 11 quarterback
team: 13 New York Giants
14 Baltimore Colts **23** San Francisco Forty-Niners

titular 7 known as, nominal **8** so-called **10** in name only, ostensible **11** in title only

Titus
surname: 6 Justus
hometown: 7 Corinth
companion: 4 Paul

Titus see **6** Tatius

Titus Andronicus
author: 18 William Shakespeare
character: 5 Aaron **6** Chiron, Marcus, Tamora **7** Alarbus, Lavinia **9** Bassianus, Demetrius **10** Saturninus

Tityus
form: 5 giant
father: 4 Zeus
mother: 2 Ge **5** Elara
home: 6 Euboea
threatened: 4 Leto
killed by: 6 Apollo **7** Artemis

tizzy 4 snit **6** dither, swivet **7** dudgeon **8** tailspin
British: 8 sixpence

Tjaden
character in: 25 All Quiet on the Western Front
author: 8 Remarque

Tlepolemus
father: 8 Hercules
mother: 10 Astyocheia
wife: 6 Polyxo
son: 8 Deipylus
killed by: 8 Sarpedon

Tmolus
king of: 5 Lydia

to 2 ad, on **3** for **4** into, near, unto, upon, with **5** about, until **6** at hand, closed, toward **7** against, forward **8** together **10** concerning, included in **11** contained in
prefix: 2 ac, ad
Scottish: 3 tae

toad
group of: 4 knot

toady 4 fawn **6** fawner, flunky, stooge, yes-man **8** hanger-on, kowtow to, parasite, truckler **9** flatterer, sycophant **10** bootlicker, curry favor **11** applepolish, lickspittle **13** applepolisher, backscratcher

To Althea, From Prison
author: 15 Richard Lovelace

to a man 3 all **8** every one **9** one and all **10** completely **12** to the last man

To a Skylark
author: 18 Percy Bysshe Shelley

toast 3 dry **4** heat, warm **5** brown, grill, honor **6** salute, warm up **9** celebrate **10** compliment **11** commemorate **12** browned bread, clink glasses **15** drink one's health

tobacco
varieties: 4 tree, wild **6** Indian **7** jasmine, Turkish **9** broadleaf, flowering, Nicotiana **12** long-flowered **16** Nicotiana rustica, Nicotiana tabacum

Tobacco Road
author: 15 Erskine Caldwell
character: 3 Ada **4** Dude **5** Pearl **6** Bessie **8** Ellie May **9** Lov Bensey **12** Jeeter Lester

To Be or Not To Be
director: 13 Ernst Lubitsch
cast: 9 Jack Benny **11** Robert Stack **12** Lionel Atwill **13** Carole Lombard, Felix Bressart
setting: 6 Poland

Tobias
father: 5 Tobit
grandfather: 6 Tobiel
son: 8 Hycranus

Tobit
father: 6 Tobiel
son: 6 Tobias

To Catch a Thief
director: 15 Alfred Hitchcock
cast: 9 Cary Grant **10** Grace Kelly **12** John Williams **17** Jessie Royce Landis
setting: 13 French Riviera

Tocharian
language family: 12 Indo-European
spoken in: 11 Central Asia

Tocqueville, Alexis de
author of: 18 Democracy in America

tocsin 4 bell **5** alarm **7** warning

today 3 now **7** this day, this era **8** nowadays, this time **9** in this era, on this day, this epoch **10** the present **11** in this epoch, modern times **13** in modern times, the present age, the present day **15** in this day and age

Todd, Richard
real name: 27 Richard Andrew Palethorpe-Todd
born: 6 Dublin **7** Ireland
roles: 13 The Hasty Heart, The Longest Day **14** The Virgin Queen **15** A Man Called Peter

toddle 6 waddle, wobble **14** take short steps, walk unsteadily

toddler 3 tot **4** babe, baby,

tyke 5 child **6** infant **9** little one

to-do 3 ado **4** fuss, stir **5** furor, noise **6** bustle, flurry, hubbub, hustle, pother, racket, ruckus, rumpus, tumult, uproar **7** turmoil **8** activity **9** agitation, commotion **10** excitement, hullabaloo, hurly-burly **11** disturbance

Toe, The
nickname of: 8 Lou Groza

to err is human
Latin: 16 errare humanum est

toff 3 nob **4** beau **5** dandy, swell **10** young blood

Toffler, Alvin
author of: 11 Future Shock **12** The Third Wave

toga 3 aba **4** garb, gown, robe **6** trabea **7** garment **12** outergarment
virilis: 9 white robe **11** manhood robe

Togo see box, p. 988

togs 4 duds **6** attire, outfit **7** apparel, clothes, threads **8** clothing, garments

To Have and Have Not
director: 11 Howard Hawks
based on novel by: 15 Ernest Hemingway
cast: 12 Dolores Moran, Lauren Bacall **13** Walter Brennan **14** Humphrey Bogart **15** Hoagy Carmichael
remade as: 13 The Gunrunners **16** The Breaking Point

To His Coy Mistress
author: 13 Andrew Marvell

toil 4 grub, moil, work **5** grind, labor, pains, slave, sweat **6** drudge, effort **7** travail **8** drudgery, exertion, hardship, hard work, industry, struggle, work hard **11** application, elbow grease **12** apply oneself, exert oneself **14** work like a horse

toiler 4 peon, serf, swot **5** navvy, prole, slave **6** drudge, flunky, menial, slavey, worker **7** grubber, laborer, servant, slogger **9** workhorse **10** wage earner **11** galley slave

toilet 2 WC **3** can, loo **4** john **5** privy **7** commode, latrine **8** facility, lavatory, men's room, outhouse, rest room, washroom **10** ladies' room **11** convenience, water closet

toilet water 5 scent **7** cologne, essence, perfume **9** fragrance

toilsome 4 hard **5** tough **6** tiring, uphill **7** arduous, onerous, tedious **8** wearying **9** difficult,

Togo
  other name: **14** French Togoland
  capital/largest city: **4** Lome
  others: **5** Badon, Kpeme **6** Anecho, Ansoho, Blitta, Klonto, Nuatja, Palime, Sokode **7** Bassari, Dopango, Pagonda **8** Atakpame, Tabligbo **10** Niamtougou
  school: **5** Benin **6** Mawull
  monetary unit: **5** franc **7** centime
  mountain: **4** Togo **7** Atakora, Koronga
  highest point: **7** Baumann
  river: **3** Oti **4** Anie, Haho, Mono, Ogou
  sea: **8** Atlantic
  physical feature:
    bight: **5** Benin
    gulf: **6** Guinea
    plain: **4** Mono
  people: **3** Ana, Ewe, Twi **4** Mina **5** Hausa **6** Akposa, Kabrai **7** Bassari, Cabrais, Kabrais, Ouatchi **8** Konkomba, Kotokoli, Lotokoli
    leader: **7** Eyadema **15** Sylvanus Olympio **16** Nicolas Grunitzky
  language: **3** Ana, Ewe, Twi **4** Mina **5** Hausa **6** French, Kabrai, Kabrie **7** Bassari, Dagomba, Ouatchi **8** Kotokoli, Lotocoli
  religion: **5** Islam **7** animism **12** Christianity

effortful, fatiguing, herculean, laborious, strenuous, wearisome **10** burdensome, exhausting **12** backbreaking

To Jerusalem and Back
  author: **10** Saul Bellow

token 4 mark, sign **5** index, proof **6** jetton, symbol **7** for show, memento, minimal, nodding, nominal, passing **8** evidence, keepsake, reminder, souvenir, symbolic **9** vestigial **10** expression, indication **11** perfunctory, remembrance, superficial, testimonial **13** manifestation

To Kill a Mockingbird
  director: **14** Robert Mulligan
  based on novel by: **9** Harper Lee
  cast: **9** John Megna **10** Mary Badham **11** Gregory Peck **12** Philip Alford
  Oscar for: **5** actor (Peck)

Tokyo
  airport: **6** Haneda
  capital of: **5** Japan
  district: **5** Ginza **6** Keihin **7** Chiyoda **8** Yokohama **10** Marunouchi **18** Tama New Town Project
  former name: **3** Edo
  island: **6** Honshu
  landmark: **8** Ueno Park **11** Meiji Shrine **12** National Diet **14** Imperial Palace, Kitanomaru Park **19** Komazawa Olympic Park
  means: **14** Eastern capital

Tola 11 Hebrew judge

Told in the Dog Watches
  author: **12** Frank T Bullen

tolerable 4 fair, so-so **7** allowed, average **8** abidable, accepted, adequate, bearable, mediocre, middling, ordinary, passable **9** allowable, endurable, innocuous, permitted **10** acceptable, admissible, fairly good, sufferable **11** commonplace, indifferent, permissible **12** run-of-the-mill **14** fair-to-middling

tolerance 7 charity **8** fairness, goodwill, patience, sympathy **9** endurance **10** compassion, sufferance **11** forbearance **13** brotherly love, fair treatment, fellow feeling, power to endure **15** lack of prejudice

tolerant 4 easy, fair, soft **7** lenient, liberal, patient, sparing **8** moderate **9** easygoing, forgiving, indulgent, unbigoted **10** charitable, forbearing, permissive **11** broad-minded, kindhearted, softhearted, sympathetic **12** unprejudiced **13** compassionate, uncomplaining, understanding

tolerate 3 let **4** bear, take **5** abide, admit, allow, brook, stand **6** endure, permit, suffer, wink at **7** indulge, stomach, undergo **8** be easy on, be soft on, sanction, submit to **9** consent to, put up with, recognize, vouchsafe

To Let
  author: **14** John Galsworthy

to life
  Hebrew: **7** lehayim **8** lechayim

Tolkien, J R R
  author of: **9** The Hobbit **12** Silmarillion **17** The Lord of the Rings
  fictional setting: **11** Middle Earth

toll 3 fee, tax **4** duty, levy, loss **6** charge, impost, tariff **7** payment, penalty, tribute, undoing **8** exaction **9** depletion, sacrifice **10** assessment, disruption, extinction **11** destruction **12** annihilation **13** extermination

Tolstoy, Leo
  author of: **11** War and Peace **12** Anna Karenina, Resurrection **17** The Kreutzer Sonata **18** Death of Ivan Ilyitch

Toltec
  tribe: **4** Itza

To Lucasta, Going to the Wars
  author: **15** Richard Lovelace

Tolumnius
  vocation: **5** augur

tom 3 cat **6** tomcat **10** male turkey

tomato 12 Lycopersicon **24** Lycopersicon lycopersicum
  varieties: **4** Husk, Pear, Tree **6** Cherry **7** Currant **10** Gooseberry, Strawberry **11** Mexican husk
  soup: **8** gazpacho
  sauce: **6** catsup **7** ketchup

tomb 5 crypt, grave, vault **8** monument **9** mausoleum, sepulcher **11** burial place **12** resting place **13** burial chamber

tomboy 3 meg **4** girl, romp **5** rowdy **6** female, gamine, hoiden, hoyden, tomrig **8** strumpet

Tom Brown's School Days
  author: **12** Thomas Hughes

tombs
  god of: **6** Anubis

tomcat 3 cat, tom **9** womanizer

To-meri *see* **5** Egypt

tomfoolery 4 play **6** antics **8** drollery, nonsense **9** high jinks, horseplay, silliness **10** goofing off, skylarking **11** foolishness **12** lollygagging, monkeyshines, prankishness **13** fooling around, messing around, playing around

Tom Jones
also: 29 The History of Tom Jones Foundling
author: 13 Henry Fielding
character: 6 Square **7** Bridget, Western **8** Mrs Honor, Thwackum **9** Mrs Miller, Partridge **11** Black George, Nightingale **12** Master Blifil **13** Lady Bellaston, Sophia Western **15** Squire Allworthy
director: 14 Tony Richardson
cast: 11 Joyce Redman **12** Albert Finney, Diane Cilento, Hugh Griffith, Susannah York **14** Dame Edith Evans
score: 11 John Addison
Oscar for: 5 score **7** picture **9** direction **10** screenplay

Tomlin, Lily
real name: 14 Mary Jean Tomlin
born: 9 Detroit MI
roles: 7 Laugh-In **8** Edith Ann **9** Ernestine, Nashville **11** The Late Show **14** Moment By Moment **27** The Incredible Shrinking Woman

Tomlinson, Mary
real name of: 12 Marjorie Main

tommyrot 3 rot **4** bosh, bull, bunk, crap, tosh **5** bilge, hokum, hooey, trash **6** bunkum, drivel, humbug **7** baloney, hogwash, spinach, rubbish, twaddle **8** buncombe, claptrap, folderol, malarkey, nonsense **9** poppycock **10** applesauce, balderdash, tomfoolery **11** foolishness **12** bullfeathers, fiddle-faddle **13** horsefeathers **16** stuff-and-nonsense

tomorrow 9 the future, the morrow **11** in the future **12** in days to come **16** the day after today **17** the next generation **Spanish: 6** manana

Tompkins, Yewell
real name of: 8 Tom Ewell

Tom Sawyer
author: 9 Mark Twain
character: 8 Huck (Huckleberry) Finn, Injun Joe **9** Aunt Polly, Joe Harper **10** Muff Potter **13** Becky Thatcher

Tom Thumb the Great
author: 13 Henry Fielding

ton
abbreviation: 1 t

tone 3 hue **4** cast, lilt, mood, note, tint **5** color, pitch, shade, sound, style, tenor, tinge **6** accent, chroma, firm up, manner, soften, spirit, stress, subdue, temper **7** cadence, quality **8** attitude, harmonic, make firm, moderate, modulate, overtone, tonality **10** inflection, intonation, make supple, modulation

Tone, Franchot
real name: 27 Stanislas Pascal Franchot Tone
born: 14 Niagara Falls NY
wife: 11 Jean Wallace **12** Joan Crawford **13** Barbara Payton **15** Dolores Dorn-Heft
roles: 10 Uncle Vanya **11** Phantom Lady **13** Three Comrades **16** Advise and Consent **17** Five Graves to Cairo, Mutiny on the Bounty **23** The Lives of a Bengal Lancer

tone up 7 make fit, shape up **9** condition **10** put in shape

Tonga see box

tongue 3 lap **4** flap, lick, spit **5** point, shaft **6** lingua, patois, speech **7** dialect, lingula **8** language **10** promontory, vernacular, vocabulary **13** organ of speech, power of speech, style of speech
  tastes: 4 salt, sour **5** sweet **6** bitter

tongue-lash 5 scold **6** berate, rail at, rebuke **7** bawl out, chew out, reprove, upbraid **8** reproach **9** castigate, reprimand **10** take to task

tongue-lashing 6 rebuke **7** censure, chiding, reproof **8** reproach, scolding **9** reprimand **10** bawling-out, chewing-out, upbraiding **11** castigation, reprobation **12** dressing-down, remonstrance

tonic 6 bracer, pickup **7** keynote **8** pick-me-up **9** analeptic, refresher, stimulant **10** invigorant **11** restorative

tonne
abbreviation: 1 t

Tono-Bungay
author: 7 H G Wells

tonsure 3 cut **4** trim **8** bald spot **11** shaven patch

too
French: 4 trop

tool see box, p. 990

too little 4 lack **6** dearth, scanty, scarce **7** paucity **8** scarcity, shortage **9** deficient, not enough, scantness **10** deficiency, inadequacy, inadequate **12** insufficient **13** insufficiency

Tonga
other name: 15 Friendly Islands
capital/largest city: 9 Nukualofa
others: 3 Mua, Pea **6** Neiafu **7** Haakame, Kolonga, Kolovai **8** Fuaamotu
division: 5 Vavau **6** Haapai **9** Tongatapu
government: 8 monarchy
head of state: 4 king
monetary unit: 6 paanga, seniti
island: 3 Eua, Kao, Ono **4** Kotu **5** Tofua, Vavau **6** Haapai, Lifuke, Nomuka **7** Otu Tolu **9** Tongatapu
highest point: 3 Kao
sea: 7 Pacific
people: 10 Polynesian
  explorer: 4 Cook **5** Bligh **6** Tasman
  king: 11 George Tupou **14** Taufaahau Tupou
  missionary: 12 Shirley Baker
  queen: 6 Salote
language: 6 Tongan **7** English
religion: 9 Methodist **12** Christianity **25** Wesleyan Free Church of Tonga
feature:
  fabric: 4 tapa
  spiritual king: 8 tui tonga

too many
French: 6 de trop

too much 4 glut **5** flood **6** excess **7** profuse, surfeit, surplus **8** fullness, overflow, plethora **9** avalanche, excessive, profusion, repletion **10** inundation, oversupply **12** overabundant **13** overabundance **14** superabundance **French: 4** trop

Toonerville Folks
creator: 11 Fontaine Fox
character: 7 skipper **13** Aunt Eppie Hogg **15** Little Scorpions, Powerful Katrina, Suitcase Simpson **20** Mickey Himself McGuire **22** Terrible Tempered Mr Bang
rode on: 7 trolley

to one side 4 over **5** aloof, apart, aside **6** aslant **14** on the sidelines

to one's liking 7 fitting **8** pleasant, pleasing, suitable **9** agreeable **10** acceptable,

tool 4 dupe, pawn 5 agent, means 6 device, medium, puppet, stooge 7 cat's-paw, machine, utensil, vehicle 8 hireling 9 apparatus, appliance, implement, mechanism 10 instrument 11 contrivance, wherewithal 12 intermediary 15 instrumentality
  carpenter's: 3 adz, awl, bit, peg, saw 4 adze, nail, rasp, vise 5 auger, brace, edger, gouge, knife, lathe, plane, ruler, screw 6 bodkin, chisel, gimlet, hammer, pliers, router, sander 7 bradawl, scraper 9 hand drill, try square 11 screwdriver
  cutting/shaping: 2 ax 3 adz, axe, saw 4 adze, burr, file, froe, frow, rasp 5 burin, croze, gouge, knife, plane, razor, shave, wedge 6 chisel, sander, shears, trepan 7 hatchet, scraper 8 scissors
  drilling/boring: 3 awl, bit, zax 4 pick 5 chuck, drill 6 gimlet, wimble 7 bradawl 11 countersink
  farmer's: 2 ax 3 axe, hoe 4 plow, rake 5 spade 6 cradle, harrow, pickax, plough, scythe, seeder, shovel, sickle, tiller, trowel 7 hayfork 9 plowshare 10 cultivator
  gripping/turning: 6 pliers, wrench 11 screwdriver
  holding: 4 vise 5 clamp
  measuring: 4 rule 5 gauge, level 6 square 7 caliper 8 dividers 10 micrometer
  mechanic's: 3 awl, zax 4 burr, file, vise 5 bevel, lathe 6 bodkin, pliers 7 bradawl, crowbar 8 calipers 9 jackscrew 11 screwdriver 12 monkey wrench
  pounding/striking: 4 maul 5 punch, wedge 6 hammer, mallet

gratifying 11 appropriate, to one's taste 12 satisfactory

toot 4 blow, honk 5 binge, blare, blast, spree 6 bender 7 trumpet 8 wingding

tooth 3 cog, nib 4 barb, cusp, fang, spur, tang, tine, tusk 5 molar, point, spike, thorn 6 canine, cuspid 7 grinder, incisor 8 bicuspid, sprocket 9 serration

toothed 6 fanged, tusked 7 dentate, notched, serrate, virgate

toothsome 6 savory 8 luscious 9 delicious, palatable 10 appetizing

Toots
  character in: 12 Dombey and Son
  author: 7 Dickens

top 3 cap, lid, van 4 acme, apex, best, brow, cork, fore, head, lead, peak 5 chief, cover, crest, crown, excel, front, noted, outdo, upper 6 better, exceed, famous, summit, tiptop, vertex, zenith 7 eclipse, eminent, highest, notable, put over, stopper, surpass, topmost 8 complete, foremost, greatest, outshine, outstrip, pinnacle, renowned 9 paramount, principal, put a top on, transcend, uppermost, upper part 10 celebrated, first place, overshadow, preeminent

topaz
  color: 4 blue 5 brown 6 yellow
  source: 5 Japan 6 Brazil, Mexico, Saxony 13 Ural Mountains 18 Cairngorm Mountains
  month: 8 November

Topaze
  author: 12 Marcel Pagnol

topaz quartz
  species: 6 quartz
  color: 4 blue, pink 5 brown, green 6 sherry

toper 3 sot 4 lush, soak 5 drunk 6 boozer 7 tippler 8 drunkard 9 alcoholic 11 dispomaniac

Top Hat
  director: 12 Mark Sandrich
  cast: 9 Eric Blore 11 Fred Astaire 12 Ginger Rogers 14 Helen Broderick 19 Edward Everett Horton
  score: 12 Irving Berlin
  song: 12 Cheek to Cheek 22 Top Hat White Tie and Tails

topic 4 text 5 theme 6 thesis 7 keynote, subject

topical 5 local 6 timely 7 current, limited 9 localized, parochial 10 particular, restricted 12 contemporary

Topkapi
  director: 11 Jules Dassin
  cast: 12 Peter Ustinov, Rob-

ert Morley 14 Melina Mercouri 16 Maximilian Schell
  setting: 8 Istanbul
  Oscar for: 15 supporting actor (Ustinov)

topknot 4 comb, tuft 5 crest 9 cockscomb, headdress, headpiece

topmost 3 top 4 head 5 chief 7 highest, leading, supreme 8 foremost 9 paramount, principal, uppermost 10 preeminent

topnotch 3 ace 4 best 5 prime 6 choice, finest, tip-top 7 supreme 8 superior, very fine 9 excellent, first-rate, nonpareil, unequaled, unrivaled 10 preeminent 11 outstanding, unsurpassed 12 incomparable, unparalleled

top of the head 4 dome, pate 5 crown 6 noggin, noodle

Topper
  director: 13 Norman Z McLeod
  based on novel by: 11 Thorne Smith
  cast: 9 Cary Grant 11 Alan Mowbray, Billie Burke, Hedda Hopper, Roland Young 16 Constance Bennett
  sequel: 13 Topper Returns 16 Topper Takes a Trip

topple 4 fall 5 crush, quash, quell, smash, upset 6 defeat, sprawl, tumble 7 abolish, shatter, tip over 8 fall over, overcome, overturn, turn over, vanquish 9 bring down, overpower, overthrow 12 pitch forward

tops 4 aces, A-one, fine 5 great, prime, super, swell 6 choice, grade-A, superb, tiptop 7 capital 8 peerless, sterling, superior, terrific, topnotch 9 excellent, first-rate, marvelous, matchless, superfine, wonderful 10 first-class, inimitable, out-of-sight, tremendous 11 outstanding, superlative 12 incomparable 13 extraordinary

top-secret 5 privy 7 private 8 eyes-only, hush-hush 12 confidential

topsoil 4 dirt, loam 5 earth

Topsy
  character in: 14 Uncle Tom's Cabin
  author: 5 Stowe

topsy-turvy 5 messy 6 untidy 7 chaotic 8 confused, inverted, reversed 9 confusing, inside out 10 disorderly, upside down 11 disarranged, wrong side up 12 disorganized

Torah 10 law of Moses

torch 5 brand 7 cresset 8 arsonist, flambeau 9 firebrand 9 set fire to 10 flashlight

torment 3 nag, vex 4 bane, pain, rack 5 agony, annoy, curse, worry 6 harass, harrow, misery, pester, plague 7 afflict, agonize, anguish, despair, scourge, torture, trouble 8 distress, irritate 9 annoyance, persecute, suffering 10 irritation

tormenter 5 bully, tease 6 despot, tyrant 7 coercer 9 oppressor 10 browbeater 11 intimidator

tormenting 7 painful, racking 9 agonizing, torturous 10 unbearable 11 unendurable 12 excruciating, insufferable

torn 4 rent, slit 5 split 6 ragged, ripped 8 ruptured, shredded 9 unraveled

tornado 4 wind 5 storm 6 funnel, squall, vortex 7 cyclone, twister, typhoon 8 outburst 9 hurricane, whirlwind, windstorm 10 waterspout 12 thunderstorm
  belt: 7 Midwest
  cloud: 4 tuba

torn apart 4 rent 6 ripped 7 asunder 8 in pieces, in shreds, shredded

toro 4 bull

Toronto
  baseball team: 8 Blue Jays
  bay: 6 Humber
  football team:
    9 Argonauts
  former name: 4 York
  harbor: 5 Inner
  hockey team: 10 Maple Leafs
  lake: 7 Ontario
  landmark: 7 CN Tower 12 Ontario Place, O'Keefe Centre 13 Dufferin Grove 14 Dominion Centre 15 Roy Thompson Hall 16 Maple Leaf Stadium, St Lawrence Centre 17 Commerce Court West 18 Royal Ontario Museum 20 Nathan Phillips Square
    park: 7 Chorley, Stanley, Trinity 8 Winthrow 9 Cedarvale 12 Center Island 16 Winston Churchill
  street: 5 Yonge
  university: 4 York

Torosaurus
  type: 8 dinosaur 10 ceratopsid

torpedo 4 sink 5 wreck 7 destroy, missile, scuttle 9 explosive 10 projectile

torpedo (marine)
  invented by: 6 Fulton

torpid 4 dull, lazy 5 inert 6 drowsy, sleepy 7 dormant, languid, passive 8 inactive, indolent, listless, sluggish 9 apathetic, lethargic, somnolent 10 half asleep, languorous, slow-moving, spiritless 12 slow-thinking 13 lackadaisical

torpor, torpidity 6 apathy 7 inertia, languor 8 dullness, laziness, lethargy 9 indolence, lassitude 10 drowsiness, inactivity, sleepiness, somnolence 11 languidness, passiveness 12 listlessness, sluggishness

torrent 4 gush, rain, rush 5 burst, flood, salvo 6 deluge, rapids, stream, volley 7 barrage, cascade, Niagara 8 cataract, downpour, effusion, eruption, outburst 9 discharge, heavy rain, rapid flow, waterfall 10 cloudburst, outpouring, white water

Torrey, John
  field: 6 botany
  developed: 16 botanical library

Torricelli, Evangelista
  nationality: 7 Italian
  discovered concept leading to development of:
    9 barometer

torrid 3 hot 4 sexy 5 fiery 6 ardent, erotic, fervid, heated, sexual, sultry 7 amorous, boiling, burning, excited, fervent, intense, lustful 8 broiling, desirous, parching, sizzling, spirited, tropical, vehement 9 hot and dry, scorching 10 passionate, sweltering 11 hot and heavy, impassioned

torte 4 cake 7 dessert 9 layer cake

tortilla 7 tostada 8 corncake 11 Mexican cake
  griddle: 5 comal

Tortilla Flat
  author: 13 John Steinbeck

tortuous 4 bent 5 snaky 6 spiral, zigzag 7 crooked, devious, sinuous, turning, winding, wriggly 8 indirect, involved, twisting, wrongful 9 ambiguous 10 circuitous, convoluted, meandering, roundabout, serpentine 11 complicated 12 full of curves, hard to follow, labyrinthine

---

tortuousness 9 sinuosity 11 indirection, sinuousness 12 convolutions 14 circuitousness

torture 4 pain, rack 5 abuse, agony, prick, smite, trial, wring 6 harrow, ordeal 7 anguish, cruelty, torment 8 distress, maltreat, mistreat 9 brutality, suffering 10 infliction, punishment 11 tribulation 12 put to the rack

torturous 5 cruel 7 galling, irksome, painful, racking 8 annoying 9 agonizing, anguished, harrowing, miserable, tormented, torturing 10 anguishing, distressed, tormenting, unpleasant 11 distressful, distressing 12 disagreeable, excruciating

tory 8 loyalist, royalist 12 conservative

Tosca
  opera by: 7 Puccini
  character: 7 Scarpia 9 Angelotti 16 Mario Cavaradossi

To Sir With Love
  director: 12 James Clavell
  cast: 4 Lulu 10 Judy Geeson 11 Suzy Kendall 13 Sidney Poitier 16 Christian Roberts
  setting: 6 London

toss 3 lob 4 cast, flip, hurl, jerk, rock, roll, sway 5 churn, fling, heave, pitch, shake, sling, throw 6 joggle, let fly, propel, tumble, wiggle, writhe 7 agitate, flounce, wriggle 8 flourish, undulate 9 oscillate

toss about 4 roil 5 bandy 6 jostle, jounce

toss back and forth 5 bandy 8 exchange

total 3 add, sum 4 full 5 add up, gross, sheer, solid, sum up, utter, whole 6 entire, figure, reckon, tote up 7 add up to, compute, perfect, total up 8 absolute, combined, complete, entirety, figure up, integral, outright, sum total, sweeping, thorough, totality 9 aggregate, calculate, downright, out-and-out, unlimited, wholesale 10 full amount, undisputed, unmodified 11 unqualified, whole amount 13 comprehensive, unconditional

totaling 8 addition, coming to 9 reckoning 10 adding up to

totalitarian 7 fascist 8 despotic 9 fascistic, tyrannous 10 autocratic, tyrannical 11 dictatorial 12 undemocratic 16 unrepresentative

totally 7 solidly, utterly **8** entirely **9** downright, out-and-out, perfectly **10** absolutely, completely, thoroughly, throughout **15** unconditionally **18** from beginning to end **20** without qualification

tote 3 lug **4** bear, cart, drag, haul, move, pack, pull **5** carry, fetch **6** convey **7** schlepp **9** transport

to the city and the world
Latin: **10** urbi et orbi
form of address used on: **10** papal bulls

to the four winds 7 all over **10** everywhere, far and wide **26** to the four corners of the world

to the letter 5 exact, right **7** correct, precise **8** accurate, explicit, specific **9** on the nose

To the Lighthouse
author: **13** Virginia Woolf
character: **4** Prue **5** James **7** Camilla **8** Mr Ramsey **9** Mr Tansley, Mrs Ramsey **11** Lily Briscoe **12** Mr Carmichael

To the North
author: **14** Elizabeth Bowen

to the point 6 direct **7** apropos, germane **8** explicit, relevant **9** pertinent **12** to the purpose

to the rear 3 aft **4** back **5** abaft **6** astern, behind **8** backward, rearward **9** backwards, sternward **10** to the stern **14** toward the stern

to the stern 6 astern, behind **8** rearward **9** sternward **10** to the stern

to the word
Latin: **8** ad verbum

to this extent
Latin: **8** quoad hoc

Toto
dog in: **13** The Wizard of Oz
author: **4** Baum

totter 4 reel, rock, sway **5** lurch, shake, waver **6** falter, teeter, waddle, wobble **7** shuffle, stagger, stumble **9** oscillate, vacillate

tottering 5 shaky **6** wobbly **7** rickety, shaking **8** insecure, topheavy, unstable, unsteady, wobbling **9** doddering, quivering, trembling **10** ramshackle, staggering

Toucan
constellation of: **6** Tucana

touch see box

touched 3 mad **4** daft, felt, nuts **5** crazy, moved, nutty **6** insane, joined **7** abutted, cracked, handled **8** demented, deranged, unhinged **10** unbalanced **12** mad as a hatter **13** off one's rocker, out of one's head **14** off one's trolley **15** mad as a March hare

Touchett, Ralph
character in: **18** The Portrait of a Lady
author: **5** James

touching 3 sad **6** moving, tender **7** pitiful **8** dramatic, pathetic, poignant, stirring **9** affecting, emotional, heartfelt, saddening, sorrowful **11** distressing, sentimental **12** heartrending **13** heartbreaking

touch me not
Latin: **13** noli me tangere

Touch of Evil
director: **11** Orson Welles
cast: **10** Janet Leigh, Ray Collins **11** Joanna Moore,

Orson Welles, Zsa Zsa Gabor **12** Akim Tamiroff, Dennis Weaver **13** Joseph Calleia **14** Charlton Heston
cameo: **15** Marlene Dietrich **19** Mercedes McCambridge

touch off 5 shoot **6** set off **7** explode, fire off, trigger **8** activate, detonate **9** discharge

touch on 4 pose **6** broach, submit **7** advance, bring up, mention, propose, suggest **9** introduce

touchstone 4 norm, rule **5** basis, gauge, guide, model, proof **7** example, measure, pattern **8** standard **9** benchmark, criterion, guideline, precedent, principle, yardstick

Touchstone
character in: **11** As You Like It
author: **11** Shakespeare

touch upon 7 apply to, concern, mention, refer to **8** allude to, bear upon, relate to **9** appertain

touchy 5 cross, huffy, surly, testy **6** bitter, crabby, grumpy **7** awkward, fragile, grouchy, peevish, waspish **8** captious, critical, delicate, petulant, snappish, ticklish **9** concerned, difficult, irascible, irritable, querulous, resentful, sensitive **10** precarious **11** thinskinned **12** cantankerous **13** quicktempered

tough 4 cold, firm, hard, hood, lout, mean, punk, wily **5** bully, cagey, canny, cruel, hardy, rigid, rough, rowdy, solid, stern **6** brutal, crafty, dogged, knotty, mulish, rugged, savage, strict, strong, sturdy, thorny, trying **7** adamant, arduous, callous, complex, durable, hoodlum, inhuman, irksome, lasting, onerous, ruffian, vicious **8** baffling, barbaric, enduring, exacting, grievous, hooligan, involved, leathery, obdurate, perverse, pitiless, puzzling, ruthless, stubborn, ticklish, toilsome **9** barbarian, confusing, difficult, enigmatic, heartless, heavy-duty, intricate, laborious, obstinate, pigheaded, resistant, roughneck, strenuous, unbending, unfeeling **10** bullheaded, delinquent, exhausting, formidable, hardheaded, inflexible, perplexing, unyielding **11** bewildering, calculating, cold-blooded, complicated, hardhearted, hard-to-solve, infrangible, insensitive,

touch 3 art, bit, paw, pet, rub, use **4** abut, cite, dash, feel, fire, form, gift, hand, hint, join, meet, melt, move, note, stir, sway, tint, work **5** equal, flair, match, pinch, rival, rouse, skill, smack, speck, style, taste, thumb, tinge, trace, unite **6** adjoin, affect, arouse, border, broach, caress, excite, finger, finish, fondle, handle, hint at, manner, method, pawing, polish, sadden, soften, strike, stroke, thrill **7** concern, consume, contact, feeling, finesse, impress, inflame, inspire, mastery, mention, quality, refer to, soupcon, surface, texture, utilize **8** allude to, artistry, bear upon, come near, come up to, converge, deal with, deftness, fineness, fondling, handling, inspirit, resort to, thumbing **9** awareness, direction, electrify, fingering, influence, palpation, pertain to, suspicion, technique **10** adroitness, intimation, manipulate, perception, sprinkling, suggestion, virtuosity **11** be in contact, compare with, familiarity, guiding hand, realization **12** acquaintance, manipulation **13** communication, comprehension, understanding

troublesome **12** bloodthirsty,
impenetrable **13** unsympathetic **14** uncompromising

toughen 4 firm **5** inure, steel
6 firm up, harden, season,
temper **7** fortify, stiffen **8** accustom **9** acclimate, habituate
10 discipline, strengthen
11 acclimatize

**Toulouse-Lautrec, Henri
Marie Raymond de**
  born: **4** Albi **6** France
  8 Albigois
  artwork: **7** Friends **13** The
  Inspection **16** At the Moulin
  Rouge **24** Au Salon de la
  Rue des Moulins **27** Jane
  Avril at the Jardin de Paris
  29 Cirque Fernando The
  Equestrienne **29** In the Par-
  lor at the Rue des Moulins
  29 The English Girl at Le
  Star Le Havre **30** La Goulue
  Entering the Moulin Rouge

toupee 3 rug, wig **6** carpet, peruke **7** periwig **9** hairpiece

tour 4 trek, trip **5** jaunt, visit
6 junket, safari, travel, voyage **7** inspect, journey **8** sightsee **9** excursion, itinerary

tourist 7 pilgrim, tripper, voyager **8** traveler, vagabond,
wanderer, wayfarer **9** journeyer, sightseer **10** rubberneck **12** excursionist,
globetrotter

tourmaline
  color: **3** red **4** blue, pink
  5 green

tournament 4 game **5** event,
match **7** contest, rivalry, tourney **11** competition

Tourneur, Cyril
  author of: **19** The Revenger's
  Tragedy

tourney 4 game **5** event,
match **7** contest, rivalry
10 tournament **11** competition

tousled 5 messy **6** mussed, untidy **7** rumpled, tangled, unkempt **8** mussed-up,
uncombed **10** disheveled,
disordered

tout 4 plug, push **5** boost, exalt, extol, vaunt **6** praise, talk
up **7** acclaim, commend, glorify, promote, tipster **8** ballyhoo, eulogize, give a tip
9 advertise, brag about, celebrate, publicize, recommend
10 aggrandize, noise about

tout a fait 8 entirely
  literally: **12** wholly to fact

tout a l'heure 7 just now
8 very soon **9** presently **14** just
a moment ago
  literally: **15** wholly to the
  hour

tout de suite 6 at once
11 immediately
  literally: **19** wholly
  consecutively

tout ensemble 11 all together

tout le monde 8 everyone
9 everybody **13** the whole
world

tovarich 7 comrade

tow 3 lug **4** drag, draw, haul,
lift, pull **5** hoist, trail

toward the end
  Latin: **5** ad fin

toward the front 5 ahead
6 before **7** forward **9** to the
fore **13** in the vanguard **14** in
the forefront

toward the rear 4 back
6 astern **8** backward, rearward **9** sternward

toward the stern 6 astern
8 rearward **9** sternward **10** to
the stern

tower 4 keep, loom, rock,
soar **5** mount, outdo, spire,
surge **6** ascend, belfry, castle,
column, exceed, pillar, refuge,
turret **7** bulwark, eclipse, minaret, obelisk, overtop, shoot
up, steeple, surpass **8** mainstay, outclass, outshine, overhang, rise high **9** bell tower,
rise above, transcend **10** foundation, overshadow, sky-
scraper, stronghold,
wellspring **12** fountainhead

towering 4 high, tall **5** lofty
6 alpine **7** soaring, sublime,
supreme **8** dominant, foremost,
mounting, peerless, snowclad,
superior **9** ascending, matchless, paramount, principal, unequaled, unmatched,
unrivaled **10** cloud-swept,
preeminent, surpassing, unexcelled **11** cloud-capped, overhanging **12** incomparable,
second to none, transcendent,
unparalleled **13** extraordinary

Tower of London, The
  author: **24** William Harrison
  Ainsworth

tower over 5 dwarf **7** surpass
8 dominate **9** rise above

town 4 burg, city **6** hamlet,
parish **7** borough, village
9 citizenry, residents **10** settlement **11** inhabitants, townspeople **12** municipality

Town, The
  author: **13** Conrad Richter

Townes, Charles Hard
  field: **7** physics
  invented: **5** maser
  awarded: **10** Nobel Prize

town hall
  German: **7** Rathaus

town house 8 row house
10 pied-a-terre **13** city
residence

township 4 town **7** village
11 subdivision **12** municipality

Toxeus
  father: **6** Oeneus
  mother: **7** Althaea
  killed by: **6** Oeneus

toxic 5 fatal **6** deadly, lethal,
mortal **7** noxious **8** poisoned,
venomous **9** poisonous, unhealthy **10** pernicious

toxin 4 bane **5** venom **6** poison **8** pathogen

toy 4 play, tiny **5** dally, pygmy,
sport **6** bantam, bauble, fiddle,
gadget, gewgaw, little, midget,
trifle **7** dwarfed, for play,
stunted, trinket **8** gimcrack
9 miniature, plaything, small-
size **10** diminutive, small-
scale **11** Lilliputian

Toy Bulldog
  nickname of: **12** Mickey
  Walker

Toynbee, Arnold
  author of: **15** A Study of
  History

to your health
  French: **11** a votre sante

toy with 8 play with **9** flirt
with **10** trifle with **16** amuse
oneself with

trace 3 bit, jot, map **4** draw,
drop, find, hint, hunt, iota,
mark, seek, sign **5** dig up,
relic, shade, tinge, token,
touch, track, trail **6** depict, flavor, trifle **7** diagram, hunt for,
look for, mark out, nose out,
outline, remains, uncover,
unearth, vestige **8** describe,
discover, draw over, evidence
9 delineate, ferret out, footprint, light upon, little bit,
search for, suspicion, track
down **10** come across, indication, suggestion **11** small
amount

trace to 6 credit **7** ascribe
8 charge to **9** attribute

Trachiniae
  author: **9** Sophocles
  characters: **4** Iole **6** Hyllus,
  Nessus **8** Deianira, Heracles

track 3 way **4** mark, path, rail,
sign, tack **5** dirty, route, scent,
spoor, trace, trail **6** course, follow **9** footprint, guide rail

track and field *see box,
p. 994*

tract 3 lot **4** area, plot, zone
5 essay **6** parcel, region
7 booklet, expanse, leaflet,

track and field
athlete: **7** Jim Ryun, Ray Ewry **8** Al Oerter, Lee Evans, Zola Budd **9** Bob Beamon, Carl Lewis, Henry Rono, Jim Thorpe **10** Ben Johnson, Bob Mathias, Bob Seagren, Edwin Moses, Grete Waitz, James Hines, Jesse Owens, John Carlos, Lasse Viren, Mac Wilkins, Paavo Nurmi, Peter Snell, Steve Ovett, Wyomia Tyus **11** Bill Rodgers, Bruce Jenner, Marty Liouri, David Wottle, Dick Fosbury, Doug Padilla, Emil Zatopek, Joni Huntley, Ralph Boston, Randy Matson, Tommie Smith **12** Dwight Stones, Frank Shorter, Harvey Glance, Jay Silvester, Kathy Hammond, Maren Seidler, Rafer Johnson, Sebastian Coe, Willie B White, Wilma Rudolph **13** Allan Feurbach, Arnie Robinson, Janice Merrill, Kathy McMillan, Kipchoge Keino, Rodney Milburn, Ronny Ray Smith, Rosalyn Bryant, William Toomey **14** Alberto Salazar, Francie Larrieu, Roger Bannister **15** Martha Rae Watson, Renaldo Nehemiah, Willie Davenport **16** Madeleine Manning, Mary Decker Slaney, Richard Wohlhuter, Steve Prefontaine **17** Alberto Juantoreno **18** Jackie Joyner-Kersee, Stephanie Hightower **21** Babe Didrikson Zaharias **22** Florence Griffith-Joyner

quarter, stretch **8** brochure, district, pamphlet, treatise **9** monograph, territory **12** disquisition

tractable 4 tame **6** docile **8** amenable, obedient, yielding **9** compliant, teachable, trainable **10** governable, manageable, submissive **12** controllable, easy to manage **13** easy to control

tractate 8 treatise **9** discourse, monograph **12** disquisition, dissertation

Tracy, Spencer
born: **11** Milwaukee WI
costar: **16** Katharine Hepburn
roles: **7** Desk Set **8** Adam's Rib, Boys' Town (Oscar) **10** Pat and Mike **12** San Francisco, Tortilla Flat **13** The Last Hurrah **14** Cass Timberlane, Inherit the Wind, Woman of the Year **15** State of the Union **16** Father of the Bride, Keeper of the Flame **17** Bad Day at Black Rock **18** Captains Courageous (Oscar), The Old Man and the Sea **19** Judgment at Nuremberg **23** Guess Who's Coming to Dinner

Traddles
character in: **16** David Copperfield
author: **7** Dickens

trade 3 buy **4** deal, line, shop, swap **5** craft **6** barter, buyers **7** calling, patrons, pursuit **8** business, commerce, exchange, shoppers, vocation **9** clientele, customers, patronize **10** buy and sell, do business, employment, handicraft, line of work, occupation, profession **12** transactions **13** merchandising **16** business dealings, buying and selling

trade commodity 5 goods, wares

trademark 6 emblem **7** feature **8** property **9** specialty **11** peculiarity **14** characteristic

trade off 4 swap **5** trade **6** barter **8** exchange

trader 6 dealer, monger, seller **7** drummer **8** merchant, retailer **10** shopkeeper, trafficker, wholesaler **11** salesperson, storekeeper **12** merchandiser, tradesperson **14** businessperson

tradesman 6 dealer, seller **8** merchant, retailer **9** craftsman **10** shopkeeper **11** storekeeper

Trade Wind
author: **6** M M Kaye

tradition 4 lore, myth, saga, tale **5** habit, usage **6** custom, legend **8** folklore, practice **10** convention **12** superstition

traditional 3 old **5** fixed, usual **7** typical **8** habitual, historic **9** ancestral, customary **10** accustomed, inveterate **11** established **12** acknowledged, conventional

traduce 5 abuse, libel, smear, sully **6** defame, malign, vilify **7** run down, slander **8** backbite, bad-mouth, besmirch **9** deprecate, disparage **10** calumniate

traffic 4 cars, deal **5** buses, ships, trade **6** barter, doings, planes, riders, trains, trucks **7** bootleg, contact, freight, smuggle **8** business, commerce, dealings, exchange, tourists, voyagers **9** commuters, relations, smuggling, travelers **10** buy and sell, enterprise, passengers **11** bootlegging, intercourse, pedestrians, proceedings **12** transactions, vacationists **13** excursionists

tragedy 3 woe **4** blow **5** grief **6** misery, sorrow **7** anguish, setback **8** accident, calamity, disaster, reversal, sad thing **9** heartache **10** affliction, heartbreak **11** catastrophe

tragic 3 sad **4** dire **5** awful, fatal **6** deadly, dreary, woeful **7** piteous, pitiful, ruinous, serious, unhappy **8** dramatic, dreadful, grievous, horrible, mournful, pathetic, pitiable, shocking, terrible **9** appalling, frightful **10** calamitous, deplorable, disastrous, lamentable **11** destructive, devastating, unfortunate **12** catastrophic **13** heartbreaking

trail 3 dog, tow, way **4** drag, draw, fall, flow, hunt, mark, path, poke, sign, tail **5** float, hound, scent, spoor, trace, track **6** be down, course, dangle, dawdle, follow, lessen, shrink, stream **7** dwindle, pathway, subside **8** decrease, diminish, footpath, grow weak, hand down, peter out, taper off **9** drag along, grow faint, grow small, lag behind **10** bridle path, drag behind, footprints, move slowly **11** beaten track **14** bring up the rear

trailblazers 7 leaders **8** pioneers **10** avant-garde, innovators **11** forerunners, originators, tastemakers **12** trendsetters

train 2 el **3** aim, set **4** line **5** break, chain, drill, focus, level, point, queue, sight, teach, trail, tutor **6** column, direct, escort, school, series, subway **7** caravan, cortege, educate, prepare, retinue **8** elevated, exercise, instruct, practice, rehearse, sequence **9** afterpart, appendage, entourage, followers **10** attendants, discipline, get in shape, procession, succession **11** bring to bear, domesticate, progression **12** continuation

Train, The
director: **17** John Frankenheimer
cast: **10** Albert Remy **11** Michel Simon **12** Jeanne

Moreau, Paul Scofield
13 Burt Lancaster

trained 4 able **6** expert, master **7** capable, skilled
8 schooled, seasoned **9** competent, qualified **11** experienced
12 accomplished

trainee 4 boot **5** cadet
6 rookie **7** private, rookie, student **9** greenhorn
10 apprentice

trainer 5 coach, tutor
7 teacher **16** athletic director

training 5 drill **8** coaching,
drilling, practice, teaching
9 education, schooling **10** discipline **11** preparation **14** apprenticeship, indoctrination

traipse 3 gad **4** roam, walk
5 range, tramp, tread **8** stroll,
trapes, wander **7** meander,
saunter **8** gadabout **9** gallivant

trait 4 mark **5** quirk **7** earmark,
feature, quality **8** hallmark
9 attribute, mannerism **11** peculiarity **12** idiosyncrasy
14 characteristic

traitor 3 rat **5** Judas, rebel
6 ratter **7** ratfink, serpent
8 apostate, betrayer, deceiver,
deserter, mutineer, quisling,
renegade, turncoat **9** hypocrite **11** false friend **12** double-
dealer **13** double-crosser, revolutionary **14** fifth columnist
15 snake in the grass **20** wolf
in sheep's clothing

traitorous 5 false **7** corrupt
8 disloyal, renegade **9** betraying, faithless **10** perfidious,
treasonous, unfaithful
11 treacherous

tramp 3 bum **4** hike, hobo,
roam, rove, slog, trek, walk
5 march, prowl, stamp, stomp
6 ramble, trudge, wander
7 floater, meander, traipse,
trample, vagrant **8** derelict
9 gallivant, itinerant **10** panhandler **11** perambulate, peregrinate **15** knight-of-the-road

trample 5 crush, stamp,
stomp **6** squash **7** flatten, run
over **14** grind under foot
15 step heavily upon

trance 4 coma, daze **5** dream,
spell **6** stupor, vision **7** reverie **8** daydream, hypnosis
9 pipe dream **10** absorption,
brown study **11** abstraction
12 sleepwalking **13** concentration, preoccupation,
woolgathering

tranquil 4 calm, cool, mild
5 quiet, still **6** gentle, placid,
serene **7** halcyon, restful
8 composed, peaceful **9** unexcited, unruffled **11** undis-

turbed, unperturbed
13 self-possessed

tranquility 4 calm, hush
5 peace, quiet **6** repose **7** concord, harmony **8** quietude, serenity **9** composure, placidity,
stillness **11** restfulness
12 peacefulness

tranquilize 4 calm, drug, lull
5 allay, quiet, relax, still **6** becalm, pacify, sedate, settle,
soothe **7** appease, assuage
9 alleviate

·transact 2 do **5** exact **6** handle,
manage, settle **7** achieve, carry
on, conduct, execute, perform
8 carry out, exercise **9** discharge **10** accomplish, take
care of **12** carry through

transaction 4 deal **6** affair
7 bargain, dealing, venture
8 exchange **9** operation **10** enterprise, settlement **11** negotiation **15** business dealing,
piece of business

transcend 5 excel, outdo **6** exceed **7** eclipse, outrank, surpass **8** go beyond, outrival,
outshine, outstrip, overleap,
overstep, surmount **9** rise
above **10** overshadow
11 outdistance

transcendence 5 merit **8** eminence **9** exceeding, greatness
10 exaltation, excellence, surpassing **11** distinction, preeminence, superiority

transcendental 5 great
6 mental **7** supreme, unusual
8 elevated, peerless, superior,
uncommon **9** exceeding, intuitive, matchless, spiritual, unequaled, unrivaled
10 surpassing **11** unsurpassed
12 incomparable, metaphysical **13** extraordinary

transfer 4 cede, deed, move,
send **5** bring, carry, shift
6 change, convey, moving, remove **7** consign, deeding, removal, sending **8** bringing,
carrying, hand over, make
over, relegate, relocate, shifting, shipment, transmit, turn
over **9** conveying, transport
10 delivering, relegation, relocating, relocation **11** consignment, transmittal
12 transporting
14 transportation

transferable 8 catching
10 contagious, infectious
12 communicable **13** transmissible, transmittable

transferal 8 delivery, transfer
10 giving over **11** handing
over, transmittal
12 transmission

transference 5 shift **6** change
7 passage, removal **9** transport **11** transmittal **12** dislodgement, displacement,
transmission **13** transmittance

transfiguration 10 conversion
13 metamorphosis, transmutation **14** transformation

transfigure 6 change **9** transform **12** metamorphose

transfix 3 pin **4** hold, stab,
stun **5** rivet, spear, spike,
stick **6** absorb, impale, pierce,
skewer **7** astound, bewitch, enchant, engross, fix fast, terrify **8** astonish, hold rapt,
intrigue **9** captivate, fascinate,
hypnotize, mesmerize, penetrate, spellbind **10** run through

transform 4 turn **5** alter
6 change, recast, remold
7 convert, remodel **8** make
over **9** refurbish, transmute
11 reconstruct, transfigure
12 metamorphose,
transmogrify

transformation 6 change **9** restyling **10** alteration, conversion, remodeling
13 metamorphosis, transmutation **15** transfiguration

transgress 3 err, sin **4** slip
5 break, cross, fault, lapse,
wrong **6** exceed, impose, offend **7** digress, infract, violate
8 infringe, trespass

transgression 3 sin **5** crime,
error, lapse, wrong **6** breach
7 misdeed, offense **8** evil deed,
iniquity, trespass **9** violation
10 immorality, infraction,
wrongdoing **11** lawbreaking
12 encroachment, infringement, overstepping
13 contravention

transgressor 5 felon **6** sinner
7 culprit **8** criminal, evildoer,
offender, violator **9** miscreant,
wrongdoer **10** lawbreaker,
malefactor, trespasser

transience 7 brevity **11** evanescence **12** ephemerality,
impermanence

transient 5 brief **7** passing
8 fleeting, soon past, temporal **9** ephemeral, momentary, short-term, temporary
10 evanescent, perishable,
short-lived, transitory, unenduring **11** impermanent
14 passing through **24** here
today and gone tomorrow

transistor
invented by: **7** Bardeen
8 Brattain, Shockley

transition 4 jump, leap
6 change **7** passage, passing
8 shifting **9** gradation, varia-

tion **10** alteration, changeover, conversion, graduation **11** progression **13** transmutation **14** transformation

transitory 5 brief **7** passing **8** fleeting, fugitive **9** ephemeral, temporary, transient **10** evanescent, not lasting, short-lived, unenduring **11** impermanent **24** here today and gone tomorrow

translate 4 turn **5** alter, apply **6** change, decode, recast, render, reword **7** clarify, convert, explain **8** decipher, rephrase, simplify, spell out **9** elucidate, interpret, make clear, transform, transmute **10** paraphrase

translucence 7 clarity **8** lucidity **10** luminosity **12** transparency **16** semi-transparency

translucent 8 pellucid **10** semiopaque, translucid **15** semitransparent

transmissible 8 catching **10** contagious, infectious **12** communicable, transferable **13** transmittable

transmission 4 note **7** message, passage, passing, sending **8** delivery, dispatch, transfer **9** broadcast **10** conveyance, forwarding, remittance **11** handing over, transmittal **12** transference, transferring **13** communication **14** transportation

transmit 4 send, ship **5** carry, issue, relay, remit **6** convey, pass on, spread **7** deliver, forward **8** dispatch, televise, transfer **9** broadcast **11** communicate, disseminate

transmittable 8 catching **10** contagious, infectious **12** communicable, transferable

transmittal 7 sending **8** delivery, transfer **10** giving over, transferal **11** handing over **12** transmission

transmutation 6 change **10** conversion **13** metamorphosis **14** transformation **15** transfiguration

transmute 5 alter **6** change **7** convert **9** transform **12** metamorphose

transparency 6 purity **7** clarity **8** lucidity **9** clearness, sheerness **11** obviousness **14** diaphanousness

transparent 4 thin **5** clear, gauzy, lucid, plain, sheer **6** glassy, limpid, patent **7** evident, obvious, visible **8** apparent, clear-cut, distinct, explicit, manifest, palpable, peekaboo,

pellucid **10** diaphanous, seethrough **11** perceptible, selfevident, translucent, unambiguous, unequivocal **12** crystalclear, unmistakable

transpire 5 arise, occur **6** appear, befall, chance, crop up, evolve, happen, turn up **7** come out, leak out **9** be met with, eventuate, take place **10** be revealed, come to pass, make public **11** become known, be disclosed, come to light, show its face

transplant 5 graft, repot, shift **7** replant **8** displace, relocate, resettle, transfer **9** transport, transpose

transport 3 bus, lug **4** bear, cart, lift, move, send, ship, take, tote **5** bring, carry, charm, fetch, train, truck **6** convey, moving, remove, thrill **7** bearing, bewitch, carting, delight, deliver, enchant, freight, removal, sending, vehicle **8** airplane, carrying, delivery, dispatch, enthrall, entrance, shipment, shipping, transfer, transmit, trucking **9** captivate, cargo ship, carry away, conveying, electrify, enrapture, freighter, overpower **10** cargo plane, conveyance **12** freight train

transportation 7 cartage, haulage, portage, removal, transit **8** delivery, dispatch, movement, shipment **9** transport **10** conveyance, transferal **12** transference, transmission **13** transmittance

transported 5 moved **6** lifted **7** charmed **8** ecstatic, thrilled, uplifted **9** bewitched, entranced **10** captivated, enthralled **11** carried away, electrified **13** beside oneself

transverse 5 cross **6** across **7** athwart, oblique, transom **8** crossbar, crossing, diagonal, traverse **9** crosswise **10** crosspiece, horizontal

transversely 9 crossways, crosswise, laterally

trap 3 net, pit **4** lure, ploy, ruse, seal, stop, wile **5** catch, feint, snare, trick **6** ambush, device, enmesh, entrap, lock in **7** ensnare, pitfall, springe **8** artifice, entangle, hold back, hunt down, maneuver **9** booby trap, stratagem **11** machination **16** compartmentalize

trappings 4 garb, gear **5** array, dress **6** attire, outfit, things **7** apparel, clothes, costume, effects, raiment, vesture **8** adjuncts, clothing, fittings

9 ornaments, trimmings **10** adornments, habiliment, investment **11** decorations **13** accoutrements, paraphernalia **14** embellishments

trash 3 rot **4** bums, crap, junk, scum **5** dregs, dross, tripe, waste **6** debris, drivel, idlers, litter, refuse, rubble, tramps **7** garbage, hogwash, loafers, residue, rubbish, twaddle **8** castoffs, leavings, nonsense, riffraff **9** poppycock, sweepings **10** balderdash **11** foolishness, ne'er-do-wells, odds and ends **15** good-for-nothings, unsavory element

trashy 4 vile **5** cheap, inane, junky, tacky **6** flashy, flimsy **7** rubbish, trivial, useless **8** riffraff, trumpery, wasteful **9** worthless **13** insignificant

trauma 4 hurt **5** shock, wound **6** injury, stress

travail 4 pain, toil **5** labor, worry **6** strain, stress **7** anguish **8** delivery, distress, drudgery, exertion, hard work, hardship **9** suffering **10** birth pains, childbirth, labor pains **11** parturition **12** accouchement

travel 2 go **4** be on, move, roam, rove, sail, tour, trek, wend **5** cross, drive, range, visit **6** cruise, junket, voyage, wander **7** journey, proceed **8** pass over, progress, sightsee, traverse **9** globetrot, hitchhike, take a trip **11** pass through, press onward

traveler 5 gypsy, nomad, rover **7** drummer, migrant, pilgrim, tourist, trekker, tripper, voyager **8** vagabond, wanderer, wayfarer **9** itinerant, journeyer, sightseer **10** vacationer **12** excursionist, globetrotter

Traveller Without Luggage author: 11 Jean Anouilh

Travels with a Donkey author: 20 Robert Louis Stevenson **donkey: 9** Modestine

Travels with My Aunt author: 12 Graham Greene

travel through 2 do **5** cover, cross, visit **8** traverse **9** negotiate **11** pass through

traverse 4 span **5** cross **6** bridge, travel **8** go across, move over, overpass **9** cross over, cut across, intersect, move along, negotiate, reach over **10** extend over, run through, travel over **11** move through, pass through, reach across

travesty 4 sham **5** farce, spoof **6** parody, satire **7** lampoon, mockery, takeoff **8** disgrace **9** burlesque **10** caricature, distortion, perversion **17** misrepresentation

Traviata, La
also: 9 The Misled **23** The Woman Who Was Led Astray
opera by: 5 Verdi
based on a story by: 14 Alexandre Dumas (fils)
  called: **7** Camille **17** La Dame aux Camelias
character: 8 Violetta **14** Alfredo Germont

Travolta, John
born: 11 Englewood NJ
roles: 6 Carrie, Grease **10** Tony Manero **11** Urban Cowboy **12** Staying Alive **14** Moment By Moment **15** Vinnie Barbarino **17** Welcome Back Kotter **18** Saturday Night Fever

trawl 3 net **4** drag, fish, haul, line **5** seine, troll **6** dredge **7** dragnet

Treacher, Arthur
real name: 11 Arthur Veary
born: 7 England **8** Brighton
roles: 11 Mary Poppins **14** National Velvet, Thank You Jeeves **16** David Copperfield **20** Magnificent Obsession

treacherous 5 false, risky **6** tricky, unsafe, untrue **7** devious **8** disloyal, perilous, two-faced **9** dangerous, deceitful, deceptive, faithless, hazardous **10** misleading, perfidious, precarious, traitorous, treasonous, unfaithful **12** falsehearted **13** untrustworthy

treachery 5 guile **6** deceit **7** perfidy, treason **8** apostasy, betrayal, trickery **9** deception, duplicity, falseness **10** disloyalty, infidelity **11** double cross **13** breach of faith, deceitfulness, double-dealing, faithlessness **15** underhandedness **17** untrustworthiness

tread 4 gait, hike, pace, roam, rove, step, walk **5** prowl, range, stamp, stomp, tramp **6** step on, stride, stroll, trudge, walk on **7** trample **8** footfall, footstep

treason 6 mutiny, revolt **7** perfidy **8** apostasy, betrayal, sedition **9** duplicity, rebellion, treachery **10** conspiracy, disloyalty, insurgence, revolution, subversion **12** insurrection

treasonable 9 faithless, seditious **10** perfidious, subversive, traitorous **11** treacherous

treasure 3 gem **4** gold **5** hoard, jewel, prize, store, value **6** esteem, jewels, regard, revere, riches, silver **7** cherish, deposit, paragon **8** bank upon, dote upon, gold mine, hold dear **11** pride and joy **14** apple of one's eye **17** pearl of great price

treasure chest 3 box **4** case **5** chest, trunk **6** coffer

treasured 4 dear **5** loved **6** adored, valued **7** beloved **8** precious **9** cherished

Treasure Island
author: 20 Robert Louis Stevenson
character: 7 Ben Gunn **8** Smollett **9** Dr Livesey **10** Jim Hawkins **14** Long John Silver **15** Squire Trelawney
director:
  1934 version: **13** Victor Fleming
  1950 version: **11** Byron Haskin
based on novel by: 20 Robert Louis Stevenson
cast:
  1934 version: **10** Lewis Stone **12** Jackie Cooper (Jim Hawkins), Wallace Beery (Long John Silver) **15** Lionel Barrymore
  1950 version: **11** Basil Sydney **12** Robert Newton (Long John Silver) **13** Bobby Driscoll (Jim Hawkins) **16** Walter Fitzgerald

Treasure of the Sierra Madre, The
director: 10 John Huston
cast: 7 Tim Holt **12** Bruce Bennett, Walter Huston **13** Alfonso Bedoya, Barton MacLane **14** Humphrey Bogart
Oscar for: 8 director **10** screenplay **15** supporting actor (Huston)

treasurer 6 banker, bursar, purser, teller **7** auditor, cashier **9** financier **10** accountant, bookkeeper, cash-keeper, controller **16** financial officer **17** minister of finance **22** secretary of the treasury **24** Chancellor of the Exchequer

Treasure State
nickname of: 7 Montana

treasury 4 bank, safe, till **5** funds, purse, vault **6** coffer **8** money box **9** anthology, exchequer, strongbox, thesaurus **10** collection, compendium, depository, repository, storehouse **11** bank account, compilation

treasury note 4 bill **8** bank note **9** greenback **12** currency note **17** silver certificate

treat 3 joy **4** blow, coat, give **5** apply, cover, favor, grant, imbue, stand **6** attend, divert, doctor, handle, manage, remedy, spring, thrill **7** comfort, delight, discuss, patch up, take out **8** consider, deal with, look upon, medicate, pleasure, relate to **9** act toward, small gift, try to cure, try to heal **10** impregnate, minister to, speak about, write about **12** prescribe for, satisfaction **13** gratification

treat as inferior 7 disdain **9** patronize **12** condescend to **18** look down one's nose at **19** discriminate against

treatise 4 text **5** essay, study, tract **6** manual, memoir, report, thesis **8** textbook, tractate **9** discourse, monograph **12** dissertation

treatment 3 way **4** cure **6** course, remedy **7** conduct, process, regimen, therapy **8** antidote, approach, handling, treating **9** doctoring, operation, procedure **10** management, medication **11** application, medical care **12** manipulation

treaty 4 deal, pact **6** accord **7** bargain, compact, entente **8** covenant **9** concordat **13** understanding **15** formal agreement **22** international agreement

tree 3 ash, elm, fir, oak **4** bush, palm, pine, wood **5** beech, birch, chase, maple, plane, plant, scrub, staff, stake, stick **6** corner, cudgel, redbud, spruce, timber, willow **7** gallows, lineage, live oak, sapling **8** ancestry, chestnut, hardwood, mahogany, pedigree, seedling **9** ailanthus, evergreen **10** cottonwood, eucalyptus

Tree Grows in Brooklyn, A
author: 10 Betty Smith
character:
  Nolan family: **5** Katie **6** Neeley **7** Francie, Johnnie
director: 9 Elia Kazan
cast: 9 James Dunn **10** Lloyd Nolan **12** Joan Blondell **14** Dorothy McGuire, Peggy Ann Garner
Oscar for: 7 special (Garner) **15** supporting actor (Dunn)

treeless 4 bald, bare **6** barren **7** denuded **8** unwooded **10** unforested

Treeplanters State
nickname of: 8 Nebraska

trek 4 hike, plod, roam, rove, sail, slog, trip 5 jaunt, march, range, tramp 6 junket, outing, travel, trudge, voyage, wander 7 journey, odyssey, passage 8 traverse 9 excursion, migration 10 expedition, pilgrimage 11 peregrinate 13 peregrination

trellis 5 arbor, bower, cross, frame, grill, trail 6 gazebo, screen 7 lattice, network, pergola 8 espalier 10 interweave 11 summerhouse

tremble 5 quail, quake, shake, waver 6 quaver, quiver, shiver 7 flutter, pulsate, shudder 9 palpitate

trembling 5 shaky 7 quaking, shaking 8 unsteady 9 doddering, quavering, quivering, shivering 10 shuddering 11 palpitating

tremblor 5 quake, seism, shock 6 tremor 8 upheaval 10 earthquake

tremendous 4 fine, huge, vast 5 giant, great, major 7 amazing, awesome, immense, mammoth, sizable, titanic, unusual 8 colossal, enormous, fabulous, gigantic, terrific, towering, uncommon 9 excellent, fantastic, first-rate, humongous, important, marvelous, monstrous, wonderful 10 formidable, gargantuan, incredible, noteworthy, stupendous 11 elephantine, exceptional 12 considerable 13 consequential, extraordinary

tremolo
music: 9 trembling, vibrating 30 rapid reiteration of a single pitch

tremor 3 jar 4 jolt 5 quake, shake, shock, spasm, throb, waver 6 quiver, shiver 7 flutter, shaking, shudder, tremble 8 paroxysm 9 pulsation, quavering, quivering, shivering, trembling, vibration 10 convulsion 11 palpitation

tremulous 5 jumpy, shaky, timid 6 wobbly 7 aquiver, excited, fearful, jittery, keyed-up, nervous, panicky, quaking 8 aflutter, agitated, atremble, hesitant, restless, wavering, worked-up 9 faltering, impatient, quivering, trembling, uncertain 10 irresolute, stimulated 13 on tenterhooks, panic-stricken

trench 3 cut, rut 4 scar 5 canal, ditch, drain, fosse, slash, slice 6 dugout, furrow, gutter, trough 7 channel, wrinkle 8 aqueduct 9 earthwork 10 depression

trenchant 4 acid, keen, tart 5 crisp 6 bitter 7 acerbic, caustic, concise, mordant, probing 8 clear-cut, distinct, incisive, scathing 9 sarcastic, scorching 10 razor-sharp 11 acrimonious, penetrating, well-defined

trend 4 bent, flow, mode 5 drift, style 7 fashion, impulse, leaning 8 movement, tendency 9 direction 10 proclivity, propensity 11 inclination

trendsetters 7 leaders 8 trendies, vanguard 10 avant-garde, innovators 11 pacesetters, tastemakers 12 advance guard, stylesetters, trailblazers

trendy 2 in 4 chic, tony 5 swank 6 modern, modish, with-it 7 current, faddish, popular, stylish, voguish 8 up-to-date 10 all the rage 11 fashionable 13 up-to-the-minute

Trenor, Gus and Judy
characters in: 15 The House of Mirth
author: 7 Wharton

Trent, Little Nell
character in: 19 The Old Curiosity Shop
author: 7 Dickens

trepidation 4 fear 5 alarm, dread, panic, worry 7 anxiety, jitters 8 cold feet, disquiet 10 uneasiness 11 butterflies, disquietude, jitteriness, nervousness 12 apprehension 13 consternation

trespass 3 sin 5 error, wrong 6 invade 7 impinge, intrude, misdeed, offense 8 encroach, infringe, iniquity, invasion 9 evildoing, intrusion, violation 10 immorality, infraction, misconduct, wrongdoing 11 delinquency, misbehavior 12 encroachment, infringement, overstepping 13 transgression, unlawful entry, wrongful entry

tress 4 curl, hair, lock, mane 5 braid, plait 6 strand 7 ringlet, wimpler 8 spitcurl

trestle 4 beam 5 board, brace, frame, table 6 timber 9 framework

trial 2 go 3 try, woe 4 care, pain, shot, test 5 agony, essay, flyer, whirl, worry 6 burden, effort, misery, ordeal, trying, tryout 7 anguish, attempt, bad luck, hearing, testing, test run, torment, trouble, venture 8 accident, distress, endeavor, hardship, vexation 9 adversity, court case, heartache, suffering 10 affliction, litigation, misfortune 11 cross to bear 12 misadventure, wretchedness

Trial, The
author: 10 Franz Kafka
character: 4 Leni 7 Joseph K 9 Titorelli 11 The Advocate

trial and error 10 experiment 13 investigation 15 experimentation 20 process of elimination

Triassic period
dinosaur from: 11 Coelophysis, Mandasuchus 12 Melanosaurus, Pisanosaurus, Plateosaurus 13 Tanystropheus 17 Heterodontosaurus

tribe see 11 ethnic group

Tribes of Israel see 6 Israel

tribulation 3 woe 4 care, pain 5 agony, grief, trial, worry 6 misery, ordeal, sorrow 7 anguish, bad luck, torment, trouble 8 distress, hardship, vexation 9 adversity, heartache, suffering 10 affliction, ill fortune, misfortune 11 unhappiness 12 wretchedness

Tribulation Wholesome
character in: 12 The Alchemist
author: 6 Jonson

tribunal 3 bar 5 bench, court, forum 6 judges 9 authority, judiciary 10 ruling body 11 judge's bench, judge's chair 14 seat of judgment

tributary 6 branch, feeder, source, stream 7 helping, subject 8 affluent 9 ancillary, auxiliary, confluent, secondary 10 subjugated, subsidiary 11 subordinate 12 contributing, contributory

tribute 3 tax 4 duty, levy, toll 5 bribe, honor, kudos 6 esteem, eulogy, excise, impost, payoff, praise, ransom 7 payment, respect 8 accolade, encomium, memorial 9 extolling, gratitude, laudation, panegyric 10 assessment, blood money, compliment, settlement 11 recognition, testimonial 12 commendation, pound of flesh 13 consideration, peace offering 14 acknowledgment

trice 3 sec 4 jiff, wink 5 blink, flash, jiffy, shake 6 minute, moment, second 7 instant 9 coup d'oeil, twinkling 11 split second

trichophobia
  fear of: 4 hair

trichoptera
  class: 8 hexapoda
  phylum: 10 arthropoda
  group: 3 fly 6 caddis

trick 3 art, gag 4 bait, dupe, feat, gift, gull, have, hoax, joke, ploy, ruse, trap, wile 5 antic, blind, bluff, caper, cheat, dodge, feint, fraud, knack, prank, put-on, skill, stunt 6 deceit, device, number, outfox, outwit, resort, secret, take in 7 deceive, gimmick, know-how, mislead, swindle 8 artifice, deftness, flimflam, hoodwink, maneuver 9 bamboozle, chicanery, deception, dexterity, imposture, sophistry, stratagem, technique 10 adroitness, hocus-pocus, manipulate, subterfuge 11 contrivance, machination, outmaneuver 13 practical joke, sleight of hand 16 prestidigitation

trickery 5 guile 6 bunkum, deceit 8 artifice, flimflam, pretense, quackery, wiliness 9 chicanery, deception, duplicity, imposture, rascality, stratagem 10 artfulness, craftiness, hocus-pocus, shiftiness 11 crookedness, deviousness 12 charlatanism, skullduggery, slipperiness 13 deceitfulness

trickiness 6 deceit 7 cunning, slyness 8 trickery 9 duplicity 10 craftiness 15 underhandedness

trickle 4 drip, leak, ooze, seep 5 exude 7 dribble, seepage 9 percolate

trickster 5 cheat, joker 6 dodger, rascal 8 deceiver, impostor, sleeveen 9 prankster

tricky 3 sly 4 foxy, wily 5 risky 6 artful, crafty, shifty, unsafe 7 cunning, devious 8 rascally, slippery, unstable 9 dangerous, deceptive, difficult, hazardous 10 touch-and-go, unreliable 11 complicated, underhanded 12 hard to handle, undependable 13 temperamental, unpredictable

trident
  form: 5 spear
  number of prongs: 5 three

trifle 3 bit, dab, jot, nip, toy 4 dash, drop, idle, iota, mite, play 5 crumb, dally, pinch, scrap, speck, tinge, touch, trace 6 bauble, dawdle, gewgaw, linger, little, morsel, sliver 7 modicum, nothing, trinket 8 fragment, gimcrack, kill time 9 bagatelle, play-

thing, waste time 10 dilly-dally, knickknack, sprinkling, triviality 11 deal lightly, small matter 12 amuse oneself, treat lightly 13 small quantity

trifler 5 flirt, idler 6 coquet 7 dabbler, dallier 8 coquette 10 dilettante

trifling 4 puny 5 petty, small, sorry, token 6 paltry, slight 7 nominal, trivial 8 beggarly, niggling, nugatory, picayune, piddling 9 worthless 10 negligible 11 unimportant 13 beneath notice, inappreciable, insignificant 14 inconsiderable 15 inconsequential

trifling circumstances
  Latin: 8 minutiae

trifling matter
  French: 10 peu de chose

trigger 5 shoot 6 set off 7 fire off 8 activate, detonate, touch off 9 discharge

trikerion 11 candelabrum, candlestick 12 candleholder

Trilby
  author: 15 George du Maurier
  character: 5 Gecko, Sandy, Taffy 8 Svengali 12 Little Billee 14 Trilby O'Ferrall

trill
  music: 7 shaking, tremolo 9 quavering

trim 3 cut, fit, lop 4 clip, crop, deck, form, lean, pare, slim, thin 5 adorn, array, lithe, prune, shape, shave, shear, shift, sleek, state 6 adjust, bedeck, border, change, fettle, kilter, limber, paring, piping, supple, svelte 7 arrange, balance, bedizen, compact, cutting, fitness, furbish, garnish, lissome, pruning, shapely, slender, willowy 8 athletic, beautify, clipping, cropping, decorate, equalize, ornament, shearing, trick out, trimming 9 adornment, condition, embellish, embroider, shipshape 10 decoration, distribute 11 streamlined 13 embellishment, ornamentation

Trim, Corporal
  character in: 14 Tristram Shandy
  author: 6 Sterne

trimming 4 trim 5 frill 7 cutting, pruning, slicing 8 clipping 9 adornment 10 decoration, shortening, truncation 11 abridgement, contraction, curtailment 12 abbreviation 13 embellishment

Trinacria see 6 Sicily

Trinidad and Tobago *see box, p. 1000*

Trinity
  author: 8 Leon Uris

trinket 3 toy 5 bijou, charm, jewel 6 bauble, gewgaw, notion, trifle 8 gimcrack, ornament 9 bagatelle, plaything 10 knickknack

trip 3 bob, err 4 flip, flub, fool, muff, pull, skip, slip, tour, trek, undo 5 caper, catch, dance, fluff, foray, jaunt, outdo, throw, upset 6 bungle, cruise, frolic, gambol, junket, outfox, outing, prance, safari, set off, slip up, voyage 7 blunder, commute, confuse, flounce, journey, misstep, release, scamper, stumble 8 activate, fall over, flounder, hoodwink, throw off 9 excursion 10 disconcert, expedition, pilgrimage 11 step lightly

Triple Crown 7 Belmont 9 Preakness 13 Kentucky Derby
  winner: 5 Omaha 7 Assault 8 Affirmed, Citation 9 Sir Barton, Whirlaway 10 Count Fleet, Gallant Fox, War Admiral 11 Seattle Slew, Secretariat

Triple Sec see 9 Cointreau

Tripoli
  capital of: 5 Libya

Triptolemos, Triptolemus
  favorite of: 7 Demeter
  inventor of: 4 plow 5 wheel
  patron of: 11 agriculture

Triquetra see 6 Sicily

triskaidekaphobia
  fear of: 14 number thirteen

Trismegistus see 5 Thoth

Tristan and Isolde
  also: 16 Tristan und Isolde
  opera by: 6 Wagner
  character: 5 Melot 8 Brangane, Kurwenal 18 King Mark of Cornwall

triste 3 sad 10 melancholy

tristesse 6 sorrow 7 sadness 10 melancholy

Tristram
  author: 22 Edwin Arlington Robinson
  character in: 16 Arthurian romance

Tristram Shandy
  author: 14 Laurence Sterne
  character: 6 Dr Slop 8 Mr Yorick 10 Toby Shandy 11 Widow Wadman 12 Corporal Trim, Walter Shandy

trite 5 banal, silly, stale 6 common 7 cliched, hum-

Trinidad and Tobago
  capital/largest city: **11** Port of Spain
  others: **4** Debe, Toco **5** Arima **6** Canaan, Coryal, Labrea **7** San Juan, Siparia **8** Rio Claro, Tunapuna **10** Roxborough **11** San Fernando, Scarborough **12** Princess Town, Sangre Grande **14** Charlotteville
  school: **6** Fatima **7** St Mary's **11** Queen's Royal
  head of state: **14** British monarch **15** governor general
  monetary unit: **4** cent **6** dollar
  island: **12** Chacachacare, Little Tobago **14** Bird of Paradise
  lake: **5** Pitch
  mountain:
    hills: **7** Trinity **10** Montserrat **12** Three Sisters
  highest point: **5** Aripo
  river: **6** Caroni **7** Ortoire **8** Oropuche, Trinidad
  sea: **8** Atlantic **9** Caribbean
  physical feature:
    bay: **5** Cocos, Guapo **6** Matura, Mayaro
    channel: **12** Dragon's Mouth **13** Serpent's Mouth
    gulf: **5** Paria
    point: **5** Radix **6** Arenal, Galera **7** Chupara, Galeota **8** Columbus
  people: **5** Irish **6** French, Syrian **7** African, Chinese, English, Spanish **8** European, Lebanese **10** East Indian, Portuguese, Venezuelan **11** Asian Indian **13** Latin American
    explorer: **8** Columbus
    leader: **8** Williams
  language: **6** French **7** Chinese, English, Spanish **10** Portuguese **12** French Patois
  religion: **5** Hindu, Islam **8** Anglican **10** Protestant **12** Christianity **13** Roman Catholic
  place:
    asphalt lake: **9** Pitch Lake
    mansions: **16** Magnificent Seven
    park: **18** Queen's Park Savannah
  feature:
    bird: **7** oilbird **8** cocorico
    clothing: **4** sari **5** dhoti
    dance: **6** Dragon, Shango
    festival: **6** Hosein, Lights
    fish: **5** guppy
    music: **7** calypso, goombay
    tree: **4** mora
  food:
    drink: **16** Angostura Bitters

drum, routine, shallow, worn-out **8** bromidic, everyday, ordinary, overdone, shopworn **9** frivolous, hackneyed **10** pedestrian, threadbare **11** commonplace, oft-repeated, stereotyped, unimportant **12** run-of-the-mill **13** platitudinous

Tritogeneia *see* **6** Athena

Triton
  god of: **3** sea
  father: **8** Poseidon
  mother: **10** Amphitrite
  shape: **6** merman
  trumpet: **10** conch-shell

triumph 3 hit, win **4** best, coup **5** smash **6** subdue **7** conquer, mastery, prevail, succeed, success, surpass, victory **8** conquest, overcome, smash

hit, vanquish **9** overwhelm **10** ascendancy, attainment, gain the day **11** achievement, superiority **12** come out on top, take the prize **14** accomplishment, get the better of

triumphal 5 proud **6** joyous **8** exultant **9** ascendant, rewarding **10** fulfilling, gratifying, successful, triumphant, victorious **11** spectacular

triumphant 6 elated, joyful **7** winning **8** exultant, jubilant **9** rejoicing **10** conquering, first-place, successful, victorious **11** celebrating **12** prizewinning

Triumph of Death, The
  author: **17** Gabriele D'Annunzio

trivia
  Latin: **8** minutiae

trivial 4 idle, puny, slim **5** banal, petty, small, trite **6** common, flimsy, little, meager, paltry, slight, two-bit **7** foolish **8** beggarly, everyday, niggling, nugatory, ordinary, picayune, piddling, trifling **9** rinky-dink, worthless **10** incidental, pedestrian **11** commonplace, meaningless, unessential, unimportant **13** inappreciable, insignificant, of little value **14** inconsiderable **15** inconsequential

triviality 5 frill **6** trifle **9** frivolity **10** paltriness **12** nonessential, unimportance **14** insignificance **18** inconsequentiality

troglodyte 5 brute **6** hermit **9** barbarian **11** cave dweller

Troilus
  father: **5** Priam
  mother: **6** Hecuba

Troilus and Cressida
  author: **18** William Shakespeare
  character: **4** Ajax **5** Priam **6** Hector **7** Ulysses **8** Achilles, Diomedes, Pandarus **9** Agamemnon

Troilus and Criseyde
  author: **15** Geoffrey Chaucer
  character: **8** Diomedes, Pandarus

trois 5 three

Trojan Horse
  made of: **4** wood
  made by: **7** Epeiosk
  contained: **8** Odysseus, warriors

Trojans, The
  also: **10** Les Troyens
  opera by: **7** Berlioz
  part one: **14** La Prise de Troie **16** The Capture of Troy
  part two: **19** Les Troyens a Carthage **20** The Trojans in Carthage
  character: **4** Dido **6** Aeneas, Hector

Trojan War
  length: **8** ten years
  combatants: **6** Greeks **7** Trojans
  cause: **5** Helen, Paris **14** Apple of Discord

Trojan Women, The
  author: **9** Euripides
  character: **5** Helen **6** Hecuba **8** Astyanax, Menelaus, Odysseus, Polyxena **9** Agamemnon, Cassandra **10** Andromache, Talthybius **11** Neoptolemus

troll 3 imp **4** ogre **5** dwarf, gnome **6** goblin
 origin: 12 Scandinavian
 form: 12 supernatural
 inhabits: 10 subterrain

trollop 4 doxy, slut **5** bitch, doxie, frump, hussy, trull, whore **6** floozy, harlot, wanton **7** baggage **8** slattern, strumpet **10** prostitute

Trollope, Anthony
 author of: 9 Orley Farm, The Warden **15** The Way We Live Now **16** Barchester Towers, Framley Parsonage
 character: 11 Phineas Finn

troop, troops 4 army, band, file, gang, herd, step, unit **5** bunch, crowd, crush, drove, flock, horde, march, press, swarm, tramp **6** parade, stride, throng, trudge **7** cavalry, company, militia **8** infantry, soldiers, soldiery, troopers **9** aggregate, gathering **10** armed force, assemblage **11** cavalry unit, fighting men, police force **12** congregation **13** military force

trop 3 too **7** too many, too much

Tropaean
 epithet of: 4 Zeus
 means: 14 giver of victory

Trophonius
 vocation: 7 builder
 father: 7 Erginus
 brother: 8 Agamedes
 god of: 5 earth
 killed: 8 Agamedes
 became: 6 oracle
  oracle called: 14 Zeus Trophonius

trophy 4 palm **5** award, booty, honor, kudos, medal, prize, relic, spoil **6** wreath **7** laurels,

memento **8** citation, souvenir **9** loving cup **10** blue ribbon **11** testimonial

tropical 5 muggy **6** sultry, torrid **8** stifling **10** sweltering **11** hot and humid

troppo, non
 music: 10 not too much

Tros
 king of: 4 Troy
 father: 12 Erichthonius
 mother: 8 Astyoche
 wife: 10 Callirrhoe
 son: 4 Ilus **8** Ganymede **9** Assaracus

trot 3 jog **9** go briskly **11** step quickly, walk smartly

troth 8 fidelity **9** betrothal **10** affiancing, engagement **12** faithfulness

Trotwood, Betsey
 character in: 16 David Copperfield
 author: 7 Dickens

trouble *see box*

troubled 5 upset **7** worried **8** bothered, careworn **9** disturbed, perturbed **10** distressed **12** heavyhearted

troublemaker 6 gossip **7** inciter **8** agitator, fomenter, provoker **9** miscreant **10** incendiary, instigator **11** rumormonger, scaremonger **12** rabble-rouser **13** mischief-maker, scandalmonger **16** agent provocateur

troublesome 4 hard **5** heavy, pesky, tough **6** cursed, knotty, taxing, thorny, tiring, trying, vexing **7** arduous, irksome, onerous, tedious **8** annoying, tiresome, unwieldy **9** demanding, difficult, fatiguing, harassing, herculean, laborious,

wearisome, worrisome **10** bothersome, burdensome, cumbersome, disturbing, irritating, oppressive, tormenting, unpleasant **11** disobedient, distressing **12** disagreeable, exasperating, inconvenient, uncontrolled **13** undisciplined

troublesomeness 5 trial **10** difficulty **11** arduousness **13** inconvenience, laboriousness, vexatiousness, worrisomeness **14** bothersomeness

Trouble with Harry, The
 director: 15 Alfred Hitchcock
 cast: 11 Edmund Gwenn **12** John Forsythe **14** Mildred Dunnock, Mildred Natwick **15** Shirley MacLaine

troubling 6 vexing **8** worrying **9** worrisome **10** bothersome, disturbing, unsettling

trough 4 duct, moat, race, tray **5** canal, ditch, flume, gorge, gully **6** furrow, hollow, ravine, trench **7** channel **8** aqueduct **10** depression

trounce 4 beat, drub, lick, trim, whip **5** cream, skunk **6** humble **7** clobber **8** vanquish **9** overpower, overwhelm **10** take care of **11** carry the day **14** get the better of

troupe 4 band, cast **5** group, troop **6** actors **7** company, players **10** performers **11** road company

trouper 5 actor **7** actress **8** thespian **9** performer **13** touring player **15** repertory player

trousers 5 jeans, pants **6** chinos, slacks **7** drawers **8** breeches, britches, jodhpurs, knickers, overalls **9** dungarees **10** pantaloons **11** bellbottoms **12** pedal pushers **14** knickerbockers

Trovatore, Il
 also: 13 The Troubadour
 opera by: 5 Verdi
 character: 7 Azucena, Leonora, Manrico **11** Count di Luna

Troy
 abducted queen: 5 Helen
 archaeologist: 6 Blegen **8** Dorpfeld **10** Schliemann
 defender: 5 Eneas **6** Aeneas
 Greek name: 5 Ilion
 hero: 6 Hector
 king: 5 Priam
 Latin name: 5 Ilium
 modern name: 9 Hissarlik
 mountain: 3 Ida
 neighboring city: 6 Albany **10** Watervliet

---

trouble 3 fix, row, vex, woe **4** blow, care, fuss, heed, mess, pain, pass, snag, work **5** agony, annoy, grief, harry, labor, pains, pinch, think, trial, upset, worry **6** affect, attend, badger, bother, burden, crisis, defect, dismay, effort, grieve, harass, misery, ordeal, pester, pickle, plague, pother, put out, scrape, sorrow, strain, strait, stress, strife, unrest **7** afflict, agitate, ailment, attempt, concern, depress, dilemma, discord, disturb, ferment, ill wind, oppress, perturb, reverse, setback, torment **8** disaster, disorder, disquiet, distress, disunity, exertion, hardship, hot water, quandary, rainy day, struggle, take time, unsettle, vexation **9** adversity, agitation, annoyance, attention, breakdown, challenge, commotion, deep water, hard times, suffering **10** affliction, convulsion, difficulty, disability, discommode, discompose, disconcert, discontent, dissension, irritation, make uneasy, misfortune, opposition **11** competition, disturbance, embroilment, instability, malfunction, predicament, tribulation **12** entanglement, exert oneself **13** inconvenience, make the effort **14** discontentment **15** dissatisfaction

river: 6 Hudson
state: 7 Alabama, New York
8 Michigan
story: 5 Iliad **7** Odyssey
surrounding region: 5 Troad,
Troas

Troy, Sergeant
character in: 22 Far From
the Madding Crowd
author: 5 Hardy

truancy 3 cut **7** absence **11** absenteeism, nonpresence
12 playing hooky **13** nonappearance, nonattendance
14 cutting classes, skipping
school

truant 4 gone **5** idler **6** absent,
dodger, evader, loafer, no
show **7** drifter, goof-off, missing, not here, shirker, slacker,
vagrant **8** absentee, deserter,
layabout **9** goldbrick **10** delinquent, malingerer,
nonpresent, not present
11 boondoggler, hooky-player
12 nonattendant, playing
hooky

truce 4 halt, lull, rest, stay,
stop **5** break, pause **7** respite
9 armistice, cease-fire **12** interruption **14** breathing spell,
discontinuance **23** suspension
of hostilities

**Trucial Oman, Trucial
States** see **18** United Arab
Emirates

truck 3 rig, van **5** lorry
15 eighteen-wheeler
type: 5 panel **6** pickup
7 trailer **8** delivery

truckle 3 bow **4** fawn **5** court,
defer, yield **6** grovel, pander,
submit **7** flatter **8** bootlick,
butter up, suck up to **9** shine
up to **10** curry favor, take orders **11** apple-polish, fall all
over **12** knuckle under **17** ingratiate oneself

truculence 8 defiance, ill humor **9** hostility, ill temper,
pugnacity, surliness **10** fierceness **11** bellicosity **12** belligerence, churlishness
14 aggressiveness

truculent 4 rude, sour **5** cross,
nasty, sulky, surly **6** fierce,
touchy **7** defiant, hostile, peevish **8** churlish, insolent, petulant, snappish, snarling
9 bellicose **10** aggressive,
ill-humored, ill-natured, pugnacious, ungracious **11** bad-
tempered, belligerent, ill-
tempered

Trudeau, Garry
creator/artist of:
10 Doonesbury

trudge 4 drag, limp, plod

5 clump, march, tramp **6** hobble, lumber **7** shamble

true 4 even, firm, full, just,
pure, real **5** exact, legal, loyal,
right, usual, valid **6** actual,
lawful, normal, proper, steady,
strict, trusty **7** correct, devoted,
factual, genuine, literal, precise, regular, staunch, typical
8 absolute, accurate, bona fide,
constant, faithful, official,
positive, reliable, rightful,
true-blue, truthful **9** authentic,
simon-pure, steadfast
10 dependable, legitimate, unswerving, unwavering
11 trustworthy
14 unquestionable

true being 4 core, soul **6** nature, psyche, spirit **7** essence

True Grit
director: 13 Henry Hathaway
based on novel by:
13 Charles Portis
cast: 8 Kim Darby **9** John
Wayne **11** Jeremy Slate
12 Glen Campbell, Robert
Duvall **14** Strother Martin
Oscar for: 5 actor (Wayne)

Truffaut, Francois
director of: 11 Day for
Night, Jules and Jim
19 Shoot the Piano Player,
The Four Hundred Blows

truism 3 saw **5** adage, axiom
6 cliche, dictum, saying
9 platitude

truly 6 indeed, in fact, really,
surely, verily **7** exactly, in
truth, no doubt **8** actually,
honestly, to be sure **9** assuredly, certainly, correctly,
factually, genuinely, literally,
precisely, sincerely **10** absolutely, accurately, definitely,
faithfully, positively, truthfully,
upon my word **11** beyond
doubt, in actuality, indubitably, so help me God **12** indisputably **13** incontestably,
unequivocally **14** beyond question, unquestionably **15** all
kidding aside, without
question

Truman, Harry S see **box**

Trumbull, John
born: 9 Lebanon CT
artwork: 21 The Battle of
Bunker Hill **26** The Resignation of Washington **28** The
Declaration of Independ-
ence **29** The Surrender of
General Burgoyne **32** The
Capture of the Hessians at
Trenton **38** The Surrender
of Lord Cornwallis at Yorktown **46** The Death of General Montgomery in the
Attack of Quebec, The

Death of General Warren at
the Battle of Bunker Hill

trumpery 5 showy, trash **6** deceit, trashy, trivia **7** rubbish,
twaddle, useless **8** frippery,
nonsense, trifling **9** deception,
worthless **11** nonsensical

trumpet 4 honk, horn **5** blare,
bugle **6** cornet **7** clarion
8 proclaim **10** hearing aid

Trumpet of the Swan, The
author: 7 E B White

trump up 4 fake **6** invent,
make up **7** concoct, falsify
9 fabricate

truncate 3 bob, lop, nip **4** clip,
crop, dock, snub, trim
5 prune **7** abridge, curtail,
shorten **8** amputate, condense,
cut short **10** abbreviate

truncheon 3 bat **4** club **5** baton, billy, stick **6** cudgel
8 bludgeon **9** billyclub

trunker 3 box, die **4** body,
bole, dado, line, main **5** chief,
pants, shaft, snout, stock,
torso **6** coffer, engine, locker,
shut up, thorax **7** baggage,
close in

Truscott-Jones, Reginald
real name of: 10 Ray
Milland

truss 3 tie **4** beam, bind, prop,
stay **5** brace, hitch, shore,
strap, tie up **6** bind up, fasten,
girder, pinion, secure **7** confine, support **8** make fast
9 constrict, framework, stanchion **12** underpinning

trust 4 care, duty, hope
5 faith, hands **6** accept, assume, belief, charge, credit,
expect, look to, rely on **7** believe, count on, custody, keeping, presume, swear by
8 credence, feel sure, reliance,
sureness **9** certainty, certitude,
count upon **10** anticipate, confidence, conviction, depend
upon, obligation, protection
11 assuredness, contemplate,
have faith in, safekeeping,
subscribe to, take on faith,
take stock in **12** guardianship
14 give credence to, responsibility, take for granted

trusted 6 trusty **8** reliable
9 unfailing **10** dependable
11 trustworthy

trustee 8 guardian **9** caretaker,
custodian, protector

trusteeship 4 care **6** charge
7 custody **10** protection
11 safekeeping
12 guardianship

trusting 8 gullible, trustful

Truman, Harry S
nickname: **15** Give Em Hell Harry
presidential rank: **11** thirty-third
party: **10** Democratic
state represented: **8** Missouri
succeeded upon death of: **9** Roosevelt
defeated: **5** (Farrell) Dobbs, (Thomas Edmund) Dewey **6** (Claude A) Watson, (Norman) Thomas **7** (Henry Agard) Wallace **8** (Edward A) Teichert, (James Strom) Thurmond
vice president: **7** (Alben William) Barkley
cabinet:
  state: **6** (James Francis) Byrnes **7** (Dean Gooderham) Acheson **8** (George Catlett) Marshall **10** (Edward Reilly) Stettinius (Jr)
  treasury: **6** (Frederick Moore) Vinson, (John Wesley) Snyder **10** (Henry) Morgenthau (Jr)
  war: **6** (Kenneth Claiborne) Royall **7** (Henry Lewis) Stimson **9** (Robert Porter) Patterson
  defense: **6** (Robert Abercrombie) Lovett **7** (Louis Arthur) Johnson **8** (George Catlett) Marshall **9** (James Vincent) Forrestal
  attorney general: **5** (Thomas Campbell) Clark **6** (Francis) Biddle **7** (James Howard) McGrath **9** (James Patrick) McGranery
  navy: **9** (James Vincent) Forrestal
  postmaster general: **6** (Frank Comerford) Walker **8** (Robert Emmet) Hannegan **9** (Jesse Monroe) Donaldson
  interior: **4** (Julius Albert) Krug **5** (Harold LeClaire) Ickes **7** (Oscar Littleton) Chapman
  agriculture: **7** (Charles Franklin) Brannan, (Claude Raymond) Wickard **8** (Clinton Presba) Anderson
  commerce: **6** (Charles) Sawyer **7** (Henry Agard) Wallace **8** (William Averell) Harriman
  labor: **5** (Maurice Joseph) Tobin **7** (Frances), Perkins (Wilson) **13** (Lewis Baxter) Schwellenbach
born: **2** MO **5** Lamar **8** Missouri
died: **2** MO **8** Missouri **10** Kansas City
buried: **2** MO **8** Missouri **12** Independence
education:
  law school: **21** Kansas City School of Law (did not graduate)
religion: **7** Baptist
interests: **5** piano **7** history
vacation spot: **2** FL **7** Florida, Key West
author: **14** Year of Decision **19** Years of Trial and Hope
political career: **8** US Senate **13** Vice President
  presiding judge of: **13** Jackson County
civilian career: **6** farmer
  owned: **9** men's store **12** haberdashery
military service: **5** major **9** World War I **15** MO National Guard **18** Army Reserve colonel
notable events of lifetime/term: **4** NATO **5** V-E Day **8** Fair Deal **9** Korean War **17** iron-curtain speech **20** assassination attempt **31** North Atlantic Treaty Organization
  act: **11** Taft-Hartley **12** Bretton-Woods
  airlift to: **6** Berlin
  conference: **7** Potsdam
  dropping of first: **5** A-bomb **8** atom bomb
  plan: **8** Marshall **9** Point Four
  signing of: **9** UN charter
  Treaty of: **12** Rio de Janeiro
  trial of: **9** Alger Hiss
father: **12** John Anderson
mother: **6** Martha (Ellen Young)
siblings: **8** Mary Jane **10** John Vivian
wife: **9** Elizabeth (Virginia Wallace)
  nickname: **4** Bess
children: **12** Mary Margaret

9 believing, credulous **12** unsuspicious

trustworthy 4 true **5** loyal **6** honest **7** ethical, trusted, upright **8** faithful, reliable, true-blue **9** honorable, steadfast **10** aboveboard, dependable, scrupulous **11** responsible **12** tried and true **13** incorruptible, unimpeachable **14** high-principled

trusty 7 trusted **8** reliable **9** unfailing **10** dependable **11** trustworthy

trusty companion 3 pal **5** buddy, crony **6** friend **8** intimate, sidekick **9** confidant **10** bosom buddy, confidante

truth 3 law **4** fact **5** facts **6** verity **7** reality **8** accuracy, fidelity, trueness, veracity **9** actuality, exactness, integrity **11** reliability **12** authenticity, faithfulness, truthfulness **15** proven principle, trustworthiness
  Russian: 6 Pravda
  also name of: 9 newspaper
  god of: 7 Mithras

truth conquers all things
  Latin: 18 vincit omnia veritas

truthful 4 open, true **5** exact, frank **6** candid, honest **7** artless, correct, factual, precise, sincere **8** accurate, faithful, reliable **9** authentic, guileless, veracious **10** aboveboard, meticulous, scrupulous **11** trustworthy, undeceitful, unvarnished **13** unadulterated **15** straightforward

truthfulness 6 candor **7** honesty **8** veracity

Truth or Consequences
  host: 10 Jack Bailey, Steve Dunne **12** Ralph Edwards

try 2 go **3** aim, use **4** risk, seek, shot, test, turn **5** crack, essay, fling, prove, trial, whack **6** effort, sample, strain, strive, tackle **7** adjudge, attempt, venture **8** endeavor **9** have a go at, partake of, undertake **10** adjudicate, deliberate, put to a test **11** opportunity **12** have a fling at, make an effort, take a crack at

Trygon
  nurse of: 9 Asclepius

trying 4 hard **5** pesky, tough **6** taxing, vexing **7** arduous, irksome, onerous, tedious **8** tiresome **9** difficult, fatiguing, harrowing, wearisome **10** bothersome, burdensome, exhausting, irritating **11** aggravating, distressing, troublesome **12** exasperating

tryout 4 test **5** trial **7** hearing **8** audition **10** experiment

try out 3 fry **6** render **7** compete **8** audition **9** give a test **11** performance

tryst 4 date **7** meeting, vis-a-vis **9** tete-a-tete **10** engagement, rendezvous **11** appointment, assignation

try the patience of 5 annoy **7** provoke **8** irritate **10** exasperate

try to equal 5 rival **7** compete, emulate

Tuatha De Danann 4 gods
origin: **5** Irish
mother: **4** Danu

tub 3 keg, kit, pot, tun, vat **4** bath, boat, butt, cask, ship, tank, tram, wash **5** barge, bathe, fatso, fatty, keeve, tramp **6** barrel, bucket, firkin, ore car, vessel **7** cistern, tankard **8** cauldron, slow boat **9** container, freighter

Tubalcain
father: **6** Lamech
mother: **6** Zillah
half-brother: **5** Jabal, Jubal
progenitor of:
12 metalworkers

tube 4 duct, hose, pipe **7** conduit **8** cylinder

tuber 3 anu, yam **4** beet, bulb, corm, eddo, root, taro **5** jalop, shoot **6** potato, turnip **8** rutabaga, swelling **11** enlargement

Tuchman, Barbara W
author of: **14** A Distant Mirror, The First Salute **15** The Guns of August, The March of Folly **17** Practicing History

tuck 3 put **4** cram **5** pleat, shove, stick, stuff **6** enwrap, gather, insert, pucker, roll up, ruffle, shroud, swathe, thrust **7** crinkle, swaddle

tucker 3 fag **4** bush, poop, tire **5** weary **7** exhaust, fatigue

tuckered out 5 all in, tired, weary **6** bushed, done in, pooped **8** fatigued **9** exhausted, fagged out

Tudor, Antony
choreographer of: **11** Lilac Garden **12** Pillar of Fire

tuebor 11 I will defend

Tuei see **6** Isleta

Tuesday
from: **3** Tiw
heavenly body: **4** Mars
French: **5** mardi
Italian: **7** martedi

Spanish: **6** martes
German: **8** dienstag

tuft 4 wisp **5** batch, brush, bunch, clump, crest, plume, sheaf **6** bundle, tassel **7** cluster, topknot

tug 3 lug, tow **4** drag, draw, haul, jerk, pull, yank **6** wrench **7** wrestle

tulip 6 Tulipa
varieties: **4** lady, star **5** globe **7** Turkish **9** butterfly, guinea-hen, waterlily **10** Sierra star **11** golden globe, purple globe **16** common late garden **17** common early garden

Tulkinghorn
character in: **10** Bleak House
author: **7** Dickens

Tullia
father: **14** Servius Tullius
husband: **7** Tarquin

Tullius see **14** Servius Tullius

Tulsa
football team: **7** Outlaws

tumble 3 mix **4** dive, drop, fall, flip, roll, toss **5** whirl **6** bounce, jumble, plunge, stir up, topple **7** descend, shuffle, stumble **9** cartwheel **10** somersault

tumbledown 5 shaky **7** rickety, run-down **8** decaying, decrepit, unstable **9** crumbling, tottering **10** broken-down, jerrybuilt, ramshackle **11** dilapidated, falling-down **14** disintegrating

tumbler 3 cog, dog **5** drier, glass, lever **6** goblet, vessel **7** acrobat, athlete, gymnast, juggler **12** somersaulter

tumbrel 4 cart **5** wagon **7** tipcart **8** dumpcart

tumbril
French: **7** fourgon

tumid 5 puffy **6** turgid **7** bloated, bulging, dilated, pompous, swollen **8** enlarged, expanded, inflated **9** bombastic, distended, edematous, tumescent **11** protuberant **12** magniloquent **13** grandiloquent

tummy 3 gut **5** belly **6** paunch, tum-tum **7** abdomen, midriff, stomach **9** bay window **11** breadbasket

tumor 3 wen **4** cyst, lump, wart **5** pride **6** cancer, growth **7** bombast, sarcoma **8** hematoma, neoplasm, swelling, tubercle **9** carcinoma, papilloma, pomposity **11** tumefaction

tumult 3 ado, din **6** bedlam, bustle, clamor, hubbub, racket, uproar **7** turmoil **8** disorder, upheaval **9** agitation, commotion, confusion **10** excitement, hullabaloo **11** disturbance, pandemonium

tumultuous 4 loud **5** noisy, rough, rowdy **6** stormy, unruly **7** chaotic, furious, lawless, raucous, riotous, violent **8** agitated, confused **9** clamorous, disturbed, turbulent **10** boisterous, disorderly, uproarious **11** tempestuous

tun 3 keg, tub, vat **4** butt, cast, drum **6** barrel **8** hogshead

tune 3 air **4** aria, line, song, step **5** adjust, ditty, motif, pitch, theme **6** accord, adjust, melody, number, strain, unison **7** concert, concord, harmony **9** agreement **10** conformity

tuneful 6 catchy, dulcet **7** lyrical, musical **9** melodious

tungsten
chemical symbol: **1** W

Tungusic
language family: **6** Altaic
includes: **6** Manchu

tunic 4 robe **5** cloak **6** jacket, mantle, poncho, tabard **7** garment, surcoat

Tunica
tribe: **10** Chitimacha

Tunis
capital of: **7** Tunisia

Tunisia see box

Tunney, Gene
real name: **17** James Joseph Tunney
nickname: **14** Fighting Marine
sport: **6** boxing
class: **11** heavyweight

Tuonela
also: **6** Manala
origin: **7** Finnish
name of: **10** afterworld
form: **6** island
lacked: **3** sun **4** moon

Tupman
character in: **14** Pickwick Papers
author: **7** Dickens

tu quoque 7 thou too

Turandot
opera by: **7** Puccini
character: **3** Liu **4** Pang, Ping, Pong **5** Calaf, Timur **8** Turandot (Princess of China)

turbid 5 muddy, murky **6** cloudy, opaque, roiled **7** clouded, unclear **8** agitated

Tunisia
  other name: 8 Carthage **9** Ifriqiyah
  capital/largest city: 5 Tunis
  others: 4 Beja, Sfax, Susa **5** Gabes, Gofsa **6** Djerba, Mateur, Nabeul, Remada, Sousse, Tozeur **7** Bizerte, Kairwan **8** Carthage, Jendouba, Kairouan, Monastir, Tebourba, Zaghouan **9** Grombalia **10** Ferryville
  empire: 8 Carthage **13** Barbary States
  school: 5 Tunis **16** Pasteur Institute
  measure: 3 saa **4** saah **5** cafiz **6** mettar **8** milerole
  monetary unit: 5 dinar **6** dollar **7** millime
  weight: 3 saa **4** rotl **5** artal, ratel, uckia
  island: 6 Djerba, Galite
  lake: 6 Achkel, Djerid **7** Bizerte
  mountain: 5 Atlas **6** Mrhila **7** Tebessa **8** High Tell, Zaghouan **12** Northern Tell **17** Dorsale Tunisienne
  highest point: 6 Chambi
  river: 8 Medjerda, Mellegue
  sea: 13 Mediterranean
  physical feature:
    cape: **3** Bon **5** Blanc **8** Rasaddar
    desert: **6** Sahara
    gulf: **5** Gabes, Tunis **8** Hammamet
    oasis: **5** Gabes, Gafsa, Nefta **6** Djerba, Tozeur **9** El Oudiane **13** El Hamma Djerid
    plains: **5** Sahel
    salt lake: **11** Chott Djerid, Shatt Djerid
    valley: **8** Medjerda
    wind: **5** chile **6** chilli **7** sirocco
  people: 3 Jew **4** Arab **6** Berber
    artist: **5** Gorgi, Turki
    dynasty: **6** Hafsid **7** Fatimid **8** Aghlabid, Almohade **10** Husseinite
    leader: **6** Ben Ali **9** Bourguiba
  language: 6 Arabic, Berber, French
  religion: 5 Islam **7** Judaism **12** Christianity
  place:
    center of Tunis: **13** Place d'Afrique
    mosque: **5** Great **7** Zitouna
    museum: **5** Bardo, Kouba **6** Sousse
    palace: **14** Dar Ben Abdallah
    ruins: **8** Carthage
    street: **14** Habib Bourguiba
  feature:
    cap: **7** chechia
    clothing: **5** jebba **7** safasri **9** babbouche
    market: **4** souk
  food:
    dish: **7** mesfouf **8** couscous
    drink: **4** iban **5** legmi
    fruit: **12** deglet en nour

9 disturbed, stirred up, unsettled

turbulence 4 fury **6** frenzy, hubbub, tumult, unrest, uproar **7** ferment, rioting, torrent, turmoil **8** disorder, violence **9** agitation, commotion **10** excitement, unruliness **11** disturbance

turbulent 5 rowdy **6** fierce, raging, stormy, unruly **7** chaotic, furious, riotous, violent **8** agitated, restless **9** clamorous, disturbed **10** blustering, boisterous, disorderly, tumultuous, uproarious

11 tempestuous

tureen 4 bowl, dish **9** casserole, container **10** receptacle

turf 3 sod **4** area, peat, plot, soil **5** divot, grass, haunt, sward, track **7** verdure **9** racetrack, territory **10** greensward

Turgenev, Ivan
  author of: 5 Smoke **9** First Love **10** Virgin Soil **14** Fathers and Sons **18** A Month in the Country **19** A Sportsman's Notebook, A Sportsman's Sketches, The Torrents of Spring

turgid 5 puffy, showy **6** florid, ornate **7** flowery, pompous,

swollen **8** inflated, puffed up **9** bombastic, grandiose, overblown **10** hyperbolic

Turkey *see box, p. 1006*

Turkic
  language family: 6 Altaic
  group: 5 Kazak, Nogai, Uigur, Uzbek, Yakut **7** Chuvash, Kirghiz **8** Turkoman **10** Karakalpak **11** Azerbaijani **14** Osmanli Turkish

Turkmenistan
  capital/largest city: 9 Ashkhabad
  head of state: 9 president
  government: 8 republic
  monetary unit: 5 ruble
  river: 8 Amu Darya
  sea: 7 Caspian
  physical feature: 13 Kara Kum Desert
  people: 7 Turkmen **10** Turkmenian
  language: 6 Turkic **10** West Turkic
  religion: 11 Sunni Muslim
  feature: 9 Altyn Depe

turmeric
  botanical name: 12 Curcuma longa
  also called: 7 tumeric **13** Crocus indicus, Indian saffron
  family: 6 ginger
  color: 6 yellow
  used as: 3 dye **6** amulet **8** cosmetic, medicine
  origin: 4 Asia **9** Caribbean, East India
  charm against: 5 ghost **10** tree spirit

turmoil 4 mess **5** chaos **6** tumult, uproar **7** ferment **8** disorder **9** agitation, commotion, confusion **10** convulsion **11** disturbance, pandemonium
  French: 14 bouleversement

turn 2 do, go **3** act, arc, lie, put **4** bend, coil, come, deed, flex, hang, look, loop, make, rest, ride, roll, send, shot, sour, spin, time, veer, walk, wing **5** alter, apply, crack, curve, drive, eject, fling, hinge, pivot, round, scare, shift, shock, spell, spoil, start, stint, swing, throw, twist, whack, wheel, whirl **6** action, become, chance, change, curdle, depend, direct, effort, fright, gyrate, invert, period, reside, rotate, sprain, stroll, swerve, swivel, wrench, zigzag **7** acidify, attempt, convert, deliver, execute, ferment, perform, reverse, revolve, service, winding **8** gyration, overturn, roll over, rotation, surprise **9** cause to go, deviation, discharge, transform **10** accomplish, alteration, revolution

Turkey
capital: 6 Angora, Ankara
largest city: 8 Istanbul
others: 4 Enos, Troy, Urfa 5 Adana, Bursa, Izmir, Konya, Maras, Siirt, Sivas 6 Aintab, Edessa, Edirne, Elaziz, Marash, Samsun, Smyrna 7 Antakya, Antioch, Erzurum, Kayseri, Mersin, Scutari, Trabzon, Uskudar 8 Stamboul 9 Byzantium, Eskisehir, Gaziantep 10 Adrianople 14 Constantinople
school: 6 Aegean, Ankara 8 Istanbul
division: 4 Pera, Sert 5 Siirt, Troad 6 Angora, Eyalet, Thrace 7 Anadolu, Beyoglu, Cilicia 8 Anatolia 9 Asia Minor, Kurdistan
measure: 3 dra, oka, pik 4 draa, khat, kile, zira 5 berri, kileh, zirai 6 arshin, chinik, fortin, halebi 7 nocktat
monetary unit: 4 lira, para 5 akcha, asper, kurus, pound, rebia 6 akcheh, zequin 7 aetilik, beshlik, piaster 8 medjidie
weight: 3 oka, oke 4 aqui, dram, rotl 5 artal, cheke, kerat, obolu, ratel 6 batman, dirhem, kantar, maunch, miskal 7 drachma, quintal, yusdrum
island: 6 Cyprus, Kibris
lake: 3 Tuz, Van 7 Egridir 8 Beysehir
mountain: 2 Ak 3 Ala 4 Alai, Dagh, Kara 5 Hasan, Hinis, Honaz, Murat, Murit 6 Ala Dag, Bingol, Bolgar, Pontic, Suphan, Taurus 7 Aladagh, Erciyas 8 Karacali 10 Kackar Dagi
highest point: 6 Ararat
river: 4 Aras, Kura 5 Araks, Dicle, Firat, Gediz, Goksu, Halys, Irmak, Kizil, Mesta, Murat, Sarus 6 Araxes, Ceyhan, Seihun, Seyhan, Seylan, Tigris 7 Kurucay, Muradsu, Orontes, Sakarya 8 Granicus, Macestus, Maeander, Menderes 9 Euphrates 13 Buyukmenderes
sea: 4 Aral 5 Black 6 Aegean 7 Marmara 13 Mediterranean
physical feature:
  cape: 4 Baba, Ince 5 Bafra 6 Anamur, Helles, Hinzir 7 Karatas, Kerempe
  gulf: 3 Cos 5 Izmir 7 Antalya
  inlet: 10 Golden Horn
  peninsula: 9 Anatolian, Gallipoli
  plateau: 9 Anatolian
  strait: 8 Bosporus 9 Bosphorus 11 Dardanelles
people: 4 Arab, Kurd, Turk 6 Seljuk
  king: 8 Mausolus
  leader: 5 Inonu, Osman 6 Ecevit 7 Demirel 8 Menderes, Suleiman 12 Kemal Ataturk
  poet: 5 Homer
language: 6 Arabic 7 Kurdish, Turkish
religion: 5 Islam 7 Judaism 12 Christianity 13 Greek Orthodox, Roman Catholic
place:
  bridge: 6 Galata
  dam: 9 Gokcekaya
  mosque: 4 Blue, Yeni 8 Selimiye 11 Hagia Sophia, Sultan Ahmed
  ruins: 4 Troy 7 Ephesus 8 Pergamum
  tomb: 12 Kemal Ataturk
feature:
  cap: 3 fez 6 calpac 7 calpack
  clothing: 6 caftan, dolman, jelick 7 yashrak 8 charshaf, maharmah, shakseer
  goat hair: 6 mohair
  grill: 6 mangal
  harem: 5 serai 8 seraglio
  musical instrument: 5 canum, kanum 6 canoon, johnie, kussir, zither 8 crescent, jingling
  pipe: 10 meerschaum
food:
  dish: 5 halva, pilaw 10 doner kebab, shish kebab
  drink: 4 boza, raki 5 airan, pasha, rakee 6 mastic
  pastry: 7 baklava
  turkey: 4 hind

turn a deaf ear to 6 ignore, slight 9 disregard

turn aside 5 avert 6 divert 7 deflect, deviate 8 turn away

turn away 5 avert 6 give up 8 alienate, estrange, send away 9 turn aside 12 turn one's back

turnback 4 fold, quit, tack 5 repel 6 defect, desert, return, revert 7 forsake, regress, relapse, repulse, retrace, retreat, reverse 9 backslide

turncoat 5 Judas 6 bolter 7 traitor 8 apostate, betrayer, defector, deserter, quisling, renegade 12 double-dealer

turn down 5 spurn 6 refuse, reject 14 lower the volume, refuse to accept

Turner, Joseph Mallord William
born: 6 London 7 England
artwork: 12 The Shipwreck, The Slave Ship, Tintern Abbey 17 Dawn After the Wreck 20 Dido Building Carthage 22 Venice S Giorgio Maggiore 24 The Sun of Venice Going to Sea 25 The Thames near Walton Bridge, Ulysses Deriding Polyphe-

mus **30** Burning of the Houses of Parliament **32** Snowstorm Hannibal Crossing the Alps **32** The Falls of the Rhine at Schaffhausen **34** The Bay of Baiae with Apollo and the Sibyl **37** Fighting Temeraire Tugged to her Last Berth **47** The Parting of Hero and Leander from the Greek of Musaeus **50** The Shipwreck Fishing Boats Endeavoring to Rescue the Crew

Turner, Kathleen
 roles: **8** Body Heat **12** Prizzi's Honor **17** Romancing the Stone, The Jewel of the Nile **18** Peggy Sue Got Married

Turner, Lana
 real name: **29** Julia Jean Mildred Frances Turner
 nickname: **11** Sweater Girl
 born: **9** Wallace ID
 discovered at: **16** Schwab's Drugstore
 husband: **9** Artie Shaw, Lex Barker **10** Bob Topping **12** Stephen Crane
 roles: **7** Madame X **11** Peyton Place **15** By Love Possessed, Imitation of Life **26** The Postman Always Rings Twice

turning 4 bend **5** curve **7** bending, curving, winding **8** pivoting, rotating, spinning, twisting, whirling **9** revolving, swiveling

turnip 12 Brassica rapa
 group: **8** Rapifera
 varieties: **6** Indian **7** Italian, Swedish **8** seven-top

turn off 4 bore, exit **5** douse, leave, repel **6** revolt, sicken **7** disgust, repulse **8** alienate, turn away **9** switch off **10** deactivate

turn of phrase 5 idiom **8** locution, phrasing **10** expression **11** phraseology

Turn of the Screw, The
 author: **10** Henry James
 character: **5** Flora, Miles **7** Mr Quint **8** Mrs Grose **10** Miss Jessel **12** The Governess

turn on 5 start, tempt **6** allure, attack, entice, excite **7** actuate, attract **8** activate, energize, interest, switch on

turn one's stomach 6 revolt, sicken **7** disgust **8** nauseate

turnout 5 crowd **6** output, throng **8** assembly, audience **9** gathering **10** assemblage, production

turn out 4 garb, oust **5** array, dress, eject, end up, evict, exile, expel **6** appear, attend, attire, banish, clothe, evolve, fit out, invest, rig out, show up, unfold **7** cast out, come out, costume, develop, kick out **8** drive out, send away **9** switch off **11** come to light

turn over 4 flip **5** upset **6** bestow, rotate **7** deliver **8** flip-flop, give over, hand over, overturn **9** surrender **10** relinquish, somersault

turn pale 4 fade **6** blanch, whiten **7** lighten

turn tail 4 flee **7** retreat, run away **8** back away **12** beat a retreat

turn to account 7 exploit, utilize **8** profit by, put to use **9** make use of **12** capitalize on

turn topsy turvy 5 upset **7** capsize, confuse, tip over **8** flip-flop, overturn, put askew **10** disarrange, turn turtle **11** disorganize

turn turtle 5 upset **7** capsize, tip over **8** flip over, keel over, overturn, turn over **14** turn upside down

turn up 4 come **6** appear, arrive, crop up, drop in, emerge, loom up, show up **7** develop, surface **11** come to light

Turnus
 father: **6** Daunus
 mother: **7** Venilia
 sister: **7** Juturna
 sought to win: **7** Lavinia
 killed by: **6** Aeneas

Turpentine State
 nickname of: **13** North Carolina

turpitude 4 evil, vice **8** baseness, lewdness, vileness **9** depravity **10** corruption, debauchery, defilement, degeneracy, immorality, perversion, sinfulness, wickedness, wrongdoing **13** dissoluteness **14** licentiousness

turquoise 4 aqua **5** stone **7** mineral, sky-blue **10** aquamarine **12** greenish-blue, Prussian-blue
 source: **12** United States

turret 5 tower **6** belfry, cupola, garret, gazebo, louver, terret **7** minaret, rotator, steeple **8** gunhouse, gunmount **9** belvedere, pepperbox **10** watchtower
 tool: **5** lathe

turtle 3 box **4** musk, wood **6** slider **7** painted, reptile,

snapper, spotted **8** slowpoke, terrapin, tortoise **10** turtledove **11** leatherback
 dorsal shell: **8** carapace
 nautical: **5** upset **6** pocket **7** capsize **8** overturn
 order: **8** Chelonia
 ventral shell: **8** plastron
 young: **7** turtlet

Turveydrop
 character in: **10** Bleak House
 author: **7** Dickens

tussle 4 fray **5** brawl, fight, melee, scrap, set-to **6** battle, fracas **7** grapple, scuffle, wrestle **8** conflict, struggle **10** donnybrook, free-for-all **11** altercation

tussock 4 hair, tuft **5** brush, bunch, clump, grass, sedge **7** bulrush, cluster, thicket **8** feathers

tutelage 8 coaching, guidance, teaching, training, tutoring **9** direction, education, schooling **10** discipline **11** inculcation, instruction, supervision, trusteeship **12** guardianship **14** indoctrination

tutor 4 guru **5** coach, drill, teach **6** master, mentor, school **7** prepare, teacher **8** instruct **10** instructor **11** give lessons

tutorial 5 class **8** didactic, edifying **11** educational, instructive **12** prescriptive

tutti
 music: **3** all **18** all players together, all singers together

Tuvalu
 other name: **13** Ellice Islands, Lagoon Islands
 capital: **8** Funafuti
 head of state: **14** British monarch **15** governor general
 monetary unit: **4** cent **6** dollar
 island: **3** Nui **6** Niutao **7** Nanumea, Vaitupu **8** Funafuti **9** Nanumanga, Niulakita, Nukufetau **10** Nukulaelae
 highest point: **5** Nuwak
 sea: **7** Pacific
 people: **6** Samoan **10** Polynesian
  leader: **5** Lauti
 language: **6** Samoan **7** English **8** Tuvaluan **10** Polynesian
 religion: **10** Protestant **12** Tuvalu Church

Tuvim, Judith
  real name of: **12** Judy
  Holliday

twaddle 3 rot **4** bosh, bunk
  5 trash, tripe **6** babble, drivel,
  gabble, jabber, piffle **7** chatter,
  prattle, rubbish **8** claptrap, idle
  talk, nonsense, tommyrot
  9 jabbering, silly talk **10** balderdash **16** stuff-and-nonsense

Twain, Mark
  real name: **13** Samuel
  Clemens
  author of: **9** Tom Sawyer
  10 Roughing It **12** A Tramp
  Abroad, The Gilded Age
  15 (Adventures of) Huckleberry Finn **18** The Innocents Abroad **20** Life on the
  Mississippi **21** The Mysterious Stranger, The Prince
  and the Pauper **29** The Man
  That Corrupted Hadleyburg
  36 A Connecticut Yankee in
  King Arthur's Court **41** The
  Celebrated Jumping Frog of
  Calaveras County

twang 9 resonance, vibration
  10 nasal sound
  13 reverberation

Tweedledee
  character in: **22** Through the
  Looking Glass
  author: **7** Carroll

Tweedledum
  character in: **22** Through the
  Looking Glass
  author: **7** Carroll

tweet 4 peep **5** cheep, chirp
  7 chirrup, chitter, twitter

Twelfth-Night
  author: **18** William
  Shakespeare
  character: **5** Feste, Maria, Viola (Cesario) **6** Olivia, Orsino **7** Antonio **8** Malvolio
  9 Sebastian **12** Sir Toby
  Belch **18** Sir Andrew
  Aguecheek

Twelve Angry Men
  director: **11** Sidney Lumet
  cast: **8** Ed Begley, Lee J
  Cobb **10** E G Marshall,
  Henry Fonda, Jack Warden
  11 Jack Klugman, John
  Fiedler **12** Martin Balsam

Twelve O'Clock High
  director: **9** Henry King
  cast: **10** Dean Jagger **11** Gary
  Merrill, Gregory Peck, Hugh
  Marlowe **15** Millard Mitchell
  Oscar for: **15** supporting actor (Jagger)

Twentieth Century
  director: **11** Howard Hawks
  based on play by: **8** Ben
  Hecht **16** Charles MacArthur
  cast: **11** Roscoe Karns
  13 Carole Lombard, John

Barrymore **14** Walter
Connolly

Twentieth Century, The
  narrator: **14** Walter Cronkite

twenty-one see **9** blackjack

Twenty Questions
  host: **10** Bill Slater, Jay
  Jackson
  panelist: **11** Herb Polesie
  12 Bobby McGuire **13** Johnnie McPhee **14** Dickie Harrison, Florence Rinard
  15 Fred Van De Venter

**Twenty Thousand Leagues
Under the Sea**
  author: **10** Jules Verne
  character: **7** Conseil, Ned
  Land **11** Captain Nemo
  22 Professor Pierre Aronnax
  submarine: **8** Nautilus

Twenty Years After
  author: **14** Alexandre Dumas
  (pere)

Twice-Told Tales
  author: **18** Nathaniel
  Hawthorne

Twightwee see **5** Miami

twilight 3 ebb, eve **4** dusk
  6 sunset **7** decline, evening,
  sundown **8** eventide, gloaming,
  moonrise **9** half-light, last
  phase, nightfall **14** edge of
  darkness

Twilight of the Gods
  8 Ragnarok
  German:
  15 Gotterdammerung

Twilight Zone, The
  host: **10** Rod Serling

twin 4 dual, like **5** alike **6** double, paired **7** matched, twofold **9** duplicate, identical

Twin 6 Thomas

twine 4 coil, cord, rope, wind
  5 braid, cable, plait, twist,
  weave **6** string, thread **7** binding, entwine **9** interlace
  10 intertwine

twinge 4 pain, pang, stab
  5 cramp, spasm, throb **6** stitch,
  tingle, twitch

twinkle 4 glow **5** blaze, flare,
  flash, gleam, shine **7** flicker,
  glimmer, glisten, shimmer,
  sparkle **11** scintillate

Twinkleton, Miss
  character in: **22** The Mystery
  of Edwin Drood
  author: **7** Dickens

Twins
  constellation of: **6** Gemini

twirl 4 spin **5** pivot, twine,
  wheel, whirl **6** gyrate, rotate
  7 revolve **9** pirouette

twist 3 arc, way **4** bend, coil,
  curl, idea, kink, knot, pull,
  roll, spin, turn, veer, wind,
  wrap, yank **5** curve, pivot,
  ravel, slant, snake, swing,
  twine, whirl, wrest **6** change,
  method, notion, rotate, spiral,
  sprain, swerve, swivel, system,
  tangle, wrench, zigzag **7** contort, distort, entwine, meander **8** approach, rotation,
  surprise **9** corkscrew, interlace,
  treatment **10** intertwine, involution **11** convolution,
  development

twisted 4 bent **6** warped
  7 crooked, gnarled **8** deformed **9** contorted, distorted,
  misshapen

twisting 7 crooked, curving,
  turning **9** contorted, revolving,
  spiraling, swiveling

twist out of shape 4 warp
  6 deform **7** contort, distort

twitch 3 tic **4** jerk **5** shake,
  spasm, throb **6** quaver, quiver,
  squirm, tremor, wiggle,
  writhe **7** tremble **8** paroxysm
  10 convulsion

twitter 4 fuss, peep, stew
  5 cheep, chirp, tizzy, tweet,
  whirl **6** bustle, flurry, pother,
  uproar, warble **7** chatter, chirrup, ferment, fluster, flutter
  8 chirping **10** turbulence
  11 chirruping

two-faced 5 false **7** devious
  8 slippery **9** deceitful, deceptive, dishonest, insincere
  10 perfidious **11** dissembling,
  double-faced, duplicitous, fork-
  tongued, treacherous, underhanded **12** dishonorable,
  disingenuous, falsehearted,
  hypocritical **13** double-dealing,
  untrustworthy

twofold 4 dual **6** double **7** two-
  part

**Two Gentlemen of Verona,
The**
  author: **18** William
  Shakespeare
  character: **5** Julia **6** Silvia,
  Thurio **7** Proteus **9** Valentine **11** Duke of Milan

Two Lands, The see **5** Egypt

two of a kind 4 pair **5** twins
  6 couple **7** doublet

two-part 4 dual, twin **6** double, paired **9** bipartite

twosome 3 duo **4** pair
  5 brace **6** couple

2001: A Space Odyssey
  author: **13** Arthur C Clarke
  director: **14** Stanley Kubrick
  character: **4** Dave **5** Steve
  computer: **3** HAL

cast: 3 HAL **10** Keir Dullea **12** Gary Lockwood **16** William Sylvester
song: 20 Thus Spake Zarathustra (Richard Strauss)
sequel: 24 Two Thousand Ten: Odyssey Two

two-time 6 betray **10** be disloyal **11** double-cross **12** be unfaithful **13** be treacherous, play false with **14** break faith with

two-timing 5 false **6** tricky **7** perfidy **8** bad faith, betrayal, disloyal, trickery **9** deceiving, deception, duplicity, falseness, treachery **10** disloyalty, perfidious **11** double-cross, duplicitous, treacherous **13** breach of faith, double-dealing, faithlessness **14** double-crossing

two-wheeler 4 bike **5** cycle **7** bicycle

Two Years Before the Mast
　author: 18 Richard Henry Dana Jr

Tybalt
　character in: 14 Romeo and Juliet
　author: 11 Shakespeare

Tyche
　origin: 5 Greek
　goddess of: 7 fortune
　corresponds to: 7 Fortuna

tycoon 4 boss **5** mogul, nabob **6** big gun, bigwig **7** big shot, magnate **8** big wheel **9** potentate **12** entrepreneur **13** industrialist **17** captain of industry

Tydeus
　father: 6 Oeneus
　mother: 8 Periboea
　uncle: 5 Melas **6** Agrius **9** Alcathous
　son: 8 Diomedes

tyke 3 kid, tad, tot **5** child **6** shaver, squirt, wee one **9** little one

Tyler, John *see box*

Tyll Eulenspiegel *see* **16** Till Eulenspiegel

Tyndall, John
　field: 7 physics
　nationality: 5 Irish
　studied diffusion of: 5 light

Tyndareus
　wife: 4 Leda
　daughter: 6 Phoebe **8** Philonoe, Timandra **12** Clytemnestra

Tyndaridae *see* **15** Castor and Pollux

type 4 font, kind, race, sort **5** brand, class, genus, group, model, order, print **6** design, family, phylum, sample **7** pattern, species, variety **8** category, division, specimen, typeface **9** archetype, prototype **10** typography

type, movable
　invented by: 9 Gutenberg

Typee
　author: 14 Herman Melville
　character: 3 Tom (Melville) **4** Toby **6** Marnoo, Mehevi **7** Fayaway **8** Kory-Kory

typewriter
　invented by: 5 Soule **6** Sholes **7** Glidden

Typhoeus
　form: 7 monster
　father: 8 Tartarus
　mother: 2 Ge
　number of heads: 10 one hundred

Tyler, John
　presidential rank: 5 tenth
　party: 4 Whig **20** Democratic-Republican
　state represented: 2 VA **8** Virginia
　defeated: 5 no-one
　　succeeded upon death of: **8** Harrison
　vice president: 4 none
　cabinet:
　　state: **6** (Abel Parker) Upshur **7** (Daniel) Webster, (John C) Calhoun
　　treasury: **4** (George Mortimer) Bibb **5** (Thomas) Ewing **7** (John Canfield) Spencer, (Walter) Forward
　　war: **4** (John) Bell **7** (John Canfield) Spencer, (William) Wilkins
　　attorney general: **6** (Hugh Swinton) Legare, (John) Nelson **10** (John Jordan) Crittenden
　　navy: **5** (John Young) Mason **6** (Abel Parker) Upshur, (George Edmund) Badger, (Thomas Walker) Gilmer
　　postmaster general: **7** (Francis) Granger **9** (Charles Anderson) Wickliffe
　born: 2 VA **8** Greenway, Virginia **17** Charles City County
　died/buried: 2 VA **8** Richmond, Virginia
　education: 14 William and Mary
　religion: 12 Episcopalian
　vacation spot: 2 VA **7** Hampton **8** Virginia
　political career: 8 US Senate **12** State Council **13** vice president **24** US House of Representatives
　　delegate to: **13** State Assembly
　　governor of: **8** Virginia
　civilian career: 6 farmer, lawyer
　military service: 19 War of Eighteen Twelve
　notable events of lifetime/term:
　　act: **6** Tariff (of 1842)
　　annexation of: **5** Texas
　　treaty: **16** Webster-Ashburton
　father: 4 John
　mother: 4 Mary (Marott Armistead)
　siblings: 7 William **8** Wat Henry **10** Maria Henry **12** Anne Contesse **14** Christina Booth **15** Martha Jefferson **18** Elizabeth Armistead
　wife: 5 Julia (Gardiner) **7** Letitia (Christian)
　children: 4 John, Mary **5** Alice, Julia, Pearl **6** Robert **7** Lachlan, Letitia **8** Tazewell **9** Elizabeth **12** Anne Contesse, Lyon Gardiner **13** David Gardiner, John Alexander **16** Robert FitzWalter

Typhon
　form: 7 monster
　father: 8 Typhoeus
　son: 5 Ladon

typhoon 4 gale, gust, wind **5** storm **7** cyclone, tempest, tornado, twister **9** hurricane, whirlwind

Typhoon
　author: 12 Joseph Conrad

typical 5 model, stock, usual **6** normal **7** average, regular **8** ordinary, orthodox, standard **9** exemplary, in keeping **10** individual, prototypal, true to type **11** distinctive, in character **12** conventional, to be expected **14** characteristic, representative

typify 5 sum up **6** embody **7** betoken, connote, pass for **8** instance, stand for **9** epitomize, exemplify, incarnate, personify, represent **10** illustrate **12** characterize

typography measure 2 em, en **4** pica **5** point

Tyr
origin: **12** Scandinavian
god of: **7** victory
father: **4** Odin **5** Othin
mother: **3** Fri **5** Frigg, Frija **6** Frigga
killed by: **4** Garm

tyrannical 7 fascist **8** despotic **9** imperious **10** oppressive **11** dictatorial, domineering **13** authoritarian

tyrannize 7 oppress **8** domineer, overlord **10** slave drive

tyrannized 9 exploited, oppressed **11** downtrodden, subservient **12** harshly ruled

Tyrannosaurus
type: **8** dinosaur, theropod
location: **7** Montana **12** North America
period: **10** Cretaceous

tyrannous 8 despotic **9** imperi-

ous **10** iron-handed, oppressive, repressive, tyrannical

tyranny 7 cruelty, fascism **8** coercion, iron fist, iron hand, iron rule, severity **9** despotism, harshness **10** domination, oppression, repression **11** persecution **12** dictatorship **13** reign of terror **15** totalitarianism

tyrant 5 bully **6** despot **8** dictator, martinet **10** persecutor, taskmaster **11** cruel master, slave driver

Tyre
king of: **5** Hiram

tyro 6 intern, novice, rookie **7** learner, recruit, trainee **8** beginner, initiate, neophyte, newcomer **9** greenhorn **10** apprentice, tenderfoot

Tyro
father: **9** Salmoneus
loved by: **8** Cretheus, Poseidon
son: **5** Aeson **6** Neleus, Pelias
grandson: **5** Jason **6** Nestor

Tyrrheus
occupation: **8** shepherd

Tyson, Cicely
born: **9** New York NY
roles: **5** Roots **7** Sounder **33** The Autobiography of Miss Jane Pittman

Tyson, Mike
original name: **7** Michael
nickname: **8** Iron Mike
born: **2** NY **8** Brooklyn **17** Bedford-Stuyvesant
wife: **11** Robin Givens
manager: **9** Cus D'Amato **10** Bill Cayton **11** Jimmy Jacobs
trainer: **12** Angelo Dundee
promoter: **7** Don King
boxing title: **3** IBF, WBA, WBC **11** heavyweight
defeated: **6** Holmes, Spinks, Thomas, Tillis, Tucker **7** Berbick
defeated by: **7** Douglas (Buster)
convicted of: **4** rape

tzimmes 4 fuss **6** uproar **10** hullabaloo
literally: **4** stew **9** mixed dish

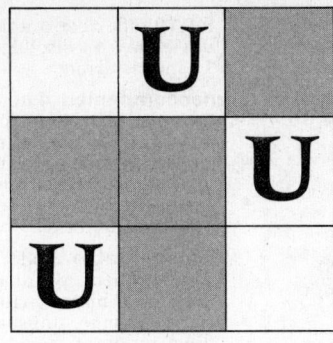

Ubangi-Shari *see* **22** Central African Republic

Ubermensch 8 superman

ubiquitous 7 allover **9** pervading, pervasive, prevalent, universal, worldwide **10** everywhere, widespread **11** everpresent, omnipresent **12** all-pervading

ubiquitously 10 everywhere **11** extensively

ubi supra 19 where mentioned above

Ucalegon
   counselor to: **5** Priam

Uccello, Paolo
   real name: **11** Paolo di Dono
   born: **5** Italy **8** Florence
   artwork: **8** The Flood **12** The Night Hunt **15** Sir John Hawkwood **18** The Rout (Battle) of San Romano **20** St George and the Dragon

Udaeus
   member of: **6** Sparti
   grandson: **8** Tiresias

Udall, Nicholas
   author of: **19** Ralph Roister Doister

Uganda *see box, p. 1012*

ugliness 8 ill-favor **9** grossness **10** homeliness **11** hideousness, monstrosity **12** unseemliness **13** frightfulness, grotesqueness, monstrousness, repulsiveness, unsightliness **14** unpleasantness **16** unattractiveness

ugly 4 foul, mean, vile **5** nasty **6** homely, horrid, odious **7** hideous, hostile, ominous **8** dreadful, horrible, menacing, unseemly **9** abhorrent, dangerous, difficult, frightful, grotesque, monstrous, obnoxious, offensive, repellent, repugnant, repulsive, sickening, unsightly **10** abominable, disgusting

ugly as sin 7 hideous **9** frightful, grotesque, monstrous, repulsive

Ugly Duckling, The
   author: **21** Hans Christian Andersen

ukase 4 fiat **5** edict, order **6** decree, dictum, ruling **7** command, mandate, statute **9** directive, manifesto, ordinance **10** injunction **12** proclamation **13** pronouncement

Ukraine
   capital/largest city: **4** Kiev
   others: **4** Lviv (Lvov), **6** Odessa **7** Donetsk, Kharkov, Lugansk (Voroshilovgrad) **8** Mariupol (Zhdanov) **9** Krivoi Rog, Zaporozhe **14** Dnepropetrovsk
   head of state: **9** president
   government: **8** republic
   monetary unit: **6** grivna **10** karbovanet
   mountain: **7** Crimean **10** Carpathian
   river: **3** Bug **6** Donets **7** Dnieper
   sea: **5** Black
   people: **7** Russian **9** Ukrainian
   language: **9** Ukrainian
   religion: **17** Ukrainian Catholic, Ukrainian Orthodox
   feature: **25** Askaniya Nova Nature Reserve

Ulan Bator
   capital of: **8** Mongolia

ulcer 4 sore **6** canker

Uller
   also: **4** Ullr
   origin: **8** Teutonic
   god of: **12** winter sports
   stepfather: **4** Thor

Ullmann, Liv
   born: **5** Japan, Tokyo
   nationality: **9** Norwegian
   roles: **7** Persona **10** Face to Face **11** Forty Carats, Lost Horizon **12** The Emigrants **16** Cries and Whispers **19** Scenes from a Marriage

Ullr *see* **5** Uller

Ulman, Douglas Elton
   real name of: **16** Douglas Fairbanks

ulna
   bone of: **8** lower arm

ulterior 6 covert, hidden, secret **7** selfish **9** concealed **10** undivulged, unrevealed **11** self-serving, undisclosed, unexpressed **13** opportunistic

ultimate 3 end **4** acme, apex, last, peak **5** final **6** height, utmost **7** extreme, maximum, supreme **8** crowning, eventual, greatest, terminal **9** at the peak, high point, last straw, long-range, resulting **10** conclusive, definitive
   French: **7** dernier

ultramodern 8 advanced, brand-new **10** avant-garde, newfangled **13** in the vanguard, up-to-the-minute

Ulysses
   author: **10** James Joyce
   character: **10** Molly Bloom **12** Blazes Boylan, Buck Mulligan, Leopold Bloom **14** Stephen Dedalus

Ulysses *see* **8** Odysseus

umber 5 brown **7** pigment **9** dark-brown **14** yellowish-brown

umbrage 5 pique, shade **6** leaves, shadow **7** foliage, offense, outrage **10** resentment

Umbrellas of Cherbourg, The
   director: **11** Jacques Demy
   cast: **10** Anne Vernon **15** Nino Castelnuovo

Uganda
  capital/largest city: **7** Kampala
  others: **4** Arua, Gulu, Lira **5** Atiak, Jinja, Mbale, Mengo **6** Kasese, Kiboga, Kitgum, Masaka, Moroto, Pajule, Soroti, Tororo **7** Entebbe, Kachung, Kilembe, Mbarara, Mombasa **8** Kyenjojo **11** Port Masindi
  school: **8** Makerere
  division: **4** Toro **6** Ankole, Busoga **7** Buganda, Bunyoro
  monetary unit: **4** cent **8** shilling
  island: **4** Sese
  lake: **5** Kioga, Kyoga **6** Albert, Edward, George **8** Victoria
  mountain: **4** Oboa **5** Elgon **7** Virunga **9** Mufumbiro, Ruwenzori **18** Mountains of the Moon
  highest point: **10** Margherita
  river: **4** Aswa, Kafu **5** Pager **7** Katonga **9** White Nile **10** Albert Nile **12** Victoria Nile
  physical feature:
    falls: **5** Owens **8** Kabalega **9** Murchison
    plateau: **6** Ankole **11** East African
    valley: **9** Great Rift
  people: **4** Alur, Gisu, Soga, Teso **5** Ateso, Bantu, Chiga, Ganda, Langi, Lango, Nkole, Pygmy **6** Acholi, Ankole, Bagisu, Bakiga, Basoga, Batoro **7** Baganda, Banyoro, Bunyoro, Hamitic, Lugbara, Nilotic, Sudanic **9** Nyoro-Toro **10** Banyankole, Karamojong
    explorer: **5** Baker, Speke **7** Stanley
    king: **6** Mutesa, Mwanga **8** Kabarega
    leader: **5** Obote **6** Mutesa **7** Omukama **11** Idi Amin Dada
  language: **5** Ateso, Ganda **7** English, Luganda, Swahili
  religion: **5** Islam **7** animism **8** Anglican **10** Protestant **13** Roman Catholic
  place:
    airport: **7** Entebbe
    dam: **10** Owens Falls
    national park: **6** Kidepo **14** Murchison Falls, Queen Elizabeth
  feature:
    clothing: **7** busuuti
    council of chiefs: **6** lukiko
    dance group: **17** Heart Beat of Africa
    king: **6** kabaka
  food:
    drink: **6** waragi

16 Catharine Deneuve
  score: **13** Michel Legrand

Umbrian
  language family: **12** Indo-European
  branch: **6** Italic

umpire **5** judge **7** arbiter, mediate, referee **8** mediator, moderate **9** arbitrate, go-between, moderator **10** adjudicate, arbitrator, negotiator **11** adjudicator, intercessor

Una
  character in: **15** The Faerie Queene
  author: **7** Spenser

unabbreviated **5** uncut **8** complete, undocked, unpruned **9** uncropped, unreduced, unsnipped, untrimmed **10** unabridged **11** uncondensed, uncurtailed, unshortened **12** uncompressed, unexpurgated

unable **5** unfit **6** cannot **8** helpless, impotent **9** incapable **10** inadequate, unequipped **11** incompetent, unqualified
  to tell pitch: **8** tone deaf

unabridged **5** uncut **6** entire, intact **8** complete **10** full-length **11** uncondensed

unacceptable **8** below par, improper, unseemly, unworthy **9** deficient, out of line, unwelcome **10** disallowed, inadequate, unsuitable **11** displeasing, intolerable **12** inadmissible, not allowable, not up to snuff **13** insupportable **14** unsatisfactory **15** not up to standard

unacceptableness **8** disfavor, disgrace, ignominy **18** unsatisfactoriness

unaccommodating **4** rude **8** churlish **9** difficult, unhelp-

ful **10** inflexible, intolerant, unyielding **11** disobliging **13** inconsiderate

unaccompanied **4** lone, solo **5** alone, apart **6** single, singly **8** isolated, lonesome, separate, solitary **9** a cappella, by oneself **10** unattended, unescorted **12** all by oneself **13** companionless

unaccountable **3** odd **4** free **5** clear, queer, weird **6** exempt, immune **7** bizarre, curious, excused, strange, unusual **8** baffling, innocent, peculiar **9** blameless, not liable, unheard-of **10** inculpable, intriguing, mysterious, surprising **11** astonishing, unexplained **12** inexplicable, unfathomable **13** extraordinary, not answerable **14** not responsible **16** incomprehensible

unaccustomed **3** new, odd **4** rare, wild **5** green, new to, novel, queer **6** quaint, unique, unused **7** amazing, bizarre, curious, foreign, not used, strange, ungiven, untried, unusual **8** original, peculiar, singular, uncommon **9** fantastic, startling, unheard-of **10** remarkable, surprising, unfamiliar, unversed in **11** astonishing, out-of-the-way, unpracticed **12** unacquainted, unhabituated, unimaginable **13** extraordinary, inexperienced **14** unfamiliar with **16** out of the ordinary

unacknowledged **9** anonymous **10** unanswered **11** disregarded **12** unidentified, unrecognized

unadorned **4** bald, bare **5** naked, plain, stark **6** simple **7** austere **11** undecorated **12** unornamented **13** unembellished **15** straightforward

unadulterated **4** pure, true **5** clear, uncut **7** genuine **9** unalloyed, untainted **14** untampered-with

unadventurous **5** chary, timid **7** careful **8** cautious, hesitant **11** circumspect

unadvisable **5** silly **6** stupid, unwise **8** unseemly **9** imprudent **11** inadvisable, inexpedient, injudicious, undesirable **15** disadvantageous

unaesthetic **9** tasteless **10** inartistic **11** insensitive **16** undiscriminating

unaffected **4** open **5** frank, naive, plain **6** candid, direct, honest, simple **7** genuine, natural, sincere, unmoved **8** innocent 9 childlike, guileless, ingenuous, unfeeling, unstirred, untouched, unworldly, wholesome 10 impervious, unbothered, unreserved 11 indifferent, insensitive, openhearted, plain-spoken, unconcerned, undesigning, undisturbed 12 unresponsive 13 unsympathetic 15 straightforward, unsophisticated

unaffectedness 4 ease 11 naturalness 12 unconstraint

unafraid 4 bold 5 brave 6 daring, heroic, plucky 7 valiant 8 fearless, intrepid, stalwart, valorous 9 audacious, daredevil, dauntless 10 courageous 11 indomitable, lionhearted, venturesome 12 stouthearted 13 adventuresome

unaggressive 3 shy 4 meek 5 timid 7 passive 8 peaceful, timorous 9 peaceable, shrinking 11 unambitious 14 unenterprising

unagitated 4 calm 6 gentle, placid, serene 8 composed, tranquil 9 collected, unexcited, unruffled 10 untroubled 11 undisturbed, unperturbed 13 self-possessed

unalloyed 4 pure 7 unmixed 11 unqualified 13 unadulterated

unalterable 5 fixed, rigid 6 stable 8 constant 9 immutable, indelible, obstinate, permanent, perennial 10 inflexible, persistent 11 irrevocable 12 indissoluble, unchangeable 13 irretrievable

unambitious 4 easy, lazy 6 humble, modest, simple 8 slothful 10 unaspiring 12 unaggressive 14 unenterprising

unamiable 4 sour 5 cross, surly, testy 6 sullen 7 grouchy, hostile, peevish 8 churlish 9 irascible 10 ill-humored, unfriendly, unpleasant, unsociable 11 bad-tempered, uncongenial 12 disagreeable

unamorous 4 cold, cool 6 frigid 8 unloving 11 passionless

unanimated 4 dull, flat, limp 5 inert, vapid 7 insipid 8 lifeless 10 insentient 11 unconscious

unanimity 6 accord 7 concord, harmony 9 agreement, consensus 11 concordance, concurrence 17 meeting of the minds

unanimous 6 allied, united

9 accordant, consonant, of one mind 10 harmonious, likeminded

unannounced 6 secret, sudden 8 surprise, withheld 10 suppressed, unheralded 11 undisclosed, unlooked for, unpublished 12 unadvertised 13 unanticipated

unanticipated 6 sudden 8 surprise 10 unexpected, unforeseen, unheralded 11 unannounced, unlooked-for, unpredicted

unappealing 10 disgusting, uninviting, unpleasant 11 displeasing 12 disagreeable, unappetizing, unattractive

unappetizing 6 horrid 7 insipid 10 bad-tasting, disgusting, uninviting 11 unpalatable 12 disagreeable

unapproachable 4 cold, cool 5 aloof 6 remote, unique 7 austere, awesome, distant, supreme 8 foremost, peerless, superior 9 matchless, nonpareil, unequaled, unrivaled 10 forbidding, inimitable, preeminent 11 beyond reach, stand-offish, unreachable 12 inaccessible, incomparable, intimidating, second to none, unattainable, unparalleled 13 beyond compare

unasked 6 wanton 8 unbidden, unsought, unwanted 9 uninvited, unwelcome 10 gratuitous 11 uncalled-for, undesirable, unrequested, unsolicited

unassertive 3 shy 5 timid 6 humble, modest 7 bashful 8 sheepish 9 diffident, shrinking

unassertiveness 7 modesty, shyness 8 docility, timidity 9 timidness 10 diffidence, humbleness 11 bashfulness 12 sheepishness

unassuming 5 muted, plain 6 homely, modest, simple 7 natural 9 easygoing 11 unassertive, unobtrusive 13 unpretentious 14 unostentatious

unattached 5 apart, split 6 single 8 detached, separate 9 separated 11 unconnected 12 disconnected

unattractive 4 dull, ugly 5 plain 6 homely 8 frumpish 11 unappealing, undesirable 12 unappetizing

unauthentic 4 fake, mock, sham 5 bogus, false, phony 6 untrue 7 dubious 8 doubtful 9 imitation, synthetic

10 fraudulent 11 counterfeit 12 questionable

unauthenticated 8 disputed 10 apocryphal, unverified 15 unsubstantiated

unauthorized 6 banned, covert 7 furtive 8 outlawed, unlawful 9 concealed, unallowed, underhand 10 prohibited, unapproved, unofficial 11 clandestine, uncertified, unpermitted, unwarranted 12 unaccredited, unsanctioned 13 under-the-table

unavailable 5 taken 6 scarce 7 lacking, married 9 not at hand 10 nonpresent 11 nonexistent

unavailing 4 idle, vain, weak 5 empty, inept 6 futile, no good 7 invalid, useless 8 bootless, impotent 9 fruitless, worthless 11 ineffective, ineffectual 12 unproductive, unsuccessful

unavoidable 4 sure 5 fated, fixed 7 certain 9 necessary, requisite 10 compulsory, imperative, inevitable, obligatory 11 inescapable 13 unpreventable 14 uncontrollable

unaware 8 heedless, ignorant, unwarned 9 in the dark, unalerted, unknowing, unmindful 10 unapprised 11 incognizant, unconscious 12 off one's guard, unacquainted, unsuspecting 13 unenlightened

unawares 8 abruptly, by chance, suddenly 9 by mistake 10 by accident, by surprise, mistakenly 11 unknowingly, unwittingly 12 accidentally, out of nowhere, unexpectedly, unthinkingly 13 inadvertently, involuntarily, unconsciously 14 without warning 15 unintentionally 16 like a thunderbolt 20 like a bolt from the blue, like a thief in the night

unbalanced 3 mad 4 daft, loco 5 batty, nutty, wacky 6 crazed, uneven, warped 7 bonkers, cracked, leaning, unequal, unglued, unsound 8 demented, deranged, lopsided, unhinged, unpoised, unstable, unsteady 9 disturbed, illogical, psychotic, unsettled 10 irrational, unadjusted 11 not all there 12 psychopathic

unbearable 11 intolerable, unendurable, unthinkable 12 inadmissible, insufferable, unacceptable 13 insupportable

unbecoming 4 ugly **6** homely, vulgar **8** improper, unfitted, unseemly, unsuited **9** offensive, tasteless, unsightly **10** indecorous, unsuitable **11** unappealing, unbefitting **12** unattractive **13** inappropriate

unbelief 5 doubt **7** dubiety **9** disbelief **10** skepticism **11** incredulity **12** doubtfulness

unbelievable 5 false **6** absurd, insane **7** amazing, asinine, idiotic **10** astounding, farfetched, incredible, irrational, remarkable, ridiculous **11** astonishing **12** preposterous, unimaginable, unreasonable **13** hard to swallow

unbeliever 7 atheist, heathen infidel, skeptic **8** apostate **10** godless one **11** disbeliever, nonbeliever

unbelieving 7 dubious **8** doubting **9** quizzical, skeptical **10** suspicious **11** distrustful, incredulous, questioning, unconvinced **12** disbelieving, nonbelieving

unbend 5 relax **6** relent, unflex **10** straighten **12** straighten up **13** straighten out

unbending 4 firm **5** rigid, stiff, tough **6** severe, strict **8** stubborn **9** obstinate **10** inflexible, stone-faced, unyielding **11** hard as nails **14** uncompromising

unbent 5 erect **7** relaxed, unbowed, upright, yielded **8** relented, straight, uncurved, unflexed **9** unstooped **12** straightened

unbiased 4 fair, just **7** liberal, neutral **8** detached, tolerant **9** impartial, unbigoted **10** fair-minded, open-minded, undogmatic **11** broad-minded **12** uninfluenced, unprejudiced **13** disinterested, dispassionate

unbigoted 8 tolerant, unbiased **10** open-minded **11** broad-minded **12** unprejudiced

unbind 4 free, undo **5** loose, untie **6** detach, loosen, ungird **7** deliver, release, undress **8** let loose, unfasten

unblamable 5 clear **8** innocent **9** blameless, guiltless, not guilty **10** inculpable, not at fault **14** not responsible

unblemished 4 pure **7** perfect **8** flawless, spotless, unmarred, unsoiled **9** unsullied **10** immaculate, unvitiated **11** white as snow **13** unadulterated **14** uncontaminated **15** clean as a whistle

unblock 4 free, open **5** unbar, unjam **6** unclog, unstop

unborn 5 fetal, later **6** coming, future, to come **7** in utero **9** embryonic **10** subsequent, succeeding **11** prospective

unbosom oneself 7 confess, confide, lay bare **15** unburden oneself

unbound 4 free **5** freed, loose **6** loosed, untied **8** detached, let loose, loosened, released **10** unconfined, unfastened **12** unrestrained

unbounded 8 absolute **9** boundless, unbridled, unlimited **12** uncontrolled, unrestrained, unrestricted **13** unconditional, unconstrained

unbreakable 5 tough **6** strong

unbroken 5 whole **6** entire, intact **7** endless **8** complete **9** ceaseless, continual, incessant, uncracked, undivided, unsmashed **10** continuous, sequential, successive, unruptured **11** consecutive, progressive, unremitting, unshattered **12** undiminished **13** uninterrupted

unbuckle 4 undo **6** loosen **7** release, unhitch, unstrap **8** uncouple, unfasten

unburden 4 free **6** reveal **7** confess, confide, relieve, unbosom **8** disclose **9** disburden **10** unencumber **11** disencumber **15** get off one's chest **18** get out of one's system

unbusinesslike 6 casual, sloppy **8** informal **11** impractical, inefficient

uncalculated 9 unplanned **10** accidental, unintended **11** inadvertent **14** unpremeditated

uncalled-for 6 wanton **7** unasked **8** needless, unneeded, unsought, unwanted **9** redundant, uninvited **10** gratuitous, unprompted **11** unjustified, unnecessary, unsolicited **12** nonessential **14** supererogatory

uncanny 5 eerie, weird **6** spooky **7** curious, strange **8** inspired **9** fantastic, intuitive, marvelous, unearthly, unheard-of, unnatural **10** incredible, mysterious, prodigious, remarkable, unexampled **11** astonishing, exceptional **12** unbelievable, unimaginable **13** extraordinary, uncomfortable

uncanonical 12 unauthorized, unscriptural

Uncas
character in: **20** The Last of the Mohicans
author: **6** Cooper

unceasing 7 endless, eternal **8** constant **9** continual, incessant, perpetual, sustained **10** continuous, persistent, without end

uncelebrated 6 unsung **7** obscure, unknown **9** anonymous **14** uncommemorated

unceremonious 4 curt, rude **5** hasty, rough **6** abrupt **7** brusque **8** informal **11** precipitate

uncertain 4 hazy **6** fitful, unsure **7** dubious, erratic, not sure, obscure, unclear **8** doubtful, hesitant, nebulous, not fixed, variable, wavering **9** debatable, undecided, unsettled **11** disputable, indefinite, indistinct, in question, irresolute, unresolved, up in the air **11** conjectural, fluctuating, not definite, speculative, unconfirmed, vacillating **12** not confident, questionable, undetermined **13** indeterminate, unpredictable

uncertainty 4 odds, risk **5** doubt **6** chance, gamble **8** quandary **9** ambiguity, confusion, hesitancy, vagueness **10** hesitation, indecision, perplexity, unsureness **11** ambivalence, vacillation **12** equivocation, irresolution, shilly-shally **14** indefiniteness

unchain 4 free **7** release, set free **8** liberate, unfetter **9** unshackle

unchangeable 5 rigid **6** stable **7** uniform **8** stubborn **9** immutable, obstinate, permanent **10** inflexible, invariable **11** unalterable **12** intransigent

unchanging 4 fast, firm **5** fixed **6** stable, static **7** abiding, durable, lasting **8** constant **9** immutable, permanent, steadfast **10** monotonous **11** everlasting **12** indissoluble

unchaperoned 10 unattended, unescorted **12** unsupervised **13** unaccompanied

uncharacteristic 8 atypical **12** out of keeping **16** unrepresentative

uncharitable 5 tight **6** stingy, unkind **7** miserly **9** illiberal, niggardly, unfeeling **10** unfriendly, ungenerous, ungracious **11** closefisted, insensitive, tightfisted **12** parsimonious **13** unsympathetic **15** uncompassionate

unchaste 4 lewd **5** loose **6** erotic, impure **7** corrupt, immoral **8** immodest **9** abandoned, debauched **10** dishonored

unchecked 4 free **5** loose **6** unruly **7** liberal, rampant **8** reinless, unreined **9** out of hand, unbridled, unmuzzled **10** unhindered **12** out of control, unrestrained, unsuppressed

uncivil 4 curt, rude **5** blunt, surly **6** abrupt, gauche **7** boorish, brusque **8** impolite **10** ungracious **11** ill-mannered **12** disagreeable, discourteous

uncivilized 4 rude **6** savage, vulgar **7** boorish, brutish, illbred, uncouth, untamed **8** barbaric, churlish **9** barbarous, obnoxious, ungenteel **10** uncultured, unpolished **12** uncultivated

unclad 4 bare, nude **5** naked **7** exposed, unrobed **8** disrobed, in the raw, starkers, stripped **9** in the nude, unclothed, uncovered, undressed **10** starknaked **15** in the altogether

unclean 4 evil, foul, tref, vile **5** dirty, dusty, grimy, messy, muddy, sooty **6** filthy, impure, soiled **7** defiled, immoral, obscene, smutted, stained **8** polluted, unchaste **9** blemished **10** besmirched

unclear 3 dim **4** hazy **5** blear, faint, foggy, fuzzy, misty, vague **6** bleary, cloudy, vapory **7** clouded, obscure, shadowy **8** shrouded, vaporous **9** ambiguous, uncertain **10** indefinite, indistinct

Uncle Remus
    author: **18** Joel Chandler Harris

Uncle Tom's Cabin
    author: **19** Harriet Beecher Stowe
    character: **5** Eliza, Topsy **10** Eva St Clare **11** Simon Legree

Uncle Vanya
    author: **12** Anton Chekhov
    character: **6** Marina **12** Mihail Astrov **13** Ivan Voynitsky (Uncle Vanya) **14** Marya Voynitsky **15** Sonya Andreyevna **16** Yelena Andreyevna **19** Alexandr Serebryakov

unclose 4 open **6** reveal, unclog, unfold, unshut, unstop, unwrap **7** unblock
    poetic: **3** ope

unclothed 4 bare, nude **5** na-

ked **6** unclad **7** exposed, unrobed **8** stripped **9** in the nude, uncovered, undressed

unclouded 5 clear, light, sunny **6** bright, serene **10** unobscured

uncollected 4 owed **5** owing, upset **6** shaken **8** agitated, troubled **9** disturbed, perturbed **11** discomposed, outstanding

uncolored 4 bald, bare, true **5** plain, stark **6** simple **9** unadorned **11** unvarnished **12** unelaborated **13** unembellished **15** straightforward

uncombed 5 messy **6** blowsy, frowzy, matted, mussed, untidy **7** ruffled, rumpled, snarled, tangled, tousled, unkempt **11** disarranged

uncomfortable 4 edgy **5** tense, upset **6** on edge, uneasy **7** awkward, keyed up, nervous, painful **8** confused, strained, troubled **9** ill at ease **10** bothersome, disquieted, irritating, out of place **11** discomfited, discomposed, distressful **13** on tenterhooks

uncommitted 9 unpledged **11** undedicated

uncommon 4 rare **5** novel **6** scarce, unique **7** bizarre, curious, notable, supreme, unusual **8** peculiar, peerless, superior **9** matchless, unmatched **10** infrequent, remarkable, unexcelled, unfamiliar **11** exceptional, outstanding, superlative **12** incomparable, unparalleled **13** extraordinary **14** unconventional **15** once in a lifetime **16** few and far between

uncommunicative 3 mum, shy **4** dumb, mute **5** quiet **6** silent **8** reserved, reticent, retiring, taciturn **9** secretive, withdrawn **10** speechless, tongue-tied, unsociable **11** untalkative **12** close-mouthed, inexpressive

uncomplicated 4 easy **5** clear, plain **6** simple **10** uninvolved

uncomplimentary 8 critical, derisive, negative **9** insulting **10** unadmiring **11** disparaging **12** disapproving, unflattering

uncompromising 4 firm **5** rigid, stiff **6** strict **8** exacting, hardline, obdurate **9** immovable, unbending, unvarying **10** inexorable, inflexible, scrupulous, unyielding **11** unrelenting

unconcealed 4 bald, bare, open **5** overt **6** in view **7** ex-

posed, in sight, obvious, visible **8** apparent, manifest, revealed **9** uncovered **11** discernible, perceivable, perceptible **12** in plain sight, out in the open

unconcentrated 4 weak **7** diffuse, diluted, thinned **9** dispersed, scattered, spread out **11** watered down

unconcern 10 dispassion **11** insouciance, nonchalance **12** indifference

unconcerned 4 cold **5** aloof **6** serene **7** distant, unaware, unmoved **8** composed, uncaring **9** apathetic, oblivious, unfeeling, unmindful **10** impervious, nonchalant, uninvolved, untroubled **11** indifferent, insensitive, passionless, unperturbed **12** unresponsive **13** unsympathetic

unconditional 5 utter **6** entire **8** absolute, complete, outright **9** downright, unlimited **10** conclusive **11** categorical, unqualified **12** unrestricted **13** thoroughgoing

Unconditional Surrender
    author: **11** Evelyn Waugh

unconfident 3 shy **5** timid **7** bashful **8** reticent, retiring, timorous **9** diffident, shrinking, uncertain

unconfirmed 7 dubious **8** unproved **10** unapproved, unverified **11** unvalidated **12** questionable **14** uncorroborated **15** unsubstantiated

unconformity 7 anomaly **9** deviation **10** aberration, divergence **11** abnormality, peculiarity **12** eccentricity, idiosyncrasy, irregularity **13** nonconformity

uncongenial 9 ill-suited, unamiable **10** dissimilar, unfriendly, unpleasant **12** disagreeable, incompatible **13** unsympathetic

unconnected 7 severed **8** detached, discrete, separate **9** uncoupled, unhitched, unrelated **12** disconnected

unconquerable 6 innate **9** ingrained **10** inveterate, invincible, unbeatable **12** impenetrable, invulnerable, undefeatable **14** insurmountable, unvanquishable

unconscionable 7 extreme **9** excessive **10** immoderate, inordinate, outrageous **11** inexcusable, unjustified, unwarranted **12** indefensible, preposterous, unforgivable, un-

pardonable, unreasonable
13 unjustifiable

unconscious 3 out **6** latent
7 in a coma, out cold **8** comatose, in a faint **9** insensate, senseless, unknowing, unmindful **10** suppressed, unrealized **11** incognizant **12** unsuspecting **14** dead to the world

unconstitutional 7 illegal
8 unlawful **12** unauthorized

unconstrained 4 bold, easy
7 natural, relaxed **8** unforced **9** abandoned **10** unaffected **11** spontaneous, uninhibited
French: **6** degage

unconstraint 4 ease **7** abandon **8** boldness, free will, openness **9** frankness **11** naturalness, spontaneity

uncontrollable 6 unruly
7 wayward **12** ungovernable, unmanageable

uncontrolled 4 free, wild
8 absolute **9** abandoned, unlimited **10** ungoverned
12 unrestrained

unconventional 3 odd **4** rare
5 crazy, kinky, nutty, queer, wacky, weird **6** far-out, quaint, unique **7** bizarre, curious, offbeat, strange, unusual **8** aberrant, atypical, bohemian, freakish, original, peculiar, singular, uncommon **9** different, eccentric, fantastic, irregular **10** newfangled, outlandish, unorthodox **11** exceptional **12** unaccustomed **13** extraordinary, idiosyncratic, nonconforming, nonconformist **15** individualistic

unconvinced 7 dubious
8 doubtful **9** skeptical, uncertain, unsettled

unconvincing 5 false, fishy
7 dubious, suspect **10** suspicious **11** implausible **12** questionable, unbelievable

uncooked
 French: **9** au naturel

uncooperative 6 ornery **7** selfish **8** perverse, stubborn **9** difficult, unhelpful, unwilling
11 intractable **12** intransigent

uncoordinated 6 clumsy
7 awkward **8** ungainly
9 graceless

uncouple 4 undo **6** detach, loosen, unhook **7** release, unhitch **8** unbuckle

uncoupled 8 detached, loosened **9** separated, unhitched
10 disengaged **11** unconnected **12** disconnected

uncourageous 5 timid **8** cow-

ardly, timorous **9** dastardly, shrinking **13** pusillanimous

uncourtly 7 ill-bred, uncivil, uncouth **9** ungallant **10** ill-behaved, ungracious, unmannerly **11** uncourteous **12** discourteous **13** ungentlemanly

uncouth 4 rude **5** crass, crude, gross, rough **6** callow, coarse
7 boorish, brutish, ill-bred, loutish, uncivil **8** barbaric, churlish, impolite **9** unrefined
10 indelicate, uncultured, unmannerly **11** ill-mannered, uncivilized **12** uncultivated

uncover 4 bare, undo **5** dig up, strip **6** denude, dig out, expose, reveal, unmask, unveil, unwrap **7** disrobe, lay bare, uncloak, undrape, undress, unearth **8** disclose, unclothe
9 make known, unsheathe
11 make visible **12** bring to light

uncovered 4 bare **5** bared, dug up, naked **7** exposed, noticed **8** detected, revealed **9** disclosed, made known **10** discovered **13** brought to view
14 brought to light

uncovering 8 exposure **9** divulging, unmasking **10** disclosure, divulgence, laying open, revelation **15** bringing to light **20** bringing out in the open

uncritical 4 dull, dumb **6** casual, obtuse, stupid **7** inexact, offhand, shallow **8** careless, ignorant, slipshod **9** imprecise, untutored **10** inaccurate, uneducated, unschooled, unthinking **11** perfunctory, superficial
12 unreflecting
16 undiscriminating

unctuous 4 oily, smug
6 smarmy **7** fawning, honeyed, servile **8** slippery, too suave
9 pietistic, too smooth **10** flattering, obsequious **11** sycophantic **12** honey-tongued, ingratiating **13** sanctimonious, self-righteous

uncultivated 3 raw **4** wild
7 uncouth **8** unfarmed, unplowed, untilled **9** unrefined
10 unimproved
11 undeveloped

uncultivated land
 god of: **8** Silvanus, Sylvanus

uncultured 5 crass **6** coarse, common, vulgar **7** low-bred
9 inelegant, unrefined **10** unpolished **12** uncultivated

uncustomary 4 rare **6** unique
7 amazing, unusual **8** singular, uncommon, unwonted
9 unheard-of **10** incredible, un-

expected **11** astonishing, exceptional **12** unaccustomed, unbelievable **13** extraordinary, unanticipated

undaunted 5 brave **6** gritty, heroic, plucky **7** unfazed, valiant **8** fearless, intrepid, resolute, stalwart, valorous **9** not put off **10** courageous, undismayed **11** indomitable, unflinching, unperturbed, unshrinking **12** stouthearted **13** undiscouraged

undeceive 8 disabuse **10** disenchant **11** disenthrall, disillusion **12** open one's eyes
13 break the spell **15** burst one's bubble **19** bring one down to earth **20** shatter one's illusions

undecided 4 open **5** vague
6 unsure **7** dubious, pending
8 not final, wavering **9** tentative, uncertain, unsettled
10 indecisive, indefinite, in abeyance, in a dilemma, irresolute, of two minds, openminded, unresolved, up in the air **11** fluctuating, vacillating
12 undetermined, unformulated **16** hemming and hawing **17** blowing hot and cold
20 going around in circles

undecorated 4 bare **5** blank, plain, stark **6** simple **7** austere **9** unadorned
13 unembellished

undedicated 11 indifferent, uncommitted

undefiled 4 pure **5** clean
6 chaste, intact, virgin **7** natural **8** innocent, spotless
9 stainless, unsullied
10 unpolluted

undemanding 4 easy **6** lowkey, simple **7** patient, relaxed
9 easygoing **10** submissive
12 easy to please, laissez-faire
14 live-and-let-live

undemonstrative 3 shy
4 cold **5** aloof **7** distant, stoical **8** reserved **9** impassive
11 unemotional **12** inexpressive, unresponsive **14** selfcontrolled

undeniable 4 sure **6** patent, proven **7** certain, obvious
8 decisive, manifest **10** conclusive **11** established, indubitable, irrefutable **12** beyond a doubt, demonstrable, indisputable **13** incontestable **14** unquestionable
16 incontrovertible

undeniably 6 surely **9** certainly **10** decisively, definitely
11 irrefutably **12** conclusively, demonstrably, indisputably
13 incontestably **14** beyond

question, unquestionably **16** incontrovertibly

undependable 6 fickle **7** erratic, flighty **8** unstable, variable, wavering **10** capricious, changeable, inconstant, unreliable **13** irresponsible, unpredictable, untrustworthy

under 3 sub **5** below, lower, neath, short **7** beneath **8** inferior, less than **9** because of **11** subordinate

undercover 3 sly **6** covert, hidden, secret **7** furtive, sub rosa **8** hush-hush, stealthy **9** concealed, disguised, incognito **10** unrevealed **11** clandestine, undisclosed **12** confidential **13** surreptitious
French: **8** a couvert

undercurrent 4 aura, hint, mood **5** sense, tinge, vibes **7** quality, riptide **8** undertow **9** undertone **10** atmosphere, intimation, suggestion, vibrations **12** crosscurrent

undercut 9 discredit, undermine, undersell **10** compromise

underestimate 7 dismiss, put down **8** belittle, minimize, misjudge **9** deprecate, discredit, disparage, disregard, sell short, underrate, undersell **10** depreciate, undervalue **11** detract from **12** miscalculate

undergarment 3 bra **4** BVDs, slip **5** pants, shift, teddy **6** corset, girdle, shorts **7** chemise, panties **8** bloomers, camisole, knickers, lingerie, skivvies **9** brassiere, petticoat, union suit **12** jockey shorts

undergo 5 brave, stand **6** endure, suffer **7** sustain, weather **8** submit to **9** encounter, go through, withstand **10** experience

undergraduate 4 coed, soph **5** frosh, plebe **6** junior, senior **7** scholar, student **8** freshman **9** sophomore, undegreed **10** degreeless, nondegreed **13** underclassman, upperclassman

underground 6 buried, covert, secret **7** sub-rosa **10** undercover **11** belowground, clandestine **12** subterranean **13** surreptitious **15** below the surface

underground chamber 4 tomb **5** crypt, vault **6** cellar **8** catacomb **9** sepulcher

underhand, underhanded 6 covert, crafty, sneaky, tricky **7** corrupt, crooked, cunning, devious, evasive, furtive,

illegal **8** sneaking, stealthy **9** conniving, dishonest, unethical **10** fraudulent **12** unprincipled, unscrupulous **13** surreptitious

underhandedness 5 guile **6** deceit **7** slyness **8** trickery **9** chicanery, deception, duplicity **10** sneakiness, trickiness **13** secretiveness

underline 6 accent, stress **7** dwell on, point up **9** emphasize, press home **10** accentuate, underscore **15** bring into relief

underling 4 serf **6** flunky, lackey, menial, minion, thrall, vassal **7** servant, subject **8** employee, hireling, inferior **9** attendant, hired hand **11** subordinate

underlying 5 basic **6** covert **7** beneath, radical **8** implicit **9** elemental, essential **10** subtending **11** fundamental

undermine 4 foil, ruin **5** erode **6** injure, riddle, scotch, thwart, weaken **7** cripple, destroy, subvert, torpedo **8** sabotage **9** eat away at, frustrate, hamstring **10** neutralize **11** burrow under, tunnel under

underneath 5 below, lower **6** bottom, hidden **9** disguised, subject to **14** misrepresented

undernourished 8 starving, underfed **12** malnourished

under obligation 5 bound **6** liable **7** obliged **8** beholden, indebted **9** obligated **10** answerable, in one's debt **11** accountable, responsible

underpart 4 sole **5** belly, tails **6** bottom **9** lower side, underside

underpin 4 bear **7** bolster, support **10** strengthen **12** substantiate

underpinning 4 base **5** basic **6** ground **7** support **9** essential **10** foundation, groundwork **11** fundamental **12** substructure

underplay 8 play down **11** deemphasize

underprivileged 4 poor **5** needy **6** in need **7** hapless, unlucky **8** badly-off, deprived, ill-fated, indigent **9** destitute, penniless, penurious **10** ill-starred, pauperized **11** handicapped, unfortunate **12** impoverished **13** disadvantaged **22** in adverse circumstances

underrate 6 slight **8** belittle, derogate, minimize **9** deni-

grate, deprecate, disparage **10** depreciate, undervalue **13** underestimate

underscore 4 mark **6** accent, deepen, play up, stress **7** feature, point up **8** heighten **9** emphasize, intensify, press home, underline **10** accentuate **15** draw attention to

underscoring 6 stress **8** emphasis **11** underlining

underside 4 back, sole **5** belly, tails **6** bottom **7** reverse **9** lower side, underpart

undersized 4 tiny **5** elfin, short, small **6** little, petite, slight **7** stunted **8** dwarfish **10** diminutive **11** lilliputian

underskirt 4 slip **7** pannier **9** crinoline, hoopskirt, petticoat

understand 3 dig, get, see **4** hear, know, read, take **5** grasp, learn **6** absorb, accept, assume, can see, fathom, gather, take it **7** be aware, discern, make out, presume, realize **8** conclude, perceive **9** apprehend, interpret, recognize **10** appreciate, comprehend, take to mean **14** sympathize with, take for granted

understandable 8 apparent **12** recognizable, unmistakable **14** comprehensible

understanding 4 pact **5** grasp **7** empathy, insight, knowing **8** sympathy, tolerant **9** agreement, awareness, intuition, knowledge, sensitive **10** cognizance, compassion, compromise, discerning, perception, perceptive, responsive **11** concordance, sensitivity, sympathetic **12** appreciation, appreciative, apprehension **13** compassionate, comprehension **17** meeting of the minds

understate 8 minimize **11** deemphasize

understated 9 minimized **10** restrained **12** conservative, deemphasized

understatement 7 litotes **10** minimizing **20** conservative estimate

understudy 3 sub **6** backup, double, fill-in, relief **7** standby, stand-in **9** alternate, surrogate **10** substitute **11** pinch hitter, replacement

undertake 3 try **5** begin, essay, start **6** assume, strive, tackle, take on **7** attempt **8** commence, embark on, endeavor, set about, shoulder **9** agree to do, enter upon **11** promise to do **13** get involved in

undertaking 3 job **4** task **6** effort **7** concern, project, pursuit, venture **8** endeavor **10** commitment, enterprise

Under the Greenwood Tree
author: **11** Thomas Hardy

under the influence 5 drunk **6** sodden, soused, wasted, zapped, zonked **7** smashed **8** besotted **9** plastered **10** inebriated **11** intoxicated **20** three sheets to the wind

under the weather 3 bad, ill **4** sick **6** ailing, sickly, unwell **9** unhealthy **10** indisposed

undertone 4 aura, hint, mood **5** scent, sense, tinge, trace **6** flavor, mumble, murmur, nuance **7** feeling, inkling, low tone, quality, whisper **8** coloring **10** atmosphere, intimation, suggestion **11** connotation, implication **12** subdued voice, undercurrent

undervalue 6 slight **8** belittle, derogate **9** discredit, disparage, underrate **10** depreciate **13** underestimate

underwear 3 bra **4** BVDs, slip **5** pants, teddy **6** briefs, corset, girdle, shorts **7** chemise, panties **8** bloomers, camisole, knickers, lingerie, skivvies **9** brassiere, petticoat, union suit **12** jockey shorts, smallclothes **14** unmentionables

underweight 4 bony, lank **5** gaunt, lanky **6** skinny **7** scrawny, spindly **8** skeletal, underfed **9** emaciated **12** skin-and-bones **13** hollow-cheeked **14** spindle-shanked, undernourished

underworld 4 Hell **5** Hades, limbo **6** the mob **8** mobsters, the Mafia **9** criminals, gangsters, purgatory **10** Cosa Nostra **11** shades below **12** the syndicate **13** bottomless pit, nether regions **14** organized crime **15** criminal element, infernal regions **16** abode of the damned
god of: **3** Dis **5** Hades, Orcus, Pluto **8** Dis Pater

under wraps 6 hidden, secret **9** concealed **10** suppressed, under cover

underwrite 3 aid **4** back **7** approve, endorse, finance, sponsor, support, warrant **8** invest in, sanction, validate **9** guarantee, subsidize **11** countersign

underwriter 5 angel **6** backer, patron **7** sponsor **8** investor **9** financier, guarantor

undeserving 3 bad **8** inferior, unworthy

undesirable 5 unfit **8** disliked, improper, unbidden, unsavory, unseemly, unwanted, unworthy **9** offensive, unpopular **10** unbecoming, uninviting, unsuitable, unwelcomed **11** distasteful, unbefitting, unwished-for **12** disagreeable, inadmissible, unacceptable, unattractive **13** inappropriate, objectionable **14** unsatisfactory

undetectable 12 unnoticeable, unobservable **13** imperceptible, unsubstantial

undetermined 6 chance **7** unfixed, unknown **8** unproved, unproven **9** uncertain, undecided **10** indefinite, irresolute **13** indeterminate, unascertained

undeveloped 3 raw **5** crude, green **6** callow, unripe **8** immature, inchoate, unformed **9** embryonic, half-baked **10** unfinished **11** rudimentary, unexploited **12** uncultivated

undignified 3 low **7** boorish **8** improper, shameful, unseemly, unworthy **9** degrading, inelegant, tasteless, unrefined **10** beneath one, indecorous, indelicate, in bad taste, unbecoming, unladylike, unsuitable **11** unbefitting **13** discreditable, inappropriate, ungentlemanly **18** beneath one's dignity
Latin: **8** infra dig **15** infra dignitatem

undiluted 4 neat, pure **5** sheer **7** unmixed **8** straight **11** unfortified **12** full-strength **13** unadulterated

Undine
form: **6** spirit
location: **5** water
sex: **6** female

undiscerning 11 insensitive **12** unperceptive **14** indiscriminate

undisciplined 4 wild **6** fickle, fitful **7** erratic, wayward, willful **8** unsteady, untaught **9** mercurial, untrained, untutored **10** capricious, changeable, inconstant, uneducated, unfinished, unreliable, unschooled **11** unpracticed **12** obstreperous, uncontrolled, undependable, unrestrained **13** unpredictable

undisclosed 6 hidden, secret **7** private **9** concealed **10** unrevealed **12** confidential

undisguised 4 open **5** clear, utter **7** evident, obvious **8** com-

plete, distinct, manifest, unhidden **9** out-and-out **10** plain as day, pronounced, unreserved **11** unconcealed **12** unmistakable, wholehearted **13** thoroughgoing **24** plain as the nose on one's face

undismayed 7 uncowed **8** unafraid, unscared **9** confident, unabashed, unalarmed, undaunted **12** unfrightened **13** undiscouraged, unintimidated

undisputed 4 sure **7** certain, granted **8** accepted **9** undoubted **10** conclusive, undeniable **11** beyond doubt, indubitable, irrefutable, past dispute, uncontested **12** acknowledged, indisputable, unchallenged, unquestioned **13** a matter of fact, incontestable **14** beyond question, freely admitted, unquestionable **15** without question **16** incontrovertible

undistinguished 5 plain, usual **6** common **7** prosaic **8** everyday, mediocre, ordinary **10** pedestrian, unexciting **11** commonplace **12** run-of-the-mill, unremarkable **13** unexceptional **18** nothing to rave about

undistracted 4 calm **6** serene, stolid **7** unfazed **9** impassive, unruffled **10** untroubled **11** undisturbed

undisturbed 4 calm, cool **5** quiet **6** placid, serene, steady **7** equable, unmoved **8** composed, peaceful, tranquil **9** collected, inviolate, unexcited, unruffled, untouched **10** of solitude, unagitated, unbothered, untroubled **11** left in order, unperturbed **13** imperturbable, self-possessed, uninterrupted

undivided 5 solid, whole **6** entire, united **7** unified, unsplit **8** complete **9** of one mind, unanimous **10** not divided, unstinting **12** wholehearted

undo 3 end **4** free, open, ruin, void **5** annul, erase, loose, quash, untie **6** cancel, defeat, loosen, offset, repair, unbind, unfold, unhook, unknot, unlace, unlock, unwrap **7** destroy, nullify, rectify, reverse, subvert, unchain, unravel, wipe out **8** demolish, overturn, unbutton, unfasten **9** disengage, eliminate, make up for, undermine **10** counteract, invalidate, neutralize **11** disentangle **13** compensate for **14** counterbalance

undogmatic 7 liberal **8** flexible, tolerant **10** open-minded **11** broad-minded

undoing 4 doom, jinx, ruin **5** upset **6** defeat **7** erasure, nemesis **8** collapse, downfall, negation, reversal, weakness **9** annulment, breakdown, overthrow, ruination, thwarting, wiping out **11** cause of ruin, destruction **12** Achilles' heel, cancellation, invalidation **13** counteraction, nullification **14** neutralization

undomesticated 4 wild **5** feral **6** ferine, savage **7** untamed **8** barbaric **9** barbarous **11** uncivilized

undone 6 ruined **9** come apart, destroyed **10** incomplete, unfastened **12** not completed

undoubted 4 sure **5** utter **7** certain **8** absolute, complete, definite, positive **11** indubitable, unequivocal **12** indisputable **13** unimpeachable **14** unquestionable

undoubtedly 6 surely **7** no doubt **9** assuredly, certainly, decidedly, doubtless **10** absolutely, definitely, positively, undeniably **11** indubitably **12** beyond a doubt, unmistakably, without doubt **13** unequivocally **14** beyond question, unquestionably **15** without question

undress 5 strip **6** nudity **7** disrobe, uncover, undrape **8** disarray, unclothe **9** nakedness **10** dishabille **18** take off one's clothes

undressed 4 bare, nude **5** naked **6** unclad **7** denuded, exposed, unrobed **8** disrobed, stripped, undraped **9** unclothed, uncovered

Undset, Sigrid
author of: **6** The Axe **20** Kristin Lavransdatter, The Master of Hestviken

undue 6 unmeet **8** impolite, improper, needless, overmuch, too great, unseemly, unworthy **9** excessive, tasteless **10** ill-advised, indiscreet, in bad taste, inordinate, not fitting, unbecoming, unsuitable **11** superfluous, uncalled-for, unjustified, unnecessary, unwarranted **13** inappropriate, objectionable

undulate 4 coil **5** slink, weave **9** fluctuate **11** rise and fall

undulating 4 wavy **5** bumpy **6** uneven

undulation 7 coiling **8** slinking,

twisting **10** contortion **11** convolution **16** rising and falling

undutiful 6 remiss **8** disloyal **11** disobedient

undying 6 steady **7** abiding, endless, eternal, lasting **8** constant, enduring, immortal, unending, unfading, untiring **9** continual, deathless, incessant, perennial, permanent, perpetual, unceasing **10** continuing **11** everlasting, never-ending, unfaltering, unrelenting, unremitting **12** imperishable, never-failing, undiminished **13** uninterrupted **14** indestructible

unearth 4 find, show **5** dig up **6** dig out, exhume, expose, reveal **7** display, divulge, exhibit, root out, uncover **8** disclose, discover, disinter, dredge up, excavate **9** disentomb, ferret out **10** come across, come up with **12** bring to light

unearthly 5 awful, eerie, weird **6** absurd **7** extreme, ghostly, phantom, strange, uncanny, ungodly, unusual **8** abnormal, ethereal, spectral, terrible **10** horrendous, unpleasant **11** disembodied, incorporeal, unspeakable **12** disagreeable, extramundane, supernatural **13** extraordinary, preternatural

unease 5 worry **7** tension **8** disquiet **9** misgiving **10** discomfort, uneasiness **11** disquietude **12** apprehension

uneasiness 5 dread **6** dismay **7** anxiety **9** agitation, misgiving **10** discomfort, foreboding **11** disquietude, distraction, nervousness **12** apprehension, discomfiture, discomposure, perturbation **16** apprehensiveness

uneasy 4 edgy **5** nervy, tense, upset **6** on edge, queasy, unsure **7** awkward, irksome, nervous, uptight, worried **8** strained, troubled, worrying **9** disturbed, ill at ease, perturbed, upsetting **10** bothersome, disquieted, disturbing, unpleasant **11** constrained, disquieting **12** apprehensive **13** uncomfortable

uneatable 8 inedible **11** not fit to eat

uneconomical 4 dear **6** costly **8** wasteful **9** expensive **10** exorbitant, high-priced, immoderate, overpriced **11** extravagant **12** unreasonable

uneducated 8 ignorant, untaught **9** unlearned, untrained,

untutored 10 illiterate, uncultured, unlettered, unschooled **12** uncultivated, uninstructed **13** unenlightened

unelaborated 4 bald, bare **5** plain, stark **6** simple **9** essential, unadorned, uncolored **11** fundamental, unvarnished **13** unembellished **15** straightforward

unembellished 4 bald, bare **5** naked, plain, stark **7** austere **9** unadorned **11** undecorated **12** unornamented

unemotional 4 cold, cool **6** formal, remote **7** distant **8** lukewarm, reserved **9** apathetic, impassive, unfeeling **11** indifferent, passionless, unconcerned **12** unresponsive **15** undemonstrative

unemployed 4 axed, idle **5** fired **6** canned, sacked, unused **7** bounced, jobless, laid-off **8** workless **9** at leisure, at liberty, booted-out, dismissed, on the dole, on welfare, out of a job, out of work **10** discharged, unoccupied **11** pink-slipped

unencumbered 4 free **6** vacant **7** unladen **8** expedite **10** unburdened, unhindered **13** unhandicapped

unending 6 steady **7** endless, eternal, lasting **8** constant, enduring **9** continual, incessant, perennial, permanent, perpetual, unceasing **10** continuous, unwavering **11** everlasting, never-ending, unremitting **12** undiminished **13** uninterrupted

unendurable 7 racking **9** agonizing, torturous **10** tormenting, unbearable **11** intolerable **12** excruciating, insufferable

unenlightened 8 ignorant **9** in the dark, unlearned **10** uneducated, uninformed **11** uninitiated **12** uninstructed

unenterprising 4 lazy **11** unambitious **12** unaggressive

unenthusiastic 8 lukewarm **10** unspirited **11** halfhearted, indifferent **13** unimpassioned

unequal 6 biased, uneven, unfair, unjust, unlike **7** bigoted, partial **9** different, disparate, unmatched **10** dissimilar, not uniform, prejudiced **11** inequitable

unequaled 7 supreme **8** peerless **9** matchless, paramount, unmatched, unrivaled **10** consummate, unexcelled **11** ne plus ultra, unsurpassed **12** incomparable, second to none,

unapproached, unparalleled
13 beyond compare **16** beyond comparison

unequivocable 4 bald **5** utter **8** outright **9** out-and-out **11** categorical, unqualified

unequivocal 5 clear, final **7** certain **8** absolute, clear-cut, decisive, definite, emphatic **11** unambiguous **12** indisputable **13** incontestable **16** incontrovertible

unequivocally 7 clearly **9** certainly, downright **10** completely, decisively, definitely, thoroughly **12** emphatically, indisputably, unmistakably **13** incontestably **14** unquestionably, wholeheartedly **16** incontrovertibly

unerring 4 sure **7** certain, precise **8** constant, faithful, reliable **9** faultless, unfailing **10** infallible, unchanging

unessential 8 nonvital **9** accessory, extrinsic **10** disposable, expendable **11** dispensable, superfluous, unimportant, unnecessary **12** nonessential

unethical 5 dirty, shady, wrong **6** shoddy, unfair **7** devious **8** unworthy **9** dishonest, underhand **10** unladylike **12** dishonorable, disreputable, questionable, unprincipled **13** ungentlemanly **14** unconscionable

uneven 4 awry, bent **5** bumpy, lumpy, rough **6** angled, coarse, craggy, curved, jagged, tilted, unfair, unjust, unlike **7** crooked, not flat, slanted, sloping, unequal **8** lopsided, not level, not plumb, onesided, unsmooth **9** different, disparate **10** dissimilar, illmatched, unbalanced

unevenness 7 oddness **9** bumpiness, lumpiness, roughness **10** jaggedness, ruggedness **11** crookedness **12** irregularity **14** changeableness

uneventful 4 dull **5** quiet, usual **6** boring **7** average, humdrum, prosaic, routine, tedious **8** ordinary, standard, tiresome **10** monotonous **11** commonplace **12** conventional **13** insignificant, unexceptional, uninteresting

unexcelled 7 supreme **8** flawless, peerless, superior, unbeaten **9** faultless, matchless, unequaled, unmatched, unrivaled **10** consummate **11** unsurpassed **12** incomparable, second to none, transcendent,

unapproached, unparalleled
13 beyond compare

unexceptional 5 usual **6** normal **7** mundane, typical **8** ordinary, standard **9** customary **12** conventional, run of the mill

unexcited 4 calm, cool **6** placid, serene **7** unmoved **8** composed, detached **9** collected, unruffled **11** undisturbed, unemotional **13** dispassionate, unimpassioned

unexciting 4 dull, flat **5** vapid **6** boring **7** insipid **10** lackluster

unexpected 6 sudden **9** startling, unplanned **10** accidental, surprising, undesigned, unforeseen, unintended **11** astonishing, unlooked-for, unpredicted **12** out of the blue **13** unanticipated, unintentional

unextinguished 5 alive **10** unquenched **12** still burning

unfaded 5 fresh **6** bright **8** undimmed **10** unwithered

unfailing 4 true **5** loyal **6** steady **7** endless **8** constant, enduring, faithful, reliable **9** continual **10** continuous, dependable, infallible, unchanging, unwavering **12** neverfailing **13** inexhaustible

unfair 4 foul **5** dirty **6** biased, unjust **7** corrupt, crooked, partial, unequal **8** not right, onesided, partisan **9** dishonest, underhand, unethical **10** not cricket, prejudiced **11** inequitable **12** dishonorable, unprincipled, unreasonable, unscrupulous **14** unconscionable

unfaithful 5 false **6** faulty, untrue **7** inexact **8** disloyal, unchaste **9** deceitful, distorted, erroneous, faithless, imperfect **10** adulterous, inaccurate, inconstant, perfidious **11** not accurate, treacherous **12** falsehearted **13** untrustworthy

Unfaithfully Yours
director: **14** Preston Sturges
cast: **10** Rudy Vallee **11** Rex Harrison **12** Edgar Kennedy, Linda Darnell **15** Barbara Lawrence

unfaithfulness 7 falsity, perfidy **9** falseness, treachery **10** disloyalty, fickleness, infidelity **11** inconstancy **13** faithlessness **14** perfidiousness

unfaltering 4 firm, sure **6** steady **8** enduring, resolute **9** obstinate, steadfast, unfail-

ing **10** dependable, persistent, unflagging, unswerving, unwavering **11** persevering, undeviating **12** never-failing, wholehearted

unfamiliar 3 new **5** novel **6** exotic, unique **7** curious, foreign, strange, unknown, unusual **9** different **10** ignorant of, unversed in **11** a stranger to, little known, out-of-theway, unexposed to, uninitiated, unskilled in **12** not well-known, unacquainted, unconversant **13** not acquainted, unpracticed in **14** unaccustomed to **15** inexperienced in, uninformed about **18** unenlightened about

unfamiliarity 9 ignorance **11** strangeness **12** inexperience **15** lack of knowledge

unfashionable 5 dated, dowdy, passe **6** frumpy, old-hat **8** outmoded **9** out-of-date, unstylish **12** old-fashioned

unfasten 4 undo **5** unpin, untie **6** detach, unbind, unbolt, unhook, unlace, unlash, unlink, unlock **7** unclose, unhitch, unlatch, unstick **8** unbutton, uncouple

unfastened 5 apart, undid **6** undone, untied **7** severed, unlaced, unstuck **8** detached, unhooked **9** unbuckled, uncoupled, unhitched **11** unconnected **12** disconnected

unfathomable 4 deep, vast **6** arcane, remote, subtle **7** complex, extreme, obscure **8** abstract, abstruse, esoteric, profound, puzzling **9** enigmatic **10** bottomless, perplexing **16** hard to understand, incomprehensible

unfavorable 3 bad **4** poor **7** adverse, unhappy **8** unsuited, untimely **9** ill-suited **10** illfavored, regretable **11** inopportune, regrettable, unfortunate, unpromising **12** inauspicious, inconvenient, infelicitous, unpropitious, unseasonable **15** disadvantageous

unfeasible 10 impossible, infeasible, unsuitable, unworkable **11** impractical **12** unachievable **13** impracticable

unfeeling 4 cold **5** cruel **9** heartless **11** hardhearted, insensitive **13** unsympathetic

unfeigned 4 real, true **7** genuine, sincere **10** unaffected

unfetter 4 free **7** release, set free, unchain **8** liberate **9** unshackle

unfilled 4 open **5** blank, empty **6** hollow, vacant **7** drained **9** available **10** unoccupied

unfinished 5 crude, rough **6** undone **7** lacking, sketchy, wanting **8** immature **9** deficient, imperfect, unnatural, unpainted, unrefined, unstained **10** incomplete, unexecuted, unpolished **11** uncompleted, unfulfilled, unlacquered, unvarnished

unfit 4 sick, weak **5** frail **6** infirm, not fit, sickly **7** not up to, unequal, unready, unsound, useless **8** delicate, disabled, unsuited **9** incapable, not suited, unhealthy, unskilled, untrained **10** inadequate, ineligible, not equal to, unequipped, unprepared, unsuitable **11** debilitated, illequipped, incompetent, ineffective, inefficient, not designed, unqualified **12** ill-contrived, not cut out for **13** inappropriate, incapacitated

unflagging 4 firm **5** fixed **6** steady **7** staunch **8** constant, enduring, resolute, tireless, unshaken, untiring **9** steadfast, tenacious, undaunted **10** determined, persistent, relentless, undrooping, unswerving, unwavering, unyielding **11** indomitable, persevering, undeviating, unfaltering, unremitting **13** indefatigable **14** uncompromising

unflappable 4 calm, cool **6** placid, serene **8** composed **9** collected **10** cool-headed **11** unexcitable **13** imperturbable, self-possessed

unflinching 4 firm, game **6** gritty, plucky, steady, strong **7** staunch **8** fearless, resolute, stalwart, unshaken **9** steadfast, tenacious, unabashed, undaunted **10** persistent, unswerving, unwavering, unyielding **11** indomitable, unfaltering, unshrinking **12** unhesitating

unfold 4 bare, show, tell **6** open up, reveal, unfurl, unroll, unveil, unwrap **7** divulge, explain, expound, lay open, open out, present, recount, uncover **8** describe, disclose, set forth **9** elucidate, explicate, make known, spread out **10** stretch out

unfolding 4 rise **5** birth, start **9** beginning, evolution, inception, unfurling **10** revelation **11** development

unforced 4 easy **5** frank **6** candid, casual **7** natural, relaxed

8 informal **9** easygoing **10** unaffected **13** unconstrained

unforeseen 6 abrupt, sudden **8** surprise **9** unplanned **10** accidental, surprising, unexpected, unintended **11** unlooked-for, unpredicted **12** out of the blue **13** unanticipated

unforeseen danger 7 pitfall **8** exigency **9** emergency **11** contingency

unforgettable 7 notable **8** eventful, exciting **9** important, memorable, thrilling **10** noteworthy **11** significant

unfortunate 5 sorry **6** cursed, jinxed, woeful **7** hapless, unblest, unhappy, unlucky **8** illfated, ill-timed, luckless, untimely, wretched **10** disastrous, ill-advised, ill-starred **11** inopportune, regrettable, unfavorable **12** inauspicious, infelicitous, unpropitious, unprosperous, unsuccessful

unfounded 4 idle **5** false **6** untrue **8** baseless, spurious **9** erroneous **10** fabricated, groundless

unfrequented 5 empty **6** lonely **7** remote, uncouth **8** isolated, solitary **9** unvisited **11** out-of-the-way **16** off the beaten path

unfriendly 4 cold **5** aloof **6** at odds, chilly **7** distant, haughty, hostile, warlike **8** inimical, snobbish **9** on the outs, reclusive, withdrawn **10** ungracious, unsociable **11** belligerent, contentious, quarrelsome, uncongenial **12** antagonistic, disagreeable, disputatious, inhospitable **13** at loggerheads, at sword's point, unsympathetic

unfruitful 4 vain **6** barren, fallow, futile **7** useless, wornout **8** infecund **9** fruitless **10** unavailing **11** purposeless, unrewarding **12** impoverished, unproductive, unprofitable **14** unremunerative

unfulfilled 8 thwarted **10** frustrated, unrealized **11** unsatisfied
  French: **6** manque

unfurl 4 open **6** expand, spread, unfold, unroll **7** develop, roll out **8** shake out **9** spread out

ungainly 5 stiff **6** clumsy, klutzy **7** awkward **9** lumbering, maladroit **10** ungraceful **13** uncoordinated

ungallant 4 rude **7** boorish, uncivil, uncouth **8** impolite **9** uncourtly **10** ill-behaved, un-

gracious, unmannerly **11** illmannered, uncourteous **12** discourteous **13** ungentlemanly

ungenerous 4 mean, near **5** close, cruel, petty, small, venal **6** greedy, shabby, sordid, stingy **7** miserly, selfish, sparing **8** churlish, covetous, cowardly, grudging **9** illiberal, mercenary, niggardly, penurious, rapacious **10** avaricious **11** small-minded **12** narrowminded, parsimonious, uncharitable

ungifted 8 mediocre **9** unskilled **10** amateurish, unskillful, untalented **14** unaccomplished

unglue 6 unseal **7** peel off, unstick **9** pull apart

ungodly 4 base, vile **5** awful **6** rotten, sinful, wicked **7** corrupt, ghastly, godless, heinous, immoral, impious **8** depraved, dreadful, terrible **9** dissolute **10** degenerate, horrendous, iniquitous, outrageous, villainous **11** blasphemous **12** dishonorable, unreasonable

ungovernable 6 unruly **7** defiant, froward, naughty, wayward **8** contrary, mutinous, perverse, stubborn **9** fractious, obstinate **10** disorderly, rebellious, refractory **11** disobedient, intractable **12** noncompliant, recalcitrant, unmanageable, unsubmissive

ungraceful 5 inept **6** clumsy **7** awkward **9** inelegant

ungracious 4 rude **5** bluff, blunt, gruff, harsh, short **6** abrupt, coarse, crusty, vulgar **7** boorish, brusque, loutish, uncivil, uncouth **8** churlish, grudging, impolite **9** uncourtly, ungallant **10** illbehaved, unladylike, unmannerly **11** bad-mannered, illmannered, impertinent, uncourteous **12** disagreeable, discourteous, inhospitable **13** disrespectful, ungentlemanly

unguarded 6 unwary **8** careless, tactless, too frank **9** imprudent, unmindful, unwatched **10** incautious, indiscreet, undefended **11** defenseless, unpatrolled, unprotected **12** undiplomatic, unrestrained **13** ill-considered, uncircumspect

unguent 4 balm **5** cream, salve **6** lotion **8** ointment **9** emollient

ungulate 2 ox **3** cow, gnu, hog, pig, yak **4** boar, calf, deer, goat, ibex **5** camel, daman, horse, llama, tapir **6** hoofed, vicuna **7** buffalo, caribou, giraffe, peccary **8** antelope, elephant, hooflike, ruminant **9** dromedary **10** hartebeest, rhinoceros, wildebeest **12** hippopotamus

unhampered 4 free **8** expedite **9** unimpeded **10** unconfined **12** unencumbered, unrestrained, unrestricted

unhandy 5 inept **6** clumsy, gauche, klutzy **7** awkward **8** bumbling, fumbling, inexpert, unwieldy **9** all thumbs, ham-handed, maladroit, unskilled **10** cumbersome, unskillful **11** inefficient **12** inconvenient, unmanageable **14** butterfingered

unhappiness 3 woe **5** grief **6** misery, sorrow **7** anguish, sadness **8** distress **9** heartache

unhappy 3 bad, sad **4** blue, poor **5** inapt, sorry **6** gloomy, somber, unwise **7** adverse, awkward, doleful, foolish, forlorn, hapless, joyless, unlucky **8** dejected, downcast, luckless, unseemly **9** depressed, imprudent, long-faced, sorrowful, woebegone **10** despondent, dispirited, ill-advised, melancholy, unbecoming, unsuitable **11** crestfallen, injudicious, regrettable, unbefitting, unfortunate **12** heavyhearted, infelicitous, unsuccessful **13** inappropriate **14** down in the mouth

unharmed 5 whole **6** unhurt **9** uninjured, unscathed, untouched **10** in one piece, unaffected **14** with a whole skin

unhealthy 3 bad **4** sick, weak **6** ailing, feeble, infirm, morbid, poorly, sickly, unwell **7** harmful, hurtful, invalid, not well, noxious, unsound **8** depraved, diseased, negative, perilous **9** dangerous, degrading, hazardous **10** corrupting, indisposed, morally bad **11** destructive, detrimental, undesirable, unhealthful, unwholesome **12** demoralizing, in poor health, insalubrious **13** contaminating

unheard-of 3 odd **4** rare **6** unique **7** amazing, curious, unknown, unusual **8** freakish, original, singular, uncommon **9** irregular, matchless **10** incredible, outlandish, outrageous, phenomenal, unexpected **11** exceptional **12** incomparable, preposterous, unbelievable, unparalleled, un-

reasonable **13** extraordinary, inconceivable, unprecedented

unheated 3 icy **4** cold **6** chilly, drafty, frosty **7** ice-cold **8** unwarmed

unheeding 7 ignored **8** mindless **12** disregarding

unhelpful 7 of no use, useless **8** in the way **9** hindering **11** disobliging **13** inconsiderate, uncooperative

unheralded 6 unsung **10** unexpected, unforeseen **11** unacclaimed, unannounced, unlooked-for **12** unproclaimed, unpublicized, unrecognized **13** unanticipated

unhesitating 5 eager, quick, ready **6** direct, prompt **9** immediate **10** unreserved **11** unflinching **12** wholehearted, without delay **13** instantaneous **18** without reservation

unhinge 6 detach **7** disrupt **8** separate, unsettle **9** disengage, dislocate, disorient, unbalance **10** disconnect **13** disarticulate

unhitch 6 detach **8** separate, uncouple, unfasten **9** disengage **10** disconnect

unhitched 8 detached **9** uncoupled **10** unfastened **12** disconnected

unholy 4 base, evil, vile **5** awful **6** rotten, sinful, wicked **7** corrupt, heinous, immoral, ungodly **8** depraved, dreadful, shocking **9** dishonest **10** horrendous, iniquitous, outrageous, villainous **12** dishonorable, unreasonable

Unholy Loves
    author: 15 Joyce Carol Oates

unhurried 4 easy, slow **7** gradual **9** leisurely **10** deliberate, slow-moving

unicorn
    form: 5 horse
    feature: 4 horn
    symbolizes: 6 purity
        8 chastity
    constellation of: 9 Monoceros

unidentified 5 vague **7** unknown, unnamed **8** nameless **9** anonymous, unlabeled **11** unspecified **12** undesignated, unrecognized

unification 5 union, unity **6** fusion, merger **7** uniting **8** alliance, junction **9** coalition, combining **11** coalescence, combination, confederacy **12** amalgamation **13** confederation, consolidating, consolidation, incorporation

uniform 4 even, garb **5** alike, array, at one, dress, equal, habit **6** attire, in line, in step, livery **7** apparel, costume, regalia, regular, similar, the same **8** agreeing, constant, in accord, of a piece, unvaried, vestment **9** consonant, identical, of one mind, unaltered, unvarying **10** conforming, consistent, harmonious, unchanging **11** regimentals, undeviating

uniformity 8 equality, monotony, sameness **10** consonance **11** consistency, equivalency, homogeneity **15** standardization

unify 3 wed **4** ally, fuse, join **5** blend, merge, unite **6** couple, link up **7** combine **8** coalesce, federate **10** amalgamate **11** confederate, consolidate, form into one, incorporate **12** lump together **13** bring together

unilluminated 3 dim **4** dark **5** murky, unlit **6** gloomy **7** obscure **8** darkened **9** lightless, unlighted

unimaginable 10 incredible **12** unbelievable **13** inconceivable **16** incomprehensible

unimaginative 4 dull **5** stale, stock, trite, usual, vapid **6** dreary **7** cliched, humdrum, prosaic, routine, tedious **8** everyday, mediocre, ordinary **9** hackneyed **10** pedestrian, uncreative, unexciting, uninspired, unoriginal, unromantic **11** commonplace, predictable **12** run-of-the-mill, unremarkable **13** uninteresting

unimpaired 4 good **5** clear, sound **6** intact, unhurt **8** unbroken, unharmed **9** uninjured, unscathed, unspoiled **10** undeformed

unimpassioned 4 calm, cool **6** placid, serene, stolid **7** unmoved **8** detached, unloving **9** apathetic, impassive, objective, unexcited **11** indifferent, unemotional **13** dispassionate

unimpeachable 4 pure **5** clean, solid **7** perfect **8** reliable, spotless, unmarred **9** blameless, faultless, inviolate, stainless, undefiled, untainted **10** immaculate, impeccable, inculpable, infallible **11** trustworthy, unblemished **12** unassailable **13** above reproach, totally honest **14** beyond question, irreproachable, unquestionable **15** beyond criticism, unchallengeable

unimportant 5 minor **6** lesser,

meager, paltry, slight **7** trivial **8** inferior, mediocre, not vital, nugatory, piddling, trifling **10** immaterial, irrelevant, low-ranking, negligible, of no moment, second-rate **11** subordinate **12** nonessential, not important **13** insignificant **14** inconsiderable **15** inconsequential, of no consequence

uninformed 6 unread **7** unaware **8** ignorant **9** in the dark, not with it, unadvised, unknowing, unlearned **10** uneducated, unschooled **12** unconversant, uninstructed **13** unenlightened

uninhabited 5 empty **6** vacant **8** deserted, forsaken **9** abandoned, unlived in, unpeopled, unsettled **10** unoccupied, untenanted **11** unpopulated

uninhibited 4 fast, free, open, rash **5** frank **6** candid, daring, madcap, not shy, unwary **8** careless, heedless, immodest, reckless, uncurbed, unreined **9** abandoned, impetuous, impulsive, outspoken, unbridled, unchecked, unguarded, unimpeded, unstopped **10** capricious, flamboyant, forthright, headstrong, incautious, indiscreet, unhampered, unhindered, unreserved **11** instinctive, plainspoken, spontaneous **12** free-spirited, uncontrolled, unobstructed, unrestrained, unrestricted **13** unconstrained **15** straightforward, unself-conscious

uninjured 5 whole **6** intact, unhurt **8** unharmed **9** unscathed, untouched **10** in one piece **14** with a whole skin

uninspired 4 dull **5** stale, stock, trite, vapid **7** cliched, humdrum, prosaic, unmoved **8** ordinary **9** hackneyed, unexcited, unstirred, untouched **10** pedestrian, unaffected, unexciting, unoriginal **11** commonplace, indifferent, predictable, unemotional, unimpressed **12** run-of-the-mill, uninfluenced, unstimulated **13** unimaginative, uninteresting

uninspiring 4 dull **5** bland, stale **6** boring **7** insipid, prosaic **10** lackluster **13** uninteresting

uninstructive 6 barren **9** unhelpful **10** unedifying **12** unproductive **13** uninformative

unintelligent 4 dull, dumb, slow **5** blank, dense, dopey, thick **6** obtuse, stupid **7** asinine, doltish, idiotic, moronic **8** retarded **9** cretinous, dim-

witted, imbecilic **10** dull-witted, half-witted, slow-witted **11** blockheaded, thickheaded **12** simpleminded

unintelligible 8 baffling, puzzling **9** confusing, illegible, insoluble **10** incoherent, perplexing **11** meaningless **12** impenetrable, inarticulate, unfathomable **14** undecipherable **16** incomprehensible

unintentional 9 unplanned, unwitting **10** accidental, fortuitous, undesigned, unintended, unthinking **11** inadvertent, involuntary, unconscious **14** unpremeditated

uninterested 5 aloof, blase **6** remote **8** heedless, listless, uncaring **9** apathetic, incurious, unmindful **10** above it all, uninvolved **11** indifferent, unconcerned **13** unimpressible

uninteresting 3 dry **4** drab, dull **5** trite, vapid **6** boring, dreary, jejune **7** humdrum, insipid, prosaic, tedious **8** lifeless, ordinary, tiresome, unmoving **9** colorless, wearisome **10** monotonous, pedestrian, uneventful **11** uninspiring **12** unsatisfying **13** insignificant

uninterrupted 8 unbroken **9** ceaseless, continual, incessant **10** continuous **11** unremitting

uninviting 8 annoying **9** offensive **10** unalluring, unpleasant, untempting **11** displeasing, distasteful, unappealing, undesirable, unwelcoming **12** disagreeable, unappetizing, unattractive

uninvolved 4 easy **5** clear **6** simple **7** neutral, obvious, outside **8** detached **9** impartial **10** unaffected **13** disinterested, dispassionate, uncomplicated

union 5 blend, guild, unity **6** fusion, league, merger **7** amalgam, joining, mixture, oneness, uniting, wedding **8** alliance, marriage, unifying **9** synthesis **10** federation, fraternity **11** affiliation, association, combination, corporation, partnership, unification **12** amalgamation **13** confederation, consolidation
　type: **5** craft, labor, trade

unique 8 by itself, peerless, singular **9** matchless, nonpareil, unequaled, unmatched, unrivaled **10** inimitable, one of a kind, surpassing, unexampled, unexcelled **11** distinctive, unsurpassed **12** incomparable, unapproached, unparalleled

unit 4 part **5** group, whole **6** entity, member **7** element, measure, package, section, segment **8** category, division, quantity **9** component **10** detachment **11** constituent, measurement **12** denomination

Unitas, Johnny
　nickname: **7** Johnny U
　sport: **8** football
　position: **11** quarterback
　team: **14** Baltimore Colts

unite 4 ally, fuse, join, pool **5** blend, merge, unify **6** couple **7** combine **8** coalesce, federate, lock arms, organize **10** amalgamate, homogenize, join forces **11** confederate, consolidate, incorporate **12** join together, lump together **13** stand together

united 3 one **5** fused **6** allied, joined, merged, pooled **7** blended, coupled, leagued, unified **8** combined **9** federated, of one mind, unanimous **10** collective **11** amalgamated, in agreement **12** consolidated, incorporated **14** joined together, lumped together

United Arab Emirates
　other name: 11 Pirate Coast, Trucial Oman **13** Trucial States
　capital/largest city: 8 Abu Dhabi
　others: 5 Ajman, Dubai, Kalba, Tarif **6** Sharja **7** Fujaira **11** Ras al Khaima **12** Umm al Qaiwain
　division: 5 Ajman, Dibai, Dubai **6** Sharja **7** Fujaira, Sharjah **8** Abu Dhabi, Fujairah **11** Ras al Khaima, Umm al Qaiwan **12** Ral al Khaimah, Umm al-Qaiwain
　monetary unit: 3 fil **6** dirham
　highest point: 5 Hafit
　physical feature:
　　desert: **10** Rub al Khali
　　gulf: **4** Oman **7** Persian
　　oasis: **7** Buraimi **9** Al Buraymi
　　peninsula: **7** Arabian
　people: 4 Arab **6** Indian **7** African, Iranian **9** Pakistani **10** South Asian
　leader: 22 Zaid Bin Sultan al-Nahayan
　language: 5 Farsi **6** Arabic **7** English, Persian
　religion: 5 Islam
　war: 4 Gulf **11** Desert Storm

United Kingdom *see*
7 England

United States *see box*

unity 5 peace, union **6** accord, entity, fusion, league, merger **7** concord, harmony, joining, oneness, rapport **8** alliance, goodwill **9** synthesis, unanimity, wholeness **10** federation, fellowship, friendship **11** affiliation, association, cooperation, partnership, unification **12** amalgamation, amicableness **13** compatibility, confederation, consolidation, understanding **14** like-mindedness

universal 7 general **9** worldwide **10** ubiquitous, widespread **11** omnipresent **12** affecting all, all-embracing, all-inclusive **13** international

Universal creator
Egyptian: **4** Ptah

universality 8 currency **10** prevalence **12** predominance **17** comprehensiveness

universe
god of: **6** Amen Ra, Amon Ra

university 6 campus, school **7** academy, college **11** institution
British: **6** Oxford **9** Cambridge
Cambridge: **7** Harvard
former: **9** alma mater
French: **8** Sorbonne
Hanover: **9** Dartmouth
lecturer: **9** prelector
New Haven: **4** Yale
New Jersey: **9** Princeton
New York: **8** Columbia
Providence: **5** Brown
session: **4** term **7** seminar **8** semester
Wit: **4** Lyly, Nash **5** Peele **6** Greene

unjust 6 biased, unfair, warped **7** partial **8** one-sided, partisan, wrongful **9** unmerited **10** prejudiced, unbalanced, undeserved **11** inequitable, unjustified, unwarranted

unjustifiable 11 inexcusable **12** indefensible

unjustly 7 falsely, wrongly **8** unfairly **10** wrongfully **11** dishonestly, faithlessly, inequitably **12** undeservedly

unkempt 5 messy **6** sloppy, untidy **7** rumpled, tousled **8** mussed-up, slovenly, uncombed **9** ungroomed **10** disheveled, disordered **11** disarranged

unkind 4 mean **5** nasty **7** abusive **8** uncaring **9** malicious, unfeeling **10** unfriendly, un-

generous, ungracious **11** insensitive, thoughtless **12** inhospitable, uncharitable **13** inconsiderate, unsympathetic

unknot 5 untie **7** unsnarl **8** untangle **11** disentangle

unknowable 12 inaccessible **13** inconceivable

unknown 7 obscure, unnamed **8** nameless **9** anonymous, unheard-of **10** unrenowned **12** uncelebrated, undesignated, undetermined, undiscovered, unidentified

Unknown authors
author of: **4** Edda (elder) **7** Beowulf **8** Everyman, King Horn, Stasimon **10** Cinderella **11** Poema del Cid **12** Panchatantra, Vercelli Book, Volsunga Saga **14** Gesta Romanorum, Sibylline Books **15** Chanson de Roland, The Forty Thieves, The Song of Roland **16** Grettir the Strong **17** The Nibelungenlied **20** Aucassin and Nicolette, Robin Hood's Adventures **23** The Dream of the Red Chamber, The Thousand and One Nights **26** Sir Gawain and the Green Knight **29** Collection of Ten Thousand Leaves **29** The Arabian Nights' Entertainment

unladylike 4 rude **6** coarse, common, vulgar **7** ill-bred, uncouth **8** impolite **10** unmannerly **12** discourteous

unlawful 7 illegal, illegit, illicit, lawless **8** criminal **9** forbidden **10** prohibited, unlicensed, unofficial **12** unauthorized **13** against the law **16** unconstitutional

unlawful act 5 crime **6** felony **10** wrongdoing **11** lawbreaking, malfeasance, misdemeanor

unleash 4 free **5** let go **7** release, set free **8** let loose, liberate **12** give free rein

unlettered 8 ignorant, untaught **9** unlearned, untutored **10** illiterate, uneducated, unschooled **11** unscholarly

unlighted 3 dim **4** dark **5** murky, unlit **6** gloomy **7** stygian, sunless **8** moonless **9** lightless **13** unilluminated

unlikable, unlikeable 7 hateful **9** offensive, unlovable **10** hard to like, unloveable, unpleasant **11** displeasing, unappealing **12** disagreeable

unlike 7 diverse, unalike, un-

equal **9** different, disparate **10** dissimilar

unlikelihood 12 doubtfulness, unlikeliness **13** improbability

unlikely 8 hopeless **10** improbable **11** unpromising **12** questionable, unbelievable, unpropitious **19** scarcely conceivable

unlikeness 8 contrast, variance **9** disparity, variation **10** difference, divergence **13** dissimilarity, dissimilitude

unlimited 4 huge, vast **5** total **7** endless, immense **8** absolute, complete, infinite **9** boundless, limitless, unbounded, unchecked **11** unqualified **12** immeasurable, totalitarian, uncontrolled, unrestrained, unrestricted **13** comprehensive, inexhaustible, unconstrained **15** all-encompassing

unload 4 dump **7** off-load **8** get rid of, unburden **9** dispose of **10** unencumber

unlooked for 6 sudden **7** unasked **8** surprise **10** unexpected, unforeseen, unheralded **11** unannounced, uncalled for, unpredicted, unsolicited **13** serendipitous, unanticipated

unlovable, unloveable 7 hateful **9** unlikable **10** hard to like, unlikeable, unpleasant **11** displeasing, unappealing **12** disagreeable

unloving 4 cold, cool **6** frigid **11** indifferent, passionless **13** unimpassioned

unlucky 6 cursed, jinxed **7** hapless, unhappy **8** ill-fated, luckless, untoward **9** ill-omened **10** ill-starred **11** star-crossed, unfortunate **12** inauspicious, misfortunate

unman 7 unnerve **8** castrate **10** discourage, emasculate

unmanageable 5 balky, bulky **6** mulish, unruly **7** awkward, unhandy, wayward, willful **8** ungainly, unwieldy **9** fractious, pigheaded **10** cumbersome, rebellious, refractory **11** disobedient, intractable, troublesome **12** incorrigible **14** uncontrollable

unmanly 5 timid **6** yellow **8** cowardly, sissyish, womanish **9** sissified, weak-kneed **10** effeminate **11** lily-livered, unmasculine, weakhearted **12** fainthearted **13** pusillanimous **14** chickenhearted

unmannerly 5 crude, gross, surly **6** coarse **7** boorish, ill-

United States
capital: 12 Washington DC
largest city: 11 New York City
others: 4 Nome **5** Miami **6** Boston, Dallas, El Paso **7** Chicago, Detroit, Houston, Memphis, Phoenix, San Jose, Seattle **8** Columbus, Honolulu, San Diego **9** Anchorage, Baltimore, Cleveland, Milwaukee **10** Los Angeles, New Orleans, San Antonio **12** Indianapolis, Jacksonville, Philadelphia, Salt Lake City, San Francisco
school: 3 MIT **4** Penn, Yale **5** Brown **6** Baylor, Drexel, Vassar **7** Amherst, Colgate, Cornell, Fordham, Harvard, Oberlin **8** Bryn Mawr, Columbia, Stanford, Wesleyan **9** Dartmouth, Princeton, Radcliffe **10** Bennington **12** Johns Hopkins, Mount Holyoke
division: 4 Iowa, Ohio, Utah **5** Idaho, Maine, Texas **6** Alaska, Hawaii, Kansas, Nevada, Oregon **7** Alabama, Arizona, Florida, Georgia, Indiana, Montana, New York, Vermont, Wyoming **8** Arkansas, Colorado, Delaware, Illinois, Kentucky, Maryland, Michigan, Missouri, Nebraska, Oklahoma, Virginia **9** Louisiana, Minnesota, New Jersey, New Mexico, Tennessee, Wisconsin **10** California, Puerto Rico, Washington **11** Connecticut, Mississippi, North Dakota, Rhode Island, South Dakota **12** New Hampshire, Pennsylvania, West Virginia **13** Massachusetts, North Carolina, South Carolina **18** District of Columbia
island: 4 Guam, Long, Maui, Oahu **5** Block, Ellis, Kauai, Lanai, Umnak **6** Hawaii, Kodiak, Niihau, Unimak, Virgin **7** Baranof, Key West, Long Key, Molokai, Nunivak, Sanibel **8** Aleutian, Hawaiian, Key Largo, Shumagin, Unalaska **9** Atka Amlia, Canal Zone, Chichagof, Kahoolawe, Nantucket, Snipe Keys **10** Islamorada, Oyster Keys, Puerto Rico, St Lawrence **11** Longboat Key **12** Santa Barbara **13** American Samoa, Marquesas Keys, Prince of Wales, Santa Catalina, Summerland Key **15** Martha's Vineyard **16** Cantout Enderbury **26** Trust Territory of the Pacific
lake: 4 Erie, Mead **5** Huron, Tahoe **6** Cayuga, Finger, George, Itasca, Oneida, Seneca **7** Iliamma, Ontario **8** Michigan, Superior **9** Champlain, Great Salt, Salton Sea, Teshekpuk, Winnebago **10** Okeechobee **11** Yellowstone **13** Pontchartrain, Wallenpaupack, Winnipesaukee **14** Lake of the Woods
mountain: 4 Hood **5** Coast, Green, Kenai, Ozark, Rocky, White **6** Alaska, Brooks, DeLong, Elbert, Helena, Mesabi, Pocono, Shasta **7** Cascade, Chugach, Foraker, Harvard, Kilauea, Massive, Olympic, Olympus, Rainier, St Elias, Whitney **8** Catskill, Davidson, Endicott, Katahdin, Mauna Loa, Mitchell, Ouachita, St Helens, Wrangell **9** Allegheny, Blue Ridge, Kuskokwim, North Peak, Pikes Peak **10** Black Hills, Blanca Peak, Grand Teton, Washington, Williamson **11** Appalachian, Santa Monica **12** Sierra Nevada **14** Berkshire Hills
highest point: 6 Denali **8** McKinley
river: 3 New, Red **4** Gila, Iowa, Milk, Ohio, Rock **5** Black, Cedar, Coosa, Flint, Grand, Green, James, Neuse, Osage, Pearl, Pecos, Snake, White, Yukon **6** Brazos, Hudson, Neches, Neosho, Nueces, Owybee, Pee Dee, Platte, Powder, Sabine, Salmon, Wabash **7** Alabama, Big Horn, John Day, Klamath, Potomac, Roanoke, San Juan, St Johns, Trinity **8** Arkansas, Big Black, Canadian, Cheyenne, Cimarron, Colorado, Columbia, Delaware, Humboldt, Illinois, Kentucky, Kootenay, Missouri, Niabrana, Ouachita, Savannah **9** Allegheny, Deschutes, Des Moines, Minnesota, Rio Grande, Smoky Hill, St Francis, Tennessee, Tombigbee, Wisconsin **10** Cumberland, Republican, Sacramento, San Joaquin, St Lawrence, Tallapoosa **11** Connecticut, Mississippi, North Platte, South Platte, Susquehanna, Yellowstone **12** Tallahatchie **14** Little Colorado, Little Missouri
sea: 6 Arctic, Bering **7** Pacific **8** Atlantic, Beaufort
physical feature:
  bay: **5** Tampa **7** Bristol, Prudhoe **8** Biscayne, Monterey **9** Apalachee **10** Chesapeake **12** San Francisco
  desert: **4** Gila **6** Mojave **7** Painted **8** Colorado, Vizcaino **9** Black Rock **11** Death Valley
  falls: **7** Niagara
  gulf: **6** Alaska, Mexico **10** California
  plain: **5** Great
  plateau: **8** Colorado, Piedmont **10** Cumberland **11** Appalachian
  strait: **6** Bering **7** Florida
people:
  architect: **4** Root **5** Davis **6** Upjohn, Wright **7** Burnham, Downing, Furness, Gilbert, Gropius, Latrobe **8** Bogardus, Holabird, Sullivan **9** Bullfinch, Jefferson **10** Richardson **14** Mies van der Rohe
  artist: **5** Henri, Homer, Leutz, Moses, Peale, Wyeth **6** Copley, Durand, Millet, Rothko, Stuart **7** Audubon, Cassatt, O'Keeffe, Pollock, Sargent **8** Whistler
  author: **3** Poe **4** Grey, Inge, Loos, Luce, West, Wouk **5** Aiken, Albee, Beach, Benet, Crane, Eliot, Frost, Guest, Harte, Hecht, James, Lewis, Oates, Odets, O'Hara, Paine, Pound, Stowe, Twain, Vidal, Welty, Wolfe, Wylie **6** Bellow, Bierce, Bryant, Cabell, Capote, Cather, Cooper, Cullen, Ferber, Holmes, Hughes, Irving, Kilmer, Lanier, London, Lowell, Mather, Millay, Miller, Norris, O'Neill, Porter, Styron, Updike, Wilder **7** Angelou, Baldwin, Clemens, Costain, Dreiser, Emerson, Gallico, Hammett, Hellman, Howells, Jeffers, Kerouac, Lardner, Malamud, Nabokov, Roethke, Stevens, Thoreau, Webster, Wharton, Whitman **8** Anderson, Bradbury, Caldwell, Cummings, Faulkner, Macleish, McCarthy, Melville, Michener, Mitchell, Morrison, Rawlings, Robinson, Sandburg, Schwartz, Sherwood, Sinclair, Teasdale, Whit-

(continued)

United States (*continued*)
tier, Williams **9** Burroughs, Dickinson, Dos Passos, Hawthorne, Hemingway, McCullers, Steinbeck **10** Fitzgerald, Longfellow, Tarkington
composer: **4** Ives, Kern **5** Cohan, Loewe, Sousa **6** Berlin, Foster, Joplin, Lerner, Porter **7** Copland, Gilbert, Rodgers **8** Gershwin, Sullivan **9** Bernstein **11** Hammerstein
explorer: **4** Byrd, Pike **5** Boone, Cabot, Clark, Lewis, Perry **6** Hudson, Joliet **7** Jolliet **8** Columbus **9** Marquette **10** Eric the Red
leader: **3** Jay **4** Clay, King, Penn **5** Bryan, Davis, Henry, Paine **6** Revere, Sumner **7** Stevens, Webster **8** Franklin, Humphrey **9** Goldwater
military leader: **3** Lee **4** Pike **5** Clark, Gates, Grant, Meade, Tyler **6** Austin, Custer, Marion, Patton **7** Bradley, Houston, Jackson, Sherman **8** Marshall, Pershing **9** MacArthur, Roosevelt, Stillwell **10** Eisenhower, Vandenburg, Washington **11** Schwarzkopf
president: **4** Bush, Ford, Polk, Taft **5** Adams, Grant, Hayes, Nixon, Tyler **6** Arthur, Carter, Hoover, Monroe, Pierce, Reagan, Taylor, Truman, Wilson **7** Clinton, Harding, Jackson, Johnson, Kennedy, Lincoln, Madison **8** Buchanan, Coolidge, Fillmore, Garfield, Hamilton, Harrison, McKinley, Van Buren **9** Cleveland, Jefferson, Roosevelt **10** Eisenhower, Washington
sculptor: **4** Rush **6** Calder, French, Rogers **7** Borglum **9** Greenough, Remington **12** Saint-Gaudens
language: 7 English, Spanish
religion: 5 Amish **6** Mormon **7** Baptist, Judaism, Shakers **8** Lutheran **9** Methodist **10** Protestant **11** Pentacostal **12** Episcopalian, Presbyterian **13** Roman Catholic **14** Church of Christ, Congregational **15** Eastern Orthodox, Latter Day Saints **19** Seventh Day Adventist
place:
national park: **4** Zion **5** Platt **6** Acadia **7** Big Bend, Glacier, Olympic, Redwood, Sequoia **8** Wind Cave, Yosemite **9** Haleakala, Mesa Verde, Multnomah **10** Crater Lake, Everglades, Grand Teton, Hot Springs, Isle Royale, Shenandoah **11** Bryce Canyon, Canyonlands, Grand Canyon, Kings Canyon, Mammoth Cave, Yellowstone **12** Mount Rainier **13** Mount McKinley, Virgin Islands **14** Lassen Volcanic, Rocky Mountains **15** Carlsbad Caverns, Petrified Forest **19** Great Smoky Mountains
possession: 4 Guam **10** Puerto Rico **13** American Samoa, Virgin Islands **14** Mariana Islands **15** Caroline Islands, Marshall Islands
feature:
colony: **7** Roanoke **8** Plymouth **9** Jamestown **11** Rhode Island **12** New Amsterdam, New Hampshire **14** New Netherlands **16** Massachusetts Bay
festival: **9** Mardi Gras
national symbol: **9** bald eagle
tree: **7** redwood, sequoia

bred, loutish, uncivil, uncouth **8** impolite **10** ungracious, unladylike **11** ill-mannered **12** badly behaved, discourteous **13** ungentlemanly

unmarked 5 clean, clear **9** undamaged, undefaced, unnoticed **10** unobserved **11** unblemished **15** undistinguished

unmarried 4 free **5** unwed **6** maiden, single **7** old maid, widowed **8** bachelor, divorced, spinster, unwedded, virginal, wifeless **9** available, fancy free **10** spouseless, unattached **11** husbandless **21** footloose and fancy-free

unmarried girl
French: **10** jeune fille
German: **8** fraulein
Spanish: **8** senorita

Unmarried Woman, An
director: **12** Paul Mazursky
cast: **9** Alan Bates **11** Cliff Gorman **13** Jill Clayburgh, Michael Murphy

unmask 4 bare, show **6** betray, expose, reveal, unveil **7** lay open, uncover **8** disclose, discover **12** bring to light

unmasking 6 baring **8** betrayal, exposure **9** discovery, unveiling **10** disclosure, laying open, revelation, uncovering **15** bringing to light

unmatched 6 unlike **7** diverse, supreme, unequal **8** peerless, variable **9** differing, disparate, matchless, unequaled **10** dissimilar **12** second to none, unparalleled **13** beyond compare

unmerciful 4 cold, evil **5** cruel, harsh **6** brutal, severe, unkind **7** brutish, extreme, inhuman **8** inhumane, pitiless, ruthless **9** excessive, heartless, inclement, merciless, unfeeling, unpitying, unsparing **10** malevolent, relentless **11** hardhearted **14** unconscionable

unmindful 3 lax **6** remiss **7** unaware **8** careless, derelict, heedless **9** forgetful, negligent,

oblivious, unheeding **11** thoughtless, unconscious

unmistakable 5 clear, plain **6** patent **7** evident, glaring, obvious **8** apparent, distinct, manifest, palpable **9** prominent **10** pronounced, undeniable **11** conspicuous, unequivocal **12** indisputable **14** unquestionable

unmistakably 7 clearly, plainly **8** palpably, patently **9** certainly, decidedly, downright, evidently, glaringly, obviously **10** definitely, distinctly, manifestly, positively, thoroughly, undeniably **11** prominently **12** indisputably **13** conspicuously, unequivocally **14** unquestionably **17** beyond all question

unmitigated 6 arrant **8** absolute, unabated, unbroken **9** downright, out-and-out **10** persistent, unrelieved **11** unqualified **12** unalleviated **13** uninterrupted

unmixed 4 neat, pure **5** sheer **6** simple **8** straight **9** unalloyed, unblended, undiluted, unmingled **13** unadulterated

unmoved 4 calm, cold, firm **5** aloof **6** dogged **7** devoted, staunch **8** resolute, resolved, uncaring, unshaken **9** dedicated, obstinate, steadfast, unfeeling, unpitying, unstirred, untouched **10** determined, inflexible, not shifted, persistent, relentless, unaffected, unswerving, unwavering **11** indifferent, unconcerned, undeviating, undisturbed, unfaltering **12** stonyhearted, uninterested, unresponsive **14** uncompromising

unmoving 4 dead, dull **5** fixed, inert, still **6** boring, serene **8** immobile **9** powerless **10** motionless, stationary **11** emotionless **13** at a standstill

unnamed 8 nameless, unsigned **9** anonymous, incognito **10** innominate, uncredited, unreported, unrevealed **11** undisclosed, unspecified **12** pseudonymous, undesignated, undiscovered, unidentified **14** unacknowledged

unnatural 4 fake **5** phony, put-on **6** forced **7** assumed, stilted, studied, unusual **8** aberrant, abnormal, affected, freakish, mannered, peculiar **9** anomalous, contrived **10** artificial, theatrical **13** self-conscious

unnecessary 5 extra **6** excess **7** surplus **8** needless, overmuch **9** auxiliary, excessive **10** expendable, gratuitous, unrequired **11** dispensable, superfluous, uncalled-for, unessential **13** supplementary

unnerve 5 daunt, scare, upset **7** agitate, unhinge **8** frighten, unsettle **10** intimidate

unnerving 5 scary **8** daunting **9** upsetting **10** enervating, unsettling **11** frightening

unnoticeable 3 dim **5** faint **6** hidden **7** obscure **9** concealed **10** indistinct, unassuming, unemphatic, unobserved **11** unobtrusive **12** undetectable **13** imperceptible, inconspicuous, insignificant, undiscernible **14** unostentatious

unnoticed 6 unfelt, unseen **7** unheard, unnoted **8** unheeded, untasted **10** not smelled, overlooked, unobserved **11** disregarded, unperceived **12** undiscovered

unobservant 4 dull **5** blind

8 unseeing **9** unmindful **11** incognizant

unobstructed 4 fair, free, open **5** clear **8** apparent **9** unimpeded **10** unhampered, unhindered **11** unprevented

unobtainable 9 hard to get **10** impossible, out of reach, out of touch **11** unavailable, unreachable **12** improcurable, inaccessible

unobtrusive 3 shy **6** humble, modest **7** bashful **8** reserved, reticent, retiring **9** diffident **10** unassuming **11** unassertive **13** inconspicuous, unpretentious **14** unostentatious

unoccupied 4 idle **5** empty **6** vacant **8** unfilled **9** abandoned, unengaged **10** untenanted **11** uninhabited

unofficial 8 informal **12** unauthorized

unorganized 5 loose **6** casual, random **7** aimless, chaotic **8** confused **9** haphazard, orderless, unordered **10** disjointed, unarranged, undirected **11** harum-scarum **12** unclassified, unsystematic **13** helter-skelter **14** unsystematized

unornamented 4 bald, bare **5** blank, naked, plain, stark **6** simple **7** austere **9** unadorned **11** undecorated **13** unembellished

unorthodox 7 erratic **9** eccentric, irregular **14** unconventional

unostentatious 3 shy **5** plain, quiet **6** humble, modest, simple **9** unadorned, unaffected **10** unassuming **11** constrained **13** inconspicuous, unpretentious **14** unpresumptuous

unpaid 3 due **4** owed **5** owing **9** in arrears **11** outstanding

unpaid debt 5 debit **7** arrears **9** liability **10** balance due, obligation **12** indebtedness

unpalatable 5 nasty **8** inedible, unsavory **9** repellent, repulsive **10** bad-tasting, unpleasant **11** displeasing, distasteful **12** disagreeable, unappetizing **13** hard to swallow

unparalleled 4 best, rare **5** alone, crack, elect **6** unique **8** gilt-edge, peerless, singular **9** matchless, superfine, unequaled, unmatched, unrivaled **10** crackajack, inimitable, unimitated **11** unsurpassed **12** unapproached **13** unprecedented **15** of the first water

unperceptive 5 blind **9** unfeeling **11** insensitive, unobservant **12** imperceptive, impercipient **13** unsympathetic

unperturbed 4 calm, cool **6** poised **8** composed, tranquil **9** collected, unexcited, unruffled **10** coolheaded, nonchalant, unagitated, undismayed, untroubled **11** levelheaded, undisturbed **13** unimpassioned

unplanned 9 impromptu **10** accidental, fortuitous, improvised, unexpected, unforeseen **11** spontaneous **12** uncalculated **13** unintentional **14** extemporaneous, unpremeditated **15** spur-of-the-moment

unpleasant 5 nasty, pesky **7** irksome, noisome **8** annoying, churlish **9** obnoxious, offensive, repugnant, repulsive, unlikable, vexatious **10** ill-humored, ill-natured **11** displeasing, distasteful **12** disagreeable, unattractive **13** objectionable

unpleasantness 8 ugliness **9** ill nature, nastiness **12** churlishness **13** obnoxiousness, offensiveness, repulsiveness **15** distastefulness **16** disagreeableness, unattractiveness

unpointed 4 dull **5** blunt **6** dulled **11** unsharpened

unpolished 3 raw **5** gawky, inept, rough **6** cloudy, clumsy **7** amateur, awkward, unwaxed **8** inexpert, unbuffed, unglazed, unshined **9** inelegant, unrefined, unskilled **10** uncultured, unfinished, unskillful **11** unburnished, unpracticed **12** uncultivated **13** inexperienced **14** unaccomplished **15** unsophisticated

unpopular 7 snubbed **8** disliked, rebuffed, rejected, slighted, unwanted **9** disdained, neglected, unwelcome **10** unaccepted **11** disapproved, undesirable **12** looked down on, unacceptable

unpopulated 5 rural **9** backwoods, unpeopled, unsettled

unprecedented 5 novel **6** unique **9** unheard-of **10** unexampled **11** exceptional **12** unparalleled **13** extraordinary **15** hitherto unknown

unpredictable 6 fitful **7** erratic **8** fanciful, unstable, variable **9** arbitrary, eccentric, impulsive, mercurial, uncertain, whimsical **10** capricious, changeable, inconstant

unprejudiced 4 fair, just 8 unbiased, unswayed 9 impartial, objective, unbigoted 10 even-handed, fair-minded, open-minded, undogmatic 11 broad-minded 12 uninfluenced 13 disinterested

unpremeditated 5 ad-lib 9 impetuous, impromptu, impulsive, unplanned 10 accidental, improvised, unintended 11 involuntary, spontaneous 12 uncalculated, unthought-out 13 unintentional 14 extemporaneous 15 spur-of-the-moment

unprepared 5 ad-lib 7 offhand, unready 8 off guard 9 extempore, impromptu 10 flat-footed, improvised 11 spontaneous, unrehearsed 14 extemporaneous 15 spur-of-the-moment

unprepossessing 4 grim 5 seedy 10 ill-favored, ill-looking 12 unattractive

unpressed 5 baggy 6 mussed, sloppy 7 creased, rumpled 8 unironed, wrinkled 9 shapeless, uncreased

unpretentious 5 plain 6 homely, humble, modest, simple 10 unassuming, unimposing 11 unelaborate, unobtrusive 14 unostentatious

unprincipled 6 amoral 12 unscrupulous 14 conscienceless, unconscionable

unproductive 4 poor 6 barren 7 sterile, useless 8 bootless 9 infertile 10 unfruitful, unyielding 11 ineffective, ineffectual, inefficient 12 unprofitable

unprofessional 6 shoddy, sloppy 7 amateur 8 bungling, careless 9 negligent, unethical 10 amateurish 11 incompetent, inefficient, unpracticed 12 unprincipled 13 inexperienced, undisciplined, unworkmanlike 14 unbusinesslike

unprofitable 4 vain 7 useless 8 bootless 11 ineffective, ineffectual

unprogressive 7 diehard 8 backward, standpat, stubborn 9 benighted, right-wing 11 reactionary, reactionist 12 conservative 17 ultraconservative

unprolific 6 barren 7 sterile 9 infertile, unfertile 10 nonbearing 12 unproductive

unpromising 5 bleak 9 ill-omened 10 forbidding 11 unfavorable 12 inauspicious, unpropitious

unpropitious 7 adverse 8 contrary 9 unfitting 10 unsuitable 11 unfavorable 12 antagonistic, inauspicious, infelicitous

unprotected 4 open 5 naked 6 unsafe 7 exposed, unarmed 8 helpless, insecure, perilous 9 dangerous, hazardous, unguarded 10 undefended, vulnerable 11 defenseless

unproven 7 in doubt 8 arguable, doubtful 10 indefinite, in question, up in the air 11 open to doubt, unconfirmed 12 experimental, inconclusive, questionable 13 unestablished 14 open to question

unpunctual 4 late 5 tardy 7 belated 10 behindhand, behindtime

unqualified 5 total, unfit, utter 8 absolute, complete, inexpert, positive, thorough, unsuited 9 downright, out-and-out, unskilled, untrained 10 consummate, undisputed, uneducated, unprepared, unschooled 11 ill-equipped, incompetent 13 inexperienced, unconditional

unquenched 8 unslaked 11 unsatisfied 14 unextinguished

unquestionable 4 sure 5 clear, plain 6 proven 7 certain, evident, obvious, perfect 8 definite, flawless 9 blameless, errorless, faultless 10 impeccable, undeniable 11 beyond doubt, irrefutable, self-evident, unequivocal 12 indisputable, uncensurable 13 uncontestable, unimpeachable 14 irreproachable

unquestionably 6 surely 7 totally 9 certainly, doubtless 10 absolutely, completely, definitely, positively, unarguably 12 conclusively, indisputably, without doubt 13 unequivocally

unravel 4 undo 5 feaze, solve 6 unfold, unfurl, unknit 7 clear up, resolve 8 decipher, separate, untangle 9 pull apart 10 disinvolve 11 disentangle

unreachable 10 impossible, out of touch 11 out of the way, unavailable, unrealistic 12 inaccessible, unobtainable 14 unapproachable

unreal 4 airy 5 dream 6 dreamy 7 ghostly, not real, phantom, shadowy 8 ethereal, illusive, illusory, imagined, spectral 9 dreamlike, fantastic, imaginary, legendary 10 chimerical, fictitious, idealistic, intangible 11 nonexistent 13 insubstantial 16 phantasmagorical

unrealistic 4 wild 5 crazy, silly 6 absurd 7 asinine, foolish 8 crackpot, delusory, fanciful 9 illogical 10 idealistic, improbable, infeasible, starry-eyed 11 impractical 12 unreasonable

unrealized 8 thwarted 10 frustrated, incomplete 11 nonexistent, unfulfilled, unsatisfied 14 unaccomplished

unreasonable 5 undue 6 absurd, biased, mulish, unfair 7 bigoted 8 obdurate, stubborn, too great 9 excessive, fanatical, illogical, obstinate, pigheaded, senseless, unbending 10 bullheaded, exorbitant, farfetched, headstrong, immoderate, inflexible, inordinate, irrational, prejudiced, unyielding 11 extravagant, intractable, nonsensical, opinionated, uncalled-for, unwarranted 12 closed-minded, preposterous, ungovernable, unmanageable 13 unjustifiable

unreasoning 8 careless, heedless 9 impulsive 10 irrational, unthinking 11 thoughtless 13 unintelligent

unrecognizable 9 disguised, incognito 10 in disguise 11 camouflaged 14 unidentifiable

unrecognized 6 unsung 7 cryptic, unknown 9 incognito, unnoticed

unrefined 3 raw 5 crude, rough 6 coarse, vulgar 7 boorish, low-bred 9 inelegant

unrehearsed 7 offhand 8 informal 9 extempore, impromptu, impulsive, unplanned, unstudied 10 improvised, off-the-cuff, unprepared 11 extemporary, spontaneous 14 extemporaneous, unpremeditated 15 improvisational, spur-of-the-moment 19 off the top of one's head

unrelated 6 not kin, unlike 7 foreign 8 unallied 10 dissimilar, extraneous, irrelevant, non-germane 11 unconnected 12 inapplicable, incompatible, unassociated 13 inappropriate

unrelenting 5 rigid 6 steady 7 adamant, endless 8 constant, unabated, unbroken 9 ceaseless, incessant, tenacious, unbending 10 implacable, inexorable, inflexible, relentless, unrelieved, unswerving, unwavering, unyielding **11** undeviating, unremitting **14** uncompromising

unreliable 4 fake **5** false, phony **6** fickle **8** fallible, mistaken, unstable **9** deceitful, erroneous, uncertain **10** capricious, changeable, inaccurate, inconstant **12** questionable, undependable **13** irresponsible, untrustworthy

unremarkable 5 usual **6** common **7** average **8** everyday, mediocre, ordinary **11** commonplace **12** unimpressive, unsurprising **13** insignificant, unexceptional **15** undistinguished

unremitting 6 dogged **8** constant, tireless, untiring **9** ceaseless, continual, incessant, unceasing **10** continuous, persistent **11** persevering

unrepentant 7 callous **8** hardened, obdurate, unatoned **9** unashamed **10** uncontrite, unexpiated **11** remorseless **12** incorrigible, unregenerate

unrepressed 4 free, open **7** liberal **8** effusive, outgoing **9** expansive, exuberant **11** extroverted, uninhibited **12** unrestrained

unreserved 4 full, open **5** frank **6** entire **11** unqualified **12** wholehearted

unresolved 4 moot **5** vague **7** pending **8** doubtful, unsolved **9** tentative, uncertain, undecided, unsettled **10** disputable, unanswered **11** contestable, speculative **12** questionable, undetermined **13** problematical, unascertained

unresponsive 4 cold, cool, dull, limp **5** inert **6** frigid **7** passive **8** lifeless **9** apathetic, unfeeling **11** cold-blooded, inattentive, indifferent, unemotional **13** dispassionate, unsympathetic

unresponsiveness 6 apathy **7** inertia **9** lassitude, passivity **11** inattention, passiveness **12** indifference

unrest 5 chaos **6** tumult **7** anarchy, discord, ferment, protest, turmoil **8** disorder, disquiet, upheaval **9** agitation, rebellion **10** discontent, turbulence **12** restlessness **15** dissatisfaction

unrestrained 8 uncurbed **9** abandoned, boundless, excessive, unbridled, unchecked, unlimited **10** immoderate, in-

ordinate, unfettered, ungoverned, unhampered, unhindered, unreserved **11** extravagant, intemperate, uninhibited, unrepressed **12** uncontrolled, unrestricted, unsuppressed **13** irrepressible

unrestraint 6 excess **7** abandon **9** uncontrol **10** unruliness **12** extravagance, immoderation, recklessness **13** excessiveness, impulsiveness

unrestricted 8 absolute, complete **9** out-and-out, unbounded, unlimited **11** unqualified **12** unrestrained **13** unconditional

unrigid 3 lax **4** easy, limp, soft **5** loose **6** giving, limber, mobile, pliant, supple **7** elastic, lenient, plastic, pliable **8** flexible, informal, merciful, tolerant, yielding **9** indulgent, malleable **11** conformable

unrigorous 4 easy **5** loose, slack **6** casual, sloppy **7** inexact **8** careless, slapdash **9** imprecise

unripe 5 green **8** immature **10** unseasoned **11** undeveloped **14** underdeveloped

unrivaled 8 superior, topnotch **9** unequaled **10** undisputed **11** unsurpassed

unroll 6 reveal, uncoil, unfold, unfurl, unwind **7** display, lay open, play out **9** spread out

unruffled 4 calm, cool, even, mild **5** quiet, still **6** placid, serene, smooth **8** composed, tranquil **9** collected **10** coolheaded, nonchalant, unagitated, untroubled **11** undisturbed, unperturbed **13** self-possessed

unruly 4 wild **5** rowdy **7** restive, wayward, willful **8** contrary, perverse **9** fractious, unbridled **10** boisterous, disorderly, headstrong, refractory **11** disobedient, intractable **12** obstreperous, ungovernable, unmanageable **13** undisciplined **14** uncontrollable

unsafe 5 risky **7** exposed **8** insecure, perilous **9** dangerous, hazardous, unguarded **10** undefended, unreliable, vulnerable **11** defenseless, treacherous, unprotected **13** untrustworthy

unsatisfactory 4 poor **5** inept, unfit **8** below par, inferior, unworthy **9** deficient **10** inadequate, ineligible, unsuitable **12** inadmissible, unacceptable **13** inappropriate

unsavory 3 bad **4** flat, foul **5** nasty **7** insipid, tainted

9 tasteless **10** bad-tasting, nauseating, unpleasant **11** distasteful, unpalatable **12** disagreeable, unappetizing

unscathed 5 sound, whole **6** entire, intact, unhurt **7** perfect **8** unharmed **9** uninjured, untouched **10** unimpaired **11** unscratched **13** all in one piece

unscholarly 8 ignorant **9** unlearned **10** illiterate, uneducated, uninformed **11** illinformed **13** unintelligent

unschooled 3 raw **5** green **6** callow **8** ignorant, untaught **9** unlearned **10** illiterate, uneducated, uninformed, unlettered, unseasoned **11** uninitiated **13** inexperienced

unscrupulous 5 sharp **6** amoral **7** crooked, devious, immoral **9** unethical **12** dishonorable, unprincipled

unseasonable 6 too hot **7** too cold, too warm **8** abnormal, untimely

unseasoned 3 raw **5** bland, green, plain **6** callow **7** untried **8** immature **13** inexperienced

unseeing 5 blind **7** unaware **9** oblivious, sightless **11** unobservant

unseemly 4 rude **5** crude, gross **6** coarse, vulgar **7** boorish, loutish **8** churlish, improper, indecent, unworthy **9** incorrect, offensive, tasteless **10** indecorous, indelicate, out of place, unbecoming, unladylike, unsuitable **11** distasteful, ill-mannered, unbefitting, undignified **12** discourteous, disreputable **13** discreditable, inappropriate, reprehensible, ungentlemanly

unselfconscious 7 artless **10** unaffected **13** unpretentious

unselfish 7 liberal **8** generous, handsome, princely, selfless **10** altruistic, benevolent, bighearted, charitable, openhanded **11** considerate, magnanimous, magnificent **12** humanitarian **13** philanthropic **15** self-sacrificing

unserviceable 7 useless **8** unusable

unsettle 5 upset **6** bother, rattle, ruffle **7** agitate, confuse, disturb, fluster, perturb, trouble, unhinge **8** bewilder, confound, disorder **9** unbalance **10** disconcert **13** throw off guard

unsettled 5 fazed 7 anxious, nervous, ruffled 8 agitated, confused, doubtful 9 disturbed, nonplused, perturbed, undecided 10 disquieted, distracted, nonplussed, up in the air 11 discomfited 12 disconcerted 16 at sixes and sevens

unshackle 4 free 7 release, set free, unchain 8 liberate, unfetter

unshakable 4 fast 6 stable 7 abiding, staunch 8 constant, enduring 9 dauntless, permanent, steadfast, unruffled 10 changeless, inflexible, unsinkable, unwavering 11 levelheaded, unflappable 13 imperturbable

unshaken 4 calm, cool 6 poised, serene, stable 7 staunch, unmoved 8 composed, constant, resolved 9 steadfast, tenacious, undaunted, unexcited, unruffled 10 controlled, determined, inflexible, relentless, unaffected, unswerving, untroubled, unwavering 11 levelheaded, undeviating, undisturbed, unemotional, unfaltering, unflinching, unperturbed 13 self-possessed 14 uncompromising

unshapely 5 baggy 9 amorphous, shapeless

unshaven 5 hairy 7 bearded, bristly, hirsute, stubbly, unkempt 9 whiskered 11 bewhiskered

unsheathe 4 bare 6 expose 7 pull out 8 withdraw

unsightly 4 ugly 6 horrid, odious 7 hideous 9 obnoxious, offensive, repellent, repulsive, revolting, sickening 11 distasteful 12 unattractive

unsigned 9 anonymous 13 bearing no name

unskilled 5 green, inept 7 untried 9 untrained 10 amateurish, apprentice 11 incompetent, unqualified 13 inexperienced

unskillful 5 inept 6 clumsy, unable 7 awkward 8 inexpert 9 incapable, maladroit, untrained 10 amateurish 11 incompetent, ineffective, unpracticed 13 inexperienced

unsmiling 3 sad 4 glum, grim 5 grave 6 dismal 7 austere, joyless, serious 9 cheerless, grim-faced

unsociable 7 haughty 9 withdrawn 10 antisocial, unfriendly, ungracious 11 introverted 14 unapproachable

unsoiled 4 pure 5 clean, fresh, white 6 chaste 8 innocent, pristine, spotless 9 unstained, unsullied 10 immaculate 11 unblemished, untarnished

unsolicited 4 free 8 unforced, unsought, unwanted 9 undesired, uninvited, unwelcome, voluntary 10 gratuitous, unasked for 11 spontaneous, unnecessary, unrequested, unwished for, volunteered

unsophisticated 4 open 5 green, naive 6 candid 7 artless, natural 8 homespun, innocent, trusting 9 ingenuous, unstudied, unworldly 10 unaffected, unassuming 11 uncontrived 13 undissembling, unpretentious 15 straightforward

unsound 3 mad, off 4 weak 5 risky, shaky, unfit, wrong 6 absurd, ailing, faulty, feeble, flawed, infirm, insane, marred, sickly, unsafe 7 foolish, invalid, rickety, tottery 8 confused, crippled, decrepit, deranged, diseased, drooping, impaired, insecure, not solid, not valid, perilous, specious, spurious, unhinged, unstable, unsteady 9 blemished, dangerous, defective, erroneous, hazardous, illogical, imperfect, incorrect, senseless, uncertain, unfounded, unhealthy, unsettled, untenable 10 disordered, fallacious, groundless, irrational, precarious, unbalanced, unreliable 11 languishing, mentally ill 12 in poor health 13 off one's rocker, unsubstantial

unsoundness 7 frailty 8 delicacy, weakness 9 fragility, frailness, shakiness 11 decrepitude, derangement, instability 12 unsteadiness

unsparing 4 full 6 giving, lavish 7 copious, liberal, profuse 8 abundant, generous 9 bountiful, plenteous, plentiful, unlimited 10 big-hearted, munificent, ungrudging, unstinting 11 extravagant, magnanimous, unqualified 13 unconditional

unspeakable 4 huge, vast 5 awful, great 6 odious 7 fearful, immense 8 enormous, shocking 9 abhorrent, frightful, loathsome, monstrous, repellent, repulsive, revolting, sickening, unheard-of 10 abominable, disgusting, incredible, nauseating, prodigious 11 astonishing, unutterable 12 overwhelming, unimaginable 13 extraordi-

nary, inconceivable, inexpressible, undescribable

unspecified 5 vague 7 general, unnamed 9 undefined, unsettled 10 indefinite 11 unannounced, unindicated, unmentioned 12 undesignated, undetermined, unpublicized, unstipulated

unspoiled 4 open 7 artless, natural, perfect 8 pristine, spotless, trusting, unharmed, unmarred 9 preserved, undamaged, unscarred, unspotted, unstudied, unworldly 10 unaffected, unassuming, unimpaired, unpampered 11 unblemished, uncorrupted 13 unpretentious 15 unselfconscious, unsophisticated

unspoken 5 tacit 6 silent 7 implied 8 implicit 9 ineffable, not voiced, unuttered 10 understood 11 unexpressed

unspotted 5 clean 8 spotless, unsoiled 9 undefiled, unstained, unsullied 11 unblemished

unstable 4 weak 5 frail, shaky, tippy 6 fickle, fitful, flimsy, wobbly 7 erratic, fragile, rickety 8 changing, insecure, shifting, unsteady, volatile 9 emotional, mercurial, tottering 10 capricious, changeable, fly-by-night, irrational 11 fluctuating, vacillating 12 inconsistent 13 irresponsible, unpredictable, unsubstantial

unstained 5 clean 8 spotless 9 unspotted, unsullied, untainted 11 unblemished, uncorrupted

unsteady 6 fickle, wobbly 7 rickety 8 doubtful, unstable 10 unreliable 12 questionable, undependable 13 untrustworthy

unstinting 11 unqualified 12 enthusiastic, unrestrained, wholehearted

unstooped 5 erect 6 unbent 7 upright 8 straight, vertical

unstudied 4 glib 6 casual 7 artless, natural 8 informal, unforced, unversed 9 guileless, unuttered 10 unaffected 11 spontaneous 12 uncalculated

unsubmissive 6 unruly 7 defiant, froward, naughty, wayward 8 contrary, mutinous, perverse, stubborn 9 fractious, insurgent, obstinate, seditious, undutiful 10 disorderly, rebellious, refractory, unyielding 11 disobedient, intractable 12 noncompliant, recalcitrant,

ungovernable, unmanageable
13 insubordinate

unsubstantial 4 airy, weak
5 filmy **6** feeble, flimsy **7** unsound **8** ethereal, fanciful, illusory **9** idealized, imaginary
10 jerrybuilt **11** lightweight
12 undetectable **13** imperceptible **17** indistinguishable

unsubstantiated 8 disputed
10 unverified
15 unauthenticated

unsuccessful 4 poor, vain
6 foiled, futile, hard up **7** baffled, hapless, unlucky, useless
8 abortive, badly off, luckless, strapped, thwarted **9** fruitless, moneyless, penniless **10** illstarred, profitless, unavailing, unfruitful **11** ineffectual, unfortunate **12** unproductive, unprofitable, unprosperous
14 unremunerative

unsuitability 9 unfitness, wrongness **11** impropriety, uselessness **12** unseemliness
13 inconsistency **15** incompatibility, unacceptability
17 inappropriateness

unsuitable 5 inapt, unfit **7** unhappy, useless **8** improper, unseemly **9** unfitting, worthless
10 inadequate, indecorous, out of place, unbecoming, unsuitable **11** incongruous, unbefitting **12** inadmissible, incompatible, inconsistent, infelicitous, out of keeping, unacceptable **13** inappropriate

unsuited 5 inapt, wrong **9** unfitting **10** out of place
13 inappropriate

unsullied 5 clean **8** spotless, unsoiled **9** undefiled, uninjured, untainted **10** unpolluted **11** unblackened, unblemished, uncorrupted, untarnished **14** uncontaminated

unsupportable 6 faulty **9** unfounded, untenable
12 indefensible

unsure 3 shy **5** timid **7** bashful **8** hesitant, insecure, reserved **9** unassured, uncertain, undecided **11** in a quandary, unconfident, unconvinced
12 self-doubting **15** selfdistrustful

unsurpassed 4 best **7** highest, supreme **8** greatest, peerless, superior **9** matchless, nonpareil, paramount, unequaled, unmatched, unrivaled **10** consummate, unexcelled **11** exceptional **12** incomparable, transcendent, unparalleled

unsuspecting 5 naive **6** unwary **7** unaware **8** gullible, off

guard, trusting **9** believing, credulous **12** overtrustful, unsuspicious **13** overcredulous

unsuspicious 5 naive **8** gullible, trustful, trusting **9** credulous **12** unsuspecting
13 unquestioning

unswerving 4 firm **6** steady, strong **7** devoted, staunch
8 faithful, resolute, resolved, unshaken, untiring **9** dedicated, steadfast, undaunted
10 determined, inflexible, unflagging, unwavering, unyielding **11** undeviating, unfaltering, unflinching, unremitting **12** single-minded
14 uncompromising

unsympathetic 7 callous
8 pitiless, uncaring **9** heartless, repellent, repugnant, unfeeling, unlikable **10** hard-boiled, unlikeable, unmerciful, unpleasant **11** coldhearted, displeasing, hardhearted, indifferent, uncongenial
12 antipathetic, unattractive
15 uncompassionate

unsystematic 6 sloppy **7** chaotic, jumbled, muddled **8** confused **9** haphazard, unplanned
10 disordered, disorderly
12 disorganized, unmethodical

untainted 4 pure **5** clear **9** unsullied **11** uncorrupted
13 unadulterated

untalented 5 inept **8** mediocre, ungifted **9** unskilled **10** amateurish, unskillful
14 unaccomplished

untamed 4 wild **5** feral **6** savage **9** unsubdued **11** uncivilized **12** uncultivated

untangle 5 solve **7** clear up, unravel, unsnarl, untwist
9 extricate **11** disentangle
13 straighten out

untarnished 6 bright **7** perfect, shining **8** flawless, polished, spotless, unsoiled **9** faultless, undefiled, unstained, unsullied, untainted **10** immaculate, impeccable, undisputed, unoxidized **11** unblackened, unblemished **12** unbesmirched **13** unimpeachable

untaught 6 unread **7** natural
8 ignorant **9** untutored **10** illiterate, uneducated, unlettered, unschooled
11 spontaneous
12 uninstructed

untenable 4 weak **6** faulty, flawed **7** invalid, unsound
8 baseless, specious, spurious
9 debatable, erroneous, illogical **10** fallacious, groundless, unreliable **11** contestable

12 indefensible, questionable
13 insupportable, unjustifiable, unsustainable
14 unmaintainable

unthinkable 11 unwarranted
12 unimaginable **13** inconceivable, insupportable, unjustifiable **16** incomprehensible, out of the question

unthinking 7 witless **8** careless, heedless, mindless, tactless
9 imprudent, negligent, senseless **11** inadvertent, insensitive, thoughtless **12** undiplomatic
13 inconsiderate, uncircumspect

untidiness 5 chaos, mix-up, upset **6** jumble **7** clutter **8** disarray, disorder, scramble, shambles **9** confusion, messiness **10** sloppiness **12** dishevelment **14** disarrangement
15 disorganization

untidy 5 dowdy, messy
6 frowsy, mussed, sloppy
7 chaotic, rumpled, tousled, unkempt **8** careless, confused, littered, mussed up, slipshod, slovenly **9** cluttered **10** bedraggled, disarrayed, disheveled, disorderly, slatternly, topsy-turvy **12** unmethodical
13 helter-skelter

untie 4 free, undo **5** loose
6 loosen, unbind, unlace
7 unchain, unstrap **8** make free, unfasten **11** disentangle

untilled 6 fallow **8** unplowed
12 uncultivated

until we meet again
  French: **5** adieu **8** au revoir
  German: **14** auf Wiedersehen
  Hawaiian: **5** aloha
  Italian: **4** ciao **5** addio
    11 arrivederci
  Japanese: **8** sayonara
  Spanish: **5** adios

untimely 5 inapt **7** unhappy
8 ill-timed, mistimed, unseemly **9** imprudent, premature, unfitting **10** ill-advised, malapropos, out of place, unbecoming, unexpected, unsuitable **11** inopportune, unbefitting, unfortunate **12** inconvenient, infelicitous
13 inappropriate

untiring 5 fresh **6** steady **7** devoted, earnest, patient, staunch, zealous **8** constant, diligent, resolute, sedulous, tireless **9** assiduous, dedicated, steadfast, tenacious, unceasing, unwearied **10** determined, persistent, relentless, unflagging
11 never tiring, persevering, unfaltering, unremitting
12 wholehearted
13 indefatigable

untold 6 myriad, secret, unsaid **7** endless, private, unknown **8** hushed up, infinite, numerous, unspoken, withheld **9** concealed, countless, limitless, unbounded, uncounted, unrelated **10** numberless, suppressed, unnumbered, unreported, unrevealed **11** innumerable, undisclosed, unexpressed, unpublished **12** immeasurable, incalculable, undetermined

Untouchables, The
  character: 7 Rossman **9** Eliot Ness, Lee Hobson **10** Cam Allison, Frank Nitti **11** Enrico Rossi **14** Martin Flaherty **18** William Youngfellow
  cast: 10 Jerry Paris **11** Bruce Gordon, Paul Picerni, Robert Stack, Steve London **13** Abel Fernandez, Anthony George, Nick Georgiade
  narrator: 14 Walter Winchell

untouched 3 new **4** pure **5** alone **6** intact, virgin **8** pristine, unharmed **9** uninjured **10** unaffected, unmolested

untoward 5 amiss **6** unruly **7** adverse **8** contrary **9** difficult **11** unfavorable **12** inauspicious, unpropitious

untrainable 6 unruly **11** intractable, unteachable **12** ungovernable

untrained 3 raw **5** green **7** untried **9** unskilled **11** unqualified **13** inexperienced

untried 3 raw **5** green **6** callow **8** immature, untested **10** unseasoned **13** inexperienced

untroubled 4 calm **6** placid, serene **7** halcyon, relaxed **8** carefree, careless, peaceful, tranquil **9** easygoing, unworried **10** unbothered **11** free-and-easy, undisturbed, unperturbed **12** happy-go-lucky, lighthearted

untrue 4 fake, sham **5** false **6** made up **7** not true **8** disloyal, spurious, unchaste **9** dishonest, erroneous, faithless, falsified, incorrect, unfounded **10** adulterous, fallacious, fictitious, fraudulent, groundless, inaccurate, inconstant, perfidious, unfaithful, untruthful **11** promiscuous, treacherous **12** meretricious **13** double-dealing

untrustworthy 5 false **6** fickle, shifty, untrue **7** corrupt, crooked, devious **8** disloyal, fallible, slippery, two-faced **9** corrupted, deceitful, dishon-est, faithless, insincere, uncertain, unethical **10** capricious, inconstant, perfidious, unfaithful, unreliable, untruthful **11** treacherous **12** dishonorable, disreputable, questionable, undependable, unprincipled, unscrupulous **13** irresponsible **15** unauthenticated

untruth 3 fib, lie **4** hoax, tale, yarn **5** fable, story **6** canard, humbug **8** flimflam **9** deception, falsehood, fish story, invention **11** fabrication **12** equivocation **13** falsification, prevarication **16** cock-and-bull story **17** misrepresentation

untruthful 5 false, lying **8** specious, spurious **9** deceptive, dishonest **10** fraudulent, mendacious

untutored 5 naive **6** native, unread **8** ignorant, untaught **10** illiterate, uneducated, unlettered, unschooled **12** uninstructed **15** unsophisticated

untypical 3 odd **4** rare **5** alien **7** bizarre, deviant, strange, unusual **8** aberrant, abnormal, atypical, uncommon **9** anomalous, irregular, unnatural **10** unfamiliar **16** unrepresentative

unused 3 new **7** strange, untried **8** left over, not given, pristine, unopened **9** remaining, untouched **10** unemployed **12** unaccustomed, unacquainted, unhabituated

unusual 4 rare **5** novel **6** unique **7** curious, offbeat, strange **8** atypical, peculiar, singular, uncommon **9** unequaled, unheard-of, unmatched, untypical **10** noteworthy, one of a kind, phenomenal, remarkable, surprising, unfamiliar **11** exceptional **12** incomparable, unparalleled **13** extraordinary, unprecedented **16** out of the ordinary

unvaried 4 even **5** fixed **6** steady **7** regular, uniform **8** all alike, constant **9** identical, unchanged **10** all the same, invariable, monotonous, unchanging **11** homogeneous, unalterable, undeviating

unvarnished 3 raw **4** bald, bare **5** blunt, crude, frank, naked, plain, stark **6** candid, direct, honest, simple **7** sincere **8** straight **9** unadorned, uncolored **10** unfinished **11** fundamental, undisguised **13** unembellished **15** straightforward **23** straight-from-the-shoulder

unvarying 4 even **6** steady **7** regular, uniform **8** constant **10** unwavering

unveil 4 bare **6** reveal **7** divulge, publish, uncloak, uncover **8** announce, disclose **9** broadcast, make known, unsheathe **12** bring to light

unveiled 5 bared **8** divulged, laid bare, revealed **9** announced, broadcast, disclosed, made known, published, uncovered **14** brought to light

unveiling 4 show **5** array **7** display, exhibit, showing **10** exhibition, exposition **13** demonstration

unverified 7 alleged, rumored **8** disputed **15** unauthenticated, unsubstantiated

unwarranted 7 illegal **8** culpable, unlawful **9** arbitrary, unfounded **10** censurable, groundless, unapproved **11** inexcusable, uncalled-for, unjustified **12** indefensible, unauthorized, unreasonable, unsanctioned

unwary 4 rash **5** hasty **7** unalert **8** careless, headlong, heedless, reckless **9** imprudent, unguarded **10** incautious, indiscreet, unwatchful **11** precipitate **12** disregardful **13** uncircumspect

unwashed 4 foul **5** dirty, grimy, muddy **6** filthy, grubby, smudgy, soiled **7** unclean **8** begrimed

unwasteful 6 frugal **7** thrifty **9** effective, effectual, efficient **10** productive

unwavering 4 firm **6** steady, strong **7** staunch **8** faithful, resolute, unshaken, untiring **9** dedicated, steadfast, tenacious **10** determined, persistent, unflagging, unswerving **11** persevering, undeviating, unfaltering, unflinching, unremitting **12** single-minded **14** uncompromising

unwelcome 7 outcast **8** excluded, rejected, unwanted **9** thankless, uninvited, unpopular **10** uncared for, unpleasant, unrequired **11** displeasing, distasteful, undesirable, unessential, unnecessary, unwished for **12** disagreeable, unacceptable

unwell 3 ill, low **4** sick **5** frail **6** ailing, infirm, laid up, poorly, queasy, sickly **7** rundown **8** delicate, qualmish **10** indisposed **11** off one's feed **15** under the weather

unwholesome 3 bad **4** evil,

foul **5** toxic **6** deadly, filthy, sinful, wicked **7** baneful, harmful, hurtful, immoral, noxious, ruinous **8** depraved, venomous **9** corrupted, danger-ous, degrading, poisonous, pol-luting, unhealthy **10** corrupting, pernicious **11** deleterious, detrimental, undesirable, unhealthful **12** demoralizing, dishonorable, insalubrious, unnourishing **13** contaminating

unwieldy 5 bulky, heavy **6** clumsy **7** awkward, weighty **8** not handy **10** burdensome, cumbersome **12** hard to han-dle, incommodious, inconven-ient **13** uncomfortable

unwilled 6 reflex **9** automatic **11** involuntary, unconscious **12** uncontrolled **13** nonvolitional

unwilling 5 loath **6** averse **7** against, opposed **9** demur-ring, reluctant, resistant **10** dissenting, indisposed, un-desirous **11** disinclined **12** not in the mood, recalcitrant **14** unenthusiastic

unwillingness 8 aversion **10** opposition, reluctance, re-sistance **13** indisposition **14** disinclination

unwise 4 dumb **5** crazy, silly **6** stupid **7** foolish, unsound **8** reckless **9** foolhardy, impru-dent, senseless **10** ill-advised **11** improvident, inadvisable, injudicious **12** shortsighted, unreasonable **13** irresponsible, unintelligent

unwitting 7 unaware, un-meant **9** unknowing, un-planned **10** accidental, undesigned, unexpected, un-thinking **11** inadvertent, invol-untary **12** unconsenting **13** unintentional **14** unpremeditated

unwonted 4 rare **7** unusual **8** atypical, uncommon **10** in-frequent, remarkable, unex-pected, unfamiliar **11** exceptional **12** unaccus-tomed **13** extraordinary

unworkmanlike 6 clumsy, sloppy **11** inefficient

unworldly 4 holy, pure **5** godly, green, moral, naive, pious **6** callow, devout, divine, sacred, solemn **7** ethical **8** ethereal, heavenly, innocent, trusting **9** aesthetic, celestial, religious, spiritual, unearthly **10** idealistic, immaterial, pro-vincial **12** intellectual, meta-physical, overtrusting **13** inexperienced, philosophi-

cal **14** transcendental **15** unsophisticated

unworried 4 calm **6** serene **7** relaxed **8** carefree, com-posed, peaceful, tranquil **9** easygoing, unruffled **10** untroubled

unworthy 5 unfit **7** ignoble **8** improper, shameful, un-seemly **9** degrading, unethical **10** unbecoming, unsuitable **11** unbefitting **12** dishonorable, disreputable, unacceptable **13** discreditable, inappropriate, objectionable

unwrap 4 open **6** loosen, un-bind **7** uncover

unwrinkled 4 even, flat **6** ironed, smooth **7** unlined **8** smoothed **9** uncreased, unrumpled

unwritten 4 oral **5** tacit, vocal **7** assumed, implied **8** implicit, inferred, unstated **9** custom-ary **10** spoken only, under-stood, unrecorded **11** traditional, unexpressed **12** unformulated, unregistered **13** by word of mouth

unwritten law
Latin: **13** lex non scripta

unyielding 4 firm, hard **5** rigid, stiff, stony, tough **6** wooden **8** resolute, rocklike, stubborn **9** obstinate, steadfast, unbend-ing, unpliable **10** determined, inexorable, inflexible, persis-tent, unswerving, unwavering **11** undeviating **14** uncompromising

up 4 atop, lift, over, rear **5** about, above, aloft, along, aside, astir, at bat, built, close, equal, erect, raise **6** apiece, as-cend, higher, lifted **7** abreast, batting, forward, promote, skyward, through **8** advanced, cheerful, increase, out of bed, overhead, standing, together, windward **9** northward **10** op-timistic **11** constructed

up and about 5 afoot, astir **6** active, mobile, roused **7** walking **8** out of bed **10** ambulatory, on one's feet

up-and-down 6 fitful, seesaw, uneven **7** bobbing **8** jouncing, wavering **11** alternating, fluc-tuating, vacillating

upbraid 5 scold **6** berate, re-buke, revile **7** bawl out, cen-sure, chew out, reprove **8** admonish, chastise, de-nounce, reproach **9** castigate, dress down, reprimand **10** tongue-lash

upbringing 7 rearing **8** breed-ing, training **10** background

upcoming 6 coming, nearby **7** looming, nearing, pending **8** imminent **9** impending, mo-mentary **11** approaching, drawing nigh, forthcoming, in the offing, prospective

update 5 amend, emend, re-new **6** recast, revamp, revise, rework **7** restore, touch up, upgrade **8** overhaul, renovate **9** refurbish **10** rejuvenate, re-organize, streamline

up for grabs 4 open **9** available

upgrade 5 raise, slope **6** ascent, better **7** advance, dignify, ele-vate, incline, inflate, promote **8** gradient

upheaval 5 flood, quake **6** blowup, tumult **7** turmoil **8** disorder, upthrust **9** cata-clysm, explosion, tidal wave **10** disruption, earthquake, rev-olution **11** catastrophe, disturbance

uphill 4 hard **5** tough **6** rising, taxing, tiring, upward **7** ar-duous, onerous **8** toilsome, wearying **9** ascending, difficult, fatiguing, strenuous, weari-some **10** burdensome, enervat-ing, exhausting **12** backbreaking

uphill work 8 struggle, tough job **10** difficulty, rough going **11** arduousness **12** hard sled-ding **13** laboriousness

uphold 4 bear, prop **5** brace, carry, raise, shore **6** defend, hold up, prop up **7** approve, bolster, confirm, elevate, en-dorse, protect, shore up, sup-port, sustain **8** advocate, buttress, champion, maintain, preserve, underpin **9** encour-age **10** stand up for, under-brace **11** acknowledge, corroborate

upholder 7 devotee **8** adherent, advocate, defender, partisan **9** supporter

up in the clouds 6 elated, joyful, joyous **8** ecstatic, eu-phoric **9** exuberant, rapturous **11** on cloud nine **15** in sev-enth heaven

Upis
goddess of: **10** childbirth

Upjohn, Richard
architect of: **13** Trinity Church (NYC)
style: **13** Gothic Revival

upkeep 4 keep **6** living **7** sup-port **8** expenses, overhead **10** management, sustenance **11** maintenance, subsistence **12** conservation, preservation

upland 4 high, rise **5** ridge **6** height **7** plateau **8** eminence, highland **9** elevation, high place, high point **10** prominence

uplift 5 edify, raise **6** better, refine **7** advance, bracing, elevate, improve, inspire, lifting, shoring, support, upgrade **8** civilize, propping **9** cultivate, elevation **10** betterment, bolstering, enrichment, refinement **11** advancement, buttressing, cultivation, edification, enhancement, improvement **12** underpinning

uplifting 9 elevating, elevation, improving, inspiring **11** improvement **12** enlightening **13** enlightenment, inspirational

upon 2 at, on **4** atop **5** about **6** toward **7** against, thereon **9** by means of, thereupon **10** after which, thereafter

upper 3 top **4** high **5** major **6** higher, inland **7** eminent, greater, topmost **8** elevated, northern, superior **9** important

upper-case letter 7 capital **9** majuscule **13** capital letter

upper class 5 elite **6** gentry, uptown **7** (high) society **8** highborn, highbred, wellborn **9** beau monde, haut monde, high-class, patrician, top drawer **10** upper crust

11 aristocracy, blue-blooded **12** aristocratic, silk-stocking **14** creme de la creme, to the manor born **15** to the manner born

upper crust 5 elite **6** gentry **7** (high) society **9** beau monde, haut monde, top drawer **10** upper class **11** aristocracy **14** creme de la creme

upper hand 4 edge, sway **5** power **7** command, control, mastery **8** whip hand **9** advantage, authority, supremacy **10** domination **12** predominance

upper house 6 Senate **12** House of Lords

uppermost, upmost 3 top **4** main **5** chief, first, major, prime **7** highest, leading, primary, supreme, topmost **8** crowning, dominant, foremost, greatest, loftiest **9** essential, paramount, principal **10** preeminent **11** predominant **12** transcendent **13** most important

Upper Volta *see box*

upright 3 rib **4** fair, good, just, pale, pier, pile, pole, post, prop **5** erect, moral, shaft, stake, strut **6** column, honest, picket, pillar **7** ethical, support, upended **8** reliable, stan-

dard, vertical **9** honorable, righteous, stanchion **10** aboveboard, high-minded, principled, standing-up, upstanding **11** trustworthy **12** on the up-and-up **13** perpendicular

uprightness 5 honor **7** dignity, honesty **8** morality **9** integrity **13** righteousness **15** trustworthiness

uprising 4 riot **6** mutiny, revolt **8** outbreak **9** rebellion **10** insurgence, revolution **12** insurrection

uproar 3 ado **4** stir, to-do **5** furor **6** clamor, tumult **7** turmoil **9** agitation, commotion **11** disturbance, pandemonium **16** state of confusion

uproarious 4 loud, wild **5** noisy **6** raging, stormy **7** furious, intense, riotous **9** clamorous, hilarious, turbulent, very funny **10** boisterous, disorderly, hysterical, tumultuous **11** tempestuous **13** sidesplitting

uproot 6 banish **7** abolish, cast out, destroy, root out, wipe out **8** dislodge, displace, force out **9** eliminate, extirpate **10** annihilate, do away with **11** exterminate

upset 3 ire, irk, mad, vex **4** beat **5** anger, annoy, crush, irked, messy, mix up, pique, quash, smash, upend, vexed, worry **6** bother, cancel, change, defeat, enrage, grieve, invert, jumble, muddle, mussed, rattle, thrash, untidy **7** agitate, angered, annoyed, capsize, chaotic, confuse, conquer, disturb, enraged, fluster, furious, grieved, incense, jumbled, mixed-up, perturb, reverse, tip over, trouble, trounce, unnerve, upended, worried **8** agitated, bothered, capsized, confused, demolish, disorder, distress, incensed, inverted, overcome, overturn, slovenly, troubled, turn over, unnerved, upturned, vanquish **9** discomfit, disturbed, infuriate, overpower, overthrow, overwhelm, perturbed **10** discompose, disconcert, disheveled, disordered, disorderly, disquieted, distressed, hysterical, overturned, tipped over, topple over, topsy-turvy, turned over, upside-down **11** disarranged, disorganize, overwrought, wrong side up **12** disorganized **13** make miserable **14** turn topsy-turvy

upsetting
  French: 14 bouleversement

upshot 3 end **6** effect, payoff,

Upper Volta
  other name: 11 Burkina Faso (Fasso)
  capital/largest city: 11 Ouagadougou
  others: 4 Kaya **7** Banfora **9** Koudougou **10** Ouahigouya
  division: 7 Yatenga **9** Tenkodogo **11** Fada Ngourma
  monetary unit: 5 franc **7** centime
  mountain: 4 Tema
  highest point: 8 Nakourou **10** Tenakourou, Tenekourou
  river: 5 Komoe **6** Mekrou, Sourou **8** Pendjari, Red Volta **10** Black Volta, White Volta
  physical feature:
    plateau: **5** Sahel **7** Sikasso, Voltaic
    wind: **9** harmattan
  people: 4 Bobo, Lobi, Samo **5** Bella, Bissa, Dyula, Fulbe, Hausa, Mande, Marka, Mossi, Puehl **6** Fulani, Senufo, Tuareg **7** Grunshi, Voltaic, Yatenga **8** Mandingo **9** Gourounsi **15** Bunsansi Gambaga
    French governor: **7** Hesling
    god: **4** Wuro **5** Tenga
    king: **4** Naba **5** Mogho
    leader: **5** Oubri, Zerbo **7** Yameogo **8** Lamizana **9** Mogho Naba
  language: 4 Bobo, Lobi, More, Samo **5** Dyula, Mande, Mossi **6** French
  religion: 5 Islam **7** animism **12** Christianity
  place:
    game reserve: **11** Arlyand Pama
  feature:
    animal: **5** hyena **6** duiker, jackal **7** gazelle, warthog **10** hartebeest
    tree: **4** shea **6** acacia, baobab, karite, locust

result, sequel **7** outcome **8** offshoot **9** aftermath, outgrowth **10** conclusion **11** aftereffect, consequence, culmination, eventuality **16** final development

upside down 7 chaotic **8** reversed **10** disorderly **11** topsy turvey **12** bottomside up **16** at sixes and sevens

upstairs 2 up **11** above stairs, second floor

upstanding 4 good, tall, true **5** erect, moral, on end **6** honest **7** ethical, upright **8** straight, truthful, vertical, virtuous **9** honorable, righteous **11** trustworthy **13** incorruptible, perpendicular

upstart 4 snip, snob, snub **6** nobody **7** bounder, parvenu **8** mushroom **9** conceited, newly-rich **10** adventurer **12** nouveau riche **13** self-assertive

upsurge 4 gain, push, rise **5** spurt **6** pickup, thrust, upturn **7** advance, upswing **8** increase **11** improvement

upswing 4 rise **6** pickup **7** upsurge **11** improvement, upward trend

uptight 5 tense **7** anxious, fearful, nervous, worried, wound up **8** insecure, neurotic, troubled **9** unbending **10** unyielding **12** apprehensive

up-to-date 2 in **3** new **5** today **6** modern, modish, timely, trendy, with-it **7** current, stylish **9** in fashion **12** contemporary **13** up-to-the-minute **French: 9** au courant

upturn 4 gain, push **6** thrust **7** advance, upsurge **8** increase **9** expansion **11** improvement

upward 4 high, more **5** above, aloft **7** skyward **9** ascending, uppermost

upward movement 4 rise **5** climb **6** ascent, rising, upturn **7** scaling, takeoff **8** climbing, mounting **9** ascension

upward trend 4 rise **5** boost **6** pickup **7** advance, upsurge, upswing **8** increase **11** improvement

Uralic
language branch: **7** Samoyed **10** Finno-Ugric

Urania
also: **9** Aphrodite
member of: **5** Muses
personifies: **9** astronomy

uranium
chemical symbol: **1** U

Uranus
mother: **4** Gaea
wife: **4** Gaea
father of: **6** Giants, Titans **8** Cyclopes **10** Titanesses **13** Hecatonchires
castrated by: **6** Cronos, Cronus, Kronos

Uranus
position: **7** seventh
satellite: **5** Ariel **6** Oberon **7** Miranda, Titania, Umbriel
color: **9** blue-green
characteristic: **5** rings

Urartu see **7** Armenia

urban 4 city, town **5** civic **8** citified **9** municipal **11** worldly-wise **12** cosmopolitan, metropolitan **13** sophisticated

urban area 4 city **9** inner city **10** metropolis **11** megalopolis **16** metropolitan area

urbane 5 civil, suave **6** polite, smooth **7** courtly, elegant, gallant, genteel, politic, refined, tactful **8** debonair, gracious, mannerly, polished, well-bred **9** civilized, courteous **10** chivalrous, cultivated, diplomatic **11** gentlemanly **12** cosmopolitan, well-mannered **13** sophisticated

urchin 3 boy, imp, lad **4** brat, waif **5** gamin, stray, whelp, youth **6** gamine, laddie **8** young pup **9** stripling, young punk, youngster **10** young rogue, young tough **11** guttersnipe

Urd 4 Norn
origin: **12** Scandinavian
form: **8** giantess
personifies: **4** past
developed from: **5** Urdar
companion: **5** Skuld **8** Verdandi

Urdar 12 original Norn
origin: **12** Scandinavian
form: **8** giantess
children: **3** Urd **5** Skuld **8** Verdandi

Urey, Harold Clayton
field: **9** chemistry
isolated: **9** deuterium
awarded: **10** Nobel prize

urge 3 yen **4** back, coax, goad, itch, poke, prod, push, spur, sway, wish **5** drive, egg on, fancy, force, press, prick, speed **6** advise, desire, exhort, hasten, hunger, motive, reason, thirst **7** beseech, counsel, craving, dictate, entreat, implore, impulse, longing, passion, push for, quicken,

request, solicit, suggest **8** advocate, appeal to, argue for, champion, convince, persuade, petition, pressure, stimulus, yearning **9** hankering, importune, incentive, plead with, prescribe, prompting, recommend **10** accelerate, inducement, motivation, supplicate **11** prevail upon, provocation

urgency 4 need, urge, want **5** press **6** stress **8** exigency, pressure **9** necessity **10** importance, insistence **11** persistence **14** imperativeness **15** importunateness

urgent 5 grave **6** ardent **7** crucial, earnest, fervent, intense, serious, weighty, zealous **8** critical, pleading, pressing, required, spirited **9** demanding, essential, heartfelt, important, insistent, momentous, necessary **10** beseeching, compelling, compulsory, imperative, obligatory, passionate **12** wholehearted **13** indispensable

urge on 4 push **5** boost **7** cheer on, pull for, root for

urging 7 bidding, counsel, goading **8** egging on **9** prompting **11** exhortation

Uriah
father: **7** Shemiah
wife: **9** Bathsheba
served: **5** David

urinary system
component: **6** kidney, ureter **7** bladder, urethra
rids body of: **5** salts, waste, water **8** minerals

Uris, Leon
author of: **5** Topaz **6** Exodus **7** Trinity **9** Battle Cry **10** Armageddon

urn 3 jar, pig **4** ewer, kist, tomb, vase **5** grave, steen **6** teapot **7** samovar **9** coffeepot
botanical: **7** capsule **11** sporebearer
in keno: **5** goose

Urn Burial
author: **15** Sir Thomas Browne

Uruguay see box, p. 1036

U S A
author: **13** John Dos Passos
character: **10** Ben Compton, Mary French **11** Joe Williams **12** Margo Dowling **13** Fainy McCreary (Mac), Janey Williams **14** J Ward Morehouse **15** Charley Anderson, Eleanor Stoddard, Eveline Hutchins **18** Anne Elizabeth Trent **22** Richard Ellsworth Savage

Uruguay
  other name: 10 Purple Land
  capital/largest city: 10 Montevideo
  others: 4 Fray, Melo 5 Minas, Rocha, Salto 6 Bentos, Riv-
    era 7 Artigas, Colonia, Dolores, Durazno, Florida, San
    Jose 8 Mercedes, Paysandu, Trinidad 9 Maldonado 10 Las
    Piedras, Santa Lucia, Tacuarembo 12 Treinta y Tres
    13 San Jose de Mayo
  measure: 4 vara 6 cuadra, suerte
  monetary unit: 4 peso 9 centesimo, centisimo
  weight: 7 quintal
  island: 5 Lobos
  lake: 5 Merin, Mirim 18 Embalse del Rio Negro
  mountain: 6 Animas 10 Grand Hills 14 Cuchilla Grande
  highest point: 15 Mirador Nacional
  river: 4 Malo 5 Mirim, Negro, Plata 6 Parana, Ulimar
    7 Cuareim, Queguay, Uruguay 8 Yaguaron 9 Cebollati
    10 Tacuarembo
  sea: 8 Atlantic
  physical feature:
    estuary: 5 Plata
  people: 4 Yaro 5 Swiss 6 Indian 7 Italian, mestizo, Rus-
    sian, Spanish 8 Charruas
    artist: 6 Figari
    author: 4 Rodo 5 Reyes 6 Onetti 7 Sanchez 9 San Mar-
      tin 10 Ibarbourou
    leader: 5 Oribe 6 Rivera 7 Artigas 9 Lavelleja 10 Borda-
      berry 14 Batlle y Ordonez
  language: 7 Italian, Spanish
  religion: 13 Roman Catholic
  place:
    resort: 12 Punta del Este
    square: 13 Independencia
  feature:
    animal: 4 puma 6 jaguar 8 capybara 9 armadillo
    bird: 4 rhea 5 nandu 7 hornero, ostrich
    cattle ranch: 8 estancia
    cowboy: 6 gaucho
    dance: 5 tango 7 milonga
    festival: 8 Carnival 13 Semana Criolla
    lasso: 10 boleadoras
    metal straw: 8 bombilla
    music: 9 candomble
    musical drama: 7 tablado
    ruling class: 10 Patriciado
  food:
    barbecue: 5 asado
    dish: 7 puchero 9 churrasco 13 asado con cuero
    drink: 4 mate

usable 5 handy 6 useful
9 adaptable 10 functional
11 serviceable

usage 3 use 4 care, mode
5 habit 6 custom, manner,
method, system 7 control
8 good form, habitude, handling, practice 9 etiquette, operation, tradition, treatment
10 convention, employment,
management 12 manipulation

use 3 aid, ply, sap 4 good,
help, work 5 apply, avail,
drain, exert, spend, treat,
usage, value, waste, wield,
worth 6 devour, employ, expend, handle, profit 7 benefit,
consume, deplete, exhaust, exploit, operate, service, utilize

8 deal with, exercise, function,
handling, profit by, put to
use, resort to, squander 9 act
toward, advantage, dissipate,
enjoyment, make use of, operation, swallow up, throw
away 10 employment, manipulate, run through, usefulness
11 application, convenience,
fritter away, utilization 12 behave toward, capitalize on
13 make the most of
14 serviceability

used 3 old 5 eaten, spent 7 ap-
plied, treated 8 actuated, consumed, depleted, employed,
occupied, operated, utilized
9 customary, exercised, exhausted, exploited, practiced

10 accustomed, habituated,
secondhand 11 implemented,
manipulated

used up 4 beat, shot 5 all in,
spent 6 wasted 7 worn out
8 depleted, tired out
9 exhausted

useful 5 handy 7 helpful
8 valuable 9 effective, practical, rewarding 10 beneficial,
convenient, functional, profitable, time-saving, worthwhile
11 serviceable, utilitarian
12 advantageous

usefulness 5 avail, value,
worth 6 profit 7 benefit, purpose, utility 9 advantage
11 convenience, helpfulness,
suitability 12 adaptability,
practicality 13 effectiveness
14 serviceability

useless 4 vain 6 futile 7 of no
use 8 bootless, unusable
9 fruitless, unhelpful, worthless 10 inadequate, profitless,
unavailing 11 incompetent, ineffectual, inefficient 12 unproductive 13 impracticable,
inefficacious, nonfunctional,
unserviceable

uselessness 6 vanity 8 futility,
idleness 9 inutility 10 inefficacy 13 fruitlessness,
worthlessness

Uses of Enchantment, The
  author: 15 Bruno Bettelheim

use sparingly 4 save 5 hoard,
stint 6 scrimp 7 cut back, dole
out 8 conserve, not waste,
preserve

use to advantage 7 exploit
8 profit by 12 capitalize on
13 turn to account

use up 5 drain, spend 6 expend, finish 7 consume, deplete, exhaust 9 dissipate
10 run through

Ushant
  author: 11 Conrad Aiken

usher 4 lead, show 5 guide,
steer 6 attend, convoy, direct,
escort, herald, launch, leader,
porter, ring in, squire 7 conduct, precede, preface 8 announce, director, proclaim
9 conductor, introduce
10 doorkeeper, gatekeeper,
inaugurate

Usnach
  also: 6 Usnech
  origin: 5 Irish
  daughter: 6 Naoise

Usnech *see* 6 Usnach

USSR *see* 6 Russia

Ustinov, Peter
  born: 6 London 7 England

roles: 7 Topkapi **8** Quo Vadis? **9** Billy Budd, Spartacus **12** We're No Angels

usual 5 stock, trite **6** common, normal, wonted **7** popular, regular, routine, typical **8** expected, familiar, habitual, ordinary, orthodox, standard **9** customary, hackneyed **10** accustomed, prescribed, threadbare **11** commonplace, established, oft-repeated, traditional **12** conventional, run-of-the-mill **15** well-established

usurp 4 grab **5** steal **7** preempt **8** arrogate **10** commandeer **11** appropriate **12** encroach upon, infringe upon

usurpation 6 taking **7** seizure **8** grabbing, stealing **10** arrogation, preemption **13** appropriation

Utah *see box*

utensils 4 gear **5** tools **6** outfit, silver, tackle **8** flatware **9** apparatus **10** implements, silverware **11** instruments **13** paraphernalia

Utgard
  origin: 12 Scandinavian
  realm of: 7 Skrymir **10** Utgardloki
  location: 9 Gatunheim

Utgardloki *see* **7** Skrymir

utilitarian 5 handy **6** usable, useful **8** sensible, valuable, workable **9** effective, efficient, practical, pragmatic **10** beneficial, convenient, functional, profitable **11** serviceable **12** advantageous

utility 3 aid, gas, use **4** help **5** avail, extra **6** backup **7** benefit, reserve, service **8** function **9** accessory, advantage, alternate, auxiliary, secondary,

surrogate, telephone **10** additional, substitute, usefulness **11** convenience, electricity **12** availability, supplemental **13** public service **14** serviceability

utilization 3 use **10** employment **11** application **12** exploitation

utilize 3 use **6** employ **7** exploit **8** profit by, put to use, resort to **9** make use of **12** capitalize on **13** bring into play, make the most of, turn to account **14** avail oneself of, have recourse to, put into service **15** take advantage of

utmost, uttermost 4 acme, best, main, peak, tops **5** chief, first, major, prime **6** tiptop, zenith **7** capital, highest, leading, maximum, primary, supreme, the most **8** cardinal, foremost, greatest, last word, ultimate **9** paramount, principal, sovereign **10** preeminent **11** predominant

Uto-Aztecan (Nahuatl)
  tribe: 4 Pima **5** Aatam, Aztec, Nahua **6** Mexica, Papago **8** Pima Alto

utopia 4 Eden **6** heaven **7** Erewhon **8** paradise **9** ideal life, Shangri-la **12** perfect bliss, perfect place **13** seventh heaven

utopian 9 visionary **10** idealistic, unfeasible, unworkable **11** unrealistic **12** otherworldly, unattainable, unrealizable **13** impracticable, insubstantial, unfulfillable

Utrillo, Maurice
  born: 5 Paris **6** France
  mother: 14 Suzanne Valadon
  artwork: 16 The Church at Deuil, The Church of Blevy **17** Church at St Hilaire **19** La Petite Communiante **22** Sacre Coeur de Montmartre

ut supra 7 as above

utter 3 say **4** emit, pure, talk, tell, yell **5** sheer, shout, speak, state, total, voice **6** entire, mutter, reveal **7** declare, deliver, divulge, exclaim, express, perfect, whisper **8** absolute, complete, disclose, outright, proclaim, thorough, vocalize **9** downright, enunciate, out-and-out, pronounce, unchecked **10** articulate, unmodified, unrelieved **11** categorical, unequivocal, unmitigated, unqualified

utterance 4 talk, word **6** an-

Utah
  abbreviation: 2 UT
  nickname: 6 Mormon **7** Beehive
  capital/largest city: 12 Salt Lake City
  others: 3 Roy **4** Moab, Orem **5** Delta, Heber, Kanab, Logan, Magna, Manti, Nepli, Ogden, Price, Provo **6** Beaver, Eureka, Kearns, Layton, Murray, Tooele, Vernal **7** Bingham **8** American **9** Bountiful **11** Brigham City
  college: 5 Weber **11** Westminster **12** Brigham Young
  feature:
    bridge: 7 Rainbow
    dam: 6 Hoover **10** Glen Canyon
    gorge: 7 Flaming
    national historic site: 11 Golden Spike
    national monument: 8 Dinosaur **14** Natural Bridges
    national park: 4 Zion **6** Arches **11** Bryce Canyon, Canyonlands, Capital Reef
    reef: 7 Capital
  tribe: 3 Ute **5** Piute, Uinta(h), Yampa **6** Navajo, Paiute **7** Gosiute **8** Paviotso, Shoshoni
  people: 7 Mormons **10** Maude Adams **11** Karl G Maeser **12** Brigham Young **13** John M Browning **15** Latter-Day Saints **16** George Sutherland **19** Daniel Cowan Jackling
    explorer: 9 Dominguez, Escalante
  lake: 4 Mead, Swan, Utah **6** Powell, Sevier **9** Great Salt
  land rank: 8 eleventh
  mountain: 4 Lena, Lion, Waas **5** Cedar, Henry, Hogup, Peale, Rocky, Trail, Uinta **6** Frisco, Navajo, Swasey, Wahwah **7** Granite, Griffin, Hawkins, Pennell, Terrace, Wasatch **8** Linnaeus **9** Confusion
    highest point: 9 Kings Peak
  physical feature:
    basin: 5 Great
    canyon: 4 Echo
    desert: 6 Sevier
    plateau: 7 Wasatch **8** Colorado, Tavaputs
  river: 4 Bear **5** Grand, Green, Weber **6** Jordan, Sevier, Virgin **7** San Juan **8** Colorado
  state admission: 10 forty-fifth
  state bird: 7 seagull
  state flower: 8 sego lily
  state motto: 8 Industry
  state song: 14 Utah We Love Thee
  state tree: 10 blue spruce

swer, remark, speech **7** opinion **9** discourse, statement **10** expression **11** declaration, exclamation **12** articulation, proclamation, vocalization **13** pronouncement, verbalization

utterly 4 just **5** fully **6** wholly **7** totally **8** entirely, outright **9** downright, extremely, perfectly **10** absolutely, completely, thoroughly **14** to the nth degree

uttermost 6 utmost **7** extreme, maximum, supreme **9** outermost, sovereign **12** extreme limit

Utu
　origin: 8 Sumerian
　god of: 3 sun

Uzbekistan
　capital/largest city: 8 Tashkent
　others: 9 Samarkand
　head of state: 9 president
　government: 8 republic
　monetary unit: 5 ruble

　river: 8 Amu Darya, Syr Darya
　sea: 4 Aral
　people: 5 Uzbek
　language: 5 Uzbek
　religion: 5 Islam **11** Sunni Muslim

Uzziah
　also: 7 Azariah
　king of: 5 Judah
　father: 7 Amaziah
　son: 6 Jotham **7** Jehoram **8** Jonathan

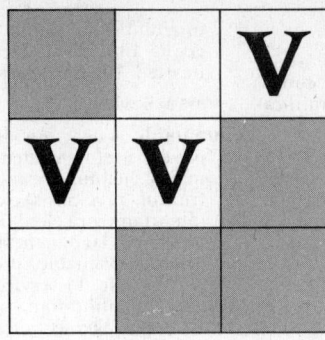

vacancy 3 gap **4** hole, void **5** abode, place **6** breach, cavity, hollow **7** crevice, fissure, housing, lodging, opening **9** emptiness, situation **10** empty space, vacantness **11** room for rent **12** house for rent

vacant 4 dull, free, idle, open **5** aloof, blank, blase, clear, empty, vapid **6** unused, wooden **7** deadpan, for rent, leisure, vacuous **8** deserted, detached, for lease, forsaken, not in use, unfilled **9** abandoned, apathetic, incurious, oblivious, poker-face, unengaged **10** tenantless, unemployed, unoccupied, untenanted **11** indifferent, unconcerned, unfurnished, uninhabited **12** unencumbered **14** expressionless **15** uncomprehending

vacate 4 quit **5** empty, leave **6** give up, resign **8** abdicate, evacuate, hand over **9** surrender **10** depart from, relinquish

vacate the throne 4 cede, flee, quit **5** yield **6** give up, resign, retire **7** abandon **8** abdicate **10** relinquish

vacation 4 rest **5** leave, R and R **6** recess **7** holiday **8** furlough, holidays **10** sabbatical **12** intermission **13** take a vacation **14** leave of absence **17** rest-and-recreation
  French: 8 vacances

vacillate 4 reel, rock, roll, sway, toss **5** pitch, shift, waver **6** falter, teeter, totter, wobble **7** flutter, vibrate **8** hesitate **9** fluctuate, hem and haw, oscillate **12** shilly-shally **14** blow hot and cold

vacillating 7 swaying **8** wavering **9** diffident, uncertain, vibrating **10** hesitating, irresolute, on the fence **11** fluctuating, uncertainty

12 irresolution **15** shilly-shallying

vacillation 7 swaying **8** wavering **9** faltering, vibration **10** indecision **11** fluctuation, uncertainty **12** irresolution **15** shilly-shallying

Vacuna
  origin: 6 Sabine
  goddess of: 11 agriculture

vacuous 4 dull, idle, void **5** blank, empty, inane, silly **6** stupid, vacant **7** fatuous, foolish **8** indolent, unfilled **9** senseless **11** empty-headed, purposeless

Vaduz
  capital of: 13 Liechtenstein

vae victis 18 woe to the vanquished

vagabond 4 hobo **5** gypsy, nomad, rover, tramp **6** roamer, roving **7** drifter, floater, migrant, nomadic, rambler, roaming, vagrant **8** bohemian, carefree, homeless, rambling, wanderer, wayfarer **9** footloose, itinerant, transient, traveling, wandering, wayfaring **10** journeying **11** beachcomber

Vagabond Lover
  nickname of: 10 Rudy Vallee

vagary 4 kink, whim **5** fancy, humor, quirk **6** notion, oddity, whimsy **7** caprice, fantasy, impulse **8** crotchet, daydream **10** brainstorm, erraticism **11** peculiarity **12** eccentricity, idiosyncrasy, passing fancy

vagrant 3 bum **4** hobo **5** nomad, rover, tramp **6** beggar, loafer, roamer, roving **7** floater, migrant, nomadic, roaming **8** homeless, rambling, vagabond, wanderer **9** itinerant, transient, wandering **10** panhandler **11** peripatetic **15** knight-of-the-road

vague 4 hazy **5** fuzzy, loose

6 casual, random, unsure **7** general, unclear **8** confused, nebulous **9** imprecise, uncertain, unsettled **10** ill-defined, indefinite, inexplicit, undetailed, unspecific **11** not definite, unspecified **12** undetermined

vaguely 5 dimly **6** hazily **7** loosely **8** dreamily, slightly, vacantly **9** obscurely, sketchily **10** nebulously **11** ambiguously **12** indistinctly

vagueness 8 haziness **9** ambiguity, confusion, fuzziness **11** uncertainty **13** lack of clarity **14** indefiniteness

vain 4 idle **5** cocky, proud, silly **6** futile **7** foolish, pompous, stuck-up, useless **8** arrogant, boastful, bootless, dandyish, egoistic, nugatory, puffed-up, trifling **9** conceited, egotistic, fruitless, pointless, worthless **10** disdainful, profitless, swaggering, unavailing **11** egotistical, ineffective, ineffectual, superficial, time-wasting **12** self-admiring, supercilious, unprofitable, unsuccessful, vainglorious **13** self-important, self-satisfied

Vainamoinen
  origin: 7 Finnish
  hero of: 8 Kalevala
  form: 8 magician
  opposes: 5 Louhi
    11 Joukahainen

vainglorious 5 cocky **7** haughty, pompous, stuck-up **8** affected, arrogant, boastful, bragging, insolent **9** conceited **10** egoistical, pretentious, swaggering **11** egotistical, swell-headed **12** narcissistic, supercilious **13** full of oneself, self-important

vainglory 6 vanity **7** conceit, swagger **9** cockiness **10** pretension **11** braggadocio

14 self-importance **16** over-bearing pride

vale 6 good-by **8** farewell

valedictory 4 last **5** final **7** parting **8** farewell, terminal, ultimate **9** departing **10** conclusive **11** leavetaking **14** farewell speech **19** commencement address

Valentine
character in: **20** Two Gentlemen of Verona
author: **11** Shakespeare

Valentino, Rudolph
real name: **16** Rodolfo (Alfonzo Raffaele Pierre Philibert) Guglielmi
born: **5** Italy **12** Castellaneta
wife: **9** Jean Acker **14** Natasha Rambova
roles: **8** The Sheik **12** Blood and Sand **16** The Son of the Sheik **17** Monsieur Beaucaire **30** The Four Horsemen of the Apocalypse

valerian 9 Valeriana
varieties: **3** red **5** Greek **6** common **7** African **8** American **11** long-spurred

Valery, Paul
author of: **7** Cahiers, Charmes **12** The Young Fate **13** Le Jeune Parque **16** Sketch of a Serpent **20** The Graveyard by the Sea

Valhalla
origin: **8** Teutonic
hall of: **4** Odin **5** Othin

valiant 4 bold **5** brave, noble **6** daring, heroic **7** gallant **8** fearless, intrepid, knightly, resolute, stalwart, unafraid, valorous **9** audacious, dauntless, undaunted **10** chivalrous, courageous **11** lionhearted, unflinching **12** bold-spirited, great-hearted, stouthearted

valid 4 good **5** legal, licit, sound **6** lawful, proper, strong **7** fitting, genuine, logical, weighty **8** accurate, decisive, forceful, official, powerful, suitable, truthful **9** authentic, effective, legalized, realistic **10** acceptable, applicable, compelling, convincing, legitimate **11** substantial, well-founded **12** well-grounded **13** authoritative, being in effect **14** constitutional, legally binding

validate 5 enact, prove, stamp **6** ratify, verify **7** certify, confirm, sustain, warrant, witness **8** legalize, sanction **9** authorize, make legal, make valid **10** make lawful **11** corroborate, countersign **12** au-thenticate, make official, substantiate

validation 8 sanction **12** confirmation, legalization, ratification **13** authorization, certification

validity 5 force, logic, power, right **6** weight **7** grounds, potency **8** accuracy, legality, strength **9** authority, soundness, substance **10** legal force, legitimacy, properness **11** suitability **12** authenticity, truthfulness **13** acceptability, applicability, effectiveness **14** conclusiveness, convincingness

valise 3 bag **4** grip **7** handbag, luggage, satchel **8** suitcase **9** briefcase, Gladstone **11** portmanteau

Valjean, Jean
character in: **13** Les Miserables
author: **4** Hugo

Valkyrie
origin: **8** Teutonic
home: **8** Valhalla
attendant of: **4** Odin **5** Othin
queen: **8** Brunhild, Brynhild **10** Brunnhilde

Vallee, Rudy
real name: **17** Hubert Prior Vallee
nickname: **16** The Vagabond Lover
born: **13** Island Point VT
played: **9** saxophone
wife: **9** Jane Greer
roles: **16** The Vagabond Lover **17** The Palm Beach Story, Unfaithfully Yours **41** How to Succeed in Business Without Really Trying

Valletta
capital of: **5** Malta

valley 3 cut, dip, gap **4** dale, dell, glen, vale **5** basin, chasm, glade, gorge, gulch, gully **6** bottom, canyon, divide, hollow, ravine **8** water gap

Valley Forge
author: **15** Maxwell Anderson

Valley of Horses, The
author: **9** Jean M Auel

Valley of the Dolls
author: **16** Jacqueline Susann

valor 4 grit, guts **5** nerve, pluck, spunk **6** daring, mettle **7** bravery, courage, heroism **8** boldness, chivalry **9** fortitude, gallantry **11** intrepidity **12** fearlessness **13** dauntlessness

valorous 4 bold **5** brave, gutsy **6** heroic, plucky **7** valiant **8** fearless, intrepid, stalwart, unafraid **9** dauntless **10** courageous **11** indomitable, lionhearted **12** stouthearted

valse 5 waltz

valuable 4 dear, good **6** costly, prized, useful, valued **7** admired, helpful **8** esteemed, fruitful, precious **9** expensive, important, priceless, respected, treasured **10** beneficial, high-priced, invaluable, profitable, worthwhile **11** serviceable, significant, utilitarian **12** advantageous

valuation 9 appraisal **10** assessment, evaluation **14** estimated value

value, values 3 use **4** cost, help, rate **5** assay, count, judge, merit, price, prize, rules, weigh, worth **6** admire, amount, assess, charge, esteem, ideals, profit, reckon, revere, size up **7** beliefs, benefit, cherish, compute, customs, respect, service, utility **8** appraise, evaluate, prestige, treasure **9** advantage, appraisal, greatness, moral code, practices, standards **10** admiration, appreciate, assessment, estimation, excellence, importance, set store by, usefulness **11** conventions, market price, superiority **12** code of ethics, institutions, significance

valued 6 prized **7** revered **8** esteemed **9** cherished, respected, treasured **11** appreciated **14** highly regarded

valueless 7 trivial, useless **9** worthless **11** of no account, unimportant **13** insignificant **14** good for nothing **15** inconsequential

vamoose 3 out **4** away, scat, shoo **5** be off, leave, scram **6** beat it, begone, depart, get out, go away **7** get lost

vamp 5 siren **9** temptress **10** seductress **11** enchantress, femme fatale **12** introduction

Vamp
nickname of: **9** Theda Bara

vampire 3 bat **7** Dracula **11** bloodsucker

van 4 cart, dray, head **5** lorry, scout, truck, wagon **6** camper, picket **7** trailer **8** sentinel, vanguard **9** first line, forefront, front rank **10** avant-garde, large truck **12** advance guard, covered truck **13** front of an army **16** foremost division
french: **7** fourgon

Van, Bobby
real name: **10** Robert King
born: **9** New York NY

roles: **10** Kiss Me Kate, On Your Toes **11** No No Nanette **12** It's Only Money, The Ladies' Man **13** Small Town Girl **23** The Affairs of Dobie Gillis

van Alen, William
architect of: **16** Chrysler Building (NYC)

Van Allen, James Alfred
field: **7** physics
invented: **18** radio proximity fuse
discovered: **22** Van Allen radiation belts

Van Buren, Martin *see box*

Vance, Vivian
real name: **11** Vivian Jones
born: **12** Cherryvale KS
roles: **9** I Love Lucy **10** Ethel Mertz

Vancouver
hockey team: **7** Canucks

vandal 6 looter, raider **7** ravag-

er, wrecker **8** marauder, pillager, saboteur **9** barbarian, despoiler, destroyer, plunderer **10** demolisher

vandalism 6 damage **10** defacement **11** destruction **17** malicious mischief

vandalize 3 mar **5** trash, wreck **6** damage, deface **7** despoil, destroy

Vanderlyn, John
born: **10** Kingston NY
artwork: **14** Ariadne on Naxos **20** The Death of Jane McCrea **28** Marius Amid the Ruins of Carthage **31** Ariadne Asleep on the Island of Naxos

Van Dyck, Sir Anthony
born: **7** Antwerp **8** Flanders
artwork: **8** Charles I (in Hunting Dress) **11** Iconography **18** Madonna of the Rosary **19** Blessed Herman Joseph, Cardinal Bentiro-

glio **20** Ecstasy of St Augustine **21** Marchesa Elena Grimaldi

Van Dyke, Dick
born: **12** West Plains MO
roles: **12** Mary Poppins **12** Bye Bye Birdie **15** Dick Van Dyke Show

Vane, Sutton
author of: **12** Outward Bound

Vanessa
author: **11** Hugh Walpole

Van Gogh, Vincent
born: **12** GrootZundert **14** The Netherlands
artwork: **10** Pere Tanguy **11** Cafe at Night, L'Arlesienne **13** The Olive Grove **14** The Starry Night **15** The Potato Eaters **16** The Bridge at Arles **18** Portrait of Dr Gachet, The Chair and the Pipe **22** Cornfield with Cypresses

vanguard 3 van **7** leaders **8** forerank **9** first line, forefront, front line, front rank, spearhead **10** avant-garde, innovators, leadership, modernists **11** pacesetters, tastemakers **12** advance guard, trailblazers, trendsetters

Van Helsing, Dr
character in: **7** Dracula
author: **6** Stoker

Vanir
origin: **12** Scandinavian
race: **4** gods
conflicting with: **4** Asar **5** Aesir

vanish 3 die, end **5** cease **6** die out, expire, perish **7** die away **8** dissolve, fade away, melt away, pass away **9** disappear, evaporate, terminate **13** dematerialize **15** become invisible

vanished 4 dead, gone, lost **7** defunct, died out, extinct **11** disappeared

vanishing 8 dying out **10** extinction, fading away **11** passing away **12** disappearing **13** disappearance **15** dematerializing

vanitas vanitatum 16 vanity of vanities

vanity 4 sham **5** folly, pride **6** mirage **7** compact, conceit, egotism, falsity, inanity **8** delusion, futility, idleness, selflove **9** emptiness, powder box, vainglory, vanity bag **10** hollowness, narcissism, self-praise, vanity case **11** makeup table, mirror table, self-conceit, uselessness **13** dressing table, fruitlessness, worthlessness

---

Van Buren, Martin
nicknames: **9** The Red Fox **17** The Little Magician **18** The Careful Dutchman
presidential rank: **6** eighth
party: **8** Democrat
state represented: **7** New York
defeated: **5** (Hugh Lawson) White **6** (William Person) Mangum **7** (Daniel) Webster **8** (William Henry) Harrison
vice president: **7** (Richard Mentor) Johnson
cabinet:
state: **7** (John) Forsyth
treasury: **8** (Levi) Woodbury
war: **8** (Joel Roberts) Poinsett
attorney general: **6** (Benjamin Franklin) Butler, (Felix) Grundy, (Henry Dilworth) Gilpin
navy: **8** (James Kirke) Paulding **9** (Mahlon) Dickerson
postmaster general: **5** (John Milton) Niles **7** (Amos) Kendall
born/died/buried: **12** Kinderhook NY
education:
Academy: **10** Kinderhook
college: **4** none
studied: **3** law
religion: **13** Dutch Reformed
vacation:
toured: **6** Europe (1853-1855)
author: **64** Inquiry into the Origin and Course of Political Parties in the United States
political career: **8** US Senate **11** state Senate **13** vice president **20** state Attorney General
governor of: **7** New York
secretary of: **5** State
minister: **12** Great Britain
civilian career: lawyer
notable events of lifetime/term: **5** Panic (of 1837)
treaty: **16** Webster-Ashburton
war: **9** Aroostook
father: **7** Abraham
mother: **5** Maria (Hoes Van Alen)
siblings: **6** Derike, Hannah **7** Abraham **8** Lawrence
wife: **6** Hannah (Hoes)
children: **4** John **6** Martin **7** Abraham **13** Smith Thompson

14 self-admiration, superficiality

Vanity Fair
author: 25 William Makepeace Thackeray
character: 10 Becky Sharp 11 Miss Crawley 12 Amelia Sedley, Joseph (Jos) Sedley 13 George Osborne, Rawdon Crawley 14 Sir Pitt Crawley 20 Captain William Dobbin

vanity of vanities
Latin: 16 vanitas vanitatum

vanquish 4 beat, best, drub, lick, rout 5 crush 6 defeat, master, subdue, thrash 7 conquer 8 overcome 9 overpower, overthrow, overwhelm, subjugate 11 triumph over

vanquisher 6 master, victor, winner 7 subduer 8 champion 9 conqueror 10 subjugator

vanquishment 6 defeat 7 mastery, triumph, victory, winning 8 conquest 10 conquering, overcoming

Van Slyke, Helen
author of: 10 No Love Lost 15 A Necessary Woman, The Heart Listens 18 Always Is Not Forever

Van Tassel, Katrina
character in: 23 The Legend of Sleepy Hollow
author: 6 Irving

Vanuatu *see box*

vapid 4 dull, flat, lame, tame 5 bland, empty, stale 7 insipid 8 lifeless 9 colorless, pointless 10 flavorless, wishy-washy 11 meaningless, uninspiring 12 unsatisfying 13 characterless

vapor 3 dew, fog 4 haze, mist, smog 5 fumes, smoke, steam 6 miasma 8 moisture

vaporize 5 dry up 7 distill 8 condense, melt away 9 dissipate, evaporate

Varden, Gabriel/Dolly
character in: 12 Barnaby Rudge
author: 7 Dickens

Vargas Llosa, Mario
author of: 13 The Green House 16 The Time of the Hero 26 Conversation in the Cathedral 27 Aunt Julia and the Scriptwriter 34 Captain Pantoja and the Special Service

variable 6 fickle, fitful, uneven, unlike 7 diverse, mutable 8 changing, shifting, unstable, wavering 9 alterable, different, spasmodic, unsettled 10 capri-

---

Vanuatu
other name: 11 New Hebrides
capital/largest city: 4 Vila
others: 5 Santo 6 Forari 10 Luganville
school: 7 Malapoa
monetary unit: 5 franc 7 centime
island: 3 Api, Epi 4 Aoba, Gaua, Malo, Tana, Vate 5 Banks, Efate, Maewo, Santo, Tanna 6 Ambrym, Mabrim, Torres 8 Aneityum, Malekula 9 Erromanga, Pentecost, Vanua Lava 13 Espiritu Santo
mountain: 6 Lopevi
highest point: 11 Tabwemasana
sea: 7 Pacific
people: 8 European 10 Melanesian, Polynesian 11 Micronesian
explorer: 4 Cook 7 Queiros
leader: 4 Lini
language: 6 French 7 Bislama, English 16 Melanesian Pidgin
religion: 7 animism 8 Anglican, John Frum 10 Protestant 12 Presbyterian 13 Roman Catholic
feature:
cult: 5 cargo

---

cious, changeable, inconstant, indefinite 11 fluctuating

variance 4 odds 6 change 7 dispute, quarrel 9 deviation, disparity 10 contention, difference, dissension, divergence, unlikeness 11 discrepancy, incongruity 12 disagreement, modification 13 dissimilarity, inconsistency

variant 7 altered, derived, takeoff 8 modified 9 departure, different, divergent, variation 10 alteration 11 transformed 12 modification 14 transformation

variation 6 change 7 variant, variety 8 mutation, variance 9 departure, deviation, diversity 10 aberration, alteration, difference, divergency, innovation 11 discrepancy 12 disagreement, modification 13 metamorphosis 14 transformation

varicolored 6 calico, motley, tartan 7 dappled, flecked, marbled, mottled, piebald 9 multi-

---

hued 10 iridescent, opalescent, variegated 11 rainbowlike, technicolor 12 multicolored, parti-colored 13 polychromatic

varied 5 mixed 6 motley, sundry 7 diverse, various 8 assorted 9 different 10 variegated 11 diversified 13 heterogeneous, miscellaneous

variegated 4 pied 6 motley 7 checked, dappled, mottled, piebald 9 checkered 12 parti-colored

variety 4 hash, kind, race, sort, type 5 brand, breed, class, genre, genus, group, stock, tribe 6 change, family, jumble, medley, motley, strain 7 melange, mixture, species 8 category, division, pastiche 9 diversity, patchwork, variation 10 assortment, collection, difference, hodgepodge, innovation, miscellany, subspecies 11 subdivision 12 denomination, multiplicity, unconformity 13 dissimilarity, heterogeneity, nonuniformity 14 classification, omnium-gatherum 15 diversification

various 3 few 4 many, some 5 other 6 divers, myriad, sundry, varied 7 diverse, several 8 assorted, manifold, numerous 9 countless, different 10 dissimilar 11 innumerable 12 multifarious 13 miscellaneous, multitudinous

varlet 3 cur 6 rascal, wretch 7 villain 9 scoundrel 10 blackguard

Varner, Will
character in: 9 The Hamlet
author: 8 Faulkner

varnish 4 gilt 5 adorn, cover, gloss, stain 6 excuse, soften 7 conceal, lacquer 8 disguise, mitigate 9 embellish, gloss over 10 smooth over

vary 4 veer 5 alter, shift 6 change, depart, differ, modify 7 deviate, dissent, diverge 8 be unlike, contrast, disagree 9 alternate, disaccord, diversify, fluctuate

vase 3 jar, jug, pot, urn 5 crock, diota 8 canister 9 container 10 jardiniere

Vashti
husband: 9 Ahasuerus
replaced by: 6 Esther

vassal 4 serf 5 helot, liege, slave 6 tenant, thrall 7 bondman, servant, subject, villein 8 retainer 9 bondslave, bondwoman, dependent 11 subordinate

vassalage 4 yoke **7** bondage, serfdom, slavery **9** servitude **11** enslavement

vast 4 huge, wide **5** great, jumbo **7** endless, immense, titanic, very big **8** colossal, enormous, far-flung, gigantic, infinite, spacious **9** boundless, capacious, extensive, limitless, monstrous, unbounded, unlimited, very large **10** monumental, prodigious, stupendous, tremendous, voluminous, widespread **11** far-reaching, measureless, significant, substantial **12** immeasurable, interminable

vastness 7 bigness **8** enormity, hugeness **9** immensity, largeness **12** enormousness

Vathek
author: **15** William Beckford

Vaticanus 16 Greek uncial codex

Vaughan Williams, Ralph
born: **7** Britain **10** Down Ampney
composer of: **3** Job **8** The Wasps **9** Flos Campi **10** Antarctica (symphony No 7), **11** Old King Cole **12** A Sea Symphony **13** Hugh the Drover, On Wenlock Edge, Sir John in Love, Songs of Travel **14** Riders to the Sea, The House of Life, The Sons of Light **15** A London Symphony, The Poisoned Kiss **16** The Lark Ascending **17** A Pastoral Symphony **18** Five Tudor Portraits, Sinfonia Antarctica **19** The Pilgrim's Progress **22** Toward the Unknown Region

Vaughn, Robert
born: **9** New York NY
roles: **7** Bullitt **12** Napoleon Solo **15** The Man from UNCLE **19** The Magnificent Seven **22** The Young Philadelphians

vault 4 arch, dome, jump, leap, safe, tomb **5** bound, clear, crypt **6** arcade, cupola, hurdle, spring **7** ossuary **8** catacomb, jump over, leapfrog, leap over, wall safe **9** mausoleum, polevault, sepulcher, strongbox **10** arched roof, spring over, strongroom **13** arched ceiling, burial chamber

vaunt 5 strut **6** brag of, flaunt **7** exult in, show off, swagger **9** crow about, gasconade, gloat over **10** boast about

vaunted 7 exalted, praised **11** gloated over, overpraised **12** boasted about

Veary, Arthur
real name of: **14** Arthur Treacher

veer 3 yaw **4** jibe, tack, turn **5** curve, dodge, drift, shift, wheel **6** swerve, zigzag **7** go about **9** come round, turn aside **15** change direction

Vegas
character: **5** Angie **6** Binzer **8** Beatrice, Dan Tanna **10** Bernie Roth **11** (Sgt) Bella Archer
cast: **10** Tony Curtis **11** Judy Landers, Robert Urich **12** Naomi Stevens, Phyllis Davis **13** Bart Braverman

vegetable 3 pea **4** bean, beet, corn **6** carrot, greens, legume, squash, turnip **7** cabbage, lettuce, parsnip, produce, spinach **8** broccoli, eggplant, lima bean, rutabaga, zucchini **10** string bean **11** cauliflower

vegetarian 5 vegan **8** meatless **9** herbivore **11** herbivorous

vegetation 5 flora, grass, sloth, weeds **6** leaves, plants, torpor **7** foliage, herbage, languor, loafing, verdure **8** dormancy, idleness, lethargy **9** flowerage, indolence, plant life, shrubbery **10** inactivity **11** hibernation, languidness, rustication **12** sluggishness
god of: **6** Dumuzi

vehemence 4 heat, zeal **5** ardor **6** fervor, warmth **7** passion **9** intensity

vehement 3 hot **4** wild **5** eager, fiery, rabid **6** ardent, fervid, fierce, heated, stormy **7** earnest, excited, fanatic, fervent, furious, intense, violent, zealous **8** agitated, forceful, frenzied, vigorous **9** emotional, fanatical, hotheaded **10** passionate **11** impassioned, tempestuous **12** enthusiastic

vehemently 5 hotly **6** wildly **7** eagerly **8** ardently, fiercely, strongly **9** earnestly, excitedly, fervently, furiously, intensely, violently, zealously **10** vigorously **11** emotionally, fanatically **12** passionately **13** tempestuously **16** enthusiastically

vehicle 3 bus, car **4** tool **5** agent, means, organ, plane, train, truck **6** agency, device, medium **7** bicycle **9** mechanism **10** automobile, conveyance, instrument, motorcycle, rocket ship **12** intermediary **14** transportation

veil 3 dim **4** hide, mask **5** cloak, cloud, cover **6** enwrap, mantle, screen, shroud **7** blanket, conceal, curtain, envelop, obscure **8** covering **10** camouflage

veiled 3 dim **5** murky **6** draped, hidden **7** muffled **8** obscured, shrouded **9** concealed, covered up, disguised, enveloped, enwrapped **11** camouflaged

veiling 3 net **4** mesh **8** cloaking, covering **9** obscurity **10** concealing

vein 3 rib, web **4** bent, hint, line, lode, mark, mood, seam, tone **5** fleck, layer, stria, style, touch **6** furrow, manner, marble, nature, strain, streak, stripe, temper, thread **7** stratum **8** tendency **9** capillary, character **10** complexion, propensity **11** blood vessel, disposition, inclination, temperament **12** predilection **14** predisposition

Veiovis
god of: **4** dead

Velazquez (Velasquez), Diego Rodriguez de Silvay
born: **5** Spain **7** Seville
artwork: **8** Philip IV **10** Las Meninas **13** Luis de Gongora, Pope Innocent X, Venus and Cupid **14** Cardinal Borgia **17** Don Gaspar de Guzman, Isabella of Bourbon **18** Adoration of the Magi, The Tapestry Weavers **19** The Infanta Margarita, The Surrender of Breda **20** Infanta Maria Theresia **21** An Old Woman Cooking Eggs **22** Portrait of a Court Jester, Portrait of Juan de Pareja **23** The Immaculate Conception **30** Prince Balthasar Carlos at the Hunt

veloce
music: **4** fast

velocity 4 pace **5** haste, speed **8** alacrity, celerity, rapidity **9** fleetness, quickness, swiftness **10** expedition, speediness

venal 5 shady **6** greedy **7** corrupt, crooked, selfish **8** bribable, covetous, grasping **9** dishonest, mercenary, rapacious **10** avaricious **11** corruptible **12** unprincipled, unscrupulous **13** moneygrubbing

venality 7 avarice **10** corruption **11** bribe-taking **13** mercenariness, money-grubbing

vend 4 hawk, sell **5** trade **6** barter, deal in, market, peddle, retail **7** auction, trade in **8** huckster **11** merchandise

Vendetta, La
author: **14** Honore de Balzac

vendor, vender 6 dealer, hawker, monger, seller, trader 7 peddler 8 huckster, merchant, purveyor, retailer, salesman, supplier 9 tradesman 10 wholesaler 12 merchandiser 13 street peddler

veneer 4 coat, mask, show 5 front, layer 6 casing, facade, facing, jacket, sheath 7 coating, overlay, wrapper 8 covering, envelope, pretense 10 outer layer

venerable 3 old 4 aged 5 hoary 6 august 7 admired, ancient, elderly, honored, revered 8 esteemed 9 respected, venerated 11 patriarchal, white-haired

venerate 5 adore, extol, honor 6 admire, esteem, hallow, revere 7 cherish, glorify, idolize, respect, worship 8 look up to 9 reverence 11 pay homage to

venerated 4 holy 5 loved 6 adored, sacred 7 honored, revered 8 hallowed 9 respected 10 reverenced, worshipped 12 paid homage to

veneration 3 awe 5 honor 6 esteem, homage, wonder 7 respect, worship 8 devotion 9 adoration, adulation, reverence 10 admiration, exaltation 11 idolization 13 glorification

venereal 6 carnal, sexual 7 genital

Venezuela *see box*

vengeance 7 revenge 8 avenging, reprisal, requital 11 malevolence, retaliation, retribution 12 ruthlessness 13 an eye for an eye, implacability 14 revengefulness, vindictiveness 15 a tooth for a tooth

veni, vidi, vici 19 I came I saw I conquered
  author: 12 Julius Caesar

venial 5 minor 6 slight 7 trivial 9 allowable, excusable 10 defensible, forgivable, not serious, pardonable 11 justifiable, unimportant, warrantable

Venice *see box*

Venn, Diggory
  character in: 17 Return of the Native
  author: 5 Hardy

venom 3 ire 4 gall, hate 5 anger, spite, toxin, virus 6 choler, enmity, grudge, hatred, malice, poison, rancor, spleen 7 ill will 8 acrimony, savagery 9 animosity, barbar-

Venezuela

name means: 12 little Venice

capital/largest city: 7 Caracas

others: 4 Aroa, Coro 6 Atures, Cumana, Merida 7 Barinas, Barines, Cabello, Guaware, Maracay, Maturin 8 Asuncion, Carupano, La Guaira, La Gyayra, Tacupita, Valencia 9 Barcelona, Maracaibo, Tacarigua 12 Barquisimeto, Puerto La Cruz, San Cristobal 13 Cuidad Bolivar, Puerto Cabello 18 Santo Tome de Guayana

division: 4 Lara 5 Apure, Sucre, Zulia 6 Aragua, Falcon, Merida 7 Barinas, Bolivar, Cojedes, Guarico, Monagas, Tachira, Yaracuy 8 Carabobo, Trujillo

measure: 5 galon 6 fanega 7 estadel

monetary unit: 4 peso 5 medio 6 fuerte 7 bolivar, centimo 8 morocota 10 venezolano

weight: 3 bag 5 libra

island: 4 Aves 7 Cubagua, Tortuga 9 La Orchila, Los Roques, Margarita 11 Los Hermanos 12 La Blanquilla

lake: 9 Maracaibo, Tacarigua

mountain: 3 Pao 4 Pava, Yair 5 Andes, Duida, Icutu 6 Concha, Cuneva, Merida, Parima, Sierra, Yumari 7 Imutaca, Masaiti, Roraima 8 Gurupira 9 Pacaraima 10 Auyan-Tepui 11 Turimiquire 18 Cordillera del Norte

highest point: 7 Bolivar

river: 3 Oro, Pao 4 Meta 5 Apure, Caura, Negro, Suata, Tigre, Unare, Zulia 6 Amazon, Arauca, Caroni, Cuyuni 7 Guanare, Guanipa, Guarico, Orinoco, Oritueo, Paragua, Suapure, Vichada, Yuruari 8 Guaviare, Manapire, Venturai 9 Cuchivero 10 Casiquiare, Portuguesa

sea: 8 Atlantic 9 Caribbean

physical feature:
  falls: 5 Angel
  gulf: 5 Paria 6 Triste 9 Venezuela
  highlands: 6 Guiana 7 Guayana, Segovia
  plains: 6 Llanos

people: 4 Bare, Pume 5 Bello, Carib, pardo, zambo 6 Arawak, Creole, Timote 7 Charoya, Guahibo, Kaliana, mestizo, mulatto, Otomaca, Timotex 8 Caquetio, Guarauno, Matilone 11 Maquiritare
  artist: 7 Marisol
  author: 5 Bello 8 Gallegos 13 Diaz-Rodriguez
  explorer: 8 Columbus
  god: 5 Tsuma
  leader: 4 Paez 5 Gomez, Leoni 6 Castro 7 Bolivar, Miranda 10 Betancourt 12 Guzman Blanco 14 Herrera Campins

language: 4 Pume 7 Spanish

religion: 5 Islam 7 Judaism 10 Protestant 13 Roman Catholic

feature:
  animal: 4 puma 5 sloth 6 jaguar, ocelot 7 manatee, peccary 8 anteater, capybara 9 armadillo
  cowboy: 7 llanero
  dance: 6 joropo 16 diablos danzantes
  folk entertainment: 10 burriquita
  musical instrument: 6 cuatro 7 maracas
  street performance: 8 parranda

food:
  black beans: 8 caraotas
  bread: 5 arepa
  dish: 7 hallaca 8 cachapos, pabellon
  soup/stew: 8 sancocho

Venice
　art exhibition:
　　8 Biennale
　artist: 7 Bellini, Codussi
　　8 Fabriano, Longhena,
　　Mantegna, Palladio,
　　Scamozzi, Veronese
　　9 Canaletto, Carpaccio,
　　Giorgione, Sansovino
　　10 Tintoretto
　capital of: 6 Veneto
　　15 Venezia province
　church: 18 San Giorgio
　　Maggiore, Santa Maria
　　dei Frari **19** Santi Gio-
　　vanni e Paolo
　Italian: 7 Venezia
　landmark: 6 Ca' d'Oro
　　9 Campanile **10** Grand
　　Canal **11** Doge's Palace
　　13 Bridge of Sighs
　　15 Libreria Vecchia
　　16 Palazzo Rezzonico,
　　Saint Mark's Church
　　20 Accademia di Belle
　　Arti **21** Palazzo dei Pro-
　　curatori **22** Scuola
　　Grande di San Rocco
　　23 Palazzo Vendramin-
　　Calergi
　port: 8 Marghera
　resort: 9 Lido Beach
　sea: 8 Adriatic
　small canal: 3 rii
　tomb: 5 Titan
　traveler: 9 Marco Polo

ity, brutality, hostility **10** bitterness, resentment
11 malevolence **12** spitefulness **13** maliciousness,
rancorousness

venomous 5 cruel, fatal, toxic
6 bitter, brutal, deadly, lethal,
malign, savage **7** abusive,
caustic, hostile, noxious, vicious **8** spiteful, virulent
9 malicious, malignant, poisonous, rancorous, resentful
10 malevolent **11** ill-disposed
12 bloodthirsty

vent 3 air, tap **4** bare, drip,
emit, flue, gush, hole, ooze,
pipe **5** exude, spout, utter,
voice **6** effuse, escape, faucet,
let out, outlet, reveal, spigot
7 air hole, chimney, debouch,
declare, divulge, express, opening, orifice, release **8** aperture,
disclose, exposure, venthole
9 discharge, let escape, pour
forth, utterance **10** disclosure,
expression, revelation, smokestack, ventilator **11** communicate, declaration

ventilate 3 air, sow **5** voice
6 aerate, air out, report, review, spread **7** analyze, de-

clare, discuss, dissent, divulge,
examine, express **9** broadcast,
circulate, comment on, criticize, oxygenate, publicize, talk
about **10** bandy about **11** disseminate, noise abroad

ventilator 3 fan **4** flue **7** aera-
tor **10** exhaust fan, smoke-
stack **14** air conditioner

venture 2 go **3** bet, try **4** dare,
risk **5** flyer, offer, wager
6 chance, gamble, hazard,
plunge, submit, tender, travel
7 advance, attempt, hold out,
presume, proffer, project **8** endeavor, make bold **9** adventure, risk going, strive for,
undertake, volunteer **10** enterprise, put forward, take a
flyer **11** speculation, uncertainty, undertaking

venturesome, adventure-
some 4 bold, rash **5** risky
6 daring, tricky, unsafe, unsure **7** dubious **8** doubtful, insecure, perilous, reckless,
ticklish **9** ambitious, audacious,
dangerous, daredevil, energetic, foolhardy, hazardous,
impetuous, impulsive, uncertain **10** aggressive, precarious
11 adventurous, speculative
12 enterprising, questionable

venturesomeness 6 daring
8 audacity, boldness **9** derring-
do **11** impetuosity
12 recklessness

Venus
　origin: 5 Roman **7** Italian
　goddess of: 6 spring
　　7 gardens
　son: 6 Aeneas
　grandson: 5 Iulus
　epithet: 7 Erycina **8** Gene-
　　trix **10** Erticordia
　corresponds to: 9 Aphrodite

Venus and Adonis
　author: 18 William
　　Shakespeare

veracious 4 true **6** honest
7 sincere **8** accurate, faithful,
truthful **10** scrupulous
11 punctilious

veracity 5 truth **6** candor, verity **7** honesty, probity **8** accuracy, openness **9** exactness,
frankness, integrity, sincerity
10 exactitude **11** correctness
12 truthfulness **13** guilelessness, ingenuousness
14 verisimilitude

Vera-Ellen
　real name: 13 Vera-Ellen
　　Rohe
　born: 12 Cincinnati OH
　roles: 9 On the Town
　　14 White Christmas

veranda
　Hawaiian: 5 lanai

verbal 4 oral, said **5** vocal
6 spoken, voiced **7** in words,
of verbs, of words, uttered
9 expressed, unwritten

verbal exchange 6 dialog
8 dialogue **10** discussion
12 conversation

verbalize 5 speak, utter, voice
7 express **10** articulate **12** put
into words

verbal thrust 3 dig **4** gibe,
jeer **5** taunt **13** cutting remark

verbatim 5 exact **7** exactly, literal, precise **8** accurate, faithful **9** literally, literatim,
precisely **10** accurately, faithfully **11** to the letter, word for
word **15** chapter and verse,
letter for letter
　Latin: 14 ipsissima verba

verbatim et literatim 21 in
exactly the same words
29 word for word and letter
for letter

verbena
　varieties: 4 moss, rose, sand
　　5 clump, lemon, shrub **7** red
　　sand **8** pink sand **9** beach
　　sand **10** desert sand, Mojave
　　sand, yellow sand **12** com-
　　mon garden

verbiage 9 logorrhea, loquacity, prolixity, verbosity, wordiness **10** volubility
11 verboseness **12** effusiveness **14** circumlocution, grandiloquence, long-windedness

verbose 5 gabby, wordy **6** prolix **7** voluble **8** effusive **9** garrulous, talkative
10 longwinded, loquacious
13 grandiloquent
14 circumlocutory

verbosity 9 diffusion, prolixity,
talkiness, wordiness **11** diffuseness **13** talkativeness
14 long-windedness

verboten 9 forbidden
10 prohibited

Verdandi 4 Norn
　origin: 12 Scandinavian
　form: 3 elf
　personifies: 7 present
　developed from: 5 Urdar
　companions: 3 Urd **5** Skuld

verdant 4 lush **5** green, leafy,
shady, turfy **6** grassy **7** mea-
dowy **8** blooming, thriving
9 luxuriant **10** burgeoning,
springlike **11** flourishing

Verdi, Giuseppe
　born: 5 Italy **7** Busseto
　composer of: 4 Aida
　　6 Otello **7** Macbeth, Na-
　　bucco, Othello **8** Falstaff
　　9 Don Carlos, Il Corsaro,
　　Rigoletto, The Misled **10** La

Traviata **11** Il Trovatore
13 The Troubadour
14 Manzoni Requiem **15** Simon Boccanegra

verdict 6 answer, decree, ruling **7** finding, opinion **8** decision, judgment, sentence **9** valuation **10** assessment, estimation **11** arbitrament, arbitration **12** adjudication **13** determination

Vere, Captain
character in: **9** Billy Budd
author: **8** Melville

Vereen, Ben
born: **7** Miami FL
roles: **5** Roots **6** Pippin **13** Chicken George **20** Jesus Christ Superstar

verge 3 end, hem, lip, rim **4** brim, edge **5** bound, brink, ledge, limit, skirt **6** be near, border, flange, fringe, margin **7** confine, extreme **8** approach, boundary, frontier, terminus **9** threshold **11** approximate **12** be on the brink

verge upon 4 abut **5** flank **6** adjoin, border **8** be next to **10** neighbor on

Vergil, Virgil
author of: **6** Aeneid **8** Bucolics, Eclogues, Georgics

verification 5 proof **7** support **9** guarantee **10** validation **12** confirmation **13** accreditation, certification, corroboration, documentation **14** authentication, substantiation

verify 5 prove **7** certify, confirm, support, sustain, witness **8** accredit, attest to, document, validate, vouch for **9** establish, guarantee, testify to **11** corroborate **12** authenticate, substantiate

verily 4 amen **5** truly **6** really **9** certainly, yes indeed **10** positively

veritable 4 real, true **5** utter, valid **6** actual **7** genuine, literal **8** absolute, bona fide, complete, positive, true-blue **9** authentic **13** incontestable, unimpeachable **14** unquestionable **17** through-and-through

Verlaine, Paul
author of: **6** Wisdom **7** Sagesse **8** Langueur **17** Songs Without Words **19** Romances sans Paroles

Vermeer, Jan
born: **5** Delft **7** Holland
artwork: **11** View of Delft **12** The Lace Maker, The Procuress **13** Drinking Scene **14** A Street in Delft,

The Head of a Girl **15** Allegory of Faith, Girl with a Red Hat **16** The Artist's Studio **18** Girl Reading a Letter, Girl with a Wine-glass **19** A Girl Asleep at a Table, A Painter in his Studio **20** A Woman Weighing Pearls **22** Maidservant Pouring Milk **23** Young Woman with a Water Jug **24** A Soldier and a Laughing Girl **31** Christ in the House of Mary and Martha

vermilion 3 red **7** scarlet **8** cinnabar **9** bright red **15** mercuric sulfide

vermin 4 ants, lice, mice, owls, rats **5** crows, fleas, foxes, pests **6** snakes, wolves **7** bedbugs, coyotes, roaches, spiders, weasels **8** termites, varmints **9** water bugs **10** centipedes, silverfish **11** birds of prey **18** pestiferous insects

Vermont *see box*

vermouth
type: **4** wine **6** brandy **8** aperitif
origin: **5** Italy **6** France

varieties: **3** dry **5** sweet
drink: **9** Boomerang **11** Bittersweet
with bourbon: **9** Allegheny
with brandy: **3** BVD
with Dubonnet: **3** BVD
gin: **5** Bijou, Bronx, Tango **6** Caruso **7** Bermuda, Caberet, Martini **10** Bloodhound
with rum: **6** Bolero **8** Apple Pie **10** Black Devil **11** Shark's Tooth
with rye: **8** Brooklyn **9** Algonquin
with scotch: **8** Affinity **10** Bobby Burns
with sherry: **6** Bamboo, Brazil
with sloe gin: **10** Blackthorn
with vodka: **8** Kangaroo **9** Corkscrew
with whiskey: **9** Manhattan

vernacular 4 cant **5** idiom, lingo, slang **6** jargon, patois **7** dialect **8** parlance, shoptalk **9** the vulgar **12** common speech, native tongue **13** natural speech **14** informal speech, native language

vernal 3 new **5** fresh, green

Vermont
abbreviation: **2** VT
nickname: **13** Green Mountain **20** Four-Season Recreation
capital: **10** Montpelier
largest city: **10** Burlington
others: **5** Barre, Stowe **7** Grafton, Newfane, Newport, Rutland **8** St Albans, Winooski **9** Bountiful, Vergennes **10** Bennington **11** Brattleboro
college: **7** Goddard, Norwich, Trinity, Windham **8** Marlboro **10** Bennington, Middlebury, St Michaels
feature:
　covered bridge: **5** Scott
　house: **15** Old Constitution
　monument: **6** Battle
people: **9** John Deere, John Dewey **10** Ethan Allen **12** Brigham Young **13** Warren R Austin **15** Stephen A Douglas
lake: **7** Caspian, Dunmore, Seymour **8** Bomoseen **9** Champlain **10** Willoughby **12** Memphremagog
land rank: **10** forty-third
mountain: **5** Green, White **7** Bromley, Hogback, Taconic **8** Prospect, Stratton
　highest point: **9** Mansfield
physical feature:
　uplands: **10** New England
　valley: **9** Champlain
president: **14** Calvin Coolidge, Chester A Arthur
river: **4** West **5** Otter, White **7** Saxtons **8** Lamoille, Nulhegan, Winooski **10** Missisquoi **11** Connecticut
state admission: **10** fourteenth
state bird: **12** hermit thrush
state animal: **11** Morgan horse
state flower: **9** red clover
state motto: **15** Freedom and Unity
state song: **11** Hail Vermont
state tree: **10** sugar maple

6 spring **8** youthful
10 springlike

Verne, Jules
  author of: 19 Five Weeks in
  a Balloon **21** From the
  Earth to the Moon
  26 Around the World in
  Eighty Days **32** Twenty
  Thousand Leagues Under
  the Sea
  character: 11 Captain Nemo,
  Phineas Fogg
  12 Passepartout

Veronese, Paolo (Cagliari)
  born: 5 Italy **6** Verona
  artwork: 12 Book of Esther
  13 The Last Supper **14** Supper at Emmaus **15** The Rape
  of Europa, Triumph of Venice **17** Mary with the Saints,
  The Finding of Moses, The
  Marriage at Cana, Wisdom
  and Strength **19** Martyrdom
  of St George, The Choice of
  Hercules **21** Esther before
  Ahasuerus **22** Feast at the
  House of Simon **24** Mars
  and Venus United in Love,
  The Feast in the House of
  Levi, The Temptation of St
  Anthony **31** Jesus and the
  Centurion of Capernaum
  32 The Family of Darius be-
  fore Alexander

Verrocchio, Andrea del
  real name: 31 Andrea di
  Michele di Francesco Cione
  born: 5 Italy **8** Florence
  artwork: 5 David **15** Boy
  with a Dolphin **17** Christ
  and St Thomas **18** The Baptism of Christ **19** Bartolommeo Colleoni **23** Christ and
  Doubting Thomas **25** Beheading of John the Baptist

versatile 3 apt **4** able **5** handy
  6 adroit, clever, expert, gifted
  7 protean **8** talented **9** adaptable, all-around, ingenious,
  many-sided **10** proficient
  11 many-skilled, resourceful
  12 accomplished, multifaceted

verse 4 poem **5** meter, rhyme,
  stave **6** jingle, poetry, stanza
  7 measure, strophe

versed 4 able **5** adept **6** expert,
  taught **7** erudite, learned,
  skilled, tutored **8** lettered,
  schooled, skillful, well-read
  9 competent, practiced, scholarly **10** at home with, instructed, proficient
  11 enlightened, experienced
  12 accomplished, familiar
  with, well-informed **14** acquainted with, conversant
  with

versifier 4 bard **6** rhymer,
  writer **8** minstrel, poetizer,
  poetling, rhymster **9** poetaster,

rhymester **10** rhymesmith,
troubadour, versemaker, verse-
smith **11** versemonger
12 balladmonger

version 4 side **5** story **6** report
  7 account **9** depiction, rendering **10** adaptation, paraphrase,
  re-creation **11** description, restatement, translation
  14 interpretation

vers libre 9 free verse

vertebral column
  bone of: 5 spine **8** backbone

vertex 3 cap, tip **4** apex, peak
  5 crown **6** summit, zenith
  8 pinnacle **12** highest point
  13 crowning point

vertical 5 plumb, sheer **7** upright **12** ninety-degree
  13 perpendicular

vertiginous 5 dizzy, giddy,
  shaky **6** whirly **7** reeling
  11 lightheaded

vertigo 7 reeling **8** fainting
  9 dizziness, giddiness **12** unsteadiness **15** lightheadedness

Vertigo
  director: 15 Alfred Hitchcock
  cast: 8 Kim Novak **12** James
  Stewart **16** Barbara Bel
  Geddes
  setting: 12 San Francisco
  score: 15 Bernard Herrmann

Vertumnus
  also: 9 Vortumnus
  origin: 5 Roman
  god of: 5 fruit **7** gardens, seasons **8** orchards
  wife: 6 Pomona

verve 3 vim, zip **4** dash, elan,
  fire, zeal **5** ardor, drive, force,
  gusto, punch, vigor **6** energy,
  fervor, relish, spirit, warmth
  7 abandon, feeling, passion,
  rapture, sparkle **8** vitality, vivacity **9** animation, eagerness,
  vehemence **10** enthusiasm,
  liveliness

Verver, Maggie
  character in: 13 The Golden
  Bowl
  author: 5 James

very 4 bare, mere, most, much,
  pure **5** exact, extra, plain,
  quite, sheer, truly **6** deeply,
  highly, hugely, mighty, really,
  simple, vastly **7** awfully, exactly, fitting, greatly, notably,
  perfect, precise, totally **8** actually, entirely, markedly, specific, suitable, terribly
  9 assuredly, certainly, decidedly, eminently, essential, extremely, immensely, intensely,
  necessary, obviously, perfectly,
  precisely, unusually, veritably
  10 abnormally, absolutely,
  abundantly, completely, defi-

nitely, especially, particular,
profoundly, remarkably, strikingly, thoroughly, uncom-
monly, undeniably
11 appropriate, exceedingly,
excessively **12** emphatically,
surpassingly, tremendously
13 exceptionally, significantly
14 unquestionably

very best
  French: 14 creme de la
  creme

Very Easy Death, A
  author: 16 Simone de
  Beauvoir

very great 4 huge **6** severe
  7 extreme, intense, mammoth,
  titanic **8** colossal, enormous,
  gigantic **9** excessive, monstrous **10** gargantuan, immoderate, inordinate, prodigious
  11 magnificent, spectacular
  14 Brobdingnagian

very nearly 6 almost **7** close
  to **9** just about **10** more or
  less, not far from
  13 approximately

very old 4 aged **6** primal **7** ancient, antique, archaic **8** primeval **10** antiquated,
  primordial **11** prehistoric
  12 antediluvian

very soon
  French: 11 tout a l'heure

vessel 3 cup, jar, jug, keg,
  mug, pot, tub, vat **4** boat,
  bowl, butt, cask, dish, duct,
  scow, ship, tube, vase, vein
  5 barge, craft, crock, flask,
  glass, liner, plate, yacht **6** artery, barrel, beaker, carafe,
  flagon, goblet, packet, tanker,
  whaler **7** caldron, collier,
  cruiser, platter, tankard, trawler, tugboat, tumbler, utensil
  8 decanter, paquebot, sailboat
  9 capillary, container, ferry-
  boat, freighter, houseboat,
  steamboat, steamship **10** ocean
  liner, receptacle

vest 3 rig **4** garb, robe **5** array,
  drape, dress **6** attire, clothe,
  enwrap, fit out, jacket, jerkin
  7 apparel, deck out, doublet,
  envelop **8** accouter **9** waistcoat

Vesta
  origin: 5 Roman
  goddess of: 6 hearth
  festival: 8 Vestalia
  corresponds to: 4 Caca
  6 Hestia

vestal 4 pure **6** chaste, maiden,
  simple, virgin **8** maidenly, virginal, virtuous **9** pure woman,
  undefiled, unmarried, unworldly **10** immaculate
  15 unsophisticated

vested 5 fixed **7** settled **8** absolute, complete **9** permanent **10** guaranteed **11** established, inalienable **12** indisputable **14** unquestionable

vestibule 4 hall **5** entry, foyer, lobby **6** lounge **7** hallway, passage **8** anteroom, corridor **10** passageway **11** antechamber, entrance way, waiting room **12** entrance hall

vestige 4 sign **5** relic, token, trace **6** record **7** memento, remnant **8** evidence, souvenir

vestments 4 garb, gear **5** dress **6** livery, outfit **7** apparel, clothes, costume, raiment, regalia, uniform **8** clothing **9** trappings **13** accoutrements

vesture 4 robe **5** robes **7** apparel, clothes, garment, raiment **8** clothing, garments **9** vestments

vetch 5 Vicia
  varieties: 3 cow **4** bard, bird, milk **5** crown, hairy, Sitka **6** bitter, common, kidney, purple, smooth, spring, tufted, winter **8** Narbonne **9** horseshoe, Hungarian, woolly-pod **12** large Russian

veteran 3 vet **6** expert, master **7** old hand **8** old-timer, seasoned **9** ex-soldier **10** campaigner, old soldier, war veteran **11** experienced **12** ex-serviceman **13** long-practiced

veto 4 deny, void **6** denial, enjoin, forbid, negate, reject **7** nullify, prevent, refusal **8** disallow, prohibit, turn down **9** rejection **10** prevention **11** disallowing, prohibition **12** disallowance **16** turn thumbs down on

vex 3 bug, irk **4** fret, gall, miff, pain, rile **5** anger, annoy, chafe, harry, pique, upset, worry **6** badger, bother, grieve, harass, hassle, nettle, pester, plague, ruffle **7** chagrin, disturb, provoke, torment, trouble **8** distress, irritate **9** displease **10** exasperate **18** ruffle one's feathers

vexation 5 pique, trial **6** hassle **7** torment **8** headache, nuisance **9** annoyance **10** affliction, harassment, irritation **11** aggravation **13** pain in the neck

vexatious 5 pesky **6** thorny, vexing **8** annoying, nettling **9** badgering, harassing, hectoring, provoking, troubling, worrisome **10** bothersome, irritating **11** disquieting, pestiferous, troublesome

vexed 5 irked, riled, testy **6** galled, miffed, piqued **7** annoyed, nettled, peevish **8** provoked **9** irritated **11** disgruntled, exasperated

viable 6 usable **8** feasible, workable **9** adaptable, practical **10** applicable **11** practicable

viaduct 4 ramp, span **8** overpass

vial 5 ampul, flask, phial **7** ampoule

via media 10 a middle way

viands 4 cate, diet, eats, fare, food **7** cuisine, edibles, vittles **8** victuals **9** provender **10** foodstuffs, provisions

vibrancy 4 fire **5** ardor **7** elation **8** vitality, vivacity **9** animation **10** enthusiasm **11** high spirits

vibrant 4 deep, loud **5** alive, eager, vital, vivid **6** ardent, bright, florid, lively **7** fervent, glowing, intense, orotund, pealing, pulsing, radiant, ringing **8** animated, bell-like, colorful, forceful, luminous, lustrous, resonant, sonorous, spirited, vehement **9** brilliant, deep-toned, energetic, quivering, thrilling, throbbing, vibrating, vivacious **10** fluttering, glittering, resounding, shimmering **11** full of vigor, resplendent, reverberant **12** electrifying, enthusiastic

vibrate 4 beat, sway **5** quake, swing, throb, waver **6** quaver, quiver, ripple, wobble **7** flutter, pulsate, tremble **8** undulate **9** oscillate, palpitate, pendulate **11** reverberate

vibration 5 quake **6** quiver, tremor **7** quaking **9** quivering, throbbing, trembling

vicar 6 cleric, parson, pastor **8** preacher **9** churchman, clergyman **12** ecclesiastic

vicarious 6 mental **7** by proxy **8** imagined, indirect **9** imaginary, surrogate **10** empathetic, fantasized, secondhand **11** at one remove, sympathetic

Vicar of Wakefield, The
  author: 15 Oliver Goldsmith
  character: 6 George, Olivia, Sophia **7** Deborah **10** Dr Primrose, Mr Burchill **14** Arabella Wilmot **15** Squire Thornhill **19** Sir William Thornhill

vice 4 flaw **5** fault **6** defect **7** blemish, failing, frailty **8** iniquity, weakness **9** depravity,

weak point **10** corruption, debauchery, degeneracy, profligacy, wantonness, wickedness **11** shortcoming **12** imperfection **14** licentiousness

vice president
  resigned: 10 Spiro Agnew **12** John C Calhoun
  accused of treason: 9 Aaron Burr **17** John C Breckinridge
  youngest elected: 17 John C Breckinridge
  elected by Senate: 14 Richard Johnson
  elected but did not serve: 11 William King
  rejected nomination: 11 Frank Lowden, Silas Wright
  lived longest: 15 John Nance Garner
  succeeded to presidency: 9 John Tyler **10** Gerald Ford **12** Harry S Truman **13** Andrew Johnson **14** Calvin Coolidge, Chester A Arthur, Lyndon B Johnson **15** Millard Fillmore **17** Theodore Roosevelt

vice versa 9 in reverse **10** conversely **12** contrariwise **16** the other way round **18** in the opposite order

vicinity 4 area **6** region **8** environs, locality, vicinage **9** adjoining, precincts, proximity **11** environment, propinquity **12** neighborhood, surroundings

vicious 3 bad **4** base, evil, foul, mean, vile, wild **5** awful, cruel, gross, nasty, surly **6** brutal, fierce, horrid, savage, sullen, wicked **7** hateful, heinous, hellish, immoral, inhuman, untamed, violent **8** churlish, depraved, fiendish, libelous, shocking, spiteful, terrible, venomous **9** abhorrent, atrocious, barbarous, dangerous, ferocious, invidious, malicious, monstrous, nefarious, offensive, predatory, rancorous **10** abominable, defamatory, diabolical, ill-humored, ill-natured, malevolent, pernicious, slanderous, villainous, vindictive **11** acrimonious, ill-tempered, treacherous **12** bloodthirsty

viciousness 4 evil **6** malice **7** cruelty **8** ferocity, savagery, villainy, violence **9** barbarity, brutality, ill nature **10** fierceness, wickedness **11** heinousness

vicissitude 6 change **8** mutation **9** variation **10** difficulty, mutability, succession **11** fluctuation

Vicomte of Bragelonne, The
  author: **14** Alexandre Dumas (pere)

victim 4 butt, dead, dupe, gull, mark, pawn, prey, tool **5** patsy **6** pigeon, quarry, sucker, target **7** injured, wounded **8** casualty, fatality, innocent **9** scapegoat

victimize 3 con **4** dupe, gull, hoax **5** bully, cheat, cozen **6** betray, delude **7** deceive, defraud **8** hoodwink **9** bamboozle

victor 6 winner **8** champion, medalist **9** conqueror **10** vanquisher **11** prizewinner

Victoria
  capital of: **8** Hong Kong **10** Seychelles

Victoria
  origin: **5** Roman
  goddess of: **7** victory
  corresponds to: **4** Nike

Victorian 4 prim, smug **6** narrow, proper, stuffy **7** insular, prudish **8** priggish **9** pietistic **10** tight-laced **11** puritanical, straitlaced **12** conventional, hypocritical **13** sanctimonious

victorious 7 winning **8** champion **10** conquering, successful, triumphant **11** vanquishing **12** championship, prizewinning

Victor Victoria
  director: **12** Blake Edwards
  cast: **10** Alex Karras **11** James Garner **12** Julie Andrews **13** Robert Preston **14** John Rhys-Davies **15** Lesley Ann Warren
  setting: **5** Paris

victory 7 laurels, success, the palm, triumph **8** conquest, the prize **9** supremacy **10** ascendancy **11** superiority
  god of: **3** Tyr
  goddess of: **4** Nike **8** Victoria

Victory
  author: **12** Joseph Conrad
  character: **4** Lena, Wang **5** Jonas, Pedro **8** Davidson **9** Axel Heyst, Schomberg **13** Martin Ricardo

victuals 4 chow, diet, eats, fare, feed, food, grub, meat **5** meals **6** fodder, forage, repast, stores, viands **7** cooking, cuisine, edibles, rations, vittles **8** supplies **9** groceries, provender **10** foodstuffs, provisions **11** comestibles, nourishment, refreshment

Vidal, Gore
  author of: **4** Burr **5** Kalki **6** Julian **8** Creation **16** Myra Breckinridge **18** Eighteen

Seventy-Six, The Judgment of Paris **19** Visit to a Small Planet

Vidar
  origin: **12** Scandinavian
  father: **4** Odin **5** Othin
  killed: **6** Fenrir, Fenris

vide 3 see

vide ante 9 see before

vide infra 8 see below

videlicet 6 namely **11** that is to say
  abbreviation: **3** viz

vide post 8 see after **10** see further

vide supra 8 see above

vide ut supra 10 see as above **16** see as stated above

Vidor, King
  director of: **8** The Crowd **12** Stella Dallas, The Big Parade **16** Northwest Passage

vie 4 life **5** fight **6** strive **7** compete, contend, contest **8** be a rival, struggle, tilt with **9** challenge

Vienna
  airport: **9** Schwechat
  area: **11** Innere Stadt
  capital of: **7** Austria
  early name: **4** Wena **9** Vindobono
  German: **4** Wein
  landmark: **7** Hofburg **10** Stadtsoper **13** Saint Stephen's **15** Albertina Museum, Belvedere Palace **16** Historical Museum, Schonbrunn Palace
  river: **6** Danube
  ruler: **8** Hapsburg
  street: **11** Ringstrasse

Vientiane, Viengchan
  capital of: **4** Laos

vi et armis 20 with force and with arms

Vietnam see box, p. 1050

view 3 eye, ken, see **4** gaze, look, note, peek, peep, scan **5** judge, scene, sight, study, vista, watch **6** behold, belief, gaze at, glance, look at, notion, regard, survey, take in, theory, vision **7** diorama, examine, explore, feeling, glimpse, inspect, observe, opinion, outlook, picture, scenery, thought, witness **8** attitude, consider, glance at, judgment, panorama, perceive, pore over, prospect **9** landscape, sentiment, spectacle **10** conception, conviction, scrutinize, think about **11** contemplate, perspective

view as 4 deem, hold **5** count,

judge, think **6** regard **7** account, believe **8** consider, take to be **10** look upon as

viewpoint 4 bias, side **5** angle, slant **6** aspect, belief **7** feeling, opinion **8** attitude, position **9** sentiment **10** conviction, standpoint **11** orientation, perspective **12** vantage point **16** frame of reference

view with disfavor 7 condemn, dislike **8** object to **9** frown upon **10** disapprove, think ill of **13** look askance at, regard as wrong **14** discountenance **15** take exception to

view with horror 5 abhor **6** eschew **8** sicken at **9** abominate, shudder at **10** recoil from, shrink from

vif
  music: **6** lively

vigilance 4 care, heed **7** caution, concern **8** prudence **9** alertness, attention **10** precaution **11** carefulness, forethought, guardedness, heedfulness **12** cautiousness, watchfulness **14** circumspection

vigilant 4 wary **5** alert, chary **7** careful, guarded, heedful, on guard, prudent **8** cautious, watchful **9** attentive, observant, wide-awake **10** on one's toes, on the alert **11** circumspect, on one's guard **12** on the lookout, on the qui vive

vigor 3 pep, vim, zip **4** dash, elan, fire, zeal **5** ardor, drive, force, might, power, verve **6** energy, fervor, spirit **7** passion, stamina **8** haleness, strength, vitality, vivacity **9** animation, hardiness, intensity, vehemence **10** enthusiasm, liveliness, robustness **11** earnestness **12** forcefulness

vigorous 4 bold, hale **5** hardy, lusty, vital **6** active, ardent, brawny, lively, mighty, robust, strong, sturdy, virile **7** dynamic, intense, vibrant **8** forceful, muscular, powerful, spirited **9** assertive, energetic **10** aggressive

vigorously 4 hard **7** briskly, lustily **8** actively, cogently, forcibly, robustly, strongly, sturdily **9** with force **10** forcefully, powerfully **11** strenuously **13** energetically

Vigrid
  origin: **12** Scandinavian
  final battlefield of: **4** gods

Viking, viking 4 Dane **6** pirate **7** mariner **8** Norseman,

Vietnam
other name: 5 Annam 15 French Indochina
capital: 5 Hanoi 6 Saigon
largest city: 6 Saigon 13 Ho Chi Minh City
others: 3 Hue, Ron 4 Ngai, Vinh 5 Dalat, Hoa Da, Hoian
6 Annhon, Cholon, Danang, Hongay 7 Bacninh, Cam
Ranh, Caobang, Donghoi, Hoabinh, Namdinh, Quinhon,
Songoan, Tayninh, Viettri, Vinhloi 8 Binhdinh, Haiphong,
Nhatrang, Panthiet, Phan Rang, Quangtri, Quangyen,
Thanhhoa, Vinhlong 9 Haiphoang, Longxuyen
11 Dienbienphu
school: 3 Hue 5 Hanoi 9 Ho Chi Minh
division: 5 Annam, North, South 6 Tonkin 11 Cochin
China
measure: 4 gang, phan, thon
monetary unit: 2 xu 4 dong 7 piaster
weight: 3 can, yet 4 uyen
mountain: 6 Badinh, Badink 7 Nindhoa, Ninhhoa 8 Fansipan, Knontran, Ngoolinh, Ngoolink, Tchepone, Tclepore
18 Annamese Cordillera
highest point: 8 Fan Si Pan
river: 2 Bo, Ca, Da, Lo, Ma 3 Chu, Gam, Koi, Red
4 Chay 5 Nhiha 6 Mekong 7 Dongnai
sea: 10 South China
physical feature:
  delta: 6 Mekong 8 Red River
  gulf: 4 Siam 6 Tonkin 7 Tonking 8 Thailand
  peninsula: 11 Indochinese
people: 3 Hoa, Man, Meo, Tai, Tay 4 Cham, Kinh, Nung,
Thai 5 Khmer, Malay, Muong 7 Chinese 8 Annamese,
Annamite 9 Cambodian 10 montagnard, Vietnamese
  leader: 5 Le Loi 8 Le Duc Tho 9 Ho Chi Minh 11 Ngo
  Dinh Diem, Pham Van Doug 14 Nguyen Van Thieu
language: 3 Yue 4 Cham 5 Khmer, Rhade 6 French
7 Chinese, English 9 Cantonese 10 Vietnamese
religion: 6 Cao Dai, Hoa Hao, Taoism 7 animism 8 Buddhism 12 Christianity, Confucianism 13 Roman Catholic
place:
  ruins: 10 Nguyen tomb
feature:
  army: 4 ARVN 5 COSVN 8 Communsi, Viet Cong, Viet
  Minh
  clothing: 5 ao dai
  new year: 3 Tet

Northman, searover 9 plunderer 12 Scandinavian
boat: 8 long ship
burial: 9 ship grave
chieftain: 4 jarl
exploration: 5 Italy, Spain
6 France, Russia 7 England,
Germany, Iceland, Ireland,
Vinland 9 Greenland
famous: 4 Eric 8 Eirikson, Ericsson 10 Eric the Red
11 Leif Ericson
governing council: 4 Ting
5 Thing 8 Folkmoot
legend: 4 Edda, saga
origin: 6 Norway, Sweden
7 Denmark, Finland
warrior: 7 beserk 9 berserker
writing: 4 rune

Vila
capital of: 7 Vanuatu

vile 3 bad, low 4 base, evil,
foul, lewd, mean, ugly 5 awful, gross, nasty 6 coarse,
filthy, odious, sinful, smutty,
sordid, vulgar, wicked
7 beastly, hateful, heinous, ignoble, immoral, obscene, vicious 8 depraved, shameful,
shocking, wretched 9 abhorrent, degrading, execrable, invidious, loathsome, nefarious,
obnoxious, offensive, perverted, repellent, repugnant,
repulsive, revolting, salacious
10 abominable, degenerate,
despicable, detestable, disgusting, iniquitous, unpleasant,
villainous 11 disgraceful, foul-
mouthed, humiliating 12 contemptible 13 objectionable

Vile Bodies
author: 11 Evelyn Waugh

vileness 4 evil 8 foulness, iniquity, villainy 9 depravity, nastiness 10 immorality,
odiousness 11 degradation,
heinousness, viciousness

12 wretchedness 13 offen-
siveness

Vili
origin: 12 Scandinavian
brother: 4 Odin 5 Othin

vilification 5 libel 7 calumny,
slander 10 defamation
13 disparagement

vilifier 5 scold 6 carper, critic
7 reviler 9 backbiter

vilify 5 abuse 6 defame, revile
7 slander 8 bad-mouth, dishonor 9 criticize, disparage
14 inveigh against

vilifying 7 abusive 8 libelous
9 malignant 10 calumnious,
defamatory, slanderous

villa, Villa 5 aldea, dacha
6 castle, Pancho 7 chateau,
mansion 9 residence 13 country estate

village 4 burg 6 hamlet, suburb 8 hick town 9 small
town 11 whistlestop
12 municipality

Village, A
author: 10 Sholem Asch

villain 3 cad, cur, rat 5 knave,
louse, rogue 6 rascal, rotter,
varlet 7 caitiff, stinker 8 evildoer, scalawag 9 miscreant,
scoundrel 10 blackguard, malefactor 11 rapscallion 12 transgressor, wicked person
15 snake in the grass

villainous 4 base, evil, foul,
vile 6 wicked 7 caddish, heinous 8 horrible, infamous
9 monstrous, nefarious
10 abominable, despicable, detestable, maleficent 12 black-
guardly 13 reprehensible

villainy 4 evil 8 vileness 9 depravity, rascality 10 wickedness 11 viciousness,
maleficence

Villa-Lobos, Heitor
born: 6 Brazil 12 Rio de
Janeiro
composer of: 6 Choros
20 Bachianas Brasileiras

Villefort
character in: 21 The Count
of Monte Cristo
author: 5 Dumas (pere)

villein 4 carl, esne, serf 5 ceorl,
churl, slave 6 drudge 7 bond-
man, peasant 9 bondwoman

Villette
author: 15 Charlotte Bronte

Villon, Francois
author of: 9 The Legacy
16 Le grand testament, Le
petit testament
quote: 25 Mais ou sont les

neiges d'antan **31** But where are the snows of yesteryear

Villuppo
character in: 17 The Spanish Tragedy
author: 3 Kyd

vim 2 go **3** pep, zip **4** dash, fire, snap, zeal **5** ardor, drive, force, might, power, punch, verve, vigor **6** energy, fervor, spirit **7** passion, potency **8** strength, vitality, vivacity **9** animation, intensity, vehemence **10** enthusiasm, liveliness

vin 4 wine

Vincentio
character in: 17 Measure for Measure
author: 11 Shakespeare

vincit omnia veritas 16 truth conquers all **22** truth conquers all things

vindicate 4 free **5** clear **6** acquit, assert, defend, excuse, uphold **7** absolve, bear out, bolster, justify, support **8** advocate, champion, maintain **9** discharge, exculpate, exonerate **11** corroborate **12** substantiate

vindication 6 excuse **7** apology, defense **11** explanation **13** justification

vindictive 6 bitter, malign **8** avenging, punitive, spiteful, vengeful **9** malicious **10** malevolent, revengeful **11** retaliative, retaliatory, unforgiving

vinegarish 4 acid, sour, tart **5** harsh **6** acidic, biting **7** acerbic, pungent **9** acidulous **10** astringent

vin ordinaire 12 ordinary wine **20** inexpensive table wine

vintage 3 era, old **4** aged, date, fine, rare **5** epoch, great, prime, prize **6** choice, period **7** ancient, antique **8** sterling, superior **9** excellent, out-of-date, wonderful **11** outstanding **12** old-fashioned

Viola (Cesario)
character in: 12 Twelfth Night
author: 11 Shakespeare

violate 4 rape **5** abuse, break **6** defile, invade, ravish **7** disobey, outrage, profane **8** dishonor, infringe, trespass **9** blaspheme, desecrate, disregard, trample on **10** contravene, transgress **12** encroach upon

violation 5 abuse **6** breach **8** trespass **9** sacrilege **10** defile-

ment, infraction **11** desecration, dishonoring **12** encroachment, infringement **13** contravention, nonobservance, transgression

violence 4 fury, rage **5** force, might, power **6** impact **7** outrage **8** ferocity, savagery, severity **9** brutality, intensity, onslaught **10** bestiality, fierceness **11** desecration, profanation **13** ferociousness, physical force **16** bloodthirstiness

violent 3 hot **4** wild **5** cruel, fiery **6** brutal, fierce, insane, raging, savage, severe, strong, unruly **7** berserk, furious, intense, rampant **8** maniacal, vehement **9** explosive, ferocious, hotheaded, murderous, unbridled **10** passionate **11** full of force, intractable, tempestuous **12** ungovernable **14** uncontrollable

Violent Bear It Away, The
author: 15 Flannery O'Connor

Violent Land, The
author: 10 Jorge Amado

violet 5 Viola
varieties: 3 dog, red **4** bush, pale, pine, rock, tree, wood **5** coast, cream, dame's, false, flame, green, marsh, pansy, sweet, water **6** Alaska, alpine, Canada, garden, German, horned, plains, stream **7** African, English, Mexican, Olympic, Persian, redwood, scarlet, striped, two-eyed **8** bird-foot, crowfoot, dog-tooth, florist's, hook-spur, Labrador, larkspur, Missouri, trailing **9** early blue, evergreen, ivy-leaved, marsh blue, sagebrush, tall white **10** Australian, great basin, Philippine, sweet white, western dog, woolly blue, yellow wood **11** Alpine marsh, American dog, arrow-leaved, Confederate, downy yellow, early yellow, lance-leaved, long-spurred, northern bog, strap-leaved **12** eastern water, great-spurred, kidney-leaved, northern blue, smooth yellow **13** common African, Halberd-leaved, northern downy, northern white, purple prairie, southern coast, white dog-tooth, yellow prairie **14** primrose-leaved, triangle-leaved **16** California golden, large-leaved white **17** round-leaved yellow, western sweet white **18** western round-leaved

violin family
instruments: 3 kit **5** cello, re-

bec, viola **7** baryton **8** bass viol, lyra viol, violetta **10** hurdy-gurdy **11** viola d'amore, violoncello **12** tromba marina, viola pomposa **13** lira da braccio **14** violino piccolo **15** hardanger fiddle

viper
group of: 4 nest

Viper's Tangle, The
author: 15 Francois Mauriac

virago 3 nag **4** fury **5** harpy, scold, shrew, vixen **6** dragon, gorgon **7** she-wolf **8** battle-ax, fishwife, harridan **9** termagant, Xanthippe

Virbius
origin: 5 Roman
god of: 6 forest **7** hunting

Virchow, Rudolf
field: 8 medicine **9** pathology
nationality: 6 German
completed formulation of:
10 cell theory

Virgil *see* **8** Vergil

virgin 4 girl, lass, maid, pure **6** chaste, damsel, maiden, unused **7** unmixed **8** pristine **9** unalloyed, undefiled, unsullied, untouched **10** unpolluted **13** unadulterated **14** uncontaminated
constellation of: 5 Virgo

Virgin *see* **4** Mary

Virginia *see box, p. 1052*

Virginian, The
author: 10 Owen Wister
character: 5 Betsy, Randy, Steve **6** Shorty **7** Trampas **9** Molly Wood **10** Judge (Henry) Garth
cast: 8 Lee J Cobb **10** Gary Clarke, James Drury, Pippa Scott, Randy Boone **11** Doug McClure **12** Roberta Shore
setting: 11 Shiloh Ranch **16** Wyoming Territory

Virginians, The
author: 25 William Makepeace Thackeray

Virgin Mary
ingredient: 11 tomato juice

Virgin Soil
author: 12 Ivan Turgenev

Virgo
symbol: 6 virgin
planet: 7 Mercury
rules: 7 service
born: 6 August **9** September

virile 4 bold **5** brave, hardy, husky, lusty, manly **6** brawny, heroic, manful, mighty, potent, robust, strong **7** valiant **8** fearless, forceful, muscular, powerful, resolute, stalwart, vigorous **9** audacious, mascu-

Virginia
 abbreviation: 2 VA
 nickname: 11 Old Dominion
 capital: 8 Richmond
 largest city: 7 Norfolk
 others: 5 Galax, Luray, Salem 6 Marion 7 Bedford, Bristol, Emporia, Fairfax, Pulaski, Roanoke 8 Danville, Hopewell, Manassas, Staunton, St Albans, Tazewell, Yorktown 9 Arlington, Lexington, Lynchburg 10 Alexandria, Appomattox, Petersburg, Portsmouth, Waynesboro, Winchester 11 Newport News 12 Hampton Roads, Martinsville, Williamsburg 13 Virginia Beach 14 Fredericksburg 15 Charlottesville
 college: 3 Lee 7 Hampton, Madison, Radford 8 Longwood, Richmond 10 Washington 11 Mary Baldwin, Old Dominion 13 Randolph Macon 14 Averett Hollins, Mary Washington, William and Mary
 feature:
  battle site: 7 Bull Run 8 Fair Oaks, Manassas, Richmond, Yorktown 10 Petersburg, Seven Pines, Wilderness 12 Spotsylvania 14 Fredericksburg 16 Chancellorsville
  dam: 4 Kerr
  historical site: 10 Monticello 11 Mount Vernon 12 Williamsburg 13 Stratford Hall
  national monument: 26 George Washington Birthplace
  national park: 10 Shenandoah 26 Colonial National Historical
 tribe: 6 Saponi, Tutelo 7 Monacan 8 Manahoac, Meherrin, Nottaway, Pamunkey, Powhatan 9 Matchotic 10 Appomuttoc
 people: 9 Henry Clay, John Rolfe, John Smith 10 Robert E Lee, Walter Reed 11 George Mason 12 John Marshall, Patrick Henry 13 Samuel Houston 14 Cyrus McCormick 15 Meriwether Lewis 17 Booker T Washington, Richard Evelyn Bird 18 Light-Horse Harry (Henry) Lee
 lake: 4 Kerr 5 Smith
 land rank: 11 thirty-sixth
 mountain: 5 Cedar 6 Clinch, Elliot 8 Baldknob 9 Allegheny, Blueridge
  highest point: 6 Rogers
 physical feature:
  bay: 10 Chesapeake
  bridge: 7 Natural
  caverns: 5 Luray
  port: 7 Norfolk 8 Richmond 10 Portsmouth 11 Newport News
  tunnel: 7 Natural
  valley: 10 Shenandoah
 president: 9 John Tyler 11 James Monroe 12 James Madison 13 Woodrow Wilson, Zachary Taylor 15 Thomas Jefferson 16 George Washington 20 William Henry Harrison
 river: 3 Dan 4 York 5 James 7 Potomac, Rapidan, Roanoke. 10 Appomattox, Shenandoah 12 Rappahannock
 state admission: 5 tenth
 state bird: 8 cardinal
 state flower: 16 flowering dogwood
 state motto: 17 Thus Ever To Tyrants
 state song: 24 Carry Me Back to Old Virginia
 state tree: 7 dogwood

line, masterful, strapping, undaunted 10 courageous 12 stouthearted

virtual 5 tacit 7 implied 8 implicit, indirect 9 essential, practical 11 substantial

virtually 8 in effect 9 in essence 11 essentially, in substance, practically

13 substantially 14 for the most part 23 for all practical purposes, to all intents and purposes

virtue 5 honor, value 6 purity, reward 7 benefit, decency, honesty, modesty, probity 8 chastity, goodness, morality, strength 9 advantage, good

point, innocence, integrity, principle, rectitude, virginity 11 strong point, uprightness

virtuosity 7 mastery 8 artistry, wizardry 14 accomplishment

virtuoso 4 whiz 6 expert, genius, master, wizard 7 artiste, prodigy 10 master hand

virtuous 4 good, just, pure 5 moral 6 chaste, decent, modest 7 ethical, upright 8 innocent, laudable, virginal 9 continent, exemplary, honorable, righteous, unsullied 11 commendable, meritorious 12 praiseworthy 14 high-principled

virtuous person
 Hebrew: 6 zaddik

Virtus
 personifies: 7 courage

virtute et armis 15 by virtue and arms
 motto of: 11 Mississippi

virulent 5 toxic 6 bitter, deadly, lethal, malign 7 harmful, hostile, hurtful, noxious, vicious 8 spiteful, venomous 9 injurious, malicious, poisonous, rancorous, resentful, unhealthy 10 malevolent, pernicious 11 acrimonious, deleterious

virus 3 bug 4 germ 7 microbe 13 microorganism

vis 5 force, power 8 strength

visage 3 air 4 face, look, mien 5 image 6 aspect 7 profile 8 demeanor, features 9 semblance 10 appearance 11 countenance, physiognomy

vis-a-vis 8 eye to eye, together 9 in company, privately, tete-a-tete 10 face-to-face, side by side 11 as opposed to 12 in contrast to 14 as compared with, confidentially 19 as distinguished from

viscera 4 guts 6 bowels 7 innards, insides 8 entrails 10 intestines

visceral 3 gut 5 crude 6 earthy 11 instinctive

viscous 5 gluey, gooey, gummy, slimy, tacky, thick 6 sticky, syrupy, viscid 9 glutinous

visibility 7 ceiling, clarity, horizon 10 definition, prominence 11 range of view 12 distinctness 14 perceptibility 15 conspicuousness, discernibleness

visible 4 open 5 clear, plain 6 in view, marked, patent

7 blatant, evident, glaring, in focus, in sight, obvious, pointed, salient, seeable **8** apparent, distinct, manifest, palpable, revealed **9** prominent **10** noticeable, observable, pronounced **11** conspicuous, discernible, inescapable, perceivable, perceptible, well-defined **12** unmistakable

vision 4 idea **5** dream, fancy, ghost, sight **6** notion **7** concept, fantasy, phantom, specter **8** daydream, eyesight, illusion **9** foresight **10** apparition, conception, perception, revelation **11** discernment, imagination **15** materialization

visionary 4 seer **6** dreamy, unreal, zealot **7** dreamer, fanatic, fancied, utopian **8** delusive, fanciful, idealist, illusory, romantic, theorist **9** imaginary, unfounded **10** chimerical, daydreamer, idealistic, starry-eyed **11** imaginative, impractical **13** insubstantial

Vision of Judgement, The
    author: **9** Lord Byron

visit 4 call, stay **5** haunt, smite **6** affect, assail, attack, befall, call on, punish **7** afflict, assault, go to see, sojourn **8** drop in on, frequent, happen to, look in on, stay with **9** sojourn at **10** be a guest of

Visit, The
    author: **19** Friedrich Durrenmatt

visitant 5 alien **7** arrival, visitor

visitor 5 guest **6** caller **7** company, tourist, tripper, voyager **8** traveler **9** journeyer, sightseer, sojourner, transient **10** house guest, vacationer

vista 4 view **5** scene **6** vision **7** outlook, picture, scenery **8** panorama, prospect **9** landscape **11** perspective

visual 5 optic **6** ocular **7** optical, seeable, visible **9** for the eye **10** noticeable, observable, ophthalmic **11** perceptible

visualize 5 fancy, image **7** dream of, foresee, imagine, picture **8** envision **9** conceive of, daydream of **16** see in the mind's eye

vital 4 life, live **5** alive, basic, chief, quick **6** lively, living, urgent, viable **7** animate, crucial, dynamic, primary, serious, vibrant **8** animated, cardinal, critical, existing, forceful, foremost, material, pressing, spirited, vigorous **9** breathing, energetic, essential, important, necessary, par-

amount, requisite, vivifying **11** fundamental, significant **13** indispensable

vitality 3 pep, vim, zip **4** zeal, zest **5** verve, vigor **6** energy **8** dynamism, strength, vivacity **9** animation, life force **10** ebullience, enthusiasm, exuberance, liveliness **13** animal spirits

vitalize 6 excite, vivify **7** animate, quicken **8** activate, energize **9** stimulate **10** invigorate, strengthen **11** bring to life

vital part 9 essential, necessity, requisite **10** key element, sine qua non **11** requirement

Vital Parts
    author: **12** Thomas Berger

vital principle 5 blood **6** source **9** lifeblood **10** sine qua non

vitals 5 belly **6** bowels **10** intestines **11** vital organs **14** liver and lights

Vita Nuova
    author: **14** Dante Alighieri

vitiate 3 mar **4** thin, undo, void **5** spoil, taint **6** blight, cancel, debase, defile, dilute, impair, infect, injure, poison, weaken **7** abolish, corrupt, pervert, pollute **8** sabotage **9** discredit, undermine **10** adulterate, depreciate, invalidate, make faulty, obliterate **11** contaminate

vitriolic 4 acid **5** acerb, nasty, sharp **6** biting **7** abusive, acerbic, caustic, cutting **8** sardonic, scathing **9** sarcastic, satirical, withering **11** acrimonious **13** hypercritical

vituperate 5 abuse **6** carp at, defame, malign, rail at, rebuke, revile, vilify **7** censure **9** castigate **10** speak ill of **14** inveigh against

vituperation 5 abuse, blame, scorn **6** insult, rebuke, tirade **7** censure, obloquy, slander **8** acrimony, scolding **9** invective **10** defamation, revilement, scurrility **11** castigation, deprecation **12** calumniation, denunciation, faultfinding, vilification **13** tongue-lashing

vituperative 5 harsh **7** abusive **8** scornful **9** insulting, maligning, vilifying **10** censorious, defamatory, scurrilous, slanderous **11** acrimonious, deprecatory

vivace
    music: **5** quick **9** vivacious

vivacious 3 gay **5** jolly, merry, sunny, vital **6** active, bright,

bubbly, cheery, genial, lively **7** buoyant **8** animated, bubbling, cheerful, spirited **9** convivial, ebullient, sparkling, sprightly **10** frolicsome, full of life **12** effervescent, lighthearted

vivacity 3 zip **4** dash, elan **5** gaity, verve, vigor **6** energy, spirit **8** buoyancy, vitality **9** animation **10** ebullience, liveliness **13** effervescence

Vivaldi, Antonio
    born: **5** Italy **6** Venice
    composer of: **10** Gloria Mass **14** L'Estro Armonico, The Four Seasons **16** Judith Triumphant **17** Juditha Triumphans, Le Quattro Stagioni **19** Harmonic Inspiration

Viva Zapata!
    director: **9** Elia Kazan
    cast: **10** Jean Peters **12** Anthony Quinn, Marlon Brando
    Oscar for: **15** supporting actor (Quinn)
    script: **13** John Steinbeck

vive 8 long live (whomever)

vive valeque 15 live and keep well

Vivian
    also: **16** The Lady of the Lake
    character in: **16** Arthurian romance
    lover: **6** Merlin

Vivian Grey
    author: **16** Benjamin Disraeli

vivid 3 gay **4** deep, loud, rich **5** clear, shiny, showy **6** bright, florid, garish, lively, moving, strong **7** glowing, graphic, intense, radiant, shining **8** colorful, definite, distinct, dramatic, emphatic, forceful, lifelike, luminous, lustrous, powerful, stirring, striking, true-life, vigorous **9** brilliant, effulgent, energetic, marvelous, memorable, pictorial, realistic **10** astounding, expressive, impressive, remarkable **11** astonishing, conspicuous, descriptive, inescapable, luminescent, picturesque, resplendent **12** unmistakable **13** extraordinary

vividness 9 intensity **10** brightness, brilliance

vivified 7 revived **8** animated, awakened **9** enlivened, quickened, vitalized **11** invigorated

vivify 6 revive, wake up **7** animate, enliven, quicken **8** vitalize **10** invigorate

vixen 4 fury **5** scold, shrew, witch **6** virago **8** fishwife, harridan, spitfire **9** female fox, termagant

Vladimir
character in: **15** Waiting for Godot
author: **7** Beckett

Vlaminck, Maurice de
born: **5** Paris **6** France
artwork: **8** Red Trees, The Storm **15** Hamlet in the Snow, Winter Landscape **17** The Bridge at Chatou **18** Picnic in the Country, Street at Marly-le-Roi **21** Landscape with Red Trees

vocabulary 4 cant **5** argot, idiom, lingo, slang, style **6** jargon, patois, speech, tongue **7** dialect, lexicon **8** language, phrasing **9** word stock **10** vernacular **11** phraseology, terminology

vocal 4 open, oral, sung **5** blunt, frank, lyric **6** candid, choral, direct, spoken, voiced **7** uttered, voluble **8** operatic **9** outspoken, vocalized **10** forthright, of the voice **11** articulated, plainspoken

vocalize 3 air, say **4** vent **5** speak, utter **7** express **9** ventilate **10** articulate **12** put into words

vocation 3 job **4** line, post, role, task **5** berth, field, stint, trade **6** career, estate, metier **7** calling, pursuit, station **8** business, lifework **9** situation **10** assignment, employment, line of work, occupation, profession

vocational 3 job **5** trade **6** career **9** technical **11** specialized **12** occupational

vociferate 4 howl, yell, yelp **5** shout, shout **6** bellow, clamor, cry out, holler, shriek, squeal **7** bluster, call out, exclaim, screech **9** ejaculate **11** make a racket **12** raise a rumpus

vociferation 3 cry **4** howl, yell, yelp **5** noise, shout **6** bellow, clamor, outcry, shriek, squeal, uproar **7** screech **11** ejaculation, exclamation

vociferous 4 loud **5** noisy, vocal **6** shrill **7** blatant **8** piercing, shouting, strident, vehement **9** clamorous, outspoken **10** boisterous, loud-voiced, uproarious **11** importunate

vodka
origin: **6** Poland, Russia
drink: **10** Moscow Mule
with amaretto: **9** Godmother
with bouillon: **8** Bullshot
with cider: **15** Brewster Special

with Cognac: **7** Cossack
with cranberry juice: **10** Cape Codder
with creme de cacao: **7** Barbara **9** Ninotchka **11** Russian Bear **12** Velvet Hammer, White Russian
with curacao: **8** Aqueduct
with Galliano: **16** Harvey Wallbanger
with gin: **15** Russian Cocktail
with kahlua or Tia Maria: **12** Black Russian
with kirsch: **12** Volga Boatman
with orange juice: **11** screwdriver
with tomato juice: **10** Bloody Mary
with vermouth: **8** Kangaroo **9** Corkscrew

Vogt, Carl Henry
real name of: **12** Louis Calhern

vogue 3 fad **4** mode, rage **5** craze, style, trend **6** custom **7** fashion **8** currency, practice, the thing **10** acceptance, popularity **11** the last word **12** popular favor **14** the latest thing **15** prevailing taste

voguish 4 chic **5** smart **6** modish **7** faddish, stylish **11** fashionable

voice 3 air, say **4** alto, bass, part, role, tone, vent, vote, will, wish **5** speak, state, tenor, utter **6** choice, desire, option, reveal, singer, speech **7** declare, divulge, express, opinion, singers, soprano **8** announce, baritone, delivery, disclose, proclaim, vocalize **9** contralto, enunciate, pronounce, ventilate **10** articulate, intonation, modulation, preference, vocal sound **11** communicate **12** articulation, mezzosoprano **13** participation, power of speech

voiceless 3 mum **4** deaf, mute, surd **6** silent **7** anaudia, aphonic, spirate

voice of the people
Latin: **9** vox populi

void 4 bare, emit, free, null, pass **5** annul, blank, clear, drain, eject, empty, purge **6** barren, cancel, devoid, recant, repeal, revoke, vacant, vacuum **7** abolish, drained, emptied, exhaust, invalid, lacking, nullify, pour out, rescind, reverse, vacuity, wanting **8** depleted, evacuate, nugatory, renounce, throw out **9** destitute, discharge, emptiness, exhausted, repudiate **10** empty space, invalidate, not in force **11** countermand, inoperative

voidance 7 voiding **8** ejection, emission **9** discharge, expulsion

Voight, Jon
born: **9** Yonkers NY
roles: **7** Joe Buck **8** The Champ **10** Coming Home (Oscar) **11** Deliverance **13** The Odessa File **14** Catch Twenty-Two, Midnight Cowboy

voila 3 see **4** look **9** there it is

volatile 4 rash, wild **5** brash, giddy, moody **6** fickle, fitful **7** erratic, flighty, gaseous **8** eruptive, reckless, unstable, unsteady, vaporous, variable **9** explosive, frivolous, mercurial, spasmodic, unsettled **10** capricious, changeable, evaporable, inconstant, irresolute, vaporizing **12** undependable **13** temperamental, unpredictable

volition 4 will **6** choice, option **8** choosing, decision, free will **10** discretion, resolution **13** determination

volley 5 burst, salvo **6** shower **7** barrage **8** outbreak, outburst **9** broadside, discharge, fusillade **10** outpouring

Volpone (The Fox)
author: **9** Ben Jonson
character: **5** Celia, Mosca **7** Bonario, Corvino, Voltore **9** Corbaccio, Peregrine **18** Lady Politic Would-Be, Lord Politic Would-Be

Volsung
origin: **12** Scandinavian
mentioned in: **8** Volsunga
grandfather: **4** Odin **5** Othin
son: **7** Sigmund
daughter: **5** Signy

Volsunga
origin: **9** Icelandic **12** Scandinavian
form: **4** saga
time: **17** thirteenth century
subject: **8** Volsungs

Volta, Alessandro, Count
nationality: **7** Italian
invented: **15** electric battery
discovered: **10** methane gas

Voltaic
also: **3** Gur
language family: **16** Niger-Kordofanian
group: **10** Niger-Congo
includes: **5** Mossi

Voltaire, Francois
real name: **19** Francois Marie Arouet
author of: **5** Zadig, Zaire **6** Alzire, Merope **7** Candide, L'Ingenu, Mahomet **11** The Henriade **16** The Maid of

Orleans **23** Philosophical Dictionary
member of: **11** Philosophes

Volturnus
origin: **5** Roman
personifies: **4** wind **8** east wind **13** southeast wind

voluble 4 glib **5** wordy **6** chatty, fluent **7** twining **8** effusive, flippant, rotating, twisting **9** garrulous, talkative **10** loquacious

volume 4 book, bulk, heap, mass, size, tome **5** folio, sound, tract **6** amount, extent, quarto **7** measure **8** capacity, loudness, quantity, treatise, vastness **9** abundance, aggregate, magnitude, monograph **10** dimensions

voluminous 5 ample, large **7** copious, massive, sizable **8** abundant **9** extensive

Volund *see* **7** Wayland

voluntary 6 willed **8** free-will, intended, optional, unforced **10** deliberate **11** intentional, volunteered **13** discretionary, noncompulsory

volunteer 5 offer **6** extend, tender, unpaid **7** advance, present, proffer, recruit **8** enlistee **9** voluntary **10** put forward **11** step forward **12** unpaid worker **13** charity worker

Volunteer State
nickname of: **9** Tennessee

Voluptas
origin: **5** Roman
goddess of: **8** pleasure

voluptuary 4 rake, roue **7** epicure, gourmet, seducer **8** gourmand, hedonist, sybarite **9** bon vivant, debauchee, high liver, libertine, womanizer **10** gastronome, sensualist **14** pleasure seeker

voluptuous 4 soft **6** carnal, erotic, sexual, smooth, wanton **7** fleshly, lustful, sensual **8** sensuous **9** debauched, dissolute, luxurious, sybaritic **10** dissipated, hedonistic, lascivious, licentious, profligate **13** self-indulgent **14** pleasure-loving **15** pleasure-seeking

vomit 4 barf, emit, puke **5** eject, expel, heave, retch **7** bring up, throw up, upchuck **8** disgorge **9** discharge, spew forth **10** belch forth **11** regurgitate **15** toss one's cookies

Vonnegut, Kurt, Jr
author of: **8** Jailbird **9** Slapstick **10** Cat's Cradle, Palm

Sunday **11** Player Piano **18** Slaughterhouse Five **20** Breakfast of Champions **22** Happy Birthday Wanda June

Von Sternberg, Josef
director of: **12** The Blue Angel

Von Sydow, Max
real name: **18** Carl Adolph von Sydow
born: **4** Lund **6** Sweden
roles: **12** The Emigrants **14** The Seventh Seal **15** The Virgin Spring **16** Wild Strawberries **24** The Greatest Story Ever Told

voracious 6 greedy **7** hoggish **8** edacious, ravenous **10** gluttonous, insatiable, omnivorous

Voragine, Jacobus de
author of: **12** Legenda Aurea (Golden Legend)

vortex 4 eddy **7** cyclone, twister **9** maelstrom, whirlpool, whirlwind

votary 3 fan **4** buff **6** zealot **7** admirer, devotee, fanatic, habitue **8** adherent, champion, disciple, follower, partisan **10** aficionado, enthusiast **11** afficionado

vote 3 say **4** poll **5** voice **6** ballot, choice, option, ticket **8** approval, decision, election, judgment, suffrage **9** franchise, selection **10** plebiscite, preference, referendum **11** cast a ballot **13** determination

vouch 4 back **6** affirm, attest, back up, uphold, verify **7** certify, confirm, endorse, support, sustain, swear to, warrant, witness **8** attest to, maintain **9** guarantee **11** corroborate **12** authenticate

voucher 4 chip, chit **5** check, proof **6** surety, ticket **7** receipt, warrant **8** warranty **9** affidavit, debenture **10** credential **11** certificate **12** verification **14** authentication

vouchsafe 4 give **5** allow, deign, favor, grant **6** bestow, convey, tender **7** concede **10** condescend

vow 4 oath, word **5** swear, troth, vouch **6** affirm, assert, assure, parole, pledge, plight, stress **7** declare, promise, resolve **8** contract **9** emphasize **11** word of honor **13** solemn promise

vox populi 14 popular opinion **16** voice of the people

voyage 4 sail **6** cruise **7** passage **8** crossing, navigate **9** ocean trip **10** sea journey

Voyage of the Beagle, The
author: **13** Charles Darwin

voyager 5 rover **7** cruiser, pilgrim, rambler, tourist **8** traveler, wayfarer **9** jet-setter, journeyer, sightseer **10** adventurer **12** excursionist, globetrotter, peregrinator **13** world traveler

Voyage to the Bottom of the Sea
character: **6** Doctor **8** Kowalsky, Stu Riley, (Cdr/Capt) Lee Crane **9** Patterson **10** (Lt Cdr) Chip Morton **11** (Chief Petty Officer) Curley Jones **12** Chief Sharkey **14** (Adm) Harriman Nelson
cast: **9** Allan Hunt, Del Monroe **10** Henry Kulky, Paul Trinka **11** Richard Bull, Terry Becker **12** David Hedison **13** Robert Dowdell **15** Richard Basehart
submarine: **7** Seaview
explorer: **7** Sea Crab
mini-sub: **10** Flying Fish

Vronsky, Count Alexei
character in: **12** Anna Karenina
author: **7** Tolstoy

Vulcan
origin: **5** Roman
god of: **4** fire **12** metalworking
epithet: **8** Mulciber
corresponds to: **10** Hephaestus, Hephaistos

vulgar 3 low **4** base, rude **5** crude, dirty, gross, rough **6** coarse, common, filthy, ribald, risque, smutty **7** boorish, ill-bred, lowbrow, obscene, uncouth **8** impolite, indecent, off-color, ordinary, plebeian **9** offensive, tasteless, unrefined **10** suggestive **11** ill-mannered, proletarian **12** pornographic, uncultivated

vulgarian 3 oaf **4** boor, lout **5** brute, yahoo **7** Babbitt **9** ignoramus **10** philistine **16** anti-intellectual

vulgarity 8 bad taste, rudeness **9** crudeness, grossness, indecency, indecorum, obscenity **10** coarseness, ill manners, indelicacy, smuttiness **11** boorishness, pornography **12** impoliteness **13** tastelessness

vulnerable 4 weak **7** exposed **8** helpless, insecure **9** sensitive, unguarded **10** easily hurt, undefended **11** defenseless, susceptible, thin-skinned, unprotected

Vye, Eustacia
character in: **17** Return of the Native
author: **5** Hardy

wacky, whacky 3 odd **4** nuts **5** crazy, kooky **6** cuckoo, insane, kookie **7** cracked, foolish, touched **9** eccentric, senseless **10** irrational **12** crackbrained

wad 3 bat, pad **4** cram, head, heap, lump, mass, tuft **5** money, stuff **6** bundle, riches, stop up **7** fortune **8** bankroll, plumbago

waddle 3 wag **4** sway **6** hobble, toddle, totter, wobble

wade 4 ford, plod, plow, toil, trek **5** labor **6** drudge, trudge **9** walk in mud **11** walk in water

wafer 4 chip **5** candy, flake **6** cookie **7** cracker **15** unleavened bread

waft 4 blow, puff **5** drift, float

wag 3 bob, wit **4** card, move, stir, wave **5** clown, droll, flick, joker, shake **6** jester, jiggle, switch, twitch, waggle, wiggle, wigwag **7** buffoon, farceur, flicker, flutter **8** comedian, humorist, jokester **9** oscillate **11** wisecracker **14** life of the party

wage 3 fee, pay **6** income, salary **7** carry on, conduct, payment, revenue, stipend **8** earnings, engage in, maintain, practice **9** emolument, undertake **10** recompense **12** compensation, remuneration

wage earner 6 worker **8** employee **9** job holder **12** hourly worker

wager 3 bet, pot **4** ante, pool, risk **5** fancy, guess, stake **6** assume, gamble, hazard **7** imagine, jackpot, presume, suppose, surmise, venture **8** make a bet, theorize **9** speculate **10** conjecture, take a flyer **11** speculation, try one's luck

12 tempt fortune **15** hazard an opinion

wages 3 bet, fee, pay **4** gage, hire **6** fights, reward, return, salary **7** engages, payment, stipend **8** conducts, earnings **9** emolument **10** prosecutes, recompense **12** remuneration

wage war 5 fight **6** combat **7** contend, make war **8** do battle **12** march against

waggery 5 chaff **6** banter, riding **7** joshing, kidding, ragging, ribbing **8** chaffing, drollery, raillery, twitting **French: 8** badinage

waggish 5 droll, funny **7** comical, puckish **8** humorous

waggle 4 wave **5** wield **8** brandish

Wagner, Honus
  real name: 15 John Peter Wagner
  nickname: 14 Flying Dutchman
  sport: 8 baseball
  position: 9 shortstop
  team: 17 Pittsburgh Pirates

Wagner, Richard
  born: 7 Germany, Leipzig
  composer of: 5 Faust **6** Rienzi **7** Die Feen **8** Parsifal **9** Lohengrin **10** Tannhauser, The Fairies **14** Siegfried Idyll **16** The Mastersingers, Tristan and Isolde, Wesendonck Lieder **17** The Flying Dutchman **20** Der Ring des Nibelungen, The Ring of the Nibelungs **27** Die Meistersinger von Nurnberg
    the Ring Cycle Part 1:
      12 Das Rheingold, The Rhine Gold
    the Ring Cycle Part 2:
      10 Die Walkure **11** The Valkyrie
    the Ring Cycle Part 3:
      9 Siegfried

    the Ring Cycle Part 4:
      15 Gotterdammerung **17** Twilight of the Gods

Wagner, Robert
  born: 9 Detroit MI
  wife: 11 Natalie Wood
  roles: 6 Switch **10** Hart to Hart **13** It Takes a Thief, Prince Valiant, The Longest Day **24** All the Fine Young Cannibals

wagon 3 car, van **4** cart, dray, tram, wain **5** coach, lorry, tonga, truck **7** caisson **10** automobile, battleship
  covered: 15 prairie schooner
  maker: 10 wainwright
  police: 10 Black Maria
  Russian: 6 telega
  sideless: 6 rolley
  track: 3 rut

Wagon Train
  character: 9 Bill Hawks **11** Barnaby West, Cooper Smith, Duke Shannon **14** Charlie Wooster, Major Seth Adams **15** Christopher Hale, Flint McCullough
  cast: 8 Ward Bond **11** Scott Miller, Terry Wilson **12** Frank McGrath, John McIntire, Michael Burns, Robert Fuller, Robert Horton

waif 5 gamin, stray **6** gamine, urchin **7** mudlark **9** foundling **10** ragamuffin, street arab **11** guttersnipe **13** homeless child **14** tatterdemalion

wail 3 cry **4** bawl, howl, keen, moan, roar, weep, yell **5** groan, shout, whine **6** bellow, bemoan, bewail, cry out, lament, outcry, plaint **7** keening, moaning, wailing **9** caterwaul **10** rend the air **11** lamentation

waist 3 top **5** shirt **6** blouse, bodice, middle **7** midriff **9** midregion, waistband, waistline **10** middle part, midsection, shirtwaist

waistband 4 belt, sash
5 cinch **6** girdle

waistcoat 4 vest **5** benjy
6 jacket, jerkin, veskit, vestee,
weskit **7** singlet
  French: gilet

wait 4 halt, stay, stop **5** dally,
delay, pause, tarry **6** linger,
put off **7** suspend **8** postpone,
stopover **9** deferment **10** suspension **11** continuance
12 postponement

wait for 6 expect **10** anticipate

Waiting for Godot
  author: 13 Samuel Beckett
  character: 8 Estragon,
  Vladimir

wait on 5 serve **6** assist, attend

waive 4 stay **5** defer, forgo, let
go, table, yield **6** give up, not
use, put off, shelve **7** forbear,
lay over **8** disclaim, forswear,
postpone, renounce
9 surrender

waiver 9 dismissal **10** abdication, disclaimer **11** abandonment **12** renunciation
14 relinquishment

Wakashan
  tribe: 6 Nootka **8** Kwakiutl,
  Puyallup

wake 4 fire, path, stir, wash
5 rally, rouse, trail, train,
vigil **6** arouse, course, excite,
kindle, revive **7** enliven, provoke, quicken **8** backwash
9 galvanize, stimulate
11 resuscitate

wakeful 4 wary **5** alert, astir
7 careful, heedful **8** cautious,
restless, vigilant, watchful
9 insomniac, observant, sleepless **10** unsleeping
11 circumspect

wake up 4 rise **5** arise **6** vivify **7** animate, enliven **8** vitalize **9** stimulate

Walcott, Joe
  real name: 18 Arnold Raymond Cream
  nickname: 9 Jersey Joe
  sport: 6 boxing
  class: 11 heavyweight

**Walden, or Life in the
Woods**
  author: 17 Henry David
  Thoreau

Wales *see box*

wander aimlessly 5 amble,
stray **6** ramble, stroll **7** meander, saunter

Wanderer, The
  author: 13 Alain Fournier

wandering 5 lapse **8** rambling,
straying **9** deviation **10** aber-

Wales
  other name: 5 Cymru **7** Cambria
  capital: 7 Cardiff
  cities: 4 Rhyl, Ross **5** Flint, Towyn **6** Amlwch, Bangor,
  Brecon, Sidney **7** Cwmbran, Herford, Newport, Rhondda,
  Swansea **8** Aberdare, Caerleon, Holyhead, Pembroke
  9 Fishguard, Glamorgan **10** Caernarvon, Caerphilly, Carmarthen **11** Aberystwyth **12** Milford Haven **13** Kidder-
  minster, Merthyr-Tydfil
  division: 5 Clwyd, Dyfed, Flint, Gwent, Powys **6** Radnor
  7 Denbigh, Gwynedd **8** Anglesey, Cardigan, Monmouth,
  Pembroke **9** Brecknoch, Glamorgan, Merioneth **10** Caernarvon, Carmarthen, Montgomery
  government: 29 constituent part of Great Britain
  measure: 5 cover **7** cantred, crannoc, listred
  island: 4 Mona **5** Caldy **8** Anglesey, Holyhead
  lake: 4 Bala **6** Vyrnwy
  mountain: 6 Berwyn **8** Cambrian **9** Prescelly **13** Brecon
  Beacons
  highest point: 7 Snowdon
  river: 3 Dee, Usk, Wye **4** Alun, Taff, Tawe, Teme, Towy
  5 Clwyd, Conwy, Dovey, Neath, Teifi **6** Conway, Severn,
  Vyrnwy
  sea: 5 Irish **8** Atlantic
  physical feature:
    bay: **7** Swansea **8** Cardigan, Tremadoc, Tremadog
    channel: **7** Bristol **9** St George's
    hills: **7** Malvern
    peninsula: **5** Lleyn
    strait: **5** Menai
    valley: **7** Rhondda
  people: 4 Celt, Kelt **5** Cymry, Kymry, Welsh **7** Brython,
  Silures, Taffies **8** Awabokal, Cambrian **9** Siluridan
    actor: **6** Burton **8** Williams
    artist: **4** John
    author: **3** Map **5** Jones, Lewis, Mapes, Parry **6** Machan,
    Thrale **9** Llewellyn **11** Dylan Thomas **14** Dafydd ap
    Gwylym
    god: **3** Deu, Dew **4** Bran, Gwyn **5** Dylan **7** Gwydion
    leader: **5** Bevan **6** Rhodri **8** Hywel Dwa **11** Cadwallader
    12 Bishop Morgan **13** Owen Glendower **16** David Lloyd
    George **18** Llewelyn ap Gruffydd
  language: 5 Welsh **6** Celtic, Cymric, Keltic, Kymric **7** Cymraeg, English
  religion: 8 Anglican **9** Methodist **10** Protestant
  12 Presbyterian
  place:
    bridge: **6** Severn
    castle: **6** Conway **7** Harlech **9** Beaumaris **10** Caernarvon,
    Caerphilly **11** Aberystwyth
  feature:
    festival: **10** Eisteddfod
    stories: **10** Mabinogion
  food:
    dish: **8** flummery

---

ration, digressive, discursive,
maundering, meandering,
roundabout **11** abnormality
12 idiosyncrasy **13** nonconformity **14** circumlocutory

Wandering Jew, The
  author: 9 Eugene Sue

Wanderings
  author: 10 Chaim Potok

wane 3 ebb **4** fade, sink
5 abate, droop, waste **6** ebbing, fading, lessen, weaken,

wither **7** abating, decline,
dwindle, subside **8** decrease,
diminish, fade away **9** dwindling, lessening, recession,
subsiding, weakening,
withering

wangle 4 worm **5** trick
6 jockey, scheme **7** finagle,
wheedle **8** engineer, intrigue,
maneuver **9** machinate
10 manipulate

wanness 6 pallor **8** grayness,
paleness **9** ashenness **10** sal-

lowness, sickliness
13 colorlessness

want 4 hunt, lack, need, seek,
wish **5** covet, crave, fancy
6 dearth, demand, desire, hunger, penury **7** be needy, craving, hope for, long for,
paucity, pine for, poverty, require, wish for **8** scarcity,
shortage, yearn for, yearning
9 indigence, necessity, pauperism, privation, requisite
10 deficiency, insolvency
11 destitution, requirement
13 impecuniosity, insufficiency,
pennilessness
14 impoverishment

Wanted: Dead or Alive
 character: 11 Josh Randall
 cast: 12 Steve McQueen
 job: 12 bounty hunter
 gun: 8 Mare's Leg

wanting 5 short **6** absent
7 lacking, missing **9** defective,
deficient, imperfect **10** inadequate **11** substandard
12 insufficient

wanton 4 bawd, fast, jade,
lewd, rake, roue, slut, tart
5 gross, hussy, loose, satyr,
whore **6** chippy, harlot,
lecher **7** bestial, immoral, lustful, obscene, seducer, trollop,
willful **8** careless, heedless,
mindless, needless, strumpet,
sybarite, unchaste **9** abandoned, adulterer, concubine,
debauched, debauchee, dissolute, lecherous, libertine, malicious, senseless, womanizer
10 deliberate, fornicator,
groundless, licentious, malevolent, profligate, prostitute, sensualist, unprovoked,
voluptuary **11** fornicatrix, promiscuous, unjustified, whore-
master **13** inconsiderate,
irresponsible

wapiti 3 elk **4** deer **11** American elk
 female: 3 cow
 literally: 9 white rump
 male: 4 bull
 species: 16 Cervus canadensis

Wapshot Chronicle
 author: 11 John Cheever

war 5 clash, fight **6** attack, battle, combat, invade **7** contend
8 conflict, fighting, struggle
10 opposition **11** hostilities
 god of: 4 Ares, Odin
  5 Othin **8** Quirinus
 goddess of: 4 Enyo
  6 Athena, Athene, Inanna,
  Ishtar, Pallas, Saitis **7** Bellona, Mylitta **11** Tritogeneia **12** Pallas Athena
  18 Alalcomenean Athena

War and Peace
 author: 10 Leo Tolstoy

 character: 7 Kutuzov **8** Napoleon **13** Natasha Rostov,
 Nikolay Rostov, Pierre Bezuhov **14** Anatole Kuragin
 15 Andrey Bolkonsky **19** Ellen Kuragin Bezuhov
 22 Princess Marya
 Bolkonsky

War and Remembrance
 author: 10 Herman Wouk

warble 4 lump, purl, sing
5 carol, larva, trill, tumor,
yodel **6** growth, quaver, ripple **7** twitter, vibrate, whistle

war cry 6 slogan **8** Geronimo

ward 4 zone **5** avert, block, repel **6** charge, thwart **7** beat
off, fend off, prevent, quarter
8 pavilion, precinct, stave off,
turn away **9** dependent,
forestall
 French: 7 protege

warden 5 guard **6** keeper,
ranger, sentry **7** curator, manager **8** guardian, watchman
9 protector **14** superintendent

Warden, The
 author: 15 Anthony Trollope

ward off 5 avert **7** prevent

wardrobe 4 togs **5** chest **6** attire, closet, outfit **7** apparel,
clothes **8** clothing, garments
10 cedar chest **12** clothespress
 French: 6 bureau **7** armoire,
 commode **10** chiffonier
 11 habillement

wares 4 line **5** stock **7** staples
8 supplies **9** inventory
11 commodities, merchandise

warfare 5 fight **6** battle, combat **8** conflict, fighting
11 hostilities

Warhol, Andy
 born: 14 Philadelphia PA
 artwork: 9 Brillo Box, Liz
 Taylor **13** Marilyn Monroe
 16 Campbell's Soup Can
 20 Green Coca-Cola Bottles

wariness 7 caution **9** alertness,
suspicion, vigilance **11** carefulness, guardedness, heedfulness **12** watchfulness
14 circumspection

warlike 7 hostile, martial, valiant **8** inimical, militant, military **9** bellicose, combative
10 unfriendly **11** belligerent,
contentious, threatening
 Indian: 8 Arapahoe

warlike attitude 9 hostility,
pugnacity **11** bellicosity
12 belligerence, belligerency
13 combativeness
14 aggressiveness

warm 3 hot **4** cook, heat, kind,
melt, thaw **5** cheer, happy,

sunny, tepid, vivid **6** bright,
heated, heat up, joyful, joyous, kindly, lively, loving,
simmer, tender **7** affable, cordial, earnest, fervent, glowing,
intense **8** animated, cheerful,
friendly, gracious, outgoing,
pleasant, spirited, vehement,
vigorous **9** brilliant **10** passionate **11** kindhearted, sympathetic **12** affectionate,
enthusiastic **13** compassionate,
tenderhearted

warmhearted 4 kind **6** genial,
kindly, loving **7** cordial **10** solicitous **11** sympathetic **12** affectionate **13** compassionate

warm-hued 3 red **4** rosy
5 ruddy, vivid **6** golden, orange, yellow **7** crimson, roseate, scarlet **8** blushing

warmish 5 tepid **7** cooling

warm oneself 4 bask **12** soak
up warmth, toast oneself

warmth 3 joy **4** fire, heat,
zeal **5** ardor, cheer, verve,
vigor **6** fervor, spirit **7** hotness,
passion **8** kindness, sympathy
9 animation, happiness, intensity, vehemence **10** affability,
compassion, cordiality, enthusiasm, excitement, joyfulness,
kindliness, liveliness, lovingness, tenderness **11** earnestness **12** cheerfulness,
friendliness, graciousness
15 kindheartedness
17 tenderheartedness

warn 5 alert **6** advise, inform,
notify, signal **7** apprise, caution, counsel **8** admonish

warning 4 hint, omen, sign
5 alarm, token **6** advice, notice, signal **7** portent, presage
8 appraisal **9** foretoken **10** intimation **12** notification

War of the Worlds, The
 author: 7 H G Wells
 invasion by: 8 Martians

war of words 7 dispute, quarrel **8** argument **11** altercation,
controversy **12** disagreement

warp 4 bend, bent, bias
5 quirk, twist **6** debase, deform, infect **7** contort, corrupt,
distort, leaning, mislead, pervert **8** misguide, misshape,
tendency **9** prejudice, proneness **10** contortion, distortion,
partiality, proclivity, propensity **11** deformation, disposition, inclination
14 predisposition

warrant 3 vow **4** aver, avow
5 swear **6** affirm, assert, assure, attest, permit, pledge
7 certify, declare, justify, license, promise **9** authorize,

guarantee **10** asseverate, permission **13** authorization

warranty 6 pledge **9** agreement **11** certificate

Warren, Robert Penn
author of: 5 Flood **7** Audubon **8** Promises **10** Now and Then **12** Incarnations **14** All the King's Men **18** World Enough and Time
member of: 12 the Fugitives

warring 7 hostile **8** battling, clashing, fighting, opposing **9** combatant **10** contending **11** belligerent, conflicting, contentious

warrior 7 fighter, soldier, veteran **9** combatant, man-at-arms **10** campaigner **11** legionnaire

Warsaw
area: 11 Stare Miasto
capital of: 6 Poland

landmark: 14 Kazimierzowski **25** Palace of Culture and Science
Polish: 8 Warszawa
river: 7 Vistula
square: 5 Rynek

warship 5 Maine, U-boat **6** corvet **7** Alabama, cruiser, frigate, gunboat, Monitor **8** Bismarck, corvette, Graf Spee, ironclad, man-of-war **9** destroyer, ironsides, Merrimack, submarine **11** dreadnought, torpedo boat **12** Constitution, Old Ironsides **13** Constellation **15** aircraft carrier **16** superdreadnought
fleet: 6 armada
part: 6 turret
plating: 5 armor

wary 5 alert **7** careful, guarded, heedful, mindful, prudent, wakeful **8** cautious, discreet, vigilant, watchful **10** suspicious **11** circumspect

War Within and Without
author: 19 Anne Morrow Lindbergh

wash 3 mop, rub, wet **4** bath, lave, soak, swab, wipe **5** bathe, clean, float, flood, rinse, scour, scrub **6** drench, shower, sponge **7** cleanse, immerse, launder, laundry, moisten, mopping, shampoo **8** ablution, cleaning, inundate, irrigate, lavation, scouring **9** cleansing **10** laundering

washbasin 3 tub **4** bowl **5** laver **6** lavabo **8** lavatory

washed out 4 drab, dull, pale **5** dingy, faded, white **6** dreary, grayed **8** bleached **9** colorless

washed up, washed-up 4 lost, shot **6** bathed, broken, ruined, undone **7** done for, preened, through **8** bankrupt, done with, fatigued, finished,

---

Washington
abbreviation: 2 WA **4** Wash
nickname: 7 Chinook **9** Evergreen
capital: 7 Olympia
largest city: 7 Seattle
others: 4 Omak **5** Pasco **6** Renton, Tacoma, Yakima **7** Ephrata, Everett, Hoquiam, Othello, Pullman, Spokane **8** Aberdeen, Bellevue, Longview, Puyallup, Richland **9** Anacortes, Bremerton, Kennewick, Vancouver, Wenatchee **10** Bellingham, Burlington, Walla Walla **11** Port Angeles
college: 7 Gonzaga, Seattle, Whitman **9** Evergreen, Whitworth **10** Puget Sound **14** Seattle Pacific **15** Pacific Lutheran
feature:
    dam: 10 Bonneville **11** Grand Coulee
    fort: 5 Lewis
    national park: 7 Olympic **12** Mount Rainier **13** North Cascades
tribe: 3 Hoh **5** Lummi, Makah, Twana **6** Cayuse, Samish, Skagit, Yakima **7** Chinook, Clallam, Clatsop, Cowlitz, Dwamish, Nooksak, Palouse, Quaitso, Sanpoil, Spokane, Squaxon, Tulalip **8** Chehalis, Chimakum, Colville, Nespelim, Nez Perce, Okanagon, Pishquow, Puyallup, Quileute, Quinault, Sahaptin, Salishan, Sinkiuse **9** Nisqually, Quinaielt, Semiahmoo, Skokomish, Swinomish **10** Senijextee, Shoalwater **11** Shahaptaine
people: 7 Seattle **10** Bing Crosby **11** Hank Ketcham **12** Elisha P Ferry **13** Marcus Whitman **15** William O Douglas **19** Isaac Ingalls Stevens
    explorer: 4 Cook, Gray **6** Heceta **9** Vancouver **13** Lewis and Clark
lake: 4 Soap **5** Moses, Union **6** Chelan, Ozette **7** Cle Elum, Cushman, Kachess **8** Crescent, Quinault **9** Keechelus, Wenatchee **10** Washington
land rank: twentieth
mountain: 4 Blue, Jack, Tunk **5** Adams, Baker, Lemei, Logan, Moses, Sloan **6** Kettle, Quartz, Simcoe, Stuart **7** Shuksan **8** Cascades, Olympics, St Helens **11** Kettle River
    highest point: 7 Rainier
physical feature:
    falls: 10 Snoqualmie
    port: 6 Tacoma **7** Everett, Seattle **10** Bellingham
    sound: 5 Puget **7** Rosario
river: 5 Snake, White **6** Yakima **7** Spokane **8** Columbia, Quinault **9** Snohomish **10** Snoqualmie **11** Pend Oreille
state admission: 11 forty-second
state bird: 15 willow goldfinch
state fish: 14 steelhead trout
state flower: 17 coast rhododendron **19** western rhododendron
state motto: 7 By and By (Alki)
state song: 16 Washington My Home
state tree: 14 western hemlock

scrubbed **9** played out, showered

washing 6 laving **7** bathing, laundry, purging, rinsing, soaking **8** cleaning, scouring **9** ablutions, drenching, scrubbing, showering **10** laundering, shampooing

Washington (state) *see box, p. 1059*

Washington, George *see box*

Washington DC *see box*

Washington Square
  author: **10** Henry James

wash one's hands of
4 deny, quit **6** give up **7** abandon, decline, disavow, forsake **8** abnegate, cast away, disclaim, forswear, renounce **9** repudiate **10** relinquish

washout 6 fiasco, fizzle **7** failure, letdown **8** disaster **14** disappointment

wash out 4 fade, fail **6** bleach **7** deplete, fatigue **8** enervate, enfeeble **10** debilitate, devitalize

wasp
  variety: **5** paper **6** cuckoo, ensign, hornet, potter, spider **12** yellow jacket

waspish 5 huffy, testy **6** crabby, cranky, ornery, shirty **7** bearish, fretful, peevish, pettish **8** petulant, snappish **9** crotchety, fractious, irascible, irritable, querulous **12** cantankerous

Wasps, The
  author: **12** Aristophanes
  character: **10** Bdelycleon, Philocleon
    dog: **5** Labes

wassail 5 drink, punch, revel, toast **6** liquor, tipple **7** carouse, revelry **8** beverage, carousal

waste 3 die, ebb, rob **4** fade, loot, melt, rape, raze, ruin,

sack, sink, void, wane **5** abate, crush, decay, drain, dregs, droop, empty, offal, smash, spoil, strip, trash, wreck **6** barren, burn up, debris, devour, litter, misuse, ravage, razing, refuse, scraps, steppe, tundra, weaken, wither **7** crumble, decline, deplete, despoil, destroy, dwindle, exhaust, garbage, looting, pillage, plunder, rubbish, shatter, subside **8** badlands, decrease, demolish, diminish, leavings, misapply, misspend, needless, prey upon, remnants, squander, wrecking **9** devastate, disappear, dissipate, emptiness, evaporate, excrement, leftovers, misemploy, ruination, sweepings **10** demolition, plundering, remainders, wilderness **11** destruction, devastation, dissipation, expenditure, fritter away, prodigality, squandering **12** despoliation, extravagance **14** misapplication

waste away 4 fail, rust **7** corrode, decline, eat into

wasted 5 spent **6** used-up **7** ravaged **9** emaciated, exhausted **12** unproductive

wasteful 8 prodigal **9** unthrifty **10** thriftless **11** extravagant, improvident, spendthrift, squandering **12** uneconomical

wastefulness 10 imprudence, lavishness **11** prodigality, squandering **12** extravagance, improvidence

wasteland 6 desert

Waste Land, The
  author: **7** T S Eliot

waste time 5 dally **6** dawdle, loiter **10** dillydally

watch 3 eye, see **4** heed, look, mark, mind, note, ogle, save, tend **5** alert, guard, scout, stare **6** attend, be wary, gaze at, guards, look at, look on, notice, patrol, peep at, peer at, picket, regard, sentry, survey, tend to **7** be chary, care for, examine, lookout, observe, oversee, protect, stare at **8** pore over, preserve, sentinel, sentries, take heed **9** attention, patrolman, vigilance **10** observance, scrutinize **11** contemplate, observation, superintend, supervision **15** superintendence

watch fire 6 beacon
  kinds: **4** bale **6** signal

watchful 4 wary **5** alert, aware, canny, chary **6** shrewd **7** careful, guarded,

Washington DC
  airport: 6 Dulles **8** National
  basketball team: 7 Bullets
  capital of: 12 United States
  designed by: 7 L'Enfant
  football team: 8 Redskins
  landmark: 4 Mall **7** Capitol, Ellipse **8** Pentagon **10** White
    House **11** National Zoo **12** Ford's Theatre, Franklin Park,
    Supreme Court **13** Lafayette Park, Rock Creek Park
    14 Farragut Square, Reflecting Pool, Watergate Hotel
    15 Lincoln Memorial, McPherson Square **16** National Ar-
    chives **17** Jefferson Memorial, Library of Congress, Na-
    tional Arboretum **18** Washington Monument **21** Frederick
    Douglass Home, Robert F Kennedy Stadium **22** Smith-
    sonian Institution **23** National Sculpture Garden **25** Ar-
    lington National Cemetery **33** Kennedy Center for the
    Performing Arts
  museum: 5 Freer **7** Renwick **8** Corcoran **9** Hirshhorn
    10 African Art **11** Smithsonian **13** Dumbarton Oaks
    15 National Gallery **17** Folger Shakespeare **18** Phillips
    Collection **23** National Portrait Gallery
  river: 7 Potomac **9** Rock Creek
  street/avenue: 4 Ohio **7** New York, Potomac **12** Constitu-
    tion, Independence, Pennsylvania **13** Massachusetts
  university: 6 Howard **8** American, Catholic **10** George-
    town **11** George Mason **16** George Washington

heedful, mindful, prudent
8 cautious, open-eyed, vigilant **9** attentive, observant
11 circumspect

watchfulness 4 care, heed
9 attention, diligence, vigilance **13** attentiveness

watchman 5 guard, scout
6 patrol, picket, sentry **7** lookout **8** sentinel **9** patrolman

Watch on the Rhine
  director: 13 Herman Shumlin
  based on play by: 14 Lillian
    Hellman
  cast: 9 Paul Lukas **10** Bette
    Davis **19** Geraldine
    Fitzgerald
  Oscar for: 5 actor (Lukas)

watch over 5 guard **6** attend
7 oversee, protect
11 superintend

watchtower 6 beacon, pharos,
signal **7** seamark **8** landmark
10 lighthouse

watchword 5 motto **6** byword,
slogan

water 3 cut, dip, sea, wet
4 damp, lake, pond, pool,
soak, tear, thin **5** douse, flood,
H two O, ocean, river, souse
6 dampen, deluge, dilute,
drench, lagoon, splash,
stream **7** immerse, moisten
8 inundate, irrigate, sprinkle,
submerge **10** adulterate
  goddess of: 4 Enki

**Water Carrier (Water
Bearer)**
  constellation of: 8 Aquarius

watercolor
  French: 9 aquarelle

watercourse 5 canal, river
6 strait **7** channel, conduit,
narrows, passage **8** aqueduct

water down 3 cut **6** censor,
dilute, weaken **7** thin out
9 expurgate **10** adulterate

watered down 4 weak **6** dilute **7** diluted **8** weakened
11 adulterated

waterfall 7 cascade, Niagara
8 cataract

waterfront 4 dock, mole, pier,
quay **5** basin, jetty, levee,
wharf **6** marina **7** landing

waterless 3 dry **4** arid, sere
6 barren **7** parched, thirsty
10 desertlike

Waterloo Bridge
  director: 11 Mervyn LeRoy
  cast: 11 Vivien Leigh **12** Lu-
    cile Watson, Robert Taylor
    13 Virginia Field
  remade as: 4 Gaby

**Water Monster (Sea
Serpent)**
  constellation of: 5 Hydra

water of life
  Latin: 9 aqua vitae

Waters, Ethel
  nickname: 19 Sweet Mama
    Stringbean

born: 9 Chester PA
roles: 5 Pinky **6** Beulah
21 The Member of the
  Wedding

Watership Down
  author: 12 Richard Adams

Water Snake
  constellation of: 6 Hydrus

watertight 9 nonporous
10 impervious **11** impermeable

waterway 5 canal, inlet, river,
route **6** gutter, strait, strake,
stream **7** channel

Water Wonderland
  nickname of: 8 Michigan

watery 3 wet **4** damp, thin,
weak **5** fluid, moist, teary
6 liquid, rheumy **7** aqueous,
diluted, tearful, tearing
11 adulterated

Watling, Belle
  character in: 15 Gone With
    the Wind
  author: 8 Mitchell

Watt, James
  nationality: 8 Scottish
  developed: 11 steam engine
    12 piston engine

Watteau, Jean Antoine
  born: 6 France
    12 Valenciennes
  artwork: 6 Gilles **8** Mezzetin
    9 La Finette **10** La Toilette
    12 Joys of Living, L'indiffer-
    ent **13** La Gamme d'Amour
    16 Company in the Park, La
    Lecon de Musique **18** En-
    seigne de Gersaint, Ger-
    saint's Signboard, La
    Comedie Francaise, La Con-
    cert de Famille **20** Le Dejeu-
    ner en plein air,
    L'assemblee dans un parc
    21 Harlequin and Colum-
    bine **23** Embarquement pour
    Cythere, Italian and French
    Theater, Jupiter Surprises
    Antiope, Les Amusements
    Champetres **24** Conversation
    in the Open Air, The Em-
    barkation for Cythera

wattle 6 Acacia
  varieties: 5 black, broom, ce-
    dar, glory, green, hairy,
    oven's, Sally, swamp
    6 frosty, golden, mudgee, or-
    ange, silver, sticky **7** bram-
    ble, buffalo, coastal, prickly,
    weeping, Wyalong **8** blue-
    leaf, cinnamon, graceful,
    screw-pod, sunshine **9** red-
    leaved **10** golden-rain, nee-
    dle-bush **11** Cootamundra,
    Mount Morgan, Wallan-
    garra **12** Sydney golden
    14 Peppermint-tree
    16 Queensland silver

Watts, Sir George Frederic
born: **6** London **7** England
artwork: **4** Hope **14** Physical
Energy **17** Paolo and Francesca **19** Anastasio
degl'Onesti **45** Caractacus
Led in Triumph Through
the Streets of Rome
54 Alfred Inciting his Sub-
jects to Prevent the Landing
of the Danes

Waugh, Evelyn
author of: **9** Men at Arms
10 Vile Bodies **11** The Loved
One **13** Black Mischief, Edmund Campion **14** A Handful of Dust, Decline and
Fall **15** A Little Learning
19 Brideshead Revisited
20 Officers and Gentlemen
22 Unconditional
Surrender

wave 4 coil, curl, file, flap,
line, rank, rise, roll, rush,
sway, tier **5** curve, flood,
pulse, shake, surge, swell,
swing, train, twirl, wield
6 billow, column, comber, deluge, motion, quiver, ripple,
roller, signal, spiral, string
7 breaker, flutter, gesture, pulsate, tremble, vibrate, winding **8** brandish, flourish,
increase, undulate, whitecap
9 advancing, oscillate, pulsation, vibration **10** salutation,
undulation **11** gesticulate,
heightening **13** gesticulation

wave at 4 hail **6** signal
7 gesture

wave on 6 beckon, signal
7 gesture **11** gesticulate

waver 4 flap, reel, sway, vary
5 pause, shake, swing, weave
6 careen, change, falter,
quiver, totter, wobble **7** flutter,
stagger, tremble **8** hesitate, undulate **9** fluctuate, vacillate
10 dillydally **12** shilly-shally

wavering 8 hesitant, waffling
9 undecided **10** hesitating, indecisive, irresolute
11 vacillating

Waverley
author: **14** Sir Walter Scott
character: **12** Flora MacIvor
14 Donald Bean Lean, Edward Waverley **15** Rose
Bradwardine **16** Baron Bradwardine **17** Evan Dhu
MacCombich **24** Fergus
MacIvor Vich Ian Vohr
25 Prince Charles Edward
Stuart

wavy 5 curly **6** coiled, curved
7 rolling, sinuous, winding
8 mazelike, rippling, tortuous
10 meandering, serpentine,
undulating **11** curvilinear
12 labyrinthine

wax 4 grow **5** swell, widen
6 become, blow up, dilate, expand, extend, thrive **7** balloon,
develop, enlarge, fill out, inflate, puff out **8** increase

way 3 far, off **4** area, form,
lane, pass, path, road, room,
wont **5** habit, means, route,
space, trail, usage **6** course,
custom, far off, manner,
method, nature, region, system **7** conduct, passage, pathway, process **8** behavior,
distance, practice, remotely,
vicinity **9** direction, procedure,
technique **12** neighborhood

wayfarer 8 traveler, wanderer
9 sojourner

Wayfaring Stranger
nickname of: **8** Burl Ives

way in 4 door, gate **5** entry
6 access, portal **7** doorway,
gateway, ingress **8** approach,
entrance

Wayland
also: **6** Volund **7** Wieland
origin: **8** European
king of: **5** elves

waylay 4 lure **5** decoy **6** ambush, assail, attack, entrap
7 assault, ensnare, set upon
8 inveigle

Wayne, Anthony
nickname: **10** Mad Anthony
served in: **10** Indian Wars
16 Revolutionary War
captured: **10** Stony Point
battle: **10** Brandywine, Ger-
mantown **13** Fallen Timbers

Wayne, David
real name: **13** Wayne
McMeekan
born: **14** Traverse City MI
roles: **6** Sakini **8** Adam's Rib
12 The Front Page **13** Mister Roberts, Tonight We
Sing **15** Huckleberry Finn
16 Portrait of Jennie **26** The
Teahouse of the August
Moon

Wayne, John
real name: **21** Marion Michael Morrison
nickname: **4** Duke
born: **11** Winterset IA
roles: **5** Hondo **6** Chisum
8 Ringo Kid, Rio Bravo, The
Alamo, True Grit (Oscar)
9 McLintock, Rio Grande
10 Stagecoach **11** The Quiet
Man, The Shootist **12** The
Searchers **14** Rooster Cog-
burn, The Green Berets
16 How the West Was
Won **17** The Sands of Iwo
Jima **27** The Man Who
Shot Liberty Valance

Way of All Flesh, The
author: **12** Samuel Butler

character: **9** Mr Overton
Pontifex family: **5** Ellen
6 Althea, Ernest, George
8 Theobald **9** Christina

Way of the World, The
author: **15** William Congreve
character: **6** Foible **7** Fainall,
Witwoud **9** Mirabell, Wait-
well **10** Mrs Fainall, Mrs
Marwood **12** Lady Wishfort,
Mrs Millamant **17** Sir Wilfull Witwoud

way of thinking 7 beliefs
9 principle **10** conviction
11 persuasions

way out 4 exit **6** egress, escape, outlet

Ways of Escape
author: **12** Graham Greene

wayward 5 balky **6** fickle, fitful, mulish, unruly **7** erratic,
restive, willful **8** contrary, perverse, stubborn, variable
9 mercurial, obstinate, whimsical **10** capricious, changeable,
headstrong, inconstant, rebellious, refractory, self-willed
11 disobedient, fluctuating, intractable, troublesome **12** inconsistent, incorrigible,
recalcitrant, undependable, ungovernable, unmanageable
13 insubordinate

Wazhazhe *see* **5** Osage

weak 4 lame, poor, puny, soft,
thin **5** faint, frail, shaky,
spent **6** feeble, flimsy, unsafe,
wasted, watery **7** brittle, diluted, exposed, fragile, insipid,
lacking, unmanly **8** cowardly,
delicate, helpless, timorous,
unsteady, wide open **9** breakable, enervated, exhausted,
frangible, powerless, spineless,
tasteless, unguarded, untenable **10** assailable, effeminate,
irresolute, namby-pamby, vulnerable, wishy-washy **11** adulterated, debilitated, defenseless,
ineffective, ineffectual, inefficient, unprotected, unsupported **12** unconvincing
13 inefficacious, unsubstantial,
untrustworthy
14 unsatisfactory

weaken 3 sap **4** fade, fail, flag,
thin, wane **5** abate, droop,
lower, unman, waste **6** dilute,
expose, impair, lessen, soften
7 cripple, dwindle, exhaust,
thin out **8** diminish, enervate,
mitigate, moderate **9** undermine **10** devitalize, emasculate

weakened 5 frail **6** dilute,
faulty, flawed, watery **7** diluted **8** delicate, disabled **9** enfeebled **10** undermined
11 adulterated, debilitated, watered down

weakling 4 twit, wimp **5** mouse, sissy **6** coward **7** chicken, milksop **9** cream puff, jellyfish **10** namby-pamby, pantywaist **11** milquetoast, mollycoddle

weak-minded 4 daft, dull **7** foolish **8** backward, mindless **10** irresolute **11** addle-headed, vacillating **12** feeble-minded, muddleheaded, thick-skulled

weakness 4 bent, bias **5** fault **6** defect, hunger, thirst **7** failing, frailty, leaning, passion **8** appetite, debility, fondness, lameness, penchant, tendency **9** prejudice, proneness, shakiness **10** deficiency, feebleness, flimsiness, proclivity, propensity **11** inclination **12** debilitation, imperfection, unsteadiness **13** vulnerability **14** susceptibility **15** ineffectiveness **16** unconvincingness, unsubstantiality **17** untrustworthiness

weak point 4 flaw **5** break, crack, fault **6** defect **10** deficiency **11** shortcoming

weak position 8 handicap **12** disadvantage

weak-willed 8 hesitant, wavering **10** hesitating, indecisive, irresolute

wealth 4 fund, mine **5** goods, means, money, store **6** assets, bounty, estate, luxury, mammon, riches **7** capital, fortune **8** chattels, fullness, opulence, property, richness **9** abundance, affluence, amplitude, plenitude, profusion, resources **10** easy street, prosperity **11** copiousness **12** independence **13** luxuriousness

wealthy 4 rich **5** flush **6** loaded **7** moneyed, well-off **8** affluent, well-to-do **9** well-fixed **10** prosperous, well-heeled

weapon 3 arm **5** guard, means **6** attack, resort **7** bulwark, defense, measure, offense **8** armament, resource, security **9** offensive, safeguard **10** protection **14** countermeasure

weaponry 4 arms, guns **8** armament, materiel, ordnance

wear 3 don, tax, use **4** duds, fray, last, tire, togs, wrap **5** drain, erode, put on, shred, weary **6** abrade, attire, damage, endure, injury, shroud, slip on, swathe **7** apparel, clothes, corrode, dress in, eat away, exhaust, fatigue, frazzle,

rub away, service, swaddle, utility **8** clothing, costumes, garments, overwork, wash away **9** disrepair **10** employment, overburden **11** application, consumption, utilization **12** dilapidation **13** deterioration **14** disintegration

wear away 4 rust **5** erase, erode **7** corrode, eat into

weariness
French: **5** ennui

wearing apparel 4 duds, garb, rags, togs, wear **5** dress **6** attire, finery **7** clothes, costume, raiment, regalia, threads **8** clothing, ensemble, garments, wardrobe
French: **11** habillement

wearing away 7 erosion **8** abrasion, friction, grinding, scraping **9** corrosion

wearing down 6 tiring **7** eroding, erosion **8** abrasion, friction, grinding, scraping **10** overcoming

wearisome 4 dull **6** boring, dreary, tiring, trying **7** arduous, irksome, tedious **8** annoying, tiresome, toilsome **9** fatiguing, laborious, vexatious **10** bothersome, burdensome, exhausting, irritating, monotonous, oppressive

wear out 4 tire **7** exhaust, fatigue **8** enervate, enfeeble **10** debilitate

weary 3 fag **4** beat, dull, tire **5** all in, blase, bored, fed up, jaded, spent, tired **6** boring, bushed, done in, drowsy, pooped, sleepy, tiring, tucker **7** annoyed, drained, exhaust, fatigue, humdrum, overtax, play out, routine, tedious, tire out, worn-out **8** dog tired, fatigued, overwork, tiresome **9** disgusted, exhausted, fatiguing, impatient, soporific, wearisome **10** dispirited, exhausting, monotonous, overburden **11** somniferous **12** discontented, dissatisfied

weather 3 dry, tan **4** face, rust **5** brave, clime, stand **6** bleach, season **7** climate, oxidize, toughen **8** confront, windward **9** withstand **11** temperature
god of: **4** Jove **7** Jupiter

weave 4 fuse, join, knit, lace, link, loom, meld, wind **5** blend, braid, curve, plait, snake, twist, unify, unite **6** mingle, writhe, zigzag **7** combine, entwine, meander, texture **9** interlace **10** criss-cross, intertwine **11** incorporate

Weaver, Earl
nickname: **15** Earl of Baltimore
sport: **8** baseball
position: **7** manager
team: **16** Baltimore Orioles

Weaver, Dennis
born: **8** Joplin MO
roles: **7** Chester, McCloud **8** Gunsmoke **9** Gentle Ben **13** Kentucky Jones

Weaver, Sigourney
born: **12** Los Angeles CA
roles: **5** Alien **6** Aliens **10** Eyewitness **12** Ghostbusters **17** Gorillas in the Mist **26** The Year of Living Dangerously

Weavers, The
author: **16** Gerhart Hauptmann

web 3 net **4** maze, mesh, trap **5** snare **6** screen, tangle, tissue **7** complex, netting, network **8** gossamer **9** labyrinth, screening

Web and the Rock, The
author: **11** Thomas Wolfe
character: **10** Esther Jack **12** George Webber

Webb, Jack
born: **13** Santa Monica CA
wife: **11** Julie London
roles: **6** The Men **7** Dragnet **9** Joe Friday **15** Sunset Boulevard

Webber, George
character in: **16** The Web and the Rock **18** You Can't Go Home Again
author: **5** Wolfe

Webb family
characters in: **7** Our Town
member: **5** Emily, Wally
author: **6** Wilder

Weber, Karl Maria Friedrich Ernst von
born: **6** Lubeck **7** Germany
composer of: **6** Oberon **9** Euryanthe **13** Der Freischutz **20** Invitation to the Dance

Weber, Max
born: **6** Russia **9** Bialystok
artwork: **11** The Geranium **17** Chinese Restaurant **18** Adoration of the Moon

Webfoot State
nickname of: **6** Oregon

Webster
character: **6** George **7** Webster **9** Katherine
cast: **10** Alex Karras, Susan Clark **13** Emmanuel Lewis

Webster, John
author of: **13** The White

Devil **17** The Duchess of
Malfi

we cannot
 Latin: **11** non possumus

we command
 Latin: **8** mandamus

wed 3 tie **4** bind, fuse, link,
 mate, meld **5** blend, hitch,
 marry, merge, unify, unite,
 weave **6** attach, commit, couple, devote, pledge, splice
 7 combine, espouse, make
 one, win over **8** dedicate
 11 incorporate

wedded 4 tied **5** bound, fused
 6 joined, linked, melded,
 merged, united **7** blended, devoted, marital, married,
 pledged, unified **9** committed,
 connected **12** incorporated

wedding 8 marriage, nuptials

---

wedding anniversaries
 first: 5 clock, paper
 second: 5 china **6** cotton
 third: 5 glass **7** crystal,
  leather
 fourth: 4 silk **5** linen
  20 electrical appliances
 fifth: 4 wood
  10 silverware
 sixth: 4 iron, wood
 seventh: 4 wool **6** copper **8** desk sets **16** pen
  and pencil sets
 eighth: 4 lace **6** bronze,
  linens
 ninth: 5 china **7** leather,
  pottery
 tenth: 3 tin **8** aluminum **14** diamond
  jewelry
 eleventh: 5 steel **11** accessories **14** fashion
  jewelry
 twelfth: 4 silk **6** pearls
  11 colored gems
 thirteenth: 4 furs, lace
  8 textiles
 fourteenth: 5 ivory
  11 gold jewelry
 fifteenth: 7 crystal,
  watches
 twentieth: 5 china
  8 platinum
 twenty-fifth: 6 silver
  21 sterling silver jubilee
 thirtieth: 5 pearl
  7 diamond
 thirty-fifth: 4 jade
  5 coral
 fortieth: 4 ruby
 forty-fifth: 8 sapphire
 fiftieth: 4 gold **13** golden
  jubilee
 fifty-fifth: 7 emerald
 sixtieth: 7 diamond

---

weddings
 god of: 8 Talassio

wedge 3 jam, ram **4** cram,
 pack, rend, rive **5** chock,
 chunk, crowd, force, press,
 split, stuff **6** cleave
 7 squeeze

wedlock 8 marriage
 9 matrimony

Wednesday
 Dutch: 8 woensdag
 French: 8 mercredi
 German: 8 mittwoch
 heavenly body: 7 Mercury
 Italian: 9 mercoledi
 name comes from: 4 Odin
  5 Woden
 observance: 12 Ash
  Wednesday
 Spanish: 9 miercoles
 Swedish: 6 onsdag

wee 4 tiny **5** dwarf, scant,
 teeny **6** little, minute, petite,
 scanty **7** itty-bitty, miniature,
 minuscule **10** diminutive,
 teeny-weeny, undersized
 11 Lilliputian, microscopic

weed 3 bur, hoe, nag, pot
 4 burr, butt, cull, dock, hemp,
 rake **5** cigar, joint, vetch
 6 darnel, harrow, pull up, root
 up, uproot **7** tobacco **8** nuisance, plantain, purslane,
 toadflax **9** cigarette, crabgrass,
 cultivate, dandelion, eliminate,
 extirpate, marijuana
 12 mourning band

weed out 6 banish **7** abolish,
 discard **8** get rid of, throw
 out **9** eliminate

Weena
 character in: 14 The Time
  Machine
 author: 5 Wells

weeny 3 wee **4** tiny **5** frank,
 small, teeny **6** hotdog, little,
 teensy, wiener
 11 frankfurter

weep 3 cry, orp, sob **4** bawl,
 bend, drip, leak, lerm, ooze,
 shed, tear, wail **5** exude,
 mourn **6** bewail, boohoo, lament, shower **7** blubber, lapwing, whimper **8** sweating
 9 exudation
 genus: 8 Vanellus

weep over 5 mourn **6** bemoan, bewail, lament

weevil
 variety: 4 boll, rice

Wegener, Alfred L
 field: 10 geophysics
  11 meteorology
 nationality: 6 German
 theory of: 16 continental
  drift

Wegg
 character in: 15 Our Mutual
  Friend
 author: 7 Dickens

weigh 4 lift **5** count, hoist,
 raise, scale **6** burden, charge,
 ponder, regard **7** balance, compare, measure **8** consider, encumber, evaluate, ruminate
 11 contemplate
 12 counterbalance

weigh anchor 4 sail **7** cast off,
 set sail, ship out

weigh down 4 load **6** anchor,
 burden **7** oppress **8** encumber,
 obligate, overload

weight 3 tax **4** heft, load,
 mass **5** value **6** burden, import, saddle, strain, stress
 7 ballast, concern, oppress,
 tonnage, urgency **8** emphasis,
 encumber, poundage, pressure **9** heaviness, influence,
 magnitude **10** importance
 11 consequence **12** significance **13** consideration,
 ponderousness

weight, unit of see box

weightlessness 8 buoyancy
 9 lightness **11** zero gravity

weighty 5 grave, heavy, hefty,
 vital **6** solemn, taxing, trying,
 urgent **7** arduous, crucial, earnest, massive, onerous, serious **8** critical, crushing,
 cumbrous, pressing **9** difficult,
 essential, important, ponderous **10** burdensome, cumbersome, oppressive
 11 significant, substantial,
 troublesome **12** considerable
 13 consequential

Weill, Kurt
 born: 6 Dessau **7** Germany
 composer of: 8 Happy End
  13 Lady in the Dark
  15 Down in the Valley
  18 The Lindbergh Flight,
  The Threepenny Opera
  19 Die Dreigroschenoper
  31 Rise and Fall of the City
  of Mahagonny **32** Aufstieg
  und Fall der Stadt
  Mahagonny

Weir, Peter
 director of: 7 Witness **9** Gallipoli **11** The Last Wave
  26 The Year of Living
  Dangerously

weird 3 odd **4** wild **5** crazy, eerie, kooky, nutty, queer **6** far-
 out, mystic, spooky **7** bizarre,
 curious, ghostly, magical,
 strange, unusual **8** abnormal,
 freakish, peculiar **9** eccentric,
 grotesque, irregular, unearthly,
 unnatural **10** mysterious, outlandish, phantasmal, unortho-

weight, unit of
  of Afghanistan: 3 pau, paw, ser, sir
  of Algeria: 4 rotl
  of Argentina: 4 last **5** grano, libra **7** quintal **8** tonelada
  of Austria: 4 marc, saum, unze **5** denat, karch, pfund, stein **7** centner, pfennig **8** vierling
    9 quantchen
  of Belgium: 4 last **5** carat, livre, pound **6** charge **7** chariot **9** esterling
  of Bolivia: 5 libra, marco
  of Borneo: 4 para **6** chapah
  of Brazil: 3 bag **4** onca, onza **5** libra **6** arroba, oitava **7** arratel, quilate, quintal **8** tonelada
  of Bulgaria: 3 oka, oke **5** tovar
  of Cambodia: 4 mace, tael
  of Chile: 5 grano, libra **7** quintal
  of China: 3 fan, fen, hao, kin, ssu, tan, yin **4** chee, chin, dong, shih, tael, tsin **5** catty, chien,
    picul, tchin, tsien **6** kungli **7** haikwan, kungfen, kungssu, kungtun **8** kungchin **9** candareen
    10 kupingtael
  of Colombia: 3 bag **4** saco **5** carga, libra **7** quilate, quintal
  of Costa Rica: 3 bag **4** caja **5** libra
  of Cuba: 5 libra **6** tercio
  of Ecuador: 5 libra
  of Egypt: 3 kat, ket, oka, oke **4** dera, heml, khar, okia, rotl **5** artal, artel, deben, kerat, minae,
    minas, okieh, pound, ratel, uckia **6** hamlah, kantar **7** drachma, quintal
  of El Salvador: 3 bag **4** caja **5** libra
  of England: 3 bag, kip, tod, ton **4** keel, last, mast, maun **5** barge, fagot, grain, maund, pound,
    score, stand, stone, truss **6** bushel, cental, fangot, firkin, fother, fotmal, pocket **7** quarter,
    quintal, sarpler
  of Estonia: 4 lood, nael, puud
  of Ethiopia: 3 pek **4** kasm, natr, oket, rotl **5** alada, artal, mocha, neter, ratel, wakea **6** wogiet
    8 farasula **9** mutagalla
  of France: 3 sol **4** gros, kilo, marc, once **5** carat, livre, pound, tonne, uckia **6** gramme, passir
    7 tonneau **8** esterlin **9** esterling
  of Greece: 3 mna, oka, oke **4** mina, obol **5** litra, livre, maneh, pound **6** diobol, dramme, kan-
    tar, obolos, obolus, stater, talent **7** chalcon, chalque, drachma **8** diobolon, talanton
  of Guatemala: 4 caja **5** libra
  of Guinea: 4 akey, piso, uzan **5** benda, seron **6** quinto **8** aguirage
  of Hungary: 7 vamfont **8** vammazsa
  of Iceland: 4 pund **5** pound, tunna **6** smjors
  of India: 3 mod, pai, ser, vis **4** dhan, drum, hoen, kona, myat, pala, pank, pice, raik, ruay,
    tael, tali, tank, tola, wang, yava **5** adpad, bahar, hubba, masha, maund, tical **6** abucco, karsha
    8 mangelin
  of Indonesia: 5 catty, ounce, thail **6** soekoe
  of Iran: 3 ser **4** dram, dung, rotl, sang, seer **5** abbas, artel, maund, pinar, ratel **6** dirhem, gan-
    dum, karwar, miscal, nakhod, nimman **7** abbassi **8** tcheirek
  of Italy: 5 carat, libra, oncia, pound **6** carato, denaro, libbra, ottava
  of Japan: 2 mo **3** fun, kin, kon, rin, shi **4** kati, kwan, niyo **5** carat, catty, momme, picul
    6 kwamme **8** hiyakkin
  of Java: 4 amat, pond, tali **5** pound **6** soekel
  of Korea: 3 won
  of Latvia: 9 liespfund
  of Libya: 3 pik, saa **4** kele **5** teman, uckia **6** gorraf, misura **7** mattaro, termino **8** kharouba
  of Malaysia: 4 chee, mace, tael, wang **7** tampang
  of Mexico: 3 bag **4** onza **5** carga, libra, marco **6** adarme, arroba, ochava, tercio **7** quintal
  of Mongolia: 3 lan
  of Morocco: 4 rotl **5** artal, artel, gerbe, ratel **6** dirhem, kintar **7** quintal
  of Myanmar: 2 ta **3** can, mat, moo, pai, vis **4** binh, dong, kyat, ruay, viss **5** bahar, behar,
    candy, tical, ticul **6** abucco **7** peiktha
  of the Netherlands: 3 ons **4** last, lood, pond **5** bahar, grein **6** korrel **7** wichtje **8** esterlin
  of Nicaragua: 3 bag **4** caha, caja **8** tonelada
  of Norway: 3 lod **4** mark, pund **9** skaalpund **10** bismerpund
  of Pakistan: 4 seer, tola **5** maund
  of Paraguay: 7 quintal
  of Peru: 5 libra **7** quintal
  of the Philippines: 5 catty, fardo, picul, punto **6** lachsa **7** quilate **8** chinanta
  of Poland: 3 lut **4** funt **5** uncya **6** kamian **7** centner, skrupul
  of Portugal: 4 grao, onca, once **5** libra, marco **6** arroba, oitava **7** arratel, quintal **9** excropulo
  of Russia: 3 lof, lot **4** dola, funt, lana, last, loof, loth, once, pood, poud **5** dolia
  of Saudi Arabia: 3 oke
  of Scotland: 4 boll, drop **5** trone **6** bushel
  of Somalia: 8 parsalah
  of Spain: 4 onza **5** frail, grano, libra, marco, tomin **6** adarme, arroba, dinero, dracma, ochava
    7 arienzo, quilate, quintal **8** caracter, tonelada

(continued)

weight, unit of (*continued*)
  of Sudan: **5** habba
  of Sweden: **3** ass, lod, ort **4** last, mark, sten **5** carat **6** nylast **7** centner, lispund **8** skalpund, skeppund **9** shippound
  of Switzerland: **4** fund **5** pfund **7** centner, quintal **12** zugthierlast
  of Syria: **4** cola, rotl **5** artal, artel, ratel **6** talent
  of Tanzania: **8** farsalah
  of Thailand: **3** bat, hap, pai, pay, sen, sok **4** baht, haph, kati, klam, klom **5** catty, chang, coyan, fuang, picul, pilul, tical **6** fluang, graini, salung, sompay **7** tamlung
  of Tunisia: **3** saa **4** rotl **5** artal, artel, ratel, uckia **6** kantar
  of Turkey: **3** oka, oke **4** aqui, dram, kile, rotl **5** artal, artel, cheke, kerat, obolu, ratel **6** batman, dirhem, kantar, maunch, miskal **7** drachma, quintal, yusdrum
  of Uruguay: **7** quintal
  of Venezuela: **3** bag **5** libra
  of Vietnam: **3** can, yet **4** uyen
  of Yugoslavia: **3** oka **5** dramm, tovar, wagon **7** satlijk

---

dox **12** supernatural **14** unconventional

weirdo 3 nut **4** kook **5** flake, freak **6** looney **7** lunatic, oddball **8** crackpot, original **9** character, eccentric, screwball **10** one-of-a-kind

Weird sisters 5 Fates, Norns

Weisenfreund, Muni
  real name of: **8** Paul Muni

Weismuller, Johnny
  real name: **20** Peter John Weissmuller
  born: **9** Windbar PA
  Olympic sport: **8** swimming
  Olympic gold medals: **4** five
  wife: **9** Lupe Velez
  roles: **6** Tarzan **9** Jungle Jim

Weiss, Peter
  author of: **10** Marat/Sade **14** Vanishing Point

welcome 4 meet **5** admit, greet **6** at home, salute, wanted **7** embrace, receive, usher in, winning **8** accepted, admitted, charming, engaging, enticing, greeting, inviting, pleasant, pleasing **9** agreeable, entertain, reception **10** delightful, gratifying, salutation **11** comfortable

Weld, Tuesday
  real name: **12** Susan Ker Weld
  born: **9** New York NY
  husband: **11** Dudley Moore
  roles: **12** I Walk the Line **14** Play It as It Lays **16** The Cincinnati Kid, Wild in the Country **19** Looking for Mr Goodbar

welfare 4 good **6** health, profit, relief **7** benefit, success, the dole **9** advantage, happiness

well *see box*

well-adjusted 6 normal, secure **8** sensible

Welland, May
  character in: **17** The Age of Innocence
  author: **7** Wharton

well-behaved 6 polite, sedate **8** decorous

well-being 4 ease, good, luck, weal **6** health, profit **7** benefit, comfort, fortune, success, welfare **8** felicity, good luck **9** advantage, affluence, happiness **10** prosperity

wellborn 8 highbred **9** patrician **10** upper-class **12** aristocratic, silk-stocking

Wellbred
  character in: **19** Every Man in His Humour
  author: **6** Jonson

well-bred 5 civil, suave **6** polite, urbane **7** elegant, gallant, genteel, refined **8** cultured, ladylike, mannerly, polished **9** civilized, courteous **10** cultivated **11** gentlemanly **13** sophisticated

well-chosen 3 apt **4** fine

5 prize **6** choice, seemly, select **7** apropos, correct, fitting, special **8** superior **9** excellent **11** appropriate

well-considered 7 careful, prudent **8** cautious **10** thoughtful **11** circumspect

well-coordinated 6 smooth **8** graceful **9** dexterous **10** effortless

well-defined 5 clear, plain **8** clear-cut, definite, distinct, palpable **10** pronounced

well-dressed 4 chic **5** natty, smart **6** dapper **11** fashionable

well-educated 7 erudite, learned **8** cultured, literate **9** scholarly **10** cultivated **13** knowledgeable

Weller, Sam
  character in: **14** Pickwick Papers
  author: **7** Dickens

Welles, Orson
  real name: **17** George Orson Welles

---

well 3 jet, run **4** flow, fund, good, gush, hale, mine, ooze, pool, pour, rise **5** amply, fount, fully, issue, lucky, right, shaft, sound, spout, spurt, store, surge **6** easily, fairly, hearty, justly, kindly, nicely, proper, robust, source, spring, stream, strong, warmly **7** chipper, fitting, healthy, readily, rightly **8** famously, fountain, laudably, properly, suitably, very much, vigorous **9** agreeably, capitally, carefully, correctly, favorable, favorably, fortunate, promising, quite well **10** abundantly, acceptably, adequately, auspicious, completely, familiarly, felicitous, intimately, personally, prosperous, splendidly, successful, thoroughly **11** approvingly, commendably **12** advantageous, auspiciously, considerably, propitiously, satisfactory, successfully, sufficiently **13** substantially **14** advantageously, satisfactorily **15** sympathetically **16** enthusiastically
  hole drilled in ground for: **3** gas, oil **5** water

born: 9 Kenosha WI
wife: 9 Paola Mori **12** Rita Hayworth
formed: 14 Mercury Theatre
radio show: 14 War of the Worlds
roles: 8 Jane Eyre **11** Citizen Kane, The Third Man, Touch of Evil
director of: 7 Macbeth, Othello **8** Falstaff **11** Citizen Kane, The Stranger, Touch of Evil **23** The Magnificent Ambersons

well-favored 4 fair **5** bonny **6** comely, pretty **7** sightly, winsome **8** fetching, handsome **9** beautiful **10** attractive **11** good looking

well-fed 5 hefty, plump, stout **6** portly, rotund **9** corpulent

well-fixed 4 rich **7** moneyed, wealthy **8** affluent **10** prosperous

well-founded 7 factual **9** supported **12** corroborated **13** substantiated

well-groomed 4 neat, tidy **5** natty **6** spruce **10** impeccable

well-grounded 5 valid **7** factual **8** reliable **9** supported **10** undeniable, undisputed, unshakable **11** irrefutable **12** corroborated, indisputable **13** incontestable, substantiated **16** incontrovertible

well-heeled 4 rich **7** moneyed, wealthy **8** affluent **10** in the chips, in the money, prosperous

Wellington
    capital of: 10 New Zealand

Wellington, Duke of
    also: 15 Arthur Wellesley
    nickname: 6 Hookey **12** The Great Duke
    nationality: 7 British
    served in: 5 India **14** Napoleonic Wars
    battle: 6 Assaye **7** Vitoria **8** Talavera, Waterloo **9** Salamanca
    served as: 13 prime minister
    memoirs: 20 Wellington Dispatches

well-kept 4 heat, neat, tidy **7** orderly **9** organized **10** systematic **11** disciplined, uncluttered

well-known 4 open **5** famed, noted **6** common, famous **7** big-time, eminent, evident, leading, obvious, popular **8** familiar, infamous, renowned **9** important, notorious, prominent **10** celebrated, scandalous, understood **11** established, illustrious, outstanding

well-lighted 5 lit up **6** ablaze, bright **11** illuminated

well-made 4 fine **7** perfect **8** executed, flawless **9** faultless **11** beautifully

Wellman, William
    director of: 5 Wings **9** Beau Geste **11** A Star Is Born **13** Nothing Sacred **15** The Story of GI Joe **16** The Ox-Bow Incident

well-mannered 6 polite **7** genteel, refined **8** cultured, decorous, ladylike, polished **9** courteous, dignified **10** cultivated **11** gentlemanly

well-matched 5 close **10** nip-and-tuck

well-off 4 rich **5** flush **6** loaded **7** moneyed, wealthy **8** affluent **10** prosperous **11** comfortable

well-padded 5 plump, stout **6** chubby, fleshy, portly, rotund **9** corpulent

well-proportioned 7 classic, elegant, shapely **8** graceful **11** symmetrical

well-read 7 erudite, learned **8** cultured, literate **9** scholarly **10** cultivated

well-reasoned 4 wise **10** perceptive, thoughtful **11** intelligent

well-rehearsed 6 smooth **7** planned **8** prepared **9** practiced

Wells, H G (Herbert George)
    author of: 5 Kipps **10** Tono-Bungay **11** Ann Veronica **14** The Time Machine **15** The Invisible Man **16** Outline of History **17** Love and Mr Lewisham, The War of the Worlds **19** The History of Mr Polly **22** The Shape of Things to Come **23** Mr Britling Sees It Through

Wells, Julia Elizabeth
    real name of: 12 Julie Andrews

wellspring 4 font **6** origin, source **9** beginning **10** birthplace **12** fountainhead

well-stocked 4 full **11** overflowing

well-suited 6 proper **7** correct, fitting **8** suitable **9** congenial, congruous **10** compatible, harmonious **11** appropriate

well-to-do 4 rich **7** moneyed, wealthy **8** affluent **10** in the chips, in the money, prosperous

well up 4 boil, rise **6** bubble **7** surface

well-ventilated 4 airy **5** windy **6** breezy, drafty

well-versed 7 knowing **9** qualified **10** conversant **11** experienced **13** knowledgeable
    French: 9 au courant

well-wisher 6 friend **8** advocate, champion **9** supported

Welsh Mythology
    goddess: 3 Don
    goddess of fire / fertility / agriculture / household / wisdom: 6 Brigit
    king: 4 Bran, Llud, Ludd, Nudd
    magician: 5 Lloyd
    paradise: 5 Annwn **6** Annfwn
    prince: 5 Pwyll **7** Kilwich
    princess: 5 Olwen
    romantic tales: 10 Mabinogian

welt 4 bump, lump, mark, wale, weal **6** bruise, streak, stripe **8** swelling **9** contusion

Weltanschauung 25 manner of looking at the world

Weltansicht 9 world view

welter 4 heap, mass, mess, pile, roll, toss **5** heave, storm **6** bustle, grovel, hubbub, jumble, racket, tumult, wallow, writhe **7** tempest, turmoil **9** commotion, confusion **10** hodgepodge, turbulence

Welter, Blanca Rosa
    real name of: 14 Linda Christian

Weltschmerz 6 sorrow **9** world pain **20** sentimental pessimism

Welty, Eudora
    author of: 12 Delta Wedding, Golden Apples **13** Losing Battles **14** The Ponder Heart **15** A Sweet Devouring **19** The Robber Bridegroom **20** The Optimist's Daughter

wench 4 doxy, girl, lass, maid, slut **5** whore **6** damsel, lassie, maiden **8** strumpet **10** prostitute

wend 4 make **5** hie to

went 3 ran **4** flew, left **5** faded, got on **6** flew by, lapsed, passed **7** elapsed, sallied **8** departed, filed off, passed by, took wing, vanished **9** proceeded, took leave **10** shuffled on, took flight **11** disappeared, forged ahead **12** sallied forth **13** pressed onward

Wentworth, Captain Frederick
character in: **10** Persuasion
author: **6** Austen

Werfel, Franz
author of: **9** Mirror Man
19 Forty Days of Musa
Dagh, The Song of
Bernadette

Werle, Gregers
character in: **11** The Wild
Duck
author: **5** Ibsen

Werner, Oskar
real name: **24** Oskar Josef
Bschliessmayer
born: **6** Vienna **7** Austria
roles: **9** Jules and Jim, Ship
of Fools **17** Voyage of the
Damned **22** Fahrenheit Four
Fifty One, The Shoes of the
Fisherman **26** The Spy Who
Came in from the Cold

Wertmuller, Lina
director of: **9** Swept Away
(by an unusual destiny in
the blue sea of August)
13 Seven Beauties

Wescott, Glenway
author of: **14** The Grandmother, The Pilgrim Hawk
16 The Apple of the Eye
17 Apartment in Athens

Wessex
fictional place created by:
5 Hardy

West, Benjamin
born: **13** Springfield PA
artwork: **17** Death on a Pale
Horse **19** Death of General
Wolfe **22** Saul and the
Witch of Endor

West, Dame Rebecca
real name: **28** Cicily Isabel
Fairfield Andrews
author of: **8** The Judge
11 Harriet Hume **13** Birds
Fall Down **15** The Thinking
Reed **19** The Strange Necessity **20** The Fountain Over-
flows **21** The Return of the
Soldier **22** Black Lamb and
Grey Falcon

West, Jessamyn
author of: **11** Leafy Rivers
13 A Matter of Time
18 Except for Me and Thee
21 The Friendly Persuasion
22 The Massacre at Fall
Creek

West, Mae
born: **10** Brooklyn NY
roles: **3** Sex **8** Sextette **9** I'm
No Angel **10** Diamond Lil
13 Klondike Annie **14** Go
West Young Man **15** Night
After Night, She Done Him
Wrong **16** Myra Breckin-

ridge **17** My Little
Chickadee
autobiography: **28** Goodness
Had Nothing To Do With It
quote: **18** Beulah peel me a
grape **22** Come up and see
me sometime

West, Morris L
author of: **7** Proteus **9** Harlequin **13** The Salamander
14 The Clowns of God
15 The Tower of Babel
17 The Devil's Advocate
22 The Shoes of the
Fisherman

West, Nathanael
author of: **12** A Cool Million **16** Miss Lonelyhearts
17 The Day of the Locust

Westcott, Edward Noyes
author of: **10** David Harum

Westenra, Lucy
character in: **7** Dracula
author: **6** Stoker

Western, Sophia
character in: **8** Tom Jones
author: **8** Fielding

Western Sahara *see box*

Western Samoa *see box*

Western Star
author: **19** Stephen Vincent
Benet

Western Sahara
other name: **13** Spanish
Sahara
capital: **6** Al Aiun **7** El
Aaiun
city: **3** Zug **5** Daora,
Smara **6** Aargub,
Dakhla, Tichla **9** As-
queimat, Bir Gandus
10 Bir Enzaran
12 Guelta Zemmur
government: **33** disputed
territory claimed by
Morocco
river: **7** Uad Atui **8** Uad
Assag **13** Saguia el
Hamra
sea: **8** Atlantic
physical feature:
cape: **6** Barbas
7 Bojador
desert: **6** Sahara
wind: **5** leste **6** gibleh
people: **4** Arab **6** Berber
language: **16** Hassaniyya
Arabic
religion: **5** Islam
feature:
political group:
14 Polisario Front

Western Samoa
other name: **17** Navigator's Islands
capital/largest city:
4 Apia
others: **6** Safotu, Sataua
7 Faleolo, Palauli, Pou-
tasi, Tuasivi **8** Faga-
malo, Falelima,
Lufilufi **9** Falealupo,
Mulifanua **10** Sama-
laeulu, Satupaitea
monetary unit: **4** sene,
tala
island: **5** Upolu **6** Manono, Savaii **7** Apolima
mountain: **4** Fito, Vaea
highest point: **13** Mauga
Silisili
sea: **7** Pacific
physical feature:
bay: **4** Asau, Salu
6 Safata **7** Lafanga,
Matautu **8** Fangaloa,
Salealua **9** Saluofata
strait: **7** Apolima
people: **6** Samoan
10 Melanesian,
Polynesian
author: **20** Robert
Louis Stevenson (Tus-
itala, Teller of Tales)
explorer: **6** Wilkes
9 Roggeveen
12 Bougainville
language: **6** Samoan
7 English
religion: **9** Methodist
10 Protestant **13** Roman
Catholic
14 Congregational
place:
observatory: **4** Apia
tomb: **9** Stevenson
feature:
chief: **5** matai
clothing: **5** pareu
8 lavalava, puletasi
dance: **4** siva
daughter of chief:
5 taupo
house: **4** fale
food:
dish: **8** palusami
drink: **3** ava

Westhus, Haie
character in: **25** All Quiet on
the Western Front
author: **8** Remarque

West Indies *see box*

Westinghouse, George
nationality: **8** American
invented: **8** air brake **12** railroad frog **20** railroad signal
system

West Indies
11 archipelago
  Associated States:
    7 Antigua, Grenada, St Lucia 8 Anguilla, Dominica 12 St Kitts-Nevis
  bird: 4 tody 6 mucaro
  channel: 7 Jamaica 9 Old Bahama
  component: 4 Cuba 5 Haiti 6 Tobago 7 Bahamas, Jamaica 8 Barbados, Trinidad 10 Hispaniola, Puerto Rico 13 Virgin Islands 14 Leeward Islands, Lesser Antilles 15 Greater Antilles, Windward Islands 17 Dominican Republic
  crop: 6 coffee 9 sugarcane
  fish: 4 pega 5 pelon
  formerly: 10 federation
  fruit: 5 papaw 6 pawpaw 7 genipap
  islands: 5 Turks 6 Caicos, Cayman, Virgin 7 Bahamas, Leeward 8 Windward
  kale: 7 malanga
  lizard: 6 arbalo
  music: 7 calypso
  passage: 4 Mona 8 Windward
  rodent: 5 hutia
  sea: 9 Caribbean
  shark: 4 gata
  sorcery: 3 obi 5 obeah
  tree: 5 genip 6 aralie
  tribesman: 5 Carib 6 Arawak 7 Ciboney
  vessel: 6 droger, drogher
  volcano: 5 Pelee

Westlake, Donald E
  author of: 8 Bank Shot 10 The Hot Rock 13 Dancing Aztecs 15 Brothers Keepers
    as Richard Stark: 9 The Hunter 10 The Seventh
    as Tucker Coe: 19 Murder Among Children

Westover, Russ
  creator/artist of: 15 Tillie the Toiler

West Side Story
  director: 10 Robert Wise 13 Jerome Robbins
  cast: 10 Rita Moreno 11 Natalie Wood, Russ Tamblyn 13 Richard Beymer 14 George Chakiris
  score: 15 Stephen Sondheim 16 Leonard Bernstein

Oscar for: 7 picture 8 director 15 supporting actor (Chakiris) 17 supporting actress (Moreno)

West Virginia *see box*

Westward Ho!
  author: 15 Charles Kingsley

west wind
  associated with: 8 Favonius, Zephyrus

wet 3 dip 4 damp, dank, rain, soak 5 humid, moist, rainy, soggy, steep, storm, water 6 clammy, dampen, drench, liquid, shower, soaked, sodden, splash, stormy, watery 7 immerse, moisten, showery, soaking, sopping, squishy, wetness 8 dampened, dampness, dankness, drenched, dripping, inundate, irrigate, moisture, sprinkle, submerge 9 exudation, liquified, moistness, rainstorm 10 clamminess 11 waterlogged 12 condensation 13 precipitation

wet blanket 4 drag 6 damper 10 spoilsport 11 party-pooper

wet down 5 spray 6 dampen 7 moisten 8 sprinkle

wettish 4 damp 5 moist 6 clammy

we who are about to die salute thee
  Latin: 19 morituri te salutamus
  said by: 15 Roman gladiators
  said to: 13 Roman emperors

whack 2 go 3 box, hit, rap, try 4 bang, belt, blow, cuff, slam, slap, slug, sock, stab, turn 5 baste, clout, crack, knock, pound, punch, smack, smite, thump, trial 6 strike, wallop 7 attempt, venture 8 endeavor

whale 4 beat, cane, drub, flog, orca, whip 6 baleen, thrash 9 bastinado
  constellation of: 5 Cetus
  group of: 3 gam, pod

West Virginia
  abbreviation: 2 WV 3 W Va
  nickname: 8 Mountain 9 Panhandle
  capital: 10 Charleston
  largest city: 10 Huntington
  others: 5 Logan 6 Elkins, Keyser, Ripley, Vienna, Weston 7 Beckley, Grafton, Spencer, Weirton 8 Fairmont, Wheeling 10 Clarksburg 11 Moundsville, Parkersburg
  college: 5 Salem 7 Bethany, Concord 8 Marshall, Wheeling 9 Bluefield 10 Charleston 14 Davis and Elkins 16 Alderson Broaddus 20 West Virginia Wesleyan
  feature:
    historical site: 12 Harper's Ferry
    national road: 10 Cumberland
  tribe: 7 Moneton
  people: 9 Pearl Buck 14 Arthur I Boreman 19 Walter Philip Reuther 24 Thomas "Stonewall" Jackson
    explorer: 12 Morgan Morgan
  island: 14 Blennerhassett
  lake: 4 Lynn
  land rank: 10 forty-first
  mountain:
    highest point: 10 Spruce Knob
  physical feature:
    cavern: 6 Seneca
    plateau: 9 Allegheny
    rock: 6 Seneca
    spring: 8 Berkeley 12 White Sulphur
  river: 3 Elk 4 Ohio 6 Gauley 7 Kanawha, Potomac, Tug Fork 8 Big Sandy, Guyandot 11 Monongahela
  state admission: 11 Thirty-fifth
  state bird: 8 cardinal
  state fish: 10 brook trout
  state flower: 11 great laurel 15 big rhododendron 17 great rhododendron
  state motto: 25 Mountaineers Are Always Free
  state song: 17 West Virginia Hills 20 This Is My West Virginia 27 West Virginia My Home Sweet Home
  state tree: 10 sugar maple

whammy 3 hex 4 jinx 5 curse 7 evil eye 9 evil spell

wharf 3 key 4 dock, pier, quai, quay, slip 5 jetty 6 marina 7 landing 10 breakwater

Wharton, Edith
author of: 10 Ethan Frome, The Old Maid 15 The House of Mirth 17 The Age of Innocence 21 The Custom of the Country

Whatever Happened to Baby Jane?
director: 13 Robert Aldrich
cast: 10 Bette Davis 11 Victor Buono 12 Joan Crawford 15 Marjorie Bennett

What Every Woman Knows
author: 12 James M Barrie
character: 9 John Shand 15 Charles Venables 18 Comtesse de la Briere, Lady Sybil Tenterden
Wylie family: 5 Alick, David, James 6 Maggie

what it takes 5 skill 7 ability, mastery 9 expertise 10 capability, competence, expertness 11 proficiency 13 the right stuff

What Mrs McGillicuddy Saw!
author: 14 Agatha Christie

What Price Glory?
author: 15 Maxwell Anderson

What's Happening!!
character: 5 Rerun 6 Dwayne 7 Shirley 9 Dee Thomas, (Mama) Mrs Thomas 11 Roger (Raj) Thomas
cast: 9 Fred Berry, Mabel King 12 Ernest Thomas 13 Haywood Nelson 15 Danielle Spencer, Shirley Hemphill

What's My Line?
host: 8 John Daly
panelist: 8 Hal Block 9 Fred Allen 10 Steve Allen 11 Bennett Cerf 13 Arlene Francis 15 Louis Untermeyer 16 Dorothy Kilgallen

wheat 8 Triticum
varieties: 4 club, rice 5 durum, dwarf, India, river 6 Alaska, common, German, Polish, starch 7 English, poulard 8 hedgehog 10 one-grained, two-grained 13 Mediterranean
product: 4 bran 5 bread, flour, pasta 6 cereal 8 macaroni 9 spaghetti

Wheat State
nickname of: 6 Kansas

wheedle 4 coax, lure 5 charm 6 cajole, entice, induce 7 beguile, flatter 8 butter up, inveigle, persuade, soft soap

wheel 4 disk, drum, hoop, ring, roll, spin 5 pivot, round, swirl, twirl, whirl 6 caster, circle, gilgal, gyrate, roller, rotate, swivel 7 revolve 9 pirouette

Wheel of Fortune
host: 8 Pat Sajak
assistant: 10 Vanna White

wheels 3 car 4 auto, heap 5 motor 6 jalopy 7 flivver, vehicle 8 motorcar 9 tin lizzie 10 automobile

wheeze 4 gasp, hiss, pant, puff 7 panting, whistle

whelp 3 boy, cub, kid, lad, pup 4 brat 5 child, puppy, youth 6 urchin 9 stripling, youngster 14 whippersnapper

whence 9 from where 10 antecedent 14 from what source

Where Eagles Dare
director: 12 Brian G Hutton
based on novel by: 15 Alistair MacLean
cast: 7 Mary Ure 12 Robert Beatty 13 Clint Eastwood, Patrick Wymark, Richard Burton 14 Michael Hordern

wherefore 2 so 3 why 7 because 13 for what reason

where I may stand
Greek: 6 pou sto

where mentioned above
Latin: 8 ubi supra

whereupon 8 upon what 10 after which 14 upon which point

wherewithal 4 cash 5 funds, means 6 assets 7 capital 9 financing, resources

whet 4 edge, hone, stir 5 grind, pique, strop, tempt 6 allure, arouse, awaken, entice, excite, induce, kindle 7 animate, provoke, quicken, sharpen 9 stimulate 11 put an edge on

whether willing or not
Latin: 12 nolens volens

which see
Latin: 2 qv 8 quod vide

which was to be demonstrated
Latin: 3 QED 21 quod erat demonstrandum

which was to be done
Latin: 17 quod erat faciendum

which was to be shown
Latin: 3 QED 21 quod erat demonstrandum

whiff 4 hint, odor, puff 5 aroma, draft, scent, smell, sniff, trace 6 breath, breeze, zephyr 7 bouquet
French: 7 soupcon

Whig Party
president belonging to: 5 Tyler 6 Taylor 8 Fillmore, Harrison

while 2 as 3 yet 4 idle, till, time, when 5 until 6 during, effort, whilst 7 filling, interim, trouble, whereas 8 although, occasion

whim 4 urge 5 fancy, quirk 6 notion, vagary 7 caprice, conceit, impulse 8 crotchet 11 inspiration 12 eccentricity

whimper 3 sob 4 pule 5 whine 6 snivel 7 blubber, sniffle, sobbing 9 cry softly, sniveling 11 sob brokenly 16 whine plaintively

whimsical 5 droll 6 fickle, fitful, quaint 7 amusing, erratic, waggish 8 fanciful, notional, quixotic 9 eccentric 10 capricious, changeable, chimerical 12 inconsistent

whimsy, whimsey 4 bent, wish 5 fancy, humor, prank, quirk 6 notion, vagary 7 caprice, fantasy 8 escapade, drollery 11 make-believe

whine 3 cry, sob 4 fret, mewl, moan, wail 6 grouse, murmur, mutter, snivel 7 grumble, whimper 8 complain 9 complaint 11 gripe meekly 12 plaintive cry 14 cry plaintively

whip 3 rod 4 beat, cane, drub, flap, flog, jerk, jolt, lash, lick, maul, rout 5 birch, flick, spank, strap, thong, whisk 6 rattan, snatch, switch 7 cowhide, rawhide, scourge, trounce 8 birch rod, vanquish 9 horsewhip, toss about 10 blacksnake, flagellate 13 cat-o'-nine-tails, defeat soundly, move violently 14 beat decisively, beat into a froth

Whip 8 scorpion

whip hand 4 sway 5 power 7 control, mastery 9 advantage, authority, dominance, supremacy, upper hand 10 ascendancy, domination

whipped 5 caned, waled 6 beaten, darted, flayed, frothy, lashed, roused 7 flogged, frothed, incited, revived, spanked, subdued, swished, whisked 8 defeated, overlaid, punished, scourged,

switched **9** chastised
10 vanquished

whir 3 hum **4** buzz, purr
5 drone **7** whisper

whirl 2 go **3** try **4** reel, spin,
stab, turn **5** crack, fling, pivot,
swirl, trial, twirl, whack,
wheel **6** circle, dither, flurry,
gyrate, rotate **7** attempt, revolve, turning **8** circling, gyration, pivoting, rotation,
spinning, swirling, twirling,
wheeling **9** feel dizzy, feel
giddy, pirouette, revolving,
turn round **10** dizzy round,
rapid round, revolution
12 merry-go-round **17** state of
excitement **18** dizzying
succession

whirlpool 4 eddy **5** swirl,
whirl **6** vortex **9** maelstrom
15 whirling current

whirlwind 4 rash **5** hasty,
quick, rapid, short, swift **7** cyclone, tornado, twister
8 headlong **9** breakneck, impetuous, impulsive
10 waterspout

whirly 5 dizzy, giddy, shaky
7 reeling **8** spinning
11 vertiginous

whisk 3 fly, zip **4** beat, bolt,
dart, dash, race, rush, tear,
whip, whiz **5** bound, brush,
flick, hurry, scoot, shoot,
speed, spurt, sweep **6** hasten,
scurry, spring, sprint
type: **4** wire **6** French
8 omelette

whiskbroom 5 brush

whiskered 5 bushy, hairy
6 shaggy **7** bearded, bristly,
hirsute **8** unshaven **11** bewhiskered, mustachioed

whiskers 5 beard **7** stubble
8 bristles

whiskey, whisky 3 gin, rum,
rye **4** corn, shot **5** booze,
hooch, Irish, juice, vodka **6** liquor, red eye, rotgut, Scotch
7 alcohol, aquavit, blended,
bourbon, spirits **8** eau-de-vie
9 aquavitae, firewater, moonshine, unblended **10** sneaky
pete, usquebaugh **11** mountain
dew **14** John Barleycorn,
white lightning
type: 3 rye **6** Scotch
7 bourbon
drink: 8 hot toddy **14** Klondike Cooler
with beer: 11 Boilermaker
with Benedictine: 10 Frisco
Sour
with Cointreau: 16 Canadian
Cocktail
with vermouth: 9 Manhattan

whisper 3 hum **4** blab, buzz,

hint, purr, sigh, tell **5** blurt,
bruit, drone, rumor **6** gossip,
murmur, mutter, reveal, rustle **7** breathe, confide, divulge,
inkling **8** disclose, innuendo,
intimate **9** undertone **10** suggestion **11** insinuation

whist
derived from: 8 triomphe
descendant: 6 bridge
number of players: 4 four
six tricks: 4 book

Whistle
author: 10 James Jones

**Whistler, James Abbott
McNeill**
born: 8 Lowell MA
artwork: 6 Etudes **9** Harmo-
nies, Nocturnes **10** Rosa
Corder **12** Arrangements,
The White Girl **13** Thomas
Carlyle **15** Cicely Alexander,
Wapping-on-Thames
24 Venetian Palaces Noc-
turnes **28** Arrangement in
Grey and Black No 1 (The
Artist's Mother) **29** Chelsea
Nocturne in Blue and
Green **31** Princess of the
Land of the Porcelain
35 Falling Rocket Nocturne
in Black and Gold **37** Cre-
morne Lights Nocturne in
Blue and Silver

whistle-stop 5 stump **8** campaign **11** electioneer

whit 3 dab, dot, jot **4** chip,
dash, drop, iota, mite, snip
5 crumb, grain, pinch, speck
6 morsel, tittle, trifle **7** modicum, smidgen **8** fragment, particle, splinter **9** scintilla

white 3 wan **4** ashy, fair, gray,
pale, pure **5** ashen, blond,
clean, filmy, hoary, ivory,
milky, pasty, pearl, smoky,
snowy **6** benign, chalky,
chaste, cloudy, frosty, leaden,
pallid, pearly, sallow, silver
7 ghostly, silvery **8** blanched,
bleached, grizzled, harmless,
innocent, spotless, virtuous
9 alabaster, bloodless, Caucasian, colorless, stainless, undefiled, unspotted, unstained,
unsullied **10** cadaverous, immaculate **11** translucent, unblemished, unmalicious

White, E B (Elwyn Brooks)
author of: 11 One Man's
Meat **12** Stuart Little
13 Charlotte's Web **14** Is
Sex Necessary? (with James
Thurber) **19** The Trumpet of
the Swan
column: 13 Talk of the
Town

White, Stanford *see* **17** Mead
McKim and White

**White, T H (Terence
Hanbury)**
author of: 15 The Book of
Merlyn **16** The Ill-Made
Knight **17** The Witch in the
Wood **18** The Candle in the
Wind, The Sword in the
Stone **20** The Once and Fu-
ture King

White Album
author: 10 Joan Didion

White Company, The
author: 19 Sir Arthur Conan
Doyle

White Heat
director: 10 Raoul Walsh
cast: 11 James Cagney
12 Edmond O'Brien, Virginia Mayo **16** Margaret
Wycherly

White-Jacket
author: 14 Herman Melville

whiten 4 pale **5** clean, frost
6 blanch, bleach, silver
7 lighten

whiteness 6 pallor **7** wanness
8 paleness **9** snowiness **10** sallowness **13** colorlessness

White Nights
director: 14 Taylor Hackford
cast: 12 Gregory Hines
18 Mikhail Baryshnikov
choreographer: 10 Twyla
Tharp

White Rabbit
character in: 28 Alice's Adventures in Wonderland
author: 7 Carroll

whitewash 6 excuse **7** absolve,
cover up, justify **8** downplay,
minimize, play down **9** calci-
mine, exonerate, vindicate
paint made by mixing:
12 lime and water

Whitewater
author: 10 Paul Horgan

whitish 4 buff, pale **6** chalky,
creamy **7** grayish

Whitman, Bert
creator/artist of: 14 The
Green Hornet

Whitman, Walt
author of: 12 Song of Myself **13** Leaves of Grass
18 Oh Captain My Captain
33 When Lilacs Last in the
Dooryard Bloom'd

Whitmore, James
born: 13 White Plains NY
roles: 4 Them **5** Bully
8 Oklahoma **9** Battlecry
10 Will Rogers **11** Black
Like Me **12** Battleground,
Harry S Truman, Tora Tora
Tora **15** Command Decision,
Give 'em Hell Harry **19** The
Next Voice You Hear

Whitney, Eli
nationality: **8** American
invented: **9** cotton gin
pioneered use of: **14** mass production

Whittier, John Greenleaf
author of: **9** Snow-Bound **10** Maud Muller **14** The Barefoot Boy **16** Barbara Frietchie

whittle 3 cut **4** clip, pare **5** carve, shave, slash **7** curtail, shorten **8** decrease

whiz 3 fly, hum, zip **4** bolt, buzz, dart, dash, hiss, race, rush, scud, tear, whir, zoom **5** adept, drone, scoot, shark, shoot, speed, spurt, sweep, swish, whine, whisk **6** expert, genius, hasten, master, scurry, sizzle, sprint, wizard **7** prodigy, scuttle, whistle **11** crackerjack

who goes there?
French: **7** qui vive

who knows?
Spanish: **9** quien sabe

whole 4 body, bulk, full, hale, unit, well **5** sound, total, uncut **6** entire, intact, robust, system **7** essence, healthy, perfect **8** complete, ensemble, entirety, totality, unbroken, unharmed, vigorous **9** aggregate, undivided, uninjured **10** assemblage, unabridged **12** completeness, quintessence, undiminished

wholehearted 4 true **7** earnest, serious, sincere, zealous **8** complete, emphatic **9** unfeigned **10** unreserved, unstinting **12** enthusiastic

wholesome 4 hale, nice, pure, well **5** clean, fresh, hardy, moral, sound **6** decent, honest, worthy **7** chipper, dutiful, ethical, healthy, upright **8** blooming, hygienic, innocent, sanitary, vigorous, virtuous **9** exemplary, healthful, honorable, uplifting **10** nourishing, nutritious, principled **11** meritorious, responsible **12** invigorating **13** strengthening

whole world, the
French: **11** tout le monde

wholly 5 fully, quite **7** totally, utterly **8** as a whole, entirely **9** perfectly **10** altogether, completely, thoroughly
Latin: **6** in toto

whoop 3 cry **4** hoot, howl, roar, yell **5** cheer, hollo, shout **6** bellow, cry out, holler, hurrah, outcry, scream, shriek **7** screech **9** hue and cry

whopper 3 fib, lie **6** big one **7** fiction **9** falsehood, fish

story, tall story **16** cock-and-bull story

whopping 4 huge **5** giant, large **8** thumping, whacking, whapping **10** incredible **13** extraordinary

whore 3 pro **4** bawd, doxy, jade, slut, tart **5** hussy, tramp **6** chippy, harlot, hooker, prosty, wanton **7** demirep, hustler, trollop **8** call girl, mistress, strumpet **9** concubine **10** prostitute **12** streetwalker
French: **9** courtesan **12** demimondaine

whorl 4 coil, curl, roll **5** helix **6** circle, spiral **9** corkscrew **11** convolution

Who's Afraid of Virginia Woolf?
author: **11** Edward Albee
director: **11** Mike Nichols
cast: **11** George Segal, Sandy Dennis **13** Richard Burton **15** Elizabeth Taylor
Oscar for: **7** actress (Taylor) **17** supporting actress (Dennis)

Who Said That?
host: **8** John Daly **11** Robert Trout **13** Walter Kiernan
panelist: **9** Bill Henry **12** Bob Considine, H V Kaltenborn, June Lockhart **14** John Mason Brown, Morey Amsterdam **17** John Cameron Swayze

Who's on First?
author: **17** William F Buckley Jr

wicked 3 bad, low **4** base, evil, foul, vile **5** acute, awful, gross, rowdy **6** cursed, fierce, impish, raging, severe, sinful **7** corrupt, extreme, fearful, galling, heinous, hellish, immoral, intense, knavish, naughty, painful, rampant, Satanic, serious, vicious **8** depraved, devilish, dreadful, fiendish, infamous, rascally, shameful **9** atrocious, malicious, monstrous, nefarious **10** abominable, bothersome, degenerate, iniquitous, malevolent, scandalous, villainous **11** disgraceful, mischievous, troublesome **12** blackhearted, dishonorable, incorrigible **13** reprehensible

wickedness 4 evil **6** infamy **8** baseness, foulness, iniquity, vileness **9** depravity, malignity **10** immorality, sinfulness **11** malevolence **13** maliciousness, nefariousness

Wicked Witch of the West
character in: **13** The Wizard of Oz
author: **4** Baum

Wickfield, Agnes
character in: **16** David Copperfield
author: **7** Dickens

Wickford Point
author: **13** John P Marquand

Wickham, Mr
character in: **17** Pride and Prejudice
author: **6** Austen

wide 4 vast **5** ample, broad, fully, great, large, roomy **7** dilated, immense **8** expanded, extended, spacious **9** boundless, capacious, distended, extensive, outspread **10** commodious, completely

wide-awake 2 up **5** alert, aware, quick **8** vigilant, watchful **9** attentive, insomniac, observant, sleepless

widely 3 far **5** broad **6** abroad **7** broadly, greatly, largely **10** by and large, far and near **11** extensively

widely known 6 common **7** popular **8** familiar **9** universal, worldwide

widen 6 expand, extend, spread **7** broaden, enlarge, stretch

widened 7 swelled, swollen **8** enlarged, expanded, extended **9** broadened, distended, stretched

wide open 4 ajar, vast **5** agape **6** gaping **7** exposed, yawning **8** extended, unfenced **9** cavernous, expansive, outspread, unbounded **12** outstretched, unobstructed

wide open spaces 7 boonies, country **9** boondocks **11** countryside, hinterlands

wide-ranging 5 broad **7** immense **8** sweeping **9** extensive, universal, unlimited **10** exhaustive **11** diversified, farreaching **12** encyclopedic **13** comprehensive

Wide Sargasso Sea
author: **8** Jean Rhys

widespread 5 broad **9** extensive, outspread, pervasive, worldwide **10** nationwide **11** far-reaching

Widmark, Richard
born: **9** Sunrise MN
roles: **4** Coma **7** Madigan **8** The Alamo **11** Kiss of Death **12** The Long Ships **16** Halls of Montezuma, How the West Was Won **19** Judgment at Nuremberg

Widow Douglas
  character in: **15** (The Adventures of) Huckleberry Finn
  author: **5** Twain

wie geht's 9 how are you?

Wieland
  author: **20** Charles Brockden Brown

wield 3 ply, use **4** wave **5** apply, exert, swing **6** employ, handle, manage **7** display, utilize **8** brandish, exercise, flourish **10** manipulate

wife 3 rib **4** mate **5** bride, squaw, woman **6** missus, spouse **7** consort, old lady **8** helpmate, helpmeet **9** companion
  French: **5** femme
  German: **4** frau

Wife of Bath
  character in: **18** The Canterbury Tales
  author: **7** Chaucer

Wifey
  author: **9** Judy Blume

wig 3 rug **4** fall **6** carpet, peruke, switch, topper, toupee, wiglet **7** periwig **9** hairpiece

Wiggin, Kate Douglas
  author of: **23** Rebecca of Sunnybrook Farm

wiggle 3 wag **4** jerk **5** shake, twist **6** quiver, squirm, twitch, writhe **7** flutter **8** writhing **9** squirming

wigwam, Wigwam 3 hut **4** tent, tipi **5** hogan, lodge, tepee **6** teepee **7** weekwam, wickiup **11** Tammany Hall

Wilcox family
  characters in: **10** Howard's End
  members: **4** Paul, Ruth **5** Henry **7** Charles
  author: **7** Forster

wild, wilds, the wild 3 mad **4** bush, rash **5** bleak, feral, giddy, madly, nutty, rabid, rough, waste **6** choppy, crazed, fierce, insane, madcap, raging, raving, rugged, savage, unruly, wooded **7** berserk, bizarre, flighty, frantic, furious, howling, lawless, natural, untamed, violent **8** barbaric, blustery, demented, desolate, fanciful, forested, frenzied, insanely, maniacal, reckless, unbroken, unhinged **9** abandoned, fanatical, fantastic, ferocious, furiously, illogical, lawlessly, naturally, overgrown, primitive, rampantly, screwball, turbulent, violently, wasteland **10** disorderly, maniacally, uninformed **11** harebrained, impractical, tempestuous,

uncivilized, uninhabited **12** uncultivated, ungovernable, unrestrained **13** rattlebrained, undisciplined **14** undomesticated

wild animal 5 beast, brute

Wild Ass's Skin
  author: **14** Honore de Balzac

Wild Bunch, The
  director: **12** Sam Peckinpah
  cast: **10** Ben Johnson, Robert Ryan **11** Warren Oates **12** Edmond O'Brien **13** William Holden **14** Ernest Borgnine

wildcat 3 cat **4** lynx **6** ocelot

Wild Duck, The
  author: **11** Henrik Ibsen
  character: **5** Werle **8** Old Ekdal **9** Gina Ekdal **12** Gregers Werle, Hjalmar Ekdal **13** Hedvig Relling

Wilde, Cornel
  real name: **19** Cornelius Louis Wilde
  born: **9** New York NY
  wife: **11** Jean Wallace
  roles: **9** Maracaibo **11** Omar Khayyam **12** Forever Amber, The Naked Prey **15** A Song to Remember **21** A Thousand and One Nights **22** The Greatest Show on Earth

Wilde, Oscar
  author of: **6** Salome **17** The Critic as Artist **18** Lady Windermere's Fan **22** The Ballad of Reading Gaol, The Picture of Dorian Gray **27** The Importance of Being Earnest

Wilder, Billy
  director of: **11** One Two Three **12** The Apartment (Oscar) **13** Some Like It Hot **14** The Lost Weekend (Oscar) **15** Double Indemnity, Stalag Seventeen, Sunset Boulevard **16** The Seven Year Itch **18** Love in the Afternoon **24** Witness for the Prosecution

Wilder, Gene
  real name: **14** Jerry Silberman
  born: **11** Milwaukee WI
  roles: **12** Silver Streak, The Producers **14** Blazing Saddles, Bonnie and Clyde **17** Young Frankenstein **22** The World's Greatest Lover **27** Start the Revolution Without Me **43** The Adventures of Sherlock Holmes' Smarter Brother

Wilder, Laura Ingalls
  author of: **26** The Little House on the Prairie

Wilder, Thornton
  author of: **7** Our Town **9** The Cabala **13** The Matchmaker **14** The Ides of March **16** The Woman of Andros **17** The Skin of Our Teeth **20** Heaven's My Destination **21** The Bridge of San Luis Rey

wilderness 4 bush **5** waste **6** barren, desert, forest, plains, tundra **7** barrens **8** badlands, wasteland **9** mountains

Wildeve, Damon
  character in: **17** Return of the Native
  author: **5** Hardy

Wild Is the River
  author: **14** Louis Bromfield

Wild Kingdom
  host/narrator: **9** Jim Fowler, Stan Brock **13** Marlin Perkins

Wild One, The
  director: **12** Laslo Benedek
  cast: **9** Lee Marvin **10** Mary Murphy **12** Marlon Brando

Wild Strawberries
  director: **13** Ingmar Bergman
  cast: **12** Ingrid Thulin **13** Bibi Andersson **14** Victor Sjostrom **17** Gunnar Bjornstrand

Wild Wild West
  character: **10** James T West **13** Artemus Gordon
  cast: **10** Ross Martin **12** Robert Conrad
  traveled by: **5** train

wile, wiles 4 coax, lure, ploy, ruse, trap **5** charm, guile **6** cajole, entice, gambit, seduce **7** cunning **8** artifice, maneuver, persuade, subtlety, trickery **9** chicanery, expedient, stratagem **10** artfulness, craftiness, subterfuge **11** contrivance, machination

Wilfer, Bella
  character in: **15** Our Mutual Friend
  author: **7** Dickens

Wilhelm, Kate
  author of: **10** City of Cain, Fault Lines **11** The Planners **14** The Infinity Box **16** The Clewiston Test **19** More Bitter than Death **26** Where Late the Sweet Birds Sang

Wilhelm Meister
  author: **6** Goethe

Wilhelm Tell
  also: **11** William Tell
  author: **17** Johann von Schiller

wiliness 5 guile **7** cunning, slyness **8** artifice, foxiness, scheming, trickery **10** artfulness, craftiness **11** machination

Wilkes family
characters in: **15** Gone With the Wind
members: **4** John **5** Honey, India **6** Ashley **15** Melanie Hamilton
author: **8** Mitchell

will 4 want, wish **5** endow **6** bestow, confer, desire **7** craving, feeling, longing, resolve, wish for **8** attitude, bequeath, pleasure, yearning **9** hankering, testament **10** conviction, preference, resolution **11** disposition, inclination **12** resoluteness **13** determination

Willard, Frank
creator/artist of: **11** Moon Mullins

Willet, John
character in: **12** Barnaby Rudge
author: **7** Dickens

willful 6 mulish, unruly **7** planned, studied **8** designed, intended, obdurate, perverse, stubborn **9** obstinate, pigheaded **10** bullheaded, deliberate, determined, headstrong, inflexible, persistent, purposeful, unyielding **11** intentional, intractable **12** contemplated, premeditated, ungovernable **13** undisciplined **14** uncompromising

Williams, Esther
nickname: **13** Mermaid Tycoon **14** Queen of the Surf **17** Hollywood's Mermaid
born: **12** Los Angeles CA
husband: **13** Fernando Lamas
roles: **13** Bathing Beauty **15** Jupiter's Darling, Ziegfeld Follies **16** Dangerous When Wet, Neptune's Daughter **20** Million Dollar Mermaid

Williams, Janey
character in: **3** USA
author: **9** Dos Passos

Williams, Myrna
real name of: **8** Myrna Loy

Williams, Robin
born: **9** Chicago IL
roles: **6** Popeye **12** Mork and Mindy **18** Good Morning Vietnam **23** The World According to Garp

Williams, Ted
nickname: **6** the Kid **16** Splendid Splinter
sport: **8** baseball
position: **8** outfield
team: **12** Boston Red Sox

Williams, Tennessee
author of: **10** Camino Real **13** The Rose Tattoo **14** Summer and Smoke **16** Cat on a Hot Tin Roof, Night of the Iguana, Sweet Bird of Youth **17** Orpheus Descending, The Glass Menagerie **18** Small Craft Warnings, Suddenly Last Summer **21** A Streetcar Named Desire **24** The Roman Spring of Mrs Stone

Williams, William Carlos
author of: **7** Tempers **8** Paterson **9** White Mule **11** Al Que Quiere **20** Pictures from Brueghel

William Tell
also: **13** Guillaume Tell
opera by: **7** Rossini
character: **6** Arnold **7** Gessler

William the Conqueror
also: **17** William of Normandy **21** William I King of England
fought against: **8** Harold II
battle: **8** Hastings
succeeded by: **6** Henry I **9** William II

Willie and Joe
creator: **11** Bill Mauldin

willing 4 game **5** ready **7** content **8** amenable **9** agreeable, compliant, not averse **10** responsive

willingly 4 gain, lief, soon **6** freely, gladly, liefly **7** eagerly, happily, readily **8** by choice **10** cheerfully, graciously **11** voluntarily **12** with pleasure

willingness 4 zeal **8** alacrity **9** eagerness, readiness **10** enthusiasm **11** inclination

Willoughby, John
character in: **19** Sense and Sensibility
author: **6** Austen

willow 5 Salix
varieties: **3** bay, red **4** bush, goat, gray, seep **5** black, crack, false, Niobe, Pekin, pussy, silky, water, white **6** Arctic, arroyo, basket, desert, golden, laurel, puzzle, woolly, yellow **7** brittle, prairie, sandbar, scouler, shining, weeping **8** creeping, florist's, polished, Virginia **9** bay-leaved, bearberry, flowering, sprouting **10** cricket-bat, dragon-claw, large pussy, small pussy **11** green-scaled, heart-leaved, peach-leaved, Port Jackson **13** halberd-leaved **16** Wisconsin weeping

willowy 5 lithe **6** limber,

pliant, supple, svelte **7** lissome **8** flexible **9** sylphlike

Wills, Chill
born: **12** Seagoville TX
group: **26** Chill Wills and the Avalon Boys
voice of: **21** Francis the Talking Mule
roles: **5** Giant **8** The Alamo **10** Way Out West **11** The Yearling **15** Meet Me in St Louis

Wills, Garry
author of: **14** Nixon Agonistes, Reagan's America **16** Inventing America

Will Scarlet
character in: **9** Robin Hood

willy-nilly 8 perforce **10** helplessly, inevitably **11** inescapably, unavoidably **12** compulsively, irresistibly **14** uncontrollably
Latin: **12** nolens volens

Wilmer
character in: **16** The Maltese Falcon
author: **7** Hammett

Wilson, Edmund
author of: **11** Axel's Castle **19** To the Finland Station

Wilson, Myrtle
character in: **14** The Great Gatsby
author: **10** Fitzgerald

Wilson, Sloan
author of: **26** The Man in the Gray Flannel Suit

Wilson, Woodrow *see box*

wilt 3 die, ebb, sag **4** fade, flag, sink, wane **5** droop **6** recede, weaken, wither **7** decline, dwindle, shrivel, subside **8** decrease, diminish, languish **10** degenerate **11** deteriorate

Wilt the Stilt
nickname of: **15** Wilt Chamberlain

wily 3 sly **4** foxy **5** alert, sharp **6** artful, crafty, shifty, shrewd, tricky **7** crooked, cunning, devious **8** guileful, scheming **9** deceitful, deceptive, designing, underhand **10** intriguing **11** calculating, treacherous

win 3 bag, get, net **4** earn, gain, sway **6** attain, induce, master, obtain, pick up, secure **7** achieve, acquire, collect, conquer, convert, prevail, procure, realize, receive, success, triumph, victory **8** conquest, convince, overcome, persuade, vanquish **9** influence **10** accomplish

win acceptance 9 establish **10** ingratiate

Wilson, Woodrow
  name at birth: 19 Thomas Woodrow Wilson
  nickname: 5 Tommy
  presidential rank: 12 twenty-eighth
  party: 10 Democratic
  state represented: 2 NJ
  defeated: 4 (Eugene Victor) Debs, (William Howard) Taft **5** (James Franklin) Hanly **6** (Allen
    Louis) Benson, (Arthur Edward) Reimer, (Charles Evans) Hughes, (Eugene Wilder) Chafin
    9 (Theodore) Roosevelt
  vice president: 8 (Thomas Riley) Marshall
  cabinet:
    state: **5** (Bainbridge) Colby, (William Jennings) Bryan **7** (Robert) Lansing
    treasury: **5** (Carter) Glass **6** (William Gibbs) McAdoo **7** (David Franklin) Houston
    war: **5** (Newton Diehl) Baker **8** (Lindley Miller) Garrison
    attorney general: **6** (Alexander Mitchell) Palmer **7** (Thomas Watt) Gregory **10** (James Clark)
      McReynolds
    navy: **7** (Josephus) Daniels
    postmaster general: **8** (Albert Sidney) Burleson
    interior: **4** (Franklin Knight) Lane **5** (John Barton) Payne
    agriculture: **7** (David Franklin) Houston **8** (Edwin Thomas) Meredith
    commerce: **8** (William Cox) Redfield **9** (Joshua Willis) Alexander
    labor: **6** (William Bauchop) Wilson
  born: 2 VA **8** Staunton
  died/buried: 2 DC **10** Washington
  education:
    college: **8** Davidson **18** College of New Jersey (later known as Princeton U)
    law School: **20** University of Virginia
    university: **12** Johns Hopkins
  religion: 12 Presbyterian
  author: 8 The State **16** George Washington **18** Division and Reunion **27** A History of the
    American People **28** More Literature and Other Essays **34** An Old Master and Other Political
    Essays **41** President Wilson's Case for the League of Nations **47** Congressional Government:
    A Study in American Politics
  political career:
    governor of: **9** New Jersey
  civilian career: 6 lawyer
    professor of history: **15** Bryn Mawr College **18** Wesleyan University
    professor of jurisprudence: **9** Princeton
    president of: **9** Princeton
  notable events of lifetime/term: 14 Fourteen Points **15** League of Nations
    Act: **7** Adamson **8** Sedition **9** Espionage **10** Child Labor **11** Liberty Loan, Panama Canal
      14 Federal Reserve **15** Federal Farm Loan **16** Clayton Antitrust, Selective Service **22** Fed-
      eral Trade Commission
    conference: **3** ABC **10** Paris Peace
    18th Amendment: **11** Prohibition
    program: **10** New Freedom
    sinking of: **9** Lusitania
    Treaty: **10** Versailles
    won: **15** Nobel Peace Prize
  quote: 34 The world must be made safe for democracy
  father: 13 Joseph Ruggles
  mother: 5 Janet (Woodrow)
  siblings: 13 Joseph Ruggles **14** Annie Josephson **16** Marion Williamson
  wife: 5 Edith (Bolling Galt), Ellen (Louise Axson)
  children: 13 Jessie Woodrow **15** Eleanor Randolph, Margaret Woodrow

wince 5 cower, quail **6** cringe, flinch, recoil, shrink **7** grimace, shudder **8** cowering, cringing, draw back, quailing **9** shrinking

wind 3 air, lap **4** bend, blow, clue, coil, curl, fold, gale, gust, hint, loop, news, puff, roll **5** blast, bluff, curve, draft, scent, smell, snake, twine, twirl, twist, whiff **6** breath, breeze, hot air, ramble, report, wander, zephyr, zigzag **7** bluster, bombast, cyclone, entwine, inkling, meander, sinuate, tempest, tidings, tornado, twaddle, twister, typhoon, whisper **8** boasting, idle talk **9** aerophone, hurricane, knowledge, whirlwind **10** intimation, suggestion **11** braggadocio, fanfaronade, information **12** intelligence
  god of: 5 Eurus, Niord, Njord, Notus **6** Aquilo, Auster, Boreas **8** Favonius, Zephyrus
  father: 8 Astraeus
  mother: 3 Eos

windfall 7 bonanza

Windhoek
  capital of: 7 Namibia

Wind in the Willows, The
  author: 14 Kenneth Grahame
  character: 4 Mole, Toad **6** Badger **8** Water Rat

windless 4 calm **5** still
8 stifling

window 3 bay **5** oriel **6** dormer **7** opening, orifice, transom **8** aperture, casement, porthole, skylight

Winds of War, The
author: **10** Herman Wouk

windstorm 4 gale **6** squall
7 cyclone, tempest, tornado, twister, typhoon **9** hurricane, whirlwind

windswept 4 bare **5** bleak
6 barren **8** desolate
13 weatherbeaten

windup 3 end **5** close **6** ending, finish **10** completion, conclusion, expiration
11 termination

wind up 3 end **4** halt, stop
5 cease, close **6** finish, settle
8 complete, conclude
9 terminate

windy 5 blowy, empty, gabby, gusty, wordy **6** breezy **7** verbose **8** blustery, rambling **9** bombastic, garrulous, talkative **10** loquacious, meandering, rhetorical
13 grandiloquent

wine
French: **3** vin
Italian: **4** vino
god of: **7** Bacchus
goddess of: **6** Libera

wine-colored 6 claret **8** burgundy, cardinal

winemaking
god of: **9** Aristaeus

Winesburg, Ohio
author: **16** Sherwood
Anderson

wing 3 ala, fly, set **4** band, clip, flap, knot, nick, soar, zoom **5** annex, graze, group **6** circle, clique, pennon, pinion **7** adjunct, aileron, coterie, faction, section, segment **8** addition, coulisse **9** appendage, extension **10** fraternity

Winged Horse
constellation of: **7** Pegasus

Winger, Debra
husband: **13** Timothy Hutton
roles: **10** Black Widow, Cannery Row **11** Urban Cowboy **17** Terms of Endearment **22** An Officer and a Gentleman

Wingert, Dick
creator/artist of: **6** Hubert

Wingfield family
characters in: **17** The Glass Menagerie

member: **3** Tom **5** Laura
6 Amanda
author: **8** Williams

Wings
director: **15** William A
Wellman
cast: **8** Clara Bow **10** Gary
Cooper **12** Richard Arlen
18 Charles Buddy Rogers
Oscar for: **7** picture

Wings of the Dove, The
author: **10** Henry James
character: **8** Kate Croy, Lord
Mark **9** Mrs Lowder
11 Milly Theale **12** Mrs
Stringham **13** Merton
Densher, Sir Luke Strett

wink at 6 ignore **7** condone,
let pass **8** overlook **9** disregard

Winkle
character in: **14** Pickwick
Papers
author: **7** Dickens

winner 5 champ **6** master, victor **8** champion **9** conqueror
10 vanquisher

Winnie-the-Pooh
author: **7** A A Milne
character: **3** Owl **5** Kanga
6 Eeyore, Piglet, Rabbit, Tigger **7** Baby Roo **16** Christopher Robin

winning 7 amiable **8** charming, engaging, pleasing **9** appealing, beguiling, disarming **10** attractive, bewitching, entrancing **11** captivating **12** ingratiating, irresistible

Winnipeg
hockey team: **3** Jets

win over 4 beat, best
5 charm **6** defeat, seduce
7 convert **8** overcome, vanquish **9** captivate, overpower

winsome 5 sweet **6** comely
7 amiable, likable, lovable
8 charming, cheerful, engaging, pleasing **9** agreeable, appealing, endearing
10 attractive, bewitching, delightful

Winter, Lady de
character in: **18** The Three
Musketeers
author: **5** Dumas (pere)

Winter, Maxim de
character in: **7** Rebecca
author: **9** Du Maurier

Winterbourne
character in: **11** Daisy Miller
author: **5** James

Winter of Our Discontent, The
author: **13** John Steinbeck

Winters, Shelley
real name: **14** Shirley Schrift
born: **9** St Louis IL
husband: **13** Tony Franciosa
15 Vittorio Gassman
roles: **11** A Double Life **12** A
Patch of Blue **14** A Place in
the Sun **16** A House Is Not
a Home **19** The Diary of
Anne Frank **20** The Poseidon Adventure

Winterset
author: **15** Maxwell Anderson

winter sports
god of: **4** Ullr **5** Uller

Winter's Tale, The
author: **18** William
Shakespeare
character: **7** Camillo, Leontes,
Paulina, Perdita **8** Florizel,
Hermione **9** Autolycus,
Polixenes

Winter Wonderland
nickname of: **8** Michigan

wintry 3 icy, raw **4** cold
5 bleak, chilly, harsh, polar,
snowy, stark **6** arctic, chilly,
dreary, frigid, frosty, frozen,
gloomy, stormy **7** glacial **8** Siberian **9** cheerless

wipe 3 dry, mop, rub **4** swab
5 apply, brush, clean, erase,
rub on, scour, scrub, swipe,
towel **6** banish, remove, rub
off, sponge, stroke

wiped out 5 broke **6** failed,
ruined **8** bankrupt, indigent,
strapped **9** destitute, insolvent,
penniless **12** impoverished

wipe out 4 ruin **5** erase
7 abolish, destroy, eclipse
8 bankrupt **9** devastate, eliminate, eradicate, extirpate, liquidate **10** annihilate,
obliterate **11** exterminate

wiping out 7 erasing **9** eclipsing, expunging **10** abolishing,
destroying **11** eliminating,
eradicating **12** annihilating,
obliterating

wire 5 cable **8** filament, telegram **9** cablegram, telegraph

wiry 4 lean **5** agile, kinky,
lanky, spare, stiff **6** limber,
pliant, sinewy **7** brittle

Wisconsin *see box*

wisdom 6 brains **8** sagacity
9 teachings **10** philosophy,
principles, profundity **11** discernment, penetration **12** apperception, intelligence
13 comprehension, judiciousness, understanding
god of: **2** Ea **4** Enki, Odin
5 Othin, Thoth
goddess of: **6** Athena, Athene, Brigit, Pallas, Saitis

Wisconsin
abbreviation: **2** WI **3** Wis
nickname: **6** Badger
capital: **7** Madison
largest city: **9** Milwaukee
others: **5** Ripon **6** Antigo, Beloit, Cudahy, Neenag, Racine, Wausau **7** Ashland, Baraboo, Bloomer, Kenosha, Menasha, Oshkosh, Portage, Shawano **8** Appleton, Boscobel, Green Bay, Lacrosse, Superior, Waukesha **9** Eau Claire, Fond du Lac, Sheboygan, Shorewood, Wauwatosa, West Allis **10** Brookfield, Janesville **12** Steven's Point
college: **5** Ripon **6** Beloit **7** Alverno, Carroll, Viterbo **8** Carthage, Lawrence **9** Marquette, Northland
feature:
　fort: **6** Howard **8** Crawford **9** Winnebago
　national lakeshore: **14** Apostle Islands
tribe: **3** Fox, Sac **4** Sauk **5** Huron **6** Oneida, Ottawa **8** Chippewa, Kickapoo **9** Winnebago **10** Potawatomi
people: **11** Orson Welles **12** Fredric March, Harry Houdini, Spencer Tracy **13** Hamlin Garland **14** Joseph McCarthy, Georgia O'Keeffe, Thornton Wilder **16** Frank Lloyd Wright **17** Robert M LaFollette
　explorer: **6** Joliet **7** Allouez, Nicolet **8** Radisson **9** Marquette **12** Groseilliers
island: **8** Madeline
lake: **6** Geneva, Poygan **7** Kenosha, Mendota, Wissota **8** Michigan, Superior **9** Winnebago
land rank: **11** twenty-sixth
mountain: **7** Baraboo **9** Sugarbush **10** Blue Mounds
　highest point: **9** Timm's Hill
physical feature:
　glacial hills: **13** Kettle Moraine
　rock formations: **8** The Dells
river: **3** Fox **4** Wolf **7** St Croix **8** Chippewa **9** Black Rock, Wisconsin **11** Mississippi
state admission: **9** thirtieth
state bird: **5** robin
state fish: **11** muskellunge
state flower: **5** pansy **6** violet **10** wood violet
state motto: **7** Forward
state song: **11** On Wisconsin
state tree: **10** sugar maple

7 Minerva **11** Tritogeneia **12** Pallas Athena **18** Alalcomenean Athena

wise 3 way **4** sage **6** manner **7** knowing, respect, sapient **8** profound **9** judicious, sagacious **10** discerning, perceptive **11** intelligent **13** knowledgeable, perspicacious, understanding

Wise, Robert
director of: **11** I Want to Live **13** West Side Story (with Jerome Robbins, Oscar) **15** The Sound of Music (Oscar)

wiseacre 4 fool, sage **5** idiot **7** tomfool **9** know-it-all, simpleton **10** smart aleck

Wise Blood
author: **15** Flannery O'Connor

wisecrack 4 jest, joke, quip

5 flash, sally **8** cut jokes **9** witticism **11** smart saying

Wise men *see* **4** Magi

wise up 5 edify **6** advise, inform **7** apprise **9** enlighten, make aware

wish 3 yen **4** hope, long, love, pine, want, whim, will **5** crave, yearn **6** aspire, desire, hunger, thirst **7** command, craving, leaning, longing, request **8** ambition, appetite, fondness, penchant, yearning **10** aspiration, partiality **11** inclination **12** predilection

wishes 11 compliments **13** felicitations **15** congratulations

wish for 4 want **5** covet, crave **6** desire

Wishfort, Lady
character in: **16** The Way of the World
author: **8** Congreve

wishful 4 avid **5** eager **6** keen on, pining **7** anxious, craving, hopeful, longing, wanting, wistful **8** aspiring, bent upon, desirous, fanciful, yearning **9** ambitious, expectant

wish well 10 felicitate **12** congratulate

wishy-washy 4 dull, weak **5** inane, vapid, wimpy **6** jejune **7** insipid **8** wavering **10** indecisive, irresolute **11** ineffective, ineffectual, vacillating **12** equivocating, noncommittal **14** tergiversating **15** shilly-shallying

wisp 4 lock, tuft **5** bunch, shred, torch, twist **6** bundle, rumple **8** fragment **10** whisk broom **11** ignis fatuus **13** friar's lantern

wispy 4 thin **5** frail **6** slight **8** fleeting, nebulous

wistaria, wisteria
varieties: **4** pink, wild **5** silky, water **7** Chinese **8** Japanese **9** Rhodesian

Wister, Owen
author of: **12** The Virginian

wistful 3 sad **6** musing, pining **7** craving, doleful, forlorn, longing, pensive **8** desirous, mournful, yearning **9** hankering, sorrowful, woebegone **10** meditative, melancholy, reflective **12** disconsolate **13** contemplative, introspective

wit 3 wag **4** gags **5** comic, humor, joker, jokes, quips, sense **6** acumen, banter, brains, jester, joking, levity, wisdom **7** cunning, funster, gagster, insight, punster, sparkle, waggery **8** comedian, drollery, humorist, jokester, judgment, raillery, sagacity, satirist, vivacity **9** funniness, intellect **10** astuteness, brightness, cleverness, jocularity, perception, shrewdness, witticisms **11** discernment, penetration, wisecracker **12** intelligence, perspicacity **13** comprehension, epigrammatist, sagaciousness, understanding
French: **8** badinage **9** bel-esprit **10** persiflage

witch 3 hag **4** fury **5** crone, scold, shrew, vixen **6** ogress, virago **7** seeress **8** battle-ax, harridan **9** sorceress, temptress, termagant **10** prophetess **11** enchantress
French: **6** beldam

witchcraft 6 hoodoo, voodoo **7** sorcery **8** black art, witchery, wizardry **9** diabolism, fetishism, voodooism **10** black

magic, divination, necro-
mancy **11** conjuration,
enchantment

with
French: **4** avec, chez

with a grain of salt
Latin: **13** cum grano salis

with a lawsuit pending
Latin: **12** pendente lite

with authority
Latin: **10** ex cathedra

withdraw 2 go **5** leave, split
6 depart, go away, recall, recant, remove, retire **7** extract,
rescind, retract, retreat, take
off, vamoose **9** disappear,
unsheathe

withdrawal 4 exit **6** egress
7 leaving, retreat **9** departure
10 retirement, retraction
14 discontinuance

withdrawn 3 shy **5** quiet **8** reserved, retiring, unsocial **9** reclusive **10** unfriendly
11 introverted
15 uncommunicative

wither 4 fade, wilt **5** abash,
blast, droop, dry up, shame
7 cut down, mortify, shrivel
9 dehydrate, desiccate,
humiliate

withered 3 dry **4** arid, sere
5 dried, faded **6** shrunk,
wilted **7** decayed, dried up,
drooped, stunned, wizened
9 petrified, shriveled
10 languished

withering 6 biting **7** caustic
8 scathing **9** shrinkage, shrinking, wrinkling **10** shriveling
11 contracting, contraction,
devastating

with few words
Latin: **12** paucis verbis

with force and with arms
Latin: **9** vi et armis

with great praise
Latin: **13** magna cum laude

withheld 4 kept **7** checked, for-
bore, refused, starved **8** kept
back **9** boycotted, refrained

with highest praise
Latin: **13** summa cum laude

withhold 4 hide, keep **6** hush
up, retain **7** conceal, cover
up **8** suppress

withhold from 4 deny **6** refuse

within 2 on **4** into **5** inner
6 during, inside **7** indoors
8 inwardly
combining form: **3** eso
4 endo
prefix: **5** intra

within an inch of 4 near
6 all but, almost, nearly

with-it 7 current **8** up-to-date
French: **9** au courant

**with one's own two
hands 7** oneself, unaided
10 unassisted

without 4 save **5** minus **6** beyond, except, unless **7** lacking,
nowhere, outside, wanting
8 exterior, external, free from,
outdoors **9** excepting
10 externally
appointment: **7** sine die
care: **8** sine cure
charge: **4** free **6** gratis **8** sine
cure
combining form: **4** ecto
doubt: **9** sine dubio
feet: **4** apod **6** apodal
French: **4** sans
horns: **7** acerous
Latin: **4** sine
law: **8** anarchic
light: **7** aphotic
life: **5** amort **9** inanimate
luster: **3** mat **5** matte
offspring: **9** sine prole
prefix: **2** in
roads: **7** invious
saddles: **8** asellate, bareback
subcalyx leaves: **9** bractless
teeth: **5** morne **8** edentate
this: **7** sine hoc
tongue, teeth, or claws:
5 morne
which not: **10** sine qua non
wings: **7** apteral **8** apterous

without a doubt 6 surely **8** of
course **9** certainly **10** absolutely, positively **11** indubitably **12** indisputably
14 unquestionably

without basis 7 unsound
9 unfounded **10** groundless,
ungrounded **11** unjustified, unsupported **15** unsubstantiated

without care
French: **9** sans souci

without charge 4 free
10 gratuitous, on the house
13 complimentary
Latin: **6** gratis

without doubt
French: **9** sans doute

without end 7 endless, eternal, forever **8** immortal, infinite, timeless, unending
9 ceaseless, continual, endlessly, eternally, perpetual
10 immortally, infinitely, time-
lessly, unendingly **11** ceaselessly, continually, everlasting,
never-ending **13** everlastingly
14 lasting forever

without equal
French: **10** sans pareil

without error 4 true **5** exact,
right **7** correct, perfect, precise, sinless **8** accurate, truthful, unerring **9** faultless
10 infallible

without exception 5 never
6 always, wholly **8** entirely
10 absolutely, completely, invariably, positively

**without fear and without
reproach**
French: **22** sans peur et sans
reproche

Without Feathers
author: **10** Woody Allen

without funds 5 broke **6** ruined **8** bankrupt, indigent,
strapped, wiped out **9** destitute, flat broke, insolvent,
penniless **10** stone broke
12 impoverished

without light 3 dim **4** dark
5 black, dusky, murky, shady
6 opaque **7** obscure, shadowy,
stygian, sunless

without limit
Latin: **11** ad infinitum

without limitation 6 wholly
7 totally, utterly **8** entirely
9 endlessly **10** absolutely, completely, definitely, positively,
thoroughly **11** boundlessly
13 unequivocally
15 unconditionally
French: **12** carte blanche

without notice 5 ad-lib **9** impromptu **10** improvised **11** extemporary **14** extemporaneous
Latin: **9** extempore

**without offspring, without
progeny**
Latin: **9** sine prole

without the day
Latin: **7** sine die

without which not
Latin: **10** sine qua non

with praise
Latin: **8** cum laude

withstand 4 bear, defy
5 brave **6** endure, resist, suffer **7** weather **8** confront, cope
with, tolerate

witless 3 mad **5** crazy **6** insane, stupid **7** fatuous, foolish,
unaware **9** slaphappy

witness 3 see **4** mark, note,
sign, view **5** proof **6** attend,
behold, look on, notice, verify **7** bear out, certify, confirm, endorse, initial, observe
8 attester, attest to, beholder,
deponent, document, evidence,
looker-on, observer, onlooker,
perceive, validate, vouch for
9 establish, spectator, testifier,
testimony **10** validation

11 corroborate, countersign
12 authenticate, confirmation, substantiate, verification
13 corroboration, documentation **14** authentication, substantiation

Witness for the Prosecution
director: **11** Billy Wilder
based on play by: **14** Agatha Christie
cast: **11** Tyrone Power
14 Elsa Lanchester
15 Charles Laughton, Marlene Dietrich

wits 4 mind **6** sanity **9** composure **14** coolheadedness

witticism 4 jest, joke, quip
5 sally **7** epigram
French: **6** bon mot **10** jeu d'esprit

witty 5 comic, droll, funny
6 bright, clever, jocose
7 amusing, jocular, waggish
8 humorous, mirthful **9** brilliant, sparkling, whimsical
11 quick-witted **13** scintillating

witty saying 4 jest, quip
6 bon mot **7** epigram **9** witticism **13** clever comment

Witwoud, Sir Wilfull
character in: **16** The Way of the World
author: **8** Congreve

wizard 4 sage, seer, whiz
5 adept, shark **6** expert, genius, oracle **7** diviner, prodigy, wise man **8** conjurer, magician, sorcerer, virtuoso **9** enchanter **10** soothsayer
11 clairvoyant, necromancer

Wizard of Id, The
creator: **10** Johnny Hart
11 Brant Parker
character: **4** King **5** Spook
6 jester, Rodney, Tyrant

Wizard of Oz, The
director: **13** Victor Fleming
author: **10** L Frank Baum
cast: **4** Toto **8** Bert Lahr (Cowardly Lion) **9** Jack Haley (Tin Woodsman), Ray Bolger (Scarecrow) **11** Billie Burke (Good Witch of the North), Frank Morgan (wizard), Judy Garland (Dorothy) **13** Clara Blandick
15 Charley Grapewin
16 Margaret Hamilton (Wicked Witch of the West), The Singer Midgets (Munchkins)
score: **9** E Y Harburg
11 Harold Arlen
remade as: **6** The Wiz
place: **6** Kansas **8** Land of Oz **11** Emerald City
Dorothy wore: **8** red shoes

wizened 3 dry **5** dried **7** dried

up **8** shrunken, withered, wrinkled **9** shriveled

WKRP in Cincinnati
character: **10** Andy Travis, Herb Tarlek, Les Nessman
12 Venus Flytrap **13** Arthur Carlson, Dr Johnny Fever
14 Bailey Quarters **15** Jennifer Marlowe
cast: **7** Tim Reid **9** Gary Sandy **10** Gordon Jump
11 Frank Bonner, Jan Smithers **12** Loni Anderson
14 Howard Hesseman, Richard Sanders

wobble 4 reel, sway **5** quake, shake, waver **6** shimmy, teeter, totter **7** quaking, shaking, stagger, swaying **8** wavering
9 shimmying, teetering, tottering **12** unsteadiness

wobbly, Wobbly 5 loose, shaky **7** doubtful **8** hesitant, insecure, unstable, unsteady, wavering **9** quavering, trembling **11** vacillating
union: **17** Industrial Workers

Wodehouse, P G (Pelham Grenville)
author of: **8** Full Moon
14 Thank You Jeeves
15 The Mating Season
character: **6** Jeeves **13** Bertie Wooster

Woden
origin: **10** Anglo-Saxon
chief of: **4** gods

woe 5 agony, gloom, grief, trial, worry **6** misery, sorrow **7** anguish, anxiety, despair, torment, torture, trouble **8** calamity, distress **9** adversity, dejection, heartache, suffering
10 affliction, depression, melancholy, misfortune **11** tribulation **12** wretchedness

woebegone 3 sad **4** glum
6 gloomy **7** doleful, forlorn
8 dejected, funereal, mournful, tortured, troubled, wretched
9 agonizing, anguished, miserable, sorrowful, suffering
10 distressed

woeful 3 bad, sad **5** awful, cruel **6** tragic **7** doleful, painful, unhappy **8** crushing, dreadful, grievous, hopeless, horrible, terrible, unlikely, wretched **9** agonizing, appalling, miserable, sorrowful
10 calamitous, deplorable, depressing, disastrous, lamentable **11** distressing, unpromising **12** catastrophic, heartrending **13** disheartening, heartbreaking

woe to the vanquished
Latin: **9** vae victis

Wofford, Chloe Anthony
real name of: **12** Toni Morrison

Wojtyla, Karol
real name of: **14** Pope John Paul II **18** Archbishop of Krakow

wolf 4 bolt, gulp **5** scarf **6** devour, gobble **7** consume
constellation of: **5** Lupus
group of: **4** pack

Wolf, The
author: **11** Frank Norris

Wolfe, Thomas
author of: **14** The Hills Beyond **16** The Web and the Rock **17** Look Homeward Angel, Of Time and the River **18** You Can't Go Home Again
character: **10** Eugene Gant
12 George Webber

Wolfe, Tom
author of: **11** Radical Chic
13 The Right Stuff **14** The Painted Word **16** The Pump House Gang **21** From Bauhaus to Our House **23** The Bonfire of the Vanities
24 Mau-mauing the Flak Catchers **26** The Electric Kool-Aid Acid Test
43 The Kandy Kolored Tangerine Flake Streamline Baby

Wollstonecraft, Mary
husband: **13** William Godwin
daughter: **25** Mary Wollstonecraft Shelley
author of: **30** A Vindication of the Rights of Women

Wolverine State
nickname of: **8** Michigan

woman 4 girl, lady, maid, wife **5** flame, lover **6** damsel, maiden, matron **7** beloved, darling, dowager, females, fiancee, sweetie **8** ladylove, mistress **9** charwoman, concubine **10** girlfriend, handmaiden, sweetheart, sweetie pie **11** chambermaid, housekeeper, maidservant
French: **5** femme **8** paramour
Latin: **9** inamorata

Woman, first
Scandinavian: **5** Embla

Woman in White, A
author: **13** Wilkie Collins

womanish 7 unmanly **8** feminine, ladylike **9** sissified
10 effeminate

womanlike 8 feminine
10 effeminate

womanly 8 feminine, matronly

Woman of Substance, A
author: 21 Barbara Taylor Bradford

Woman of the Year
director: 13 George Stevens
cast: 10 Fay Bainter 12 Reginald Owen, Spencer Tracy 16 Katharine Hepburn

Woman's Life, A
author: 15 Guy de Maupassant

Women, The
director: 11 George Cukor
based on play by: 15 Clare Boothe Luce
cast: 11 Hedda Hopper 12 Joan Crawford, Joan Fontaine, Marjorie Main, Norma Shearer 15 Paulette Goddard, Rosalind Russell
remade as: 14 The Opposite Sex

Women at Point Sur, The
author: 15 Robinson Jeffers

Women in Love
director: 10 Ken Russell
based on novel by: 10 DH Lawrence
character: 11 Gerald Crich 12 Rupert Birkin 14 Gudrun Brangwen, Ursula Brangwen
cast: 9 Alan Bates 10 Oliver Reed 11 Eleanor Bron 12 Jennie Linden 13 Glenda Jackson
Oscar for: 7 actress (Jackson)

wonder 3 awe 4 gape 5 sight, stare 6 marvel, ponder, rarity 7 miracle 8 cogitate, meditate, question 9 amazement, spectacle, speculate 10 conjecture, phenomenon 11 fascination 12 astonishment, stupefaction

wonder child
German: 10 wunderkind

wonderful 4 fine, good 5 great, super 6 divine, superb, tiptop, unique 7 amazing, capital 8 fabulous, singular, smashing, striking, terrific 9 admirable, excellent, fantastic, marvelous 10 astounding, incredible, miraculous, phenomenal, staggering, surprising 11 astonishing, crackerjack, fascinating, magnificent, sensational, spectacular 13 extraordinary

Wonderland State
nickname of: 5 Maine

wonderstruck 4 agog 6 amazed 8 thrilled 9 astounded, stupefied 10 astonished, enthralled, spellbound 11 dumbfounded 13 flabbergasted

Wonder Woman
character: 9 (Corp) Etta Candy 11 Diana Prince, Joe

Atkinson, (Maj) Steve Trevor 13 Gen Blankenship
cast: 11 Lynda Carter 12 Lyle Waggoner 13 Beatrice Colen, Normann Burton 14 Richard Eastham

wont 3 apt, use 4 used, vain 5 habit, haunt, usage 6 custom, desire 8 accustom, inclined, practice 10 accustomed

wonted 3 apt 5 prone 6 likely 7 given to 10 accustomed, habituated

woo 3 sue 5 chase, court 6 cajole, pursue 7 address, entreat, solicit 8 petition 9 importune

wood 3 log 4 bush 5 brake, brush, copse, grove 6 boards, forest, lumber, planks, siding, timber 7 thicket 8 firewood, kindling 9 clapboard, wallboard 10 timberland

Wood, Grant
born: 9 Anamosa IA
artwork: 12 Spring in Town 13 Stone City Iowa 14 American Gothic 15 Woman with Plants 16 Parson Weems' Fable 18 Dinner for Threshers, John B Turner Pioneer 21 Daughters of Revolution

Wood, John, Sr
architect of: 6 Circus (Bath)

Wood, Natalie
real name: 13 Natasha Gurdin
born: 14 San Francisco CA
husband: 12 Robert Wagner
roles: 5 Gypsy 10 Brainstorm 12 The Great Race, The Searchers 13 West Side Story 17 Inside Daisy Clover 18 Rebel Without a Cause, Splendor in the Grass 19 Sex and the Single Girl 23 This Property Is Condemned 25 Love with the Proper Stranger 27 Miracle on Thirty-fourth Street

wooded 5 treed 8 forested

wooden 4 dull 5 frame, rigid, stiff 6 clumsy, vacant 7 awkward, deadpan 8 lifeless, ungainly 9 impassive, unbending 10 inflexible, ungraceful 11 unemotional 14 expressionless

Woodhouse, Emma
character in: 4 Emma
author: 6 Austen

woodland 5 copse, grove, treed 6 forest 7 coppice, thicket 8 forested

wood of life
Latin: 11 lignum vitae

woods
god of: 8 Silvanus, Sylvanus

Woods, Sara
real name: 13 Sara Bowen-Judd
author of: 11 Done to Death 12 My Life Is Done 13 Yet She Must Die 15 A Show of Violence, Knives Have Edges 16 And Shame the Devil 17 The Third Encounter, Trusted Like the Fox 18 Bloody Instructions
character: 15 Anthony Maitland

Woodstock
also called: 11 The Cavalier
author: 14 Sir Walter Scott

Woodstock
director: 15 Michael Wadleigh
cast: 6 The Who 7 Santana 8 Joan Baez 9 Joe Cocker 12 Richie Havens 13 John Sebastian, Ten Years After 17 Jefferson Airplane 19 Crosby Stills and Nash 20 Country Joe and the Fish, Sly and the Family Stone
Oscar for: 11 documentary

Woodward, Bob
author of: 4 Veil 19 All the President's Men (with Carl Bernstein)

Woodward, Joanne
born: 13 Thomasville GA
husband: 10 Paul Newman
roles: 12 A Fine Madness, Rachel Rachel 15 Three Faces of Eve (Oscar) 16 The Long Hot Summer 43 The Effect of Gamma Rays on Man-in-the-Moon Marigolds

woodwind instrument
4 oboe 5 flute 7 bassoon, piccolo 8 clarinet 9 bass flute 10 cor anglais 12 bass clarinet 13 double bassoon

wooer 4 beau, love 5 flame, lover, swain 6 adorer, suitor 7 admirer, courter 8 paramour 10 sweetheart

wool
fabric: 4 felt 5 crepe, llama, serge, tweed, twill 6 alpaca, angora, boucle, covert, faille, melton, vicuna, woolen 7 challis, doeskin, Donegal, worsted 8 cashmere, homespun, shetland 9 Astrakhan, camelhair, gabardine, sharkskin 10 hopsacking 11 Harris tweed, herringbone

Woolf, Virginia
author of: 7 Orlando 8 The Waves, The Years 10 Jacob's Room 11 Mrs Dalloway

14 A Room of One's Own
15 To the Lighthouse
member of: 15 Bloomsbury Group

wool-gather 8 daydream, muse idly

woolly, wooly 5 downy, furry, fuzzy, hairy, sheep, vague **6** fleecy, lanate, lanose **7** blurred, muddled, unclear **8** confused, floccose, peronate **10** flocculent, indistinct **12** disorganized

woozy 4 hazy **5** dizzy, faint, foggy, fuzzy, giddy, shaky **6** punchy **7** muddled **9** befuddled **11** light-headed

word, words 3 vow **4** chat, dirt, news, poop, term **5** edict, order, rumor, set-to, voice **6** advice, avowal, decree, gossip, letter, notice, phrase, pledge, remark, report, ruling, signal **7** command, comment, dictate, dispute, explain, express, hearsay, lowdown, mandate, message, promise, quarrel, summons, tidings **8** argument, audience, bulletin, chitchat, colloquy, decision, describe, dialogue, dispatch, locution, telegram **9** assertion, assurance, bickering, direction, discourse, interview, sobriquet, ultimatum, utterance, wrangling **10** articulate, communique, conference, contention, discussion, expression **11** altercation, appellation, declaration, designation, information, scuttlebutt **12** consultation, intelligence, tittle-tattle **13** communication, pronouncement
French: 9 tete-a-tete

word for word and letter for letter
Latin: 19 verbatim et literatim

wordiness 9 diffusion, prolixity, verbosity **11** diffuseness, profuseness

wording 8 language, phrasing **11** phraseology

wordless 4 dumb, mute **5** tacit **6** silent **8** implicit, taciturn **10** speechless **11** unexpressed

word of honor 3 vow **4** oath **6** pledge **9** assurance

word play 6 banter **7** jesting, kidding
French: 8 badinage, repartee

Words, The
author: 14 Jean-Paul Sartre

Wordsworth, William
author of: 7 Michael **9** Ode to Duty **10** The Prelude **12** Tintern Abbey **14** Lyrical

Ballads (with Coleridge) **16** The Ruined Cottage **24** Intimations of Immortality **25** Resolution and Independence
home: 11 Dove Cottage

wordy 5 windy **6** prolix, turgid **7** fustian, gushing, verbose **8** effusive, mumbling **9** bombastic, garrulous, redundant, talkative **10** discursive, loquacious, rhetorical, roundabout **12** tautological **13** grandiloquent

work, works 2 do, go **3** act, job, run, win **4** book, deed, duty, feat, form, gain, line, make, mill, mold, move, shop, song, task, toil, yard **5** beget, cause, chore, craft, enact, labor, opera, piece, plant, shape, slave, solve, sweat, trade **6** drudge, effect, effort, office, output **7** achieve, calling, drawing, execute, exploit, factory, fashion, foundry, innards, insides, operate, perform, produce, product, pursuit, succeed, trouble **8** building, business, concerto, contents, creation, drudgery, endeavor, engender, exertion, function, industry, maneuver, painting, progress, symphony, transmit, vocation **9** originate, sculpture, structure **10** assignment, employment, enterprise, manipulate, occupation, production, profession **11** achievement, composition, performance, transaction
Latin: 4 opus
French: 6 metier

work, artistic or literary
French: 6 oeuvre

workaday 5 plain **6** common **7** humdrum, prosaic, routine **8** ordinary **10** unexciting **11** commonplace

work at 3 try **5** essay **6** tackle **7** attempt **8** endeavor

workbench 5 board, table **7** counter

work conquers all
Latin: 16 labor omnia vincit
motto of: 8 Oklahoma

worker 4 doer, hand **5** grind **6** drudge, toiler **7** artisan, hustler, laborer, plodder

8 achiever, employee, producer **9** craftsman, performer **11** breadwinner, eager beaver, proletarian

work for 6 assist **7** support **8** champion

working 3 job **4** duty, toil **5** labor, tasks **6** action, chores, fluent, usable, useful **8** business, drudgery, employed, exertion, industry, laboring **9** effective, operation, operative, practical **10** employment, occupation, profession **11** assignments, functioning, performance

Working
author: 11 Studs Terkel

working-class 5 labor **8** plebeian **10** blue-collar **11** proletarian

working class 9 commoners, common man **11** blue collars, proletariat
Greek: 9 hoi polloi

workmanlike 5 adept **8** skillful **9** efficient **10** productive

workmanship 5 skill **9** handcraft, handiwork, technique **10** handicraft **11** manufacture **12** construction

work out 5 solve, train **6** figure, reckon **7** compute, resolve **8** exercise, practice **9** ascertain, calculate, determine

Works and Days
author: 6 Hesiod

work saver 9 appliance **11** convenience

work-saving 4 easy **6** simple **9** efficient

worktable 4 desk **5** bench, board, table **7** counter

work together 5 unite **7** pitch in, share in **8** take part **9** cooperate **11** collaborate, participate

work toward 3 try **4** seek **6** aim for **7** attempt **8** aspire to, endeavor, reach for

work up 4 goad, urge **5** upset **6** excite **7** agitate, ferment, provoke

work with 5 coach, drill, teach, train **6** assist **8** exercise, instruct **9** cooperate **11** collaborate

world 3 age, era, orb **4** gobs, lots, star **5** class, Earth, epoch, globe, group, heaps, realm, times **6** domain, nature, oodles, people, period, planet, sphere, system **7** mankind, society **8** creation, division, du-

ration, everyone, humanity, industry, universe **9** everybody, humankind, macrocosm **10** profession
Latin: 6 cosmos
Russian: 3 mir

World According to Garp, The
author: 10 John Irving
director: 13 George Roy Hill
cast: 10 Glenn Close, Hume Cronyn **11** John Lithgow **12** Jessica Tandy, Mary Beth Hurt **13** Robin Williams

World Enough and Time
author: 16 Robert Penn Warren

worldly 5 blase **6** astute, shrewd, urbane **7** callous, earthly, fleshly, knowing, mundane, profane, secular **8** material, physical, temporal **9** corporeal, mercenary **11** experienced, terrestrial **12** cosmopolitan **13** sophisticated

world pain
German: 11 Weltschmerz

world view
German: 11 Weltansicht

world-weary 5 blase, bored, jaded **9** unexcited

worldwide 4 rife **6** global **8** catholic, ecumenic, globular, planetal, sweeping **9** universal

worm 4 edge, inch **5** crawl, creep, steal **6** writhe **7** wriggle **9** penetrate **10** infiltrate
kinds: 4 inch, tape **5** angle, earth

worn 4 weak **5** dingy, drawn, faded, seedy, spent, tired, weary **6** frayed, shabby, wasted **7** abraded, haggard, pinched, rickety, wearied **8** battered, decrepit, dog-tired, drooping, fatigued **9** enfeebled, exhausted **10** threadbare, tumbledown **11** debilitated, dilapidated

worn-out 4 dead, shot **5** spent, tired **6** beat-up, effete, shabby, used-up **7** run-down **9** exhausted **10** threadbare **11** dilapidated **12** deteriorated

worn thin 9 motheaten **10** threadbare **11** dilapidated

worried 6 afraid, scared **7** anxious, fearful **9** concerned **10** distressed **12** apprehensive

worrisome 5 fussy, pesty **6** trying, uneasy, vexing **7** anxious, fretful, irksome **8** annoying **10** bothersome, despairing, disturbing, irritating, tormenting **11** aggravating, troublesome **12** apprehensive

worry 3 vex, woe **4** care, fret,

stew **5** agony, beset, dread, grief, harry, upset **6** badger, bother, dismay, harass, hector, misery, pester, plague **7** agitate, agonize, anguish, anxiety, bugaboo, concern, despair, disturb, perturb, problem, torment, trouble **8** distress, vexation **9** misgiving, persecute **10** difficulty, uneasiness **12** apprehension **13** consternation

worsen 4 fail, slip **5** erode, lapse, slide **7** decline **10** degenerate, retrogress **11** deteriorate **12** disintegrate

worsening 7 setback **9** inflaming **10** increasing, regressing, regression **11** aggravating, heightening **12** exacerbating, intensifying **13** retrogressing, retrogression

worship 5 adore, exalt, extol **6** admire, esteem, praise, pray to, revere **7** adulate, glorify, idolize, lionize **8** dote upon, venerate **9** adoration, reverence **10** exaltation, veneration **11** devotionals

worshipful 5 pious **6** devout **8** reverent

worshiping 7 adoring **8** exalting **9** adoration, adulation, adulating, idolizing, reverence **10** exaltation, glorifying, magnifying, venerating, veneration **11** idolization **13** glorification, magnification

worst 3 bad **4** beat, best, rout **5** floor, outdo **6** defeat, lowest, outwit **7** conquer, poorest, triumph **8** inferior, overcome, vanquish **9** discomfit **10** overmaster, unpleasant

worth 3 use **4** cost, good **5** merit, price, value **6** assets, estate, wealth **7** benefit, effects, utility **8** holdings **9** appraisal, resources, valuation **10** importance, usefulness **11** consequence, possessions

worth having 8 valuable **9** desirable

Worthing, Jack
character in: 27 The Importance of Being Earnest
author: 5 Wilde

worthless 6 futile, paltry **7** trivial, useless **8** bootless, piddling, unusable **9** fruitless, meritless, pointless **10** unavailing **11** ineffectual, undeserving, unimportant **12** meretricious, unproductive **13** insignificant **14** good-for-nothing

worthless objects 4 junk

5 trash **7** garbage, rubbish **8** discards **11** odds and ends

worthwhile 4 good **6** usable, useful **8** valuable **9** rewarding **10** beneficial, profitable

worthy 3 fit, VIP **4** good, name **5** moral, noble **6** bigwig, decent, honest, leader, proper **7** big shot, ethical, fitting, notable, upright **8** big wheel, great man, immortal, laudable, luminary, official, reliable, suitable, virtuous **9** admirable, befitting, deserving, dignitary, estimable, excellent, honorable, personage, reputable **10** creditable **11** appropriate, commendable, meritorious, respectable

worthy of imitation 5 model **9** emulative, exemplary

Wotan
origin: 8 Germanic
chief of: 4 gods
corresponds to: 4 Odin **5** Othin

Wouk, Herman
author of: 13 The Winds of War **14** The Caine Mutiny **17** War and Remembrance **19** Marjorie Morningstar
character: 12 Captain Queeg

wound 3 cut **4** gash, harm, hurt, pain, slit, tear **5** slash, sting **6** bruise, damage, grieve, injure, injury, lesion, offend, pierce, trauma **7** anguish, mortify, torment **8** distress, lacerate, vexation **9** contusion **10** affliction, irritation, laceration **11** provocation

wounded 3 cut **4** hurt **6** mauled **7** damaged, injured, pierced, stabbed **8** impaired, ruptured, stricken **11** traumatized

wrack 4 kelp, ruin **5** ruins, trash **6** clouds, refuse **7** destroy, seaweed, torment **8** downfall, eelgrass, wreckage **9** cloud rack **11** destruction, storm clouds

wraith 5 ghost, shade, spook **6** spirit **7** phantom, specter **8** phantasm **10** apparition **15** materialization
Irish: 7 banshee
German: 12 doppelganger
French: 8 revenant

wrangle 4 tiff **5** argue, brawl **6** bicker **7** dispute, quarrel **8** squabble

wrangling 6 strife **7** arguing, discord **8** clashing, friction **9** bickering **10** contention **11** quarrelling

wrap 4 bind, cape, coat, fold, gird, hide, mask, veil, wind

5 cloak, cover, scarf, shawl, stole 6 bundle, clothe, encase, enfold, girdle, jacket, mantle, shroud, swathe 7 conceal, enclose, envelop, sweater 8 surround

wrapper, wrapping paper
4 case 6 casing, jacket, sheath 8 covering, envelope, slipcase 9 container

wrapping 6 caping, hiding 7 veiling 8 cerement, bundling, swathing 9 embracing, packaging, shrouding 10 engrossing, enswathing, enveloping 11 enshrouding, surrounding

wrap up 3 end 4 pack 6 finish, wind up 7 engross, envelop, involve, package 8 bundle up, complete, conclude 9 polish off 11 dress warmly

wrath 3 ire 4 bile, fury, gall, rage 5 anger 6 animus, choler, rancor, spleen 8 vexation 9 animosity, hostility 10 irritation, resentment 11 displeasure, indignation 13 irritableness

wrathful 3 mad 5 angry, irate 6 bitter, raging 7 furious 8 incensed, virulent

wreak 4 vent, work 5 visit 7 execute, indulge, inflict, unleash

wreak vengeance 6 avenge 7 get even, revenge 9 retaliate

wreath 5 crown 6 diadem, laurel 7 chaplet, coronet, festoon, garland
  Hawaiian: 3 lei

wreathe 4 bend, coil, wind 5 curve, twist 7 entwine, envelop 8 encircle 10 intertwine, interweave

wreck 3 end 4 mess, raze, ruin 5 break, crash, death, level, ruins, smash, total, upset 6 finish, ravage, wretch 7 breakup, crack-up, destroy, shatter, undoing 8 demolish, derelict 9 devastate, overthrow 10 disruption 11 destruction, devastation, dissolution 12 annihilation

wreckage 4 ruin 5 ruins 6 jetsam 7 flotsam, remains 8 shambles 11 destruction

Wren, P C
  author of: 9 Beau Geste

wrench 3 rip 4 jerk, pull, tear, warp 5 force, twist, wrest, wring 6 sprain, strain 7 distort, pervert 12 misrepresent
  type: 6 monkey, socket 7 spanner

wrest 3 get, rip 4 earn, gain, grab, jerk, make, pull, take,

tear 5 force, glean, twist, wring 6 attain, obtain, secure, wrench 7 achieve, extract, squeeze

wrestle 4 toil 5 labor 6 battle, strive, tussle 7 contend, grapple, scuffle 8 struggle 10 struggling

wrestling
  athlete: 8 Dan Gable

wretch 3 cur, pig, rat 4 hobo, waif, worm 5 knave, louse, rogue, swine, tramp 6 misfit, rascal, rotter, varlet 7 castoff, outcast, stinker, villain 8 derelict, scalawag, sufferer, vagabond 9 scoundrel 10 blackguard 11 unfortunate

wretched 3 low 4 base, mean, vile 5 awful, lousy, sorry 6 abject, gloomy, rotten, shabby, sleazy 7 crushed, doleful, forlorn, hapless, pitiful, scruffy, unhappy, worried 8 dejected, downcast, dreadful, hopeless, inferior, pathetic, pitiable, terrible 9 cheerless, depressed, miserable, niggardly, sorrowful, woebegone, worthless 10 abominable, despairing, despicable, despondent, melancholy 11 crestfallen, unfortunate 12 contemptible, disconsolate, disheartened, inconsolable 13 brokenhearted

wretchedness 4 pain 6 misery, sorrow 7 despair, torment, trouble 8 distress, hardship 9 adversity 10 affliction, melancholy, misfortune 11 unhappiness 12 hopelessness

wriggle 5 twist 6 squirm, wangle, writhe 7 meander

Wright, Archibald Lee
  real name of: 11 Archie Moore

Wright, Frank Lloyd
  architect of: 8 Taliesin (Spring Green WI) 10 Robie House (Chicago) 11 Martin House (Buffalo NY), Unity Church (Oak Park IL) 12 Fallingwater (Kaufmann House Bear Run PA), Taliesin West (near Phoenix AZ) 13 Imperial Hotel (Tokyo) 16 Guggenheim Museum (NYC) 22 Marin County Civic Center (CA) 35 Larkin Company Administration Building (Buffalo NY) 45 S C Johnson and Son Wax Company Administration Center (Racine WI)
  style: 6 Modern 7 Organic, Prairie

Wright, Orville and Wilbur
  invented: 8 airplane

first plane: 6 Flyer I 9 Kitty Hawk

Wright, Richard
  author of: 8 Black Boy 9 Native Son 17 Uncle Tom's Children

wring 4 hurt, pain, rend, stab 5 choke, force, press, twist, wrest 6 coerce, grieve, pierce, sadden, wrench 7 agonize, extract, squeeze, torture 8 compress, distress

wrinkle 4 fold, idea 5 crimp, fancy, pleat, slant, trick 6 crease, device, furrow, gather, notion, pucker, rimple, rumple 7 crumple, gimmick 9 crow's-feet, viewpoint 11 corrugation

wrinkled 3 old 4 aged 5 lined 6 folded, ridged, rucked, rugate, rugose, rugous, seamed 7 creased, crimped, rimpled, rippled, ruckled, rumpled 8 crimpled, furrowed, puckered 9 shriveled

writ 10 court order 11 sealed order 14 mandatory order

write 3 pen 4 copy, show 5 draft 6 author, draw up, record, scrawl 7 compose, dash off, jot down, make out, produce, set down, turn out 8 inscribe, scribble 10 transcribe

write down 3 jot 4 note, post 5 enter 6 record

write in full 5 add to 6 expand, extend, pad out 7 amplify, augment, stretch 9 expatiate

write out 6 expand, extend 7 amplify, enlarge, stretch 8 lengthen

writer 4 hack, poet 6 author, critic, penman, scribe 7 copyist 8 essayist, novelist, reporter, reviewer, scrawler 9 columnist, dramatist, scribbler 10 journalist, librettist, playwright, songwriter 11 penny-a-liner 12 calligrapher, newspaperman 13 correspondent 14 newspaperwoman
  French: 11 litterateur

write to 7 address 8 send word 9 drop a line, send a card, send a note 10 correspond 11 send a letter

write-up 4 item 5 piece, story 7 article

write up 5 cover 6 report

writhe 4 jerk 5 flail 6 squirm, thrash, thresh, wiggle 7 contort, wriggle

writing 4 book, play, poem,

tome, work **5** diary, essay, novel, print, story **6** column, letter, report, script, volume **7** article, copying, journal, penning **8** critique, document, drafting, libretto, longhand **9** authoring, composing, editorial, recording **10** inscribing, manuscript, penmanship **11** calligraphy, composition, publication **12** transcribing **Latin: 4** opus

writings
Hebrew: 7 Ketubim

written agreement 6 treaty **7** compact **8** contract

written law
Latin: 10 lex scripta

written-out form 9 extension **12** augmentation **13** amplification

wrong 3 bad, sin **4** awry, bilk, evil, harm, hurt, ruin, vice **5** abuse, amiss, cheat, crime, false, inapt, kaput, unfit **6** faulty, fleece, injure, injury, ruined, sinful, unfair, unjust, untrue, wicked **7** crooked, defraud, illegal, illicit, immoral, inexact, inverse, misdeed, offense, reverse, swindle, unhappy, unsound **8** criminal, dishonor, evil deed, ill-treat, immodest, improper, iniquity, maltreat, mistaken, mistreat, opposite, trespass, unlawful, unseemly, villain **9** dishonest, erroneous, felonious, illogical, incorrect, injustice, unethical, unfitting **10** dishonesty, fallacious, illegality, immorality, inaccurate, indecorous, indelicate, iniquitous, malapropos, mistakenly, sinfulness, unbecoming, unfairness, unsuitable, wickedness, wrongdoing **11** blameworthy, erroneously, incongruous, incorrectly, inexcusable, unbefitting, undesirable, unwarranted **12** dishonorable, inaccurately, infelicitous, unlawfulness **13** inappropriate, reprehensible, transgression, unjustifiable **15** unrighteousness

wrongdoer 5 crook, felon, knave, rogue **6** rascal, sinner **7** culprit, misdoer, villain **8** evildoer, offender **9** miscreant, scoundrel **10** blackguard, delinquent, lawbreaker, malefactor, trespasser **11** perpetrator **12** transgressor

wrongdoing 3 sin **4** evil, vice **5** crime **8** misdeeds **10** misconduct **11** delinquency, malfeasance, misbehavior

wrongful 3 bad **6** unfair, unjust **7** illegal **8** criminal, un-

lawful **10** iniquitous, inequitable **12** illegitimate
act: 4 tort
dispossession: 6 ouster

wrongheaded 3 wry **8** perverse, stubborn **9** misguided

wrong side out 9 backwards **10** topsy-turvy

wrought 4 made **6** beaten, formed, worked **7** crafted **8** hammered **9** fashioned **11** constructed, handcrafted

wrought-up 7 excited **8** agitated **9** emotional **10** hysterical

wry 3 dry **5** askew, droll **6** bitter, ironic, warped **7** amusing, caustic, crooked, cynical, satiric, twisted **8** perverse, sardonic **9** contorted, distorted, sarcastic

Wunderkind 11 wonder child **12** child prodigy

Wurster, William
architect of: 13 Cowell College (UC Berkeley) **17** Ghirardelli Square (San Francisco CA)

Wuthering Heights
character: 9 Ellen Dean **10** Heathcliff, Mr Lockwood **11** Edgar Linton **14** Isabella Linton **15** Catherine Linton, Frances Earnshaw, Hareton Earnshaw, Hindley Earnshaw **16** Linton Heathcliff **17** Catherine Earnshaw
director: 12 William Wyler
author: 11 Emily Bronte
cast: 10 David Niven **11** Donald Crisp, Flora Robson, Leo G Carroll, Merle Oberon (Cathy) **15** Laurence Olivier (Heathcliff) **19** Geraldine Fitzgerald

Wyatt, James
architect of: 8 Pantheon

Wyoming
abbreviation: 2 WY **3** Wyo
nickname: 8 Equality
capital: 8 Cheyenne
largest city: 6 Casper
others: 4 Cody, Lusk **7** Bighorn, Buffalo, Laramie, Rawlins, Worland **8** Gillette, Greybull, Kemmerer, Riverton, Sheridan, Sundance **11** Rock Springs
feature:
  center: **11** Buffalo Bill
  dam: **8** Shoshone
  fort: **7** Laramie
  historical preserve: **11** Fort Bridger
  national grassland: **11** Tunder Basin
  national monument: **11** Devil's Tower, Fossil Butte
  national park: **10** Grand Teton **11** Yellowstone
  reservoir: **12** Flaming Gorge
tribe: 4 Crow **5** Kiowa, Sioux **7** Arapaho, Bannock **8** Cheyenne
people: 11 Buffalo Bill **14** Jackson Pollock **16** Nellie Tayloe Ross **18** Francis Emroy Warren
  explorer: **6** Colter, Stuart **7** Bridger **10** Bonneville
lake: 7 Jackson **11** Yellowstone
land rank: 5 ninth
mountain: 3 Elk **5** Cloud, Moran **6** Absaro, Hoback, Tetons **7** Bighorn, Fremont, Laramie, Rockies **8** Atlantic, Sheridan **9** Wind River **10** Black Hills **11** Rattlesnake
  highest point: **11** Gannett Peak
physical feature: 11 Jackson Hole
  basin: **7** Wyoming
  cave: **8** Shoshone
  hot springs: **11** Thermopolis
  plains: **5** Great
river: 4 Bear, Wind **5** Green, Snake **6** Platte, Powder, Tongue **7** Bighorn **8** Cheyenne, Shoshone **10** Sweetwater **11** Yellowstone **12** Belle Fourche
state admission: 11 forty-fourth
state bird: 17 western meadowlark
state flower: 10 painted cup **16** Indian paintbrush
state motto: 11 Equal Rights
state song: 7 Wyoming
state tree: 10 cottonwood

(London) **9** Lee Priory
(Kent) **10** Stoke Poges
(Buckinghamshire) **13** Font-
hill Abbey (Wiltshire)
14 Dodington House (Gloucestershire) **15** Heveningham
Hall (Suffolk) **16** Sandleford
Priory (Berkshire)
style: 13 Gothic Revival

Wyatt, Jane
born: 9 Campgaw NJ
roles: 9 Boomerang **11** Lost
Horizon **15** Father Knows
Best **17** Great Expectations
19 Gentleman's Agreement
21 None But the Lonely
Heart

**Wyatt Earp, The Life and
Legend of**
character: 10 Morgan Earp,
Virgil Earp **11** Ben Thompson, Doc Holliday **12** Bat
Masterson, Bill Thompson
13 Old Man Clanton
cast: 9 Hal Baylor **10** Denver
Pyle, Dirk London, Hugh
O'Brien **12** John Anderson
13 Douglas Fowley **14** Trev-
or Bardette **20** Mason Alan
Dinehart III

setting: 8 OK Corral **9** Dodge
City, Ellsworth, Tombstone
Wyatt's pistols: 15 Buntline
Special

Wyeth, Andrew Newell
born: 2 PA **10** Chadds Ford
father: 7 N C Wyeth
artwork: 9 Grape Wine, River
Cove **12** Nick and Jamie
14 Christina Olson, Distant
Thunder **15** Christina's
World **22** Winter Nineteen
Forty-six

Wyler, William
director of: 6 Ben Hur (Oscar) **7** Jezebel **9** Dodsworth,
Funny Girl, The Letter
10 Mrs Miniver (Oscar), The
Heiress, These Three **12** Roman Holiday **14** The Little
Foxes **15** Counsellor-at-Law
16 Wuthering Heights
18 Friendly Persuasion
22 The Best Years of Our
Lives (Oscar)

Wylie, Philip
author of: 13 Opus Twenty-
one **19** A Generation of
Vipers

Wyman, Jane
real name: 14 Sarah Jane
Fulks
born: 10 St Joseph MO
husband: 12 Ronald Reagan
daughter: 13 Maureen
Reagan
son: 13 Michael Reagan
roles: 5 So Big **9** Pollyanna
11 Falcon Crest, The Blue
Veil, The Yearling
13 Johnny Belinda (Oscar)
14 Angela Channing, The
Lost Weekend **17** The Glass
Menagerie **20** Magnificent
Obsession

Wyndham, John
real name: 16 John Beynon
Harris
author of: 14 The Kraken
Wakes **15** Consider Her
Ways **17** The Midwich
Cuckoos, Trouble with Li-
chen **19** The Day of the
Triffids

Wyoming *see box*

Wyss, Johann Rudolf
author of: 22 The Swiss
Family Robinson
adaptation of: 14 Robinson Crusoe

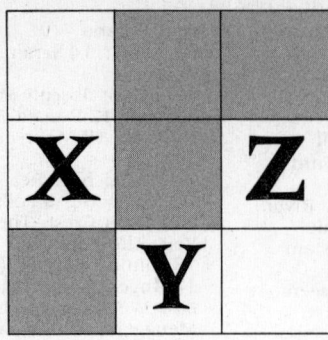

Xanthippe, Xantippe 3 hag
4 fury 5 scold, shrew, vixen
6 dragon, virago 7 scolder
8 spitfire 9 termagant
 husband: 8 Socrates

Xanthus and Balius
 horses of: 8 Achilles
 trait: 8 immortal

Xenia
 epithet of: 6 Athena
 means: 10 hospitable

Xenoclea
 form: 9 priestess

xenon
 chemical symbol: 2 Xe

xenophobia
 fear of: 9 strangers

Xerxes *see* 9 Ahasuerus

x-ray 9 radiogram 10 radio-
graph 13 roentgenogram
14 roentgenograph

X-ray tube
 invented by: 8 Coolidge

Xuthus
 father: 6 Hellen
 mother: 6 Orscis
 wife: 6 Creusa
 son: 3 Ion 7 Achaeus

yacht 4 boat, race, sail, ship,
yawl 5 ketch, sloop 6 cruise,
cutter 7 catboat 8 schooner
 race: 11 America's Cup

yachting
 athlete: 9 Ted Turner
 11 Lowell North

yahoo 4 lout 5 brute, yokel
7 lowbrow 9 barbarian, ignoramus, vulgarian

Yahoos
 fictional people in: 16 Gulliver's Travels
 author: 5 Swift

Yahweh 3 God 4 Lord 5 Jahve,
Jahwe, Yahve 6 Author, I am
I am, Jahveh 7 Creator, Eternal, Jehovah 8 Absolute, Almighty, Infinite
 component: 2 he 3 yod, vav
 pronunciation: 6 Adonai, Elohim 9 forbidden
 transliteration: 4 YHVH

Yale, Linus, Jr
 invented: 12 cylinder lock
 27 dial-operated combination
 lock

yam 9 Dioscorea 14 Ipomoea
batatas
 varieties: 4 wild 5 Negro, water, white 6 Attoto, potato,
 yellow 7 Chinese 11 sweet
 potato

Yamasaki, Minoru
 architect of: 14 St Louis Air-
 port (MO) 16 World Trade
Center (NYC) 21 Woodrow
Wilson Building (Princeton
NJ)

yammer 3 cry 4 carp, harp,
howl, wail, yell 5 whine
7 grumble, whimper
8 complain

yank 3 tug 4 jerk, pull 5 pluck,
wrest 6 snatch, wrench 7 draw
out, extract, pull out

Yankee, Yank 2 GI 5 teddy
6 gringo 8 American, doughboy 10 Northerner
 Spanish: 6 yanqui

Yankee Doodle Dandy
 director: 13 Michael Curtiz
 cast: 10 Joan Leslie
 11 James Cagney (George M
 Cohan) 12 Irene Manning,
 Walter Huston
 Oscar for: 5 actor (Cagney)

yanqui 6 Yankee 9 US citizen

Yaounde
 capital of: 8 Cameroon

yap 3 yip 4 blab, gush, rave,
talk, yawp, yelp 5 scold
6 babble, gabble, gossip, jabber, rave on, tattle 7 blather,
chatter, lecture, palaver, prattle 8 complain, converse

Yaqui
 language family: 6 Cahita
 location: 6 Mexico, Sonora
 7 Arizona

yard 4 lawn 5 close, court
6 garden 7 confine, grounds,
pasture 8 compound 9 enclosure, three feet
 abbreviation: 2 yd

yardbird 3 con 5 felon 7 convict 8 prisoner

yard goods 5 cloth 6 fabric
8 material, textiles

Yard of Sun
 author: 14 Christopher Fry

yardstick 4 rule 7 measure
8 standard 9 criterion

Yaren District
 capital of: 5 Nauru

yarn 4 tale 5 story 7 account
8 anecdote 9 adventure, narrative 10 experience

Yastrzemski, Carl
 nickname: 3 Yaz
 sport: 8 baseball
 team: 12 Boston Red Sox

Yates, Peter
 director of: 7 Bullitt
 12 Breaking Away

yawn 3 gap 4 bore, gape
5 chasm 8 open wide, oscitate

yawp 4 roar, yelp 5 noise
6 clamor, squawk, yammer

Yaz
 nickname of: 15 Carl
 Yastrzemski

Yazoo
 author: 12 Willie Morris

year, years 3 age, era **4** time
5 cycle, epoch **6** period
abbreviation: **2** yr

Yearling, The
director: **13** Clarence Brown
author: **22** Marjorie Kinnan
Rawlings
cast: **9** Jane Wyman **10** Chill
Wills **11** Gregory Peck
14 Claude Jarman Jr
character: **9** Ora Baxter
10 Jody Baxter **11** Oliver
Hutto, Penny Baxter
12 Grandma Hutto
14 Twink Weatherby
19 Fodder-Wing Forrester

Year of Living Dangerously, The
director: **9** Peter Weir
cast: **9** Linda Hunt (Billy
Kwan), Mel Gibson
15 Sigourney Weaver
setting: **7** Jakarta
Oscar for: **17** supporting actress (Hunt)

year of wonders
Latin: **14** annus mirabilis

yearn 4 ache, long, pine, sigh,
want, wish **5** crave **6** hanker,
hunger, thirst **8** languish

yearning 3 yen **4** ache, want,
wish **5** fancy **6** desire, hunger,
thirst **7** craving, longing, passion **9** hankering **10** aspiration **11** inclination

Yeats, William Butler
author of: **7** A Vision **8** The
Tower **9** Last Poems **14** Leda
and the Swan **15** The Winding Stair **18** Sailing to Byzantium **19** Among School
Children, The Wild Swans
at Coole **21** Easter Nineteen
Sixteen **22** The Lake Isle of
Innisfree **29** An Irish Airman Foresees His Death

yegg 6 bomber **9** cracksman
11 safecracker

yell 3 boo, cry **4** bawl, hoot,
howl, roar, yowl **5** cheer,
hollo, shout, whoop **6** bellow,
clamor, cry out, holler, hurrah, huzzah, outcry, scream,
shriek, squall, squeal **7** screech

yellow 4 gold **5** blond, lemon,
ocher **6** afraid, canary, craven,
flaxen **7** chicken, fearful, saffron **8** cowardly, timorous
10 frightened **12** apprehensive,
fainthearted **13** pusillanimous
14 chickenhearted

yellow-belly 6 coward **7** caitiff,
chicken, dastard **8** poltroon

Yellowhammer State
nickname of: **7** Alabama

yellowish 4 buff **5** blond,
cream **6** blonde, creamy,
flaxen

Yemen, North
other name: **4** Sana
capital/largest city:
4 Sana **5** Sanaa
others: **4** Moka, Taiz
5 Dahhi, Damar, Jibla,
Mocha, Mukha, Taizz,
Umram **7** Hodeida,
Hudayda
monetary unit: **4** fils,
rial **5** riyal
island: **5** Zugar **6** Hanish
highest point: **6** Shuayb
river: **5** Abrad, Zabid
6 al-Jawf, Surdud
sea: **3** Red
physical feature:
desert: **10** Rub al
Khali
gulf: **4** Aden
lowlands: **6** Tihama
peninsula: **7** Arabian
strait: **11** Bab el
Mandeb
people: **4** Arab **5** Zaidi
6 Shafai, Yemeni
8 Yemenite
leader: **16** Ali Abdallah Saleh **19** Abd al-
Aziz Abd al-Ghani
language: **6** Arabic
religion: **5** Islam
place:
ruins: **5** Marib
feature:
dagger: **7** jambiya
king: **4** imam
kingdom: **4** Saba
5 Sheba **11** Arabia
Felix
tree: **3** fig **5** carob,
mango, myrrh
food:
coffee: **5** mocha

Yellow Kid, The
creator: **10** R F Outcault
trademark: **10** nightshirt
place: **5** slums **11** Hogan's
Alley
coined term: **16** yellow
journalism
first: **10** comic strip

yelp 3 yap, yip **4** bark, howl
5 shout **6** clamor, holler,
scream, shriek, squeal
7 screech

Yemen, North *see box*

Yemen, South *see box*

yen 4 ache, long, pine, sigh,
want, wish **5** crave, fancy,
yearn **6** aching, desire, hanker,
hunger, relish, thirst **7** craving, longing, passion **8** appetite, languish, yearning
9 hankering **10** aspiration
11 inclination

Yemen, South
capital: **4** Aden **14** Madinat al-Shaab
largest city: **4** Aden
others: **5** Ahwar, Shihr,
Tarim **6** Balhaf,
Damqut, Seiyun,
Shabwa, Shibam, Za-
makh **7** Mukalla
monetary unit: **4** fils
5 dinar
island: **5** Perim **7** Ka-
maran, Socotra
mountain: **7** Djehaff
highest point: **6** Thamir
river: **4** Bana **6** Tibban
7 Masilah **9** Hadramaut
sea: **6** Indian **7** Arabian
physical feature:
desert: **10** Rub al
Khali **12** Empty
Quarter
gulf: **4** Aden
peninsula: **7** Arabian
valley: **9** Hadramawt
people: **4** Arab
language: **6** Arabic
religion: **5** Islam
feature:
animal: **4** ibex, oryx
clothing: **4** futa

yenta 3 hen **6** gossip **8** busybody **12** blabbermouth

Yentl
director: **15** Barbra Streisand
based on story by: **19** Isaac
Bashevis Singer
cast: **13** Mandy Patinkin
15 Barbra Streisand

**Yeobright, Thomasin and
Clym**
characters in: **17** Return of
the Native
author: **5** Hardy

yeoman 4 chap, exon **5** churl,
clerk, swain **6** farmer, fellow
7 granger, plowman, servant
8 graycoat, retainer **9** beefeater **10** freeholder **12** petty
officer

Yerby, Frank
author of: **8** Fair Oaks
10 Health Card **11** Griffin's
Way **12** Pride's Castle
16 The Foxes of Harrow
21 Hail the Conquering
Hero

yes 3 aye, yea **4** amen, okay,
true **5** truly **6** assent, indeed,
it is so, just so, really, so be
it, surely, verily **7** consent, exactly, granted, no doubt **8** approval, of course, to be sure
9 agreement, assuredly, certainly, doubtless, precisely
10 acceptance, positively **11** af-

firmation, undoubtedly **12** ac- quiescence, emphatically **13** affirmatively, authorization
 French: 3 oui
 German: 2 ja
 Spanish: 2 si

yesterday 7 the past **10** by- gone days, days of yore, olden times, time gone by **11** former times **13** the recent past **14** the good old days **17** the day before today **22** on the day preceding today

yet 3 but **4** also, even, then, up to **5** again, still, while, until **6** no less, though **7** besides, earlier, even now, further, however, thus far **8** although, hitherto, moreover **9** pres- ently **10** eventually, ulti- mately **12** nevertheless **15** notwithstanding

yew 5 Taxus
 varieties: 4 plum **5** Irish **6** golden **7** Chinese, English, Florida, Western **8** Ameri- can, Japanese, Southern **11** Chinese plum, Plum- fruited **12** Japanese plum, Prince Albert **14** Harrington plum

Yggdrasil
 also: 9 Iggdrasil
 origin: 12 Scandinavian
 kind of tree: 12 evergreen ash
 roots: 5 three
 binds: 6 Asgard **7** Midgard **8** Niflheim **10** Mithgarth

yield 3 pay, sag **4** bear, crop, earn, gain, give **5** beget, break, burst, defer, droop, forgo, grant, spawn, split, waive **6** accede, cave in, give in, give up, kowtow, render, return, submit, supply **7** bow down, concede, forbear, fur- nish, give way, harvest, pay- ment, premium, produce, product, provide, revenue, suc- cumb, truckle **8** collapse, cry uncle, earnings, generate, in- terest, proceeds, renounce **9** acquiesce, gleanings, pro- create, surrender **10** capitulate, relinquish

yielding 3 lax **4** soft **6** ceding, spongy **7** sagging **8** flexible, obedient **9** compliant **11** com- plaisant **13** accommodating

Yigdal 22 Jewish liturgical prayer
 literally: 12 becomes great

Yizkor 33 Jewish service to commemorate the dead
 literally: 9 be mindful

Ymir
 origin: 12 Scandinavian
 progenitor of: 6 giants

earth made from: 5 flesh
 water made from: 5 blood
 heavens made from: 5 skull

yogi 5 Hindu **6** mystic **7** ascetic

Yogi Bear
 creator: 12 Hanna-Barbera
 character: 6 BooBoo
 setting: 14 Jellystone Park

yoke 3 tax **4** bond, join, link, load, pair, span, team **5** brace, clasp, hitch, trial, unite **6** at- tach, burden, collar, couple, fasten, strain, weight **7** bond- age, coupler, harness, serfdom, slavery **8** distress, pressure, troubles **9** servitude, thralldom, vassalage **10** oppression **11** enslavement, tribulation

yokel 4 clod, hick, rube **7** bumpkin, hayseed, peasant, plowboy **10** clodhopper, provincial

yolk 6 yellow

yonder 3 yon **5** there **6** far-off **7** faraway, farther, thither

Yorick
 skull in: 6 Hamlet
 author: 11 Shakespeare

Yorick, Mr
 character in: 14 Tristram Shandy
 author: 6 Sterne

York, Michael
 born: 6 Fulmer **7** England
 roles: 6 Tybalt **7** Cabaret **11** Lost Horizon **14** Four Musketeers, Romeo and Ju- liet, The Forsyte Saga **15** Three Musketeers **19** The Island of Dr Moreau **24** The Last Remake of Beau Geste

York, Susannah
 real name: 23 Susannah Yo- lande Fletcher
 born: 6 London **7** England
 roles: 5 Freud **6** Images **8** Jane Eyre, Tom Jones **12** The Awakening
 author of: 18 In Search of Unicorns

Yossarian
 character in: 14 Catch- Twenty-two
 author: 6 Heller

You Asked for It
 host: 8 Art Baker **9** Jack Smith

You Bet Your Life
 host: 11 Groucho Marx
 announcer: 14 George Fenneman

You Can't Go Home Again
 author: 11 Thomas Wolfe
 character: 10 Esther Jack **11** Lloyd McHarg **12** George Webber **13** Else von Kohler **14** Foxhall Edwards

You Can't Take It With You
 author: 8 Moss Hart **14** George S Kaufman
 director: 10 Frank Capra
 cast: 10 Jean Arthur, Mischa Auer **12** Edward Arnold, James Stewart **15** Lionel Barrymore
 Oscar for: 7 picture **8** director

young 3 cub, pup **4** baby, kids **5** child, issue, minor, whelp **6** boyish, callow, junior, kit- ten, youths **7** budding, girlish, growing, progeny, puerile, teenage **8** childish, children, immature, juvenile, underage, youthful **9** beardless, infantile, juveniles, offspring, teenagers **10** adolescent, descendant, sophomoric, youngsters **11** ad- olescents, undeveloped **13** inexperienced
 god of: 7 Angus Og
 goddess of: 4 Hebe

Young, Chic
 creator/artist of: 7 Blondie

Young, Denton True
 nickname: 2 Cy **7** Cyclone
 sport: 8 baseball
 position: 7 pitcher
 team: 12 Boston Braves, Bos- ton Red Sox **16** Cleveland Indians, St Louis Cardinals

Young, Loretta
 real name: 13 Gretchen Young
 husband: 12 Grant Withers
 roles: 13 Cause for Alarm **14** The Bishop's Wife **15** Come to the Stable **18** The Farmer's Daughter (Oscar) **20** Rachel and the Stranger

Young, Robert
 born: 9 Chicago IL
 roles: 10 Relentless **11** H M Pulham Esq **13** Marcus Welby M D **15** Father Knows Best **16** Strange Interlude

Young Adventure
 author: 19 Stephen Vincent Benet

Young Frankenstein
 director: 9 Mel Brooks
 cast: 8 Teri Garr **10** Gene Wilder, Peter Boyle **11** Gene Hackman **12** Madeline Kahn, Marty Feldman **14** Cloris Leachman
 score: 10 John Morris

young girl
 French: 10 jeune fille

young lady
 German: 8 fraulein

Young Lonigan
 author: 13 James T Farrell

Young Manhood of Studs Lonigan
author: 13 James T Farrell

youngster 3 boy, kid, tot
4 baby, girl 5 child, minor,
youth 7 progeny 8 juvenile,
teenager 9 fledgling, offspring
10 adolescent

young Turks 6 rebels 8 radi-

cals, upstarts 9 activists 10 in-
surgents 15 revolutionaries

young woman
French: 10 demoiselle

you're welcome
German: 5 bitte

Your Show of Shows
regular: 9 Bill Hayes, Jerry
Ross, Sid Caesar 10 Carl

Reiner 11 Imogene Coca
12 Howard Morris, Nellie
Fisher 13 James Starbuck,
Robert Merrill 16 Margue-
rite Piazza

youth 3 boy, kid, lad 4 kids
5 bloom, child, minor, prime,
teens 6 heyday 7 boyhood
8 children, girlhood, juvenile,
minority, teenager 9 child-

Yugoslavia
other name: 8 Dalmatia 34 Kingdom of the Serbs Croats and Slovenes
capital/largest city: 7 Beograd 8 Belgrade
others: 3 Nis 4 Pola, Pula, Savo, Zara 5 Agram, Bosna, Budva, Fiume, Kotor, Pirot, Rieka,
Rtanj, Senta, Split, Tuzla, Uskub, Zadar 6 Bitola, Bitolj, Ca Haro, Maglaj, Morava, Mostar,
Osijek, Prilep, Ragusa, Rijeka, Skopje, Trogir, Visoko, Zagreb 7 Cetinje, Laibach, Maribor,
Novisad, Skoplje, Spalato 8 Monastir, Pristina, Sarajevo, Subotica, Titograd 9 Banja Luka, Dubrovnik, Ljubljana, Podgorica, Smederevo
division/former division: 6 Bosnia, Serbia 7 Croatia 8 Crna Gora, Slovenia 9 Macedonia,
Vojvodina, Voyvodina 10 Montenegro 11 Hercegovina, Herzegovina 14 Kosovo-Metohija
measure: 3 oka, rif 4 akov, ralo 5 donum, khvat, lanaz, plaze, stopa 6 motyka, ralico
9 danoranja
monetary unit: 4 para 5 dinar
weight: 3 oka 5 dramm, tovar, wagon 7 satlijk
island: 3 Rab 4 Arbe, Brac, Cres, Hvar, Pago 5 Mljet, Solta, Susac, Susak 7 Korcula
lake: 4 Bled 5 Ohrid 6 Prespa 7 Ochrida, Scutari
mountain: 5 Karst 6 Balkan 7 Rhodope 8 Crna Gora, Durmitor 9 Sar-Pindus 10 Karawanken
  Alps: 6 Carnic, Julian 7 Dinaric 9 Slovenian 16 Northern Albanian
highest point: 7 Triglav
river: 3 Una 4 Drim, Drin, Ibar, Krka, Kupa, Sava, Tisa 5 Anube, Bosna, Cazma, Drava, Drina,
Raska, Tamis, Timok, Tisza, Vrbas 6 Danube, Morava, Vardar, Velika 7 Neretva 9 Vojvodina
sea: 8 Adriatic
physical feature:
  bay: 5 Kotor
  cave: 8 Postojna
  channel: 7 Narento
  gulf: 5 Kotor 7 Kvarner, Trieste
  hot springs: 16 Krapinske Toplice
  peninsula: 6 Balkan 7 Istrian
people: 4 Serb, Slav 5 Croat 7 Slovene 8 Albanian 10 Macedonian 11 Montenegrin
  author: 6 Andric, Djilas, Krleza 7 Dedijer
  leader: 4 Tito 5 Dusan, Pasic 6 Djilas 7 Nemanja 9 Milosevic, Obrenovic 13 Mikhailovitch
  ruler: 5 Peter 9 Hapsburgs 12 Ottoman Turks
  sculptor: 9 Mestrovic
language: 7 Bosnian, Slovene 8 Albanian, Croatian 9 Hungarian, Slovenian 10 Macedonian
11 Montenegrin 13 Herzegovinian, Serbo-Croatian
  alphabet: 5 Latin 8 Cyrillic
religion: 5 Islam 13 Roman Catholic 15 Eastern Orthodox, Serbian Orthodox
place:
  amphitheater: 4 Pula
  bridge: 9 Stari Most
  fortress: 10 Kalemedgan
  monastery: 8 Sopocani
  mosque: 6 Begova 15 Bajrakli Dzamija
  ruins: 14 Hadrian's Palace
  square: 8 Republic
feature:
  coffee house: 7 kafanas
  fields: 5 polje
  military governor: 7 vojvodi
  musical instrument: 5 gusla
  poems: 5 pesme
  slippers: 6 opanki
food:
  dessert: 4 pita
  drink: 5 rakia 6 rakija 7 maraska 9 slivovitz 10 sljivovice 13 Turkish coffee
  meat: 7 shaslik 9 cevapcici 10 culbastija
  soup: 6 corbas

hood, fledgling, juveniles, schoolboy, stripling, teenagers, youngster **10** adolescent, pubescence, youngsters **11** adolescence, adolescents

youthful 5 fresh, young **6** boyish, callow **7** girlish, puerile, teenage **8** childish, immature, juvenile **10** adolescent, sophomoric **12** enthusiastic, lighthearted **13** inexperienced

yowl 3 bay, cry **4** bawl, roar, wail, yelp **5** shout, whine **6** bellow, holler, scream, shriek, squeal **7** screech **9** caterwaul

yucca
varieties: **4** blue **6** banana

Zachariah
father: **4** Babi, Elam **9** Barachias
wife: **9** Elizabeth
son: **3** Abi **14** John the Baptist
succeeded: **8** Jeroboam
visitor: **7** Gabriel

zaddik 14 virtuous person **15** righteous person

Zadkine, Ossip
born: **6** Russia **8** Smolensk
artwork: **4** Stag **6** Christ **7** Orpheus **9** Musicians **10** The Prophet **13** Woman with a Fan **14** Mother and Child **16** The Destroyed City

Zadok
father: **5** Baana, Immer **6** Ahitub
son: **7** Shallum
daughter: **7** Jerusha
served: **5** David

zaftig 5 buxom, plump **6** bosomy

Zagreus
form: **5** child, deity
father: **4** Zeus
mother: **6** Semele **10** Persephone

Zaire see box

Zambia see box

zany 3 nut **4** wild **5** balmy, batty, booby, buffo, clown, comic, crazy, cutup, daffy, dizzy, goofy, inane, nutty, silly, wacky **6** jester, nitwit, screwy, weirdo **7** buffoon, half-wit, lunatic **8** bonehead, clownish, imbecile, lunkhead, numskull **9** blockhead, eccentric, harlequin, ludicrous, pantaloon, simpleton, slapstick **10** nincompoop, noodlehead, outlandish **11** nonsensical person
French: **7** farceur

9 San Angelo, spineless **11** twisted-leaf

Yugoslavia see box, p. 1089

Yuit see **6** Eskimo

Yukon Territory
border: **6** Alaska **15** British Columbia, Selwyn Mountains **18** Mackenzie Mountains
capital: **10** Whitehorse
country: **6** Canada
event: **8** gold rush (1897)
Indian: **4** Dene **6** Eskimo **7** Kutchin **8** Loucheux **9** Athabasca
lake: **6** Kluane **9** Great Bear

Zapotec
language family: **5** Otomi **6** mixtec
location: **6** Mexico, Oaxaca

mineral: **4** gold **6** silver
mountain: **3** Joy **5** Logan **6** Harper **7** Kennedy **8** Campbell
region: **8** Klondike
river: **5** Pelly **9** Porcupine
sea: **8** Beaufort
town: **4** Elsa, Faro, Mayo, Snag **5** Rocky **6** Dawson **8** Franklin, Wernecke **9** Mackenzie

yule 4 Noel **9** Christmas

Yule, Joe, Jr
real name of: **12** Mickey Rooney

Yuman
tribe: **6** Mohave, Mojave **8** Hualapai

zapped 5 drunk **6** killed, soused, wasted, zonked **7** smashed **9** destroyed, plastered **10** inebriated

Zaire
other name: **5** Congo **12** Belgian Congo **13** Congo-Kinshasa **17** Congo-Leopoldville
capital/largest city: **8** Kinshasa
others: **4** Baya, Boma, Lebo **5** Aketi, Ilebo **6** Banana, Kamina, Kasaji, Kikwit, Matadi, Sandoa **7** Butembo, Kananga, Kolwezi **8** Bakwanga, Yangambi **9** Kisangani **10** Lubumbashi, Luluabourg, Mutshatsha **12** Port-Francqui, Stanleyville **14** Elisabethville
school: **5** Zaire **8** Lovanium
division: **4** Kivu **5** Kasai, Shaba **7** Equator, Katanga **8** Oriental
monetary unit: **5** zaire **6** makuta
lake: **4** Kivu **5** Mweru, Tumba **6** Albert, Edward, Upemba **9** Mai-Ndombe **10** Tanganyika
mountain: **7** Crystal, Mitumba, Virunga **9** Ruwenzori **10** Nyaragongo **18** Mountains of the Moon
highest point: **10** Margherita
river: **4** Ruki, Uele **5** Congo, Dengu, Ibina, Kasai, Lindi, Zaire **6** Likati, Lomami, Lukuga, Ubangi **7** Aruwimi, Lualaba, Lulonga
sea: **8** Atlantic
physical feature:
    falls: **4** Kivu **6** Tshopo **7** Stanley
    forest: **5** Ituri
    valley: **9** Great Rift
people: **4** Kuba, Luba, Yaka **5** Bantu, Bashi, Bemba, Kongo, Lulue, Lunda, Mongo, Pygmy **6** Azande, Baluba, Watusi **7** Bakongo, Nilotes, Tshokwe **8** European, Mangbetu, Sudanese
    explorer: **3** Cao **7** Stanley
    leader: **6** Mobutu (Sese Seko) **7** Lumumba, Tshombe **8** Kasavubu
    ruler: **7** Belgium, Leopold
language: **5** Bantu **6** French **7** Chiluba, Kikongo, Lingala, Swahili **8** Sudanese, Tshiluba
religion: **5** Islam **7** animism, Kimbang **10** Protestant **13** Roman Catholic
place:
    dam: **4** Inga **9** Le Marinee **10** Del Commune
    national park: **6** Albert, Upemba **7** Garamba
feature:
    animal: **5** hyena, okapi **7** giraffe, gorilla **10** rhinoceros
    fish: **11** electric eel

Zambia
 other name: 16 Northern Rhodesia
 capital/largest city: 6 Lusaka
 others: 4 Kafu **5** Choma, Isoka, Kabwe, Kitwe, Mansa,
 Mbala, Mongu, Mpika, Mumba, Ndola **6** Mwenda **7** Chi-
 pata, Luapula, Mankoya **8** Balovale, Chingola, Luanshya,
 Mazabuka, Mufulira, Mulobezi **11** Livingstone
 division: 7 Puapula **10** Copperbelt **11** Barotseland
 monetary unit: 5 ngwee **6** kwacha
 lake: 5 Mweru **6** Kariba **9** Bangweulu **10** Tanganyika
 mountain: 8 Muchinga
 highest point: 12 Mafinga Hills
 river: 5 Congo, Kafue **7** Luangwa, Luapula, Zambezi
 8 Chambezi **9** Chambeshi
 physical feature:
  cave: **5** Nsalu **14** Chifabwa Stream
  falls: **7** Kalambo **8** Victoria
  gorge: **6** Kariba
  plateau: **7** Zambian
  swamp: **7** Lukanga **9** Bangweulu **12** Mweru Wantipa
  valley: **8** Chambezi **9** Great Rift
 people: 4 Lozi **5** Bantu, Bemba, Ngoni, Tonga
  developer: **6** Rhodes
  explorer: **11** Livingstone
  hero: **11** Chitimukulu
  leader: **6** Kaunda
 language: 4 Lozi **5** Bemba, Lunda, Tonga **6** Luvale,
 Nyanja **7** English **9** Afrikaans
 religion: 5 Hindu, Islam **7** animism **10** Protestant **13** Roman Catholic
 place:
  botanical garden: **10** Munda Wanga
  dam: **5** Kafue **6** Kariba
  game reserve: **6** Valley
  library: **20** Hammerskjold Memorial
  museum: **11** Livingstone
  national park: **5** Kafue, Sumbu **12** South Luangwa
 feature:
  canoe: **10** nalikwanda
  king: **7** litunga
  king's aide: **5** sungu, twite **8** inabanza
  taxi: **6** zamcab

11 annihilated, intoxicated

zeal 4 fire, zest **5** ardor, gusto, verve, vigor **6** fervor, relish **7** passion **8** devotion, industry **9** animation, eagerness, intensity, vehemence **10** enthusiasm, fanaticism, fierceness, intentness **11** earnestness

zealot 3 fan, nut **4** buff **5** bigot, crank **6** pusher **7** devotee, fanatic, hustler **8** believer, champion, crackpot, go-getter, live wire, partisan **9** extremist **10** enthusiast

zealous 5 eager, rabid **6** ardent, fervid, fierce, gung ho, raging, raving **7** devoted, earnest, fanatic, fervent, intense **8** animated, vehement, vigorous **10** passionate **11** impassioned, industrious **12** enthusiastic

Zebedee
 wife: 6 Salome
 son: 4 John **5** James

Zeboim
 destroyed with: 5 Admah, Sodom **8** Gomorrah

Zebulun
 father: 5 Jacob
 mother: 4 Leah
 brother: 3 Dan, Gad **4** Levi **5** Asher, Judah **6** Joseph, Reuben, Simeon **8** Benjamin, Issachar, Naphtali
 sister: 5 Dinah
 descendant of: 10 Zebulunite

Zechariah
 father: 5 Bebai, Hosah **6** Jehiel, Pashur **7** Isshiah **8** Jehoiada, Jonathan **9** Berechiah **11** Jeberechiah, Meshelemiah
 grandfather: 4 Iddo
 mother: 6 Merari
 son: 8 Jahaziel
 daughter: 6 Abijah

Zeffirelli, Franco
 director of: 14 Romeo and Juliet **19** The Taming of the Shrew **20** Brother Sun Sister Moon

Zeitgeist 18 the spirit of the time

Zelos
 origin: 5 Greek
 personifies: 4 zeal **9** emulation
 father: 11 Titan Palles
 mother: 4 Styx
 brother: 3 Bia **6** Cratus
 sister: 4 Nike

Zemeckis, Robert
 director of: 15 Back to the Future **17** Romancing the Stone

zenith 4 acme, apex, best, peak **6** apogee, climax, summit, vertex **7** maximum **8** pinnacle **11** culmination

Zenobia (Zeena)
 character in: 10 Ethan Frome
 author: 7 Wharton

Zephaniah
 father: 8 Masseiah
 son: 3 Hen **6** Josiah
 succeeded: 8 Jehoiada
 deathplace: 6 Riblah

zephyr 8 west wind **9** puff of air **10** gentle wind **11** breath of air, light breeze

Zephyrus
 personifies: 8 west wind
 father: 8 Astraeus
 mother: 3 Eos
 loved: 10 Hyacinthus
 son: 6 Balius **7** Xanthus

Zeppelin, Ferdinand Graf von
 nationality: 6 German
 invented: 9 dirigible **21** rigid dirigible airship
 famous ship: 10 Hindenberg

Zernbbabel
 father: 7 Pedaiah **9** Shealtiel

zero 2 no **3** nil, zip **5** aught, nadir, zilch **6** cipher, naught **7** nothing **8** goose egg **11** nonexistent, nothingness

zero hour 5 onset, start **7** liftoff **9** beginning **12** commencement

zest 3 joy, zip **4** salt, tang, zeal, zing **5** gusto, savor, spice, taste, verve **6** flavor, relish, thrill **7** delight, passion **8** appetite, piquancy, pleasure **9** eagerness, flavoring, seasoning **10** enthusiasm, excitement **12** exhilaration, satisfaction

zestful 6 active, lively **7** dynamic, vibrant **8** animated, spirited, vigorous **9** vivacious **12** invigorating

zesty 5 spicy, tangy 7 piquant 9 flavorful

Zetes
origin: 5 Greek
member of: 9 Argonauts
father: 6 Boreas
mother: 8 Orithyia
twin brother: 6 Calais

Zethus
father: 4 Zeus
mother: 7 Antiope
wife: 5 Thebe
twin brother: 7 Amphion

Zeus *see box*

zigzag 4 awry, tack 6 angles, forked, jagged 7 chevron, crankle, crooked, notched, sinuous, stagger 8 crotched, serrated, sideling, traverse 9 bifurcate 10 circuitous, deflection

Zillah
husband: 6 Lamech
son: 9 Jubal-cain, Tubul-cain

Zilpah
slave of: 4 Leah
concubine of: 5 Jacob
son: 3 Gad 5 Asher

Zimbabwe *see box*

Zimbalist, Efrem, Jr
born: 9 New York NY
father: 14 Efrem Zimbalist
mother: 9 Alma Gluck
daughter: 18 Stephanie Zimbalist
roles: 3 FBI 13 Wait Until Dark 15 By Love Possessed 16 The Chapman Report 62 Seventy-seven Sunset Strip

Zimmerman, Ethel Agnes
real name of: 11 Ethel Merman

zinc
chemical symbol: 2 Zn

zing 3 pep, vim, zap, zip 4 dash, snap, tang, whiz, zest 5 gusto, speed, vigor, whine 6 energy, spirit 7 liven up 8 satirize, vitality 9 animation, criticize 10 enthusiasm, liveliness

zingara, zingaro 5 gypsy

Zinnemann, Fred
director of: 5 Julia 8 High Noon, Oklahoma 9 The Search 12 The Nun's Story 13 The Sundowners 17 A Man for All Seasons (Oscar) 18 From Here to Eternity (Oscar)

Zion 6 utopia 9 city of God 11 City of David 13 ancient Israel
hill in: 9 Jerusalem
built on the hill: 6 Temple

Zeus
also: 7 Cenaean 9 Atabyriam, Ithomatas 10 Anchesmius 11 Panomphaeus 12 Cithaeronian
birthplace: 5 Crete
brother: 5 Hades 8 Poseidon
corresponds to: 4 Amen, Amon, Jove 5 Ammon 6 Amen Ra, Amon Ra 7 Jupiter
daughter: 4 Hebe 6 Athene 10 Eileithyia, Persephone
epithet: 5 Areus, Arius, Sotor 6 Aqueus, Nemean, Philus 7 Alastor, Apemius, Ctesius, Lycaeus, Polieus, Stenius 8 Agoraeus, Aphesius, Apomyius, Catharius, Chthonius, Coccygius, Hecaleius, Lecheates, Mechaneus 10 Cataebates, Coryphaeus, Homagyrius, Laphystius, Meilichius 11 Eleutherius 12 Panhellenius
father: 6 Cronus
form: 5 deity
god of: 7 heavens
lover: 4 Leto 7 Demeter
mother: 4 Rhea
position: 7 supreme
sister: 4 Hera 6 Hestia 7 Demeter
son: 4 Ares 6 Apollo, Hermes
wife: 4 Hera 5 Metis

Zimbabwe
other name: 8 Rhodesia 16 Southern Rhodesia
capital/largest city: 6 Harare 9 Salisbury
others: 5 Gwelo, Gweru 6 Kariba, KweKwe, Mutare, QueQue, Umtali 7 Gatooma, Rusambo, Selukwe, Shabani 8 Bulawayo, Zimbabwe 10 Beitbridge
monetary unit: 4 cent 6 dollar
lake: 4 Kyle 6 Kariba
mountain: 5 Vumba 6 Manica 7 Inyanga 11 Chimanimani, Matopo Hills
highest point: 9 Inyangani
river: 4 Sabi, Save 5 Lundi 6 Shashi 7 Limpopo, Umniati, Zambezi
physical feature:
  falls: 8 Victoria
  grassland: 4 veld
  plateau: 8 Highveld 11 Mashonaland
people: 3 Ila 4 Sena 5 Asian, Bantu, Bemba, Sotho, Tongo, White 6 Indian 7 Barotse, Chinese, English, Mashoma, Mashona, Ndebele 8 Coloured, Japanese, Matabele 9 Afrikaner 10 Balokwakwa
  developer: 6 Rhodes
  explorer: 11 Livingstone
  king: 9 Lobengula, Mzilikaze
  leader: 5 Nkomo 6 Mugabe 7 Sithole 8 Muzorewa 9 Ian D Smith
language: 3 Ila 5 Bantu, Shona 7 English, Ndebele
religion: 7 animism 8 Anglican 12 Christianity, Presbyterian 13 Dutch Reformed, Roman Catholic
place:
  dam: 6 Kariba
  national park: 6 Hwange, Wankie 7 Matopos 9 Inyangani 13 Victoria Falls
  ruins: 5 Khami 6 Temple 8 Zimbabwe 9 Acropolis 13 Valley of Ruins
feature:
  cattle pen: 5 kraal
  game: 5 tsoro 7 mandani
  hut: 4 kaia
  kingdom: 5 Rozwi 10 Monomotapa
  tree: 4 teak 6 baobab, mopani

zip 3 fly, nil, pep, run, vim
4 buzz, dart, dash, hiss, life,
nada, rush, zero, zest **5** aught,
close, drive, force, gusto,
hurry, power, punch, speed,
verve, vigor, whine, zilch
6 cipher, energy, impact,
naught, spirit, streak **7** nothing, whistle **8** goose egg,
strength, vitality, vivacity
9 animation, intensity **10** enthusiasm, exuberance, liveliness **13** effervescence

zipper
    invented by: **6** Judson

Zipporah
    father: **5** Reuel **6** Jethro
    husband: **5** Moses
    son: **7** Eliezer, Gershom

zircon
    source: **5** Burma **6** Ceylon
    8 Cambodia, Sri Lanka
    9 Kampuchea

zirconium
    chemical symbol: **2** Zr

zodiac 4 belt, zone **5** stars
    7 circuit
    fire sign: **3** Leo **5** Aries
    11 Sagittarius
    earth sign: **5** Virgo **6** Taurus
    9 Capricorn
    air sign: **5** Libra **6** Gemini
    8 Aquarius
    water: **6** Cancer, Pisces
    7 Scorpio

    division: **4** sign **5** decan
    6 trigon
    number of houses: **6** twelve
    falling between two signs:
    4 cusp

Zoimo, Vincent Edward
    real name of: **12** Vince
    Edwards

Zola, Emile
    author of: **4** Nana **7** The
    Soil **8** Germinal **10** L'As-
    sommoir **11** The Downfall,
    The Dram Shop **13** Therese
    Raquin **14** The Human Ani-
    mal **20** The Experimental
    Novel

zone 4 area, belt, ward **5** tract
    6 region, sector **7** quarter, sec-
    tion, terrain **8** district, locality,
    location, precinct **9** territory

zonked 5 drunk **6** soused,
    wasted, zapped **7** smashed
    9 plastered **10** inebriated
    11 intoxicated

zoo 8 vivarium **9** menagerie

zoom 3 fly, zip **4** buzz, race,
    rise, soar **5** climb, flash, shoot,
    speed **6** ascend, rocket, streak
    7 advance, take off **9** skyrocket

zoophobia
    fear of: **7** animals

Zophar
    friend: **3** Job **5** Elihu **6** Bil-
    dad **7** Eliphaz

Zorba the Greek
    director: **17** Michael
    Cacoyannis
    based on the story by:
    11 Kazantzakis
    cast: **9** Alan Bates **11** Irene
    Pappas, Lila Kedrova
    12 Anthony Quinn
    score: **16** Mikis Theodorakis
    Oscar for: **17** supporting ac-
    tress (Kedrova)

Zosteria
    epithet of: **6** Athena
    means: **20** one who girds
    with armor

zucchini 5 gourd **6** squash
    12 summer squash

Zuck, Alexandra
    real name of: **9** Sandra Dee

Zuckerman Unbound
    author: **10** Philip Roth

Zurich
    festival: **12** Sechselanten
    landmark: **8** Rietberg
    9 Kunsthaus **15** CG Jung In-
    stitute **17** Centre Le Corbu-
    sier, Fraumunster Kirche
    21 Grossmunster Cathedral
    religious figure: **7** Zwingli
    9 Bullinger
    river: **6** Limmat
    Roman name: **7** Turicum

Zweig, Arnold
    author of: **7** Claudia **24** The
    Case of Sergeant Grischa